P9-CSB-667
TERRY FOX
MARATHON
OF
HOPE
Crowfoot
Susanna Moodie
Jeanne Sauvé
Victoria Cross
Alex Baumann
Ned Hanlan
Sir Frederick Banting
CANADA
FIVE 5 CENTS
1927
Tom Thomson
Tom Longboat

THE CANADIAN ENCYCLOPEDIA

VOLUME I
A - For

Hurtig Publishers
Edmonton

Hurtig Publishers Ltd.
10560 – 105 Street
Edmonton, Alberta
Canada T5H 2W7

Every attempt has been made to identify and credit sources for photographs. The publisher would appreciate receiving information as to any inaccuracies in the credits for subsequent editions.

Canadian Cataloguing in Publication Data

Main entry under title:
The Canadian Encyclopedia

Editor in Chief: James H. Marsh.

ISBN 0-88830-269-X (set). — ISBN 0-88830-270-3 (v. 1). — ISBN 0-88830-271-1 (v. 2). — ISBN 0-88830-272-X (v. 3)

1. Canada – Dictionaries and encyclopedias.
I. Marsh, James H.
FC23.C36 1985 971'.003'21 C84-091250-1
F1006.C36 1985

Designed, typeset and manufactured
in Canada

SPECIAL ACKNOWLEDGMENT

Publication of *The Canadian Encyclopedia* would not have been possible without the generosity and foresight of the Government of Alberta.

To commemorate the 75th anniversary of Alberta's entry into Confederation, the Province donated four million dollars towards the research and development of the first comprehensive reference work on modern Canada and its people. This generous assistance has financed five years of intensive research, writing, editing and verification. It was the Alberta Government's faith in the project that made possible this vivid new portrait of our country.

In addition, the Government of Alberta is providing a free set of the encyclopedia to schools and libraries across Canada and to diplomatic posts abroad.

Hurtig Publishers and the Province have provided French-language rights free to Les Éditions Internationales Stanké Ltée, which will publish *L'Encyclopédie du Canada* in 1987.

Special thanks are due to the Honourable Peter Lougheed, Premier of Alberta, the Honourable Mary LeMessurier, the Honourable Horst Schmid and the Honourable Robert Dowling, whose enthusiastic support has made possible this worthy and enduring gift to all Canadians from the people of Alberta.

Hurtig Publishers
gratefully acknowledges
a major gift from

NOVA, AN ALBERTA CORPORATION

whose financial support made possible the acquisition of the cartography, artwork and illustrations which appear throughout these three volumes. Without NOVA's timely and generous assistance the inclusion of colour illustrations and maps in *The Canadian Encyclopedia* would not have been possible.

Hurtig Publishers
gratefully acknowledges the support
and co-operation of

THE UNIVERSITY OF ALBERTA

faculty and staff, whose enthusiastic assistance and encouragement played an indispensable support role in the preparation of *The Canadian Encyclopedia*.

Special thanks are owing to Myer Horowitz, President; Lorne Leitch, VP; Ron Phillips, VP; David Norwood, Assistant VP; Len Young, Bernard Cordell, Douglas Martin and Bernadette Quenneville of Printing Services; Dale Bent and Ron Senda of Computing Services; Mrs. G. White, Supervisor, University Library; the University Libraries; Faculty of Library Science; and the academic and support staff of the departments of the University of Alberta. The co-operation provided by the university community exceeded anything the publisher could reasonably have expected and is a reflection of the University of Alberta's commitment to research, scholarship and education.

FOREWORD

Hurtig Publishers' concept of a new, comprehensive, affordable encyclopedia of modern Canada dates back to the early 1970s. Everyone we approached agreed without hesitation (especially teachers, students and librarians) on the need for and importance of such a reference work. But, despite determined effort, the seed money for the research, writing and editorial development required for such a huge undertaking could not be found. Premier Peter Lougheed and the Alberta government changed that in 1979 with a generous grant. Without their confidence and support *The Canadian Encyclopedia* would never have been published.

Almost a full year of detailed research and planning culminated with the appointment of James Marsh as editor in chief and the hiring of our editorial, research and clerical staff from across Canada. *The Canadian Encyclopedia* is the product of thousands of skilled contributors and dozens of dedicated staff. But the principal credit for its high editorial quality, after 5 years of intensive, demanding effort, must go to James Marsh. Few who were not intimately connected with the project can conceive of the immense difficulties, the unanticipated problems, the pressure, and the massive volume of work faced by our editors, researchers and support staff. I believe the encyclopedia speaks for itself, and the superb efforts of our editor in chief and his staff.

Two other colleagues must be singled out. Managing Director Frank McGuire developed the technical systems and managed the day-to-day scheduling, administration, production and planning that allowed *The Canadian Encyclopedia* to be published on time and close to budget, despite the numerous unexpected costs, pitfalls and problems that arose during the 5 years of development. Dr. Harry Gunning, past president of the University of Alberta and Chairman of our National Advisory Board, provided invaluable advice and assistance. Without the special skills of Frank McGuire and Harry Gunning, the entire project could have been in jeopardy on more than one occasion. All members of the National Advisory Board provided valuable guidance through the difficult early stages and several hundred consultants lent their expertise throughout the editorial process.

When it became clear that additional funds would be needed to maintain the high standards we had set, NOVA, AN ALBERTA CORPORATION stepped in to help with no hesitation. Dianne Hall, Senior Vice-President of NOVA, and Bob Blair, President, gave *The Canadian Encyclopedia* crucial support just when it was needed most.

From the very beginning the University of Alberta played a significant role. Dr. Myer Horowitz, President, and Vice-President Lorne Leitch, the academic staff and many others at the University provided unfailing support, co-operation, enthusiasm and encouragement.

The Canadian Commercial Bank believed in the encyclopedia whereas numerous other bankers had dismissed the project as being too risky. President Gerald McLaughlan, Greg Fraipont and Barry Hicks were instrumental in arranging the millions of dollars in loan capital required to print and bind these volumes and to pay for all the other expensive costs of production.

Special recognition and thanks are due not only Minister of Culture, Mary LeMessurier, but also to John S. O'Neill, John Patrick Gillese and others in Alberta Culture who administered the province's R & D grant.

Hurtig Publishers also greatly appreciates the co-operation and assistance of the Department of Energy, Mines and Resources in Ottawa in making available materials vital to the compilation of some 300 maps appearing throughout these volumes.

To all the thousands of contributors we extend our deepest gratitude. There is not space enough to name all of those who contributed so much without proper recognition and accolades. However, special recognition is due David Shaw and his design staff; Senior Editors Adriana Davies, Patricia Finlay, Mary McDougall Maude, James Ogilvy and Rosemary Shipton; and Rick Checkland, Lillian Wonders, Ken McVey, Patricia Fong, Huguette Labelle, Anne Scotton, Timothy Porteous, José Druker, Elizabeth Munroe, Sharon Burton, Jan Steckly, Glen C. Hyatt, and Peter Freeman.

By the time you read this, some 5000 Canadians from across our country will have been involved in producing these 3 volumes. The articles were written in every province and territory. While centred in Edmonton, editorial work was also carried out in Calgary, Ottawa, Toronto and London, Ont. Colour separations and pre-preparation work were performed in Vancouver and printing in Montréal. The cloth was produced in Cornwall, Ont; binding was done in Toronto and packaging in Oshawa, Ont.

It will have taken ten months to print, bind and package this reference set. As a result, some of the material, as in all encyclopedias, contains information that will have been changed by events. In the future, encyclopedias such as this will certainly continue to be available in book form, but not very many years from now *The Canadian Encyclopedia* should be available via electronic means as well, with immediate updates, via your television set, home computer, telephone, or perhaps video laser discs.

It is difficult to forecast the future of *The Canadian Encyclopedia*. If this edition is well received and is a financial success then a second, revised, expanded and updated edition will likely be published in 1988, and we hope at regular intervals thereafter. As this is being written, work on a second edition has already commenced.

In retrospect we can now see that the task we set out to accomplish in 1979 was immensely more difficult than we had anticipated. Perhaps, had it been somehow available, we could have spent millions of dollars more in development funds and taken several additional years for editorial preparation. However, our intent from the very beginning was to produce a first-class Canadian encyclopedia that would go on sale to the public at a low price so that all Canadian families could afford to purchase the set for their own homes. We are pleased to have achieved this goal and to have provided a valuable reference work on our country. I sincerely hope you will be happy with Canada's new national encyclopedia and that it will make an important contribution to Canadians' understanding of one another and to our pride in our country.

Mel Hurtig

MEL HURTIG

INTRODUCTION

The production of an encyclopedia is an undertaking with a long and noble tradition stretching back to ancient Greece. Though the grand "circle of knowledge," from which the word *encyclopedia* is derived, has expanded beyond the scope of any single enterprise, the attempt to draw together the overwhelming accumulation of human knowledge remains a worthy goal that tempts each generation. *The Canadian Encyclopedia* differs greatly from the last encyclopedic work on Canada, published a generation ago. It portrays a country more mature in its literature and arts, more aware of its regional and ethnic diversity, more sophisticated in its politics and foreign policy, and yet still a nation in the making, searching for new solutions to its economic, social and linguistic problems and still struggling to realize the potential of a land of unimaginable size, variety and resources. The entries in *The Canadian Encyclopedia* provide an intricate sketch of Canada, drawn by its finest scholars and writers, that will provide not only an invaluable reference tool and repository for information, but a portrait of its time that will continue to be interpreted by future generations.

The development of a list of articles is the central creative act in the planning of an encyclopedia. The editors sought to provide coverage of all aspects of life in Canada, of all regions, over a vast time scale from the geological formation of the most ancient rocks to the most recent political events. Because there exists no cohesive framework that would easily encompass all provinces of knowledge, the process of identifying topics and assigning them weight in relation to the boundless variety of other subjects was one of intensive planning and constant revision. The master article list continued to grow as the editors received reports from the project's 250 consultants, as new topics were uncovered in the course of editing and as events changed Canada over the 4 years of the editorial process. The lists included all major subjects that any reader would expect to find in a Canadian encyclopedia, such as populated places, the provinces and territories, leading cultural and political figures, political themes such as federalism, Canada's flora and fauna, its ethnic groups and its artistic endeavours. The final list of over 8000 entries also includes numerous topics of particular Canadian character, such as the voyageur, birchbark canoe, ice hockey, Northwest Coast Indian art and Inuit sculpture, as well as many unusual subjects that illuminate lesser-known aspects of Canada, such as ice worms, duels, birchbark biting, cemeteries, La Corriveau and Zouaves. Entries on a representative sample of Canadian literary works, such as *The Apprenticeship of Duddy Kravitz* and *Kamouraska*, are provided in hope that they will introduce readers to good Canadian books. Some 3500 biographies were chosen to provide information on people from all periods, regions and subject areas, while emphasizing those who, including contemporary Canadians, have made lasting contributions to (or impressions on) Canadian society. Based on advice from consultants, criteria for inclusion varied according to what was appropriate to the area under consideration. For instance, in the case of contemporary painters, limited space required that an age criterion be imposed. In all areas the biographies are representative of a far greater number worthy of study. Some emphasis has been placed on including the innovators rather than the facilitators. An effort has been made to include the results of current research, for example, in native and women's studies. In all subject areas, contributors were asked to stress the Canadian aspect of their subject. In discussing fields of study, such as anthropology, economics or physics, some background information was required to explain Canadian research and accomplishment, though limitations of space prevented extensive treatment of material more appropriate to general reference works or textbooks.

The editors decided early in the planning that the encyclopedia would be written by specialists who were best able to explain the finer points of their subjects and could impart to the encyclopedia the distinctive quality of representing the country as a whole. This approach places great demands on editors to mold the writing of thousands of contributors into a coherent reference work, but it rewards the reader with expert writing, a broad scope and sparks of individuality. We were very fortunate in attracting some 2500 authorities from all major Canadian universities, federal and provincial public services, scientific institutions, museums, galleries, newspapers, magazines and private industry, as well as numerous free lances. Many of these contributors did original research on subjects as diverse as snowshoeing and Sikhism. Many entries, such as those on theatre, sculpture, printmaking, the print industry, philosophy and cartography, are the first reliable syntheses of their subject in Canada.

All articles were evaluated by consultants and expert readers to ensure that controversial issues were treated fairly, that interpretations were based on sound research and that different views of important questions had been explained. The signed entries of the encyclopedia reflect the diversity of the people who have created it. The readers, editors and researchers endeavoured to check every statement for accuracy, to ensure reasonable conformity to the compact style of a reference work, and to make every entry as readable and as current as possible. To ensure that the encyclopedia remained a manageable size and met the guidelines for length (established to keep the price of the encyclopedia low enough to encourage the widest possible distribution among Canadians), the entries had to be concise, and submissions that dealt less specifically with Canada or that duplicated material covered elsewhere had to be dropped. The 3.2 million words published in the encyclopedia were distilled from over 10 million words submitted to the editors, who were grateful for the advancements in computer technology that helped keep track of every article and contributor and facilitated the countless changes and updates made to the text.

The humanist and scholar Dr. Samuel Johnson wrote, in reference to his great dictionary, that "the world is little solicitous to know whence proceeded the faults of that which it condemns." An encyclopedia is a difficult undertaking because of its magnitude and because expectations are so great that it will fulfil so many contrasting demands. *The Canadian Encyclopedia* is delivered in the spirit in which it has been created by its staff, contributors, advisers, consultants, cartographers, photographers, artists, indexers and technical staff, who have sought to bring to Canadians a deeper knowledge about themselves and their diverse country. I express our gratitude to the many Canadians from every part of Canada who have generously given us their time and their support for a project they believed to be of great importance to our nation. My final acknowledgement is to Mel Hurtig, who set us all on the greatest enterprise of our lives. He believed that all Canadians would be drawn together in this national project, and his faith in Canada is reflected in these pages.

James H. Marsh

JAMES H. MARSH
Editor in Chief
Edmonton, Sept 1985

USING THE ENCYCLOPEDIA

Organization The content of the encyclopedia has been organized in entries which are listed alphabetically. The entry titles, which appear in boldface type (eg, **Humorous Writing in English**), have been chosen to aid the reader in the search for information on particular subjects. This system has the advantage of providing quick access to information and a convenient means of dealing with topics that students or general readers might encounter in their daily readings. Such an arrangement tends to scatter information throughout the alphabet, but through cross-references the editors have tried to maintain the connections between entries and to lead the reader quickly to related articles, as from the biography of J.S. Woodsworth to entries on Social Gospel, Co-operative Commonwealth Federation, etc. Readers should look first among the article titles for the topic they seek, and, if there is not a separate entry, then among the 30 000 subjects listed in the Index at the end of Volume III. The cross-references within the entries themselves (marked in small capitals, eg, IRON ORE) are provided when they might lead to greater understanding of the main subject of the entry and are not always exactly in the form of the article to which they refer; for example, "Department of EXTERNAL AFFAIRS leads the reader to the article **External Affairs, Department of**, and the cross-references AGRICULTURE or NATIVE PEOPLE may lead to several entries that begin with that title.

The major subject areas have generally been broken down into several types of entries to meet the varying needs of the reader. For example, the field of architecture is dealt with in an overview, in an entry describing the profession (**Architectural Practice**), in an historical essay (**Architectural Development**) and in a series of articles on types of architecture (**Government Building** or **Religious Building**), styles, issues (**Heritage Conservation**), and specific buildings (**Massey College**); in addition, biographies of important architects (**Arthur Erickson, Douglas Cardinal**) are presented. The entries have been designed to present basic facts, explain central concepts and, space permitting, describe their subjects in greater detail. Through this organization and this variety of approaches the editors hope to have satisfied the different demands that are placed on an encyclopedia.

Alphabetical Arrangement The entries of the encyclopedia have been alphabetized using the "word-by-word system," in which headings are arranged according to the letters of the first word. Second and subsequent words are used for determining the order of the entries only when two or more headings begin with the same word. Hence, entries beginning with a short word appear before entries with the same short word forming the opening letters of a longer word; for example, **Ice Cap** appears before **Icebreakers**, and **Forteau** and **Fortification** follow **Fort Smith, Fort Steele** and **Fort Walsh**. For the sake of convenience, all the names beginning with "Mac" and "Mc" have been sorted as though they were spelled "Mac"; and those beginning with "Saint," "Sainte," "St" or "Ste" as though they were spelled "Saint." Numbers are listed as if they were spelled out; for example **4-H Clubs** is sorted as if it were "Four-H Clubs."

Personal Names In the interests of convenience it was decided to enter biographies under the name by which a person is commonly known. Thus, in the case of French compound names or titles, a biography will be found under the name a person used; for example, Louis de Baude, Comte de Frontenac, is placed under **Frontenac**; René-Robert Cavelier de La Salle, under **La Salle**. However, Guy Carleton, First Baron Dorchester, is found under **Carleton** and John Buchan, First Baron Tweedsmuir, under **Buchan**, since that is how they are best known to posterity. Writers are placed under their own name rather than their pen name, for example, Ralph Connor is listed under **Gordon, Charles William**. Indians of the historical period have been entered under their English name, for example, **Poundmaker**. Nuns are generally found under their name in religion, for example, **Marie de l'Incarnation**. Le, La, Du, Des, but generally not de, are considered part of French names and are capitalized.

Place-names Most entries on specific physical features, such as **Saguenay River** or **Helmcken Falls**, follow the style and spelling of the *Gazetteer of Canada* in inverting generic terms that precede the formal name; for example, entries on Lake Erie and Mount Logan are listed under **Erie, Lake** and **Logan, Mount**. Populated places are not inverted under their formal names, for example, the town of **Lake Louise**. The encyclopedia has also adopted the policy of the *Gazetteer of Canada* in using the form of geographic names used within each province; hence, **Trois-Rivières, La Grande Rivière** and **Montréal** are used in preference to Three Rivers, Grand River and Montreal.

Readings Lists of readings that should be easily accessible in libraries are included at the end of many entries for those readers who want to pursue a subject in greater depth. It was often not possible to include readings for short entries, but many will be found at the end of the longer overview articles. Those wishing further information on 17th-, 18th- and 19th-century biographical subjects should consult published volumes of the *Dictionary of Canadian Biography*.

Currency The primary function of an encyclopedia is to provide information that will be of enduring value. The time required to produce such a large and complex work makes it impossible to present the reader with a book as up-to-date as the daily newspaper. The contributors and editors have used the most recent and most reliable information and statistics available to them, and have drawn heavily on the results of the 1981 census. Every attempt has been made to provide consistent data for comparison; for example, population figures of cities and towns are given, whenever possible, from the same year. The results of the 1984 federal election have been incorporated and an attempt has been made in the case of biographies to include up-to-date information to the fall of 1984.

THE CANADIAN ENCYCLOPEDIA

Managing Director
Frank O. McGuire

Publisher
Mel Hurtig

Editor in Chief
James H. Marsh

SENIOR EDITORS

Sciences
Adriana Albi Davies

Social Sciences
Patricia Finlay

Biographies
Mary McDougall Maude

Humanities
James A. Ogilvy

Arts
Rosemary Shipton

EDITORIAL STAFF

Places Editor
John St. James

Translation Editor
Penny Williams

Former Arts Editor
Diana Selsor Palting

Editor-Researchers
Nancy Brown Foulds
Kim Patrick O'Leary
Gilda Sanders
Natalie Sharpe

Editor-Proofreader
David Evans

Assistant to the Editor in Chief
Micaela Gates

Research Assistants
Bill Johnston
Alan Knight
Margaret Filshie Leask
James McCormick
Evelyn R. Phillips
Mary Potrebenko
Charlotte Stevenson
Nancy Toth
Janet Wason
James Williams
Robert Winslow
Peter Wons

Illustrations Editors
Carol Woo
Debra MacGregor

Illustrations Co-ordinator
Karen Gall

Proofreaders
John Rasmussen
Peggy McCallum

Free-lance Editors
Mary P. Bentley
Robert D. Bott
Lydia Burton
Wendy Cameron
Barbara Czarnecki
Lydia Dotto
Diane Egerton
R. Gayle Fraser
Catherine Frost
M. Jean Houston
Susan Kent
Carlotta Lemieux
Martin K. McNicholl
Gordon Morash
Barbara Sutton
Jean L. Wilson
Douglas Worts
Robert Wuetherick

ADMINISTRATIVE STAFF

Project Co-ordinator
Carol Holowach

Assistant to the Managing Director
Irene Evans

Secretarial
Gail Dawson
Rose Litzenberger
Elizabeth Nay
Mary Ann Semeniuk

Word Processing
Sheila Birmingham
Avril Glen
Julie Marseu
Robyn Ross
Fay Wong

DESIGN

Book Design
David Shaw

Assembly
J. Harrison Shannon
Martha Staigys

Artists
Claire Tremblay
Danielle Baum
John Crosby
Charles Douglas
Aleta Schueler
Shirley Stacey

Endpapers
Tom McNeely

CARTOGRAPHY

Hosford Publishing

Cartographic Consultant
Rick Checkland

Cartographic Editors
Peter Whitehead
Lillian Wonders

Cartographers
Michel Lavoie
Mariko Patrie

INDEXING

Eve Gardner
Ron Gardner
Gardner Indexing Services

TRANSLATION

Charles Strong
Quality Language Services

COMPUTER/TECHNICAL

Bernard H. Cordell
Douglas Martin
Glen Miller
Bernadette Quenneville
Ron Senda

NATIONAL ADVISORY BOARD

CONSULTANTS

Fulford, Robert
Editor, Saturday Night
Toronto

Gadacz, René Robert
Dept of Anthropology
University of Alberta
Gagnon, François-Marc
Professeur d'histoire de l'art canadien
Université de Montréal
Gall, Gerald L.
Associate Professor of Law
University of Alberta
Gander, Lois
Director, Legal Resource Centre
Faculty of Extension
University of Alberta
Gendron, Pierre R. (deceased)
Consultant
Hudson, Qué
Gillott, Cedric
Professor of Biology
University of Saskatchewan
Gingras, Yves
Institut d'histoire et de sociopolitique des sciences
Université de Montréal
Goa, David J.
Curator of Folk Life
Provincial Museum of Alberta
Edmonton
Godard, Barbara Thompson
Associate Professor of English
York University
Govier, George W.
President
Govier Consulting Services Ltd
Calgary
Graham, John Finlayson
Professor of Economics
Dalhousie University
Granatstein, J.L.
Professor of History
York University
Grant, John Webster
Professor of Church History (retired)
Emmanuel College
Victoria University, Toronto
Grant, Peter S.
Partner, McCarthy & McCarthy
Barristers & Solicitors, Toronto
Gregg, Robert J.
Professor Emeritus of Linguistics
University of British Columbia
Griffiths, Anthony J.F.
Professor of Botany
University of British Columbia
Gruchy, Charles G.
Assistant Director
Collections & Research
National Museum of Natural Sciences
Ottawa

Haber, Erich
Assistant Curator of Vascular Plants
National Museum of Natural Sciences
Ottawa
Hall, Frederick A.
Associate Professor of Music
McMaster University
Hamelin, Jean
Professeur d'histoire
Université Laval
Handling, Piers
Writer, Toronto
Harker, W. John
Professor of Education
University of Victoria
Harris, Walter E.
Professor Emeritus of Chemistry
University of Alberta
Hayne, David M.
Professor of French
University of Toronto
Heron, Craig
Assistant Professor of Social Science & History
York University
Heyman, Richard D.
Professor of Sociology of Education
University of Calgary
Hiller, Harry H.
Professor & Head of Sociology
University of Calgary
Hillmer, Norman
Senior Historian
Directorate of History
Dept of National Defence, Ottawa
Hogg, Helen Sawyer
Professor Emeritus of Astronomy
University of Toronto

Jackel, David
Professor & Chairman of English
University of Alberta
Jackel, Susan
Assistant Professor of Canadian Studies
University of Alberta
Jackson, Harold
Professor of Food Microbiology
University of Alberta
Jackson, John N.
Professor of Applied Geography
Brock University
Jarrell, Richard A.
Associate Professor of Natural Science
Atkinson College, York University
Jewett, Pauline
Member of Parliament
New Westminster-Coquitlam, BC
Joffe, Anatole
Centre de recherche mathématiques appliquées
Université de Montréal
Johnstone, Rose M.
Professor & Chairman of Biochemistry
McGill University
Juteau-Lee, Danielle
Professeure agrégée de sociologie
Université de Montréal

Kalbach, Warren E.
Professor of Sociology
University of Toronto
Kallmann, Helmut
Chief, Music Division
National Library of Canada, Ottawa
Kalman, Harold D.
Consultant in the History & Conservation of Architecture
Ottawa
Kapelos, George Thomas
President, Society for the Study of Architecture in Canada
Toronto
Kealey, Gregory S.
Professor of History
Memorial University of Newfoundland
Klymasz, Robert B.
Curator, Slavic & East European Programme
Canadian Centre for Folk Culture Studies
National Museum of Man, Ottawa
Kula, Sam
Director, National Film, Television & Sound Archives
Public Archives of Canada, Ottawa
Kupsch, Walter O.
Professor of Geology
University of Saskatchewan

Lacroix, Laurier
Professeur d'histoire de l'art
Université Concordia
Laine, Mabel H.
Administrator
Encyclopedia of Music in Canada
Toronto
Lambert, James H.
Rédacteur-Historien
Dictionary of Canadian Biography
Québec
Land, R. Brian
Director
Ontario Legislative Library Research & Information Services;
Professor of Library & Information Science
University of Toronto
Larin, Gilles-Normand
Professeur d'économique
Université de Sherbrooke
LaSalle, Pierre
Energie et Ressources, Québec
Laycock, Arleigh H.
Professor of Geography;
Director, Water Resources Centre
University of Alberta
Legget, Robert F.
Consultant, Ottawa
Lemieux, Vincent
Professeur de science politique
Université Laval
Lessard, Claude
Professeur agrégé des sciences de l'éducation
Université de Montréal
Levy, Julia G.
Professor of Microbiology
University of British Columbia

Linteau, Paul-André
Professeur d'histoire
Université du Québec à Montréal
Lithwick, N.H.
Professor of Economics & Public Administration
Carleton University
Lord, Guy
Professeur titulaire de droit
Université de Montréal

McBryde, W.A.E.
Professor of Chemistry
University of Waterloo
McCardle, Bennett
Writer, Ottawa
McCue, H.A.
Director, Education Services
Cree School Board, Chisasibi, Qué
McFadyen Clark, Annette
Chief, Canadian Ethnology Service
National Museum of Man, Ottawa
McGillivray, Donald G.
National Economics Editor
Southam News, Ottawa
McKenna, Sister Mary Olga
Associate Professor of Education
Mount Saint Vincent University
Mackie, George O.
Professor of Biology
University of Victoria
McKillop, A.B.
Associate Professor of History
University of Manitoba
McLeod, Lionel E.
President, Alberta Heritage Foundation for Medical Research
Edmonton
MacMillan, Keith
Professor of Music
University of Ottawa
McMillan, Barclay
Broadcaster & writer, Ottawa
McMordie, Michael
Professor of Architecture
University of Calgary
McNicholl, Martin K.
Naturalist & ornithologist, Toronto
McNulty, Jean
Research Associate of Communication
Simon Fraser University
Mailhot, Laurent
Professeur de littérature
Université de Montréal
Major, Jean-Louis
Professeur titulaire des lettres françaises
Coordonnateur associé
Corpus d'éditions critiques
Université d'Ottawa
Mann, Kenneth H.
Director, Marine Ecology Laboratory
Government of Canada
Fisheries & Oceans
Dartmouth, NS
Martin, Gérard-B
Doyen, Faculté des sciences de l'agriculture et de l'alimentation
Université Laval
Martin, Sandra
Writer, Toronto
Melody, William H.
Professor of Communication
Simon Fraser University
Miller, Mark
Journalist, Toronto
Moir, John S.
Professor of History
University of Toronto
Morrison, Alexander
Assistant Deputy Minister
Health Protection Branch
Dept of National Health & Welfare
Ottawa
Murray, Joan
Director
The Robert McLaughlin Gallery
Oshawa, Ont

Naldrett, Anthony J.
Professor of Geology
University of Toronto
Nelles, Henry Vivian
Professor of History
York University
Nelson, Joseph S.
Professor of Zoology
University of Alberta
Nielsen, N. Ole
Professor of Veterinary Pathology
University of Saskatchewan

Nitecki, André
Professor of Library Science
University of Alberta
Nursall, J. Ralph
Professor of Zoology
University of Alberta

Officer, Jillian M.
Assistant Professor of Dance
University of Waterloo
Ogilvie, John R.
Director, School of Engineering
University of Guelph
Orpwood, Graham W.F.
Science Adviser
Science Council of Canada, Ottawa
Ostiguy, Jean-René
Conservateur chargé de recherches
Galerie nationale du Canada, Ottawa
Ouellet, Henri
Chief, Vertebrate Zoology Division;
Curator of Birds
National Museum of Natural Sciences
Ottawa
Owram, D.R.
Associate Professor of History
University of Alberta

Palmer, Howard
Associate Professor of History
University of Calgary
Panitch, Leo Victor
Professor of Political Science
York University
Parsons, John
Teacher of Newfoundland Culture
Booth Memorial Regional High School
St John's
Pawluk, Steven
Professor of Soil Science
University of Alberta
Perks, William T.
Professor of Urbanism & Planning
University of Calgary
Phillips, Ruth B.
Assistant Professor of Art History
Carleton University
Phillipson, Donald J.C.
Historian of Science, Ottawa
Pickard, George L.
Professor Emeritus of Oceanography
University of British Columbia
Plant, Richard L.
Associate Professor of Drama
Queen's University
Porter, Arthur
Professor Emeritus of Industrial Engineering
University of Toronto
Preston, Richard J.
Professor of Anthropology
McMaster University

Quarterman, C. David
President, Alexander Bay Associates
Ottawa

Rea, J.E.
Professor of History
University of Manitoba
Redmond, Gerald
Professor of Recreation & Leisure Studies
University of Alberta
Reed, F. Leslie C.
Forest Policy Consultant
Vancouver
Reid, John G.
Associate Professor of History
Mount Allison University
Reid, Robert G.B.
Associate Professor of Biology
University of Victoria
Richardson, Douglas
Associate Professor of History of Art
University of Toronto
Riley, Barbara
Curator, History Division
National Museum of Man, Ottawa
Robertson, Ian Ross
Associate Professor of History
University of Toronto
Robinson, J. Lewis
Professor of Geography
University of British Columbia
Rocher, Guy
Professeur titulaire de sociologie
Université de Montréal

Rodway, Margaret R.
Associate Professor of Social Welfare
University of Calgary
Roland, Charles G.
Professor of the History of Medicine
McMaster University
Rose, Phyllis
Graduate Student
University of Toronto
Rouillard, Jacques
Professeur d'histoire
Université de Montréal
Rousseau, Louis
Professeur de religiologie
Université du Québec à Montréal
Routledge, Marie
Research & Documentation Co-ordinator
Inuit Art Section
Indian & Northern Affairs Canada
Ottawa
Roy, Patricia E.
Associate Professor of History
University of Victoria
Ruppenthal, Karl M.
UPS Foundation Professor & Director
Centre for Transportation Studies
University of British Columbia
Rutter, Nathaniel W.
Professor & Chairman of Geology
University of Alberta

Saddlemyer, Ann
Professor of English & Drama
Victoria College & Graduate
Centre for Study of Drama
University of Toronto
Sales, Arnaud
Professeur agrégé de sociologie
Université de Montréal
Scobie, Stephen A.C.
Professor of English
University of Victoria
Scott, Anthony
Professor of Economics
University of British Columbia
Sebert, Louis M.
Canada Land Surveyor, Ottawa
Shadbolt, Doris
Curator Emeritus
Vancouver Art Gallery
North Burnaby, BC
Shaw, Robert F.
Consultant, Montreal Engineering
Company, Limited, Montréal
Shebeski, Leonard H.
Dean Emeritus
University of Manitoba
Shortt, Samuel E.D.
Associate Professor of Family Medicine;
Associate Professor of History
Queen's University
Simeon, Richard
Professor of Political Studies
Queen's University
Sinclair-Faulkner, Tom
Associate Professor of Religion
Dalhousie University
Sirois, Antoine
Professeur de littérature
Université de Sherbrooke
Slater, Peter
Professor of Theology
Toronto School of Theology;
Centre for Religious Studies
University of Toronto
Slaymaker, Olav
Professor of Geography
University of British Columbia
Smith, David C.
Professor & Principal of Economics
Queen's University
Smith, Derek G.
Associate Professor of Sociology &
Anthropology
Carleton University
Smith, Donald B.
Associate Professor of History
University of Calgary
Smith, Peter J.
Professor of Geography
University of Alberta
Stairs, Denis
Professor & Chairman of Political
Science
Dalhousie University
Stamp, Robert
Writer, Toronto
Stanbury, W.T.
Professor of Policy Analysis
University of British Columbia
Steeves, Taylor A.
Professor of Biology
University of Saskatchewan
Stelck, Charles R.
Professor Emeritus of Geology
University of Alberta
Stevenson, John T.
Associate Professor of Philosophy
University of Toronto
Stewart, Wilson N.
Professor Emeritus of Botany
University of Alberta
Strate, Grant
Professor of Dance
Simon Fraser University
Strong-Boag, Veronica
Associate Professor of History &
Women's Studies
Simon Fraser University
Studnicki-Gizbert, Konrad W.
Economic Commission for Latin America
United Nations, Santiago de Chile
Sutherland, Stuart R.J.
Toronto
Swinton, George
Adjunct Professor of Art History
Carleton University

Tartar, John
Professor of Computing Science
University of Alberta
Taylor, C.J.
Historian, National Historic Parks
& Sites Branch
Parks Canada, Ottawa
Taylor, William E., Jr
President
Social Sciences & Humanities Research
Council of Canada, Ottawa
Tepperman, Lorne
Professor of Sociology
University of Toronto
Thomas, Morley K.
Former Director General
Canadian Climate Centre
Downsview, Ont
Thompson, Dixon A.R.
Professor of Environmental Science
University of Calgary
Tupper, Allan
Associate Professor of Political
Science
University of Alberta
Tweedie, Katherine
Assistant Professor of Photography
Concordia University

Vachon, Auguste
Chief
Medal, Heraldry & Costume Section
Public Archives of Canada, Ottawa
Vallee, Frank G.
Professor of Anthropology & Sociology
Carleton University
van Zyll de Jong, Constantinus G.
Curator, Mammalogy Section
National Museum of Natural Sciences
Ottawa
Véronneau, Pierre
Historien
Cinémathèque québécoise/Musée du
cinéma, Montréal
Vézina, Claude
Directeur adjoint
Institut Armand-Frappier
Laval, Qué

Wagner, Anton
Association for Canadian Theatre
History, Toronto
Waite, P.B.
Professor of History
Dalhousie University
Weinrich, Peter H.
Executive Director
Canadian Crafts Council, Ottawa
West, J. Thomas
Curator, Canada's Sports Hall of Fame
Toronto
Whitaker, Reginald
Professor of Political Science
York University
Whyte, Donald R.
Professor of Sociology & Anthropology
Carleton University
Wilkin, Karen
Independent curator & critic, Toronto
Wilkinson, Bruce W.
Professor of Economics
University of Alberta
Williams, William M.
Birks Professor of Metallurgy
McGill University
Williamson, Mary F.
Fine Arts Bibliographer
York University
Wilson, J. Donald
Professor of History of Education
University of British Columbia
Wise, S.F.
Professor of History;
Dean of Graduate Studies & Research
Carleton University
Wolfe, Morris
Ontario College of Art, Toronto
Wolfe, Roy I.
Professor of Geography (retired)
York University
Wonders, William C.
Professor of Geography
University of Alberta
Woodcock, George
Writer, Vancouver
Wyczynski, Paul
Titulaire de recherche des
lettres françaises
Université d'Ottawa
Wyman, Max
Author and critic, Vancouver

Young, Walter D.
Professor of Political Science
University of Victoria

Zeller, Suzanne E.
PhD Student of History
University of Toronto

CONTRIBUTORS

Abbott, Caroline Louise
Writer & photographer, Montréal
Abella, Irving
Professor of History
Glendon College
York University
Abler, Thomas S.
Associate Professor of Anthropology
University of Waterloo
Abu-Laban, Baha R.
Professor of Sociology;
Associate Vice-President (Research)
University of Alberta
Acton, Donald
Agriculture Canada, Saskatoon
Adams, Peter
Professor of Geography
Watershed Ecosystems Program
Trent University
Adie, Peter A.
Former Head, Biomedical Section
Defence Research Establishment
Suffield, Alta
Ahearn, Catherine
Author & Poet Laureate of Ottawa
(1982-84), Ottawa
Aiken, David E.
Research Scientist
Dept of Fisheries & Oceans
St Andrews, NB
Albert, Jim
Associate Professor of Social Work
Carleton University
Aldrich, Frederick A.
Professor of Biology
Memorial University of Newfoundland
Allaire, Gratien
Professeur d'histoire
Faculté Saint-Jean
University of Alberta
Allard, Jacques
Professeur de littérature
Université du Québec à Montréal
Allen, A. Richard
Member of the Ontario Legislative
Assembly;
Professor of History
McMaster University
Allen, Karyn Elizabeth
Curator of Art
The Nickle Arts Museum, Calgary
Allen, Max
Curator
The Museum for Textiles, Toronto
Allen, Robert S.
Deputy Chief
Treaties & Historical Research Centre
Dept of Indian & Northern Affairs
Ottawa
Allen, Willard F.
Professor of Chemistry
University of Alberta
Alt, Marlene Michele
Writer, Banff
Amatt, John
President
One Step Beyond Adventure Group
Canmore, Alta
Anctil, Pierre
Researcher
Institut québécois de recherche sur
la culture, Montréal
Anderson, Donald W.
General Secretary
Canadian Council of Churches, Toronto
Anderson, Doris H.
President
National Action Committee on the Status
of Women, Toronto
Anderson, Duncan M.
Associate Professor of Geography
Carleton University
Anderson, Frank W.
Historian, Saskatoon
Anderson, Grace Merle
Professor of Sociology & Anthropology
Wilfrid Laurier University
Anderson, Peter S.
Research Associate of Communication
Simon Fraser University
Andreae, Christopher A.
Historica Research Limited
London, Ont

Andrès, Bernard
Professeur d'études littéraires
Université du Québec à Montréal
Andrew, Sheila
Graduate Student
University of New Brunswick
Andrews, Florence
Associate Professor of Sociology
Carleton University
Andrus, Donald F.P.
Associate Professor of Art History
Concordia University
Anisef, Paul
Associate Professor of Sociology
York University
Anstey, Thomas H.
Agrologist, Ottawa
Applebaum, Louis
Composer & conductor;
Chairman, Federal Cultural Policy
Review Committee (1980-82), Toronto
Archer, Christon I.
Professor of History
University of Calgary
Archer, David J.W
Archaeologist, Vancouver
Archibald, Clinton
Professor of Administration
University of Ottawa
Archibald, Mary
Writer
Shelburne, NS
Arima, Eugene
Ethnologist, Ottawa
Arlett, Allan
Executive Director
The Canadian Centre for Philanthropy
Toronto
Armour, Leslie
Professor of Philosophy
University of Ottawa
Armstrong, G.H.M.
President, Law Society of
Saskatchewan (1977);
President, Federation of Law
Societies of Canada (1980-81), Regina
Armstrong, Pat
Professor of Sociology & Women's
Studies
Vanier College, Montréal
Arnason, John T.
Associate Professor of Biology
University of Ottawa
Arsenault, Georges
Visiting Professor in Acadian
Studies
University of Prince Edward Island
Arseneault, Céline
Botaniste (Bibliothécaire), Jardin
botanique de la Ville de Montréal
Arthur, Eric R. (deceased)
Architect & writer, Toronto
Artibise, Alan F.J.
Director, Institute of Urban Studies
University of Winnipeg
Asch, Michael I.
Associate Professor of Anthropology
University of Alberta
Asimakopulos, Athanasios
Professor of Economics
McGill University
Asselin, Alain
Professeur de phytopathologie
Université Laval
Atchison, John
Lecturer in History
Armidale College of Advanced
Education
Armidale, NSW, Australia
Atwood, Margaret
Writer, Toronto
Aubrey, Irene E.
Chief, Children's Literature Service
National Library of Canada, Ottawa
Aun, Karl
Professor Emeritus of Political
Science
Wilfrid Laurier University
Austin-Smith, Peter J.
Non-game Biologist
Dept of Lands & Forests, Nova Scotia

Austman, Helgi H.
Agricultural consultant
Gimli, Man
Avery, Donald H.
Associate Professor of History
University of Western Ontario
Ayer, William A.
Professor of Chemistry
University of Alberta
Ayers, Hugh D.
School of Engineering
University of Guelph
Ayles, G. Burton
Director of Research
Dept of Fisheries & Oceans, Winnipeg
Ayre, John
Writer, Guelph
Aytenfisu, Maureen
Student, Edmonton

Babcock, Douglas R.
Research Officer
Historic Sites Service, Edmonton
Babcock, Robert H.
Professor of History
University of Maine
Babe, Robert E.
Associate Professor of Communication
University of Ottawa
Bachynski, Morrel P.
President, MPB Technologies Inc
Ste-Anne-de-Bellevue, Qué
Baglole, Harry
Historian, PEI
Bai, David H.
Associate Professor of Anthropology
University of Alberta
Baigent, Margaret J.
Associate Professor of Nutritional
Sciences
University of Toronto
Baird, David M.
Director
Tyrrell Museum of Palaeontology
Drumheller, Alta
Baird, Patricia A.
Professor of Medical Genetics
University of British Columbia
Baker, Allan J.
Curator-in-charge
Dept of Ornithology
Royal Ontario Museum;
Associate Professor of Zoology
University of Toronto
Baker, G. Blaine
Assistant Professor of Law
McGill University
Baker, Melvin
Researcher, House of Assembly
Province of Newfoundland
Baldwin, Douglas O.
Assistant Professor of History
University of Prince Edward Island
Baldwin, John R.
Kingston, Ont
Bale, Gordon
Professor of Law
Queen's University
Bandoni, Robert J.
Professor of Botany
University of British Columbia
Banfield, Paul A.
Queen's University
Barber, Marilyn J.
Associate Professor of History
Carleton University
Barbour, Douglas F.
Professor of English
University of Alberta
Barker, Clifford A.V.
Professor of Theriogenology (retired)
Ontario Veterinary College
Guelph, Ont
Barlow, Jon C.
Curator of Ornithology
Royal Ontario Museum;
Professor of Zoology
University of Toronto

Barman, Jean
Canadian Childhood History Project
University of British Columbia
Barnard, David T.
Associate Professor of Computing &
Information Science;
Director of Computing Services
Queen's University
Barnes, John
Associate Professor of Law
Carleton University
Barr, Elinor
Writer & researcher
Thunder Bay, Ont
Barr, John J.
Director of Public Affairs
Syncrude Canada Ltd, Edmonton
Barratt, Robert F.
Editor, Food in Canada *magazine*
Toronto
Barrett, Tony
Investment banker & environmentalist
Toronto
Barrie, H.J.
Schomberg, Ont
Barris, Ted
Writer, Edmonton
Barry, George S.
Energy, Mines & Resources Canada
Ottawa
Bartlett, Donald R.
Professor of English
Memorial University of Newfoundland
Basinger, James F.
Assistant Professor of Geology
University of Saskatchewan
Baskerville, Peter A.
Associate Professor of History
University of Victoria
Baszczynski, Marilyn J.
Dept of French
University of Western Ontario
Batten, Alan H.
Senior Research Officer
Dominion Astrophysical Observatory
Victoria
Herzberg Institute of Astrophysics
Baudouin, Jean-Louis
Professeur de droit
Université de Montréal
Baum, Carol
Canadiana Dept
Royal Ontario Museum, Toronto
Bazin, Jules
Historien d'art, Montréal
Bean, Gladys
Sports historian, Montréal
Beard, William R.
Lecturer in Film
University of Alberta
Beaton, Belinda A.
Writer, Toronto
Beaudoin-Ross, Jacqueline
Curator of Costumes & Textiles
McCord Museum
McGill University
Beaudoin, Gérald-A.
De l'Académie canadienne-française
Faculté de droit
Université d'Ottawa
Beaudoin, Réjean
Assistant Professor
University of British Columbia
Beaudry, Louise
Historienne de l'art, Montréal
Beauregard, France
Université Laval
Beaven, Brian P.N.
Visiting Assistant Professor
University of Western Ontario
Beck, J. Murray
Professor Emeritus of Political
Science
Dalhousie University
Beckman, Margaret
Chief Librarian
University of Guelph
Beckwith, John
Composer, Toronto
Bedard, Roger
Professeur d'horticulture
Université Laval

Beer, Don
Senior Lecturer in History
University of New England
Armidale, NSW, Australia
Behiels, Michael D.
Associate Professor of History
Acadia University
Béland, Madeleine
Centre d'études sur la langue, les arts et les traditions populaires (CELAT)
Université Laval
Béland, Mario
Etudiant en histoire de l'art (maîtrise)
Université Laval
Bélanger, Guy
Etudiant en histoire
Université de Montréal
Bélanger, Réal
Professeur d'histoire
Université Laval
Bélanger, René
Historien
Sillery, Qué
Bélisle, Jean
Professor of Visual Arts
Concordia University
Bell, Norman W.
Professor of Sociology
University of Toronto
Bellan, Ruben C.
Professor of Economics
University of Manitoba
Belleau, André
Professeur de littérature
Université du Québec à Montréal
Belzile, René J.
Professeur d'alimentation animale
Université Laval
Bennett, Gerry
Writer
Woodbridge, Ont
Bennett, John
Writer, Ottawa
Bensley, Edward Horton
Professor Emeritus of Medicine; Honorary Osler Librarian
McGill University
Bentley, D.M.R.
Professor of English
University of Western Ontario
Bercuson, David J.
Professor of History
University of Calgary
Bergen, John J.
Professor of Educational Administration
University of Alberta
Berger, Jeniva
President
Canadian Theatre Critics Association; Theatre journalist & editor, Toronto
Berger, Thomas R.
Professor of Law
University of British Columbia
Bergeron, Claude
Professeur d'histoire d'architecture
Université Laval
Bergerud, A.T.
Honorary Professor of Biology
University of Victoria
Berkowitz, Norbert
Professor of Fuel Science
Dept of Mineral Engineering
University of Alberta
Bernard, André
Professeur de science politique
Université du Québec à Montréal
Bernard, Frank R.
Fisheries & Oceans
Pacific Biological Station
Nanaimo, BC
Bernard, Jean-Paul
Professeur d'histoire
Université du Québec à Montréal
Bernard, Jean-Thomas
Professeur d'économique
Université Laval
Bernier, Jacques
Professeur agrégé d'histoire
Université Laval
Bernier, Marc
Directeur des relations publiques
Université de Sherbrooke
Bernier, Silvie
Sherbrooke, Qué
Bernshaw, Nicole
Ste Thérèse, Qué

Berry, Jonathan
Business Manager
Chess Federation of Canada, Ottawa
Berry, Michael J.
Director
Division of Seismology & Geomagnetism
Earth Physics Branch, Ottawa
Berry, Ralph
Professor of English
University of Ottawa
Berton, Pierre
Writer & broadcaster, Toronto
Besner, Neil
English Instructor
Mount Royal College, Calgary
Bessai, Diane E.
Professor of English
University of Alberta
Betke, Carl
Chief of Research
Historic Sites Service
Alberta Culture, Edmonton
Betz, Roger
Ontario Trappers Association
North Bay, Ont
Bewers, John Michael
Bedford Institute of Oceanography
Dartmouth, NS
Beylerian, Onnig
Montréal, Qué
Bezeau, M. Vincent
Historian, Directorate of History
Dept of National Defence, Ottawa
Bibby, Reginald W.
Associate Professor of Sociology
University of Lethbridge
Bibeau, Gilles
Professeur d'anthropologie médicale
Université de Montréal
Bickell, Ivan B.
Vice-President & Marketing Manager
Gillis Quarries Ltd, Winnipeg
Bigauskas, Julius
Energy, Mines & Resources Canada
Ottawa
Bilaniuk, Petro B.T.
Professor of Theology
University of St Michael's College; Professor of Religious Studies
University of Toronto
Bird, Carolyn J.
Associate Research Officer
National Research Council of Canada
Halifax
Bird, Michael S.
Associate Professor of Religious Studies & Fine Arts
Renison College & University of Waterloo
Bird, Richard M.
Professor of Economics
University of Toronto
Birrell, Andrew
Director
National Photography Collection
Public Archives of Canada, Ottawa
Bishop, Carol Anne
Writer, Toronto
Bishop, Charles A.
Professor of Anthropology
State University of New York
Oswego, NY
Bishop, Mary F.
Research Associate of Health Care & Epidemiology
University of British Columbia; Historian, Vancouver
Bissett-Johnson, Alastair
Professor of Law
Dalhousie University
Black, Conrad M.
Chairman
Argus Corporation Limited, Toronto
Black, Joseph Laurence
Professor of History
Carleton University; Director, Institute of Soviet Studies
Black, M. Jean
Assistant Professor
University of North Carolina
Chapel Hill, NC
Black, Naomi
Associate Professor of Political Science
York University
Blackadar, Robert G.
Director
Geological Information Division
Geological Survey of Canada, Ottawa
Blackburn, Robert H.
Librarian Emeritus
University of Toronto

Blackwell, John D.
Lecturer in History
Queen's University
Blair, Alex M.
Associate Professor of Geography
York University
Blair, Robert
Professor of Animal & Poultry Science;
Executive Director
Prairie Swine Centre
University of Saskatchewan
Blais, André
Professeur de science politique
Université de Montréal
Blakeley, Phyllis
Provincial Archivist for Nova Scotia
Public Archives of Nova Scotia
Halifax
Bleakney, J. Sherman
Professor of Biology
Acadia University
Blevis, Bertram C.
Director General
Research Policy & Planning
Dept of Communications
Communications Research Centre
Ottawa
Bliss, L.C.
Professor of Botany
University of Washington
Bliss, Michael
Historian, Toronto
Blodgett, E.D.
Professor of Comparative Literature
University of Alberta
Blodgett, Jean
Freelance curator, Ottawa
Blue, Arthur W.
Professor of Native Studies
Brandon University
Boadway, Robin W.
Professor of Economics
Queen's University
Boag, David A.
Professor of Zoology
University of Alberta
Bocking, Douglas H.
Associate Provincial Archivist
Saskatchewan Archives Board
University of Saskatchewan
Boddington, J.
By-Law Officer, Edmonton
Boddy, Trevor
Lecturer, School of Architecture
University of British Columbia
Bodner, John M.
All-Breed Judge;
Western Canada Regional Director
American Cat Fanciers Association
Winnipeg
Boer, George J.
Chief, Numerical Modelling Division
Canadian Climate Centre
Atmospheric Environment Service
Downsview, Ont
Bogart, James P.
Associate Professor of Zoology
University of Guelph
Boggs, Jean Sutherland
Chairman & Chief Executive Officer
Canada Museums Construction Corporation Inc, Ottawa
Boileau, Gilles
Département de géographie
Université de Montréal
Boivin, Aurélien
Professionel de recherche
Dictionnaire des oeuvres littéraires du Québec
Université Laval
Boivin, Bernard
Herbier, Louis-Marie
Université Laval
Boivin, Jean
Professeur de Relations Industrielles
Université Laval
Bolduc, André
Conseiller, Vice-présidence Information
Hydro-Québec, Montréal
Bolduc, Yves
Professeur de littérature québécoise
Université de Moncton
Boles, Glen W.
Waterworks Planner, City of Calgary
Bolger, Francis W.P.
Professor of History
University of Prince Edward Island

Bollinger, Kenneth E.
Professor of Electrical Engineering
University of Alberta
Bonavia, George
Journalist, Ottawa
Bondurant, Flint
BC Hydro, Vancouver
Bonenfant, Joseph
Professeur titulaire
Département d'études françaises
Université de Sherbrooke
Bonish, Gayle
Graphic Co-ordinator
Imax Systems Corporation, Toronto
Bonisteel, Roy
Broadcaster & journalist
Trenton, Ont
Boonstra, Rudy
Associate Professor of Zoology
University of Toronto
Bothwell, Robert
Professor of History
University of Toronto
Bott, Robert D.
Writer, Calgary
Bouchard, Randy & Dorothy Kennedy
British Columbia Indian Language Project, Victoria
Boucher, Michel A.
Economiste (mines et métaux)
Secteur de la politique minérale
Energie, Mines et Ressources, Canada, Ottawa
Boulet, Gilles
Président
Université du Québec
Boulet, Roger H.
Author & curator;
Director, Burnaby Art Gallery
Burnaby, BC
Bourassa, André G.
Professeur de théâtre
Université du Québec à Montréal
Bourbonnais, Nicole
Professeure de lettres françaises
Université d'Ottawa
Bourgault, Pierre L.
Vice-Rector, Administration
University of Ottawa
Bovey, Patricia E.
Director
Art Gallery of Greater Victoria
Victoria
Bowker, Wilbur Fee
Professor Emeritus of Law
University of Alberta
Bowles, Roy T.
Professor of Sociology
Trent University
Bowsfield, Hartwell
Associate Professor of History
York University
Boyanoski, Christine
Assistant Curator of Canadian Historical Art
Art Gallery of Ontario, Toronto
Boyce, Farrell M.
Research Scientist
Environment Canada
Burlington, Ont
Bradt, Oliver A.
Research Scientist (retired)
Horticulture Research Institute of Ontario
Vineland Station, Ont
Brady, William J.
Station Manager, CFPL AM & FM
London, Ont
Braiden, Chris
Inspector
Edmonton Police Dept, Edmonton
Brander, F. Gerald
President Emeritus
Tourism Industry Association of Canada, Toronto
Brassard, Guy R.
Associate Professor of Biology
Memorial University of Newfoundland
Brasser, Ted
Ethnologist
Canadian Ethnology Service
National Museum of Man, Ottawa
Bray, R. Matthew
Associate Professor of History
Laurentian University
Breen, David H.
Associate Professor of History
University of British Columbia
Bregha, François
Energy analyst, Ottawa

Brehaut, Willard
Professor of History & Philosophy of Education
Ontario Institute for Studies in Education, Toronto

Brennan, J. William
Associate Professor of History
University of Regina

Brennan, Paul W.
Senior Milling Technologist
Canadian International Grains Institute, Winnipeg

Brierley, John E.C.
Sir William Macdonald Professor; Dean, Faculty of Law
McGill University

Briggs, Jean L.
Professor of Anthropology
Memorial University of Newfoundland

Brillinger, David R.
Professor of Statistics
University of California at Berkeley

Brink, Jack
Senior Archaeologist
Archaeological Survey of Alberta
Edmonton

Brinkhurst, Ralph O.
Chief, Ocean Ecology Laboratory
Institute of Ocean Sciences
Canadian Federal Dept of Fisheries & Oceans
Sidney, BC;
Adjunct Professor
University of Victoria;
Associate, Royal Ontario Museum
Toronto

Brochu, André
Professeur de lettres
Université de Montréal

Brodo, Irwin M.
Curator of Lichens
National Museums of Canada, Ottawa

Brodribb, Somer
Dept of Sociology in Education
Ontario Institute for Studies in Education, Toronto

Brookes, Alan A.
Associate Professor of History
University of Guelph

Brookes, Ian A.
York University

Brooks, David B.
Marbek Resource Consultants Ltd
Ottawa

Broughton, Robert S.
Professor of Agricultural Engineering
McGill University

Brown, David
PhD Student of Physical Education & Sport Studies
University of Alberta

Brown, Desmond H.
Dept of History
University of Alberta

Brown, Jennifer S.H.
Associate Professor of History
University of Winnipeg

Brown, R.G.B.
Research Scientist
Canadian Wildlife Service
Dartmouth, NS

Brown, Robert Craig
Professor of History
University of Toronto

Brown, Roy I.
Professor of Educational Psychology
University of Calgary

Brown, Thomas E.
Alberta Culture
Lethbridge, Alta

Bruce, Lorne D.
Reference Librarian
Social Science Division
University of Guelph Library

Brumley, John H.
President, Ethos Consultants Ltd
Medicine Hat, Alta

Brunger, Alan G.
Associate Professor of Geography
Trent University

Brust, Reinhart A.
Professor of Entomology
University of Manitoba

Bryan, Rorke Bardon
Professor of Geography & Forestry
Scarborough Campus
University of Toronto

Bryant, Giles Bradley
Organist & Master of the Choristers
St James' Cathedral, Toronto

Brzustowski, Thomas A.
Professor of Mechanical Engineering
University of Waterloo

Buchignani, Norman
Associate Professor of Anthropology
University of Lethbridge

Buck, Ruth Matheson
Writer, Regina

Buckner, Phillip A.
Professor of History
University of New Brunswick

Budden, Geoff
Professor of History
Memorial University of Newfoundland

Buggey, Susan
Chief, Historical Research
Parks Canada, Winnipeg

Buisson, Lise
Montréal

Bumsted, J.M.
Professor of History
St John's College
University of Manitoba

Burant, James
Curator
Collections Management Section
Picture Division
Public Archives of Canada, Ottawa

Burke, Joan
Royal Ontario Museum, Toronto

Burke, Robert D.
NSERC University Fellow & Adjunct Assistant Professor
University of Victoria

Burnet, Jean
Professor of Sociology
Glendon College, York University

Burnett, David
Independent curator & writer, Toronto

Burnett, Marilyn (Schiff)
Researcher & writer, Toronto

Burnham, Dorothy K.
Research Associate, Textile Dept
Royal Ontario Museum, Toronto

Burns, Eedson Louis Millard
Adjunct Professor of International Affairs
Carleton University

Burns, Robert J.
Parks Canada, Ottawa

Burns, Robin
Associate Professor of History
Bishop's University

Burton, Ian
Director
Institute for Environmental Studies
University of Toronto

Buteux, Paul
Associate Professor of Political Studies
University of Manitoba

Butler, Frank Taylor
Assistant Professor of Physical Education
Memorial University of Newfoundland

Butler, K.J. (Jack)
Painter, Winnipeg

Butts, Edward
Writer
Mississauga, Ont

Butts, Robert E.
Professor of Philosophy
University of Western Ontario

Cadotte, Marcel
Professeur agrégé de pathologie
Université de Montréal

Callaghan, John C.
Clinical Professor of Surgery;
Director, Division of Thoracic & Cardiovascular Surgery
University of Alberta Hospital

Callahan, John W.
Associate Professor of Paediatrics & Biochemistry
Research Institute, The Hospital for Sick Children, Toronto

Camerlain, Lorraine
Cahiers de théâtre Jeu, Montréal

Cameron, Bill
Writer, Saskatoon

Cameron, Christina
Chief, Canadian Inventory of Historic Building
Parks Canada, Hull

Cameron, Elspeth
Co-ordinator, Canadian Literature & Language Programme
University of Toronto

Cameron, Wendy
Toronto, Ontario

Campbell, A. Barrie
Agriculture Canada, Research Station
Winnipeg

Campbell, Beverly
Biosystematics Research Institute
Ottawa

Campbell, Douglas F.
Associate Professor of Sociology
Erindale College
University of Toronto

Campbell, Gordon
Professor of Education
University of Lethbridge

Campbell, Ian A.
Professor of Geography
University of Alberta

Campbell, J. Milton
Biosystematics Research Institute
Ottawa

Campbell, Neil John
Director-General, Marine Sciences & Information Directorate
Dept of Fisheries & Oceans, Ottawa

Campbell, Percy I.
Chief, Water Survey of Canada
Hull, Qué

Campbell, Sandra
National Arts Centre, Ottawa

Campion, Richard
Technical Director
Canadian Weightlifting Federation
Ottawa

Cannon, William T.
Associate Professor of Business
Queen's University

Cantin, Pierre
Professeur
Collège de l'Outaouais, Hull

Caplan, Usher
Editor, Ottawa

Carasco, Emily F.
Associate Professor of Law
University of Windsor

Carbin, Clifton F.
Executive Director, Deaf Children's Society of British Columbia;
Vice-President
American Society for Deaf Children

Cardy, Patrick Robert Thomas
Associate Professor of Music
Carleton University

Carefoot, Thomas H.
Professor of Zoology
University of British Columbia

Careless, J.M.S.
Professor Emeritus
Massey College
University of Toronto

Carlisle, Jock Alan
Proprietor, Carlisle Consultants
Deep River, Ont

Caron, Laurent G.
Professeur de physique
Université de Sherbrooke

Carpenter, Carole H.
Associate Professor of Humanities
York University

Carpenter, Ken
Associate Professor of Art History
York University

Carrière, Gaston
Archiviste, Archives Deschâtelets
Ottawa

Carroll, Carman V.
Public Archives of Canada, Ottawa

Carter, Brian G.
Associate Professor of Immunology
University of Manitoba

Carter, George E.
Professor of Economics
Ryerson Polytechnical Institute & Atkinson College, York University

Carter, Margaret
Heritage research consultant, Ottawa

Cashin, Richard J.
President, Newfoundland Fishermen, Food & Allied Workers Union
St John's

Casselman, Ian
Historian, Toronto

Cavers, Paul B.
Professor of Plant Ecology
University of Western Ontario

Chabot, Richard
Professeur d'histoire
Université du Québec à Montréal

Chagnon, Roland
Professeur de sciences de la religion
Université du Québec à Montréal

Chambers, Edward J.
Professor of Economics
University of Alberta

Chambers, Francis J.
Chief Pilot PISCES IV
Institute of Ocean Sciences
Sidney, BC

Chambers, Robert D.
Professor of English Literature
Trent University

Champagne, Michel
Conservateur de l'art moderne
Musée du Québec, Québec

Chapman, James K.
Professor of History
University of New Brunswick

Chapman, John D.
Professor of Geography
University of British Columbia

Charbonneau, Louis
Professeur de mathématiques
Université du Québec à Montréal

Charlton, Murray Norman
National Water Research Institute
Aquatic Ecology Division
Burlington, Ont

Chartrand, L. Margaret
Novice historical researcher
Winnipeg

Chartrand, Luc
Journaliste, Radio-Canada
Montréal

Chartrand, René
Senior Military Advisor/Curator
Parks Canada, Ottawa

Chatterton, Brian D.E.
Professor of Geology
University of Alberta

Cheff, Michel Vincent
Galerie Nationale du Canada, Ottawa

Childers, Walter R.
Agriculture Canada (retired)
Ottawa

Chimbos, Peter D.
Associate Professor of Sociology
Brescia College
University of Western Ontario

Chisholm, Alexander J.
Director, Atmospheric Processes Research Branch
Environment Canada
Downsview, Ont

Choquette, Robert
Professeur agrégé
Université d'Ottawa

Chorniawy, Catherine
Research historian, Edmonton

Christian, Timothy J.
Associate Professor of Law
University of Alberta

Christian, William E.
Associate Professor of Political Studies
University of Guelph

Christie, Carl A.
Historian, Directorate of History
Dept of National Defence, Ottawa

Christie, Innis
Associate Dean & Professor of Law
Dalhousie University

Chubey, B. Bert
Research Scientist
Agriculture Canada
Morden, Man

Churcher, Charles Stephen
Professor of Zoology
University of Toronto;
Research Associate
Royal Ontario Museum, Toronto

Chute, Janet
Graduate Student, Doctoral Program
McMaster University

Chutter, S. Donald C.
Ottawa Bureau Chief
Revay & Associates Limited, Ottawa

Cinq-Mars, Jacques
Commission archéologique du Canada
Musée national de l'Homme, Ottawa

Clague, John J.
Geological Survey of Canada
Vancouver

Clandinin, Michael Thomas
Associate Professor of Nutritional Biochemistry
University of Toronto

Clark, A. McFadyen
Chief, Canadian Ethnology Service
National Museum of Man, Ottawa

Clark, Howard C.
Professor of Chemistry;
Vice-President Academic
University of Guelph

Clark, Lovell
Professor of History
University of Manitoba
Clark, Robert H.
Professional engineer, Ottawa
Clark, T. Alan
Professor of Physics
University of Calgary
Clark, Thomas H.
Professor Emeritus of Geological Sciences
McGill University
Clarke, R. Allyn
Bedford Institute of Oceanography
Dartmouth, NS
Clarkson, Stephen
Professor of Political Economy
University of Toronto
Clement, Wallace
Professor of Sociology
Carleton University
Clerk, Nathalie
Analyste en architecture
Parcs Canada
Hull, Qué
Clermont, Norman
Département d'anthropologie
Université de Montréal
Clermont, Yves W.
Professor of Histology
McGill University
Clifford, Howard
Consultant on Day Care
Health & Welfare Canada, Ottawa
Clippingdale, Richard
Director, Canadian Studies
Carleton University
Cloutier, Nicole
Curator of Early Canadian Art
Montréal Museum of Fine Arts
Clowes, Gigi
Writer, Vancouver
Coad, Brian W.
Associate Curator of Fishes
National Museum of Natural Sciences
Ottawa
Coakley, John P.
National Water Research Institute
Burlington, Ont
Coates, Donna
Instructor of English
Mount Royal College, Calgary
Cochran, Bente Roed
Art historian & writer
Athabasca University
Cody, William James
Curator, Vascular Plant Herbarium
Biosystematics Research Institute
Agriculture Canada, Ottawa
Cogswell, Dale R.
Government Records Archivist
Provincial Archives of New Brunswick, Fredericton
Cogswell, Fred
Professor Emeritus of English Literature
University of New Brunswick
Cohen, Stanley A.
Counsel, Human Rights Law
Dept of Justice, Ottawa
Cole, Susan G.
Writer, Toronto
Coleman, Patricia H.
Nutritional Sciences
Research Officer
University of Toronto
Collard, Elizabeth
Consultant on Ceramics
National Museum of Man, Ottawa
Collins, Malcolm M.C.
Head, Power Engineering Section
National Research Council, Ottawa
Colombo, John Robert
Writer, Toronto
Condemine, Odette
Professor of French Canadian Literature
Carleton University
Connelly, M. Patricia
Associate Professor of Sociology
Saint Mary's University
Connor, James T.H.
Historian
London, Ont
Conolly, Leonard W.
Professor of Drama
University of Guelph
Conover, Robert J.
Research Scientist
Bedford Institute of Oceanography
Dartmouth, NS

Conrad, Margaret
Associate Professor of History
Acadia University
Conron, A. Brandon
Professor Emeritus
University of Western Ontario
Conway, Brian E.
Professor of Chemistry;
Killam Research Fellow (1984)
University of Ottawa
Cooch, F. Graham
Senior Research Science Advisor
Canadian Wildlife Service, Ottawa
Cook, Eung-Do
Professor & Head of Linguistics
University of Calgary
Cook, Francis R.
Curator, Herpetology Section
National Museum of Natural Sciences
Ottawa
Cooke, O.A.
Senior Archival Officer
Directorate of History
Dept of National Defence, Ottawa
Cope, Gordon William
Professor of Geology
University of Calgary
Corbeil, Pierre
Professeur d'histoire
CEGEP de Drummondville, Qué
Corcoran, Frank
Assistant Director
Public Programming
National Museum of Man, Ottawa
Cormier, J. Clement
Founding President (1963-67);
Chancellor (1973-78)
University of Moncton
Cornell, Peter McCaul
Director, Economic Council of Canada
Ottawa
Cosentino, Frank
Professor of Physical Education & Athletics
York University
Cosper, Ronald L.
Associate Professor of Sociology
Saint Mary's University
Cotnam, Jacques
Professeur de littérature québécois
York University
Coupland, Robert T.
Professor of Plant Ecology
University of Saskatchewan
Courchene, Thomas J.
Professor of Economics
University of Western Ontario
Courtney, John C.
Professor of Political Science
University of Saskatchewan
Cove, John J.
Associate Professor of Anthropology
Carleton University
Cowan, Jeff G.
Partner, Weir & Foulds
Toronto
Coward, Harold G.
Professor of Religious Studies
University of Calgary
Cox, Bruce
Associate Professor of Anthropology
Carleton University
Cox, Diane Wilson
Professor, Research Institute
The Hospital for Sick Children;
Depts of Paediatrics, Medical Genetics & Medical Biophysics
University of Toronto
Crabb, Michael F.
Freelance writer & broadcaster
Toronto
Cragg, Laurence Harold
President & Professor Emeritus of Chemistry
Mount Allison University
Craig, Mary M.
La Fédération des Coopératives du Nouveau-Québec, Montréal
Craig, Terrence L.
Assistant Professor of English
University of Western Ontario
Crain, Ian K.
Canada Land Data Systems
Environment Canada, Ottawa
Crane, Brian A.
Barrister & Solicitor
Gowling & Henderson, Ottawa

Crane, David
Director of Corporate Affairs
Canada Development Investment Corporation, Toronto
Cranmer-Byng, John L.
Professor Emeritus of History
University of Toronto
Cranstone, Donald A.
Energy, Mines & Resources Canada
Ottawa
Craven, David L.
Associate Professor of Art History
State University of New York
College at Cortland, NY
Crawford, Roy D.
Professor of Animal & Poultry Genetics
University of Saskatchewan
Creery, Tim
Journalist, Ottawa
Crine, Philippe
Professeur de biochimie
Université de Montréal
Crookell, Harold
Professor of Business
University of Western Ontario
Cross, Michael S.
Dean of Continuing Education;
Professor of History
Dalhousie University
Crossley, Diane
Victoria, BC
Crossman, E.J.
Curator-in-Charge
Dept of Ichthyology & Herpetology
Royal Ontario Museum, Toronto
Croteau, Omer
Professeur titulaire de sciences çomptable
Ecole des hautes études commerciales
Montréal
Crowe, A. David
Head, Tree Fruits Program
Agriculture Canada
Kentville, NS
Crowe, Keith Jeffray
Senior Negotiator
Office of Native Claims
Dept of Indian & Northern Affairs
Ottawa
Cruden, David M.
Professor of Civil Engineering & of Geology
University of Alberta
Cruickshank, David A.
Professor of Law
University of Calgary
Crunican, Paul
Professor of History
University of Western Ontario
Cůješ, Rudolf P.
Professor of Sociology
St Francis Xavier University
Cumming, Carman W.
Professor of Journalism
Carleton University
Cumming, Leslie Merrill
Research Scientist
Geological Survey of Canada, Ottawa
Currie, Philip J.
Assistant Director (Curatorial)
Tyrrell Museum of Palaeontology
Drumheller, Alta
Currie, Raymond F.
Associate Professor of Sociology
University of Manitoba
Curtis, Christopher G.
Historian
Parks Canada, Ottawa
Curtis, James
Associate Professor of Sociology
University of Waterloo
Cusack, Leonard J.
History Teacher
Kinkora Regional High School, PEI
Cutler, Maurice
Director, Public Affairs
Office of the Auditor General of Canada
Cybulski, Jerome S.
Curator of Physical Anthropology
National Museum of Man, Ottawa
Czypionka, Joachim B.
Historian & writer, Edmonton

d'Agincourt, Lorraine G.
Writer, California
D'Allaire, Micheline
Professeur agrégé d'histoire
Université d'Ottawa

Dagg, Anne Innis
Freelance wildlife biologist
Waterloo, Ont
Dahl, Edward H.
National Map Collection
Public Archives of Canada, Ottawa
Dahlie, Hallvard
Professor of English
University of Calgary
Dahms, Moshie E.
Reference Librarian
Humanities Division
University of Guelph Library
Dale, Hugh Monro
Professor of Botany
University of Guelph
Dale, Ralph
Librarian, Central Region Libraries
Grand Falls, Nfld
Dales, John H.
Toronto
Daly, Eric W.
Manager Administration
Metro Toronto Region
The Canada Trust Company, Toronto
Dansereau, Pierre
Professeur d'écologie
Université du Québec à Montréal
Danys, Ruth
Freelance writer, Toronto
Darnell, Regna
Professor of Anthropology
University of Alberta
Daubeny, Hugh
Research Scientist
Agriculture Canada, Vancouver
Davenport, Paul
Associate Professor
McGill University
David, Gilbert
Ecrivain, Montréal
David, Hélène
Chercheure
Institut de recherche appliquée sur le travail, Montréal
David, Peter P.
Professeur titulaire de géologie
Université de Montréal
Davidson, William A.B.
Editor (retired)
Canadian Textile Journal, *Montréal*
Davies, Gwendolyn
Associate Professor of English;
Associate of the Centre for Canadian Studies
Mount Allison University
Davies, John A.
Professor of Geography
McMaster University
Davis, Ann
Freelance curator
London, Ont
Davis, Chuck
Writer & broadcaster, Vancouver
Davis, Richard C.
Dept of English;
Arctic Institute of North America
University of Calgary
Dawe, Michael J.
Archivist
Red Deer & District Archives
Red Deer, Alta
Day, John M.
Management Consultant, Vancouver
Day, Lawrence
Toronto
de Jong, Nicolas J.
Provincial Archivist of Prince Edward Island, Charlottetown
de Pencier, Honor
Curatorial Assistant, Canadiana Dept
Royal Ontario Museum, Toronto
Dearden, P.
Assistant Professor of Geography
University of Victoria
DeBresson, Chris
Professeur Invité, Histoire et Socio-Politique des Sciences
Université de Montréal
Decarie, Malcolm Graeme
Associate Professor of History
Concordia University
Deeg, Bart F.
Recreation Planning Consultant
Bart Deeg & Associates, Edmonton
Deeprose, Ronald K.
Director
Technical Services Division
Alberta Environment, Edmonton

DeFelice, James
Professor of Drama & writer
University of Alberta
Del Buono, Vincent M.
Chief, Police Powers Project
Dept of Justice, Ottawa
Delorme, L. Denis
National Water Research Institute
Environment Canada
Burlington, Ont
Dempsey, Hugh A.
Assistant Director (Collections)
Glenbow Museum, Calgary
Dempsey, L. James
Graduate Student
University of Calgary
den Otter, A.A.
Associate Professor of History
Memorial University of Newfoundland
Derome, Jacques F.
Associate Professor of Meteorology
McGill University
Derry, Duncan R.
Consulting geologist
Derry, Michener, Booth & Wahl
Toronto
Derry, Ramsay
Editor, Toronto
Desbarats, Peter
Dean, Graduate School of Journalism
University of Western Ontario
Deschênes, Donald
Ethnomusicologue
Moncton, NB
DesGranges, Jean-Luc
Chercheur scientifique
Service canadien de la faune
Région du Québec
Désilets, Andrée
Professeur d'histoire
Université de Sherbrooke
Desloges, Yvon
Agent de recherche
Parcs Canada, Québec
DeSorcy, Gerald L.
Energy Resources Conservation Board
Calgary
Dick, Lyle
Historian, Parks Canada
Winnipeg
Dickie, Lloyd Merlin
Research Scientist
Bedford Institute of Oceanography;
Adjunct Professor of Oceanography
Dalhousie University
Dickin McGinnis, Janice
Calgary
Dickinson, John A.
Professeur d'histoire
Université de Montréal
Dickinson, W. Trevor
Professor of Hydrology
University of Guelph
Dimić, Milan V.
Professor of Comparative Literature
University of Alberta
Dion, Gérard
Professeur de relations industrielles
Université Laval
Dionne, René
Professeur titulaire de lettres
françaises
Université d'Ottawa
Dirks, Gerald E.
Associate Professor of Politics
Brock University
Dirks, Patricia G.
Assistant Professor of History
Brock University
Diubaldo, Richard J.
Associate Professor of History;
Director, Centre for Mature Students
Concordia University
Dobbin, Murray
Writer, Saskatoon
Dobell, Rodney
Professor of Public Administration
University of Victoria
Dodd, Dianne
PhD Candidate
Carleton University
Dodman, Donald A.
Parish Priest
St Albert, Alta
Doerr, Audrey D.
Indian & Northern Affairs, Ottawa
Doiron, Allen
Archiviste
Archives provinciales du
Nouveau-Brunswick, Fredericton

Dolman, Claude Ernest
Professor Emeritus of Microbiology
University of British Columbia
Dompierre, Louise
Associate Curator
Agnes Etherington Art Centre
Kingston, Ont
Donaldson, Mairi
Victoria
Donaldson, Sue Anne
Associate Professor of Environmental
Design
University of Calgary
Donelan, Mark A.
Research Scientist
Environment Canada
Burlington, Ont
Donnelly, Margaret Mary
Barrister & Solicitor, Edmonton
Donner, John
Brampton, Ont
Donneur, André
Montréal, Qué
Doob, Penelope B.R.
Associate Professor of English
& Multidisciplinary Studies
York University
Doody, Peter K.
Barrister & Solicitor, Ottawa
Doolittle, Joyce
Professor of Drama
University of Calgary
Dorcey, Anthony H.J.
Assistant Director
Westwater Research Centre
University of British Columbia
Dorion, Gilles
Professeur titulaire des littératures
Université Laval
Dotto, Lydia
Science writer, Toronto
Doucet, Roger A.
Agronome, Ministère de l'Agriculture
des Pêcheries et de l'Alimentation du
Québec
Doucette, Leonard E.
Professor of French
Scarborough College
University of Toronto
Dougall, Charles
Dictionary of Canadian Biography
Toronto
Dougan, Jane L.
Research Assistant
University of Guelph
Douglas, W.A.B.
Director, Directorate of History
Dept of National Defence, Ottawa
Dowbiggin, William F.
Executive Sport Publications Ltd;
Publisher, Edmonton
Downey, R. Keith
Principal Research Scientist
Agriculture Canada Research Station
Saskatoon
Doyle, Arthur T.
Political historian, Fredericton
Doyle, Denzil J.
President, Doyletech Corporation
Ottawa
Doyle, Richard
Editor, the Globe and Mail
Toronto
Doyon, Pierre
Professeur d'histoire de l'art
Université de Montréal
Drache, Sharon
Writer, Ottawa
Drager, Derek C.
Writer, Edmonton
Drake, W.M.
Toronto
Draper, James A.
Dept of Adult Education
Ontario Institute for Studies in
Education, Toronto
Draper, Wayne
Environment Canada, Ottawa
Dreisziger, Nandor Fred
Associate Professor of History
Royal Military College of Canada
Drinkwater, Kenneth F.
Marine Ecology Laboratory
Bedford Institute of Oceanography
Dartmouth, NS
Driscoll, Bernadette
Associate Curator of Inuit Art
The Winnipeg Art Gallery, Winnipeg

Drolet, Jean-Paul
Mining engineer, Ottawa
Drover, Glenn
Professor of Social Work
University of British Columbia
Drummond, Ian M.
Professor of Economics
University of Toronto
Drummond, R. Norman
Associate Professor of Geography
McGill University
Dryden, Jean E.
Provincial Archives of Alberta
Edmonton
Drysdale, Patrick D.
Lexicographer
Toronto & Abingdon, England
Dubois, Jean-Marie M.
Professeur de géographie
Université de Sherbrooke
Dubro, James R.
Investigative Journalist
Norfolk Research Unit, Toronto
Ducharme, Léo
Professeur, Faculté de droit
Section de droit civil
Université d'Ottawa
Duchesne, Raymond
Professeur d'histoire des sciences
Télé-université, Université du Québec
Duchesneau, François
Professeur titulaire de philosophie
et d'histoire des sciences
Université de Montréal
Duciaume, Jean-Marcel
Professeur de littérature et
civilisation québécoise
University of Alberta
Ducrocq-Poirier, Madeleine
Docteur d'Etat es lettres
(littérature québécois)
Université de Paris - Sorbonne
Centre national de la recherche
scientifique, France
Duffy, J. Dennis
Professor of English;
Principal of Innis College
University of Toronto
Dufresne, M.R.
Ex-Medical Director (retired)
Pharmaceutical Industry
Duley, Walter W.
Professor of Physics
York University
Dulong, Gaston
Professeur titulaire de linguistique
Université Laval
Dumont, Micheline
Professeure d'histoire
Université de Sherbrooke
Dunbar, Max
Professor of Oceanography
McGill University
Duncan, Graham W.
Secretary, Canadian Billiards &
Snooker Referees' Association
Willowdale, Ontario
Duncan, Neil J.
Special Lecturer in Mining
Engineering
University of Alberta
Dunlop, Marilyn E.
Medical writer, Toronto Star
Toronto
Dunton, Davidson
Fellow, Institute of Canadian Studies
Carleton University
Duperreault, Jean R.
School of Human Kinetics
University of Ottawa
Dupont, Jean-Claude
Professeur d'ethnologie
Université Laval
Durocher, René
Professeur d'histoire
Université de Montréal
Dussault, Gabriel
Professeur agrégé de sociologie
Université Laval
Dyck, Noel
Associate Professor of Anthropology
Simon Fraser University
Dyer, Charles C.
Associate Professor of Astronomy
University of Toronto
Dykes, James
Toronto

Eagle, John A.
Associate Professor of History
University of Alberta
Eakins, Peter R.
Associate Professor of Geology
McGill University
Eaman, Ross
Assistant Professor of Journalism
Carleton University
Eastman, Harry C.
Professor of Economics
University of Toronto
Eber, Dorothy Harley
Writer, Montréal
Eccles, William John
Professor Emeritus
University of Toronto
Eddie, Christine
Chercheure en communications, Québec
Edwards, Oliver Edward
Chemistry Division
National Research Council of Canada
Ottawa
Edwards, Peggy
Fitness consultant, Ottawa
Ehrhardt, Roger B.
North-South Institute, Ottawa
Eichler, Margrit
Professor of Sociology
Ontario Institute for Studies in
Education, Toronto
Einarson, Neil
Manitoba Culture
Heritage & Recreation, Winnipeg
Elder, R. Bruce
Lightworks, Toronto
Elford, Jean
Writer, Sarnia
Elias, Peter Douglas
Prince Albert, Sask
Eliot, C.W.J.
Professor of Classics
Mount Allison University
Elliott, David R.
Historical contractor
Nanoose Bay, BC
Elliott, James A.
Research Scientist
Bedford Institute of Oceanography
Dartmouth, NS
Elson, John A.
Professor of Geological Sciences
McGill University
Emery, George
Associate Professor of History
University of Western Ontario
Emmerson, Donald W.
Consultant, Ottawa
Emmons, Douglas B.
Food Research Institute
Agriculture Canada, Ottawa
Emond, Maurice
Professeur de littérature
Université Laval
Empey, William F.
Vice President & General Manager
Data Resources of Canada, Toronto
English, John R.
Professor of History
University of Waterloo
Enkin, Murray W.
Professor of Obstetrics & Gynecology,
Clinical Epidemiology & Biostatistics
McMaster University
Enros, Philip C.
Toronto
Epp, Frank H.
Professor of History
Conrad Grebel College
University of Waterloo
Erb, Robert Bruce
Executive Vice President
Canadian Automobile Association
Ottawa
Erskine, Anthony J.
Canadian Wildlife Service
Sackville, NS
Evans, Brian L.
Professor of History
University of Alberta

Fahey, Curtis
Dictionary of Canadian Biography
Toronto
Fall, Valerie J.
Executive Director
The Catholic Women's League of
Canada, Winnipeg
Fallis, A. Murray
Professor Emeritus of Parasitology
University of Toronto

Fankboner, Peter V.
Associate Professor of Biology
Simon Fraser University
Farr, D.M.L.
Professor of History
Carleton University
Farr, Dorothy M.
Curator
Agnes Etherington Art Centre
Queen's University
Farrell, Fred
Archivist
Provincial Archives of New Brunswick
Feder, Alison
Professor of English
Memorial University of Newfoundland
Fedoroff, Sergey
Professor & Head of Anatomy
College of Medicine
University of Saskatchewan
Fee, Margery
Writer, Victoria
Fehr, Kevin O'Brien
Pharmacologist
Addiction Research Foundation
Toronto
Feindel, William
Director
Montreal Neurological Institute
Montréal
Feldman, Seth R.
Associate Professor of Film Studies
York University
Fenna, Donald
Professor of Applied Sciences in Medicine
University of Alberta
Fennell, William O.
Professor Emeritus
Emmanuel College, Toronto
Fenton, M. Brock
Professor of Biology
Carleton University
Fenton, Terry L.
Director, The Edmonton Art Gallery
Edmonton
Ferguson, Bob
Author, Who's Who in Canadian Sport*;*
Sports Writer, Ottawa Citizen, *Ottawa*
Ferguson, Howard L.
Director General
Canadian Climate Centre
Atmospheric Environment Service
Environment Canada
Downsview, Ont
Ferron, Jean
Professeur de biologie
Université du Québec à Rimouski
Fetherling, Doug
Author, Toronto
Field, George
Institute of Law Research & Reform
University of Alberta
Field, John L.
Historical consultant
Niagara Historical Society
Niagara-on-the-Lake, Ont
Field, Richard Henning
Independent curator & writer
Halifax, NS
Findlay, Leonard M.
Professor of English
University of Saskatchewan
Fink, Howard R.
Professor of English;
Director, Radio Drama Project
Concordia University
Finklestein, Maxwell
Parks Canada, Ottawa
Finlayson, Douglas A.
Graduate Studies in Geography
University of Alberta
Finn, Gérard
Historien, Ottawa
Fisher, Richard S.
Moncrieff Management Ltd, Montréal
Fisher, Robin
Professor of History
Simon Fraser University
Fisher, Stan C.
Canadian Handball Association
Sherwood Park, Alta
Fitsell, John Walter (Bill)
Historian, International Hockey Hall of Fame & Museum
Kingston, Ont
Fitzgerald, Patrick J.
Professor of Law
Carleton University
Flaherty, David H.
Privacy Project
University of Western Ontario

Flanagan, Thomas
Professor of Political Science
University of Calgary
Fleming, R.B.
Graduate Student
University of Saskatchewan
Flitton, Marilyn G.
Researcher, Vancouver
Fong, David G.
Mineral Economist
Mineral Policy Sector
Energy, Mines & Resources Canada
Ottawa
Foran, Maxwell
School Principal
Calgary Board of Education
Forbes, Ernest R.
Professor of History
University of New Brunswick
Forbes, R.E.
Industrial Commissioner
Brandon, Man
Forbes, William B.
Executive Editor
Canadian Printer & Publisher
Maclean Hunter Ltd, Toronto
Forbis, Richard G.
Professor of Archaeology
University of Calgary
Forcese, Dennis P.
Professor of Sociology & Anthropology;
Dean, Faculty of Social Sciences
Carleton University
Ford, Anne Rochon
National Field Director
DES Action: Canada, Toronto
Ford, Clifford
Executive Secretary
Canadian Musical Heritage Society
Ottawa
Ford, Derek C.
Professor of Geography
McMaster University
Ford, Gillian
Devonian Botanic Garden
University of Alberta
Ford, Susan
Ballenford Architectural Books
Toronto
Forest, Bertrand
Agricultural Consultant
Roche Associés Ltée, Québec
Forrester, Ronald W.
President
Canadian Jiu-jitsu Association
Oakville, Ont
Forrester, Warren D.
Oceanographic consultant, Ottawa
Forsey, Eugene Alfred
Retired senator, professor & trade union official, Ottawa
Forsyth, Frank R.
Horticultural consultant
Berwick, NS
Forsyth, Peter A.
Professor of Physics
University of Western Ontario
Fortin, Claire-Andrée
Études québécoises
Université du Québec à Trois-Rivières
Fortin, Gérald
Professeur, Institut national de la recherche scientifique
INRS-Urbanization, Montréal
Forward, Charles N.
Professor of Geography
University of Victoria
Forward, William F.
Research Associate
Science Council of Canada, Ottawa
Foss, Brian F.
Lecturer
Dawson College, Montréal
Foster, Franklin
Kingston, Ont
Foster, J. Bristol
Ecological consultant, Victoria
Foster, John E.
Associate Professor of History
University of Alberta
Foster, Michael K.
Iroquoian Ethnologist
Canadian Ethnology Service
National Museum of Man, Ottawa
Foulds, Glenn B.
Edmonton

Fowke, Edith M.
Professor of English
York University
Fowler, Marian
Writer
Shelburne, Ont
Fox, Paul W.
Principal, Erindale Campus
University of Toronto
Mississauga, Ont
Fox, Richard C.
Professor of Geology & Zoology
University of Alberta
Fox, Rosemary J.
Vice-President
Canadian Nature Federation;
Director, Friends of the Stikine
Smithers, BC
Francis, Daniel
Writer, Ottawa
Francis, Diane
The Toronto Star, *Toronto*
Frank, David
Associate Professor of History
University of New Brunswick
Frank, Julius F.
Animal health consultant
Manotick, Ont
Franklin, Colin Athol
Director General
Applications Program
Dept of Communications, Ottawa
Franks, C.E.S.
Associate Professor of Political Studies
Queen's University
Fransen, David
Historian, Directorate of History
Dept of National Defence, Ottawa
Franson, Robert T.
Associate Professor of Law
University of British Columbia
Frappier, Armand
Retired director & consultant
Institut Armand-Frappier
Laval-des-Rapides, Qué
Fraser, Kathleen D.J.
Doctoral Student
University of Western Ontario
Fraser, Robert Lochiel
Senior Manuscript Editor
Dictionary of Canadian Biography
Toronto
Fréchette, Pierre
Professeur d'économique
Université Laval
Fredeen, Howard Townley
Research Scientist,
Animal Breeding (retired)
Lacombe, Alta
Freedman, Benjamin
Associate for Bioethics, Westminster Institute for Ethics & Human Values
London, Ont
Freeman, Gordon Russel
Professor of Chemistry
University of Alberta
Freeman, Mac
Professor of Education
Queen's University
Freeman, Milton M.R.
Henry Marshall Tory Professor
University of Alberta
Freeman, Minnie Aodla
Writer, Edmonton
Freeman, Roger D.
Clinical Professor of Psychiatry
University of British Columbia;
Psychiatric Consultant
Western Institute for the Deaf
Freitag, Walter H.P.
Professor of the Church in Historic Witness & Biblical Interpretation
Lutheran Theological Seminary
Saskatoon
French, Carey
The Globe and Mail, *Toronto*
French, Hugh M.
Professor of Geography & Geology
University of Ottawa
Frideres, James S.
Professor of Sociology
University of Calgary
Friesen, Gerald
Associate Professor of History
University of Manitoba
Friesen, James D.
Professor of Medical Genetics
University of Toronto

Frost, Stanley Brice
Director, History of McGill Project
McGill University
Fuerstenberg, Adam G.
Professor of English
Ryerson Polytechnical Institute
Toronto
Fulford, Robert
Saturday Night *magazine, Toronto*
Fuller, Anthony (Tony) M.
Associate Professor of Rural Development
University of Guelph
Fuller, George R.
Professor of Interior Design
University of Manitoba
Fuller, William A.
Professor of Zoology
University of Alberta
Fullerton, Douglas H.
Retired Chairman
National Capital Commission;
Consultant & writer, Ottawa
Furniss, Ian F.
Economist, Ottawa
Fyfe, Richard
Environment Canada
Canadian Wildlife Service
Edmonton
Fyfe, William S.
Professor of Geology
University of Western Ontario

Gadacz, René Robert
Dept of Anthropology
University of Alberta
Gaffield, Chad
Associate Professor of History
University of Victoria
Gagan, David
Professor of History
McMaster University
Gagnon, François-Marc
Professeur d'histoire de l'art
Université de Montréal
Gaizauskas, Victor
Herzberg Institute of Astrophysics
National Research Council of Canada
Ottawa
Galarneau, Claude
Professeur d'histoire
Université Laval
Gale, Peggy
Independent curator, Toronto
Gall, Gerald L.
Professor of Law
University of Alberta
Gallacher, Daniel T.
Curator of Modern History
British Columbia Provincial Museum
Victoria
Gallagher, Paul
Principal, Capilano College
North Vancouver
Galloway, Strome
Writer, Ottawa
Ganapathy, Natarajan
Metric Commission Canada, Ottawa
Ganzevoort, Herman
Associate Professor of History
University of Calgary
Gardner, David E.
Actor, director & theatre historian
University of Toronto
Gardner, Norman
President
CPCI - Canadian Productivity Consultants Inc, Ottawa
Garrett, Christopher J.R.
Professor of Oceanography
Dalhousie University
Garrett, John F.
Institute of Ocean Sciences
Sidney, BC
Gaskell, Jane
Associate Professor of Education
University of British Columbia
Gauvin, Lise
Professeur de littérature
Université de Montréal
Gauvin, M.J.
Nonferrous Commodities Division
Minerals & Metals Strategy Branch
Energy, Mines & Resources Canada
Ottawa
Gayler, Hugh J.
Associate Professor of Geography
Brock University
Geekie, Douglas A.
Director of Communications
Canadian Medical Association, Ottawa

Geiger, John Grigsby
Journalist, Edmonton
Geist, Valerius
Professor of Environmental Science
University of Calgary
Gellner, John
Magazine editor & writer, Toronto
Gendreau, Paul
Regional Co-ordinating Psychologist
Ontario Ministry of Correctional Services, Toronto
Gendron, Ghislain
Professeur de phytologie
Université Laval
Gerrath, Joseph F.
Associate Professor of Botany
University of Guelph
Gersovitz, Julia
Architect;
Auxiliary Professor
McGill University
Gessler, Trisha
Curator
Queen Charlotte Islands Museum
Queen Charlotte City, BC
Getty, Ian A.L.
Research Director
Nakoda Institute, Stoney Tribe
Morley, Alta
Ghostkeeper, Elmer N.
President
Alberta Federation of Métis Settlement Associations, Edmonton
Giard, Jacques R.
Associate Professor of Industrial Design
Carleton University
Gibb, Sandra
Head, Exhibition Development
National Museum of Man, Ottawa
Gibbons, Kenneth M.
Assistant Professor of Political Science
University of Winnipeg
Gibson, Lee
Freelance researcher & volunteer archivist
Provincial Archives of Manitoba
Winnipeg
Gibson, William C.
Chairman, Universities Council of BC
Vancouver
Giffen, Perry James
Professor of Sociology
University of Toronto
Gignac, Elizabeth Hollingsworth
Former Head of Communications
Canadian Museums Association, Ottawa
Giguère, Richard
Professeur de littérature
Université de Sherbrooke
Gilchrist, C.W.
Former Managing Director
Roads & Transportation Association of Canada
Gillese, John Patrick
Director, Film & Literary Arts
Government of Alberta, Edmonton
Gillespie, Beryl
Iowa City, Iowa
Gillespie, Bill
Journalist, St John's
Gillett, John M.
Curator Emeritus
National Museums of Canada, Ottawa
Gillett, Margaret
Macdonald Professor of Education
McGill University
Gilliss, Geraldine
Director, Research & Information Services
Canadian Teachers' Federation, Ottawa
Gillmor, Alan
Associate Professor of Music
Carleton University
Gillott, Cedric
Professor of Biology
University of Saskatchewan
Gilson, J.C.
Professor, Agricultural Economics
University of Manitoba
Gingras, Yves
Historian of science, Montréal
Girouard, André
Dept de français
Université Laurentienne

Glendenning, Burton
Supervisor, Historical Division
Provincial Archives of New Brunswick
Fredericton
Gnarowski, Michael
Professor of English
Carleton University
Goa, David J.
Curator of Folk Life
Provincial Museum of Alberta
Edmonton
Godard, Barbara
Associate Professor of English
York University
Godby, Ensley A.
Director General
Canada Centre for Remote Sensing
Ottawa
Godfrey, W. Earl
Curator Emeritus of Ornithology
National Museum of Natural Sciences
Ottawa
Godfrey, William G.
Associate Professor & Head of History
Mount Allison University
Godwin, R. Bruce
Executive Director
Prairie Provinces Water Board, Regina
Gonick, Cy
Professor of Economics
University of Manitoba
Gonzales, Cecilia A.
Associate Professor of Clothing & Textiles
University of Manitoba
Gooch, Bryan N.S.
Pianist;
Associate Professor of English
University of Victoria
Gooding, S. James
Director, Museum Restoration Service
Bloomfield, Ont
Goodis, Jerry
Toronto
Goodman, John T.
Director, Dept of Psychology
Children's Hospital of Eastern Ontario, Ottawa;
Professor of Psychology
University of Ottawa
Gordon, Donald C., Jr.
Research Scientist
Bedford Institute of Oceanography
Dartmouth, NS
Gordon, Walter L.
Chairman
Canadian Institute for Economic Policy, Toronto
Gorham, Deborah
Associate Professor of History
Carleton University
Gorham, Harriet R.
Writer, Ottawa
Gorham, Stanley W.
Honorary Research Associate
Central New Brunswick Woodmen's Museum
Boiestown, NB
Gotlieb, Calvin Carl
Professor of Computer Science;
Faculty of Library & Information Science
University of Toronto
Gottesman, Daniel H.
Thalassa Research Associates
Victoria
Gough, Barry Morton
Professor of History
Wilfrid Laurier University
Gough, Joseph B.
Editor, Canadian Fishing Report
Ottawa
Gouin, Judy
Artist, Toronto
Gould, Allan M.
Writer, Toronto
Goulet, Henri
Research Scientist
Biosystematics Research Institute
Ottawa
Gourd, Benoît-Beaudry
Directeur de la recherche
Productions Abitibi-Témiscamingue Inc
Rouyn, Qué

Gow, James Iain
Professeur de science politique
Université de Montréal
Gowans, Alan
Professor of History in Art
University of Victoria
Graham, J. Wesley
Dean of Computing & Communications
University of Waterloo
Graham, Jane E.
Associate Editor
Dictionary of Canadian Biography
Toronto
Graham, John F.
Professor of Economics
Dalhousie University
Graham, Katherine A.
Assistant Professor of Public Administration
Carleton University
Graham, Roger
Professor Emeritus of History
Queen's University
Grainger, E.H.
Arctic Biological Station
Ste-Anne-de-Bellevue, Qué
Granatstein, J.L.
Professor of History
York University
Granger, Alix
Investment Manager
F.H. Deacon, Hodgson Inc
Vancouver, BC
Granger, Luc
Professeur titulaire de psychologie
Université de Montréal
Grant, John A.G.
Chief Economist
Wood Gundy Inc, Toronto
Grant, John Webster
Professor of Church History (retired)
Emmanuel College
Victoria University, Toronto
Grant, Peter
Writer, Victoria
Gray, Carolyn Elizabeth
McMaster University
Gray, David Robert
Associate Curator, Ethology
National Museam of Natural Sciences
Ottawa
Gray, Earle
Writer
Woodville, Ont
Gray, G. Ronald
General Manager
Technical Manpower Development
Syncrude Canada Ltd, Edmonton
Gray, James
Associate Professor of Geography
University of Montréal
Greaves, D'Arcy M.
Classical guitarist, Edmonton
Green, J. Paul
Professor of Music Education
University of Western Ontario
Green, Leslie C.
Professor of Political Science
University of Alberta
Green, Mel
Barrister, Toronto
Green, Richard
Writer
Bramalea, Ont
Greenberg, Reesa
Associate Professor of Art History
Concordia University
Greene, John P.
Teacher, St John's
Greenfield, Thomas B.
Professor
Ontario Institute for Studies in Education, Toronto
Greenhous, Brereton
Historian, Directorate of History
Dept of National Defence, Ottawa
Greenland, Cyril
Professor, School of Social Work;
Associate Professor of Psychiatry
McMaster University
Greenshields, John Edward Ross (deceased)
Director
Canada Agriculture Research Station
Saskatoon
Greer, Allan
Assistant Professor of History
University of Maine at Orono
Gregory, Patrick T.
Associate Professor of Biology
University of Victoria

Gregory, Robert W.
Professional engineer, Calgary
Grey, Julius H.
Associate Professor of Law
McGill University
Gridgeman, Norman T.
Science writer, Vancouver Island
Griezic, Foster J.K.
Associate Professor of History
Carleton University
Griffin, Herbert L.
Visiting Research Professor
Institute of Canadian Studies
Carleton University
Griffin, John D.M.
Former General Director
Canadian Mental Health Association
Toronto
Griffiths, Anthony
Professor of Botany
University of British Columbia
Griffiths, Graham C.D.
Honorary Research Associate of Entomology
University of Alberta
Griffiths, Naomi E.S.
Dean, Faculty of Arts
Carleton University
Grinstein, Sergio
Research Institute
The Hospital for Sick Children
Toronto
Grove, Jack W.
Professor of Political Studies
Queen's University
Gruber, Patrick D.
Midland, Ont
Gruen, Hans E.
Professor of Biology
University of Saskatchewan
Guest, Dennis
Associate Professor of Social Work
University of British Columbia
Guest, Hal J.
Historical resource consultant
Winnipeg
Guilmette, Armand
Professeur de lettres
Université du Québec à Trois-Rivières
Guilmette, Bernadette
Chargée de cours (lettres)
Université du Québec à Trois-Rivières
Gundy, H. Pearson
Professor Emeritus of English Language & Literature
Queen's University
Gunnars, Kristjana
Writer, Winnipeg
Gunner, S.W.
Health Protection Branch
Health & Welfare Canada, Ottawa
Gunning, Harry Emmet
Killam Professor of Chemistry (retired)
University of Alberta
Guy, Allan
Professor of Educational Administration
University of Saskatchewan
Gwyn, Julian
Professor of History
University of Ottawa
Gwyn, Richard J.
The Toronto Star
Ottawa Columnist

Haanappel, Peter P.C.
Associate Professor of Law
McGill University
Haber, Erich
Assistant Curator of Vascular Plants
National Museums of Canada, Ottawa
Hacker, Carlotta
Author of The Indomitable Lady Doctors
London, Ont
Hackler, Jim
Professor of Sociology
University of Alberta
Haddad, Yvonne Yazbeck
Associate Professor of Islamic Studies
Hartford Seminary
Hartford, Conn
Haehling von Lanzenauer, Christoph
Professor of Business Administration
University of Western Ontario
Hage, Keith D.
Professor of Geography
University of Alberta

Haliburton, G. Brenton
Public Archives of Nova Scotia
Halifax
Hall, David J.
Professor of History
University of Alberta
Hall, Frederick A.
Assistant Professor of Music
McMaster University
Hall, John W.
Agrologist, Winnipeg
Hall, Roger
Dept of History
University of Western Ontario
Hallett, Mary E.
Associate Professor of History
University of Saskatchewan
Halliday, Hugh A.
Canadian War Museum, Ottawa
Halliday, Ian
Herzberg Institute of Astrophysics
National Research Council of Canada
Ottawa
Halloran, Mary
Toronto
Hallowell, Gerald
Editor, University of Toronto Press
Toronto
Hallworth, Beryl M.
Herbarium, Dept of Biology
University of Calgary
Halpenny, Francess G.
Professor Emeritus of Library & Information Science
University of Toronto
Halpin, Marjorie M.
Associate Professor of Anthropology;
Curator of Ethnology
University of British Columbia
Hamacher, Vincent Carl
Professor of Electrical Engineering & Computer Science
University of Toronto
Hamelin, Louis-Edmond
Géographe
Université du Québec à Trois-Rivières
Hamilton, Donald G.
Director-General (retired)
Research Branch, Agriculture Canada
Ottawa
Hamilton, Sally A.
Mineral Policy Sector, Ottawa
Hamilton, William B.
Winthrop Pickard Bell Professor of Maritime Studies
Mount Allison University
Hamre, Brent M.
General Manager, Canadian Farm & Industrial Equipment Institute
Burlington, Ont
Hancock, Geoffrey
Editor-in-Chief
Canadian Fiction Magazine, *Toronto*
Handling, Piers
Writer, Toronto
Hanrahan, James
President, St Thomas More College
University of Saskatchewan
Hansen, Asbjorn T.
Senior Research Officer
National Research Council of Canada
Ottawa
Harbron, John D.
Foreign Affairs Analyst
Thomson Newspapers, Toronto
Harcourt, Peter
Professor of Film Studies
Carleton University
Hardwick, David F.
Research Associate
Biosystematics Research Institute
Ottawa
Hardy, Jean-Pierre
Historien, Musée National de l'homme
Ottawa
Hardy, René
Professeur d'histoire
Université du Québec à Trois-Rivières
Hare, F. Kenneth
Provost, Trinity College
University of Toronto
Hargittay, Clara
Art critic
Oakville, Ont
Hargreaves, J. Anthony
Professor & Director
Graduate Studies & Research;
Faculty of Dentistry
University of Alberta
Harper, Alex M.
Senior Research Scientist
Agriculture Canada Research Station
Lethbridge, Alta
Harper, J. Russell (deceased)
Writer;
Former Professor of Canadian Art History
Concordia University
Harris, Peter
Research Scientist
Agriculture Canada, Regina
Harris, R. Cole
Professor of Geography
University of British Columbia
Harris, Stephen
Historian, Directorate of History
Dept of National Defence, Ottawa
Harris, Stuart A.
Professor of Geography
University of Calgary
Harrison, Lionel G.
Professor of Chemistry
University of British Columbia
Harte, Peter J.
Privacy Project
University of Western Ontario
Harvey, David D.
Writer, Ottawa
Hatch, Fred J.
Aviation Historian
Directorate of History
Dept of National Defence, Ottawa
Haufe, Wilbert O.
Head, Animal Parasitology Section
Research Section
Lethbridge, Alta
Hauser, Jo
Physician, Health & Welfare Canada
Ottawa
Haycock, Ronald G.
Associate Professor of History
Royal Military College of Canada
Hayden, Michael
Professor of History
University of Saskatchewan
Hayes, Florence C.
Music Research Assistant
National Library of Canada, Ottawa
Hayne, David M.
Professor of French
University of Toronto
Haynes, R.H.
Professor of Biology
York University
Hayter, Carol
Fine Arts Dealer
Movements In Time Ltd, Toronto
Heald, Henry F.
Writer
Nepean, Ont
Heaver, Trevor D.
UPS Foundation Professor of Transportation
University of British Columbia
Hebda, Richard J.
Archaeology Division
British Columbia Provincial Museum
Victoria
Hébert, Gérard
Professeur titulaire
Université de Montréal
Heidenreich, Conrad E.
Professor of Geography
York University
Helleiner, Frederick M.
Professor of Geography
Trent University
Helling, Rudolph (deceased)
Professor of Sociology
University of Windsor
Helm, June
Professor of Anthropology
University of Iowa
Heming, Bruce S.
Professor of Entomology
University of Alberta
Hénault, Odile
Architecte et critique d'architecture, Montréal
Henderson, William B.
Barrister & Solicitor, Toronto
Hendry, Tom
Writer, Toronto
Hennessy, Ralph L.
Executive Director (retired)
Standards Council of Canada
Henripin, Jacques
Professeur de démographie
Université de Montréal
Henry, Michael M.
Ophthalmologist, Toronto
Henteleff, Yude M.
Barrister & Solicitor
Buchwald Asper Henteleff, Winnipeg
Herbert, Frank A.
Professor of Pulmonary Medicine
University of Alberta
Herman, Alex
Research Scientist
Bedford Institute of Oceanography
Dartmouth, NS
Heron, Craig
Assistant Professor of Social Science & History
York University
Herperger, Don J.
Saskatchewan Archives Board, Regina
Herrero, Stephen M.
Professor of Environmental Science & Biology
University of Calgary
Hessel, Ingo
Ottawa
Hewett, Phillip
Minister
Unitarian Church of Vancouver
Vancouver
Hexham, Irving
Assistant Professor of Religion
University of Manitoba
Heydenkorn, Benedykt
Vice-Director & Editor
Canadian Polish Research Institute
Toronto
Hickcox, Edward S.
Associate Professor of Educational Administration
The Ontario Institute for Studies in Education, Toronto
Hickman, Michael
Professor of Botany
University of Alberta
Higgins, Donald
Associate Professor of Political Science
Saint Mary's University
Higgs, David
Professor of History
University of Toronto
Hildebrandt, Walter
Historical Research
Parks Canada, Winnipeg
Hill, Charles Christie
Curator of Canadian Art
National Gallery of Canada
Hill, Harry M.
Director General
Prairie Farm Rehabilitation Administration
Agriculture Canada, Regina
Hill, Tom
Woodland Indian Cultural Centre
Brantford, Ont
Hiller, James K.
Associate Professor of History
Memorial University of Newfoundland
Hillmer, Anne Trowell
Dept of External Affairs, Ottawa
Hillmer, Norman
Senior Historian
Directorate of History
Dept of National Defence, Ottawa
Hindsgaul, Ole
Assistant Professor of Chemistry
University of Alberta
Hirose, Akira
Professor of Physics
University of Saskatchewan
Hlus, Carolyn
Writer, Edmonton
Hobbs, Helen
Graduate student, Vancouver
Hobbs, R. Gerald
Associate Professor of Church History
Vancouver School of Theology
Vancouver
Hodgetts, John Edwin
Professor Emeritus
University of Toronto
Hodgins, Bruce W.
Professor of History
Trent University
Hodgins, J.W. (deceased)
Professor Emeritus of Engineering
Memorial University of Newfoundland
Hoeniger, Judith F.M.
Associate Professor of Microbiology
University of Toronto
Hogan, J.J.
Ottawa
Hogg, Helen Sawyer
Professor Emeritus of Astronomy
University of Toronto
Holdsworth, Gerald
Environment Canada, Calgary
Holman, H.T.
Solicitor, Ottawa
Holmes, C. Janet
Royal Ontario Museum, Toronto
Holmes, Jeffrey
Director of Information
Social Sciences & Humanities Research Council of Canada, Ottawa
Holmes, John W.
Counsellor
Canadian Institute of International Affairs, Toronto
Holmgren, Eric J.
Historian, Edmonton
Hong, Alvin George
Executive Director
Canadian 5-Pin Bowlers Association
Ottawa
Hopwood, Peter
Ottawa
Horn, Michiel
Professor of History
Glendon College, York University
Hourston, Alan S.
Fisheries Biologist
Nanaimo, BC
Houston, C. Stuart
University of Saskatchewan
Houston, James
Author & artist
Queen Charlotte Islands, BC
Howard, Ross K.
National Reporter, The Toronto Star
Toronto
Howard, Victor M.
Professor of English
Michigan State University at East Lansing
Howell, Colin D.
Associate Professor of History
Saint Mary's University
Hudon, Raymond
Professeur de science politique
Université Laval
Hudson, Douglas R.
Instructor of Anthropology
Fraser Valley College
Abbotsford, BC
Huel, Raymond J.A.
Associate Professor of History
University of Lethbridge
Hughes, Richard David
Public Services Librarian
Cariboo College
Kamloops, BC
Hulse, Elizabeth
Thomas Fisher Rare Book Library
University of Toronto
Humber, William
Director, Continuing Education
Seneca College, Toronto
Hume, Stephen
Editor, The Edmonton Journal
Edmonton
Hummel, Monte
Executive Director
World Wildlife Fund (Canada), Toronto
Humphries, Charles W.
Associate Professor of History
University of British Columbia
Humphrys, Edward William
Consultant, Ottawa
Hunt, Geoffrey
Architectural Historian, New York
Hunt, John R.
Research Scientist
Agriculture Canada
Agassiz, BC
Hunter, Kenneth E.
President, Conestoga College of Applied Arts & Technology
Kitchener, Ont
Huston, Mervyn J.
Professor Emeritus
University of Alberta
Hutcheon, Linda
Associate Professor of English
McMaster University
Hutchinson, Gerald M.
Minister, United Church of Canada
Thorsby, Alta
Hutchinson, Roger C.
Associate Professor of Religious Studies, Victoria College
University of Toronto
Huyda, Richard J.
Public Archives of Canada, Ottawa

Hyatt, A.M.J.
Professor of History
University of Western Ontario

Indra, Doreen Marie
Dept of Anthropology
University of Lethbridge
Ingolfsrud, Elizabeth
Author & consultant, Toronto
Isaacs, Avrom
Director & art dealer
The Isaacs Gallery, Toronto
Isaacs, Colin F.W.
The Pollution Probe Foundation
Toronto

Jackel, David
Professor of English
University of Alberta
Jackel, Susan
Assistant Professor of Canadian Studies
University of Alberta
Jackman, Sydney W.
Professor of History
University of Victoria
Jackson, Bernard S.
Curator, The Memorial University Botanical Garden at Oxen Pond
Memorial University of Newfoundland
Jackson, Graham
Toronto
Jackson, Harold
Professor of Food Science
University of Alberta
Jackson, John D.
Professor of Sociology
Concordia University
Jackson, John James
Professor & Dean of Education
University of Victoria
Jackson, John N.
Professor of Applied Geography
Brock University
Jackson, Lionel E.
Research Scientist
Geological Survey of Canada
Vancouver
Jackson, Robert J.
Professor of Political Science
Carleton University
Jackson, Roger C.
Professor & Dean of Physical Education
University of Calgary
Jackson, Stephen O.
Social Studies Teacher
Booth Memorial Regional High School
St John's
Jaenen, Cornelius J.
Professor of History
University of Ottawa
James, Donna
Writer
Kingston, Ont
James, Ellen
Associate Professor of Art History
Concordia University
James, Ross D.
Associate Curator of Ornithology
Royal Ontario Museum, Toronto
Jameson, Sheilagh S.
Writer & historian
Calgary
Jamieson, Stuart M.
Professor Emeritus of Economics
University of British Columbia
Janisch, Hudson N.
Professor of Law
University of Toronto
Janssen, Christian T.L.
Professor of Business
University of Alberta
Janus, Lorraine L.
Assistant to the Senior Scientist
National Water Research Institute
Canada Centre for Inland Waters
Burlington, Ont
Jarrell, Richard A.
Associate Professor of Natural Science
Atkinson College, York University
Jean, Marguerite, s.c.i.m.
Secrétaire générale
Congrégation des Soeurs du Bon-Pasteur de Québec;
Historienne et docteur en droit canonique
Jeeves, Alan H.
Associate Professor of History
Queen's University

Jekyll, Robert
Artist, Toronto
Jenkin, Michael
Science Adviser
Science Council of Canada, Ottawa
Jensen, Phyllis Marie
Dept of Sociology
University of Toronto
Jensen, Vickie D.
Curriculum designer, Vancouver
Jenson, Jane
Associate Professor of Political Science
Carleton University
Jerry, L. Martin
Director
Tom Baker Cancer Centre & Southern Alberta Cancer Program;
Clinical Professor of Medicine
University of Calgary
Jessop, Alan M.
Energy, Mines & Resources Canada
Ottawa
Jobb, Dean
Newspaper reporter, Halifax
Jofriet, Jan C.
Professor of Engineering
University of Guelph, Ont
Johansen, Peter
Assistant Professor of Journalism
Carleton University
Johns, Timothy
Graduate Student of Biological Sciences
University of Michigan at Ann Arbor
Johns, Walter H.
Professor Emeritus & former President, University of Alberta
Johnson, J.K.
Professor of History
Carleton University
Johnson, Peter Wade
Director, Agriculture Canada Research Branch, Research Station
Delhi, Ont
Johnston, Alfred G.
Resource Analyst
Energy, Mines & Resources Canada
Ottawa
Johnston, C. Fred
Associate Professor of Education
Queen's University;
Canadian Canoe Association
Johnston, Charles M.
Professor of History
McMaster University
Johnston, Frances E.M.
President & Chief Executive Officer
The Museum of Promotional Arts
Toronto
Johnston, Hugh
Professor of History
Simon Fraser University
Johnston, Richard
Associate Professor of Political Science
University of British Columbia
Johnston, W. Stafford
RR2, Mitchell, Ont
Johnston, William
Directorate of History
Dept of National Defence, Ottawa
Jones, Brian
Curator, Paleontological Collections
University of Alberta
Jones, David Phillip
Professor of Law
University of Alberta
Jones, Elwood Hugh
Professor of History
Trent University
Jones, Gaynor G.
Faculty of Music
University of Toronto
Jones, Laura
Writer & photographer, Toronto
Jones, Richard A.
Professeur d'histoire
Université Laval
Jopling, Alan V.
Professor of Geography & Geology
University of Toronto
Jose, Colin
Writer
Hamilton, Ont

Jotham, Neal R.
Executive Director
Canadian Federation of Humane Societies, Ottawa
Jungkind, Walter
Professor of Visual Communication Design
University of Alberta

Kadulski, Richard
Past Chairman
Solar Energy Society of Canada Inc
Vancouver
Kage, Joseph
Consultant
Outremont, Qué
Kahil, A.A.
Manager of Energy Alternatives
Novacorp Engineering Services Ltd
Calgary
Kaiser, Patricia
Freelance journalist, Toronto
Kalbach, Warren E.
Professor of Sociology
University of Toronto
Kaliski, Stephan Felix
Professor of Economics
Queen's University
Kallmann, Helmut
Chief, Music Division
National Library of Canada, Ottawa
Kallweit, Karen Danelle
Faculty of Architecture
Technical University of Nova Scotia
Kalman, Harold D.
Consultant in the history & conservation of architecture, Ottawa
Kapelos, George
City Planner, Toronto
Kaplan, William Edward
Toronto
Kaprielian, Isabel
Ontario Institute for Studies in Education, Toronto
Kareda, Urjo
Artistic Director
Tarragon Theatre, Toronto
Karsten, Peter
Executive Director, Calgary Zoo, Botanical Garden & Prehistoric Park
Calgary
Kartzmark, Elinor Mary
Professor of Chemistry
University of Manitoba
Kattan, Naim
Head, Writing & Publication Section
Canada Council, Ottawa
Kaufmann, Martin L.
Head, Plant Breeding, Pathology & Forage Section
Agriculture Canada Research Station
Lacombe, Alta
Kawamura, Leslie S.
Professor & Head of Religious Studies
University of Calgary
Kealey, Gregory S.
Professor of History
Memorial University of Newfoundland
Keane, David R.
History of Medicine
McMaster University
Kearns, King S.
Executive Assistant to the President
The Winnipeg Commodity Exchange
Winnipeg
Keen, Michael J.
Director, Atlantic Geoscience Centre
Geological Survey of Canada
Dartmouth, NS
Keenlyside, David L.
Atlantic Provinces Archaeologist
National Museum of Man, Ottawa
Keillor, Elaine
Associate Professor of Music
Carleton University
Keith, W.J.
Professor of English
University of Toronto
Keizer, William Stirling
Graduate Student
Queen's University
Kelley, Frances C.
Director, Footwear Bureau of Canada
Montréal
Kelly, Louis Gerard
Professor of Linguistics
University of Ottawa
Kemp, David D.
Associate Professor of Geography
Lakehead University

Kemp, Walter H.
Professor of Music
Dalhousie University
Kendall, Kay
Director of Communications
Association of Canadian Distillers
Ottawa
Kendle, John Edward
Professor of History
University of Manitoba
Kennedy, J.E.
Professor of Physics
University of Saskatchewan
Kennedy, John L.
Assistant TV Program Director
CBC-Toronto
Kennell, Elizabeth H.
Graduate Art History Student
Concordia University
Kentfield, John A.C.
Professor of Engineering
University of Calgary
Kenyon, John P.B.
Associate Professor of History
Scarborough Campus
University of Toronto
Kenyon, Walter A.
Archaeological & historical consultant, Toronto
Kernaghan, Kenneth
Professor of Politics & Administration
Brock University
Kernaghan, Lois Kathleen
Historical researcher & editor
Boutilier's Point, NS
Kerr, Adam J.
Director
Canadian Hydrographic Service
Atlantic Region
Kerr, Gordon R.
Regional Director
Canadian Wildlife Service, Edmonton
Kerr, Robert B.
Professor Emeritus of Medicine
University of British Columbia
Kerr, Stephen R.
Research Scientist
Bedford Institute of Oceanography
Dartmouth, NS
Kestelman, Paula
Researcher, Montréal
Kesteman, Jean-Pierre
Professeur d'histoire
Université de Sherbrooke
Kesterton, Wilfred H.
Professor Emeritus of Journalism
Carleton University
Ketchen, Keith
Senior Scientist (retired)
Dept of Fisheries & Oceans
Pacific Biological Station
Nanaimo, BC
Kevan, Douglas Keith McEwan
Professor of Entomology;
Director, Lyman Entomological Museum
Macdonald College Campus
McGill University
Kevan, Peter G.
Associate Professor of Environmental Biology
University of Guelph
Kew, J.E. Michael
Associate Professor of Anthropology
University of British Columbia
Keyes, John
Historian, Québec
Kidd, Bruce
Associate Professor of Physical Education
University of Toronto
Kierans, Thomas W.
Professional Engineer & President
Atlantic Progress Ltd, St John's
Killan, Gerald
Professor of History
King's College
University of Western Ontario
Kingsmith, Ray A.
Calgary
Kirschbaum, Stanislav J.
Associate Professor of Political Science
Glendon College, York University
Kirton, John James
Associate Professor of Political Science
University of Toronto

Klaassen, Walter
Professor of History
Conrad Grebel College
University of Waterloo
Klamkin, Murray S.
Professor of Mathematics
University of Alberta
Klar, Lewis N.
Professor of Law
University of Alberta
Klinck, Harold R.
Professor of Agronomy
McGill University
Klymasz, Robert B.
Curator
Slavic & East European Programme
Canadian Centre for Folk Culture Studies
National Museum of Man, Ottawa
Knapton, Richard W.
Assistant Professor of Biological Sciences
Brock University
Knelman, Judith
Writer, Toronto
Knight, Alan R.
Dept of English
University of Alberta
Knight, David B.
Professor of Geography
Carleton University
Knowles, Robert Hugh
Professor of Plant Science
University of Alberta
Knudsen, Brian M.
Dept of Natural Resources, Winnipeg
Koennecke, Franz M.
Morriston, Ont
Koepke, Wray E.
Energy, Mines & Resources Canada
Ottawa
Koltun, Lilly
Chief, Acquisition & Research
National Photography Collection
Public Archives Canada, Ottawa
Koroscil, Paul M.
Associate Professor of Geography
Simon Fraser University
Koslow, J. Anthony
Assistant Professor of Oceanography
Dalhousie University
Kostash, Myrna Anne
Writer, Alberta
Krajina, Vladimir J.
Professor Emeritus & Honorary
University of British Columbia
Kranck, Kate
Research Scientist
Dept of Fisheries & Oceans
Bedford Institute of Oceanography
Dartmouth, NS
Krasnick, Cheryl
Doctoral Candidate of History
Queen's University
Krats, Peter V.
PhD Candidate
University of Western Ontario
Krebs, Charles J.
Professor of Zoology
University of British Columbia
Krenz, F. Henry
Director, Abrico Energy Management Services Ltd
Lakefield, Ont
Kristof, Andrea
Architect, Toronto
Krossel, Martin
Toronto
Kulisek, Larry L.
Associate Professor of History
University of Windsor
Kupsch, Walter O.
Professor of Geology
University of Saskatchewan
Kushner, Eva M.
Professor of French & Comparative Literature
McGill University;
Vice-President
Social Sciences & Humanities Research Council of Canada, Ottawa
Kuyt, Ernie
Wildlife Biologist
Canadian Wildlife Service, Edmonton
Kwavnick, David
Carleton University
Kyer, C. Ian
Lawyer
Fasken & Calvin, Toronto

Labelle, Micheline
Professeur de sociologie
Université du Québec à Montréal
Laberge, Danielle
Professeur de sociologie
Université du Québec à Montréal
Lacombe, Michèle
Assistant Professor of English
Mount Allison University
Lacoursière, Estelle
Professeur de biologie
Université du Québec à Trois-Rivières
Lacroix, Laurier
Professeur d'histoire de l'art
Université Concordia
Laferrière, Michel
Associate Professor of Education
McGill University
Lafrance, Guy
Professeur de philosophie
Université d'Ottawa
Laidlaw, William G.
Professor of Chemistry
University of Calgary
Laine, Mabel H.
Administrator
Encyclopedia of Music in Canada
Toronto
Laing, Gertrude M.
Ex-Commissioner
Royal Commission on Bilingualism & Biculturalism
Lajeunesse, Claude
Director of Targeted & University-Industry Programs
Natural Sciences and Engineering Research Council of Canada, Ottawa
Laliberté, G-Raymond
Professeur de sciences politiques
Université Laval
Lalonde, André
Professor of History
University of Regina
Lamb, W. Kaye
Former Dominion Archivist
Public Archives of Canada
Lambert, Geoffrey
Associate Professor of Political Studies
University of Manitoba
Lambert, James H.
Rédacteur-Historien
Dictionnaire biographique du Canada
Québec
Lammers, George E.
Curator of Paleontology
Manitoba Museum of Man & Nature;
Associate Professor of Museology
University of Winnipeg
Lamonde, Yvan
Professeur d'histoire
McGill University
Lancaster, Peter
Professor of Mathematics
University of Calgary
Land, R. Brian
Director, Legislative Library
Research & Information Services
Toronto
Professor of Library & Information Science
University of Toronto
Landreville, Pierre
Professeur titulaire de criminologie
Université de Montréal
Lane, E. David
Aquaculture & Fisheries
Malaspina College
Nanaimo, BC
Lane, Robert B.
Lane & Lane Ltd
Consultant, Vancouver
Langlands, Robert P.
Professor of Mathematics
The Institute for Advanced Study
Princeton University
Lapins, Karlis O.
Agriculture Canada, Research Station
Summerland, BC
Lapointe, Pierre Louis
Historian
Hull, Qué
Laquian, Eleanor R.
Researcher & writer, Ottawa
Larkin, Peter Anthony
Professor of Zoology
University of British Columbia
Larmour, Jean B.D.
Historical researcher, Regina
LaRocque, Emma D.
Lecturer of Native Studies
University of Manitoba

Larose, Serge
Centre de recherches Caraibes
Université de Montréal
Larouche, Jeannette
Historienne
Chicoutimi, Qué
Larter, Edward N.
Professor of Plant Science
University of Manitoba
LaSalle, Pierre
Energie et Resources, Québec
Latouche, Daniel
Professeur agrégé de science politique
Université McGill
Launay, Viviane F.
Executive Director
Canadian Federation for the Humanities, Ottawa
Laurence, Gérard
Professeur d'histoire des communications de masse
Université Laval
Laurence, Karen
Free-lance writer, Toronto
Laurendeau, Marc
Political columnist, La Presse;
Broadcaster on radio & television
Montréal
Lauzon, Michael
Editor, Corpus Chemical Report
Toronto
Lavallée, Omer
Corporate historian & archivist
Canadian Pacific Limited, Montréal
Laverty, Kathleen
The Hett Gallery Ltd, Edmonton
Lavery, Kenneth R.
President
Brewers Association of Canada, Ottawa
Lavigne, Marie
Historienne
Aylmer, Qué
Lavigueur, Patricia Johnston
Consultant, Canadian Federation of Independent Business (CFIB), Montréal
Lavkulich, Leslie M.
Professor of Soil Science
University of British Columbia
Lavoie, Pierre
Théâtrothèque
Université de Montréal
Law-West, Don G.
Minerals & Metals Strategy Branch
Mineral Policy Sector
Energy, Mines & Resources Canada
Ottawa
Law, Charles
General Manager
CHEM info Services Inc
Laxer, Jim
Associate Professor of Political Science
Atkinson College, York University
Laycock, Arleigh H.
Professor of Geography;
Director, Water Resources Centre
University of Alberta
Laycock, David H.
Assistant Professor of Political Science
University of Saskatchewan
Layne, Richard E.C.
Research Scientist
Tree Fruit Breeding
Agriculture Canada
Harrow Research Station, Ont
Lazerson, Marvin
Professor of Education
University of British Columbia
Le Roy, Donald J.
Ottawa
LeBlanc, Hugues
Agronome
l'Assumption, Qué
Leblond, C.P.
Professor of Anatomy
McGill University
LeBlond, Paul H.
Professor of Oceanography
University of British Columbia
LeBlond, Sylvio
Professor Emeritus of Clinical Medicine & History of Medicine
Laval University
Lechasseur, Antonio
Historien, Institut québécois de recherche sur la culture
Rimouski, Qué

Lecraw, Donald J.
Professor of Economics
School of Business Administration
University of Western Ontario
Ledoux, Johanne
Montréal
Leduc-Park, Renée
Professeure de littérature
Queen's University
LeDuc, Lawrence
Professor of Political Science
University of Windsor
Lee, David
Historian
Parks Canada, Hull
Lee, John Alan
Associate Professor of Sociology
University of Toronto
Leech, Robin
Research Biologist, Edmonton
Leefe, John G.
Minister of Fisheries, Nova Scotia
Legendre, Camille
Professeur de sociologie
Université de Montréal
Legge, Russel D.
Associate Professor in Religious Studies
University of Waterloo
Legget, Robert F.
Consultant, Ottawa
Leiper, Jean M.
Professor of Physical Education
University of Calgary
Lemaire, Michel
Professeur de littérature
Université d'Ottawa
Lemay, J-P
Professeur de zootechnie
Université Laval
Lemieux, Pierre H.
Professeur de littérature
Université d'Ottawa
Lemieux, Raymond U.
University Professor
University of Alberta
Lemieux, Vincent
Professeur de science politique
Université Laval
Lemire, Guy
Professeur de criminologie
Université de Montréal
Lemire, Maurice
Professeur de littérature québécoise
Université Laval
Lemire, Robert
Centre Canadien d'Architecture
Montréal
Lemon, Robert E.
Professor of Biology
McGill University
Lenarcic, Dorothy A.
Communications Co-ordinator
Canadian Jewellers Association
Lennards, Jos L.
Associate Professor of Sociology & Education
Glendon College, York University
Lepage, Yvan G.
Professeur de littérature française
Université d'Ottawa
LeRoy, Rodney L.
Technical Director, Electrolyser Inc
Etobicoke, Ont
Leslie, Peter M.
Director, Institute of Intergovernmental Relations
Queen's University
Lessard, Claude
Professeur agrégé et vice-doyen aux études des sciences de l'education
Université de Montréal
Letheren, Carol Anne
Partner, Mathieu, Williams Letheren
Toronto
Levere, Trevor H.
Professor of History of Science
University of Toronto
Levin, Malcolm
Associate Professor of Education
Ontario Institute for Studies in Education, Toronto

Levine, Allan E.
Librarian & historian, Ottawa
Levine, Gilbert
Research Director
Canadian Union of Public Employees
Ottawa
Levitt, Joseph
Professor of History
University of Ottawa
Lewis, Brian S.
British Columbia Sports Hall of Fame & Museum, Vancouver
Lewis, John B.
Director, Institute of Oceanography
McGill University
Lewis, Joyce C.
Administrative Assistant
The Ontario Historical Society
Toronto
Lewis, Laurie
Design Dept
University of Toronto Press
Leyton, Elliott H.
Professor of Applied Anthropology
Memorial University
Lightbody, James W.
Associate Professor of Political Science
University of Alberta
Lightstone, Jack N.
Associate Professor of Religion
Concordia University
Lindberg, Gary M.
Director
National Aeronautical Establishment
National Research Council of Canada
Ottawa
Lindquist, Evert E.
Senior Research Scientist
Biosystematics Research Institute
Agriculture Canada, Ottawa
Lindsay, Peter L.
Professor of Physical Education & Sport Studies
University of Alberta
Lindsey, Joseph D.
Toronto
Linteau, Paul-André
Professeur d'histoire
Université du Québec à Montréal
Lipkin, Mary-Jane
Communications Officer
Canadian Advisory Council on the Status of Women, Ottawa
Lister, Marilyn
Ottawa
Lister, Rota Herzberg
Associate Professor of English
University of Waterloo
Lit, John
Professor & Chairman of Physics
Wilfrid Laurier University
Litman, Moe M.
Associate Professor of Law
University of Alberta
Livingstone, Donna
Glenbow Museum, Calgary
Lochhead, Douglas G.
Director of Canadian Studies
Mount Allison University
Lochnan, Carl J.
Consultant & writer, Ottawa
Lock, Anthony R.
Canadian Wildlife Service
Bedford Institute of Oceanography
Dartmouth, NS
Locke, Jack L.
Herzberg Institute of Astrophysics
National Research Council of Canada
Ottawa
Loken, Gulbrand
Associate Professor of Educational Administration
University of Calgary
Loney, D. Edwards
Professor Emeritus
Queen's University
Lord, Kathleen
Secondary Teacher, Wemindji
James Bay, Qué
Lorimer, James
Publisher
James Lorimer & Company Ltd, Toronto
Lortie, Marcel
Professeur de foresterie
Université Laval

Loughton, Arthur
Director
Horticultural Experiment Station
Ontario Ministry of Agriculture & Food
Simcoe, Ont
Lovick, Laurence Dale
Instructor of English & Canadian Studies
Malaspina College
Nanaimo, BC
Lowes, Raymond Nicholson
Honorary President
Bruce Trail Association
Hamilton, Ont
Lown, Peter J.M.
Professor of Law
University of Alberta
Lowry, W. Mark
Executive Director
Canadian Amateur Diving Association
Ottawa
Lozowski, Edward P.
Professor of Meteorology
University of Alberta
Lumsden, D. Paul
Master of Norman Bethune College
York University
Lumsden, Harry G.
Research Scientist, Ontario Ministry of Natural Resources
Maple, Ont
Lumsden, Ian Gordon
Director, Beaverbrook Art Gallery
Fredericton
Lund, John
Professor of Metallurgical Engineering
University of British Columbia
Lupul, Manoly R.
Professor of Canadian Educational History
University of Alberta
Lussier, Réal
Historien de l'art, Montréal
Lynch, Gerald
University of Western Ontario
Lyon, Deborah Maryth
Writer, Winnipeg

McAfee, R. Ann
Housing Planner, City of Vancouver
Vancouver
Macadam, William I.
Executive Producer
Norfolk Research Unit
Norfolk Productions Ltd, Toronto
McAllister, Don E.
Curator, Ichthyology Section
National Museum of Natural Sciences
Ottawa
McAndrew, William J.
Historian, Directorate of History
Dept of National Defence, Ottawa
Macartney, J. Malcolm
University of Victoria
Macartney-Filgate, Terence
Film & television producer, Toronto
McBean, D.S.
Cerealist, Research Station
Agriculture Canada
Swift Current, Sask
McBryde, W.A.E.
Professor of Chemistry
University of Waterloo
McCall, Christina
Writer, Toronto
McCalla, Douglas
Professor of History
Trent University
MacCallum, Hugh
Professor of English
University of Toronto
MacCallum, Ian
Dept of Geography
Memorial University of Newfoundland
McCallum, Margaret Elizabeth
University of Toronto
McCann, Lawrence D.
Associate Professor of Geography
Mount Allison University
McCann, S.B.
Professor of Geography
McMaster University
McCardle, Bennett
Archivist
Public Archives of Canada, Ottawa
McCart, Peter J.
Aquatic Environments Limited, Calgary

McCarthy, Michael J.
Social Studies & Language Arts Co-ordinator
Roman Catholic School Board
Ferryland District, Nfld
McClellan, Catharine
Professor Emeritus
University of Wisconsin
McConnell, W.H.
Professor of Law
University of Saskatchewan
McCormack, A. Ross
Vice-President (Academic)
University of Winnipeg
McCracken, Jane
Alberta Culture
Historic Sites Service, Edmonton
McCue, H.A.
Director, Education Services
Cree School Board
Chisasibi, Qué
McCulloch, James A.W.
Director General
Central Services Directorate
Atmospheric Environment Service
McCullough, A.B.
Parks Canada, Hull
Macdonald, Cathy
Sport historian, Edmonton
MacDonald, G. Edward
Sessional lecturer
University of Prince Edward Island
MacDonald, Heather
Historical researcher, Halifax
MacDonald, Les
Social Sciences & Humanities Research Council of Canada, Ottawa
MacDonald, Martha
Associate Professor of Economics
Saint Mary's University
McDonald, Michael
Associate Professor of Philosophy
University of Waterloo
Macdonald, R.H.
Author & journalist
Saskatoon
Macdonald, Roderick A.
Professor of Law
McGill University
MacDonald, Stewart D.
Curator, Vertebrate Ethology
National Museum of Natural Sciences
Ottawa
Macdonald, Valerie Isabel
Western Regional Coordinator
National Association of Underwater Instructors, Vancouver
McDougall, Allan K.
Associate Professor of Political Science
University of Western Ontario
McDougall, Anne
Writer, Ottawa
MacDougall, April J.
The Rubber Association of Canada
Mississauga, Ont
MacDougall, Heather
Assistant Professor of History
University of Toronto
McDougall, John N.
Professor of Political Science
University of Western Ontario
McDougall, Robert L.
Professor Emeritus of English
Carleton University
McDowall, Duncan
Senior Research Associate
The Conference Board of Canada
Ottawa
MacDowell, Laurel Sefton
Assistant Professor of History
University of Toronto
Mace, Thomas F.
Homemaker, Victoria
MacEwan, Grant
Writer, Calgary
McEwen, Alec C.
Commissioner
International Boundary Commission
Ottawa
McEwen, Freeman L.
Dean, Ontario Agricultural College
University of Guelph
McFadden, K.D.
Professor of Anatomy
University of Alberta
McFall, Jean
York Pioneer & Historical Society
Toronto

McFarlane, Pat
Pollution Probe Ottawa-Carleton
Ottawa
McFeat, Tom
Professor of Anthropology
Scarborough Campus
University of Toronto
McGahan, Elizabeth W.
Assistant Professor of History
University of New Brunswick
McGee, Harold Franklin, Jr.
Professor of Anthropology
Saint Mary's University
McGee, Timothy J.
Associate Professor of Music
University of Toronto
McGhee, Robert
National Museum of Man, Ottawa
McGill, William B.
Professor of Soil Science
University of Alberta
McGillivray, Donald G.
National Economics Editor
Southam News, Ottawa
MacGillivray, Royce
Associate Professor of History
University of Waterloo
McGinn, Roderick Alan
Assistant Professor of Geography
Brandon University
MacGregor, James G.
Writer, Edmonton
McGregor, Pauline
Southern Alberta Curling Association
Calgary
McGuinness, Eric
Environment Canada
Canada Centre for Inland Waters
Burlington, Ont
MacInnis, J.B.
Undersea Research Limited
Toronto
McIntosh, Dave
Departmental Historian
National Revenue, Customs & Excise
Ottawa
McIntyre, W. John
Teaching Master
Seneca College of Applied Arts & Technology, Toronto
McKay, Alexander G.
Professor of Classics
McMaster University
McKay, Gordon A.
Environment Canada
Atmospheric Environment Service
Downsview, Ont
McKeague, J. Alex
Soil Scientist
Agriculture Canada, Ottawa
McKee, Jon
Artist, Toronto
McKendry, Ruth
Writer
Elginburg, Ont
McKenna, Barbara A.
Instructor in History
University of Western Ontario
McKenna, Brian
Writer-producer
Montréal
MacKenzie, David C.
Toronto
Mackenzie, Hector M.
(Post-Doctoral) Research Fellow in History
University of Toronto
MacKenzie, Robert C.
MacKenzie Environmental Consultants
Edmonton
MacKenzie, Ross G.
Associate Professor of Anatomy (retired)
University of Toronto
McKenzie, Ruth
Writer, Ottawa
MacKenzie, William C.
Consultant, Ottawa
Mackey, William Francis
CIRB Research Professor
Laval University
Mackie, George O.
Professor of Biology
University of Victoria
McKillop, A.B.
Jackman History Project
Victoria University, Toronto
Mackinnon, C.S.
Associate Professor of History
University of Alberta

MacKinnon, Frank
Professor of Political Science
University of Calgary
MacKinnon, William R.
Archivist
Provincial Archives of New Brunswick
MacLachlan, Bruce B.
Associate Professor of Anthropology
Southern Illinois University at Carbondale
McLachlan, J.
Senior Research Officer
National Research Council, Halifax
McLaren, Angus
Professor of History
University of Victoria
McLaren, Ian A.
Professor of Biology
Dalhousie University
MacLaren, Roy
Former Minister of State
Dept of Finance Canada, Ottawa
McLaughlin, Kenneth
Associate Professor of History
University of Waterloo
McLay, Catherine M.
Associate Professor of English
University of Calgary
MacLean, Raymond A.
Professor of History
St Francis Xavier University
McLellan, A. Anne
Associate Professor of Law
University of Alberta
McLeod, Cam
Writer, Toronto
MacLeod, Kenneth Ogilvie
National Advertising Manager
Henry Birks & Sons, Montréal
MacLeod, Malcolm
Associate Professor of History
Memorial University of Newfoundland
Macleod, Roderick C.
Professor of History
University of Alberta
McLuhan, Elizabeth
Curator, National Exhibition Centre &
Centre for Indian Art
Thunder Bay, Ont
McMaster, Gerald R.
Curator, Contemporary Indian Art
National Museum of Man, Ottawa
McMillan, Barclay
Broadcaster & writer, Ottawa
MacMillan, Carrie
Associate Professor of English
Mount Allison University
McMillan, Donald Burley
Professor of Zoology
University of Western Ontario
MacMillan, Keith
Professor of Music
University of Ottawa
McMordie, Michael
Professor of Architecture
University of Calgary
McMullen, Lorraine
Professor of English Literature
University of Ottawa
McMullin, Stanley E.
Associate Professor of Canadian Studies
University of Waterloo
McMurray, William C.
Professor & Chairman of Biochemistry
University of Western Ontario
McNabb, Debra A.
MA Graduate Student of Geography
University of British Columbia
McNamara, Anne
Writer, Calgary
McNaught, Kenneth
Professor of History
University of Toronto
McNicholl, Martin K.
General Manager
Long Point Bird Observatory
Port Rowan, Ont
McNulty, Jean
Mass Communications Programme
York University
Macpherson, Andrew H.
Regional Director-General
Environment Canada, Edmonton
McPherson, Hugo A.
Grierson Professor of Communications
Dept of English
McGill University
MacPherson, Ian
Professor of History
University of Victoria

Macpherson, Kay
Past President, Voice of Women
Canada, Toronto
Macqueen, Roger W.
Professor of Earth Sciences
University of Waterloo
MacRae, Donald A.
Professor of Astronomy
David Dunlap Observatory
University of Toronto
McRae, Sandra F.
Institute for the History &
Philosophy of Science & Technology
University of Toronto
Mc Shane, King G.
Adjunct Professor of Law
Carleton University
McTaggart Cowan, Ian
Chancellor
University of Victoria
McVetty, Peter B.E.
Assistant Professor of Plant Breeding
& Genetics
University of Manitoba
McWhinney, Ian
Professor of Family Medicine
University of Western Ontario
Magnin, Anthony A.
Assistant Director-Research Project
Management
Connaught Research Institute
Willowdale, Ont
Magnusson, Warren
Assistant Professor of Political
Science
University of Victoria
Mailhiot, Gilles-D.
Président, Collège dominicain de
philosophie et de théologie
Ottawa
Mailhot, Laurent
Professeur de littérature
Université de Montréal
Mailhot, Pierre
Institut d'aménagement
Université de Sherbrooke
Maini, J.S.
Director General, Policy Directorate
Corporate Planning Group
Environment Canada, Ottawa
Maisonneuve, Lise
Université de Montréal
Major, Jean-Louis
Professeur titulaire des lettres
françaises
Université d'Ottawa
Major, Robert
Département des lettres françaises
Université d'Ottawa
Malkin, Peter
Art historian, Vancouver
Malloch, David
Professor of Botany
University of Toronto
Mann, Cedric R.
Director-General
Institute of Ocean Sciences
Dept of Fisheries & Oceans
Sidney, BC
Mann, Kenneth H.
Dept of Fisheries & Oceans
Bedford Institute of Oceanography
Dartmouth, NS
Mann, Martha
Designer (ADC), Toronto
Marchand, J.R.
Ministry of State for Science &
Technology, Ottawa
Mardiros, Anthony
Professor Emeritus of Philosophy
University of Alberta
Margolis, Leo
Research Scientist
Pacific Biological Station
Dept of Fisheries & Oceans
Nanaimo, BC
Markham, Philip de Lacey
Professional engineer, Ottawa
Markham, W.E.
Ice Branch, Atmospheric Environment
Service
Downsview, Ont
Marsh, John S.
Associate Professor of Geography;
Chairman, Environmental & Resource
Studies Program
Trent University
Marshall, J. Stewart
Professor Emeritus of Physics &
Meteorology
McGill University

Marshall, Victor W.
Associate Professor of Behavioural
Science
University of Toronto
Martin, Douglas
General Secretary
Baha'i Community of Canada, Toronto
Martin, Jean-Claude
President
Canadian Hospital Association
Ottawa
Martin, John E.H.
Manager, Canadian National Collection
(Zoology)
Biosystematics Research Institute
Research Branch, Agriculture Canada
Ottawa
Martin, Sandra
Writer, Toronto
Martineau, André
Chief, Public Relations
Public Archives of Canada, Ottawa
Maskow, May
Consultant, Toronto
Maslove, Allan M.
Director, School of Public
Administration
Carleton University
Masters, Donald C.
Professor Emeritus
University of Guelph
Matheson, John Ross
Judge
Perth, Ont
Matheson, William A.
Associate Professor of Politics
Brock University
Mathews, Robin
Professor of English
Carleton University
Mathewson, William G.
Associate Professor of Animal Science
Nova Scotia Agricultural College
Mathien, Thomas
Transitional Year Programme
University of Toronto
Mathieson, J.R. (John)
Regional Director, Pacific Region
Atmospheric Environment Service
Vancouver
Mathieu, Jacques
Professeur d'histoire
Université Laval
Matthews, Keith
Professor of History;
Chairman, Maritime History Group
Memorial University of Newfoundland
Matthiasson, John S.
Associate Professor of Anthropology
University of Manitoba
Mattison, David
Archivist, Provincial Archives of
British Columbia
Victoria
Maule, Christopher J.
Professor of Economics &
International Affairs
Carleton University
Maurer, Alfred R.
Research Scientist
Vegetable Physiology
Agassiz Research Station, BC
Maybank, John
Principal Research Scientist
Saskatchewan Research Council
Saskatoon
Maycock, Paul F.
Professor of Botany
Erindale College
University of Toronto
Maze, Jack
Professor of Botany
University of British Columbia
Mealing, Stanley R.
Professor of History
Carleton University
Medjuck, Sheva
Associate Professor of Sociology
Mount Saint Vincent University
Medovy, Harry
Professor Emeritus of Pediatrics
University of Manitoba
Meen, Sharon P.
Social historian, Vancouver
Melançon, Benoît
Université de Montréal
Melody, William H.
Professor of Communication
Simon Fraser University
Melvin, James R.
Dept of Economics
University of Western Ontario

Merilees, Philip E.
Canadian Climate Centre
Environment Canada, Toronto
Messenger, Ann
Associate Professor of English
Simon Fraser University
Metcalf, George
Associate Professor of History
University of Western Ontario
Metcalfe, David R.
Agriculture Canada, Research Station
Winnipeg
Mežaks, Jānis (John)
Archivist, Archives of Ontario
Toronto
Michael, T.H. Glynn
Executive Director
The Chemical Institute of Canada
Ottawa
Michon, Jacques
Professeur agrégé d'études françaises
Université de Sherbrooke
Middlebro', Tom
Associate Professor of English Literature
Carleton University
Millar, James Francis Verchere
Professor of Archaeology
University of Saskatchewan
Miller, Carman
Associate Professor of History
McGill University
Miller, Elizabeth
Associate Professor of English
Memorial University of Newfoundland
Miller, J.R.
Professor of History
University of Saskatchewan
Miller, John A.
Canadian Music Centre, Toronto
Miller, Judith N.
Policy Development & Planning Officer
Medical Research Council of Canada
Ottawa
Miller, Mark
Writer, Toronto
Miller, Mary Jane
Associate Professor of Fine Arts
Brock University
Miller, Orlo
Writer
London, Ont
Millin, Leslie
Gondolin Consulting Services
Vancouver
Millman, Peter M.
Herzberg Institute of Astrophysics
National Research Council Canada
Ottawa
Millman, Thomas R.
Former Archivist
Anglican Church of Canada, Toronto
Mills, Charles A.
Quality assurance engineer
Hamilton, Ont
Mills, David
Assistant Professor of History
University of Alberta
Mills, Eric L.
Professor of Oceanography & Biology
Dalhousie University
Mills, Isabelle Margaret
Professor of Music
University of Saskatchewan
Milne, David A.
Associate Professor of Political
Studies
University of Prince Edward Island
Milne, William J.
Professor of Engineering
Memorial University of Newfoundland
Milner, Marc
Historian, Directorate of History
Dept of National Defence, Ottawa
Milton, David G.
Executive Director
Canadian Institute of Treated Wood
Ottawa
Milton, Janice
Research assistant, Halifax
Minnes, Gordon
Canadian Pulp & Paper Association
Montréal
Miquelon, Dale
Professor of History
University of Saskatchewan
Mitchell, Edward
Research Scientist
Dept of Fisheries & Oceans
Arctic Biological Station
Ste-Anne-de-Bellevue, Qué

itchell, K.R.
Professor of English
University of Regina
itchinson, Wendy
Associate Professor of History
University of Windsor
ohr, Johann W.
Professor of Law & Sociology
York University
oir, John S.
Professor of History
University of Toronto
olnar, George Dempster
Professor & Chairman of Medicine
University of Alberta
oncrieff, Patrick M.
Senior Manager, Agriculture
Bank of Montreal, Toronto
onet, Jacques, s.j.
President, Regis College
Toronto
ontagnes, Ian
Assistant Director & Editor-in-Chief
University of Toronto Press, Toronto
oodie, D. Wayne
Professor of Geography
University of Manitoba
oody, Barry M.
Associate Professor of History
Acadia University
oogk, Peter N.
Associate Professor of History
University of British Columbia
ooney, Kathleen A.
Assistant Professor of Anthropology
University of Victoria
oore, Christopher
Historian
Burlington, Ont
oore, James G.G.
Dept of Language & Literature
Booth Memorial Regional High School
St John's
oore, Keith L.
Professor & Chairman of Anatomy;
Associate Dean of Basic Sciences
University of Toronto
oore, Teresa
Public Relations Co-ordinator
Canadian Figure Skating Association
Ottawa
oriarity, Andrew J.
Medi-Edit Ltd, Toronto
orinis, E. Alan
Anthropologist, Vancouver
orisset, Pierre
Professeur de biologie
Université Laval
orissette, Yves-Marie
Associate Professor of Law
McGill University
orlan, Richard E.
Curator, Plains Archaeology
Archaeological Survey of Canada
National Museum of Man, Ottawa
orley, J. Terence
Assistant Professor of Political Science
University of Victoria
orley, Patricia A.
Professor of English & Canadian Studies
Concordia University
orris, Cerise
Professor of Social Service
Dawson College, Montréal
orris, Peter
Associate Professor of Film Studies
Queen's University
orrison, David A.
National Museum of Man, Ottawa
orrison, Jack W.
Director General, Research
Agriculture Canada, Ottawa
orrison, Jean
Historical Research Officer
Old Fort William
Thunder Bay, Ont
orrison, Kenneth L.
Historical writer
Thunder Bay, Ont
orrison, Rod
Administrator, Victoria
orrison, W. Douglas
Professor of Animal & Poultry Science
University of Guelph
orrison, William R.
Associate Professor of History
Brandon University

Morrow, Don
Associate Professor of Physical Education
University of Western Ontario
Morton, Desmond
Professor of History
Erindale College
University of Toronto
Morton, John K.
Professor of Biology
University of Waterloo
Moscovitch, Allan
Associate Professor of Social Work
Carleton University
Moss, John
Professor of English
University of Ottawa
Mossman, Mary Jane
Associate Professor
Osgoode Hall Law School
York University
Motut, Roger
Professor Emeritus
University of Alberta
Mowat, Farley
Writer, Port Hope
Mowat, Susanne
Ottawa
Moyer, David S.
Associate Professor of Anthropology
University of Victoria
Moyles, R. Gordon
Associate Dean of Arts
University of Alberta
Muehlen, Maria
Curator, Inuit Art Section
Indian & Northern Affairs Canada
Ottawa
Muise, Del
Associate Professor of History
Carleton University
Muldoon, Francis C.
Federal Court of Canada, Ottawa
Mummery, Robert M.
Photographer, Edmonton
Munawar, Mohiuddin
Research Scientist
Great Lakes Fisheries Research Branch
Fisheries & Oceans
Canadian Centre for Inland Waters
Burlington, Ont
Munn, R.E.
Institute for Environmental Studies
University of Toronto
Munro, J. Ian
Professor of Computer Science
University of Waterloo
Murray, Joan
Director
The Robert McLaughlin Gallery
Oshawa, Ont
Murray, Robert G.E.
Professor of Microbiology & Immunology
University of Western Ontario
Mutimer, Brian T.P.
Associate Professor of Physical Education
St Francis Xavier University
Mycio, Luba
Canadian Wildlife Federation
Ottawa
Myles, John
Associate Professor of Sociology
Carleton University

Nadeau, Robert
Professeur de philosophie
Université du Québec à Montréal
Nadeau, Vincent
Professeur de littérature
Université Laval
Naidoo, Josephine C.
Associate Professor of Psychology
Wilfrid Laurier University
Nasgaard, Roald
Chief Curator
Art Gallery of Ontario, Toronto
Nason, Roger
Bicentennial Co-ordinator
City Hall, Fredericton
Nattrass, Susan M.
Edmonton
Navin, Francis P.D.
Associate Professor of Civil Engineering
University of British Columbia
Neal, Margaret
Co-ordinator
Standardbred Canada Library
Canadian Trotting Association
Toronto

Neary, Peter
Professor of History
University of Western Ontario
Neatby, H. Blair
Professor of History
Carleton University
Neatby, L.H.
Author;
Professor of Classics (retired)
Saskatoon
Neave, Edwin H.
Professor of Finance
Queen's University
Needler, A.W.H.
St Andrews, NB
Needler, George T.
Director
Atlantic Oceanographic Laboratory
Ocean Science & Surveys Atlantic
Dept of Fisheries & Oceans
Bedford Institute of Oceanography
Dartmouth, NS
Neelin, James M.
Professor of Biology & Biochemistry
Carleton University
Neill, Robin F.
Associate Professor of Economics
Carleton University
Nelles, H. Vivian
Professor of History
York University
Nelson, Joseph S.
Professor of Zoology
University of Alberta
Nepveu, Pierre
Professeur de littérature
Université de Montréal
Nettleship, David N.
Research Scientist
Seabird Research Unit
Canadian Wildlife Service
Bedford Institute of Oceanography
Dartmouth, NS
Neufeld, Edward Peter
Senior Vice President & Chief Economist
The Royal Bank of Canada, Montréal
Neufeldt, Ronald W.
Associate Professor of Religious Studies
University of Calgary
Neuman, Shirley
Associate Professor of English
University of Alberta
New, William H.
Professor of English;
Editor, Canadian Literature
University of British Columbia
Newark, Michael J.
Meteorologist, Environment Canada
Newell, Dianne
Assistant Professor of History
University of British Columbia
Newlands, David L.
Museum Studies Program
University of Toronto
Newman, Peter C.
Author
Cordova Bay, BC
Nicholson, Norman L.
Professor of Geography
University of Western Ontario
Nicks, John
Reynolds Alberta Museum
Wetaskiwin, Alta
Nicolson, Murray
Lecturer of History
Wilfrid Laurier University
Nielsen, N. Ole
Professor of Veterinary Pathology
University of Saskatchewan
Niosi, Jorge E.
Professeur de sociologie
Université du Québec à Montréal
Nkemdirim, Lawrence C.
Professor of Geography
University of Calgary
Noble, William C.
Professor of Anthropology
McMaster University
Nonnecke, Ib
Professor & Chairman of Horticultural Science
University of Guelph
Norrie, Kenneth H.
Professor of Economics
University of Alberta
Novak, Barbara
Writer
London, Ont

Nursall, J. Ralph
Professor of Zoology
University of Alberta
Nuttall, V. Walter
Agriculture research scientist (retired), Winnipeg

O'Brien, Allan
Professor of Political Science
University of Western Ontario
Occhietti, Serge
Professeur de géographie physique
Université du Québec à Montréal
O'Dea, Shane
Associate Professor of English
Memorial University of Newfoundland
O'Dor, Ronald K.
Professor of Biology
Dalhousie University
Officer, Jillian M.
Assistant Professor of Dance
University of Waterloo
O'Grady, Jean
Collected Works of John Stuart Mill
University of Toronto Press, Toronto
Oke, Timothy R.
Professor of Geography
University of British Columbia
O'Neill, Patrick
Associate Professor of Drama
Mount Saint Vincent University
Onyszchuk, Mario
Professor & Chairman of Chemistry
McGill University
Orford, Robert R.
Executive Director, Alberta Workers' Health, Safety & Compensation;
Associate Clinical Professor of Health Services Administration & Community Medicine
University of Alberta
Orkin, Mark M.
Lawyer & writer, Toronto
Orlikow, Lionel
Consultant, Winnipeg
Ormsby, Margaret A.
Professor Emerita
Vernon, BC
Osborne, Brian Stuart
Professor of Geography
Queen's University
Ouellet, Fernand
Professeur d'histoire
Université d'Ottawa
Ouellet, Henri
Chief, Vertebrate Zoology Division
National Museum of Natural Sciences
Ottawa
Ouellet, Réal
Département de littérature
Université Laval
Owens, John N.
Professor of Biology
University of Victoria
Owram, D.R.
Associate Professor of History
University of Alberta

Packer, John G.
Professor of Botany
University of Alberta
Page, Donald M.
Historian, Dept of External Affairs
Ottawa
Page, Garnet T.
Consultant, Calgary
Page, James E.
Canadian Studies Program
Secretary of State
Hull
Page, Malcolm
Associate Professor of English
Simon Fraser University
Paikin, Lee
Visiting Assistant Professor of Law
University of British Columbia
Paikowsky, Sandra
Associate Professor of Art History;
Curator, Concordia Art Gallery
Concordia University
Pain, Howard
Writer, Toronto
Painter, Michael F.
Consultant forester, Vancouver
Palardy, Jean
Historien
Fondation Macdonald-Stewart, Montréal
Palay, Murray S.
Barrister & solicitor, Winnipeg
Palmer, Bryan D.
Associate Professor of History
Simon Fraser University

Palmer, Howard
Associate Professor of History
University of Calgary
Palmer, Tamara Jeppson
Instructor of General Studies
University of Calgary
Paltiel, Khayyam Zev
Professor of Political Science
Carleton University
Panitch, Leo
Professor of Political Science
York University
Pannekoek, Frits
Alberta Culture, Edmonton
Panting, Gerald Ernest
Professor of History
Memorial University of Newfoundland
Paradis, Jean-Marc
Professeur d'histoire
Université du Québec à Trois-Rivières
Pariseau, Jean
Historien en chef
Service historique de la défense nationale, Ottawa
Parker, George L.
Professor of English
Royal Military College of Canada
Parker, Graham
Professor of Law
Osgoode Hall Law School
York University
Parry, Keith
Associate Professor of Anthropology
University of Lethbridge
Parsons, John
Teacher of Newfoundland Culture
Booth Memorial Regional High School
St John's
Parsons, Timothy R.
Professor of Oceanography
University of British Columbia
Pastore, Ralph T.
Associate Professor of History
Memorial University of Newfoundland
Patching, Thomas H.
Professor Emeritus of Mineral Engineering
University of Alberta
Paterson, Donald G.
Professor of Economics
University of British Columbia
Paterson, W. Stan B.
Quadra Island, BC
Patterson, E.P.
Associate Professor of History
University of Waterloo
Patterson, G. James
Professor of Anthropology
Eastern Oregon State College at La Grande
Payment, Diane Paulette
Historian, Parks Canada
Winnipeg
Peacey, John G.
Head, Dept of Chemical Engineering
Noranda Research Centre
Pointe Claire, Qué
Peacock, Gordon B.
Professor of Drama
University of Alberta
Peake, Frank A.
Professor of History (retired)
Laurentian University
Pease, Jane H.
Professor of History
University of Maine at Orono
Pease, William H.
Professor of History
University of Maine at Orono
Pederson, Diana
Doctoral Candidate of History
Carleton University
Pedwell, Susan
Writer, Toronto
Peel, Bruce
Chief Librarian Emeritus
University of Alberta
Peers, Frank W.
Professor of Political Science
University of Toronto
Pelletier, Gérard
Chairman of the Board of Trustees
National Museums of Canada, Ottawa
Pelletier, Jacques
Professeur de littérature québecoise
Université du Québec à Montréal
Pelletier, Réjean
Professeur agrégé de science politique
Université Laval

Peltier, W. Richard
Professor of Physics
University of Torônto
Penelhum, Terence
Professor of Religious Studies
University of Calgary
Penner, Norman
Professor of Political Science
York University
Penton, M. James
Professor of History
University of Lethbridge
Percy, Michael B.
Associate Professor of Economics
University of Alberta
Perks, William T.
Professor of Urbanism & Planning
University of Calgary
Perla, R.
Research Scientist
National Hydrology Research Institute
Canmore, Alta
Persaud, Trivedi V.N.
Professor & Head of Anatomy
University of Manitoba
Peters, Erik J.
The Hett Gallery Ltd, Edmonton
Peters, Robert Henry
Associate Professor of Biology
McGill University
Peterson, Jeannie
Contract researcher
Dartmouth, NS
Peterson, R.L.
Curator, Mammalogy
Royal Ontario Museum
Toronto
Peterson, Thomas E.
Associate Professor of Political Studies
University of Manitoba
Petryshyn, Jaroslav
Instructor of History
Grande Prairie Regional College
Phaneuf, Louis-Philippe
Professeur
Université de Montréal
Phelan, P.P.
National Defence Headquarters
Directorate of Cadets, Ottawa
Phelps, Edward
Librarian, Regional Collection
University of Western Ontario Library
Phillips, Carol
Director
Norman Mackenzie Art Gallery
University of Regina
Phillips, David W.
Climatologist, Environment Canada
Downsview, Ont
Phillips, Paul
Professor of Economics
University of Manitoba
Phillips, Roy A.
President & Executive Director
The Canadian Manufacturers' Association, Toronto
Phillips, Ruth Bliss
Assistant Professor of Art History
Carleton University
Phillips, Truman P.
Associate Professor of Agricultural Economics & Extension Education
University of Guelph
Phillipson, Donald J.C.
Historian, Ottawa
Picard, Ellen I.
Professor of Law
University of Alberta
Piché, Victor
Professeur de démographie;
Directeur du Centre de Recherches Caraibes
Université de Montréal
Pickard, George L.
Professor Emeritus of Oceanography
University of British Columbia
Pierce, Richard A.
Professor Emeritus of History
Queen's University
Pierre-Deschênes, Claudine
Historienne, Montréal
Pierson, Ruth Roach
Associate Professor of History & Philosophy; & Sociology in Education
Ontario Institute for Studies in Education, Toronto
Pill, Juri
General Manager, Planning
Toronto Transit Commission, Toronto

Pirozynski, K.A.
Palaeomycologist
National Museums of Canada, Ottawa
Pitt, David G.
Professor of English Language & Literature
Memorial University of Newfoundland
Pitt, Janet E.M.
Researcher, St John's
Pitt, Robert D.
Educational Television Centre
Memorial University of Newfoundland
Pivato, Joseph
Associate Professor of Humanities
Athabasca University
Plamondon, Réjean
Directeur des communications
Université de Montréal
Plant, Richard L.
Associate Professor of Drama
Queen's University
Ploeg, Jozinus
Associate Director
Division of Mechanical Engineering
National Research Council, Ottawa
Plouffe, Hélène
Rédactrice & recherchiste, Montréal
Plunkett, T.J.
Professor of Public Administration
Queen's University
Poiker, Thomas K.
Professor of Geography & Computing Science
Simon Fraser University
Polèse, Mario
INRS-Urbanization
Université du Québec
Polnaszek, Frank
Hartford, Conn
Ponting, J. Rick
Associate Professor of Sociology
University of Calgary
Pool, Annelies M.
Writer
Yellowknife, NWT
Pope, Carol Ann
Burnaby, BC
Porteous, Hugh A.
Manager, Issues Coordination
Corporate Planning
Via Rail Canada Inc, Montréal
Porter, Arthur
Professor Emeritus
University of Toronto
Porter, John R.
Professeur d'histoire de l'art
Université Laval
Porter, Marion
Researcher, Ottawa
Posluns, Michael
Hoople, Posluns & Associates
Ottawa
Pothier, Bernard
Canadian War Museum, Ottawa
Potvin, Gilles
Critique musical
Le Devoir*, Montréal*
Poulin, Gabrielle
Ecrivain, Ottawa
Powell, Deborah J.
Ottawa
Powell, Jay (James V.)
Associate Professor of Anthropology
University of British Columbia
Prang, Margaret E.
Professor of History
University of British Columbia
Pratt, Larry
Professor of Political Science
University of Alberta
Pressman, Norman E.P.
Associate Professor of Urban & Regional Planning
University of Waterloo
Preston-Thomas, Hugh
Associate Director
Division of Physics
National Research Council, Ottawa
Preston, Richard A.
Professor Emeritus of History
Duke University at Durham, NC
Preston, Richard J.
Professor of Anthropology
McMaster University
Price, John A.
Professor of Anthropology
York University
Pringle, Alexander D.
Barrister & Solicitor, Edmonton
Pritchard, Gordon
Professor of Biology
University of Calgary

Pritchard, John
Research Director
Haisla Aboriginal Rights Program
Victoria
Proctor, John T.A.
Professor of Horticultural Science
University of Guelph
Pugh, Garth Charles
Research Officer II
Dept of Culture & Recreation, Regina
Punch, Terrence M.
Vice President
Royal NS Historical Society;
Chairman, Genealogical Association of NS, Halifax
Putt, Eric D.
Professional Agrologist
Creston, BC
Pylyshyn, Zenon W.
Professor of Psychology & Computer Science
University of Western Ontario

Qualter, Terence H.
Professor of Political Science
University of Waterloo
Quamme, Harvey A.
Research Scientist
Agriculture Canada
Summerland, BC
Quayle, D.B.
Marine zoologist
Nanaimo, BC

Ralston, H. Keith
Assistant Professor of History
University of British Columbia
Ramraj, Victor J.
Associate Professor of English
University of Calgary
Ramsay, Donald A.
Principal Research Officer
National Research Council, Ottawa
Ramsden, Peter G.
Associate Professor of Anthropology
McMaster University
Raney, R. Keith
Deputy Director
RADARSAT Project Office
Canada Centre for Remote Sensing
Ottawa
Rapp, Egon
Professor of Agricultural Engineering
University of Alberta
Rasmussen, Mark A.
Historical geographer, Edmonton
Rasporich, Anthony W.
Professor of History
University of Calgary
Rasporich, Beverly J.
Assistant Professor of General Studies
University of Calgary
Rawlyk, George A.
Professor of History
Queen's University
Ray, Arthur
Professor of History
University of British Columbia
Rayburn, Alan
Executive Secretary
Canadian Permanent Committee on Geographical Names, Ottawa
Rea, J.E.
Professor of History
University of Manitoba
Read, John H.
Professor of Community Health Sciences & Pediatrics
University of Calgary
Redmond, Gerald
Professor of Recreation & Leisure Studies
University of Alberta
Reed, Austin
Canadian Wildlife Service
Ste-Foy, Qué
Reed, F. Leslie C.
Forest Policy Consultant, Vancouver
Reeves, Randall R.
Arctic Biological Station
Ste-Anne-de-Bellevue, Qué
Regan, Ellen M.
Associate Professor
The Ontario Institute for Studies in Education, Toronto
Regehr, T.D.
Professor of History
University of Saskatchewan

Reid, Alison M.
Consulting biologist
Victoria
Reid, David
Associate Professor of Surgery (orthopaedic);
Consultant in Sports Medicine
University of Alberta
Reid, Ian A.
Special Surveys Engineer
Water Survey of Canada, Ottawa
Reid, John G.
Associate Professor of History
Mount Allison University
Reid, M.H. (Lefty)
Director & Curator
Hockey Hall of Fame & Museum, Toronto
Reid, Richard
Associate Professor of History
University of Guelph
Reid, Robert G.B.
Professor of Biology
University of Victoria
Reilly, Nolan
Assistant Professor of History
University of Winnipeg
Reilly, Sharon
Curator of History & Technology
Manitoba Museum of Man & Nature
Winnipeg
Reiswig, Henry M.
Associate Professor of Biology
McGill University
Rémillard, Gil
Professeur titulaire de droit constitutionnel
Rennie, Donald Andrews
Professor of Soil Science
University of Saskatchewan
Rennie, Jim
Publisher
Jim Rennie's Sports Letter
Collingwood, Ont
Ricard, François
Professeur agrégé de littérature
Université McGill
Richards, John
Assistant Professor
Simon Fraser University
Richards, William D.
Assistant Professor of Communication
Laboratory for Computer & Communication Research
Simon Fraser University
Richardson, Eric Harvey
Principal Research Officer
National Research Council of Canada
Dominion Astrophysical Observatory
Victoria
Richardson, Keith W.
Programme Officer
Social Sciences & Humanities Research Council, Ottawa
Richardson, W. George
Associate Professor of History of Engineering
Queen's University
Richman, Alex
Professor of Psychiatry;
Community Health & Epidemiology
Dalhousie University
Rickwood, Roger R.
City Solicitor's Dept, City Hall
Hamilton, Ont
Ricou, Laurie
Associate Professor of English
University of British Columbia
Riddell, W. Craig
Associate Professor of Economics
University of British Columbia
Rider, Peter E.
Atlantic Provinces Historian
National Museum of Man, Ottawa
Ridington, Robin
Associate Professor of Anthropology
University of British Columbia
Riedel, Walter E.
Associate Professor of German
University of Victoria
Riegert, Paul W.
Professor of Biology
University of Regina
Riggs, Bert
Writer, St John's
Ritchie, J.C.
Professor of Botany
University of Toronto

Robb, S. Andrew
Assistant Professor of History & Canadian Studies
University of Prince Edward Island
Robert, Jean-Claude
Professeur d'histoire
Université du Québec à Montréal
Robert, Lucie
Chargée de recherche
Dictionnaire des oeuvres littéraires du Québec
Université Laval
Roberto, Eugène
Professeur de lettres françaises
Université d'Ottawa
Roberts, John S.
Interim General Manager
Canadian Payments Association, Ottawa
Roberts, William
Shirley Leishman Books, Ottawa
Robertson, Ian Ross
Associate Professor of History
University of Toronto
Robertson, J.A.L.
Director of Program Planning
Atomic Energy of Canada Limited
Research Company Head Office, Ottawa
Robertson, Raleigh John
Professor of Biology
Queen's University
Robidoux, Réjean
Professeur titulaire de littérature
Université d'Ottawa
Robillard, Denise
Journaliste et écrivain, Montréal
Robinson, Bart T.
Writer, Equinox *magazine*
Camden East, Ont
Robinson, J. Lewis
Professor of Geography
University of British Columbia
Robinson, Sinclair
Associate Professor of French
Carleton University
Robson, Tom W.
Director of Development
University of Winnipeg
Roby, Yves
Professeur d'histoire
Université Laval
Roche, Douglas
Author & journalist;
President, United Nations Association in Canada
Rocher, Guy
Professeur titulaire de sociologie
Université de Montréal
Rodney, William
Professor of History & Dean of Arts
Royal Roads Military College
Victoria
Rodrigo, Russell G.A.
Professor of Chemistry
Wilfrid Laurier University
Rodriguez, Juan
Writer, Montréal
Roeder, Robert C.
Lazenby Professor of Physics
Southwestern University at Georgetown, Tex
Rogers, Jacob
Priest
Goulds, Nfld
Rogerson, Robert J.
Associate Professor of Earth Sciences & Geography
Memorial University of Newfoundland
Roland, Charles G.
Professor of the History of Medicine
McMaster University
Romaniuk, Eugene W.
Professor of Educational Psychology
University of Alberta
Romanow, Joseph R.
President, Machinery & Equipment Manufacturers' Association of Canada
Ottawa
Romanowski, Barbara
Director, Social Hygiene Services
Alberta Social Services & Community Health, Edmonton
Rome, David
Dept of Religion
Concordia University
Ronald, Keith
Professor of Zoology
University of Guelph
Ronish, Donna Yavorsky
Historian, Montréal
Rose, Albert
Professor of Social Work
University of Toronto

Rose, Phyllis
Graduate Student
University of Toronto
Rosen, Earl
Executive Director
Canadian Independent Record Production Association, Toronto
Rosenberg, Ann C.
Instructor of Fine Arts
Capilano College, North Vancouver
Ross, Alexander M.
Professor (retired)
University of Guelph
Ross, Catherine Sheldrick
Assistant Professor of Library & Information Science
University of Western Ontario
Ross, David I.
Director of Operations
NORDCO Limited (Newfoundland Oceans Research & Development Corporation)
St John's
Ross, David P.
Social economic consultant, Ottawa
Ross, Henry U.
Professor Emeritus of Metallurgical Engineering
University of Toronto
Rostoker, Gordon
Professor of Physics
University of Alberta
Rothney, Gordon Oliver
Honorary Fellow, St John's College
University of Manitoba
Rothrock, George A.
Professor of History
University of Alberta
Rothstein, Samuel
Professor of Librarianship
University of British Columbia
Rotstein, Abraham
Professor of Economics
University of Toronto
Roueche, Leonard R.
Manager, Research
British Columbia Ferry Corporation
Victoria
Rouillard, Jacques
Professeur d'histoire
Université de Montréal
Rousseau, Guildo
Professeur de littérature
Université du Québec à Trois-Rivières
Rousseau, Henri-Paul
Professeur d'économie
Université Laval
Routledge, Marie
Research & Documentation Co-ordinator
Inuit Art Section
Indian & Northern Affairs Canada
Ottawa
Rowat, Donald Cameron
Professor of Political Science
Carleton University
Rowberry, R. Geoffrey
Professor of Horticulture
University of Guelph
Rowe, Frederick W.
Senator
Rowe, John Stanley
Professor of Plant Ecology
University of Saskatchewan
Rowe, Kenneth
Fellow of the Royal Philatelic Society of Canada, Toronto
Rowe, Percy A.
Travel Editor, Toronto Sun
Toronto
Rowland, Gordon G.
Crop Development Centre
University of Saskatchewan
Rowley, Diana
Editor, Ottawa
Rowsell, Harry C.
Professor of Pathology;
Executive Director, Canadian Council of Animal Care, Ottawa
Roy, David J.
Director, Centre for Bioethics
Clinical Research Institute of Montréal, Montréal
Roy, Fernande
Professeur d'histoire
Université du Québec à Montréal
Roy, Patricia E.
Associate Professor of History
University of Victoria
Roy, Reginald H.
Professor of Military & Strategic Studies
University of Victoria

Rozee, Kenneth Roy
Professor of Microbiology
Dalhousie University
Rubenstein, Lorne
Journalist, Toronto
Rubin, Ken
Public interest researcher & consultant, Ottawa
Rubin, Leon J.
Professor of Chemical Engineering
University of Toronto
Rubio, Gerald J.
Assistant Professor of English
University of Guelph
Rubio, Mary H.
Co-Editor
Canadian Children's Literature
Dept of English
University of Guelph
Ruddel, David-Thiery
Historian, National Museum of Man
Hull, Qué
Ruff, Norman J.
Assistant Professor of Political Science
University of Victoria
Ruiz, Wilson
Journalist & broadcaster, Toronto
Rukavina, Norman A.
Geologist
National Water Research Institute
Burlington, Ont
Runnalls, Oliver John Clyve
Chairman, Centre for Nuclear Engineering;
Professor of Energy Studies
University of Toronto
Rupert, Robert John
Associate Professor of Journalism
Carleton University
Ruppenthal, Karl M.
UPS Foundation Professor;
Director, the Centre for Transportation Studies
University of British Columbia
Rushdy, Roger
Agronome
Station de Recherche Deschambault
Deschambault, Qué
Russell, Dale A.
Curator of Fossil Vertebrates
National Museum of Natural Sciences
Ottawa
Russell, Hilary
Parks Canada, Hull
Russell, Loris S.
Curator Emeritus
Royal Ontario Museum, Toronto
Russell, Peter A.
Resident Tutor, Fircroft College
Birmingham, England
Russell, Victor L.
Manager, City of Toronto Archives
Toronto
Rutherford, Paul Frederic William
Professor of History
University of Toronto
Rutter, Nathaniel W.
Professor & Chairman of Geology
University of Alberta
Ryan, Douglas E.
McLeod Professor of Chemistry
Dalhousie University
Ryan, James T.
Professor of Chemical Engineering
University of Alberta
Ryan, John
Professor of Geography
University of Winnipeg
Ryan, Shannon
Associate Professor of History
Memorial University of Newfoundland
Ryder, June M.
Geologist, Vancouver
Ryerson, Stanley-Bréhaut
Professeur invité d'histoire
Université du Québec à Montréal

Saarinen, Oiva W.
Associate Professor of Geography
Laurentian University of Sudbury
Sabina, Ann P.
Mineralogist
Geological Survey of Canada, Ottawa
Sager, Eric W.
Assistant Professor of History
University of Victoria
Saint-Jacques, Bernard
Professor of Linguistics
University of British Columbia

Saladin-d'Anglure, B.
Professor of Anthropology
Université Laval
Sales, Arnaud
Professeur agrégé de sociologie
Université de Montréal
Sallot, Jeff
The Globe and Mail, *Ottawa*
Salter, Liora
Associate Professor of Communication
Simon Fraser University
Sameoto, Douglas D.
Research Scientist
Bedford Institute of Oceanography
Dartmouth, NS
Sanderson, Marie E.
Professor of Geography
University of Windsor
Sandison, Margaret J.
Executive Director
Saskatchewan Sports Hall of Fame
Regina
Sangster, Joan
Lecturer
Trent University
Santink, Joy L.
Doctoral Student of History
University of Toronto
Sarjeant, A. Margaret
Saskatoon
Sarjeant, William A.S.
Professor of Geological Sciences
University of Saskatchewan
Sarty, Roger
Historian, Directorate of History
Dept of National Defence, Ottawa
Sauchyn, David J.
Assistant Professor of Geography
University of Regina
Saul, John S.
Professor of Social Science
Atkinson College, York University
Sauriol, Pierre
Agronome
Ministère de l'agriculture du Québec
St-Rémi, Qué
Savard, Pierre
Professeur d'histoire
Université d'Ottawa
Savile, D.B.O.
Research Associate Emeritus
Biosystematics Research Institute
Ottawa
Savishinsky, Joel S.
Professor of Anthropology
Ithaca College, NY
Savitt, Ronald
Professor of Marketing
Michigan State University at East Lansing
Sawatsky, Rodney J.
Associate Professor of Religious
Studies & History
Conrad Grebel College
University of Waterloo
Sawatsky, Ronald G.
Centre for Religious Studies
University of Toronto
Sawula, Lorne William
National Volleyball Coach (Women)
Regina
Sawyer, Deborah C.
Information Plus Inc, Toronto
Saywell, John T.
University Professor
York University
Scarfe, Christopher M.
Professor of Geology
University of Alberta
Scargill, M.H.
Professor Emeritus of Linguistics
University of Victoria
Schaefer, Otto
Director
Northern Medical Research Unit
Medical Services
Health & Welfare Canada, Edmonton
Schau, Barbara Ann
Sessional Lecturer
Carleton University
Schipper, Sidney S.
Dean, Fashion Technology Division
George Brown College;
Adjunct Professor of Fashion
Ryerson Polytechnical Institute
Toronto
Schledermann, Peter
Director
Arctic Institute of North America
University of Calgary

Schlesinger, Benjamin
Professor of Social Work
University of Toronto
Schmitz, Nancy
Professeur d'anthropologie
Université Laval
Schoenauer, Norbert
Macdonald Professor of Architecture
McGill University
Schrodt, Barbara
Associate Professor of Physical
Education (Sport History)
University of British Columbia
Schultz, George A.
Professor of History
University of Manitoba
Schwartz, Joan M.
National Photography Collection
Public Archives of Canada, Ottawa
Schweizer, Elizabeth J.
Editorial Assistant
Studies in History & Politics
Bishop's University
Schweizer, Karl W.
Associate Professor of History
Bishop's University
Schwier, Charles
Research Associate, Canadian
Institute of Guided Ground Transport
Queen's University
Scobie, Stephen
Professor of English
University of Victoria
Scott, David S.
Executive Director
Institute for Hydrogen Systems
Mississauga, Ont
Scott, Peter J.
Associate Professor of Biology
Memorial University of Newfoundland
Scott, Stephen A.
Professor of Law
McGill University
Scott, W. Beverly
Senior Scientist
Huntsman Marine Laboratory
St Andrews, NB;
Professor Emeritus of Zoology
University of Toronto
Scudder, Geoffrey G.E.
Professor & Head of Zoology
University of British Columbia
Seager, Allen
Assistant Professor of History
Simon Fraser University
Sealey, D. Bruce
Professor of Education
University of Manitoba
Sealey, Gary
Chief, Interpretation & Visitor
Services, Parks Canada
Hull
Sealy, Spencer G.
Professor of Zoology
University of Manitoba
Sebert, Louis M.
Canada Land Surveyor, Ottawa
Segall, Harold N.
Assistant Professor of Medicine
McGill University
Segger, Martin
Director
Maltwood Art Museum & Gallery
University of Victoria
Séguin, Normand
Professeur d'histoire
Université du Québec à Trois-Rivières
Sehon, Alec H.
Professor of Immunology
University of Manitoba
Selwood, H. John
Associate Professor of Geography
University of Winnipeg
Semple, Neil A.
Assistant Archivist
United Church of Canada
Victoria University, Toronto
Senda, Yoshio
National Coach;
Technical Director, Judo Alberta
Senior, Elinor
Assistant Professor
McGill University
Senior, Hereward
Professor of History
McGill University
Serne, Robert Allan
Regional Manager
Canadian Portland Cement Association
Prairie Provinces Region, Edmonton

Sewell, John
Former Mayor of Toronto;
Journalist, Toronto
Seymour, Christopher M.
Executive Secretary
Canadian Tobacco Manufacturers'
Council, Montréal
Seymour, Patrick D.
Director, Devonian Botanic Garden
University of Alberta
Shadbolt, Doris
Curator Emeritus
Vancouver Art Gallery
North Burnaby, BC
Shadbolt, Douglas
Professor of Architecture
University of British Columbia
Shaffer, Ed
Professor of Economics
University of Alberta
Shaker, Fouad E.
Writer, historian, TV commentator &
international correspondent
Greenfield Park, Qué
Shannon, Elizabeth E.
Associate Professor of Clothing &
Textiles
University of Manitoba
Shapiro, Bernard J.
Director & Professor of Education
Ontario Institute for Studies in
Education, Toronto
Shaver, Frances M.
Research consultant
Laval, Qué
Shaw, Gordon C.
Professor of Administrative Studies
York University
Shaw, Murray C.
President
Canadian Ski Marathon, Ottawa
Shearing, Clifford D.
Associate Professor of Criminology &
Sociology
University of Toronto
Sheehan, Carol
Ethnologist & art historian
Calgary
Sheehan, Nancy M.
Associate Professor of Educational
Policy & Administrative Studies
University of Calgary
Sheffer, Harry
Former Vice-Chairman
Defence Research Board, Ottawa
Sheffield, Edward (Ottawa)
Professor Emeritus of Higher
Education
University of Toronto
Sheinin, Rose
Professor of Microbiology
University of Toronto
Shek, B.-Z.
Professor of French
University of Toronto
Shelest, Jaroslaw
Research historian, Edmonton
Shephard, Roy J.
Director, School of Physical & Health
Education;
Professor of Applied Physiology
University of Toronto
Sheppard, R. Ronald
Edmonton, Alta
Sheppard, Robert
Correspondent, The Globe and Mail
Edmonton
Shifrin, Ellen
Dance researcher, Toronto
Shih, Chang-tai
Curator of Crustaceans
National Museum of Natural Sciences
Ottawa
Shoyama, Thomas K.
Visiting Professor
University of Victoria
Shuter, William L.H.
Professor of Physics
University of British Columbia
Sidor, Nicholas
CRTC, Hull
Siegel, Arthur
Professor of Social Science
York University
Silcox, David P.
Writer, Toronto
Sillanpaa, Lennard
Orleans, Ont
Silverman, Eliane Leslau
Assistant Professor of Women's
Studies
University of Calgary

Silversides, C. Ross
Forestry consultant
Prescott, Ont
Simeon, Richard
Professor of Political Studies
Queen's University
Sinclair-Faulkner, Tom
Associate Professor of Religion
Dalhousie University
Sirois, Antoine
Professeur de littérature
Université de Sherbrooke
Sisler, Rebecca
Sculptor & writer, Ottawa
Sitwell, O.F.G.
Associate Professor of Geography
University of Alberta
Skeoch, Alan Edward
Head of History
Parkdale Collegiate Institute
Toronto
Skogstad, Grace
Associate Professor of Political
Science
St Francis Xavier University
Slater, Peter
Professor of Theology
Toronto School of Theology;
Centre for Religious Studies
University of Toronto
Slavutych, Yar
Professor of Slavic Languages
University of Alberta
Slaymaker, H. Olav
Professor of Geography
University of British Columbia
Sloan, W.A.
Instructor, Canadian History
Selkirk College
Castlegar, BC
Slocombe, D. Scott
Graduate Student of Planning
University of British Columbia
Slonecker, Charles E.
Professor & Chairman of Anatomy
University of British Columbia
Sly, Peter Gerent
National Water Research Institute
Dept of the Environment
Burlington, Ont
Smart, Patricia
Associate Professor of French
Carleton University
Smith, André
Associate Professor of French
McGill University
Smith, Barry L.
Chief, Regulatory Affairs
Food Directorate
Health Protection Branch, Ottawa
Smith, David B.
Professor of Biochemistry
University of Western Ontario
Smith, David E.
Professor of Political Science
University of Saskatchewan
Smith, Denis
Dean of Social Science
University of Western Ontario
Smith, Derek G.
Associate Professor of Sociology &
Anthropology
Carleton University
Smith, Donald A.
Associate Professor of Biology
Carleton University
Smith, Donald B.
Associate Professor of History
University of Calgary
Smith, Douglas A.
Associate Professor of Economics
Carleton University
Smith, Frances K.
Curator Emeritus
Agnes Etherington Art Centre
Queen's University
Smith, James G.E.
Curator of North American Ethnology
Museum of the American Indian
Heye Foundation, New York City
Smith, James N.M.
Associate Professor of Zoology
University of British Columbia
Smith, Kenneth V.
National Sport & Recreation Centre
Ottawa

nith, Maurice V.
Adjunct Professor of Environmental Biology
University of Guelph
nith, Peter C.
Research Scientist
Atlantic Oceanographic Laboratory
Bedford Institute of Oceanography
Dartmouth, NS
nith, Peter J.
Professor of Geography
University of Alberta
nith, Shirlee Anne
Keeper
Hudson's Bay Company Archives
Provincial Archives of Manitoba
Winnipeg
nith, T. Bradbrooke
Barrister & Solicitor
Burritt's Rapids, Ont
nith, William Young, Jr.
Historian, Fredericton
nucker, Joseph
Associate Professor of Sociology
Concordia University
ıider, D. Laureen
Associate Professor of Sociology
Queen's University
ıow, Dean R.
Professor of Anthropology
State University of New York at Albany
ıowdon, James D.
Sessional Lecturer of History
Acadia University
ɔcknat, Thomas P.
Assistant Professor of History
Queen's University
landt, Omond M.
Consultant
Bolton, Ont
ɔmerville, Margaret A.
Associate Professor of Law & Medicine
McGill University
ɔper, James Herbert
Curator Emeritus, Botany Division
National Museum of Natural Sciences
Ottawa
ɔrfleet, John R.
Associate Professor
Concordia University
uthcott, Mary E.
Artist & writer
Mississauga, Ont
ɔuther, Jack G.
Research Scientist
Geological Survey of Canada
palding, David A.E.
Vice-President, Kanata Heritage Research & Presentation Corporation
Edmonton
peisman, Stephen A.
Director, Toronto Jewish Congress & Canadian Jewish Congress
Ontario Region Archives
pencer, Andrew N.
Associate Professor of Zoology
University of Alberta
pencer, Deirdre
Craft contractor, Calgary
pencer, Don
Assistant Archivist/Registrar
The Seagram Museum
Waterloo, Ont
pencer, John F.T.
Research Associate of Biology
Goldsmiths' College
University of London;
School of Biological Sciences
Thames Polytechnic
London, England
pencer, John H.
Professor & Head of Biochemistry
Queen's University
pettigue, Douglas O.
Professor & Head of English
Queen's University
pragge, Godfrey L.
Associate Professor of Urban & Regional Planning
Queen's University
prague, D.N.
Associate Professor of History
University of Manitoba
pray, William A.
Vice-President (Academic)
St Thomas University
ɔry, Irene M.
Professor Emeritus of Economics
University of Ottawa

St-Hilaire, Marc
Groupe saguenéen des chercheurs en histoire
Chicoutimi, Qué
St-Laurent, Gaston
Professeur de nutrition
Université Laval
Stacey, C.P.
University Professor Emeritus
University of Toronto
Stacey, Robert
Writer, editor & exhibition curator
Toronto
Stager, John K.
Professor of Geography
University of British Columbia
Stagg, Ronald J.
Professor of History
Ryerson Polytechnical Institute
Toronto
Stahl, Elvira
Director, Biomedical Editorial & Translation Services
Montréal
Stairs, Denis
Professor of Political Science
Dalhousie University
Stairs, Douglas G.
Professor of Physics
McGill University
Stamp, Robert M.
Writer, Toronto
Stanbury, W.T.
UPS Foundation Professor of Regulation & Competition Policy
University of British Columbia
Stanley, David M., s.j.
Professor of New Testament Studies
Regis College, Toronto
Stanley, Della M.M.
Historian, Halifax;
Part-time History Professor
Saint Mary's University
Stanley, George F.G.
Professor Emeritus of History
Royal Military College &
Mount Allison University
Stanley, Laurie C.C.
Writer, Cluny House
Kingston, Ont
Stanton, Charles R.
Writer, Ottawa
Starr, Gail
Professor of Law
University of Calgary
Staveley, Michael
Dean of Arts & Professor of Geography
Memorial University of Newfoundland
Stayner, Margaret M.
Education Consultant
Social Hygiene Services, Edmonton
Stead, Gordon W.
Vancouver
Steele, James
Associate Professor of English
Carleton University
Steeves, Taylor A.
Professor of Biology
University of Saskatchewan
Stefansson, Baldur R.
Professor of Plant Science
University of Manitoba
Stein, Janet R.
Professor of Botany
University of British Columbia
Stein, Michael B.
Professor of Political Science
McMaster University
Stelter, Gilbert A.
Professor of History
University of Guelph
Stenning, Philip C.
Senior Research Associate
Centre of Criminology
University of Toronto
Stepney, Philip H.R.
Assistant Director (Natural History)
Provincial Museum of Alberta
Edmonton
Steppler, Howard A.
Professor of Agronomy
Macdonald College of McGill University
Ste-Anne-de-Bellevue, Qué
Sterling, Theodor D.
Professor of Computer Science
Simon Fraser University
Stern, H.H.
Professor Emeritus
Ontario Institute for Studies in Education, Toronto

Stevens, Peter
Professor of English
University of Windsor
Stevenson, Charlotte
Toronto
Stevenson, Garth
Professor of Political Science
University of Alberta
Stevenson, John T.
Associate Professor of Philosophy
University of Toronto
Stewart, J. Douglas
Professor of Art History
Queen's University
Stewart, John B.
Professor of Political Science
St Francis Xavier University
Stewart, John R.
Assistant Archivist
Kamloops Museum & Archives
Kamloops, BC
Stewart, Kenneth W.
Professor of Zoology
University of Manitoba
Stewart, Lillian D.
Parks Canada, Winnipeg
Stiles, Michael E.
Professor of Foods & Nutrition
University of Alberta
Stocking, John R.
Associate Professor of Art History
University of Calgary
Stoddart, Jennifer
Director of Research
Canadian Advisory Council on the Status of Women, Ottawa
Stoicheff, Boris Peter
University Professor &
Professor of Physics
University of Toronto
Stone, Kay F.
Associate Professor of Folklore
University of Winnipeg
Stonehouse, Donald H.
Energy, Mines & Resources Canada
Ottawa
Storgaard, Anna K.
Professor of Plant Science
University of Manitoba
Stortz, Gerald J.
Assistant Professor of History
University of Western Ontario
Story, George Morley
Professor of English
Memorial University of Newfoundland
Stott, Jon C.
Professor of English
University of Alberta
Strate, Grant
Director, Centre for the Arts
Simon Fraser University
Strausz, Otto P.
Professor of Chemistry
University of Alberta
Stringham, Elwood W.
Professor of Animal Science (retired)
University of Manitoba
Strong-Boag, Veronica
Associate Professor of History & Women's Studies
Simon Fraser University
Struthers, J.R. (Tim)
Writer
London, Ont
Struthers, James
Associate Professor of Canadian Studies
Trent University
Stuart, Richard
Regional Historian, Parks Canada
Calgary
Stuart, Ross
Associate Professor of Theatre
York University
Studnicki-Gizbert, Konrad W.
Economic Commission for Latin America
United Nations, Santiago de Chile
Sturino, Franc
Assistant Professor of History
York University
Stursberg, Peter
Adjunct Professor
Centre for Canadian Studies
Simon Fraser University
Stursberg, Richard
Director General
Dept of Communications, Ottawa

Sullivan, Brian E.
Assistant Deputy Minister
Alberta Dept of Economic Development
Edmonton
Summers, William F.
Professor of Geography
Memorial University of Newfoundland
Sunahara, Ann G.
Lawyer, Edmonton
Sung, Shan-Ching
Professor
Division of Neurological Sciences
University of British Columbia
Sutherland, Maxwell
Chief, Historical Research Division
Parks Canada, Hull
Sutherland, Neil
Professor of Social & Educational Studies
University of British Columbia
Sutherland, Sharon L.
Associate Professor of Public Administration
Carleton University
Sutherland, Stuart R.J.
Toronto
Sutnik, Maia-Mari
Photographic Co-ordinator
Art Gallery of Ontario, Toronto
Suzuki, David Takayoshi
Professor of Zoology
University of British Columbia
Swainson, Donald
Professor of History
Queen's University
Swainson, Neil A.
Professor of Political Science
University of Victoria
Sward, Robert
Writer, Toronto
Sweeny, Alastair
Writer, Port Hope & Ottawa
Swinton, George
Artist & scholar
Morrisburg, Ont
Swinton, William Elgin
Professor Emeritus of Zoology
University of Toronto
Swyripa, Frances
Canadian Institute of Ukrainian Studies
University of Alberta
Sykes, T.
Canadian Association of Manufacturers of Medical Devices, Toronto
Sylvain, Philippe
Professeur titulaire d'histoire (retraité)
Université Laval
Sylvestre, Guy
Honorary Librarian
Royal Society of Canada, Ottawa
Symington, Rodney
Associate Professor of German
University of Victoria
Syms, E. Leigh
Curator of Archaeology
Manitoba Museum of Man & Nature
Winnipeg
Szathmary, Emöke J.E.
Professor of Anthropology
McMaster University

Talman, James J.
Professor of History
University of Western Ontario
Tanner, Adrian
Associate Professor of Anthropology
Memorial University of Newfoundland
Tardif, Louis-Paul
Associate Executive Director
Canadian Trucking Association
Ottawa
Tarnopolsky, Walter Surma
Justice, Ontario Court of Appeal
Tarr, Leslie K.
Professor of Communications
Central Baptist Seminary, Toronto
Taschereau, Sylvie
Chercheur en histoire
Université du Québec à Montréal
Tatum, Jeremy B.
Associate Professor of Astronomy
University of Victoria
Tausky, Thomas E.
Associate Professor of English
University of Western Ontario
Taylor, C.J.
Historian, National Historic Parks & Sites Branch
Parks Canada, Hull

Taylor, Charles
Writer, Toronto
Taylor, Christopher Edward
Director, Policy Dept
Immigration Group, Canada
Employment & Immigration Commission
Ottawa
Taylor, J. Garth
Arctic Ethnologist
National Museum of Man, Ottawa
Taylor, J. Mary
Affiliate Scientist, Oregon Regional
Primate Research Center
Portland, Ore
Taylor, Jeff
PhD Candidate of History
University of Manitoba
Taylor, John H.
Associate Professor of History
Carleton University, Ottawa
Taylor, John Leonard
Writer & consultant, Ottawa
Taylor, M. Brook
Willowdale, Ont
Taylor, Philip S.
Habitat Biologist
Canadian Wildlife Service, Saskatoon
Taylor, Roy Lewis
Director of the Botanical Garden;
Professor of Plant Sciences
University of British Columbia
Taylor, Sylvia
Botanical Garden
University of British Columbia
Taylor, William Clyne
Professor of Pediatrics
University of Alberta
Taylor, William E. (Jr)
President
Social Sciences & Humanities
Research Council of Canada, Ottawa
Tehrani, Ghassem
Horticultural Research Institute
Vineland Station, Ont
Telewiak, Robert
Mineral Economist
Energy, Mines & Resources Canada
Ottawa
Templin, R. John
Head
Low Speed Aerodynamics Laboratory
National Research Council
Ottawa
Tennyson, Brian D.
Associate Professor of History
University College of Cape Breton
Tepperman, Lorne
Professor of Sociology
University of Toronto
Terasmae, Jaan
Professor of Geology
Brock University
Théberge, Pierre
Chief Curator
Montréal Museum of Fine Arts
Thesen, Sharon
Writer, Vancouver
Thiessen, George J.
Distinguished Visiting Scientist
National Research Council, Ottawa
Thiesson, Stuart A.
Executive Secretary
National Farmers Union
Thivierge, Marîse
Historienne
Institut québécois de recherche sur
la culture
Thivierge, Nicole
Professeur d'histoire
Université du Québec à Rimouski
Thomas, Ann
Assistant Curator of Photographs
National Gallery of Canada, Ottawa
Thomas, Clara
Professor of English
York University
Thomas, Eileen Mitchell
Barrister & Solicitor
Ottawa
Thomas, Gregory
Interpretive Planner
Parks Canada, Winnipeg
Thomas, Morley K.
Climatologist, Toronto;
Director General (retired)
Canadian Climate Centre
Downsview, Ont
Thomas, Paul G.
Associate Professor of Political
Studies
University of Manitoba

Thompson, Andrew Royden
Professor of Law;
Director, Westwater Research Centre
University of British Columbia
Thompson, Dixon A.R.
Professor of Environmental Science
University of Calgary
Thompson, John R.
Editor
Athabasca University
Thompson, Teresa
General Synod Archivist
Anglican Church of Canada, Toronto
Thompson, William Paul
Associate Professor of Architecture
University of Manitoba
Thomson, Alex J.
Senior Financial Economist
The Royal Bank of Canada, Montréal
Thomson, Malcolm M.
(Retired), Ottawa
Thomson, Reginald George
Dean, Atlantic Veterinary College
University of Prince Edward Island
Thomson, Stanley
Professor of Civil Engineering
University of Alberta
Thorburn, Hugh G.
Professor of Political Science
Queen's University
Thorpe, Frederick J.
Chief, History Division
National Museum of Man, Ottawa
Thuro, Catherine M.V.
Lighting Historian, Toronto
Tiedje, John L.
Manager, Research Dept
Esso Petroleum Canada
Sarnia, Ont
Tiessen, Herman
Professor of Vegetable Physiology
University of Guelph
Tinic, Seha M.
Professor of Finance
University of Alberta
Todd, Ewen C.D.
Food-borne Disease Reporting Centre
Health & Welfare Canada, Ottawa
Toguri, James M.
Professor of Metallurgy
University of Toronto
Tomkins, George S.
Professor of Education
University of British Columbia
Tomović, Vladislav
Associate Professor of Sociology
Brock University
Toner, Peter M.
Associate Professor of History
University of New Brunswick
Tousignant, Pierre
Professeur agrégé d'histoire
Université de Montréal
Town, Harold B.
Artist, Toronto
Townsend-Gault, Charlotte
Writer & anthropologist
Halifax
Townsend, Joan B.
Professor of Anthropology
University of Manitoba
Townsend, Richard G.
Associate Professor of Educational
Administration
The Ontario Institute for Studies in
Education, Toronto
Travill, Anthony A.
Professor of Anatomy
Queen's University
Tremblay, Gaëtan
Professeur de communications
Université du Québec à Montréal
Tremblay, Jean-Yves
Director
Industrial Minerals Division
Energy, Mines & Resources Canada
Ottawa
Tremblay, Marc-Adélard
Professeur d'anthropologie
Université Laval
Trépanier, Pierre
Professeur agrégé d'histoire
Université de Montréal
Triggs, Stanley G.
Curator, Notman Photographic Archives
McCord Museum, Montréal
Trofimenkoff, Susan Mann
Professor of History
University of Ottawa

Troper, Harold
Professor of History
The Ontario Institute for Studies in
Education, Toronto
Trott, Elizabeth A.
Writer, Toronto
Truax, Barry D.
Associate Professor of Communication
& Centre for the Arts
Simon Fraser University
Trudel, Marc J.
Professeur d'horticulture
Université Laval
Trudel, Marcel
Professeur émérite
Université d'Ottawa
Trueman, Mark E.H.
Atmospheric Environment Service
Downsview, Ont
Tuck, James A.
Professor of Archaeology
Memorial University of Newfoundland
Tucker, Albert V.
Professor of History
Glendon College, York University
Tuinman, Jaap
Professor of Education
Simon Fraser University
Tunnicliffe, Verena J.
Assistant Professor of Biology
University of Victoria
Tuomi, Archie L.W.
Senior Advisor Recreational Fisheries
Dept of Fisheries & Oceans, Ottawa
Tupper, Allan
Associate Professor of Political
Science
University of Alberta
Turner, H.E.
Associate Professor of History
McMaster University
Turner, Nancy J.
Research Associate, Botany Division
British Columbia Provincial Museum
Victoria
Turnock, William J.
Research Scientist
Agriculture Canada, Winnipeg
Tweedie, Katherine
Assistant Professor of Photography
Concordia University
Tyler, Christopher D.
Author, potter & craft administrator
Halifax
Tyrchniewicz, Edward W.
Professor & Head of Agricultural
Economics
University of Manitoba

Urquhart, M.C.
Sir John A. Macdonald Professor of
Political & Economic Science
Queen's University

Vachon, Auguste
Chief
Medal, Heraldry & Costume Section
Picture Division
Public Archives of Canada, Ottawa
Vagt, G. Oliver
Mineral Economist
Energy, Mines & Resources Canada
Ottawa
Valaskakis, Gail C.
Associate Professor of Communication
Studies
Concordia University
Vallee, Frank G.
Professor Emeritus of Sociology &
Anthropology
Carleton University
Vallières, Marc
Professeur agrégé d'histoire
Université Laval
van Everdingen, Robert O.
National Hydrology Research
Institute, Calgary
van Ginkel, Blanche Lemco
Professor of Architecture
University of Toronto
van Nus, Walter
Associate Professor of History
Concordia University
Van Roey-Roux, Françoise
Professeur de français
Collège de Maisonneuve, Montréal
Van Wagner, Charles E.
Research Scientist, Forest Fire
Canadian Forestry Service
Chalk River, Ont

Van Wart, Alice
Dept of English
University of Alberta
van Zwamen, Christine
Canadian Nature Federation, Ottawa
van Zyll de Jong, Constantinus G.
Curator, Mammalogy Section
National Museum of Natural Sciences
Ottawa
Vanasse, André
Professeur titulaire d'études littéraires
Université du Québec à Montréal
Vanderburgh, Rosamond M.
Associate Professor of Anthropology
University of Toronto
Varley, Christopher
Toronto
Vastokas, Joan M.
Professor of Anthropology
Trent University
Vaughan, Frederick
Professor of Political Science
University of Guelph
Vaz, Edmund W.
Professor of Sociology
University of Waterloo
Veatch, Richard
Professor of Political Science
University of Winnipeg
Veeman, Michele M.
Professor of Agricultural Economics
University of Alberta
Veeman, Terrence S.
Professor of Economics & Agricultural
Economics
University of Alberta
Vermeirre, André
Professeur d'histoire
Université de Montréal
Véronneau, Pierre
Responsable publications et recherches
Cinémathèque québécoise
Vézina, Claude
Assistant Director
Institut Armand-Frappier
Laval-des-Rapides, Qué
Vézina, Raymond
Historien d'art
Gouvernement du Canada, Ottawa
Vick, Roger
Curator, Devonian Botanic Garden
University of Alberta
Vigod, Bernard L.
Professor of History
University of New Brunswick
Vincent, Aubrey R.
Teacher, St John's
Vincent, Thomas B.
Associate Professor of English
Royal Military College of Canada
Vita, Kati
Critic, Montréal
Vladykov, Vadim D.
Professor Emeritus of Biology
University of Ottawa
Voice, Douglas
Associate Professor of Music
University of Ottawa
Voisine, Nive
Professeur titulaire d'histoire
Université Laval
Volkoff, George M.
Dean Emeritus, Faculty of Science
University of British Columbia
Vollmer, Michael
Yacht designer
Burlington, Ont
Voyer, Roger D.
Principal
Nordicity Group Ltd, Ottawa

Wachna, Pamela S.
Associate Curator
Market Gallery of the City of Toronto
Archives, Toronto
Waddams, Stephen M.
Professor of Law
University of Toronto
Wagg, Susan
Art historian, Montréal
Wagner, Anton
Association for Canadian Theatre
History, Toronto
Waiser, W.A.
Historian, Parks Canada
Winnipeg
Waite, P.B.
Professor of History
Dalhousie University

Walcroft, Michael John
Technical Projects Director
Connaught Laboratories Limited
Willowdale, Ont

Walden, David B.
Professor
University of Western Ontario

Walker, Deward E., Jr
Dept of Anthropology
University of Colorado at Boulder

Walker, James W. St.G.
Associate Professor of History
University of Waterloo

Walker, John P.
Professor of Animal & Poultry Science
University of Guelph

Walker, Susan
Publisher
Quill & Quire, *Toronto*

Walkom, Tom
Ottawa, Ontario

Wallace, Birgitta Linderoth
Staff Archaeologist, Parks Canada
Atlantic Region, Halifax

Wallace, Carl M.
Associate Professor of History
Laurentian University, Sudbury

Wallace, Hugh N.
Associate Professor of History
Mount Saint Vincent University

Wallace, P.R.
Professor Emeritus of Physics
McGill University;
Principal, Science College
Concordia University

Wallot, Jean-Pierre
Professeur titulaire d'histoire
Université de Montréal

Walsh, Susan
Vancouver

Wanzel, J. Grant
Associate Professor of Architecture
Technical University of Nova Scotia

Ward, Norman
Britnell Professor of Political Science
University of Saskatchewan

Ward, Philip R.
Conservator, Ottawa

Ward, W. Peter
Associate Professor of History
University of British Columbia

Ware, Tracy
Doctoral Candidate
University of Western Ontario

Warkentin, John
Professor of Geography
York University

Warner, John Anson
Long Beach, Calif

Waterman, A.M.C.
Professor of Economics
University of Manitoba

Waters, Janice
Ottawa

Waterston, Elizabeth
Professor of English
University of Guelph

Watkins, Mel
Professor of Economics
University of Toronto

Watson, Lorne
Professor of Piano
Brandon University;
Artistic Director, Eckhardt-Gramatté
National Competition for the
Performance of Canadian Music

Watt, Robert D.
Director
The Vancouver Museum, Vancouver

Waugh, Douglas
Executive Director (retired)
Association of Canadian Medical
Colleges, Ottawa

Waugh, Earle H.
Associate Professor of Religious Studies
University of Alberta

Wayman, Morris
Professor of Chemical Engineering & Forestry
University of Toronto

Weait, Christopher
Co-principal bassoonist
The Toronto Symphony, Toronto

Weaver, John C.
Professor of History
McMaster University

Webb, James L.
Endocrinology Laboratory
St Mary's Hospital;
Dept of Pathology
McGill University

Webster, D.B.
Curator, Canadian Dept
Royal Ontario Museum, Toronto

Webster, Douglas R.
Director
Urban & Regional Planning Programme
University of Calgary

Webster, Gloria Cranmer
Curator, U'mista Cultural Centre
Alert Bay, BC

Webster, Helen R.
Mineral Resource Analyst
Mineral Policy Sector
Energy, Mines & Resources Canada
Ottawa

Wegenast, William G.
Associate Professor of Engineering
Memorial University of Newfoundland

Weinrich, Peter H.
Executive Director
Canadian Crafts Council, Ottawa

Weir, Thomas R.
Professor of Geography
University of Manitoba

Weisbord, Merrily
Writer, Montréal

Wellburn, G. Vernon
Manager, Western Division
Forest Engineering Institute of
Canada, Vancouver

Welsh, Harry L.
Professor Emeritus of Physics
University of Toronto

Wenaas, Carl J.
Writer, Winnipeg

Werner, Leo H.
Executive Director
International Maple Syrup Institute

Wertheimer, Douglas
Newspaper Publisher, Calgary

Weseloh, D.V. Chip
Canadian Wildlife Service
Burlington, Ont

West, J. Thomas
Curator
Canada's Sports Hall of Fame, Toronto

West, Roxroy
Writer, Winnipeg

Weston, Marla L.
Paleobiology Division
National Museum of Natural Sciences
Ottawa

Whalen, Linda D.
Writer, St John's

Whebell, C.F.J.
Associate Professor of Geography
University of Western Ontario

Wheeler, John O.
Geological Survey of Canada
Vancouver

Whitaker, Reginald
Professor of Political Science
York University

White, Clinton Oliver
Associate Professor of History
Campion College, University of Regina

White, M. Lillian
Calgary, Alberta

Whitehorn, Alan
Associate Professor of Politics
Royal Military College of Canada

Whiteson, Leon
Architecture critic & author
Toronto

Whiteway, James R.
Research Analyst
Public Relations Division
Ontario Hydro, Toronto

Whitmore, Gordon Francis
Professor of Medical Biophysics
University of Toronto;
Head, Physics Division
Ontario Cancer Institute, Toronto

Whyte, Donald
Professor of Sociology & Anthropology
Carleton University

Wickberg, Edgar
Professor of History
University of British Columbia

Wien, Thomas
PhD Candidate
McGill University

Wiggins, Ernest J.
Consultant, Edmonton

Wight, Darlene
Inuit art consultant, Ottawa

Wilcox, Betty
Victoria, BC

Wilimovsky, Norman J.
Professor & Curator of Fisheries
University of British Columbia

Wilkin, Karen
Independent curator & critic
Toronto

Wilkinson, Bruce William
Professor of Economics
University of Alberta

Willey, Robert C.
Editor, Canadian Numismatic Journal
Espanola, Ont

Williams, David Ricardo
Adjunct Professor of Law
University of Victoria

Williams, Glyndwr
Professor of History
Queen Mary College
University of London, England

Williams, Patricia Lynn
Archivist & historian, Saskatoon

Williams, Richard M.
Adviser,
Uranium & Nuclear Energy Branch
Energy, Mines & Resources Canada
Ottawa

Williams, S. Ridgeley
Assistant Director
National Museum of Natural Sciences
Ottawa

Williams, Sydney B.
President, Hays & Williams Ltd
Calgary

Williams, W.M.
Birks Professor of Metallurgy
McGill University

Williamson, Mary F.
Fine Arts Bibliographer
York University

Williamson, Moncrieff
Director Emeritus of Confederation
Centre Art Gallery & Museum
Charlottetown

Willis, Christopher J.
Professor of Chemistry
University of Western Ontario

Willis, Norman M.
Curator, National Medal Collection
Public Archives of Canada, Ottawa

Willmot, Rod
Chargé de cours
Université de Sherbrooke

Wilson, Bruce G.
Chief, London Office
Public Archives of Canada
London, England

Wilson, H.E.
Associate Professor of History
University of Alberta

Wilson, Ian E.
Provincial Archivist
Saskatchewan Archives Board, Regina

Wilson, J. Donald
Professor, History of Education
University of British Columbia

Wilson, J. Tuzo
Director General
Ontario Science Centre
Don Mills, Ont

Wilson, Jean
Editor, Vancouver

Windwick, Brent
Health Law Project
University of Alberta

Winks, Robin W.
Professor of History
Yale University

Wirick, Gregory
Journalist, Ottawa

Wirick, Ronald G.
Professor of Economics
University of Western Ontario

Wise, S.F.
Professor of History & Dean of
Graduate Studies & Research
Carleton University

Withrow, William J.
Director, Art Gallery of Ontario
Toronto

Wittenberg, Henry
President, Canadian Toy Manufacturers
Association

Wolfe, Leonhard S.
Professor of Neurology & Neurosurgery
Montréal Neurological Institute
McGill University

Wonders, William C.
University Professor of Geography
University of Alberta

Wood, Bernard
Director, North-South Institute, Ottawa

Woodcock, George
Writer, Vancouver

Woodruff, M. Emerson
Professor of Optometry
University of Waterloo

Woods, Robert James
Professor of Chemistry
University of Saskatchewan

Wright, Glenn
Public Archives of Canada, Ottawa

Wright, Harold E.
Partridge Island Research Project
Saint John, NB

Wright, J.F.C.
Alberta Consumer & Corporate Affairs
Edmonton

Wright, J.V.
Archaeological Survey of Canada
National Museum of Man, Ottawa

Wright, Janet
Parks Canada, Hull

Wright, Kenneth O.
Former Director
Dominion Astrophysical Observatory
National Research Council of Canada
Victoria

Wright, Roy A.
Ethnohistorian, Ottawa

Wyczynski, Paul
Titulaire de recherche
Université d'Ottawa

Wyman, Max
Author & critic, Vancouver

Wynn, Graeme
Associate Professor of Geography
University of British Columbia

Yaffe, Leo
Macdonald Professor of Chemistry
McGill University

Yalden, Maxwell F.
Commissioner of Official Languages
Ottawa

York, Derek
Professor of Physics
University of Toronto

Young, A.J. (Sandy)
Professor of Physical Education
Dalhousie University

Young, C. Maureen
MA Graduate Student of History
University of Victoria

Young, David A.
Head of Museum Advisory Services
Royal Ontario Museum, Toronto

Young, Gayle
Composer & writer
Grimsby, Ont

Young, H. Brig
Almonte, Ont

Young, Jane
Curator, Surrey Art Gallery
Surrey, BC

Young, Jeffery
Research Assistant
Canadian Institute of Guided Ground
Transport
Queen's University

Young, John H.
Clergy
Upper Rawdon, NS

Young, Roland S.
Consulting Chemical Engineer
Victoria

Young, Walter D. (deceased)
Professor of Political Science
University of Victoria

Zack, Manuel
Assistant to the President
McMaster University

Zeller, Suzanne E.
PhD Student of History
University of Toronto

Zeman, Jarold K.
Professor of Church History
Acadia University

Zemans, Joyce
Associate Professor of Art History
York University

Zepp, Norman W.
Assistant Curator
Mackenzie Art Gallery, Regina

Ziegel, Jacob S.
Professor of Law
University of Toronto

Ziff, Bruce
Assistant Professor of Law
University of Alberta

Zingrone, Frank D.
Associate Professor of Communication
York University

Zoltai, Stephen C.
Research Scientist
Canadian Forestry Service, Edmonton

Zuk, Louise
St Albert, Alta

ABBREVIATIONS

" inch
µ micron
a are (unit of metric land measure)
A/C/M Air Chief Marshal
A/M Air Marshal
A/V/M Air Vice-Marshal
AAA Amateur Athletic Association
Adm Admiral
Ala Alabama
alt altitude
Alta Alberta
approx approximately
Apr April
ARC Alberta Research Council
Ariz Arizona
Ark Arkansas
Assn, assn Association, association
Asst Assistant
Atty Gen Attorney General
Aug August
b born
BA Bachelor of Arts
bap baptized
Batt Battalion
BBC British Broadcasting Corportion
BC British Columbia
BComm Bachelor of Commerce
Bdy, bdy Boundary, boundary
BEd Bachelor of Education
BLitt Bachelor of Literature
BMus Bachelor of Music
BNA British North America
Bor Borough
Brig-Gen Brigadier-General
BSc Bachelor of Science
BSW Bachelor of Social Work
Btu British thermal unit
bu bushels
C City
c census
c circa
CA Chartered Accountant
CAF Canadian Armed Forces, Canadian Air Force
Calif California
CAPAC Composers, Authors and Publishers Association of Canada
Capt Captain
CAUT Canadian Association of University Teachers
CBC Canadian Broadcasting Corporation
CBE Companion of the Order of the British Empire
CCCL Canadian Catholic Confederation of Labour
CCF Co-operative Commonwealth Federation
CCL Canadian Congress of Labour
Cdn Canadian
CDPT Collège dominicain de Philosophie et Théologie
Cdr Commander
CEF Canadian Expeditionary Force
CEGEP Collège d'enseignement général et professionnel
CFB Canadian Forces Base
CFDC Canadian Film Development Corporation
CGA Certified General Accountant
Chan Channel
cm centimetre
CMA Census Metropolitan Area
CMG Companion of the Order of St Michael and St George
CNR Canadian National Railways
CNTU Confederation of National Trade Unions
Co, co Company, company
Col Colonel
Coll College
Colo Colorado
Comm Community
Conn Connecticut
Const constable
Corp, corp Corporation, corporation
COTC Canadian Officer Training Corps
CPCGN Canadian Permanent Committee on Geographical Names
Cpl Corporal
CPR Canadian Pacific Railway
CRBC Canadian Radio Broadcasting Commission
CRTC Canadian Radio-Television and Telecommunications Commission
CTC Canadian Transport Commission
Czech Czechoslovakia
Cy County
d died
Dak Dakota
Dan Danish
db decibel
Dec December
Del Delaware
Dept, dept Department, department
DEW Distant Early Warning
DFC Distinguished Flying Cross
DIAND Dept of Indian Affairs and Northern Development
Dir, dir Director, director
Dist, dist District, district
Div Division
DM District Municipality
DMus Doctor of Music
DSC Distinguished Service Cross
DSO Distinguished Service Order
DSW Doctor of Social Work
dwt deadweight, deadweight tons
E east
e estimate
ed editor, edited, edited by, edition
eds editors
EEC European Economic Community
eg (*exempli gratia*) for example
elev elevation
EMR Dept of Energy, Mines and Resources
Eng England
est established
etc (et cetera) and so forth
F/O Flying Officer
fd founded
Feb February
fl (floriat) flourished
Fla Florida
Flt Lt Flight Lieutenant
Flt Off Flight Officer
Flt Sgt Flight Sergeant
Fr Father
Fri Friday
FRSC Fellow of the Royal Society of Canada
Ft Fort
g gram
Ga Georgia
GATT General Agreement on Tariffs and Trade
GDP Gross Domestic Product
Gen General
Ger German, Germany
GHz gigahertz
Gk Greek
GNP Gross National Product
Gov Gen, gov gen Governor General, governor general
govt government
GSC Geological Survey of Canada
GW gigawatt
h hour; hecto
ha hectare
Ham Hamlet
HBC Hudson's Bay Company
hg hectogram
hL hectolitre
hm hectometre
HMCS Her Majesty's Canadian Ship
hp horsepower
hr hour
Hz hertz (one cycle per second)
I, Is Island, Islands
ie (*id est*) that is
Ill Illinois
Inc Incorporated
Ind Indiana
Insp Inspector
Inst, inst Institution, institution
Int, int International, international
IR Indian Reserve
Ire Ireland
Jan January
k kilo
Kans Kansas
KB Knight of the Bath
KC King's Counsel
KCMG Knight Commander of St Michael and St George
kg kilogram
kHz kilohertz
kL kilolitre
km kilometre
km/h kilometres per hour
kPa kilopascal
kW kilowatt
kWh kilowatt-hour
kW/m kilowatts/metre
Ky Kentucky
L litre
La Louisiana
Lab Labrador
Lat Latin
lat latitude
LC Lower Canada
LID Local Improvement District
LLD Doctor of Laws
Lk, lk Lks, lks Lake, lake, Lakes, lakes
long longitude
LRCP Licentiate of the Royal College of Physicians
Lt Lieutenant
Lt-Gov Lieutenant-Governor
Ltd Limited
Ltée Limitée
m metre
m/s metres per second
MA Master of Arts
Maj Major
Man Manitoba
Mar March
Mass Massachusetts
MBE Member of the Order of the British Empire
Md Maryland
MD Doctor of Medicine
Me Maine
MEng Master of Engineering
mg milligram
Mgr Monseigneur
mHz megahertz
Mich Michigan
MIL Military Reserve
min minute
Minn Minnesota
Miss Mississippi
mj megajoule
mL millilitre
MLA Member of Legislative Assembly
mm millimetre
MNA Member of National Assembly
Mo Missouri
Mont Montana
MP Member of Parliament
MPP Member of Provincial Parliament
MRCS Member of the Royal College of Surgeons
MSc Master of Science
MSW Master of Social Work
Mt Mount
Mt A Mount Allison University
Mtn, mtn, Mts, mts Mountain, mountain, Mountains, mountains
Mw megawatt
N north
N Dak North Dakota
N Mex New Mexico
NB New Brunswick
NC North Carolina
NDHQ National Defence Headquarters
NDP New Democratic Party
NEB National Energy Board
Nebr Nebraska
NEP National Energy Policy
Nev Nevada
NFB National Film Board
Nfld Newfoundland
NH New Hampshire
NHL National Hockey League
NJ New Jersey
No, no Number, number
Nor Norwegian
NORAD North American Air Defense
Nov November
NRC National Research Council
NRCC National Research Council of Canada
NS Nova Scotia
NSAC Nova Scotia Agricultural College
NSCAD Nova Scotia College of Art and Design
NTS National Topographic Survey
NWC North West Company
NWMP North-West Mounted Police
NWT North-West Territories (before 1905) Northwest Territories (since 1905)
NY New York

OAC Ontario Agricultural College
OBE Order of the British Empire
Oct October
OECD Organization for Economic Cooperation and Development
Okla Oklahoma
OMI Oblates of Mary Immaculate
Ont Ontario
OPEC Organization of Petroleum Exporting Countries
Oreg Oregon
Pa Pennsylvania
PAC Public Archives of Canada
PC Progressive Conservative
PCO Privy Council Office
PEI Prince Edward Island
Pen, pen Peninsula, peninsula
pH hydrogen-ion concentration
PhD Doctor of Philosophy
PM Prime Minister
PMO Prime Minister's Office
PO Petty Officer; Post Office
pop population
POW Prisoner of War
PQ Parti Québécois
Prem Premier
Pres President
pseud pseudonym
Pt Point, Port
publ published
QC Queen's Counsel
Qué Québec
R & D Research and Development
R River
RAF Royal Air Force
RCAF Royal Canadian Air Force
RCN Royal Canadian Navy
RD Rural District
Rear-Adm Rear-Admiral
Reg Regiment
repr reprinted
rev revised
RFC Royal Flying Corps
RI Rhode Island
RIA Registered Industrial and Cost Accountant
RM Rural Municipality
RMC Royal Military College of Canada
RN Registered Nurse
RSC Royal Society of Canada
Ry Railway
Ryerson Ryerson Polytechnical Institute
S South
s second; section (in reference to Criminal Code)
S Dak South Dakota
Sask Saskatchewan
SC South Carolina
Scot Scotland
Sen Senator
Sept September
SFU Simon Fraser University
Sgt Sergeant
SI Système International des Unités
Soc, soc Society, society
Sol Gen Solicitor General
Span Spanish
Sqn Cdr Squadron Commander
Sqn Ldr Squadron Leader
SS Ship Title (Steamship)
St Saint
St FX Saint Francis Xavier University
Staff-Sgt Staff-Sargeant
Ste Sainte
Str Strait
Supt Superintendent
Switz Switzerland
T Town
t tonne
TCA Trans-Canada Airlines
Tenn Tennessee
Terr, terr Territory, territory
Tex Texas
TLC Trades and Labor Congress
tr translated, translation
trans translated
TV Television
TWh terawatt hours
Twp Township
U University
U de M Université de Montréal
U Leth University of Lethbridge
U Man University of Manitoba
U of A University of Alberta
U of C University of Calgary
U of O University of Ottawa
U of T University of Toronto
U Vic University of Victoria
U Wpg University of Winnipeg
UBC University of British Columbia
UC Upper Canada
UCC United Church of Canada
UCCB University College of Cape Breton
UK United Kingdom
UK£ United Kingdom pound
UMWA International Union, United Mine Workers of America
UN United Nations
UNB University of New Brunswick
UNESCO United Nations Educational, Scientific and Cultural Organization
UP Unincorporated Place
UPEI University of Prince Edward Island
UQ Université du Québec
UQAC Université du Québec à Chicoutimi
UQAM Université du Québec à Montréal
UQAR Université du Québec à Rimouski
UQTR Université du Québec à Trois-Rivières
US United States of America
USSR Union of Soviet Socialist Republics
Va Virginia
Vl Village
vol, vols volume, volumes
VP Vice-President
Vt Vermont
W West
Wash Washington
Wis Wisconsin
WLU Wilfrid Laurier University
WO Warrant Officer
WWI World War I
WWII World War II
Wyo Wyoming
YMCA Young Men's Christian Association
yrs years
YT Yukon Territory
YWCA Young Women's Christian Association

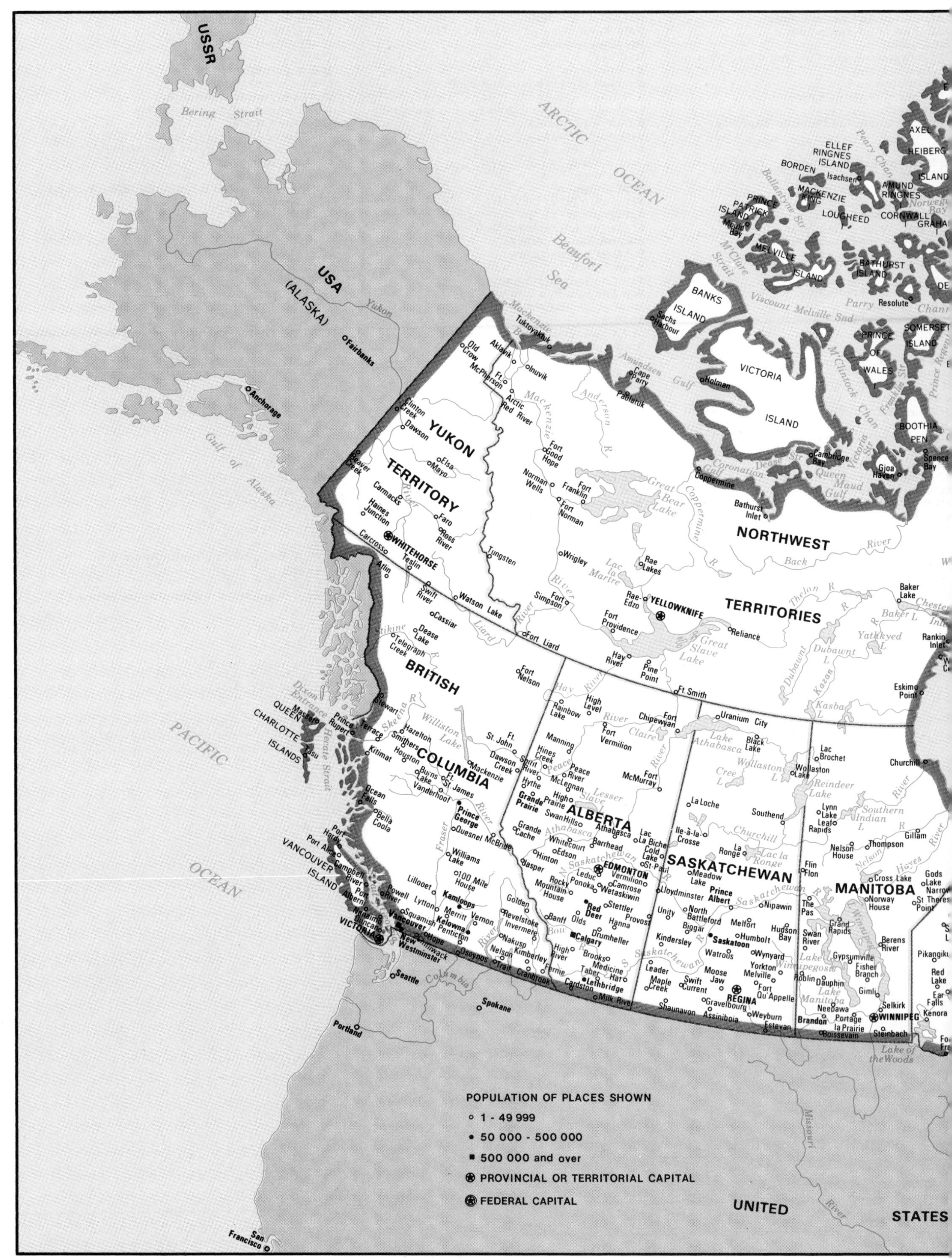

POPULATION OF PLACES SHOWN
1 - 49 999
50 000 - 500 000
500 000 and over
PROVINCIAL OR TERRITORIAL CAPITAL
FEDERAL CAPITAL
YUKON TERRITORY
NORTHWEST TERRITORIES
BRITISH COLUMBIA
ALBERTA
SASKATCHEWAN
MANITOBA
USA (ALASKA)
USSR
UNITED STATES
PACIFIC OCEAN
ARCTIC OCEAN
Beaufort Sea
Bering Strait
Gulf of Alaska
WHITEHORSE
YELLOWKNIFE
VICTORIA
EDMONTON
REGINA
WINNIPEG
Calgary
Vancouver
Saskatoon

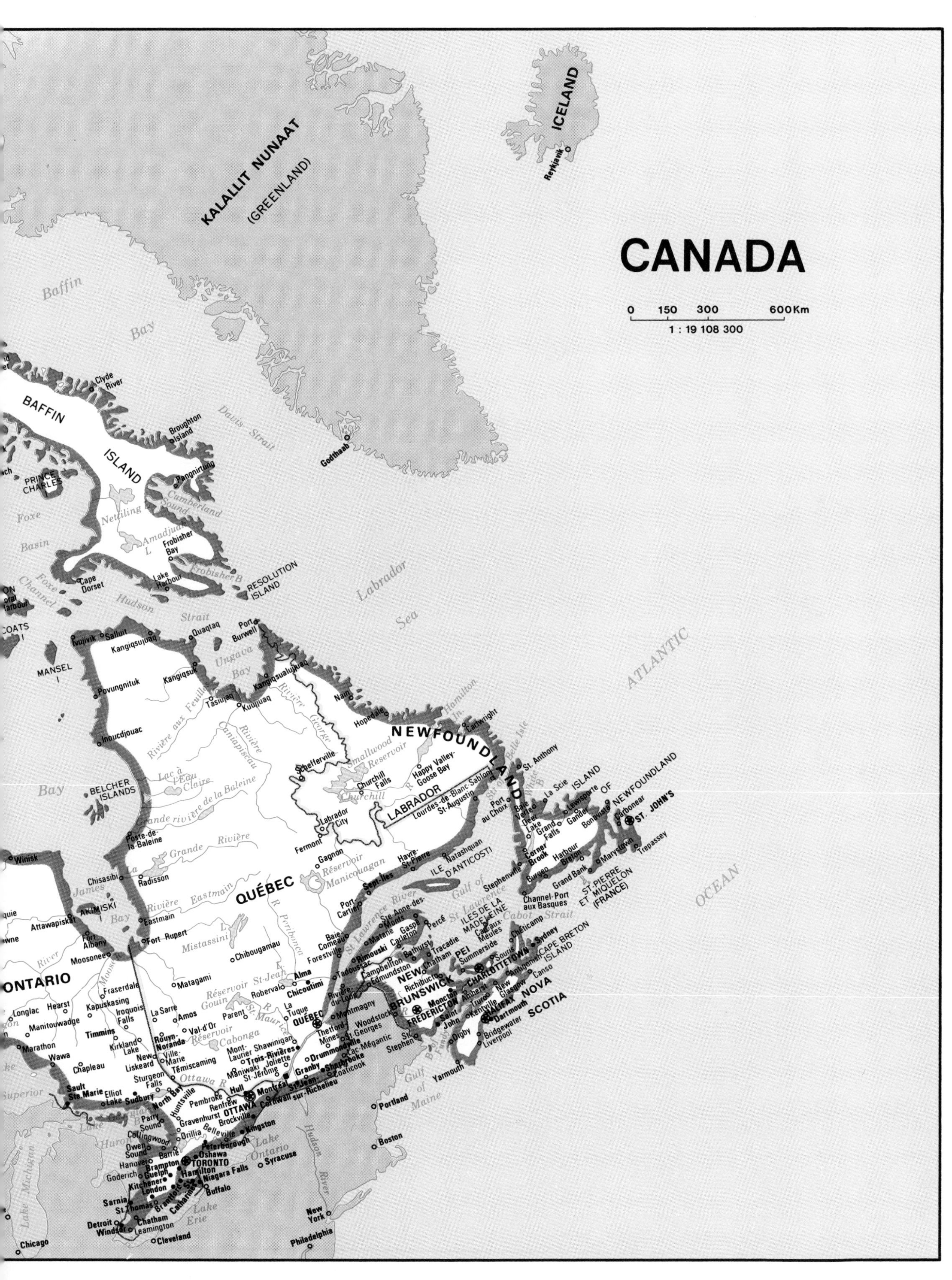
CANADA
0 150 300 600Km
1 : 19 108 300

THE CANADIAN ENCYCLOPEDIA

A Mari usque ad Mare ("From Sea to Sea"), Canada's motto, was derived from Psalm 72:8, which reads in Latin "Et dominabitur a mari usque ad mare, et a flumine usque ad terminos terrae," and in the King James version, "He shall have dominion also from sea to sea, and from the river unto the ends of the earth." Attention was first directed to the verse when, apparently at the suggestion of Samuel Leonard TILLEY, the term "dominion" was chosen to represent Canada as a whole when the British North America Act was drafted. "From sea to sea" could not apply to Canada until 1871, when BC joined Confederation and the Dominion extended from Atlantic to Pacific. In 1872 Rev George Monro GRANT crossed the country as secretary to Sandford FLEMING, who was then in charge of the Pacific railway surveys. The next year he published *Ocean to Ocean*, his journal describing the journey. The title is akin to "from sea to sea" and strong tradition insists that thereafter Grant preached in many centres using Psalm 72:8 as his text and advocating the adoption of "from sea to sea" as Canada's motto. The first official use came in 1906, when the phrase was engraved on the head of the mace of the Legislative Assembly of the new Province of Saskatchewan. This would be known to Joseph Pope, undersecretary of state at the time, and the phrase evidently impressed him. In 1919 Pope was named to a 4-member committee appointed by the federal government to recommend a new design for the Arms of Canada. No motto was included in the old design, but one was to be included in the new arms. A draft design, which included the motto, was approved by Cabinet in Apr 1921 and by King George V in May. Maj-Gen W.G. Gwatkin, one of the committee members, had proposed that the motto be *In memoriam in spem* ("In memory, in hope"), but Pope's counterproposal was adopted. On 29 Sept 1921, after viewing the final design, he wrote in his diary: "Our Arms are very handsome . . . everything that can be desired. The motto 'A Mari usque ad Mare,' which is an original suggestion of my own, I regard as very appropriate." *See* EMBLEMS OF CANADA; HERALDRY. W. KAYE LAMB

The single Canadian species of abalone (*Haliotis kamtschatkana*) is called the Japanese, pinto or northern ear shell, depending on the locale (*photo by Hälle Flygare*).

Abalone (*Haliotis*), genus of primitive, marine, gastropod MOLLUSCS with over 70 species world wide. The single Canadian species (*Haliotis kamtschatkana*) is called the Japanese, pinto or northern ear shell, depending on locale. This large (up to 12 cm), limpetlike snail prefers semiprotected waters between the low intertidal zone and 18 m depth. The abalone uses its powerful foot to fasten itself to rock surfaces. *H. kamtschatkana* is a gregarious species which grazes on drift and surface algae. Its ear-shaped shell has a wavy texture and bears, on its outer whorl, 4-5 respiratory pores which also act as exit ports for spawn and excreta. The shell's outer surface is mottled red-green. The blue-green iridescence of its inner pearly surface has made it popular with Northwest Coast Indians as material for jewellery and inlays. The abalone's soft, muscular parts (tenderized and grilled as steak or ground up for bisque) are a choice gourmet food. Its only other predators are sea stars and, occasionally, sea otters. PETER V. FANKBONER

Abbotsford, BC, District Municipality, pop 12 745 (1981c), area 13 856 ha, inc 1972 from amalgamation of the District of Sumas and village of Abbotsford, is located on the S bank of the FRASER R between MATSQUI and CHILLIWACK. The area's traditional agricultural economy has declined, while there has been a marked increase in industrial activity as firms have moved from VANCOUVER seeking less congested areas. The manufacturing sector includes feed and food products, brick and tile. The former village of Abbotsford (likely named after Henry Abbott, CPR superintendent) serves as a retail trade and service centre for the surrounding districts; commercial development has now moved into the adjacent district of Matsqui. Continued growth as an industrial and residential suburb of Vancouver is assured. Abbotsford is served by a newspaper, the *Express*. Each year the famous Abbotsford Air Show brings thousands of visitors to the area from all over the Pacific Northwest. ALAN F.J. ARTIBISE

Abbott, Sir John Joseph Caldwell, lawyer, professor, politician, prime minister (b at St Andrews East [St-André-Est], Lower Canada 12 Mar 1821; d at Montréal 30 Oct 1893). A graduate of McGill College, he was admitted to the Bar 1847 and taught at McGill from 1853, serving as

Sir John Joseph Caldwell Abbott, 3rd prime minister of Canada, 1891-92 (*courtesy Public Archives of Canada/PA-33933*).

dean of the law faculty 1855-80. Although he signed the Annexation Manifesto in 1849, he quickly recanted and during the *Trent* crisis of 1861 he raised and commanded a militia force to patrol the border with the US. He sat in the legislative assembly, and later in the House of Commons from 1860 until he was appointed to the Senate in 1887, except for the period 1874-1880. Solicitor general for Canada East in the short-lived administration of J.S. MACDONALD and L.V. SICOTTE 1862-63, he entered the federal Cabinet in 1887 as government leader in the Senate and minister without portfolio. (He was also mayor of Montréal 1887-89.) In 1891 he succeeded Sir John A. MACDONALD as PM. His was largely a caretaking administration and in 1892 he turned over the government to Sir John S.D. THOMPSON. CARMAN MILLER

Reading: C. Ondaatje and D. Swainson, *The Prime Ministers of Canada 1867-1968* (1968).

Abbott, Maude Elizabeth Seymour, pathologist (b at St Andrews East [St-André-Est], Qué 18 Mar 1869; d at Montréal 2 Sept 1940). Though she graduated in arts from McGill (1890), she was barred from medicine because of her sex, so she earned Bishop's CM, MD (1894); ironically McGill awarded her MD, CM (honoris causa, 1910) also LLD (1936). As asst curator, McGill Medical Museum (1898) and curator (1901), she introduced the use of the museum in teaching pathology. A disciple of William OSLER, she contributed to his text *Modern Medicine* (1908) the chapter on "Congenital Heart Disease," which he declared the best thing he had ever read on the subject. Apart from 2 years, her whole career was at McGill where, though world famous, she was never promoted beyond the rank of assistant professor. She served as permanent international secretary of the International Association of Medical Museums and editor of its journal (1907-1938), and published many papers on pathology as well as histories of medicine and nursing. A trifle eccentric in later life, she was generous, active, always involved and sometimes known as "The Beneficent Tornado." MARGARET GILLETT

Reading: Margaret Gillett, *We Walked Very Warily: A History of Women at McGill* (1981).

Abduction, literally leading away, historically meant the seizure of a wife from her husband, or a female infant or heiress from her parent or lawful guardian, for marriage, concubinage or prostitution. From Edward I's time abduction was a criminal offence, and the husband or guardian was entitled to monetary damages for the woman abducted. Under the Canadian Criminal Code abduction occurs when, without her consent, a female of any age is taken out of the possession of her parent or guardian for marriage or illicit sexual intercourse with anyone; or a girl under 16 is unlawfully taken away from anyone with lawful authority over her. In the case of unlawful sexual intercourse with a girl under 16 the accused may be acquitted if there is evidence that she was more to blame than he, or if he can convince the court that he honestly believed she was over 16, but no such defence exists with abduction. Nor does her consent provide her abductor with a defence. It is also abduction to take away a child under 14 years of age with intent to deprive a parent or other lawful guardian of possession of that child, or with intent to steal anything on or about the person of such a child. *See* KIDNAPPING. L.C. GREEN

Abenaki take their name from a word in their own language meaning "dawn land people" or "easterners." In 1600 the Eastern Abenaki occupied what is now the state of Maine, except for its northern and easternmost portions. The Western Abenaki lived in the rest of northern New England, from New Hampshire to Lk Champlain. The Western and Eastern Abenaki spoke closely related Algonquian languages, each having various local dialects. Eastern Abenaki had at least 4 such dialects, Pequawket (Pigwacket), Arosaguntacook, Kennebec and Penobscot. All Abenaki were part of the Eastern Algonquian cultures and were separated from other Algonquians to the W and N by an intrusion of Iroquoian-speaking cultures over 2000 years ago.

Around 1600, there were nearly 14 000 Eastern Abenaki and 12 000 Western Abenaki, but Old World diseases, particularly measles and smallpox, reduced these numbers by 78% and 98%, respectively, within a few decades. Surviving Western Abenaki, often called Sokoki or Penacook, withdrew into refugee communities and many eventually moved to the villages of Bécancour and St Francis in Québec. The Eastern Abenaki were not as devastated by warfare and disease, and over 800 Penobscot survive on a reservation near Old Town, Maine; many Pequawket, Arosaguntacook and Kennebec people moved to Québec settlements during the colonial period.

The Abenaki are prominent in the journals of CHAMPLAIN and other explorers and missionaries. They survived the colonial wars of the following 200 years by balancing contending French and English interests, and remained politically important even though reduced in number. The fall of NEW FRANCE left the Abenaki with little defence against English expansion after 1760, forcing them into a weak alliance with other tribes formerly allied with the French. The American Revolution split the Eastern Abenaki from the Western Abenaki, who were by this time living in Québec. The Penobscot sided with the Passamaquoddy of eastern Maine in holding the eastern frontier of New England for the Americans. The Abenaki remained divided in their loyalties through the WAR OF 1812.

In 1600 all Abenaki were hunters, fishermen and gatherers. Attempts to adopt agriculture did not succeed until after the FUR TRADE developed. Consequently, the population density of the Abenaki was only about a tenth that of agricultural Algonquians in New England. They adapted quickly to the fur trade and a world economy. They traditionally lived in villages near falls on major rivers during the seasons when migratory fish could be harvested. During other seasons they dispersed in family groups to the coast or to small camps on interior tributaries. These camps became the bases of trapping territories during the heyday of the fur trade. When the trade declined, many turned to the lumbering industry, CANOE manufacture and basketry. Today, most Abenaki are engaged in the mainstream occupations of Québec and New England. They continue to be known for the quality of their split basketry and their lively folkore. The culture hero Gluskabe figures importantly in Abenaki tales. However, the stories are now told in English or French, for Abenaki dialects are nearly extinct. *See also* NATIVE PEOPLES, EASTERN WOODLANDS and general articles under NATIVE PEOPLE. DEAN SNOW

Reading: F. Speck, *Penobscot Man* (1970); B.G. Trigger, ed, *Handbook of North American Indians*, vol 15: *Northeast* (1978).

Abercromby, James, army officer (b at Banffshire, Scot 1706; d at Glassaugh, Scot 23 Apr 1781). A career soldier, he came to N America in 1756 and was appointed commander-in-chief of British forces. He led an army of about 15 000 men up Lk Champlain, and by early July 1758 approached Ft Carillon, where French commander MONTCALM was hastily entrenching with a much smaller army. After a series of futile assaults on July 8 and the loss of nearly 2000 men, Abercromby retreated hastily. Recalled immediately, he was succeeded by Jeffery AMHERST. STUART R.J. SUTHERLAND

Aberdeen and Temair, Ishbel Maria Gordon, Marchioness of, née Marjoribanks (b at London, Eng 15 Mar 1857; d at Aberdeen, Scot 18 Apr 1939). Married to the earl of ABERDEEN in 1877, she accompanied him to Ireland when he was lord lieutenant, and to Canada, where he was governor general 1893-98. Lady Aberdeen was deeply involved in the political crises involving the governor general from 1894 to 1896. Far more important, however, was her work with women's organizations. A staunch Presbyterian and Gladstonian Liberal, a woman of great poise and boundless energy, she was an aristocrat-democrat with a strong social conscience. She believed that women represented an enormous, unused capacity in Canada, and that they could be a civilizing force in an untamed country. She was instrumental in forming the Canadian branch of the NATIONAL COUNCIL OF WOMEN. Despite fierce opposition from the medical establishment, she created the VICTORIAN ORDER OF NURSES. The social family compact in Ottawa, Montréal and Toronto opposed and ridiculed her projects. Her attempts to use Rideau Hall to cool the racial and religious passions of the 1890s and to break down social barriers did not endear her to the local establishment. JOHN SAYWELL

Reading: J.T. Saywell, ed, *The Canadian Journal of Lady Aberdeen* (1960).

Lady Aberdeen was a woman of great poise and boundless energy; during her stay in Canada she was instrumental in forming the Canadian branch of the National Council of Women and the Victorian Order of Nurses (*courtesy Public Archives of Canada/C-22760*).

Aberdeen and Temair, John Campbell Gordon, 1st Marquess of, governor general of Canada 1893-98 (b at Edinburgh, Scot 3 Aug 1847; d at Tarland, Scot 7 Mar 1934). John Campbell was educated at St Andrews U and University Coll, Oxford. A Liberal, he entered the House of Lords in 1870 upon the death of his elder brother. Made lord lieutenant of Aberdeenshire in 1880, he served as lord lieutenant of Ireland briefly in 1886 and again 1905-15. Aberdeen had visited Canada twice before becoming its governor general in 1893. A social crusader of great zeal and piety, he and Lady ABERDEEN, his irrepressible wife, devoted much of their vice-regal time in Canada to good works. Their sympathies for Liberals in Britain and Canada, however, made relations with Conservative governments in Canada difficult. Aberdeen's refusal to accept appointments made by Sir Charles TUPPER, following his electoral defeat in

896, produced great controversy. A section of ne Aberdeens' reminiscences, *We Twa*, 2 vols 1925) is devoted to their Canadian experiences.

CARMAN MILLER

berdeen Lake, 1101 km², elev 80 m, max ength 91 km, is located in the NWT, 213 km S f the Arctic Circle. It is part of a closely linked chain (W to E: Lks Beverly, Aberdeen and chultz) of elongated lakes that, together with aker Lk, form a 2849 km² drainage basin for ne THELON R before it empties into Hudson Bay ia the 160 km long CHESTERFIELD INLET. BAKER AKE, the only community within close proximity (106 km E) is the sole inland settlement of ne Inuit in the NWT. Aberdeen Lk was named or Gov Gen Lord Aberdeen (1893-98) by geoloist J.B. TYRRELL.

DAVID EVANS

berhart, William, "Bible Bill," radio evanelist, premier of Alberta, 1935-43 (b in Hibbert wp, Perth County, Ont 30 Dec 1878; d at Vanouver 23 May 1943). An important influence n religious sectarianism in western Canada, berhart headed the first SOCIAL CREDIT government. He was trained as a school teacher at Aitchell Model School and the Normal School n Hamilton, Ont. Wanting to become a Presbyerian minister, he began studying for an extraural BA from Queen's (completed 1911, after e had moved to Alberta) while he was principal of Central Public School in Brantford. In Ontario he became an active lay preacher and ible-class teacher and was highly influenced y the *Scofield Reference Bible* and its dispensaional system of interpretation.

In 1910 Aberhart moved to Calgary to become school principal. His popular Bible class at Grace Presbyterian Church was transferred to Wesley Methodist Church in 1912 after he was mbroiled in a dispute which probably involved oth his theology and his personality. In 1915 e became the unofficial minister of Westourne Baptist Church. In spite of attempts by aptist leaders to remove Aberhart from the hurch, his congregation remained loyal. After brief association with a Pentecostal minister in 920, Aberhart began introducing "charismatic" ractices and doctrines into the church, much to he consternation of the local Baptist ministers. He identified with the fundamentalist movement and became increasingly antagonistic to nainstream denominations.

Aberhart realized the possibilities of radio nd began broadcasting Sunday afternoon servces in 1925. By 1939 over 9000 children across he Prairies were enrolled in his Radio Sunday chool. He opened a school to train ministers nd missionaries for the furtherance of fundamentalism. As early as 1923 he was teaching night-school classes in theology in the basement f Westbourne Baptist Church, but he needed larger facility to house the school and the rowds which were attracted to his meetings. He erved as dean of the Calgary Prophetic Bible nstitute, opened in 1927, and taught many of its classes, administered the church and preached over the radio. In 1929 Aberhart founded his own sect, the Bible Institute Baptist Church, after most of the Westbourne congregation had split from him.

The GREAT DEPRESSION was devastating for the farm-based western economy and misery was widespread. The inability of political parties to find solutions to the problem of "poverty in the midst of plenty" drove Albertans to seek alternative remedies, and they were attracted to the ideas of Aberhart. Previously non-political, in 1932 Aberhart became interested in the monetary-reform doctrines of a British engineer, Maj C.H. Douglas, who believed that conventional capitalism would founder because private control of credit would lead to a chronic insufficiency of mass purchasing power. The solution, he believed, was state supervision of credit and

William "Bible Bill" Aberhart. As Alberta premier from 1935 until his death in 1943, he was leader of Canada's first Social Credit government (*courtesy Public Archives of Canada/C-16477*).

the issuance of consumer discounts to balance consumption with full production. Aberhart modified and popularized this doctrine into a proposal that each citizen be given a $25-a-month "basic dividend" to purchase necessities. Aberhart built a grass-roots movement, the Alberta Social Credit League, to promote his ideas. When the existing political parties showed little interest, he took the league into the political arena. In Sept 1935, Social Credit took 56 of 63 seats in the Alberta legislature and swept the United Farmers of Alberta from office.

After becoming premier, Aberhart found he could not fulfil his pre-election promises. His moratorium on debt collections saved some farms and homes, but his concept of Social Credit was never realized. In 1937, after a major crisis in his caucus, he was forced to accept assistance from Major Douglas's emissaries from England. The monetary legislation they introduced was quickly disallowed by the federal government and precipitated the Rowell-Sirois Commission on DOMINION-PROVINCIAL RELATIONS.

Aberhart died in office in 1943. He was succeeded by Ernest C. MANNING, the first graduate of the Calgary Prophetic Bible Institute.

DAVID R. ELLIOTT

Reading: J.A. Irving, *The Social Credit Movement in Alberta* (1959); L.P.V. Johnson and Ola J. MacNutt, *Aberhart of Alberta* (1970).

Abitibi, Lake, 932 km², straddles the Québec-Ontario border about 280 km S of James Bay. Irregularly shaped and about 75 km long, it is actually 2 lakes joined by a narrows. It drains W and N through the Abitibi R and Moose R to the bottom of James Bay. The region is heavily forested and supports a pulp-and-paper industry centered at IROQUOIS FALLS, W of the lake. Gold mining has been important and the wild natural setting attracts a growing number of tourists. The lake was a fur-trade centre from 1686 when the Chevalier de TROYES established a post as he passed on his way overland from Québec to attack forts on the bottom of the bay. The name comes from an Indian word meaning "halfway water" and was adapted by the French to describe the lake's location between Hudson Bay and their posts on the Ottawa R.

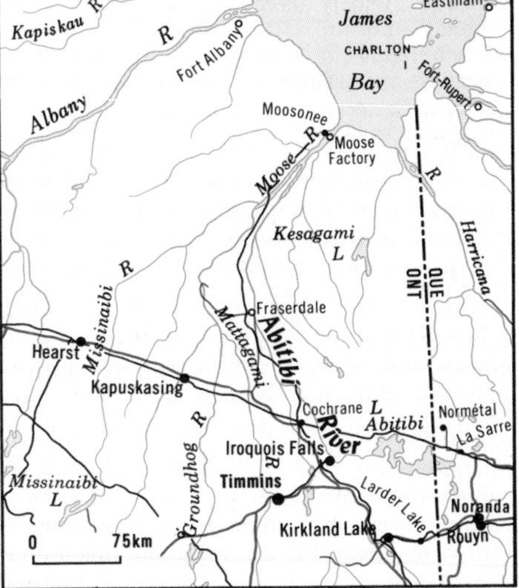

DANIEL FRANCIS

Abitibi-Price Inc is a major manufacturer of paper and related products, with head offices in Toronto. The company was incorporated as Abitibi Power & Paper Company Ltd in 1914 to acquire Abitibi Pulp & Paper Company (fd 1912). It acquired extensive timber, waterpower and mineral rights, and became Abitibi Price Company Ltd in 1965. It adopted its present name in 1979 and now makes a variety of papers and building products in Canada and the US. Sales or operating revenues were $1.6 billion in 1982 (ranking 52nd in Canada), assets $1.6 billion (ranking 56th) and the company employed 15 000. The major shareholder is Olympia and York Developments Ltd, which owns 93%.

DEBORAH C. SAWYER

Aboriginal Rights in Canada derive from the long-term use and occupation of lands by aboriginal peoples prior to European colonization. They are most commonly thought of as rights to the lands and resources themselves, but there is a growing emphasis on societal issues such as cultural rights, legal recognition of customary practices and self-determination.

Since 1982 the INDIAN, INUIT and MÉTIS of Canada have been able to look to section 35 of the Constitution for recognition and affirmation of their existing aboriginal rights. Further provision has been made for a series of constitutional conferences to identify and define the rights of the aboriginal peoples. In order to achieve constitutional recognition, however, it must be shown that an aboriginal right existed prior to colonization and that it has not been extinguished since that time. These issues have traditionally posed great difficulty for Canadian courts.

Sources of Aboriginal Rights Three principal sources have been drawn upon to establish legal recognition of aboriginal rights: international law, the Royal PROCLAMATION OF 1763 and specific court cases. International law has, since the 16th century, discussed legal issues connected with colonization. Those discussions, generally, do not seem to have influenced Canadian thinking or practice on aboriginal rights.

The Royal Proclamation of 7 Oct 1763 recognized the land rights of Indians and established that the rights could only be purchased by the Crown. A loosely described "Proclamation Line" separated the lands reserved as Indian hunting grounds from those which could be opened for settlement. The Proclamation, however, does not state the exact western extent of these reserved lands, nor does it refer explicitly to the Maritime provinces.

In 1889 the British Privy Council was called upon as the highest Canadian court to decide the *St Catherines Milling* case, a dispute between Canada and Ontario over jurisdiction of resources in the Treaty No 3 territory. This land had been within the ambit of the Proclamation prior to the treaty, and the Privy Council implied that the Proclamation was the sole source of the aboriginal title, vaguely described as a "usufruct" (*see* INDIAN TREATIES; NATIVE PEOPLE, LAW). In the *Calder* case, decided by the Supreme Court of

Canada in 1973, Nishga in BC argued that their aboriginal title was confirmed by the Proclamation as well. The Supreme Court was divided on that point, but held that aboriginal title depended on traditional use and occupation, not solely on the Proclamation. In the *Baker Lake* case, decided by the Federal Court Trial Division in 1979, it was held that the aboriginal title was proven if the claimants and their ancestors were members of an organized society; if the society occupied the specific territory in respect of which title is claimed; if its occupation of the territory excluded that of other organized societies; and if its occupation was an established fact at the time Britain asserted sovereignty. Aboriginal rights other than land rights would likely require a similar provenance in order for a Canadian court to recognize them.

Extinguishment of Aboriginal Rights Prior to the CONSTITUTION ACT, 1982, Parliament had the clear power to pass a law extinguishing any or all aboriginal rights. Parliament had never exercised this power, at least not directly, although statutes such as the Migratory Birds Convention Act (1970) have been held to limit certain aboriginal or treaty hunting rights implicitly. Native groups have not accepted that Parliament's powers were so sweeping, and the Constitution now affords the opportunity to question earlier court decisions.

The *Calder* case dealt with the issue of extinguishing aboriginal title indirectly by pre-Confederation regulation of resources inconsistent with recognition of aboriginal rights. The *Calder* case was inconclusive: 3 judges said there must be direct extinguishment; 3 said extinguishment could be implied from the historical circumstances. Another method of extinguishing aboriginal title, if not all aboriginal rights, is to enter into a treaty, purchase or LAND-CLAIMS settlement with potential native claimants (see JAMES BAY AGREEMENT). Under the new constitutional arrangement, rights not extinguished prior to 1982 are protected from statutory and indirect extinguishment. Extinguishment now must be effected directly by treaty, land-claims settlement or constitutional amendment.

Summary Canadian courts have had difficulty in defining and recognizing aboriginal rights, especially those not strictly relating to land, but the Constitution Act, 1982, will stimulate many more cases to which new constitutional considerations will apply. At the same time, there is a political process in place for the identification and definition of aboriginal rights which are to have express constitutional protection. Land-claims negotiations may also bring into the Constitution new kinds of rights, aboriginal only in the sense that they can be claimed by the aboriginal peoples of Canada. WILLIAM B. HENDERSON

Reading: P. Cumming and N. Mickenburg, *Native Rights in Canada* (2nd ed, 1972); K. Lysyk, "The Indian Title Question in Canada: An Appraisal in Light of Calder," *Canadian Bar Review* 51 (1973); D. Sanders, "The Rights of the Aboriginal Peoples of Canada," *Canadian Bar Review* 61 (1983); B. Slattery, *Ancestral Lands, Alien Laws: Judicial Perspectives on Aboriginal Title* (1983).

Abortion, termination of pregnancy, especially if deliberately induced. Abortion has been widely practised throughout history as a means of birth control. Abortion after "quickening" (approximately 14 weeks after conception) may have traditionally been a common-law offence, but only in 1803 was abortion before quickening made a statutory offence in England. This and subsequent laws were aimed at abortionists and made abortion a capital crime only if it was performed by someone other than the mother, although theoretically the laws permitted prosecution of the mother herself as "aidor and abettor." There are no reported Canadian cases which considered this question; however, the Offences Against the Person Act (1861) made it a crime in Britain for a woman to perform an abortion on herself. Canadian legislation on the same point predated the English, eg, the 1849 New Brunswick Statute Act to Consolidate . . . the Criminal Law and the 1851 Nova Scotia Law of Offences Against the Person. The Canadian legislation was probably based upon an 1845 New York statute. Growing concern over a falling birthrate among English Canadians at the turn of the century and anxiety over "race suicide" linked opposition to abortion with all forms of birth control and gave rise to further legislation making it an indictable offence to sell or advertise drugs or articles "intended or represented as a means of preventing conception or causing abortion" (s179, Criminal Code, 1892). Nevertheless, significant numbers of women continued to seek abortions from doctors or quacks or to self-abort using dangerous folk methods. The issue was brought to public attention in 1908 in a Toronto newspaper article entitled "Race Suicide," which charged that some doctors were growing rich performing abortions. Several doctors were subsequently charged, but the extent of the practice is unknown because cases usually only came to public attention when something went wrong. The medical profession continued to support the notion that abortion was morally as well as legally wrong.

Pressure to legalize abortion on some or all grounds intensified in various parts of the world after WWII. Impetus was gained by broadening support for women's rights as well as growing concern about the personal and social consequences of unwanted children and the high maternal death rates associated with illegal abortion. By the mid-1960s, restrictions lessened in many parts of the world, particularly in Japan, Eastern Europe, Scandinavia and Great Britain. In 1973 the US Supreme Court ruled that even in the second trimester of pregnancy abortion is a private matter between a woman and her physician. Under the Canadian Criminal Code, an attempt to induce an abortion by any means is a crime, whether committed by the woman herself, or by another. Because intervention and intent constitute the crime, it may be committed even if the attempt is unsuccessful, or if the woman is not pregnant. The maximum penalty is life imprisonment, unless the woman herself is convicted, in which case it is 2 years. The law, which was liberalized in 1969 with an amendment to the Criminal Code allowing that abortions are legal if performed by a doctor in an accredited or approved hospital after a therapeutic abortion committee has certified that "the continuation of the pregnancy of such female person would or would be likely to endanger her life or health," has been interpreted in a widely divergent manner by various hospital committees. One approach has been to apply a defence of necessity, which excuses an otherwise unlawful act where the harm avoided by doing the act exceeds the harm which it inflicts, and in which there is no other reasonably available course of conduct. This defence was used in the Morgentaler Case, in which the Supreme Court of Canada concluded that "it is manifestly difficult to be categorical and state that there is a law of necessity, paramount over other laws. . . . If it does exist it can go no further than to justify noncompliance in urgent situations of clear and imminent peril when compliance with the law is demonstrably impossible." The Supreme Court overturned the jury finding in favour of Henry MORGENTALER, and he was forced to serve his prison term. However, in Québec, the Liberal government that prosecuted Morgentaler was replaced by a Parti Québécois government which decided not to press further charges and later extended this immunity from prosecution to the publicly financed health clinics in Québec. Morgentaler later opened abortion clinics in Winnipeg and Toronto. He and 2 colleagues were charged under Ontario law with conspiracy to perform abortions but were acquitted Nov 1984.

The new abortion law has not been applied uniformly throughout Canada. Many hospitals have not established therapeutic abortion committees, and because the law does not define "life" or "health," each committee must make its own rules. Furthermore, committees are placed in the questionable position of granting "sick" women legal abortions, while "healthy" women are refused. Case by case, it is impossible to predict how much a woman will suffer if she is compelled to remain unwillingly pregnant. The earlier an abortion, the safer; Canadian law has no limit on the gestation period after which an abortion is illegal, but in practice most physicians and hospitals will not, except in rare cases, perform abortions after 20 weeks' gestation. The national (1980) total was 65 751, or 17.9 abortions per 100 live births, ranging from 32.9 abortions for each 100 live births in BC to 1.2 per 100 in PEI.

Abortion remains a controversial and divisive issue in contemporary society. It is still condemned by some religious groups as contrary to church law and teachings. Roman Catholic canon law condemns abortion except when it results indirectly from a medical procedure intended for another purpose, eg, removal of a cancerous uterus. On the other hand, the United Church of Canada supports the position of freedom of choice. A diverse group bases its opposition to the trend to liberalize abortion law on the rights of the unborn. For opposing groups, the issue centers on a woman's right to choose whether or not to terminate a pregnancy and is based on the premise that abortion is a moral issue to be decided by individuals, not the state. The issue of abortion raises complex medical and legal questions. The present law was criticized by a joint commission of the Canadian Medical Assn and the Canadian Bar Assn because it fails to make clear the potential grounds for abortion; fails to make any distinction in the age or degree of development of the conceptus; has on occasion caused hospital-board elections to become political and thus, by allowing the board decisions to be influenced by the preconceived notions of those elected, subverted the Criminal Code provisions; is violated by several independent abortion clinics; and is applied unequally across Canada.

Challenges to the law have come from both anti-abortion and pro-choice groups. An anti-abortionist group in May-June 1983 challenged the 1969 amendment before the Saskatchewan Court of Queen's Bench on the grounds that a fetus, from conception, deserves protection under section 7 of the CANADIAN CHARTER OF RIGHTS AND FREEDOMS, which states that "everyone has the right to life," but the court of first instance held that the Charter does not conflict with s251 of the Criminal Code. Forces seeking further liberalization of the law have also invoked the Charter on the grounds of a woman's right to the security of her person in a challenge to the Supreme Court of Ontario. Decisions in these cases will be crucial to future developments.

Academic Freedom commonly means the freedom of professors to teach, research and publish, to criticize and help determine the policies of their institutions, and to address public issues as citizens without fear of institutional penalties. Other meanings include the autonomy of the university in running its internal affairs, and the freedom of students to function within the academic programs they have chosen. The Canadian Association of University Teachers (CAUT) argues that "the common good depends upon the search for truth and its free exposition. Academic freedom is essential to these purposes." Demands for academic freedom in primary and secondary education have had little success.

The most serious threats to academic freedom have come from those who hold the purse strings — wealthy benefactors, church bodies or provincial governments. Governing boards and academic administrators have transmitted such threats, the strongest being the loss of employment, to individuals. Threats to the freedom of professors have also come from colleagues or students unwilling to tolerate ideological or methodological diversity. Notable incidents in the development of academic freedom in Canada were the dismissals of Salem BLAND from Wesley College, Winnipeg, in 1917, and of John King GORDON from United Theological College, Montréal, in 1933, and the unsuccessful attempt in 1941 to fire Frank UNDERHILL from University of Toronto. The dismissal of Harry Crowe from United College, Winnipeg, in 1958 led CAUT (fd 1951) to address issues of academic freedom for the first time. Since 1959 CAUT's Academic Freedom and Tenure Committee has investigated and helped resolve many cases across Canada. None was more complicated than the dismissal of several professors from Simon Fraser University in the late 1960s. CAUT's ultimate sanction, if attempts at negotiation fail, is to urge faculty association members not to take employment at the censured institution.

Silence on controversial subjects largely characterized the years before 1960. Since then, increasing freedom for professors has been due partly to the development of academic TENURE into tenure during good behaviour rather than during pleasure of the governing board. Professors generally cannot be dismissed except for just cause, to be demonstrated before an impartial tribunal. Faculty unionization has tended to transform tenure into a seniority system; its relation to academic freedom is thus becoming less clear at a time when financial constraint is endangering that freedom in all its meanings.

MICHIEL HORN

Reading: Michiel Horn, "Professors in the Public Eye," *History of Education Quarterly* 20 (1980).

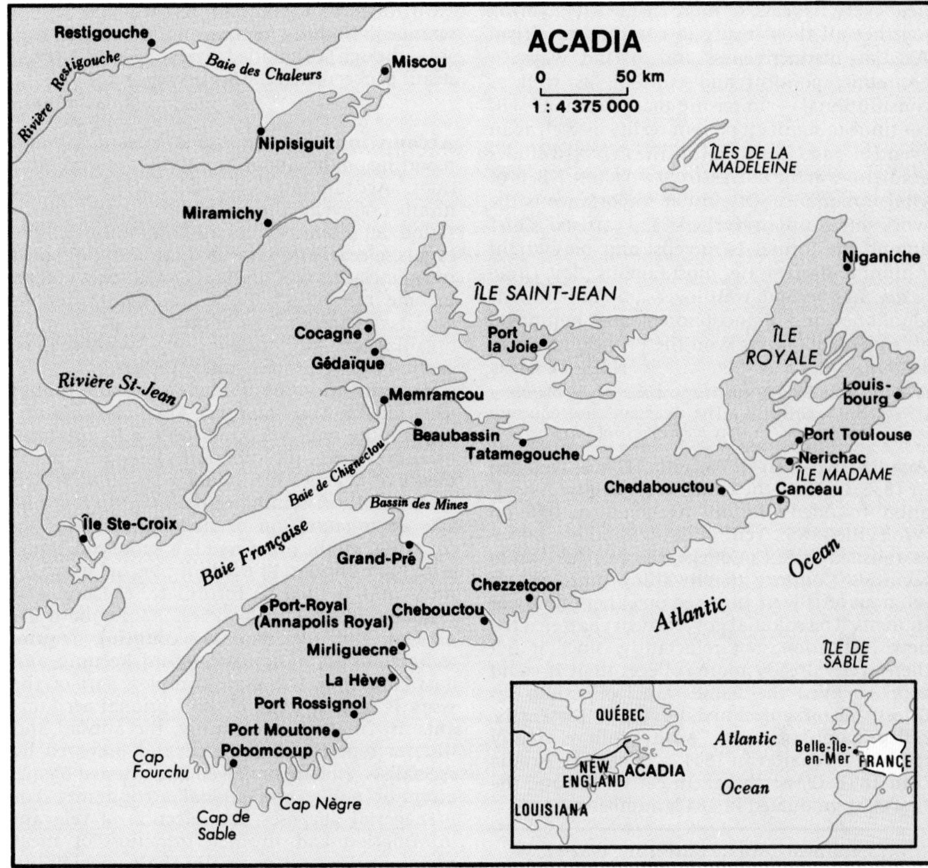

Acadia, the name given towards the end of the 16th century to lands now forming the SE part of Québec, eastern Maine, and NB, NS and PEI. The word may have come from "Arcadia," a name suggested by the classical land of rustic peace and assigned to this region by VERRAZZANO. It has also been claimed to derive from the Micmac word *quoddy*, meaning "land" or "territory." The first serious European attempt to colonize the area was made by the French. In 1603, Henry IV of France commissioned Pierre Du Gua de MONTS as his viceroy and lieutenant-general in this part of the world. The official documents spelled the region's name in various ways (Lacadie, La Cadie, Accadie) and were unclear about the actual boundaries to be claimed. Minimal headway had been made in establishing the colony when in 1621 the Scots laid a rival claim to the territory, naming it NOVA SCOTIA. From then until the TREATY OF PARIS (1763), international treaties always referred to the lands as "Acadie or Nova Scotia."

The colonists of the 17th century became known as Acadians and were predominantly French-speaking Roman Catholics, although some had Protestant beliefs and a number were English-speaking. The rival claims to the colony, along with its geographical position as a significant part of the border between NEW FRANCE and New England, made life eventful for its settlers. They were ruled by France and then by England until, by the terms of the 1713 TREATY OF UTRECHT, Acadia changed hands for the last time and became an English possession. By this time there were nearly 2000 Acadians, closely bound by kinship and acutely aware that their homeland was the frontier between 2 hostile empires. During the next 45 years the Acadians attempted to define themselves as neutral. They were successful insofar as they were frequently called by both English and French "les Français neutres" — "the neutral French." But their position was precarious, especially at a time when religious and linguistic prejudices were strong. The French considered that Acadian oaths of neutrality could be no more than a device to "buy" time, since the Acadians were French-speaking Catholics whose loyalties ought to be with France. The English considered Acadian insistence on neutrality a flimsy cover for a fundamental disaffection, and thought that speaking French and worshipping as Catholics implied a basic Acadian untrustworthiness, an Acadian penchant for France.

As the mid-18th century continued the Acadians developed their communities, saw their population expand nearly fourfold and attempted to convince both French and English that Acadian identity was unique, based on the acceptance of neutrality as the only path to independent survival. The intensification of the struggle between Britain and France for the control of N America, however, brought matters to a bitter climax. In 1755 the lieutenant-governor of Nova Scotia, Col Charles LAWRENCE, under considerable pressure from the government of Massachusetts and from British Adm Boscawen, who was in Halifax, decided with the colonial council that the Acadians posed too great a threat to the security of the British cause. Their continued obduracy against swearing the oath of loyalty, their willingness to promise only neutrality, not active military aid against the French, seemed to Lawrence grounds enough to send the Acadians into exile. Between 1755 and 1763, therefore, over three-quarters of the Acadian population, some 10 000 men, women and children, were deported. The community which had grown during the last 150 years was fragmented. As the boats left with their cargoes of humanity, bound for destinations in the other British N American colonies (including some in the present-day US), it looked as if Acadia had been brought to an end and the Acadians' future would be only the memory of tragedy.

However, the Acadians withstood exile with great fortitude. Their forced travel, their incarceration in prisoner-of-war camps and the ravages of smallpox and typhoid epidemics severely reduced their numbers, but their sense of independent community remained undiminished. After England and France came to terms in 1763, Acadians built their future in 3 ways. Some became assimilated into the societies where they then were; today one can find descendants of those Acadians deported to places as far apart as Belle-Île-en-Mer, France; Annapolis Royal, NS; Maryland; and elsewhere. Some of the exiles travelled farther to settle in Louisiana, and the outlines of some of their journeyings formed the basis of Longfellow's EVANGELINE. By far the most significant proportion of the exiles, however, sought to return to their former homelands. In 1764 Acadians were once more granted the right to own land in NS, and by 1800 the population of Acadians in NS, NB and PEI was 8000; by 1901 it was 139 006, and by 1951, 286 868. In 1983 Acadians numbered 37% of the population of NB, 10.2% of the population of NS and 13.7% of the population of PEI. Today in Louisiana the Acadian culture is also flourishing, and those of Acadian descent ("Cajuns") form a significant proportion of the population of that state.

From 1881 to the present the Acadians in the Maritimes have used "conventions nationales," held every 10 years, or more frequently, to bring together all those ready to continue to affirm Acadian distinctiveness and to find ways — economic, political and cultural, as well as constitutional — to ensure that "Acadian" will continue to signify a present reality as well as an eventful past. In this effort the Centre d'études acadiennes at the UNIVERSITÉ DE MONCTON, NB, is of vital importance. Of similar importance is the work of Acadian writers and artists. Chief among the former is novelist and playwright Antonine MAILLET. Her most famous play, *La Sagouine*, has become well loved among both Anglophones and Francophones, and her novel PÉLAGIE-LA-CHARRETTE won the Prix Goncourt in 1979. N.E.S. GRIFFITHS

Reading: Jean Daigle, ed, *The Acadians of the Maritimes* (1982); N.E.S. Griffiths, "The Acadians" (introductory essay), *Dictionary of Canadian Biography*, vol IV (1979).

Acadia University, Wolfville, NS, was founded in 1838. In 1828, the Nova Scotia Baptist Association founded Horton Academy in Horton [Wolfville], NS. Ten years later the BAPTISTS established Queen's College, sharing the Horton facilities. Contrary to prevailing practices, no religious tests were imposed on either faculty or students. The colonial government chartered the new institution, but reluctantly, since it felt there were already more colleges than it could support. Even the name raised objections, as Queen Victoria declined having a Dissenters' college named after her. "Acadia College" finally received its charter in 1841, and became Acadia U in 1891. Classes began in early 1839 and the first class graduated in 1843, numbering 4.

Enrolment: Acadia University, 1982-83
(Source: Statistics Canada)

Full-time Undergrad	*Full-time Graduate*	*Part-time Undergrad*	*Part-time Graduate*
2 989	89	641	90

A theology department was soon added, although Acadia continued to emphasize liberal arts. The Associated Alumni of Acadia College, est 1860, provided crucial early financial support. Still very active, it is one of the oldest alumni organizations in Canada. In the 1860s a Ladies' Seminary was established; by 1880 women were attending college classes, although informally. In 1884 Acadia's first woman graduate received her degree. Other areas of concentration have been added to the liberal-arts program. Besides the faculties of arts and science, there are schools of computer science, home economics, business administration, music, recreation and physical education, applied science, education, secretarial science and graduate studies. In 1966 the Baptists relinquished control, although retaining a strong presence on the board of governors. The affiliated Divinity College, established 1968, serves that denomination's theological needs. BARRY M. MOODY

Acadian Trail, a 117 km long-distance coastal trail following the breathtaking W coast of CAPE BRETON I in Nova Scotia. It is hoped that this trail will continue inland through NS, connect with the Fundy Trail in New Brunswick, and eventually join the 3200 km long Appalachian Trail that begins in Maine. The trail traverses the rugged coast across the Cape Breton Highlands, passing over beaches, grasslands, spruce forests and wilderness sections. BART DEEG

Accommodation, first successful steamboat built entirely in N America. It was launched 19 Aug 1809 at Montréal, its engines having been constructed at the FORGES SAINT-MAURICE, Trois-Rivières. The ship was propelled by 2 open-side paddle wheels, though a sail could be raised if the engine failed. John MOLSON and partners paid £2000 for the *Accommodation* but by 1810 losses of £4000 had accrued and it was scrapped. Nothing remains of the pioneering ship, though it signalled a new age. By 1819, 7 steam packets plied the St Lawrence R.
JAMES MARSH

Accounting is the process of measuring and reporting on the financial activities of organizations. Accountants must select from a large number of events those which affect an organization and can be measured financially; the events selected and measured are then presented in financial reports. Users of accounting reports include managers within an organization as well as outsiders who are interested in what the organization has achieved, eg, shareholders, creditors, governments and investors.

Accounting can be divided in 2 subdisciplines (correlated to user category). Financial accounting is more widely known because it produces balance sheets, income statements and statements of changes in financial position, which are generally disseminated both within and outside an organization or firm. Managerial accounting, on the other hand, is more concerned with the information needs of internal management and is used to formulate, execute, and evaluate plans and policies. While both financial and managerial accounting require technicians for systematic record keeping and data collection, the more complex part of the work is usually done by professional accountants. In financial accounting, the annual and interim reports are designed and prepared by specialists, and are reviewed and attested by auditors or public professional accountants. For managerial purposes, the selection of relevant information and the determination of measurement rules are normally the responsibility of highly qualified accountants.

Accounting is centuries old and has evolved from a strict custodianship function to one concerned with taxation, auditing, information systems, economics, etc. However, although record keeping can be traced back to Babylon, and double-entry bookkeeping was used as early as 1494, the accounting professions in N America are fairly recent. The first known official meeting of N American accountants was held in Montréal in June 1879, for the purpose of establishing a society to promote the profession. Three large associations now exist in Canada. The oldest, established in 1902 as the Dominion Association of Chartered Accountants, is now called the Canadian Institute of Chartered Accountants; members of the institute are designated as CAs. The Society of Management Accountants (RIAs) was originally formed in 1920 under the name of the Canadian Society of Cost Accountants. The Canadian Certified General Accountants Association (CGAs) was incorporated in 1913 as the General Accounting Association. Each association has a national organization but, since education is under provincial jurisdiction, each has provincial organizations (known as institutes, orders, associations or societies) to establish and control education and entry requirements.

Each association imposes professional examinations and practical experience requirements. The chartered accountants were the first, in 1970, to require a university degree of their members. In addition to a degree, candidates must complete a program of advanced professional study, pass a nationwide final exam and complete a 2- or 3-year term of service with an approved public accounting firm. The certified general accountant candidates can complete their university degrees before or after the professional examinations and must have practical experience in a business firm or in government. Although it is possible to become an RIA with high school, a very large proportion of candidates take university courses. All major Canadian universities offer courses that prepare candidates for the professional examinations.

Private accounting offers a variety of job opportunities, ranging from the technical aspects of bookkeeping to the more complex processes of administrative planning. Private accountants work for specific organizations, eg, governments, hospitals and universities. In medium-sized as well as in large business corporations, important financial positions (eg, controller, chief accountant, treasurer, internal auditor) are usually held by professional accountants.

Public accounting includes activities such as auditing, management consulting, reporting on other financial information for creditors or governments, and perhaps serving as trustees in bankruptcy cases. Auditing is related to the attest function — the expression of an opinion about the fairness of accounting reports, which is a legal requirement for public corporations. Auditing is reserved, in some provinces, for chartered accountants. Consulting on accounting, taxation, information systems and finance, etc, has expanded rapidly in the last few decades and will probably continue to do so.

The 3 major accounting associations each publish a professional journal: the *CA Magazine*, *Cost and Management* and the *CGA Magazine*.
O. CROTEAU

Reading: R. Skinner, *Accounting Principles* (1972).

Acid Rain, the wet or dry deposition of acidic substances and their precursors on the Earth's surface. Wet deposition refers to RAIN, snow, HAIL, drizzle and other familiar forms of visible precipitation. Dry deposition, mostly invisible, occurs through gravitational settling of large particles and uptake of gases and small particles at the Earth's surface. Rain and other precipitation may be defined as acidic or alkaline depending on chemical composition. The degree of acidity is usually measured on the pH scale, a logarithmic measure of the concentration of hydrogen ions (H^+) in precipitation. Values range between 0 (maximum acidity) and 14 (maximum alkalinity); 7 represents a neutral solution. A value of pH 5.6 is often used as a standard, because it is that of a clean water sample in equilibrium with the level of atmospheric carbon dioxide. The pH of a precipitation sample represents the net hydrogen-ion content of its various chemical constituents (acidic or alkaline, natural or anthropogenic).

Current annual measurements of the average pH of precipitation in the Northern Hemisphere range from about 4.0-7.0. The lower, highly acidic values occur primarily over and immediately downwind of industrialized areas in northeastern N America and Europe. Higher pH values are found over less-industrialized plains with large amounts of alkaline dust in their atmospheres, but even these areas are showing increased acidity. The association of relatively acidic precipitation with industrial regions leads to the conclusion that anthropogenic (human-generated) emissions of sulphur oxides (SO_x) and, to a lesser extent, nitrogen oxides (NO_x) are key elements of the acid-rain phenomenon, an inference increasingly supported by scientific evidence. Current annual emissions of SO_x amount to about 24 million t in the US and about 4.8 million t in Canada. Thermal ELECTRIC-POWER plants (coal fired) produce 66% of US emissions and about 15% of Canadian. Nonferrous smelters, producing such metals as NICKEL and COPPER, account for about 45% of Canada's SO_x emissions. Emissions of these substances have been controlled by building taller stacks with POLLUTION-control devices, primarily to reduce local air concentrations to levels consistent with the protection of human health (*see* AIR POLLUTION). A result of taller stacks has been the dispersal of SO_x and NO_x over increasingly large regions. These acid-rain precursors can be transported thousands of kilometres through the atmosphere and transformed into sulphuric acid (H_2SO_4) and nitric acid (HNO_3).

When acid rain reaches the Earth's surface it can be detrimental to aquatic ecosystems, FORESTRY, AGRICULTURE, buildings, automobiles and human health. Aquatic effects depend on the acid-reduction capability of receiving surfaces (eg, vegetation, soils, rock structures). In areas where this buffering capacity tends to be low (eg, the Canadian SHIELD), acidic deposition over several years has led to increased acidity of rivers and lakes and to accelerated leaching of aluminum and heavy metals (eg, mercury, cadmium, lead) from soils. As the pH of surface waters falls below about 5.0, the diversity of such aquatic life as vegetation, zooplankton, amphibians and fish is reduced. Most fish populations are eradicated when the average pH of a lake drops to about 4.5; spring runoff and periods of high activity are times of highest vulnerability. Hundreds of lakes in eastern N America and Scandinavia are devoid of fish because of water acidification; thousands more are threatened. Rivers, too, have shown adverse effects (eg, the marked decline of Atlantic salmon in the Maritimes). Birds and other fish predators may decrease because of reduced food. The effects of acid rain on forests and agricultural crops, although less well documented, are potentially serious, including direct damage to plant foliage, retardation of growth, deterioration of plant roots associated with the leaching of soil constituents and, possibly, uptake of newly soluble harmful chemicals. Since the Canadian forest industry is valued at $20 billion annually, even a small reduction in productivity is economically significant. Forest animals may be affected indirectly through reduced quality or quantity of nutrients for their young.

Potential effects of acid rain on human health take several forms. Higher local concentrations of heavy metals in GROUNDWATER and wells may be harmful. Acidified drinking water may become further contaminated by leaching of copper, lead and other metals from delivery pipes. Increased concentrations of heavy metals in acidified rivers and lakes can lead to their accumulation in food chains, thus posing a problem for populations consuming large quantities of freshwater fish.

As a first step in controlling acid rain, in 1982 Canada formally proposed to the US a target loading of 20 kg of wet sulphate per hectare per year. It is estimated that a reduction of current deposition rates to this value would protect moderately sensitive ecosystems and could be achieved over N America by reducing SO_x emissions by about 50%. Canada "imports," through the atmosphere, about 3 to 4 times as much sulphur as it "exports" to the US. Canada is taking steps to reduce the problem, which in some areas is rated by an "acid-rain index" in weather forecasts. Available control methods include use of low-sulphur coal, removal of sulphur from fuel and feeder ore, production of sulphuric acid and use of flue-gas desulphurization techniques. The cost of reducing N American SO_x emissions by 50% would amount to several billions of dollars per year, but a 1981 study indicates that, apart from the intangible benefits of a cleaner environment and longer-term human health security, the current economic benefits of controlling acid rain are comparable to the costs of control. *See* ENDANGERED ANIMALS; HAZARDOUS WASTES. H.L. FERGUSON

Reading: R. Howard and M. Perley, *Acid Rain: The North American Forecast* (1981).

Acorn, Milton, poet (b at Charlottetown 30 Mar 1923). Acorn's strong left-wing views and working-class sentiments are translated into an aggressive and polemical quality in his writing that, in his own words, "without apology or embarrassment makes use of Marxist and existentialist ideas." He began to publish in *New Frontiers* in 1952. His first collection of verse, *In Love and Anger* (1956), was privately issued in Montréal, where he coedited the poetry magazine *Moment* (7 issues, Feb 1960 to June 1962), first with A.W. PURDY and later with Gwendolyn MACEWEN, to whom he was married. Passed over for the Gov Gen's Award for his major collection, *I've Tasted My Blood* (1969), Acorn was honoured by fellow poets with the "Peoples' Poet Award." Other books by him are *More Poems for People* (1972) and *The Island Means Minago* (1975). MICHAEL GNAROWSKI

Acoustics is the SCIENCE of sound and factors affecting hearing. It can be divided into various subfields, including physical acoustics, practical acoustics, architectural acoustics, musical acoustics, physiological and psychological acoustics. Physical acoustics studies airborne, audible sound, infrasound (below audible frequencies or 16 Hz) and ultrasound (above audible frequencies or 16 000 Hz). It examines propagation and absorption of all frequencies in air and other gases, liquids, semisolids and solids. In gases, only longitudinal waves (ie, those with perpendicular displacement) are important; in liquids and, especially, in solids, shear waves (which cause changes in shape but not in volume) and surface waves occur. Thus, seismic waves (whether on the Earth or the moon) are a legitimate part of acoustics. The large field of sound production, recording and reproduction, with all attendant electronic elements and measuring instruments, is an important part of practical or engineering acoustics. Knowledge of the physical principles of acoustics has further practical application in planning recreational and other developments to reduce the adverse effects of NOISE. Sound production, by one or more live players, vocalists or lecturers, whether assisted by loudspeakers or not, is greatly affected by the character of the room in which it takes place. Architectural acoustics aims to maximize the acceptability of MUSIC or intelligibility of speech in concert or lecture halls. Musical acoustics considers the workings of physical and electronic musical instruments. Since the ear is such an important detector and modifier of audible sounds, its operation is studied in physiological acoustics. Psychological acoustics studies the brain's signal-processing function, which is necessary for a sound to be heard or interpreted. A practical application of this branch would be the study of the elements important to achieving a stereophonic effect. Because of its importance as a modern environmental health problem, noise and its control are treated as a separate subdivision of acoustics. Bioacoustics studies all aspects of acoustic behaviour in animals.

In Canada acoustics research takes place in government laboratories (eg, NATIONAL RESEARCH COUNCIL), the universities (eg, Concordia, McMaster, Toronto) and industry. Canadian research into the transmission of sound in the atmosphere has been extensive; areas studied include the effect of temperature gradient, turbulence, obstruction, ground reflections and ground impedance. This research has applications in ARCHITECTURE, for designing buildings to meet noise-reduction provisions of BUILDING CODES; in URBAN AND REGIONAL PLANNING, for siting of buildings, expressways, airports, sound barriers, etc; in industrial health, for designing provisions of codes relating to noise in the workplace. More esoteric work, such as measuring the velocity and absorption of high ultrasonic sound in various liquids to deduce the detailed architecture of their constituent molecules and the energy needed to change their structure, has application in various fields of ENGINEERING. Such work is related to the use of SONAR and RADAR techniques to determine the structure of media (water and air) and the position of objects in them, to seismic techniques used in PETROLEUM EXPLORATION and to the use of ultrasound in MEDICINE. The effect of the complex shape of the outer ear on transmission of sound has been studied by segments of the record player, radio and television receiver industry concerned with the development of high-fidelity earphones. Industrial work has also been done on the effect of room shape and furnishings on music reproduced through loudspeakers. Means have been developed for assessing loudspeakers subjectively in normal rooms and correlating the results with standard, objective anechoic-chamber (ie, echo-free) measurements. G.J. THIESSEN

Act (Statute), law passed by Parliament or a provincial legislature. A federal Act must pass 3 readings in the HOUSE OF COMMONS and in the SENATE, and must receive royal assent. Assent is given by the SOVEREIGN (rarely), or, in his name, by the GOVERNOR GENERAL or (usually) his deputy (a judge of the SUPREME COURT OF CANADA), in the Senate Chamber. A provincial Act must pass 3 readings in the legislature and receive the LIEUTENANT-GOVERNOR'S assent. Royal assent has never been refused to a Dominion bill, but lieutenant-governors have refused assent 28 times, the last time in 1945. EUGENE A. FORSEY

Act of Union Reunification of UPPER CANADA and LOWER CANADA under one government was a recommendation of the 1839 DURHAM REPORT. The necessary legislation to establish the PROVINCE OF CANADA was introduced in the British Commons in May 1839. In Sept Charles Poulett Thomson (later Lord SYDENHAM) was sent as governor general to acquire Canadian consent, which he obtained from Lower Canada in Nov and from Upper Canada in Dec. The resolutions of both Canadian legislative bodies were fused by Lower Canada Chief Justice James Stuart early in 1840. After passage in the British Parliament, July 1840, the Act of Union was proclaimed on 10 Feb 1841 in Montréal.

Its main provisions were establishment of a single parliament with equal representation from each constituent section; consolidation of debt; a permanent Civil List; banishment of the French language from official government use; and suspension of specific French Canadian institutions relating to education and civil law. The Act naturally aroused considerable opposition. In Upper Canada, the FAMILY COMPACT opposed union, and in Lower Canada religious and political leaders reacted against its anti-French measures. In fact, the Act was unfair to Lower Canada with its larger population and smaller debt. However, both Canadas agreed to work within the Act, especially under the liberal influence of the united Reform Party led by Louis LAFONTAINE and Robert BALDWIN. Within 15 years many unjust clauses had been repealed, and prosperity and RESPONSIBLE GOVERNMENT had modified many of the Act's financial and constitutional provisions. Nevertheless, the full unifying intent of the Act was not realized until CONFEDERATION. JACQUES MONET, S.J.

Action française, L', a monthly magazine published 1917-28 in Montréal. It was the voice of a group of petit bourgeois priests and nationalists who comprised the Ligue des droits du français, an organization formed in 1913 to protect the French language. In 1920 Abbé Lionel GROULX became the group's leader, and in 1921 it became the Ligue d'action française. In 1922 the magazine flirted with the idea of political independence but by 1927 had come out in favour of greater respect for the rights of the French Canadian minority within Canadian confederation. League members deplored the economic weakness of their compatriots and the growth of American investments in Québec; but, worried by the social changes wrought by INDUSTRIALIZATION and urbanization, most of them argued that agriculture was the way to promote the economic independence of French Canadians. The group published the annual *Almanach de la langue française*, intended for a broader public, and ran a publishing house and a bookstore. FERNANDE ROY

Reading: Susan Mann Trofimenkoff, *Action française* (1975).

Action libérale nationale Founded in 1934 by discontented Liberals under Paul GOUIN, this third party in Québec politics quickly gained the support of radical FRENCH CANADIAN NATIONALISTS such as Philippe Hamel and Ernest Grégoire. Its program, based on social, economic and political reform, generated wide popular interest. In a nearly successful bid to upset the incumbent Liberal government of Louis-Alexandre TASCHEREAU in the 1935 provincial elections, the ALN joined forces with the Conservatives, led by Maurice DUPLESSIS, to form the UNION NATIONALE. In the following months, Duplessis maneuvered to ensure his supreme leadership of the coalition. After the UN's striking victory in the 1936 elections, most of the well-known nationalists formerly linked to the ALN broke with Duplessis, whom they accused of refusing to implement the party's program. Paul Gouin, who had not even been a candidate in 1936, unsuccessfully attempted to revive the ALN in the 1939 elections. RICHARD JONES

Action nationale, L', founded in 1933 by economist Esdras Minville as the voice of the Ligue d'Action nationale, is the oldest journal of opinion in Québec. As a continuation of *L'Action française* (1917-28) and *L'Action canadienne-française* (1928) which represented the "Québec-first" nationalist doctrine of Lionel GROULX, *L'Action nationale* has always fought for autonomy, against the centralizing thrust of the federal government into fiscal matters (Rowell-Sirois Commission) and culture (Massey Commission). In the 1930s-50s it attracted nationalist youth, including editor André LAURENDEAU (1937-42, 1948-54), and in the 1960s progressively radicalized its stand on constitutional matters from one of provincial autonomy to associate-state to outright independence. Directed by Minville and François-Albert Angers, the magazine stressed economics, the continuity of French language and culture, the Catholic church and Laurentian history. It criticized certain reforms of the QUIET REVOLUTION, especially in education. Though it has declined in influence, the magazine has avoided partisan ties and pursues the same objective for which it was founded: free and energetic intellectual effort on behalf of a people and their culture. *See also* MAGAZINES. PIERRE TRÉPANIER

Actualité, L', a French-language monthly magazine published in Montréal, was founded in 1909 as *Bulletin paroissial* and edited until 1945 by the Jesuit Armand Proulx. The review changed its name many times: to *L'Action paroissiale* (1932), *Ma paroisse* (1949), *L'Actualité* (1960) and *L'Actualité magazine* (1967). Monthly circulation was 140 000 in 1958, 107 000 in 1965, and 225 000 in 1984.

Traditionally, the magazine supported the ideas of the UNION NATIONALE PARTY, and featured the work of many leading Québec writers and journalists. Editor Jean-Louis Brouillé (1960-72) endeavoured to make it the foremost Québec publication, reflecting the interests of the typical French Canadian Catholic family. Following a serious financial crisis in 1972, which resulted in major changes in staff and content, the magazine was sold in 1976 to MACLEAN HUNTER as part of a merger between *L'Actualité* and the French edition of MACLEAN'S (founded 1961). Former *Maclean's* editor Jean Paré has edited *L'Actualité* since 1976. The magazine presents a variety of news and feature stories in a glossy and colourful design, and appeals to an affluent and well-educated readership. *See also* MAGAZINES.

ANDRÉ DONNEUR AND ONNIG BEYLERIAN

Adams, David, ballet dancer (b at Winnipeg 16 Nov 1928). Known primarily as the NATIONAL BALLET OF CANADA's first principal male dancer, he played an important role in establishing the company. He began his training and performing career with Gweneth LLOYD's Winnipeg Ballet (later ROYAL WINNIPEG BALLET) and matured as a fine classical dancer in England and Canada. He performed as lead soloist in both countries, notably with the National Ballet of Canada 1951-61, the London Festival Ballet 1961-69 and the Royal Ballet 1970-76, excelling in the great classical male roles. He returned to Canada as ballet master to the Alberta Ballet 1977-79 and in 1984 was teaching at the Edmonton School of Ballet. JILLIAN M. OFFICER

Adams, Frank Dawson, geologist (b at Montréal 17 Sept 1859; d there 26 Dec 1942). A member of the GEOLOGICAL SURVEY OF CANADA 1880-89, Logan Professor of Geology at McGill 1892-1922, dean of applied science at McGill 1905-19, and acting principal and VP there 1919-22, Adams was Canada's most eminent geologist of the first half of the 20th century. Applying petrographic techniques learned at Heidelberg, where he obtained his PhD, he laid the foundations of modern igneous and metamorphic petrography in Canada. His experimental work on the flow of brittle rocks proved as revolutionary in geology as the work in physics of his colleague Ernest RUTHERFORD, establishing him as the founder of modern structural geology.

A prominent educator, Adams strongly promoted development of graduate studies in Canada. In 1918, as a lt-col overseas, he became deputy director of Khaki U, an innovative Canadian plan to further the education of troops awaiting demobilization. After retiring in 1922 he produced the first geological map of Ceylon and his definitive history, *The Birth and Development of the Geological Sciences* (1938).

P.R. EAKINS

Adams, Thomas, planner (b near Edinburgh, Scot 10 Sept 1871; d in Sussex, Eng 24 Mar 1940). A leading British planning pioneer, Adams subsequently became one of the founders of the Canadian planning movement. Adams became acquainted with Patrick Geddes and the Garden City movement headed by Ebenezer Howard and was one of the founders and first president of the British Town Planning Inst. In 1914 he became planning adviser to the Canadian Commission of Conservation, established in 1909. Adams provided great impetus to Canadian planning and promoted the creation of comprehensive legislative, institutional and professional structures. He wrote extensively in *Town Planning and Conservation of Life* and in 1917 published *Rural Planning and Development*. He founded the Civic Improvement League in 1915 and the Town Planning Inst of Canada in 1919. His achievements include planning the town of Kipawa (now Témiscaming), Qué, and drafting an urban-renewal scheme for Halifax. Adams's influence declined following the demise of the Commission of Conservation in 1921. From 1921 to 1923 he was occupied with projects for the National Parks Division and between 1923 and 1930 was director of the regional plan for New York C and environs. Though recognizing his important historical role, recent assessments have diminished his contribution to Canadian URBAN AND REGIONAL PLANNING. O.W. SAARINEN

Reading: Michael Simpson, "Thomas Adams in Canada, 1914-1930," *Urban History Review* XI, 2 (1982).

Adaskin, Harry, musician, educator, broadcaster (b at Riga, Latvia 6 Oct 1901), elder brother of Murray and John ADASKIN. An orchestral and chamber violinist, he formed a duo in 1923 with his future wife, pianist Frances Marr, which toured widely in Canada and abroad, often premiering Canadian compositions. Adaskin established the music program of UBC in 1946, teaching there until 1973. An excellent raconteur whose musical insights were enriched by a knowledge of painting and literature, he was host of several CBC Radio series. In 1975 he was made an Officer of the Order of Canada.

BARCLAY MCMILLAN

Adaskin, John, musician, radio producer, administrator (b at Toronto 4 June 1908; d there 4 Mar 1964), younger brother of Harry and Murray ADASKIN. He was an enthusiastic supporter of young musicians and Canadian composition, and his CBC Radio productions, "Opportunity Knocks" and "Singing Stars of Tomorrow" (in which he also performed as conductor), helped many aspiring artists establish careers. Appointed executive secretary of the Canadian Music Centre in 1961, Adaskin promoted the use of Canadian music in the schools by commissioning composers to write music suitable for student performers.

BARCLAY MCMILLAN

Adaskin, Murray, composer, educator, violinist, conductor (b at Toronto 28 Mar 1906), brother of Harry and John ADASKIN. An orchestral and chamber musician, he turned to composition in the mid-1940s after studies with John WEINZWEIG. His compositions for a wide variety of performance media, including opera, employ a highly personal neoclassical idiom, frequently using Canadian folk material. In 1952 he became head of music at U Sask. He was conductor of the Saskatoon Symphony Orchestra 1957-60. A most effective spokesman for Canadian music, Adaskin was named an Officer of the Order of Canada in 1981. BARCLAY MCMILLAN

Administrative Law is one of the 3 basic areas of public law dealing with the relationship between government and its citizens, the other 2 being CONSTITUTIONAL LAW and CRIMINAL LAW. The major purpose of administrative law is to ensure that the activities of government are authorized by Parliament or by provincial legislatures, and that laws are implemented and administered in a fair and reasonable manner. Administrative law is based on the principle that government action, whatever form it takes, must (strictly speaking) be legal, and that citizens who are affected by unlawful acts of government officials must have effective remedies if the Canadian system of public administration is to be accepted and maintained.

The complex nature of the modern STATE is such that elected representatives are not capable of passing laws to govern every situation. Many of their lawmaking powers, as well as the power to administer and implement the laws, are therefore delegated to administrative agencies. These agencies are involved in virtually every area of government activity and affect ordinary citizens in many ways, whether these citizens be homeowners needing a building permit to erect a new room, injured employees seeking workers' compensation, farmers selling their produce, or owners of a trucking company wishing to transport goods between Vancouver and Montréal.

Government activity is controlled in various ways. First, according to the Canadian Constitution, elected politicians may pass any laws they please, provided such laws do not infringe upon the rights and liberties guaranteed by the CANADIAN CHARTER OF RIGHTS AND FREEDOMS and do not attempt to regulate legislative activity reserved for another level of government. Administrative authorities, as inferior bodies to whom the power to interpret and implement such laws is delegated, are also subject to these constitutional limitations. Second, delegating legislation defines the powers to be allocated to the agency (or minister) and sets forth the requirements to be met before the authority may act. For example, if entitlement to a government benefit depends upon the establishment of certain disputed facts or the interpretation of an ambiguous statute, the applicable legislation will sometimes provide for a hearing before another group of officials (constituted as a "board" or "tribunal") who will make the final decision. In some cases, a decision of the board or ADMINISTRATIVE TRIBUNAL can be appealed to the courts if there is an error of law or a more serious error of fact. Third, certain COMMON-LAW principles, derived originally from the courts of England and subsequently developed by Canadian courts, impose limits or obligations upon tribunals. The best example is the principle that administrative authorities must act in accordance with "natural justice," which imposes certain procedural obligations that an authority must meet in exercising power. Common-law doctrine only operates where no statutory legislation covers the matters at issue.

If citizens feel that an administrative authority has made a decision affecting them that violates a constitutional, statutory or common-law principle, they may ask a court of law to review the actions of the authority. Canadian courts will only exercise their control over administrative authorities if the authority exceeds its jurisdiction (*see* ULTRA VIRES), if it commits an error of law, or if it follows improper or unfair procedures.

According to the concept of jurisdiction, government bodies must act within the scope of the powers delegated to them by their enabling legislation. If these bodies take action without legal authority, they are said to have exceeded their jurisdiction and their action may be reversed by the courts. It is the role of the courts to interpret the enabling legislation and to determine whether it permits the action which the tribunal proposes to take.

In some cases, the power granted to administrative authorities is subject to express limits found in the enabling legislation. For example, the power given to a tribunal to regulate rents in apartment buildings of 10 units or more does not give it jurisdiction to regulate rents in buildings with only 4 units. A further example deals with the delegation of power by authorities. Courts have required that powers be exercised only by those to whom they are entrusted. Thus, members of a tribunal empowered to grant liquor licences to restaurants may not delegate this power to a staff member or an outside person.

In other cases, the legislation contains no defined limits on an authority's power; the courts will imply limits to prevent what is termed the "abuse of power" or to ensure that the power can be properly exercised. For example, in the case of the rent tribunal, a court will not permit the tribunal, as part of its power to regulate rents, to require the landlord to supply certain appliances. On the other hand, where ministers have the power to issue visas to foreign visitors, the vast number of applications and the nature of the task implies that subordinate officials may perform this duty in place of the minister.

The concept of jurisdiction does not address the merits of the decision made by government officials. Generally, it is not the function of the courts to intervene in the conduct of government. However, courts may intervene where an authority has abused its power. There are several examples of this. A decision must be made on the basis of relevant considerations; reliance upon irrelevant considerations or the failure to consider relevant ones will enable a court to review the decision. Further, an authority cannot exercise its power for a purpose other than the purpose for which the power was intended. For example, if a minister had the power to close a hospital only for sanitary or safety reasons, he could not use this power for financial and budgetary reasons. A tribunal may not bind itself or limit its discretion by making general rules that apply to every case. Each case must be decided on its own merits. In addition, there must be some evidence before a tribunal to justify decisions of fact. Finally a decision cannot be unreasonable to the extent that it is one which no reasonable person in the position of the decision maker would have made.

The third ground of judicial review of administrative action deals with procedure. Administrative agencies must follow proper procedure in arriving at their decisions. The various procedures stem from the basic requirement of the "right to be heard." In some cases, a statute or regulation will set out the basic procedures that govern the process of decision making, such as what notice must be given of a hearing and to whom, the right to have counsel, the right to call evidence and to cross-examine witnesses. Where a statute establishes no procedures, administrative law will enforce certain common-law principles to ensure that all persons subjected to government action are treated fairly. These are the previously mentioned principles of "natural justice." They have 2 basic objectives: that no person shall be condemned without a hearing, and that any decision must be made by a person or tribunal who is impartial and not biased.

What constitutes procedural fairness will depend upon the nature of the power being exercised, the party affected, the consequences of the intended action, and the practicalities of requiring time-consuming procedures. In serious cases affecting individuals, such as revoking a doctor's licence to practise medicine, procedures similar to those found in a court of law will be imposed. In other cases, such as the decision to terminate a lease in a public-subsidized apartment building, the courts have held that there is only a "duty to act fairly," which is satisfied if the tenant is informed of the complaints made against him or her and is provided with an opportunity to answer or to remedy them. In a few cases, such as a Cabinet decision on a petition from a tribunal that awarded a rate increase to a large private utility, the courts have held there is no duty of fairness to be followed because the decision maker, the Cabinet, was performing a legislative function of a political nature.

The ability of the citizen to challenge administrative decisions in court depends upon the availability of appeal or judicial review and the status of the individual who comes before the court. As far as the former is concerned, rights of appeal to the courts are often provided by legislation. In other situations, the historic and constitutional ability of the "superior" courts of law to review the actions of "inferior" administrative bodies must be relied upon. In the past, the procedure invoked to seek judicial review was by way of historic "prerogative" remedies, each with its own technical legal requirements. Today, in some provinces, statutory reforms have simplified these procedures into the single remedy of "judicial review," which encompasses all of the historical remedies yet provides the courts with the discretion not to intervene in administrative activity if relief is not justified. The superior courts in each province are responsible for granting these remedies where provincial administrative action is challenged. The decisions or actions of a federal administrative agency are reviewed by the Federal Court of Canada.

The second factor affecting the ability of individuals to obtain judicial review of administrative action is related to the status of the individual to sue. In many cases, the individual is directly affected by a particular decision, such as the termination of a disability pension, and this does not present a problem. In other cases, individuals challenging the constitutionality of legislation may seek to represent a broader public interest. Nevertheless the courts have generally permitted such citizens to proceed where they can show that a serious doubt exists about the validity of the legislation and where there is no other reasonable or effective means of bringing the issue before the courts.

In most cases, a citizen's remedy is restricted to having an administrative decision reversed. The court will, in some instances, grant the relief requested (eg, granting a licence where one is refused) or, as is more likely, will send the matter back to the administrative agency to be decided upon by a proper interpretation of a statute or of proper and relevant facts. In rare cases, eg, when the administrative action was not only illegal but was taken in bad faith, damages will be awarded. In RONCARELLI V DUPLESSIS the Supreme Court of Canada held the premier of Québec liable for $25 000 for wrongfully cancelling a liquor licence because he did not approve of the religious activity of the licence-holder.

In some situations, a statute will provide that the decision of the tribunal cannot be appealed to or reviewed by the courts. Often this occurs in fields of specialized expertise, such as labour relations, where it is felt the courts do not possess the experience or understanding necessary for making final decisions. Such restrictions on appeals have not prevented the courts from reviewing the decisions of these tribunals where there is an excess of jurisdiction. However, the courts have recognized that these tribunals may make decisions that the court, if it were deciding the issue, would not make, either because of its interpretation of the relevant statute or because of its view of the facts. In such cases, the Supreme Court of Canada has stated that the tribunal has acted outside its jurisdiction only if it has reached a decision that is "patently unreasonable." Even where administrative agencies are not protected by such clauses, the courts have tended not to interfere in areas of specialized or technical expertise, such as health professions, securities, urban planning and nuclear energy. J.G. COWAN

Administrative Tribunals exercise powers delegated by Parliament or a provincial legislature. Examples include the National Energy Board, the Alberta Liquor Control Board, the CANADIAN RADIO-TELEVISION AND TELECOMMUNICATIONS COMMISSION, the Immigration Appeal Board and the Ontario Municipal Board. Usually permanent, tribunals deal with a specialized subject and are frequently established in such a way that their activities are beyond partisan politics or direct government control. Because tribunal members generally are not judges, they do not enjoy total judicial immunity and their activities are subject to judicial review (*see* ADMINISTRATIVE LAW). Only the legislative branch can amend or repeal legislation establishing the tribunal or its terms of reference. Frequently, no appeal on the substantive merits of a tribunal decision is permitted, but when there is such an appeal it may have to be made to another administrative tribunal. Parliament need not make provision for appeals to the courts (although the legislative branch may specifically create such an appeal), but the superior courts always retain their constitutional right to determine whether the tribunal's actions lie within the latter's jurisdiction. DAVID P. JONES

Admiralty (short for Board of Admiralty), a British government department which, between its inception in the early 18th century and its amalgamation into the Ministry of Defence in 1964, was responsible for the conduct of naval affairs. In all matters concerning colonial defence, including the defence of Canada, the Admiralty was a necessary participant because of its role in transporting supplies and ensuring maritime security. *See also* COLONIAL OFFICE.

STUART R.J. SUTHERLAND

Adoption, the legal process severing ties between a child and its biological parents (or "birth parents" as they are called today) who are unable or unwilling to care for it, and creating new ties between a child and people who are not its natural parents.

Adoption, which is governed by provincial law, was introduced into Canadian common law (*see* FAMILY LAW) beginning in New Brunswick in 1873 to save "illegitimate" children from the stigma of illegitimacy and place them with couples unable to have their own children (though some provinces, eg, Ontario, have recently amended their laws to remove the status of "illegitimacy"). Because more unwed mothers now keep their own children, those adopted are often older, sometimes physically or mentally handicapped and sometimes from disadvantaged groups, although increasing numbers of legitimate children are being adopted from families that ended in divorce. There are usually different stages in the adoption process, eg, the screening of applicants by welfare authorities before a child is placed (although in some provinces independent adoptions are possible, provided no payment is involved); a court hearing to determine the advisability of the adoption; the temporary placement of a child in an adoptive home; and the final adoption order granting the adoptive parents legal guardianship of the child. The child acquires succession rights and the family name of the adoptive family. The adoption process normally requires the consent of the natural parents, though that of the father of an illegitimate child is not always necessary; the court has power to dispense with the need for such consent in specified circumstances. If the child is of a specified age (often 12 years) its consent is also necessary. In Québec the Civil Code governs adoption with much the same effect as does the common law in the rest of Canada.

Adoption is a social as well as a legal process. The practice of adoption has changed in response to changing social attitudes and needs, but the legal process has not kept pace with these changes. There is now mounting pressure from adopted persons for contact with their birth parents to be made possible, and vice versa. Some provinces, such as Ontario, operate a system (the Voluntary Disclosure Registry) to facilitate voluntary disclosure, where adopted persons, having attained the age of majority, can indicate to the registry that they would like to contact their birth parents, and if the birth parents have registered the same request the connection will be made. Before adopted persons reach the age of majority the adoptive parents can veto contact with the birth parents. Other current issues include the debate over the child's right to consent to adoption (at present in Ontario, for example, a child 7 years of age or older must consent); the possibility of subsidized adoptions to facilitate adoption by parents who otherwise could not financially support a child; and the consideration, in recent years, of the concept of open adoption in which birth parents and adoptive parents would co-operate constructively in the adoption process. ALASTAIR BISSETT-JOHNSON

Adult Education in Canada is both a field of practice and (since the 1960s) a field of study. According to UNESCO, as a field of practice adult education denotes the entire body of organized educational processes, whatever the content, level or method, whether formal or informal, and whether the processes prolong or replace initial education in schools, colleges, universities or apprenticeship systems. The term "adult" usually means someone beyond the legal school-leaving age. Other than that, there is no upper age limit for learning.

Adult education as a field of study was originally interdisciplinary, borrowing from psychology, sociology, history, philosophy and the medical sciences. Like other fields of study, it has a particular body of knowledge and areas of specialization. University academic programs in adult education are concerned with teaching as well as research. At present, 8 universities in Canada offer a master's degree in adult education, and 3 (the universities of BC, Montréal and Toronto) offer a doctorate. These courses and programs prepare people as instructors, counsellors, community workers, administrators, evaluators, trainers and as professional development co-ordinators. Adult education is therefore really a generic term, variously used to mean a program, a movement, a subject matter, and sometimes a method. In particular, it reflects a specific philosophy about learning and teaching based on the assumption that adults can and want to learn, that they are able and willing to take responsibility for that learning, and that the learning itself should respond to their needs.

Origins Adults have always been engaged in learning, whether for survival, creativity, communal and individual interaction, or personal growth. In the 1800s the mechanics' institutes in Ontario, Québec and Nova Scotia provided information and learning opportunities to workers. Before Confederation, 1867, Queen's University was involved in extramural or extension work by offering public lectures, and the YMCA offered night classes for adults and educational programs for the military. Farmers' institutes were established, and by the late 1800s the National Council of Women had been founded; home and school associations had expanded; public lectures were being given in many communities; women's institutes had been established, and educational programs were being organized by religious and other groups. All these programs were developed in response to adult needs and interests.

Where organizations offering appropriate programs did not already exist, new organizations were created or existing ones changed their mandate of responsibility. An important related development was the establishment of and the rapid increase in publicly supported LIBRARIES.

In 1899 Frontier College was established to extend learning opportunities to those adults (mostly men) who lived and worked in remote communities, such as logging, mining and railway camps (*see* LITERACY). Much later, Frontier College and other organizations extended educational services to people in prisons, factories and farm kitchens, and to fishermen, rural people and immigrants.

From 1900 to 1925 programs for adults continued to expand. Khaki University was organized in England for Canadian military personnel returning to Canada after WWI. During this time the Workers' Education Association, which provided opportunities for working people, was introduced to Canada from the UK. With the growth of the West, universities extended their educational services to rural and remote communities by means of lectures, debating competitions, musical concerts and motion pictures. Indeed, U of A and U Sask were originally set up to offer extension courses. In the mid-1920s U of A used radio for EDUCATIONAL BROADCASTING and in the early 1930s established the BANFF CENTRE SCHOOL OF FINE ARTS. The efforts of SAINT FRANCIS XAVIER UNIVERSITY in Antigonish, NS, were especially effective in helping people stricken by the Great Depression, culminating in the establishment of an extensive CO-OPERATIVE MOVEMENT (*see* ANTIGONISH MOVEMENT).

Experimental work in public broadcasting the formation of the Institute of Public Affairs at Lake Couchiching (*see* COUCHICHING CONFERENCE), the founding of the NATIONAL FILM BOARD (1939), and 2 national radio forums in the 1940s — Citizen's Forum (1943) and Farm Radio Forum (1944) — all made use of media technology for learning and educating . Later developments included the use of satellite and television.

In 1958 the establishment of the Quetico Residential Conference and Training Centre in northwestern Ontario provided adults with further opportunities for learning. From the 1930s to the 1960s, educational programs were initiated by the Canadian Chamber of Commerce; the Labour College of Canada was established in Montréal (1962); and there was increased government support for training and education, eg, the Technical and Vocational Training Assistance Act in 1960 and the Agricultural Rehabilitation and Development Act in 1961 (*see* EDUCATION, TECHNICAL).

Internationally, Canadians contributed to the development of adult education through such organizations as the International Congress of University Continuing Education, and UNESCO. With support of participants from the UNESCO conference in Tokyo (1972), and under the leadership of a Canadian adult educator, Dr J. Roby KIDD, the International Council for Adult Education (ICAE) was established in 1973. After Dr Kidd died in 1982, the ICAE established an annual Roby Kidd Award for significant and innovative work in Adult Education. *Convergence*, the journal of the ICAE (begun in 1968), is now published in 4 languages and circulated to 76 countries from its Toronto headquarters.

Four national adult-education associations have been founded in Canada: the Canadian Association for Adult Education (CAAE, 1935); the Institut canadien d'education des adultes (ICEA, 1952), which primarily serves the French-language sectors of adult education in Canada; the Canadian Association for University Continuing Education (CAUCE, 1954); and the Canadian Association for the Study of Adult Education (CASAE, 1981).

Structures and Agencies Continuing education has become a way of life for many adults in Canada. Organized nonformal learning exists at all levels of government and within trade unions, co-operatives, industrial and commercial enterprises, hospitals, prisons, religious as well as cultural organizations, and health and fitness programs. Adult education takes place in factories, offices, gymnasiums, lecture halls, classrooms, libraries, museums, residential centres and churches, through a wide variety of teaching and learning methods.

Adult education also takes place in formal settings, as part of credited programs within schools, colleges and universities. Such agencies also engage in adult education nonformally through their departments of continuing education and extension. For example, the rapid expansion of the COMMUNITY COLLEGE and CEGEP systems in the 1960s and 1970s added greatly to the educational resources available to adults. Usually the structure of adult education is the responsibility of an instructor or a planner, or in the case of industry and government, a person in charge of professional development. Increasingly, these persons are beginning to see themselves as adult educators.

Participation The first national survey of adult education in Canada (1934) revealed the wide variety of activities and the large numbers of people that were involved in some kind of purposeful learning. Research by TVOntario indicated that 75% or more of the adults surveyed were or wished to be involved in further learning. A 1982 Gallup study for CAAE and ICEA of

Canadians 18 years and over revealed that 34% were involved in some kind of formal or nonformal educational program. However, most surveys document the participation of adult learners in visible and publicly supported institutions such as schools and colleges, but a large number of adults are involved in some form of purposeful learning outside these institutions. Nevertheless, many adult Canadians do not participate in any available education programs. The implications of this are especially important to Canada, which has one of the highest levels of functionally illiterate adults of any industrialized country. The 1981 census documented that of the Canadian population 15 years and over and not attending school full-time, 22% had less than 9 years of formal schooling. Greater efforts are being made to extend the educational opportunities of this group of adults.

Issues and Implications The attempts to develop government and institutional legislation that will economically support adult education parallel the increasing involvement of adults in educational programs. Also, many barriers, such as geographical distances and physical handicaps, prevent certain groups (eg, the handicapped, the isolated, the elderly, the undereducated, certain cultural groups, and women with small children) from participating in these programs (*see* DISTANCE LEARNING).

As adult education develops as a field of practice and a medium for research and study, participation and support will also have to increase. Within the context of adult education itself, the varied ways of learning that have been developed have blurred the formerly rigid roles of teacher and student, a fact that has been held up as proof that all adults, whether teachers or students, have something to teach (from life experience or from training) as well as something to learn from each other. Adult education as a field of practice and study has made an indelible contribution to society through its expression of respect for adults as responsible learners, as instigators of their own learning processes, and as valuable resources. JAMES A. DRAPER

Reading: D.H. Brundage and D. MacKeracher, *Adult Learning Principles and Their Application to Program Planning* (1980); J.R. Kidd, *How Adults Learn* (1976).

Advertising, the paid use of selected space or time in a communications medium by an identified organization or individual to present a message, is essentially a 20th-century development. Advertisers want to persuade people that certain goods or services are worth buying, to enhance the advertiser's image or to present a viewpoint. Advertising and the communications media have developed together; as technology and communications have progressed, the forms and uses of advertising have changed. In style and content, advertising provides an index of the political, social, economic and artistic climate of the times.

The first formal advertisement in Canada was an offer of butter for sale that appeared in 1752 in an official government publication, the *Halifax Gazette*. In 1764 the *Quebec Gazette* (later renamed the *Chronicle-Telegraph*) was founded, as much to carry news of merchandise as events. To reach Canada's 5 million people in 1900, advertisers could choose among 4 print media: 121 daily newspapers serving 570 000 subscribers; general-interest magazines; special-interest magazines; and street posters, which delivered inexpensive and graphic messages, often at or near retail stores. The most effective vehicle for fostering a national market was the mail-order catalogue, especially Eaton's. Not an advertising medium in the strict sense (because space was not for sale), the seasonal catalogues reached millions of farm and town people with advertising for a wide range of merchandise.

By 1889 newspapers were carrying enough advertising to encourage Anson McKim to open an office in Montréal to arrange the placement of advertisements in Ontario newspapers. He created a completely new type of business. Because the papers paid him a commission, his company became Canada's first advertising agency. He brought some order to the newspaper advertising business and deflated newspapers' exaggerated circulation claims by publishing the *Canadian Newspaper Directory*. Another early agency was McConnell Advertising, launched in London, Ont, about 1900.

In 1919 Canada issued its first radio-transmitting licence to Marconi's experimental wireless telephony station in Montréal (CFCF), and by 1928 more than 75 radio stations had been licensed to operate. Radio became an extremely successful advertising medium; by the end of the 1920s Canadians were complaining of too much broadcast advertising. In 1932 the federal government, deciding that broadcasting should not be left entirely to private enterprise, created the Canadian Radio Broadcasting Commission, later renamed the CANADIAN BROADCASTING CORPORATION, with authority to own stations in major cities and a monopoly to operate radio networks. In 1953 the government stopped collecting the annual licence fee, funding the CBC directly from public funds. By 1980-81 CBC radio and TV cost the taxpayer $550 million, or $22 per person per year, and advertising had been dropped entirely from CBC radio stations.

Soon after WWII, TV signals started flowing into Canada from US border cities. Alarmed at the number of Canadian antennae tuned to US stations, CBC opened TV stations in Toronto and Montréal in 1952 and licensed privately owned stations for other centres (*see* BROADCASTING, RADIO AND TELEVISION). TV's persuasive blend of sight, sound and motion (and later colour) made it a powerful advertising medium. Within 8 years, advertisers were spending $50 million a year in TV. Canadians' appetite for TV led to the construction of huge CABLE TV systems in the 1970s, multiplying the number of channels available in millions of homes. Advertisers wanting to reach a mass audience must now spread their expenditures among many stations. Cable networks may have a powerful impact; 2-way TV, for instance, could turn TV advertising into a direct-response process that would allow viewers to order a product by pushing a button on a home control unit. PAY TELEVISION, which relies on direct charges to the viewer rather than on advertising or government funding, will also alter the advertising patterns for broadcast media.

In 1980 advertisers spent about $4.2 billion, or $170 for every man, woman and child in Canada, in the various media. Most items sold in supermarkets are packaged goods; by means of media advertising, manufacturers try to influence shoppers in their selection of products from the shelves. Two of the largest companies, General Foods and Procter & Gamble, spent $45 million on advertising in Canada in 1980. Other big spenders are tobacco and alcohol manufacturers, automobile and oil companies, banks and fast-food chains.

Advertisers are classified as either national or local. National advertisers sell their products or services in more than one market, usually in the major markets across the country. The local advertiser, typically a retailer, serves one market only and restricts advertising to that audience. In the early 1980s a fast-growing segment of advertising aimed to promote ideas. "Advocacy advertising" is undertaken by corporations, professional associations, special-interest groups or labour unions that want to communicate their viewpoints in space where they have control of the message, rather than relying on the news media to interpret and carry their views. Elections are advocacy advertising campaigns, but politicians already in power also use advertising to explain their programs and policies. Governments have become big advertisers; the various departments of the federal government were Canada's largest advertiser in 1980, spending $42 million; the Ontario and Québec governments spent $35 million. Advertising by other provinces and by crown corporations added several more millions of dollars.

Major Advertising Media There are 118 daily NEWSPAPERS in Canada, with total circulations of 5.2 million; they enter 70% of all households. Daily newspapers receive 20% of the dollars spent on advertising. Without advertising, they would cost readers 5 times as much to buy, for 20% of their revenue comes from the selling price and the remaining 80% from the sale of national, local and classified advertising. In 1979 total advertising revenues for all daily newspapers in Canada reached $828 million, a gain of more than 50% in 6 years. National advertising accounted for 19% of the total and local advertising for 54%.

TV is another major advertising medium. Canadians are avid TV viewers; over half of their homes have more than one set and more than 80% of the population view TV at least once every day (*see* TELEVISION PROGRAMMING). Advertisers channel 18% of their total spending into TV. The Bureau of Broadcast Measurement divides Canada into 52 TV markets, which are reached by 122 commercial stations, most of them connected to one of the 2 French or 3 English networks. The 20 stations owned by CBC earned $100 million in advertising revenues in 1980. The privately owned stations that year earned $141 million in selling time to local advertisers, $290 million in direct sales to national advertisers and $79 million as their share of the networks' advertising revenues; 90% of their revenue is from advertising. Advertising expenditures have been climbing faster for TV than for any other medium: 114% from 1976 to 1981. A 30-second commercial on the CTV network's 16 stations cost $7200 in 1983.

Radio was forced to redefine its strengths with the advent of TV. Today it is again successful as an advertising medium. Comparatively inexpensive, it is useful to advertisers who want to repeat their messages frequently. Used creatively, it can invoke the listener's own imagination. Canada's 503 private radio stations earned $391 million in advertising revenues in 1980, 75% of that from local advertisers. Radio receives about 12% of all advertising expenditures, and commercials provide 99% of the revenue of private radio stations (*see* RADIO PROGRAMMING).

The number of consumer MAGAZINES in Canada, aimed at general and leisure interests rather than business or professional interests, rose from 250 in 1975 to 396 in 1981. Consumer magazines have 2 methods of distribution: paid circulation magazines are those available only to a paying audience; controlled circulation magazines are provided free to selected audiences whom the publishers believe to be valuable to advertisers. Although controlled circulation has been common among business publications, it was only in the 1970s that the technique was adopted for many consumer magazines. The later 1970s saw the advent of local TV and entertainment magazines produced by daily newspapers as part of their weekend packages. Total national advertising revenues for consumer magazines climbed from $94 million in 1975 to $157 million in 1980.

Community newspapers, usually published once or twice a week, have changed their role since the 1950s, when most were owned by local printing plants. By 1981 about 175 of the estimated 900 community newspapers were group owned, serving population segments within or surrounding cities. One such newspaper, *Mississauga News*, has a circulation of 70 000. Except for English weeklies in Québec, community newspapers have grown in number, size and stature as a result of citizen participation and of economies afforded by computerized typesetting and offset printing techniques. Advertising revenues of $55.6 million in 1971 climbed to an estimated total of $227 million by 1981. Most of this advertising (77%) is local, another 11% is classified and only 12% comes from national advertisers.

Canada has more than 500 business publications, with circulations ranging from a few thousand to more than 100 000. They carry advertising and editorial content of interest to people in business or the professions. The majority of business publications are produced by a half-dozen publishing houses, the 2 largest being MACLEAN HUNTER LIMITED and SOUTHAM Business Publications. Many magazines offer their advertisers other services and activities, such as trade shows and seminars. Revenues have increased from $55 million in 1975 to $105 million in 1980, or about 3% of all advertising.

Outdoor advertising, the billboards offered by 36 organizations across the country, has a total annual business of about $60 million. In the 1970s the "outdoor industry" faced a challenge to its existence, when Canadians became increasingly concerned to protect all aspects of the environment. In self-defence, the companies and the advertising industry turned to strict self-regulation. They eliminated some signs, restricted others to commercial thoroughfares, declared a 0.4 km setback from highways and improved design. By the early 1980s most Canadians seemed to accept outdoor advertising. The industry has expanded in other directions: advertising in bus shelters and on shopping-mall posters, and spectacular displays with moving parts and elaborate lighting. Outdoor advertising is an economical medium. The advertiser can make a prominent statement at low cost, often to supplement advertising in other media, but the sales message must be effective even when seen for only a moment. Transit advertising, located inside and outside of vehicles and in subway, bus and commuter stations, is widespread. Point-of-purchase communication includes both sign and package advertising. Not an advertising medium in the usual sense, it offers a reminder message in or near the retail outlet, in the form of window or shelf stickers and special display cases.

Advertising Agencies Though many of the largest advertisers have advertising departments within their companies, and a few even have their own in-house agency operations and place advertising themselves, most national advertising is prepared and placed by ad agencies. Some of the largest local advertisers also employ agencies. Agencies are complex organizations that offer clients a range of services: media planning and placement, account management, graphic design and copywriting, production and research to study audience reaction and response. A number of major research organizations have been set up by agencies, advertisers and media to provide objective audience data. The Bureau of Broadcast Measurement, for example, provides regular studies of radio and TV audiences. These surveys estimate how many people of each sex in different age categories listen to or watch various programs. The Print Measurement Bureau analyses the readership of 50 consumer magazines and provides demographic information on readers' age, education, income, marital status, occupation and product usage. Other research companies specialize in measuring the degree to which people remember advertising they have watched, heard or read.

Advertising Regulation Advertising in Canada is highly regulated. The practice of advertising law has become a profitable legal specialty. The provinces regulate liquor, pharmaceutical, business and professional advertising; the federal government regulates every area that comes under its jurisdiction, such as food and drugs. Because government licences are required for all radio and TV stations, broadcasting is regulated more than the print media. The CRTC requires pre-clearance of all commercials for beer, wine, cider, food, drugs, cosmetics, medical devices and children's products. Beer and wine advertising is also examined by Health and Welfare Canada and by provincial liquor boards. Food commercials are studied by the Dept of Consumer and Corporate Affairs. Health and Welfare looks at commercials for drugs, cosmetics and medical devices. Children's commercials are checked by an Advertising Standards Council that includes representatives of the Consumers' Assn of Canada, advertisers, agencies, media and the CRTC. The CBC has its own commercial acceptance process and the CTV, Global and Atlantic TV networks are similarly served by a Telecaster Committee. Beyond these clearly regulated areas is a misty region of taste, sense and judgement. Here there are self-regulatory codes prepared by the Canadian Advertising Advisory Board (CAAB) in conjunction with governments and manufacturers. Through its Advertising Standards Council, CAAB previews advertising on request and bans any advertising in breach of its codes.

Careers in Advertising Advertising includes business, show business, science and art. The industry offers a range of work, in agencies, advertising departments of large companies and among the media and suppliers. No single course of education covers them all. Employers often require university, or at least community college, education. They want commerce and business administration graduates for account-management work, art-college training for art directors and illustrators, sociology and psychology majors for market research, journalism or English literature backgrounds for copywriting. Several industry associations offer night courses in advertising. The Institute of Canadian Advertising, an association of advertising agencies, sponsors a 3-year night course leading to designation as a certified advertising agency practitioner, open to those with at least one year's practical experience. There are more than 400 ad agencies in Canada, ranging in size from large offices which employ up to 500 people in several branches to one-person operations, and including specialized companies such as creative boutiques and media-buying services. The 65 member agencies of the Institute of Canadian Advertising claim to handle 80% of all national advertising.

JERRY GOODIS

Aeolian Landform, a feature of the Earth's surface produced by either erosive or constructive action of the WIND. The word derives from Aeolus, the Greek god of the winds. Wind EROSION processes consist of abrasion, ie, the scouring of exposed surfaces by the sand-blasting action of wind-borne material; and deflation, ie, the removal of sand-sized and smaller particles by the wind. Sand is transported short distances to form dunes; finer silt is transported farther to form loess. Wind transportation causes attrition of the moving particles, which rub one another and develop characteristic surface frosting and pitting. Wind abrasion produces faceted pebbles (ventifacts) found in certain parts of Canada; furrowed bedrock surfaces common in N Saskatchewan; and yardangs (sharp-crested ridges carved from soft but coherent deposits) found mainly in desert regions. Deflation produces wind pits, deflation depressions and basins, all common in dune areas in Canada. Large-scale wind erosion contributed to the formation of preferentially oriented valleys or coulees in S Alberta. The process of winnowing through deflation, whereby the smaller grains are carried off by the wind, leaves behind a layer of pebbles and boulders called lag gravel or reg which protects the ground surface from further erosion. These layers are common in some dune areas in Canada, the most spectacular ones occurring S of Lk ATHABASCA.

Sand dunes are not limited to desert regions, since aeolian features that were once active and are now stabilized are widespread in many temperate and cold zones. Sand-dune areas cover about 26 000 km^2 or approximately 0.27% of the total area of Canada: Alberta has 45%; Saskatchewan, 36%; Manitoba, 10%. The concentration of dune areas on the prairies results from the availability of suitable sandy deposits left behind by GLACIERS, the frequent occurrence of dry, westerly winds and the openness of the region. The dry, westerly winds produced the easterly oriented dunes. Elsewhere in Canada, less effective dry winds produced local dune areas. In the ICE AGES, the ice sheet controlled the distribution of air masses and produced northwesterly oriented dunes in N Saskatchewan and Alberta and southwesterly oriented dunes in the St Lawrence Lowlands, Qué. Most of Canada's dune areas are stabilized by vegetation; relatively few are active, except in the area S of Lk Athabasca. This region contains 385 km^2 of barren sand surfaces, recognizable on satellite photos, with beautiful, active sand dunes producing breathtaking scenery. This large-scale aeolian activity is not climatically controlled but is due to the prevailing local GROUNDWATER conditions. In Canada only about 2.5% of the total dune area is active; 95% of that total occurs in the above-mentioned region.

One common feature of almost all sand dunes in Canada, which distinguishes them from desert dunes, is that they show some parabolic form, concave upwindward. This form develops if moisture is present in the dunes. Individual dunes may have simple or complex forms, depending on the mode and duration of their development. The dune areas of Canada have been grouped into a series of regional zones according to differences in dune form. Each zone has distinct environmental characteristics. In every dune area, local aeolian activity began as soon as sandy surfaces became exposed to the air after the disappearance of the ice. In more humid regions, activity lasted for only a short time. Dry winds blowing from one direction or another accumulated the sand to form either transverse or parabolic dunes. Transverse dunes persisted as long as the sand in them remained dry. When moistened by rainfall, they broke up into parabolic dunes. In one region in central Alberta, dunes showing stages of this transformation have been preserved by stabilization. In drier regions where activity continued and dunes migrated downwind, vegetation invaded the interdune areas. When the climate became humid, the dunes were gradually stabilized by vegetation, and soils developed on them. This process occurred in the southern PRAIRIES only after a few thousand years of activity. Later, periodic CLIMATE fluctuations caused many of the dunes to become partly active from time to time, and buried parts of their stabilized surfaces and soils. Radiocarbon dating of organic material extracted from buried soils has helped to show that more than 10 periods of renewed aeolian activity have occurred in the last 5000 years. These periods correlate well with other climate-sensitive phenomena such as tree-ring development. In Canada, loess deposits are generally small in area and usually occur downwind from dune areas. They represent the silt-sized portions of aeolian transportation. Other, still less extensive aeolian deposits include the so-called cliff-top deposits formed by sediments that were deflated from barren, cliffy slopes exposed to the winds. Occurrences of these on the southern prairies have been the sites of past volcanic-ash deposition (*see* VOLCANO). P.P. DAVID

Aerodynamics, branch of ENGINEERING concerned with gaseous fluids (usually air) in motion and, in particular, with the effects of this motion on rigid or flexible bodies. The forces acting on the surface of a body moving through air, or (what is the same thing) the pressure exerted by air flowing past a body at rest, are affected mainly by the shape and size of the body, the relative speed of the flow, and the density, viscosity and compressibility of the gas. Viscosity is the ability of a flowing liquid or gas to develop internal shear stresses that resist flow. In air, viscous forces are generally small in comparison with inertia forces, a condition which leads to flow instability and turbulence. Thus, WINDS near the rough surface of Earth are generally turbulent, as is the flow in the thin boundary layer next to the skin of an airplane in flight. The problem of turbulence has never been completely resolved although, for most engineering purposes, its effects are reasonably predictable.

The compressibility of air determines the speed of sound or the speed at which pressure changes are transmitted through the flow field. The speed of sound is about 340 metres per second at sea level, 296 m/s in the stratosphere. If the speed of a body exceeds the speed of sound, the pattern of flow changes drastically and pressure waves tend to pile up into shock waves. The Mach number is the ratio of the body speed to the speed of sound. The design of efficient aircraft shapes for flight at transonic and supersonic speeds (Mach number near or greater than 1) remains one of the most challenging problems in aerodynamics.

Viscosity and compressibility are the most troublesome factors in theoretical aerodynamics and the steady development of aerodynamics during this century has been possible only through a close association between experimental and theoretical research. The main laboratory tool of the aerodynamicist, the wind tunnel, is a specially designed tube or duct in which air is made to flow under precisely controlled conditions. Many of the engineering departments in Canadian universities have small or medium-sized tunnels that are used for various research purposes. Large, general-purpose wind tunnels (suitable for investigation of aerodynamic design problems of aircraft and road vehicles, and the testing of large-scale models of engineering structures) typically cost tens of millions of dollars to design and build, and are comparatively rare. The largest tunnels in Canada are at the NATIONAL RESEARCH COUNCIL, Ottawa: one is capable of speeds up to about 55 m/s and has a test section 9 m^2; another, with a 1.5 m^2 test section, is capable of speeds up to 4 times the speed of sound. The design of large wind tunnels is a highly specialized field in which one Canadian consulting engineering firm, DSMA International, has developed a worldwide reputation. DSMA's engineers have designed and supervised construction of many tunnels for automotive research and high- and low-speed aircraft development in N America, Europe and Asia.

The needs of aircraft design have prompted many advances in aerodynamics. For example, DE HAVILLAND AIRCRAFT OF CANADA LTD have designed a famous line of STOL (short take off and landing aircraft): the DE HAVILLAND BEAVER, OTTER Twin Otter, DASH 7 and Dash 8. De Havilland's success has resulted, in part, from the company's steady progress in design of high-lift wing flap systems and of means of maintaining precise control at unusually low flying speeds. However, the applications of aerodynamics extend far beyond the needs of aeronautics. For example, the University of Western Ontario pioneered development of a specialized wind tunnel, with a very long test section, to model the turbulent characteristics of natural winds over Earth's surface. It has been used to check the design of large structures, including some of the tallest buildings in the world. The Universities of British Columbia and Moncton and a private consulting firm, Morrison Hershfield Ltd, in Guelph and Edmonton, all have tunnels of this type for the investigation of such problems as bird flight, PESTICIDE-spray diffusion and snow drifting. NRC's large tunnels have been used to measure pressures and aerodynamic forces on downhill skiers, cars, high-rise buildings, model ships and trains, a flexible stadium roof, an offshore oil platform, snowmobiles, motorcycles and parachutes, as well as on nearly all the aircraft designed in Canada. NRC aerodynamicists have also revived a forgotten French invention: the vertical-axis wind turbine (VAWT), which looks like a large egg-beater. R.J. TEMPLIN

Aerospace Industry has specialized capabilities for the design, research, development, production, marketing, repair and overhaul of aircraft, aero engines, aircraft and engine subsystems and components, space-related equipment, and air- and ground-based avionic systems and components. It is economically impractical for the Canadian industry to meet the diverse commercial and defence aerospace-product needs of the Canadian market. Through selective specialization, the industry has developed products in response mainly to export-market demands; 70-80% of its sales are in export markets. Approximately 100 companies are engaged in significant manufacturing. The main centres of production are Montréal, Toronto and Winnipeg. Employment in 1981 was 41 000, with sales of $2.6 billion.

History Canadair Ltd, the principal aircraft-manufacturing company, started in the 1920s as the Aircraft Division of Canadian Vickers Ltd in east Montréal. Canadair designed and manufactured a series of airplanes, starting with the Vedette, the first Canadian flying-boat design. The company was relocated at the Cartierville airport in the Montréal suburb of St Laurent during WWII and, under Canadian government ownership, was an important centre of military aircraft production for amphibious Canso aircraft. In 1947 the government sold Canadair to the US Electric Boat Co, only to repurchase the company in 1976. Canadair has become an important source of executive jet aircraft, represented by the Challenger aircraft series.

Another major aircraft manufacturer, DE HAVILLAND, has been active in Canada since 1928. Originally, as a subsidiary of the de Havilland Aircraft Co of England, it sold and serviced aircraft designed in the UK. Manufacturing came later, culminating in large-scale production of Anson, Mosquito and Tiger Moth aircraft during WWII. The first serious design venture of the Canadian engineering team was the Chipmunk trainer, followed in 1947 by the famous DE HAVILLAND BEAVER light aircraft. The Beaver initiated a sequence of short-takeoff-and-landing aircraft (STOL): the DE HAVILLAND OTTER, CARIBOU, Buffalo, DASH 7, Dash 8 and Twin Otter. In 1974 the government purchased de Havilland to secure the development and production of the Dash 7 aircraft and the continued operation of the company as an aircraft manufacturer in Canada.

The first modern aero-engine design unit in Canada was started in Toronto. Acting on the recommendations of a government technical mission, the National Research Council of Canada (NRC) established Turbo Research Ltd in 1944 in Leaside, a suburb of Toronto. A specification for a turbojet was drawn up and work began on the design of the TR 4 engine, later called the Chinook.

In 1945 A.V. Roe, Canada, was formed to provide a domestic aircraft- and engine-design manufacturing capability, particularly for defence. The new company took over the assets of Victory Aircraft Ltd, at Malton, Toronto, which had produced Lancaster bombers during WWII. The Turbo Research team joined the group at Malton a year later. In the summer of 1946 the Royal Canadian Air Force requested the design and development of a turbojet engine, the Orenda, with a thrust equal to that of any contemporary engine under design abroad. By 1951 the team of engineers and technicians had expanded and a new manufacturing plant was constructed; it was opened in 1952. Within 17 months some 1000 Orendas had been delivered to the RCAF and production eventually reached 3824.

A.V. Roe began work on the design and development of a supersonic engine, later called the Iroquois, in 1953. This engine was chosen to power the AVRO ARROW (CF-105) supersonic all-weather fighter. On 20 Feb 1959, just a few weeks before the first Iroquois-engined Arrow was to take to the air, the government cancelled the aircraft and engine programs. The termination of the Arrow was a watershed in the history of the Canadian aerospace industry, and of A.V. Roe in particular. Over one weekend the work force at A.V. Roe shrank from 5000 to 1000 workers, with a total of 14 000 workers losing employment throughout the industry. Since that time Canada has not sought to be self-sufficient in aerospace weapon systems. The Malton aircraft facilities of A.V. Roe continued under de Havilland direction until 1963, when the Douglas Aircraft Co assumed ownership to produce wings for its DC-9 commercial jet aircraft. Later the Douglas parent company was taken over by the McDonnell (US) Co and the Malton facility became McDonnell Douglas Canada Ltd. The Canadian entity has developed into an important manufacturer of wings for the DC-9, the DC-9 Super 80, the DC-10 and the KC-10 aircraft.

The largest company in the Canadian Aerospace Industry is Pratt and Whitney Aircraft of Canada (PWC), designers and manufacturers of a highly successful series of jet and propjet aero engines with over 50% of the world market for civil turbine engines. Pratt and Whitney established the Canadian company in 1929 as a parts and overhaul facility for Wasp radial engines. During WWII the business grew, owing to the substantial use of Pratt and Whitney engines by the military. Studies during the mid-1950s indicated that the piston-engine business would decline, and it was decided that PWC would organize a team to design and develop gas turbine engines for the general aviation market. An engine specification for a propjet of about 500-shaft horsepower and designated the PT-6 was developed. The engine has since become preeminent in its class. Later engines have included the JT-15 fan-jet and the A-50 series used for the de Havilland Dash 7 and other aircraft. By 1978 there were 50 models of the PT-6 and the JT-15D in production and both engine families had set the standard for general aviation engines around the world.

This historical view of the industry would be incomplete without reference to the development of Canadian Aircraft Electronics. CAE has grown from a fledgling company in Montréal in 1945 to a corporation with subsidiary aerospace companies across Canada engaged in the design and manufacture of aircraft simulators, avionics (aviation electronic equipment), and aircraft components and subsystems.

In space-related activities, Canada's industry is modest by comparison with the US, Russian and European industries, but it is first-rate in special fields. The industry originated in the 1920s with ground-based research projects for the study of the Earth's upper atmosphere conducted by scientists from U of Saskatchewan. An extension of these researches, using high-altitude balloons, was initiated in the 1950s by DRB, and led to work with sounding rockets, developed by Bristol Aerospace, Winnipeg, using the Black Brant rocket. In 1954 the Canadian Army conducted the first series of rocket firings at Fort Churchill, Man.

At the end of 1958 the US National Aeronautics and Space Administration (NASA) accepted a DRB proposal to create jointly a sounding satellite, the Alouette I, which was supported by a network of Canadian ground stations at Ottawa, Prince Albert and Resolute Bay and 10 other stations around the world. The satellite was launched in 1962 and was a significant technological success. This entry into the field of space technology aroused considerable interest in using the technology for communications satellites. In Sept 1969 Telesat Canada was formed to provide domestic communications services by satellite throughout the country. Hughes Aircraft Corp (US), with Northern Electric and SPAR Aerospace, designed and developed the ANIK I, II and III satellites, launched in Nov 1972, April 1973 and May 1975 respectively. Canada became the first country in the world to own and operate a domestic SATELLITE COMMUNICATIONS system.

In order to develop the capabilities of its space industry, Canada undertook in the mid-1970s to provide a Remote Manipulator Arm for the US space shuttle. The arm was successfully deployed during the second flight of the space shuttle Columbia in 1982, and gained world recognition for the technological capability of SPAR Aerospace and the NRC.

The Modern Industry has a hierarchy of 3 tiers of capabilities and products. In the first tier are the principal companies with integrated design and production capability for complete aircraft and engines. The second-tier companies manufacture components and subsystems for the principal companies in Canada and abroad. The third tier comprises machine shops, heat treatment shops, foundries, forges and other companies whose business is predominantly the aerospace industry. All aerospace companies must ensure a very high quality and reliability of products, and as a result the companies have a high cost structure specific to aerospace. They tend not to serve general markets, other than nuclear engineering, which has similar quality and reliability demands.

The 3 tiers are not integrated; rather, the companies are interdependent with other N American aerospace companies. This interdependence results from the international nature of the world airline business, from the US as the principal trading partner, from foreign ownership (mainly US) of about 50% of the companies, and particularly from a defence-sharing agreement between Canada and the US. Although Canadian military sales had declined as a proportion of total sales from 66% in 1963 to 22% in 1981, the Canada-US Defence Production Sharing Agreement (DPSA) and its associated Canadian financial-assistance program, the Defence Industries Productivity Program for industry and market development, have been very significant in shaping the industry's development since the demise of the Arrow program. The DIPP has helped to finance both defence projects and civilian projects handled by the defence industry. The Dash 7 aircraft and the civilian PT-6 and JT-15 aero engines were partially funded by DIPP. In the period 1971-82, $430 million of DIPP funds were applied for research and development, for establishment of Canadian industrial sources and for modernization with advanced production equipment. Another major source of funding for the government-owned aircraft companies has been the provision of

The Canadian-built Challenger series has made Canadair an important source of executive jet aircraft (*courtesy Canadair*).

guarantees for loans from the private sector, authorized by Parliament.

For the 20-year period ending in 1981, there was a rough balance between the imports and exports of commercial and defence aerospace products. This balance was assured for military products by adoption of a government policy to seek industrial-benefit offsets for the Canadian industry against major procurements. Until the 1980s commercial aircraft imports were also, in part, kept in balance through industrial-benefit arrangements with Boeing, Lockheed and McDonnell. However, a Civil Aircraft Agreement of 1980 under the General Agreement on Tariffs and Trade, to which Canada is a signatory, now forbids including offset requirements as a part of a civil aircraft transaction, although it does not prevent negotiating offsets as long as the sale is not conditional upon these offsets. The same agreement removed all tariffs on commercial aircraft trade, and the DPSA referred to earlier has effectively eliminated tariffs on defence trade. The industry now operates with a nonprotected status. This has the twin effect of causing the industry to remain competitive in world terms but leaving it vulnerable against foreign industries, which receive some protection through receiving directed defence procurements.

Aerospace products, such as complete aircraft, aero engines and the electrical, electronic and mechanical subsystems, represent a complex and highly demanding application of advanced technology. The requirement for maximum safety and performance, with minimum weight, is a major reason why aerospace continues to emphasize the use of new and improved materials and new design and production technologies. The industry is a leader in the application of computer-integrated design and manufacturing technologies. The skill rating of engineers, technologists and production workers reflects the high design and quality standards of this industry. One disturbing feature is a pattern of cyclical employment caused by changing personnel requirements at succeeding phases of the relatively few major Canadian aerospace projects. As a result, immigration of engineers has frequently been relied upon to meet intensive demands, and few Canadian universities offer aerospace-related courses. The notable exceptions are U of Toronto, Ryerson and SAIT. The larger companies in the industry are unionized and labour relations are generally satisfactory. The main unions are the United Auto Workers and the International Association of Machinists and Aerospace Workers.

Institutions and Societies The aerospace industry is represented nationally by the Air Industries Assn of Canada, which exists mainly as a lobby group to assure the continuance of federal government financial support for its member companies. It has also sponsored valuable co-operative projects for productivity improvement and for the enhancement of labour relations and training arrangements with unions, academic establishments and provincial and federal government departments. The technical society for the industry is the Canadian Aeronautics and Space Institute (CASI).

NORMAN GARDNER

Reading: G.A. Fuller, J.A. Griffin and K.M. Molson, *12 Years of Canadian Aeronautics* (1983); K.M. Molson, *Canadian Aircraft Since 1909* (1982); R.D. Page, *Avro Canuck CF-100* (1982); D. Watson et al, *Avro Arrow* (1980).

Affaires, Les, the main French-language business newspaper in Canada was founded in 193 in Montréal where it is still published. A weekly, it has a circulation of about 57 000 mainly in Québec. It is published by Publications Les Affaires (1979) Inc. The publisher of *Les Affaires* is Claude Beauchamp; Jean-Paul Gagné is editor. *Les Affaires* is noted for its coverage of Québec investments, its advice to readers in everyday language, a section of brokers' analysis and a weekly company profile.

D. MCGILLIVRAY

Affleck, Raymond Tait, architect (b at Penticton, BC 20 Nov 1922). Educated at McGill and in Zurich, Switz, he began independent practice in 1953 and in 1955 joined in forming the firm of Affleck Desbarats Dimakopoulos Lebensold Sise, from 1970 called Arcop Associates, Architects and Planners. While his firm participated in many important projects from St John's (Arts and Culture Centre, 1967) to Vancouver (Queen Elizabeth Theatre, 1955) Affleck is particularly associated with the Montréal development Place Bonaventure (1964-68), PLACE VILLE MARIE (1956-65) and more recently Maison Alcan (1983). Affleck's concern for the quality of life in a northern climate is expressed in Place Bonaventure and other projects that interweave many different strands of urban activity with indoor pedestrian streets and atria. The Maison Alcan joins a restored historic hotel and grey stone houses on Sherbrooke St to the reticent but entirely modern glass and aluminum clad headquarters behind by means of a glazed atrium.

MICHAEL MCMORDIE

AFL-CIO The American Federation of Labor (est 1886) consisted of skilled craft unions that disagreed with the reform policies and organization of the KNIGHTS OF LABOR. The AFL involved Canadian workers from the beginning, and between 1898 and 1902 the first Canadian organizer, John FLETT, chartered over 700 locals. Most Canadian unions were affiliated with the TRADES AND LABOR CONGRESS OF CANADA, which was associated with, and dominated by, the AFL. During the 1920s the AFL hewed to craft union interests, ignoring unskilled workers in the new mass-production industries (steel, auto, electrical). In Nov 1935, these workers set up what later became the Congress of Industrial Organizations, organizing by industry rather than by craft. The CIO won several spectacular strikes in Canada (*see* OSHAWA STRIKE), openly engaged in politics and bickered with the AFL. New challenges such as automation after WWII persuaded labour leaders in the US to settle their differences and merge in 1955; their Canadian affiliates merged a year later. Although the AFL-CIO remains a powerful blue-collar pressure group in the US, it has not succeeded in winning much support from expanding white-collar occupations.

ROBERT H. BABCOCK

Africans The term "African" includes indigenous Negroid-Blacks of West, East and Southern Africa, the Hamito-Semites of Ethiopia, and people of other ethnocultural origins who view Africa as home by virtue of several generations of settlement on the African continent. Chief among these latter groups are Europeans of British, Portuguese, Afrikaner-Dutch and Jewish ethnocultural origins, people of mixed descent and Asian Indians of Muslim, Hindu and Goan Christian religious-cultural background.

The vast continent of Africa and its complex array of peoples has not had a close relationship with Canada. BLACK Africans, in particular, comprise a very small, scattered and almost unknown group of newcomers to Canada, although Africans of European and Asian ancestry have a clearer presence. However, little formal documentation exists on any of these groups.

Historically, Canadian IMMIGRATION POLICY has not favoured immigration by Asians and Africans. From 1946 to 1950 Africans comprised only 0.3% of new immigrants to Canada, a figure that rose to an average of only 1-2% over the next 20 years. With the 1966 White Paper on immigration and the attempt to introduce a nondiscriminatory screening process the proportion of African immigrants rose to an average of approximately 2% from 1968 to 1970, indicating that while the new system was more objective, it was highly selective. It also favoured certain countries, including the black countries of Nigeria and Ghana. In 1972-73, with Canada's acceptance of some 7000 Ugandan Asians, the proportion of immigrants rose from 6.8% of total immigration, and it remained at an average of about 5.2% from 1975 to 1978, corresponding to the movement of Portuguese and British settlers to Canada after Angola and Mozambique (1975) and Zimbabwe (1980) achieved independence. From 1973 to 1983, some 16 000 South Africans, mainly of non-black ethnic origins, entered Canada. The steady, relatively high immigration from Tanzania and Kenya, too, reflects Asian Indian rather than black African migration.

The introduction of the Green Paper on Immigration (1976) had the effect of restricting the entry of potential landed immigrants in the "independent" class. This regulation seriously curtailed movement of people from black African countries, and it is aggravated by the fact that there are just 3 Canadian Employment and Immigration offices in Africa. The office located in Abidjan, capital of the Ivory Coast, serves 23 widely dispersed neighbouring countries; that in Nairobi, capital of Kenya, serves 19 equally dispersed countries in the northeastern part of the continent. By contrast, the office located in Pretoria, the administrative capital of the Republic of South Africa, serves just 5 countries at Africa's southern tip.

The 1976 Immigration Act, however, has had the positive consequence of allowing Canadian citizens to sponsor close relatives. This stipulation has been especially beneficial for landed immigrants from the Republic of South Africa, and from Tanzania, Kenya, Uganda, Angola, Zimbabwe, and, to a lesser degree, Nigeria and Ghana. In 1983, 3624 people (comprising 4.1% of Canada's total immigration) immigrated to Canada from Africa. Most of the immigrants from this group in the "independent class" came from the Republic of South Africa and the Malgasy Republic. At the present time Canada is looking for entrepreneurs and self-employed immigrants with the funds to establish business operations capable of employing Canadian citizens. Such entrepreneurs are more likely to emerge from the affluent European-Asian African groups than from black African groups. Overall, most Africans in any of the ethnocultural groups are drawn from the former English-speaking colonies of Africa; a smaller number originate in the former French-speaking colonies of Africa, chiefly from Mali, Senegal, Zaire, Malagasy Republic and the Ivory Coast.

It is estimated that only about 10% of people classified as REFUGEES in Africa would be classified as such according to the UN definition of the term, but all groups may count among their numbers self-exiled persons, or persons seeking greater personal freedom for themselves and their families. These subgroups are difficult to identify except where offical data exist on immigrant refugee status, eg, with Ugandan Asian Indians and the Ethiopians of Eritrea. The 1976 Immigration Act established a new "refugee class." For 1983 Canada accepted 818 refugees from Africa (compared to 372 in 1982), and 415 from Ethiopia, 79 from Uganda, 69 from Sudan, 49 from Algeria, 40 from Nigeria, 35 from South Africa and 131 from other countries. The federal government sponsored 79.6% of these refugees; 20.4% were privately funded.

Migration and Settlement

According to the 1981 census, there are 45 215 persons of African origin in Canada, comprising a mere 0.19% of the total population. Most Africans settled in Ontario, followed by Québec, Alberta, Nova Scotia and BC. Approximately 1500 people speak African languages, eg, Ashanti (Ghana), Hausa, Yoruba and Ibo (Nigeria), Kru (Liberia-Sierra Leone), Amharic (Ethiopia), Tigrinya (Eritrea), Sotho, Tswana and Zulu (South Africa), Bamhara, Malnike (Mali-Ivory Coast), Wolof and Dyola (Senegal), in their home settings, but all Africans who come to Canada have a good knowledge of either English or French.

Social and Cultural Life

Black Africans From 1963 to 1967, Africans immigrated from Ethiopia (641), Ghana (113), Kenya (548), Nigeria (175), Rhodesia (641), Republic of South Africa (3512), Tanzania (242), Uganda (153), Zaire (18), Zambia (424). Many African countries attained independence about that time: Zambia (1964), Tanzania (1962) and Uganda (1961), Kenya and Nigeria (1960). White Rhodesia unilaterally declared its independence from Britain in 1965, and South Africa declared itself a republic and withdrew from the COMMONWEALTH in 1961. Given these changes it is difficult to judge the ethnic mix that entered Canada at the time. Many newcomers may have been European settlers emigrating from a changing Africa, but it seems certain that black Africans as well began to settle in Canada in the 1960s.

Ethiopian refugees accepted into Canada in recent years comprise a linguistic-cultural group distinct from other Africans with whom they tend to have only peripheral contact. Refugees from the secessionist Red Sea province of Eritrea tend to be well educated and skilled. Many speak Italian as a consequence of the WWII Italian occupation of Ethiopia. An interesting but tiny Ethiopian subgroup (about 10 000-12 000 people) are the Falashas ("Black Jews"), who come from the northwest provinces of Ethiopia. They practise an ancient form of Judaism, but they have no knowledge of Hebrew and their priests use Ge'ez, the Semitic-Sabaean script originating in the 4th century AD, as their liturgical language. Most Africans in Canada are Christian or Muslim.

As a group black Africans generally share only one area of common experience — that of PREJUDICE AND DISCRIMINATION and RACISM in the host country. Contrary to liberal credo held in Western societies, discrimination does not necessarily disappear in boom periods of the economy. White attitudes regarding racial issues are mostly independent of traditional sociodemographic variables such as age, education and income.

Ugandans and Other Asians In 1972, with the so-called "Africanization" of Uganda, some 50 000 Ugandan Asians were expelled. Approximately 7000 were invited to settle in Canada. Given the variety of skills and professional background they brought with them, coupled with their initiative and enterprising attitudes, most Ugandan Asians have made steady socioeconomic progress in Canada. They have settled primarily in Ontario (40% in Toronto), BC and Québec.

The largest group of Ugandan Asians in Canada are the Ishmailiyah (Ismailis), a sect of the Shiah branch of Islam. A smaller Islamic sect in Canada are the Ithna-Ashariyah. The Ismailis, and to a lesser degree the Ithna Asheri, have developed strong ethnocultural and religious groups that have contributed to their sociopsychological integrity and their economic progress.

The Gujarati Hindus, traditionally a business caste in India and East Africa, have been successful in business and professional occupations in Canada. They tend to be a conservative people, practising the Hindu-Gandhian teachings of Ahimsa (nonviolence), asceticism and respect for all life. They are mostly vegetarian; marriages are endogamous within similar castes and are frequently arranged by parents.

The Goan Indians originated in the Portuguese-dominated province of Goa on the Malabar Coast, 402 km south of Bombay. Many contemporary Goans have some Portuguese background, have Portuguese names, and are Roman Catholic. When ousted by Idi Amin in 1972, many came to Canada, settling mainly in Toronto. They have their own organizations, apart from people coming directly from Goa, and apart from the large Portuguese community in Toronto. Today they are uniformly English speaking.

All the Asian Indian subgroups have more bonds of kinship with people from India and Pakistan and with the religions and cultures of those countries than with black Africans.

Angola-Mozambique Portuguese In 1976-77, 2100 "returnees" (white and coloured Portuguese) from the newly independent territories of Angola and Mozambique were admitted into Canada, even though they did not qualify as genuine refugees since they held Portuguese passports. The Portuguese settlers in Africa had remained Portuguese citizens. Two factors contributed to this "humanitarian" gesture by Canada: pressure from the Portuguese Canadian community and requests from the Portuguese ambassador to Canada to help ease the burden of returning white colonials. Most returnees entered Canada in 1978-79 under contract as skilled workers to firms in Canada. These returnees have prospered, and do not seem to rely on the support of Portuguese aid societies. They are viewed as having integrated well into the larger society, possibly because of their fluency in English.

South Africa and Zimbabwe By far the largest number of people that have entered Canada from any sub-Saharan country have been those originating in the Republic of South Africa. Between 1964 and 1983, 35 851 immigrants, including a large number of English-speaking, British and Jewish people, and small groups of Afrikaners (Dutch-French Huguenot), coloureds (mixed descent), Asian Indians and a handful of black Africans, left South Africa for Canada. Professionals of all types, eg, university professors, medical doctors, school teachers, writers, artists and some skilled artisans, are to be found in all the groups.

The political climate of South Africa is characterized by tension and uncertainty. The white elite leave the country at a steady rate of about 1500 per year. Former white Rhodesians as well have found a wintry haven in Canada. Most white South Africans in Canada are liberal minded, but the barriers to intergroup communication imposed by apartheid seem to continue in the host country. Each racial group has at least some loose bonding within its own group, but little across groups, even where people originate from the same cities and towns.

Only a sprinkling of well-educated black Africans have any chance of enjoying the climate of political and personal freedom afforded by Canada. Even blacks who seek refugee status in

Canada must prove they would be persecuted if they returned to South Africa. Living under apartheid does not qualify an individual as a refugee. JOSEPHINE C. NAIDOO

Agar, Carlyle Clare, helicopter pioneer (b at Lion's Head, Ont 28 Nov 1901; d at Victoria 27 Jan 1968). In 1905 Agar moved to Edmonton, where he was educated and learned to fly. He joined the RCAF in 1940 and was awarded an Air Force Cross for contributions as a flight teacher. He attempted to set up an air service in Penticton and Kelowna, BC, and in 1947 flew the first commercial HELICOPTER into Canada, spraying orchards with insecticide. He perfected helicopter flying in mountainous terrain and carried out aerial surveys. In 1949 he airlifted construction material, equipment and personnel to the mountainside Palisade Lk Dam. In 1951 he performed a similar task for the Aluminum Co of Canada's giant smelter complex at Kitimat, BC. His company, Okanagan Air Service, became one of the largest commercial helicopter operations in the world. He was awarded the MCKEE TROPHY in 1950. JAMES MARSH

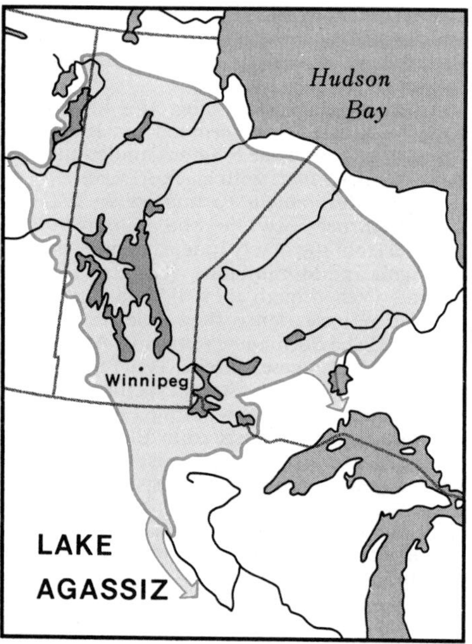

Agassiz, Lake The largest glacial lake in N America formed 11 500 years ago in front of the northeastwardly retreating Laurentide Ice Sheet, which acted as a dam. The lake covered much of Manitoba, NW Ontario, parts of eastern Saskatchewan and North Dakota, and NW Minnesota. At its largest, Lake Agassiz was about 1500 km long, over 1100 km wide and about 210 m deep. Its history is complicated by the behaviour of the ice sheet, which at times readvanced and affected lake levels and drainage systems. Several outlet channels and about 35 beach ridges at different elevations have been identified. Some of these, such as the prominent Campbell Beach Ridge, can be traced for hundreds of kilometres. For the first 500 years, drainage was southward through the Minnesota R Valley. As glacial retreat continued into NW Ontario, the lake lowered and drainage shifted eastward into Lk Superior via various channels in the Lk Nipigon basin area. About 9900 years ago, a readvance blocked the eastern outlet, raising the lake to earlier levels. Between 9500 and 9200 years ago, the ice sheet rapidly disintegrated and eastern outlets were once again opened. As deglaciation continued, lower lake levels were established until the drainage shifted N into Hudson Bay. The final drainage of the lake occurred about 7700 years ago. Only remnants, eg, Lk WINNIPEG, remain today. The former lake basin and sediments have provided valuable agricultural land. *See* GLACIER; GLACIATION. N. W. RUTTER

Agawa Bay is located 90 km NW of Sault Ste Marie, Ont, on the N shore of Lk Superior. The area was sacred to the OJIBWA and the name is Indian for "sacred place." The magnificent beach is strewn with innumerable pebbles, worn smooth by the waves. Nearby bands of rock, some 1 billion, some 2.5 billion years old, lie twisted in layers like hardened candy. The famous PICTOGRAPHS are on the sheer rock face above. Located by Selwyn Dewdney in 1959, the red ochre and grease paintings are thought to celebrate a safe passage across the lake, or possibly a war victory of a great chief, some 200 years ago. Among the images are a fabulous panther, a serpent and a rider and galloping horse. JAMES MARSH

Aging for individuals is a continual biological, psychological and social process from infancy to old age. Conventionally, the term narrowly refers to the transition from adulthood to old age. Population aging refers to a decline in relative numbers of young people and an increase in relative numbers of old people. With brief interruptions, the Canadian population has been aging from its inception.

Historical Context The social character of old age has undergone a remarkable transformation in the 20th century. In the past, the elders of the community were defined less by chronological age than by institutional seniority, particularly within the family. To be old meant to hold a particular position within a system of generations — having adult children and grandchildren — rather than to be a member of an age group defined by its date of birth. Therefore, the age at which individuals were actually recognized as being old varied. The contemporary practice of designating all those above age 65 as old is historically unique and derives from another unique 20th-century practice of retiring elderly workers at a fixed age without regard to physical ability or mental capacity. Until well into this century, most people continued to work until death or the onset of extreme DISABILITY. Retirement was a privilege of the wealthy. In 1921, 60% of all males over the age of 65 were actively engaged in the LABOUR FORCE. By 1951, this figure had declined to 40% and by 1981 to 14%. Retirement as a general principle of labour-force management was made possible through the development of a system of retirement wages, eg, OLD-AGE PENSIONS, both public and private. The transition into old age is now defined primarily by the individual's relation to the economy; only in this context is it possible to understand the contemporary conventional practice of defining the elderly as all those above the age of 65.

Social Composition of the Elderly In 1981 there were 2 360 980 persons aged 65 and over in Canada, 57% of whom were women. By 1961, elderly women began to outnumber elderly men, and this trend has continued as a result of the changing sex composition of international migration to Canada and changes in life expectancy. In the early part of this century, more men than women immigrated to Canada, but between 1931 and 1948 more women than men arrived, many joining husbands and families. By the 1960s men and women were immigrating to Canada in approximately equal numbers. As these migrants age, females in the older age groups will become even more marked, because although increases in life expectancy have benefited both men and women, the gap in life expectancy between the sexes has widened. In 1976 the average life expectancy of a 65-year-old male was 13.95 years; for a female it was 18 years.

Sexual differences in longevity imply that the social experience of aging differs greatly for men and women. Most men live out their lives in a family, with a wife; most women become widows. In 1981, 76% of elderly men were married but only 40% of elderly women; in contrast only 14% of elderly men were widowed, compared to 49% of elderly women. About 66% of all elderly household heads live in their own homes. The remaining 34% is composed of renters, lodgers and those in institutions for the elderly. There is no consensus about the proportion of Canada's institutionalized elderly population; estimates range between 6% and 10%. Over time there has been a trend among the widowed, divorced and single elderly to live on their own rather than with family or friends, a trend that is usually interpreted as the result of a rising standard of living. Both residential patterns and surveys indicate that most elderly persons wish to live close to, but not with, their children.

Economic Status of the Elderly While the real standard of living of the elderly has reflected the rising standard of living in Canada as a whole, the relative economic position of Canada's elderly remains low, reflected in the number of elderly persons who qualify for support under the federal government's Guaranteed Income Supplement. The widespread coverage under this program also indicates the prevalence of poverty among the elderly. In 1979, 52.6% of all elderly couples received such benefits, and among unattached women over the age of 65 70.3% were receiving benefits. There is also evidence indicating that the relative economic position of the elderly has recently deteriorated. Between 1951 and 1971 the percentage of the elderly in the bottom 2 income quintiles increased from 68.5% to 75.1%; in the same period the percentage in the highest quintile decreased from 11.7% to 6.4%. Such a trend would be expected if rising levels of retirement were not met by compensating increases in retirement benefits to offset the loss of labour-force income. It is now commonly agreed that Canada's retirement-income system is inadequate in this regard, for both current and future retirees (*see* SOCIAL SECURITY). PENSION programs were designed on the premise that government should provide a basic minimum of income security beyond which additional income needs in retirement would be met through private-sector pension plans negotiated between employers and employees, but this additional coverage was not, and is unlikely to be, forthcoming.

Health and Health Services The elderly tend to suffer from more illnesses, both physical and mental, and make greater use of health-care practitioners and facilities than do younger age groups. Unlike the young, however, the elderly tend to suffer primarily from such chronic conditions as heart disease, arthritis and physical impairments of various types. Although 75% of the elderly population suffer from at least one chronic condition, 80% are functionally capable of independent living. Traditional medical practice, which has focused on the acute, short-term conditions typically experienced by the young, cannot be applied appropriately to the medical needs of the growing numbers of the elderly. While many of the elderly require temporary hospitalization, health care is primarily a matter of providing ongoing services and assistance to minimize the consequences of long-term or permanent disability. In the absence of sufficient community-based, home-care services, many elderly persons are required to seek access to institutional care prematurely. Consequently, provincial governments during the last decade have emphasized the provision of homemaker, handyman and home-meal services, adult day-care centres and other services not traditionally considered part of health care.

Adaptation to Aging Discovering the secret

of a "happy old age" has preoccupied men and women throughout history, but it remains a secret. Like the young, the elderly find multiple routes to happiness, but again like the young, the elderly experience misery from illness, poverty and social isolation. Popular perceptions to the contrary, considerable research has indicated that retirement has not noticeably affected the well-being of the elderly in a negative way. If retirement is accompanied by sufficient income to prevent a significant decline in living standards, it is experienced by many as liberation from tedious and debilitating working conditions. Indeed, what most distinguishes the contemporary character of old age is the fact that it is no longer necessary for elderly men and women to work until they fall ill or die.

Population Aging In 1851, 65 000 persons in Canada were age 65 or older, comprising less than 3% of the population. Today, more than 10% of the population is old by this conventional definition, and this figure may rise to 20% by 2031. Population aging began to occur as early as the 19th century in countries such as France and Sweden and since 1900 has become characteristic of all highly industrialized nations. Increased longevity has had only a marginal impact on this development. The major factor contributing to population aging is the supply of young people. The 2 principal sources of the supply of young people are migration and fertility. International migrants tend to be young adults seeking to improve their economic situation. Any increase in immigration to Canada will considerably alter the projected size of Canada's elderly population in the next century. The exceptionally high level of fertility after WWII accounts for the relatively large numbers of old people expected in the next century. The BABY-BOOM generation, born during the 1950s and early 1960s, is like a bubble moving through the age pyramid. By the year 2031, the last of this generation will have reached age 65.

As a result of unusually high postwar levels of immigration and fertility, the process of population aging has advanced more slowly in Canada. In countries such as Sweden, Austria and Germany, the elderly already constitute more than 16% of the population. Within the industrialized world, only Japan has a significantly younger population than that of Canada. The problems frequently imputed to an aging society in the popular media and in academic circles are both social and economic. The increased costs of supporting an elderly population, the effects on productivity and the blocked mobility channels for younger workers, it is argued, will serve to generate new social conflicts between the old and young. The experience of European nations where this process is already quite advanced, however, does not substantiate this view. Sweden, Austria and Germany were among the most successful countries in surviving the severe economic recession of the past decade and were also among those countries least likely to experience growing popular resistance to rising social expenditures, even though national old-age pension systems in these countries tend to be considerably more generous than those in Canada. These countries have also adapted with relative ease to a large elderly population because, while the elderly population has been increasing, the size of the youthful population below working age has been declining. As a result, the ratio of the nonworking to the working-age population has also declined, so that expenditures on the old have been offset by declining expenditures on the young. A similar trend is projected for Canada. In 2031 the ratio of those over age 65 and under 18 to the working-age population will reach 67%. This is somewhat higher than the 1981 figure of 60% but considerably lower than the 87% of 1961.

Old age has long been a source of private troubles for men and women. In the late 20th century it has also become a public issue. National and social institutions, generally designed to serve a youthful population, will have to adjust to the needs of an aging population. But history has not come to an end and it would be presumptuous to assume that the character and experience of old age will mean the same thing in the next century as it does in this one. The social, legal and political constituency we now call the elderly was created by social, political and economic forces, and it can be dramatically altered by these same forces.

J. MYLES

Reading: Victor Marshall, *Aging in Canada: Social Perspectives* (1980).

Agnew, John Lyons, mine executive (b at Pittsburgh, Pa 28 July 1884; d at Copper Cliff, Ont 9 July 1931). Agnew attended Pittsburgh schools and worked as a labourer in the steel mills before joining International Nickel's Canadian operations at Copper Cliff in 1904. As general superintendent in WWI, he was closely connected with rapid increases in the company's NICKEL production for allied armament manufacturers. During the 1920s, first as president of the International Nickel Co of Canada (INCO), a subsidiary of the American parent firm, and later as VP when the Canadian company became the senior enterprise, Agnew was instrumental in promoting nickel for peacetime products, directing the construction of new smelting and refining plants and developing the Frood Mine, later one of the world's largest nickel producers. He was president of the Canadian Institute of Mining and Metallurgy and a director of several corporations. J. LINDSEY

Agribusiness With the farm as the centre, agribusiness is that sector of the economy that includes all firms, agencies and institutions that provide inputs to the farm and procure commodities from the farm for processing and distribution to the consumer. Traditionally, agribusiness focused on farm inputs (ie, supplies such as farm machinery, feed, PESTICIDES) and services (eg, financial institutions). The modern definition includes firms that buy raw farm commodities (eg, milk, hogs, grain, oilseeds) and process and distribute the wide range of resulting products through numerous channels to domestic and foreign consumers. Examples include firms involved in meat packing, flour and canning companies and retail food stores. Agribusiness differs from other sectors of the economy because of the seasonality of crop and livestock production and, of course, weather. Many specialized institutions, such as AGRICULTURAL MARKETING BOARDS and specialized government agencies (eg, Canadian Livestock Feed Board), play a role in controlling and directing the system. The many transactions surrounding the world's precarious food balance make it likely that the agribusiness sector of the AGRICULTURE AND FOOD system will continue to expand.

P.M. MONCRIEFF

Agricultural Aid, the provision of agricultural products or technology by one nation to another, normally by developed to developing countries. Aid will continue to be required because in many developing countries 4 out of 10 persons are malnourished; developing countries now grow only 87% of their own food needs and may be able to produce only 74% by the year 2000; and their deficits of wheat, rice and coarse grains are expected to be over 77 million t by 1988.

Contributions to the UNITED NATIONS's technical-assistance program in 1949 marked the beginning of Canadian aid to developing countries. Initially the departments of External Affairs, Trade and Commerce, and Finance administered aid programs. In 1968 the CANADIAN INTERNATIONAL DEVELOPMENT AGENCY (CIDA) was created and charged with the responsibility of managing Canada's overseas development programs. In 1970 Parliament established the INTERNATIONAL DEVELOPMENT RESEARCH CENTRE (IDRC), a public corporation created to "initiate, encourage, support and conduct research into the problems of developing regions of the world." By 1982-83 aid disbursements by these 2 institutions were $1386.75 million, ie, 83% of Canadian Official Development Assistance (ODA) and 0.38% of the GROSS NATIONAL PRODUCT. Canada is thus the eighth-highest donor among members of the Organization for Economic Cooperation and Development. In 1982-83, 16% ($273.21 million) of Canadian ODA was distributed as food aid through one of the following 4 programs.

Bilateral Aid is provided to specific countries or groups of countries. In 1982-83 bilateral aid accounted for 43% of ODA and 20% of total food aid (over $141 million).

Multilateral Aid, 35% of ODA in 1982-83, is usually given to international agencies. In that year it had a food-aid component valued at $122.04 million, most of which was channelled through the World Food Program.

Special Programs Aid refers to monies given to nongovernmental organizations (NGOs). The $9.7-million food-aid budgets of the NGOs, in 1982-83, were handled primarily by the Canadian Hunger Foundation, CARE Canada, Inter Pares International Development Service, and Oxfam Canada. NGOs tended to promote food-aid programs directed at alleviating local problems. In addition, Canada provided $12.58 million in support of 14 international agricultural research centres.

International Development Research Centre IDRC's contribution to agricultural aid differs from CIDA's to the extent that IDRC promotes the development of a scientific and technical base which developing countries can use to improve their agricultural output. IDRC's agricultural aid is handled by 2 bodies: the Agricultural, Food and Nutrition Science Division, with an annual budget of approximately $18 million; and the section of the Social Science Division dealing with Economics and Rural Modernization, with a budget of approximately $2 million.

Canada's agricultural aid includes the assignment of advisers abroad and the training of students from developing countries in Canada. In the period 1968 to 1978 Canadian universities supplied at least 314 person years (28 annually) in aid to developing countries. One-third of these person years were spent on projects in sub-Sahara Africa. The largest group of projects (using 43% of person years) was directed at improving institutions (universities, national research centres, government units) in developing countries. Production and rural development received 35%. Thirty-three Canadian universities were involved in these activities. The 8 university faculties or colleges of agriculture or veterinary medicine supplied 78% of this advisory time. In 1982 most of the 262 Canadian advisers working in the areas of economic planning and renewable resources dealt with agricultural problems. Similarly, many of the 348 students from developing countries supported by CIDA to study in the areas of economics and administration or renewable resources were actually studying agriculture. TRUMAN P. PHILLIPS

Agricultural Economics, is a field of study related to the application of ECONOMICS theory to problems and issues surrounding the production, processing, distribution and consumption of agricultural food and fibre products. Agricultural economics differs from the study of crop science or animal science primarily because of its relation to human behaviour. In crop science it is possible to study the effects of nitrogen fertilizer on crop growth by holding all other aspects of growth constant. In agricultural economics it is virtually impossible to study one aspect of human behaviour in such a strict manner. Economics is that SOCIAL SCIENCE concerned with the allocation of scarce resources among competing uses to satisfy human wants. As people generally have more wants than can be satisfied at any given moment, decisions must be made about the importance and cost of each; thus, each person must allocate scarce resources (frequently money) among alternative wants to obtain most satisfaction. By studying such choices as they relate to farmers, the farm production process and the distribution of farm commodities to consumers, agricultural economists can learn about the nature of the demand for farm products and the price for which they can be sold.

In Canada the discipline probably had its origin in the application of economic thinking to problems of physical agriculture in courses taught in the agricultural colleges. Farm management and marketing courses were among the first courses taught that related strictly to agricultural economics. In 1926 a Department of Farm Economics, headed by J.E. Lattimer, was established at Macdonald College, McGill University. The Ontario Agricultural College at Guelph offered undergraduate courses in the discipline; graduate programs were offered with the help of the Department of Political Economy at the University of Toronto. The U of T had appointed its first professor of Rural Economics, T. Jackman, in 1921. At the federal level, establishment in 1929 of the Economics Branch of the then Dept of Agriculture was a response to the need for research into pressing agricultural problems, problems which worsened with the GREAT DEPRESSION. Although an agricultural economics department did not then exist at University of British Columbia, courses in the field were being offered as early as 1920. The University of Manitoba established a Department of Farm Management and Co-operative Marketing in 1915; U Man's Department of Agricultural Economics had a 4-year agricultural-business program and awarded the first master's degree in the field in 1932. In 1982, degrees in agricultural economics were offered at the bachelor level at Nova Scotia Agricultural College, and at the bachelor and postgraduate levels at Laval, McGill, Guelph, Manitoba, Saskatchewan, Alberta and British Columbia. Various agricultural colleges also offer training in agricultural economics.

Teaching practice, theory and research in the field were influenced by American universities (eg, Cornell, Wisconsin, Minnesota). Course content was originally concerned with production at the individual farm level. Thus, agricultural economics was essentially problem-oriented and, in the search for conceptual tools to address specific problems, general economics theories such as welfare economics and those outlined in KEYNESIAN ECONOMICS gradually came to influence thought in agricultural economics. Agricultural economists have also made contributions to general economics theory. The most outstanding example, former Harvard professor John Kenneth GALBRAITH, was trained at U of T as an agricultural economist and developed the theory of "countervailing powers," ie, that competition is less a restraint on corporations than are interest groups on the opposite side of the market. Agricultural economics as a field of study is divided into various subfields, each concerned with a specific major problem area. Common to all activities of the agricultural economist is the need for progressive improvement in the state of agriculture and rural living in the context of the Canadian economy.

Farm-Production Economics

Historically the first major problem area addressed was farm-production economics. In this subfield, significant questions pertain to how a greater farm net income may be attained; how production costs may be reduced; which combination of farm inputs is best; and which product or commodity should be produced. These general questions may be translated into very practical terms. Should I plant wheat, corn or barley this year? Would I be better off feeding calves to slaughter weight or buying heavy feeders? Farm production economics addresses choice among inputs as well as decisions regarding what to produce when prices, weather, technology, institutions and people change, thus influencing farm profits or losses.

In the past, agricultural economists used 2 perspectives to answer farm-production questions: the farm-management approach and a conceptual approach based on theoretical models. The first approach addressed production questions by analysing the prices of goods bought and sold. Farm surveys were used to determine production costs among groups of similar farms to gain an appreciation of which type of farm was most successful. Recommendations could then be made to all farmers to change their practices to match more closely those of successful farmers. Unfortunately, this approach could not be applied universally because of geographic and temporal variations. The conceptual approach was based on the application of existing economic theory to agriculture. Economists using this method approached farm problems through economic models developed using quantitative research. The development of farm models to serve as theoretical ideals for comparison with real situations required statistical study of large numbers of farms to ensure that basic farm input-output relationships were statistically sound. Today, sophisticated COMPUTER analysis techniques are important to the theoretical agricultural economist. The major criticism of this type of analysis is that results are too theoretical and too far removed from the practicalities of farming.

Farm-Welfare Economics

Farm-welfare economics is concerned both with the needs of farmers and with those of society as they are influenced by developments in agriculture or by the decisions of individual farmers. Questions addressed in farm-welfare economics relate to the overall efficiency of agricultural resource use, ie, the provision of cheap and plentiful food within the context of the political forces at work within Canada. This is the arena of AGRICULTURE AND FOOD POLICY, the roots of which are in agricultural economics.

At one time, Canadian farmers were largely self-sufficient, producing food and fibre for their own families with little surplus for sale. Farms were largely labour oriented and all family members participated in production. As educational opportunities grew, many farm children gained an education and left the farm for urban areas. At the same time, new technologies were being adopted, eg, use of high-yield, disease-resistant, quick-growing seed and of tractors instead of horses, which allowed one farmer to work a much larger acreage. Specialization also occurred as some farmers became experts at grain production while others raised poultry or hogs. These changes were not accidental; farmers pursued them in an effort to reduce costs and increase sales and gross revenue. Success or failure depended on management capability as well as on differences in basic farm resources (eg, soil productivity). Hence, some areas of Canada have not progressed as much as others and it has been increasingly difficult for smaller farms to achieve incomes above the POVERTY line.

Agricultural economists have attempted to understand the reasons for this evolution and to develop alternative policies and programs that ease the adjustment of those leaving agriculture and strengthen the agricultural capability of rural areas (*see* RURAL SOCIETY).

Agriculture and Rural Development

Many people believe that agriculture can play a much larger role in Canada's economy than it does today. The AGRIBUSINESS sector provides farm inputs and procures farm commodities for processing and distribution to consumers. Employment in this sector is 3-4 times greater than on-farm employment. Agricultural economists have been involved in the design and evaluation of programs to encourage the further processing of farm products and to establish distinctive agriculture and food systems in rural areas. For example, the Canada/Alberta Nutritive Processing Program provides special grants to firms that establish food-processing operations in the province. Other regions and provinces have set up programs to encourage self-sufficiency in agricultural production, often through joint federal-provincial programs under the Agricultural and Rural Development Act (ARDA) or through special sectoral agreements between provinces and the federal Dept of Regional Industrial Expansion. Provinces such as PEI and Newfoundland have attempted to produce more foodstuffs locally, thereby reducing the flow of funds to other provinces. Enhanced production also results in growth of provincial economies with increased employment and income. Special grants encouraging farm development have been incorporated into education-extension programs. Many programs are devoted to building necessary infrastructures such as improved roads, storage facilities, veterinary clinics, etc. In Ontario, emphasis has been placed on improving FARM DRAINAGE to enhance soil productivity.

Agricultural economists have also been involved in international development work, especially through the CANADIAN INTERNATIONAL DEVELOPMENT AGENCY (CIDA) and the World Bank. The World Bank has a detailed program analysis process that specifies beforehand the overall benefits to a country's national economy and the financial benefits to farmers and other participants that may be expected from an agricultural and rural-development program. For example, one of the larger foreign-aid programs is the Canadian wheat program, which introduced large-scale mechanized grain farming to Tanzania in eastern Africa.

Agriculture Policy

The agricultural sector is constantly undergoing change as a result of new technology, shifting demands, international agreements and disagreements and changing pressure groups. These changing conditions necessitate the periodic re-evaluation of farm policies. The task of objectively analysing alternative policies frequently requires the expertise of agricultural economists (working in the universities, provincial and federal agriculture departments, etc). Political parties and the many farm and commodity groups often hold conflicting positions. As a result of the actions of such groups, and those of individual farmers, rural residents and urban sympathizers, governments (provincial and federal) have had to design policies to address their concerns. These policies and programs have taken many forms, from direct subsidies on commodities, through actuarially sound insurance plans, to control over production and prices. For example, programs such as the interest-rate rebate plans of provinces in the early 1980s, direct payments per head of cattle marketed and formation of AGRICULTURAL MARKETING BOARDS to control production and prices of specific commodities addressed the problems of adequate return and income stability. Agricultural economists have been very influential in prescribing the workings of each scheme as well as in the ongoing management of the systems established.

Agricultural Marketing

In Canada, agricultural marketing is an increasingly important field of endeavour in agricultural economics. This subdiscipline has focused largely on the marketing process from farm gate to consumer; the sale of farm inputs to farmers receives much less attention. Much of economic theory is based on the concept of the free market; however, farmers usually have found themselves competing to sell their commodities to one or, at best, a few buyers. Agricultural-economics studies have focused on forms of industrial organization and the means by which markets and participants can be judged to be performing marketing tasks efficiently. Such information, combined with farmers' perceptions that their bargaining power is weak against industries such as grain companies and meat-packers, has fostered the development of farmer co-operatives, boards and associations to redress alleged faults in the marketing process (*see* CO-OPERATIVE MOVEMENT). Agricultural economists have also played a role in defining standard grades of products; for example, Canadian hog- and cattle-grading systems serve as world-recognized models (*see* COMMODITY INSPECTION AND GRADING). Such definitions are vitally important to trade.

Agricultural economists are also interested in designing least-cost procurement systems for farm commodities. Thus, instead of each farmer delivering small units of produce to major market areas, collection systems have been set up to minimize transportation costs and improve the cost efficiency of the marketing process. Examples include control of fluid milk pickup by milk-marketing boards and establishment of local, centralized hog-assembly yards.

One of the basic assumptions underlying the operation of a free market is perfect information. Many farm commodities are marketed outside of a rigidly controlled process; thus the provision of market information for such commodities as CORN, WHEAT, HOGS, cattle and OILSEEDS is important. An area of specialization has developed within agricultural economics to provide market outlooks and analyses. Such specialists study past cyclical trends, current weather behaviour in key producing countries, general demand conditions and government policies in order to make projections on prices in coming months. Agricultural production cannot be turned on and off at will; it occurs in patterns based on seasonality and livestock-production cycles. Therefore, market forecasts are essential to farm-management decisions.

Land-Resource Economics

The applied nature of agricultural economics is nowhere more evident than in the subfield of land economics, a specialized area of production economics that focuses on LAND, the major factor in farm production. Agricultural economists study both the actual productive value of land and its market value. In most instances farmland cannot generate sufficient return to warrant the price paid because the market price of land is usually higher than its productive value. This discrepancy results from expectations about future increase in value. The theoretical base of professional land and real-estate appraisal is in land economics, which embraces the establishment of rental rates, land taxation and other property-rights considerations. The balance between personal and public rights over property has long been in debate. For example, does the Crown have the right to expropriate farmland for airports, urban expansion or recreational purposes and, if so, what price should be paid? Intermingled in these issues are public concerns over land use, eg, zoning of agricultural land for food production and laws regarding weed-control or SOIL-CONSERVATION practices. Many agriculturists believe that farmers are custodians of the land, holding it for future generations. Unfortunately, high interest rates and low farm-commodity prices have led some farmers to exploit their land to the fullest to survive. This exploitation has resulted in charges that they are mining the soil of its nutrients to the detriment of the land resource. The impact of economics and public TAXATION measures on these problems are frequent subjects for study by agricultual economists.

It is a small step from land to other land-based natural resources, and agricultural economists have studied the conflicting needs of farmers, wildlife species, foresters and outdoor recreationists. Similarly, as water availability and quality become increasingly important to agriculture, the economics of water use also increases in importance. A complicating factor in the resolution of problems related to land use is the lack of definition regarding the ownership of natural resources. Wildlife eat hay and other crops belonging to farmers (eg, it is estimated that in 1979 waterfowl consumed or destroyed about $3.6 million worth, ie, 1%, of crops), but the wildlife may belong to the Crown or society at large. Land may be privately held, but hunters may pursue wildlife in season. Management of conflicts and of common-use natural resources is yet another area of agricultural-economic endeavour. Benefit-cost analysis has developed from natural-resource economics and the need to quantify decisions. This methodological tool has played an important part in analysing public-sector questions and in ranking projects in which governments can invest. *See* FARM LAW.

P.M. MONCRIEFF

Agricultural Education in Canada occurs formally at at least 4 levels: school system, diploma (sub-degree) level, university bachelor-degree level, and postgraduate-degree level (master's and doctoral). In addition, another informal level (ie, extension activities) operates as the link between scientific findings, technological developments and the farmer. Agricultural education in primary and secondary schools generally consists of a course designed to acquaint the student with the complexities of modern agriculture. Usually taught in high school, it is aimed at developing an awareness of the role of agriculture in society. Formal post-secondary education and extension activities constitute Canada's most significant agricultural-education efforts.

Agricultural education began in NEW FRANCE in 1670 at the Petit Séminaire at Saint-Joachim, an "industrial" school which provided some training in agriculture. Training was most probably directed to practical experience on the school farm, which was described as having good pastures, woods, an area of tillable land and 150 head of cattle. This program, begun by Bishop LAVAL, continued until 1715. Two additional schools, initiated in Québec early in the 19th century, lasted for only one year. In 1859 the School of Agriculture of Sainte-Anne-de-la-Pocatière, sponsored by Abbé Pilote, opened with Emile Dumais as professor of agriculture. It offered a diploma and later a degree program. In 1962 it became part of the Faculty of Agriculture of Laval University.

The first English-language agricultural school was established at Guelph, Ont, in 1873 and received its first students in 1874. It began with a 1-year, practical, work-oriented program. In 1880 a 2-year diploma program was instituted and the school underwent a name change, from Ontario School of Agriculture to Ontario Agricultural College and Experimental Farm (OAC). In 1887 a third year was added to the program, and in 1888 the OAC was affiliated with University of Toronto, thus achieving degree-granting status. A fourth year was added to the program in 1902. In 1964 OAC affiliated with University of Guelph.

In 1885 a school of agriculture was established at Truro, NS, followed 8 years later (1893) by a school of horticulture at Wolfville. Both were absorbed by the Nova Scotia Agricultural College (NSAC), which officially opened at Truro in Feb 1905, gaining degree-granting status in 1980.

The last agricultural school established in the 19th century was the School of Agriculture of Oka, founded in 1893 by the Trappist Fathers of the abbey of Oka, Qué. In 1908 it affiliated with Laval and changed its name to the Agricultural Institute of Oka. In 1962 it became a part of Laval's new Faculty of Agriculture.

Contemporary Degree-Granting Institutions

Schools of agriculture differ markedly in their affiliation and sponsors. There is no Canadian equivalent of the US Land Grant Act, which established land-grant agricultural colleges throughout that country. Early Québec schools were sponsored by religious groups, while McGill's Macdonald College was endowed by Sir William MACDONALD. NSAC, OAC and the Manitoba Agricultural College (MAC) were established by their respective provincial ministries of agriculture, while the faculties of agriculture of Saskatchewan, Alberta and BC are part of provincial universities. Those schools established as integral faculties of a university did not provide instruction in many of the basic arts and science subjects (eg, literature, chemistry, physics, mathematics); students instead took service courses offered in the arts and science faculties. The MAC and OAC initially provided these basic courses, relinquishing them when the university moved onto the agriculture campus in Manitoba in the former case, and when a university was established on the OAC campus in the latter. Macdonald College, while always a part of McGill, has, by reason of physical separation of the 2 campuses, provided instruction in the basic sciences by its own specialized staff.

The subject areas deemed appropriate to agriculture have changed significantly. The early schools all offered courses in CROP and ANIMAL production, SOIL SCIENCE, agricultural engineering and AGRICULTURAL ECONOMICS were also a part of many early curricula. The development of AGRICULTURAL RESEARCH and its associated disciplines has broadened the offerings of all faculties. Most faculties now address the processing of agricultural products as well as primary production, and some include WILDLIFE and FORESTRY as a part of natural-resource management training.

Nova Scotia Agricultural College operates as an interprovincial college providing agricultural education to students from NS, NB, PEI and Nfld. In 1980 the NSAC received approval to offer a 4-year program leading to a BSc in Agriculture (in plant science, animal science, agricultural economics and plant protection). Before 1980 the college had offered a 2-year university-level program which prepared students for the final year of a degree program at the OAC, Macdonald or University of Maine; it still offers 2-year programs which permit students to enter areas of specialization available at these institutions but not at NSAC. The NSAC does not offer a program leading to postgraduate degrees.

Laval University The Faculty of Agriculture and Food Sciences currently offers an 8-trimester (4-year) program following the CEGEP (COLLÈGE D'ENSEIGNEMENT GÉNÉRAL ET PROFESSIONNEL, ie, senior matriculation). Students receive a BScA degree with specialization in agroeconomy; bio-agronomy with concentration in soil/plant, animal science or agricultural MICROBIOLOGY; agricultural engineering; or food science. Through the School of Graduate Studies, MSc degrees are available in DIETETICS, rural economy and agricultural engineering; MSc and PhD degrees in plant science, agricultural microbiology, soils, food science and animal science; and a PhD in nutrition.

Macdonald College, McGill University, located at Ste-Anne-de-Bellevue, Qué, was built, endowed and staffed through the benefaction of Sir William Macdonald. Construction began in 1905, the first students enrolling in the fall of 1907. An earlier McGill agriculture program was begun by Principal J.W. DAWSON, who in 1864 published *First Lessons in Scientific Agriculture for Schools.* Macdonald is unique among faculties of agriculture in N America in being part of a largely privately endowed university. The faculty currently offers 3 undergraduate degrees through 3-year (6-term) programs following completion of the CEGEP diploma. The areas of specialization for the BSc (Agr) are agricultural chemistry, agricultural economics, animal science, general agriculture, plant science (with emphasis on agronomy, horticulture or plant protection), soil science, environmental BIOLOGY, microbiology, ENTOMOLOGY, community resource development, land planning and CONSERVATION of environmental and wildlife resources. Areas of specialization for the BSc in Food Science are consumer services, nutrition, food administration, dietetics and food science. A BSc in Agricultural Engineering is also awarded. The faculty co-operates with the Faculty of Education to offer the BEd degree in HOME ECONOMICS and with the Faculty of Management to give a BComm in food services administration.

All departments offer MSc and PhD degrees through the Faculty of Graduate Studies and Research. Programs of study and directed research are given in agricultural chemistry and physics, agricultural engineering, animal science (including animal GENETICS, animal physiology and nutrition), entomology, microbiology, plant science (including agronomy, plant breeding, horticulture, plant genetics and plant pathology), soil science and wildlife biology.

Ontario Agricultural College From 1888 until 1964 the OAC degree of BSA was awarded by U of Toronto. Since 1964 the degree has been awarded by U of Guelph. The OAC currently offers a 4-year, post-senior-matriculation program leading to the BSA degree.

All OAC students take the same courses in their first year, after which they may specialize in agricultural business, agricultural economics, agricultural mechanization, animal and poultry science, applied microbiology, crop science, dairy science, entomology-apiculture, environmental biology, horticultural science, plant protection, resource economics and rural development, RESOURCE MANAGEMENT or soil science.

MSc degrees are offered in agricultural business, extension education and rural development. A Master of LANDSCAPE ARCHITECTURE degree is also offered. Programs of study and directed research leading to MSc and PhD degrees are offered in agricultural economics, agrometeorology, animal and poultry science, crop science, dairy science, earth science and geology, engineering, entomology-apiculture, food science, horticulture science, microbiology, plant protection and pathology, resource economics, resources management and soil science.

Manitoba Agricultural College In 1906 the MAC was established as an outgrowth of a dairy school operated by the Manitoba Department of Agriculture since 1894. In 1924 MAC was transferred from the Dept of Agriculture to the Board of Governors of University of Manitoba. The various BSA programs of the university's Faculty of Agriculture require 4 years of study following senior matriculation. All students take common courses in the first year. In years 2-4 they may specialize in agricultural economics and farm management, agricultural engineering (students preparing for the professional association register for the agricultural engineering program in the Faculty of Engineering), agricultural sciences, animal science, entomology, food science, plant science or soil science. MSc and PhD programs are offered in agricultural economics and farm management, animal science, entomology, food science, plant science (including cereal chemistry) and soil science.

University of Saskatchewan The Faculty of Agriculture of Saskatchewan was established in concert with the university. The university's location within Saskatoon was, in fact, determined by its suitability for an agricultural college (ie, it had adequate land for a farm and experimental field work). University of Saskatchewan's first agriculture classes were held in 1912. The faculty offers a BSc in Agriculture. All programs consist of 4 years following Saskatchewan Division IV or grade 12. In the first year all students follow a common curriculum. Later they may specialize in agricultural biology, agricultural chemistry, agricultural economics, agricultural mechanics, agricultural microbiology, agronomy, animal science, crop science, dairy and food science, horticultural science, plant ecology, parks and recreation, poultry science or soil science. The College of Graduate Studies and Research offers various graduate degrees: the MAgr, a nonthesis degree, in animal and poultry science and agricultural economics; an MSc in agricultural economics; MSc and PhD programs in animal science, poultry science, crop science, dairy and food science, plant ecology and soil science. The degrees of MEng, MSc and PhD in agricultural engineering are offered in the College of Engineering.

University of Alberta The Faculty of Agriculture of University of Alberta began instruction in 1915; this program, like Saskatchewan's, was an integral part of the new university. In 1970 a FORESTRY program was added and the faculty's name was changed to the Faculty of Agriculture and Forestry. Two other Alberta institutions, the Vermilion and Olds schools of agriculture, were established in 1913.

The faculty currently has a 4-year post-senior-matriculation program leading to a BSc in Agriculture. A modified first year is also offered at University of Calgary, University of Lethbridge and at affiliated junior colleges. Students specialize after the first year in general agriculture, rural economics (agricultural economics and rural sociology), agronomy, livestock science, poultry science, grazing management, plant protection, plant science or soil science. The faculty also co-operates with the Faculty of Engineering to offer a program leading to a BSc in Agricultural Engineering and with the Faculty of Home Economics to offer a BSc in Food Science. A nonthesis Master of Agriculture is given in agricultural engineering, animal science, food science, soil science and rural economy. A Master of Engineering is offered in agricultural engineering and in food science. A thesis MSc is offered in agricultural engineering and in home economics; MSc and PhD programs are offered in animal science, entomology, food science, forest science, plant science, soil science and rural economy.

University of British Columbia The Faculty of Agriculture received its first students in 1915 and was assisted in its development by Professor L.S. Klinck of Macdonald College. The faculty requires 4 years of study following senior matriculation. The degree of BSc (Agr) is offered in agricultural economics, bio-resource engineering (through the Faculty of Applied Science), agricultural mechanics, animal science, plant science, poultry science and soil science. The degree of Bachelor of Landscape Architecture is also offered. At the graduate level the MSc degree is offered in agricultural economics, agricultural extension and agricultural mechanics. Both MSc and PhD degrees are offered in animal science, food science, plant science, poultry science, resource management (interdisciplinary) and soil science.

Non-Degree-Granting Institutions

At least 4 schools which evolved from practical, non-degree programs are still operating, namely the diploma programs of NSAC, Macdonald College, OAC and University of Manitoba's Faculty of Agriculture. There are 21 institutions offering post-secondary work in agriculture. Of these, 5 offer programs in French (one in NB, 3 in Qué, one in Ont); the remaining 16 offer programs in English (one each in NS, Qué, Man and Sask; 2 in BC; 4 in Alta; and 6 in Ont). All but 5 of the schools are independent of their provincial university faculties of agriculture. These are the diploma schools of NSAC, Macdonald College, OAC and the faculties of agriculture of University of Manitoba and University of Saskatchewan. All these schools offer production-oriented courses to prepare young farmers for modern farming. In addition, many offer programs to prepare graduates for jobs as technicians in various agricultural industries. Most programs are of 2-year duration, although some offer a third year.

Subject matter mirrors the changes that have taken place in agriculture. Production courses, which previously emphasized instruction on plowing or home slaughtering of beef or poultry, may now provide information on agricultural chemicals for pest control, farm accounting and use of computers in feed formulation, and adjustment and management of highly complex farm machinery.

Agricultural Extension

The process of transferring new developments in technology and farming techniques from researchers to farmers is called "extension." Those responsible for this process in Canada are called agricultural representatives (agrologists) or, in Québec, agronomes. The need to engage in extension activity has long been recognized. The former Manitoba Agricultural College organized special "Better Farming Trains" which toured the province with demonstrations, lectures, exhibits and staff consultants. A similar technique was used by Macdonald College, which in addition appointed graduates as "demonstrators" and stationed them in rural areas. This function was later taken over by the provincial extension service.

Extension educational and advisory activity is a major responsibility of provincial ministries of agriculture. The educational role is fulfilled by organizing and, in many cases, conducting short courses, workshops, etc, and by the preparation of interpretative bulletins, press releases, etc, for farmer use. Extension services are staffed by agricultural professionals and specialists in various agricultural production problems. The agricultural representative can play a key role in identifying problems at the local level and in relaying these problems to the research scientist. In many instances the representative co-operates with the research scientist in the conduct of "local" tests of new technology.

HOWARD A. STEPPLER

Agricultural Exhibitions probably began as bazaars or fairs. Through the centuries these gatherings diverged somewhat from their original function and became primarily competitive showplaces for livestock and produce and settings for the display of new agricultural technology, as well as social events. Canadian agricultural exhibitions derive much of their character from the agricultural fairs of England nd Scotland. Canada's first such fair was held ı NS in 1765. Fairs continue to make important ›ntributions to Canada's RURAL SOCIETY by pro- iding social and educational opportunities, nd to all Canadians by helping to improve ag- culture through competition.

Contemporary agricultural exhibitions vary reatly: the majority are country "fairs" lasting ne or 2 days and featuring a cross section of ag- cultural products and local crafts. Regional ex- ibitions, lasting 3-4 days, are less common, en- ɔmpass areas served by several local fairs and tisfy the desire for larger events featuring reater competition. A third type of fair, the rovincial exhibition, draws exhibits from a ill larger geographic area and tends to be more ommercial" in that dealers in farm machinery nd other farm technologies display their wares. n the interprovincial or national level, To- onto's Royal Winter Fair, probably Canada's est-known agricultural exhibition, serves a reat cross section of the industry. Other well- nown exhibitions are the Royal Manitoba Vinter Fair at Brandon and the CALGARY STAM- EDE. Most recently, large specialized shows have ppeared. For example, well over 1000 head of attle are exhibited at the annual Agribition in askatchewan and Ag Ex in Manitoba. The An- ual Farm Progress Show in Regina represents nother type of specialization: agricultural quipment worth millions of dollars and repre- enting the most modern agricultural technol- gy is exhibited.

The main agricultural product exhibited in nost of the regional, interprovincial or national xhibitions is livestock, although grain, fruit, oultry, pets, vegetables, flowers and crafts are mportant features. The spirit of competition of hese events has contributed to improvements in ivestock breeds. The horse show is an important ivestock exhibit because of its entertainment alue and the quality of product displayed. Ex- ibition activities have been largely responsible or the development of keen national and inter- ational equestrian competition. Standards of esirability in the appearance of commercial ivestock (eg, cattle, SHEEP, HOGS) change as con- umer diet preferences change. Swine, for exam- ɔle, have been bred over a period of many years o be long and lean rather than short and fat, as onsumers opt for less fat in their diets. Simi- arly, size and breed of BEEF cattle have changed o reflect perceived production efficiencies ass- med to be inherent in the more rapid weight ncrease of larger breeds.

Exhibitions have played a special role in per- onal development through the promotion of -H CLUB programs. The 4-H movement really tarted when, early in the century, exhibitions egan sponsoring livestock competitions for outh. Exhibitions continue to change along vith the public's desire to observe new de- elopments in the AGRICULTURE AND FOOD system, o remain current in standards of excellence and o enjoy the opportunity to socialize with people rom a cross section of the community at large. See CHAUTAUQUA; CANADIAN NATIONAL EXHIBITION.

R.E. FORBES

Agricultural Implements Canadian agricul- ure changed rapidly between 1850 and 1900, nd changes in agricultural implements both aused and reflected changes in other sectors.

Machinery

In addition to the spade, hoe and rake famil- ar to modern gardeners, early hand tools used n farming included the seeder, a perforated vooden trough carried by means of a strap round the neck and used in broadcast seeding; he sickle and the scythe, one- and 2-handed nives, respectively, used for cutting field crops nd hay; the flail, 2 wooden rods attached by a trap and used to thresh out the kernels of grain; he winnowing tray, a 2-handled, half-moon-shaped receptacle used to cast flailed grain into the air so that the chaff could be blown away; the fork, used for pitching hay or shovelling manure; the wooden grain shovel; the hay knife and hay hook; and the grafting froe, a knife used to split branches in grafting. Most of these implements were superseded; others (eg, the plow) underwent substantial modification.

Plow From early wooden-moldboard, single-handled, home-made machines, plows became chilled-steel, mass-produced, scientifically designed 2-handled walking plows; then single-moldboard riding plows, double-moldboard riding plows, and finally giant machines with up to 16 moldboards. These alterations occurred as the source of power changed from oxen (best for root-strewn pioneer farms) to teams of HORSES, then multiple teams of horses (up to 16 to a hitch), steam-driven traction engines with the power of 50 or more horses, and finally lighter, more versatile but equally powerful gasoline tractors.

Threshing Machinery underwent the most dramatic and expensive changes. In 1850 most farmers cut their grain with cradle scythes, and the few short weeks of the harvest dictated the amount grown. In winter, cut grain was threshed on the BARN floor, by beating with flails or treading with horses' hooves until the kernel fell free of the straw and was scooped up and winnowed, by the wind or by an artificial wind created by a fanning mill. More efficient machines (eg, the generation of reapers triggered by the inventions of Cyrus McCormick and Obed Hussey in the US and Patrick Bell in England) allowed farmers to harvest larger and larger amounts of grain. Larger threshing machines, initially powered by one- or 2-horse treadmills, and later by immense steam-driven traction engines, began to appear. Mechanical threshers were manufactured by Waterloo, Sawyer-Massey, Hergott, Lobsinger, Moody and other Canadian manufacturers.

Seed Drills changed from primitive, arm-held broadcast seeders to precisely engineered 11, 13 and 15 run, horse-drawn grain drills that punched seeds into nicely tilled ground at precise depths and intervals.

Tillage Machinery was also improved. Harrows made from tree branches, with IRON spikes driven into them, were replaced by various steel-spring harrows that were able to tear freshly turned sod into a weed-free seedbed in much less time.

The Industry

Rapid change provided opportunities for industrialists. The tiny local BLACKSMITH shops of Canadian villages began to increase in size as the demand for iron increased, particularly after the railway boom of the 1850s, which allowed cheap iron to move more easily from England and the US. The demand for iron for engines, rolling stock and track led to the establishment of a sophisticated iron industry in Hamilton, Ont. Earlier ironmakers (eg, the Van Normans) had relied on poor-grade bog iron. In the 1850s higher-quality iron stimulated the growth of local foundries.

Horse-drawn mowing machine, *c*1859 (*courtesy National Library of Canada/Rare Books Div*).

Iron began to replace wood in farm implements. Implement-makers grew in number, particularly around the western end of Lk Ontario, where MASSEY, Verity, Patterson, Wilkinson, Sawyer, Cockshutt, Wisner, HARRIS and others established their factories, making plows, cutting boxes, fanning mills, seed drills, reapers, mowers, threshing machines and steam engines. Because it was cheap and plentiful, wood was used wherever possible. Iron, however, was essential for cutting and moving parts in general. Larger- and larger-scale implement makers seemed to sprout up overnight; some of these companies, eg, those that were conservative or undercapitalized, disappeared as quickly; others thrived and continue to dominate the farm machinery industry into the late 20th century.

As one machine was rendered obsolete by the invention of an improvement (eg, the wire binder replacing the sail-reaper and itself replaced by the twine binder), the pace of competition accelerated. A few Canadian companies, eg, the plow maker William H. Verity, specialized in one implement; however, most of the big implement makers produced full lines of farm equipment. The Massey Manufacturing Co (originally established at Bond Head and later relocated at Newcastle, then Toronto, because of the need for a railway supply and delivery system) only made about 50-odd implements in 1847. In 1860 it was making 2 classes of implements: simple machines of Canadian design (eg, straw cutters, harrows, wheelbarrows, fanning mills) and more complicated machines copied from American patents (eg, Manny's Combined Reaper and Mower, Wood's New Self-Raking Reaper, Pitt's Horse Power, Ketchum's Patent Mower). The manufacture of American machines in Canada was a matter of considerable pride and the absence of a PATENT law, until 1869, encouraged Canadian implement makers to make annual trips to the US in search of new ideas and special rights to manufacture new American inventions.

Ontario Markets were strongest in western Ontario, where the rural majority in the 1850s had been able to set aside capital from the high grain prices caused by the Crimean War. In eastern Ontario the number of manufacturers was smaller but still significant, the most prominent being Frost and Wood of Smiths Falls, which survived the period of intense competition in the 1890s. Herring of Napanee, which marketed fanning mills and reapers, eventually folded, as Massey-Harris machines moved into a wider and wider market area after 1891. Not all implement makers stayed in that line of production; for example, the Gibbard Co of Napanee initially made fanning mills and coffins, then began making fine furniture, eventually dropping implement manufacturing completely.

The Maritimes Machine makers in the Maritimes also had a period of growth; however, the market was small and was eventually dominated by the larger Ontario manufacturers, who spread their wares eastward following CONFEDERATION. Connell Brothers (Woodstock, NB) and Harris and Allen (Saint John) were successful manufacturers in the LOYALIST farming centres. Others could be found in PEI and NS.

Québec implement makers were more influenced by European machine patterns and the medieval 2-wheeled plow remained a common sight on Québec farms throughout the 19th century. Since many French Canadians were at least partially agricultural throughout the 19th century, implement makers had many opportunities. Doré and Fils (La Prairie) and Mathew Moody and Sons (Terrebonne) were successful makers of stationary threshing machines and horsepower treadmills in the 20th century; examples of their machines can still be found in eastern Canada.

Western Canada The growth of prairie agriculture was a 20th-century phenomenon and, although Winnipeg did attract some implement makers, by the time the prairie market opened up, the eastern implement makers (protected by the high tariffs of the NATIONAL POLICY) were ready to provide the latest open-end binders pioneered by the Harris, Massey and Toronto Reaper companies. The popularity of self-propelled steam traction engines after 1900 demanded a high level of technological sophistication, and American companies (eg, Case, Deere, International Harvester) competed stiffly with Ontario manufacturers. These companies were quick to design and construct bigger and bigger steam-engine tractors for the rich prairie grainfields. The threshing-machine industry expanded to meet the increased power provided by these steam-engine tractors. Again Ontario implement makers, with their head start in implement TECHNOLOGY, were able to capture most of the new western market and Waterloo, Lobsinger, Sawyer-Massey, Hergott and Bell were soon shipping larger and larger portable threshing machines to the West. Although wooden bodied to begin with, these new dinosaurs of the western prairies soon were made with galvanized metal, and thus were better able to withstand the ravages of time. Many can still be seen abandoned on prairie farms, while their offspring, the combine harvesters, chew their way across the ripening fields of wheat.

ALAN SKEOCH

Agricultural Implements Industry comprises establishments involved in MANUFACTURING a range of farm machinery, including combines, cultivators, harrows, harvesters, threshing machines, etc. Canada's farm equipment industry had its beginnings in the mid-19th century, when the establishment of local iron foundries stimulated development of farm implement manufactories. Some of the earliest of these companies (including Massey, Harris, etc) were established in the Lk Ontario district. Many early manufacturers failed or were absorbed into larger companies, while other new companies opened. In the 1980s literally hundreds of manufacturers and distributors of farm equipment market their products in Canada. These enterprises range from large, multinational companies that produce a broad range of machinery and implements to smaller, specialty-line manufacturers.

In 1982 there were 197 manufacturers of agricultural implements in Canada, employing over 9000 workers. Only 2 establishments employed more than 1000 workers; two-thirds of establishments employed fewer than 100 workers. Of the larger, "full-line" manufacturers, most are branch plants of US companies. The more innovative, smaller establishments, which specialize in a small range of equipment (ie, "short-line" manufacturers), are Canadian owned. Many of these are found in the Prairie region. Workers in the industry belong to either national unions (eg, United Steelworkers of America, Teamsters Union) or regional ones. Value of shipments in 1982 was $1.08 million.

The Modern Industry

Canada's farmers buy over $2-billion worth of machinery and implements annually, including an average of some 27 000 tractors, 7500 swathers, 7000 hay balers, 7000 grain combines and a host of plows, diskers and other tillage tools. A large proportion of the industry's products, particularly tractors and other major machines, is still manufactured outside the country. However, Canada's manufacturing sector is growing rapidly, with a base of short-line manufacturers in various locations across the country. The larger multinationals are also decentralizing some of their major manufacturing to Canadian-based plants. The industry is represented by the Canadian Farm and Industrial Equipment Institute, Burlington, Ont, and the Prairie Implements Manufacturers Assn, Regina.

Farm equipment markets in N America have always been cyclical in nature, with predictable 5-to-7-year cycles. However, with the economic downturn which began in the early 1980s, farm equipment sales began a downward spiral that proved to be particularly severe. For example, in 1979, sales of farm tractors in the 2-wheel drive category, 40 HP and over, totaled 23 383 units; in 1983, 12 584 units were sold, a difference of 42.6%. Similarly, some 5000 large, self-propelled combine harvesters were sold in 1979; this figure fell to 3200 in 1983. Most other lines of farm equipment have suffered similar sales reductions in the same period, but an industry report predicted continuing improved sales for the balance of the decade. During the depressed period 1980-83, machinery and equipment were purchased only when absolutely necessary. Although all manufacturers and distributors suffered, some of the large companies, such as MASSEY-FERGUSON INDUSTRIES LTD, International Harvester, the White Farm Equipment organization and others, found themselves in particularly severe financial difficulties. They were forced to cut production, lay off large numbers of employees and close some manufacturing facilities. Massey-Ferguson was totally restructured, with unprofitable divisions sold off or simply disbanded. White Farm also experienced similar difficulties in maintaining its operations in Canada and the US. It has been placed in receivership twice and only recently was restructured to begin operations again. International Harvester's financial difficulties prompted the company to lay off employees and sell off nonagricultural divisions.

Other changes in the farm equipment industry in N America have been the result of the economic depression in AGRIBUSINESS. Many full-line companies that had produced a broad range of agricultural machines and implements are now concentrating on manufacturing a limited line of key products. Many companies are also "jobbing out" specialty lines previously built in-house, thus freeing capital, reducing overhead and providing better inventory planning.

Products

In the last 50 years, the number of people engaged in farming has declined radically and hectarages farmed have increased dramatically. These changes have been made possible by developments in farm machinery that permit Canadian farmers to till, seed and harvest ever larger hectarages with less expenditure of time and labour.

Tilling Equipment In the past, farmland were continually cultivated and many passes were made across the field to prepare the ground for seeding. Modern tillage practices seek to minimize disturbance of the soil surface to conserve vital topsoil and its nutrients (*see* SOIL CONSERVATION). Tilling implements have been designed to prepare seedbeds with little disturbance of the surface. Thus, while the moldboard plow continues to be used in farming areas where a deep seedbed is required (eg, for cereal crops, corn, soybeans), the modern chisel plow, which features a series of cultivating chisel points for preparing a seedbed while disturbing the ground surface only minimally, is becoming more popular. The industry has also developed tillage implements that leave stubble from previous crops in place, thus retaining the nutrients that such residues provide and helping control EROSION.

Seeding Equipment To complement changing tillage practices and equipment, modern seeding implements (eg, air seeders) inject seed into the prepared earth through pneumatic injectors. Air seeders have only recently entered the marketplace and have already proven to be efficient in seeding through previous crop stubble, particularly in dry-land farming areas in western Canada.

Hay and Forage Equipment Farmers managing large dairy or beef feedlot operations operate highly mechanized businesses. Traditional baling machines which produced a compact, rectangular bale of hay weighing about 45 kg have given way to machines that produce large round bales of up to 680 kg. This new technology provides for better storage capability and improved drying and curing of harvested forage materials. Similarly, FORAGE CROPS may be cut and conditioned using highly efficient forage harvesters. Grinder mixers, machines that prepare silage for proper consistency and exact portioning, as well as adding vitamins, etc, are also available.

Modern combine in operation near Winnipeg, Man (*photo by Jim Merrithew*).

Harvesting Equipment Modern combine harvesters are capable of harvesting a broad range of crops, including wheat, barley, corn, soybeans, etc. They can cut and harvest a swath as much as 15 m wide in a single pass, thus allowing the farmer to harvest hundreds of hectares per day. Technological advances include computerized monitoring systems to provide the operator with information on grain loss, damage and rate of speed for optimum performance.

Swathers or windrowers, machines designed to cut grain and leave the grain stooks in windrows, are widely used in areas where ripened grain requires some drying prior to harvesting (eg, in western Canada). When farmers judge the time is appropriate, they harvest the precut crop with a special conveyor type of combine pickup table and the final harvesting steps take place.

Tractors Technological advances in tractor manufacturing during the last 20 years have been dramatic. The typical modern farm tractor is diesel powered (over 90% of all self-propelled farm machines have diesel engines), with a rating of about 90 HP, although models ranging from small 9 HP units up to large 4-wheel-drive units of over 400 HP are being marketed. Many of these provide a wide range of computerized operating features, eg, digital gauges that report wheel slippage, recommended gear settings and information regarding fuel efficiency and productivity. Although industry engineers have been experimenting with alternative fuels to power machinery, most believe that the conventional diesel engine (with modification) will continue in use to the end of the century.

BRENT M. HAMRE

Agricultural Marketing Board, a statutory body which acts as a compulsory marketing agent, performing or controlling one or more of the functions of marketing on behalf of producers of specific agricultural commodities. Boards may be established and operated under legislation passed by either provincial or federal governments, depending on whether the products they market or regulate are produced and sold within a province (intraprovincially) or are sold interprovincially or to export markets. Some boards are subject to the jurisdiction of both levels of government. In 1980-81 there were 121 agricultural marketing boards in Canada. Marketing boards operate in every province and regulate a wide variety of agricultural products.

The first boards developed from farmers' efforts to gain market power through joint action and as a reaction to unstable farm prices and incomes. Efforts early in this century to organize co-operative AGRICULTURAL MARKETING ventures grew into attempts by some producers' groups to achieve compulsory, centralized marketing through boards. Disruption of marketing channels during and after WWI led to centralized GRAIN HANDLING AND MARKETING by temporary government agencies from 1917 to 1920. However, the first Canadian producer-controlled agricultural marketing boards were introduced in BC in the late 1920s. In 1931 the Supreme Court of Canada found that the legislation under which these early producer marketing boards were established infringed upon the authority of the federal government in interprovincial trade, and that the boards themselves constituted an indirect tax. Pressure for national legislation permitting establishment of marketing boards increased as farm prices and incomes fell during the GREAT DEPRESSION of the 1930s. Federal legislation for this purpose was passed in 1934, but was also found to be unconstitutional because it interfered with the authority of the provinces in intraprovincial trade. Subsequent provincial and federal legislation recognized the respective jurisdictions of the 2 levels of government.

Provincial marketing Acts generally establish supervisory boards or councils which develop provincial commodity marketing plans and oversee the introduction and operation of boards and commissions which administer these plans. Directors of commodity commissions are generally government appointed, but board directors are commonly elected by producers. Commodity marketing plans are implemented following a favourable vote by producers of the commodity. Under the Agricultural Products Marketing Act of 1949, the federal government can authorize boards established under provincial marketing Acts to regulate interprovincial and export sales. Eighty such provincial boards were in operation in 1980-81.

Potato harvesting, New Haven, PEI (*photo by Wayne R. Barrett/Masterfile*).

Conflicts arising from efforts by some provincial supply-management boards to control the inflow of products from other provinces contributed to passage of the Farm Products Marketing Agencies Act in 1972. This Act provided for the establishment of the supervisory National Farm Products Marketing Council, for the development of national or regional marketing plans, and for the establishment and operation of national marketing agencies or boards. By 1978 there were national boards for eggs, turkeys and broiler chickens, operating in conjunction with the provincial boards for these commodities. National agricultural marketing institutions acting under separate legislation include the CANADIAN WHEAT BOARD (CWB), marketing agency for major prairie grains, which has been in operation since 1935; and the Canadian Dairy Commission, which was established in 1966 and which, together with provincial milk boards, administers the national dairy program for industrial milk and cream.

There is substantial variation in the legislatively sanctioned powers held and exercised by boards and considerable difference in the activities they undertake in pursuit of their objectives. The major objectives of marketing boards are to enhance producers' prices and incomes and to reduce variability in them. Some boards are also concerned that access to market opportunities be shared equitably among producers and that there be standardized terms of sale for the product which they regulate. Boards are empowered to enforce compliance with the marketing regulations they administer and may have power to license processors and handlers of the product they regulate. Boards usually have powers to conduct or sponsor research, information or product-promotion activities and most are empowered to purchase and sell the product they regulate. Some are specified as the sole buyer from producers and the sole seller on their behalf. For example, the CWB is the sole seller in export markets of prairie WHEAT, BARLEY and OATS. Some boards are empowered to pool producer prices or market returns by grade of product (eg, the CWB, many of the HOG boards and some VEGETABLE boards). Some boards have the power to schedule producers' deliveries to the marketing system through delivery quotas. The CWB performs this activity and also regulates shipments of grain through the transportation system to terminal grain elevators or mills. Some marketing boards negotiate prices and other terms of sale with processors or handlers, eg, some hog boards and some of the boards for FRUITS.

The strongest marketing powers held by boards are those to determine prices, when enforced by the power to apply supply-controlling quotas. Such quotas involve control over the entry of new producers and over the amount of the product produced or marketed. The use of these pricing- and supply-control mechanisms by provincial and national boards for POULTRY and DAIRY products is controversial. Advocates note that these programs have reduced variability in farm prices and increased producers' incomes; critics say the programs have contributed to increased food prices and higher consumer expenditures and that the method of administration has created economic inefficiencies in production and marketing. Boards which do not possess or exert these supply-control powers have given rise to much less controversy and are more widely accepted.

M.M. AND T.S. VEEMAN

Reading: Sidney Hoos, ed, *Agricultural Marketing Boards: An International Perspective* (1979).

Agricultural Products Board, federal government department est 1951 under the Emergency Powers Act to administer contracts with other countries for the purchase or sale of agricultural products and conduct other commodity operations, eg, purchase of surplus Canadian commodities, where required. Some of these commodities are donated as international aid to fulfil Canada's commitments to the UN Food Administration Organization. The board reports to the minister of agriculture.

Agricultural Research and Development The Canadian agri-food industry has become an effective producer and processor of food and feed as the result of the work of innovative, hardworking farmers, good land-resources management, and the application of the technology derived from agricultural research and development or operational research work. Canadian agriculture is a complex of many independent farms which differ in size and types of production. Farmers operate on a rather small scale, under differing CLIMATE, SOIL and other conditions. They cannot afford to finance, organize and conduct research; thus, because such work is in the public interest, most farming and food research is financed directly or indirectly by governments.

The greatest challenge to agricultural research lies in the primary production of food. However, the AGRICULTURE AND FOOD system also includes those industries involved in the food-processing, supply and AGRICULTURAL-MARKETING sectors. Because agricultural products must meet human nutritional needs, food research complements conventional agricultural production research to provide abundant yields of a wide variety of high-quality foods.

History

The need for agricultural research in Canada was recognized more than 100 years ago. The first step in the organization of research took place in 1874 with the establishment of the Ontario School of Agriculture, later the Ontario Agricultural College and Experimental Farm, at Guelph. While the research conducted at the school was useful, Canada's varied soil and climatic conditions limited its applicability. A decade later, agricultural methods were proving inadequate and resulting in soil impoverishment and poor crop yields. The prevailing agricultural depression brought home the need for agricultural research and, in 1886, Parliament passed a bill establishing 5 experimental farms.

The RESEARCH STATION and experimental farm system has expanded to include over 40 research establishments from coast to coast. Provincial research bodies have been established, and university and industrial research programs have proliferated. During a century of research, plant varieties and animal strains have been improved; good SOIL CONSERVATION practices have been implemented; losses by INSECT PESTS, PLANT DISEASES, animal DISEASE, DROUGHT and frost have been reduced or overcome; economical methods of storage and food preservation have been discovered; and better means of using food CROPS and animal products have been developed. These types of research serve to make Canadian farmers more secure in their undertakings and provide consumers with better products.

Responsibility for Research

In Canada, both provincial and federal governments may legally undertake research. Responsibility for overall adequacy rests with federal authorities, while the provinces have jurisdiction over agricultural teaching and extension. The research function is shared among Agriculture Canada and other federal agencies, provincial departments of agriculture, provincial research councils, university faculties of agriculture and VETERINARY MEDICINE and private industry. The respective roles of these organizations were considered and defined by representatives of the institutions and departments involved at a series of meetings held in 1964. Representatives agreed that all agencies engaging in agricultural research must be at liberty to undertake any or all types of investigation falling within their competence. About 2000 researchers are engaged in agricultural research work, full-time or part-time.

Two major national committees made up of representatives of provincial and federal governments, universities and other organizations involved in research are responsible for the co-ordination of agricultural research. The Canadian Agricultural Services Co-ordinating Committee (est 1932, reorganized 1964) co-ordinates research, extension and education services, and is responsible for assessing immediate and future research needs and developing appropriate proposals. Provincial and regional committees assess and make recommendations regarding agricultural research and education within provinces. The Canadian Agricultural Research Council (est 1974) is the primary adviser to the government on the state of agricultural research in Canada.

Agriculture Canada, the largest of the public research agencies, has assumed the major share of responsibility for agricultural research, directly conducting over 50% of all agricultural research in Canada. The program is largely concentrated in the Research Branch, but funds are also provided for research at universities and other public and private institutions. The Research Branch was formed in 1959 by integrating 2 research services of the Canada Dept of Agriculture, ie, the Experimental Farms Service and the Science Service. Agriculture Canada employs over 800 scientists at its various research institutions.

Provincial Departments of agriculture play a vital role in intraprovincial research. Because of their close contacts with farmers, especially through their extension personnel, provinces can readily identify research needs. They also participate in research advisory committees at provincial and national levels. Agricultural research activities vary from province to province as a result of historical development in Canada, including differences in the economic importance and nature of agricultural products in the various provinces. In the West the provinces do relatively little research, instead relying to a greater or lesser extent on universities and federal agricultural research stations. In Ontario and Québec provincial departments sponsor research services, farms and stations and also support agricultural research at the university level. The Atlantic provinces, with only one degree-granting agricultural institution, rely more heavily on federal research programs than do other regions of Canada. Alberta, Ontario and Québec have provincial agricultural research councils to identify research needs, plan and co-ordinate their research programs and make research grants.

Universities across Canada conduct agricultural research programs necessary in the training of research scientists, and act as research institutions for federal and provincial governments to a greater or lesser extent. University researchers (at 11 faculties of agriculture and veterinary medicine) comprise the second-largest single group of agricultural scientists in Canada.

Successes and Goals

Review and adjustment of agricultural research policy is a continuous process. Changes in the structure and organization of research must keep pace with changes in agriculture. Success in agricultural research results in part from linkages between scientific discovery, technological development and application. Results of research are usually disseminated through agricultural extension services of provincial departments of agriculture, although results which can be incorporated immediately into farming practice are sometimes disseminated by the organization which conducted the research.

Canadian successes in plant breeding, disease control, ANIMAL BREEDING, etc, have won international renown. Among the most significant of these achievements are the various developments in WHEAT, from Red Fife (1840s) to Marquis (1903) and beyond to rust-resistant forms (eg, Selkirk). Rust research is undertaken at the Dominion Rust Research Laboratory, Winnipeg (est 1925). The creation of CANOLA as a source of VEGETABLE OIL and oil cake that are safe for human and animal consumption, respectively, was a major success of the postwar period. Researchers at University of Manitoba were largely responsible for the production of an entirely new, man-made cereal crop, TRITICALE, a fertile cross between 2 different genera of cereals, wheat and RYE. Less dramatic but economically very important developments include improvements in SOYBEANS, SUNFLOWERS, TOBACCO, and various FRUIT and VEGETABLE crops to increase both the area in which the crop may be successfully grown and the yield. Perhaps the best-known success in animal breeding is the development of the Lacombe HOG at the Agriculture Canada experimental farm at Lacombe, Alta. Work is also proceeding on POULTRY (for meat and egg yield), BEEF and DAIRY cattle, etc. Such work involves important research into genetic and congenital defects of animals, which may have applicability to the study of human GENETIC DISEASE.

Agricultural methods have changed, but the responsibility of the Canadian agriculture and food system is still to provide the population with an adequate supply of nutritious and wholesome food. The growing awareness of food quality control has focused attention on agricultural research needs. Emphasis must also be placed on use and conservation of RESOURCES (especially soils) and on developing new sources of ENERGY. *See* AGRICULTURAL AID.

BERTRAND FOREST

Agricultural Soil Practices Development and management of SOIL RESOURCES for agricultural production requires consideration of land-clearing methods, SOIL and CROP practices (including EROSION control) and environmental impact.

Land-Clearing Methods

Development of land for agriculture frequently requires clearing of brush-covered or forested land. Such clearing aims to remove unwanted material efficiently and economically, minimize topsoil displacement and degradation, and leave a seedbed sufficiently well cleared and graded to allow use of cultivating, planting and harvesting equipment. Methods selected for surface clearing depend on the nature, density and extent of the cover VEGETATION. Harvesting of marketable timber, if present, constitutes the first stage and may involve individual trees or a stand. Logs may be cut, stripped and piled with tree harvesters; trees may be knocked down, lifted and moved with tree-dozers. Stumpers are often preferred to bulldozers for removing stumps and large stones as they minimize topsoil disturbance. Heavy-duty bar mowers, rotary brush mowers and brush beaters are used to cut, chop and shred brush. When such a device produces a mulch, trash disposal is eliminated. Selective herbicides are used to remove specific plant species; nonselective or contact herbicides, for defoliation. Plants with deep root systems are removed with an undercutting or root-cutting and clearing implement. Soil is cleared to below plowing and cultivation depths. Root rakes and similar specialized equipment allow thorough combing of surface-cleared areas to remove roots, stump fragments, small brush and undergrowth. Final finishing is done with heavy disc plows and harrows; land levellers are used where grading is required for improved surface drainage.

Soil and Crop Practices

Establishment of an agricultural program requires careful selection of soil and crop management practices to optimize long-term yields, while minimizing soil loss, compaction and degradation. Throughout Canada erosion of topsoil and subsoil is increasing. Cropping practices dependent on continuous cultivation of a single crop have also precipitated soil degradation across the country.

Water Erosion Sheet and rill erosion occur in fields as a result of improper soil and crop management, erodible soil conditions, and excessive surface drainage and field runoff. Spring snowmelt and summer convective storms in western Canada cause most damage. Upland cultivated soils across Canada are subject to soil loss by sheet, rill and gully erosion. Conservation tillage and cropping systems provide the most cost-effective remedial measures. Terraces can be used to form a series of diversions down a SLOPE or to change a steep slope to a series of gentler slopes. Grassed waterways can be developed on sloping cultivated areas where surface runoff concentrates or where it has produced severe rill damage. These waterways may also be used as outlets for contour strips or contour diversions.

Spraying tomatoes (*courtesy Agriculture Canada*).

ncentrated surface flows can lead to gully formation; water seepage out of the developed nks often aggravates this problem. Small gulls can be regraded and revegetated, but larger es may require installation of surface dirsions (to divert runoff laterally from the ope), check dams (to slow velocity of concentated flow) or drop structures (eg, rock chutes, bsurface drop inlets, surface drops). Seepage ains can be installed in banks to control oughing and bank mining (*see* FARM DRAINGE).

Wind Erosion results in serious soil loss here inappropriate soil and crop management stems are used, fields are exposed to an extenve WIND run, or topographic features are vulerable. Late winter and early spring are critical asons in western Canada, where as much as)% of cultivated land is left fallow and, thus, is bject to wind erosion. Land-management sysms for SOIL CONSERVATION include keeping the rface of soils in a rough condition (eg, by minnizing tillage operations); keeping vegetation, sidue and trash on the surface; using manures, een manures and crop rotations; cropping and rip-cropping at right angles to the prevailing ind; and providing wind barriers (eg, tree elterbelts, grass strips, fence rows).

Streambank and Ditchbank Erosion can be used by water running over the surface of the ank on its way to the drainageway or stream, y soil instability resulting from subsurface epage or other locally high soil-water condions, by shear stresses imposed on the bank by e stream flow, and by land-management acvities (eg, pasturing animals on banks, cultiating land immediately adjacent to banks). In a cent inventory of agricultural WATERSHEDS in ntario, erosion is shown as occurring on 37% f the banks and rotational slumping on 25%. ıch problems can be controlled with revegetaon, runoff diversions, vegetated buffer strips nd drop structures. Soil stability problems can e alleviated with regrading and revegetation, ank drainage, limiting animal access and conructing retaining walls. Problems linked to igh stream velocities or localized turbulence n be controlled with vegetative and rock ripp linings; more serious problems require gabins, concrete blocks or asphalt linings.

Environmental Impact

Accelerated soil erosion on fields and banks uses damage not only in the immediate area ut also downstream, as the transported soil articles clog stream channels, silt ponds and servoirs, or cover fish-spawning beds. Where e capacity of a channel is reduced by sedimention, flood waters may be forced to reroute verland. Agricultural sediments can be transort agents for potential contaminants (eg, hosphorus, heavy metals, herbicides). Susended solids can be controlled at the erosion urce or in the flow system. Sediment traps at eld drainage outlets or in waterways are used intercept sediment-laden surface runoff.

W.T. DICKINSON

gricultural Stabilization Board, established nder the federal Agricultural Stabilization Act f 1958, is empowered to stabilize the prices of gricultural products to maintain a fair relaonship between the prices received by farmers nd the cost of goods and services they buy. unds for board operations come from an anual appropriation through the budget of the ederal minister of agriculture. The board has 2 eans of stabilizing the prices of designated agcultural products: it may offer to purchase any ommodity deemed to be in excess supply; or it ay make a deficiency payment to producers of product the market price of which is below ome designated minimum support price. The oard is assisted in its work by an advisory comittee of farmers or representatives of farm organizations, all of whom are appointed by the federal minister of agriculture. Under the original Agricultural Stabilization Act (which replaced the 1944 Agricultural Prices Support Act), the support price for designated commodities was set at 80% of the average price for the preceding 10 years. The Act was amended in 1975 to provide a guaranteed price of 90% of the 5-year average weighted price for cattle, hogs, sheep, industrial milk and cream, corn and soybeans, and for oats and barley produced outside the CANADIAN WHEAT BOARD designated area of the Prairies.

J.C. GILSON

Agriculture, Department of Originally the Bureau of Agriculture (est 1852), it was established by an Act of Parliament in 1868 to concentrate on the urgent need of the time to control livestock diseases and prevent their entry into Canada. The department is responsible for federal policies relating to agriculture and food, including grading and inspection, seed certification, regulations on pesticides and fertilizers, market development programs, scientific research and dissemination of information. The minister is responsible for initiating and administering all federal legislation relating to AGRICULTURE and for operations of the AGRICULTURAL PRODUCTS BOARD, Canadian Dairy Commission, Canadian Grain Commission, CANADIAN LIVESTOCK FEED BOARD and National Farm Products Marketing Council. The Research Branch, located on the Central Experimental Farm in central Ottawa, is the principal research organization serving Canadian agriculture. The branch has 38 other establishments across Canada to serve areas of varied soil and climatic conditions. The department's 1984-85 budget was $1.2 billion.

Agriculture, Federal Task Force on, est 1967 to advise the federal minister of agriculture on problems of Canadian agriculture and to recommend policies. Surplus production and lagging incomes in the wheat and dairy industries had precipitated threats of a strike by angry dairy farmers and led to a march on Parliament Hill in May 1967 (*see* NATIONAL FARMERS UNION). The task force delivered its report, *Canadian Agriculture in the Seventies,* in 1969. It found widespread dissatisfaction with low farm incomes, uncertain markets and prices, overproduction, small nonviable farms and diminishing export markets. It recommended that the government should reduce its direct involvement in agriculture and phase out subsidies and price supports; that the farm population should be reduced; and that younger low-income farmers should leave farming while older nonviable farmers should be assisted to achieve a better standard of living. Convinced that the surpluses of wheat and dairy products would continue in the 1970s, the commissioners recommended that farmers shift to producing other commodities.

The major AGRICULTURE AND FOOD POLICIES of the 1970s that grew out of this report were ironically characterized by greater interdependence between government and agriculture rather than by the looser ties the task force had recommended.

GRACE SKOGSTAD

Agriculture and Food Many structural and technological changes have occurred in Canadian farming in the period 1951 to 1981 and, although national trends are discernible, significant regional differences exist. In the following profiles of Canadian farming, the principal farming regions described are the Atlantic region (Nfld, PEI, NS, NB), Québec, Ontario, the Prairie region (Man, Sask, Alta) and British Columbia. Data for the territories are included when relevant.

Since WWII Canada has changed from a semirural society to a largely industrialized and urban one. As INDUSTRIALIZATION proceeded, the rural sector rapidly declined in proportion, but it appears that the population engaged in farming has stabilized at its 1981 level. The process of agricultural industrialization has been accompanied by important changes in the farming sector, including larger farms, greater capital investment and more sophisticated business management. In many ways the rural sector has almost disappeared as a separate social entity.

The most profound changes in farming have been economic and social in nature. For example, mixed farming has declined as farmers increasingly specialize in a single CROP or type of livestock. This specialization has led to increased market risk for farmers as evidenced by the higher rates of farm business failures in the 1980s. Such structural changes have taxed existing marketing and financial institutions and contributed to increased stress for the farming community. Other kinds of changes have been more modest: the crops which farmers grow and the livestock they raise have changed only slightly. Perhaps the most notable changes in crop production in the period included the expansion of grain-corn production in eastern Canada and, in the West, the development of an edible OILSEED crop — CANOLA. In ANIMAL AGRICULTURE, highly concentrated and specialized poultry, meat and egg production became the norm and, in beef production, leaner animals have become the preferred consumer product.

Stage of Development

Under the impetus of allied wartime demands for food and fibre and as a consequence of the reduced labour supply, Canadian farms rapidly became mechanized, larger in size and more specialized in operation, a trend which continued after the war. During the period 1951 to 1981, the amount of improved land farmed in Canada (principally land in crops, improved pasture and summer fallow) increased 18%, from 39 million ha to 46 million ha. In the same interval the real (1971 constant dollar) investment in farm machinery rose 80%, from $3.8 billion in 1951 to $6.9 billion in 1981. This investment increased, relative to that in land, buildings and livestock, from 15% of total farm capital in 1951 to 20% in 1981. In the latter year the machinery portion of total investment was highest in the Atlantic and Québec regions (24-25%) and lowest in BC (12%). Canadian farms became more intensively cultivated, with the real (1971 constant dollar) investment in machinery increasing from $96/ha of improved farmland in 1951 to $151 in 1981. The most rapid increase in the machinery/land ratio was in Québec; the least rapid, in BC. The greater amount of machinery on Canadian farms has resulted in a smaller farm labour force operating larger farms. Total farm size increased by 83%, from an average of 113 ha in 1951 to 207 ha in 1981. The increase in average farm size in this period was greatest in the Atlantic region (89%) and least in Ontario (30%).

Subsistence farming in Canada largely disappeared in the postwar years and was replaced by the new phenomenon of increased remunerative work by farmers and farm-family members off their own farms. This off-farm work included work for other farmers and nonagricultural employment (eg, operating a school bus). By 1981, 39% of all farm operators in Canada were engaged in some form of paid employment off their own farms for an average of 171 days a year. The highest proportion of farmers doing off-farm work was in BC (51%); the lowest, in Québec (32%). Overall, 13% of the off-farm work by Canadian farmers in 1981 consisted of work for other farmers, but the largest proportion, 87%, was in nonagricultural employment. These proportions were generally consistent in all regions.

Farm Capital

The total capital value of Canadian farms in

1981 was $130 billion in current (nominal) dollars, more than double the amount just 5 years earlier and over 13 times the level of 1951. Average capital value was $409 000 per farm in 1981, compared with only $15 000 in 1951. The highest regional average value per farm in 1981 was in the Prairie region ($508 000); the lowest, in the Atlantic region ($184 000). Much of the nominal increase in capital value in the 30-year period was in real-estate values. Across Canada the value of farm real estate rose from almost $260/ha in 1951 to over $375/ha in 1981, increasing most rapidly in Ontario. More recently (1976-81) the increase in Ontario real-estate values was only 7%, with values increasing more rapidly in all of the other regions, the highest rate (43%) being in the Prairies.

Farming Inputs

Modern farming includes the increased use of technical inputs such as chemical fertilizers. The average application rate of the primary fertilizer nutrients (nitrogen, phosphate for phosphorus, and potash for potassium) increased almost 5 times between 1960-61 and 1980-81, from 14 kg/ha to 67 kg/ha for Canada as a whole. Regional differences in fertilizer application reflect differing SOILS, CLIMATES and crops. The highest rates of fertilizer use are in the more humid eastern Canadian regions; the lowest, in the generally drier Prairie region. Farmers reporting use of fertilizers increased from 38% of all farmers in 1971 to 59% in 1980, with the most rapid increase occurring in the Prairie region. During this same brief period, land area which was treated with commercial fertilizers increased from 16% of all improved farmland to 40%. The Canadian fertilizer market is now relatively mature and increases in rates of use in all regions will probably be more moderate in future.

Recent trends in incidence of use and areas treated with PESTICIDES have been generally similar to those for fertilizers. In 1970, 45% of Canadian farmers reported using pesticides; by 1980 this figure had increased to 53%. Farmland area treated with pesticides rose from 12% in 1970 to 23% in 1980. Regionally the highest incidence of pesticide use in 1980 was in Ontario (62%); the lowest, in BC (29%). As with fertilizer use, regional differences reflect differences in crops grown, intensity of cultivation and the severity of INSECT PEST infestations.

The use of sophisticated electronic COMPUTERS has increased in farming in the past decade, although no statistical information is available to measure the extent of use. Many farmers have adopted computer technology to obtain daily price information on crops and livestock and to prepare cost analyses and financial summaries. Governments and private institutions have developed programs to encourage the use of computer technology, perhaps the most well-known being the CANFARM system, which allowed farmers to submit data for analysis. CANFARM began as a federal-provincial-university program but is now privately operated.

Tenure and Business Organization

Owner-operated farms were the principal form of land tenure in 1951 (79%); although still dominant in 1981, they had fallen to 63% of all farms. In 1981 Québec had the highest proportion of owner-operated farms (80%); the Prairie region, the lowest (54%). The proportion of Canadian farms operated by tenants has remained almost unchanged, 7% in 1951 and 6% in 1981. Part-owner, part-tenant farms increased from 14% of all farms in 1951 to 31% in 1981. Regardless of land tenure, however, family-operated farms in all regions remain the overwhelming practice of farm business organization (99.3% of all farms in 1981).

Farm Population

Canada's total population climbed from 14 million in 1951 to 24 million in 1981. Farm population, however, fell from less than 3 million in 1951 (about 21% of the total) to just over one million in 1981 (4% of the total). The greatest regional declines in the farm share of the total population in the 30-year period occurred in the Atlantic region and Québec; the least, in BC. The Prairie region continued to have the highest proportion (11%) of its population on farms in 1981 (compared with 38% in 1951).

Area and Condition of Farmland

The total area of Canada is nearly 1 billion ha. Farms occupied less than 7% of this area in 1981 (66 million ha). The rest is forest, lakes, mountains, swamps and arctic tundra (*see* SOIL CLASSIFICATION). Improved farmland area in 1981 was even less (46 million ha or over 4%) of Canada's total area. While the 1981 total area in farms has declined by over 6% from 70 million ha in 1951, improved farmland has increased by 7 million ha since then. Thus the proportion of improved land in farms increased from almost 56% of all farmland in 1951 to 70% in 1981.

Changes between 1951 and 1981 in area and condition of farmland differ by region. In eastern Canada, both total and improved area has decreased in all 3 regions, especially in Atlantic Canada. In the West, however, both total and improved-farm areas increased in both regions. In BC improved farmland area more than doubled in the 30-year period. Canada's Prairie region, the largest single agricultural region, accounted for 80% of the national total area in 1981 and 82% of the improved farmland area. In 1951, the region accounted for 71% and 74%, respectively.

Types of Farms

There were 318 000 farms of all sizes and types in Canada in 1981, compared to 623 000 in 1951. In 1981 about 50% were in the Prairie region; 30 years earlier the region had held 40%. The Atlantic region had fewest farms, 4% of the 1981 total. Since WWII total farm numbers declined more slowly in BC than elsewhere: the province had 4% of all farms in 1951; 6% by 1981. The most rapid 30-year decline in farm numbers occurred in the Atlantic region, almost 80%.

There are 4 main types of farm: livestock (including DAIRY), field crop, FRUIT and VEGETABLES, and combinations of types or specialty farms. Between 1951 and 1981 the principal change in these categories has been a decrease in the relative numbers of livestock farms and an increase in the proportions of field-crop and fruit and vegetable farms. Regionally the dominant farm types in 1981 were distributed as follows: Atlantic — dairy (27%), cattle and HOGS (32%); Québec — dairy (50%), cattle and hogs (22%); Ontario — dairy (19%), cattle and hogs (36%), small grains, including WHEAT (21%); Prairie region — cattle and hogs (22%), small grains, including wheat (63%); BC — cattle and hogs (36%), fruit and vegetables (21%).

Regionally the most important shifts in farm

Livestock and Poultry Numbers, Selected Years, 1951-81[1]

(Source: Agriculture Canada, *Selected Agricultural Statistics for Canada,* 1978 and 1982; Statistics Canada, *Census of Canada: Agriculture*)[2]

	No of Head[3]	*1951*	*1961*	*1971*	*1981*
Cattle and Calves	10^3	8 363	11 934	13 271	13 502
Hogs	10^3	4 914	5 331	7 624	9 875
Sheep and Lambs	10^3	1 461	1 548	851	817
Poultry	10^6	68	78	101	104

[1] At midyear, June 1 or July 1

[2] Newfoundland data are included in 1981 but not in other years

[3] 10^3 = thousand head; 10^6 = million head. Totals may not sum because of rounding

types since 1951 occurred in Ontario and BC. Ontario small-grain farms were relatively fe in 1951, but increased to over one-fifth of types in 1981 primarily because of increas corn production. In BC, dairy farms were dom nant in 1951; by 1981 they accounted for few than 10% of all farm types as dairy operatio increased their size of business and became mc specialized.

Crops and Livestock

There are 7 crops grown in Canada which, t gether with summer fallow, have accounted f about 80% of all improved farmland throug out the 1951-81 period: wheat, oats, barle corn, canola, potatoes and tame hay. The pri cipal national changes included increases areas of wheat, corn, barley, canola and tan hay; the area in oats decreased sharply.

Areas of Selected Principal Field Crops (thousand h

(Source: Statistics Canada, *Census of Canada: Agricultur*

Crop	*1951*	*1961*	*1971*	*19*
Wheat	10 220	10 245	7 854	12 4
Oats for grain	4 815	3 457	2 765	1 5
Barley	3 173	2 238	5 658	5 4
Corn for grain	127	162	571	1 1
Canola/Rapeseed	2	287	2 147	1 4
Potatoes	115	124	108	1
Tame hay	4 265	4 949	4 878	5 1
Summer fallow	8 279	11 275	10 613	9 7
Total	31 446	32 737	34 594	36 9

[1] Newfoundland data are included in 1981 but not in ot years

Although there has been a general trend wards larger areas planted to crops in th period, wide variations have occurred. In t Atlantic region the area of oats and tame h declined, while the potato area increased. Québec the oats area declined but corn increase In Ontario the area under corn for grain a silage increased sharply. In the Prairie regi the wheat area increased, as did barley, tan hay and canola, the latter from 2000 ha in 19 to almost 3 million ha in 1976. In BC, are planted to barley and tame hay were mu greater in 1981 than in 1951.

As the population grew, per capita incom generally rose, as did the demand for most me and livestock products. Livestock numbers va ied over the review period depending on t stage of the beef and hog cycles; however, 1981 there were 61% more cattle and calv hogs had doubled and poultry increased by 53 In the Atlantic region and Ontario, hog a poultry numbers increased sharply; in Québ they more than tripled; in BC, hog numbers i creased fivefold and poultry numbers almc fourfold. In the Prairies the numbers of cat and calves doubled. Sheep and lamb numbe were down by 44% nationally, as Canadia generally preferred other meats and lamb pr ducers faced strong competition in the sma Canadian market from lower-cost Australia and New Zealand producers.

Sources of Farm Income

Cash receipts of Canadian farmers from farn ing operations totalled $18.7 billion in 198 almost 7 times greater than the amount earn in 1951. About two-thirds of this increase r sulted from higher prices; one-third, fro greater quantities being marketed. The relati importance of income from crops rose from 42 of the total in 1951 to 48% in 1981; that from t sale of livestock and products fell from 56% 48%. In the same interval, payments made b governments to farmers under various price an income stabilization and other programs i creased from 2% of total cash receipts in 1951 4% in 1981 (*see* AGRICULTURAL MARKETING). Wi respect to particular commodities, the propo tion of total cash receipts derived from whe

Principal Sources of Farm Cash Receipts (Millions$)[1]
(Source: Statistics Canada, *Farm Cash Receipts*)

Region	*Source*	*1951*	*1961*	*1971*	*1981*
Atlantic	Crops	19.7	25.3	46.2	233.4
	Livestock[2]	80.9	78.0	104.0	370.3
	Other[3]	9.5	5.4	6.0	31.5
	Total[4]	110.1	108.7	156.3	635.2
Québec	Crops	33.4	44.6	70.0	343.4
	Livestock	318.7	353.3	551.8	2110.6
	Other	24.0	19.6	68.1	258.8
	Total[4]	376.2	417.5	689.9	2712.8
Ontario	Crops	179.4	257.1	458.7	1748.6
	Livestock	597.6	608.7	920.7	3004.3
	Other	7.1	6.7	38.5	200.5
	Total[4]	784.1	872.5	1417.9	4953.4
Prairie	Crops	885.4	747.9	1111.7	6375.1
	Livestock	460.6	604.7	917.9	2985.4
	Other	12.0	37.3	32.8	185.8
	Total[4]	1358.0	1389.8	2062.5	9546.3
British Columbia	Crops	33.3	41.6	71.6	304.8
	Livestock	72.2	91.5	147.0	523.6
	Other	1.7	2.0	3.3	35.5
	Total[4]	107.2	135.1	221.9	863.9
Canada	Crops	1151.2	1116.4	1758.3	9005.2
	Livestock	1530.1	1736.2	2641.4	8994.3
	Other	54.3	71.0	148.7	712.1
	Total[4]	2735.5	2923.7	4548.5	18711.6

[1] Newfoundland data are included in 1981 but not in other years
[2] The livestock category includes livestock products
[3] The "other" category includes forest and maple products and payments made to farmers under various federal and provincial programs
[4] Totals may not sum because of rounding

sales decreased slightly; that from canola increased from virtually zero to over 3% of the total. The shares of cattle and dairy products were relatively unchanged, but the proportion contributed by hogs, poultry and eggs declined on a national basis.

In the Atlantic region, potatoes, dairy products, poultry, eggs, hogs, cattle, calves, fruits and vegetables accounted for 80% of farm cash receipts in both 1951 and 1981. Potatoes, fruits and vegetables doubled in relative shares; cattle and calves dropped by half. Total cash receipts from all sources rose 5.5 times, but about 28% of the increase was a result of greater quantities marketed.

In Québec about 80% of farm cash receipts in both years were derived from dairy products, hogs, poultry, eggs, cattle and calves, but the relative importance of cattle and calves decreased by half. Total cash receipts from all sources rose 7 times; about 29% of the increase occurred because more of the product was being marketed.

The 80% share of Ontario farmers' total cash receipts came from a diverse range of products, with cattle and calves accounting for the largest share (about one-quarter) in both 1951 and 1981. Grain corn and SOYBEANS increased in importance; hogs, poultry and eggs declined. Cash receipts from all sources increased sixfold; about [illegible]5% of the increase was attributable to increased output.

In the Prairie region, wheat sales accounted for 45% of total cash receipts in 1981, down from a 49% share in 1951. The proportion of total receipts attributable to canola increased from virtually zero in 1951 to 6% in 1981; the share from cattle and calves also rose, but that from hogs fell. Of the 3 Prairie provinces, Manitoba remained the most diversified in 1981. Total cash receipts in the Prairie region from all sources increased sevenfold in the 30-year period; 37% of the increase resulted from greater production.

In BC 80% of total farm cash receipts were derived from dairy products, fruits, vegetables, cattle, calves, poultry, eggs, floriculture, nursery stock and hogs. Dairy products, floriculture, nursery stock and hogs increased in relative shares; cattle and calves decreased. Total farm cash receipts from all sources were up eightfold between 1951 and 1981; 31% of the increase resulted from greater output. *See* AGRIBUSINESS; BANKRUPTCY; FARM LAW; FOOD AND BEVERAGE INDUSTRIES; RURAL SOCIETY.

IAN F. FURNISS

Agriculture and Food Policy Federal agricultural policy is intended to serve national economic and political goals as well as the interests of those directly involved in and affected by Canadian agriculture — primarily producers, food processors, distributors, retailers and consumers. The Task Force Report on AGRICULTURE, official publications such as *Canadian Agriculture in the Seventies* (1969); *A Food Strategy for Canada* (1977); and the 4-volume *Orientation of Canadian Agriculture* (1977) identify the national goals as economic development, rising and stable incomes, full employment and harmonious international and federal-provincial relations. Specific agricultural goals include stable and fair producer returns, adequate supplies of high-quality nutritious food at stable and reasonable prices, and rural development and resource conservation. Over the next decade the focus will be on increased food production and processing and the promotion and expansion of agricultural exports.

From Confederation until the late 1950s, federal agricultural policy was designed to secure Canada's control over the West and produce food for Canada, her trading partners and war allies. Governments encouraged the production and export of grain. The freight rates at which grain grown on the Prairies moved to export markets were fixed as early as 1897 in the CROW'S NEST PASS AGREEMENT. The grain-handling system was regulated and a CROWN CORPORATION, the CANADIAN WHEAT BOARD, given monopoly authority in 1943 over the marketing of Prairie wheat, and between 1949 and 1973 over oats and barley.

The GREAT DEPRESSION forced governments to consider problems of agriculture itself, particularly low and unstable incomes. Programs were introduced to increase productivity and efficiency and thereby ostensibly raise and stabilize commodity prices. The Farm Improvement Loans Act (1944) and the Farm Credit Corporation Act (1959) made credit available and encouraged the mechanization and growth in size of farms. The Agricultural Prices Support Board (1944) and later the Agricultural Stabilization Board (1958) gave farmers a measure of protection from the fluctuating competitive marketing system by guaranteeing a base price for selected farm commodities (*see* AGRICULTURAL MARKETING BOARD).

Federal expenditures to support and stabilize prices of dairy products expanded significantly in the 1970s, accounting for 80% of federal price and income maintenance payments, and became permanent with the creation of the Canadian Dairy Commission in 1966 (*see* NATIONAL FARMERS UNION). A joint provincial-federal crop insurance program begun in 1959 reduced the financial impact of natural disasters. Federal-provincial co-operation in the Agricultural and Rural Development Act (1960) and Fund for Rural Economic Development (1966) were designed to distribute incomes more equitably within the farm sector.

Federal programs prior to the 1970s interfered as little as possible with the competitive market system of pricing. Farmers received market prices; the stabilization programs shored up farm incomes when prices fell below average, but did so at levels that minimally distorted the operation of the market system. While the Canadian Wheat Board instituted order in grain marketing and equity in pricing, grain prices themselves were established by changing world market factors. Provincial governments had allowed producers to pool their products and sell through provincial marketing boards or cooperatives which could negotiate higher prices. When the federal legislation to permit national marketing boards was declared unconstitutional (the *Natural Products Marketing Reference*, 1937), the federal government passed the Agricultural Products Marketing Act (1949). Provincial boards could be delegated federal authority to regulate the outward movement of commodities into export and interprovincial trade but could not restrict the inflow of commodities from other provinces or countries, and were thus unable to control completely the supply and, therefore, the price of the regulated commodity.

The unusually turbulent markets and a serious cost-price squeeze for many farmers in the 1970s led provincial governments to initiate and the federal government to extend income maintenance programs. Québec, BC and Ontario passed comprehensive stabilization legislation and several other provinces undertook to protect hog and cattle producers from unstable markets and depressed prices. The federal government amended the Agricultural Stabilization Act in 1975 and passed the Western Grain Stabilization Act in 1976. The former guaranteed government support of the prices of industrial milk and cream, corn, soybeans, slaughter cattle, hogs, sheep, and oats and barley raised outside the Canadian Wheat Board region at 90% of the previous 5-year average. The latter stabilized the net profit from the sale of oats, barley, wheat, canola, flaxseed and rye. These programs consumed almost 40% of federal agricultural spending and meant most commodities were protected.

The most innovative policy in the 1970s allowed producers to fix and determine the price of commodities. The Farm Products Marketing Agencies Act (1972) authorized 3 national marketing agencies — the Canadian Egg Marketing Agency (1972), the Canadian Turkey Marketing Agency (1973) and the Canadian Chicken Marketing Agency (1979) — to control supply nationally and to administer prices. Supply management had been implemented earlier in the dairy industry. Between 1970 and 1972, a market-sharing quota system was created that attempted to balance industrial milk and cream supplies with domestic demands; in conjunction with import controls (in place since 1951) and federal subsidies, it has significantly raised and stabilized dairy farmers' incomes. Longstanding policies include the research program, 50% of which is now the responsibility of the Department of AGRICULTURE.

Another policy, intended to stimulate regional development, of subsidizing the storage and transportation of feed grains from western Canada, originated in 1941. This policy changed considerably in 1973 and since 1976 has placed a ceiling price on feed grain for eastern Canadian buyers.

By the 1980s, although federal expenditures on agriculture were twice those of the provinces, several provinces were no longer willing to leave agricultural policy primarily to the federal government. There was also widespread commitment at both levels to increase farmers' bargaining power by direct intervention in the marketplace through production controls and administered pricing. In Dec 1981 a bill to establish Canagrex, a Canadian agricultural exporting agency, was introduced by the federal minister of agriculture, Eugene Whelan. A crown corporation, Canagrex is designed to help offset Canada's net trade deficit in nongrain agricultural products and to negotiate with the many countries that prefer state-trading associations to private traders. An 11-member board of directors, representative of government, the private sector and the agriculture industry, will manage Canagrex with its $12.3-million budget. As an element in the Agri-Food Strategy, Canagrex is meant both to help the private sector and marketing boards in the export of agricultural products and services and to buy agricultural commodities and services and sell them to foreign buyers.

Policy Formation and Implementation Despite shared federal and provincial jurisdictions over agriculture, federal legislation is paramount in the event of conflict. Authority over marketing is divided: the federal government regulates export and interprovincial marketing, while the provincial governments legislate marketing within their borders. Provincial agricultural and food policy is almost entirely the work of provincial departments of agriculture. However, while Agriculture Canada initiates most agricultural legislation and is primarily responsible for serving producers' interests, a number of federal departments and agencies make and affect agricultural and food policy. The minister of agriculture supervises several AGRICULTURAL AGENCIES that carry out agricultural policies, including the National Farm Products Marketing Council (an umbrella organization whose prime responsibility is to advise the minister), the CANADIAN LIVESTOCK FEED BOARD, the Canadian Dairy Commission, the Farm Credit Corporation and the Agricultural Stabilization Board. He shares with the minister of consumer and corporate affairs the task of representing consumer interests in food policy. The minister of transport supervises grain transportation by rail and water, as well as government grain elevators, and administers the Crow's Nest Pass rates. Another minister is in charge of the Canadian Wheat Board. The Dept of Industry, Trade and Commerce negotiates tariffs, promotes trade in foodstuffs and assists the food-processing and manufacturing industries.

Critique of Policy A major complaint since the early 1970s is that Canada does not have a food policy, only an agricultural policy preoccupied with producers' concerns. Consumers and others feel they have no say in food policy since they are not represented, for example, on the marketing boards which determine prices of dairy and poultry products. The Food Prices Review Board, established to monitor food prices between 1973 and 1975, recommended a long-term national food policy. In response, the federal government issued *A Food Strategy for Canada* (1977) and convened a National Food Policy Conference in the same year to which all interested groups were invited. However, these discussions failed to produce a consensus, and the criticism remains that Canada lacks a long-term national food policy, that agricultural policy is ad hoc and often contradictory, and that consumer food concerns are ignored.

The dairy- and poultry-marketing boards with supply-management powers are criticized as monopolistic agencies which have allowed farmers to be inefficient, have barred young farmers from entering the poultry and dairy industry by inflating quota values and thus raising the cost of farming operations, and have increased food costs to consumers. Interprovincial tensions have developed as provinces with growing populations seek to increase their share of the available market while provinces with stagnant or declining populations resist decreases in their share. The tendency to protect local consumer markets for local producers distresses the federal government, which advocates the geographical distribution of production on the basis of natural comparative advantage.

In western Canada the grain-handling and rail system and the grain freight rates are outstanding issues. Western provinces view federal expenditures to upgrade the rail and grain-handling system as insufficient. The provinces argue that the railways' desire to abandon branch lines will mean the death of small rural communities. Within the region there is a heated debate about the costs and benefits of the Crow's Nest freight rates. Finally, agricultural policy is criticized for its failure to help low-income farmers, its inattention to land-use planning and environmental considerations, and its ineffectiveness in restricting concentration in the food-processing and retail industries. Problems of rural poverty, income instability and market uncertainty, particularly in the beef and hog sectors, remain to be solved. Government failure to redress consumer and producer grievances has stimulated the formation of several pressure groups, including the Prairie Farm Commodity Coalition and the National Farmers Union; antagonism to supply management heightened the political role of the western Canadian cattle and grains commodity groups; and in the 1980s high interest rates led to the formation of the Canadian Farmers Survival Association. GRACE SKOGSTAD

Agriculture History Canadian agriculture has experienced a markedly distinct evolution in each region. A varied CLIMATE and geography have been largely responsible, but, in addition, each region has been settled at a different period in Canada's economic and political development, with a range of national and international forces being exerted. The principal unifying factor has been the role of government: from the colonial era to the present, agriculture has been largely state directed and subordinate to other interests.

Before 1000 BC, Indians of the lower Great Lakes and St Lawrence regions received horticulture from the S or W. IROQUOIS and related cultures practised slash-and-burn farming, but no group depended on agriculture totally for subsistence. The HURON planted 2 types of maize (Indian CORN), SQUASH and BEANS in row hills. The Indians practised seed selection and elementary principles of forcing but were not aware of the value of manuring. Long before the appearance of French traders, agricultural Indians traded maize for skins and meat obtained by woodland hunters. After the advent of the FUR TRADE, Algonquian middlemen traded maize with more distant bands for prime northern pelts, and traded furs, in turn, with the French. Indian agriculture was important in provisioning the fur trade until the late 18th century.

Maritimes Maritime agriculture dates from the establishment of PORT-ROYAL by the French in 1604. ACADIAN settlers diked marshland in the Annapolis basin and used it for growing wheat, flax, vegetables and pasturage. After the signing of the TREATY OF UTRECHT (1713), France withdrew to Plaisance, Nfld; Île Royale [Cape Breton I]; and Île St-Jean [PEI]. They intended that Île St-Jean would serve as a source of grain and livestock for their naval and fishing base on Cape Breton. Few Acadians moved from their homeland to Île St-Jean before the 1750s. By midcentury the predominantly fishing population in Île Royale was cultivating small clearings with wheat and vegetables, and possessed a variety of livestock.

After acquiring Acadia in 1713, Britain promoted Maritime agriculture in pursuit of objectives of defence and MERCANTILISM. Provisions were needed to support Nova Scotia's role as a strategic bulwark against the French. Britain also promoted agriculture to supply provisions for the West Indies trade, and hemp for its navy and merchant marine. Financial incentives were offered to Halifax settlers to clear and fence their land, but the lack of major markets kept the area in a state of self-sufficiency. The Acadians continued to supply produce to the French on Île Royale, an act which contributed to their expulsion by the British in 1755. Some Acadians were later asked, however, to instruct the British in marshland farming. The influx of LOYALIST settlers in the 1780s increased demand for marshland produce. Since the American states provided stiff competition in flour and grains, the Fundy marshlands were largely turned to pasture and hay for cattle production. On PEI the British government attempted to promote agricultural settlement by granting 66 lots of 8094 ha to private individuals.

Between 1783 and 1850 agriculture was dominant in PEI, but subordinate to the cod FISHERY and the trade with the West Indies in NS, and secondary to the TIMBER TRADE and shipbuilding in NB. With Loyalist immigration, the area of agricultural settlement in the Maritimes expanded from the marshlands to include the shores of rivers, especially the SAINT JOHN. Although the new areas were suited to cereal production, settlers tended to engage in mixed farming for cultural, agricultural and marketing reasons. Most full-time farmers concentrated on livestock raising, which required less manpower than did cereal growing. Before 1850 both NS and NB remained net importers of foodstuffs from the US. PEI alone achieved an agricultural surplus, exporting WHEAT to England as early as 1831.

Agricultural development in the early 19th century was limited by the skills post-Loyalist immigrants possessed. Most of these settlers were Highland SCOTS who were ill-prepared for clearing virgin forest, and the standard of agricultural practice was low. In 1818 John YOUNG, a Halifax merchant using the name "Agricola," began agitating for improved farming methods. As a result, agricultural societies were formed with a government-sponsored central organization in Halifax. Young's efforts had virtually no impact, however, since merchants were not involved in local farming. Hence there was little economic incentive for farmers to produce a surplus for sale. Nonetheless, agricultural lands and output grew gradually, and by mid-century the farming community was a political force, demanding transportation improvements and agricultural protection.

After 1850 Maritime agriculture was affected by 2 principal developments: the transition throughout the capitalist world from general to specialized agricultural production and, especially after 1896, the integration of the Maritime economy into the Canadian ECONOMY. The last 2 decades of the 19th century witnessed an increase in the production of factory cheese and creamery butter and a rapid increase in the export of APPLES, especially to Britain (*see* FRUIT AND VEGETABLE INDUSTRY). After 1896 the boom associated with Prairie settlement opened the Canadian market to fruit (especially apples) and POTATOES. By the 1920s the British market for NS apples was threatened by American, Australian and BC competition, notwithstanding improvements introduced by Nova Scotia producers to increase efficiency. The Canadian market for potatoes was supplemented by markets in

Cuba and the US. Although Cuba moved to self-sufficiency after 1928, PEI retained some of the market by providing seed stock.

Those sectors of Maritime agriculture dependent on local markets began to suffer in the 1920s. Difficulties in the forest industries contributed to the disappearance of markets, and the introduction of the internal combustion engine diminished the demand for horses and hay. Meat from other parts of Canada supplanted local production. In the 1930s the potato export market suffered as American and Cuban markets became less accessible. These factors, coupled with problems in the silver fox industry (*see* FUR FARMING), were catastrophic for PEI; its agricultural income dropped from $9.8 million in 1927 to $2.3 million in 1932. Only the apple export market remained stable, a result of British preferential tariff on apples from the empire. In response to various difficulties during the 1930s, many farmers turned to more diversified self-sufficient agriculture, a change reflected in increased dairy, poultry and egg production.

Newfoundland In Newfoundland agriculture was never more than marginally viable. Nonetheless, fishermen practised subsistence agriculture along the creeks and harbours of the East Coast, and commercial farming developed on the Avalon Peninsula and on parts of Bonavista, Notre Dame and Trinity bays. Newfoundland's agricultural history really began with the food shortages associated with the American Revolution, when 3100 ha were prepared for agriculture in the St John's, Harbour Grace and Carbonear areas. In the early 19th century a number of factors combined to give an impetus to agriculture: the arrival of Irish immigrants with agricultural skills, the growth of St John's as a market for vegetables, a road-building program, and an 1813 authorization allowing the governor to issue title to land for commercial use.

In the late 19th and early 20th centuries the government intensified its efforts to interest the people in agriculture. By 1900, 298 km^2 were under cultivation and there were some 120 000 horses, cattle and sheep in the colony. Through the Newfoundland Agricultural Board (formed 1907) the government established agricultural societies (91 in 1913) which provided assistance in such things as land clearing and the acquisition of seed and farm implements. In the 1920s the government imported purebred animals to improve the native stock. In the 1930s, in order to mitigate the hardship of the economic depression the government responded to the urgings of the Land Development association, a private group, by providing free seed potatoes, in an effort to promote "garden" cultivation. Upon joining Confederation in 1949, Newfoundland took advantage of federal government funding to establish agricultural measures such as a loan program, a land-clearing program, and the stimulation of egg and hog production. Since WWII, in keeping with the general Canadian trend, the number of Newfoundland farms has decreased while the average farm size has increased.

Québec In 1617 Louis HÉBERT began to raise cattle and clear a small plot for cultivation. Small-scale clearing ensued as settlers planted cereal grains, peas and Indian corn, but only 6 ha were under cultivation by 1625. Beginning in 1627 the French Crown granted fur monopolies to a succession of companies in exchange for commitments to establish settlers. The charter companies brought some settlers, who used oxen, asses and later horses to clear land, but agricultural self-sufficiency was realized only in the 1640s and marketing agricultural produce was always difficult during the French regime. In 1663 Louis XIV reasserted royal control and with his minister Colbert promoted settlement by families. Intendant Jean TALON reserved lots for agricultural experimentation and demonstration, introduced crops such as hops and hemp, raised several types of livestock and advised settlers on agricultural methods. By 1721 farmers in New France were producing 99 600 hL of wheat and smaller amounts of other crops annually, and owned about 30 000 cattle, swine, sheep and horses (*see* SEIGNEURIAL SYSTEM).

After 1763 and the arrival of British traders, new markets opened for Canadian farm produce within Britain's mercantile system. Francophone HABITANTS predominated in the raising of crops, but they were joined by anglophone settlers. British subjects purchased some seigneuries, which they settled with Scottish, Irish and American immigrants. New Englanders also settled the Eastern Townships and other areas. Anglo-Canadians promoted some new techniques of wheat and potato culture through the press and in 1792 formed an agricultural society at Québec. While the focus of the government's promotional activity was in Upper Canada [Ontario] and the Maritimes, Lower Canada [Québec] enjoyed a modest growth of wheat exports before 1800. Nevertheless, Lower Canadian wheat production lagged far behind that of Upper Canada in the first half of the 19th century. The failure of Lower Canadian agriculture has been blamed by some on the relative unsuitability of the region's climate and soils for growing wheat, the only crop with significant export potential; soil exhaustion; and the growth of the province's population at a faster rate than its agricultural production in this period. Because there was little surplus for reinvestment in capital stock, Lower Canada was slow to develop an inland road system, and transport costs remained relatively high.

By the 1830s Lower Canada had ceased to be self-sufficient in wheat and flour, and increasingly began importing from Upper Canada. The mid-century gross agricultural production of Canada East [Québec] totalled $21 million — only about 60% of Canada West's [Ontario's] production. Both modernizing and traditional farms contained more children than they could adequately support, and widespread poverty induced thousands of habitants to migrate to Québec's cities and to New England (*see* FRANCO-AMERICANS). As well, spurred by religious colonizers, settlement pushed N of Trois-Rivières, S of Lac Saint-Jean and S along the Chaudière R. However, little commercial agriculture was practised in these areas.

Later 19th-century Québec agriculture was marked by increases in cultivated area and productivity, and a shift from wheat production to dairying and stock raising. From the 1860s government agents worked to educate farmers to the commercial possibilities of dairying, and agronomists such as Edouard Barnard organized an agricultural press and instituted government inspection of dairy products. Commercial dairies, cheese factories and butteries developed around the towns and railways, most notably in the Montréal plain and the Eastern Townships. By 1900 dairying was the leading agricultural sector in Québec. It was becoming mechanized in field and factory and increasingly male-oriented as processing shifted from the farm to factories. By the end of the century 3.6 million kg of Québec cheese were being produced, an 80-fold increase since 1851.

By the 1920s, however, agriculture accounted for only one-third of Québec's total economic output. WWI had artificially stimulated production, and new mining, forestry and hydroelectric ventures opened up new markets; but they also contributed to and symbolized the shift from agricultural to industrial enterprises in the Québec economy. By the 1920s Québec soil was again becoming exhausted due to a lack of fertilizer which stemmed from a lack of credit. Farmers' political organizations, such as the Union catholique des cultivateurs (fd 1924), addressed the problem of lack of credit and other issues.

Like their counterparts elsewhere in Canada, Québec farmers suffered during the 1930s. In areas removed from urban markets there was a return to noncommercial agriculture, with a consequent increase in the number of farms. During the decade farm income decreased more drastically than did urban wages. WWII marked a return to widespread commercial agriculture, and postwar trends included a decrease in the number of farm units and in farm population, and an increase in the average size of farm holdings.

Ontario American independence in 1783 both created a potential security threat on British North America's southern border and cut off Britain's principal agricultural base in N America. The British channeled Loyalists into the lower Great Lakes region, where Gov SIMCOE suggested settling soldiers along the waterfront for defence, with other settlers filling in the land behind. The authorities initially promoted hemp culture as an export staple to stimulate British manufacturing and contribute to defence. However, scarcity of labour in relation to land inhibited its production. Between 1783 and 1815 settlement filled in along the lake shores and the St Lawrence, where some cereal grains and vegetables were grown, chiefly for subsistence.

Agriculture in what is now Ontario was dominated 1800-60 by wheat production. Wheat was the crop most easily grown and marketed and was an important source of cash for settlers. Apart from limited internal demand from such sources as British garrisons, canal construction crews and lumber camps, the principal markets were Britain and Lower Canada. Between 1817 and 1825 Upper Canadian farmers shipped an average of 57 800 hL to Montréal. Dependence on wheat culture was reflected in a boom-and-bust economy. The application of the CORN LAW restrictions in 1820 effectively shut BNA wheat out of British markets, causing a disastrous drop in wheat prices and land values. Prices and export volumes rallied in the 1820s, but the market collapsed in 1834-35. Crop failures in the late 1830s resulted in near starvation in many newly settled areas. Despite the American tariff, similar failures in the US created a temporary market for surplus Upper Canadian wheat. Meanwhile, transportation improvements facilitated shipments out of the region. As a result of these improvements, favourable climate conditions and growth in markets, wheat exports increased from 1 million hL in 1840 to 2.25 million in 1850.

After 1850 Canada West's agriculture became increasingly diversified. Repeal of the Corn Laws in 1846 promoted instability in wheat prices, but higher American prices after the discovery of California gold helped producers overcome trade barriers to livestock, wool, butter and coarse grains. Favourable trading conditions continued with the RECIPROCITY Treaty, 1854-66. Moreover, a price depression in 1857 and crop destruction by the midge in 1858 hastened the switch to livestock. In 1864 factory cheesemaking was introduced, and by 1900 Canadian cheddar cheese, largely from Ontario, had captured 60% of the English market. At the organizational level, both the Grange (after 1872) and the Patrons of Industry (after 1889) reflected a developing producer consciousness among Ontario farmers.

Technological developments assisted both the grain and livestock sectors in the 19th century. Field tillage was improved by the introduction of copies of American cast-iron ploughs after 1815. To control weeds biennial naked summer-fallow was generally practised between about 1830 and 1850, when crop rotation became prevalent. Government authorities also promoted the British technology of covered drains to reclaim extensive tracts of swampy or bottom land, averting the use of furrow and ditch drainage that impeded mechanization. The reaper diffused rapidly in the 1860s, permitting increased grain production. Widespread use of the cream separator by 1900 promoted butter production, while refrigeration was a catalyst to the beef and pork industry.

In the late 19th and early 20th centuries Urbanization expanded the demand for market gardening around cities and more specialized crops in different regions. These included orchard farming in Niagara Peninsula, Prince Edward and Elgin counties, and tobacco in Essex and Kent counties. Dairying developed on the fringes of cities and cash crop acreages declined in favour of feed grains and fodder, while beef producers were unable to meet the domestic demand. Throughout rural Ontario there were farm-initiated associations of stockbreeders, dairy people, grain growers, fruit growers, etc, as well as the government-initiated Farmers' Institutes and Women's Institutes. The associations reflected a faith in farm life in the face of rural depopulation and an industrializing society. Various farmer-initiated groups worked in the UNITED FARMERS OF ONTARIO movement which formed the provincial government in 1919 under E.C. DRURY.

During the 1920s Ontario farmers experienced a taste of prosperity as prices increased on various agricultural commodities. One result of this prosperity was a decline in the drift to the cities. By 1931, however, Ontario farm receipts had decreased 50% from 1926. Although Ontario escaped the drought conditions of the Prairies, farmers were unable to market much of their produce, and surplus meat, cheese, vegetable and apples were shipped west. The government responded to the crisis with regulation, with dairying the most important example. The Ontario Marketing Board was formed in 1931 with a 5-year plan instituted in 1932. In return for government loans, producers improved their herds and modernized their barns. By WWII Ontario agriculture was diversifed for an urban market, with both AGRICULTURAL MARKETING BOARDS and farmer-owned co-operatives playing important roles.

The Prairies In western BNA, Scottish settlers practised river-lot agriculture at RED RIVER COLONY after their arrival in 1812. While the survey system was French Canadian, agricultural practices followed the Scottish pattern. Land adjacent to the river was cultivated in strips in the manner of the Scottish "infield," with pasturage reserved for the "outfield" behind. The MÉTIS alternated agriculture with the seasonal activities of the BUFFALO HUNT and freighting. Red River came to assume a role in provisioning the fur trade alongside Indian and company agriculture.

Confederation was the spur to the agricultural development of the PRAIRIE WEST. In the mid-19th century central Canadian businessmen were seeking investment opportunities to complement central Canada's industrial development. The prospect of agricultural expansion in the western interior was very appealing. Canada proceeded to purchase the Hudson's Bay Company's RUPERT'S LAND (1870), repress Métis resistance (1870 and 1885), displace the Indian population, and survey the land for disposal to agricultural settlers (*see* DOMINION LANDS POLICY). Wheat quickly established its economic importance. However, continuing low world prices, culminating in a worldwide depression in the early 1890s, halted development until 1900. Western Canada's dry climate and short growing season were the most serious stumbling blocks. Genetic experimentation, leading to the development of Marquis wheat in 1907, in combination with the Dominion government's promotion of summer-fallowing to conserve soil moisture and control weeds, helped remove the technical barriers to continued agricultural expansion. Large-scale RANCHING on leased land began in what is now southern Alberta and Saskatchewan in the 1870s and 1880s. The area's dry climate was practically overcome by small-scale irrigation from the 1870s on and the introduction of a Dominion irrigation policy in 1894. Western agriculture received the necessary economic stimulus from an overall decline in transportation costs (*see* CROW'S NEST PASS AGREEMENT) and a relative rise in the price of wheat in the late 1890s.

Under Clifford SIFTON's great immigration schemes, the Dominion effectively completed the agricultural settlement of the Prairies. Mechanization of the wheat economy with steam, gas tractors, gang ploughs and threshing machines contributed to huge production surpluses. An unprecedented boom in wheat prices during WWI promoted cultivation of new lands. Price depressions in 1913 and after WWI precipitated many bankruptcies by overcapitalized farmers. Nevertheless, between 1901 and 1931 the amount of land under field crop on the Prairies jumped from 1.5 to 16.4 million ha.

The collapse of wheat prices after WWI had serious consequences for Prairie farmers. Many operators who had purchased implements and more land at high prices during the war defaulted and lost their farms. Throughout the 1920s and 1930s operators of farms on poorer soils consistently lost money, as did farmers in the dry belt of SW Saskatchewan and SE Alberta. Drought, grasshoppers and crop disease further worsened conditions for farmers in the 1930s; the government responded with the PRAIRIE FARM REHABILITATION ADMINISTRATION. Technological advances such as the development of the combine harvester resulted in both more efficient agriculture and the forcing off the land of farmers lacking sufficient capital to purchase the new technology. The mechanization process in Prairie agriculture as a whole was essentially halted during the 1930s, to be dramatically resumed after WWII.

From the early settlement era western farmers depended on central Canadian business to provide their production inputs and to finance, purchase and transport their grain. In order to gain some control over the economic forces which controlled them, organizations were formed to advance their interests. Early agrarian movements in Manitoba and the North-West Territories espoused the virtues of co-operation and criticized Dominion tariff policy, freight rates and federal disallowance of railway charters to the CPR's rivals. After forcing the government in 1899 to ensure better service from the railways, farmers formed GRAIN GROWERS' ASSOCIATIONS in the Territories in 1901-02 and in Manitoba in 1903. These organizations carried on educational work among farmers, promoted provincial ownership of inland elevators and, ultimately, campaigned for the co-operative marketing of grain. This latter objective was achieved in 1906 with the formation of the Grain Growers' Grain Co (now the United Grain Growers).

The Grain Growers' Grain Co is representative of the first phase of Prairie co-operative grain marketing. In the context of heightened farmer and worker consciousness after WWI it came under criticism for having become too business-oriented. A radical wing developed in the Prairie farm movement, led by H.W. Wood of the UNITED FARMERS OF ALBERTA. In 1923-24 farmers organized compulsory pools — a new form of co-operative marketing — in the 3 Prairie provinces (eg, *see* SASKATCHEWAN WHEAT POOL). Pools were successful throughout the 1920s, but collapsed after the Depression struck in 1929. Although the federal government moved to save the pools and stabilize the wheat market, it did so by appointing a manager from the private grain trade. Thus the original co-operative design of the pools was undermined. As a further attempt to stabilize the market the government in 1935 introduced the CANADIAN WHEAT BOARD, which farmers had been demanding since their wheat board experience of 1919-20. Again, however, this board was dominated by the private grain trade and reflected its interests as much as those of farmers. In 1943 the wheat board was made compulsory for the marketing of western wheat, and in 1949 the board's authority was extended to western barley and oats.

The agrarian movement in western Canada was more than an economic phenomenon. People in the pools, the grain growers' associations and farm political parties intervened and were influential in Prairie culture, society and politics, as well as in economics. Farm-movement women, for example, were active in the TEMPERANCE crusade, the WOMEN'S SUFFRAGE movement, child welfare and rural education, as well as in the economic and political struggles they shared with farm men. Political protest movements which developed in the 1920s around the pooling crusade, such as the Farmers' Union of Canada, eventually entered the CO-OPERATIVE COMMONWEALTH FEDERATION as an important component of the Canadian socialist tradition.

British Columbia Agriculture in British Columbia was first developed to provision the fur trade. In 1811 Daniel Harmon of the North West Co started a garden at Stuart Lake, and later HBC factors planted small gardens on Vancouver I, at Ft St James, Ft Fraser and Ft George. The HBC also helped establish the Puget's Sound Agricultural Co to assist in provisioning. Commercial demand for agricultural products was spurred by GOLD RUSHES after 1858. However, while ranching was established in the interior along the Thompson and Nicola valleys and some farming settlement occurred, newcomers were more attracted to the lure of gold than to agricultural opportunities. Production lagged far behind demand.

Railway production camps in the early 1880s provided a domestic market for agricultural products, but the establishment of Canadian rail linkages destroyed the early wheat industry, which could not compete with Prairie wheat, either in quality or in price. In the 1890s the establishment of the Boundary and Kootenay mining industries created new markets. Lumbering and fish-packing industries also stimulated agriculture although producers dependent on local industry suffered when lumber camps moved on or mines or canneries closed. Large-scale farming continued in districts such as the Cariboo and Similkameen, while smaller-scale specialized agriculture developed in the Okanagan and Fraser valleys. By the 1880s the Okanagan Valley had developed a specialized fruit industry while market gardening and dairying flourished in the lower Fraser Valley as urban markets increased.

The British Columbia Fruit-Growers' Assn, fd 1889, was the first formal organization of producers in the province. Its objectives were to investigate potential markets on the Prairies and methods of controlling fruit marketing. In 1913 economic difficulties obliged Okanagan fruit growers to set up a co-operative marketing and distribution agency, financed largely by the provincial government. The agency helped eliminate eastern Canadian and American competition on the Prairies. The depression of 1921-1922, however, signalled the beginning of an 18-year search for more permanent stability. A 1923 plan called on fruit growers to agree to sell for a 5-year period through a central agency. Only 80% of producers supported the plan and competition among shippers kept prices low. Various government and private schemes were tried without success between 1927 and 1937. In 1938 the provincial government established the Tree Fruit Board to be the sole agency for apple marketing. The following year producers set up Tree Fruits Ltd as a producer-owned central selling agency. In 1939-40 farmers' co-operatives in BC (of which Tree Fruits Ltd was the most important) did a combined business of nearly $11 million. Although there were some difficulties for BC agriculture in WWII, with the export market being cut, a combination of government assistance and improved purchasing power on the Prairies contributed to the creation of a seller's market by 1944.

The North Agriculture N of 60°N lat began with European contact, since the region was beyond the range of native cultivation techniques. Following Peter POND's 1778 experiment in gardening near Lake Athabasca, the HBC established crops and livestock along the Mackenzie R at Ft Simpson, Ft Norman and Ft Good Hope, and at Ft Selkirk at the junction of the Pelly and Yukon rivers. Missionaries developed livestock, gardens and crops at a number of missions in the late 19th and early 20th centuries. During the KLONDIKE GOLD RUSH, some miners grew their own vegetables in the relatively fertile Dawson City soil, but most supplies were imported. The pattern that emerged from the gold rush period and came to characterize northern agriculture in the 20th century was one of small market gardens and part-time farming, subordinate to mining. In the Yukon, ranches developed on the Pelly River and along the Whitehorse-Dawson trail. The mining area around Mayo provided a demand for market gardening. In Mackenzie District the significant agricultural activity was undertaken by Oblate missionaries at Ft Smith, Ft Resolution and Ft Providence. During the 20th century the federal government studied the agricultural potential of the North through co-operative experimental work with selected farmers (such as the Oblate missionaries) and, after WWII, in their own substations. The consensus which developed was that agriculture was not commercially viable. Transportation improvements allowed southern produce to undercut potential northern production and climate has been a continuing impediment. LYLE DICK AND JEFF TAYLOR

Reading: D.H. Akenson, ed, *Canadian Papers in Rural History*, 3 vols (1978-82); C. Chatillon, *L'Histoire de l'agriculture au Québec* (1976); V.C. Fowke, *Canadian Agricultural Policy* (1946) and *The National Policy and the Wheat Economy* (1957); R.L. Jones, *History of Agriculture in Ontario, 1613-1880* (1946); J. McCallum, *Unequal Beginnings* (1980); I. MacPherson, *Each for All* (1979); G.E. Reamon, *A History of Agriculture in Ontario*, vol 1 (1970); N. Séguin, *Agriculture et colonisation au Québec* (1980); L.A. Wood, *A History of Farmers' Movements in Canada* (1924; reproduced with new materials, 1975).

Ahearn, Thomas, electrical engineer, businessman (b at Ottawa 24 June 1855; d there 28 June 1938). A telegraph operator at 14, by 25 Ahearn was Ottawa branch manager of the telegraph and telephone companies. In 1882, with W.Y. Soper, he started an electrical contracting business that grew into a network of companies controlling electricity supply, streetcars and streetlights in Ottawa. Ahearn reputedly invented the electric cooking range, installed in the Windsor Hotel. In 1899 drove the first automobile (electric) in Ottawa. Rich by 1900, Ahearn became a director of the Bank of Canada and other leading institutions and a prominent local philanthropist. Chairman of the Ottawa Improvement Commission (later the NATIONAL CAPITAL COMMISSION) from 1926 to 1932, he established Ottawa's parkway system and personally financed the Champlain Bridge over the Ottawa R in 1928. That same year he was appointed to the Privy Council. DONALD J.C. PHILLIPSON

Ahenakew, Edward, Anglican clergyman (b at Sandy Lake IR, Sask; buried there July 1961). A gifted speaker and writer in Cree or English, Ahenakew stirred his people to a sense of their worth as Indians. Through almost 50 years he travelled from one reserve to another in the Saskatchewan diocese and to church synods across Canada. He collaborated in the publication of a Cree-English dictionary and edited a monthly newsletter in Cree syllabics. During the 1920s he was active in efforts to form a national league of Indians. His "Cree Trickster Tales" appeared in *American Folklore* in 1925. After his death, other articles from his unfinished manuscripts were edited for *Saskatchewan History* and *The Beaver;* and in 1974 *Voices of the Plains Cree*, a collection of his writings, was published. He died en route to Dauphin, Man, to help in a summer school for Indian lay readers. RUTH M. BUCK

Aid to (or of) the Civil Power, the calling out of military troops by the civil authorities to help maintain or restore public order. ACP is not to be confused with martial law (military takeover of government), the WAR MEASURES (restrictions of civil liberties imposed by Parliament in times of emergency), military assistance to civil authorities in case of disasters, or assistance to ROYAL CANADIAN MOUNTED POLICE, penitentiaries, customs, etc. It is now considered part of Internal Security Operations, a broader term which comprises RCMP surveillance of enemy agents on Canadian soil and related activity.

In England, a 1360 statute authorized justices of the peace to restrain, arrest and imprison rioters. The first modern Riot Act was proclaimed in 1714. Until 1829, parish constables were responsible for maintaining public order, but they were so few and so poorly trained that army troops had to be called out to repress serious riots. The London Metropolitan Police was created in 1829 to help prevent, rather than repress, public disorders, and in 1856 the Police Act was passed, with specific military functions distinguished from those of the police and magistrates.

Following the acquisition of ACADIA in 1713 and Canada in 1760, the British Army garrison troops in BNA replied to requests for ACP in accordance with their military regulations. In 1868 Canadian laws concerning the police, illegal assembly and riots were enacted, and the MILITIA ACT authorized calling out Canadian troops in ACP. British practice generally remained the model. Regulations and Orders for the Canadian Militia replaced the British ones in 1870. In 1924 the power of calling out troops was moved from local authorities to provincial attorneys general.

From 1796 to 1870 British troops, occasionally helped by local militiamen, provided ACP roughly 100 times. Since then Canadian troops have helped maintain or restore public order 140 times and have helped repress penitentiary riots 20 times. Half the former occurred before 1900, usually because of absence, shortage or improper training of police. Since 1933, troops have not been involved in strikebreaking except under the War Measures Act, and all callouts except one have taken place in Ontario and Québec, which are the only provinces not policed by the RCMP. Over half the penitentiary callouts have occurred since 1962, and in most cases the army did not have to use force. Recent research has helped to prove that Canadian history has witnessed violence; at the same time, military interventions have not usually resulted in the use of undue force. *See* ARMED FORCES (MILITIA). JEAN PARISEAU

Aide-Créquy, Jean-Antoine, priest, painter (b at Québec City 5 Apr 1749; d there 6 Dec 1780). The first Canadian-born painter, he was the son of a master mason. He was ordained in 1773 and became parish priest at Baie St-Paul. In June 1780, because of delicate health, he went to Québec's Hôtel-Dieu hospital, where he died several months later. His artistic training is unknown, but he learned by studying the work of Frère LUC in local churches and the European works found in the seminary and religious communities of Québec City. His paintings showed these influences, yet bore his own personal stamp. Most of his paintings were for churches, including those at L'Islet, St-Roch-des-Aulnaies, St-Joachim and Île-aux-Coudres (today in the bishopric of Chicoutimi). Aide-Créquy followed the French tradition already established in Canada and his works are representative of the era following 1763. RÉAL LUSSIER

Aikins, William Thomas, surgeon, educator (b at Toronto Township, Upper Canada 4 June 1827; d at Toronto 25 May 1897). The son of Protestant Irish immigrants, he studied at John ROLPH's Toronto School of Medicine and Jefferson Medical Coll, Philadelphia. Graduating in 1850, he became anatomy instructor in Rolph's school. In 1856 the staff wrested control of the school from the overbearing Rolph; Aikins, then professor of surgery, became president, remaining so until 1887 when, through his efforts, the TSM became the U of T medical faculty. Aikins served as dean until 1893. A superb surgeon and early exponent of Lister's antiseptic methods, he was an inspiring teacher and able administrator under whose direction the TSM and university's medical school acquired national reputations. Moreover, as a leading member of the Council of the Ontario Coll of Physicians and Surgeons (1866-), he helped raise provincial standards for medical education. DAVID R. KEANE

Ailleboust de Coulonge et d'Argentenay, Louis d', governor of New France 1648 to 51 (b at Ancy-le-Franc, France 1612?; d at Montréal May 1660). He was a nobleman and military engineer who sailed in 1643 to play a leading role in the newly established Catholic outpost of Ville-Marie [Montréal]. Named governor of all Canada in 1648, he was powerless to prevent the dominant Iroquois from annihilating all but a few of his Huron allies. After 1651, d'Ailleboust remained in New France, serving as acting governor 1657-58. ALLAN GREER

Air Canada, a commercial airline based in Montréal, created in 1937 as TRANS-CANADA AIRLINES. In 1965 the name Air Canada was adopted and today the company offers regular passenger, mail and commodity service to centres in Canada, the US, Europe, Bermuda and the W Indies, with charter passenger and cargo services also available. In 1979 Air Canada acquired just under 86.5% of outstanding Nordair shares. Plans call for the restoration of Nordair to the private sector and Air Canada is looking at possibilities for such a transfer. Wholly owned subsidiaries of Air Canada are Touram Inc, specializing in package tours and other travel-related services, and Airline Maintenance Buildings Ltd. It also owns 30% of Innotech Aviation, involved in the general aviation field. In 1983 Air Canada had sales or operating revenue of $2.3 billion (ranking 35th in Canada), assets of $2.1 billion (ranking 39th), and 21 584 employees. The Canadian government owns 100% of the company. DEBORAH C. SAWYER

Air Law and Space Law are separate and distinct branches of LAW, although they are occasionally treated as one ("Aerospace Law"). Air law, the older of the 2, is the body of public and private law, both national and international, that regulates aeronautical activities and other uses of airspace. Space law, on the other hand, regulates activities of states in outer space, primarily the use of satellites. The essential difference between air law and space law stems from the legal status of airspace and of outer space. Whereas airspace, except over the high seas and Antarctica, is under the sovereignty of subjacent states, outer space is governed by the regime of freedom. The question of boundaries between outer space and airspace is awaiting international agreement; it is virtually certain, however, that the boundary will not be placed higher than 100 km above sea level.

Space Law The origin of space law can be traced to the launching on 24 Oct 1957 of Sputnik I, the first artificial Earth satellite. Since that time the legal regulation of outer-space activities has been largely centered in the UN Committee on the Peaceful Uses of Outer Space. In contrast to air law, the bulk of space law consists of norms incorporated in international treaties. The most important is the 1967 Treaty on Principles Governing the Activities of States in the Exploration and Use of Outer Space, including the Moon and Other Celestial Bodies (also known as the Outer Space Treaty). The major principles of the treaty are freedom of access to, and use of, outer space; prohibition against national claims to sovereignty in any part of outer space; and a ban on the placing of weapons of mass destruction anywhere in outer space.

Air Law In Canada legal regulation of air navigation is the exclusive competence of Parliament. The major, relevant legislation includes the Aeronautics Act (the cornerstone of the Canadian civil aviation regulatory system); the National Transportation Act (setting up the Canadian Transport Commission as the principal organ for the economic regulation of air transport); the Carriage by Air Act (governing the liability of air carriers relating to international carriage by air); and the Air Canada Act (establishing a crown corporation to operate air transport services).

Because much air navigation takes place internationally, many legal norms governing the technical aspects of air navigation have been developed internationally and are implemented by national legislation. The International Civil Aviation Organization (ICAO), headquartered in Montréal, was established pursuant to the Convention on International Civil Aviation (Chicago, Ill, 1944). ICAO has a membership of 152 states. The exchange of commercial rights in international air transport is regulated mainly by hundreds of bilateral agreements, along with the multilateral International Air Services Transit Agreement of 1944 and certain provisions of the Chicago Convention.

The Warsaw Convention of 1929, amended by the Hague Protocol of 1955, is widely accepted and governs the liability of air carriers with respect to the international carriage by air of passengers, baggage and cargo. Canada is a party to the amended convention and has implemented it through the Carriage by Air Act. The rules of Canadian domestic law govern air carriers' liability relating to carriage by air in Canada not covered by the Carriage by Air Act and claims for damage to third parties caused, for example, through aerial collisions, excessive noise, and aerial spraying.

Another important aspect of air law is concerned with offences and certain other acts committed on board aircraft (the Tokyo Convention of 1963), the suppression of unlawful seizure of aircraft (the Hague Convention of 1970) and the suppression of unlawful acts against the safety of civil aviation (the Montréal Convention of 1971). Each of these conventions has been accepted by many states, including Canada.

Air Pollution Air pollutants are substances that, when present in the atmosphere in sufficient quantities, may adversely affect people, animals, vegetation or inanimate materials. The sources of air pollution include industry, vehicles, domestic activities (eg, heating, cooking), agriculture (slash burning, blowing dust, farm odours) and natural events (forest fires, VOLCANOES, dust storms, salt from sea spray, pollen). Water vapour released from combustion of natural gas may cause ice FOG in winter in such northern cities as Edmonton, and thus might be considered a pollutant in those circumstances. Air pollutants occur in minute quantities, mostly measured in parts per million or parts per trillion parts of air. Some chemicals causing highly objectionable odours occur at such low concentrations that they cannot be measured.

Types of Pollutants

Pollutants include total suspended particulate matter (TSP), sulphur dioxide (SO_2), oxides of nitrogen (NO_2 and NO), ozone (O_3), carbon monoxide (CO), hydrogen sulphide (H_2S), hydrogen fluoride (HFl) and LEAD (Pb). Many of these result from the burning of fossil fuels (eg, coal, oil, gasoline). There are also a few highly toxic pollutants such as PESTICIDES, MERCURY and PCBs (polychlorinated biphenyls). Occupational and indoor pollutants include factory dust and cigarette smoke. Other pollutants of concern are the sulphate and nitrate fractions of TSP (*see* ACID RAIN), carbon dioxide, chlorofluoromethanes and ionizing radiation.

Air Pollution Pathways

The initial behaviour of a pollutant depends on the nature of its source, which may be a chimney releasing gases at high temperature and exit velocity, or the tail pipe of a moving vehicle. Subsequently, the pollutant moves with the WIND and is diluted by wind eddies. In some cases, chemical transformations into new forms of pollutants may take place, eg, SO_2 may change to sulphates. Pollution is often carried long distances by the wind but is finally removed by wet and dry deposition. Scientists have predicted that, if all man-made pollution sources were turned off suddenly, the atmosphere would return to a pristine state within a few days. Despite the atmosphere's seemingly limitless capacity to accept and dilute the waste products of society, meteorological conditions occasionally lead to serious air-pollution episodes. For ground-level sources, these episodes are associated with light winds and temperature inversions (ie, temperature increasing with height, a condition reducing wind gusts and pollutant dilution rates), which result in smog. For emissions from tall chimneys, pollution episodes are associated with strong, steady winds and also with fumigations (inversions aloft and vigorous mixing near the ground caused by surface heating). The most serious recorded air-pollution episode in Canada is the "Grey Cup smog" of Nov 1962, which lasted 5 days. It caused increased hospital admissions throughout southern Ontario and postponement of the football game in Toronto because of poor visibility.

Effects of Air Pollutants

Adverse effects to human and animal health include respiratory ailments (silicosis, pneumonia, asthma, emphysema, bronchitis and hay fever) caused by particles (SO_2, NO_2, O_3, pollens); carboxylhemoglobin, a condition that interferes with the ability of hemoglobin to combine with oxygen, resulting from carbon monoxide uptake by the bloodstream; eye watering and skin irritation caused by ozone; damage to internal organs from lead, mercury, pesticides, etc. It is suspected that lung CANCER and other chronic diseases may be caused or exacerbated by air pollution. Direct damage to vegetation includes necrosis (tissue death), chlorosis (whitening of leaves) and premature aging; indirect damage may result from soil acidification by acid rain. Metal corrosion, caused mainly by SO_2 and sea spray, takes the form of increased rust and metal fatigue. Damage to fabrics, paint and rubber, caused mainly by NO_2, O_3 and H_2S, results in shortened life span, discoloration, cracking and peeling. Soiling of materials, caused by soot, necessitates increased washing, dry cleaning and painting. Climatic effects of pollution can be regional and immediate (eg, ice fogs in Edmonton, large-scale regional hazes) or global and long-term. The main trace substances involved are water vapour, sulphate particles, CO_2, TSP and chlorofluoromethanes.

Air-Resource Management and Pollution Control

Strategies used to control air pollution are varied. Emissions can be reduced by means of burning less or cleaner fuel (eg, gas instead of coal), more efficient burning of fuel (ie, at higher temperatures or with oxygen added) and installation of pollution-control devices. The use of tall chimneys, such as the "superstack" erected by Inco Ltd at Sudbury, Ont, may solve local problems but tends to enlarge the affected area. Meteorological episode control involves reduction of emissions (eg, switching to low-sulphur fuels) when atmospheric dispersal is poor. Other strategies include regional land-use planning, development of pollutant-resistant strains of vegetation, and development of paint, metals, etc, with increased life expectancies in polluted environments. Emission control is of primary importance, but some sources may be technologically or economically difficult to manage. Most air-resource programs, therefore, use a combination of strategies.

Most Canadian provinces and the federal government have Clean Air Acts that specify emission standards (maximum permissible rates of release of designated pollutants from particular types of sources) and ambient air-quality standards (maximum permissible concentrations of designated pollutants in the outdoor environment). Under the Canadian Constitution, health is a provincial responsibility, with air-pollution control undertaken largely by the provinces. However, the federal government has jurisdiction over pollution from trains and ships, regulates lead content of gasoline, and can intervene when air pollution crosses the US-Canada border. The Atomic Energy Control Board regulates ionizing radiation. The federal government also plays an important co-ordinating role, through federal-provincial committees and task forces, in setting standards, and monitoring criteria, research and engineering programs. Indoor pollutants are regulated mostly by industrial hygiene authorities. Some cities broadcast smog alerts and pollution indices. *See* ENVIRONMENTAL LAW; POLLUTION. R.E. MUNN

Reading: D.V. Bates, *A Citizen's Guide to Air Pollution* (1973); A.F. Friedlaender, ed, *Approaches to Controlling Air Pollution* (1978).

Aird, Sir John, banker (b at Longueuil, Canada E 15 Nov 1855; d at Toronto 30 Nov 1938). Aird, the president of the Canadian Bank of Commerce, is best known for his role as chairman of the Royal Commission on Radio Broadcasting that reported in 1929. He joined the bank in 1878 and rose to become president in 1924. Mackenzie KING's government put him at the head of the broadcasting royal commission in 1928, and Aird's report recommended that a public body regulate private broadcasters and air its own programs. The Canadian Radio Broadcasting Commission, the forerunner of the CBC, came into existence in 1932 as a result. J.L. GRANATSTEIN

Airport, an aerodrome that has received a licence from the federal Dept of Transport to handle commercial air traffic. There are more than 3200 aerodromes in Canada (1983), of which approximately 1210 are licensed as airports by Transport Canada. Each aerodrome is an installation on land or water, where aircraft can take

erial view of Terminal 2 at Toronto-Lester B. Pearson ternational Airport, Canada's most active airport. It andles over 14 million passengers a year (*courtesy National Film Board/Photothèque*).

'f or land, and has facilities available for hanling passengers and cargo.

Development of Airports Before WWII, airorts, aerodromes and emergency fields were esblished across Canada, mainly to follow the oute patterns of existing railroad systems as ell as to accommodate new developments in olated areas. After the war, a number of milary aerodromes built in support of Canada's ar effort and municipal airports taken over uring the war were either handed back to local overnments or taken over by the federal Dept f Transport (now called Transport Canada).

With the advent of jet aircraft in the 1950s, the eed, range and capacity of transport aircraft ore than doubled. Airport facilities rapidly beme overburdened and requirements for the xpansion and modification of airport facilities nd systems became increasingly difficult to ccommodate through the 1960s and 1970s. uring this period, some local governments ould not meet the demand or the considerable x burden generated by growth needs, and deite federal-government funding efforts (and some cases provincial support) some munipal airports reverted to federal ownership. thers continued to maintain operation but ith substantial subsidization.

Together with the growth of passenger and rgo volumes there was increased activity and chnological change in the field of general AVITION, which includes private flying for purposes of recreation, instruction and business. hese activities have been accommodated at priate, provincial, municipal, Transport Canada nd, to a small extent, military airports. Most of e 20 000 aircraft registered in Canada and the ajority of the more than 50 000 licensed pilots re associated with general aviation.

Major Airports in Canada Nineteen of the ajor airports account for over 82% of all schedled traffic, which includes 100% of internaonal travel and over 90% of all interprovincial avel. Eight of these airports are designated as ternational under agreements reached with ember nations of the International Civil Aviion Organization (ICAO), and are located at ancouver, Calgary, Edmonton, Winnipeg, Tonto, Montréal (Mirabel), Halifax and Gander. oronto International Airport (now Torontoester B. Pearson International Airport) is the most active, handling over 14½ million passengers in 1981.

Self-Supporting Airports There are 23 major airports owned and operated by Transport Canada that are called self-supporting or revolving-fund airports. The fund refers to an accounting mechanism first introduced in the fiscal year 1969-70 at Toronto and Montréal. A revised Airports Revolving Fund was introduced on 1 April 1979, and the 23 airports are managed financially through this mechanism. The 23 airports are meant to be jointly self-supporting, with cross-subsidization an integral feature of the fund.

Traffic Control The Air Traffic Services Branch of the Canadian Air Transportation Administration (CATA) provides a complete range of traffic control for aircraft operating under Instrument Flight Rules (IFR) and Visual Flight Rules (VFR). The branch staffs all control towers at Transport Canada airports and some municipal airports, as well as area control centres that handle en-route and overflight traffic. These responsibilities are part of the provisions of an air-traffic control system in the international air space for which Canada has accepted responsibility through ICAO.

Security Legislation and standards concerning security are developed and enforced by the regulatory services within CATA. The Airports Services and Security Branch is responsible for establishing levels of service provided, for applications from airport users, and for the interrelated policing and emergency services at the airports. The X-ray and electronic-gate inspection of luggage and passengers is obligatory, as it is for all nations belonging to ICAO. Various precautionary measures have been established at all major airports to deal with the threat of aircraft hijacking or terrorist attacks.

Terminal Buildings and Design Every airport comprises a relatively large industrial complex and, in proportion to other industries in the city or area it serves, is usually one of the largest facilities in the locale. As an example, the total number of employees (including airlines staff, concessionaires, cargo handlers, Transport Canada staff, etc) at Dorval Airport exceeded 14 000 in the early 1980s. The terminal building, with adjacent car parks, access roads and aircraft parking and loading facilities, contains a wide variety of conveniences for travellers and employees. Accommodations for airlines, air traffic, weather and communications services, customs, immigration, health, security and various administrative activities are also provided within the terminal buildings at most major airports.

Growing demand for further expansion of airport facilities has aroused controversy because of the high costs, questions of efficiency and convenience, and environmental concerns. Public opposition prevented the building of a second major airport in Toronto. Both Mirabel and Calgary International airports have been criticized for their high costs and rental fees. The need to operate airports efficiently as well as to keep costs down has led Transport Canada to research new functional designs without frills.

See AIRPORT ARCHITECTURE. H. BRIG YOUNG

Airport Architecture The Aeronautics Act of 1919 made provision for the construction of airports (or "air harbours"), but for many years airplanes used landing fields equipped with few facilities. In 1927 the federal government provided incentives for private flying clubs to develop airports with hangars and workshops. Winnipeg's Stevenson Field, for example, which opened in 1928, had been the aerodrome of the Winnipeg Flying Club. The principal building was a simple rectangular structure; within a few years it was replaced by a larger wide-span hangar with a low-arched roof and a shed to the side for the waiting room and offices, the typical airport design of the early 1930s.

A new wave of construction was inspired by the formation of the Dept of Transport in 1936 and the inauguration of Trans-Canada Air Lines (now AIR CANADA) in 1937. Calgary's McCall Field, built by the city in 1938, and Dorval Airport near Montréal (1940) represented the new breed of airports. The passenger terminal, now separate from the hangar, featured a ticket lobby and general waiting area, not unlike the familiar arrangement of a RAILWAY STATION.

The Department of Transport introduced the severe international style in its airports of the 1950s. Two of the most distinguished were Ottawa International Airport (architect W.A. Ramsay, 1955-60), with passenger handling areas located to either side of a central waiting area and a control tower above, and the larger Winnipeg International Airport (Green, Blankstein and Russell, with W.A. Ramsay, 1960). The new Dorval Airport (Illsley, Templeton, Archibald, and Larose and Larose, 1960) had, in addition to "fingers" against which the airplanes docked, a remote quay linked to the main terminal by an underground moving sidewalk.

After 1960 there were several experiments in improving passenger convenience. Lester B. Pearson (Toronto) International Airport's Terminal 1 (John B. Parkin Associates, with W.A. Ramsay, 1962) is circular in plan to provide the maximum perimeter space for aircraft while offering a short walk for passengers; a large parking garage is situated over the Aeroquay, and the administration building and control tower (both John B. Parkin Associates, with W.A. Ramsay, 1962) are separate structures. Mirabel Airport, near Montréal (Papineau, Gèrin-Lajoie, LeBlanc, Edwards, 1975) is shallow in plan so that passengers need walk only a short distance to the departure gate, whence they board wheeled passenger vehicles that transport them to the airplanes. Calgary International Airport (Stevenson, Raines, Barret, Hutton, Seton and Partners, 1977) has a more conventional plan with a 3-storey central terminal area leading to fingers at either side. The new terminals incorporate security barriers, remote lounges and loading bridges, features which have been added to many earlier airports and have obscured the clarity of their design.

In the 1970s Canada exported airport design; a number of Canadian firms designed facilities abroad, including the airports at Kabul, Afghanistan, and the island of Saint Kitts.

HAROLD D. KALMAN

Aitken, Robert Morris, flutist, composer (b at Kentville, NS 28 Aug 1939). After several orchestral appointments — most remarkably with the Vancouver Symphony Orchestra where, at age 19, he was its youngest-ever principal flute — Aitken left orchestral work in 1971 to concentrate on solo performance and chamber music. He appeared frequently with harpsichordist Greta Kraus and with the Lyric Arts Trio, which he founded in 1964. Widely sought after as a soloist by orchestras in N America, Europe and Asia, he has often given premiere performances of contemporary Canadian works. To his own compositions Aitken brings the virtuoso performer's delight in sound, experimenting adventurously with instrumental timbre, electroacoustical colour and oriental techniques to produce music of high originality. Several of his compositions have been recorded.

BARCLAY MCMILLAN

Aitken, William Maxwell, 1st Baron Beaverbrook, financier, politician, author, publisher (b at Maple, Ont 25 May 1879; d at Cherkley, Mickleham, Eng 9 June 1964). The son of a Presbyterian minister, Beaverbrook later claimed that his religion lay at the root of his worldly success. In 1880 his family moved to Newcastle, NB. A clever if mischievous boy, "Max" displayed a passion for moneymaking. He dabbled in journalism and sold insurance before becoming a clerk in a Chatham, NB, law office. There he began his lifelong friendships with R.B. BENNETT and James DUNN. In 1897 he abandoned law school to follow them to Edmonton, where he operated a bowling alley before returning to the Maritimes. In 1900 he began selling bonds, particularly those of expanding industries and Canadian-based utilities. He established the Royal Securities Corp in 1903 and within 5 years was a millionaire. He moved to Montréal and concentrated on promoting new companies and merging old ones, his most notable creations being Stelco and Canada Cement.

In 1910 he moved to London, Eng, where he pursued his business interests and entered politics. Guided by Andrew Bonar LAW, Aitken won a seat for the Conservatives in the second general election of 1910. He championed tariffs and imperial unity and was knighted in 1911. During WWI he represented the Canadian government at the front and wrote *Canada in Flanders*. His aptitude for political tactics was revealed by his part in Lloyd George's accession as PM. In 1917 he was made a peer, taking the title Beaverbrook after a stream near his Canadian home. He became minister of information in 1918.

Max Aitken (Lord Beaverbrook). He began selling bonds in 1900 and was a millionaire before he was 30. In 1910 he moved to England, where he became involved in politics and the newspaper business. During WWII he was minister of aircraft production in Churchill's wartime government (*courtesy Public Archives of Canada/PA-6467*).

After the war, Beaverbrook left politics and established a chain of British newspapers. He bought the *Daily Express* and the *Evening Standard* and created the *Sunday Express*. He also wrote books on his wartime experiences. In 1929 he spearheaded the Empire Free Trade movement, though the idea found little support in the protectionist climate of the 1930s.

As minister of aircraft production in Churchill's wartime government, Beaverbrook galvanized the aircraft industry. Other wartime appointments followed, but despite his bullish determination Beaverbrook lacked the temperament for lasting political success and left politics in 1945. After the war, he supervised his newspapers and wrote political memoirs and biographies of his influential friends.

DUNCAN MCDOWALL

Reading: A.J.P. Taylor, *Beaverbrook* (1972).

Aklavik, NWT, Hamlet, pop 721 (1981c), is located near the mouth of the MACKENZIE R, 1143 air km NW of YELLOWKNIFE. The name, of Inuit origin, means "where there are bears." It was a major centre of the Mackenzie Delta region in the 1950s, but owing to serious flooding most facilities were relocated to the nearby INUVIK site in 1961. The community is called "the town that wouldn't die" by the Inuvialuit and Loucheux DENE, who refused to relocate. In 1931-32 it was a base for the pursuit of the "Mad Trapper of Rat River," Albert Johnson. Most residents subsist on hunting, trapping and fishing.

ANNELIES M. POOL

Alabama, Confederate warship constructed in Britain during the AMERICAN CIVIL WAR. The US sought to have the ship detained there, but it escaped. Until it was sunk in June 1864, it attacked Union (Northern) shipping, inflicting great losses. American claims for compensation from Britain, submitted to arbitration in 1871, were omitted from negotiations for the TREATY OF WASHINGTON, despite an American suggestion that compensation might be made by cession of some Canadian territory. In 1872 a Geneva tribunal awarded $15.5 million in gold to the US.

ROBIN W. WINKS

Alarie, Pierrette, soprano, teacher (b at Montréal 9 Nov 1921). She studied with Jeanne Maubourg, Albert Roberval and Elisabeth Schumann, and in the studio of Salvator Issaurel. In 1945 she appeared with New York's Metropolitan Opera after having won the Opera's Auditions of the Air. As a soloist, and with her husband Léopold SIMONEAU, she sang on the great European and N American stages. She and her husband received the 1959 Prix de musique Calixa-Lavallée and the diploma of honour from the Canadian Conference of the Arts (1983), and their record of *Mozart concert Arias and Duets* won the Grand Prix du disque from the Académie Charles-Cros in Paris in 1961. Together they founded the Victoria chamber opera company, Canada Opera Piccola (1978), and the Advanced Training Opera Centre (1982).

HÉLÈNE PLOUFFE

Alaska Boundary Dispute, between Canada and the US over the boundary of the Alaska Panhandle running S to latitude 54°40′ N on the coast of BC. When the US purchased Alaska from Russia in 1867, it inherited the Russian position on the boundary, first defined in the 1825 Anglo-Russian treaty. The US claimed a continuous stretch of coastline, unbroken by the deep fiords of the region. Canada demanded control of the heads of certain fiords, especially the Lynn Canal, which gave access to the Yukon. The KLONDIKE GOLD RUSH after 1896 brought the smouldering dispute to a head. When direct negotiations in the JOINT HIGH COMMISSION of 1898-1899 failed, the problem was referred to an international tribunal, whose 3 American and Canadian members were frankly partisan. The sixth, Lord Alverstone, Lord Chief Justice of England, supported the American claim for a boundary running behind the heads of the inlets, but agreed to the equal distribution of 4 islands at the mouth of Portland Canal. In protest the Canadian judges refused to sign the award and violent anti-British feeling erupted in Canada.

Irritated at the decision, PM Sir Wilfrid Laurier asserted that Canada's lack of TREATY-MAKING POWER made it difficult to maintain its rights internationally, but he took no immediate action. Canadian anger gradually subsided, although suspicions of the US provoked by the award may have contributed to Canada's rejection of free trade in the 1911 "reciprocity election." Nevertheless, the Alaska settlement promoted better understanding between the US and Britain that worked to Canada's advantage in WWI.

D.M.L. FARR

Alaska Highway, constructed 1942-43 from Dawson Creek, BC, to Fairbanks, Alaska. In the face of a serious threat of a Japanese invasion a preliminary road was rammed through forest wilderness and 5 mountain ranges in only 8 months. Called the Alcan Military Hwy, it ran 2333 km from Dawson Creek to Big Delta, Alaska. Groups of US Army engineers working from several starting points built up to 13 km a day. The following year it became a permanent all-weather, gravel-surfaced road, 7 to 8 m wide, 2451 km long, from Dawson Creek, BC to Fairbanks, Alaska — the result of the labour of 11 000 soldiers and some 16 000 Canadian and American civilians. There were 133 bridges 6 m or longer and several thousand culverts. The US invested $147.8 million in the project for men, materials and equipment. Canada provided the right of way and on 3 April 1946 took over the 1954-km portion of the road from Dawson Creek to the Alaska border. Canada paid the US $108 million to cover airfields and flight strips, buildings, telephone systems and other assets, but not construction of the highway itself. Opened to unrestricted travel in 1947 the road was regraded and widened by Canadian army engineers during the next 17 years until it was turned over (1964) to the federal dept of public works, which has continued to improve it. Although in 1982 less than one quarter of the road was paved, hundreds of kilo netres were bituminous surface-treated to carry he traffic, which ranged from 220 vehicles a lay in isolated areas to 1700 a day near White-orse. Expenditures were about $35 million a ear. Maintenance is a continual battle against ature: floods and landslides in spring, blizards and extreme cold in winter, when temeratures of -48°C can cause bulldozer blades to rack like glass. Although originally built for nilitary purposes, the highway has helped the orestry, oil, mining, tourist and trucking inlustries. It provided an important impetus to he development of Edmonton as a supply entre and, as an enduring link to northern BC nd the Yukon, has had the psychological beneit of ending the isolation of the North.

C.W. GILCHRIST

Albani, Dame Emma, stage name of Marie-ouise-Cécile-Emma Lajeunesse, soprano (b at Chambly, Canada E 1 Nov 1847; d at London, ng 3 Apr 1930). Her parents were her teachers n Chambly, Plattsburgh and Montréal, where he gave her first concert in 1856. She was to beome the first Canadian-born artist to disinguish herself in the international world of pera, oratorio and concert singing. After studes in Paris and Milan, she made her opera debut t Messina, Italy, as Oscar in *Un Ballo in maschera* 1869), but her first real triumph came soon afer, as Amina in *La Sonnambula*. This was to be er debut role in London (1872), Paris (1872) nd New York (1874). Though attached to Covnt Garden, London, she steadily pursued her nternational career in many countries. In 1891-892 she sang at the Metropolitan Opera in New ork. By the time she retired from the opera tage in 1896, she had sung 43 leading roles. he made about a dozen enthusiastically received Canadian tours, 1883-1906. Her remarkble voice has been preserved on a Rococo 5255 ecord, on which she sings 8 titles, including urn-of-the-century songs and three Handel rias.

GILLES POTVIN

Albany River, 982 km long, issues from Lk St oseph, NW Ontario, and flows E to Eby Falls, where it drops over the rocky ledge of the Canaian SHIELD onto the clay lowlands and into AMES BAY near Ft Albany (est 1684). It has a RAINAGE BASIN of 134 000 km^2 and a mean disharge of 1420 m^3/sec. Named for the Duke of Albany, later King James II, it was an active UR-TRADE ROUTE, though less favoured than the AYES R because of its poorer links to other river ystems. Main tributaries are the Ogoki and Kenogami rivers.

JAMES MARSH

Alberta

Capital: Edmonton
Motto: *Fortis et Liber* ("Strong and free")
Flower: Wild rose (also known as prickly rose)
Largest Cities: Edmonton, Calgary, Lethbridge, Red Deer, Medicine Hat, St Albert, Fort McMurray
Population: 2 238 000 (1981c); rank fourth, 9.2% of Canada; 77.3% urban; 14% rural nonfarm; 8.7% farm; 3.5 per km^2 density; 20.4% increase from 1976-81; Jan 1984e pop, 2 345 100
Languages: 91.7% English; 1.3% French; 7% Other
Entered Confederation: 1 Sept 1905
Government: Provincial — Lieutenant-Governor, Executive Council, Legislative Assembly of 79 members; federal — 6 senators, 21 members of the House of Commons
Area: 661 185 km^2; including 16 796 km^2 of inland water; 6.66% of Canada
Elevation: Highest point — Mount Columbia (3747 m); lowest point—shores of Lake Athabasca and Slave River
Gross Domestic Product: $53.1 billion (1982e)
Farm Cash Receipts: $3.8 billion (1982)
Electric Power Generated: 28 990 994 MWh (1983)
Sales Tax: None (1984)

Alberta, the westernmost of Canada's 3 Prairie rovinces, shares many physical features with ts neighbours to the E, SASKATCHEWAN and MANTOBA. The Rocky Mts form the southern portion f Alberta's western boundary with BRITISH COUMBIA. Alberta's western location places it at onsiderable distance from the traditional ecoomic and political power centres of Canada; owever, the province possesses the country's argest deposits of oil and natural gas, and expansion of the petroleum industry from 1947 to 983 made it the fastest-growing province in hat period, producing a westward shift of ecoomic power in Canada. The reordering of the elationship between Alberta and central Canda, in which Alberta has been a supplier of raw materials to the more highly industrialized Onario and Québec, has become an important provincial priority.

The province was named after Princess Louise Caroline Alberta, 4th daughter of Queen Victoia. Alberta then was one of 4 provisional disricts of the North-West Territories, and inluded only that part of the present province S of 5°N lat and W of 111° long. Alberta's current oundaries were determined in 1905 when it beame a province. Though appearing quite homogeneous, Alberta may be divided into 2 distinct sociocultural regions — southern Alberta, with Calgary as its focal point; and central and northern Alberta, with Edmonton as the metropolitan centre. This division has deep historic roots. Southern Alberta was once the domain of the Blackfoot nation; farther north the Cree and various woodland tribes held sway. In the early days of white settlement, the south welcomed the rancher, while the grain farmer opened the central agricultural region. Calgary and southern Alberta were first linked to the east by the Canadian Pacific Railway, Edmonton and the north by the Grand Trunk Pacific and Canadian Northern railways. Later, Calgary became the administrative and financial headquarters for the province's petroleum industry, Edmonton its exploration and production centre. Politically, while both regions voted strongly Progressive Conservative in the 1970s and early 1980s, opposition in the north tends to coalesce around the New Democratic Party provincially, while in the south it gravitates to right-of-centre candidates.

Land and Resources

Physiography, climate, soil and vegetation combine to delineate 4 biophysical regions within Alberta. The prairie region includes most of southern Alberta, more precisely the land S and E of an arc stretching from Waterton in the SW corner to a point along the Saskatchewan border E of Red Deer. This gently rolling grassland is relatively dry and mostly treeless. The terrain varies locally, in places broken by deep river valleys, and rising from less than 300 m in the NE to 1200 m in the CYPRESS HILLS in the SE. The parkland region predominates in central Alberta, forming a crescent to the W and N of the prairie region and including most of the N SASKATCHEWAN R drainage basin. This area varies from the flatland of old lake bottoms to rolling landscape with numerous lakes and depressions. It contains both treed and grassy terrain, with soil and climatic factors favourable to agriculture. The boreal-forest region covers the northern half of the province. Here great rivers and lakes dominate the landscape, draining northward to the Arctic Ocean. Soil and climatic factors militate against agriculture, except in the PEACE R region of the NW, where parkland conditions create the world's most northerly graingrowing area. West of the plains an area of FOOTHILL ridges rise to the Rocky Mts W of Grande Prairie and along the southern portion of Alberta's western boundary with BC. Here is found some of Canada's most spectacular natural scenery, with peaks rising to 3600 m.

Geology Alberta's oldest surface landscape is its extreme northeastern part, E of the Slave and lower Athabasca rivers, where crystalline rocks formed during the Precambrian era (3500 to 600 million years ago) appear at the surface. This small outcrop of the Canadian SHIELD does not end in the NE, for its rocks form a basement under the rest of the province, sloping down to 6000 m in the SW. During the Paleozoic era (600 to 225 million years ago) Alberta alternated between dry land and sea, and life evolved from simple plants and animals to vertebrates and dry-land vegetation. The decay of this plant and animal life, especially during the Devonian period (400 to 350 million years ago), formed the basis of most of the province's oil and naturalgas deposits. The Mesozoic era (225 to 70 million years ago) also subjected Alberta to alternating upraisings of the land and infloodings of ocean waters. This was the era of the dinosaurs, the period that bequeathed the BADLAND formations of the Red Deer R valley, and laid down most of the province's coal resources. The Cenozoic era (70 million years ago to the present) saw the uplifting of the Rocky Mts and the establishment of the province's physiographic framework. About 35 000 years ago the last advance of polar ice scoured the terrain and destroyed vegetation. Only the highest parts of the Rockies, the Cypress Hills and the Porcupine Hills escaped. The final retreat of the ice age, beginning about 13 000 years ago, created the current river systems and soils.

Surface The prairie region of southern Alberta includes both short-grass and mixed-grass characteristics. The short-grass area of the SE corner features short, drought-resistant grasses, such as blue gramma, growing on light brown SOIL deficient in nitrogen and phosphorus, and about 12 cm deep. Annual water deficiency and wind erosion cause considerable soil drifting.

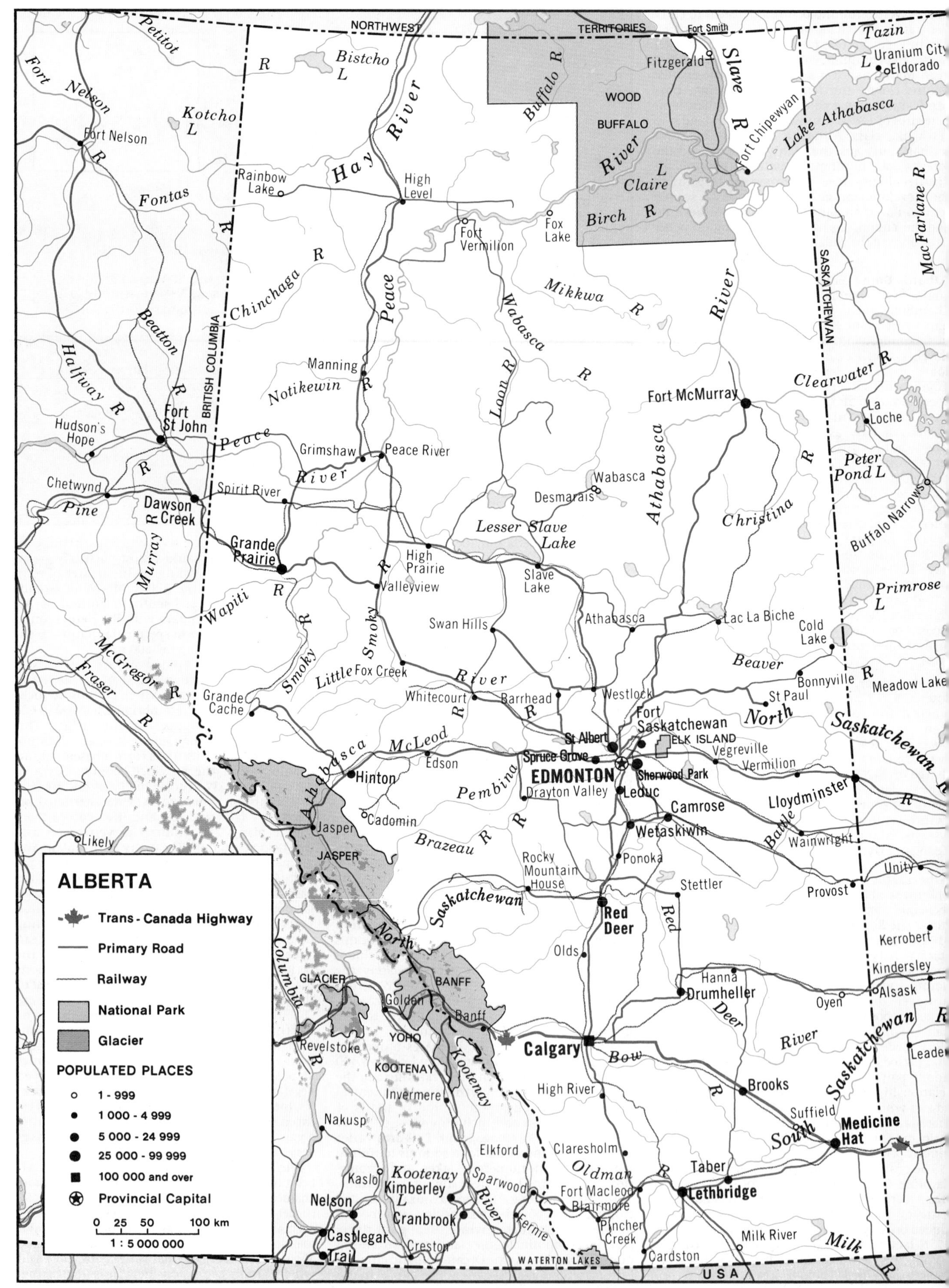
ALBERTA
Trans-Canada Highway
Primary Road
Railway
National Park
Glacier
POPULATED PLACES
1 - 999
1 000 - 4 999
5 000 - 24 999
25 000 - 99 999
100 000 and over
Provincial Capital
0 25 50 100 km
1 : 5 000 000
NORTHWEST TERRITORIES
BRITISH COLUMBIA
SASKATCHEWAN
USA
EDMONTON
Calgary
Red Deer
Lethbridge
Medicine Hat
Fort McMurray
Grande Prairie
St Albert
Sherwood Park
Spruce Grove
Fort Saskatchewan
Leduc
Camrose
Wetaskiwin
Lloydminster
Drumheller
Brooks
Peace River
High Level
Fort Chipewyan
Fort Smith
Fort Vermilion
Slave Lake
Athabasca
Lac La Biche
Hinton
Jasper
Banff
Edson
Whitecourt
Barrhead
Westlock
Vegreville
Vermilion
Wainwright
Ponoka
Stettler
Olds
Hanna
High River
Claresholm
Fort Macleod
Pincher Creek
Cardston
Taber
Milk River
Suffield
Oyen
Provost
WOOD BUFFALO
JASPER
BANFF
GLACIER
YOHO
KOOTENAY
WATERTON LAKES
ELK ISLAND
Lake Athabasca
Lesser Slave Lake
Peace River
Athabasca River
North Saskatchewan River
South Saskatchewan River
Bow R
Red Deer River
Oldman R
Milk R

The mixed-grass area, forming an arc to the W and N of the short-grass region, contains more fertile, dark brown soil, while western wheat grass and other taller grasses provide the natural vegetation. The parkland regions of central Alberta and the Peace R country are characterized by a natural vegetation cover of tall grasses and aspen trees. The central parkland contains fertile black soils, while the black, grey black and dark brown soils of the Peace R area are slightly less fertile. The boreal region of northern Alberta contains forest vegetation varying from predominant aspen and white birch in the S to white spruce, tamarack and black spruce farther N. Balsam, fir and jack pine are also found in eastern areas, with alpine fir and lodgepole pine in the W. Nutrient-deficient grey soils underlie the forest cover. Alpine fir, white spruce and lodgepole pine dominate the lower elevations of the Rocky Mts. At higher elevations, scattered stands of black spruce and alpine larch are interspersed with lichens and alpine flowers in lovely alpine meadows. Rock, permanent snow cover and glacial ice dominate the very highest elevations.

Water The small MILK R basin in SE Alberta drains through the Missouri and Mississippi rivers S to the Gulf of Mexico. The rest of southern Alberta is drained by the S and N Saskatchewan river basins E to Hudson Bay via the Nelson R system. These rivers carry 75% of the water that flows E. Northern Alberta is dominated by the Athabasca, Hay and Peace river basins, which drain N through the Mackenzie R to the Arctic Ocean. Low annual precipitation, high evaporation rates and fast runoff produce chronic water deficits in southern Alberta, varying from a moderate deficiency in the parkland region to a severe shortage in the short-grass prairie area. Irrigation has been used in the latter area since the late 19th century; over 162 000 ha are part of formal irrigation systems. Yet the amount of water available for irrigation is itself limited by the water flow in the S Saskatchewan R basin. There have been recurrent proposals to divert water southward from the Peace and Athabasca rivers.

Lk Claire and Lesser Slave Lk are the 2 largest lakes entirely within Alberta.

Climate Alberta's northerly latitude, stretching between 49° N and 60° N, puts the province in the northern cool-temperate zone. Thus cold winters and relatively short, cool summers are to be expected. Yet the most important factors in determining both temperatures and precipitation are the height and width of the Rocky Mts and the direction of the prevailing winds. The mountain ranges intercept air moving in from the Pacific and drain it of moisture. Thus the Rockies' eastern slopes are in a rain shadow, and Alberta's skies are predominantly clear. Precipitation is low, ranging from about 30 cm annually in the SE to 40-45 cm in the N. Alberta is Canada's sunniest province, ranging from 1900 annual hours of sunshine in the N to 2300 in the S. Air funnelling through the Rockies also produces the warm, dry CHINOOK winds, especially strong and prevalent in SW Alberta. Chinooks can raise temperatures dramatically within hours, melting snow and exposing grass, and providing welcome respite during the cold winter.

The influence of the Pacific air mass weakens in eastern Alberta, giving way to continental air masses originating in the Arctic and midwestern US. These air masses bring Jan mean temperatures ranging from -8°C in the S to -24°C in the N, and July mean temperatures ranging from 20°C in the S to 16°C in the N. The growing season lasts about 120 days in southern Alberta, decreasing to 60 days in the N. In the N the shorter season is offset by longer days and lower altitudes and wheat is grown as far N as the Peace R.

Resources Alberta is the foremost energy-resource province in Canada. Proven remaining recoverable reserves were estimated in 1980 as follows: conventional crude, 720 million m^3; synthetic crude, 3.9 billion m^3; natural gas, 1747 billion m^3; and liquid natural gas, 294 million m^3. Life indexes for conventional crude have been estimated at about 13 years and 26 years for natural gas. COAL has even longer-term potential. About 70% of Canada's proven remaining coal reserves lie within Alberta, estimated at 13.5 billion t in 1978, with a life index of 1000 years at current levels of production. The province's total potential of hydroelectric energy is estimated at 4.8 million kW.

The province possesses an estimated 2.661 million ha of land suitable for agriculture. Alberta's forests total 330 830 km^2, and have a potential annual yield of 15 million m^3 (coniferous) and 13 million m^3 (deciduous). Traditional fur and fisheries resources of northern Alberta have declined in recent years, while recreational resources have increased in importance with population growth and urbanization. Within Alberta approximately 54 000 km^2 of land are reserved as national parks, 7700 km^2 as provincial parks and 250 000 ha as provincial wilderness areas.

Conservation The Environmental Council of Alberta (formerly the Environment Conservation Authority) was established by provincial legislation (1970) to review government policies and programs on environmental matters, and to hold inquiries and public hearings at the request of Cabinet or upon public representations. The council has subsequently addressed questions of resource exploitation, environmental impact of commercial development, environmental education, water, air and noise pollution, and water and hazardous-waste management. Because its role is advisory rather than regulatory, its recommendations are not always acted upon by government, to the displeasure of environmental groups.

Two of Alberta's national parks began as wildlife sanctuaries. ELK ISLAND (E of Edmonton) and WOOD BUFFALO (44 thousand km^2 straddling the border with the NWT) were created to help the species whose names they bear, but in both cases the most spectacular success has been in preserving the bison of the plains. A number of provincial parks and wilderness areas function as wildlife reserves, including Cypress Hills Park in the SE, Sir Winston Churchill Park on Lac La Biche and Willmore Wilderness Park N of Jasper.

People

Settlement of Alberta took place primarily in the 1896-1914 period. By 1901 the population of the future province was 73 022; in 1911 it reached 373 943. Settlers arrived from eastern Canada, the US, Great Britain and continental Europe. The rate of growth declined in subsequent years, with total population reaching 584 454 in 1921, 796 169 in 1941 and 1 331 944 in 1961. Growth was slowest during the GREAT DEPRESSION of the 1930s. The rate increased after WWII, through immigration from overseas and the movement of people from other parts of Canada to a visibly prosperous Alberta. From July 1973 to July 1984 the province experienced its most rapid growth, from 1 768 500 to 2 367 400. However, from July 1983 to July 1984 the population declined to 2 361 300.

Urban Centres Alberta's population is classified as 77.3% urban, 14% rural nonfarm and 8.7% farm. Rural population reached its peak in the late 1930s, with 530 000 people accounting for two-thirds of the provincial total. The trend to urbanization quickened during WWII and sharply accelerated in the postwar boom years. By 1951 the rural figure had fallen to 490 000 and the proportion to 52%. The most notable feature of urban growth is concentration in 2 metropolitan centres. In 1946, 27% of Alberta's population lived in EDMONTON and CALGARY; by 1981 this had increased to 56.5%. Edmonton, the provincial capital and administrative centre, had a metropolitan population of 657 057 in 1981; Calgary, the petroleum and financial centre, was second with 592 743. By June 1983 Edmonton numbered 698 600 and Calgary 619 814. Calgary's immediate wholesale and retail hinterland includes all of the province S of Red Deer, plus a portion of southeastern BC. Edmonton's hinterland includes the rest of Alberta and parts of the Peace R region of northeastern BC. Alberta's secondary urban centres have been affected by the metropolitan growth of Edmonton and Calgary. LETHBRIDGE, RED DEER and MEDICINE HAT in the S have been able to preserve their trading areas only at the expense of smaller communities. ST ALBERT, Sherwood Park, LEDUC and Ft Saskatchewan are virtually satellite towns within Edmonton's orbit. Only FORT MCMURRAY in the NE and GRANDE PRAIRIE in the NW, because of distance and regional resource development, have escaped the direct metropolitan influences of the 2 largest cities.

Labour Force The number of persons employed in Alberta in July 1984 was 1 294 000. The province's unemployment rate in 1981 was 3.8%, less than half the national average. For many years Alberta had Canada's lowest unemployment rate, but in 1982 the province had the second lowest, behind Saskatchewan, with 7.5%; its rate was over 10% in 1983-84. Significant trends in the provincial labour force include growth in the service industries (a 50% increase from 1975 to 1980) and an expanding female-participation rate (up from 39.4% of total work force in 1971 to 56.7% in 1980). The distribution of the labour force, by industry, in Sept 1983 was recorded as follows: service 30.9%, trade 17.0%, agriculture 8.6%, transportation 8.6%, construction 8.1%, manufacturing 8.0%, other primary industries 5.6% and finance 5.4%. Over the previous 5-year period, service (+74 000), public administration (+22 000) and trade (+19 000) showed the greatest growth; construction (-5000) showed the only decline. The average weekly earnings in May 1983 was $463, second only to BC and $46 above the national average.

Ethnicity, Language, Religion Alberta's population is characterized by diversity of ethnic group, language and religion. Native peoples predominated until the 1880s, but were quickly outnumbered by the first influx of English-speaking Protestants and French-speaking Catholics from eastern Canada. The greatest diversity in population dates from the 1896-1914 wave of immigration, which drew from northern, central and eastern Europe tens of thousands of settlers, speaking a variety of languages and representing many religious groups. The major ethnic groups represented in 1981 were British 962 790 or 43.5%; German 233 175 or 10.5%; Ukrainian 136 710 or 6.2%; Scandinavian 78 560 or 3.5%; French 111 870 or 5%; Dutch 65 060 or 2.9%; native peoples 60 005 or 2.7%; Polish 37 660 or 1.7%. Other groups include Austrian, Chinese, Czech, Finnish, Hungarian, Italian, Japanese, Jewish, Russian, Slovak and West Indian. The population by mother tongue in 1981 was overwhelmingly English: 1 794 915 or 81%. Yet other tongues persisted as earlier non-British immigration was supplemented by post-WWII arrivals. German was the mother tongue of 90 410 or 4.2% of the total population; Ukrainian 66 680 or 3%; French 60 900 or 2.7%.

The largest religious group in Alberta in 1981 was the Roman Catholic Church with 573 645 members or 25.9% of the total population. Churches next in order were United with 525 480 or 23.7%; Anglican with 202 265 or

Byzantine church near Wasel, Alta (*photo by Pat Morrow*).

9.1%; Lutheran 144 675 or 6.5%; Baptist 66 370 or 2.9%; Presbyterian 63 895 or 2.8%; Eastern Orthodox 49 270 or 2.2%; Ukrainian Catholic 40 280 or 1.8%. Minor religious groups of greater prominence in Alberta than elsewhere in Canada include the MORMONS (42 980 or 1.9%), MENNONITES (20 545 or 0.9%) and HUTTERITES (7395).

This diversity has affected popular attitudes and public policies in education and multiculturalism. The split between French Catholics and English Protestants in the years prior to provincehood in 1905 led to the formation of publicly funded, local separate school boards for the Catholic (or sometimes Protestant) religious minority. In later years religious groups such as Hutterites, Mennonites and the Christian Reformed Church gained their own educational privileges, either within the framework of public education or through self-supported private schools. While English has remained the predominant language of instruction in Alberta schools, both provincial and local jurisdictions have tolerated, even encouraged, the use of French, German, Ukrainian and Indian languages as teaching languages.

The high percentage (51.5% in 1981) of people of neither British nor French origin in the province gave rise to criticism of the federal government's English-French bilingual and bicultural policies of the 1960s and 1970s, and a preference for multicultural and multilingual policies.

Economy

Alberta's economy has followed a pattern of rimary-resource exploitation and dependence on external markets, with prices and revenues largely determined by outside economic and political forces. This pattern was established with the FUR TRADE of the 18th century and continued in the 19th century with ranching and then grain growing. The completion of the CPR in 1885 provided market routes for Alberta grain, as well as aiding the penetration of eastern Canadian manufactured goods. Agriculture remained the dominant economic activity until the discovery of oil in the Leduc field in 1947 and has since been surpassed in net product value by mining and manufacturing as well.

Alberta's gross domestic product in 1981 amounted to $42.4 billion. Nearly one-fifth of this total, or $8.3 billion, was contributed by mining, dominated by oil and natural gas. The financial sector (including insurance and real estate) stood second at $9.1 billion, or 21.4%, followed by the service sector (community, business and personal services) at $6 billion, or 14%; retail and wholesale trade at $3.8 billion, or 8.9%; construction at $3.4 billion, or 8%; manufacturing at $3.1 billion, or 7%; transportation at $2.9 billion, or 6.8%; and agriculture at $1.9 billion, or 4%. By 1982 Alberta's GDP had increased to $52.1 billion. Private and public investment in Alberta grew by 126% between 1977 and 1982 to reach $20.9 billion, representing a per capita investment of $8928. Total personal income increased 78.7% between 1976 and 1981 to a figure of $12 459, compared with the Canadian average of $11 520. The consumer price index (1981=100) for 1983 stood at 117.2 for Edmonton and 117.1 for Calgary.

Despite the unprecedented growth of the late 1970s, the Alberta economy was particularly hard hit by the recession of the early 1980s.

Agriculture Alberta's agricultural industry remains of major importance to the province, the nation and — in grain exports — to the world. In 1981, with 9.2% of Canada's population, Alberta produced 20% of the nation's food. Between 1975 and 1980 the value of farm cash receipts increased by 65% and in 1982 reached $3.8 billion. Most of the overall increase came through the sale of livestock (chiefly cattle) and their products, which rose by 84.9% over the period to $1.7 billion, slightly less than half the total farm cash receipts. Cereal crops — led by WHEAT, CANOLA and BARLEY — totalled $1.9 billion in receipts, roughly half the total in 1982. Other crops, such as sugar beets, potatoes and vegetables, made up the remainder.

Around the metropolitan areas of Edmonton and Calgary, and in the corridor between the 2 cities, are dairy and poultry operations, cattle, and hog and sheep farms. Wheat and small grain farmers are located particularly in the Peace R region, the Edmonton, Camrose and Lloydminster areas, and in a belt from Red Deer SE to the US boundary. Mixed enterprises are again found in the crescent sweeping NW from Lethbridge to Calgary and Red Deer, then NE to Camrose and Lloydminster, plus the counties N of Edmonton. The black and brown soils of the mixed-grass prairie and parkland regions provide the environment with the greatest potential for mixed farming. Away from this fertile crescent, especially in the SE, lie the more specialized ranching and wheat operations, which compensate for their marginal soils with larger size. Irrigated farming, centred in Lethbridge, produces sugar beets, potatoes and vegetables.

Industry Alberta's manufacturing economy contributed 13% ($3.1 billion) towards the total census value added in goods produced during 1981. Manufacturers in Alberta tend either to process local raw materials (petroleum, agricultural, wood or nonmetallic mineral commodities) or to engage in custom manufacture and fabrication for the resource-development and construction sectors. During the 1970s the most rapidly expanding manufacturing area was the PETROCHEMICAL INDUSTRY, notably ethylene at Joffre and vinyl chloride monomer, ethylene and chloralkali at Ft Saskatchewan. Provincial policies aimed at diversification in the manufacturing industry have enjoyed some limited success, such as the beginning of a steel industry.

Construction was one of the most important industrial activities between 1955 and the early 1980s with the oil and gas industry accounting for a consistently large proportion of this expansion. The estimated total value of construction work in Alberta in 1983 was $13.4 billion, almost 15% higher than 1980. Engineering construction increased by 20%, while total building construction was up 7.3% (a 28% increase in nonresidential construction and a 14.5% decline in residential construction). Edmonton and Calgary, as Canada's fastest-growing cities, were the centres of commercial and residential construction during the 1970s. However, after 1982 the engineering and petroleum servicing industries, along with the province's architects, were very hard hit by the recession.

Tourism is a third major sector of Alberta's industrial economy. Year-round recreational pursuits in the Rocky Mts — particularly in BANFF and JASPER NATIONAL PARKS — draw hundreds of thousands of tourists annually from all over the world. Local attractions include the annual CALGARY STAMPEDE and Edmonton's Klondike Days, week-long extravaganzas emphasizing aspects of Alberta history.

Mining The estimated total value of minerals produced in Alberta during 1983 was $22.2 billion, amounting to 61.7% of the Canadian total. The value of fuels, by far the major component of mineral production (96.7% in 1983), reached $21.4 billion, or 86% of total national value. Between 1975 and 1980 the volume of crude oil produced in Alberta decreased overall, while the volume of natural gas produced annually increased.

The volume of coal produced in Alberta rose by 67% between 1975 and 1980 to reach 20.1 million t, increasing to 21.6 million t in 1983. Coal formed the basis of Alberta's first mining endeavour, in the Lethbridge region in 1870. By the time of WWI, coal mining was a major economic activity in the Lethbridge, Crowsnest Pass

Cowboys round up white-faced Hereford cattle for branding, near the Red Deer R in southern Alberta (*photo by Richard Harrington*).

Massive bucket wheel extracting bitumen from the Athabasca tar sands. It is estimated that the tar sands contain more oil than the Gulf of Arabia (*courtesy Suncor Ltd*).

and Drumheller areas. Following an initial decline in the 1920s, and a drastic loss of domestic consumers in the 1950s, Alberta's coal industry reached its lowest point in the early 1960s. Since then a slight increase in the domestic market, plus the negotiation of long-term leases to supply the Japanese steel industry, have pumped new life into the industry. Alberta produces limited quantities of salt, sodium sulphate and peat moss, plus a number of minerals used in the construction industry, such as limestone, sand, clay and gypsum. The province is the world's largest producer of elemental sulphur from hydrocarbon sources. Small amounts of gold and other metallic minerals are mined, and the province possesses deposits of low-grade iron ore and uranium in the Lk Athabasca region.

Forestry Although nearly one-half of Alberta is covered by forest, a combination of low provincial demand and low-quality timber (compared, for example, with neighbouring BC) results in only a small fraction of the forest potential being exploited. In 1981 forestry accounted for just 0.1% ($51 million) of the province's gross domestic product. Timber quotas and other aspects of forest management are controlled by the Alberta Forest Service, a government agency. The production of sawn lumber, chiefly spruce, totals about 1.6 million m³ (370 million board feet) annually. Pulp mills are located at Hinton and Grande Prairie.

Fisheries The commercial fishing catch (about half of it whitefish) in Alberta's northern lakes averaged 2 million kg in the mid-1970s, with an annual value of about $800 000. In 1983 the catch was 2.4 million kg, with a market value of $3 million.

Finance The expansion of the petroleum industry after WWII, particularly during the 1970s, produced a westward shift of financial power within Canada, with Alberta the major beneficiary. During the 1970s, Calgary consolidated its position as the major provincial financial centre and emerged as a contending national centre. Between 1978 and 1980 the Calgary-based Alberta Stock Exchange increased its number of company listings by 182, reaching almost 300, the vast majority of new members being small oil and gas companies. Dollar volumes traded on the exchange grew from $95 million to $470 million during the same period. By 1980 Calgary housed offices of 22 foreign banks (with 8 more scheduled by 1985), and had become the third-largest head-office location for major Canadian companies, behind only Toronto and Montréal. Two Canadian banks, the Canadian Commercial Bank and the Bank of Alberta, are headquartered in Edmonton. The Treasury Branches, which only loan to Alberta-based businesses, have played an important role in the Alberta economy.

Transportation While river transportation provided the communication network for the 18th- and early 19th-century fur trade, it was rail transportation that opened Alberta to extensive settlement in the late 19th century, and tied the region's economy into that of the nation. Southern Alberta is served chiefly by the CPR, central Alberta by the CNR, and northern regions by the Alberta Resources Ry, the Northern Alberta Ry and the Great Slave Ry. CPR and CNR lines transport virtually all of Alberta's grain crop E and W to international markets. So important are these routes to the province's economic well-being that railway issues, such as abandoning branch lines, the CROW'S NEST PASS RATE AGREEMENT, and the upgrading of main lines and terminal facilities, are important political as well as economic concerns.

The importance of Alberta's highways to the movement of both people and goods has increased since the end of WWII. The most heavily travelled route is the 4-lane Highway 2 between Edmonton and Calgary. Important interprovincial routes include Highway 1, the TRANS-CANADA HIGHWAY from Medicine Hat through Calgary to Banff; Highway 16, the Yellowhead Highway, from Lloydminster through Edmonton to Jasper; and the Mackenzie Highway running N from the Peace R country to the NWT. Calgary is the headquarters of Greyhound Lines, the largest intercity bus system in Canada, with a network of over 22 500 km.

Alberta's 2 international airports, located at Calgary and Edmonton, experienced the largest annual increases in passenger traffic among all major Canadian airports during the 1970s. Regular passenger service to other parts of the country and abroad is provided by Air Canada, Canadian Pacific Airlines, Pacific Western Airlines, plus a number of American and European carriers. Wardair of Edmonton is Canada's largest charter airline, providing both national and international services. Air travel within the province is dominated by Pacific Western Airlines and Time Air.

Alberta has over 100 000 km of PIPELINES carrying oil and gas to both internal and external markets. Oil moves E through the Interprovincial line (completed from Alberta to Lk Superior in 1953, later to Montréal) and W through the Trans Mountain line to the Pacific. NOVA CORPORATION built the pipelines that deliver gas to Alberta's boundaries, where it enters interprovincial or American lines. Nova is the principal partner in the Foothills Pipeline consortium, formed to deliver Alaskan natural gas to the continental US, although only the southern portion has been completed.

Oil pump west of Edmonton, Alta. The discovery of oil at Leduc in 1947 transformed the province's economy (*photo by Pat Morrow*).

Energy The oil industry in Alberta began with the discovery of the Turner Valley field in 1914. However, apart from a brief flurry of activity in the late 1930s, the industry remained small until the discovery of the Leduc field in 1947, followed by the opening of the Woodbend, Redwater and Pembina fields. The more than 17 000 producing wells are distributed over most of the province. Alberta production, as a proportion of the Canadian total, increased from about 79% in 1972 to 84% in 1983. In 1983, 15.5% was exported to the US, 63.7% to other provinces, while only about 21.3% was consumed within the province. Oil, however, is the largest single source of energy within Alberta (43%), the majority being used as industrial feedstock. The natural-gas industry is older than oil, dating from 1885 discoveries near Medicine Hat. The more than 17 000 producing gas wells are distributed throughout all areas of the province, except the NE. Alberta produced the bulk of Canada's natural gas through the 1970s, varying from 83% in 1973 to 88.1% in 1983. Provincial markets use 22.3% of production, with 34% exported to the US in 1983, and 39.9% consumed elsewhere in Canada. Within the province, natural gas is used to generate electricity and as fuel for industrial, commercial and residential purposes. Natural gas is also the feedstock on which the petrochemical industry is based. Alberta also possesses reserves of heavy crude (in the Lloydminster and Cold Lake areas) and the vast tar sands of the Ft McMurray region. Only since the 1960s have rising prices for oil made the tar sands a commercially viable operation. The first 2 plants to exploit the tar sands for conversion into synthetic crude oil were Great Canadian Oil Sands (now Suncor) and Syncrude. The development of further MEGAPROJECTS was halted by the economic recession of the early 1980s, although there are some 20 to 30 pilot projects underway in 1984, and the huge Husky Heavy Oil development at Lloydminster was announced in 1984.

Since 1947 the petroleum industry has brought prosperity to both the public and private sectors, transforming Alberta from a "have-not" to a "have" province. While Edmonton became the centre for petroleum servicing, production and transmission, Calgary remained the exploration, administrative and financial centre, owing in part to its proximity to the original

Turner Valley field. Royalties from petroleum production swelled provincial coffers, allowing the Social Credit government of the 1950s and 1960s and the Conservatives of the 1970s to keep taxes low. Yet disputes over petroleum pricing and export levels have led to acrimonious debates between Alberta and the federal government, and have produced strong provincial-rights and even quasi-separatist political movements. By the mid-1980s, while most disputes had been at least temporarily resolved, the slowdown in the economy had had a severe impact on the Alberta-based petroleum industry.

Government and Politics

Legislative power is vested in a LIEUTENANT-GOVERNOR (appointed by the federal government and representing the Crown) and a 79-member, single-chamber, elected Legislative Assembly. However, the traditional powers of the lieutenant-governor have in practice lapsed. Executive power is exercised by a Cabinet of responsible ministers selected by the PREMIER, the leader of the political party commanding a majority in the legislative assembly. Each minister presides over one or more departments of government. The senior division of the judiciary is the Court of Queen's Bench, whose justices are appointed by the federal government. The Trial Division of the Queen's Bench hears both civil and criminal cases, usually the more severe ones, while the Appeals Division hears appeals from both the Queen's Bench and the Provincial Court. This Provincial Court, with its judges appointed by the province, hears the great majority of both civil and criminal cases in the first instance.

Local Government Local municipal authority is derived from the province and based on various municipal acts. MUNICIPALITIES provide local services such as police and fire protection, garbage and sewage disposal, water and other utilities, road maintenance and public transportation, and parks and recreational services. Urban municipalities include cities, towns, "new towns" (with special borrowing powers), villages and "summer villages" (resort areas). Rural authorities include municipal districts (averaging 30 TOWNSHIPS) and COUNTIES (averaging 40 townships). The difference between these 2 forms of rural municipality lies in the responsibility for public education. In municipal districts, public school boards are discrete entities, whereas in counties the public schools are administered by a committee of the county council. A third type of rural municipality is the improvement district — outlying areas which do not elect their own councils but are directly administered by the Department of Municipal Affairs.

Federal Representation Alberta has 6 seats in the Senate (a fixed number, constitutionally determined) and 21 seats in the House of Commons in 1984 (a flexible number, subject to REDISTRIBUTION after each decennial census). The Liberal Party won the majority of Alberta's seats in the first 2 federal elections following provincehood, in 1908 and 1911. Conservatives won the province in the 1917 federal election, Progressives from 1921 to 1930, and Social Credit from 1935 to 1957. Beginning with John Diefenbaker's sweep of 1958, Alberta has voted overwhelmingly Conservative. The elections of 1972, 1974, 1979, 1980 and 1984 saw the Conservatives take every Alberta seat, with the popular vote ranging from 58% to 69%. Such bloc support for the Conservatives, while the majority of Canada returned Liberal governments, had, until 1984, left Alberta on the Opposition side in the House of Commons since 1963, except during the short-lived government of Alberta native Joe CLARK, 1979-80.

Public Finance Residents of Alberta have paid the lowest income taxes in Canada (although only by 0.5% in 1984), and pay no provincial gasoline or retail-sales taxes. The province depends instead on various fees, rentals and royalties from oil, natural gas, coal and other mineral companies; this income accounts for more than 45% (1981-82) of total government revenue. Before 1976 all revenue became part of the general budgetary fund used to finance the total range of government expenditures. Following the energy-pricing crisis of the mid-1970s, however, revenues increased dramatically and the government was faced with vast potential surpluses. The result was the creation in 1976 of the ALBERTA HERITAGE SAVINGS TRUST FUND, into which 30% (reduced to 15% in 1982) of the nonrenewable resource revenue was set aside. The Heritage Fund is intended primarily to earn a maximum return on equity, to provide financial resources for periods when resource income declines, to strengthen and diversify the provincial economy, and to undertake special capital projects, such as health-care facilities, irrigation and recreation projects, and the development of oil-sands technology.

Health In July 1969 Alberta entered the federal medicare scheme and operates the universal Alberta Health Care Insurance Plan. Negotiations between the province and the medical profession over fee schedules under this plan have at times been heated, with a number of practitioners opting for "balanced billing" or "extra billing." Welfare services within the province include public assistance to the aged, disabled and handicapped, with an increasing emphasis on preventive social services. Heritage Fund money has financed medical research through the $300 million endowment fund, Alberta Heritage Foundation for Medical Research, and increased the stock of hospital beds. The 2 largest capital projects are the new Health Sciences Centre in Edmonton and the enlarged Alberta Children's Hospital in Calgary. There is a variety of health-care institutions in the province, including large general hospitals in the major urban centres, smaller rural hospitals, auxiliary hospitals specializing in extended-care treatment, provincial mental and psychiatric hospitals, and nursing homes for senior citizens.

Premiers of Alberta 1905-1984

	Party	Term
Alexander Cameron Rutherford	Liberal	1905-10
Arthur Lewis Sifton	Liberal	1910-17
Charles Stewart	Liberal	1917-21
Herbert Greenfield	United Farmers of Alberta	1921-25
John Edward Brownlee	United Farmers of Alberta	1925-34
Richard Gavin Reid	United Farmers of Alberta	1934-35
William Aberhart	Social Credit	1935-43
Ernest Charles Manning	Social Credit	1943-68
Harry Edwin Strom	Social Credit	1968-71
Peter Lougheed	Conservative	1971-

Politics Alberta provincial politics is characterized by governing parties commanding huge majorities in the legislature, remaining in power for lengthy periods, and then being decisively beaten and virtually eliminated by a new political force. This pattern was established by the Liberals under Alberta's first premier, Alexander C. RUTHERFORD, who took 22 of 25 seats, with 61% of the popular vote, in the first provincial election in 1905. Similar Liberal victories were recorded in 1909, 1913 and 1917 under Rutherford and his successors, A.L. SIFTON and Charles STEWART. The UNITED FARMERS OF ALBERTA, fuelled by agrarian unrest at the end of WWI, swept to power in the 1921 provincial election with 38 of 61 seats and 44% of the popular vote. Under premiers Herbert GREENFIELD and John BROWNLEE, they repeated this pattern in 1926 and 1930. But in 1935 yet another new provincial force, the SOCIAL CREDIT League under William ABERHART, took 56 of 63 seats with 54% of the popular vote. Under Aberhart and his successors, Ernest MANNING and Harry STROM, Social Credit governed for 36 years, not to be swept aside until the victory of Peter LOUGHEED and the Conservatives in 1971, with 49 of 75 seats and 46% of the popular vote. Lougheed and the Conservatives crushed all opposition in 1975, 1979 and 1982. Since the United Farmers of the 1920s successful provincial political parties in Alberta have often opposed policies of the federal government, particularly on issues of taxation, natural resources and the nature of the Canadian confederation.

Lieutenant-Governors of Alberta 1905-1985

	Term
George Hedley Vicars Bulyea	1905-1
Robert George Brett	1915-2
William Egbert	1925-3
William Legh Walsh	1931-3
Philip Carteret Hill Primrose	1936-3
John Campbell Bowen	1937-5
John James Bowlen	1950-5
John Percy Page	1959-6
John Walter Grant MacEwan	1965-7
Ralph G. Steinhauer	1974-7
Frank C. Lynch-Staunton	1979-8
Helen Hunley	1985-

Education

The first schools in Alberta were founded by Catholic and Protestant missionaries in the mid-19th century. The North-West Territories School Ordinance of 1884 established a dual confessional system of Catholic and Protestant schooling based on the Québec model. Subsequent Protestant settlement and the determination of territorial political leader F.W.G. Haultain saw the gradual weakening of religious duality in education. Alberta entered Confederation in 1905 with a system based on the Ontario model — one provincial educational system, allowing local provision for the dissenting religious minority, known as separate schools, but excluding province-wide duality. Ontario also provided the initial model for programs of study, course content and grade structures, a model that lasted until the 1930s. That decade, however, was a particularly innovative one in education, and saw the introduction of social studies, the junior high school and the large unit of rural school administration, plus expansion in adult education and steps towards the economic and professional betterment of teachers.

Administration Public education in Alberta is a shared responsibility of the provincial government and local public and separate school boards. The provincial department of education (Alberta Education) has overall jurisdiction in areas such as curriculum and teacher certification, while local boards employ teachers and operate schools at the elementary (grades 1-6), junior high (7-9) and senior high (10-12) levels. Funding is provided by a combination of provincial grants and local property taxes. In 1982-1983, 462 109 students were enrolled in grades 1-12. Pre-grade 1 education is available, though not compulsory, through Alberta Early Childhood Services (ECS), a unique interdepartmental holistic approach to child development, in partnership with local school board or community ECS operators.

Institutions Post-secondary education is under the jurisdiction of Alberta Advanced Education and Manpower. Provincial grants account for approximately 85% of funding, the balance coming from tuition fees and private grants. The province's 4 universities — Alberta, Calgary, Lethbridge and Athabasca (a unique DISTANCE-LEARNING institution) — are all public nondenominational institutions, enrolling a total of 46 797 graduate and undergraduate students in 1983-84. Other components of the public, post-secondary sector include Northern Alberta Institute of Technology in Edmonton and Southern Alberta Institute of Technology in Calgary (11 476 students combined in 1983-84) and 10 public colleges (14 503 full-time and 8678 part-time in 1983-84). The colleges offer a variety of university transfer, vocational and high-school upgrading courses.

Cultural Life

Cultural life in Alberta has had to combat 2 major negative forces: the persistence of a "frontier ethos" that emphasizes economic materialism and rugged individualism; and a cultural dependency on external metropolitan centres such as New York, London, Toronto and Los Angeles. Yet it has had advantages: a rich physical landscape that has influenced both painters and writers; a diverse population that perpetuates various ethnic cultures; plus recent governmental, corporate and private affluence, which has benefitted the cultural sector.

The Arts Until the 1960s, visual arts in Alberta were centered in Calgary around the Provincial Institute of Technology and Art (now the Alberta College of Art), and dominated by a British-inspired school of landscape painters. From W.J. PHILLIPS through H.G. GLYDE, W.L. Stevenson and Illingworth KERR, they painted the prairie, foothills and mountain countryside. Calgarians Maxwell BATES (also an architect) and Marion Nicol were 2 modernist exceptions. During the 1960s, abstract expressionist painting of the New York school began to influence Alberta painters through the Edmonton Art Gallery. The leading public galleries are the Edmonton Art Gallery and the Glenbow-Alberta Institute in Calgary. Provincial government support for the visual arts includes the Alberta Art Foundation, which purchases works for its permanent collection.

The professional performing arts are centred in Edmonton and Calgary, with most critics giving the artistic edge to the capital city. The EDMONTON SYMPHONY and the Calgary Philharmonic dominate orchestral music; there are 2 opera companies, the Edmonton Opera Association and Calgary's Southern Alberta Opera Association; and 2 ballet companies, the ALBERTA BALLET COMPANY and the Alberta Contemporary Dance Theatre, both of Edmonton. Dramatic groups include the CITADEL THEATRE in Edmonton and Theatre Calgary. Many Alberta playwrights (including nationally acclaimed John Murrell and Sharon Pollock) have worked with Alberta Theatre Projects, a Calgary company that has encouraged local writers and indigenous themes. Major facilities for the performing arts include the twin Jubilee auditoriums in Edmonton and Calgary (built for the 50th anniversary of provincehood in 1955), Edmonton's Citadel Theatre and Calgary's new civic-built Centre for the Performing Arts. The BANFF CENTRE SCHOOL OF FINE ARTS is emerging as a nationally and internationally renowned training centre for young professionals in the performing arts.

A number of commercially successful and critically acclaimed writers of both fiction and nonfiction are based in Alberta, including novelists Robert KROETSCH (whose works take an irreverent, surrealistic look at 20th-century Alberta life), W.O. MITCHELL, and Rudy WIEBE (who has explored the ethnic diversity of prairie life). Younger talents have been encouraged by the provincial government's annual Search-for-a-New-Alberta-Novelist competition. Nonfiction writing is dominated by regional historians who appeal to both the academic and the popular reader; these include Grant MACEWAN, James Gray and Hugh Dempsey of Calgary, and James MacGregor and A.W. Cashman of Edmonton. The University of Calgary library houses one of Canada's best collections of contemporary writers' papers; Mitchell and Wiebe are represented, as well as many out-of-province writers.

Communications Daily newspaper publishing in Alberta is dominated by chain ownership; 6 of the 9 dailies are parts of Toronto-based national chains. These are the Edmonton *Journal*, Calgary *Herald*, and Medicine Hat *News* (Southam newspaper group); the Edmonton *Sun* and Calgary *Sun* (owned by Maclean Hunter); and the Lethbridge *Herald* (part of the Thomson newspaper empire). Bowes Publishers Ltd, a regional chain, publishes the Grande Prairie *Daily Herald-Tribune* and Fort McMurray *Today*. The Red Deer *Advocate*, though independent of Canadian chains, is Canada's only foreign-owned daily newspaper; it is controlled by the Liverpool Post and Echo group in Britain. There are approximately 100 weekly or community newspapers serving metropolitan, suburban and rural areas of Alberta. Magazines published in the province include the neo-conservative, provincial-rights oriented *Alberta Report* and the arts-oriented *NeWest Review* (both independently owned and published in Edmonton), the leisure- and life-style-oriented *Calgary* and *Edmonton* magazines (owned by Pacific West Press of Vancouver), plus a number of trade journals serving the petroleum and other industries.

The 11 television stations in Alberta include a mixture of national and local ownership. The CBC has network stations in Calgary and Edmonton, and affiliated stations in Red Deer, Lloydminster and Medicine Hat. CTV has affiliated stations in Calgary, Edmonton, Lethbridge and Lloydminster. Independent stations are CFAC Calgary and CITV Edmonton. Most of urban Alberta is also served by cable TV systems, which offer additional American and local channels to subscribers. Alberta Independent Pay Television of Edmonton is the regional pay-TV licensee for the province. The approximately 35 AM and 12 FM radio stations in the province are privately owned. Exceptions are the CBC network stations in Calgary and Edmonton, the U of A student station, CJSR, and the provincially owned CKUA, part of the ACCESS network that utilizes both radio and television primarily for educational broadcasting.

Historic Sites Historic sites in the province are concentrated around early exploration, fur-trade, missionary, mounted police and settlement activity. The provincially funded Alberta Historical Resources Foundation assists local groups in heritage-preservation activities. The major museums are the GLENBOW MUSEUM in Calgary, the Provincial Museum of Alberta in Edmonton, and a paleontological museum under construction at Drumheller. The major historical archives are found at the Provincial Museum in Edmonton and the Glenbow-Alberta Institute, Calgary. The Historical Society of Alberta has active chapters in Calgary, Edmonton and Lethbridge.

History

In the late 18th century southern Alberta was occupied by the BLACKFOOT, BLOOD, PEIGAN and Gros Ventre. The Kootenay and other trans-mountain peoples made regular buffalo-hunting expeditions into the area, while more southerly tribes came on warring raids. Along the N Saskatchewan R were the SARCEE, though there is some question whether they existed there before the fur trade; farther N were the BEAVER, and beyond them the SLAVEY. These Indians felt the effects of European culture long before they saw their first Europeans. Metal tools and weapons brought by the HUDSON'S BAY COMPANY were traded and retraded westwards across the Prairies; similarly the horse moved N from Spanish Mexico in the early 1700s. Gradually tribes close to Hudson Bay became dependent on trade goods and began to penetrate westwards in search of furs to use as barter. The Cree and Assiniboine (including the Stoney) moved up the N Saskatchewan R in the 18th century, forcing the Sarcee and Blackfoot tribes S and the Beaver N. The Chipewyan entered the NE corner of Alberta, pushing the Beaver back towards the mountains. By the early 1800s, the Gros Ventre had moved S into the US.

Exploration The first European known to have reached present-day Alberta was Anthony HENDAY, an HBC employee who, accompanied by a band of Cree, likely wintered near the present site of Edmonton in 1754. Competition between the HBC and the Montréal-based NORTH WEST COMPANY dominated the region in the late 18th and early 19th centuries. In 1778 Peter POND, an aggressive Nor'wester, travelled down the Athabasca R and established the first fur-trading post in the province. Ft Chipewyan on Lk Athabasca was founded in 1788 and served as the jumping-off point for Alexander MACKENZIE's trip down the Mackenzie R in 1789, and his journey up the Peace R and through the Rocky Mts to the Pacific 4 years later. The HBC countered by sending Peter FIDLER and David THOMPSON to explore and map the Athabasca and Saskatchewan rivers in the 1790s and early 1800s. The 2 companies built competing posts throughout northern and central Alberta until 1821, when the rival companies merged.

By the middle of the 19th century, Christian missionaries in search of Indian souls had begun to challenge the fur traders for possession of the territory. Methodist Robert RUNDLE in 1840 became the first resident cleric in what is now Alberta, followed 2 years later by the Roman Catholic Father Jean-Baptiste Thibault. Missionary activity peaked in the third quarter of the century, with such illustrious names as Albert LACOMBE among the Catholics and the Methodist father-and-son team of George and John McDougall. The persistent advance of the European frontier challenged the HBC's continued control over the territory. Anticipating the termination of the company's licence and curious about the suitability of the territory for general settlement, both the British and Canadian governments commissioned expeditions in 1857 to explore and report on the Prairies. Capt John PALLISER headed the British expedition, while the moving spirit of the Canadian party was Henry Youle HIND, whose optimistic reports balanced the less enthusiastic findings of Palliser and ultimately influenced Britain to refuse renewal of the HBC licence.

Settlement On 1 Nov 1869 the Canadian government purchased the entire HBC territory, including all of the future province of Alberta. The following year the region between the new province of Manitoba and the Rocky Mts was organized as the North-West Territories of Canada, with its administrative centre first at Winnipeg, then at Battleford, and finally at Regina. The DOMINION LANDS ACT of 1872 laid the basis for the quarter-section homestead survey. Two years later the NORTH-WEST MOUNTED POLICE established their first Alberta post at Ft Macleod. The North-West Territories Act of 1875 provided for a lieutenant-governor and legislature (first an appointed council, gradually replaced by an elected assembly). A series of treaties was subsequently signed with Indian groups: Treaty No 6 in 1876 covered the Cree lands of central Alberta; Treaty No 7 in 1877 brought in the Blackfoot, Sarcee and Stoney of southern Alberta; Treaty No 8 in 1899 covered most of northern Alberta (*see* LAND CLAIMS).

Settlement was still slow to materialize during the 1880s, despite the arrival of the CPR in Calgary in 1883 and its transcontinental completion 2 years later. By 1881 only some 1000 non-native settlers resided within the boundaries of the present province of Alberta; 10 years later it was just 17 500. The great influx of settlement at the end of the century followed the development of fast-maturing varieties of hard

Waterton Lakes National Park, southwestern Alberta. The area was once a Blackfoot stronghold and was discovered by Europeans in the 1850s. Situated 276 km SW of Calgary, the park was united with Montana's Glacier National Park in 1932 to form the world's first international peace park (*photo by Richard Vroom*).

spring wheat, the exhaustion of good available land in the American West, the easing of the 22-year economic depression that had gripped N America, and the vigorous immigration policy of the federal government under the direction of Clifford SIFTON. From 1896 to WWI, Alberta and other parts of the Canadian Prairies were the beneficiaries of one of the most important and dramatic population migrations in modern N American history. Settlers poured onto the open prairie farmlands and into its bustling towns and cities. Many came from Ontario and other parts of eastern Canada, others from the US and Great Britain, and others from continental Europe; the great variety of linguistic and religious backgrounds imposed an indelible, multicultural stamp on Alberta life. Alberta's population rose from 73 022 in 1901 to 373 943 in 1911 and 584 454 in 1921.

Development The creation of the province of Alberta on 1 Sept 1905 was the logical result of the great immigration boom, and an answer to the political campaign for autonomy that had developed in the North-West Territories. Political controversies at the time of provincehood centred on the rights of the Roman Catholic minority to publicly funded separate schools, the boundary with the new sister province of Saskatchewan (Albertans sought 107° W long but had to settle for 110°), and Edmonton's victory over Calgary for the site of the new provincial capital. While these issues left a legacy of bitterness towards perceived federal interference in local matters, none was as contentious as Ottawa's decision to retain control of Crown lands and natural resources. Not till 1930 were these responsibilities transferred to provincial control.

Fortune smiled on the new province of Alberta during its first decade. Immigration accelerated; grain harvests were bountiful; new communities sprang up, and a network of railway lines rapidly expanded. Yet resentment grew among farmers, who believed that their status as independent entrepreneurs was being jeopardized by the railways, banks and grain-elevator companies. The rise of the United Farmers of Alberta as a political party, and their victory over the Liberals in the 1921 provincial election were in part a manifestation of this unrest. Yet the UFA government had to cope with a provincial economy in the 1920s and early 1930s that was much weaker than the pre-1914 boom years. Grain prices fluctuated and the once-important coal-mining industry declined. The worldwide depression of the 1930s, accompanied by prairie drought, soil drifting and grasshopper plagues, accelerated an economic decline that had begun a year earlier. The Social Credit League won the 1935 provincial election by promising to fight the Depression (and the perceived eastern control of Alberta's economy) with a mixture of religious fundamentalism and radical monetary theory.

The discovery of oil at Leduc in Feb 1947 began the process of transforming Alberta's economic base from agriculture to petroleum. The resulting exploitation of oil and natural-gas resources produced an ever-accelerating flow of royalties to augment provincial revenues, brought prosperity to most segments of the population, and transformed the cities of Edmonton and Calgary into prosperous metropolitan centres. The 1973 worldwide oil-pricing crisis brought an even greater prosperity that lasted until the general economic recession of the early 1980s.

ROBERT M. STAMP

Reading: B.M. Barr and P.J. Smith, eds, *Geographical Dimension of Settlement and Livelihood in Alberta* (1983); John Barr, *The Dynasty: The Rise and Fall of Social Credit in Alberta* (1974); Carlo Cardarola, ed, *Society and Politics in Alberta* (1979); W.G. Hardy, ed, *Alberta: A Natural History* (1967); John Irving, *The Social Credit Movement in Alberta* (1959); James G. MacGregor, *A History of Alberta* (1972); C.B. MacPherson, *Democracy in Alberta: Social Credit and the Party System* (1953); W.E. Mann, *Sect, Cult, and Church in Alberta* (1955); University of Alberta, *Atlas of Alberta* (1969); Rudy Wiebe, *Alberta, A Celebration* (1979). *See also* the journal *Alberta History.*

Alberta Ballet Company, an Edmonton ballet company founded in the late 1950s by Ruth Carse as a small performing group. From this came the Edmonton Ballet Co (incorporated 1961), reconstituted as a professional classical ensemble, the Alberta Ballet Co, in 1966. Brydon Paige, who became artistic director of the company (12-14 dancers) in 1976, has choreographed *The Nutcracker, The Firebird* and *Cinderella.* The repertoire also includes the modern works *Promenade, A Soldier's Tale* and *Sundances* by Lambros Lambrou, resident choreographer since 1979.

SUSAN PEDWELL

Alberta Energy Company Ltd was established as a CROWN CORPORATION by the Alberta government under the Alberta Energy Company Act (1974). After an offering of public shares in 1975 (including an Alberta Priority Period of 2 weeks to allow Albertans to invest first in the company), by 1982 AEC was a public company with more than 50 000 shareholders owning 56% of the outstanding common shares. AEC invests in exploration and development of gas and oil resources (including tar and drilling operations). It maintains investments in pipelines, an electric utility, forest products and the coal and steel industry.

Alberta Heritage Savings Trust Fund Established in 1976 with the passage of the Alberta Heritage Savings Trust Fund Act, the purpose of the Heritage Fund is to save and invest revenues from Alberta's oil and gas. From 1976 to 1982-83 the Heritage Fund derived its funds from an annual transfer of 30% of Alberta's non-renewable resource revenues and retention of the Fund's investment earnings. In 1983 the Act was amended to allow the proportion of nonrenewable resource revenues to be specified annually. In 1983-84 the Fund received 15% of these revenues, totalling $720 million. Since mid-1982, the Fund's investment income has been transferred to the province's budget. In 1983-84, $1.47 billion was transferred, providing support equal to 2 months out of 12 of budgetary expenditures. Money from the Fund has been invested in capital projects to provide long-term benefits to Alberta, eg, Alberta Oil Sands Technology and Research Authority ($250 million to 1983-84), the Walter C. Mackenzie Health Sciences Centre ($268 million), Kananaskis Country Recreation Development ($183 million) and major irrigation projects ($284 million). Investments intended to strengthen or diversify Alberta's economy include the debentures of provincial crown corporations, such as the Alberta Opportunity Co ($168 million to 1983-84), Alberta Agricultural Development Corporation ($847 million), Alberta Home Mortgage Corporation ($2.5 billion) and Alberta Housing Corporation ($907 million). Investments in development projects include participation in the Syncrude project ($443 million) and loans for the Prince Rupert grain terminal ($117 million). Prior to 1982-83, the Fund also provided loans to other Canadian provinces ($1.9 billion in debentures were held at the end of 1983-84). As of 31 March 1984, the financial and deemed assets of the Heritage Fund were $13.17 billion.

Alberta Oil Sands Technology and Research Authority, an Alberta CROWN CORPORATION funded by the ALBERTA HERITAGE SAVINGS TRUST FUND, was established in 1975 to promote the development and use of new technology for oil-sands and heavy-oil production, with emphasis on reduced costs, increased recovery and environmental acceptability. Enhanced recovery of conventional crude oil was added to AOSTRA's mandate in 1979. AOSTRA reports to the minister of energy and natural resources. Projects are selected by a 7-member, government-appointed board consisting of Alberta residents with experience in PETROLEUM development and technology management. AOSTRA operates primarily through projects, the costs of which are shared with industry; the resultant technology is available to any user at fair market value. AOSTRA also supports research at Canadian universities and research institutions, provides grants to inventors, and funds the operation of a technical information system. Educational assistance is provided through scholarships and fellowships. AOSTRA expects to spend more than $400 million over the life of the program, with comparable expenditures by industry. This expenditure makes AOSTRA one of the largest single-purpose research and development programs in Canada. AOSTRA's head office and information centre is in Edmonton; a second office is in Calgary.

E.J. WIGGINS

.lberta Press Act Reference (1938) also alled Reference Re Alberta Statutes, concerned n Alberta bill which would have compelled ach newspaper in the province, when called pon to do so by a government official, to publsh the government's rebuttal of criticism of the overnment that had appeared in the newsaper. The Supreme Court of Canada judged that e bill was ULTRA VIRES of the province, ie, that exceeded the power of the provincial legisture. Five of the 6 judges gave as their primary eason that the bill was ancillary to and deendent upon other, invalid legislation. Two dges, however, added that free political disussion was too important to Canada as a whole) be treated as a local and private matter, and ne other judge argued that legislation affecting eedom of the press in discussing public affairs 'as within the CRIMINAL LAW power of Parliaient. Three judges declared that free public disussion is the breath of life for our parliamenry institution derived from Great Britain and hat our constitution is similar in principle to hat of the UK. GÉRALD-A. BEAUDOIN

.lberta Research Council (ARC), the oldest nd best-funded provincial research organizaon, was established by order-in-council as the cientific and Industrial Research Council of .lberta in 1921. In 1930 a provincial Act forhalized the council's mandate to inventory and romote development of natural resources. The overnment could not fund ARC during the REAT DEPRESSION, and the council was governed y UNIVERSITY OF ALBERTA from 1933 to 1942. In 951 a revised Act formally established it as inependent of the university and appointed its irst research director, Nathaniel GRACE. Research acilities were built on the university campus in 954-55; laboratory and office space has been stablished in Nisku, Devon, Red Deer, Calgary, ethbridge and Edmonton. ARC is recognized or expertise in COAL LIQUEFACTION, oil-sands geoogy and chemistry and other resource-extracion technologies. Research is planned in the reas of computer technology and BIOTECHNO-OGY. ARC is a CROWN CORPORATION, responsible or advising the government, providing techical advice to industry and promoting ecoomic and social development through reearch. The president, appointed by provincial xecutive council, presides over about 500 staff. 'he council now consists of 15 members from usiness, university and government, and is haired by a member of the provincial legisature. Funding is primarily through provincial rants and contracts, with smaller business and ederal input. *See* ALBERTA OIL SANDS TECHNOLOGY AND RESEARCH AUTHORITY. MARTIN K. MCNICHOLL

Alberta Wheat Pool, with head offices in Calary, is an agricultural CO-OPERATIVE formed in 1923 when the open-market system of selling wheat began to weaken in response to a recesion in prices. All original members of the Alberta Wheat Pool contributed $1 per share; when legislation governing the pool was enacted, this money was refunded and the pool became a service association with ownership esting with the operating grain farmers. Today he Alberta Wheat Pool handles seed and ferilizer distribution, and the interests of its grainproducing members come before profits. As of July 1982, it had annual sales or operating revenue of $1.5 billion (ranking 61st in Canada), including grain purchased for and delivered to the CANADIAN WHEAT BOARD; assets of $464 million (ranking 137th); and 2094 employees. The shares are held by co-operative members.
DEBORAH C. SAWYER

Alcan Aluminium Limited, with head offices in Montréal, is a Canadian producer and fabricator of ALUMINUM. In 1902 the Northern Aluminium Company was incorporated in Shawinigan Falls, Qué, as a Canadian subsidiary of the Aluminum Company of America. In 1925 it became the Aluminium Company of Canada, Ltd. In 1928 it became a corporation by acquiring all outstanding stock from its parent, and eventually emerged as a major competitor to the Aluminum Company of America. The present name was adopted in 1966.

Alcan is the third-largest aluminum producer in the noncommunist world and is involved in all phases of the aluminum business, with bauxite holdings in 7 countries and smelters in 8. The company generates electricity from its own hydroelectric facilities and handles mining and processing facilities. As well, Alcan has joint ventures in Brazil, Jamaica, Spain and Ireland. In 1982 it had sales or operating revenue of $5.7 billion, converted from US dollars (ranking 7th in Canada), assets of $8.2 billion (ranking 6th) and 71 567 employees. Shares are widely held and foreign ownership stands at 49%. DEBORAH C. SAWYER

Alcoholism is a behaviour pattern characterized by uncontrolled drinking of alcoholic beverages to the extent of impairing health and social functioning. Alcoholism is thus one extreme in a range of drinking patterns that vary among individuals in degree of dependency and tolerance, and in a host of other ways, eg, timing, beverage choice. Groups and countries also differ in drinking patterns, norms and standards, and forms of regulation and control. The term "problem drinker" is used to refer to persons not necessarily physically addicted to alcohol but experiencing (or causing) health, social, and other problems.

History of the Use of Alcohol The process of fermenting sugar-containing liquids to make alcohol has been known since the beginning of recorded history and is today practised by many preliterate people around the world. The ancient Egyptians drank both wines and beers, as did earlier peoples elsewhere in the Middle East. Of 139 societies around the world, at least 121 apparently consume alcohol in some beverage form. Stronger drinks, produced by distilling fermented liquids, first appeared during the Middle Ages in the Middle East or South Asia (*see* DISTILLING INDUSTRY).

Sociologists have found that the amount of drinking differs among the societies of the world, and that this variation can be explained by technological complexity and other factors. Although more advanced societies are more likely to use alcohol, drunkenness is more widespread among less complex societies, apparently because of anxiety induced by the uncertainties and other hazards of subsistence. The introduction of distilled beverages from Europe has also tended to disrupt traditional drinking practices in non-Western societies. More controlled drinking is associated with tighter social organization, particularly where alcohol use is incorporated symbolically into collective ceremonies. In industrial societies, the greater personal freedom people enjoy, together with the requirement for more organized and tightly scheduled work activity, has led to pressure to regulate and limit alcohol use.

Scientific Perspectives on Alcohol Use Ethanol, popularly known as "alcohol," is actually one of a class of organic compounds consisting of a hydroxyl group attached to a carbon atom. Ethyl alcohol (CH_3CH_2OH) is the principal pharmacological ingredient of alcoholic beverages. Other alcohols and related substances are present in small quantities, and these may contribute to the physiological and psychological effects of alcohol, including the "hangover." One ingredient, thujone, a component of wormwood oil, is a potent intoxicant present in absinthe and in lesser quantities in vermouth. In wines, yeast acts on natural sugars to produce ethanol; wines are made not only from grapes, but from many other fruits as well, and have a maximum alcohol content of about 14%, as this is the concentration at which yeast is killed (*see* WINE INDUSTRY). Fortification, in which a portion of the must is distilled and then returned to the original liquid, can increase the alcohol content of wine, as in the production of sherry. BEERS are typically lower in alcohol content and are produced from starchy plants by first breaking down, with the help of an enzyme, the complex carbohydrates into simpler sugars. Finally, beverages containing up to 95% alcohol can be produced by distillation, ie, the heating of a fermented liquid to the point that the portion containing ethanol will evaporate and condense back to a liquid state. Popular distilled beverages in Canada include rum, made from sugar cane, and whisky, produced from barley and other grains.

An alcoholic beverage is absorbed rapidly into the bloodstream through the stomach wall and the small intestine because it does not undergo any digestive processes. The rate of absorption can be modified by, among other factors, the type and amount of food present in the stomach. Recent ingestion of a fatty meal substantially slows absorption of alcohol. From the blood, alcohol is distributed to all parts of the body and absorbed until an equilibrium is achieved between the alcohol in the blood and that in various organs. Alcohol is eliminated slightly (10%) through expiration, perspiration and urination, but most of it is metabolized in the liver, ultimately producing water, carbon dioxide and energy.

The degree of intoxication produced by ethanol reflects the concentration of alcohol in the blood, which is primarily a function of the amount ingested, the volume of blood in the body, rates of absorption and metabolism, and time since ingestion. Depending on body weight, an adult male could have a blood alcohol concentration of 0.06% after 3 typical drinks of an alcoholic beverage. Findings on physiological and psychological correlations of these small doses of ethanol are inconsistent, but at larger doses there is no doubt that alcohol becomes a central nervous-system depressant. The evidence suggests that a blood alcohol level of 0.1% affects some of the motor areas of the brain, eg, speech, balance and manual dexterity. An alcohol concentration of 0.2% depresses all the motor centres and that area concerned with emotions. At 0.45% the entire area concerned with perception is depressed and coma results. At 0.7% the centres controlling heartbeat and breathing are depressed and the person dies.

In general, the findings of psychological studies of the effects of ethanol, particularly at lower doses, on complex behaviour (eg, aggression, sex) are difficult to interpret. Research on the effects of alcohol on emotions and "moods" are likewise inconclusive. Many laboratory studies have ignored the situational variables, eg, the presence of others, social relationships with these people, and so forth, that set the context for drinking in everyday life. There is also evidence that a person's expectations of the effects of alcohol play a large part in the quality of the drinking experience.

Studies of national drinking patterns and cross-cultural research on alcohol use have revealed considerable societal variation in behavioural responses to alcohol. The definitions held by a group or a society about the functions, uses and effects of alcohol almost certainly significantly affect the responses of persons to dietary alcohol. In some societies, eg, Italy, where alcohol is defined largely as a food, wine is consumed with meals and seems to have little disruptive effect on behaviour. In Scandinavia, especially Finland, alcoholic beverages are traditionally defined as intoxicants, and the consumption of distilled beverages, largely apart from meals, can lead to explosive or violent episodes. In beer-drinking countries of Europe and N America, alcohol is largely defined as a facilitator of social interaction. However, it would be premature to conclude that the strength or type of beverage is the direct or indirect cause of behavioural response. Among certain rural Bolivians, for instance, the normal beverage contains 95% alcohol, and yet the response to gross intoxication in social situations to this unusually strong drink is passiveness, and disruptive behaviour is extremely rare.

Alcoholism and Alcohol Abuse Researchers approach the problem of alcoholism from a variety of perspectives: biological (how alcohol affects the body), psychological (how it affects the mind) and sociological (how alcohol is provided and consumed in society). It is clear that some persons develop a tolerance for alcohol, ie, increasing amounts are required to achieve the same degree of perceived intoxication. Some people also become dependent on alcohol; a change occurs in their body cells, which have become adapted to alcohol. Withdrawal symptoms include craving, shakiness and increased anxiety (the hangover can be considered a mild form of withdrawal). More extreme reactions to cessation of long periods of heavy drinking can include nausea, vomiting and seizures. Delerium tremens ("DTs"), which combines several of these withdrawal symptoms, can include hallucinations and other unpleasant sensations.

Some chronic problems resulting from prolonged heavy drinking are considered manifestations of alcoholism; these include nutritional deficiencies, digestive problems, inflammation of the liver and pancreas, anemia, impotence, neurological dysfunctions and the newly discovered fetal alcohol syndrome. Other problems related to heavy drinking include motor vehicle crashes, other forms of accidental death and injury, suicide and crime.

Despite much research, the causes of alcoholism remain obscure. Alcoholism, in fact, is better conceived as a set of related problems, each of which differs somewhat in characteristics, causes, prognosis and treatment. Cultural factors, eg, religion, attitudes toward alcohol, and drinking problems, are related to rates of alcoholism. Social phenomena, such as the practices of family and friends and the nature and strength of punishments and rewards for drinking, also affect alcohol use and abuse. Limitations or inducements regarding the availability of alcohol, such as income, regulations on manufacture, distribution and sales, appear in some studies to influence the extent of drinking and alcohol problems. Individuals also differ in their predisposition to alcohol intoxication and dependence, and for this reason much psychological and physiological research has been conducted. There is little evidence, however, that certain personality types are predisposed to alcoholism.

Drinking in Canada More than 80% of Canadian adults consume alcoholic beverages at least occasionally. Canada has been classified internationally as a beer-drinking country, as beer and ale account for more than 50% of the consumption of absolute alcohol. Another 35% represents use of distilled spirits. Although in countries such as Turkey, Poland and Israel the majority of alcohol consumed is in the form of spirits, in absolute terms Canadians are among the world's leaders in spirits consumption also, since many of the countries specializing in spirits have relatively low levels of alcohol consumption overall. Canadians on average drink only 8 litres of wine apiece annually, compared with 166 in Portugal and 142 in France. In general, however, the drinking patterns of the countries of the world are becoming more similar to one another; in Canada this means that consumption of beer has been declining and that of wine increasing.

Canadians now drink about 12 litres of absolute alcohol per adult per year, and the amount has been increasing. In 1950 the figure was less than 7 litres per capita. Nevertheless, alcohol use in most countries, including Canada, is relatively moderate today compared with that of the 18th and 19th centuries. In the 1870s, for example, Canadians drank, on the average, about 15 litres annually. Moreover, the type of beverage consumed has been changing, reflecting a long-range trend away from distilled beverages and towards milder beverages. The TEMPERANCE MOVEMENT of the 19th-century seems to have had considerable impact on moderating drinking practices, although it could have merely reflected a trend already underway in society. Canada is generally similar to northwestern European industrial countries in alcohol consumption levels.

It has been estimated that there are approximately 700 000 alcoholics in Canada (about 5% of adult drinkers), a figure calculated from the known incidence of mortality caused by cirrhosis of the liver, and therefore probably a conservative estimate. International comparisons of alcoholism generally rely on data on cirrhosis of the liver (the "Jellinek formula"), and it is known that cirrhosis rates are highly correlated with overall consumption levels. Therefore, rates of alcoholism for the countries of the world generally reflect consumption levels, so alcoholism in Canada is about average for Western countries. About 2700 persons annually die in Canada from cirrhosis of the liver, which is equivalent to a death rate per year of 17 per 100 000 population age 20 and over. A few hundred more die of other alcohol-related conditions (poisoning, automobile accidents, etc). Rates of death caused by cirrhosis of the liver increase markedly with age and are higher in urban areas and in the West and North, the areas with the highest levels of alcohol consumption in Canada.

Canada is a complex and varied country and it manifests considerable variation in drinking practices. Canadians say they have about 6 drinks per week on the average, although this is undoubtedly an underestimation. Men, however, drink 3 times as much alcohol on the average as do women. In the more traditional Atlantic region the sexes differ by a factor of 4, whereas in BC the sex difference in drinking is less. English-speaking Canadians drink more than linguistic minorities. For males, alcohol consumption peaks in the fifth and sixth decade of life, whereas the amount of drinking declines steadily with age for women. Married people drink less than the single, divorced or separated.

Other factors appear to influence alcohol use, in particular social class and religion. For women, increases in the level of education, income and occupational skill lead to a greater use of alcohol, although studies suggest that a higher proportion of female heavy drinkers are found in the low-income population. Men in the intermediate levels of occupation and education have the highest levels of alcohol consumption. Jews are the least likely to abstain from alcohol of any religious group, but they also have the lowest rates of alcoholism. This immunity to addiction seems to result from the ritual uses that alcohol is put to in orthodox religious practice. Persons with no religious affiliations are the heaviest drinkers. For men, recent illness is more common among heavier drinkers, whereas the reverse is true for women; this difference probably merely reflects, however, the increase in illness with age and the different effects of alcohol on age for men in contrast to women.

Responses to Alcohol Problems Prior to the 19th century in Canada, the use of alcohol w largely taken for granted, and cider, beer a wine were consumed every day. Addiction alcohol was ignored, since regular use of be erage alcohol was the accepted norm. The e ception to this generalization was the ea attempts (by both French and British autho ties) to regulate the drinking of native peop The drinking of distilled spirits had becor more common by the turn of the 19th centu and temperance movements in Britain and t US advocated moderation in the use of alcoho beverages. The churches, particularly the Ba tists and Methodists, became active in the ter perance cause, which eventually advocated to abstention from alcohol and the legal pr hibition of the "liquor traffic." At this poi conflict between social groups (eg, religious, et nic and political) began to affect the debate, a plebiscites for prohibition revealed large inte provincial differences in support of the me sure. Québec was overwhelmingly opposed prohibition, while PEI and NS were heavily favour. Prohibition of spirits became nation policy during WWI, although much illicit ma ufacture and evasion occurred. Shortly aft WWI the provinces began replacing prohibito legislation with a system of government-co trolled distribution and licensing. The ostensib purpose of this role for government was maint nance of public health and order, but the actu function today is largely one of raising reven and dispensing political patronage. Researc does show, however, that the pricing polici and the control of the hours and days of sale c have some impact on alcohol consumption ar problems.

Treatment of Alcoholism A variety of pr grams to treat alcohol-related problems exis in Canada. Some programs treat alcoholics d rectly, while others offer referrals to treatme facilities, provide counselling for families alcoholics or provide programs on alcoholis prevention, drinking and driving, etc. Alcoho ics Anonymous (AA) and a variety of gover ment-sponsored programs (some affiliated wit health-care institutions, others existing only treat alcoholism) are directly concerned wit providing assistance to alcoholics. Governme programs have been classified as, first, detox fication, ie, inpatient care for 2 or 3 days; se ond, short-term residential, ie, inpatient trea ment or rehabilitation for a few days or week third, long-term residential; and fourth, ou patient clinics. Outpatient clinics account f over 33% of facilities; 30% of programs are lon term residential and include halfway hous and rural retreats. Nationally, there are abo 350 such programs, which admit about 200 ne cases per facility annually. About 10% of Car ada's addicted population is treated annually b one or another of the alcoholism program Males are 6 times as likely as females to b admitted and the mean age of admission is 4 years.

The annual cost in Canada for the treatmer of alcoholism borne by the provinces in 197 was about $50 million, or $543 per case. B comparison the provinces earn some $2 billio in profits from their liquor monopoly. The ec nomic costs of alcohol abuse include, howeve lost production in industry (which for male amounts to about $4 billion annually), and est mated total health-care costs (including hospita days) amount to over $3 billion annually. Th cost of traffic accidents resulting from alcoh abuse may amount to over $1.6 billion annu ally. Alcohol abuse has been linked to fires (e from lighted cigarettes), child abuse and violen crime. These and other costs are difficult to esti mate.

Types of Therapy Therapies for alcoholisn include drugs (eg, Antabuse), which cause un pleasant reactions in the drinker; individua psychotherapy; behavioural techniques (eg, learned aversion); and group therapy. The efficacy of these therapies is controversial.

Typically, about 33% of alcoholics appear to recover or improve after treatment, but estimates may only reflect the fact that the severity of a drinking problem tends to fluctuate and individuals generally seek treatment during acute phases of their condition. There is really not even a consensus on what constitutes "improvement." Although a few researchers have claimed that alcoholics can tolerate "social" drinking, this notion runs counter to the ideology of AA, a widespread and reportedly successful self-help organization for alcoholics. Among its tenets is a firm emphasis on helping other alcoholics, which contributes to morale and solidarity among AA members.

RONALD L. COSPER

Reading: J. Royce, *Alcohol Problems and Alcoholism* (1981); W. Schmidt, R. Smart and M. Ross, *Social Class and the Treatment of Alcoholism* (1968).

Alder, TREE or shrub of genus *Alnus* of BIRCH family. The 30 known species are found mainly in the Northern Hemisphere; 3 are native to Canada. Speckled alder (*A. rugosa*) is a transcontinental shrub and the most common Canadian alder. Red alder (*A. rubra*) is a small, short-lived tree of western BC. Green alder (*A. crispa*) is a transcontinental northern shrub; the very closely related Sitka alder (*A. crispa sinuata*) is found in BC mountains. Genus displays birch-like characteristics, eg, shallow roots, horizontal bark markings (lenticels) and elongated spring catkins (cylindrical reproductive structures). Alders occupy moist sites and have nitrogen-fixing root nodules. They are distinguished by stalked buds, twig cores somewhat triangular in cross section, and fruiting bodies resembling miniature cones. Healer, artisan and warrior used alders: bark for throat medicine, dyes and tannin; wood for cabinets and for bridge foundations because of endurance under water; and charcoal for gunpowder.

ROGER VICK

Speckled alder (*Alnus rugosa*), with male flowers (left), female flowers (centre) and cones on the right (*artwork by Claire Tremblay*).

Alderdice, Frederick Charles, businessman, politician (b at Belfast, Ire 10 Nov 1872: d at St John's 26 Feb 1936). He was twice prime minister of Newfoundland, Aug-Nov 1928 and June 1932-Feb 1934, and the last person to hold that office before confederation with Canada. A prominent St John's businessman, he entered the Legislative Council in 1924 and assumed the Liberal-Conservative party leadership and the prime ministership on the retirement of Walter MONROE in 1928. Alderdice was defeated by Richard SQUIRES in the ensuing general election but remained leader of the opposition United Newfoundland Party. Newfoundland had been in financial difficulties since WWI and by 1932 international credit had all but disappeared. On 5 Apr 1932, in a climate of unemployment, widespread distress and accusations of government misconduct, there was rioting in St John's outside the legislature. The House was subsequently prorogued, and in the June elections Alderdice's party defeated Squires 25 seats to 2. With Newfoundland facing imminent bankruptcy, Alderdice appealed to Britain for financial aid and the appointment of a royal commission to consider Newfoundland's future. The resulting Amulree Report of 1933 recommended the temporary suspension of responsible government. The Newfoundland legislature agreed, and on 16 Feb 1934 a COMMISSION OF GOVERNMENT was instituted and continued for 15 years, composed of 3 Newfoundlanders, 3 Britishers and the governor. Alderdice was appointed a commissioner.

ROBERT D. PITT

Alderfly, small, dark, soft-bodied INSECT of order Megaloptera, family Sialidae, found in freshwater habitats bordered by ALDER. It is characterized by 2 pairs of veined, membranous wings, chewing mouthparts, large eyes and long, many-segmented antennae. Adults may not feed and are short-lived. Alderflies are most active at midday. They deposit 200-500 dark brown eggs in rows forming large masses on branches or other objects near water. Larvae hatch in 10-14 days and drop or make their way to water. Larvae are aquatic, preferring muddy bottoms. They have chewing mouthparts and are predaceous. The larval stage may require 2-3 years to complete. Fully grown larvae pupate in a cell in soil, moss, under stones, etc, usually near water. About one month is spent in the pupal period. Adults appear in early summer and are feeble fliers. Of the 10 species found in Canada, *Sialis velata* is the most widely distributed (BC to Qué). Larvae and adults are food for many freshwater fish and bait for anglers.

J.E.H. MARTIN

Alert Bay, BC, Village, pop 626 (1981c), inc 1946, is located on Cormorant I, off Vancouver I, 288 km N of VANCOUVER. Its sheltered bay first attracted KWAKIUTL Indians who used the area as a winter dwelling; the village has a striking collection of TOTEM POLES, including the tallest in the world. It is one of the most important fishing areas in BC and is also supported by logging, mining and tourism.

ALAN F.J. ARTIBISE

Alexander, Harold Rupert Leofric George, 1st Earl Alexander of Tunis, army officer, governor general (b at London, Eng 10 Dec 1891; d at Slough, Eng 16 June 1969). The last British governor general of Canada (1946-52) was born into the Irish aristocracy. A regimental officer in the Irish Guards during WWI, he had once hoped to be a professional artist, but the war made him a committed soldier. By 1937 he was the youngest major-general in the British army. He led the 1st Division in France in 1940 and the rearguard at Dunkirk, directed the British-Chinese army's retreat from the Japanese invasion of Burma (1942), and from Aug 1942 was senior army commander in the Mediterranean. He was slated to become chief of the Imperial General Staff after the war, but British PM Winston Churchill claimed that "Canada is a much more important post." Handsome, athletic, elegant, and assisted by a popular wife, Lady Margaret, Alexander made a strong public impression as governor general. At ease in an essentially ceremonial role, he travelled widely and led a relaxed life, with ample time to ski, fish and paint. On his return to England he was unenthusiastic minister of defence in the Churchill government, 1952-54.

O.A. COOKE AND NORMAN HILLMER

Alexander, William, Earl of Stirling, poet, courtier, colonizer (b at Menstrie, Scot *c*1577; d at London, Eng 1640). Although he never visited N America, he is remembered for his nationalistic foresight, and for providing Nova Scotia with its name, flag and coat of arms. Sir William envisaged colonization as an answer to Scottish expansion, comparable to the contemporary, successful English ventures. Enjoying the support of both James I and Charles I, he was granted territory (1621), necessary funding through the sale of knight-baronetcies (1624), and armorial bearings for the province (1626). Financial problems, the reluctance of Scots to emigrate and French territorial claims all hampered development. Although Sir William's son established 2 brief settlements, in Cape Breton and at PORT-ROYAL (Annapolis Royal), the entire grant was sacrificed to the French in 1632 in return for full payment of Charles I's marriage settlement.

LOIS KERNAGHAN

Reading: John G. Reid, *Acadia, Maine and New Scotland* (1981).

Alexandria, Ont, Town, pop 3271 (1981c), inc 1903, located midway on the CNR rail line between Montréal and Ottawa. Father Alexander Macdonell, later bishop of Upper Canada, began the town (first known as Priest's Mills) as a mill site a few years after the War of 1812. In 1890 it became the seat of the Roman Catholic diocese of Alexandria (later relocated at Cornwall). Around that time it showed much promise in carriage manufacturing. After economic setbacks in the Great Depression and earlier, Alexandria since WWII has regained a considerable degree of prosperity with a concentration on textiles, footwear, milk processing and trucking. It continues its early role as a merchandising and services centre for the surrounding farm community. About two-thirds of the population are French Canadian, but both English and French are spoken. St Finnan's Cathedral, the Bishop's Palace and the Monastery of the Precious Blood are of architectural interest.

ROYCE MACGILLIVRAY

Reading: Royce MacGillivray and Ewan Ross, *A History of Glengarry* (1979).

Alfalfa, or lucerne (genus *Medicago*), herbaceous perennial belonging to the LEGUME family and grown as a FORAGE CROP. It evolved in central Asia, an area with cold winters and hot, dry summers, and spread to Europe, East Asia, Africa and the New World. The major commercial species are *M. sativa* and *M. falcata*. Alfalfa flowers range from purple to yellow and are borne on a long raceme (ie, structure composed of short stalks spaced equally along a central axis). The seed pods are spiral shaped; small, kidney-shaped seeds are produced. The trifoliate leaves are arranged alternately on the stem. The root system is characterized by a deep taproot which, under favourable drainage conditions, may penetrate 7.5 m. The erect stems usually grow 60-90 cm high; regrowth after cutting is very rapid, even in hot summers. When alfalfa is cut for silage or hay, at the later flower-bud stage, the protein content may vary from 10% to 20%. Since 1950, many improved cultivars have been bred to increase alfalfa use in Canada. The yellow-flowered *M. falcata* has been developed for dry-land prairie; blue-flowered *M. sativa* has been made disease and insect resistant to maintain hectarages in areas of Canada with favourable temperature, drainage and soil acidity. Yield varies greatly with temperature and moisture conditions: eg, in the Edmonton area, 2 cuts yield 5136 kg/ha; in Winnipeg, 6787 kg/ha; in Guelph, 3 cuts yield 13 619 kg/ha. Alfalfa will continue to be the most important forage for DAIRY cattle.

W.R. CHILDERS

Algae, aquatic organisms that manufacture food by photosynthesis and have relatively simple morphology and unprotected reproductive structures. When conducting tissue is present, it does not contain lignin (compound typical of cell walls of woody plants). The algae, a heterogeneous group, were once included entirely in the PLANT kingdom; however, the present-day 5-kingdom division categorizes BLUE-GREEN ALGAE as monerans, others as protistans. Most researchers still consider certain algae to be properly classed as plants.

Classification

Algae are classified primarily on the basis of biochemical and cytological (cell) differences, which show that some algae are not related as closely to one another as to other organisms. Features used include pigments present (in addition to chlorophyll *a*; storage reserves; nature of cell covering; and presence and location of organelles (cell parts analogous to organs). The generally accepted classification scheme recognizes 4 divisions, primarily based on the presence of specific cell organelles. Within each division, classification is based on biochemical features and cell details. Not all phycologists [Gk, *phykos,* "seaweed"; *logos,* "discourse"] accept this system; there is a tendency to recognize more divisions (7-12), each with fewer classes. The lack of membrane-bound organelles distinguishes the blue-green algae. Rhodophyta are characterized by the complete absence of flagella (organelles for motility). Chromophyta and Chlorophyta are differentiated by pigmentation. The traditional divisions, each containing several classes, are discussed below.

Rhodophyta [Gk, *rhodo,* "red"] occur mostly in marine habitats, often dominating lower intertidal and subtidal regions. Most red algae consist of rows of intertwining cells, linked in a series end to end (as filaments). Cells have a characteristic appearance as cell walls are very thick and swell at death. Individual cells appear to be interconnected by thin strands penetrating the cell walls. Sexual reproduction is common for most species with a complex life history. Cell walls contain agar and carrageenan, used in various industries to stabilize emulsions, coat various materials, etc. Carrageenan is harvested from coastal areas in PEI and NS. The NATIONAL RESEARCH COUNCIL has actively encouraged the establishment of SEAWEED farming of IRISH MOSS. Coralline red algae, an integral component of living CORAL reefs, deposit calcium carbonate in their cell walls. In the Orient one red alga, *nori,* is a prized food. An attempt has been made to provide high-quality *nori* from BC for Japanese markets.

Chromophyta [Gk, *chroma,* "colour"] have a yellow-brown colour resulting from the dominant pigments, including certain carotenoids and chlorophyll c_2. All Chromophyta have complex flagella. The number, form and insertion of these flagella are used to distinguish classes. In some classes, sexual reproduction is unknown. Most classes are primarily unicellular, and are an important component of phytoplankton (small, drifting aquatic plants). Bacillariophyceae (diatoms) occur not only as PLANKTON, but also as benthic (bottom-dwelling) forms. Cell walls contain silica; massive amounts of diatom walls form deposits of diatomaceous earth, used for grinding and polishing or as insulating material. One member of class Xanthophyceae, mustard alga, is known to swimming-pool owners. Another well-known organism, *Euglena* (Euglenophyceae), with both animallike and plantlike features (motility and photosynthesis, respectively), has been variously classified as Chromophyta, Chlorophyta or Euglenophyta.

The Phaeophyceae [Gk, *phaios,* "dusky"], or brown algae, largest group of Chromophyta, dominate cold coastal waters. Intertidal and subtidal Canadian waters abound with representatives of this class; 2 orders are particularly obvious, Laminariales (kelps) and Fucales (rockweeds). Various marine animals live in the large kelp beds. In arctic and subarctic regions, kelps and rockweeds predominate. The largest and most structurally complex algae belong to these classes; specialized conducting and reproductive cells are present. Sexual reproduction occurs commonly and the life history is usually plantlike, showing alternation of generations or phases. Cell walls contain algin, especially in the kelps abundant along BC coasts. The BC government is studying the possibility of commercial harvesting. In China and Japan kelps (*kombu* and *wakame*) are used as food.

Fucus, a brown algae commonly called rockweed (*courtesy National Museum of Man/National Museum of Natural Sciences*).

Chlorophyta [Gk, *chloros,* "green"] contain most genera and show most diversity. They may be divided into several classes, separated primarily by morphological and cytological features. Green algae in freshwater and terrestrial habitats are generally microscopic and morphologically simpler than those growing in marine habitats. Masses of green algae form pond scums. Commonly, the algal component of LICHENS is a member of class Chlorophyceae. The life history of the freshwater green algae involves extensive asexual reproduction; the zygote is often only a resistant stage, able to last through periods unfavourable for growth and reproduction. Most marine green algae have either the typical plantlike or animallike life history and lack the resistant zygote.

Charophyceae (stoneworts) occur in the FOSSIL record as calcified remains of female reproductive structures. Stoneworts are restricted to freshwater and some estuarine habitats and are generally microscopic. They are probably similar to the progenitors of vascular plants. As a class, the Charophyceae might be be expanded to include some of the Chlorophyceae that have cell features more similar to vascular plants than to the majority of green algae.

Cyanophyta, or blue-green algae, are monerans, ie, prokaryotic cells lacking membrane-bound nuclei. Many researchers consider them to be a special class of bacteria.

Structure and Function

Algal cells may be covered by rigid walls, series of plates, strips or scales. The basic wall consists of carbohydrates, often combined with proteins. Wall composition may involve inorganic materials (eg, silicon, calcium). Certain compounds, phycocolloids [Gk, *kollodes,* "glue"], abundant in cells of red and brown algae, are commercially marketed (ie, agar, algin, carrageenan). Storage reserves are also usually carbohydrates (eg, glucose, starch). Fats, oils and proteins may be present but less is known about them.

Chlorophyll *a* is the principal photosynthetic pigment, but accessory pigments allow absorption of light energy at different wavelengths; such energy is transferred to chlorophyll *a* for photosynthesis. Accessory pigments may be soluble in water or organic compounds (eg, alcohol). Water-soluble pigments, the phycobiliproteins [Lat, *bilis,* "bile"], are restricted in occurrence; organic-soluble pigments occur in all algae.

Cytological variation among algae includes presence and nature of flagella on some cells. Reproductive cells commonly are flagellated, as are some vegetative cells. A flagellum may be smooth or may have tubular hairs along most of its length. The way the flagella are inserted on the cell is also important in classification.

Many algae reproduce primarily by asexual means, often producing great numbers of organisms in a relatively short time. Such occurrences are termed blooms. Many algae have sexual reproduction as a normal part of their life history. Cells producing reproductive cells have no protective covering of sterile tissue and vegetative cells often become reproductive. Gametes (sex cells) may be identical in appearance or different enough to be considered male and female. In the latter instance the smaller, often motile gamete is male. Gametes are normally dispersed freely in water; the zygote is unprotected by parent cells. Some algae, primarily those growing in marine environments, produce 2 multicellular generations, as do terrestrial plants. Other algae produce only one recognizable stage. Some of these have a life history similar to that of most animals, in which gametes are produced by meiosis or reduction division (ie, cells have half of the genetic makeup of the parent cell); hence, fertilization is necessary. Still other algae, primarily those in freshwater habitats, produce gametes by mitosis; the resultant complete single cell of the zygote has the same genetic makeup as the parent cell.

Distribution

Algae have worldwide distribution, growing wherever light and water are present. Their most obvious occurrences are on rocky coasts of all continents (except Antarctica) and as scums of lakes and ponds. Canada's Pacific Coast has a richer algal flora than the Atlantic Coast, which generally has fewer and smaller species. Distribution on the inner coast differs from that of the open coast, primarily because of differences in salinity. Subarctic and arctic marine algae are more restricted in all ways; there is little growth in unprotected areas. In Canadian marine areas, summer is characterized by the presence of large numbers of algae, the increase being especially noteworthy wherever ice masses occur in winter. The depths to which algae grow depend on light penetration. In coastal estuaries, algae have reduced reproductive potential and are morphologically different from those of open waters.

Open waters, marine or fresh, contain forms too small to be seen without a microscope. Usually unicellular and known as phytoplankton [Gk, *phyton,* "plant"; *planktos,* "wandering"], they are primary food producers for ZOOPLANKTON [Gk, *zoe,* "life"]. Phytoplankton are usually not present in large masses and must be concentrated to be studied. Members of the Chromophyta are the most common phytoplankton, Dinophyceae and Bacillariophyceae predominating. Phytoplankton can form blooms, eg, red tides composed primarily of Dinophyceae. In inshore waters, such as some BC coastal inlets, the Bay of Fundy or St Lawrence estuary, dinoflagellate blooms produce a toxin which may be concentrated by shellfish feeding on them. Eating the shellfish can cause paralysis and death to seabirds and mammals (including humans).

Canada contains more than 25% of the Earth's fresh water, mainly in lakes and rivers. Phytoplankton in lakes generally are limited to open water, unless the shoreline slopes gradually and contains areas of sediment where rooted aquatic plants can grow. Generally, the larger the ratio of sediment surface to water volume, the more productive the water body. Productivity refers to the number of organisms present and to their physiological activities of growth and reproduction. As phytoplankton are food for zooplankton, which in turn are eaten by fish, attempts to increase phytoplankton production have been undertaken in lakes where commercially important fish live or reproduce.

Studies done in BC and Ontario show that increases in fish size and numbers occur when nursery lakes are fertilized with nitrogen and phosphorus (*see* AQUACULTURE). Rocky or sandy lake shores provide few nutrients for algal growth. The cool, acidic waters of sphagnum bogs are relatively rich in certain of the Chlorophyceae, Chrysophyceae and Xanthophyceae (*see* SWAMP, MARSH AND BOG). In general, large rivers are poor habitats for algae, except in backwater areas or along shores. Slower-moving rivers may have some phytoplankton and some algal growth along shores if sediment is sufficiently stable. Fast-moving mountain streams usually have a specific algal flora, although large populations are rarely present.

Algae can also live in habitats where water occurs only as condensation, eg, dry soil, desert areas, rocks. In moist areas, some algae grow on trees and shrubs, stone, concrete and man-made objects. Some algae grow in hot mineral SPRINGS; some unicellular Chlorophyceae grow in ice and snow, eg, red snow seen in summer in old, melting snowbanks in the mountains of BC and Alberta. A few grow in high concentrations of various chemicals (eg, sodium, magnesium, chlorine, sulphur) as in prairie water bodies that lose water only by evaporation. A few algae live on or in other organisms. *See* VEGETATION REGIONS.

JANET STEIN

Reading: F.E. Round, *Ecology of Algae* (1981).

Algoma Steel Corporation Limited Algoma started producing steel in SAULT STE MARIE, Ont, to make rails for Canada's transcontinental railroads. On 18 Feb 1902 the first steel was tapped and several months later the first rails rolled in Canada were produced. The plant then consisted of a 550 tpd (tonnes per day) Bessemer steel converter and a 900 tpd rail mill. Rails now account for less than 10% of the company's annual steel shipments of nearly 2.5 million t. Algoma, a fully integrated steel producer, has 5 BOSFs (basic oxygen steelmaking furnaces) and Canada's largest blast furnace, which is over 30 storeys high and has a production capacity of over 5000 tpd of pig iron. Algoma's modern rolling facilities include a 422 cm wide plate mill, the widest in Canada, and over half its steel is sold as plate and sheet. Algoma is a long-established producer of structural shapes for the domestic CONSTRUCTION INDUSTRY. *See* IRON AND STEEL INDUSTRY.

JOHN G. PEACEY

Algonquin (Algonkin) are a group of communities of Algonquian-speaking people living in western Québec and adjacent Ontario, centering on the OTTAWA R and its tributaries. They call themselves *Anissinapek* (*Anishinabeg*) or by the name of their local community. The Algonquin have been known to Europeans since 1603, when they were allies of the French and of the MONTAGNAIS-NASKAPI and HURON against the IROQUOIS. This conflict, which had its origins in the competition over the European FUR TRADE, lasted throughout much of the historic period.

Algonquin has been classified as a dialect of Ojibwa, one of the languages of the Algonquian family. As the dialects of Ojibwa merge one into another, it is not possible to establish a definite linguistic boundary between other Ojibwa dialects and Algonquin. However, the Algonquin are politically distinct from the OJIBWA. Neighbours of the Algonquin include CREE, OTTAWA, Huron and Iroquois. Since Algonquin bands or local communities were largely independent of one another, relations between an individual Algonquin band and other groups depended largely on local conditions. Marriages took place between Algonquin and other groups and generally relations between neighbouring bands were tempered by kinship ties regardless of language or tribal designations. Relationships with the Iroquois fluctuated, with hostilities most pronounced during the 17th and 18th centuries; however, some Algonquin resided alongside Catholic Iroquois at Oka, a mission reservation near Montréal.

The Algonquin were hunters who lived in bands consisting of related families. The bands were egalitarian, with leadership provided by respected individuals and heads of families. In the southern portion of their area where both climate and soils permitted, some bands practised gardening. During the historic period they became involved in the fur trade. Summer encampments near trading posts became larger and, as time spent trapping for furs increased, some necessities were purchased from the traders to supplement hunting and fishing. Their skills have led to employment in forestry and other industries in recent years. During the 19th century, modern INDIAN RESERVES and communities emerged, often near the former trading posts. Hostilities with Iroquoians ceased as Algonquin and Iroquois worked together for the betterment of conditions for Indians as a whole. More recently the Algonquin have joined with the Cree and others to strive for mutual goals as various development projects threaten their traditional way of life. A calculated estimate places the contemporary Algonquin population at 4600. *See also* NATIVE PEOPLES, EASTERN WOODLANDS and general articles under NATIVE PEOPLE.

MEREDITH JEAN BLACK

Reading: B.G. Trigger, ed, *The Handbook of North American Indians*, vol 15: *Northeast* (1978).

Algonquin Provincial Park (est 1893, 7600 km²), the oldest provincial park in Ontario, is located 210 km N of Toronto. The area, which lies across the southern edge of the Canadian SHIELD between Georgian Bay and the Ottawa R, consists mainly of Precambrian granites, smoothed and gouged by ice sheets that receded 10 000 years ago. The rolling topography is dissected by numerous rivers and some 2500 lakes, which provide access by boat to the interior. Poor soils, a harsh climate and fires have produced a varied and changing second-growth FOREST, including pine, fir, birch and poplar. The PARK is famous for its wolves, and other species (eg, deer, moose, bear, raccoon) are common. About 240 bird species have been recorded, including the gray jay, spruce grouse, brown thrasher, scarlet tanager and loon. The cold, deep, nutrient-poor lakes are especially suited to trout, and smallmouthed bass; pike, muskellunge and walleye are also found. Extensive logging, especially for white PINE, began in the 19th century; today 75% of the park is still subject to controlled logging. Recently, land-use pressures and park planning have led to considerable public debate regarding the appropriate use and designation of the park. Much research (primarily on ecosystems) has occurred in Algonquin, and an astronomical OBSERVATORY is situated in the park. Facilities include a museum and pioneer logging exhibit, lodges, campgrounds, scenic drives, trails and 1600 km of lake and river canoe routes.

JOHN S. MARSH

Algonquin Provincial Park, Ont, established in 1893 as a result of concern about the depletion of natural resources and the growing need to provide recreation in a natural setting (*courtesy Ontario Ministry of Natural Resources*).

Algonquin Radio Observatory, *see* OBSERVATORY.

Alien Question Most of Upper Canada's earliest settlers were from the US, but following the WAR OF 1812 American immigration was discouraged by Gov Francis GORE. The problem was to determine the loyalty of immigrants from the recent enemy; the law stated that anyone might claim full naturalization by swearing loyalty to Britain after 7 years' residency in the colony. By implication, those who had not gone through these proceedings — approximately half the population of UC — were alien, and were vulnerable to dispossession, disenfranchisement and disqualification from office. The confused state of affairs reached a crisis in 1820-21 when American-born Barnabas BIDWELL and his son, Marshall, sought election to the House of Assembly and faced opponents who claimed they were ineligible to hold office. If the Bidwell's were aliens, so was the majority of UC's population. The controversy was settled in Feb 1827 when a new instruction from the COLONIAL OFFICE retroactively corrected any defects in the citizenship of all UC officeholders and landowners who had arrived before 1820.

D.N. SPRAGUE

Alikomiak and **Tátimagana,** Inuit hunters from the central Arctic, were the first of their race to be condemned and executed (1 Feb 1924) under Canadian law. They had murdered 4 Inuit at Coronation Gulf in Aug 1921 in a dispute over women, and Alikomiak, while under arrest at Tree River had shot and killed W.A. Doak of the RCMP and Otto Binder of the Hudson's Bay Co. A judicial party travelled from Edmonton to Herschel I in the summer of 1923, and the 2 men were convicted of murder and sentenced to death. It was decided that the earlier policy of leniency had not sufficiently impressed the Inuit with the seriousness of such offences; thus, despite appeals in the press, for the first time in such a case the sentences were not commuted, and the men were hanged in the transport shed of the RCMP detachment at Herschel I.

W.R. MORRISON

Alimony refers to the right of one spouse to receive financial support from the other during marriage. On divorce, a similar right to receive "maintenance" arises. Historically, only a wife was able to obtain alimony and this right was dependent on her proving to a superior court that her husband had been guilty of matrimonial misconduct, eg, adultery, physical cruelty or desertion. However, even if misconduct could be proven, the wife might be disentitled where it could be demonstrated that she had also been guilty of specified misconduct or had connived at or condoned her husband's action, or where some other defence was available. Alimony could also be awarded by a court as an additional remedy where, for example, the wife received a court order for judicial separation.

Many of these original concepts have been reformed and there is considerable diversity regarding alimony among the provinces. Alberta, Newfoundland, Saskatchewan, NS and the NWT have retained vestiges of the old fault-based approach, and in the latter 3 jurisdictions certain rights to receive alimony remain available only to the wife. The modern trend, adopted in the other Canadian jurisdictions, is to place the husband and wife on equal terms and to replace the requirement of matrimonial misconduct with a simpler notion of a duty to provide support in cases of financial need.

The provision of maintenance or support involves a money payment, paid either in a lump sum or periodically. The amount ordered depends on a variety of factors, including financial needs, means and the standard of living of the spouses. Reallocation of property ownership cannot be ordered as alimony, although all provinces possess separate statutory provisions which permit such orders (*see* FAMILY LAW; PROPERTY LAW). BRUCE ZIFF

Allan, Andrew Edward Fairbairn, radio-drama producer, actor, writer (b at Arbroath, Scot 11 Aug 1907; d at Toronto 15 Jan 1974). Seeing radio as the national theatre of Canada, through his taste, judgement and intelligence he brought the art of radio drama to new heights during his long career with the CBC, and set standards internationally. Allan came to Canada at age 17 and graduated from U of T, where he edited the *Varsity*. His first radio job was with CFRB Toronto. He was working for the BBC in England when war broke out in 1939 and was returning to Canada with his father on the *Athenia* when it was torpedoed and sunk. His father was killed. Allan joined the CBC in Vancouver 1942, and produced the Stage series of over 400 dramas in Toronto 1944-56. It included some classics and some newly created works by writers such as Lister Sinclair, Ted Allan, Len Petersen, Tommy Tweed, Mavor MOORE and many others who wrote scripts for emerging stars Lorne GREENE, Lloyd Bochner, Budd Knapp, Jane Mallett and John Drainie. Robert FULFORD has observed that Allan's CBC Stage "gave many of us . . . our first hint that there were Canadian writers who had something interesting to say." He retired in 1962, unable to transfer his great talents to TV. He was the first artistic director of the SHAW FESTIVAL at Niagara-on-the-Lake, Ont, 1963-65, and continued writing, acting and directing for TV and radio until his death in 1974. JOHN L. KENNEDY

Reading: A. Allan, *A Self Portrait* (1974).

Allan, Sir Hugh, shipping magnate, railway promoter, financier (b at Strathclyde, Scot 29 Sept 1810; d at Edinburgh 9 Dec 1882, buried at Montréal). Allan immigrated to Montréal (1826) and obtained employment through relatives as a clerk in a general merchandising firm. Ten years later, Allan became a partner, and with financing from his father and brothers in Scotland, bought steamers and sailing ships to extend the firm's shipping business. As president of the Montreal Board of Trade (1851-54), Allan persuaded the Canadian government to use mail contracts to subsidize regular steamship lines between Montréal and Britain (1853). Allan, with technologically advanced ships built in Clyde, Scot, and the help of Conservative political friends, was able to wrest the contract from competitors in 1856. By the 1870s, Allan's company, the Montreal Ocean Steamship Co, also held government contracts to carry passage-assisted immigrants. Taking advantage of the Québec government's subsidies for colonization railways, Allan expanded into railway building. An Allan-organized syndicate, including some Americans and incorporated in 1872 as the CANADIAN PACIFIC RAILWAY Co, obtained the contract to build the railway to British Columbia that was promised that province when it joined Confederation. Meanwhile, Allan contributed over $400 000 to the Conservative election fund. Suspicions that Allan had bought the railway contract led to the PACIFIC SCANDAL and Sir John A. MACDONALD's only post-Confederation electoral defeat in 1873. Allan acquired coal mines on mainland Nova Scotia, and factories for textiles, shoes, iron and steel, tobacco and paper in central Canada. He used his banking and insurance interests to secure favourable press coverage through generous loans to editors. Although a Presbyterian, he successfully cultivated the leading French Canadian clergy, and once had a priest relieved of his parish duties to participate in a campaign to obtain municipal subsidies for an Allan railway. Allan was knighted by Queen Victoria in 1871. *See* RAILWAY HISTORY; SHIPPING INDUSTRY.

MARGARET E. MCCALLUM

Allan, Sir Hugh Andrew Montagu, banker, shipowner, sportsman (b at Montréal 13 Oct 1860; d there 26 Sept 1951), second son of Sir Hugh ALLAN. To avoid confusion with his cousin Hugh Andrew Allan (1857-1938), he changed his name to Hugh Montagu in 1878. His business career began when at age 21 he entered the firm of Hugh and Andrew Allan, shipbrokers and builders. He was chairman of the ALLAN LINE of steamships, 1909-12, shortly before it was purchased by Canadian Pacific, but his principal interest was in banking. He served as the last president of the Merchants' Bank of Canada, 1902-22. In 1921 it had 400 branches and assets of $190 million, but its loans were overextended and, to avoid its collapse, Allan arranged for its amalgamation into the Bank of Montreal. He was also president or director of numerous financial and manufacturing companies. Allan was an enthusiastic sportsman, president of the Montreal Jockey Club for many years, his horses winning the QUEEN'S PLATE, the Montreal Hunt Cup and other trophies. He donated the ALLAN CUP, for competition in amateur hockey, in 1910. He was honorary lieutenant-colonel of the Black Watch (Royal Highland Regiment) of Canada, and was knighted in 1904. Of his 4 children, his son was killed in WWI and 2 daughters drowned in the *Lusitania* sinking, 1915. The surviving daughter, Marguerite Martha Allan (1895-1942), founded the Montreal Repertory Theatre, an influential amateur dramatic group between the wars.

D.M.L. FARR

Allan, William, businessman, politician (b near Huntly, Scot 1770; d at Toronto 11 July 1853). Between 1795 and 1822 Allan established himself as a prosperous merchant in York [Toronto], as a government officeholder and as a land speculator. From 1822 to 1835 he was the first president of the BANK OF UPPER CANADA, an institution so successful that it was attacked both politically as the too-powerful tool of the FAMILY COMPACT and commercially for its banking monopoly in Upper Canada. Allan served on the board of the Welland Canal Co, was co-commissioner of the Canada Co 1829-41, and governor of the British America Fire and Life Assurance Co 1836-53. As well, Allan served on the Legislative Council 1824-41 and on the Executive Council 1836-41. His reputation was made in business, however, and rests on his contribution to Ontario banking. WENDY CAMERON

Allan Line was a Scottish-Canadian shipping company founded by Capt Alexander Allan (1780-1854) with his newly purchased brigantine, *Jean*, which sailed from Greenock, Scot, to Québec in 1819. In 1826 his son, Hugh ALLAN, came to Montréal and established the family business in Canada; other sons established offices in Greenock and Glasgow. In 1854 the Allan consortium formed the Montreal Ocean Steamship Company, which in 1855 won the government mail contract to Britain. With innovative engineering and design the Allan ships prospered on the Atlantic and other trade routes. The first steel liner to sail the Atlantic

Copy of a brochure advertising Allan Line Royal Ma Steamships sailings for summer season, 1881 (*courte Public Archives of Canada/C-4127/R. Inness Coll*).

was the Allan Line's *Buenos Ayrean* in 1880. Aft the turn of the century the company ha difficulty financing new ships and was so to CANADIAN PACIFIC Ocean Services in 1909. S SHIPPING INDUSTRY.

PETER HOPWO

Reading: Thomas E. Appleton, *Ravenscrag* (1974).

Allard, Charles Alexander, businessma medical doctor (b at Edmonton, 19 Nov 1919 Allard graduated in medicine from U of A i 1943. From 1955 until 1969 he was a surgeo and then chief surgeon at the General Hospita in Edmonton. He began his career as an entre preneur when he constructed a clinic to hous his own practice in 1947. He established Allarc Developments, one of the largest REAL-ESTAT companies in Canada, and was its president an chairman of the board until he sold it to Carm Developers of Calgary for $130 million in 198 He has been active in finance (North West Trust life assurance (Seaboard Life Insurance) and th media (Allarco Broadcasting) and is a membe of the board of directors of Allarco Develop ments. JORGE NIO

Allard, Jean-Victor, soldier (b at Saint-Mo nique de Nicolet, Qué 12 June 1913). He wa commissioned in the Non-Permanent Activ Militia in 1933, served during WWII at th Canadian Army Staff College, Kingston, and i England, Italy, (Royal 22e Régiment), Belgium the Netherlands and Germany (6th Infantr Brigade), finishing with the rank of brigadie From 1945 to 1948 he was military attaché i Moscow; in 1953 he commanded the 25th In fantry Brigade in Korea and represented Canad at the armistice sign-ing in Panmunjom. He wa the first commander of Mobile Command an in July 1966 was promoted to general and ap pointed chief of defence staff, the first Frenc Canadian to be thus recognized. JEAN PARISEA

Allen, Ralph, journalist, editor, novelist (b a Winnipeg 25 Aug 1913; d at Toronto 2 De 1966). One of the best-loved and most influ ential editors of his day, Allen was justly fa mous for his work at *Maclean's* (1946-60) an the *Toronto Star* (1964-66). Reared in Oxbow Sask, he began his career with the Winnipe

Tribune and was a distinguished war correspondent for the Toronto *Globe and Mail*. He also wrote 5 novels, of which *The Chartered Libertine* (1954), a satirical look at the CBC, is best known, and a popular history of Canada, *Ordeal by Fire* (1961). He is credited with implementing many editorial techniques and procedures still in use today. DOUG FETHERLING

Allergies In a biological sense, the term "immunity" refers to the capability of individuals to resist or overcome infection. The protective response of an individual's system to a foreign agent consists of the production either of selective antibodies (blood proteins), also called "immunoglobulins," or of cells that can recognize and subsequently neutralize the offending agent, or both. The foreign agent that triggers the immune response is referred to as an "antigen." The term "allergy" refers to an altered immunological reactivity of the host to a foreign substance that leads to diverse harmful effects on re-exposure to that substance; more precisely, allergies include those reactions in which immunoglobulin E, a protein produced in white blood cells, is involved. The foreign substance responsible for a given allergy is called an "allergen."

The immunoglobulins, or antibodies, comprise a heterogeneous family of proteins, classified as IgM, IgD, IgG, IgA or IgE. The IgE antibodies are responsible for allergies of the immediate type, eg, allergies to the constituents of various pollens, house dusts, foods, animal danders and hairs, parasites, insect venoms, various pharmaceutical preparations (eg, penicillin) and some industrial chemicals.

IgE antibodies are unique in that they bind with very high affinity to white blood cells (basophilic leukocytes) and to mast cells found in a variety of tissues. Thus, basophils and mast cells (abundant in respiratory and gastrointestinal tracts) in a person who has produced IgE antibodies become coated with these molecules, which are oriented on the cell membrane in such a way that they can still combine with the inciting allergen. Subsequent exposure of such allergic individuals to the allergen results in its combination with the IgE antibodies on the cell surface and the subsequent release from the basophils and mast cells of inflammatory compounds, eg, histamine and leukotriene, which can profoundly affect smooth muscles and blood vessels (causing constriction or dilation leading to abnormal heart rate), mucous secretion and breathing. Allergic reactions of the immediate hypersensitivity type can range in severity from a local skin wheal with reddening of the surrounding area to systemic effects involving a profound drop in blood pressure, swelling, choking and anaphylactic shock. For example, a significant number of people die each year from the systemic effects of drugs such as penicillin, or of the constituents of honeybee venom present in a sting.

It is possible that the capacity to produce IgE reflects a protective function of this immunoglobulin; however, to the sufferers from hayfever and rhinitis the production of IgE results in disease. Normal persons also produce IgE antibodies, but only some of these individuals develop IgE-mediated immediate-type allergies. Therefore, a person who is allergic may be distinguished from one who is not by the sensitivity of their respective systems, ie, the amount of IgE produced, and not the production itself. The release of histamine and leukotrienes from mast cells and basophils in an allergic person causes a quantitatively different effect from that in normal individuals, allergic persons being extremely sensitive to minute quantities of allergen.

A second type of allergic reaction, qualitatively different from that mediated by IgE antibodies, is typified by the response to POISON IVY and poison oak. If a cellular response has caused a harmful rather than a beneficial reaction, the allergic manifestations seen in, for example, allergic contact dermatitis, can follow direct skin contact with the offending allergen. Drugs such as ampicillin and ordinary and industrial chemicals such as formaldehyde and trimellytic anhydride fall into this category. Potentially allergenic compounds may also be found in topical skin creams.

Types of Allergic Reactions
(Source: P. Young, *Asthma and Allergies: An Optimistic Future*, NIH Publications, Washington, DC, 1981)

Type	*Mechanism*	*Examples*
Type I Immediate hypersensitivity or anaphylactic	IgE antibody on mast cells reacts with antigen resulting in release of mediators.	hay fever, anaphylaxis
Type II Cytotoxic	IgG antibody reacts with cell membranes or antigen associated with cell membranes	transfusion of incompatible blood types
Type III Arthus	antigen and antibody bind together to form immune complexes in walls of blood vessels or kidneys	serum sickness, drug reactions
Type IV Delayed hypersensitivity or cell mediated	White blood cells interact directly with antigen	poison ivy, graft rejection

Allergic disorders are widespread in N America, although the actual distribution of disorders varies with the nature of the allergic response. Allergic diseases such as hay fever and extrinsic asthma afflict about 17% of the Canadian population. Clearly, the distribution of allergies caused by environmental allergens such as RAGWEED pollen, house dust or pet animal dander is determined by the distribution of the allergen itself. Allergies to ragweed pollen occur mainly in the eastern provinces; those to grass pollens throughout Canada; and those to western red cedar in BC. Allergies to dietary components occur throughout the country.

In those cases in which the offending allergen can be identified, the obvious treatment is avoidance. If the allergen cannot be avoided, two basic strategies of therapy are currently employed. One attempts to induce, through a series of hyposensitizing injections of the offending allergen, the production of the protective immunoglobulin of the IgG class and the concomitant reduction in IgE antibodies. The other involves the administration of drugs, such as antihistaminics, which ameliorate the symptoms of allergy without, however, curing the disease.

Efforts to improve the effectiveness of allergy treatment have met with little success over the last 70 years. It is only since 1966, when the husband and wife team of Kimishige and Teruko Ishizaka (then working in Denver) discovered the class of IgE antibodies, that real progress has been achieved in the understanding of the molecular and cellular mechanisms underlying immediate hypersensitivity. It is anticipated that through intensified research more effective cures for allergic diseases will be discovered in the foreseeable future. In Canada, research on the various facets of allergic diseases is being conducted at most medical schools, primarily with the financial support of the Medical Research Council of Canada. In particular, in recognition of the specialized expertise available in related biomedical sciences among researchers in the Department of Immunology at University of Manitoba, the MRC established in 1973 a Group for Allergy Research, consisting of a coordinated team of 6 senior investigators, their assistants and trainees, all working toward the elucidation of the chemical nature of some of the common pollen allergens and of the basic mechanisms responsible for the regulation of IgE antibody production. The group has recently shown that allergens can be modified chemically to products which are tolerated better by patients than the standard allergenic extracts used for hyposensitization therapy. Recent clinical trials in Scandinavia with honeybee venom, which had been modified according to the procedures developed in Winnipeg, have demonstrated that the patients treated with the modified allergens could tolerate the intravenous injection of a dose of venom equivalent to that delivered by a bee without any untoward effect. Clearly, as with all other diseases, progress in allergy treatment can be achieved only on the basis of a better understanding of the fundamental mechanisms responsible for the disease. B.G. CARTER AND A. SEHON

Alline, Henry, evangelist, hymnist, theologian (b at Newport, Rhode I 14 June 1748; d at N Hampton, NH 2 Feb 1784). An itinerant evangelical preacher in the Maritimes, Alline wrote hymns, religious tracts and a *Life and Journal*. He began his career as a saddlebag preacher in Falmouth, NS, and spent most of his life touring NS and NB. Although self-educated, he was a prolific writer and speaker committed to music as a part of religious worship. He worked unceasingly from 1776 to 1783 to create and sustain a religious revival known as the "New Light" movement. His followers, who were based mainly in NS, were referred to as "Allinites." Alline, despite the uneasiness he aroused in established church communities, was a persuasive preacher. He succeeded in his self-appointed mission to awaken many settlers to religion and is looked upon as a major influence in the establishment of the BAPTIST Church in the Maritimes. Besides his *Life and Journal* (1806) and *Hymns and Spiritual Songs* (1786), he published 5 religious pamphlets and his major theological work, *Two Mites on Some of the Most Important and Much Disputed Points of Divinity* (1781). In this latter work he expresses his personal beliefs on many religious points, including his strong anti-Calvinist stand.

DOUGLAS LOCHHEAD

Reading: J.M. Bumsted, *Henry Alline* (1971).

Allison Pass, elev 1352 m, is located at kilometre 60, highest point on the Hope-Princeton Hwy (opened 1949) through the CASCADE MTS of southern BC. It was named for John Fall Allison, commissioned by Gov J. DOUGLAS about 1860 to inspect gold strikes on the Similkameen R. He returned to report finding a new, low pass between the Skagit and Similkameen rivers. Allison mined near HOPE and was later a pioneer rancher in the Princeton area. Manning Prov Pk headquarters is situated 9 km E of the pass.

GLEN BOLES

Allotment of Time, rules of the House of Commons, Standing Orders 75A, 75B and 75C, often confused by the media with the CLOSURE rule, S.O. 33. Since 1968 most bills pass the committee stage in the standing COMMITTEES and may be amended at the report stage, but S.O. 33 applies only in the House and in committees of the whole House and works inefficiently when there are several distinct motions at a stage. The standing orders were passed by the House on 24 July 1969 amid great controversy, which was terminated by the use of closure. The new rules established procedures by which the House may set a time schedule for a bill at one or more stages of the legislative process. S.O. 75A applies when all party house leaders agree, and 75B when the Government house leader has the support of a majority of the parties; 75C allows the Government to propose, and the House to determine, after a 2-hour debate, the reasonable time to be allotted for a bill at a stage, eg, the second-reading stage. When the fixed time (eg, 2 days) elapses, divisions are called; consequently, allotment of time is often called "guillotine closure." *See also* FILIBUSTER. JOHN B. STEWART

Alma, Qué, City, pop 26 322 (1981c), inc 1979, located at the head of the SAGUENAY R near Lac SAINT-JEAN, 230 km N of Québec City. County seat of Lac Saint-Jean Est, headquarters of the judicial district of the same name, the present city contains 5 former municipalities: Alma, Riverbend, Isle-Maligne, Naudville and the parish of Alma. Born of the lumber industry in 1860, Alma quickly became a prosperous agricultural parish. It burst into the industrial age in 1923 with the start of construction of the Isle-Maligne hydro station on the Grande Décharge. When completed in 1926, the station supplied power for the Arvida aluminum works and the Price paper mill in Alma. Population multiplied fivefold 1921-31. During WWII ALCAN built an aluminum plant there that was expanded during the 1950s. In that same era Alma became a tertiary centre for the Lac Saint-Jean area (commerce, professional services, hospital, college). Geographic centre of the Saguenay-Lac Saint-Jean region, it is the site of various regional organizations. Alma is also the departure point for Lac Saint-Jean cruises.

MARC ST-HILAIRE

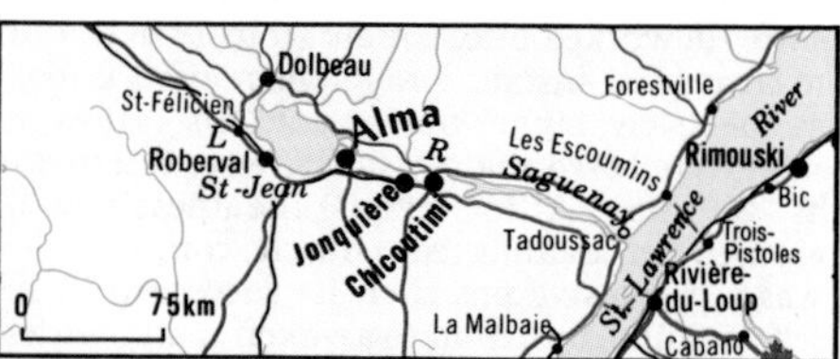

Almanacs, annual compilations in sheet or book form which included a calendar, with saints' days and other significant dates, and astronomical phenomena, such as eclipses, phases of the moon and transits of the planets, were a well-established tradition in Britain and the American colonies by the mid-18th century. Canada's first printers brought this tradition with them adapting it to the French, English or Indian market. The almanac was a local publication since astronomical tables were calculated according to the longitude and latitude of a particular geographical area. Other information of local interest, such as lists of church and civic officials, postal and customs regulations, and stagecoach and ferry services, was also frequently included. Cheap, practical and annually in demand, the almanac was a "bestseller" for early printers and an important source of revenue.

Many of the earliest almanacs printed in Canada no longer survive. The Brown and Gilmore office in Québec City is known to have issued a sheet almanac each year from at least 1765 and an almanac for the Indian trade from the following year, but most of these early wall calendars are known only from the printers' records. There had been a printing office in Halifax as early as 1751, but it is not known if an almanac was produced there. Brown and his successor, John Neilson, later published the popular *Almanach de Québec* for over 60 years beginning in 1780. Anthony Henry of Halifax printed Canada's oldest surviving almanac, *The Nova-Scotia Calendar* for 1770. In 1788 Henry began the publication of a second almanac, *Der Neuschottländische Calendar*, for German-speaking settlers of the colony. It is believed to be the first German-language publication printed in Canada. Christopher Sower printed New Brunswick's first almanac (1786); and the oldest surviving almanac printed in Ontario is *Tiffany's Upper-Canada Almanac, for the year 1802*, published by Silvester Tiffany at Niagara (Niagara-on-the-Lake). The King's Printers at York (Toronto) published almanacs with increasing regularity in the early years of the 19th century. Of particular interest today are those issued by Charles Fothergill in the 1820s because of the "Sketch of the Present State of Canada" included each year. Few almanacs seem to have been produced in the Prairie provinces, perhaps because of the relatively late arrival of printing there. Some almanacs published in the American northwest included information about Vancouver I and the mainland, but *The British Columbia Almanac*, published in Victoria (1895-98), is the only one known to have been produced in the province.

The use of the almanac as a vehicle for political opinion has a long history in English-speaking countries. A Canadian example is William L. MACKENZIE's *Caroline Almanack* for 1840, published while the rebel leader was in exile in Rochester, NY. Special-interest groups — religious, political, professional, labour and commercial — used the almanac to sell their ideas. Particularly prolific in the late 19th and early 20th centuries were the almanacs issued by patent-medicine manufacturers, in which the calendar itself is lost in a sea of advertisements and testimonials. Canada's oldest continually published almanac, *The Canadian Almanac & Directory*, first issued by Hugh Scobie of Toronto for 1848, still retains a small calendar and astronomical section. As quick reference sources for information about all aspects of Canadian life, this directory is still consulted, as are similar works such as the *Corpus Almanac & Canadian Sourcebook*. ELIZABETH HULSE

Almighty Voice, or Kah-kee-say-mane-too-wayo, meaning Voice of the Great Spirit, also known as Jean-Baptiste, Cree, outlaw (b near Batoche, Sask 1874; d there 30/31 May 1897). Almighty Voice's tragic confrontation with the NWMP resulted in the last battle between whites and Indians in N America. He grew up on the One Arrow Reserve near Batoche. In Oct 1895 he was arrested for illegally butchering a cow. Stories conflict, but shortly after his arrest Almighty Voice escaped from the Duck Lk jail and shot and killed NWMP Sgt Colin Colebrook. For 19 months he evaded police but he was finally cornered with 2 young relatives in a poplar bluff. For 2 days the fugitives fought a force of 100 police and civilian volunteers, killing Cpl C.H.S. Hockin and Const J.R. Kerr of the NWMP, and Ernest Grundy, Duck Lk postmaster. The bluff was bombarded with cannon-fire, resulting in the 3 Indians' deaths.

EDWARD BUTTS

Almond, Paul, filmmaker (b at Montréal 26 Apr 1931). Educated at McGill and Oxford, Paul Almond joined the CBC in 1954. He directed numerous dramas, "The Hill" (1954), "Under Milk Wood" (1959) and "Point of Departure" (1960). All won Ohio awards. In 1968 he made his first feature, *Isabel* (1968), which starred his wife, Geneviève BUJOLD. Two films also starring Bujold followed, *Act of the Heart* (1970) and *Journey* (1972). The unique trilogy, displaying Almond's interest in the irrational and mystical, constitute his best work and a distinctive contribution to Canadian film. In 1980 he was called in to direct the ill-fated *Final Assignment* (1980). He then went on to produce and direct *Ups and Downs* (1983). PIERS HANDLING

Almonte, Ont, Town, pop 3855 (1981c), inc 1871, is located on the Mississippi R, 54 km SW of Ottawa. The site was granted to David Shepherd for a gristmill and sawmill (1819) and like most pioneer towns was given several names, including Shipman's Mills, after Daniel Shipman, who is regarded as the town's founder. The name Almonte was chosen (1856) in honour of the Mexican general Juan Almont whose championing of Mexican independenc in the face of American aggression appealed t the citizens of the town. In 1827 Almonte wa made administrative centre for Irish imm grants, but its chief subsequent importance wa for woollen textiles. Power was drawn from th scenic falls within the town. Today, it is a agricultural-supply, electronics and textile manufacturing centre. It is the birthplace of R Tait MCKENZIE, surgeon and sculptor, who re stored an old gristmill (*c*1830) outside the tow and used it as a studio; the mill survives as Mi of Kintail Museum and contains 70 of McKen zie's works. Robert Young House (*c*1835) was th boyhood home of James NAISMITH, inventor c basketball. The weekly newspaper is the *Gazett*

K.L. MORRISO

Althouse, John George, educator (b at Ails Craig, Ont 10 Apr 1889; d at Temagami, Ont Aug 1956). Educated at U of T, he was appointe headmaster of U of T Schools 1923, dean of th Ontario Coll of Education 1934 and chief direc tor of education for Ontario 1944. Though a sup porter of moderate progressivist influences du ring the 1930s, he became the principal agent fo Premier George DREW's conservative shift in On tario education in the 1940s. President of the Ca nadian Education Assn 1948-49, he was the au thor of *The Ontario Teacher: An Historical Sketch c Progress, 1800-1910* (1929). ROBERT M. STAM

Altschul, Rudolf, professor of anatomy, sci entist, author (b at Prague [Czech] 24 Feb 1901; d at Saskatoon 4 Nov 1963). He received his medi cal degree in Prague and did postgraduate work in Paris and in Rome. In 1928 he began the prac tice of neuropsychiatry in Prague, but in 1939 he and his wife fled the Nazi occupation and made their way to Canada and U Sask where he wa first an instructor and, by 1955, head of the department of anatomy. Altschul was a mar of broad culture: photographer, linguist, connoisseur of the arts, a born raconteur and superb teacher. He was the author of 103 scientific papers dealing with a wide variety of subjects including the pathology of the nervous system skeletal muscle degeneration, cell division and, in particular, arterial degeneration, the subject of his books: *Selected Studies on Arteriosclerosis* (1950), and *Endothelium — Its Development, Morphology, Function and Pathology* (1954). His later research led to niacin therapy for lowering blood-serum cholesterol and in 1964 to the publication of *Niacin in Vascular Disorders and Hyperlipemia*. S. FEDOROFF

Aluminum (Al), silvery, ductile metal which acquires a dull lustre on exposure to air, caused by the formation of a film of aluminum oxide that adds corrosion resistance. Aluminum is light (its density about 1/3 that of copper), nonmagnetic and melts at 660°C. It is a good conductor of heat and electricity. The element was isolated in 1825 and the first ingot was produced in 1854, but an economic method of commercial production (Hall-Héroult electrolytic process) was discovered only in 1886. Abundant hydroelectric power enables Canada to produce primary aluminum from 6 smelters in Québec and one at KITIMAT, BC, the main producer being the ALCAN ALUMINIUM LIMITED. Refined metal is fabricated by casting, rolling and extrusion. Manufactured products include doors, windows, house siding, beverage cans, foil, cooking utensils, electrical wiring, etc. Pure aluminum is soft but may be hardened by mechanical working and by the addition of alloys such as copper, magnesium, manganese and zinc.

Canada produced 1 124 874 t of primary aluminum in 1981, about 7% of world output, valued at 0.56% of the GNP. Since Canada consumes only about a quarter of its production, a large amount is exported as primary metal,

ostly to the US. Aluminum is the most abunant metal in the Earth's crust but does not occur ncombined. The principal source of the metal, auxite, contains about 50-60% alumina (aluinum oxide, Al_2O_3) and forms by the weatherg of aluminum-rich rocks under tropical onditions. Bauxite is imported from Brazil, uinea, Guyana and Australia. Aluminum is roduced by separating pure alumina from auxite in a refinery, then treating the alumina y electrolysis. An electric current flowing rough a molten electrolyte, in which alumina as been dissolved, divides the aluminum oxide to oxygen, which collects on carbon anodes nmersed in the electrolyte, and aluminum etal, which collects on the bottom of the arbon-lined cell (cathode). *See* METALLURGY.
A. JOHNSTON

madjuak Lake, 4140 km², is one of 2 lakes tuated in the Great Plain of the Koukdjuak, in -central BAFFIN I. This lower-lying area has merged only recently from beneath the waters f FOXE BASIN. Amadjuak Lk is the fourth-largest n the NWT. High inland cliffs are unusual in e Arctic and the lake is noted for the 30 m igh limestone cliffs that overlook it. They ark the scarp edge of the cuesta plain and are eepened and swept clear of debris by the action f the lake's waves. DOUG FINLAYSON

mbridge, Douglas White, engineer, busiessman (b at Mexico City, Mexico 5 Jan 1898; d t Toronto 16 Nov 1976). Educated at Lower anada College and McGill, Ambridge held varous positions in the pulp and paper industry in e 1920s and 1930s and helped construct Onrio Paper Co's plant at Baie Comeau, Qué, 937. In WWII, as a member of the Production oard and director general of the Naval Shipuilding Branch in Ottawa, he played a major ole in industrial mobilization. He directed the onstruction of crown-owned Polymer Corp's ynthetic rubber plant in Sarnia, Ont, and was, uccessively, its VP, president and chairman. In 946 he was created CBE. He became president of bitibi Power and Paper 1946, and presided ver its recovery and expansion, retiring from e presidency 1963 and from the chairmanship 967. He was appointed chairman of the Onrio Deposit Insurance Corp in 1967. J. LINDSEY

mbrose, Tommy, pop singer, composer (b at oronto 19 Oct 1939). The creator of many of anada's most successful advertising jingles, mbrose is also well known as a club performer nd broadcaster. He began his career at age 5 ith gospel-singing appearances at Toronto outh for Christ rallies and on local radio. Priarily a singer of popular music since 1957, he as been host of several CBC TV series: "While Ve're Young" (1960-61), "The Tommy Ambrose how" (1961-63) and the gospel music show Celebration" (1975-76), which first appeared on BC Radio (1971-74). Ambrose also has several ecords to his credit. BARCLAY MCMILLAN

merican Civil War, 1861-65, sectional conlict between the Northern US states (Union) and e Southern states that seceded and formed the onfederacy. It was important in the development of a separate Canadian identity. Canaian opinion was generally anti-Northern, and e Washington government, aware of this, was ostile to both Britain and British North Amera. Britons and Canadians, predicting a Southrn victory, anticipated an attack on Canada by e Northern army, which many thought ould seek territory in compensation. Resulting ension along the border led to numerous minor ncidents, much misunderstanding and 4 sigificant crises, including the ALABAMA, TRENT, nd *Chesapeake* incidents. The fourth, raids on t Albans, Vt, in fall 1864 by Confederates based n Montréal, brought pursuing Northern troops onto Canadian soil. Confederates hoped to draw the North into violating British neutrality in Canada, with a view to inciting Britain to declare war on the North, but the attempt failed. Immediately after the war a series of FENIAN raids heightened tensions along the border; they likely would not have been tolerated by the Americans had there not been a legacy of hostility left between Canada and the Union, notwithstanding the enlistment of many Canadians in the Northern armies. This hostility led to the American abrogation of the 1854 RECIPROCITY Treaty at the earliest possible opportunity, in Mar 1866.

In analysing the causes of the war John A. Macdonald blamed the excessive power given to the states under the American Constitution, and he determined that the BNA Act would not repeat this flaw. He also established a border patrol, forerunner to the NORTH-WEST MOUNTED POLICE. Perhaps most important, the threat of American invasion, made explicit by the aftermath of the ST ALBANS RAID, led the British to favour CONFEDERATION of the BNA colonies for more effective defence. Thus the war contributed directly to both the timing and the form of Confederation. ROBIN W. WINKS

Reading: Robin W. Winks, *Canada and the United States* (1971).

American Revolution (also known as American War of Independence), 1775-83, struggle by which the Thirteen Colonies won independence from Britain. Disputes over taxes, administration and the territorial provisions of the PROCLAMATION OF 1763 and the QUEBEC ACT, simmering since the TREATY OF PARIS, 1763, broke into open war at Lexington, Mass, 18 Apr 1775. Prominent American colonists signed the Declaration of Independence on 4 July 1776.

An effective propaganda campaign conducted by the Americans succeeded in eliciting some support, particularly in Montréal, where there was some pro-American activity. The French Canadian clergy, seigneurs and leading citizens adopted a policy of support for the British, but most of the common people remained neutral and reluctant to become involved. Bishop Briand issued an episcopal mandate denouncing the rebels and urging the people to more active support, but Gov Sir Guy CARLETON (Lord Dorchester) had little success raising the militia. In Sept 1775 Gen Richard Montgomery led American forces northward, seizing Ticonderoga, Crown Point and FORT CHAMBLY. When Ft Saint-Jean capitulated in Oct, Carleton abandoned Montréal and the Americans took possession Nov 13/14. Meanwhile, Gen Benedict ARNOLD managed, despite hardships and desertions, to bring some 700 men via the Kennebec and Chaudière rivers to Québec. Montgomery joined him in early Dec with another 300 men and during a snowstorm on 31 Dec 1775 launched a desperate assault. Arnold and his men penetrated some distance into Lower Town but surrendered under counterattack. Montgomery and his leading officers were killed in their attack from the other side of Lower Town. The remaining Americans kept up their desperate siege through the winter, but were easily routed when the spring thaw brought British reinforcements. They abandoned Montréal May 9.

The failure of the American invasion left bitter memories among Canadians and drove many sympathizers into exile. However, there had been little active support for the Americans: clergy and seigneurs remained staunchly loyal and, after some equivocation, so did the merchants. Most HABITANTS remained determinedly neutral, in defiance of Bishop Briand and Carleton. Gen BURGOYNE led a British counterinvasion southward via Lk Champlain, but he overextended himself and, in the first great victory for the Americans, surrendered at Saratoga 17 Oct 1777.

As in previous conflicts, Nova Scotia remained an uncertain battleground during the Revolution. The provincial Assembly voted addresses of loyalty, but illegal town meetings gave secret support to New England. Nearly every important outpost outside Halifax suffered from American PRIVATEERING. In 1775 rebels seized Partridge I in Halifax harbour and made a futile attack on Ft Cumberland (FORT BEAUSÉJOUR) in 1776, but by 1779 the British had cleared the Bay of Fundy of privateers.

After a protracted struggle, British forces surrendered in Oct 1781, and the TREATY OF PARIS, 1783, formally recognized the United States of America. The failure of the American invasion and the influx of some 40 000 LOYALIST refugees into Nova Scotia and Québec determined that the development of the remaining British colonies would differ profoundly from their southern neighbours. D.N. SPRAGUE

Reading: J.B. Brebner, *The Neutral Yankees of Nova Scotia* (1937); M. Jensen, *The Founding of a Nation* (1968); G. Lanctot, *Canada and the American Revolution* (trans 1967); G.F.G. Stanley, *Canada Invaded, 1775-1776* (1973).

Americans Migration between the US and Canada has usually been treated as a natural event — diffusion through a semipermeable border. But any act of migration is an adventure and the adventuring spirit has at times characterized even the American migrant. The interpenetration of Canadian and American peoples has been such that no Canadian can have escaped its influence. That only 1.4% of the total population in 1971 was American born is deceptive, for the American is one of the oldest and — for all its fluctuations — one of the most enduring stocks in Canada. Perhaps 3 million Americans have immigrated to Canada since the first English settlements of the mid-18th century. Two million of these (about 20% of all immigrants) arrived in the 20th century.

Complex and polyglot as the movement from the US has been, Americans are generally considered as transients — technicians and managers doing a turn of garrison duty in the "northern hinterland" before returning home. Americans are less willing than other immigrants to assume Canadian citizenship: less than half of the Americans who immigrated to Canada in this century have become Canadian citizens. Some retain American citizenship as insurance against a possible return; others, though permanently resident in Canada, prefer to think of themselves as "North Americans." The ease with which American immigrants can return to the US has of course probably qualified their willingness to seek Canadian citizenship, as has their exposure to American nationalism. Unfortunately, because no official statistics of return migration exist (*see* EMIGRATION), it is impossible to calculate how many Americans remain in Canada, even though sometimes their numbers on arrival (eg, draft dodgers in the 1960s and 1970s) can be roughly estimated. For the same reason, there is no way of knowing the average length of residence of American branch-plant managers (*see* CANADIAN-AMERICAN ECONOMIC RELATIONS).

Since the arrival of the LOYALISTS in Canada, American migration has characteristically been heterogeneous. Americans have also tended to migrate as individuals rather than groups, although movements of a few ethnic and religious groups occurred in the 19th century. Even during the 4 best-known migration periods (Loyalists, BLACKS, farmers and draft dodgers), Americans have tended to seek individually for land, alternative resources, opportunities and freedom.

Americans have emigrated from all regions of the US (but particularly from eastern border states) and from all ethnic groups (but especially those of British and northern European stock). Canada has traditionally welcomed Americans who emigrate with property and who possess technical skills, a welcome reflected officially in IMMIGRATION POLICY. However, not all Americans have been considered ideal immigrants; since the late 1800s immigration policy has managed to exclude most American blacks and the urban poor.

Migration Between 1901 and 1914, as the railways opened up the West and as cheap land became scarce in the US, American farmers began to pour into Canada, supplying nearly as many western settlers as did the British Isles. This is the midpoint and apex of American migration so far, and some of its effects are measurable. In 1926, American-born farm operators still comprised 16% of all those in western Canada. Among all US immigrants, though, the proportion of American farmers intending to farm decreased 1922-26 from 50% to 42%, whereas the proportion of all immigrants intending to farm increased from 35% to 50%. But Americans had all along sought and found land in Canada (eg, clearing the Queen's Bush in Ontario; following the Red River's contours into Manitoba), bringing their experience to bear on land that was only dimly sensed to be foreign. As late as 1951, 24% of the American-born labour force was involved in agriculture, as compared to 17% of the foreign-born labour force as a whole. In 1971 the 10 895 American-born farmers in Canada comprised 14% of all foreign-born farmers.

American settlers have been involved in many Canadian adventures, including the early FUR TRADE, EXPLORATION, resource discovery and exploitation, early industrialism, railway and bridge building and modern scientific research. American labour leaders have exerted whatever impact they have had by visiting Canada and not by settling here, with the exception of the leaders of agrarian protest in the West, such as Henry Wise WOOD (*see* POPULISM). The American religious contribution was important in the early part of the 19th century, eg, with the founding and development of the major branches of Protestantism and with the migration of certain groups such as the Quakers. The churches became Canadianized after the REBELLIONS OF 1837 and most Americans withdrew from positions of authority. At the end of the century, HUTTERITES, MENNONITES and members of the MORMON CHURCH migrated from the US, generally to western Canada. Religious migration has since settled into a steady trickle.

Most American schoolteachers, along with the Methodist circuit riders, departed after 1837, and not until the academic explosion of the 1960s were Americans strongly represented in the Canadian education system. In 1961, 597 American-born academics resided in Canada; this number increased to 3580 in 1971 and continued to grow rapidly until the mid-1970s. American artists too, in all media, were very scarce before that decade.

The migration of the nonprofessional, nonmanagerial workers from the US is comparatively difficult to trace. From time to time Canada has needed labour but has not always been able to import it from the US, mainly because of a lack of competitive wages. Since WWI the number and proportion of skilled and unskilled worker immigrants from the US has declined steadily. American-born workers in the pulp and paper industry, for instance, calculated as 4.5% of all workers in 1921, rose to 5.8% by the end of that expansive decade, but by 1971 accounted for a mere 0.9%.

After entering Canada, Americans seem to scatter more than other immigrants. Lack of regional economic opportunity is less likely to discourage an American than other immigrants because an American is more likely to be seeking a retirement home or a refuge from urban decay. There has been steady and increasing American settlement in the Atlantic provinces.

Economic Life American settlers in Canada have traditionally included a disproportionately large and abnormally transient managerial and proprietary element. These settlers have been found more in industries and in areas where American-owned companies are particularly active. For example, many Americans have moved to Alberta since the late 1940s to direct gas and oil operations, either independently or as employees of American-owned companies. The number of low-skilled Americans working in the Alberta oil fields, however, has remained miniscule and the American-born population of Alberta has declined absolutely since 1951.

As the Gray Report observed in 1972, American investors (who would include some potential immigrants) "have seen Canada as a logical extension of their markets, given the cultural and social similarities, political stability, physical proximity, benefits of advertising spillover, and the increased ease of access as communications and transportation improve." Both investors and immigrants from the US have, at least in the present century, concentrated in resource extraction. US ownership of the oil and gas, mining and forest-product industries has averaged close to 50% since WWII. American-born managers overall account for an average of 3.1% of all managers in Canada but 8.2% of all managers in extractive industries. Manufacturing is also an important area of investment for Americans. American-born managers working in Canada comprise 4% of all managers in manufacturing, specializing in such industries as rubber and chemicals. Areas in which American influence seems obvious, however (eg, fast-food restaurants), are often those that attract few American immigrants, managerial or otherwise.

American managerial immigrants (not identified as such in official reports until 1954) comprised, between 1954 and 1979, a high of 69% of all managerial immigrants (in 1961) and a low of 19% (1977). During these years, about 1000 American managers immigrated annually (35% of all American immigrants), yet the proportion of American-born to foreign-born and to the total number of managers in Canada dropped 1961-71. The rate of transience may be increasing; it is at least apparent that fewer and fewer Americans are involved in managing American-owned operations in Canada. This probably reflects the maturing both of the companies and the Canadian managerial force (*see* BUSINESS MANAGEMENT).

Many former Americans, though, have put in much more than "a tour of garrison duty" in Canada. American industrial founders helped establish the potteries and forges of early Québec and Ontario and some helped create whole towns, eg, Walkerville, Ont; Moodyville, BC; and Hull, Qué, founded by Philemon WRIGHT. Less tangible but no less real and vital are legacies such as the brain mapping carried out by Wilder PENFIELD in Montréal and the shaping of modern liberalism in Canada by C.D. HOWE. Despite a general reticence on the subject, many Americans have acknowledged an identification with Canada, though none so colourfully as William VAN HORNE. "Building that railroad," he said, "would have made a Canadian out of the German Emperor."

DAVID HARVEY

Amérique française, magazine fd 1941 by former Collège Jean-de-Brébeuf students led by Pierre Baillargeon, following Collège publications by François Hertel and his colleagues, accurately reflected the artistic ideals of a certain Québec intellectual elite. Its contributors, worried about the future of letters and culture in Québec, worked for the recognition of French culture in America. The magazine covered the various arts, but favoured literature. Its goal was to promote the growing French Canadian writing movement.

The magazine lost some of its dynamism in 1945, when Gérard Dagenais, the new director broadened its scope to include social and economic issues. The result lacked a coherent guiding philosophy and attracted few readers. In 1947 Hertel left the magazine to Corine Dupuis-Maillet, who tried unsuccessfully to turn *Amérique française* into a prestigious literary review. Her daughter, Andrée Maillet, took over in 1951 and devoted the magazine almost entirely to new writing until its demise in 1955. It had published 4-12 issues every year since 1941. A number of authors made their first appearance in its pages, including Jacques FERRON and Anne HÉBERT. In 1963 Maillet relaunched the magazine, but only one issue appeared. *See* LITERARY PERIODICALS IN FRENCH.

LISE MAISONNEUVE

Ames, Sir Herbert Brown, businessman, civic reformer, politician (b at Montréal 27 June 1863; d there 31 Mar 1954). Ames was a successful businessman who wrote books about, and worked for civic reform, and who also worked in the interests of imperial trade and international peace. Employed in his father's firm of Ames, Holden and Co, he was elected a Montréal alderman in 1898 and worked for reform, particularly in health and education. He served as a Conservative MP 1904-20. From 1919 until 1926 he was financial director of the secretariat of the League of Nations in Geneva, and he also held other posts with the league. His book, *The City Below the Hill* (1897), is one of the earliest sociological descriptions of the working-class districts of Montréal.

T.D. REGEHR

Amherst, NS, Town, pop 9684 (1981c), inc 1889, is located near the border with New Brunswick, 15 km E of SACKVILLE, NB. Settlement began in the 1830s, but it was not until shortly before WWI that Amherst became an important regional centre. It boasted a railway-car factory with 2000 workers and an engineering company with an international reputation, as well as factories making woollen goods, enamel products, footwear and pianos. Its population was almost as large in 1914 as it is today. After WWI, the town's economy collapsed along with that of many Maritime centres, as a result of economic policies that favoured central Canada. In the 1920s thousands of Amherst residents left in search of work in New England and western Canada. The town has never really recovered from this crisis. Today, it survives as a service centre for the surrounding agricultural community and supports some light industry. Tourism is important and Amherst residents always have a warm welcome for the many visitors who take advantage of its location as a gateway to Nova Scotia.

NOLAN REILLY

Amherst, Jeffery, 1st Baron Amherst, British army officer (b near Sevenoaks, Eng 29 Jan 1717; d near Sevenoaks 3 Aug 1797). Less recognized than James WOLFE, Amherst was the ultimate conqueror of Canada in the SEVEN YEARS WAR. Influential patrons gained Amherst command of an expedition against LOUISBOURG in 1758. He obtained the town's surrender on 27 July by a careful but slow siege by his overıelming forces. Made commander in chief in America, he undertook a methodical but cau-ıus advance up Lk Champlain in 1759, which d little effect on French efforts to halt Wolfe's erations and ended abruptly after the fall of ıébec City in Sept. But in 1760 Amherst anned a campaign that saw 3 armies grind wn French resistance in converging on Mon-al. The capitulation of Montréal on 8 Sept arked the end of French rule in Canada. Am-rst left N America in Nov 1763 for Eng-ıd, where his handling of the earlier PONTIAC ırising provoked criticism. Knighted in 1761 d ennobled in 1776, he twice served as com-ander in chief of the British army before re-ing in 1796 as a field marshal. A formal and ıiturn man, Amherst made his reputation in America, and he owed much of his later ad-ıncement to this success. STUART SUTHERLAND

mherstburg, Ont, Town, inc 1878, pop 5685 981c), located on Detroit R near Lk Erie. First ttled 1784, it became the new base for the Brit-ı after they evacuated Detroit. In 1796, Ft Mal-n was established, and LOYALIST refugees laid t a townsite. General BROCK used the fort as a se to capture Detroit (1812), but it was under merican occupation 1813-15. In 1837-38 Am-rstburg was attacked 4 times by Rebel sup-rters of William Lyon MACKENZIE and was mbarded by the schooner *Anne*, which later n aground and was captured. The British gar-on remained until 1851. Today there are veral secondary industries, including soda ash ining, in the town, and it is the centre for ma-ıe salvage. At Ft Malden Historical Pk, origi-l earthworks, stone buildings and a block-use have been restored. Christ Church dates om 1818, and Bellevue, a beautiful Georgian ansion, from *c*1819. JAMES MARSH

mi, Henri-Marc, paleontologist, prehistorian at Belle-Rivière, Qué 23 Nov 1858; d at Men-n, France 4 Jan 1931). The son of a Swiss pas-r, Ami studied science at McGill, notably un-r John William DAWSON. He worked for the OLOGICAL SURVEY OF CANADA 1882-1911. Ami is st known for his work on geological for-ations in Québec and the Maritimes. His bibli-raphy contains over 200 titles. He was editor the *Ottawa Naturalist* 1895-1900. In 1900 he as elected to the RSC, and the Geological Soc of ndon honoured him with the Bigsby Medal 05. His comfortable financial situation and arriage to Clarissa Burland, from a prominent ontréal family, allowed Ami to resign from e Geological Survey in 1911 to concentrate on ehistorical studies. After moving to France, he unded the École canadienne de préhistoire, an stitution jointly funded by the French govern-ent and the RSC. RAYMOND DUCHESNE

ading: Morris Zaslow, *Reading the Rocks* (1975).

mnesty Act, 1 Feb 1849, offered a pardon to l those involved in the 1837-38 REBELLIONS. It iginated Mar 1838, when a conditional par-on was extended to minor participants. In 343, with Colonial Office authority, Gov Gen etcalfe issued a special pardon to any exiled bels who petitioned. By early 1844 all 58 rebels ho wanted to end their exile had received ardons, and in Jan 1845 they began returning Canada from Australia and Bermuda. That ear Louis-Joseph PAPINEAU, in exile in France nce 1839, also returned. Four years later, the aldwin-Lafontaine ministry introduced its mnesty bill. Only William Lyon MACKENZIE, the ıe rebel who had not been given a special par-on in 1843, returned to Canada under the Act. CURTIS FAHEY

mos, Qué, Town, pop 9421 (1981c), inc 1925, located 75 km NE of Rouyn-Noranda in north-estern Québec. It owes its existence to its vourable location in the heart of the Abitibi gion at the junction of the transcontinental railway and the Rivière Harricana, one of the region's major waterways. The area used to be called Harricana, an Algonquin expression meaning "place where bark dishes are obtained for cooking." Founded in 1914, Amos became in the mid-1920s the most important town in Abitibi and the county town of this newly settled region of Québec. It tooks its name from Alice Amos, the wife of Sir Lomer Gouin, premier of Québec. Amos assumed a leading role in the region because of its many sawmills and the surrounding rich agricultural lands lying among the Harricana. It is also the site of a new papermill belonging to Normick-Donahue. A short distance from Amos, the Abitibiwini ("people of the high ground," an Algonquin band) live in the Indian village of Pikogan.

BENOÎT-BEAUDRY GOURD

Amphibian, member of a class of VERTEBRATE animals derived from FISH and ancestral to REPTILES. Amphibians are represented by 3 living orders: Anura (FROGS), Caudata (SALAMANDERS) and Gymnophiona (caecilians or burrowing LIZARDS). Frogs have one extinct and 23 living families; salamanders, 5 extinct and 8 living families; and caecilians, 4 living families. Amphibians are tetrapod (4-legged) or, in the case of some limbless salamanders and caecilians, derived from tetrapod ancestors. They have a moist, glandular skin without epidermal scales, feathers or hair. Frogs lack a true tail as adults and have disproportionately long hind legs and exaggerated mouths. Most salamanders have a more typical vertebrate body, with elongated bodies and tail and relatively even-sized front and hind legs. Although easily identified by their lack of scales, salamanders are sometimes mistaken for lizards. All frogs and most salamanders have 4 toes on the forefeet, 5 on the hind feet; some salamanders have fewer toes or lack limbs entirely. Caecilians are limbless and have little or no tail. They usually have folds or grooves which give the body a segmented, wormlike appearance.

Green frog (*Rana clamitans*) shown in pond environment with water star grass, tuberous water lily and (lower left) frog egg mass (*artwork by Claire Tremblay*).

Canada has 40 species of native amphibians: 21 frogs and 19 salamanders. None are unique to Canada and most have more extensive ranges in the US. None occur in the northern tundra, but several are abundant in the boreal forest. The deciduous forests of SW Ontario, the coastal rain forest and interior valley grasslands of BC and the central plains of Saskatchewan and Alberta contain many species that barely range into Canada. No amphibians survived GLACIATION in Canada; therefore, this fauna has been here less than 18 000 years. Amphibians are of minimal direct economic importance. Some frogs are caught for food, particularly the bullfrog native to southern parts of eastern Canada and introduced in BC. Small frogs are used for fishing bait. The largest use may be of bullfrogs, leopard frogs and mudpuppies in university and high-school dissection and experimental physiology.

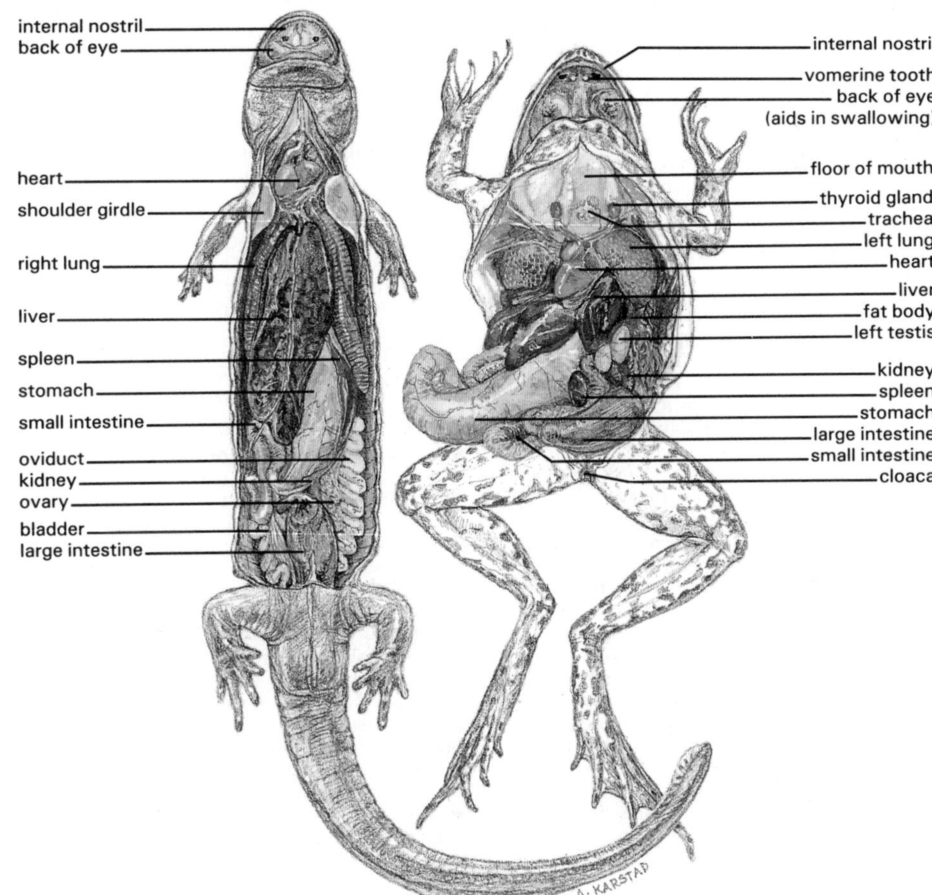

Internal organs of a salamander (left) and green frog (*artwork by A. Karstad Schueler*).

Amphibians are, however, a vital part of the ecosystem, forming a significant part of the terrestrial, aquatic and semiaquatic biomass and acting as a biological control on INVERTEBRATE members. They have recently been found useful as indicators of the effects of ACID RAIN.

F.R. COOK

Reading: F.R. Cook, *An Introduction to Canadian Amphibians and Reptiles* (1984).

Amund Ringnes Island, 5255 km², located between Ellef Ringnes and Axel Heiberg islands in the ARCTIC ARCHIPELAGO. It is flat (highest point about 610 m) and windswept; in winter its coasts are virtually indistinguishable from the surrounding ice. It was discovered 20 April 1900 by Gunerius Isachsen, a member of the Norwegian SVERDRUP expedition, and named for a member of the brewery that financed the expedition. It was surveyed 1916 by V. STEFANSSON, who found coal and gypsum on the island.

JAMES MARSH

Amundsen, Roald, arctic explorer (b at Sarpsborg, Norway 16 July 1872; d between Norway and Spitsbergen 18 June 1928). Amundsen went to sea as a young man. Determined to navigate the NORTHWEST PASSAGE, he purchased the *Gjoa*, readied it for arctic waters and embarked in 1903. After 2 icebound winters, *Gjoa* emerged in the Beaufort Sea, the first ship to cross the top of N America. In 1911 Amundsen reached the S Pole and in 1920 he sailed through the Northeast Passage. Then he turned his attention to air exploration and in 1926 flew over the N Pole in an airship piloted by Umberto Nobile. Amundsen disappeared in 1928 on his way to search for Nobile, missing on another arctic flight.

DANIEL FRANCIS

Amyot, Francis, Frank, paddler (b at Thornhill, Ont 14 Sept 1904; d at Ottawa 21 Nov 1962). His father, Dr John A. Amyot, was federal deputy minister of health. In Ottawa Amyot canoed at the Rideau Aquatic Club and the Britannia Boating Club. A large man at 188 cm and 84 kg, he required a custom-made racing shell and paddle to accommodate his long, powerful body stroke. He won 6 national senior single-blade singles championships between 1924 and 1935. In 1936 he was coach, manager and a member of the first Canadian Olympic canoeing team and at Berlin won a gold medal in the 1000 m Canadian Singles. He served in the RCN during WWII and later was an organizer of the Rideau Canoe Club.

C. FRED JOHNSTON

Anabaptists, religious and social dissenters in 16th-century Europe. In Switzerland Anabaptists arose out of the humanistically oriented Reformation in Zürich in 1525; in south and central Germany, out of joint streams of medieval mysticism and apocalypticism (the expectation that the end of the world is imminent) in 1526; in the Netherlands, out of sacramentarianism (the belief that the sacraments are merely outward symbols) and apocalyptic perfectionism in 1530. Major leaders in Switzerland were Conrad Grebel, Michael Sattler and Balthasar Hubmaier; in Germany, Hans Denck, Hans Hut, Jacob Hutter (*see* HUTTERITES) and Pilgram Marpeck; in the Netherlands, Melchior Hoffman, Bernhard Rothmann, Dirk Philips, Menno Simons (*see* MENNONITES) and David Joris. The movement was relatively small in numbers, but it appeared in most German-speaking areas of Europe as well as in France, England, Poland, Moravia and Italy. It quickly came under intense pressure everywhere because of its radical departure from traditional beliefs and polity, and it was regarded as socially and politically dangerous. At least 6000 Anabaptists were executed by 1578.

Although not organizationally linked, the 3 originating groups shared characteristics. The first was emancipation from the tutelages of the past and an insistence upon the freedom of laymen to make their own spiritual choices. The authority of papal and academic hierarchies was rejected in favour of the exclusive authority of Scripture, and scriptural interpretation became the prerogative and obligation of the congregation. Every function of civil government in the congregation was rejected. Anabaptists insisted upon religious liberty and most eschewed participation in government and military service (*see* PACIFISM). All adopted a congregational structure with voluntary internal discipline. The church was seen as the continuing presence and activity of Christ in the world.

The second major shared characteristic was rejection of the LUTHERAN doctrine of salvation by God's grace alone, and an insistence that the believer's faith must be proven and supplemented by deeds: man must bear the cross of discipleship, thus participating in the atonement. Infants were not baptized because they could not make their own commitment to Christian discipleship. Conscious, deliberate human participation in the process of salvation was symbolized in adult ("believer's") baptism; hence the name "anabaptism" [Gk *anabaptizein*, "to baptize again"]. The emphasis on good works produced a strong strain of perfectionism. Christ, who was to return soon, was to find his bride (the church) without spot or wrinkle. Perfectionism led to frequent schisms, such as the Amish schism of 1693 in which the main issue was church discipline.

Some 236 000 Canadians (1981c) are members of groups that arose within the Anabaptist tradition: Mennonites, Hutterites, BRETHREN IN CHRIST (Tunkers) and The Missionary Church. *See also* EVANGELICAL AND FUNDAMENTALIST MOVEMENTS.

WALTER KLAASSEN

Reading: H.S. Bender, ed, *The Mennonite Encyclopedia*, 4 vols (1955-59); G.H. Williams, *The Radical Reformation* (1962); Walter Klaassen, *Anabaptism in Outline* (1981).

Anarchism, the political doctrine which teaches that government is evil and unnecessary and that society should be recognized on the basis of voluntary mutual-aid associations. In Canada it has never generated much support, although small groups of activists have existed sporadically in larger cities and anarchist ideas have lightly influenced a number of writers. The movement's most famous theoretician, Peter Kropotkin, visited Canada in 1897; it was on his recommendation that Tolstoy and others decided to settle the DOUKHOBORS on the Canadian Prairies, 1898-99. Anarchist Emma Goldman, after a militant career in the US and USSR, died in Toronto in 1940. Among Canadian anarchists is activist-writer George Woodcock, who in 1962 published *Anarchism*, a history of the movement.

Anatomy of Criticism: Four Essays, by Northrop FRYE (Princeton, 1957), has had a powerful international influence on modern critical theory. Frye is a learned and eloquent spokesman for the view that literature constitutes an autonomous system, an order of works and words to be studied through a systematic and classificatory approach, as articulated in the essays comprising the "anatomy." Following his formidable "polemical introduction," Frye sets out 4 critical approaches and their corollary theories, upon which he constructs an elaborate typology: "Historical Criticism: Theory of Modes"; "Ethical Criticism: Theory of Symbols"; "Archetypal Criticism: Theory of Myths"; and "Rhetorical Criticism: Theory of Genres." Frye's work has been attacked by critics who see in his approach a dangerous tendency to dehistoricize both literature and criticism; and it has been praised by those who see his as the most powerful arguments to locate "human desire" at the centre of the literary universe. Frye's long-held view that the Bible stands as the originating document of masterwork of Western literature informs T*Great Code* (1982) which, with its projected companion volume, may in time supersede *Anatom of Criticism* as Frye's major work. *Anatomy of Criticism* has been translated into French as *Anatom de la critique* (Paris, 1969) and into German an Italian.

NEIL BESN

Anciens canadiens, Les (1863), a Canadia classic combining the appeal of historical ro mance and local realism, was written by Phili AUBERT DE GASPÉ, Sr, in his seventies in response the call by the journal *Les* SOIRÉES CANADIENN for the preservation of the past. Set in rur Québec at the time of the CONQUEST, the actio juxtaposes the lives of 2 friends doomed to fig each other: Jules d'Haberville, future seigne at St-Jean-Port-Joli, and Archibald Camero of Locheill, an exiled Highlander in love wi Jules's sister Blanche. Walter Scott's novels mer with French Canadian folklore in Gaspé's fi tionalized memoir; his anecdotal style blen historical materials with legends, such as t story of La CORRIVEAU, in a nostalgic, ultimate heroic portrait of New France. The definiti tenth French edition was published by Fides i 1975; Georgina Pennée's translation (1864) surpassed by Charles G.D. Roberts's *The Canadia of Old* (1890).

MICHÈLE LACOM

Anderson, David, Church of England bishop at London, Eng 10 Feb 1814; d at Clifton, ne Bristol, Eng 5 Nov 1885). Grandson of a Presb terian minister and son of an East India C surgeon he was educated at Edinburgh and O ford (BA 1836, MA 1839, DD 1849). At school h met Archibald Campbell Tait, later bishop London and archbishop of Canterbury, an partly through his influence decided to seek o ders in the Church of England. After curacies i Liverpool he was on the staff of St Bees Theolo ical College until 1846, then served briefly perpetual curate of All Saints', Derby. Large through the influence of members of the Cla ham Sect, he was nominated first bishop of th diocese of RUPERT'S LAND. Consecrated in Ma 1849 he proceeded to his new diocese centered the RED RIVER COLONY, accompanied by his sist and 3 sons, his wife having died 2 years befor He was bishop and HBC chaplain until 186 during which time the church's missiona work was extended towards James B and in the Mackenzie and Yukon valleys.

F.A. PEA

Anderson, Frank Ross, international che master (b at Edmonton, Alta 3 Jan 1938; d at Sa Diego, Calif 18 Sept 1980). Bedridden for 5 yea with arthritis, he discovered CHESS at age 15. H first steps outside led to the chess club. Anderso won the Canadian championship 1953 an 1958, but his greatest success was at the Che Olympics. In 1954 at Amsterdam and again i 1958 at Munich he won the gold medal on 2n board. He would have gained the grandmaste title in Munich, but reaction to an incorrect pre scription prevented him from appearing for th final game. In the late 1960s he moved to Sa Diego, where he ran a tax consulting business.

JONATHAN BERR

Anderson, James Thomas Milton, educato author, premier of Saskatchewan (b at Fai banks, Ont 23 July 1878; d at Saskatoon 29 De 1946). After teaching in the Yorkton distric Anderson was appointed inspector of schoo 1911 and director of education among ne Canadians 1918 — the year he published *The E ucation of the New Canadian.* In 1924 he becam leader of the Conservative Party and in 192 was elected MLA for Saskatoon City. Followin the defeat of J.G. GARDINER's ministry on 6 Se 1929, Anderson formed the Co-operative go ernment, a coalition of Conservatives, Pro gressives and Independents. The controvers urrounding the 1930-31 amendments to the chool Act obscured his administration's legislative record. Two years after his government's ushing defeat in 1934, Anderson retired from olitics and managed an insurance company efore being appointed acting superintendent of he School for the Deaf, Saskatoon, in 1944.

RAYMOND J.A. HUEL

nderson, Rudolph Martin, zoologist, explorer, conservationist (b near Decorah, Iowa 30 une 1876; d at Ottawa 22 June 1961). He participated in explorations of Alaska with the American Museum of Natural History, then served as cond to Vilhjalmur STEFANSSON in the Canadian Arctic Expedition from Alaska to Bathurst let (1913-16), editing its 16-volume findings. is conservation efforts started then, when he ointed out declines of caribou and muskoxen the North. In 1916 he was part of a government advisory board that drafted the Migratory irds Convention Act. As head of the biology vision of the National Museum of Canada 920-46, he published an important catalogue Canadian mammals and a guide to collecting nd preserving vertebrates still in wide use. He as also associate editor of the *Canadian Field-aturalist* 1918-55.

MARTIN K. MCNICHOLL

nderson River, 692 km long, originates in a roup of lakes N of GREAT BEAR LK in the NWT nd meanders N and W to empty into Liverpool ay, an arm of the Beaufort Sea, just E of the lackenzie Delta. Its lower reaches were originally inhabited by Inuit who were decimated by n epidemic of scarlet fever in 1865. During the 860s the HBC operated a trading post at its outh, where the modern settlement of Stanton located. It is named after James Anderson, an BC factor formerly in charge of the district.

DANIEL FRANCIS

ndré, Brother, né Alfred Bessette, faith-ealer, religious counsellor (b at St-Grégoire-'Iberville, LC 9 Aug 1845; d at Montréal 6 Jan 937). Although he was functionally illiterate, nimposing in speech and stature, and never dvanced beyond the most lowly positions ithin his religious order, the Congregation f the Holy Cross (CSC), Brother André became e most popular religious figure in Québec in e 20th century. Tens of thousands attributed eir miraculous healings to André's intervention with his patron, St Joseph, the husband of the Virgin Mary. His work scandalized many priests, physicians and sophisticated Catholics; but in 1904 his admirers, many from blue-collar families, helped him to build a small oratory in honour of Joseph on the slopes of Mount Royal. Some years later the church hierarchy became involved. A basilica, still Montréal's most imposing landmark, was constructed during 1924-55. The church organized pilgrimages and the oratory became the liturgical centre for the Catholic trade-union movement of Québec. Half a million visitors still come to the oratory every year — the only major urban shrine in Canada.

: Joseph's Oratory, constructed 1924-55 on the site of a nall chapel built by Brother André on the slopes of lount Royal. The basilica is the only major urban rine in Canada and is visited by half a million pilrims a year (*photo by Perry Mastrovito/Reflexion*).

Despite his reputation as a faith healer, Brother André's primary concern was to promote the worship of the suffering Christ through the patronage of St Joseph. Afflicted by poor health throughout his life, André encouraged his closest followers to accept their suffering rather than to seek healing, since suffering brings one closer to Jesus on the Cross. He was beatified on 23 May 1982.

TOM SINCLAIR-FAULKNER

Reading: Henri-Paul Bergeron, *Brother André, Apostle of Saint Joseph* (1958).

Andre, Harvie, politician (b at Edmonton 27 July 1940). Educated at the California Inst of Technology and U of A (PhD 1963), Andre taught chemical engineering at U of Calgary 1966-72. Elected to the House of Commons for Calgary in 1972, he was a key supporter of Joe CLARK's successful bid for the PC leadership in 1976. A trusted Clark adviser thereafter, Andre was a vocal opponent of PETRO-CANADA and the National Energy Program. He also developed an expertise on defence questions, pushing as Opposition defence critic for a stronger, better-equipped Canadian Armed Forces. He was named minister of supply and services by Brian MULRONEY in Sept 1984.

NORMAN HILLMER

Anemone, or wind flower, perennial, herbaceous PLANT of genus *Anemone*, family Ranunculaceae. The genus contains 120-150 species, most found in temperate and subarctic regions. The usually single, goblet-shaped flower lacks petals but has 5-20 petallike sepals. Colours range from white through purple to red. Anemones have a dry, one-seeded fruit (achene). Of the 20 N American species, 11 are native to Canada. The white-blossomed Canada anemone (*A. canadensis*), the most widespread species in moist locations, is found throughout Canada, excluding Newfoundland. *A. patens*, Manitoba's PROVINCIAL FLORAL EMBLEM since 1906, is commonly but incorrectly known as the prairie crocus. Its purple-tinged sepals are a beautiful sight on the Prairies early in spring. The most familiar cultivated forms are the fall-blooming Japanese anemone (*A. hupehensis*) and the spring-blooming florist's anemone (*A. coronaria*). Anemones require well-drained soil and partial shade. They are grown from seed or propagated by division.

CÉLINE ARSENEAULT

Angéline de Montbrun (1882), novel by Laure Conan (pseudonym of Félicité ANGERS), is French Canada's first psychological novel and one of its first novels by a woman. In it Angers adapts epistolary fiction, religious meditations and the private lady's journal to narrate the tragedy of a young girl, raised by her godlike father in the isolated village of Valriant, who cannot, after his death, transfer her affections to her fiancé Maurice. Her beauty having been symbolically disfigured in a fall, Angéline renounces the world and her lover. In contrast to her friend Mina, a *mondaine* ("worldly woman") turned Ursuline nun, she struggles in a private agony and ecstasy of regret, eagerly awaiting death and the joys of afterlife. Angers transmutes autobiographical details into a powerful psychological study of the role played by religion in

Prairie crocus (*Anemone patens*), Manitoba's floral emblem (*photo by Julie O. Hrapko*).

19th-century family life. *Angéline* was serialized in *La Revue canadienne* (1881-82), published in 1884 and reissued several times. It was translated into English by Yves Brunelle in 1974.

MICHÈLE LACOMBE

Angers, Félicité, pen name Laure Conan, writer (b at La Malbaie, Qué 9 Jan 1845; d at Québec C 6 June 1924). A witness to her times and the first French Canadian female novelist, Conan's writings followed the triple imperative of family, nation and religion. *Un Amour vrai* (1878-79) is only a long story, but ANGÉLINE DE MONTBRUN (1881-82) is an original novel: its form and structure (correspondence, narrative, diary) respond to personal needs and the characters are more than traditional stereotypes. Its first critics called it pious, some modern ones call it unhealthy, others note its fine psychological analysis and daring form. The heroines of *La Vaine foi* (1921) and *L'Obscure souffrance* (1919), both in domestic service, give deeper expression to the sorrow and faith of Angéline de Montbrun. Carried along by the literary current of the day and influenced by François-Xavier GARNEAU's *Histoire du Canada*, Conan wrote 3 historical novels. In *A l'oeuvre et à l'épreuve* (1891), the Christian hero, Garnier, renounces his youthful love to become a Jesuit and dies a martyr's death. In *L'Oublié* (1900), Closse is obedient to familial duty but still dies a hero's death for the homeland. *La Sève immortelle* (1925) demonstrates the courage of 2 young people who give up their foreign loves to marry each other and better serve their country.

GABRIELLE POULIN

Anglicanism is that tradition in CHRISTIANITY whose members are in full communion with the see of Canterbury, Eng. Originally confined to the British Isles, the Church of England has spread to almost every corner of the world, with some 2.4 million adherents in Canada (1981c). Anglicanism considers itself to stand within the primitive catholic tradition, preserving a solid scriptural basis; a ministry of bishops, priests and deacons in unbroken succession from the time of the Apostles; a sacramental order; and a recognition of church tradition which is nevertheless freed from medieval excesses and superstitions. Anglicanism is both catholic in this sense and a product of the 16th-century Reformation. The word "Protestant" is sometimes applied to it, but this is confusing because the same word is also applied to the nonepiscopal bodies that appeared at the time of the Reformation. In Scotland, the US and elsewhere, Anglicans are also known as Episcopalians.

Anglicanism stands in the Greco-Gallican tradition; its nature is to emphasize community and loving relationship as distinct from the legal conformity emphasized by the Latin (Roman Catholic) tradition. It has been concerned with reunifying the Christian faith and has a long history of what are now known as ecumenical encounters. In Canada, discussion among vari-

St Anne's Anglican Church, Toronto. The church is a scaled-down model of the Byzantine masterpiece Hagia Sophia in Istanbul. In 1923 J.E.H. MacDonald was hired to direct the beautification and many of the panels were executed by Group of Seven members (*courtesy St Anne's Anglican Church*).

ous Protestant bodies in the late 19th century were precursors to the formation of the UNITED CHURCH OF CANADA in 1925. Anglicans took no part in these early negotiations, but began discussions with the United Church in the 1940s and from 1969 included the CHRISTIAN CHURCH (DISCIPLES OF CHRIST). The resulting "Plan of Union" proposed that the Protestant bodies accept the episcopal church structure, and attempts were made to deal with differences in theology. Limited practical co-operation included sanctioning a joint calendar and a common hymn book. But by the early 1970s enthusiasm had cooled, and in 1975 the Anglican Church formally withdrew from negotiations, on the grounds that the nonepiscopal group had failed to recognize that they were not dealing with another Protestant denomination.

There has been a greater possibility of understanding between Anglicanism and the Church of Rome, although it has been hindered by doctrinal differences and, since the first Vatican Council (1870), Rome's refusal to recognize Anglican ordinations. However, in 1983 the Anglican-Roman Catholic International Commission (ARCIC), established in 1970, issued a final report on the first stage of its deliberations indicating the possibility of agreement on the Eucharist, ordination and the nature of authority in the church. The talks were continuing in 1984.

In its modern form Anglicanism has been a religion of 2 books: the Bible and the Book of Common Prayer. It understands the Bible as *fons et origo* of Christian truth but also as subject to interpretation by the church; tradition plays an important part in its understanding. Anglican scholars have been in the forefront of biblical studies. Anglicanism is also liturgical in its worship. The first prayer book, which appeared in 1549 and was largely the work of Archbishop Thomas Cranmer, was a compilation of ancient biblical and Catholic worship. Current revisions used throughout the world still reflect Cranmer's influence. Anglicanism emphasizes a ministry of Word and Sacrament. The Book of Common Prayer has been described as the Bible arranged for public worship. The Eucharist, in theory and increasingly in practice, is the principal Sunday service. There has been some tension between scriptural and sacramental emphasis, the evangelical (low-church) position emphasizing the ministry of the Word and personal religious experience, the catholic (high-church) position seeing the church as a divine society, the Body of Christ, administering the grace of God through the sacraments.

There has always been flexibility in Anglican theology, and hence Anglicanism has not always seemed to present the same face to the world. But because wide differences of interpretation and practice are possible within Anglicanism, schisms have been rare. In "Old Dissent" the principal examples, CONGREGATIONALISTS (or Separatists) and ANABAPTISTS (who originally included those later called BAPTISTS), represent not so much a dissent from Anglicanism itself as a doctrinal divergence from catholicism in general. The outstanding example of "New Dissent" was METHODISM, in which the differences were less doctrinal than practical and behavioural, and the schism was due to misunderstanding and intransigence on both sides.

More recently the only schisms of note have been those of the Reformed Episcopal movement and the Anglican Catholic group. The Reformed Episcopal Church, fd 1843 in the US to protest against "ritualism," appeared in England the following year as the Free Church of England, and in Canada, chiefly in Ontario and BC, about the same time. It was distinctively evangelical and strongly opposed to what it considered to be romanizing tendencies. It has virtually disappeared in the 20th century. The Anglican Catholic Church, which gained a small following in Canada, was born of a reaction against what was regarded as liberalization in the Episcopal Church of the US in the 1970s. Particular objection was taken to proposed revisions of the prayer book and to the admission of women to holy orders.

Anglicans have always been interested in education and have been active in the establishment and support of schools and colleges. Many Canadian universities were originally either Anglican foundations or have been strongly supported by Anglicans.

History in Canada The first known service in what is now Canada was performed by Robert Wolfall, a chaplain in Sir Martin FROBISHER's expedition, in Frobisher Bay on 2 Sept 1578. Thereafter Anglicanism spread through immigration from the British Isles and the coming of LOYALISTS, many of whom were Anglicans, after the American Revolution. In the British colonies it was tacitly assumed that, without special legi lation, the Church of England was the esta lished, or "official," church, with the same stat and limitations as in the mother country. Th was not always understood by the people, pa ticularly non-Anglicans, or by the authoritie Establishment was a thorny issue, hotly debate throughout early Canadian history (*see* CLERG RESERVES). The purpose of 18th-century Nov Scotia legislation was not to "establish" the C E, since that was taken for granted, but to assu Protestants of freedom of worship and to e clude Roman Catholics. Establishment impose certain responsibilities in the conduct and regi tration of baptisms, marriages, and burials, im portant in the days before state registration vital statistics. It did not imply that the churc had coercive powers to compel support, nor th it derived financial advantage — even pay fo clergy — from the state.

In early Canada there was no local churc organization. C of E clergy had been sent by th missionary societies or were military chaplain only after 1787 were bishops appointed. I keeping with the principle of establishment, th governor was the ordinary (chief ecclesiastic officer) and made necessary organizational de cisions which might include appointments parishes and the issue of marriage licences; h had no sacramental or specifically ecclesiastic powers.

Missions were the work of the Society for th Propagation of the Gospel (SPG), fd 1701, an ex tension of the Society for Promoting Christia Knowledge (SPCK), fd 1698; the Church Mis sionary Society (CMS), fd 1799; and the Coloni and Continental Church Society (CCCS or "Col. Con."), fd 1838. The 2 former societies underto the whole of Anglican missionary work amon native peoples in BNA until the 1905 formatio of the Missionary Society of the Church in Can ada, and continued to support a large part unt the 1940s. CCCS was an evangelical societ which concentrated on ministering to settler Beyond that, its greatest single work was mai taining Emmanuel College, Saskatoon, for th training of clergy, 1914-54.

The first Anglican bishopric in BNA was tha of Nova Scotia, established in 1787 with Loyalis Charles INGLIS as bishop. Although he was style bishop of Nova Scotia, his jurisdiction include Newfoundland, Bermuda, PEI, and Lower an Upper Canada. His load was lightened in 179 with the creation of the Diocese of Quebec wit Jacob MOUNTAIN as bishop. By 1860 the 6 dio ceses then existing, Nova Scotia, Quebec, To ronto, Fredericton, Montreal and Huron, ha combined to form the Provincial Synod of th Church of England and Ireland in Canada. Afte formation of the General Synod in 1893, the in stitution was officially the Church of Englan in Canada until 1955, when it became the An glican Church of Canada.

The Provincial Synod of RUPERT'S LAND was th second to be formed. In 1875 it combined th dioceses of Moosonee (fd 1872) and Athabasc and Saskatchewan (fd 1874) into an ecclesi astical province. A bishop was elected in eac province to act as presiding bishop, or met ropolitan, and in 1893 it was decided that the should receive the title "archbishop." That yea also saw the formation of the General Synod o the Church of England in Canada, a legislativ and administrative body with clerical and la representatives from each diocese. Its presidin bishop was accorded the title Primate of Al Canada. The first sessions took place in Sep 1893 at Trinity College, Toronto. In 1912 th dioceses existing in Ontario were separated fro the old ecclesiastical province of Canada to for a new one. Similarly, in 1914 the dioceses of BC previously without any provincial organiza tion, combined in the ecclesiastical province o BC. The modern Anglican Church of Canada i ıde up of 30 dioceses, which are distributed in rovinces, each with an archbishop.

In the 19th century, Anglican missionaries en failed to distinguish between evangeltion and acculturation, tacitly assuming that be Anglican was to be English. This led to ficulties in later years. In the 20th century, re has been tension between the claims of rituality and those of social welfare. The urch has always been concerned for the needy England it was for many years the only ency for the relief of the poor). In 1908 a comttee on Moral and Social Reform (later the pt of Social Service) was set up by the Canan General Synod. It laboured long to awaken d inform the social conscience of Canadian nglicans. Organizational structures at the nanal level have changed, but the church conues to be actively involved in social issues ch as ABORTION and BIRTH CONTROL, social and onomic problems, the PEACE MOVEMENT and tive rights. Although there is considerable pport for such activities, some members fear at the church's mission is in danger of being storted and misunderstood: economic wellng does not necessarily imply membership in e Kingdom of God. F.A. PEAKE

ading: T.C.B. Boon, *The Anglican Church from the Bay to Rockies* (1962); J. Fingard, *The Anglican Design in Loyal-Nova Scotia* (1972); J.L.H. Henderson, *John Strachan* 69); T.R. Millman, *Jacob Mountain* (1947); F.A. Peake, *Anglican Church in British Columbia* (1959).

nglin, Margaret, actress (b at Ottawa 3 Apr 76; d at Toronto 7 Jan 1958). Daughter of mothy W. Anglin, Speaker of the House of mmons, she was born in the Speaker's Chamrs. She made her professional debut in 1894 *Shenandoah* in New York and was an early ccess as Roxanne in *Cyrano de Bergerac* (1898), the title role in *Mrs. Dane's Defence* and in *The eat Divide* (1906). She had her own classical mpany in 1913, playing Shakespeare's Viola, salind and Cleopatra. In Greek tragedy she as dynamic as Antigone, Medea, Electra and higenia. She retired after *Watch on the Rhine* 943). She toured once to Australia and freently performed in Canada. DAVID GARDNER

nguhadluq, Luke, Inuit artist (b at Chanty Inlet, NWT 1895; d at Baker Lk, NWT 8 b 1982). A powerful camp leader of the Uthikhalingmiut people, Anguhadluq had 2 ult sons to hunt beside him, a rare good forne during the years of starvation among the land CARIBOU INUIT. When he moved into ker Lk at age 73, too old to hunt, he turned to awing as a source of income. His drawings dect a world view unique to hunting peoples d reminiscent of prehistoric art. When Angudluq made drawings of the drum dance, he ade the skin drum enormous and yellow like e sun, dominating the centre of the picture. nall, static Inuit men and women spiral ound the drum like rays emanating from their amanic source. When drawing, he laid the par between his outstretched legs and turned the awing as he worked, conceiving his image e a map, looking down on his subject, with e continuous horizon line formed by the ges of the paper. K.J. BUTLER

ngus, Henry Forbes, educator, public servant at Victoria 19 Apr 1891). A professor of ecomics at UBC, 1919-56, Angus was a key memr of the Royal Commission on DOMINION-OVINCIAL RELATIONS, 1937-40, and an official in e Dept of External Relations 1940-45. He orked for full rights for JAPANESE Canadians in e interwar years and vigorously opposed their ternment during WWII. He also championed ternational co-operation, particularly among oples and nations bordering on the Pacific. *nada and Her Great Neighbor: Sociological Surveys Opinions and Attitudes in Canada Concerning the United States* (1938) and *Canada and the Far East, 1940-1953* (1953) are his best-known publications. NORMAN HILLMER

Anhalt, István, composer, educator (b at Budapest, Hungary 12 Apr 1919). One of Canada's most individual composers, whose work is strongly influenced by his study of the psychology of speech, Anhalt combines traditional instruments, electronics and the human voice in the textures and sonorities of a highly complex musical language. He came to Montréal in 1949 and joined McGill's music theory department. He founded and directed its Electronic Music Studio 1964-71, and then went to Kingston as head of Queens's music department. Representative of his works are *Symphony No. 1* (1958), *Symphony of Modules*, for orchestra and tape (1967), *Foci* (1969) and *La Tourangelle* (1975), a musical based on the life of the 17th-century Ursuline MARIE DE L'INCARNATION. BARCLAY MCMILLAN

Animal Animals are many-celled, responsive herterotrophs (eaters of various things). Herbivores eat plants; carnivores eat flesh; omnivores, such as man, eat nearly everything. Parasites inhabit and subsist in other organisms. The shape of animals, the way they move, how they sense and seize and swallow food suggest that the need to find an organic food source is the most important characteristic of their lives. The EVOLUTION of animal structure has resulted in a vast number of adaptations, so that there are now more kinds of animals than of all other living things combined. It is impossible to keep track of all species that have been formally described, but there are more than a million. Two thousand to 4000 new species are found annually, usually small and inconspicuous, often from remote places (eg, Canada's ARCTIC ARCHIPELAGO).

The animal kingdom is divided into 33 groups (phyla), each one of which has characteristics setting it apart from all others. The FOSSIL record shows that animals have existed for more than 600 million years. Although their origins are obscure, they undoubtedly evolved from animallike PROTISTA. Patterns of structure link the members of each phylum. Species within a phylum differ by individual modifications which have evolved to serve different modes of life. During the history of life, perhaps 10 times as many forms as now exist have arisen. Most species of animals persist for millions of years but, invariably, each is supplanted by another, better adapted to the conditions within which it lives.

Animal distribution depends on geography, climate and historical events. Each continental mass has a unique fauna which has evolved largely independently. Within each continent are distinctive associations isolated by features such as mountains, deserts or forests. Events of the past, such as GLACIATION or the shifting of land (*see* PLATE TECTONICS), have strongly influenced the adaptations of animals. Thus, there are more kinds of animals in the tropics than in the high latitudes, because of more equable climatic conditions, and because conditions have been stable for longer periods, allowing for more complete exploitation of available habitats. The fauna of Canada, like its PHYSIOGRAPHIC REGIONS and VEGETATION, reflects its N American association, and the effects of the GLACIERS which only 10 000 years ago covered about 97% of Canada's surface.

Some animals are found nearly everywhere in Canada, eg, northern pike, walleye, whitefish, Canada goose, mallard, ruffed grouse, beaver, muskrat, moose, black bear, weasel. Others are restricted, and almost unique to Canada, eg, muskoxen in the Arctic Lowlands; mountain goats in the Cordillera; pronghorns in the Interior Plains; lake trout around the Shield; snow geese across the Shield and eastern Arctic. The rich assemblage of animals in the St Lawrence Lowlands, a northern extension of southern forms, includes bowfins among the fish, more amphibians and reptiles than anywhere else in Canada, the opossum and many birds.

Canada's animals have influenced its history through their effects on the FUR TRADE, FISHERIES and settlement, as well as story and song. Canada's heritage includes tales of fierce mosquitoes and black flies, vast herds of bison, calls of loon and coyote, busyness of beavers and friendliness of whiskey jacks. The fear inspired by grizzly bear and timber wolf, the sight of killer whale and sea otter, the skill needed to catch Atlantic salmon and the pleasure of dining on Winnipeg goldeye are legendary. It is a rich heritage that must be preserved.

Reading: C. P. Hickman, et al, *Integrated Principles of Zoology* (1984).

Animal Agriculture Domesticated animals are those of which the maintenance and reproduction are, to some degree, controlled by humans. Certain behavioural traits are needed if an animal is to be adapted to domestication, including the ability to live in groups, reasonably rapid reproduction rates and the ability to thrive on available food. With domestication, came a redesigning of the animal to meet human needs (eg, for food, transportation, work or companionship). Modern BEEF and DAIRY cattle, HOGS, HORSES, GOATS, SHEEP and POULTRY are the results of breeding programs extending over centuries (goats were domesticated as early as 7000 BC). Thus, even within poultry (*Gallus domesticus*), the ability to produce large quantities of eggs is carried by certain breeds, while rapid growth (ie, meat deposition) is carried by others.

Besides being important sources of various foods, animals also supply mankind with many other items. About 40% of the live ruminant, 60% of the live hog and 70% of live poultry are used as human food. The average Canadian dairy cow produces about 5600 kg of milk annually; the average chicken lays about 260 eggs per year. Animals also provide wool, LEATHER and feathers. By-products include INSULIN, bone meal, glycerol, etc.

Since the 1970s Canadian food consumption patterns have changed markedly: beef, pork and poultry consumption has increased substantially, and fruit, vegetable and sugar consumption has also gone up; consumption of dairy products and eggs has decreased, as has that of wheat flour and, to a slight degree, potatoes. The figures indicate only the amount of product purchased ("disappearance of product"); actual consumption is difficult to determine, as a good deal of wastage occurs after purchase. Per capita disappearance of animal products is as follows: beef, 41 kg; pork, 32 kg; poultry, 23 kg; milk solids, 25 kg; eggs, 12 kg. Total animal products disappearance approximates 135 kg per person per year. Canadians eat very little veal, lamb or mutton; per capita totals do not normally exceed 3-4 kg.

In 1981 livestock and products accounted for 48% of farm income in Canada, ie, $8.96 billion. An estimated 14 million cattle and calves were held on Canadian farms, including 2.4 million milk cows and dairy heifers and 5.4 million beef cows and heifers. Over 9 million pigs and 748 000 sheep and lambs were kept. The poultry population is difficult to estimate, but about 488 million dozen eggs and 431 000 t of eviscerated fowl and poultry were produced. In the Atlantic region, livestock and livestock products contributed $370 million or 58% of total farm cash receipts; in Québec, $2 billion or 78%; in Ontario, $3 billion or 61%; in the Prairie region, $3 billion or 31%; in BC, $524 million or 61%.

It is often argued that animals produced for food compete with humans for available food and should, therefore, be reduced or eliminated as the world population continues to increase. Some competition for food does occur; for example, domestic animals consume cereal grains, some of which would be suitable for humans. However, ruminants are able to utilize materials not useful to humans and even nonruminants can use some forage-type material. Much of the world's agricultural land is unsuitable for intensive crop production. In Canada, about 18 million ha is classified as unsuitable for any agricultural use, beyond the production of perennial FORAGE CROPS, because of its topography, climate, soil type, etc. This land can be harvested only by grazing and animals raised on such land do not compete with humans but, rather, contribute greatly to the human dietary.

Furthermore, animals can convert poor-quality protein into high-quality protein, which is of particular significance to the diet of small children. The use of cereal and legume by-products for animal foods is an integral part of Canadian agriculture. Economic competition for these products determines the degree to which they are and will be used for animal feed. Waste is a feature of all phases of food production. About 30% of wheat milled is by-products, eg, middlings, shorts and bran (*see* FLOUR MILLING INDUSTRY). In the production of oatmeal, about 60% of the original oat becomes by-product. The extraction of oil from soybeans and rapeseed yields vast amounts of by-products, useful primarily as protein sources for livestock. When corn, wheat, oats or barley are harvested for grain, the remaining stalk or straw can be used as an energy source for ruminants. Residues from vegetable and fruit crops, low-quality fruit, vegetables and grain, and many other items, including garbage, can also be used. Ruminants can eat the manure produced by nonruminants (especially poultry), if it is properly treated and handled. The use of manure as feed is not inhumane since feces are consumed readily and many animals routinely practise coprophagy.

Livestock and Soil Conservation

Specialization of production has been a continuing trend in Canadian agriculture for many years. Factors contributing to the trend include the development of skills in crop production, housing of animals and applications of technology, combined with the availability of vast amounts of power, access to large markets, etc. Specialization in plant growing has led to one or 2 particular crops being grown year after year on the same land, dependence on purchased fertilizers and chemicals, large fields, large equipment, etc. Increased destruction of SOIL has followed. The presence of livestock allows greater variety in crop production (ie, forage crop production, the use of legume forages in rotation with grains) and the application of manure, an important fertilizer, to the land. No substitute for such procedures, suitable for maintaining the integrity of the soil, has been found. Thus, livestock production contributes to the long-term integrity of the agricultural system.

Other Uses

Animals kept for pleasure include common pets, recreational animals (ie, horses) and even some food-producing animals. All are important to Canada's society and economy. The racing, riding and workhorse industries alone employ thousands of people and are worth billions of dollars. It is estimated that there are half as many horses in Canada now as when they were used as a primary power source; their main use now is for pleasure. In some parts of Canada, notably Waterloo County, Ont, horses still serve as a power source for farmers, eg, for tilling and transportation. In western Canada the horse is a key factor in efficient RANCHING. Horses consume large amounts of forages and by-product materials and some cereals. The cat- and dog-food business is also of great economic significance as are VETERINARY services, grooming materials, etc. Cats and dogs compete with humans for food to some degree, but many are fed scraps and table wastes.

W.D. MORRISON

Animal Management

Animal management involves integrating the proper feeding, breeding, health care, housing and handling of domestic animals to optimize their productivity. The animal manager requires knowledge and skill to operate within the limits imposed by the available resources of land, labour and capital.

Feeding Animals require food for maintenance, growth, production and reproduction. Farm livestock includes ruminant mammals (cattle, sheep, goats), nonruminant mammals (horses, hogs, furbearers) and poultry. Ruminant animals have a 4-compartmented stomach, the compartments being the rumen, reticulum, omasum and abomasum. Within the rumen and reticulum a vast population of bacteria and protozoa live in symbiosis with their ruminant host. With the help of its microbial "partners" the ruminant is able to digest considerable portions of fibrous materials such as hay, straw and silage, feeds which are unsuitable for pigs or poultry. (The horse, while a nonruminant, possesses a microbial population in the hindgut that permits digestion of fibre to a comparable degree.) The microbes are also able to synthesize the right kind of amino acids (components of protein) from dietary protein in which such acids are missing (or present in inadequate amounts) or, to a limited extent, from nonprotein nitrogen in the diet. They are also able to synthesize some vitamins, notably those of the B group. Nonruminants do not have these capabilities; thus, nonruminant rations must provide all essential vitamins, minerals and amino acids. This consideration also applies in the feeding of calves, lambs and kids, since the young of ruminant species do not possess a developed rumen until they are some months old.

The food requirements of animals differ according to their activities and condition. For example, a cow at peak lactation requires 3-4 times as much food as during her dry period; the requirement of a ewe suckling twins is comparably greater than when she is dry. Working horses require higher quality food than do horses at pasture; pregnant horses also need better food. Good managers adjust both quantity and quality of feed according to these needs, but make the changes gradually.

In Canada, feeds are normally classified as roughages (pasture, hay, straw, silage), basal feeds (grain, grain by-products) and protein supplements (mainly residues of OILSEED crops and products of animal origin, eg, fish meal). Roughages are normally the cheapest feeds and, therefore, form the basis of all ruminant and horse diets. Roughages other than pasture are cut in summer and stored for winter use. Production of quality hay requires early cutting and, in some parts of Canada, the use of a barn drier to eliminate excess moisture. Hay declines greatly in feeding value if cutting is delayed; the somewhat increased volume harvested does not compensate. Thus, adequate and easily accessible storage is important. On-farm storage is also necessary for grains and other purchased feed inputs. For some classes of livestock (eg, sheep), grain is best fed whole but, for most other classes, rolling or grinding with or without pelleting is desirable. In general, such processing facilitates mixing, increases digestibility and reduces waste. Hay and straw too may be chopped and incorporated in a total mixed ration.

All species and, especially, lactating animals and poultry at peak of laying, require access to plentiful clean water at all times. Although not a source of energy, water is the medium i which most foodstuffs are metabolized ar their products transported in blood and urin Water also plays important roles in lubricatic of joints and regulation of body temperatur Livestock obtain water from feed as well as b drinking; consequently, the amount drunk d pends on the type of food consumed. For exan ple, water represents 90% of the green weight turnips or kale, 65-70% of most silages and 10 of hays. Water deprivation results in reduce food intake and, thus, lowered productivity.

Successful and profitable feeding of farm liv stock involves the provision of foodstuffs th supply the requisite nutrients in the cheape possible form, in amounts permitting the an mal to produce (meat, milk, eggs, wool, wor etc) up to their genetic potential but witho wasting feed by oversupply. The major advanc in COMPUTER technology applied to animal ope ations simplify efficient feeding as well as oth processes (eg, identification, ventilation, recor keeping). Since practical and economic consi erations dictate that most farm animals a maintained and fed as groups, it is importa that the individuals grouped have similar fee requirements.

Not all of the energy in a foodstuff contribut to growth, production or reproduction; variab proportions, according to the particular feed, a lost in the feces, urine and gas produced. F example, a feedlot steer weighing 450 kg w produce about 23 kg of urine and feces dail The energy value of different foodstuffs is com monly expressed as either percent "Total Digest ble Nutrients" (ie, kg/100 kg feed) or as calori of digestible energy. For health, safety and en vironmental reasons, it is very important th adequate manure management procedures be standard part of all animal-management ope ations.

Health and Handling Livestock cannot b productive unless healthy; thus, managers any animal enterprise must be knowledgeab about the signs of good or ill health. They mu know in what circumstances to take appropria action and when to call for skilled veterinar help. They must have a good relationship wi a veterinarian who, in turn, knows the farm farmer and livestock; such partnerships tak time to develop. Both partners must practise th tenets of preventive medicine; the use of dru is often the result of failure to achieve ideal hu bandry standards. One of the most characterist features of modern livestock farming is intens fication, especially in the aspect of housing. In tensification increases the inherent health ha ard; thus, in designing buildings for livestoc strict attention must be paid to sanitation, vent lation and temperature control, as well as co and operational ease.

Effective disease control requires avoidan of stress, quarantine of new additions and sic animals, preventive vaccination against som bacteria (eg, those of genus *Clostridium*, whic cause tetanus, blackleg, etc) and strict sanitiz tion of such equipment as milking machine Cleanliness of feed troughs, the animals them selves and of attendant personnel is importan External parasites are controlled by dippin spraying or dusting; internal parasites (e roundworms, tapeworms, flukes) can be con trolled by pasture rotation or other measures break the parasite's life cycle, accompanied b strategic deworming.

Many potential pathogens (eg, intestin worms, coccidia) normally live within far livestock at a level of host-parasite balanc Only when stress or some other factor rende the host weakened or vulnerable does the para site multiply, often very rapidly, producin symptoms of illness in the host. Such stress ca occur, for example, at parturition, during period of under feeding, or as a result of som extraneous event (eg, chasing of sheep by dogs). Thus, to minimize stress, livestock should always be handled quietly with the aid of such facilities (eg, corrals, chutes, headgates, etc) as will make matters easy for both operator and stock. Knowledge of the natural behaviour of the particular species is used in siting and design of handling facilities.

Agriculture Canada (*see* AGRICULTURE, DEPARTMENT OF) is responsible for legislation to protect Canada's livestock from diseases identified by law as reportable. Scrupulous adherence to such legislation and good management have made Canadian livestock breeders and farmers among the most successful in the world and Canadian livestock (both breeding stock and that intended for human consumption) much sought after.

Marketing

Proper management aims to meet market demands. Production of many commodities (eg, milk, eggs, pork, chicken) is controlled by national or provincial regulatory boards, which may set requirements for health and nutrient content and may also regulate output (*see* COMMODITY INSPECTION AND GRADING; FOOD LEGISLATION). For example, milk for sale must be produced on premises meeting strict sanitary standards. It is priced according to its butterfat content and produced according to a quota system, with a differential pricing structure to discourage oversupply or undersupply. Similarly, hogs are marketed at a standard weight (100 kg live weight) and overweight or overfat hogs suffer discount pricing. Among farm livestock, beef cattle, hogs, sheep, goats, horses and fur animals can now be produced in Canada without imposed restrictions of output. Here too, however, the effective manager must keep in mind current market conditions and strive to foresee coming changes to modify production accordingly. Good management must therefore include a responsible and co-operative attitude toward the inspection of products and premises as well as strict observance of such matters as drug use and drug-withdrawal periods. W.G. MATHEWSON

Animal Breeding The science of animal breeding belongs entirely to the 20th century but the art and practice were ushered in by those who first attempted domestication of wild species. The first attempts to develop captive herds capable of supporting permanent settlements occurred in the Neolithic era (about 25 000 years ago) and marked the beginning of human intervention in the natural EVOLUTION of animal species.

Amenability to handling was undoubtedly the first selection criterion but, judging from cave paintings that have survived, attention was also paid to hair colour, horn size, hair length, etc. In the absence of written records, there is no certain knowledge of the evolution of animal breeding practices but written documents dating back more than 4000 years indicate that humans appreciated the significance of family resemblances in animal mating schemes, recognized inbreeding hazards and enforced their selection decisions by castrating males not desired for breeding. One consequence of this process was the development of diverse types (breeds) within each domesticated species. In addition, a wide geographical redistribution of species occurred as invading armies, migrating peoples and traders transported livestock into new lands.

The Englishman Robert Bakewell, who lived in the 18th century, was the first to introduce progeny testing to determine the breeding worth of young males, and vigorously promoted such concepts as "like begets like," "inbreeding produces prepotency" (ie, superiority), and "breed the best to the best." His successes attracted imitators, who established diverse British breeds of BEEF and DAIRY cattle, SHEEP and HOGS, and initiated breed societies and pedigree herd books. Most modern breeds originated in the 1790-1860 period.

Animal Breeding in Canada Important early cross-breeding studies were performed at University of Saskatchewan before 1930, under the direction of J.W. Grant MACEWAN and L.M. Winters. Since 1940, the major research centres have been the Agriculture Canada RESEARCH STATIONS at Lacombe, Alta, Brandon, Man, and Ottawa; the major educational centres, the universities of Alberta, Manitoba, Guelph and McGill. The relative scarcity of scientists and research centres in this area reflects the high cost of breeding research on large animals.

Notable ongoing crossbreeding studies include the investigations of Roy Berg (U of A) and Howard FREDEEN and associates (Lacombe Research Station). Inbreeding studies with pigs ended at Lacombe in 1960 but continue with laboratory species (mice) at several locations, including Lacombe. Canadian studies on quantitative genetics were initiated by Jack Stothart (1934). He and his successors have used field data to augment and extend the theory and practice of livestock population genetics. Stothart was also the first to evaluate this theory empirically through controlled selection experiments with pigs. His results, since augmented by studies with poultry by Robert Gowe (Ottawa), beef cattle by Jack Newman (Lacombe) and John Lawson (Lethbridge, Alta), and beef cattle and pigs by Gunther Rahnefeld (Brandon) and Howard Fredeen (Lacombe), were in full accord with theoretical expectations. Practical application of population genetics theory by Stothart and Fredeen led to development of the Lacombe breed of pigs, the first livestock breed developed in Canada, and now propagated in 24 countries. Other applications of their theoretical and applied research have been the national performance testing programs for pigs and beef cattle, and practical performance selection programs for the livestock industry.

Show-ring standards, once considered authoritative criteria for potential breeding merit, have given way to performance tests that objectively measure differences among contemporary animals or progeny groups for the quantitative traits of growth rate and production of eggs, milk, wool and meat. Livestock exhibitions now serve primarily to promote and sell animals that have met performance test criteria (*see* AGRICULTURAL EXHIBITIONS).

Quantitative genetic variability is gradually decreased and selection effectiveness diminished in animal populations subjected to prolonged, intense selection. This fact does not impose an insurmountable barrier to continued genetic improvement; research has demonstrated that genetic variability can be restored by a period of relaxed selection or by the crossing of plateaued lines. A potential barrier, however, is the presence of genes or gene complements that enhance performance for one desired trait but have detrimental effects on others; eg, the single major gene (or linkage group) that causes muscular hypertrophy and simultaneously increases susceptability to stress. Muscular hypertrophy is desirable because it enhances the shape and muscle content of specific carcass cuts; however, associated stress susceptibility diminishes reproductive rate, increases incidence of death through cardiovascular failure, and promotes undesired postmortem biochemical changes in muscle tissue.

GENETIC ENGINEERING techniques are being applied in research at the Veterinary Infectious Disease Organization (VIDO), U of Sask campus, to create new vaccines for livestock diseases. There is optimism that application of this technology to large animals will clarify the multiple effects caused by specific genes and, with pigs, for example, permit development of stock possessing muscular hypertrophy without stress susceptibility.

Animal breeding research in Canada proceeds on several fronts. Work at McGill emphasizes the genetics of congenital defects in MAMMALS, particularly humans (*see* GENETIC DISEASE). Guelph has specialized in refinement of mathematical techniques for predicting potential breeding worth. Work at other research centres, notably the western universities and units of the Research Branch, embraces both theoretical and applied aspects of population genetics in studies of mating systems, performance selection techniques and the biological interpretation of genotypic and phenotypic variance. Results are published in numerous international journals, including the *Canadian Journal of Animal Science* and the *Canadian Journal of Genetics and Cytology*. HOWARD FREDEEN

Animal Issues The close relationship between man and animals has persisted since prehistoric times but societies for the protection of animals have been in existence for only about 100 years in the Western World. During the Victorian era, the antivivisection movement developed to oppose science's use of animals in biomedical research. The battle between vivisectionists and antivivisectionists resulted in the UK's Cruelty to Animals Act of 1876. This legislation heralded a clear victory for the antivivisection movement and imposed upon Britain's medical scientists a system of licensing, inspection and bureaucratic practices which is still under debate.

After WWII, biomedical research escalated tremendously. New drugs, treatments and techniques were discovered at a pace that permitted the health sciences to prevent and treat conditions previously thought to be incurable, to prolong life and relieve suffering. In Canada, since 1968 surveillance of the ethical use of the 2 million experimental animals used annually in biomedical research has been the responsibility of the Canadian Council on Animal Care. The CCAC pioneered the requirement of local institutional animal-care committees, a concept now being considered elsewhere. Approximately 20 million animals are used annually for research in the US and 4.3 million in the UK. However, numbers are decreasing because of high cost and development of alternative techniques, such as tissue culture and computer simulation. Although animal experiments have resulted in medical and surgical advances for humans and for animals themselves, criticism of the use of animals remains. In 1975, clinical psychologist Richard Ryder coined the term "speciesism," ie, a bias favouring one's own species. This bias has been criticised by philosophers who opposed the Judeo-Christian concept of man's "dominion" over animals and held that animals had rights similar to those of humans (eg, living without suffering and use inflicted by the human animal). Peter Singer, James Mason and others extended the discussion of animal liberation to include a "new ethics" for the treatment of animals. They widened their fields of concern to domesticated animals raised under new, intensive livestock-management practices; those in entertainment such as RODEOS, circuses and ZOOS; and those hunted for sport or for their skins. Animal activist groups conducted acts of vandalism against scientists, research laboratories and "factory farms." Butchers' windows were labelled "Meat is Murder." Protests often culminated in violent acts and arrests which in many instances gave to the perpetrators a sense of martyrdom and accomplishment.

HUMANE SOCIETIES and other less militant animal-welfare groups have been willing to discuss differences in a rational, nonpolarized manner. Some consider the efforts of the activists "misdirected humaneness". Of the 34 organizations devoted to animal welfare in Canada, the Canadian Federation of Humane Societies (CFHS) has the largest membership (200 000, including affiliates). Unfortunately, the proliferation of special-interest groups (eg, "Save Our Seals") has diluted the overall objectives of the animal-welfare community. This splintering effect has sometimes hindered those who take a moderate stand in their attempts to protect animals and eliminate cruel practices. No one, as yet, has defined "humaneness," but the question has been addressed by philosophy professor Bernard E. Rollin in his book *Animal Rights and Human Morality* (1981).

Many symposia have sought to define the problems associated with pet animals. Discussions have focused on disease, dog bites, the fouling of parks, lawns and gardens, animal control and euthanasia of surplus animals. Despite symposia, books, spay-neuter clinics and public education on responsible pet ownership, pounds and humane societies are still obliged to kill excessive numbers of surplus dogs and cats. In Canada, approximately 500 000 unwanted companion animals are destroyed annually. The livestock industry, in developing modern methods of animal production to produce a profit for the farmer and an economical product for the consumer, has developed some intensive livestock-management practices which are being questioned by those concerned about animal welfare (*see* ANIMAL AGRICULTURE). Although legislation covering these practices is not forthcoming, the federal government, aided by the animal welfare movement, industry, animal scientists and veterinarians is developing codes of practice for handling the various domestic animals.

The dilemma associated with man's relationship to animals is discussed in the book by Oxford biologist Marion Stamp Dawkins, *Animal Suffering: The Science of Animal Welfare* (1980). It provides an outline of the biological approach to animal welfare. Unfortunately, we lack much knowledge about what constitutes pain or distress and about how to recognize latent or masked suffering. To understand the suffering of animals it is necessary to understand better their ethological or behavioural needs, awareness and perception. The closer examination of man's relationship to and use of animals has resulted in the development of scientific recognition of the human-companion animal bond. A prominent international organization, the Delta Society, was established in 1981 to promote the health and well-being of people and animals by investigating the relationship between them and with their environment. Researchers studying the bonds between humans and companion animals have suggested that such humans benefit from reduced stress, lower blood pressure and enhanced socialization. The use of dogs to assist the handicapped (eg, blind and hearing impaired) is already familiar. New knowledge acquired through biomedical research, or through man's understanding of and responsibility toward animals themselves, can only lead to an improvement in the health and well-being of both man and animals.

H.C. ROWSELL

Reading: Canadian Council on Animal Welfare, *Guide to the Care and Use of Experimental Animals* (1980); W.J. Dodds and F.B. Orlans, eds, *Scientific Perspectives on Animal Welfare* (1983); J. Mason and P. Singer, *Animal Factories* (1980); R.D. Ryder, *Victims of Science: Use of Animals in Research* (1975).

Animals, Endangered, *see* ENDANGERED ANIMALS.

Animals in Winter In the Canadian temperate zone, cold-blooded (poikilothermic) animals, those incapable of regulating body temperatures internally, become dormant in winter. A period of arrested growth and development

Ptarmigan in winter (*photo by Harry Savage*).

(diapause) characterizes the life cycle of most INSECTS that overwinter in egg, larval, pupal or, uncommonly, adult stages. Some insects produce organic compounds (antifreeze) to protect cells and tissues. To escape sub-zero temperatures AMPHIBIANS lie dormant in swamp and pond mud, in soil or under debris. SNAKES enter rock dens or burrows where, alone or in clusters, they slip into a cold stupor. Warm-blooded (homeothermic) animals survive cold and food-short seasons by adjusting metabolic rates, varying insulation and blood circulation, and modifying behaviour. Winter dormancy in animals (hibernation), during which metabolism may be only 1-5% of normal, is marked by very low body temperatures (hypothermia). Respiration and heart rates drop to low levels and become irregular. Hibernators, eg, jumping mice, nonmigratory bats and ground squirrels (including woodchucks and marmots), accumulate body fat for insulation and to survive dormant periods up to 6 months or longer. Energy-rich brown fat is used by hibernants for internal heat production (thermogenesis) during frequent intervals of arousal. Black bears are deep sleepers because their temperatures remain nearly normal, although respiration and heart rates decrease sharply. Bears, raccoons, skunks and chipmunks awaken on mild, midwinter days to seek food or change dens. MAMMALS and BIRDS rely on heavy, efficient insulating coats and thick fat deposits to meet the stresses of northern winters. They respond to cold by fluffing out fur or feathers (piloerection) to capture air between outer coat surface and skin. Air trapped in the fur of beaver, muskrat, mink and river otter increases tolerance to cold water. White winter coats of ptarmigan, weasels and hares also serve as concealing coloration (camouflage). Physiological reactions of animals to chilling include raising heat production (metabolism), reducing blood flow to skin (vasoconstriction), and producing heat by muscle tremors (shivering). Some animals have complex vascular networks in limbs to move heat from warmer arteries to cooler veins for return to deeper tissues.

Animals use snow as a travel surface and insulating blanket. Thickly feathered feet of ptarmigan and wide, densely furred paws of snowshoe hare and lynx are adaptations for moving over snow. Fringed toes of grouse enable them to grip snow-covered branches firmly. Grouse, ptarmigan and some small birds burrow into snow to reduce heat losses. Other birds conserve heat at night by roosting together under eaves, conifer boughs or in tree cavities. In deep snow, deer and moose gather in areas of softwood shelter and hardwood browse. In mountains, herds of mule deer and elk seek less severe conditions by moving down south-facing slopes. Much winter activity of shrews and small rodents, including breeding, occurs under the snow (subnivean), which offers a stable, windless microclimate with less extreme temperatures than those prevailing above. Runways and tunnels, trampled through ground litter and granular snow, connect food caches with nests of dead grasses where animals curl up (alone or together) to conserve heat. Few small mammals could survive winter above the snow since energy costs of doing so are 15-50% greater than those of remaining below. Yet they sometimes emerge briefly, above that protective cover, exposing themselves to predators while moving from one area to another.

P.J. AUSTIN-SMITH

Anka, Paul Albert, singer, songwriter (b at Ottawa 30 July 1941). Of Lebanese Canadian origins, Anka became famous in his teens with such songs as "Diana" (the second-highest selling record in history), "You Are My Destiny," "Puppy Love" and "Lonely Boy." He has written over 400 songs, displaying an uncanny ability to create hit songs, including Frank Sinatra's "My Way," "She's a Lady" for Tom Jones and the theme for *"The Tonight Show"* on television. Frequent appearances in concert and on TV continue to prove his talent.

ALLAN M. GOULD

Anna Wyman Dance Theatre was launched professionally as the Anna Wyman Dancers with a series of performances at the Vancouver Art Gallery in 1971. AWDT is considered one of Canada's principal modern-dance companies. It grew from an amateur demonstration and performing troupe created by the Austrian dancer, choreographer, and teacher, Anna Wyman (b 1928), after she settled in Vancouver in 1967. The repertoire has consisted exclusively of Wyman choreography. Her style, evolved from lengthy ballet training and modern-dance training in Austria and England, is abstract and highly theatrical, often relying heavily on technical effect. The company, which has received operational support from the Canada Council since 1973, has toured extensively. In 1973 it took part in the International Young Choreographers' Competition in Cologne, Germany, where Wyman's *Here at the Eye of the Hurricane* (music Stockhausen) was named one of the 3 most outstanding entries. AWDT's 1975 cross-Canada tour was the first national tour by a modern company. Successes at the Montréal Cultural Olympics (1976) and the Montréal and Toronto dance festivals (1978) were followed by a tour of the People's Republic of China (1980), the first visit to mainland China by a modern-dance company from the Western world.

MAX WYMAN

Annand, William, politician, publisher, premier of NS (b at Halifax 10 Apr 1808; d at London, Eng 12 Oct 1887). Elected to the NS House of Assembly in 1836, Annand supported the Reform movement. Defeated in 1843, he bought and edited Joseph HOWE's *Novascotian*, then began the *Morning Chronicle* the next year, while continuing the *Novascotian*. Re-elected in 1851 Annand held his seat until 1867, despite rumours of self-aggrandizement. His vacillation on the Confederation issue weakened his role and leadership of the anticonfederates passed to Joseph Howe. After his defeat, Annand was appointed to the Legislative Council and maneuvered to become premier. Weak and indecisive, he was replaced in 1875 by Philip Carteret Hill. Annand spent his remaining years in London, first as Canada's agent general, then an agent for Nova Scotia.

LOIS KERNAGHAN

Annapolis Lowlands, situated in Digby, Annapolis and King's counties, NS, extends 155 km from the E shore of ST MARY'S BAY eastward to the W shore of MINAS BASIN. Geologically founded upon weak, mainly red, sedimentary rocks of Triassic age (about 230 million years old), its elevation ranges from sea level at its western and eastern ends to about 35 m in the centre, rising to about 60 m on N and S flanks. It is overlooked on the N by the basalt escarpment of North Mtn which rises to 180-240 m, and on the S by the granite upland of South Mtn, rising to 150-210 m. Following the retreat of glacial ice, about

3 000 years ago, the lowlands were nearly ompletely flooded by the sea to a height of 0 m. Subsequent isostatic uplift caused withrawal of the sea, but in the last 6000 years seavel rise has led to the growth of extensive salt narshes at each end of the lowlands, through vhich the Annapolis and Cornwallis rivers low in broad meanders. These marshes were ne focal area of ACADIAN French settlement rom the founding of PORT-ROYAL (1605) to the nid-18th century. Dikes were built by Acadians regulate tidal flooding of the marshes and to ermit their drainage for use as rich hayfields. owards the centre of the lowlands, wellrained, stone-free soils on undulating topograhy free of spring frosts form the basis of apple rchards and dairy farming. Principle towns inlude KENTVILLE, home of an Agriculture Canada xperimental station; DIGBY, terminal for ferries SAINT JOHN, NB, and a fishing port; and WOLFLLE, home of Acadia U. The name derives from NNAPOLIS ROYAL (for England's Queen Anne), e renamed settlement of Port-Royal.

I.A. BROOKES

Annapolis Royal, NS, Town, pop 631 (1981c), nc 1893, is located on the south side of the Anapolis R, about 10 km from its mouth near the estern shore of Nova Scotia. The entire basin vas named PORT-ROYAL by Champlain and de Monts when they discovered the area in 1604. he site was amenable for settlement, offering a mperate climate and arable land, and was perct for military purposes, protected by surunding hills. BIENCOURT de Poutrincourt established a small group of farmers there in 1606 nd Acadian settlement spread slowly along the asin and river. The habitation was destroyed in 613 by Samuel Argall and the English erected fort nearby in 1628-29. In 1632 the French rernned and about 1636 d'Aulnay de Charnisay uilt a small fort at the present site of Ft Anne. It as captured by Sedgwick in 1654 and reocupied by the French in 1670. Ft Anne was been in 1687 and after its completion was strong nough to stave off 2 invasions from New ngland colonials in 1704 and 1707. Francis ICHOLSON changed the name to Annapolis in onour of Queen Anne when he captured the rt in 1710, and the fort was garrisoned until 854. The settlement was the capital of Nova Scotia until the founding of Halifax in 1749. After the deportation of the ACADIANS, the area was resettled by New Englanders and LOYALISTS. The old and new names gradually merged to become the official name, Annapolis Royal. Shipping became an important industry in the 19th century, with timber an important export, and an ironworks was established. Today the town is the shipping centre for the apple industry of the Annapolis Valley. Ft Anne was restored and in 1917 became Fort Anne National Historic Park.

HEATHER MACDONALD

nnapolis Royal, NS. French settlement in the area ates from the early 17th century; today the town is the ipping centre for the Annapolis Valley's apple indusy (*photo by John deVisser*).

Anne of Green Gables, novel by Lucy Maud MONTGOMERY, published in Boston, 1908; its first Canadian edition appeared in Toronto, 1943. The first of 8 novels about Anne, this has remained Montgomery's most popular work. Its appeal lies in Anne's development as a volubly imaginative, overarticulate, spontaneous but sensitive child-heroine. Rescued from an orphanage, she finds ample "scope for the imagination" at Green Gables, where she wins the hearts of Matthew and Marilla Cuthbert, and in Avonlea, where she wins the community's affection. Anne's bright passage from childhood into adolescence has won for the novel international acclaim; it has gone through numerous editions, has been translated into at least 15 languages and has twice been made into a film. A musical version of the story has played annually in Charlottetown, PEI, since 1965.

NEIL BESNER

Annelida, phylum of segmented worms with a true body cavity (coelom) separating gut from body wall. Annelids probably evolved from unsegmented coelomates which became segmented to allow continuous, active burrowing. In turn they give rise to arthropods. the phylum is divided into 3 classes: Polychaeta (mainly marine worms); Oligochaeta (EARTHWORMS and many freshwater worms); and Hirudinea (LEECHES). More than 9000 annelid species are known worldwide. In Canada, more than 150 marine and freshwater oligochaete species and 20 earthworm species are known, although many must remain to be described. There are probably 600 polychaete species and 45 species of leech in Canada and the adjacent US.

Annelids are mostly vermiform (wormshaped), with an anterior (frontal) mouth preceded only by the prostomium, bearing sensory organs; anus is posterior. Most have bristles (chaetae or setae), usually arranged in 4 groups on each segment. Frontal brain has 2 major connections running around the esophagus to the first of a long series of segmental ganglia (nerve masses) along lower side of worm. In earthworms the ventral nerve cord has 3 special, large fibres that allow emergency messages to pass quickly from one end of the worm to the other along the otherwise rather slow conducting system. These fast pathways enable worms to make quick escape movements, eg, if bitten. Worms were the first ANIMALS to evolve closed blood vessels, some of which have become enlarged to act as pumps or simple hearts. Very simple eyes and some tentacles may form a head. Some worms bear gills on various body parts, but most breathe through moist skin. There are few internal organs. Worms excrete through the body surface and by tubular nephridia (kidneylike organs). Their simple guts may have a few special organs, and there may be areas for storage (crop) and for breaking up food (gizzard). Only leeches have teeth, used to chew live prey or pierce skin for bloodsucking. Although annelids mate, oligochaetes, leeches and many polychaetes are hermaphroditic.

Some polychaetes [Gk, *poly*, "many"; *chaetes*, "bristles"] have jaws or teeth of cuticle. These may be on the end of a pharynx that can be rapidly pushed out to seize or bite prey (eg, blood worm, *Glycera*). Many tube-dwelling polychaetes have elaborate tentacles for capturing food particles. Polychaetes are nearly all found in the sea or in estuaries; a very few, including the Canadian *Maniyunkia*, are found in fresh water. Worms with fewer bristles, oligochaetes [Gk, *oligo*, "few"], live mainly on land in moist burrows. These include earthworms (Lumbricidae family and allies) with 8 setae per segment. Other similar but smaller oligochaetes have up to 120 bristles per segment; fewer (about 24), arranged in 4 bundles, are usual. These forms may live in the deep sea, along shorelines, in rivers and lakes, in moist soils, in water trapped in plants or on glaciers (ICE-WORMS). Small, white enchytraeids are familiar denizens of compost heaps, and are raised commercially as fish food. Oligochaete food ranges from bacteria in soil to algae, vegetable matter and some animal remains; one species eats live prey. Leeches (Hirudinea) always have 34 segments but no bristles. They move about using 2 suckers. They live in fresh or salt water, or on land in the tropics. Many are external parasites of vertebrates; some eat snails and worms.

R.O. BRINKHURST

Annexation Association, fd 1849 to promote Canada-US political union. In Oct and Dec it published 2 versions of the "Annexation Manifesto." Most of those who signed it were from the powerful English-speaking business community in Montréal and Québec and the French Canadian radical nationalist movement led by Louis-Joseph PAPINEAU. The businessmen were disappointed at Britain's abolition of preferential duties on Canadian lumber, wheat and flour products and by its decision to consent to the REBELLION LOSSES BILL; the nationalists were republicans who preferred American political institutions. Strongly opposed by the BRITISH AMERICAN LEAGUE and by followers of Louis-Hippolyte LA FONTAINE, the movement died out after the 1854 RECIPROCITY Treaty was signed.

JACQUES MONET, SJ

Anson Northup, the first of many steamers to navigate the RED R from Minnesota to the RED RIVER COLONY. Shortly after its arrival in Ft Garry in June 1859, the *Anson Northup* was purchased by the HBC and entrepreneur J.C. Burbank, who renamed it the *Pioneer*. It went into general service, according preferred rates to the HBC. STEAMBOATS on the Red R heralded the end of HBC dominance in the North-West: bulk cargoes could now be transported into and out of the region, and the region's agricultural and commercial potential was seen in a much more favourable light by Canada, which after 1867 moved quickly to acquire the area. J.E. REA

Ant, common name for small, mostly ground-dwelling, social INSECTS of family Formicidae, order Hymenoptera. Ants are the most numerous insects. An estimated 12 000 species occur worldwide, about 186 in Canada. They are black, red, brown or yellow; smooth, hairy or spined; and characterized by a slender waist at the base of the abdomen, bearing 1 or 2 beadlike enlargements. Heads are large with elbowed antennae and, usually, well-developed mouthparts. Workers are wingless; reproductives are usually winged, mating in flight. After mating, the queen sheds her wings and excavates a chamber where she lays eggs. The first larvae are tended by the queen; later broods, by workers. Ants are the most diverse and specialized social insects. They occur from the tropics to the arctic tundra, and on most islands. Nests of some primitive ants may never contain more than 12 individuals, while those of highly social species may comprise millions. Ants prey on other insects, eat seeds, tend aphids for honeydew excretions or cultivate fungus gardens. Some ants raid nests of other species, capturing slaves which they carry back to work in their own nests. Certain species are specialized social parasites, existing only in nests of other ants. M.V. SMITH

Antelope, *see* PRONGHORN.

Anthony Island Provincial Park situated on the most southerly of the Queen Charlotte Is, BC, holds the remaining fragments of a rich culture. Ninstints, village of the Kunghit HAIDA, reveals a 2000-year history to archaeologists. The inhabitants of Ninstints were encountered in the late 18th century by European explorers interested in trade. The 2 groups traded peacefully in the 1780s, but bitter conflicts erupted in 1791 and 1795. Smallpox, rather than war, however, took the lives of most of the inhabitants, and the population was reduced from 300 to 30. The village was finally abandoned in the late 1800s.

Today, overgrown with lush vegetation, the remains of Ninstints's LONGHOUSES and TOTEM POLES pay silent homage to their creators. Complex conservation programs to protect the remaining structures and keep them clear of vegetation will help to ensure the future of this UNESCO World Heritage Site. *See also* NORTHWEST COAST INDIAN ART. LILLIAN STEWART

Reading: G.F. MacDonald, *Ninstints, Haida World Heritage Site* (1983).

Anthropology is the comparative study of past and contemporary cultures, focusing on the ways of life and customs of all peoples of the world. Specialty subdisciplines have developed within anthropology, owing to the amount of information collected and the variety of methods and techniques used in anthropological research. These subdisciplines are physical anthropology, archaeology, linguistic anthropology, ethnology and theoretical anthropology, and applied anthropology.

Physical Anthropology is the study of the evolution and physical varieties of humankind. It includes the physical measurement of skeletal remains and of living people (anthropometry); the study of human genetics, with comparisons to the genetic makeup of other primates; the study of primate behaviour for a detailed description of their social behaviour and comparative generalizations about primate social organization. Research of this kind indicates how the social behaviour of early human groups might have been organized (*see* ANTHROPOLOGY, PHYSICAL).

ARCHAEOLOGY studies the prehistory, and some of the history of mankind through digging up and analysing the remains of past cultures. Archaeology also dates the origins of human occupations in various parts of the world, the origins of tools, other artifacts, art and structures that have developed over the ages. Archaeologists seek to reconstruct the development and total cultures of past peoples.

Linguistic Anthropology, or ethnolinguistics, is the study of the organization of language, including the identification and analysis of units of speech, from the simplest units of sound to the complex and various combinations of sound and meaning that are used in the thousands of languages spoken in the world today. Historical and comparative study also makes it possible to reconstruct languages that are no longer spoken, and to establish the relationships among languages. The linguistic anthropologist may also study nonverbal forms of communication and the rules for the proper use of speech (pragmatics) (*see* ANTHROPOLOGY, LINGUISTICS).

Ethnology and theoretical anthropology are the scientific core of anthropology and are described in detail in this entry. Anthropology evolved partly from the specialties mentioned above, and partly from the description of particular, living cultures (ethnography). As our knowledge of prehistory, history and the present varieties of culture increased, anthropology developed as a science that aimed at elaborating comprehensive explanations of social life (theoretical anthropology). Through the comparative analysis of individual behaviour and culture patterns, the science has tried to formulate generalizations and universal tendencies (ethnology). This development followed from improvements in research tools and practical models from which to describe reality. Ethnography is associated with exploration and descriptive work, often among distinctive, non-European tribes, whereas theoretical anthropology employs abstract hypotheses and perspectives from other disciplines, as well as more abstract tools of observation and analysis. Ethnology puts the 2 together, using theoretical models and a wide empirical knowledge of different cultures to allow for comparisons and the formulation of general cultural norms.

Applied Anthropology is the use of anthropological knowledge for solving practical problems of human groups. This application has been tried mostly in small communities struggling with problems of poverty, or of rapid cultural, technological or economic change. It is also concerned with developing new forms of education to help people cope with rapid change, or with more effective ways of improving the health of the community.

Anthropology is a young science with high ambitions to describe, understand and explain the origins, varieties and purposes of mankind's customs, beliefs, languages, institutions and lifeways; to find general cultural norms; and to provide practical guidance for humankind.

Historical Development of Anthropology Curiosity about the lifeways and customs of different peoples is probably as old as humankind. People everywhere learn to recognize as relatives or friends those whose actions, language and dress are familiar. We learn to notice cultural differences, because these differences of speech, appearance and activities define for us what it is to be a "stranger." An enduring record of different customs has been made as far back as the earliest known written records, in ancient Greece, Mesopotamia, China and other centres of civilization. Travellers and philosophers in many parts of the world speculated about the origins of humanity, the use of fire, language, the rise of cities and kingdoms, laws, religion, metals, war, art, agriculture, music and so on. The European age of discovery brought a renewal of interest in the "strange" peoples and customs that were observed by explorers, traders and missionaries.

Anthropology as a profession, as a study by people dedicated to the science of culture, arose during the late 1800s, with the main theoretical interest being cultural evolution, or the determination of when and where human civilization appeared for the first time and how civilizations spread and developed. Cultures, according to this view, are natural systems, developing in organization and content according to natural laws and progressing gradually towards "high" culture — ie, technical, intellectual and moral excellence. Each person and society was thought to be engaged in this progressive change, but at different rates. Those at the slowest rates remained at the level of savagery, those at medium rates had entered the stage of barbarism (typically as horticulturalists or pastoralists), and those progressing at the fastest rates achieved literacy and finally an industrial economy. This concept of culture was thought to be universal, applying to all humankind. The force behind this progress was thought to be absolute, inevitable and irreversible, sometimes called "the psychic unity of mankind" or human nature.

The next major theoretical interest to develop in anthropology was called historicism. Where evolution held that all cultures necessarily passed through the same stages towards the same goal, the culture historians thought this scheme too simple and uniform to fit the reality of human variations. These historians set out to identify, for each culture, what was invented and what was borrowed (diffusion), a distinction which raised a number of questions requiring researched and documented answers. How were the various hunting tools developed? How did the different pastoral economies form? How did agricultural practices in different parts of the world come about? How did the development of villages with permanent occupation aid the growth of a complex agricultural economy? When did the ability to make metal tools appear? Specific questions were asked about particular cultures and the answers were brought together to give a composite picture of the development of cultural traditions. Each composite was viewed as an emergent system — a system developing according to its own circumstances and with its own direction, integrating items that were borrowed over the years from neighbouring cultures or even from distant cultures. People did not repeatedly reinvent their ways of life, but rather learned their cultures automatically, as a part of what we call "received tradition" — thoses things that people of a society have always known to be useful, true or good. Anthropological historicists, or ethnohistorians, have continued to contribute to our understanding of cultures by reconstructing particular histories.

Another basic interest in theoretical anthropology, strong in the period between the world wars, was the search for universal functions (useful, integrating relationships) that exist in all cultures. The focus of attention is the process by which groups adapt themselves to their natural environment and promote collective activities that ensure the fulfilment of human needs Basic survival needs are those related to metabolism, reproduction, bodily comforts, safety, movement and health. Secondary needs arise from the ways that people in groups deal with the basic needs, establishing institutions that will function to fulfil economic, kinship, political and other needs by regulating the norms of behaviour and the selection of members for these activities. Symbolic needs are satisfied through communication norms, religious beliefs and ceremonies, and expressions of art, including myths and tales. These anthropologists termed "functionalists," try to understand how each culture met these needs and what kinds of social institutions were customarily used.

Similar to the functionalists' interest in universal human needs, the interest of the culture and personality theorists centered on the old controversy of the relation of nature to nurture, with special attention to the cultural foundations of personality. The characteristics of child rearing and temperament were found to vary a great deal from one culture to another. Some cultures, for instance, were remarkably permissive; others were restrictive. Some were characterized by a strong show of emotions and others by little emotional expression. Some showed great consistency in the way that children were treated while others showed little predictability in response to children's behaviour. The various combinations of these norms for child rearing were found to lead to different adult characteristics, and to contribute to the norms of adult behaviour (such as aggressive, placid, friendly, suspicious) for each culture. The ways that persons in each culture mature from infancy through old age is of great interest to many anthropologists today. More recent work in cognitive anthropology has emphasized variability of individual responses to cultural socialization.

By comparison, structural anthropology looks for universal rules of human thought, usually far from our normal awareness, in unconsciously learned (and used) regularities in the mind. The example of language is helpful; we make sentences as we talk with each other, and our sentences always follow rules of grammar, yet we are scarcely aware of the rules we use. We don't think to ourselves, "first the noun, then the verb" as we talk to each other. Much of our behaviour is similarly guided by rules in our deep unconscious, which we use intuitively and easily. In this way we organize our social relations, enjoy the meaning in a book or story, and sense the "rightness" of a ritual such as a wedding, a funeral or a church service. Structural anthropologists believe that all rules of this sort are variations on a few universal "deep" rules, which they are trying to discover. Once again, the interest is in defining human nature or psychic unity.

In Neo-Marxism, or historical materialism, the emphasis is placed on economic systems, modes of production and exchange of goods. Neo-Marxists believe that these economic, production and exchange factors are the products of confrontations between various elements of the social system. They are trying to prove that in the capitalist mode of production, labourers are exploited by the interests of capital, and that as a result they benefit only in small measure from their efforts at production.

A more recent approach to social analysis is cognitive anthropology, the study of units of thought and their combinations. Cognitive anthropologists seek the rules by which different cultures organize their knowledge in their own distinctive styles. The point is to understand cultural features as they are understood by the people within the particular culture and to explain these features to a wider audience outside the culture.

Early anthropologists investigated communities of people in isolated places cut off from the modern world. Since WWII the isolation of these small groups has ended. The study of stability and change has concentrated on cultural contacts, urbanization, industrialization, the effect of media and schools, and other dynamic factors that are transforming even the most remote peoples of the world. There is a renewed interest in cross-cultural studies, using the comparative method to derive general norms and universals of culture, whether in child rearing, mental health or religion. The emphasis is no longer on single items of culture as they are distributed around the world but on the relationships among many items, or clusters of cultural traits and their dynamic interdependency.

Concept of Culture The classic definition of culture, still widely accepted, was published over 100 years ago by E.B. Tylor. It is "that complex whole which includes knowledge, belief, art, morals, law, custom, and any other capabilities and habits acquired by man as a member of society." From an anthropological perspective, virtually every mature human being is thoroughly endowed with his or her culture. Everyone knows a language; knows how to act towards relatives, friends or strangers; how to take a place in society; how to use many of the basic tools; how to make an exchange of goods or services; how to regard the persons who have political power or social prestige; when to evaluate things, actions or ideas as good or bad; and how one's particular world is arranged in size, shape and purpose. People know these things, and they have a sense of what is excellent in each of these aspects of their culture; perhaps a sense of what an ideal person should be. But what is ideal to an 18th-century Montréal gentleman is a far cry from the ideal for a Vancouver artist or a prairie farmer, a Maritime fisherman or an Inuit mother. In order to deal with these differences, the concept of culture is divided into major segments such as technology, economics, kinship and social organization, value systems and ideology.

Technology refers to the things manufactured and the knowledge and skills required to make them. Technology is responsive to the physical environment and to the level of cultural development, so that a northern hunting culture, for example, will be different from a tropical farming culture.

Economics refers to exchange and trade and may involve goods and services, or a less tangible exchange of rights and privileges. This trade may be within a community or among different groups. Often the trade is more than simple exchange, giving a stable and dependable bond, or alliance, to the group.

Kinship and social organization refer to the relations among the people of a group, and include the way an individual knows how to act and what to expect in his relationships to others, as well as whom he may or may not marry, from whom he may inherit property or other rights, and to whom he should will his estate and responsibilities.

Value systems and religious belief and behaviour are the aspects of culture that are closest to the human significance or meanings of events, beyond the events themselves. Birth, reaching adulthood, marriage and death are charged, in the minds of most people, with special value, and often with spiritual meaning. This is also true of the aspects of life that are most closely linked with getting a living, such as rituals of hunting, agriculture or pastoralism. Ideologies, world view and cultural imperatives provide people with their sense of the way the world is constituted or arranged, and how the persons must act to be in harmony with the world, rather than at risk of harm through being in conflict with the natural order. Ideologies are maps or images of what the arrangement of society should become, a statement of the ideal toward which the group should strive.

Each of these major segments of culture has attracted many studies, both at the level of describing how that segment is defined for particular cultures and also how similar or different it may be when viewed cross-culturally. Information about particular cultures, and for cross-cultural comparisons, arises from the basic anthropological activity — field studies.

Field Research was once left to the travellers, traders and missionaries who cared to write about peoples and their cultures. The first anthropologists were social philosophers and intellectuals who understood cultures through the "armchair studies" of historical and travel documents. Only in the last decades of the 1800s did anthropology become a discipline based upon fieldwork and the accumulation of firsthand observations. Training in field methods of observation is an important part of anthropological apprenticeship. Data are usually gathered through systematic observation of daily events, and participation observation in events and situations that are of special importance to the people (such as economic activities, social relationships and ritual acts). The anthropologist seeks out and interviews people who possess special and relevant knowledge and who communicate with accurate detail and completeness (key informants). Every fieldworker develops a method for recording and classifying his data so that he can draw upon accurate and appropriate information in writing up his scientific reports. Anthropologists often stay in the field for a year or more, in order to establish good relations with the people they are studying and to be thorough and accurate in making a record of what people say and do. This kind of field research requires special human skills as well as skill in anthropological theories, concepts, methods and techniques. The observer must also explain who he is, what he is doing, the reasons for doing his research, the use that he will make of the information he collects, how long he will stay, and other questions that are a part of honesty and courtesy towards one's hosts. He must not only abide by the ethical principles of his profession, but also by the ethical principles of the people he is living with and then writing about.

Anthropology in Canada The fathers of Canadian anthropology were the missionaries who lived in French Canada in the 1600s. These men, such as Fathers LeClercq, Le Jeune and Sagard, were deeply interested in knowing the lifeways and beliefs of the native people they lived among, and they provided the detailed descriptions that were used by professional anthropologists, from the early "armchair" social philosophers to the historically oriented anthropologists of today. Canadian anthropology grew from records written by dedicated individuals whose profession was religion (Jesuits and other missionaries), or who were explorer-traders such as Lescarbot, or 2 centuries later teachers in our early universities, such as Sir Daniel Wilson at Toronto or John William DAWSON at McGill (in the mid-1880s). Government employees, in particular with the GEOLOGICAL SURVEY OF CANADA, made important records of their travels, including details about the native people they met and observed in the course of their work. The most important of these men is George Mercer DAWSON, who was employed by the Geological Survey from 1875 and rose to be its director in 1895. It was his sustained support more than that of any other one person that resulted in the establishment of a professional basis for Canadian anthropology, though he died before it was given formal recognition.

In 1910 PM Wilfrid Laurier established a Division of Anthropology within the Geological Survey, marking the beginning of professional anthropology in Canada. Offices were in the Victoria Memorial Museum in Ottawa, and professionally trained men were recruited from England and the US. From Professor Boas came Edward SAPIR, who had just completed his doctorate and was embarking on a brilliant career in anthropology. From Oxford's Professors Tylor and Marett came Charles Marius BARBEAU, a Rhodes scholar born in rural Québec. Barbeau's work at the NATIONAL MUSEUM (as it became known) was only one part of his contribution to Canadian anthropology. Les Archives de folklore at U Laval originated in his great collections of French Canadian material culture, songs, stories and tales, and in his students', especially Luc Lacourcière's, work to establish the archives

(1944). Barbeau also recruited to the museum a fellow student from Oxford, Diamond JENNESS. Sapir and Barbeau both made ethnographic studies and collections of the cultures of the Indians of the Northwest Coast, following George Mercer Dawson and Boas in this area. Jenness is best known for his research in the Arctic among the COPPER INUIT. But each also worked in many other areas of Canada, recording traditions and songs, studying native languages, and collecting artifacts for the museum. William WINTEMBERG and Harlan Smith worked archaeological sites to build the collections of prehistoric artifacts. These men, with a very few others, had nearly sole responsibility for the development of the profession in Canada from 1910 until 1925, when Sapir left Canada and Thomas MCILWRAITH took the first academic position in anthropology at a Canadian university. Five years later, McIlwraith was still the sole member of his department, and the very slow growth of anthropology is shown by the fact that the next universities to hire anthropologists, UBC and McGill, did so only in 1947. The first doctoral dissertation that is distinctly anthropological was appropriately based upon the Jesuit records and other documents on the subject, "The Conflict of European and Eastern Algonkian Cultures, 1504-1700: A Study in Canadian Civilization." The author, Alfred G. BAILEY, received his degree in history because in 1934 there was no anthropology doctoral program. The first PhD in anthropology was granted in 1956, with only a few more being granted until the late 1960s. The 1970s brought a boom in university development and in professional anthropology, and by 1980 about 400 people with doctorates in anthropology were employed in Canada, and many more with a master's degree. Harry Hawthorn built the department at UBC and set a standard for the use of anthropological research as a guide to policy in his classic report to the federal government, coauthored by M.-A. Tremblay, *A Survey of the Contemporary Indians of Canada* (1966, 1967). K.O.L. Burridge and C.S. BELSHAW at UBC, and R.F. SALISBURY at McGill, did internationally admired research in Melanesia on the religion and other beliefs and the economics of the colonized native people of the area. Research in Africa has been undertaken by nearly 100 anthropologists, of which the work of R.B. Lee of U of T on the political economy of the bushmen is probably the best known.

Common trends dominate the development of anthropology in Canada, in spite of differences in language or distances between the various universities and museums. Part of the reason for this uniformity is the widespread influence of the ideas of Boas and his students. Moreover, anthropology in English Canada is built on an interest in the native people of Canada, who lived in small, isolated communities. This fact led to anthropological emphasis on the empirical field-study tradition, with participant observation and interviews with key informants, and resulted in reports that described the technology, economics, social organization, values and world view of each particular community. In many of these communities, people were conscious of their past history, sometimes from a sense of discontent with their present situation and with a concern that the past was slipping away from them without a satisfactory or secure new way of life to replace the old. The anthropologist's interest in traditions could then be an occasion to record the past before it was forgotten. Since the early studies by Boas, Jenness and others of small, tradition-oriented communities in the Arctic, and since the studies by Boas, Barbeau, Sapir and others of Northwest Coast Indian communities, the empirical study of small and isolated communities has continued to occupy the interests of many Canadian anthropologists.

In French Canada anthropology has built upon rural and small-town studies of the Québec region and its people, again emphasizing the study of small and relatively isolated groups. The development of anthropology in Québec is based upon the classic studies of French Canadians by early sociologists. The most important figure is Leon GERIN, whose "L'Habitant de St-Justin" illustrated how, in rural Québec, the old European patriarchal system continued in organizing the community's lifeways. The American Everett C. Hughes also influenced Québec anthropology with his *French Canada in Transition* (1943), a study of the process of industrialization in the town of Drummondville. Another American, Horace Miner, wrote *St-Denis: A French Canadian Parish* (1939), which became a model for community studies in Québec. Miner, an anthropologist, and the sociologists Gerin and Hughes all made extensive use of participant observation and key-informant interviewing during their field research.

Anthropology expands by learning about people, and the particular people that anthropologists study have an important influence upon the general and theoretical ideas that are developed. In English Canada the development of anthropology was guided by the studies of small communities of native people, with research in other areas of Canada and the world gradually increasing during the 1960s and 1970s. This wider horizon gives a valuable broadening of empirical and theoretical materials to Canadian anthropology, while the original interests in native peoples continues to develop as well. In Québec the studies of rural and small-town communities added to the cultural "mapping" of more isolated areas that continued through the 1960s, especially at U de Montréal and at Laval. The anglophone McGill U supported this research, but also developed a research program on social change among the James Bay Cree. In the 1970s the regional studies continued, but with more defined focus upon socioeconomic disparities and Marxist interpretations. Laval and Montréal also became interested in the James Bay Cree, and McGill sponsored research in Africa and Latin America. Applied anthropology has grown partly in response to the needs of native people and organizations during the 1970s.

During the 1970s and 1980s increasing specialization within anthropology has provided more refined methods and precision in research, but this specialization has meant that some topics have not received the attention they deserve. In both English Canada and Québec, the study of urban centres is barely begun, and their size and complexity will continue to challenge anthropologists to develop method and theory. Many of the less densely settled areas of Canada still remain to be studied. The emphasis on economic and ecological aspects of culture has resulted in too little emphasis on the family, on male-female relationships, the social and value aspects of work, beliefs and ideology, and the organization of industrial, professional and bureaucratic groups. The feminist perspective may provide a critical and corrective effect on research in all regions, and in all aspects of study. Canada has developed excellent resources for training professional anthropologists who may do this work. As of 1980 there were graduate programs leading to the PhD in anthropology at 9 universities across Canada: Alberta, British Columbia, Laval, McGill, McMaster, Manitoba, Montréal, Simon Fraser and Toronto. There were at least 14 professional organizations in Canada representing anthropologists, of which the Canadian Ethnology Society, founded in 1973 and publisher of the journal *Culture*, is the most broadly representative. There are over 20 other journals or monograph series.

Anthropology is a young discipline, although it is one of humankind's oldest interests. In th past century, the study of human variety and o the universal human qualities that underlie th variety has developed successfully in Canad and in other areas of the world. Much has bee done; much remains to be done. If we are to un derstand human nature, we must be able to un derstand the many ways that this nature is ex pressed, and the new ways that will develop i the future. When our knowledge has the accu racy and completeness that a science of human kind works to provide, this understanding ca give reliable guidance for efforts to improve th condition of all people, everywhere. Anthro pologists study humanity and serve human in terests and values.

R.J. PRESTON AND M.-A. TREMBLA

Anthropology, Linguistics in Canada LINGUIS TICS exists as a fully autonomous disciplin represented by about 12 independent program as well as by linguistic research within depart ments of English, various other language area education, philosophy, psychology, sociolog and anthropology. In spite of this disciplinar diversity, linguistics within anthropology con centrates particularly on the study of America Indian languages. Within N American anthro pology, linguistics has been included tradition ally as one of the subdisciplines, along wit ANTHROPOLOGY, PHYSICAL; ARCHAEOLOGY; socio-cul tural ANTHROPOLOGY, and applied anthropology In the early 1980s 26 Canadian university de partments of anthropology had at least on linguist on staff. Eight of the 9 PhD program offered studies in linguistics and 6 museum were actively engaged in linguistic research.

There are historical precedents for the Cana dian study of American Indian languages. Ed ward SAPIR, the foremost linguist among th students of Franz BOAS, served as director of an thropological research in Ottawa from 1910 t 1925, under the auspices of the Geological Sur vey, Dept of Mines. This program is now th Canadian Ethnology Service of the NATIONA MUSEUM OF MAN and retains Sapir's linguistic in terests. During his tenure, Sapir encouraged de tailed fieldwork on particular languages, stress ing phonology (sound system) and morpholog (word structure). Not content with description Sapir classified N American Indian language into a small number of stocks of related familie comparable in time depth to Indo-European Five of Sapir's 6 basic N American stocks — Eskimo-Aleut, Na-Dene (including Athapascan Haida and Tlingit), Algonquian-Wakashan Penutian and Hokan-Siouan — are spoken i Canada. Moreover, Sapir pioneered in recon struction of cultural history from linguistic evi dence, demonstrating, for example, the Alaskar and northwestern Canadian origin of the Na vajo and Apache tribes of the American SW.

More recent Amerindian studies have con tinued to focus on descriptive linguistics an language classification. Linguists have becom more specialized in method and theory, al though many have remained within anthro pology. The traditional study of phonology and morphology has expanded to include synta (sentence structure) and semantics (meaning). A few anthropological linguists have moved from the study of meaning to the socio-cultural con text of language use within a particular culture

Applied linguistics has focused on the de velopment of writing systems for Indian lan guages, some based on the Roman alphabet and others on syllabics (combinations of consonan and vowel which function together in the con struction of words). Much of this work has been carried out in collaboration with Canadian native communities concerned with the mainte nance and preservation of their languages.

Linguistics within anthropology remains an essential part of the training of anthropologists and of their potential contribution to the communities they study, particularly in native-language teaching. Simultaneously, anthropological linguistics has maintained its ties to general linguistics, which it enriches by its understanding of less familiar languages spoken today by many native Canadians (*see* NATIVE PEOPLE, LANGUAGES). REGNA DARNELL

Anthropology, Physical, has no single definition acceptable to all its practitioners, but most agree that the major focus of the field is on problems of human evolution and variation. The foundations of modern physical anthropology, like those of modern biology, rest on Neo-Darwinian evolutionary theory, which provides the common background for a diverse discipline that lacks a common set of methods. Physical anthropologists recognize that interaction between human culture and human biology has shaped and maintained our species, and that full understanding of the processes responsible requires consideration of both biology and culture. Reflecting this interdisciplinary concern, most physical anthropologists work in university departments of anthropology. Many, however, are employed in departments of anatomy, dentistry, human kinetics, and zoology.

Human biological history is most directly told by the fossil record. Although hominid remains (fossils in the human line) are not found in the Western Hemisphere, Canadians have contributed to PALEONTOLOGY. Foremost among them was Davidson BLACK, who named and studied the fossils called "Peking Man" (*Sinanthropus pekinensis = Homo erectus pekinensis*). Studies on nonhuman primates (prosimians, monkeys, apes) have ranged from the earliest fossils to the living. Though research in primate behaviour is valuable in itself, these works are also used to provide inferences about behaviours that may have been present in the forms from which nonhuman primates and humans are descended.

The greatest contribution of Canadians over the period since 1871 has been in human osteology. Descriptions of the size and shape of skeletons of archaic and prehistoric Inuit and Indian peoples have been superseded by analyses of past population distributions, assessments of group composition by age and sex, and determination of contemporary and earlier population relationships. The effects of nutrition, diseases, climate, culture and genetics on past populations are routinely investigated with techniques borrowed from biochemistry, pathology, epidemiology, demography, radiology and statistics. Tools such as the scanning electron microscope are used to discern age-associated changes in the bone. The U of Toronto has led osteological research; strong contributions are also being made at the universities of Manitoba, Winnipeg, Queen's, Guelph, McMaster, and the National Museum of Man.

Studies of living peoples have included assessment of cold adaptation in indigenous groups, determination of adult body composition, and study of the growth and development of children. The U of Montréal is preeminent in research on human morphologic and genetic variation. The impact that specific microevolutionary forces (genetic drift, gene flow) and social factors (marriage patterns) have on the genetic features of populations have been examined in groups as diverse as subarctic Indians and Caribbean island isolates. The effect of gene flow on genetic relationships within Amerindians and the demonstration of genetic linkages between Siberian and N American populations have received emphasis at McMaster. Demographic studies of religious isolates and hunting-gathering groups are increasing in the search to document the action of microevolutionary forces on human groups.

Canadian universities offering a doctoral program in physical anthropology are Simon Fraser, Alberta, Toronto and Montréal. In addition to universities already mentioned, Victoria, Calgary, Saskatchewan and Memorial each have training and research centres. The professional organization is the Canadian Assn for Physical Anthropology. EMŐKE J.E. SZATHMARY

Anticosti, Ile d', 8000 km^2, 225 km long and 56 km at widest point, is located in the GULF OF ST LAWRENCE, athwart the entrance to the St Lawrence R. The name likely derives from the Indian word *natiscosti,* meaning "where bears are hunted." There is logic in the suggestion that it comes from the Spanish *ante* (before) and *costa* (coast), but no real evidence. Though considerably larger than PEI, its population is only about 300. Most of the coastline is dominated by steep limestone cliffs, and several of its rivers cut through deep canyons. The eastern end is an enormous bog. Most of the inhabitants trace their ancestry to Newfoundland, St Pierre and Miquelon, and the Îles de la Madeleine. Entirely French speaking, they have made their living as fishermen, trappers, farmers, lumberjacks and lighthouse keepers. In 1909 over 800 ha were under cultivation, but no farms remain. The lighthouses are now all automatic.

Discovered by Jacques CARTIER in 1534 (he took it for a peninsula), the island was granted as a seigneury 1680 to Louis JOLLIET in recognition of his exploration of the Mississippi R. After the fall of New France, it was annexed to Newfoundland, but in 1774 returned to Canada. In 1872 a Montréal land company was bankrupted trying to colonize the island, and in 1884 it was sold at auction for $101 000 to Francis Stockwell, an English businessman, who also went bankrupt trying to develop it. In 1895 Henri Menier, a millionaire French chocolate manufacturer, bought the island to develop as a private sports preserve. It was sold again 1926 to Consolidated Bathurst Inc, and a pulpwood industry flourished, more or less, particularly in the late 1920s, when the population rose to 3000. These operations were shut down 1972 because of transportation costs and forest fires. The first permanent village was located at Baie-Ste-Claire. Menier developed it as a model town, but it was abandoned in the 1920s for Port-Menier, or Baie Ellis, the only settlement on the island today. Outside Port-Menier lie the ruins of the island's once-famous landmark, Château Menier, a luxurious villa. It was deliberately set on fire in 1953.

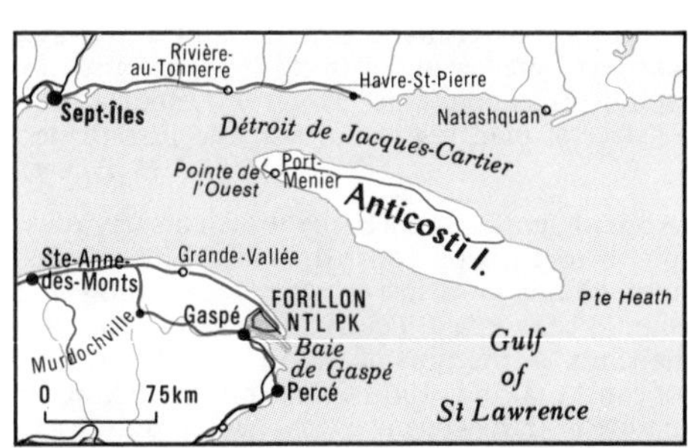

The island has a rich variety of wildlife, the most notable being the more than 100 000 Virginia white-tailed deer — the progeny of 220 brought by Menier in 1896. Deer hunting is a main attraction. Thousands of ships pass the island each year, and its treacherous reefs have given it the nickname "Graveyard of the Gulf." It is estimated that some 400 ships have foundered on the reefs, most in the 18th and 19th centuries, before the establishment of lighthouses. Ships still run aground occasionally despite navigational aids.

A controversy broke out in 1937, when a group of Germans took out an option to buy the island and develop the forest industry. Pressure from the federal and Québec governments aborted the attempt. JAMES MARSH

Antigonish, NS, Town, pop 5205 (1981c), inc 1889, is situated on a small plain about 1.6 km from Antigonish harbour. Located midway between HALIFAX and SYDNEY, it is a quiet college and residential community. With no major industry, Antigonish relies on being the market centre for surrounding communities. In 1785 a group of British soldiers first settled the area, then known as Dorchester. Population increased during the Napoleonic Wars, when Antigonish supplied much-needed timber to Britain. From 1821 onward the town was known as Antigonish. The name derives from the Micmac *Nalegitkoonechk* ("where branches are torn off"). In 1855 SAINT FRANCIS XAVIER U was opened. In the 20th century the university led in the founding of the ANTIGONISH MOVEMENT, a program of ADULT EDUCATION and self-help; the Coady Institute, which provides education for Third-World leaders; and the CO-OPERATIVE MOVEMENT in NS. Antigonish is also home to the Highland Games, a celebration of Scottish dance and sports. HEATHER MACDONALD

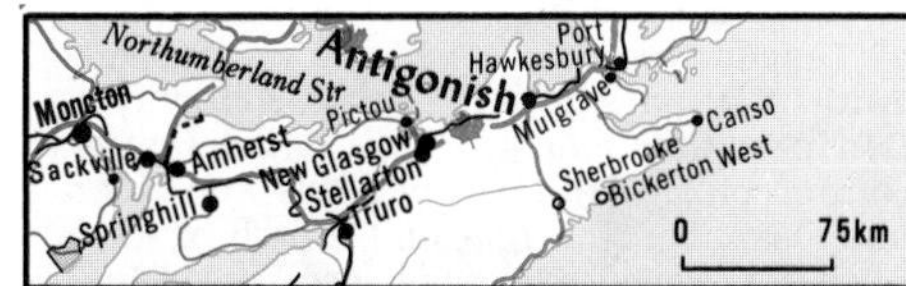

Antigonish Movement, a social and economic movement sponsored by the Extension Dept of SAINT FRANCIS XAVIER UNIVERSITY, Antigonish, NS. During the 1920s, following several decades of adversity in fishing, mining and agriculture in eastern Nova Scotia, St FX became involved in a series of social and economic programs, and in 1928 it established the Extension Dept. The department was under the direction of Father Moses COADY, but it relied heavily on the inspiration of Father J.J. "Jimmy" TOMPKINS and on the organizing zeal of Coady's assistant, A.B. MACDONALD.

The "Antigonish Movement" was unusual — a liberal Catholic movement at a time when conservatism was dominant in the Roman Catholic Church (*see* CATHOLICISM; CATHOLIC ACTION). It focused on ADULT EDUCATION as a means towards social improvement and economic organization. Typically, one of the movement's organizers would enter a community, use whatever contacts could be found and call a public meeting to assess the community's strengths and difficulties. A study club would be created and a program for a series of meetings developed. Usually, at the end of these meetings, one or more co-operatives would be established to help overcome the difficulties that had been discussed. The CREDIT UNION was most common, but the movement also organized co-operatives for selling fish, retailing consumer goods, building homes and marketing agricultural produce.

During the 1930s the Antigonish Movement spread to, or was imitated in, many areas of ATLANTIC PROVINCES. It also became well known in other parts of Canada and in the US, publicized by its own leaders, the churches and the credit union movement. During the 1940s a series of articles and books made the movement known in Europe, Latin America and Asia. In the 1950s adult educators and social activists began coming to study the movement in Antigonish, and in 1960 the Coady International Institute was established. The institute, a training centre for adult education and social action, soon attracted students for courses on the Antigonish method. Thousands of community organizers have studied in Antigonish. Upon returning to Asia,

Latin America and Africa they have attempted, with differing degrees of success, to duplicate the movement's early accomplishments in Nova Scotia. In recent years the movement has played an important role in Canada's FOREIGN AID programs.

Locally the Antigonish Movement has found its study club approach difficult to sustain since the 1950s. The arrival of television, road improvements and a gradually increasing standard of living have made it difficult to assemble groups for sustained study and community activism. The movement has been forced to embrace new media, such as television, and to face current issues, most of which are not resolved through co-operatives, in order to maintain its momentum. The success of these efforts is not as easily demonstrable as were the very concrete accomplishments of the 1930s and 1940s. *See also* DISTANCE LEARNING; CO-OPERATIVE MOVEMENT.

IAN MACPHERSON

Reading: Gregory Baum, *Catholics and Canadian Socialism* (1980); M.M. Coady, *Masters of Their Own Destiny* (1963); A.F. Laidlaw, ed, *The Man from Margaree* (1971).

Anti-Inflation Act Reference (1976), temporary and extraordinary measure instituted by the Trudeau government to control high unemployment and inflation. The Supreme Court of Canada upheld the validity of the federal Anti-Inflation Act (1975), and therefore of certain peacetime emergency powers designed to control profits, prices, dividends and salaries and to combat INFLATION, on the basis of the implicit emergency power (defined by Mr Justice Beetz as a concurrent and paramount power over matters normally under provincial jurisdiction) recognized in, eg, the FORT FRANCES decision. The court held by a majority that Parliament need not make a ritual statement that a state of emergency exists. GÉRALD-A. BEAUDOIN

Anti-Inflation Board, established by Act of Parliament in late 1975 to administer a wage-and-price-control program. Although the program was phased out during 1978, the AIB did not cease all operations until 1979. Because of its examination of company profits, close to $323.1 million was returned to the marketplace by hundreds of companies. The wide-ranging mandate of the board was highly controversial; it examined auto, fuel-oil and gas prices, Bell Canada employee wages, insurance premiums, beef prices, etc. The board's consequent recommendations resulted in rebates, wage rollbacks and price increases. Amendments were made to the Anti-Inflation Act to ensure that prices and wages did not automatically jump when the control period (and therefore the AIB's recommendations) came to an end.

Antimony (Sb), silvery white, brittle, lustrous metallic element, with a melting point of 630°C. It is a poor conductor of heat and electricity. The most important source of antimony is the MINERAL stibnite. Stibnite and antimony metal have been used since 4000 BC, for example, stibnite as eyebrow pigment. Antimony is used in alloys, especially to impart hardness and strength to lead. Lead-acid batteries are a major but diminishing use; newer, maintenance-free batteries use cadmium-lead instead. Other uses of lead-antimony alloys include cable sheathing, bearing alloys and type metals. Antimony compounds are used in flame retardants, paints, ceramics, enamels and glass. Most antimony ores are upgraded by flotation. Antimony is extracted from concentrates by roasting and reduced to metal by addition of scrap iron and salt. Some antimony is recovered from complex ores by leaching and electrolysis. Antimony is recovered from LEAD ores as antimonial lead (*see* METALLURGY). The major antimony producing countries have been China, Bolivia, the USSR, Thailand, Turkey and Yugoslavia. Antimony minerals are common in the Cordilleran and Appalachian regions of Canada, where antimony is recovered as a lead by-product. Canada's most recently worked antimony mine, near Lk George, NB, closed in 1981 but could be reopened. In 1980 Canada's antimony production was valued at $6 million. J.J. HOGAN

Anti-Reciprocity Movement A number of organizations were formed to oppose the RECIPROCITY agreement of Jan 1911 between Canada and the US. Most prominent was the Canadian National League, headed by Toronto lawyer Zebulon LASH. Others were the Canadian Home Market Assn, a branch of the Canadian Manufacturers' Assn which was active in distributing propaganda literature and in raising funds for the campaign; and the Anti-Reciprocity League, established in Montréal in late Feb. Claiming to be politically nonpartisan, this league launched a door-to-door petition campaign and held rallies throughout the country. A leading figure in the antireciprocity agitation was Clifford SIFTON, formerly minister of the interior in the Liberal government. CURTIS FAHEY

AOSTRA, *see* ALBERTA OIL SANDS TECHNOLOGY AND RESEARCH AUTHORITY.

Aphid, or plant louse, small, soft-bodied INSECT that sucks plant sap. Aphids belong to order Hemiptera, suborder Homoptera, and may be red, pink, brown, yellow, green, purple or black. Over 3900 species are known worldwide; over 600 in Canada. Aphids appear to have originated about 280 million years ago. In Canada, a fossil aphid over 78 million years old has been found preserved in amber. Aphids can migrate great distances (up to 1300 km) and are very prolific. In autumn, fertilized females lay overwintering eggs. The following spring these eggs hatch into wingless females that reproduce without mating, giving birth to live female offspring. Throughout the summer, several generations of unfertilized, daughter-producing females may occur. In late summer winged males and females are produced. These mate, producing fertilized, overwintering eggs. Often the asexual generations live on a different host plant from the sexually reproducing generation. In warm climates, aphids do not usually produce males, sexual females or eggs. Aphids may be polymorphic with winged and wingless forms in the same species. They are major INSECT PESTS which stunt or kill plants, cause plant galls, reduce yield and vigour, contaminate edible parts, and transmit plant viruses. They are controlled by climatic factors, land and water barriers, predaceous insects, fungus diseases, aphid-resistant plants, irrigation, modification of time of planting or harvest, and insecticides.

A.M. HARPER

Appeal, judicial process by which a party complains to a higher court that a decision against him or her by a lower court was wrong and should be reversed. The availability of an appeal depends on the type of case involved, the level of court making original determination and the nature of that determination. Each province has its own appeal court and the FEDERAL COURT of Appeal hears certain matters of federal jurisdiction; decisions from these courts can be appealed only to the SUPREME COURT of Canada. Appeal courts in Canada almost always sit in panels of odd numbers of judges to ensure a majority decision in favour of one party or another.

LEE PAIKIN

Apple (*Malus domestica*), the orchard apple, a cultivated species of the ROSE family, is Canada's most important FRUIT crop. It resulted from centuries of selection from wild species (eg, *M. sylvestris, M. prunifolia, M. pumila*), with interspecies hybridization. Over 75 wild species have been recognized, but many are hybrids among 17 or more true species (3 of which are native to Canada). Probably originating in the Caucasus, cultivated varieties were recognized in the 3rd century BC. Apple growing was brought to France and Britain by the Romans and from there to the New World. Early records show apple trees growing at LaHave, ACADIA, by 1635. The Fameuse cultivar, arising from a seed or seedling brought from France, has been grown in Québec for over 150 years. The showy flowers are borne in terminal clusters, chiefly on short, lateral woody shoots (spurs) on spreading trees of modest size. Trees may reach 12 m by 6 m in spread and height, although smaller trees are preferred. Tree size is controlled by choice of rootstock, cultivar (commercial variety), site and soil, and by management practices (eg, pruning). Fruit development depends upon cross fertilization. Cultivars must be propagated by vegetative methods (eg, grafting); however, many fruiting trees have been grown from seed and provide a rich source of new cultivars. Of the thousands of cultivars named, only a few hundred can now be found and only about a dozen are important. McIntosh, Red Delicious, Spy, Spartan, Cortland, Golden Delicious, Idared, Newtown, Winesap and Gravenstein are important in Canada. Apples are the preferred fruit of Canadians and are used fresh or cooked. Large volumes of juice are consumed; lesser quantities are converted into fermented products and vinegar. After juice extraction, the remains (pomace) may serve as a source of pectin or may be fed to livestock.

Adapted to temperate zones, apple trees must have a dormant period of about 1000 hours below 5°C but do not survive winter temperatures below −40°C. Sites near water are preferred. In Canada, the growing regions are in NS, southern NB and Québec, near the lakes in Ontario, and in the southern valleys of BC. After planting several years of care are necessary before production of break-even crops. Care includes pruning, spraying, providing bees for POLLINATION, irrigation and controlling rodents and deer. Most apples are carefully hand picked. Maturity is important and sprays to control maturation and preharvest drop may be necessary. Harvested fruit is cooled promptly and control of storage atmosphere helps maintain quality. Apples are sold by variety and, for marketing, are graded by size and quality. Below-grade fruit is usually used for juice. In 1980, 552 589 t, valued at $84.9 million, were produced in Canada. A.D. CROWE

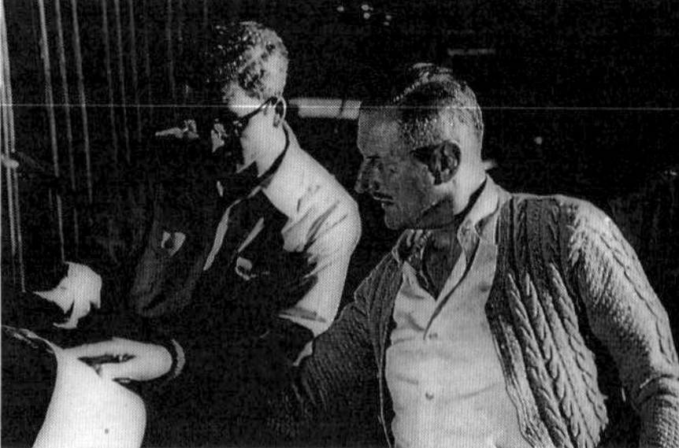

Louis Applebaum (left), one of Canada's most prodigious composers, has written and conducted hundreds of scores for film, theatre, and radio and TV drama *(courtesy Public Archives of Canada/PA-122729/NFB/W.A. Curtin).*

Applebaum, Louis, composer, conductor, administrator (b at Toronto 3 Apr 1918). After studies at the Toronto Conservatory of Music and U of T with Boris BERLIN, Healey WILLAN and Sir Ernest MACMILLAN, Applebaum went to New York to study composition. By the mid-1940s he had moved to Hollywood, where his film scores were in great demand, but in 1949 he returned to Canada. One of Canada's most prodigious composers, he has written and conducted hundreds of scores for film, theatre, and radio and TV drama. His concert pieces, ballets and fanfares, frequently commissioned, are always admired as strong and appropriate, qualities that reflect his awareness of the need for the artist to be pragmatic and conscious of developments in his art. In addition to his busy career as a working composer, Applebaum's administrative skills have made him a consultant for organizations, including the National Film Board, the Canada Council and the CBC. He has served on numerous committees, such as CAPAC-Canadian Association of Broadcasters, for the promotion of Canadian music, and as an adviser on the formation of music faculties, opera and ballet companies. He established the music wing of the STRATFORD FESTIVAL and in 1965 he chaired a government-commissioned committee whose report led to the formation of the National Arts Centre Orchestra. He was executive director of the Ontario Arts Council 1970-79, when he became co-chairman, with Jacques Hébert, of the Federal Cultural Policy Review Committee. MABEL H. LAINE

Apprenticeship, as a form of instruction in which a novice learns from a master of a craft or art, has existed for thousands of years. The craft guilds of western Europe, which developed in the 7th and 8th centuries, formalized the apprenticeship system and retained control of it until the 16th century. Until the late 19th-century, apprenticeship was the sole means for people to acquire the skills for almost all occupations.

In early 19th-century Canada, apprenticeship training was carried on by the skilled tradesmen who immigrated from Europe (*see* WORK). The training was sporadic and it varied even within a particular trade, but as long as a supply of skilled people was readily available through immigration, the lack of training presented no urgent problem; but as Canada became industrialized, it was necessary to develop a Canadian apprenticeship program. As a result of strong pressures from the building trades, led by Joseph Piggott, Ontario passed the first Apprenticeship Act in 1928, providing for regulation and support of apprenticeship. BC (1935) and Nova Scotia (1936) passed Apprenticeship Acts modeled on the Ontario legislation.

In 1944, under the Vocational Training Co-ordination Act, the federal government arranged to enter into an agreement with any province to provide financial assistance for apprentice training. As a result, the majority of provinces enacted legislation establishing apprenticeship programs. Generally provincial legislation provides for the regulation of apprentice training, the establishment of trade-advisory committees and the appointment of a director of apprenticeship.

By 1984 the apprenticeship system was being practised in several hundred trades. The provinces have established a co-operative Interprovincial Standards Program to provide for acceptance of certification in all provinces for apprentices who meet the interprovincial standard.

Apprenticeship is founded on a contractual relationship between an employee and an employer, in which the employer agrees to provide opportunities for the employee-apprentice to earn the skills required for a trade under the supervision of someone already qualified in that trade. The period of training is usually from 3 to 5 years and follows a structured training program or curriculum. Up to 90% of the training occurs in the workplace; some of the concomitant theoretical knowledge is taught at an institution, generally a COMMUNITY COLLEGE or institute of technology. The apprentice's progress is monitored by the director of apprenticeship in each province, who also certifies the successful completion of the training by issuing a Certificate of Qualification.

Apprentices are generally paid a percentage of the certified journeyman's wage, which increases throughout the apprenticeship period. The costs of the in-school portion of the training are paid by the federal government, which also provides apprentices with a living allowance or unemployment-insurance payments. Employers receive a return from the apprentices' labour. In certain trades that are considered critical to the Canadian economy, the federal government provides substantial subsidies to employers of apprentices. The subsidies for women apprentices have been increased to encourage the training of women in nontraditional occupations.

Under the apprenticeship system, a fixed number of hours must be devoted to the practical and theoretical aspects of the curriculum, on the grounds that an employer can thus recover part of the costs of training by having an apprentice with some of the skills of a journeyman for a period of time at less cost than the full journeyman rate. It is also contended, particularly by unions, that competence is best achieved by allowing apprentices to practise their skills in a work setting over a period of time. Recently, however, the adoption of a competency-based system has been proposed, ie, a system under which apprentices could be certified at whatever point in the training they could demonstrate competency.

The regulation of apprentice wage rates as a percentage of a journeyman's wages has been criticized as a barrier to the entry of young people into apprenticeships. It is argued that the rates are too high or too inflexible for current labour market conditions. Various alternatives have been proposed, including complete deregulation (which would permit apprentice wage rates to be set by collective bargaining in unionized industries or by labour-market forces) and a system of using the minimum wage as a base and of raising wages by percentage through the period of apprenticeship.

Another major issue concerns the current requirement for comprehensive training. Many smaller companies cannot offer instruction in all the necessary skills of a trade. In some cases therefore apprentices are contracted to associations of employers who move the apprentices from company to company to learn the full range of skills. Another strategy — the modular curriculum system — is used widely and successfully in the mining industry and is being extended to industrial trades. The modules outline training in discrete packages. Apprentices are credited for the completion of each module and on completing all modules receive a certificate of qualification. The critics of the modular approach fear that its widespread use will lead to fragmentation of the trades into narrow specialities.

It is well documented that there are many more well-qualified young people in Canada who wish to enter apprenticeship than there are available openings, and that the major barrier to apprenticeship is the unwillingness of employers to offer such training.

KENNETH E. HUNTER

Apprenticeship in Early Canada Until the mid-19th century, apprenticeship was a system of training that enabled young men or, more rarely, women to acquire the skills of a particular trade or profession. The 3 major means of access to apprenticeship were through institutions, the family or an agreement with a craftsman or professional, ratified by a notarial deed. Although the last form is that most often mentioned in historical accounts, the training of one family member by another appears to have been at least as widespread and was preferred by merchants and the professions (eg, doctors, lawyers, notaries). Very few apprentices were trained in institutions. In the formal and family systems, training was essentially practical and was given in the craftsman's workshop or the professional's office.

European and Canadian System

From the Middle Ages or earlier, many trades in France and other European countries organized themselves into communities which came to be known as corporations or guilds. The guild system was characterized by the creation among craftsmen of a hierarchy comprising apprentices, journeymen and masters. The masters headed the guilds and elected juries responsible for drawing up and implementing regulations. Among these regulations were those governing apprenticeship and access to mastership: a long training period and an often rigorous entry procedure were imposed on apprentices; journeymen wishing to become masters had to pay a large fee and produce an original work of superior quality, ie, a masterpiece.

When the first French craftsmen arrived in NEW FRANCE in the 17th century, they soon discovered that it was impossible to carry on their strict guild traditions and regulations. There was too much to be done in the new country for them to concentrate solely on their own trade; their time was divided among exercising their craft, clearing the land, fishing and trading furs. When the first villages sprang up and the training of a core group of craftsmen became necessary, the French system was no longer suitable, because 17th- and 18th-century Canada lacked specialized manpower. Guilds, as they had existed in France, were abandoned; however, the hierarchy and system of practical training were maintained. Members of the professions enjoyed better conditions: already favoured by a higher social rank, they came to Canada in fewer numbers and were able to devote most of their time to their professional duties.

Certain characteristics of the apprenticeship system in England, France, the US, Québec and the Maritimes bear striking resemblances, particularly the age of apprentices and the duration of apprenticeship. With the exception of many anglophone masters, who hired their apprentices at a younger age and for a longer period, most masters hired apprentices around the age of 16½ for a 3-year period. Training was generally completed around the age of 21 but there were some exceptions, notably in the case of apprentices who were orphans. Authorities used official apprenticeship as a means of placing orphans in families and ensuring that they received training in a particular trade. Orphans generally began their training at a much younger age and worked for longer periods than other apprentices. The age of apprentices in the professions was essentially the same as that of craft apprentices, but the length of the training differed considerably. For example, legislation established the training period of lawyers and notaries at 5 years.

Working conditions reveal the characteristics of apprenticeship and the marked differences between craftsmen and professionals. Among 17th and 18th century craftsmen, the traditional organization of production and work dominated. With the exception of items produced at the FORGES SAINT-MAURICE and a few large workshops, each piece was the work of one craftsman, master or journeyman, sometimes assisted by an apprentice. Craftsmen generally worked in small workshops (often attached to their homes) and owned all their tools. Work was usually done to order and division of labour was almost nonexistent. The major sources of energy were still muscle power and water; raw materials were processed mainly by hand tools.

Under this system, working relations were

not defined solely on the basis of labour supply and demand as today but also in terms of rights, obligations, and personal relationships which were often very authoritarian in nature. Contracts stipulated that the apprentice obey the master, work on his behalf and strive to learn his trade. In return, the master agreed to reveal all the secrets of his craft and provide accommodation, food, clothing and a small annual salary, paid either in cash or in kind. The apprentice worked 6 days a week, his hours varying depending on the trade and whether it was practised indoors or outdoors. Working days were generally from 5 AM to 8 or 9 PM, with a minimum of 2 hours for lunch and dinner. Apprentices worked 12-14 hours a day, a little longer than the journeyman or master, since they had to prepare the others' work before the shop opened and clean up after closing. Some apprentices in the 17th and 18th centuries received religious and academic as well as technical training.

Once the apprenticeship period was over, young workers might work for a few years as journeymen and then open their own shop when they had enough money; others inherited their father's shop. The journeyman's salary was 4-6 times greater than that of the apprentice. At this intermediate stage, the journeyman entered the job market and made products of his own. Some journeymen trained apprentices or were responsible for the internal operation of the workshop in the master's absence. The working conditions of apprentices to merchants or in the professions were very different from those of craft apprentices. Apprentices to the professions usually came from wealthier families, worked fewer hours, received some education before beginning their apprenticeship and were not required to perform domestic duties.

Changes in the Nineteenth Century

The economic boom of the early 19th century, certain British influences and the process of urbanization provoked irreversible changes in MANUFACTURING, work organization and conditions of apprenticeship. In order to meet the competition from imported products in the expanding local market, many master craftsmen also acted as merchants and manufacturers and modified their production methods. They used machine tools, grouped several craftsmen together under the same roof, shared tasks and were thus able to hire unskilled labour to make products on a large scale. This development marked the transition from individual artisan to workshop and, subsequently, to factory production in urban centres. The transition was a long and complex process spread over nearly the entire 19th century and craftsmen's workshops and factories co-existed for a long time. These major changes affected the role of traditional apprenticeship in the work force and society. Apprentices gradually became a source of cheap manpower and were hired more for their labour than for training purposes. They were hired at increasingly younger ages and their contracts were prolonged and expanded to embrace several tasks so that they could be used as cheap labour for longer periods. The traditional responsibilities of masters (support and moral and religious education) were replaced by a cash payment. Some masters failed to teach apprentices "the secrets of the trade"; others mistreated them. Apprentices often ran away, since they had difficulty breaking their contracts. If caught, they were prosecuted, rarely winning their case.

While the traditional apprenticeship system deteriorated, other institutions increased in importance. At the beginning of the 19th century, evening schools began to replace the education previously given by the master and his wife. In order to have more control over the education of apprentices and young journeymen, masters and merchants followed the example of their counterparts in Great Britain and established technical institutes in the major cities of eastern Canada (Halifax, Québec City and Montréal). These institutes were viewed by the authorities as training centres where workers could learn respect for the establishment, discipline in the workplace and proper social behaviour. Sunday schools and temperance groups, established during the first half of the 19th century, supported the institutes in the pursuit of a common goal: to teach workers how to use their leisure time so that they would put more effort into their work. During the second half of the 19th century, technical institutes partly replaced workshops as the place in which training was provided.

The founding of the first unions in the 1830s and professional corporations in the late 1840s resulted, in part, from a desire to control access to occupations and to protect their members. With the exception of the construction trades and the professions, which succeeded in limiting the number of apprentices, trades (eg, shoe making, coopering, tinsmithing) were threatened by technological change. Schools gradually took over responsibility for training professionals; hence, the creation of professional associations (eg, of doctors and notaries) gave professionals an opportunity to control not only the quality of education but also the number of graduates (*see* EDUCATION HISTORY). Although government authorities first feared giving so much power to doctors and notaries, these 2 professional groups were granted such powers (in 1845 and 1847, respectively) after applying considerable pressure.

JEAN-PIERRE HARDY AND DAVID-THIERY RUDDEL

Apprenticeship of Duddy Kravitz, The, by Mordecai RICHLER, was published in London and Boston, 1959, and Toronto, 1969. Duddy Kravitz is a brash Jewish Montréal kid determined to make it — whatever "it" is, whatever "it" takes. Acting on his grandfather's maxim that a man is nothing without land, Duddy schemes and dreams to develop his first brainstorm, a lakeshore property in the Laurentians. Duddy is an attractive figure, bursting with chutzpah, but he is also driven to exploit others in his drive to succeed. Richler frames Duddy's initiation within a pungently satiric sendup of Jewish and Wasp middle-class gentility as seen from the sharp-eyed, tough-minded St-Urbain Street perspective that has become one of Richler's trademarks. Duddy's eventual triumph is also his downfall, costing him more in lost love than he will ever realize in money. Richler's most popular novel, *The Apprenticeship of Duddy Kravitz* has been translated into French as *L'Apprentissage de Duddy Kravitz* (Elisabeth Gille-Nemirovsky, Paris, 1960; Jean Simard, Montréal, 1976). A movie was made in 1974 and Duddy made his stage debut in Edmonton in 1984. NEIL BESNER

Apps, Charles Joseph Sylvanus, Syl, hockey player (b at Paris, Ont 18 Jan 1915). He excelled at football and represented Canada in pole vaulting in the 1934 British Empire Games and 1936 Berlin Olympics. He played centre for Toronto Maple Leafs 1936-43 and 1945-48, scoring 201 goals and 231 assists in 423 games and a further 25 goals and 28 assists in 69 playoff games. A fast, graceful skater and superb playmaker, he was honoured for his team play and leadership. He was elected MPP for Kingston in 1963 and has been a member of Cabinet in the Ontario government. JAMES MARSH

Apricot, common name for certain members of genus *Prunus* of the ROSE family, which produce sweet, round or oblong, nearly smooth FRUIT (resembling a small PEACH), with a large, flat stone. The 6 or more wild species are distributed throughout Asia, Asia Minor and southeastern Europe, mostly in dry areas. Most cultivars (commercial varieties) originated from the common apricot, *P. armeniaca.* Apricots were brought to Greece and Italy in the 4th century AD and to the American continent in the early 18th century. Apricot trees are large and spreading; leaves are large, heart shaped and dark green; flowers are white. The kernels are poisonous in some cultivars; in others they are sweet. Apricots are cultivated mainly for their fruit, though some species are grown as ORNAMENTALS. In Canada apricots are grown primarily in the dry, warm southern interior of BC. Factors that limit successful cultivation include sensitivity of blossoms to spring frosts, susceptibility of trees and fruit to diseases in humid climates, and high temperature requirements in summer. Canadian plantings total 150 ha. Principal cultivars are Wenatchee, Tilton and Blenheim. Apricot fruit is rich in minerals and in vitamins A and B. The fruit is used dried and as a canned product and, to a lesser extent, fresh.

K.O. LAPINS

Aqjangajuk Shaa (Axangayu), artist (b at Shartoweetuk camp near Cape Dorset, NWT 17 Mar 1937). Aqjangajuk, who began carving in stone in the 1950s, does not do a great deal of detailing; instead he works for a total effect, concentrating on spatial interaction, expressive qualities and overall form. While some of his carvings of human and animal subjects are compact, robust, solid and static, others are more open, outwardly thrusting, dynamic forms. His only print, *Wounded Caribou* (1961), is a very effective portrayal of an animal stricken by a hunter's arrow. JEAN BLODGETT

Aqjangajuk Shaa, *Figure with Ulu* (*c* 1967), green stone 38.5 x 47.0 x 6.0 cm (*reproduced by permission of the Wes[t] Baffin Eskimo Co-operative, Cape Dorset, NWT/Art Gallery [o]f Ontario. Gift of the Klamer family, 1978*).

Aquaculture is the human-controlled cultivation and harvest of freshwater and marine PLANTS and ANIMALS. Synonyms include aquiculture, fish farming, fish culture, mariculture, fish breeding and ocean ranching. Throughout the world, aquaculture operations constitute an integral part of FISHERIES and aquatic RESOURCE MANAGEMENT. Organisms as varied as trout, carp and tuna (ie, finfish), shrimps and oysters (ie shellfish) and seaweed are grown, using ponds, tanks or nets, in salt, brackish and fresh waters.

In 1980 total worldwide aquaculture production amounted to about 8.7 million tonnes, ie roughly 12% of the total world fish production. Of aquaculture production, 37.1% was finfish, 36.7% molluscs (eg, oysters, mussels); 25.4% seaweeds (eg, kelp); and 8% crustaceans (eg, lobsters, shrimp). Almost every country has some form of aquaculture. The world's major producers are China (46%), Japan (11%), India (10%), Korea (5%) and the USSR (4%). From 1971-80 there was a 73% increase in total production. If achieved, a projected doubling of production b

Canadian Aquaculture Production (in tonnes) by Region and Commodity Group

(Source: Dept of Fisheries and Oceans, Ottawa, 1982)

Region	*Trout*	*Salmon*	*Other Finfish*	*Molluscs*
BC	84	129	–	1 400
Prairies	169	–	3.5	–
Ontario	750	–	0.6	–
Québec	350	–	0.3	–
Atlantic Provinces	125	160	59	800
Total	1 478	289	63.4	2 200

* Tuna

** Figures are estimates only

1990 will substantially reduce the projected demands a growing population will place on the world's natural fish stocks, many of which are already overfished.

In the major aquaculture regions of the world, the emphasis has been on species that find wide acceptance among all social groups, eg, trout and salmon in N America and Northern Europe, carp in Eastern Europe and Israel, mussels in France and Spain, prawns and milkfish in the Philippines, Asian species of carp in SE Asia, and seaweeds in Japan and Korea. In some areas, there has been some emphasis on luxury products, eg, freshwater prawns, for specific markets or export, but the total production of such items remains low.

The origins of aquaculture go back thousands of years. Oysters in Japan and fish in Egypt were cultured before 2000 BC. In China, domestication of carp, the most commonly cultured fish, began 5 centuries earlier than in Europe. The first book on fish culture was reportedly written by a Chinese scholar, Fan Li, in the 5th century BC. Carp were introduced to Europe from the Danube R by the Romans in the 1st to 4th centuries AD. Culture techniques were refined by monks during the 14th to 16th centuries. Trout were first raised in a hatchery in Germany in 1741, and the first attempts at commercial trout culture were made as early as 1853 in the US. Rainbow trout, once found only in N America, are now cultured throughout the world.

The originator of Canadian aquaculture was Samuel WILMOT, who developed techniques for salmon and trout in the 1860s and 1870s that were so successful that nearly a century elapsed before significant changes were made in Canadian trout hatcheries. Most Canadian aquaculture operations have been operated by government. Starting in the 1960s, the value of non-government production rose, and it is now higher than government production. Between 1972 and 1982, finfish production has doubled. Government production of finfish (now about 40% of the total) has involved, almost exclusively, the hatching and rearing of young fish in hatcheries for release in the wild for commercial and sport fisheries. Private or commercial aquaculture production is for direct sale as food and for private sportfishing.

Aquaculture practices may be categorized by the degree of human control over production. The following arrangement is in order of increasing control.

Release of Young into the Wild A well-known practice, the stocking of lakes and streams with young trout, is commonly used by federal and provincial hatcheries, and involves rearing the fish in a hatchery from a few weeks to over a year. Once stocked, the fish are exposed to all the hazards of nature, such as predatory fish and birds.

Raft Culture of Molluscs and Seaweed In this type of culture, ropes or nets are suspended from floating rafts. The animals or plants become attached to the ropes or nets and obtain food and nutrients from the water. The organisms are not fed, but they are protected from bottom-dwelling predators and are not as subject to crowding as they would be in nature.

Cage Culture of Finfish Significant advantages can be obtained by growing fish in floating cages. For example, in Norway, Atlantic salmon are confined in large (20 m x 20 m), nylon-mesh cages. The cages, held in specially chosen areas of the fjords, are supplied daily with specially prepared foods. Safe from birds and other fish, the salmon grow rapidly and most survive to a marketable size.

Pond Culture of Fish By growing fish in man-made earthen ponds, even greater control can be maintained. Trout, carp, catfish and numerous other species are supplied with food, either prepared diets or natural food produced by fertilizing the pond waters. The fishes' environment can be improved by adding or aerating water, or treating it with chemicals.

Intensive Tank Culture While most federal and provincial hatcheries produce fish for stocking, virtually the same techniques are used to grow fish from eggs to market size. In the most intensive systems, as many aspects of the environment are controlled as is technically possible. Pumps supply a constant flow of water at controlled temperatures. Food is given at specified times from automatic feeders. Specially bred, disease-free stocks of fish are used.

The types of aquaculture operations in Canada vary considerably from region to region. On the West Coast, there has been a 5-6 fold increase in the rearing and stocking of Pacific salmon, as part of the Canada-BC Salmonid Enhancement Program. The goal of this program is to double commercial and sport harvest of salmon. Private cage-culture operations, for growing salmon for market, have also been established, and preliminary cage culture of other fish (eg, sable fish) is being attempted. On the Prairies, several thousand farmers regularly stock small prairie pothole lakes with rainbow trout fingerlings in spring and harvest pan-size fish in fall. The production is mainly for private use, but increasing numbers are being marketed commercially. Significant numbers of walleye and whitefish fry are stocked from government hatcheries into large lakes in attempts to enhance and rehabilitate important commercial fisheries. In Ontario and Québec, rainbow and brook trout are reared in ponds and tanks. The major production of fish, for direct sale to stores and restaurants, is in these 2 provinces, but there is also significant production of trout for stocking of private fishing ponds. The Ontario government has been stocking Pacific salmon and various species of trout in the Great Lakes in order to rehabilitate the fisheries there. In the Atlantic provinces, the federal government has been stocking hatchery-reared Atlantic salmon and trout since the 1880s. Recently, cage culture of Atlantic salmon and rainbow trout has been established in the Bras d'Or Lakes and the S coasts of NS and NB. Perhaps the most unusual aquaculture operation in Canada is the small but successful cage culture of bluefin tuna in St Margaret's Bay, NS. Large tuna (275-500 kg) are captured in nets, then held in cages and fed daily for several months. The much larger tuna (350-650 kg) are harvested and shipped directly to Japanese markets. MOLLUSC culture is primarily of oysters, although there is some mussel production in the Atlantic provinces. Operations are gradually introducing new techniques such as the culture of shellfish on suspended ropes and traps.

The success of aquaculture operations in Canada will depend on the availability of land, water and capital, on technologies employed, market acceptance and the technical and business competence of the entrepreneur.

G. BURTON AYLES

Aquin, Hubert, novelist (b at Montréal 24 Oct 1929; d there 15 Mar 1977). Best known for his 4 complex modernist novels, Aquin also influenced contemporary Québec culture as political activist, essayist, filmmaker and editor. Brilliant, tormented and deeply committed to a Québec whose contradictions he seemed to embody, Aquin had a flair for drama and public gesture; he once declared: "It is my life that will turn out to have been my super-masterpiece."

Aquin received a licentiate in philosophy from U de M in 1951. From 1951 to 1954 he studied at the Institut d'études politiques in Paris and on his return to Montréal worked for Radio-Canada (1955-59). From 1960 to 1968 he was a colourful and influential figure in the growing movement for Québec independence. While supporting himself by work at the Montreal Stock Exchange (1960- 64) and the National Film Board (1959-63), he was an executive member of the first independentist political party, the Rassemblement pour l'Indépendance nationale (RIN), 1960-69. During the same period, as an editor of *Liberté*, he engaged in debate with Pierre TRUDEAU on the question of Québec independence. In 1964 he declared in a press release that he was going "underground" to work for independence through terrorism; he was arrested shortly afterwards and detained 4 months in a psychiatric institute, where he wrote his first novel, *Prochain épisode* (1965), the story of an imprisoned revolutionary. In Dec 1964 he was acquitted of illegal possession of a firearm.

The publication of *Prochain épisode* established Aquin as perhaps the most important cultural figure in Québec of his generation, but he continued to assert his inability to compromise with any established order. In 1966 he was expelled from Switzerland and wrote that the expulsion was due to RCMP influence. In 1969 he became the first Québec writer to refuse the GOVERNOR GENERAL'S AWARD, offered to him for *Trou de mémoire* (1962). In the same year he denounced Pierre BOURGAULT's decision to merge the RIN with René LÉVESQUE's Mouvement pour la souveraineté-association and resigned from the party.

The following years seem to have been marked by a growing despair linked to Aquin's sense of separation from the political centre of his beloved Québec. In 1969 he published *L'Antiphonaire*, which unlike his previous 2 novels has no explicit political content. In 1971 he resigned from the editorial board of *Liberté*, claiming that its reliance on CANADA COUNCIL support had kept it silent on the events of the OCTOBER CRISIS of the previous year. In 1974 appeared Aquin's final novel, *Neige noire*, a modern version of Hamlet integrating film, music and painting techniques into its sustained philosophical reflection on time, love, death and the sacred. In Mar 1975 he became literary director of Éditions La Presse, a position which because of its links with POWER CORPORATION was seen by some as a contradiction of his earlier "revolutionary" stance. But Aquin had always claimed he became a revolutionary because as a Québecois he was denied the opportunity of being a banker, and his time at Editions La Presse was marked by conflicts over money he wanted to invest in "unprofitable" Québec literary ventures. In Aug 1976 he resigned, accusing his superior Roger LEMELIN of "colonizing Quebec from the interior," and entered a period of financial insecurity and severe depression which ended in his suicide.

PATRICIA SMART

Arabs, or more specifically, Syrian-Lebanese immigrants, began to arrive in Canada in small numbers in 1882. Their immigration was relatively limited until 1945, after which time it increased progressively, particularly in the 1960s and 1970s. Today about one out of every 2000 Canadians is Arabic in origin. At present, the label "Arab Canadian" does not refer to one religious affiliation, country of origin or distance from the immigrant generation but to the mixture of characteristics, beliefs, etc, that some 125 000 Canadians of Arab origin have inherited from the past or acquired in Canada.

Origins The Arab world extends from the Arabian Gulf through N Africa to the shores of the Atlantic Ocean. It is a region diverse in physical geography, climate and natural resources, but its inhabitants share cultural traditions and the Arabic language.

The early wave of Arab immigrants originated from Syria and what is now known as Lebanon. More than 90% were Christians seeking freedom from poverty and the Ottoman (Turkish) colonial regime. The post-WWII wave of Arab immigrants comprised a broader mixture of Christian groups and a substantial number of Muslims and Druzes (*see also* ISLAM) who were motivated by the desire to escape unfavourable social, economic and political conditions in their homelands.

The 2 waves of immigrants came from markedly different social and political contexts — the early immigrants from an economically less-developed Arab world, colonized by the Ottoman Turks, the postwar immigrants from a decolonized Arab world undergoing rapid socioeconomic development. These differences are expressed through different world views, attitudes and behaviour.

Migration By 1901 Canada had about 2000 Syrian immigrants, by 1911 about 7000. For the next 40 years relatively few Syrian immigrants were admitted to Canada because of severe restrictions on the admission of immigrants from Asia (*see* PREJUDICE AND DISCRIMINATION), but between 1946 and 1975, 48 619 immigrants arrived, particularly from Egypt (18 115), Lebanon (16 333), Morocco (7234), Syria (3713), Jordan (737) and Tunisia (583). Others came from Algeria, Saudi Arabia, Kuwait, Iraq, Libya, Sudan, Bahrain, Qatar, United Arab Emirates, Somalia, Mauretania, Yemen and Oman. Many of these more recent Arab immigrants arrived as highly educated married couples with children. At present, about 50% of the Arab ethnic group in Canada are of Syrian-Lebanese origin; 25% are of Egyptian origin and the remainder are from other Arab states. The number of Christians exceeds that of Muslims by a ratio of 3 to 1.

Settlement Patterns Canadians of Arab origin always tended to settle in urban areas but not in neighbourhood concentrations. Since the turn of the century, Québec and Ontario have consistently attracted the majority of Arab immigrants; 80% of Arab Canadians are about equally divided between these 2 provinces. In Québec the heaviest concentration of Arab Canadians is in metropolitan Montréal; in Ontario, they are to be found largely in Toronto and vicinity, but also in Ottawa, Windsor, London and Hamilton. The Arab communities of Alberta and Nova Scotia rank third and fourth in size, but are much smaller than those of Québec and Ontario.

Economic Life Many of the early Syrian immigrants entered the labour force through pedlary, an independent but relatively low status occupation. Through hard work, frugality and reciprocal support, the economic fortunes of pedlars often rose and they expanded their entrepreneurial activities. The postwar immigrants, however, arrived with higher average educational and occupational qualifications, the majority of them planning to follow professional and other white-collar careers.

Religion and Community Life Both the early and postwar immigrants were involved in institution building, particularly religious institutions. At the beginning of this century, several Eastern Christian churches were founded: Antiochian Orthodox, Melkite (Catholic) and Maronite (Catholic). The Coptic Orthodox Church was established in 1965, following the arrival of large numbers of Coptic immigrants from Egypt.

Muslim institutions developed more slowly, because of the small size and dispersal of this religious group. The first mosque in Canada, Al Rashid Mosque, was built in Edmonton in 1938. Since the 1950s mosques have been established in virtually all major urban centres.

Secular associations were also established by both the early pioneers and later immigrants to serve social, cultural, charitable and political needs. Memberships are usually mixed; in a few cases they are confined to youth, women, university students or professionals. Some national groups, eg, Lebanese, Syrians, Palestinians, Egyptians, have established their own distinct associations. Only the Canadian Arab Federation is national in scope and membership. Several Arab Canadian associations have sponsored the publication of multilanguage (Arabic, English, French) periodicals; some newspapers are published by individual Canadian Arabs.

Education Arab immigrants value education highly, both for themselves and for their children. Except for "Saturday" Arabic-language schools they have not established their own community-based schools. The educational attainment of Arab Canadians is comparable to the Canadian average; they are to be found at all levels of the occupational hierarchy and some have achieved renown in their respective fields.

Politics No particular political ideology or political party is dominant among Arab Canadians. They are involved in the political process at the municipal, provincial and federal levels. Arab ethnicity has not been a prominent feature of their political involvement in Canada, except in pressure-group politics involving Canada's Middle East policy.

Group Maintenance Arab immigrants have had to learn a new language, establish new social networks, integrate themselves into the economic system, learn new cultural norms and values and discard some of the ways of the country of origin. The Canadian-born generations have naturally been even further assimilated into Canadian society. At the same time, however, a moderate degree of institutional development within the Arab ethnic group reflects a tendency towards preserving ethnic traditions. Maintaining the Arabic language, for example, is important, and the family and the community language school helped this process with varying degrees of success. Whether or not an Arab Canadian knows Arabic, links with the ancestral heritage can be, and have been, maintained through Arabic food, music, dances, mass-media exposure, visits to the "Old Country" and correspondence with friends and relatives left behind. Generally, the immigrant generation was more likely to maintain links with the cultural heritage than its Canadian-born counterpart, but although many Canadians of Arabic origin have probably lost contact with the past the majority are aware and proud of their ethnic origins. BAHA ABU-LABAN

Reading: Baha Abu-Laban, *La présence arabe au Canada* (1981) and *An Olive Branch on the Family Tree: The Arabs in Canada* (1980).

Arachnida, large class of chelicerate arthropods (segmented, jointed-limbed animals) including orders Araneae (SPIDERS), Scorpiones (SCORPIONS), Opiliones (harvestmen), Pseudoscorpiones (pseudoscorpions), Solifugae (wind scorpions) and Acari (MITES and TICKS). Second only to INSECTS in species numbers, an estimated 300 000 arachnid species may occur worldwide, about 12 000 in Canada. The great majority are mites; spiders are next most common. Characteristically, arachnids have 4 pairs of legs, two pairs of mouth parts, and, if present, simple eyes on the body above the first 2 pairs of legs. Arachnids are an ancient lineage: the earliest known fossils are of 420 million-year-old scorpions. All major living groups had originated by at least 300 million years ago. Mites and spiders occur throughout Canada, including the Arctic. Ticks, pseudoscorpions and harvestmen are transcontinental, excluding arctic regions. Scorpions and wind scorpions live only in southernmost, western Canadian desert areas. Most arachnids are predators of other arthropods, although some harvestmen feed on dead organic matter; ticks are parasites of VERTEBRATES, and mites have diverse feeding habits. EVERT E. LINDQUIST

Arbitration is a process of legal decision making, usually under a contract, in which the people affected have agreed who will act as judge by naming a person or agreeing upon a means of selecting an individual or tribunal. Arbitrators who are usually but not necessarily lawyers, are paid by the people who choose them. In every province there is an Arbitration Act or other statutory instrument (eg, Labour Relations Act) that regulates the process to some extent and provides for review by the ordinary courts or another superior tribunal in the event of serious errors by the arbitrators. Labour arbitration is more common than all other kinds together perhaps because grievance arbitration is required by most Canadian labour-relations statutes. In the public sector, interest arbitration may be substituted for the right to strike. *See* STRIKES AND LOCKOUTS; LABOUR LAW. INNIS CHRISTIE

Arboretum [Lat, *arbor*, "tree"], special garden or part of a BOTANICAL GARDEN devoted to growing TREES and other woody perennials. Specimens are usually planted in groups reflecting botanical relationships or habitat preferences, in a manner producing a pleasing, parklike landscape. There may be only a few woody PLANTS or up to several thousand different kinds, some in special plantings such as rose gardens, lilac dells, azalea and rhododendron beds, hedge gardens, shrub borders and displays of woody climbers. Representative specimens are usually labelled with their common and scientific names; family name and the country of origin may appear as well. The parents of hybrids may be indicated. Educational programs are often developed in conjunction with local schools and regional horticultural societies. A well-equipped arboretum has a library, HERBARIUM and facilities for research. Alternatively, a relationship may be established with a nearby university or RESEARCH STATION which has these facilities. The main functions of an arboretum are to grow and to display effectively as large a selection of named woody plants as possible. Basic research involves discovering and recording characteristics, correct name, botanical relationships, origin, distribution, habitat requirements, economic importance and cultural uses of each kind of plant. Practical research includes testing for hardiness, studying methods of propagation, examining seed production and viability and carrying out breeding experiments to produce new and better varieties. Introduction of plants brought back from expeditions to other parts of the world or obtained by exchange of seeds and propagating stock is an important function. Research programs and publications centre around the collections. Arboretums serve as information centres and to train students in horticulture. The preservation of diverse plants as living specimens and worldwide exchange of seeds guarantee a material basis for the continuing search for new sources of fuel, food and medicine. Research results provide information to foresters, fruit growers, nurserymen, landscape architects, urban planners, park administrators and professional and amateur botanists and gardeners.

The Dominion Botanic Garden and Arboretum, on the Central Experimental Farm, Ottawa, dates from the late 1890s, when tests on hardiness of woody plants were carried out by the Department of Agriculture. Other botanical gardens and arboretums appeared more recently in Canada. The Jardin Botanique, Montréal, and the Royal Botanical Gardens, Hamilton (est 1931 and 1941, respectively) both include arboretums. Morgan Arboretum, Macdonald College, Québec, containing woody plant species, is essentially a project in forest conservation and SILVICULTURE. Québec also has a network of 21 arboretums established since 1969 by its Ministère des terres et forêts. Several universities maintain arboretums on or near campus, eg, Guelph, Western Ontario, Laurentian, Alberta and BC. Other arboretums include Ross Arboretum, Indian Head, Sask; Niagara Parks Commission Apprentice School for Gardeners, Niagara Falls, Ont; Agricultural Research Station, Morden, Man; Van Dusen Botanical Garden, Queen Elizabeth Park, Vancouver, BC; Metropolitan Toronto Zoo; and a number of forest nursery stations in various provinces. JAMES H. SOPER

Arcand, Denys, filmmaker (b at Deschambault, Qué 25 June 1940). One of Québec's most politically aware filmmakers, he worked for PARTI PRIS before studying history at Université de Montréal, where he co-directed *Seul ou avec d'autres* (1962) with Denis HÉROUX and Stéphane Venne. He joined the NFB 1963, where his feature-length documentary on the textile industry, *On est au coton* (1970), was so controversial it was suppressed for 6 years. He made another documentary, *Québec: Duplessis et après . . .* (1971), before leaving the NFB for the private sector. *La Maudite Galette* (1972), *Réjeanne Padovani* (1973) and *Gina* (1975) were distinctive views of Québec society, original and provocative. He then moved to TV, scripting the "Duplessis" series for Radio-Canada and directing 3 episodes of "Empire Inc." He returned to the NFB to make a feature documentary on the 1980 referendum, *Le Confort et l'indifférence* (1982), which won the Québec Critics Prize. PIERS HANDLING

Archaeological Survey of Canada, established in 1971, is the component of the NATIONAL MUSEUM OF MAN that deals with the archaeological heritage of Canada. Its major goals are the preservation of archaeological sites, research into the PREHISTORY of Canadian aboriginal peoples and informing the public of the results of archaeological research through publications and exhibitions. As the lead federal agency involved in the management of archaeological resources, it co-ordinates the protection and rescue of threatened sites on federal lands. Its Mercury Series of monographs is the main outlet for reporting of archaeological research in the country. Its exhibitions, both in the National Museum of Man and smaller exhibits which travel across the country, are designed to contribute to public understanding of the prehistory and traditions of the native peoples of the country.

ROBERT MCGHEE

Archaeology represents the study of past human cultures; the past can be separated into 2 broad periods: the historic and the prehistoric. The historic period is characterized by the availability of written documents, whereas the prehistoric spans some 2 million years from the time man first became a tool-maker. In Canada, the known prehistoric record extends back about 30 000 years (*see* PREHISTORY); the historic begins about 1000 years ago with the NORSE VOYAGES but more concertedly begins with the appearance of European fishermen, explorers and traders on the E and W coasts after 1500 AD. Often, European material items, particularly ironware, penetrated far inland through native traders to distant Indians who had not yet seen the Europeans. Archaeologically, this is known as the protohistoric, a transitional period between the late prehistoric and the historic when direct contacts were continuously made between NATIVE PEOPLES and Europeans.

Archaeology strives to reconstruct the past lifeways of mankind, largely through material remains found preserved on former sites. Such remains are often limited to relatively imperishable artifacts made of stone, antler or fired clay, but sometimes remarkable cases of preservation occur in dry caves, bogs or PERMAFROST. Post-mold patterns, rock alignments, hearths, rock paintings and petroglyphs can furnish important details about past camp sites, villages, and ceremonial-religious features. Burials yield information not only about mortuary practices, but often provide direct biological facts about the past people themselves. Dietary practices can be reconstructed from preserved faunal and floral remains, and some archaeologists even attempt to determine past economic, social, religious and political life of ancient populations.

An archaeological site constitutes any locality that exhibits the material remains of a former people. Site sizes can range from a single artifact, to kill-spots, tipi rings, and more complex cemetery and habitation settlements such as hamlets, villages, towns and FORTIFICATIONS. In Canada, our largest aboriginal sites and monuments include some of the RAINY RIVER BURIAL MOUNDS, the drive lanes for the HEAD-SMASHED-IN BUFFALO JUMP, and certain of the late Ontario Iroquois and historic BC settlements that measure up to 6 ha.

Initially, one of the field archaeologist's main problems lies in determining the nature of a given site. Was it used only once (ie, a single component), or was the site recurrently occupied by the same or a different series of peoples (ie, multi-component)? Determining contemporaneity of houses or other features on a site, let alone contemporaneity of several sites, also poses important problems for the archaeologist. Throughout Canada, known historic and prehistoric archaeological sites are usually locally named, but since 1952 they also have been nationally recorded according to Charles E. Borden's Uniform Site Designation scheme. The Borden system enumerates Canadian archaeological sites according to their latitude-longitude position within the country.

Contemporary Canadian Archaeology

Archaeologists interested in reconstructing past lifeways work in conjunction with scholars in many fields. They collaborate with geologists, geographers, biologists, physical anthropologists, palaeontologists, chemists, astronomers, mathematicians, physicists, historians, sociologists and anthropologists. The association of archaeologists with social scientists is of long standing, and many Canadian archaeologists affiliated with museums and universities still consider their field to be a specialty discipline within the wider context of ANTHROPOLOGY. Indeed, archaeology is usually taught within anthropology departments across Canada.

Canadian professional archaeology has its origins within the late 19th-century museum movement and is associated in particular with David BOYLE in Ontario. Nevertheless, it was only in 1938 at U of T, Dept of Anthropology, that a trained archaeologist, Philleo J. Nash, began teaching formal courses in the subject. His pioneering endeavours were continued after WWII by the 30-year tradition of J. Norman EMERSON. In the West, Borden initiated the first archaeology courses at UBC in 1949. The first separate department of archaeology established in N America was founded by Richard S. MacNeish and Richard G. Forbis at U of Calgary in 1964; SFU opened the second separate department in Canada and inaugurated a doctoral program in 1971.

Four types of professional archaeologists practise today in Canada. The first 2 represent the traditional, academic research scientists and educators associated with the nation's major universities and museums. Since 1972, 2 additional areas have had a phenomenal growth: the personnel hired by provincial government agencies to undertake cultural resource management and conservation programs made necessary by new heritage, antiquities, and cultural resource legislation; and archaeologists affiliated with business consulting firms vying for government and industrial contracts. Basically, the new consulting and managerial archaeologists represent applied archaeology as opposed to the traditional research-academic archaeology in Canada.

History of Canadian Archaeology

The Origins of Canadian archaeology lie in early 19th-century antiquarianism as practised in central to eastern Canada. The pre-Confederation era of relic hunting for exotic art objects and valued metal wares saw destruction of many native burial grounds on properties newly cleared by Euro-Canadian settlers. Ontario's NIAGARA PENINSULA stands out, for it was here that historic NEUTRAL cemeteries were dug into as early as 1828, and some of the sites attained international fame. Such was the case for the

Prehistoric turtle effigy at Minton, Sask (*photo by Richard Vroom*).

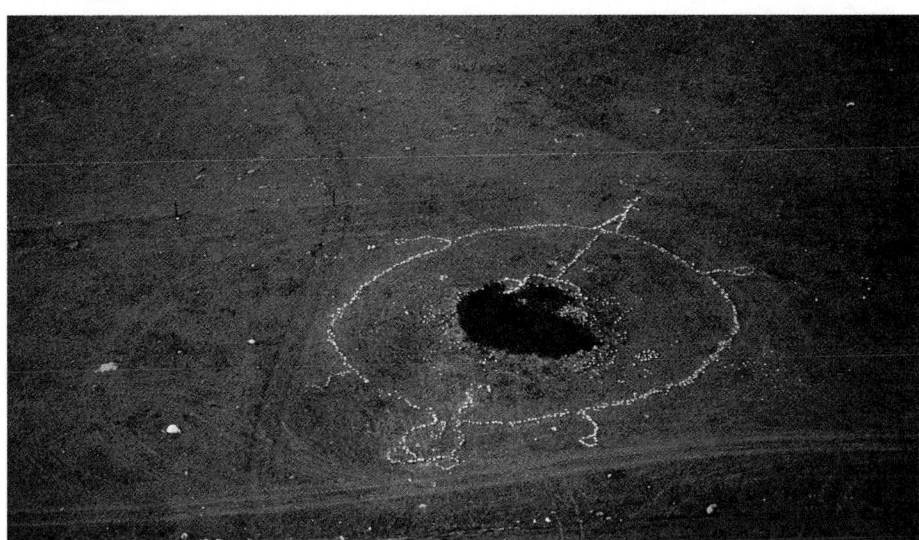

Dwyer ossuaries N of Hamilton. Opened prior to 1836, Dwyer attracted many men of letters including Sir Daniel WILSON. Their individual interests ranged from relic collecting and preservation of native culture to specific artifact interpretation.

In 1842 Sir William E. LOGAN founded the GEOLOGICAL SURVEY OF CANADA in Montréal. This Survey later produced many famous scientist-explorers who traversed the vast expanse of Canada making invaluable observations on archaeological remains, historic forts, native traditions and other natural history.

From 1867 to 1914 considerable archaeological interest developed across Canada, except in the sparsely populated Saskatchewan, Alberta and northern territories. The E and W coasts attracted collectors to the large shell middens, while southern Manitoba and Ontario had conspicuous burial mounds that evoked interpretations about a vanished race of "Mound Builders" with recognizable ties to the elaborate mounds of the Mississippi and Ohio drainages. In southern Ontario, desecration of HURON burial pits became common Sunday afternoon sport for looters, despite reasoned pleas from concerned intelligentsia. In Québec, concerted attention was paid to identifying HISTORIC SITES, particularly HOCHELAGA at Montréal by Sir John W. DAWSON, and in New Brunswick Loring W. BAILEY and William F. Ganong synthesized known prehistoric and historic sites.

The post-Confederation era was one of intensive archaeological and ethnographic collecting for new museums and universities. Photographic collecting also made a debut. Local naturalist, historic and scientific societies flourished and from them provincial governments were stimulated to establish museums and other educational programs promoting archaeology. NS opened the first provincial museum in 1868 at Halifax, while Ontario and BC sponsored formal museums in 1886. It was primarily from these museum and university milieus that the first generation of professional Canadian archaeologists began doing field work, initiating research, and generally setting standards.

Notables such as T.G.B. Lloyd, William Gossip, Bernard Gilpin, Harry Piers, Spencer Baird, George Matthew, Henry Montgomery, George Laidlaw, Andrew Hunter, Frederick Waugh, Marvin Schultz, George Bryce, Charles HILL-TOUT and James TEIT all contributed to a new archaeological excellence, but paramount among them was Ontario's David Boyle. Once a blacksmith and public-school teacher, Boyle rose to become provincial archaeologist in 1886, a post he held until his death in 1911. He established the first journal in Canada expressly devoted to archaeology and ethnography in 1886, the *Annual Archaeological Reports of Ontario*, and this series continued until 1928. Internationally renowned in Britain and the US, Boyle was an indefatigable worker widely revered as the leading figure in Canadian archaeology and museology.

The Modern Era Of the second generation of professional archaeologists in Canada, 2 individuals became most prominent: Harlan I. Smith and William J. WINTEMBERG. Smith began a distinguished career in BC as a member of the 1898 Jessup North Pacific Expedition organized in New York by Franz BOAS. Wintemberg commenced his researches in southern Ontario as a protégé of Boyle in 1900. In 1911-12 both Smith and Wintemberg joined the Victoria Memorial Museum in Ottawa. This Geological Survey of Canada museum, later renamed the National Museum of Canada in 1927, opened in 1911 with a newly created Anthropological Division headed by linguist, poet and administrator Edward SAPIR. Shortly after, Diamond JENNESS, Canada's most distinguished anthropologist, joined the museum as did C. Marius BARBEAU. Smith and Wintemberg worked together on various sites across the country and initiated exploratory surveys. As of 1912, Ottawa became the primary centre for Canada-wide archaeological research.

Commencing in 1913, concerted research was directed towards far northern Canada as a result of the interdisciplinary Canadian Arctic Expedition of 1913-18. Vilhjalmur STEFANSSON became interested in prehistoric and modern commerce among the arctic coast Inuit, while Jenness developed the first detailed information about the Coronation Gulf Copper Eskimos (*see* COPPER INUIT), and their material culture. The Stefansson-Anderson Arctic Expedition also recovered various harpoons and darts that were analysed in 1919 by Clark Wissler. In the eastern Arctic, professional archaeological ground was first broken by Therkel Mathiassen, dedicated archaeologist with the Danish Fifth Thule Expedition, 1921-24, organized by Knud Rasmussen, who traversed Canada's entire northern mainland from Greenland to Alaska.

Questions about Inuit origins proved popular during this time, and Kaj Birket-Smith proposed his now defunct hypothesis of an inland origin for Inuit culture in north-central Canada. He and others were unsuccessful with such ideas because they attempted to solve an essentially archaeological problem with the data and techniques of ethnology. In 1925, Jenness made a major breakthrough with his analysis and definition of the prehistoric DORSET Eskimo culture. Its dating was contested by Henry B. Collins until 1948, when Collins found stratigraphic proof that Dorset predated THULE Eskimo at the Crystal II site, Frobisher Bay, Baffin I. This find confirmed many of Jenness's early claims.

In southern Canada, Smith and Wintemberg worked together in 1913-14 in NS; Frank G. SPECK discovered the TADOUSSAC site in 1915; and in Ontario, the Provincial Museum was renamed the ROYAL ONTARIO MUSEUM in 1914 with quarters in a new building. Rowland B. Orr became the second and last provincial archaeologist for Ontario from 1911 until his death in 1933. Also in Toronto, Canada's first archaeological society for professionals and laypersons, the Ontario Archaeological Assn, was founded in 1919 but survived for only a decade. In 1926 Thomas F. MCILWRAITH formed the first department of anthropology in Canada, at U of T. Specializing in Canadian studies, this department maintained close ties with the ROM, where it had its main offices from 1926 until 1961.

In the West, second-generation professional archaeology was alive but not as vibrant or expansionist as within the Toronto and Ottawa centres. Manitoba saw extensive excavation of burial mounds by William B. Nickerson in 1914, but afterwards, archaeological interest generally waned. The same was true for Saskatchewan and Alberta, although interested individuals did form the early Saskatchewan Archaeological Society in 1935 under William J. Orchard. West of the mountains, the main concern was with collecting art objects, particularly TOTEM POLES and their motifs. Some petroglyphs were also studied in 1912-35 (*see* PICTOGRAPHS AND PETROGLYPHS).

1945-60 The immediate postwar era of Canadian archaeology, 1946-55, is characterized by formal training of students, new dating methods, new analytical techniques, increased public awareness and involvement in archaeology, and the development of a personal, closely-knit group of professionals across the country. Of this third generation of Canadian archaeologists, Ontario's Emerson largely led the way in the East, along with Kenneth E. Kidd, while in the West Borden stands out. For northern Canada, Henry B. Collins of the Smithsonian Institution maintained an active program between 1948 and 1955 that introduced various students to arctic archaeology, including William E. Taylor, Jr. Taylor became director of the new NATIONAL MUSEUM OF MAN in 1967 and together with James V. Wright established the ARCHAEOLOGICAL SURVEY OF CANADA in 1971.

The growing cadre of trained individuals and nonprofessional archaeologists during the 1950s included Elmer Harp in Newfoundland; Edward S. Rogers in Québec; J. Douglas Leechman of the National Museum as well as Thomas E. Lee and MacNeish; Wilfrid Jury, James F. Pendergast, Clyde C. Kennedy, Richard B. Johnston, Frank Ridley in Ontario; and Taylor in the Arctic. Emerson's students, James V. Wright, Walter A. Kenyon, Kenneth C.A. Dawson and Helen E. Devereux, were beginning to staff new programs. All were instrumental in bringing new research concerns and character to the archaeology of northeastern Canada.

Five large-scale archaeological projects in Ontario illustrate the new directions, techniques and training in Canadian archaeology during this third generation. The excavations at the Jesuit site of STE MARIE AMONG THE HURONS, first by K.E. Kidd in 1941 and later by Jury in 1948, saw concerted effort to recover and restore one of Canada's early historic missions. Thomas Lee's 1951-53 excavation at the Sheguiandah site, MANITOULIN I, revealed one of the largest Paleoindian quarry sites known anywhere in N America, and Emerson's 1956-57 work along the route of the impending ST LAWRENCE SEAWAY marked the first major salvage archaeology in eastern Canada (*see* ARCHAEOLOGY, SALVAGE). From 1955 to 1960 the ROM fielded a party under Johnston that provided the first detailed knowledge about a burial mound in Canada, in this case the famed SERPENT MOUND near Peterborough. Kenyon also cut new ground with his near total excavation of the Miller Pickering village in 1958-59. Such advances marked different types of archaeological firsts in Canada.

In the Arctic, something of a "golden era" fluoresced during this third generation of Canadian archaeology. New Paleoeskimo cultures were discovered, and new refinements were geographically added concerning Dorset, Thule and SADLERMIUT INUIT. To these ends the work of Henry B. Collins, Taylor, Jørgen Meldgaard and Moreau S. Maxwell stands particularly paramount. In the adjacent Barren Lands and northern forests of the Yukon and the NWT MacNeish and Harp undertook pioneering reconnaissances and archaeological excavations that are still useful. Canada's far northern archaeologists have never been numerous, but the use of aircraft has greatly enhanced access to this vast, difficult but beautiful tract of Canada.

Western Canada also experienced exciting new archaeological developments during the years 1946-60. In Manitoba, MacNeish undertook excavations that provided a chronological scheme that augmented the local endeavours of Chris Vickers and Walter M. Hlady. Thomas and Alice B. Kehoe investigated south-central Saskatchewan, while Boyd N. Wettlaufer surveyed portions of southern Saskatchewan and Alberta. The year 1955 saw new directions in Alberta archaeology with the establishment of the Glenbow Foundation directed by Leechman. He introduced various professionals for formal archaeological surveys throughout the province, including H. Marie Wormington, William Mulloy, E. Mott Davis and Richard G. Forbis. Significantly, the Glenbow Foundation, established by Eric L. HARVIE, represented the first private institution to sponsor archaeology in Canada (*see* GLENBOW MUSEUM).

In BC, Borden began his dedicated career with that province's archaeology in 1945, digging the Point Grey site. His later work at Marpole on the lower Fraser R, 1948-57, is most significant, as was the salvage archaeology within Tweedsmuir Park, 1951-52. This work, done in the face of the Kemano power reservoir (near KITIMAT), marks Canada's earliest salvage archaeology projects. Roy L. Carlson and Wilson DUFF were trained during this period, and 1960 saw passage of a provincial Archaeological and Historic Sites Protection Act in BC.

Expansionism: 1960-75 The pace of Canadian archaeology significantly changed after 1960. This fourth period was characterized by attempts to define regional sequences, increased interdisciplinary and specialty analyses, expansion of university programs, the development of archaeological field schools, wide-ranging canoe surveys through the boreal forest, and a time when problems of culture history and past peoples motivated considerable research. New funding sources opened, including the CANADA COUNCIL, which began supporting archaeology in 1961, followed by the SOCIAL SCIENCES AND HUMANITIES RESEARCH COUNCIL OF CANADA. This was also the period when Québec archaeology came into its own, with the 1962 establishment of the Société d'archaéologie du Québec. Parks Canada also undertook new programs in both prehistoric and historic archaeology. The mid to late 1960s proved most dynamic on all archaeological fronts in Canada.

Expansionism occurred at the NATIONAL MUSEUMS OF CANADA and in universities, paralleling a greater public interest in Canada's national heritage following CENTENNIAL YEAR. To the group of Taylor, Wright, George F. MacDonald, and William N. Irving at the National Museum in Ottawa were added Donald G. MacLeod, Roscoe Wilmeth, Robert McGhee, Donald W. Clark, David Sanger, Richard E. Morlan, William J. Byrne, Roger Marois, Bryan H. Gordon and David L. Keenlyside. In extreme eastern Canada James A. Tuck, Devereux, William W. Fitzhugh, Urve Linnamae, John S. Erskine, David Sanger, MacDonald, Christopher Turnbull and Richard N. Pearson contributed significantly to our archaeological knowledge of that region. In Québec Jacques Cinq-Mars, Charles A. Martijn, René Ribes and Gilles Tassé initiated new dimensions to the discipline. Ontario saw a steady stream of students produced by Emerson that included MacDonald, Romas Vastokas, Donald G. MacLeod, Michael W. Spence, Morgan J. Tamplin, McGhee, William C. Noble, William A. Russell, Alan E. Tyyska, Peter G. Ramsden and William D. Finlayson. Also in Ontario, Kenyon pursued investigations along Rainy R, as well as at historic Ft Albany.

In the West, expansionism was also apparent. The U of Manitoba established an archaeological MA program under William J. Mayer-Oakes. Eugene M. Gryba, E. Leigh Syms, Jack Steinbring, Gary A. Dickson, Leo F. Pettipas and Ronald J. Nash became noteworthy contributors, while in Saskatchewan Ian G. Dyck, George Arthur and James F.V. Millar established important archaeological centres at Regina and Saskatoon, respectively. The U of Calgary became a major archaeological focus with its specialized department, and graduated its first archaeology PhDs in 1968 including Albertan resident Barney O.K. Reeves. At Edmonton, Ruth Gruhn undertook local excavations as did Robert Kidd and Clifford Hickey. In BC, James J. Hester, Philip M. Hobler, Donald Mitchell, Carlson, Sanger, Turnbull and Knut Fladmark all represent prominent contributors during this fourth period of Canadian archaeological development.

The northern sectors of Canada received almost continuous attention during the 1960-75 period. Wright undertook numerous surveys and excavations through Ontario westward to Alberta and the District of Keewatin that required a stamina reminiscent of the 19th-century GSC scientist-explorers. Guy Mary-Rousselière opened new ground in the Canadian Arctic, as did McGhee, while Noble, Clark, Morlan and Gordon investigated the northern forests and margins.

Archaeology in Canada attained some measure of maturity during this period. Not only did the number of practising archaeologists rise from a mere dozen to nearly 100, but an interested public helped stimulate formation of the nationwide Canadian Archaeological Assn in 1968. This organization has become the official watchdog and forum for archaeology in Canada, and it initiated a *Bulletin* publication series in 1969. This series was later transformed into a major Canadian archaeological serial under the editorship of McGhee, and retitled the *Canadian Journal of Archaeology* in 1977. In 1978, the CAA established the "Smith-Wintemberg Medal," and this prestigious award was given to C.E. Border and J.N. Emerson in 1978, and R.G. Forbis in 1984.

The Archaeological Survey of Canada also inaugurated its archaeological Mercury Series in 1972, thereby superseding the National Museum of Man *Bulletin* series, the *Contributions to Anthropology* and their *Anthropological Papers*. Parks Canada introduced a series on the Canadian Historic Sites Service that included reports on LOUISBOURG, LOWER FORT GARRY and ROCKY MOUNTAIN HOUSE. Clearly, the discipline of archaeology had become firmly established in most parts of Canada during this innovative period.

The Legal Era: 1975-Present The year 1975 signals a significant turning-point in Canadian archaeology. Legalities and legislation, initiated in most cases by professional archaeologists, changed the conduct and responsibilities for archaeology in most of Canada's provinces. While legislation concerning archaeological sites existed in Ontario as early as 1952 and in BC in 1960, it was not until after 1975 that forceful legalities came into effect. Not only were licensing procedures introduced, but comprehensive archaeological reporting measures became mandatory. Most provincial governments, activating constitutional powers, assumed a new responsibility for ownership, conservation and disposition of archaeological and other heritage resources. They also developed their own individual systems to manage such matters. By so doing, the role of the National Museum of Man became increasingly restricted to archaeology within federal jurisdictions such as the northern territories, national parks, airports and harbours.

Since 1975 the new legislation has required that lands to be developed, inundated or otherwise disturbed must first be investigated for their archaeological potential. This could lead to mitigation followed by salvage or rescue excavations. In large, the new Canada-wide forms of provincial heritage legislation has resulted in the emergence of new applied archaeologists, a surge in site inventorying, and a plethora of reports. Unfortunately, many of the new reports are unavailable and often written as impact studies without wider integration with current research syntheses.

The future directions of Canadian archaeology cannot be precisely forecast, but already it is apparent that the number of new applied archaeologists far exceeds the traditional teaching/research specialists. Indeed, there are simply too many to name individually here. It is to be hoped, however, that the various factions of the fifth-generation Canadian archaeologists will recognize specific merits in each other, and not lose sight of the ultimate goals of archaeology, namely, the study of Canada's past peoples. Much of Canada still remains only spot checked from an archaeological perspective, and no comprehensive, authoritative volume has been written detailing Canadian archaeology as a whole.

R.G. FORBIS AND W.C. NOBLE

Reading: D. Jenness, "Fifty Years of Archaeology in Canada" in *Royal Society of Canada, Anniversary Volume 1882-1932* (1932); G. Killan, David Boyle: *From Artisan to Archaeologist* (1983); W.C. Noble, "One Hundred and Twenty-Five Years of Archaeology in the Canadian Provinces" in *Canadian Archaeological Association Bulletin*, 4 (1972).

Archaeology, Industrial A type of interdisciplinary history that promotes understanding of the industrial era by focusing on physical remains, whether above ground or below, and by combining the insights of fieldwork and historical research. The name is recent in origin but already is well established throughout the world. Industrial archaeology originated in Great Britain, birthplace of the Industrial Revolution, in the late 1950s as a response to the alarming rate at which the nation's industrial and ENGINEERING heritage was being destroyed, and as a celebration of the lives and works of industrialists, engineers and inventors of the early industrial period. N Americans formed the Society for Industrial Archeology in 1971 and, while there is no separate Canadian organization, Canada is represented on the International Committee for the Conservation of the Industrial Heritage, created in 1978. An independent regional group was organized in Ontario in 1981.

The field everywhere is interdisciplinary and focuses on a wide range of industrial objects, structures and sites. However, the industrial experience and contemporary social, economic and political priorities within various countries naturally have shaped the work of industrial archaeologists along individual national lines. In European countries and the US, for example, sites and structures of importance to the Industrial Revolution have received the most attention. These include power sources and transmission systems, CANALS and RAILWAYS, and sites devoted to the TEXTILE INDUSTRY and IRON AND STEEL production. In addition to the strictly industrial and engineering structures, European practitioners pay considerable attention to industrial villages and workers' housing. In Canada and in Scandinavian countries the early industrial era was more closely associated with staple RESOURCE extraction and primary processing. Thus, sites devoted to MINING, FORESTRY, FISHERIES, iron making, BREWING and DISTILLING are favoured for study. In Europe, where there is interest in teaching industrial archaeology, the field attracts mostly academic historians of TECHNOLOGY or ARCHITECTURE; in N America work is carried on mainly by museum and HISTORIC-SITES personnel, or historic preservationists, including historians, curators, architects, archaeologists, planners, photographers and teachers.

With such diversity in practice and practitioners, the field has yet to develop a coherent methodology and theoretical framework. In general the research involves fieldwork, comprising recording through photography and measured drawings, oral interviews and site plans. So much tangible evidence of early INDUSTRY and industrial technology remains above the surface that actual excavation is seldom necessary. The insights of fieldwork are then combined with historical research to provide a record and understanding of what the Industrial Revolution entailed, more complete than that provided by written documents alone. When the subject matter is particularly threatened by loss or destruction, fieldwork resembles salvage archaeology. Threats arise because industrial and engineering structures frequently become functionally obsolete; sometimes they are found in unattractive surroundings or in poor condition; many are even seen in a negative light as symbolic of human misery and exploitation. Thus the goal may be simply to preserve knowledge of the site or structure for posterity. In Canada, there has been less interest in projects devoted to recording and inventorying or in developing industrial archaeology as an academic discipline. Instead, work on industrial museums and historic industrial sites has been of much more importance. There are over 690 industrial and 100 TRANSPORTATION and COMMUNICATION museums alone. Numerous industrial archaeological sites are administered by the various levels of government, the most significant being the historic national park of the FORGES SAINT-MAURICE. Located just N of Trois-Rivières, Qué, it is the site of Canada's oldest industrial complex (1729-1883). *See* INDUSTRIALIZATION. DIANNE NEWELL

Archaeology, Salvage, the rescuing of archaeological sites and their contents from destruction threatened by natural or human means. The remains of past human cultural activity are like other nonrenewable resources; they are limited in number and cannot be recreated once they are destroyed. The archaeological record may take thousands of years to form, but sites may be obliterated in hours, even minutes. The destruction of sites and removal of artifacts by indiscriminate surface collection or by improper or unauthorized excavation has reached a critical stage in N America. Canada is no exception. Archaeologists are concerned that few opportunities will remain for studying archaeological materials in their original contexts.

Sites and artifacts can be uncovered and destroyed in many ways, eg, by oil pipeline construction, road and railway extension, agricultural practices, housing and industrial expansion, natural erosion, flooding or vandalism. Emergency or salvage archaeology is being done in the MACKENZIE VALLEY PIPELINE corridor and in the paths of the Dempster and Mackenzie highways in the Yukon and NWT. In BC, salvage operations took place when Prince Rupert harbour was expanded. CFB Suffield in Alberta was surveyed and excavated because military exercises resulted in land disturbance which threatened known and unknown sites. Over 1100 prehistoric and historic sites were discovered in one 400-km^2 survey area at Suffield.

Background archival work and rapid aerial reconnaissance are 2 procedures that facilitate the evaluation of potential sites. At the Draper site near the new Lester B. Pearson Airport, Toronto, a Huron village of over 32 longhouses dating to 1500 AD was uncovered. In Arctic Canada, coastal erosion threatens sites, and vandalized Inuit burials on Baffin I require salvage. The Thule Archaeology Conservation Project, begun in 1972, monitors the destruction of Thule sites on Baffin I, Somerset I and elsewhere. Here, quantities of whalebone accumulated by Thule hunters 1000 years ago are being "mined" to supply bone for the Inuit carving industry. Important evidence of Thule houses and domestic life is lost when raw bone and ancient artifacts are indiscriminately gathered.

International concern generated action by Canadian federal and provincial governments to ensure that Canada's nonrenewable cultural heritage is adequately researched and recorded, and, if possible, that examples are preserved (*see* CONSERVATION OF MOVABLE CULTURAL PROPERTY). UNESCO recommendations inspired such Canadian legislation as the National Museums Act and the Cultural Property Export and Import Act. One result of the ratification in Canada of the 1970 UNESCO recommendation was the establishment of the ARCHAEOLOGICAL SURVEY OF CANADA (1971). The ASC assumes responsibilities for the survey and rescue of prehistoric sites endangered by federal land development, as well as general regional research, curatorial work and the establishment of a National Prehistoric Site Inventory. By the 1970s most provinces had some form of archaeological-resources management agency and program, including their own salvage projects, staffed by professionals. Legislation relating to archaeological resources is not uniform from province to province, but generally builders, developers or other individuals are required to report to provincial agencies any discovered sites or cultural materials. Access to archaeological sites is controlled; provisions are made for halting construction to allow surveying or excavation; and penalties are imposed for violation of regulations pertaining to archaeological sites. Salvage archaeology is public archaeology. Its importance will continue to increase as Canada experiences more urban and industrial growth and as the public becomes more aware of the value of preserving cultural heritage. RENÉ R. GADACZ

Archaic culture is characterized by archaeologists as the seasonal selective exploitation of forest and woodland resources preceding or paralleling the establishment of horticulture. Though the culture is universal across N America, dating between about 6000 BC and 500 AD, and follows the earlier PALEOINDIAN stage, artifact styles are not identical wherever it is found. In technology, the Archaic stage is typified by specialized varieties of woodworking implements such as axes, gouges and knives. Pottery is found in some areas; formalized burial sites occur in others, but there is little evidence of any housing. The cultivation and domestication of maize, the grain eventually cultivated by all N American tribes, took place during the Archaic in the Mexican highlands. *See also* PREHISTORY. RENÉ R. GADACZ

Archambault, Louis, sculptor (b at Montréal 4 Apr 1915). He studied at the École des Beaux-Arts in Montréal, receiving the prestigious Prix du Ministre 1939. In 1948 he joined with others, including Alfred PELLAN, to sign the manifesto *Prisme d'Yeux*. From 1955 to 1968 he received numerous awards, including the Royal Architectural Institute of Canada's medal of honour (1958) and the Centennial Medal (1967). He created major pieces for the Canadian pavilions at the Brussels (1958) and Montréal (1967) international expositions, and has done commissioned works for Place des Arts, Montréal, the Ottawa and Toronto airports and the Ottawa city hall. His work is found in many Canadian and foreign museums, and has been seen in many one-man and group shows. His contribution to the growth and renewal of sculpture in Canada makes him the greatest Canadian sculptor of his generation. MICHEL CHAMPAGNE

Archer, Violet, composer, educator (b at Montréal 24 Apr 1913). A composer of marked individuality, widely recognized for her command of both traditional and contemporary techniques, she studied composition with Claude CHAMPAGNE and Douglas CLARKE in Montréal and in New York with Béla Bartók and Paul Hindemith. Archer has produced a large body of music embracing most of the vocal and instrumental performance media, including a comic opera, *Sganarelle* (1973), and a documentary-film score (*Someone Cares*). Her *Piano Concerto no 1* (1956), which demands great virtuosity from soloist and orchestra alike, is considered one of the finest concertos composed by a Canadian. After appointments at universities in the US (1950-61), where she also adjudicated state and national young-composer competitions, Archer returned to Canada and taught theory and composition at U of A from 1962 until retirement in 1978. BARCLAY MCMILLAN

Archery As a fighting and hunting weapon, the bow and arrow was widely used in prehistoric times and throughout the Middle Ages. Archery became a recreational sport in England in the 15th and 16th centuries, after the decline of the bow and arrow as a military weapon. There are 2 general types of longbow: the ordinary, straight-ended bow and the recurved bow. The latter (made of laminated wood, plastic and fibreglass) is most commonly used in archery competition, of which the most popular forms are target archery (shooting at a standard-size target) and field archery (shooting at targets at random distances in the field).

In Canada, archery clubs were formed in the mid-1800s. In 1864, in Ontario, the Yorkville Archery Club staged a tournament, the first record of archery as a sport in Canada. Little is known about organized competition until 1927, when the Canadian Archery Assn (later Federation of Canadian Archers) was formed. The first Canadian championships were held in 1931. Ontario was the principal archery province for some years, and it was not until 1951 that the CAA became truly national. Canadians have done well in international competition. A team was first entered in the 1963 world championships, and the Canadians placed 5th in 1967. Dorothy Lidstone became the first Canadian to earn a world title — the 1969 women's world target archery championship; the Canadian women's team placed 2nd that year, In 1971 the men's team was 3rd in the world and Emmanuel Boucher set a world record for the double 30-m distance. At the 1973 Championships of the Americas, Les Anderson and Wayne Pullen were gold-medal winners in field archery, and Anderson placed 2nd overall. Lucille Lessard won the 1974 women's field archery world title and the 1975 Championships of the Americas field archery event, and placed 5th in the 1976 Olympics. Canadian men's and women's teams were 2nd in the 1979 Pan-American Games and the 1980 target Championships of the Americas. The 1982 Championships of the Americas were held in Canada for the first time, in Joliette, Québec. BARBARA SCHRODT

Archibald, Edgar Spinney, agriculturalist (b at Yarmouth, NS 12 May 1885; d at Ottawa 23 Jan 1968). Archibald's greatest contribution to Canadian agriculture was his dedicated and active support of scientists in the Experimental Farms Service, of which he was director 1919-51. Although his training was in livestock, he recognized the importance of all disciplines contributing to food production. He chaired the Tobacco Enquiry Committee (1928), the program committee for the World Grain Exhibition and Conference at Regina (1933), and helped form the Prairie Farm Rehabilitation Administration, which developed successful soil-conservation practices between 1935 and 1951. He received 3 honorary degrees and several fellowships and other honours, including Companion of the Order of Canada. A mountain in the Yukon is named after him. T.H. ANSTEY

Archibald, Edith Jessie, née Archibald, socialite, feminist, author (b in Newfoundland 1854; d at Halifax 1936). Educated in New York and London, Eng, Archibald married in 1874 Charles Archibald, mining engineer and later president of the Bank of NS. She was president of Maritime WOMAN'S CHRISTIAN TEMPERANCE UNION from 1892 to 1896, president of the Halifax Local Council of Women from 1896 to 1906, president of the Halifax VON from 1897 to 1901, and, as vice-president of the NS Red Cross in 1914, chaired the department responsible for Canadian prisoners of war overseas. An ardent suffragist, Archibald advised a shift from confrontation to more subtle maternal feminist tactics after the defeat of the suffragist campaign in the early 1890s. She led the suffrage delegation to the legislature in 1917 and later chaired the Halifax Conservative Women's Auxiliary. An eloquent speaker, with a fine writing style, she published articles, pamphlets, songs, plays and several books, including one about her father, *Life and Letters of Sir Edward Mortimer Archibald* (1924), and *The Token* (1930). ERNEST R. FORBES

Archibald, Edward William, surgeon, scientist, educator (b at Montréal 5 Aug 1872; d there 17 Dec 1945). Archibald was a gifted surgeon who recognized that advance in surgery must come through scientific research, and he changed the character of surgical education at McGill and elsewhere from the purely clinical to the scientific. Part of his early schooling was in Grenoble, where he became bilingual and laid the foundation of lifelong ties with France. A McGill medical graduate, he became associated with the Royal Victoria Hospital in Montréal shortly after its opening. Eventually, he became surgeon in chief of the hospital and professor of surgery at McGill. Archibald had his faults; they included an almost incredible degree of absentmindedness, with an inability to keep track of time. But even his faults seemed merely to increase the affection of his colleagues. One of them wrote, "O Edward you would be sublime/ If only you could be on time." EDWARD BENSLEY

Archibald, John Smith, architect (b at Inverness, Scot 14 Dec 1872; d at Montréal 2 Mar 1934). He came to Canada in 1893 and was employed as supervising architect in the office of Edward MAXWELL in Montréal. From 1897 to 1915 he practised in partnership, and thereafter under his own name. He was known for his administrative ablility and expertise in construction methods. He tried to promote economy in relation to architecture through a series of articles distributed across Canada. During the 1920s the CNR commissioned him to design large hotels across Canada from Halifax to Vancouver. In his best works in Montréal — Emmanuel Congregational Church, Montréal Technical School, Masonic Memorial Temple — Archibald adhered to the classical tradition of symmetry and monumental grandeur. He was president of the Royal Architectural Institute of Canada 1924-25 and was elected a fellow in 1930. ROBERT LEMIRE

Architectural Competitions have been used successfully for many years to select architects or designs for major projects of regional or national importance. Qualified architects are invited to submit designs, based on a fixed program of requirements and a specified set of procedures, which are then assessed by a jury of distinguished architects and representatives of the sponsor. The competition may be used to select an architect or design; to provide an opportunity for participation to architects who might not otherwise be considered; to obtain the best talent available in a given locale, region or nation; or to make an architectural statement.

A competition can take several forms. In open competitions, invitations to participate are extended to all qualified architects within a specified locale, region or nation, or even internationally. Closed competitions are limited by the sponsor to specially qualified or selected architects. In 2-stage competitions the first stage is open, and used to obtain concepts for the design of a project, discover new talent, or to select architects who have credentials appropriate to the project; the second stage is used to obtain a final design for the project.

Architectural competitions are run by architects' professional organizations, such as the Royal Architectural Institute of Canada (RAIC) and the provincial associations. The rules of a competition govern the basis and terms of participation, the fee structure, the eligibility and qualifications of candidates, and the process to be followed should the project not proceed or should a partnership or joint venture be required. The first prize usually consists of the award of a contract to implement the winning design. The PARLIAMENT BUILDINGS in Ottawa, and many other important heritage buildings, were designed in competition. However the history of competitions is fraught with controversy, with many examples of winning designs that are so radical or experimental that the sponsor decided not to proceed.

Vincent Massey, chairman of the Royal Commission on NATIONAL DEVELOPMENTS IN THE ARTS AND LETTERS AND SCIENCES in 1951, recommended that all major public buildings in Canada be designed through architectural competition. In 1952 the federal government held a national competition for the NATIONAL GALLERY OF CANADA, an example followed by several other major projects, including Toronto City Hall and Winnipeg City Hall (both international), Winnipeg Art Gallery (national), Massey College, U of T (closed), Simon Fraser U (master plan, local), the Mendel Art Gallery, Saskatoon (national) and, more recently, city halls for Edmonton, Calgary and Mississauga.

In 1953 the Massey Foundation sponsored a series of prestigious design awards. The Massey gold medal was awarded to a building considered to be the most important contribution to Canadian architecture in the preceding 3-year period; and 20 silver medals were awarded for other buildings. The Massey medals, which were awarded 8 times at 3-year intervals, had a major impact on the quality of architecture in Canada by virtue of the intense competition they generated. Since 1982 they have been superseded by the Governor General's medals for architecture, administered by the RAIC. The Canadian Housing Design Council introduced a design award competition to stimulate the quality of HOUSING design in Canada and several building materials manufacturers have sponsored similar design award programs. *See also* ARCHITECTURAL PRACTICE. DOUGLAS SHADBOLT

Architectural Practice An architect designs and superintends the construction of buildings. The process by which buildings are constructed and put into use can be divided into 9 stages, each requiring specific approvals and funding commitments. The stages are as follows: *opportunity identification,* in which the purpose, nature and scope of the facility is determined and the general location is established; *feasibility,* in which various options are examined and evaluated, and a site is determined; *project definition,* in which the requirements of the facility are determined in detail; *design development,* in which the conceptual design is prepared and further processed into a detailed design; *working documents,* during which the detailed contract drawings, specifications, and other contract documents are completed; *tendering and procurement,* in which the contract documents are used to obtain bids from contractors to construct or provide the facility; *construction,* in which the facility is built; *commissioning,* in which the facility is turned over from the contractors to the owner's organization, and put into use; *operation and maintenance,* in which the owner operates the facility throughout its useful life. The process will vary in complexity and in the length of time it takes to complete the facility. The project may be divided into a number of sub-projects, but each of these will roughly follow the stages outlined above. The knowledge and expertise required at each stage also varies. For example, for a small single-family house, one person, such as the architect, can provide almost everything required to complete or co-ordinate each task at each stage. At another scale, a complex facility, such as a large hospital building, would require several hundred experts at various stages, a multi-disciplinary team with careful, highly skilled, specialized management and co-ordination.

Buildings are initiated by individual clients or by a group representing a public or private institution or corporate entity. The architect is selected by the client for his skills and capability to lead and manage the implementation and for his ability as a designer and specialist in design quality control. Architectural firms are able to provide specialized services demanded by clients for particular building types, such as schools, hospitals, office buildings, commercial facilities, recreational facilities and churches.

A typical small architectural practice will have 1 or 2 registered architects, with up to 10 or more assistants who may or may not be fully qualified architects. The principal architects are usually generalists with the experience, knowledge and personal capability to handle all stages of small and medium-sized projects. A large architectural practice will be based on one or more principals, with several senior associates or junior partners, all registered architects. The practice may employ 50-200 architects, technologists or draftsmen. Frequently, large practices will include or organize teams with other professional disciplines, such as structural, mechanical, electrical or civil engineers. They are then able to provide the expertise required for large, complex projects.

The practice of architecture in Canada is controlled by the profession under the terms of provincial legislation. Each province has an association or institute of architects which monitors and regulates practice by controlling the licensing of individual architects through admission requirements and procedures, and by disciplining members who transgress the rules of practice. Only members of the provincial association or institute are allowed to call themselves architects or to practise architecture. The association may prosecute other persons who do so. Individual members of a provincial association may join the Royal Architectural Institute of Canada (RAIC). Educational requirements consist of a professional degree of Bachelor of Architecture (or equivalent), followed by supplementary coursework provided by the professional association prior to a pre-registration examination. A candidate may also meet those requirements by completing the RAIC Minimum Syllabus program, which is predominantly a self-study program allowing the candidate to qualify while employed in an architect's office. The RAIC Certification Board screens and approves the education status of all candidates. Architecture schools in Canada have been established at the following universities: British Columbia, Calgary, Manitoba, Carleton, Laval, McGill, Montréal, Toronto, Waterloo, and at the Technical University of Nova Scotia in Halifax. In addition to the educational requirements, a candidate for admission to the profession must have completed 2 or 3 years of practical experience in an architect's office acceptable to the provincial association with which the candidate wishes to register. On completion of these requirements, and with established residency, the candidate will be accepted and registered.

Mobility for registered architects is provided for by arrangements for reciprocal recognition of credentials, which may include provisions for special examination (eg, where language or legal systems differ) or proof of residence. Mobility for students who may wish to reside in another province or country to complete their professional qualifications is provided in Canada by the national purview of the RAIC Certification Board, and internationally by the recognition of different schools of architecture by bodies such as the Commonwealth Association of Architects, and the Royal Institute of British Architects. DOUGLAS SHADBOLT

Architectural Styles are a conscious aesthetic response to the challenge of building. It implies academic knowledge on the part of the designer — be he architect, engineer or builder. The succession of architectural styles that have touched Canada reflects the complex political, social and economic influences that have shaped the

In the foreground, Place Royale, Québec City, shows the ordinary form of 17th- and 18th-century Québec townhouses with their steeply pitched roofs and dormer windows; the Château Frontenac beyond embodies the fanciful château style. Both styles were drawn from the same French traditions (*courtesy Yves Tessier/Reflexion*).

country. Historically, building design in Canada grew out of western European culture: the early French tradition was supplanted in the 19th century by British and later by American fashions. In the 20th century, however, the influence has become international.

The *French baroque* style reached Canada late in the 17th century and held sway — at least for RELIGIOUS BUILDING and GOVERNMENT BUILDING — for almost a century. The Archbishop's Palace in Québec City (1693-97, demolished) by architect Claude BAILLIF, and the Château de Vaudreuil in Montréal (1723-27, demolished) by engineer Gaspard CHAUSSEGROS DE LÉRY, though reduced in scale and grandeur when compared to their prototypes in France, captured the essential characteristics of baroque taste in the outpost of NEW FRANCE: classical vocabulary including columns, pilasters, domes and pediments from the Italian Renaissance masters, steep roofs alive with tiny round dormer windows and tall chimneys, sweeping double staircases and enclosed courtyards called *cours d'honneur*.

The neoclassical façade of the Bank of Montreal, Montréal, Qué (John Wells, 1846-48; later alterations, 1903), lends commerce the dignity of a Roman temple (*courtesy Notman Photographic Archives, McCord Museum*).

In the second half of the 18th century the influx of British immigrants and LOYALISTS from the American colonies implanted a more discreet and sober version of classical taste, influenced by Italian architect Andrea Palladio. Imbued with a sense of balance and harmonious proportions, the *Palladian* style in Canada, often called the Georgian style, can be identified by such features as a central pediment, rusticated ground storey, lateral wings, accentuated second storey, and the characteristic Venetian or flanked window. Best illustrated by PROVINCE HOUSE, Halifax (1811-18), Palladianism thrived in the Atlantic provinces and Québec, and to a lesser extent in Ontario, until about 1820.

Neoclassicism, inspired by archaeological discoveries in Greece and Italy, implied a re-evaluation of classical taste and called for strict accuracy in the imitation of original classical structures. Reaching Canada through British and American architectural publications and a new generation of British-trained architects such as George BROWNE, William Footner and John OSTELL, the *neoclassical* style modified the delicate refinement of the Palladian idiom to create smoother, starker forms featuring baseless colonnades or pilasters springing from ground level, and a Greek revival repertoire of scrolls, flat-headed flanked windows, and squat Doric columns. KINGSTON CITY HALL (1842-44) by George Browne and Laval U in Québec City (1854-57) by Charles BAILLAIRGÉ illustrate the varied facets of neoclassicism in Canada.

The *Gothic revival* style was inspired by buildings from the "dark ages" of medieval Europe. Initially introduced in Canada by Irish architect James O'Donnell at NOTRE-DAME DE MONTREAL (1823-29), Gothic revival persisted across Canada for over a century, especially in religious architecture. Identified by features such as the pointed or ogival arch for door and window openings, buttresses and pinnacles, the style evolved through various stages: the rational phase promoted by a group of British theologians known as the Ecclesiologists is best illustrated by CHRIST CHURCH CATHEDRAL, Fredericton (1846-53), by architects Frank Wills and William Butterfield. The High Victorian Gothic phase, which sanctioned polychromy, asymmetry, texture and picturesque effects, find expression in the Library of Parliament in Ottawa (1859-76) by Fuller and Jones (*see* PARLIAMENT BUILDINGS). The beaux-arts phase, which witnessed a return to symmetry and monumentality, is exemplified by early U of Saskatchewan buildings (about 1912-20) by architect David K. Brown and Hugh Vallance.

Superimposed upon these distinct styles in the first half of the 19th century was the *picturesque* movement, an 18th-century British taste which had an impact particularly on domestic architecture in Québec, Ontario and the Atlantic provinces. Not a style in itself, architecture of the picturesque typically enhanced and took account of informal landscape settings. Cottages and villas like Colborne Lodge in High Park, Toronto (1836), by architect John George HOWARD had characteristic features of the picturesque: careful siting to explore the vistas, asymmetrical placement on the building lot, broken roofline with raised towers or tall chimneys, bow, bay or French windows, and a verandah with exotic treillage or delicate posts.

By mid-century the traditional stylistic categories gave way to eclecticism and variety. New sources of inspiration were sought and several fashions coexisted simultaneously. The *Italianate* style, eg, made popular in the 1850s and 1860s by the American architectural pattern books, appeared in several guises: BANKS and government buildings such as the Kingston Custom House (1856-57) and Post Office (1856-59), both designed by the Montréal firm of Hopkins, Lawford and Nelson, featured heavy rusticated ground storeys, nearly flat roofs, and semicircular headed openings; Italianate houses such as the rectory of St Mark's Church in Niagara-on-the-Lake (about 1858) acquired irregular plans, tall square towers, overhanging eaves with paired brackets and groups of semicircular windows; and a select group of buildings like the Don Jail in Toronto (1858-65) and the Halifax County Court House (1858-60) by William THOMAS and Sons added tortuous forms and vermiculated stonework to the other Italianate features.

With an increasing taste for pompous and imposing forms in the second half of the 19th century, Italianate gave way to Second Empire influence, a style that began in France during the reign of Emperor Napoleon III (1852-70) and flowered in the US. The *Second Empire* style is a modification of the Italianate style, made more massive through the addition of pavilions, towers and mansard roofs. Adopted by the federal Dept of Public Works in the 1870s, this style was disseminated across the country in public buildings like the Saint John Custom House (1877-81) by supervising architects McKean and Fairweather, and the Toronto Post Office (1871-73) by supervising architect Henry Langley. Though well suited for the houses of the bourgeoisie who deemed the bombastic forms to be appropriate expressions of their wealth, conservative values and social standing, Second Empire fell out of fashion by the end of the 1880s.

In their quest for novelty, architects in the late 19th century turned to unexploited historical periods for inspiration, leading to the brief flowering of styles such as Romanesque revival, Château and Queen Anne revival. Drawn from the work of American architect H.H. Richardson, the *Romanesque revival* appeared in Canada in the 1890s, well illustrated by the old Toronto City Hall (1890) designed by E.J. Lennox, with its rugged wall surfaces, squat columns, massive semicircular arches, round and square towers, and carved foliage and gargoyles. The *Château* style, an adaptation of French 16th-century castles in the Loire Valley, also reached Canada from the US, this time at Québec

City where American architect Bruce Price created the Château Frontenac (1892), the first of the smooth-surfaced, steep-roofed and round-towered palaces that came to symbolize Canadian railway hotels (*see* HOTEL). The *Queen Anne revival* style, though theoretically modeled on late 17th-century English buildings, was typical of its period in its asymmetrical composition and profusion of detail. Especially popular for domestic architecture in all regions of Canada, this style encouraged the use of materials such as brick, stone and shingle for their polychromatic and textural contrasts, and the eclectic agglomeration of heterogeneous details from all periods of design, including Flemish gables, Venetian windows, Tudor mullions, Gothic revival ribbed chimney stacks and corner towers.

In contrast to these fussy historical revivals, the *beaux-arts* movements, named for the École des beaux-arts in Paris, offered a refreshing alternative. Important public buildings in Canada in the early 20th century, such as the SASKATCHEWAN LEGISLATURE BUILDING in Regina (1908-12) by Montréal architects Edward and William MAXWELL, demonstrated well-articulated and rigorously symmetrical facades, axial planning of interior space, and an imposing monumentality. CHRISTINA CAMERON

Art deco, or *Art moderne* (both names drawn from the 1925 Paris *Exposition internationale des arts décoratifs et industriels modernes*), brought simplified, more geometric, versions of traditional historic ornament as well as some that were purely abstract, without historic reference, and with bold, often jarring colours. At its extreme, this brash and (for its time) startling style, most evident in interior design, created a suitable setting for the frenetic gaiety of the Jazz Age. The Marine Building, Vancouver (McCarter and Nairne, 1929-30), especially the main entrance and lobby, is the supreme public work, while Ernest CORMIER's own house in Montréal (1931) is a sensitive and subtle domestic example.

Influencing transitional styles, through the 1930s and early 1940s, was the superficial application of "streamlining," the sleek rounded forms of the advanced aircraft of the period, to a variety of objects from automobiles to furniture. The result, sometimes called *moderne,* further propagated rounded corners and horizontal stripes. A fine, sedate example is Page and Steele's Garden Court Apartments, Toronto (1939). The epitome of the mixture appeared in the movie theatres, justifying the term Odeon style; its characteristics were flowing curves, grooves and stripes, indirect lighting and pastel colours.

Behind these superficial fashions was a profound revolution in design which, from the turn of the century, began to produce an increasing number of fully realized "modern" buildings. The term "modern," indicating "of the present" or "contemporary," makes no precise reference to style but has generally meant design and construction that adheres closely and obviously to the requirements of utility and efficiency. These objectives inspired early Canadian modernists Peter Thornton, R.A.D. Berwick and C.E. Pratt on the West Coast, and Marcel Parizeau and Robert Blatter in Québec in the 1930s.

Despite the wide variety of forms and approaches called "modern," the version which became most closely identified with the modern movement in architecture was named the *international style* by H.R. Hitchcock and Philip Johnson in their 1932 book of that name. It was characterized by generally cubic forms, unadorned white surfaces, large often horizontal windows, and asymmetrical massing in response to the "functional" arrangement of interior volumes. Not only was there little or no decorative relief but any visual reference to historic style was absolutely proscribed.

As the architects associated with the international style came to design larger buildings after WWII, particularly commercial offices and apartments, a modern version of the late 19th-century office tower emerged which emphasized the regular repetitive structure and the impersonality of the process by which it was produced and inhabited. The result is exemplified at its most distinguished by the Toronto Dominion Centre in Toronto (Mies van der Rohe, consultant, John B. PARKIN Associates and BREGMAN AND HAMANN, 1963). Variations on this ubiquitous and usually anonymous "international modern" style became characteristic of downtown business districts as they expanded from the 1950s to the 1980s.

By the mid-1960s a significant broadening of international modern had begun, together with the first signs of direct reaction to its abstraction and austerity. First to come were bolder forms earlier associated with European expressionism, especially the pursuit of personal or symbolic expression through sculptural modelling, as in the works of Douglas CARDINAL, Clifford WIENS, Étienne GABOURY, P.M. Côté and Roger D'Astous (eg, Château Champlain, Montréal). Then followed a revived interest in the form and detail of earlier buildings. *Post-modernism,* more a catch-all tag for a mood or attitude than an identifiable style, covers this change of direction. It includes the renewed use of identifiable historic elements from classical Greek or Roman orders to the decorative features of ordinary 19th-century rural houses (as in Peter Rose's Bradley House, North Hatley, Qué, 1977), especially the search for local or regional inspiration. MICHAEL MCMORDIE

Architecture The transfer of European architectural traditions to Canada began with the arrival of French settlers in the early 1600s. The buildings of Inuit and Indians had little effect on European structures, because native construction proceeded from an entirely different matrix (*see* HOUSE); its symbolic mimetic shapes meant nothing to white settlers, and its technology was too primitive to be usefully borrowed. Even the simplest techniques employed by N America's first European settlers turn out upon investigation to be European in origin rather than indigenously borrowed; indeed, N American architecture has within the last decade or so provided evidence for survivals in Europe of early techniques previously believed to have been lost ages before settlement of N America began.

The concourse of Union Station, Toronto (Ross & Macdonald, Hugh Jones and John M. Lyle, 1915-20), shows the beaux-arts adaptation by Lyle of the vaulted hall of a Roman bath for a 20th-century gathering place (*photo ©1984 Hartill Art Associates*).

What appeared in NEW FRANCE was a typically colonial architecture. Composed almost totally of medieval and baroque forms and techniques familiar from the homeland, which thus served as instruments to transplant that culture to the New World, this architecture only gradually and to a surprisingly small degree adapted to the new land's particular climatic conditions. The typical Québecois house was the farmhouse of Normandy, Maine or Anjou, the provinces of origin of most of New France's earliest settlers. Examples are the Heureux house at Charlesbourg, the Athanase Denis house at Neuville, or the Marcotte house at Cap Santé. Church and palace architecture, eg, the Basilica or Jesuit Church in Québec City or the Château de Vaudreuil in Montréal (now gone or totally altered, but known from photos and drawings), was only minimally adapted to the New World, and more by necessity than choice, in that ornament was less elegant and abundant, symmetry less rigorous and scale smaller, corresponding to the colony's generally limited resources.

Only 2 basic building types from the Old Regime in New France survived the Conquest of 1759-60: the parish church and the peasant homestead. Associations from the Old Regime attaching to these forms made them visual metaphors of, and hence instruments to promote, Québecois *survivance* in the face of successive waves of English-speaking immigrants. Thus, a standardized type of church loosely modelled on the parish churches of Bishop Laval's 17th-century seigneuries gave both visual and social focus to more than 30 communities in the Montréal area from 1800 to 1840, stamping them as "French." A corresponding number appeared in the Québec City area; as refined and developed in the French classical tradition by Thomas BAILLAIRGÉ, protegé of Jérôme DEMERS, vicar-general of Québec, they came to represent one of the great lasting accomplishments of Canadian arts. The church-type so established in the early 19th century continued to serve as an instrument promoting French survival in variant but readily recognizable forms well into the 20th century, not only in Québec but wherever French-speaking Canadians went, in northern Ontario, Manitoba, Saskatchewan, northern NB and northern Québec (*see* RELIGIOUS BUILDING).

The British element in Canadian life was represented in the first half of the 19th century by elaborate edifices in a rather old-fashioned British style, which was perpetuated until the mid-19th century. Victoria Hall in Cobourg, of huge size for this small town, was dedicated by the Prince of Wales (the future Edward VII) in 1860 (*courtesy Parks Canada/Heritage Recording Service*).

The Québecois house-type continued to be built, generation after generation, in ever-increasing numbers for an ever-increasing population. Its materials varied from stone to timber; it sometimes had a porch and sometimes not; it could be small (the Laurier "birthplace" at St-Lin) or large (Symmes Inn, Aylmer), but its basic proportions and distinctive shapes remained recognizable. Later house-types, such as the flat-topped duplex with outside staircases lining Montréal and Québec City streets and reproduced extensively in expansion towns of the 1890-1920 period in St-Jérôme or Joliette, never entirely displaced it. Today, the popular/commercial "Maison du patriote" continues the tradition.

Following the change in administration in 1763, a number of British administrators, officers and merchant-adventurers settled in the colony, followed 20 years later by streams of dispossessed LOYALISTS from the newly independent American colonies. In the depressed post-Waterloo decades wave upon wave of Britons arrived to populate the English-speaking provinces of Upper Canada and NB, to complete the anglicization of NS and PEI, and create a large English minority in Lower Canada. As French Canadian culture stressed its French and Catholic origins, English Canada manifested an admiration for British institutions — a dependence clearly revealed in architecture.

Immigrants from the old British colonies in N America brought with them the Georgian style of 18th-century America, an architecture influenced by the classical tradition. NIAGARA-ON-THE-LAKE and Queenston show plentiful examples built in wood or stone, as does the old Bath road from Cataraqui to Picton; older Canadian cities have isolated examples, eg, the Campbell house in Toronto or the MacMartin house in Perth. Newer immigrants who began arriving directly from Britain in the 1820s built in the Georgian style of their homeland, commonly in stone, with heavier proportions that gave old Loyalist towns (Kingston, Prescott, Brockville, Halifax) distinctive streets of cutstone Georgian façades. Local builders quickly fused the 2 types. This style, marked by symmetry and order, can be seen in PROVINCE HOUSE, Halifax, and the Colonial Building, St John's; courthouses in Napanee and Brockville, Kingston and Saint John; city halls in Perth, Kingston and Sandwich (*see* KINGSTON CITY HALL); and in commercial complexes like the ST LAWRENCE HALL in Toronto, Bonsecours Market in Montréal and Victoria Hall in Cobourg. In contrast to the US, where public and commercial buildings in Georgian style had acquired distasteful connotations of colonialism and had been superseded by Roman and Greek classical temple-styles, in English Canada in 1850 the symbolism of Georgian was still valid and the style alive. Vestigial traces of this "First British Empire" style can be discovered in houses and public buildings of the Canadian West as late as the 1920s, as in the Court House at Nicola, BC.

Revivals of Gothic and other medieval styles (Elizabethan, Tudor) began to appear in Canada early in the 19th century. Broadly speaking, the connotations of this style were continuity of traditions (church, state), as contrasted to revolutionary breaks with the past fostered by the French and American revolutions and proclaimed in French and American classical revivals. In Britain, castles built in Gothic to proclaim hereditary family roots appeared from the 1770s on; Windsor Castle was refurbished after 1815 as a memorial to Waterloo and the concomitant survival of the British monarchy; in the 1830s London's Westminster New Palace (Houses of Parliament) was swathed in Gothic forms which imaged the historical authentication and vindication of English parliamentary government. It was the Gothic revival in France that came first to Canada, in the form of the 1823-29 rebuilding of NOTRE-DAME, the original (1722) parish church of Montréal. Why Gothic was chosen for this huge church (for long the largest Gothic church in N America) has been much disputed; but certainly a major factor was the contemporary revival of Gothic in France to proclaim the restoration of French traditions of monarchy and Catholicism, exemplified by the restored Bourbons' tombs and completion of Ste-Croix Cathedral (1230, destroyed 1568, rebuilding began 1601, completed 1823-29) in Orléans. In English Canada the Gothic revival appeared in houses such as Chief Justice Boulton's "Holland House" in Toronto, which proclaimed British loyalties via a central section emulating Windsor Castle's huge crenellated keep-tower, a tradition climaxed in 1911 by Sir Henry PELLATT's evocation of Balmoral in Casa Loma (Toronto). In the PARLIAMENT BUILDINGS in Ottawa, the picturesque spires, pinnacles, pointed arches and textured walls of the Gothic revival style proclaimed the continuity of British institutions from medieval to modern times, in Canada as in Britain. No other provincial parliament building followed the Ottawa example (in striking contrast to the US where almost all 50 state capitols are recognizable variants of the federal capitol in Washington), perhaps a metaphor of FEDERAL-PROVINCIAL RELATIONS in Canada.

After the mid-19th century, Gothic *per se* was often mixed with elements of other picturesque styles, a process initiated in the remarkable main building of U of T (UNIVERSITY COLLEGE) and perpetuated in many customs houses and post offices sporting French Second Empire mansards, Italianate pediments or Tudor half-timberings.

Distinctively Canadian too are the patterned brick Ontario farmhouses and their row-house counterparts in Ontario cities built from the 1860s into the 1880s; though not consistently Gothic Revival in detail (many round-headed windows, Italianate pediments, Second French Empire mansards), they were fundamentally Gothic Revival in spirit, revealing continuity with the Old Country (especially Scotland and Ulster) in their verticality, textural variety and assymmetry. Variants of the type, most commonly in wood, appear in other English-speaking provinces. Towards the end of the 19th century these house-styles were superseded in popularity by a picturesque Tudor style favoured for suburban building, 1900-30; Westmount, Montréal; Rosedale, Toronto; Shaughnessy, Vancouver; and Mount Royal, Calgary, all have fine examples, but the finest appear in Oak Bay, Victoria, created by Samuel MACLURE. In due course medieval styles filtered down to middle- and lower-class levels, and they survive in popular/commercial speculative building.

Gothic Revival churches flourished in Canada's 19th-century cultural climate, and each major denomination developed distinctive variants. Anglican churches expressed British ties either by ostentatious correctness (the strict ecclesiological cathedrals in St John's and Fredericton, *see* CHRIST CHURCH CATHEDRAL) or "British atmosphere" (from the brass-plaque-studded walls of St James' Cathedral, Toronto, or Christ Church, Montréal, to the tiny "rustic Gothic" churches of the Gulf Islands or Prairies, to the

Up to the 1950s, anglophone Canadians generally tended to find their identity, as distinct from Americans, in belonging to the British Empire. That feeling climaxed in the 1900-20 period, and to that time belong major Canadian buildings in revived Roman style, like this Alberta Legislature Building in Edmonton. The British Empire was often favourably likened to the Roman, as a civilizing influence (*courtesy Public Affairs Bureau, Government of Alberta*).

For many years the dominant element on the landscape of the Canadian prairies was supplied by the railways which, in a real sense, created Canada: water tanks, stations, grain elevators. A typical complex is seen here at Glaslyn, Sask (*courtesy National Images of North America, Washington, DC*).

inventive wooden Gothic of the Maritimes). Also to be noted is the distinctive Gothic style introduced by the Presbyterian Church in Canada. This denomination was often, in Ontario at least, the biggest in town and built bold, inventively designed exteriors (Centre Presbyterian, Brockville) and interiors with dramatic space mouldings, curving balconies and pews, and unique abstract geometric windows, thereby belying the popular association of Scottish Presbyterianism with an austere indifference to aesthetic concerns.

Canada's famous chateau-style hotels were basically Gothic revival in spirit and frequently in specific forms as well, as in the dining room and library of the Empress Hotel in Victoria. Their Gothic was polished with academic allusions both to Scottish castles and to French châteaux on the Loire, eg, the Château Frontenac in Québec City, the Château Laurier in Ottawa, the Fort Garry in Winnipeg and the Bessborough in Saskatoon (*see* HOTEL).

Between 1890 and 1914 the British Empire became more self-consciously imperial than before — a development which tended to be exaggerated in Canada because it was as members of the British Empire that English-speaking Canadians identified themselves *vis-à-vis* Americans. Visible manifestation of this self-consciousness came in an academic (ie, correct) revival of Imperial Roman (2nd-4th centuries AD) architectural style; patriotic Britons thought of themselves as latter-day Romans gone forth to civilize the natives of rude regions of the earth, as Rome had civilized Gaul, Spain and Britain. A similar sense of mission, though with a lesser element of self-identification, possessed Americans and British at this time; grandiose buildings in Imperial Roman (or beaux-arts, "City Beautiful" — there are many names) rose everywhere in Anglo-American cities. Canada's principal representatives of this style are the legislature buildings of the Prairie provinces (mainly first decade 20th century, *see* GOVERNMENT BUILDING); Toronto's and Vancouver's RAILWAY STATIONS from the century's second decade (they belong to the "Columbian Exposition" family of Roman-bath city monuments that included stations in Washington, New York, Philadelphia, St Louis); BANKS in the classical temple-style introduced early in the 19th century in the US, now built in a much grander and archaeologically more correct manner (eg, Bank of Montreal at Portage and Main in Winnipeg, by the premier American firm of McKim, Mead & White, 1913; Bank of Nova Scotia on Sparks St in Ottawa, 1924; Bank of Nova Scotia in Halifax by John LYLE, 1929, a pioneer in introducing Canadian ornament to architecture); and that plethora of monuments to the Great War of 1914-18, most of them in recognizable vestiges of "Imperial Bombast" style (as academic Roman has been well called in such contexts), which are one of the most melancholy yet distinctive features of Canadian cityscapes ("died for the Empire" is their most common inscription).

These many different expressions were overwhelmed by the wave of modernism that swept across Western architecture after 1945, to remain unchallenged until the late 1970s. Modernism being by definition not a style but a way of building that is universally and eternally valid, it tended to obliterate regional and national traditions. What distinguished modernism in Canada was a utopianism more unrestrained than elsewhere. Without carrying much of the burden of its own defence, and freer of economic problems than most other countries, Canada provided ideal nourishment for the utopianism that was everywhere latent in modernism. Utopian faith in universities as agents to promote human perfectibility has rarely been so effectively imaged as in BC's SIMON FRASER U (Arthur ERICKSON) or Toronto's Scarborough College (John Andrews), both designs winning international awards. Nor has the idea of culture being something you can create through art ever been more effectively expressed than in the veritable efflorescence of theatre complexes in Canada of the 1960s, the GRAND THÉATRE in Québec City, Confederation Centre in Charlottetown, or the NATIONAL ARTS CENTRE in Ottawa.

Not the least interesting aspect of modernism in Canada is the way its formal evolution has followed a general pattern set in the US and Europe at about a 10-year lag. International-style Bauhaus modernism, introduced in the US in the late 1930s, appeared first in Canadian architecture schools (U of T) in the late 1940s, brought back from Harvard by Toronto students including John C. PARKIN; thence it spread across Canada in the early 1950s. Plastic and brute styles of modernism appearing in Europe in the late 1950s (eg, Corbusier's Ronchamp, reviving Mendelsohn's 1920s moulded concrete) became popular in Canada in the late 1960s (eg, Douglas CARDINAL'S ST MARY'S CHURCH in Red Deer, Alta, 1968; Moshe Safdie's "Habitat" at EXPO 67). The multiple glass box popular in the US in the early 1960s had its notable Canadian realizations in the 1970s (eg, Erickson's Bank of Canada headquarters in Ottawa (1979) and Robson Square Law Courts in Vancouver, 1979). The stark technocratic style of the late 1960s in Europe appeared in Canada in the 1970s (eg, McMaster Health Science Centre, Hamilton, by ZEIDLER Partnership, 1972). Obviously this pattern is a cultural expression, reflecting the national psyche. The dominant and controlling element in Canadian society has from the beginning been cautious and nonexperimental when confronted with new ideas — whether those ideas were early 19th-century British conservatism, late 19th-century British liberalism, or 20th-century European modernism. If one had to cite a single area of modern architecture of consistently high quality it would have to be churches. Some modern churches in Canada have received wide publicity, eg, Étienne GABOURY'S Precious Blood Church in St Boniface, Man (1968), but at least equally satisfactory is his parish church of St Claude in Manitoba (1961) that is rarely mentioned. There are literally dozens of churches that deserve far more attention than they get, such as the cathédrale/presbytère/évêché complex in Nicolet, Qué (Gérard Malouin, 1961). *See also* ARCHITECTURAL STYLES; ARCHITECTURE, DEVELOPMENT. ALAN GOWANS

Reading: C. Ede, *Canadian Architecture 1960-1970* (1971); Alan Gowans, *Building Canada* (1966); L. Whiteson, *Modern Canadian Architecture* (1983).

Architecture, Development ARCHITECTURE, a consciously intellectual and aesthetic activity, and utilitarian building are both shaped by the materials, technology, money and time available to the designer; the particular activities to be housed; the climate to be tempered; the organization of design and construction; and the ideas about appropriate form held at the time. All these factors have varied significantly through the nearly 4 centuries of European settlement in Canada.

1000-1700 The earliest European buildings so far traced in Canada are simple, crude constructions similar in technique to the stone, earth and timber dwellings of some NATIVE PEOPLES (*see* HOUSE). It is generally accepted that the remains at L'ANSE AUX MEADOWS in Newfoundland are those of an early 11th-century settlement by a small group of Norse adventurers who lived a communal, nearly tribal life crowded together in a few great houses. The buildings were roughly built of logs and stone, with roofs thatched with branches and reeds. Open fires on the beaten earth floors of the houses gave what heat there was, the smoke finding its way out through the textured thatch. In the wake of the Vikings came BASQUES and British seamen who regularly crossed the Atlantic to fish the Grand Banks, and who established homes and villages on the Newfoundland coast. No buildings survive from these settlements, but contemporary illustrations of French settlements in the Atlantic region show low structures built of sod and of upright posts planted in the ground.

New France In the early 17th century French navigators, merchants and missionaries, following Samuel de CHAMPLAIN, established 2 permanent spheres of influence in Canada: on lands known as Acadia on the Bay of Fundy, and in the settlements on the N shore of the St Lawrence that became Montréal and Québec City. Champlain's first buildings in Québec were gable-roofed timber constructions, joined by a gallery at the second level, and protected by a moat and a wall with pointed bastions where cannon were placed. The habitation at PORT-ROYAL was similar.

The French were the first Europeans to plant their culture in Canada, a transatlantic exten-

Ste-Famille, Ile d'Orléans, Qué (1743-49, clochers added in 1809 and 1843). More monumental than earlier parish churches, with towers and niches for sculpture, it has the usual steeply pitched roof, bell-cast gables, and combination of rough and finely dressed stonework (*photo by John deVisser*).

sion of metropolitan France that comprised social organization, economy, religion, art and architecture. The establishment of a full panoply of governmental and religious institutions in Québec City and, to a lesser extent, Montréal meant that occasionally high-style buildings, such as the Archbishop's Palace (Claude Baillif, 1692) or Notre-Dame Cathedral (Claude Baillif, 1684-97) in Québec City, were erected in a simplified version of the currently popular French baroque taste. The palace was built in rendered stone with a curved baroque gable to the chapel. The reredos, described by a contemporary, Bacqueville de La Potherie, as a simplified version of that at Val-de-Grace Church, rivalled the beauty of palaces in France. The vast majority of the population was agricultural, settled along the St Lawrence on narrow, long strips of land; the settlers required simple utilitarian structures to shelter them from the harsh climate (*see* SEIGNEURIAL SYSTEM). Plain rural churches were built of rubble masonry, with perhaps cut-stone trim around doors and windows, and protected from moisture by a white stucco rendering called *crépi* (St François Church, Île d'Orléans). Farm houses, though sometimes built of stone, most often were made from wood, either solid log or heavy wooden frame filled with stone called *colombage pierroté* and increasingly of wood-filled frame (*pièces-sur-pièces*). Like their counterparts in France, these early farmhouses had low walls, steep roofs (covered with shingles, boards or thatch), small casement windows, and few interior partitions (eg, maison Girardin, Beauport). The problems of survival imposed by the severity of the climate in NEW FRANCE left little opportunity for elaborate decoration.

Severed politically from France by the British conquest of 1759-60, and isolated from European revolutionary upheavals, the original New France culture flourished. The remarkably conservative building traditions of New France — where methods and styles brought from the mother country were repeated with only slight modifications — endured until the end of the 18th century. Though British and US developments began to make inroads in the 19th century, French Canadian traditions persisted into the 20th century in 3 characteristically Québecois architectural types: the church, seigneurial manor and rural house (*see* RELIGIOUS BUILDING). Québec churches retained their vaguely Louis XVI design and decorative schemes until well into the century. The house form gradually adapted itself to the Québec climate through such changes as the raised ground storey (to allow for snow accumulations), multiple chimneys and dormers, and the extension of the bell-cast eaves (intended to keep moisture off the walls) to become the roof of the cantilevered, picturesquely carved verandah.

Manoir Mauvide Genst, St-Jean, Ile d'Orléans, Qué, 1743. A substantial low-ceilinged timber-beamed stone house built by the royal surgeon, Jean Mauvide (*photo by M. McMordie*).

British and Loyalist Building British colonization of the Canadian territories began on the Atlantic coast late in the 17th century from both England and the American colonies, followed by LOYALIST settlement after 1776 from the East Coast through Québec into present-day Ontario. In the early 19th century UPPER CANADA became the recipient of large numbers of US immigrants. The British immigrants brought their direct experience of Georgian, then, later, Victorian architecture from the British Isles, while those arriving in Canada from the US brought their experience of the adapted Georgian or "federal" architecture.

Both groups had a desire to reproduce familiar surroundings in what was often, particularly for the European immigrants, a harsh and unfamiliar setting. Their neat, rectangular buildings of stone, timber or brick had at least a superficial symmetry and the carefully proportioned sash windows of the Georgian originals. Depending on the availability of money, skills and materials, structures such as the Matheson House (Perth, Ont, 1840), PROVINCE HOUSE (Halifax, John Merrick?, 1811-18), and St Paul's Church (Halifax, 1750) carried the classical detail of the prototypes — the columns or pilasters, decorative friezes, Palladian windows and other trimmings whose origins went back from Georgian England to the Florentine Renaissance and beyond to the ancient architecture of Greece and Rome.

In Halifax, Georgian England had a direct presence, even to the Palladian-influenced country estate the duke of Kent laid out at Bedford Basin at the end of the 18th century. Its only surviving structure is the tidy, circular, white, classically ordered rotunda with its simple Tuscan columns. In Québec the new English presence was established within the matrix of French building by structures such as Holy Trinity Anglican Cathedral of Québec (by military engineers Robe and Hall, 1800-04, roof raised about 1816). The cathedral's austere Ionic pilasters and blind arches outside, vaulted ceiling and galleries raised on Ionic columns inside, must have seemed an intrusion set among the very different buildings of the Québecois tradition.

Much of the building from this early period of British settlement has gone, decayed, been demolished or, in the case of towns with flammable wooden buildings built side by side, burned in the fires that were a recurrent feature of older, timber settlements. Some of the buildings, such as the Barnum House (Grafton, Ont, about 1817) featuring a central pedimented block with flanking wings, and some of the quality of the towns — houses, streets, trees and gardens — survive. NIAGARA-ON-THE-LAKE in Ontario, eg, retains traces of the early 19th-century townscape (houses on Queen St, early 1820s).

St Paul's Anglican Church, Halifax, NS (1750, extensively altered 1812). Based on the Palladian church designs of English architect James Gibbs, it was built from a frame fabricated in New England (*photo by Sherman Hines/Masterfile*).

Some buildings from this period have been reassembled in museum villages such as UPPER CANADA VILLAGE in Ontario or KING'S LANDING in NB.

In Britain architecture became greatly enriched in the early Victorian period, when lively irregularity became more fashionable than regular and restrained Georgian. The early 19th century is the period of the picturesque, of Gothic revival and neoclassicism as well as a variety of other ARCHITECTURAL STYLES retrieved from the remote corners of architectural history and geography. Both Gothic revival and Neoclassical were important styles in Canada through the mid-19th century. The classical style was now represented by direct recreation of ancient Greek and Roman features, on the Bank of Montreal, Montréal (John Wells, 1846-48) and the simpler, baseless Doric of St Andrew's Presbyterian Church, Niagara-on-the-Lake (Cooper, 1831).

Competing with classicism, particularly in the Ottawa PARLIAMENT BUILDINGS and the Anglican churches for which it had become the preferred style in England, was revived Gothic: the architecture of pointed arches, ribbed vaults and flying buttresses that seized the imagination of some theorists of church architecture. Examples are CHRIST CHURCH CATHEDRAL of Fredericton NB (William Butterfield and Frank Wills 1846-53) and the Cathedral of St John the Baptist in St John's, Nfld (George Gilbert Scott, from 1846), both designed by leading English architects. Along with this elaborated Gothic inspired by the great cathedrals and parish churches of medieval England came a renewed interest in the more modest traditional architecture of the English countryside, from which came the steep pitched gables and the decorated bargeboards which could be found both in elaborate public buildings and in ordinary town and country houses.

As the 19th century advanced, these changes in the taste and style of building were encouraged and propagated by even more profound social changes: increased population, improved agriculture and industry, in both Europe and the New World. The harnessing of steam power and the new and sophisticated exploitation of such old materials as cast and wrought iron

Ioly Trinity Anglican Cathedral, Québec City (Hall and Robe, 1800-04). The first Anglican cathedral built outide the British Isles, it was designed by two army offiers in a simplified Palladian style inspired by James Gibbs's St Martin-in-the-Fields, London (*photo © Hartill Art Associates*).

ccelerated the changes in the way people lived. team-powered transportation on land and at ea encouraged the concentration of people and ndustry, and began to make practicable extenive factories, cities and even large-scale agriculure. In Canada these developments were exmplified by Montréal, Toronto and Hamilton, vith industrial complexes like the Massey-Iarris agricultural machinery factories in Toonto (from 1879). Cast-iron building componts became commonplace. Developments in ron-framed construction reached their symolic culmination in the Crystal Palace in London (1851), which spawned a generation of rystal palaces around the world, including Toronto and Montréal (the Toronto example was designed by Sir Sandford FLEMING and Sir Collingwood Schreiber, 1858; then altered and moved to Exhibition Park, 1879). In the 1850s New York entrepreneurs created and distributed prefabricated cast-iron storefronts, one of which still stands at the Coombs store on Granville St, Halifax. In Victoria, BC, mid and late 19th-century cast-iron facades survive from both San Francisco and local iron foundries.

1867-1918 As INDUSTRIALIZATION advanced, new kinds of buildings appeared to serve the ndustrial and commercial economies — factory buildings and warehouses, RAILWAY STATIONS, HOTELS, office buildings. The most spectacular development was the high office building. Its first Canadian appearance in Montréal and Toronto depended on newly developed solutions to the problems of tall construction, vertical transportation and fire protection. High buildings in masonry (in brick or stone) required immensely thick supporting walls at the lower levels as the superimposed load of the high structure increased. The street level, however, was the most desirable for commercial purposes and commanded the highest rents. Stronger, and yet more slender metal-frame structures offered obvious advantages, but the iron that had been used through the middle of the century was brittle and unsuitable for structures that had to give with slight movements induced by wind and settling. Cast-iron columns and beams had to be cast to final shape before erection and could not be adjusted on the building site. Both these problems were eliminated as structural steel became available through the 1860s. Strong in bending as well as under compression, steel had the necessary elasticity and could be altered to accommodate changes or errors in the building design. The Temple Building (Bay and Richmond Sts, designed by George W. Gouinlock, 1895) was one of the last tall office buildings in Toronto to have a cast-iron frame. Iron and steel, however, were both vulnerable to the heat of building fires. The answer was found with the enclosure of the exposed steel structure within thick masonry or a surface of plaster, to insulate the steel long enough to permit the fire in a burning building to be controlled. An early example with a structural steel skeleton was the old Board of Trade Building (Yonge and Front Streets, Toronto, designed by James and James of New York, 1889).

Finally, with the invention of the Otis elevator (1856), buildings could exceed the walk-up height limit of 4-6 storeys. The New York Life Insurance Co Building on the Place d'Armes, Montréal (Babb, Cook and Willard, 1887), 8 storeys, was described as the first Montréal skyscraper. Equity Chambers (Adelaide and Victoria Streets, Toronto, 1878, demolished 1960s), 5 storeys, was described as "the first business block in the city to introduce the elevator." These developments were combined in such early fireproofed steel-framed buildings as the Robert Simpson Co store on Yonge St in Toronto, a rebuilding in 1895 of the store opened in 1894 and destroyed by fire. The second time the steel columns and beams were encased in concrete, and fire-resistant floor construction was used. Another early fireproofed steel frame was used for the Federal Building in Vancouver, 1905-10 (701 West Hastings St) designed by the Dept of Public Works. Similarly, reinforced concrete became a useful material for large-scale buildings from the end of the century (60 Front St W, about 1900, was said to be the first in Toronto), not only for framed structures but also for dams and for buildings with structural walls such as silos. Grain elevators in Montréal, Toronto, Port Arthur and Calgary were an inspiration to the Europeans Walter Gropius and Le Corbusier.

Corinthian capital of a cast-iron shopfront on Wharf St, Victoria, BC, 1861-85. Elaborate forms developed in stone could be reproduced cheaply using prefabricated cast-iron elements (*photo by M. McMordie*).

At the same time, the technological revolution in the construction of ordinary wood buildings affected the fabric of every town, village and large urban centre. Traditional construction of preindustrial buildings was either completely in timber frame or a combination of load-bearing brick or stone with heavy timber beams. Two inventions of the early 19th century, economical machine-made nails and light machine-sawn timbers, revolutionized building in wood, and led to a system called "balloon framing." It was fast, economical, flexible and extremely efficient, providing great strength with economy of material. The strength came from the combination of frame with the wood sheathing that covered it. Cladding could be wood, brick or stone, though these were no longer a necessary part of the building structure but merely an exterior surface resisting the weather and giving an attractive appearance. This industrially based framing replaced the older braced timber frame of the eastern settlements as the ordinary construction of late 19th- and 20th-century Canada. It spread across the West, leaving expensive and prestigious solid stone and brick construction for the more elaborate buildings.

In contrast to the long architectural tradition in eastern and central Canada, the architecture of the West was just beginning as the 19th century closed. The exceptions were the forts and trading posts of the FUR TRADE and the first planted settlements on Vancouver I and the RED RIVER COLONY. Usually built in horizontal logs or the so-called Red River Frame (vertical posts grooved to receive tongued horizontal logs, an earlier Québec technique called *pièces-sur-pièces*), and occasionally in stone, examples can be seen at LOWER FORT GARRY, nucleus of the settlement (1830s-50s), and FORT LANGLEY (completed 1841). Otherwise the settlement and the architecture of the West belong to the industrial era. This is particularly true of the ordinary buildings of the farms, towns and cities, where machine-sawn lumber, prefabricated ornament and decoration chosen from the mail-order catalogues offered the cheapest and often the best way to build.

A recurrent theme of western Canadian architecture is the contrast between local buildings, modest and relatively unsophisticated, and those of eastern interests, the branch BANKS and branch stores (the Hudson's Bay Co or Birks) designed usually by Toronto or Montréal architects according to prevailing international standards. The most striking example was the château-style railway hotels, originating with the Banff Springs Hotel designed by the CPR's Boston architect, Bruce Price (1888). They are variously described as medieval French, Québecois, Edwardian, Scottish and beaux-arts classical in inspiration, but all capped by the steeply pitched roofs, often with multiple dormers that suggest a romantic retreat. The effect is most successful at Banff in its wild mountain setting, and most fully developed at Château Frontenac on Cap Diamant overlooking the St Lawrence R (1892-1920).

Another feature of western Canadian architecture was its variety, arising from the diversity of the population. Whereas settlement in the East up to Confederation had been British or French in origin, the open territory of the West attracted settlers from northern Europe, Russia, Ukraine, Germany, Scandinavia, Iceland and China. Each group brought its distinctive traditions, tastes and skills, expressed in buildings ranging from the thatched and stuccoed Ukrainian houses to the striking domed and towered churches of the Orthodox religious traditions (ELK ISLAND NATIONAL PARK and Ukrainian Cultural Heritage Village, Alberta) to the detail and ornament of Chinatown buildings everywhere (especially in downtown Vancouver).

The formation of the province of Manitoba in

1870, the extension of Confederation to include BC in 1871, and the creation of new provinces in Saskatchewan and Alberta in 1905 created occasions for the most elaborate early buildings of the West, the provincial parliament buildings (*see* GOVERNMENT BUILDING). The BC legislature building was designed by Francis Mawson RATTENBURY in what he called a "free classical style" (1893-97, 1912-16), while the Saskatchewan building is an American beaux-arts version of English baroque by the Montréal firm Edward and William S. Maxwell (completion 1908-12).

In the 1890s outstanding American architects had an impact on the design of the central structures in the growing cities of Canada. H.H. Richardson influenced E.J. Lennox's design of the Toronto City Hall (1890), and Louis Sullivan and the "Chicago School" the early skyscrapers, the Grain Exchange, Calgary (1909) and the Tegler building, Edmonton (H.A. Magoon, 1911). As well, the influence of the British arts and crafts movement inspired architects across the country from Eden Smith in Toronto to Samuel MACLURE in Victoria. By the First World War, however, the example of such outstanding original figures as Frank Lloyd Wright of the United States, Charles Rennie Macintosh of Scotland and Peter Behrens of Germany had made little impact on Canadian architecture. Wright's close associate, Francis C. Sullivan, followed his lead with a few innovative buildings around Ottawa, and in the Montréal suburb of Maisonneuve, Wright's example also influenced such remarkable buildings as the Recorder's Court (1913).

Many important commissions in Canada were won by American architects or by immigrant Britons. This competition became an incentive to Canadians to institute more formal and sophisticated arrangements for the education of architects (the first professorship was created in the School of Practical Science in Toronto in 1890 and the first full department at McGill in 1896) and to organize the profession with legislative authority. The Ontario Assn of Architects was established in 1889 and the Province of Quebec Assn of Architects in 1890, followed by other provincial associations. In 1907 these associations formed a national organization which in 1909 became the Royal Architectural Institute of Canada (*see* ARCHITECTURAL PRACTICE).

1918-39 In architecture, the period between the wars was one of experiment and innovation as designers in Europe and America responded to the challenge of new building technology and to the sense of living in a new age of machinery, electricity, rapid travel and communication. Walter Gropius's Bauhaus buildings in Dessau, Germany (1925-26), and Le Corbusier's Villa Savoie in France (1929-30) became the touchstones of the new international style. The core of both Chicago and New York underwent an amazing high-rise development. The new design style, art deco, and technological "streamlining" began popular fashions in decoration. In Canada, however, clients and the profession remained generally conservative in their tastes. The Toronto architect John LYLE modified the classical forms of established beaux-arts architecture to create more up-to-date art deco ornament in such buildings as his Bank of Nova Scotia branch in Calgary (1930), and, in response to growing national pride, incorporated decorative motifs drawn from the region: ranchers and cattle, wheat and the derricks of the oil industry. Percy NOBBS, who came from Britain to head McGill's architecture school in 1903, worked across the country with fine buildings from Montréal to Edmonton (campus plan, early buildings for U of Alberta), as did many other Montréal architects. Darling and Pearson's head office building for the Canadian Bank of Commerce

The entrance arch and elevator lobby of McCarter and Nairne's Marine Building, Vancouver (1929-30), displays the rich form and colour possible with terra-cotta decoration in the art-deco style (*photo by M. McMordie*).

in Toronto (1929-31) was the finest of the skyscrapers and for several decades the tallest building in the Commonwealth. Its symmetrical, stepped back tower contrasted plain limestone surfaces with rich Romanesque detail. The Marine Building in Vancouver (McCarter and Nairne, 1929-30) was a splendidly decorated exercise in art deco, built in brick and stone with terra cotta reliefs of contemporary transportation. A major practitioner, the Paris-trained Montréal architect Ernest CORMIER, designed the main block at U de Montréal (1924-42) and the Supreme Court, Ottawa (1938-39, the château-style roof at PM Mackenzie King's insistence). Perhaps the finest example of art deco is Cormier's own home, with boldly abstract forms in stone terrazzo and plaster (1418 Pine Avenue, Montréal, 1930-31).

The first signs of a wholehearted move in Canada to adopt European and US modernism in architecture came with slow economic recovery from the mid-1930s and particularly in the years after WWII. Swiss immigrant Robert Blatter and Québec-born Marcel Parizeau designed the first international-style houses. In the late 1930s Peter Thornton, Robert Berwick and C.E. Pratt (later THOMPSON, BERWICK, PRATT AND PARTNERS) set up practices in Vancouver, and John B. PARKIN (later joined by the younger, unrelated, John C. PARKIN) in Toronto. These architects were significant as representatives of a new generation who contributed to the gradual eclipse of design based on historical styles in favour of an architecture of abstract form, exposed structure and plain materials (often glass, steel or aluminum, concrete, sometimes stone, tile or wood) used without decorative enrichment and with a stern simplicity of treatment.

1940-84 The war years saw a significant demand for utilitarian buildings, economical and efficient construction, and so promoted the ideals and technology in which the mainstream of modern architecture was based. In Canada, it was in industrial buildings that the new technology was first employed, and the need for the rapid erection of a large number of structures, eg, aircraft hangers, encouraged an innovative approach to design and construction. A government agency, Wartime Housing Ltd, constructed a distinctive, simple, standardized housing for workers in defence-related industries.

After 1945 Canada began to respond to th new architecture of the 1920s and 1930s. Th return of service people and a surge in the fo mation of new families created great oppo tunities for architectural development. Housin was needed and Wartime Housing Ltd was r placed by Central Mortgage and Housing Co poration (*see* CANADA MORTGAGE AND HOUSING CO PORATION) in 1946. As the children of th postwar BABY BOOM reached school age they cr ated a demand for schools that followe through in successive waves of building el mentary schools, secondary schools, technica colleges, community colleges and universities.

While traditional historical architecture co tinued to be designed and built, particularly b older architects before the war, a new generatio of younger architects (Parkin, Berwick, Prat Thornton), believed that the appropriate way t build was in the directions established by th leaders of modernism. These Canadian innova tors were increasingly successful in persuadin school boards, government departments, indus trialists and other important clients to trust the vision of architecture as simple, efficient, ad vanced in construction and services, and fre of all historical styles. This vision was to b supported with a new level of technical com petence. One of the leading architectural firm John B. Parkin Associates, sought to bring a the skills and technical knowledge togethe under one roof as part of a comprehensive, co porate design firm which could offer everythin from structural and mechanical engineerin architectural design, detailing and supervisio through to design of interiors, landscape and th design of the signs required for a new buildin (Aeroquay, Lester B. Pearson Airport, Toront 1957-65). This view of design as a comprehen sive professional service which covered ever aspect of the building, its setting and its furnish ing, was pursued by many other firms in collab oration with sympathetic consultants.

New architects rose to prominence and som older firms gained new vigour. In Vancouve the leaders were Thompson, Berwick and Prat Gardiner and Thornton; and McCarter, Nairn In Winnipeg a distinguished group include Moody, Moore and Partners; Green, Blankste and Russell; and Smith, Carter and Searle. I Toronto, among a number of others, the Parki firm achieved the greatest prominence nation ally and internationally. John BLAND, for man years head of McGill University School of Ar chitecture, also distinguished himself in practic in Montréal, as did a younger group, Affleck Desbarats, Dimakopoulos, Lebensold, Sise. A host of younger, smaller firms followed an architects such as Barry DOWNS in Vancouve Douglas CARDINAL in Edmonton, Clifford WIEN in Regina, Étienne GABOURY in Winnipeg, an Roger D'Astous in Montréal established them selves as outstanding figures. The 1950s an 1960s became a period of great architectural ex citement.

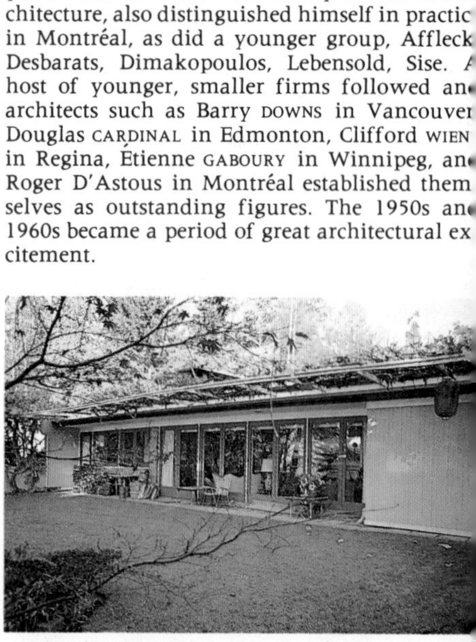

Among the pioneers of modern architecture was B.C Binning, better known as a graphic artist. He designed number of houses including his own (above), built i West Vancouver *c* 1940 (*photo by M. McMordie*).

International Recognition The postwar growth ' architecture in Canada was marked by the ıilding of a number of major structures, many ıe result of ARCHITECTURAL COMPETITIONS and vards. Among the early triumphs of modern ·sign was the choice of the John B. Parkin firm › design the new headquarters building for the ntario Assn of Architects (1954). Other mile- one structures included the Ottawa City Hall / Rother, Bland and Trudeau (1958); the BC ectric Building (now BC Hydro) in Vancouver / Thompson, Berwick and Pratt (1955-57); ıd the new TORONTO CITY HALL designed by the nnish architect, Viljo Revell, and carried out ı association with the Parkin firm (opened)65). Arthur ERICKSON and Geoffrey Massey 'on the commission for the new SIMON FRASER in Burnaby, BC (1963-65). Ron THOM, after a ıstinguished career in Vancouver, moved to)ronto, establishing an independent practice 'ith such buildings as MASSEY COLLEGE at U of (1963), Shaw Festival Theatre, Niagara-on- ıe-Lake (1978), and TRENT U, Peterborough 963-71). Through the 1950s and 1960s many ınadian architects were recognized in the in- rnational architectural press and began to gain ›mmissions that carried their work overseas.

EXPO 67 merits particular attention for its ar- ıitecture. The contribution of Canadian archi- ·cts was multiple and significant; individually : in groups they designed or supervised the)nstruction of the national and corporate pavi- ons but made their mark most obviously with ıe design of the facilities for the Canadian)vernment. Affleck, Desbarats, Dimakopoulos, ·bensold and Sise were responsible for several markable theme pavilions based on massive trahedral space frames carried out in exposed ructural steel. Erickson designed the Man ıd Health and Man and Community pavil- ›ns, lighter and more delicate in atmosphere, 'ith carefully planned landscaping and inte- ›or lighting. John Andrews was responsible for lively and attractive cluster of spaces designed › house displays by a number of developing)untries.

Architectural Education Through this same ›stwar period there was an expansion of Cana- ıan architectural education. In 1984 architec- ıral degree programs were offered in 10 Cana- ıan universities (there were just 5 in 1945), and variety of programs in architectural technol- gy and drafting was available at technical in- itutes and colleges across the country.

The pattern of architectural education has ıanged. The system established before WWII : McGill, Toronto and Manitoba was a 5-year ndergraduate program leading to the BArch egree. These programs held a traditional view ' architectural education that emphasized the esign studio (timetabled for perhaps half of a 5- or 28-hour week of programmed time) and a ·ries of technical subjects including materials ıd methods of construction, structures, acous- cs, illumination, heating, ventilating and air)nditioning, as well as varying amounts of rchitectural theory and history. Through the)60s this emphasis on technical and profes- onal education, on formal architectural de- gn, came to seem inadequate. There was an in- ·easing concern with the response of users to ıe buildings that were designed for them, and 'ith a variety of social and political issues. At of T under Peter Prangnell and at UBC under enry Elder, both English-trained architects hough Prangnell also studied at Harvard), rchitectural programs were altered to become ıuch broader in their direction, both in giving udents choice of subjects and in a strong em- hasis on social issues and personal responses ıther than on formal and technical content. ollowing US precedents, U of Manitoba created new Bachelor of Environmental Studies de- ree, common to students of architecture, INTERIOR DESIGN and LANDSCAPE ARCHITECTURE, to be followed for the architects by the professional MArch degree. Admission to the UBC architecture program was changed to require first a bachelor's degree, followed by a 3-year BArch degree. The Faculty of Environmental Design at U of Calgary, which admitted its first students in 1971, also required a first degree for admission, followed by interdisciplinary work bringing together students in architecture, urban planning and environmental science (and, more recently, INDUSTRIAL DESIGN), as well as more purely architectural work (*see* URBAN DESIGN; ZONING). The consequence of all these changes was, by the 1970s, a much more varied, experimental educational program.

Changing Patterns of Practice Along with divergent trends in design and education throughout the 1960s and 1970s came increasing variety in the ways architecture was practised and the actual design and construction of building projects. Costs, time and quality control became issues of prime importance during a period of increasing inflation and greater complexity of building functions. Traditionally an architect prepared a design which, when approved, was developed into a full set of working drawings and specifications; then a contractor was selected, often by competitive tendering, to construct the building under the architect's overall supervision. New alternatives included "package deals," "fast tracking" of constructions; and project management systems. In package deals, the building user is offered the design and construction of new facilities for a fixed sum or under some lease arrangement by an entrepreneur who might be a building contractor or simply a broker who arranges finance, site acquisition, design and construction. In fast tracking, the project designers and building contractor are selected together or in close succession at the inception of a project and construction begins on the basis of a sequential design process in which the rapid overall preliminary design of a building is followed by detailed design from the lower levels up; excavation and construction of foundations proceeds before design of the upper levels is complete. Project management involves the placing of design and construction under the overall supervision of a new group of professionals — management experts, cost accountants, professional engineers, and, in some cases, architects who undertake on behalf of the client to control the cost and scheduling of the project from beginning to end (*see* CONSTRUCTION INDUSTRY). These developments were interpreted by many architects as a challenge to their professional competence. Architects' professional associations now require further training prior to professional certification, through monitored practical experience, short courses and professional practice examinations.

Toronto Dominion Centre, Toronto (Mies van der Rohe, consultant, with John B. Parkin Associates and Bregman and Hamann, 1964-68). The success of the international modern style — severe, impersonal, highly disciplined — depends largely on proportion and detail (*photo by M. McMordie*).

Diversity in forms of practice paralleled these developments. There remained a preponderance of small firms and individual architects who continued to offer services of the traditional sort to clients who wished to alter or build private houses, smaller schools and institutional buildings, or small- to medium-sized commercial structures. Some architectural firms began to specialize, eg, in highly complex and demanding building types, particularly hospitals and health-care facilities. A small number of firms incorporated within their own organization all the design competence required to offer a comprehensive service. Most architects, however, continued to employ a variety of independent consultants, to avoid a high degree of specialization in a few types of buildings, and to work in smaller groups which allowed the senior members of the firm a greater degree of involvement in each of the firm's projects. Even within these firms, however, architects and architectural technicians emerged with specialized roles in design, drawings and specifications, project supervision, legal contracts, or management.

Present Trends Widespread allegiance to an international modern style of architecture continues, particularly for commercial buildings which are remarkably similar from country to country, regardless of distinctive historical traditions, climate, landscape and society. As well, a much greater diversity of approaches became evident in the 1960s. This variety affected the designs of new buildings and encouraged the study and conservation of older ones. Place Bonaventure, Montréal (Affleck, Desbarats, Dimakopoulos, Lebensold, Sise, 1967) signalled a new emphasis on buildings combining many different uses under one roof. The organization of the building around a large internal "atrium" space became a feature of these and other buildings, eg, EATON CENTRE, Toronto (ZEIDLER PARTNERSHIP, 1977); Metro Library, Toronto (Raymond MORIYAMA, 1977). Climate-protected pedestrian systems began to appear in Canadian cities, either below ground, as in Toronto and Montréal, or above ground, as in Calgary's Plus 15. Some architects are best known for their association with particular developments. Colin Bent of Toronto, eg, is recognized for his innovative designs for Arctic conditions (Polaris Mine Project, Little Cornwallis I, NWT, 1981). Webb, Zerafa, Menkes, Housden, based in Toronto but with offices across the country and internationally, has become the country's largest practice through the design of office and retail complexes, including the golden glazed Royal Bank Plaza, Toronto (1976) and the triangular Calgary Municipal Building (completion 1985). Zeidler Partnership, also of Toronto, again a general practice, has specialized in high technology health-science work (McMaster Health Science Centre, Hamilton, 1972; Walter C. Mackenzie Health Science Centre, Edmonton, 1982).

A new emphasis on regional and national culture, in traditional architecture, resulted in Canada in the restoration and conservation of the architecture of New France, Acadia, the British, Loyalist and American settlers, Ukrainians and similar groups. On the national level the federal government, through Parks Canada, initiated the Canadian Inventory of Historic Build-

The grand multilevel daylit interior space, as at the Eaton Centre, Toronto, revives a 19th-century building form and adapts it to the northern climate (*photo by M. McMordie*).

ing in 1970 to survey and study architecture across the country, in order to support the work of the Historic Sites and Monuments Board of Canada. A high degree of sophistication in the actual technical documentation and preservation of buildings was established. HERITAGE CANADA FOUNDATION was founded in 1973 as a publicly endowed but independent national society to promote interest, knowledge and preservation of Canada's architectural and urban heritage, and a new national society, the Society for the Study of Architecture in Canada, emerged to provide a forum and stimulus for the efforts of academics, professionals and laymen. Provincial and, in some cases, local governments moved to enact legislation and bylaws to promote HERITAGE CONSERVATION. In Montréal, the Canadian Centre for Architecture, an institution of international scope and quality devoted to the study of architecture, was founded in 1979 by architect and conservationist Phyllis Lambert. Numerous local and regional societies were reinvigorated or newly formed to promote the conservation, preservation and rehabilitation of Canada's architectural heritage, both public and private.

In design, the influence of this new wave of historical interest can be seen in the work of younger architects such as Peter Rose of Montréal, whose buildings explicitly draw upon regional traditions in design and on occasion employ elements from historical styles. There is a renewed emphasis on traditional forms, a feeling that setback and detached towers like the TD Square in Toronto or the BC Electric Building in Vancouver represent a tendency that threatens to destroy the coherence of a closely knit, lowrise city of continuous street facades contrasted with more open city squares. Both these concerns were addressed in the program written for a competition for a new city hall for Mississauga, Ont, by George Baird of U of T (1982) and evidenced in the winning scheme by J. Michael Kirkland and Edward Jones. Norman Hotson's Granville I, Vancouver (1979-), combines lively urban design and imaginative conservation in the transformation of an old industrial area into a mixed-use commercial and recreational district.

The future directions suggested by present-day trends might include the revival of older traditions, conservation of heritage buildings, concern for energy efficiency, respect for locality, promotion of traditional qualities of cities, re-establishment of the street as a place to be defined by continuous facades of moderate height and, in general, a renewed sense of urbanity in Canadian architecture.

CHRISTINA CAMERON AND MICHAEL MCMORDIE

Reading: E. Arthur, *Iron: The Story of Cast and Wrought Iron in Canada from the Seventeenth Century to the Present* (1982) and *Toronto No Mean City* (1974); A. Barratt and R. Liscombe, *Francis Rattenbury and British Columbia: Architecture and Challenge in the Imperial Age* (1983); T. Boddy, ed, *Prairie Architecture* (1980); *Canadian Architect*, 1-(1955-); *Canadian Architect and Builder*, 1-22 (1888-1908); *Canadian Heritage*, 1- (1975-); M. Carter, ed, *Early Canadian Court Houses* (1983); R. Cawker and W. Bernstein, *Building with Words: Canadian Architects on Architecture* (1981) and *Contemporary Canadian Architecture* (1982); *Construction*, 1-27 (1907-34); N. Clerk, *Palladian Style in Canadian Architecture* (1984); B. Downs, *Sacred Places: British Columbia's Early Churches* (1980); A. Duffus et al, *Thy Dwellings Fair: Churches of Nova Scotia 1750-1830* (1982); C.M. Ede, *Canadian Architecture 1960/70* (1971); F. Gagnon-Pratte, *L'Architecture et la nature à Québec au dix-neuvième siècle: les villas* (1980); A. Gowans, *Building Canada* (1966) and *Church Architecture in New France* (1955); R. Greenhill, K. Macpherson and D. Richardson, *Ontario Towns* (1974); H.D. Kalman, *The Railway Hotels and the Development of the Château Style in Canada* (1968), *Exploring Ottawa* (1983) and *Exploring Vancouver* (1974); M. Lessard and H. Marquis, *Encyclopédie de la maison québecoise* (1972); M. MacRae and A. Adamson, *The Ancestral Roof: Domestic Architecture of Upper Canada* (1963), *Cornerstones of Order: Courthouses and Town Halls of Ontario 1784-1914* (1983) and *Hallowed Walls: Church Architecture in Upper Canada* (1975); L. Maitland, *Neoclassical Architecture in Canada* (1984); J.C. Marsan, *Montreal in Evolution* (1981); Newfoundland Historic Trust, *Ten Historic Towns: Heritage Architecture of Newfoundland* (1978) and *A Gift of Heritage: Selections from the Architectural Heritage of St. John's, Newfoundland* (1975); L. Noppen, *Les Églises du Québec (1600-1850)* (1977); L. Noppen, C. Paulette and M. Tremblay, *Québec: trois siècles d'architecture* (1979); J.I. Rempel, *Building with Wood and Other Aspects of Nineteenth-Century Building in Central Canada* (1980); T. Ritchie, *Canada Builds 1867-1967* (1967); I.L. Rogers, *Charlottetown: The Life in its Buildings* (1983); Royal Architectural Institute of Canada, *Architecture Canada*, 1-50 (1924-73); M. Segger and D. Franklin, *Victoria: A Primer for Regional History in Architecture* (1979); Society for Study of Architecture in Canada, *Selected Papers from the Society of Architecture in Canada* (1976-84); D. Stewart and I.E. Wilson, *Heritage Kingston* (1973); J. Veillette and G. White, *Early Indian Village Churches: Wooden Frontier Architecture in British Columbia* (1977); L. Whiteson, *Modern Canadian Architecture* (1983); J. Wright, *Architecture of the Picturesque in Canada* (1984).

Archives The term "archives" has 2 meanings. Archives are usually defined as the permanent records. In this sense, archives constitute that coherent body of recorded information created or received by a government, corporate body or organization in the course of its business, or by an individual in his activities, and which is then maintained, preferably in continuous authorized custody, as a record of that business or activity. Given the myriad forms in which information can now be recorded, archives grow correspondingly complex. Archives today range in physical format from traditional paper files, minute books, ledgers, diaries, letters and reports, to microfilm, photographic images, cartographic materials, architectural drawings, motion-picture film, sound recordings, videotape and machine-readable data files. It follows, too, from this definition, that the archival record is not constant but is continuously created and augmented. In any modern administrative body, whether a large government or a local voluntary association, information is recorded for some administrative purpose. It may then be kept for reference or for audit and legal reasons. When it is no longer current, the designated archivist of that administrative body selects records of enduring value for preservation. Larger governments, institutions and corporations maintain their own archives. The archives of smaller bodies are often deposited under formal agreement with an appropriat public archives, federal, provincial, municipal or university. Similarly, individuals in an walk of life may create records of permanen value to society. In Canada, such personal collections are treated as archival, complementin the official record and documenting the diversity of Canadian society. Most of the public archives as well as some universities and librarie actively seek out such private materials relate to their areas of interest.

"Archives" has yet a second meaning. It refer to the institutions or organizational units responsible for maintaining the archival record An archive in this sense has 4 functions. First it appraises recorded information for its value selects that which is permanent, and acquire this portion through formal transfer. Second the archive conserves the record, by preservin intrinsically valuable documents in their original physical form or by transferring the information to a permanent documentary form Third, an archive arranges and describes the records in its keeping. The archival principles o arrangement, "provenance" and "respect de fonds," recognize that the archival record is mos appropriately kept in its original order, reflecting the manner and context in which it cam into being. The tools of archival description ar collectively and appropriately termed "findin aids" and include main entry card catalogues indices, file and shelf lists, inventories, institutional guides and, in Canada, the *Union List o Manuscripts in Canadian Repositories* (2 vols, 197 and supplements) and the *Guide to Canadian Photographic Archives* (1984). Finally, a functionin archive endeavours to make its records publicly accessible. On occasion, access to archives may be limited by terms, usually of defined duration imposed to protect recent confidential information, by regulations respecting the protectio of personal privacy, or by copyright considerations. However, for the most part, Canadia archives are open to all, encouraging those seriously interested in research to draw on thei resources. Most Canadian archives respond to written inquiries and provide copies of thei records at cost to assist research. Some are able to provide extended research hours or engage in exhibition, adult education and publicatior programs.

Archives are an essential aspect of contemporary society for several reasons. The ancien role of archives remains: documenting the rights of governments, corporate bodies and individuals within society. Proof of persona property rights, or eligibility for pension benefits as much as international boundary disputes have rested on the integrity of the archival record. Government, in all its forms, has played a substantial role in the life of every citizen From the broad development of public policy, to taxation and spending, to government decisions on immigration, conscription, social assistance development grants, municipal zoning, and a host of other matters affecting individuals, official records show how the government has fulfilled the public trust. In a democratic society there exists a basic right to have such records appropriately preserved and to have public access to the government's archives. Archives when linked to records management programs perform a valuable administrative function. By applying a systematic approach to handling often bulky administrative information, government and corporate archives have reduced the need for office space and records storage equipment, while simplifying reference to previous decisions or policies. Finally, archives form a basic cultural resource. They preserve in the most direct way possible the thoughts of previous generations. Ideally, an archive mirrors the organization or community on which it is based. Its collections attempt to reflect all aspects the complex past. Like any memory, it can drawn upon in diverse ways, providing the undation for virtually all historical activity.

The Canadian archival tradition derives from e dual administrative and cultural roles of chives in society. The natural concern of gov-nment to preserve essential records for admin-rative and legal purposes can be traced to NEW ANCE, with a proposal for the appointment of custodian of the archives in 1724 and a sug-stion by the intendant, Gilles Hocquart, for a ecial archive building in 1731. The Legislative ouncil of Quebec passed an ordinance in 1790 or the Better Preservation and due Distribu-on of the Ancient French Records" to gather cords concerning property and "to give cheap d easy access to them." Such initiatives were oradic and isolated. At Confederation, the ept of the Secretary of State was assigned the ancellery responsibility "to keep all State cords and papers." An official, Henry J. Mor-n, was duly appointed to this Records Branch, d served from 1875 to 1883.

The Quebec Literary and Historical Society as formed in 1824 and began an active pro-am of research and publication, assisted in 332 by the first of a series of grants from the egislative Assembly of Lower Canada. Mem-rs of the society visited Paris, London and ew York in their efforts to locate and tran-ribe historical documents relating to Canada. uring the 1850s, the Library of Parliament be-me closely involved in these efforts, extend-g the search to include pioneer reminiscences Upper Canada and the WAR OF 1812.

Canada was not the only province interested archival matters prior to Confederation. The S legislature approved a motion by Joseph OWE, leading to the appointment of T.B. Akins records commissioner in 1857.

Four years after Confederation, the Quebec iterary and Historical Society again took the itiative by petitioning the new federal govern-ent to establish an archive to assist "authors nd literary inquirers." In 1872 the government sponded. An Archives Branch was formed in e Dept of Agriculture and a journalist, Doug-s Brymner, was appointed. Brymner, regarded Canada's first Dominion archivist, brought xtraordinary enthusiasm and zeal to the task. ntil his death in 1902, Brymner pursued is "noble dream," seeking to "obtain from all urces private as well as public, such docu-ents as may throw light on social, commer-al, municipal, as well as purely political his-ory." With the limited resources available to im, the archivist obtained a major series of ar Office records and acquired or located cords, papers and pamphlets. Brymner ex-nded earlier sporadic efforts with a program transcribe, by hand, the records of Canada's olonial past in the British Museum, the Public ecord Office and the Archives nationales. alendars of many of these institutions were ublished in the archive's annual reports. As udents and scholars took up the study of Cana-ian history they found a significant resource in e growing archives and a willing colleague in rymner.

The Public Archives of Canada Following the ecommendations of a federal commission con-erned about the state of government records, e 2 archival programs, the Records Branch the Dept of the Secretary of State and the rchives Branch of the Dept of Agriculture, erged in 1903. Arthur G. DOUGHTY was ap-ointed in 1904 as both Dominion archivist and eeper of the records, with a mandate as inclu-ive as Brymner's "noble dream."

Over the next 31 years, under Doughty's lively eadership, the Archives expanded in size, scope nd staff. The program was recognized by stat-te in 1912, giving the PUBLIC ARCHIVES OF CANADA ull departmental status. A fireproof archive building, opened in 1906 and expanded in 1926, quickly filled. The overseas copying program grew more systematic and the search for Canadian materials expanded to other European repositories. The descendants, French and English, of colonial governors, administrators and generals responded generously to Doughty's fervent appeals for historical records. Within Canada, the Archives established offices for a time in Montréal, Québec City, Trois-Rivières, Saint John, Halifax and Winnipeg, locating, copying or acquiring archival materials. Maps, pictures of all kinds, and even nonarchival museum objects formed part of Doughty's "storehouse" of Canadian history.

Government records began being transferred to the PAC in quantity. A royal commission in 1912 recommended a more formal records program for the federal government, but the outbreak of war in 1914 postponed the construction of a suitable records storage building. Despite repeated efforts, a formal records program eluded the Archives until the 1950s.

Even so, the growing collection had its impact on the teaching and writing of Canadian history. The advice of historians was sought through the Historical Manuscripts Commission (formed 1907) and in editing a new series of documentary publications. One of Doughty's own dreams for a new approach to Canadian HISTORIOGRAPHY was realized in 1914 with the publication of the ambitious 23-volume series CANADA AND ITS PROVINCES. From 1911 to 1920 scholarships were offered to senior university students to spend the summer at the PAC studying original sources. This was followed in the next 2 decades by a graduate course in Canadian history held at the Archives. For the generation of historical scholars after WWI, the Archives became their summer meeting place, to research, exchange ideas, organize the profession, plan new publications, and renew enthusiasm before returning to their winter vigils teaching Canadian history, often alone, at scattered universities.

The Archives' programs slowed with the GREAT DEPRESSION. Doughty retired in 1935, honoured by a knighthood; and, at his death, by a statue. His successor, Gustave Lanctôt, shifted the Archives' acquisition focus slightly to emphasize post-Confederation materials and introduced new documentary media with motion-picture film and sound recordings.

Supported by the obvious magnitude of the postwar proliferation of records and by the strong recommendations of the Massey Commission (1951), a new dynamic Dominion archivist, W. Kaye Lamb, succeeded in giving the

Archives, as storage places for permanent records, may contain paper files, minute books, ledgers, diaries, letters, motion-picture films, architectural drawings, videotapes, medals, photographic images, machine-readable files and cartographic materials (*courtesy Public Archives of Canada*).

archives a central role in a modern records management system for the federal government. The opening of a federal records centre in Ottawa (1956), followed in recent decades by similar regional records centres across Canada, marked a new era for the PAC. The merging of a multimedia cultural archives and a government record office, begun in 1903, became reality. The Archives, under Dr Lamb, his successor Wilfred I. Smith, and their increasingly numerous and professional staff, flourished. Canada's CENTENNIAL YEAR provided the occasion for a long-awaited move to an elegant new building, shared with the NATIONAL LIBRARY OF CANADA. Traditional programs were given new life, as the acquisition of private manuscripts and records was placed on a more systematic basis. Earlier efforts were formalized as the National Map Collection, the National Photography Collection, the National Film, Television and Sound Archives, architectural archives, ethnocultural archives, and conservation services assumed greater importance. New technologies were adapted to archival service. In the 1950s microphotography enabled the Paris and London offices to obtain complete and accurate copies of records series in place of the selective and fallible handwritten copies so painstakingly produced since 1880. Microfilm also provided an economical means of duplicating unique records for security or for consultation across the country. More recently, the establishment of a Machine Readable Archives and experiments in applying digitized laser disc recording to preserving information have made the PAC a world leader in the archival implications of new technology.

The Archival System The early example of the PAC was not lost upon the provinces. Indeed, its achievements and emphases provided a pattern followed by many of our provincial, municipal and institutional archives. NS's pre-Confederation archival initiatives were reconfirmed by a statute in 1929 and the opening of an archive building in 1931. Ontario established a provincial archive in 1903 and reinforced its program with an archives Act in 1923. The Bureau des archives du Québec (now the Archives nationales du Québec) was established in 1920 and embarked on an impressive program of acquisitions and publications. In other provinces — BC, Alberta, Saskatchewan, Manitoba, PEI and NB — archival activity began in their legislative libraries through the more or less formal interest of their librarians. The BC archives emerged as an identifiable unit in 1908, but for the others, archival activity was rudimentary through the 1920s and 1930s.

The explosion of administrative records both in volume and in physical form, which provided the impetus for the federal archives' growth after WWII, has been equally noticeable in provinces, municipalities, businesses, universities and, indeed, in all administrative agencies. To cope with this growth, many organizations have established archives and records management programs. Where earlier archives may have grown from cultural inspiration, administrative necessity has loomed large in the proliferation of archives in recent years.

Archival legislation in Saskatchewan in 1945 and 1955 provided a model for others in dealing with provincial records. Ontario, particularly in the decade 1965-75, developed an excellent records management program. By 1968, each of the provinces had established archives and, since that date, each has obtained new or renovated facilities with suitable environmental and security controls (*see* CONSERVATION OF MOVABLE CULTURAL PROPERTY). Significant legislative advances have been achieved with the passage of new archives Acts in NB (1977), Québec (1983) and Newfoundland (1983). Only BC remains without archival legislation. The provincial archives have been joined by archives in the Yukon (1972) and the NWT (1979). Indeed, the last 2 decades have witnessed a considerable expansion of archival activity. The Archives nationales du Québec has established 8 regional offices in the province. Several larger cities now have significant archives programs (Toronto, Vancouver, Edmonton, Calgary, Ottawa). Most universities have archives to preserve their own records while a number, either through their archives or libraries, have developed major research collections: FOLKLORE archives have been gathered at Memorial, Laval and Laurentian; literary papers at Queen's, McMaster and Calgary; and regional collections have evolved at Moncton, Queen's, Western Ontario, Manitoba, Brandon and UBC. Churches, banks, insurance corporations and oil companies have formed corporate archives, while a number of museums, historical societies and libraries have endeavoured to provide archival service to their communities.

A report, *Canadian Archives*, published by the SOCIAL SCIENCES AND HUMANITIES RESEARCH COUNCIL OF CANADA in 1980, highlighted the widening interest in archives and the importance of archives to Canadian studies. While archival activity has increased, so have both the complexity and volume of the archival record and the research demands placed on the system. The traditional scholarly archival clientele is now outnumbered by the genealogists, local historians, heritage activists, teachers, radio and television producers and journalists, all of whom archivists have encouraged. To cope, the 1980 report recommended the formation of provincial networks of archives to share reference information and specialized facilities, supported by various federal services co-ordinated by the PAC. Federal-provincial agreement on the structure of a more interdependent archival system was secured in 1983-84 and various co-operative projects have been started.

The proliferation of archives in recent years has been accompanied by the emergence of an archival profession. An Archives Section was formed within the Canadian Historical Assn in 1956. It encouraged the development of an archives course at Carleton U and began publication of *The Canadian Archivist*. In 1967 the Assn des archivistes du Québec was formed, bringing professional and amateur archivists together in a vigorous association with its own publication, *Archives*. The Archives Section evolved into the Assn of Canadian Archivists (1975), and its journal, *Archivaria*, has grown in scope and content. Both associations, loosely joined in the Bureau of Canadian Archivists, and the emerging provincial archival associations have devoted considerable attention to basic problems: education, training, descriptive standards, copyright, freedom of information and government policies as they affect archives. For entry into the profession, a Master of Archival Studies program has developed at UBC and various courses and diploma courses are available in library schools, universities and colleges. IAN E. WILSON

Reading: Archives, Libraries and the Canadian Heritage: Essays in Honour of W. Kaye Lamb, Archivaria 15 (winter 1982-83); *Archives: Mirror of Canada's Past*, intro by W.I. Smith (1972); *Canadian Archives*, Report to the Social Sciences and Humanities Research Council of Canada, by the Consultative Group on Canadian Archives (1980); C. Couture and J-Y. Rousseau, *Les archives au XXe siècle. Une réponse aux besoins de l'administration et de la recherche* (1982); H. Jenkinson, *A Manual of Archive Administration* (2nd ed, 1937); T.R. Schellenberg, *Modern Archives: Principles and Techniques* (1956).

Arctic Animals are animals that have adapted, physically and behaviourally, to the particular conditions of life in the most northerly region of Earth. The Arctic can be defined in various ways. Geographically, it is that part of the world lying N of the ARCTIC CIRCLE (66° 30′ N lat) beyond which there is at least one day in the year in which the sun never sets and one in which it never rises. Ecological definitions invoke the major discontinuities: on land, the major break is the TREELINE; in the sea, it is where the characteristically low-salinity arctic waters meet Atlantic and Pacific waters in zones of upwelling and mixing. Typically, the lives of terrestrial and aquatic members of the arctic fauna are closely linked. The sea provides a food source for land birds (from snow buntings to whistling swans) that forage in spring on seaweed windrows on storm beaches; winter ice provides access to marine life for arctic foxes, wolves and polar bears. Conversely, many marine animals (from murres to walrus) use parts of the land for mating and raising young; others, such as the ringed seal and the ivory gull, can raise their young on ice and can thus be independent of the terrestrial environment.

The arctic land fauna resembles more familiar faunas of the northern temperate zones; fewer species are present, but they are generally of the same orders and families as those farther south. The deficiencies arise for several reasons. On land, mean annual temperatures are below freezing and the ground remains frozen at depth; therefore, no warm layer persists near the surface through the winter. Hence, REPTILES and most hibernating MAMMALS are not found N of the line of continuous PERMAFROST. Because trees are absent, certain boreal-zone INSECTS, RODENTS, carnivores and BIRDS that depend on them for food and shelter disappear. Open water is scarce in the Arctic throughout most of the year. Except where rapids and tide-rips occur, solid ice or dense pack generally forbids access to the aquatic environment. Animals wintering on the arctic TUNDRA must quench their thirst with snow. Fish-eating birds and mammals typically migrate for the winter to areas providing better access to prey; the remainder concentrate at the scattered polynya (ice-free refuges).

The characteristic that most restricts opportunities for animal life may be the brevity of the arctic growing season. The land VEGETATION produced in the few, but long, days of the arctic summer must sustain life over an extended, harsh and demanding winter. It is hardly surprising that the most mobile animals pass the winter elsewhere: birds on ocean coasts farther S and in interior plains and forest lands; and many barren-ground caribou on lichen pastures of the open boreal forest. The short growing season tends to squeeze certain species out of arctic ecosystems entirely. Beyond the edge of the barrens, it is rare to encounter the plagues of blackflies inevitable in the boreal forest. The absence of bats and swallows might be attributed to the lack of flying insects necessary to these animals in rearing their young.

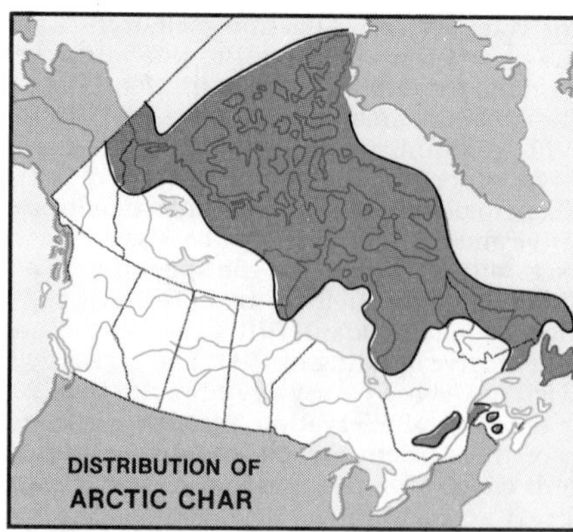

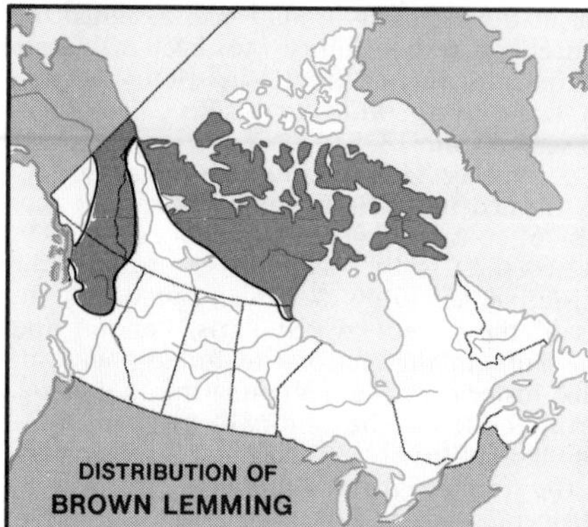

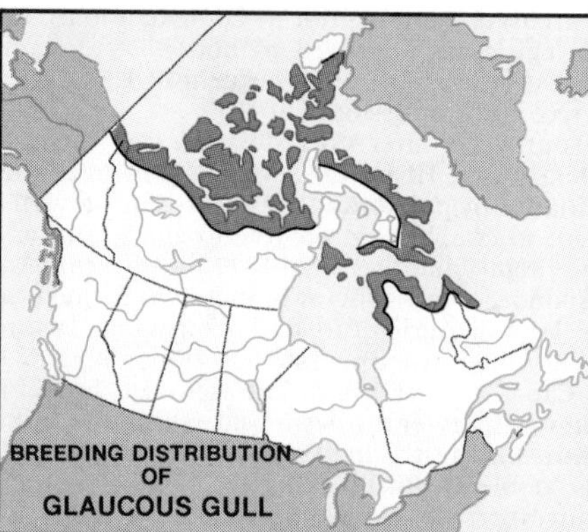

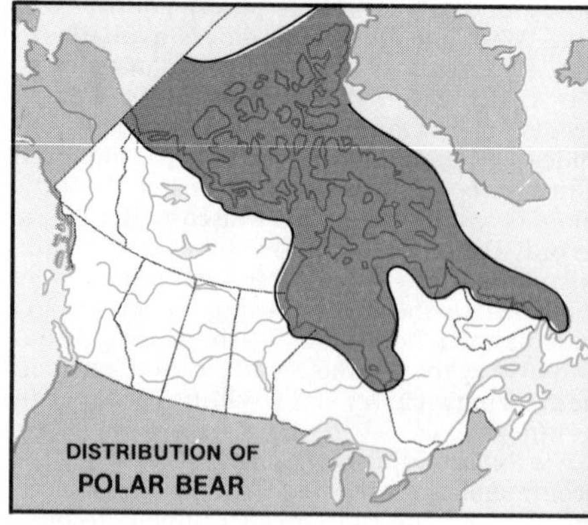

Another serious constraint is the dangerous heat loss caused by low winter temperature and high windchill. This factor imposes on warm-blooded animals the need for a thick, dense

.sulating coat, which means that surface-intering arctic animals must generally be rge. The larger the animal, the greater the ody-mass to skin-surface ratio and the smaller e relative heat loss. Northern ravens and arctic xes are the smallest animals found above the ow surface during the arctic winter. Hard-acked snow denies the use of drifts for shelter groups, from grouse to ungulates, which use e softer drifts of the boreal zone for that pur-se. Animals using the solid arctic snow drifts r shelter include the collared or varying lem-ing, which grows special winter claws for the urpose, and the polar bear, which burrows in r its winter and maternity dens. The ringed al is unique in constructing its maternity den snow on the surface of land-fast sea ice.

Although food sources may be few, sparse nd evanescent, combinations of many provide vings for several successful arctic animals. ost arctic species are quite opportunistic. To e south, insects typically feed on one plant ecies only and birds and mammals have re-tively fixed diets; in the Arctic, exploitation broader food resources (ie, trophic niches) is ommon. The polar bear provides one example. ears are typically omnivorous. Polar bears e amphibious and able to subsist on very iverse and meagre resources, both terrestrial nd aquatic, for long periods each year. Among irds, the long-tailed jaeger is equally well dapted, being for the brief arctic summer an ter of terrestrial arthropods (especially spiders nd midges), bird hunter (particularly of nest-ngs), lemming catcher, sea-food gatherer of the dal flats and carrion seeker.

The modern Canadian arctic land fauna may e traced back to the Pleistocene epoch (*see* ICE GE). A few thousand years ago, during the last ontinental GLACIATION, thick sheets of ice cov-ed most of Canada and much of the northern S. Arctic animals have descended from species at occupied land revegetating after the retreat f the ice. At least 2 sources of origin are evident: e west, where ice-free land extended from the T and Alaska, under what is now the Bering a; and the south, which can be visualized as a one, like that near the foot of a modern glacier, ubject to cycles of improvement and deterior-tion. Presumably, the brown lemming, grizzly ear and barren-ground caribou came from the est; the tundra vole, red fox and moose from e south. Polar bears and arctic foxes are so at ome on sea ice that they live wherever the ice ack has reached the shore.

Compared to the land, sea and lake waters re-ain within a narrow temperature range year ound. However, the seasonal fall in temper-ture affects the aquatic environment pro-undly by causing surface water to freeze to a epth of 2 m or more. Ice, particularly when vered with snow, impedes penetration into ater of the solar radiation necessary for photo-ynthesis. Furthermore, bottom freezing and ouring by drifting ice floes greatly reduces the roductivity of arctic intertidal and near-shore arine zones. Marine productivity is compara-vely low, limited by temperature and the vailability of nutrients and light. Because of mited winter productivity, several populations f marine mammals winter in more productive pen seas.

Marine vegetation includes benthic and plank-onic algae (ie, seafloor and free-floating forms) nd algae that live within the lower levels and oat the submerged surfaces of floating ice. This ving material feeds the zooplankton preyed pon by arctic and polar cod, birds such as urres and guillemots, and marine mammals ich as the ringed seal. Algae also feed molluscs hich sustain the walrus. The predators highest the food chains of the arctic seas are polar ears and killer whales; important scavengers iclude glaucous gulls, amphipod crustaceans (which attack fish and seal carcasses left too long in nets) and Greenland shark (lethargic fish attaining lengths of about 3 m). The arctic char, the most important arctic food fish, lives its first year in lakes but, where passage exists, takes up an anadromous habit in later life: ie, it migrates to coastal waters for the summer to feed voraciously on crustaceans and other small marine animals, and returns to spawn in lakes in autumn.

The arctic fauna are the basis for local subsistence economies and, being partially migratory, support food, trade and recreation elsewhere in the world. Snow geese hatched in the Canadian Arctic are hunted as far S as the rice fields of Texas; harp seal populations, which summer in arctic waters, are harvested in the Gulf of St Lawrence. The earliest known arctic peoples used small stone blades and points suitable for killing thin-skinned game, eg, caribou and birds. Later cultures depended on sea mammals, particularly the bowhead or Greenland right whale. This, the largest arctic species, was greatly reduced by American and Scottish WHALING in the late 1800s, and is now the only truly endangered arctic mammal. The Inuit of the historical era have all been dependent on sea mammals, particularly the ringed seal, which stays in the frozen arctic bays and straits all winter, scratching breathing holes through the ice. The hunter would wait at a hole and harpoon the animal as it rose to the surface. Seals provided fuel (seal oil), skins (used for summer boots and tents) and meat. Warm clothing had always been essential in the Arctic; the bearskin winter trousers of the Greenland hunter were as distinctive as the guardsman's busby. Caribou killed in Aug, when the hair is still short and fine, provided the most popular clothing skins. Muskox robes and skins of caribou killed in winter were used for bedding. The trade in arctic fox furs began in earnest in the early 1900s. Because both the fox populations and the value of the furs fluctuate so greatly from year to year, trapping in the Arctic yields an uncertain return.

With social and industrial development, CONSERVATION of arctic fauna has demanded increased attention. Recent developments include restrictions by the US on the import of sea-mammal products; imposition by the International Whaling Commission of quotas on the take of bowheads by Alaskan Eskimos; signing of an international convention on the conservation of the polar bear (particularly on the high seas) by the US, Norway, Denmark, the USSR and Canada; and the development of means in Canada to involve northerners more directly in the conservation of the barren-ground caribou vital to their lives. The growing interest in oil exploration and production, offshore drilling and year-round shipping is of the greatest concern to environmentalists and native groups. Other threats to arctic animals may include the impact of pollutants, industrial and military, from the south on more fragile ecosystems, and more harvesting pressure as human populations grow. *See* ANIMALS IN WINTER. A.H. MACPHERSON

Reading: F. Bruemmer, *Encounters with Arctic Animals* (1972).

Arctic Archipelago Lying N of mainland Canada, these islands, the largest group in the world, cover 1.3 million km^2 with their intervening waters. They contain 6 of the world's 30 largest islands, including BAFFIN I, the fifth largest. They are separated by "channels," some of which would qualify as seas elsewhere in the world. PARRY CHANNEL which runs from LANCASTER SOUND to M'Clure Str and divides the northern QUEEN ELIZABETH ISLANDS from the rest, is an important part of the NORTHWEST PASSAGE. The main islands, and groups of islands, are BANKS, VICTORIA, PRINCE OF WALES, SOMERSET and Baffin islands and the Queen Elizabeth group including the SVERDRUP and PARRY islands and ELLESMERE I).

Some of the islands, especially those towards the E, are mountainous, with peaks over 2000 m. The higher land on these islands is commonly occupied by ice caps that contain most of Canada's glacier ice and from which flow Canada's largest GLACIERS. The southeastern archipelago consists of north-thrusting prongs of the Canadian SHIELD, separated by fairly flat-lying Paleozoic rocks. The northern part, including most of the Queen Elizabeth Is, consists of younger, heavily folded sedimentary rocks, producing mountains on islands such as AXEL HEIBERG and parts of DEVON and Ellesmere in the centre and E. This geological variety produces spectacular variations in scenery, with rugged "old" and "new" mountains and high and low plains of various ages and rock types. Perhaps it is the sedimentary rocks that make this area of Canada so distinctive; elsewhere most of arctic and subarctic Canada is dominated by

Bache Peninsula on the east coast of Ellesmere Island, NWT, 3rd-largest island in Canada and most northerly in the Artic Archipelago (*photo by Stephen J. Krasemann/ DRK Photo*).

the Shield. The sedimentary rocks contain few metallic minerals, but may well contain huge deposits of oil and natural gas as well as the coal discovered by early explorers.

Apart from Greenland, which is almost entirely ice covered (and geologically an extension of the archipelago), the Canadian Arctic Archipelago forms the world's largest high-arctic land area. By any measure, this is a truly polar environment. In the northern islands, night lasts 3 or 4 months in winter and day lasts the same period in summer. The Queen Elizabeth Is are a polar desert, with often much less than 13 cm of precipitation a year. The average annual temperature may be as low as -20°C in the N and -6°C in southern Baffin I, with extreme low temperatures in the order of -50°C. Summer temperatures may rise above freezing for one or 2 months. The PERMAFROST exceeds 550 m in thickness and may in places reach 1000 m.

The vegetation is formed largely of low sedges, mosses and grasses, with occasional dwarf willows. At some favoured locations plant life can be lush and in the short flowering season the vegetation is quite beautiful. Only 17 species of land mammals live in the archipelago, generally in small numbers restricted to certain areas. The island CARIBOU — the special Peary Caribou that are smaller and whiter than the mainland variety — live in small herds and do not migrate like their mainland cousins. Other large animals in the archipelago are the MUSKOX, arctic fox, WOLF, LEMMING and white arctic hare. Only 64 species of birds spend the summer in the high-arctic islands and only 6 species overwinter there. The surrounding seas are home to the polar bear, the walrus and various types of seal and whale, including the narwal and the beluga.

The high arctic has been occupied by the INUIT and their predecessors for thousands of years. Today, they live in settlements scattered throughout the islands, generally on the sea. Ancient links with the Greenlandic people are still maintained. Evidence has been found of contact between the Vikings, who lived in Greenland during the Middle Ages, and the islands (*see* NORSE VOYAGES). The non-Inuit population is made up of government and military personnel in settlements such as FROBISHER BAY, RESOLUTE and ALERT. PETER ADAMS

Arctic Archipelago Channels

The seawaters of the Arctic Archipelago were first sighted by William BAFFIN, who sailed into Smith Sound and northern BAFFIN BAY in 1616 and who first recorded Jones Sound and Lancaster Sound, which is the eastern entrance to the Northwest Passage. In 1819 Sir William Parry sailed through the W as far as M'Clure Str, where he was stopped by ice. The Northwest Passage was finally sailed by Roald AMUNDSEN 1903-06 and again by Sgt LARSEN of the RCMP 1940-42 (W-E) and 1944 (E-W). The waters N of Baffin Bay, now known as Nares Str, were explored from 1852 on. Very little scientific OCEANOGRAPHY was done in the Arctic Islands until after WWII, although an excellent pioneer expedition under Otto SVERDRUP 1898-1902 produced important geological and biological results. Danish expeditions and US Coastguard *Marion* in 1928 made oceanographic studies in Smith, Jones and Lancaster sounds.

The depths of the channels range from less than 200 m to about 800 m in eastern Lancaster Sound. The most important sill (minimum) depths, related to water transport, are 140 m in Barrow Str and 250 m in Nares Str. The continental shelf varies from over 550 m in depth in the W and N to 200 m in the E. In spite of low tidal ranges, which decrease from E to W, tidal currents can be strong in certain narrow passages, such as Bellot Str, Fury and Hecla Str and Hell Gate. The dominant water flow through the islands is from the Arctic Ocean southward through Nares Str and eastward through Lancaster Sound and Fury and Hecla Str. The first 2 currents flow into Baffin Bay and the latter into Foxe Basin, Hudson Bay and Hudson Str. The most recent estimate of the total transport of Arctic Ocean water through the islands is 2.1 million m^3/s, but there is probably considerable annual variation. The depth and extent of the channels offer commercial possibilities (for submarine tankers) as well as some strategic concern (as an avenue of approach for submarines).

Ice cover, with an average thickness from 1.6 m to 2 m, is complete in winter throughout the archipelago, with the exception of several recurring polynyas (areas of open water surrounded by sea ice), the largest of which are in northern Baffin Bay and in the southeastern BEAUFORT SEA. These polynyas, which freeze late and thaw early, are a focus for marine and bird life and there is evidence of early human habitation, by the THULE and DORSET peoples, on the landmasses adjoining them. Biologically the waters of the archipelago are rich in mammals and birds (in summer) and poor in fishes. The plankton is typical of that of the upper 250 m of the Arctic Ocean. M.J. DUNBAR

Arctic Circle, a parallel of latitude 66° 32′ N; similarly, the Antarctic Circle is the parallel of latitude 66° 32′ S. Between these circles the SUN rises and sets daily. N of the Arctic Circle the sun remains above the horizon at midnight at midsummer and never rises at midwinter. Since light rays are bent by the Earth's atmosphere, the sun can be seen when it is slightly below the horizon. Thus, the midwinter sun can be seen at places slightly N of the circle. The number of days the sun stays above (or below) the horizon increases the farther N one goes until, at the pole, the sun never sets for 6 months and never rises during the other 6. These effects occur because the Earth's axis of rotation is tilted relative to the plane of its orbit around the sun. During the northern winter, when the Northern Hemisphere is tilted away from the sun, the Earth's curvature creates an area of permanent shadow centered on the North Pole. This area starts to form at the fall equinox (Sept 22), grows to a maximum at midwinter, then decreases, vanishing by the spring equinox (Mar 21). For the remainder of the year, when the Northern Hemisphere is tilted towards the sun, an area of permanent sunlight centres on the pole. Because the tilt of the Earth's axis is about 23.5°, the Arctic and Antarctic circles lie at latitudes of about 66.5°. The Arctic Circle is not a climatic boundary. Trees grow N of it in the Mackenzie Delta; in Nouveau-Québec the TREELINE is 1000 km farther S. INUVIK, NWT, is the only moderately large Canadian settlement lying N of the circle. W.S.B. PATERSON

Arctic Exploration began in the Elizabethan era when English seamen sought a shortcut to the Spice Is of the Far East by the seas north of America — the so-called NORTHWEST PASSAGE. Martin FROBISHER in 3 voyages (1576, 1577 and 1578) found the way blocked by Baffin I. Seeking to round this obstacle, John DAVIS (1585, 1586 and 1587) explored Cumberland Gulf (now Sound) and found the entrance to Hudson Str, which was to conduct Henry HUDSON (1610) into his bay. In 1616 Robert Bylot and William BAFFIN explored Baffin Bay, sighting the westward-leading channels of Jones and Lancaster sounds. Owing to ice-covered seas and mirage, they mistakenly judged them to be closed bays, a common error among arctic explorers. The arctic littoral of N America remained unexplored for the next 2 centuries. Samuel HEARNE (1771) by the Coppermine R, and Alexander MACKENZIE (1789) by the Mackenzie R, barely reached arctic tidewater and learned nothing of

Skirmish with Eskimos by John White, who accompanie[d] Martin Frobisher on his second voyage to the Arctic i[n] 1577. White's paintings created tremendous intere[st] about the New World, and his works are now recog[-]nized as masterpieces of their kind (*courtesy Trustees of th[e] British Museum*).

adjoining coasts. Of the vast ARCTIC ARCHIPELAG[O] to the N, only isolated stretches of Baffin I's shore had come to light.

In 1818 the British ADMIRALTY renewed i[ts] search for the NW Passage. That year John Ros[s] rounded Baffin Bay but, like Baffin, believe[d] that Lancaster Sound was just a bay. In 1819-2[0] W.E. PARRY proved the sound to be the gatewa[y] to unknown western seas. Hampered by ic[e] he sailed 800 km along Parry Channel (Lan[-]caster Sound, Barrow Str and Viscount Melvil[le] Sound) to Melville I, where he wintered. Acros[s] the ice-choked Viscount Melville Sound he ob[-]tained a distant view of Banks I. On a later voy[-]age he entered Prince Regent Inlet, where he los[t] a ship in the ice. The summers were very shor[t] and it was found that a sailing ship could sta[y] at sea for barely 2 months before being immo[-]bilized by ice.

To the S, between 1819 and 1839, canoe an[d] boat parties under John FRANKLIN and late[r] Thomas SIMPSON explored a channel along th[e] continental shore from Bering Str to Boothi[a] Isthmus. In 1845 Franklin sailed from Englan[d] to link this channel with Parry Channel, in[-]tending thus to complete the NW Passage. His ships never returned, and were for several year[s] unreported. Numerous rescue parties were sen[t] (1848-54) by Britain and the US. The search fo[r] the missing crews could not be done thoroughl[y] by ships icebound for most of the year. Smal[l] parties hauling equipment and supplies o[r] sledges sought evidence. Although unsuccess[-]ful in their assigned task, these parties mappe[d] much of the Canadian archipelago.

John RAE and Richard Collinson explore[d] and mapped the island coasts nearest the con[-]tinental shore, while 4 crews of Capt Horati[o] Austin's squadron (1850-51) did the same o[n] both sides of Parry Channel. Other expedition[s] mapped parts of Somerset and Victoria islands and gave shape to the S coasts of Devon, Bath[-]urst and Melville islands. Sir Edward BELCHER explored (1852-54) the N shores of the latter 3. The great sledge traveller Leopold MCCLINTOCK helped by G.F. Mecham, discovered Eglinto[n] and Prince Patrick islands in a return journey o[f] over 2100 km.

The most dramatic voyage in polar histor[y] was made by the rescue ship *Investigator*. Havin[g] sailed from Plymouth, Eng, on 20 Jan 1850, i[t] rounded S America and entered the Arctic Ocea[n] by way of Bering Str. Its captain, Robert MCCLURE discovered Prince of Wales Str and travelle[d] through it to the NE angle of Parry's Banks I — thus completing the NW Passage. McClur[e] had, by an alternate route, accomplished wha[t]

ʌS *Assistance* and HMS *Pioneer*, engaged in the search ꞉ Franklin under the command of Sir Edward Belcher, own in winter quarters, Devon I, 1853. The Franklin ırch led to a great expansion of knowledge of the ctic (*courtesy Public Archives of Canada/C-41305*).

anklin had died attempting: he had connected ırry's voyage of penetration from the E with anklin's coastal survey from the W. However, rashly put his ship into the heavy ice pack, hich had stopped Parry. His ship was repeatly thrown over on its side by gale-driven ice asses. In Sept 1851 he found refuge in the Bay Mercy on Banks I's N shore, where the *Invesator* was frozen in for 18 months. Its crew was duced to extreme want, and would have perıed but for the timely arrival of a detachment Belcher's squadron under Capt Henry Kellett. This and other strenuous endeavours conıued the search for Franklin. Rae (1851) and llinson (1853) had come near success but had rned back at the approach of winter. In 1854 ıe learned from Inuit that years previously any Europeans had died on western King Wilım I and on the adjacent mainland. In 1859 cClintock reached the island by ship and edge and ascertained that Franklin's vessels ıd been frozen in in that region. The crews had rished of hunger and scurvy while trekking r the mainland. McClintock also filled in cerin gaps in his predecessors' maps, tracing alost completely the coasts in the archipelago up 77° N.

Discovery farther N was largely the work of mericans and Scandinavians. Englishman A. Inglefield and Americans E.K. Kane, I. ayes and C.F. Hall opened up the channel beveen Greenland and Ellesmere I, and the sury of Ellesmere's E shore was completed by e 1875-76 British polar expedition under G.S. ares. In 1876 P. Aldrich rounded the top of lesmere and named the northernmost point of hat is now Canadian territory Cape Columbia. orwegian Otto SVERDRUP explored the W shore Ellesmere I (1898-1902) except for a gap filled by American Robert Peary in 1906. Norweans in separate groups also surveyed the entire ɔast of Axel Heiberg I, and to the W discovered ıd mapped the 2 Ringnes islands and King hristian I, the latter a promising source of natral gas in the 1980s. Sverdrup had accomlished a vast amount with a minimum of misap or danger. The Norwegians' use of skis and eir familiarity with the northern climate gave em a great advantage over their British predessors. This was illustrated in the 1913-18 joureys of Vilhjalmur STEFANSSON, which opened to Europeans the last lands in the Canadian North previously unknown to them. In the employ of the Canadian government he took his ship through Bering Str, where it was crushed in the ice. With ready adaptability he organized a foot party and crossed the hazardous moving ice of the Beaufort Sea to Banks I. Taking to the ice again he put the finishing touch to McClintock's survey of Prince Patrick I, and went NE to discover Brock and Borden islands. The latter was afterwards found to be 2 islands: Borden and Mackenzie King. With the discovery of Meighen I in 1916 Stefansson made the last substantial addition to Canadian territory.

The NW Passage had been traced but its navigation was long deferred, as no sailing ship could hope to get through, nor could a steamer stow enough coal to wrestle its way through the ice pack that was certain to be encountered. In 1903-06 the Norwegian explorer Roald AMUNDSEN, when engaged in a magnetic survey, made use of the internal combustion engine to propel his 80-ton *Gjoa* through from ocean to ocean. The voyage of the US tanker *Manhattan* in 1969 made it plain that the most nearly usable NW Passage is by way of Parry Channel and Prince of Wales Str.

These explorations have done more for general science than for material interests. There has been little success in extracting seemingly abundant fossil fuels from the northern islands, but the attraction of petroleum and mineral deposits has provided a fresh impetus, and aerial photographs and more detailed maps improved tools, for a new phase of exploration on this Canadian frontier. *See* EXPLORATION; CARTOGRAPHY. LESLIE H. NEATBY

Reading: A. Cooke and C. Holland, *The Exploration of Northern Canada 500-1920* (1978); Leslie H. Neatby, *In Quest of the North West Passage* (1958), *Conquest of the Last Frontier* (1966) and *The Search for Franklin* (1970).

Arctic Oceanography The study of OCEANOGRAPHY reveals information about the origin, composition and movements of marine waters; OCEAN basins; interactions with the atmosphere; and the living organisms of the sea, ie, the plants and successive levels of animals that feed on them (*see* MARINE ECOLOGY). The seas of the Canadian Arctic (here defined as reaching from the LABRADOR SEA in the E to the BEAUFORT SEA in the W) are covered by ice for more than half the year. Cold, arctic surface water, originating in the upper 200-300 m of the Arctic Ocean, flows out of the Arctic basin through the Canadian ARCTIC ARCHIPELAGO and between Canada and Greenland towards the Atlantic Ocean. In Baffin Bay, Davis Strait and neighbouring regions, it mixes with warmer water from the Atlantic to form subarctic water. The Subarctic covers a relatively large area in eastern Canada; its western counterpart, formed where Pacific and Arctic waters meet and mix, is restricted to a narrow band along the shore of the Beaufort Sea (*see* COASTAL WATERS). Oceanographic information is obtained from the Arctic for many users, including navigators, hunters and fishermen, petroleum and mine developers, traders and climatologists.

Danish scientists aboard the vessel *Godthaab* and Americans on the *General Greene* began oceanographic investigation of waters bordering the eastern Canadian Arctic long before comparable Canadian efforts were launched. In 1930 the Hudson Bay Fisheries Expedition (under H.B. HACHEY), supported by the federal government, provided the first extensive account of circulation and general PHYSICAL OCEANOGRAPHY of the Canadian Arctic. In 1948 the Canadian government responded to a need for expanded Canadian oceanographic effort in the Arctic with establishment of the Eastern Arctic Investigations (now the Arctic Biological Station, Ste-Anne-de-Bellevue, Qué). The 15 m research vessel *Calanus* was built in NS in 1948, and a program, mainly of BIOLOGICAL OCEANOGRAPHY, was begun in the eastern Arctic. M.J. DUNBAR was in charge of the survey. In the Western Arctic, G.L. PICKARD in 1949 participated in a program in the Bering and Chukchi seas with the US Naval Electronics Laboratory. Co-operative research with United States oceanographers began in the early 1950s in the Beaufort Sea. W.M. Maxwell, of the Defence Research Board, played a significant role in this research and survey work. In 1954 HMCS *Labrador* completed a cruise that linked the eastern and western Arctic through the NORTHWEST PASSAGE, culminating in a circumnavigation of North America; a series of eastern arctic cruises followed.

The Polar Continental Shelf Project began in 1959, supporting a wide variety of arctic research projects, including oceanography; this organization continues to provide valuable service. In the same decade, Canadians joined American oceanographers on Ice Island T-3 in the Arctic Ocean. In the 1960s the Frozen Sea Research Group began work; the group is now based at the Institute of Ocean Sciences, Victoria. The BEDFORD INSTITUTE OF OCEANOGRAPHY participated in oceanographic surveys in the eastern and central Arctic during the early 1960s, and in 1969-70 continued with the more spectacular *Hudson* cruise around the Americas. A portion of that cruise was spent in the Beaufort Sea. The *Hudson* (built 1963) was the first Canadian vessel specially built for oceanographic research. More recently, multidisciplinary ship-based studies have been carried out by the Bedford Institute in the eastern Arctic.

The 1970s saw the beginning of a period of oceanographic study encouraged, at least partly, by questions of possible effects of OIL AND NATURAL GAS exploration on the environment. Studies were concerned with the effects of ocean currents, ocean waves and SEA ICE on vessels and fixed installations, and conversely with the impact of vessels and drill sites on the environment (eg, consequences of oil spills on the biota of arctic seas). The period marked appearance of a high level of nongovernment funding of oceanographic research and the growth of private consultants in a field largely occupied until that time by government-sponsored researchers. The first major study of the new era was the Beaufort Sea Project, jointly sponsored by government and the PETROLEUM INDUSTRY and comprising some 40 projects dealing with all major divisions of oceanography. Other studies have followed, including the Eastern Arctic Marine

Environmental Studies program (EAMES) in Baffin Bay and Davis Strait, the Offshore Labrador Biological Studies program (OLABS) and the Baffin Island Oil Spill project (BIOS).

In recent years, Canadian oceanographers have participated in a number of arctic studies outside Canadian waters, most of them being international co-operative undertakings. Among them are AIDJEX (Arctic Ice Dynamics Joint Experiment), a Canada-US oceanographic program in the Beaufort Sea; LOREX (Lomonosov Ridge Experiment), FRAM (a series of studies named after the vessel of arctic explorer Fridtjof Nansen), EUBEX (Eurasian Basin Survey) and CESAR, all located in the Arctic Basin; and MIZEX (Marginal Ice Zone Experiment), involving several countries off the East Greenland and Alaskan coasts. E.H. GRAINGER

Arctic Red River, NWT, UP, pop 120 (1981c), is situated at the confluence of the Arctic Red and MACKENZIE rivers, 1011 air km NW of YELLOWKNIFE. This tiny community is on a site that was probably a seasonal fishing camp for Loucheux DENE many centuries before European contact. The settlement remained isolated until the late 1970s when construction of the Dempster Hwy gave its residents access to larger centres. ANNELIES POOL

The high kick, one of the Arctic Winter Games' unique events (*photo by Jim Merrithew*).

Arctic Winter Games, biennial games initiated 1970 to provide northern athletes with opportunities for training and competition and to promote cultural and social interchange among northern peoples. The first games drew 710 participants from Alaska, the YT and the NWT to Yellowknife. Athletes from northern Québec and observers from the Soviet Union and Greenland joined the 1972 games. Subsequent events were held in Anchorage, Alaska, 1974; Schefferville, Qué, 1976; Hay River and Pine Point, NWT, 1978; Whitehorse, YT, 1980; Fairbanks, Alaska, 1982; Yellowknife, NWT, 1984; and Whitehorse, YT, 1986. Events include badminton, cross-country skiing, curling, figure skating, hockey, indoor soccer, shooting, snowshoeing, speedskating, triathlon and volleyball. The most unusual events are traditional arctic sports, developed over the years by Inuit to test stamina, strength and endurance (for example, the high kick in which athletes leap into the air with one foot or both feet).

Argenson, Pierre de Voyer d', governor of New France 1658-61 (bap in France 19 Nov 1625; d 1709? in France). There was an Iroquois attack the day following Gov d'Argenson's arrival at Québec, and negotiations with and defence against these powerful enemies were his major preoccupations. He devoted almost as much energy to his public quarrels with Bishop Laval and the Jesuits. Also concerned about the fragility of the Canadian economy, he urged a monopoly control over the fur trade and an increased agrarian population, but his advice was not heeded. ALLAN GREER

Argentia, Nfld, founded in the late 1600s. A US navy base served the largest US task force in the Atlantic in WWII (*photo by Janet Green/Masterfile*).

Argentia, Nfld, UP, pop 93 (1981c), is located on the W coast of the AVALON PENINSULA. Formerly the fishing community of Little Placentia (*Petit Plaisance*) founded by the French in the late 1600s, it was the site of English merchant premises by the 1700s. A small silver-lead mine, opened near the community in the 1880s, operated sporadically until 1925; consequently Little Placentia was renamed Argentia around 1900. In 1940 the US leased most of the small peninsula for a naval base. Argentia residents were resettled in nearby communities. The base served the largest US task force in the Atlantic, 12 403 personnel in 1943. Near this base, in Placentia B, US Pres Roosevelt and British PM Churchill met aboard the USS *Augusta* to negotiate the historic Atlantic Charter in 1941. The construction of the base created work for up to 15 000 Newfoundlanders, but it was phased down in 1969; in 1947 the air station was abandoned and in 1975 the naval station was closed. A small Canadian and American oceanographic facility remains. J.E.M. PITT AND R.D. PITT

Argue, Hazen Robert, politician (b at Moose Jaw, Sask 6 Jan 1921). He was MP from 1945 to 1963 for Assiniboia (formerly Wood Mountain), Sask, and was Parliament's youngest member when he entered. Argue was the only Opposition member from Saskatchewan to survive the DIEFENBAKER sweep in 1958. He became House leader of the 8-member CO-OPERATIVE COMMONWEALTH FEDERATION caucus that year. In 1960 he was elected national leader of the CCF. When the CCF and the Canadian Labour Congress formed the NEW DEMOCRATIC PARTY in 1961, T.C. DOUGLAS easily defeated Argue for the leadership. Six months later, Argue shocked the NDP by resigning, charging that its structure gave too much power to the unions. He was reelected to the Commons in 1962 as a Liberal but was defeated in 1963. Over the objections of some Saskatchewan Liberals of longer standing, Argue was named to the Senate in 1966. He was appointed to PM TRUDEAU's Cabinet in 1980 as minister of state responsible for the CANADIAN WHEAT BOARD. BILL CAMERON

Argus Corporation Ltd, with head offices in Toronto, is a specialized investment and holding company, incorporated in 1945. Attracting little interest to itself or its activities for much of its history, Argus was thrust into the spotlight in 1978 when members of the Black family acquired majority control through the acquisition of 2 blocks of Ravelston shares from the estates of J.A. (Bud) MCDOUGALD and Eric PHILLIPS. Argus has become a large investment company, holding shares in manufacturing and merchandising concerns and maintaining substantial minority interests in enterprises with long-term growth potential. Among its other holdings it owns 40% of DOMINION STORES LIMITED. In 1982 it had sales or operating revenue of $7 million, assets of $114.2 million and 18 employees. Ravelston Corporation Ltd holds 88% of Argus shares; chairman Conrad M. BLACK and his brother, G. Montegu Black, a company directo are said to own 96% of Ravelston. D.C. SAWY

Arluk, George, artist (b in the Keewatin regio NWT 5 May 1949). An Inuit sculptor now li ing in Baker Lake, NWT, Arluk began to tea himself how to carve soapstone at age 9. In th 1960s he was influenced by sculptors TIKTA and KAVIK and John PANGNARK. By the mi 1970s he had developed a unique style of sem abstraction. His subjects sometimes include spi its and arctic animals, but his main theme is th human figure. He depicts single figures such hunters and mothers with babies in their hood Most often he groups figures together to for abstracted compositions of gently curving form that undulate rhythmically. His sculptures o ten have antler parts added that protrude complex patterns from the stone. D. WIGH

Armaments, fighting tools, including devic for surveillance and reconnaissance. The fir armaments were probably jagged pieces rock (missile weapons) and crude wooden clu (shock weapons), both instinctive adaptations food-gathering implements. Eventually a com bination created a battle-axe or spear, whic like most weapons could be used either offen sively or defensively. Wood or leather in th form of shield or body armour was purely de fensive and of little value by itself.

Defensive armaments now range from space and layered steel and ceramic armour on tank to airborne warning and command system (AWACS). Offensive weapons have becom more complex and deadly, with greater rang accuracy and hitting power. Modern missil weapon systems can be conveniently broke down into 3 components: a transportation an launching platform, a delivery mechanism an the missile itself. They range from the fo soldier carrying an automatic rifle to the nu clear-powered submersible bearing submarine launched ballistic missiles (SLBMs) with mul tiple, independently targeted re-entry vehicle (MIRVs) with atomic warheads, and aircraf loaded with napalm, bombs or target-seekin missiles. The high-technology aspect of som current armaments, such as satellite reconnais sance and computerized laser range-finding an communications, makes it extremely difficul to distinguish in some instances between arma ments and industrial tools.

Archaeological evidence suggests that prehis toric armaments in N America developed in th same sequence as in other parts of the world The earliest written evidence comes from th 14th-century *Greenlanders' Saga*, which recount that NORSE adventurers armed with axes, explor ing the N Atlantic coast about 1000 AD, fough with "skraelings" (perhaps BEOTHUKS) who use bows and arrows. These were still the dominan weapons when Europeans began to infiltrat the continent again in the 16th century, bring ing with them the age of gunpowder. Jacque CARTIER used primitive hand guns ("fire lances" to impress Indians in the Baie des Chaleur during the summer of 1534, and mounted can non on the ramparts of his Québec fort in th winter of 1535. In 1609 Samuel de CHAMPLAIN allying himself with Huron and Algonqui Indians, killed 2 Iroquois with his harquebu (a matchlock musket), thus initiating a long lived enmity. Pehr KALM, a Swedish traveller reported 140 years later that there was scarce ly a French Canadian "who was not a cleve marksman and who did not own a rifle. He also noted the production of cannon an mortars at the FORGES SAINT-MAURICE near Trois Rivières. Some Indians were armed with mus kets by that time, although the bow and toma hawk remained more popular.

As the indigenous inhabitants were subdued driven farther west or killed, fighting in N

American-designed, Canadian-built Grizzly armoured personnel carrier (*courtesy National Defence Headquarters*).

America between people of European descent relied increasingly upon more sophisticated missile weapons, and the limited Canadian production of armaments ceased. In the early 19th century the flintlock musket gave way to the breech-loading rifle, while an ever smaller proportion of people possessed weapons. Some magazine rifles from the US were used by the Canadian Militia to repel the FENIANS in 1866 and 1870, and an American Gatling machine gun was used in suppressing the NORTH-WEST REBELLION of 1885. However, the militia continued to rely upon British rifles and artillery. The DOMINION ARSENAL began to produce small-arms ammunition in 1882, but the first Canadian-built, breech-loading, magazine rifle issued to the militia was the Ross (a variation on the Austrian Mannlicher), which first went into production in 1903. An excellent sporting rifle, it proved unsatisfactory under the rigours of active service in 1915, and production ceased in Mar 1917. In the CANADIAN EXPEDITIONARY FORCE it was replaced with the British Lee-Enfield rifle. Militiamen were again issued Ross rifles for home defence during WORLD WAR II.

For that war Canada manufactured a wide range of armaments, including combat aircraft such as the de Havilland Mosquito and Avro Lancaster bombers, armoured vehicles, artillery and naval guns, landing craft, convoy escorts, radios, RADAR, SONAR, small arms and enormous quantities of ammunition, explosives and pyrotechnics. Few, however, were of Canadian design, nor were Canadian forces necessarily equipped with them. One of the rare Canadian design initiatives, the Ram tank, was not a success and was never used in action; Ram hulls, however, with the turrets removed, were used in NW Europe in 1944 as the first armoured personnel carriers (APCs).

Since WWII Canada has continued to rely largely upon armament designs of its allies, sometimes modified to meet Canadian needs, for major weapon systems (*see* BOMARC MISSILE CRISIS). For example, the British Centurion served as the Canada's main battle tank for 25 years, 1952-77. Exceptions have been the AVRO CF-100 fighter aircraft and the various classes of small warships in the naval service, most notably the "Tribal" Class destroyers and "St Laurent" Class destroyer escorts. Advanced and complex projects such as the *Bobcat* APC, the AVRO ARROW fighter and the *Bras d'Or* hydrofoil have had to be abandoned because of restricted marketing possibilities and excessive design costs. Canada has had more success in producing high-technology components for American weapon systems. NATO allies employ Canadian-designed CRV-7 air-to-ground rockets, "Elsie" antipersonnel mines and extended-range, full-bore (ERFB) artillery rounds. Canadian forces depend heavily upon the Hornet fighter and Twin Huey, Kiowa and Sea King helicopters (all American) and the Leopard C 1 tank (W German), armed with a variety of appropriate missiles, for their tactical launch-ing platforms. Small arms currently carried by the Canadian infantryman (who rides in American-designed, Canadian-built APCs) include Belgian rifles and light machine guns, American heavy machine guns and antitank and antiaircraft missile launchers.

As part of the NORAD agreement, nuclear-tipped air-to-air missiles under American control have been held in Canada to be used by Canadian aircraft in case of need. With the adoption of the CF-18 Hornet during the 1980s, these are to be phased out of service. Canadian forces in Europe are also backed by American nuclear-weapon systems, but Canada has renounced nuclear armaments of her own, a decision that in 1970 removed the Honest John missile, acquired 1961, from the Canadian weapon inventory. Meanwhile, arguments over the offensive or defensive nature of weapons systems such as the Cruise missile and the Stealth bomber rage fruitlessly, since — as in prehistoric times — their use is largely a function of the intentions of those who wield them. The "quality or quantity" debate is now receiving much attention within the terms of Lanchester's N-Square Law: for the odds to be equal the effectiveness of the numerically weaker side has to be raised by the square of the ratio of the numbers involved; ie, against twice as many the weaker side needs to be 4 times as good in order for it to stand an even chance. Should weapon systems be simplified at the cost of effectiveness in order that more may be available? Among the superpowers the US has consistently favoured effectiveness while the USSR has emphasized numbers. *See* DISARMAMENT.

BRERETON GREENHOUS

CF-18 aircraft in flight (*Canadian Forces photo*).

Armed Forces, the combined land, naval and air forces prepared to engage in a nation's defence or in warfare. Canada's indigenous armed forces have evolved from the earliest militia through the establishment of the regular army, navy and air force to the modern Canadian Armed Forces.

Militia and Army

Militias, part-time forces organized for defence, date from the early Middle Ages — in England from the Anglo-Saxon *fyrd* (the national militia before the Norman Conquest). By the 18th century the few *milices* left in France were almost exclusively ceremonial, but in New France the system was revitalized to meet the Indian and English menaces. In Canada the name "militia" covered both part-time and regular forces until WWII. In the 1950s the militia became the part-time RESERVE FORCE. From about 1883 to 1940 the regulars were called the Permanent Force, or Permanent Militia. Thereafter, until unification in 1968, they were the Canadian Army.

In 1669 Louis XIV, expanding on earlier experience with militia training in Québec, Montréal and Trois-Rivières, advised that the militia system should be adopted throughout New France. Gov FRONTENAC later appointed a captain of militia in each parish, and required all males 16-60 to train for 1 or 2 months annually. The honorary *capitaines de milice* were highly respected by the habitants, and were leaders in both military and civil spheres. New France's militia was more effective than those in the English colonies, since it was skilled in the *petite guerre:* swift movement through the forest and surprise attack — tactics borrowed from the Indians. It made some notorious raids on New England settlements. Along with the TROUPES DE LA MARINE, or colonial regular troops, the militia protected the colony until the SEVEN YEARS' WAR brought regular regiments from France. The militia also provided CORVÉE labour to build roads, bridges and FORTIFICATIONS. When Gen James WOLFE threatened Québec in 1759 the militia was called out in a *levée en masse,* and several thousand militiamen were incorporated into the regular army that Montcalm had brought from France. After the capitulation of Montréal in 1760, the British used the militia captains in the administration of the country. They called up Canadien militia for service during PONTIAC's rebellion of 1763 and when the Americans invaded in 1775.

In Nova Scotia captains of militia were appointed as early as 1710, and there was a militia in Halifax in 1749. But the chief sources of support for the British garrisons in the Maritimes during the AMERICAN REVOLUTION were regiments raised for local defence, or fencibles enlisted for service anywhere in N America.

In 1793 provincial regiments were raised in Montréal and Québec. Disbanded in 1802, these Lower Canadian units were replaced in 1803 by the training of 1200 militiamen in service battalions. In 1791 Upper Canadian Lt-Gov John Graves SIMCOE raised a permanent corps of veterans, the Queen's Rangers, for defence and public works. It was disbanded in 1802 and replaced in 1811 by a fencible regiment. Simcoe had also attempted to establish a compulsory militia based on counties, but there was no provision for training it until 1808. During the WAR OF 1812 Canadian militia were assigned transport and labour duties. Volunteers fought alongside British regulars and provincial regiments. Canada was saved by British regulars, but the militia played an important role and Canadian legend later gave it credit for the victory.

Militia volunteers aided in suppressing the 1837 REBELLIONS, and some companies were kept together for several years. With the unification of the Canadas in 1841 the British government raised the Royal Canadian Rifles, a regiment of veterans, for garrison duties. Cavalry raised by Toronto's Denison family, the Montréal Fire Brigade (which doubled as an infantry battalion), the Halifax Militia Artillery and the "Uniform" Companies of Artillery in New Brunswick trained in peacetime at little cost to the government. In 1855 the MILITIA ACTS retained the principle of compulsory enrolment in the Sedentary Militia, but also authorized paid volunteer units. Thus the voluntary principle was accepted as the basis of Canadian defence. It proved so popular that it led to the formation of many historic units, but compulsory enrolment remained the theory, though not the practice, for 2 more decades.

When the AMERICAN CIVIL WAR raised fears of an American attack on Canada, an attempt to introduce compulsory training failed. In 1863 the volunteer militia that could be paid was increased to 10 000 and the number that could be trained but not paid was to be 35 000. None were trained in the Canadas before the war ended, but 34 800 men trained for 5 days in the Maritimes, and officers' schools were established. In 1865, 1100 Canadian officers attended a 3-week camp at La Prairie, Qué. In 1866, 20 000 volunteers faced FENIAN raiders and some fought them at Ridgeway. Militia infantry attended camps of instruction at Thorold (Ont), where they were brigaded with the British regulars. Cavalry and artillery camped at Toronto.

After Confederation the militia system continued. Forty thousand volunteers in cavalry, infantry, rifle and artillery units were to train annually for 8 to 17 days. In 1870 two militia battalions accompanied British regulars sent to suppress the RED RIVER REBELLION. In 1871 artillery schools opened at Kingston and Québec. A British general officer commanding (GOC) was appointed to the militia in 1874, and the Military College was established in 1876 at Kingston. From 1883 the staffs of 3 artillery schools (another was in Victoria, BC), a cavalry school at Québec, infantry schools at Fredericton, St Jean, Toronto, and later at London, and a mounted-infantry school at Winnipeg were the beginnings of the Permanent Force (PF). Under a British GOC, Frederick MIDDLETON, almost 8000 Canadian troops helped to suppress the NORTH-WEST REBELLION in 1885. Shortcomings revealed in training, equipment and organization had been caused by the government's failure to make adequate provision for defence except in times of crisis, such as the Russian scare of 1878, when the threat of war between Britain and Russia suggested the possibility of Russian attacks on Canadian ports.

Maj-Gen Ivor HERBERT, GOC 1890-95, secured approval of much-needed reform. Headquarters staff was expanded, officers were sent to England for training and, at the time of the 1895 Venezuela crisis (when the US threatened war with Britain over the determination of Venezuela's boundary with British Guiana), the PF infantry received a new rifle, the long Lee-Enfield. This was the last occasion on which fear of an American attack led to military preparations in Canada. In 1898, 200 PF volunteers went to the Yukon to help police and customs officers maintain order during the KLONDIKE GOLD RUSH. Before the YUKON FIELD FORCE returned in 1900, English Canadians induced PM Sir Wilfrid Laurier to send 1000 men to the SOUTH AFRICAN WAR. Militia volunteers, their numbers stiffened by regulars, formed a special service battalion of Royal Canadians under PF officer Lt-Col W.D. OTTER. A second contingent drew heavily on the permanent staff of the cavalry school and on the NORTH-WEST MOUNTED POLICE. Canada also raised an infantry battalion to relieve the British garrison in Halifax for war service.

The Canadian Militia was riddled with political patronage. Three reforming GOCs, Herbert, E.T.H. HUTTON and the earl of Dundonald, fought against it and ended their Canadian tours of duty abruptly. Nevertheless, Sir Frederick BORDEN, minister of militia and defence 1896-1911, was sincerely anxious for reform. In 1904 the British GOC was replaced by a Militia Council and the way was cleared for a Canadian chief of the general staff. The first was Otter in 1908. Ancillary corps were added: Medical, Army Service Corps, Ordnance, the Canadian Corps of Guides (for intelligence), Engineers and Signals. The infantry was re-equipped with a Canadian-made rifle, the Ross. In 1909 Canada agreed at an imperial (defence) conference to standardize organization and equipment on British models and to accept imperial general staff officers. By 1914 Canada's PF numbered 3000 and there were almost 60 000 partially trained militia. A mobilization plan had been prepared. But instead of using this during WORLD WAR I, Minister of Militia Sir Samuel HUGHES created the CANADIAN EXPEDITIONARY FORCE (CEF) by appealing for volunteers.

By the end of the war Canada had organized 5 divisions for overseas service. The Canadian Corps was commanded by a Canadian, Lt-Gen Sir Arthur CURRIE, and it was staffed by Canadians in all but a few key positions. After the war the number of PF infantry regiments was raised from 1 to 3, and the total PF establishment was 10 000. Actual strength remained around 4000 and Canada had no tanks or modern guns. Militia units were largely self-financed and self-equipped. At the height of the Depression only a few more than 2000 men went to camp, and then for only 4 days. The deteriorating international situation brought reorganization in 1936. Non-Permanent Active Militia (NPAM) establishment was reduced from a paper figure of 134 000 in 15 divisions to 86 557 in 7. Some cavalry units were mechanized, and by 1939 the number of artillery units had been increased from 97 to 155. The militia began to get new uniforms and equipment to replace WWI issue, and for the first time the men received service boots.

In WORLD WAR II Canada fielded an army of 3 infantry and 2 armoured divisions, and raised 3 divisions for home defence. Nearly three-quarters of a million men and women served. In June 1940 the NATIONAL RESOURCES MOBILIZATION ACT authorized the government to requisition Canadians' services for home defence. After the NRMA was amended in Nov 1944 to permit CONSCRIPTION for overseas service, some 2500 conscripts actually went into operational units during the last months of the war.

The Canadian Army establishment was fixed in 1946 at 25 000. In 1951 Canada sent troops to support the UNITED NATIONS forces in the KOREAN WAR, and almost 22 000 eventually served there. In 1952 the Canadian Army establishment was raised to 52 000 to meet Canada's obligations to NATO. In the 1950s the militia of 6 divisions was renamed the Reserve Force, but its assignment to security duties and civil defence, along with the disbandment of some ancient units, weakened morale. By 1977 it numbered only 15 000; and of those, barely 3000 were ready to reinforce the regulars. *See* REGIMENTS. RICHARD A. PRESTON

Navy

Indigenous naval forces in N America can be traced to the colonial period. Until the late 19th century, armed flotillas met specific colonial, provincial or national needs, both on the coasts and on the Great Lakes (*see* PROVINCIAL MARINE). Anglo-German naval rivalry nourished the idea that the fisheries-protection vessels of the Dept of Marine and Fisheries should become a separate organization, and on 29 Mar 1909 Parliament approved expenditure on a Canadian naval service to co-operate with Britain's Royal Navy. On 4 May 1910 the NAVAL SERVICE ACT brought the Royal Canadian Navy (RCN) into being. The navy was a major political issue, and it suffered severe setbacks under Conservative rule between 1911 and 1914. Divided between Halifax, NS, and Esquimalt, BC, it was directed from a distant headquarters in Ottawa. L.P. Brodeur, the first minister, George J. Desbarats, deputy minister, and Rear-Adm Charles E. KINGSMILL, RN (retired), director, were transferred from the Dept of Marine and Fisheries; they understood the navy's problems, but the naval staff sometimes failed to appreciate the fleet's needs, and often could not explain them to government. After WWI, Conservative and Liberal administrations alike starved the navy. Commodore Walter HOSE, director of the naval service 1921-28 and chief of the naval staff (CNS) 1928-34, had to resist efforts by the militia to subordinate and even disband it. Forced to close Royal Naval College of Canada in 1922, Hose established the ROYAL CANADIAN NAVAL VOLUNTEER RESERVE in 1923. Rear-Adm Percy NELLES, CNS 1934-43, built on this foundation when international tension in the late 1930s at last, and almost too late, aroused Ottawa to the need for an effective navy.

In both world wars, U-BOAT threats in the western Atlantic led to the unexpected growth of the RCN. In 1917-18 this simply meant diverting to Canada's East Coast resources previously allocated to the Royal Navy. In 1941 it meant creating a major oceanic fleet through a massive program of shipbuilding and recruiting. Anticipated commitments in the Pacific compounded the problem in 1943. The RCN grew from 13 warships and about 3000 men in 1939 to some 365 warships and 100 000 personnel in 1945. At first expansion diluted efficiency, especially in the navy's main function, convoy escort. When in 1943 the naval staff lost touch with chang-ing operational requirements in the fleet, Angus L. MACDONALD, minister of national defence for naval services 1940-45, replaced Nelles with Rear-Adm G.C. Jones. Partly because Naval Service Headquarters mounted skilful shore-based control of shipping, radio-intercept and intelligence operations, and partly because Canada provided half the escorts on the N Atlantic routes (*see* BATTLE OF THE ATLANTIC), Britain and the US agreed to establish a new theatre of operations, the Canadian Northwest Atlantic. On 1 May 1943 Rear-Adm L.W. MURRAY, who with other Canadian officers resented subordination in that region to the US Navy, became the theatre's commander in chief, an appointment unique in Canadian history. From 1943 to 1945 the RCN became the third-largest navy among the Allies, and satisfactorily carried out a wide variety of operations in many theatres.

Canadians often saw the RCN as a pale imitation of the RN; PM Mackenzie KING suspected that the Canadian service was a mere instrument of the British ADMIRALTY. Nevertheless, to preserve a continuing oceanic fleet, in 1945 his government approved a small permanent navy of 2 aircraft carriers, 2 cruisers and 12 destroyers. However, there was no rush to join the regular navy and it was necessary to extend the service of some reserve personnel who had joined during the war. Relations between officers and men soured under the pressures of adjustment to peacetime, which for many old hands meant resuming the merely routine prewar activities. After 3 mutinies in 1949, Rear-Adm E. Rollo MAINGUY presided over a commission that eloquently urged casting off certain inappropriate British customs. Its report, which was received with mixed feelings by the naval profession, became the RCN's Magna Carta.

In the Korean War, 1950-53, the RCN kept a highly professional force of 3 destroyers in Korean waters. By 1964, fed by COLD WAR tensions, the navy had grown to 1 aircraft carrier (the BONAVENTURE), 22 Canadian-designed and Canadian-built destroyers, 17 ocean escorts of WWII vintage, 10 coastal minesweepers and 21 500 personnel, committed for the most part to antisubmarine operations in NATO. Unification followed in 1968. Bitter opposition came from naval officers, many of whom resigned; Rear-Adm W.M. LANDYMORE was so vocal and indiscreet that he was dismissed. Greatly reduced in size and capability in the 1970s, and less readily identified than the RCN with its British progenitor, Maritime Command of the Canadian Armed Forces still derives much professional knowledge from the RN and remains one of the principal antisubmarine forces in NATO. W.A.B. DOUGLAS

Air Force

The Royal Canadian Air Force came into existence on 1 Apr 1924, and lost its distinct identity with the unification of the Canadian Armed Forces in 1968. Before 1914 military aviation in Canada did not exist; it was a matter for greater world powers. J.A.D. MCCURDY and F.W. "Casey" BALDWIN, members of Alexander Graham BELL's Aerial Experiment Association, arried out flight trials of the SILVER DART and *Baddeck-I* in Aug 1909 at Petawawa, Ont, but roused little interest in the Dept of Militia and Defence. Military and naval aviation underwent extraordinary development after WWI began, but the reluctance of the Canadian government to develop a distinct air force persisted until late in the war. Over 20 000 Canadians served as pilots, observers and ground support staff in the British ROYAL FLYING CORPS, the ROYAL NAVAL AIR SERVICE and, after 1 Apr 1918, the Royal Air Force, in every theatre of the war. The publicity given to Canadian participation in the air war, and especially to the exploits of such outstanding fighter pilots as W.A. BISHOP, W.G. BARKER, Raymond COLLISHAW and D.R. MACLAREN, helped to build pressure for the establishment of a distinctly Canadian service. So did the fact that German long-range submarines were a threat to shipping on Canada's East Coast. The Borden government accordingly authorized the creation of 2 small forces: the ROYAL CANADIAN NAVAL AIR SERVICE, for coastal defence, and the Canadian Air Force, which was intended to work with the Canadian Expeditionary Force on the Western Front. Both organizations were short-lived, the RCNAS being disbanded in Dec 1918 and the CAF in mid-1919.

Before the fledgling CAF was dissolved, steps had already been taken to formulate a national aviation policy. An air board, chaired by Minister of Customs A.L. SIFTON, was appointed in June 1919 and given the task of advising government on future aviation policy. This board laid the foundation for the development and regulation of civil aviation and, on the assumption that military aviation strength really depended upon a strong commercial sector, envisaged the formation of only a small, temporary military air force. The Canadian Air Force was thus established in Apr 1920, but it was soon clear that something more permanent was required. Under the National Defence Act of 1922 the Air Board was absorbed by the new Department of National Defence, and its civil and military air arms were united under the director, CAF, who reported to the army chief of staff (later chief of the general staff). The CAF was now a permanent force. Not until Nov 1938 did the air force's senior officer become chief of the air staff, directly responsible to the minister of national defence. In 1923 the CAF was designated "Royal," and on 1 Apr 1924, when the King's Regulations and Orders for the Royal Canadian Air Force came into effect, it adopted the RAF ensign, motto, UNIFORMS and rank structure, and even the same official birthdate.

Despite these colonial trappings, the RCAF was a Canadian service in personnel and function. Until the early 1930s about half the RCAF's manpower performed civil air operations. Forest spraying and fire patrol, fisheries and customs surveillance on both coasts, mercy flights and aerial photography (which contributed greatly to the mapping and geological survey of remote areas) were the bulk of the RCAF's duties. Its aircraft, such as the Canadian Vickers Vedette flying boat, were designed for such missions. In 1928 the force purchased a few Siskin fighters and Atlas army co-operation aircraft from Britain to replace its long-retired military aircraft. No further important purchases were made during the GREAT DEPRESSION. For the first half of the interwar period, therefore, Canada had a military flying service in name only, although connections with the RAF, through exchanges, a liaison staff and the posting of Canadian officers to British staff schools, ensured a degree of professionalism and some acquaintance with the evolution of air doctrine.

When WWII began in 1939, the RCAF had no first-class aircraft or other equipment, with the exception of some Hawker Hurricanes. Nevertheless, a framework for future expansion had been established. Western and Eastern Air Commands were responsible for coastal air defence, and Training Command was centered at Trenton, Ont. Eight Permanent Active Air Force squadrons and 12 Auxiliary Active Air Force squadrons had been organized.

The key to wartime expansion was the BRITISH COMMONWEALTH AIR TRAINING PLAN. This vast program graduated 131 553 aircrew by its close, of whom 72 835 were Canadian. Despite the Canadian government's commitment to training Commonwealth aircrew, it did not accord the RCAF an independent status commensurate with that of the Canadian Army during the war. Although the BCATP Agreement contained a British undertaking that Commonwealth aircrew "shall . . . be identified with their respective Dominions," the Canadian government failed to provide financially for the ground crew needed to support Canadian aircrew overseas, or for full financing of Canadian aircrew serving abroad, or even for the support of Canadian air units overseas. As a result, Canadian pilots, navigators, air gunners and other aircrew found themselves dispersed throughout the RAF, rather than being concentrated in RCAF groupings. Minister for National Defence for Air C.G. POWER, with the assistance of the RCAF senior officers, prevailed upon the RAF to permit the formation of more RCAF squadrons as the war progressed.

Of 250 000 men and women in the wartime RCAF, 94 000 served overseas. Most airmen flew with the RAF, but 48 separate Canadian squadrons took part in operations around the globe, from No 1 (later 401) Squadron's participation in the BATTLE OF BRITAIN to 435 and 436 (Transport) Squadrons' missions in India and Burma during the final days of the conflict with Japan. 417 Squadron and 331 Wing fought in N Africa, and the former went on into Italy. Canadian squadrons played a part in all RAF operational home commands. They formed a group of their own, 6 Group (RCAF) in Bomber Command, and contributed half the strength of the RAF's 83 Composite Group in the Second Tactical Air Force. Airmen such as Air Vice-Marshals C.M. "Black Mike" MCEWEN and G.E. Brookes, Group Capts W.R. MacBrien and G.R. McGregor and Wing Cdrs George Keefer and Stan Turner became noted air leaders. Wallace McLeod, "Buck" McNair and George "Buzz" BEURLING carried on the tradition of Bishop, Barker, Collishaw and MacLaren.

From the beginning, the RCAF was deeply involved in the Battle of the Atlantic. Squadrons from East Coast bases carried out convoy duties and antisubmarine patrols, flying Lockheed Hudsons and Venturas, Catalinas, Cansos and Liberators. RCAF squadrons participated with American forces in the defence of Alaska against Japanese incursions. In addition, the RCAF flew on antisubmarine duties in the Far East.

Bomber Command was the largest RAF operational command. Into it were poured thousands of Canadian BCATP graduates to take part in the massive area-bombing campaign. Canadians were involved from the start, but the first Canadian unit was 405 Squadron, which was operational in mid-1941 and was part of the elite Pathfinder group. In Jan 1943, 6 Group became operational, commanded first by Brookes and then by McEwen. (These were the highest operational commands held by Canadian airmen in WWII.) Wing Cdr J.E. FAUQUIER was the leading Canadian bomber pilot. Casualties were heavy; of the more than 17 000 fatal casualties suffered by the RCAF during WWII, nearly 10 000 were sustained in Bomber Command.

By late 1946 the RCAF had dwindled to 13 000 all ranks. The permanent force resumed such duties as transport, search and rescue, and survey patrols. Jet flight did not enter the service until 1948, when some British Vampires were purchased. In the Korean War, Canada's official air contribution was limited to the transport duties of 426 Squadron, although some RCAF pilots flew with the US Air Force. It was the Cold War threat that reversed the trend towards reducing the RCAF's size. In Feb 1951 the Canadian government committed an air division of 12 fighter squadrons to Europe as part of its NATO involvement. In 1958 Canada and the US joined in the formation of the North American Air Defence Command (NORAD): in addition to substantial home defence commitments, this new orientation in Canadian defence policy meant that a Canadian became deputy commander. The first to serve was Air Marshal C.R. SLEMON.

Canadian air defence in the post-1945 period relied heavily upon foreign-produced aircraft, a policy underlined by the cancellation of the AVRO ARROW in 1959. The tendency to respond to outside initiatives, a long-term characteristic of the RCAF, did not end with the disappearance of the force when the armed services were unified in 1968. In today's Canadian Armed Forces, signs of the RCAF remain, as in its numbered squadrons and in the less tangible, but no less real, air force spirit. S.F. WISE

Unification and After

The Canadian Forces Reorganization Bill, proclaimed 1 Feb 1968, abolished the RCN, the Canadian Army and the RCAF, and created a single service, the Canadian Armed Forces, with regular and reserve components and the potential for a special force to meet NATO, United Nations or other external commitments. The experiment of unification was unique to Canada and was not imitated by other countries. Within a decade the 3 service identities had to some degree re-emerged.

Integration had been a recurrent policy since the establishment of a single National Defence Headquarters in 1922. Under Brooke CLAXTON, minister of national defence 1946-54, Canada's MILITARY COLLEGES and systems of military law had been unified, as had other aspects of military administration. During the years of John Diefenbaker's Conservative government (1957-63), medical, legal and chaplains' services were integrated. The armed forces expected major changes when the Liberals returned to power in 1963. Military leaders could not escape some responsibility for the indecision and confusion in defence policies which had helped bring down the Diefenbaker government. The Glassco Royal Commission (1963) was highly critical of inefficiency and triplication of administration. It seemed reasonable to blame administrative waste for part of the rapid decline of capital spending in the defence budget, from 42.4% in 1954 to 18.9% in 1962. In Opposition, the Liberals had dropped their earlier arguments against nuclear warheads, but promised a searching review of defence policy and an easing out of alliance roles involving nuclear arms.

Toronto businessman Paul HELLYER had been defence critic in Opposition, and as minister of defence he first undertook the promised policy review. When his report appeared in Mar 1964, adjectives like "mobile," "flexible" and "imaginative" and an emphasis on PM Lester Pearson's favourite accomplishment, PEACEKEEPING, did not conceal a continuing commitment to NATO, to continental air defence and to domestic security. Almost overlooked was the one-line promise of "a single unified defence force."

Unification had not been Hellyer's policy initially. The idea grew on him as he tried to deal with 3 service chiefs, each struggling for his own service. The Glassco Commission had found over 200 interservice committees, few of them collaborating. In future, Hellyer believed, the services would have to work closely together. His first step, approved by Parliament on 7 July 1964, was full integration of National Defence Headquarters under a single chief of the defence staff. Staff functions were divided among 4 branches: operations, personnel, logistics and finance. There was little criticism. Even the services welcomed a streamlined headquarters if it would fulfil the promise of badly needed new equipment. On 7 June 1965, navy, army and air force commands were replaced by 6 functional commands, most of them with regional responsibilities. Maritime Command took over the RCN's ships and the RCAF's antisubmarine squadrons on both coasts. Mobile Command at St-Hubert, Qué, was to control the army's brigade groups and militia and the RCAF's ground-support squadrons. Training Command and Material Command integrated tri-service functions, while Air Defence and Air Transport Commands passed unaltered from the RCAF. Communications Command was added later; Canada's ground and air forces in Europe reported directly to Ottawa. On 1 May 1966 camps, stations and the navy's land-based "ships" became 39 Canadian Forces Bases. Unified training schools and a single pay system took shape.

Many senior officers now expected a breathing space, but Hellyer's commitment to unification was undiluted. Institutional changes had gone far to make unification natural. When senior officers protested, Hellyer regarded their opposition as verging on a challenge to civil supremacy over the military. Politicians, editors and cartoonists often ridiculed the officers' objections. The public was reminded that several who resigned in protest enjoyed generous pensions. By appointing Gen Jean-Victor ALLARD as chief of the defence staff, Hellyer secured an enthusiast for unification and for eliminating many British features of the forces. Although debate over the Reorganization Bill was prolonged and sometimes rancorous, the legislation passed the Commons with NDP and Social Credit support. Within a year, members of the Canadian forces had begun to appear in new green uniforms modelled on those of the US Air Force, with rank badges recognizable to American as well as Canadian personnel.

The public spectacle of integration and unification overshadowed government efforts to find new roles and equipment for its revamped military organization. Instead of reducing international roles to fit reduced strength, the government committed major forces to peacekeeping in Cyprus in 1964 — a "brief" task which had not ended by 1984. The search for a nonnuclear role in NATO led to a promise to send forces to Norway if NATO's northern (and nonnuclear) flank was threatened. The ill-equipped Canadian brigade group in Germany did not receive armoured personnel carriers until 1967 or modern tanks until 1977. When air force advisers asked for American-built F-4 Phantoms, the government chose the CF-5, a cheaper, less sophisticated aircraft. A navy program of 8 general-purpose frigates was cancelled and replaced by construction of 4 helicopter-equipped destroyers for antisubmarine work and a costly refit of the single aircraft carrier, the *Bonaventure*.

Well aware that public opinion and most colleagues favoured defence cuts, Hellyer had negotiated a fixed budget of $1.5 billion a year for his department. His drastic reorganization, with the accompanying drop in personnel, was a trade-off for modernization. Inflation ate up most of the savings. A destroyer worth $20 million in 1960 cost $50 million by 1967. Canadian apathy regarding defence spending grew with the decade and with criticism of American involvement in Vietnam. Domestic concerns, inflation, unemployment and Québec SEPARATISM preoccupied Canadians.

On 26 June 1968, Canadian voters gave their confidence to a new Liberal leader, P.E. Trudeau, who promised systematic policymaking and a cure for the "strategist's cramp" that had bound Canadian defence since WWII. On 3 Apr 1969 the new prime minister proclaimed new defence priorities: surveillance of Canadian territory and coastlines (protection of sovereignty); defence of N America in co-operation with the US; fulfilment of NATO commitments; and performance of any international peacekeeping roles Canada might assume. The list turned Hellyer's 1964 priorities upside down. Peacekeeping, the justification for Hellyer's unification, was lowest; "surveillance" was now on top. Hellyer's successor as minister of national defence, Léo Cadieux, went to Brussels to warn of drastic cuts in Canada's NATO force. In Aug 1969 Canada's NATO contingent of 10 000 was halved and the remaining ground forces were transferred from British to American command. In Parliament, Cadieux announced that Armed Forces strength would fall from 110 000 to 80-85 000. *Bonaventure*, newly refitted, was scrapped. Five regular regiments vanished from the active list. Most CF-5 fighters went into storage. The new policies were costly and military leaders took the blame. Disposal of the costly aircraft carrier, the mothballing of an experimental hydrofoil and delivery of the now-inappropriate new destroyers made Maritime Command look foolish. One consequence of criticism was a 1972 policy of "civilianization" in NDHQ.

The government's policies, summarized in *Defence in the Seventies* (1970), elaborated the military role in ensuring Canadian sovereignty, not merely in the Arctic and on the oceans but in AID TO THE CIVIL POWER. This last was a historic but half-forgotten role for Canadian forces, but urban violence in the US and potential peacekeeping roles had justified planning and training. In Oct 1969 troops were rushed to Montréal when rioting accompanied a police strike. A much more massive intervention occurred during the OCTOBER CRISIS: on 14 Oct 1970 troops were ordered to Ottawa to protect public buildings and prominent figures. On Oct 16 the prime minister proclaimed the WAR MEASURES ACT, and more than 10 000 troops in battle order were soon deployed in Montréal, Québec and Ottawa. It was a dramatic and dangerous exercise of power. Some officers recognized that such activity posed great danger for the Armed Forces as an institution. The troops were fortunate that they could withdraw as early as Nov 12 without suffering or inflicting casualties.

The October Crisis heightened awareness of the importance of making the Canadian forces more representative of an essentially bicultural nation. The Royal Commission on BILINGUALISM AND BICULTURALISM had demonstrated that the Armed Forces remained typical of federal institutions which frustrated French-speaking Canadians. Outside of a few army units, the forces had operated almost entirely in English. Few French Canadians had ever reached the highest ranks. In 2 world wars, unilingualism of the forces had contributed to bitterly divisive conscription crises. The Trudeau government was determined to make federal agencies effectively bilingual, and the Armed Forces were an obvious place to start.

New policies included expansion of language training, recruiting and promotion policy to achieve proportional representation through the rank structure, separate training for French-speaking personnel covering most of the 300 specialist trades, and French-language ships, flying squadrons and ground-force units. The program, coinciding with sharp reductions in overall strength, a weak budget and allegations of political interference, was acutely unpopular with the English-speaking majority. French-language units often made the Armed Forces look as divided as the country they served. Time patience and new generations of personne would gradually make bilingualism, like uni fication, seem more natural.

Both experiments had been easier because i was unclear how Canadian forces could be use in a world that seemed to be moving toward détente. But in the 1970s the world began t appear more dangerous. The creation of th Organization of Petroleum Exporting Countrie and its power to raise oil prices revealed un expected vulnerability among Western indus trialized countries. The growth of a powerfu Soviet fleet with a potential global reach adde to a threat hitherto limited to massive armoure forces and powerful missile batteries. The Cana dian government, seeking to improve commer cial relations with Europe, discovered the cost o the 1969 decision to halve the NATO contingen not only could the remnant not be removed, bu its obsolete tanks and aircraft had to be replace to assuage the anger of NATO partners. Despit painful and costly delays, Canada began re equipping (*see* ARMAMENTS). During the 7-yea process of choosing a maritime patrol plane, th price rose from $300 million to more than $ billion. The search for a new fighter airplane le to the McDonnell-Douglas F-18D, essentially a unproven aircraft. The decisive consideratio was the amount of business the deal would dis tribute to Québec and Ontario industries. Whil the aging ships and aircraft of Maritime Com mand spent long periods in harbour awaitin repairs, delivery dates for 6 patrol frigates re ceded into the late 1980s and the 1990s.

The reluctant commitment to re-equip re flected a belated realization that Canada's influ ence in the world was not improved by the de bilitated state of its Armed Forces. Purchases o German Leopard tanks and American aircraf served as much a diplomatic as a military pur pose. Even domestic opinion appeared to sup port a modest strengthening of the forces. Be fore the 1979 election, the Trudeau governmen promised to add 4700 men and women to a uni formed strength that had fallen to 78 000 and t add a capital-spending program equal to at leas 20% of the defence budget. The commitmen was endorsed by Joe Clark's Conservative gov ernment, which won the election. Clark's gov ernment also established a task force to repor on the possible unscrambling of unification.

The task force reported to a renewed Libera government. Unification was not to be undone Its original rigour had already begun to fade The functional commands had been modifie by 1975 to restore a shadow of the original services: Maritime Command, Mobile Com mand and Air Command. Officers in charge isolated in Halifax, St-Hubert and Winnipeg were granted improved access to NDHQ. Dis tinctions developed in the training and caree planning of members of each command, but i took the 1984 victory of the Conservatives and new minister, Robert Coates, to revive 3 separate service uniforms. By then the green uniform had become their own tradition to four-fifth of serving personnel, and the new uniform seemed strikingly irrelevant to Canadian secu rity or the Armed Forces' own priorities.

Rearmament reflected the fading of détent with the USSR, and was a response to the ag gressive, confrontational style of the US's Rea gan administration, which was elected in Nov 1980. Like many European allies, Canadian leaders regarded the right-wing philosophy of this American government as simplistic and dangerous. Paradoxically, to influence Wash ington and to show solidarity with other NATO allies, Canada had to strengthen its conven tional military capacity. Almost symbolically Reagan's first visit to Ottawa in Mar 1981 wa the occasion to renew the NORAD agreement fo the third time.

Canada's sovereignty has always been limited by military dependence, first on Britain and then on the US. In peacetime few Canadians have worried about an arrangement which most have felt to be inevitable. A few have argued that Canada should scrap all armed forces in a splendid commitment to PACIFISM. Since this would force the Americans to defend their N American frontier, it would be an ultimate surrender of national sovereignty. The alternative might be an armed neutrality patterned on Sweden's, but the vastness of Canada's geography would make the cost almost prohibitive.

Defence policy of the early 1980s continued in a tradition set since Confederation: first, to work for peace between 2 powerful and suspicious neighbours; second, to maintain various alliances as insurance against disaster; third, to prepare for self-defence, which has never been seriously contemplated in peacetime. Although unheroic and modest, such policies have had the merit of success. Canada's premium for defence insurance has been and remains small. In the early 1980s, among NATO allies Canada stood 13th of 15 in military effort, spending 1.8% of the gross domestic product on defence compared to a NATO average of 3.8%. Only 1% of Canada's labour force was in uniform, while its allies had an average of 2.8%. Canada's forces, among the best paid in the world, had much obsolete and worn-out equipment. The inflated rank structure evident in 1984 — too many senior officers, not enough privates — would be justified if Canada could count on leisurely expansion in event of war. In fact, it was a symptom of costly peacetime careerism and a lack of tough realism which can be understood only against the background of Canada's defence history.

DESMOND MORTON

Reading: James Boutilier, ed, *The RCN in Retrospect 1910-1968* (1981); Canada. Army Headquarters, Historical Section, *The Regiments and Corps of the Canadian Army* (1964); B. Cuthbertson, *Canadian Military Independence in the Age of the Superpowers* (1977); James Eayrs, *In Defence of Canada*, 5 vols (1964-83); D.J. Goodspeed, *The Armed Forces of Canada* (1967); S. Kostenuk and J. Griffin, *RCAF Squadron Histories and Aircraft, 1924-1968* (1977); K. Macpherson and J. Burgess, *The Ships of Canada's Naval Forces, 1910-1981* (1981); Desmond Morton, *Canada and War* (1981); Leslie Roberts, *There Shall Be Wings* (1959); G.F.G Stanley and H.M. Jackson, *Canada's Soldiers 1604-1954* (1954); G.N. Tucker, *The Naval Service of Canada*, 2 vols (1951).

Armenians The Armenian Soviet Socialist Republic, the only Armenian political unit in existence today, comprises only a portion of historic Armenia. Most of the Armenian students and factory recruits who started the chain of Armenian migration to Canada in the 1880s were born in the territories occupied by the Ottoman Empire. In the 1890s some Armenians immigrated to Canada from the US. By 1915 there were approximately 1000 Armenians in Canada, largely sojourning men of peasant class from Anatolia. From 1915 to 1922 over 1.5 million Armenians perished as a result of the Turkish government's policy of genocide. Canadian immigration restrictions passed in 1909 effectively barred all but 1500 survivors of the Genocide from entering Canada between 1919 and 1939. Liberalization of Canada's immigration regulations in the 1950s and the end to the classification of Armenians as Asiatics, led to an influx of Armenian immigrants, almost exclusively from the Mediterranean countries. It is estimated that today there are about 50 000 Canadians of Armenian descent.

Most Armenians in Canada are now entrepreneurs and professionals. About 60% of Armenians live in metropolitan Montréal, 35% in the Toronto-Hamilton megalopolis, and the remainder in other urban centres.

The majority of Armenians belong to the Armenian National Apostolic Church; others adhere to the Catholic or Protestant churches. In addition to administering to the religious needs of the community, the churches are also engaged in social and cultural functions.

The Armenian National Committee is the umbrella organization of the Armenian Revolutionary Federation, which was founded in Canada in 1902, and has been the major nationalist party in Canada for over 80 years. The Democratic Liberal (Ramgavar) and the Social Democrat Hnchagian parties also have followers. Along with the Armenian General Benevolent Union, the parties organize cultural, social, charitable, athletic, and scout and guide activities. The Armenian language press, including a large number of bulletins and newsletters, and the weeklies, *Horizon* and *Abaka*, play an important role in language retention.

The Genocide and the fear of ultimate national extinction have spurred Armenians to powerful efforts to preserve their ethnic heritage, especially through Armenian schools. At least 1100 children in Montréal and Toronto attend 4 full-time elementary day schools based on a trilingual curriculum. ISABEL KAPRIELIAN

Armstrong, Ernest Howard, journalist, lawyer, politician (b at Kingston, NS 27 July 1864; d at Bridgewater, NS 15 Feb 1946). Educated at Acadia and Dalhousie (LLB, 1888), Armstrong edited the Weymouth *Free Press* from 1889 to 1892, and later moved to Yarmouth where he held various administrative posts. He was MLA for Yarmouth County (1906-20) and held the public works and mines portfolio in the Liberal government of Premier G.H. MURRAY 1911-23. A hardworking but unimaginative politician, Armstrong sought retirement to the bench when, as senior Cabinet member, he succeeded to the premiership (1923-25). Although the Liberals' rout in the June 1925 election was basically the result of regional depression, Armstrong's misreading of the MARITIME RIGHTS movement and mishandling of labour problems in the coal mines contributed to the Conservative landslide. ERNEST R. FORBES

Armstrong, John, printer, labour leader (d at Toronto, 22 Nov 1910). The major Conservative labour spokesman in Toronto in the 1880s, Armstrong was active in the Toronto Trades and Labor Council and in the TRADES AND LABOR CONGRESS OF CANADA. Fired from the Toronto *Mail* after the unsuccessful 1884 strike, Armstrong helped lead Toronto workers away from the Tories briefly. Sir John A. MACDONALD's timely intervention allowed Armstrong to arrange a truce between the printers and the *Mail*. Appointed to the Royal Commission on the Relations of Labour and Capital, he led a pro-labour faction which issued a separate report. When the Conservatives came to power in Ontario, Armstrong was named secretary of the Ontario Bureau of Labour. G.S. KEALEY

Armstrong, John Archibald, business executive (b at Dauphin, Man 24 Mar 1917). A geologist, he graduated from University of Manitoba and worked 42 years for Imperial Oil, Canada's largest oil company, including 4 as president and 8 as chairman of the board, before retiring 1982. His tenure as president and chairman was a difficult time for Canada's oil industry and Imperial. After nearly 30 years of rapid growth, the industry had entered a period of declining supplies, production rates and consumer demand, with sharply higher prices and national controversy over revenue sharing between the oil companies, oil-producing provinces and the federal government. Under Armstrong's administration, Imperial appeared to cope with these difficulties with more success than most oil companies. EARLE GRAY

Armstrong, William, civil engineer, artist, photographer (b at Dublin, Ire 28 July 1882; d at Toronto, Ont 8 June 1914). He immigrated to Toronto in 1851, and his work as a railway engineer gave him opportunities to indulge his hobby of painting in not yet settled parts of the country. He painted native life in the style of Paul KANE and his sketches of troops in the RED RIVER REBELLION (1870) appeared in the *Canadian Illustrated News*. He was a competent watercolourist and in works such as *The Arrival of the Prince of Wales at Toronto* (1860) he has left a valuable record. He was much admired in his day and, as drawing master at the Toronto Normal School for 26 years, had a lasting influence. He was associate member of the Royal Canadian Academy at its founding. Armstrong was also one of the earliest collodion wet-plate practitioners, but few of his photographs have survived. JAMES MARSH

Army Benevolent Fund Board, est under the Army Benevolent Fund Act (1947) to administer funds in special accounts existing in the Consolidated Revenue Fund. The board comprises 5 members, nominated from each of the National Council of Veterans Associations in Canada and from the ROYAL CANADIAN LEGION. The funds represent a source of relief for WWII veterans and their dependants when help is not available from other veterans' programs or social programs. Educational assistance is also provided subject to evidence of need and continued progress. The board reports to Parliament through the minister of veterans affairs.

Arnold, Benedict, soldier (b at Norwich, Conn 14 Jan 1741/42; d at London, Eng 14 June 1801). After service in the Seven Years' War, he enlisted in the American Revolutionary Army. He captured Ticonderoga, 10 May 1775, and with Richard Montgomery attacked Québec that Dec. On Montgomery's death, Arnold became commander of American forces in Canada, and led the retreat, via Montréal, in the spring of 1776. Pleading unfair treatment at the hands of the Americans, Arnold deserted to the British 1780. He served in the British army until 1781 and spent the rest of his life in obscurity. His name is synonymous with treachery in the US.

DAVID EVANS

Arnprior, Ont, Town, pop 5828 (1981c), inc 1892, located at the confluence of the Madawaska and OTTAWA rivers, 56 km W of Ottawa. The community was founded by the despotic Scots laird Archibald MCNAB in 1823, and the site was named after the ancestral home (Arnpryor) of his Buchanan kinsmen. McNab lost his settlement rights in 1840, and the site was deserted until 1851, when Daniel McLauchlin began large-scale lumbering operations on the Madawaska. Lumber and textiles dominated the economy for a long time. Now helicopters and tourism are important, and the Canadian Civil Defence College is located here. Memorabilia of McNab's days are displayed at the Arnprior and District Museum, and his summer home, Waba Lodge, is recreated 10 km SW. The 2 weekly newspapers are the *Guide* and the *Chronicle*.

K.L. MORRISON

Aroostook War, a point of crisis in the Maine-New Brunswick boundary dispute which in early 1839 saw both sides send troops into the valley of the Aroostook, a tributary of the SAINT JOHN R. By the TREATY OF PARIS, 1783, the boundary was supposed to run N from the ST CROIX R to an undetermined height of land. At stake were the Acadian settlements of Madawaska, communication between the British provinces, and rich timber resources. Serious conflict was avoided through compromise and the dispute was resolved by the ASHBURTON-WEBSTER TREATY of 1842.

ERNEST R. FORBES

Arpent, a French measure of length and area. Numerous regional variants of the arpent coexisted in 17th-century France; of these, the *arpent*

de Paris came into use in Canada before 1636 as part of a system of measures. The *arpent de superficie*, or square arpent (equivalent to 0.342 ha), remained the standard measure of land area in the old seigneurial districts of Québec until supplanted by the metric system in the late 1970s.

TOM WIEN

French Unit	*English Equivalent*	*Metric Equivalent*
pied	1.066 ft	.325 m
toise (6 pieds)	6.40 ft	1.95 m
perche (3 toises)	19.18 ft	5.85 m
arpent (10 perches)	191.8 ft	58.5 m
lieue (84 arpents)	16 111.2 ft (3.051 mi)	4.91 km

Arsenault, Angèle, singer, songwriter (b at Abrams, PEI 1 Oct 1943). A collector and singer of Acadian folk songs, she was encouraged by her impresario Lise Aubut to write and sing her own songs in English and French (1973-74). She was cofounder (1974) of the Société de production et de programmation de spectacles (SPPS). Her long-playing record *Libre* won the 1979 ADISQ Gala Award for best-selling album. She changed her image to a more natural style in the early 1980s, but her rhythmic songs are still the vehicle for her own special brand of humour.

HÉLÈNE PLOUFFE

Arsenault, Aubin-Edmond, lawyer, politician, premier of PEI (b at Abrams Village, PEI 28 July 1870; d at Charlottetown 29 Apr 1968). In 1917 Arsenault became premier of the Island, the first Acadian premier of any Canadian province. Son of Joseph-Octave Arsenault, a longtime provincial member and the first and only PEI Acadian named to the Senate, Aubin-Edmond sat in the PEI assembly 1908-21. He was successively minister without portfolio, premier and attorney general and 1919-21 leader of the opposition. From 1921 to 1946, Arsenault served as judge of the Supreme Court of PEI.

GEORGES ARSENAULT

Art The native people of Canada excelled in all forms of art (*see* INDIAN ART; INUIT ART; NORTHWEST COAST INDIAN ART; PREHISTORY), but their great achievements are beyond the scope of this article. Early Canadian art in the European tradition cannot be separated from European artistic production of the same period. From the time they arrived in Canada, French colonists attempted to reproduce an architectural environment that reminded them of their motherland (*see also* ARCHITECTURE). Before launching more ambitious projects, they erected a system of protection used in Europe since the late Middle Ages: the fortified manor. Early construction at PORT-ROYAL; Champlain's residence in Québec City (1608); and Maisonneuve's Pointe-à-Callières fort in Montréal (1642) were built on these lines, though in materials such as wood which were available and easily worked. Construction methods borrowed nothing from indigenous habitations.

Objects of curiosity as well as of conquest, the native people of the New World were first depicted on maps by illustrators who had no direct knowledge of their subject. They reflected more the traditional preconceptions about peoples who were supposed to inhabit the far reaches of the known world than the actual accounts of the discoverers, who themselves were not without prejudice. Books about Canada were more accurate. Champlain's *Works*, for instance, were illustrated by a few engravings based on his drawings, which gave a relatively good view of some aspects of Huron life, such as hunting, healing rituals and funerary practices. The portraits of Inuit painted by John White during Martin FROBISHER's expedition are astonishingly accurate. Drawings by the Jesuit Louis Nicolas, now known as the *Codex canadensis*, took their inspiration from François Du Creux's *Historia canadensis*. . . (1664), but they added so many details to their models that they contribute immensely to knowledge of the first inhabitants of Canada, particularly the Algonquin.

Ex voto of Marquis de Tracy (1666). Mercantilism made the development of indigenous painting virtually impossible during the French regime. Ex voto painting was among the few exceptions (*courtesy Basilique Ste-Anne-de-Beaupré*).

Population growth, while much slower than in New England during the same period, soon made it necessary to construct more permanent dwellings. Towns began to flourish. QUÉBEC CITY had taken shape by the end of the 17th century, its major buildings already in locations they occupied during the French regime (to 1760). Cathedrals, convents and the headquarters of the governor and the intendant occupied the best land on Cape Diamond or, as it was then called, "la haute ville." The commercial lower town developed around the small Notre-Dame-des-Victoires Chapel (1688), in front of which a bust of the king graced a small square. Built according to plans drawn up by engineers Claude Baillif, Levasseur de Néré and Chaussegros de Léry, if not by professional architects, these buildings were solid constructions in stone, recalling the style of provincial France of the same period.

Founded a little later, MONTRÉAL followed a similar development. Maisonneuve's old fort was abandoned, and the city spread out along the St Lawrence R between the parish church, almost where Notre-Dame is today, and the Bonsecours Chapel, construction of which began in 1657. A fortified wall was built in an attempt to establish the town boundaries. A striking example of 18th-century military architecture, the massive fortress of LOUISBOURG on Cape Breton I was designed by Jean-François de VERVILLE to follow Sébastien Le Prestre de Vauban's system of FORTIFICATIONS and proved extremely costly to build. After 1960 it was rebuilt by Parks Canada in meticulous detail.

At the same time as this urban development was taking place, the SEIGNEURIAL SYSTEM was creating rural habitations along the river. Villages, the centre of which was always the parish church, were slow to develop. By the 18th century the countryside was dotted with churches that imitated the splendid town churches, which in turn were reminiscent of French provincial churches. Québec's Notre-Dame and the churches of the Jesuits and Récollets had a determining influence on these rural churches. Houses around Québec, in contrast, resembled those on Norman farms, and houses elsewhere recalled those found in Maine, Perche or Anjou, the native regions of most of the colonists. In contrast to New England architecture, stone and wood were used frequently, but brick was never employed.

By the late 17th century, sculptors were commissioned to adorn the churches with high altars in carved and gilded wood. Unlike church paintings, which were created on canvas and could be rolled up and transported by ship, the more cumbersome sculptures were produced locally by tradesmen who passed their knowledge down through the generations from master to apprentice. The most famous were the Levasseurs and BAILLAIRGÉS of Québec, Philippe Liébert and, later, Louis QUÉVILLON of Montréal. In style these sculptors were catching up to the prevalent trends in France — Louis XV, rococo, neoclassical — though with some delay owing to the difficulties in communication between the metropolis and the colony (*see also* SCULPTURE).

France's MERCANTILISM made it more difficult for PAINTING to develop. With the exception of ex-voto paintings (*see* VOTIVE PAINTING) and a few portraits of nuns (especially posthumous portraits) and officers done in New France, paintings dating from the French regime were imported. Frère LUC might be considered an exception, but he spent only 15 months in Canada. On one level these difficult conditions contributed to the quality of early painting in Canada, for they have a spontaneity and naïvety not always found in sculpture.

The British Conquest in 1760 did not immediately alter the face of architecture in Lower Canada. Buildings damaged during the war were reconstructed and churches were built according to traditional plans, now slightly more formalized under the influence of Abbé Conefroy's plan for the Boucherville Church (1801). Later under the influence of Jérôme Demers, a professor of architecture at the seminary in Québec architects such as his pupil Thomas Baillairgé became receptive to French neoclassicism. Demers was a devoted follower of French architects like Vignole and Blondel.

The arrival of the British in N America had an immediate effect on painting. English officers trained at the Military Academy in Woolwich showed their enthusiasm for the Canadian landscape by producing many TOPOGRAPHIC PAINTINGS and ornamental landscapes which were often engraved in London. Thomas Davies was one of the earliest and the most famous of these English watercolour artists. His works have a freshness not found in those of Richard Short or James Patison Cockburn, which are of a more documentary nature.

New waves of colonists had a profound influence on the arts. Like the French before them the British tended to prefer the style which they knew best, Georgian, which for a long time thereafter symbolized allegiance to the British Crown. The LOYALISTS brought art objects and ideas with them from the US, including silver engravings and paintings, as well as the memories of the architecture of various regions. By 1800 an expanding economy favoured growth of a middle class and several garrison communities. Portraits of merchants and their families of soldiers, government officials and the clergy were in demand. After spending 14 years as a portrait artist in the US, Robert Field lived for 8 years in Halifax, where he continued in this genre; his English background and training made him a polished painter, familiar with the styles and techniques fashionable during this period.

The turn of the century saw the beginning of what is sometimes called the Golden Age of Québec painting. New stimuli became available Québec artists went to Europe to study, and European artists continued to arrive in Canada François Beaucourt, Antoine PLAMONDON and

Théophile HAMEL belonged to the former group, William BERCZY and Cornelius KRIEGHOFF to the atter. Joseph LÉGARÉ, however, never set foot in Europe; his interest in art and collecting developed parallel to his pictorial records of landscapes, dramatic events in the history of Québec and occasional bursts of pictorial fantasy.

Stylistically, European influence in Canada remained strong, but subject matter in painting broadened. In small precise paintings Peter RINDSBACHER showed what it meant to a young Swiss to sail into Hudson Bay and settle in the Red River Colony. Working out of Upper Canada, Paul KANE can really be called an artist/adventurer; he was inspired by the American George Catlin to make a journey across Canada n 1846, recording Indians, the portages and the cenery in 240 sketches and 100 paintings, still mall in format and stylistically dense.

As in the US during the first half of the 19th entury, Canada too was sensitive to a variety of rchitectural styles. British architects such as ohn Wells (Bank of Montreal, 1848) and John OSTELL (Notre-Dame-de-Grace, 1851) used a neolassical style in their buildings in Montréal, whereas James O'Donnell and his patrons avoured the neogothic for the Church of NOTRE-DAME (1829) in the same city. Both stylistic endencies were also employed in Halifax, Kingston and Toronto.

In 1796 York (named Toronto in 1834) became the capital of Upper Canada. Growing prosperity attracted portrait painters such as G.T. BERTHON, landscape painters such as Robert R. Whale, and explorers and genre painters such as William HIND, whose sketches are as interesting as his paintings. All were precursors of the more important Lucius O'BRIEN, John A. FRAER and Allan EDSON, who, like American painters of the same period, favoured a romantic approach to landscape, with richer brushwork and ubtler use of colour. These men were the first to ttempt to convey on canvas the majesty of the ocky Mts or the atmospheric effects of the Atantic Coast.

With Confederation in 1867, the urge to xpress a new sense of Canada as a unified ountry was felt in the arts. The Parliament uilding in Ottawa was completed in 1865; obert HARRIS was commissioned to paint his amous group portrait, *The Fathers of Confederation*, on his return from Italy in 1882. The oyal Canadian Academy of the Arts and the ATIONAL GALLERY OF CANADA were created in 880 by the marquis of Lorne (*see* ARTISTS' ORGANIATIONS).

Following a brief slowdown caused by the economic crisis in 1873, Canadian architecture rew at an unprecedented rate and, in the East at east, reflected the evolution from an essentially ural to an industrial economy. The period 873-1914 witnessed a new taste for historicism, s if each architect felt the need to compete with is colleague in his ability to quote some archictural elements of the past: Gothic spires or indows were linked to French mansards, Italnate elements with Tudor styles. Public buildngs (churches, RAILWAY STATIONS such as Windsor Station in Montréal, "château"-style HOTELS uch as the Frontenac in Québec City and the mpress in Victoria) as well as domestic archicture, particularly in rural Ontario, showed his eclecticism. In the midst of this "revival" enzy a new feeling for modern architectural pace, and innovative materials such as cast on, glass and, later, cement appeared, leading basic structural changes in Canadian architecre.

At the turn of the century, painting was arked by such major figures as James Wilson ORRICE, the father of Canadian modernism; zias LEDUC, who divided his time between amtious church decorations and exquisite still es and landscapes of St-Hilaire; Homer WATSON, who presented a more intimate vision of the Canadian landscape; and George REID and Paul PEEL, who were closer to the academic tradition. Nevertheless, with the exception of Morrice, who was an avid admirer of Matisse as early as 1908, and perhaps William BRYMNER, the influence of the *école de Paris* was not felt until later.

The Amphitheatre of Lutetia (1953), oil on canvas, 81 x 106.4 cm, by Paul-Émile Borduas. Borduas gathered together a number of young painters and formed a group called Automatistes whose 1948 manifesto marked the emergence of modern thinking in art in Canada (*courtesy Paul-Emile Borduas/National Gallery of Canada/Gift of the Douglas M. Duncan Collection*).

In the meantime, sculpture, which up to then had simply continued along traditional lines, began to change. New materials were explored, wood being replaced by bronze and plaster. New needs were answered: historical monuments in town squares, particularly war monuments in many towns and cities following WWI; ornamentation of the façades of new buildings, such as Louis-Philippe HÉBERT's project for the legislature building in Québec City; elaborate TOMBSTONES in cemeteries. New subject matter was attempted: Indian subjects, and figures from folklore and Canadian history. As in the past, new styles appeared emulating European trends: academism, art nouveau, symbolism (Alfred LALIBERTÉ) and, later, art deco. Sculpture became public (*see* PUBLIC ART) and, in Québec, less exclusively religious.

The early 1920s were great years for Canadian painting. The Toronto-based GROUP OF SEVEN, completely committed to the task of giving Canada a truly national form of painting, sought in the Canadian landscape their source of inspiration. They responded to its grandeur and captured it in decorative patterning and bold colours, without falling into the naturalism of the previous generation. Despite his short career, Tom THOMSON left behind a remarkable group of paintings and oil sketches. Concurrently with this Canadian "coast to coast" movement, a regionalist painting style developed in Québec. It was less a reflection of nature than of the French Canadian's 3-century attachment to the land. On the West Coast, Emily CARR expressed her unique response to both Northwest Coast Indian art and the BC landscape. Influenced by Fauvism and the mysticism of Lawren HARRIS, she made a contribution of her own and was the first woman artist to achieve eminence in Canadian art.

John LYMAN, a great admirer of Morrice, attempted after his return from Europe in the early 1930s to realign the art movement with the *école de Paris*. In 1939 he created the CONTEMPORARY ARTS SOCIETY and organized the modernist offensive in Canadian painting. WWII coincided with unprecedented growth in painting in Québec. In 1940 Alfred PELLAN returned from Paris and soon exhibited the strong influence that Cubism and especially Picasso had made on him. Paul-Émile BORDUAS gathered a number of young painters, including Jean-Paul RIOPELLE and Fernand LEDUC, and formed the AUTOMATISTES. Their 1948 manifesto, REFUS GLOBAL, had considerable ideological repercussions even beyond Québec's artistic world. It marked the emergence of modern thinking, free of the old conformism, religious or otherwise. After this breakthrough, one movement followed another in Québec, where painting tended to be more theoretically defined than in the other provinces. In reaction to automatism, the PLASTICIENS, Guido MOLINARI and Claude TOUSIGNANT, freed painting from its surrealistic attachments and directed it toward formal research. From then on, painters became concerned with structural and colour problems.

Similar concerns were surfacing in Toronto. PAINTERS ELEVEN, of whom the most famous were Harold TOWN and Jack BUSH, moved from the abstract expressionism practised in New York to formalism. In general, the problem of contemporary Canadian painting is to maintain its originality in the face of strong American influences. Michael SNOW, with his remarkable original contributions to contemporary cinema, and the London, Ont, group with Greg CURNOE and Jack CHAMBERS, were particularly successful in differentiating their work from American art of the 1960s. The same concern has haunted young Canadian sculptors such as Armand Vaillancourt, Robert Roussil and Robert MURRAY.

At first sight, modern architecture in Canada may look more international in style than do painting or sculpture. Climate and tradition, however, have led architects to achieve a style with a specific Canadian character. Foreigners are more thrilled than Canadians by the extent of Canadian subterranean architecture in cities like Montréal or Toronto, where it is possible to go from hotel to shopping centre to living quarters without stepping outside into the cold. Arthur ERICKSON at Simon Fraser U in Vancouver and John Andrews at Scarborough College, U of Toronto, have achieved buildings of great elegance and distinction.

What, then, is distinctive about Canadian art? From the beginning, artists in Canada have refused to operate in a vacuum, to cut themselves off from their European roots, whether French, English, Scottish, Irish or Ukrainian. At the same time, freed from a heavy weight of traditions, they display a certain inventiveness, imposed by isolation, by adaptation to difficult physical conditions. In many respects the Canadian experience in art may seem to parallel the American one, but the French influence, completely lacking in the US, is too overwhelming in Canadian art not to maintain an essential distinction between the art forms of the 2 countries. This quality is true not only for Québec and French Canadian artists, but for all Canadian artists. Moreover, federal institutions like the CANADA COUNCIL, the Art Bank and the National Gallery have succeeded in creating among contemporary Canadian artists a sense of community that goes beyond the language barrier and seeks a specific Canadian answer to the problems of art in our day. FRANÇOIS-MARC GAGNON

Reading: D. Burnett and M. Schiff, *Contemporary Canadian Art* (1983); A. Gowans, *Building Canada* (1966); J. Russell Harper, *Painting in Canada* (1977); D. Reid, *A Concise History of Canadian Painting* (1973); L. Whiteson, *Modern Canadian Architecture* (1983).

Art, Contemporary Trends Contemporary art in Canada, as elsewhere, is marked by a questioning of the nature of art — what art has been about historically, what it ought to be about and who its intended audience is to be. This questioning has been accompanied by experimentation and innovation. The resulting work varies in content from the intensely personal to the public investigation of social and political issues; it ranges in form from the intellectually disciplined to the free and intuitive; and differs in production from the solitary to the collective.

As traditional art forms were discarded, contemporary art tested its limits as seldom before: it explored the link between means and ends, reset the boundaries between art and "reality," and redefined the art object in its aesthetic, social and economic contexts. The art processes have gained momentum and direction from forces as varied and contradictory as developments in computer and communications technology, oriental mysticism, and new thinking in the social and behavioural sciences, in philosophy and linguistics, including the work of Marshall MCLUHAN; and from the international flow of ideas about art, coming during this period largely from the US — but, as modernism has given way to post-modernism, increasingly coming again from Europe. The need to experiment has been met by the new materials and tools made available by technological advance — plastics, computers, lasers, holograms, and the communications media — which by their nature suggested alternative contexts for art and access to a wider audience.

In Canada the diversity of contemporary trends has been compounded by the distance between centres of art activity and by their different histories, resources and responses to outside influences. This isolation has been offset by official support for alternative spaces and by the growing number of avant-garde art magazines with a national circulation: *Vanguard, Parachute* and *Parallelogramme*, the organ of the artist-run centres.

Both Fusion des Arts in Montréal (fd 1964) and Intermedia in Vancouver (fd 1967) grew out of this climate. They were loose groupings of artists working in different media (film, music, dance, poetry) and in the traditional categories of painting and sculpture, which were perceived by many to be pointlessly restricting when isolated. Glenn Lewis, Glenn Toppings, Dennis Vance, Dallas Sellman, Gary Lee Nova, Evelyn Roth, Gerry Gilbert and many others were associated with Intermedia, although they often worked co-operatively or anonymously through pseudonyms. The artists of Fusion, whose founders were Richard Lacroix, François Soucy, François Rousseau and Yves Robillard, also pooled resources and shared ideas. The resulting happenings and performances — works combining touch and sound, vision and movement to experiment with sensory awareness, located as often outside as in an art gallery — exuded a sense of optimism about the anticipated social benefits to be gained from the arts now that they were speaking a common and, it was hoped, comprehensible language.

In forming the N.E. Thing Co (1966), Iain and Ingrid BAXTER, who were among the founding members of Intermedia, demonstrated multimedia and interdisciplinary principles by setting up categories of their own, departments of their company which would deal with its multifarious products — the vacuum-formed still lifes, the inflatable plastic landscapes, works transmitted by telex, photographs of found images bearing the N.E. Thing Co's ACT (Aesthetically Claimed Thing) or ART (Aesthetically Rejected Thing) seals, and all of it to stimulate the GNG (Gross National Good), which was far more important than the GNP (Gross National Product). A company button proclaimed the message "Art is all over" — meaning that art can literally be anything at all, or else nothing special. It was a logical extension of the gesture, newly influential in the 1960s, made in 1913 by French artist Marcel Duchamp when he mounted a bicycle wheel on a stool and displayed it in an art gallery along with other "Readymades." In demonstrating that art could be a business with a product (Visual Sensitivity Information) the N.E. Thing Co was trying to demystify art, to link it to the real world, to show, as Duchamp had done, that art is in the eye of the beholder.

Despite its mimicry of capitalist business practices, the N.E. Thing Co shared the conviction of many progressive artists of the time that art should not be understood primarily as a marketable commodity. Among numerous suggestions Les Levine has made since the late 1960s, as to how else art might be understood, were his Disposibles (1968-69). These brightly coloured, vacuum-formed plastic modules were intended to be disposable, had no inherent value as objects, and could be arranged and rearranged at the whim of their owners. Levine's idea was the art; how it looked was up to anyone else. Michael SNOW, like Levine, was living in New York at this time. In their different ways they were responsible for channelling the ideas of conceptual art into Canada, though by its nature it easily travelled through the mail, the magazine and word of mouth.

Bill Vazan's *World Line* was realized with the help of a civil engineer and people in 25 locations around the world, casting an imaginary zigzag line around the globe (*courtesy Bill Vazan*).

Conceptual art maintained that if the traditional forms of painting and sculpture were bankrupt and abstraction merely an irrelevant attenuation, then the object in making art was to isolate some essential "artness" which existed independently of any form it might take. The main result of conceptual art in Canada has been a way of thinking about art rather than any notable works, though the most memorable ideas were those that were given some kind of form and, therefore, were not properly conceptual. Snow has centered his work on an internally consistent exploration of the camera's potential, a process which has resulted in films and works both on and off the wall, of great poetry and coherence. Snow's work, which has an international following, has been an inspiration for many other artists, especially those for whom art stands or falls by the strength of its idea or concept.

In the early 1970s the NOVA SCOTIA COLLEGE OF ART AND DESIGN in Halifax was the focus for conceptual art in Canada. Characteristic of work by influential staff at NSCAD was Eric Cameron's *Camera Inserted in my Mouth* (1973-76), in which the camera lens, inserted into the artist's mouth for the duration of a standard 30-minute tape with the only visible record on an otherwise black monitor being the shadowy trickle of saliva, used the medium to clarify an idea about the ultimately self-reflexive nature of art.

In *One Million Pennies* (1980) Gerald Ferguson gave vivid realization to the critical notion that art and money might be synonymous, no other way having been devised to indicate value, in a work that consisted of a heap of one million pennies, newly minted, on a gallery floor. The paintings of Garry Neill Kennedy are also typical of a later development of conceptual art. Intending a comment on the irreducible nature of paintings as art objects, Kennedy perversely located it in format and pigment. He systematically analysed the colours and sizes of 32 paintings from the permanent collection of the Art Gallery of Ontario. The result was a parallel and entirely schematic series of drawings, *Canadian Contemporary Collection - The Average Size - The Average Colour* (1978), the thirty-third item representing the average of the total.

While conceptual art remained concentrated in eastern Canada, body art, in which the artist's person is interpreted as both the source of all ideas about art and the ultimate tool in their realization, was the related form which gained the widest following. In Vancouver it became part of the aesthetic of anarchic satire and expressive indulgence which characterized the work of Al Neil and the artists of the Western Front; in Toronto it served to release the interest of many artists in the exploration and expression of the individual. Everywhere it was used to further the feminist cause. Montréal artist Sorel Cohen gave graphic summation to the physical activities (bed making, window cleaning) and social role (organizer and homemaker) traditionally expected of women. In accord with the pared-down sensibilities of minimal and conceptual art, Cohen's photographic sequences reproduced the physical experience directly, without poetry or drama.

In *Smile*, a videotape made by Albert McNamara in 1971 while a student at NSCAD, the particularity of an individual's smile is lost in a half-hour-long contemplation of a generalized cliché about the body and its expressiveness. Video, with its unique blend of privacy in the making and infinite publicity for the product adapted well to the concerns of body art. In *Birthday Suit*, Lisa Steele scrutinized the scars and defects of her body while recounting their history. Vincent Trasov, whose work for 5 years consisted of disguising his body as a peanut, ran, as Mr Peanut, for mayor of Vancouver in 1974; his campaign — an artist/politician encased in his image in the public arena — put in a nutshell the predicament of art and artist in taking meaningful roles in society.

Awareness of the person is extended in environmental art into the person's awareness of the environment. Reality "out there" is thought to have more presence, more potency, than any representation in paint or other traditional medium. The artist intervenes only to appropriate the existing qualities. Since the late 1960s this very durable strategy has been employed to very different ends. For a number of years, Irene Whittome has been installing in galleries objects and colours that she has made to be metaphors for her feelings about a particular place, room or city, so that the original atmosphere is recreated. In 1971 Bill Vazan's *World Line*, which was realized with the help of a civil engineer and many people in 25 different locations around the world, cast an imaginary, zigzag line around the globe. Its only visible form was 25 angles in black tape on 25 floors, the arms of each leading geodetically on to the next point on the line. *World Line* invited us to consider (as did another work of Vazan's which put Canada in parentheses, with brackets drawn on beaches in PEI and Vancouver I) some of our strongest preconceptions about an environment that we are hardly able to conceive. In *Defunct* (1982), Rita McKeough installed in the gallery of the Alberta College of Art replicas which she had built of old houses of Calgary. In the evenings she came into the gallery to destroy them, acting out her strong feelings about the wanton destruction of our urban environment. In *Destruck* (1983) the houses have evolved arms with which to defend themselves, but the ensuing fight with the bulldozers only prolongs the death throes. The architectural environment also concerns Melvin CHARNEY, Montréal architect/artist, who, in the street gallery, recreates versions of the vernacular architecture which he feels we overlook and destroy at our peril; when we lose the past which is written on our buildings, however humble, we risk losing our identity in the present. In 1976 Charney orchestrated "Corridart," in which Sherbrooke St, Montréal's main processional axis, was transformed by responses to the street and its history from many of the city's artists. In a vivid demonstration of the power of art, Mayor Drapeau, within a week of its installation and before the Olympic visitors arrived, ordered the destruction of what was perceived as a threat.

Krzystof Wodiczko's "Public Projections" reveal that we see a building or locale as a myth in an interplay with changing social and cultural circumstances. Using slide projectors, he temporarily projects images of this myth on the physical structures themselves. The images he threw onto the façade of the Art Gallery of Ontario in 1981 suggested the collusion of art, business and cultural bureaucracy. The myth which we construct around mountains, and the very different ones around nuclear weapons, together with the announcement of the planned testing of the US cruise missile in Alberta, led to the projection of the image of that missile on a rock face near Banff.

Correspondence art, art that uses the postal system for its distribution, provides another method of circumventing the confines of art object and art gallery. Chuck Stake (Don Mabie), who has been mailing out of Calgary for 10 years, and Anna Banana are 2 of Canada's most prolific links in a global network of those who make and share art for the price of postage.

Rita McKeough's *Defunct* (1981) mixed media installation and performance. McKeough installed replicas of old Calgary houses in the gallery of the Alberta Coll of Art, and in the evenings she destroyed them, bit by bit, acting out her strong feelings about the destruction of the urban environment (*courtesy Rita McKeough/photo by Charlie Fox*).

Collage, the random assemblage of found images in such a way that the whole has impact and meaning that is greater than the sum of its parts, has complex roots in Duchamp, dada and the early surrealists. It fits a contemporary notion that we have no grounds for discriminating between one object or image and another, or between one interpretation and another, since all have a part to play in the way we construct our view of the world. This idea is also a component of structuralism, an approach to knowledge made widely accessible through the writings of the French anthropologist Claude Levi-Strauss. His remark, "The decision that everything must be taken into account facilitates the creation of an image bank," provoked Michael Morris and Vincent Trasov to initiate Image Bank in Vancouver — a flow of images and requests for images which circulated around an international network of visual artists, poets, writers and musicians, thereby extending the chance of random relationships and juxtapositions in a scheme of things where everything was worth something. These same ideas inspired Glenn Lewis to initiate the *Great Wall of 1984* (1973). He invited 165 people to contribute the content of 365 plexiglass boxes, resulting, when stacked along the wall, in a huge co-operative collage to intrigue passersby at the National Science Library in Ottawa.

The re-emergence of collage has been followed by the return of imagery and, with it, illusion, drama and narrative. In these pluralist circumstances, which were prevailing by the late 1970s, one response has been analysis. An intellectual and highly self-aware analysis of how contemporary art can proceed and claim meaning and status for itself, echoing similar procedures elsewhere, is offered in the work of 2 Vancouver artists, Jeff Wall and Ian Wallace. They use photography to scrutinize the value of images, their own and those of the mass media, and to ask how the "art" version of them is distinguishable from any other version.

Performance art, and the often related installations, has been one of the most significant of the hybrid art forms, variously betraying its origins in the political urgency of agitprop, the high spirits of dada cabaret, the spontaneity of the happening and, in a concern with the processes through which images and ideas acquire meaning or have their meaning eroded, in its relationship with conceptual art. Bruce Barber, in carefully didactic performances, offers a reproof to both senders and receivers of the implicit sociopolitical content offered in the mass media. Elizabeth Chitty shows how we can meet the essentially sensory blandishments of those same media, while Marcella Bienvenue in her performances re-enacts the philosophical confusion into which the individual must inevitably be thrown by the barrage. In these instances, and many others, performance has been an effective vehicle, though by no means the only one, for the concerns of feminism.

An outrageous parody of this society and its promotional styles has been evolved through an ongoing series of performances, videotapes, installations and more by General Idea, the alias of 3 Toronto artists, A.A. Bronson, Felix Partz and Jorge Zontal: all art needs some kind of promotion and must make or find for itself a context if it is not to be socially meaningless.

Edward Poitras in his mixed-media installation *Stars in Sand* (1982) conveyed the wry poetry that results from the ambivalence of Indian artists towards their ancestry and the art forms of their ancestors. Many native artists from all parts of the country, wishing to communicate with society at large, are searching for forms that combine elements from traditional arts and mythology with their own responses to the present. They are often in the company of those other artists who take the risk of creating a personal mythology. Gathie FALK's *tableaux vivants*, like her work in other media, show that it is possible to communicate effectively through a set of highly idiosyncratic symbols.

The personal poetry found in recent performance works by Bruce Parsons is used to point up a message of the widest relevance: the imbalance between man's use and abuse of the natural world in advanced industrial societies. Among the growing number of artists who are prepared to appropriate any means, including the so-called "revival" of painting, to make uncompromising response to a troubled world, 2 should be mentioned: Jamelie Hassam, who, in *Desaparecidos* (1981), recreated in all its desperate anguish the protest of the grandmothers of the "disappeared ones" of Argentina, and Ron Benner, whose works deal with the plunder of nature by man, of one society by another.

How artists can operate at all in the compromised role allowed by their historically privileged position is the question that Carol Condé and Karl Beveridge have attempted to answer in photographic installations, which deal with specific social issues such as the personal consequences of strike action and the role of women in the work place. For Brian Dyson, who founded Syntax (Calgary International Artists' Contact Centre) in 1980, and his colleague Paul Woodrow, the only solution to the predicament of art, the only way to meet their social responsibilities, has been to stop making art and devote their energies to animating broadly based cultural activities in their local Calgary community of Hillhurst-Sunnyside. They believe that today direct social action is the only effective way for artists to give form to their ideas and perceptions. *See also* PAINTING; VIDEO ART.

CHARLOTTE TOWNSEND-GAULT

Reading: R. Bringhurst et al, eds, *Visions: Contemporary Art in Canada* (1983); D. Burnett and M. Schiff, *Contemporary Canadian Art* (1983).

Art Conservation and Restoration, *see* CONSERVATION OF MOVEABLE CULTURAL PROPERTY.

Art Dealers in Canada have served as art dealers everywhere, not only as sellers of art but as tastemakers. Since they act as a link between the work of art and the art-buying public, they have an important role in the identification of who is important in Canadian art. By their sales, they help determine how much fame the artist will have, at least in the marketplace. In recent years, many of the more prominent members of the profession, such as G. Blair Laing in Toronto and Walter Klinkhoff in Montréal, Kenneth G. Heffel in Vancouver, the Masters Gallery in Calgary, the Hett Gallery and Woltjen/Udell in Edmonton, and Loch Gallery in Winnipeg, as well as Geoffrey Joyner at Sotheby's in Toronto significantly affected the field through their connoisseurship. To be successful, a dealer must act responsibly, not only towards the field but towards the artist and the public. The Professional Art Dealers Assn (fd 1966) maintains basic guidelines and ethical standards for the operation of commercial art galleries.

Until the mid-19th century, dealers in Canada were forced to diversify their stock so that they carried art along with other salable items. James Spooner in Toronto, for instance, ran a small picture gallery with works by Daniel FOWLER, John FRASER, Paul PEEL and Homer WATSON in the rear of his tobacco shop on King St East. By the 1930s, however, several important galleries had been established — Leroy Zwicker in Halifax; Robertson and Ensor in Ottawa; Mellors Fine Art, Lange and Roberts in Toronto; William R. Watson in Montréal. All these galleries sold mostly 19th-century English and European paintings. Some art dealers, however, played a significant role as pioneers in supporting young Canadian artists, eg, Douglas DUNCAN who opened the Picture Loan Society in Toronto in 1936, and in the 1950s Agnes Lefort and Denyse Delrue in Montréal and Dorothy Cameron in Toronto (her Here and Now Art Gallery opened in 1959). Success did not come easily. PAINTERS ELEVEN, with the help of Jack BUSH who showed with Roberts Gallery in Toronto, managed to have 2 shows there in 1954 and 1955. Though critics were interested and, by the second show, there was considerable public attention, sales were few. Avrom Isaacs in Toronto opened the Greenwich Gallery as a framing shop in 1955. By 1959 he had changed the name to the Isaacs Gallery and begun to foster a group of young artists that included Michael SNOW and Graham COUGHTRY who are now part of Canadian art history.

In the 1960s, with the growing enthusiasm for Canadian art and increasing affluence, there was a proliferation of art dealers, particularly in Toronto. The audience by now counted among its ranks the corporate sector. Businesses such as CIL, the Toronto Dominion Bank, and various oil companies, particularly Imperial Oil, began collections. The CANADA COUNCIL Art Bank program, established in 1972 with a budget of $1 million a year, and the program of the Department of Public Works (1964-78), in which 1% of the cost of all government buldings had to be spent on art, added substantially to the funds available (*see* PUBLIC ART).

The 1960s also saw the emergence of a new kind of dealer, the co-operative gallery or "alternate" space. A Space in Toronto, SAW in Ottawa, and other artist-run centres in a network across the country operate art galleries dedicated to promoting contemporary artists and sales, with no stigma of "commercialism." They meet a need created by a more diversified art scene — art that involves performance, VIDEO ART or large installations. Many contemporary dealers, eg, Ydessa Handeles in Toronto who opened her business in 1980, have gone along with the new trend. They consider their role more one of finding sponsors than of actively selling, though selling, particularly to the NATIONAL GALLERY OF CANADA, is important too. *See* ART, CONTEMPORARY TRENDS.

Dealers have had a significant role in influencing public taste and promoting the unusual. Galleries across Canada have been largely responsible for the promotion and sale of the art of native people. Max Stern's Dominion Gallery in Montréal introduced the sculpture of Henry Moore to Canada. He was also the first gallery to give contracts to artists, beginning with Goodridge ROBERTS in 1949.

The commercial relationship between artist and dealers is usually based on commission (usually 40% or even 50% to the gallery, though it may be as low as 30% for established artists) and most work is sold on consignment. Some dealers, such as Walter Moos in Toronto, may buy an artist's production for several years and market it accordingly. Sales by commission are difficult for the unknown artist, who often must help pay for the opening and associated expenses. The dealer provides the exhibition space and sometimes a modest catalogue or flyer as well as the cost of advertising. Some dealers show remarkable intuition for the future market value of an artist's work. They may hold works of art until an artist dies and then dictate market value. Max Stern bought many works by the unrecognized Emily CARR, and Walter Klinkhoff, among others, is still able to show exhibitions of the work of Goodridge Roberts.

JOAN MURRAY

Reading: Douglas Duncan: A Memorial Portrait, ed A. Jarvis (1974); G. Blair Laing, *Memoirs of an Art Dealer*, 2 vols (1979, 1983); J. Morris, *Adrift on Course* (1979); W.R. Watson, *Retrospective: Recollections of a Montreal Art Dealer* (1974).

Art Education and the training of artists in Canada are directly related to the changing status of art in our society. Art education, whether for personal or professional purposes, corresponds to the development of psychological and pedagogical knowledge and to the current definition of a work of art. The development of creativity has only recently been defined as a separate activity and is part of that larger debate over whether an artist is born or trained. The role of the art school — whether it should simply teach the techniques which allow innate talent to develop or should actively redefine the nature of a work of art — remains an open question. Early art education in Canada was based mostly on the APPRENTICESHIP system. The myth that Bishop Laval established Canada's first school of arts and crafts at St Joachim in 1685 has been discredited. Most early artists received their training before they arrived — FRÈRE LUC, Louis Dulongpré, William BERCZY — though some colonists, such as Mother Marie Madeleine Maufils de St Louis, received individual tutoring from artists who were passing through. In the apprenticeship system a master artist would train a young apprentice in exchange for assistance. Apprenticeship first appeared in the woodcraft and decorative art fields — woodworking, cabinetmaking, tinsmithing, ironmongery, silversmithing — fields for which the demand was greatest and which helped meet the need for repair work on imported objects. Apprenticeship is intrinsically a conservative system in which knowledge and methods in the arts and crafts are passed on relatively unchanged through several generations. While these artists/craftsmen were rarely innovative, there was some response to new techniques, stylistic influences and competition, mostly from abroad.

The apprenticeship system served a purpose: it established traditions of local practice and culture which survived over several generations. Some of the most important early centres of creativity owed their existence to the apprenticeship system, especially in SCULPTURE and ARCHITECTURE. The Levasseur and BAILLAIRGÉ family dynasties dominated art activity in Québec and passed on a tradition of high achievement clearly based on French models and subject matter, but with its own characteristics of technical sophistication, human warmth and simplicity. In silversmithing in Québec there is a connection from Laurent Amyot to Françoi Sasseville and Pierre Lespérance; in Nova Scoti a preference for English or American styles ca be seen in works by Peter Norbeck, Michael Sep timus Brown and Thomas Brown. In paintin the most prestigious of these lineages is tha which runs from Joseph LÉGARÉ to Louis Philippe HÉBERT, via Antoine PLAMONDON, Thé ophile HAMEL and Napoléon BOURASSA. The in digenous art production of the 19th century i indebted to this system.

Apprenticeship played a relatively small rol in the fine arts, developing only at the end of th 18th century in a combination school an workshop where the training was adapted t small groups. François Baillairgé's studio wa functioning like a school when it offere courses in drawing, painting and sculptur Louis QUÉVILLON used his workshop in the sam way to train woodworkers and sculptors, com plementing art lessons with academic studies The type of education proposed by Baillairg was basic and generalized, and its aim was les the formation of artists than of technicians an amateurs appreciative of the arts. In this sense art education moved further away from th ideal of a school modelled on the Europea academies.

A system of private art instruction develope throughout the 19th century as the number o itinerant artists declined and many immigran artists settled in the colony. Most of the a teachers who advertised in the papers prior t 1850 stressed their teaching abilities, and in struction was an important source of revenu for people like William Eagar in Halifax an George Theodore BERTHON in Toronto. Despit the frequency and quantity of the courses, w have little information about their content, styl and clientele. It seems that most students wer young, cultured and socially privileged ladies Instruction was specialized by medium (crayon watercolours, pen and ink, oils), genre (land scape, still life) or style (learning to paint like known artist). Drawing was basic, and the stu dents learned to copy various themes and frag ments of artistic works. Imitation was consid ered a way to transmit artistic knowledge Students learned to reproduce the pictorial con ventions found in certain works and trans mitted either by engravings or by examples pro vided by the art master.

Private educational establishments (colleges universities, convents) also offered courses b local artists. Charles Mondelet, in his well known *Letters of Elementary and Practical Educatio* (1841), made no mention of art instruction i his plan for public and normal schools; suc courses had to wait another decade. Art edu cation, which until then had been availab only to the privileged classes, underwent a pro cess of democratization and simplification. Edu cation officials in Upper and Lower Canada es tablished art-education programs in the schools based on the principle that instruction in draw ing is as essential as instruction in reading an writing and should be taught to all childrer This recognition of the fundamental impor tance of drawing led to the creation of exercise intended to stimulate the child's visual vocab ulary. The *Dominion Drawing Books* appeared, sys tematizing both the methods and the materia to be used.

In the 19th century the Industrial Revolutio brought a new awareness of the relationship be tween form and function in manufactured ob jects (*see* INDUSTRIAL DESIGN). In England and Eu rope this development led not only to th creation of schools of art and design with indus trial application, but also to a rejuvenation o arts and crafts. This influence spread to Canad in the 1860s and, in succeeding years, variou schools of applied art and technology wer established, eg, the Board of Arts and Manufacturers, and Joseph Chabert's Institution nationale, founded in Montréal in 1870. Such colleges offered a complete program that included freehand drawing and technical drawing (mechanical, architectural), decorative painting, lithography, modelling and wood sculpture; since these programs were aimed at specialized workers, they sensitized a new social group to artistic techniques and the application of aesthetic principles to the environment. The courses, however, emphasized technical qualities (correct drawing, harmonious colours, balanced composition) rather than expression and formal research, and increased the conceptual gulf between applied art and fine art. Consistent efforts were made well into the 20th century, as at École du Meuble founded in 1937, or by Donald Buchanan at the National Industrial Design Council after 1946, to keep strong ties between design and fine arts, and today numerous schools and university departments, one of which is the NOVA SCOTIA COLLEGE OF ART AND DESIGN, offer both programs.

Apprenticeship and private art schools were replaced in the late 19th century by schools founded and directed by societies of artists and amateurs which had come into being about 25 years earlier. The Ontario Society of Artists, the Art Assn of Montreal and the Royal Canadian Academy established courses which tended to be adaptations of academic European models (*see* ARTISTS' ORGANIZATIONS). Their methods taught respect for tradition, the hierarchy of different media and genres and the supremacy of drawing. Art colleges and the Toronto Normal School under Egerton Ryerson collected plaster castings, photographs and engravings of European works. Some European-trained teachers taught in and led their schools for more than 30 years, and so influenced several generations of students. William Brymner at the Art Assn of Montreal school, George Reid at the Ontario College of Art, John Hammond at the Owens Art Institute of both Saint John and Sackville, NB, were particularly well known. Art studies often led to a stay abroad, in the US or Europe. It was essential to see, study and copy the masterpieces and to meet foreign colleagues in the hope of winning professional recognition for careers in Canada.

The basic structure of the professional art schools remained unchanged until the mid-20th century, despite internal developments (eg, the Ontario College of Art after 1912) and proliferation (eg, the École des beaux-arts in Québec City, 1920, and in Montréal, 1923). The relationship between fine arts and applied arts continued. Young Canadian artists preparing for a career turned increasingly to the US because the range of courses was broader and instruction more specialized. Many students continued to be wealthy young women whose training was seen as a complement to their general education, though the status of female artists developed more quickly in English Canada. The Beaver Hall Hill Group, which consisted mainly of graduates of the Art Assn of Montreal school, helped pioneer recognition of female artists in 1920-21.

In the 1940s there was a major reform in the specialized schools. The structures which had been put in place 70 years earlier gave way to a variety of methods of instruction. The dissolving of the link between art and industry, the downgrading of the importance of art from the past in favour of the development of the artist's own values, and the predominant role of colour and gesture to express individuality, all characterized the art produced after WWII and affected the kinds of courses being offered. Two major reactions followed. One was to return to individualized training, with exchanges between artists of different ages and statures. This system took various forms such as workshops, symposiums and seminars, as at Emma Lake or the BANFF CENTRE SCHOOL OF FINE ARTS, where professionals shared their beliefs and experience with younger people.

The other major reaction, as the university took responsibility for the training of a large number of artists in the humanist tradition, was to expand the student's awareness in areas other than his immediate interests. Since the first Bachelor of Fine Arts was awarded in 1939 at Mount Allison U in Sackville, NB, many institutions of higher learning across the country have established their own programs, offering a rich academic structure with great social and aesthetic value as well.

Art education as a SOCIAL SCIENCE, a system based on the psychological development of the child, was also developed in the 1940s. Arthur LISMER is considered the pioneer of this form of art education in Canada. He put the principles into practice at the Art Gallery of Toronto after 1919 and in the Montréal Museum of Fine Arts after 1941. For Lismer, art education meant placing individuals in a situation in which their natural creativity could blossom. The needs, resources and limits of each person were considered, and the role of the educator was to facilitate the creativity. This approach, developed in Europe, had considerable success and was integrated into art education in the public schools. In Montréal, Irène Senécal introduced this method at the École des Beaux-Arts.

Historical, theoretical and practical reflection on art education, begun by C.D. Gaitskell in his book *Arts and Crafts in the Schools of Ontario* (1948) and continued by various royal commissions on the status of the arts in Canada (eg, Rioux Report; NATIONAL DEVELOPMENT IN THE ARTS, LETTERS AND SCIENCES, ROYAL COMMISSION ON), has been the concern of relevant university research departments. Based on the most recent psychological, aesthetic and pedagogical information, they try to expand the range and quality of artistic experiences offered to the student, making innovative use of museums and galleries and other art activities available outside the classroom. LAURIER LACROIX

Reading: F.W. Rowe, *Education and Culture in Newfoundland* (1976); J.D. Wilson, *Canadian Education* (1970).

Art Galleries and Museums are institutions that collect, preserve, study and present permanent collections of heritage objects to the public.

Although authentic documentation of the early history of Canadian museums is meager, it is known that 18th-century religious institutions in Québec and the Maritimes had natural history collections that were used by the priests-educators. These same church schools accumulated religious relics, curiosities and VOTIVE PAINTINGS, which marked the beginnings of immigrant art in Canada. Laval U had mineralogical collections as early as the 1790s, followed soon after by other universities, but museums as formally organized institutions were unknown. In the early 1800s mechanics' institutes in the Maritimes accumulated collections for teaching purposes; in addition, models that illustrated physical phenomena and the means by which machinery functioned were constructed. Also during this time, miscellaneous collections were garnered from exhibitions, teaching collections or personal "cabinets of curiosities" and assembled in LIBRARIES or government buildings for temporary show or special events.

The first museum in Canada seems to have been opened by Thomas Barnett, who advertised his personal museum of local and foreign specimens at NIAGARA FALLS in 1831. Soon after, a less commercial museum opened at Niagara-on-the-Lake, and Dr Abraham GESNER founded his museum at Saint John, NB, in 1842. Museums were formally established at Laval U and the Canadian Institute in Toronto in 1852, followed by one at McGill U in 1856. Nova Scotia opened the first provincial museum in 1868 in Halifax, based on collections assembled in a local mechanics' institute, and BC and Ontario sponsored formal museums in 1886.

It was not until after Confederation, 1867, however, that the museum movement swept across Canada, becoming a hallmark of the late 19th century. An outline of the early history of the National Museum of Canada illustrates the blend of private initiative, government support and opportune circumstances that marked the development of museums. In 1842 William LOGAN became provincial geologist of Québec, and by 1845 he had amassed and catalogued a large comparative collection of specimens. After the collection was exhibited in London in 1851, Logan and the government were encouraged to found a permanent geological museum. By mid-century, developers and the government recognized the value of national collections in encouraging exploration and resource development. In 1853 Logan wrote a report to Parliament that eventually generated a grant of $28 000 for the maintenance of the collection and for publications. In 1881 Logan's museum was moved to Ottawa to be a part of the research collection and museum of the GEOLOGICAL SURVEY OF CANADA. A long period of underfunding and lack of organization followed, though in 1911 the museum moved into the new Victoria Memorial Museum Building. In 1927 the museum was formally recognized as the National Museum of Canada. The NATIONAL GALLERY OF CANADA was established in 1880 (*see also* NATIONAL MUSEUMS OF CANADA).

Numbers of Museums by Province and Territory, 1984

Alberta	139	Ontario	543
BC	217	PEI	26
Manitoba	115	Québec	233
NB	69	Saskatchewan	167
Newfoundland	48	NWT	4
NS	121	YT	11

It was in the first half of the 20th century that small community museums and the remaining provincial museums were founded (*see* ART GALLERY OF ONTARIO; GLENBOW MUSEUM; ROYAL ONTARIO MUSEUM). The earliest museums were situated in eastern Canada, but as immigrant settlers moved to the West, pride in the varied ethnic origins gave birth to many collections that eventually became community or regional museums. The growth of museums was slow and 2 major reports, the Miers-Markham Report of 1932 and the Massey Report of 1951, showed little development over a 20-year period.

CENTENNIAL YEAR in 1967 and several provincial and metropolitan birthdays in the 1960s gave a marked impetus to museum development. Provinces and communities alike chose to commemorate their heritage by starting new museums or modernizing old ones. A second reason for the expansion of museums was the secretary of state's announcement in 1972 of massive aid to the cultural sector, primarily to "decentralize and democratize" our national heritage in museums. This influx of money allowed museums to reach new audiences with new programs, and brought about a growing cultural awareness. By 1984, according to the Canadian Museums Assn, there were approximately 1700 museums, art galleries and related institutions in Canada.

Museums are funded with tax dollars in the form of a budget, if a part of a larger governing body, or by grants if funding is from outside the direct line of responsibility. Some 21 major museums receive substantial direct federal funding as "associates" of the National Museums of Canada and all other permanent, nonprofit, public museums are eligible to receive grants under the National Museums' Museum Assistance Programs. Consequently, the source of museum funding may be federal, provincial, municipal or self-generated, and occasionally private. Frequently, contributions may be derived from several of these sources. Museums are also confronted with the responsibility of raising a large part of their money through fund raising or marketing the unique services a museum can offer. *See* ARTS FUNDING. GEORGE LAMMERS

Reading: B. Dixon et al, *The Museum and the Canadian Public* (1974); A.F. Key, *Beyond Four Walls: The Origins and Development of Canadian Museums* (1973); T. Poulos, ed, *Conference Proceedings for 2001: The Museum and the Canadian Public* (1977).

Art Gallery of Ontario, founded in 1900 as the Art Museum of Toronto, became the Art Gallery of Toronto in 1919 and, in 1966 — reflecting an expanded role in the province — the Art Gallery of Ontario. The 10 000 paintings, sculptures, prints and drawings of the permanent collection include examples from the Old Master traditions, the Impressionists and early 20th-century movements — paintings by such masters as Rembrandt, Hals, Poussin, Chardin, Delacroix, Renoir and Picasso, and sculptures by Rodin, Degas and Matisse. The gallery's Henry Moore Sculpture Centre holds the largest and most comprehensive public collection of Moore works anywhere. More than half the permanent collection is the work of Canadian artists dating from the 18th century to the present day. The gallery averages about 40 special exhibitions each year. Major international shows in recent years have included Treasures of Tutankhamun, and, organized by the gallery, collections of works by J.M.W. Turner, Vincent van Gogh, William Blake, Lawren HARRIS, Alex COLVILLE and Gershon ISKOWITZ. Other exhibitions have explored 20th-century international sculpture, from Paul Gauguin to Henry Moore, and the northern landscape painting in Europe and N America, with a focus on the Canadian tradition.

Lectures, films, tours and concerts are regularly scheduled. In the Activity Centre, children and adults enjoy art-related activities or take classes in the Gallery School. The Edward P. Taylor Reference Library and the Audio-Visual Centre are invaluable information centres for researchers, art historians and students. The original gallery home, The GRANGE, is a restored Georgian mansion and a museum of life in Upper Canada in the 1830s. Reaching into communities across Ontario and Canada, Extension Services offer touring exhibitions, studio programs, and advisory services to community centres and contribute to the Ontario Ministry of Citizenship and Culture Festival Program.

The gallery's collection, facilities and programs have attracted a strong membership of 30 000, the largest per capita in N America. In recent years, annual attendance has averaged 500 000 visitors. The gallery receives about 51% of its annual operating costs from the province of Ontario, supplemented by grants from federal and municipal governments. The remainder of the budget is earned from membership support, program fees, retail shops, a restaurant, and by private gifts and corporate donations. All works of art in the collection have either been donated or purchased with income from donations.
WILLIAM WITHROW

Art Ross Trophy is awarded annually to the player who leads the NATIONAL HOCKEY LEAGUE in scoring points during the regular season. If there is a tie at the end of the season, the trophy is awarded to the player with the most goals. It was first presented in 1947 by Arthur Howie Ross, former manager of Boston Bruins. Gordie HOWE won it 6 times, Phil ESPOSITO 5, Stan MIKITA 4, Guy LAFLEUR 3 and Wayne GRETZKY in 3 of his first 4 seasons. JAMES MARSH

Art Writing and Criticism is a new field in Canada, dating for the most part from the 1950s. A distinction must be made between art criticism, which is a qualitative judgement of works of art, and the philosophy of art, which is concerned with interpreting works, with discovering the nature, significance and symbolism of art in general. There is, however, a reciprocity in the relationship of art criticism and the philosophy of art: every evaluation of quality always includes an explicit or implicit interpretation of the meaning of the work, and every interpretation implies a previously formulated qualitative judgement.

Art criticism can address various aspects of the visual arts such as qualitative judgement in public and private collecting, architecture, the decorative arts, patronage of artists, art dealings, conservation of art and organization of exhibitions. Much Canadian art criticism has been of a fairly practical nature. The vast increase in the number of artists, public and commercial galleries, and art patrons since WWII reveals an expansion of artistic discernment. Written art criticism has increased at a comparable rate.

The first art writing and criticism in Canada was published as short articles in daily and weekly newspapers, or general interest periodicals. The earliest of these periodicals included the short-lived *L'Abeille canadienne*, a Montréal fortnightly published 1818-19, the *Halifax Monthly Magazine* of 1830 and the Upper Canadian *Canadian Literary Magazine* of 1833. Later *La Revue canadienne, The Week, Foyer domestique* and the *Canadian Home Journal* devoted regular columns to art. These articles usually examined current exhibitions, discussing the works in fashionably flowery language in relation to Victorian ideals rather than pictorial qualities. By the end of the 19th century, longer studies, such as Sherwood's chapter in Hopkins's *Canada: an Encyclopaedia of the country*, made an appearance. However, it was only in the 1920s that books devoted exclusively to art were published, including those by Georges Bellerive and Newton MacTavish. Despite this interest, neither authors nor critics could make a living on art writing alone.

In the early 20th-century this economic factor continued to affect the types of authors who published. A considerable number of authors were artists, some were curators employed at public galleries and a few were professional critics. Practising artists such as Arthur LISMER, Lawren S. HARRIS and C.W. JEFFERYS produced important articles; Eric Brown, director of the National Gallery of Canada, added writing to his many duties, a practice continued by Donald W. Buchanan, a coeditor of *Canadian Art* and later staff member of the National Gallery. Robert Ayre furthered the tradition of sparetime writer; while fulfilling his duties with the CNR Public Relations Department, he wrote for the *Montreal Standard* and subsequently the *Montreal Star*. Some professional art journalists did exist. One of the earliest of note was Hector Charlesworth, who wrote on many subjects, including art. In the post-WWI period Jean Chauvin contributed perceptive pieces in the French press, as did Pearl McCarthy in the 1950s and early 1960s at the Toronto *Globe and Mail*. Journalists such as Newton MacTavish and F.B. Housser wrote some of the few early books on Canadian painting. Little effort was made at dispassionate, rational criticism, with the notable exception of those, like Ayre and McCarthy, who wrote regular columns.

The first changes, evident in the 1950s, occurred as a result of the expansion of public galleries (*see* PAINTING). At that time these institutions experienced a considerable growth in number, staff and programs. A greater interest developed in historic overviews, especially in book form, through the influence of research-oriented curators such as R.H. Hubbard, Gérard Morisset and J. Russell Harper. Their books on the history of Canadian art were characterized by the use of extensive primary materials; they revolutionized the field, opening it to serious study. Within a decade other surveys and specialized studies appeared, such as Alan Gowan's *Looking at Architecture in Canada*, F.M. Gagnon's *Premiers peintres de la Nouvelle France* and Jean Palardy's *The Early Furniture of French Canada*. Themes were enlarged to include more thorough studies of the arts of the native peoples of Canada. Marius Barbeau's and Diamond Jenness's pioneer works on Canadian Indians were expanded by scholars such as Wilson Duff. The art of the Inuit, having been seriously neglected, was first promoted by James HOUSTON and then analysed by George Swinton. After 1960 contemporary art began to have its advocates, too many to be listed; approaches tended to be formalist, sometimes Maoist. These studies, however, are only the beginning, for many areas remain untouched; we lack informative studies of Canadian sculpture, Maritime architecture, patrons, dealers and critics, and most of the decorative arts.

The second dynamic expansion in gallery activity, occurring in the mid-1970s and caused by an injection of federal funds, garnered an increased public and stimulated art writing. Galleries themselves were becoming more numerous and more specialized. Viewers could attend public or commercial art galleries and artist-run spaces, all producing exhibitions and, potentially, catalogues (*see* ART, CONTEMPORARY TRENDS). These new shows in turn provoked reviews and articles in newspapers, general periodicals and specialized art journals. In the popular press, the amount of space devoted to the visual arts remained relatively small and the level of reportage remained descriptive. Museum newsletters became more numerous, influential and diverse. *ArtsAtlantic* (1977) introduced the concept of co-operative sponsorship, for the publication is supported by 11 Maritime galleries and museums. The Vancouver Art Gallery's *Vanguard* began in 1972 as a tabloid newspaper, but in 1979 changed its format to a magazine style and extended its scope to the national scene.

The increasing exhibition activity was reflected in the expanding number of specialized art journals, which, since WWII, have added important dimensions to the art field. *Canadian Art*, initiated in 1943 and renamed *artscanada* in 1967, was followed by *Vie des arts* in 1956; both publications concentrated on contemporary issues. In 1983 financial problems precipitated the demise of *artscanada* and *Artmagazine* (fd 1969), but the next year, 2 new periodicals, *C* and *Canadian art*, went to press. Only with the National Gallery's *Bulletin* and the 1974 creation of *RACAR* and the *Journal of Canadian Art History* have historical issues received continuing attention. Recently, numerous magazines have appeared written and published by artists. Many of these emanate from artist-run galleries, including the *Only Paper Today* from Toronto's A Space, *Centrefold* from Calgary's Parachute Centre, and *Virus* published by Montréal's Véhicule. Others come from art groups, such as General Idea's *File*. Some are broadly based, including *Parachute*, a magazine devoted to fine contemporary criticism. Specialized and more commercial publications such as *Video Guide, Canadian Architect* and *Photo Canada* are addressed to a restricted readership.

With this considerable increase in art writing came a change in the types of writers who published. The artist was still an important contributor, acting both as commentator and critic; the professional art critic, though often working part-time, became more prominent; and the university-trained art historian, a new generation of specialist, added considerably to the dialogue.

As catalogues became more common, they also became more varied and complex. Introductions gradually shifted from being straightforward biographical information to more probing analytic appraisals, complemented by an increasing number of reproductions. The approaches used are as diverse as the material covered. Alvin Balkind's soft-cover catalogue *17 Canadian Artists: A Protean View* accomplished its educational aim through the use of many illustrations and an evocative text. Working with a more defined subject, David MILNE's prints, Rosemarie Tovell effectively led the reader through the development of this important aspect of Milne's art (1980). Unfortunately, in this the largest area of art writing, distribution remains a major problem; some galleries are experimenting with copublishing certain catalogues as trade books through established publishers.

In books the trends are somewhat different. Biographies are favoured. These, including F.M. Gagnon's impressive *Borduas*, contain much solid research. But the greatest proportion of books published are of the coffee-table variety, a format eminently suited to lavish and large colour illustrations and a moderate amount of popular text. Recently this trend has been pushed further to the production of limited editions, collector volumes selling for thousands of dollars and dealing with well-known artists such as Christopher PRATT and KENOJUAK. Writers are drawn from the same pool that produces most of the catalogues and articles, although academics are gradually becoming more involved.

Along with the increased amount of art writing and criticism being done in Canada, there is a new professionalism and an expanded range of approach. This is due, in part, to the recent attention universities and galleries have accorded Canadian art history. The erstwhile norm — nonevaluative, first-person documents and biographical data — is gradually being expanded to produce interpretive or critical catalogues and journal articles. While one single philosophy of art has not become dominant in Canada, imported concepts, such as American critic Clement Greenberg's formalist approach, have attracted adherents. Yet there is increasing recognition of the politico-cultural nature of art and the global dimension of the contemporary artist's environment. Writers are acknowledging these individual and cultural values in particular works rather than seeking values through the application of rules formulated in advance; they are more conscious too of current literary theories. On the whole, Canadian art writing is becoming more analytic and more critical, seeking both new interpretations and better methods of evaluation. ANN DAVIS

Reading: K. McKenzie and M.F. Williamson, eds, *The Art and Pictorial Press in Canada* (1979).

Arthabaska, Qué, Town, pop 6827 (1981c), inc 1903, is located on the Rivière Nicolet in the Piedmont Appalachians, 5 km SE of VICTORIAVILLE and halfway between Québec City and Sherbrooke. The name is derived form the Cree word *Ayabaskaw*, meaning "place of the bulrushes and reeds." The founder, Charles Beauchesne, who arrived in 1834, was impressed by the size of the trees and quality of the soil. The first industries were potash and maple-sugar production. Establishment of the Arthabaska Convent (1870), the Arthabaska Commercial College (1872) and Collège St-Joseph (1905) made the town a popular centre of culture and education. Sir Wilfrid LAURIER began his law career here in 1867. His summer home has been converted into a museum. By 1882 cigar manufacturing, tanneries, flour mills and sawmills had been established. Furniture manufacturing was introduced around 1948. Located in the heart of a dairy and lumber-manufacturing region, Arthabaska is known as the "Capitale des Bois-Francs." Mont St-Michel, called "Monte Cristo" by the first settlers, dominates the town. JEAN-MARIE DUBOIS AND PIERRE MAILHOT

Arthritis, from the Greek *arthron* ["joint"] and *itis* ["inflammation"]. The word encompasses a wide range of disorders involving the various joints of the body, but always signifies the existence of varying degrees of inflammation which, if left unchecked, or if persisting over sufficient time, causes pain and ultimate destruction of the joint surfaces. Rheumatism, from the Greek *rheumatismos* ["flowing condition"], is used by the public (but rarely by medical practitioners) to describe any acute or chronic aching or stiffness of muscles, tendons, ligaments and joints, including arthritis and painful muscle conditions.

The rheumatic diseases are important both clinically and economically. About 1 in 50 Canadians by the age of 75 years (in a female to male ratio of 65.4% to 34.6%) will have suffered some form of rheumatic complaint. Although between 7% and 10% of visits to doctors' offices relate to musculoskeletal problems (ranking only behind circulatory, respiratory and endocrine disorders), this percentage does not reflect the prevalence of the disease, because as many as 75% of individuals with rheumatic complaints do not seek medical attention.

The campaign against rheumatic disease is conducted by professional societies, voluntary health organizations and official governmental agencies. The International League Against Rheumatism was founded in 1927. The Pan-American League is one of its subdivisions, and in Canada the Canadian Arthritis Association co-ordinates and supports much of the work and research at all levels.

Osteoarthritis and rheumatoid arthritis are the most prevalent forms of arthritis. Osteoarthritis is characterized by morning stiffness, pain proportional to activity, swelling and grating of the joints with movement, and a gradual loss of motion. The articular surface gradually thins and the joint becomes mechanically unsound. It is most common with the elderly, but it is unclear if it is simply a manifestation of aging. It is usually classed as a degenerative condition and occurs mainly in the chief weight-bearing joints, eg, hips and knees. Treatment can include the use of anti-inflammatory medications (eg, aspirin), physiotherapy and walking aids. Total replacement of a joint, particularly the hip, by an artifical joint is possible.

Rheumatoid arthritis is a chronic inflammatory disorder of unknown cause, although it may be related to the body's immune system. It affects approximately 1% of the N American population over the age of 15 years with an overall female-to-male ratio of 3 to one. Although rheumatoid arthritis affects the joints, it is a systemic illness and affects most other tissues of the body to varying extents. This disease, which usually starts with swelling, warmth, pain and stiffness in one or more joints, is classically symmetrical, ie, it affects the small joints of the hands, wrists and feet but tends, except in its severe, progressive forms, to spare the hips and spine. Treatment can include anti-inflammatory medications, such as gold therapy, rest, splints, walking aids and physiotherapy. Artificial joints made of a combination of metal and various plastics and silastic materials can also be implanted.

Of the less common forms of arthritis a particularly virulent type, juvenile rheumatoid arthritis, commonly affects children (male and female) between the ages of one to 5 years. Characterized by a high fever, a rash, joint pains and sometimes heart trouble, the disease may destroy many of the joints.

Other arthritides include ankylosing spondylitis, psoriatic arthritis and Reiter's syndrome. Ankylosing spondylitis, a genetic disease to which native peoples seem particularly vulnerable, primarily affects young men, particularly their spines and large pelvic joints. Psoriatic arthritis, an inflammatory arthritis, is associated with the skin disease psoriasis. Reiter's syndrome is associated with infections of the urinary tract or bowel.

Gout, in which the body's inefficiency to handle certain chemicals allows the precipitation of crystals of uric acid (monosodium urate) in and around joints, is the best-known metabolic cause of arthritis. Other crystals identified as causing arthritis include calcium pyrophosphate, which leads to a disease called "pseudogout" because of the similarity of the symptoms to gout. Gouty infections affecting joints lead to rapid destruction of the articular surface because the enzymes liberated by the body's white blood cells. These enzymes digest the substance of the joint surface, depriving it of its mechanical properties. DAVID C. REID

Reading: S.P. Blau and D. Schultz, *Arthritis: Complete Up-to-date Facts for Patients and their Families* (1974).

Arthur, Eric Ross, architect, author (b at Dunedin, New Zealand 1 July 1898; d at Toronto 1 Nov 1982). Educated in England, Arthur came to Canada in 1923 to become an associate professor of architecture, U of T. Throughout his career, he was concerned with the preservation of Toronto's architectural heritage. He was a founder of the Architectural Conservancy of Ontario (1932) and thereafter actively involved in numerous restoration projects in Toronto, including the ST LAWRENCE HALL (1967). He was author and coauthor of several books on architecture. His best known, *Toronto: No Mean City* (1964), is a standard reference on the city and its architectural past. He was named a companion of the Order of Canada in 1968. (*See* BARNS; TOMBSTONES.) SUSAN FORD

Arthur, Sir George, soldier, colonial administrator (b at Plymouth, Eng 21 June 1784; d at London, Eng 19 Sept 1854). After an undistinguished military career and 2 minor colonial appointments, he became lt-gov of Upper Canada in 1838. An early decision to execute 2 prisoners taken in the REBELLION OF 1837 made him seem a bloodthirsty Tory. More lenient in reality than his advisers and the Assembly, he remained a moderate even after the border was set aflame by American raids, restraining Upper Canadians from retaliation. Though sympathetic to the FAMILY COMPACT, he introduced important administrative reforms. After the arrival of Gov Gen C.E.P. Thomson (SYDENHAM) 1839, he became largely a figurehead. He returned to England in 1841 and served as governor of Bombay 1842-46. P.A. BUCKNER

Reading: A.G.L. Shaw, *Sir George Arthur* (1980).

Artists' Organizations The history of visual artists' groups in Canada is filled with short-lived societies which have had a major influence on both professional and amateur artists. All kinds of associations have existed at one time or another, with artists grouped by age, region, aesthetic idea, medium, profession or even by gender. Artists' organizations have often been founded to meet specific needs (to form pressure groups, organize exhibitions, improve representation in the market) and are generally the product of one person's labour, someone who leads the group as its president or secretary.

The mixed associations created before the 1840s paid little attention to the visual arts, but through their meetings artists were integrated into a network of intellectual exchanges.

The Halifax Chess, Pencil and Brush Club (1787-1817) is considered the first artists' organization in what is now Canada, though its mandate extended beyond art to polite pursuits. The Society for the Encouragement of Art and Science in Canada (Québec, 1827) joined with the QUEBEC LITERARY AND HISTORICAL SOCIETY in 1829 and was composed mainly of military personnel, members of the clergy and liberal professions with scientific, historical and literary interests. The artists in this group were mostly amateurs or young professionals, as in the Society of Artists and Amateurs of Toronto (1834). At irregular intervals, the Toronto Society of Arts (1847) and the Montreal Society of Artists (1847) brought artists together with a public that could give them entry to the wealthiest circles, those few who were commissioning works.

The Montréal association was revived in 1860 as the Art Assn of Montreal, but its artists became increasingly inactive. Collectors dominated the association and rented space once a year to show their collections and the works of the few member artists and guests, most of them part of the ephemeral Society of Canadian Artists (1867). In 1879 the art association acquired permanent premises, which enabled it to hold annual exhibitions based on the model of the Paris salons, to host the Royal Canadian Academy exhibits and to use some artists as instructors and members of committees. Artists benefited from these activities, but when the art association became a museum its values changed for many artists. However, the school continued to have good teachers, it attracted many promising students and was an important forum for art educators (*see* ART EDUCATION).

The founding of the Royal Canadian Academy of Arts (RCA) in 1880, under the impetus and patronage of Governor General the marquis of Lorne and Princess Louise, marked an important stage in the recognition of the artist's status in Canadian society. The RCA adopted several regulations from European and British academies, such as the election of members by nomination and the artist's donation of an admission work; these works became the core of the collection of the NATIONAL GALLERY OF CANADA. The RCA continued to play a most important role in the history of Canadian art. It became the arbiter of taste in established art circles; its annual exhibitions, held in a few towns throughout the country, became national events; its competitions promoted the development of PUBLIC ART; it was responsible for showing Canadian art abroad at British Empire exhibitions and world fairs; and all the while it sponsored courses as a means of improving the quality of artwork in Canada.

The RCA was less effective in meeting the specific needs of artists in various regions. While its members were selected on a national basis, their representativeness was questionable. It had limited means and a structure constantly hampered by large distances and administration. From its foundation the RCA was challenged by artists who questioned its hold on the aesthetic standards of the nation. Other societies became important to Canadian painters, sculptors, graphic artists and architects.

The Ontario Society of Artists (OSA), founded in 1872, was always dynamic. It created its own collection, had annual exhibitions and founded the Art Union of Canada to encourage collectors to acquire its members' works. In co-operation with the Ministry of Education, the OSA founded a school of art known today as the ONTARIO COLLEGE OF ART; OSA members planned the curriculum and taught at this school.

As the number of trained and professional artists increased in a society that was expanding both demographically and economically, new artists' organizations appeared, most of which tended to be more specialized. Toronto had many such organizations, less prestigious than the RCA or the OSA, but different goals attracted people who wanted to share their specialities with others of the same mind. The Toronto Art Students' League, founded in 1886, was not only a school but a setting where members met to draw, discuss, comment on each other's work and create projects together. Most of its members were illustrators, as in the Pen and Pencil Club of Montréal. The Art Students' League gave rise to the Graphics Art Club, which played an important role in the development of graphic art, even before becoming the Canadian Society of Graphic Art in 1933.

Specialized groups were established whose membership included only professionals, people interested in one medium. The short-lived Assn of Canadian Etchers (1885) was revived on a more solid basis in 1916 as the Society of Canadian Painter-Etchers and Engravers. The Toronto Camera Club (1891) and the Montréal Sketching Club (1899) had premises for meetings and exhibitions and published texts and catalogues. The large number and membership of these associations indicate how strongly artists felt the need to meet with their colleagues (*see also* PHOTOGRAPHY; PRINTMAKING).

In contrast to highly structured groups like the RCA or the Women's Art Assn of Toronto (1890), there were clubs such as the Arts and Letters Club of Toronto (1908), the Mahlstick Club (1899), l'Arche and the Arts Club of Montréal (1912). Members were usually friends who met together when they felt like it, came from the same social class and had the same tastes. Meetings were pleasant; people discussed freely, each in turn presenting his works for friendly criticism. Resources were pooled in order to organize private or public shows, dinners, excursions or exhibitions. The Canadian Art Club (1907) in Toronto was simply a group of well-known artists, some of them members of the RCA, whose sole purpose was to organize exhibitions of members' works and thus to lobby collectors more effectively.

At the turn of the century, artists' groups appeared in the West. The Winnipeg Art Society (1902), the British Columbia Society of Artists (1909) and the British Columbia Art League (1920) were evidence of the country's growth and of the desire of artists and amateurs in these regions to stimulate each other and enliven their activities. In the years after WWI new groups were added to the network: the Manitoba Society of Artists (1925), the Women Painters of Western Canada and the Alberta Society of Artists (1931).

The Maritimes were also active with associations multiplying there as well. The Maritime Art Assn, founded in 1935, drew on the experience of earlier Maritime groups (for example, the Nova Scotia Society of Artists, Newcastle Art Club, Moncton Arts Society, Art Society of Prince Edward Island). In 1940 the Maritime group was unified and strengthened by the publication *Maritime Art*, which helped to spread news of artists' work. The magazine unexpectedly developed into a national magazine, *Canadian Art*, coedited by some curators from the National Gallery of Canada and finally became the independent Toronto publication *artscanada*.

New national groups were established in the spirit of their predecessors. The Canadian Society of Painters in Watercolour (1925) focused on and renewed interest in watercolours, a medium already very popular in the 19th century. The Council of the Guild of Sculptors (1896) was revived and transformed to become the Sculptors' Society of Canada (1928).

The GROUP OF SEVEN (1920-33) was typical of other associations formed later in the century, in that it was organized by several artists who shared an aesthetic ideal. Together they searched for a Canadian iconography based on landscape, yet individually each artist sought to distinguish himself from the Group. The Seven were succeeded by the Canadian Group of Painters (1933), which drew its members from across Canada; it was open to men and women and was concerned with modernism and figure painting as well as the landscape, with "the right of Canadian artists to find beauty and character in all things."

Many artists resented the "national institution" the Group of Seven had become and in the ensuing climate of protest several new groups were formed, particularly in Québec. The Beaver Hall Hill Group (1924) in Montréal, mainly women painters from the Art Assn school, explored contemporary art trends, and psychological and formal aspects were of utmost importance in their compositions. The Eastern Group of Painters (1938) included 7 active Montréal artists whose common interest was painting, not a nationalist theory. The CONTEMPORARY ART SOCIETY (1939-48) was founded in Montréal by John Lyman to defend modern art. The society was composed of artists and a few intellectuals who did not necessarily share the same style or thinking but who wished to show their support of nonacademic art. In 1948 both the AUTOMATISTE and the Prisme d'yeux movement published manifestos which adopted opposing attitudes to artistic creation and caused the demise of Lyman's group.

Nonfigurative art was established across Canada by the Calgary Group (around 1947), the PLASTICIENS (manifesto published in 1955), the Non-figurative Artists Assn of Montreal (1956-61), PAINTERS ELEVEN (1953-60) in Toronto and the REGINA FIVE (early 1960s). These groups did not attempt to define a new artistic current. Rather, by concentrating on a particular element of their work, from the creative process (individuality of gesture, spontaneity) to the enhancement of certain formal and pictorial elements (surface, space, light, line, colour), artists gave a new perspective to art, while at the same time being part of an international movement. The groups provided a forum for debate among artists concerned with the common issues of the role of art and its meaning in a postindustrial civilization (*see also* PAINTING).

The militancy of Western society in the 1960s and early 1970s was reflected in the types of artists' organizations established. The 1960-80 period saw the consolidation of existing societies and the creation of new groups that attempted to increase governmental and public awareness of the artist's role and needs. Artists became more politically and socially involved through their associations, seeking to become part of current debates while affirming the professional aspect of their careers. Groups of artists appeared that were stimulated by the development of a common aesthetic and art such as General Idea in Toronto and N.E. Thing Co in Vancouver (*see* ART, CONTEMPORARY TRENDS). Existing groups generally tried to become more cohesive and more effective in action. The Society of Canadian Painter-Etchers and Engravers, for example, joined with the Canadian Society of Graphic Art to form the Print and Drawing Council of Canada in 1976.

The need for an increasingly international and competitive market led artists to analyse more objectively their associations' goals and the means at their disposal. The Society of Cooperative Artists (1957), which in 1967 became the Society of Canadian Artists, began publishing *artmagazine* in 1969 in order to give the public better information on its members' work and the activities of other institutions and associations. Supersocieties were formed on a national scale to represent visual artists throughout Canada on terms different from those of the RCA. The Professional Artists of Canada (PAC) was created in 1969 as an association of associations comprising 7 existing societies that wished to join together to make themselves heard by the public, whose opinion they were increasingly seeking.

PAC's founding was a reaction by existing associations to the establishment, at the end of 1967, of a more demanding group, the Canadian Artists Representation/Front des artistes canadiens (CAR/FAC). Created through the initiative of Jack Chambers, CAR/FAC was a decentralized structure from the outset which attempted to unite its members on the basis of professional demands, such as royalty payments to artists for the reproduction of their works and a schedule of rates paid for works hung in exhibitions. In 1957 the Canadian Conference of the Arts had raised the issues of copyright, tax reform and social security for visual artists who had no agents or regular incomes. With the exception of copyright, these problems remain unsolved, and it appears that artists as a group are not strong enough to ensure that their most elementary demands are met.

Recent formations such as Western Front in Vancouver or Art Metropole in Toronto, although socially aware, exist primarily to provide members and their guests with an organization similar to many "parallel galleries" and artist-run centres across Canada. They give artists facilities and space in which to realize and show their experimental and often unmarketable work.

Québec artists always remained a separate group within the umbrella associations, though in the 1970s they belonged to specialist artist groups. Sculptors and engravers were particularly active (Association des sculpteurs du Québec, 1961-76; Conseil de la sculpture, 1978; Association des graveurs du Québec, 1971; Conseil de la gravure, 1978, which prepared a code of ethics for its members). As within the other Canadian associations, efforts for the long-term unification of Québec artists (Société des artistes professionels du Québec, 1966) have had mixed results because of the lack of general interest and solidarity on the part of the artists as a whole. Since each artist is at a different level of political awareness and professional development, individual interests take precedence over the interests of the group.

The most constructive and active groups in the history of art in Canada appear to have been the small, organic ones in which natural affinities have appeared and artists have put the elements of a common aesthetic ideal into practice. These natural associations enable the artist to compare his opinions and works with those of a few colleagues and friends, through direct and informal exchanges, thus helping him face the hesitations and isolation of the studio with more assurance and confidence.

LAURIER LACROIX

Reading: D. Reid, *A Concise History of Canadian Painting* (1973).

Arts Funding Artistic activities in Canada are funded by a variety of sources, including self-generated earnings, private and corporate donations, and governments at the federal, provincial, regional and municipal levels. The federal government has been providing the services of institutions such as the National Gallery, the National Museum and the Public Archives for over 100 years, and this long-standing commitment has been matched by many provincial and local governments. In contrast, orchestral and theatrical companies that were active before the end of WWI sustained themselves without government help, through monies earned at the box office supplemented by gifts from benefactors. The TORONTO SYMPHONY ORCHESTRA, then a semi-professional ensemble supported by a group of businessmen, began to give concerts in 1908. The Calgary Symphony dates from 1913 and the Société (now Orchestre) Symphonique de Québec from 1906. Most theatrical companies were amateur groups until the 1950s, inhibited by the absence of appropriate theatres. Occasionally a wealthy patron donated a building or hall to the community, which might stimulate professional services, as with MASSEY HALL in Toronto.

Individual and Corporate Donations In recent years government tax policies have sought to encourage corporate and private donations to arts operations. In 1917 the federal government instituted the Income War Tax Act which allowed deductions, without limit, for private donations to activities that could help the war effort. In 1929 a ceiling of 10% was placed on deductions applied to churches, hospitals, universities and educational institutions. "Educational" donations often included arts and cultural activities. The Income Tax Act of 1948 retained the ceiling on deductions for charities. From then on, private donations and gifts began to have a significant effect on communities across the country. In 1957 an optional deduction of $100 for charities was instituted, together with a rise in the level of deductible corporate donations. In 1972 the charitable deductions ceiling was raised to 20%, but has had little effect on donations.

Of all donations for charitable purposes, only a small part reaches the arts community though totals did rise from $73.4 million ($62.5 million for individuals and $10.9 million for corporations) in 1946 to $328.1 million ($268.4 million and $59.7 million) in 1970. In 1979 the totals were $884.8 million and $171 million. Of the 419 835 corporations operating in Canada in 1979, fewer than 4% (15 619) claimed any tax-deductible charitable donations; nearly all such gifts were directed to welfare, health, religion and education. In dollars only one-twentieth of the 5% claimed, on average, went to arts and cultural activities. Some companies offer supplies and personal services as supplements or alternatives to donations of cash, often out of operational rather than donation budgets. New buildings, equipment and other capital expenditures are attractive to donors seeking visible recognition for their gifts.

Corporate donations are affected by annual profits, and nonprofit arts companies find this source of income unstable and unreliable. Priorities for giving within a single corporation often shift with changing times and interests. In recent years in Canada the order of priorities for corporate donations has been as follows: symphonic music, museums and galleries, theatre, dance, opera, choral music, libraries, ethnic groups, archives. Patrons and donors must respond to the competition for funds between well-established and new ventures, large and small operations within cities and towns, professional and amateur activities, national and regional programs, and organizations and individuals.

Government Support to arts programs is provided in both direct and indirect ways. Direct support includes grants, loans and subsidies, information services, and the proprietorship and operation of galleries, museums, libraries, archives, parks and historic sites. Federal government support for the arts was for many years centered in the Dept of the Secretary of State, but the Arts and Culture Branch was shifted to the Dept of Communications in 1980. Most arts agencies now report through that ministry and the department itself operates a number of support programs. Many other federal departments, including External Affairs, Indian Affairs, Environment, Employment and Immigration, and Supply and Services play important roles in arts activities also.

Some federal agencies are, in effect, government-owned operators of arts programs. These include the National Arts Centre, the CANADIAN BROADCASTING CORPORATION, the NATIONAL FILM BOARD, the NATIONAL MUSEUMS OF CANADA, the NATIONAL LIBRARY and the PUBLIC ARCHIVES OF CANADA. Decisions of the CANADIAN RADIO-TELEVISION AND TELECOMMUNICATIONS COMMISSION also affect the interests of the arts community. Other federal agencies have been created to provide grants, subsidies, investments and scholarships: the CANADA COUNCIL, the SOCIAL SCIENCES AND HUMANITIES RESEARCH COUNCIL, the CANADIAN FILM DEVELOPMENT CORPORATION and the National Museums Corporation. Federal ministries and their provincial counterparts often provide grants directly, though some provinces have established independent granting councils or boards. In the 1981-82 fiscal year, provincial government expenditure on culture totalled $802.9 million, of which 33.7% was spent in Ontario, 31.7% in Québec, 10% in BC, 9% in Alberta and the remainder in the other provinces and territories. Income from lotteries is also used by federal and provincial bodies in support of the arts.

Governments often buy artistic services in the form of concerts which they offer free to the public, the purchase of books for library distribution and of works of art to enhance government buildings and offices (*see* LIBRARIES; PUBLIC ART). In architectural design and decor, governments exert a significant influence on the artistic and industrial communities: in contracts worth hundreds of millions of dollars each year they build, furnish and decorate office buildings, courthouses, council chambers, embassies and post offices (*see* GOVERNMENT BUILDING).

Indirect support is provided mostly through forgone taxes, as in the case of the 50% capital-cost allowance for investments in Canadian film and videotape production, and deductions from taxes of the value of donations to the arts. Help also comes through internal subsidies such as those provided by the Dept of Communications to the post office to reduce the cost of mailing books, MAGAZINES and NEWSPAPERS (*see* POSTAL SYSTEM). Government regulations can significantly change the artistic climate for some cultural industries, as happened to the recording industry when the CRTC regulated the amount of Canadian-originated recordings played on Canadian radio stations. Similarly, Canadian-content regulations imposed on TV and PAY-TELEVISION broadcasters has residual impact on FILM and TV-production companies, their artists and performers (*see* BROADCASTING, RADIO AND TELEVISION; RADIO PROGRAMMING; TELEVISION PROGRAMMING). Both the federal and provincial governments have been urged to enact other regulations to stimulate the production of Canadian theatrical films.

Federal Expenditures on Culture, 1982-83 (in Millions$)

Canada Council	59.9
CBC	737.4
Canadian Film Development Corporation	4.5[1]
CRTC	5.4
National Arts Centre	15.8
National Film Board	53.0
National Library of Canada	32.1
National Museums Corporation	62.5
Public Archives of Canada	31.2
Social Sciences and Humanities Research Council	57.0
Arts & Culture Branch, Dept of Communications	237.8[2]
Secretary of State for Multiculturalism	13.0
Official Language Minorities	1.3
Historic Parks of Canada	53.5
Others, for cultural programs	76.8
Total	$1 373.4
Cultural net costs as percentage of government net costs	1.9%

[1] Supplemented by $35 million for TV production in 1983
[2] Includes Post Office subsidy

The Canada Council In 1949 the federal government formed a Royal Commission on NATIONAL DEVELOPMENT IN THE ARTS, LETTERS AND SCIENCES and named Vincent MASSEY as chairman. The report, published in 1951, had a marked effect on government attitudes and many of its programs. It brought the federal government into direct support of universities and recommended the establishment of new institutions, notably the National Library in 1953 and the Canada Council for the Arts, Humanities and Social Sciences in 1957. The Council at first subsisted on income of under $2.4 million (1957-58) from a $50-million endowment established by the government, with a mandate "to foster and promote the study and enjoyment of, and the production of works in the arts." By 1965 the Council requested and was allocated its first additional government appropriation, an assignment of $10 million to be disbursed over the period of 3 years. In 1983-84 the Council's budget had grown to $77.5 million. The Council directs its funds to individual artists, arts companies and support services. Most grants are made on the advice of peer groups and juries of experts in the various arts disciplines. In 1978 the Humanities and Social Sciences division was separated from the original Council, and the new Social Sciences and Humanities Research Council deals with the academic community.

Grants by the Canada Council have become vital to the continued good health and aspirations of professional arts companies and are divided for 1983-84 approximately as follows: writing and publishing, 14%; music, 19.7%; theatre and mime, 21.4%; dance, 12.3%; visual arts, including the Art Bank and film and video, 12.5%; explorations (a miscellaneous regional program), 3.3%; touring, 4.9%; multidisciplinary, 0.3%; with the remaining 11.6% going to the individual artists. The budget of the Canada Council represents only a small part of the federal government involvement in arts support. Cultural programs are assigned about 2% of federal expenditures, the largest single item being government appropriation to the CBC.

All provinces have government departments and agencies through which they fund arts activities and provide support. A province's goals may vary from those enunciated by the federal government, and its clientele may be somewhat different, often including amateur groups and ethnic activities, for example. Nevertheless, the basic patterns for offering assistance and funds to arts groups are essentially similar to those described. Municipal granting decisions, with few exceptions, are made by governing councils without benefit of outside advice or independent citizen boards. In some areas, mostly in the West, provincial and local community foundations have been active in the arts. Though funding by municipal governments is still relatively meagre, the level seems to be rising steadily.

Arts companies are hard pressed to assign staff and provide the expertise necessary to deal with this complex funding process. Though administration would be easier if funded by a single patron, most arts companies agree that the present system enables them to achieve freedom in artistic planning and development. This they seem to value more than a reduced work load. The report of the Federal Cultural Policy Review Committee (1982) endorses the principle of multiple sources of funding for similar reasons.

LOUIS APPLEBAUM

The commissioners of the Royal Commission on National Development in the Arts, Letters and Sciences (from left to right) Arthur Surveyer, Rev Georges-Henri Lévesque, Rt Hon Vincent Massey, Hilda Neatby, Norman A.M. MacKenzie *(courtesy Public Archives of Canada/Canadian Assn for Adult Education)*.

Arvida Strike began 24 July 1941, when some 700 workers in the Aluminum Co of Canada (Alcan) in Arvida, Qué, spontaneously walked off the job. The next day the strike spread to 4500 workers, who decided to occupy the plant. Since the industry had been classified as essential to the war effort, the strike was illegal under federal law. A commotion resulted when Minister of Munitions and Supply C.D. HOWE told the press that 300 men had seized the factory and enemy sabotage was suspected. Two companies of soldiers were sent to Arvida to protect the factory.

Work resumed 4 days later and negotiations began, with the union as intermediary, assisted by federal conciliators. A subsequent royal commission rejected the sabotage theory, concluding that the strike had been the result of workers' frustration over their long struggle for better salaries and working conditions. The immediate catalysts to the strike had been deductions from the July 23 pay envelopes and a stifling heat wave. The company made amends several days later by giving a slight increase in salaries and in cost-of-living bonuses.

JACQUES ROUILLARD

As For Me and My House, novel by Sinclair ROSS (New York, 1941; Toronto, 1957), explores the spiritual, social and natural forces which threaten to crack a strained marriage. Philip Bentley, a thwarted artist turned minister, and his wife have just moved to Horizon, a small Saskatchewan town struggling through the 1930s. Their story is told in diary form by Mrs Bentley, whose descriptions of Horizon's false-fronted stores become increasingly suggestive of the Bentley's false-fronted lives. She also records the bleak oppression of a pretentious and puritanical social ambience, and of a constantly threatening natural environment which assaults the town's flimsy structures with seasonal cycles of heat and cold, dust and snow. The novel closes with the Bentleys adopting Philip's illegitimate child, determined to make a new life beyond Horizon. Ross depicts the trials of small-town life on the Prairies with a starkly repetitive style and beautiful clarity.

NEIL BESNER

Asbestos, generic term normally used to describe 6 MINERALS, some of which are asbestiform, ie, separable into long, silky, flexible fibres. The 3 main minerals are chrysotile, amosite and crocidolite. Of these, chrysotile is by far the most important commercially and is the only type produced in Canada. Asbestos is valuable because of its fibrous structure, high tensile strength and resistance to high temperature and chemical attack. The Romans used asbestos cloth for wrapping the dead for cremation over 2000 years ago. Asbestos was first discovered in N America in 1860, in the Des Plantes R region of

Asbestos mine, Advocate Mines Ltd, Nfld *(photo by J.A. Wilkinson/Valan)*.

Québec. Canadian production began in 1878 at Thetford-Mines, Qué. Subsequent discovery of large reserves in the Eastern Townships led to establishment of 5 mining towns, making up the present Québec asbestos region. Asbestos is used in over 3000 products serving the CONSTRUCTION, TRANSPORTATION, ELECTRICAL APPLIANCE, equipment and other industries. Asbestos-cement pipe and sheet account for about 60% of world consumption; other uses include flooring and roofing products, friction products (brake linings and clutch facings), coatings and compounds, special papers and insulation. The asbestos content of products ranges from 10-90%.

Canada, the world's second-largest producer of asbestos, accounted in 1980 for about 25% of estimated world production of 5.1 million t. The USSR accounted for about 50%. About 5% of Canadian production is used by manufacturing plants, mainly in Québec and Ontario; the remainder is exported. Asbestos-fibre shipments in 1981 were valued at nearly $548 million or 0.2% of GNP; Québec accounted for 85% of Canada's production of 1.12 million t; BC for about 8%; and Newfoundland for about 6%. In Canada a mechanical dry-milling process separates fibres from rock by repetitive breaking and return of nondisintegrated rock, drying, separation of fibres from rock by suction at each step, cleaning, grading and packaging. The Canadian grading system divides mine products to crude asbestos; hand-selected, cross-vein aterial, which may comprise up to 10% or ore of the rock; and milled asbestos, all grades oduced by mechanical treatment of ore. Past gh-level exposure to airborne asbestos dust in e workplace has been a health hazard. Long-ne employees (10-29 years), exposed to the ghest dust levels in asbestos mines and mills, ffered excess mortality mainly from asbes-sis, a lung disease. Conditions are now care-lly monitored and workers undergo regular edical examinations. G.O. VAGT

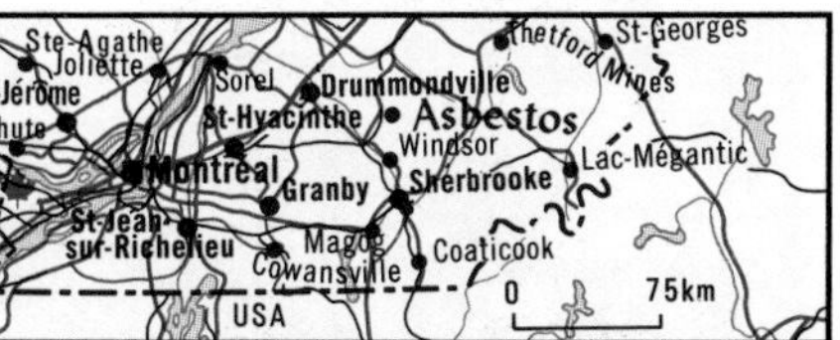

sbestos, Qué, Town, pop 7967 (1981c), inc 37, is located in the Lower Appalachian pla-au 63 km N of Sherbrooke and 55 km SE of ummondville. John Manville discovered an BESTOS deposit in 1881 on the present site, hich has been mined and expanded ever since. e Jeffrey mine is the largest open-face asbes-s mine in the world, measuring 330 m in pth and 1.2 km in diameter. The mill has an nual capacity of 545 000 000 kg of fibre. The gion has also been the site of copper, iron and te mines, the latter having been used in the anufacture of school blackboards. On 14 Feb 49 a strike of asbestos-industry workers began at involved 5000 miners, lasted for 120 work-g days and became a turning point in Québec's cial history (*see* ASBESTOS STRIKE.) The mine's eady growth has transformed the town's land-ape; some streets and homes were eliminated 1975 to allow further industrial develop-ent. The added presence of wood-product and ectrical-equipment manufacturers has enabled sbestos to become the major economic centre of chmond County. The town has a mineralogy d mining history museum and is host to the nual Festival des Gourmands.
JEAN-MARIE DUBOIS AND PIERRE MAILHOT

sbestos Strike began 14 Feb 1949 and for the xt 4 months paralysed major asbestos mines Québec, the most important of which were merican owned. From the start, this strike of 00 workers affiliated with the CCCL (later NFEDERATION OF NATIONAL TRADE UNIONS) esented a challenge to the entire union move-ent, anglophone management in Québec, the ovince's political system and the Roman tholic Church, and disrupted their former lationships. It began illegally, and thus broke ith the CCCL's long tradition of co-operation ith management. The asbestos fight also pro-uced unprecedented inter-union solidarity. nions had previously formed a common front battle an anti-union bill of the UNION NATION-LE government, and now the CCCL, the Féd-ation provinciale du travail du Québec (FPTQ, ter part of QFL) and unions affiliated to the CL and CIO organized strike-support meetings roughout Québec. The church also backed the rikers. This put the bishop's office in direct nflict with Prem Maurice DUPLESSIS, whose po-ce, based in mining-company offices, were in nflict with the strikers. The strike became a istorical and political event of symbolic import at introduced Québec to an era of embittered bour conflict and presaged the QUIET REVOLU-ON. HÉLÈNE DAVID

sh (*Fraxinus*), genus of TREES or SHRUBS of olive mily (Oleaceae). About 60 species occur world-ide, primarily in cold temperate regions; 4 are ative to Canada. Native ashes (white, red, blue d black) grow in the East; some forms of red

White ash (*Fraxinus americana*), with male flowers and fruit (*artwork by Claire Tremblay*).

ash reach southeastern Alberta. Trees are of medium height with generally straight, slender trunks. The large compound leaves, consisting of 5-11 leaflets, occur in pairs on the twig. The small, dark flowers are grouped in clusters. Ashes produce large amounts of fruit in the form of winged seeds, which remain on the tree well into winter and are an important food source for birds and squirrels. Ashes prefer the rich, moist soils of swamps and riverways. Except in black ash, the wood is heavy, hard, tough and strong and widely used for sporting goods, tool handles and furniture. *See* PLANTS, NATIVE USES. ESTELLE LACOURSIÈRE

Ashburton-Webster Treaty (Treaty of Washington), 9 Aug 1842, negotiated by Alexander Baring, First Lord Ashburton, for Britain, and US Secretary of State Daniel Webster. Several sources of friction between the 2 countries were removed, especially regarding those boundaries between BNA and the US which remained in doubt following the TREATY OF GHENT. A particular problem had been the 12 000 mi (approx 31 000 km) disputed between NB and Maine, 5000 mi (approx 13 000 km) of which went to NB. The treaty also provided for the surveying, mapping, and marking of the agreed NB-Maine boundary, completed June 1847. It made some minor adjustments along the northern boundaries of Vermont and New York, and described for the first time the boundary from Lake Huron to Lake of the Woods. N.L. NICHOLSON

Ashcroft, BC, Village, pop 2156 (1981c), is situated on a flat bench above the THOMPSON R in the interior of southern BC, about 90 km W of Kamloops. The name originally applied to Ashcroft Manor, a stopping house built on the old CARIBOO ROAD in 1863 by Clement and Henry Cornwall, ranchers who named the place after their English ancestral home. Clement became a member of both provincial and federal parliaments, was a senator and served as BC's lt-gov 1881-87. In 1883 a townsite was surveyed a few km from the manor in anticipation of the construction of the CPR, completed 1885. First called St Cloud, it became an important transportation centre after a bridge was built over the Thompson in 1884 — the railhead for the north and mile "0" for the Cariboo Road. Ashcroft was prosperous and busy until completion of the Pacific Great Eastern Ry, now BC Ry, from Vancouver after WWI. Since the decline in mining in the Cariboo, Ashcroft mainly serves the CPR and CNR and acts as a supply centre for nearby open-pit copper mines. JOHN R. STEWART

Asparagus (*Asparagus officinalis*), perennial VEGETABLE of the LILY family. Of Eurasian origin, asparagus was grown for food and medicinal purposes over 2000 years ago. The crop spread throughout Europe and later to N America. The spears, cut when 15-18 cm high, are relished as a cooked or raw vegetable. The crop is established from one-year-old crowns (grown from seed in a nursery), set out in spring in a 15 cm deep furrow, and covered with 5 cm of soil. The emerging spears of a newly established field are harvested for about 2 weeks in the spring of the third year; the full cutting season (6-8 weeks) is achieved the fifth year. An established field can produce for 15-20 years; one commercial field in BC is over 50 years old. After harvest, spears are permitted to grow into ferns (1.5-2.5 m high) for the manufacture of carbohydrates, which are stored in the fleshy roots and used to produce new growth in spring. The fern, killed by frost, is left to trap snow and insulate roots. Asparagus beetles in eastern Canada and aphids in the OKANAGAN VALLEY, BC, are the principal INSECT PESTS. The major disease is *Fusarium* wilt; asparagus rust is a problem in humid regions of eastern Canada. Asparagus varieties include Mary and Martha Washington, Viking, Beacon, Centennial and Washington State University hybrids. The main growing areas in Canada are Ontario, 1880 ha; BC, 325 ha; Québec, 550 ha; and Manitoba, 90 ha. H. TIESSEN

Aspen, deciduous, hardwood TREE in genus *Populus* of WILLOW family. Trembling aspen (*P. tremuloides*) and largetooth aspen (*P. grandidentata*) are native to Canada; the former, found from TREELINE to northern Mexico, is the most widely distributed tree in N America. Trembling aspen grows on most soils, doing best on well-drained, moist, sandy or gravelly loams. It is shade-intolerant and short-lived (about 60 years). A "pioneer" tree, it colonizes areas disturbed by logging or fire, propagating by root suckers rather than seeds. It also acts as "nurse tree" to softwood or hardwood forest taking over a site. On the Prairies, it may be the only tree. Leaves are nearly circular, with a short tip; the flattened stalk makes them tremble in the wind. Twigs are slender, shiny and brownish grey, the bark smooth, waxy and pale green to chalky white in colour. Trees reach 12-18 m in height. Open grown specimens have a profusely branched, globular crown; forest trees have long, cylindrical trunks with short, rounded crowns. Largetooth aspen, less widespread, is found in Canada from southeastern Manitoba to the Atlantic Provinces. It resembles trembling aspen in form and habit; the coarse-toothed, almost circular leaves also tremble.

Quaking aspen (*Populus tremuloides*), with female flowers (left) and male flowers (right) (*artwork by Claire Tremblay*).

Assembly of First Nations is the national political organization representing Canada's status Indians (*see* INDIAN). The AFN is the culmination of efforts to form a national Indian organization which go back as far as the 1920s. It succeeds both the National Indian Advisory Council (fd 1961, *see* NATIVE COUNCIL OF CANADA) and the National Indian Brotherhood, which was active in representing Indian interests throughout the 1960s and 1970s under leaders Walter DEITER, George MANUEL and Noel Starblanket. In the late 1970s the increase of power at the local level of Indian government, the need to react to federal constitutional proposals, and the ideology of "Indian nationhood" led to calls for reform. Thus the Assembly of First Nations was founded by chiefs representing a majority of bands during a meeting in Ottawa in 1980. The chiefs declared their assembly the one and only voice of the First Nationals of Canada, referred to as Indian bands in the INDIAN ACT. The AFN replaced the National Indian Brotherhood (which had been based on an executive chosen from the provincial Indian organizations) with a new structure based on the common vote of individual Indian local governments. The NIB corporate structure was retained for legal transactions. The chiefs outlined their objectives for the new organization in the Declaration of First Nations.

Although the AFN does not have a formal constitution, it agreed in Apr 1982 to elect a national chief for a 3-year term to manage the assembly's ongoing work. The chief is assisted by 6 regionally elected vice-chiefs. A Confederacy of Nations meets from time to time as an interim executive committee, and the chiefs meet in assembly at least once a year to determine policy and direction.

The new organization immediately faced formidable challenges. It was recognized by the federal government as the organization to represent Indian people in the First Ministers' conferences held to identify and define ABORIGINAL RIGHTS in Canada's patriated constitution. Disputes in Mar 1983 over what the official position would be, and whether the AFN should even participate, caused the withdrawal of a number of chiefs representing about 15% of Canada's Indian population. In May 1984 many chiefs from Alberta also withdrew when they objected to an AFN resolution on proposed changes to the Indian Act regarding discrimination against Indian women and their children (*see* Jeannette LAVELL).

The main thrust of the AFN has been the entrenchment of the right of Indian self-government in Canada's constitution and recognition of aboriginal title and rights. It has made representations on these subjects to UN commissions. When a Parliamentary Task Force on Indian Self-Government was struck in 1982, the AFN was invited to have an ex-officio member work with the committee with all privileges except that of voting. In Ottawa, AFN officials lobby MPs and ministers of government to make sure its positions are considered in the formulation of government policy. Secretariats in such areas as education, health, social services and economic development carry on consultations, develop policy and assist individual First Nations. *See also* LAND CLAIMS; NATIVE PEOPLE, POLITICAL ORGANIZATION AND ACTIVISM. MICHAEL POSLUNS

Assiniboia, a name derived from the ASSINIBOINE Indians, applied to 2 political units in the 19th century, and still in use. The first territory in RUPERT'S LAND delimited for governmental purposes, as distinct from trading districts, was the 1811 HBC grant of 116 000 square miles to Lord SELKIRK. This District of Assiniboia (RED RIVER COLONY) was supervised by a governor and council until Nov 1869, when Louis RIEL's resistance effectively ended its life. The second provisional government of the Red River resistance, convened 9 Mar 1870, named itself the Legislative Assembly of Assiniboia and, in its third List of Rights to Ottawa, requested that "Assiniboia" become Canada's fifth province. However, without consulting the assembly, Riel suggested to Ottawa the name Manitoba to avoid confusion. To ensure Manitoba's smooth transition to Canadian authority, Col Garnet WOLSELEY persuaded Donald SMITH, HBC representative, to revive the original council and greet Lt-Gov A.G. Archibald formally on 6 Sept 1870. The first Assiniboia then ceased to have an official existence.

A settler's home near Carberry, Assiniboia. Painting by Edward Roper (*courtesy Public Archives of Canada/C-11030*).

On 8 May 1882 the federal government created 4 "provisional districts" in the North-West Territories. The southern district, present-day southern SASKATCHEWAN, was called Assiniboia (see ALBERTA, ATHABASCA). The districts, designed "for the convenience of settlers and for postal purposes," were roughly equal in size and natural-resource distribution. Along the CPR, Assiniboia developed rapidly. With the 1886 grant of 2 seats in the federal Parliament and the use of the district boundaries to determine representation in the Territorial Assembly, a district consciousness developed. When provincial status and new boundaries were being considered in 1904-05, Assiniboia and Saskatchewan were potential names. Minister of the Interior Clifford SIFTON preferred Assiniboia but, when residents of the northern district asked that their choice be used, he acquiesced.

Today the name applies to a rural municipality and provincial constituency in Manitoba, and to a town and federal constituency in Saskatchewan. This riding was prominent in 1919, when an independent farmers' candidate defeated a former provincial Liberal Cabinet minister, and again in 1935 when it sent former premier James G. GARDINER to Ottawa to become federal minister of agriculture. GERALD FRIESEN

Assiniboine received their name from an OJIBWA word for their practice of boiling food by dropping heated rocks into water. They were first described in the *Jesuit Relations* as having split off from the Yanktonai Sioux sometime prior to 1640. From a homeland around the Mississippi headwaters, they moved northwestwards, to the Lake of the Woods and towards Lk Winnipeg. At the peak of their power their territory ranged from the Saskatchewan and Assiniboine river valleys in Canada to the region N of the Milk and Missouri rivers in the US. Linguistically they belong to the Siouan family, speaking a dialect of Dakota.

Trading with the HUDSON'S BAY COMPANY from the late 17th century, they were noted for their PEMMICAN production and their role as mi dlemen, trading European goods to the dista Plains tribes. Through the 19th century th were closely allied with the CREE, while int mittently in conflict with the BLACKFOOT, t Gros Ventres, and their Siouan relatives to the They suffered greatly from European diseas especially smallpox. From an estimated pop lation of 10 000 in the late 18th century, th number declined to 2600 by 1890. Numbers b gan to increase only in the 1920s, owing to bett health and living conditions.

The Assiniboine culture exhibited most of t classic Plains Indian traits. They were noted f their expertise in constructing buffalo poun and made a greater use of dogs, having few horses than other Plains tribes. Their ima among white traders and settlers was general positive, with frequent reports of their hos tality.

In Canada the White Bear and Carry the Ket bands were signators to Treaty No 4 (1874), a the Mosquito-Grizzly Bear's Head bands we signators to Treaty No 6 (1876), while the bands residing south of the international bord signed the Judith R Treaty (1855). In Cana they are now located on 3 Saskatchewan serves: Carry the Kettle (shared with a Sio group); Mosquito-Grizzly Bear's Head; a White Bear (shared with Ojibwa and Cree). 1980 the total population on these reserves w 2641. Those found in Alberta are known STONEY. In the US Assiniboine reside on the Belknap and Ft Peck reservations. *See also* NAT PEOPLES, PLAINS and general articles under Nati People. IAN A.L. GET

Reading: E.T. Denig, *Five Indian Tribes of the Upper Misso* (1961); D. Kennedy (Ochankugahe), *Recollections of Assiniboine Chief*, ed J.R. Stevens (1972); R.H. Lowie, "T Assiniboine," American Museum of Natural Histo *Anthropological Papers* 4, Pt 1 (1909).

Assiniboine, Mount, elev 3618 m, the high mountain between the Trans-Canada Hwy a the US border in the ROCKY MTNS, is often call "The Matterhorn of the Canadian Rockies." Sit ated on the continental divide, 35 km S of Ban its western slopes are in Mt Assiniboine Pr Pk, the eastern slopes in Banff National Pk. was named in 1885 after the Stoney Indians Dr G.M. DAWSON, director of the Dominion Ge logical Survey. Father de Smet and his guid were probably the first white men to see t peak in 1845. After several other attempts climb the peak, Sir James Outram, with Swi guides, made the first ascent in 1901. It is easy ascent by today's standards, but numero accidents have occurred on the mountain. GLEN BOI

Assiniboine River, 1070 km long, rises in Saskatchewan, fed by the Etomami and Whi sand rivers, swells into Lake of the Prairies ar flows SE across the Manitoba border, where it is joined by the QU'APPELLE R and, 30 km SE of BRANDON, the SOURIS R. Joining the RED R at the "forks" in Winnipeg, it cuts a wide, scenic valley through the Manitoba Escarpment, and drains a broad, fertile plain that is one of Canada's prime wheat-growing areas. LA VÉRENDRYE built Fort La Reine (1738) on the river near present-day PORTAGE LA PRAIRIE. Its route was well travelled by fur traders, and after 1850 settlement crept W from the forks, where light, dry soil offered excellent farming prospects. The river is navigable for some 500 km, and before the railway came, 7 stern-wheelers plied its course from Winnipeg to Fort Ellice. The name, meaning "those who cook by placing hot stones in water," was taken from the Assiniboine Indians and was later applied to the Dist of ASSINIBOIA. JAMES MARSH

Association for Canadian Studies, fd 1973, has grown into a distinctive LEARNED SOCIETY with over 100 institutional and 500 individual members. Its formal emphasis is to encourage teaching, research and publication about Canada, and it has attempted to translate into reality T.H.B. SYMONS's study, *To Know Ourselves* (2 vols, 1975). The association views Canadian studies as an interdisciplinary exploration of all aspects of Canada's social, cultural and physical environment, its economic system and its place in the world; it generally supports thematic studies of Canada as an entity, rather than discipline-based scholarship or regional studies (*see* CANADIAN STUDIES). ACS has organized conferences on national themes (the Canadian North, Canada and the Sea), supported projects on ethnohistory, multiculturalism and film, and promoted archival development. James E. Page, formerly of Seneca College, Willowdale, Ont, was the driving force until 1982, and through ACS he was able to initiate the International Council for Canadian Studies. PAUL GALLAGHER

Association of Universities and Colleges of Canada (AUCC) dates from 1911 and assumed its present name in 1965. Most of the universities and some university-level colleges are members, as are the 2 provincial and 2 regional associations of universities. A voluntary organization with a secretariat in Ottawa, the AUCC promotes co-operation among universities, coordinates some of their activities (eg, collective relations with governments), assists in their international relations, administers central services such as scholarship programs, and serves as a clearing house of information on Canadian higher education. Its publications include a monthly newsmagazine, *University Affairs*, and a biennial *Directory of Canadian Universities*.

EDWARD SHEFFIELD

Associations are voluntary, nongovernmental, nonprofit organizations composed of personal or institutional members, with or without federal or provincial incorporation, formed for some particular purpose or to advance a common cause, especially of a public nature. Related terms include foundation, society, institute, federation, alliance, club and union. The freedom of association is one of the fundamental freedoms guaranteed by the Canadian Charter of Rights and Freedoms. It is estimated that individual Canadians on average are associated with 3.6 organizations such as business, trade and professional associations, chambers of commerce and boards of trade, labour organizations and unions, health and welfare groups, religious organizations, athletic associations, political organizations, learned societies, cultural groups, fraternal organizations and service clubs, and community and neighbourhood groups.

In 1982 there were approximately 4200 active nonprofit organizations incorporated at the federal level, many of which were associations, and about 1000 boards of trade and chambers of commerce incorporated federally. In addition, thousands of associations are incorporated under provincial law. Ontario, for example, reported about 16 000 active nonprofit corporations in 1982. There are also hundreds of associations operating without federal or provincial incorporation.

Historical Background The history of associations in Canada dates from 1604, when Samuel de Champlain founded the ORDRE DE BON TEMPS for the promotion of recreation and relaxation on Ste Croix I, the first French settlement in N America. A few Canadian associations still in existence can trace their origins back to the 18th century. For example, the Halifax Board of Trade was founded in 1750; the Grand Lodge of Upper Canada of the Ancient Free and Accepted Masons was established in 1792; and the Law Society of Upper Canada was organized in 1797. (Most dates given in this article are formation dates, not incorporation dates.)

Associations formed before Confederation include the Montréal Board of Trade (1822); the Nova Scotia Barristers' Society (1825); the Toronto Board of Trade (1845); the Barristers' Society of New Brunswick (1846); Le Collège des Médecins et Chirurgiens de la Province de Québec (1847); the Royal Canadian Institute (1849); Le Barreau du Québec (1849); the Medical Society of Nova Scotia (1854); the Nova Scotia Board of Insurance Underwriters (1857); the Ontario Fruit Growers' Assn (1859); the Ontario Educational Assn (1861); the Nova Scotian Institute of Natural Science (1862); the Law Society of British Columbia (1863); the Nova Scotia Fruit Growers' Assn (1863); the Entomological Society of Canada (1863), the first national association formed in the sciences; the College of Physicians and Surgeons of Ontario (1866); the CANADIAN MEDICAL ASSN and the Ontario Dental Assn (1867).

From 1867 to 1900 many new associations were established at both the national and provincial level. Examples of national associations formed during this period and still in existence are the CANADIAN MANUFACTURERS ASSN (1871); the ROYAL SOCIETY OF CANADA (1882); the Canadian Institute of Surveying (1882, as the Assn of Dominion Land Surveyors); the Engineering Institute of Canada (1887, as the Canadian Society of Civil Engineers); the Canadian Electrical Assn (1889); the Royal Astronomical Society of Canada (1890, as the Astronomical and Physical Society of Toronto); the CANADIAN BANKERS' ASSN (1891); the Canadian Education Assn (1892); and the Canadian Institute of Mining and Metallurgy (1898). From 1900 to the end of WWII there was a steady increase in the number of associations. The period of greatest growth coincided with the economic prosperity of the 1960s. More than one third of the 1500 nonprofit corporations incorporated under federal legislation from 1900 to 1970 were incorporated in the 5-year period 1966-70.

The headquarters of national associations are concentrated heavily in the vicinities of Toronto (about 38%), Ottawa (about 27%) and Montréal (about 11%). The Vancouver, Edmonton and Winnipeg areas have smaller concentrations of association headquarters.

Origins and Growth A number of Canadian associations owe their origins to foreign parents, particularly American or British. When Canadian membership in foreign associations has increased to a significant number, members have withdrawn to form their own associations with headquarters in Canada. There are still scores of foreign associations with Canadian chapters or divisions, such as the American Society of Mechanical Engineers, New York, and the Royal Commonwealth Society, London. In addition, several international associations such as the International Air Transport Assn have their headquarters in Canada. Many Canadian labour unions are affiliated with international unions headquartered in the US. By 1981, however, the percentage of total union membership affiliated with international unions had declined to less than 45%, a drop of 17% in 10 years, as new national unions and independent local organizations were organized in Canada.

The proliferation of associations is a result of the growth in population, the expansion and diversification of the economy, and greatly increased government activity, especially in health care and social services, as well as the desire for communication with others sharing common interests.

Types There have been various attempts to classify associations into types according to purpose, function and structure. No classification has been satisfactory because of the diversity in membership, objectives, structure, methods of operation and concerns. One classification makes a distinction between those associations that function primarily for the benefit of the public (charitable organizations) and those that carry on their activities primarily for the benefit of their members (membership organizations). Another distinguishes between corporate-type and federation-type organizations. The latter may bring together associations devoted to the same subject, or to several different subjects. It is also possible to classify associations according to their principal activity. *The Directory of Associations in Canada* uses more than 800 subject classifications ranging from accounting to zoology to describe the activities of the associations listed.

Incorporation is often advantageous or necessary for nonprofit corporations to carry out certain of their activities. The principal advantages of incorporation as a nonprofit corporation without share capital are that it provides greater continuity and permanency for the organization, frees members from liability for the debts and obligations of the corporation, and facilitates certain activities such as the holding of real estate. Such corporations must be conducted without pecuniary gain for the members.

Federal nonprofit corporations in Canada include many of the large charitable and membership organizations and virtually all the boards of trade and chambers of commerce incorporated under the Boards of Trade Act. For associations carrying on activities within a single locality or province, provincial incorporation as a nonprofit corporation is sufficient. Each province has its own requirements and procedures for incorporation.

Organization and Operation The board of directors of an incorporated nonprofit corporation manages its business and affairs. The board is legally responsible for holding the constitution and bylaws, for making policy to further the attainment of its stated goals and objectives, and for appointing the chief executive officer. A small group of board members, including the officers, constitutes the executive committee, which sits between board meetings to make decisions on behalf of the board.

The usual officers of an association are the president, vice-president, treasurer and secretary. The officers may be selected by the membership or appointed by the board, and their duties are set out in the bylaws or established by the board. The chief executive officer or executive director (the title may vary) performs duties assigned by the board of directors. This officer executes policies as prescribed by the board, selects employees for the operation of the association office, prepares budgets, approves expenditures and attends all meetings of the board and its executive committee.

The committee structure of associations usually reflects its goals and objectives. Typical committee responsibilities include membership, nominations, education, research, publishing, public and government relations. Officers and directors are expected to render a periodic account of their stewardship, usually in the form of an annual report. The requirements for membership are usually stated in the bylaws of the association and there may be several classes of membership, such as member, associate, student and honorary member. Some associations admit anyone interested in its activities; others, such as professional associations, have specific requirements for membership. In general, charitable organizations rely for their income on grants from government and on donations from business and the general public, whereas membership organizations obtain most of their income from fees and dues.

Contribution to Society Associations registered federally as charitable organizations are legally obligated to provide services beneficial to the community at large. Although membership associations have the advancement of the interests of their members as their primary aim, they too may respond to changing conditions in society by engaging in programs and activities in the public interest. Associations have an important role in building consensus in society by providing the mechanism for their members to reach agreement on social values, on objectives to be pursued and on the means to achieve objectives. Through interaction with government, associations participate in shaping public policy. National associations, many of which are bilingual, can contribute to the strengthening of national unity by improving communications and understanding among the different peoples and regions of Canada. Associations are also important as sources of information about hundreds of specialized activities in our society. By helping those in need, supporting and publishing worthwhile research, educating members of the public, contributing to the personal development of citizens and pressing for just and humanitarian causes, associations are making a significant contribution to Canadian society. *See also* FOUNDATIONS.

R.B. LAND

Aster [Lat, "star"], common name applied mainly to 2 herbaceous genera (*Aster* and *Cal listephus*) of flowering PLANTS in family Compositaeor Asteraceae. Over 250 species of true *Aster* are known worldwide. Of 52 *Aster* species native to Canada, about 40 have been brought under cultivation. *A. alpinus* and *A. campestris* of the Rocky Mts are most popular for alpine gardens. Canadian species are mostly perennial, late-season flowering and, usually, blue, purple, pink or white. Plants have alternate, simple leaves and large clusters of showy flower heads, usually comprising a central disc surrounded by showy rays. Wild asters are found in prairie, forest and desert areas. Some species are woody at base. China aster (*Callistephus chinensis*), introduced from China in 1731, is now among the most popular of cut flowers, being diverse in form and providing blue shades, rare in the related chrysanthemum. Infusions of *Aster* roots were used by some Canadian Indians as remedies for cuts, heart ailments or eye problems. *See* ORNAMENTALS; PLANTS, NATIVE USES.

ROGER VICK

Astman, Barbara, photographer, multimedia artist (b at Rochester, NY 12 July 1950). Astman is a graduate of Rochester Institute of Technology (1970) and Ontario College of Art (1973). Her camera works and sculptural installations are a mixture of various traditional art forms — drawing, painting, photography, sculpture — which are redefined by a contemporary sensibility. A fascination with current technological developments has resulted in images of remarkable colour, texture and scale. Her *Red* series (1980) represented a breakthrough on several levels — symbolism, content and form. The artist is posed frontally amidst a carefully balanced composition of objects, each spray-painted red, which because of their redness assume a variety of implications at once playful and vaguely threatening. In the *Places* series (1982) she explored the traditional dimension of sculptural assemblage — mixed-media construction of linoleum, wood and plastics. *Settings for Situations* (1984) consist of formal sculptural wood constructions mounted on the wall and placed on the floor. Astman's use of material and technology place her in the forefront of post-modern activity. Her work is not only technically and aesthetically exquisite but it also reaches for the deepest mysteries of the self.

From Barbara Astman's "red" series, ektacolour mural of woman reading a book, holding a mug (*courtesy Barbara Astman/Sable Castelli Gallery Ltd*).

KARYN ELIZABETH ALLEN

Astronaut [Gk *astron*, "star"; *nautikos*, "sailor"], or cosmonaut, individual involved in flight beyond Earth's atmosphere. Both the US and the USSR have well-established spaceflight programs. American astronaut trainees were initially test pilots selected from the military services. In the US the National Aeronautic and Space Administration (NASA, est 1958) is in charge of manned flights; in the USSR, the Academy of Sciences. Manned spaceflight became possible only after a series of unmanned flights, the first being that of the Earth-orbiting SATELLITE Sputnik 1, launched by the USSR on 4 Oct 1957. Yuri Gagarin piloted the first manned Earth-orbiting spacecraft, Vostok 1, launched on 12 Apr 1961 from Kazakhstan, USSR. The first American to orbit Earth was John Glenn, in Friendship 7, on 20 Feb 1962.

Although Canada has been involved in the development of SPACE TECHNOLOGY since the early 1960s (the US launched the Canadian-built scientific satellite Alouette 1 on 29 Sept 1962), its direct participation in manned flight is very recent. In 1983, as a result of Canada's contributions to the American space program (eg, development of the CANADARM), NASA offered to fly Canadian astronauts as "payload specialists" aboard the Space Shuttle. In June 1983, the NATIONAL RESEARCH COUNCIL OF CANADA began a 6-month, nationwide hunt to fill 6 positions in a program to train Canada's first astronauts. The 5-member screening committee was made up of representatives from the NRC, the Department of National Defence and the Ministry of State for Science and Technology. Almost 4300 people applied; 68 applicants were interviewed between 18 Oct and 9 Nov 1983. The 19 finalists were interviewed again in Ottawa, participated in orientation sessions and technical briefings, and underwent medical examinations. The final selection was made in the first week of Dec 1983. Candidates were chosen on the basis of their academic background, technical expertise and physical fitness. The astronauts, who will be employed by the NRC for terms of up to 3 years, will perform experiments aboard the US Space Shuttle during 3 flights, in Oct 1984, late 1985 and early 1986. One set of experiments involves studying space motion sickness and disorientation in zero gravity; another, development of an advanced "machine vision" system to help astronauts maneuver the Canadarm.

Brief biographies of members of the Canadian Astronaut Program follow. Ken Money (b 1935 at Toronto, grew up Noranda, Qué), a physiologist with the Defence and Civil Institute of Environmental Medicine, Dept of National Defence, Toronto, is an expert on space motion sickness. He has been involved in shuttle experiments with US scientists and was co-designer of the Canadian motion sickness and disorientation experiments. Money is a former Olympic athlete and a jet pilot who has flown search and rescue missions. Roberta Bondar (b 1945 at Sault Ste Marie, Ont), a neurologist at McMaster University's Medical Centre, was an assistant professor and director of the Multiple Sclerosis Clinic when selected. She is a pilot and has been active in the Canadian Society for Aviation Medicine. Marc Garneau (b 1949 at Québec City), an electronics expert, worked with the DND as head of the Communications and Electronic Warfare section. He attended the Royal Military College, Kingston, Ont, and received his PhD in ELECTRICAL ENGINEERING from University of London in England. When chosen, Steven MacLean (b 1955 at Ottawa) had just received his PhD in PHYSICS from York University. He was a postdoctoral student at Stanford University in California, working under Nobel Prize winner Arthur Schawlow on LASER research that will be applicable to his work on Canadian shuttle experiments. Robert Thirsk (b 1953 at New Westminster, BC) was a medical doctor at Montréal's Queen Elizabeth Hospital and has a degree in MECHANICAL ENGINEERING (biomedical) from the Massachusetts Institute of Technology. Bjarni Tryggvason was a research officer with the NRC, specializing in AERODYNAMICS and METEOROLOGY. Born in Iceland (1945), Tryggvason grew up in BC and is a Canadian citizen. He took his PhD in engineering at University of Western Ontario. He is a pilot and flying instructor. In Mar 1984 Marc Garneau and Robert Thirsk were chosen as prime and backup crew for the Oct 1984 shuttle flight. Garneau became the first Canadian to cross the "last frontier" when the US Space Shuttle Challenger took off from the Kennedy Space Centre, Florida. Various space sickness and space vision experiments were successfully completed by Garneau in the 8-day mission, during which Challenger circled the Earth 132 times.

LYDIA DOTTO AND ADRIANA A. DAVIES

Astronomy, science that studies the SUN, the solar system, the remote stars, distant GALAXIES and all other detectable bodies in the universe. Its major subdisciplines include astrophysics, the closely related field of SPECTROSCOPY and COSMOLOGY. Astronomy is often regarded as the oldest SCIENCE, since more than 5000 years ago motions in the sky were used to predict events such as the annual flood on the Nile. During the era of modern exploration, astronomy had practical applications in navigation, SURVEYING and timekeeping. Modern astronomy, however, is more concerned with the physical and chemical nature of matter beyond Earth, where conditions of temperature and pressure, and gravitational and magnetic fields allow astronomers to observe matter under extremes unattainable in terrestrial laboratories. Astronomy is closely related to PHYSICS, CHEMISTRY, MATHEMATICS, GEOLOGY, ENGINEERING and COMPUTER SCIENCE.

The earliest astronomical observations in

what is now Canada were scattered observations made as early as 1612 by arctic explorers and occasional sightings of COMETS and eclipses recorded by Jesuit missionaries, starting in 1618. There may be some disagreement about the earliest astronomical OBSERVATORY, depending on the definition adopted. Perhaps the earliest observatory in N America was that built by the Marquis de Chabert 1750-51 at LOUISBOURG. Chabert produced maps and astronomical observations as well as a report, *Voyage fait par ordre du roi en 1750 et 1751 dans l'Amerique septentrionale.* Unfortunately, nothing remains of this observatory. There is evidence that Joseph Frederick Wallet DESBARRES built a small observatory in 1765 at Castle Frederick, NS, for testing his surveying instruments. The building probably also housed astronomical telescopes. Nothing remains of this structure. The Toronto Magnetic Observatory began observations in 1840, but the astronomical instruments intended for it were never received. In 1850 an observatory was constructed on the Citadel at Québec City to support the requirements of marine navigation, but neither the original structure nor its successor, built on the Plains of Abraham in 1874, survives today. An astronomical observatory was built in 1851 on the campus of University of New Brunswick and an official plaque, unveiled in 1955, identifies this building as the "First Astronomical Observatory in Canada." A public observatory was built in Kingston in 1856; an observatory for TIME determination followed in Montréal in 1862; and modest telescopes were erected in other towns and cities in the next 3 decades. The federal government became involved in 1885 because of the urgent need to survey lands adjacent to the transcontinental railway, since astronomical techniques were required in mountainous regions.

The determination of longitude (relative to the meridian of a city in western Europe) for a ship at sea, a recently discovered island or a colony in the Americas, was a major problem during the voyages of discovery. The invention and perfection of the marine chronometer by John Harrison in 1761 solved the practical problem. Before this, however, various astronomical methods were used in attempts to determine longitude: in New France the Jesuits observed more than a dozen eclipses between 1632 and 1694; 5 lunar eclipses observed at Québec City or at STE MARIE AMONG THE HURONS (Midland, Ont) were also observed in Europe, and some useful longitudes were derived. Although some solar eclipses were observed quite well, the theory of the time was inadequate to derive accurate longitudes from the observations.

By the 19th century, interest in eclipses had shifted from the determination of longitudes to the study of the sun; therefore, total solar eclipses became the events of interest. Eclipse expeditions involve careful planning and frequently difficult journeys to remote locations, such as that made by an American expedition to northern Manitoba to observe the total eclipse of 17 July 1860. The party, which included Simon Newcomb, an American astronomer born in NS, suffered the fate common to later expeditions: clouds on the crucial day. The 20th century has produced 8 total solar eclipses in Canada, which have been studied by ground parties and, since 1945, from aircraft and even rockets. The most significant Canadian expedition, however, remains the one led by C.A. CHANT to Australia in 1922, during which observations were made of the displacement of stars near the eclipsed sun. These measurements helped provide observational support for the theory of relativity.

Few stories in the history of astronomy can rival those associated with early observations of the transits of Venus. On the rare occasions when Venus is directly between Earth and the sun, it is seen to transit the solar disk over the course of several hours. It was realized in the 17th century that accurate timing of such transits (which come in pairs, 8 years apart, once every 122 years) could be used to establish the scale of the solar system. Immense efforts were made to observe the transit of 1769, including an arduous expedition to the area of CHURCHILL, Man, by the astronomer William Wales and another English observer. After a frightening winter, they made successful observations of the transit. An attempted observation from Île aux Coudres, 100 km downstream from Québec City, was incomplete because of clouds. In 1882 there were plans to observe the transit from more settled areas of Canada, including substantial observatories in Woodstock, Ont (which was clouded out at crucial times), and Kingston, Ont (where useful observations were made). These international campaigns were moderately successful, but observational problems limited the accuracy of the final result.

Canadian astronomy shows a pattern of parallel development in universities and federal government agencies. The provinces have been involved indirectly through their general support of university development. The federal government made its first provision for astrophysical research with the establishment of the Dominion Observatory in Ottawa (1905), a facility equipped with a refracting telescope and a reflecting solar telescope, in addition to transit instruments for positional astronomy. Government research facilities expanded in 1918, when the Dominion Astrophysical Observatory near Victoria, BC, was opened. Its telescope was the world's largest at the time of its installation (1918). Facilities at Victoria have been upgraded with the addition of a second telescope and continuous modernization of detecting equipment. Major observatories for radio astronomy have been built near Penticton, BC, and in ALGONQUIN PROVINCIAL PARK, Ont. In recent years the most important instrument for Canadian optical astronomers has been the Canada-France-Hawaii Telescope on Mauna Kea in Hawaii, opened in 1979. All government astronomical research programs were placed under the aegis of the NATIONAL RESEARCH COUNCIL in 1970. The NRC's Herzberg Institute of Astrophysics was formed in 1975, adding programs in laboratory astrophysics and space science.

The first Canadian department of astronomy was established at U of T in 1904 and, in 1935, through the efforts of Dr Chant, the university acquired the David Dunlap Observatory. In 1971, U of T inaugurated the first Canadian telescope operating in the Southern Hemisphere, at Las Campanas, Chile. The University of Western Ontario, Queen's University, York University, University of Calgary, University of Alberta and University of Victoria also have their own observatory facilities. The Université de Montréal and Laval share facilities at Mont Mégantic, Qué. Undergraduate training only is available from the following universities: Laurentian, Laval, Lethbridge, Manitoba, McGill, Saskatchewan and Simon Fraser. The universities of Alberta, British Columbia, Guelph, Lakehead, Montréal, Queen's, St Mary's, Toronto, Victoria, Waterloo, Western Ontario and York offer both undergraduate and graduate training.

The first major planetarium in Canada was the Queen Elizabeth Planetarium opened in Edmonton, Alta, in 1962. Several major cities in Canada now have planetariums which offer the public visual instruction in astronomy for a moderate fee.

Despite its small size, the Canadian astronomical community has included many eminent scientists renowned for their contributions to international astronomy, among the most prominent being C.S. BEALS, Sidney VAN DEN BERGH, C.A. Chant, Arthur COVINGTON, W.E. HARPER, Frank HOGG, Helen HOGG, W.F. KING, J.L. LOCKE, Andrew MCKELLAR, Peter MILLMAN, Joseph PEARCE, R.M. PETRIE, J.S. PLASKETT, R.M. STEWART and R.K. YOUNG.

Societies and Journals

Active astronomical societies, the members of which are professional astronomers or amateur enthusiasts, flourish today at local, national and international levels. The earliest Canadian astronomical society was the Toronto Astronomical Club, formed in 1868 through the initiative of Andrew Elvins. The club was an outgrowth of the Canadian Institute and, after 2 decades of variable vitality, became the Astronomical and Physical Society of Toronto in 1890. The name was changed to the Royal Astronomical Society of Canada (RASC) in 1903, and local centres have joined until at present there are 20 centres in major cities across Canada. The membership of nearly 3000 includes both professional and nonprofessional members. Each centre operates its own program of lectures and many have constructed fine observing facilities. An annual general assembly attracts members from throughout the country for a 3-day meeting to exchange ideas and reports on achievements. Not all local astronomy clubs are part of the RASC. Several autonomous clubs exist in various cities and towns and there is an association of French-language clubs in Québec, l'Association des groupes d'astronomes amateurs (AGAA). More than a dozen clubs belong to the AGAA, including the 2 French-speaking centres of the RASC; total membership is about 1000. The Canadian Astronomical Society (CAS) was formed in 1970 as the society of professional astronomers in Canada and has over 200 members. The society conducts an annual meeting for the presentation of research results and represents astronomers in matters of national concern.

Astronomical papers appeared as early as the 1850s in the *Canadian Journal,* published by the Canadian Institute. The first *Transactions of the Astronomical and Physical Society of Toronto* were published in 1891; this annual publication was superseded by the *Journal of the Royal Astronomical Society of Canada* in 1907. The journal has published at least 6 issues per year since then. The periodical is designed to be of interest to both amateurs and professionals and has a substantial circulation abroad. The society also publishes annually the *Observer's Handbook,* a compendium of forthcoming sky events and astronomical data. The RASC, many of its individual centres, the AGAA, the CAS and other clubs also publish newsletters on a regular basis.

IAN HALLIDAY

Reading: Donald Fernie, *The Whisper and the Vision: The Voyages of the Astronomers* (1976); Helen S. Hogg, *The Stars Belong to Everyone: How to Enjoy Astronomy* (1976).

Atchison, John D., architect (b at Monmouth, Ill 1870; d after 1930). Atchison was the most prominent member of the "Chicago School" of architects who practised in Winnipeg. He worked in Chicago for William Le Baron Jenney and had his own firm there 1894-1904. He then moved to Winnipeg, remaining there until 1922 when he left for California. During this Manitoba period he designed nearly 100 buildings in styles varying from the progressive Wardlaw Block (1905) to the historically eclectic Great-West Life Assurance Building (1911). A professional of high competence, Atchison brought Winnipeg a connection with the most progressive architectural centre in N America at that time, and helped building there advance technically and stylistically. WILLIAM P. THOMPSON

Athabasca, Alta, Town, pop 1731 (1981c), is located on the Athabasca R, 150 km N of Edmonton. It was known until 1904 as Athabasca Landing. First established as a fur-trade post in

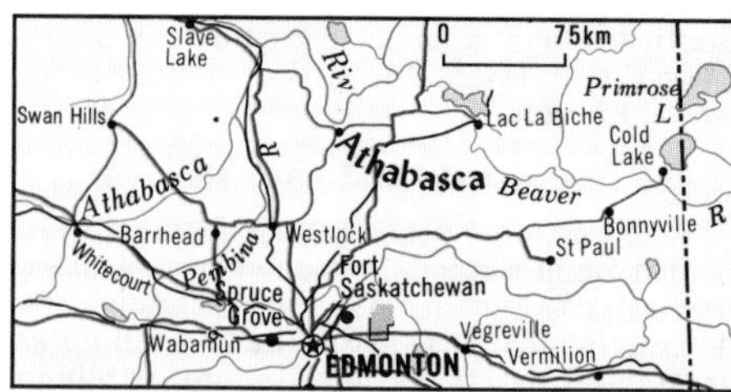

1848 by the HBC, and terminus of the ATHABASCA LANDING TRAIL, the town became popular from 1883 to 1912 as a distribution centre for goods shipped overland from Edmonton to Athabasca, then northwards by scow or steamboat for the Mackenzie R or through Lesser Slave Lk for the Peace. The town also served as a collection point for furs and other commodities bound for southern markets. Athabasca reached its zenith during the Klondike era and was incorporated as a town in 1911. However, the CNR reached Athabasca in 1912, and with the completion of the Alberta and Great Waterways Ry and the Edmonton Dunvegan and BC Ry in 1919, the town's importance waned. It became a local agricultural service centre, and is today the home of ATHABASCA U. It has also been the seat of the Anglican diocese of Athabasca since 1884.

FRITS PANNEKOEK

Athabasca, Lake, 7936 km^2, elev 213 m; located in NE Alberta and NW Saskatchewan, at the edge of the Precambrian SHIELD, fourth-largest lake entirely in Canada. It is fed by the ATHABASCA and PEACE rivers, and drains N via the SLAVE R into GREAT SLAVE LAKE. The lake was a pivotal point in the fur-trade system, being as far W as canoes could go and still return before the ice. Northern brigades returned from the Arctic via the Mackenzie and Slave rivers, and western brigades from the Pacific via the Peace or Athabasca. Ft Chipewyan (est 1788) was the meeting point, and is still a centre of trade. Camsell Portage, URANIUM CITY and Eldorado are on or near the northern shore. The lake was discovered by Samuel HEARNE (1771). Its name is of Cree origin and might mean "where there are reeds" or "meeting place of many waters." The lake has a good stock of whitefish, which was used in earlier days to feed the fur traders.

JAMES MARSH

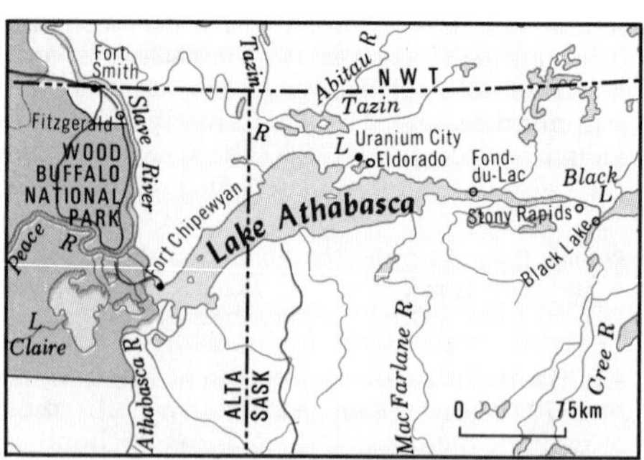

Athabasca Landing Trail was est 1875 by HBC between Edmonton and Athabasca Landing to improve and expand northern transportation. This 161 km portage, which links the N Saskatchewan R with the Mackenzie R system, played a vital role in the development of northern Alberta, the YT and the NWT. Surveyed in 1879, the trail was Canada's busiest northern route for 40 years, during the transformation of the area from fur-trade monopoly to a modern, diversified economy; the settlement of Western Canada; and the evolution of modern transportation. The development of railways (Athabasca, 1912; Grande Prairie, 1916; and Ft McMurray, 1917) diminished the trail's importance. The trail experienced a brief revival with the building of the ALASKA HIGHWAY during WWII, but modern highways now bypass most

Athabasca River, Jasper National Park, Alta, the southernmost headstream of the Mackenzie R system (*photo by Hälle Flygare*).

of the historic route. What remains of the trail today begins at Gibbons, Alta.

J.B. CZYPIONKA

Athabasca Pass, elev 1748 m, a solitary spot now visited rarely by hikers and mountaineers, is situated on the extreme SW boundary of JASPER NATIONAL PK, on the BC-Alberta border. It is reached from the E by gentle slopes from the Whirlpool R, an Athabasca R tributary. Its W side drops steeply down Pacific Cr to Wood R, a Columbia R tributary. Its first recorded crossing was by David THOMPSON and his party in 1811. Thereafter the pass was used for several years as a main fur-trade route across the ROCKY MTNS, though heavy snow caused voyageurs some hardship during late spring crossings. A small lake at its summit was named the Committee's Punch Bowl after the governing body of the HBC.

GLEN BOLES

Athabasca River, 1231 km long, rises in the COLUMBIA ICEFIELD, flows N through Jasper National Park, then NE past FT MCMURRAY, Alta, to LAKE ATHABASCA; it is the southernmost headstream of the MACKENZIE R, and its chief tributaries are the Pembina, Lesser Slave and McLeod rivers. In NE Alberta, it passes through huge deposits of oil sands containing BITUMEN. Near the river, the oil sands are close to the surface, and outcrops can be seen on its escarpment. Peter POND wintered on the river 1778; and the first freight route to the Rockies followed the Athabasca to Jasper and then by pack horses over ATHABASCA PASS. Goods were later moved by horse N from Edmonton to Athabasca Landing and then by barge along the river. This route fell into disuse when the railway was built from Edmonton to Waterways (1917).

JAMES MARSH

Athabasca University, Athabasca, Alta, was established 1972 in Edmonton to provide DISTANCE EDUCATION at the university level. Athabasca's mandate is to make university education accessible to adults seeking the benefits of

Enrolment: Athabasca University, 1982-83
(Source: Athabasca U)

Full-time Undergrad	*Full-time Graduate*	*Part-time Undergrad*	*Part-time Graduate*
—	—	6 610*	—

* Enrolment for fiscal year Apr 1982-Mar 1983

an open education, not campus-based. Hom study, supplemented by tutor support, is centr to most courses. Athabasca provides courses i administrative studies, social sciences, natur sciences and humanities, and undergraduate d grees in administration, arts and general studie The university was moved to new facilities i Athabasca in 1984.

B. BEATC

Athans, George, Jr, water-skier (b at Kelown BC 6 July 1952). Athans began competiti waterskiing at age 12, and at 15 won the slalon Before his career was ended in 1975 by a kn injury, he was 10 times Canadian champio 1965-74 and set 5 Canadian records. He won th world overall title at Banolas, Spain, in 197 and again in 1973 at Bogota, Colombia. In 197 he became the first non-US skier to win the cov eted US Masters title. He has been Canadian am ateur, BC and Quebec athlete of the year and i 1974 he was awarded the Order of Canada.

REG BARN

Atheism and Agnosticism An atheist believ there is no God. An agnostic believes we a unable to know whether or not there is a Go Although the word "agnosticism" was invente by T.H. Huxley (1825-95), the position is ve old, going back to the Greek Sceptics. Since i practice the agnostic cannot commit himself t religious belief any more than the atheist ca believers seldom distinguish between then Both views are widespread today, for 3 mai reasons. First, the enormous growth of scientif knowledge has required no use of the idea God: there is no Christian physics or chemistr Since claims about God cannot be tested by sc ence, atheists reject them, and agnostics say w cannot decide about them. Second, the power technology has reduced the human sense of d pendence on outside forces, and so lowered th psychological barriers to scepticism. Third, th study of religion itself by science and history ha suggested that it, too, can be understood witho assuming the reality of God.

In Huxley's time, the atheist or agnostic wa probably someone brought up as a Christia who would retain a deep interest in religio even after rejecting it. This is less commonly tru today, and religious thinkers have now to spea to a world where doubt and denial are com bined with widespread indifference. One aca demic expression of this is the philosophical po sition popularly known as positivism, whic argues that claims about God are not merely b yond knowledge, but cannot even be state early. In Canada the decline of RELIGION may ave been held back by the thinness of popuation and by ethnic loyalties; but while religion emains a potent force, scepticism is a widepread view. *See* PHILOSOPHY. TERENCE PENELHUM

Athlone, Alexander Augustus Frederick Villiam Alfred George Cambridge, Earl of, oldier, governor general of Canada 1940-46 (b t Kensington Palace, London, Eng 14 Apr 1874; at London 16 Jan 1957). Athlone was the secnd member of the royal family (after the duke f CONNAUGHT) to be governor general of Canada. His wife, the Princess Alice, was a grandaughter of Queen Victoria. Retiring from his areer as a soldier after WWI, Athlone took an nterest in education and medical research, and vas governor general of S Africa, 1923-30. He vas to have been appointed governor general of Canada in 1914, but requested that his name be vithdrawn because of WWI. Although thinkng himself too old when asked again during WWII, he served more than a full term. He and 'M Mackenzie KING were fellow fussbudgets nd got along well, the more so because Athlone vas unfailingly discreet, cautious and without ffectation. Even so, King found it difficult to hare the spotlight with a head of state "not beonging to one's own country." NORMAN HILLMER

Atikokan, Ont, pop 4389 (1981c), UP in northrn Ontario on the Atikokan R, 220 km W of Thunder Bay. The name derives from an Ojibwa vord for caribou bone. It was a small bush setlement until the 1940s, when huge iron-ore deosits were opened on nearby Steep Rock Lk. After WWII it was one of several prosperous ommunities on Ontario's mining frontier, alhough the late 1970s brought a decline in minng activity. It is at the centre of a popular wilderness recreation area and is a jumping-off spot or nearby Quetico Provincial Pk. DANIEL FRANCIS

Atlantic Development Council, est 1969, uner the Government Organization Act, is based n St John's, Nfld, and consists of up to 11 memers. Members of the council advise the minister of Regional Industrial Expansion with regard to proposals and programs for fostering economic expansion in the Atlantic Provinces.

Atlantic Provinces NOVA SCOTIA, PRINCE EDWARD ISLAND, NEW BRUNSWICK and NEWFOUNDLAND constitute the Atlantic provinces. The 3 MARITIME PROVINCES (NS, PEI and NB) have much in common; among other things they share a historical and cultural heritage, and their residents have remarkably similar attitudes towards Canada, the US and Britain. Newfoundland development and Newfoundlanders have been shaped by quite different forces and personalities. Until 1949 most Newfoundland residents had few emotional and economic ties with the Maritimes in particular and Canada in general. Throughout the 18th and 19th centuries Newfoundland, unlike the Maritime provinces, was not an integral part of the economic, cultural and political system of N America. Rather, it was the western vantage point of a British way of life, providing a powerful undercurrent for Newfoundland's unique brand of local patriotism. CONFEDERATION in 1949 began the difficult process of transforming Newfoundlanders into Canadians.

Population in the Atlantic Provinces (000s)

	NS	*NB*	*PEI*	*Nfld*
1871	388	286	94	147
1911	492	352	94	243
1951	643	516	98	361
1981	847	696	123	568

Since 1949 many attempts have been made to draw the Atlantic provinces closer. Possibly most important was the 1954 establishment of the Atlantic Provinces Economic Council. APEC was to have united economic thinking in Atlantic Canada and projected a positive regional image. But despite APEC and many similar organizations, few residents of the Atlantic provinces see themselves as parts of such a region. In the Maritimes there has been strong support for Maritime Union, but there has been little enthusiasm, as the Task Force on Canadian Unity discovered in 1978, for Atlantic Union. Newfoundland has never been interested in Atlantic Union and the discovery of the Hibernian oil field off its E shore has merely strengthened its resolve to remain apart. GEORGE A. RAWLYK

Atlantic Salmon (*Salmo salar*) are found in some 300 rivers along the eastern coast of Canada (*courtesy National Museum of Natural Science*).

Atlantic Salmon (*Salmo salar*), probably the best-known member of the Salmonidae family, occurs on both sides of the Atlantic Ocean. In Canada, Atlantic SALMON are found in some 300 rivers from Ungava Bay southward along the Labrador coast to Québec and the Maritimes, notably the RESTIGOUCHE R and MIRAMICHI R (NB), HUMBER R and GANDER R (Nfld), Matane and Bonaventure rivers (Qué) and the Eagle and Forteau rivers (Lab). Until the late 1800s, they were abundant in Lk Ontario, and they still occur, landlocked, in lakes in Eastern Canada. Atlantic salmon have a streamlined body, soft-rayed fins and an adipose (fatty) fin. Specimens may attain weights of over 27 kg, but fish over 13.5 kg are uncommon. Commercially caught fish average about 4.5 kg. Atlantic salmon are renowned for leaping in their attempts to ascend falls to reach spawning grounds. A very high percentage of salmon return to their natal streams to spawn. Spawning occurs in autumn and the large eggs overwinter. Young spend 1-3 years in the river before going to sea as "smolts." Salmon returning to the river after one year at sea are called grilse and may weigh about 2.2 kg; salmon at sea for 2 years will weigh 4.5-6.7 kg. Not all Atlantic salmon die after spawning and some spawn more than once. *See* TROUT. W.B. SCOTT

Atlin Lake, 774 km^2, is a long, narrow lake in northwestern BC touching the Yukon border. The source of the YUKON R, it was inundated by prospectors during the KLONDIKE GOLD RUSH 1898-99. The town of Atlin is on the E shore. Once isolated behind high mountain ranges, it is now linked to Whitehorse by highway, and is the centre of an extensive mining and hunting region. The name corresponds to an Indian word meaning big or stormy water. DANIEL FRANCIS

Atmospheric Environment Service, *see* CLIMATE INFORMATION.

Atomic Energy of Canada Ltd was incorporated as a crown agency in 1952 under the Atomic Energy Control Act to take over the Chalk River project from the National Research Council. Reporting to Parliament through the minister of ENERGY, MINES AND RESOURCES, the company is involved in heavy-water production and most applications of NUCLEAR ENERGY in Canada. AECL undertakes more than 90% of nuclear-energy research and development in Canada to support the design, development and construction of CANDU (Canadian Deuterium Uranium) nuclear power stations. It has subsidiaries operating under the names AEC Radiochemical Co. (Commercial Products), AEG Engineering Co and AEC Chemical Co. *See* NUCLEAR SAFETY.

Attawapiskat River, 748 km long, formed by the confluence of the Pineimuta, Trading and Otoskwin rivers at Attawapiskat Lk, in NE Ontario, flows E, jogs N and runs E to the flatland by JAMES BAY. Its drainage area is 50 200 km^2 and its mean discharge 626 m^3/s. Its mouth, mired in bog and marsh, is a migratory stopover for great numbers of ducks and geese. The whole course is largely uninhabited except for a few trading posts and the small Cree settlement of Attawapiskat at the river mouth. The name, from the Indian *atawabiskat*, meaning "rock bottom," refers to its limestone bed, once the bottom of an ancient sea. JAMES MARSH

Attikamek (Tête-de-Boule) Around 1972 the CREE-speaking Indians in the Bouclier region of the upper St-Maurice R in Québec decided to readopt the name Attikamek (White Fish) used by their predecessors in the 17th century, and to abandon the name Tête-de-Boule, of uncertain origin, which had been applied to them since 1697. This name change does not necessarily imply a close ethnic relationship between the Attikamek of the 17th century and those of today. Following various social upheavals linked to epidemics at the time of contact and during the violent IROQUOIS WARS in the mid-17th century in these regions, a complete reorganization took place among nomadic hunters in Québec, and various groups, hitherto distinct, began to band together. It is known that ethnic boundaries remained relatively flexible over the years and that today's Attikamek have discovered genealogical links with several neighbouring groups. Although these people numbered 500-550 in the mid-17th century, by 1850 there were only about 150 scattered over 7000 km^2 and divided into 2 major bands, the Kikendatch and the Weymontachingue. The Manouane band appeared a little later (around 1865-75) as an offshoot of the Weymontachingue.

Over the centuries, the Attikamek of the St-Maurice region have led a hard life of hunting, fishing, trapping and wild-berry picking around trading posts established in their region in the late 18th and early 19th centuries. They placed a high value on maintaining the autonomy of each nuclear family, but families combined into small winter co-operative or hunting groups, each with an experienced leader. Their economic activities were a compromise between traditional, seasonal activities and economic dependence upon the FUR TRADE.

Despite a long history of involvement in the fur trade, continuous contact with missionaries did not begin until about 1837. After 1830 Attikamek ancestral lands were actively coveted by lumber merchants. In 1910 the railway reached Weymontachingue and the harnessing of the St-Maurice and Manouane rivers added to environmental and social pressures. A wage-earning class appeared during WWII, along with various social-security benefits. In 1983 the 2800 Attikamek of the St-Maurice region, located in the 3 villages of Manouane, Weymontachingue and Obidjiwane (formerly the Kikendatch band), were fighting to preserve their traditional cultural autonomy and a role in society equal to the non-Indian Québec culture. Since 1975, they have joined with the MONTAGNAIS-NASKAPI to form the Attikamek-Montagnais Council. *See also* NATIVE PEOPLES, SUBARCTIC and general articles under NATIVE PEOPLE. NORMAN CLERMONT

Reading: Norman Clermont, *La Culture matérielle des indiens de Weymontachie* (1982) and "Qui étaient les Attikamèques?" in *Anthropologica* 16, 1 (1974); J. Helm, ed, *Handbook of North American Indians*, vol 6: *Subarctic* (1981).

Attorney, someone appointed to represent another or to act in his place. Power of attorney is the legal document appointing this representative. Before 1574 attorneys-at-law were persons permitted to practise in the superior courts of English common law as representatives of suitors who did not appear. After 1873 the term attorney was replaced by "Solicitor of the Supreme Court of Judicature." In N America attorney and attorney-at-law have become synonymous with lawyer. The federal minister of justice is ATTORNEY GENERAL for the Queen in Canada.

K.G. MCSHANE

Attorney General, office of, is essentially that of the chief law officer of the Crown. In that capacity, the attorney general is responsible for the conduct of prosecutions of offences on behalf of the Crown and serves as solicitor to the Crown in respect of any civil matters. Regarding the former function, there have recently been several constitutional cases involving the division of prosecutorial authority between federal and provincial authorities. However, the bulk of prosecutions conducted in Canada are done under the auspices of a provincial attorney general. In that capacity, the attorney general has the discretion, based on the evidence presented to him or to his agent, to prosecute or not to prosecute in a given instance. With respect to certain offences, such as the hate propaganda provisions of the CRIMINAL CODE, the direct consent of the attorney general is necessary before his office can commence a prosecution.

Regarding the latter function, any communication between the office of the attorney general with other offices of government is privileged under the solicitor-client privilege at common law.

In all provinces, the office of the attorney general is established under the authority of Section 92(14) of the Constitution Act, 1867, which gives the provincial legislatures authority over "the administration of justice." However, the attorney general of a province may be formally designated as the attorney general or as the provincial minister of justice (as in Québec, for example) or both. Federally the attorney general is both the attorney general of Canada and the minister of justice of Canada. In some provinces, the attorney general's office may incorporate the functions of the office of the SOLICITOR GENERAL, or in other provinces, the 2 offices may be separate and distinct with a division of responsibilities. Federally the 2 offices are separate.

Recently, some cases have arisen under the CANADIAN CHARTER OF RIGHTS AND FREEDOMS which test the independence of provincial court judges and justices of the peace, given their legal attachment to the office of the attorney general and their constitutional requirement of independence under the new entrenched Charter.

G. GALL

Atwood, Margaret Eleanor, "Peggy," poet, novelist, critic (b at Ottawa 18 Nov 1939). A varied and prolific writer, Atwood is one of Canada's major contemporary authors. She studied at Victoria Coll, U of T, 1957-61, where the influence of Jay MacPherson and Northrop FRYE directed her early poetry towards myth and archetype as exemplified by *Double Persephone* (1961). Her poetic reputation was established when *The Circle Game* (1966) was awarded the Gov Gen's Award. In 1969 she published *The Edible Woman*, a novel in which themes of women's alienation echo those in her poetry. In *Procedures for Underground* (1970) and *The Journals of Susanna Moodie* (1970), her next books of poetry, the irrational cannot be accepted. The inadequacy of language to come to terms with experience is extended in *Power Politics* (1971) to sexual politics where words are a refuge of weak women against male force. In the 1970s Atwood

Margaret Atwood, a varied and prolific writer who has captured the issues of her time in the satirical, self-reflexive mode of the contemporary novel (*photo by Graeme Gibson*).

was involved with nationalist cultural concerns as an editor of House of Anansi Press 1971-73. She published *Survival: A Thematic Guide to Canadian Literature* in 1972, the same year as *Surfacing*, her best-known novel, in which the technology-nature conflict is cast in political terms, Americans against Canadians. As in her other novels, the Atwood protagonist goes through an archetypal retreat to the wilderness, the irrational, before reintegrating into society.

Continued critical success marked her publication of *You are Happy* (1974) and her third novel *Lady Oracle* (1976). In these years Atwood also worked less successfully in new genres, writing several TV scripts and screenplays. She published a history, *Days of the Rebels: 1815-1840* (1977) and short stories, *Dancing Girls* (1977) and *Bluebeard's Egg* (1983). Two books followed in 1978: *Two-Headed Poems*, which continued to explore the duplicity of language, and *Up in the Tree*, a children's book, which introduced Atwood the artist. *Life before Man* (1979) is a more traditional novel than most of her fiction, developing a series of love triangles through exposition rather than image.

In 1980 Atwood became vice-chairman of the WRITERS' UNION OF CANADA. She worked on a TV drama, *Snowbird* (CBC, 1981), and published another children's book *Anna's Pet* (1980). Always interested in civil rights, she was active over several years in Amnesty International, and this activity had an impact on *True Stories*, a book of poetry, and *Bodily Harm*, a novel appearing in 1981. In both works she "bears witness," breaking down distinctions she herself makes between poetry (at the heart of her relationship with language) and fiction (her moral vision of the world). Her collected criticism, *Second Words* (1982), contained some of the earliest feminist criticism written in Canada. Her involvement with the revised *Oxford Book of Canadian Poetry* (1982), which she edited, marked her central position among Canadian poets of her generation. In all her writing her careful craftsmanship and precision of language, which give a sense of inevitability and a resonance to her words, are recognized. In her fiction, Atwood has explored the issues of our time, capturing them in the satirical, self-reflexive mode of the contemporary novel. Atwood has had continued critical success since the mid 1960s; her many honours include the MOLSON PRIZE in 198

BARBARA GODAR

Reading: S. Grace, *Violent Duality* (1980); A.E. Davidso and C.N. Davidson, eds, *The Art of Margaret Atwo* (1981).

Aubert de Gaspé, Philippe-Ignace-François journalist (b at Québec City 8 Apr 1814; d at Halifax 7 Mar 1841). He wrote the first French Canadian novel. After attending the Séminaire de Nicolet, Aubert de Gaspé became a stenographe and journalist. In Nov 1835 he was imprisone for a month following an altercation with member of the assembly, and he avenged him self by planting a stinkpot in the vestibule of th Québec House of Assembly. Obliged to take ref uge at St-Jean-Port-Joli, he amused himself b composing a novel, *L'Influence d'un livre* (1837 One chapter at least (chap 5) appears to hav been contributed by his father, Philippe-Joseph AUBERT DE GASPÉ, who later wrote *Les Anciens Cana diens* (1863). Young Aubert de Gaspé defende his novel against charges of sensationalism an lack of realism, but when the book was repub lished posthumously in 1864 as *Le Chercheur d trésors*, Abbé Henri-Raymond CASGRAIN tone down many passages and deleted others.

DAVID M. HAYN

Aubert de Gaspé, Philippe-Joseph, novelis (b at Québec City 30 Oct 1786; d there 29 Ja 1871). Scion of an old seigneurial family, Aube de Gaspé studied law under Jonathan SEWEL and was admitted to the bar in 1811. That yea he married Susanne Allison, by whom he sub sequently had 13 children, and began to practis law. In 1816 he was named sheriff of Québe City, but was removed from office in 1822 fo faulty accounts. He retired to the ancestra manor house at St-Jean-Port-Joli, and was late imprisoned for debt (1838-41), being released b a special Act of Parliament. While he was i prison, his son, Philippe-Ignace-François AU BERT DE GASPÉ, died at Halifax. After his releas Aubert de Gaspé spent the summers on his estat and winters in Québec City, participating in th capital's social and literary life and frequentin Octave CRÉMAZIE's bookstore, — a meeting plac of writers. In 1863 he published his historica romance *Les Anciens Canadiens*. It was an immedi ate success and is considered the first classic o French Canadian fiction. Three years later Au bert de Gaspé published his *Mémoires*, containin recollections of early 19th-century French Cana dian life; a further collection, *Divers* (1893), ap peared posthumously.

DAVID M. HAYN

Philippe Joseph Aubert de Gaspé. In B. Sulte, *Histoire de canadiens-français*, Vol VI, 1882 (*courtesy Public Archives Canada/C-14256*).

Aubut, Françoise, married name Pratte, organist, educator (b at St-Jérôme, Qué 5 Sept 1922). She was one of the first performers to play the works of Marcel Dupré and Olivier Messiaen widely in Canada. She studied at the Conservatoire national in Montréal with Eugène Lapierre and Antonio Létourneau, at the New England Conservatory (Boston) and at the Paris Conservatory with Dupré and Messiaen. In 1945 she returned to Canada, having won the Grand Premier Prix, awarded for the first time to a N American. As well as giving numerous recitals, she taught at the U de M, the Conservatoire de musique du Québec à Montréal and at the École Vincent-d'Indy. Her repertoire has included the works of Canadian composers Jean PAPINEAU-COUTURE and Roger Matton. She received the 1961 Prix de musique Calixa-Lavallée.

HÉLÈNE PLOUFFE

Auditor General of Canada, Office of, est 1878 to audit the accounts of the federal government's departments, agencies and many of its CROWN CORPORATIONS. The auditor general is independent of the government and reports results of annual examinations of government financial statements to the House of Commons. The office also conducts comprehensive audits of individual departments and agencies and government-wide issues such as management of human resources, contracting and the use of computers. The Audit Office operates under the Auditor General Act of 1977, which requires the auditor general to examine and report on whether public funds have been spent economically and efficiently and whether audited organizations are in a position to measure whether the funded programs are effective.

MAURICE CUTLER

Auditory Impairment (or hearing impairment) is more common in Canada than is generally realized. According to Health and Welfare estimates in 1976 (based on US rates) some 1.5 million Canadians had trouble hearing in one or both ears, but this is not a true measure of the impact of auditory impairment, which often results in impairment of speech as well. Approximately 745 000 Canadians (or 3.2%) suffer significant bilateral impairment. Those who are deaf (cannot hear or understand speech) number almost 300 000. This figure includes those who lost their hearing before age 19 (some 47 000) and those who were deaf before age 2 or 3 (some 23 000). The more severe the hearing loss and the earlier the onset, the more speech development will be affected. Even in adult life the onset of deafness is likely to produce some speech defect.

Auditory impairment may be caused by infections, drugs, heredity, injuries, tumours and NOISE. Readings of sound are made in decibels (db). For example, a conversation is 60 db, ordinary city traffic is 80 db. Hearing damage (after sustained exposure) begins at 85 db (lawnmowers, garbage trucks, motorcycles are all above this level). A typical rock band emits 110 db of sound, which after 15 minutes can harm unprotected ears. The pain threshold (125 db) is exceeded by the discharge of shotguns and jet engines.

For practical purposes, those termed "deaf" demonstrate severe or profound losses on hearing tests, while those termed "hard-of-hearing" do not suffer the same severity of impairment. Methods of instructing the deaf have been disputed from the time Alexander Graham BELL, who like his father Alexander Melville BELL taught the hearing impaired, debated the preferable method of instructing the deaf — the oral or sign language — with Thomas H. Galludet.

The majority of deaf Canadians who lost their hearing before age 2 are so severely impaired in hearing and speech that they prefer sign language for comfortable communication. American Sign Language is the major sign language used in Canada; French Canadian Sign Language is related to it, with some significant differences. Both languages differ from the spoken language in many ways. Although sign language or some form of signing has always existed in schools for deaf children, its officially permitted use has only become widespread recently because of the mistaken idea that it would impair speech development. There has been a major shift to the inclusion of "signing" in US programs for deaf children, but Canada has followed this development unevenly.

Deaf people have their own cultural interests, eg, theatre, mime, jokes and sports, while sharing many of the interests of hearing Canadians. Official organizations for the deaf include the Canadian Cultural Society of the Deaf (1940), Canadian Cultural Society for the Deaf (1970) and the Federation of Silent Sports (1959) now the Canadian Deaf Sports Association. The Canadian Co-ordinating Council on Deafness was founded in 1975; 50% of its board members are hearing impaired. In comparison with American deaf people, however, deaf and hard-of-hearing Canadians are not well organized, although this is changing.

The earliest schools for deaf children in Canada were those established in Montréal for French boys in 1848 and for French girls in 1851. A Protestant school was founded in Montréal by a deaf immigrant from Yorkshire in 1870. Recent educational changes include early intervention programs (*see* SPECIAL EDUCATION), integration into ordinary schools, better amplification and the use of sign language.

Technical aids are now highly developed, and include telecommunication devices for the deaf ("TDDs").

R. D. FREEMAN AND C. F. CARBIN

Augustus, or Tattanoeuck, Inuk hunter, interpreter (b N of Churchill, NWT early 1800s; d near Rivière-à-Jean Feb or Mar 1834). Noted for his loyalty, integrity and outstanding capabilities as an interpreter, Augustus accompanied FRANKLIN and BACK on their early northern explorations. He was employed as a hunter for the HBC at Ft Churchill from 1816 until 1822 when he was chosen to accompany Franklin's first land expedition. On Franklin's second expedition, Augustus averted almost certain disaster by venturing alone to speak with 40 hostile Inuit who had pillaged Franklin's boats. So impressed were the Inuit by Augustus's bravery and loyalty to his officers that no harm came to the party. In 1834 Augustus met an untimely death journeying overland to join Back at Ft Reliance.

HARRIET GORHAM

Augustyn, Frank, ballet dancer (b at Hamilton, Ont 27 Jan 1953). Widely praised as a classical dancer and greatly admired for his elegant bearing, Augustyn trained at the NATIONAL BALLET SCHOOL, joined the NATIONAL BALLET OF CANADA in 1970 and swiftly became a soloist in 1971 and principal dancer in 1972. He and frequent partner Karen KAIN won the award for best *pas de deux* at the 1973 Moscow International Ballet Competition, and more recently the 2 have starred in several Norman CAMPBELL films, performed *Giselle* at Moscow's Bolshoi Theatre and toured widely. In 1979 Augustyn was invested as Officer of the Order of Canada. In 1980 he joined the Berlin Opera Ballet, returning to the National Ballet in 1982.

PENELOPE DOOB

Auk (Alcidae), family of highly specialized SEABIRDS that contains auks (including the now extinct GREAT AUK), auklets, MURRES, murrelets, RAZORBILLS, dovekies, guillemots and PUFFINS. The 23 species of this ancient and diverse group occupy a special niche in nearshore and offshore northern polar and temperate waters. Alcids are diving birds which pursue small fish and invertebrates by "flying" underwater. They have a chunky appearance and are 15-65 cm long. Plumage is typically black or dark brown above, white underneath. Wings are short. Alcids come ashore only during breeding season. Most species are colonial and breed at a few coastal sites (often islands) which are free of predators and near an adequate food supply. They are long-lived, breed first at 4-5 years, and normally lay only one egg annually. Depending on the species, eggs are laid on exposed ledges on steep sea cliffs, in rock crevices or between large boulders, or in burrows. Both parents incubate eggs and rear young; incubation and chick-rearing usually last a total of 10 weeks. Of the 21 species breeding in N America, 11 breed in Canada. The common and thick-billed murres (*Uria aalge* and *U. lomvia*) breed in Atlantic and Pacific oceans; razorbills (*Alca torda*), black guillemots (*Cepphus grylle*) and Atlantic puffins (*Fratercula arctica*) in the Atlantic and parts of the Arctic Ocean; pigeon guillemots (*Cepphus columba*), marbled and ancient murrelets (*Brachyramphus marmoratus, Synthliboramphus antiquus*), Cassin's and rhinoceros auklets (*Ptychoramphus aleuticus, Cerorhinca monocerata*), and tufted puffin (*Lunda cirrhata*) breed in the Pacific. Four other species are non-breeding visitors: dovekie (*Alle alle*), horned puffin (*F. corniculata*), Xantus' murrelet (*Endomychura hypoleuca*) and parakeet auklet (*Cyclorrhynchus psittacula*).

D.N. NETTLESHIP

Authors and Their Milieu Only a handful of professional authors in Canada survive on the royalties from their books, a situation documented in the first survey of writers undertaken by Statistics Canada in 1979. Of 1045 writers sampled (representing the 4479 writers who were then members of writers' unions), 71% lived in Ontario and Québec; 24% earned over $20 000 annually and 42% under $5000; and only 311 were employed full-time as writers. Authors are not motivated by profits alone, yet the payment they receive for their intellectual labours encourages them to contribute to our cultural life, and payment is determined by their relations with publishers, the state, their audiences in schools and the public at large.

Commercially successful or not, professional writers must be devoted to their craft, for a manuscript can take a year or longer to finish. Then follows the lengthy process of finding a publisher (a literary agent may be hired to do this). If the publisher's readers respond favourably to the manuscript, the publisher determines the retail price of a book by estimating expenses for editing, design, printing, binding and distribution. Distribution costs include a 20-50% discount to jobbers and retailers. Sometimes these expenses are shared with another publisher when foreign publication is arranged. The author, whose royalty may be 5-15% of the retail price, is usually the last to profit from such ventures but is paid for every copy sold. Publishers normally expected to break even when about 70-80% of an edition is sold.

Because the survival of our national literature cannot be left to the vagaries of the marketplace, it is generally accepted that authors' incomes need to be supplemented. In the absence of private patronage and writers with private means of support, the obligation to fund writers has fallen to agencies of the federal and provincial governments. This situation evolved because historically Canada's geography and economy, along with foreign competition, made the market for local books and magazines precarious. Distribution is costly because Canada's small population is stretched along a 6500 km ribbon. British and American publishers, who recoup their distribution costs here through their larger markets, gained control of Canada's market in the late 19th century by establishing branches in Toronto, the centre of English-language publishing. In so doing, they effectively denied Canadian publishers direct access to their markets, and they retained the lucrative world and subsidiary rights to Canadian and other authors. Much original publishing in Canada was possible only because books were issued jointly with a foreign house — a common international practice. Sometimes the decision to publish a Canadian author in Canada was made in another country. However, even authors who publish both at home and abroad do not necessarily make a living from book sales.

Writers' fortunes are affected by those of their publishers. The Toronto book trade prospered in the 1950s and 1960s, but since 1970 inflation and recession have severely shaken the major locally owned houses. Ryerson and Gage were sold to American firms (Gage was repatriated in 1978); Macmillan changed owners twice; others went into receivership or verged on bankruptcy. Government investigations of foreign control of publishing and distribution caused both Ontario and Québec to give financial aid to their publishing industries. Federally, foreign takeovers were slowed down with the establishment of the FOREIGN INVESTMENT REVIEW AGENCY (1974). Meanwhile, production and distribution costs climbed, and retail prices skyrocketed. Provincial textbook budgets were cut, public and college libraries reduced their purchases, and new products vied for consumers' money.

These circumstances would have been far harder on authors had it not been for the 1951 Royal Commission on NATIONAL DEVELOPMENT IN THE ARTS, LETTERS AND SCIENCES (Massey Commission), which recommended government support for publishing and authorship. As a result, the CANADA COUNCIL was created in 1957, and similar arts councils were later established in all the provinces. Although government aid is welcomed by authors and publishers, it has meant some regulation and intervention in creative matters by the vast bureaucracies that administer the programs. In the early 1970s the federal government began to assist in the promotion of Canadian books abroad, and in 1979 it established the Canadian Book Publishing Development Program to provide direct grants to the publishing industry. In recent years most federal funds have come from the Dept of COMMUNICATIONS, as direct subventions to publishers for individual titles or as grants for the subsistence of writers. The Canada Council also sponsors the annual national Book Festival for the promotion of books and reading, and it administers the Governor General's Awards. The provincial arts councils operate in a similar way. The councils, as well as some cities, universities and publishers, also offer LITERARY PRIZES, which can stimulate sales of individual authors' books.

The most thorough re-examination of government involvement in the arts was the 1980-82 Federal Culture Policy Review Committee, chaired by Louis APPLEBAUM and Jacques Hébert, whose *Report* (1982) recommended increased government patronage in support of publishers and writers, while reaffirming writers' freedom from political control. In the early 1980s the federal government was preparing a comprehensive new copyright Act (to replace the 1921 Act), consulting with the book trade, authors and librarians on such complex problems as international copyright, the free flow of books across international borders, unauthorized photocopying and compensation for library borrowings ("payment for public use"). A white paper on COPYRIGHT LAW appeared in 1984.

Copyright problems inspired the establishment of the Canadian Society of Authors (1899) and the Canadian Authors' Association (1921). Besides copyright, more recent organizations such as the League of Canadian Poets (1966) and the WRITERS' UNION OF CANADA (1973) have lobbied for the "Canadianization" of publishing and distribution, for more funds for literary translation, and for income-tax adjustments and increased earnings to authors from library circulation of their books. In 1975 the Writers' Union protested when the large retail chains, Coles and W.H. Smith, sold remaindered American editions of Canadian authors whose own Canadian editions were still in print. Such importing was possible because court injunctions were slow and penalties for infringement of copyright were minimal.

The grim economic circumstances surrounding the major publishers and the disappearance of well-paying outlets like the *Star Weekly, Family Herald* and *Weekend Magazine* were offset by the greatest flourishing of regional publishing since Confederation. SMALL PRESSES were established from coast to coast in the 1960s and the 1970s. They awakened a new interest in regional literature, and in spite of harsh economic conditions, many of them managed to survive and grow.

Canadian writers have received critical and popular acclaim at home and abroad, especially since WWII. Canadian literature courses have become more numerous in schools and universities, facilitated by reprint series and anthologies and by tapes and records of authors reading from their works. Many colleges offer writer-in-residence programs which are supported by the institutions and by various arts councils. Literary and intellectual research flourishes in LITERARY PERIODICALS; bibliographies, biographies, collections of letters and surveys all help to locate our writers in the panorama of Canadian life, a situation which hardly existed before 1960. Authorship has been a central topic at the Canadian Writers' Conference (Queen's University, 1955), the State of English Language Publishing in Canada (Trent University, 1975), the Conference on the Canadian Novel (University of Calgary, 1978) and similar gatherings.

Although the writer's situation is subject to many economic variables, the growing recognition of Canadian writing and its creators is an encouraging sign, with both intellectual and economic benefits for writers, that our society is beginning to acknowledge their importance in its culture. *See* BOOK PUBLISHING; LITERATURE IN ENGLISH; LITERATURE IN FRENCH. GEORGE L. PARKER

Reading: Paul Audley, *Canada's Cultural Industries* (1983); W.J. Keith and B.Z. Shek, eds, *The Arts in Canada* (1980).

Autobiographical Writing in English Letters, journals, diaries, memoirs and autobiographies are all ways of saying to the reader, "I was there." Although differing in many ways, these forms are alike in having an authoritative "I" who recounts events and impressions experienced amid a specific social context, and a "there" that can be readily located in time and space. Because they speak in such personal tones, these records and narratives are rich in human interest. Social and intellectual historians find them especially valuable sources, and they are sometimes studied by literary historians and critics as well.

The circumstances of colonial life particularly favoured the writing of journals, diaries and letters. Explorers, fur traders, missionaries, surveyors, government officials and army and law-enforcement officers were all obliged by their superiors to keep daily records of their work (*see* EXPLORATION AND TRAVEL LITERATURE). Emigrants and travellers, especially women, wrote long letters home to their families and friends, and many kept diaries and journals. Although seldom written with publication in mind, these documents occasionally reached print because they contained information and commentary of use or interest to a wider readership. Written on the spot, they are a treasure trove for historians seeking to reconstruct the daily lives of private individuals. Literary scholars recognize in them a means by which newcomers to Canada practised putting into words whatever they found new and noteworthy in the landscape, climate, inhabitants, institutions, customs or speech of British North America. Although all 3 forms are now almost lost arts, the journals, diaries and letters of earlier generations of Canadians are becoming increasingly available in modern editions and reprints.

By contrast, memoirs and autobiographies continue to appear regularly. Unlike letters and diaries, they view events in retrospect and are often written with publication and posterity in mind. These works are more limited in historical reliability — the writer will have forgotten or suppressed a good deal — but the author has greater opportunities for achieving a shaped and finished narrative. Memoirs are more loosely constructed than autobiographies, and reveal more of external circumstances than of inner development. Often appearing under the simple title *Memoirs* or a variant (*Recollections, Reminiscences, Forty Years in . . .*), they are characteristically anecdotal and episodic, with the focus dispersed among the many interesting people and places the writer has known. Autobiography, on the other hand, downplays the context and highlights the unfolding drama of self-knowledge and growth, thus drawing in the literary critic, who analyses the autobiography's projection of a narrative persona, the deployment of dramatic, descriptive and narrative skills, and the achievement of structure, pattern or design in the whole.

A cluster of books describing Upper Canada [Ontario] before 1850 shows all these forms in their characteristic 19th-century guises. Elizabeth SIMCOE, wife of Lt-Gov John Graves Simcoe, kept a diary from 1791 to 1796 that was published in 1911 and then reedited in 1956 by Mary Quayle Innis as *Mrs. Simcoe's Diary*. Describing life in official circles at York [Toronto], it is at a far remove from *Our Forest Home* (1889), based on the letters and journals of Irish emigrant Frances Stewart, who settled in the 1820s on the Otonabee R near Peterborough. Among Stewart's neighbours were Samuel Strickland, author of *Twenty-Seven Years in Canada West* (1853), and his more famous sisters, Catharine Parr TRAILL and Susanna MOODIE. Traill's letters to her family in England were published as *The Backwoods of Canada* in 1836 for the information of intended middle-class British emigrants; it is now one of the classics of Canadian literature. Moodie wrote autobiographically of her years of *Roughing It in the Bush* (1852) and her later *Life in the Clearings* (1854). British author and feminist Anna Jameson visited her attorney general husband in York and then used her journals as the basis for *Winter Studies and Summer Rambles in Canada* (1838), giving the observations and opinions of a sophisticated and adventurous visitor.

Other times and places yield their quota of firsthand accounts. Labrador is the scene for journals by Capt George CARTWRIGHT (1911), recollections by Lambert de Boileau (1861) and Capt Nicholas Smith (1937), and autobiographies by Sir Wilfred GRENFELL (*A Labrador Doctor*, 1919; *Forty Years for Labrador*, 1932) and Elizabeth GOUDIE (*Woman of Labrador*, 1973). Col William Baird recorded his *Seventy Years of New Brunswick Life* (1890) but was overtopped by New Brunswick Baptist minister Joshua N. Barnes in *Lights and Shadows of Eighty Years* (1911). Sir Andrew MACPHAIL's *The Master's Wife* (1939) is a polished and memorable vignette of Prince Edward Island life in the later 19th century.

Travel and adventure in the North and West have likewise proved fertile themes. Accounts by fur traders include John MCLEAN's *Notes of a Twenty-five Years' Service* (1849) and P.H. Godsell's *Arctic Trader* (1934). Missionary work lies behind the letters and journal of Charlotte Selina Bompas, edited in 1929 by S.A. Archer as *A Heroine of the North*, and memoirs in 5 volumes by thodist John C. MCDOUGALL, including *Path-ing on Plain and Prairie* (1898) and *In the Days of Red River Rebellion* (1903). Early Mounted icemen of a reminiscent bent include John G. nkin (*Trooper and Redskin in the Far Northwest,* 9) and Col Sam STEELE, who wrote of his untie days and much else in *Forty Years in ada* (1915). Of many Klondike books, 2 that nd out are Martha Louise Black's *My Ninety rs* (1976; first published in 1938 as *My Seventy rs*) and Laura B. Berton's *I Married the Klondike* 54).

HOMESTEADING on the Prairies generated doz-s of first-person settlers' accounts and mem-s. Mary Georgina Hall wrote letters home de-ibing *A Lady's Life on a Farm in Manitoba* (1884), d E.A. Gill told of his days as *A Manitoba Chore* (1912). *Wheat and Woman* (1914) is Georgina nnie-Clark's self-portrait as a woman grain mer in Saskatchewan. In *Northwest of 16* 58) J.G. MacGregor describes growing up on Alberta frontier; the journals and letters of ah Ellen Roberts, whose family also home-aded in Alberta, were edited for publication Latham Roberts under 2 titles, *Of Us and the en* (1968, Canadian ed) and *Alberta Homestead* 71, US ed). An unusual and striking story is ntained in the letters of Hilda Rose, written m near Fort Vermilion, Alta, first published the *Atlantic Monthly* in 1927 and issued as *The mp Farm* a year later. *Homesteader* (1972), the le James M. Minifie chose for his recollections a Saskatchewan boyhood, speaks for an entire nre.

Although the majority of autobiographers d memoirists have some other, previously es-lished, claim to fame, a few have written in role of spokespersons for the unknown and sung. G.H. Westbury published *Misadventures a Working Hobo in Canada* in 1930, just as the eat Depression began to make hoboes of many en. *Saints, Devils, and Ordinary Seamen* (1946) re the subjects of memoirs by Lt W.H. Pug-y, while Norman B. James made his mark in story with his *Autobiography of a Nobody* (1947). yllis Knight, through tape recording and edi-g by her son Rolf, has shown us the extraor-nary dimensions of *A Very Ordinary Life* (1974). aria CAMPBELL's moving story in *Halfbreed* 73) represents a side of Canadian life too little own or understood.

Prime ministers occasionally write memoirs, t seldom autobiographies; their private letters d diaries are often useful correctives to their ficial" selves that appear in state papers. Two lumes of Robert BORDEN's *Memoirs* were pub-hed in 1938; John G. DIEFENBAKER's *One Canada* peared in 1975. Lester B. PEARSON's *Mike* (3 ls, 1972-75) is autobiographical, although the st 2 volumes were ghostwritten after his ath. *Affectionately Yours* (1969), edited by J.K. hnson, is an attractive little collection of let-s by, and occasionally to, Sir John A. MAC-NALD. The diaries of PM Mackenzie KING, nning to many volumes, have raised more estions than they answer. But the "inside ry" provided by slightly lesser lights in poli-s and public life can entertain. Judy LAMARSH d Humphrey Carver both published interest-g autobiographies in 1975; hers was *Memoirs of ird in a Gilded Cage,* his *Compassionate Landscape.* eanwhile, Charles Ritchie continues to prove at superb diarists are not altogether extinct: *e Siren Years: A Canadian Diplomat Abroad* was blished in 1974, to be followed by *An Appetite Life* (1977), *Diplomatic Passport* (1981), and *rm Signals* (1983).

Literate and shapely autobiographies often st on long years of practice in prose writing. urnalists such as James M. Minifie and Grat-n O'LEARY (*Recollections of People, Press, and Poli-s,* 1977) have the fluency and wit of profes-nals. Florence Bird is another longtime urnalist and public figure with an important story to tell; the fact that she tells it under the title *Anne Francis, An Autobiography* (1974) will confuse some younger Canadians until they read her book. Full-fledged men and women of letters having until recently been rare in Canada, we have few accounts of a literary life, but those few are worth seeking out, especially John GLASSCO's *Memoirs of Montparnasse* (1970), a *tour de force;* Lovat Dickson's 2 autobiographical volumes, *The Ante-Room* (1959) and *The House of Words* (1963); and George WOODCOCK's *Letter to the Past* (1983). Scholars read and write a good deal, but like prime ministers they are generally too discreet to lay bare their inmost thoughts and feelings in autobiography. Notable exceptions are historian Arthur Lower, with *My First Seventy-Five Years* (1967) and Victoria College's Kathleen Coburn, who, while disclaiming autobiographical intent, nevertheless charts a fascinating course in *In Pursuit of Coleridge* (1977). Emily CARR was a painter before she turned to writing, and her style in both art forms is distinctively her own. Carr's sketches in *The Book of Small* (1942), her autobiography *Growing Pains* (1946) and her journals, *Hundreds and Thousands* (1966), are the work of a major talent.

It is generally assumed that autobiographers, having chosen to tell their life stories, may write selectively and with some dramatic colouring, but will not deliberately mislead the reader as to essential facts. Thus it was something of a literary scandal when noted naturalist and conservationist Grey Owl, whose autobiographical *Pilgrims of the Wild* appeared in 1935 (2nd ed, 1968), was revealed at his death in 1937 as English-born Archie BELANEY. Much the same excitement attended Douglas Spettigue's unmasking of novelist Frederick Philip GROVE, a development that put large parts of Grove's much-admired autobiography *In Search of Myself* (1946) into the category of fiction.

There are several once-popular Canadian authors who have written autobiographies that seem more durable than their poetry and fiction. James Oliver Curwood and Ralph Connor (Charles W. GORDON) sold millions of copies of their novels in the early 20th century; Curwood's *Son of the Forests* was published in 1930, Gordon's *Postscript to Adventure* in 1938, shortly after his death. Nellie MCCLUNG, although now best known for her early feminist activism, first made her name as a writer of stories. Her 2 volumes of autobiography, *Clearing in the West* (1935) and *The Stream Runs Fast* (1945) convey a warm and attractive personality. Laura Goodman Salverson was an Icelandic-born novelist who won a Governor General's Award for her 1939 autobiography *Confessions of an Immigrant's Daughter,* and Frederick NIVEN's reflections on his life in *Coloured Spectacles* (1938) have more artistry and interest than his long historical novels. It seems probable, however, that Stephen LEACOCK's *The Boy I Left Behind Me* (1946) will always rank below his satiric sketches, and poet Robert SERVICE added nothing to his fast-dimming lustre in *Ploughman of the Moon* (1945) and *Harper of Heaven* (1948). Whether Mazo DE LA ROCHE will be remembered for her novels, her autobiography *Ringing the Changes* (1957), both, or neither, is for posterity to decide. These authors and hundreds more Canadians have put it on record that, like Edith Tyrrell in 1938, *I Was There,* and in so doing they have added imaginative texture and depth to Canadian prose writing. SUSAN JACKEL

Reading: Jay Macpherson, "Autobiography," in Carl F. Klinck, ed, *Literary History of Canada* (2nd ed, 1976), 616-23.

Autobiographical Writing in French The golden age of personal literature (*littérature intime*) in the Western World occurred in the late 18th and early 19th centuries. Examples of the genre are not found in Québec before the mid-19th century. Québec writers, timid about self-revelation, were extremely discreet about their personal lives. Their characteristic reserve, which led writers to speak more comfortably of others than of themselves, was typical of the literature until the late 1950s.

Those diaries which were not straightforwardly external in orientation revolved around the dominant theme that had provoked their existence in the first place. The subject was war for Octave CRÉMAZIE's *Journal du siège de Paris* (1870-71) and for Simone Routier's *Adieu, Paris!* (1940). It was the stifling effect of prison life, 1948-51, for Marcel Lavallé's *Journal d'un prisonnier* (published posthumously, 1978). Clear-eyed introspection marked this book, as it did the typical adolescent diary, Fadette's *Journal d'Henriette Dessaulles, 1874-80* (published posthumously, 1971). Poet Saint-Denys GARNEAU offered an analysis tinged with mysticism in his *Journal* of the period 1935-39 (published posthumously, 1954; tr *The Journal of Saint-Denys Garneau,* 1962), and the analysis in *Notes pour une autre fois* (1983) by Jean-Ernest Racine was coloured by the imminence of death.

Memoirs are an older genre in French Canada, though their intimacy is sometimes debatable. They concentrate on career development and are often avowedly didactic. There are numerous political memoirs, though not one of a really prominent person. Most such memoirs are partisan pleadings that completely ignore the subject's private life. The truly autobiographical and literary qualities of the *Mémoires* (3 vols, 1969-73) by Georges-Émile LAPALME are in striking contrast to the banality prevalent in the field. These disillusioned memoirs of the unfortunate adversary of the all-powerful Maurice DUPLESSIS help to illuminate the *Chronique des années perdues* (1976) of Lapalme's close collaborator, Guy Frégault. The actor Palmieri (J. Sergius Archambault) used pleasant little anecdotes to evoke theatrical life in *Mes souvenirs de théâtre* (1944); sculptor Alfred LALIBERTÉ (1878-1950) illuminated the plastic arts with his more revealing *Mes souvenirs* (published posthumously, 1978). Intellectual life was represented in the *Souvenirs* (1944-55) of Édouard MONTPETIT and the impressive *Mes mémoires* (4 vols, 1970-74) of Lionel GROULX, who described almost a century of evolution in Québec society. Finally, the aristocratic style of life evoked in the 19th-century *Mémoires* (1866) of Philippe AUBERT DE GASPÉ, Sr, found its 20th-century echo in the *Testament de mon enfance* (1952; tr *Testament of my Childhood,* 1964) and *Quartier Saint-Louis* (1966) by Robert de Roquebrune.

Like memoirs, volumes of remembrances were intended to keep the national heritage alive and to instruct future generations. They developed themes already familiar in journals: war, whether through civilian eyes (Marcel Dugas, *Pots de fer,* 1941) or military ones (Joseph-Damase Chartrand, *Expéditions autour de ma tente,* 1887); a humourous account of prison life by Jules Fournier (*Souvenirs de prison,* 1910); the profession of writing discussed in the singularly unconfiding *Confidences* (1959) of Olivier Maurault and of Ringuet (Philippe PANNETON, 1965). Authors also described their traditional Québec childhoods. These "collective" remembrances painted an idyllic picture of the past and of rural family life: best known were *Les Rapaillages* (1916) by Lionel Groulx and *Chez nous, chez nos gens* (1924) by Adjutor Rivard. Though there were happy exceptions to the rule, eg, Louis-Honoré FRÉCHETTE's *Mémoires intimes* (treating the period 1839-1903 and published posthumously, 1961), the earlier of these childhood remembrances usually followed this model, whereas later ones built new stereotypes around city life.

Since true autobiography requires the author to centre his account on his own evolution, the genre was practically nonexistent in Québec until 1960. The celebrated trilogy by Claude Jasmin, *La Petite Patrie* (1972), *Pointe-Calumet, Boogie-Woogie* (1973) and *Sainte-Adèle, la vaisselle* (1974), combined autobiography with collective remembrances. The various writings of Paul Toupin gathered together in *De face et de profil* (1977) dealt strictly with his personal life and his writing career; both the *Souvenirs en lignes brisées* (1969) by J.E. Racine and the *Journal dénoué* (1974) by Fernand OUELLETTE dug into the author's personality in a painful search for a deeper level of the self. This kind of search can veer from its original intent to produce an activist work such as *Nègres blancs d'Amérique* (1968; tr *White Niggers of America*, 1971) by Pierre Vallières or an awakening to the feminine condition, such as *La Vie défigurée* (1979) by Paule Saint-Onge. In more popular autobiographies, self-revelation is a pretext for denunciation of social injustice.

An overview of Québec personal literature would be incomplete without examples of private correspondence. Three poets are included among those whose letters were posthumously accorded the honour of publication: Octave Crémazie, Nérée Beauchemin and Saint-Denys Garneau. If to this list is added *Lettres d'un artiste canadien: Napoléon Bourassa* (1929), one has the only virtually complete published editions of private correspondence: the most personal writing of all.

Québec society was long turned in on itself. It gave its writers no privileged status and demanded that they exercise the greatest possible discretion about their private lives. However, writers of the 1980s, now at the height of their powers, seem determined to live more openly and so to join the international literary mainstream. FRANÇOISE VAN ROEY-ROUX

Automatistes, Les The painter Paul-Émile BORDUAS, inspired by the stream-of-consciousness writing (*écriture automatique*) of French poet André Breton, transposed this idea onto canvas, PAINTING spontaneously and without preconception. The Automatiste movement was born when Borduas showed 45 of these gouaches at the Ermitage Theatre in Montréal from 25 Apr to 2 May 1942. He gained a few followers from among his students at the École du Meuble, including Marcel BARBEAU, Jean-Paul RIOPELLE and Roger Fauteux; others, such as Pierre GAUVREAU and Fernand LEDUC, came from the École des beaux-arts in Montréal, and Jean-Paul MOUSSEAU came from the Collège Notre-Dame. The group met in Borduas's studio to discuss Marxism, surrealism and psychoanalysis, all subjects looked down on by the church. The Automatistes held a number of exhibitions, notably in New York in 1946 and in Paris in 1947. Their first Montréal exhibition was on Amherst St in Apr 1946, and they were designated as "Automatistes" at their second Montréal showing, on Sherbrooke St in Feb 1947. What had begun as a dissident student group was now an important cultural movement.

In 1948 Borduas released the manifesto REFUS GLOBAL, which served as a preface for a series of texts by Claude GAUVREAU (poet and brother of Pierre), Françoise Sullivan (a dancer), Bruno Cormier and Fernand Leduc, and expressed the views of the Automatistes. It extended the movement's aesthetic intuitions into the political field, "resplendent anarchy" being the mirror of the spontaneous painting encouraged by the group. The group dispersed after the manifesto was published, for Riopelle and Leduc had already left for Paris. Their last show — "La Matière Chante" organized by Claude Gauvreau — took place in 1954. FRANÇOIS-MARC GAGNON

Reading: D. Burnett and M. Schiff, *Contemporary Canadian Art* (1983); François-Marc Gagnon, *Paul-Emile Borduas. Biographie critique et analyse de l'oeuvre* (1978). J. Russell Harper, *Painting in Canada* (1977); D. Reid, *A Concise History of Canadian Painting* (1973).

Automobile Few inventions have had as great an impact on the world as the automobile. The first Canadian automobile, built in 1867 by Henry Seth Taylor, was regarded as a novelty, as were the single-cylinder vehicles that were imported from the US in 1898. In 1904 Canada's AUTOMOTIVE INDUSTRY began with the establishment of Ford Motor Co of Canada, Ltd. By 1913 there were some 50 000 motor vehicles in Canada; 70 years later the number had increased to some 14 million — one vehicle for every 1.7 persons. With the world's second-highest ratio of automobiles to inhabitants, Canada is often regarded as automobile dependent. Today the automobile is used for about 80% of all "journey-to-work" trips, about 85% of all pleasure travel and about 90% of all intercity travel. Canadian vehicles travel some 15 billion km per year on some one million km of highways, roads and streets.

The number of vehicles in each province generally reflects provincial population, with Ontario having the most vehicles (5 million in 1982) and PEI (68 000) the fewest.

Early automobiles were used by the wealthy for racing and amusement. Although these vehicles had engines, they truly were "horseless carriages" — little more than lightweight buggies with motive power. They were unreliable, expensive and sometimes dangerous. The earliest automobiles were hand made and sometimes built to order. Ransom Olds conceived the idea of interchangeable components, which made assembly-line production possible. By thus reducing costs, the automobile was made available to many customers for whom the price had previously been too high. As automobile sales increased, so did production. Detroit, Mich, which became the automotive centre of the world and nearby Windsor, Ont, prospered. Automobiles made it easier for people to travel, enabled salesmen to cover more territory and encouraged travel. They allowed people to live farther from work and consequently had a profound effect on URBAN DESIGN. Automobiles created the demand for more streets, highways and freeways. They spawned service stations, garages, insurance underwriters and numerous other types of services.

Today the automobile, together with its suppliers, infrastructure and supporting industries, represents an important component of the economy, notably the CONSTRUCTION INDUSTRY. Transport consumes about half of all the petroleum used in Canada, and automobiles take half of that quantity — as much as all of the other modes of transport combined.

The enormous impact of the automobile has not been without costs. Roads, highways and freeways require land that might otherwise be used for housing, parks or agriculture. Concern over the loss of land to the automobile has led to pressures by environmental groups. Their pressures resulted in the cancellation of plans to build the Spadina Freeway in Toronto and plans to expand highways in national parks in the West.

Each year Canadian cars produce millions of tonnes of carbon dioxide, carbon monoxide, various particulants and other types of gas. They contribute to the smog that plagues many Canadian communities (*see* AIR POLLUTION; POLLUTION). Auto-emission standards are more lax in Canada than in the US. Many of the vehicles sold in

Auto-related Accidents, Deaths and Injuries 1960-82

Year	*Accidents*	*Fatalities*	*Injuries*
1960	247 829	3 283	90 186
1970	198 839	5 080	178 501
1980	184 302	5 461	262 977
1981	183 643	5 383	260 658
1982	156 779	4 169	225 717

Casualty Rates in 1982 per 100 Million Vehicles/k

	Fatalities	*Inju*
Canada	2.3	123
Newfoundland	1.8	77
PEI	1.9	79
NS	2.9	73
NB	3.6	91
Québec	2.7	113
Ontario	1.7	140
Manitoba	2.1	143
Saskatchewan	2.5	88
Alberta	2.3	97
BC	2.8	158
YT	0.7	48
NWT	1.0	43

Canada do not meet the minimum requiremen of the US Environmental Protection Agency.

Far more Canadians are injured in auto mobiles than by any other mode of transpor Young persons are often the victims: in 1982, fo example, 52% of all persons killed in auto related accidents were between the ages of and 34. For many years the number of auto related accidents increased almost without in terruption, but in recent years the number o persons killed and injured has declined. (Befor 1980 the accident statistics included all auto mobile accidents that were reported; after th date the statistics gathered by the provinci governments included only those accidents th resulted in death or serious injury.) In 1982 th YT had the fewest number of fatalities pe vehicles/km and NB the highest. The NWT ha the best record of injuries per vehicle/km and B the worst.

In recent years, most of the provinces hav passed legislation that makes the use of seat bel mandatory. Safety experts believe that their us has reduced auto-related deaths and the severit of injuries sustained. Since focus on the value o seat belts has intensified, increasing numbers o drivers have used them. The number of seat-be users in Canada increased nearly 14% betwee 1982 and 1983.

Today, most Canadian automobiles are ga oline powered; a smaller number use diese engines. Some vehicles (principally taxicabs an fleet vehicles) are powered by propane, liquefie natural gas and other petroleum product While alcohol can be used as vehicle fuel, it generally more expensive than gasoline. Pro ponents of electric-powered vehicles see a gre future for them, but thus far their use has bee limited, because of their cost, the weight of the batteries and their restricted range. *See also* AUTO MOBILE ASSOCIATIONS. K.M. RUPPENTHA

Automobile Associations The first tourin clubs and associations were for people travellin by cycle, train or on foot. Automobile club were formed later when the automobile becam more widely used and distributed. The club were mainly social in nature, and almost en tirely confined to Europe until the end of th 19th century. At the beginning of the 20th cen tury, the owners of automobiles throughout Eu rope and N America felt the need to meet an discuss their problems: laws that restricted the activities, the organization of races, the de velopment of the motor car as a practical mean of conveyance, the encouragement of technica progress, and their defence against a hostile pub lic. In Canada, the establishment of the Cana dian Automobile Assn (1913) united every non profit provincial and municipal motor club t promote a better understanding of the auto mobile and to improve roads and motoring con ditions in general. Today, there is a worldwid network of about 200 motoring and touring as sociations and clubs with a common bond – the promotion of travel and tourism. Each o these individual organizations consists of man mponent clubs and branch offices located in ery community where there are motor vehi-s and tourists. The main purpose of such an filiated network, comprising thousands of fices in over 100 countries, is to ensure that embers of the various clubs have access to club rvices and assistance wherever they may avel. ROBERT ERB

utomobile Racing in Canada can be said to ve originated during the last 3 decades of the th century with the great popularity of CLING. The tremendous interest in developing alternative mode of personal transportation that provided by the horse led to the rapid olution of technological innovations. Such ventions as the pneumatic tire and the drive aft, which appeared on early bicycles, even-ally found their place on the automobile. lso, the early supporters of cycling formed ubs, engaged in tours and races, and cam-igned for good roads. Many carried this en-usiasm into the 20th century with the arrival the automobile.

The earliest automobile racing took the form speed trials and tours. In 1900, F.S. Evans set a cord of 3 hrs, 20 min, driving an automobile e 60 km between Toronto and Hamilton. Both ronto and Winnipeg witnessed many tours d "runs" by the automobile owners of their ties during this time, but the first automobile ce took place in the latter city. There, in 1901, e driver of a 12-horsepower Ford won the first tomobile race in Canada. Four years later, the innipeg Automobile Club was holding regu-r night races for passenger and light touring rs. In Toronto, automobile racing appears to ve found its earliest home at the CANADIAN TIONAL EXHIBITION. In 1913, a form of auto-obile polo was staged at the CNE's grandstand, d the following year races and hurdling in tomobiles were added to increase the popu-rity of the show. In 1917, Gaston Chevrolet ced successfully in an automobile against an rplane flown by Ruth Law, a noted aircraft pi-t of the time. In 1919, Ralph De Palma was in-ted to drive the world's fastest car in a time test the CNE's track. From 1920 to 1928, a series of ces were held with prizes totalling $9000.

Despite its early start, automobile racing has ot been a premier sporting event in Canada. nly in the past decade, with the advent of the an-Am series of races and the annually staged anadian Grand Prix for Formula One cars, has e sport aroused broader interest. For many ars it was confined to a number of quarter-d eighth-of-a-mile oval tracks of asphalt or rt construction. The cars used were greatly odified passenger vehicles known as "stock" rs. Competition was localized and there was ttle success at establishing national races, let one international events like those occurring many other sports. This form of racing con-nues to this day. More recently, stock-car races, nctioned by the US Automobile Club (USAC), ave been held at the better-established race acks in Canada, and a few Canadians have ied to find success on the very popular US rand National Circuit organized by NASCAR. nother form of US racing which enjoyed great opularity in the 1950s and 1960s in Canada is ag racing. Two drivers race their cars against ch other and the clock from a standing start ver a quarter-mile straight track. By 1965, there xisted a dozen sanctioned Canadian drag acks.

The real impetus to involve Canada and Cana-ian drivers in international racing has come om road racing, which takes place on closed rcuits featuring a variety of turns and straight-ways. A wide variety of cars, divided into dif-rent classes, from small sedans and sports cars the more exotic open-wheeled formula racers, re raced on these tracks. The roots of this form of racing can be found in the interest that developed in N America after WWII in the small sports cars brought back from Europe by returning servicemen. The availability of abandoned air strips provided the facilities to race these automobiles. In fact, the first road race in Canada took place on the Abbotsfield Airfield in BC in 1949. One of the first tracks in Ontario was created in Edenvale, near Stayner, in the vicinity of Georgian Bay. In Winnipeg, the old Netley Airport was the scene of racing activity, starting in 1955. Although similar racing spread across the West, the centre of Canadian road racing was southern Ontario. These early years of racing on airport strips were without much organization or professionalism. In 1951, the Canadian Automobile Sports Club was formed as a federation of auto sports clubs across Canada.

By 1959, a growing disagreement between those who raced for fun and those who believed the sport could only be developed through competitions between well-known drivers lured by substantial cash prizes led to the formation of the Canadian Racing Drivers Assn. In May 1956 the British Empire Motor Club opened Harewood Raceway near Jarvis, Ont. Here many of Canada's top drivers of the 1960s got their start. A major development, however, was the construction of Mosport, a 2.46-mile (4 km) road-racing circuit N of Bowmanville, Ont. On 24 June 1961 a crowd of 40 000 spectators gathered to watch Britain's Stirling Moss defeat an international field in the first Player's 200 race. Further efforts were made to develop the sport. Edmonton International Speedway and LeCircuit at Ste Jovite, Qué, were opened in the years that followed. In 1963, Don Hunt of Toronto developed the concept of a Canadian-American challenge series for unrestricted sports cars and, 3 years later, the first Can-Am race was held. Each year a series of races is held over a number of road courses in Canada and the US. Although American drivers have won most of the races, in 1968 John Cannon of Montréal won the last Can-Am race prior to the complete domination of the event until 1974 by the McLaren team of Britain.

On 27 Aug 1967, the first Canadian Grand Prix for Formula One cars was held at Mosport Park. The race has been a highlight of the automobile racing season since. In 1978, it was moved to Montréal, where it was won for the first time by a Canadian, Gilles VILLENEUVE — for whom the course is now named. The first Canadian to compete at the Formula One level was Peter Ryan of Mont-Tremblant, Qué. A highly promising young driver, his career ended tragically on 2 July 1962 when he was killed while racing in Europe. In 1969 and 1970, George Eaton of Toronto drove for the BRM team in N America and in selected European events. By far the most successful Canadian driver was Gilles Villeneuve. After a brilliant career in N America, he joined the Ferrari racing team in 1977. From then until his death in 1982, he won 6 world-championship races, including, in 1981, the crown jewel of the sport, the Monaco Grand Prix. Other successful Canadian drivers include Earl Ross, who was NASCAR's rookie of the year in 1974, and Gary BECK of Edmonton, who won the 1974 world drag-racing championship.

In spite of these successes, Canadian automobile racing remains at the periphery of the sport worldwide — perhaps reflecting Canada's relation to the automobile industry, based in the US, Europe and Japan. J. THOMAS WEST

Reading: Len Coates, *Challenge: The Story of Canadian Road Racing* (1970).

Automotive Industry in 1982 comprised some 500 establishments, producing almost $20 billion in vehicles and parts; it ranked first among Canada's manufacturing industries. The first horseless carriage in Canada was built by Henry Seth Taylor in 1867 in Stanstead, Qué. Taylor's steam pleasure carriage was considered a novelty, but as other pioneers built steam, electric and gasoline engines in the late 19th century, the automobile began to find a place in personal and goods TRANSPORTATION. The automotive industry began in Canada when a group of young businessmen in Windsor, Ont, led by Gordon M. McGregor, formed the Ford Motor Co of Canada, Ltd (1904), only a year after Henry Ford, the promotor and inventor, had begun production in Detroit. Cars were assembled in the works of the Walkerville Wagon Co, Ltd, as parts were ferried by wagonload across the Detroit R. Canadian Fords were soon being shipped to most parts of the far-flung British Empire. Col R.S. MCLAUGHLIN, Canada's pioneer in the industry, converted the family's thriving carriage and sleigh production in Oshawa, Ont, to the new horseless carriage with its noisy internal-combustion engine. In 1908 McLaughlin arranged with William C. Durant, the financial wizard who formed General Motors, to use David Buick's engines. Buick engines with McLaughlin-designed bodies gained world renown. Later, Durant offered McLaughlin the Canadian rights to the Chevrolet "Classic Six," a 5-passenger touring car designed by racing-car driver Louis Chevrolet. General Motors of Canada Ltd was formed in 1918, under the presidency of McLaughlin, when McLaughlin Motor Co Ltd and Chevrolet Motor Co of Canada Ltd merged. Detroit, just across the Detroit R from WINDSOR, became the world centre for automotive production at the beginning of the century. The reasons for Detroit's predominance seem to have been based on its well-established carriage, bicycle and boat-engine industries and the excellent road system in the surrounding region. Windsor became the Canadian extension of Detroit because of 2 inducements: a 35% tariff on carriages of all kinds entering Canada and a preferential tariff entry to British countries.

The development work in automotive technology was done in Europe; even the name "automobile" is French. A French army captain, Nicholas Cugnot, built a steam-artillery tractor, the first self-propelled land vehicle, and another Frenchman, Jean-Joseph-Étienne Lenoir, first used a gas engine in a vehicle to drive on a highway. Steam and electric vehicles offered many advantages, but the internal-combustion engine has dominated. Nicolaus A. Otto, a German engineer, developed the 4-stroke engine, the foundation of the industry which has produced the 400 million cars and trucks on the roads of the world today. Gottlieb Daimler and Wilhelm Maybach worked together at the end of the 19th century to produce a practical, Otto-cycle automobile engine. Emile Levassor, of Panhard and Levassor, conceived the central frame structure suited to carrying an engine. By adding pneumatic tires, most of the obstacles to the beginning of motoring had been removed. It was the master mechanics of Detroit who turned the luxury plaything into a mass-produced, low-priced, reliable convenience for common use. Ransom E. Olds was the first successful mass producer in the US, with his rakish, curved-dash "merry" Oldsmobile. Important contributions were made by Ford, Charles and Frank Duryea, Henry Leland, Walter Chrysler, Charles Nash and Charles "Boss" Kettering, who invented the self-starter which made motoring less dangerous and more reliable.

In the early years, thousands of automobiles were introduced but few survived. In Canada these included the LeRoy, the popular Russell, the Tudhope, the Thomas, the Galt and many others. But no independent Canadian automobile company survived; Canada did not have enough people to support a native industry. The motor vehicle industry, however, burgeoned because of the demands of the first mechanized war. As a result, from 1918 to 1923 Canada was the second-largest vehicle producer in the world and a major exporter. Those Canadian manufacturers who succeeded were allied to successful US companies.

The form and size of today's automotive industry was shaped by the first "Canadian-content" legislation in 1926, the Tariff Board hearings of the mid-1930s, the Royal Commission on the Automotive Industry of 1960, the subsequent CANADA-US AUTOMOTIVE PRODUCTS TRADE AGREEMENT (APTA or Autopact) of 1965, and the Iranian oil crisis of 1979 which ushered in the automotive depression of the early 1980's. One result of the Autopact is continental, conditional free trade in motor vehicles and original equipment parts. The agreement contains safeguards requiring that APTA producers in Canada maintain levels of assembly related to the value of their sales here. At present, over 80% of the vehicles produced in Canada are exported.

In the early 1980s the automotive industry accounted for about 6% of total direct manufacturing employment in Canada and 10% of the value of total manufacturing shipments. The industry consumed 37% of iron foundry production, 17% of rubber products, 15% of machine-shop products, 13% of wire goods, 14% of processed aluminum, 8.5% of carpeting and fabrics and 8% of glass products. The Canadian automotive industry is the final destination of over 20% of all domestic steel shipments, representing over 10 000 jobs in the Canadian steel industry. There are 9 producers of cars and trucks in Canada, and Canada is the sixth-largest producer in the world. These vehicle assemblers also produce half of the value of parts and components going into vehicle production. One-third of these original equipment parts is produced by some 450 Canadian-owned parts companies, and the remaining 17% is produced by the 10 largest, independent multinational parts companies. Ontario continues to be the centre for vehicle assembly with 83%; about 12% of assembly is in Québec; and smaller facilities are maintained in BC, Manitoba and NS. Original equipment-parts plants are also concentrated in Ontario (80%) and Québec (10%). After-market parts production, which is about one-quarter that of original equipment parts, is located in Ontario (68%), with 16% each in Québec and Western Canada. The automotive industry also includes a distribution system of about 3500 dealers employing almost 80 000 persons.

Canada's automotive industry is not independent but is a fully integrated N American industry bound by the Autopact. The effects have been generally positive for Canada, creating more jobs, higher wages and lower car prices for Canadians. The Canadian industry has also grown more efficient since the agreement and plants in Oakville, Oshawa and Windsor are competitive with those in Detroit. However, several developments of the 1970s put the N American industry in a crisis. The most visible sign of change was the growing sales of Japanese and European cars, as Canadian consumers turned to smaller, more fuel-efficient cars. Nevertheless, while the Japanese have implemented self-imposed restrictions on cars exported to Canada, recent models from General Motors, Ford and Chrysler have begun to regain the confidence of consumers as well as car enthusiasts. The issue of import restraints has been

Leading Canadian Automobile Manufacturers, 1983

Company	*Sales*	*Rank among Cdn companies*	*Employees*	*Foreign Company ownership*
General Motors	$9.5 bill	2	36 500	100%
Ford	$5.7 bill	6	34 700	92%
Chrysler	$3.6 bill	16	11 176	100%

Spare tires being placed in a car trunk on the assembly line by a semi-automatic arm at the Ford plant, Oakville, Ont (*courtesy National Film Board/Photothèque*).

controversial, with the 1983 Federal Task Force on the Canadian Automotive Industry claiming that they are necessary to protect jobs and consumer groups claiming that they restrict choice and cause an overall rise in car prices.

In Canada about $5 billion was spent on new plants and equipment between 1978 and 1983. Huge sums went into single projects; eg, about $1 billion to renovate and expand GM's transmission plant in Windsor, over $700 million on Ford's new engine plant, and $500 million spent by Chrysler to renovate production in the continent's most robotized assembly plant. Management methods and organization, as well as relationships with labour and suppliers have been revamped in attempts to promote greater productivity and quality. Governments are also involved in the automotive industry. The federal government is using its impressive $25-million test track and facilities at Blainville, Qué, and Ontario has established 6 technology centres, an Automotive Parts Technology Centre in St Catharines, and a Robotics Technology Centre in Peterborough. In future years there will be many innovations in this revitalized, restructured industry.

JAMES G. DYKES

Autonomy Bills, 1905, became the Acts creating the provinces of Alberta and Saskatchewan. The federal government refused to accept the scheme proposed by North-West Territories Prem F.W.G. Haultain, which envisaged a single province controlling its own lands, resources and educational policy, and instead created 2 provinces. The legislation defined the boundaries of the provinces, granted them the same status as other provinces (except that public lands and resources remained under feder[al] control until 1930), provided for representatio[n] in the federal Parliament and for local RESPONS[I]BLE GOVERNMENT, spelled out federal subsidie[s] and ensured the continuation of Catholic an[d] Protestant schools originally provided for in th[e] NORTH-WEST TERRITORIES ACT of 1875. The bil[ls] proved so controversial that they occupied a[l]most 10 weeks of debate between Feb and Jul[y] 1905 and led to the climax of the NORTH-WE[ST] SCHOOLS QUESTION and to continuing resentme[nt] of an allegedly semicolonial status for the Pra[i]rie provinces within Confederation.

DAVID J. HA[LL]

Autopact, *see* CANADA-US AUTOMOTIVE PRODUC[TS] AGREEMENT.

Auyuittuq National Park (est 1972), locate[d] on the Cumberland Pen of BAFFIN I, is Canada['s] first national PARK located N of the Arctic Circl[e]. It is a harsh land of barren TUNDRA, jagge[d] mountain peaks, deep FJORDS and ice. The Penn[y] Ice Cap covers over 25% of the park's 21 50[0] km^2. vegetation is sparse, although in the bri[ef] arctic summer flowers such as white mountai[n] avens, yellow arctic poppy and purple saxifrag[e] colour the sand. Wildlife is not abundant; herbi[-] vores, including arctic hare, lemming and a fe[w] barren-ground caribou, are preyed upon b[y] wolves, arctic fox and weasel. The coast is hom[e] for millions of SEABIRDS. Glaucous gulls, fulma[rs] and black guillemots nest on sheer cliffs. Pola[r] bears, seals, walrus, beluga and narwhals patr[ol] the icy coastal waters. Stone-age DORSET peop[le] lived here over 2500 years ago. Norse explore[rs] visited but did not linger. In the 12th centur[y] ancestors of the present Inuit arrived. Thes[e] Thule people hunted whales and caribou. Eng[-] lish explorers arrived in 1585, but contact wit[h] European culture was not established until th[e] mid-1800s, when whalers set up shore station[s] on Baffin I. From April to July, the park pro[-] vides wilderness camping, hiking and moun[-] taineering challenges for enthusiasts.

LILLIAN STEWAR[T]

av Paul, Annette, ballet dancer (b at Stock[-] holm, Sweden 11 Feb 1944). Trained at th[e] Royal Swedish Ballet School, she was chose[n] from among company apprentices to dance th[e] lead in *The Stone Flower* in 1962. For 10 years sh[e]

Auyuittuq National Park, Baffin I, est 1972, was Can[-] ada's first national park N of the Arctic Circle; Crater L and Mt Odin are shown (*courtesy Parks Canada/Prairie R[e]gion*).

ained with the Royal Swedish Ballet as prin- al dancer and danced as guest ballerina with ROYAL WINNIPEG BALLET, Harkness Ballet, Nor- gian Ballet and other companies before join- Les GRANDS BALLETS CANADIENS in 1973. She ught beauty, vast experience and artistic ma- ity to the many roles created for her, includ- those by her husband, choreographer Brian CDONALD. She retired in 1984.

JILLIAN M. OFFICER

alanche, rapid, downslope movement of w, ICE, WATER, ROCK, SOIL, vegetation, etc, xed in various proportions. The term is used st often when snow or ice is the major com- ent (*see* LANDSLIDE, ROCKSLIDE). Numerous ava- ches fall annually in the mountains of Al- ta, BC, NWT and the YT. They are less quent in the rounded mountains and hills of East; however, a fatal avalanche burial thin the Toronto city limits shows the vulner- lity of any place where snow and a suitable pe occur. In Canada avalanches kill an aver- of 7 people annually (usually mountaineers skiers). Occasionally, avalanches cause major ASTERS: 60 killed near Dyea, BC-Alaska, 3 Apr 98; 58 near Rogers Pass, BC, 5 Mar 1910; 57 in k and snow avalanches near Britannia Mine, , 27 Mar 1915; and 26 near Granduc Mine, , 18 Feb 1965.

The order-of-magnitude estimates of ava- che size and corresponding effects are as fol- vs: a large avalanche which could destroy a lage or forest would fall about 1000 m (up to 00 m in extreme cases, as on Mounts Logan or Elias), deliver over 100 000 m^3 of snow, ice, , and impact with pressures exceeding 100 a; a medium-sized avalanche capable of de- oying a house or car would fall about 100 m, iver about 1000-10 000 m^3 and impact at out 10 kPa; a small avalanche which could ry, injure or kill a human could descend less n 100 m, with volumes of 10-100 m^3 and im- ct at about 1 kPa.

Avalanche paths consist of 3 zones: starting, ck and runout deposition. Most starting zones large avalanche paths are high-angle bowls, ques and open slopes, oriented to prevailing nds to trap and accumulate blowing snow. A rting zone would normally include at least e section where slope steepness exceeds 25°, hough slush avalanches may release on more ntle slopes (5-10°). Ice avalanches typically rt at the snout of a GLACIER or tributary ice eam, advancing or retreating over a cliff face. ow or ice released from the starting zone urs into the track (an open slope or, more of- , a gully confining and directing the flowing ss). As the avalanche accelerates, additional ow, ice, water, rock, soil, vegetation, etc, may entrained into the flow. Maximum ava- che speed depends on steepness, length, ape and roughness of track; flow height; operties of flowing material; and other fac- s. The NATIONAL RESEARCH COUNCIL has mea- red maximum speeds of about 50 m/sec for ge, dry-snow avalanches at Rogers Pass. A st-moving, dry-snow avalanche is character- d by a spectacular "powder cloud" and "wind asts" causing damage in front and to the sides moving snow. Wet snow and slush ava- nches normally flow at slower speeds and do t have powder clouds or wind blasts.

The runout-deposition zone occurs where the alanche decelerates because of decreasing epness, widening or termination of a gully to an open slope or alluvial fan, or a zone of creased surface roughness. In the Alps, ava- nches sometimes outrun historically recorded undaries, destroying buildings standing for nturies. By contrast, most damage in Canada curs at relatively new constructions (build- gs, powerlines, bridges, railroads) placed in e runout zone of avalanche paths for which little or no historic information is available. Economic consequences of avalanches are especially felt in BC where, in addition to causing damage and fatalities, avalanches block highway and railroad traffic.

Powder avalanche crosses the highway in Kootenay National Park, BC. The path of a previous avalanche can be seen in the background (*photo by Jim Davies, Banff*).

Snow avalanches begin in either of 2 ways. A small volume (less than 1 m^3) of loose snow can slip out from the snow surface in the starting zone. As this initial mass descends it entrains an ever-widening, triangular area of snow, giving the impression from a distance that the avalanche initiated at the upper vertex point of the triangle; hence, this type of avalanche is sometimes called a point avalanche. Conversely, a cohesive snow slab can release almost instantaneously over a relatively wide area of shear weakness (100-100 000 km^2). Slabs could be as little as 0.1 m thick, or could involve the entire snowpack (5 m thick in extreme cases). Slab avalanches are particularly hazardous because a large amount of snow is set in motion almost simultaneously. After slab failure, sharply defined fracture surfaces remain at the starting zone.

A snow slab fails when the slab's load exceeds the shear strength of supporting layers. Such failure of snow is most common during or immediately after heavy snowstorms when potentially weak layers cannot strengthen fast enough through crystal-to-crystal bond formation (sintering) to keep up with the increasing load of new snow. Slabs also release when thaw and creep deformation lower the strength of a weaker layer. A weakness may originate as the snow recrystallizes deep within the pack. One weakness, depth hoar, is a layer of weak, coarse grains recrystallized in the presence of strong temperature gradients. Another, surface hoar, develops when atmospheric water vapour deposits directly onto the snow surface, growing cohesionless, feathery crystals. Slab instability occurs when a heavy layer of new snow is added to a snowpack weakened by an existing layer of depth or surface hoar. Slab avalanches tend to release on ice crusts or smooth grassy slopes, especially when bonds are weakened by a thaw.

Snow-slope instability is evaluated from observations of weak layers and from meteorological data (snowfall, WIND, temperature). At Rogers Pass, avalanche forecasters operate several mountain meteorological and snow-study stations. New snow loading is observed during critical periods and the shear strength of potentially weak layers is evaluated with shear frames, ram penetrometers, and by simulating shear failure on miniature inclined planes. Observers also record avalanche activity because often, once avalanches start to run on certain slopes (test slopes), the activity will continue and possibly intensify. If snow-slope instability is suspected, authorities may restrict public access and then artificially release avalanches by explosive blasting of the starting zone. Avalanche defences (eg, concrete sheds and wedges, earth mounds and dams) are sometimes placed in the runout-deposition zone.

About 50% of victims buried in avalanche debris suffocate in the first half-hour. On the other hand, victims buried favourably (within air pockets) have survived lengthy burials (even days). Thus, rescue is attempted whenever possible by trained teams using probe poles and avalanche dogs. A victim equipped with a transmitting device (audio-induction field, Rf field, magnetic field) can be located relatively quickly by search parties equipped with a compatible receiver.

R.I. PERLA

Reading: C. Fraser, *Avalanches and Snow Safety* (1978).

Avalon Peninsula, 10 360 km^2, is a spreading peninsula thrust out into the rich fishing grounds of the N Atlantic, forming the SE corner of insular Newfoundland. The orientation of the land tends to be NE, following folds in the peninsula's Precambrian, Cambrian and Ordovician structures. The Isthmus of Avalon, less than 5 km at its narrowest, joins the peninsula to the rest of the island. From Grates Pt in the N to Cape Freels-Cape Pine in the S, the peninsula stretches 180 km and spans nearly 100 km E-W. The peninsula is, and has been since the settling of the island, its most populous region. By the early 1800s it was home to more than three-quarters of the colony's population and today about 40% of Newfoundlanders live here, more than half in the ST JOHN'S metropolitan area.

The peninsula's rugged coastline was the earliest settled in the province and its 4 major bays, TRINITY, CONCEPTION, ST. MARY'S and PLACENTIA, were among the earliest fished. Newfoundland's first formal colony was begun at CUPIDS, Conception B, in 1610, followed by several other chartered "plantations" around the Avalon. Sir George CALVERT was granted a portion of the

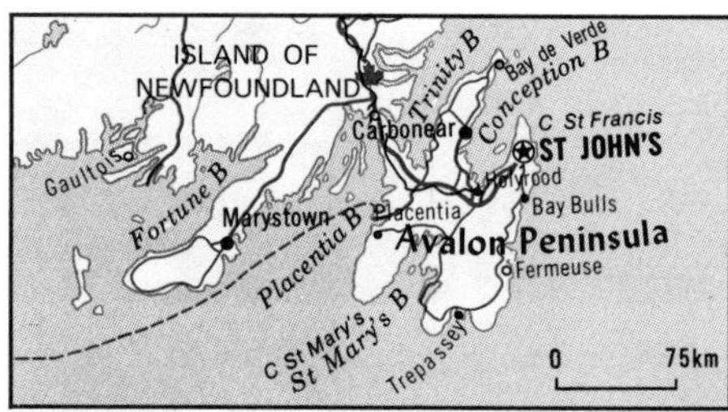

peninsula 1623 and lived there 1627-29, with his headquarters at FERRYLAND on the "Southern Shore." It was his holding, called Avalon after the legendary site where Christianity was introduced to England, for which the peninsula was named. During the 1600s and 1700s the peninsula saw conflicts between the French and English with France establishing PLACENTIA on the SW coast as its capital in the 1660s. Today, in addition to being the principal commercial and administrative region of the province, the peninsula is the location of many historic sites, 3 national historic parks, several provincial parks, a nature park near Salmonier, a spectacular seabird sanctuary at CAPE ST MARY'S, and a 862 km^2 wilderness area in its SE quadrant.

ROBERT D. PITT

Reading: J.J. Manion, ed, *The Peopling of Newfoundland* (1977).

Aviation, the art and science of flying, has been a practical reality only since the early 20th century. Canadians have participated in its development almost from its inception. Significant early research was initiated by Rupert TURNBULL, who built the first wind tunnel in Canada in 1902, and by the farsighted Alexander Graham BELL, who founded the Aerial Experimental Assn in 1907 and recruited 2 U of T graduates, John MCCURDY and F.W. BALDWIN, as well as 2 Americans, Glenn Curtiss and Tom Selfridge. Working from laboratories in Hammondsport, NY, near Curtiss's engine factory, and BADDECK, NS, just W of Sydney, the team developed several aircraft. The *Red Wing*, designed by Selfridge and completed in 1908, made 2 successful flights, piloted by Baldwin, at Hammondsport before crashing. Baldwin thus became the first Canadian to fly, albeit in the US. Next the *White Wing*, also piloted by Baldwin, took to the air. Curtiss's *June Bug* was third, and this craft became the first to remain airborne for a full 1000 m. Finally, after an initial attempt at Hammondsport, McCurdy's SILVER DART was shipped to Baddeck, and on 23 Feb 1909 he made the first powered, heavier-than-air flight in Canada.

In Aug 1909, in an attempt to find additional financing, McCurdy flew both the *Silver Dart* and the *Baddeck I* (the first aircraft to be made in Canada) before an assembly of militia officers at Camp Petawawa, Ont. Though both aircraft performed well in the air, neither survived its encounter with the rough landing field. Despite this setback, interest in aviation survived, and more experimental craft were built. In 1911 McCurdy flew from Key West to Havana, the longest overwater flight to that date. John Porte was preparing to fly from Newfoundland to Ireland in 1914, but the attempt was cancelled by the onset of war.

Commercial Aviation The first commercial cargo flight in Canada took place in Oct 1913, when Montréal newspapers were carried from Montréal to Ottawa. Unfortunately the aircraft crashed on the return takeoff. In 1919 the CANADIAN PACIFIC RAILWAY requested parliamentary approval to amend its charter to include air transportation. The government extended regulation to cover the fledgling industry by passing the Aeronautics Act (1919), which created the Air Board to consider such requests.

The first commercial passenger flight took place in 1920, when 2 bush pilots flew a fur buyer north to The Pas, Man, from Winnipeg. One month later, the first regular services were initiated when Imperial Oil chartered several Junkers aircraft to ferry men and supplies from Edmonton to the newly discovered oil fields at Ft Norman, NWT.

From 1920 to 1937 air transport expanded rapidly, although it was still composed of a large number of small carriers, operating predominately north-south routes, feeding traffic from the railways to the interior (*see* BUSH FLYING). Although long-distance airmail services were tested as early as 1920, it was not until 1927 that the Post Office authorized air delivery in cases where surface transportation was interrupted by the onset of winter.

In 1936 Parliament transferred control of civil aviation from DND to the newly created Dept of Transport, then under the aegis of C.D. HOWE. Faced with applications from US investors who wished to open a transcontinental passenger air route, and pressure from several Commonwealth countries that wanted the same system established as part of a more grandiose all-British, round-the-world network, Howe approached the 2 major railways and Canadian Airways, requesting that they participate in a nonprofit, government-guaranteed national carrier. CPR and Canadian Airways backed away over the issue of government representation on the board of directors, and Howe's preference shifted to the establishment of an all-government carrier. Thus, Trans-Canada Air lines was formed in 1937 as a wholly owned subsidiary of the CNR. In 1964 the name was changed to Air Canada, and in 1977 the Air Canada Act transferred share ownership from CN to the Crown. The government has been reluctant to license services in direct competition with it and the crown corporation is now Canada's largest airline.

CPR acquired 11 aircraft operating companies during 1941 and continued operations under the name United Air Services Ltd. The name was changed 24 Mar 1942 to Canadian Pacific Air Lines Ltd. In 1944 it applied for transcontinental status, which it was not granted until 1958 when it was allowed to operate a single daily service. The terms were gradually extended and in 1979 it was given the transcontinental route without restriction. Hampered by government in its attempt to fly domestically, CPAir expanded internationally from its Vancouver base, appropriating routes that Air Canada, which had the right of first refusal on all external services, did not visualize as being profitable. Flights were inaugurated to Australia, Japan and Hong Kong (1949); to South America (1953); and to Europe (1955), pioneering the transpolar Vancouver-Amsterdam route.

Four major regional carriers also supply airline services to the Canadian public. Central BC Airways was formed in 1946. In 1953 it was renamed PACIFIC WESTERN AIRLINES Ltd and later absorbed Queen Charlotte Airlines and Associated Airways. PWA is now Canada's third-largest airline. With headquarters in Calgary, it flies scheduled routes within the territory bounded by Toronto, Seattle, Inuvik and Resolute Bay. PWA was purchased by the Alberta government in 1974, but 85% of its shares were sold in 1983. Nordair, the youngest of the regional airlines, was formed in 1957. Its route structure was originally based on Arctic resupply flights from a Montréal hub, but by 1983 its scheduled services reached as far W as Winnipeg. In 1978 Air Canada purchased an 85% holding, but continued to operate the airline as a separate entity. In Feb 1953 Rimouski Airlines Ltd changed its name to QUEBECAIR. Operating an extensive route pattern within Québec, it has obtained traffic rights to Toronto. Eastern Provincial Airways, based in GANDER, Nfld, was formed in 1949. In Oct 1963 it purchased Maritime Central Airways, which traced its origins back to 1941. EPA serves A lantic Canada with routes from St John's as f W as Toronto. WARDAIR, a charter airline wi headquarters in Edmonton, was formed in 19 as a bush charter company and started the ove seas charter business in 1962. In 1983 it operat 7 wide-bodied jets on international charter se vices, and its revenue equalled that of any of t regionals.

In 1983 domestic scheduled flights of all ai lines carried 14 million passengers, more tha double the number in 1970. The 5 major rout were Toronto-Montréal, Calgary-Edmonton, T ronto-Ottawa, Toronto-Vancouver and Calgar Vancouver. Over 7.5 million passengers we carried between Canada and the US, aga roughly double the 1970 level. The 5 maj routes were Toronto-New York, Montréal-Ne York, Montréal-Miami, Toronto-Chicago ar Vancouver-Los Angeles. In that same year 2 million passengers were carried on intern tional charter flights, up from 850 000 in 19 and split roughly 50/50 between US and ove seas destinations. Detailed 1980 statistics are n available for other international scheduled se vices, but it is estimated that they carried b tween 4 and 5 million passengers.

Although most of the airlines remain profi able, expenses have been rising faster than rev nues, and net income has been decreasing. T primary factor has been the rapid rise in t price of fuel, from 3.5 cents per litre in 1970 over 21 cents in 1980. Fuel costs, only 22% operating expenses in 1970, had risen to 48% the 1980 total.

General Aviation General aviation has b come a major force in Canada. In mid-19 there were 24 437 civil aircraft registered in Ca ada, or one for every thousand persons. Of th total, only about 200 were owned by the 7 maj airlines. The total number, which more tha doubled over the previous decade, breaks dow into 22 199 airplanes, 1476 HELICOPTERS and abo 762 miscellaneous craft such as gliders, gyr planes and BALLOONS. About 17 500 registratio (72%) were for private use only, 6500 (25%) we for commercial use and the remainder we either experimental craft or were operated b government agencies. Corporations owned an operated about 1000 private aircraft for e ecutive transportation. The other 16 500 priva planes were used for both business and re reational purposes, generally owner-operate Canada had 61 340 licensed pilots in 1981, a 50 increase over the previous decade.

Commercial general aviation is a major i dustry in Canada. In 1980 this sector, exclusiv of the 7 major airlines, comprised 853 comp nies employing more than 10 000 people. 1979 Transport Canada estimated that over 2 million hours were flown. The major categori of use included charter flights (39.5%), flyir training (29.5%), nonprofit flying clubs (13 and unit toll services (6.5%). Other categories i cluded crop spraying, fire fighting, constru tion, aerial photography and sightseeing.

Government Regulation Most countries, i cluding Canada, consider that aviation has su ficient inherent risks to warrant governme controls to ensure that minimum standards safety are met and minimum levels of pr ficiency demonstrated (*see* TRANSPORTATION REG LATION). The government has also determin that commercial aviation is in effect a publ utility and that the public interest must ther fore be protected. In a Supreme Court decision 1932, aviation was deemed to be wholly wit in federal jurisdiction; consequently, provinci regulation is minimal.

Responsibility for air safety is exercised b TRANSPORT CANADA through one of its agenci the Canadian Air Transport Administration. addition to providing and maintaining airport air navigation facilities and air traffic contr services, CATA is charged with the licensing of personnel (pilots, mechanics, controllers) and equipment, registration of aircraft, and accident investigation.

Economic regulation is carried out by the Air Transport Committee, part of the CANADIAN TRANSPORT COMMISSION, which grants licences for the provision of commercial air services, including scheduled and charter carriage of passengers, freight and mail, as well as specialty services such as pilot training, crop spraying and fire control.

The Future When Canada's newest international airport, MIRABEL, was being planned during the late 1960s, air traffic in Canada had been growing at the rate of about 15% per year and was expected to increase indefinitely. Provision was made in the design to handle such expected improvements as the supersonic transport (SST) and the 800-passenger stretched double-deck jumbo jet. In 1983 long-term projections of traffic growth had fallen to about 4% per year; the super jumbo was still on the drawing boards; and the SST was losing money. Aircraft designs and airline operations are being developed to suit reduced traffic expectations, and the emphasis is on fuel economy and operational efficiency, through improved aerodynamics, engine design, structural weight and operational control procedures. Cost will be the primary consideration in all changes in aviation in the future. *See also* MCKEE TROPHY; MILITARY AVIATION AND AIRCRAFT. RICHARD FISHER

Reading: F. Ellis, *Canada's Flying Heritage* (1954, rev 1968); G.A. Fuller, J.A. Griffin and K.M. Molson, *125 Years of Canadian Aeronautics* (1983); L. Milberry, *Aviation in Canada* (1979); K.M. Molson, *Pioneering in Canadian Air Transport* (1974); K.M. Molson and H.A. Taylor, *Canadian Aircraft Since 1909* (1982).

Avison, John Henry Patrick, conductor, pianist (b at Vancouver 25 Apr 1915; d there 30 Nov 1983). After beginning a career as a solo pianist and accompanist, Avison accepted appointment as first conductor of the CBC Vancouver Chamber Orchestra in 1938. During 42 years under his versatile direction, this proficient orchestra performed works of all periods, specializing in the 18th-century repertoire and premiere performances of new Canadian works. BARCLAY MCMILLAN

Avison, Margaret, poet, librarian, social worker (b in Galt [Cambridge], Ont 23 Apr 1918). Educated at Victoria Coll, U of T, Avison began her writing career with a poem in the *Canadian Poetry Magazine* in 1939. She was a Guggenheim fellow in 1956, and her first collection, *Winter Sun* (1960), won the Gov Gen's Award. Avison is an intensely private poet whose images and constructs challenge the reader. The outward complexities of her writing mask a deeply religious and vulnerable sensibility, perhaps best revealed in her second book, *The Dumbfounding* (1966). In 1978 she published *Sunblue*, a collection that combines her sense of the everyday, minutely recollected, with poems that are a continuing restatement of faith. Among her other works are *History of Ontario* (1951), for young people, and a collaboration, *The Plough and the Pen: Writings from Hungary 1930-1956* (1963). MICHAEL GNAROWSKI

Avocet (order Charadriiformes, family Recurvirostridae), large, long-legged SHOREBIRD, about 40 cm long, with striking white-and-black plumage. The 4 species (one in each of N and S America, Eurasia and Australia) breed in small, loose colonies in coastal saltmarshes and shallow, alkaline inland lakes. Avocets feed on small crustaceans, worms and other benthic animals. Their long, slender, upward-curving bills are well adapted to their hunting technique. The birds wade slowly through shallow water, sweeping their bills from side to side just above the muddy bottom and seizing whatever prey is stirred up. Avocet numbers have declined with reclamation of their marshy habitats. However, their reestablishment in Britain, since the 1940s, is a classic example of successful conservation of an ENDANGERED SPECIES through habitat management. The American avocet (*Recurvirostrata americana*), with a yellow neck and bright blue legs, breeds in southern Alta, Sask and Man, and south to California and Texas, wintering in Texas, California and Central America. R.G.B. BROWN

Avro Arrow (CF-105), an advanced, supersonic, twin-engined, all-weather interceptor jet aircraft developed by A.V. Roe of Canada from 1949 until the government's controversial cancellation of the project in 1959. Encouraged by A.V. Roe's success in developing the AVRO CF-100 CANUCK and recognizing the need for an aircraft to counter the threat of Soviet bombers over the demanding Canadian North, enthusiastic RCAF officers, defence scientists and defence-industry officials had persuaded the Liberal government by Dec 1953 to authorize 2 prototype airframes in anticipation of a production run of up to 600 aircraft costing $2 million apiece. Canada was also forced to develop the Arrow's engine, and fire-control and missile systems, and estimated costs rose to $12.5 million per aircraft. Test flights indicated that, with the proper engines, the plane could well be the world's fastest and most advanced interceptor. However, doubts mounted as the government's order shrank to 100 and unit cost rose. In Oct 1958, to cut costs, the new Conservative government terminated Canadian fire-control and missile development, and renewed efforts to sell the aircraft to the US, just when the US was promoting BOMARC MISSILES and the USSR's launch of an ICBM missile was raising doubts about the priority of the Soviet bomber threat. After export efforts again failed, the project was cancelled on 20 Feb 1959. A.V. Roe bitterly fired 14 000 employees; the government ordered all plans and prototypes destroyed; and many Canadians bemoaned the devastation of Canada's aircraft industry, the resulting flight of scientists and engineers to the US, and Canada's renewed dependence on the US for interceptor aircraft. JOHN KIRTON

Avro CF-100 Canuck, first jet fighter designed and built in Canada. After 4 years' development, it first flew Jan 1950, and 792 were built. It became operational April 1953 and served 10 years in NORAD and NATO squadrons. It was not as fast as contemporary fighters, but its good climb rate, excellent radar, twin-engined reliability and all-weather capability made it suitable for defence in the extreme conditions of the Canadian North and in the cloud of W Germany. Fifty-three were sold to Belgium. Two are preserved in the National Aviation Museum, one in Calgary Centennial Planetarium and others in parks and bases across Canada. The name "Canuck" was considered inappropriate for a fighter and was not generally used. JAMES MARSH

Avro Jetliner (C-102), N America's first jet airliner, designed in Canada by James Floyd. It first flew on 10 Aug 1949, exceeding 800 km/h, the first flight of a jet transport in N America, second in the world. (The de Havilland Comet flew on 27 July 1949.) In April 1950 it made the first international jet-transport flight in N America, from Toronto to New York. It aroused much interest in the US and was one of the outstanding aeronautical achievements of its day, but it never saw production. TRANS-CANADA AIRLINES lost interest even before the first flight, and in the Cold War atmosphere C.D. HOWE insisted that Avro concentrate on the CF-100 fighter. The RCAF, the first air force to operate jet transports, ordered 2 Comets in November 1951. The Jetliner was sold for scrap 1956; only the nose section and engines survive in the National Aviation Museum. JAMES MARSH

Axel Heiberg Island, 43 178 km², third-largest in the Arctic QUEEN ELIZABETH IS and seventh-largest in Canada, is separated from ELLESMERE I to the E by Eureka and Nansen sounds. Mountains of the Princess Margaret Range rise precipitously on the W, reaching a height of 2211 m. Ice fields and glaciers cover 14 733 km² of the mountains. The eastern part is hilly, with local plains. Vegetation is scant, but well-vegetated spots occur in the lowlands. Arctic hares are the most common mammals. Muskoxen occur in the lowlands, but caribou are scarce. The island was discovered in 1899 by a Norwegian expedition led by Otto SVERDRUP who named it after the Norwegian consul. S.C. ZOLTAI

Axelrad, Arthur Aaron, histologist (b at Montréal 30 Dec 1923). Educated at McGill (MD, CM 1949; PhD 1954), Axelrad has been professor and head of histology in the anatomy department at U of T since 1966. He has achieved international acclaim for his research in hemopoiesis and leukemia. Axelrad's research group is known worldwide for its studies on various aspects of blood cell differentiation, with special reference to the myeloproliferative disorders. The group's work is focused on finding growth regulatory molecules that can control the response of hemopoietic stem cells. Axelrad has published over 80 scientific papers. He was elected a fellow of the RSC in 1982. KEITH L. MOORE

Axworthy, Norman Lloyd, politician (b at North Battleford, Sask 21 Dec 1939). He was a Princeton PhD and left-wing political activist. He taught at U of Winnipeg and directed its Institute of Urban Affairs before serving as Manitoba MLA 1973-79. He was elected to the House of Commons for Winnipeg in 1979 and again in 1980. A combative parliamentarian, tough-minded administrator and assiduous constituency politician, Axworthy was the sole elected Cabinet minister from the West in PM P.E. TRUDEAU's last government and served as minister of employment and immigration 1980-83, and minister of transport, 1983-84. He was the only Prairie Liberal to win a parliamentary seat in the 1984 election. NORMAN HILLMER

Aylmer, Qué, City, pop 26 695 (1981c), inc 1975, is located on Lac Deschênes in the OTTAWA R, 10 km SW of HULL. Created through a legislative merger of Aylmer (inc 1847 and named to honour Lord Aylmer, gov gen of Canada), Lucerne (1878) and Deschênes (1920), this suburban municipality is spread over a large territory and is a golfer's paradise (6 golf courses) and the home of the Connaught Race Track. Its oldest built-up area, the original town of Aylmer, was the administrative centre of Hull Township for most of the 19th century. Aylmer is the most bilingual city of the National Capital Region: 59.3% of its citizens have French as their mother tongue, 36.9% English (1981c). PIERRE-LOUIS LAPOINTE

Aylmer, Matthew Whitworth-Aylmer, 5th Baron, colonial administrator (b 24 May 1775; d at London, Eng 23 Feb 1850). After a distinguished military career he was appointed governor general of British N America in 1830. Despite his efforts to pacify the francophone majority, the Assembly of Lower Canada became increasingly radical and in 1834 passed the 92 Resolutions of grievance, one of them demanding his recall. Embittered, he inclined to the anglophone minority and thus exacerbated ethnic divisions. Blamed for the failure of conciliation, he was dismissed in 1835. Without doubt he was politically inept but much criticism of him was unfair. He cannot be held responsible for the crisis in Lower Canada that led to the REBELLION OF 1837. P.A. BUCKNER

Babiche is made from rawhide and has multiple uses. Hide is denuded of hair through a soaking process, stretched until dried, and cut into long narrow strips. Named by the early French traders, these thongs were used for fishing and harpoon lines, lacing for SNOWSHOES, bowstrings, gill nets, tumplines and headbands, rackets and drumheads. Bags of fine workmanship were knit of babiche. Braided babiche was used in making halters and carrying straps. The hides of land and aquatic animals were made into babiche and varied, according to animal, in thinness, colour and strength. RENÉ R. GADACZ

Baby, François, businessman, militia officer, politician (b at Montréal 4 Oct 1733; d at Québec City 6 Oct 1820). A fur trader from Montréal during the 1750s, Baby was taken prisoner to England in 1760. He returned from France in 1763 to set up as a merchant at Québec. In 1773-1774 he travelled to London as an influential defender of the constitutional proposals of Governor CARLETON [Dorchester], eventually adopted as the QUEBEC ACT. His resistance to the American invasion of 1775-76 and political conduct thereafter earned him appointment to the Legislative Council in 1778, and he lived the rest of his life on revenues from landed property, life annuities and government salaries. Baby backed Governor HALDIMAND's opposition to the colonial merchants' demands for an elective assembly, and later opposed attempts by the PARTI CANADIEN to extend the assembly's authority over colonial finances. A bright light in Québec's worldly high society, Baby was nevertheless a devout Roman Catholic, whose conduct secured him the admiration of the censorious Bishop PLESSIS. JAMES H. LAMBERT

Baby, James (bap Jacques), officeholder, politician, militia officer (b at Detroit, Mich 25 Aug 1763; d at York [Toronto] 19 Feb 1833). Son of wealthy Detroit merchant Jacques Baby, *dit* Dupéront, he was an obvious choice when Lord Dorchester recommended adding "one or two Canadians" from Detroit to the lists of executive and legislative councillors for the proposed province of Upper Canada. Appointed to both councils in 1792, he sat for life. Described by John Graves SIMCOE as a "French Gentleman of indisputable loyalty," Baby was regarded as the perfect liaison with the French-speaking, Roman Catholic community in the western extremity of the province. He held a plurality of offices during his lifetime, the most important being inspector general. On his appointment in 1816 he moved to York. Assiduous in his attention to duty, he was of limited abilities. "A man of most Gentlemanly manners tho' rather slow of apprehension" was how John STRACHAN put it. Although not a cipher, Baby was susceptible to Strachan's bullying on important issues. On one famous occasion, noted by William Lyon MACKENZIE, the affable and gentle Baby was reduced to tears by Strachan's tactics.
ROBERT L. FRASER

Baby Boom The GREAT DEPRESSION of the 1930s prolonged the decline in Canada's birthrate (*see* POPULATION) as it did in most Western countries. The low point was reached in Canada in 1937, when the gross birthrate (the annual number of live births per 1000 inhabitants) was 20.1. Improved economic conditions caused a recovery that accelerated during WWII. By 1945 the birthrate had risen to 24.3 per 1000 inhabitants; by 1946 it had jumped to 27.2 per 1000 inhabitants, and it remained between 27 and 28.5 per 1000 until 1959, after which time it gradually fell. The baby boom began (1950-52) with a number of births that had been postponed during the Depression, but 2 other factors affected it as well. First, a larger proportion of adults married, and those who did had more children. Taking married and single women together, those born in 1911 and 1912 had an average of 2.9

children, whereas those born between 1929 and 1933 had an average of 3.3. This is called "completed fertility." These 2 generations are separated by 20 years and, between the older and the younger, the number of children per woman increased by 0.4 (13%). Second, more than 50% of baby-boom births can be attributed to what demographers call "timing phenomena." More young adults married at a younger age (the median age for a woman's first marriage was 23.2 years in 1940 and 21.1 years in 1965), and between the end of the war and 1965, young couples tended to have their children during the first few years of married life.

Between 1940 and 1965 the number of births in Canada rose from 253 000 in 1940 to 479 000 in 1960 but dropped to 419 000 in 1965. Over a period of 25 years, the baby boom produced 1.57 million more births than would otherwise have occurred (about 8.65 million), an increase of more than 18%. By 1965, however, people were marrying at a later age and were waiting longer to have children, partly because more women were entering the work force and partly because there was general access to better contraceptive measures. JACQUES HENRIPIN

Back, Frederic, film-animation artist, graphic designer, teacher (b at Sarrebruick, Territoire de la Sarre, France 8 Apr 1924). Internationally acclaimed for his many animated films for children produced by the French-language division of the CBC, he attended the École des Beaux-Arts in Rennes, France, and immigrated to Canada in 1948. Hired by the CBC, Montréal, in 1952, he designed graphics and models for various TV series. He was encouraged to develop his animation skills and in 1970 proceeded to create several short animated films, primarily for young children, usually with a message associated with ecology or conservation or Québec nationalism. He won the Academy Award Oscar for *Crac* in 1982. JOHN L. KENNEDY

Frederic Back, internationally acclaimed Montréal film animator (*courtesy Canapress*).

Back, Sir George, Arctic explorer, naval officer, artist (b at Stockport, Eng 6 Nov 1796; d at London, Eng 23 June 1878). Back made his first voyage N in 1818 and thereafter spent much of his life exploring the Arctic. He was stationed in Halifax in 1814 and accompanied Lt John FRANKLIN to the Coppermine R in 1819. His heroism in saving comrades' lives during this expedition is recorded. In 1824 he accompanied Franklin overland to Great Bear Lk and the Arctic coast. On a search mission for John ROSS in 1834, Back found and travelled the Thlew-ee-choh R, later named for him. Though his final expedition (1836) was aborted because of severe ice conditions, Back's lifetime accomplishment was honoured with the medal of the Royal Geographical Society and a knighthood (1839).

Back is said to have learned watercolour techniques while a prisoner of war in France (1809-14), and he was the most important Arctic topographer of his day. Using a camera lucida, he sketched forest fires, rapids, rock formations, campsites and native life along the routes. Records of the second Franklin expedition and Back's overland expedition up the Thlew-ee-choh R are preserved in the Public Archives of Canada. JAMES MARSH

View of the Arctic Ocean from the mouth of the Coppermine R at midnight, 20 July 1821, by Sir George Back, aquatint (*courtesy Public Archives of Canada/C-41288*).

Back River, 974 km long, rises in Contwoyto Lk, N of GREAT SLAVE LK, NWT, and flows NE across the barren lands to Chantrey Inlet, S of King William I. It has a drainage area of 107 000 km² and a mean discharge of 612 m³/sec. The river is turbulent in its upper course, but as it enters a broad plain, it widens to form Lks Pelly, Garry and MacDougall. On its final leg it narrows to cut through another rocky section to the coast. The river is named for Sir George BACK (1796-1878), who first explored the river in 1833-35. The original Indian name was *Thlew-ee-choh*, "great fish river." He named the lakes after Sir John Henry Pelly and Nicholas Garry, governor and deputy governor of the HBC, and his friend Lt-Col MacDougall of the 79th Highlanders. JAMES MARSH

Backwoods of Canada: Being Letters From the Wife of an Emigrant Officer, Illustrative of the Domestic Economy of British America, The, by Catharine Parr TRAILL, was published 1836 in London. Traill's letters to her mother in England provide a perennially optimistic account of her day-to-day life in the "backwoods" of UPPER CANADA. The letters describe her month-long voyage to Canada with her husband, and their travels to the "interior" to settle near Peterborough, where Traill lived for over 60 years. The letters, particularly vivid in natural description, give us both a portrait of a persevering, buoyant and resourceful woman adapting to a new life and place, and an encyclopedic cataloguing of the details of her new surroundings. Whether describing Indians, Americans, wildlife, natural scenery, illnesses or Canadian customs, or providing recipes for soft soap, candles, vinegar or pickles, Traill's letters brim with vigour and with her eviden leasure at discovering the nature of her adopt-d homeland. *Backwoods* was translated into rench as *Les Forêts intérieures du Canada: lettres :rites par la femme d'un officier émigrant sur la vie omestique des colons américains* (Paris, 1843). A elected English edition, ed Clara Thomas, ap-eared in Toronto in 1966. NEIL BESNER

addeck, NS, UP, pop 972 (1981c), is located on he N shore of BRAS D'OR LK, 77 km W of SYDNEY. It s the beginning and end of the Cabot Trail, and vas the summer home of inventor Alexander raham BELL, as well as the site of the first air-lane flight in the British Empire (1909). The light of the SILVER DART and many of Bell's nventions are brought to life in the Alexander raham Bell Museum. The early settlers of the rea were LOYALISTS, although the first land grant vas to an English settler in 1819. Nineteenth-entury Baddeck supplied the surrounding areas vith manufactured goods. There were also gold nd gypsum mines, gristmills and a major ship-uilding industry. Modern Baddeck relies heav-ly on its reputation as a vacation haven. The nuseum, beautiful scenery and sailing are ma-or attractions. Luxury yachts are built now in-tead of commercial vessels. H. MACDONALD

adger The American badger (*Taxidea taxus*) is ne only N American WEASEL specialized for bur-owing and capturing prey underground. The ody is squat; legs, short and heavily muscled; eet, large with long, heavy claws. Adult males nay reach 11.4 kg in weight and 80 cm in ength. The head is small, triangular and flat-ened, with prominent snout and ears. The long, oarse pelage on the body is silvery yellowish, nderparts are paler and feet are black. The head s brown with white crescents on the face. A arrow white stripe runs from muzzle to shoul-ers. Badgers inhabit grassland and open wood-nd of the southern Prairie provinces and BC, xtending southward through the prairies and emideserts of the US and northern Mexico. The adger is primarily nocturnal, resting by day in xtensive burrows, usually alone or a female vith kits. Food is mostly burrowing rodents. Aating occurs July-Aug. Litters (1-4 young) are orn Mar-Apr. Young are independent in 2-3 nonths and mature early; females may breed at months, males usually not until 7 months. oth sexes hibernate. Over-hunting and preda-or control have reduced the badger to the verge f extinction in Canada. *See* ENDANGERED ANI-ALS. IAN MCTAGGART COWAN

adger (*Taxidea taxus*), squat, muscular weasel special-ed for burrowing and capturing prey underground hoto by Tim Fitzharris).

adlands, barren, intricately eroded and deeply issected landscapes, largely devoid of vegeta-on and characterized by steep slopes and nar-ow, winding channels and gullies. The name nay derive from the French *terres* ("land") *mau-aises* ("bad"), as the French were among the ear-est European explorers in interior western N merica, where badlands are common. Bad-nds form where relatively unconsolidated, oft or geologically weak, horizontally layered SEDIMENTARY ROCKS (eg, clays, silts, shales) and poorly cemented sandstones are exposed to vigorous EROSION by rain and running water. They tend to occur in semiarid areas where precipitation, although small in total annual amount, often falls in short, intense convectional rainstorms. Badlands are areas of very rapid erosion, often several millimetres a year. Dense vegetative cover is discouraged by the semiarid climate and the rapidity of erosion, for it is difficult for the plants to take root, grow and survive to reproduce. Moreover, the typical badlands rocks weather into rather infertile soil and do not support a dense plant cover. As a result, large areas are unprotected from rainfall impact and rapid surface runoff is encouraged. Subsurface flow of water is aided by the growth of deep desiccation cracks in summer, and eventually large sinkholes and pipes may form. This process is assisted by the presence of certain clay minerals which undergo rapid expansion as they get wet and contraction as they dry. Badlands occur in many countries including China, Turkey, Spain, Israel and Italy. Areas of badlands are found in many of the western states, especially S Dakota. In Canada, badlands can be seen in several locations in southern Alberta. Especially extensive are the Red Deer R badlands of Drumheller and DINOSAUR PROVINCIAL PARK, where they are associated with world-famous dinosaur-fossil remains. I.A. CAMPBELL

Typical badland landscape, in Dinosaur Provincial Park, SE Alberta (*courtesy Provincial Museum of Alberta*).

Badminton is a game played on a rectangular court divided into equal halves by a 5-ft-high (1.5 m) net, by 2 players (or 4 players in doubles) whose object is to hit the shuttlecock ("shuttle") with their racquets so that it touches the opponent's side of the court. Very light racquets are used to hit the specially designed shuttlecock with great speed or skilful deception. Top-class play demands a wide range of motor skills, excellent eye-hand co-ordination and superb physical fitness. It is likely that badminton originated about 2000 years ago in China and Siam. Some sources say it was British army officers serving in Poona, India, who adopted the ancient game, possibly bringing it home when on leave during the 1860s. It may have first been played in England at the duke of Beaufort's country estate, called Badminton House. The game was adopted at several English seaside resorts, and soon after in the London suburbs. The Badminton Assn of England was founded in 1893 and wrote the laws of the game, which have changed very little since.

Military personnel introduced badminton to Vancouver, BC, in the late 1890s. It was slow to spread to other regions, though there is evidence of it being played in Ottawa in 1900 and the first Canadian club was founded in Montréal in 1907. The first open tournament was the BC Championships (1913-14 season). After WWI, the Canadian Badminton Assn (CBA) was founded (1921-22) and the first Canadian Championships were held in Montréal (1922). The tournament was only for Canadians at first, but was opened to the world in 1957, and is now regarded as a major international tournament. The greatest initial stimulation to the game in Canada came in the fall of 1925 when a British team toured the country and provided the impetus to erect specially built halls in many cities. Five years later a similar tour was arranged; both British teams were captained by Sir George Thomas, who donated the Thomas Cup to the International Badminton Federation (IBF) in 1939. During the 1930 tour Jack PURCELL of Guelph, Ont, defeated the 4 best British players and, in 1933, he was world professional champion. Dorothy WALTON dominated Canadian women's play in the 1930s and won the All-England women's singles title in 1939. Canada has been active and successful in the badminton tournaments played at the Commonwealth Games. Jamie Paulson (Calgary) won the gold medal at the 1970 Edinburgh Games and the silver 4 years later in Christchurch, NZ, while Canadians won 2 silver and 2 bronze medals at the 1978 Edmonton Games.

There are 30 facilities in Canada built for badminton (1983), though most play occurs in school gymnasia, church halls or community centres. It is estimated that over 1 million Canadians play badminton recreationally, while 60 000 are registered members of the CBA, which continues aggressively to promote recreational and elite badminton for the benefit of all interested people. JOHN J. JACKSON

Reading: Canadian Badminton Association Handbook; Badminton Canada (available at 333 River Road, Ottawa, Ont, K1L 8B9).

Baer, Erich, chemist, educator (b at Berlin, Ger 8 Mar 1901; d at Toronto 23 Sept 1975). He studied at U Berlin under Hermann O.L. Fischer with whom he worked until 1948, from 1937 at U of T. Baer became a professor in 1951 and professor emeritus in 1969. His work dealt with the synthesis of substances based on glycerol. One of such compounds became known as the Fischer-Baer ester, which plays a central role in the metabolism of carbohydrates. To arrange atoms in molecules in the right order and have them assume the proper configuration in 3-dimensional space, Baer made use of the configuration already available in natural sugar alcohols in a simple and most elegant way. The glycerol derivatives thus obtained were the starting materials for the synthesis of a series of phospholipids, fatlike substances containing a substituted phosphate group. These are essential structural elements of the cell membrane of all living organisms. Baer published well over 100 scientific papers and received many honours and awards. His legacy includes a generation of well-trained scientists. LEON J. RUBIN

Baffin, William, explorer (b at London? 1584?; d 1622). One of the most proficient navigators of his time, he sailed aboard the DISCOVERY in 1615 in search of the NORTHWEST PASSAGE, examining the entrance to Hudson Str, and turning back at sight of land named Baffin I by W.E. PARRY. On this voyage he obtained the first longitude figured at sea. In 1616, he discovered Baffin Bay, Jones Sound and LANCASTER SOUND. He was killed in the Middle East at the siege of Hormuz. JAMES MARSH

Baffin Bay, 689 000 km², is a deep body of water located between Greenland and BAFFIN I. Water depths are generally less than 1000 m, but reach a maximum 2400 m near its centre. The bay is connected to the Arctic Ocean in the N through Nares Str, Jones and LANCASTER sounds, and to the LABRADOR SEA in the S by DAVIS STR. Discovered by Robert Bylot in 1615, the bay was named after his lieutenant, William BAFFIN. Circulation is generally anticlockwise; off Greenland, relatively warm, salty water moves N, while along Baffin I, cold, fresher water originating from the Arctic Ocean flows S. Icebergs, formed by calving off the Greenland glaciers, appear year-round, but are most numerous in Aug. Extensive coverage by pack ice occurs seasonally Nov to July. In the N there is a recurring polynya, or area of open water ("north water"), the reason for which is still unknown. Between 1650 and 1900, intensive fishing by Europeans and Americans depleted the bay's large whale population. Exploitation of other mammals (seals, walrus) as well as fish (cod, halibut, haddock, herring) has been minimal.
ALLYN CLARKE AND KEN DRINKWATER

Baffin Island, NWT, 507 451 km², 1500 km long and 200-700 km wide, is the largest island in Canada and the fifth-largest island in the world. Located in the ARCTIC ARCHIPELAGO, it is separated from Greenland by DAVIS STRAIT and BAFFIN BAY, from Northern Québec by HUDSON STRAIT, and from the Melville Pen by Foxe Basin and the narrow Fury and Hecla Str. The island's immensity and bewildering coastline confused early explorers and concealed its geography until recent times. It was likely here that one of the great ice sheets that covered most of Canada originated some 18 000 years ago, and ice lingered on the island until almost 1500 years ago; vast areas are still sheathed in ice year-round. Geologically, Baffin I is a continuation of the eastern edge of the Canadian SHIELD, which tilts upward in the E to form a mountainous spine, sloping away into plateaus and lowlands in the W. A desolate plateau in the N comprises Brodeur and Borden peninsulas, separated by Admiralty Inlet — thought to be the world's largest FJORD. From S of the Hantzsch R to Fox Pen is the remarkable Great Plain of the Koukdjuak, consisting of a coastal strip of flat, grassy marshland and a slightly higher plain showing a series of old beaches. The Foxe Pen is rocky in the S and drops over dramatic bluffs

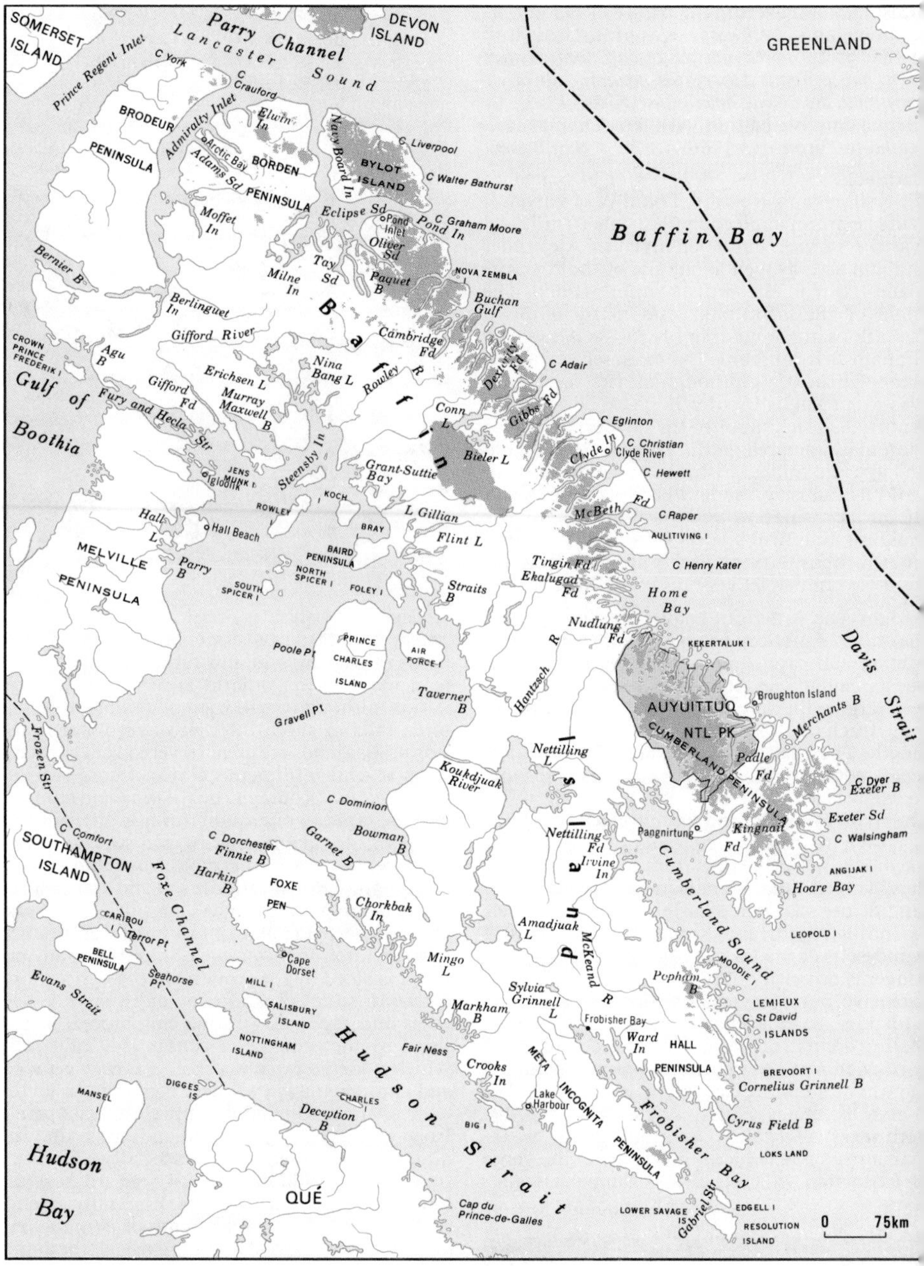

Community of Pond Inlet, located on NE Baffin Island, NWT, the largest island in Canada and the 5th largest in the world (*photo by Stephen J. Krasemann/DRK Photo*).

to the sea on the W coast. There are numerous freshwater lakes on the island, including NETTILING (5543 km²) and AMADJUAK (3116 km²). Baffin Bay is the wintering ground for narwhal, walrus, beluga, bowhead whales and bearded harp seals. The island is the nesting ground for millions of birds: thick-billed murres, kittiwakes and fulmars. A sanctuary at Cape Dorset protects eiders, guillemots, gulls, buntings, water pipits and redpolls.

The Dorset people likely settled around Cumberland Pen about 1500 years ago. In the 12th and 13th centuries the THULE spread over the island (*see* BAFFIN ISLAND INUIT). It was probably visited by NORSE seafarers in the 10th and 11th centuries, and is likely the Helluland of the Viking sagas. Martin FROBISHER reached the island in 1576 and made 2 more voyages (1577 and 1578), carting back loads of worthless ore he thought was gold. John DAVIS explored Cumberland Sound (1585-87); William BAFFIN, for whom the island is named, charted the E coast 1616; and Luke FOX penetrated Foxe Channel 1631. But the island's bays and fjords continued to perplex navigators seeking a NORTHWEST PASSAGE, and Baffin Bay was not rediscovered until 1818. W.E. PARRY explored the W coast 1821-23, followed by Scottish and New England whalers, who established shore stations around Cumberland Sound. Sailors' graves and relics of the WHALING, which lasted until the early 20th century, have been uncovered at Kivitoo on the Davis Coast. German scientists built a meteorological station on Cumberland Sound 1882-83. Franz BOAS wintered at Kekertuk 1884 and was able to sketch a reasonably accurate map of the whole island. J.E. BERNIER wintered at Pond Inlet (1906-07) and Arctic Bay (1910-11), and from the latter base J.E. Lavoie traced the coastline from Admiralty Inlet to Fury and Hecla Str. The whaling stations at Kekerton and Blackhead I were the first European settlements. The Anglican Church set up missions at the stations and the HBC established its first post on the island at Lake Harbour (1911). Today the largest settlement is Frobisher Bay (pop 2333, 1981c). Significant quantities of lead, zinc and silver are mined at Nanisivik and shipped to smelters in southern Canada. The hamlet of Pangnirtung is the southern gateway to AUYUITTUQ NATIONAL PARK (21 500 km²), Canada's first national park N of the Arctic Circle. The park contains some of the island's most spectacular scenery, including Pangnirtung Pass — a 100 km U-shaped trench — glaciers, lakes, waterfalls and the 2200 m peak, Mt Odin. JAMES MARSH

Baffin Island Inuit occupy BAFFIN I, the largest island in the ARCTIC ARCHIPELAGO, and they display considerable regional diversity in both dialect and culture. Those in the extreme N belong to the IGLULIK INUIT, who also live on the mainland. The remaining groups, often lumped together and referred to as the Inuit of S Baffin Island, are concentrated along the rugged E coast, including Cumberland Sound and Frobisher Bay, and along the N shore of Hudson Strait. The latter share many cultural traits with the LABRADOR INUIT on the other side of Hudson Strait, which was frequently crossed for trading purposes. The Inuit of Baffin I became known to the outside world as early as 1576, when Martin FROBISHER met and fought with some of them in the bay which now bears his name. Throughout the 18th and early 19th centuries Inuit along the S coast had occasional trade contacts with European exploration and supply vessels that stopped briefly on their way through to Hudson Bay. Farther N, the Inuit of Davis Strait did not encounter outsiders in any numbers until after 1820, when Scottish and American whalers started making annual visits to Baffin I through the heavy drift ice of western Baffin Bay. Inuit material culture was greatly modified by the increased flow of trade goods, including firearms, and by the large supply of wood provided by frequent shipwrecks. Contact with Europeans increased during the late 19th century when whalers started to establish permanent shore stations. Although the Inuit may have welcomed regular trade and occasional employment, it is thought that their population declined rapidly because of dietary changes and exposure to European diseases.

After the decline of commercial whaling in the early 20th century, the Inuit of Baffin I turned increasingly to fox trapping in order to satisfy their dependence on European manufacturers. Since the 1950s the Inuit have become much more sedentary, moving into modern communities such as FROBISHER BAY, the transportation hub and largest settlement on the island. One of the best-known communities on Baffin Island is CAPE DORSET, now recognized around the world for the outstanding soapstone carvings, prints and drawings of its Inuit artists. *See also* NATIVE PEOPLES, ARCTIC. J. GARTH TAYLOR

Reading: Peter Pitseolak and Dorothy Eber, *People From Our Side: An Inuit Record of Seekooseelak* (1975).

Baggattaway, *see* LACROSSE.

Bagot, Sir Charles, governor general of British N America 1841-43 (b at Ruguley, Eng 23 Sept 1781; d at Kingston, Canada W 19 May 1843). Educated at Rugby and Oxford, he was elected to the British Parliament in 1807. He served as undersecretary of state for foreign affairs and successively as minister to France and to the US, as well as ambassador to Russia and to The Netherlands. In 1817 he negotiated with the American secretary of state, Richard Rush, an agreement providing for disarmament on the Great Lks and Lk Champlain (RUSH-BAGOT AGREEMENT).

In Jan 1842 Sir Charles arrived in Kingston as governor general of Canada. By September it was apparent that the administration of his predecessor, Lord SYDENHAM, was about to lose the confidence of the majority in the assembly. Bagot invited the French Canadian leader, Louis-Hippolyte LAFONTAINE, to join the Executive Council, which he did along with Robert BALDWIN. Although Bagot had not fully conceded the principle of RESPONSIBLE GOVERNMENT, his invitation to La Fontaine was not fully approved in London, and his policy was repudiated by his successor, Sir Charles METCALFE.

Although for many months before his death Bagot was bedridden and unable to play an active part in government, he was severely criticized by Tory leaders. However, his popularity among Reformers, especially French Canadians, remained strong. It was aided by his fluency in French, his charm as a speaker and his great gift for diplomacy in politics. His wife, Lady Mary Wellesley-Pole, a niece of the Duke of Wellington, was very popular in the social circles of Kingston and Québec. JACQUES MONET, SJ

Reading: J.M.S. Careless, *The Union of the Canadas* (1967); Jacques Monet, *The Last Cannon Shot* (1969).

Bagshaw, Elizabeth Catherine, physician (b near Cannington, Ont 18 Oct 1881; d at Hamilton, Ont 5 Jan 1982). One of Canada's first woman doctors (MB, U of T 1905), she had a successful 60-year practice but is best known for her 30 years as medical director of the Hamilton Birth Control Clinic. Cheerful and courageous, she accepted the post in 1932 despite opposition from medical colleagues and local clergy, and worked with dedicated volunteers to provide Hamilton women with inexpensive and reliable contraceptives. She received numerous honours throughout her long life, including an honorary doctorate from McMaster.

DIANNE DODD

Baha'i Faith, a world religion with followers in 340 countries and territories, and with 132 National Spiritual Assemblies. The 1981 census shows 7955 Baha'is in Canada. Although its forerunner, the Babi movement, had its roots in Shi'ah IRAN, the Baha'i faith is independent rather than a sect of another religion, and derives its inspiration from its own sacred scriptures. These consist primarily of the writings of the founder, Baha'u'llah (1817-92), who Baha'is believe is the Messenger of God to our age, the most recent in a line stretching back beyond recorded time and including Abraham, Moses, Buddha, Christ and Muhammad. The central teaching of Baha'u'llah is that mankind is one human race, and that the age for the unification of this race in a global society has arrived. Among the principles of justice on which it is based are equality of the sexes, the right of all people to education, the abolition of all forms of prejudice and the need for the establishment of a world government with its own PEACEKEEPING force.

Baha'is believe that all great religions of the past have been stages in the progressive revelation of what Baha'u'llah called "the changeless Faith of God." God himself is unknowable. From age to age he reveals himself through his messengers, whose lives and teachings reflect God's qualities. These successive revelations provide the chief impulse in the evolution of all civilization. Other messengers will follow Baha'u'llah so long as the universe exists, but the challenge of the next thousand years will be to realize Baha'u'llah's vision of world unity. For the individual, the purpose of life is to know and worship God. This lifelong process occurs as the individual learns to serve mankind and in the process develops his own spiritual, moral and intellectual capacities. Prayer, meditation on the creative Word and the discipline of one's physical nature are necessary aids to this effort. The soul is immortal and continues to evolve after death.

The Baha'i Faith began in 1844 in Persia [Iran], with the announcement of the new age by Baha'u'llah's forerunner, known as the Bab ("The Door"). The Bab (1819-50) and some 20 000 early Persian followers, regarded as heretics, were persecuted and killed, and in 1868 Baha'u'llah was exiled to the Turkish penal fortress of Akko, on the bay of Haifa in present-day Israel. The shrines where the Bab and Baha'u'llah lie buried are today the focal points of a vast complex of gardens and institutions. By 1983 over 2000 ethnic groups were represented in the 120 000 Baha'i centres established worldwide. At that time Baha'is in Iran who refused to recant their faith were subject to punishment under the regime of the Ayatollah Khomeini.

Baha'is have no clergy. The affairs of the community are governed by democratically elected councils locally, nationally and internationally. At the lower 2 levels the councils, known as Spiritual Assemblies, are elected each year. The supreme governing body, the Universal House of Justice, whose seat is at the faith's world headquarters on Mount Carmel, Haifa, is elected every 5 years. Because of its beliefs, the Baha'i Faith has placed great importance on co-operation with all efforts toward world unity. The body which represents it in international affairs, the Baha'i International Community, holds consultative status as one of the nongovernmental organizations at the UNITED NATIONS, and takes an active part in the UN's many humanitarian and educational activities.

Baha'i Faith in Canada Canada has played an unusually important role in Baha'i history. After a brief visit here in 1912 the founder's son, Abdu'l-Baha, gave US and Canadian believers joint responsibility for expansion of the Baha'i Faith around the world. Canadian Baha'is responded enthusiastically, and today their community shoulders the second-largest burden of responsibilities for international activities. Two

Québec architects, Jean-Baptiste Louis Bourgeois and William Sutherland Maxwell, designed the 2 most important of the many shrines and houses of worship erected by Baha'is: the first House of Worship in the western world, Chicago, Ill, and the Shrine of the Bab on Mt Carmel in Haifa. One of the community's members, W.S. Maxwell's daughter Mary, in 1937 married the great-grandson of the founder of the Baha'i Faith, Shoghi Effendi Rabbani, who served in the central role of Guardianship until his death in 1957.

Canadian Baha'is work in countless community-development projects undertaken by their faith around the world, and their National Assembly collaborates with the CANADIAN INTERNATIONAL DEVELOPMENT AGENCY on a range of such activities. The Canadian community pioneered the concept of an international organization for Baha'i studies to bring together scholars and students in an application of Baha'i principles to various social concerns. The Association for Baha'i Studies, fd 1977, has its headquarters in Ottawa.

The faith has attracted members from all Canadian provinces and territories and from every ethnic group and social class. Some 60 of the faith's 350 elected Local Spiritual Assemblies are on Indian reserves and others, with Inuit members, are in remote Arctic centres. The Canadian National Spiritual Assembly was the first Baha'i institution in the world to be incorporated formally by a special Act of a sovereign parliament, an example since followed in many other countries. The Baha'i National Centre is located in Thornhill, Ont, and the former Maxwell home in Montréal is maintained as a Baha'i place of PILGRIMAGE. J. DOUGLAS MARTIN

Baie-Comeau, Qué, Town, pop 12 866 (1981c), inc 1937, is located on the N shore of the St Lawrence R, at the mouth of the Rivière MANICOUAGAN, about 420 km NE of Québec City. At the start of the 20th century, the area was still a huge hunting and fishing land of the MONTAGNAIS-NASKAPI, completely isolated and without transportation routes. Its geographic advantages (deep bay, neighbouring rivers with strong flows, huge forestry resources) led Col Robert R. McCormick, publisher of the Chicago *Tribune*, to build a paper mill and create a town in 1936. It took the name of Napoléon-Alexandre Comeau, a celebrated N-shore naturalist. During the 1950s, Baie-Comeau grew rapidly: the Quebec North Shore Paper Co enlarged and renovated its paper factory, a huge aluminum company (Reynolds) came in 1958 and grain silos (Cargill Grain Co) in 1960. The economic growth of the town and region was stimulated by the 1960 construction of a 448 km highway linking N-shore towns and the 1959-79 harnessing of the hydroelectric potential of the Outardes and Manicouagan rivers. The Manic-Outardes complex built by HYDRO-QUÉBEC supplies Québec City's electricity. The Daniel Johnson Dam (Manic 5), 210 km N of Baie-Comeau, is one of the world's largest. Baie-Comeau is also endowed with a deepwater sea port. An historical museum houses a collection of native artifacts. Baie-Comeau is the birthplace of Brian MULRONEY, prime minister of Canada, 1984- .
CLAUDINE PIERRE-DESCHÊNES

Baie des Chaleurs Scandal In 1890-91, when only about 100 km of the 320 km Baie des Chaleurs Railway had been built, serious questions arose about relations between the contractors and the sponsoring governments. The railway had received subsidies from both federal and Québec Liberal governments, and on 4 Aug 1891 the Conservatives launched a Senate inquiry. It turned out that the Québec government had been bribed with its own railway subsidy, the money probably having been used to pay off election expenses. A royal commission was established by the province, and the dismissal of Honoré MERCIER's government followed on 16 Dec 1891. P.B. WAITE

Bailey, Alfred Goldsworthy, poet, historian, man of letters (b at Québec City 18 Mar 1905). Bailey was educated at UNB, U of T and the London School of Economics. His life has been directed towards scholarship, and he is best known for *The Conflict of European and Eastern Algonkian Cultures, 1504-1700: A Study in Canadian Civilization* (1937). Bailey's first collection of verse, *Songs of the Saguenay* (1927), was privately issued at Québec, and shows him as a young but rather traditional craftsman. In 1952 appeared a second collection, *Border River*. Here poetry is more modern in tone and freer in form. His collected poems, *Miramichi Lightning* (1981), shows the closing of the circle of Bailey's growth and development as a poet. From conservative beginnings he has evolved into a contemporary voice that echoes the surrounding reality and keeps its intellectual spirit in play. In 1972 Bailey published a collection of his essays, *Culture and Nationality*, which gives a measure of his role as cultural historian. MICHAEL GNAROWSKI

Bailey, Loring Woart, geologist, educator (b at West Point, NY 28 Sept 1839; d at Fredericton 10 Jan 1925). Son of a professor at the US Military Academy, Bailey was educated at Harvard and Brown and knew many important scientists. At UNB he taught chemistry and natural science 1861-1900 and biology and geology 1900-07. Bailey pursued interests in geology, biology, anthropology and applied physics. In 1863 and 1864, accompanied by G.F. Matthew and C.F. Hartt, he undertook mineralogical and geological surveys of NB. They discovered the Silurian (Cambrian) age of the rock formations, not Precambrian as had been believed, and laid the foundations for elucidating the entire geological region, including New England. From 1868 Bailey contributed summer fieldwork to the Geological Survey of Canada. A RSC charter member (1882), he retired as professor in 1907; then as a member of the Biological Board he continued his earlier researches on Canadian diatoms. SUZANNE ZELLER

Reading: M. Zaslow, *Reading the Rocks* (1975).

Bailiff, sheriff's deputy employed for execution of judgements (eg, seizure of judgement debtor's goods, repossession of chattels, and evictions); also, officer of the court having custody of prisoners under arraignment. Individuals may be appointed to carry on business as bailiffs in counties where they are needed for the public convenience. K.G. MCSHANE

Baillairgé Family, architects, sculptors and painters active in Québec for 5 generations until well into the 20th century, the most prominent of whom are Jean, François, Thomas and Charles.

Baillairgé, Jean, master carpenter, joiner, sculptor, architect (bap at Blanzay, France 31 Oct 1726; d at Québec C and buried 6 Sept 1805). Brought to New France in 1741 by Bishop Pontbriand, Jean Baillairgé possessed technical competence in carpentry and joinery as well as a rudimentary grasp of French academic classicism. For 60 years he executed and occasionally designed woodwork for shops, houses, public and religious buildings. Of particular note was the interior sculpture for churches in and around Québec, especially the pulpit, churchwardens' pew and steeple (1768) and retable (1786-93, with his son) for Notre-Dame cathedral in Québec. A man "stern in matters of religion, duty and authority" but "cheerful in character," he fought in the militia of New France in 1759 and with the British garrison against the American invasion in 1775-76. He fostered a love of the building arts among his contemporaries and founded a dynasty of architects, sculptors and painters.

Baillairgé, François, sculptor, architect, painter, city treasurer (b at Québec C 21 Jan 1759, d there 15 Sept 1830). François Baillairgé surpassed his father Jean in the quality of his craftsmanship, especially ornamental sculpture At a time when Québec was cut off from the mother country, he renewed contact with the French classical principles of the Louis XVI period. Recognizing François's talents early, Jean and the Séminaire de Québec sent him to study in Paris 1778-81 at the Académie royale de peinture et de sculpture. On his return, François produced altarpieces and retables for many parish churches as well as large religious canvases, ships' figureheads and fanciful works such as the coat of arms for the duke of Kent's carriage. Working first with his father and later with his son, François excelled in the design and execution of richly carved and classically inspired church interiors. Among the best are those at L'Islet (1782-86), St-Ambroise de la Jeune Lorette (1810-16), St-Joachim at Montmorency (1816-29) and Baie St-Paul (1818-28). To François can be attributed the introduction of the baldaquin and the Louis XVI domed tabernacle to Québec altarpieces.

His academic training is evident in the classes he offered in painting, sculpture and mathematics, as well as his application of theoretical knowledge found in the architectural treatises he had purchased in France. He consciously used principles from the 1568 book by Philibert de L'Orme, that French interpreter of Italian Renaissance taste, in his solutions for the tabernacle of Notre-Dame cathedral in Québec and the façade of the Québec prison (1808-14). With his son Thomas and Abbé Jérôme DEMERS, François Baillairgé set the stage for the full flowering of Québec academic neoclassicism.

Baillairgé, Thomas, architect, sculptor, painter (b at Québec C 20 Dec 1791; d there 9 Feb 1859). Thomas drew on the architectural inheritance of his father François and grandfather Jean to bring architecture of the Québec church to its most perfect form. His practice witnessed the gradual shift from execution to design. He collaborated closely with Abbé Jérôme Demers, who attempted to set down the rules and guidelines for architectural design and practice in his *Précis d'architecture* (1828). This course outline on architecture, supplemented by Thomas's plates and carved models of the classical orders, is the first architectural treatise written in Canada.

Thomas Baillairgé synthesized his Renaissance inheritance with a blend of French and English neoclassicism to produce a series of harmonious and monumental church designs. Both the striking 3-dimensional interior at St-Joachim in Montmorency (1816-29) and the twin-towered churches exemplified by the façade design for Notre-Dame cathedral in Québec (1843), Ste-Geneviève de Pierrefonds (1844) and St-Roch de Québec (1845) reveal his ability to capture the spirit of classicism by the rigorous integration of all design elements into a unified ensemble.

True to family tradition, he maintained a professional practice, training apprentices in architecture and sculpture and certifying their competency after 3 years' practical work, formal classes and reading in his splendid library. An affable, music-loving bachelor, he often entertained the French Canadian elite at social evenings where discussions ranged from politics to science and history. The greatest church architect of French Canada, he influenced religious architecture for almost a century.

Baillairgé, Charles, architect, civil engineer, surveyor, mathematician, inventor, writer (b at Québec C 29 Sept 1826; d at Québec C 10 May 1906). Member of the fourth generation of this rchitectural dynasty, he broke with the classi-al tradition of his forebears to become an ec-ectic designer well-versed in the technological hanges and stylistic diversity of his own era. pprenticed to his father's cousin Thomas, harles qualified as an architect, civil engineer nd provincial land surveyor by age 22. The ransition from craftsman to designer was then omplete, for Charles, unlike the previous Bail-airgés, did not execute his own work. An am-itious and intellectually curious individual, he uickly put aside the neo-classicism of his entor to produce unusual and innovative uildings. Two of the earliest, a Gothic Revival hapel with triple balconies for the Sisters of harity (1850-54) and the Bilodeau shop with m high Doric columns and interior floating ezzanine (1849-50), startled architecturally onservative Québec.

During the 1850s he secured important com-issions including the Québec Music Hall 851-53), U Laval (1854-57), the church at Ste-Marie de Beauce (1854-60) and the Québec rison (1860-63). Such was his reputation that e was called to Ottawa in 1863 to supervise the ARLIAMENT BUILDINGS and departmental build-ngs. His private ambition to transform his ppointment as associate architect into the po-ition of chief architect of public works was uined by the corruption that he encountered at ttawa. Instructed to prepare evidence against ne contractors, Charles Baillairgé was abruptly ismissed so that his testimony could not be eard. He returned to Québec C where he re-laced his father as city engineer, a post he oc-upied 1866-98.

An avid reader, Charles Baillairgé augmented rançois's and Thomas's architectural library y collecting a wide variety of books from Eng-nd, France, Belgium and the US. He himself rote extensively in both English and French n architecture, engineering, language and ma-hematics. His Stereometrical Tableau, a mathe-atical formula for measuring volumes, won im international recognition. His love of study nd mechanical bent of mind led him to invent steam-propelled automobile at age 17, an lectro-chromatic rotating fountain and an iron iffel Tower for London. Restless and hard-vorking, Charles Baillairgé designed over 180 uildings, wrote more than 250 books and arti-les, and fathered 20 children. His son William-uval succeeded him as city engineer, thereby xtending the family's influence on the Québec uilding scene to the fifth generation.

CHRISTINA CAMERON

aillie, James Little, ornithologist, naturalist, vriter (b at Toronto 4 July 1904; d there 29 May 970). Employee of the Royal Ontario Museum or 48 years, Baillie's profession and avocation vere devoted to the study and interpretation of rnithology. At his death, he was assistant cura-or of ornithology at the ROM. He had also been egistrar, cataloguer and custodian of the mu-eum's ornithological collections. His activities nd accomplishments in his field were innu-erable. He served on the Council of the Ameri-an Ornithologists' Union; acted as secretary-reasurer of the Canadian Audubon Soc; was a ounding member of the Toronto Ornithological lub; was president of the Toronto Field Natu-alists; for 29 years wrote a weekly bird column n the *Toronto Telegram;* and lectured on orni-hology at U of T. Baillie wrote many papers n ornithology published by the ROM. He also ompiled volumes of data on N American natu-alists now at U of T. The Toronto Field Natural-sts' Club acquired 36 hectares of land near xbridge, Ont, for the Jim Baillie Nature Re-erve.

G. BENNETT

aillie, Thomas, soldier, administrator (b at lanwell, Eng 4 Oct 1796; d at Boulogne, France 0 May 1863). After a stint in the British infan-try, Baillie secured an appointment as commis-sioner of crown lands and surveyor general of NB in 1824, and for 2 decades he was at the cen-tre of controversy in that province. Required to collect taxes from the expanding TIMBER TRADE, Baillie gave wide powers to loosely controlled subordinates in enforcing what were regarded as tyrannical regulations. Arrogant and osten-tatious, he soon antagonized local politicians and timber traders. He even circumvented the governors and came to be seen as representing all that was wrong with the colonial system. Eventually the united effort of his opponents forced the British to curtail his powers in 1837. Undaunted, Baillie continued to fight for ex-ecutive control of development. Personal bank-ruptcy in 1839 should have finished him, but he recovered, was elected to the Assembly in 1846, and became a member of the Executive Council. Compelled to resign in 1848, he remained sur-veyor general until 1851 when he retired to Eng-land.

CARL M. WALLACE

Baillif, Claude, builder/architect (b *c*1635; d in the West Indies 1698 or 1699). The SÉMINAIRE DE QUÉBEC hired Baillif, a Parisian, as a stonecutter for 3 years and he arrived in Canada Sept 1675. After 1678 he was a building contractor for walls, houses, churches, gun batteries, a cathe-dral tower and the bishop's palace. For colonial craftsmen, versatility was essential for survival. Baillif's designs were guided by books on civil and military architecture. He had 2 partners 1682-83, then worked independently, employ-ing subcontractors and his own journeymen or apprentices. This builder and his wife had only a small home and little in movable effects. He carried 2667 *livres,* however, when he sailed for France Oct 1698. After a shipwreck in the Caribbean, Baillif died on another vessel off St Martin.

PETER N. MOOGK

Reading: Alan Gowans, *Church Architecture in New France* (1955).

Bait Acts During the early 1880s the New-foundland salt-fish trade was in trouble as the product's market value declined. A principal cause was increased competition from Norwe-gian and French fishermen, the latter heavily subsidized by the French government. Although Newfoundland could not affect the Norwegian fishery, the local government felt it could in-fluence the French. The GRAND BANKS fishery was the largest French operation in Newfound-land waters, requiring fresh bait generally pur-chased from Newfoundland fishermen on the S coast. The government that took office in 1885 decided to use bait as a lever to reduce French competition in foreign markets by prohibiting the sale of bait to French fishermen if subsi-dization continued. The first Bait Act was intro-duced in 1886, but Britain refused to give the necessary assent until it was modified in 1887. This Act and subsequent variations did not noticeably curtail the French, who found alter-native supplies. During the 1890s and the early 20th century, Newfoundland tried to use Bait Act provisions to control the sale of bait to both Canadian and American fishermen. The Acts did not solve Newfoundland's economic problems, and the colony returned to seeking solutions in railway development and industri-alization. *See* FISHERIES HISTORY.

SHANNON RYAN

Baker, Carroll, singer, songwriter (b at Bridge-water, NS 4 Mar 1949). Baker's electric per-formance of Conway Twitty's "I've Never Been This Far Before," on the 1976 Juno Awards tele-cast established her as a talent to be reckoned with. Performing since age 4, at 16 she moved to Ontario and by the time she was 19 she had started to sing with country bands. After meet-ing country manager Don Grashey, she started on a professional career, recording first for Grashey's Gaiety label (1971-75) then for RCA Records (1976-82). Throughout the late 1970s she had a string of hit records. She dominated the Big Country Awards and won the Juno in 1976, 1977 and 1978 as top female country singer. In 1983, in an effort to establish her ca-reer in the US, she left RCA and signed with Tembo Records.

RICHARD GREEN

Baker Lake, NWT, Hamlet, pop 954 (1981c), is situated 946 km NE of Yellowknife. It is 160 km E of the TREELINE, at the NW end of Baker Lk (1888 km^2), and is approximately at the geo-graphic centre of Canada. The only inland Inuit community in the NWT, its people, the CARIBOU INUIT, have evolved a life-style dependent on caribou and fish of the interior rather than on the sea mammals that sustain other Inuit groups. The community developed rapidly after WWII, when it was an advance base for the Canadian Army's "Operation Muskox" snow-mobile expedition. In the late 1970s the hamlet made national headlines in a landmark aborigi-nal-rights court case, when its residents con-tested the right of companies to mine URANIUM in the area. Although the majority Inuit popu-lation still subsists on traditional hunting and carving activities, today the community has a hotel, arts and crafts centre, general store and airstrip.

ANNELIES POOL

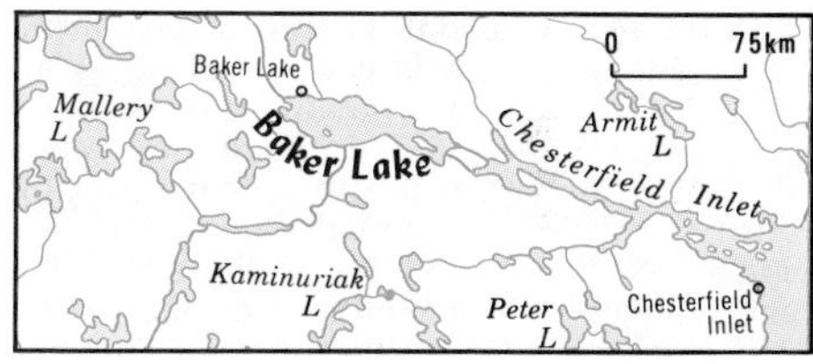

Baking Industry The Canadian baking indus-try consists of companies that manufacture bread, cakes, pastries and similar perishable bakery products. MANUFACTURING of breadlike products goes back to antiquity, but the first known production of leavened bread occurred in Egypt after the process of fermentation was discovered about 4000 years ago. Modern breads only began appearing a little over 100 years ago. In early Canada, bread was produced in the home. As communities appeared, small bakeries were established to supply village needs; some of these bakeries gradually evolved into today's major commercial baking establishments. It has been estimated that in 1900 only 8% of Cana-dian housewives bought bread; by the early 1960s, more than 95% of homemakers regularly purchased bread and the bulk of their bakery requirements from commercial bakeries.

The Canadian baking industry has a sound reputation for product improvement. For exam-ple, during WWII government concern about the lack of iron in the diets of some Canadians led to the decision to add iron to the bread sup-ply. Canada became one of the first countries to adopt this standard. Then, in 1953, the Cana-dian industry introduced vitamin-enriched bread. Bread proved to be the ideal food to de-liver extra, necessary vitamins such as thia-mine, riboflavin and niacin to consumers.

During the last 40 years, dramatic changes have occurred in the baking industry. There has been a steady decline in the number of commer-cial baking operations: in 1939 the number of producing baking plants was reported at 3231; by 1961, there were 2600; by 1973, 1690; and by 1981, 1431. Modern technology has led to in-creasingly larger and more sophisticated pro-duction operations, which in turn have created excess production capacity in many parts of the country. At the same time, road and rail im-provements have increased distribution capabil-ity. Finally, efficient, new packaging systems and materials have greatly extended the "shelf life" of many bakery products. Thus, a modern wholesale baking company can easily supply many products to markets 500 miles from a central plant base. Consequently, smaller regional plants have been phased out.

Published statistics on the baking industry include only the production from commercial or wholesale baking operations, ie, the output of the major Canadian baking companies. The statistics exclude the production of small local bakers, that of institutional baking facilities (eg, hotels, restaurants) and that of franchised bakeries and in-store bakeries of chain stores. In short, published information on the Canadian baking industry is understated. For example, it is estimated that there are 1000-2000 in-store bakeries in operation and that, at a minimum, each produces and sells nearly 3000 kg of bread a week.

As is the case with all other sectors of the FOOD AND BEVERAGE INDUSTRY, the baking sector must comply with a great many federal, provincial and municipal government regulations (*see* FOOD LEGISLATION). For example, packaging guidelines have been established by Consumer and Corporate Affairs Canada; the Health Protection Branch of Health and Welfare Canada is concerned with plant sanitation and related subjects. At the national level the industry is represented by the Bakery Council of Canada in Toronto.

Of the 1431 wholesale baking establishments in Canada in 1981, Nfld had 11; PEI, 4; NS, 42; NB, 27; Qué, 423; Ont, 452; Man, 76; Sask, 61; Alta, 130; BC, 204; and the YT and the NWT, 1. In 1973, with 1690 plants in operation, the industry achieved an annual value of factory shipments of about $598.4 million. Materials and supplies for bread and related bakery products cost over $259 million. Cost of fuel and electricity was $11.9 million. At that time the industry employed more than 28 000 workers. By 1981, although the industry was operating 259 fewer production units than in 1973, its sales reached about $1.36 billion. Materials and supplies cost $613 million in that year; fuel and electricity, $37 million. Employment had declined to 26 347 workers. ROBERT F. BARRATT

Balaklava Island, 8 km^2, situated off the N coast of VANCOUVER I, is located between Nigei and Hurst islands, and is flanked by Queen Charlotte Str in the N and Goletas Channel in the S. It is 15 km NW of PORT HARDY, BC. This tiny island has a lighthouse at Scarlett Pt (1905) to aid shipping. It was named after the Battle of Balaklava (Crimean War) by Capt Pender of the *Beaver*. DAVID EVANS

Balance of Payments, an accounting statement of the economic transactions between residents and governments of 2 countries during a specified time, usually yearly or quarterly; also refers to the difference between receipts and payments in some category of international transactions, often merchandise trade or the current account. The balance of payments statement is based on double-entry bookkeeping in which each economic transaction gives rise to a credit and a debit. A credit shows a decrease in assets or an increase in liabilities, a debit the opposite. If residents of 2 countries bartered goods, for example, declining inventory of exported goods would constitute a credit, while an increasing inventory would constitute a debit. Residents are likely to be paid for their exports with an increase in a bank balance or an increase in the indebtedness of the foreign residents and decline of their own indebtedness. The increase in the bank balance and loans to foreign residents or the decrease in liabilities to the foreign residents would be debits that matched the credit created by the exported goods. When transactions without payment occur (eg, exports of personal gifts, unrequited foreign aid or remittances by immigrants to relatives at home), the debit side is recorded to

Balance of Payments Current Account

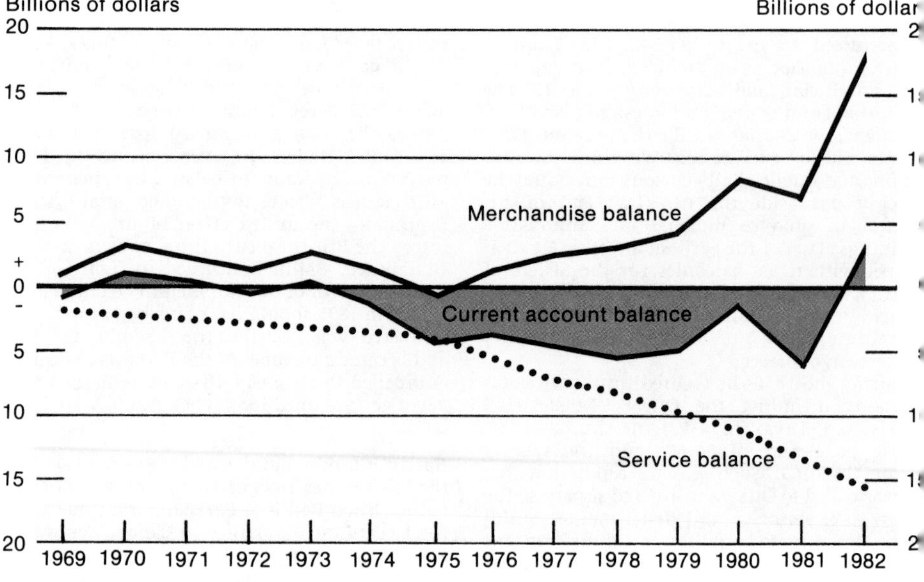

Source: Catalogue F1-21/1982E Dept. of Finance Canada.

maintain the equality of credits and debits. A difference between the sum of credits and debits can only occur for one category of transactions; because some transactions are incorrectly recorded and others are not recorded at all, a difference between recorded credits and debits arises which is offset by an arbitrary balancing entry entitled "errors and omissions." In Canadian statistics, credits are receipts (identified with a plus sign), debits are payments with a negative sign (excepting the Net Official Monetary Movements account).

Transactions in the Canadian balance of international payments comprise the current account, which records international transactions in goods and services and unilateral transfers (*see also* INTERNATIONAL TRADE); the capital account, which records international transactions in assets and liabilities; and official monetary movements, which record the federal government's stock of gold and foreign currencies resulting from its interventions in the market for foreign exchange. The most important current transactions are those for merchandise trade, eg, in 1980 exports accounted for 83% of current receipts and imports for 74% of current payments. Other current transactions are for services. In 1982 Canada's merchandise trade surplus rose to $17 billion from $7.4 billion in 1981. The current account may be in surplus by up to $3 billion — the first time since 1973 that there has been a surplus. The principal receipts of Canadian residents were for the provision of travel and freight services to foreign residents. Canadian residents also made payments to foreigners for travel and freight, but the largest nonmerchandise payments, in the form of interest and dividends, went to nonresidents for the use of their capital in Canada.

A country's purchases of goods and services from other countries need not equal its sales. Canada usually incurs more current payments than receipts. The current balance is financed by net borrowing or lending or by the purchase or sale of equity (capital that represents ownership). Canadian residents, including governments, are net debtors internationally. The capital account records the net international transactions in different types of assets. In 1980 there was a net inflow (receipt) of direct investment capital into Canada of $535 million. This net flow resulted from large gross flows in each direction comprising increases of ownership in Canadian enterprises by foreign residents who either established new firms or purchased exist ing Canadian-owned firms and of purchases b Canadians of interests of foreign residents i Canada. In 1980 Canadian residents made majc net direct investments in foreign countries, re sulting in a net outflow of $2.7 billion, 60% c which went to the US. (Canadian direct invest ment abroad was substantially greater than fo eign direct investment in Canada, but must b considered in relation to the size of the econo my.) Direct-investment transactions by both Ca nadian and foreign residents in Canada an abroad led to net payments on that capital item but were compensated for by the sum of portfo lio transactions, short-term investments (th purchase of shares and bonds for income or cap ital gains) and other capital movements. Th balance on capital account resulted in a net capi tal inflow (a decrease in the stock of assets hel by Canadians and therefore a credit or receipt) c $2.6 billion. In 1980 the surplus on capital ac count covered the recorded deficit of $1.5 billio on current account, but there was also an esti mated debit of $2.5 billion owing to errors an omissions, and therefore a deficit of over $1 bil lion. This overall deficit was covered by a credi or receipt of an official monetary movemen which reduced the government's assets by $1. billion. The sums of all credits and debits or al receipts and payments were, as required, equal.

MERCANTILIST policy, dominant until the en of the 18th century, advocated the developmen of a surplus of receipts over payments in a coun try's merchandise trade or on current accoun Foreign residents paid the surplus with gold o silver and therefore increased the stockpile c precious metals considered the measurement o a nation's wealth. International flows of pre cious metals were the only kind of capital trans action recognized at the time. This is the origi of the term "favourable" balance of payments t denote a surplus, and "unfavourable" to denot a deficit on merchandise or current accoun Other mercantilists believed that a surplus cre ated employment, and advocated policy t create a merchandise surplus for that reason. I 1752 the Scottish philosopher David Hume un dermined the theoretical basis of the mercan tilist balance-of-payments policy by explainin that a permanent surplus on current accoun was impossible to achieve, because the inflov of gold and silver necessary to finance it woul increase the money supply and so raise domesti prices, with a resulting increase in imports an ecrease in exports. The current-account deficit r surplus is basically determined by where eople choose to hold their assets; eg, when a ountry's residents decide to increase their holdngs in foreign bonds, the foreign currency eeded is obtained by selling more goods and ervices abroad than are bought, creating a urrent-account surplus. The currency finances ne net accumulation of capital assets from oreign sources — a capital-account deficit. According to modern Keynesian analysis, a urrent-account surplus stimulates employment ecause exports add more to earned incomes, nd therefore to domestic expenditures, than nports lose abroad. However, if one country atmpts to create a surplus, other countries may etaliate. Balance of payments is also viewed as means of distributing the world's capital reources. Residents in an area of high capital roductivity will import more goods and serices than they export and use that balance to uild up domestic productive capacity.

H.C. EASTMAN

aldoon, settlement fd 1804 for Highland SCOTS y the earl of SELKIRK on the swampy north hore of Lk St Clair on the Chenail Écarté R, pper Canada (near present-day Wallaceburg, nt). Selkirk chose the site on his 1803-04 tour f UC because of its isolation and its apparently rategic location, and named it after a recently old family estate in Scotland. He projected a rge sheep farm there. The first 102 settlers eached Lachine, Qué, on the *Oughton*, on 19 July 804, and travelled overland to Baldoon, only arrive during the annual malaria season. Many soon joined in sickbed members of the dvance party led by William Burn (who himlf succumbed). Sheriff Alexander MACDONELL, elkirk's agent, struggled for years at considrable expense to the earl to make a success of ne venture, but found the swampy land and ne difficulty of sheep farming to be serious obacles. Macdonell's problems, combined with ne UC authorities' lack of enthusiasm for Selirk's settlement schemes, encouraged Selkirk transfer his efforts to the RED RIVER COLONY. aldoon staggered on until the WAR OF 1812, hen the earl's farm was ravaged by the inading American army of Gen Isaac Hull. Alnough this spelled an end to the settlement, ome of the original Highlanders remained in ne area.

J.M. BUMSTED

aldwin, Frederick Walker, "Casey," aviator, nventor (b at Toronto 2 Jan 1882; d at Nearagh, NS 7 Aug 1948). He completed engineering udies at U of T. In 1907 he became a founding ember of the Aerial Experiment Assn with .G. BELL, J.A.D. MCCURDY and 2 Americans. After working on the design and construction of neir first aircraft, on 12 Mar 1908 he became the rst British subject to pilot an aircraft, at Hamnondsport, NY. He and McCurdy formed the anadian Aerodrome Co at Baddeck, NS, and onstructed 2 more aircraft. He also piloted the LVER DART on 12 Aug 1909. He developed methds of transmitting sound through water and erfected a hydrofoil. He was elected to the NS egislature in 1933.

JAMES MARSH

aldwin, Robert, lawyer, politician, office older (b at York [Toronto] 12 May 1804; d Yorkville [Toronto] 9 Dec 1858). The eldest on of William Warren BALDWIN was called to ne bar in 1825. Temperamentally and intellecually unlike his gifted father, the shy, introective Robert entered politics in 1829 as a eformer, winning a seat in the Assembly in a y- election. Defeated the following year he reed to private life. Melancholic, withdrawn, rtured by doubts and demons, his life and appiness revolved around his family and most specially his wife (they were married in 1827). er death on 11 Jan 1836 shattered him emotionally and may explain the severe depressive illness that plagued him in later years. Despite his grief and a profound distaste for public life he was impelled to accept office as an executive councillor the following month by his Christian sense of duty. The resignation in Mar 1836 of Baldwin and the other councillors over Lt-Gov Francis Bond HEAD's refusal to consult them plunged the colony into the gravest political and constitutional crisis prior to the REBELLION OF 1837. Baldwin remained neutral during the uprising but became the rallying figure in rebuilding the postrebellion Reform opposition and forging an alliance with L.H. LAFONTAINE's Lower Canadian liberals. Although not a natural politician or a towering intellect, Baldwin commanded respect and exercised moral leadership by reason of his character. In a preindustrial society that revered the code of gentlemen, he embodied the cherished virtues of adherence to honour, duty and principle. Each time he gained office he left it by resignation rather than compromise his principles. Solicitor general in Gov Gen Lord SYDENHAM's ministry and an executive councillor in 1841, Baldwin resigned that June when the governor refused to implement RESPONSIBLE GOVERNMENT. In the Assembly, Baldwin and LaFontaine steadily attracted members to the cause of responsible government until they had built a majority. They attained office in 1842-43 and again in 1848-51, the latter the so-called "Great Ministry." The first government was active and successful but a conflict with Governor METCALFE over his refusal to consult them on patronage led to their resignations in Nov 1843. During this, and the subsequent ministry Baldwin served as co-premier and attorney general (Upper Canada). In the second ministry his great accomplishments were the formal attainment of responsible government and its confirmation during the REBELLION LOSSES crisis of 1849, establishment of UNIVERSITY OF TORONTO, reform of the Upper Canadian judiciary, and establishment of an adequate system of municipal govenment in the upper province. Baldwin's hold on power was weakened, however, by a left-wing revolt in the party (by the CLEAR GRITS), his own deteriorating health, and differences over economic policy with Francis HINCKS. Discouraged and wracked by depression Baldwin resigned on 30 June 1851. Later that year he sought re-election but was defeated. The tormented figure withdrew to his home, to give himself over to the rituals of his preoccupation with his dead wife. As a man Baldwin was little understood or loved by contemporaries, or historians. He had failed to preserve the social order he sought to defend, but his reputation is secure as the popularizer of responsible government and one of the first, if not the first, proponents of a bicultural nation.

MICHAEL S. CROSS AND ROBERT L. FRASER

Reading: J.M.S. Careless, ed, *The Pre-Confederation Premiers* (1980); M.S. Cross and R.L. Fraser, "'The Waste that Lies Before Me': The Public and the Private Worlds of Robert Baldwin," *Historical Papers* (1983).

Baldwin, William Warren, doctor, lawyer, politician (b at Knockmore, Ire 25 Apr 1775; d at Toronto 8 Jan 1844). He arrived in Upper Canada in 1799, eventually settling at York [Toronto]. Urbane, talented, and in due course wealthy, Baldwin established a comfortable and distinguished law practice. His enduring reputation derives from his political activity. Although he served only 2 terms as an assemblyman he made a signal contribution to the cause of political reform and organization. Baldwin was an 18th-century man, an Irish whig who supported aristocracy, primogeniture, ministerial responsibility, and the civil and religious liberties of the British constitution. His great cause was RESPONSIBLE GOVERNMENT, that "the English principles of responsibility be applied to our local Executive Council." The fight was carried on by his eldest son Robert BALDWIN, whom he had instilled with a sense of providential mission. Baldwin was remembered by Charles Durrand as "a haughty, prejudiced, Protestant Irish gentleman . . . very rough and aristocratic in his ways."

ROBERT L. FRASER

Balfour, St. Clair, publisher (b at Hamilton, Ont 30 Apr 1910). Balfour is chairman of Southam Inc, one of Canada's largest newspaper chains. He attended Trinity College School and U of T. He served with distinction in the Royal Canadian Navy during WWII, winning a Distinguished Service Cross. In 1955 he became executive vice-president of Southam and in 1970 chairman. Balfour was instrumental in diversifying the company's interests into radio and TV.

J.L. GRANATSTEIN

Balfour Report, 1926, the conclusions of an Imperial Conference committee under the chairmanship of Lord Balfour, a British cabinet minister and former prime minister, on relations between the self-governing parts of the empire-COMMONWEALTH, a pivotal document in Canada's evolution to fully self-governing nationhood. The report declared that Britain and the Dominions of Canada, South Africa, Australia, New Zealand and the Irish Free State were "autonomous Communities within the British Empire, equal in status, in no way subordinate one to another in any aspect of their domestic or external affairs, though united by a common allegiance to the Crown, and freely associated as members of the British Commonwealth of Nations." Incorporated verbatim in the conference proceedings, the report led directly to the legislative recognition of dominion autonomy in the 1931 STATUTE OF WESTMINSTER.

NORMAN HILLMER

Ball Hockey is a fast, skilful sport, with leagues operating in all Canadian provinces. The game traces its ancestry to the simple stick-and-ball games of the Middle Ages. Ball hockey became popular in the 19th century, using some of the techniques of ice HOCKEY but replacing the puck with a tennis ball, and was played informally in streets or back alleys across Canada. With the invention, in 1969, of a hollow, no-bounce, plastic ball, ball hockey developed as a separate sport. The first organized league in Canada was formed in New Westminster, BC, in 1958, and the Canadian Ball Hockey Assn was founded in 1976. All ages participate, and games are played in hockey arenas, lacrosse boxes and gymnasia.

BARBARA SCHRODT

Ballard, Bristow Guy, research engineer (b at Fort Stewart, Ont 19 June 1902; d at Ottawa 22 Sept 1975). Ballard was educated at Queen's and worked for 5 years on Westinghouse high-speed electric locomotives before joining the NATIONAL RESEARCH COUNCIL staff in 1930. He became director of the Radio and Electrical Engineering Division in 1948, VP (scientific) in 1954, and president in 1963. His appointment as president took place in the last days of the DIEFENBAKER government, and Ballard told several friends he had neither wanted nor asked for the post, which he was reluctant to accept since his deafness had inhibited his making himself well known among Ottawa "mandarins." He had a clear aim, to stimulate Canadian ENGINEERING to catch up with Canadian science in its disciplinary development, but his attempts to achieve this were frustrated. In 1955, when he convened a conference of university deans of engineering to offer them the array of research grants and scholarships available to scientists, his proposals were rebuffed. When as NRC president he attempted to reorient the Council towards industrial engineering, he was overborne by the academics who then made up the majority of the Council. Ballard's policies were largely implemented by his successors, W.G. SCHNEIDER and Larkin KERWIN.

DONALD J.C. PHILLIPSON

Ballet, in strictest terms, is an artistically stylized form of theatrical dance based on a codified system of movement. Combined with music, sets and costumes it can be used to tell a story, evoke a mood, illustrate a piece of music or, simply, to provide a presentation of theatrical movement that is entertaining or intriguing in dance terms alone. Today, the word ballet is used more loosely to describe not only the classic academic dance with its well-defined technique but also more contemporary, free-ranging forms of theatrical dancing. Ballet, in its traditional form, has evolved from the early court entertainments of Renaissance Italy. These dances were brought to France by Italian masters in the 16th century. The *ballet de cour* (court ballet) developed from social dancing for the aristocracy to become elaborate, spectacular, and highly theatrical presentations used to demonstrate the wealth and power of French monarchs. The most notable was *Le Ballet comique de la Reine Louise*, mounted in Paris (1581) as part of 2 weeks of celebration marking an important royal marriage. The 5-hour performance was remarkable in offering a continuous dramatic narrative. Although these court dances continued, the development of ballet as a theatrical art gained momentum with the emergence of the popular opera-ballet in late 17th-century France. Dance interludes were placed between the vocal scenes. Ballet increasingly became a professional activity for trained dancers. The opera-ballet allowed little room for the independent development of ballet and in the 18th century, dance masters began to create dances which alone would carry a story.

The work of French choreographer and theorist Jean-Georges Noverre (1727-1810) was particularly influential in advancing the cause of the *ballet d'action*. His *Letters on Dancing and Ballets* (1760) rejected the subservient role of dancing within the tradition of the opera-ballet and strongly advocated the more dramatic style. This required a more expressive style of dancing than the rather formal dance movements of the opera-ballet. The *ballet d'action* had as its aim the establishment of dance as a discrete theatrical art. Passages of dancing continued to be included in operas but ballet slowly exerted the right to its own place in the theatre. *La Fille mal gardée* (1789) is among the earliest ballets from this period to have survived into our age, in an updated form.

The first half of the 19th century witnessed important developments in ballet. The Italian dancer, choreographer and teacher Carlo Blasis (1797-1878) wrote extensively about his theories of ballet and published an important codification of its technique. At the same time, European middle-class audiences flocked to see such famous ballerinas as Marie Taglioni, Fanny Elssler and Carlotta Grisi. Indeed, as the century progressed, the art of ballet in France and much of Europe came to be dominated by the ballerina, with male dancers taking a secondary role. Although the intellectual and aesthetic movement known as the Romantic Movement was slow to touch ballet, works such as *La Sylphide* (1832) and *Giselle* (1841) captured the public imagination and remain audience favourites even today. Ballet in France degenerated artistically during the latter part of the 19th century but thrived in Denmark under the brilliant ballet master August Bournonville (1805-79) and in Russia, where the French-born Marius Petipa created, among many others, such enduringly popular ballets as *The Sleeping Beauty* and *Swan Lake*.

A great Russian impresario, Serge Diaghilev, helped to restore the art of ballet in western Europe by bringing groups of Russian dancers to Paris and other leading capitals in the years before WWI. His excellently trained dancers performed exciting new works by such innovative choreographers as Vaslav Nijinsky (also a dancer of legendary gifts) and Mikhail Fokine. After the Russian Revolution of 1917, many important figures of the Russian ballet settled in Europe and N America, doing much to advance ballet wherever they went. Even after Diaghilev's premature death in 1929, groups of Russian dancers continued to make extensive tours of N America until the 1950s. Under Diaghilev's auspices, great artists, writers, composers and choreographers were brought together to create new works in which theme, steps, decor, costumes and music formed an authentic whole. This did much to fortify ballet's right to be considered a true theatrical art form, not just entertainment. Even as Diaghilev was helping to restore and rejuvenate ballet in the West, other very different forms of theatrical dance were being developed in Europe and N America. In large part these forms rejected what was perceived as the rigidity, and therefore artistic limitations, of traditional ballet. What came to be known as modern dance grew from a different set of ideas about movement and produced its own distinct type of dance theatre. In recent years, however, the boundaries that used to separate ballet from modern dance have been eroded. A process of cross-fertilization has seen a partial blending of techniques and styles. Choreographers of ballet now often draw on ideas and movements that find their origin in modern dance.

Ballet thus began its life in Europe and, until the middle of the 20th century, Canadians were generally spectators of the art. The French colonization of the St Lawrence Valley from the 17th century onwards saw the introduction of dance masters to Canada but their activities were directed mostly to teaching children of the rich. The real beginnings of professional ballet in Canada date from the 1930s, when such important teachers as Boris VOLKOFF in Toronto, Gwendolen Osborne in Ottawa, Gerald Crevier in Montréal, and June Roper in Vancouver began to produce dancers equipped to pursue professional careers. Without Canadian companies for them to dance in, however, these talented young artists had to find work abroad. Patricia Wilde from Ottawa and Melissa Hayden from Toronto are 2 outstanding examples. Both rose to international stardom dancing in American ballet companies. More than a decade later Lynn SEYMOUR, who was born in Alberta and initially trained in Vancouver, felt it necessary to pursue her career overseas, in England. As a dancer in the Royal Ballet she came to be hailed as one of the century's greatest dramatic dancers.

In 1938, however, 2 English ballet teachers, Gweneth LLOYD and Betty FARRALLY, established what later (1949) was to become Canada's first truly professional company, the Winnipeg Ballet. In Toronto, a distinguished British dancer and choreographer, Celia FRANCA, founded the NATIONAL BALLET OF CANADA (1951); and 7 years later Les GRANDS BALLETS CANADIENS was founded in Montréal by Ludmilla CHIRIAEFF. These major companies provide work for about 13[illegible] dancers. Each has developed its own identity. The ROYAL WINNIPEG BALLET has long been considered one of N America's most popular ballet troupes. The works it performs are selected to appeal to audiences without sacrificing artistic integrity. The dancers are notable for their extraordinary energy and obvious desire to perform always to the fullest extent of their capacities. The National Ballet, in contrast, has followed the traditions of the great European classical repertory companies and, although it has a large repertoire of one-act works, is particularly noted for its lavish, full-length productions of such ballets as *Swan Lake* and *The Sleeping Beauty*. Le

Karen Kain with Frank Augustyn dancing *Romeo and Juliet* (courtesy National Ballet Archives).

Grands Ballets Canadiens, like the Royal Winnipeg Ballet, has for the most part avoided costly productions of full-length story ballets with elaborate sets and costumes. The company has been particularly distinguished in recent years by its willingness to experiment with the work of new choreographers (many of them Canadian) and to include a number of works by leading modern-dance choreographers. The NATIONAL BALLET SCHOOL and the schools attached to the Royal Winnipeg Ballet and Les Grands Ballets Canadiens are leaders in the provision of professional training to young dancers. Despite its short history, ballet in Canada has established firm roots. Leading Canadian companies have toured overseas and Canadian dancers have won recognition at important international ballet competitions. For many years, concerned observers have regretted the apparent lack of good Canadian choreography and have sometimes blamed the large companies, particularly the National Ballet, for a lack of commitment to creativity. The shortage of first-rate ballet choreographers is, however, felt by companies around the world, and Canada has an increasing number of choreographers of proven worth who may help earn Canada its own special place in the world of ballet. MICHAEL CRABB

Ballets Jazz de Montréal, Les, is a dynamic dance company devoted to ballet-jazz, based on strong ballet technique and jazz music. The company was formed (1972) by Eva von Gencsy, Genevieve Salbaing, and Eddy Toussaint, with a nucleus of dancers from the dance school founded by Hungarian-born von Gencsy in Montréal in 1962. Today, that school, together with others in Québec City and Toronto, provides the major financial support for the company. In 1977, Salbaing took over complete artistic direction. Choreographers Brian MACDONALD, Rael Lamb, Lynne Taylor-Corbett, Buzz Miller and Herb Wilson have created original works for the company, which was also the first group to perform jazz works from the archives of New York's American Dance Machine company. Les Ballets Jazz has received critical acclaim throughout Canada and abroad.
CAROL BISHOP

Balloon, vehicle that can rise within Earth's atmosphere because its total weight is less than that of the air it displaces. This principle was first enunciated by Greek mathematician and inventor Archimedes. The necessary lift or buoyancy is obtained by filling an envelope with a gas lighter than air (eg, HYDROGEN, helium, heated air). The first manned balloon flight was made over Paris on 21 Nov 1783 by François Pilâtre de Rozier and the Marquis d'Arlandes in a gondola beneath a cloth and paper envelope, inflated by air heated by a fire hung below it. The balloon was constructed by the Montgolfier brothers. Ten days later, French scientist J.A.C. Charles and his assistant flew about 43 km suspended beneath a hydrogen-filled silk-and-rubber balloon, returning safely to Earth. This balloon incorporated many features of a modern gas-filled balloon, eg, an open-necked envelope allowing for gas expansion, a top-mounted gas-release valve and a supply of ballast for altitude control. Many significant flights followed, as ballooning developed military, sporting and scientific applications.

Early military use included tethered observation posts from which battles could be directed. Free balloons were used as somewhat unpredictable delivery systems for passengers, bombs and messages during long sieges. In WWI, bombing of civilian and military targets from airships changed the nature of warfare. Tethered barrage balloons protected strategic targets from low-level aircraft attack during WWII.

Launch of a modern scientific balloon and payload from Churchill, Man, under sponsorship of the National Research Council (*courtesy T.A. Clark*).

In this century, powered airships were used extensively for passenger transportation, until the *Hindenburg* disaster in 1937 demonstrated the danger of using highly flammable and explosive hydrogen as lift gas. Balloons are still used as heavy-lift vehicles in remote, inaccessible areas (eg, logging operations in BC forests). Modern variants of the airship are used as platforms for television cameras at sporting events. New designs, using the inert gas helium, are being tested in Canada for potential use as bulk-cargo carriers.

Balloon-flying has always had a sporting component, with rallies, races and long-duration flights catching the public imagination. In the 1960s, development of the modern hot-air balloon, with a strong, light nylon envelope inflated by hot air from a reliable propane burner, led to a resurgence of interest in the sport. The many long flights made in gas-filled balloons culminated in crossings of the Atlantic and Pacific oceans by American teams (1978 and 1981, respectively). So far, attempts to circumnavigate the globe in a free balloon have been unsuccessful.

In science, routine meteorological soundings (atmospheric temperature, moisture content, wind speed and direction) by small instrument packages on rubber balloons are an essential part of modern global WEATHER FORECASTING. The modern scientific balloon is a huge but extremely thin polyethylene envelope, reinforced with nylon tapes and inflated with helium. It can place instruments within the layers of interest for atmospheric studies or above absorbing and turbulent layers for astronomical observations. Balloon-borne instrumentation has led to advances in atmospheric POLLUTION studies, cosmic ray research, X-ray and infrared ASTRONOMY and high-resolution photography of astronomical sources, including the sun. X-ray measurements from smaller balloons during auroral displays have been important in unravelling the complex interactions of the solar wind with Earth's magnetic field, which cause the NORTHERN LIGHTS. In biology, balloons have often provided silent platforms for the observation of wild animals in their undisturbed habitat.

In Canada, ballooning is supported by the NATIONAL RESEARCH COUNCIL through the Canada Centre for Space Science and its Space Research Facility, Gimli, Man. A series of flights is launched each year from Gimli in support of university research programs. Several universities, particularly Calgary, Saskatchewan and York, have been active in astronomical, atmospheric and aeronomical research from balloons for many years. T.A. CLARK

Bancroft, Henry Hugh, organist, composer (b at Cleethorpes, Eng 29 Feb 1904). Educated in England, Bancroft arrived in Canada in 1929 to serve as organist-choirmaster at St Matthew's and All Saints' Anglican churches, Winnipeg, and later at Christ Church Cathedral, Vancouver. In 1948 he moved to Sydney, Australia. He returned to Winnipeg in 1953 and then moved to Nassau, Bahamas. In 1958 he became organist-choirmaster at All Saints' Cathedral, Edmonton, retiring in 1980. In 1977 he received the Lambeth degree from the Archbishop of Canterbury and in 1980 an honorary LlD from University of Alberta. ERIC J. HOLMGREN

Band, an *ad hoc* Canadian Indian political unit, which may be bound together by blood relationships and marriage bonds, even though membership and territorial limits are fluid. Local bands may number 50 persons and regional bands 200-500, but there is little co-operation in such activities as politics, religion and economics. The size, activities and membership of bands depends on fluctuations in the availability of hunting and gathering resources. The Canadian government recognizes 573 Indian bands whose social and territorial boundaries do not necessarily coincide with those of Indian people. *See also* INDIAN RESERVE; NATIVE PEOPLE, DEMOGRAPHY. RENÉ R. GADACZ

Band, The, internationally popular rock band (1968-76), began *c*1960 as the Hawks, backing "rockabilly" singer Ronnie HAWKINS in southern Ontario, and subsequently (as the Crackers) toured the world (1965-66) with Bob Dylan. The Band, based in the US, was known for musically kaleidoscopic albums and for such hits as "The Weight" and "Up on Cripple Creek." Canadian members were guitarist and songwriter Robbie Robertson, bassist Rick Danko, organist Garth Hudson, pianist Richard Manuel; drummer Levon Helm was born in Arkansas.
MARK MILLER

Banff, Alta, UP, pop 4208 (1981c), is located on the Bow R, 130 km W of Calgary. Founded 1883 in an attempt to eliminate a tunnel on the CPR main line, the first town, 3 km from present-day Banff, was known as Siding 29. Renamed 1883 for an ancient resort town in Scotland,

and relocated 3 years later, the new townsite grew to 300 residents that first year. Banff's development has always been determined by the federal government, tourism and the railway. In 1885 a national reserve, which in 1887 became BANFF NATIONAL PARK, was created around the town, spurring the most significant event in its history, the opening of Banff Springs Hotel, June 1888. Home to famous Albertans, such as Mary Schaffer Warren, Walter Phillips, Earle Birney, Carl Rungis, as well as Lt-Gov Brett, owner of the Park Sanitarium Hotel, Banff early established itself as one of Alberta's main cultural centres. This position was further evidenced by the establishment of the BANFF CENTRE SCHOOL OF FINE ARTS in 1933, and later the Whyte Museum of the Canadian Rockies, which comprises an archives, gallery and heritage collection. FRITS PANNEKOEK

Banff Centre School of Fine Arts began in 1933 as a special summer program sponsored by the U of Alberta's Division of Continuing Education and was intended to provide cultural enrichment for beginners and serious amateurs in drama, music and art. Under the able leadership of the first 2 directors, Donald Cameron and David Leighton, this school had evolved by the 1980s into a leading world centre for continued learning, serving advanced students and professionals with a year-round curriculum of depth and variety.

The Banff Centre is located in one of the choicest locations in N America, nestled on the side of Tunnel Mt and overlooking the ski resort of BANFF and the picturesque Banff Springs Hotel. It provides participants with the advantages of a wilderness setting, combined with highly developed modern facilities in the performing arts, visual arts and music. Over the years, a faculty of internationally recognized fine-arts instructors and a generous scholarship endowment have ensured the enrolment of a student body of well-demonstrated potential and competitive spirit.

Although diplomas are given for successful completion of the various specific programs offered, the basic concept of education at the Banff Centre differs, through insistence on independent research, from that found at most art schools, conservatories or university fine-arts graduate programs. The Centre assumes that the participant has already mastered the fundamentals of technique or craft and is seeking a fresh start as a mature and creative artist in a serene and vitalizing environment. J.R. STOCKING

Reading: D. Cameron, *Campus in the Clouds* (1956); D. and P. Leighton, *Artists, Builders and Dreamers* (1982).

Banff National Park (6640 km^2), Canada's first and most heavily visited national park, is located 125 km W of Calgary in the Rocky Mts, and stretches 240 km along the eastern slope of the Continental Divide. Originally set aside in 1885 to preserve sulphur hot springs for public use, Banff's blend of towering peaks and flower-strewn meadows makes it among Canada's most exhilarating holiday areas. The GLACIERS still clinging to upper mountain slopes have helped shape the park's landscape, creating numerous lakes, waterfalls and broad, U-shaped valleys. Forests of lodgepole pine, Engelmann spruce and alpine fir soften the flanks of the mountains and are home to many large mammals, including cougar, wolf, moose, elk, black bear and the awesome grizzly — the park's most formidable resident. Bighorn sheep, mule deer and other wildlife can often be seen alongside park roads. Campgrounds, resorts, alpine and cross-country skiing, and 1100 km of hiking trails radiate from BANFF townsite. LILLIAN STEWART

Banff National Park, showing Bow Valley, Mt Rundle and the Banff townsite viewed from Mt Norquay (*photo by Tom W. Parkin/Pathfinder*).

Bank Architecture Institutionalized banking came to British N America in 1820, when the Bank of New Brunswick at Saint John was granted a charter by the provincial government. In 1822 the BANK OF MONTREAL, in operation since 1817, was chartered by the Province of Lower Canada. By year's end, there were 5 chartered banks in the provinces; on the eve of Confederation there was a total of 28 in the provinces of Canada, NS and NB.

Because banks — both family businesses and those under government charter — competed for clients, they recognized the value of an architectural image that would attract customers. They adopted chiefly Greek and Roman architectural forms, which symbolized wealth, integrity, endurance and confidence. In 1818 the Bank of Montreal constructed a stolid 3-storey building on St James St, with a portico consisting of a classical pediment supported by Doric columns. The BANK OF UPPER CANADA on Toronto's Adelaide St (architect W.W. Baldwin, 1830) resembled a respectable London town house and featured a Doric portico.

As the century progressed, imposing institutional structures, predominantly in the classical revival styles, characterized most big-city banks.

Bank of Upper Canada, Toronto, built in 1830 and restored in 1982 (*photo ©1984 Hartill Art Associates*).

Montréal's St James St was the financial heart of Canada, where stood the Bank of Montreal headquarters (John Wells, 1846-48), Molson's Bank (George Browne, 1866) and the Merchants Bank (Hopkins and Wily, 1870). Smaller cities followed Montréal's lead; the Commercial Bank in London (F. Kortum and William Hay, 1859-61) had a refined Italian Renaissance revival façade.

The opening of impressive bank buildings in Winnipeg early in the 20th century proclaimed that the prairie city had achieved a dominant financial position. A series of imposing banking structures around Portage and Main streets included the large neoclassical regional centres of the Bank of Montreal (McKim, Mead and White, 1913) and the Canadian Bank of Commerce (Darling and Pearson, 1910), the 10-storey Bank of Hamilton Building (J.D. Atchison, 1916), and the smaller but sophisticated Bank of Toronto (H.C. Stone, 1906) and ROYAL BANK OF CANADA (Carrière and Hastings, 1910). All featured superb banking halls as well.

Branch banking had been legalized in 1841, and by 1900 there was a proliferation of branch operations. Many branches were designed from a central office. In order to remain competitive in the rapidly expanding West, the Canadian Bank of Commerce hired the Toronto firm of Darling and Pearson to design prefabricated branches in 3 sizes; between 1906 and 1910 the B.C. Mills Timber and Trading Co produced almost 70 structures which, shipped from Vancouver by rail to their destination, could be erected in a single day. Architect John M. Lyle designed both large and small banks for the BANK OF NOVA SCOTIA in the 1920s and 1930s. The templelike Bank of Nova Scotia (1924) on Sparks St, Ottawa, with its freestanding columns and decorated frieze, represents the height of Lyle's classical bank designs.

After 1945 major changes occurred in the attitude of banks towards their buildings, as reputations established in the preceding decade removed the need to be identified by impressive symbolic architecture. Efficiency became paramount as the policy of centralized, standardized design intensified. Old branches were judged obsolete and replaced with new ones designed by the banks' architectural staffs. Each bank had its preferred material — the Banks of Commerce and Montreal chose brick, and the Royal Bank black granite. Most were single-storey plain, rectangular structures. In contrast to the era when banks dominated their surroundings, standing as the symbols of a town's sense of wealth and worth, recent branch banks are frequently understated buildings.

National and regional head offices have continued the tradition of assertive designs. Since the 1960s, a number of banks have occupied large portions of distinguished high-rise tower in the international style. Most noteworthy are the Toronto Dominion Centre in Toronto (Ludwig Mies van der Rohe, with John B Parkin Associates, and Bregman and Hamann 1964-68), the Royal Bank in Montréal's Place

ʼille Marie (I.M. Pei and Associates, with Affleck, Desbarats, Dimakopoulos, Lebensold and ise, 1963) and Royal Bank Plaza, Toronto Webb, Zerafa, Menkes, Housden Partnership). ʼhe Bank of Canada, the regulator of the naion's money, has enlarged its original neolassical headquarters (Marani, Lawson, and ʼlorris, with S.G. Davenport, 1937) by wrapping he building with twin 12-storey towers of nirrored glass (Arthur Erickson, with Marani, ,ounthwaite and Dick, 1974-79). *See also* URBAN ESIGN. HAROLD D. KALMAN

ank of British Columbia, a bank chartered n 1966 with headquarters in Vancouver. It has ver 2000 employees and maintains 50 branches n BC and Alberta, as well as offices in the Cayıan Is, the US and Hong Kong. As of Oct 1982 nnual sales or operating revenues were $504 ıillion and assets were $3.3 billion (ranking 9th among banks and financial institutions in ʼanada). DEBORAH C. SAWYER

ank of Canada, wholly owned by the Government of Canada, is Canada's central bank or nonetary manager. Established in 1935, it is reponsible for issuing paper currency, for acting s fiscal agent and banker for the federal govrnment, for setting the BANK RATE and for imılementing and helping to formulate MONETARY OLICY. As banker and fiscal agent the bank nanages the issue and redemption of federal overnment securities and the payment of INEREST they accrue. It also operates in the foreign xchange market as the government's agent to xert a stabilizing influence on the Canadian ollar EXCHANGE RATE. It does not engage in comnercial BANKING activity.

According to the BANK OF CANADA ACT, the ssential purpose of money management is to elp achieve price, employment and economic rowth conditions that are "in the best interests of the economic life of the nation." As monetary nanager the bank controls the growth of bank leposits (the main component of MONEY supply), n different ways. Each chartered bank is reuired to maintain minimum cash (computed s a percentage of its deposits) reserves in the orm of notes or deposits with the Bank of Canda. Each bank is also required to maintain secndary reserves in the form of excess cash reerves, treasury bills and day-to-day loans to nvestment dealers. The Bank of Canada may ary this reserve ratio from 0-12% of deposits. ʼhe Bank of Canada can alter chartered-bank ash by buying or selling securities in the open narket. Cash reserves will increase as soon as he cheque in payment of the securities is cleared nd deposited in a chartered bank's account vith the Bank of Canada. It can similarly manage cash reserves by transferring Government of ʼanada deposits between the chartered banks nd itself. Through its control over cash reserves he bank influences the supply of money and onsequently the level of interest rates and vailability of credit. As lender of last resort, it an also make advances to some financial instiutions (including banks) for temporary periods o relieve unusual financial pressures. On rare ccasions the bank has used moral suasion, ie, it as persuaded institutions to act in a certain vay. For example, it might indicate to the charered banks its views on a particular lending acivity. These views are taken seriously by the anks.

The Bank of Canada is managed by a senior overnor, a senior deputy governor and 12 irectors. In addition the deputy minister of inance is a nonvoting member of the board. Directors are appointed by the federal minister of finance, with Cabinet approval, for 3-year erms. In turn the directors appoint the governor nd senior deputy governor, again with Cabinet pproval, for 7-year terms. The Bank of Canada as had 4 governors: G.F. Towers, J.E. COYNE, L. Rasminsky and G.K. Bouey. Although the bank enjoys substantial independence, the Bank of Canada Act gives the finance minister the right to issue a formal, written policy directive to the Bank of Canada if, after consultation, disagreement on policy persists. It was the resignation of J.E. Coyne in 1961, over differences with the government, that influenced the introduction of the legal provision clarifying that ultimate responsibility for policy rests with the government. E.P. NEUFELD AND A.J. THOMSON

Bank of Canada Act, 3 July 1934, created the BANK OF CANADA 1935 in response to the 1933 Royal Commission on Banking and Currency. The Bank of Canada was at first privately owned, but was nationalized by 1938. The Act and associated revisions to the Bank Act also changed the legal framework for Canada's chartered banks, which were now obliged to maintain a specified ratio (not less than 5%, usually 10%) between liabilities to the public (current and savings accounts) and their claims on the national monetary authorities (Bank of Canada paper currency, plus deposits with the Bank of Canada). The banks lost the right to borrow on demand from the government as had been permitted under the 1914 FINANCE ACT. Instead they could borrow from the Bank of Canada, which would also hold the main accounts of the Dominion and lend to it, while in general managing the national monetary system. It would do this by issuing paper currency, changing the rate of INTEREST at which it would lend to the chartered banks, or by buying and selling bonds in the securities markets so as to affect the supply of credit and the demand for it, or by buying and selling gold and foreign monies so as to affect the demand-supply balance in the foreign-exchange market, where Canadian dollars are exchanged for foreign monies. Through such operations the Bank of Canada can and does affect the cost and availability of credit, but it has never fixed interest rates for the public at large or rationed the supply of credit directly. During WWII it helped the Dominion in financing the war effort. Under later legislation its powers were extended and modified, but not changed in essentials. It also acquired a subsidiary, the Industrial Development Bank, est 1945. The Bank of Canada may be called Canada's central bank, because of its special functions in relation to the chartered banks, the international environment and the federal government.
IAN DRUMMOND

New Bank of Canada building in Ottawa, designed by Arthur Erickson, with its exterior a facade of mirrored glass. The old building is shown bottom right, integrated with the new *(courtesy National Film Board/ Photothèque).*

Bank of Montreal, with head offices in Montréal, is Canada's oldest chartered bank. Founded in 1817, the Bank of Montreal participated in many of the developments spurring the growth of Canada: the first CANALS, the TELEGRAPH, the CANADIAN PACIFIC RAILWAY, major hydroelectric projects and the development of Canada's ENERGY and MINING industries. It was the banker in Canada for the Canadian government from 1863 until the founding of the BANK OF CANADA in 1935. It was also the first Canadian bank to establish representation outside the country, with correspondent agencies started in London and New York in 1818. In 1893 it was named the Canadian government fiscal agent in Britain, a function it still performs. Between 1903 and 1962 the Bank of Montreal purchased the assets and business of smaller banks, mainly in Atlantic Canada. Today, it has over 1300 branches in Canada and overseas, and it offers corporate, government, merchant and personal banking services with a variety of commercial and international services. The Bank of Montreal also promotes Canadian trade abroad. In Oct 1983, it had revenue of $7.4 billion with as-

One-penny decimal coin issued by the Bank of Montreal in 1842 after the union of Upper and Lower Canada *(courtesy Currency Museum, Bank of Canada/Jas. Zagon).*

sets of $63 billion (ranking 3rd among banks and financial institutions in Canada) and 29 125 employees. DEBORAH C. SAWYER

Bank of Nova Scotia, fd 1832 in Halifax, is Canada's second-oldest chartered bank. Its first branches were in the Maritimes, but it expanded into Winnipeg and Minnesota in the 1880s as the CPR was built. Between 1883 and 1919 it amalgamated with smaller banks, beginning with the Union Bank of Prince Edward Island and ending with the Bank of Ottawa. It was the first Canadian bank to operate in the Caribbean, opening a branch in Jamaica in 1889; it also established a branch in London in 1920.

During the 1960s the bank again diversified internationally; it operates over 200 branches and subsidiaries in 45 countries, as well as its more than 1000 branches in Canada. It offers a variety of financial services, including gold and silver trading, mortgage loans, leasing, real-estate and trust services. Now known familiarly as "Scotiabank," it pioneered several financial services to simplify banking for the ordinary consumer. In 1981 it became the first Canadian bank to offer complete branch services in Japan and it also participated in a test of the business applications of satellite communications. Although the general office was moved to Toronto in 1900, the head office is still in Halifax. As of Oct 1983, it had annual revenue of $5.8 billion, assets of $54.8 billion (ranking 4th among banks and financial institutions in Canada) and 25 537 employees. DEBORAH C. SAWYER

Bank of Upper Canada, chartered 21 Apr 1821, commenced operations at York [Toronto] July 1822. It owed its origins to pressure from the commercial community, to close links with the FAMILY COMPACT, and to the local government's hope that a bank would provide it with sorely needed capital. William ALLAN, president for 12 of the bank's first 13 years, adapted British banking theory to the reality of a capital-starved frontier and provided generally sound leadership. Thomas Gibbs Ridout, cashier (general manager) 1822-61, and William Proudfoot, Allan's successor (1835-61), were less successful. During the REBELLIONS OF 1837-38 the bank annoyed local commercial interests and, partly as a result, the Commercial Bank of the Midland District expanded more rapidly in the 1840s. During the 1850s, the bank held the government account, provided significant short-term capital for railroad development and, in the boom years, recklessly speculated in land and railways. The bank never recovered from the 1857 economic collapse, losing the government account in 1864 and entering trusteeship in Nov 1866. Despite its great contribution to the development of Canadian commerce, it became a casualty of the very process it had helped facilitate: the transition from MERCANTILISM to an industrial economy. PETER A. BASKERVILLE

Bank Rate, the BANK OF CANADA's minimum interest rate on short-term loans to the chartered banks, to savings banks under the Québec Savings Bank Act, to other members of the CANADIAN PAYMENTS ASSOCIATION that maintain deposits with the Bank, and to investment dealers. The bank rate often indicates the Bank of Canada's preferences concerning the level of short-term interest rates, but it is generally higher than other rates of short-term credit in order to encourage borrowers to obtain funds elsewhere. The rate has been fixed throughout most of its history, but at present it has been set at one-quarter of one percent above the average yield on 90-day Government of Canada treasury bills sold at the latest weekly auction. Hence, the bank influences bank rate indirectly each week through its own tender price for treasury bills (*see also* BANKING). E.P. NEUFELD AND A.J. THOMSON

Banking, a financial process carried out by an institution that accepts deposits, lends money and transfers funds. The 2 principal types of banks are central banks and commercial banks, or chartered banks as the latter are called in Canada. A central bank such as the BANK OF CANADA operates as an arm of the federal government, carrying out its MONETARY POLICY, acting as a lender of last resort to the commercial banks, holding deposits of governments and chartered banks and issuing notes or money. Chartered banks accept deposits from the public and extend loans for commercial, personal and other purposes. Other financial institutions, known as "near-banks," perform some of these functions, but banks are the only financial institutions that can increase or contract the basic money supply.

History of Banking In one of the earliest codes of law, compiled by Hammurabi, king of Babylon from 1792 to 1750 BC, several paragraphs were devoted to banking. By *c*1000 BC in Babylon the transfer of bank deposits to a third party was common, and the palace or temple extended loans from its own assets. The Greeks established private banks, which accepted deposits and acted as agents in the settlement of debts. Pasion of Athens, a famous 4th-century-BC banker, invested his own funds and those of his depositors in commercial ventures. Roman bankers acted as money changers, auctioneers, discounters and creditors; they formed a banking association and maintained something similar to a modern current-accounts system.

"Bank" derives from the Italian word *banco,* the bench on which money changers sat to conduct their business, and from the 5th to the 11th century bankers acted primarily in this capacity. With the advent of the Crusades, the Lombards, N Italian merchants, formed merchant guilds; they accepted deposits, granted advances and made payments, preferring to operate where they were not required to pay taxes. In the 12th century, the Lombards established themselves in London, and Lombard Street remains a symbol of financial power. From the 14th to the 19th century various banks were established in countries such as Italy, Holland, Spain, France, Germany and England. The Bank of Amsterdam was established in 1609 and acted as a guarantor of coinage, since it would accept coins only at what it perceived as their real value. The Bank of Stockholm, founded at about the same time, issued receipts for deposits that were circulated for purchasing goods and as bills of exchange, in effect, the first bank notes. The Bank of England was established in 1694 as a private bank (remaining so until 1946) under a royal charter to raise money for war. Banking history in England is distinguished by the early development and use of the cheque; on the continent the limitations of the nonnegotiable cheque precluded extensive use of deposit credit until well into the 19th century.

Under the French regime, barter had generally been the method of trade. The coins and merchandise customarily sent from France returned there for the purchase of imports. One year (1685), when a shipment did not arrive, signed playing cards were issued as legal tender, redeemable in coins and merchandise (when they arrived), and the colonists were ordered to accept the cards as money. Later due bills redeemable not in real coins or merchandise but in card money were issued. By 1760 the colony was 80 million livres in debt, much of it in worthless *ordonnances* issued by Bigot. After the CONQUEST the British used Mexican, Spanish, Portuguese, French and German coins to pay their troops, which, with trade goods, became the coin of the realm.

In 1782 Montréal merchants formed the Canada Banking Company, but because it could not obtain permission to issue bank notes it failed as did 2 other similar ventures in 1807 and 1808. During the War of 1812 the governor issued "army bills" that bore interest and could be exchanged for cash, government bills of exchange in London or more army bills. In 1817 the BANK OF MONTREAL (a joint-stock operation owned by a handful of men) opened its doors in Canada, but because of delays in the approval of its charter until 1822, 2 other banks — the Bank of New Brunswick in 1820 and the Chartered Bank of Upper Canada in 1821 — were granted a head start. The Bank of Upper Canada was controlled by the FAMILY COMPACT and the legislature of the time refused charters to any group unless some of its members belonged to the oligarchy. Another bank, the Bank of the People, was established by the enterprising Francis HINCKS, who became prime minister of the Province of Canada and later John A. Macdonald's finance minister. He was responsible for ensuring the passage of Canada's first Bank Act (1871) and was later named president of the Consolidated Bank. (He was also brought to trial on various offences and convicted of fraud, although the conviction was reversed on appeal.)

The Bank of Montreal's charter was similar to that of the first Bank of the US, established to be the creature and agency of the national government under the new federal constitution but Canadian and American banking systems developed quite differently. Canadian banking has been described as "a branch plant of English commercial banking," and, as one historian notes, "it was the model least suited to promoting industrial development in the colony." Regional growth suffered as well. For example by 1912, in one area of the Maritimes, only 5 cents of every dollar deposited in the bank was loaned locally and 95 cents was transferred to central Canada.

Many of Canada's first bankers, eg, Samuel Zimmerman, who was involved in the Great Southern Railway swindle, were not examples of probity, and until the 1920s banks in Canada were generally unstable. (Between 1867 and 1914 the failure rate of Canadian banks was 36% as opposed to that of the US of 22.5%, costing Canadian shareholders 3½ times more than was lost to American shareholders; of the 26 failures in this period, 19 resulted in criminal charges against bank officers or employees.)

In the US, in contrast, where banking was fiercely competitive and regionally oriented, 2 types of banks developed. Eastern banks favoured stability and gradual expansion, while those burgeoning in the West were more venturesome. The number of banks in Canada was restricted by high capital requirements and vested interests allied to the legislators. Attempts by westerners to form their own bank were vetoed by the Canadian Bankers' Association, officially incorporated in 1901. As a result the Canadian banking system became characterized by the creation of a few dominant banks with many branches, compared to the American practice of encouraging many unit banks and restricting or prohibiting branches. Until 1867 charters were issued by Upper Canada and Lower Canada and subsequently by the federal government. Canadian banks were also regulated by law in considerable detail, eg, the fixing of a minimum paid-up capital ($100 000 in 1871 and $250 000 since 1890). Twenty-eight banks were chartered by 1867 and 38 by 1886. This number changed little until WWI when it declined sharply, until by 1964 only 8 remained, of which 5 were nationally significant. As a result of legislative changes and economic expansion of the West, the number of domestic banks increased to 12 and the number of foreign-owned banks to 59. In contrast, Denmark, with a population of 5 million, has about 40 commercial banks and 200 savings banks a well as a number of foreign banks; Austria has about 38 joint-stock banks, 10 private banks, 165 savings banks, 1279 rural co-operatives, 10 provincial mortgage banks and a postal savings bank; and the US has about 14 700 banks. The Canadian banking system remains basically a banking oligopoly dominated by the "Big Five" (*see* BUSINESS ELITE), banks large not only by Canadian but by world standards. Ranked by size of deposits in 1982, in a list of the largest banks in the free world, the ROYAL BANK ranked seventeenth; the CANADIAN IMPERIAL BANK OF COMMERCE, thirty-first; the Bank of Montreal, thirty-third; the BANK OF NOVA SCOTIA, forty-fifth; and the TORONTO DOMINION BANK, fifty-sixth. The "Big Five" control about 85% of bank assets in Canada.

The development of the ECONOMY also changed banking practices. In the 19th century, the banks issued their own notes, which were used as money, but gradually governments supplanted this privilege until finally only the Bank of Canada could issue legal tender. Lending practices evolved from the primary banking function of making commercial loans that were self-liquidating within a year to making loans on grain secured by warehouse receipts, on proven reserves of oil in the ground and in the form of mortgages on real estate.

Other financial institutions providing some of these banking functions also began appearing early in Canadian history. Mortgage loan companies patterned after building societies in the UK opened in the 1840s and evolved into "permanent" companies, eg, the Canada Permanent Mortgage Company, selling debentures and investing in mortgages. TRUST COMPANIES were also formed during this time to act as trustees and professionally manage estates and trusts; they gradually assumed banking functions, eg, providing savings and chequing accounts, and became major participants in the mortgage market. Savings banks first appeared in 1846 to collect savings from the public but that form of near-bank is relatively insignificant in the financial system.

The other major type of near-bank is the savings and credit co-operative, called a CREDIT UNION in most of Canada and a CAISSE POPULAIRE in some areas. After a slow start in the first half of the 20th century, credit unions grew rapidly by using deposits to extend loans to their members.

Role of Banks As is true with all financial institutions, the basic function of banks is to channel funds from individuals, organizations and governments with surplus funds to those wishing to use those funds, which is why they are called financial intermediaries. But banks also have a premiere position in this financial intermediation because of their role in providing the payment system while acting as the vehicle for Canadian monetary policy and the federal government's instrument for some social and political policies. Consequently the actions of the banks have a major impact on the efficiency with which the country's resources are allocated. In addition to these wider roles, the banks also have an obligation to their shareholders to earn an adequate return on their equity and pay sufficient dividends. If these goals are neglected, investors will withdraw their capital from the banking system and force either a contraction of the money supply or government ownership.

The experience of the early 1980s reveals the conflict that can arise among these purposes and goals in the Canadian banking system. The federal government encouraged the banks to extend huge loans to Canadian companies wishing to take over subsidiaries of foreign companies, especially in the oil and gas industry, in defiance of sound banking practice and wider economic implications, such as the misallocation of credit resources, pressure on the Canadian dollar and an inflationary expansion of the money supply. As a result the domestic loan portfolio of the banks began deteriorating sharply in 1982 to what was probably its worst condition in the postwar period. Loans to the highly cyclical real-estate industry accounted for about 120% of bank capital; loans to oil and gas companies such as DOME, Sulpetro and Turbo, to forest product companies such as Western Forest Products, and to MASSEY-FERGUSON and International Harvester also imperilled the financial strength of the banks.

International lending practices of Canadian banks were equally disastrous. Brisk demand and wide profit margins encouraged the larger Canadian banks to pursue international borrowers vigorously with the result that their foreign assets increased from $21.7 billion in 1973 to $156.7 billion in 1983. Many of these loans were made to governments or government-guaranteed borrowers on the theory, which any student of history knows is incorrect, that governments do not default on loans. By the summer of 1983, over 40 countries had agreed to or had applied for rescheduling of their debt or had accumulated substantial arrears in interest payments. Furthermore, banks began extending new credits to foreign lenders to enable them to pay interest on older loans. This sleight of hand is good for the reported earnings of the banks but does little or nothing to resolve the serious problem of international debt.

Predictably, the result of both the domestic and international lending policies was huge losses for the banks and intensified malaise and costs for Canadians. In an effort to combat the impact on bank earnings, the margin or difference between the prime rate and the cost of funds was pushed to the highest level in many years. In 1980 the banks' prime rate was 15.5% and the rate on bank savings deposits was 12.5%, a "spread" of 3%, but 2 years later, the prime rate was at the same level while the savings account rate had dropped to 11%, a spread of 4.5%. Borrowers were therefore paying a higher than normal price for money while savings received less than normal. In addition to these penalties, the high proportion of bank assets tied up in nonproductive loans restricted the banks' flexibility in accommodating credit-worthy borrowers.

Source of Assets and Liabilities When a bank or other financial institution is incorporated, it begins operations by selling shares to investors and the funds raised in this manner become the shareholders' equity. The bank will then try to attract deposits from the public in the form of demand deposits, which can be withdrawn by cheque at any time and which normally pay no interest; savings accounts, which pay a variable rate of interest and have restrictions on their withdrawal; and deposits with a fixed term of a few days to 5 years, paying a fixed rate of interest. In 1983 the banks held $19.5 billion in demand deposits, $66.1 billion in savings accounts and $79.9 billion in term deposits. All of this deposit money is a liability or debt of the bank, used to acquire assets that can generate profits and pay the interest and operating costs. Public demand and government regulations require that the banks keep some of their assets in the form of cash and investments, eg, treasury bills, which can be quickly converted into cash. Most of the remaining financial resources are invested in securities such as bonds and term-preferred shares and in loans and mortgages. In 1983 Canadian banks held $2.4 billion in cash, $26.5 billion in securities, $111.3 billion in Canadian loans, $34.2 billion in mortgages and $111.7 billion in foreign currency loans.

Banks, trust companies and credit unions have historically concentrated their assets and liabilities in different areas but this has been changing over the past 10 years. The banks monopolized the market for demand accounts because at one time they were the only deposit institution offering bank accounts with chequing privileges; they still control the huge corporate accounts, but the trust companies and credit unions have been taking a larger slice of the market for personal chequing accounts. The market shares for savings accounts have changed little over the past decade. On the liability side, banks are still the predominant lenders to business and government but have also recently grabbed a big share of the consumer credit and mortgage market.

Profits The profits of the Canadian banks rose rapidly between 1972 and 1982 because of a combination of factors. First, the assets of the banking system increased 5.8 times (domestic assets 4.5 times and foreign assets 9.6 times). The increase in foreign assets (from 26% to 43% of total assets) was largely responsible for rising profits because their rate of return rose from 0.58% in 1975 to 0.69% in 1980. In contrast the rate of return on domestic assets fell from 0.68% to 0.42% during the period. Second, the banks increased their assets faster than they increased their shareholders' equity. As a result of this higher leverage, the assets-to-capital ratio rose from 22.3 in 1972 to 29.8 in 1982. This trend increased both the potential for profit and the degree of risk in the banking system. Third, the wider spread between the lending and borrowing rates coupled with increased bank charges for services such as chequing, safety deposit boxes and lending fees became more important in boosting profits towards the end of the decade. Fourth, loan losses have been the only significant depressant to profits. The banks stated that their actual loan loss rose from $364.4 million in 1978 to $2.42 billion in 1982, but there is enormous variation in the way different banks account for problem loans. Earnings of the different banks were consequently overstated by 20-45% depending on the problems they encountered. Fifth, the 41% increase in bank profits in 1981 and continued gains in early 1982 created such a public outcry that the federal government attempted to mollify the public by appointing a parliamentary committee to examine bank profits. Not unexpectedly, the committee reported that the apparent excess profit resulted from higher leverage, rapid asset growth and international operations. Profits were not excessive, and the low rate of income tax was largely the result of government policy. The committee also recommended a number of measures to strengthen the banking system, increased disclosure of their financial condition, and the provision of some means for resolving consumer complaints. The inspector general of banking has acted on some of these recommendations, particularly in the areas of loan loss provisions and directives regarding the adequacy of the capital base and the leverage ratios.

Banking Structure and Operation Canadian commercial banks, like other investor-owned organizations, are managed by a board of directors, headed by a chairman, which oversees a president and vice-presidents representing special areas of the bank. Boards of banks, however, are considered the most prestigious boards of all; they are large (35 to 50 members) and their members are generally also members of boards of other major companies. Sixty-three directors of the 5 largest banks sit on the boards of the 16 largest life insurance companies, controlling 83% of that industry. The directors of the Royal Bank and the Bank of Montreal also sit on the boards of 44% of the companies that rank among the 250 largest nonfinancial, nonbanking companies in Canada. Eighteen out of the 33 large insurance companies have 70 "interlocking directorships" with 20 trust companies. At one time, many bank directors were also directors of trust companies, but interlocks between banks and trust companies are now forbidden — a restriction that has had little practical effect in loosening the control of the many by the few.

The structure of Canadian banking is also distinguished by the system of branch banking; Canadians have one of the highest ratios of banking branches to population in the world, with one deposit branch for every 1800 Canadians. Fifty percent of the branches, however, belong to 5 banks. In addition, there is a strong trend toward the reduction of branches and the cutting of their personnel.

In the last revision (1980) of the Bank Act, 2 types of banks were defined in Canada: Schedule A banks are banks that are Canadian owned and Schedule B banks are foreign owned. There are now 58 Schedule B banks in Canada, concentrating and competing heavily in the market for loans to medium- and small-scale business.

Regulation of Banking According to the CONSTITUTION ACT, 1867, banking is regulated by the federal government and property and civil rights are provincial responsibilities. The first Bank Act, virtually drafted by the Bank of Montreal, put Maritime banks under the control of federal banks. In 1894 the Bankers Association (later the CBA) was founded. A powerful lobby group, it was given the right to determine the fitness of bankers seeking charters, and under the regimes of both Macdonald and Wilfrid Laurier, bankers effectively chose the ministers of finance by threatening to excite financial crises if the candidates suggested by the prime ministers were approved.

In 1964 the Royal Commission on BANKING AND FINANCE (Porter Commission) recommended "a more open and competitive banking system," but most of its suggestions for reform (eg, that banking be legally defined to prevent banks from straying into other areas) were not followed. The 1967 Bank Act revision lifted the 6% per annum interest-rate ceiling banks could charge and allowed banks to enter the mortgage field. As a result, banks increased their mortgage portfolio in 3 years from $825 million to $18.6 billion. The 1967 Act also barred the previously legal practice of collective rate setting by banks, required banks to inform borrowers better about the real cost of loans, and provided $20 000 of federal deposit insurance for each account in banks and near-banks. Provincially chartered institutions, eg, trust companies and credit unions, were gradually protected in a similar way by provincial governments. The federal government has increasingly encroached on this area of provincial responsibility, particularly with the establishment of the Canada Deposit Insurance Corporation. (For the provinces' part, the takeover of Crown Trust by the Ontario government is an example of a provincial government's ability to abrogate the rights of shareholders of provincially incorporated institutions.)

The 1977 Bank Act revisions were delayed until 1980. In 1977 a legislative proposal that would have required banks to provide better disclosure of interest charges was defeated. As a result of changes in the Bank Act of 1980 the CANADIAN PAYMENTS ASSOCIATION was established as the agency responsible for the cheque clearing system; reserve requirements were reduced, increasing bank assets by millions of dollars; the minister of finance became the sole arbiter deciding which new banks could be established; foreign banks were allowed to establish themselves and required to keep reserves but their growth was restricted in various ways; banks were allowed to become involved in the business of leasing large equipment; banks were allowed to become involved in factoring; and banks (but not their subsidiaries) were limited to a 10% holding of residential mortgages. The

Total Assets of the Canadian Banking System
(Source: Bank of Canada)

	1973 Millions$	*1983 Millions$*	*Compound Annual Increase 1973-1983*
Banks	$79 754	$368 628	16.5%
Trust Companies and Mortgage Loan Companies	16 446	92 291	18.8
Credit Unions	8 814	37 111	15.5
Savings Banks	805	5 255	20.6
Total	105 819	503 285	16.9

banks are also regulated by the Bank of Canada under the authority of the Bank of Canada Act. The Bank of Canada regulates principally by controlling its cash reserves — the principal factor determining ability of the chartered banks to expand credit and increase their deposits. The Bank of Canada also uses its moral suasion to persuade banks to pursue certain desired courses of action.

Future of Banking The major structural change in banking, still in its formative stage, is the move towards an electronic funds transfer system. The old paper trail provided by cheques, passbooks and handwritten or hand-entered data is being replaced by computerization of the banking system through automatic teller machines, automatic clearinghouses, preauthorized payments and automatic depositing of government cheques, payroll and bond interest. For the user of banking services, resulting advantages include multibranch banking, increased hours of access to the banking system and a wider range of banking services and products. Disadvantages include problems in correcting errors and assigning responsibility for them and infringements on personal PRIVACY by both banks and governments through easy access to the enormous data banks. Bank customers are also discovering that computerization has enabled banks to assign costs more accurately to individual banking transactions and then charge for these costs. ALIX GRANGER

Reading: H.H. Binhammer, *Money, Banking and the Canadian Financial System* (1982); D.E. Bond et al, *The Economics of the Canadian Financial System* (1983); Alix Granger, *Don't Bank on It* (1981); T. Naylor, *The History of Canadian Business*, vol 1 (1975);

Banking and Finance, Royal Commission on (Porter Commission), est 1961 (after the governor of the Bank of Canada, James COYNE, had publicly disagreed with the federal government's economic policies), to examine and to make recommendations for the improvement of "the structure and methods of operations of the Canadian financial system, including the banking and monetary system and the institutions and processes involved in the flow of funds through the capital markets."

The commission, which included several representatives of BANKING institutions, made many recommendations in its 1964 report, including the abolition of the 6% interest rate ceiling on bank loans; disclosure of bank-loan costs; entry of banks into conventional mortgage financing; and legislation to prevent banks from agreeing to set common interest rates, chequing costs and other customer charges. It also recommended that trust companies, finance companies, creditors and other "near banks" be brought under the authority of the BANK OF CANADA; that the Bank Act be amended so that the government could overrule the central bank on MONETARY POLICY; and that government regulations be established to control mergers between banks and TRUST COMPANIES or bank takeovers of other financial institutions. Some of the recommendations were incorporated into the 1967 Bank Act revisions. MARTIN KROSSEL

Bankruptcy, a legal process that provides financial relief for debtors and a protection for creditors. When an individual or a corporation goes bankrupt, an accountant (called a trustee) is appointed to take control of the debtor's assets and distribute them among the unpaid creditors. Once this process is completed the debtor is released from any further obligation to pay those debts. The bankruptcy process can be initiated either by the debtor or by one or more creditors. The debtor whose debts become unmanageable may go bankrupt so that he can be released from his debts and get a fresh start.

A debtor commences the process by making an "assignment in bankruptcy," which is essentially an agreement to turn over all of his assets to a trustee for sale and distribution to his creditors. Creditors can also "petition" a debtor into bankruptcy. There are several reasons why they would do this. Debtors are sometimes overoptimistic, spending all their remaining assets in an unrealistic hope of success. Sometimes they try to hide or sell property to keep a personal benefit and defeat creditors' claims. The appointment of a trustee in bankruptcy can prevent this. Creditors can petition the Bankruptcy Court (a division of the Supreme Court or Court of Queen's Bench in the common law provinces and of the Court Superior in Québec) and if they establish the individual or corporation's insolvent status then the court will grant a "receiving order," ie, a court order giving a trustee in bankruptcy control of the bankrupt's assets.

If the bankrupt is an individual, the trustee acquires control of all the assets except those that under the law of the province are exempt from seizure; if the bankrupt is a corporation, the trustee takes control of all its assets. Each province has slightly different exemptions, but most allow a debtor to keep a basic stock of clothing, furniture, tools and sometimes a car or truck and a basic equity in a home. A wage earner who declares bankruptcy or is petitioned into bankruptcy can continue to work and earn money, but the trustee or the court may require that some payments be made to the trustee for the creditors before the final discharge is granted. The amount will depend on the income of the debtor and his degree of fault in becoming bankrupt. A corporation cannot resume business under its own control until or unless it pays all its debts. A bankruptcy deals only with unsecured debts; secured creditors with mortgages or liens remain free to enforce their security, and the trustee can only take what remains on behalf of the unsecured creditors.

Consumer bankruptcies have been increasing steadily in recent years, passing the rate of 3000 per month, for the country as a whole, in Sept 1982. This trend is partly explained by the fact that there is now less stigma attached to bankruptcy in Canadian society. In addition, the recession of the early 1980s has meant that, stigma or not, many more people have been forced to bankruptcy as a last resort solution to problems of indebtedness. The incidence of bankruptcies tends to follow widespread crop failures, plant closures, mine shutdowns and local or general market collapses. There is also a marked "domino" effect, especially in single-industry towns and in cities heavily dependent on one form of economic activity.

The Bankruptcy Act provides a rehabilitative scheme for consumers short of bankruptcy called the "orderly payment of debts" plan. Under the plan, individuals with non-business debts have their debts frozen. They work out a budget with a counsellor and make one monthly payment which is distributed among the creditors, who receive all their principal but over a longer period, and with interest reduced to a low rate. This plan (or an equivalent), offered through a provincial Consumer Affairs Department, is available in most provinces.

An increasingly used procedure under the ankruptcy Act is a "proposal." A person or corporation in financial trouble can make a formal roposal to the creditors to pay them less money ver a longer period of time in satisfaction of eir debts. If the creditors agree, no bankruptcy ccurs, leaving the individual in control of his ssets. If they disagree or if a default is made in ese lesser payments, bankruptcy occurs automatically. This allows some businesses to reructure their debts and continue to operate ithout going bankrupt. It is still, however, the ast popular of the 2 alternatives: in Sept 1982 ere were only 58 proposals across Canada but 30 business bankruptcies.

anks, Harold Chamberlain, "Hal," tradenion leader (b at Waterloo, Iowa 28 Feb 1909). tough and ruthless seamen's leader, Banks as invited to Canada in 1949 by shippingompany interests acting with the support of e federal government and organized labour. hey intended him to oust the communistontrolled Canadian Seamen's Union. Within 2 ears the Canadian District of the Seafarers' Inrnational Union had, under Banks, won conol of the collective-bargaining rights of almost ll of Canada's sailors. While Banks achieved npressive gains in wages and working conditions for his members, he also ran the SIU in a ictatorial manner. His attempt to expand his nion's jurisdiction to represent mates and engineers brought him into conflict with other nions and ultimately with the CANADIAN LAOUR CONGRESS. This conflict precipitated bloody attles at Canadian ports and a general disruption in shipping. The federal government appointed a commission of inquiry under BC ourt of Appeal Justice T.G. Norris. In his report Norris described Banks as a hoodlum and bully, and following a conviction for conspiracy to assault, Banks fled the country. Extradition was refused by the American government. WILLIAM EDWARD KAPLAN

anks Island, 70 028 km^2, fifth-largest island n Canada, westernmost island of the ARCTIC RCHIPELAGO. It is bordered on the W by the eaufort Sea and separated from Melville I on he N by M'Clure Strait and from Victoria I on he E by Prince of Wales Str. The SE coast is arked by dramatic cliffs of yellow, white and

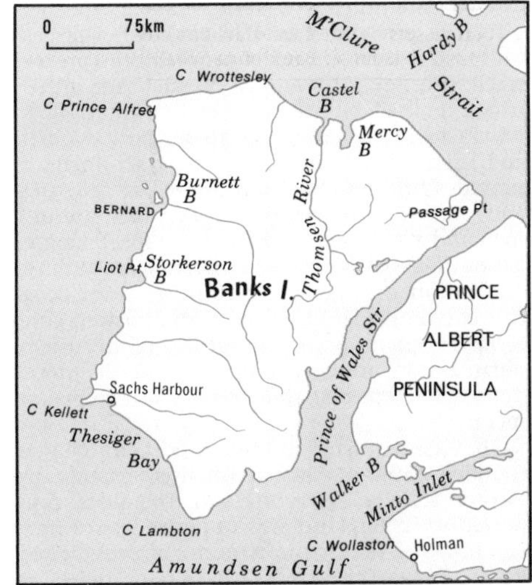

red quartzites. The low W coast is characterized by long, sandy offshore bars, rising at the SW tip to the spectacular Nelson Head cliffs (425 m) of Precambrian rock almost 2 billion years old — 325 million years older than any other part of the island. Limestone cliffs rise at Cape M'Clure and Cape Crozier on the N coast. Along the E coast the land slopes up from the beach into mud, sand and gravel cliffs. The highest point is Durham Heights (almost 730 m). The central portion is a level plain, cut by valleys of the larger rivers that rise near the E side. Seams of hard, impure coal underlie the NE plateau, and softer coal has been found around Mercy Bay. On the E side, which was glaciated, lakes are numerous and glacial till covers the hills.

Banks I was first sighted by Lt F.W. Beechey, a member of the W.E. PARRY expedition, Aug 1820, and named for Sir Joseph Banks, president of the Royal Society. R.J. McClure landed on the S coast 1850. V. STEFANSSON reached the island across the ice of the Beaufort Sea and established a base near Cape Kellet. The island was inhabited by Inuit at least 500 years ago, but except for an air base at Sachs Harbour, it is now uninhabited except for trappers. There is a large arctic fox population, as well as caribou, polar bears, wolves, muskoxen, arctic hare, lemmings, wolverines, seal and occasionally grizzly bears. White and bowhead whales are common offshore. Numerous species of birds are found, including some 200 000 lesser snow geese, black brant, eiders, whistling swan, snowy owls, rough-legged hawks and ravens. Arctic char have been taken at the mouths of the Sachs, De Salis and Thomsen rivers; whitefish and trout at the Thomsen. The only biting insect is the mosquito. JAMES MARSH

anks Island, NWT, the 5th-largest island in Canada nd the westernmost island of the Arctic Archipelago *photo by Lyn Hancock*).

Bannatyne, Andrew Graham Ballenden, businessman, politician (b on South Ronaldsay, Orkney Is 31 Oct 1829; d at St Paul, Minn 18 May 1889). Bannatyne was one of Red River's most prominent businessmen whose concern for the future led him, in 1869-70, to support Louis RIEL and the hope for a multiracial society. He entered the service of the HBC at 14, but left it in 1851 to set up as a free trader with his father-in-law Andrew McDermot. By the late 1860s, Bannatyne and his new partner, Alexander BEGG, were the largest retail and wholesale merchants in Red River. When Riel began his resistance in 1869, Bannatyne supported the demand for a negotiated entry into Canada and tried with some success to act as a liaison between whites and mixed bloods. There were some stormy scenes with the erratic Riel, but Bannatyne brought stability as a member of the provisional government. In 1873-74, he abetted Riel's elections to the House of Commons and, after Riel was declared an outlaw and his seat of Provencher vacated, Bannatyne was elected by acclamation in 1875.

Bannatyne had little interest in federal politics and did not seek reelection. During the 1870s, he sold his business and turned to land speculation, at which he prospered; but his fortunes were shattered when the western land boom collapsed in 1882. J.E. REA

Reading: A. Begg and W.R. Nursey, *Ten Years in Winnipeg* (1879).

Bannock [Old English *bannuc,* "morsel"], a form of bread that served as a staple in the diets of early settlers and fur traders. It took the form of a flat round cake or pancake. Ingredients included unleavened flour, lard, salt, water and sometimes baking powder. Bannock derives from the cookery of Scotland and northern England. JOHN ROBERT COLOMBO

Banting, Sir Frederick Grant, codiscoverer of INSULIN (b at Alliston, Ont 14 Nov 1891; d near Musgrave Harbour, Nfld 21 Feb 1941). Youngest of 6 children of a middle-class farm family, Fred Banting persevered through high school, failed first year in arts at U of T and then enrolled in medicine. He graduated in 1916 with above average grades, served as a medical officer in France, where he was wounded in action and decorated for valour, and in 1919-20 completed his training as an orthopedic surgeon. In July 1920 he began the practice of medicine in London, Ont.

On the night of 31 Oct 1920, after reading a routine article in a medical journal, Banting wrote down an idea for research aimed at isolating the long-sought internal secretion of the pancreas. He received support for his proposed research at U of T, where he began work on 17 May 1921 under the direction of J.J.R. MACLEOD and assisted by C.H. BEST. Banting's and Best's experiments were crudely conducted and did not substantiate Banting's idea, which was physiologically incorrect. But their apparently favourable results encouraged greater efforts, which culminated in the winter of 1921-22 in the discovery of insulin by a team of researchers that included Macleod, Banting, J.B. COLLIP and Best.

Insulin was immediately and spectacularly effective as a lifesaving therapy for DIABETES MELLITUS. Banting was hailed as the principal discoverer of insulin because his idea had launched the research, because of his prominence in the early use of insulin, and because he and his

Sir Frederick Banting, co-discoverer of insulin and recipient of the Nobel Prize *(courtesy Public Archives of Canada/PA-123481/Arthur S. Goos)*.

friends carried on a campaign to discredit his senior collaborators, Macleod and Collip, with whom he was temperamentally incompatible. On learning that he was to share the 1923 Nobel Prize for physiology or medicine with Macleod, Banting gave half his prize money to Best. He was awarded a life annuity by the federal government, appointed Canada's first professor of medical research at U of T and knighted in 1934.

Banting supervised important research into silicosis and problems in aviation medicine before his death on a flight to England in 1941 to look into the state of medical research there. But his own research was trivial, for he was not in fact a skilled or well-trained scientist. The burden of his fame weighed heavily on an insecure but determined man, leading to a turbulent personal life and considerable unhappiness. He became an accomplished amateur painter, whose work strongly reflects the influence of his friend and sketching companion, A.Y. JACKSON. He was survived by his second wife and by a son from his first marriage. In several magazine polls during his lifetime, he was judged the most famous living Canadian. MICHAEL BLISS

Reading: Michael Bliss, *Banting: A Biography* (1983) and *The Discovery of Insulin* (1982).

Baptists, originally ANABAPTISTS ("rebaptized"), persons and groups who, during the 16th-century Protestant Reformation, rejected infant baptism and (re)baptized adult believers upon profession of faith. The 2 terms later came to signify divergent traditions. Baptists accept the Bible as the reliable record of God's revelation to mankind and as the only norm for Christian beliefs and practices. They have produced many confessions of faith, but such statements are not regarded as binding interpretations of the Bible. Ideally, every believer and every congregation has "soul liberty," freedom to interpret the Scriptures and to seek guidance from the Spirit of God on all matters. The local church is seen as a fellowship of believers who have made a commitment to follow Christ, usually in an experience of spiritual rebirth or conversion, and have made a public confession of faith, in the rite of "believer's baptism." Only such persons may join the church. Since the 1640s Baptists have used immersion of the whole body under water as the only form of baptism. The second ordinance (seldom described as a sacrament) is communion, a simple commemoration of Christ's sacrifice on the cross observed by most Baptist churches on the first Sunday of each month. Ministry is conceived as a service to which all disciples are called in order to make use of their gifts (the priesthood of all believers). The pastor's task is seen as a full-time calling to preach, teach, counsel, train and co-ordinate the ministries exercised by all members. Ordination, to which in many Baptist churches both women and men are admitted, is not a sacrament; it provides for public recognition of the call, gifts and training for ministry. Deacons are lay men and women elected from the local congregation to assist with pastoral care, communion celebration and general administration. Local churches enjoy freedom to make decisions concerning beliefs, practices, calling of ministers, organization and property. Democratic procedures are accepted at all levels of church government.

The first English-speaking Baptist church was founded 1609 in Amsterdam, Netherlands, by Puritan refugees from England. The oldest congregation in England was organized 1612 near London, and the first in America at Providence, RI, in 1639. The original Baptist churches in Canada were formed under ministers from Massachusetts, at Sackville, NS (now in NB), in 1763 and Horton (now Wolfville), NS, in 1765. Both congregations ceased to exist in the mid-1770s, although the church in Wolfville was recovenanted in 1778. The GREAT AWAKENING in Nova Scotia, and revivals in the 19th century led to rapid growth in the Maritimes. In New Brunswick Baptists became the largest Protestant denomination. Originally, the majority adhered to the Regular (CALVINIST) theological orientation while a minority endorsed the opposing Free Will (Arminian) position, maintaining the possibility of salvation for all. The two groups merged in 1906 to form the United Baptist Convention of the Maritime Provinces. In 1963 "Maritime" was changed to "Atlantic" (UBCAP) to include Newfoundland, where Baptist churches were introduced in the 1950s. Churches organized in the African United Baptist Assn (part of UBCAP) have been important in the large black community in NS. Only in the Atlantic provinces have Canadian Baptists avoided organizational schism. In Upper and Lower Canada Baptist life was shaped from the beginning by conflicting convictions and traditions among immigrants from the US and Britain. The first churches were planted by American ministers (Caldwell's Manor in the Eastern Townships, Lower Canada, in 1794, and a church near Beamsville, Upper Canada, in 1796). They excluded non-Baptists from communion. Newcomers from England endorsing "open communion" influenced the development of Baptist churches in Montréal and eastern Ontario. From 1815 on, immigrants from the Scottish Highlands brought the revivalist tradition of James and Robert Haldane to the Ottawa Valley. Controversy over communion practice and other disagreements hindered co-operation in missionary work and education for several decades. In 1888 two regional bodies united in the Baptist Convention of Ontario and Quebec (BCOQ). The Ontario mosaic was enriched by many racial and ethnic groups. From the 1820s on, slaves escaping from the southern US by the UNDERGROUND RAILROAD established a network of black congregations. In the 1830s, French-speaking immigrants from Switzerland arrived in Québec, and under Henriette Feller (1800-68) initiated Baptist work in Montréal and the Eastern Townships (the Grande Ligne Mission). In 1969 the French churches organized their own Union d'églises baptistes françaises au Canada (UEBFC).

Photo of the rite of baptism, Minitonas, Man, Aug 1929 *(courtesy Canadian Baptist Archives)*.

In 1873 Ontario Baptists sent a minister to Winnipeg. The First Baptist Church was established there in 1875, and in 1884 the Baptist Convention of Manitoba and the North-West Territories was organized. Meanwhile, churches were founded on the Pacific coast, in Victoria (1876) and New Westminster (1878). The Convention of Baptist Churches in BC was formed in 1897. Ten years later the churches in the western provinces formed the Baptist Convention of Western Canada, renamed the Baptist Union of Western Canada in 1909. Many affiliated congregations worshipped in languages other than English, but German- and Swedish-speaking churches eventually severed their BUWC links.

Repeated calls for a national fellowship finally led in 1944 to the Baptist Federation of Canada. Affiliation with any of the unions or conventions implies membership in BFC. Its primary concerns are national, international and interdenominational. BFC also co-ordinates work done by the 4 constituent bodies in such areas as EVANGELISM, Christian education and chaplaincies, and it sponsors an extensive program of relief and development overseas. The only other national agency related to BFC is the Canadian Baptist Overseas Mission Board, fd 1912. In 1982 it assisted churches in 7 countries and supported 120 Canadian missionaries. BFC's 133 000 members are in 1138 congregations.

The Fellowship of Evangelical Baptist Churches in Canada, the second-largest Baptist body, dates back to the 1953 merger between the Union of Regular Baptist Churches, fd 1927 and the Fellowship of Independent Baptist Churches, fd 1933. Both groups appeared in the aftermath of the fundamentalist-modernist theological controversy of the mid-1920s, led by Dr Thomas Todhunter SHIELDS, pastor of Jarvis Street Baptist Church in Toronto (*see* EVANGELICAL AND FUNDAMENTALIST MOVEMENTS). About one-seventh of the churches in BCOQ left the convention and formed 2 groups. In 1965 the Convention of Regular Baptists of BC, fd 1927, and the Prairie Regular Baptist Missionary Fellowship, fd 1930, joined FEBC. Total membership in 426 affiliated churches is estimated at 55 000.

The North American Baptist General Conference is a fellowship of originally German-speaking churches. The oldest such congregation was organized in Bridgeport, Ont, in 1851. Until the 1920s the churches enjoyed dual affiliation with the NABGC, which includes churches in the US and Canada, and with one of the regional conventions which are now parts of BFC. The 104 Canadian churches in NABGC, redominantly in the western provinces, have ome 15 700 members. Baptist General Confernce was organized by Swedish immigrants in anada and the US. In the early 1890s churches vere founded in Waterville, Qué, and Winnieg. Apart from a few churches in northwestern ntario, all congregations today are in western anada. Before 1948 they maintained dual affilition with the BGC and the BUWC. The BGC as approximately 5600 members in 69 congreations.

Among the smaller Baptist groups, which tol some 80 churches with an estimated 8000 nembers, is the Alliance of Reformed Baptist hurches, fd 1888 in NB as part of the Holiness Movement. It merged with the Wesleyan Methdist Church in 1966, which in 1968 joined the ilgrim Holiness Church to become The Wesyan Church. The Primitive Baptist Conference f New Brunswick traces its origin (about 1875) the leadership of George W. Orser. Recently his conference established links with the Naional Assn of Free-Will Baptists in the US. The ssn of Regular Baptist Churches (Canada), rganized 1957, comprises a small cluster of hurches led by Toronto's Jarvis Street Baptist hurch. Canadian Baptist Conference (Southern aptist) is a fellowship of about 30 churches n western Canada and 3 in southern Ontario vhich are affiliated with the Southern Baptist onvention through its state conventions adjaent to the Canadian border. There are several ther small groups, such as Bible Baptist hurches, Reformed Baptist Churches, Seventh ay Baptist Churches and the Gospel Missionary ssociation (Alta). In most cases, such congreations relate to the corresponding bodies in the JS.

Apart from these formal affiliations, there are nany independent congregations, representing he most radical application of the principle f local church autonomy. In 1982 the total Bapist constituency in Canada, combining indeendent and affiliated churches, was some 1917 ongregations with over 227 000 members; worhip is in over 20 languages. Membership statisics do not include children and adherents who ave not as yet joined the church. The 1981 ensus reported 696 850 persons as Baptists, substantial increase from 422 312 in 1921. Nevertheless, Baptists, like other major Protesant denominations, declined as a proportion of he total population from 4.8% in 1921 to 2.9% n 1981. Several conventions or conferences o-operate in the Baptist World Alliance. With 125 member conventions in 90 countries, the BWA reports total membership of 32 million adults. Baptists were among the earliest advocates of religious freedom and of separation between church and state. They participate in the political, economic and cultural life, and seek to implement the lordship of Christ in all spheres of life. Recently Baptists have been divided in their attitudes to ecumenical relations. Many Canadian congregations co-operate with other churches in evangelism, joint services and social ministries, and many support the EVANGELICAL FELLOWSHIP OF CANADA. Within Canada, the BFC was a member of the CANADIAN COUNCIL OF CHURCHES from its founding in 1944. In 1980, however, it terminated its affiliation because of lack of consensus among its 4 constituent conventions. Only BCOQ remains in the CCC. No Canadian Baptist body joined the World Council of Churches.

In the second quarter of the 19th century Baptists fought for equal educational opportunities for all citizens. Acadia College in Wolfville, NS, was the first post-secondary institution in Canada which did not impose denominational tests for students or teachers. In Ontario Baptists gave leadership in the struggle over CLERGY RESERVES and the establishment of a nonsectarian provincial university in Toronto. Baptists founded several colleges: Acadia College (1838), later ACADIA UNIVERSITY; Canada Baptist College, Montréal (1838-49); Woodstock College, Woodstock, Ont (1881) and Toronto Baptist College (1881), both to be replaced by MCMASTER UNIVERSITY; and Brandon College (1899-1938), now BRANDON UNIVERSITY. All have passed from Baptist control. Today the different conventions and conferences operate one junior college, 10 seminaries, and several schools for lay training. Among the many Baptist educators and scholars 2 deserve special mention: George P. Gilmour, pres of McMaster U (1950-61), and Watson Kirkconnell, pres of Acadia U (1948-64). In politics, several leaders enjoyed close association with the Baptist fellowship: PMs Alexander MACKENZIE, Charles TUPPER and John DIEFENBAKER; and premiers William ABERHART, Ernest MANNING and Thomas DOUGLAS. J.K. ZEMAN

Reading: J.E. Harris, *The Baptist Union of Western Canada* (1976); Stuart Ivison and Fred Rosser, *The Baptists in Upper and Lower Canada before 1820* (1956); George Edward Levy, *The Baptists of the Maritime Provinces 1753-1946* (1946); Robert G. Torbet, *A History of Baptists*, 3rd ed (1973); J.H. Watt, *The Fellowship Story* (1978); Jarold K. Zeman, *Baptist Roots and Identity* (1978), and ed, *Baptists in Canada* (1980).

Barachois Pond Provincial Park (est 1962, 35 km^2), one of the largest of over 70 parks in Newfoundland and Labrador, is located at the head of St Georges Bay, 70 km S of Corner Brook along the Trans-Canada Highway. It occupies part of the Appalachian Mts, known in the area as the Long Range, formed over 450 million years ago. Subsequent EROSION reduced the peaks to less than 400 m and glaciers gouged out the valley now filled by Barachois Pond. The area is forested, predominantly with spruce, fir, larch and aspen, although stands of black ash and white pine (rare in Newfoundland) occur, as do many ORCHIDS. Mammals include snowshoe hare, beavers, caribou and the elusive pine marten. Over 100 species of birds inhabit the park, including the rare arctic three-toed woodpecker. For generations the area was used by moose, caribou and rabbit hunters, and by loggers and local residents seeking fuel wood. The area is now dedicated to nature protection and recreation. There is a modern campsite and opportunities for swimming, motorboating, canoeing, fishing and hiking (the trail to Erin Mt offering fine views). In winter, no services are provided but the park is available for skiing, snowshoeing, snowmobiling and ice fishing. JOHN S. MARSH

Barbeau, Charles Marius, ethnologist, folklorist, ethnomusicologist (b at Ste-Marie-de-Beauce, Qué 5 Mar 1883; d at Ottawa 27 Feb 1969). Founder of professional FOLKLORE studies in Canada, he worked at the National Museum from 1911 to the late 1960s, collecting a vast archive of traditional songs, texts and artifacts — especially of French Canadian and native peoples. Taught at home by his parents until age 12, he entered training for the priesthood at 14, but then went on to study law at Laval. After law school, he studied as a Rhodes scholar at Oxford, where he became intrigued by anthropology. With his diploma in anthropology he was recommended for a post at the newly formed National Museum in Ottawa. Barbeau made his most enduring contribution as a collector of folk traditions, with nearly 1000 publications and many more thousands of texts and songs now preserved in archives.

His first loyalty was to his homeland in Québec, and he was sure that rural Québec had preserved folk traditions reaching back to medieval times. Nevertheless, he worked in the US and across Canada, in particular with the TSIMSHIAN in BC. Two themes are prominent in his life — homeland and journeys — and the Tsimshian myth of an ancient migration from a distant homeland convinced him that they had journeyed as a tribe from Asia within living memory. While anthropologists no longer accept this hypothesis, it was a powerful motive for Barbeau's activity over the years, aided by Tsimshian William BENYON, in recording the tribe's traditional lore in order to preserve the legacy of a fading past in the face of the pressures of the industrial age.

Marius Barbeau. He collected a vast archive of French Canadian and Indian songs, texts and artifacts, and was the founder of professional folklore studies in Canada (*courtesy National Film Board/Photothèque*).

Barbeau also founded the Archives de Folklore at Laval and several folklore groups, and was especially successful in bringing ethnology and folklore to the Canadian public, through several prizewinning books and tireless lecturing and teaching. He received many honours and awards, including honorary doctorates from Montréal, Laval and Oxford, and was made a Companion of the Order of Canada. R.J. PRESTON

Reading: C.M. Barbeau, *The Downfall of Temlaham* (1928) and *Quebec: Where Ancient France Lingers* (1936); Barbeau and Edward Sapir, *Folk Songs of French Canada* (1925).

Barbeau, Jean, dramatist (b at St Romuald, Qué 10 Feb 1945). He is best known for his humorous but sympathetic treatment of *joual*, the popular idiom of Québec, in such plays as *Manon Lastcall* (1972) and *Joualez-moi d'amour* (1972), the latter a brilliant description arising from Québec's linguistic and cultural dichotomy. *Le Chemin de Lacroix* (1971), *0-71* (1971) and *Ben-Ur* (1971) also deal, in less amusing fashion, with the psychological victims of his province's malaise. Barbeau's more recent works deal with broader themes, as in *Le Jardin de la maison blanche* (1979), a stinging criticism of the materialistic values of contemporary N American society. He is one of the most productive and most popular of current playwrights in Québec. L.E. DOUCETTE

Barbeau, Marcel, painter, sculptor, filmmaker (b at Montréal 18 Feb 1925). An active member of the AUTOMATISTES led by Paul-Émile BORDUAS, Barbeau is a widely exhibited, innovative artist. His early training was thorough. As well as studying drawing at the École du Meuble, Montréal, he worked with Borduas, with architect Marcel Parizeau and art historian Maurice Gagnon. He travelled extensively 1962-74, living and exhibiting in Paris, New York and California, and his style changed, moving from the lyrical abstracts of the Automatiste period towards a more geometric mode. By the 1980s, however, he had returned to the free-form, all-over surface activity that he had favoured before. Barbeau is also a filmmaker, producing *Désirs-mouvements* (1977), and a performance artist. ANN DAVIS

Barber and Barber, Winnipeg's most prolific architectural firm 1876-88. Founded 1876 by Charles Arnold Barber (b at Irish Creek, near Athens, Canada W *c*1847; d 1916) and joined in 1882 by his brother, Earle William Barber (b 1855; d 1915), the firm designed over 100 buildings in Manitoba in little more than a decade. Apparently neither brother had professional or academic architectural training, and by the mid-1880s their style began to lose favour in competition with better educated architects. After a scandal over contracting estimates for Winnipeg City Hall, the brothers left town (1887) and set up practice in Duluth, Minn, and Superior, Wis. WILLIAM P. THOMPSON

Barber, Clarence Lyle, economist (b near Wolseley, Sask 5 May 1917). His experience of prairie farm life during the GREAT DEPRESSION gave him a commitment to improving Canadian economic policy, and a concern for the needs of farmers. After study at the universities of Saskatchewan, Clark and Minnesota and 2 years in the RCAF, Barber joined the Dominion Bureau of Statistics in 1945, moving to McMaster in 1948 and in 1949 to the University of Manitoba, where he has remained. Barber has written many articles and monographs on economic theory and policy in a Canadian context. He directed the research which led to the Greater Winnipeg Floodway, served as UN adviser to the Philippines; and, from 1966 to 1970, conducted a one-man Royal Commission on Farm Machinery. In 1984 he was a member of the Macdonald Commission. In 1977 he was elected to the RSC. A.M.C. WATERMAN

Barker, William George, "Billy," fighter pilot (b at Dauphin, Man 3 Nov 1894; d at Ottawa 12 Mar 1930). He was credited with 53 aerial victories during WWI, but is mostly remembered for the epic, single-handed combat against some 60 German aircraft that won him the Victoria Cross on 27 Oct 1918. After the war he joined W.A. BISHOP in an ill-conceived commercial aviation venture in Toronto, but in June 1922 he accepted a commission in the Canadian Air Force and briefly became the first director of the RCAF. He was fatally injured when his Fairchild aircraft crashed at Rockcliffe air station, Ottawa. BRERETON GREENHOUS

Barkerville, BC, is a restored gold-rush town in the BC interior. The Fraser R GOLD RUSH, the first of several in BC, reached the area (125 km SE of PRINCE GEORGE) in 1862 when William Barker, a Cornish sailor, made a huge strike there. The CARIBOO ROAD, completed 1864-65, brought large freight wagons and stagecoaches to the town, making it part of the Cariboo district, a long corridor of contiguous development. Barkerville soon numbered almost 3000 people, though most miners still wintered in Victoria or San Francisco. Its permanent residents included merchants, hoteliers, builders and bankers. As the region's population stabilized, Barkerville began to develop a cultural life. Sunday labour was stopped; the miners unionized for shorter shifts; a Masonic Hall was built (1866); an HBC store set up (1867); resident preachers became prominent in the town; entertainment shifted from horse racing and variety to legitimate plays (1868); and gambling was outlawed. Government offices were maintained there owing to the occasional mining "excitement" in the district, but by 1900 the town had faded considerably. During the 1930s it became a satellite of Wells, site of the Cariboo Gold Quartz mine. In 1958 the provincial government undertook to restore the historic town as part of its centennial celebrations. In 1959 Barkerville was made a provincial historic park. ALAN F.J. ARTIBISE

Barley, common name for members of genus *Hordeum* of the GRASS family (Gramineae). Many wild and cultivated forms occur and, since all cultivated forms and some of the wild ones are interfertile, they are assumed to belong to one species, *H. vulgare*. Because of its ability to adapt to a wide range of SOIL and CLIMATE conditions, barley is widely grown in many parts of the world and was one of the earliest cultivated CROPS. Although the centre of origin is not known, barley has been gathered or cultivated for thousands of years in the Middle East, Far East, North Africa and east-central Africa.

The barley PLANT has a cylindrical stem which is hollow, except at the nodes (solid areas from which the leaves arise). The spike or head is composed of spikelets attached to the nodes of a zig-zag structure known as a rachis. Each spikelet consists of 2 husks or hulls, enclosing male and female floral parts. The rachis nodes may have either one or 3 spikelets, giving the spike the appearance of having 2 or 6 rows of kernels; hence, the names 2-rowed and 6-rowed barley.

Barley is referred to as having either a spring or a winter habit of growth. Spring-sown types, which mature in 80-90 days, predominate in Canada. Slightly acid, well-drained loams or clay loams are preferred. Barley can be attacked by fungal PLANT DISEASES (eg, stem rust, smuts), bacterial blight and VIRUS diseases (eg, yellow dwarf). It is also prone to agronomic problems (eg, weak straw, head shattering). In Canada, plant scientists working to improve barley are producing new strains (cultivars) with genetic resistance to disease, higher yield and improved agronomic and quality features.

Most of the 4.8 million ha devoted to barley production in Canada is located on the PRAIRIES. Approximately 13.5 million t of barley are produced annually: about one-half is marketed through commercial channels; the remainder is kept on the farm for livestock feed or for seed. A large proportion of marketed barley is made into malt for beverages or malt-enriched food products (*see* BREWING INDUSTRY). Barley can also be made into pearled grain for soups, into flour for flatbread or can be eaten as porridge. Canada exports approximately one-half of the barley it markets (currently 3.5 million t annually), representing about one-quarter of world exports. *See* GRAIN HANDLING AND MARKETING.

D.R. METCALFE

Barnacle, common name for marine INVERTEBRATES of subclass Cirripodia, class Crustacea. Barnacles, the only sessile CRUSTACEANS, have adopted an odd life-style: they stand on their heads and kick food into their mouths. Six appendages (cirri), operating like a miniature net, filter food from the water. The eyes and second antennae are absent and the body reduced; the carapace (shell) is covered with calcareous plates. Acorn barnacles are common on Canadian intertidal rocks; some members of this group are specialized for life attached to whales. The stalked goose barnacle is named for its resemblance to a bird neck and head. Aggregates of some species reproduce simultaneously and, in spring, intertidal rocks are coated with spat (spawn) cementing themselves in place. The cement can withstand enormous pressure. In Canada, the barnacle's main economic importance is as a fouling organism: extensive growth on ship hulls can greatly slow vessels. Although barnacles are delicacies in some countries, even the larger ones are rarely sampled in Canada.

V. TUNNICLIFFE

Barnard, Édouard-André, agronomist and journalist (b at Trois-Rivières, Qué 30 Sept 1835; d at Varennes, Qué 19 Aug 1898). An important Québec agronomist in the second half of the 19th century, Barnard had abandoned his studies early to go into trade. In 1856 his interest turned to agriculture, however, and for several years he was also involved with the army, organizing 2 companies of volunteers in Trois Rivières during the TRENT AFFAIR in 1861. He became involved in the ZOUAVES movement and in 1868 went to Rome. He returned to Trois Rivières and ran *La Semaine agricole* from 1869 to 1872 before settling in Varennes and giving speeches on farming. He then spent a year in Europe, encouraging emigration to Canada and studying European agriculture. Upon his return he held various senior positions in the Dept of Agriculture and in 1877 founded *Le Journal d'agriculture*. JEAN-CLAUDE ROBERT

Barnes, Howard Turner, physicist (b at Woburn, Mass 21 July 1873; d at Burlington, Vt 4 Oct 1950). Graduating from McGill in 1893 in applied sciences, he was initiated into research work by his physics professor Hugh L. Callendar, an authority in electrical precision measurements. Applying the techniques of his teacher to a peculiarly Canadian problem, Barnes devoted his life work to the study of the physical properties of ice. In 1906 he published *Ice Formation*. In the years following he tackled the applied side of the problem and published his results in *Ice Engineering* (1928), a few years before his retirement in 1933. His ability in precision measurements led to his election to the Royal Soc of London in 1911. He delivered the coveted Tyndall Lectures in 1912 at the Royal Inst in London on his favourite subject "Ice Formation in Canada, Physical and Economic Aspects." A member of the Royal Soc of Canada since 1902, he became president of Section III in 1908. That same year he was named Macdonald Professor of Physics at McGill, succeeding Ernest RUTHERFORD. YVES GINGRAS

Barns, like certain of our native birds and animals, have joined the ranks of "endangered species." No funds from wealthy societies, heritage trusts or governments are spent on the purchase and preservation of our oldest barns, and their demise can be expected within the next decade. Changes in agricultural economy have caused hundreds of farmers in Canada to go bankrupt and farms to be abandoned. On farms that are still prosperous, new barns have often been built that lack the cultural and architectural interest of barns from earlier years.

Barn design has always been affected by regional inherited customs and by available building materials. Building materials were often timber, brick and stone for exteriors; wood shingles, slate and thatch for roofs. Though slate is rare, thatch in Québec is extinct. It was never as durable or weather resistant as thatch in countries where reeds were used in the composition; Canadian thatch was usually straw. For the barn enthusiast with a camera it is rewarding to find a well-designed old barn built with any of these materials on walls and roof; and nothing is more shocking than to see a barn, perfect in form, covered by a galvanized roof or with walls protected by shining aluminum sheathing. The all-aluminum sheeted barn is now a common sight, and the barn of the future will likely be of metal or other weatherproof, prefabricated material.

In form and function Canadian barns are classified as English and Pennsylvania Dutch. In all eastern regions, barns that are circular or polygonal are infrequent except in Québec, where many examples abound, immaculately maintained and painted in the brightest hues. The connected barn is of ancient origin and few remain in Canada. Of the types mentioned, the Pennsylvania is most common except for the little English barn. The majority are sheeted in mber planks, but there are superb examples in one and more permanent materials. However, is not for their construction that they are nportant, but for their form and function. A pical site is one with a southerly exposure on sing ground. The barn is built with its great oors opening at the upper level onto what is lled the threshing floor, which is actually a oad aisle flanked by stout, squared timbers bays stretching from floor to ceiling. The anary, opening off the threshing floor, is neat, ell-built in consideration of its precious connts, and is divided into 6-8 bins separated by a assage. At the close of the season, the threshing oor is filled with farm machinery. During the utumn and winter, hay is lowered by chute to e cattle below.

For the housing of animals, the Pennsylvania arn is outstanding. Usually the upper structure, mow, is cantilevered as much as 2.4 m, an adirable invention because of the shelter it gives e cattle in the byre behind the barn. Nearly all anadian Pennsylvania barns are built of pine lanks, but in Pennsylvania some of the finest re stone or brick, or combinations of stone brick gable-ends with timber vertically or orizontally nailed on the projecting mow. The utch barn can be seen at its best on each side of e Hudson R, but there are Canadian examples. s plan can be easily remembered — the only arn type with main doors at the end and not n the side. This barn plan, sometimes called asilican, has a "nave" or threshing floor and isles, on one side for cattle and on the other side or horses. Historically, in Holland, women serants slept over the cattle and men over the orses. A fascinating historic feature of the early utch barns in Holland was the living space at he "sanctuary" end of the Basilican prototype. here, furniture could be arranged around a entrally placed fire and flanked on 2 sides by edrooms or built-in beds which would be lowred for sleeping. The farmer could be seated so hat he had supervision over the threshing floor, orses and cattle. One barn has been saved for PPER CANADA VILLAGE, and though it has the entral door, the structure has been anglicised y eaves that are higher than the prototypes in olland or the Hudson R region.

A very curious survival of the ancient plan is barn built (1906) at Weyburn, Sask. Externally shows no signs of the traditional type with ow eaves and central door, but the family lived nder the same roof as their animals; living uarters were 6 m in depth and consisted of 2 toreys, the upper being bedrooms. The ground loor had a door and windows overlooking the hreshing floor.

The ubiquitous little English barn gets its ame from one of identical use and form in Britain. It has a central threshing floor, with pace to the left for threshed grain and on the ight for unthreshed grain. This barn, whose neasurements were often as little as 16.8 x 7.6 n, flourished at a period when wheat cultivaion dominated agriculture. When more room or storage became necessary after a bountiful harvest, the threshing floor was extended by one bay with a loft overhead. To achieve this, a pine beam of awesome dimensions was cut from the kind of tree then to be found in the primeval forest. Square holes show where joists were once fitted to hold the floor and its load. Farmers were reluctant to use part of the barn for cattle during a period of agricultural change, and after the old barn was left to its original uses, a small cattle barn was built at right angles to the old, or with still further need, a third barn for horses would be added to form a 3-sided court. At Carleton Place, Ont, the ultimate was reached with a piggery which filled the gaps and created an inner court, a sheltered place with many uses. At one time the house was attached to the barn. The idea of having the farmer in such an intimate relationship to his animals and storage was good, but fires could be devastating. The only remaining example in Canada is the barn in Weyburn, Sask.

The French Canadians showed much ingenuity and a love of primary colours in barns. Their barns were usually long and low, with a surprising number of circular and polygonal shapes adding variety to the traditional singlestorey rectangles. They had tight-tongued and grooved, painted walls. Where wooden barns elsewhere relied for ventilation on shrinkage of boards, the Québecois provided it by cupolas placed on ridges. In clapboard walls on barns outside of Québec City the cracks allowed the free passage of air and permitted a host of pigeons, numerous owls, swallows, mice and cats to enter. The Québec barn is preeminent for decoration in paint, and its plain surfaces give the farmer ample opportunity for the display of colour. In many old barns outside of Québec City, farmers take advantage of flat areas to demonstrate the raison d'être for their operations, and large faded paintings of cows or horses are a rewarding sight. One very spirited painting of horses in motion can be seen at Petit Chocpiele in NB. It is a mural and approaches the standards of fine art rather than the vernacular (*see* FOLK ART).

Carved stone lintels on wooden barns were used for decoration. An excellent example still exists. Lettering in stone has been moved from a barn in Erin Township, Ont, to a stone wall at Rockwood Academy, Rockwood, Ont. The inscription (1863) reads: "When your barn is well filled all snug and secure, Be thankful to God and remember the poor." ERIC ARTHUR

Reading: Eric Arthur and Dudley Witney, *The Barn* (1972).

Barr, Murray Llewellyn, anatomist, geneticist (b at Belmont, Ont 20 June 1908). A major contributor to the establishment of the science of human cytogenetics, Barr was educated at Western and was a member of its faculty 1936-73. From 1939 to 1945 he was an RCAF wing commander. In 1949 he co-discovered the sex chromatin, the presence of which distinguishes cells of normal females from those of normal males. A simple buccal-smear sex-chromatin test, introduced with K.L. MOORE, identified persons with abnormal sex-chromosome complexes and the exact nature of the error was established by chromosome studies (karyotyping). This research contributed substantially to understanding the cause of various cogenital syndromes. Barr wrote *The Human Nervous System* and *A Century of Medicine at Western*. He is a fellow of the Royal Soc of London and has received many other honours. In 1962, he received the Joseph P. Kennedy Jr Foundation Award from President John F. Kennedy for his work in mental retardation. W.J. BRADY

Barr Colonists arrive at Saskatoon (*courtesy Public Archives of Canada/PA-38667*).

Barr Colonists In 1902 the Rev Isaac Barr secured a huge land tract between the present-day Alberta-Saskatchewan border and Maidstone (Sask). In Mar 1903 he brought approximately 2000 colonists from England. Arriving Apr 17 in Saskatoon, they spent 2 weeks bickering and reorganizing before embarking on an easy 270 km wagon trip to the colony. Many discontents left to form their own communities. Tired of continual criticism, Barr resigned, went to Toronto to sort out his money problems, and moved to the US and eventually Australia. Leadership passed to his rival, the Rev George Lloyd, after whom the colony's first town was named LLOYDMINSTER in July 1903. Despite initial setbacks, the Barr colonists opened up the vast area west of Saskatoon. In 1905, Alberta and Saskatchewan were created (*see* AUTONOMY BILLS), and the interprovincial boundary passed through Lloydminster. Although the CANADIAN NORTHERN RAILWAY, which arrived that year, placed its station on the less populated Alberta side, the colonists continued to develop the Saskatchewan side. Not until the 1970s oil boom did the western portion match the eastern side. FRANK W. ANDERSON

Barre du jour, La (*BJ*), magazine fd 1965 by Nicole BROSSARD, Marcel Saint-Pierre, Roger Soublière and Jan Stafford, to stimulate writing through writing and to transform both the production and the reading of literature. In 1977, *BJ* was reorganized as *La Nouvelle Barre du jour* (*NBJ*) by Brossard (who left in 1979), Michel Gay and Jean-Yves Collette, and by Dec 1983 it had published 133 issues. Despite a change of management in Sept 1981 to Hugues Corriveau, Louise Cotnoir and Lise Guèvremont, the magazine's purpose has remained unchanged. From the start, *BJ* wanted to combine formal research with appreciation for a certain tradition, and so it presented the unpublished works of Charles GILL, Louis-Joseph QUESNEL, Nérée Beauchemin, Saint-Denys GARNEAU, Gaëtane de Montreuil and Émile NELLIGAN. By abandoning the "cult of the soil" as subject matter (*see* NOVEL IN FRENCH) and skirting revolutionary politics, *BJ* distinguished itself from both *Hexagone* and PARTI PRIS. *BJ* favoured articles about theory and formalism; *NBJ* prefers fiction and applied literary theory, and publishes on the theory and practical battles of feminism. There have been various series, dealing with such subjects as literary history and literary theory, and special issues devoted to such genres as fantasy and science fiction. *NBJ* is a laboratory of creation and research, a permanent writing workshop, drawing in contributors as the need arises. It has not merely echoed current literary trends in Québec; it has pioneered their creation. Although it has at times been repetitive in dealing with themes and issues, the publication has played an important part in Québec literature. *See* LITERARY PERIODICALS IN FRENCH. JOSEPH BONENFANT

Barrett, David, social worker, politician, premier of BC (b at Vancouver 2 Oct 1930). From a working-class Jewish family, he pursued university studies in the US in philosophy (Seattle U) and social work (St Louis U), returning to BC 1956 to work for the Dept of Corrections. He won a seat for the CCF in the 1960 provincial election, was re-elected for the NEW DEMOCRATIC PARTY (1963, 1966 and 1969), and was chosen provincial leader in 1969 when his opponent, Tom BERGER, failed to be re-elected. The NDP won the 1972 election and initiated many reforms, notably a freeze on the conversion of agricultural land, a mineral-royalties tax, the establishment of a powerful labour-relations board and an expanded public sector. Opposition to the government's zealous approach and declining revenues enabled the Social Credit Party to defeat the Barrett administration in 1975. Barrett returned to the Assembly in a 1976 by-election and remained leader of the Opposition. He announced his resignation as leader of the provincial NDP after another general-election defeat in May 1983 and in 1984 hosted a radio talk show in Vancouver. He is noted for his emotional, entertaining platform style and informal manner. J. T. MORLEY

Barrett, Silby, labour leader (b at Bishop's Cove, Conception B, Nfld 27 Sept 1884; d at Toronto 9 Aug 1959). Barrett fished with his father and worked in the coal mines in Cape Breton and Ohio before settling in GLACE BAY in 1908. He became president of the United Mine Workers of NS in 1916 and of the Amalgamated Mine Workers of NS in 1917; when the miners affiliated as District 26, UMWA, in 1919, Barrett became international board member, a post he held repeatedly until 1942. Despite his early reputation as a "red," Barrett soon became a staunch ally of international UMWA president John L. Lewis. When District 26 was suspended in 1923, Lewis appointed Barrett the district's provisional president, and in 1936 Lewis appointed Barrett Canadian director of the Steelworkers' Organizing Committee. A founder of the CANADIAN CONGRESS OF LABOUR in 1940, Barrett was elected to the executive annually until 1955. Moving to Toronto in the 1940s, he became director of District 50, UMWA. A strong backer of the CCF, Barrett was famed in labour circles for his political shrewdness and salty wit: whatever he had to confess, he boasted, "I never cast a Liberal nor a Tory vote." DAVID FRANK

Barrette, Antonio J., politician, premier of Québec (b at Joliette, Qué 26 May 1899; d at Montréal 15 Dec 1968). He began his political career by winning the Joliette seat for the UNION NATIONALE Party in the 1936 election that brought Maurice DUPLESSIS to power. He was easily re-elected 6 times between 1939 and 1960. Because of his labour experience — as a mechanical engineer and leader of the Conseil régional du travail — he served as minister of labour 1944-60, and was responsible for applying his party's labour policies, including some that were clearly antiunion. Upon Paul SAUVÉ's death in Jan 1960, he was chosen the new party leader and thus became Québec premier, remaining in office only until the June election that year, won by the Liberals. He finished his public career as Canadian ambassador to Greece 1963-66. DANIEL LATOUCHE

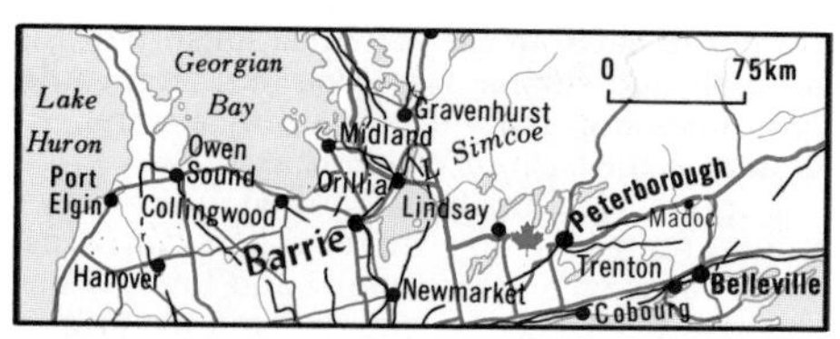

Barrie, Ont, City, pop 38 423 (1981c), inc 1959, seat of Simcoe County. Located at the head of Kempenfelt Bay on Lk SIMCOE, 70 km N of Toronto, it lay along an important supply route, inaugurated during the War of 1812, linking York (Toronto) on Lk Ontario to British military posts on the upper Great Lakes. The name refers either to Commodore Robert Barrie, a British naval officer on Lake Ontario, or to Capt Barry, commander of the 15th Regiment of York. Settlement began in 1833. Barrie enjoys excellent highway connections with Toronto. Its economy is based on diversified manufacturing — principally appliances, hardware and electronics. In winter it is a favourite spot of ice fishermen and hosts an annual winter carnival. A campus of Georgian College of Applied Arts and Technology is located here. DANIEL FRANCIS

Barrister, member of legal profession in England who has exclusive right of audience in high and superior courts. Usually retained by a solicitor, barristers have unique legal status. In Canada the term is used informally to describe lawyers who appear in higher courts, but all Canadian common lawyers are both barristers and solicitors, although some provincial legislation refers to the 2 categories. In Québec CIVIL LAW the distinction is made between "notaires" (NOTARY) and "avocats." K.G. MCSHANE

Barter is the exchange of one commodity or service for another without the use of money as a medium of exchange. A barter agreement (also called "countertrade") among countries calls for the exchange of stated amounts of goods.

Trading nations, such as Canada, increasingly find that customers who cannot pay insist on matching imports with exports for balance-of-trade purposes. Within Canada as well, bartering is used by struggling companies. For example, a radio station may offer its weekly commentators a week's holiday, including free flights and hotels. This trip is paid for by a travel agency, which receives a discount on its advertising rates on the station. In the 1960s, because of the growing use of such cashless commerce, the Canadian federal tax authorities began to restrict the practice of barter. Now companies giving individuals cashless benefits must issue a slip stating the value of the goods or services for income tax purposes. If such benefits are not reported as taxable income, the tax burden shifts to other Canadian workers who receive only monetary remuneration.

While increasing taxes and tough economic times have spawned the growth of barter and the so-called UNDERGROUND ECONOMY within Canada, the deteriorating world economy has resulted in an increase in the amount of barter, or countertrade, between nations.

Countertraders accept payment in the form of goods or services. The countertraders must not only sell their own goods, but they must accept and sell someone else's too. Countertrade is therefore also known as "triangulation" because it requires at least 3 parties: buyer, seller and customers. It has been estimated that as much as 30% of world trade during the 1970s and early 1980s has been conducted by countertrade.

In 1983 the world's largest single countertrade deal involved the Canadian federal government, a crown corporation, dozens of Canadian corporations and the government of Romania. That year, the Romanians agreed to buy a Candu reactor for $1 billion from ATOMIC ENERGY OF CANADA. Romania, however, was su[ffering] from huge debts and poor prices for i[ts] exports. Subject to strict controls from banke[rs] on how much it could spend on imports, th[e] Romanian government had to pay for the r[e]actor in goods and services.

Ottawa's Export Development Corporati[on] became involved as a form of banker and insu[r]ance company. It undertook to lend Romani[a] most of the money needed to pay Atomic E[n]ergy and its dozens of suppliers and manu[]facturers as they complete and ship componen[ts] to Romania. The companies, which inclu[de] Canadian General Electric and Canadian Wes[t]inghouse, will be furnished with a monthl[y] list of Romanian goods from which they ca[n] choose. The goods will pay for the component[s] and may either be used by the manufacture[rs] themselves or may be resold elsewhere for cash. Proceeds will be used to repay the federal gov[]ernment.

Such sophisticated dealings are conducte[d] elsewhere in the world by gigantic trading com[]panies such as Mitsubishi in Japan or Phibr[o] Salomon Corp in New York City, the world['s] largest trading company.

The Royal Bank of Canada became the fir[st] Canadian bank to create a division to facilitat[e] cashless transactions. A Canadian company sel[]ling computer equipment and programmin[g] services may have to accept teak from Thailan[d] in exchange for its commodities. The bank find[s] a buyer for the teak, and pays the Canadia[n] company cash for its goods and services whe[n] they are sent or completed. The bank, in tur[n] makes a profit by paying the Canadian com[]pany slightly less than it obtains for the teak.

Many large Canadian companies with world[]wide operations, eg, Massey-Ferguson Ltd, Gen[]eral Motors of Canada, Noranda Mines Ltd, Bat[a] Shoes and the Potash Corp of Saskatchewan employ their own countertrade specialists. DIANE FRANC[IS]

Bartlett, Robert Abram, arctic mariner (b a[t] Brigus, Nfld 15 Aug 1875; d at New York C 2[8] Apr 1946). A sealer and merchant seaman from his youth, Bartlett began his arctic career i[n] 1898, joining the first of Robert Peary's 3 at[]tempts to reach the N Pole. On Peary's last at[]tempt in 1908-09, Bartlett accompanied him t[o] within 250 km of the pole. In 1913 Bartlett com[]manded *Karluk,* supply ship of the Canadia[n] Arctic Expedition lead by Vilhjalmur STEFANS[]SON. The ship was wrecked near Wrangel I nort[h] of Siberia and Bartlett made a daring sled tri[p] across the ice to Alaska to seek help. Later h[e] commanded the *Effie M. Morrisey* on scientifi[c] voyages to the Arctic spanning 2 decades. DANIEL FRANCI[S]

Bartlett, William Henry, artist, author, trav[]eller (b in Kentish Town, Eng 26 Mar 1816; [d] at sea off Malta 13 Sept 1854). As a boy Bartlet[t] served an apprenticeship (1822-29) under Joh[n] Britton during which he showed ability as [a] draftsman and landscape artist. In 1832 h[e] met William Beattie, who remained his lifelon[g] friend and biographer and who arranged fo[r] him to make sketches for his travel book, *Swit[]zerland Illustrated* (1836). From this time until hi[s] death, Bartlett travelled widely in the Middl[e] East, Europe and America, making hundreds o[f] sketches for engravings in more than 40 books 12 of which he wrote himself. His popularit[y] owed much to his architectural training which when combined with his penchant for the pic[]turesque and the sublime, guaranteed that th[e] reader saw scenes he could recognize as charm[]ing, impressive and representational.

Bartlett spent several months in Canada i[n] 1838 sketching prominent sights such as th[e] falls at Montmorency and Niagara, the fis[h] market at York [Toronto], the view over Mon[-]

'imber Slide at Les Chats, Bytown, Upper Canada (c 1838), brown wash by William Henry Bartlett, one of the artist's many depictions of Canadians at their daily work (*courtesy Public Archives of Canada/C-40331*).

réal, and the locks on the Rideau Canal at Ottawa. As well, he showed Canadians at their daily work: clearing the forest, fishing, rafting on the Ottawa, excavating the Long Sault Canal, bringing in nets at Wellington in Prince Edward County, ferrying cattle in the Eastern Townships, and building the esplanade at Québec C. The many engravings that illustrate the 2 volumes of *Canadian Scenery* (1842) constitute an important and attractive documentation of living conditions in the Maritimes and the Canadas in 1838. ALEXANDER M. ROSS

Reading: Alexander M. Ross, *William Henry Bartlett* (1973).

Baseball is a game played with a bat and ball between 2 teams (of 9 players each), which alternate between being at bat and in the field. The object is to score runs by advancing players counter-clockwise around 4 bases, each 90 feet (27.5 m) apart. Games of bat and ball have their roots in ancient religious rites celebrating spring's return and appear throughout history. The game in N America is a descendant of English rounders. In New England, rounders evolved into a popular regional sport, known as townball, played at public meetings in the early 19th century. From these informal games emerged 2 interpretations of baseball, each with its own written rules and organized teams. These 2 styles competed for popularity until the American Civil War. The "Massachusetts game" was closest in form to townball and allowed 10 to 14 men on the field. A variation of this game was played in Beachville, Ont, on 4 June 1838 at a celebration to mark the previous year's victory by government forces over insurgents. This was the first recorded baseball-type game in Canada and predated by 7 years the establishment by Alexander Cartwright and his team, the New York Knickerbockers, of the "New York game" with 9 men on the field.

The early history of organized baseball in Canada is closely associated with southwestern Ontario. The first Canadian team was the Young Canadians of Hamilton, formed in April 1854. A local clerk, William Shuttleworth, was instrumental in its development. Other early teams included the Burlingtons of Hamilton (1855), a London team (1856) and a St Thomas team (1858). The Massachusetts game rules were favoured. The New York rules were introduced in 1859 in Hamilton. The popularity of the 9-man game in the US and the beginning of international play in 1860, with Buffalo's victory over the Burlingtons, led to its rapid adoption in Ontario. The Young Canadians of Woodstock awarded themselves a silver ball in 1863 and it became an annual prize for the Canadian champion. Woodstock's lineup included 7 Ontario-born players whose occupations ranged from carriage maker and cooper to blacksmith, printer and grocer. In 1864 they were defeated by the American champions, the Brooklyn Atlantics, at a Rochester, NY, tournament. In 1867 Woodstock, Hamilton and Ingersoll entered the world baseball tournament in Detroit, Mich, and Ingersoll won the junior class team championship. By 1868 large financial rewards induced some teams to move toward a semiprofessional status, with team members sharing tournament prizes. In 1869 the Guelph Maple Leafs replaced Woodstock as Canadian champions. The Guelph team was the first to import American professionals, who together with such Canadians as star pitcher William Smith, a local jeweller, won the Guelph world semiprofessional baseball championship in 1874 in Watertown, NY.

Guelph's president George Sleeman, a local brewer and future mayor, and Harry Gorman, a London newspaperman, formed the first Canadian League in 1876, with members in Kingston, Toronto, Hamilton, Guelph and London. The London Tecumsehs dethroned Guelph as Canadian champions, in no small part through signing one of baseball's first curveball pitchers, Fred Goldsmith, and 5 other American professionals. That same year several large American cities formed an exclusive National League to monopolize the best baseball talent. In 1877 a number of smaller American industrial centres organized the reform-minded International Assn. London and Guelph joined and the Tecumsehs won the first championship with a season-ending victory over the Pittsburgh Alleghenys. London then rejected membership in the National League, owing to the league's restrictions on games with nonleague teams, and was the lone Canadian entry in the 1878 Assn. Financial difficulties led to the Tecumsehs' mid-season collapse. Organized baseball in Ontario lacked clear direction again until the 1885 formation of another Canadian League based in the province. Toronto's decision to join an American minor league in 1886 led to the end of professional baseball's independent character in Ontario, since the Ontario teams became subservient to the interests of American major league organizations.

Baseball gained in popularity in other parts of Canada. In 1865 a bylaw was passed in Montréal preventing the playing of baseball in city parks or public places. In a more positive vein, the game spread to the Maritimes from New England and the first Canadian-born major league player, William Phillips of Saint John, NB, played for Cleveland in 1879. In western Canada a crude form of baseball had been played at Red River in the 1840s, but the modern game did not appear until 1874 in Winnipeg. Its growth followed the railroad and many of the early promoters were associated with companies anxious to move players and fans along the rails. Rail workers and a future Saskatchewan premier, Walter SCOTT, were among those who enjoyed the amateur game in the 19th century. American professionals contributed to the game's spread as did eastern Canadians such as James Ross, a member of London's champion amateur team of 1877. He took the game west, becoming a rancher and later a member of the Canadian Senate. By 1904 baseball was so popular in the Yukon that a 2-game international championship was played and won by Whitehorse over the Alaskan town of Skagway. In 1907 the Western Canada League, a minor professional organization, was formed in Alberta and 2 years later included teams from Saskatchewan and Manitoba. The league led a financially troubled and brief existence, duplicating the history of other minor professional sports organizations in Canada. The Cape Breton Colliery League, based in coal-mining towns in NS, survived from 1937 to 1939. The Provincial

Captain Robert Pearson of the YMCA, umpiring behind the plate at a baseball match held in the Canadian lines, Sept 1917 (*courtesy Public Archives of Canada/PA-1921*).

Montreal Expos' former catcher, Gary Carter, traded in 1984 (*courtesy Expos, Montreal Baseball Club Ltd*).

Toronto Blue Jays' outfielder Lloyd Moseby at bat. The Blue Jays joined the American League in 1977 and drew 6 million fans in their first four seasons, a major-league record (*courtesy Toronto Blue Jays*).

League in Québec, at times an outlaw league outside the control of major league baseball, lasted from 1935 to the early 1960s. Several French Canadian stars such as Roland Gladu and Jean-Pierre Roy were developed in this league.

Toronto and Montréal had teams in the International League, a respected minor league, for periods of 78 and 55 years, respectively. Montréal developed a reputation as a good baseball town and the team's ownership included, at one time or another, Canadian baseball star "Tip" O'NEILL and Charles Trudeau, father of the future Canadian prime minister. In 1946 Jackie Robinson became the first black player in modern "organized" baseball when he played for the Montreal Royals. He was a crowd favourite, leading the Royals to the minor league baseball championship. A new era began in 1969 with the introduction of major league baseball to Montréal. In 1977 the MONTREAL EXPOS moved from the comfortable surroundings of Jarry Park to Olympic Stadium where they have drawn crowds of over 2 million in one season. A second Canadian major league franchise began in 1977 when the TORONTO BLUE JAYS joined the American League. They attracted over 6 million fans in their first 4 seasons, a major league record. Each season these teams play an exhibition game for the Pearson Cup, with funds going to Canadian amateur baseball.

The amateur game in Canada is overseen by a hierarchy of local and provincial organizations, such as the Ontario Baseball Assn founded in Hamilton in 1918. At the national level, the Canadian Federation of Amateur Baseball co-ordinates in such areas as coaching programs and national amateur teams. There were 115 000 registered amateur players in Canada in 1981 in the senior, junior, bison, midget and under-midget categories. Québec with 43 000 players and BC with 29 000 lead the provinces. Since 1871, 138 Canadians have made it to major league baseball, including Bob Emslie, Mooney GIBSON and Phil MARCHILDON; of these only 81 were trained in Canada, but their ranks include such contemporary stars as pitcher Ferguson JENKINS and outfielder Terry Puhl. Baseball remains identified as the national game of the US, but its popularity has spanned many generations in Canada and the 2 very different societies of the 19th and 20th centuries. The Canadian Baseball Hall of Fame opened at Exhibition Place, Toronto, in 1983. Its first inductees were Phil Marchildon, Tip O'Neill and George Selkirk (players); John Ducey and Frank Shaughnessy (builders); and Lester PEARSON (honorary).

Softball is a variation of baseball in which a larger ball is delivered in an underhand motion to the batter. Two types of softball are played in Canada: fast pitch, in which the ball is delivered to the batter in a rapid motion; and slow pitch, in which the ball is tossed in an arc. The game began as a form of indoor baseball in the 1890s in the US, but soon came to Canada where it has become a popular summer recreation for men and women. The Ontario Amateur Softball Assn, formed in 1923, was the first such organization anywhere. Softball has since spread throughout the world. Canadians are credited with introducing it into Holland during WWII. In 1949 Tip Top Tailors of Toronto won the N American championship in Little Rock, Ark. In 1972, represented by the Richmond Hill Dynes of Ontario, Canada won the men's world championship in Manila, and in 1976 another Canadian team, Victoria Bate Construction of BC, tied for the men's world title with the US and New Zealand at the tournament in New Zealand. Softball is overseen by local and provincial organizations, and the Canadian Amateur Softball Association acts as a nationwide co-ordinating body responsible for 7 annual national championships. Over 567 000 men and women play organized softball on close to 40 000 teams across Canada. WILLIAM HUMBER

Reading: L. Cauz, *Baseball's Back in Town: A History of Baseball in Toronto* (1977); William Humber, *Cheering for the Home Team: The Story of Baseball in Canada* (1983); H. Seymour, *Baseball*, vols 1, 2 (1960, 1971).

Basil, *see* HERBS.

Basketball is a team sport, invented by Canadian James A. NAISMITH in 1891, which has spread throughout the world. The game had its origin at the YMCA International Training School, now Springfield College, in Springfield, Mass. Naismith, a psychology student at that time and then an instructor at the school, responded to a need for an indoor winter recreational activity that could be easily learned and played in teams. Naismith tried to find a way of using a ball without the football tackle and of throwing it with skill instead of force. The result was a team sport whose object was to score by throwing a large ball into a basket place horizontally about 3 m above the floor. Havin conceived this idea Naismith defined specif rules for orderly play. From the original gam with 13 basic rules, basketball has progresse to a highly skilled sport, with an intricate blen of timing, intuition and co-operation. Record indicate that basketball was played in Canad prior to 1900; photographs of the Vancouve YMCA basketball team of 1900-01 are on display at the Pacific National Exhibition in Vancouver.

Graduates of the former YMCA School exported the sport throughout the world. B the 1930s it was played in over 50 countries prompting its acceptance as an official Olympi competition in the 1936 Berlin Games. It ha already appeared as a demonstration sport a the 1904 St Louis Olympics and, through th EDMONTON GRADS, a women's team, at the 1924 1928 and 1932 Olympic Games. Canada's tean at Berlin, the Windsor Ford V8s, made up c players primarily from Windsor, Ont, an strengthened by players from the West Coast won the silver medal. Canada did not pla Olympic basketball again until 1976 in Montréal. The women's team finished last in th 6-team tournament, while the men were 4t among 12 teams, losing the bronze medal gam to the USSR.

Canada's record in other international competition is highlighted by the achievements o Edmonton Grads under J. Percy PAGE. Fron 1915 to 1940 they dominated basketball with world championships and a record 502 wins i 522 games, of which 78 were consecutive. Sinc 1976, Canada's men's national team has consistently placed among the top 6 amateur teams i the world, winning a gold medal in the 197 Commonwealth Cup, the gold medal in th 1983 World University Games and finishin fourth in the 1984 Los Angeles Olympics. I 1981 the women's national team was ranke 4th in the world behind USSR, the US and Cuba

The official governing body for basketbal in Canada is the Canadian Amateur Basketball Assn, now called Basketball Canada, formed in Dec 1928 in Port Arthur (now Thunde Bay), Ont. Its initial main function was to assis with national championships, but its programs beyond men's and women's national championships, now include men's and women's national team development; technical development with coaching, official and player certification; youth programs; a Hall of Fame educational services; promotion and revenu generation. In 1973 Basketball Canada voted t adopt the international playing rules of th International Amateur Basketball Federation (FIBA). With the formation of a National Assn of Basketball Officials (NABO), the transition t international rules has been relatively smooth although Canadian universities and some high schools have maintained the former rules.

FRANK T. BUTLER

Basques were expert fishermen and sailors from the SE corner of the Bay of Biscay. With the Portuguese, they were early arrivals to Newfoundland's GRAND BANKS. Around 1525 they began WHALING and fishing for COD off Newfoundland, along the N shore of the St Lawrence R from the Str of Belle Isle to the Saguenay R, and in places where similar conditions attracted such northern marine life. The Basques controlled the entire NE coast for over a century. Every spring until about 1626 they sailed to their N American whaling stations, where they set up scaffolding to dry codfish and built stone ovens to prepare whale oil, a commodity that was highly prized in Europe. Their encounters with natives, particularly MICMAC, were friendly. In Dec or Jan, when ice conditions began to worsen, the Basques returned home.

Basque activities in the St Lawrence estuary ached a peak in the period 1550-80. In the arly 17th century a combination of factors ventually ended their voyages. These included decrease in the whale population, a weakning of Spain's influence during its war with rance, English-Dutch competition in northern aters, increased Inuit hostility and the growg strength of NEW FRANCE.

Samuel de CHAMPLAIN encountered Basque shermen during his early voyages and beneted from their knowledge of the N shore of the Lawrence. He had close ties with those who ame from France, despite their protests over the ounding of Québec. With Marc LESCARBOT, hamplain described the major Basque setement at Lesquemin (Les Escoumins, Qué); at or Bay (NS) he met an experienced Basque fishrman who had come there every year since 565. He described the Str of Belle Isle as an area equented by Spanish Basques.

The Basques left many traces of their presence n our shores, including place-names such as ingan (Qué) and Ingornachoix, Port au Choix nd Port au Port (Nfld). French Canadians dopted the Basque word *orignal* for the Canaian MOOSE. Recent archaeological work at RED AY, Nfld, has uncovered important evidence of asque habitation, including an abundance of ed roof tiles (used for ballast), pottery, glassvare and skeletons. Five Basque shipwrecks ave been located in the area; the earliest, the *an Juan*, dates from 1565. RENÉ BÉLANGER

eading: Harry Thurston, "The Basque Connection," *quinox* (Nov-Dec 1983).

ass, name applied to members of 3 FISH famies: temperate bass (Percichthyidae) with 4 spees in Canada (white perch, white and striped ass, wreckfish); sunfish (Centrarchidae) with 2 species in Canada (including largemouth, ock and smallmouth basses); and sea bass erranidae) with 3 species in Canada (yellowfin ass, black sea bass, snowy grouper). It can be en that some members of bass families are not alled bass. Anglers also use the word for several nrelated species. Temperate basses are found in arine, brackish or fresh waters of eastern Canda, with striped bass occurring along the BC oast as a result of introductions. Like sunfish, emperate basses have teeth in the mouth and piny fins. They are distinguished by a spine on ne gill cover and 2 dorsal fins (the spiny dorsal n is separate from the soft-rayed dorsal). Temerate basses are occasionally fished commerally and as sport fishes. The white perch has ecently become established in Lk Ontario, inading northwards from the US. This species as a high fecundity and tends to become verabundant, with many stunted individuals. unfish family members are freshwater fishes ound in lakes, ponds and slow-moving, warm treams of southern Canada. They are native to astern waters but have been introduced into acific drainages. They are characterized by aving bands of teeth on the roof of the mouth nd tongue, as well as on the jaws; by spines in he anal fin and in the continuous dorsal fin; nd ctenoid (rough-bordered) scales. They feed n insects, crayfish and other fishes. The largenouth and smallmouth basses are important game fishes. Sea bass family members are found along the Atlantic coast, but little is known about them in these waters. The yellowfin bass has only recently been reported in Canada. BRIAN W. COAD

argemouth bass (*Micropterus salmoides*), an important anadian game fish (*courtesy National Museum of Man/ ational Museum of Natural Sciences*).

Bassett, Carling Kathrin, tennis player (b at Toronto 9 Oct 1967). In 1981 she won the Canadian junior indoor title and in 1982 was ranked first among world juniors after wins in Tokyo and Taipei. Also in 1982, at age 14, she became the youngest winner of the Canadian closed championship, winning the title again in 1983, the year in which she turned professional. By age 16 she had emerged as Canada's premier tennis player, scoring victories over several top international players and winning the Gunze Invitational at Osaka, Japan. She lost to Chris Evert Lloyd in the final of a World Tennis Assn championship and in 1983 advanced to the quarterfinals of the French Open, Australian Open and Wimbledon. She was a semifinalist in the 1984 US Open. JAMES MARSH

Bat, nocturnal MAMMAL of order chiroptera. Bats are the only flying mammals. Two families are known from Canada: Vespertilionidae, smooth-faced bats; Molossidae, free-tailed bats. The 19 Canadian species range in size from the 5 g small-footed bat (*Myotis leibii*) to the 35 g big free-tailed bat (*Tadarida macrotis*). Although all bats can see, most fly and hunt using echolocation or biosonar. In summer Canadian bats consume daily up to 50% of their body weight in insects. In winter they hibernate or migrate to warmer areas. Bats annually produce one litter of 1-2 (rarely 3-4) young. Most Canadian species mate in autumn; females store sperm over winter. Ovulation and fertilization occur when females leave hibernation in spring; young are born 50-70 days later. Newborn bats are about 25% of their mothers' mass and grow very quickly, feeding on their mothers' milk until they are large enough to fly and hunt insects. Young little brown bats (*M. lucifugus*) may fly by age 3 weeks. Bats may be longlived; a little brown bat banded in Ontario had survived over 30 years in 1977. Banding studies indicate that some Canadian bats migrate several hundred kilometres to summer roosts. In summer Canadian bats roost in trees, cliffs or buildings; in winter most select caves or old mines as hibernation sites. Only big brown bats (*Eptesicus fuscus*) regularly hibernate in buildings. In Canada bats occur from the US border to the TREELINE, although a vagrant red bat (*Lasiurus borealis*) was reported from Southampton I in the Arctic. In the tropics, many species occur including some that feed on fruit or nectar and pollen and spectacular carnivorous species taking fish, birds, frogs, mice and even other bats. The most infamous bats are the vampires. Three species of these blood-feeders occur in Central and S America. Razor-sharp incisor teeth are used to cut into prey and an anticoagulant in vampire saliva keeps blood from clotting. These bats do not occur in Canada. M.B. FENTON

Bata, Thomas John, shoe manufacturer (b at Prague, Czech 17 Sept 1914). Son of Thomas Bata, owner of the world's largest shoe manufacturing companies, he began his career as apprentice in his father's factory at Zlin, Czech, in 1929. In 1935 he went to England as assistant general manager of British Bata Shoe Co. He came to Canada in 1939 and built a new plant at Batawa, Ont. At that time the company was established in more than 30 countries. In 1983 it had factories, stores and related enterprises in 95, employed 88 000 people, made and sold more than one million pairs of shoes daily and was the world's largest shoemaker. Bata is the president of Bata Ltd, and a director of IBM Canada, CP Air Lines and IBM World Trade Corp. JORGE NIOSI

Bateman, Robert McLellan, painter (b at Toronto 24 May 1930). Bateman received his early training as a naturalist at Toronto's Royal Ontario Museum and studied painting and drawing with Gordon Payne and Carl SCHAEFER. Bateman's work relates both to traditional wildlife illustrators, such as Fuertes and Allen Brooks, and to the GROUP OF SEVEN and contemporary realist artists. For about 20 years until 1976, he taught high-school geography and art in Toronto and Burlington, Ont, and travelled widely. Throughout the 1950s and early 1960s he painted mainly in abstract and semiabstract styles, though he continued to sketch plants, birds and mammals. Then, after seeing an Andrew Wyeth exhibition in 1963, he began producing realistic paintings in which wildlife is the central or incidental subject, often within a richly worked environment. These achieved international success, and there have been major showings of his work in Canada and abroad. RAMSAY DERRY

Reading: Ramsay Derry, *The Art of Robert Bateman* (1981).

Bates, John Seaman, chemist, environmentalist (b at Woodstock, Ont 9 June 1888). A graduate of Acadia U, Bates obtained the first PhD in chemical engineering granted by Columbia U. In his first career, in the pulp and paper industry, he was one of the first to apply scientific principles to pulp processing. At an age when most have retired, Bates moved to government and consulting work in the water supply and environment field in NB, NS and PEI. Bates is probably best known for his contributions to the establishment of scientific and technical societies such as the Technical Section of the Canadian Pulp and Paper Assn and the Chemical Institute of Canada. T.H.G. MICHAEL

Bates, Maxwell, artist, architect, author, poet (b at Calgary 14 Dec 1906; d at Victoria 14 Sept 1981). Apprenticed in his father's architectural office in 1924, he attended life classes at the Calgary Art Club and studied painting at the Provincial Institute of Technology and Art 1926-27, identifying strongly with French postimpressionist painters. He lived in London, Eng, 1931-39, exhibiting regularly. His book *A Wilderness of Days* (1978) details his experience of internment in a German prisoner-of-war camp 1940-45. He returned to Calgary in 1946 and joined his father's architectural firm; with partner A.W. Hodges he designed Calgary's St Mary's Cathedral, a unique prairie monument. He was part of the Calgary Group of artists formed by Jock (J.W.G.) MACDONALD and others (1947). Although suffering a severe stroke that left him partially paralysed in 1961, he moved to Victoria and continued to paint landscapes and boldly coloured, dynamic and expressive figure studies (*Cocktail Party I*, 1965). His poetry collection *Far Away Flags* was published in 1964. JOYCE ZEMANS

Bates, Patricia, née Martin, artist (b at Saint John 25 June 1927). She studied art in Belgium, France and New York, as well as Mt Allison U, NB. Her principal medium has always been PRINTMAKING, and she is one of the few artists to exploit embossing techniques successfully. Highly innovative, her work includes 2-sided prints meant to hang away from the wall. They are usually perforated, and may employ laminations and embroidery. Her colour, which is limited to black, white and silver, is used symbolically, as is her imagery — geometric compositions inspired by the cosmology of the Islamic Middle East or the Zen Buddhist mandala. JUDY GOUIN

Batfish, underwater vehicle designed to carry oceanographic instruments and sensors. It is towed behind a ship in a sawtooth, undulating pattern. The Batfish can dive or ascend by rotating its hydroplanes ("wings") on ship command,

and is capable of diving between the surface and approximately 400 m. Control power, used to activate the wings, is derived from an impellor-driven hydraulic pump within the Batfish. The core of the armoured towing cable contains 7 electrical conductors through which electronic information is transmitted to the surface from sensors mounted on the Batfish. The information is transferred to a shipboard computer and stored on magnetic tape. The Batfish was developed at the BEDFORD INSTITUTE OF OCEANOGRAPHY, Dartmouth, NS, and manufactured by Guildline Instruments Ltd, Smiths Falls, Ont. It has been equipped with 3 sensors: a conductivity-temperature-depth probe, used to measure physical oceanographic features; a fluorometer (mounted atop the Batfish) measuring chlorophyll *a* fluorescence, the indicator of phytoplankton or plant biomass; and an electronic zooplankton counter (mounted below the Batfish), measuring small marine copepods or bugs (approximately 0.5-4 mm long) which consume mainly marine plants. Information from the biological sensors is used in fisheries studies of the marine food chain. *See* ECOLOG.

ALEX W. HERMAN

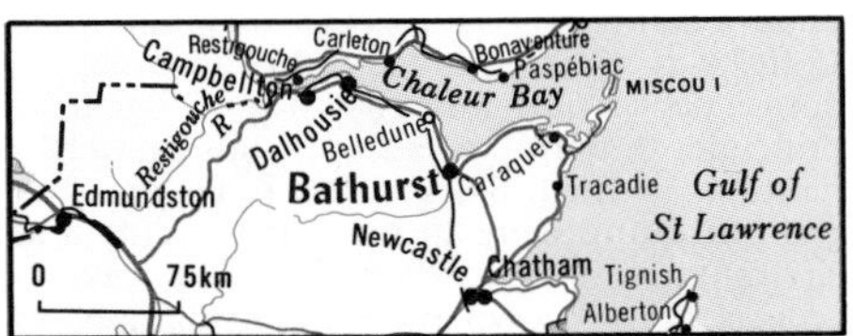

Bathurst, NB, City, pop 15 705 (1981c), inc 1966, administrative centre of Gloucester County, is located on Bathurst harbour at the mouth of the Nepisiguit R in northern NB. Founded by Nicolas DENYS in 1652, the site was abandoned after his death in 1688. The next settlers were dispossessed ACADIANS (1757) and English traders (1776). First called Nepisiguit, then St Peters, it was renamed Bathurst in 1828 after the colonial secretary. Lumbering and shipbuilding, begun here in the 1820s, and sawmills dominated the economy until a pulp mill opened in 1914; it was expanded to make paper in 1923 and underwent major renovations in 1983. The discovery of sizable base-metal deposits in 1953 in the surrounding region spurred the city's development. The area has 40% of Canada's reserves of silver, lead and zinc; its mine-mills process 10 000 tonnes of ore daily. The community is primarily English and French speaking (51%/47%, 1981c), and besides English and French high schools, has a bilingual trade and technology community college.

BURTON GLENDENNING

Bathurst Inlet, a SE extension of CORONATION GULF, penetrating the arctic shore for some 200 km. The hamlet of Bathurst Inlet is located at the mouth of the Burnside R, which drains Contwoyto Lk to the SW. The inlet was named by Sir John FRANKLIN in 1821 for the third earl of Bathurst, then secretary of the colonies. Some of its numerous islands have rocky cliffs that nest peregrine falcons and golden eagles.

JAMES MARSH

Bathurst Inlet, NWT, still icebound in mid-July (*photo by Richard Harrington*).

Bathurst Island, NWT, discovered in 1819 by Admiral Parry; the final shape of the island was revealed only after aerial reconnaissance by the RCAF in 1947 (*photo by Stephen J. Krasemann/DRK Photo*).

Bathurst Island, over 18 000 km^2 (including its offshore islands), is located in the ARCTIC ARCHIPELAGO, NWT. The present position of the N Magnetic Pole is near its northern end. Its physiography is greatly influenced by a geological structure of relatively undisturbed sedimentary strata. The island's form is a low-relief plateau, sloping to the S and W, with few parts higher than 330 m in elevation. Widespread surface exposure of the shale and siltstone formations supports abundant vegetation for this latitude and has given Bathurst I a prolific wildlife population compared to other arctic islands. Although discovered by PARRY as early as 1819, and later explored by search parties seeking traces of the FRANKLIN EXPEDITION, it was only after aerial reconnaissance by the RCAF in 1947 that its final shape was revealed. The "peninsula" forming the western coast was discovered to be in reality a series of islands. Parry named the island for the earl of Bathurst, longtime

Map of Batoche, the site of the last major battle of the North-West Rebellion (1885). The map was drawn by Capt H. Haig shortly after the battle and was published in 1886 (*courtesy Public Archives of Canada/NMC-48690*).

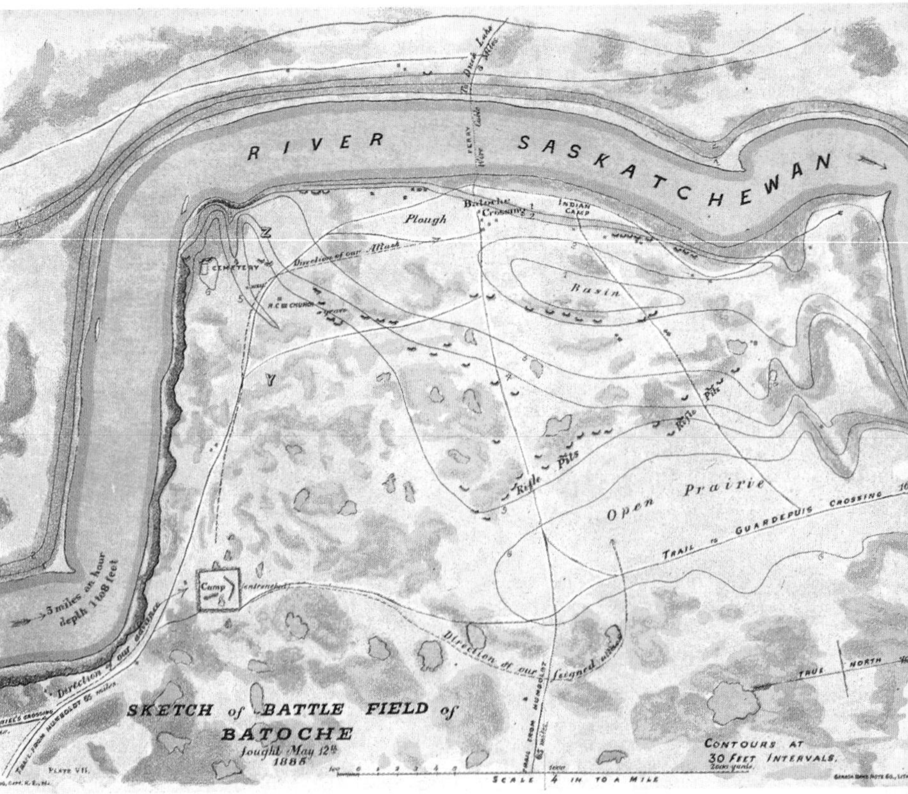

:itish minister of war and the colonies in the ırly 19th century. DOUG FINLAYSON

atoche, national historic site 44 km SW of :ince Albert, Sask; Métis community and scene a major confrontation, 9-12 May 1885, durıg the NORTH-WEST REBELLION. Maj-Gen Frederick IDDLETON with 800 men attacked approximate- 175 MÉTIS and Indians on 2 fronts: by river, om the HBC steamer *Northcote,* and by land. ıe strategy failed when the Métis lowered a rry cable, decapitating the *Northcote*'s smokeack and leaving the steamer to float harmssly downstream. The Métis also effectively sisted Middleton's land forces until May 12, hen Middleton's forces — two 9-pounders, a atling gun and about 130 men — feinted orth, drawing the Métis out of their rifle pits ound St Antoine-de-Padoue Church and toards the Gatling gun. A strong wind prented Lt-Col Van Straubenzie from hearing the ıns and co-ordinating his attack on the church ith Middleton's action, but Lt-Col Williams as able to break through weakened Métis ıes. Middleton's North-West Field Force swept ast the Métis, who were firing nails and stones om their rifles. The battle was over and the irit of the rebellion broken. Over 25 men from oth sides were killed. Louis RIEL was appreended a few days later, Gabriel DUMONT fled to ıe US, and other participants were captured nd held for trial. WALTER HILDEBRANDT

aton Broadcasting Incorporated, a diversied Canadian communications company, is ontrolled by the EATON family (Eaton's of Can- da) through Telegram Corporation Ltd. Baton perates radio stations in Saskatoon, Ottawa and Vindsor (Ont), and television stations CFQC-TV, skatoon, and CFTO-TV, Toronto's largest priate TV station. Through its subsidiary Glen Varren Productions Ltd, Baton operates facilies in Toronto for the production of television rograms, commercials and movies. Other holdıgs include a broadcast sales company and usiness forms, graphics and packaging operions. Total assets of Baton in 1983 were $105 illion, with revenues of $140 million. PETER S. ANDERSON

attle, Helen Irene, zoologist, educator (b at ondon, Ont 31 Aug 1903). A pioneering Canaian zoologist and much-loved teacher, she has een emeritus professor of ZOOLOGY at Western nce 1972. As one of the first zoologists actively ıgaged in laboratory (as opposed to field) rearch in marine biology, she demonstrated that ıe methods of the histology and physiology boratories could provide answers to marine roblems. Many of her papers are beautifully lustrated with her own ink drawings. One of ıe first women to enter a field dominated by ıen, she campaigned to improve the place of vomen in universities and encouraged many to ke up careers in science. She was selected by ıe National Museum of Natural Sciences in ttawa as one of 19 outstanding women scintists in Canada and was represented in a travlling exhibit to mark International Women's ear. Many honours have accrued to her. Her rst love was her teaching, which spanned ome 50 years. Her students have become leaders ı Canadian biology and her influence has been elt worldwide. DONALD B. MCMILLAN

attle of Amiens took place 8-11 Aug 1918, W f Amiens, France. A co-ordinated assault, pearheaded by the Australian and Canadian orps, involving aircraft, tanks, artillery, cavlry, and infantry, it was subsequently charcterized by the German Gen Ludendorff as he black day of the German army." The Allied orces won a major victory. The 4 Canadian diisions defeated parts of 15 German divisions, outing 4, at a cost of some 9000 casualties. Their uccess initiated the "hundred days" which saw the Germans repeatedly driven back all along the Western Front, and which culminated in the armistice of 11 Nov 1918. *See* WORLD WAR I. BRERETON GREENHOUS

Battle of Britain, 10 July to 31 Oct 1940, the first battle in history to be fought exclusively in the air, resulted in the Royal Air Force's Fighter Command compelling the German Luftwaffe to abandon its attempt to establish air superiority over S and E England. Without that superiority, a German invasion of Britain was impracticable. Only one Canadian unit participated, although many more Canadians serving in the RAF were in the forefront. No. 1 (Fighter) Squadron (later No. 401), flying Hawker Hurricanes and commanded by Sqn Ldr E.A. McNab, first met the enemy on Aug 25. When withdrawn on Oct 9 the squadron had been credited with 30 enemy aircraft destroyed and 8 "probables." Three Canadians had been killed and 10 wounded or injured in crash landings. *See* WORLD WAR II. BRERETON GREENHOUS

Battle of Châteauguay, fought 26 Oct 1813 between the leading elements of an American army of invasion and a smaller Canadian force consisting principally of the VOLTIGEURS, a French Canadian fencible corps under Lt-Col Charles de SALABERRY. The field of battle was along the Châteauguay R about 50 km S of Montréal. Through innovative devices and scare tactics, including the blowing of horns in the woods to suggest a large force of defenders, the Canadians confused the Americans, who became overly cautious and soon retreated. Montréal was not seriously threatened for the remainder of the WAR OF 1812. ROBERT S. ALLEN

Battle of Paardeberg, first major British success in the SOUTH AFRICAN WAR since "Black Week," 10-15 Dec 1899. Faced by a reorganized British offensive directed at their capitals, the Afrikaners made a stand at Paardeberg, a point on the Modder R some 130 km from Bloemfontein. Canada's 1st contingent fought first at Paardeberg Drift on 18 Feb 1900 where, after hours under fire in the scorching sun, they were ordered to make a suicidal assault. Their second engagement took place on Feb 27, 3 km from the Drift. The Canadians, attacking before dawn, faced withering Afrikaner rifle fire. Although the regiment was ordered to retreat, 2 companies from the Maritimes, who failed to hear or heed the order, maintained their position and returned the fire. Shortly thereafter Gen Piet Cronje and almost 4000 exhausted Afrikaners surrendered. The battle for Paardeberg cost Canada 31 men; another 92 were wounded. CARMAN MILLER

Battle of Ste-Foy, fought during the SEVEN YEARS' WAR on the road to Ste-Foy, a village 8 km W of Québec. In late Apr 1760 François de LÉVIS and his French force of 5000 engaged 3900 British troops under Col James MURRAY outside the city walls, soundly defeating them. Lévis then laid siege to the town while awaiting reinforcements from France. However, British ships arrived first. Lévis was forced to raise his siege and retreat to Montréal. W.J. ECCLES

Battle of the Atlantic, phrase used 6 Mar 1941 by British PM Winston Churchill to describe efforts to defeat attacks by the German navy on Allied shipping between America and Europe during WORLD WAR II. By that time German forces had sunk some 6½ million tons, of which only a third could be replaced. In May 1941 British cryptographers solved the German naval Enigma code, giving Britain the advantage in the E Atlantic. After June, Allied naval escorts provided continuous convoy protection, and in Sept American forces were committed to the task. Terrible losses continued, but by Nov 1942 ship construction overtook sinkings. Tactical skill and air cover eventually drove U-boats into mid-Atlantic, beyond the range of shore-based aircraft. Further cryptographic breakthroughs in Dec 1942 and Mar 1943, roving support groups, and very long-range and carrier-borne aircraft closed the gap. In the first 3 weeks of May 1943 escorts sank 31 U-boats, forcing Germany to abandon the N Atlantic convoy routes; an attempted comeback in Sept failed.

Canada provided about half the naval escorts in the Newfoundland (later Mid Ocean) and Western Local Escort Forces, most land-based air coverage from Newfoundland and the Maritimes, and 7 RCAF squadrons used elsewhere by Britain's Coastal Command. Desperately short of equipment and training, Canadian forces eventually reached adequate operational standards, winning responsibility for the new Canadian Northwest Atlantic theatre. By war's end 25 421 convoyed merchant ships had crossed the Atlantic successfully, and the RCN and RCAF received credit for 47 of the 788 U-Boats and 2 Italian submarines destroyed. W.A.B. DOUGLAS

Joseph Legaré's painting of *The Battle of Ste-Foy* (*c* 1854). Levis defeated the British but was forced to retreat to Montréal when British reinforcements arrived (*courtesy National Gallery of Canada*).

Battle of the Plains of Abraham, 13 Sept 1759, during the SEVEN YEARS' WAR, fought upstream from Québec on a tract of land that is thought to have been named after Abraham Martin, to whom it was granted 1635-45. A powerful British force under Maj-Gen James WOLFE and Vice-Adm Charles Saunders was sent up the St Lawrence to capture Québec. The French, commanded by Lt-Gen the Marquis de MONTCALM, at first held the British at bay. Having sailed upstream past the city on Sept 5 and 6, Wolfe's army landed without opposition on Sept 13, climbing the cliffs a few km above Québec. Montcalm's communications with his source of supplies were threatened; he felt obliged to accept battle and impulsively attacked without waiting to collect all his forces. The armies actually on the field seem to have been about numerically equal — some 4500 each — but the British were all regulars, whereas many of the French were ill-trained militia. The French attack was broken by British infantry fire, and the French retired in disorder. Both Wolfe and Montcalm were mortally wounded. The French field army retreated up the St Lawrence by a circuitous route that night. Québec surrendered on Sept 18. A French attack early in 1760 failed to recover the city, and later in the year the British captured Montréal and NEW FRANCE fell. C.P. STACEY

Battle of the Rhineland, 8 Feb-10 Mar 1945, fought by FIRST CANADIAN ARMY (with XXX British Corps under command) and Ninth US Army while forcing back the Germans to the Rhine R. For the Canadians it involved attacking over inundated ground in the first phase (Operation *Veritable,* Feb 8-21) and through the Hochwald forest in the second (Operation *Blockbuster,* Feb 22-Mar 10) against stubborn opposition as the Germans defended German soil. Throughout the month poor weather robbed the Allies of much of their accustomed tactical air support, while mud frequently immobilized their armoured forces. Nevertheless, the W bank of the Rhine was cleared as far S as Düsseldorf in some of the bitterest fighting of WWII. Allied casualties totalled nearly 23 000, the Canadians losing 5300. The Germans lost approximately 90 000 men, of whom some 52 000 were taken prisoner. By 23 Mar 1945 the Allies were on the Rhine from Strasbourg, France, to Nijmegen, Netherlands. *See* WORLD WAR II.
BRERETON GREENHOUS

Battle of the Somme, 1 July-late Nov 1916, during WORLD WAR I, saw British, Imperial, and French troops hammering German defence lines N of the Somme R in one of the most futile and bloody battles in history. The 1st Newfoundland Regiment was virtually wiped out at Beaumont Hamel on the first day of the battle. The Canadian Corps entered the battle on Aug 30, and during its attacks in Sept was supported by the first tanks used in action on the Western Front. The machine guns, barbed wire, trenches and massive use of artillery resulted in hard fighting and heavy casualties, especially in the capture of Regina Trench, Courcelette, Thiepval and Ancre Heights. Rain, snow, and sleet brought the battle to an end. After 5 months' fighting the Allies had penetrated about 13 km along a 35 km front. Allied losses were estimated at 623 907, of whom 24 713 were Canadians and Newfoundlanders. German losses were estimated at 660 000. R.H. ROY

Battleford, Sask, pop 3565 (1981c), inc 1910, is located at the confluence of the N SASKATCHEWAN and Battle rivers, 155 km NW of Saskatoon, and was once among the most important of early settlements in western Canada. While little more than a small fur-trade post and surveyor work camp, the settlement was named capital of the vast North-West Territories in 1876. A large government complex and nearby North-West Mounted Police post were then established, as well as a townsite. Its trade and government functions grew rapidly, but in 1882 the capital seat was moved to Regina and the CPR main line, which had been projected for Battleford, went to southern Saskatchewan. During the North-West Rebellion (1885), Métis and native problems further damaged settlement prospects for the region.

In 1905 a rail line finally reached the area, but the Canadian Northern Ry had chosen to bypass Battleford, an event that eventually led to the creation of the adjacent community of North Battleford. Battleford prospered as a government centre for land title registration, a judicial district and an Indian Affairs office, but never fulfilled its earlier expectations. Today Battleford and North Battleford, with a combined population of 17 595 (1981c), form a service centre for the surrounding region, which depends largely on agriculture and some oil and gas development. MARK RASMUSSEN

Baumann, Alex, "Sasha," swimmer (b at Prague, Czech 21 Apr 1964). Soon after he arrived with his family at Sudbury at age 9, he began setting age-group records in swimming under coach Jeno Tihanyi. In 1978 he won the 200 m individual medley (IM) at the Darmstadt International meet (butterfly, breaststroke, backstroke, freestyle) and won numerous national and international meets in the 200 IM, 400 IM, freestyle, backstroke and butterfly before setting a Commonwealth record in the 400 m IM 28 July 1981 and a world record in the 200 m IM the next day. Forced out of swimming for 10 months because of a chronic shoulder problem, he returned to lower the Commonwealth record in the 400 m IM and the world record in the 200 m IM at the COMMONWEALTH GAMES in Brisbane, Australia, Oct 1982. He won the 400 m and 200 m IM events at the WORLD UNIVERSITY GAMES in Edmonton, July 1983, and lowered the 400 m IM world record to 4:17.53 at the Olympic trials. His 2 gold medals at the Los Angeles Olympics (200 m IM, world record 2:01.42; 400 m IM, world record 4:17.41) made him one of only 4 Canadians to win 2 Olympic gold medals (along with George HODGSON, Percy WILLIAMS, Gaetan BOUCHER). He was a political science student at Laurentian U in 1984. JAMES MARSH

Alex Baumann with one of his two gold medals at the 1984 Los Angeles Olympics (*courtesy Athlete Information Bureau/Service Information-Athlètes*).

Baxter, John Babington Macaulay, lawye politician, premier and chief justice of NB at Saint John 16 Feb 1868; d there 27 Dec 194 Baxter played a leading part in the develo ment of the Conservative Party in NB and w a leader in the Maritime Rights movement the 1920s. He was a city councillor (1892-191 attorney general of NB (1915-17), federal mini ter of customs (1921), premier 1925-31 and chi justice 1935-46. He was the author of *Historic Records of the New Brunswick Regiment, Royal Art lery* (1896), the unit he had commanded fro 1907 to 1912. ARTHUR T. DOY

Baxter, Joseph Iain Wilson, artist (b at Mi dlesborough, Eng 16 Nov 1936). Brought to Ca ada by his parents in 1937, Iain Baxter began h artistic career as a painter, but by 1965 he w creating plastic bas-reliefs of such objects as pla tic bleach, milk and detergent bottles. *Bagg Place* (1966), a 4-room furnished apartment, e ery part and item of which was bagged in pla tic, contained psychological and sociologic overtones. In 1966 he and his wife Elaine (fro 1971 she used Ingrid), formed what became t N.E. Thing Co Ltd. The NETCO collaboratio continued until 1978 and produced ACTs (Ae thetically Claimed Things), ARTs (Aesthetical Rejected Things), conceptual works that de with ways of perceiving the environment, co struction analogues, works using comm nication media as extensions of man, and pa ticipatory pieces. Since 1978 he has prepare photo works and mixed-media pieces, incorp rating polaroid photos, drawings, painting an sometimes objects. An uninhibited attitude t wards art and a partiality for common "thing are combined with sureness of line and som times sensual colour in works enriched as muc with ambiguity, wit and inventive play as t his persistent aesthetic questioning.

Reading: M. L. Fleming, *Baxter²: Any Choice Works* (198

Bay Bulls, Nfld, UP, pop 1081 (1981c), is locat on the E coast of the AVALON PENINSULA. O of the earliest settlements, it has the earlie known English place-name in Newfoundlan (The name may have come from the bull or t ice bird.) First used by the French, it was the si of wintering English fishermen by 1635, fort fied by Gov David KIRKE 1638 and attack by Dutch Admiral De Ruyter 1665. The sem permanent fishing settlement was attacked the French 5 times, 1696-1796, during Angl French rivalry over Newfoundland's fishery. year-round fishing community of mainly Iri immigrants was established by 1800. Reside merchants established thriving fish firms du ing the 1800s and Bay Bulls became a local bu ness centre. A fisheries research station was e tablished 1931, and during WWII the area w leased to Canada as a naval repair base. Mode Bay Bulls is a fishing and fish-processing cent and the site of an RCA-Bell Canada microwa satellite station. J.E.M. PITT AND R.D. P

Bay d'Espoir is a fjordlike arm of Hermitage on Newfoundland's S coast, entered betwe West Head and Dawson Point, 3 km NW. Mo than 50 km from mouth to head, ice-free Ba d'Espoir (French for "hope"), has sheer cliffs an steep-sided hills rising 180 to 300 m. The ba divides into 2 principal arms to the N, and N beyond 14 km long Bois I. Because of t tremendous watershed from a surrounding gl cial plateau, the area was chosen as the si of a hydroelectric power development, bui 1964-1977, at 600 MW the largest in insul Newfoundland. Until 1964 Bay d'Espoir w sparsely settled by Newfoundlanders origina ing in PLACENTIA B in the 1700s, and by MICMA who established the Conne River settlement the mid-1800s. Today fishing, lumbering an construction work are the area's main sources employment. JANET E.M. P

Bay Roberts, Nfld, Town, pop 4512 (1981 inc 1951, is located on the W shore of CONCEPTI

y. Established by the late 1600s by English shermen, Bay Roberts is probably named for a ench family name, Robert. The inshore fishy and later the Labrador fishery and seal hunt ntributed to the growth of Bay Roberts as a ading fishing, trading and commercial settleent by the 1800s. With CARBONEAR and HARUR GRACE, Bay Roberts became an important rvice, supply and communications centre with imerous wholesale companies and small-scale dustries. Today, it is the largest salt-fish procing centre in Newfoundland, supplying Eupean, Brazilian and Caribbean markets. In the 70s the original settlement expanded to inude several nearby communities.

JANET E.M. PITT AND ROBERT D. PITT

ayefsky, Aba, artist, teacher (b at Toronto 7 pr 1923). Bayefsky studied at Central Techcal School, Toronto, 1937-42, then enlisted in e RCAF. As an official war artist he produced visual record of Belsen concentration camp. He udied in Paris (1948) and later travelled to Ina (1958) and Japan (1960, 1969, 1982). Besides s well-known watercolour and oil works decting Toronto market scenes and portraits of iends, Bayefsky has done several large-scale urals and created portfolios of lithographs ised on Canadian Indian legends and mytholgy and Hebrew religious themes. Throughout s career the human figure has been the basis his work; most recently he completed a large ries of paintings depicting tattooed people in anada and Japan. Since 1957 he has been an structor at the Ontario College of Art, Toronto. 1979 he was appointed to the Order of Canla; he has achieved international recognition r his watercolours and graphics.

PAMELA WACHNA

ayfield, Henry Wolsey, naval officer, hydroaphic surveyor (b at Hull, Eng 21 Jan 1795; at Charlottetown 10 Feb 1885). At age 11, Bayeld joined the Royal Navy. In 1816 he was igaged by Capt W.F.W. Owen to assist in surying Lk Ontario. On Owen's recall to England 1817, the Admiralty instructed Bayfield to rvey Lk Erie and then Lks Huron and Supeor. After completing these surveys, Bayfield as appointed surveyor of the St Lawrence. orking from Québec City 1827-40, he surcyed and charted the Québec shores of the St awrence R and Gulf, part of the Labrador coast, so the E coast of NB; and from Charlottetown, 341-56, the PEI coastline, most of the NS coast nd part of Newfoundland's coast. His surveys icluded the main river estuaries; the harbours f Montréal, Québec, Halifax and Charlottewn; and Anticosti, Sable and the Magdalen Is. lotivated by a desire to prevent shipwrecks and ss of life, he took pride in the accuracy of his iarts. Bayfield was promoted rear-admiral 856, vice-admiral 1863 and admiral 1867. His iling directions were published as *The St Lawnce Pilot* (1860) and *The Nova Scotia Pilot* (1856, 860).

RUTH MCKENZIE

azalgette, Ian Willoughby, aviator (b at Calary 19 Oct 1918; d in France 4 Aug 1944). He ined the Royal Air Force in 1941 and was warded the Distinguished Flying Cross for allantry in 1943. He was awarded the VICTORIA ROSS posthumously for a courageous attack on a rget at Trossy St Maxim, France, despite heavy ntiaircraft fire. He managed to land his crippled Lancaster bomber but perished in an exlosion. In 1949 a mountain in Jasper National ark was named in his honour.

JAMES MARSH

C Hydro Formed by provincial legislation in 962, BC Hydro and Power Authority, a CROWN ORPORATION, was given a mandate to provide a cure ENERGY future for British Columbia. Toay, the company serves more than 90% of the opulation and is responsible for the overall lanning, generation and supply of ELECTRIC POWER for the province. In addition to developing British Columbia's hydroelectric potential, BC Hydro provides a natural-gas distribution system in the lower mainland and a liquid petroleum-gas (LPG) distribution system in Greater Victoria. BC Hydro also operates a rail freight service on the SW tip of the lower mainland. Until 1980, the utility operated city transit services in Greater Vancouver and Greater Victoria and, before 1979, an interurban bus service on the lower mainland and Vancouver I. BC Hydro employs approximately 8500 people. Its headquarters are in Vancouver.

In 1962 most of the province's 443 000 electric customers were served by the BC Electric Company and the provincially owned BC Power Commission. The provincial government had acquired BC Electric in 1961, and the 2 utilities were amalgamated the following year as BC Hydro. BC Electric began its hydroelectric and electric-railway operations in the late 1890s. The Power Commission was established by the provincial government in 1945 to consolidate the operations of many small utilities outside the BC Electric service areas.

After amalgamation, BC Hydro began developing the hydroelectric potential of the Peace and Columbia rivers. The W.A.C. Bennett Dam on the PEACE R is among the largest earthfill structures in existence, and the project's 2400 megawatt (MW) Gordon M. Shrum Generating Station was the world's largest underground powerhouse when it started operating in 1968. The 1964 signing of the COLUMBIA RIVER TREATY between Canada and the US opened the way for construction in BC of 3 dams, Duncan, Keenleyside and Mica, to regulate the flow of the Columbia R, enabling BC and the US to construct large power plants along the river and its tributaries. Only the Mica project, which has an ultimate capacity of 2604 MW, included generating facilities. The 810 MW Seven Mile project on the Pend d'Oreille R and the 700 MW Peace Canyon project on the Peace R began operations in 1980. The 2700 MW Revelstoke project on the Columbia R, due for completion in 1984, will bring BC Hydro's total installed generating capacity to 10.6 million kW.

Most of BC Hydro's existing generating capacity of approximately 8800 MW is produced at 32 hydroelectric-generating plants, which have a total capacity of 7500 MW. The remainder is generated by conventional thermal, gas turbine and stationary diesel plants. To meet anticipated future demands, BC Hydro is considering various hydroelectric options. The proposed projects, none of which is expected to come into service until the mid to late 1990s, include major developments on the Peace and Columbia rivers. *See* ELECTRIC UTILITIES.

FLINT BONDURANT

Beach, *see* COASTAL LANDFORM.

Beals, Carlyle Smith, astronomer (b at Canso, NS 29 June 1899; d at Ottawa 2 July 1979). Astronomer and assistant director of the Dominion Astrophysical Observatory, Victoria, BC, until 1946, Beals was Dominion Astronomer in Ottawa until his retirement in 1964. While at Victoria, he made important contributions to the observation and interpretation of emission lines in the spectra of certain hot stars, to the understanding of the nature of the gas clouds in interstellar space and to the development of instrumentation for astronomy. As Dominion Astronomer he guided the postwar development of astronomical and geophysical research in Canada. Combining his knowledge of ASTRONOMY and his interest in geophysics, he initiated a highly successful program in the identification and study of meteorite craters in Canada. Recognized internationally as one of the leading astronomers of his day, he was the recipient of many honours including the Order of Canada.

J.L. LOCKE

Beam, Carl, artist (b West Bay, Manitoulin I, Ont 1943). He graduated from U Vic 1976 and then studied at U of A. Beam works on a large format, canvas or paper, with acrylics. He abstracts realistic details from life and by repetition and juxtaposition of various elements forces the viewer to find meaning. His deep concern is to keep alive traditional Anishnabe (Ojibwa) cultural values.

MARY E. SOUTHCOTT

Bean, Green (*Phaseolus vulgaris*) There are at least 6 classes of green bean, and many cultivars (commercial varieties) are available within each class. Common types include the "snap" bean (green or wax) and kidney beans. The fruit is a pod, round or flat, curved or straight. Plant breeders have perfected a tender, round, fleshy, stringless pod with minimum fibre in the walls. Green beans are either quick-growing bush types or pole types, requiring a long growing season. Bush types are low growing, self supporting and nonclimbing. Pole types, with never-ending stem elongation, must be supported by string or posts. The bean plant is shallow rooted and requires adequate moisture. Bush-bean pods mature in a concentrated manner and successive plantings every 14 days are necessary for continuous podding; given optimum growing conditions, they are harvested 45-65 days after seeding. Pole-bean pods begin maturing 55-75 days after seeding; one planting will give continuous podding. Green beans (especially bush types) grow well throughout temperate parts of Canada. Main areas of commercial production are Québec, Ontario and BC. Yields of 4-6 t/ha are not uncommon for bush beans and pole types give considerably higher yields. The estimated annual worth of green beans grown in Canada exceeds $8-10 million; imports (mostly from southern US) are of about equal value.

I.L. NONNECKE

Bear (family Ursidae), stocky, bob-tailed MAMMAL with 5 clawed toes on each paw. Three species inhabit Canada: POLAR BEAR (*Ursus maritimus*), GRIZZLY BEAR (*U. arctos horribilis*) and black bear (*U. americanus*). Grizzly and black bears are omnivores, eating flesh or vegetable matter in season; polar bears prey mainly on seals. Black bears, the most common and widespread in Canada, may also be brown or cinnamon. Males weigh 80-250 kg; females are 10% lighter. Bears occupy coniferous forest, deciduous forest and swamp habitats, and occur over most of Canada except tundra and arctic regions. Recently, they have moved near settled areas. Breeding begins at 3 years, with mating in June-July. Embryos do not develop until Dec because of delayed implantation. In delayed implantation the fertilized egg develops slowly, while floating in the uterus. Eventually it becomes attached to the wall of the uterus and development continues until birth. In Jan-Feb, after 200-225 days gestation, usually 2 (range, 1-3) cubs are born in dens. Cubs become independent after about one year. In winter, bears sleep in dens but do not truly hibernate. Adults are solitary and are dangerous when no longer afraid of man. Bear skins are used as rugs and covers; their flesh is eaten.

C.S. CHURCHER

Bearberry, or kinnickinnick, trailing, evergreen shrub of heather family. Flexible, rooting branches grow up to 2 m long, are covered with reddish, shreddy bark and bear alternate, dark green, oval leaves. Small, waxy, urn-shaped flowers are white or pink, tipped with red. They grow in small clusters at branch ends, in late spring and early summer, and develop into bright red, fleshy fruits. Genus name, *Arctostaphylos*, derives from Greek *arctos* "bear," *staphylos*, "bunch of grapes"; species name, *uva-ursi*, from Latin *uva*, "bunch of grapes," *ursus*, "bear" — literally "bearberry, berry-bear." Bearberry grows across Canada on dry sandy soils (often called sandberry), but is also found on gravel terraces, sand dunes and in the boreal forest, and is valuable as ground cover for checking erosion on watersheds. It is less common above TREELINE. Kinnickinnick [Algonquian, "that which is mixed"] leaves were combined with tobacco and smoked by Blackfoot and other Indian groups in religious ceremonies. Bearberry extract has a high content of tannic and gallic acids which make it an astringent. It also contains arbutin, which becomes a germicide in the renal tract. The Thompson Indians of BC used it for kidney diseases, and the Blackfoot made an infusion for sore gums, and salve for skin diseases.

BERYL HALLWORTH

Beardy, Jackson, artist (b Quentin Pickering Jackson Beardy at Island Lake, Man 24 July 1944; d at Winnipeg 8 Dec 1984). He was educated at a government residential school and studied art at the Winnipeg Technical Vocational High School and U of Man. In his twenties he struggled with episodes of serious illness. His art draws on a deep knowledge of his native Cree tradition gained from a close childhood relationship with his grandmother and from his systematic collection of myths and legends in northern Manitoba during the mid-1960s. In 1972 he joined with ODJIG, MORRISSEAU, RAY, JANVIER, Cobiness and Sanchez to form the "Group of Seven." Although Beardy's early work often narrates specific legends, his mature art expresses fundamental cosmological and spiritual concepts such as balance in nature, regeneration and growth, and the interdependence of all things. His distinctive graphic style is characterized by precisely defined flat areas of warm colour and curving ribbons of paint. From 1982 to 1983 he was senior arts adviser to the federal Dept of Indian Affairs and Northern Development.

RUTH B. PHILLIPS

Bearlake are Athapaskan-speaking people who live near GREAT BEAR LK in the NWT. Their trading post and settlement is Ft Franklin, at the western end of the lake. The Bearlake were not considered a distinct people by self-designation or by outsiders until the 20th century. Historically, and probably before records exist, Great Bear Lk was exploited by various small bands of HARE, DOGRIB and SLAVEY intercepting the caribou herds and fishing the shores and tributaries. An aboriginal enemy of the Athapaskan peoples were the INUIT, who sometimes approached the NW area of the lake in pursuit of caribou. Occasionally this may have produced open hostilities, but mutual fear was generally handled by avoidance, and hostility was gradually reduced during the historical period.

Ft Franklin, on Keith Arm near the entrance of Great Bear R, is close to one of the few fishing sites open all year at this latitude. It was an obvious place for friendly neighbouring peoples to enjoy a dependable resource and to mingle socially. With the coming of the FUR TRADE, and a trading post intermittently active since 1804, there was increased contact among Indian groups. Through the 19th century and into the 20th, these groups gradually began to consider themselves "Bear Lakers" as a larger unit. They also developed their own dialect, incorporating features from Dogrib, Hare and Slavey-Mountain languages. In 1978 the population was 680, twice the number estimated in the early 20th century. In the late 1920s uranium and silver were discovered at the eastern end of Great Bear Lk. Uranium mining during the 1940s brought some involvement in the Canadian economy for the Bearlake, but by the 1950s this involvement was minimal. The Bearlake still rely on traditional hunting and fishing activities, with trapping and limited employment providing cash for other necessities.

BERYL C. GILLESPIE

Beatty, Sir Edward Wentworth, lawyer, railway official (b at Thorold, Ont 16 Oct 1877; d at Montréal 23 Mar 1943), son of Henry BEATTY. After studying at Upper Canada College, U of Toronto and Osgoode Hall, Beatty articled with a law firm in Toronto. When A.R. Creelman, a partner in the firm, was appointed CPR general counsel in 1901, he took Beatty to Montréal as his assistant. Beatty's ability impressed President Thomas SHAUGHNESSY. He was appointed general counsel in 1913 and became the first Canadian-born CPR president in 1918. The CPR faced competition from the CNR, particularly in accommodation and construction of prairie branch lines in the 1920s. Beatty strengthened the system, which he had inherited from Shaughnessy, and in 1942 created Canadian Pacific Airlines. He was knighted in 1935.

JOHN A. EAGLE

Reading: D.H. Miller-Barstow, *Beatty of the C.P.R.* (1951).

Beatty, Henry, businessman, pioneer transportation official (b at Cootehill, Ire 1 May 1834; d at Toronto 10 Apr 1914). Beatty immigrated with his parents to Thorold, Canada W, when he was 9. In 1857, apprenticing in the hardware business, he travelled widely and, seeking adventure, struck gold in the Cariboo. In 1870 he became a partner in his uncle's steamship firm. Under Beatty's management the firm expanded from one to 5 steamships and extended its operations from Sarnia to Port Arthur, Ont, and Duluth, Minn. In 1882 he was appointed manager of lake transportation for the CPR. One of his first duties was to supervise construction in Scotland of 3 vessels that became the nucleus of CPR Steamships. A man of unusual executive ability and vision, he served as marine adviser to the CPR after his retirement (1892).

JOHN A. EAGLE

Beatty, Patricia, dancer, choreographer (b at Toronto 13 May 1936). She trained at Bennington College, Vt, and in New York and Connecticut with Martha Graham and Pearl Lang. She then danced with Lang's company 1960-65 before returning to Canada. In 1966 she founded the New Dance Group of Canada, which gave its first performance 1967 with guest artists Peter RANDAZZO and David EARLE, and in 1968 Beatty became co-director with them of the TORONTO DANCE THEATRE. Much of her early choreography focused on the relationship between the sexes. More recent dances, such as *Seastill* (1979) and *Skyling* (1980), both designed by Aiko SUZUKI, and *Emerging Ground* (1983), a collaboration with Graham COUGHTRY, have found inspiration in the natural world.

GRAHAM JACKSON

Beau, Henri, painter (b at Montréal 27 June 1863; d at Paris, France 15 May 1949). After his first design and painting lessons in Montréal, he left for the US in 1884, ending up in San Francisco where he did coloured engravings. Returning to Montréal in 1886, he went on to Paris, studying at the Académie Julian and the École des Beaux-Arts. He had his first showings in the 1890s and in 1900 won third prize for painting at the Universal Exhibition. Beau appeared regularly in exhibitions in Europe and America. In Canada the Salon du Printemps of the Art Assn and the Royal Canadian Academy frequently hung his works. He was official painter of the Public Archives of Canada 1915-38. An active member of several French art societies, he was made an officer of the French Academy.

With his brother Paul, a fine-arts ironworker, Beau left a definite mark on Canadian art, heralding the coming young generation of painters. Yet, with his French academy training and French tastes, he was one of the last representatives of a dying age. Among his important works are *Les Noces de Cana* (1894) in the Sacré Coeur chapel of Notre-Dame de Montréal, *La Dispersion des Acadiens* (1900) at St Joseph's U, Moncton, NB, and *L'Arrivée de Champlain à Québ*[ec] (1908) at the Musée du Québec.

MICHEL CHAMPAG[NE]

Beauchemin, Micheline, tapestry weaver (b [at] Longueuil, Qué 24 Oct 1930). Beauchemin be[gan] her career making stained-glass window[s] but early turned to the vibrant colours found i[n] skeins of wool to hook, weave and embroid[er] spectacular wall hangings. She then studied [at] the École des Beaux-Arts in Montréal, winnin[g] a scholarship to study with Ossip Zadkine i[n] Paris (1953). Travels to N Africa and Greece in[spired] her to embroidery, a favourite occupatio[n] as a child, sending *Visage de Mistra* to Chartre[s] 1954. Back in Canada in 1957 she used a tumu[lt] of wool, acrylic, gold and silver threads, an[d] aluminum, for some 60 tapestries, floatin[g] walls, and forms in space, found in Place d[es] Arts (Montréal, 1963), the National Arts Cent[re] (Ottawa), Tokyo, San Francisco and cities acro[ss] Canada. Beauchemin has travelled and studie[d] in Japan, China, India, the Canadian Arctic an[d] the Andes, adding depth and mystery to h[er] love of light, water, wings and nets.

ANNE MCDOUGA[LL]

Beauchemin, Yves, writer (b at Noranda, Qu[é] 26 June 1941). Before becoming a Radio-Québ[ec] researcher, Beauchemin taught and worked i[n] publishing. His first novel, *L'Enfirouapé* (1974) was a burlesque replay of certain events of th[e] 1970 OCTOBER CRISIS. *Le Matou* (1981) describes th[e] crazy, tragic adventures of a young Montréal[er] who decides to free himself from the collectiv[e] history of economic dependence by running [a] restaurant. That *Le Matou* became one of Québ[ec] literature's best-sellers is because of its lucid ob[servation] of individuals and societies, its su[btle] delineation of colourful personalities, its de[tached] tone, in which humour tempers irony and its teeming life, conveyed by a quick, exu[berant] and controlled style.

GABRIELLE POUL[IN]

Beauchêne, Robert Chevalier, dit, adven[turer], privateer (b at Pointe-aux-Trembles [Mon[tréal] 23 Apr 1686; d at Tours, France Dec 1731. As a young man, Beauchêne served as a VOYA[GEUR] and on raiding expeditions against th[e] English colonies. In 1707 he joined an Acadia[n] privateer. He later crossed the Atlantic, wan[dered] through western France and was killed i[n] a brawl in Tours. His memoirs, with many ex[aggerations] and inaccuracies, were published i[n] 2 vols by Alain-René Lesage as *Les Aventures d[e] monsieur Robert Chevalier, dit de Beauchêne, capitai[ne] de flibustiers dans la Nouvelle-France* (1732).

ALLAN GREE[R]

Beaucours, Josué Dubois Berthelot de, mil[itary] officer, engineer, governor of Trois-Rivières and Montréal (b in France *c*1662; d a[t] Montréal 9 May 1750). Beaucours came to Ne[w] France 1688 as an infantry officer but is bette[r] known for his work in fortifications: at Trois-Rivières (1690-91), Québec (1692-93, 1710-1[1] and 1713-14), Chambly (1709-11), Montréa[l] (1702 and 1707-09) and LOUISBOURG (1715-16). Strongly supported by colonial governors an[d] administrators for his practicality, he was les[s] well regarded at Versailles for the technica[l] quality of his work, which remains a subject o[f] debate. His appointments as chief engineer fo[r] Canada (1712-14) and Île Royale [Cape Breton] (1715-16) were brief, but after 1716 he slowl[y] climbed the administrative ladder, becomin[g] governor of Trois-Rivières in 1730 and of Mon[tréal] in 1733. He retired from the latter pos[t] 1748.

F.J. THORP[E]

Beaudet, Jean-Marie, conductor, pianis[t], administrator, organist, teacher (b at Thetford Mines, Qué 20 Feb 1908; d at Ottawa 19 Ma[r] 1971). As a conductor and administrator, h[e] promoted Canadian music at home and abroad. He held several positions with the CBC 1937-6[...]

d was responsible for giving music a larger le in CBC programming. During this time he o conducted several concerts for the CBC. ter serving as the CBC's representative in Paris 957-59), he returned to Canada as executive cretary of the Canadian Music Centre 959-61). In 1964 he was appointed music di- ctor for the National Arts Centre where he as- mbled the centre's permanent orchestra.
HÉLÈNE PLOUFFE

audin, Jean, filmmaker (b at Montréal 6 Feb 39). After studying at École des Beaux-Arts, ontréal, and the School of Design, Zurich, audin joined the NFB 1964. His first experi- ental feature, *Stop* (1970), was followed by *Le able est parmi nous* (1971), which he made in the ivate sector. He returned to the NFB, making 4 autiful dramatic shorts, including *Cher Théo* 975), before directing *J.A. Martin photographe*, a ccès d'estime for which Monique Mercure won e best actress award at Cannes. The film's suc- ss enabled him to make *Cordélia* (1980) for the FB, a feature film based on a well-known urder case. PIERS HANDLING

aufort Sea can be taken to include the whole the clockwise gyre of the Canada Basin of the rctic Ocean N of Alaska, the Yukon and the ackenzie Delta coast, bounded on the E by NKS I and PRINCE PATRICK I. In a more restricted, ficial sense, it has been defined as that part of e Arctic Ocean lying S and E of a line con- cting Point Barrow, Alaska, and Lands End, ince Patrick I. In this narrower definition it s an area of 450 000 km^2. The coast is low- ing, with barrier islands and sandspits, and is bject to considerable scouring by ice and ero- n by storm surges. The inshore waters are allow (the line of 200 m in depth varying om about 80-200 km from shore), and the elf is much wider in the Canadian than in the section. From the edge of the shelf (200 m) e bottom deepens fairly rapidly to 3500 m, the ain Canada Basin to the N being close to 4000 at its deepest.

Tides are predominantly semidiurnal (twice a y), with a small range from 0.3 to 0.5 m. In- ore currents in the ice-free zone in summer are riable and chiefly wind driven, dominated by ternating NW and easterly winds. NW winds, hanced by the effect of the Earth's rotation, use the MACKENZIE R discharge, laden with sed- ment, to turn eastward along with the general sterly flow of seawater. Easterly winds tend reverse this current. Dominant features in mmer are a northwesterly flow of water E of erschel I and an easterly flow along the Tuk- yaktuk Peninsula. Farther offshore, in the ice- vered region, the general Beaufort Sea Gyre kes over in the form of a westerly flow. The water is typically Arctic Ocean water, low in temperature and salinity, but a Pacific influence is discernible, originating in the Bering Sea and reflected in the fauna, which include Pacific herring and salmon.

The region is rich in seabirds in summer and is an important breeding ground and migration staging area. The general level of biological production is fairly high, subarctic rather than arctic, and seals and whales form an important element in the native economy. Exploration for oil and gas on the Canadian shelf began in 1976, although the first drilling permits were issued as early as 1960. The Beaufort Sea is regarded as the most promising region for oil and gas production in the Canadian Arctic. M.J. DUNBAR

rtificial oil-drilling island in the shallow waters off e Mackenzie Delta in the Beaufort Sea *(courtesy Petro- um Resources Communication Foundation).*

Beauharnois, Charles Beauharnois de La Boische, Marquis de, governor of New France 1726-47 (b at La Chaussaye, near Orléans, France 12 Oct 1671; d at Paris, France 12 July 1749). Beauharnois brought long experience as a naval officer in the wars of Louis XIV to the difficult task of checking British colonial expansion. With the help of allied Indian nations, he successfully defended strategic points on the Acadian boundary, on Lk Ontario and in the West despite peacetime financial restrictions. The spread of the War of the Austrian Succession to N America in 1744 resulted in a shortage of trading items, which severely strained the French network of alliances with the Indians. After Beauharnois's departure in 1747, several of his recommendations, such as the fortification of Québec City and the reinforcement of French might in the West, were approved.
JEANNETTE LAROUCHE

Beauharnois de La Chaussaye, François de, Baron de Beauville, INTENDANT of New France 1702-05 (bap 19 Sept 1665 near Orléans, France; d there 9 Sept 1746). Beauharnois, a protégé of the minister of marine, faced a difficult situation on his arrival in New France. The fur trade was in decline, following a price slump in Europe, and war had broken out between England and France. He tried, with subsidies to the Compagnie de la Colonie, to save the fur trade and also to develop agriculture, but his brief stay gave him no opportunity for significant achievements. His 3 years as intendant were undoubtedly an apprenticeship that put him in line for promotions in France, culminating in his appointment as intendant of the marine at Rochefort. JEANNETTE LAROUCHE

Beaulieu, Victor-Lévy, journalist, novelist, essayist, playwright, publisher (b at St-Paul-de-la-Croix, Qué 2 Sept 1945). A well-known figure, Beaulieu is important to Québec literature as much for his various activities as his own respected writing. He has won many literary prizes: Grand prix littéraire de la Ville de Montréal (*Les Grandes-pères*, 1971), Gov Gen's Award (*Don Quichotte de la démanche*, 1974), Prix France-Canada (*Monsieur Melville*, 1978) and Prix Jean-Béraud-Molson (*Satan Belhumeur*, 1981). Beaulieu loves to experiment with various literary styles and shatter their usual boundaries. *Blanche forcée* (1976) is a story; *N'évoque plus que le désenchantement de ta ténèbre, mon si pauvre Abel* (1976), a lamentation; *Sagamo Job J* (1977), a hymn; *La Tête de Monsieur Ferron* (1979), a humorous epic. As an essayist he is as interested in his literary ancestors (*Pour saluer Victor Hugo*, 1971; *Jack Kérouac*, 1972) as in forgotten Québec writings (*Manuel de la petite littérature du Québec*, 1974). He has written 2 TV series (*Les As* and *Race de monde*, an adaptation of the first novel in the "Vrai Saga des Beauchemin") and several plays (including *Ma Corriveau*, 1976, and *Monsieur Zéro*, 1977). After working for Éditions du jour and Éditions de l'Aurore, he started his own publishing company, VLB éditeur, in 1976; and has published poetry, novels and plays, each with equal attention to detail. Constantly evolving, Victor-Lévy Beaulieu's work testifies to his exploration of a real and literary homeland. BENOÎT MELANÇON

Reading: G. Bessette, *Trois romanciers québécois* (1973).

Beaulne, Guy, director (b at Ottawa 23 Dec 1921). His father was artistic director and director of an Ottawa theatre company, Le Groupe Beaulne. After graduating from U of O, he studied drama under Denis d'Inès in Paris while working as a correspondent for Radio-Canada and a theatre critic for *Le Droit*. Returning home, he worked as a radio drama producer for Radio-Canada until 1956, and in TV until 1963. He then joined the Québec Dept of Cultural Affairs where he was executive director of artistic education until 1970; first director of the Grand Théâtre de Québec until 1976; and member of the Délégation générale du Québec in Paris until 1979. In 1981 he was appointed director of the Conservatoire d'art dramatique de Montréal. Beaulne founded the Association canadienne du théâtre d'amateurs in 1958 and served as its director until 1963. He is credited with the creation of the radio program *La Famille Plouffe*, and followed Jean-Paul Fugère as producer of the TV program of the same name. In the area of experimental drama, he worked on a radio program entitled "Nouveautés dramatiques" as well as the English-language TV program, "Shoe string theatre." ANDRÉ G. BOURASSA

Beautiful Losers (Toronto and New York, 1966; London, 1970) is a novel by Leonard COHEN. Cohen's scholar-narrator researches the history of Catherine (Kateri) TEKAKWITHA, an Iroquois saint, and broods over his memories of his dead Indian wife, Edith, and his dead male lover, mentor and genius, the mysterious, all-knowing "F." The recreation of Catherine's ascent toward sainthood coalesces with the narrator's contemporary beatification as he descends from F's treehouse, hitchhikes to Montréal and is miraculously transformed in front of gaping crowds on St Lawrence Boulevard. The language of *Beautiful Losers* plays seriously, sensually and poetically over Tekakwitha's history as a saving source of inspiration for the "beautiful loser" who invokes her life as a prayer for his own body and soul. *Beautiful Losers* has been translated into Japanese, German, Dutch, Swedish, Italian, Danish, Norwegian and Spanish, as well as French (*Les Perdants Magnifiques*, Paris, 1972, 1973). NEIL BESNER

Beaven, James, philosopher (b at Westbury, Eng 9 July 1801; d at Niagara, Ont 8 Nov 1875). Educated as an Anglican clergyman, he arrived at King's Coll, Toronto, in 1843. He published the first philosophical work written in English Canada, *Elements of Natural Theology* (1850). Beaven sought a rational basis for belief. His design theory of the universe, emphasizing order in all things, set a trend in Canadian thinking that was continued by his philosophical and literary successors. Although Daniel WILSON, president of U of T at the time, called him a "dry old stick," Beaven's wit was well known in class. His sensitivity to the environment and concern for native peoples are evident in his travel journal, *Recreations of a Long Vacation* (1846).
ELIZABETH A. TROTT

Beaven, Robert, businessman, politician, premier of BC (b at Leigh, Eng 20 Jan 1836; d at Victoria 18 Sept 1920). He was attracted west from Toronto by the gold rushes and went into business in Victoria. During the agitation for BC's union with Canada he was secretary of the Confederation League. Elected in 1871 to the BC legislature, he served in the DE COSMOS and WALKEM Cabinets, and in 1882 succeeded Walkem as premier. On losing the July 1882 election, he clung to office until defeated in the legislature, Jan 1883. Beaven continued to sit in the Assembly until 1894, part of the time as leader of the Opposition. He also served as mayor of Victoria in 1892, 1893 and 1896.

H. KEITH RALSTON AND BETTY WILCOX

Beaver are Athapaskan-speaking people of the PEACE R area of BC and Alberta. They were called Beaver by early explorers, after the name of a local group, the tsa-dunne, and call themselves Dunne-za ("our people"). In the later 1970s there were about 900 status Indians who spoke Beaver dialects. Before contact there may have been more than 1000 in an area of about 194 250 km². Their neighbours are the Athapaskan SEKANI and SLAVEY to the W and N, and the Algonquian CREE who invaded the eastern part of their territory in historic times. Fur-trading posts were established along the Peace R in the 1790s, and Roman Catholic missionaries won many Beaver converts after 1850.

The Beaver traditionally lived in small nomadic hunting bands of 25-30 people. They came together into larger groups along the Peace R for summer ceremonials, at which they sang, danced and played the hand game, a guessing competition between teams of men. Most food came from hunting large game animals: bison in the prairie country near the Peace R, moose in the muskeg and forests, caribou near the mountains, and bears. Before they obtained firearms from fur traders, hunting was often done by groups of people who surrounded animals or drove them over cliffs (*see* BUFFALO HUNT). These communal hunts were led by religious leaders or prophets known as "Dreamers." Beaver children were sent into the bush on vision quests to gain supernatural power from the animals. The introduction of rifles made individual hunters more efficient and led to a decline in game populations, particularly bison, which became extinct in the area by 1900. The Dreamers tried to help their people understand and anticipate the changes brought about by white people. Although most Beaver are Roman Catholic and some now accept evangelical Protestantism, most also retain their traditional beliefs.

The Beaver signed Treaty No 8 in 1899, 1900 and 1910, formalizing their right to live by hunting and trapping (*see* INDIAN TREATIES). They now live on INDIAN RESERVES in BC and Alberta. Much of their former land is developed for farming and petroleum production, but hunting and trapping are still possible in the northern part of their territory. These activities are important sources of food and income, and help to maintain a sense of identity. *See also* NATIVE PEOPLES, SUBARCTIC and general articles under NATIVE PEOPLE.

ROBIN RIDINGTON

Reading: P. Goddard, *The Beaver Indians* (1917); J. Helm, ed, *Handbook of North American Indians*, vol 6: *Subarctic* (1981); R. Ridington, *Swan People: A Study of the Dunne-za Prophet Dance* (1978).

Beaver (*Castor canadensis*), Canada's largest RODENT (15-35 kg). Its thick-set body is covered with dark, reddish brown fur consisting of coarse guard hairs over dense, soft underfur. The black tail is horizontally flattened, paddle shaped and scaly. Large, webbed hind feet are powerful paddles for swimming. Beavers are superb swimmers, and can stay underwater for 15 minutes. When alarmed, they slap the water with their tails, warning others to take refuge underwater. Beavers inhabit forested regions across Canada and N to TREELINE, but are infrequent on the prairies. Typically, they occupy slow-flowing streams where they construct dams of sticks, logs, debris and mud. These dams protect their lodges, which are built of the same materials and have entrances below water level and ramps leading up to living quarters above water. Beavers gather their building materials by collecting wood and felling trees and they often build canals for floating logs. The dams maintain a water supply to protect the lodges and also provide greater access to the beaver's major food items: leaves, buds, twigs and bark of deciduous and (rarely) coniferous trees. Beavers also eat herbaceous pond vegetation. They do not hibernate but store branches for food in a submerged mass beside the lodge. Each lodge normally contains an adult pair, newborn kits and yearlings born the previous year, and a colony may consist of a cluster of lodges. Beavers breed in Jan-Feb, have a gestation period of 3½ months, and give birth to 2-4 young. Beaver was once considered the most valuable fur, particularly when felt hats made from the underfur were symbols of prestige. The pursuit of the beaver from the Maritimes to the Mackenzie Valley led to the exploration of vast regions of what became Canada. Although the beaver almost became extinct at that time, thriving populations now occur across Canada. It is rightly Canada's national emblem. One other species exists, the European beaver (*C. fiber*). *See* FUR TRADE.

R. BOONSTRA

Beaver (*Castor canadensis*), Canada's national emblem. The beaver was trapped almost to extinction during the fur-trade era, but thriving populations now occur across Canada (*photo by Al Williams*).

Beaver, wooden paddle steamer — the fi steamship on the Northwest Coast. It was bu in 1835 near London, Eng, and sailed to t Columbia R in 204 days. The *Beaver* served a supply ship for the HBC until the Fraser R GO RUSH of 1858, when it entered passenger a freight service between Victoria and the mai land. From 1862 to 1874 the HBC trader becar Her Majesty's Hired Survey Ship *Beaver*. Aft the HBC sold the ship in 1874, it was used a workhorse and tow until 1888, when it w wrecked in the First Narrows in Vancouv harbour. Only a few relics remain.

J. MAR

Beaver Club, Montréal club, fd in 1785. A mission was restricted to FUR TRADE veterans the PAYS D'EN HAUT. The club embraced as mem bers wealthy fur merchants, retired traders a well-connected WINTERING PARTNERS (principall but not exclusively, from the NORTH WEST CO PANY); as honorary members, ships' captai and army officers; and as guests, illustrious pe sons. It embodied the heart of Montréal societ with winter bacchanalian feasts its principal a tivity. The club evidently ceased functioni around 1825, to be revived briefly in 1827. motto was "Fortitude in Distress."

JEAN MORRISO

Beaver Pelts were divided into 2 maj classifications in the FUR TRADE: coat beaver ar parchment. Coat beaver (*castor gras*) pelts we processed and worn by the Indians before bei traded. The inner sides were scraped and rubbe with animal marrow; the pelts were then sew into robes. After several months of wear, th long guard hairs fell out, their roots loosened the scraping, and the skins became oiled an pliable. The under fur or beaver wool (*duvet* consisting of barbed hairs that could form a du able, luxurious felt, was of prime importanc to the European hat industry until the 1830 when silk hats became fashionable. The woo could easily be removed from the skins, whic yielded a useful leather.

Parchment (*castor sec*) pelts were sun dried im mediately after skinning. Once in Europe, the required combing to remove the guard hair Indians trading to the St Lawrence Valley fu nished pelts mostly of this type. In the late 1600 the HBC successfully tapped new supplies c coat beaver from northern Indians, touching of intense English-French rivalry for these desi able furs. Indian-white relations were some times strained as traders sought to match thei coat and parchment beaver-pelt inventorie with changing European market requirements

JENNIFER S.H. BROW

Beck, Sir Adam, manufacturer, politician power-authority commissioner (b at Baden Canada W 20 June 1857; d at London, Ont 1 Aug 1925). Feared and revered as an empir builder, Beck dominated Ontario politics for generation as he built and expanded the Ontari Hydro-Electric Power Commission into the larg est publicly owned power authority in th world. Son of a German Lutheran foundryma and miller, Beck made his name as a manu facturer of cigar boxes, outstanding athlete mayor and MPP in London. As mayor he led movement of Ontario municipalities and board of trade to get cheap electric power from NIAGARA FALLS. In 1905 James P. WHITNEY mad Beck head of a public inquiry that ultimatel recommended creating a municipally owned provincially financed, co-operative hydro electric distribution system. Supported by bipar tisan public ownership advocates, the Ontari Hydro-Electric Commission was formed.

The system began in a small way in 1910, bu through Beck's aggressive promotion of "Powe At Cost," thousands of new industrial, retail an household customers soon were gained. B charging initial low rates to induce a large de and, then building huge, efficient generating stations whose low costs permitted further rate reductions, Beck rapidly expanded his system and drove most of his private competitors out of business. He also browbeat balky municipalities, tyrannized provincial governments with his powerful following and abused his regulatory authority to hamper private rivals. Eventually he overreached himself and E.C. DRURY's government cancelled his electric railway scheme; G. Howard FERGUSON also kept Beck and Hydro on a short leash.

As principal founder and guiding genius of ONTARIO HYDRO, Beck helped establish the public enterprise tradition in Canada, though his methods did little to render such enterprises more politically accountable. H.V. NELLES

Reading: H.V. Nelles, *The Politics of Development* (1974); J. Sturgeon, *Adam Beck* (1982).

Beck, Gary, drag race driver (b at Seattle, Wash 8 Jan 1941). Beck raced stock cars for 12 years before becoming a drag racer, operating from his home in Edmonton, Alta. He was an outstanding competitor in this sport during the 1970s. He won the National Hot Rod Assn championship at Indianapolis, Ind, in 1972, and in 1974, his finest year, he won an unprecedented 3 NHRA and 2 American Hot Rod Assn events, was world champion, and was named *Car Craft* top fuel driver of the year and *Drag News* driver of the year. Beck also won several 1975 events, including the Canadian Open.

GERALD REDMOND

Beck, Tom, conservationist, oil-field environmental and social-management consultant (b at Bishaws, Scot 11 Mar 1932). Beck pioneered environmental protection and management in the Canadian PETROLEUM INDUSTRY. Twenty years in the Alberta oil business led to his appointment in 1970 as environmental co-ordinator for Elf Oil and later Aquitaine. From 1980 to 1982 he was director of Environmental and Social Affairs for Petro-Canada. Dedicated to maintenance of natural environments and to sensitive development of natural resources, Beck has had wide influence. He was a founder of the Alberta Wilderness Assn, governor of the Arctic Inst, and became chairman of the Canadian Environmental Advisory Council in 1978.

IAN MCTAGGART COWAN

Beckwith, John, composer, educator (b at Victoria 9 Mar 1927). One of the most distinctively English Canadian voices among Canada's composers, Beckwith has created a wealth of music rooted in his sensitive experience of the Canadian environment. Although he has composed much instrumental music, the majority of his important works are for voices, often settings of texts by Canadian writers. Several of Beckwith's most eloquent works have emerged from his long collaboration with poet-playwright James REANEY, among them the operas *Night Blooming Cereus* (1953-58) and *The Shivaree* (1965-78). His *Sharon Fragments* (1966) for unaccompanied choir, commemorating the Children of Peace, a music-loving 19th-century Ontario religious sect, is one of the most frequently performed of his works based on historical themes. Widely read and highly articulate, Beckwith is well known as a writer, lecturer and broadcaster. He has written music criticism for Toronto newpapers and has contributed articles on various aspects of Canadian musical life to periodicals and books of reference. He planned and wrote several music series and documentaries for CBC radio. On the faculty of U of T since 1955, he was dean of music 1970-77. In 1984 he was appointed first Jean A. Chalmers Professor of Canadian Music and first director of the Institute for Canadian Music at U of T.

BARCLAY MCMILLAN

Reading: Peter Such, *Soundprints* (1972).

Bedford Institute of Oceanography (BIO) is operated by the federal Dept of FISHERIES AND OCEANS and includes units of the Dept of the Environment and Dept of Energy, Mines and Resources. Founded in 1962, it is the principal oceanographic institution in Canada, comparable to the Scripps and Woods Hole institutions in the US. The BIO performs long-term research in all fields of the marine sciences over a wide geographic area; undertakes shorter-term research in response to national needs; carries out surveys and cartographic work to ensure a supply of navigation charts for the region from Georges Bank to the Northwest Passage; and responds with all relevant expertise to any marine emergency. To this end it is organized into groups devoted to PHYSICAL OCEANOGRAPHY, marine ecology, HYDROGRAPHY, marine geology FISHERIES and environmental protection. The BIO has one medium and 2 large research vessels, several smaller craft and a central library and computer system. Research results are published in international scientific journals and in the official reports of the various government departments. K.H. MANN

Bedford Magazine Explosion, 18-19 July 1945, initiated when an ammunition barge blew up at the naval magazine jetty on Bedford Basin, Halifax harbour. Fire spread quickly to adjacent piles of ammunition, which had been temporarily stored outside because of overcrowding in the main compound. A chain reaction of fire, explosion and concussion rocked Halifax for a day. Contingency plans existed for such an accident, and by late July 18, much of Halifax's northern half had been evacuated smoothly. None of the explosions approached the force of the 1917 HALIFAX EXPLOSION, but shattered windows, cracked plaster, occasional minor injuries and one death were reported. The community felt a lingering resentment towards the navy after the VE-DAY RIOTS, but voluntary firefighting by naval personnel at the ammunition depot largely offset this feeling.

LOIS KERNAGHAN

Bee, member of INSECT order Hymenoptera characterized by branched hairs on the body, chewing mouthparts (sometimes modified for lapping or sucking), transparent wings with few veins, enlarged hind appendages with stiff hairs for gathering pollen, and a large crop (honey stomach) for storing and carrying nectar. The sting at the tip of the female's abdomen is connected to poison glands. The stings of worker honeybees are barbed and, when removed, usually tear the bee's body, causing death. The queen's sting is used only against other queens. Bees may be solitary (eg, carpenter, plasterer, leafcutting, burrowing), social (bumblebees, stingless bees, honeybees) or parasitic. Most species are adapted for gathering nectar and pollen from blossoms. Of an estimated 20 000 species worldwide, about 1000 occur in Canada. Most bees are solitary in habit. Most short-tongued bees excavate tunnels in soil where they construct nest cells. Leafcutting bees fashion cells from precisely shaped leaf pieces; carpenter bees nest in holes drilled in dead wood. Some members of genus *Anthophora* (mining bees) fashion unique, clay nest cells. Females of all these species provision each cell with pollen and nectar, deposit an egg, and leave offspring to develop independently.

Relatively few species (*c* 500) are social, ie, have communal nests, co-operative brood care, and a caste system. Caste structure and behaviour is regulated by external secretions (pheromones), which induce behavioural or developmental responses. Pheromones are used to mark trails to food sources, although honeybees also use "dance" language to communicate direction. The most widely studied social bee is the honeybee (*Apis mellifera*). The precise architecture of the honeycomb, the complex social behaviour of the colony, the honey and beeswax they provide (*see* BEEKEEPING), and their efficiency in POLLINATION of fruit and seed crops, make honeybees among the most fascinating and useful insect friends of man. Honeybees were introduced to N America by European settlers during the 17th century.

Bumblebees, many of which are native to N America, are primitively social bees with annual societies. They are large and well adapted to temperate climates, where they are most numerous. In Canada, 42 free-nesting bumblebee species are found, several above the Arctic Circle. Some stingless bees have large social colonies. These are mostly tropical and semitropical in distribution. In the New World they occur from Mexico through Central and S America. These are the only honey-producing bees native to the western hemisphere, and have been kept for centuries by local beekeepers. They produce relatively little honey compared to honeybees.

Some bees have evolved into parasites of their relatives and have lost the ability to gather food and rear their own offspring, eg, bees of genus *Psithyrus* of the bumblebee family. The *Psithyrus* queen seeks out an established bumblebee nest and either replaces or lives alongside its original queen. She lays eggs which the host workers rear. *Psithyrus* bees produce only reproductives. Some solitary bees, eg, cuckoo bees, are also parasitic, depositing their eggs in nests of other bees. M.V. SMITH

American beech (*Fagus grandifolia*), with male flowers (bottom left), female flowers (top left) and nut on bottom right (*artwork by Claire Tremblay*).

Beech (*Fagus*), genus of TREES of beech family (Fagaceae). Ten species occur worldwide; one, American beech (*F. grandifolia*), is native to N America. In Canada, this species is found primarily in the East. American beech has a straight trunk covered with thick, smooth, bluish grey bark and can attain 30 m in height. The leaves are alternate, single, long ovals with saw-toothed edges. Leaves of young trees often remain on the twigs throughout winter. The edible beechnut is an important food source for a number of animals, particularly squirrels. American beech is usually found with sugar maples on temperate, well-drained slopes. Its leaves decompose very slowly, forming a thick leaf litter which acidifies soil and makes regeneration of sugar maple increasingly difficult. European beech (*F. sylvatica*) is planted as an ORNAMENTAL in Canada. Varieties include copper beech, weeping forms, variegated leaf forms. The heavy, hard, tough wood is used for tool handles, floor planks and furniture.

ESTELLE LACOURSIÈRE

Beechey Island is on the N side of LANCASTER SOUND off the SW corner of DEVON I at the entrance to Wellington Channel in the ARCTIC ARCHIPELAGO. At low water it is joined to the larger island by a narrow gravel isthmus and forms the NW side of Erebus Bay. Sir John FRANKLIN's ships are believed to have spent the winter of 1845-46 at the island, and during the subsequent search for Franklin it was used as a supply depot and rendezvous. The island is small, only 2.5 km across, but its steep shores, rising to a flat plateau 244 m high, make it a prominent landmark. DANIEL FRANCIS

Beecroft, Norma, composer, broadcaster (b at Oshawa, Ont 11 Apr 1934). A composer of the avant-garde, she has created music for a variety of performance media, combining traditional instruments, voice and electronically produced or altered sounds, with appealing individuality. *From Dreams of Brass* for soprano, narrator, choir, orchestra and tape, one of her best-known works, is typical of Beecroft's style. Like *Rasas II* and *The Living Flame of Love*, it uses text written or translated by her sister, poet and painter Jane Beecroft. An enthusiastic promoter of Canadian music, Beecroft has produced programs for CBC radio and became widely known as host of "Music of Today." She has also been active in promoting concert performances of new music. BARCLAY MCMILLAN

Reading: Peter Such, *Soundprints* (1972).

Beef Cattle Farming Cattle (family Bovidae, genus *Bos*) were first brought to Canada by French settlers. In 1677 there were 3107 in NEW FRANCE; in 1698, 10 209; by the mid-18th century, 50 013. Cattle were valuable as a food source (milk, cheese, butter, meat) and for their hides, used in LEATHERWORKING. Cattle farming spread across the country with settlement, and RANCHING became particularly important in the RANGELANDS of western Canada. The importance of beef cattle to Canadian agriculture has increased steadily since WWII. In 1981 there were an estimated 13.8 million cattle and calves on Canadian farms, 5.3 million of which were beef cows and heifers. Cattle slaughtered totaled 3.2 million, an increase of 4% from 1980.

Most of Canada's veal and young beef comes from a 3-phase system involving the cow-calf enterprise to produce weanling calves, the stocker or holding enterprise and the finishing (usually feedlot) operation. Two or 3 of these operations may be combined on a single farm or ranch. The triple combination, most common where breeding-herd size is small, is often a subsidiary enterprise of a mixed farming operation.

Cow-Calf Enterprise

The cow-calf enterprise involves maintaining a breeding herd to produce the heaviest weight of weaned calves possible. Breeding-herd size varies considerably, from a few cows on small mixed farms to several hundred in large range herds. The larger units (averaging 38 breeding females) are located in the 4 western provinces, where over two-thirds of Canada's breeding herds are located. However, about one-sixth of Canada's supply of veal and young beef comes from unneeded male and female calves of dairy herds, most of which are located in Ontario and Québec.

The western emphasis on beef production probably stems from the fact that the cow-calf operation is usually based on a low-cost pasture resource, eg, sparsely vegetated areas, nonarable land (12 ha required per cow), or very intensively cultivated and irrigated pastures (0.5 ha per cow). Some of the largest operations are found on predominantly natural pastures requiring 8 ha or more per cow. In such areas, the winter feed supply may be purchased but most often comes from improved native meadows or intensively managed arable land.

The breeding herd usually consists of cows and heifers of one breed or crossbred from breeds likely to produce hybrid vigour in the various maternal characteristics; and performance tested, purebred bulls from breeds noted for their post-weaning growth and carcass characteristics (*see* ANIMAL BREEDING).

Shorthorn, originating in NE England and S Scotland, was the first beef breed to be established and the first to arrive in Canada (1832). Its superior growth and fattening propensity (over the nondescript cattle of the day) quickly made it popular. Reds, roans, whites, and red and whites are common colours in purebred herds, reds being the most popular. Mature cows weigh over 600 kg and bulls, 900 kg. A dual purpose or milking Shorthorn strain has frequently been used in beef herds. A polled (hornless) mutant of the breed has become popular.

Hereford, originating in the county of that name, is a well-muscled, hardy breed. Well known for its foraging abilities under difficult range conditions, the breed quickly established itself as western Canada's main commercial breed. Its attractive, predominantly white face, underline and other white markings on a red body became a trademark ("white face" or "baldy") among cattle producers. A polled strain was developed in Canada and the US from mutants.

Aberdeen Angus, a smoothly finished black-coloured Scottish breed, has persistently found a place in beef production. Noted for its ease of calving and the easier delivery of Angus-sired calves, the breed also has other valuable characteristics in crosses (eg, early maturity, marbling quality of meat). A frequently occurring red mutant has now been developed as a separate strain.

Other British breeds, including Galloway (polled and dun, black or white-belted black), Black Welsh, Lincoln Red (of Shorthorn origins), South Devon, Devon and Luing, have appeared over the years but have not been significant in Canadian beef production.

Over the past 3 decades, the emphasis on growth and the hybrid vigour produced by crossing has resulted in considerable interest in continental breeds ("exotics"), especially since new quarantine regulations were adopted to facilitate importation.

Charolais, a very large white or creamy white breed of east-central France, was one of the earliest introduced. Its exceptional growth rate and muscling make it particularly valuable in crossing. Mature bulls average over 1000 kg and cows, 700 kg. A polled strain is being developed.

Limousin, a yellow-brown horned breed about the size of a Hereford, was the second continental breed to arrive in Canada and is valued for its excellent ratio of lean to fat and bone, a characteristic persisting in crosses.

Simmental, one of the most popular European breeds, is a dual-purpose (predominantly dairy) breed. Of Swiss origin, this large red and white breed is known under various names throughout Europe. For beef production valuable characteristics are rapid growth and milk production.

Other continental breeds popular in crossbreeding are Maine d'Anjou, a large red and white breed from NW France; Blonde d'Aquitaine, from southern France; 3 white breeds from Italy, ie, Chianina, equal in growth rate and mature size to the Charolais, and its smaller sister breeds Romagnola and Marchigiana; Gelbvieh, a large, red German breed; and Salers, a smaller red breed of central France.

Summer grazing is usually controlled by distribution of watering facilities and trace-mineralized salt licks, pasture rotation, or movable electric fences. Calves, "identified" at birth, run with cows. If not naturally polled, they are usually dehorned and vaccinated against common diseases (eg, blackleg) early in the pasture season. Male calves are generally castrated. If range is limited or extra gain is economically warranted, calves may have access to grain.

Breeding takes place in summer, preferably during a 6-week to 2-month period when cows are exposed to fertility tested bulls (approximately one bull to 30 cows). Yearling heifers (approximately 15 months old), if well grown (300 kg), are bred to sires known to produce easily delivered calves. High conception rates are extremely important but seldom exceed 85-90%. Calves are weaned from early Oct to mid-Nov, usually just before winter feeding. At 6 months, calves from British breeds and their crosses usually average 200 kg for males and 185 kg for females. Earlier-born calves or crosses with "exotics" may be 50-100 kg heavier. Male calves and those females not needed for breeding are transferred to stocker operations, as are cows that failed to become pregnant or produced poorer calves.

Wintering requires feeding in most areas, although pasture or cash crop residues may be used, weather permitting. In some areas, eg, CHINOOK belt, winter grazing of mature herds on specially reserved pastures is normal. Feed is supplied only under severe weather conditions and before calving. The herd is usually broken into 3 or 4 groups so that replacement heifer calves, pregnant yearling heifers and 2-year-olds expecting their first calves can be fed to facilitate growth. In large herds, bulls are usually fed separately, but allowed to run with mature cows. Winter feed is usually home-grown hay or silage from GRASSES, legumes and CEREAL CROPS. Grain and protein concentrates may augment poor-quality feeds; mineral mixtures and vitamin A supplements are the main purchased feeds. The average cow will consume 2% of its body weight in dry feed (eg, hay) per day; hence, wintering a mature cow normally requires 2 t of feed.

Stocker Operation

The stocker operation is normally attached to the cow-calf or the finishing enterprises, being essentially a period of growth between weaning and the finishing phase for slaughter (6-12 months). It is roughage and pasture based, aiming at getting as much efficient youthful growth of skeleton and muscle as possible. As a single enterprise, it is highly speculative and is usually a "grasser" operation for individuals with ample pasture but no winter feed. These farmers buy wintered steer and heifer calves in spring, and sell them in late summer or fall to feedlot operators.

Finishing Operation

Finishing, the final step in preparing animals for slaughter, aims to increase body weight and value. While some cow-calf operators may carry out this enterprise after a stocker phase for their own calves, most finishing is now done in specially designed units, holding several hundred or thousands of animals. Some farmers, eg, a few in Ontario, traditionally used the feedlot to enhance the value of their home-grown crops and to provide a winter occupation. Larger units may be equipped with feed-preparation mills and most use mixing and unloading trucks to distribute the feed in long troughs, twice daily. Profits arise from 2 sources: price margin, ie, the difference between the buying and selling price (the original 300 kg weight of a steer purchased for $1.80/kg and sold for $2.00/kg has produced a profit of $60.00 through the $0.20/kg price margin); and feed margin, ie, the difference between the cost of a kilogram of gain and the selling price of that gain. Thus, if it cost $1.90/kg to put on 200 kg in the feedlot and the 500 kg finished steer sold for $2.00/kg, the operator has had a gain of $20.00 through a positive $0.10/kg feed margin.

Astute and fortunate buying and selling ma

overn price-margin profits, but feed margin is ependent on cattle that are efficient users of ed and on low-cost rations. Calves, 6-8 months ld, are the most efficient converters of feed (7-8 nits of feed per unit gain) but are the slowest ainers (1.0-1.1 kg/day) and require the longest eding period. Yearlings are less efficient (8-9 nits of feed per unit gain) but gain faster .1-1.3 kg/day) and usually require 140 days in e feedlot. Heifers usually gain slightly more owly in the feedlot and finish at lighter eights.

The key in finishing is high-energy feed (eg, ains of BARLEY, CORN and, to some extent, HEAT and OATS) fed with bulky roughages (eg, rn silage, hay, straws). In local areas, some fuse or by-products (eg, distillers' slops, brew-s' grains, BEET pulp and molasses, milling and nning crop residues) may form the basis of ss efficient but profitable feeds. Lower-quality eds are usually used in the first part of the nishing period. As the animal increases in eight, each new unit of gain requires more or etter feed, and higher-energy feed is needed to roduce economical gains. In most parts of Can-la, finishing cattle on grass alone is not eco-omical, as top grades can seldom be reached be-use of the yellow colour of the fat in most reeds or the lack of sufficient fat covering in earling or younger cattle. It is very effective nd more economical, especially for yearling eifers, if the last 60 days are spent in dry lot.

In spite of the vagaries of price fluctuations nd increasing costs, beef farming has persisted, beef is the meat preferred by most consumers. ver the long term, it has produced reasonable turns; however, since the annual operating osts are high, because of the large capital in-olved in land and cattle, many operators can-ot withstand years of low returns and high terest rates. ELWOOD W. STRINGHAM

eekeeping The art of keeping BEES for honey nd beeswax evolved from honey hunting. Eu-opean and African cave paintings indicate that eople raided wild honeybees' nests for their veet bounty at least 15 000 years ago. Egyptian ecords show that, as early as 3000 BC, bees were rovided with domiciles and kept for honey roduction. Early Greek and Roman writers ention apiculture. The products of the hive ere so sought after that the Romans sometimes vied taxes of honey and beeswax. Many refer-nces to bees and honey occur in the Bible. Hon-ybees were kept in clay pots or cylinders, hol-w logs, wicker baskets and straw skeps (hives). owever, management for honey production as very limited until the mid-19th century, hen the Rev L.L. Langstroth, in the US, inven-d the movable-frame hive. It was then possi-e to open the hive, examine it, and remove oney without destroying the combs. This vention increased honey production and ade possible the development of the modern eekeeping industry. European settlers, coloniz-g N and S America, Australia and New Zeal-nd during the 16-19th centuries, introduced oneybees from their homelands. The bees did ell in the new environments; these areas now ave important beekeeping industries. In 1981, 9 980 Canadian beekeepers kept 633 500 hon-ybee colonies with a total honey production of 4.7 million kilograms.

Honey is obtained commercially from 4 spe-es of genus *Apis: A. mellifera*, the most im-ortant and widely used honeybee, native to Eu-ope, Asia Minor and Africa; *A. cerana*, the most nportant Asian species; *A. dorsata* and *A. florea*, lso Asian species, which cannot be kept in ives, but from the nests of which wild honey is ometimes harvested. Several species of stingless ees, mainly of families Meliponidae and Tri-onidae, are also used. Stingless bees, which oc-ur only in tropical and semitropical areas, are sometimes kept in log hives or specially designed nest boxes, where they produce limited amounts of honey. All of these bees form perennial societies, and store considerable amounts of honey to help the colony survive periods of dearth. This characteristic makes it possible for the beekeeper to harvest surplus honey. Many other wild bees (eg, bumblebees) feed on nectar but do not store it in excess and are not useful for honey production. In midsummer, a strong honeybee colony will contain one queen, as many as 60 000 to 80 000 workers (undeveloped females) and some hundreds of drones (males). The queen may lay as many as 2000 eggs daily, mostly fertilized eggs which develop into worker bees in 21 days. Under special circumstances, bees can develop a few of the fertilized eggs into queens in 16 days, by rearing them in large peanut-shaped queen cells and feeding the developing larvae on a glandular secretion, royal jelly. A mated queen can withhold fertilization when laying, the unfertilized eggs developing into drones. A drone completes development in 24 days. Although honeybees are kept in hives and are often selected and bred for superior honey-producing characteristics, they cannot be considered domesticated. They retain their wild instincts and can be managed only within limits.

Most Canadian beekeepers winter their bees. In winter, bees cluster together and generate enough heat to keep warm. The beekeeper must ensure that the bees have sufficient food and protection from cold. Most honeybee colonies are wintered outside, but some are moved into unheated cellars (particularly in Québec). Many beekeepers in the western prairies kill their bees in fall and purchase packaged bees (a queen and about 10 000 workers in a screen cage) from the southern US in spring. Interest in the wintering of colonies is increasing in western Canada, despite severe winters.

By seeing that the bees have adequate food and space, are kept healthy and have a productive young queen, the beekeeper tries to bring the colony to its maximum population in time for the "honey flow" — the period (usually during June, July and Aug) when many flowers are in bloom and bees gather and store excess nectar. Stored nectar is converted into honey through the evaporation of water and by the conversion of sucrose in the nectar to the simple sugars, dextrose and levulose.

Prior to 1900 honey was consumed mainly in the comb. Today, extracted honey commands most of the market. Full combs of honey are taken from the hive, the wax cappings removed, and the combs placed in an extractor where honey is separated from the cells by centrifugal force. Honey that has been heated and strained will remain liquid for several months and is often marketed in this form. Over a period of time, the dextrose in the honey tends to crystallize, forming granulated honey. The granulation process can be controlled by adding a small amount of previously granulated honey to liquid honey and storing it at a lower temperature (14°C). This speeds up the crystallization and results in a smooth, creamy honey. Granulated honey can be returned to the liquid state by heating it (not above 60°C) until the crystals are completely melted. The colour and flavour of honey depends on the blossoms from which it is derived. Honey from clover, alfalfa, rapeseed, fireweed and basswood is white; that from sunflower, goldenrod and aster tends to be golden; buckwheat honey is quite dark. In general, darker honeys tend to be somewhat stronger in flavour, but this does not mean they are inferior in quality. Most honeys are blends, since the bees visit many different plant species in collecting nectar.

Honeybees derive their food almost entirely from flowering PLANTS. Nectar is gathered in minute quantities from each blossom and carried back to the hive in the bee's honey stomach. Pollen is transported as pellets in pollen baskets on the bee's legs. Pollen is not used in making honey but serves as a protein source for the developing larvae and for the adult workers. To obtain the large amounts of nectar and pollen required, bees from each colony visit millions of blossoms in a season. While foraging, they act as agents of POLLINATION and provide a vital service to agriculture, a service estimated to be worth 10-20 times the value of the honey and beeswax harvested by the beekeeper. Because their numbers can be controlled and they can be readily transported, honeybee colonies are often rented and moved to areas where fruit and seed crops are grown commercially. The complex social organization, the biology, and the industrious nature of honeybees have long fascinated people. This may be why an increasing number of Canadians are becoming hobbyist beekeepers. With only a few hives to manage, they have time to observe more closely the behaviour of these most interesting and beneficial social insects. M.V. SMITH

Beers, William George, lacrosse player, dentist (b at Montréal, Canada E 5 May 1843; d 26 Dec 1900). He was the prime mover in organizing and popularizing LACROSSE; he also founded and edited Canada's first dental journal and was dean of Canada's first dental college. Introduced to lacrosse at age 6, he was chosen at 17 to represent Montréal as goalkeeper in the match played before the Prince of Wales. In 1867 he campaigned to have lacrosse accepted as Canada's national game. Though unsuccessful, his efforts helped raise the number of clubs from 6 to 80 that year, as did a national convention he organized in Kingston, Ont. He was elected secretary of the National Lacrosse Assn which originated there. The rules Beers had published in 1860 to help standardize the game were also adopted at this convention. In 1869 he published *Lacrosse: The National Game of Canada*. He played a continuing role in the sport's development, accompanying teams to England in 1876 and 1883. PETER LINDSAY

Beet (*Beta vulgaris*), biennial herbaceous plant of the Chenopodiaceae family. There are 4 cultivated varieties: red or vegetable beet, fodder beet (mangel-wurzel), chard and sugar beet. Beets originated in the Mediterranean basin where *B. maritima*, forerunner of *B. vulgaris*, still grows wild. All beets are adapted to temperate climates with optimal growing temperatures of 18-28°C and rainfall of 500-700 mm over a 5-7 month growing season. They develop bulbous, sugary roots and many long-stalked leaves during the first year. The roots must be exposed to prolonged periods of frost before the plant flowers in its second year. Fodder beets have been in existence for thousands of years and are used as cattle feed in northern Europe. Red beets have been eaten from time immemorial, either cooked or pickled, and are grown in all temperate and subtropical countries. The root is spherical (up to 10 cm in diameter) and coloured by betaine, a dark red pigment. Red beets are a popular market garden vegetable throughout Canada. GHISLAIN GENDRON

Sugar Beets produce a large, succulent, white, cone-shaped root and a rosette of large leaves in the first year. If they overwinter, they produce large, branched seed stalks up to 2 m high the second year. They are pollinated by wind and will cross readily with other members of the species. In 1747 Andreas Margraff, a German chemist, proved that the sugar extracted from beets was identical to that from sugar cane. The first sugar-beet processing plant was built in Silesia in 1802. In 1840 sugar beets supplied 5% of the world's sugar. Today, 40% of the sugar used worldwide and 10% of Canadian requirements are produced from them. Sugar beets are adaptable to a wide range of soils and climates. In N America they are grown commercially from Canada (Alta, Man, Qué) to the Mexican border. Specialized machinery is used to plant the seed, apply PESTICIDES, cultivate and harvest beets. Seedling diseases are controlled by treating seeds with fungicide. Other diseases are not an economic problem in Manitoba and Alberta; however, *Cercospora* leaf spot can cause severe damage in Québec. In Canada INSECT PESTS include cutworm, wireworm, flea beetle and webworm.

Sugar beets are grown under irrigation in Alberta and under natural rainfall conditions in Manitoba and Québec. The yield is 25-60 t per hectare, depending on the growing season and rainfall. An average of 125 kg of granulated white sugar is produced from a tonne of beets. The leaves that remain in the field are fed directly to livestock or worked into the soil as green manure. When dry, beet pulp, the part of the sugar beet remaining after the sugar is extracted, equals about 6% of the weight of the roots; molasses, the dark, heavy, viscous liquid that remains after the sugar is extracted from the beet juice, equals about 5%. Both products are excellent livestock feed. Molasses is also used extensively for YEAST production. J.W. HALL

Swiss Chard (*B. vulgaris* var. *cicla*) is a foliage beet: it develops no edible root but is grown for its large, fleshy leafstalks and very broad leaves. It is one of the best summer potherbs because it is very heat tolerant. Chard plants grow 50-100 cm high. Common types have crumpled green leaves and greenish white stalks. The newer cultivar (commercial variety), Rhubarb, has crimson stalks. In the cultivar Burgundy, the deep red in the stalk, midrib and main veins makes it a suitable ORNAMENTAL in mass border plantings. If harvested frequently, a spring planting is productive until fall frosts; therefore, Swiss chard is a good substitute for spinach. It is a good source of vitamin A. Leafstalks and midribs can be cut and eaten like asparagus; leaves can be frozen or canned like spinach. Commercial production is limited, but Swiss chard is a popular garden crop. V.W. NUTTALL

Beetle, term referring to the INSECT order Coleoptera [Gk, "sheath wing"], the largest order of living organisms. Beetles occur in a wide variety of terrestrial and aquatic habitats and use many different types of food. It is estimated that of the 3 million insect species worldwide, 30-40% are beetles. In Canada 6750 species are known; an estimated 2400 have not yet been recorded. Familiar beetles include scarabs (sacred symbol of early Egypt), weevils, and tiger, ground, blister, June and leaf beetles. Beetles are well represented as FOSSILS, the earliest known being Upper Permian forms (280-225 million years old). Representatives of all 4 modern suborders occur in Lower Triassic deposits (225-190 million years old). With so diverse a group a specific description is difficult, but most beetles share the following characteristics. They pass through a complete metamorphosis (ie, have distinct egg, larval, pupal and adult stages). Larvae and adults generally have chewing mouthparts. Adults have 2 pairs of wings; the outer, horny or leathery pair (elytra) cover the inner, membranous flight wings to form a straight line down the back when at rest. The adult body is usually hardened; antennae usually have 11 or fewer segments. The first segment of the thorax is free; the dorsal surface, large and shieldlike. Size ranges from 0.25 mm to over 10 cm. Most Canadian beetles are brown or black, although an extremely wide range of colours and patterns occurs. Colour may be produced by structural modifications to the cuticle (waxy covering), producing metallic greens and blues, etc; or by pigments in the cuticle, producing oranges, reds, yellows, etc.

Convergent ladybug beetle (*Hippodamia convergens*). This and related species feed, both as larvae and adults, on soft-bodied insects. They are a very important agent in natural control of aphids (*artwork by S. Stacey*).

The number of beetle species becomes markedly reduced approaching higher latitudes: only 300-400 species extend into the Canadian Arctic. Coleoptera probably is not the largest insect order in this country; however, beetles occupy extremely varied habitats and occur throughout Canada except in the northernmost Arctic islands. Since mobility is often somewhat restricted, the habitat of a given species is directly related to its food. Many families are primarily phytophagous, feeding on plant material; many are predacious, feeding on other invertebrates; relatively few are parasitic on vertebrates. Many species are carrion, dung or pollen feeders. Larvae and adults of a species may feed on the same host; or adults may have strikingly different feeding habits from larvae, not feeding at all, or using a different food source.

Beetles are of immense economic importance, since they include many of the most destructive INSECT PESTS known. Many species attack household and stored products (eg, carpet beetles, confused flour beetle, granary weevil). Plant feeders destroy crop foliage, attacking virtually all cultivated crops. Wood borers attack nearly all trees and shrubs (eg, bark beetles, apple bark borers, poplar borers, etc). Others transmit disease: Dutch elm disease is caused by a fungus transmitted by the elm bark beetle. Coleopterids do very little direct damage to humans and domestic animals although, in rare cases, domestic animals (eg, horses) may die from eating hay containing dead blister beetles. Several species give off toxic chemicals which cause blisters on contact with skin. Some beetles are beneficial. Many predatory species feed on destructive insects, eg, ladybird beetles have been introduced to control aphids and scale insects attacking crops. Families such as ground and rove beetles contain hundreds of species that feed on destructive insects and regulate their populations. Some species considered highly beneficial in one stage may cause damage in another (eg, some larval blister beetles feed on grasshopper eggs, but adults are leaf-feeders, attacking legumes and other plants). Other species are of considerable benefit as pollinators, or in the decomposition of dead and waste organic material.

BEVERLY CAMPBELL AND J.M. CAMPBELL

Begbie, Sir Matthew Baillie, judge, first chief justice of BC (b at the Cape of Good Hope 9 May 1819; d at Victoria 11 June 1894). Sent from England in 1858 to be the first judge of the ne colony of British Columbia, he quickly esta lished his reputation as a resolute, but fair, u holder of British law and order in the scatter mining camps of the colony, the white pop lation of which was largely American. His e forts and those of Governor James DOUGL ensured that the colony remained British, to b come part of Canada. Upon BC entering CONFE ERATION in 1871, Begbie became its first chi justice. He guided the judicial system of t province to an era of considerable sophis cation, displaying characteristics unexpected a Victorian judge: espousal of the rights of Ch nese and Indians; a lifelong interest in pr gressive law reforms and a tendency to take t side of the "little man." In later years he was t social lion of the genteel society of Victor where he lived in bachelor comfort.

DAVID RICARDO WILLIA

Reading: David R. Williams, *The Man For a New Countr Sir Matthew Baillie Begbie* (1977).

Begg, Alexander, writer, historian (b at Québ City 19 July 1839; d at Victoria 6 Sept 189 Educated at St John's, Québec C and Aberdee Scot, Begg was trading in manufactured goods the RED RIVER COLONY in 1867. After a brief peri in journalism, he worked for the Manitoba go ernment as auditor, deputy treasurer ar queen's printer from 1877 to 1884. He becan immigration agent of the CPR, but later r turned to journalism at Seattle in 1884 and th Victoria as editor of the *Daily Colonist* in 189 Drawing upon his firsthand knowledge of t events of the Red River Rebellion and the cr ation of the province of Manitoba, Begg pu lished several historical works, including *T Creation of Manitoba* (1871), *Ten Years in Winnip* (1879), *The Great Canadian North-West* (1881) ar *History of the North-West* (1894-95). DAVID EVA

Reading: Alexander Begg, *Red River Journal*, ed W Morton (1969).

Bégon de La Picardière, Michel, INTENDANT New France 1712-26 (b at Blois, France 21 M 1667; d at La Picardière, France 18 Jan 174 When he arrived, the economy of New Fran was suffering from depression in the beav trade and inflation caused by the use of PLAYIN CARD MONEY. His superiors accepted Bégon's pr posal to redeem the card money in installmen at half face value. He failed in attempts to libe alize the fur trade and to establish industri capable of overcoming the colony's defic Extensively involved in private trade and su pected of embezzlement, he was recalled France in 1723. FRANCE BEAUREGA

Belaney, Archibald Stansfeld, alias *Grey Ow* writer, conservationist (b at Hastings, Eng Sept 1888; d at Prince Albert, Sask 13 Apr 193 Raised by 2 maiden aunts and his grandmoth Belaney had an unhappy childhood. As a b he was fascinated with N American Indians a dreamed of becoming one. At 17 he left f northern Canada where, apart from his w service, he spent the remainder of his li Through his association with the Ojibwa northern Ontario he learned about the wilde ness. Shortly after his arrival he imaginative presented himself as the son of a Scot and Apache and began to use the name Grey Owl. Grey Owl he published his first book *The Men the Last Frontier* (1931). Anahareo, his Iroqu wife, convinced him of the need for CONSE VATION, and that became the central theme of h writings. Appointed to Riding Mountain, a later to Prince Albert National Park to look aft a beaver conservation program, he wrote books in western Canada: *Pilgrims of the W* (1934), *The Adventures of Sajo and her Beaver Peo* (1935) and *Tales of an Empty Cabin* (1936). H work was extremely popular, especially in Br ain, where he made 2 lecture tours. After h

onservationist Grey Owl (Archibald Belaney) feeding baby beaver in Riding Mountain Park, 1931 (*courtesy ntario Archives*).

ath the press discovered his English birth, d in the ensuing uproar his contributions as conservationist were forgotten. Only a generion later were they again recognized.

DONALD B. SMITH

ading: Lovat Dickson, *Wilderness Man* (1973).

elcher, Sir Edward, naval surveyor, explorer at Halifax 27 Feb 1799; d at London, Eng 18 ar 1877). As a surveyor he participated in ajor British naval expeditions to Bering Str, frica, the Americas and the Far East. He oved able, though quarrelsome and vindicve. In 1852 he was given charge of 5 ships iling in search of Sir John FRANKLIN. Belcher's pedition rescued Robert MCCLURE and his men, arooned for 3 winters during their own arch, but his ships were icebound and in sumer 1854 he ordered 4 abandoned. Back in Engnd he was rebuked but not court-martialled. e spent the rest of his life in literary and scitific pursuits. DANIEL FRANCIS

elcher, Jonathan, lawyer, chief justice, eutenant-governor of NS (b at Boston, Mass 23 ly 1710; d at Halifax 30 Mar 1776). Educated Harvard, Cambridge and the Middle Temple ondon, Eng), Belcher served at the English d Irish bars until appointed in 1754 as first ief justice of NS, an office he held, with that president of the governor's council, until his ath. The first formally trained law officer apinted in the province, he established orderly urts, English as opposed to Massachusetts lel precedents, and solidly drafted legislation. s administrator and lieutenant-governor (Oct 60-Sept 1763), he found himself in open conct with the elected House of Assembly over sues affecting its mercantile leaders. His connuance of Governor Charles LAWRENCE's enuragement to New England settlements in NS as fruitful, but he also repeated, in 1762, his edecessor's inhumane expulsion of ACADIANS. lcher's lack of political judgement and fiancial ineptitude left him subject to the persive power of Joshua MAUGER. Learned, welltentioned but pompous, Belcher contributed ost significantly as a jurist. SUSAN BUGGEY

elcher Islands, totalling some 13 000 km², loted in SE HUDSON BAY about 100 km from the outh of the Grande Rivière de la Baleine. The lands are low-lying and are underlain by masve deposits of iron ore. First sighted by Henry DSON 1610, they were surveyed by W.E.C. dd 1915. The name is sometimes ascribed to Edward BELCHER, who led a search for Sir hn FRANKLIN, but is likely derived from James lcher, captain of an HBC vessel. Like all the isnds of Hudson Bay, they are part of the WT. JAMES MARSH

Belgians are citizens of Belgium, a European country divided linguistically into those in the N who speak a Dutch dialect (the Flemish) and those in the S who speak a French dialect (the Walloons). There is also a small German-speaking community along the eastern border of the country. Belgian immigration to Canada (with a few individual exceptions) did not really begin until 1880. In 1901 there were 2994 Belgians in Canada; in 1981 more than 50 000 Canadians of Belgian orgin were listed in the census.

Migration and Settlement Belgian immigration was particularly active before WWI and between 1951 and 1961, when some 2500 Belgians immigrated annually. Québec and western Canada were particularly attractive to Belgians at the end of the 19th century. The Québec government, under premiers Mercier and Gouin, encouraged Belgians to settle in rural areas. In the cities, they became tradesmen, small businessmen, teachers and musicians. Belgian financiers invested in the real estate and paper industries and in the mines.

Most Flemish Belgians went to the West, where they were primarily involved in agriculture. Some largely Belgian communities developed in Saskatchewan, Alberta and in Manitoba (eg, St-Boniface). Some 100 Belgian peasants settled in the Vancouver region around 1900; a decade later Belgian investors were attracted to the vineyards of the Okanagan Valley. In Ontario Belgians moved into sugar-beet and tobacco cultivation (eg, in Chatham, Delhi, Wallaceburg). Prior to WWI, some Belgian miners worked in the coal mines of Nova Scotia, New Brunswick and Alberta.

Belgians have distinguished themselves in every aspect of Canadian life — music, painting, higher education, business and municipal politics. There are several Belgian bishops within the Canadian Roman Catholic Church. Belgians established the Redemptorist (1879), Benedictine (1912) and Premonstratensian (1949) orders in Canada; the Belgian oblates are known for their work in the Far North. Belgians have integrated easily into the Canadian population, probably because they are few in number, widely dispersed and culturally very similar to French and English Canadians. There are Belgian associations in Québec, Ontario and Manitoba; some of the oldest are the Union belge in Montréal (1902), the Club belge de St-Boniface (1905) and the Société belge de bienfaisance (1921).

ANDRÉ VERMEIRRE

Beliveau, Jean, hockey player (b at Trois-Rivières, Qué 31 Aug 1931). He learned to skate in the backyard of his home in Victoriaville and played junior hockey at Québec City. Idolized by fans who packed the Québec Colisée to watch him play, Beliveau played 2 more years with Québec Aces, despite the entreaties of the Canadiens. He finally joined MONTREAL CANADIENS in 1953, signing the most lucrative contract to that time. By 1956, when he won the NHL scoring championship and HART TROPHY (most valuable player), he had become the dignified leader of the most powerful team in history. In 18 seasons and 1125 games he scored 507 goals and 1219 points. In 162 playoff games he scored 79 goals (second all-time) and a record 176 points. He retired 1970-71 and became a VP of the Canadiens. JAMES MARSH

Bell, Alexander Graham, inventor (b at Edinburgh, Scot 3 Mar 1847; d at Baddeck, NS 2 Aug 1922). Generally considered second only to Thomas Alva Edison among 19th- and 20th-century inventors and, through their inventions, originators of social change, Bell came from Scotland with his parents in 1870 to Brantford, Ont. There he and his father worked as speech therapists for the deaf. A scientific approach to their work, awareness of the electric

Alexander Graham Bell arrived in Brantford, Ont, in 1870. He was the inventor of the telephone and was also instrumental in the early development of aviation in Canada (*courtesy Public Archives of Canada/C-17335*).

telegraph, and invention of a successful microphone led to the invention of the telephone 1874-76. By then Bell was teaching at a deaf school in Boston, Mass, and spending his summers with the family at Brantford. He patented the telephone and energetically promoted its commercial development in the US, founding the Bell Telephone Co in 1876. Victory in a number of lawsuits over telephone patents made him rich by age 35. By then he had moved to Washington, DC, to watch over his business interests. In 1890 he bought land at Baddeck and later built himself a house there named Beinn Bhreagh ("beautiful mountain" in Gaelic).

Bell spent the rest of his life in scientific research, both in person and by paying for the experiments of others. In the US he collaborated with S.P. Langley, builder of a steam-powered aircraft in the 1890s, and funded the early atomic experiments of A.M. Michelson. Bell himself worked on the photoelectric cell, the iron lung, desalination of seawater, and the phonograph, and attempted to breed a "super race" of sheep at Baddeck. His wife, Mabel Gardiner Hubbard (1857-1923), whom Bell first met owing to her deafness, shared his scientific as well as his philanthropic interests. She was a full member of the Aerial Experiment Assn, undertook her own horticultural experiments, and with their 2 daughters lobbied from at least 1910 for women's right to vote.

The Aerial Experiment Assn was formed by Bell in 1907 in partnership with J.A.D. MCCURDY, F.W. BALDWIN and a few other young engineers, such as Glenn H. Curtiss, an American builder of motorcycle engines. After early experiments with man-lifting kites, the AEA turned to gasoline-powered biplanes (which they called "aerodromes") and built several successful aircraft. The flight of the SILVER DART at Baddeck 23 Feb 1909 is generally accepted as the first manned flight in Canada. The AEA worked simultaneously on "hydrodromes" or hydrofoil boats from 1908. The HD-4, built in 1917, set a world water-speed record of 114.04 km/h in 1919 that was not approached by any other boat for more than a decade.

The HD-4 and other Bell memorabilia have been preserved at the National Historic Site at Baddeck. There are many biographies of Bell; the basic technical history of the AEA is *Bell and Baldwin* by J.H. PARKIN (1964).

DONALD J.C. PHILLIPSON

Bell, Alexander Melville, educator, founder of the Canadian telephone industry (b at Edinburgh, Scot 1 Mar 1819; d at Washington, DC 7 Aug 1905). He was the father of Alexander Graham BELL. Prior to moving his family to Tutela Heights near Brantford, Ont, in the 1870s, he was professor of elocution at the universities of London and Edinburgh. He invented "visible speech," a written code especially useful to the deaf, which indicates exactly how all human vocal sounds are made, and he authored several texts on this subject. Receiving 75% of the Canadian patents to the telephone in 1877, Bell proceeded to hire agents to solicit telephone rentals; the instruments were to be attached to private lines owned by the lessees. Failing to find a Canadian buyer for the patents, he sold them to National Bell (US) in 1880. In Canada he was professor of elocution at Queen's Coll, Kingston, Ont, before moving to Washington, DC, in 1881. ROBERT E. BABE

Bell, Alistair Macready, graphic artist (b at Darlington, Eng 21 Oct 1913). He moved to Vancouver in 1929, where he enrolled at the School of Art in 1935. A draftsman in a structural steel plant until 1967, he worked in his free time as an artist, becoming a fine draftsman and an adept in the graphic media drypoint, etching, wood engraving and woodcut. His spare, sometimes stark designs express the essence of his favourite subjects — birds and animals, ships, bare landscapes — and elevate them into moving abstractions of form. He has travelled in Europe and N America in search of inspiration, and has exhibited in Europe, Latin America, Canada and the US; his works are in the Victoria and Albert Museum in England and the National Gallery in Ottawa. Major retrospectives were held at the Burnaby Art Gallery (drawings and graphics, 1971) and the Art Gallery of Greater Victoria (prints, 1981). GEORGE WOODCOCK

Bell, John Howatt, lawyer, politician, premier of PEI (b at Cape Traverse, PEI Dec 1846; d at Los Angeles, Calif 29 Jan 1929). Member of the PEI Legislative Assembly 1886-98 and MP 1898-1900, Bell, a Liberal, was reelected provincially in 1915 and was premier 1919-23. The thrust of his government's activity was road building. During his office the provincial vote was extended to women in 1922. NICOLAS J. DE JONG

Bell, Marilyn, swimmer (b at Toronto, Ont 19 Nov 1937). Under the tutelage of coach Gus Ryder, Bell began building a reputation in marathon swimming at 15. Although she later became the youngest to swim the English Channel and conquer the Str of Juan de Fuca, she won fame as a 16-year-old schoolgirl in 1954. In Sept that year, braving numbing cold and lamprey eels, she was the first to swim the 52 km span of Lk Ontario from Youngstown, NY, to Toronto. Fleetingly, she ruled the aquatic world and captured the imagination of Canadians. BOB FERGUSON

Marilyn Bell, whose marathon swimming feats are part of Canada's national sports lore. Her 1954 swim across Lk Ontario in 21 hours captured the admiration of people across Canada (*courtesy Canada's Sports Hall of Fame*).

Bell, Robert, geologist, explorer (b at Toronto 3 June 1841; d at Rathwell, Man 19 June 1917). In 1857 Bell was junior assistant to the GEOLOGICAL SURVEY OF CANADA. He obtained a BSc from McGill (1861) and in 1862 was made a member of the prestigious Geological Soc of London in recognition of the Canadian contribution to the London Exhibition. Following George LAWSON, he was interim professor of chemistry and natural science at Queen's 1863-67. In 1869 Bell was employed full-time by the survey, and began a series of northern and western explorations, mapping rivers draining into HUDSON BAY and reconnoitring the route for a transcontinental railway. A GSC assistant director 1877, charter member of the ROYAL SOCIETY OF CANADA (1882) and an MD (McGill) by 1878, Bell in 1884-85 was medical and science officer aboard 2 government expeditions to explore HUDSON STR. He called Hudson Bay "the Mediterranean of N America" and advocated its utilization as a natural highway between western Canada and Europe. In 1889 he was a member of the Royal Commission on the Mineral Resources of Ontario and in 1890 became chief geologist of the GSC. In 1897 he explored BAFFIN I and in 1899 GREAT SLAVE LK.

Despite many honours and his remarkable exploration of many areas of geology, zoology, ethnology, botany and forestry over a vast and previously unknown terrain, Bell never realized his ambition to become GSC director. Appointed acting director 1901, he retired in 1906. After living in Paris 1912-14, Bell and his family moved to the Assiniboine R in Manitoba. SUZANNE ZELLER

Bell Canada Enterprises Inc (BCE) is a multinational holding company and parent firm to over 80 companies known collectively as the Bell Group. Its subsidiaries include Bell Canada, Canada's largest telephone operating company, and Northern Telecom, a multinational communications equipment manufacturer. BCE attained this position in 1983 through a corporate reorganization initiated by Bell Canada, hitherto the parent firm of the Bell Group. Bell Canada, the telephone operating company, was incorporated under federal charter in 1880 as the Bell Telephone Company of Canada. Its charter authorized the company to offer telephone service throughout Canada. Although Bell Canada's telephone operations today are limited to Ontario, Québec and portions of the NWT, other members of the Bell Group provide service in the Atlantic provinces (New Brunswick Telephone Co, Maritime Telegraph and Telephone Co serving NS, Island Telephone Co serving PEI, and Newfoundland Telephone Co). Bell Canada itself accounts for over 10 million telephones, or 60% of the Canadian total.

Since 1906 Bell Canada has been subject to regulation by various federal regulatory boards, currently the CANADIAN RADIO-TELEVISION AND TELECOMMUNICATIONS COMMISSION. The CRTC's mandate is to ensure that Bell's rates are "just and reasonable." Federal regulatory jurisdiction extends to Bell Canada by virtue of the company's charter, and does not extend to the parent firm, BCE. A major reason cited by Bell Canada for reorganizing was to remove certain activities from regulatory authority. Major regulatory issues over the years have included Bell's less than arm's-length dealings with its affiliated equipment supplier, Northern Telecom, and the comingling of revenues from monopolized an competitive services making the justness of monopolized prices difficult to ascertain. *See als* ECONOMIC REGULATION; MEDIA OWNERSHIP; UTILITIES. ROBERT E. BAB

Bell Island, 34 km², the largest island in CONCEPTION BAY, off Newfoundland's AVALON PENINSUL is a flat outcropping of Ordovician sandston and shale interbedded with red hematite, a iron ore. Its high, red-stone cliffs are visib from Portugal Cove to the E from which a ferr runs the 5 km to the island. Off-lying Bell Roc gave the 9 km long, 3 km wide island its nam First settled in the mid-1700s, the island experienced a drastic change in its economy in th 1890s, when iron-ore mining was begun ther The mine site at Wabana in the N became i largest community. Nova Scotia Steel first operated the mine but ownership eventually passe to Dominion Steel Corp and finally to Hawke Siddeley Canada. Until the beginning of operations in Labrador, the Bell I mine was the largest producer of iron ore in Canada; during its lif it was the world's most extensive submarin iron mine. The ore was smelted at SYDNEY, N until competition and declining markets led t the cessation of mining on Bell I in 1966. Th island suffered economic difficulties and a los of residents as a result; many of the work forc now commute to nearby ST JOHN'S. ROBERT D. PI

Bell-Smith, Frederic Marlett, painter (b a London, Eng on 26 Sept 1846; d at Toronto 2 June 1923). Bell-Smith received his early a training in London and came to Montréal i 1867. He worked in photographic firms in Montréal and then in Hamilton, Ont, and Toront and exhibited primarily watercolours of sporing subjects. In 1881 he was appointed art dire tor at Alma College in St Thomas, Ont, and i the 1880s sketched in Québec, Maine and th Rocky Mts. From 1888 his income was derive from sales of his work, and he exhibited regularly. His attempts to obtain official governme patronage in 1895 and in 1897, on the occasio of Queen Victoria's Jubilee, were unsuccessfu Nevertheless, he did achieve some notoriety being granted a sitting by the queen in 189 Bell-Smith was a popular and prolific artist. H was especially known for his landscapes fro the Rocky Mts and the Selkirk Range, where h often travelled, as well as for London and Par street scenes. ROGER H. BOUL

Reading: Roger H. Boulet, *Frederic Marlett Bell-Smit 1846-1923* (1977).

Bella Bella, or Heiltsuk, is the language spoke by the older people in the Indian villages o Bella Bella and Klemtu situated on islands alon the BC central coast. The present residents o Bella Bella (which had an on- and off-reserv membership of 1300 in 1980) are most descendants of 4 separate groups of Indians wh amalgamated towards the end of the 19th century. Klemtu (with an on- and off-reserve population of 315 in 1980) is composed of India who have ancestral ties either with a Coast TSIMSHIAN-speaking group from farther N or Heiltsuk-speaking group from Kynoch Inlet, of Klemtu.

Bella Bella (Heiltsuk) is part of the N Wakashan division of the Wakashan language family and is closely related to Oowekyala, the language of the Oowekeeno (Owikeno) people o Rivers Inlet, SE from Bella Bella. The Bella Bel still maintain close cultural and social ties wit the Rivers Inlet people (population 158 in 1980

Like other peoples of coastal BC, the Bel Bella and Oowekeeno cultures were chara terized by elaborate POTLATCHES, cedar plan houses, TOTEM POLES and concern with soci

ella Bella deer mask (*courtesy National Museums of* *anada/National Museum of Man/S82-39*).

ınking. These 2 groups differ from one another ı that the Oowekeeno live primarily in a fresh-ʼater environment, while the Bella Bella are on ıe ocean and participate in a sea-life economy.

Information concerning the traditional social ystem of the Bella Bella (and of the Oowekeeno) ; scant, though it seems to have been based n unilineal clans, each composed of a number f family groups or lineages occupying one or ıore houses. However, influence from the ıatrilineal clans to the north resulted in the ella Bella favouring descent reckoned along ıe mother's line. There were 4 or more clans, ıcluding Raven, Eagle, Blackfish and Wolf. ach clan owned its own resource-gathering ıtes and shared in hosting ceremonials. Winter eremonials were dominated by the Tsaika HAMAN's) dance series, which included the lamatsa or cannibal dances. Some researchers elieve the Hamatsa dance, well known ıroughout Wakashan, Tsimshian and HAIDA reas, originated among the Bella Bella.

First contacts with non-Indians were in the 790s. A HUDSON'S BAY CO fur trading post, Ft 1cLaughlin, operated in Bella Bella territory be-ween 1833 and 1843 and involved the native eople in the maritime FUR TRADE. The focus of ·ade shifted in 1849 with the establishment of t Rupert near the northeastern end of Van-ouver I. By the 1880s a mission and hospital ʼere located in Bella Bella. The people became ıccessful commercial fishermen in the early 900s and many of them continue to play an nportant role in the industry.

Since the early 1970s, the Heiltsuk Cultural entre, sponsored by the Bella Bella Indian and administration, has been involved with ınguage and culture programs. Other band rojects include the operation of a hotel and a tore, and the development of an airport. rogress in economic development, and in the ıaintenance and teaching of language and cul-ıre, has also been made by the Oowekeeno un-er the direction of their band council. *See also* ATIVE PEOPLES, NORTHWEST COAST and general arti-les under NATIVE PEOPLE.

eading: R. Olson, "Social Life of the Owikeno Kwa-iutl," *Anthropological Record* 14, 3 (1954) and "Notes on ıe Bella Bella Kwakiutl," *Anthropological Record* 14, 5 955).

ella Coola live in an isolated fishing village n the central West Coast of BC. In 1980 their egistered population was 756. The term "Bella oola" once referred collectively to the Bella oola, Talio, Kimsquit and some Kwatna who ıhabited villages around North Bentinck Arm and the Bella Coola Valley, South Bentinck Arm, Dean Channel and Kwatna Inlet, respectively. By the 1920s they had abandoned all their other village sites and amalgamated on the present reserve at the mouth of the Bella Coola R. Since the late 1970s the Bella Coola have called themselves the "Nuxalk Nation," derived from the native term that in earlier times referred exclusively to the people of the Bella Coola Valley. They speak a Coast Salish language known as Bella Coola that is isolated from the other Salish languages of the coast and forms a linquistic island surrounded by Athapaskan and Wakashan languages. Culturally the Bella Coola are most similar to their Wakashan neighbours, the Heiltsuk (BELLA BELLA).

Villages traditionally consisted of descent groups who traced their lineage to a group of mythical first ancestors. Each group of ancestors, equipped with tools and ceremonial knowledge, descended from a mountaintop and established a village at its base. Through marriage, a network of descent groups developed that linked the villages. Most people chose to live in their fathers' villages. However, they were also related to their mothers' descent groups, if different. The multiple-family cedar-plank dwellings were large enough to house as many as 6 couples and their children. Members of the household, which included elderly relatives, supported one another in potlatching and economic pursuits.

The most prominent characteristic of Bella Coola life was its extremely rich and complex ceremonialism, dominated by the POTLATCH and 2 secret societies, the sisaok and the kusiut. Membership in the sisaok was limited to the children and certain relatives of chiefs. Initiation included a period of seclusion, followed by a public display of a masked figure representing the initiate's crest. They performed at potlatches and funerals and occasionally at less important ceremonials. Bella Coola winter ceremonials were dominated by the kusiut. Each member possessed a special kusiut name and had a supernatural patron whose dance he or she imitated.

Bella Coola was a fishing, hunting and gathering society. Salmon and eulachon ("candlefish") fishing in the Bella Coola R continues to be important (*see* SMELT). Each year, eulachons are netted, rendered into grease and traded. The fish are smoke-dried in the traditional manner (*see* SMOKEHOUSE), canned and frozen. Band administration, a band-operated commercial fish-smoking plant, and salmon-enhancement programs provide employment.

The first recorded encounter with the Bella Coola occurred briefly in the summer of 1793 when Captain George VANCOUVER entered their waters. He was followed only weeks later by an overland exploration team headed by Alexander MACKENZIE. This historic occasion became incorporated into Bella Coola oral tradition and the story of the welcome they gave Mackenzie is still a source of Bella Coola pride. *See also* NATIVE PEOPLES, NORTHWEST COAST and general articles under NATIVE PEOPLE.

DOROTHY KENNEDY AND RANDY BOUCHARD

Reading: T.F. McIlwraith, *The Bella Coola Indians*, 2 vols (1948).

Bella Coola women cutting salmon for smoke drying, 1976 (*courtesy Dorothy Kennedy*).

Belleville, Ont, City, pop 34 881 (1981c), inc 1877, seat of Hastings County, located on the Bay of Quinte, an arm of Lk Ontario about 180 km E of Toronto at the mouth of the Moira R. The original inhabitants were fur traders, but the settlement's founder is considered to be the Loyalist, Capt John Meyers, who built a grist-mill beside the river in 1790. The village of Meyers' Creek grew up at the site. In 1816 it was officially surveyed and the name was changed to Belleville after Arabella, wife of Francis Gore, lt-gov of UC. As the forests of the hinterland were logged, Belleville became an important sawmilling centre. The GRAND TRUNK RY passed through in 1855 and the town became a divisional point; the GTR station, dating from the 1850s, is a well-preserved example of the early railway era. Logging died out in the 1870s, but the city developed a thriving cheesemaking industry and in this century an economy based on diversified light manufacturing. The Hastings County Museum and campus of Loyalist College are located here. DANIEL FRANCIS

Bellevue House, built between 1838 and 1840 for businessman Charles Hales, was one of several elegant villas built on the outskirts of Kingston in the mid-19th century. Its spacious landscaped gardens, vista over Lk Ontario, and

Bellevue House, one of the elegant villas built on the outskirts of Kingston, Ont, in the mid-19th century. It was leased to John A. Macdonald 1848-49 (*photo by Richard Vroom*).

its slightly exotic Italianate design with an irregular plan, tower, verandahs and decorative eave fringe reflect the picturesque taste both in architecture and landscape design. In 1848-49 Bellevue was leased to John A. MACDONALD, then a member of the Legislative Assembly and receiver general for the Province of Canada. Bellevue was purchased by Parks Canada in 1964 and is now operated as a national historic park. It has been restored to the late 1840s period.

JANET WRIGHT

Beluga Whale, or white whale (*Delphinapterus leucas*), grows to a maximum length of about 6 m and is widely distributed in the Arctic, with a few small populations in subarctic areas. Most N American populations are migratory and are identified by their summer grounds, eg, Cook Inlet (Alaska), Bristol Bay, Beaufort Sea, Lancaster Sound (especially Cunningham Inlet), Cumberland Sound, E and W Hudson Bay, Ungava Bay and St Lawrence R. Like the closely related NARWHALS, belugas are often found near ice. They have long been hunted by northern natives for meat and oil, and by commercial whalers for hides and oil (*see* WHALING). Belugas prey on various marine organisms and some fishermen have considered them serious competitors for salmon and cod. During the 1930s an extermination program carried out in the St Lawrence R by the Québec government included payment of a bounty for each *marsouin blanc* (beluga) killed. Today, the St Lawrence population is severely depleted, as are those in Cumberland Sound, Ungava Bay and SE Hudson Bay. Adults are distinctively white except for margins of flippers and tail flukes. There is no dorsal fin. The high, rounded forehead ends in a short, broad beak. Calves and juveniles are grey to blue, but otherwise resemble adults. Belugas have a remarkably varied vocal repertoire and have been called sea canaries. Their biosonar system, used for echolocation in navigation and hunting, is among the most sophisticated found in nature.

R. REEVES AND E.D. MITCHELL

Belzberg, Samuel, financier (b at Calgary, 26 June 1928). Educated at U of A, Belzberg was active in oil and gas investment and all aspects of real-estate development. In 1962 he founded City Savings and Trust in Edmonton in response to the need in western Canada for real-estate development financing. Belzberg moved to Vancouver in 1968 and, with his partners (including brothers Hyman and William), formed Western Realty, an amalgamation of 16 private companies. The sale of Western Realty in 1973 enabled the Belzbergs to buy Far West Financial Corp of California, which brought them national attention. In 1970 First City Financial Corp was formed as parent company to City Savings and by 1984 it was a diversified holding-investment company with assets in excess of $3 billion and operations throughout Canada and the US. City Savings and Trust, renamed First City Trust Company in 1978, had grown by 1984 to a $2.9 billion corporation with 30 offices in Canada. The Belzbergs, many of whose relatives died during WWII, financed the Simon Wiesenthal Center at Yeshiva U, Los Angeles, which conducts studies of the holocaust and is being expanded to include a Museum of Tolerance. Belzberg also established in 1977 the Dystonia Medical Research Foundation with joint headquarters in Vancouver and Los Angeles and clinics at UBC, Columbia U and in London, Eng.

CHUCK DAVIS

Bengough, John Wilson, political cartoonist (b at Toronto 7 Apr 1851; d there 2 Oct 1923). One of the first substantial figures in editorial cartooning, he started off on George BROWN's *Globe* in 1871 but left to found the satirical weekly *Grip* (1873-94), which established itself by ridiculing PM John A. MACDONALD during the PACIFIC SCANDAL. Indeed, our mental picture of Macdonald, with his sly posture, witty mouth and whisky nose, owes much to Bengough's treatment. He is also of secondary interest as a 19th-century social radical, to whom communalism, vegetarianism, feminism, antivivisectionism and prohibition combined in one vast utopian ideal. In later life he returned to journalism, and was a much-loved but little-listened-to public scold, frequently honoured in Canada and abroad for his lectures, called "chalk talks," and books. Selections from *A Caricature History of Canadian Politics* (1886) were reprinted in 1974.

DOUG FETHERLING

Bengough, Percy, labour leader (b at London, Eng 1883; d at Vancouver 10 Aug 1972). Bengough came to Canada in 1905, worked at his trade as a machinist and joined the Amalgamated Soc of Engineers. In 1916 he joined the International Assn of Machinists and held many offices in that union. From 1921 to 1942 he was secretary of the Vancouver Dist Trades and Labor Council. He was elected VP of the TRADES AND LABOR CONGRESS in 1931 and president between 1943 and 1954. He actively supported the merger with the Canadian Congress of Labour to create the CANADIAN LABOUR CONGRESS in 1956. In 1949 Bengough helped found the International Confederation of Free Trade Unions and served on its executive board. During the war he served on several government advisory committees, for which he was awarded a CBE.

LAUREL SEFTON MACDOWELL

Bennett, Charles James Fox, merchant, politician, premier of Nfld 1870-74 (b at Shaftesbury, Eng 11 June 1793; d at St John's 5 Dec 1883). Bennett was one of the wealthiest merchants in mid-19th-century Newfoundland. Besides involvement in the fish trade, he started a brewery, a distillery, a foundry and a shipbuilding yard. He commissioned extensive mineral surveys along the coasts, and in the 1860s developed the prosperous copper mine at Tilt Cove (Notre Dame Bay). Bennett was also an important leader of the anticonfederate party in the late 1860s. He was largely responsible for the overwhelmingly successful campaign mounted against the confederates (led by Frederick B.T. CARTER) in 1869. The anticonfederate government of 1870 to 1874 managed the colony's affairs with reasonable efficiency, but the premier could not maintain party unity. Bennett's resignation in Jan 1874 ended his effective political career, although he remained an MLA until 1878.

J.K. HILLER

Bennett, Richard Bedford, Viscount, businessmen, lawyer, politician, prime minister (b at Hopewell Hill, NB 3 July 1870; d at Mickleham, Eng 27 June 1947). He led the Conservative Party, 1927-38, and was prime minister of Canada, 7 Aug 1930 to 23 Oct 1935. After graduating from Dalhousie in 1893, Bennett went to Cal[gary] and became the law partner of Senato[r] James A. LOUGHEED. In 1898 he won election as [a] Conservative to the Assembly of the North-Wes[t] Territories, but failed in bids to enter federal pol[itics] in 1900 and the new Alberta legislature i[n] 1905. Through his associations with Loughee[d] and Max AITKEN, Bennett prospered, and b[y] 1909, when he was elected in Alberta, he was fi[nancially] independent. In 1911 he went to Ot[tawa] as the Conservative member for Calgary. He became discouraged when PM Borden di[d] not appoint him to the Cabinet and, expecting t[o] be appointed to the Senate, he did not stand fo[r] re-election in 1917. In 1921 Arthur MEIGHEN, who disliked Bennett but respected his influ[ence], named him minister of justice. Bennet[t] was defeated in the 1921 general election, bu[t] won in 1925 in Calgary W. In Meighen's brie[f] 1926 government he was minister of finance.

In 1927 Bennett gained the Conservative lead[ership] at the party's first convention. An excel[lent] parliamentary debater, he strengthened th[e] party, but it was the GREAT DEPRESSION which as[sured] victory in the 1930 election. He promise[d] aggressive action to combat the Depression, bu[t] once in office found it difficult to develop a co[herent] program. His business instincts did no[t] serve his political interests. His major initiative[,] to persuade the British Empire to adopt prefer[ential] tariffs, brought some economic relief t[o] Canada but not enough. His establishment of re[lief] camps for single men lost him much popu[larity]. By 1933, the nadir of the Depression, h[e] seemed indecisive and ineffective. He becam[e] the butt of endless jokes. Cars towed by horse[s] because owners could not afford gasoline wer[e] dubbed "Bennett buggies." In 1934 he was in[creasingly] isolated and faced major dissent bot[h] in the party and the country. Early in 1935 h[e] dramatically announced that he supporte[d] "government control and regulation." He calle[d] for progressive taxation, unemployment insur[ance], health insurance, and other major socia[l] reforms. Unfortunately for Bennett, Canadian[s] did not find his New Deal as convincing a[s] Americans found Roosevelt's. In Oct 193[5] Mackenzie KING's Liberals swept the Conser[vatives] out of office.

Bennett continued ineffectively as oppositio[n] leader until 1938, when he bitterly abandone[d] Canada and bought an estate in Surrey, Eng. Hi[s] British friends, notably Aitken (Lord Bea[verbrook]

R.B. Bennett, 11th prime minister of Canada, 1930-3[5] (*courtesy Public Archives of Canada/C-687*).

erbrook), secured a viscountcy for him in 1941. e never forgave Canada for failing him, and, ignoring his career, Canadians, it seems, have ot forgiven Bennett. *See* BENNETT'S NEW DEAL.

JOHN ENGLISH

ennett, William Andrew Cecil, merchant, olitician (b at Hastings, NB 6 Sept 1900; d t Kelowna, BC 23 Feb 1979), premier of BC 952-72, a period of unparalleled economic xpansion. Educated in NB schools, in 1930 he ought a Kelowna hardware store which beame successful. He was elected Conservative 1LA for Okanagan in 1941, sitting as a Coalion backbencher and serving on the Post-War ehabilitation Council. He crossed the floor 1951 and sat as an independent, but was -elected as a SOCIAL CREDIT candidate in the consed June 1952 provincial election and subquently chosen caucus leader. The lieutenantovernor called him to form a government 1 ug 1952.

During 2 decades of prosperity, Bennett's adinistration took credit for the construction nd improvement of highways, the northern xtensions of the Pacific Great Eastern Ry and ajor hydroelectric projects on the Peace and olumbia rivers. Although Bennett espoused ee enterprise, he expropriated the province's rgest privately owned hydroelectric firm in 961; took over the Black Ball ferry line and creed the BC Ferry Corp in 1958; and attempted to stablish the BANK OF BRITISH COLUMBIA with 25% rovincial ownership.

From 1953 on, Bennett acted as his own fiance minister. Following a "pay as you go" poly that closely watched spending and transrred debts or "contingent liabilities" to agencies ich as the Toll Highway and Bridge Authority, ennett claimed in 1959 that the province was ebt free. His administration curbed the power f labour unions, limited social-welfare spendg, kept the civil service trim but expanded ost-secondary educational facilities. Bennett roclaimed himself a Canadian but had pronged disputes with the federal government ver the COLUMBIA RIVER TREATY, tax sharing and onstitutional reform.

In Aug 1972, BC elected an NDP government nder David BARRETT. Subsequently, Bennett signed as MLA and leader of the Social Credit arty and was succeeded by his son, W.R. BENETT.

PATRICIA E. ROY

ennett, William John, businessman (b at chreiber, Ont 3 Nov 1911). After graduating om U of T in 1934, Bennett became private ecretary to C.D. HOWE. When Howe became inister of the Dept of Munitions and Supply 939, Bennett became his executive assistant, position he held until he was appointed VP nd general manager of Eldorado Mining and efining Ltd, a crown corporation responsible r the production of uranium in Canada. Uner Bennett, Eldorado brought its Beaverlodge ranium-ore deposit into production in 1953. s president of both Eldorado and Atomic Engy of Canada Ltd in the 1950s, Bennett played key role in expanding Canada's NUCLEAR ENRGY industry and in developing the nuclear chnology which formed the basis of the Candu actor. Retiring from Eldorado and AECL in 958, he became VP of the Iron Ore Co in 1960 nd president in 1965. He retired in 1977.

J. LINDSEY

ennett, William Richards, businessman, olitician, premier of BC (b at Kelowna, BC 14 pr 1932), son of W.A.C. BENNETT. After leaving igh school, Bennett devoted his efforts to a caer in business and with his brother made a ccess of various real-estate and other specutive ventures. In 1973 he sought and won the CIAL CREDIT nomination in the Okanagan S seat left vacant by his father's resignation and shortly became leader of the party. He was able to rebuild the party membership and provided a rallying point for opposition to David BARRETT's NDP government. His party was returned to power late in 1975 and he became premier. He did not enjoy an easy time in office. Before 1983 his government was marred by minor scandals and suggestions that some of his leading ministers were actually in control. In recent years it has been plagued by a stagnant economy. After the May 1983 election in which Social Credit increased its majority, Bennett responded to the economic situation and rising unemployment by attempting to cut government spending and encourage private investment. The controversial restraint program he introduced was met by large-scale demonstrations mounted by the Solidarity Coalition of trade unions and community organizations. In compromise, late in 1983, the government abandoned a number of proposals introduced in that summer's budget but continued its resolve to reduce government spending.

J.T. MORLEY

Bennett's New Deal In the mid-1930s, at the height of the GREAT DEPRESSION, Prime Minister R.B. BENNETT's political demise seemed inevitable. Seeking to reverse the tide running against his Conservative Party, on 2 Jan 1935 he began a series of live radio speeches outlining a "New Deal" for Canada. It promised a more progressive taxation system, a maximum work week, a minimum wage, closer regulation of working conditions, unemployment insurance, health and accident insurance, a revised old-age pension and agricultural support programs. Nevertheless, Bennett lost the Oct 1935 general election, and in Jan 1937 the JUDICIAL COMMITTEE OF THE PRIVY COUNCIL declared most of the "New Deal" ULTRA VIRES.

JOHN ENGLISH

Benoît, Jacques, writer (b at Lacolle, Qué 1941). In 1967 Benoît published *Jos Carbone*, a short narrative, blending violence with the fantastic, which won the Québec Literary Competition in 1968. Encouraged by this success, Benoît published in rapid succession *Les Voleurs* (1969), *Patience et Firlipon* (1970) and *Les Princes* (1973). He then turned to scriptwriting and produced *La Maudite Galette, Réjeanne Padovani* (co-writer; both directed by Denys ARCAND) and *L'Affaire Coffin*. As a journalist with *La* PRESSE, Benoît won the 1976 Judith Jasmin Award for a series of articles entitled "Il était une fois dans l'est" ("Once upon a time in the East"). In 1981 Benoît published *Gisèle et le serpent*, which established him as an undisputed master of the fantasy novel.

ANDRÉ VANASSE

Benoît, Jean, surrealist artist (b at Québec C 1922). He studied at the École des beaux-arts in Montréal where he taught for a time. He became involved in the 1945 "cadavres exquis" experiments with Léon Bellefleur, Albert DUMOUCHEL, Jean Léonard, Mimi Parent and Alfred PELLAN, and in 1948 signed the free art "Prisme d'yeux" manifesto using the pseudonym "Je Anonyme." He later settled in Paris with Mimi Parent. Benoît became famous for his costume-sculptures, in particular one designed for the 1959 surrealist ceremony, "Executing the Will of the Marquis de Sade." Parts of this costume were exhibited at the 8th international surrealist exhibition held that year. In 1963, he published sketches of costumes for Fernando Arrabal's play *Le Communion solennelle*, in the surrealist review *La Brèche*. One of these costumes, "Le Nécrophile," was created for "L'Écart absolu" exhibition in 1966. His work has been praised on numerous occasions by writer André Breton. The manuscript of *Les Champs magnétiques*, the first surrealist text, written by Breton and Philippe Soupault, is kept in one of Benoît's "objects," a sculptured casket.

ANDRÉ G. BOURASSA

Benson, Clara Cynthia, professor of chemistry (b at Port Hope, Ont 1875; d there 24 Mar 1964). Associated with U of T for 50 years, she was the first woman to graduate in CHEMISTRY (1899), optimistic that there would be many openings for women selecting this area. She became one of the first 2 women awarded a PhD at Toronto (1903). Appointed science instructor in the Lillian Massey School of Household Science, she assisted her colleagues in their struggle for academic recognition of this area. A capable teacher, stimulator of research and friend of her students, Benson served as professor and head of the Dept of Food Chemistry, Faculty of Household Science 1926-45. She was honoured by a scholarship in her name. The Benson Building at U of T was named in recognition of her efforts to obtain better athletic facilities for women students.

PATRICIA H. COLEMAN

Bentley, Maxwell Herbert Lloyd, Max, hockey player (b at Delisle, Sask 1 Mar 1920; d at Saskatoon 19 Jan 1984). He played senior hockey at Drumheller, Alta, and Saskatoon and turned professional with Chicago, where he played 5 years as centre of the "Pony Line," with brother Doug on left wing and Bill Mosienko on right. He was traded for 5 players to Toronto 1947, after winning the scoring title the previous 2 years. He played 6 years for TORONTO MAPLE LEAFS and one for New York Rangers. Bentley was a masterly stickhandler and a quick, darting skater — one of the most skilled players of his era. He retired to operate the family wheat farm in 1954. He scored 245 goals and 544 points in 646 games, and 18 goals, 45 points in 52 playoff games.

JAMES MARSH

Beny, Roloff, photographer (b Wilfred Roy at Medicine Hat, Alta 7 Jan 1924; d at Rome, Italy 16 Mar 1984). Beny took up photography as a child. He also painted and had a watercolour show at age 15. After studying fine arts at U of T and State U of Iowa, he concentrated on painting and printmaking. In the mid-1950s, however, he turned to photography, having his first show in 1955 in London, Eng. After that Beny had many exhibitions and produced over a dozen lavishly illustrated books based on his travels, including *To Everything There Is a Season: Roloff Beny in Canada, Japan in Colour, India, Odyssey: Mirror of the Mediterranean* and *Forty Countries in Forty Years*. His honours included the gold medal at the 1968 Leipzig International Book Fair. He made his home in Rome for many years.

LOUISE ABBOTT

Beothuk ("the people" or "true people") were the now-extinct inhabitants of Newfoundland. Word lists, transcribed in the 18th or early 19th centuries, have been thought by some to indicate an Algonquian linguistic affiliation; others argue that the language cannot be proven to be related to any native N American language family. At the time of European contact the Beothuk occupied at least the S and NE coasts of Newfoundland. They may have numbered no more than 500 to 1000; population is difficult to estimate owing to a contraction in their territories in the early contact period and the absence of surviving documentation.

Archaeological evidence suggests that the Beothuk inhabited Newfoundland long before European colonization and that they may be descended from earlier people who occupied the Island for several thousand years. In prehistoric times, they seem to have been primarily a coastal people organized in small bands throughout the various bays to fish and hunt seals, other sea mammals and birds. They also may have visited interior locations to take caribou at river crossings, but the pattern of a winter-long interior occupation does not seem to have occurred until postcontact times. In both the prehistoric and historic periods the Beothuk dwelt in bark- or skin-covered tents in summer and in semisubterranean houses during the cold months. Bows and arrows, harpoons and spears were used in hunting, which often took place from seaworthy bark canoes with a high prow and stern, and a sheer which rose markedly amidships. However, the most distinctive of Beothuk artifacts are carved bone, antler and ivory pendants intricately decorated with incised patterns. Many of these items were recovered from grave sites in caves or rock shelters in the late 19th and early 20th centuries. Another notable feature of Beothuk culture was the people's lavish use of powdered hematite, or red ochre, with which they painted their canoes, other artifacts and even their bodies. Since these people were the first N American aborigines encountered by Europeans, it is possible that their custom of using red ochre was responsible for the sobriquet "Red Indians," which was later applied to all native peoples on this continent. As a result of European encroachment, slaughter and diseases to which they had no natural resistance, the Beothuk's numbers diminished rapidly following contact. The last known surviving Beothuk, SHAWNANDITHIT, died of tuberculosis in St John's in 1829. JAMES A. TUCK

Reading: J.P. Howley, *The Beothuks or Red Indians* (1915); F.W. Rowe, *Extinction: The Beothuks of Newfoundland* (1977).

Berczy, William, painter, architect, colonizer (b Johann Albrecht Ulrich Moll in Wallerstein [Germany] and bap 10 Dec 1744; d at New York C 5 Feb 1813). He spent his youth in Vienna, studied in Italy and worked in England before leading a group of colonists to New York state in 1792 and, in 1794, to Markham, UC. Thereafter he considered himself a Canadian and, from 1805, relied exclusively on painting for his living, first in York [Toronto] and later in Montréal. He became a popular portraitist, and also did some church decoration and architectural work, including the design of Christ Church in Montréal in 1803. He is best known for 2 portraits in oil: the dramatic full-length portrait of Joseph BRANT (c1805) in colourful costume, and the group portrait *The Woolsey Family* (1809), remarkable for composition and architectural detailing and regarded as one of the masterpieces of early Canadian art.

ROSEMARY SHIPTON

The Woolsey Family (1809) by William von Moll Berczy; oil on canvas. As well as being one of the masterpieces of early Canadian painting, it is a valuable representation of the family values and dress of early Canada (*courtesy National Gallery of Canada/Gift of Major Edgar C. Woolsey, 1952*).

Beresford-Howe, Constance, novelist (b at Montréal 10 Nov 1922). The author of 7 novels and various magazine pieces, Beresford-Howe was educated at McGill (BA, 1945, MA, 1946) and at Brown U (PhD, 1965). A member of the McGill department of English (1949-71) she wrote 4 novels exploring the emotional lives of young women while at McGill: *The Unreasoning Heart* (1946); *Of This Day's Journey* (1947); *The Invisible Gate* (1949); and *My Lady Greensleeves* (1955). In 1971 Beresford-Howe moved to Toronto and has taught English at Ryerson Polytechnical Inst. Three more novels have been published: *The Book of Eve* (1973), *A Population of One* (1977) and *The Marriage Bed* (1981). These novels concern the daily lives of contemporary women. *Eve*, a stage adaptation by Larry Fineberg of *The Book of Eve*, premiered at the STRATFORD FESTIVAL in 1976.

JEAN WILSON

Berger, Thomas Rodney, lawyer, judge, humanitarian (b at Victoria 23 Mar 1933). Berger practised law in Vancouver 1957-71. He was NEW DEMOCRATIC PARTY MP for Vancouver-Burrard 1962-63 and MLA and leader of the BC NDP 1966-69. From 1971 to 1983 he served as justice of the Supreme Court of BC, and from 1974 to 1977 as commissioner of the MACKENZIE VALLEY PIPELINE Inquiry. His report, *Northern Frontier, Northern Homeland* (1977), recommended eloquently against a pipeline across the northern Yukon and for a 10-year moratorium on pipeline construction in the Mackenzie Valley to permit prior settlement of native LAND CLAIMS. Berger's 1981 criticism of the federal-provincial constitutional accord for its removal of aboriginal rights and of the Québec veto resulted in 1982 in formal criticism of his "indiscretion" by the Canadian Judicial Council. In Apr 1983 he resigned in disagreement with the council's view that judges should not comment on matters of great public concern. That July he agreed to return to many of the issues raised by the pipeline inquiry as head of the Alaska Native Review Commission, a 2-year inquiry sponsored by the Inuit Circumpolar Conference into the effects of the 1971 Alaska Native Claims Settlement Act. DENIS SMITH

Reading: T.R. Berger, *Fragile Freedoms* (1982).

Bering, Vitus Jonassen, explorer (b at Hor ens, Denmark 1680; d on Bering Island 8 D 1741). An officer in the Russian navy, Berin was appointed in 1725 by Peter the Great explore the Siberian coast. After 3 years' dela Bering sailed from Okhotsk and passed throug Bering Str, proving that Asia and America we not joined. On a subsequent expedition in 174 he sailed from Siberia eastward into the Gulf Alaska and was the first navigator to sig mainland Alaska. On the return voyage his sh was delayed by storms and had to put in Bering I, where he died of scurvy.

DANIEL FRANC

Bering Sea Dispute During the 1880s, whi Americans hunted seals on the Pribilof I which the US had acquired from Russia in 186 Canadians conducted SEALING in the open w ters. In 1886 American revenue cutters, clain ing to protect "American property," began sei ing Canadian sealing vessels. An internation tribunal in 1893 upheld the Canadian right hunt seals in international waters, but impose certain restrictions. In 1911 an internation conference banned pelagic sealing in the Berin Sea but provided handsome compensation Canada. N.F. DREISZIGI

Beringia is a landmass including portions of modern nations (Canada, US and USSR) and ex tending from the Siberian Kolyma R and Kam chatka Pen, through Alaska and YT, to th Mackenzie R in the NWT. Near the centre of th region is Bering Str for which it was named. To day, this strait links the Arctic and Pacif oceans, but in the past lowered sea levels, resul ing in part from growth of continental GLACIER exposed portions of the continental shelves form a broad land bridge between notheast As and northwest N America. The importance Beringia is twofold: it provided a pathway fo intercontinental exchanges of PLANTS and AN MALS during glacial periods and for interocean exchanges during interglacials; it has been centre of EVOLUTION and has supported appa ently unique plant and animal communitie The history of Beringia is important not only i the evolution of landscapes but also in that plants and animals.

Beringia is a land of great beauty with th highest mountains in N America overlookin broad plateaus and meandering rivers. It ex tends from frozen arctic coasts on the N to Pa cific coasts warmed by the Japanese Current o the S. The temperatures range from some of th coldest on the Earth in winter to uncomfortabl warm in summer. Twenty-four-hour summe days contrast with long periods of winter dark ness. Because of its aridity, much of Beringia re mained unglaciated during the ICE AGES. Th stratigraphy of long sequences of nonglaci sediment exposed at various sites can be co related with alpine and continental glacial ad vances elsewhere. FOSSILS from such sedimen are often exceptionally abundant and well pre served. They include pollen grains, plant fossil INVERTEBRATES and VERTEBRATE bones. Studies fossils and of the sediments in which they occu have permitted tentative reconstructions paleo-environments in western and easter Beringia.

Beringia is of special importance in the stud of human PREHISTORY since it is most likely th area through which man first entered the Wes ern Hemisphere, presumably following th migrations of large MAMMALS, known from fo sil evidence to have roamed eastward acro the Bering Land Bridge. Portions of wester Beringia (now eastern Siberia) may have bee occupied by humans at least 35 000 years ag Artifacts of comparable age have been te tatively identified in eastern Beringia on the ba sis of broken and butchered mammal bones, b e oldest secure evidence of human occupation Alaska or YT dates to only 15 000 years ago. ermanent settlement of Beringia depended pon the invention and perfection of a complex ray of cultural and technological skills. Tailred skin clothing, secure dwellings, control of re, special methods of food procurement and orage and possibly some form of watercraft to oss large, cold-water bodies were prerequisites human life in these latitudes. Some writers ave suggested that the ancient colonization of eringia represented a technological achieveent equivalent to the penetration of such envinments as Antarctica, the deep sea and the oon. RICHARD E. MORLAN

erkeley, Edith, née Dunington, biologist (b at albagh, S Africa 6 Sept 1875; d at Nanaimo, BC Feb 1963) and **Cyril**, chemist (b at London, ng 2 Dec 1878; d at Nanaimo, BC, 25 Aug 1973). lith and Cyril met as undergraduates at Lonn U, married in 1902, and went to Bihar, Ina, where Cyril studied the culture and prossing of indigo. Moving in 1914 to BC, they rmed for 2 years near Vernon; both taught at e new UBC, and in 1919 settled at the Nanmo Biological Station. Following her lead, ey became world authorities on the classication of marine polychaete worms and deep respected members of the station's scientific mmunity. In recognition of their achieveents Cyril was granted an LlD by U of Victoria 1968. Both were enthusiastic gardeners, colcting rhododendron species and developing ew species of irises. A.W.H. NEEDLER

erkinshaw, Richard Coulton, company exetive (b at Toronto 2 Sept 1891; d there 4 May 70). Berkinshaw attended Upper Canada Colge, U of T and Osgoode Hall. After serving in WI he practised corporate law with a Toronto m until 1920, when he joined the Goodyear re and Rubber Co of Canada. He became genal manager and treasurer in 1933. He played a ajor role in Canada's industrial mobilization ring WWII as chairman of the Wartime Instries Control Board, president of Polymer rp and director general of the Priorities anch of the Department of MUNITIONS AND SUPY. He was created a CBE in 1946. Berkinshaw turned to Goodyear 1945, becoming president 52 and chairman 1959. He was chancellor of inity College, Toronto, and president of the NADIAN NATIONAL EXHIBITION, the Queen Elizath Hospital and the Toronto Board of Trade. J. LINDSEY

ernardi, Mario, conductor (b at Kirkland ke, Ont 20 Aug 1930). Considered the leading nadian-born conductor of his generation, ernardi has appeared widely in Canada and road. A career as pianist and accompanist, ben after study in Italy and Toronto, gradually ve way to conducting, following his CANAAN OPERA CO debut in 1957. He conducted opera tensively in Canada before becoming a musil director of the Sadler's Wells Opera Co in ndon (1966-68). First conductor of the Naonal Arts Centre Orchestra, formed in Ottawa 968), Bernardi created a disciplined, finely lanced ensemble, internationally praised for nsitive playing and transparent sound. Leavg Ottawa in 1982, he accepted the music directorship of the Calgary Philharmonic Orchestra fective 1984. He was named a Companion of e Order of Canada in 1972. BARCLAY MCMILLAN

ernier, Joseph-Elzéar, arctic mariner (b at Islet, Qué 1 Jan 1852; d at Lévis, Qué 26 Dec 34). Captain of the government steamship *ctic*, Bernier led seagoing expeditions into the ctic between 1904 and 1911, certifying Canla's claim to the northern archipelago. Bernier ft school at age 14 to sail as a cabin boy on his father's ship. Three years later he was captain of his own ship carrying timber from Québec to England. For 25 years he commanded sailing vessels all over the world. In 1895 Bernier became governor of the Québec jail, a position which gave him leisure to pursue his interest in polar navigation. He devised a plan for reaching the N Pole, a feat not yet accomplished, but at the last moment in 1904 he and his ship *Arctic* were pressed into government service patrolling the eastern Arctic. On annual cruises Bernier explored the archipelago and collected customs duties from whalers and traders. In July 1909 he unveiled a plaque on Melville I which officially claimed the Arctic Islands for Canada. After 1911 Bernier carried on private trading on Baffin I and during WWI he commanded an Atlantic convoy ship. After the war he returned to the arctic patrol, retiring in 1925. During his career Bernier commanded over 100 ships, crossing the Atlantic 269 times. He knew more about navigating the difficult arctic waters than any contemporary mariner. His 3 *Reports on the Dominion Government Expeditions to the Arctic Islands and Hudson Strait, 1906-1910 (1910-11)* are classics of Canadian arctic literature. DANIEL FRANCIS

Sylvie Bernier in action at the 1984 Los Angeles Olympics, where she won Canada's first gold medal in diving *(courtesy Athlete Information Bureau/Service Information-Athlètes).*

Bernier, Sylvie, diver (b at Québec C 31 Jan 1964). She won a silver medal in the 3 m springboard DIVING event at the 1982 COMMONWEALTH GAMES in Brisbane, Australia (478.83 points), a bronze at the 1983 WORLD UNIVERSITY GAMES (462.48 points) and a bronze at the 1983 PAN-AMERICAN GAMES (473.97 points). She finished first at the Ft Lauderdale International (506.52 points) in May 1984 and continued her rapid improvement to win a gold medal in 3 m springboard diving (530.70 points) at the 1984 Los Angeles Olympics — Canada's first gold medal in Olympic diving. JAMES MARSH

Bernstein, Harold Joseph, physical chemist (b at Toronto 26 Aug 1914). After graduating PhD from U of T (1938), he moved to U of Copenhagen on a scholarship. Picked up by the Nazi invaders of Denmark 1940, he underwent the devastating experience of a 5-year internment in Germany. After the war he joined the NATIONAL RESEARCH COUNCIL in Ottawa 1946, established a molecular SPECTROSCOPY section, opened up a study of nuclear magnetic resonance — with W.G. SCHNEIDER and J.A. Pople he wrote an important text, *High Resolution Nuclear Magnetic Resonance* (1959) — and pioneered a new field called resonance Raman spectroscopy. His long career brought international recognition and many honours and awards have accrued to him. He retired in 1978. N.T. GRIDGEMAN

Berries, Cultivated The most important small or soft FRUITS produced in Canada are strawberries (*Fragaria ananassa*), red raspberries (*Rubus idaeus*), highbush and lowbush blueberries (*Vaccinium corymbosum* and *V. angustifolium*, respectively) and cranberry (*V. macrocarpon*). Blackberries (various *Rubus* species), also an important N American soft fruit, are not produced commercially in Canada. Within Canada, southwestern BC is the most important production region for all berries except lowbush blueberries. Strawberries are an important crop in Ontario, Québec and the Maritime provinces, and are produced in localized areas outside urban centres in the Prairie provinces. In recent years, red raspberry production has increased dramatically in BC (making it the leading producing area in the world) but has declined in eastern Canada. Production of highbush blueberries has increased in BC and has remained stable in localized areas of Ontario, Québec and the Maritimes. Lowbush blueberry production, which is restricted almost entirely to the Maritimes, has increased.

Strawberries are grown under one of 2 cultural systems. In the hill-row system, all runner plants are removed; fruit production is entirely from the original mother plants, which are spaced 30-35 cm apart in rows 2.7-3 m apart. In the matted-row system, predetermined numbers of runner plants are allowed to root; thus, both mother and runner plants produce fruit. The original plants are spaced 50-75 cm apart in rows 2.7-3 m apart. Fruit from hill rows usually is larger and goes to fresh-market outlets; the smaller fruit from matted rows goes to processing market outlets.

Red Raspberry plants, which are usually planted in early spring as one-year-old dormant canes, are spaced 75 cm apart in rows 3 m apart. In established plantations as many as 12 canes are left per plant or stool. The spent fruiting canes are removed in winter. In early spring, the current year's fruiting canes are pruned to 1.5 m.

Blueberries Highbush blueberries are spaced 1.5-1.8 m apart in rows 3 m apart. Annual pruning, which removes the older wood and weaker canes, is done in winter. Since most lowbush blueberry plantations are developed from natural stands, there are no spacing recommendations. Pruning is done in late fall or early spring by burning with oil-, propane- or straw-fuelled fires.

Cranberries are grown from 7-10 cm long vines and are planted at a rate of 1700-2200 kg/ha. Pruning is not required.

Insects and Diseases

All small fruit crops are attacked by insects and various disease-causing organisms. Strawberries and red raspberries are particularly susceptible to both preharvest and postharvest fruit-rotting FUNGI, which can be at least partially controlled by a combination of chemical sprays and genetic resistance in the plants. VIRUS diseases, which are transmitted by APHIDS, can seriously affect strawberry production. Some cultivars (commercial varieties) are more resistant than others and this resistance, combined with chemical control of aphids, can help to prevent spread of the viruses. Viruses also can affect red raspberry production but resistance has been relatively successful in controlling them. Root problems in both crops can be caused by insects and NEMATODES as well as by fungi. Fungi often are controlled by improving soil drainage and, thus, increasing aeration in the root region. Insects and nematodes, which attack the roots, usually are controlled by chemical PESTICIDES applied as fumigants or drenches.

Serious fungal diseases of blueberry and cranberry are mummyberry and cottonberry, respectively. In both, infected fruits contain a white cottonball-like mass of fungi mycelia surrounding the seeds. Control is either by chemicals or by sanitary methods, ie, destruction of infected fruits. Blueberries usually are not seriously affected by INSECT PESTS. Insects can be serious on cranberries; however, most can be controlled by cultural methods that involve flooding the bogs. In recent years, the high cost of hand labour has made it necessary to use chemical methods of WEED control in all of the crops. Recommendations vary for crop and location.

The future of small fruit production seems assured in Canada because of a number of interrelated factors including development of more efficient, labour-saving cultural practices (eg, machine harvesting, improved training methods); new products (eg, yogurt, juice); and alternative marketing systems (eg, "U-pick" operations, farmers' markets). Increased production has been stimulated by the desire for more self-sufficiency in fruit production and by the knowledge that small fruit products can be satisfactory nutritional substitutes for products derived from imported fruit. More self-sufficiency means greater need for stable production in recognized and marginal production regions. The demand for increased production should stimulate CROP RESEARCH efforts in all aspects of small fruit culture. HUGH A. DAUBENY

Berries, Wild Over 200 species of small, fleshy, wild FRUITS occur in Canada. Most people consider them all "berries" but, technically, they are classed in different categories, including drupes (eg, cherries, elderberries), pomes (eg, saskatoon berries), true berries (eg, gooseberries, blueberries) and aggregate fruits (eg, raspberries, strawberries). Here "berry" is used in its less technical connotation. Some berries are poisonous; some are of doubtful edibility or unpalatable. No rules exist for distinguishing poisonous from edible types. People wishing to harvest wild berries must familiarize themselves with species in their area and learn how to prepare them. Almost all edible species in Canada were used by native peoples. Many were dried or preserved in water or oil for off-season use. They added variety and, because many were rich in vitamins and minerals, played a vital nutritional role in the traditional diet. European settlers also valued wild berries, using them for desserts, confections, preserves, juices and wines. Canadians still enjoy using them, often preferring their flavour to that of commercial types. The following are favourite Canadian wild berries.

Blackberries (genus *Rubus,* rose family, Rosaceae); over 12 species occur in woods and clearings, mainly in eastern provinces and southern BC. They are choice fruits, raw or cooked, making excellent pies, jams, jellies and wines.

Blueberries, Bilberries, Huckleberries (genus *Vaccinium,* heath family, Ericaceae); some 18 species, including bog cranberries (discussed separately), occur in Canada. All are shrubs, with edible fruits which vary in colour from red through blue to black. Cultivated varieties have been developed from wild species.

Buffaloberries (genus *Shepherdia,* oleaster family, Elaeagnaceae); silver buffaloberry (*S. argentea*) and russet buffaloberry or soapberry (*S. canadensis*) are deciduous shrubs with small, reddish orange fruits. In Canada, the former grows mainly on the prairies, the latter from coast to coast. Fruits are bitter but good in jelly; those of *S. argentea* were used by Indians to flavour buffalo meat. BC Indians whip soapberries with water to make a favourite confection.

Wild berries found in Canada, clockwise from top left: blueberry (*Vaccinium myrtilloides*), garden goosebe (*Ribes grossularia*), red raspberry (*Rubus strigosus*), cranberry (*Viburnum tribobum*), buffaloberry (*Shepherdia canadens* Saskatoon berry (*Amelanchier alnifolia*), chokecherry (*Prunus virginiana*) and strawberry (*Fragaria vesca*) (*artw by Claire Tremblay*).

Chokecherries (*Prunus virginiana,* rose family, osaceae), shrubs or small trees, which occur cross southern Canada, northwards to the YT. ruits, ranging from red to black, grow in long lusters. They have large stones and can be as-ingent, but are excellent in jellies, juices or syr-ps. Six other species of *Prunus* (4 cherries and 2 lums) are native.

Cranberries (genus *Vaccinium,* heath family, ricaceae), low, vinelike perennials growing in uskeg and peat bogs. Three or 4 closely related pecies are identified, one of which is the fore-unner of the cultivated cranberry. Berries are rt but good in sauces and desserts. Lowbush ranberry (*V. vitis-idaea*) is related, but has maller, clustered berries. Highbush cranberries *Viburnum opulus,* honeysuckle family, Ca-rifoliaceae) are tall shrubs with tart, clustered ruits.

Currants (genus *Ribes,* family Saxifragaceae, ooseberry subfamily, Grossularioideae); some 4 species are found in Canada, most of which esemble garden varieties and are used simi-arly. Fruits range from red to bluish to black. urrants lack spines or prickles and are thus dis-nguished from gooseberries.

Gooseberries (genus *Ribes,* Saxifragaceae fam-y, gooseberry subfamily, Grossularioideae), piny or prickly shrubs related to currants. ooseberries occur almost everywhere in Can-da except the Far North. At least 12 species are ound. The reddish to dark purple berries are rt and, like their cultivated relatives, are best n jellies and preserves.

Raspberries (*Rubus idaeus strigosus,* rose fam-y, Rosaceae); found in woods and clearings rom Newfoundland to BC and in northern erritories, wild raspberry was used to develop ultivated varieties. Relatives of raspberry in-lude black raspberry (*R. occidentalis*), blackcap R. *occidentalis leucodermis*), cloudberry (*R. chamemorous*), arctic raspberry (*R. arcticus*), thimble-erry (*R. odoratus, R. parviflorus*) and salmonberry R. *spectabilis*).

Salal (*Gaultheria shallon,* heath family, Eri-aceae), an evergreen shrub, restricted mainly to oastal BC. Salal has clustered berrylike fruits which, mashed and dried for winter storage, were, and still are, a major Northwest Coast In-ian food. Four other species of *Gaultheria* occur n Canada.

Saskatoon berry (*Amelanchier alnifolia,* rose amily, Rosaceae), a deciduous shrub that grows rom western Ontario to BC and the YT. The city f Saskatoon takes its name from a Cree word or the sweet, fleshy fruits, which were of prime mportance to Indians and early settlers. On the rairies, saskatoons were a major constituent of EMMICAN. They are still enjoyed and plant reeders are developing varieties for commercial roduction. Some 15 related species, all with ed-ble fruits, occur in Canada.

Strawberries (genus *Fragaria,* rose family, osaceae); 3 species are native to Canada, grow-ng in woodlands, meadows, clearings and oastlines. All are herbaceous perennials with eaves in 3 parts, and they closely resemble do-nesticated strawberries, which were derived rom 2 wild species. Despite their softness and mall size, their delicate flavour makes wild trawberries a favourite. *See* BERRIES, CULTIVATED; LANTS, NATIVE USES. NANCY J. TURNER

eading: Adam F. Szczawinski and Nancy J. Turner, *dible Wild Fruits and Nuts of Canada* (1979).

Berthon, George Théodore, portrait painter b at Vienna, Austria 3 May 1806; d at Toronto 8 Jan 1892). Son of René Théodore Berthon, ourt painter to Napoleon, George Berthon was a lassical European portraitist, trained by his fa-her and influenced by Jacques-Louis David. He worked in England 1827-40, where he taught ne of Sir Robert Peel's daughters. Settling in To-onto *c*1841, he had a successful career doing formal portraits of Upper Canada's business and judicial establishment, now hanging in Osgoode Hall and Trinity Coll, Toronto, and the Senate Chamber, Ottawa. His masterpiece is considered the portrait of Chief Justice Sir John Beverley ROBINSON. ANNE MCDOUGALL

Berton, Pierre, journalist, historian, media personality (b at Whitehorse, YT 12 July 1920). Berton is arguably Canada's best-known living writer and is particularly well regarded as a serious popularizer of Canadian history. He worked on the Vancouver *News-Herald* beginning in 1942, on *Maclean's* beginning in 1947 and on the Toronto *Star* beginning in 1958. Since the late 1950s he has been a staple of Canadian TV as host of his own shows or as a panelist. His first important book was *Klondike* (1958), a narrative of the KLONDIKE GOLD RUSH of 1898, an event in whose long shadow Berton had lived for years, being the son of a gold-seeker and having grown up in Dawson amid the debris of the stampede.

But for more than a decade following *Klondike,* Berton's name was represented with books drawn from his enterprising *Star* column and his interview programs and with such polemics as *The Comfortable Pew* (1965) and *The Smug Minority* (1968), which attacked the Anglican Church and the business-political axis, respectively. It was not until the 1970s that he attempted to pick up the serious thread of *Klondike* and resume work as a popular historian. His subject was the building of the CPR, as treated in *The National Dream* (1970) and *The Last Spike* the following year. The subject was well suited to Berton's strengths: patriotic verve, the marshalling of colourful detail and above all a driving narrative.

The Dionne Years (1977) carried him nearer social history and a smaller canvas. In turning to the WAR OF 1812 in *The Invasion of Canada* (1980) and *Flames Across the Border* (1981) Berton again dealt with events large enough to contain his heroic vision of what the past should be, and the smell of gunpowder quickened his pace without often leading to narrative excesses. Other historical works have included *My Country* (1976) and *The Wild Frontier* (1978), collected sketches of characters and events. If the railway and War of 1812 books reveal Berton at his exciting best, *Hollywood's Canada* (1975) shows a failure to penetrate beneath the surface. The book examines the way Hollywood films misrepresented Canada, but fails to follow through with any discussion of differing mythologies or to make a connection to the world of general or specific ideas. *Drifting Home* (1973) is an unexpected slice of autobiography in the form of an account of a northern rafting trip. *The Promised Land* (1984) is a history of the settling of the Canadian West.

Pierre Berton's mastery of narrative history, infused with colourful detail and patriotic verve, has made him one of the most widely read Canadian authors (*photo courtesy Michael Bedford*).

Bertrand, Jean-Jacques, politician, premier of Québec (b at Ste-Agathe-des-Monts, Qué 20 June 1916; d at Montréal 22 Feb 1973). Elected UNION NATIONALE member for Missisquoi in 1948, and re-elected several times between 1952 and 1970, he was always seen as a leader of the party's progressive wing. Minister of resources 1954-58, and of lands and forests 1958-60, he lost to Daniel JOHNSON in his bid for the party's leadership after the party's defeat in 1960. When his party returned to power in 1966, he became minister of education and was largely responsible for continuing the Liberals' educational reforms. Upon Johnson's death in 1968 he was chosen party leader and so became premier. He had to handle the first symptoms of the language crisis — particularly the school issue in St-Léonard, battleground for supporters and opponents of French schools — proposing BILL 63, which guaranteed parents' right to choose their children's schools. An ardent nationalist and defender of Québec rights, he was one of the main architects of Québec's demands for constitutional reform. His party lost the 1970 election to the Liberal Party of Robert BOURASSA. He continued as leader of the Opposition until 1971. DANIEL LATOUCHE

Bessborough, Vere Brabazon Ponsonby, 1st Earl of, governor general of Canada 1931-35 (b at London, Eng 27 Oct 1880; d at Stansted, Eng 10 Mar 1956). He was the only prominent British businessman ever to be governor general and as such something of a surprise appointment. Born into the Irish peerage and trained as a lawyer, he was a staff officer in WWI, and an MP in 1910 and again 1913-20, when he went to the House of Lords. In the 1920s he headed the San Paulo Ry and the Margarine Union and was deputy chairman of De Beers. He and his French wife were enthusiastic amateur actors, having built a theatre at their Sussex home. In Canada they inaugurated the DOMINION DRAMA FESTIVAL. The handsome, rich, well-fed and impeccably dressed aristocrat must have been an incongruous sight at the height of the GREAT DEPRESSION, but he showed his sympathy with the plight of Canadians in small ways, and was granted his wish for a 10% cut in salary. NORMAN HILLMER

Bessette, Gérard, novelist, critic (b at Ste-Anne-de-Sabrevois, Qué 25 Feb 1920). Bessette graduated from the École normale Jacques-Cartier in 1944 and obtained a doctorate in French literature from U de M in 1950. He was already a poet: his poem "Le Coureur" had taken 2nd prize at the Concours littéraires du Québec (1947) and he had been Canada's representative at the 1948 Olympic Games (poetry section). He went on to publish novels about Québec and Montréal society of the 1950s — *La Bagarre* (1958), *Le Libraire* (1960) and *Les Pédagogues* — in which he denounced the stifling influence of tradition on social and aesthetic standards. Bessette became a pioneer in psychoanalytic literary criticism in Canada with *Une Littérature en ébullition* (1968), *Trois romanciers québécois* (1973) and *Mes romans et moi* (1979). The development of this body of work was substantially influenced by a teaching career that took its author from U of Sask (1946-49) to Duquesne U (1951-58), to RMC, Kingston (1958-60), and then to Queen's, from which he retired in 1979. Two works are directly linked to Bessette's teaching career: an anthology, *De Québec à Saint-Boniface: récits et nouvelles du Canada français* (1968) and *Histoire de la littérature canadienne-française* (1968), which he coauthored. Since his novel, *L'incubation* (1965, Prix du Québec and Gov Gen's Award), critics have more fully recognized the richness and originality of his writing, which experiments in an ironic way with intimist and contemporary forms of expression. These forms are found in Bessette's more recent fiction: *Le Cycle* (1971) and *Les Anthropoïdes* (1979). A fellow of the RSC since 1966, Bessette received Québec's most prestigious literary award, the Prix David, in 1980 for the entire corpus of his work. JACQUES ALLARD

Best, Charles Herbert, physiologist, codiscoverer of INSULIN (b at West Pembroke, Maine 27 Feb 1899; d at Toronto 31 Mar 1978). The son of a Canadian-born physician, Charles Best had just completed his BA in physiology and biochemistry at U of T in the spring of 1921, when his summer employer, Professor J.J.R. MACLEOD, assigned him to work on a project devised by Frederick BANTING. Best won a coin toss with one of his classmates to see who would start with Banting; later the other student was not interested in taking Best's place. Banting's and Best's exciting experiments in the summer of 1921 persuaded Macleod to support and expand the research, and by the spring of 1922 a well-trained, well-funded team of researchers, including Macleod, Banting, J.B. COLLIP and Best, had discovered the internal secretion of the pancreas, which they named insulin. As corecipient (with Macleod) of the 1923 Nobel Prize for physiology or medicine for the discovery of insulin, Banting announced that he would share his half of the prize money with Best.

After graduate training in England, Best succeeded Macleod as professor of physiology at U of T in 1929. He was an active researcher and director of students, publishing important studies of choline, heparin and histaminase, as well as much further work on carbohydrate metabolism. He coauthored a widely used physiology text and in later life was honoured throughout the world for his contribution to the discovery of insulin. MICHAEL BLISS

Reading: Michael Bliss, *The Discovery of Insulin* (1982).

Charles Herbert Best, who won a coin toss to see who would start work with Frederick Banting on research that led to the discovery of insulin *(courtesy Public Archives of Canada/PA-112972).*

Best-Sellers in English Canadian books that have maintained high circulation over the years (such as L.M. MONTGOMERY's *Anne of Green Gables*, 1908) reveal persistent tastes in a wide readership; books with sudden sharp sales show shorter-lived fashions. Some authors, such as Arthur HAILEY, have produced one best-seller after another. Lists of best-sellers, both fiction and nonfiction, first appeared in 1888 in *The Canadian Bookseller*, and have been published since 1970 in the *Toronto Star* and since 1975 in *Maclean's*. The numbers vary widely: in fiction, the same list of best-sellers may include, in the top 10, books that have sold only 3000 copies together with others that have sold 75 000-100 000; the range in nonfiction is more likely to be between 20 000 and 40 000, although a few have reached 100 000 copies. Since publishers, bookstores and authors are sometimes reluctant to furnish exact figures and the research is not strictly scientific, such lists give only a partial record. Nor do they include textbooks, although these are frequently sold in great quantities. Nevertheless, both the current and the long-range lists are important indicators of changing tastes and interests among Canadian readers.

Some Canadian books have not only sold well in Canada but have also reached masses of readers abroad. Canadian authors discovered early that international popularity does not depend on the use of non-Canadian settings. T.C. HALIBURTON's *The Clockmaker* (1836) quickly found a large readership in Britain and the US. Nova Scotian Margaret Marshall Saunders's *Beautiful Joe* (1894) was carefully set in New England, but other early best-sellers carried images of Canadian places to the world: Gilbert PARKER's *The Seats of the Mighty* (1896) was set in old Québec City, Ralph Connor's *Black Rock* (1898) in the Rockies, Robert SERVICE's *Songs of a Sourdough* (1907) in the Yukon, Montgomery's *Anne of Green Gables* in Prince Edward Island and Stephen LEACOCK's *Sunshine Sketches of a Little Town* (1912) in Ontario.

A successful author's reputation often guarantees large sales for subsequent books. Parker, Connor (pseudonym of C.W. GORDON), Montgomery, Service and Leacock topped best-seller lists year after year until the 1920s, each new book catering to established tastes. Montgomery's *Anne*, for instance, with its imaginative use of language and its central character's free spirit and vivid response to nature, portrayed an idealized Canadian childhood that had worldwide appeal. By 1918 more than 750 000 copies had sold in the US; in 1983 in Japan and Poland *Anne* was still among the top 3 best-selling books for children.

At the end of WWI R.C. STEAD's *The Cow Puncher* (1918) was very successful in Canada, though not so well received abroad. The next worldwide best-seller to come from Canada was Mazo DE LA ROCHE's *Jalna* (1927), which portrayed a passionate family in an attractive Ontario setting. By the early 1980s, De la Roche's Jalna series had sold over 9 million copies. A huge public in the 1920s and 1930s also enjoyed less elegant Canadian fare: Luke Allan's books, such as *Blue Pete: Half Breed* (1921), Frank Packard's Jimmy Dale stories, and murder stories such as Hulbert Footner's *Easy To Kill* (1931). These books rivaled the sales of quieter rural idylls like Patrick Slater's *The Yellow Briar* (1933) and historical novels like Frederick NIVEN's *The Flying Years* (1935).

History dominated the lists at the beginning of WWII, in Canada as elsewhere. Canadian offerings included F.D. McDowell's *Champlain Road* (1939), Allan Sullivan's *Three Came to Ville Marie* (1941) and the more sentimental *Thorn-Apple Tree* (1942) by Grace Campbell. No Canadian books had worldwide success after *Jalna*, however, until Gwethalyn Graham's *Earth and High Heaven* (1944), a story of family tensions stirred by anti-Semitism in wartime Montréal. Ethnic conflicts also form the base of Hugh MACLENNAN's best-selling novel of 1945, *Two Solitudes*. Both books sold well in the US despite their Canadian settings, and Graham's book was among the top 6 on American lists for the year. Morley CALLAGHAN's *The Loved and the Lost* (1951), with a Montréal setting and interracial conflict, took advantage of the taste established by Graham and MacLennan.

In the postwar years, war stories came into mass circulation, eg, Lionel Shapiro's *The Sealed Verdict* (1947), Ralph ALLEN's *Home Made Banners* (1946) and Earle BIRNEY's *Turvey* (1949). But a social history of the 1950s would also have to note the proliferating sales of romances such as Thomas RADDALL's *The Nymph and the Lamp* (1952), comic sketches such as Eric NICOL's *Th Roving Eye* (1950) and CHILDREN'S LITERATURE, in cluding W.O. MITCHELL's *Who Has Seen the Win* (1947) and Farley MOWAT's *Lost in the Barren* (1956).

In 1959 the Canadian fictional best-seller wa Mordecai RICHLER's *The Apprenticeship of Dudd Kravitz*, set in Montréal, whereas in 1960 Davi WALKER's *Where the High Winds Blow* showe there was still a market for tales of adventur in Canada's barren North. In the 1960s the read ing and buying habits of Canadians change under the impact of television and a surg in paperback publication. The New Canadia Library, book clubs and authors' reading tour all boosted sales. Between 1960 and 1970 th number of English Canadian books in prin increased by about 250%, although no singl Canadian book became a worldwide best-selle In the early 1970s, world best-sellers illustrate shifting attitudes toward violence, feminism race relations, drugs and family life, and Cana dian writers tried plots featuring the new atti tudes. But traditional formula fiction also flour ished (*see* POPULAR LITERATURE); Canadia novelists turned out Harlequin romances abou spunky, beleaguered working girls and thei struggles (in exotic settings) toward luxury an married happiness. Publishers faced difficul inflationary times and rejoiced in clever autho like Richard Rohmer, whose fiction capitalize on current sensations in finance and politics Nonfiction lists featured Pierre BERTON's *Th National Dream* (1970) and *The Last Spike* (1971) and Peter C. NEWMAN's *The Canadian Establishme* (1975).

A list of best-sellers since the 1970s woul probably include political memoirs and bio graphies, eg, J.G. DIEFENBAKER's *One Canad* (1975), L.B. PEARSON's *Mike* (1972-75) and Rich ard Gwyn's *The Northern Magus* (1980); adventur stories such as William Stevenson's *A Man Calle Intrepid* (1976); humour such as Don HARRON' Charlie Farquharson books; financial guide such as Morton Shulman's "How To Invest series; novels such as Robertson DAVIES's Dept ford trilogy, especially *Fifth Business* (1970), an Margaret LAURENCE's Manawaka novels, espe cially *A Jest of God* (1974; sales were increased b the movie version, *Rachel, Rachel*); Alice MUNRO' story sequences, especially *Lives of Girls and Wo men* (1971); and entertaining tales by Harr BOYLE and Constance BERESFORD-HOWE. Margare ATWOOD's cool, honest and acidly funny novels especially *Life before Man* (1981), have had ver wide sales. The best-seller lists reflect Canadia choices, and perhaps Canadian needs: the nee for escape, for unavailable pleasures, for infor mation and guidance on urgent questions. Best seller lists reveal not what Canadians shoul read, but what they do read.

ELIZABETH WATERSTO

Reading: Mary Vipond, "Best Sellers in English Canada 1899-1918," *Journal of Canadian Fiction* 24 (1979).

Bethune, Charles James Stewart, clergyman entomologist, educator (b in W Flamboroug Twp, Upper Canada 11 Aug 1838; d at Toront 18 Apr 1932). He was a graduate of Toronto' Upper Canada Coll and U of Trinity Coll (BA 1859) and was ordained an Anglican priest i 1862. After serving parishes for 9 years, he wa appointed headmaster of Trinity Coll School Port Hope, which he turned into one of the mos prestigious boys' schools in Canada. As pro fessor and head of the entomology dept at th Ont Agricultural Coll (U of Guelph) 1906-20, h pioneered the instruction of the science of in sects at the university level. Always an arden collector of insects, he cofounded with William SAUNDERS the Entomological Soc of Canada i 1863, served for 11 years as its president an edited its journal, the *Canadian Entomologist*, fo about 30 years. At Guelph he developed th ɘaching of economic ENTOMOLOGY based on ɔund scientific principles, promoted the col-ɛction and careful identification of insects, and ublished widely on the lives of insects and on ɿeir control. P.W. RIEGERT

ethune, Henry Norman, surgeon, inventor, olitical activist (b at Gravenhurst, Ont 3 Mar 890; d at Huang Shiko, N China 12 Nov 1939). ethune's fame in Canada has resulted from his atus as a hero in the People's Republic of China nd the impact of this on Sino-Canadian rela-ons. Son of the manse, Bethune took up the rofession of his surgeon grandfather. He inter-upted his medical studies in Toronto to be a bourer-teacher at Frontier Coll (1911-12) and serve in 1915 as a stretcher-bearer in WWI. ollowing a stint in the Royal Navy, post-raduate training in Britain and private practice Detroit, Mich, he was found in 1926 to have ontracted pulmonary tuberculosis. After this ersonal crisis, he devoted himself to other tu-erculosis victims and to thoracic surgery in ontréal at the Royal Victoria Hospital and ter at the Hôpital du Sacré-Coeur, Cartierville, ué. Between 1929 and 1936 he invented or re-esigned 12 medical and surgical instruments nd wrote 14 articles describing his innovations thoracic technique. He became increasingly isillusioned with surgical treatment and con-erned with the socioeconomic aspects of the isease. He challenged his profession and pro-osed radical reforms of medical care and health ervices in Canada.

orman Bethune; a portrait taken in Spain during the panish Civil War, in which he organized the first obile blood-transfusion service (*courtesy Public Archives of Canada/PA-114788*).

After a visit to the Soviet Union in 1935 Be-hune joined the Communist Party. This com-itment took him to the Civil War in Spain in 936 where he organized a mobile blood-ransfusion service, the first of its kind, to oper-te on a 1000 km front. He returned to Canada 1937 to raise money for the antifascist cause Spain and soon turned his attention to the var being waged by communist forces against he Japanese invaders in China. "Spain and hina," he wrote, "are part of the same battle." ethune left Canada for the last time in 1938 to in the 8th Route Army in the Shanxi-Hobei order region. There, he was a tireless and in-entive surgeon, teacher and propagandist, and e adopted the cause and the people as his own. is accidental death from septicemia evoked Mao Zedong's essay "In Memory of Norman Be-hune," which urged all communists to emulate his spirit of internationalism, sense of responsibility and devotion to others. One of 3 prescribed articles during the Cultural Revolution, the essay made Bethune's name almost synonymous with Canada in China. HILARY RUSSELL

Reading: T. Allan and S. Gordon, *The Scalpel, the Sword: The Story of Dr. Norman Bethune* (1971); W. MacLeod et al, *Bethune: The Montreal Years* (1978); R. Stewart, *Bethune* (1973) and *The Mind of Norman Bethune* (1977).

Betula Lake, Man, is a freshwater lake and resort area in Whiteshell Provincial Park, 145 km by road NE of Winnipeg. Opened to cottage development in the 1950s, Betula is a popular swimming, waterskiing and fishing area. Its cultural history is especially notable, for located in the area are petroforms — boulder mosaics created by prehistoric peoples. These outlines, made of rocks weighing up to several hundred kg, are laid on open granite tablerock. Turtle and snake effigies predominate, but circles, human effigies and geometric patterns have also been found. The petroforms are thought to stem from the Laurel Culture (500 BC to AD 800). Some may have been used to mark portages, but the more remote sites were likely used for religious ceremonies and rituals. Some alignments correspond to astronomical phenomena. Their creators may have been ancestors of Algonquian-speaking peoples who continued to arrange petroforms after moving W to the High Plains. Systematic study of the Whiteshell mosaics began in the late 1960s. D.M. LYON

Beurling, George Frederick, "Buzz," fighter pilot (b at Verdun, Qué 6 Dec 1921; d at Rome, Italy 20 May 1948). He destroyed 28 enemy aircraft in 4 months while serving as a sergeant-pilot with 249 Sqdn, RAF, on Malta in 1942 and was commissioned and promoted flying officer. Wounded in 1942, he transferred to the RCAF as a flight lieutenant. Flying with 403 and 412 Sqdns, he was credited with 3 more victories for a total of 32. He rebelled against service discipline and was released in Oct 1944. Lost in a world without air combat — "It's the only thing I can do well; it's the only thing I ever did I really liked" — he joined the Israeli Air Force in 1948, and died when the aircraft he was ferrying to Palestine crashed. BRERETON GREENHOUS

Beynon, Francis Marion, journalist, feminist social reformer (b at Streetsville, Ont 21 May 1884; d at Winnipeg 5 Oct 1951). The Beynon family moved from Ontario to Manitoba during her childhood, and she worked in advertising and as a journalist in Winnipeg. She was active in the Canadian Women's Press Club and helped to organize the Political Equality League of Manitoba, the province's chief women's suffrage organization. In her column for the GRAIN GROWERS' GUIDE, where she was woman's page editor 1912-17, she took a wide-ranging view of the "Woman Question," discussing, in addition to suffrage, women's work and the structure of marriage and the family. When war broke out, Beynon took a pacifist position. This stand forced her resignation from the *Grain Growers' Guide* in 1917. She then left Winnipeg for the US, where she remained for the rest of her active life. DEBORAH GORHAM

Beynon, William, Nishga hereditary chief, ethnographer (b at Victoria 1888; d 1958). Initially ambiguous about his native heritage, Beynon became increasingly involved in it through research. From 1915 until 1956, he worked as an interpreter and field researcher among the Tsimshian, Nishga and Gitksan of BC. With Marius BARBEAU, he prepared an ethnographic census of those cultures, particularly their social organization and mythology. For brief periods he also assisted Franz BOAS and Philip Drucker. Despite a lack of formal training in anthropology, his field notes supply major data for these cultures. J.J. COVE

Biard, Pierre, Jesuit missionary (b at Grenoble, France 1567 or 1568; d at Avignon, France 17 Nov 1622). After long preparation for missionary work, Biard left for Acadia in early 1611. Determined and resourceful as a missionary to the MICMAC and MALISEET, Biard nevertheless incurred the enmity of French colonial promoters such as Charles de BIENCOURT, whose methods he criticized as selfish and materialistic. In July 1613, as he was attempting with 3 other Jesuits to set up a religiously based colony on the Maine coast, he was captured by an English raiding party, and subsequently returned to France. Biard's *Relation de la Nouvelle-France* (1616) was a perceptive appraisal of the problems facing early European colonizers. JOHN G. REID

Reading: John G. Reid, *Acadia, Maine and New Scotland* (1981).

Bible Schools, colleges and institutes represent a strong involvement in Christian education by the so-called EVANGELICAL Protestant churches in Canada (although a CATHOLIC Bible school, influenced by the CHARISMATIC movement, is planned for western Canada). The first 2 Bible schools in N America were begun by the Canadian founder of the Christian and Missionary Alliance Church, A.B. Simpson (Nyack, NY, 1882) and by evangelist D.L. Moody (Moody Bible Institute, Chicago, 1887). Toronto Bible Training School (later Ontario Bible College), est 1894, the first permanent Canadian Bible school and the third in N America, was modelled on Moody's institute. The purpose of Bible schools, institutes and colleges is to prepare students for Christian ministries through biblical and practical training. Most were founded by evangelicals reacting against the "liberalism" of established theological colleges. These church colleges trained ministers at a graduate level, whereas Bible schools and colleges were primarily post-secondary institutions for laity involved in the local church or in foreign and home missionary work. Evangelicals suggest that these institutions represent a resurgence of Protestant spirituality in reaction to secular humanism and agnosticism, and a return to the central concern of Christian education: the implementation of Christ's commission, "Go ye into all the world, and preach the gospel to every creature." Social scientists draw attention to economic and social factors, noting that the great periods for the establishment of Bible schools and colleges (particularly in western Canada) followed the Great Depression and WWII. For instance, William ABERHART, fundamentalist radio preacher and charismatic founder of the SOCIAL CREDIT Party, started the Prophetic Bible Institute in Calgary in the 1930s.

No single term describes the variety of Bible institutions. All offer Bible-centered day and evening programs, teach evangelical theology, stress Christian service (SUNDAY SCHOOL teaching and personal evangelism), promote overseas and home missions, and encourage personal devotional piety. Bible colleges offer 4-year undergraduate degrees in theology, whereas Bible schools or institutes generally offer only 3-year diploma programs. The term "Bible training schools" appears to have been applied only to a few schools in the early 20th century. Although many Bible schools or institutes have faculty with baccalaureates, a considerable number have some faculty who are essentially self-taught clergy or returned missionaries without extensive formal education. The colleges, in contrast, require faculty to have bachelor or even postgraduate degrees, and have maintained generally higher academic standards. Since 1959 about 40 Canadian Bible schools and colleges have organized as the Association of Canadian Bible Colleges (ACBC, inc 1968) to foster higher standards of learning. Most Bible schools and colleges offer 4 categories of specialization: General Bible (theological), Christian Education,

Missions and Church Music. Some also offer a pastoral program leading to the ministry. This Bible-centered curriculum (the Bible is, in fact, the "textbook") is augmented by structured programs requiring students to participate regularly in Christian service. Also, virtually all of these institutions originally emphasized biblical prophecy from a premillennial and dispensational point of view (*see* MILLENARIANISM).

Since 1894 more than 120 Bible institutions have been established in Canada, including part-time day or evening schools with under 10 students and full-time institutions with enrollments up to 900. It was only after 1920, however, that the movement burgeoned across Canada. In total, 69% of the institutions have been in western Canada, 22% in Ontario and Québec, and 9% in the Maritimes. In 1960, 47 Bible schools and colleges reported 3417 students, and in 1981 the ACBC reported over 60 such schools with a total enrolment over 9000.

Most Bible schools and colleges have a direct denominational affiliation, but approximately 15% are interdenominational (operated by an independent board of directors). MENNONITES have the largest number, followed by PENTECOSTALS, HOLINESS CHURCHES, BAPTISTS, Church of Christ, Church of God (Anderson, Indiana), Missionary Church, and Christian and Missionary Alliance. Some of the interdenominational institutions such as Prairie Bible Institute (Three Hills, Alta), Briercrest Bible Institute (Caronport, Sask) and Ontario Bible College (Toronto) have achieved national and international attention, especially through missionary endeavours. Prairie Bible Institute, the largest Bible institution in Canada (with a peak enrolment of 900 in 1949) was also one of the largest and most respected in N America. RONALD G. SAWATSKY

Reading: S.A. Witmer, *The Bible College Story* (1962).

Bic, Île du, uninhabited island, 14 km^2, is located in the ST LAWRENCE R, 30 km W of Rimouski, Qué. Because of its advantageous position at the mouth of the St Lawrence near the natural harbour of Bic, it played a key military role under the French regime. From the time Québec was captured by the KIRKE brothers in 1629, Île du Bic served as a communications base for vessels operating between the colony's outposts (Gaspé, Tadoussac, Québec City) and as a port for fleets during the French-English and Anglo-American wars. Missionaries also used the island as a rallying point. Before and after the Conquest, 1760, several development projects for the Bic harbour were successively devised and abandoned. Because of the many hazards for shipping in the river, during the French regime many sailors became pilots for transatlantic vessels. James MURRAY, the governor of Québec, regulated pilot activities on the river and established a pilotage station on the island. The pilots built several small houses at what came to be called Anse-des-Pilotes. In 1905 the station moved 40 km downstream to Pointe-au-Père. Countless tales are told of this island's enigmatic past and of the many shipwrecks on its reefs.
ANTONIO LECHASSEUR

Bickell, John Paris, mining executive (b at Molesworth, Ont 26 Sept 1884; d at New York City, NY 22 Aug 1951). A Toronto broker, Bickell invested in a Porcupine gold property that formed the basis of McIntyre-Porcupine Mines Ltd, of which he was president and later chairman. During the 1930s, Bickell championed the interests of Ontario mine owners and made newspaper headlines with his airplanes, fast cars and close friends, including Premier M. HEPBURN. In WWII he served in England's Ministry of Aircraft Production under Lord Beaverbrook (Max AITKEN) and in Canada's Dept of Munitions and Supply, where he was president of Victory Aircraft Ltd. Bickell became the first president of Maple Leaf Gardens (the annual trophy awarded to the outstanding player on the Toronto Maple Leafs is named for him) and helped to establish the Toronto Art Gallery (later Art Gallery of Ontario). He was a senior partner of Thomson, McKinnon, members of the New York Stock Exchange. The J.P. Bickell Foundation, provided for in his will with a capital fund of $13 million, was established chiefly to assist medical and mining research in Ontario.
J. LINDSEY

Bickert, Edward Isaac, jazz guitarist (b at Hochfeld, Man 29 Nov 1932). Canada's best-known jazz guitarist, Bickert began his professional career about 1955 in Toronto, working with Ron COLLIER, Rob MCCONNELL, Don Thompson and, for more than 25 years, Moe KOFFMAN. Developing a unique, understated style of considerable harmonic sophistication, he achieved international prominence through his work 1974-76 with US saxophonist Paul Desmond. His emergence was supported by his own early recordings 1975-78 and by those with McConnell's Boss Brass. Bickert's reticence has kept him in Toronto, where he has remained a popular accompanist to visiting jazzmen and has had a marked influence on the city's younger guitarists. MARK MILLER

Biculturalism This neologistic term came into public consciousness with the appointment of the Royal Commission on BILINGUALISM AND BICULTURALISM in 1963. On examining its terms of reference the commission could not find the word in a dictionary. It knew, however, that "biculturalism" had been used as far back as 1929 when Graham SPRY in a speech to the Canadian Club of Québec had spoken of the "bicultural character of the Canadian nation." The commission concluded that the term referred to the existence in Canada of 2 principal cultures — that associated with the English language and that associated with the French. Its function was to examine the state of each of the 2 cultures, and the opportunity for each to exist and flourish; and also the set of conditions that would enable members of the 2 cultures to cooperate effectively. Commission members did not think the term had an implication about individuals becoming bicultural, which seldom happens. They believed rather that an important factor would be whether both cultures are properly represented in common institutions and whether persons participating in these institutions have the opportunity to conserve and express their own culture.

Members of the commission rejected the notion that culture was determined by ethnic descent. They considered current language and a sense of belonging to be much more important factors. It noted that many Canadians whose ancestors came from countries other than the British Isles participate fully in the culture of English-speaking Canada, and some whose forebears were not from France in that of French-speaking Canada. It also noted that some groups, bound by ties of common ethnic origin, desired to maintain and foster their particular cultural heritages, in most cases while also taking a full part in the life of the Canadian society around them. The commission wrote extensively about these "cultural groups" and made recommendations about assistance in preserving their languages and support for their cultural activities. These observations gave rise to the federal government's statement about MULTICULTURALISM in 1971.

The concept of biculturalism, although the term was not then used, goes back to the origins of modern Canada. After the CONQUEST the British authorities allowed French Canadians full use of their language and system of civil law, and gave freedom to the Roman Catholic Church, a mainstay of their culture. In 1839 Lord Durham held in his report (*see* DURHAM REPORT) that French Canadians should be assimilated through the joining of Upper and Lowe Canada into a single entity. But after 184 French Canadian politicians in the eastern por tion of the new PROVINCE OF CANADA played thei hands cleverly and vigorously. French was soo recognized as an official language by the legis lature, and a structure for public education wa established that in effect gave full protection fo French education in Canada East. There the as similative process foreseen by Lord Durham di not develop and a distinct French Canadian cul ture continued to flourish.

Under the CONFEDERATION arrangements o 1867 the Province of Québec, with its large francophone majority, gained full control over education and other matters affecting culture. Basi support for French Canadian culture in tha province was henceforth assured. But by th 1960s it was plain that many French-speakin Canadians were dissatisfied with the place o their language and culture in Canada. Man thought both were threatened by the dominanc of English and English speakers in the industrial and commercial life of Québec; by the ob stacles to Francophones working in the federa administration while still keeping their ow culture; and by the plight of French-speakin minorities outside Québec, whose language an culture had nothing like the support enjoyed b the anglophone minority in Québec.

Since then much has happened. In Québec francophone cultural life has developed vigor ously. There have been remarkable achieve ments in education, literature, theatre, tele vision, radio, films and other fields. And mor and more Francophones take their culture a well as their language to work in senior posi tions in business. However, Québec's 1977 lan guage legislation, BILL 101, diminished the bi cultural nature of that province by rendering i officially unilingual. Outside Québec man groups of both Anglophones and Francophone now have access to public education in French, a choice that did not exist 25 years ago. And man Francophones have some much-needed form of support for their culture: French televisio and radio, newspapers and periodicals, and cul tural organizations. It seems evident today tha Canada has 2 principal cultures — that associ ated with the English language and that associ ated with the French. It is still debatabl whether each has fully equal opportunities fo development. *See* BILINGUALISM.
A. DAVIDSON DUNTO

Reading: Royal Commission on Bilingualism and Bi culturalism, Report (preliminary, 1965; final, 6 vols 1967-70).

Bidwell, Barnabas, lawyer, teacher, politicia (b at Monterey, Mass 23 Aug 1763; d at Kings ton, Upper Canada 27 July 1833), and his son **Marshall Spring Bidwell,** lawyer, politicia (b at Stockbridge, Mass 16 Feb 1799; d at New York C, NY 24 Oct 1872). Barnabas Bidwell wa a Massachusetts politician who fled to UC in 1810 when charged with forgery and embez zlement. He actively opposed the Kingston Tor establishment during the Robert GOURLAY agita tion and probably introduced the label "Famil Compact." Elected to the UC Assembly for Len nox and Addington in 1821, he was expelled be cause he was a criminal and an alien. The Torie maintained that Americans who had arrive before 1812 had to be naturalized to secure prop erty and political rights. Marshall Spring at tempted to replace his father in the Assembl but was declared ineligible as an alien. Th younger Bidwell emerged as a Reform leader sitting in the Assembly 1824-36. He rejecte the radicalism of William Lyon MACKENZIE an played no role in the rebellion, but was advise by Lt-Gov Bond HEAD to leave the province i

Dec 1837 because he was "disloyal." *See* ALIEN QUESTION. DAVE MILLS

Biéler, André Charles, painter and teacher (b at Lausanne, Switz 8 Oct 1896). He immigrated with his family to Montréal 1908 and served with the Princess Patricia's Canadian Light Infantry in WWI. He studied 1920-26 at the Art Students League, Woodstock, NY, in Paris and in Switzerland with his artist-uncle Ernest Biéler. From 1927 to 1930 he lived on Île d'Orléans, Qué, painting the life of the Québec habitants with fresh insight. Having established a studio in Montréal in 1930, he survived by teaching and taking commercial art work. Invited to Queen's 1936, he remained as professor of art until retirement in 1963.

His concern for the position of the artist in Canada led him to organize the first Conference of Canadian Artists (1941), from which emerged the Federation of Canadian Artists with Biéler as first president. More importantly, it set in motion ideas and actions that led to the establishment of the CANADA COUNCIL in 1957. He was chiefly responsible for the founding of the Agnes Etherington Art Centre, Kingston, in 1957 and was its first director. Nevertheless, painting has dominated Biéler's life. An energetic and prolific artist, he has drawn his subject matter from life experience. Stylistically, much of his work relates more to modern French painting, especially of the "School of Paris," than to contemporary Canadian movements. He has made sculpture in various media, and in 1968 invented a unique pneumatic press for printmaking. In later years his painting has been concerned with light and colour as he reinterprets thousands of early sketches. FRANCES K. SMITH

Reading: Frances K. Smith, *André Biéler: An Artist's Life and Times* (1980).

Biencourt, Charles de, Baron de Saint-Just, colonizer in ACADIA (b in Champagne, France 1591 or 1592; d in Acadia 1623), eldest son of Jean de BIENCOURT DE POUTRINCOURT. He accompanied his father on colonizing expeditions to Acadia in 1606 and 1610, and then took charge on his father's behalf at PORT-ROYAL (Annapolis Royal, NS). He was given command of the colony in 1615. As a young man, Biencourt was reputedly tactless in dealing with others, and his violent quarrels with Jesuit missionaries undoubtedly harmed the colony. His determination, however, was crucial to the survival of the French presence in Acadia after a disastrous English raid in 1613. He struggled for 10 years thereafter to promote the colony's recovery. JOHN G. REID

Biencourt de Poutrincourt, Jean de, Baron de Saint-Just, colonizer in Acadia (b 1557; d at Méry-sur-Seine, France 1615). As a young army officer, he fought in the French Wars of Religion, then entered the service of King Henry IV 1593. After Henry's grant of the colony of Acadia to Pierre Du Gua de MONTS 1603, Poutrincourt set sail with de Monts the next year. Their expedition had some success, but the colony was abandoned 1607 after the revocation of its trading monopoly. Poutrincourt, who had received a seigneurial land grant at PORT-ROYAL (Annapolis Royal, NS), was determined to return to Acadia, and finally did so 1610 with an expedition that included his sons CHARLES and Jacques. Returning to France 1611 to raise money for the colony, Poutrincourt visited Port-Royal for the last time in 1614, only to find it devastated by English raiders. Nevertheless, a few colonists remained in Acadia with Charles, thus maintaining a continuous French presence there. Poutrincourt was killed during renewed civil strife in France in 1615. JOHN G. REID

Bienville, Jean-Baptiste Le Moyne de, governor of Louisiana (bap at Montréal 23 Feb 1680; d at Paris, France 7 Mar 1767). Louisiana was New France's offshoot and the Canadian Le Moyne family were its godparents. A naval midshipman under his brother d'IBERVILLE, searching for the Mississippi's mouth in 1698 to 1699, Bienville was left as second-in-command at the Biloxi post and became acting governor in 1701. For the next 40 years, he was frequently Louisiana's senior administrator because the nominal governors were absent or ineffectual. Officially, he was commandant general 1717-25 and royal governor 1732-43. He founded New Orleans in 1718 and secured Louisiana's frontiers by military prowess, experience, ability to negotiate with Indian allies and diplomacy, keeping a small, sickly French colony caught between the Spanish and British empires alive. He retired voluntarily to France in 1743. PETER N. MOOGK

Bienville, Lac, 1248 km^2, elev 427 m, max length 89 km, is located in a sparsely populated region of northern Québec. This elongated lake, dotted with numerous islands, is fed by Lacs La Forest, Louet, Brésolles, Ossant, Roz and De La Noue. It drains W, via the 334 km Grande Rivière de la Baleine (Great Whale R), into Hudson Bay. After the Sieur d'IBERVILLE's successful assault on Ft Nelson in the bay region in 1697, the lake was named for his younger brother, Jean-Baptiste Le Moyne, Sieur de Bienville. DAVID EVANS

Big Bear (Mistahimaskwa), Plains CREE chief (b near Ft Carlton, Sask 1825?; d on the Poundmaker Reserve 17 Jan 1888). By the 1870s Big Bear had emerged as a head man of about 65 lodges. He was concerned with the disappearance of the buffalo, the increasing numbers of European settlers, and impossible treaty conditions that seemed to ensure perpetual poverty and the destruction of his people's way of life. In 1876 he refused to sign Treaty No 6 and maintained that position until 8 Dec 1882, when with the last buffalo gone, starvation was a reality. He wanted to take a reservation near Ft Pitt, but when he saw the poverty of his friends there, he worked to wring further concessions from the federal government. In an attempt to unite the Northern Cree, several meetings were held at Battleford, the largest in 1884 when over 2000 Indians joined in Big Bear's thirst dance at Poundmaker's reserve. The event nearly erupted into violence, but through the efforts of the NWMP and Big Bear peace was maintained.

Big Bear (Mistahimaskwa), Plains Cree chief who refused to sign Treaty No 6 in 1876 because he felt that the treaty conditions would ensure the destruction of his people's way of life (*courtesy Public Archives of Canada/C-1873*).

As a result of the federal government's refusal to negotiate with Big Bear, he lost the support of his more extreme followers. By 1885 they had become dominant and, led by Little Bad Man (Ayimisis) and Wandering Spirit (Kapapamahchakwew), they killed 9 whites at Frog Lake, burned Ft Pitt, and were defeated at LOON LK. Big Bear, in the background at these events and always counselling peace, surrendered at Ft Carlton on 2 July 1885. He was tried for treason-felony, found guilty and served a 3-year sentence in Stoney Mountain Penitentiary. A broken, sick man, he was released on 4 Mar 1887. FRITS PANNEKOEK

Biggar, Sask, Town, pop 2561 (1981c), inc 1911, is located in W-central Saskatchewan, 100 km W of SASKATOON. Established by the GRAND TRUNK PACIFIC RAILWAY, it was named for W.H. Biggar, general counsel of the GTPR. The community's initial development was based on the railway's decision to establish a divisional point at that location. It has continued its role as a railroad centre and serves as the commercial hub of a good grain-farming area. Its well-known slogan "New York is Big, but this is Biggar" greets visitors as they enter the town. DON HERPERGER

Biggar, Oliver Mowat, lawyer, public servant (b at Toronto 11 Oct 1876; d at Ottawa 6 Aug 1948). An authority on patent law, Biggar moved between private legal practice and positions of public trust in war and peace under both Conservative and Liberal regimes. He was a member of the Military Service Council (which implemented conscription), 1917-18; judge advocate general, the militia's top lawyer, 1918-19; trusted adviser to PM Robert BORDEN at the Paris Peace Conference, 1919; vice-chairman of the Air Board, 1919-22, and hence a crucial player in the early development of Canadian aviation; chief electoral officer, 1920-27; and the first chairman of the Canadian section of the PERMANENT JOINT BOARD ON DEFENCE, from its creation in 1940 until the end of WWII. NORMAN HILLMER

Bighorn Sheep, *see* MOUNTAIN SHEEP.

Bigot, François, financial commissary of Île Royale 1739-45, intendant of New France 1748-60 (bap at Bordeaux, Fr 30 Jan 1703; d at Neuchâtel, Switz 12 Jan 1778). Traditionally Bigot has been remembered for administrative fraud so massive as to cause the CONQUEST of New France by the British during the SEVEN YEARS' WAR.

After the British capture of Louisbourg in 1745 Bigot was sent back to Canada in 1748, against his personal wishes, to assume chief responsibility for the civil government of New France. Soon merchants began to complain that only Bigot's friends were receiving contracts to supply the government. Recalled to France in 1754 to answer these charges, his explanations apparently were satisfactory, since he was reassigned to Canada in 1755.

Government spending on Canada during the Seven Years' War rose from just over 6 million *livres* in 1755 to over 30 million in 1759. The French government believed Bigot and his associates (*see* GRANDE SOCIÉTÉ) stole much of the money. Following a show trial in Paris, referred to as the "Affaire du Canada," Bigot was sentenced to "restore" 1.5 million *livres* to the French Crown in 1763. He paid the money and ended his days in relative poverty and disgrace in exile in Switzerland. Ever since historians have debated the degree to which Bigot's dealings were criminal. The recent consensus is that his behaviour was typical of the period and that skyrocketing expenditures resulted from the war and the British blockade. In fact, Bigot was an extremely able administrator. He also presided over magnificent banquets and balls that scandalized the clergy in Canada, and his gambling bouts were notorious. HUGH A. PORTEOUS

Bilingualism is the ability to speak or write fluently in 2 languages. In Canada the term has taken on a more particular meaning: the ability to communicate (or the practice of communicating) in both of Canada's official languages, English and French. It has been formalized in LANGUAGE POLICY, in an attempt by government to respond to a difficult social question: to what extent is it possible to make legal and practical accommodations that will allow the 2 official language communities to preserve their cultural distinctiveness and at the same time pursue common goals? "Institutional bilingualism" refers to the capacity of state institutions to operate in 2 languages and should not be confused with a requirement that everyone be bilingual.

Historically, institutional bilingualism has recognized the facts of how Canada was settled and developed. Implicit in the founding of the Canadian federation was the idea that the English- and French-speaking communities should not only coexist but should complement each other. The BRITISH NORTH AMERICA ACT of 1867 established English and French as legislative and judicial languages in federal and Quebec institutions. It also set out the right to denominational schooling, which at that time was closely associated with the anglophone (Protestant) and francophone (Roman Catholic) linguistic and cultural traditions.

The development of the bilingual and bicultural nature of the Canadian federation soon experienced setbacks, however, partly as a result of the uneven application of principles and partly from a simple lack of linguistic tolerance. Although the BNA Act and the Manitoba Act (1870) accorded the French language official status in Quebec and Manitoba respectively, no such recognition was granted to the substantial French-speaking populations of Ontario and New Brunswick. Furthermore, in the late 19th and early 20th centuries a series of legislative enactments across Canada seriously restricted French-language education and virtually eliminated the use of French in provincial legislatures and courts outside Quebec.

Although the effects of these and other measures understandably linger in the minds of many Canadians, Canada has, since WWII, found a new concern for the official status of English and French and the destiny of minority language communities throughout the country. At the same time, demographic patterns, and particularly the tendency of Francophones outside Quebec to become assimilated to the English-speaking community, have increased the polarization between the official-language groups. This in turn has brought attention to the relationship of linguistic justice and national unity. Increasingly the enhancement of the French language and culture in Canada and a reaffirmation of the rights of the English language and culture in Quebec are seen as fundamental to maintaining a reasonable degree of national integrity.

The problems and demands of bilingualism within the national framework were clearly set forth by the Royal Commission on BILINGUALISM AND BICULTURALISM (1963-69). Central to the commission's recommendations was the premise that the English and French minorities throughout Canada, when of reasonable size, should be assured public services in their own language and afforded as much opportunity as possible to use their mother tongue. The commission also urged that French become a normal language of work, together with English, in the federal administration and that government documents and correspondence be generally available in both languages. Moreover the commission stressed that there was room within an officially bilingual state for other forms of linguistic and cultural pluralism, so that bilingualism and MULTICULTURALISM might complement each other.

The commission's work culminated in the adoption of the federal OFFICIAL LANGUAGES ACT (1969), designed to be the cornerstone of institutional bilingualism in Canada. The Act, which declares the "equality of status" of English and French in Parliament and the Canadian government, applies to all federal departments, judicial and quasi-judicial bodies, and administrative agencies and crown corporations established by federal statute. In addition to prescribing federal reforms and establishing the office of Commissioner of Official Languages to see that they are carried out, the Act has prompted initiatives beyond the federal administration. With encouragement and financial assistance from Ottawa, provincial governments and parts of the parapublic and private sectors have begun to reexamine their linguistic policies, at least in the services they offer, and have made some effort to pursue a policy of institutional bilingualism.

The success of any Canadian policy on bilingualism is closely tied to the co-operation of the provinces. Provincial powers in the fields of justice, public services and education can be influenced only indirectly by federal policies. To complete the picture, numerous administrative, judicial, social and educational services need to be provided by municipal and provincial authorities in regions where there are large minority-language populations. New Brunswick passed an Official Languages Act in 1969 giving equal status, rights and privileges to English and French; since the early 1970s, Ontario has increased the use of French in its courts and other provincial services; and Manitoba, as a result of a 1979 Supreme Court ruling, is moving towards the translation of its statutes into French and the transformation of its courts into bilingual institutions. In 1983 and 1984 the extent of Manitoba's compliance with its constitutional requirements became the focus of a heated political debate both inside and outside the province, leading the federal government to refer those questions to the Supreme Court of Canada for clarification. Quebec has recognized French as its sole official language since 1974. Although a number of government services are available in English (usually on request) the province has the peculiarity of being institutionally bilingual at the constitutional and federal levels while giving official recognition only to French at the level of provincial institutions. All provinces, helped to some extent by the federal Official Languages in Education Programme, now have minority-language education programs. Furthermore, SECOND-LANGUAGE INSTRUCTION has made remarkable gains across Canada, most conspicuously through the expansion of French-immersion programs in primary schools.

In Apr 1982 the CANADIAN CHARTER OF RIGHTS AND FREEDOMS came into force. The charter reinforces previous constitutional principles regarding language use in federal courts and the courts of Quebec and Manitoba, reaffirms the availability of bilingual services in the federal administration and confirms New Brunswick as the only completely bilingual province. It also breaks new ground by entrenching minority-language education rights in Canada, guaranteeing the right of children of Canadian citizens who find themselves in an official-language minority situation to an education in their own language wherever numbers warrant it. This guarantee represents a recognition that minority language education rights may be the key to the survival of minority language communities across the country.

The charter defined what was possible at the time of its enactment in the realm of institutional bilingualism, but its provisions may be developed and extended. The leadership of federal and provincial authorities in this respect is essential to achieving the underlying goal of language reform in Canada: the possibility for individuals of either anglophone or francophone background to move from province to province without forgoing their fundamental language rights and cultural identity. *See* FRANCOPHONE-ANGLOPHONE RELATIONS.

MAXWELL YALDEN

Reading: Canada, Commissioner of Official Languages, Annual Reports; Royal Commission on Bilingualism and Biculturalism, *Report* (6 vols, 1967-70).

Bilingualism and Biculturalism, Royal Commission on, often referred to by the names of its cochairmen, Laurendeau-Dunton. It was commissioned to examine existing BILINGUALISM and BICULTURALISM, and to recommend ways of ensuring wider recognition of the basic CULTURAL DUALISM of Canada. The commission was established in response to the growing unrest among French Canadians in Québec, who called for the protection of their language and culture and the opportunity to participate fully in political and economic decision making. It had 3 main areas of inquiry: the extent of bilingualism in the federal administration, the role of public and private organizations in promoting better cultural relations and the opportunities for Canadians to become bilingual in English and French. The commissioners used as their guiding principle the concept of "equal partnership" — equal opportunity for Francophones and Anglophones to participate in the institutions affecting their individual and collective lives. The commissioners were also to report on the cultural contribution of other ethnic groups and the means of preserving this contribution. In addition to a preliminary report (1965), a final report in 6 books was published, titled *The Official Languages* (1967), *Education* (1968), *The Work World* (Socio-economic Status, the Federal Administration, the Private Sector) (1969), *The Cultural Contribution of the Other Ethnic Groups* (1969), *The Federal Capital* (1970), and *Voluntary Associations* (1970). Ten commissioners representing Canada's cultural-linguistic composition were chosen. All spoke English and French and commission business was conducted in both languages. Education is a provincial responsibility, so the cochairmen called on all provincial premiers to obtain their co-operation in that section of the inquiry.

The royal commission to examine Québec's dissatisfaction had first been suggested by the editor in chief of *Le Devoir*, André LAURENDEAU, and it was established later under PM Lester B. Pearson. Laurendeau and A. Davidson DUNTON were appointed co-chairmen of the commission. Laurendeau died in 1968 and his post was assumed by M. Jean-Louis Gagnon. For many Québecois, the RCBB was a maneuvre to obscure the political issues. For many Anglophones, especially in western Canada, it was an attempt to force the French language on an unwilling population. The inquiry, however, revealed that Francophones did not occupy in the economy, nor in the decision-making ranks of government, the place their numbers warranted; that educational opportunities for the francophone minorities were not commensurate with those provided for the anglophone minority in Québec; and that French-speaking Canadians could neither find employment nor be served adequately in their language in federal-government agencies.

Recommendations to correct these and other serious weaknesses were implemented with unusual alacrity. Educational authorities in all 9 anglophone provinces reformed regulations concerning French minority education and moved to improve the teaching of French as a second language with financial assistance from the federal government. NB declared itself officially bilingual; Ontario did not, but greatly extended its services in French. French-language rights in the legislature and courts of Manitoba, disallowed by statutes passed in Manitoba in 1890, were restored by decision of the Supreme Court of Canada in 1979. A federal department of multiculturalism was established. Institutional bilingualism at the federal level became a fact with the passing of the OFFICIAL LANGUAGES ACT (1969) and the appointment of a Commissioner of Official Languages. However, the RCBB did not examine constitutional questions even though it indicated it would do so in the introduction to the final report, and the movement toward independence in Québec continued. G. LAING

Bill 22, *Loi sur la langue officielle*, passed by the Québec Liberal government of Robert Bourassa (1974), made French the language of civic administration and services, and of the workplace. Only children who could demonstrate sufficient knowledge of another language of instruction would be exempted from receiving their instruction in French. Increasing social unrest and a rise in nationalist sentiment had led to the repeal of BILL 63 and the introduction of this more comprehensive bill which, in parliamentary committee, attracted 160 written submissions. Nationalist and labour groups thought the law did not go far enough and rejected it. Anglophone and ethnic groups thought the language tests imposed by the law were unjust, and showed their displeasure in the provincial election of Nov 1976 by denying the Liberals their traditional support. R. HUDON

Bill 63, *Loi pour promouvoir la langue française au Québec* (Nov 1969), required children receiving their education in English to acquire a working knowledge of French and required immigrants to enroll their children in French-language schools. In 1967, the school board of Saint-Léonard (Montréal) had insisted that children of immigrants within its jurisdiction receive unilingual French education. Anglophone opposition caused the UNION NATIONALE government to introduce Bill 85, which never passed the parliamentary committee stage. The Gendron Commission was then established to investigate language problems in Québec, but when a compromise proposed by the Saint-Léonard school board trustees led to violent demonstrations, the government introduced Bill 63 without awaiting the commission's recommendations. Bill 63 aroused unprecedented opposition among Québec's francophone population who believed it was too weak a measure. It was eventually repealed and replaced by the more comprehensive BILL 22. R. HUDON

Bill 101, *Charte de la langue française* (1977), marked the culmination of a debate that had produced BILL 63 (1969) and BILL 22 (1975). It made French the official language of the state and of the courts in the province of Québec, as well as making it the normal and habitual language of the workplace, of instruction, of communications, of commerce and of business. Education in French became mandatory for immigrants, even those from other Canadian provinces, unless a "reciprocal agreement" existed between Québec and that province. For the PARTI QUÉBÉCOIS government a new language law was a high priority. After publishing a WHITE PAPER on the subject (1977), it introduced Bill 1, which was strongly supported by nationalist and union groups among others, and was just as sharply opposed by management circles and the province's anglophone population. The bill, withdrawn because of pressure from the Liberal opposition, reappeared as Bill 101. In 1980 the Supreme Court of Canada supported a judgement of the Québec Superior Court that struck down the section of *Charte* which declared French the language of the legislature and courts, and in1984 ruled that the CANADIAN CHARTER OF RIGHTS AND FREEDOMS (article 23) limited the bill's power to regulate the language of instruction. R. HUDON

Billiards games have been played for several hundred years and have been popular in N America since the early 1800s. In Canada, snooker is the most popular of these games, with some pool and varieties of billiards also being played. The game of billiards, while using the same equipment of the rectangular table, balls and leather-tipped cue, has developed into several variations. English billiards is usually played by 2 players, using a set of 3 balls (one red and 2 white). A player scores by pocketing his cue ball after striking another ball, by pocketing another ball by striking it with the cue ball, or by striking both other balls with his cue ball. Canadian Cyrille Dion was world champion in 1873 of a pocketless variation of billiards, in which the scoring is entirely by caroms.

In snooker 22 balls are used: a white (cue) ball, 15 red balls and 6 numbered colours — yellow (2), green (3), brown (4), blue (5), pink (6) and black (7). Two players usually compete. A player must strike a red first and if it is potted (1 point) may then choose one of the "colours" which, if potted, is replaced on the table and another red is attempted. When all the reds have been potted the colours must be played in order of value. The winner has the most points when all the balls have been potted. A match will consist of a number of games. The word "snooker" refers to a position in which a player cannot hit the ball that he is required to play because of the obstruction of another ball. The performance of George CHENIER from the mid-1940s to mid-1960s raised the status of billiards and snooker in Canada. The maximum run (or "break") possible in snooker is 147. The first and youngest Canadian to run 147 was the 17-year-old Vic Kireluk (1926-81) in Oshawa (1944). The first Canadian to run 147 in a competition was Bernie Mikkelsen in 1977. Cliff THORBURN with 21 perfect games has the most by any Canadian. In England in 1983 he scored the first perfect run in World Championship play. Only 2 women players in the world, both Canadians, have made runs of over 100: Natalie Stelmach with 109 (1977) and Sue LeMaich, 11 times, with a high run of 123.

Billiards games are played in clubs, private homes and in public "pool halls." There are about 2500 public rooms in Canada and over 250 000 regular players. The social stigma of the pool hall is fading as many rooms are now well furnished, respectable centres for family recreation. The term "pool" includes more than 60 games played on the American tables and is sometimes "loosely" applied to snooker. The major pool games are 8-ball, 9-ball and 14-1 (or straight pool). In 8-ball and 9-ball the winner is determined by the first player to pocket the 8 or 9 ball: in 14-1 the winner is the first player to pot the agreed number of balls. The pool games use a set of 15 object balls numbered 1 to 15 and a white cue ball.

In the 1970s the nationwide organization of games began. The major governing bodies are Canadian Snooker Control Council (formed 1975), Canadian Billiards and Snooker Referees Assn (1974), Canadian Professional Snooker Assn (1979) and Women's Snooker Assn of Canada (1979). GRAHAM DUNCAN

Billings, Elkanah, paleontologist (b at Gloucester, Upper Canada 5 May 1820; d at Montréal 14 June 1876). Billings's interpretation of fossils belonging to the GEOLOGICAL SURVEY OF CANADA was partly responsible for that organization's early success. He started professional life as a lawyer (1844-52), subsequently devoting himself exclusively to natural history. He contributed articles to the Bytown [Ottawa] *Citizen* and the *Canadian Naturalist and Geologist*, which he founded in 1856. His publications on fossils came to the attention of W.E. LOGAN, director of the GSC, who appointed him survey paleontologist in 1856. The study of fossils collected by the survey occupied him for the rest of his life. His insight into the stratigraphic value of fossils helped to identify the formations visited by GSC field parties, and provided Logan with information upon which he later based his concept of the "great overlap" (first published description of thrust faulting), and contributed to the success of Logan's monumental work *Geology of Canada* (1863). Of Billings's scientific writings, 2 items stand out: *Figures and Descriptions of Canadian Organic Remains* (1858-59) and *Palaeozoic Fossils* (1865-74). T.H. CLARK

Billion Dollar Gift, the Canadian government's first comprehensive attempt to finance British requirements in Canada during WORLD WAR II. The effort was made necessary by Britain's lack of gold and dollar reserves and by the dependence of Canadian war production — the key to Canada's wartime prosperity — on British orders. Canada gave its ally "munitions of war" worth $1 billion, in an act of unprecedented generosity. Announced in Jan 1942 and accompanied by an interest-free loan of $700 million and other assistance, the grant was expected to last approximately 15 months. Instead, it was depleted before the year ended. Emphasis on the gift's monetary value, rather than on the goods produced and provided, distorted its perception by the public. The gift was hence politically unpopular, especially in Québec, where it was depicted as tribute to "perfidious Albion." Nonetheless, it dramatically illustrated the importance of Canada's material contribution to the common cause. It was succeeded in May 1943 by MUTUAL AID. HECTOR M. MACKENZIE

Binning, Bertram Charles, painter (b at Medicine Hat, Alta 10 Feb 1909; d at Vancouver 16 Mar 1976). B.C. Binning, as he signed his work, came of a line of architects, but during years of adolescent illness he turned to drawing. In 1927 he began studying at the Vancouver School of Art under F.H. VARLEY. In the 1930s he studied in New York and London, under Mark Gertler, Amédée Ozenfant and Henry Moore. In 1934 Binning was first appointed to the Vancouver School of Art, and in 1949 to the UBC School of Architecture; shortly afterwards he founded the Dept of Fine Arts, which he headed for a quarter century.

Binning built an international reputation as a draftsman before taking to oil painting in 1948; he thought of drawing as "the most revealing expression of the artist" and his drawings, with their disciplined yet joyfully wandering lines, are his most valued work. His first paintings were of boats, and were characterized by gay colour and the use of the painting's flatness as a structural element. His continuing interest in architecture led him to design large mosaic murals for public buildings. His later paintings became stylized seascapes and, by the 1960s, purely abstract forms seeking to express what he called "the great quiet spatial ideas." His late years were shadowed by illness, and he painted little. The 1973 retrospective exhibition in Vancouver was his last. He was one of the first modernist painters in western Canada and a rare classicist among Canadian artists. GEORGE WOODCOCK

Biochemistry, study of the chemical nature of living material and of the chemical transformations that occur within it. Living things consist of many types of molecules (biomolecules) which, when isolated and examined, have no particular "living" characteristics, but behave in ordinary chemical ways. The properties of some of these molecules, especially large ones, are complex and subtle but are the result of the operation of chemical and physical laws. The special characteristics of living things arise from the ways in which these biomolecules are assembled within the cell. The methodology of biochemistry originated largely in PHYSICS, CHEMISTRY, IMMUNOLOGY and GENETICS.

History in Canada

Biochemistry began to emerge in Canada and the world during the last decades of the 19th century. Topics in early biochemistry were usually taught in medical schools by chemists. For example, a course in clinical and physiological chemistry was established by R.F. Ruttan and William OSLER at McGill in 1883. The department of biochemistry organized at the University of Toronto under Archibald B. MACALLUM was the first in the country and the second in the British Empire. Maud L. MENTEN, a student of Macallum's, worked with German biochemist Leonor Michaelis to clarify the kinetics of enzyme reactions; the basic equation used in enzyme kinetics is called the Michaelis-Menten equation.

During the first 3 decades of the century, biochemistry research was conducted primarily at the universities. In this early period, courses in biochemistry were established at the following universities: Manitoba, 1909 (dept, 1923); Montréal, 1911 (dept, 1951); Queen's, 1914 (dept, 1937); Alberta, 1915 (dept, 1922); Saskatchewan, 1916 (dept, 1946); Western Ontario, 1921; Dalhousie, 1924; British Columbia, 1927 (dept, 1950); Laval, 1928 (dept, 1940). Most Canadian universities now offer courses in biochemistry, through faculties of medicine, science and agriculture. In addition, many of the agricultural colleges offer plant biochemistry programs (*see* AGRICULTURAL EDUCATION).

Canadian reseachers have done excellent basic research in all areas of biochemistry, from studies of the proteins in cereal grains to studies of substances that inhibit neural (ie, brain) responses. Medical biochemists have made significant contributions in the study of hormones (endocrinology), blood fractions and the metabolism of chemical elements (eg, zinc, sulphur) and proteins. The outstanding early biochemical event in Canada was the first successful extraction from pancreas tissue of INSULIN and its application to the alleviation of diabetes. F.G. BANTING, C.H. BEST and J.J.R. MACLEOD were involved in the discovery, for which Banting and Macleod received a Nobel Prize in 1923. J.B. COLLIP was largely responsible for the purification procedures which made possible the use of insulin on human patients. Other Canadian research with direct application to medical practice included early studies in toxemias and nausea in pregnancy by V.J. HARDING (McGill, U of T), which led to the use of glucose therapy; research into the production of glandular extracts by E.W. McHenry (Connaught Laboratories, U of T), which led to a procedure for preparing active liver fractions for oral (later intramuscular injection) use in pernicious anemia; studies in steroids by J.S. Browne and Eleanor Venning (McGill) and in protein metabolism in shock victims by Browne; immunological research by J.S. Colter (U of A), A. Sehon (McGill, U Man), L.C. Vining (Dalhousie) and others; and research into malignancies and cancers by J.H. QUASTEL (Montreal-McGill General Hospital Research Inst), J.S. Colter, M.J. Fraser (U Man, Ontario Cancer Inst, McGill) and others. M. Chrétien, Institut de recherches cliniques de Montréal, has done pioneering work on peptide hormones. Some Canadian biochemists have attempted to elucidate the biochemical processes in brain tissue (eg, K.A.C. ELLIOTT, McGill; R.J. Rossiter, U of Western Ontario) and potential biochemical abnormalities associated with epilepsy (eg, E.A. Hosein, McGill) and mental illness (eg, J.H. Quastel). Other medically oriented research conducted in Canada relates to genetics and GENETIC ENGINEERING. Canadian university researchers have also made major technological innovations; for example, K.A. Evelyn, then a research fellow at McGill, developed a photoelectric calorimeter with filters, manufactured commercially and used until the 1950s.

Beginning in the late 1930s, biochemists working at federal research institutions have made substantial contributions to biochemical knowledge, many of which have had immediate, practical effects. Biochemistry research was first undertaken at the NATIONAL RESEARCH COUNCIL OF CANADA after the establishment of biochemical laboratory facilities in 1932. Initially, NRC's research was very practically oriented dealing, for example, with the processing and preservation of food, the effect of hormones on wheat and, later, the preservation of human blood fractions. Later research dealt with more diverse subjects and the early food-processing orientation became of minor importance. More recently, research has also involved biochemical processes in MICROORGANISMS (eg, relating to lipoproteins, ribosome structure). ATOMIC ENERGY OF CANADA LTD has facilities for biochemical research into the effects of radiation. Environment Canada has biochemical laboratories in each of its major divisions (eg, Fisheries, Forestry). Health and Welfare Canada maintains extensive facilities across the country to conduct the analyses necessary for enforcement of the Food and Drugs Act. Agriculture Canada has been responsible for much significant research in various areas, including the protein content of grains and means to enhance protein content and the baking properties dependent upon it; the metabolism of plant toxins; pathogenic fungi; fatty acids in oilseeds; synthesis of hormones in animals species; and animal disease. Some biochemical research is carried on by the provincial research organizations; the earliest provincial biochemical research program was established by the ALBERTA RESEARCH COUNCIL (1951).

Various special, largely medically oriented, institutions undertake some biochemical work, eg, Montreal-McGill General Hospital Research Institute, Allan Memorial Institute of Psychiatry (Montréal), Montreal Neurological Institute, Banting Institute (U of T), Hospital for Sick Children Research Institute (Toronto) and National Cancer Institute (research units across Canada).

In industry, biochemistry research has been largely confined to the drug manufacturing companies, eg, Ayerst Laboratories, Frosst, CONNAUGHT LABORATORIES, INSTITUT ARMAND-FRAPPIER, Veterinary Infectious Disease Organization (University of Saskatchewan). Biochemistry has important practical applications in the FOOD AND BEVERAGE INDUSTRIES; hence, many industries have quality control laboratories and some, notably Canada Packers and Labatts, also operate research laboratories. Several BIOTECHNOLOGY companies have opened across Canada since 1980, and this field will continue to expand.

Research in Canada is largely federally funded. Grants (primarily to individual researchers and to the universities) are co-ordinated principally by the MEDICAL RESEARCH COUNCIL of Canada.

With the exception of the Royal Society of Canada, the first national society with substantial representation among biochemists was the Canadian Physiological Society (est 1934); the Canadian Biochemical Society was an offshoot of this association. In 1957 the Canadian Federation of Biological Sciences was established. Biochemists have also supported and been represented by chemical associations (eg, Chemical Institute of Canada, est 1945) and nutritionists' associations (eg, Nutrition Society of Canada, est 1957). Canadian biochemists contribute to various national and international journals, the principal national journal being the *Canadian Journal of Biochemistry and Cell Biology* (formerly the *Canadian Journal of Biochemistry*).

DAVID B. SMITH

Reading: W.C. Murray, *A Synopsis of Human Biochemistry* (1982); E. Gordon Young, *Development of Biochemistry in Canada* (1976).

Bioethics, from the Greek word for life (*bios*) and the traditional word for systematic study of right conduct (ethics). Bioethics is one of society's attempts to manage new and far-reaching powers over life, powers coming from quite recent advances in MEDICINE, GENETICS, MOLECULAR BIOLOGY, reproductive BIOLOGY and other specializations in the life sciences. The most extensive developments and applications of these sciences have occurred in pluralistic societies, ie, those composed of a number of communities holding different moralities and philosophies of life. These communities differ on questions of right and wrong and often take conflicting positions on how advances in the life sciences may, should or should not be applied. The conflict may arise from differences about governing beliefs and assumptions concerning human life (ethos), fundamental and dominant values (morality) or the norms and methods to be used in resolving value conflicts (ethics). Such moral and ethical issues may arise in any domain of activity; however, those created by developments in the life sciences have been most prominent in attracting public attention and mobilizing societal reflection over the past 15 years. The principal issues have come from questions about research involving experimentation on human subjects; withholding or withdrawing various forms of life-support treatment from critically ill patients; euthanasia; ABORTION; prenatal diagnosis, genetic screening and selective abortion; sterilization of the mentally handicapped, BIRTH CONTROL, artificial insemination, *in vitro* fertilization and surrogate motherhood; transplantation of organs and implantation of artificial organs; definition of DEATH; psychosurgical, psychopharmacological and conditioning approaches to the control of human behaviour; recombinant DNA technology (RDT), GENETIC ENGINEERING and genetic therapy; and finally the just distribution of limited resources.

During the late 1960s and early 1970s, a number of ethics institutes, law-reform commissions and public-policy commissions promoted the interdisciplinary study and resolution of these issues. The principal organizations that have contributed to the development of bioethics are the Institute of Society, Ethics, and the Life Sciences (Hastings-on-Hudson, NY, est 1969), Kennedy Institute of Ethics (Georgetown University, Washington, DC, 1971), Society for the Study of Medical Ethics (London, Eng, 1972), National Commission for the Protection of Human Subjects of Biomedical and Behavioral Research (Washington, 1974), Center for Bioethics of the Clinical Research Institute of Montréal (1976), Protection of Life Project of the Law Reform Commission of Canada (Ottawa, 1976), Westminster Institute for Ethics and Human Values (London, Ont, 1978) and President's Commission for the Study of Ethical Problems in Medicine and Biomedical and Behavioral Research (Washington, 1978).

Biomedical innovations in genetics, human embryology, fetal medicine, geriatrics, gerontology and the neurosciences will continue to raise such questions. Uncertainties and conflicts will challenge those working in bioethics in the coming decades to clarify systematically the philosophical and social foundations of policies designed to harmonize individual welfare and the common good for present and future genertions, in the context of both national and international relations. *See* MEDICAL ETHICS.

DAVID J. ROY

Reading: T.L. Beauchamp and LeRoy Walters, eds, *Contemporary Issues in Bioethics* (1978); Warren Reich, ed, *Encyclopedia of Bioethics*, 4 vols (1978).

Biogeoclimatic Zone, large ecosystem that is geographically limited and controlled by a special ("single") macroclimate. The same predominant soil-forming processes determine the zone's SOIL and, consequently, its vegetation and animal life. Such a zone encompasses a number of smaller, vegetationally and environmentally more uniform ecosystems, which differ in those components that develop in response to conditions which are drier or moister than the zone's mesic (average) environment. The stable community of plants which develops in response to the climatic conditions of mesic sites is the most significant characteristic community of a biogeoclimatic zone. If common enough, edaphic plants, ie, those that develop in response to soil rather than climatic conditions, may also be significant. In Canada, the soils most commonly used for zonal soil characterization are those that have developed since GLACIATION from glacial drift or its outwash or from at least several-thousand-year-old lacustrine (lake), alluvial (running water) or aeolian (wind) deposits. Below the zonal level are subzones or their variations; above are higher units, ie, biogeoclimatic regions and formations. Biogeoclimatic zones have been studied in Canada (BC, Alta and the YT), the Hawaiian Is, Japan (Hokkaido I) and Indonesia.

V.J. KRAJINA

Biogeography studies all aspects of the adaptations of an organism to its ENVIRONMENT, considering systematically the origins, MIGRATIONS and associations of living things. Hence, it aims for a synthesis of data from nonbiological and biological disciplines: GEOLOGY, PHYSICAL GEOGRAPHY, GEOMORPHOLOGY, CLIMATOLOGY and METEOROLOGY, on the one hand; BIOLOGY, taxonomy, GENETICS and physiology, on the other. Biogeographical relationships cannot be understood except from an ecological perspective which tries to explain the exchanges between an organism and its environment. Ecology is subdivided into 3 fields of study: autecology (relations of individual species or populations to their milieu), synecology (composition of living communities) and dynecology (processes of change in related communities). Therefore, in its widest compass, biogeography concerns itself with the EVOLUTION of species, with changes in their ranges and with their extinctions. The principal factors influencing evolutionary development are climatic and edaphic (ie, soil-related) constraints, genetic adaptation and social integration.

Ultimately, biogeographic phenomena are explicable only as resolutions of conflicts between heredity and environment. The macroenvironment must contain resources that meet the requirements of individual organisms. Hence, the living population must be viewed as existing in nested environments of increasing magnitude that contain the positive and negative forces that act upon it. From smallest to largest these environments may be designated niche, ecotope, community, ecosystem, landscape and bioclimate. The defining of orders of magnitude in the environment permits the identification of providers of resources and factors of constraint. At its lowest spatial level, the niche, the organism encounters an accumulation of all environmental impacts. Such impacts can usually be traced to larger spatial units and to higher orders of control. For example, the tiny annual plant *Koenigia islandica* and the summer-breeding Lapland longspur occupy different ecotopes of a Baffin I sedge community, which itself is part of a larger marsh ecosystem (flats that undergo inconstant flooding) in an otherwise varied landscape under the severe stress of a high arctic bioclimate.

	Organism	*Requirement*	*Tolerance*	*Efficiency*
Eastern forest	sugar maple	H moist-cold climate; deep well-aerated soil; constant summer shade	H very cold winters; early and late frosts; insect parasites	H abundant yearly seeding; good growth rate; dominance
Grassland	aspen	L open areas for establishment	H variety of soil types; resistance to fire, insect parasites	H intensive vegetative propagation; rapid growth
Southern cattail marsh	red-winged blackbird	L marshes for nesting; varied landscape for feeding	H fluctuations of water level; changes in marsh dynamics	H territoriality; high reproductive rate; gregariousness
High northern marsh	whooping crane	H narrowly limited marsh area at each end of migration path	L competition with other birds	L vulnerability to habitat change, predators; low reproductive rate
Maritime arctic tundra	Inuit	H extremely high fat and protein diet	H cold; scarcity of vegetable food	L survival requires considerable cultural skills and occasional innovation
Southern industrial town	factory worker	L minimal food and shelter	H substandard living conditions	V survival depends on a patterned, mostly imposed technology

The ultimate explanation of plant and animal behaviour and of the fitness of an individual population to its habitat must be sought at each level. Questions concerning the relative importance of, for example, climate/soil, acidity/alkalinity (of soil), sun/shade, may be irrelevant if not set in a frame that will allow the assessment of cumulative effects. For example, climatic effects are most significant in determining the range limitations of many species. Consequently, present-day climatic limitations and knowledge of past circumstances can provide information about the place of origin of species and the migrations that have resulted in their present position.

The principle that must be kept in sight is that each kind of PLANT and ANIMAL (including man) has an individual ecological strategy that makes it more or less fit to survive in its environment. An estimation of fitness depends on 3 factors: requirements (R), tolerance (T) and efficiency (E). The table lists responses in some Canadian plant, animal and human populations and shows outstanding features of their ecological strategy. Marginal notations give an overall estimation: H (high), L (low), V (variable). The table does not provide an inventory of the living conditions wherein the life cycle of each organism unfolds, but it draws attention to some of the responses that result from R, T and E in each case. Two species having the same requirements and tolerance do not necessarily have the same efficiency. Thus, where sugar maple and beech grow together (eg, in the eastern Canadian forest), the maples seed more regularly and abundantly and usually far outweigh the beeches in the total biomass. Several nesting birds share cattail marshes with the red-winged blackbird, but do not equal its numbers or stability. Inuit populations in contact with southern Canadians rapidly increase their efficiency by applying their ability to learn new technology and move into a storage-exchange economy.

The study of all existing species of plants and animals in a given area (a forest stand, a lake, a region) often reveals the presence of units that have come there from many diverse areas. Thus, some very old geological events have left closely related species very far apart: northeastern Asia and eastern N America have very similar pairs of deciduous trees (eg, birches, maples, beeches, walnuts, tulip trees); the plains and deserts of N and S America harbour similar species long isolated from one another; Argentina and New Zealand have forests and grasslands dominated by closely related units (eg, *Nothofagus*, *Podocarpus*); the mammals and fishes of northern Europe and Canada show many affinities (eg, moose, pike).

Undoubtedly, the geological episode that has cast its stamp most visibly on Canada's landscape is the Pleistocene ICE AGE, the last million years or so (*see* GLACIATION). Several successive vegetation sequences followed the retreat of the ice sheet (from 18 000 years ago to the present). For example, the following table describes the vegetation sequences of the Mt Shefford area of southern Québec. It is especially interesting to note the temporary prevalence of vegetation types (eg, aspen parkland) that no longer exist in contemporary eastern N America.

The living flora of southern Québec contain many species that originated in the great Tertiary (from 65 million to 2.5 million years ago) eastern deciduous forest (sugar maple, beech, white trillium, bloodroot, woodland frog, ovenbird, white-tailed deer, etc); other species are closely linked to the boreal transcontinental spruce-fir (or Canadian) forest (white spruce, bunchberry, twinflower, feather mosses; brook trout, moose, purple finches, etc). Some have midwestern affinities (creeping ferns, cork elms, mud pickerel, evening grosbeaks, etc). Atlantic coastal-plain elements are rarer (grey birch, candleberry, broom crowberry, etc). Truly arctic-

Vegetation Sequences of Mt Shefford Area, Qué
(Source: Unpublished data from Pierre Richard)

Years Ago	*Vegetation Sequence*	*Description*
11 500	quasi DESERT	minimal life, intense cold, frost action on rock, PERMAFROST, no soil
11 400	herbaceous TUNDRA	arctic herbs, lichens, heaths, lakes in low areas
11 400-11 200	shrub tundra	dwarf birch, alder
11 200	forestation	trembling aspen plus birch, alder, conifers
11 200-10 500	subarctic parkland or taiga	dominated by black spruce
10 500-8 000	mixed forest	fir and white birch
8 000-4 350	deciduous forest	mixed maple, yellow birch, pine
4 350	temperate forest	maple dominant, peat formation in low areas
1 980	agricultural development	cultivation, roads, established forest on peatland

alpine species (eg, purple saxifrage, mountain avens) are generally restricted to higher altitudes. There are, of course, many widespread organisms (aspens, raspberries, crows), and some that have a nearly worldwide range (bracken ferns, reeds, cattails, etc). None of the above include the introduced WEEDS (eg, dandelion, crabgrass, galinsoga) or pests (eg, starlings, rats) that are completely naturalized (capable of fulfilling their life cycle unaided).

Similar regional units in Canada or elsewhere, if analysed floristically, would also reveal a composite picture reflecting the history of past fluctuations. Plants of the southern PRAIRIES belong to several units that witness more or less unresolved conflicts. The tall-grass prairie (big bluestem), mixed-grass prairie (blue grama, wheatgrass) and short-grass prairie (fescue) have repeatedly moved N and S and left traces. The spotty occurrence of N American halophytes (plants that grow in salty soil, eg, samphire, atriplex, greasewood) and of Great Basin desert plants (umbrella plant) also points to fluctuation of drought and high temperatures. Western boreal-forest elements (Murray pine, Alberta spruce, western prince's pine, devil's paintbrush) and eastern ones (twinflower, bunchberry, bearberry) come together in the cooler highlands. Some eastern deciduous forest species (American elm, false Solomon's seal, sweet cicely) migrate far W along the bluffs and floodplains.

The patterns of geographic distribution of plants and animals are, therefore, very revealing of past fluctuations in the displacement of the communities that harboured them, and indeed of whole bioclimatic areas that have shifted across continents. The biogeography of Canada must be seen as a whole, not solely as patterns of key species of plants and animals. This perspective requires the broader framework of world units. Worldwide, 20 bioclimatic formation classes have been identified, based on the 2 more or less independent variables, heat and moisture: tropical rain forest, temperate rain forest, tropical deciduous forest, summer-green deciduous forest, needle-leaved evergreen forest, evergreen hardwood forest, tropical woodland, temperate woodland, tropical savannah, temperate and cold savannah, thornbush, tropical scrub, temperate and cold scrub, tundra, prairie, steppe, meadow, warm desert, cold desert and crust vegetation. These classes are very unevenly distributed on the planet.

An extreme combination of heat and moisture favours the development of tropical rain forest; an extreme combination of heat and drought, warm desert. Extreme cold (almost always very dry as well) allows only snow or bare rock, or at best crust or tundra. The order in which one formation class will replace another is predictable and depends on warming or cooling trends, changes in moisture, or both (*see* CLIMATE). During the last million years, the unglaciated parts of Canada have undergone periodic shifts from summer-green deciduous forest through needle-leaf evergreen forest, temperate woodland, temperate savannah and meadow to tundra and back again, depending on warmth; from needle-leaf evergreen forest through temperate savannah, temperate woodland and prairie to steppe and back again, depending on moisture; and from steppe through temperate scrub to warm desert and back, depending on both factors. The extreme north has experienced relatively stable conditions of cold desert and crust during the entire period. Hence, when the temperate rain forests of BC are included, modern Canada contains 12 of the 20 possible bioclimatic formations.

Biogeography operates with broadly based working hypotheses that have been variously tested. It provides an essential background to cultural geography and to human ecology. In earlier stages of its development, it was more concerned with the impact of landscape on man. Fortunately, in recent years the ever-swinging oscillation of physical/cultural ANTHROPOLOGY and the emergence of human ecology as an increasingly autonomous discipline have rendered the notions briefly outlined above more relevant to human studies, ENVIRONMENTAL PLANNING and landscape management. Human activity is proving to be a very significant factor in the distribution of plant and animal species. In Canada the historical regression of many important animal species is well documented, eg, wapiti and mountain lion that were once present in the East, salmon that used to reach Lk Ontario. On the other hand, the white-tailed deer has extended its range greatly; the beaver has made several comebacks. But extinction of the great auk is forever, and there are many endangered species. PIERRE DANSEREAU

Maple grove. Each kind of plant and animal has an individual ecological strategy that makes it more or less fit to survive in its environment. The sugar maple requires a cold, moist climate, summer shade and well-aerated soil; it has a high tolerance for very cold winters and early and late frosts and seeds more regularly and abundantly than competing species (*artwork by Claire Tremblay*).

Reading: Pierre Dansereau, *Biogeography: An Ecological Perspective* (1957) and "Vegetation Zones, World" in *McGraw-Hill Encyclopedia of Science and Technology*, Vol 14 (1971); I.G. Simmons, *Biogeography, Natural and Cultural* (1979).

Biography, the written record of a person's life. Canada's search for an identity has been long, continuous, sometimes so fervent that it becomes notorious, at its best positive as an effort of understanding. Part of knowing what we are is knowing who we are, and biographical writing in Canada, in its several forms, has taken up this question. Biography has shown itself to be an approach which appeals to readers of differing tastes and experience, partly perhaps because they can satisfy curiosity about the past, even secure light upon the present, through the lives of people who actually existed in a real and pressing world. Answers about who Canadians are are still far from plentiful, but many have been attempted over the last century or so.

Obituaries, eulogies and biographical accounts of essay length and style are forms of biography in brief that began to appear in the 19th century. Obituaries of some fullness, in which appear the leading facts and some effort at interpretation that goes beyond the litany of funeral rhetoric, have remained important sources. The most valuable often appear in publications of societies or year books, such as the *Proceedings* of the Royal Society of Canada. Memorials of book length, some of which provide useful documentary evidence along with the prevailing appreciation, appeared in the mid 19th century, eg, in John Carroll's celebration of Methodist preachers, *Case and His Cotemporaries* (5 vols, 1867-77), Henry Scadding's *The First Bishop of To-*

nto (1868) for John Strachan, and Fennings aylor's *Thos. D'Arcy McGee* (1868).

In the latter half of the 19th century, coinding with one of the periods when interest in e nature of the Canadian identity was strong, ere were a number of efforts to compile colections of short accounts. Henry James Morgan the revered early name with *Sketches of Celerated Canadians* in 1862, the year he also began e first continuing publication of biographical terest, the *Canadian Parliamentary Companion.* is works include *Types of Canadian Women* (1901) nd the important *Canadian Men and Women of the ime* (1898; rev ed 1912). This work, including nly persons alive at the time of publication, vas the ancestor of the Who's Whos that began ppearing at the turn of the century. Morgan's *len and Women* was, in fact, incorporated into *he Canadian Who's Who,* first published in 1910. nother pioneer of the short biographical ketch was Fennings Taylor, who collaborated vith William Notman to produce *Portraits of ritish Americans* (3 vols, 1865-68). To the 1880s elong the works of J.C. DENT, with *The Canadian ortrait Gallery* (4 vols, 1880-81), and G.M. Rose, d, *A Cyclopaedia of Canadian Biography* (2 vols, 886, 1888). Hundreds of other compilations ave appeared, sometimes as part of larger vorks, and presenting national, regional, local r topical coverage. An example is *A Standard ictionary of Canadian Biography* by Sir Charles .D. Roberts and A.L. Tunnell (1934-38). These fforts to bring together brief accounts of men nd women continue to be made. They are genrally useful, but are not usually literary works.

Since its first appearance in 1926, W. Stewart VALLACE's *Dictionary of Canadian Biography,* beause of its comprehensiveness, has taken pride f place among the collections and has retained through several revisions. It assumed the title *Macmillan Dictionary of Canadian Biography* when he DICTIONARY OF CANADIAN BIOGRAPHY/DICTIONAIRE BIOGRAPHIQUE DU CANADA published its first volume, in English and French editions, in 966. This large project's scholarship and refernce strengths are complemented by readability, nd a special contribution of its "life and times" ccount of Canada is the large number of biographies of persons hitherto known only fleetngly and unlikely to command attention on heir own from biographers.

Biographical series were another early form f presenting the "doers" of Canada. From 1903 o 1908 appeared the "Makers of Canada" series 20 vols), edited by literary men Duncan Campell Scott and Pelham Edgar. The "Chronicles of Canada" (1914-16) allotted 13 of 32 volumes to ndividuals. Lorne PIERCE, pursuing his redoubtable efforts to encourage Canadian writing, set up the "Makers of Canadian Literature" series 11 vols, 1923-26). Activity of this type came again in the 1970s, when a number of series were launched. These include "Canadian Biographical Studies" (UTP), "Canadian Lives" (Oxford), and the National Gallery's "Canadian Artists," all of which make particular use of scholarly research; "The Canadians" (Fitzhenry and Whiteside), designed especially for students; and Lorimer's paperback reprint series "Goodread Biographies." In 1971 the province of Ontario started a major historical studies series including biographies of premiers, two of which have appeared to date.

Significant individual volumes of biography began to appear sporadically around the turn of the century: G.E. Fenety's *Life and Times of the Hon. Joseph Howe* (1896), J.S. Willison's *Sir Wilfrid Laurier* (2 vols, 1903; rev 1926), C.R.W. Biggar's *Sir Oliver Mowat* (2 vols, 1905), James Cappon's *Roberts and the Influences of His Time* (1905), and W.D. LeSueur's *Count Frontenac* (1906) — all by established writers and dealing with major figures. In the 1920s attention to the genre quickened, with O.D. Skelton's *The Life and Times of Sir Alexander Tilloch Galt* (1920), V.L.O. Chittick's *Thomas Chandler Haliburton* (1924); William Kennedy's *Lord Elgin* (1926); Chester New's *Lord Durham* (1927); G.P. deT. Glazebrook's *Sir Charles Bagot,* Lorne Pierce's *William Kirby,* Carl Y. Connor's *Archibald Lampman* (1929) and James Cappon's *Bliss Carman* (1930).

From the 1950s to the 1970s, biographies appeared in numbers that escape easy enumeration. Figures associated with the governance of Canada received major attention from a growing company of Canadian historians using documentary holdings to give reinterpretations and fullscale accounts that went beyond the "life and letters" approach favoured by earlier writers. The magisterial title is Donald CREIGHTON's *John A. Macdonald* (2 vols, 1952, 1955), which became, and has remained, a landmark. Many important political figures have still not found book-length biographers, but the field has had significant entries that continue to be viewed as "classics" for Canada: C.B. Sissons, *Egerton Ryerson* (2 vols, 1937, 1947); William Kilbourn, *The Firebrand: William Lyon Mackenzie* (1956); Kenneth McNaught, *A Prophet in Politics: J.S. Woodsworth* (1959); W.J. Eccles, *Frontenac* (1959); Roger Graham, *Arthur Meighen* (3 vols, 1960-65); J.M.S. Careless, *Brown of "The Globe"* (2 vols, 1959, 1963); Dale Thomson, *Alexander Mackenzie* (1960); George F.G. Stanley, *Louis Riel* (1963); John Morgan Gray, *Lord Selkirk of Red River* (1963); Margaret Prang, *N.W. Rowell* (1975); Robert Craig Brown, *Robert Laird Borden* (2 vols, 1975, 1980); and J. Murray Beck, *Joseph Howe* (2 vols, 1982, 1983). The extensive source material for William Lyon Mackenzie KING and the enigmas of his long career have attracted an unusual number of biographical approaches, from Bruce Hutchison's *The Incredible Canadian* (1952) through the 3 "official" volumes of MacGregor Dawson and H. Blair Neatby (1958-76) to a psycho-biographical study by Joy Esberey in 1980.

Entries into biography from academic historians are now rarer, except for the major cross-country efforts elicited by the DCB/DBC. Historical interests change over time, and the newer fields of business history, labour history, women's studies, native studies and ethnic studies have often led to group portraits rather than to those of individuals. Business history is one "new" area which has attracted the attention of a number of biographers. In the 1960s came Ross Harkness's *J.E. Atkinson of the Star* (1963) and Alan Wilson's *John Northway* (1965), early entries in a field that now includes major studies such as Michael Bliss's *A Canadian Millionaire: The Life and Business Times of Sir Joseph Flavelle* (1978). With his *Sir Frederick Banting* (1984), Bliss has moved on to science, another growing field of interest for biographers accompanying recent scholarly examinations of the history of science and technology in Canada. Norman BETHUNE's colourful medical career, for instance, has continued to provoke curiosity since Ted Allan and Sydney Gordon published a first study in *The Scalpel and the Sword* (1952); Roderick Stewart followed in 1973 with *Bethune.*

In recent years journalists have been prominent in the field of biography. In 1963 came Peter C. Newman's *Renegade in Power: The Diefenbaker Years,* inaugurating a series on recent leaders that includes Richard Gwyn's *Smallwood* (1968; rev 1972) and *The Northern Magus* (1980) and Geoffrey Stevens's *Stanfield* (1973). Joseph SCHULL has made valuable contributions to biography in his *Laurier* (1965) and *Edward Blake* (2 vols, 1975, 1976). Such accounts fall in with a long tradition of popular biography that has embraced writers of other backgrounds on subjects as various as James Fitzgibbon and Laura Secord, "Tiger" Dunlop and D'Arcy McGee, Josiah Henson, Pauline Johnson and L.M. Montgomery, Emily Murphy, Sara Jeannette Duncan, J.S. Woodsworth and C.D. Howe. The University of British Columbia established a medal for contributions to popular biography in 1951. The list of winners shows that any attempt to draw a line between popular and scholarly biography hardly holds, and the medal is now given simply for "biography."

The literary biography of Canadian writers has been slow to emerge, and the explanation undoubtedly lies in the delayed appearance of serious attention to Canadian literature in the universities. Collections began to appear in the 1960s and 1970s: Guy Sylvestre, Brandon Conron and Carl Klinck, *Canadian Writers/Écrivains canadiens* (1964, 1966), and Clara Thomas and Frank Davey, *Our Nature — Our Voices* (1973, 1974), are examples. Lengthier treatments have appeared in series already mentioned and in such undertakings as the Twayne World Authors series (from the 1960s onwards) or the ECW series of "Candian Writers and Their Works," which provide biographical accounts in support of literary analysis and criticism. Literary biographies, as such, are still few. Contemporary examples are Norman Shrive's *Charles Mair* (1965), Clara Thomas's study of Anna Jameson, *Love and Work Enough* (1967), and Lovat Dickson's several accounts of Grey Owl. A quickening pace is discernible with Douglas Spettigue's *FPG: The European Years* (1973), Elspeth Cameron's *Hugh MacLennan* (1981), Usher Caplan's portrait of A.M. Klein, *Like One that Dreamed* (1982), *William Arthur Deacon: A Canadian Literary Life* by Clara Thomas and John Lennox (1982), and David G. Pitt's first volume of *E.J. Pratt* (1984). Canadians have also made significant contributions to the biography of writers elsewhere, eg, Lovat Dickson, *H.G. Wells* (1969) and *Radclyffe Hall* (1975); George Woodcock, *The Crystal Spirit* (1966), on George Orwell; Phyllis Grosskurth, *John Addington Symonds* (1964) and *Havelock Ellis* (1980); and Michael Millgate, *Thomas Hardy* (1982).

The same delayed response, and the same reliance on biographical material as part of something else, has characterized the attention given to artists. Single volumes have, however, appeared, eg, Moncrieff Williamson's *Robert Harris* (1971), Maria Tippett's *Emily Carr* (1979) and J. Russell Harper's *Krieghoff* (1979).

Since the 1960s libraries and archives have rapidly acquired documents and papers relating to Canadian writers and other cultural figures, the majority of whom are still living and working. Indeed, no account of biography, in any field, can ignore the major contribution made to it by the development, particularly since WWII, of library and archival collections in all parts of Canada and the sharing of them made possible by interlibrary loan, microfilm and microfiche. Because of these resources, biography can be sounder and surer in its documentation of the events of a life.

It still remains, however, that biography is a literary art. Any author attempting it is challenged to call upon gifts of understanding and interpretation, of choosing and shaping, of style and colour to give life and truth to the subject. For this reason, the work of biography is never done, and new readings of individuals are inevitable over the years. Biography, one of the "great observed adventures of mankind," as Henry James put it, is not likely to lose its power to attract the talents of writers and the curiosity of readers.

FRANCESS G. HALPENNY

Biological Oceanography, branch of OCEANOGRAPHY that studies living organisms (ie, the biota) in the sea in relation to their environments. The subject is interdisciplinary, requiring an understanding of the interactions among different marine organisms and of how the physical and chemical processes of the sea affect its living communities. The biota is generally taken to include 3 major groups of organisms, ie, the PLANKTON (pelagic plants or animals that float or drift almost passively in the water), the nekton (swimming pelagic animals) and the benthos (seafloor organisms). Biological oceanography is often viewed as a series of food chains in the sea. Phytoplankton (planktonic plants), the primary producers, are consumed by the ZOOPLANKTON (planktonic animals) or secondary producers. Plankton-eating fish (planktivores) form the third level of production and above these are the fish-eating fish which consume the planktivores. A typical example of such a food chain would consist of diatoms (phytoplankton) eaten by copepods (zooplankton) which are consumed by herring (planktivorous nekton) which in turn are eaten by dogfish (piscivorous nekton). Such a representation is convenient but it oversimplifies actual relationships, since there are many more interconnections than are implied. Furthermore, physical and chemical characteristics of the water govern the amount of food transferred up the food chain. For example, the amount of nutrients available to primary producers is a property of the nutrient content and movement of any particular water mass over time.

The biological oceanography of the Pacific and Atlantic regions of Canada is governed by the subarctic water lying off both coasts. The subarctic communities of these water masses are characterized by a strong seasonal progression of plankton blooms, starting in spring and ending in fall. Production of larval and juvenile fishes is generally associated with the spring bloom; MIGRATION of adult fishes takes place in spring and fall. The release of benthic larvae is also generally associated with the spring phytoplankton bloom. The eventual settlement of some benthic organisms in relatively shallow areas is an important connection in the food chain for the commercially important FISHERIES found on the GRAND BANKS and other continental shelf areas. In the Arctic Ocean a single summer pulse of plankton occurs after the break up of fast ICE. This bloom, which may last for several months, supports an extensive food chain including zooplankton, fish, seals, polar bears and humans. However, the quantity of commercially available fish in the Arctic Ocean is very small compared to Canada's subarctic waters where plankton production is greater for a longer period of the year.

Recent developments in biological oceanography have included the REMOTE SENSING of biological events from space, also the remote sensing of deepwater communities from SUBMERSIBLES capable of descending to the greatest ocean depths (below 10 000 m). Satellite studies have been used to show the amount of plankton in different water masses, as determined by the chlorophyll concentration which influences the colour of the water. Deep submersible studies have recently shown the existence of biological communities which feed off energy-rich compounds that are given off at thermal vents in the seafloor (ie, deep-sea INVERTEBRATES). Other new techniques include the outfitting of commercial vessels for biological monitoring; the use of large plastic bag enclosures (over 1000 t) to study the ecology of the sea; and scuba-diving techniques allowing direct observation of delicate forms of plankton and direct experimentation with benthic communities.

In Canada, biological oceanographic studies are performed in the Atlantic, Pacific and Arctic oceans by university departments of oceanography and government oceanographic institutes, and at a large number of federal fisheries stations. Recently, consulting companies have taken part in biological oceanographic studies in connection with environmental planning. This last area is of growing importance since the possible dire effects of man-made POLLUTION on the oceans have become recognized in certain limited environments, eg, when oil spills occur in coastal water or urban or industrial sewage systems discharge into the sea (*see* WATER TREATMENT). The biological oceanography of these altered environments differs with each location. *See* ARCTIC OCEANOGRAPHY.

T.R. PARSONS

Biological Product, substance derived from a living organism and is used for prevention or treatment of disease. Biologicals are too complex for chemical synthesis. These products include antitoxins, bacterial and viral vaccines, blood fractions and hormone extracts. Organizations active in the production of biologicals in Canada include CONNAUGHT LABORATORIES LTD of Toronto, INSTITUT ARMAND-FRAPPIER of Montréal and the Winnipeg Rh Institute.

Vaccines

Viral Vaccines The original vaccination procedure employed by Edward Jenner made use of a VIRUS that caused a mild form of cowpox. Acquired immunity to this disease also gave protection against smallpox, a far more virulent virus. Such vaccines provided good protection because the body was responding to a replicating virus. During this early period, knowledge of virus structure and mechanism of action was gradually acquired; however, until the development of tissue culture, there was no way of growing viruses in the laboratory. Some cells had been grown in culture before 1945, but the principal breakthrough occurred when Dr Raymond Parker at the then Connaught Medical Research Laboratories discovered a defined chemical-nutrient medium in which cells would grow and replicate. Parker's discovery permitted Jonas Salk to develop his polio vaccine. Salk vaccine was produced largely in Toronto for field trial in Canada and the US: virus was grown in monkey kidney cells, then separated from the cells, concentrated and killed with formalin. The success of the new killed-virus vaccine was soon apparent and the annual polio epidemics disappeared. The Sabin polio vaccine, an attenuated vaccine also grown in monkey kidney cells and given orally, was developed a few years later.

In recent years human diploid fibroblast cells (which, in the body, develop into connective tissue) have been grown in culture. The cells have been more rigorously defined than monkey kidney cells and have permitted the preparation of more highly purified viral vaccines (eg, Salk and Sabin polio, rabies, measles, mumps, rubella). The first killed rabies vaccines were prepared in neural tissues (eg, mouse brain) and later in duck embryo. The vaccine is given both prophylactically and after exposure. The injections are painful and multiple doses are required. With the diploid-cell-grown vaccine, fewer doses are required and adverse reactions are decreased.

Other attenuated viral vaccines in use include ERA rabies veterinary strain, developed at Connaught, and the measles and rubella strains currently in favour. Future viral vaccines will be of 2 types: traditional whole virus vaccines, which are highly purified from defined cell substrates; and split or single-antigen vaccines, prepared by GENETIC ENGINEERING (eg, foot and mouth disease vaccine), extraction or chemical synthesis.

Bacterial Vaccines are of 3 basic types: whole organisms or bacterins, including pertussis (whooping cough) and vaccines for veterinary or fish use; single-antigen vaccines prepared by extraction or genetic engineering, eg, a new vaccine for calf scours; and toxoids. Many bacteria, such as those that cause tetanus or diphtheria, release toxins that cause cellular damag These toxins have been purified and treated t make them inactive, ie, toxoids. When injecte toxoids cause the formation of antibodies to th original toxin. Other bacterial vaccines pr duced include typhus, typhoid, cholera, pneu mococcal, meningococcal and bacille Calmett Guérin (BCG, used for the prevention an testing of tuberculosis). Veterinary vaccines in clude those for household pets, farm animal and other cultivated species, such as mink o fish. The vaccination of fish is a new approac necessitated by the crowding of fingerlings i AQUACULTURE operations. Administered by injec tion, immersion or spray, such vaccines are re markably effective.

Blood Fractions and Serums

Beginning in the 1930s and stimulated b WWII, blood serum was collected and freeze dried. When reconstituted, this product was o some use in the treatment of blood loss an shock following trauma. A method of fraction ating blood plasma (noncellular fluid) was de veloped in the US and, subsequently, introduce to Canada, allowing the Canadian Red Cros Transfusion Service to use blood for many pur poses. Products prepared from donated bloo include red cells, white cells, platelets, albumin immune serum globulins (including specialis products such as tetanus, Rh and rabies immu noglobulins), and coagulation factor concen trates for the treatment of hemophilias A and B

Hormones

The principal peptide hormone products pre pared in Canada are INSULIN and human growth hormone. The latter, extracted in Winnipe from donated human pituitary glands, is use to prevent dwarfism. The product is in ex tremely short supply. Recently, success has been reported in attempts to prepare human growth hormone by genetic engineering. Insulin was first isolated in Toronto by Frederick G. BANTING and Charles H. BEST in 1921-22 and has been prepared there ever since. It is currently made by extraction of bovine or porcine pancreas Seven insulin formulations of each type are available to Canadian diabetics. Recently, genetically engineered human insulin has been tested clinically. *See* ESTROGEN.

A.A. MAGNIN

Biology [Gk *bios* "life," *logos* "discourse" or "reasoning"] is the science of life, embracing all studies of living organisms and, as such, is inherently interdisciplinary. Attempts by some specialists to use the term in a narrow sense are shortsighted and damaging.

Theory and History

Biological studies of individuals and groups of organisms can occur at various levels (eg, molecular, cellular, anatomical, functional, behavioural, ecological and evolutionary). Great strides, notably in BIOCHEMISTRY and electron microscopy, have strongly influenced classification at all taxonomic levels in the last 40 years. Many organisms placed together on the basis of form and structure (gross morphology) are now seen to be unrelated, and it is clear that living beings are better classified as monera, protista, FUNGI, PLANTS or ANIMALS, rather than simply as plants or animals, the classical division. The 5 kingdoms are placed in 2 "super kingdoms": Prokaryota (cells having no membrane-bound nuclei); and Eukaryota (cells having true membrane-bound nuclei). Other distinctions correlate with nuclear structure to make the separation conspicuous and absolute.

Prokaryota include only the kingdom Monera, made up of groups of bacteria (including the so-called BLUE-GREEN ALGAE, better termed cyanobacteria). The lower boundary of Monera is ill-defined because the viruses, which are not cellular in structure, may or may not be inluded. Some viruses are so simple that they are little more than self-replicating molecules, and cannot yet convincingly be defined as "living." The simplest eukaryotic kingdom is Protista, primarily one-celled organisms with organized nuclei and other organelles which function in photosynthesis, cellular respiration, metabolism, etc. The kingdom is somewhat miscellaneous; however, protists nearly always reproduce by some form of mitotic nuclear division (ie, the nucleus divides to form 2 new nuclei, each having the same number of chromosomes as the parent nucleus). The cells are usually considerably larger than those of prokaryotes.

Protista evolved from Monera by processes not wholly understood. Current theory states that the specialized cell parts (organelles) evolved from separate entities which lived inside the one-celled body of the moneran, in symbiosis with it. This theory of "symbiotic origins" is convincing for chloroplasts (photosynthetic organelles): those of red algae deriving from cyanobacteria; those of green algae from a green prokaryote like the recently discovered *Prochloron;* and those of other algal groups from extinct or undiscovered photosynthetic prokaryotes. Although less convincing for other organelles, the theory is more plausible than some proposed alternatives. The protistan level may have been reached more than once from different Monera. Protista is not a convincingly "natural" kingdom but, rather, a convenient repository for organisms at similar evolutionary levels.

The 3 "higher" kingdoms (Animals, Plants, Fungi) arose from different groups of protistans. Defining the boundaries between Protista and the "higher" kingdoms is a major problem. For example, although slime molds (Myxomycetes) seem closer to protozoa than to true fungi, they shed dry spores, form fruiting bodies and have been studied mainly by fungal specialists (mycologists), so that most collections are in mycological HERBARIA. A more contentious case involves the Chytridiomycota (microscopic, aquatic organisms), included in Protista by some theorists, but grading imperceptibly into typical fungi and studied exclusively by mycologists. Such problems demonstrate that classifications are man-made rather than completely natural. Except at their lower limits the 3 higher kingdoms are clearly distinct.

The terms taxonomy and systematics have become nearly synonymous through careless use. "Taxonomy," coined in 1813, covers the bases, principles and rules of classification and nomenclature (naming), including the hierarchic framework, and refers not to a research discipline but to a supporting methodology. Modern "systematics" (the actual arranging, grouping and naming of organisms) began with the work of 18th-century Swedish botanist Carl von Linné (Linnaeus), who developed "binomial" nomenclature (with separate names for genus and species), which both assigns to each organism a unique scientific name (in Latin form) and indicates relationships among organisms. Advances in systematization were slow until the re-emergence of GENETICS and the growth of cytology (study of cell contents). Botanists especially made increasing use of cytogenetic data in their groupings. Through Julian Huxley and others, the "new systematics" sprang into prominence about 1940, and was soon rechristened "biosystematics," defined as the scientific study of kinds and diversity of organisms and of any and all relationships between them. The general approach to systematics for most kinds of organisms uses all appropriate disciplines, although choice varies with organisms involved, eg, cytogenetics, which studies chromosome sets within cells, clearly cannot be used routinely with many fungi whose chromosomes are scarcely detectable.

Although attempts have been made to restrict it, biosystematics is well established as using any discipline that may complement morphology and anatomy, eg, cytology, genetics, biochemistry, ecology, BIOGEOGRAPHY, reproductive biology, host-parasite relationships, ethology (animal behavior) and, with the advent of computers, mathematical analysis of data. A student taking a higher degree in plant systematics must now complement morphology with one or more subsidiary approaches and advanced students must usually be familiar with methods of statistical analysis and computer programming. Biosystematics is thus the focal point of all biology, linking all disciplines and demonstrating EVOLUTION in action, although the complexity of biology makes its complete unification difficult, if not impossible.

Biological exploration began early in Canada, but collectors returned their specimens to Europe for study. Inevitably, systematics had a late start in Canada, but early in this century the pace increased. The rise of biosystematics found systematists in Canadian universities and research institutions ready to embrace the broadened discipline. Canadian contributions have been perhaps most conspicuous in studies of some groups of flowering plants, insects and fungi.

Disciplines

The terms for the study of each of the 5 kingdoms (bacteriology, protistology, mycology, BOTANY and ZOOLOGY) are too sweeping to be considered individual disciplines, except at the introductory level. The following is a reasonably comprehensive list of biological academic disciplines (omitting specifically medical disciplines): anatomy (internal structure of organisms), biochemistry, biogeography, biometry and biostatistics, cytology, cytogenetics, ecology, embryology, ENTOMOLOGY, ethology, evolution, fisheries biology, genetics, GENETIC ENGINEERING, histology (study of cellular tissues), limnology (aquatic biology, especially freshwater), marine biology, microbiology, MOLECULAR BIOLOGY, morphology (forms of whole organisms), PALEONTOLOGY (including micropaleontology and PALYNOLOGY), PARASITOLOGY, pathology (diseases of man, other animals or plants), physiology, taxonomy and systematics, toxicology and pharmacology, and ultrastructure (detailed structure of cell organelles). Some disciplines (eg, ecology, genetics and microbiology) may be variously divided, and others tend to overlap (eg, biogeography with ecology). Many disciplines are applicable to organisms in more than one kingdom. The number of potential fields of study is thus enormous. Evolution, included in the above list because courses are taught under this title, is not a discipline but, rather, a theory which informs all biological disciplines.

Multidisciplinary Successes

Almost all organisms are influenced by several fluctuating physical factors, notably light, temperature, humidity, precipitation, wind, soil texture and nutrients, erosion and fire. The total ecology of an organism potentially involves all these factors as well as interplay with all other organisms in the community. As a result, most biological problems involve far more variables than are usually dealt with in a problem in the physical sciences. All atoms of a chemical element are identical, but all individuals of sexually reproducing organisms are different. Very often only a partial solution of a biological problem is possible; but a biologist alert to the factors involved can usually interpret the phenomena under study.

The rapid growth and increasing complexity of biology favour narrow specialization even among beginning students; but, since many problems require contributions from several biological disciplines and from the physical sciences, some compromise must be made. In advanced studies, the team approach is popular. Several examples of Canadian contributions to multidisciplinary successes are described below.

With the help of a mathematician, a botanist-mycologist having some knowledge of aerodynamics and meteorology, gained an understanding of the "splash cup" mechanism, found in various plants, which uses falling water to disperse seeds or spores. They found, surprisingly, that a 4-4.5 mm drop, such as falls from foliage, has greater momentum after less than 1 m of fall than a typical 2 mm raindrop at terminal velocity. It was then clear why golden saxifrage (*Chrysosplenium*) flourishes in arctic marshes where fog and drizzle cause drops to fall scarcely 0.5 m from nodding grasses and sedges, and why bird's nest fungi grow beneath dwarf shrubs in the Peruvian desert where fog is the only precipitation.

Elementary aerodynamics enabled an amateur ornithologist to show that the extinct Jurassic bird, *Archaeopteryx*, was not a powered flier, but surely a good glider. Its wing form and function were shown to be similar to those of most modern passerines. Paleontologists had tried to explain the wings, which had no anchorage for powerful pectoral muscles, as paddles to beat down insects, and the feathers as a shawl to keep the bird warm.

Study of various parasites throws light on plant relationships, and requires combining studies in plant systematics with mycology, entomology or nematology. Rust fungi and their host plants reflect one another's ages of origin because compatible gene complements are most likely to occur in hosts and parasites in the evolutionary youth of each group. This explanation developed through years of combined studies on the ecology and biogeography of hosts and parasites and finally yielded increased understanding of the relationships and relative ages of many plant groups.

The collared LEMMING usually has a fairly regular 4-year population cycle but, in parts of the high arctic, the population fluctuates irregularly. Wildlife zoologists, combining microclimatological and ecological studies, found that scanty and irregular snow cover in these regions may keep burrow temperatures so low that the lemmings do not achieve breeding condition.

Arctic botanical studies, which started in early spring when SEA ICE was still intact and wind-packed snow was smooth and very hard and which applied elementary aerodynamic principles, showed that seeds of most arctic plants are easily blown long distances during most of the year even if they lack wings or plumes, and that they tend to accumulate on desirable sites at the foot of banks. Elucidation of this means of dispersal allowed an explanation of the high uniformity of the relatively young arctic flora.

Applied Biology

Biology can be classified as basic research, applied research and the applications of research, but the 3 intergrade completely. A good example of the process occurs in WHEAT production. Cultivated wheat has been hybridized from wild species. Further improvements depend on accurate information on wild species that may possess useful characteristics. Such information must be supplied by the systematic botanist. The cereal geneticist must develop techniques to transfer the appropriate genes into a wheat plant. The breeder must secure a balance of desirable characteristics to produce a new variety. Finally, propagators must increase stocks of the new variety for release to farmers. Although much agricultural research is "applied," it may be necessary to revert to basic studies to solve problems, eg, in crop protection, food storage, plant pathology or veterinary medicine. The failure of early attempts to control wheat stem rust (*Puccinia graminis*) led to establishment of the Rust Research Laboratory in Winnipeg, where basic studies led to new understanding of wheat genetics, and the genetics and life history of the pathogen (agent of disease). Further information on the biology of rusts resulted from systematic studies of rusts of native plants. For agricultural crops in general, a botanist, chemist or mycologist may supply data to the geneticist and breeder; after full testing, the improved variety is propagated commercially.

Among other examples of successful interaction are the propagation of leaf-cutter bees to induce seed set in alfalfa, a practice which developed from pollination biology; the growth of the antibiotics industry from many years of laboratory testing and experiment; the field of genetic engineering, which developed from basic studies in microbial genetics and molecular biology — the new techniques developed help both industry and medical research, as in the identification and manipulation of potentially cancer-inducing genes. Fields that involve mainly applied research include ANIMAL BREEDING, animal diseases, WILDLIFE CONSERVATION AND MANAGEMENT, economic entomology, forest research, plant breeding, the study of PLANT DISEASES, soil survey and testing. Several fields are almost wholly commercial, calling on research only when trouble arises, eg, BEEKEEPING, brewing and winemaking, cheesemaking, farming, fish-hatchery operation, horticulture, industrial fermentation and MUSHROOM CULTIVATION. Other applied fields mainly serve education or research: biological illustration and modelling, specimen cataloguing, commercial specimen preparation, laboratory technical work, maintenance and operation of parks or botanical and zoological gardens, taxidermy.

Research Organizations Most biological investigation in Canada is centered in university biology departments, national and provincial museums, or institutes and laboratories of Agriculture Canada, Fisheries Research Board, Forestry Service, NATIONAL RESEARCH COUNCIL and Wildlife Service. Research may be published in bulletins, eg, of the National Museum of Natural Sciences or the Wildlife Service, monographs of Agriculture Canada, or a wide range of journals. Some papers are published in foreign or interdisciplinary journals, but the main Canadian journals (not including medical publications) are *Canadian Entomologist, Canadian Field-Naturalist, Canadian Jnl of Animal Science, Canadian Jnl of Botany, Canadian Jnl of Forest Research, Canadian Jnl of Genetics and Cytology, Canadian Jnl of Microbiology, Canadian Jnl of Plant Pathology, Canadian Jnl of Plant Science, Canadian Jnl of Zoology*, and *Le Naturaliste canadien*.

D.B.O. SAVILE

Reading: L. Margulis, *Symbiosis in Cell Evolution* (1981); E. Mayr, *The Growth of Biological Thought* (1982).

Biomass Energy, or bioenergy, is the ENERGY stored in nonfossil organic materials such as wood, straw, vegetable oils, animal tissues, human and animal excrement, and municipal and mill wastes. Like the energy in fossil fuels, bioenergy is derived from SOLAR ENERGY that has been stored in PLANTS through the process of photosynthesis; the principal difference is that fossil fuels require thousands of years to be converted into usable forms, while properly managed biomass energy can be used in an ongoing, renewable fashion. PEAT is also a form of biomass and continues to have considerable potential as an energy source. After direct solar energy and HYDROELECTRICITY, biomass is one of the most important renewable energy forms (wood and dung burning account for about 14% of the world's energy supply) and its use in Canada involves both the oldest and the newest of energy technologies.

Although biomass accounted for only 0.2 EJ (exajoules) of Canada's secondary energy use of 6.0 EJ in 1978, the potential use by the year 2000 has been estimated as high as 1.6 EJ, rising to as high as 2.8 EJ by the year 2025. Federal government policy has set a target of tripling the proportion of biomass energy in Canada's energy supply, from 3.5% of primary energy production in 1980 to 5% in the year 2000 and 10% in 2025. Biomass already provides more of Canada's energy supply than NUCLEAR POWER, accounting for 2% of secondary energy use by the residential sector and 8% of energy use in the industrial sector, mainly in the forest industries. Including lumber and pulp and paper, FORESTRY accounts for 7% of Canada's total energy consumption; forest industries meet more than one-quarter of this demand with biomass. The forest industries have been increasing their use of wood wastes that otherwise would be burned, buried or left on the forest floor. Principal uses include firing boilers in pulp and paper mills and providing heat for lumber-drying kilns. In some areas (eg, northern Ontario, PEI, NB) forest industries supply wood chips and pellets to nearby industrial, commercial and residential customers. In addition, wood is the principal heating fuel for more than 100 000 Canadian homes and a supplemental (though largely decorative) heating source in several million others. Most official estimates understate the residential consumption of wood fuel because a large proportion is harvested and used locally and does not appear in tax records or government statistics. The other major sources of biomass are AGRICULTURE, food-processing residues, industrial wastes, municipal sewage and household garbage. Energy-from-waste projects include steam production or electricity generation from garbage in Hamilton, Québec City, Montréal, and Charlottetown.

Biomass-energy products may be in solid, liquid or gaseous form, permitting a wide range of applications. At present, virtually all of Canada's biomass energy is supplied in solid form (eg, logs, chips, sawdust, pellets, charcoal, garbage), but there is also considerable potential for liquid and gaseous forms. The emphasis of much current research is in the conversion of biomass to alcohol for use as a transport fuel (to extend or replace gasoline and diesel oil). For example, at present the production of alcohol from cellulose is a 2-stage process: converting cellulose into sugars and then the sugars into alcohol through fermentation. A new symbiotic co-culture containing 2 kinds of bacteria performs both functions to make possible a one-step production of alcohol from cellulose. Another Canadian development is the discovery of a YEAST with the capacity to convert 5-carbon sugars (pentoses) to alcohol. These sugars cannot be converted to alcohol by ordinary brewer's yeast. The development of special membranes for concentrating dilute solutions by reverse osmosis is another breakthrough. Ethanol concentrations of up to 75% have been achieved and this process can displace conventional energy-intensive distillation processes.

Liquid forms of biomass energy include methanol (wood alcohol), ethanol (grain alcohol) and vegetable oils. When methanol or ethanol is mixed with gasoline, the product is sometimes called "gasohol." Methanol, produced by the distillation of wood and forest wastes, may provide an alternative fuel for transportation and industry at prices competitive with fuels from BITUMEN and COAL LIQUEFACTION. Ethanol, although it is also a viable fuel, is more expensive to produce and uses potential food supplies for raw materials. Vegetable oils might substitute for diesel fuel under certain circumstances, eg, if high-yielding, nonfood canola were grown on farmland that otherwise would lie fallow. The gaseous form of biomass energy is called biogas, a methane-based gas with a low heating value. It is typically derived from the anaerobic (ie, without the presence of oxygen) digestion of organic material, such as municipal sewage or animal manure.

Forest Biomass To meet the goal of 5% of Canada's primary energy requirements a 3-stage program of development of forest biomass has been proposed. The first stage would use all logging and mill wastes created by existing forest industries (ie, on-site residues that may even have a negative value at present because of disposal costs). This material is being increasingly used, generally with considerable savings, as a substitute for fossil fuels. Economics are usually favourable as the material is concentrated and costs of handling and transport are carried by the primary forest product of which this material is the residue. The second stage would be use of residues and residuals not currently used in conventional forest-harvesting operations. Residues are tree components left behind after merchantable material (eg, sawtimber, pulpwood) has been removed. Residuals are unmerchantable species of trees as well as defective, dying and dead trees currently unusable. The forest industry might use this material for producing steam or steam-generated electricity for on-site consumption; surplus electricity might be fed to the power grid. The third stage would be based upon extensive unused forest stands, along with serious consideration of establishment of energy plantations.

Although conventional forest industries have expressed the concern that increased use of forest biomass for energy might infringe on the production and cost of their raw material, the available supply of forest material for biomass energy has been estimated at 5 times the amount of wood now harvested by all the Canadian forest industries. Harvesting energy from forest biomass could be an economic boon for the forest industries: all cellulosic material now thrown away (ie, branches, bark, boles and stumps, and crooked, diseased, insect-infested, fire-damaged, dying and dead trees) could become valuable energy products. Use of forest biomass for energy also affords the opportunity to liquidate low-grade stands and replace them with productive stands of more valuable species. In some areas (eg, BC), it has been estimated that forest-industry wastes alone could provide enough solid and liquid fuels to replace much of the current oil consumption.

In other parts of Canada, eg, the Prairie provinces and eastern Canada, energy plantations would be needed to provide enough biomass for significant oil displacement. Marginal and submarginal agricultural land, as well as nonagricultural land (eg, wetlands), could be used for high-yield "forest farming" with rotations of less than 10 years between harvests (*see* SILVICULTURE). The tree species under trial in Canada are primarily POPLAR hybrids and include larch, green ash, willow, alder and soft maples. By selection of species, provenances and phenotypes and by cloning, it is possible to increase yield greatly and to develop disease resistance and frost hardiness. A concern of recent research is to reduce or eliminate the need for nitrogen fertilizers, a major cost in such plantations. The interplanting of nitrogen-fixing species in tree farms is one possibility under study; another is inoculating root systems of fast-growing species to make them nitrogen fixing. Plantations of poplar and willow, already under intensive culture, have produced yields 5 to 10 times the normal production of natural forests.

Agricultural Biomass Agricultural biomass includes animal manure, cellulosic crop residues, fruit and vegetable cells and food-processing effluents. Potential energy crops include high-yielding, high-carbohydrate crops such as sweet sorghum, Jerusalem artichoke and fod er beet, vegetable-oil crops such as canola and unflower, and hydrocarbon plants such as nilkweed and gumweed. Agricultural biomass as a much more limited potential than forestry iomass in Canada. Most agricultural residues ave alternative uses as animal fodder or soil onditioners and typically have a much lower nergy intensity than wood (ie, 1 m^3 of wood ontains as much energy as 5-10 m^3 of baled ield residues). Agricultural biomass is also usu- lly only available at one time of year, while orests can be harvested year round. The average nventory on forestland is about 20 times the nnual yield from cropland. However, agricul- ural biomass does have a place in farm-scale or ocalized operations. Biogas from animal ma- ures can be used to heat farm buildings or, if crubbed and compressed, to power farm vehi- les. The use of animal and food-processing vastes can abate pollution and reduce disposal roblems as well as produce energy. Straw can e burned in a specially designed furnace to dry rain and heat farm buildings. The use of canola il in farm diesel engines is undergoing con- inual development (*see* AGRICULTURAL IMPLE- IENTS INDUSTRY).

The Future Including the additional supplies otentially available from municipal wastes, iomass resources are well dispersed across the ountry. Their increased use for energy would essen the regional disparities that now cause o much friction between energy-producing nd energy-consuming regions of Canada and vould reduce the amount of money paid for oreign oil. The production of biomass-energy eedstocks provides employment; it requires in- estment in the purchase of capital equipment nd this in turn generates a multiplier effect in he economy.

The main problems facing expansion of bio- nass energy are the relatively high costs of new acilities and the need to make the industry ruly renewable. The cost barrier may be over- ome by government policy and rising prices f conventional energy sources; however, care- ul attention is also needed for problems of RE- ORESTATION, LAND USE, WATER USE, SOIL quality, ROSION and POLLUTION. Producing energy, in ddition to lumber and paper, could put new tress on the renewability of a forest-resource ase that is already endangered by past practices f the forest industries. Biomass energy must be armed, not mined; otherwise it will merely join oal, oil and natural gas as yet another non- enewable energy source.

Various federal government departments and ederal and provincial research organizations re involved in studying proposals to develop he potential of biomass energy. For example, NFOR, the federal Energy from the Forest Pro- ram, has received strong backing, and the Dept f Energy, Mines and Resources is in charge f the Biomass Conversion Program begun by he Canadian Forestry Service of Environment anada. In 1981 Mohawk Oil converted a dis- illery in Minnedosa, Man, to the production of thyl alcohol from grain. The plant, based on a easibility study done by Art Meyer of RDC Re- earch Development & Consulting Ltd, Edmon- on, serves Mohawk's Manitoba service stations vith gasohol (a mix of one part alcohol to 9 arts gasoline). A basic 3-cent-per-litre tax ex- mption from the Manitoba government allows Iohawk to sell the fuel at the same price as asoline. One bushel (25 kg) of grain yields 10.4 of ethanol and 9 kg of a high-protein by- roduct, marketable as cattle feed. Driver re- ponse to the fuel has been positive.

C.R. SILVERSIDES

BIONESS (*B*edford *I*nstitute of *O*ceanography *N*et and *E*nvironmental *S*ampling *S*ystem) is a multiple-net sampler for ZOOPLANKTON and mi- ronekton (pelagic animals 1-10 cm in length). It uses a new design concept, with nets arranged horizontally rather than vertically as in earlier multiple-net samplers. The 10 one metre square nets open sequentially and are towed from a ship at a speed of 3-6 knots on a conductor cable that transmits and receives information. The sampler supports sensors for temperature, conductivity, depth, illumination, pitch, roll, yaw and net closure, together with internal and external flowmeters and a 35 mm camera with a strobe light. This system can collect biological samples and environmental data simultaneously and can photograph animals in front of the sampler. The sampler can operate to depths of 2500 m. It weighs 782 kg and is best handled from an A-frame or large crane on a ship's stern. The towing wire and depressor attachments can be adjusted so that, at any towing speed up to 4 knots, the mouth is vertical. The sampler's weight, combined with the depressor, makes the depth variation during towing small, 0.2 m up or down in seas with waves of 1-2 m. The mouth area to surface area of the nets is 1:10; the mesh size, normally 243 ½μm. Nets are dark green and all surfaces are painted dark grey to make the sampler as inconspicuous as possible. Catches consist of animals ranging from 0.3 mm copepods to krill, squid and fish up to 20 cm long. Advantages of BIONESS include its ease of handling, its steep towing angle at high speeds and its reduced front profile. Data first collected by this sampler has made it possible to explain the ecological relationships between zooplankton, the micronekton that prey on them and the physical environment. For example, a dense layer of zooplankton at 500 m depth will not be preyed upon by a population of fish at 700 m depth because of the 200 m separation. Older methods of sampling did not reveal this fact. Such information is being used to explain the abundance and distribution of commercial species of fish.

D. SAMEOTO

Biotechnology was defined by the 1981 Federal Task Force on Biotechnology (Brossard Committee) as the "utilization of biological processes, be they microbial, plant, animal cells or their constituents, for the provision of goods and services." In some respects, biotechnological techniques represent elaborations of familiar industrial processes (eg, fermentation). While such processes were used initially to produce potable alcohol, organic acids, solvents and other products (eg, antibiotics, amino acids, vitamins, gums, steroids), recent spectacular advances in MOLECULAR BIOLOGY and GENETIC ENGINEERING have extended their range of application. Throughout the world, programs are being vigorously pursued to develop means of using biotechnology in fuel production; recovery of raw materials; crop fertilization and plant breeding; waste treatment and POLLUTION control; development of more effective health-care products, new feedstuffs and new sources of industrial chemicals; and pest control. Hence, a number of countries (eg, West Germany, France, UK, Japan) have mounted special long-term, government-financed programs in biotechnology, and the US has a commanding lead in the basic biomedical sciences. Although individual Canadian scientists have made major contributions, to date there has been little industrial participation in the commercial opportunities offered by these processes. Indeed, the task force stated that a biotechnology industry is practically nonexistent in Canada.

Techniques

Biotechnology is strongly interdisciplinary, its current strength based on key techniques spawned by interdisciplinary advances in BIOCHEMISTRY, CHEMISTRY, ENGINEERING, GENETICS, MATHEMATICS, MICROBIOLOGY and PHYSICS. These techniques include genetic engineering, industrial enzyme systems, cell fusion, plant cell culture, and biological process and systems engineering.

Genetic Engineering, based on recombinant DNA technology, provides the capability to select DNA fragments or genes (from selected organisms or plant and animal cells, or the products of chemical synthesis), join them to other pieces of DNA, and transfer them to an appropriate host production cell. The resultant MICROORGANISMS thereby acquire novel genetic properties that endow them with the ability to create new products or use and transform new substrates in fermentation-type processes. Present and future areas of application include production of human insulin, interferon and growth hormone, improved manufacture of alcohols, and utilization of cellulose. Fundamental studies in molecular biology and nucleic acids over the past 30 years have provided the biochemical explanation of the genetic process, which now provides the basis for genetic engineering. In Canada, research capabilities in this field presently reside almost exclusively in the universities and in federal government laboratories. Considerable expertise has been developed but the number of trained researchers remains seriously inadequate; furthermore, effective mechanisms for transferring technology from laboratories to industry have not yet been developed.

Industrial Enzyme Systems Enzyme use in industry and health care has increased in the past 2 decades. Traditionally, enzymes from various natural sources have been used in food production in Japan, the US and Europe; no comparable industry has developed in Canada. Now that enzymes are produced microbiologically and by genetic engineering, "tailor-made" products can be expected. Enzyme immobilization is a crucial part of this technology, and the use of immobilized bacteria, yeast, FUNGI, plant and animal cells will provide increasingly sophisticated multi-enzyme systems. New and existing products will increasingly be made with enzyme processes and Canada, as a major food producer, cannot afford to overlook the field.

Cell Fusion Development of cell fusion techniques has opened up new opportunities in agriculture, forestry and health-care products. In agriculture and forestry, cell fusion can produce hybrid plants exhibiting faster growth, atmospheric nitrogen-fixing capabilities, and greater resistance to disease and climatic factors (eg, cold, drought). Canada's major economic dependence on the agriculture and forest industries should make the application of these techniques a high priority. Other hybrid cell techniques result in the production of monoclonal (ie, derived from a single cell) antibodies, which are already being used to produce more specific diagnostic reagents, to treat patients with autoimmune reactions, in the immunotherapy of cancer and for more effective industrial purification of a variety of products.

Plant Cell Culture Plants have always been a rich source of medicinal agents and the development of techniques for culturing plant cells *in vitro* makes possible the production of a wide variety of PHARMACEUTICAL products. The Prairie Regional Laboratory of the NATIONAL RESEARCH COUNCIL OF CANADA possesses world-class expertise in plant cell culture, and this research is now being better exploited as the laboratory has been designated a national centre, and greater resources are being allocated to research.

Biological Process and Systems Engineering The very nature of biological or microbiological products and processes requires special handling techniques and procedures. These specialized biotechnology process and engineering systems are therefore central to eventual commercialization. The present paucity of large-scale biotechnology exploitation in Canada leads to a serious shortage of process and bio-engineering expertise. The task force stated that development of such expertise is urgent, and the provision of training will represent a major task for NRC's Biotechnology Centre Laboratories, under construction in Montréal.

Applications

Five major biotechnology process applications are of particular interest to Canada's resource industries: biological nitrogen fixation, cellulose utilization, waste treatment and use, development of new plant strains and mineral leaching.

Biological Nitrogen Fixation is increasingly important because of the escalating cost of nitrogen fertilizers. Plant breeding and genetic engineering techniques are expected to produce plants (eg, cereals) capable of symbiosis with nitrogen-fixing bacteria. Legumes are the only major family of food plants that naturally possess this ability.

Cellulose Utilization Canada's large agricultural and forestry resource base offers important and novel opportunities for the use of cellulose (ie, for BIOMASS ENERGY). Cellulose pretreatment processes, coupled with microbiological or enzyme hydrolysis methods, are receiving industrial attention throughout the world. Cellulose use would be attractive to Canada because of the size of the forestry industry, which makes a net annual contribution of nearly $12 billion to Canada's balance of trade; however, Canada's extensive fossil fuel reserves and consequent relatively low energy prices are expected to provide serious competition to commercial development of cellulose as an energy feedstock for some time.

Waste Treatment and Use Detoxification of effluent and the transformation of waste to useful products is increasingly important in the evolution of an industrial society (*see* RECYCLING). Biological processes offer particular advantage in adapting to varying waste compositions and conditions of degradation.

Mineral Leaching Microbiological action on mineral sulphides and conversion to more soluble forms have been known for centuries; these methods have already been adapted to the recovery of copper and uranium and will eventually be used for such metals as nickel and zinc (*see* METALLURGY). The one obvious advantage of biotechnological techniques is their very low energy requirements.

Plant Breeding Genetic engineering and cell fusion techniques will prove essential for the future economic development of Canada by providing new plant strains capable of fixing atmospheric nitrogen and exhibiting greater pest resistance, with earlier maturation, higher nutritional value and greater tolerance to a variety of climatic conditions.

Other Uses Some chemical feedstocks, presently derived from petroleum or coal, will be supplied by biological processes, including cellulosics, microbial polysaccharides, lignin derivatives, lactic and other organic acids, ethanol, acetone, butanol, vegetable oils for plasticizers, lubricants and RUBBER. In addition, certain FOOD ADDITIVES, proteins, fragrances and monomers for specialty PLASTICS and related substances, may best be produced by biotechnological techniques. It is anticipated that plants and plant cells will eventually be designed to produce predominantly single complex chemicals. Because of the rising cost of petroleum-based insecticides and the adverse effect of many of these on the environment, more highly specific biological control agents will be developed (*see* INSECT PESTS). Use of insect virus pathogens is increasingly being explored. The production of new and existing pharmaceuticals by biotechnological techniques has already started in other countries. However, Canadian pharmaceutical industry research and development is underdeveloped, largely because of present compulsory licensing provisions of the Canadian Patent Act. The original intention of the act was to reduce the cost of pharmaceuticals to consumers; the actual result has been a stunting of the industry in this country, with a major loss of HIGH-TECHNOLOGY jobs.

Because the development of biotechnology is just beginning and its full economic impact has not yet been felt, the Biotechnology Task Force proposed a Biotechnology Development Plan that would create a climate appropriate for establishment and growth of various industries. A National Biotechnology Committee has been organized, under the Ministry of State for Science and Technology, with the crucial responsibility of co-ordinating and catalyzing a nationwide effort. This committee represents the various sector interests in Canada, and holds regular meetings focusing on problem areas. A number of information networks, with their own newsletters, have been formed in the key sectors and have proved very useful for information exchange and in fostering collaboration. An inventory of biotechnology activities is presently being updated and consideration is being given to the publication of a national information letter.

The development of biotechnology in Canada is very exciting, paralleling growth in other countries. Biomedical applications, the most advanced, have already resulted in the organization of a number of new pharmaceutical and diagnostic companies, and in the expansion and extension of university based research and production institutes. Problem areas have been identified, and attempts are being made, at the academic level, to train more fermentation technologists and biotechnology oriented business graduates. The provinces have organized major efforts, with some provincial research agencies taking on a leading role.

In some respects, biotechnology has been the first and prime beneficiary of the federal government's new technology policy. This development seems only appropriate as it has been estimated that biotechnology products and processes will be involved, one way or another, in up to 70% of Canada's GROSS NATIONAL PRODUCT by the year 2010. ANDREW J. MORIARITY

Birch (*Betula*), genus of TREES and shrubs of birch family (Betulaceae). About 50 species are found in Arctic and N temperate regions worldwide. Ten species are native to Canada: 6 trees and 4 shrubs. Several species, especially the white or paper birch, are widespread throughout the country; other birches are regional (yellow and grey, East; cherry, Ontario; Alaska and water, Northwest). Leaves are alternate, oval to triangular in shape and veined, and have teet[h] of 2 sizes on the margins. Birches are bes[t] known for their paperlike bark. Most specie[s] prefer well-drained soils and good lighting. Pa[per] and grey birches are pioneering species i[n] abandoned fields and burned-over areas. Euro[pean] silver or weeping birch is a popular ORNA[MENTAL]. Canadian Indians used birches, especi[ally] paper birch, for CANOES, baskets and kitche[n] utensils. Today the wood is widely used for fur[niture] and veneers. *See* PLANTS, NATIVE USES.
ESTELLE LACOURSIÈR[E]

Paper, or "canoe," birch (*Betula papyrifera*), with cones and flowers (*artwork by Claire Tremblay*).

Birch-Bark Biting is the art of dentally per[forating] designs on intricately folded sheets o[f] paper-thin bark. The technique is known t[o] have been practised by OJIBWA (or Chippewa), CREE and Algonquian groups who utilized birc[h]bark extensively in fabricating domestic con[tainers], architectural coverings, CANOES and pic[tographic] scrolls. Bark biting was a casual a[rt] among Indian women, a means of experiment[ing] with designs that might later be translate[d] into porcupine quill or bead appliqué on bar[k] containers or hide clothing (*see* QUILLWORK). I[t] was a form of recreation or friendly competi[tion]. More recently, through the work of Cre[e] artist Angelique Merasty of Beaver Lk, Man, bark biting has achieved the status and marke[t] of a fine art. Merasty's own technical virtuosit[y] and visual repertoire have greatly amplified th[e] traditional range of rudimentary geometric de[signs] to include rich curvilinear floral, insect, animal and human figures. *See also* INDIAN ART.
ELIZABETH MCLUHA[N]

Birchbark Canoe, *see* CANOE, BIRCHBARK.

Bird, Florence Bayard, née Rhein, pen nam[e] Anne Francis, senator, journalist, broadcaster, author (b at Philadelphia, Pa 15 Jan 1908). Sh[e] moved to Canada in 1931 and established her[self] as a broadcaster and journalist. From 194[6] to 1966 Bird was a news commentator for th[e] CBC, also producing documentaries on women'[s] rights and international affairs. In 1967 PM Pearson appointed her chairman of the Roya[l] Commission on the STATUS OF WOMEN IN CANADA. Tabled in 1970, the report of the commissio[n] made 167 recommendations to eliminate sexua[l] inequality in Canada and sparked the formatio[n] of several women's groups to push for imple[mentation]. Bird was appointed to the Senate i[n] 1978. She is the author of *Anne Francis: An Auto[biography]* (1974) and *Holiday in the Woods* (1976). Bird was made a companion of the Order o[f] Canada in 1971. CERISE MORRI[S]

Bird, member of a unique group of VERTEBRATES, Class Aves. The FOSSIL record, comparative anat[omy] and embryology indicate that birds have a common ancestry with REPTILES. Paleontologist[s] believe that, among living reptiles, crocodilian[s] may be the closest relatives of birds. Birds ar[e] unique because they possess 2 major anatomica[l] adaptations: feathers, probably evolved fro[m] reptilian scales, which provide an insulatin[g] coat and give them the ability to maintain a constant body temperature, independent of th[e] temperature of the air surrounding them; and considerably modified forelimbs, from the five[-]fingered form of their probable reptilian ances[tors] to a wing covered with specially adapte[d] feathers, which give birds the power of flight. Additional adaptations include modification[s] to the skeleton that lessened its weight, throug[h] the evolution of air-filled, hollow bones; in[creased] its rigidity, through fusion of its part[s] (eg, sections of the vertebral column); and pro[vided] bony projections (processes) to whic[h] flight muscles attach, eg, the keel (projectin[g] ridge) on the sternum (breastbone). The lung[s] evolved a series of associated air sacs, whic[h] penetrate into bones and between muscles. Thi[s] respiratory system both decreases body mass an[d] creases gas exchange efficiency by permitting continual flow of fresh air over the respiratory urfaces. Body weight was reduced further hrough the ability of birds to excrete a nitrogeous waste (uric acid) that requires little water or its discharge, making it unnecessary for irds to carry this water. The reproductive sysem is functional only seasonally, becoming nlarged and heavy during the brief period of eproduction. In females of most species, it is presented by only a single ovary and oviduct hat produce the shelled eggs, which allow the oung to develop outside the mother's body and lso help reduce weight.

These adaptations in form, function and asociated behaviour have enabled birds to surmount what were, for other vertebrates, impassable geographic barriers, and to exploit irtually every habitat from arctic tundra and esert wastes to tropical forests and ocean solitudes. In Canada, about 417 species of birds have een recorded as breeding. Throughout most of he country, most species are migratory, arriving n spring to nest and rear their young, and departing for more hospitable climates in autumn. At least a few species are resident throughout he year, even in the Arctic to which such birds s the common raven, glaucous gull and rock tarmigan have become adapted to exploit the meagre food resources available during the ong, dark winters. Farther S in Canada, visitors rrive in late autumn from breeding grounds in he arctic islands, northern tundra and boreal orest to winter along the seacoasts, in the deciduous hardwood forests and on the central lains. Such birds as oldsquaw (ducks), redpolls, ine grosbeaks and snow buntings fall into this ategory.

Birds usually are most conspicuous during heir reproductive cycle. This is the time when most species undertake complex behavioural patterns that involve courtship display and ong. The breeding plumage, characteristically triking in breeding males, makes them visually onspicuous as they undertake their ritualized isplays. Perhaps the most spectacular example s the courting peacock. Birds are also conspicuous at this time through the sounds they produce, particularly when males of many species are advertising their occupancy of territory y singing. Most birds appear to establish nesting territories, ranging from relatively large reas in which most foraging and nesting occur, s in the American robin, to very small spaces, hat encompass only the nest sites, as in colonial pecies like the ring-billed gull. Territories are efended against trespass by other individuals of the same species and, in some cases, of other losely related species. The nest is built and the lutch of eggs is deposited within the territory. he size of the clutch varies considerably, from one egg in cliff-nesting seabirds like the northrn gannet, to about 18 in game birds like the ray partridge. The young hatch from the eggs fter periods of incubation varying from about 2 weeks in small songbirds like swallows and parrows, to about 9 weeks in large birds like lbatrosses. The hatchlings require parental attention for some time. For those species (eg, house wrens and American robins) the young of which hatch naked and remain in the nest until hey make their first flight, both parents bring ood during the entire nesting period. For them, ood availability is a factor of major importance. Other species (eg, ruffed grouse and Canada geese) produce chicks that are able to feed themelves shortly after hatching. In these forms, the young soon leave the nest, always accompanied by their parent(s). Their ability to avoid predators before they learn to fly is of major importance, as is suggested by the marvellous amouflage created by the colours and patterns of their downy plumage.

Birds have evolved the ability to use a great

Canada goose (*photo by Bill Brooks / Masterfile*).

variety of foods. Some species are largely herbivorous: geese graze on herbaceous plants; grouse browse on the leaves and needles of woody plants; many tropical birds live largely on fruit; and one group, which includes the hummingbirds, uses flower nectar. At the other end of the food spectrum are birds that are largely carnivorous: loons live principally on fish; hawks and owls prey primarily on terrestrial vertebrates such as rodents; and a large group of small birds has evolved to exploit the populations of insects that exist throughout the terrestrial sphere. Among these are such diverse forms as swifts and swallows, which feed on aerial insects, wood warblers, which glean leaves of trees for the arboreal insects they harbour, and dippers, which enter fast streams to feed on aquatic insects living among the bottom sediments.

D.A. Boag

Bird Classification and Evolution *Archaeopteryx*, the oldest BIRD yet discovered, is known from 5 FOSSILS recovered from fine slate deposits in Bavaria. This crow-sized animal lived during the Jurassic period (140 million years ago) in a tropical environment. *Archaeopteryx* possessed reptilian features (solid forearm bones, toothed bill, unfused backbone, claws on 3 fingers, etc). It would probably be classified as a REPTILE or small DINOSAUR but for the feathers (resembling those of modern birds), and fused furcula (wishbone), unique among Jurassic animals. The solid bones and lack of a keel on the breastbone limited its powers of flight, making it more a glider than a powered flyer. The 2 theories of bird origins currently recognized differ in tracing the details of bird evolution. Both agree that pseudosuchian thecodonts, long-tailed, scaly reptiles of the Triassic period (225-190 million years ago), are ancestral, directly or indirectly. The number of fossil birds is small (about 900 species known to date) because bird bones are fragile and have been preserved only under very favourable conditions. This makes tracing the ancestry and relationships of modern birds difficult. Fossil birds, generally, are so much larger than modern species that they can often be viewed as giant relatives. Less than 30 species are known from the Cretaceous period (140-65 million years ago). Most appear to be aquatic, with great similarities to modern grebes, flamingoes, cormorants and loons. The Paleocene period (65-54 million years ago) has yielded few bird fossils; however, the ancestors of modern families (including perching birds) appeared during this period.

Although bird classification is better known than that of any other animal group, new species are still discovered almost yearly. Current research provides new information permitting scientists to understand better the relationships between species, genera, families and orders. Over 9020 species of recent birds are recognized. These belong to 2045 genera, 160 families and 24 orders. About two-thirds of known species (5274 species in 1104 genera and 60 families) belong to the order Passeriformes (perching birds). The remaining 3746 species belong to 23 orders divided into 100 families and 941 genera. The following summary of orders currently recognized by ornithologists indicates the extent of diversity displayed by birds.

Ratites (6 families, 58 species; none Canada). Ostriches, rheas, cassowaries, emus, kiwis, tinamous. Large birds, except kiwis and tinamous; flightless and cursorial (running), except tinamous.

Sphenisciformes (one family, 18 species; none Canada). Penguins. Medium-sized to large diving birds with flipperlike wings; Southern Hemisphere.

Gaviiformes (one family, 4 species; 4 breeding species in Canada). Loons. Large diving birds with 3 webbed toes and straight, pointed bill; Arctic and Subarctic.

Podicipediformes (one family, 20 species; 5 Canada). Grebes. Small to large diving birds with lobed feet and straight, pointed bills; worldwide distribution.

Procellariiformes (23 families, 104 species; 2 families, 4 species Canada). Albatrosses, shearwaters, fulmars, petrels, storm-petrels, divingpetrels. Very small to very large oceanic birds

Northern flicker (*Colaptes auratus*) with young in a maple grove (*artwork by Claire Tremblay*).

with tubular nostrils; found on all oceans; nest on land.

Pelecaniformes (6 families, 62 species; 3 families, 6 species Canada). Tropicbirds, pelicans, boobies, gannets, cormorants, snakebirds, frigatebirds. Medium-sized to large aquatic birds with 4 webbed toes, throat pouches, pointed or hooked bills; primarily colonial nesters; worldwide distribution.

Ciconiiformes (5 families, 114 species; 2 families, 8 species Canada). Herons, bitterns, hammerkops, storks, ibises, egrets, spoonbills. Small to very large wading birds with long legs and necks; bill varies from long and spearlike to broad, flat and shovellike or decurved; all continents except Antarctic.

Phoenicopteriformes (one family, 6 species; none Canada). Flamingoes. Large wading birds with long legs and necks; bill thick with lamellae and bent sharply downward at midpoint; toes webbed; colonial nesters.

Anseriformes (2 families, 150 species; one family, 38 species Canada). Screamers, ducks, geese, swan, teals, mergansers, widgeons. Worldwide, medium-sized to very large swimming birds with 3 webbed toes and lamellate bill, except screamers (restricted to S America) which have unwebbed feet, chickenlike bills, wading habits, spurs on wings. The Labrador duck, formerly found in Canada, is extinct.

Falconiformes (5 families, 288 species; 3 families, 19 species Canada). Vultures, secretary birds, kites, hawks, eagles, osprey, falcons, caracaras. Very small to very large diurnal BIRDS OF PREY; legs short to very long; wing shape highly variable from very pointed to broad and rounded; hunters or carrion feeders; worldwide distribution.

Galliformes (4 families, 269 species; one family, 16 species Canada). Megapodes, mallee fowl, curassows, guans, chachalacas, grouse, pheasants, quails, peafowls, partridge, turkeys, hoatzins. Small to very large chickenlike birds occurring almost worldwide.

Gruiformes (12 families, 210 species; 2 families, 8 species Canada). Mesites, button quails, hemipodes, cranes, limpkins, trumpeters, rails, sun-grebes, kagus, cariamas, bustards. Very small to very large birds; structure and habits diverse; worldwide distribution.

Charadriiformes (16 families, 329 species; 6 families, 83 species Canada). Jaçanas, painted-snipes, crabplovers, oystercatchers, avocets, thick-knees, pratincoles, plovers, sandpipers, jaegers, skuas, gulls, sheathbills, skimmers, auks. Small to large birds; many species with long legs, cursorial habits; some with webbed feet and aquatic or diving habits; structure and habits diverse; worldwide distribution. Great auk, which nested in Canada, is extinct.

Columbiformes (3 families, 322 species; one family, 4 species Canada). Sandgrouse, dodos, pigeons, doves. Very small to very large birds; worldwide distribution; solitary to highly gregarious; arboreal or terrestrial. Dodo, native to the Mascarene Is, and passenger pigeon, formerly very common in Canada, are extinct.

Psittaciformes (3 families, 340 species; none Canada). Parrots, lories, parakeets, budgerigars. Very small to large tropical birds with brightly coloured plumage, strong hooked bill; 2 toes in front, 2 behind. Carolina parakeet, formerly of N America, is extinct.

Cuculiformes (2 families, 147 species; one family, 2 species Canada). Plantain-eaters, turacos, cuckoos. Small to large birds with long tail; 2 toes in front, 2 behind, or fourth reversible; many species have parasitic nesting habits; mostly arboreal, few terrestrial species; worldwide distribution.

Strigiformes (2 families, 146 species; 2 families, 15 species Canada). Barn owls and owls. Small to large birds; primarily nocturnal and arboreal; raptorial habits, noiseless flight; large eyes directed forward; worldwide distribution, except Antarctic.

East coast horned puffin (*Fratercula corniculata*) (*photo by Stephen J. Krasemann/DRK Photo*).

Caprimulgiformes (5 families, 105 species; one family, 4 species Canada). Oilbirds, frogmouths, goatsuckers, nightjars, nighthawks, potoos. Small to medium-sized birds; bill usually with wide mouth surrounded with bristles; small weak feet; nocturnal or crepuscular insect or fruit eaters; worldwide distribution.

Apodiformes (3 families, 428 species; 2 families, 7 species Canada). Swifts, crested swifts, hummingbirds. Small birds with weak feet. Swifts, distributed worldwide, have long, strong wings; hummingbirds restricted to New World have slender, pointed, long to very long bills, and bright, iridescent plumage.

Coliiformes (one family, 6 species; none Canada). Colies. Small African birds with long tails; gregarious and arboreal.

Trogoniformes (one family, 37 species; none Canada). Trogons. Small to medium-sized tropical birds with long tails, red or yellow underparts and iridescent upperparts; solitary and arboreal.

Coraciiformes (10 families, 200 species; one family, one species Canada). Kingfishers, todies, motmots, bee-eaters, rollers, hoopoes, hornbills. Small to large birds; usually solitary or in pairs; bill highly variable, from long, straight and pointed to heavy, curved and adorned with casque; some toes fused at base; worldwide distribution.

Piciformes (6 families, 383 species; one family, 13 species Canada). Jacamars, puffbirds, barbets, honey guides, toucans, woodpeckers, piculets, wrynecks. Small to large birds; most species solitary and arboreal; bill highly variable, from short, straight and pointed to very large; 2 toes in front, 2 behind, some species have only 3 toes; worldwide distribution. Ivory-billed woodpecker, formerly of N America, is extinct.

Passeriformes (60 families, 5274 species; 19 families, 188 species Canada). Perching birds. Comprises more species than all other orders together; highly diversified; adapted to perching, 3 toes in front, one behind; 9-10 primary wing feathers, 12 tail feathers; small to medium size; contains all songbirds; worldwide distribution. HENRI OUELLET

Bird Distribution and Habitat Animals' lives are circumscribed by 2 imperatives: finding food for survival, growth and reproduction; and avoiding becoming prey before reproducing. For an ANIMAL to occupy a habitat, it mu be able to survive and reproduce within it. Bird have evolved many ways of meeting these chal lenges. Their feeding structures (feet, bills, gas trointestinal tracts) are adapted to take availabl foods. Plumage structure, colour and patter protect them from their physical environmen and camouflage them from potential predator and sometimes from potential prey. Their be haviour patterns use these physiological adap tations to meet the 2 imperatives and, at th same time, enable each species to recognize i own kind. For example, the birds of Canada' S-central plains are adapted for the zone short, sparse vegetation. Their feet are adapte for walking (not hopping). Food, mainly plan parts or INVERTEBRATES, is taken with bills adapt ed to clip vegetation, crush seeds or pick up in vertebrates. Many species forage in flock thereby enhancing their efficiency in findin food and perhaps increasing their relative safe ty. Plumage, characteristically dull coloured often with darker streaks and vermiculation (wavy lines), allows them to blend with thei habitat; contrasting colours, usually confined t underparts or flight feathers, become apparen only when the bird is in flight. Most species (eg long-billed curlew, horned larks and chestnut collared longspurs) advertise their occupancy o space to prospective mates and competing mem bers of the same species through aerial display that are unique for each species. These displays which are accompanied by song, make use o special flight patterns that show off contrastin colours.

The power of flight has enabled birds to over come barriers to dispersal (eg, deserts, moun tains, oceans) and establish themselves i the breeding fauna of continents and island throughout the world. Often, they have appar ently been aided in colonizing new habitats b accidents, eg, being blown off course by storm during migration or, more recently, by huma activities, eg, transport of species into area where they did not exist previously.

Distribution of any given species is limited b availability of appropriate habitat. The numbe of species of breeding birds, greatest in th tropics where habitats have had most time t diversify, diminishes towards the poles, moun tain tops and islands farthest from continenta shores. For example, 1556 species of birds hav been recorded breeding in the tropical forests o Colombia (5° N), whereas on Ellesmere I (82° N breeding species fall to 14. The distribution o birds is constantly changing: some species ex pand their range; others exhibit an ever-con tracting distribution; still others fluctuate, ex panding for a while, then declining again. Tw major factors influence such changes: huma activities and prolonged shifts in CLIMATE. Bot influence availability of food and protectiv cover that enable birds to survive and reproduce

Canada's avifauna now consists largely o species believed to have evolved elsewher and subsequently invaded habitats available i northern N America. Wood warblers, blackbird and flycatchers are among families that appar ently evolved in tropical America and spread N via the Isthmus of Panama and Caribbean Is to inhabit various habitats across Canada eac spring and summer. By contrast many othe families (eg, grouse, thrushes and finches), ar believed to have originated in Eurasia and the invaded N America via BERINGIA. Many specie in these families reside or winter in the mor southern parts of Canada. D.A. BOA

Bird Sanctuaries and Reserves At the turn o the century with bird populations severely de pleted by uncontrolled HUNTING, attempts t protect BIRDS focused on the establishment o bird sanctuaries, areas in which hunting wa prohibited at all times of the year. More re ntly, with hunting under control but with ı increasing and industrialized human population encroaching on forests and wetlands, the ocus has shifted to include protection of habats. Protection may be achieved by various ieans, including land-use zoning, long-term greements with landowners and outright acuisition of land by wildlife agencies. Protected nd areas may be designated as national wildfe areas, conservation areas, game reserves, c. Where habitat protection is the main goal, unting may be permitted or prohibited deending on circumstances at the site. Both types protection seek the same end — conservation Canada's heritage of birds and other wildlife. t present, 82 migratory bird sanctuaries are lministered by the federal Canadian Wildlife ervice: Nfld has one; PEI, one; NS, 8; NB, 2; Qué, 5; Ont, 12; Sask, 15; Alta, 4; BC, 7; NWT, 14; one raddles the NWT-Ont border; another that of WT-Qué. Some of the most renowned of these e described below.

Sable I (NS), the only breeding site of the rare swich sparrow, also has important populaons of breeding gulls and terns.

Machias Seal I (NB), home of many nestg SEABIRDS including common puffins, arctic rns, razorbills and Leach's storm-petrels.

Bonaventure I (Qué), spectacular concentraons of northern gannets, black-legged kittiakes, common murres and other cliff-nesting abirds.

Upper Canada (Ont), stopping-off area for anada geese.

Last Mountain Lk (Sask), set aside in 1887 as America's first bird sanctuary, hosts many iigrating ducks, geese, swans and cranes and a breeding ground for sharp-tailed grouse, ommon terns, American avocets, mallards and iany others.

G.C. Reifel Sanctuary (BC), now part of a omplex of protected sites near the mouth of e Fraser R, harbours many species of WATERWL and SHOREBIRDS during migration and is sed by wintering lesser snow geese, American idgeon and American coots.

Bylot I (NWT) Greater snow geese nest on uthwestern outwash plain; thick-billed murs, black-legged kittiwakes and other seabirds n its northern and eastern shores.

Most provincial wildlife agencies have also stablished bird sanctuaries within their boundries; of particular importance are Newfoundnd's seabird sanctuaries and the pelican and rouse refuges in Man, Sask and Alta.

Important migratory bird habitats are procted in the Canadian Wildlife Service's 39 ational Wildlife Areas in 8 provinces. They inude the following well-known sites.

Tintamarre (NB), area of salt marsh at the ead of Bay of Fundy, used by migrating and reeding waterfowl.

Cap Tourmente (Qué), freshwater, tidal marsh nd adjacent meadows harbour a high proporon of the world's greater snow geese during iigration.

Long Point (Ont), along the N shore of Lk rie, part of a complex of sites protected by federal, provincial and private organizations, is n exceptional gathering location for migrating ongbirds and waterfowl.

Alaksen (BC), part of the Fraser R complex hich includes the Reifel Sanctuary.

Provincial wildlife agencies have also set side several wildlife habitat areas, many chosen specifically for their variety and richness as ird habitats. Several other important bird areas e protected and managed jointly by federal nd provincial wildlife departments. For example, in the Creston Valley Wildlife Management rea, BC, provincial and federal governments, ı collaboration with private agencies and indiiduals, protect and manage a rich wetland area nportant to migrating waterfowl.

Birds and their habitats are protected in Canada's national parks and in most provincial parks. Of special interest is WOOD BUFFALO NATIONAL PARK (Alta-NWT border), the only known nesting area of the endangered WHOOPING CRANE. Municipalities, private institutions, bird clubs and individuals have also done much to protect important areas, eg, Ile-aux-Basques, a nesting island for eiders, gulls and herons in the St Lawrence estuary, purchased in 1927 by the Provancher Society of Natural History; J.T. MINER's Sanctuary near Kingsville, Ont, which has attracted flocks of Canada geese for over 50 years; and Alf Hole's goose sanctuary near Rennie, Man.

Migratory birds regularly travel across national boundaries and must be considered an international heritage. In signing the Ramsar Convention for the Conservation of Wetlands of International Importance as Waterfowl Habitat (1981), Canada pledged to protect several important wetlands, including such sites as Alaksen, Cap Tourmente and the Queen Maud Gulf (NWT), an important breeding ground for Ross's, lesser snow, and Brant geese and many other waterbirds. Although Canada enjoys an enviable reputation for establishing bird sanctuaries and reserves, reason for concern remains. Pollution, disturbance, habitat destruction and hunting continue to threaten bird populations.

AUSTIN REED

Bird Watching, the field observation of BIRDS. The popularity of bird watching has burgeoned, especially since WWII, probably because of increased leisure, a rich literature of books and periodicals, more organizations and better educational and travel facilities. Few Canadian cities do not have at least one bird club and there are international organizations that cater to all levels of expertise. People watch birds for recreation. Many who become highly efficient at field identification compete with one another, locally and internationally, for highest numbers of species identified in a given period and specified area. However, thousands of dedicated bird watchers produce more useful information. The National Audubon Society's bimonthly *American Birds* is devoted almost entirely to publishing data provided by bird watchers. Each season one issue monitors and summarizes masses of distributional and numerical data gathered by US and Canadian birders. One issue publishes results of breeding censuses and winter censuses in ecologically defined habitats. Another is devoted to the continentwide Christmas Bird Count, begun in 1900, and now the most highly organized event of the bird watcher's year. In the 81st count, 33 802 observers reported on 1358 carefully defined areas. Such long-term records are invaluable sources of information on species distribution, population trends, periodic fluctuations, etc. Such counts quickly alert conservation officials to any species whose numbers are becoming perilously low. The notebooks, field lists, nest-record cards and banding data of bird watchers also contribute a vast body of vital information on migration, life histories, behaviour, food, economic status and ecology. It is often said that more is known about birds than any other class of animal. For this, bird watchers may claim much of the credit.

W. EARL GODFREY

Birds of Prey could be defined as birds that prey on other living animals; however, the term is usually reserved for species with hooked bills and large, strong, sharp talons. These birds include HAWKS, EAGLES, FALCONS and their relatives (order Falconiformes) and OWLS (order Strigiformes). Representatives of both orders are found almost worldwide. Although these groups are distantly related, their behavioural and anatomical similarities appear to result from parallel evolution. Some significant differences result from the diverse strategies required by day-hunting and night-hunting birds.

Fifteen species of owl are found in Canada, including the large, reclusive great gray owl (*Strix nebulosa*) (*photo by Wayne Lankinen/DRK Photo*).

Falconiformes

This order includes 287 species of mostly diurnal hunters. They are grouped into 5 families: the Cathartidae, comprised of the 7 living New World VULTURE and condor species, all principally carrion feeders; the Falconidae, 60 species including the caracaras, forest falcons and falcons; the Sagittaridae, one species of secretary bird; the Pandionidae, one species of osprey; and the Accipitridae, 218 species of kites, eagles, Old World vultures and hawks. Although many of the Falconiformes are superficially alike, each family is highly specialized and individuals vary widely in habitat requirements and food preferences. The birds range in size from the diminutive falconets, barely larger than sparrows, to the giant condors, with wingspans exceeding 3 m. All have keen day vision; many are fierce predators, spotting small animal prey while in flight or perching and then swooping to kill.

The turkey vulture (*Cathartes aura*) is the sole representative of the Cathartidae to breed as far N as Canada. The falcons are well represented in the Northern Hemisphere; 5 species breed in Canada. They are most easily identified in flight by their long, pointed wings and rapid flight. The only pandionid, the osprey, a fish-eating bird, breeds in Canada. The Accipitridae are represented by one species of kite, 2 eagles and 10 "hawks." Hawk is a general name given to several predatory birds that are smaller than eagles. The Canadian hawks can be subdivided into 3 species of forest hawks; 6 buteos, large, soaring hawks; and one harrier, ground-nesting hawks of open fields and marshes. R.W. FYFE

Strigiformes

Strigiformes, the owls, are predominantly nocturnal. This order contains 133 species classified in 2 families, Tytonidae (barn owls and relatives) and Strigidae (typical owls). Owls have superb night vision made possible by enormous pupils and light-efficient retinas. The large eyes do not move in their sockets, but an owl can rotate its head more than 180°. Acute hearing allows an owl to locate its prey by sound, as when a great gray owl plunges through deep snow to catch mice it cannot see. Soft feathers permit almost noiseless flight.

C. STUART HOUSTON

Birge, Cyrus Albert, industrialist (b near Oakville, Ont 7 Nov 1847; d at Hamilton, Ont 14 Dec 1929). After early careers as a merchant and an accountant for the Great Western Ry, Birge became manager of the American-owned

Canada Screw Co at Dundas, Ont in 1882. Five years later he moved the plant to Hamilton and in 1898 bought out American interests. Meanwhile he allied with other Hamilton businessmen to promote local enterprise. When Canada Screw was absorbed in the new Steel Co of Canada in 1910 he became that corporation's VP. By this point Birge held directorships in insurance and trust companies and eventually in the Canadian Bank of Commerce. He was a leader in the Canadian Manufacturers' Assn and in the Methodist Church, whose Victoria College he supported generously. CRAIG HERON

Birks, Henry, silversmith, founder of Henry Birks and Sons (b at Montréal 30 Nov 1840; d there 16 Apr 1928). He graduated from Montreal High School in 1856 and spent the next winter perfecting his French. In Apr 1857 he joined Savage and Lyman, a large firm of watchmakers and jewellers. On 1 Mar 1879, he opened the first Birks store on St James St in Montréal. Six years later he moved to larger premises on the same street. In 1893, since 3 sons were active in the business, the company name was changed to Henry Birks and Sons. The following year the store was moved to their new building at the corner of St Catherine and Union streets. The Birks building still stands on Phillips Square and houses the organization's head office. Since its founding in 1879, 5 successive generations of the Birks family have been involved in the company. K.O. MACLEOD

Birney, Alfred Earle, poet (b at Calgary 13 May 1904). Beginning with *David and Other Poems* (1942), Birney's poetry has consistently explored the resources of language with passionate and playful curiosity. He was educated at UBC, U of T, Berkeley and U of London, where his primary interests were in Old and Middle English, culminating in a dissertation on Chaucer. Throughout his career he has been an experimental poet, publishing over 20 books of verse that vary as widely in form and voice as they do in subject. His poems reveal his constant concern to render his encyclopedic experience — be it of Canada's geographical or cultural reaches, of nature, of travels, or of the trials of love by time — into a language marvelously dexterous and supple, always seriously at play.

Birney has also had an important career as a teacher of creative writing and literature, and as a playwright, novelist and editor. He taught at several universities, most notably at UBC (1946-65), where he founded and chaired the first Canadian department of creative writing in 1963. But his greatest contribution has been to modern Canadian poetry. In long poems and lyrics, sight poems, sound poems and found poems, whether on the page or in his recent collection of recorded poems with the percussion ensemble Nexus (1982), Birney demonstrates his deep commitment to making language have meaning in every possible and eloquent way. He has won the Gov Gen's Award for poetry twice (for *David*, 1943, and for *Now Is Time*, 1946), the Stephen Leacock Medal for his novel *Turvey* (1949) and the Lorne Pierce Medal for Literature (1953). NEIL BESNER

Birth Control Attempts by humans to control their own fertility have included continence, contraception, induced ABORTION and infanticide. "Birth control" is a term coined in 1914, and at that time it meant voluntary control of conception by mechanical or chemical means, or by both. Today, hormonal and "fertility awareness" methods and surgical sterilization are also recognized as techniques of contraception.

Before WWI, a few Canadians advocated birth control as a health measure, but organized groups to foster it did not appear until the 1920s. Like groups in Britain and the US, they argued that every child should be wanted and nurtured. Birth control could free women from debilitating annual pregnancies and reduce the incidence of illegal abortion. It could improve marital relations, maternal and child health, and FAMILY welfare. Canadian advocates did not, however, make the claim that it was the panacea of POVERTY. Supporters were, generally, educated men and women. Some were inspired by the SOCIAL GOSPEL, and some were feminists. Their occupations were varied, and their political biases ranged from socialism to conservatism.

Under the 1892 Criminal Code, birth control was obscene, "tending to corrupt morals." Unless an accused could prove that its advocacy had been "for the public good," he or she was liable to serve a 2-year jail sentence. Contraception was opposed by pronatalist business, religious, and political interest groups. Their attacks on the "birth controllers" were frequent and defamatory.

Nevertheless, by the 1920s, foreign research in human sexuality was creating interest in Canada, the 1892 law was being questioned, and family size among those in higher socioeconomic brackets was shrinking. Informed couples could limit their fertility by "under-the-counter" purchases of commercially made contraceptives, or with materials for homemade methods. High fertility persisted among the less educated poor, however, and the birth controllers urged that contraception should be free for all who wanted it. Politicians quoted the law to evade the issue, but scattered groups of determined volunteers made referrals to a few courageous physicians or provided information themselves to married women. The first advocacy organization in Canada was formed in Vancouver in 1923, and the first birth-control clinic was started in Hamilton in 1932.

From 1930 onwards a birth control program for low-income women was also provided by a philanthropist, A.R. Kaufman of Kitchener, Ont. From his Parents' Information Bureau (PIB), clients could obtain simple contraceptives by mail order and could get referrals to selected physicians for diaphragms and for contraceptive sterilization. When one of the PIB field workers, Dorothea Palmer, was arrested in 1936 in a predominantly French-speaking, low-income suburb of Ottawa, Kaufman's lawyers won her acquittal, arguing that her work was not for profit but "for the public good." The PIB was soon helping 25 000 clients a year. The landmark verdict reassured other advocacy groups, but until the 1960s they were unable to match the popularity of Kaufman's program.

After WWII and the BABY BOOM, public acceptance of birth control increased rapidly. In 1955 SERENA (Service de régulation des naissances) was started in Lachine, Qué, by Gilles and Rita Breault to teach "natural methods" of birth control. The growth of other volunteer groups was speeded by news stories of the birth-control pill and the plastic IUD (intrauterine device) and by word of the world population "explosion." In 1963 the Canadian birth-control activists, Barbara and George Cadbury, organized a federation of the Vancouver, Winnipeg, Hamilton, Toronto and Ottawa birth-control societies and arranged for its membership in the International Planned Parenthood Federation (IPPF). Its objectives were "responsible parenthood" and population education. New groups in Edmonton, Montréal and Calgary joined, but the PIB and SERENA refused invitations. The Canadian federation was first titled Canadian Federation of Societies for Population Planning, but in 1967 it changed its name to the Family Planning Federation of Canada and in 1975 to Planned Parenthood Federation of Canada (PPFC).

Member groups in Vancouver and Winnipeg won United Way grants. Since 1967 the Québec government has financed instruction for French-speaking trainers and service providers, and has also provided funds to SERENA. Early in 1969, the BC government granted funds to the Family Planning (now Planned Parenthood) Association of BC.

Robert W. Prittie led the cause in Parliament; and with informal support from the Anglican, Presbyterian, United and Unitarian churches, and later the Canadian Home Economics Association and the Salvation Army, the PPFC pressed the Canadian government to remove contraception from the Criminal Code. The Canadian Medical Association and other respected national voluntary organizations joined the campaign. The Canadian Catholic Conference of Bishops stated that it would not oppose the amendment. The law was changed in 1969.

Beginning in 1971, with grants from Health and Welfare Canada, the PPFC also undertook to act as the catalyst for government-funded birth-control information and services across Canada. It grew from 8 to 80 advocacy and service organizations, and in response, some provincial governments began to offer their own programs. The PPFC also raised money for the IPPF. The Canadian government began to meet Third World requests for help and made grants also to the IPPF and the United Nations Fund for Population Activities. These forms of international birth-control assistance continue. SERENA received a sustaining grant and has developed a network of "fertility awareness" groups both in Canada and abroad.

Health and Welfare Canada established its own Family Planning Division (FPD) as a promotional and grants-distributing agency. It sponsored a large and representative national conference in 1972. PPFC members conducted demonstration projects and a national publicity campaign, produced multilingual educational materials, and trained professionals in counselling and service delivery.

In 1976 the federal government's assistance for birth-control services diminished. Funding for the PPFC and SERENA was drastically reduced, the department was reorganized and the FPD weakened. Birth-control education and services have become political issues, and a hodgepodge of public and privately owned programs has emerged. Many observers attribute the rise in unplanned pregnancies (especially among teenagers) and in legally induced abortions to the decline in support of education and birth-control services.

Although PPFC members continue working to inform all Canadians of the benefits of education for responsible parenthood and the services to implement it, Canada now lags behind many Third World countries in co-operation between governments and nongovernmental agencies for this socially significant health promotion program. MARY F. BISHOP

Birthing Practices in Canada during the past half century have been largely determined by 4 periods of sequential, although overlapping emphasis. The first concern was the high mortality rate associated with childbirth and the need to make labour and delivery safer for the mother. Obstetrical research and training improved, and birth moved from the home to the hospital. Maternity care also benefited from advances in other medical fields, such as safe blood transfusion and the use of antibiotics. Maternal survival rates rose from 9942.4 per 10 000 births in 1930 to 9999.8 in 1982.

The relief of pain in childbirth became a second major concern. Heavy narcosis during labour and general or spinal anesthesia for delivery became the normal practice, but they were gradually eliminated because of adverse effects both on mothers and babies. Psychological preparation of the expectant mother during th prenatal period became increasingly popular, as did epidural anesthesia.

The focus of concern then shifted from the mother to the baby and perinatal survival rates increased from 940.1 per 1000 births in 1930 to 989.9 in 1982. Electronic and chemical surveillance of the fetus and intensive care of the premature or sick newborn improved their chances of survival, but this improvement was not achieved without cost. Obstetrical technology and intervention became almost routine. Caesarean section rates rose from 4.8% in 1960 to 16.1% in 1980 and are still rising. Inevitably, this led to the fourth phase, a resurgence of concern about both the short-term and long-term effects of the psychological factors associated with childbirth.

The medicalization of childbirth has led many individuals, including providers of maternity care, to search for alternatives that may provide psychological satisfaction without sacrifice of physical safety. Interest has been expressed in a revival of midwifery as an independent profession. Although midwifery training for outpost nurses who work in isolated areas of the country is provided in 3 Canadian universities (U of A, Dalhousie and Memorial), birth in Canada can legally be attended only by physicians. Canada remains one of only 8 countries in the World Health Organization that have not officially recognized midwives. Professionals on the whole have strongly opposed any move to out-of-hospital alternatives. Attempts to establish freestanding birth centres in Canada have so far been unsuccessful. Attendance at home births has been forbidden to physicians in one province and is actively discouraged in the others.

The major effect of consumer involvement in childbirth has been a change in hospital policies. Family-centered birth practices have been advocated in many Canadian hospitals, although the degree to which these practices have been implemented varies widely. Almost all hospitals allow fathers in the labour and delivery room, but less than half permit grandparents, and fewer than 10% allow siblings to be present. While most hospitals still move women to a separate delivery room for birth, combined labour and delivery ("birthing") rooms are becoming increasingly available.

MURRAY W. ENKIN

Reading: V.H. Elkins, *The Birth Report* (1983); S. Kitzinger, *The Complete Book of Pregnancy and Childbirth* (1980).

Bishop, William Avery, "Billy," fighter pilot (b at Owen Sound, Ont 9 Feb 1894; d at Palm Beach, Fla 10 Sept 1956). He was the top scoring Canadian and Imperial ace of WWI, credited with 72 victories. A fellow pilot accurately described him as "a fantastic shot but a terrible pilot."

A flamboyant extrovert, he was the first Canadian airman to win a VICTORIA CROSS, awarded him for a single-handed dawn attack on a German airfield on 2 June 1917. His last victory came on 19 June 1918 when he claimed 5 enemy aircraft. In Aug he was promoted lt-col and sent to England to help organize an abortive 2-squadron Canadian Air Force. After the war Bishop and W.G. BARKER operated a commercial flying enterprise before Bishop went into sales promotion in England and Canada. During WWII he was an honorary air marshal in the RCAF.

BRERETON GREENHOUS

Reading: W.A. Bishop, *The Courage of the Early Morning* (1966).

Bishop's University, Lennoxville, Qué, was founded 1843 under the sponsorship of G.J. MOUNTAIN, third Anglican bishop of Québec. Bishop's was to provide a liberal education for English-speaking Lower Canada (Eastern Townships), and to train Anglican clergy. In 1853

Enrolment: Bishop's University, 1982-83
(Source: Statistics Canada)

Full-time Undergrad	*Full-time Graduate*	*Part-time Undergrad*	*Part-time Graduate*
831	3	664	16

it received a royal charter to grant degrees. In 1871 a medical faculty was established, which in 1905 merged with MCGILL U Faculty of Medicine. The 1920s saw specialized programs in professional education and natural sciences introduced. In 1947 Bishop's became nondenominational. Since then, extensive campus development has taken place with public support. Bishop's offers undergraduate degrees in arts, sciences and business administration, and graduate diplomas in education and collegial teaching. Now part of a provincially supported system of higher education, Bishop's has shared its campus with Champlain College, a pre-university institution (CEGEP), since 1971.

K. AND E. SCHWEIZER

Bison, hoofed MAMMAL of the cattle family (Bovidae), variously classified by mammalogists in one or 2 species. European bison (*Bison bonasus*) is known as the wisent. The N American species, better known as buffalo, has 2 subspecies: prairie bison (*B. bison bison*) and wood bison (*B. b. athabascae*). Both have curved horns, beard, shoulder humps, short tail and mane of hair around head and neck. Bulls attain adult size at 6-8 years; cows, at approximately 4 years. Bison can live in excess of 20 years. Canada's most conspicuous CONSERVATION successes and blunders are associated with bison. The population of prairie bison is estimated to have been 50-60 million in 1800, declining to about 40 million by 1830. Huge herds grazed the prairies and, by their somewhat unpredictable movements, offered periods of feast or famine for their predators. Bulls and cows were segregated; bulls were less mobile, congregating on choice feeding areas, and were more likely to stand against predators. Herds were food for wolves, plains grizzlies and scavengers, as well as for Plains Indians and Métis. They also fed white settlers in the 19th century and sustained a short-lived hide industry. By 1885, prairie bison were virtually extinct, except for some captive

The population of prairie bison (*bison bison*) is estimated to have been 50-60 million in 1800, but by 1885 they were virtually extinct (*photo by Tim Fitzharris*).

individuals and a small herd in Yellowstone National Park (northwestern US). The Canadian government bought specimens to establish a park at Wainwright, Alta.

Wood bison lived in lowland meadows and deltas of the Athabasca, Peace and Slave rivers, several hundred kilometres from the plains bison. Larger than the plains bison, the wood bison also differed in pelage, having no long hair chaps on its front legs, shorter beard, long hairlock hanging from between its horns, shorter head hair and shorter, darker, less extensive robe. Wood bison lived in smaller groups, were notoriously more flighty and apparently lacked major migratory movements. WOOD BUFFALO NATIONAL PARK, the world's largest national park, was established in 1922 to protect the subspecies, and all went well until some 6673 animals, some of which were diseased, were transferred from Wainwright in 1925, resulting in hybridization that almost destroyed the wood bison as a separate subspecies. Today, the park shelters a hybrid population. In 1957 Dr N.I. Novakowski of the Canadian Wildlife Service discovered a remnant population of apparently pure wood bison in the park. Animals from this herd were transferred to the N shores of Great Slave Lk where a vigorous, expanding population now thrives. Others were transported to ELK ISLAND NATIONAL PARK where a captive population now exists.

The buffalo's excellent meat and superb hide, combined with its winter hardiness and unequalled ability to exist and even gain weight on poor forage, have prompted attempts at domestication and cross-breeding with cattle. Male "cattalo" are sterile, but females make excellent, long-lived, breeding stock. Experimental work on cattalo was unsuccessful, because of male sterility and market requirements for fat carcasses. Today, lean, meaty carcasses are again preferred, and interest in buffalo ranching has increased. Ironically, bison may again become a source of meat for human consumption on the prairies.

VALERIUS GEIST

bissett, bill, poet, artist, performer, publisher (b at Halifax 23 Nov 1939). James Reaney calls bissett "a one-man civilization," a fitting description of this multimedia explorer of alternate cultural visions. His work is strongly anti-establishment, even in its refusal to obey normal spelling and grammar rules. Today, bissett is internationally recognized as a performing sound poet; he has published almost 50 books of poetry; his paintings and drawings are energetically primitive analogues to his poetic vision; and his blewointment press continues to publish new writers.

DOUGLAS BARBOUR

Bitumen is the heaviest, thickest form of PETROLEUM. The 2 largest-known bitumen sources (in Alberta and Venezuela) each contain more petroleum than the entire proven conventional oil reserves of the Persian Gulf. Synthetic crude oil produced from bitumen accounts for over 10% of Canada's total oil production. Compared to conventional oil (obtained from traditional, easily accessible sources), however, synthetic crude from bitumen is expensive and complicated to produce.

There are 4 major bitumen deposits in Alberta: Athabasca, Cold Lake, Peace River and Wabasca, and various smaller ones, eg, Buffalo Head Hills. The 31 000 km^2 Athabasca deposit around Fort McMurray is largest and nearest the surface. The ATHABASCA R cuts a channel through the oil sands in places, and Indians used the tarry bitumen to caulk canoes before the first Europeans arrived in the late 18th century. Since the late 19th century, people have schemed to tap the petroleum wealth of the oil sands. Some Edmonton streets were paved with bitumen early in this century. The International

Bitumen Co and Abasand Oils Ltd produced asphalt from the Athabasca sands in the 1930s. Until recently, Alberta's bitumen deposits were commonly known as "tar sands," but industry and government now prefer the more descriptive term, oil sands.

In the NE corner of the Athabasca deposit, several ore bodies lie within 46 m of the surface. About 12% of the deposit's approximately 100 billion m^3 of bitumen occurs here. About 6 billion m^3 of bitumen, corresponding to 4.2 billion m^3 of synthetic crude and equivalent to more than 40 years of Canadian oil consumption at the 1982 rate, was considered recoverable under economic conditions prevailing in 1982. This area contains the world's only 2 commercial oilsands operations; both use the hot-water process, developed by Karl Clark of the ALBERTA RESEARCH COUNCIL in 1948, for separating bitumen from oil sands. In 1967 Great Canadian Oil Sands Ltd, now part of Suncor Ltd, opened the first, modern upgrading plant, and now produces 9200 m^3/day of high-quality synthetic crude oil. Syncrude Ltd, which opened in 1978, currently produces 18 900 m^3/day.

Unlike conventional crude oil, bitumen does not flow freely: it is heavier than water and more viscous than molasses. Most of the hydrocarbons in bitumen are heavier than pentane, and about half are very heavy molecules with a boiling point over 525°C. The light fractions are high in naphthenes (used in making gasoline and PETROCHEMICALS); the heavy fractions are high in asphaltenes (used in making asphalt for paving and roofing). Most deposits contain mixtures of bitumen (up to 5% sulphur by weight), sand, water, small amounts of heavy metals and other contaminants. In its natural state, bitumen is suitable only for paving roads. Compared to conventional crude oil, bitumen contains too much carbon and too little hydrogen. In making synthetic crude oil, special refining processes are used to remove impurities and correct the carbon-hydrogen imbalance.

Mining of Oil Sands

Because of the contaminants and the high viscosity, the first problem in exploiting bitumen is bringing it to the surface. Both Suncor and Syncrude use open-pit MINING techniques to extract oil sands. However, only about 3% of Alberta's bitumen can be reached by surface mining; the remainder requires *in situ* recovery techniques. Of the several dozen pilot projects testing *in situ* techniques, most involve applying heat so that the bitumen will flow through wells to the surface. The Esso Resources Canada Ltd *in situ* pilot plant at Cold Lake has been producing commercial quantities of bitumen for a number of years. The $200-million, 1100 m^3/day Wolf Lake project, being built by PETRO-CANADA and BP Resources Canada Ltd in the Cold Lake area, will be the second commercial operation using *in situ* recovery. Esso Resources Canada Ltd had proposed a large *in situ* project at Cold Lake, but shelved it in 1981 because of uncertainty about inflation, interest rates and world oil prices (*see* ENERGY POLICY). In 1982, for similar reasons, the Alsands consortium dropped its plans for a large surface-mining project near FORT MCMURRAY. Both Esso and Alsands planned 22 000 m^3/day operations, with capital costs estimated at $12 billion each; their proposals indicated that the economics of surface and *in situ* extraction are very similar.

At Suncor and Syncrude the ore bodies are 30-70 m thick and buried at depths of 15-35 m. The overburden consists of varying proportions of Cretaceous silts, clays and shales (Clearwater formations, 65-140 billion years old) overlying the McMurray oil sands, and Pleistocene (10 000-2.5 million year old) sands and gravels deposited unconformably on the Clearwater formations. MUSKEG, up to 5 m in thickness, covers about 40% of the terrain. Muskeg-free areas are generally covered by bush.

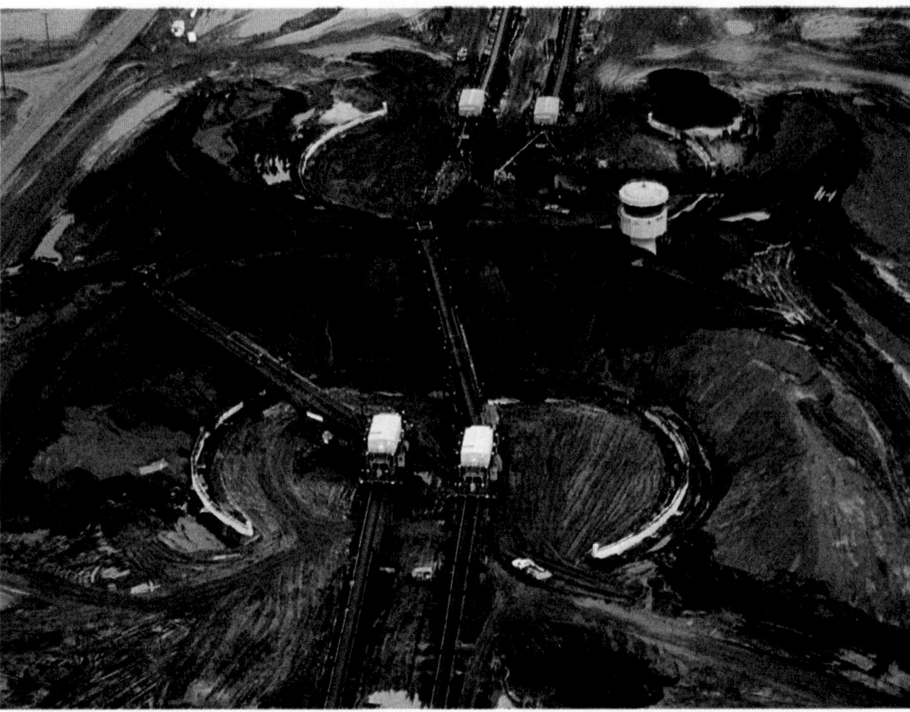

Mining the oil sands (*courtesy Alberta Oil Sands Technology and Research Authority*).

Areas to be mined are cleared of trees, then drained. The muskeg is removed during winter and stockpiled for reclamation use. At Suncor, overburden is removed by a bucket-wheel excavator which strips the material and loads it into trucks. About 80% is used to construct haulage roads and tailings dikes. At Syncrude, part of the overburden is cast directly into the mined-out area by draglines, but most is removed by two 15 m^3 hydraulic shovels, a fleet of twelve 170 t electric trucks, and other earth-moving equipment. Suncor mines the oil sand with 3, huge bucket-wheel excavators operating on benches 20 m high. The oil sand is dynamited before excavation to facilitate digging and prolong the life of digging teeth and buckets. It is transferred to the extraction plant by a system of belt wagons and conveyors. Mining at Syncrude is performed by four 61 m^3 draglines, 2 moving east, the others west, on 2 faces 4500 m long. The oil sand is piled in windrows behind the draglines, then loaded onto conveyor systems by 4 bucket-wheel reclaimers. Generally speaking, oil sands containing less than 6% (Syncrude) or 8% (Suncor) bitumen are discarded as unprofitable. Direct operating costs of mining (excluding utilities) account for 25-35% of the total direct costs (excluding interest, royalties and taxes).

The Athabasca deposit contains an estimated 100 billion m^3 of bitumen lying under 0-520 m of overburden; Cold Lake contains 26 billion m^3 and Peace River 12 billion m^3, each at depths ranging from 300-600 m; Wabasca contains 14 billion m^3 buried under 75-750 m of cover. Surface mining, currently limited to overburden depths of less than 46 m, might ultimately be feasible up to 80 m. Successful *in situ* experimentation, notably by Esso at Cold Lake, has created expectations that a significant portion of the bitumen lying below 300 m might be recovered.

Esso Resources has been experimenting continuously with *in situ* techniques at Cold Lake since 1964. Pilot plant production had reached 2200 m^3/day by 1982 and was being increased. Esso's method, called "huff and puff," involves injection of high-pressure steam for 1-2 months to heat the formation. Injection is then discontinued for 4 or more months. The bitumen seeps back to the injection wells, which now become production wells operated by pumping. Cold Lake bitumen is 2-3° API (American Petroleum Institute specific gravity scale) lighter than Athabasca bitumen and this relative lightness facilitates recovery. Initial recovery is about 20% of the in-place reserves, but it is expected that communication between wells will be established eventually, increasing recovery efficiency.

For the substantial Athabasca and Wabasca reserves lying between 80 and 300 m, however, an alternative form of technology must be developed. Mine-assisted *in situ* production (MAISP) is a promising technique. In this scheme, patterned after one at Yarega, Siberia, horizontal tunnels would be driven under the deposit and closely spaced vertical collector wells drilled upward into it. Low-pressure steam would be injected into the deposit from above to raise the temperature of the heavy oil and lower its viscosity, enabling it to flow into collector wells. Shell Canada Resources Ltd's Peace River lease is unique in that it contains a 24 m layer of uniform oil sand over a 3 m water layer. Shell's pilot-plant technique has been to inject steam into the water layer and allow the heat and pressure to spread into the oil sands through a series of wells extending upward from the water layer. Following an extensive pressurization period, steam injection is discontinued; the heated bitumen then flows down the injection wells into the water layer and is recovered by production wells.

At Gregoire Lake, Amoco Canada experimented for many years with a process, referred to as COFCAW (combination of forward combustion and waterflood), based on injecting air to heat the formation, followed by water to generate steam and loosen the bitumen. A lengthy test was terminated in 1982 after repeated failures to establish communication between wells.

Bitumen Extraction

Oil sand, as mined commercially, contains an average of 10-12% bitumen, 83-85% mineral matter and 4-6% water. Most of the mineral matter is coated by a film of water and this property permits extraction by the hot-water ocess. The oil sand is put into massive rotating ums and slurried with hot water and steam. ecks of bitumen separate from the grains of nd and attach themselves to tiny air bubbles. onditioned slurry is screened and put into rge, conical separation vessels where the aer-ed bitumen is skimmed off as a froth contain-g about 65% oil, 25% water and 10% solids. e coarse sand settles and is pumped to dis-sal sites. Some of the smaller bitumen and ineral particles remain in an intermediate wa-r layer, called middlings, which is withdrawn d pumped to secondary flotation cells. Gener-ly, 88-95% of the bitumen is recovered in the ocess. Coarse sand from the primary sepa-tors is used to build dikes, forming the large ilings ponds needed to contain the effluent. these ponds the fine particles settle slowly, oducing clarified water that is reused in the traction process. The fine particles do not con-lidate to their original density, so every cubic etre of oil sand mined creates 1.4 m^3 of mate-al for disposal. Removal of the contaminants om the froth stream is achieved through dilu-n with naphtha followed by 2 stages of cen-ifugation. About 98% recovery is achieved in e froth treatment process. The water needs of large project like Syncrude are substantial, nounting to about 0.2% of the average flow of e Athabasca R (*see* WATER TREATMENT; WATER LLUTION).

Economic and environmental incentives still ist to improve recovery, reduce heat and water quirements, and shrink or eliminate tailings nds. Consequently, many alternatives have en investigated over the years, including re-rting, solvent extraction, addition of chem-als, spherical agglomeration and the use of eophilic sieves. Since the hot-water process has en demonstrated successfully on a commer-al scale and accounts for only about 10% of the itial capital investment of a total oil-sands oject, radical new technologies will probably introduced only when they demonstrate suf-ient advantages.

Bitumen Upgrading

Suncor and Syncrude both use coking pro-sses to remove carbon from the heavy frac-ns of bitumen. Coking involves thermally cking the heavy fractions (at 468-498°C) to oduce lighter fractions (eg, gasoline, fuel gas) d petroleum coke (used as fuel in the coking ocess or sold). Syncrude's fluid coking process oduces less coke and more liquid hydro-rbons than the delayed coking used by Suncor. uid coking, however, is a very capital-inten-e process and the quality of the distillate is wer. The aborted Cold Lake project planned use Flexicoking, a modified version of fluid king, which incorporates a gasification step to nvert the net coke to a low-heating-value fuel s. The sulphur in the coke, instead of being idized to sulphur dioxide, is reduced to hy-ogen sulphide which can be more readily noved with conventional technology and nverted to elemental SULPHUR.

Hydrocracking processes, which add HYDRO-N, offer higher liquid yields, better distillate alities and lower emission levels of sulphur oxide (*see* ACID RAIN). However, short cata-t life from contamination by organometallic npounds, large energy requirements and the ed to obtain hydrogen from natural gas pe-lize the hydrocracking schemes. So far no nmerical bitumen upgraders have used hy-ocracking, but a continuing surplus of natural s has made this technology more attractive d Syncrude Canada Ltd has proposed a capac-addition program incorporating it.

To make the primary distillates into synthetic de, a process called hydrotreating is used to nove additional sulphur, nitrogen and oxy-, and to enhance the hydrocarbon molecular characteristics. Hydrotreating involves costly ancillary processes such as hydrogen-manufacturing plants, sour-gas scrubbing facilities and sulphur-recovery units.

Total direct operating costs for the 2 existing commercial oil-sands plants (mining, extraction, upgrading, utilities and off-site facilities, subsidized housing, research and development, administration and corporate management) in 1982 were in the order of \$125/m^3 (\$20/barrel) of synthetic crude. With world oil prices considerably higher than that, the oil sands hold out the promise of Canadian self-sufficiency.

G.R. GRAY

Biyiasas, Peter, chess grandmaster (b at Athens, Greece 19 Nov 1950). He moved to Canada as a child, began to play seriously in Vancouver in the late 1960s, and won the BC championship 1968-71. He played as a reserve on the Canadian student team which won a bronze medal in the World Student Games at Mayaguez, Puerto Rico, in 1971. In 1972 he won the Canadian Closed Championship in Toronto and repeated as champion in 1975 in Calgary. He received the grandmaster title in 1978 for his results in 3 tournaments: Olympiad (Haifa) 1976, Lone Pine 1978 and New York 1978. He played on Canadian Olympiad teams in 1972, 1974, 1976 and 1978 before emigrating to the US.

LAWRENCE DAY

Bjarni Herjolfsson, merchant, trader (*fl* 986). Bjarni was likely the first European to sight the E coast of N America. In the summer of 986 he headed to Iceland and then Greenland to join his father. Driven off course by stormy weather he sighted land, which he described as wooded and hilly, and continued northward sighting mountainous land and mountains partly covered with snow. Realizing these lands did not fit the description of Greenland, he changed course and eventally reached his father's estate. Scholars generally agree that Bjarni sighted Newfoundland, Labrador and Baffin I, though some argue that he strayed as far S as Maine. A few years later LEIF ERICSSON bought Bjarni's ship and rediscovered the new lands, which he named Helluland, Markland and Vinland.

JOHN PARSONS

Black, Conrad Moffat, financier (b at Montréal 25 Aug 1944). The son of an affluent but unconventional Montréal businessman, Black received a BA from Carleton and a law degree from Laval. For his MA at McGill he wrote a biography of Maurice DUPLESSIS, later published as *Duplessis* (1977). In 1969 he and a few partners began buying small English-language newspapers, building the Sterling chain. In 1978, after the death of Bud MCDOUGALD, Black, through intricate corporate and financial maneuvres, achieved control of Argus Corp, a holding company controlling a large number of Canadian corporations. This takeover gave him national prominence and a leading position in the Canadian BUSINESS ELITE.

CHRISTOPHER G. CURTIS

Black, Davidson, anatomist, anthropologist (b at Toronto 25 July 1884; d at Peking, People's Republic of China 15 Mar 1934). Professor and head of the Department of Anatomy, and honorary co-director of the Cenozoic Research Laboratory of Peking Medical Union College, Black identified a new species of ancient human, *Sinanthropus pekinensis,* from fossils found at Chou Kou Tien (Zhoukoudian) near Peking. His research on "Peking Man" formed the basis for contemporary knowledge about human evolution. Internationally acclaimed for his work, he also published extensively on more recent prehistoric human groups in China and on modern anatomy and neuroanatomy. He was little recognized in Canada during his lifetime, but is now honoured by a commemorative plaque at U of T, his alma mater.

JEROME S. CYBULSKI

Black, Martha Louise, née Munger, naturalist (b at Chicago, Ill 24 Feb 1866; d 29 Oct 1957). Despite her ladylike veneer, she was remarkably tough. In 1898 she abandoned Chicago society to join the KLONDIKE GOLD RUSH. Fascinated by the North, she returned in 1901 to open a milling business and support her 3 sons by her first marriage. In 1904 she married George Black and instantly became a loyal Canadian Conservative. When Black was appointed commissioner of the Yukon (1912-16), Martha reigned as first lady. She followed Black to England during WWI; there she received an OBE for her aid to Yukon servicemen and became a fellow of the Royal Geographical Soc for her work with Yukon flora. When George Black was unable to defend his Commons seat in 1935, Martha ran instead. At 70, she campaigned the vast Yukon constituency — often on foot — to become the second woman ever elected to the Canadian Parliament. Martha Black had style and spirit; northerners appreciated these qualities and made her a legend.

MARGARET CARTER

Reading: M.L. Black, *My Ninety Years,* ed F. Whyard (1976) and *Yukon Flowers* (1936).

Black, Samuel, fur trader, explorer (b at Pitsligo, Scot 3 May 1780; d at Kamloops, New Caledonia [BC] 8 Feb 1841). He joined the XY CO, which was absorbed by the NORTH WEST CO in 1804. A fierce opponent of the HUDSON'S BAY CO, he was one of the few Nor'Westers rejected by it at the 1821 union of the companies. But in 1823 he was admitted as clerk and in 1824 became chief trader. That year he explored the Finlay R, leaving a journal of his findings. Stationed at Kamloops in 1830, he became chief factor over all Thompson R District posts in 1837. Never popular with the Indians, he was murdered by one after a dispute.

ERIC J. HOLMGREN

Black, William, Methodist clergyman (b at Huddersfield, Eng 10 Nov 1760; d at Halifax 8 Sept 1834). Black settled near Amherst, NS, with his family in 1775. In 1779 he became a Methodist and began preaching throughout present-day NS and NB, stressing the Methodist creed of the sinfulness of man and the need for regeneration through faith. By 1784 he had communicated with Methodist leaders in the US who sent missionaries to help him. In 1789 Black was appointed bishop and superintendent for the Maritimes and Newfoundland, a position he held until he retired in 1812. He is considered the founder of Methodism in the Maritimes. When he died, the church numbered some 6000.

DEAN JOBB

Reading: E.A. Betts, *Bishop Black and his Preachers* (1976).

Black Creek Pioneer Village, North York, Ont, depicts life as it was in rural Ontario before 1867. The nucleus comprises 5 buildings constructed on the site by Daniel Stong, including a 3-room cabin built 1816. The other buildings were moved to the site, including a school, gristmill, church, inn, blacksmith shop and others. The Dalziel Barn Museum, a huge cantilever barn, contains the largest collection of 19th-century toys in Canada.

JAMES MARSH

Black Fly, small INSECT belonging to order Diptera, family Simuliidae. Black flies are small, 1-5 mm long. Not all species are black; some are yellowish orange or brownish grey. More than 1250 species are known worldwide; at least 110 in Canada. Black flies occur nearly anywhere that rivers and streams are present for juvenile stages, including arctic regions, and are especially abundant in northern, wooded regions. Juveniles (larvae) live in flowing water, gathering food by straining the water with their head fans. Females have biting mouthparts with toothed stylets for cutting skin. Males do not bite and are rarely observed. Both sexes require nectar for flight energy; females use blood for egg development. Eggs (150-600 per female) may be laid on substrates in water or dropped as females fly over water. Larvae attach to rocks or vegetation and complete development in 3-14 days, depending on water temperatures. Pupae are inactive and do not feed. Adults may emerge from any water depth, floating upward in a bubble of air generated during emergence. They are ready to fly when they break the surface. Average life span is about 3 weeks. In Central America, tropical S America and Africa, black flies frequently transmit NEMATODES causing river blindness (onchocerciasis) in humans. In Canada, black flies cause human suffering and are a scourge to livestock. In the Athabasca R region of northern Alberta, weight loss in cattle caused by black fly attacks in one outbreak (1971) amounted to 45 kg per animal; 973 animals were killed in one area alone by *Simulium arcticum*, a species whose saliva contains a toxin causing anaphylactic shock and death in cattle. In Saskatchewan, 1100 cattle were killed by this black fly during the outbreak years of 1944-47. Black flies also prevent many human activities in northern Canada during the summer and, together with MOSQUITOES, present a barrier to northern development. For example, forest workers in northern BC and Québec demand black fly control as part of their work contract. R.A. BRUST

Reading: M. Laird, *Black Flies* (1981).

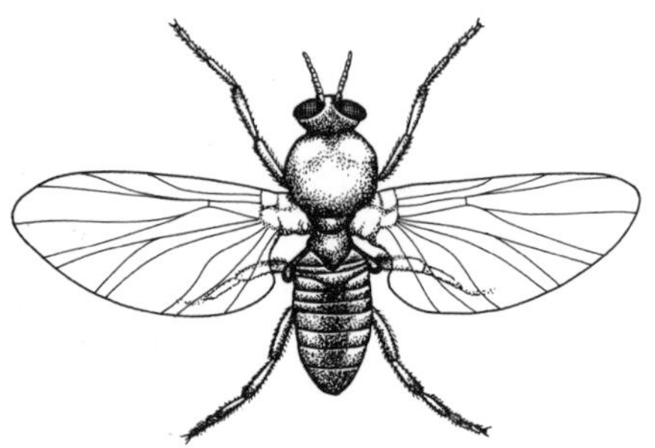

Black fly (*Simulium* sp) (*artwork by S. Stacey*).

Black Hole The notion of black holes originated with the English physicist John Michell and later with the French mathematician Pierre Simon de Laplace, who realized that if light was composed of particles, a sufficiently compact gravitating astronomical body could have such a high surface gravity that light particles (photons) could not escape from its surface, resulting in a black star. Einstein showed that no material particle could travel faster than the speed of light; therefore, neither light nor matter could escape from Laplace's black star (hence the modern name, black hole). Einstein's General Theory of Relativity is used to study black holes, since the older Newtonian theory of gravity does not provide an adequate basis for discussing the curved space-time near them. The black hole consists of a spherical surface, called the event horizon, which separates the part of space accessible to an outside observer from the inside of the black hole from which nothing can escape. The radius of this sphere, called the Schwardschild radius in honour of the German astrophysicist who derived the first black-hole solution to Einstein's equations in 1916, is proportional to the mass of the object that collapsed to form the black hole. For an object with mass equal to that of the sun, this radius is about 3 km.

Werner Israel of University of Alberta conjectured in 1967 that, once formed, a black hole can be described by a very small set of parameters, which have been shown to be total mass, and the charge and angular momentum of any matter that went into it. Kayll Lake of Queen's University and Robert Roeder of University of Toronto have shown that a compact object falling into its own black hole appears as a ring that dims very rapidly.

The existence of black holes outside the realm of theory has not yet been demonstrated. It has been assumed that a sufficiently massive star will not be able to resist its own self-gravitation forever and must eventually become a black hole. Most discoverers of black holes have based their claims on this assumption, including University of Toronto's Thomas Bolton who postulates a black hole in Cygnus x-1. Bolton's is the best candidate so far. Sun Kwok of the Herzberg Institute of Astrophysics, NATIONAL RESEARCH COUNCIL OF CANADA, has shown that, by large-scale mass loss, many massive stars may be able to avoid collapse to a black hole.

In 1974 Stephen Hawking of Cambridge University, UK, demonstrated theoretically that a black hole radiates at a temperature inversely proportional to its mass. For a solar-mass black hole the temperature of radiation is about 10^{-7} Kelvin, much below observable limits, but for a mass the size of a large mountain, the temperature is about 10^{11} K. This theory results in the consideration of such mini black holes as sources for highly energetic cosmic radiation. Primordial black holes, much less massive than these, would probably have had time to evaporate since the beginning of the universe. The size of a primordial black hole is such that the theories of gravitation and of quantum mechanics must both be used in its description, and it is hoped that this work may provide the long-sought link required to unify these theories. *See* PHYSICS. CHARLES C. DYER

Reading: Iain Nicolson, *Gravity, Black Holes and the Universe* (1981).

Blackberry, *see* BERRIES, WILD.

Blackbird, common name for several species of BIRDS of the New World subfamily Icterinae (which also includes MEADOWLARKS, ORIOLES, cowbirds and grackles). Blackbirds are medium-sized songbirds, about 20 cm long, with sharply pointed beaks. While black predominates, bright reds and yellows are conspicuous on several species. The red-winged blackbird (*Agelaius phoeniceus*), the most common blackbird in Canada, may be the most abundant bird in N America. Other blackbirds in Canada include yellow-headed, Brewer's and rusty blackbirds (*Xanthocephalus xanthocephalus, Euphagus cyanocephalus, E. carolinus*, respectively). Blackbirds display diverse breeding systems. Red-winged and yellow-headed blackbirds nest in colonies in marsh vegetation or in more widely spaced nests in upland habitats. One male often has a harem of 3-8 females nesting in his territory. The female incubates the 3-5 eggs and feeds the nestlings. Males help feed the young after they leave the nest. Rusty blackbirds are monogamous, solitary nesters in marsh edge or evergreen habitat; Brewer's range from solitary pairs to a few monogamous pairs nesting in a loose colony. In red-winged and yellow-headed blackbirds, males and females differ in form, the brigh ly coloured male being conspicuously larg than the more neutrally coloured female. Re winged blackbird populations have expande in recent decades. In early spring and la summer, tens of thousands of birds may roo together. During the day, they feed in flocks i nearby grain fields, causing economic losse However, they also eat deleterious insects, wee seeds and waste grain, thereby compensatin for damage caused. Grackles and cowbirds a sometimes referred to as blackbirds. The com mon grackle (*Quiscalus quiscula*), a black bi with iridescent green-blue head, and the brow headed cowbird (*Molothrus ater*), the male blac with a brown head and the female grey, a often found in flocks with red-winged blac birds and STARLINGS. Cowbirds are brood par sites, depositing their eggs in nests of oth species and relying on the host to raise th nestlings. R.J. ROBERTSC

Red-winged blackbird (*Agelaius phoeniceus*) on speckled alder (*artwork by Claire Tremblay*).

Blackfoot prehistoric buffalo effigy (*courtesy Glenbow A chives*).

Blackfoot, the smallest of the 3 tribes th make up the BLACKFOOT NATION. In their own la guage, they are called *siksikaw*, meaning "blac foot" or "black feet." They are of Algonquian li guistic stock and speak the same language the BLOOD and PEIGAN, with only slight dialect variations.

Occupying hunting grounds on the Battle and Red Deer R, the Blackfoot were the mo northerly of the 3 tribes making up the natio As a result, they were the first to be met by f traders, and it is likely that this caused the tribal name to be applied to the whole natio Although they ranged as far S as the Missouri they were considered to be British Indians ar were not usually involved in American tradir or treaties. Their population during the nomad period varied between 2000 and 3000 and w officially registered as 2249 in 1879.

During the nomadic period, the Blackfo were buffalo hunters and warriors, their ma enemies being the CREE and ASSINIBOINE. The leading chief in the late 1700s was The Swa who was succeeded by Gros Blanc. By the mi 19th century, Old Swan, Old Sun and Three Su were the head chiefs, and they in turn were r placed by Old Sun, Junior and CROWFOOT. Cro foot was destined to become the great lead of the tribe, taking them successfully from nomadic life to existence on an INDIAN RESERVE

In 1877 the Blackfoot signed Treaty No 7 ar took a reserve at Blackfoot Crossing, E of Ca gary. There they settled down to become farme and ranchers, with some finding employme in their own coal mine. In 1912 and 1918 t Blackfoot gained a unique status when they so about half their reserve for approximately $1 million, making them the richest tribe in we ern Canada. They obtained new houses, regul interest payments and other services. Howeve the advantages were only temporary, for by t end of WWII their funds were expended a they had little to show for their wealth except smaller reserve and some aging houses. The population in 1980 was about 3000. *See al*

NATIVE PEOPLES, PLAINS and general articles under NATIVE PEOPLE. HUGH A. DEMPSEY

Reading: Hugh A. Dempsey, *Crowfoot, Chief of the Blackfoot* (1972) and *Indian Tribes of Alberta* (1979).

Blackfoot Nation is made up of 3 tribes, the BLOOD, PEIGAN and BLACKFOOT. In addition, both the SARCEE and the Gros Ventre were allied to them in the nomadic period, forming the Blackfoot Confederacy. The term Blackfoot is accepted in Canada, and Blackfeet is common in the US. The Blackfoot nation called itself *soyi-tapix*, meaning "prairie people."

The territory of the Blackfoot Nation from the mid-1700s to the settlement period was roughly from the Battle R in the N to the upper Missouri R, and from the foothills to roughly the Alberta-Saskatchewan border. Thus, the Blackfoot hunting area included the rich buffalo ranges of southern Alberta and northern Montana. Their population varied over this period, ranging as high as 11 200 in 1823 and as low as 6350 after the 1837 smallpox epidemic. By the 1980s, their population had risen to more than 18 000, almost equally divided between INDIAN RESERVES in Alberta and Montana. Linguistically the Blackfoot are Algonquian and are thus related distantly to the CREE and Gros Ventre. However, their language is distinctive, with only slight variations in dialect among the 3 tribes. The Blackfoot claim a long plains occupancy, a tradition confirmed by archaeological research. Their culture is based entirely upon a buffalo economy.

The Blackfoot felt the influence of the white man before the first explorers met them in the mid-1700s. The HORSE, which had been brought to the New World by the Spanish, reached them from the S about 1725, at the same time as they received the gun from Cree middlemen. Throughout most of the 18th and 19th centuries, the equestrian Blackfoot dominated their hunting area and were constantly at war with the Cree, ASSINIBOINE, Crow, DAKOTA, Nez Percé, Shoshoni and other enemy tribes. They frequented the HUDSON'S BAY CO and NORTH WEST CO posts on the N Saskatchewan R, but carried on an incessant war with American trappers and free traders in the S until peace was made in 1831. From that time on, the Blackfoot divided their trade between the British and Americans. In 1855 the Blackfoot signed a treaty with the Americans, and in 1877 Treaty No 7 was signed with the Canadian government. Most of the Peigan settled on a reservation in Montana, and the Blackfoot, Blood and N Peigan tribes each took a reserve in southern Alberta.

Because of the size of their reserves, the Blackfoot tribes were able to retain much of their culture and language, although both have rapidly diminished in the post-WWII era. The reserves rely upon ranching and farming as their main industries, with small factories and plants being operated from time to time. *See also* NATIVE PEOPLES, PLAINS and general articles under NATIVE PEOPLE. HUGH A. DEMPSEY

Reading: Hugh A. Dempsey, *Indian Tribes of Alberta* (1979); J.C. Ewers, *The Blackfoot, Raiders of the Northwestern Plains* (1958).

Blacks have lived in Canada since the beginnings of transatlantic settlement. Africa is the ancestral homeland of all Canada's black population, but very few arrived in Canada from there. The earliest arrivals were slaves brought from New England or the West Indies. Between 1763 and 1865 most blacks migrating to Canada were fleeing slavery in the US. Until the 1960s the majority of blacks had emigrated from the US. Today they constitute about 2% of the Canadian population.

Migration Olivier Le Jeune is the first black to have been transported directly from Africa to Canada. He was sold in 1629 in Canada as a slave, but apparently died a free man. From then until the British Conquest (1759-60) approximately 1000 blacks brought from New England or the West Indies were enslaved in New France. Local records indicate that by 1759 there were 3604 slaves in New France, 1132 of whom were blacks. Most of the slaves lived in or near Montréal. SLAVERY, which prospered in economies dependent upon one-crop, mass production and gang labour, did not develop strongly among these colonists, but under British rule it was given new life. The English civil and criminal law which was introduced into Québec in 1763 (and which remained in force until the 1774 Quebec Act restored French civil law) contained no strictures against slavery.

The Negro Volunteer Military Company, formed around 1860-62 in Victoria, BC, under encouragement of the HBC, and disbanded 1863-64 (*courtesy Public Archives of Canada / C-22626*).

The LOYALISTS brought about 2000 black slaves with them into British N America, but 3500 free blacks, who had won their freedom through allegiance to Britain, emigrated at the same time, settling in Nova Scotia and New Brunswick. Within 2 decades, slavery had virtually disappeared among the Loyalists.

In 1793 Upper Canada became the only colony to legislate for the abolition (though gradual) of slavery. With no prospect of new imports, slavery declined steadily. By 1800 courts in other parts of British N America had effectively limited the expansion of slavery, except in New Brunswick, PEI and Cape Breton (which was a separate colony until 1820). As late as 1816 in New Brunswick, an advertisement for a runaway slave appeared in the *Royal Gazette*. On 28 Aug 1833 the British Parliament passed a law abolishing slavery in all British N American colonies.

Black migration to British N America included, in 1796, a band of Jamaican Maroons, descendants of black slaves who had escaped from the Spanish before the British conquest of Jamaica and who were feared and respected for their courage and cruelty. Then, between 1813 and 1816, 2000 slaves who had sought refuge behind British lines during the War of 1812 were taken to Nova Scotia. The largest number of American blacks arrived in Canada via a system known as the UNDERGROUND RAILROAD, a loose network of abolitionists, probably predominantly Quaker, who through communications with each other made known various places where fugitive slaves might seek refuge on their journey northward. In many areas in the northern US the Railroad did not work clandestinely and was well known to newspapers and law officers. By the time of the American Civil War it is estimated that around 30 000 slaves had found their way to Canada.

With the end of American slavery in 1865, many thousands of Canadian blacks returned to the US, although in response to American legal inequalities small groups of black Americans continued to move into Canada. From Oklahoma about 1000 blacks moved into Alberta 1909-11. The black population in Canada did not increase substantially, however, until the 1960s, when changes in the Immigration Act removed a bias against nonwhite immigrants and permitted large numbers of qualified WEST INDIANS and AFRICANS to enter Canada. This major influx of black people has greatly outnumbered the original black population in every Canadian region except the Maritimes (between 1960 and 1980 there were about 200 000 immigrants from the West Indies and over 90 000 from Africa — including persons of Asian and European descent).

Settlement Patterns Most of the Loyalist blacks, Maroons and refugee blacks in the Maritimes were located, by government policy, in segregated communities on the outskirts of larger white towns. Many of the slaves of Loyalists were taken to the Eastern Townships of Québec. Halifax, Shelburne, Digby and Guysborough in Nova Scotia and Saint John and Fredericton in New Brunswick had all-black settlements in their immediate neighbourhoods. In Ontario the Underground Railroad fugitives also tended to concentrate in settlements, less as a consequence of government policy than for the sake of mutual support and protection against white Canadian PREJUDICE AND DISCRIMINATION and American kidnappers. Most of Ontario's black settlements were in and around Windsor, Chatham, London, St Catharines and Hamilton. Toronto had a black district, and there were smaller concentrations near Barrie, Owen Sound and Guelph. Migrants to Alberta early in the 20th century established several rural settlements around Edmonton. Until recently, most of Canada's black population was relatively isolated not only from whites but from other black communities. The pattern began to break down in the 1930s and 1940s as rural blacks migrated to the cities in search of jobs. Many of the original black settlements were abandoned or considerably depopulated. The new black migration from the West Indies and Africa has been overwhelmingly directed towards the cities. Blacks are now among the most urbanized of all Canada's ethnic groups. White Canadian attitudes have been changing in the generation since World War II, and although urban blacks still face discrimination the pressures for segregation no longer apply.

Economic Life The Loyalist blacks, the Maroons and the refugees met with various obstacles in trying to establish themselves in the Maritimes. The first group knew relatively little about farming the thin soils of the Maritimes. Unless they had served actively in the Black Pioneers (a corps of free blacks) for the British, they received substantially smaller allotments of farmland than the white settlers. They were almost always segregated. Forced to seek occasional labouring jobs in neighbouring whites' towns, the blacks were vulnerable to exploitation and discrimination in employment and wages. Black settlement did not prosper in Nova Scotia; outside Shelburne County there were misunderstandings over the nature and size of promised land grants. In New Brunswick blacks received lower wages than whites. Generally the blacks throughout the Maritimes lived in poverty and near peonage.

Partly as a result of poor conditions in their new country substantial numbers of blacks in 1791-92 and again in 1800 left Nova Scotia for Sierra Leone in the "back to Africa" movement. In both instances between 33% and 50% of the blacks involved had actually been born in Africa and in both instances white men organized and financed the ventures in response to the desire by blacks to live elsewhere than Nova Scotia. In 1792 almost 1000 blacks gathered in Halifax for the journey. Although many died during and immediately after the voyage, the colony survived as an identifiable group into the 20th century. The second group (about 550 persons) were Maroons and did not leave voluntarily. At least 26 died during the voyage. On arriving they helped quell an insurrection led by the Nova Scotian emigrants who had preceded them.

Of the REFUGEE blacks, described by one historian as "the jetsam of the War of 1812," some 95 sailed from Halifax in 1820 for Trinidad. Of those that remained, the vast majority lacked the skills that could have helped them adapt to life in Nova Scotia. They had arrived at the worst of times — cheap white labour was abundant, the land they had been given was poor (they were, they said, tied to the land without being able to live upon it) and the early winters were extremely cold. They became wards of the state and victims of growing RACISM. The majority of present-day blacks in Nova Scotia are descendants of these refugees.

The fugitive blacks who had arrived in Ontario via the Underground Railroad typically arrived destitute, and without government land grants were usually forced to become labourers on the lands of others, although some farmed their own land successfully, and some worked for the Great Western Ry.

Many individual fugitives, particularly those who migrated to Victoria, BC, in the 1850s because of discrimination in California, brought skills or savings which enabled them to establish small businesses. Many also worked on farms or in shops on the new wharf at Esquimalt, BC. Until well into the 20th century, however, most Canadian blacks were employed in the lower-paying service categories or as unskilled labour. Many young blacks are now entering businesses, professions and trades, but in 1971 black Canadians as a group still received substantially lower wages than white Canadians. Recent West Indian and African immigrants have generally possessed a high level of skills, education and experience, and are found in every occupational category.

Community and Cultural Life In their concentrated settlements the early blacks had the opportunity to retain cultural characteristics and create a distinct community. Styles of worship, music and speech, family structures and group traditions developed in response to the conditions of life in Canada. The chief institutional support was the separate church, usually BAPTIST or Methodist (*see* METHODISM), created when white congregations refused to admit blacks as equal members. The churches' spiritual influence pervaded daily life and affected the vocabulary, routines and ambitions of their members. Inevitably, they assumed a major social and political role and the clergy became the natural community leaders. The many fraternal organizations, mutual-assistance bands, temperance societies and antislavery groups formed by 19th-century blacks were almost always associated with one of the churches. In the 20th century the churches led the movement for greater educational opportunity and for civil rights.

In slavery black women were forced to work to support themselves, and economic circumstances perpetuated this tradition in Canada. Black women have always played an important economic role in family life and have experienced considerable independence as a result. Raised in a communal fashion, frequently by grandparents or older neighbours, black children developed fraternal relationships throughout the local community. A strong sense of group identity and mutual reliance, combined with the unique identity provided by the churches, produced an intimate community life and a refuge against white discrimination.

A tradition of intense loyalty to Britain and Canada developed among blacks from the beginning of their settlement in Canada. The black Loyalists fought to maintain British rule in America, and their awareness that an American invasion could mean their re-enslavement prompted them to participate in Canada's military defence. Black militiamen fought against American troops in the War of 1812, were prominent in subduing the REBELLIONS OF 1837 and later helped to repel the FENIAN incursions. For a period in the 1860s the largely self-financed Black Pioneer Rifle Corps was the only armed force protecting Vancouver I, although it was later denied the opportunity to participate in the Vancouver Island Volunteer Rifle Corps. During WWI, blacks were initially rejected by recruitment offices, but persistent volunteering finally resulted in the creation of a separate black corps, though it went overseas as a construction battalion rather than a fighting force.

Urbanization and increasing secularization have changed the role of the church and the local community, and the new immigrants are bringing their own Caribbean and African heritages to Canada, though they too are adapting them to the conditions of Canadian life. There is no longer a single black Canadian tradition, but the historic values of a people who sought freedom in Canada continue to influence black institutions and attitudes today.

Education British charitable organizations sponsored schools in most of the Maritime black communities beginning in the 1780s and, during the 19th century, British and American societies established schools for blacks throughout Ontario. In addition the governments of both Nova Scotia and Ontario created legally segregated public schools. Although almost every black community had access to either a charity or a public school, funding was inadequate and education tended to be inferior. When combined with residential isolation and economic deprivation, poor schooling helped to perpetuate a situation of limited opportunity and restricted mobility. In 1965 the last segregated school in Ontario closed.

With urbanization black children were admitted into integrated city schools. Until recently the average black person had a lower educational level than whites, and this is still true in the Maritimes. The new migration is changing this situation dramatically. Blacks in every Canadian region except the Maritimes now have a higher standard of educational achievement than whites, and though they still tend to receive lower wages this may be a symptom of immigrant adjustment rather than overt prejudice.

Politics The law in Canada, with few major exceptions, has insisted on the legal equality of blacks. Until Confederation this meant English law, and black voters were inclined to support Conservative candidates committed to the preservation of British ties. Since Confederation blacks have been active in every political party and over the past 20 years have been elected as Conservatives, Liberals and New Democrats.

Though blacks have never formed a large enough group to wield direct political influence, several individual blacks have made significant contributions to political affairs. There have been black municipal councillors and school trustees for more than a century, most notably Mifflin Gibbs, who sat on the Victoria City Council in the 1860s and was a delegate to the Yale Convention deliberating BC's entry into Confederation, and William Hubbard, who served as councillor, controller and acting mayor of Toronto 1894-1907. Leonard Braithwaite was the first black in a provincial legislature when he was elected in Ontario in 1963, and Lincoln Alexander from Hamilton became the first black federal member in 1968. Emery Barnes and Rosemary Brown were both elected in the 1970s to the BC legislature.

Group Maintenance Historically the rural black community served to buffer the effects of discrimination and in its protective atmosphere a distinctive black identity evolved. The co-operative strength of community life enabled continual probings against racial limitations, but because the communities were localized and scattered their efforts were never successful in destroying the barriers entirely.

The diversified origin of today's black population makes a unified group identity less than apparent, yet whatever their background blacks face a typical set of problems. Opinion surveys and provincial human-rights commission reports reveal that racism survives and that blacks still face discrimination in employment, accommodation and public services. This creates the basis of a common experience and encourages a common response. Fostered by black newspapers and magazines, community centres and such organizations as the National Black Coalition of Canada, and enriched by greater numbers and cultural variety, a new and broader black community is being developed in the modern Canadian city. JAMES W. ST. G. WALKER

Reading: James W. St. G. Walker, *The Black Loyalists* (1976) and *A History of Blacks in Canada* (1980); Daniel G. Hill, *The Freedom Seekers, Blacks in Early Canada* (1981); Norman Sheffe, ed, *Many Cultures, Many Heritages* (1975); Robin W. Winks, *The Blacks in Canada: A History* (1971).

Blacksmithing, French Canada Until the mid-18th century, few ironsmiths practised their trade full-time. Those who repaired arms and tools in the forts and trading posts also engaged in the FUR TRADE. During the same period other metalworkers became established in the towns and countryside. These craftsmen included locksmiths, gunsmiths, nailsmiths, cutlers, edge-tool makers and farriers, who shod draught horses and oxen, polished runners, put metal rims on wheels and repaired various objects. All these workers practised a TECHNOLOGY that came from the great French craft tradition; their highly skilled art derived from trade guild knowledge, instruction and scientific treatises. APPRENTICESHIP, usually lasting 3 years, was rigorous and entry to the trade was virtually re-

ıe smithy's shop, such as this one in Vermilion, Alta, ı 1910, was the unofficial social centre at which to tch up on world events — and local gossip (*courtesy 'enbow Archives*).

ricted to the sons of ironsmiths, the descen-ants of other tradesmen, orphans under reli-ious guardianship and the sons of protected ABITANTS.

Metalworkers were important in society and t up business mainly in the major centres, ustering in the same parts of the town. At e end of the 17th century, they incorporated rming and animal husbandry into their trade. round the mid-18th century, about one-quar-r of these artisans changed occupations to ecome carpenters, masons, merchants or con-actors.

The various craftsmen produced work of high esthetic and technical quality: their products ere as remarkable for their symmetry and pro-ortional motifs as for their complex mortice-nd-tenon joints, reinforced by dowels and anges. Their work drew its inspiration from ligious symbols or copies of well-known mo-fs. Their customers were mainly religious com-unities, factories, administrators, merchants nd wealthy families. In the early 19th century, ost of the iron trades in rural areas tended to e performed by separate craftsmen. Around 850 the blacksmith's shop became the new ality: here a single craftsman performed all e varied forms of ironwork that could no nger support those who practised the individ-al crafts. Although the blacksmith made ob-cts that were less refined than those of his pre-ecessors, he built a unique technology based n knowledge derived from the various iron ades and from skilled habitants, blacksmiths om Ireland, Scotland and England, and arti-ns who had worked with metal in small merican industries (eg, quarries, brickworks).

The smith's basic means of working the etals were physical and chemical: air from the ellows, fire from the forge, water for temper-g and tools operated by hand. Transformation rocesses were heating, hammering and tem-ering (mainly with water). Besides shoeing orses and sometimes trading in them as well, e blacksmith made and repaired all the tools eeded for agriculture, cattle rearing, fishing, restry, heating and transportation. He also shioned objects with decorative motifs (eg, eur-de-lys, rattail, leaf, heart, cross, sun, oster). Blacksmiths also practised VETERINARY EDICINE and, in some areas, doctored humans s well. In rural Québec in the 19th and early 0th centuries, blacksmiths practised a magico-religious medicine based on vaguely scientific notions, combined with folk beliefs and superstitions.

The village smithy was always brimming with activity. It was a meeting place where men held their stag parties, learned to drink, played power and parlour games and discussed politics. The blacksmith indulged in certain popular practices: he was called to re-establish order in the village; he struck the new fire of Holy Saturday in his forge and carried it into the church; he headed the labour group and maintained the fire used in flax crushing; his horses drew the hearse. The blacksmith himself, the theme of tales, legends and songs, held a privileged place in folklore. The end of the 19th century and the first half of the 20th century saw the development of the country blacksmith's role. At that time, there was an average of one blacksmith for every 100 families, 3-5 blacksmiths per village. The blacksmith enabled the community to save money. Inhabitants paid a fixed price for the year and could have their horses shod as often as they wished. Clients used a barter system and paid in kind with farm or forest products. Sometimes the blacksmith lent money at interest; sometimes he resold grains, vegetables, meats and other produce that he received in payment.

When the colony of New France was established, there was a movement to set up associations similar to those found in France; however, the best that could be done was to form societies of artisans that were more symbolic than corporate in nature. These associations had no control over the quality and conditions of work. The masterpiece required for entry to the trade was never a tradition in Québec; in the early days of the colony, the only requirement was an agreement between the master and his apprentice, drafted by a notary. In the 19th and 20th centuries, the terms of engagement were less and less official. By the turn of the century, toolmaking machines had already been in use for a long time and complex implements were produced industrially. Gradually, horses were replaced by traction engines for most draught purposes. Blacksmiths became garage mechanics or wandering smiths, shoeing horses at forest work sites or setting up in an area where race or riding horses were found. In the traditional shop, machine tools had been adopted by the mid-19th century to accelerate production and organize human energy; however, except for a general decline in knowledge of the trade and some diversity in manual tools, the physical nature of the blacksmithing trade changed little up to its final disappearance in the 1950s. The country blacksmith has left behind him the memory of a strongly individualistic, boasting, swearing, noisy man who associated mostly with other men and worked with percussion tools. The urban smith, working first in a shop and then in industry as a worker, belongs to an era characterized by scientific knowledge. If he persisted in his trade, the city smith had to adapt to the evolving industrial process of working with cast IRON AND STEEL. *See* AGRICULTURAL IMPLEMENTS; FIREARMS; TOOLS, CARPENTRY. J.C. DUPONT

Blackwood, David Lloyd, printmaker, painter (b at Wesleyville, Nfld 7 Nov 1941). Although Blackwood lives in Port Hope, Ont, his attachment in his subject matter is to his Newfoundland past, and particularly to Wesleyville, on Bonavista Bay. Around this setting, he has created an almost epic story celebrating the community's 63 skippers and 12 captains. Blackwood sees himself as part of Newfoundland tradition, as a balladeer who tells a story in visual images. Blackwood studied PRINTMAKING, and today he is considered one of Canada's important etchers. Since graduating in 1963 from Toronto's Ontario College of Art, he has taught drawing and painting at Trinity College School in Port Hope. From 1969 to 1975 he was artist in residence at U of T. JOAN MURRAY

Bladen, Vincent Wheeler, economist (b at Stoke-on-Trent, Eng 14 Aug 1900; d at Toronto 26 Nov 1981). Bladen came from Balliol to U of T in 1921. Teacher, scholar, department head and dean, he was also an adviser to government, and his policy papers were responsible indirectly for the Canadian-American Autopact (1965). His writings treated the auto industry, university financing, Canadian economic affairs, industrial organization and "the literature of political economy," the topic for which generations of undergraduates remember him. As chairman of political economy and then dean of arts, he presided over U of T's expansion in the 1950s and 1960s, taking a special interest in area studies and graduate work, where he favoured Canadian self-reliance. A man of immense energy, he founded the *Canadian Journal of Economics and Political Science,* and found time to interest himself in cooking, horsemanship and the NATIONAL BALLET OF CANADA. IAN DRUMMOND

Blair, Andrew George, lawyer, politician, premier of NB (b at Fredericton, NB 7 Mar 1844; d there 25 Jan 1907). First elected MLA for York in 1878, he became leader of the Opposition in 1879, premier and attorney general in 1883, and molded his coalition into the NB Liberal Party. He formalized election campaigning and party platforms. In 1892 he suffered personal defeat in York over religious education but was reelected for Queens. He resigned in 1896 to serve as minister of railways and canals in the LAURIER Cabinet, and sat as MP for Queens-Sunbury 1896 and Saint John City 1900. Opposed to Laurier's plan to build the Grand Trunk Pacific Ry, he resigned in 1903; in 1904 he was associated with a political conspiracy to defeat Laurier. DELLA M.M. STANLEY

Blair, Sidney Robert, Bob, industrialist (b in Trinidad 13 Aug 1929). He rose to national prominence in 1977 when his Alaska Highway pipeline proposal defeated a powerful consortium of large oil and gas companies sponsoring a MACKENZIE VALLEY PIPELINE. A champion of Canadian-owned and western-based industries, Blair traces his nationalistic roots to schooling in the US and 10 years with the Canadian subsidiary of an American gas company. Under his aggressive leadership, NOVA (formerly Alberta Gas Trunk Line) grew rapidly in the 1970s by diversifying into gas marketing, petrochemicals, manufacturing and resource development, and now ranks as one of Canada's largest corporations. FRANÇOIS BREGHA

Blais, Marie-Claire, author (b at Québec C 5 Oct 1939). One of Québec's finest contemporary writers, Blais grew up in the Québec C working-class district of Limoilou. Educated by Roman Catholic nuns, she became increasingly disillusioned with school as she became absorbed in her early literary endeavours. She decided to quit her academic program and take a year's commercial training. She then worked at a variety of jobs for 3 years before moving in 1958 to the Quartier Latin near U Laval, where she attended lectures on French literature and was befriended by professors Jeanne Lapointe and Father Georges-Henri LÉVESQUE. Her first novel, *La Belle Bête,* published in 1959, was highly acclaimed as well as being criticized for its lack of conventional morality. It was published in France in 1960 and was translated into English (*Mad Shadows*), Spanish and Italian. A second novel, *Tête blanche* (1960) soon followed (English tr 1961). The young novelist then spent a few moody months in Paris and wrote a poetical novel *The Day is Dark*. Back in Montréal Blais met American critic Edmund Wilson and was awarded 2 Guggenheim fellowships that enabled her to live in New England with friends, painter Mary Meigs and journalist Barbara Deming. Perhaps her best novel, UNE SAISON DANS LA VIE D'EMMANUEL (1965) was awarded the Prix France-Canada and the prestigious Prix Médicis, and brought her a much wider international audience with translations into 13 languages. Over 2000 books, theses, articles, reviews and interviews have been written on it, and the critical contradictions they express are a tribute to the novel's rich intricacy. Blais moved to Brittany with Meigs in 1972 and, after some years in Europe, settled in Montréal where she continues to write at a steady pace. She has published some 25 books, critical editions, translations, plays and radio and TV scripts. Her honours include 2 Gov Gen's Awards (*Les Manuscripts de Pauline Archange,* 1968, *Le Sourd dans la ville,* 1979) and Québec's Prix David in 1982. She is a companion of the Order of Canada. In her novels, drama or poetry, Blais writes about mankind's success or failure, in reality or through fantasy, in redeeming human suffering in a material, moral or spiritual way.

VINCENT NADEAU

Blaise, Clark, novelist, short-story writer (b at Fargo, N Dak 10 Apr 1940). A graduate of Denison U (1961) and U of Iowa (1964), he moved to Montréal and, acquiring Canadian citizenship in 1966, taught at Sir George Williams U (now Concordia) and then at York U, Toronto. In 1984 he taught at Skidmore Coll, NY. Blaise's fiction sympathetically explores various conditions of alienation, isolation and displacement. His characters typically find themselves (as he often has) at odds in a foreign culture and place; their keen sense of wonderment at the sharply observed details of their immediate environment — oppressively eccentric or pedestrian, exotic or banal — emphasizes their private disorientation. His first book of stories, *A North American Education* (1973) was followed by *Tribal Justice* in 1974. *Days and Nights in Calcutta,* a fascinating joint autobiographical account of Blaise's year in India written with his wife, novelist Bharati Mukherjee, appeared in 1977. He has also written the novels *Lunar Attractions* (1979) and *Lusts* (1983).

NEIL BESNER

Blake, Edward, lawyer, politician, premier of Ontario (b in Adelaide Twp, Upper Canada 13 Oct 1833; d at Toronto 1 Mar 1912), son of William Hume BLAKE. Edward was an unhealthy child and received, according to his mother, "a desultory sort of education for some years — and in the morning while dressing [his father] gave him his Latin lesson." A tutor and his mother taught him other subjects. Blake then

Edward Blake, second premier of Ontario. He became leader of the federal Liberal Party in 1880 but lost the elections of 1882 and 1887. He resigned the leadership 1887 — the only Liberal leader who never became prime minister (*courtesy Public Archives of Canada / PA-27030*).

attended Upper Canada College and U of T, receiving a BA in 1854 and an MA in 1858. He studied law simultaneously and was admitted to the bar in 1856, becoming a successful and wealthy equity lawyer in Toronto. In 1858 he married Margaret Cronyn, daughter of the first Anglican bishop of Huron.

Blake entered politics in 1867 as a Liberal. He held South Bruce provincially 1867-72 and sat in the federal House of Commons 1867-91. In 1868 he became leader of the Ontario Liberal Party, and in 1871 ousted Premier John Sandfield MACDONALD to become the second premier of Ontario. He left provincial politics in 1872, but during his brief tenure as premier established the Liberal dynasty that ruled Ontario from 1871 to 1905. In 1873 Blake refused the leadership of the federal Liberal Party, but agreed to join Canada's first Liberal government under Alexander MACKENZIE. Minister without portfolio (1873-74), minister of justice (1875-77) and president of the Privy Council (1877-78), he succeeded Mackenzie as party leader in 1880 but lost the elections of 1882 and 1887, resigning the leadership in 1887 and leaving Canadian politics in 1891. In 1892 he entered the British House of Commons as an Irish Nationalist MP. Blake retired to Canada in 1906 and for many years served U of T as senator or chancellor.

The only Liberal leader who never became prime minister, Blake never attained the prominence his abilities warranted. He did, however, leave his mark, encouraging the CANADA FIRST movement and English Canadian nationalism, and recruiting Oliver MOWAT (his successor as premier of Ontario) and Wilfrid LAURIER (his successor as federal leader), 2 of Canada's most effective and electorally successful politicians.

DONALD SWAINSON

Reading: M.A. Banks, *Edward Blake* (1957); F.H. Underhill, "Edward Blake," in C.T. Bissell, ed, *Our Living Tradition* (1957); Joseph Schull, *Edward Blake* (2 vols, 1975-76).

Blake, Hector, "Toe," hockey player and coach (b at Victoria Mines, NS 21 Aug 1912). He joined MONTREAL CANADIENS in 1936 and won the HART TROPHY (most valuable player) and scoring championship 1938-39. Later he played left wing on the effective "Punch Line," with Maurice RICHARD and Elmer Lach. He broke an ankle in 1948 and retired. He was a tenacious, pr ductive player, with 235 regular season goa and 62 points in 57 playoff games. Part Frenc Canadian, he coached in Valleyfield, Qué, b fore taking over the Canadiens in 1955. He i herited perhaps the most talented team in hi tory, but he encouraged them to work as a tear and achieved unprecedented results. In his seasons, Montréal finished first 9 times an won the STANLEY CUP 8 times, including straight 1956-60. He was an emotional coac often abrasive and boisterous, and coachir strained him. He retired in 1968 and was a pointed a VP of the team.

JAMES MAR

Blake, William Hume, lawyer, politicia judge (b at Kiltegan, Ire 10 Mar 1809; d at T ronto 15 Nov 1870), father of Edward BLAK Though now largely forgotten, Blake, a leadir lawyer of his time and a pioneer in LEGAL ED CATION at King's Coll, Toronto, initiated signif cant reforms in the Upper Canadian judici system. Of a devout Anglo-Irish gentry famil Blake attended Trinity Coll, Dublin, and in migrated to Canada in 1832 with family ar friends. After a brief attempt at farming, Blal and his accomplished wife, Catherine Hum settled in Toronto, where he began legal studie The spirited and ambitious Blake rose quickly professional, political and provincial life. 1848 he was elected to the Legislative Assembl and as solicitor general West in the tumultuo second government of Robert BALDWIN and L.I LA FONTAINE, piloted long overdue legislation reorganize the senior provincial courts. Blal ably served as first chancellor of the reform Court of Chancery 1849-62, when poor heal forced his retirement. He returned briefly public life in 1864.

JOHN D. BLACKWE

Blakeney, Allan Emrys, lawyer, civil servan politician, premier of Saskatchewan (b Bridgewater, NS 7 Sept 1925). Blakeney came politics as an experienced civil servant with strong commitment to state-led economic d velopment and extensive social-welfare pr grams. He was born and raised in conservativ NS and spent 2 decades in the politically inn vative environment of Saskatchewan before b coming premier. Recruited by T.C. DOUGLAS 1950, the Rhodes scholar became one of the CC government's most valuable civil servants, fir as a legal adviser to the province's embattle crown corporations, then as a senior official the Treasury Dept. He spent 2 years in priva law practice and after his first election victory 1960 rose to the position of a senior minister i the education, finance and health portfolios the Douglas and W.S. LLOYD Cabinets. Blakene was a key figure in the Opposition 1964-70, an was elected NEW DEMOCRATIC PARTY leader i 1970. He led his party to a decisive victory ov Ross THATCHER's Liberals in 1971, and to r election in 1975 and 1978. In 1982 the NDP lo badly to the successfully rebuilt Conservativ Party.

Blakeney's major achievements were the e tablishment of a long-term, state-led econom development strategy, the creation of a natior ally admired provincial administration and th forceful articulation of western interests in suc national matters as regional economic deve opment and constitutional change. Blakene came to be recognized as one of the most capab and intelligent advocates of a more decer tralized yet equitable federal system in Canad and as the political architect of a stronger an more diversified Saskatchewan economy.

DAVID LAYCOC

Blanchard, Hiram, lawyer, politician, premi of NS (b at West River, NS 17 Jan 1820; d Halifax 17 Dec 1874). Blanchard began his leg career at Port Hood, moving to Halifax on after election as Reform (Liberal) member f

Inverness County in 1859. His support of CONFEDERATION resulted in his appointment as attorney general and government leader (succeeding Sir Charles TUPPER) in the new Cabinet of July 1867. The Reform Party was defeated in the Sept general elections, however, and Blanchard served as Opposition leader 1871-74.

LOIS KERNAGHAN

Blanchet, François, doctor, politician (b at St-Pierre-de-la-Rivière-du-Sud, Qué 3 Apr 1776; d at Québec City 24 June 1830). Blanchet studied in Québec and New York. He practised medicine in Québec and held a variety of posts: superintendent of hospitals for the Lower Canada militia, doctor at the Hôpital des Émigrés, health officer for the port of Québec, and member of the office of medical examiners. He was involved in various public health projects and medical education projects. He helped set up the first medical society in Québec and the first medical journal in Canada. He also was active in politics and was a spokesman for the PARTI CANADIEN in the House of Assembly where he represented Hertford 1809-16 and from 1818 to his death. He fought, among other causes, for the democratization of administrative structures in the colony and the development of education. With P.S. BÉDARD, he was among the Parti canadien supporters imprisoned by Gov CRAIG in 1810.

JACQUES BERNIER

Bland, John, architect, town planner, author, educator (b at Lachine, Qué 13 Nov 1911). He graduated as an architect from McGill in 1933, and then studied town planning in London, Eng. In 1941 he became director of McGill's School of Architecture, a position he held until 1972. He reorganized the school to accord with contemporary design-teaching principles and expanded it to accommodate postwar students. Many of his students have become known internationally as architects, educators and researchers. Professor Bland has served on the councils of architects' associations and on several commissions appointed to safeguard Canada's historical and cultural heritage. In private practice and in various partnerships, he has been involved in the design of Ottawa's city hall and several large developments. He has written books on architectural history, housing and community planning and coauthored several major planning reports on Canadian cities. In 1984 he was curator of McGill's Canadian Architecture Collection and continued to lecture on the history of Canadian architecture.

NORBERT SCHOENAUER

Bland, Salem Goldworth, Methodist (later United Church) minister, author (b at Lachute, Canada E 25 Aug 1859; d at Toronto 7 Feb 1950). A leading popularizer of liberal theology and the SOCIAL GOSPEL, Bland held a succession of churches in the St Lawrence and Ottawa valleys, then taught at Wesley College, Winnipeg, from 1903 until he was dismissed in controversial circumstances in 1917. A CHAUTAUQUA lecturer and columnist for the GRAIN GROWERS' GUIDE (1917-19), he returned to the pulpit ministry in Toronto in 1919 and became a regular columnist in the reform *Toronto Star*, under the byline "The Observer."

Always in the reform wing of the church and immensely popular with young people, Bland mixed temperance, sabbath observance and church-union advocacy with moderately socialist views. He spoke widely in the West. A favourite of the labour movement and farmers' organizations, he was an early advocate of a third party for Canada, helping to form the CO-OPERATIVE COMMONWEALTH FEDERATION in Ontario in the 1930s. He was a founder and mentor of the Fellowship for a Christian Social Order in 1934, a participant in Popular Front organizations in the mid-1930s (a children's home in Spain was named after him), and an ardent supporter of the Allied cause in WWII. He wrote *The New Christianity* (1920) and *James Henderson D.D.* (1926).

RICHARD ALLEN

Blaser, Robin, poet, editor, essayist, translator (b at Denver, Colo 18 May 1925; Canadian citizen 1972). Blaser's poetry and poetics were central to the San Francisco renaissance of the 1950s and 1960s, reclaiming for poetry a voice other than the subjective. He grew up in Idaho and attended Berkeley. In 1966, he joined the faculty of Simon Fraser U in Vancouver and brought important energy and insight to the many influences prominent among Canadian writers at the time. He has edited *The Collected Books of Jack Spicer* (1975), the *Selected Poems* of George BOWERING (1980), and the selected poems of Louis DUDEK. His essays have appeared in journals and anthologies in the US and Canada. His work is characterized by passionate commitment to and examination of the experience of beauty. His poems have been published in anthologies such as *The New American Poetry* (1960), *The Long Poem Anthology* (Michael Ondaatje, ed, 1979) and *The Postmoderns* (1982), as well as in broadsides and journals.

SHARON THESEN

Bleus, *see* PARTI BLEU.

Blewett, George John, philosopher (b at St Thomas, Ont 9 Dec 1873; d at Go Home Bay, Georgian Bay, Ont 15 Aug 1912). English Canada's first native-born philosopher, he turned down job offers from the US, preferring to teach at Victoria College, Toronto (1906-12). His books *The Study of Nature and The Vision of God* (1907) and *The Christian View of the World* (1912) reflect the developing Canadian culture in their emphasis on the concept of community and on nature as a life force in need of protection. Blewett's students influenced succeeding generations and his works are still quoted by teachers, clergymen and philosophers.

ELIZABETH A. TROTT

Bley, Paul, jazz pianist (b at Montréal 10 Nov 1932). An important and influential participant in New York avant-garde jazz in the 1960s, Bley began working as a teenager in Montréal before commuting 1950-53 to New York's Juilliard School of Music. He was a principal in the Montréal Jazz Workshop in 1953; thereafter he worked in the US. After associations with several great jazz musicians (Ornette Coleman, Charles Mingus, Sonny Rollins) he emerged in 1963 as a personal, introspective improviser. Working largely in trio or solo formats and, after 1968, employing the synthesizer, he has sustained an international following. His music has been documented by more than 30 recordings, the earliest from 1953.

MARK MILLER

Blind River, Ont, Town, pop 3444 (1981c), is located at the mouth of the Mississagi R on the North Channel of Lk HURON, 132 km SE of SAULT STE MARIE. Named by early VOYAGEURS because it was difficult to detect from Lk Huron, the site was important for the FUR TRADE from the mid-17th to the mid-19th century. From 1853, when the first sawmill was constructed, until the closure of McFadden Lumber Co in 1969, lumbering was the main economic activity of the community. More recently the town has benefited from the URANIUM mining boom in nearby ELLIOT LAKE, from the establishment of the Eldorado uranium refinery and from the continuing growth of tourism.

MATT BRAY

Blindness and Visual Impairment In Canada, as well as in many other countries, blindness is defined for legal and administrative purposes in such a way as to include persons who have some sight. The expression "6/60" means that persons considered blind must come within 6 metres of an object in order to see it, while persons considered sighted (ie, 6/6 vision) can see that same object from 60 metres. Those with approximately 10% or less of normal vision are therefore considered "blind." This definition of blindness provides a practical model for organizations such as social service agencies, and educational, medical and government institutions.

In Canada the largest agency using the legal definition of blindness is the Canadian National Institute for the Blind (CNIB), which has 8 major divisions throughout Canada and over 40 regional offices. The CNIB was founded "to ameliorate the condition of the blind of Canada and to prevent blindness." It operates a variety of rehabilitative and social programs, as well as prevention of blindness and public-education programs. Other organizations providing services to the blind and the visually impaired include the Montreal Association for the Blind, which houses a small elementary school for the blind. Other schools for the blind exist in Brantford (W. Ross Macdonald School), Montréal (l'Institut Nazareth et Louis Braille) and Halifax (Sir Frederick Fraser School).

Persons who feel that the term "blind" has certain psychological and social implications that do not apply to them because they retain some residual vision prefer the term "visual handicap" or "visual impairment." Many groups of visually impaired persons, including the Blind Organization of Ontario with Self-Help Tactics (BOOST), the Manitoba Federation of the Visually Handicapped, and Regroupement de l'association des amblyopes et aveugles du Québec (RAAQ), have played an important role in the development of these new conceptions.

Statistics on the number of blind and visually impaired Canadians are kept within a CNIB registry, to which individuals voluntarily give their names. According to this registry, there are about 40 332 blind and visually impaired persons in Canada (1983). CNIB officials estimate that approximately 90% of these persons have some residual vision. The registry's figures are approximate because many blind or visually impaired Canadians may choose not to register with the CNIB.

Causes of Blindness

There are roughly 4 major causes of blindness and visual impairment in Canada: macular degeneration (39%); diabetic retinopathy (11%); glaucoma (9%) and cataracts (6%). The remaining 35% of blindness and visual impairment is caused by various diseases, genetic predispositions and accidents.

Macular Degeneration The macular is a small spot near the centre of the retina, the light-sensitive innermost coat of the eye. This area is responsible for sharpest vision. If the macular deteriorates, the centre of the person's field of vision becomes blurred, and the ability to read is lost. Macular degeneration seems to be part of the normal aging process.

Diabetic Retinopathy The retina contains the light-sensitive nerve cells and fibres that transmit images to the brain. It is nourished by a network of blood vessels. In some diabetics, these fine blood vessels become more fragile and likely to bleed, causing loss of sight (*see also* DIABETES MELLITUS).

Glaucoma is an eye disease associated with abnormal pressure in the eye causing degeneration of the optic disk and defects in the field of vision.

Cataracts A cataract is a clouding of the crystalline lens of the eye. The purpose of the lens is to bring the light rays entering the eye to a focus on the retina. When the lens becomes cloudy, the light rays cannot get through and the person loses sight. The only treatment for a cataract is surgical removal of the lens (*see also* OPHTHALMOLOGY).

Treatment of Blindness

There are many new surgical techniques that have been developed to help visually impaired individuals. Children with congenital cataracts are treated with surgery before they are a year old and are fitted with contact lenses. The laser is being used in some cases of diabetic retinopathy, glaucoma and macular degeneration. Many persons with partial sight can make use of various technological aids.

Blindness and visual impairment do not restrict a person from living a full life. Many blind persons have productive careers, attend schools and universities, and participate in recreational activities. On the other hand, there are many blind and visually impaired Canadians who have not been as successful in their adaptation and who require extensive rehabilitation and social services. The attitude of blind or impaired individuals towards their handicap will largely determine the sort of life they live.

Blizzard, major snowstorm accompanied by strong WINDS and low visibility. These 2 features determine the severity of the storm more than does the temperature, which may be only just below freezing, or the amount of fresh snow involved. In Canada the official national meteorological service definition of a blizzard is a period of 6 or more hours with winds above 40 km/h, visibility reduced to below 1 km by blowing or drifting snow, and windchills over 1600 W/m^2 (watts per square metre). A blizzard is part of a low-pressure storm system, created as an inflow of mild air from the S is rapidly displaced by a cold front sweeping through from the N or W. The system tends to travel from W to E across the country, and may last up to a week. Blizzards may occur in any region of Canada, except the southwestern districts of BC; the Prairie and Maritime provinces are most frequently and severely affected. Blocked highways and rail lines, electrical-power disruption, stranded motorists and lost livestock are the predictable results of large blizzards.

J. MAYBANK

Bloc populaire canadien, a federal and Québec provincial political movement formed Sept 1942 in reaction to the NATIONAL RESOURCES MOBILIZATION ACT, which removed the existing ban on CONSCRIPTION for military service overseas. The Act violated promises made specifically to Québec in 1939, and followed a plebiscite in which a majority in every province except Québec had voted in favour of releasing the government from its commitments restricting "the methods of raising men for military service." Inspired by Henri BOURASSA and led by Maxime Raymond, MP, the Bloc included in its basic program Canadian independence and neutrality, provincial autonomy, English-French equality, a co-operative economy and family-based social reforms such as provincial health insurance. By 1944, 5 MPs belonged to the Bloc.

Led provincially by André LAURENDEAU, the Bloc was a distinct third party in the Québec legislature until the 1948 provincial election, which it did not contest. In Ottawa, the Bloc had supported Canadian membership in the UNITED NATIONS, considering it to be a genuine world organization, but in Mar 1949 its 2 remaining federal members voted against participation in NATO because "it is an armaments race." When Parliament dissolved on 30 Apr 1949, the Bloc populaire canadien ceased to exist. Among its leaders had been René Hamel, later a provincial Liberal Cabinet minister and judge; Roger Duhamel, who became Queen's Printer at Ottawa; Jean Martineau, afterwards chairman of the CANADA COUNCIL; André Laurendeau, later co-chairman of the commission on BILINGUALISM AND BICULTURALISM; and Jean DRAPEAU, the longtime mayor of Montréal.

GORDON O. ROTHNEY

Blood, one of 3 tribes which make up the BLACKFOOT NATION. In their own language they are called *Kainai,* which is a corruption of the term *a-kainaw,* meaning "many chiefs." They are of Algonquian linguistic stock and speak the same language as the BLACKFOOT and PEIGAN, with only slight variations in dialect. The Blood once occupied hunting grounds from the Red Deer R to the Belly R, but by the mid-19th century they had moved farther S to the Pakowki Lk, Belly R and Teton R regions. They often ranged far into Montana and traded as frequently with the American Fur Co as they did with the HUDSON'S BAY CO. They were a nomadic buffalo-hunting tribe (*see* BUFFALO HUNT), with complex religious societies and the reputation for being fierce warriors. Their enemies included the CREE, KOOTENAY, Shoshoni and Crow tribes. The population of the Blood during the nomadic period was 2500-3500, dropping to a low of 1750 people after the 1837 smallpox epidemic.

The leading chief of the tribe in the late 1700s was Bull Back Fat, who was succeeded by 2 descendants bearing the same name. The second Bull Back Fat made peace with the Americans in 1831, permitting them to open trading posts on the upper Missouri R. In 1855 the Blood, under Father of Many Children, Bull Back Fat and Seen From Afar, signed a treaty with the Americans. In 1877 Seen From Afar's nephew, RED CROW, was the tribe's chief signer of Treaty No 7 with the Canadian government and remained leader of the tribe until his death in 1900.

Initially the Blood were given a reserve adjacent to the Blackfoot on the Bow R, but in 1880 they moved to a new site between the St Mary R and Belly R, where they established the largest INDIAN RESERVE in Canada. In the 1890s the Blood launched a successful ranching industry, and after the turn of the century they became large-scale farmers. Over the years, they gained the reputation of being hardworking, proud people who retained many of their cultural values. Like other tribes, they faced the stresses of integration and social breakdown, but have been relatively more successful in dealing with these problems. *See also* NATIVE PEOPLES, PLAINS.

HUGH A. DEMPSEY

Reading: Hugh A. Dempsey, *Indian Tribes of Alberta* (1979); Mike Mountain Horse, *My People the Bloods* (1979).

Bloody Falls, rapids located about 15 km above the mouth of the COPPERMINE R in the central Arctic, is named for the massacre of local INUIT by CHIPEWYAN led by MATONABBEE, accompanying Samuel HEARNE on his exploration of the area in 1771. In later times the area was used as an important summer fishing site by the COPPER INUIT, as well as a stop on the route to the interior in order to obtain native copper and wood from the forests that begin 20 km upstream. ARCHAEOLOGY has discovered traces of Inuit occupation dating to about 1500 AD. The area was also occupied by Paleoeskimos about 1300 BC, and by Indian caribou hunters between roughly 500 BC and 500 AD. For over 3000 years this site has probably marked a zone of tension between Indian and Inuit cultures. *See also* PREHISTORY.

ROBERT MCGHEE

Bloore, Ronald, painter (b at Brampton, Ont 29 May 1925). Bloore studied at U of Toronto (BA 1949) and in the US and England. Appointed director of the Norman Mackenzie Art Gallery in Regina in 1958, he brought in important, progressive exhibitions, and he introduced his students at the Regina Coll of Art to the work of the American abstract expressionists. Bloore was instrumental in inviting Barnett Newman to lead the summer workshop at Emma Lake, Sask, in 1959, an event of lasting influence on the Regina art scene. Also in 1959 Bloore organized an exhibition of a group, including himself, that became known as the REGINA FIVE. Their work still influential, was seen as the expression of the new painting emerging in the Canadian West. Bloore achieved a remarkable control and resolve in his painting early in his career confining himself to the limited subject matter of "symbol-like elements" and a severely restricted palette. The paintings come alive by the play of light and shadows on the raised textured surfaces. In 1966 Bloore became a professor at York U.

CLARA HARGITTAY

Blue-green Algae (phylum Cyanophyta) are the only ALGAE characterized by cells which lack a distinct nucleus (prokaryotes). They include unicellular, colonial and filamentous forms. FOSSILS of blue-green algae make up layered formations (stromatolites) 3 billion years old in South Africa, up to 2.5 billion in the Canadian Shield. They were probably the first oxygen producing organisms and are thought to have been responsible for the early accumulation of oxygen in the atmosphere.

Their cell structure places blue-green algae in the same kingdom (Monera) as bacteria; hence they are called cyanobacteria by some scientists. Unlike most true bacteria, blue-green algae can photosynthesize chemical nutrients. Their photosynthetic machinery, including both chlorophyll and phycobiliprotein pigments, is contained in platelike membranes scattered throughout the cell; hence, they differ from "eukaryotic" algae and higher PLANTS, in whic

Ronald Bloore, *Painting* (1959), stovepipe enamel on masonite (*courtesy Ronald Bloore / Galerie Dresdnere*).

photosynthesis occurs in distinct organelles (chloroplasts). Blue-green algae contain glycogen as a stored carbohydrate. In general, a gelatinous sheath of varying thickness envelops the cell or colony. It can be red or blue depending on whether the species grows in highly acidic or basic conditions, respectively. The cell wall resembles that found in "gram-negative" bacteria (ie, those which are sensitive to penicillin) both in construction and chemistry, and contains amino acids and sugars. Some unicellular species "fix" atmospheric nitrogen, another characteristic they share with bacteria. Gas pockets (vacuoles), visible in many free-living PLANKTONIC forms, act as flotation chambers to aid cell buoyancy. Many filamentous species move when in contact with a solid surface. This movement occurs without evident organs of locomotion. Motile blue-green algae, on submerged sediments, move to the sediment surface in daytime and descend into the upper few millimetres at night (vertical migration rhythm).

Most blue-green algae reproduce by cell division. In certain filamentous forms, specialized fragments of the filament (hormogonia) serve in reproduction. Several unicellular reproductive agents (eg, akinetes, endospores, exospores and heterocysts) are also formed by many filamentous types. Heterocysts function mainly as the site of nitrogen fixation, but in a few species (eg, *Gloeotrichia ghosei*) they will germinate like spores. Sexual reproduction does not occur, but evidence exists showing that genetic recombination may take place through the joining of 2 cells which then exchange DNA. This "conjugation" is also found in bacteria.

Blue-green algae are very widespread, occurring in waters varying greatly in salinity, nutrient status and temperature; and in planktonic, benthic and aerial communities. In general, they are more abundant in neutral or slightly alkaline habitats. They occur in alkaline hot SPRINGS at temperatures approaching 73-74°C. In nutrient-rich (eutrophic) lakes, several species (eg, *Microcystis aeruginosa, Anabaena flos-aquae, Aphanizomenon flos-aquae*) are members of water "blooms" in late summer. Genetic strains of the first 2 species are responsible for poisonings of various animals. In stagnant waters, excessive growth may also cause noxious odours. Many species form symbiotic relationships with other organisms in which they supply nitrogen. Partners include FUNGI (to form LICHENS), MOSSES, FERNS, SEED PLANTS and ANIMALS. *See* WATER POLLUTION. MICHAEL HICKMAN

Bluebell, common name for several PLANTS with bell-shaped flowers of Campanulaceae and Boraginaceae families. Common bluebells, genus *Campanula* [Lat, "bell"], are perennial, herbaceous plants with milky juice, native to north temperate and arctic regions. More than 230 species are known worldwide; 9 species are native to Canada, 5 others have been introduced as garden escapes. The best-known Canadian species, *C. rotundifolia*, found from the YT to the Atlantic Provinces (in PEI, it is an escape), is the "bluebell" of Scotland or "harebell" (contraction of heatherbell). Bluebells grow in stony tundra, rocky crevices, roadsides, rich meadows and woods, from low elevations to alpine habitats. The plants flower June-Aug, and the petals are joined into bell shape. The nodding bells are blue or purple, sometimes white. The mature female element (pistil) resembles a bell clapper. Insect POLLINATION is normal but, if it does not occur, the mature pistil bends backward and self-pollinates from pollen at the base of the bell. The fruit develops pores on the side which open to release many seeds. Lungworts, sometimes also called bluebells, belong to genus *Mertensia*, borage family.

Blueberry, *see* BERRIES, CULTIVATED; BERRIES, WILD.

Bluebird (genus *Sialia*), common name for 3 species of THRUSHES occurring in North and Central America. Males have bright blue heads, backs, wings and tails. Females, although similar in size, are much greyer overall, but have blue wings and tails. They breed in open country, one species across SE Canada and all 3 in parts of the West. Nesting in natural and woodpecker cavities or birdhouses, usually at shrub level, they lay 4-5 pale blue eggs, which are incubated about 14 days. Long trails of nest boxes have been established for them, especially in the Prairie provinces. They are primarily insectivorous but eat some small fruits. R.D. JAMES

Bluefish Caves contain the oldest undisturbed archaeological evidence in Canada. Located on a limestone ridge overlooking the upper Bluefish R in the Keele Range of the northern YT, the caves consist of 3 small cavities in which loess accumulated during late Pleistocene time. Buried in these aeolian deposits are the bones of mammoths, horses, bison, caribou, sheep and many other mammals, birds and fish. Numerous large mammal bones exhibit butchering marks made by stone tools. Associated with the bones, some of which have been dated to between 12 000 and 18 000 years ago, are the lithic remains of a burin and MICROBLADE technology akin to that found in the American Paleoarctic tradition. The paleoenvironmental reconstruction based on pollen, macrofossil, pedological and micro-mammal evidence is in keeping with that obtained from other eastern Beringian regions for the period of the late Wisconsinan maximum and subsequent millennia. *See also* ARCHAEOLOGY; PREHISTORY. JACQUES CINQ-MARS

Bluenose, The, Canada's most famous ship, was launched at LUNENBURG, NS, in 1921 and named with the common sobriquet first applied by T.C. HALIBURTON to natives of NS. The schooner was designed by William J. Roué to fish the Grand Banks and to race. Skippered by Capt Angus J. Walters against the fastest American schooners, it won the International Fisherman's Trophy, emblematic of the sailing championship of the fishing fleets of the N Atlantic, in 1921, 1922 and 1923. Its only defeat was by the Boston schooner *Gertrude L. Thebaud* in the Lipton Cup in 1930, but it outraced the *Thebaud* for the Fisherman's Trophy in 1931 and 1938. The *Bluenose* also held the record for the largest catch of fish brought into Lunenburg. It came to an ignominious end, sold in 1942 to a West Indies trading company and wrecked off Haiti in 1946. A sculptured profile of the *Bluenose* has been reproduced on the Canadian dime since 1937. A replica, *Bluenose II*, was built in the same Smith and Rhuland shipyards in Lunenburg and launched in 1963 amid nostalgia for the lost golden age of sail. JAMES MARSH

Schooner *Bluenose*, 1921 (*courtesy Knickle's Studio, Lunenberg*).

Blumenfeld, Hans, urban and regional planner, educator, author, consultant (b at Osnabrück, Ger 18 Oct 1892). Appointed to the Russian State City Planning Institute from 1930 to 1933, Blumenfeld left the USSR in 1937 for the US where he worked primarily for the Philadelphia Planning Commission. He came to Canada in 1955 as assistant director of the Metropolitan Toronto Planning Board and was instrumental in shaping Toronto and its hinterland. In 1961 he became a private consultant and in 1964 a professor at U of Toronto. He is the author of numerous acclaimed articles and books, including *The Modern Metropolis* (1967) and *Metropolis and Beyond* (1979). His most significant contribution has been his vision of the "metropolis" as a new urban organism whose unique scale and structure require diagnosis and treatment. Acknowledged as one of the leading figures in 20th-century URBAN AND REGIONAL PLANNING, he is a fellow of the Canadian Institute of Planners, has received honorary degrees from U de Montréal and Waterloo and is a recipient of the American Institute of Planners Distinguished Service Award. He has had a lifelong involvement in the world peace movement. NORMAN PRESSMAN

Blyth Festival in SW Ontario specializes in Canadian plays. Started by director James Roy and board president Keith Roulston in 1975, the festival produces plays aimed first at local audiences and secondarily at visitors, and enjoys strong community support. Theatre Passe Muraille's popular *Farm Show* had been developed around nearby Clinton. Janet Amos, who succeeded Roy in 1979, was a *Farm Show* veteran, as have been many other Blyth Festival artists. The festival has restored the Memorial Hall, which was built 1919-20 but allowed to fall into disrepair. Many Blyth plays have dealt with local history (eg, *The Blyth Memorial History Show*) or rural issues (eg, Ted Johns's *He Won't Come In From the Barn*). Some have been adapted from the stories of regional writers Harry BOYLE and Alice MUNRO. However, a growing number of Blyth Festival plays have attracted national attention. Peter Colley's often-produced thriller *I'll Be Back For You Before Midnight* premiered there. So did Anne Chislett's award-winning drama about Mennonite family life before WWII, *Quiet in the Land*. ROSS STUART

Boas, Franz, anthropologist, ethnologist, folklorist, linguist (b at Minden, Westphalia 9 July 1858; d at New York City, NY 21 Dec 1942). He developed with his students the professional and intellectual direction of American anthropology, emphasizing the method of empirical culture history. His work stressed the cumulative historical factors that blend to give each society its distinctive character. Boas's first interest was in historical geography, but his pioneering work with the BAFFIN ISLAND INUIT (1883-84) showed him that people's ways are not merely a matter of geography, and that they often act against the constraints of their environment. His field research shifted permanently in 1886 to the Northwest Coast Indians. Their rich art and mythology further convinced him of the need to take into account psychological characteristics as well as geographical environment. These characteristics develop through centuries of borrowing traits from other cultures, modifying them and integrating them within the new culture. Boas's many students were his greatest legacy. His most brilliant student, Edward SAPIR, became the first chief of what is now the NATIONAL MUSEUM OF MAN. For many years Boas reigned at the hub of American professional anthropology, and was the mentor of most of the first women in the profession, Ruth Benedict and Margaret Mead among others. He worked effectively and tirelessly to move the public away from its belief in race and towards a scientific conception of culture as the basis for explaining the most significant human differences. R.J. PRESTON

Reading: Franz Boas, *The Mind of Primitive Man* (1938, rev 1965) and *Race, Language, and Culture* (1940).

Boat People, *see* SOUTHEAST ASIANS.

Boating Canadians are among the most active boaters in the world: over 50% or 13 million people go boating each year in some form of recreational craft. Canadians own almost 2.3 million boats, ranging from canoes to yachts over 20 m — more than twice the number of boats per capita compared with the US. Each year, boating generates over $2 billion of direct expenditure.

Despite the limitations on year-round boating imposed by climate everywhere except on the West Coast, Canada has many natural resources that encourage this activity. Canada has more fresh water than any other nation, dotted in a myriad of lakes and streams across the country; some of the longest rivers in the world, which stretch into the far corners of the land; and sea coasts bordering on 2 large oceans.

Historically, Canadians lived by and travelled on the water. The first inhabitants developed many unique boat designs ranging from skin or bark CANOES to magnificent ocean-going boats capable of extended voyages. The early explorers and traders were quick to realize the usefulness of native craft and adopted them as their own. Each year the HUDSON'S BAY CO, NORTH WEST CO and others arranged coast-to-coast shipment of their goods by water and, by necessity, began to modify the canoe to their needs. The first boat factories utilizing specialized production-line techniques were set up in the late 18th century in Québec to meet the demands for canoes.

By the mid-19th century, boating flourished at all levels of society. While many people enjoyed the pleasures of a canoe or pulling boat, those of more substantial means lavished money on sleek racing craft and the wagers accompanying them. Clubs catering to these pleasures were formed for all types of boats, and organized competitions for members became common. Not content with local endeavour, Canadians soon became prominent on the world stage. Ned HANLAN won the world champion sculling competition in 1880; Canada challenged twice for the America's Cup, in 1876 and 1881; and in 1896 a yacht appropriately named *Canada* won a trophy on the Great Lakes, emblematic to this day of yachting rivalry between Canada and the US (*see* YACHTING).

Boating became mechanized around the turn of the century. Factories were built using sophisticated methods to satisfy the increasing demand for boats, and engines became available to propel craft of all kinds. Though small steam boats had been used for some time, the gas engine revolutionized boating and culminated in the outboard motor we know today. Materials and techniques developed for other uses, particularly fiberglass and aluminum, were adapted to boat construction. In 1950 there were 72 558 licensed boats in Canada. Only those boats with engines over 7.4 kW (10 hp) require a licence, so this figure represents but a portion of the boats. However, by 1981, 1 744 902 licences had been issued. Almost all of these boats have been constructed in either fiberglass or aluminum.

In the early 1980s the small outboard was the most popular boat, accounting for about 45% of the total. Easily operated or transported, it provides millions of fishermen, hunters, water-skiers and casual boaters with enjoyment. The canoe comprises 30% of all Canadian boats; it can go almost anywhere and is inexpensive. Rowboats, long in the shadow of powerboats, are finding new interest among fitness devotees. Sailboats, often the most dramatic and visible of all watercraft, total 10% of Canada's fleet. Once the preserve of the wealthy or the working fisherman, sailboats were revolutionized by the use of fiberglass. Thousands of people now have access to sleek, well-designed, economical and durable boats. In this field, in particular, Canadian manufacturers have been quite successful; one of every 2 boats built in Canada is exported, generating $60 million each year in foreign sales. Larger powerboats with inboard-outboard or inboard engines make up about 6% of all boats. Various concerns about fuel consumption have led to improvements in hull design, and careful attention to styling and detail have created new demand.

Boaters in Canada operate under the Canada Shipping Act and Small Craft Regulations. Both these statutes are administered by the federal Dept of Transport through the CANADIAN COAST GUARD, though in many instances local enforcement is carried out by police forces. These groups, in conjunction with the Dept of National Defence and many volunteers, provide search-and-rescue services across Canada. Working in close conjunction with the government are several associations of boaters often grouped by interests into national bodies. The Canadian Yachting Assn and the Canadian Power Squadrons, eg, cater to sailors and powerboaters from coast to coast and have developed broad courses for teaching seamanship and navigation. Other groups involved in similar activities include the Canadian Boating Federation, which also governs powerboat racing in Canada, the Canadian RED CROSS SOCIETY and the Royal Life Saving Society Canada.

In addition to their interests in teaching boating, several of these groups also administer the sporting aspects of boating. Recent victories by Canadian sailors have put them in the forefront of Olympic and Pan American competition. Canada again challenged for the America's Cup in 1983 and had a creditable finish among the contenders. A new challenge is planned for 1987. Canadian athletes have seen considerable success in CANOEING and ROWING competitions. In 3 successive years, 1959-61, *Miss Supertest* won the Harmsworth Trophy for unlimited hydroplanes.

Canada's geography provides unequalled opportunities for boating, which Canadians have taken up without reservation. MICHAEL VOLLMER

Reading: Better Boating; Canadian Yachting; Pacific Yachting; Sailing Canada Magazine.

Bobak, Bronislaw Josephus, "Bruno," artist, arts administrator (b at Wawelowska, Poland 28 Dec 1923). Bobak has maintained a lifelong devotion to the figure, landscape and still life while extending the expressionist attitude of the early 20th century. He was Canada's youngest official war artist when commissioned in 1944. His WWII art used an expressive-realist mode, derived from his training with Carl SCHAEFER. After the war he lived in BC (1947-59) where he developed a "surrealist" style in response to the mystical qualities of BC's interior landscape. Following visits to Europe (especially Norway), he settled in NB (after 1960) and joined a passionate response for the art of Edvard Munch and Gustave Vigeland with an admiration for Oskar Kokoschka. The result was a series of powerful oils (*Wheel of Life*, 1966), drawings and woodcuts dealing with the figure and landscape. He has exhibited throughout Canada, the US and Europe. In 1962 he became director of the Art Centre, UNB. D.F. ANDRUS

Bobak, Molly Joan, née Lamb, painter (b at Vancouver 25 Feb 1922), daughter of Harold MORTIMER-LAMB. Molly Lamb's early interest in the creative arts, drawing and writing in particular, was largely due to her home environment. She studied at the Vancouver School of Art (1938-41) under Jack L. SHADBOLT, who had a profound influence upon her, joined the army (1942) and became the only woman to be appointed a war artist (1945). With her husband Bruno BOBAK she moved to Fredericton in 1959 and began to teach at UNB in 1960. The depth of her perceptions and the richness of her imagery are demonstrated as much through her writing and her work on radio and TV as through her painting. IAN GORDON LUMSDEN

Reading: Molly Lamb Bobak, *Wild Flowers of Canada* (1978).

Bobcat (*Lynx rufus*, family Felidae), medium-sized, carnivorous MAMMAL, also known as wildcat or bay lynx. It is distinguished from the similar Canada LYNX by its relatively small feet, ears tuftless or with very short tufts, and bobbed tail, white below. The coat is of one colour or spotted; fur behind the jaws and elsewhere is shorter than in lynx. Colours, more varied than in lynx, range from light grey to reddish brown. Bobcats vary greatly in size (5-18 kg), males being larger than females. Bobcats have a more southern distribution and occupy a wider range of habitats than lynx. They spread into parts of southern Canada following European settlement. Bobcats and lynx coexist in spruce-pine forests of northern and southwestern Ontario, southern Québec, NB and NS. Their chief prey is hares, but other small mammals, birds and, occasionally, even deer are taken. Bobcats may purr or mew but, unlike lynx, cannot be tamed. Like lynx, bobcats breed late Feb to early Mar, have a 50-day gestation period, and bear 1-4 young. Newborn kittens weigh 285-370 g, are spotted with strong facial markings, and are cared for by both parents. Bobcat fur is less valuable than lynx. C.S. CHURCHER

Bobsledding is a winter sport in which a sled is guided down a specially built course as rapidly as possible. The sled has 2 axles and 2 pairs of runners, is steered with a rope or wheel and operated by teams of 2 or 4 racers. Luge, or tobogganing, uses a single sled (a 1 or 2 seater) with the rider lying back from a sitting position, or in Cresta tobogganing, lying prone. The winter pastime of sledding/tobogganing developed in eastern Canada among Indian tribes who used their transportation sledges for occasional fun. It was refined by groups such as the Montreal Tobogganing Club, the first such club in Canada, formed in 1881. Most sleds could take as many as 4 riders; some accommodated 12. Tobogganing was one of Canada's prime winter sports in the 19th century. The Montmorency Ice Cone, outside Québec City, was a popular site for recreational sledding.

When the sport grew less popular in Canada after the 1880s, the original toboggan runs were abandoned. No new runs were built in the 20th century and competitors practised in Europe or at Lake Placid, NY. In the mid-1950s, Canadians competed in Europe; in 1954 Douglas Connor set a world record in the Cresta run at St Moritz, Switzerland. The Canadian Amateur Bobsleigh and Luge Assn was formed in 1957 and the first Canadian team entered international competition in 1959. In 1962, a 4-man team, led by Lamont Gordon, won the Commonwealth bobsled championship. In 1957, the EMERY brothers, Victor and John, formed the Laurentian Bobsledding Assn and began racing in the world competition in 1959. By 1964, with Douglas Anakin and Peter Kirby, they had gained the experience necessary to challenge the world's best at the Olympic Games. Despite few opportunities to practise, they set a record time in their first run and won the gold medal. The Canadian team, again led by Vic Emery, retained its title at the 1965 world championships.

In 1967 Canada's first luge team was formed and the first Canadian championships were staged. A luge team entered the 1968 Olympics and Linda Crutchfield won the 1968 N American women's luge championship. Canada finally gained modern facilities in 1976 with a 213 m luge run built in Etobicoke, Ont. In 1977 Carol Keyes and Bjorn Iverson won the N American women's and men's luge singles championships; Larry Arbuthnot won the men's championship in 1978. Czech-born Mirlav Zajonc, racing for Canada, won the world ge championship in 1983. BARBARA SCHRODT

odega y Quadra, Juan Francisco de la, aval officer, explorer, administrator (bap at ma, Peru 3 June 1743; d at Mexico City 26 Mar '94). In 1775 he made a difficult voyage of ploration from San Blas, Mexico, to 58°30′ N d Bucareli Sd, Alaska. In 1779 he commanded e frigate *Favorita* to Alaska in the expedition of nacio de Arteaga. Following naval duty, he as given command in 1789 of the naval de-rtment of San Blas, which controlled Spanish tivities on the NORTHWEST COAST. In 1792, he ok charge at the Nootka post and negotiated ith Capt George VANCOUVER over implemen-tion of the 1790 Nootka Convention. Bodega y uadra was polite but firm in defending Span-h sovereignty. He returned to Mexico in 1793, here he died suddenly. CHRISTON I. ARCHER

odsworth, Fred, nature writer (b at Port Bur-ell, Ont 11 Oct 1918). Before turning to book-ngth fiction Bodsworth was a journeyman urnalist, particularly with *Maclean's* and later e Toronto *Star*, and much of the technical pertise of the professional magazine writer is ident in his complex yet simply written wil-rness parables. *The Last of the Curlews* (1954), his st and best-known book, centres on the pass-g of traditional Inuit life. Less well known *The Atonement of Ashley Morden* (1964), an anti-ar novel whose plot revolves around germ arfare experiments. In their subjects both oks were ahead of their time. *The Sparrow's ll* (1967), a tale of survival in the wilderness, ings Bodsworth's concerns with ethics and ligion nearer the surface. He has also written on-fiction in the natural history field.

ois-Brûlé [French, "charred wood" or "burnt ood"], a 19th-century term for a mixed-blood dian or a MÉTIS, especially the descendant of an dian and a French Canadian. The expression ferred to the brownish skin colour of the étis. JOHN ROBERT COLOMBO

oldt Castle, fantasy built by George Boldt, a rman immigrant who had made a fortune in w York. In the 1890s he bought one of the OUSAND ISLANDS, had it reshaped as a heart eart I) and began construction of an ornate stle for his wife. Boldt ordered the work aban-oned when his wife died, leaving a bizarre in and curious memorial. JAMES MARSH

olt, Carol, née Johnson, playwright (b at innipeg 25 Aug 1941). A socially committed amatist, Carol Bolt is widely known for her litical, women's and children's plays. In the adition of Antonin Artaud's opposition to asterpiece theatre, she rejects the continuing nphasis on international classics in Canadian eatres; nevertheless, her own aesthetic is thor-ughly traditional in its insistence upon de-ghtful instruction. Even thrillers like *One Night and* (1977) and meta-theatre comedies like *Es-pe Entertainment* (1981) evoke the social malaise contemporary urban rootlessness while pro-ding laughter and suspense. Allan King's TV rsion of *One Night Stand* won 3 Canadian File wards in 1978.

Her best-known plays, *Buffalo Jump* (produced 71, publ 1972), *Red Emma — Queen of the Anar-ists* (1974) and *Shelter* (1975), successfully com-ne the methods of Brechtian epic drama with ose of collective creation. She is one of the Ca-adian writers creating *Fraggle Rock*, CBC's chil-en's show. ROTA HERZBERG LISTER

omarc Missile Crisis In the fall of 1958 M Diefenbaker's Conservative government nounced an agreement with the US to deploy Canada 2 squadrons of the American ramjet-owered "Bomarc" antiaircraft missile. This con-oversial defence decision was one of many flowing from the 1957 NORAD agreement with the US. It was argued by some that the surface-to-air guided missile, with a range of 640 km, would be an effective replacement for the manned AVRO ARROW, which was scrapped at the same time. Fifty-six missiles were deployed at North Bay, Ont, and La Macaza, Qué, under the ultimate control of the commander in chief, NORAD. Unfortunately, the Canadian government did not make it clear that the version to be acquired, the Bomarc-B, was to be fitted with nuclear warheads. When this became known in 1960 it gave rise to a dispute as to whether Canada should adopt nuclear weapons. In the end, the government could not bring itself to accept nuclear warheads for the Bomarcs, a reluctance which contributed to poor CANADIAN-AMERICAN RELATIONS in this period. With the Conservatives' fall in 1963 and the Liberals' return to power under PM Pearson, a decision was finally made to accept nuclear warheads for Canadian nuclear-capable forces, and the Bomarc warheads were delivered to their sites on 31 Dec 1963. Nevertheless, the decision was made reluctantly, and in 1969 PM Trudeau's new Liberal government announced that Canada would withdraw its ARMED FORCES from their nuclear roles. As part of this process the Bomarc missile was phased out of service by 1971. PAUL BUTEUX

Bombardier, J. Armand, inventor of the snowmobile (b at Valcourt, Qué 1908; d at Sherbrooke, Qué 18 Feb 1964). Like many other inventors, Bombardier first tried as a teenager to realize his idea of an all-terrain vehicle, equally reliable on soft ground (eg, muskeg) or snow. The specific invention that made his machine of 1937 a success was the principle of steering by skis in front of a tracked drive. A decade later, based partly on wartime research, he made a 12-passenger machine, for which there was a small market, chiefly military. In 1959 Bombardier's firm offered the Ski-Doo, creating a new type of vehicle, a new sport and a new market. What was different about the Ski-Doo was its size, an analogue of the motorcycle instead of the car or truck, and propulsion by a single track as wide as the whole machine, behind the steerable skis. Within a decade it transformed the social life of Inuit and arctic communities, creating a demand for gasoline, oil and spare parts. Competing SNOWMOBILE producers threatened to overwhelm the Bombardier family firm in the early 1970s, but it survived and expanded. DONALD J.C. PHILLIPSON

Bombardier Inc is a Canadian manufacturer with headquarters in Montréal. Bombardier Limited was founded in 1942 by J. Armand BOMBARDIER, inventor of the SNOWMOBILE; in 1975 it purchased majority interest in MLW-Worthington Limited (fd 1902) and, after financial consolidation in 1976, the present name was adopted in 1978. Developing, manufacturing and selling transportation and recreation products worldwide, including Ski-Doo snowmobiles, Bombardier is also involved in heat-transfer products, aerospace components and engines. The company operates 17 plants in Québec, Austria, Iceland and the US. In Jan 1983 it had annual sales or operating revenue of $551 million (ranking 132nd in Canada), assets of $338 million (ranking 169th) and 5300 employees. Its major shareholder, Les entreprises de J. Armand Bombardier Limitée, owns 66% of the company. DEBORAH C. SAWYER

Bompas, William Carpenter, Church of England missionary, bishop (b at London, Eng 20 Jan 1834; d at Cariboo Crossing [Carcross], YT 9 June 1906). Bompas left England in 1865 and spent the next 40 years in the Canadian North, becoming the first bishop of Athabasca in 1874, first bishop of Mackenzie R in 1884 and first bishop of Selkirk (Yukon) in 1891. In response to his appeals, a detachment of NWMP was sent to the Yukon in 1894. A prolific writer, his works included *The Diocese of Mackenzie River* (1888), *Northern Lights on the Bible* (1892) and *The Symmetry of Scripture* (1896). HAL GUEST

Bonaventure, light fleet aircraft carrier purchased 1952, commissioned 17 Jan 1957 as HMCS *Bonaventure*, the name of an island bird sanctuary in the Gulf of St Lawrence. With the latest equipment, jet fighters, helicopters, and propellor-driven antisubmarine patrol aircraft, it spent its career training naval air pilots, participating in naval exercises, and patrolling the Canadian coast. In 1964 it ferried a Canadian Army UN PEACEKEEPING contingent to Cyprus. Political controversy arose after a major refit in 1966-67, for which $8 million had been budgeted, cost $12.5-$17 million, according to different accounting methods. As an economy measure, the government sold *Bonaventure* for scrap in 1970, although it could have had another 10 years of usefulness. It was not replaced. All Canadian fixed-wing naval aircraft have since operated from shore. ROGER SARTY

HMCS *Bonaventure*, the controversial Canadian aircraft carrier, seen off Belfast, Northern Ireland *(courtesy Public Archives of Canada/PA-114454)*.

Bonavista, Nfld, Town, pop 4460 (1981c), inc 1964, is located on the tip of the Bonavista Pen on the Island's NE coast. Its name may have come from the Italian *O Buon Vista* ("Oh happy sight"), attributed to John CABOT, as it is traditionally thought he made his first landfall in the New World at Cape Bonavista in 1497. The community, one of the oldest in N America, was established on a flat, rocky plain SW of the cape in the late 1500s. Settled by English West Country fish merchants, it was attacked on several occasions by the French; the cape became the northeastern terminus of the FRENCH SHORE by the Treaty of Utrecht, 1713, but was returned to the English by the Treaty of Paris, 1763. In 1726 the Church of England built in Bonavista what is claimed to be Newfoundland's first school. Bonavista was from its founding the major fishing centre of Bonavista Bay and was later important in the Labrador fishery and seal hunt. In the 20th century it has become a major fish-producing centre. It is the northern terminus of the Bonavista branch of the Newfoundland Ry and the Cabot Hwy. Bonavista has remained a regional social services, transportation and marine services centre, although its importance as a port has declined with the increase in land-based transportation. JANET E.M. PITT

Bonavista Bay is an inlet on the Atlantic coast of Newfoundland between Cape Freels and Cape Bonavista. Roughly 65 km wide, it contains a large number of densely forested islands that shelter the mainland from northeasterly winds and create hundreds of kilometres of virtually landlocked waters. A portion of this attractive and historic area has been set aside as TERRA NOVA NATIONAL PARK. Several fishing villages, the largest of which is BONAVISTA, lie along the bay's rugged, deeply indented coastline. The Labrador Current sweeps past Cape Freels, regularly filling the outer bay with water cooler than -1°C and occasionally depositing an iceberg. Nonetheless, the protected inner bay warms up sufficiently for propagation of lobsters and supports an important inshore cod fishery. Apart from fishing, lumber and transportation are the major industries of the area. Over the years the waters of the bay have been the scene of scientific investigations on cod distribution relative to temperature and on fishing methodology. Cape Bonavista is the starting point for a series of hydrographic sections (the "Bonavista Triangle") carried out by the US Coast Guard Ice Patrol to monitor the Labrador Current and help forecast iceberg movement.

P.C. SMITH AND R.J. CONOVER

Bond, Sir Robert, politician (b at St John's 26 Feb 1857; d at Whitbourne, Nfld 16 Mar 1927). Bond was largely educated in England. Returning to Newfoundland about 1874, he articled but never practised law. He entered the assembly in 1882. A nationalist, Bond believed in Newfoundland's economic potential and independent future. Bond joined Sir William WHITEWAY's Liberal Cabinet in 1889 as colonial secretary. He became Liberal leader himself in 1897 and premier in 1900. His failure to achieve reciprocity with the US led eventually to a prolonged dispute with the US and UK over fishery rights. The 1908 election saw a tie between him and Sir Edward MORRIS's People's Party, from which the latter emerged victorious. Bond led the Opposition until 1914 when he retired from political life.

J.K. HILLER

Bond-Blaine Treaty In the 1880s, parts of Newfoundland's government and mercantile community felt that RECIPROCITY with the US would solve growing economic problems by providing new markets for dried cod. In 1890 Robert Bond, a minister in the colonial government, negotiated an agreement with American Secretary of State James Blaine that stipulated lower duties on imports from Newfoundland in return for access by American fishermen to the colony's bait supplies. The treaty was not ratified by Britain because of objections from Canada, which believed any such agreement should be for all British North America, and feared American expansionism. *See* BAIT ACTS.

SHANNON RYAN

Bonheur d'occasion (1945), novel by Gabrielle ROY. Set in the Montréal slum of St-Henri during WWII, it is French Canadian literature's first example of urban realism. The inhabitants greet the war as a source of salvation, rescuing them from unemployment. Florentine Lacasse, a dime-store waitress, is seduced by Jean Lévesque, a successful but selfish engineer; pregnant, she marries Emmanuel Létourneau, an innocently idealistic soldier. Her mother, Rose-Anna, is a modern *mater dolorosa,* giving birth to yet another child only to lose her husband to the war. Florentine's young brother, Daniel, dying of leukemia in a hospital, experiences material comfort for the first time, helplessly surrounded by new toys. Their dreams about to be shattered, all are presented with sympathy and insight. Roy's talent for describing the sights, smells and sounds of St-Henri is complemented by her skills as an ironist. The novel won the Governor General's and other awards, and has been translated twice as *The Tin Flute,* by Hannah Josephson (1947) and Alan Brown (1981).

MICHÈLE LACOMBE

Bonhomme is the generic term for a figure (bonhomme de sucre, "sugar baby"; bonhomme de neige, "snowman") used in several combinations in French Canada: Bonhomme Carnaval, the Québec carnival snowman mascot figure; Bonhomme de sable, "the sandman"; and Bonhomme Sept-Heures (from the English "bonesetter"), a frightening figure.

NANCY SCHMITZ

Book Clubs Canada's first book club was started in 1928 when the T. EATON CO offered its customers "a selective literary service." A committee of literary authorities made a monthly selection of titles — sold to the membership at an average price of $2.00 — which was announced in advance of publication. Although the Eaton Book Club at one time had 5000 members, it lasted only 4 years.

The Readers Club of Canada, launched by Peter and Carol Martin in 1959, was the only book club in Canada to offer its members an entirely Canadian book selection. When the club got into financial difficulty in 1978, it was sold to New Leaf, the holding company that owned SATURDAY NIGHT magazine. New Leaf president Ed Cowan ran the club for 3 years. Substantial investments in promotion failed to raise the club's membership from 6000 to a target 20 000, and it was closed down by *Saturday Night*'s next owner, Norman Webster.

Three major American-owned book clubs operate in Canada. The Book Club Division of Doubleday Canada first recruited members for its book clubs, including The Literary Guild and the Doubleday Book Club, in 1944. With some 250 000 members in Canada (1984), the club offers a wide selection of titles — 14 times a year — at discounts ranging from 10% to 60% off list price. An average of 125 Canadian titles are selected annually by an internal editorial committee. The New York-based Book-of-the-Month Club has served Canadian members since its founding in 1926. It publishes a separate catalogue for Canada and offers Canadian members, numbering about 100 000 in 1984, about 100 Canadian titles in the 14 annual mailings. Scholastic TAB Publications Ltd operates book clubs for preschoolers up to high-schoolers out of its marketing division, which orchestrates mailings into the classroom and the home. Approximately 15% of their offerings are Canadian titles. *See also* BOOK PUBLISHING.

SUSAN WALKER

Book Publishing, English-Language Severe obstacles impeded the growth of a publishing industry in early Canada. A large territory with a small, scattered population made distribution difficult and expensive; unfavourable competition from US publishers not bound by imperial copyright laws often swamped the market with cheap imported editions; successful Canadian authors usually published through established foreign companies and avoided the stigma of a colonial imprimatur; major British and American publishers established branch offices in Canada after 1890 and returned most profits to the parent company; local firms acted as agents for foreign publishers and promoted agency books to the neglect of indigenous, original publishing; finally, Canadian publishers were unable to get international rights and secure profits from subsidiary rights, and were, in effect, forced to operate only inside Canada.

In colonial times there were no clear distinctions between printing and publishing, and pioneer printers performed the roles of editors, publishers, distributors, stationers and booksellers. William Brown and Thomas Gilmore, who set up the first press in Québec City in 1764 and published the province's first newspaper, the *Quebec Gazette/La Gazette de Québec,* also published its first books, including an ABC primer, legal works by F.J. Cugnet, a 180-page catechism, and *Abram's Plains,* a poem by Thomas Cary. Hugh C. Thomson of Kingston went on from newspaper publishing to issue 2 volumes of verse and a 2-volume novel, *St. Ursula's Convent* (1824), by Julia Beckwith HART — the first fiction published by a Canadian-born author. John Neilson of Québec published the *History of Canada; from its First Discovery, to the Peace of 1763* in 1826. Joseph HOWE of Halifax published the first major literary talent in British North America, Thomas C. HALIBURTON, whose *The Clockmaker* (1836) sold rapidly and gained international sales when it was pirated in London, Philade phia and Paris; Howe claimed he made litt profit from the book. By 1851 there were sever printer-publishers in Montréal and Toron and publishing received impetus from a bu ding interest in Canadian history. F.X. GA NEAU'S 4-volume *Histoire du Canada* appeared Québec 1845-52, and provoked a Tory respon in Robert Christie's 6-volume *History of the L Province of Lower Canada* (1848-55), published Thomas Cary, Jr, and John Lovell. John Merc McMullen of Brockville compiled and pu lished on his own a *History of Canada* (185 which sold steadily for 2 decades.

John Lovell and Son was the most succes ful original publisher of the 19th century Canada. Lovell inaugurated the *Literary Garla* in 1838 and published, among others, Willia KIRBY, Michel Bibaud, Charles SANGSTER, Rosa na LEPROHON, Catharine Parr TRAILL and tran lations of F.X. Garneau. His closest counterpa was George Maclean Rose, a printer who, wi bookkeeper Robert Hunter, founded Hunte Rose and Co in Québec City in 1861, moving Ottawa in 1865 and Toronto in 1871. Ro joined briefly with Alexander Belford, who ha made a great success of pirating American au thors and flooding the US market with chea editions of such books as Mark Twain's *To Sawyer.* Rose-Belford published *Rose-Belford's C nadian Monthly* (1878-82), a continuation of th *Canadian Monthly* (1872-78), and continued th book piracy. Rose brought out 2 volumes of th *Cyclopedia of Canadian Biography* 1886-88. In 18 a new American copyright law and the su sequent Anglo-American Copyright Agreeme effectively ended book piracy in the US an Canada.

The most influential Canadian publishir house in the 1890s was the Methodist Book an Publishing House, called the RYERSON PRESS aft 1919 in honour of its first book steward, Egerto RYERSON. Established in 1829, it published rel gious books and some trade books until the Re William Briggs took over in 1879 and widel expanded the trade publishing, bringing o 37 new titles in 1897 alone. Briggs publishe numerous important Canadian writers, inclu ing Kirby, Traill, Nellie MCCLUNG, Charles G.I ROBERTS, J.W. BENGOUGH, Charles MAIR, Isabel Valancy CRAWFORD, Robert W. SERVICE and Pa line JOHNSON. The Methodist printing plant pr duced early Ralph Connor (Charles W. GORDO novels for the Westminster Press. Althoug Connor went on to sell in the millions outsic Canada, the pattern in which profits derive from selling foreign (agency) books rather tha Canadian books was already well established.

Schoolbooks had also become important. Th earliest texts were mostly imported from the U but in 1846, 31 titles were adopted from the Iris National School series. This series was used f decades, but there were Canadian series as we John Lovell's Series of School Books (1858) co tained Canadian texts, and James Campbell Canadian National Series included locally wri ten as well as British adoptions. When the O tario Readers began in 1884, the textbook ma ket across the country passed to the control Thomas Nelson, Edinburgh, William J. Ga and, soon after, Copp Clark. Canadian edition of foreign texts have continued to the present a significant branch of the publishing industr

Over a dozen new publishing houses were e tablished between 1876 and 1913 — a period confident expansion in all areas of Canadia life. Among them were Musson Book Co (189 G.N. Morang (1897), McLeod & Allen (1901 University of Toronto Press (1901), Oxford Un versity Press (1904), John C. Winston (190 Macmillan Co of Canada Ltd (1905), McClella and Goodchild (1906, later MCCLELLAND AND STE ART), Cassel and Co Ltd (1907), J.M. Dent an Sons (1913) and Thomas Nelson and Sons L

(1913). Many of the new firms were Canadian branches of US or British houses, and all Canadian publishers were agents for foreign books. This period saw 3 significant enterprises in the publishing of Canadian history and biography: the Makers of Canada, in 20 vols (Morang 1903 to 1908); the Chronicles of Canada, in 32 vols (Glasgow, Brock and Co 1914-16); and the monumental Canada and its Provinces, in 23 vols (Glasgow, Brock and Co 1914-17).

WWI provided a major impetus to publishing to fill the demand for books on the great events and their participants. Patriotic poems, notably John MCCRAE's *In Flanders Fields* (1919), were popular, as were firsthand accounts such as Billy Bishop's *Winged Warfare* (1918). The 1920s brought a slump from overproduction, but also saw the emergence of 3 important figures in publishing, Lorne PIERCE, Hugh Eayrs and John McClelland. Pierce, who became editor of the Ryerson Press in 1920, believed that the new sense of national identity fostered by Canada's war effort could be channelled into a literary revival. He edited a new anthology and the multivolume Makers of Canadian Literature in 1923 (only 12 appeared), and compiled *An Outline of Canadian Literature* (1927). Eayrs became president of Macmillan (a British firm) in 1921 and also encouraged Canadian literature, notably Mazo DE LA ROCHE and Morley CALLAGHAN. McClelland published more Canadian authors than almost all other publishers combined. The 1920s also saw brief careers for 2 new publishers outside Toronto; Graphic Publishers was started by Ottawa printer Henry C. Miller in 1924 and published perhaps 34 titles before bankruptcy in 1932; Louis Carrier founded his firm in Montréal in 1927 but closed soon after.

Hard times during the Depression of the 1930s saw salaries cut and original Canadian publishing slump, as popular foreign books were promoted. However, Clarke Irwin and Co was formed in 1930, first as an agency and later as a vigorous publisher, and some new Canadian authors were first published in these years, including Hugh MACLENNAN and Sinclair ROSS. There was a brief recovery late in WWII, but recession in the book industry lasted into the 1950s. A flood of inexpensive British and American paperbacks hit the Canadian market, and more British and US subsidiaries opened branches. Nevertheless the publishing industry experienced dramatic growth in supplying textbooks to a growing student population. McClelland and Stewart was at the centre of a virtual renaissance in Canadian literature, publishing Irving LAYTON, Leonard COHEN, Mordecai RICHLER, Margaret ATWOOD, Al PURDY and others. M & S undertook a new 18-volume history of Canada, the Canadian Centenary Series, and published best-selling authors such as Pierre BERTON and Farley MOWAT. Jack MCCLELLAND succeeded in marketing many indigenous BEST-SELLERS, such as Berton's *Comfortable Pew* (1965), and established the reprint series New Canadian Library (1958) and the Carleton Library series (1963). Most of the publishing industry was centered in Ontario and Québec, notably Toronto, but during the 1960s and 1970s numerous publishers sprang up across the country: Oberon (Ottawa), Harvest House (Montréal), Fiddlehead Books (Fredericton), Douglas & McIntyre (Vancouver), Western Producer Prairie Books (Saskatoon), Breakwater (St John's), Hurtig (Edmonton), Talonbooks (Vancouver), and James Lorimer, Anansi, New Press, Peter Martin and Women's Press (Toronto) (*see* SMALL PRESSES).

Between 1969 and 1981 the sales revenue of the Canadian book-publishing industry rose from roughly $222 million to $932 million. However, the industry has been widely publicized because of its financial difficulties, some of which are chronic. The market for English-language Canadian books is relatively small and faces powerful competition from American and British books. As costs increase, the chances that a publisher can print and sell 5000 to 10 000 copies of a Canadian book at a profit become less certain. Even in their most independent and lucrative era, most Canadian publishers depended on sales of foreign books to survive. Since the 1950s, more and more of this "agency" business has been removed from Canadian firms as growing numbers of the foreign publishers have established their own subsidiaries or branches in Canada. By 1980 foreign-controlled publishers and distributors accounted for about 75% of the industry's sales revenue. This development unfortunately amounted to a skimming of profits from the industry, with foreign-controlled firms generating profit from imported books while leaving the financially weakened Canadian-owned companies to publish new Canadian titles, incurring greater and greater debt as they did so. Canadian-controlled publishers still produce over 80% of the new titles in Canada (4731 of 5668 in 1981). In 1979 foreign-owned publishers accounted for 70% of overall sales but only 3% of new titles in English-Canadian literature. To the extent that foreign-controlled firms have become involved in publishing Canadian books, they have produced mainly for the textbook market, which involves lower risks, or where provincial government policies encourage Canadian-authored texts; however, they are also active in trade publishing.

By 1970 the situation of many of the Canadian companies was critical. The venerable Ryerson Press, $2.8 million in debt, was sold to McGraw-Hill (a US firm) in 1970. The Ontario Royal Commission on Book Publishing, chaired by lawyer and author Richard Rohmer, was established to examine the industry. The Ontario government put into place its recommendation of a loan-guarantee system for Canadian publishers, although many other recommendations made by the commission were not acted upon. However, the guarantees failed to save Clarke Irwin in 1983; it went into receivership but was subsequently resurrected by John Irwin.

It is difficult to isolate the problems of foreign control from other generic problems of Canadian publishing, and governments have been uncertain about what, if anything, should be done. There are programs in virtually every province, ranging from modest to generous, to fund book publishing, and most entail eligibility requirements for Canadian ownership, recognizing that foreign-owned firms are committed primarily to selling foreign books and returning maximum profits to the parent company. Without Canadian-controlled firms, Canadian authors will not have reasonable opportunities for publication, and provincial governments will not have available to them textbooks which fulfil the needs of their curricula.

The federal government has provided support for Canadian publishing through the Canadian Book Publishing Development Program (est 1979 to 1980 and administered by the Dept of Communications), the CANADA COUNCIL and the SOCIAL SCIENCES AND HUMANITIES RESEARCH COUNCIL. Echoing an earlier concern with Canadian sovereignty in NEWSPAPER and MAGAZINE publishing, the federal government stated as its objective in 1979 that the Canadian-controlled sector of the book-publisher/agent industry should play a dominant role in both language markets in Canada. In 1981-82, $13 million was disbursed to publishers, or 1.3% of federal expenditures on culture.

Meanwhile the educational market for Canadian texts has become more fragmented than in the past, with Ontario, for example, eliminating its provision of specific funding for textbook purchases, offering more courses with smaller enrolments and approving a greater number of texts for each course. In principle, however, the various provincial governments continue to require that Canadian texts be available for use in their school systems. Because of the historical practice of sales to retail bookstores, especially the policy of allowing returns of virtually unlimited quantities of unsold books, the weakness and foreign control of BOOK CLUBS, mass paperback and wholesale distribution, and the reluctance of Canadian banks to lend money to publishers, Canadian-owned firms continue to live a precarious existence.

English-speaking Canadians do not lack for books. With some 75 000 books a year published in the US and Great Britain, there is almost an embarrassment of choice. However, the continuing domination of the industry by foreign-controlled firms that devote only a small portion of their profits to publishing Canadian authors casts grave doubts on the future of a critical area of Canadian cultural expression. *See also* AUTHORS AND THEIR MILIEU. JAMES MARSH

Reading: P. Audley, *Canada's Cultural Industries* (1983); Dept of Communications, *Summary of briefs and hearings* and *Report of the Federal Cultural Policy Review Committee* (1982); Dept of Secretary of State, *The Publishing Industry in Canada* (1977); J.M. Gray, *Fun Tomorrow* (1978); H. Pearson Gundy, *Book Publishing and Publishers in Canada before 1900* (1965); Ontario Royal Commission on Book Publishing, *Background Papers* (1972) and *Canadian Publishers and Publishing* (1973); L. Pierce, *House of Ryerson* (1954); State of English-Language Publishing in Canada, special issue of *Journal of Canadian Studies* (May 1975); Statistics Canada, Culture Statistics, *Book Publishing: An Industry Analysis* (catalogue item 87-601), *A Cultural Analysis* (87-602), *Textbooks* (87-603) and *A Financial Analysis* (87-604).

Book Publishing, French-Language It is generally agreed that there was no publishing in New France. William Brown and Thomas Gilmore installed the first presses in Québec City, 1763-1764, and Fleury Mesplet in Montréal in 1776. These presses were used primarily for NEWSPAPERS, but also filled some printing contracts for the government, the army, the clergy and various merchants. Thus the first French-language or bilingual publications were official government texts, pastoral letters from the bishop, religious books, textbooks and advertisements. During the 19th century most books continued to be imported and commerce was largely controlled by the British under terms of the Navigation Acts, which were not finally abolished until 1844.

Few literary works were published in any quantity. Most 19th-century literature appeared in newspapers or MAGAZINES, the exceptions being publications such as *Épitres, satires* by Michel Bibeau (1830), *L'Influence d'un livre* (1837) by Philippe-Ignace-François AUBERT DE GASPÉ, and *Les Fiances de 1812* (1844) by Joseph DOUTRE. Since authors had to show guaranteed sales before they could get a contract with a publisher, many writers were involved in founding literary magazines; J.O. Letourneux, for instance, established *La Revue canadienne* in 1845, its *L'Album* devoted to literature, and the newspaper *La Minerve* launched *L'Album littéraire et musical de la Minerve* in 1846. James Huston, in *Répertoire national* (1848), published a collection of literature which had appeared first in newspapers, and Henri-Émile Chevalier founded *La Ruche littéraire* in 1853 for the same reason. Then came the great national literary magazines: LES SOIRÉES CANADIENNE (1861), *Le Foyer canadien* (1864) and *La Revue canadienne* (1864) (*see* LITERARY PERIODICALS IN FRENCH).

Expansion of schools and universities after 1860 greatly stimulated book publishing. Beauchemin of Montréal was founded in 1842, but Québec City became the publishing centre. Bookmakers, progressing from mere printer to printer-publisher or publisher-bookseller, no longer merely provided publishing materials, but took charge of the text. Georges-Hippolyte

Cherrier, in his preface to *Charles Guérin* (1853), was one of the first to define publishing as a career.

The state gave the church responsibility over education, and the religious communities, as they consolidated their position in the mid-19th century, took over the production and distribution of textbooks. The Frères des écoles chrétiennes founded their bookstore in 1877, followed by the Congrégation de Notre-Dame (1881), the Librairie Saint-Viateur (1887), the Frères de l'instruction chrétienne (1900), and the Frères du Sacré-Coeur (1902). The pattern continued until 1960, making school texts the backbone of Québec publishing until the establishment of the Ministry of Education in 1964. The situation left room for the kinds of abuses named in the Bouchard Report (1964), which described how the publishers of school texts were often the same people who recommended that these texts be included in the official lists of the Comité catholique de l'instruction publique.

Except for a nationalist revival, there were no major changes in Québec publishing in the early 20th century. The founders of various small papers, such as *Le Nationaliste*, *Le Semeur*, *La Libre Parole* and, especially, *Le* DEVOIR (1910), all promoted a kind of literature which appealed primarily to the collèges classiques. The zenith of this movement was the founding in 1917 of ACTION FRANÇAISE by Lionel GROULX. The bookstore, Librairie de l'Action française, soon became the outlet for nationalist publications. However, Groulx had to cease his publishing activities when Pope Pius XI denounced the movement in France. In 1926 Albert Lévesque took up the cause and became the main publisher of nationalist works. The movement had its opponents, however, exemplified in the founding of magazines such as *La Relève* and *Les Idées* in 1934. That same year, Albert Pelletier started his Editions du Totem, a milestone in the history of Québec publishing. Still, major works including *Les Engagés du Grand Portage* by Léo-Paul DESROSIERS, *Né à Québec* by Alain GRANDBOIS and *Trente arpents* by Philippe PANNETON were all published in Paris.

The defeat of France in 1940 was a turning-point in Québec publishing. Many writers who fled the Vichy regime to preserve their freedom of expression turned to publishers in New York and São Paulo, but most chose Montréal. Between 1940 and 1946, 21 million books came off the Montréal presses. Though Fides and Variétés dominated the market, new publishing houses sprang up: l'Arbre, le Lévrier, Lumen, Mangin, Parizeau, Pascal, Pilon, Serge, Valiquette. At war's end, however, some French writers denounced the hold exercised by Montréal publishers, a charge answered by Robert CHARBONNEAU in his book, *La France et nous* (1942). Although the postwar years were difficult for Montréal publishers, resulting in several bankruptcies, the experience had been beneficial. Québec publishers had gained experience in their craft and freedom from the control of the clergy and nationalist movements.

With the return of peace, publishing again centered on educational work. General prosperity increased the number of students, the main customer, at all levels. Established publishers, eg, Beauchemin, Granger and Fides, were joined by the Centre pédagogique (1940), the Centre de pédagogie et de psychologie (1945), the Centre éducatif et culturel (1959), the Éditions du pélican, the Éditions pédagogiques (1960), and the Presses de l'université Laval (1950).

The success of novelists Gabrielle ROY and Roger LEMELIN proved that Québec publishers could produce books other than school texts. Fides generally avoided fiction, but added Robert Rumilly's *L'Histoire de la province de Québec* and the historical works of Guy Frégault, Marcel Trudel and others to its lists. Pierre Tisseyre founded the Cercle du livre de France, a book club which guaranteed an audience for works of fiction and awarded an annual prize, and launched Françoise LORANGER, André LANGEVIN and others whose works have become classics.

Despite this success, Québec publishing had serious problems. There was no proper distribution system. Bookstores were concentrated in Montréal and Québec City, while some cities of 10 000 inhabitants lacked even a single bookstore. The large firms of Beauchemin, Fides, Granger and Dussault and a few newer houses sold more than 70% of their production directly to the educational institutions. Regional bookstores could not survive on the remainder. Moreover, the public library system was in its infancy, and educational institutions tightly controlled their students' reading material. The book market was just too small to support more than strictly pedagogic materials.

Literature continued to move ahead, however. During the 1960s some publishers played a major role in the QUIET REVOLUTION. Gaston MIRON, who founded les Éditions de l'hexagone in 1953, gathered together Québec poets celebrating the fact they belonged to the "land of Québec." The *Écrits du Canada français* brought out, in magazine form, many literary works. The publications of Éditions parti pris took on an anticlerical and anticolonial tone. A number of smaller houses, eg, Éditions Erta and Éditions Orphée, concentrated on poetry; Leméac published theatrical works exclusively. Other publishers explored nonscholastic markets. Les Éditions de l'homme and les Éditions du jour, stressing news and politics, brought literary mass-marketing to Québec. They used agencies to escape the narrow bookstore world and move into tobacco shops, supermarkets, drugstores, train stations. Even so, publishers were still in trouble.

By the end of the 1960s, publishers depended more than ever on government. Their association, founded in the 1940s, had met with the new provincial Ministry of Cultural Affairs in 1961, which responded the following year with a guarantee Act to assist publishing. A Direction des lettres et des arts was established, which led to the formation of a Conseil supérieur du livre, a federation of publishers' and booksellers' associations, to advise the ministry on publishing issues. The Bouchard Report on the dissemination of culture, tabled in 1964, suggested among other things the creation of a central book organization. A 1965 law setting the framework for bookstore accreditation took the first steps toward creating a government book policy, but was shortsighted in not eliminating wholesalers. Circumstances, however, forced the government to take more effective measures.

After 1960 major French publishers took an interest in the Québec market, which was growing at an annual rate of 12%. In 1968 Hachette, through the intermediary of Messageries internationales (MIL), forced all Québec bookstores to buy their French books from their company, alarming the Conseil supérieur du livre, which feared that French-language publishing and distribution in Québec would fall into foreign hands. Those fears were confirmed when Hachette bought out the Garneau bookstore chain. The Québec government did not act until 1973, when 3 laws were passed obliging establishments receiving Québec-government subsidies to buy their Québec and foreign books from accredited bookstores more than 50%-owned by Québec interests. This second step toward an official book policy reached fruition in the 1976 green paper by Jean-Paul L'Allier, clearly dissecting the main problems of Québec publishing: market penetration by major foreign houses; lack of foreign sales outlets; an inadequate network of public and educational libraries; the high cost of books; the poor protection afforded authors; lack of an appropriate distribution network; the government's unsatisfactory efforts to develop an effective book policy. This analysis was largely repeated in the 1978 white paper, *La Politique québécoise du développement culturel*. A shortage of money prevented the implementation of these recommendations, however, and publishers began looking more to Ottawa than to Québec City.

With the establishment of the CANADA COUNCIL in 1957, the federal government had taken a timid step into the field of culture, hitherto a provincial jurisdiction. At first its budgets were too modest to cause offence, but over time, and especially with the rising separatist movement in Québec, its subsidies grew and became the most accessible source of publishing assistance. Publishers, beneficiaries of 2 sources of income, federal and provincial, expanded their lists enormously during the 1970s. In 1968, 819 titles were published; in 1977, 3997. This increase was not solely due to publishing grants. Since they were taking fewer risks, publishers grew less selective about their titles. Some critics felt quantity had not improved quality, yet the situation probably had more to do with social change than with quality. After 1968, literature took second place to the human and social sciences as the vehicle for ideas, for society's trends and aspirations. The new generation of readers, many of whom were college graduates, worked in educational and cultural fields such as the civil service, radio, television, newspapers and the universities. Specialized books on administrative and political science took their place alongside literary and pedagogic works. University presses (and, later, publisher Gaëtan Morin) took a large part of this market, but other publishers tried to balance their lists with a mixture of theoretical, practical and fictional titles. New houses such as la Presse, HMH, Québec amérique, les Quinze, Alain Stanké and VLB éditeur still emphasize literature, but publish in a broad range of subject areas.

Despite the protection offered by government policy, large subsidies and growing readership, Québec publishing is still in difficulty, mainly because of its limited market. A recession, such as that experienced in 1982, can have serious repercussions on many publishers.

MAURICE LEMIRE

Reading: I. Cau, *L'Édition au Québec, de 1960 à 1977* (1981); G. Laberge and A. Vachon, "Book Publishing in Quebec," in Ontario Royal Commission on Book Publishing, *Background Papers* (1972); Y. Lamonde, éd, *L'Imprimé au Québec: Aspects historiques, 18e-20e siècles* (1983); Maurice Lemire, *Introduction à la littérature québécoise (1900-1939)* (1981); A. Pontaut de Bellefeuille et al, *La Bataille du Livre au Québec* (1972).

Books in Canada (1971-) is a trade journal of Canadian BOOK PUBLISHING, distributed to bookstores throughout English-speaking Canada; it appears 10 times a year. It was founded by its first editor, Val Clery, as the result of a report on the promotion of books in Canada that Clery prepared for the Book Publishers' Council. *Books in Canada* publishes extensive reviews of current books, together with interviews with and profiles of authors, and special columns on paperbacks, children's books and other topics.

GEORGE WOODCOCK

Bookselling No official figures exist for the actual number of retail stores in English Canada selling new publications. According to the best sources available, *Book Trade in Canada* (1983), there are at least 1800. Of these, about 605 are independently owned, 466 are members of a chain operation, 127 are college or university outlets specializing in texts and scholarly books, 290 are religious bookstores, and approximately 319 are retailers who sell books as a sideline. About 45% of these stores are located in Ontario, by far the argest market for new books in Canada; BC bout 25%, and the Prairie region, perhaps 0%. The remaining 10% are thinly distributed hroughout the Maritimes and Québec, though, s elsewhere, there are some excellent individ-al bookstores in the eastern provinces. Almost ll of these bookstores will also retail other mer-handise, usually stationery or gift items, and vill frequently carry MAGAZINES.

The selling of educational books (textbooks nd learning aids) is left almost entirely to ollege and university outlets. Most booksellers re concerned with what are known as "trade ooks," which are sold by publishers to book-ellers in hardcover or paperback format and vhich cover any subject — novels, biography, ookbooks, self-help, art, etc. Trade books have een categorized as books that people do not ave to buy for educational or professional pur-oses, though some trade books do find their vay into the educational market. Specialization s increasing among Canadian bookstores and it s common to find a bookstore devoted entirely o science fiction, cookbooks, theatre or some ther specific subject.

Most Canadian booksellers rely to a great de-ree on imported — mainly American — books or their sales. In 1983 about 70% of all books old in bookstores in English Canada were of US rigin; Canadian books accounted for about 0%, and the rest were mainly British. Canadian ooks comprise a vital and positive element in ookstore sales, often monopolizing the fall and Christmas best-seller lists and making the dif-erence between annual profit and losses for the ook retailers. The great majority of American nd British books purchased by Canadian book-ellers arrives through exclusive Canadian agen-ies or the Canadian subsidiaries of foreign pub-ishers. Virtually all US or UK publishers of any ize have either a Canadian office or an agency rrangement, though a few booksellers buy heir foreign titles directly from the US or UK vholesalers.

There are virtually no Canadian wholesalers elling to booksellers except in the mass-market ield, where some booksellers prefer to deal with a local wholesale supplier. Canadian titles are ought from the publishers, who either have a Canadian publishing program as well as agency US, UK) lines or devote themselves entirely to he publishing of Canadian books.

The Canadian Retail Booksellers Assn, foun-ded in 1952, has a healthy and steadily growing membership of about 450 (1983). It also offers associate nonvoting memberships to publishers and agents. Each year in June, a large and lively annual convention takes place, usually in To-ronto or Vancouver, along with a trade fair at which publishers display their new titles in preparation for the major fall and Christmas season. Booksellers from across Canada make their buying decisions during the CBA trade fair. Since the 1970s a few regional buying fairs have been organized to take place after the CBA National Book Fair and provide a strictly business environment with little or no social activity.

About half of all the trade books bought in Canada are sold by chain bookstores, and their share of the total book market appears to be growing. The reasons for this trend are complex but have mainly to do with the chains' greater ability to finance the cost of space in high-traffic areas such as major shopping malls. Because of pressure from chain expansion and in imitation of their US counterparts, Canadian independent booksellers are showing an interest in more co-operative activity. The Canadian Booksellers Co-operative (1980), a member-owned entity which makes large-scale purchases at higher discounts than those available to individual members, re-sells to its members and passes on some of the extra discount.

New developments centering around sophis-ticated electronic ordering systems and im-proved physical distribution are seen as being of great importance in the immediate future. Cana-dian booksellers seem collectively to give every indication of regarding the next decade as the most challenging and potentially rewarding in the history of Canadian bookselling. *See also* BOOK PUBLISHING. WILLIAM ROBERTS

Booth, John Rudolphus, lumber manufac-turer, railroad builder (b near Waterloo, Lower Canada 5 Apr 1827; d at Ottawa 8 Dec 1925). In 1857 Booth took over a small shingle mill in Ottawa, which he gradually expanded until he held the most extensive timber limits in Canada and was the foremost manufacturer of lumber for American and British markets. In 1904 he entered the pulp and paper industry and de-veloped a far-flung transportation network. Booth, William Perley and George Noble com-pleted the Canadian Atlantic Ry after persuad-ing PM John A. MACDONALD of its value to the lumber trade and their value to the Conservative Party. Booth then added the Ottawa, Arnprior and Parry Sound Ry, and a fleet of Great Lakes boats. He avoided politics, although he actively campaigned against the Taft-Fielding RECIPROC-ITY agreements of 1911. He was co-founder of the Dominion (Canadian) Forestry Association and contributed to various charities.

RICHARD REID

Boothia, Gulf of, NWT, is entered through Prince Regent Inlet. To the E it is bounded by the NW coast of BAFFIN I, and to the W by the BOOTHIA PEN. Depths are generally about 275 m, decreas-ing southward. The gulf was named after Felix Booth, a wealthy London distiller, who in 1829 sponsored the Sir John ROSS expedition, which first explored the gulf in an ill-fated attempt to find the NORTHWEST PASSAGE. In fact the Boothia Pen bars any passage farther W from the gulf.

DOUG FINLAYSON

Boothia Peninsula, 32 300 km², northernmost tip of mainland N America, juts some 200 km N into the ARCTIC ARCHIPELAGO, separated from SOMERSET I by Bellot Str, which is a mere 2 km wide. It is joined to the mainland by a narrow neck almost severed by 2 deep inlets and a chain of large lakes. To the E, across the GULF OF BOO-THIA, is BAFFIN I. PRINCE OF WALES I lies NW, across Franklin Str. The desolate, treeless peninsula is formed on a central spine of Precambrian rock, flanked by flat-bedded limestone lowlands. Dis-covered in 1829 by John ROSS, it was named for Felix Booth, a distiller who had financed the ex-

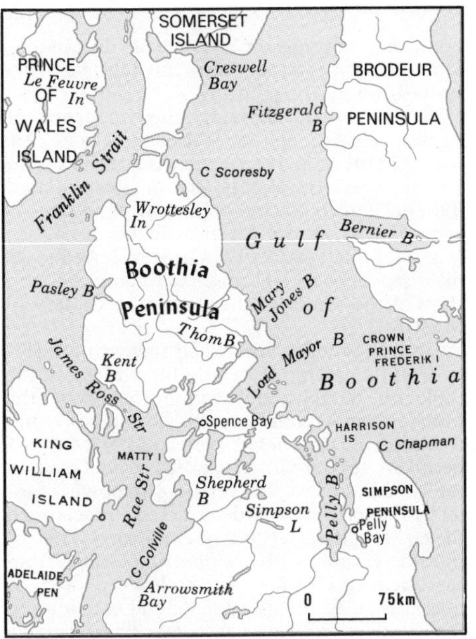

pedition. Imprisoned in the ice for 3 winters, Ross was forced to abandon his ship *Victory* and return on foot. His nephew, James C. Ross, later confirmed that Boothia is a peninsula and dis-covered the N magnetic pole near Cape Ade-laide. (The pole has since migrated northward.) Roald AMUNDSEN travelled the W coast by sledge in 1904, and H.A. LARSEN wintered at Pasley Bay on his successful voyage through the NORTHWEST PASSAGE 1941-42, journeying all around the pen-insula by sledge. There is a post and airfield at Spence Bay, on the isthmus, and a mission at Thom Bay. JAMES MARSH

Borden, Canadian Forces Base, Ont, 80 km NW of Toronto, was named after Sir Frederick BORDEN, Laurier's militia minister (1896-1911). Camp Borden was created 1916 on 60 km² of sandy plain as training grounds for flyers and soldiers in WWI. This dual role continued for the next 2 decades, with medical, service corps and infantry schools, and the first armoured school established in the 1930s. During WWII over 185 000 personnel trained here. After 1945 the school role intensified and the camp became more urban with the construction of permanent military and civilian support facilities. Unifi-cation of the armed forces gave the camp its present name. Occupying 85 km², it can house 8000 residents and in the early 1980s had an annual payroll of over $81 million. Its 15 000 yearly graduates have made it Canada's largest training centre for military trades and classifi-cations. R.G. HAYCOCK

Borden, Sir Frederick William, physician, merchant, politician (b at Upper Canard, NS 14 May 1847; d at Canning, NS 6 Jan 1917). As minister of militia and defence 1896-1911, he reorganized the Canadian Militia. Borden repre-sented King's County as a Liberal 1874-1911, except for 1882-87. A merchant in the carrying trade, Borden also acquired large corporate as-sets. While he was minister of militia, Canada sent troops to serve in the SOUTH AFRICAN WAR and expanded, reorganized and reformed its mi-litia to create an autonomous, self-contained, decentralized, citizen army capable of contrib-uting to imperial defence. CARMAN MILLER

Reading: Carman Miller, "Sir Frederick William Borden and Military Reform," *CHR* (1969).

Borden, Henry, businessman, public servant (b at Halifax 25 Sept 1901). Educated at McGill, Dalhousie and Oxford, Borden became one of Toronto's most prominent corporate lawyers. At the outbreak of WWII he was appointed to the War Supply Board in Ottawa and in 1942 was made chairman of the War Industries Control Board. Borden and C.D. HOWE, the minister of munitions and supply, worked well together and became friends. In 1943 Borden returned to his law practice and became chief fund raiser for the Conservative Party. From 1946 until 1963 he was president of Brazilian Light and Power Co; vice-chairman (1947-64) and chairman (1964-68) of the board of governors of U of To-ronto. Borden coauthored *Handbook of Canadian Company Law* (1931) and edited 2 books origi-nally drafted by his uncle: Sir Robert BORDEN's *Memoirs* (1938) and *Letters to Limbo* (1971).

ROBERT BOTHWELL

Borden, Sir Robert Laird, lawyer, politician (b at Grand Pré, NS 26 June 1854; d at Ottawa 10 June 1937). The eighth prime minister of Can-ada, Borden was a Halifax lawyer, leader of the Liberal-Conservative Party 1901-20, architect of the Conservative victory in the "Reciprocity Election" of 1911, PM during WWI and a lead-ing figure in the achievement of "Dominion Sta-tus" and the transition from the British Empire to the British Commonwealth of Nations.

Borden was a self-made man. After a brief formal education, he spent 5 years teaching at private academies in NS and New Jersey.

Returning to NS in 1874 to article in law, he was admitted to the Bar in 1878 and by 1890 headed a prestigious Halifax law firm. He was elected to Parliament in 1896 and in 1901 was selected by the Conservative caucus to succeed Sir Charles TUPPER as leader of the Liberal-Conservative Party. Over the next decade he worked to rebuild the CONSERVATIVE PARTY and establish a reform policy (the Halifax Platform of 1907). In 1911 he led the opposition to the Reciprocity Agreement negotiated by Sir Wilfrid LAURIER's government with the US and forced a general election. By skilful political management Borden brought together a coalition of anti-Laurier groups (Liberal businessmen opposed to RECIPROCITY, French Canadian *Nationalistes* opposed to the Naval Service Act, Conservative provincial administrations and his own parliamentary party) which defeated the Liberal Party.

Borden's leadership during WWI was remarkable. At home, his wartime government was responsible for the Emergency War Measures Act (1914), the first measures of direct taxation by the Ottawa government (the Wartime Business Profits Tax, 1916, and the "temporary" Income Tax, 1917), the nationalization of the Canadian Northern Ry as the first step in the creation of the CNR and, after the collapse of the voluntary recruiting system, the Military Service Act, 1917. Conscription was accompanied by the creation of a UNION GOVERNMENT of pro-conscriptionist Conservatives and Liberals which won the bitterly contested general election of 1917.

Overseas, the Canadian Expeditionary Force grew from one division to a full Canadian Corps commanded after 1917 by a Canadian, Lt-Gen Sir Arthur William CURRIE. Borden believed that the distinguished record of the CEF at Ypres, Vimy Ridge and Passchendaele and in the final 100 days was the ultimate proof of the maturity of Canadian nationhood. Principal author of Resolution IX of the Imperial War Conference of 1917, he argued that Canada and the other dominions deserved recognition "as autonomous nations of an Imperial Commonwealth." As leader of the Canadian delegation at the Paris Peace Conference in 1919, he was primarily responsible for international recognition of the autonomous status of the dominions. Borden retired as PM in 1920. In his last years he was recognized as an international statesman and firm advocate of the League of Nations. He pursued a successful career in business and served as chancellor of Queen's, 1924-30. ROBERT CRAIG BROWN

Reading: H. Borden, ed, *Robert Laird Borden: His Memoirs* (1938) and *Letters to Limbo* (1971); R. Borden, *Canadian Constitutional Studies* (1922) and *Canada in the Commonwealth* (1929); R. Craig Brown, *Robert Laird Borden*, 2 vols (1975, 1980).

Borden Island, 2795 km², is one of the Queen Elizabeth group in the high Arctic. Discovered by Vilhjalmur STEFANSSON in 1916 during the Canadian Arctic Expedition, its NW coast fronts on the Arctic Ocean. A generally low shoreline, cut by several streambeds, rises to a hilly interior. The island, named after Sir Robert BORDEN, prime minister 1911-20, is uninhabited.

DANIEL FRANCIS

Borduas, Paul-Émile, painter (b at St-Hilaire, Qué 1 Nov 1905; d Paris 22 Feb 1960). Leader of the AUTOMATISTES and author of REFUS GLOBAL, he had a profound influence on art in Canada. Ozias LEDUC encouraged young Borduas to study at the École des Beaux-Arts in Montréal (1923-27) and helped arrange his first stay in Paris (1928-30) at the Ateliers d'Art Sacré, directed by Maurice Denis. Upon his return to Canada, the economic crisis forced Borduas to abandon his dream of becoming, like "Monsieur Leduc," a church decorator, and to survive he had to settle for teaching drawing in Montréal. In 1937 he obtained a post somewhat closer to his aspirations, that of professor at the École du Meuble. Throughout this period, he painted little and destroyed much. His painting was figurative and gradually began showing the influence of Renoir, Pascin, James Wilson MORRICE and, later, Cézanne. In 1942, under the influence of the surrealism of André Breton, he produced some 60 nonfigurative gouaches, of which 45 were shown at the Théâtre de l'Ermitage in Montréal that year. In 1943 he transferred to oil the discoveries he had made with gouaches and showed the results at the Dominion Gallery in Montréal.

Paul-Emile Borduas, *Etoile noire* (1957), oil on canvas. At the end of his life, Borduas's painting became simplified to contrasts of black and white, and *Etoile noire* is probably his masterpiece (*courtesy Montreal Museum of Fine Arts*).

From then on, Borduas had increasing influence on the young, especially his students at the École du Meuble, and became leader of the Mouvement Automatiste which had showings in makeshift galleries in 1946 and 1947. In 1948 he drew up a manifesto called *Refus Global* in which, denouncing the suffocating power of established thinking in Québec, he proclaimed the right to total freedom of expression. The authorities responded by removing Borduas from his teaching position. The following year, he unsuccessfully attempted to defend his views in the autobiographical pamphlet, *Projections libérantes*, but to no avail. He was never to return to teaching. All that remained to him was painting, and he became completely immersed in his work.

Borduas moved to New York and lived there 1953-55. His pictorial goals expanded under the influence of Action painting. Always dissatisfied, he left for Paris in 1955. Toward the end of his life, his painting became simplified to contrasts of black and white. *L'Étoile noire* (1957) is probably his masterpiece. Though always successful with Canadian collectors, he had difficulty penetrating the Parisian milieu. Increasingly lonely, he dreamed of returning to Canada but died in Paris in 1960, leaving behind an outstanding life and body of art. The National Gallery of Canada and the Musée d'Art Contemporain and the Musée des Beaux-Arts in Montréal contain examples of his work.

FRANÇOIS-MARC GAGNON

Reading: François-Marc Gagnon, *Paul-Émile Borduas* (1978).

Boreal Forest, *see* VEGETATION REGIONS.

Bornstein, Eli, artist, educator (b at Milwaukee, Wis 28 Dec 1922). He was educated at U Wis and in 1950 began teaching at U Sask, becoming head of the art department in 1963. His works of the 1950s started from small, low-form, white reliefs and progressed towards larger, more complex works, with planes projecting further into space and utilizing primary colours. In 1954 he was introduced to the works of Charles Biederman, an experience which reaffirmed his direction and his major influences — Claude Monet/Paul Cézanne and cubism/constructivism. In 1957, when in Europe, Bornstein met Jean Gorin, Joost Baljeu, Anthony Hill, Kenneth and Mary Martin, Victor Pasmore and Georges Vantongerloo and returned to Saskatoon committed to the exploration of form-colour-structure relationships through 3-dimensional works. He began to work with a coloured ground plane and an expanded colour range in the 1960s. In 1966 he made his first double-plane reliefs and then went on to explore multiplane reliefs. Bornstein's structurist works combine elements of both painting and sculpture to develop and extend the landscape tradition. A Canadian citizen from 1972, he founded and edited *The Structurist* (1960-), an international art publication.

Botanical Garden A botanical garden is distinguished from a public park or display garden (eg, Butchart Gardens, BC) by having a documented collection of woody or herbaceous PLANTS on which scientific research and teaching are conducted. Arrangement of plants within a botanical garden is often made according to a botanical evolutionary sequence, or by geographic origin, special use or function. Modern botanical gardens typically serve 3 functions: education, research and public information. In Canada, most gardens are federal, provincial or municipal institutions or, most frequently, are associated with a university. If the collection consists primarily of woody plants, it may be called an ARBORETUM. Canadian gardens form part of the American Assn of Botanical Gardens and Arboreta and participate in the International Assn of Botanical Gardens.

History

The early herbal or physic gardens were created by physicians and students of medicine to grow plants having medicinal or pharmaceutical properties. The first botanical gardens devoted to broader studies of plants, including those of both economic and horticultural significance, were developed in Italy: in Pisa (1543) and Padua (1545). Shortly thereafter, botanical gardens were established in Leipzig, Germany (1580); Leyden, Holland (1587); and Montpellier, France (1593). In the 17th and 18th centuries, many gardens were founded to examine scientifically new plants introduced to Europe. Governments saw the potential of developing these plants as crops. The importance of botanical gardens in the introduction of new crop plants is exemplified by the Royal Botanic Garden, Kew, England (est 1759), which pioneered the development of rubber, banana, tea, pineapple, coffee and cacao. Many botanical gardens continue to introduce new plants, emphasizing both economic and ORNAMENTAL varieties. The tradition of systematic BOTANY (classifying and identifying plants) continues, and recent ecological studies are providing a better understanding of plant resources, particularly of rare and ENDANGERED SPECIES.

Development of Canadian Botanical Gardens

The first botanical garden was established in 1861 by George Lawson at Queen's College (now Queen's University), Kingston, Ont, but it lasted only until the 1870s. In 1886, the Experimental Farms Act of the federal Dept of Agriculture was passed and, one year later, an Arboretum and Botanical Garden was initiated at the Central Experimental Farm, Ottawa. Other research- and display-oriented gardens were later developed by the department at other stations. The second university botanical garden was established at Vancouver by John Davidson in 1916. It continues to thrive as a separate academic service department of UBC. The city of Montréal established the Jardin Botanique before WWII; it is now one of the major world gardens. The Royal Botanical Gardens, Hamilton, were established in 1941. The postwar period saw several new gardens develop as population centres increased. A review of some Canadian botanical gardens follows.

British Columbia UBC Botanical Garden (44.5 ha), including Nitobe Memorial Garden, Lohbrunner Alpine Garden, Asian Garden and BC Native Garden, operates a program of plant introduction to the nursery industry and an active educational research program. Van Dusen Botanical Display Garden (est 1972, 22 ha), operated by Vancouver Board of Parks and Recreation, specializes in displays of ornamental plants and offers educational programs with the Vancouver Botanical Garden Assn.

Alberta Devonian Botanic Garden, University of Alberta, Edmonton (est 1959, 77 ha), devotes special attention to alpine and native plants and conducts research on the hardiness of ornamental perennials and woody plants.

Saskatchewan Ross Arboretum, Indian Head (est 1946, 10 ha), operated by Agriculture Canada, specializes in the development of hardy trees for the Prairie region; planting began in 1902.

Manitoba Morden Research Station Arboretum (est 1930, 254 ha), operated by Agriculture Canada, specializes in selection and introduction of cold-hardy ornamental cultivars of herbaceous perennials, trees and shrubs.

Ontario University of Guelph Arboretum (est 1970, 133.5 ha) houses a research and evaluation collection of conifers and hardwoods, including shrub roses, nut-bearing trees and ornamental shrubs; the collection includes natural woodland. Royal Botanical Gardens, Hamilton (809 ha), comprises a series of attractively landscaped gardens within a larger natural woodland setting, including Katie Osborne Lilac Garden, Iris Garden, Centennial Rose Garden, Rock Garden and Trail Garden of Annuals. The Garden includes extensive natural areas and operates active educational and research programs. Erindale College Arboretum, Mississauga (est 1973, 73 ha), specializes in trees, shrubs and woody ornamentals for urban regions; natural woodland forms part of the Arboretum. Agriculture Canada Arboretum and Botanic Gardens, Ottawa (est 1887, 55 ha), has some of the oldest cultivated woody specimens in Canada that have been evaluated for hardiness. Rose, hedge and rock garden annual and perennial test gardens are also present. Laurentian University Botanical Garden, Sudbury (est 1972, 7 ha), specializes in native plants of the region. Lakehead University Arboretum, Thunder Bay (est 1975), contains a special collection of woody plants, particularly conifers, junipers and lilacs, which are used as part of the campus landscape.

Québec Jardin Botanique, Montréal (est 1931, 73 ha), operated by Service des Parcs de la Ville de Montréal, includes outstanding conservatory displays and extensive outdoor display gardens featuring such specialties as a taxonomic and medicinal garden. Morgan Arboretum, Macdonald College, Qué (est 1948, 243 ha), contains a collection of native Canadian trees, with special emphasis on birch.

Newfoundland Oxen Pond Botanic Park, Memorial University, St John's (est 1972, 34 ha), contains specialized display gardens, including a garden to attract butterflies, set in a natural woodland setting. ROY L. TAYLOR

Botany, the study of PLANTS and plant life, is both a descriptive and an experimental science. It began with the collection of medicinal herbs; in the process, herbalists identified many plants not used in healing. In the Middle Ages, plants known to be effective as medicines were cultivated in herb gardens (*see* BOTANICAL GARDEN). Drugs derived from such plants were important articles of long-distance trade. Botany now studies all aspects of plant life, from the BIOCHEMISTRY of plant pigments to the measurement of total plant production for the planet.

Subdivisions The study of plant life is organized in 3 ways, which are also applicable to zoological material.

The first scheme divides botanical material into a hierarchy of plant systems based on progressively larger units: molecules, organelles, cells, tissues, organs, whole plants, populations, communities, ecosystems, landscapes, biomes and the biosphere. Examples of levels of organization are large molecules, eg, DNA or chlorophyll; organelle systems, eg, nucleus or chloroplast; cells; tissue systems consisting of several types of cell; and whole plants, which may be as different as tiny planktonic plants and lofty Douglas firs. Within the hierarchy, each organizational system contains components, including more basic systems and nonliving features (eg, air spaces, oil vacuoles or space between individual plants). Each level, however, is individually integrated, and an understanding of simpler systems does not imply an understanding of higher ones, eg, the behaviour of a whole plant cannot be predicted from knowledge of its cells. The attributes of life (growth, metabolism, reproduction, movement, responsiveness to environment) are equally obvious at each level.

In the second scheme, botanical material is studied as part of a particular group of plants, eg, GRASSES, LICHENS, MOSSES, FERNS, TREES, WEEDS.

In the third scheme, botanical material belonging to a particular type of system in the hierarchy and to a particular group of plants is studied from one of several perspectives. Each may be examined in its composition, structure, function, heredity, relation to environment, development, history, classification and distribution. At the whole plant level, these divisions are termed, respectively, anatomy, morphology, physiology, GENETICS, ecology, genesis, evolution, taxonomy and plant geography.

In Canada, interest in plant identification, classification and distribution developed early; however, there are still vast areas for which plant inventories are incomplete. One important historical factor affecting the distribution of plant populations and VEGETATION in Canada is GLACIATION. Some botanists believe that the 10 000 years since the retreat of the last ice sheet is too short a period for some plants to have recolonized the whole range of available habitats. Mapping the migration of these returning plants, and the movement of alien weeds into open or disturbed habitats, gives a historical perspective, as does analysis of fossil pollen (PALYNOLOGY), which traces sequences of types of vegetation inhabiting different parts of Canada since glacial times. Study of evolutionary changes in pigments, cells and tissues gives a historical view at other levels. The development of a single organism at early stages (embryogenesis) may occur in a few days; at the vegetation level, development (succession) may take place over several hundred years.

The ecological focus, a more recent development, attempts to assess the influence of environmental factors on populations, individuals, cells and organelles. Not only well-known environmental factors (eg, temperature, water, energy as food or radiation, minerals, air and harmful or beneficial animals), but also chemical pollutants (eg, ACID RAIN) must now be included as specific environmental factors that operate in concert to affect development, structure and functioning at the various levels of plant organization.

Plant genetics began early with the selection of CROP and ORNAMENTAL plants for yield, flavour, beauty, perfume or medical value. This remains an active area of research for scientists convinced that the balance between food production and increasing human populations can be achieved through the development of more efficient plants. Plant breeders are at the forefront of the "green revolution." Correct environment, with adequate mineral nutrients and water, also contributes to higher crop yields, while crop protection methods ensure that the output survives for human use.

The study of plant genetics has led to successful plant-breeding programs in crop species. For example, the Canadian range of corn has been extended to areas formerly thought to have too short a growing season, and plant breeders can now tailor a specific variety of corn to a particular geographic area. For many plants, multiplication and propagation are solely vegetative, resulting in a large clone of very uniform genetic material. For example, all important varieties of apple are propagated by grafting or budding, and potatoes are seldom produced from seed. Less welcome results of vegetative propagation can be seen in great overgrowths of pondweeds in waterways (eg, Trent and Rideau systems) and in the Okanagan Valley. These large "nuisance" populations are produced from fragments which separate from parent plants. Although vegetative propagation is common in plants, it is impossible in nature for vertebrate animals in which each individual develops from a fertilized egg.

All life on earth is dependent on green plants storing energy in chemical bonds and producing oxygen, and on nongreen plants making available the minerals that are essential for growth. Nongreen plants (like most other living things) are "heterotrophic" and must get energy for life processes in the form of chemical compounds. Green plants' energy requirements are met through photosynthesis. Examination of the process of energy use by green plants has shown, however, that up to 50% of all energy fixed by at least some green plants "leaks out" again and is lost. Until a clearly defined function for these "escaped" substances is found, the system must be considered inefficient.

An understanding of the development of plant structure contributes to our view of the functions of cells, tissues, plants and vegetation, and may lead to better control of growth. Techniques developed for the electron microscope, in which electrons are either passed through thin tissue sections or bounced off plant material, are used to examine composition, structure and development. Many details of plant structure at the tissue and cell level, formerly hidden because of small size, have been revealed by these methods, and new techniques continue to be developed to display further the elegance of life within cells. All institutions in Canada that research plant structure use both transmission electron microscopes and scanning electron microscopes.

Applications Natural drugs, dyes, flavours and spices produced by plants have been important since ancient times. Recently, many of these have been replaced by synthetic copies. Aspects of agriculture dealing with plants that have botany as a foundation include crop production, horticulture, pasture renovation, market gardening, crop breeding, FORESTRY, flower production, LANDSCAPE ARCHITECTURE and WILDLIFE CONSERVATION AND MANAGEMENT. In addition, many POISONOUS PLANTS must be understood so that their deleterious effects can be reduced. Botany, therefore, contributes in various ways to the health, welfare and happiness of Canadians.

Fields of Work Botanists are employed by federal and provincial governments and as consultants in industry. They also teach in universities, colleges and schools. Their endeavours may be academic ("pure" research) or applied to solving problems of economic or other significance. Frequently, they co-operate with zoologists, meteorologists, soil scientists, oceanographers or other scientists.

Societies Studies undertaken by botanists are diverse and depend upon level of hierarchy, type of plant material and focus of interest. As a result, membership of the several botany-related societies in Canada does not fully reflect the botanical interests of Canadian botanists, who also belong to international societies. If a botanist classifies lichens, he is likely to join a society where he will meet individuals from other countries (eg, Australia or Finland) primarily interested in lichens, rather than joining a Canadian society of less specific focus. The botanist studying population dynamics of algae would have more in common with members of a society dealing with populations (plant and animal) than a society devoted to algae classification. Some Canadian associations that include botanists in their membership are the Canadian Botanical Assn, Royal Soc of Canada, Canadian Soc of Plant Physiologists, Canadian Phytopathological Soc, Assn of the Scientific, Engineering and Technological Community of Canada, Assn canadienne-française pour l'avancement des sciences, Agricultural Inst of Canada, Arctic Inst of N America, Canadian Forestry Assn, Canadian Inst of Forestry, Canadian Soc for Cell Biology, Canadian Soc of Cytology, Canadian Soc of Environmental Biologists, Canadian Soc of Microbiologists, Genetics Soc of Canada, Canadian Biochemical Soc, Canadian Soc of Landscape Architects, Canadian Ornamental Plant Foundation, Jeunes biologistes du Québec, and the various provincial institutes of agrologists. There are 80 local or provincial naturalists' clubs. Journals published in Canada include *Canadian Jnl of Botany, Canadian Jnl of Plant Science, Canadian Jnl of Microbiology, Canadian Jnl of Genetics and Cytology, Canadian Jnl of Plant Pathology, Canadian Jnl of Forest Research, Le Naturaliste canadien, Canadian Field Naturalist, Ontario Field Biologist. See* ANIMAL; BIOLOGY; FUNGUS.

HUGH DALE

Botany History Long before formal study of PLANTS began in Canadian academic institutions, they were studied by explorers and talented amateurs. The vegetation of Canada was first known through descriptive reports of travellers, then through the importing of seeds and bulbs for cultivation in Europe, and finally through collection and distribution of HERBARIUM specimens. The first references are a few names in vernacular in Icelandic sagas; the NORSE are now known to have travelled as far as northern Newfoundland. From descriptions and vernacular names in the reports of Jacques CARTIER's voyages, it is possible to recognize 35-40 species of eastern Canadian plants. Cartier also brought back seeds and is known to have introduced white PINE *(Pinus strobus)* and white CEDAR *(Thuja occidentalis)* to European gardens. Further progress was slow, but in 1576 Clusius provided the first formal descriptions of the following Canadian plants: common MILKWEED *(Asclepias syriaca)* and PITCHER PLANT *(Limonio congener*, now known as *Sarracenia purpurea)*.

In 1623 a series of 27 Canadian species were given scientific names by C. Bauhin; identification was based on cultivated materials, and specimens are found today in the herbarium at Uppsala, Sweden. The source is stated to be an unnamed apothecary, but circumstantial evidence points to Louis HÉBERT, the first European to cultivate land on the St Lawrence R, who resided in Paris for a few years after his travels in Acadia. About 60 Canadian plants were described, named and illustrated by Jacques Cornuti in his *Canadensium Plantarum Historia* (1635). The descriptions were based on material cultivated in the garden of V. Robin, and brought over by a French navigator (probably CHAMPLAIN, who took with him plants from his garden when he left Québec in 1629). Other plants are occasionally noted in the reports of T. Sagard and other travellers and in the JESUIT RELATIONS. The next principal source is *Histoire véritable et naturelle . . . de la Nouvelle-France . . .* (1664), by Pierre BOUCHER, in which about 50 (mainly woody) plants are discussed. His botany was analysed by Jacques ROUSSEAU in 1964.

Herbaria originated in Europe around 1550, but this research tool was not to play a role in Canada until a century and a half later. Michel SARRAZIN, appointed Médecin du Roi for NEW FRANCE and correspondent of the French Academy, took his post at Québec in 1697. He collected his first herbarium specimens at Plaisance in southern Newfoundland. Every year Sarrazin sent written observations and specimens to his correspondents at the Paris Academy. From his first shipment, J.P. Tournefort in 1700 described 8 new plant species. Later shipments went to Sébastien Vaillant and B. Jussieu. Some 16 new species were published from 1700 to 1716; otherwise, Sarrazin's botanical work remained largely unpublished. It is now known from a manuscript draft of about 1708, which describes about 225 species, and was annotated and published in 1977. Sarrazin's specimens are in the Muséum d'Histoire Naturelle, Paris.

Sarrazin's contemporary, W. Hay, a ship's surgeon, collected in Newfoundland in 1699; his specimens are at the British Museum, London. The same year, another surgeon Dièreville came to Acadia and collected some 25 specimens, one of which is now known as *Diervilla lonicera*, the bush HONEYSUCKLE. The 3-volume *Histoire de la Nouvelle-France* (1744) by P.F.X. de CHARLEVOIX contains some plant information, including a botanical appendix (largely based on Cornuti) and describes 3 new species contributed by Sarrazin.

The next king's physician, J.F. GAULTHIER, arrived in 1742. A few of his botanical discoveries were published by D. DuMonceau but his botany is mostly known through 400 pages of surviving manuscripts. He accompanied Pehr KALM during his 1749 Canadian expedition, which provided C. Linnaeus with most of his Canadian material (about 200 species) included in his *Species Plantarum* (1753). In 1755 the Hôtel-Dieu, Québec City, was destroyed by fire. Losses apparently also included the herbarium of Sarrazin and Gaultier. Duplicate specimens have been found at the Muséum d'Histoire Naturelle, Paris.

André MICHAUX arrived in N America in 1785, primarily to study TREES, and was responsible for introducing to Europe various native Canadian species. In 1792 he spent 3 summer months collecting plants in LOWER CANADA and as far N as Lk MISTASSINI. Returning to France in 1796, Michaux took with him a large herbarium, a manuscript FLORA and a monograph on oaks. The flora contains 1720 species, hundreds of them new and about 520 from Lower Canada and the Illinois country. The Michaux flora, published posthumously in 1803, seems to have evoked little interest in Canada, but in the US it was a pattern-making publication and the source of an intellectual explosion. By providing better coverage of the vegetation and by eliminating all extraneous species, it was more practical than the world floras then in use. Within 11 years, Frederick PURSH came out with a flora of N America containing more than 3000 species. Pursh moved to Canada intending to prepare a flora of Canada, but died in Montréal (1820) without completing it. A.F. Holmes, founder and future dean of the Faculty of Medicine at McGill, collected plants in the Montréal area from 1821 to 1825. His herbarium remained in Canada (McGill). The only earlier surviving one retained in Canada, that of Mrs Percival, is now with Agriculture Canada, Ottawa.

William J. Hooker was a man of encyclopedic botanical knowledge. His personal herbarium (about one million sheets) was acquired by Kew Gardens, London, in 1867. In about 1820, Hooker became interested in the flora of Canada and contacted local amateurs (eg, A.M. Percival, Harriet and William Sheppard and Lady Dalhousie, who collected in NS, starting in 1816, then in Québec, in 1820 and later). With the cooperation of the Hudson's Bay Company, he was able to send a number of natural-history explorers to N America, including John Goldie, T. DRUMMOND, D. DOUGLAS, D. THOMPSON and J. RICHARDSON. From this accumulated material, Hooker produced a 2-volume flora in 1840; because of its high cost, it was out of reach of all but the wealthiest amateurs. Léon PROVANCHER's flora was published in 1862; the catalogue of John MACOUN in 1883-1902. Macoun's herbarium, Canada's largest at the time, now forms the basis of the National Herbarium, Ottawa.

Canada's first botanical society, founded at McGill in 1855, was short-lived. The Botanical Society of Canada was founded in Kingston, Ont, in 1860 and in 1861 inaugurated the *Annals of the Botanical Society of Canada*. This society and 2 later ones were also short-lived. In contrast, the Botanical Club of Canada, Halifax, lasted from 1891 to 1910. The Field Botanists of Ontario 2 or 3 years later was founded in the 1890's.

An outstanding characteristic of Canadian botany in the 19th and early 20th centuries is the domination by American botanists (F. Pursh, T. Nuttall, J. Torrey, A. Gray, A. Wood, N.L. Britton, M.L. Fernald, P.A. Rydberg, L. Abrams, etc). Other foreign contributors were also important: a flora of Labrador was published in Germany by E. Meyer; the Yukon was included in a 10-volume flora by E. Hultén, a Swede; Hooker has already been noted; N. Polunin, a British citizen of Russian origin, wrote a flora of the eastern Arctic; I. Hustich, a Finn, compiled a list and physiogeographic study of Labrador.

Canadians were not, however, totally absent from the scene. George LAWSON was appointed professor of chemistry and natural history at Queen's in 1858. He was primarily interested in botany and was instrumental in founding the Botanical Society of Canada before leaving to become professor of chemistry at Dalhousie. H. Reeks compiled a list of the flora of Newfoundland in 1873. In 1893 A.C. Waghorne began publishing a list for Labrador, Newfoundland and Saint-Pierre and Miquelon. J.W. DAWSON, an outstanding paleobotanist, published mainly in the *Memoirs of the Royal Society of Canada*. A.W. Lindsay published a list of NS plants in 1875. Various lists and studies of vascular plants of NS were also published, mainly by G.U. Hay and A.H. MacKay. A group of amateurs studied the flora of NB and the results were compiled by W.J. Fowler in lists published in 1878 and 1885. PEI was the last Atlantic province to have its list published (by F. Bain in 1890). Most provinces and territories now have their own flora: southern BC since 1915; a manual for SW Qué, 1931, and a broader and more elaborate flora, 1935; the YT, 1941-50; NS, 1947 and 1966-69; Man, 1957; Alta, 1959; PEI, 1961; the NWT, 1957 and 1979. A flora of the Prairie provinces in 5 parts came out from 1967 to 1981. Two items of national scope should be noted: an *Enumération* published in 1966-67 provides distributions by provinces and extensive bibliographies, while H.J. Scoggan's 4-volume *The Flora of Canada* (1978-79), National Museum of Natural Sciences, supplies keys and synonymy.

Thus, at the turn of the century, Canadian botanists were still primarily concerned with lists and inventories. Not much had been done outside the field of floristics (except for Dawson's work in paleobotany). Another noted 19th-century paleobotanist was D.P. Penhallow of McGill, who also authored papers on botanical history and bibliography. In the early 20th century numerous local centres of activity arose gradually in each province: most in universities some in museums and a few in government laboratories. In the late 19th century in Canadian universities, broad scientific disciplines (eg, natural history, natural sciences, physical sciences) began to be divided into more specialized subject areas. Plant studies first came under the auspices of BIOLOGY departments, which subsequently split, in some universities, into departments of botany and ZOOLOGY.

In mycology (the study of FUNGI) the main centre has been the Dept of Agriculture (now Agriculture Canada) in Ottawa, recently with D.B.O. SAVILE as principal mycologist (1957-75). For a time, University of Manitoba was also very active. Under A.H. Buller (appointed professor of botany in 1904) and G.R. Bisby much research was carried out and basic surveys of the fungi of Manitoba and Saskatchewan were published. Buller's *Research in Fungi* (7 vols, 1909-34) became a standard authority. An outstanding amateur, John Dearness, of London, Ont, had a herbarium of 50 000 specimens and published taxonomic papers, while participating in the studies of the Winnipeg group. More recently, R. Pomerleau has published a monumental work *Flore des Champignons au Québec*. Bryology (the study of LIVERWORTS and MOSSES) and lichenology (study of LICHENS) have attracted professionals and amateurs. Among the amateurs, Ernest LEPAGE, an outstanding botanical explorer (Labrador to Alaska), contributed to both bryology and lichenology. His herbarium and botanical library were left to Laval. Algology (study of ALGAE) is currently a very active field on both coasts. Desmids were the subject of major contributions by Irénée-Marie, starting in 1939. Cytotaxonomy is practised in many places, especially in Ottawa where H.A. Senn assembled an active team soon after WWII. The outstanding team of A. and D. Löve worked in Winnipeg and then Montréal before moving to the US in 1962. In these and other fields, workers are scattered across Canada in university departments of botany or biology and government laboratories.

Amateurs have also contributed to scientific botany, mainly in the fields of floristics, taxonomy and ecology. J. Dearness and E. Lepage have already been mentioned; others include A.H. Brinkman, a bryologist working in Craigmyle, Alberta; H. Dupret, also a bryologist, in the Montréal area; W.C. McCalla, a school teacher, amateur photographer and outstanding plant collector in southern Ontario and Alberta; Rolland-Germain, a keen field botanist and constant companion of Frère MARIE-VICTORIN, whose Québec and Ontario collections are outstanding; N.B. Sanson, a park naturalist in Banff; G.H. Turner, a retired physician in Fort Saskatchewan, Alta. At least 10 others have herbaria of 10 000 or more specimens. Many amateurs eventually became leading professionals, eg, Macoun, A.E. PORSILD and Marie-Victorin. Marie-Victorin's herbarium (65 000 specimens) is now part of the herbarium of the Université de Montréal's Institut Botanique which, with holdings of 500 000 specimens, is the largest outside Ottawa. *See* BOTANICAL GARDEN; CROP RESEARCH. B. BOIVIN

Botterell, Edmund Harry, neurosurgeon, medical educator (b at Vancouver, BC 28 Feb 1906). Graduation in medicine from U Man was followed by neurosurgical training at U of T and research at Yale. During WWII Botterell served as senior neurosurgeon to No 1 Canadian Neurological Hospital, Basingstoke, Eng. On returning to Toronto he became committed to the rehabilitation of paraplegic veterans. In 1952 he was appointed chief of neurosurgery at the Toronto General Hospital and he was chairman of U of T's division of neurosurgery 1953-61. Between 1962 and 1971 Botterell served as dean of medicine and then vice principal (health sciences) at Queen's. His personal magnetism and enthusiastic leadership stimulated unprecedented expansion in teaching, research and patient care in Kingston. He was later commissioned to study health-related matters in penitentiaries. A.A. TRAVILL

Botulism, a severe but rare type of acute FOOD POISONING occurring in humans, various mammals and birds. The disease results from the consumption of food containing the potent botulinum toxin. The causative organism is *Clostridium botulinum*, an anaerobic, rod-shaped bacterium that produces heat-resistant spores. The spores are universally distributed, occurring in soils, freshwater and marine sediments and the intestinal tract of many animals. For an outbreak of botulism to occur, the spores must get into food and germinate. The germinated cells must then multiply and secrete the toxin. After the contaminated food is consumed, the toxin is absorbed from the small intestine. The characteristic symptoms usually develop in 8-72 hours. The toxin is a neurotoxin affecting nerve terminals of the parasympathetic nervous system; accordingly, the symptoms present a type of progressive paralysis. Gastrointestinal symptoms (eg, nausea, vomiting, diarrhea) may be evident before the neurological symptoms appear. Neurological symptoms are weakness, dizziness and vertigo, followed by blurred vision and difficulty in speaking and swallowing. Death may result from asphyxiation caused by paralysis of the diaphragm and chest muscles. The fatality rate has declined from over 60% to about 30%, in part because antitoxin is administered promptly in suspected cases and because mechanical respirators are used.

Control of botulism is based almost entirely on thermal destruction of the spores. Through the establishment and enforcement of strict, standardized time-temperature treatments, the commercial food-canning industry has been so successful in preventing botulism that it has become almost insignificant as a source of the disease. Home canning may lead to botulism because the time-temperature treatment of foods may be insufficient to kill the spores, especially in "low-acid" foods (eg, corn, peppers, green beans, mushrooms). Home canners should use approved pressure-cooker processes for such products. An additional safeguard is boiling these foods for 10-15 minutes before serving; this process will inactivate the botulinum toxin, if present. Some traditional foods of the native peoples of Canada, including whale, seal and walrus meat and salmon eggs, present special problems. The foods *per se* are not hazardous, but when they are preserved in various dried and fermented forms conditions conducive to the growth of *C. botulinum* are created. H. JACKSON

Bouchard, Télesphore-Damien, journalist, politician (b at St-Hyacinthe, Qué 20 Dec 1881; d at Montréal 13 Nov 1962). After several years as a journalist, Bouchard became virtually permanent mayor of St-Hyacinthe (1917-44) and simultaneously, perpetual Liberal MLA (1912-44). He became Speaker of the Québec legislature in 1930 and entered the Taschereau government in 1935. Bouchard became Opposition leader in 1936, entered the government of Joseph-Adélard GODBOUT in 1939, and in 1944 was appointed by PM Mackenzie KING to the Senate. Bouchard was best known for his 1944 charges that a French Canadian secret society, the ORDRE DE JACQUES CARTIER, was a danger to Canadian society. ROBERT BOTHWELL

Boucher, Frank, hockey player (b at Ottawa 7 Oct 1901; d at Kemptville, Ont 12 Dec 1977). He played for the RCMP, Ottawa and Vancouver before joining New York Rangers in 1926. He was the playmaking centre on the famous line with Bun and Bill COOK. Respected for his clean play, he won the LADY BYNG TROPHY 7 times in 8 seasons; it was finally given to him and another one made. JAMES MARSH

Boucher, Gaetan, speed skater (b at Charlesbourg, Qué 10 May 1958). Boucher began SPEED SKATING as an adjunct to hockey. By the time he was 14 he had won his first of many Canadian championships. A sixth place in the 1000 m at the 1976 Innsbruck Winter Olympics established him as a top international competitor. In 1977 he was World Indoor Speed-skating Champion and in 1978, 1980 and 1982 he finished second at the more prestigious World Sprint Speed-skating Championships. At the 1980 Lake Placid Winter Olympics he finished behind American Eric Heiden to win the silver in the 1000 m, one of only 2 Canadian medals that year. The 1984 Sarajevo Olympics saw Boucher return from a broken ankle suffered the previous year to record the greatest performance by a Canadian in the Winter Olympics. With a fine technique developed because of his small stature, he won gold medals at 1000 and 1500 m and a bronze in the 500. He followed this by capturing the 1984 World Sprint Speed-skating Championship. DEREK DRAGER

Boucher, Pierre, interpreter, soldier, seigneur (bap at Mortagne, France 1 Aug 1622; d at Boucherville 19 Apr 1717). He lived in HURONIA 1637-41, assisting the missionaries, living among the Indians and learning their dialects. From 1645, he lived in Trois-Rivières, distinguishing himself in its defence against IROQUOIS raids. He became captain of Trois-Rivières 1649, and governor 1654. Boucher was sent to France 1661 to plead for help, returning with soldiers and supplies and a commitment to make NEW FRANCE a crown colony. He built his seigneury of Boucherville into one of the most prosperous in the colony. His memoirs contain a valuable record of the FUR TRADE, the Indians, and his remarkable life. JAMES MARSH

Boucherville, Sir Charles-Eugène Boucher de, doctor, politician, premier of Québec 1874-78 and 1891-92 (b at Montréal 4 May 1822; d there 10 Sept 1915). A Conservative member of the Assembly of the Province of Canada, he was appointed to the Québec Legislative Council in 1867. He was premier of the province from 1874 until Mar 1878 when Liberal Lt-Gov Luc Letellier de Saint-Just, in a move labelled a *coup d'état* by the Conservatives, removed him from office and replaced him with Liberal Henri-Gustave JOLY de Lotbinière. Boucherville's administration brought in electoral reform and in 1875 abolished the Dept of Public Instruction, replacing it with an appointed superintendent of education. In 1891 after MERCIER's government had been tainted by the BAIE DES CHALEURS SCANDAL, Boucherville again became premier but he resigned a year later. DANIEL LATOUCHE

Boudreau, Walter, composer, saxophonist (b at Montréal 15 Oct 1947). At age 19 he formed his own jazz band and at 20 led various jazz groups during Expo '67. In 1969 he founded Infonie with Raôul Duguay. Boudreau was associated with this mixed-media ensemble until 1973, giving performances of both avant-garde and classical music arranged as pop numbers. Infonie also made 3 albums, one of which presented Boudreau's own composition *Paix*. Largely self-taught initially, Boudreau studied composition and theory intensively in the 1970s. He won the CBC National Radio Competition for Young Composers in 1973 with *Variations I* for chamber ensemble, derived from one of several earlier film scores. ANN SCHAU

Bouey, Gerald Keith, banker (b at Axford, Sask 2 Apr 1920). He became governor of the BANK OF CANADA in Feb 1973 and guided the country's MONETARY POLICY through the inflationary difficulties of the early 1980s. A quiet man, Bouey emerged from wartime service in the RCAF and from university education at Queen's to join the Bank of Canada in 1948. He succeeded Louis RASMINSKY as governor in 1973, turned the bank's policy in monetarist directions, and struggled to control interest rates at the beginning of the 1980s. Many disagreed with his policy prescriptions, but few doubted his integrity ánd determination. J.L. GRANATSTEIN

Bougainville, Louis-Antoine de Bougainville, Comte de, soldier, sailor (b at Paris, France 12 Nov 1729; d there 20 Aug 1811). After studying law and mathematics, he published a *Traité de calcul intégral* (1754-56) and was elected to the Royal Society (London). Having entered the military in 1750, he was posted to Québec in 1756 as aide-de-camp to MONTCALM. Bougainville was involved in the campaigns of the SEVEN YEARS' WAR leading up to the Battle of the Plains of Abraham. Although he failed to bring reinforcements in time to alter the outcome, some considered Bougainville one of Montcalm's abler officers. In 1763 he entered the French navy and proceeded to found a short-lived colony composed mostly of ACADIANS, on the Falkland Islands. His scientific expeditions, 1766-69, were written up in *Voyage autour du monde* (1771; tr *A Voyage Round the World*, 1772), and the tropical vine "bougainvillaea" was named after him. DAVID EVANS

Boulton, Henry John, lawyer, politician, judge (b at Kensington, Eng 1790; d at Toronto 18 June 1870). Although Boulton was an office-holder in the 1830s, he is remembered chiefly for his controversial role in both Upper Canada and Newfoundland. Coming to Canada around 1800, Boulton studied law in York [Toronto] 1807-11 and continued his education in England until 1816. Returning to Upper Canada, he was welcomed into the governing circles of the FAMILY COMPACT, being appointed solicitor general in 1818 and attorney general in 1829. An "independent," he was elected to the Assembly for Niagara in 1830 and took a leading part in the expulsion of William Lyon MACKENZIE from the assembly in 1831 and 1832. When ordered in 1832 to reinstate Mackenzie, Boulton sharply criticized the Colonial Office, which promptly dismissed him. The following year he was named chief justice of Newfoundland, where he was again controversial and was recalled in 1838 . He resumed his law practice in Toronto, was elected to the Assembly in 1841, and by 1847 had moved within the Reform orbit of LA FONTAINE and BALDWIN. An individualist, by 1850 he had broken with the Reformers; he gave up politics in 1851 and retired from his law practice in 1861. HEREWARD AND ELINOR SENIOR

Boundaries The political boundaries that concern Canada today are the international boundaries primarily with the US and Greenland and, because they are of more than local importance, the boundaries of the provinces and territories. The evolution of both types involved 2 distinct stages. After political decisions were made on the allocation of territory, such territories were delimited and the boundaries described in state documents. Then, usually some time later, the boundaries were surveyed and marked on the ground (the process of demarcation). The beginnings of international and internal boundary delineations can be traced to the 1763 TREATY OF PARIS, which produced a great rearrangement of boundaries in N America. For this reason the SEVEN YEARS' WAR (1756-63) between Britain an France, which immediately preceded the treat is sometimes called the "War of the Boundar Lines." All of eastern N America except SAI PIERRE AND MIQUELON became British, and th boundaries of the various colonies were adjuste to accommodate the changed circumstance Later, as a result of the AMERICAN REVOLUTION, th colonies S of Newfoundland, Nova Scotia an the Province of Quebec, as well as that part Quebec between the Ohio and Mississippi rive were lost to Britain; hence Canada's prese boundaries with the US began to emerge aft the 1783 TREATY OF PARIS.

International Boundaries In 1783 the bound ary between the US and BRITISH NORTH AMERIC was described as running from the mouth of th St Croix R on the Bay of Fundy to its sourc thence along a line drawn due N to the "north west angle" of Nova Scotia (today northwester NB), thence along the watershed between th Atlantic and the St Lawrence to the northwe head of the Connecticut R, from there along th river to 45° N and along this parallel to the S Lawrence R. The boundary continued up the S Lawrence and through Lk Ontario, the Niagar R, Lk Erie, Lk St Clair, Lk Huron and Lk Superio to the Pigeon R, and thence to Lake of th Woods. From the northwest point of that lak the boundary was to run due W to the Missis sippi R. This description, based on a map of N America first published in 1755 by John Mit chell, and inaccurate in many respects, led to a least 9 boundary problems. In 1794 JAY'S TREAT began to clarify these problems.

The first controversy developed over the exac location of the St Croix R because 3 rivers existe where the Mitchell map showed only 2. Arbi trators favoured what is now the Schoodic R but it had 2 branches, and when the easter branch was selected, a line drawn N from it al most cut off the Maritime provinces from Lowe Canada. Commissions and arbitrations in 181 and 1831 could not reach an acceptable solution During the following period of tension, a clas occurred between lumbermen from NB an Maine in the disputed area (*see* AROOSTOOK WAR) The dispute ended only when a compromis was reached through the ASHBURTON-WEBSTE TREATY of 1842.

Another difficulty developed when it wa discovered that a line drawn due W from th northwestern point of Lake of the Woods di not encounter the Mississippi R, which rose far ther S than was indicated on the Mitchell map This difficulty was resolved by the CONVENTIO OF 1818: the FORTY-NINTH PARALLEL, accepted as th southern boundary of the HUDSON'S BAY COM PANY's territories between Lake of the Wood and the Rocky Mts, very roughly approximate the northern watershed of the Mississippi-Missouri drainage system embraced by Louisiana Territory, which had been acquired by th US from France in 1803.

West of the Rocky Mts the British were unwilling to relinquish control of the Orego country then in the hands of the HBC. Britai and the US therefore agreed to occupy Orego jointly for 10 years. In 1827 this comprimise wa reaffirmed for an indefinite period. However, i the 1840s American settlers in large numbers began to enter the area and demand exclusive US jurisdiction as far N as 54°40′ N, the souther limit of Russian territory on the Pacific coast Although "fifty-four forty or fight" became a American election campaign slogan in 1844, th British proposal to divide the area by extendin the boundary along the 49th parallel westwar to the coast and then through the Str of Juan d Fuca was incorporated into the OREGON TREATY 2 years later. This treaty did not precisely describ the water boundary, and further controvers was ultimately resolved by arbitration in 187 (*see* TREATY OF WASHINGTON).

The boundary between Russian and British territory was described in 1825, well before the American purchase of Alaska in 1867. The 141st meridian was chosen as the northern part of the boundary, probably because it ran N from Mt St Elias, one of the few outstanding and unmistakable features in a relatively unknown area, and because it separated the maritime interests of the Russians from the land interests of the HBC. South of Mt St Elias to Prince of Wales I, Russian territory extended inland from the coast for 10 marine leagues (about 55.6 km). Difficulties in interpreting the exact location of this boundary arose after the KLONDIKE GOLD RUSH. The crucial question was whether the Anglo-Russian Convention of 1825 called for a boundary drawn around the heads of the coastal inlets (favoured by the US), or one which followed the summits of the mountains paralleling the general trend of the coast and cut across all inlets and fjords (which Canada advocated). The problem was referred to a joint commission and later a tribunal, which described the boundary as it exists today (*see* ALASKA BOUNDARY DISPUTE). The boundary follows the American contention, so the Alaska Panhandle shuts Canada off from direct access to the Pacific Ocean in the north and is regarded as one of the circumstances limiting the development of MINING and HYDROELECTRICITY in northwestern BC.

Between 1870 and 1880 Canada's northern limits coincided with those of the former HBC territory. Britain transferred its rights to the arctic islands to the federal government. In 1907 the claim to the sector between 141° W and 60° W was first made, although it was not officially supported until 1925. The dividing line or "line of allocation" between Canada and Greenland from 61° N northward was agreed upon with Denmark in 1974.

Canada's seaward limits embrace the territorial sea, and generally include the marginal seas within 3 nautical miles (5.5 km) of the baselines on the coast. The most notable exceptions are in the Arctic, where Canadian sovereignty includes the waters between islands. Canadian coastal fishing zones extend seaward 200 nautical miles (about 371 km), as do those of many other nations.

Interprovincial and Interterritorial Boundaries The present-day boundaries of NS, PEI and NB resulted from circumstances that were significant only when these regions were created British colonies in the 18th and 19th centuries. After 1763, Nova Scotia included the present provinces of Prince Edward Island and New Brunswick. Prince Edward Island, practically deserted by the French by that time, was resettled, but the inconvenience of having to refer judicial and legal matters to Halifax and the relative inaccessibility of the Island, especially in winter, resulted in separate government in 1796. After the American Revolution, thousands of LOYALISTS moved into the Saint John R valley and along the N shore of the Bay of Fundy. They also created administrative and judicial problems, and so New Brunswick was created a separate province in 1784 with a southern boundary across the Chignecto Isthmus from Cumberland Arm to Baie Verte.

Almost all of LABRADOR has been under the jurisdiction of Newfoundland since 1763, except from 1774 to 1809 when it was governed from Québec. But its boundaries on the landward side were never precisely delimited, and in 1902, when Newfoundland granted timber-cutting leases in the area between Lk Melville and Grand Falls (now Churchill Falls), Québec maintained that the area was properly under its jurisdiction. The federal government believed that Labrador extended only one mile (1.6 km) inland from the high-water mark along the coast. In 1927 the JUDICIAL COMMITTEE OF THE PRIVY COUNCIL decided that the boundary for the most part followed the watershed of those rivers flowing into the Atlantic Ocean. In the S, however, the boundary runs N from a point just E of Blanc Sablon to 52° N, thence westward to and up the Romaine R to the watershed portion of the boundary. This means that the headwaters of such rivers as the Romaine, Natashquan, Petit Mécatina, St-Augustin and St-Paul which drain through Québec into the Gulf of St Lawrence are in Newfoundland (*see* LABRADOR BOUNDARY DISPUTE).

Québec, like Nova Scotia, became the home of thousands of Loyalist refugees. Most settled along the N shores of the St Lawrence R and Lakes Ontario and Erie in the area between Montréal and what is now Windsor, Ont. The French SEIGNEURIAL SYSTEM of land tenure was unfamiliar to these newcomers, who were accustomed to holding their land in free and common socage (ie, leasing or renting the land). They also resented the absence of popular government, delays in administration owing to the great distance from Montréal to Windsor, the lack of any connecting road, and the tedious, precarious (and, during the winter, nonexistent) water route linking them. Petitions for their own government were heeded, and in 1791 the province was divided into UPPER CANADA and LOWER CANADA. The boundary between them ran northward from the St Lawrence R, following the westernmost limits of the seigneuries to and up the Ottawa R to Lk Timiskaming, and then due N to HBC property. However, this arrangement was not entirely satisfactory, largely because the trade of both provinces was through the St Lawrence and because the division of revenues caused dissatisfaction. In 1841 the 2 provinces were united into the PROVINCE OF CANADA. Following the passage of the BRITISH NORTH AMERICA ACT of 1867, the Province of Canada was divided into the provinces of Ontario and Québec by the same boundary that had been established in 1791. Their northern limits followed the watershed of the rivers draining into the Great Lakes-St Lawrence system. When RUPERT'S LAND was acquired by the federal government in 1870, and the province of Manitoba was created from part of it, both Manitoba and Ontario claimed the area between Lake of the Woods and what is now Thunder Bay. The controversy was not settled until 1889, when the boundary of Ontario was extended northward generally to follow a series of lakes and waterways and the Albany R to James Bay. Similarly, in 1898 the northern boundary of Québec was extended northward to follow the Eastmain R and a series of smaller waterways to the boundary of Labrador.

The colony of Vancouver's Island was established in 1849. Soon after, GOLD RUSHES on the mainland led to the establishment of the colony of BRITISH COLUMBIA in 1858 and STIKEEN TERRITORY in 1862. All three were united into British Columbia in 1866 with boundaries as they now exist. The boundaries were intended to embrace all the rivers and creeks from which it was thought that alluvial gold might be obtained, not only to control the mining itself, but so that proper jurisdiction might be exercised over miners. Similar considerations later led to the boundaries of the Yukon Territory, which were first established in 1895. Substantial sections of the eastern boundaries of BC and the Yukon followed the watershed of those rivers draining into the Pacific Ocean.

Meanwhile, the North-West Territories were being peopled and more of the area came to be divided into provisional districts for administrative and postal purposes — the District of Keewatin in 1876; Saskatchewan, Assiniboia, Alberta and Athabaska in 1882; and Ungava, Yukon, Mackenzie and Franklin in 1895. Their boundaries were almost invariably straight lines and were expressed in terms of the Dominion Lands Survey system devised to facilitate settlement. By 1905 much of the area was deemed ready for provincial responsibilities. It was felt that the area N of 60° was unfit for agriculture, without which there could be little hope of the "thick and permanent settlement" necessary for stable provincial government, and that the area S of this parallel was too large for a single province when compared with the other provinces. Most of the southern area was therefore divided by 110° W into 2 provinces of approximately equal size when Alberta and Saskatchewan were established in 1905. The fact that these 2 provinces extended to 60° N encouraged Manitoba, Ontario and Québec to request northward extensions. Both Manitoba and Ontario claimed the area between the Albany and Churchill rivers. In 1912 the boundary divided this area more or less equally between them, the extensions came into force, and Québec was extended northward to the shores of Hudson Str and Hudson Bay.

The demarcation of Canada's boundaries began in 1771 when the 45th parallel was marked as a boundary between Québec and New York. But the work was crude and the need to resurvey was accentuated by the American Revolution, when this boundary, originally between British provinces, became an international boundary. The demarcation of Canada's international boundaries was largely completed by 1913. The methods varied from region to region. The earliest boundaries in forested areas were merely compass lines marked by blazes on trees or by heaps of stones. In the prairie West they were mounds of sand or grass sod and later iron posts. Where a boundary crossed wooded land, a path or "vista" was usually cut on each side of the surveyed line. Provincial boundaries are marked in a similar way but their demarcation proceeded more slowly, usually only when it was administratively expedient. By 1962 the establishment of boundaries had essentially been completed, except for the Québec-Newfoundland boundary.

N.L. NICHOLSON

Reading: H.G. Classen, *Thrust and Counterthrust* (1965); H. Dorion, *La Frontière Québec-Terre-Neuve* (1963); Energy, Mines and Resources Canada, *"Canada Then and Now"* in *The National Atlas of Canada* (5th ed, 1982); J.A. Munro, *The Alaska Boundary Dispute* (1970); N.L. Nicholson, *The Boundaries of the Canadian Confederation* (1979).

Boundary Waters Treaty, 11 Jan 1909, between Canada and the US, resulted from a need to settle and prevent disputes regarding the uses and apportionment of waters along the international boundary. The treaty established the INTERNATIONAL JOINT COMMISSION, the first permanent joint organization between Canada and the US, to fix and apply the rules of boundary water resource use. Negotiated for Canada mainly by George C. Gibbons, the treaty also prohibited the diversion of these waters without the commission's approval, proclaimed certain general principles of boundary water resource development, and called for an end to cross-boundary pollution. It failed, however, to impose sanctions against polluters or to prevent the diversion or damming of waters crossing the boundary.

N.F. DREISZIGER

Bourassa, Henri, politician, journalist (b at Montréal 1 Sept 1868; d there 31 Aug 1952). His family was one of the most prominent in the province; his father was a well-known painter, and his grandfather, Louis-Joseph PAPINEAU, was a celebrated folk hero of the REBELLIONS OF 1837. Bourassa got an early start in politics when he was elected mayor of the town of Montebello at age 22. Six years later, in 1896, he entered federal politics, where he stayed until 1907. He resigned his seat to enter provincial politics. He was elected to the Québec Assembly in 1908 and served until 1912. Meanwhile, in 1910 he founded *Le* DEVOIR, one of the great and influential

Canadian newspapers, and remained its editor until 1932. In 1925 he was again elected from his old federal constituency of Labelle and remained a member until defeated in 1935. Because of his sensitivity to long-term issues fundamental to French Canadian society, his ability to articulate them and his courage in speaking on them, Henry Bourassa inspired the growth of a vigorous nationalist movement in French Canada around 3 main themes: Canada's relationship with Great Britain, the relationship of French to English culture, and the values that should guide economic life.

Bourassa's career coincided with a time when most Anglo-Canadians were strongly emphasizing the British nature of the country (*see* IMPERIALISM). But did this mean that Canada was automatically at war when Great Britain went to war? It was over this issue that Bourassa, a young and promising Liberal MP, came to prominence in Oct 1899 when he resigned his seat to protest the Liberal Cabinet's decision to send Canadian troops to aid the British in the SOUTH AFRICAN WAR without consulting Parliament. By 1900 he was back in the House, having won his by-election by acclamation. There he tried to establish that Parliament was the only authority that could declare war on behalf of Canada. Although his resolution was voted down, the question at issue would be fundamental to Canadian politics for the next 40 years.

In 1910 Bourassa opposed the government's naval bill because it allowed the Cabinet to turn over its proposed Canadian Navy to the British Admiralty without the permission of Parliament. Over this issue, he succeeded in the federal election of 1911 in organizing an anti-Liberal campaign effective enough to lead to a considerable depletion of Laurier's electoral strength in Québec.

After some hesitation, Bourassa came to oppose Canadian participation in WWI because the Conservative government under PM Robert BORDEN had announced the Dominion's entry without consulting Parliament. Such action, he feared, would strengthen the claim of both Canadian and British imperialists that Canada should automatically take part in all British wars. Bourassa became notorious in 1917 because both major parties used him as a symbol of extreme FRENCH CANADIAN NATIONALISM for their own political purposes. Liberal leader Wilfrid LAURIER was unwilling to agree to CONSCRIPTION because he was afraid of handing over Québec to Bourassa. Later in their victorious election campaign of that year, Borden's UNION GOVERNMENT warned that if the Liberals led by Laurier were elected, Bourassa would be the real ruler and would take Canada out of the war. But this was the last time that Bourassa would be a serious factor in Canadian politics. Mackenzie KING, who replaced Laurier as leader of the Liberal Party in 1919 and dominated the era between the wars, took up Bourassa's idea that the Canadian Parliament alone could declare war. He kept Canada legally neutral for 7 days after the British went to war against Germany in 1939, thus fulfilling the program first set out by Bourassa at the turn of the century.

Another side of Bourassa's nationalist program was his insistence that Canada ought to be an Anglo-French country. French culture must resist assimilation and have equal rights throughout the country. In 1905 he became publicly identified with what came to be called biculturalism in the 1960s through his unsuccessful campaign for Catholics to control their own schools in the new provinces of Saskatchewan and Alberta. He warned that the equality of cultures was an absolute condition for French Canadians to continue to accept Confederation. Later, after Ontario issued Regulation 17 in 1912 severely limiting the use of French as a language

Henri Bourassa, founder of *Le Devoir* and its editor until 1932. He came to prominence opposing Canadian participation in the South African War and inspired the growth of a vigorous nationalist movement in French Canada (*courtesy Public Archives of Canada / C-27360 / Henri Bourassa Coll*).

of instruction in elementary schools, Bourassa opposed the measure before English audiences as well as French (*see* ONTARIO SCHOOLS QUESTION). He only called off his campaign in Sept 1916 when the pope counselled moderation in the struggle for Franco-Ontarian rights. But it was not until the late 1920s that this offensive regulation was repealed.

In the early 1920s Bourassa found his conception of a Canadian nation, one that would be Anglo-French in nature, under attack by Québec nationalists led by Abbé Groulx. In 1922 Groulx raised, in a tentative and theoretical way, the idea of a separate Laurentian state as a desirable goal for French-speaking Quebeckers. Bourassa vehemently opposed even this vague ideal of a separate state, and his prestige was such that he was virtually able to deny it respectability.

Although his nationalist program had the greatest political impact, Bourassa believed that his most important work was to help his people be a beacon of light for Catholicism in N America. His greatest ambition was to prevent the Americanization of Canada and resist placing the accumulation of wealth above the worship of God as the dominant value of Canadian society. Although he accepted private property as essential to man's liberty, he believed that in economic matters the public good should prevail.

He was much troubled by the coming of big industry. He believed that the profit of a large enterprise was immoral but that of a small firm, comprising perhaps 5 or 10 people, was legitimate. He always considered small businessmen as the social class that by instinct and interest was best prepared to conserve Catholic values. He seems to have thought that the growth of big business was due not to economic efficiency but to greed, and that if Catholic teachings were accepted, this trend might be halted or reversed. Occasionally, he dreamed that society would revert back to one in which the rural sector was all important and the economy was one of small firms. This viewpoint was an important reason for his inability to develop a realistic program to regulate the powerful influence of big business in economic life. JOSEPH LEVITT

Bourassa, Napoléon, architect, author, painter, sculptor (b at L'Acadie, Lower Canada 21 Oct 1827; d at Lachenaie, Qué 27 Aug 1916). One of the finest Canadian artists of the 19th century, as is evident from his drawings, portraits and murals, and his architecture, Bourassa was influenced by the French neoclassicist, Ingres, and by historic painting. His most complete work was for the Notre-Dame de Lourdes Church, Montréal, though the Montebello church and the St-Hyacinthe Dominican Convent are also fine examples of his architecture. Other major projects, never completed or now destroyed, included decorative work for the Nazareth Chapel, Montréal, the St-Hyacinthe Cathedral, and the Apothéose de Christophe Colomb. He taught drawing for many years and Louis-Philippe HÉBERT, Olindo Gratton and Édouard Meloche were among his students. His correspondence and lectures are valuable documents deserving publication. He became vice-president of the Canadian Academy of Fine Arts on 6 Mar 1880. RAYMOND VÉZINA

Bourassa, Robert, politician, premier of Québec (b at Montréal 14 July 1933). Admitted to the Québec Bar in 1957, and a graduate of Oxford (1959), he was successively (1960-66) fiscal adviser to the Dept of National Revenue, a professor at U of Ottawa, Laval and U de M, and research director for the Bélanger Commission on fiscal policy. He was elected MNA for Mercier in the Québec provincial elections of 1966.

Despite his youth, Bourassa was chosen to succeed Jean LESAGE as leader of the Québec Liberal Party in Jan 1970. In 1968 he had been a prime instigator of the party's decision to reject the constitutional proposals of René LÉVESQUE. Immediately after becoming premier he was faced with the OCTOBER CRISIS and the FRONT DE LIBÉRATION DU QUÉBEC agitations. Although he was re-elected in 1973 with a majority of 102 of 110 seats, his second term saw a weakening of Québec's position within Confederation, caused in part by his refusal to sign the constitutional agreement reached in Victoria in 1971. Accused of scandal and corruption, the party lost the 1976 election to the Parti Québécois; Bourassa himself was defeated. After a long stay abroad, he returned to support the *Non* side during the 1980 REFERENDUM campaign. He was re-elected leader of the Liberals in the fall of 1983, replacing Claude RYAN. DANIEL LATOUCHE

Bourdon, Rosario, conductor, cellist, record-company executive (b Joseph Charles at Longueuil, Qué 6 Mar 1885; d at New York City, NY 24 Apr 1961). Bourdon toured Europe as a child prodigy and enjoyed early success as an orchestral cellist and recitalist in Canada and the US. In 1909 he began a versatile career with the Victor Talking Machine Co. As cellist or piano accompanist he appeared on recordings with many famous artists. As Victor's music director he conducted its house orchestras and Sousa's band, and in 1923 also became music director for NBC radio. He left Victor in 1931 to work with other record companies. BARCLAY MCMILLAN

Bourgault, Pierre, journalist, politician, professor (b at East-Angus, Qué 23 Jan 1934). After a career as a radio and TV announcer and actor, he joined the Rassemblement pour l'indépendance nationale (RIN), becoming its president in 1964. A formidable orator, he used every avenue to promote and popularize the idea of political independence for Québec. The RIN won almost 6% of the vote in the 1966 elections and in 1968 agreed to merge with the PARTI QUÉBÉCOIS. For a while a member of the PQ's national executive, Bourgault slowly withdrew from active political life. Since 1976 he has been a professor of communications at UQAM.

Bourgeau, Eugène, botanical collector (b at Brizon, France 20 Apr 1813; d at Paris, France Feb 1877). His interest in plants began early and as a young man he attracted the interest of the director of the Botanical Gardens at Lyons, where he learned the rudiments of botany. He collected plants in the Canary Is, Spain, North Africa and Algeria. In 1857 he was appointed collector to the British North American Exploring Expedition under John PALLISER. His enthusiasm and ability to co-operate with others drew praise from Palliser. During the expedition (1857-60) Bourgeau collected some 1200 species from western Canada. ERIC J. HOLMGREN

Bourgeois, according to an 18th-century writer, were not nobles, ecclesiastics or magistrates, but city dwellers who "nevertheless by their properties, by their riches, by the honorable employments which adorn them and by their commerce are above the artisans and what is called the people." By extension, it meant the owner of a ship, the man who gave artisans work and, in Canadian usage, the FUR TRADER employing hired men. In economic and social theory the word means the businessman — the trader or banker of the 17th and 18th centuries, and in Karl Marx's capitalist system, the member of a class (the bourgeoisie) employing labourers in a system of wage slavery. German economist Werner Sombart described the bourgeois as a psychological type combining entrepreneurial flair, industry and rectitude. Such theorizing has produced the notion that the development of a bourgeois class with a progressive outlook has made the modern world. From this it is postulated that a society cannot progress from feudalism to capitalism (modernity) without the intervention of such a class. In Canada, this has precipitated a debate over whether the British CONQUEST in 1760 snuffed out a developing bourgeoisie and thus condemned French Canadian society to stagnation (an injustice separatism would cure), or whether French Canadian society by its nature failed to produce Sombartian bourgeois types and condemned itself to that fate. DALE MIQUELON

Bourgeoys, Marguerite, founder of the Congrégation de Notre-Dame de Montréal (b at Troyes, France 17 Apr 1620; d at Montréal 12 Jan 1700; canonized 31 Oct 1982). In 1640 Marguerite Bourgeoys joined a non-cloistered congregation of teachers attached to a Troyes convent directed by the sister of Governor Maisonneuve of VILLE-MARIE (Montréal); she sailed for Canada in 1657 and a year later opened a girls' school in a stable on Montréal I. Besides chaperoning girls sent from France as brides for settlers (FILLES DU ROI), she recruited French and Canadian girls as teachers, organized a boarding school for girls in Montréal, a school for Indian girls on the Sulpician reserve of La Montagne, and a domestic arts school. Her "sisters" began teaching in rural parishes. Bishop LAVAL refused to permit them to take vows, but his successor Bishop SAINT-VALLIER invited them to open a school on the Île d'Orléans. Soon they had a domestic arts school and a primary school in Québec City. On 1 July 1698 the secular sisters took simple vows and became a recognized non-cloistered religious community. Marguerite Bourgeoys spent her last 2 years in meditation and prayer, already revered as a saint by the colonists when she died. CORNELIUS J. JAENEN

Marguerite Bourgeoys, founder of the Congrégation de Notre-Dame de Montréal. Already revered as a saint when she died in 1700, she was canonized in 1982 *(courtesy Public Archives of Canada / C-12340).*

Bourget, Ignace, second Roman Catholic bishop of Montréal (b at Lauzon, Qué 30 Oct 1799; d at Sault-au-Récollet, Qué 8 June 1885). Bourget studied theology and taught at the Séminaire de Nicolet for 3 years before being appointed secretary to Bishop Jean-Jacques Lartigue in 1821, who ordained him in 1822. Energetic, a tireless worker and possessed of good judgement, Bourget gained the confidence of his superior who placed him in charge of construction of the bishop's palace and St-Jacques Cathedral. Bourget saw both completed by 1825. Lartigue recommended Bourget to Rome and on 25 July 1837 Bourget was installed as his coadjutor with right of succession, which took effect at Lartigue's death on 19 April 1840.

His vast diocese covered the area from the American border to James Bay and encompassed the 22 000 Roman Catholics of Montréal, 79 parishes, 34 mission churches and 4 Indian missions; in all a population of 186 244 souls. Faced with a task that would have discouraged anyone else, the new bishop assigned the training of future priests to the Sulpicians and established a newspaper, *Les Mélanges religieux,* to spread "good principles." His greatest achievement lay in persuading French religious orders to come from Europe to help promote the "Christianization" of his diocesans. In addition, he supplemented their efforts with the work of indigenous religious institutions that he either inspired or founded. Under Bourget's leadership, the clerical hold on the population of the Montréal diocese increased over the years. Male and female religious orders were given an increasingly important role in both elementary education and the classical colleges that he personally directed; hospitals and charitable organizations were also administered by religious orders.

The activity inspired by Bourget met with a heated reaction from the sector of the lower middle class that had been converted to the liberal principles of the INSTITUT CANADIEN and the democratic PARTI ROUGE. Two ideological groups struggled to be the dominant influence on French Canadian society. Bourget led the ultramontanes who maintained that the state should be linked to and dominated by the church (*see* ULTRAMONTANISM), while his liberal opponents demanded separation of church and state, and the exclusion of the clergy from politics. After 30 years of struggle, victory went to Bourget who repeatedly attacked the Institut until it was virtually annihilated by 1885.

No other Canadian bishop of the time was as attentive to the directives from Rome or as fervent a supporter of the papal cult. Bourget's zeal inspired the raising of 507 ZOUAVES, who in 1868 were sent from his diocese to defend the papal state.

Despite his attachment to Rome, Bourget did not always obtain the support of the religious orders. In addition to his struggle with the Sulpicians over the subdivision of the parish of Notre-Dame, his most significant failure lay in his efforts to obtain an independent university in Montréal. Following pressure from the Séminaire and the archbishop of Québec, Rome agreed only to the establishment of a "satellite" of Laval U. This failure, and the controversy surrounding ultramontane involvement in politics, led to Bourget's resignation as bishop of Montréal in Sept 1876. In poor health, he celebrated his diamond sacerdotal anniversary on 9 Nov 1882 and retired from public life.

The monument erected in Bourget's honour in the centre of the memorial chapel of bishops and archbishops of Montréal is a visible symbol of the key role he played in the history of the diocese. Current historiography is increasingly critical of his religious and political views. But despite his shortcomings, his achievements make him one of the great architects of Québec society. PHILIPPE SYLVAIN

Bourinot, Sir John George, writer, historian (b at Sydney, NS 24 Oct 1837; d at Ottawa 13 Oct 1902). Bourinot graduated from Toronto's Trinity University in 1857 and then settled in Halifax, where he founded the *Herald* and became its editor. He joined the HANSARD staff in Ottawa in 1868 and in 1873 was appointed assistant clerk to the House of Commons, becoming chief clerk in 1880. One of a number of Canadian intellectuals attracted to Ottawa after Confederation, Bourinot avidly sought to define the character of the new country. He became a leading expert on Canadian government and history, writing a number of books, including *How Canada is Governed* and *Parliamentary Procedure and Practice*. A founder of the ROYAL SOCIETY OF CANADA, he was its president in 1892. C.J. TAYLOR

Bourinot's Rules *Parliamentary Procedure and Practice with an Introductory Account of the Origin and Growth of Parliamentary Institutions in the Dominion of Canada,* by Sir John George BOURINOT, Clerk of the Canadian House of Commons, was published in 1884, with 3 later editions — 1892, 1903 and 1916. It was the first Canadian book on the subject, and is still the basic authority on PARLIAMENTARY PROCEDURE. Arthur Beauchesne's later work is a handbook for ready reference by MPs. EUGENE A. FORSEY

Bourns, Arthur Newcombe, professor of chemistry, university administrator (b at Petitcodiac, NB 8 Dec 1919). Educated at Acadia and McGill (PhD, chemistry), he began teaching at Acadia and Saskatoon and continued at McMaster for 35 years. An inspiring teacher and a researcher internationally known for his contributions to physical organic chemistry, he also showed exceptional administrative skills. He became successively graduate studies dean, department chairman, VP and president (1972-80). In times particularly difficult for university presidents, he gave strong leadership marked by sound judgement, fair-mindedness and breadth of understanding and concern. These qualities brought appointment to scores of important scientific and educational bodies. He has acted as a scientific and educational adviser to governments in Canada and abroad. L.H. CRAGG

Boutroue d'Aubigny, Claude de, chevalier, INTENDANT of New France 1668-70 (b at Paris, France 1620; d in France 1680). A Parisian judge and member of the *noblesse de robe,* Boutroue became intendant of Canada between Jean TALON's first and second terms. He was reported to be assiduous in his duties and attempted to suppress the brandy trade with the Indians. Though he quarrelled with the governor, Rémy de COURCELLE, Boutroue continued to enjoy the patronage of Colbert, the French minister in charge of colonies. ALLAN GREER

Bovell, James, physician, educator, clergyman (b in Barbados 28 Oct 1817; d at Charlestown, Nevis, W Indies 15 Jan 1880). Bovell studied medicine at London, Edinburgh, Glasgow and Dublin. Licensed in 1839 by the Royal Coll of Physicians, London, he immigrated to Toronto in 1848, becoming prominent as a physician-educator, devout high churchman and synodical secretary. He was dean of Trinity College's medical faculty from 1851 until the school dissolved in 1856 following disputes with Bishop John STRACHAN. Bovell then lectured in physiology at the Toronto School of Medicine and (after 1864) at Upper Canada Veterinary Coll. He cofounded a professional journal, published medical articles and religious works, denounced inebriety and cholera-promoting filth. Bovell practised microscopy at Trinity Coll School with warden William Arthur Johnson and William OSLER, head prefect in 1866, whom he profoundly influenced. Returning to the W Indies in 1871, Bovell was ordained in 1871 and served various Anglican parishes before a stroke incapacitated him. C.E. DOLMAN

Bow River, 644 km, rises in Bow Lk, fed by glacial meltwater from the Bow Glacier (Wapta Icefield) in the Waputik Mtns in Banff National Park, Alta. It flows S and E from the Rockies through BANFF townsite and CALGARY to join the OLDMAN R, forming 2 main tributaries of the S SASKATCHEWAN R in Alberta. It drains an area of 25 300 km^2, encompassing a wide variety of physiographic and vegetational regions, from alpine ice fields and tundra, through dense conifer forest and aspen parkland, to semiarid shortgrass prairie. Several dams have been built in its middle and lower reaches for hydroelectric power (325 MW developed), flood control and irrigation. Calgary, the Eastern and Western Irrigation Districts and the Bow R Development are important beneficiaries. The name may derive from a Cree word referring to the good bow-making wood along its banks. IAN A. CAMPBELL

Sir Mackenzie Bowell, 5th prime minister of Canada, 1894-96 (*courtesy Public Archives of Canada/PA-27161*).

Bowell, Sir Mackenzie, prime minister of Canada, 1894-96 (b at Rickinghall, Eng 27 Dec 1823; d at Belleville, Ont 10 Dec 1917). Editor and owner of the Belleville *Intelligence* and an active Orangeman, Bowell was first elected as a Conservative to the House of Commons in 1867, representing North Hastings until 1892 when he became a senator, retiring finally in 1906. Bowell held several important Cabinet portfolios before he became PM in 1894. Dissatisfaction with his leadership soon forced his resignation, and Sir Charles TUPPER actually led the Tories to defeat in 1896. Although Bowell was not politically active after his resignation, he led the Opposition in the Senate 1896-1906. J.M. BUMSTED

Bowering, George, poet, fiction writer, editor, critic (b at Penticton, BC 1 Dec 1935). Although recognized as one of the foremost Canadian writers of his generation, Bowering has yet to receive the critical attention his large and varied body of work deserves. After RCAF service, Bowering attended UBC, where with Frank Davey, David Dawson, James Reid, Fred Wah and others he studied the new poetics of Creeley, Duncan and Olson, and founded the poetry newsletter *TISH*. He taught in Calgary, London and Montréal before returning to Vancouver to teach at SFU. He founded *Imago* (1964-74) and is a contributing editor to *Open Letter*. A prolific writer, whose poetry, both lyric and extended, seeks to capture flux in the rhythms of its open structures, and whose fiction seeks to subvert realist conventions through self-conscious textual invention, Bowering has published over 40 books. A witty sense of play animates his vision in them all. His poetry includes *Rocky Mountain Foot* (1969) and *The Gangs of Kosmos* (1969), for which he won his first Gov Gen's Award; *The Catch* (1976), *Selected Poems: Particular Accidents* (1980), *West Window* (1982) and *Kerrisdale Elegies* (1984). Of his fiction, *A Short Sad Book* (1977) and *Burning Water* (1980), a novel about George VANCOUVER's voyages of discovery, for which he won his second Gov Gen's Award, stand out. He has also published 2 collections of critical essays: *A Way with Words* (1982) and *The Mask in Place* (1983). The best introduction to his work is Robin Blaser's essay in *Particular Accidents*. DOUGLAS BARBOUR

Bowling, Indoor, game in which a player attempts to knock down pins by propelling a ball down a wooden lane. Similar games were played as early as 5000 BC in Egypt. The 10-pin version was developed in the US in the 19th century; and 5-pin bowling was invented in Canada in 1908 or 1909 by Thomas F. RYAN. Ryan owned a 10-pin bowling club in downtown Toronto, and tried a number of experiments to regain the interest of his elite patrons, who found the 10-pin ball too heavy and the game too strenuous. Finally, he had his father shave a regulation pin on a lathe, placed 5 of these pins on the 10-pin floor, and introduced the use of a duckpin ball (roughly 2 kg in weight and 13 cm in diameter). Ryan then developed a scoring system in which the pins were numbered from 1 to 5, making it possible to score 15 points if all pins were bowled over in each player's turn (called a frame). The player was allowed 3 balls per turn. In order to add a challenge to the game, Ryan made it obligatory to knock down the left corner pin (4 pin) before the player could be awarded any points. With 3 balls per frame and 10 frames per game, the player aimed at a perfect score of 450 points. Since the pins were very light, they easily flew through the air following contact with the ball, and the game was far noisier than before. In 1912, Ryan solved both problems by adding a thick rubber band to the belly of the pin, a feature still used today. Five-pin bowling soon became one of the most popular sports in Canada and the northern US. The first international competition was held in 1913.

In 1918, Alfred Shrubb bowled the first 400 game, and in 1921, Bill Bromfield became the first player to score a perfect 450. In 1927, 500 bowlers gathered in Toronto's King Edward Hotel to found the Canadian Bowling Assn. Over the next few years, several governing groups were formed throughout the country, but in 1978 they amalgamated to form the Canadian 5-Pin Bowlers' Assn, which now services over 250 000 members from coast to coast by organizing tournaments, providing instructional aids and granting awards. In 1956, Double Diamond, Ltd, invented a machine to set pins up automatically, thus replacing the "pinboy." The invention of a string pinsetter followed in 1963, reducing mechanical expenses and adding speed and smoothness to the game. The game remains essentially the same, and is played by more than 1 million Canadians in over 700 bowling centres each year. It is easy for children to play, and thousands of men and women participate annually in tournaments and in provincial, national and international championships. Five-pin bowling is Canada's own game and is the number-one participant sport in this country.

Ten-pin bowling has remained popular in Canada and it is now claimed to be the largest participation sport in the world. Several Canadians have excelled in international competition, notably Graydon Robinson of Toronto, who won the world championship in Tokyo, 1969; Ray Mitchell, originally from Alberta, who won the world's master championship in Hamburg, W Ger, 1972; and Cathy Townsend of Montréal, who won the women's World Cup in Manila, 1975. A.G. HONG

Bowring, Benjamin, silversmith, watchmaker, merchant (b in Devonshire, Eng; d at Liverpool, Eng June 1846). One of a large number of Devonshire tradesmen who immigrated to St John's, Bowring first visited Newfoundland in 1811; in 1815 he sold his shop in Exeter and opened a store in St John's. A careful, prudent man, he avoided the bankruptcies endemic in Newfoundland between 1815 and 1840. By the late 1820s, he had entered the general import trade of the colony and was speculating in the seal hunt. When his sons came of age in the 1830s, Bowring moved to the company's new head office in Liverpool. In 1839 he gave up active involvement in the company, which under his sons became known as "Bowring Brothers." His sons made the decisions that resulted in the family's great fortunes, but Benjamin, by moving to St John's and by careful and frugal management, gave them the base from which to start. KEITH MATTHEWS

Bowser, William John, lawyer, politician, premier of BC (b at Rexton, NB 3 Dec 1867; d at Vancouver 25 Oct 1933). A graduate of Dalhousie, Bowser moved to Vancouver in 1891 and practised law. First elected to the legislature in 1903 as a Conservative, he remained an MLA until his defeat in 1924. Attorney general from 1907, when he succeeded Sir Richard MCBRIDE as premier on 15 Dec 1915, Bowser inherited a divided party and an unpopular administration, and his government was soundly defeated in the 1916 provincial election. From 1916 to 1924 he led the Opposition. In 1933 he emerged from retirement to lead an independent non-partisan group, but died during the election campaign. PATRICIA E. ROY

Boxing is a contest between 2 opponents wearing padded gloves who attempt to win by rendering their opponents unable to continue, or by winning a judge's decision at the end of a prearranged number of rounds. Boxers may hit only with their fists and from the waist up. Boxing as a sport was introduced by the Greeks in the OLYMPIC GAMES about 686 BC.

The first bouts in Canada were "bareknuckle" fights. Gloves began appearing regularly around the turn of the century, primarily to protect the fists of the boxer rather than the fighter being hit. It was not unusual for Canadian bouts before 1900 to be scheduled for 40 rounds. The early bouts with gloves were said to be governed by the Marquis of Queensbury rules, though many think that reference was made to the "Marquis" to give the sport respectability. Early Canadian boxing was governed by each province, many of 'hich outlawed its existence. It was frequently aimed that police interfered only when bouts 'ere not going the way the promoters intended. he military, especially in "garrison towns" like alifax, could hold bouts; but with rare exceptions, such as the "Gentlemen's Sparring Club of ttawa" in the 1880s, promoted fights were ought to be "outlaw" events. Canadian boxing egan its climb to respectability in the 1890s. Today, despite the controversy that surrounds the port because of its violence, boxing draws large owds in many Canadian cities. Most of its ompetitors have come from less affluent sections of big cities such as Vancouver, Toronto nd Montréal and from poorer areas such as the laritimes. Sam LANGFORD, who was born in alifax, has often been called the greatest iddleweight of all time. As a lightweight he eat the renowned Joe Gans of the US. Though 'eighing only 71 kg he boxed 15 rounds with 4 kg Jack Johnson. Another Halifax fighter, eorge Dixon, is considered the greatest bantamweight boxer ever. He won the bantamweight title in London in 1890 and the atherweight championship the next year. ommy BURNS from Hanover, Ont, and Jimmy CLARNIN from Vancouver have also been world hampions. Though never world champion, eavyweight George Chuvalo of Toronto held anadian and Commonwealth titles and in a career in which he fought most of the great heavy'eights was never knocked down.

The Canadian Amateur Boxing Assn oversees) provincial boxing associations and one from ach of the territories. While most excellent Canadian amateurs eventually turn pro, many retain their amateur standing and aim for specific oals such as the Olympics or world amateur hampionships. Bert SCHNEIDER (1920) and Lefty WYNNE (1932) were Olympic gold medal winners. Shawn O'Sullivan of Toronto gained Canada's first world boxing championship in 1981, 'inning the World Cup Amateur Boxing lightiddleweight competition. O'Sullivan and Villie de Wit, of Grande Prairie, Alta, won silver medals at the 1984 Los Angeles Olympics. rofessional title bouts are governed by the Canadian Professional Boxing Federation, with local commissions controlling other professional oxing. A.J. "SANDY" YOUNG

oyd, Alfred, merchant, politician (d in Eng 909). Described as a "native of Canada," Boyd as operating a general store at Red River prior the troubles of 1869-70. He was elected to the onvention of Forty, which met on 28 Jan 1870 decide the fate of the RED RIVER COLONY. In Sept 870 he was appointed provincial secretary by t-Gov Adams George Archibald. Elected as ILA for St Andrew's N on 30 Dec 1870, he 'as appointed minister of public works and agriculture on 10 Jan 1871. He resigned 9 Dec 1871 make way for a representation of the halfreed population and was succeeded by John ORQUAY. Boyd acquired considerable business nd real-estate interests in Winnipeg before he ttled in England about 1890. LOVELL C. CLARK

oyd, Liona, classical guitarist (b at London, ng 11 July 1950). After moving to Toronto 'ith her parents in 1958, Boyd began years of udy with Eli Kassner, followed by 2 years with lexandre Lagoya. Her first Canadian album, *he Guitar — Liona Boyd* (1974), sold more than 0 000 copies. She has a rare ability to play both e Segovia and Lagoya methods of fingering nd is noted for extremely clean guitar interretations. Boyd won a Juno Award in 1978.

ALLAN M. GOULD

oyd, Mossom, lumberman (b in India in 814; d at Bobcaygeon, Ont 23 July 1883). A ember of the Anglo-Irish gentry, Mossom oyd emigrated to the Sturgeon Lk area of Upper anada in 1834. He became assistant to Thomas Need, owner of the Bobcaygeon sawmill and took over the mill when Need returned to England in 1843. Boyd quickly developed it into a multifaceted lumbering enterprise with sawnlumber sales in Albany, NY, local retail outlets in the Kawartha region and timber sales in Great Britain. By the 1870s Boyd's enterprise was among the largest in the region. An enthusiastic promoter of local economic development, Boyd was a constant proponent for the Trent Valley canal. After his death in 1883 the family business was run by Mossom Rater Boyd, who extended its operations to Québec and Vancouver I as well as moving into steamboating, stock raising and railway development.

CHRISTOPHER G. CURTIS

Boyd, William, pathologist, educator, author (b at Portsoy, Scot 21 June 1885; d at Toronto 10 Mar 1979). Bill Boyd obtained his medical degree in 1908 at Edinburgh and published his first book, *With a Field Ambulance at Ypres,* in 1916. He was professor of pathology at U Manitoba, 1915-37, U of T, 1937-51, and UBC, 1951 to 1954. His first pathology textbook was *Surgical Pathology* (later called *Pathology for the Surgeon*), published in 1925. Later textbooks were *Pathology of Internal Disease* (1931; later *Pathology for the Physician*), *Textbook of Pathology* (1932) and *An Introductionto Medical Science* (1937). His books were enormously popular with students all over the world for their clarity, fine prose and infectious enthusiasm for the subject matter; translated into many languages, they ran into innumerable editions. He was greatly sought after as a speaker at scientific meetings and social occasions for he could capture his audience with wit and a fine delivery. He was made a companion of the Order of Canada in 1968. H.J. BARRIE

Boyd's Cove, in eastern NOTRE DAME BAY, Nfld, has been occupied intermittently for about 2000 years. Late 17th — early 18th-century BEOTHUK pit houses have yielded diagnostic stone tools in association with European artifacts which have established a link between the Beothuk and their prehistoric ancestors. Faunal analysis indicates a late-winter to fall occupation and a subsistence pattern balanced between marine and land resources. Numerous fur-bearing animal remains and a number of trade beads hint at a fur trade. Other evidence, however, suggests that most European goods were stolen. Retaliation for such theft, and a growing white population, eventually forced the Beothuk away from sites such as Boyd's Cove and into the interior, where, hungry and sick, they became extinct in the early 19th century. *See also* ARCHAEOLOGY.

RALPH T. PASTORE

Boyle, David, blacksmith, teacher, archaeologist, museologist, historian (b at Greenock, Scot 1 May 1842; d at Toronto 14 Feb 1911). Although apprenticed as a blacksmith on arriving in Canada in 1856, Boyle became internationally prominent as Canada's premier archaeologist before WWI. Motivated by the artisan self-improvement ethic, he became a rural Ontario teacher in 1865 and a principal in Elora (1871-81). He was a practitioner of the radical child-centered theories and methods of Swiss educator Johann Pestalozzi. Subsequently, Boyle became curator-archaeologist of the Canadian Institute Museum (1884-96) and the Ontario Provincial Museum (1886-1911), laying the groundwork for development of Ontario ARCHAEOLOGY as a systematic and scientific discipline. From 1887 to 1911 he published his *Annual Archaeological Reports for Ontario,* the first Canadian periodical devoted primarily to the study of the archaeological record. Boyle was also an avid history buff and preservationist and the author of a book of nonsense poetry for children. GERALD KILLAN

Boyle, Harry J., broadcaster, author (b at St Augustine, Ont 7 Oct 1915). He worked alternately as a free-lance writer and radio reporter in southwestern Ontario before joining the CBC in Toronto in 1942. He held various positions, including radio producer and department head, at the CBC until 1968, when he left to take a seat on the CANADIAN RADIO-TELEVISION AND TELECOMMUNICATIONS COMMISSION. He has published several collections of light essays and a number of realistic yet nostalgic novels, such as *The Great Canadian Novel* (1972) and *The Luck of the Irish* (1975).

Boyle, John Bernard, painter (b at London, Ont 23 Sept 1941). Self-taught, Boyle, whose aim in youth was to be a writer, began painting around 1962 with the support of friends Greg CURNOE and Jack CHAMBERS. Boyle favours primary colours and bold handling. His work, which includes heavily painted portraits, often huge, of well-known Canadian figures such as Tom THOMSON, POUNDMAKER and Stephen LEACOCK, express his determined Canadian nationalism. He has also experimented with baked porcelain on steel. His paintings of the male and female nude (often himself or his wife) are as bold as any in contemporary art. JOAN MURRAY

Boyle, Joseph Whiteside, Joe, soldier of fortune (b at Toronto 6 Nov 1867; d at London, Eng 14 Apr 1923). Boyle is famous as a neglected hero who made a fortune in the KLONDIKE GOLD RUSH. He remained there until WWI, when he organized his own detachment and did intelligence work in Russia. Later he was said to be the confidant of Romania's Queen Marie, a distinction many others claimed but none on such good evidence. On 29 June 1983 his body, which had been buried in Britain, was reinterred at Woodstock, Ont, his boyhood home.

DOUG FETHERLING

Reading: W. Rodney, *Joe Boyle* (1974); L. Taylor, *The Sourdough and the Queen* (1983).

Boyle, Robert William, physicist (b at Carbonear, Nfld 2 Oct 1883; d at London, Eng 18 Apr 1955). The first PhD in physics from McGill (1909), Boyle is best known for his work on the properties of ultrasonic waves and his contribution to the development of an echo method for detecting submarines during WWI. He began research on the radioactivity of RADIUM under Sir Ernest RUTHERFORD at McGill and continued his work in Manchester, Eng, 1909-11. In 1912 he became head of physics at U of A and started research on ultrasonics. During WWII he supervised research on radar at the NATIONAL RESEARCH COUNCIL. He was elected to the RSC in 1921 and awarded the Flavelle Medal in 1940. He was director of physics at the NRC, 1929-48.

YVES GINGRAS

Brachiopoda, phylum of bivalved marine INVERTEBRATES, sometimes called lamp shells. Brachiopods attach to the seabed by a stalk and feed on particles caught in currents that are generated by their ciliated crown of tentacles (lophophore). The approximately 260 living species are relicts of some 30 000 FOSSIL forms which inhabited Continental Shelf areas, especially during the Paleozoic era (570-225 million years ago). They are important to geologists in establishing stratigraphic sequences useful in oil exploration and in determining shorelines and depths of ancient seas. The living genus *Lingula* differs little from a Cambrian fossil relative over 500 million years old. Brachiopodlike forms are represented in the BURGESS SHALE, BC. *See* GEOLOGY.

J.R. NURSALL

Bracken, John, politician (b at Ellisville, Ont 22 June 1883; d at Ottawa 18 March 1969). A graduate of the Ontario Agricultural College, he worked for federal and provincial governments in the West until 1910, when he became a professor of field husbandry at U Sask. In 1920 he moved to Manitoba Agricultural College, joined the Progressive movement, and became premier in 1922. For the next 2 decades he led a careful government, dealing as well as anyone could with the problems of the GREAT DEPRESSION. In 1942 the Conservative Party called on him to be leader, a task he accepted on condition the party add "Progressive" to its name. Bracken's appeal was limited, in part because of a halting speaking manner and his unwise decision to remain out of Parliament for almost 3 years. In 1945 he led the party to defeat and he resigned in 1948. J.L. GRANATSTEIN

Reading: J. Kendle, *John Bracken* (1979).

Brady, James Patrick, prospector, MÉTIS leader (b at Lac St Vincent, Alta 11 Mar 1908; disappeared in the Foster Lks area, Sask after 7 June 1967). A grandson of one of RIEL's soldiers, self-educated in politics and history, Brady became a leader among the Métis of northern Alberta and Saskatchewan. A disciple of the radical politics of the 1930s and a lifelong communist, he directed his political energies on behalf of the Métis, trying in vain to persuade the CCF in Saskatchewan to implement progressive native policies. He was a major figure in the Association des Métis d'Alberta et des Territoires du Nord Ouest and a patient and influential political teacher. He disappeared on a prospecting trip. MURRAY DOBBIN

Brampton, Ont, City, pop 149 030 (1981c). Located on the Etobicoke R 32 km NW of Toronto, it was established as a crossroads hamlet in the 1830s. It was originally called Buffy's Corners and was renamed for a town in Cumberland, Eng, when it was incorporated as a village in 1853. Economic development was spurred by the arrival of the GRAND TRUNK RY in 1856. Brampton was chosen county seat of Peel County in 1867 and was incorporated as a town in 1873. The horticultural business was begun in 1860 and remains important today, along with a number of manufacturing industries. Brampton is the birthplace and home of longtime Ontario premier, William DAVIS.

Brandon, Man, City, pop 36 242 (1981c), inc 1882, the province's second-largest city and economic hub of its SW region, is located on the ASSINIBOINE R, 200 km W of Winnipeg. It is governed by a mayor and 10 aldermen.

History From 1793 to 1832, 3 HBC posts — each called Brandon House after the Duke of Brandon, an ancestor of Lord Selkirk — were established in the Brandon area. Permanent settlement began in the late 1870s at Grand Valley, 3 km E, and the Brandon Hills. Ontario and Maritime Protestants were among the first arrivals, followed by British and American immigrants. Brandon became a divisional point on the CPR in 1881, and soon was the transportation, distribution, service and trade centre for the surrounding hinterland. Industry also had an early role in the economy as manufactured goods were produced in the 1880s and 1890s. Brandon was a judicial and regional medical centre and, by the end of the 19th century, had a federal agricultural research station, provincial jail, mental hospital, school of nursing, industrial school for Indians, and Baptist-sponsored Brandon College (post-secondary).

After WWI, labour unrest and unfavourable economic conditions occurred. Both the city and Brandon College faced financial crises. During WWII thousands of armed-forces personnel trained in the city or at nearby Shilo and Commonwealth air schools. Following the war, economic and physical growth was steady. Brandon College became a provincial university in 1967 (*see* BRANDON UNIVERSITY); Assiniboine Community College was established; petrochemical manufacturers set up plants; a regional library, arts centre and museums were developed; and facilities such as the Keystone arena-convention complex were built.

Economy Agriculture, commerce, health care and administration are the economic mainstays of Brandon. Important industries include petrochemicals, processed foods, metal products, woolens, electrical and farm equipment and publishing. Medical and educational institutions, the CPR, CNR and government agencies are among the major employers. Brandon's regional trade population (130 000) extends to Portage la Prairie, eastern Saskatchewan, the international boundary and Dauphin.

Cityscape Brandon has ready access to some of Manitoba's most attractive natural recreation areas — Spruce Woods Provincial Forest and Park to the E, Turtle Mtn Provincial Park (S), Riding Mtn National Park (N) and Brandon Hills Wildlife Management Area. In 1979 the city hosted the Canada Winter Games. It also is known for its agricultural shows — the Royal Manitoba Winter Fair, the Provincial Exhibition of Manitoba and the Ag-Ex, Manitoba's largest livestock show and sale. Brandon has numerous cultural, social and sports organizations. Musical activity is centered at Brandon U's School of Music. D.M. LYON

Reading: G.F. Barker, *Brandon: A City 1881-1961* (1977); W. Leland Clark, *Brandon's Politics and Politicians* (1981); Mary Hume, ed, *Brandon: Prospect of a City* (1981).

Brandon University, Brandon, Man, was founded in 1967. Brandon College, developed by the Baptist Convention of Manitoba in 1898, was affiliated with the UNIVERSITY OF MANITOBA until 1911, and then with MCMASTER UNIVERSITY, 1911-38. It became nondenominational in 1938 and rejoined U of Manitoba until 1967, when it received its own charter. Brandon U offers undergraduate courses in arts, science, education and music, and a master's degree in music (performance and music education). B. BEATON

Enrolment: Brandon University, 1982-83
(Source: Statistics Canada)

Full-time Undergrad	*Full-time Graduate*	*Part-time Undergrad*	*Part-time Graduate*
1 386	1	1 567	9

Brandtner, Fritz, painter (b at Danzig [Gdansk, Poland] 28 July 1896; d at Montréal 7 Nov 1969). Generally considered to have introduced German expressionism to Canada, Brandtner was trained in Berlin and came to Winnipeg in 1928. He worked as a house painter until L.L. FITZGERALD, principal of the Winnipeg School of Art, encouraged him to exhibit his own experimental paintings. In 1934 he moved to Montréal, where he found greater scope for his "modern" approach. He was associated there with John LYMAN and the CONTEMPORARY ART SOCIETY and later with the Canadian Group of Painte and with Marian SCOTT, with whom he taugh children's art classes. A strong sense of desig exuberant colours and characteristic slashin black diagonals marked his work in oil, wate colour graphics and linoleum, the latter used fo panels for the Queen Elizabeth Hotel and Jaspe Park Lodge. Murals by Brandtner are in Saska toon and Boston. ANNE MCDOUGAL

Brandy Parliament, an assembly of 20 nota bles of NEW FRANCE, who on 10 Oct 1678 we asked their opinion of the sale of brandy to th Indians. (The title was bestowed in 1921 by his torian W.B. Munro.) The Jesuits, as well as th colony's clergy, saw liquor as the chief obstacl to the success of missionary activity, wherea some colonial administrators were halfhearte when it came to banning the traffic. Colbert, th minister of marine, rejected proposals tha might lead to a decline in French exports o brandy and the customs revenue of the Cana dian administration. He asked that a meeting o notables be convened, leaving little doubt abou the verdict he desired. At the meeting, 15 o the 20 spokesmen favoured retention of th brandy trade. Although a royal edict of 24 Ma 1679 forbade the sale of liquor to Indians out side the settlements, alcohol continued to flov westward. TOM WIE

Branscombe, Gena, composer, conductor (b a Picton, Ont 4 Nov 1881; d at New York City, N 26 July 1977). Through a long and vigorous lif she composed music for piano, voice, orchestr and choir, winning particular recognition fo her music for women's voices. Her choral dram *Pilgrims of Destiny* was acclaimed by the Leagu of American Pen Women in 1928 as the fines work composed by a woman. Though she live in the US, several of her compositions embrac Canadian themes: eg, the orchestral *Quebec Sui* and the choir piece "Our Canada from Sea t Sea." In 1960 the RCN adopted her hymn "Arm that Have Sheltered Us." She founded the Brans combe Chorale of New York in 1934 and re mained its conductor for 20 years. BARCLAY MCMILLA

Brant, Joseph, or Thayendanegea, Mohaw war chief, Loyalist, statesman (b at Cayahog [near Akron, Ohio] *c* Mar 1742/43; d at Burl ington Bay, UC 24 Nov 1807), brother of Mar BRANT. Joseph Brant saw limited action durin the SEVEN YEARS' WAR and was with Sir Willian JOHNSON in the expedition against Ft Niagara i 1759. In 1761 Johnson sent him to Moor's In dian Charity School at Lebanon, Conn, where h stayed for 2 years. In 1765 Brant married a Oneida and settled in Canajoharie in the Mo hawk Valley. For nearly a decade, he acted as a interpreter for Johnson and his successor in th British Indian Dept, Guy Johnson, aided mis sionaries in teaching Christianity to the Indians and helped translate religious materials int Mohawk. With the outbreak of the AMERICA REVOLUTION, Brant immediately rallied to th royal cause, and he visited England in 177 with Guy Johnson. On his return Brant fough throughout the war with an Indian-loyalis band. He was greatly admired as a soldier an was commissioned a captain by the British i 1780, but fought as a war chief. Beginning i 1783 and through the mid-1790s Brant worke to form a united confederation of Iroquois an western Indians in order to block American ex pansion westward. His dream ultimately wa undermined by jealousies among the Indian na tions, by American and finally British opposi tion.

About 1779 Brant married Catharine, a Mo hawk from a prominent family. In May 178 following the war, Brant led the Mohawk LOY ALISTS and other native peoples to a large tract o land on the Grand R [Ont] granted them in com

Portrait of Joseph Brant by English painter George Romney, *c*1776 (*courtesy National Gallery of Canada*).

pensation for their losses in the war. Convinced that Indians would have to learn white agriculture to survive and thinking that the tract was too small for hunting, Brant wanted to lease or sell land to whites, which would provide an income as well. A complicated controversy with the government over the nature of Indian land tenure then arose; at the same time there was discontent among some of the Grand R Indians over disposition of the money. In his later years Brant lived quietly in his magnificent house at Burlington in an English style and translated parts of the Bible into Mohawk.
ROBERT S. ALLEN

Brant, Mary, or Konwatsi'tsiaiénni, meaning "someone lends her a flower," Mohawk, (b *c*1736; d at Kingston 16 Apr 1796). Mary, or Molly Brant as she was generally known, was one of the most important women in N American Indian history. From her influential position as head of a society of Six Nations matrons, she enjoyed a much greater status than her more colourful younger brother, Joseph BRANT. She was consulted by the Indians on all matters of importance. Much of her power also came from her relationship with Sir William JOHNSON, first superintendent of the northern Indians of British N America, whom the Six Nations honoured as a good friend and adviser.

In her late teens Molly became Johnson's consort. The attractive and intelligent woman presided over his household with great ability, and managed his estate in the Mohawk Valley, NY, during his frequent absences. After his death (1774), she and her brother Joseph remained staunch LOYALISTS. Molly rendered invaluable assistance to the Crown by encouraging the Six Nations to keep their alliance with England. At the end of the war she moved to Cataraqui [Kingston, Ont]. DONALD B. SMITH

Brantford, Ont, City, pop 74 315 (1981c), inc 1877, seat of Brant County, located on the Grand R, 104 km SW of Toronto. Originally inhabited by the NEUTRAL, the surrounding area was part of a large land grant of the British government in 1784 to the Six Nations Indians in gratitude for their loyalty during the American War of Independence and in compensation for the loss of their land in the Mohawk Valley (*see* IROQUOIS). In 1827 the centre of the settlement was named Brant's Ford after Mohawk leader Joseph BRANT. Non-native settlers were welcomed by the Indians, who surrendered title to the townsite in 1830. With the arrival of the railway, it became the distribution centre of a rich agricultural area. In this century manufacturing has flourished. It is the site of the first Protestant church in Ontario, St Paul's, Her Majesty's Chapel of the Mohawks, built 1785 with a grant from George III; Brant is buried in the churchyard. Alexander Graham BELL worked on the invention of the telephone at his home nearby and in Aug 1876 made the first long-distance call, from Brantford to Paris, Ont, 11 km away. The Bell Homestead (1858) has been restored, as has Henderson House — the first telephone office in Canada (1871). DANIEL FRANCIS

Bras d'Or Lake, 1098 km^2, is an arm of the Atlantic Ocean occupying the centre of CAPE BRETON I that nearly divides the island in 2. On the N it is linked to the ocean by 2 narrow channels down either side of Boularderie I. On the S it is divided from the ocean by a low strip of land that is breached by a ship canal at ST PETERS. The lake is about 70 km long and is circled by high hills. MICMAC were the earliest inhabitants and in 1650 a French trading post was built at St Peters. Late in the 18th century, LOYALISTS settled along its shores, followed by Scottish immigrants. The lake has long been known for good fishing and today is popular for water recreation of all kinds. BADDECK, on the N shore, has been a shipbuilding centre. The name is a corruption of "labrador," a term applied by Portuguese explorers to a large part of Nova Scotia.
DANIEL FRANCIS

Brascan, Ltd, formerly Brazilian Traction Light and Power Co, Ltd, is a major natural-resources company with substantial consumer product interests and extensive holdings in the financial services of the Canadian, American and Brazilian economies. In 1899 William MACKENZIE and others took over an old mule-drawn tramway in São Paulo and reorganized it as the São Paulo Tramway, Light and Power. In 1904, the same promoters created the Rio de Janeiro Tramway, Light and Power Co. Ownership of these 2 companies was assumed in 1912 by the newly created Brazilian Traction, Light and Power Co, a holding company known to Brazilians as "the Light." It furnished Brazil's industrial southeast with electric-power, tramway, telephone and gas services until late 1978, when these assets were sold to the Brazilian government. Its early ownership was primarily in European and American hands. By 1954 it was 51% Canadian owned; by 1975, 54%. The company's first major investment in Canada was John Labatt, Ltd. From its Toronto head office it controls assets of $3.3 billion (1983). Its annual sales revenue of $3.4 billion ranked it 19th among Canadian corporations, and it is 82% Canadian owned.
DUNCAN MCDOWALL

Brassard, François, composer, ethnomusicologist, organist, critic, teacher, pianist (b at St-Jérôme [Métabetchouan], Qué 6 Oct 1908; d at Québec City 26 Apr 1976). He studied music primarily with Claude CHAMPAGNE and Léo-Pol MORIN. From time to time, 1930-70, he was organist at St-Dominique church in Jonquière. The author of numerous essays, as well as analyses and harmonizations of French Canadian folk songs, Brassard is closely linked with Laval's Archives de folklore. In 1946 he was appointed to the archives' publications committee and in 1971 joined its research centre. He also wrote articles using the noms de plume Braz Arpiani and Thibaut de Champagne. In 1974 he received the Canadian Music Council Medal.
HÉLÈNE PLOUFFE

Brault, Cédia, mezzo-soprano (b at Ste-Martine, Qué 4 Jan 1894; d at Montréal 27 June 1972). She studied voice with Céline Marier and Salvator Issaurel and harmony with Rodolphe MATHIEU. She made her debut as Carmen with tenor Victor Desautels in 1918 and, in 1920, married him. Carmen was also her last role (1939). She performed in the premiere of Guillaume COUTURE's *Jean le Précurseur*. One of the first to perform the works of Ravel, Casella and Milhaud in Canada, she also gave the Canadian premiere of Léo-Pol MORIN's *Chants de sacrifice* and of Debussy's *Proses lyriques*. In 1928, on a visit to Montréal, Ravel praised her interpretation of his *Chansons madécasses*.
HÉLÈNE PLOUFFE

Brault, Jacques, writer (b at Montréal 29 Mar 1933). Brault is a major poet of contemporary Québec. He studied at the Collège Sainte-Marie (Montréal), U de Montréal and the Sorbonne (Paris), before becoming a professor at U de M in 1960. He has written for various magazines, notably *Liberté*, and is a literary critic and producer of literary radio programming for Radio-Canada.

Born to a poor family, Brault in his poetry and plays has expressed his attachment to the humble realities of life and his search for a simple and basic wisdom. His collection, *Mémoire* (which won the Prix de Poésie du Québec, 1965, and the Prix France-Canada, 1968), containing "Suite fraternelle," made him famous as a poet of contemporary urban life and of a country as yet unbuilt. His poetic works continued with *La Poésie ce matin* (1971), *Poèmes des quatre côtés* (1975), *L'en dessous l'admirable* (1975) and *Trois fois passera* (1981). Playwright (*Trois partitions*, 1972) and essayist (*Alain Grandbois*, 1968; *Chemin faisant*, 1975), he won a Gov Gen's Award in 1971 and the Prix Duvernay in 1979. MICHEL LEMAIRE

Brault, Michel, filmmaker (b at Montréal 25 June 1928). A professional photographer, Brault filmed the series *Les Petites Médisances* with Jacques Giraldeau in the early 1950s. He joined the NFB as a cameraman in 1956 and worked on the *Candid Eye* series. Quickly moving into film directing, he became a leading figure in direct cinema, using a light, portable camera. Noted for the quality of his cinematography, he went to Europe to work with directors of the *cinéma-vérité* school. Returning to Canada, he worked as director of photography on productions by Québec filmmakers such as Claude JUTRA, Anne Claire POIRIER and Francis MANCKIEWICZ. At the same time, as a film director, he collaborated with Pierre Perrault on 3 feature films, including the classic *Pour la suite du monde* (1963). His ability to combine the documentary impact of direct cinema with the emotional richness of fiction films is demonstrated in *Entre la mer et l'eau douce* (1967) and especially in *Les Ordres* (1974), a documentary dramatization of the 1970 OCTOBER CRISIS that won first prize at Cannes in 1975. Since 1976 he has produced and co-directed films with André Gladu for the series *Le Son des Français d'Amérique;* he was for many years president of the Syndicat national du cinéma. Brault has been an inspiration to a generation of filmmakers. PIERRE VÉRONNEAU

Breadalbane is a ghost ship, a 3-masted barque lying beneath the ice of the NORTHWEST PASSAGE. Sunk in 1853, she is the world's northernmost known shipwreck and the best-preserved wooden ship yet found in the ocean. Built in Scotland in 1843, she was a merchant ship sailing to Europe's great seaports carrying wine, wool, grain and essentials of the new Industrial Age. In spring 1853 the *Breadalbane* was called into service by the Royal Navy and sent to the Arctic to carry supplies to Sir Edward BELCHER's expedition which, since 1852, had been searching for the ships and men of the FRANKLIN EXPEDITION. Sir John Franklin had been lost while seeking the Northwest Passage, which had eluded Europeans for almost 3 centuries. Belcher's squadron was the Royal Navy's last and largest search expedition.

The *Breadalbane* was about 40 m long, generously built, a square-rigged ship typical of the hundreds that linked the great oceans during the reign of Queen Victoria. But she was no match for the Arctic. In spite of her sturdy wooden hull and the skill of her crew, she was trapped in the polar ice. On 21 Aug 1853, just after midnight, a slab of ice knifed through her starboard bow. The 21-man crew scrambled over the side to safety. Within 15 minutes the *Breadalbane* was headed for the bottom. The crew were picked up by her surviving sister ship, the *Phoenix*.

For 127 years she remained where she was, hidden below the grinding polar pack, cloaked by freezing currents. She lay on the seafloor in the darkness, hard on her keel, her broken bowsprit pointing E, towards home and England. Joseph B. MACINNIS's first expedition to find the ship (Aug 1978) was prompted by research by arctic marine historians Stuart Hodgson and Maurice Haycock. Available documents included eyewitness accounts from the archive of the Scott Polar Research Institute, Cambridge, England.

She was found in 1980 after 3 years of searching the waters S of Beechey I. On 13 August the *Breadalbane* ghosted onto the screen of the side-scan SONAR, her hull intact, 2 of her masts still standing. In 1981 the expedition went back for a more detailed look, supported by the CANADIAN COAST GUARD, the National Geographic Society and other institutions. A remotely piloted SUBMERSIBLE was lowered into the lethally cold water. One hundred metres down, with still and video cameras, colour photographs were taken. Her bow, masts, rudder and anchor could be seen; the green copper sheathing that still protected her hull looked like new. In a small cabinet hanging on her deckhouse were her compass and a signal light; nearby was the big wooden wheel that had guided her across the stormy N Atlantic. Seeing the *Breadalbane* was like looking through time at another century, at a sailing ship that had gone to the bottom before the American Civil War, before Canada became a Dominion.

Like all historical artifacts, the *Breadalbane* will take time to study, and special problems are raised by her position in the Arctic. She lies under an unpredictable barrier of ice. Marine geologists and sea-ice morphologists, under the guidance of senior scientist Steve Blasco of the BEDFORD INSTITUTE OF OCEANOGRAPHY, wish to study ice formation over the ship and the effects of ice scouring on nearby sediments. This information is of interest to all parties working in northern waters, including oil companies (*see* ARCTIC OCEANOGRAPHY; OCEAN INDUSTRIES). Yet the *Breadalbane* lies far below the depths at which marine archaeologists can work. To unlock her secrets, new DIVING and photographic techniques specific to the Arctic are being developed. The new technology includes the Sea-Otter submersible, a lock-out diving system and WASP, a physiologically protective diving suit. All are operated by Can-Dive Services, Vancouver.

The *Breadalbane* is unique among shipwrecks, being beautifully preserved by arctic waters. For scientists, she is a drowned benchmark, an opportunity to learn more about arctic BIOLOGY and GEOLOGY and about the SEA ICE that floats over her masts. Historically, she is a time capsule: some of her cargo and working tools and personal effects of the crew are still on board. Diving down to her, studying her remains, is an excursion into Canada's past and into our future. JOSEPH B. MACINNIS

Reading: Joseph B. MacInnis, *The Breadalbane Adventure* (1983).

Breau, Lenny, jazz guitarist (b at Auburn, Maine 5 Aug 1941; d at Los Angeles, Calif 12 Aug 1984). As a boy, he was taken to Winnipeg by his parents, country singers Hal Lone Pine and Betty Cody. His youthful virtuosity, eclecticism and technical innovation drew attention in Toronto as early as 1962, but his career was hampered by personal problems, including a lengthy drug addition. Early recordings — *Guitar Sounds, The Velvet Touch* — made Breau something of a legend outside Canada, and in 1975 he returned to the US. His career and influence subsequently grew with further recordings in jazz and country contexts. MARK MILLER

Brébeuf, Jean de, Jesuit missionary, author of *Relations des Jésuites,* 1635, 1636 (b at Condé-sur-Vire, France 25 Mar 1593; martyred at St-Ignace in HURONIA 16 Mar 1649; canonized 16 Oct 1940). Brébeuf came to Canada in 1625 as a missionary to the nomadic Montagnais. Sent to the HURON near Georgian Bay in 1626, he learned their language and preached there until 1629, when Québec was captured by the KIRKE brothers and the Jesuits were forced to return to France. He returned in 1633 and was in charge of the Huron mission for 4 years. Brébeuf, an accomplished linguist, supervised the preparation of a Huron grammar and dictionary. In 1640, following a devastating smallpox epidemic, the Huron attacked him and his companion, beat them and damaged their mission. In 1640-41 he began a mission among the NEUTRAL, but they regarded him as a sorcerer. In 1644 he returned to Huronia, remaining there until 16 Mar 1649 when he was captured by invading IROQUOIS at the St Louis mission, taken to St-Ignace and brutally killed. His bones are buried at the Martyrs' Shrine near Midland, Ont. CORNELIUS J. JAENEN

Brebner, John Bartlet, historian (b at Toronto 19 May 1895; d at New York C, NY 9 Nov 1957). Educated at U of T, Oxford and Columbia U, he taught 1921-25 at U of T and then moved to Columbia U for the rest of his academic life. Here he established his reputation as a historian and teacher; he was also very active in the Carnegie Endowment for International Peace. Brebner's most influential books are *New England's Outpost* (1927), *The Neutral Yankees of Nova Scotia* (1937), *The North Atlantic Triangle* (1945) and, with M.L. Hansen, *The Mingling of the Canadian and American People* (1940). His explanation for the expulsion of the Acadians in 1755 and the neutrality of Nova Scotia during the American Revolution is still widely regarded as the "classic account." G.A. RAWLYK

Breeze, Claude Herbert, painter (b at Nelson, BC 9 Oct 1938). Breeze was taught by Ernest LINDNER in Saskatoon (1954-55) and then studied at Regina with Kenneth LOCHHEAD and Arthur MCKAY. After graduating in 1958, he spent a year at the Vancouver School of Art. One of the important West Coast painters, Breeze was the first in Canada to depict the violence shown by the media, especially television. In many ways his work of the early 1960s, particularly his series Lovers in a Landscape, with its probing content and dry handling, anticipates the work of the young contemporary figure painters. Breeze has recently completed a number of lithographs based on his fascination with aikido, a Japanese martial art. He has taught at York U in Toronto since 1976. JOAN MURRAY

Bregman, Sidney (b at Warsaw, Poland); **Hamann, George Frederick** (b at Toronto 14 June 1928); architects. The partnership, founded in Toronto in 1953, is active across N America primarily in the design and construction of health-care facilities (Mount Sinai Hospital, Toronto, and the Ottawa General Hospital) and of commercial and retail space. Alone or in joint venture, the firm has designed over 2.8 million square metres of office accommodation, much of it in downtown Toronto: the Toronto Dominion Centre with J.B. PARKIN Associates; the EATON CENTRE with the ZEIDLER Partnership; Harbour Square; the Simpson Tower; and the 72-storey First Canadian Place.
GRANT WANZEL AND KAREN KALLWEIT

Bren Gun Scandal Before WWII the British government was anxious to acquire new, secure sources for weapons production. The Canadian government was reluctant to co-operate, fearing isolationist opinion, especially in Québec. In 1938, however, the deputy minister and minister of national defence recommended a Canadian appliance manufacturer, John Inglis, and the British and Canadian governments awarded his firm a contract for production of the Bren light machine gun. Impropriety was alleged, and a royal commission was appointed. Although it found no evidence of corruption, it recommended that civilian business advice be sought in future. This report helped lead to civilian control over war production in WWII (*see* MUNITIONS AND SUPPLY, DEPARTMENT OF). Bren gun production was very successful: some 200 000 were made in Canada. ROBERT BOTHWELL

Brener, Roland, sculptor (b at Johannesburg, S Africa 22 Feb 1942). His sculptural style has been influenced by Constructivist theories and by his instructor, Anthony Caro, at St Martin's School of Art, London. This school has taught a nontraditional approach to sculpture since the early 1960s, centering on syntatical construction rather than techniques of modelling. Brener uses prefabricated materials such as pipes and scaffolding in his abstract sculptures, allowing him to build linear sculptures on a large scale. Yet, because of their logical structural order, their visual shape belies their complexity. In 1973 Brener began teaching in the visual arts dept, U Vic. KATHLEEN LAVERTY

Brethren in Christ (identified as "Tunkers" in Canada in the 19th century) were a group of Christians who shared the ANABAPTIST belief in adult baptism. They trace their origins to 1770 when concerned members of the MENNONITE, LUTHERAN and BAPTIST churches in Lancaster County, Pa, broke with the formalism of their parent churches. The organization of the new group was very loose and various small independent groups emerged, the most important of which were probably the so-called River Brethren. After the American Revolution, many of the Brethren, who had taken a PACIFIST position in that conflict, emigrated to what is now Ontario, where their pacifist convictions were officially recognized and respected in the Militia Act of 1793. Canada's roughly 2500 adult Brethren in Christ participate in the international relief activities of the Mennonite Central Committee, but their church has retained a separate denominational identity in Canada and the US.
T.D. REGEHR

Brett, George Sidney, philosopher (b at Briton Ferry, Wales 5 Aug 1879; d at Toronto 27 Oct 1944). Educated at Oxford and having taught in India, he moved from teaching classics (1908) at Trinity Coll and University Coll, U of T, to the department of philosophy, where he was chairman 1927-44. His 3-volume *A History of Psychology* (1912-21) assesses the philosophy of mind theories; Brett presents PSYCHOLOGY as the study of the immediate data of the inner life, distinguishes it from other sciences, and resists the new experimentalist approach. *The Government of Man* (1913) traces political stages in societies. Freedom is seen here to emerge from the relation between man's inner life and changing social orders. Brett's commitment to historical modes of understanding led him to be seen by some as the founder of the "Toronto School of Intellectual History." He guided courses and appointments in Toronto for many years. A fellow of the Royal Soc of Canada, he founded the *Canadian Journal of Religious Thought,* served as an edi-

r for the *Journal of General Psychology* and the *In-rnational Journal of Ethics,* and was first editor of e *University of Toronto Quarterly.*
ELIZABETH A. TROTT

rewing Industry Brewing began in Canada ith the first settlers and traders. At first, beer aking was a cottage industry, but in 1668 Can-la's first commercial brewery was built by the tendant Jean TALON at Québec City. Its aims ere to promote temperance (by offering an al-rnative to strong imported French liquors), eep currency from leaving the country for im-orted beverages and make use of the abun-ance of grain available in the New World.

In its early development period the industry nsisted of small, independent breweries scat-red throughout the country. As a result of odern distribution systems, quality control nd rising costs, production became centralized nd most local breweries disappeared (although s a result of the "real ale" movement in Europe, nall "brew pubs" are beginning to enjoy a naissance, so far, only in BC). Today, Canada's rewing industry comprises Carling O'Keefe reweries of Canada Ltd, Labatt Brewing Co Ltd nd MOLSON Breweries of Canada Ltd, each of hich has plants in 9 of the 10 provinces; and rge regional breweries: Old Fort Brewing Com-any Ltd in BC, Rocky Mountain Breweries Ltd Alberta, Northern Breweries Ltd and Amstel rewery Canada Ltd in Ontario, and Moosehead reweries Ltd in NS and NB. In 1983 there were 8 brewing plants operating across Canada in 9 rovinces (PEI has no breweries). Because of rovincial legislation, beer is generally mar-eted locally (ie, beer brewed outside a province annot be sold at "domestic" prices). In the 1970s arling O'Keefe, Labatt and Molson supplied bout 80% of the beer sold in Canada.

Canadians consume about 20.5 million hL f beer annually. Consumption per capita is pproximately 85 L. In the early 1970s Canada anked tenth among the nations of the world in er capita consumption; in 1983, twelfth. Lager as become the preferred type of beer consumed, ccounting for almost 63% of the market; ale ac-ounts for most of the remainder. Twenty years go the shares of ale and lager were reversed, ith ale accounting for 59% of sales. Beer is used s a generic term and includes both lager and le. The difference between the 2 is that lager is ade by fermenting with a type of yeast that rops to the bottom of the fermenting tank and s lighter in taste; whereas more hops are used to rew ale and the yeast usually rises to the top of e tank. Less than 1% of the remainder of beer s sold as stout (heavy-bodied darker and weeter beer brewed with roasted malt and a igher percentage of hops) and porter (weaker tout). Light beers, containing 4% alcohol by olume, were introduced in Canada in the late 970s. Brands of this nature are becoming in-reasingly popular in the 1980s. Regular-trength Canadian beers contain 5% alcohol by olume.

The production, distribution and sale of beer ontributed $6.3 billion to Canada's GROSS NA-IONAL PRODUCT in 1982. This figure represents .8% of the GNP and illustrates the impact on he economy of beer consumption. Export vol-me accounted for 9.8% of beer production (Ca-adian beer is particularly popular in the US). ver 98% of the beer consumed in Canada was roduced by Canadian brewers. The brewing in-ustry's annual purchases of domestic materials nd supplies were substantial ($515 million in 982). For example, BARLEY malt cost over $140 nillion; bottles bought in Canada came to over 44 million; and cartons and labels amounted to ver $130 million.

Salaries, wages, commissions and employee ecurity benefits paid by the industry amounted o over $639 million. However, this item is a small part of the wage bill when the total em-ployment arising from the brewing and market-ing of beer is considered. There are 18 122 persons employed directly by the brewing in-dustry; an additional 72 358 are employed in jobs related to distribution and sales. Further in-direct employment is generated from brewing and marketing: the earnings of an additional 103 330 persons depend indirectly on the pro-duction, distribution and sale of beer. Thus, total employment amounts to 193 810 jobs, account-ing for 1.6% of Canada's labour force.

Calcutt Brewery, Ashburnham, Ont (near Peterborough), *c*1900-10. Photo shows Henry Calcutt, proprietor, in buggy *(courtesy Public Archives of Canada / C-21195).*

Revenue to all levels of government gener-ated by the brewing and marketing of beer amounted to about $2.3 billion in 1982. Just over $1.2 billion came from federal excise duty and sales tax and provincial liquor-board prof-its and sales taxes; the remainder represented various taxes paid to the different levels of gov-ernment by the employees and companies in-volved.

Advertising of alcoholic beverages is strictly controlled by provincial governments (NB and PEI have banned it on radio and television). This restriction, combined with others (eg, uni-formity of price, distribution outlets and, until recently, packaging), has caused the industry to seek innovative and distinctive promotional op-portunities. Today, breweries sponsor a range of sporting events (eg, cycling, downhill skiing) and Carling O'Keefe, Labatts and Molson own sports teams (eg, Montreal Canadiens, Toronto Argonauts and Quebec Nordiques). *See* Sir John CARLING; John Sackville LABATT; Eugene O'KEEFE.
KEN LAVERY

Brewster, Elizabeth Winifred, writer (b at Chipman, NB 26 Aug 1922). Since 1972 Brewster has taught English at U of Sask, but before that she was a librarian and cataloguer in NB, Ontario, Alberta and BC. She was educated at UNB, Radcliffe Coll, U of T and Indiana U. Winner of several awards and honours, Brewster has written 13 books, most of them poetry collections. Her first book of poetry was *East Coast* (1951) and since then she has produced 8 others, including *Passage of Summer* (1969), *Sunrise North* (1972), *Sometimes I Think of Moving* (1977) and *The Way Home* (1982). As well, she has written 2 novels and 2 story collections.
JEAN WILSON

Brewster, Harlan Carey, politician, premier of BC (b at Harvey, NB 10 Nov 1870; d at Calgary 1 Mar 1918). Educated in NB and Boston, Mass, and qualified as a printer and deep-sea naviga-tor, Brewster moved to BC about 1893. Succes-sively employed as ship's purser, accountant and salmon cannery manager, he eventually be-came owner of the Clayoquot Sound Cannery in 1907. In 1909 he was elected Liberal MLA for Alberni. In 1912, as leader of the Opposition, he ran against Premier Richard MCBRIDE in Victoria but, like all other Liberals, was defeated. He re-turned to the legislature through a Vancouver by-election in 1916 and was re-elected in the general election, serving as premier until his de-ath. His brief administration introduced such reforms as WOMEN'S SUFFRAGE and PROHIBITION and attempted to clean up political corruption, es-pecially surrounding the Pacific Great Eastern Ry.
PATRICIA E. ROY

Bridges have always been important in Cana-dian TRANSPORTATION, if only because of the many waterways to be crossed by roads and rail-ways. Logs cut from the local forests had to suf-fice for stream crossings on primitive trails be-fore the advent of truss designs early in the 19th century. In winter the frozen surfaces of rivers and lakes provided safe crossings when ice had gained sufficient thickness. Ice bridges are still used; carefully designed crossings (with ice arti-ficially built up) served, for example, on the long access road to the JAMES BAY PROJECT during the winter of 1971-72 prior to the erection of permanent bridges. More remarkable was the use of an ice bridge across the St Lawrence R in the winters of 1880-81 and 1881-82, from Ho-chelaga to Longueuil [Montréal], to carry a standard-gauge railway; from Jan to March in each of those winters a small train, weighing 60 tons, safely used this unique bridge.

Covered bridges, still to be seen on secondary roads in eastern Canada, were important in ear-ly Canadian bridge building. First used in 1805 in Philadelphia, and long known as "kissing bridges" (for the most obvious of reasons), they came into wide use by the end of the century. There were then at least 1000 in Québec and more than 400 in NB. Today, there are probably not more than 200 in either province, and spe-cial efforts have been made in NB for their pres-ervation. The covered bridge over the Saint John R at HARTLAND, NB, is 385 m long, renowned as "the longest covered bridge in the world."

Covered bridges were all built of timber, vari-ous types of trusses enabling steadily increasing span lengths to be used after the first US patent for trusses was taken out in 1830. Three years earlier, using a European design, John BY had incorporated a 60 m span truss bridge across the Big Kettle of the Chaudière at Bytown [Ottawa] in the Union Bridge across the Ottawa R, the first link between Lower and Upper Canada, built at the start of work on the RIDEAU CANAL. On the associated Ottawa R canals, engineer of-ficers of the Royal Staff Corps had used pre-fabricated timber bridges even before 1827. Tim-ber has continued in use for bridges in Canada to the present day, some of the most notable exam-ples being the great timber trestle bridges used in early railway construction in the West, now generally replaced by steel structures.

It was a common practice to use timber for bridges in early railway building in Canada. An exception was the INTERCOLONIAL RY, completed in 1876. The chief engineer, Sir Sandford FLEM-ING, insisted on masonry piers for all his bridges and wrought iron for his bridge spans, as in the 2 multispan bridges across the Miramichi R, NB. Steel trusses now replace the original wrought iron spans; the piers, however, are the originals from over a century ago. Even more significant were some of the bridges erected in the 1850s for the GRAND TRUNK RY from Montréal to Toronto, particularly the Victoria Bridge (1860) across the St Lawrence R at Montréal, even today one of the world's great bridges (2742 m long). Its origi-nal spans, and those of the bridge carrying the track over the Ottawa R at Ste Anne de Bellevue, were wrought iron rectangular boxes, later re-placed by steel trusses.

By the end of the century, steel was used widely. Its capability for bridges is well shown by the Interprovincial Bridge over the Ottawa R at Ottawa, the longest cantilever span in the world when built, still in active use although now for road traffic rather than rail. Down-stream, the Jacques Cartier Bridge at Montréal (opened in 1929) is another fine cantilever struc-ture. The Quebec Bridge, further downstream

Covered bridge, Gatineau R at Wakefield Qué (*photo by John deVisser*).

still, is Canada's most famous bridge. Designed to carry the National Transcontinental Railway across the St Lawrence, it was started in 1906 as the longest steel cantilever bridge of the world. It failed, with tragic loss of life, during erection in Aug 1907 (*see* QUEBEC BRIDGE DISASTERS). A new start was made and the finished bridge was opened on 22 Aug 1919. The accident was studied to good effect by an expert royal commission, and its report, a classic of structural engineering, has benefitted bridge design around the world.

A suspension bridge for road traffic now parallels the Quebec Bridge, one of a small number of such graceful structures found at strategic spots in Canada: across the Lion's Gate at Vancouver; the international section of the St Lawrence; and linking Halifax with Dartmouth across its harbour entrance. So successful was the latter that it has now been duplicated. The first bridge over the Niagara R, below the falls, was an elaborate suspension bridge carrying not only highway traffic but also the GREAT WESTERN RY. It was replaced later by the first of a series of fine steel-arched bridges.

Repair of bridges without disrupting traffic has been a significant part of Canadian bridge engineering. One of the most famous examples was the reinforcing of the steel arched truss bridge over Stoney Cr on the CPR main line through the Rocky Mts. In the 1950s, similar well-planned changes were made to some of the bridges crossing the ST LAWRENCE SEAWAY in order to give adequate clearance beneath them. Equally notable was the replacement of the fixed centre spans of 3 bridges over the Beauharnois power canal with vertical-lift bridges to permit passage of seaway traffic, this feature having been incorporated in the original designs 20 years before.

Reinforced concrete was first used in bridge construction in the early 20th century, eg, the Hurdman Bridge in Ottawa built in 1906. Today, probably the majority of small highway bridges are of reinforced concrete, an increasing number built of prefabricated units. Some quite large bridges have been constructed of this versatile material, as in the multi-span, arched Broadway Bridge across the S Saskatchewan R at Saskatoon. The Broadway Bridge and the earlier University Bridge, also multi-span arched, add greatly to the distinctive appearance of the central part of this prairie city. Some older bridges can hardly be considered beautiful, but the use of reinforced concrete has had a beneficial effect on bridge aesthetics. The elegant lines of the rigid frame bridges on major Ontario highways, eg, are believed to have influenced similar designs in the US and the UK. ROBERT F. LEGGET

Brier Island is a small island off the end of Digby Neck at the entrance to the BAY OF FUNDY in SW Nova Scotia. It is the last link in a broken chain of land separating the larger bay from St Mary's Bay. The coastline is marked by tall columns of rock that descend in steps to the water. Fishing is the main activity on the island; the main settlement is the village of Westport (pop 380). Capt Joshua Slocum, who became the first person to sail alone around the world in 1895-98, was a native son. DANIEL FRANCIS

British American Land Company, chartered 20 Mar 1834 and promoted by John GALT, CANADA COMPANY founder; Edward ELLICE, Lower Canada's largest absentee landowner; and others. It purchased 343 995 ha of crown land in the Eastern Townships (Qué) for £120 000. Before 1844 its activities satisfied no one: the few settlers who came to the relatively inaccessible holdings complained of high land costs and harsh company policy; local politicians resented the fact that control over the purchase of money went to the executive branch of the government; and British shareholders demanded dividends. After ceding 206 898 ha to the government in 1841 in lieu of overdue payments, the company appointed Alexander T. Galt, John Galt's son, as local commissioner (1844-55). He increased land prices, but allowed a longer payment time. General immigration and local land sales increased. Urged by Galt and his successor, R.W. Heneker, the company invested in railways and industrial pursuits to stimulate sales. Although it operated until the 1950s, most of its land had been sold by 1910. PETER BASKERVILLE

British Block Cairn and Suffield Tipi Rings, located in the open prairie of southeastern Alberta, consist of a central stone cairn 10 m in diameter and 2 m high surrounded by a 24 m diameter stone circle. Between the central cairn and the surrounding ring is a human figure outlined in stone. In the immediate vicinity are numerous smaller stone circles, or "tipi rings," used by Indians to hold down the edges of their lodges. The site is the largest known example of one type of ceremonial aboriginal structure found rarely throughout the Northern Plains and included in the general category of MEDICINE WHEELS. Although the specific ceremonial function of structures such as the British Block is unknown, research indicates that their construction began about 4000 to 5000 years ago and that they continued to be enlarged and added to intermittently until the early historic period. *See also* ARCHAEOLOGY; PREHISTORY.

JOHN H. BRUMLEY

British Columbia Canada's most westerly province is a mountainous area whose population is clustered in the southwestern corner. It is a land of diversity and contrast within small areas. Coastal landscapes, characterized by high, snow-covered mountains rising above narrow FJORDS and inlets, contrast with the broad forested upland of the central interior and the plains of the NE. People live around the shores of sheltered Georgia Strait in the SW and are dispersed in linear patterns along the N-S valleys in the southern half of the province. With an area of 948 600 km^2, BC is Canada's third-largest province, after Québec and Ontario. The provincial population of 2 744 467 in 1981 is third in numbers in Canada, after Ontario and Québec. The intense "Britishness" of earlier times is referred to in the province's name, which originated with Queen Victoria and was officially proclaimed in 1858. The province is closely tied to the American Northwest with which it shares locational continuity.

Land and Resources

Regions British Columbia has 2 main regions, loosely called "the Coast" and "the Interior," with numerous contrasts and variations within each. The so-called "Lower Mainland," dominated by metropolitan Vancouver, contains 55% of the province's population and is its commercial, cultural and industrial centre. A slightly broader region, sometimes called the Georgia Strait region, includes Victoria and the SE coast of Vancouver I; this area holds 70% of the population. The vast interior is dominated by parallel mountain ranges and population is strung north-south along valleys, notably the Okanagan and the Kootenay. Nodes of population are dispersed, as at Kamloops and Prince Georg in the interior or Prince Rupert and Kitimat o the northern coast, each the centre of a separa subregion and each depending more on worl markets than on local markets. Much of th evolution of resource-based economic activity i the province has been concerned with linkin together these separate regions into a broad provincial economy. The northern half of th province is virtually uninhabited N of Princ Rupert and is cut off from the Pacific by th Alaska Panhandle. The PEACE RIVER LOWLAND c the NE is actually an extension of the Interic Plains and more closely resembles neighbourin Alberta than the rest of the province.

Landforms, Geology and Drainage The Co dilleran mountain system of western N Americ covers most of British Columbia, except for th Peace R area of the NE. The ROCKY MOUNTAINS ris abruptly about 1000-1500 m above the foothil of Alberta, and some of their snow- and ic covered peaks tower more than 3000 m abov sea level; the highest peak, Mt Robson, W of Ja per, Alta, is 3954 m. In the southern Rockies, th sharp, jagged sedimentary-rock peaks of mainl Paleozoic geological age differ from the mo rounded, lower peaks of Proterozoic age to th N. The Rocky Mountains terminate S of th LIARD R in northeastern BC and do not exten into the Yukon or Alaska — contrary to som foreign maps and atlases. The western boundar of the Rocky Mountains is the narrow ROCK MOUNTAIN TRENCH — the longest valley in America, extending more than 1500 km alon the length of BC from Montana to the Yuko Out of the trench flow the headwaters of th Kootenay, COLUMBIA, FRASER, Parsnip, Finla Kechika and Liard rivers, each separated fro another by low drainage divides.

Two other mountain systems lie W of th Rocky Mountain Trench: the COLUMBIA MOU TAINS to the S and the Cassiar-Omineca Mou tains to the N. The Columbia Mountains (a co lective name seldom used in BC) consist c 3 parallel, N-S ranges (Purcell, Selkirk, Mo ashee) which have sharp peaks of 2000-3000 m separated by long, narrow valleys occupied b Kootenay Lk and the Columbia R. These mour tains consist mainly of sedimentary and intru sive rocks of Cretaceous, Triassic and Jurass ages, and they have been well mineralized. Th fourth range of the group, the Cariboo Mour tains NW of the Thompson R, is composed c sedimentary rocks of Proterozoic age which ap pear to be less mineralized.

The broad, gently rolling uplands of the Inte rior Plateau covers central British Columbia. Th region can be considered a basin because it surrounded by higher mountains. Many of th rocks are lavas of Cretaceous and Tertiary geo logical ages with apparently little mineral ization except around the plateau edges. Th Fraser R has cut deeply into the bedrock in th southern part to form the spectacular FRASE RIVER CANYON. Northward the Stikine Plateau another upland area of mainly Jurassic lav rocks, with some recent volcanoes, containin the headwaters of the Stikine R. Average alt tudes of both the Interior and Stikine platea are about 1000 m above sea level.

The western section of the Cordillera consis of 2 mountain systems along the coast and th offshore Insular Mountains. The northern en of the Cascade Mountains of Washington sta terminates at the Fraser R, and then the high snow- and ice-covered peaks of the Coast Mour tains extend northward to the Yukon. These sce nic mountains have peaks up to 3000 m in th southern part, with Mt Waddington, the highes peak, rising to 4016 m. Numerous long, twist ing, deep fjords penetrate into the mountai mass along the coast. The rocks are mostly gran itic intrusions of Cretaceous and Tertiary age and there are some recent volcanoes. The lowe

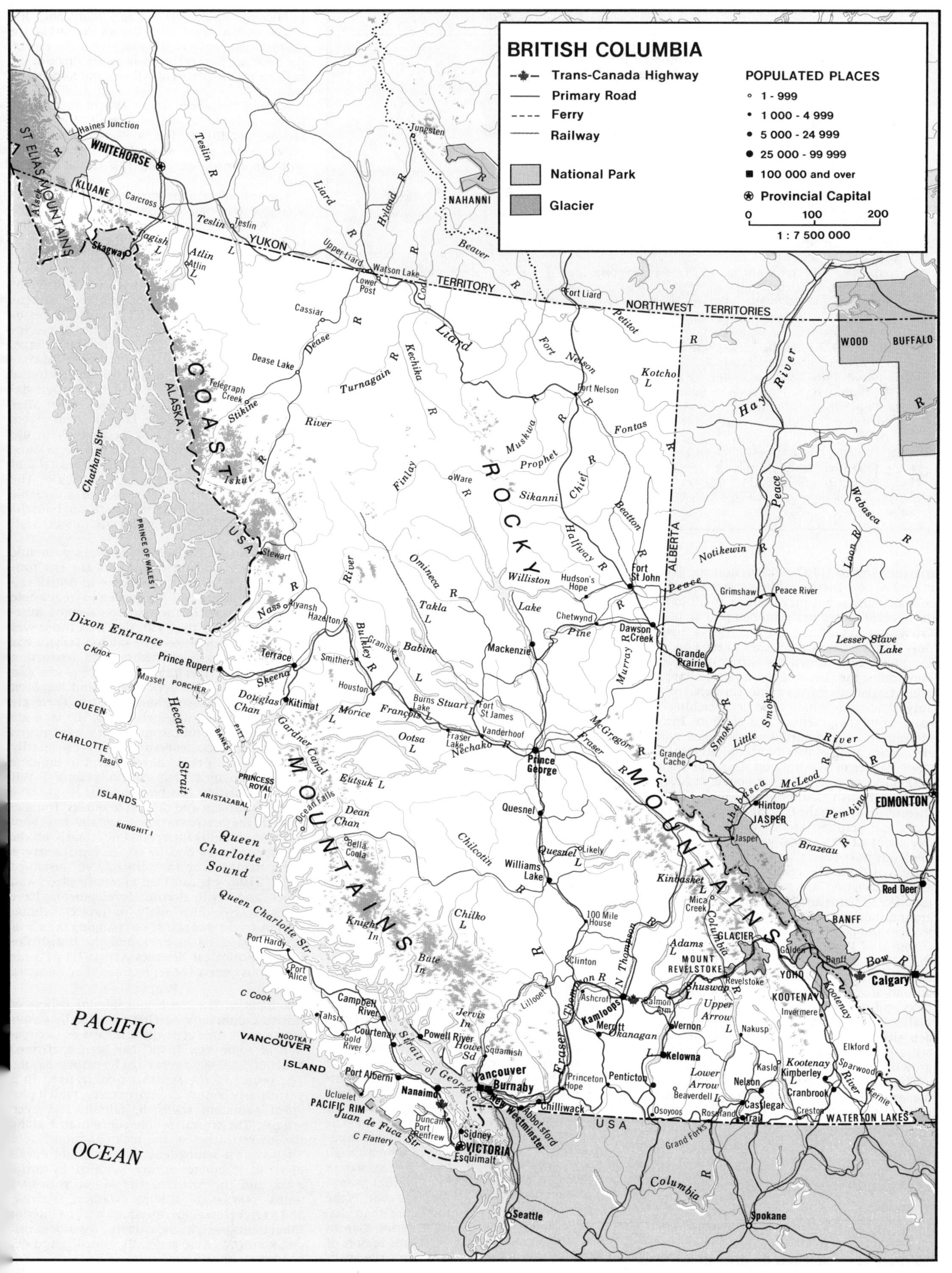
BRITISH COLUMBIA
Trans-Canada Highway
Primary Road
Ferry
Railway
National Park
Glacier
POPULATED PLACES
1 - 999
1 000 - 4 999
5 000 - 24 999
25 000 - 99 999
100 000 and over
Provincial Capital
0
100
200
1 : 7 500 000
YUKON
TERRITORY
NORTHWEST TERRITORIES
ALBERTA
ALASKA
USA
PACIFIC
OCEAN
COAST
MOUNTAINS
ROCKY
MOUNTAINS
ST ELIAS MOUNTAINS
WHITEHORSE
Haines Junction
KLUANE
Carcross
Skagway
Tagish L
Atlin
Atlin L
Teslin
Teslin L
Teslin R
Tungsten
NAHANNI
Watson Lake
Lower Post
Upper Liard
Fort Liard
Cassiar
Dease Lake
Telegraph Creek
Stikine
Iskut R
Stewart
Nass R
Aiyansh
Hazelton
Prince Rupert
Terrace
Kitimat
Smithers
Houston
Burns Lake
Fort St James
Vanderhoof
Fraser Lake
Prince George
Mackenzie
Williston Lake
Hudson's Hope
Fort St John
Chetwynd
Dawson Creek
Fort Nelson
Ware
Grande Prairie
Grimshaw
Peace River
Lesser Slave Lake
WOOD BUFFALO
Grande Cache
Hinton
JASPER
Jasper
EDMONTON
Red Deer
Calgary
BANFF
YOHO
KOOTENAY
GLACIER
MOUNT REVELSTOKE
WATERTON LAKES
Quesnel
Likely
Williams Lake
100 Mile House
Clinton
Lillooet
Ashcroft
Kamloops
Salmon Arm
Revelstoke
Vernon
Kelowna
Penticton
Merritt
Princeton
Hope
Chilliwack
Abbotsford
New Westminster
Vancouver
Burnaby
Squamish
Powell River
Courtenay
Campbell River
Port Hardy
Port Alice
Tahsis
Gold River
Port Alberni
Nanaimo
Ucluelet
PACIFIC RIM
Duncan
Port Renfrew
Sidney
VICTORIA
Esquimalt
Seattle
Spokane
Nakusp
Kaslo
Nelson
Castlegar
Trail
Rossland
Grand Forks
Osoyoos
Beaverdell
Kimberley
Cranbrook
Creston
Invermere
Golden
Elkford
Sparwood
Fernie
Mica Creek
Masset
Tasu
Bella Coola
Ocean Falls
Dixon Entrance
Hecate Strait
Queen Charlotte Sound
Queen Charlotte Str
QUEEN CHARLOTTE ISLANDS
VANCOUVER ISLAND
Strait of Georgia
Juan de Fuca Str
C Flattery
C Cook
C Knox
Chatham Str
PRINCE OF WALES I
PORCHER I
BANKS I
PITT I
PRINCESS ROYAL I
ARISTAZABAL I
KUNGHIT I
NOOTKA I
Douglas Chan
Gardner Canal
Dean Chan
Knight In
Bute In
Jervis In
Howe Sd
Liard R
Hyland R
Beaver R
Petitot
Fort Nelson R
Kotcho L
Hay River
Turnagain R
Kechika R
Dease R
Muskwa R
Prophet R
Fontas
Chief R
Sikanni
Beatton R
Halfway R
Finlay R
Omineca R
Takla L
Babine L
Stuart L
François L
Nechako R
Ootsa L
Eutsuk L
Morice L
Bulkley R
Skeena
Peace R
Pine R
Murray R
Smoky R
Little Smoky R
McGregor R
Fraser R
Notikewin R
Wabasca R
Loon R
Athabasca R
McLeod R
Pembina R
Brazeau R
Chilcotin R
Quesnel L
Chilko L
Kinbasket L
Columbia R
Adams L
N Thompson R
Thompson R
Shuswap L
Upper Arrow L
Lower Arrow L
Okanagan L
Kootenay L
Kootenay R
Bow R
Columbia R

British Columbia

Capital: Victoria
Motto: Splendor Sine Occasu ("Splendour without diminishment")
Flower: Pacific dogwood
Largest Cities: Greater Vancouver, Greater Victoria, Prince George, Kamloops, Kelowna, Nanaimo, Penticton
Population: 2 744 000 (1981c); rank third, 11.3% of Canada; 77.9% urban; 19.9% rural nonfarm; 2.2% farm; 2.9 per km² density; 10% increase from 1976-81; Jan 1984e pop, 2 851 700
Languages: 91.7 English; 1.5% French; 6.8% Other
Entered Confederation: 20 July 1871
Government: Provincial — Lieutenant-Governor, Executive Council, Legislative Assembly of 57 members; federal — 6 senators, 28 members of the House of Commons
Area: 948 596 km²; including 18 068 km² of inland water; 9.5% of Canada
Elevation: Highest point — Fairweather Mountain (4663 m); lowest point — sea level along coasts
Gross Domestic Product: $44.7 billion (1982e)
Farm Cash Receipts: $945 million (1982)
Value of Fish Landings: $223.7 million (1981); $191 million (1982)
Electric Power Generated: 47 278 801 MWh (1983)
Sales Tax: 7% (1984)

COAST MOUNTAINS (1500-2000 m) near the Skeena R are less of a barrier to the penetration of Pacific air masses, but they increase in altitude to the N, culminating in the highest peak in BC, Mt Fairweather (4663 m), on the Alaska border. Only 3 major rivers, the Fraser, Skeena and Stikine, have cut through the barrier of the Coast Mountains; the first 2 of these valleys have become important topographic funnels for the only land-transportation routes reaching the coast from the interior. The offshore Insular Mountains are the partially submerged northern continuation of the Olympic Mountains and Coast Ranges of Washington state. The highest peak on Vancouver I is GOLDEN HINDE, at 2200 m.

All of British Columbia was under a thick sheet of ice during the Glacial Age. Some coastal areas, and perhaps interior valleys, became ice free about 12 000-15 000 years ago, and coastal lowlands have been rising, relative to sea level, since that time. The results of continental and alpine glaciation are seen everywhere in the province in fjords and cirques in the mountains, ground moraine across the Interior Plateau and terraces and benches along interior rivers.

Soils and Vegetation It is estimated that less than 5% of British Columbia has soils suitable for agricultural production. As in most mountainous areas, only the narrow floodplains, terraces and deltas of the river valleys have alluvial soils on which crops can grow. Glacial deposition on the middle slopes of the mountains provides sufficient soil to support tree growth.

The coniferous trees of coastal British Columbia are the tallest, broadest trees in Canada. DOUGLAS FIR, western CEDAR, balsam, HEMLOCK and Sitka SPRUCE grow very well in the mild, wet climate and are the basis for the province's most valuable primary industry, FORESTRY. Similar trees, plus lodgepole and ponderosa PINE and ASPEN, occupy the middle slopes of the interior mountains and plateaus. Depending on local conditions of slope and exposure, the upper treeline across southern BC is about 2000 m and declines to about 1000 m in the N. In contrast, grassland cover indicates the drier climate E of the Coast Mountains and in the lower valleys of the rivers across the southern third of the province.

Climate There are wide variations in climatic conditions within small areas in mountainous British Columbia. The major climate contrast is between the coast and the interior, but there are also significant variations between valleys and uplands, and between the northern and southern parts of the province. Relatively warm air masses from the Pacific Ocean bring mild temperatures to the coast during the winters, while cold water keeps coastal temperatures cool in the summer. The barrier of the Coast Mts hinders these moderating conditions from being carried inland. Average Jan mean temperatures are close to 0°C at most coastal stations — the mildest in Canada — and July averages are about 15°C. In contrast, the interior may be covered in winter by cold air masses pushing S from the Yukon or Alaska, particularly in the northern part of the province. Average daily mean January temperatures are -10°C to -15°C across the central interior and are a cold -20°C or more on the northeastern plains. The southern interior valleys may heat up during the summer, recording July average monthly temperatures of more than 20°C, but farther N stations at higher altitudes on the central Interior Plateau average about 15°C in midsummer.

The air masses which cross the Pacific bring ample rainfall to the coast, particularly in the autumn and winter. On the lee (eastern) side of the mountains, the interior valleys receive much less precipitation. The west-facing mountains of Vancouver I receive more than 250 cm of annual precipitation, whereas the east-coast lowland records only about 70 to 100 cm. The western slopes of the interior mountains accumulate 100 to 200 cm annually, of which a high percentage is snowfall; but the OKANAGAN VALLEY receives a mere 25 cm of annual precipitation. The frost-free season on the coast is the longest in Canada, averaging more than 200 days; in contrast, the central Interior Plateau is handicapped by a short frost-free season of only 75 to 100 days. In summary, the well-publicized, mild, wet winters and cool, dry summers associated with British Columbia are characteristic only of the southwest; the rest of the province has temperature conditions similar to those on the plains of Alberta and Saskatchewan.

Natural Resources About 55% of British Columbia is forested, and as a result of excellent growth conditions for coniferous trees, the province has about 40% of the merchantable wood in Canada on about 15% of the forested land.

The geology of most mountainous areas is favourable to mineralization, and BC is no exception. A wide range of metals has been discovered throughout the Cordilleran part of the province, including lead, zinc, gold, silver, molybdenum, copper and iron. The Interior Plains, NE of the Rocky Mountains, have a different geological base consisting of younger, sedimentary rocks which have been the sources of petroleum, natural gas and coal. The heavy precipitation, steep mountain slopes and large, interior drainage basins are ideal physical conditions for the production of hydroelectric power, and BC has the second-largest provincial potential for ELECTRIC-POWER GENERATION, after Québec; but some of the large interior rivers have not been harnessed because their use would damage the habitat of the PACIFIC SALMON, which spawn in the headwaters of coastal and interior rivers flowing into the Pacific. The physical environment of BC is itself a valuable resource, attracting visitors from throughout the world, as well as giving pleasure to local residents.

Conservation The balance between economic development and preservation of the environment is particularly troublesome in British Columbia, which relies heavily on non- renewable resources. Many of the resources seemed inexhaustible, but by the 1930s the Coast forest was being rapidly depleted. The salmon fishery has been threatened by overfishing and destruction of marine and river habitats in some places, and some of BC's scarce agricultural land has been lost to roads, housing and industry. There are those who argue that such uses of the land are more productive (of income) than is agriculture.

Early provincial governments were primarily concerned with rapid development to promote local employment, but especially since WWII much legislation has been enacted to preserve the environment and natural resources. The success of the REFORESTATION program has been questioned and is interpreted differently by the forestry industry and by critics, but forestry is being managed by the principle of "sustained yield." Fishing is confined to certain places and times and hydroelectric developments have been delayed indefinitely to protect salmon runs. A freeze was placed on changing the use of agricultural land in 1971, and the British Columbia Ecological Reserves Act (1971) set aside numerous reserves of representative ecosystems.

People

Settlement The coasts and interior valleys of British Columbia were first occupied by NATIVE PEOPLE some time after the last Ice Age. Occupation of some sites in BC has been confirmed at about 6000-8000 years ago by carbon dating. The people of the NORTHWEST COAST lived in a particularly bountiful environment, which provided abundant shellfish, salmon and even whales. The coastal people concentrated along the lower reaches of the major salmon rivers. They were a semisedentary people and developed an elaborate culture, typified by TOTEM POLES and the POTLATCH (*see* TAGISH; TSIMSHIAN; HAIDA; WAKASHAN; TLINGIT; KWAKIUTL; NOOTKA; and NATIVE PEOPLE, NORTHWEST COAST). The interior inhabitants, such as the CARRIER, Interior SALISH and KOOTENAY were generally nomadic and depended on hunting.

The first permanent European settlement came with the development of the FUR TRADE in the early 19th century. A flurry of activity followed the discovery of gold on the lower and middle Fraser R, resulting in a system of supply and transportation inland along the Fraser R to the Cariboo Mts. More permanent mining towns began to dot the valleys of the SE area by the 1880s — each supported by local forestry, small farms and complex rail, road and water transport. In contrast, settlement was more urban and commercial on the SW coast. VICTORIA, the capital, was the main administrative and commercial settlement and the supply centre for interior and coastal resource development during the period 1860-90. After VANCOUVER, on Burrard Inlet N of the mouth of the Fraser R, was selected as the site for the western terminal of the CPR in 1886, it soon replaced Victoria as the commercial centre and became the main port through which both coastal and interior products moved to world markets.

Thus, British Columbia developed contrasting coastal and interior settlement patterns, which remained the same throughout the 20th century, although densities increased. Population has always been primarily urban, and in 1981 [illegible]0% of the population was so classified. With [illegible]0% of the provincial population in the southwestern region, no other province has a concentration of population in such a relatively small area. The remaining population is dispersed in linear patterns across the southern half of the province, mainly occupying the N-S valleys or in resource-based settlements along the main transportation lines. The only major groups of farming population live in the Okanagan Valley and dispersed along the highway between Kamloops and Prince George. These linear population clusters are separated from each other by unoccupied mountain ranges. Few people live N of Prince George and Prince Rupert, except for an urban and agricultural cluster in the Peace R area of the NE.

Urban Centres Metropolitan Vancouver is the largest city in the province and ranks third in population among the metropolitan cities of Canada. Victoria is the only other BC metropolitan city larger than 100 000 population. These 2 cities and many nearby municipalities have most of the secondary and consumer-goods manufacturing in the province; the main water, road, rail and air transportation and transfer facilities; most of the head offices and commercial and financial offices; and most of the cultural and entertainment attractions. These cities and their activities are supported by the largest number of farmers in the province, in the adjoining Lower Fraser Valley and along the E coast of Vancouver I.

Other large cities are resource-based processors and service and supply centres for subregions dispersed throughout the province. They had populations of about 50 000-70 000 in 1981 and included PRINCE GEORGE, KAMLOOPS, KELOWNA and NANAIMO. A number of smaller cities with populations of 20 000-40 000 include CRANBROOK-KIMBERLEY, TRAIL-CASTLEGAR, PENTICTON, VERNON, DAWSON CREEK-FORT ST JOHN, PRINCE RUPERT and PORT ALBERNI.

Labour Force People in business, finance, trade, service and manufacturing make up around 60-65% of the work force. Those in primary industries total only about 7%. They include forest workers (but not those in sawmills and pulp and paper mills), fishermen (but not those in fish-processing plants), miners (but not those in mineral processing) and farmers. In periods of expanding economy and rapidly increasing population prior to 1982, it was not surprising that there were as many labourers in the construction industries (7%) as in the primary, resource-based industries. Many people are needed in transportation, both to move people and products within the large cities and to move natural resources in partially processed form to the coastal ports or to central Canadian and American markets. Such workers constitute slightly less than 10% of the work force.

Osoyoos — lake, valley and town in the southern Okanagan in southcentral BC (*courtesy Elliott and Nicole Bernshaw / Bernshaw Photography*).

British Columbia is a separate and distinct labour complex and has experienced patterns of industrial conflict sometimes different from the rest of Canada. A much higher percentage of workers belong to UNIONS, and STRIKES have been frequent and prolonged. Various reasons have been suggested for this, for example, that BC is an extension of the Pacific Northwest region of the US — the most unionized area in that country — and the province's workers have been influenced by their more highly paid American neighbours; and that the concentration of economic life in Vancouver has led to centralization of unions and bargaining. Finally, it has been argued that the rapid but erratic pattern of economic growth in the province has led to bitter dispute, particularly in the forest and construction industries, which are already vulnerable to seasonal and cyclical fluctuations.

Languages, Ethnicity and Religion In the early part of this century more than 75% of the residents were of British origin and most of the population spoke English as their first language. In the late 19th century the only group of non-British settlers were the CHINESE who were brought in as labourers for the building of the CPR. Afterwards many of them settled in Vancouver where they formed the largest Chinese community in Canada. A smaller "Chinatown" also arose in Victoria. Most Chinese worked in service or commercial occupations. JAPANESE also settled in southwestern BC prior to 1940. They were a significant group in the fishing industry, in Fraser Valley farming and in a small commercial core in Vancouver. The native Indian population was recorded as about 82 000 in 1981, of whom about 19 000 were classified as nonstatus Indians. Most of the status Indians live on INDIAN RESERVES dispersed throughout the province. One of the few distinctive social groups that did not settle in southwestern BC was the DOUKHOBORS. In the 1920s and earlier this religious group migrated to South-central BC from the Prairies and settled on small, communal farms in the Kootenay, Slocan, Columbia and Kettle valleys.

As in other parts of Canada, the percentage of people of British origin declined rapidly from 1950 to 1981. After 1970 the influx of large numbers of East and SOUTHEAST ASIANS and SOUTH ASIANS particularly affected BC. Some were REFUGEES; others sought better opportunities in service and business occupations. These demographic changes in BC's population are reflected in the cityscapes, in the variety of restaurants and the areas known as "Chinatown," "Little Italy" and the "Greek Village." English as a second language was a major subject in the province's primary schools in the 1970s. The French Canadian share of the population and language is minor in BC.

The figures for ethnic and national origins may be misleading because most of the BC population in 1981 was born within the province. Most people are therefore at least second- or third-generation residents. In addition to immigrants who have recognizably distinct cultures and physical characteristics, there were even larger numbers (as recorded in the period 1971-76) who migrated to BC from other parts of Canada. The "newness" of BC and its rapid population growth contrast with those of the Atlantic provinces and Québec, most of whose population was born within the eastern region.

Since the majority of people are of British national origin and English speaking, as in other parts of Canada they are predominantly CHRISTIAN within the UNITED, ANGLICAN and Roman CATHOLIC churches. The variety of other cultures and second languages can be seen in the relative significance of other religions such as SIKHISM and ISLAM.

The earlier part of the province's history was marred by RACISM, particularly the anti-Asiatic riots of 1907 and the KOMAGATA MARU incident of 1914. Stirred up by politicians of all parties, fears were rampant that British Columbia's future as a "white province" was threatened. The population of Japanese and Chinese was less than 40 000 in 1921, but their concentration in Vancouver made them conspicuous. Forced to take lower wages and hardworking, they were considered unfair competition by the unions. The campaign of the Asiatic Exclusion League (est 1921) and others resulted in the Chinese Immigration Act of 1923, which effectively ended Chinese immigration. The Japanese were evicted from their coastal fishing villages during WWII and placed in INTERNMENT camps — a bitter episode in their history in Canada.

Economy

Resource-based activities have been the basis of BC's economy throughout its modern history. The Indians depended on the animal population of land and sea for their food, clothing and exchange. The first items of trade desired by Europeans were sea-otter pelts from the coast and animal furs from the interior. Settlers of European origin were primarily attracted by mineral resources, notably gold in the central interior and SE, but also coal was mined on Vancouver I, near Nanaimo. By the 1880s the tall, straight coniferous trees of the coast forest were being cut for lumber to supply other Pacific Rim settlements, and salmon were being canned at numerous river-mouth canneries to be shipped throughout the world. In the 19th century the natural resources of BC were utilized to supply markets elsewhere in Anglo-America or in East Asia or Europe. Local manufacturing consisted mainly of some first-stage processing of these resources.

As population increased in the 20th century and concentrated in or near the ports in the SW, consumer-goods manufacturing became possible in the southwestern cities, aided by the high cost of transporting manufactured goods from eastern Canada and United States, and by an ample supply of inexpensive hydroelectric power. Agricultural settlement expanded across the lowland and delta of the Lower Fraser R. The management and financial activities concerned with resource developments remained in the coastal cities, mainly Vancouver, maintaining the long-established contrast between the primary activities of the N coast and interior, and the commercial business and assembly activities of the southwestern cities.

Forestry Forestry has been the main component of BC's economy throughout this century. Forest products rank first in value among provincial primary industries, and BC produces 70% of Canada's sawn lumber, most of its plywood and 25% of its chemical pulp. The industry employs 14% of the labour force (1981). Commercial logging began in the 1840s on Vancouver I and spread to the Lower Fraser after the gold rush of 1858. Lumber mills were established in the SW after the middle of the 19th century to supply the building needs of the growing settlements and to export to nearby Pacific settlements. Temporary SAWMILLS also operated near all of the scattered mining communities in the interior; some of these mills, located on the 2 main railway lines, were able to export lumber eastward to the growing Prairie towns in the early 20th century. Lumber production expanded rapidly along the coast after WWI, as the newly opened Panama Canal made eastern US and European markets more accessible to West Coast mills. Most lumber companies made operational decisions to extend their logging camps northward along the coast and to transport the logs by a variety of water transport means to large sawmills around the Georgia Strait region. With minor exceptions, such as near Prince Rupert, this pattern of N coast primary cutting and S coast processing and export has been maintained.

Pulp and paper mills were established at a few places around Georgia Strait early in the 20th century, but these mills did not have large consuming markets for newsprint and paper similar to the markets in the eastern US available for eastern Canadian mills at that time. Unlike eastern mills, the pulp and paper mills of BC became integrated into existing sawmill operations and received much of their wood fibre raw material from product residue such as sawdust and chips from adjoining lumber mills. The pulp and paper industry remained coastal until the mid-1960s, when mills were opened in several places across the interior. This interior expansion was part of the general spread of the forest industry into the interior of the province, stimulated by increased foreign markets, improved interior road and rail transport, new government concessions and cutting rights to forested areas, and a concern for possible depletion of the coast forest reserves.

Throughout the 1970s the interior produced about half of the value of provincial forest products. Small sawmills disappeared along the coast early in this century and across the interior after 1950, and were replaced by very large, centrally located sawmills, sometimes with adjoining pulp and paper or paper mills. Although water transport, often in self-dumping log barges, is still the chief means of transporting logs to the mills along the coast, water transport is rarely used in the interior — unlike the river-based log transport system which evolved in eastern Canada, eg, on the MIRAMICHI and OTTAWA rivers. Interior logs and finished forest products are all moved by road or rail and therefore all forestry-based settlements are located on the main railways or highways.

In 1978 the BC Legislature passed 3 new Acts dealing with the responsibilities of the Department of Forests in managing, protecting and conserving the forest resource. Pressures on the industry, which is hard pressed in recessionary times, increase as demands grow for preservation of the forests for recreation, wildlife and aesthetic screens, and as a resource for future generations. *See also* FOREST; FOREST ECONOMICS; FOREST HARVESTING; FOREST REGIONS; and FORESTRY EDUCATION.

Mining Mining and mineral processing employ about 3% of the labour force (1981), but yield about 20% of the value of the products of the major industries of BC. Coal and copper account for about one-half of the total and others in order of importance are oil, zinc, natural gas and molybdenum. Mining became important in BC in 1858 with the Fraser GOLD RUSH and later discoveries in the Cariboo region. Between 1890 and 1910 the Kootenay region of southeastern BC became one of the most important mining areas of Canada. The huge smelter-refinery at Trail receives ore from BC, the Yukon and the NWT.

Coal was first mined near Nanaimo on Vancouver I in the mid-19th century. Immense coal deposits in the Fernie-Crowsnest Pass area were used by the Trail smelter and by the railways until they converted to diesel fuel. Both metallurgical and thermal coal are now exported from southeastern BC to Japan and elsewhere. The younger, sedimentary rocks of northeastern BC, like those of the interior plains of Alberta, are the sources of coal, petroleum and natural gas. The latter 2 products are transported by pipelines to urban markets in southwestern BC and the adjoining northwestern states of the US.

Metal mines have opened and closed across the southern interior from Grand Forks to Princeton throughout this century. In the early 1980s mining in the area was highlighted by large, open-pit copper mines SW of Kamloops. Other metal mines have produced intermittently across the Interior Plateau from near Williams Lake to Babine Lake in the NW. Mines have also operated intermittently along the coast of BC for more than a century. Base-metal mines opened and closed near Stewart, NE of Prince Rupert, and at several places on Vancouver I. Iron ore and copper, to name just 2 examples, have been exported to Japan from coastal mines. Because nearly all of the mineral production of BC is consumed outside of the province, the fortunes of the mining industry are largely determined outside the province.

Fisheries Commercial fishing and sportfishing in the many large lakes in the interior of the province are minor compared with the river-mouth, alongshore and deep-sea FISHERIES of the coast. The most valuable fishery is for the 5 species of Pacific salmon, which have 2- to 5-year cycles of river spawning, sea migration and return to the same spawning rivers. As the returning fish approach and concentrate off river mouths they are caught by large, modern fishing vessels. Although most coastal rivers produce some salmon the largest catches are obtained off the mouths of the Fraser and Skeena. Early in this century salmon canneries were dispersed all along the BC coast, close to the catching areas because salmon were perishable. However, the gradual introduction of improved boats, with longer ranges and refrigeration, resulted in the closing of most canneries on the central coast and the concentration of fish processing into a few large plants near Prince Rupert and Vancouver.

Other fish caught along the coast and offshore include HERRING (and a valuable by-product herring roe), halibut and other groundfish such as COD and sole. The physical character of fjorded, submerged coastal BC provides numerous shelters and harbours for fishing vessels, but the province lacks the broad, shallow offshore continental shelf which is a favourable fish habitat off East Coast Canada.

Emily Carr, *Shoreline* (1936), oil on canvas. One of BC's great artists, Carr was affected both by the province's great natural beauty and its native heritage (*courtesy The McMichael Collection / Gift of Mrs H.P. DePencier, 1966*).

Wycliffe Prairie, near Kimberley in southeastern BC (*photo by Pat Morrow*).

Agriculture In cultivated land as a percentage of total provincial area, BC ranks second lowest in Canada, behind Newfoundland; however, BC produces 5% of Canada's total agricultural products on less than 2% of Canada's agricultural land. Farming began in BC to supply the trading posts in the mid-19th century. The growing cities of Vancouver and Victoria stimulated agricultural expansion in the Fraser Valley and on Vancouver I. In the 1890s fruit and vegetable growing were established in the Okanagan and beef ranching in the Cariboo region.

The largest area of cultivated land is in the Peace R area, which accounts for about 90% of the grain harvested in BC. Aided by the longest frost-free season in Canada, the small farms of the Lower Fraser R produce dairy and livestock products, vegetables, small fruits and specialty crops such as blueberries, cranberries and flower bulbs. In the dry southern interior, agriculture flourishes only where irrigation systems have been established. The narrow benches and terraces above Okanagan Lk comprise one of Canada's 3 main fruit-growing regions and one of 2 grape-growing areas. The small, intensive farms produce apples, pears, peaches, cherries, plums, grapes and apricots. Cattle ranching is carried on across small areas of grassland on the southern Interior Plateau, but not enough meat is produced to supply even the Vancouver market.

Despite the scarcity of high-quality agricultural land in BC, in the period from 1966 to 1971 urban sprawl was consuming over 6000 ha per year of prime agricultural land. About 20% of the prime agricultural land of the Lower Fraser and 30% of the Okanagan had already been converted when the Environment and Land Use Act (1971) froze the agricultural land. In 1973 the Land Commission Act was established to preserve agricultural land, but there is great demand for it for housing, industry, hobby farms and country estates.

Improved land area in BC, by region, 1981
(regions defined by combinations of census divisions)

Region	*Hectares*	*Number of farms*
Peace River	376 000	1 870
Prince George-Skeena	130 000	1 640
Okanagan	103 000	5 300
Thompson	101 000	950
Cariboo	91 000	1 020
Lower Mainland	81 000	6 130
Kootenay	36 000	1 020
Vancouver I	26 000	2 075

Energy British Columbia produces a surplus of energy in the form of electrical power, coal, petroleum and natural gas. The latter 2 come entirely from the interior plains of the NE and are transported by pipeline to the Vancouver market and beyond to the northwestern US. The small, accessible coalfields on eastern Vancouver I and in the southwestern interior plateau were worked out early in the 20th century. The coalfields in the southern Rocky Mts were developed at the beginning of this century to supply smelters in the Kootenay region. Beginning in the 1960s technological improvements in open-pit mining, unit trains and new port facilities made it possible for both thermal and metallurgical coals to be mined in the SE in larger amounts for export to Japan. In addition, other coal mines were opened in the 1980s in the Rocky Mountains and foothills of northeastern BC, also for export. Because both areas are far from ocean transport the rail system had to be improved to move such large quantities of coal into world markets.

British Columbia is well endowed with steep and rugged landforms and ample precipitation, which together produce enormous seasonal runoffs in numerous rivers and vast amounts of potential hydroelectric power. Hydroelectric power was first produced at the close of the 19th century from small rivers in the SW for urban consumers in Victoria and Vancouver. The largest single power site in the SW prior to 1940 was developed on Bridge R, just E of the Coast Mountains. The southwestern power sources were sufficient for industrial and residential markets in the Georgia Str region until the 1960s. Around the turn of the century, the Kootenay and other rivers in the SE were dammed to produce electric power for the many local mines and towns. This power was ample until the 1960s. Following international agreement, the Columbia R was dammed at Mica Creek in the "Big Bend" N of Revelstoke in the late 1960s to help even out the flow of the river and make American downstream power plants more efficient (*see* COLUMBIA RIVER TREATY). In the 1970s, turbines were installed in the dam to produce electric power for metropolitan Vancouver.

In the northwest, a special power project was completed in 1954 to supply cheap power for a large aluminum smelter at Kitimat. In this project the headwaters of the Nechako R, a non-fish-spawning tributary of the Fraser R, were dammed and the water diverted through a tunnel in the Coast Mountains to a large subterranean power plant at Kemano on the coast. The northeastern section of the province was the last to be developed for hydropower. As a result of technological improvements in long-distance transmission facilities, it became possible to dam the Peace R where it spilled out of the Rocky Mountains and to send the power about 1000 km to the growing markets in metropolitan Vancouver. The Fraser R, occupying the central part of the province, is the greatest potential source of hydroelectric power, but technology has not yet solved the problem of using the river for both fish and power.

Transportation Land transportation has been funnelled into the narrow river valleys across the southern half of the province. The 2 transcontinental railways used the Fraser and Skeena valleys to cross through the western mountain barrier to reach the coast. Only 4 passes through the Rocky Mts have been used by the railways and, later, roads to enter BC from the E. From S to N these strategic passes are CROWSNEST, KICKING HORSE, YELLOWHEAD and PINE. The only S-N railway, the BRITISH COLUMBIA RY (originally called the Pacific Great Eastern), is owned by the provincial government. In the 1950s it was extended from Vancouver through Prince George to the Peace R area in the NE; another extension of the railway into the unoccupied area NW of Prince George was halted in the 1970s.

British Columbia lacked an interconnected highway system in the interior until the 1950s. The first paved road entirely across the province, the TRANS-CANADA HIGHWAY, was not completed until 1962. Most roads still follow the valley floors — where people and settlements are — and therefore have a general S-N pattern, with fewer E-W links. The provincial government is responsible for the construction and maintenance of all public roads in unorganized territory and for classified arterial highways through incorporated areas. Several parts of BC have little or no land transportation lines. There are no roads along the long section of mainland coast between Powell River and Prince Rupert because of extremely high construction costs around the innumerable fjords, plus the lack of permanent settlements. Only one gravel road crosses northwestern BC from Prince Rupert (and Stewart) to Cassiar and the ALASKA HIGHWAY; the latter is the only road across northeastern BC.

Coastal British Columbia is served by an extensive ferry service, which moves freight, cars and passengers across the Strait of Georgia. Small coastal boats, tugs and barges move natural resources, supplies and people along the sheltered "Inside Passage" between Vancouver I and the mainland and northward to Prince Rupert, the Queen Charlotte Is and the Alaska Panhandle. Early in this century, shallow-draft lake vessels operated during summer on the long, narrow lakes of the central and SE interior, but they gradually disappeared after all-season highways were built.

All major cities in British Columbia are served by airlines, which, like rail, road and water transportation, further reinforce the dominance of metropolitan Vancouver and the densely occupied southwestern corner of the province.

Tourism and Recreation British Columbia is known internationally for the extent and diversity of its opportunities for outdoor recreation, particularly sportfishing, CAMPING, HIKING, boat cruising, driving for pleasure, SKIING and HUNTING. Most tourists come by car, with the heaviest flow via Revelstoke, Kamloops and the Fraser Canyon or S from Salmon Arm down the Okanagan. Much of northern BC still lacks a network of roads and therefore attracts relatively few people. Most of the visitors come from the Prairies — three-quarters of all Canadians visiting BC come from Alberta — with significant traffic from the states of Washington, Oregon and California.

The spectacular mountain scenery and varied local physical environments are most accessible in the many provincial and federal parks. The national parks are mainly in the mountains of eastern BC and include YOHO, KOOTENAY, GLACIER and MOUNT REVELSTOKE. PACIFIC RIM NATIONAL PARK on western Vancouver I has the longest continuous stretch of sand beach in the province. BC had 367 provincial parks and recreation areas in 1982, totalling more than 4.5 million hectares. These are classified into 4 types: 29 recreation areas; 286 class A parks, which are usually campsites and picnic grounds; 6 larger class B parks and 46 class C parks, which include very large areas such as GARIBALDI, STRATHCONA and Tweedsmuir.

Government and Politics

British Columbia is governed by a legislative assembly of 57 members (1983) elected from one- and 2-person ridings. Electoral districts are redefined after each major census to maintain representation in proportion to current population distribution. A LIEUTENANT-GOVERNOR, appointed by Canada's GOVERNOR GENERAL, is the head of provincial government in title only; power resides with the PREMIER of the province, who is the leader of the political party winning the most seats in the legislature at elections, which must be held at least every 5 years. A CABINET is chosen by the premier from the majority party and government service is provided by a civil service, headed by deputy ministers, with headquarters in Victoria. BC has 6 appointed senators in the federal SENATE and 28 elected members in the federal HOUSE OF COMMONS in Ottawa. This representation is proportionate to BC's population, which is 11% of Canada's total.

The highest court in BC is the Court of Appeal, made up of the chief justice and 10 puisne justices. The Supreme Court is lower than the Court of Appeal; it has a chief justice and 26 puisne justices. There are 8 COUNTY courts, although the term "county" is not used to define an administrative unit. Magistrates and justices of the peace may preside over provincial courts, which may deal with family matters and juvenile delinquents. The Governor General-in-Council (the Crown, in effect) appoints all provincial judges. The attorney general is the chief law officer of the province, empowered to act in all litigation in which the province is a party; the ministry is responsible for the administration of justice, policing and the provision of legal services.

Premiers of British Columbia 1871-1983

	Party	Term
John Foster McCreight		1871-72
Amor De Cosmos		1872-74
George Anthony Walkem		1874-76
Andrew Charles Elliott		1876-78
George Anthony Walkem		1878-82
Robert Beaven		1882-83
William Smithe		1883-87
Alexander Edmund Batson Davie	Conservative	1887-89
John Robson	Liberal	1889-92
Theodore Davie		1892-95
John Herbert Turner		1895-98
Charles Augustin Semlin	Conservative	1898-1900
Joseph Martin	Liberal	1900
James Dunsmuir	Conservative	1900-02
Edward Gawler Prior	Conservative	1902-03
Sir Richard McBride	Conservative	1903-15
William John Bowser	Conservative	1915-16
Harlan Carey Brewster	Liberal	1916-18
John Oliver	Liberal	1918-27
John Duncan MacLean	Liberal	1927-28
Simon Fraser Tolmie	Conservative	1928-33
Thomas Dufferin Pattullo	Liberal	1933-41
John Hart	Coalition Govt	1941-47
Byron Ingemar Johnson	Coalition Govt	1947-52
William Andrew Cecil Bennett	Social Credit	1952-72
David Barrett	New Democratic Party	1972-75
William Richards Bennett	Social Credit	1975-

Lieutenant-Governors of British Columbia 1871-1983

	Term
Sir Joseph William Trutch	1871-76
Albert Norton Richards	1876-81
Clement Francis Cornwall	1881-87
Hugh Nelson	1887-92
Edgar Dewdney	1892-97
Thomas Robert McInnes	1897-1900
Sir Henri Gustave Joly de Lotbinière	1900-06
James Dunsmuir	1906-09
Thomas Wilson Paterson	1909-14
Sir Francis Stillman Barnard	1914-19
Edward Gawler Prior	1919-20
Walter Cameron Nichol	1920-26
Robert Randolph Bruce	1926-31
John William Fordham Johnson	1931-36
Eric Werge Hamber	1936-41
William Culham Woodward	1941-46
Charles Arthur Banks	1946-50
Clarence Wallace	1950-55
Frank MacKenzie Ross	1955-60
George Randolph Pearkes	1960-68
John Robert Nicholson	1968-73
Walter Steward Owen	1973-78
Henry Pybus Bell-Irving	1978-83
Robert Gordon Rogers	1983-

Local Government Most people in British Columbia live in communities with local government, but most of the area of the province has no local government, or people, and the resources and lands of this unorganized territory are administered by departments in the provincial government. Less than 1% of the provincial area is incorporated into (in 1982) 33 cities, 38 district municipalities, 12 towns, 57 villages and 28 regional districts with various forms of local government. These incorporated areas include about 80% of the provincial population. In all MUNICIPALITIES, local voters elect a mayor and members of a council. In the 99% of the provincial area classified as Unorganized Territory, there is no specific local government except for the 28 regional districts. Each regional district has a board made up of local elected and nominated members, plus provincial government representation. Regional districts are established by Cabinet partly to assist the joint financing of certain services such as water, sewers, regional parks and transportation among a group of municipalities. These districts may do regional planning but the implementation of the plans is the responsibility of the local municipalities. BC does not have township and county administrative units, as have other parts of Canada.

Public Finance Most of the revenue of the provincial government comes from taxes levied on a wide range of property, sales and incomes of citizens, companies and corporations. For example, there are taxes on nonmunicipal lands, gasoline, liquor and tobacco, and a general sales tax; provincial licences and permit fees include charges for the right to cut timber on crown land and for the use of other natural resources. The province receives a share of income tax which is collected by the federal government and returned to the province as part of various federal-provincial tax-sharing arrangements. Most of the expenditures of the government go to education, and health and social services, the latter including hospitals, medical care, welfare and social-assistance payments. Part of public expenditure pays the salaries of civil servants who administer the government bureaucracy and provide services to citizens. The government also maintains ferries, which are more important in British Columbia than in other provinces, as well as roads and bridges.

Health British Columbia's health services were provided through 17 health districts and 5 municipal health departments in 1982. The provincial government provides all personnel working within the health districts. All permanent residents of the province qualify for benefits under the Hospital Insurance Act, including hospital care and doctors' fees. This medical service is partly paid for by premiums paid by all residents. The Ministry of Health also operates long-term care programs, care for mental patients and a subsidized ambulance service.

Politics The federal party lines of Liberal and Conservative were not introduced to the province until 1903, when Richard MCBRIDE, the first Conservative leader, became premier. The Liberal Party formed its first government in 1916, led by H.C. BREWSTER, and the Conservatives regained power in 1928 under Simon TOLMIE. Many labour leaders had come from Great Britain, bringing experience as organizers, and they gained early success in BC when legislation for improved working conditions and social services was introduced. Various third parties were active. The Labour Party elected members in 1920, 1924, 1928 and 1933. Progressive and Socialist parties emerged with the serious economic difficulties of the GREAT DEPRESSION, and the Conservatives were virtually wiped out in 1933, Tolmie holding their single seat; the new CO-OPERATIVE COMMONWEALTH FEDERATION (CCF) won 7 seats and 31% of the vote. The new Liberal government ruled for the next 20 years, under premiers T.D. PATTULLO, John HART and Byron I. JOHNSON.

In 1952 a new party led by W.A.C. BENNETT broke away from the Conservative Party and called itself SOCIAL CREDIT, after a similar party in Alberta. This party then governed the province for 20 years during a period of enormous resource development and growth, particularly in the interior of the province, which was being better interconnected internally and linked to the SW coast by road-building programs and the northern extension of the British Columbia Rwy to the Peace R area. The NEW DEMOCRATIC PARTY (formerly CCF) became the official Opposition in the 1960s with the virtual disappearance of the provincial Liberal and Conservative parties. The NDP was elected to government for the first time in 1972, led by David BARRETT. The electorate has tended to polarize in roughly equal numbers around the 2 parties, with Social Credit advocating free enterprise and government restraint, and the NDP advocating moderate socialism and government economic and social involvement. Social Credit regained power in 1975, led by William BENNETT, son of W.A.C. Bennett, and was re-elected in 1983.

Education

Elementary schools were established in Victoria about 1853, a few years after a fort was built there by the HBC, and they were maintained by the colonial government after 1858. The Public School Act of 1872 established a free provincial school system. The first secondary schools (then called high schools) were available in Victoria in 1876 and in Vancouver in 1890. Education is free and compulsory for children from 7 to 15 years of age. Children who live in isolated areas may be taught through correspondence courses provided by the Ministry of Education. Elementary and secondary schools are administered by local boards, made up of elected local citizens, with financial support mainly from the provincial government, in addition to local taxes on property. British Columbia was divided into 75 school districts in 1981. There are a few private schools, modelled on the British system, and some schools supported by religious groups. These schools charge fees for attendance and also receive limited government financial support. The provincial government provided special programs for the hearing impaired in 41 school districts in 1981, and also operated a residential school for the deaf in Vancouver. The curricula for school courses and programs are established by civil servants in the Ministry of Education and are usually similar throughout all schools in the province. This uniformity allows for student transfers from one district to another. Within this structure, however, individual schools and classes may adapt or change the curriculum for local needs.

Post-secondary education is offered by 4 universities, and an Open Learning Institute which supplies correspondence courses. The original university in the province was UNIVERSITY OF BRITISH COLUMBIA, located on a scenic peninsula adjoining the western edge of Vancouver. Victoria College, affiliated with UBC, supplied the first 2 years of university education to residents of Victoria; it was expanded to university status in 1963. A new university, SIMON FRASER, was built in Burnaby in 1965 to accommodate the greatly increased population of metropolitan Vancouver. A former religious college, Trinity Western, in the Lower Fraser Valley near Langley, was granted a charter to offer university-level courses through 4 years in 1979. The BC Institute of Technology in Burnaby provides a wide range of technical and vocational courses for post-secondary students and the province operates 4 other vocational schools. Teacher-training programs are offered at each of the 3 large provincial universities. The smaller cities in the rest of the province, and suburban metropolitan Vancouver, are served by a system of 14 community colleges offering first- and second-year university-level courses and vocational and technical programs. Academic courses in the colleges receive transfer credit to the major provincial universities.

Cultural Life

The culture of the people of BC has evolved from the traditions of the people who migrated to the region. British influences were strong in the 19th century, being brought by settlers and entrepreneurs from England, who came directly to the colonies and the new province. In the 20th century British cultural characteristics were diversified by people from eastern Canada who had second- or third-generation British origins. These eastern influences became more dominant after 1950 when internal migration from eastern Canada rapidly increased BC's population and brought the institutions, societies and cultural events and activities found across the rest of Canada to BC. Many of Canada's finest writers, such as Phyllis WEBB, George BOWERING and Michael ONDAATJE, are resident in BC. The mix of BC's culture is different from that of the rest of Canada in 2 notable ways. First, the mixture of people from India, Pakistan, Malaysia, the Philippines, Hong Kong, Japan and China brings distinct forms and activities to West Coast culture. At one time these characteristics were visible in turbans, saris, etc, but distinctive clothing has now virtually disappeared except for special cultural or religious events. "Chinatown" remains an enduring part of the urban landscape of central Vancouver. West Coast Indians, the second distinct culture group, had a highly developed culture (*see* NORTHWEST COAST INDIAN ART). Indian arts and crafts have been revived in recent decades and have left their imprint on the broader society. The province's most famous artist, Emily CARR, was profoundly influenced by Indian art.

The BC government gives financial assistance to cultural and ethnic groups, publishers and community organizations through the BC Cultural Fund (est in 1967). Additional activities are also aided by grants from the Western Canada Lottery Foundation.

Major museums, archives and art galleries are located in Vancouver and Victoria and, in addition, local museums are maintained in several smaller cities in the interior. The Vancouver Museum and Planetarium, located on the waterfront in the western part of the city, adjoins the City Archives and the distinctive Maritime Museum; the latter, in which the famous RCMP schooner ST ROCH is preserved, emphasizes the importance of the sea in Vancouver's past and present. The Provincial Museum in Victoria is noted for its lifelike panoramas and displays and for the several floors of material illustrating the natural environment and Indian and early European settlements. The UBC Museum of Anthropology, designed by Arthur ERICKSON, houses an impressive collection of Northwest Coast Indian artifacts.

Numerous theatrical companies perform in Victoria and Vancouver, and some of the productions are taken on tour to coastal and interior cities. The geographical problem of the concentration of cultural, social and athletic events in the southwestern corner of the province and their scarcity elsewhere is a well-known theme in BC. The VANCOUVER CANUCKS have been in the NHL since 1971 and the BRITISH COLUMBIA LIONS in the CFL since 1954; the latter now play in BC Place — Canada's only covered stadium. The Vancouver Whitecaps were Canada's most successful professional soccer franchise in attracting fans until their demise in 1984.

All of the major cities have daily newspapers and the smaller coastal and interior cities publish weekly newspapers. Similarly, the major television and radio stations are in Vancouver and Victoria, but many smaller communities have their own radio and television stations, which are often fed programs from the main networks. Most of the province's book and magazine publishers are in Vancouver, which is in the peculiar position of being an attractive market for eastern publishers and media but also having just a large enough share of the British Columbia population and income to be a sufficient market for local firms.

HISTORIC SITES include FORT LANGLEY, the first fur-trading post in the Lower Fraser Valley, BARKERVILLE and FORT STEELE. The provincial government has numerous historical signs at scenic pull-off sites along all major highways.

History

British Columbia was one of the last frontiers of discovery in N America. In 1774 Spaniards under Juan PÉREZ HERNANDEZ were probably the first Europeans to see the coast of BC. They did not land, but Perez claimed the region for Spain. Four years later James COOK took his 2 British ships into NOOTKA SOUND on the W coast of Vancouver I. Within a few years British traders came by sea and developed a flourishing fur trade with coastal Indians. In 1789 Spain and Britain disputed ownership of West-Coast N America. The Spanish had established a trading post at Nootka Sd and seized British ships there. This NOOTKA SOUND CONTROVERSY was settled by the Nootka Conventions of 1790-92, which gave equal trading rights to both countries but did not determine ownership. British claims were strengthened after 1792 when ships under George VANCOUVER carried out a careful 3-year mapping of the coast from Oregon to Alaska. Vancouver named many of the bays, inlets and coastal landform features. In this period of worldwide European colonialism there was no concern among European governments and businessmen that this area was already occupied by the native peoples.

In 1793 the first European report about the interior of BC was made by the NORTH WEST CO fur trader, Alexander MACKENZIE. He entered the region from the E via the Peace and Upper Fraser rivers, exploring westward across the Chilcotin Plateau and through the Coast Mountains to the long inlet at Bella Coola. Two other members of the NWC, Simon FRASER and David THOMPSON, explored other parts of the interior early in the 19th century and opened fur-trade posts supplied from Montréal — the first permanent settlements in the province. In 1808 Fraser reached the mouth of the river which now bears his name, and Thompson found the mouth of the Columbia R in 1811, after exploring the river routes of southeastern BC. For about 50 years, while eastern N America was being occupied and settled by agricultural people and dotted with commercial cities, the mountainous western part of the continent remained little-known territory on the fringes of fur-trade empires controlled from eastern cities.

During the first half of the 19th century, the British-owned HUDSON'S BAY COMPANY controlled the western fur trade, including the area of present-day Washington and Oregon. As American settlers moved into the southern part of this region in the 1830s they refused to recognize the authority of the British company. Conflicting territorial claims (the US claimed N to 54°40') were settled in the 1846 OREGON TREATY, establishing the southern boundary of BC along the 49th parallel, except for Vancouver I. In anticipation of this result, the HBC moved its headquarters to newly established Fort Victoria in 1843.

In 1849 the British government granted Vancouver I to the HBC for colonization, and in 1851 James DOUGLAS, an official of the company, became governor of the colony. In 1856 Douglas established a legislative assembly for Vancouver I. At mid-century the only white settlements in what was to become British Columbia were fur-trade posts on the coast, such as Victoria, Nanaimo and Ft Langley, and in the interior, such as Kamloops, Ft (later Prince) George and Ft St James.

Development This quiet period of history ended in 1857 when gold was discovered in the sand bars along the Lower Fraser R. The ensuing GOLD RUSHES brought thousands of fortune hunters, mainly from the California goldfields, but also from other parts of the world. Many came by boat from San Francisco, crowding into inadequate facilities in Victoria to buy supplies and receive permits. Prospecting proceeded upstream along the banks and bars of the Fraser R during 1858. The town of YALE was established as a transshipping centre at the S end of Fraser Canyon and the eastern end of water transport from the Fraser R mouth. Gold seekers walked the tributaries of the Fraser R and major finds were made E of Quesnel. The boomtown of Barkerville arose at the western edge of the Cariboo Mountains as the chief service town for the Cariboo goldfields. At its peak in the early 1860s Barkerville probably held a fluctuating population of about 25 thousand, making it the largest settlement in western Canada.

In order to establish government and maintain law and order around the goldfields, the British established the mainland colony of British Columbia in 1858 under the authority of James Douglas who remained governor of Vancouver I. The new settlement of NEW WESTMINSTER, located slightly inland on the N bank of the Fraser R delta, was proclaimed capital of the new colony in 1859. This administrative centre controlled river traffic entering the Fraser R en route to the interior. In the early 1860s the amazing feat of building the CARIBOO ROAD along the walls of the Fraser Canyon was accomplished in order to move supplies to interior settlements.

With gold production declining and people

Classic U-shaped valley in the Coast Mountains of BC (*photo by Tom W. Parkin/Pathfinder*).

leaving, the British government united the 2 colonies in 1866 to reduce administrative costs. New Westminster was the capital of the combined colony for 2 years before protests from the older capital, Victoria, resulted in the seat of government being moved there in 1868. The resulting physical separation of the capital from the majority of the people and economic activity on the mainland created later communication problems for the region. Many government services and offices had to be duplicated on the mainland.

After 1867 the British colony on the West Coast debated whether it should join the new CONFEDERATION of eastern provinces known as Canada. In 1871 the 12 000 white residents of BC agreed to enter the Dominion of Canada on the condition that the federal government build a transcontinental railway to link it with the East. The new province was to wait, rather impatiently at times, for 15 years before the CANADIAN PACIFIC RY reached the SW coast. The union with Canada was an unhappy one at first. The new province ran heavily into debt; the cost of governing a large mountainous area with few people was very high and revenues from resource users were low. More than one-third of the province's white residents lived in or near Victoria. Even by 1881 the white population of 24 000 was less than the estimated 25 000 Indians. The hoped-for expansion of trade with East Asia did not develop immediately with the arrival of the CPR in 1885. But the railway did bring people to the port of Vancouver and by 1901 that city surpassed Victoria in population. Vancouver's population of almost 30 000 in 1901 had been achieved in 15 years, whereas Victoria had only 21 000 people after 58 years of occupation.

Entrepreneurs came to British Columbia around the turn of the century to exploit the province's vast resources. A salmon-cannery industry was established along the coast. Sawmills were in operation all around the shores of Georgia Str and particularly along eastern Vancouver I. The first pulp and paper mill was built at Powell River in 1912. The major expansion of the forest industry came, however, after WWI when the opening of the Panama Canal gave access to markets around the N Atlantic region. BC attracted a different type of settler from those who settled on the land on the Prairies and across eastern Canada. A need for capital and access to natural resources for export were more important than ownership of farmland.

In the 1890s the major resource development and settlement in interior BC centered on the mining activity in the Kootenay region of the SE. Prospectors, mainly from mining camps in western Montana and Idaho, moved northward along the valleys and discovered gold and base metals in the area W of KOOTENAY LAKE. Mining camps arose in the Slocan Valley, at ROSSLAND, near Grand Forks and elsewhere. NELSON became the main service, supply and administrative centre, with a population of about 4500 in 1911. Railways extended northward into the region from the US, and the CPR built a line westward through the Crowsnest Pass in 1899 to bring coal from FERNIE to smelters in the mining centres. By about 1914, however, many of the mines had closed and some towns were abandoned, although other mines opened in later years. The extension of the Kettle Valley branch of the CPR to the coast during WWI came after the peak of mining activity in the Kootenay region.

Agriculture brought settlers to the S-central interior. At the time of the Cariboo Gold Rush, ranching was established in the grassland valleys and rolling basins across the southern interior plateau. Irrigation was developed early in the century west of Kamloops and in the northern Okanagan Valley. Irrigation for orchards that spread S from Vernon aided settlement projects for returning soldiers after WWI (*see* VETERANS' LAND ACT).

The building of the Grand Trunk Pacific Rwy W from Edmonton through the Upper Fraser, Bulkley and Skeena valleys in 1907-14 was intended to give Canada a second gateway through the mountains to the Pacific coast. Prince George then became a minor sawmill centre, with rail access eastward to the growing housing market in the Prairie provinces. But the port and rail terminal at Prince Rupert never developed the anticipated volume of traffic, partly because there was little need for incoming freight. The small town remained mainly a fisheries centre, with continuing hopes.

Resource-based activities suffered serious economic decline in BC during 1930-45 because of the loss of world markets. After about 1950, however, the improved transportation system did much to integrate the interior resource economies and settlements with coastal collection, processing and management centres. Increased hydroelectric-power production from the interior supplied relatively cheap power for local manufacturing. Thousands of Canadians migrated to BC, attracted by the mild climate and perceived economic opportunities, joining thousands of other immigrants from Asia. These people were not only labour and management for the growing commercial and service occupations, they were also consumers of goods, services and entertainment. J. LEWIS ROBINSON

Reading: G.P.V. and H.B. Akrigg, *British Columbia Chronicle, 1847-71* (1977); Mary L. Barker, *Natural Resources of British Columbia and Yukon* (1977); M.L. Cuddy and J. Scott, *British Columbia in Books* (1974); Albert L. Farley, *Atlas of British Columbia* (1979); Robin Fisher, *Contact and Conflict* (1977); Margaret A. Ormsby, *British Columbia* (1958); H.K. Ralston and J. Friesen, eds, *Historical Essays on British Columbia* (1976); J. Lewis Robinson, *British Columbia* (1973); Marie Tippett and Douglas Cole, *From Desolation to Splendour* (1977).

British Columbia Lions, FOOTBALL team. The BC Lions played their first game on 11 Aug 1954 in Vancouver's Empire Stadium. Under coach and general manager Annis Stukus they achieved only one victory in their initial season and did not make the Western Conference playoffs until 1959. In 1963, coached by Dave Skrien and led by the quarterbacking of Joe Kapp, the Lions appeared in their first GREY CUP, losing 21-10 to Hamilton but coming back in 1964 to defeat the Tiger-Cats 34-24. The Lions were to wait 19 years before they returned to the national final. In 1983, under Coach Don Matthews, they posted their best record to date (11-5) while playing in their new 60 000-seat home,

Vancouver's 60 000-seat BC Place stadium, built in 1983, is the home of the BC Lions. It is the only completed covered football stadium in Canada (*photo by Al Harvey/Masterfile*).

B.C. Place (Canada's first covered stadium), where they finished the season with a narrow Grey Cup loss to the Toronto Argonauts.

DEREK DRAGER

British Columbia Railway was incorporated as the Pacific Great Eastern Railway in 1912 to build a line from North Vancouver to Prince George, where it was to link up with the GRAND TRUNK PACIFIC RAILWAY. Initially it was privately owned, but financial .difficulties developed quickly and in 1918, after only 283 km of track from the coastal port of Squamish to the head of the inland river transport at Quesnel had been built, the Pacific Great Eastern was taken over by the BC government. The remaining mileage from North Vancouver to Squamish and from Quesnel to Prince George was not completed until 1956. Two major northern extensions and several branch lines were built after that date. A northeastern extension through the Peace R country reached Ft Nelson in 1971. A northwestern extension to Dease Lk remains incomplete. Significant portions of the line have been electrified to expedite the carriage of coal. The British Columbia Railway serves the resource industries of the northern interior of the province, operating about 1609 km of track which were built at a cost of more than a billion dollars in public funds.

T.D. REGEHR

British Columbia Research Council, nonprofit society incorporated in 1944 to provide facilities for technological research and industrial development in BC. BC Research, a technical wing of the council, comprises scientific, engineering and technical laboratory facilities. Under its mandate to enable small BC firms to improve their competitive position in Canadian and world markets, BCR attempts to balance short-term contract work for primary industries with longer-term "core" investigations, often in co-operation with university researchers and funded through provincial and federal grants. BCR is recognized internationally for expertise in microbial leaching of MINERALS from low-grade ores and concentrates; it is also strong in FISHERIES technology, COAL LIQUEFACTION and bioengineering. About 160 staff members, under an executive director, work in laboratories located at UNIVERSITY OF BRITISH COLUMBIA campus. Research is conducted in 4 divisions. Almost half of BCR income is derived from industry. Cooperative ventures include the provision of free information to business in collaboration with the NATIONAL RESEARCH COUNCIL, and the establishment of the Western Foundation for Advanced Industrial Technology, jointly with industry. Three scholarships are awarded annually.

MARTIN K. MCNICHOLL

British Columbia Sports Hall of Fame and Museum was founded to pay tribute to those British Columbians who have brought special honour to the province through their sports accomplishments. Opened in 1966, it is one of the largest multi-sport museums in N America, and preserves BC's rich sports heritage. In its displays, photos, scrapbooks, newspaper clippings, memorabilia, trophies and film theatre, visitors can view the development of sports in BC from before the turn of the century and learn about the hall's honoured members. Located in Vancouver, the hall is also used as a research and education centre for students.

BRIAN S. LEWIS

British Commonwealth Air Training Plan, an agreement of 17 Dec 1939 between Canada, the UK, Australia and New Zealand, making Canada the focus of a British Empire-wide scheme to instruct aircrew. It was a major Canadian contribution to Allied air superiority in WORLD WAR II. Called the "Aerodrome of Democracy" by US Pres F.D. Roosevelt, Canada had an abundance of air training space beyond the range of enemy aircraft, excellent climatic conditions for flying, immediate access to American industry, and relative proximity to the UK via the N Atlantic shipping lanes.

Canada had been the home of a major recruiting and training organization in WORLD WAR I, and the British again looked to it for aviators after 1936. Prime Minister W.L.M. KING's peacetime caution about such schemes evaporated after the declaration of war in 1939: a training program would keep Canadians at home, ward off demands for a large expeditionary force and bury the politically divisive issue of overseas CONSCRIPTION.

Negotiating the agreement was difficult. Canada agreed to accept most of the plan's costs but insisted that the British consent to a public pronouncement that air training would take precedence over all other aspects of the Canadian war effort. The British expected that the Royal Air Force would absorb Canadian air training graduates without restrictions, as in WWI. The King government demanded that Canadians be identified as members of the RCAF by their shoulder badge. Nevertheless, Article 15 of the agreement, providing for the possible organization of Canadian "units and formations" overseas, was vague and unsatisfactory, the more so because of Ottawa's understandable reluctance to pay both for training and for the maintenance of an operational force abroad. Most RCAF personnel overseas served with the RAF, not their national air force, and the process of creating distinctly Canadian squadrons was slow and painful.

Canada administered and controlled the plan in accordance with standards and overall policy set by the RAF. The training program was carried out by the RCAF, supported by the Canadian Flying Clubs Assn, commercial aviation companies and the federal Department of Transport. Training began on 29 Apr 1940, but was hampered by a shortage of aircraft, instructors and completed airfields. After the fall of France in June 1940, the plan was accelerated, and the first of a series of transfers of RAF aircrew schools to Canada took place. In 1942, after renewal of the agreement and reorganization of the plan, all British units in Canada were integrated formally into the BCATP.

At the plan's peak, there were 107 schools and 184 ancillary units at 231 sites. The aircraft establishment stood at 10 906 and the ground organization at 104 113 men and women. The Canadian government paid more than $1.6 billion, three-quarters of the total cost. Graduates totalled 131 553 pilots, navigators, bomb aimers, wireless operators, air gunners and flight engineers from the 4 founding partners, other parts of the COMMONWEALTH, the US and countries of occupied Europe. Almost half the total aircrew employed on British and Commonwealth flying operations were products of the BCATP. Canadian graduates numbered 72 835, providing crews for 40 RCAF home defence and 45 overseas RCAF squadrons, as well as constituting about 25% of the overall strength of RAF squadrons. This major commitment to the air war overseas, and particularly to Bomber Command, inevitably exacted a very heavy toll in Canadian casualties, a result very different from Mackenzie King's original aim.

F.J. HATCH AND NORMAN HILLMER

Reading: F.J. Hatch, *Aerodrome of Democracy* (1983).

British North America, the term usually applied to the British colonies and territories in N America after the US became independent in 1783 until CONFEDERATION in 1867. At first it consisted of the provinces of Quebec, NOVA SCOTIA, St John's I [PEI], NEWFOUNDLAND, the HUDSON'S BAY COMPANY territories, and lands belonging directly to the Crown. The influx of LOYALIST settlers from the US into NS resulted in the creation of NEW BRUNSWICK and CAPE BRETON I as separate colonies in 1784. The division of the PROVINCE OF QUEBEC into UPPER CANADA and LOWER CANADA in 1791 separated the people of predominantly British and American origin in the west from those of mainly French origin in the east. In 1799 St John's I was renamed PRINCE EDWARD ISLAND. In 1820 Cape Breton I was reunited with NS and in 1841 Upper and Lower Canada were united to form the PROVINCE OF CANADA. On the west coast the HBC colony of Vancouver's I was established in 1849 and what is now southern British Columbia became another crown colony in 1858. In 1866 the 2 were united as BRITISH COLUMBIA, a single colony with enlarged boundaries.

N.L. NICHOLSON

Reading: N.L. Nicholson, *The Boundaries of the Canadian Confederation* (1979); R.C. Harris and J. Warkentin, *Canada Before Confederation* (1974).

British North America Act, statute enacted 29 Mar 1867 by the British Parliament providing for CONFEDERATION. In Sept 1981 it was renamed the CONSTITUTION ACT 1867 as part of the movement toward "patriation" of the Constitution.

W.H. MCCONNELL

Britnell, George Edwin, political economist, professor (b at London, Eng 9 June 1903; d at Saskatoon 14 Oct 1961). Head of the Dept of Economics and Political Science at U Sask from 1938 until his death, Britnell also served as university administrator, government adviser and royal commissioner and was Canadian delegate to 3 international economic conferences. For 16 years he was special adviser on transportation to the Saskatchewan government and, with V.C. FOWKE, won retention of the CROW'S NEST PASS AGREEMENT on grain rates. In addition to a distinguished academic publishing career, he was also president of the Canadian Political Science Assn 1956-57, chairman of the Canadian Social Science Research Council 1956-58 and representative to the International Economic Assn. Elected fellow of the Royal Soc of Canada 1950, he was the first Harold Innis Visiting Research Professor of Political Economy at U of T in 1954.

PAUL PHILLIPS

Reading: G.E. Britnell *The Wheat Economy* (1939) and (with V.C. Fowke) *Canadian Agriculture in War and Peace* (1962).

Brittain, Donald, filmmaker (b at Ottawa 10 June 1928). After several years with the *Ottawa Journal,* he joined the NFB in 1955. He soon became one of the most respected Canadian documentary filmmakers. In 1962 he produced the 13-part series, *Canada at War.* Two years later, with John Kemeny, he co-directed *Bethune,* a film that marked the beginning of his approach to portraying controversial figures. In his lively, humorous, original and often biting style he portrayed such personalities as Leonard COHEN, Lord THOMSON of Fleet, Ferguson JENKINS, Malcolm LOWRY and the Dionne quintuplets. It was *Volcano: An Inquiry into the Life and Death of Malcolm Lowry* (1976) that firmly established his international reputation. Perhaps because of his training as a journalist, Brittain selected sensitive, topical subjects. In *The Champions* (1978) he took on the political careers of Pierre TRUDEAU and René LÉVESQUE. He ruffled bureaucratic feathers with *Paperland — The Bureaucracy Observed* (1979), chosen film of the year at the Canadian Film Awards. In 1974 he directed his first full-length film on the history of Canadian cinema 1895-1939, *Dreamland,* and provided the commentary for a follow-up film entitled *Has Anybody Here Seen Canada?* (1978). The quality and variety of his output has placed Brittain among leading documentary filmmakers.

PIERRE VÉRONNEAU

Brittain, Miller Gore, painter (b at Saint John, NB 12 Nov 1912; d there 21 Jan 1968). His early paintings, inspired by life in Saint John, were in the style promoted by the Art Students League,

New York, which he attended 1930-32. Depicting labourers at work, local citizens on crowded streetcars or derelicts congregated outside drinking establishments, his paintings earned him the label "the Canadian Brueghel." During WWII Brittain served in the RCAF and worked briefly as a war artist. In 1946 he returned to Saint John, and the balance of his life he devoted to painting works with surrealistic overtones: figurative compositions of tortured bodies, pastel landscapes that pictured flowers, heads and bodies set in strange lunar landscapes, and portraits of frenzied religious subjects. J. RUSSELL HARPER

Broad Bean, *see* FABA BEAN.

Broadbent, John Edward, political theorist, MP (b at Oshawa, Ont 21 Mar 1936). Born to a family of auto workers in a company town, he is said to have been carried on the picket line during the 1937 strike against General Motors. After studies at U of T (PhD, 1966) and the London School of Economics, he joined the political science department at York U in 1965. He was elected to the House of Commons in 1968 as NEW DEMOCRATIC PARTY member for Oshawa-Whitby, winning the seat by a tiny margin. In his early years as MP he was identified with the party's left wing. Unsuccessful in his first attempt to win the leadership in 1971, he became a serious contender in 1974 when party leader David LEWIS lost his seat while Broadbent's own majority increased enormously. After some hesitation he again offered himself and was elected July 1975. As leader he emphasized economic issues and helped the party recover from its disastrous 1974 defeat. In 1980 the NDP made its best showing ever, but Broadbent soon faced a caucus revolt (mainly centered in Saskatchewan) against his support for the patriation of Canada's Constitution. The party convention in 1981 endorsed his position, but some discontent remained, and at the 1983 convention prairie delegates circulated a manifesto implicitly critical of Broadbent's leadership. Although NDP support appeared to decline prior to the 1984 election campaign, Broadbent waged a brilliant campaign, emphasizing tax reforms, lower interest rates, and equality for women. The NDP emerged with 30 seats, only 10 fewer than the Liberals, including an unprecedented 13 seats in Ontario. GARTH STEVENSON

Broadcasting, Educational, *see* EDUCATIONAL BROADCASTING.

Broadcasting, Radio and Television In a northern land marked by long winters, vast distances and a fragmented population, the communication provided by Canadian radio and TV is crucial. Broadcasting has not only become a principal source of entertainment, it also links the citizen to what is going on outside the home and has helped to develop a sense of community. Canada has a more elaborate and advanced physical structure for delivering radio and TV programs than is found in any comparable country in the world. For example, in 1979 the US had 982 transmitters in operation, but Canada, with a tenth of the population, had 1045 (including rebroadcasting transmitters), a number that grew to 1225 in 1981. Canada was a pioneer in SATELLITE COMMUNICATIONS, and was the first to use geostationary satellites in domestic COMMUNICATIONS. The national broadcasting service, the CANADIAN BROADCASTING CORPORATION, distributes most of its programs nationally by satellites, also using them in the assembling of programs. TV services to the Canadian North are almost completely dependent on satellites and earth stations. As a result of these technical developments, 99% of the population has a choice of 2 TV channels, 91% has 3 channels, and over 50% has 8 or more. The weak element in the broadcasting system lies not in the physical

Broadcast of Madge Macbeth's play "Superwoman" from Ottawa radio station CNRO, Ottawa, in the 1920s (*courtesy Public Archives of Canada/C-29468*).

facilities but in the amount of original Canadian programming (*see* RADIO PROGRAMMING; TELEVISION PROGRAMMING; MUSIC BROADCASTING). The CBC produces an impressive number of radio and TV programs in English and French, many of high quality; but the private TV stations broadcasting in English have depended mostly on imported foreign (principally US) programs for prime time. Many of these imported programs have been popular, but such dependency has led to a continuing struggle to devise public policies that would ensure a more distinctively Canadian broadcasting service. For the past 50 years, Canada has employed a combination of public and private enterprises, falling somewhere between the strong state-owned element of the British system and the less regulated private-enterprise system of the US. The stages in this evolution can be related to successive Acts of Parliament and to the regulating bodies set up to license stations and to establish and administer the rules.

The Pioneer Stage (1913-28) Under the Radiotelegraph Act of 1913, a government minister (for most of this period, the minister of marine and fisheries) had the power to license radio broadcasting stations and to charge a $1 licence fee on each receiving set. About 60 stations were in operation, most of them of low power or providing intermittent service. Regulations were minimal.

Emergence of Public Ownership and Regulations (1928-36) By 1936, the present pattern in the ownership and control of broadcasting had emerged. In 1928 the government established a royal commission, under the chairmanship of Sir John AIRD, to advise on the future of broadcasting in Canada. Canadian radio development had been rudimentary, and many listeners were tuning to American stations and the newly established US networks. Moreover, Canadian stations were experiencing greater interference from unregulated frequencies in the US. There were also many complaints about intrusive advertising on the commercial stations, in both Canada and the US, and some saw a possible model in the British Broadcasting Corporation. The Aird Commission's report (1929) proposed a publicly owned corporation not unlike the BBC, and its main recommendations were taken up by an active group of citizens organized as the Canadian Radio League. Broadcasting, they argued, should be regarded as a national public service rather than merely as a profit-making industry, and its ownership and operating structure should be organized to recognize this principle. Québec, supported by Ontario, contested the right of the federal government to assume control of broadcasting, and a reference was made to the SUPREME COURT OF CANADA with a subsequent appeal to the JUDICIAL COMMITTEE OF THE PRIVY COUNCIL. Its judgement (1932) confirmed federal jurisdiction over radio communication and content of programs; and a special parliamentary committee was appointed to devise the means for implementing the Aird Commission's recommendations.

An Act creating the Canadian Radio Broadcasting Commission (CRBC) was passed with all-party support on 26 May 1932. The 3-man commission was empowered to regulate, control and carry on broadcasting in Canada; to originate and transmit programs; to lease, purchase or construct stations; and eventually to assume complete ownership of all Canadian broadcasting, if the means were provided. In its term of office, the commission was beset by many difficulties. In the depths of the Depression, the government of R.B. BENNETT never gave the commission the money to carry out its programming responsibilities satisfactorily. The CRBC managed to establish outlets in only 5 centres; in most cities privately owned stations distributed the commission's network programs. Thus the mixed system, combining public and private stations in one network, was established. It characterizes CBC radio and TV to the present day.

The CBC as Operator and Regulator (1936-58) The weaknesses of the Radio Commission and growing criticism in Parliament led to a new broadcasting Act when the Liberals under W.L. Mackenzie KING took office in 1935. The commission had been regarded as too dependent on government; suspicions were aroused that some of its decisions had been influenced by partisan considerations. The new prime minister, at the urging of the Radio League, determined to revise the legislation to reflect more fully the Aird Report and to bring it up to date.

By 1936, the year the revised Canadian Broadcasting Act was passed, conditions were considerably altered. The number of homes purchasing licences for their radios had increased from ½ million in 1931 to 1 million by the end of 1936. Canadians had become accustomed to receiving their own network programs, in English or French, for at least a few afternoon and evening hours. There was no thought in government of abandoning the national experiment. But the private radio stations had not only survived, they had prospered. Private radio provided music, weather and community information. Most private stations also carried popular American entertainment programs, with which Canadian advertisers were eager to be associated. In Nov 1936 the Canadian Broadcasting Corporation, with a board of 9 governors, replaced the Radio Commission, and it enjoyed much greater autonomy. Financed by an increased licence fee, the CBC took vigorous steps to increase Canadian coverage through high-powered regional transmitters. It also expanded the national program services by broadcasting many more hours each week, incorporating in its schedule some imported programs from the US networks. By 1944 it operated 3 radio networks, 2 in English (Trans-Canada and Dominion) and 1 in French. The private radio stations were not allowed to form their own national network, although under the rather liberal regulations of the CBC they indeed thrived. There were some complaints about the CBC's alleged monopoly position, but successive parliamentary committees and the Royal Commission on NATIONAL DEVELOPMENT IN THE ARTS, LETTERS AND SCIENCES (Massey Commission) all expressed approval of the governing system and the contribution of the CBC to Canada's cultural life.

The arrival of TV in 1952 foreshadowed an end to the system under which the CBC was at once the regulatory authority and the principal Canadian programmer. TV began under CBC auspices, as the Massey Commission had recommended, but the twin responsibilities for program production and national distribution were so expensive that the government of Louis St Laurent decided against construction of CBC outlets in every province. CBC TV could not be self-sufficient as was BBC TV in Britain. Once more, private-station licensees were expected to distribute the national programs provided by the CBC. It must be said that the policy adopted by the government in the mid-1950s, of authorizing only one station, public or private, in the principal Canadian cities, was extraordinarily successful in spreading TV service rapidly across the land. However, appetites for additional TV outlets were so quickly stimulated that a one-station policy for each city could not be maintained, and a Royal Commission on Broadcasting in 1955-57 (Fowler Commission) led to new legislation.

Regulation by the BBG (1958-68) The Broadcasting Act of 1958, replacing the legislation of 1936, was introduced by the Conservative government of John Diefenbaker. During the previous decade the Canadian Assn of Broadcasters, representing most private radio and TV stations, had conducted a vigorous campaign to convince the public that it was unjust to have the same public body (the CBC) as operator and as regulator of its private competition. This argument persuaded the Progressive Conservative Party to abandon its support of the 1936 legislation and to proceed with the new Act. It continued to treat all broadcasting in Canada as a single system, with a 15-member Board of Broadcast Governors (BBG) assigned the responsibility of regulating "the activities of public and private broadcasting stations in Canada and the relationship between them" and "ensuring the continued existence and efficient operation of a national broadcasting system." The BBG was to hear applications for new stations and make recommendations to the government minister who issued such licences. Despite the BBG's regulatory authority, the CBC continued to have its own board of directors under the Act, and continued to report directly to Parliament. Under the BBG, the TV system expanded rapidly, and radio became more a local and community service, except for the radio networks of the CBC. A second TV network, CTV, consisting of second stations in the larger Canadian cities, began operations in 1961, and the CBC TV networks in English and French continued to distribute programs, partly commercial and partly unsponsored, through CBC-owned stations and a larger number of private affiliates.

Broadcasting under the CRTC (1968-present) The 1958 legislation had brought about disputes between the 2 public agencies, the BBG and CBC, and in 1968 a new Act was passed to correct some of the ambiguities. The authority to issue licences was delegated to the Canadian Radio-Television Commission, and the new legislation brought CABLE TV, already securely established in a number of cities, under the authority of the new regulatory body, the CRTC (in 1976 renamed the CANADIAN RADIO-TELEVISION AND TELECOMMUNICATIONS COMMISSION, also CRTC). The CRTC has been more active than the BBG in trying to ensure that radio and TV stations and networks (in the words of the Act) "should be effectively owned and controlled by Canadians so as to safeguard, enrich and strengthen the cultural, political, social and economic fabric of Canada," and also that the programming provided should be "of high standard, using predominantly Canadian creative and other resources." The CBC has had no difficulty in meeting or exceeding the Canadian-content quotas imposed by the CRTC, but the private stations and networks have barely met the minimum standards, especially in prime time. Added to the effect of importing American TV by cable, the result of these minimum standards has been that more US than Canadian programs are available to Canadian audiences.

The CRTC clearly did not intend to increase the share of viewing time going to American TV programs, but that has happened. There are several explanations. Most important was the decision, influenced by public demand, to license cable systems in all parts of Canada to import 2, 3 or more US channels, thus making full US network services available almost everywhere. There was also a decision to license a regional Canadian network in the most populous Canadian province, Global Television in Ontario, which did not have the resources to schedule as many attractive Canadian programs as the 2 national networks, CBC and CTV. Moreover, because of the CRTC's loose definition of prime time as the hours from 6 PM to midnight, the private broadcasters were able to cluster their American programming within the peak hours, between 7 and 11 PM. All this has increased the share of audience watching US programs to about 70% for English-language programs. The situation is not as serious in French-speaking Canada, where about 60% of TV programs are Canadian in origin. Even in Québec, however, the share of non-Canadian viewing has been growing.

The CBC continues to distribute a great deal of Canadian programming. It has been said that it produces more original TV and radio programming than any other broadcaster, public or private, anywhere in the world. Also, the CRTC has licensed 2 other public services producing many of their own programs, TV Ontario and Radio-Québec, each as an educational service financed by the province it serves. Their evening programs attract a substantial general audience. The private TV network in Québec, TVA, with 9 stations, is a very important source of French-language programs and complements the service of the CBC French network.

Whether broadcasting will help preserve Canada's cultural sovereignty is still unresolved; the question will grow in complexity as technology advances. Canada has built the biggest physical system in the world, but in large part has turned it over to the US entertainment industry. Canadian governments are now searching for a way to establish a national information grid using all the possibilities of a modern TELECOMMUNICATIONS system. As for broadcasting, there is the prospect of several dozen TV channels, or even 100, in place of the 10 or 20 so far employed, and it is not clear how many of these can be programmed in Canada. Another unresolved issue, as technology changes, is how much will be regulated and controlled by a federal authority and how much by the provinces. The provincial governments have sought a larger place in CABLE TELEVISION, PAY TELEVISION, determination of program content, and regulation of common carriers. Whether these claims will be resolved by redefining jurisdictions, or by concurrency or interdelegation is yet to be determined (*see also* COMMUNICATIONS IN QUÉBEC; COMMUNICATIONS IN THE NORTH).

FRANK W. PEERS

Reading: David Ellis, *Evolution of the Canadian Broadcasting System* (1979); Frank W. Peers, *The Public Eye* (1979).

Broadcasting, Royal Commission on (Fowler Commission) established (1955) under Robert Fowler, shortly after the development of private television in Canada, to consider the problems of financing the Canadian BROADCASTING system and the roles of public and private broadcasters in solving them. It rejected private broadcasters' arguments that cultural goals should be met primarily by the CBC and suggested the establishment of minimum cultural standards for private broadcasting and the creation of an independent regulatory agency to supervise broadcasting. The 1958 Broadcasting Act, which was based on the report, was replaced (1967-68) by a new Act establishing the CANADIAN RADIO-TELEVISION COMMISSION (CRTC).

NICK SIDOR

Broccoli (*Brassica oleracea*, Botrytis Group), annual or biennial VEGETABLE belonging to the Cruciferae family. The species is native to the Mediterranean region. In Europe the term "broccoli" is used for the cold-tolerant overwintering CAULIFLOWER and what is known in N America as broccoli is often called "calabrese." Broccoli is cultivated for its tightly packed flowering head and upper stalks, which are consumed when the flowers are in bud. It is becoming an increasingly important vegetable crop in Canada and is particularly well suited to parts of the Maritimes and BC. The crop does not perform well if temperatures are excessively high. Traditional cultivars were harvested July-Sept; European and Japanese cultivars selected in BC have extended the season from June to the first heavy frost. Broccoli is grown for both the fresh and processing markets. In 1979 the Canadian processing crop was worth $1.18 million, of which $0.8 million came from BC; the BC fresh market crop was worth $0.6 million. Canadian fresh market production amounted to only 12.5% of the quantity imported.

A.R. MAURER

Brock, Sir Isaac, military commander, administrator of Upper Canada (b at St Peter Port, Guernsey 6 Oct 1769; d at Queenston Heights, UC 13 Oct 1812). He arrived in Canada in 1802 with his regiment, the 49th Foot. He was promoted maj-gen in 1811, and in the absence of Francis GORE was made provisional administrator of UPPER CANADA. At the outset of the WAR OF 1812, Brock's bold initiatives in ordering the capture of Michilimackinac and in leading attacks on AMHERSTBURG and Detroit raised the confidence of the militia. He was killed by a sharpshooter when leading troops against an American battery on Queenston Heights. The memory of Brock, the fallen hero and saviour of Upper Canada, remained extraordinarily strong in Ontario history. His body was moved in 1824 to the summit of Queenston Heights under an imposing monument (destroyed in 1840, but replaced that year by the stately monument that dominates the battlefield today).

ROBERT S. ALLEN

Brock University was founded in 1964 in St Catharines, Ont. It is named after Maj-Gen Sir Isaac BROCK, who led British forces in the WAR OF 1812 in a battle fought 8 km from the site of the campus. The university offers programs in the arts and sciences, and has specialized schools of administrative studies, physical education, recreation, urban and environmental studies, child studies and education. All of the university's facilities are modern and include a science complex, completed in 1983, a physical education complex with an Olympic-size pool, and residence accommodation for 650 students. The campus is located on the edge of the Niagara Escarpment overlooking the city.

Enrolment: Brock University, 1982-83
(Source: Statistics Canada)

Full-time Undergrad	*Full-time Graduate*	*Part-time Undergrad*	*Part-time Graduate*
3 360	77	3 510	418

Brockington, Leonard Walter, first chairman, CANADIAN BROADCASTING CORP (b at Cardiff, Wales 6 Apr 1888; d at Toronto 15 Sept 1966). Having immigrated to Edmonton in 1912 he was called to the bar in 1919. As chairman of the CBC 1936-39, an unpaid office, he oversaw the establishment of a national network of high-powered regional transmitters and significant increases in program production. Brockington established for the CBC the principles of nonpartisanship and nonsponsored broadcasts. He felt free speech was best promoted through the free apportionment of time to competent speakers on various sides of controversial issues, as opposed to the sale of time to individuals or commercial concerns. He became special assistant to PM Mackenzie KING 1939-42, and adviser on Commonwealth affairs to the British minister of information, 1942-43. Subsequently, he became president of Odeon Theatres in Canada and rector of Queen's.

ROBERT E. BABE

Brockinton, archaeological site located along the SOURIS R of southwestern Manitoba. It has yielded 3 distinctive occupations: an early bison-butchering pound about 800 AD, a Blackduck culture occupation about 1200 AD, and the first excavated evidence of the Williams culture, about 1600 AD. The Blackduck occupation demonstrated the adaptation of WOODLAND Indians adjusting to seasonal bison hunting. The Williams occupation showed the reliance upon bison by a Plains tribe; it is distinguished by uniquely decorated pottery consisting of small bowls, some with incurved rims, decorated with 2-strand cords impressed in the clay and zones of punctates made by using hollow tubes such as quills of bird feathers. *See also* ARCHAEOLOGY; PREHISTORY. E. LEIGH SYMS

Brockville, Ont, City, pop 19 896 (1981c), inc 1962, located on the St Lawrence R, 80 km E of Kingston. An important transshipment centre in the past, it remains a divisional point on the CNR and, as gateway to the Thousand Islands, a major tourist centre. Founded as a LOYALIST settlement 1784 by William Buell and Daniel and Charles Jones, it was called Elizabethtown and renamed in 1813 for Lt-Gov Sir Isaac BROCK. The railway encouraged growth, and Canada's oldest railway tunnel was built (1854-60) to provide access to the riverfront. For a time foundries and machine shops were active, but these have been replaced by electrical, electronic, pharmaceutical and chemical industries. Many fine old houses survive, and the massive stone Brockville Courthouse (1841-44) is one of Ontario's oldest public buildings. Nearby Blockhouse I was used as a rebel base (1837), and as a quarantine station during a cholera epidemic (1832). Newspaperman R. Ogle Gowan founded the Grand Lodge of British N America 1830, and the daily *Recorder and Times* has been published since 1821, longer than any newspaper in Canada. A campus of St Lawrence College of Applied Arts and Technology is located here, and as "gateway to the THOUSAND ISLANDS" Brockville is a major tourist centre. K.L. MORRISON

Broda, Walter, "Turk," hockey player (b at Brandon, Man 15 May 1914; d at Toronto 17 Oct 1972). He was an outstanding goaltender with TORONTO MAPLE LEAFS 1936-52, winning the VEZINA TROPHY in 1941 and 1948, and sharing it with Al Rollins in 1951. He played his best under pressure, allowing only 2.09 goals per game in 101 playoff games. He had 61 shutouts in regular season play, and another 13 in playoffs. JAMES MARSH

Brodeur, Louis-Philippe, barrister, politician (b at Beloeil, Qué 21 Aug 1862; d at Québec C 1 Jan 1924). He was the son of Toussaint Brodeur, a rebel of 1837. He was educated at the Collège de St-Hyacinthe and Laval and called to the bar in 1884. He entered Parliament as MP for Rouville in 1891, served as Speaker 1901-04, and as minister of inland revenue under Wilfrid LAURIER in 1904. He was a staunch advocate of Canadian autonomy, his most important portfolio being marine and fisheries 1906-11; as minister he introduced legislation founding the Royal Canadian Navy. He sat on the Supreme Court of Canada from 1911 until becoming lieutenant-governor of Québec in 1923. MARC MILNER

Broley, Charles Lavelle, banker, ornithologist (b 7 Dec 1879; d at Delta, Ont May 1959). A banker in Winnipeg, he was also active in ornithology and conservation. In 1939 he "retired" to winters in Florida and summers in Ontario. In Florida he began a raptor-banding study, in 8 years banding 814 bald eagles. Recoveries showed that eagles dispersed northwards after nesting prior to southern migration, the first study to demonstrate this phenomenon with large numbers. Declining hatching success during his study resulted in one of the first alerts to science of the dangers of insecticides. Broley was to assume membership in a special conservation committee on bald eagles when he died fighting a brushfire. He was honoured for his work by a life membership in the Natural History Soc of Manitoba. MARTIN K. MCNICHOLL

Reading: M.J. Broley, *Eagle Man* (1952); J. Gerrard, *Charles Broley, An Extraordinary Naturalist* (1983).

Bronfman Family Descendants of a prosperous Russian immigrant, Ekiel Bronfman, members of the Bronfman family own and control huge financial empires that have been built from the profits of the family liquor business. Until recently the best-known member of the family was Samuel Bronfman (b at Brandon, Man 4 Mar 1891 according to one source and b en route from Russia in 1889 according to another; d at Montréal 10 July 1971). Samuel was instrumental in taking over Joseph E. Seagram and Sons in 1927, merging it with Distillers Corp and building the new company into the world's largest distilling corporation.

Soon after their arrival in 1889, the Bronfman family left their homestead near Wapella, Sask, for Brandon, where Ekiel started a wood-fuel delivery business with sons Abe (b in Russia 15 Mar 1882; d at Safety Harbor, Fla 16 Mar 1968), Harry (b at Napouda, Russia 7 Apr 1886; d at Montréal 12 Nov 1963) and Samuel. In 1903 the family borrowed money to buy the Anglo-American Hotel in Emerson, Man. Business boomed with the construction of the CPR and by the middle of WWI the family was running 3 profitable hotels in Winnipeg. It was Harry Bronfman's imagination and momentum that carried the family into the liquor trade. His credit allowed the family to purchase large stocks of liquor which was sold at a good profit in the interprovincial package trade during PROHIBITION in Canada. A similar move prior to prohibition in the US gave the family a large stock for export into that country. During prohibition in the US Samuel Bronfman travelled throughout the country developing contracts and arranging deliveries. When prohibition ended in 1933 the Bronfmans and SEAGRAMS were ready with huge amounts of their own well-aged and carefully blended liquors which they sold bottled to the consumer through a network of distributors, a marketing approach developed by Samuel, who had become the driving force in Seagrams. Success in the US brought huge profits and led to the company's expansion throughout the world. Seven Crown and Seagram's VO became the largest selling brands of whisky in the world. Under Samuel's leadership the company invested in wineries and distilleries and by 1965 was operating in 119 countries with sales over $1 billion.

Samuel and Saidye Bronfman in the early 1930s (*courtesy Winnipeg Free Press*).

In 1984 Seagrams was owned by Samuel's descendants through their control of Cemp Investments Ltd (an acronym for Samuel's children, Charles, Edgar, Mindel and Phyllis). Edgar M. Bronfman (b at Montréal 20 June 1929), Samuel's oldest son, was chairman of the board and chief executive officer of the Seagram Company Ltd. He ran the US operations from New York and was involved in Democratic politics. Samuel's second son, Charles Rosner (b at Montréal, Qué 27 June 1931) was deputy chairman and chairman of Cemp Investments Ltd. A Canadian nationalist, Charles ran the Canadian operations and owned the Montreal Expos baseball club. In 1984 Cemp controlled directly and indirectly $38.5 billion in assets. For example, Cemp owned 51% of Cadillac-Fairview Corp, one of N America's largest real-estate companies.

Financiers in their own right were Peter (b at Montréal 2 Oct 1929) and Edward (b at Montréal 1 Nov 1927), the sons of Allan Bronfman (b at Brandon 21 Dec 1895; d at Montréal 26 Mar 1980). Samuel excluded his brother Allan's family from Seagrams and most of the family fortune. However, Peter and Edward have, through Edper Investments, built their own financial empire considered by many to rival Cemp. For example, in 1984, Edper indirectly controlled Canada's largest forestry company and largest trust company. CHRISTOPHER G. CURTIS

Reading: Peter Newman, *The Bronfman Dynasty* (1978).

Bronson, Erskine Henry, manufacturer, politician (b at Bolton, NY 12 Sept 1844; d at Ottawa 19 Oct 1920). His father Henry Franklin BRONSON moved the family to Bytown [Ottawa] in 1853 during an influx of Americans attracted by cheap waterpower at the Chaudière Falls. In 1867 he entered the Bronson and Weston Lumber Co, assuming control in 1889 on his father's death. His concern for forestry conservation drew him into provincial politics in 1886, and 3 years later he joined Oliver MOWAT's Reform Cabinet as minister without portfolio, a position he held in the HARDY Cabinet until 1898.

During the 1890s Bronson diversified his business concerns into a corporate empire based on hydroelectric and traction utilities. He believed that only large corporations with immense capital working in co-operation with government could develop Canada's industry. This philosophy, and his interests in the Ottawa Electric Co (director) and Ottawa Power Co (president), involved him in a 1905 public utilities plebiscite in Ottawa, which he lost. His prestige and influence declined swiftly and he retired in 1910 a frustrated and disillusioned man. RICHARD REID

Bronson, Henry Franklin, lumber manufacturer (b at Moreau Twp, Saratoga County, NY 24 Feb 1817; d at Ottawa 7 Dec 1889). In 1852 Bronson and his partner John Harris moved to Bytown (Ottawa) to exploit the timber reserves of the Ottawa Valley. Utilizing modern mills, they were among the first to ship lumber from Ottawa to American markets. Abijah Weston replaced Harris, and the Bronson-Weston Lumber Co became one of the largest in Canada. Although Bronson retained his American citizenship, he became a leading Ottawa citizen, a major philanthropist and a supporter of the Reform Party. RICHARD REID

Brooke, Frances, née Moore, novelist, dramatist, essayist (christened at Claypole, Eng 24 Jan 1724; d at Sleaford, Eng 23 Jan 1789). In London, Frances moved in literary and theatrical circles. She published a weekly *The Old Maid* (Nov 1755 - July 1756) and a tragedy *Virginia* in 1756. Turning to fiction, in 1760 she translated a novel of sensibility, 3 years later publishing her own such novel, *The History of Lady Julia*

Mandeville. That year she sailed for Québec, where her husband, the Reverend John Brooke, was military chaplain. Here she wrote the first Canadian novel, *The History of Emily Montague* (1769), which she enriched with descriptions of landscape and climate, current events and inhabitants of the new colony. Returning to England in 1768, she continued her literary career with 2 translations from the French and several novels. From 1773 she, with tragic actress Mary Ann Yates, managed the Opera House, and she finally achieved theatrical success with her tragedy *The Siege of Sinope* (1781) and 2 comic operas, *Rosena* (1783) and *Marian* (1788).
LORRAINE MCMULLEN

Brooker, Bertram Richard, artist, novelist, poet, journalist, advertising executive (b at Croydon, Eng 31 Mar 1888; d at Toronto 21 Mar 1955). He emigrated to Portage la Prairie, Man, in 1905 and worked with the Grand Trunk Pacific Ry. He then owned and operated a motion picture theatre in Neepawa, Man, subsequently working on newspapers in Manitoba and Saskatchewan. Brooker moved to Toronto in 1921 as an advertising executive. As an artist — working in oil, watercolour, pencil, ink and print media — he executed both abstracts and realistic works. Brooker became the first Canadian artist to exhibit abstracts in 1927; *Sounds Assembling* (1928) and *Alleluiah* (1929) are early important paintings. As a novelist he won the first Gov Gen's Award for fiction in 1937 with *Think of the Earth*. He initiated, introduced and edited *The Yearbook of the Arts in Canada 1928-1929*, and a second volume in 1936. Brooker was an active member of Toronto's cultural life, painting, writing both prose and poetry, and regularly reviewing contemporary art and literature.
PATRICIA E. BOVEY

Brooker, Todd, alpine skier (b at Paris, Ont 24 Nov 1959). He began skiing at 4 and by 12 was racing throughout Ontario and Québec. An extremely aggressive skier, he has experienced both spectacular wins and devastating injuries. In 1979, his first year on the elite team, he injured a knee and was sidelined for over a year. In 1982-83, he won 2 World Cup events and ended the season with the number-one Fédération internationale du ski ranking in downhill. In 1983-84, despite several crashes, he achieved 2 World Cup second-place finishes.
MURRAY SHAW

Brooks, Alta, Town, pop 9421 (1981c), inc 1911, is located 185 km SE of Calgary on the Trans-Canada Hwy. In signing Treaty No 7 (1877), the BLACKFOOT yielded their traditional hunting grounds to cattle ranchers. A CPR siding was built on the site (1883), but when a townsite was surveyed in 1907, the population was only 9, including divisional engineer E.M. Brooks, after whom the town is named. In 1914 the CPR built a dam on the BOW R at Bassano (50 km NW), irrigating much of the surrounding country and encouraging settlement. Today a 3 km long canal irrigates more than 40 000 ha of prosperous farmland, the water being carried by a siphon under the CPR tracks. The Provincial Horticultural Research Station is located in the town, and to the S is Kinbrook Island Prov Pk, located on Lk Newell, Alberta's largest artificial lake, which serves as an irrigation reservoir. DINOSAUR PROV PK (40 km NE) has some of the world's most extensive fossil remains.
ERIC J. HOLMGREN

Brooks, Allan Cyril, naturalist, artist, soldier (b at Etawah, India 15 Feb 1869; d at Comox, BC 3 Jan 1946). Born to a prominent naturalist family, he received his early education in England. His family moved to Milton, Ont, in 1881, and then to Chilliwack, BC, in 1887. Brooks spent most of his remaining life in the Okanagan Valley and on Vancouver I. Drawings of birds, some of which survive from his fifth year, form his greatest legacy; he was illustrator of TAVERNER's books on Canadian birds and of several American ornithological and popular works. An ardent hunter and collector, he carefully prepared bird skins as taught by T. MCILWRAITH and mounted his own big-game heads, selling many specimens to museums. His scientific publications number about 130 and concentrated on faunistics and taxonomy. He travelled widely, especially in N America, and was known for his boundless enthusiasm. In WWI he quickly rose to the rank of major and received the DSO.
MARTIN K. MCNICHOLL

Reading: H.M. Laing, *Allan Brooks: Artist Naturalist* (1979).

Brooks, Lela Alene, speed skater (b at Toronto, Ont 7 Feb 1908). Encouragement from speed skating parents, strong self-motivation and a fierce competitive instinct enabled Brooks to succeed. Without formal coaching, she learned to leave the starting post quickly and had the stamina to hold her lead. Between 1921 and 1935 she won all the speed skating titles available to women, from provincial to world levels, and set new records at most of these levels. She was named to the 1936 Olympic team but opted for marriage and retirement.
BOB FERGUSON

Brooman Point Village, archaeological site located at the tip of a long peninsula extending from the eastern coast of BATHURST I in the High Arctic. Although the site shows traces of Paleoeskimo occupations between about 2000 BC and 1 AD, the major prehistoric settlement occurred from about 900-1200 AD. Archaeological excavations have revealed the presence of a late DORSET Paleoeskimo village, the remains of which were almost totally obliterated by early THULE-culture Inuit who built a village on top of the Dorset site and incorporated many Dorset artifacts into the wall-fill of their houses, thus preserving them in PERMAFROST. These artifacts include one of the largest known collections of Dorset carvings in wood, ivory and antler (*see* INUIT ART). The Thule village is radiocarbon dated to about 1100 AD and consists of 20 winter houses, of which only 4 or 5 were occupied at one time. The bones of at least 20 bowhead whales, used in house construction, indicate that the local Thule people efficiently exploited an environment much richer than that which exists in the area today. *See also* ARCHAEOLOGY; PREHISTORY.
ROBERT MCGHEE

Brossard, Nicole, writer, publisher (b at Montréal 27 Nov 1943). Brossard is a leading exponent of so-called formalist poetry in Québec and a major theoretician and promoter of literary and cultural feminism. In 1965 she founded *La* BARRE DU JOUR, a literary magazine which rebelled against nationalist-inspired poetry. Her poetry, in collections such as *Le Centre blanc* (1970) and *Suite logique* (1970), is abstract and antilyrical, and influenced the young poets of the magazine *Les Herbes rouges*. Brossard has also written novels. In 1975 her career took on a feminist dimension, the same year her *Mécanique jongleuse* won the Gov Gen Award. She founded the feminist paper *Les Têtes de pioche* (1976-79) and the magazine *La Nouvelle Barre du jour* (1977-) and has participated in many conferences in Canada and abroad about women's writing or Québec literature. An active member of the Union des écrivains québécois, she took up publishing in 1979, at first being responsible for Editions Quinze and then running her own company, l'Intégrale, founded 1982.
PIERRE NEPVEU

Brott, Alexander, conductor, composer, violinist, educator (b at Montréal 14 Mar 1915). Early success as a violinist led to a teaching appointment at McGill in 1939. There, Brott founded the McGill Chamber Orchestra (1945), which he still conducted in 1984. Concertmaster (1945-58) and at various times (1948-61) assistant conductor of ORCHESTRE SYMPHONIQUE DE MONTRÉAL, he was artistic director of the Kingston Symphony 1965-81 and has guest conducted most major Canadian orchestras. On frequent conducting tours abroad, he has been an enthusiastic champion of the music of Canadian composers. Brott's own output as composer for a variety of instrumental and vocal media is large. A skillful craftsman with a sure mastery of form, he uses counterpoint as his primary construction technique. Much of Brott's music is distinguished by good humour, elegant wit and satire.
BARCLAY MCMILLAN

Alexander Brott, conductor and composer. On conducting tours abroad, he is an enthusiastic champion of the music of Canadian composers (*courtesy National Film Board / Photothèque*).

Brott, Boris, conductor, violinist (b at Montréal 14 Mar 1944), son of Alexander BROTT. After his debut as a violinist at age 5, youthful conducting studies and award-winning performances in prestigious conducting competitions, Brott became assistant conductor of the TORONTO SYMPHONY (1963-65), then conductor of England's Northern Sinfonia at Newcastle upon Tyne (1964-68). Artistic director and conductor of the Hamilton Philharmonic Orchestra since 1969, as well as conductor of the BBC Welsh Orchestra (from 1972) and the CBC Winnipeg Orchestra (from 1975), Brott is known for musicianship, artistic flair and innovative programming concepts successful in audience building, not least in the domain of contemporary music.
BARCLAY MCMILLAN

Brown, Arthur Roy, fighter pilot (b at Carleton Place, Ont 23 Dec 1893; d at Stouffville, Ont 9 Mar 1944). A flight commander with 209 Squadron, Brown has often been credited with killing Manfred, Freiherr von Richthofen, the famed "Red Baron," on 21 Apr 1918. It is more likely, however, that von Richthofen was killed by ground fire from Australian machine gunners. Credited with 11 victories, Brown survived a serious flying accident in July 1918 and left the RAF a year later. He subsequently engaged in various businesses involved with flying.
BRERETON GREENHOUS

Brown, Edward Killoran, professor, critic (b at Toronto 15 Aug 1905; d at Chicago, Ill 24 Apr 1951). E.K. Brown was educated at U of T and U of Paris, and he taught at U of T, U of Man, Cornell and U of Chicago. His most important contributions to Canadian criticism were his well-known study *On Canadian Poetry* (1943, rev ed 1944); his annual surveys of Canadian poetry in the UNIVERSITY OF TORONTO QUARTERLY 1936-50; and his edition of Duncan Campbell SCOTT's poems (1951). At home in French and English, Brown was the first modern Canadian critic to establish a context for the study of 19th- and 20-century Canadian POETRY by identifying Canada's major poets (Archibald LAMPMAN, D.C. Scott and E.J. PRATT), tracing their influences and closely defining the strengths of their verse.
NEIL BESNER

Reading: E.K. Brown, *Responses and Evaluations: Essays on Canada*, ed D. Staines (1977).

Brown, Eldon Leslie, mining engineer, executive (b at Toronto 19 Aug 1900). After working as an engineer for the Mond Nickel Co, Brown joined Sherritt Gordon Mines Ltd in 1927, becoming president and managing director 1946. He also served as manager of God's Lake Gold Mines Ltd, consulting engineer of Madsen Red Lake Gold Mines and VP and general manager of Michipicoten Iron Mines Ltd. A brilliant mine engineer, he played a key role in the discovery and development of Sherritt Gordon's Lynn Lk nickel-cobalt mine, brought into production in the early 1950s, employed airborne geophysical equipment to locate the Fox mine 1960 and encouraged the development of complex chemical and metallurgical extraction processes. He retired as chairman 1968. He served as president of the Canadian Metal Mining Assn 1950 and received University of Toronto's Engineering Alumni Medal. J. LINDSEY

Ernest Brown (*courtesy Provincial Archives of Alberta/E. Brown collection*).

Brown, Ernest, photographer (b at Middlesborough, Eng 1877; d at Edmonton 1951). He arrived in Edmonton in 1904 and recorded the quick growth of the city during the boom years 1904-14. His business collapsed in 1914 and in 1920 he was forced to vacate his premises. Embittered, he ran unsuccessfully as Labour Independent in the 1921 provincial election. Having set up his former assistant Gladys Reeves as a photographer, he spent 8 years in Vegreville photographing, cataloguing his collection and writing a history, "The Birth of the West." He returned to Edmonton in 1929 and operated the Pioneer Days Museum 1933-39, exhibiting his artifacts and photographs. In 1947 the province purchased his museum artifacts and his collection of 50 000 negatives (now housed in the Provincial Archives of Alberta). E.J. HOLMGREN

Brown, George, journalist, politician (b at Alloa, Scot 29 Nov 1818; d at Toronto 9 May 1880). Raised in Edinburgh, he emigrated with his father to New York in 1837. They moved to Toronto in 1843 and began a paper, the *Banner*, for Upper Canadian Presbyterians. The next year George launched the Toronto *Globe* to back Reform efforts for RESPONSIBLE GOVERNMENT. He helped win the Reformers' victory of 1848, and made his *Globe* a vigorous force in Upper Canada. New issues rising there in church-state relations (notably Catholic demands for state-aided separate schools) led him into the Assembly as member for Kent in 1851. In the then PROVINCE OF CANADA, Brown's pronouncements against church-state ties drew favour in its predominantly Anglo-Protestant Upper Canadian half, but animosity in largely French-Catholic Lower Canada. Moreover, in 1853 he took up the idea of representation by population, which would give the more populous Upper Canada a majority of seats in the legislature. Beset by sectional strains, the Reform regime collapsed in 1854. The Liberal-Conservatives took office, while Brown sought to rebuild Reform.

He won over the Clear Grit radicals, strong in rural Upper Canada, whom he had formerly opposed for their sweeping American-style democracy. In Jan 1857 a reorganized Upper Canadian Reform Party adopted his policies of "rep by pop" and annexation of the Northwest, the fur trade expanse beyond the Great Lakes. This potent combination of Toronto leadership, the *Globe* and agrarian Grit numbers swept the Upper Canada elections of late 1857. In Aug 1858 Brown even formed a government with A.A. DORION, head of the Lower Canada Liberals; but sectional balances were too shaky, and it swiftly fell. The Upper Canada leader then steered a Reform Convention of 1859 in Toronto to the concept of a federal Union of the Canadas as a remedy for sectional division. Yet his concept did not carry Parliament, and in 1861, ill and temporarily defeated, he withdrew to recuperate. In 1863 he returned as member for S Oxford, after a visit to Britain where he married Anne Nelson, daughter of a prominent Edinburgh publisher.

A restored, deeply happy Brown explored more conciliatory means to achieve reform of the Union. In 1864 he chaired an all-party parliamentary committee on that subject, which on 14 June reported in favour of the "federal principle" to overcome the sectionalism which by then had brought political deadlock. When on the same day a last, ineffectual Conservative ministry broke down, he offered to support a new government ready to pursue constitutional changes. In consequence, he joined with his chief Conservative rivals John A. MACDONALD, A.T. GALT and G.E. CARTIER, to form a coalition which would seek a federal union of all the British provinces or, failing that, Canadas. Through this strong new coalition, stemming from Brown's crucial initiative, the movement to CONFEDERATION now surged ahead. He played a major role at the CHARLOTTETOWN CONFERENCE and the QUEBEC CONFERENCE that formulated the plan, was first to carry it to the British government in Dec 1864, and spoke compellingly for it in the 1865 Confederation Debates in the Canadian Assembly. In Dec 1865, however, he resigned from the coalition cabinet over internal dissensions. He continued to support Confederation nonetheless and ran in the first federal elections in fall 1867. Defeated, he then left Parliament. He felt satisfied still that his chief aims had been realized and retired to the *Globe* office, his warm family life with wife and 3 children, and the Bow Park estate near Brantford which he developed as a large-scale cattle-breeding enterprise.

Brown remained a power in Liberal circles as elder statesman and director of a formidable mass-circulation journal. He was active in Ontario party affairs, a Canadian senator from 1874, and close to Alexander MACKENZIE, his former chief lieutenant, federal prime minister 1873-78. Brown's death came in 1880 by tragic accident. A dismissed *Globe* employee, George Bennett (whom he had never known), accosted him in his office and shot him in a sudden struggle. The seemingly minor leg wound grew infected and finally brought his death.

J.M.S. CARELESS

Reading: J.M.S. Careless, *Brown of The Globe* (1959-63).

George Brown. His initiative in forming a coalition with his Conservative rivals was crucial in the movement towards Confederation. Brown was killed by a disgruntled former employee at the *Globe*, which Brown had founded in 1844 (*courtesy Public Archives of Canada/C-26415*).

Brown, James Sutherland, "Buster," soldier (b at Simcoe, Ont 28 Jun 1881; d at Victoria 13 Apr 1951). Brown joined the militia in 1896, transferred to the Royal Canadian Regiment in 1906, and served in a number of staff appointments overseas during WWI. Of LOYALIST stock, the outspoken Brown was deeply suspicious of the US and a champion of Canada's British heritage. In the 1920s, as director of military operations and intelligence, he drafted Defence Scheme No 1, Canada's contingency plan for defence in a war between the British Empire and the US. The scheme was dropped in 1931 by the chief of the general staff, A.G.L. MCNAUGHTON, who knew the Americans would inevitably win such a war. Brown commanded Military District 11 in BC, 1929-33, when he retired following a clash with McNaughton over the administration of the unemployment relief camps managed by the Dept of National Defence. He took refuge in Victoria, running unsuccessfully for office as a Conservative and railing against socialism and other "isms" he considered disruptive of society.

S. HARRIS AND NORMAN HILLMER

Brown, John George, "Kootenai," army officer, prospector, constable, whisky trader, buffalo hunter, wolfer, dispatch rider, guide, scout, driving force in establishing WATERTON LAKES NATL PK (b at Ennistymon, Ire 10 Oct 1839; d at Waterton Lks, Alta 18 July 1916). Through his grandmother's persistence Brown was commissioned in 1857 "without purchase" as an 8th Regiment ensign. After service in India 1858-59, he sold his commission and in 1862 set out for the Cariboo goldfields of BC. There he prospected unsuccessfully, trapped and served briefly as constable at Wild Horse Cr. In 1865 he travelled through the Rocky Mts to Waterton (Kootenay) Lks, which enchanted him and from which ultimately his nickname was derived.

Continuing across the prairie to Ft Garry, he was wounded by marauding Blackfoot, then traded whiskey in the Portage area. Employed briefly by a private company carrying mail for the US Army in the Dakota and Montana territories, Brown remained with the military as a civilian "tripper." Despite capture and near death at the hands of SITTING BULL in 1869, he continued dispatch riding until 1874. Brown then joined his wife's people — he had married a Métis in 1869 — hunting buffalo and wolfing. In 1877, at Ft Benton, Montana, Brown quarrelled with and killed Louis Ell, a celebrated hunter. Acquitted by a territorial jury he settled at Waterton Lks, where he traded and established a reputation as guide and packer. During the 1885 NORTH-WEST REBELLION, he became chief scout for the Rocky Mt Rangers.

Brown early foresaw the need to preserve the Waterton area and campaigned strenuously on its behalf. With the establishment of the Kootenay Forest Reserve in 1895 he became fishery officer and, in 1910, forest ranger. In 1914 his dream of further CONSERVATION was realized when the reserve became Waterton Lks Natl Pk, was enlarged and made contiguous with the international boundary and Glacier Natl Pk in the US. WILLIAM RODNEY

Brown, William, journalist, printer (b at Nunton, Scot *c*1737; d at Québec C 22 Mar 1789). In partnership with Thomas Gilmore he published the first issue of the *Quebec Gazette/La Gazette de Québec* 21 June 1764. The *Gazette* was the first periodical in the PROVINCE OF QUEBEC and began with the ideal of informing the public with impartiality. However, mention of the revolutionary events in the Thirteen Colonies was censored by Gov Guy CARLETON after 1768 and publication was suspended during the American invasion of 1775-76, resuming thereafter as, in Brown's description, "the most innocent gazette in the British Dominions." Brown and Gilmore also published the first books in Québec, including a catechism, legal works and *Abram's Plains* (1789), a collection of poems by Thomas Cary.
JAMES MARSH

Browne, George, architect (b at Belfast, Ire 5 Nov 1811; d at Montréal 19 Nov 1885). He created some of 19th-century Canada's finest buildings. In the 1830s he designed houses in Québec City and Montréal. With the union of Upper and Lower Canada (1841) and the establishment of the new capital at Kingston, Browne (then a government architect) did considerable work, including many private, commercial and civic buildings. Mostly in local limestone, they show a sophisticated handling of mass and texture. Their style, which might be called "heroic primitive," expresses the triumphant character of a society just emerging from the pioneering stage. The finest example is Kingston City Hall. Browne moved with the capital to Montréal in 1844, where his splendid Second-Empire-style Molsons Bank of 1864-66 (now Bank of Montreal) survives.
J. DOUGLAS STEWART

Browne, George, Jr, architect (b at Montréal, Canada E 1852 or 1858; d at St Petersburg, Fla 20 June 1932). After study with his father, a prominent Montréal architect, Browne travelled in Europe and went to South Kensington School of Art, London. He returned to Montréal in 1877 and in 1879 came to Manitoba. His design of the Massey Block (1885) in Winnipeg for the implement company of that name established a unique Manitoba style of commercial buildings by its use of local materials and a primitive Romanesque classicism in style. He also built Wesley Coll (U Winnipeg) in 1895, the finest Richardsonian Romanesque building extant in Winnipeg. Browne left for New York C in 1910 and later retired to Florida. W. P. THOMPSON

Brownell, Peleg Franklin, painter, teacher (b at New Bedford, Mass 27 July 1857; d at Ottawa 13 Mar 1946). After studying at the Boston Museum of Fine Arts, he went to Paris to study under Robert-Fleury, Bouguereau and Bonnat. In 1886 he became principal of the Ottawa Art School and subsequently headed the Woman's Art Assn of Ottawa (later Ottawa Art Assn), retiring 1937. He also painted in the West Indies, the US, the Gaspé and the Gatineau. Besides highly keyed landscapes, he produced portraits, flower studies, marines and genre scenes in oil, watercolour and pastel. A founder-member of the Canadian Art Club (1907), he was represented in the exhibitions of several art associations and showed internationally at the 1893 Chicago World's Columbian Exposition; the 1900 Paris World's Fair, at which he won a bronze medal for his RCA diploma work, *The Photographer*, 1896; the Louisiana Purchase Exhibition, St Louis, 1904; and the British Empire Exhibition, 1924-25. His paintings are found in major Canadian collections. Perhaps his best-known canvas is *The Beach, St. Kitts* (1913).
ROBERT STACEY

Brownlee, John Edward, lawyer, politician, executive, premier of Alberta (b at Port Ryerse, Ont 27 Aug 1883; d at Calgary, Alta 15 July 1961). He was one of Alberta's most effective premiers and for 5 decades a major voice in western farmer organizations. Son of a small-town merchant and a devout Methodist teacher, he moved to Calgary in 1909 to pursue a career in the booming West. He became solicitor for the fledgling UNITED FARMERS OF ALBERTA and played an important part in the amalgamation of United Grain Growers in 1917. When the UFA won the 1921 Alberta election, he became attorney general and helped organize the Alberta Wheat Pool. After a well-mannered back-stairs revolt, he became premier in Nov 1925, and his most significant achievement was his negotiation of the transfer to Alberta of control over its natural resources, an agreement drafted by him and signed 14 Dec 1929. During the Depression, Albertans became frustrated with his fiscal restraint, cautious assistance programs and political conservatism. A lonely voice against the tide of SOCIAL CREDIT, and undermined by charges of personal scandal under the Alberta Seduction Act, he and the UFA were devastated in 1935. In 1948 he rejoined UGG as president and general manager, modernizing the company's financial structure and rationalizing the elevator system by closing smaller, inefficient operations and concentrating on larger delivery points. FRANKLIN L. FOSTER

Bruce, Herbert Alexander, surgeon, military officer, politician (b at Blackstock, Ont 28 Sept 1868; d at Toronto 23 June 1963). Founder of Toronto's Wellesley Hospital (1911), he was appointed special inspector-general of the Canadian Army Medical Corps overseas by Sir Sam HUGHES in 1916. His *Report on the Canadian Army Medical Service* recommended a complete reorganization, including segregation of Canadian wounded in Canadian facilities. Although many of his ideas were subsequently implemented, Bruce and his report were disowned by the government. He later published his charges in *Politics and the Canadian Army Medical Corps* (1919). As lieutenant-governor of Ontario, 1932-37, he struggled to maintain his office against Mitch HEPBURN, the Liberal premier elected on a promise to reduce government expenditure. As a Conservative MP, 1940-46, Bruce was an outspoken proponent of wartime CONSCRIPTION. His lively memoirs, *Varied Operations* (1958), recount his medical, military and political careers.
O.A. COOKE

Bruce Peninsula, 100 km long, 38 km wide at base, juts NW from OWEN SOUND to Tobermory, thus forming GEORGIAN BAY in Lk HURON, Ontario. Composed of NIAGARA ESCARPMENT strata, it has a gentle tilt from the cliffs on Georgian Bay to the flat sand and clay plains on Lk Huron's shore. Owen Sound and Colpoys Bay form fjordlike harbours on Georgian Bay. Cape Croker, projecting 10 km into the bay, is an Ojibwa IR. Adjacent Hope Bay is famous for its sheer limestone cliffs and sandy beach. At Lion's Head a jagged rock formation, 51 m high, gives the site its name. At Tobermory the clear waters and numerous shipwrecks have produced a diving centre, and Fathom Five Provincial Park (11.7 ha) has been established. In addition, in 1980 the federal government bought 14 Tobermory islands as part of GEORGIAN BAY ISLANDS NATIONAL PARK. Called "the N American rendezvous of plants," the Bruce is a paradise for botanists, containing northern, transitional and southern tree species, approximately 49 orchid species and 30 species of ferns. The BRUCE TRAIL follows the rugged wilderness of the Georgian Bay side, much of which was recommended for preservation in the Niagara Escarpment Plan.
RAYMOND N. LOWES

Bruce Trail is a continuous, 720 km footpath on the NIAGARA ESCARPMENT connecting QUEENSTON, near NIAGARA FALLS, with the village of Tobermory in the BRUCE PENINSULA, Ontario. The trail follows the escarpment cliff through the fruit lands of Niagara and the city of HAMILTON, across the Dundas Valley, N through the Caledon Hills to the Blue Mts, then NW across the Beaver Valley to OWEN SOUND and onward, seldom out of sight of Lk Huron's GEORGIAN B, to Tobermory. This opportunity to explore Ontario on foot has been grasped by thousands, making the trail an important tourist attraction for Canada and encouraging the Ontario government to take steps towards preserving the escarpment. Public-spirited landowners gave permission for the Trail route to cross their properties; volunteer members of the Bruce Trail Assn built the trail and now maintain it. The idea for a nature trail across Ontario leading to "the Bruce," a paradise for naturalists, was proposed by Ray Lowes, a Stelco metallurgist, in 1960, and from this idea the BTA grew into a dedicated organization that manages the trail and channels the efforts of its members into maintenance, appropriate hiking behaviour, nature appreciation and respect for landowners' property.
RAYMOND N. LOWES

Bruhn, Erik Belton Evers, ballet dancer, choreographer (b at Copenhagen, Denmark 3 Oct 1928). As a dancer Bruhn has excelled in roles with many ballet companies, and his many awards include the Nijinsky Prize 1963 and the Diplôme d'honneur of the Canadian Conference of the Arts 1974. Since staging *La Sylphide* for the NATIONAL BALLET OF CANADA in 1964, Bruhn has been closely associated with the company (and its school) as guest artist, choreographer, teacher, resident producer and (from 1983) artistic director. His works for the company, including the controversial psychological *Swan Lake*, are mainstays of the repertoire, and his impeccable classical style and dramatic intelligence have influenced numerous Canadian dancers.
PENELOPE DOOB

Brûlé, Étienne, explorer, interpreter (b probably at Champigny-sur-Marne, France *c*1592; d in Huronia *c* June 1633). In 1610 Brûlé went to live among the HURON. He became a skilful interpreter and intermediary. Travelling with his adopted people, Brûlé was likely the first European to see Lks Ontario, Huron and Superior and on a mission to the Susquehannock he roamed as far as Chesapeake Bay. He was captured by the Iroquois and ritually tortured but was released, likely on a promise to promote an alliance with the French. In 1623 he travelled northward and reported the rapids at Sault Ste Marie. Unfortunately Brûlé left no account of his career and reports of the missionaries were coloured by their contempt for his native lifestyle. The original COUREUR DE BOIS, he was an independent, adventurous spirit. In 1629 he deserted to the KIRKE brothers when they attacked Québec. Accused of treason by CHAMPLAIN, he returned to Huronia. Despite lurid speculations that he was tortured and eaten, Brûlé was likely murdered for political reasons, possibly because of his dealings with the Seneca or another tribe feared by the Huron. JAMES MARSH

Brunet, Louis-Ovide, priest, teacher, botanist (b at Québec City 10 Mar 1826; d there 2 Oct 1876). After working as a parish priest for 10 years, Brunet was offered a position as a science teacher at his alma mater, the Séminaire de Québec. In 1862 he succeeded Thomas Sterry HUNT as professor of natural history at Laval. His numerous botanical field trips in Québec and Ontario, as well as 2 years spent in Europe visiting herbaria and attending courses given by experts at the Muséum national d'histoire naturelle in Paris, provided him with basic training in botany, which was completed when he developed close contacts with Canadian and American botanists. He published his first original work in 1865. By 1870 Brunet had become an expert botanist and was expected to undertake a study of Canada's flora. Strongly encouraged in this endeavour by the great American scholar Asa Gray, Brunet assembled an extensive set of notes which unfortunately were never published, his promising career having been cut short by illness. RAYMOND DUCHESNE

Brunette Island, 30 km^2, is situated at the mouth of Fortune B on Newfoundland's S coast, 18 km S of Connaigre Head. The island, roughly triangular, measures 11 km E-W and 6 km N-S. A steep ridge backs the NW shore, at one point rising to 160 m. From the early 1800s the island supported a fishing community at Mercer's Cove in the SE until the islanders were resettled, with government assistance, in the late 1950s. Brunette I then became a provincial wildlife reserve and the site of experimental colonies of caribou, moose, Arctic hare and bison, the latter brought from Alberta in 1964 in a unique but unsuccessful attempt to introduce the animal to Newfoundland. ROBERT D. PITT

Brussels Sprouts (*Brassica oleracea,* Gemmifera Group), biennial VEGETABLE of the Cruciferae family. Brussels sprouts are native to western Europe. The plant develops small heads or sprouts at the leaf axils along the stem, rather than one large head. A long-season crop, Brussels sprouts mature in autumn and early winter. Some cultivars are more cold tolerant than others and can be overwintered in temperate areas. The crop is best suited to the Maritimes and coastal BC, and requires a high level of fertilization and adequate soil moisture throughout the season. Most cultivars grown in Canada are first-generation hybrids developed in Japan or Holland. They are produced for the fresh and processing markets. Although some of the fresh-market crop is still hand harvested, mechanization is developing rapidly. In 1982 the Canadian processing crop was worth $3.354 million, of which $3.056 million originated in BC. Canadian production for the fresh market amounts to 62% of the quantity imported. A.R. MAURER

Bryce, Peter Henderson, physician (b at Mount Pleasant, Canada W 17 Aug 1853; d at sea 15 Jan 1932). He served as first secretary of the Ontario Board of Health 1882-1904 when he joined the federal Dept of Immigration as its chief medical officer. A man of strong opinions, Bryce agitated for health reform, concentrating his attack on tuberculosis. His condemnation of Indian boarding schools as breeding grounds of the disease caused official embarrassment. Retired in 1921, Bryce studied Canadian letters and finished a manuscript on the life of Sir Oliver MOWAT shortly before dying on a voyage to the West Indies. JANICE DICKIN MCGINNIS

Reading: P.H. Bryce, *The Illumination of Joseph Keeler* (1915) and *The Value to Canada of the Continental Immigrant* (1928).

Bryce, Robert B., public servant (b at Toronto 27 Feb 1910). An engineering graduate from U of T, Bryce studied economics at Cambridge (under J.M. Keynes) and at Harvard. He joined the federal Dept of Finance in 1938, and over the next decade his abilities contributed significantly to the department's pre-eminence in Ottawa and to its concentration of power there. He was appointed clerk of the Privy Council and secretary to the Cabinet in 1954. He served there throughout the DIEFENBAKER government and was remarkable for his ability to win the trust and co-operation of an often difficult PM. In 1963 he became deputy minister of finance, and in 1971 Canadian executive director to the INTERNATIONAL MONETARY FUND. His last major position was the chairmanship of the Royal Commission on CORPORATE CONCENTRATION. R. BOTHWELL

Brymner, William, painter, teacher (b at Greenock, Scot 14 Dec 1855; d at Wallasey, Eng 18 June 1925). Brymner's father was the first Dominion archivist. William is remembered as Canada's first great art teacher. His respect for academic training and his own delicate painting skill, combined with a gentle way with others' talent, influenced many men and women studying in Montréal in the early 1900s. Educated at Richmond, Qué, Brymner went to Paris to train for architecture. While there he decided to paint. In 1886 he was appointed director of art classes at the Art Assn of Montréal. The same year he became a full RCA member. He painted the human figure and interiors in a representational style; he also did watercolours on silk, and murals, as found in the old Porteous house on Île d'Orléans. He sketched landscape with J.W. MORRICE and Maurice CULLEN, his 1899 *Early Morning in September* illustrating a fine palette of glowing sensual colour, while the pastoral scene holds a lingering touch of Europe in its settled tranquility. ANNE MCDOUGALL

BTO, Bachman-Turner Overdrive, rock band including Robin Bachman, Randy Bachman, Blair Thornton and Fred Turner. They were internationally popular during the mid-1970s. BTO's third album "Not Fragile," spawned the million-selling single "You Ain't Seen Nuthin' Yet." By 1977, when Bachman left, 20 million records had been sold worldwide. BTO continued touring and recording. Until 1979 it was one of the most successful Canadian rock bands; it reunited in 1984 and toured Canada. JOHN GEIGER

Buchan, John, 1st Baron Tweedsmuir, author, governor general of Canada 1935-40 (b at Perth, Scot 26 Aug 1875; d at Montréal 11 Feb 1940). Buchan published 6 books of fiction, poetry and history while an Oxford undergraduate. He was briefly an administrator in S Africa, a political journalist and tax lawyer, and then was chief literary adviser (later a director) of publishers Thomas Nelson and Son 1906-29. This, and the books that he produced at a prodigious rate all his life, including historical biographies, such as *Lord Minto* (1924), and fast-paced thrillers, such as *The Thirty-Nine Steps* (1915), gave him a creative outlet and comfortable income. There was always a tension in Buchan between his desire to live quietly and his ambition to be a part of bigger things. Despite serious illness, he went to France in WWI as an intelligence officer. He was a popular MP 1927-35 but was too lacking in partisan fervour for a Cabinet post. In Canada Buchan had time to indulge his contemplative side. He loved the variety, beauty and adventure of a big land, and tried to convey a sense of community and unlimited potential on his frequent tours, which included the first by a governor general to the Arctic. Horrified by WWII, he worked with US President Roosevelt and PM Mackenzie KING in their peace initiatives of the late 1930s. Although admiring King more politically than personally, Buchan forged strong links with the PM. King noted the governor general's weaknesses — his self-importance and love of titles — but he deeply appreciated Buchan's "real support . . . sterling rectitude and disinterested purpose." Buchan's autobiography, *Memory Hold-the-Door* (1940), was completed shortly before his death. He instituted the GOVERNOR GENERAL'S LITERARY AWARDS in 1937. NORMAN HILLMER

Buchanan, John MacLennan, lawyer, politician, premier of NS (b at Sydney, NS 22 Apr 1931). Elected to the NS Assembly 1967 and appointed to the Cabinet 1969, Buchanan was chosen provincial Conservative leader 1971. He lost the election of 1974, but led his party to victory in 1978 and added to its majority in 1981. As premier, his concerns have been revitalizing Sysco, the publicly owned steel plant, controlling domestic energy costs, increasing coal production by opening new mines, and developing offshore mineral resources. His government has also promoted a pilot tidal project at the head of the Annapolis Basin, the first step towards harnessing Fundy tides. J. MURRAY BECK

Buck, Gary, singer, songwriter, administrator, record producer (b at Thessalon, Ont 21 Mar 1940). Besides being a successful country music singer-songwriter, his recording of "Happy to Be Unhappy" (1963) was an international hit. Buck managed Capitol Record's Beechwood Music 1970-71 and in 1971 established his own recording and publishing firm, Broadland Music, which handled some of the top names in Canadian music before being taken over by Quality Records in 1976. A director of the Country Music Assn in Nashville 1971-75 and founder of the Canadian country music organization ACME, Buck won Juno Awards 1964-66 and in 1975 won the Big Country Awards for "top male singer" and "top producer." RICHARD GREEN

Buck, Tim, machinist, trade unionist, communist leader (b at Beccles, Eng 6 Jan 1891; d at Cuernavaca, Mexico 11 Mar 1973). Like many skilled British workers, Buck immigrated to Canada in 1910 in search of a better living. He was soon immersed in radical working-class politics in Toronto. Buck later claimed to have been a founding member of the COMMUNIST PARTY OF CANADA, organized in a secret 1921 meeting in a barn near Guelph, and soon became a leading architect of its trade-union policy. In 1929, after a struggle against party leaders who supported Trotsky's critique of developments in the international communist movement, Buck emerged as the party's general secretary, a post he held for 32 years. He published many articles, pamphlets and books. He spent over 2 years in jail 1932-34 and 3 years underground during WWII when his party was banned. In 1971 he received the Order of the Great October Revolution from the USSR. CRAIG HERON

Bucke, Richard Maurice, psychiatrist, author (b at Methwold, Eng 18 Mar 1837; d at London, Ont 19 Feb 1902). Brought to Upper Canada when one year old, Bucke was raised and educated on the family farm near Hamilton. Following an adventurous youth in the American West, he graduated in medicine from McGill in 1862, studied abroad for 2 years and then began his practice in Sarnia, Canada W. He was appointed superintendent of the Asylum for the Insane in Hamilton in 1876 and of the London asylum in 1877. He was a founder of the School of Medicine at U of Western Ontario. His theories on the causes and treatment of mental diseases and his advocacy of the "moral restraint" of the insane attracted widespread attention. Bucke corresponded voluminously with Walt Whitman and became Whitman's official biographer and ultimately one of his literary executors. He found in Whitman's poetry a confirmation of his belief that the mystical experience, once the preserve of the few, will become accessible to the many. To this end he published his popular *Cosmic Consciousness* (1901), which attempts to demonstrate that man is on the verge of a psychic revolution. The book has enjoyed a vast readership. Bucke's papers are in the library at Western. JOHN ROBERT COLOMBO

Buckler, Ernest, novelist (b at Dalhousie West, NS 19 July 1908; d at Bridgetown, NS 4 Mar 1984). Buckler showed a remarkable sensitivity to the landscape and human character of his native Annapolis Valley. One of his principal strengths was his lyrical and metaphorical prose style. After studying at Dalhousie and U of Toronto, Buckler worked for 5 years as an actuarial mathematician in Toronto before ill health prompted him to return to NS. He began his writing career by contributing short stories and essays to *Esquire* and *Saturday Night*. His major achievement, however, *The Mountain and the Valley* (1952), is a novel about a gifted, ambitious boy who remains so deeply attached to life in rural NS that his creativity becomes stifled. *The Cruelest Month* (1963) explores the unhappy passions of a group of intellectuals. Buckler returned to his youthful community life in *Ox Bells and Fireflies* (1968), a "fictional memoir" (Buckler's term). *Nova Scotia: Window on the Sea* (1973) again uses elements of fiction and lyrical description, this time to accompany Hans Weber's photographs. *The Rebellion of Young David and Other Stories* (1975) is a collection of 1940s and 1950s stories. *Whirligig* (1977), a volume of light verse and prose, won the Leacock Award for Humour (1978). THOMAS E. TAUSKY

Buckley, Kenneth Arthur Haig, economist, professor (b at Aberdeen, Sask 16 July 1918; d at Saskatoon 30 May 1970). After graduating from U of Toronto and London School of Economics, Buckley returned to the Dept of Economics and Political Science at U of Saskatchewan 1945. He was a Canadian pioneer in quantitative economic history. His first major work, *Capital Formation in Canada, 1896-1930* (1955), was a study of the impact of the wheat economy on Canadian economic growth, and influenced a generation of economic historians. His later work encompassed a wide range of subjects — from a critique of the STAPLE THESIS to historical estimates of internal migration. He was well known to students for the text *Economics for Canadians*, written with Helen Buckley (1960), and (with M.C. Urquhart) the monumental *Canadian Historical Statistics* (1965). PAUL PHILLIPS

Buckwheat (genus *Fagopyrum*), broad-leaved, erect annual belonging to the buckwheat family (Polygonaceae). The cultivated species, common buckwheat (*F. esculentum*) and tartary buckwheat (*F. tataricum*), are grown as field crops. Wild buckwheat (*Polygonum convolvulus*), a common WEED, is distantly related. Buckwheat originated in Asia and was introduced to Europe and N America. The plant consists of a single main stem (smooth, grooved and hollow), several branches and a shallow taproot system. The dark green leaves are heart shaped. Flower clusters (usually white, sometimes pink) are found at branch ends or arise from axils of leaves. The seed, an achene (dry one-seeded fruit), is triangular and varies in colour from brown to grey to black. Buckwheat is grown mainly for human consumption (eg, flour for pancake mixes, bread and ethnic dishes, breakfast cereal) and is also used for livestock and poultry feed, as a green-manure crop, as a smother crop and as a source of buckwheat honey. In Canada it is grown mainly in Manitoba (85%) and in Québec (15%). In 1981 total production was 53 000 t valued at $20.5 million. Its importance as a cash crop has decreased. About one-third of the crop is consumed in Canada; the remainder is exported. B.B. CHUBEY

Buctouche, NB, village, pop 2476 (1981c), is located 40 km N of MONCTON. This Northumberland Str port draws its name from the Micmac word for "big bay." ACADIAN families returning from exile settled here as early as 1784, followed by the English after 1800. The current population is 93% French speaking (1981c). Fishing, lumbering and shipbuilding were the main industries, and construction of a branch railway to Moncton (1888) spurred local commerce until it was abandoned in the 1960s. While the traditional primary industries remain important, future prosperity is seen to lie in the field of high technology. Completion of a plant to manufacture computer parts in the early 1980s was expected to relieve the area's chronic unemployment. Buctouche is the birthplace of 2 prominent Canadians — Antonine MAILLET, internationally renowned Acadian author, and millionaire industrialist K.C. IRVING. DEAN JOBB

Buddhism, a major world religion encompassing various systems of philosophy and ethics, with about 52 000 adherents in Canada (1981c). It was founded around 500 BC by a prince of the Sakya clan, Siddhartha Gotama, who came to be known as Gotama the Buddha. Though accounts of the founder's life vary, the Northern (Sanskrit) and Southern (Pali) traditions agree that Siddhartha was born in Lumbini Garden (present-day Nepal), attained enlightenment at Bodhgaya (India) began preaching in Benares (Varanasi) and entered *nirvana* (passed away) at Kusinara (Kasia, India). At the age of 29 Siddhartha turned his back on his life as a prince in order to seek enlightenment. After 6 years as an ascetic he became Buddha (Sanskrit *bodhi*, "enlightened" or "awakened"), and now recognized the principle of relativity (the interdependence of all phenomena), which implied that nothing lasts forever (*anitya*); everything will eventually become dissatisfying (*duhkha*); nothing has a nature of its own (*anatman*); and, when attachment to calculated and established values is extinguished (*nirvana*), bliss (*santi*) is gained. Thus to become a Buddha does not mean that one becomes divine. A Buddha is one who recognizes that nothing, including his soul, has an eternal essence. Wishing to share his insight (*dharma*), Gotama Buddha preached his first sermon on the Middle Path and on the Four Noble Truths: the unsatisfactoriness of life, the origin of that unsatisfactoriness, its cessation and the path leading to its cessation. The 5 monks who attended him were the first Buddhist congregation (*sangha*) in Gotama Buddha's 45 years of preaching.

After his death a schism arose between those determined to emulate the religious practices that led Gotama to enlightenment, and others stressing the experience of enlightenment itself. Gradually 2 distinct traditions appeared. The Theravada system, developed by those holding the former view, bases its philosophy and ethics on the Pali texts compiled by Buddhists in southern India. It spread through Burma, Sri Lanka, Cambodia, Thailand and other SE Asian countries. The latter system, the Mahayana tradition, bases its philosophy and ethics on the Sanskrit texts from northern India. It spread to Korea, Vietnam, Japan and other E Asian countries by way of China and Tibet. As each tradition spread, it changed to accommodate the language, culture, customs and attitudes of the new country. As well, some Buddhist teachings have influenced, or become integral to, various NEW RELIGIOUS MOVEMENTS.

Buddhism in Canada JAPANESE immigrants probably brought Buddhism to Canada during the late 1800s. Because it was identified with a particular ethnic group, this form of Buddhism did not become integrated into the Canadian milieu. More recently, Buddhism has come to Canada with both Asians and non-Asians, and is rooted doctrinally in either the Theravada or Mahayana (including the Vajrayana) tradition. Among new immigrants and their children, Buddhism often takes on an organizational structure holding little religious significance, but designed to fulfil requirements for incorporation under the Societies Act. Membership is normally open, although most Buddhist societies expect commitment to the Buddha, the dharma (teaching) and the sangha in a manner consistent with each society's understanding of these terms. Buddha is considered to be an understanding celestial being by some, an earthly being by others. Dharma is law to some, to others a guiding principle. For some, sangha is a community of ordained monks, for others the community of monks and laity. Some societies require the layman's vows of refraining from the 3 physical acts of taking life, taking what has not been given, and sexual excess; the 4 speech-related actions, lying, slandering, foolish talk and harsh talk; and the 3 mental actions, selfishness, malice and seeing wrongly. With increasing intermarriage, the predominantly Asian societies have had to adapt their ways to retain non-Asians as members.

Each society is centered on a leader known by different titles in different groups: *bhikkhu, lama, sensei*, monk, spiritual director, *roshi*, spiritual adviser, teacher, *oya*, minister, *geshe, tulku*, master or reverend. In some groups the leader acts as social worker, foreign-language teacher and family counsellor, while attempting to transmit something about the religion to his or her congregation. Such groups are usually "closed systems," in which the leader is closely aligned with the parent culture. In other groups, especially those whose members wish to devote their lives to meditation, the leader oversees and supervises the members' spiritual growth. Such members are very dependent, yielding themselves to the leader's charismatic power and establishing a close bond. Groups continuing from Asian parent organizations use English translations of their scriptures in the belief that the younger generations of "hyphenated Canadians" (Japanese-Canadians, TIBETAN-Canadians, etc) will thus learn to appreciate their religious and cultural history. In practice, however, many translations make little more sense to the younger generation than do the originals.

Although Sunday has no ecclesiastical meaning for Buddhists it is set aside for religious observances because in Canada it is difficult to attend services on weekdays. Special religious days are New Year's Day, Nirvana or Parinirvana Day (Feb 18), Wesak (Full Moon, Apr-May) or Hanamatsuri Day (Flower Festival, Apr 8), Founder's Day, Organization Day, Bodhi Day (Dec 8), Special Anniversary Day and New Year's Eve. Buddhists also celebrate specific times in life: birth, naming, confirmation or ordination, marriage and death. These are considered religiously significant because they are especially conducive to reflecting upon the principle of relativity, or dependent co-arising. Ceremonies associated with the techniques of meditation include those related to daily activities such as eating, shaving and bathing.

The Toronto Mahavihara (Buddhist Centre), est 1978, was the first Theravada temple in Canada. It continues the tradition established at the Mahavihara in Anuradhapura, Sri Lanka, begun in the third century BC. The Sri Lankan government, through its High Commission in Ottawa, donates funds for the basic needs of the resident bhikkhus. Membership is open. In Vancouver a Theravada Buddhist Society, Dhamma, is devoted to self-development through moral living, Vipassana (insight) Meditation and methodical study of the Abhidhamma philosophy of Buddhist scriptures as handed down in the Pali canon. The Ariya Theravada Society, fd 1981 in Calgary, has expanded into Vancouver. This group, which follows the Pali tradition, promotes Buddhist teaching and practice through meditation and retreats. These last 2 societies are led by occidentals who were trained and ordained in India and Thailand, respectively.

The Ambedkar Mission, fd 1979 in Scarborough, Ont, follows the religious and social philosophy of Dr Ambedkar, who rose from among the untouchables to become one of India's most respected Buddhist leaders. The society promotes social justice, peace and understanding. Membership is open, although the group was originally made up mostly of people of Indian origin.

Within the second tradition, the Mahayana, was developed the doctrine of *bodhisattva*, which includes the belief that the historical Buddha was a brief manifestation of an eternal, absolute Buddha. Mahayana Buddhist organizations in Canada can be categorized according to the parent group's country of origin. Before Tibet became an "autonomous region" of the People's Republic of China, there were 4 major orders of Tibetan Buddhism (Gelugpa, Sakyapa, Nyingmapa and Kagyupa), of which the Kagyupa and the Gelugpa are best represented in Canada. Organized in Canada as the Karma Kargyu Society, the Karma-Kagyupa lineage was headed by is Holiness Rangjung Rigpe Dorje, the 16th Gyalwa Karmapa (1924-81). The Gelugpa, which has no national organization, is headed by His Holiness Tenzin Gyatso, the 14th Dalai Lama (b 1934).

The Marpa Gompa Meditation Society, fd 1979 in Calgary, studies, practises and promotes the teachings of the Kargyu order of Tibetan Buddhism. It is officially headed by Karma Tinley Rinpoche, founder of Toronto's Mikyo Dorje Institute and Khampo Gangra Drubgyudling meditation centre. At the Dharmacakra Centre, also in Calgary, members hold meetings to meditate and to study the 5 traditional subjects: Prajnaparamita scriptures, Abhidharma texts, Madhyamaka texts, logic and disciplinary codes. At the Gaden Chöling in Toronto, fd 1980, members learn Gelugpa meditation practices, Tibetan language and Madhyamaka philosophy, and occasionally take part in retreats. The Tibetan children are instructed in traditional songs, dances, music and language. Many meditation centres have been organized under the Venerable Chögyam Trungpa. His centres, easily identified by the name "Dharmadhatu," are predominantly Kagyupa in meditative practices, but members may also be introduced to the Nyingmapa tradition.

In China in the 6th century AD, Zen became a separate school of Buddhism when Bodhidharma stressed that Buddhist life should emphasize meditation. Zen Buddhism in N America is usually associated with Japanese culture. However, the Zen Lotus Society, a "lay monastery," was incorporated in 1980 under Samu Sunim, a Korean Zen monk, who came to Montréal in 1968 and moved to Toronto in 1970. Special days observed are Buddha's enlightenment, lunar new-year celebration, *kido* (chanting scriptures for a week), all in Jan; spring equinox; Buddha's birthday; and ancestral day and autumn equinox in Sept. In spring and autumn, captive animals are taken to the countryside and, after a special ceremony, set free to symbolize the intention "not to kill but to cherish all living beings."

Soto Zen was transmitted to Japan from China in the 13th century. The Edmonton Buddhist Priory, inc June 1979, has close spiritual bonds with the Soto Zen Church of Japan. A priory of the Order of Buddhist Contemplatives (OBC), established by and for Western followers of Soto Zen, is a Western expression of Zen practice based on the teachings of Roshi Jiyu-Kennett, founder and spiritual director of Shasta Abbey at Mt Shasta, Calif.

Basically a Pure Land Buddhist group, the Universal Buddhist Church, est 1968 in Vancouver, comprises an all-Chinese congregation which practises a Buddhism having Pure Land, Zen and Yogacara flavours with strong Confucian and Taoistic tendencies. Among other interests, this group studies meditation and parapsychology.

The highly organized and progressive Reiyukai (Spiritual Friendship Society) was founded in Japan by Kakutara Kubo (1892-1944). Within 60 years this lay association has established offices throughout the world. The Reiyukai encourages individuals to seek and develop their inner character through *senzo-kuyo* (unselfishly caring for ancestors) and *michibiki* (sharing the personal experience with others unfamiliar with the Reiyukai teaching). The society's office in Canada is The Reiyukai Society of BC, Vancouver.

The Soka Kyoiku Gakkai (Value-Creation Education Society), which became the Soka Gakkai in 1946, was formed to promote peace among mankind by bringing happiness and harmony to individuals. Members of this lay organization propagate by means of *shakubuku* ("break and subdue") the teaching that all individuals are already Buddhas. The method is derived from Nichiren (1222-82), founder of the Nichiren sect of Japanese Buddhism. Nichiren Sho-shu of Canada (NSC) was established in Toronto in 1961; in 1983 there were about 1200 members.

During WWII the removal from BC and the INTERNMENT of people of Japanese ancestry almost eradicated Japanese Buddhism from Canada. Although adherents had likely resided in BC as early as 1889 when the first Japanese consulate was established, the first recorded assembly of Japanese Buddhism in Canada took place in Vancouver in 1904, when 14 Buddhists met to request a minister from the Honpa Honganji Temple in Kyoto, Japan (mother temple of the Jodo Shinshu sect). In 1905 the first resident minister, Rev Senju Sasaki of the Vancouver Nihon Bukkyo-kai (Japanese Buddhist Association), began preaching, and the Nihon Bukkyo-kai was incorporated in 1909 with about 650 members. By 1926 the mother temple in Kyoto had sent 7 ministers to the Vancouver area. By 1941, 11 ministers were serving 16 temples in BC. Administration for the period 1904-32 was from San Francisco, but in 1932 the Canadian body requested independence, and until the evacuation of 1941 the churches were governed by a ministerial superintendent. The lifting of the WAR MEASURES ACT in 1949 restored Japanese freedom of movement throughout Canada; some Japanese Buddhists returned to BC and others settled elsewhere.

A national conference of Japanese Buddhists was held in 1955 in Toronto, and from that meeting arose the Buddhist Churches of Canada (BCC). BCC churches follow the interpretation of the Buddha-dharma according to Shinran (1173-1262), the founder of Jodo Shinshu Buddhism, who promoted the principle of dependent co-arising as the basis for individual salvation. Shinran attempted to understand the *dharma* in view of his own existence and thus derived the *Nembutsu* (recitation of *Namu Amida Butsu*) teaching, which he emphasized as an expression of gratitude and joy in realizing the interrelated nature of human existence. At the conference that created the BCC the question of a national headquarters was an important issue, but by 1983 that idea had not materialized. In 1956, 6 ministers were serving 18 congregations comprising 3500 members; in 1983 a bishop presided over 11 ministers administering 18 congregations comprising 3110 active members, most of them in the Vancouver and Toronto areas and southern Alberta. In 1975 the BCC adopted English and parliamentary procedure for meetings so that younger delegates, not proficient in Japanese, could attend national meetings.

Other Buddhist groups include the International Buddhist Foundation, formed in 1982 to encourage scholarly research in studies related to Buddhism. The Toronto Buddhist Federation fd 1982, resulted from an earlier gathering of Buddhists in Toronto that was preparing to attend a peace conference. Membership, limited to registered Buddhist charitable organizations, includes Buddhists from Burma, Cambodia, Canada, China, India, Japan, Korea, Laos, Sri Lanka Thailand, Tibet, the US and Vietnam.

LESLIE S. KAWAMURA

Reading: Government of India, *2500 Years of Buddhism* (1956); Leslie S. Kawamura, *Golden Zephyr* (1975) Emma McCloy Layman, *Buddhism in America* (1976) K.W. Morgan, *The Path of the Buddha* (1956); Walpola Rahula, *What the Buddha Taught*, 2nd ed (1974); R.H Robinson and W.L. Johnson, *The Buddhist Religion* (1982). The Buddhist Library in Oshawa, Ont, was established in 1979 to provide the public with information on Buddhist philosophy.

Budgetary Process is designed, at all levels of government, to ensure that there is control, accountability and planning. In theory, the preparation by the executive (usually annually) of a budget for presentation to and approval by the legislature makes possible the exercise of popular control over spending. The budget statement must include all the annual revenues and expenditures. As a planning instrument, the budget, again in theory, allows a government to analyse the revenue and expenditure implications of its current and proposed programs and the financial interrelationships among them. Federally, the budgetary process also serves to stabilize the economy.

In the Canadian government there are really 2 budgets (revenue and expenditure) and 2 budgetary processes. The revenue budgetary process culminates with the presentation of the budget speech to Parliament by the minister of finance. In it and in accompanying documentation, the minister reviews the current and projected state of the economy and the government's financial situation, and announces any specific changes in tax rates and tax structures. Following the budget debate, the House of Commons votes to accept or reject the budget. This vote is a matter of confidence. If the revenue budget is rejected by the Commons the government resigns and an election may be called, which happened with the MINORITY GOVERNMENT budgets of May 1974 and Dec 1979.

Considering the crucial importance to the ruling government of a budget speech, the process of budgetary preparation is rather odd. Traditionally, the revenue budget is prepared in strict secrecy by the minister of finance and a relatively small group of his officials. With the possible exception of the prime minister, the rest of Cabinet is seldom informed of its contents until just before the budget speech. The ostensible reason for this secrecy and for the lack of consultation is that prior knowledge of a budget's contents might enable some individuals to profit unfairly at the expense of others. However, in recent years several ministers of finance have acknowledged the desirability of pre-budget consultations and have considered easing the secrecy surrounding the budget's preparation. The preparation of the expenditure budget is much less secret, at least within the government. Tabled in the House each Feb for the fiscal year beginning the following Apr, it is officially called the Estimates, and unofficially the Blue Book. General direction and priority setting in the budget are prepared by the CENTRAL AGENCIES who then negotiate adjustments, reconcile budget submissions of individual departments and prepare the total expenditure budget for submission to Parliament by the president of the Treasury Board.

Prior to 1971 Parliament was asked to approve everything from salaries to supplies to old-age pensions to travel expenses for public servants. The most important determinant of expenditures on most items in one year was the levels of spending on those items in the previous year. The prevailing view among those who participated in or studied the budgetary process was that the expenditure budget did not enable Parliament to exercise meaningful control or allow the Cabinet to plan effectively. In many cases members of Parliament could not see any links between the planned spending of a particular department and the services the department provided. In addition, information was provided only for the fiscal year under consideration, so MPs were unable to gauge the potential expenditure implications of a budget item for subsequent years. The same factors made it difficult for the government and its officials to relate its policy and program planning to its expenditures. It had no satisfactory way of determining the impact on spending of new programs under consideration. The reverse was also true; problems were exacerbated by the inevitable interdependencies among departments, because the spending of one department could reinforce, duplicate or cancel that of another.

Significant reform was attempted in the early 1970s by PM Pierre TRUDEAU's government, which adopted a "scientific" or "rational" budgeting and decision-making process in the form of a Planning-Programming-Budgeting System (PPBS). As its name implies, PPBS was intended to integrate the policy-planning and budgetary processes. Rather than focusing on inputs or objects of expenditure, PPBS focused on outputs, the ultimate effects of government activities on Canadians. Departmental activities were classified into programs and subprograms. A program was defined in relation to a particular aspect of special welfare, eg, health, justice, safety or national security, and all activities with an impact on that area were to be part of that program. In practice, the classification of activities into programs was never clear-cut. Theoretically, under the PPBS system, the Cabinet and the relevant central agencies (principally the PRIVY COUNCIL OFFICE) were to plan and decide priorities as programs. Departments were to submit budget requests within the same framework and to conduct analyses showing how their activities contributed to the objectives of the various programs. Unsatisfactory activities could be altered or eliminated and interrelationships among departments' activities would be taken into account explicitly.

In operation, PPBS never fulfilled its promise, largely because the analysis, integral to the system, required massive quantities of data, including not only financial statistics, which were usually obtainable, but less readily available reliable information on program operations and effects. In many cases the basic social science and other knowledge necessary to evaluate the impact of programs does not exist, eg, it is very difficult to gauge, even conceptually, how expenditures for drug testing, a public medical-care system, the promotion of better nutrition, or health-related education actually affect the population's health, even if a level of health could be measured. PPBS ignored the political realities of the budgetary process. A budget represents a compromise among competing interests and objectives both inside and outside government. Whether more money is spent on national defence or on social programs is fundamentally a question of social values and requires a political decision. Once these decisions are made, it is extremely costly and disruptive to fight all the bureaucratic and political battles anew each year. That is why, traditionally, budgetary processes have concentrated attention on the margins; except in exceptional circumstances, the bulk of government expenditure remains basically undisturbed and discussion centres on the allocation of new or incremental spending. PPBS, if it had worked as planned, would have involved negotiating the entire budget every year. PPBS did, however, result in some modest improvements in the budgetary process. Analysis of the impacts of programs and activities is now commonplace. The format of the Blue Book presented to Parliament, while far from perfect, is more useful to MPs and fosters more informed debate.

A more recent reform in the federal budgetary process was instituted in 1979 by the Conservatives under PM Joe CLARK and was continued by the Liberal government elected in 1980. Known as PEMS, Policy and Expenditure Management System, its purpose is the integration of priority-setting and budgeting (as was the case with PPBS), the increase of ministerial control over policy and planning, and the establishment of an adequate schedule in the planning and budgetary processes. To operate PEMS the Cabinet is divided into 6 committees: 2 central committees (Priorities and Planning, and Treasury Board) and 4 policy committees (Economic Development, Social Development, Foreign and Defence Policy, and Government Operations). The Priorities and Planning Committee, chaired by the prime minister, establishes the general policy directions for the government. It approves the fiscal plan prepared by the Department of Finance. The fiscal plan reviews the existing and projected state of the economy and the revenue and expenditure implications of various policy alternatives, and decides the total spending limit of the government for the upcoming and subsequent fiscal years. The fiscal plan is the chief link between the revenue and expenditure budgetary processes (*see* FISCAL POLICY).

All government spending is divided into a number of policy sector resource "envelopes," or sectoral budgets, which are managed by the Priorities and Planning Committee and the 4 policy committees. In setting the fiscal plan, the Priorities and Planning Committee determines how much of the government's total spending will be allocated to each of the resource envelopes. Each policy committee develops plans for its policy sector within the general policy goals established by the government, guides the departments reporting to it in the preparation of their plans and budgets, and manages the envelope(s) for which it is responsible. Only in exceptional circumstances can the total allocation of a sectoral resource envelope be exceeded; if ministers want to increase spending on one program, they may have to pay for it by decreasing spending on other programs in the same envelope. PEMS is meant to strengthen the decision-making power of the elected Cabinet ministers with whom, according to the principles of responsible government, such power should reside. All of the planning and budgeting in PEMS is conducted in 5-year plans which include the current year, the upcoming year for which the expenditure budget is being prepared, and the following 3 years. ALLAN M. MASLOVE

Buffalo, *see* BISON.

Buffalo Child Long Lance, writer, actor, impostor (b Sylvester Long at Winston-Salem, NC 1 Dec 1890; d at Arcadia, Calif 20 Mar 1932). Of mixed Indian and white (and possibly black) ancestry, he was able to escape the segregated southern US because he looked "Indian." Presenting himself as a Cherokee he gained entry to the famous Carlisle Indian School in Pennsylvania. As "Sylvester Long Lance" he fought in the Canadian Army in WWI and then settled in Calgary. In the early 1920s he worked for several western Canadian newspapers. Adopted by the BLOOD as Buffalo Child in 1922, he began a free-lance writing career as Chief Buffalo Child Long Lance. In 1928 he published his fictitious "autobiography," *Long Lance*, which won acclaim as a Blackfoot reminiscence of growing up in the last days of freedom on the plains. In 1930 he starred in *The Silent Enemy*, a feature film about northern Canadian Indians before the Europeans. His fortunes turned as rumours of his true origins began circulating and early in 1932 he took his own life. DONALD B. SMITH

Reading: Donald B. Smith, *Long Lance: The True Story of an Impostor* (1982).

Buffalo Hunt, the means by which the primary food resource of the Plains Indians and MÉTIS was harvested. In addition to approaching the BISON herd stealthily, and occasionally using subterfuges such as cloaking themselves in prairie wolf skin or bawling like calves, hunters co-operated in funnelling the herd towards a

A Buffalo Rift (1867), by A.J. Miller, illustrates a method of buffalo hunting used by the Blood, Peigan, Cree and Sarcee (*courtesy Public Archives of Canada/C-403*).

cliff (buffalo jump) or a strongly built corral (pound), permitting a large kill. Deep snows or marshy ground enabled hunters to close with their floundering quarry. With the introduction of the horse, about 1730, the charge and the surround became additional hunting methods. The hunt was the basis of the Plains Indian way of life, since it provided the essentials: the meat was food, sinew and bone became tools, and hides became clothing and shelter. The hunt and its products gave rise to and supported complex social, political and cultural institutions. The hunt was also essential to the FUR TRADE. Provisioning posts along the Red, Assiniboine and N Saskatchewan rivers acquired dried meat and PEMMICAN, and fresh buffalo meat in season. After the mid-19th century, hides were used to make industrial drive belts.

The increase in the Indian and Métis population, the demands of industrial centres and the incompatibility of free-running herds with agricultural settlement have been cited as explanations of the extinction of the bison. The use of the horse may also have been critical: pedestrian hunters harvested buffalo with little discrimination as to sex and age, but the horse hunters could focus on the favoured heifer or young cow. By the early 1880s the prairie bison were virtually extinct; a few wood bison survived in northern forests. JOHN E. FOSTER

Buffaloberry, *see* BERRIES, WILD.

Bug, name properly applied to a member of the Hemiptera, the most diverse order of INSECTS having incomplete metamorphosis. Over 55 000 species have been described worldwide; about 3080 species (of a probable 4230), in Canada. Bugs are most closely related to THRIPS and probably shared a common ancestor in the Carboniferous era (over 300 million years ago). They range from 0.1-9 cm long and are classified into 2 suborders: Heteroptera (true bugs) and Homoptera (including cicadas, leafhoppers, APHIDS, SCALE INSECTS and mealy bugs). All have piercing and sucking mouthparts. Most bugs feed on vascular tissues of higher PLANTS but many true bugs eat other insects or take blood from vertebrates, including humans (eg, bedbug, *Cimex lectularius*). Bugs are widely distributed across forested and prairie regions of Canada but few species occur in the Arctic or Subarctic. In a given area, species diversity is usually related to host plant diversity, since most bugs are host specific. Although bugs are generally terrestrial, some (eg, back swimmers and water boatmen) are aquatic. Most semiaquatic bugs (eg, pond skaters and saldids) prey on other small ARTHROPODS.

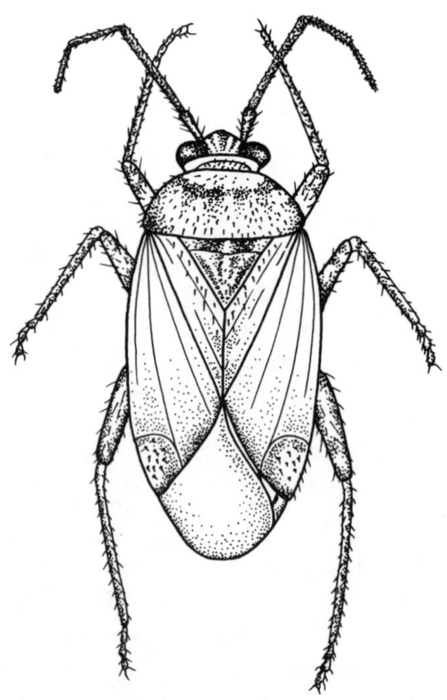

Lygus bug (*Lygus lineolaris*). These insects feed by sucking plant sap and may cause extensive damage to alfalfa and other forage crops (*artwork by Shirley Stacey*).

Most adult bugs have 2 pairs of wings, 2 large, compound eyes, and 2 or 3 dorsal ocelli (simple eyes), but a few are wingless or vary in wing length and have their eyes reduced accordingly. Forewings in heteropterans are hemielytra: the basal half opaque and stiff, the apex transparent. These are folded flat over the abdomen when not in use. Forewings in homopterans are either transparent or opaque throughout and are folded, rooflike, over the body. True bugs have 5 juvenile stages, homopterans 3-7. Whiteflies and male scale insects have 1 or 2 nonfeeding, "pupal" stages. Female scale insects reproduce while still juvenile. Males lack functional mouthparts and are short-lived. Most bugs have separate sexes and deposit eggs, but some (eg, aphids) are parthenogenetic (eggs develop without fertilization), and viviparous (deposit live young).

In Canada, 112 species of Hemiptera, including plant bugs, aphids, leafhoppers, psyllids, and scale insects, have been recorded as crop pests (*see* CROP PROTECTION). Their feeding can kill or deform seedlings, reduce plant vigour, and lower seed set by damaging flowers or seeds. Many aphids and leafhoppers transmit plant diseases. Large populations of aphids and scale insects excrete "honey dew" onto leaves of host plants, providing a substrate for growth of photosynthesis-inhibiting "sooty mold." Many predatory heteropterans are beneficial to man because they feed on INSECT PESTS. B.S. HEMING

Reading: J.A. Slater and R.M. Baranowski, *How to Know the True Bugs* (1978).

Bugnet, Georges-Charles-Jules, pseudonym Henri Doutremont, editor, writer, botanist (b at Chalon-sur-Saône, France 23 Feb 1879; d at St Albert, Alta 11 Jan 1981). A homesteader in Alberta from 1905, Bugnet rarely found favour in the eyes of Québec literary critics. Nevertheless, the range of his writing, as well as its religious intensity, places it among the most important work in French published in Canada in the 1930s. His work in the hybridization of roses earned him the Chevalier de l'ordre des palmes académiques in 1970. Bugnet was founder and president of the Association canadienne-française de l'Alberta, as well as editor of *Union*. This interest in French pioneers in Alberta is reflected primarily in his celebrated novel, *La Forêt* (1935; tr *The Forest*, 1976). His knowledge of, and sympathy for, the Métis is developed in *Nipsya* (1924). After Gabrielle ROY, Bugnet may be considered the major francophone writer of the Canadian West. E.D. BLODGETT

Buhay, Rebecca, "Becky," political activist, educator (b at London, Eng 11 Feb 1896; d at Toronto 16 Dec 1953). She emigrated to Canada in 1912 and became active in Montréal socialist causes during WWI. After studying at the radical Rand School of Social Sciences, New York, she became an organizer in Montréal garment unions. She joined the Workers (Communist) Party of Canada and in 1922 was elected to its national executive. In the 1920s and 1930s she toured and lectured, taught at party schools and took a women's delegation to Russia. During WWII she worked to free interned communists. After the war she resumed her educational work, stressing women's role in the struggle for socialism. She was revered among colleagues for her abilty to communicate radical ideas and her loyalty to political friends and the communist movement. JOAN SANGSTER

Buies, Arthur, bap Joseph-Marie-Arthur, journalist, chronicler, essayist (b at Montréal 24 Jan 1840; d at Québec City 29 Jan 1901). A lucid witness to and passionate participant in the late 19th-century ideological battles, Buies left behind a body of exceptional works which are not well known. Buies was educated in Québec and Paris. In 1860 he enrolled in Garibaldi's army and rashly sang its praises upon returning to Montréal in 1862. Buies was the most radical member of the INSTITUT CANADIEN's second generation. He never involved himself in active politics, but participated in all the ROUGES' intellectual crusades. He handled words with ease and vigour. His *Lettres sur le Canada* (1864, 1867) raised crucial social issues and denounced obscurantism, prejudice, laziness and fanaticism. After another stay in Paris, Buies founded in 1868 *La Lanterne canadienne*, an anticlerical, nationalist and democratic paper which was condemned by Québec's bishops. Gradually he moved beyond polemical writing to a more relaxed, refined and subtle prose style — his 3 collections of *Chroniques* being excellent 19th-century literary works. Humour came to temper his irony and his ideas turned into impressions. After meeting with Antoine LABELLE in 1879, Buies became an explorer and geographer and described the regions of Québec then being opened up to settlement. LAURENT MAILHOT

Building Codes and Regulations Under Canadian law the regulation of buildings is a provincial responsibility and is carried out through various laws, Acts, codes and regulations, often administered at the municipal level. Provincial legislation empowers government agencies or departments to regulate different aspects of buildings, depending on the objectives of the specific law or Act. Such legislation permits the establishment of detailed regulations by which the objectives of the law are to be met, or may refer to other documents. For example, laws protecting the safety and health of building occupants usually refer to building codes for additional requirements. Building codes generally apply to new construction and have traditionally been concerned with fire safety, structural sufficiency and health of the building's occupants. More recent codes have dealt with accessibility for handicapped persons and with energy conservation.

Zoning and planning legislation plays an important role in regulating buildings by restricting the type, size, spacing, setback and use of buildings and by controlling general land use in a community. Its purpose is to maintain certain neighbourhood characteristics and to allow for a community's orderly development. Such legislation, enacted at a local or regional level, is tailored to the aims and objectives of the area (*see* URBAN AND REGIONAL PLANNING).

In addition to building codes, there are various miscellaneous Acts aimed at specific building types or at specific services within buildings. Liquor-licensing, hotel, theatre and factory Acts, for example, may affect construction or use of specific types of buildings. Regulations under such Acts may parallel, or even conflict with, building-code provisions, although the trend is to rely on building codes where practicable. Plumbing, electrical, elevator and boiler and pressure-vessel codes are examples of STANDARDS aimed at particular building services and may be enacted separately or combined in a single Act.

Fire-prevention bylaws or fire codes regulate the ongoing safety of existing buildings. They regulate maintenance provisions for the purpose of fire safety, control the handling and storage of flammable materials in buildings, control furnishings (where appropriate) and regulate hazards related to certain industrial processes. The fire-prevention bylaws or fire codes take over where building codes stop. While building codes are generally administered by building departments, fire-prevention bylaws and fire codes are administered by the fire services.

History

Although the regulation of buildings now falls within provincial jurisdiction, past governments delegated this responsibility to municipalities, with the result that building regulations diversified. Since municipal resources varied widely, the quality and efficiency of building regulations also varied; before WWII building regulation was nonexistent in many areas.

To promote uniformity, a model set of requirements, the National Building Code of Canada, was published in 1941 under the auspices of the NATIONAL RESEARCH COUNCIL. By 1980, 8 editions had been published. From its inception, the National Building Code had a major unifying influence on building-code requirements, although it had no legal status unless adopted by an authority having jurisdiction. By the 1970 edition, an estimated 75-85% of construction in Canada was built in conformity with the National Building Code or an adaptation of it. Provincial authorities took an increased interest in building regulations and began reversing the process of delegating the development of code requirements to municipalities. Mandatory provincial codes were introduced: by 1980, BC, Alta, Man, Ont and Qué had adopted provincial codes based on the National Building Code; Sask and NB did not have provincial codes, but their legislation required that a municipality adopting a building code use the National Building Code. In those provinces without provincial codes, the National Building Code was in general use by the larger municipalities. Local authorities may amend or revise the requirements of the National Building Code to meet local conditions.

The National Fire Code has a shorter historical development. First published in 1963 by the NRC (4th edition, 1980) its general acceptance has lagged behind that of the National Building Code and provincial acceptance has been fairly recent. It has been adopted or has formed the basis of fire prevention requirements in BC, Alberta and Manitoba; is referred to in the legislation in several other provinces; and has been adopted by many municipalities where a provincial code does not exist.

Development

The associate committees responsible for providing the National Building Code and the National Fire Code are appointed by NRC. A number of technical committees operate under their direction with the assistance of the NRC to produce these documents. The Associate Committee, National Building Code, also produces the Canadian Plumbing Code, Canadian Farm Building Code, Residential Standards, and Measures for Energy Conservation in New Buildings. With the exception of Residential Standards, all are written as model legislation for adoption by authorities having jurisdiction. Residential Standards, developed for buildings constructed under the National Housing Act, is based on the National Building Code and contains additional requirements for mortgage purposes.

A number of standards-writing agencies produce standards on various aspects of building, which are referred to in building codes or in other regulations. The National Building Code, for example, refers to 182 such standards, including standards for construction materials, design, installation, equipment and testing. Provincial Acts also refer to such standards or base their regulations on them. For example, the Canadian Electrical Code, produced by the Canadian Standards Association, forms the basis for electrical requirements in every province. Other standards-writing bodies in Canada include the Canadian General Standards Board, Underwriters Laboratories of Canada and the Canadian Gas Association. All such bodies are privately financed, except the Canadian General Standards Board, which operates out of the Dept of Supply and Services. The standards produced by these bodies play a major role, along with building codes, in regulating the construction of buildings in Canada. *See* ARCHITECTURE; CONSTRUCTION INDUSTRIES; HOUSING. A.T. HANSEN

Bujold, Geneviève, actress (b at Montréal 1 July 1942). Since 1965, when she appeared in Alain Resnais's *La Guerre est finie*, Bujold has had an international career, starring in *Le Roi de coeur* (1966), *Anne of a Thousand Days* (1969), *Earthquake* (1974) and *Murder by Decree* (1978). Her first important Canadian role was in Michel BRAULT's *Entre la mer et l'eau douce* (1967) and she starred in *Kamouraska* (1973) by Claude JUTRA. However, it is on 3 of Paul ALMOND's films — *Isabel* (1968), *Act of the Heart* (1970) and *Journey* (1972) — that her personality and presence are imprinted. Her most remarkable successes have been in roles in which her vulnerable feminine appearance is contrasted with powerful passions and impulses. PIERRE VÉRONNEAU

Bulau, Horst, ski jumper (b at Ottawa 14 Aug 1962). Trained at Camp Fortune, he began skiing at 2½, competing in alpine events at 5. Entering national ski-jumping competition for the first time in Thunder Bay, Ont, in 1975, he won handily, demonstrating outstanding potential with his explosive takeoff. In 1979 he won the World Junior Ski Jumping Championship, the first world nordic title for a Canadian. Since that time, he has 13 World Cup wins in 4 years and has been ranked 2nd or 3rd in the world for 3 of those years. Although he became famous in Europe long before his achievements were fully appreciated in Canada, his successes have won him a number of sports excellence awards and attracted a great deal of Canadian attention to the sport. MURRAY SHAW

Bull, Gerald Vincent, scientist (b at North Bay, Ont 9 Mar 1928). Orphaned at 3, Bull displayed scientific brilliance early and earned a PhD in aerodynamics at only 23. He worked for the Defence Research Board at Valcartier, near Québec C, 1950-64, specializing in the development of guns to shoot instrument packages into the upper atmosphere and beyond. (In the early years of space technology, rockets were both unreliable and too expensive for most countries to develop.) Bull's High Altitude Research Project (HARP) was transferred from the DRB to McGill in 1964. Bull installed a giant 16-inch cannon (made of US naval guns fastened end to end) on Barbados and developed production workshops near Atwater, Qué. When Canadian and US government support ended, he formed the Space Research Corp in 1971 to continue HARP, funded by offering scientific services to countries unable to afford national space programs and by selling the products of SRC's special workshops. These products extended to shells for 155 mm artillery. (Bull had earlier designed a cannon shell shape that offered significant advantages over conventional designs.) In 1980 Bull was convicted in US courts of exporting munitions to the Republic of Africa, contrary to the UN arms embargo, and was sentenced to 6 months in prison, SRC was declared bankrupt and liquidated. DONALD J.C. PHILLIPSON

Buller, Annie, née Guralnick, political activist, union organizer (b in Ukraine 9 Dec 1895; d at Toronto 19 Jan 1973). Her Jewish parents emigrated to Montréal when she was a child. During WWI she became active in the Socialist Youth Movement, and after studying Marxism at the Rand School of Social Sciences, New York, established the Montréal Labour College with Becky BUHAY and Bella GAULD. She joined the COMMUNIST PARTY OF CANADA in 1922 and devoted herself to full-time party organizing and managing party publications. In the early 1920s she went to Cape Breton to organize mine workers. She organized for the communist-led Industrial Needle Trades Workers Union in Toronto and Winnipeg in the early 1930s. Because of her organizing work among coal miners in Estevan, Sask, in 1931, Buller was jailed after a riot in which 3 strikers were killed by the RCMP. While working as a business manager of the *Western Clarion* in 1939, she was again arrested and was interned until 1942. After the war she was business manager of the *Tribune* and *National Affairs* and participated in a consumer campaign to roll back prices. She retired from full-time party work in the late 1950s, but remained politically active until her death. JOAN SANGSTER

Bunkhouse Men During the 19th century massive capital projects gave rise to a demand for large labour pools. Canadian IMMIGRATION policy was developed to import manpower. Irish workers were brought in to build the canals and railways of central Canada, Chinese to help build the CPR. At the same time, a pattern of bush work grew up among French Canadians servicing the burgeoning TIMBER TRADE of the Maritimes and central Canada. The term "bunkhouse men" is typically applied to some 50 000 workers who constituted a labour pool for the booming Canadian economy in the first 3 decades of the 20th century. They lived in frontier work camps and provided unskilled labour in logging, harvesting, mining and construction. Mainly single and "foreign," they experienced brutal exploitation. Partly as a result of this, but primarily because jobs moved around, bunkhouse men were highly mobile, tramping within regions and sometimes across the country to find work. They were also often at the forefront of labour radicalism. *See* COMPANY TOWN; REVOLUTIONARY INDUSTRIAL UNIONISM; INDUSTRIAL WORKERS OF THE WORLD. A. ROSS MCCORMACK

Bunting, common name for several, not particularly closely related members of the SPARROW family (Emberizidae). Four species nest in Canada: indigo bunting (*Passerina cyanea*) in open deciduous forests and parkland from SW Québec, across southern Ontario to southern Manitoba; its western counterpart, lazuli bunting (*P. amoena*), in brush country from southern BC to southern Saskatchewan; lark bunting (*Calamospiza melanocorys*) locally in open grassy prairies of southern Saskatchewan, Alberta and SW Manitoba; and snow bunting (*Plectrophenax nivalis*), a circumpolar species, on tundra, wintering in open country in southern Canada and northern US. Male indigo buntings are blue all over; male lazuli buntings have blue heads and backs, 2 white wing bars and cinnamon breasts shading to white on the abdomen. Female indigo and lazuli buntings have quite similar, dull brown plumage. The female lazuli bunting has 2 wing bars. Both species are around 14 cm long. Hybrids have been discovered where ranges overlap. Both species are migratory, wintering in Mexico and Central America. Male lark buntings are all black with large, white wing patches; females are brown with dark streaks and light wing patches. Their numbers and breeding-range boundaries fluctuate considerably from year to year. Males often sing in flight, holding their wings at an angle above the body and circling slowly back to earth while uttering a long and varied song of whistles, trills and buzzes. Snow bunting males are immaculate in breeding plumage; white with black back and black patches on wings and tail. Females, and males outside the breeding season, are slightly duller. In Canada, snow buntings are among the most northerly of nesting birds, breeding up to northern Ellesmere I. Flocks of snow buntings are a familiar sight in most of southern Canada in winter, usually over weedy fields and stubble. RICHARD W. KNAPTON

Bunyan, Paul, mythical giant lumberjack. Tales of how Bunyan and his blue ox Babe created the Great Lks, the Rocky Mountains and the tides of the Bay of Fundy are related in E. Shepard, *Paul Bunyan* (1924) and J.D. Robins, *Logging with Paul Bunyan* (1957). The Bunyan mythology first appeared in print in columns of the Detroit *News Tribune* (1910), but a Canadian origin has often been claimed. It may have originated in the French Canadian folk tradition of 'Tit-Jean or Jean Bonhomme, or possibly from the lumber woods of NB and Maine, where the legendary feats of the hero GLOOSCAP were well known. JAMES MARSH

Buoy, floating object, usually anchored but occasionally allowed to float freely or to be dragged by sea anchor. Buoys are widely used as navigation markers to indicate channels, the presence of shoals, etc. In OCEANOGRAPHY buoys function to protect or mark the position of equipment and as platforms to hold instruments. Instrumented buoys range in size from 10 m diameter, discus-shaped hulls moored to the seafloor and weighing many tens of tonnes to small, 10 cm diameter, free-drifting cylinders weighing a few kilograms. Large hulls, with mast heights of up to 10 m, are used at open-ocean sites such as continental shelves; smaller hulls, of discus, boat, spar or spherical shape, are suitable nearshore or in lakes. Sensors on buoys monitor environmental parameters, such as air and water temperature, wind, ocean currents and ocean wave motion. Information can be recorded on board or telemetered to a shore station, directly or through a geostationary SATELLITE. Data from buoys support research, forecasting, monitoring and emergency measures. For example, buoy networks on the East and West coasts monitor sea state to provide wave-climate information. Canada has developed open-ocean "drifters" which use a polar orbiting satellite for tracking and communication. They have circumnavigated Antarctica, drifted across the Pacific and followed the circulation pattern around and across the N Atlantic. Similar drifters track spilled oil, SEA ICE and ICEBERGS. Nearshore drifters can be tracked using a VHF beacon. J.A. ELLIOTT

Burbidge, George Wheelock, lawyer, jurist, author (b at Cornwallis, NS 6 Feb 1847; d at Ottawa 18 Feb 1908). Hard working and dedicated, Burbidge was a complex individual who typified the 19th-century legalist in being fair and a staunch supporter of the rule of law, but uncompromising and elitist. As deputy minister of justice 1882-87, he blocked the 1884 plan of Sir Matthew BEGBIE, chief justice of BC, to bar Canadian-born Chinese from inheriting or purchasing land. In 1885 he was the federal government's chief strategist in the trial of Louis RIEL. His *Digest of the Criminal Law of Canada* successfully collected Canadian penal law in one volume and was superseded only by the Criminal Code of 1892, of which Burbidge was coauthor with Robert SEDGEWICK. When elevated to the bench in 1887 as the first justice of the Exchequer Court, he organized that tribunal and developed much of the procedure it follows today. D.H. BROWN

Bureaucracy may be defined as the system of authority, persons, offices and methods that government uses to achieve its objectives. This definition avoids the derogatory use of the word as synonymous with red tape, ie, with delay, inefficiency and inflexibility. It does, however, reflect the common association of bureaucracy with the growth of government activities and expenditures and with the consequent increase in the number and power of government or public sector employees, also called bureaucrats, public servants or civil servants (*see* PUBLIC SERVICE).

The activities of Canadian governments have expanded rapidly since 1945. Governments are primarily involved in providing services and in regulation. To support these services and regulatory functions they conduct research on matters ranging from new ways of sorting mail to the inspection of food and drugs. From Confederation to WWII growth in the level of government expenditures and the number of government employees was relatively small, but the increasing scale and complexity of government activities (with newer responsibilities such as consumer and environmental protection, medicare and atomic energy research) has resulted in an enormous growth in public expenditures and public sector employment. As a proportion of the Gross National Product (GNP), the total combined expenditures of the federal, provincial and municipal levels of Canadian government increased from 32.5% in 1961 to 45% in 1982. The federal percentage of total expenditures has decreased steadily since 1945, but expenditures by provincial and municipal governments have increased, mainly because of the increased demand for services within the provinces' constitutional jurisdiction, notably in the fields of health, education and transportation.

By 1981 the number of public-sector employees (ie, employees in regular departments at all 3 levels of government, the armed forces, persons employed in educational institutions and hospitals, and employees of government enterprises) had reached 2.5 million or 21.6% of the employed labour force. Since 1945, the number of employees, like the level of expenditures, has increased more rapidly in the provincial governments than in the federal and local governments.

Organization of the Bureaucracy To carry out their responsibilities, governments use a variety of administrative organizations, the 2 major forms being departments and nondepartmental bodies. The federal government has about 30 departments, ranging from traditional departments, eg, Agriculture, External Affairs and Justice, to newer ones, eg, Consumer and Corporate Affairs, and Environment. The federal government also has several hundred nondepartmental bodies known as Crown agencies, including CROWN CORPORATIONS and various boards, commissions and tribunals, and several important administrative units generally described as CENTRAL AGENCIES which are responsible for co-ordinating the activities of departments and, to a lesser extent, nondepartmental bodies. Similar administrative organizations exist in the provincial and local governments.

Power of the Bureaucracy Because government activities are too large and too complex for all powers to be exercised by elected representatives and the courts, much discretionary power is granted to public employees. Senior bureaucrats are often responsible for the initiation of policy proposals (to which end they frequently work closely with the representatives of powerful PRESSURE GROUPS) and for the implementation of legislation. The subject matter of many laws is very technical, eg, atomic energy, and very complicated, eg, tax reform. Moreover, the implications of many laws are widespread and their full consequences are unpredictable. Elected representatives are therefore obliged to pass laws written in general and sometimes vague language and to delegate to public employees the authority to interpret and enforce these laws (*see* ADMINISTRATIVE TRIBUNALS). Similarly, judges have neither the time to hear all the cases requiring interpretation of the law nor the knowled needed to understand and to interpret correct laws involving very technical matters. Parlia ment therefore delegates to public employees th power to pass regulations that have the force o law, to enforce these regulations and to penali those who do not obey them. As a result the employees now exercise powers of a legislativ and judicial nature traditionally exercised b the legislatures and the courts (*see* REGULATOR PROCESS). Public employees also have power t influence the content of laws. Since electe politicians do not have as much knowled as public employees about the subject matt or implications of the many laws propose they must rely heavily on the advice of the em ployees.

Image of the Bureaucracy The negative atti tude of many Canadians towards public em ployees has several causes. Governments, be cause of their size, their pursuit of politica objectives and their focus on service rather tha profit, tend to operate less efficiently than busi ness enterprises. Citizens who believe that the receive too few government services for thei tax dollars and that there is too much govern ment regulation often blame public employee as well as politicians. There is also a widesprea public perception that public employees some times misuse their discretionary powers. Contr and influence over public employees are exe rcised by elected politicians, judges, journalist pressure group representatives, individual citi zens, and other public employees, but publi employees will continue to exercise a large mea sure of discretionary power.

KENNETH KERNAGHA

Reading: Kenneth Kernaghan, ed, *Public Administration i Canada* (1982).

Bureaucracy and Formal Organization Th term BUREAUCRACY is traditionally associate with the administration of government and it various agencies. (The definition of the wor *bureaucratie* in the dictionary of the French Acad emy, 1789 supplement, was "power, influenc of the heads and staff of government bureaux." Bureaucracy is also basic, however, to the oper ation of private corporations, political parties unions, churches and any other large moder organization. Its association with routine, pa perwork, lengthy procedures, and a centralize and rigid hierarchy has given the term a pejora tive meaning. Technically, however, in the SO CIAL SCIENCES, the term generally refers to the de velopment of formal organizations.

Bureaucracy is first of all a form of social or ganization. The common denominator of bu reaucratization lies in the quest for a "rationa model for administration. Mass organization meet their objectives through an elaborate divi sion of labour which results in compartmental ization and diversification of duties, which i turn leads to specialized functions, ie, imple mentation, management and special expertise This multiplicity of functions clearly require the establishment of a co-ordinated structure and of regulations, administrative procedure and standards that define the responsibilities o each position and its relation to other positions Such specialization by function itself increase the need for centralized control and adminis tration, and thus the establishment of a hier archy that integrates each function in a chain o command. Authority is delegated within spe cific areas of competence and is subject to a fina authority that defines the organization's policie as a whole and monitors, or controls, the mate rial or symbolic results at a central point. Thi final authority is more political than adminis trative in nature, and is therefore not purel bureaucratic. Bureaucracy as a whole is organ ized as a pyramid, as may be seen from th sometimes very complex organization chart used to describe large modern organizations. Within this structure, emphasis is given to vertical channels rather than to horizontal channels of communication between individuals. Similarly, indirect communications are common because individuals must transmit information to the higher levels of organization through a superior. This reduction in personal contacts, which is viewed as an element of efficiency, is also the cause of communication breakdowns and "red tape."

Recruitment in bureaucratic organizations is usually conducted according to recognized rules, eg, the competition system in the PUBLIC SERVICE. While positions involving the most routine tasks are occupied by personnel with relatively few qualifications, the executive, management and specialized positions are occupied by individuals who usually have a university degree. These individuals are sometimes hired or appointed, however, not for their skills but out of political considerations, eg, as PATRONAGE for past favours. In contrast a considerable number of positions in BUSINESS MANAGEMENT are occupied by individuals who do not have a university degree, but are trained by the company. A system of hierarchically organized titles corresponding to the organization chart is used to define the status of the individuals and to project his or her probable "career path."

The modern theory of bureaucracy, which derives largely from the German sociologist Max Weber, sees it as a formal codification of the idea of rational organization and the major element in the rationalization of modern capitalism. In the bureaucracies of private firms as well as government, objectives are set by rational, systematic, standardized techniques, thereby eliminating the effects of interpersonal relationships. Bureaucratic organization thus reflects the belief that maximum efficiency can be achieved through logical planning and calculation.

Considerable doubt is cast on the validity of this belief in contemporary theory. Studies have revealed many malfunctions in bureaucratic systems, including lack of dynamism resulting from their ritualistic behaviour. Problems and conflicts tend to be resolved through the imposition of new controls and rules which, ultimately reinforce the bureaucracy (bureaucracies also tend to reproduce themselves, to divert energy into maintaining their own existence rather than fulfilling their original purpose). It is questionable as well whether the technical rationality of bureaucracy, expressed strictly as goals and means, is suitable to all types of organization. Even if it seems to apply easily to companies that espouse the fundamental logic of maximizing profit and to some routine governmental activities, this same rationality becomes inefficient and harmful when applied to government activities that cannot be reduced to pure repetition and controls. It is impossible to administer schools, hospitals, public housing and community service centres bureaucratically and without distortion because these services, which are dependent upon social needs and political decisions, cannot be determined strictly on the basis of rational abstract forecasts.

Bureaucracy cannot exist without bureaucrats; therefore the term denotes not only an organizational structure but a social group. Such a group is found in every large organization, and in the government it ranges from individuals responsible for administrative functions (eg, "paper pushers," who are traditionally assigned generally routine subordinate tasks and whose situation is rapidly changing as a result of computerization) to the "mandarins" in the senior echelons of the public service, who are often held in awe by new ministers. But the heart of any bureaucracy is the executive and middle managers, who represent the true power base.

In Western societies, bureaucracies differ in nature because of the substantial autonomy of individual institutions. Public and private bureaucracies are clearly distinct, notwithstanding their common characteristics and a degree of interpenetration that results from the movement of senior and middle managers from one sector to the other. In Canada there is significantly more movement from private to public than vice versa. Although they participate in the power system, the bureaucracies in Western countries cannot take it over entirely and become a class unto themselves as has happened in the Soviet Union, where political and economic power blend in the name of technical rationality. History has shown the importance of resisting the dynamics of bureaucratic growth and of maintaining heterogeneous bureaucracies to preserve a democratic order and social freedom.

ARNAUD SALES

Reading: K. Kernaghan, ed, *Public Administration in Canada* (1982); M. Weber, *Economy and Society*, vol 3 (1968).

Burgeo, Newfoundland, Town, pop 2504 (1981c), inc 1950, is a principal fishing and fish-processing centre on the SW coast of insular Newfoundland. The name is a corruption of Virgeo ("a thousand virgins") first applied to the Burgeo Is. The main part of the community is on 2.5 km long Grandy I, connected to the mainland by a causeway. Settled since the late 1700s, the community's only link with the rest of Newfoundland was by sea until 1979, when a road connected Burgeo to the Trans-Canada Hwy.

ROBERT D. PITT

Burgess Shale Site in YOHO NATIONAL PARK, BC, shows the beginnings of life in fossil-bearing rock formations. In 1909 Charles Doolittle Walcott, while searching for fossils, accidentally and literally stumbled upon a block of shale bearing the imprints of soft-bodied organisms. Most FOSSIL remains result from the imprint of a hard structure (a shell or a skeleton) being preserved. This site, with its INVERTEBRATE fossil remains, is unique. More than 120 species of marine invertebrates have been discovered: sponges, sea worms and tiny "sea monsters" like the 5-eyed Opabinia and the Halluciegenia with its 7 pairs of stiltlike spines and 7 tentacles. Many of these species are rare, resembling nothing else so far discovered in fossil sites. Burgess Shale has been declared a World Heritage Site.

LILLIAN STEWART

Burglary became a crime under English COMMON LAW in the Middle Ages; it was once punishable by death. Burglary is prohibited by provisions in the Canadian CRIMINAL CODE (s306-308) against "breaking and entering." If convicted, a person is liable to life imprisonment if the burglarized place is a dwelling, or 14 years if it is not. There are 3 major elements to the crime. First, there must be a breaking; someone lawfully entering a place through an open door cannot be liable. Secondly, there must be an entry into the place, an intrusion of some part of the offender's body or an instrument being used by the offender. Finally, the person must either intend to commit a serious (indictable) offence as he is making his intrusion, or actually commit such an offence once inside. Although the crime of burglary once referred specifically to intrusions at night, under present provisions of the Criminal Code this is no longer true. *See* ROBBERY.

LEE PAIKIN

Burgoyne, John, army officer (b in Eng 1722; d at London, Eng 3 Aug 1792). A distinguished cavalry officer and public figure, Burgoyne arrived in Québec in 1776 with large reinforcements, and served during the successful campaign of that year. In summer 1777, he led a force of 9000 soldiers southward along the Lk Champlain-Hudson R route with the objective of severing New England from the other colonies. After a series of costly battles, he was forced to surrender at Saratoga, NY, 17 Oct 1777, an event which led perhaps to the eventual American victory.

STUART R.J. SUTHERLAND

Burka, Petra, figure skater (b at Amsterdam, Netherlands 17 Nov 1946). While competing in the 1962 Canadian figure-skating championships at age 15, Burka became the first woman skater to complete the triple salchow jump in competition. In 1964 she won the Canadian championships and placed 3rd in the Olympics and the world championships. Burka won the 1965 Canadian, N American and world championships. She received the LOU MARSH TROPHY that year as Canada's top athlete. After a 2nd-place finish in the 1966 world championships, she turned professional and toured with an ice show until 1969.

BARBARA SCHRODT

Burka, Sylvia, speed skater, cyclist (b at Winnipeg 4 May 1954). Through hard work and determination, she overcame a visual handicap to become a world-class athlete in 2 sports. Despite losing an eye in a childhood accident, Burka was Canada's national junior SPEED-SKATING champion by age 15. Four years later, in 1973, she won the world junior championship. Ill during the 1976 Winter Olympics, her best result was a 4th in the 1500-m event. However, she recovered to win the world championship 2 weeks later. In 1977 she won the world sprint speed-skating title. Her speed-skating accomplishments also included 2 world records. She has also competed in international cycling competitions, finishing 4th in the individual pursuit event at the 1977 world championships and setting a world record while training in 1982. She is married to cyclist Jocelyn Lovell.

J. THOMAS WEST

Burke, Johnny, poet, playwright, songwriter (b at St John's 1851; d there Aug 1930). While working at a variety of jobs, Burke moonlighted as a poet, writing hundreds of broadsheet ballads about events in St John's, printing them on his own press and selling them for 2 to 5 cents a copy. He was said to have used an old-fashioned gramophone with a huge horn to attract customers. His first songbook was published in 1901. Some of his most famous songs are "Cod Liver Oil," "The Trinity Cake" and "The Kelligrews Soiree." His musical comedies include *The Battle of Foxtrap, The Topsail Geisha* and *Cotton's Patch.*

JAMES G.G. MOORE

Reading: P. Mercer, ed, *The Ballads of Johnny Burke* (1974).

Burnaby, BC, District Municipality, pop 136 494 (1981c), area 10 682 ha, inc 1892. It adjoins VANCOUVER on the W, COQUITLAM on the E and NEW WESTMINSTER on the SE. Named after Robert Burnaby, a businessman and legislator of the 1860s, it features Burnaby Mtn (365 m), Burnaby Lk, the Fraser R and Burrard Inlet. Burnaby is governed by a mayor and 8 aldermen and is a member of the Greater Vancouver Regional Dist. Originally a sparsely populated rural district — with a population of 400 in 1900 — it developed into a residential community for workers in Vancouver and New Westminster. Industrial development and construction of large wholesale and retail outlets followed, and urbanization has continued in recent years. Burnaby ranks second in the region to Vancouver in industrial diversity, employment and output. Its industries include steel fabrication, manufacturing of trucks and telecommunications equipment, lumber and shin-

gle operations, and commercial fishing and fish processing. Residential and industrial developments have almost eliminated agriculture. Its educational facilities include SIMON FRASER U, and the BC Institute of Technology (with over 300 full-time and 8000 extension students). Attractions are Heritage Village (recreating a typical 1890-1925 community), Ismaili Mosque, Barnet Marine Park, the Burnaby Art Gallery and one of the world's largest indoor skating and hockey complexes. ALAN F.J. ARTIBISE

Burns, Eedson Louis Millard, soldier, diplomat, author (b at Westmount, Qué 17 June 1897). After graduating from RMC in 1915, Burns fought on the Western Front with the Royal Canadian Engineers, 1916-18. Between the wars he attended the School of Military Engineering, Chatham, Eng, and the Staff College at Quetta, British India, and was an instructor at RMC. From 1931 to 1936 he was in charge of the Geographical Section of the General Staff, where he made a major contribution to the development of Canadian military mapping. In 1939 he was a lt-col attending the Imperial Defence College, London, Eng.

After staff appointments in England and Canada, he commanded the 4th Canadian Armoured Brigade and 2nd Canadian Infantry Division in England, and then the 5th Canadian Armoured Division and 1st Canadian Corps in Italy. He led the corps during operations in the Liri Valley (May 1944) leading to the capture of Rome, and in the highly successful attack on the Gothic Line (Aug/Sept 1944). A subtle sense of fun, well disguised beneath a dour exterior, accompanied his formidable intellect. However, he could not win the confidence of his subordinates and a "him or us" ultimatum brought about his relief in Nov 1944.

Burns retired from the army in June 1947 and began a second career as a public servant. In Aug 1955 he joined the Dept of External Affairs and was loaned to the UN, becoming commander of the UN Emergency Force in the Middle East, 1956-59 (*see* PEACEKEEPING). From 1960 to 1969 he was chief adviser to the Canadian government on DISARMAMENT conferences. He was a professor of strategic studies at Carleton 1972-75. His books include *Manpower and the Canadian Army, 1939-1945* (1956), *General Mud: Memoirs of Two World Wars* (1970), *Between Arab and Israeli* (1962), *Megamurder* (1966) and *A Seat at the Peace Table: The Struggle for Disarmament* (1972). BRERETON GREENHOUS

Burns, Patrick, meat packer, rancher (b at Oshawa, Canada W 6 July 1856; d at Calgary 24 Feb 1937). A farm boy without much formal schooling, Burns joined the vanguard of Ontario farmers moving to Manitoba after the RIEL uprising. In 1878 he walked 250 km from Winnipeg to the homestead he had selected near Minnedosa. To earn working capital, Burns began to freight goods from Winnipeg and trail neighbours' cattle to the Winnipeg market. By 1885 he was buying cattle full time and in 1886 he got his first contract to supply beef to a railway construction gang. His business grew with the railway boom and he expanded aggressively into ranching, packing and the retail meat trade. By WWI Burns was established internationally and had become one of Canada's most successful businessmen. In 1928 he sold his packing business for $15 million but retained his vast cattle ranches. He was made a senator in 1931 and is honoured as one of the "Big Four" western cattle kings who started the CALGARY STAMPEDE. DAVID H. BREEN

Reading: Grant MacEwan, *Pat Burns, Cattle King* (1980).

Burns, Tommy, boxer (b Noah Brusso at Hanover, Ont 17 June 1881; d at Vancouver, BC 10 May 1955). Starting as a welterweight in 1900, Burns became, 6 years later, the only Canadian to hold the world heavyweight championship when he beat Marvin Hart. Known as a tenacious boxer and strong hitter, the 170 cm, 79.4 kg French Canadian defended his title 10 times in 33 months before losing to Jack Johnson in Sydney, Australia, on 25 Dec 1908. His defences included victories over the heavyweight champions of England and Australia. He knocked out the Irish champion, Jem Roche, in 1 min, 28 secs, the shortest title defence ever. The $30 000 he received for fighting Johnson was the beginning of "big" money for boxers. A.J. "SANDY" YOUNG

Tommy Burns, Canada's only world heavyweight champion. He lost only 4 of 60 fights and defended his crown 10 times in less than 3 years before losing to the formidable Jack Johnson (*courtesy Public Archives of Canada/C-14092*).

Burpee, Lawrence Johnston, civil servant, librarian, author (b at Halifax 5 Mar 1873; d at Oxford, Eng 13 Oct 1946). He entered the Canadian civil service in 1890 and served as private secretary to 3 ministers of justice. From 1905 to 1912 Burpee was librarian of the Ottawa Public Library, and from 1912 until his death was Canadian secretary to the INTERNATIONAL JOINT COMMISSION. Burpee was a founder of the Canadian Historical Assn and honorary secretary 1926-35 and president 1936-37 of the Royal Soc of Canada. A prolific writer, he published many articles and works on Canadian studies. DAVID EVANS

Burt, George, labour leader (b at Toronto 17 Aug 1903). Burt became a journeyman plumber, but during the Depression he moved to Oshawa to work for General Motors. He was the first treasurer of Local 222 United Automobile Workers (UAW), organized just before the historic 1937 OSHAWA STRIKE. In 1939 he was elected Canadian director of the UAW over C.H. MILLARD. Burt was a VP of the Canadian Congress of Labour, a general VP of the Canadian Labour Congress, and was president 1951-53 of the Ontario Federation of Labour. He led the Canadian UAW from its militant infancy until 1968, when it was the second-largest and most socially conscious union in Canada. Burt was involved in labour politics and gained support from communist and CO-OPERATIVE COMMONWEALTH FEDERATION factions in his union at different times. He was a member of the NDP's founding committee. LAUREL SEFTON MACDOWELL

Burton, Dennis, painter (b at Lethbridge, Alta 6 Dec 1933). Burton achieved renown in 1965 for his "Garterbeltmania" — large paintings of women in garterbelts. He had become interested in drawing the nude and abstraction at the Ontario College of Art (1952-56) and was influenced by William RONALD's work. In 1960 his images of genitalia first became obvious in *Smokeshop Sex Marauder*. With Joyce WIELAND and Michael SNOW, he represents a rigorous exploration of erotic themes in Canadian art. His paintings, figurative, abstract or "calligraphic," are full of dashing energy. JOAN MURRAY

Burton, Eli Franklin, physicist (b at Green R, Ont 14 Feb 1879; d at Toronto 6 July 1948). Educated at U of T and Cambridge, Burton spent his whole career at U of T, succeeding J.C. McClennan as head of the physics department in 1932. He was a council member of the NATIONAL RESEARCH COUNCIL 1937-46 and served on the board of Research Enterprises Ltd, the secret wartime radar factory. His most notable achievement was building the first electron microscope in N America, with Cecil Hall, James Hillier and A.F. Prebus at Toronto in the late 1930s. Hillier and Prebus went on to scientific careers in the US, where the electron microscope was manufactured by RCA Ltd. DONALD J.C. PHILLIPSON

Burton, Ralph, army officer (b at Hull Bank, Eng 1724; d at Scarborough, Eng 1768). He came to N America in 1754 and saw extensive service during the SEVEN YEARS' WAR, including action at Louisbourg (1758) and Québec (1759). He was appointed military governor of Trois-Rivières in 1760 and later of Montréal. In 1764 he was appointed commander of the British forces in Québec, but after quarreling with Governor MURRAY, he was recalled (1766). STUART R.J. SUTHERLAND

Burwash, Nathanael, Methodist minister, university chancellor (b 25 July 1839 at St Andrew's, Qué; d at Toronto 30 Mar 1918). Theologically moderate, he trained a generation of Methodist ministers and undergraduates to pursue enlightened research in theology and the humanities. Raised in Baltimore, Canada W, he was educated at Victoria College, graduated 1859, and was ordained 1864. He began teaching science 1866 at Victoria College. In 1871 he became professor and in 1873 dean of the newly created Faculty of Theology. He became chancellor (president) of Victoria 1887 and oversaw the university's move from Cobourg to Toronto. He retired 1913 but taught theology until his death. While he was not an original scholar, his writings and lectures became the standard for generations of Methodist clergy and laity. Committed to the scientific method and free enquiry, he played a conciliatory role in the debate over EVOLUTION and higher criticism. He was also widely respected in the Canadian intellectual and religious community and was an active supporter of ecumenism. His published books include *Wesley's Doctrinal Standards* (1881); *A Manual of Christian Theology on the Inductive Method* (1900) and *The History of Victoria College* (1927). NEIL SEMPLE

Bus Transportation The word "bus," short for omnibus, refers to any self-propelled road vehicle capable of carrying more persons than a private automobile. The terms coach and bus are used interchangeably, although, strictly speaking, buses are outfitted for short-distance travel and coaches have more comfortable seating and other amenities for longer journeys. Buses are the most common means of public conveyance within and between cities and towns in Canada and often the only public service. For busy intercity markets with distances of under 500 km, the bus offers more frequent service and lower-priced tickets than do air or rail carriers.

Self-propelled bus service began in 1892 in Hamilton, Ont, as an adjunct to urban tramways. Bus operation in the countryside developed as a replacement for horse transportation enterprises, with companies such as Brewster Transport (Alta, BC) and Penetang-Midland (Ont) operating both systems in the early 20th century. The intercity/rural bus industry flowered in the late 1920s and the network of services has developed since that time in keeping with additions and improvements to the road system. Within urban areas, bus services began in the early 1920s and, after WWII, motor buses and electric trolleybuses replaced STREET RAILWAY services. The growth of suburban areas in the past 2 decades has resulted in a major growth in the bus network.

Types of Bus Service Most people are familiar with the scheduled or regular route service: a bus runs according to a fixed timetable, serving set points along specific roads. Anyone may ride, upon payment of a set fare, and packages may be sent on intercity/rural services. Most buses are used for scheduled route service. Charter services represent another common type of bus operation in which people pay as a group for transportation directly to the place and at the time of their choosing. Tour services are a form of bus transportation and may operate on a regular schedule; alternatively the tour may follow a circuit covering a major part of the country, with arrangements for meals and lodging included. Hundreds of bus companies are engaged in the charter and tour fields. Industrial bus systems provide scheduled services for commuters to a particular job location not covered by public transportation, particularly in BC and Alberta. Most commonly these services are paid for by the employer, both to assist the worker and as an alternative to maintaining parking areas. Some industrial fleets have hundreds of buses. In the BC lumber industry there are more buses in industrial service than in the Vancouver urban motor bus fleet.

Airport bus services, similar to the railway "station bus" of an earlier era, link airports with the downtowns of major cities. They may also provide a direct ride to smaller cities nearby.

Route Network The present network of intercity and rural scheduled bus services developed from many origins: as outgrowths of earlier horse-transport enterprises; as replacements for infrequent branch-line passenger trains; as transit systems reaching out from cities to surrounding towns; and, following the rapid expansion of the highway system during the 1960s, as altogether new links in Canada's network — a process still continuing in the North. Though most regions of Canada have good route coverage, there is one striking omission from networks in both Canada and the US: the virtual absence of short-distance rural routes. In Canada, these movements are handled by special-purpose services: yellow school buses, minibuses for the elderly or the handicapped and industrial contract runs for workers. In Europe these various travel demands are usually handled on one system.

Bus Transportation Companies There are over 1000 companies providing bus service, but most routes are operated by the "big 10" of scheduled service: Acadian Lines, Canada Coach, Gray Coach, Grey Goose, Greyhound Lines of Canada, Pacific Coach Lines, SMT Eastern, Saskatchewan Transportation, Terra Transport (Canadian National) and Voyageur. Half of these companies are privately owned and the remainder are crown corporations. The nature of the territory, frequency of service and growth rate of the economy in the area served determine whether any given company makes a profit.

Technology and Manufacturing Buses come in many types: the standard rear-engine, 2-axle bus, found in every city, and its 2- or 3-axle motorcoach equivalent for intercity service; the school-type bus, employing a truck chassis with the engine out front; the articulated bus, of extra length and hinged for easier cornering; and the doubledecker, used on many sightseeing routes. Electric trolleybuses have been used since the beginning of bus transport, with 4 major cities possessing modern fleets at present.

Historically, many small firms were engaged in bus manufacturing, such as Sunnyside Auto Body Works (Alta), Laurie Wagon (Man), Smith Brothers (Ont), St Lin Bodies (Qué) and Middle West Pubnico Bus Builders (NS). As time passed, a reduced number of larger companies met Canadian domestic and export needs. For city transport, General Motors Diesel Division, Flyer Ltd, and Ontario Bus Industries dominate. For intercity and rural applications, 3 builders are noteworthy, each of which has evolved some special feature: Prevost Car (Qué), Motor Coach Industries (Man) and Western Flyer (Man). Prevost has developed a cost-effective way of providing large windows that curve up into the roof of a coach, which is of special appeal to tour and charter operators. Motor Coach Industries, through its link with Greyhound Lines of Canada, has developed a coach that can produce 2 or more million kilometres of service at low cost and high reliability, resulting in its widespread use in scheduled service. Until 1966, Western Flyer (which now, as Flyer Industries, deals only in city transit) built an exceptionally rugged coach in its "Canuck" series. Designed to operate at top highway speeds over the network of gravel roads in western and northwestern Canada, in temperatures as low as -50°C, these coaches provided excellent service over a 25-year period.

Regulation of bus transportation rests with the provincial governments. The Supreme Court of Canada has ruled that the federal government has the right to regulate interprovincial bus transportation, but for practical reasons the individual provinces undertake this function in consultation with each other.

Scheduled services are closely regulated. Most rural routes lack sufficient population to support more than one carrier. Busier city-to-city lines are usually restricted to one carrier, so that profits earned there can supplement service to thinly populated territory. Fares, as well as entry and exit from the marketplace, are controlled. Charter and tour services are also regulated, though in some jurisdictions the restriction on the number of authorized carriers has been eased. For all practical purposes, operating authorities are granted in perpetuity.

Airports usually have insufficient bus-traffic potential to warrant more than one carrier, so monopolies are awarded. An important element of competition is introduced every 5 to 10 years, when open bidding is held by airport authorities to choose a carrier for exclusive operation over the subsequent period.

Future Prospects Canada may be a nation of automobile owners, but for surface travel its people have a strong propensity to use public transport. Canadians use scheduled bus lines and railway services more than 3 times as often as their US neighbours. Similar results are found when urban-transit ridership is compared between the 2 countries for cities in comparable population groups. With the widespread network of services and bargain-priced fares, Canadians are likely to continue their support of this safe and energy-efficient form of transport. *See also* ROADS AND HIGHWAYS; URBAN TRANSPORTATION.

BRIAN SULLIVAN

Bush, John Hamilton, Jack, painter (b at Toronto 20 Mar 1909; d there 24 Jan 1977). Internationally acclaimed as Canada's leading abstract painter in the 1960s and 1970s, Bush established his local reputation as a radical in the 1950s as a member of PAINTERS ELEVEN.

He obtained his formal training in Montréal and Toronto 1926-28. For most of his life he was a successful advertising artist, which he said allowed him great freedom in his own work. His earliest paintings, small landscapes and cityscapes, aspired to the manner of the GROUP OF SEVEN, but by the late 1930s he had established a personal figurative style that won him access to Canada's official painting societies. He was a member and frequently an officer of the Canadian Society of Painters in Water Colour, the Ontario Society of Artists, the Royal Canadian Academy and the Canadian Group of Painters (1940-64). In the late 1940s, dissatisfied with his work, he produced a group of stylized, expressionist figure paintings with emotional and religious themes. About this time, too, he became interested in American abstract expressionism. His painting was completely abstract but still expressionist and gestural by the early 1950s, and, with like-minded artists such as William RONALD, Harold TOWN, Oscar CAHÉN, Alexandra LUKE and Jock MACDONALD, Bush found himself in opposition to standard Toronto painting. He exhibited with 6 of these colleagues in "Abstracts at Home" at Simpsons department store in 1953. With some additions, they exhibited as Painters Eleven 1954-60, including a showing at New York's Riverside Museum in 1956. A 1957 visit from American art critic Clement Greenberg to the group confirmed Bush's interest in thinner, simpler painting (and introduced him to a lifelong friend). Despite this support, Bush did not fully explore this mode for several years. His first solo show in New York (1962), however, consisted of "Thrust" pictures which stated themes that would preoccupy him for the rest of his life: thin radiant colour, eccentric shapes and expansive compositions — evidence of his deep admiration for Matisse. In "Flags" and "Sashes" (1962-63) — probably his best-known series — he simplified structure even further, to allow colour more autonomy. His paintings of the later 1960s and 1970s rely increasingly on his remarkable colour sense, culminating in the rich orchestrations of innumerable colour strokes in his last "musical title" series. At the same time, he explored subtle vari-

Jack Bush, *School Tie* (1965), oil on canvas (*courtesy Edmonton Art Gallery*).

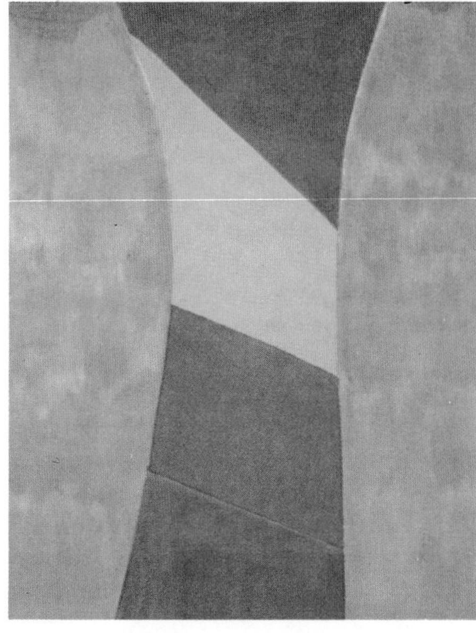

ations in surface in the rollered and sponged ground pictures of the 1970s.

From the mid-1960s on, Bush travelled fairly often to Europe and the US, making friends with many international artists of similar beliefs. Though quick to respond to what he saw, he always remained highly individual. After 1965 he exhibited with these international contemporaries in the new David Mirvish Gallery in Toronto. (As though to indicate his new, nonofficial, nonprovincial status, he had resigned from all societies in 1964.) Despite his growing international fame, however, Bush remained interested in and accessible to younger artists. His encouragement and his work influenced many of the present generation of Canadian painters and sculptors. He represented Canada at the 1967 São Paulo Bienal and has been included in many prestigious international exhibitions. In 1972 his one-man exhibition opened the new contemporary galleries of the Boston Museum. The Art Gallery of Ontario organized a 1976 retrospective that toured Canada. Bush's awards include a John Simon Guggenheim Foundation fellowship and the Order of Canada.

KAREN WILKIN

Reading: Terry Fenton, *Jack Bush, A Retrospective* (1976); Karin Wilkin, ed, *Jack Bush* (1984).

Bush Flying In Canada, the word "bush" has been used since the 19th century to describe the hostile environment beyond the clearings and settlements. In bush flying it has been used to refer to flying in adverse, if not hostile, conditions in the remote expanses beyond the ribbon of settlement in southern Canada, into the "bush" of the SHIELD and the barren Arctic. By the end of WWI most of southern Canada had been linked by railways, but the North remained as inaccessible as ever by land. Its innumerable lakes and rivers did, however, provide alighting areas for water-based aircraft in summer and ski-equipped aircraft in winter. Winter flying began in 1917-18 and the first winter bush flying in Canada was undertaken by Fairchild Aerial Surveys (of Canada). In 1926 H.A. "Doc" Oaks flew supplies from Hudson, Ont, to Narrow Lake, Ont, on 27 Dec for Bathurst Mines. Under Oaks's directions, methods of engine heating and maintenance in difficult winter conditions were developed. The Elliot Brothers of Sioux Lookout, Ont, are credited with the development of special skis for landing on snow or ice. Early navigation was basically by recognition as pilots followed the course of rivers.

Bush flying began as aerial reconnaissance for spotting forest fires. Laurentide and other paper companies hired ex-RNAS pilot, Stuart GRAHAM, in 1919 to fly forest-fire patrols over the St Maurice R valley. Using 2 war-surplus Curtiss HS-2L flying boats, Laurentide extended their patrols from Lake-of-the-Woods to James Bay. These early operations were succeeded by a general air service, Laurentide Air Service Ltd, which carried out operations in both Québec and Ontario, including the first regular Canadian air-mail, passenger and freight service from Haileybury, Ont, to Rouyn, Qué (1924). Laurentide ceased operation in 1925 and from then to 1927 the major bush-flying organization in Canada was the Ontario Provincial Air Service, established in 1924 and devoted almost entirely to forestry operations.

The usefulness of aircraft in northern mining operations was demonstrated after the gold strike in the Red Lk district of northwestern Ontario (1925). Patricia Airways and Exploration Ltd carried passengers, freight and mail to the remote area. In 1928 Northern Aerial Mineral Exploration began prospecting by air vast areas of Ungava and the Yukon. Western Canada Airways (renamed Canadian Airways 1930) was formed in 1926 by James A. RICHARDSON, a wealthy Winnipeg grain merchant. One of WCA's pilots, Leigh Brintnell, set out from Winnipeg in 1929, dropped off prospector Gilbert LABINE at Great Bear Lk, flew on to Aklavik, across the Richardson Mts to Whitehorse and Prince George, then to Edmonton and back to Winnipeg — some 15 000 km. (Labine found pitchblende, striking it rich.) By Jan 1929, WCA had established a regular air service down the Mackenzie R from Ft McMurray. One of the most dramatic events of the late 1920s was the flight of 2 aircraft, led by Lt-Col C.D.H. MacAlpine, north from Churchill, Man. The planes got stranded on Queen Maude Gulf. With the help of local Inuit, the men made their way safely overland to Cambridge Bay. In 1930 an expedition piloted by Walter Gilbert flew up the Boothia Pen and found a cairn containing artifacts of the FRANKLIN EXPEDITION. Bush pilots made major surveys of the proposed route of the HUDSON BAY RY in 1926, and, in 1927, 7 aircraft were ferried to Southampton I in the Arctic to gather information on the navigation of HUDSON STR.

Bush pilots at Great Bear Lake, NWT. Bush flying was important in the discovery and exploitation of the radium and uranium in the area (*courtesy City of Edmonton Archives*).

The use of bush flying in the development of mining continued even through the GREAT DEPRESSION. By the mid-1930s more freight was being moved by air in Canada than in all the rest of the world combined. The scale of bush flying was greatly expanded during the development of iron ore reserves in Québec and Labrador. Hollinger Ungava Transport (HUT) hauled fuel, food, dissassembled bulldozers and even cement for dams in the late 1940s. With up to 96 aircraft arrivals per day, HUT carried 170 000 passengers in 10 000 flights before the project ended. In the mid-1950s, Maritime Central Airlines made some 28 000 flights in 29 months during construction of the DEW line across northern Canada. More recently, the JAMES BAY PROJECT depended entirely on bush planes in its early stages, while massive Hercules transports delivered huge loads of food, fuel and equipment.

Bush flying transformed the North. It became possible by the 1930s to charter an aircraft and fly almost anywhere. Aircraft services became available to trappers and missionaries as well as to geologists and surveyors. Moreover, victims of accidents or illness could be brought out quickly for medical attention. The first such incident occurred on 28 Aug 1920, when J.W. Thompson was flown out for a mastoid operation from Moose Factory on James Bay to Cochrane, Ont, by W.R. Maxwell in a Curtiss HS-2L. By the late 1920s and through the 1930s such flights were common; the longest such flight occurred from 27 Nov to 20 Dec 1939, when W.E. Catton flew a Junkers W-34 from Winnipeg to Repulse Bay, NWT, and returned to bring out a man with frozen, gangrenous hands. In the postwar period, air strips have been built in the larger northern settlements, HELICOPTERS have been introduced, and good radio and navigation facilities have been established along with up-to-date weather information services. All this has greatly changed northern Canada and bush flying, but aircraft equipped with floats or skis continue to serve all those who live and work in remote areas. *See also* NOORDUYN NORSEMAN, DE HAVILLAND BEAVER, DE HAVILLAND OTTER.

Bushnell, Ernest L., pioneer broadcast executive (b near Lindsay, Ont 19 Nov 1900). He trained as a singer at the Toronto Conservatory but turned to announcing and then station management. He managed CFRB and CKCN in Toronto 1929-33, then started Canada's first advertising agency for radio. With the CBC 1945-58, he retired as a vice-president. In 1983 he was honorary chairman of Bushnell Communications Ltd.

Reading: P. Stursberg, *Mister Broadcasting* (1971).

Bushtit, *see* CHICKADEE.

Business Cycles are fluctuations in economic activity that occur in most modern economies. They trace out a wavelike pattern with a length of between 3.5 and 7 years. Since 1945 the duration of periods of above-average economic performance has usually been greater than that of below-average performance with a general rise in the long-term average. The peaks in economic activity are normally higher in successive cycles.

Business cycles are divided into phases which describe economic activity as it moves from a peak to a trough and back. They describe the behaviour of a variety of economic indicators which reflect basic business conditions, although in complex economies the government role in establishing such conditions is necessarily measured at the same time. Important indicators are industrial production, exports, imports, railway freight loadings, construction contracts awarded and bank clearings. Occasionally monetary indicators are also included as descriptive statistics. To achieve precision ıese data are taken weekly or monthly; to-ether they trace out a reference cycle which ıaps the congruence of peaks and troughs in an :tempt to indicate average business cycle be-aviour. Some indicators persistently tend to eak and trough before others and are described ; leading (as opposed to lagging) indicators. In anada, exports and construction contracts are ading indicators because of the export orien-tion of the economy and the important role layed by the construction industry in natural source development. Although this analysis is ormally applied to the economy at large, there evidence of significant difference in business ycle behaviour between the various regions of anada in both the timing of cycles and their verity.

Business cycles are a phenomenon of rela-vely developed and diversified economies. hey are thought to originate from the timing of :al investment and the adjustment of inven-ries of goods, particularly those with some ıanufacturing component. In Canada's open :onomy these influences are both domestic and reign. Marxist interpreters hold that business cles are inherent in the capitalist system and e generated by the method of appropriating ırplus value; they are simply one set of a struc-ıre of cycles, some of which are thought to be very long duration. Non-Marxists view the ısiness cycle as being independent of the na-ıre of business ownership and more deeply oted in investment, its inevitably lumpy na-ıre, and the nature of both domestic and inter-ational trade. Marxists and non-Marxists gree that the Kuznets cycle of 15 to 25 years uration, evident in the international economy the late 19th and early 20th centuries, and the ısiness cycle are linked.

Probably the first evidence of a business cycle henomenon in Canada occurred 1854-59. A ak in economic performance, associated with ıe demand growth brought about by the Cri-ıean War and the RECIPROCITY Treaty with the S, was followed in 1857 by a recession brought out by factors which included a slackening in ıe pace of railway construction. The recovery hase was brought about by both an increase in omestic investment and a revived export de-ıand. The post-1850 business cycle was the roduct of growing market integration, itself nked to the new transport and communica-ons forms: steamships, railways and tele-aphs. The Canadian economy grew in size and ope as a result of this integration, and the first opearance of the business cycle was concomi-nt with the first major signs of industrial di-ersification.

Some 19th-century business cycles were al-ıost wholly domestic. The best example is that und in the 1880s which was almost exclu-vely dominated by the pace of transcontinen-l railway construction; the cycle peaked in 885, the last year of major new construction on ıe CPR (*see* RAILWAY HISTORY). Many business cles were, in contrast, associated with both oms and crises in the international economy. rosperity immediately following Confed-ation was brought to an end by a domestic re-onse to the worldwide financial crisis of 371-72 and its consequent restriction on the vailability of investment capital. A trough in 889 coincided with a similar but less severe in-rnational crisis. Business cycles were also gov-ned by noncrisis international forces such as ıe peak in British lending to the international pital market in 1913.

All evidence suggests that before 1914 there as a growing coincidence of business cycles in ınada and the US, Canada's major trading ırtner. However, between the world wars the ansmission mechanism weakened. The GREAT EPRESSION, the most famous of all business cy-es, was brought about by more than the usual influences of cyclical motion: the instability of the international structure of both trade and payments mechanisms, inappropriate exchange rate policies, and world instability in certain commodity markets. Since 1945 there has been an increasingly similar pattern of business cy-cles in Canada and the US. Cycles transmitted from the US with both a shorter lag and an in-creasingly similar amplitude have been the dominant feature of recent Canadian business cycle history. Business cycles often become asso-ciated with particular events: the KOREAN WAR expansion and a natural resource boom in Can-ada in the early 1950s; the Eisenhower recession of 1959; the oil crisis of the early 1970s; and the monetary contraction of the early 1980s. The trough in economic activity in 1982, while part of a wavelike pattern, has been accentuated by policies which acted to deepen the business cycle beyond what otherwise might have occurred. Such policies included the high nominal and real interest rates introduced by most Western governments during this period.

DONALD G. PATERSON

Reading: W.L. Marr and Donald G. Paterson, *Canada: An Economic History* (1980).

Business Education In the 1981-82 school year there were 45 900 full-time and 31 700 part-time students enrolled in bachelors programs in busi-ness offered by Canadian universities, amount-ing to 12.9% and 14.4% of undergraduate enrol-ment respectively. Full-time community college enrolment in business subjects was 65 200, or 39% of total enrolment in these institutions. A vast variety of continuing-education courses in all areas of business, available through post-secondary institutions, professional bodies, eg, the Institute of Chartered Accountants and the Canadian Bankers' Association, management consulting firms and in-house organizations, are offered to practising managers in the private and public sectors of the economy. In recent years female enrolment in these programs has increased significantly. For example, in the pe-riod 1970-71 women represented only 9.5% of total business undergraduate involvement. By 1981-82 this proportion had increased to 39%. These changes are indicative of the shifts that will occur in the next 20 years in the sex compo-sition of managerial occupations.

In Canada university undergraduate degrees in business administration are generally de-signated as bachelors of commerce (B Comm). The first B Comm degree in Canada was granted by Queen's University in 1919, 2 years after a commerce program was introduced. Forty-eight Canadian universities now offer undergraduate business degrees. Undergraduate business edu-cation prior to the mid-1960s was heavily, though not exclusively oriented to training peo-ple for ACCOUNTING, particularly those intending to become chartered accountants. While sub-stantial numbers of commerce graduates still as-pire to professional accountancy, the design of university business programs changed as a res-ult of two 1959 reports (Gordon-Howell and Pierson, sponsored respectively by the Ford and Carnegie foundations) on business education. The reports emphasized that the primary objec-tive of higher education in business should be student development of the requisites for mana-gerial competence. The present curriculum fo-cuses on problem identification and problem solving, and their relationship to managerial decision making. As well, the recognition that many factors external to an organization (eg, fiscal and monetary policies, government pro-grams and regulations, changes in statutes and new interpretations of constitutional law) will strongly influence the options open to manage-ment has revolutionized business education, and has resulted in major curriculum reform, a significant increase in the academic qualifica-tions of teaching staff and an increase in re-search, which had been almost totally lacking.

Students in undergraduate business courses are required to take a program incorporating courses in general education with others more narrowly professional. General education courses, eg, those in the humanities, social sci-ences (including economics) and in quantitative analysis and analytical reasoning, will typically comprise about 40-60% of the student's pro-gram. The core of the curriculum will include the study of behaviour in organizations, the de-sign and structure of organizations, managerial and financial accounting, finance, marketing and production management. A student may major in any one of these areas, or may choose to pursue a general business degree. Courses con-cerning law, business-government relations and business policy and strategic planning are man-datory. In Canada there is also an increasing tendency to regard a course in international business as mandatory.

In the 1981-82 school year, there were 3766 full-time and 4275 part-time students enrolled in MBA programs (13.6% and 18.4% enrolment respectively of all master's programs). Of those in MBA programs, 28% were female. There are now 28 Canadian universities offering MBA programs. This is a professional rather than an academic graduate degree, and is designed for students of differing educational backgrounds, eg, in liberal arts, science, engineering, who wish to pursue a professional career in manage-ment. The MBA is a 2-year degree. The first year covers the core foundation and functional areas of managerial training (quantitative reasoning, organizational structure and behaviour, mana-gerial and aggregative economics, accounting, finance and marketing); the second year nor-mally combines required courses in organiza-tional policy formation and execution, and in the impact of public policy upon the business organization, with a number of elective options.

Business Education in the Future Business schools have been praised for producing superb analysts and business theorists (for applying the tools of rational analysis to decision making), but severely criticized for failure to encourage innovative and experimental thinking, to come to grips with the process of making decisions, and in general for failing to recognize that man-agement is also an art. What is likely to emerge in business programs is an effort to reconcile the past Gordon-Howell and Pierson emphasis on rational analysis with the need to remedy these identified deficiencies.

EDWARD J. CHAMBERS

Business Elites The role of business ELITES has never been as straightforward in Canadian soci-ety as it has in countries with longer histories and more clearly defined class systems. The Canadian "Establishment" (also known as the Economic Elite, Corporate Elite and Business Elite) is really a loosely knit group of contenders for economic, political and cultural power. Al-though its structure and sources of authority are constantly in flux, the members of the group tightly control the country's decision-making processes.

Economic power in Canada has shifted ac-cording to the way money has been made, eg, furs, railways, banking, mining, oil, microchips and fast food. At the same time, Canada's eco-nomic centre of gravity has shifted from Mont-réal to Toronto, where it largely remains, despite some movement westward.

The very existence of an Establishment — a cabal of power brokers bent on what Lord Rus-sell called "the production of intended effects" — runs contrary to the traditional notion of Can-ada as a land of freely accessible opportunities. To reinforce this notion, even the most out-spoken power wielders strenuously disavow any mutual benefits deriving from their elitist credentials. In fact, they seldom need to conspire among themselves because their interests so seldom conflict.

Most Canadians tend to view the class system — if they think of it at all — as a reference to ways of life or levels of sophistication. The common misconception that everyone belongs to what George Orwell called "the lower-upper-middle class" — a class that can provide its offspring with the advantages of education but not much in the way of inherited wealth or social position — was not challenged until 1965, when John PORTER published his monumental VERTICAL MOSAIC, a detailed examination of Canada's power structure in the 1950s. Porter revealed dramatic inequalities of income and opportunity among Canadians, demonstrating that only about 10% of Canadian families could actually afford the middle-class life-style then considered average. He argued that the corporate elite (only 6.6% of whom were French Canadian) was rooted in 183 dominant corporations that controlled the majority of economic activities. Power was held by a predominantly Anglo-Saxon economic elite of only a few hundred; ethnic origin was virtually as significant in determining membership in the elite in 1951 as it had been in 1885 and 1910.

Porter also demonstrated that the majority of Canadian political leaders were middle class in origin. He wrote, "The upper class doesn't seem attracted to the turbulence of politics and, in any case, the privileges they enjoy are not threatened by the holders of political power. Nor is there any tradition of working-class participation in politics. I think the real problem with Canada is that its political system is ineffective to cope with national problems. It leaves the definition of major goals — and therefore the power — to the corporate elite. . . Although it has a class structure peculiar to its own history and geography, Canada is probably not unlike other Western industrial nations in relying heavily on its elite groups to make major decisions and to determine the shape and direction of its development. . . Power arises because of the general social need for order. Everyone in society has a set of expectations about how others will behave. Among such ordered relationships are those which grant the right to a few people to make decisions on behalf of the group." Porter's original thesis was expanded and brought up to date a decade later by Wallace Clement, who concluded that "Canada has been and remains a society controlled by elites. With increasing economic concentration over the past twenty years, the structure has become increasingly closed, thus making it more difficult for those outside the inner circles of power to break through."

Because they have deliberately set themselves apart from the politicians, members of Canada's business elite exercise a mandate virtually bereft of public accountability. Many of the wealthiest individuals escape to offshore tax havens; others lobby strenuously for the protection of their privileges (*see* PRESSURE GROUPS) and, in fact, their efforts have not been unsuccessful. Canada has one of the lowest corporate tax rates of any industrialized country. Although collectively the corporate elite endow universities, preserve landmarks, donate artworks and raise money for appropriate charities, the impulse toward creative generosity is hardly overwhelming; corporate charitable donations account for only 2% of corporate profits.

Canada's Establishment is composed of overlapping rings of power. While no social compact exists, a confederacy of regional elite groupings — loosely knit yet interlocking — comprises a psychological entity. Its members share habits of thought and action and similar beliefs, values and enemies.

Unlike the power of the political and cultural elites, economic power is usually handed down from generation to generation. Cradled in an Indian summer of extended adolescence, the sons and daughters of the rich learn early that established family wealth (with its palace guard of legal retainers, chartered accountants and investment counsellors) is not so much for spending on private fripperies as for influencing positions and events.

By the early 1980s the hereditary pews of the business Establishment were filled with a new breed of ambitious crown princes, symbolized by the death of John Angus "Bud" MCDOUGALD in 1978 and the capture of his Argus empire by Conrad BLACK. "Canada is widely assumed to be an egalitarian society, but the extent to which rich men's sons dominated the financial news in the 1970s was absolutely astonishing," Alexander Ross noted in *Canadian Business*. "It was almost as though control of major portions of the Canadian economy were being passed on, like family memberships in the Granite Club."

Like the charter members of every elite, Canada's decision makers disavow the possession of power even if they value its exercise. They are accustomed to running things, promoting those men (and very occasionally those women) recognized as reliable. Much of this process operates through negative sanctions; the overly ambitious or unsuitable interloper is blocked by invisible but unbreachable barriers. This system of sanctions operates through the exclusive clubs, private schools and other elite institutions that close and open their doors according to sets of unspoken values that can be called Canadian mainly because they cannot properly be described as anything else. There are certain people who, no matter how many deals they make with Establishment firms, no matter how often they best their competitors, will never be part of its world. They and many others are the victims of the Establishment's most potent weapon: the power to exclude. This ability to withhold favours is most frequently exercised through the "Big Five" chartered banks — the Royal, the Commerce, the Bank of Montreal, The Toronto-Dominion and the Bank of Nova Scotia (*see* BANKING). Even during the depths of the recession of the early 1980s, when their own balance sheets looked shaky, the bankers continued to exercise papal control over the Canadian economy. The executive board meetings of the 5 largest banks represent the greatest source of nongovernmental power in Canada. During these deliberations, personal relationships through which the economic elite consolidates its existence and swells its authority are formed, strengthened and multiplied.

Canada is held together through the influence of a relatively tiny coterie of power wielders, but power is a difficult commodity to isolate in Canadian society. The definition of it as the "ability to compel obedience" is not broad enough to describe how it is exercised in Canada; neither is Max Weber's view of power as "the chance of a man or a group or a number of men to realize their own will in a communal action, even against the resistance of others who are participating in it." C. Wright Mill's "power elite" theory is not really relevant, because Canada has no significant military industrial complex — no group of centurions sliding in and out of a Pentagon, a state department, a White House or the equivalent of a Ford Foundation or Council on Foreign Relations. There is no cabal comparable to the Pittsburgh Mellons strong enough to control any region, although the McCains and Irvings approach that stature in the closed duchy of NB.

Atlantic industrialist K.C. Irving (left) and Calgary construction magnate Frederick C. Mannix (right) at their induction into the Canadian Business Hall of Fame, 1979 (*courtesy Canapress*).

The Canadian business elite is also distinguished by the fact that so much important decision making is exercised by surrogates. Two-thirds of Canada's 100 largest corporations are owned outside the country. Even if local managers exercise apparent autonomy, their authority is not final — they answer to outside boards of directors. The chief executive officers who run these companies must act as colonial administrators. Most, though not all, American companies treat Canada as a slightly backward acreage of their northern sales territories, reflecting the comment by Jacques Maisonrouge, head of the IBM World Trade Corporation, that "for business purposes, the boundaries that separate one nation from another are no more real than that of the equator."

Few members of Canada's business elite have resisted Canada's Americanization. In fact, it may be the only national elite in history that has cheerfully participated in its own demise. The attitude of E.P. TAYLOR, one of the most successful Canadian entrepreneurs of his day, was typical: "If it weren't for the racial issue in the US and the political problems they have, I would think that the two countries could come together. . . . I'm against this trend of trying to reduce American ownership in Canadian companies. I think nature has to take its course."

This let's-surrender-with-profit syndrome has prevented Canada's capitalist class from attaining any clear perspective of itself and its long-term role. Northrop FRYE has interpreted this colonial attitude as frostbite on the roots of the Canadian imagination. "Colonialism," he has written, "produces a disease for which I think the best name is prudery. By this I do not mean reticence in sexual matters. I mean the instinct to seek a conventional or commonplace expression of an idea." Frye's description of the prudery of spirit, the snobbish modesty and the reluctance to take risks characterizes Canada's elite. National power grids of enormous corporations have replaced traditional family control of wealth and power (except in the Maritimes). Many of the most influential men in Canadian cities and towns no longer belong to local power clusters but are instead the ambassadors of large multinational or transnational corporations. Their loyalty to Canada is at best ambivalent; their dollars seek the highest rate of return regardless of the implications that this may have for the country.

Because they believe so implicitly in themselves, most members of the corporate elite are seldom able to distinguish between the public interest and their own. However, for an Establishment to flex its muscles freely requires the kind of compliant political authority Canada has not always elected. The private sector's leaders demand that their parliamentary representatives "maintain investor confidence," ie, laws should be enacted and enforced for the business community's benefit. The business elite believes that the only good government is one willing to grant their efforts unbridled rein. Occasionally this happens, eg, the business-government axis forged during WWII by C.D. HOWE.

By the 1980s, the conflict between government and the private sector was growing bitter. The business community reacted to the initiatives of the TRUDEAU government with self-righteous rage. The federal LIBERAL PARTY, determined to find policy initiatives that might maintain them in their accustomed perch of power, abandoned their traditional stance which in the past had allowed them to strike the most marketable balance between elitism and egalitarianism. Their new mood was reflected in the National Energy Program, designed to restore some of the control of Canada's most vital industry to Canadians (*see* ENERGY POLICY). The business elite, interpreting such actions as massive inteference in the "free" flow of market forces, reacted with outraged threats of exodus. The more sensitive among its members, however, realized that the issue symbolized a basic contradiction inherent in any democratic capitalist society. Capitalism is concerned above all with the promotion of economic efficiency, but social democracies are concerned with other objectives as well, eg, a more equitable distribution of wealth. With governments less willing to sponsor indiscriminate corporate handouts and businessmen becoming increasingly opposed to satisfying the demands for the expansion of social services, the 2 value systems continued to drift apart. In Sept 1984 Canada elected a Conservative government that promised to be more responsive to the Canadian business community. PETER C. NEWMAN

Reading: W. Clement, *The Canadian Corporate Elite* (1975); Peter C Newman, *The Canadian Establishment*, 2 vols (1975, 1981).

Business History, defined as the written record of the activities of individuals and enterprises seeking private profit through the production of goods and services, has deep roots in Canadian history, although it has matured only recently.

The evolution of Canada's business structure — encompassing enterprises, businessmen and business practices — dates from the earliest European contact with the continent. The Atlantic FISHERIES and the FUR TRADE were developed by French and English merchants exercising their metropolitan influence through such companies as the COMPAGNIE DES CENT-ASSOCIÉS (fd 1627) and the HUDSON'S BAY COMPANY (fd 1670). The progressive development of fur, timber and wheat staples provided the backbone of early Canadian business development, eg, large fur trading companies (the NORTH WEST COMPANY, *c*1780-1821), timber companies (Mossom Boyd and Company, *fd c*1848) and wheat traders (the Richardson family of Kingston). From these central enterprises, ancillary activities developed. Diversification stimulated the emergence of BANKING (BANK OF MONTREAL, 1817), early manufacturing (Montreal Nail and Spike Works, 1839) and service industries (John Molson's Montréal brewing, banking and steamboat enterprises, *c*1810).

Early Canadian entrepreneurs did not function in an environment of unbridled free enterprise. The state exercised a formative role from the beginning. Mercantilist legislation (the English NAVIGATION ACTS), commercial policy (Galt's 1859 tariff) and financial guarantees (GUARANTEE ACT, 1849) all influenced the businessman's risk-taking. In this light, Confederation may be viewed as the equipping of the federal government with powers to create a transcontinental commercial nation. Tariff increases in the NATIONAL POLICY of 1879 stimulated Canadian manufacturing, partly Canadian-owned (Massey, 1847) and partly foreign-owned (Canadian Rand Drill Company, 1889). The combination of turn-of-the-century prosperity, new staples such as western wheat and pulp and paper, and the impact of URBANIZATION fostered the creation of new enterprises. HYDROELECTRICITY, for instance, prompted the establishment of Canadian Westinghouse in 1903. The period saw the creation of new companies through mergers (STELCO, 1910).

The 20th century has seen the elaboration of the established pattern of staples exploitation (nickel, iron ore) together with the introduction of new technologies (automobiles, aviation, electronics). Manufacturing has generally remained the preserve of central Canada, where indigenous industry has been overshadowed by FOREIGN INVESTMENT. The state continued to influence business through competition, taxation and labour policies as well as entering the marketplace itself through crown corporations (TRANS-CANADA AIRLINES, est 1937). Canadian companies have prospered as conglomerates (Power Corporation, GEORGE WESTON LIMITED) or as purveyors of unique technology (BOMBARDIER INC, est 1942) or in specified precincts such as broadcasting and banking.

Historians have interpreted these developments in a variety of ways. The central role of staple trades attracted early attention. D.G. CREIGHTON'S *The Commercial Empire of the St. Lawrence* (1937) and H.A. INNIS'S 1930 study, *The Fur Trade in Canada*, followed in 1940 by *The Cod Fisheries*, placed businessmen and their aspirations and activities in a broad national framework. Although akin to ECONOMIC HISTORY in their macroeconomic reach, these works contained much detail on Canada's earliest large enterprises. Such thematic treatments have been perpetuated by journalists (Peter NEWMAN, *The Canadian Establishment*, 1975), sociologists (Wallace Clement, *The Canadian Corporate Elite*, 1975) and economists (R.T. Naylor, *History of Canadian Business*, 1975), all of whom seek to portray the business community as the tightly knit, all-powerful upper stratum of Canadian society.

On a microeconomic level, Canadian business historians have produced a varied collection of company histories and biographies which range from hagiography to credible scholarship. Such company-sponsored histories as William Kilbourn's *The Elements Combined* (1960) on Stelco, E.P. Neufeld's study of MASSEY-FERGUSON (*A Global Corporation*, 1969) and Shirley E. Woods's, *The Molson Saga* (1983) set a high standard. Journalistic company histories, such as those of Merrill Denison (*The People's Power*, 1960) frequently verge on uncritical exercises in public relations. Others appearing at times of corporate crisis (Peter Cook, *Massey at the Brink*, 1981; Peter Foster, *Other People's Money: The Banks, The Government and Dome*, 1983), display competence but often treat historical research as a backdrop to examining present business problems. Few industry studies exist, an exception being O.W. Main's 1955 study, *The Canadian Nickel Industry*. Recent biographies of Sir Joseph FLAVELLE (Michael Bliss, *A Canadian Millionaire*, 1978) and C.D. HOWE, a businessman in politics (William Kilbourn and Robert Bothwell, *C.D. Howe*, 1980) serve to reverse the past tradition of business biography as puffery. Royal commissions (CORPORATE CONCENTRATION, 1978) frequently contain useful sections of business history.

Research in business history has generally been impeded by business suspicion, academic condescension and archival neglect. Furthermore, the writing of business history in Canada has tended to focus too exclusively on the forward and backward linkages of the staple trades, ignoring other areas of economic growth (eg, the spread of Canadian banking and electric utilities abroad). Despite the contributions of expatriate Canadians such as N.S.B. Gras (1884-1956) and H.G.J. Aitken (1922-) to the study of business enterprise abroad, Canadian business history lags behind its British and American counterparts. Many gaps exist; studies of business failure, individual companies, business-government relations, the role of foreign investment, the evolution of corporate law and management and labour relations all merit attention.

Innovative work has nonetheless been produced. H.V. Nelles's 1974 study, *The Politics of Development*, on the Ontario hydroelectric industry, and Tom Traves's 1979 examination, *The State and Enterprise*, of the interaction of business and the state after WWI, both break new ground (eg, in analysing the businessman's dynamic role in FEDERAL-PROVINCIAL RELATIONS). Popular business histories such as Philip Smith's *The Treasure-Seekers* (Home Oil, 1978) and Donald MacKay's *Empire of Wood* (MacMillan Bloedel, 1982) have broadened business history readership. Labour historians frequently touch on business concerns, such as the fractious labour-management relations of the Cape Breton steel industry. Québec business historians have tended to focus on broad themes such as the province's "economic inferiority" (Yves Roby, *Les Québécois et les investissements américains*, 1976, and Durocher and Linteau, *Le "Retard" du Québec et l'infériorité économique des Canadiens français*, 1971). The Montreal Business History Project (est 1976) is the first collective attempt to chronicle the evolution of business in one of Canada's leading commercial centres.

Despite these advances, no journal of business history or dictionary of business biography exists in Canada. Future development will depend on greater interest and co-operation from the business community, the pursuit of academic excellence in the field and, possibly, the growth of business history as "public history" (eg, corporate archives, use of business history as a facet of business administration programs).

DUNCAN MCDOWALL

Reading: R.W. Hidy, "Business History," *International Encyclopedia of the Social Sciences*, vol 6 (1968); D.S. Macmillan, ed, *Canadian Business History: Selected Studies, 1497-1971* (1972); G. Porter and R. Cuff, eds, *Enterprise and National Development* (1973).

Business Management is the co-ordination and control of the functional activities of a firm: production, marketing, finance, accounting, personnel, and research and development within the context of the firm's overall competitive strategy. Business managers must not only be knowledgeable about and have experience in the 5 functional areas of the firm, but must also be able to take into account the political, economic, social, technological and international environments that may affect the firm's operations and business strategy. These characteristics of business management are important for all firms in all countries, irrespective of their economic system.

Business management is important for the Canadian economy. In the early 1980s, 11.1 million of Canada's 12-million labour force were employed in the private sector. Businesses accounted for about 85% of nonresidential gross fixed capital formation in Canada, and for almost all of Canada's exports and imports.

Each of the functional areas of business management (as well as overall business strategy) is crucial to the success of a firm. Production managers purchase and take inventory of raw materials and semifinished inputs, manage the use of these inputs in the production process, and control final goods inventory and the shipping, transportation and distribution of final products. Marketing managers conduct market research to determine which products will be in demand and at what prices and quantities, and manage the advertising, promotion and sale of products. Personnel managers hire, train, evaluate, promote and chart the careers of the firm's production, administrative and management personnel. Financial managers raise capital for the firm from external sources such as banks, the stock market, individuals and the public-debt market, manage the internal flow of funds, and evaluate the profitability of capital expenditures for plant and equipment, and research and development. Management accountants collect cost data on wages and on equipment and materials inputs, and combine them with sales data to calculate profits and taxes. Research and development managers develop and acquire new process technology to increase production efficiency and new product technology to improve and expand the range and quality of a firm's products.

Top business managers assess the strengths and weaknesses of the firm in relation to its competitors at home and abroad in order to formulate and implement the firm's competitive strategy. A successful business strategy may involve the development of new products and markets either by internal growth or by mergers and acquisitions. Top management also influences the corporate management style and "corporate culture." Interpersonal relations can range from formal, closed, rigid and hierarchical to informal, open, flexible and group oriented. Ensuring that all employees possess the information, skills, attitudes and motivation to use their full potential in furthering the firm's success is one of the most important aspects of business management.

If one area of management fails, it is difficult for a firm to survive. In the early 1980s, the after-tax profits of Canadian firms were only about 5% of sales; consequently, small errors in any of the functional areas could easily lead to losses and bankruptcy, and about 1% of all businesses in Canada went BANKRUPT each year. However, although each aspect of business management is important, the relative emphasis on each within a firm depends on the firm's competitive strategy, the industry and country in which it operates, and also on the economic, political and social context. For example, business management differs among banks, retail stores and steel companies, and among businesses in Canada, the US, Japan, France, the Soviet Union and China. Business management in Canada has developed unique characteristics because of Canada's geography, economy, and political, social and cultural system.

Business Management in Canada Canada is large geographically but has a small, dispersed population; therefore, government has been involved extensively in the development of infrastructure — roads, railroads, transportation, electric power — and in industrial development. Government influence is more pervasive at the firm, industry and economy-wide level in Canada than in the US: the decisions of business managers in Canada are more circumscribed by government regulation, but Canadian business managers are also more likely to seek government assistance than are their American counterparts.

Canada's relatively small, dispersed markets and its proximity to the large, high-income US market may explain why Canadian business managers are relatively averse to taking risks. New products and processes have often been developed and introduced in the US and subsequently transferred to Canada. Even when a new product or process has been developed in Canada, it is often marketed first in the US. Research and development expenditures as a percentage of GROSS NATIONAL PRODUCT (GNP) in Canada are less than half those of Canada's major trading partners. This relatively low level of technological development, combined with the relatively small-scale firms and plants needed to serve Canada's protected domestic markets, has led to a relatively low level of productivity and productivity growth in the manufacturing sector. High wages have further reduced the ability of Canadian firms to compete at home and abroad. There are many successful Canadian firms in the banking, manufacturing, natural-resource and service sectors that are competitive internationally, but in general Canadian business managers look inward to the Canadian market rather than outward toward world markets.

Under the NATIONAL POLICY of PM John A. Macdonald, relatively high tariffs were placed around Canada's MANUFACTURING sector to protect it and to promote industrial development. Foreign, especially American, firms invested in Canada to circumvent this tariff and sell their products in the Canadian market and to gain access to Canada's plentiful natural and agricultural resources (*see* CANADIAN-AMERICAN RELATIONS, ECONOMIC). Consequently, FOREIGN INVESTMENT in Canada's mining and manufacturing sectors is extensive (almost 60% of total assets in early 1980), but this percentage has slowly declined since the mid-1960s, partly because of government programs to promote Canadian-owned firms. Foreign ownership has often had the effect of reducing the scope, independence, authority and flexibility of Canadian business managers in foreign-owned subsidiaries — over key decisions concerning research and development, investment, the introduction of new products, pricing and international trade — because these decisions are frequently made abroad at the head offices of a multinational enterprise. Some critics of the high level of foreign ownership in Canada have also charged that it has stunted the development of Canadian entrepreneurs and Canadian-owned businesses; foreign-owned firms often hire the "best and the brightest" of Canadian managers, and have had the effect of reducing investment by Canadians, who feel threatened by the perceived technological, financial and management superiority of foreign-owned subsidiaries.

Compared with Canadian-owned firms, US firms have a larger percentage of managers with university education and with formal education in business and commerce at the undergraduate and master's level. In Canada, and especially in Canadian-owned firms, promotion to the top ranks of business management has often been based more on experience with the firm and on family background than on educational achievement, performance and initiative (*see* ELITES). This situation has been changing as the number of business school graduates has increased in Canada. Yet by the early 1980s Canada had less than 5% of the number of bachelor's and master's graduates in commerce and business administration that the US had, and only 1% of doctoral graduates in business administration.

INDUSTRIAL RELATIONS is another distinctive feature of business management in Canada. Canadian business has a poor record of days lost to STRIKES and work stoppages, for several reasons. A high percentage of workers, especially in the public service, are unionized in Canada, and unions tend to be more militant in Canada than in the US; management tends to be more rigid, formal and confrontational and less progressive in its relations with workers than management in the US, Europe (with the exception of the UK) and Japan.

Future of Business Management Canada is a trading nation (30% of its output of goods and services is exported and an equal percentage of domestic consumption is imported) and INTERNATIONAL TRADE has become more competitive as transportation and communications costs and tariff and nontariff barriers to trade have fallen and as the production and export capabilities of countries around the world have increased. This trend will challenge Canadian business management to increase the productivity of capital, labour and raw materials utilization; to introduce and develop an increasing number of new products and processes; and to become more export oriented in business operations.

DONALD J. LECRAW

Reading: P.F. Drucker, *Managing in Turbulent Times* (1980); R.H. Waterman and T.J. Peters, *In Search of Excellence* (1982); J.A. Humphrey, et al, *An Introduction to Business Decision Making* (1981).

Butchart, Robert Pim, industrialist (b at Owen Sound, Canada W 30 Mar 1856; d at Victoria 27 Oct 1943). Educated in Owen Sound, he joined his father's hardware business. In 1888 he began the Owen Sound Portland Cement Co. He moved to BC in 1904, and at Tod Inlet, near Victoria, established the first Portland cement plant in BC. He eventually had interests in several cement mills in Canada, including mills at Calgary and Montréal, and in the US. During WWI he directed the Shipbuilding Dept of the IMPERIAL MUNITIONS BOARD in BC. In 1884 he married Jennie Foster Kennedy of Toronto. She turned the abandoned quarries surrounding her home into Butchart Gardens, now a famous tourist attraction.

PATRICIA E. ROY

Butler, John, army officer, Indian agent (b at New London, Conn, bap 28 Apr 1728; d at Newark, Upper Canada 13 May 1796). Interpreter and Indian agent in colonial New York, Butler led groups of Indians against Ft St-Frédéric (near Crown Point, NY), Ft Carillon (Ticonderoga, NY) and Ft Frontenac (Kingston, Ont) during the SEVEN YEARS' WAR. During the AMERICAN REVOLUTION he moved to Canada and raised a force of rangers that raided American frontier settlements. A key figure in Indian affairs in BNA, Butler was one of the original settlers and a prominent local official in Lincoln County, Upper Canada.

CARL A. CHRISTIE

Butler, Sir William Francis, military officer, author (b at Ballyslateen, Suirville, Ireland 31 Oct 1838; d at Bansha Castle, Ireland 7 June 1910). As intelligence officer to the 1870 Red River Expedition, Butler preceded the force to the settlement, then travelled by canoe and YORK BOAT to Ft Frances to meet Sir Garnet WOLSELEY. Commissioned to report on conditions in the Saskatchewan R country, he made a 6000 km trip to Ft Carlton and Rocky Mountain House which he recounted in THE GREAT LONE LAND (1872). Another trip from Ft Garry to Ft St John, through the Rockies, and down the Fraser R to the Pacific inspired *The Wild North Land* (1873).

O.A. COOKE

Buttercup, common name for several herbaceous PLANTS of genus *Ranunculus*, family Ranunculaceae [Lat, "little frog," from wet habitat]. An estimated 600 species occur in north temperate and arctic regions, with a few species in tropical alpine zones. In Canada 45 species occur, of which 7 are introduced Eurasian WEEDS. Buttercups have alternate, simple or deeply divided, compound leaves, the latter being the source of another common name, crowfoot. A few are aquatic, bearing much-divided leaves. About 40 species are cultivated as ORNAMENTALS, 2 or 3 of these being double-petalled forms. Buttercups are acrid in taste, or even poisonous. Flowers are usually yellow, but may be white or, rarely, red. The shiny petals have a nectar pit or scale at the base. Stamens and pistils are numerous, pistils being arranged spirally on an elongated axis or receptacle. After fertilization, the pistils ripen into hard fruits (achenes). *See* POISONOUS PLANTS.

J.M. GILLETT

Butterfly, term referring to INSECTS of order Lepidoptera [Gk, "scaly wings"]. The Canadian fauna includes 272 known species, compared to 695 known from N America as a whole, and over 20 000 worldwide. Possibly about 60 species remain to be discovered or recorded in Can-

iger Swallowtail butterfly (*photo by Mary W. Ferguson*).

da. Butterflies are characterized by having an-ennae that are knobbed or hooked at the tips. hey fly by day and are usually brightly col-ured. Species found in Canada are varied in ze, wingspans ranging from under 2.5 cm to .5 cm. Adults have a long, hollow tongue (pro-oscis) and usually feed on nectar. Larvae of all utterflies in Canada feed on vegetation. The life ycle of a given species may require from a few veeks to 2 years to complete, and it involves a omplete metamorphosis through egg, larva aterpillar) and pupa (chrysalis) to adult. Dif-erent families have characteristically shaped nd marked eggs, which are usually laid on a ost plant, singly or in batches of up to 300. Spe-ies differ in ways of overwintering: most pass e winter in the egg, larval or pupal stage, but a w (eg, mourning cloak and Milbert's tortoise-hell) overwinter as adults. Butterflies inhabit ll areas of Canada where flowering plants oc-ur. Their numbers diminish northwards, down about 16 species in the Arctic. Although some pecies (eg, red admiral and common sulphur) re widely distributed, others are confined to articular habitats or geographical regions. Monarch and painted lady butterflies migrate to anada from the US.

Butterfly populations are controlled by incle-ent weather, diseases, parasites, predators and abitat suitability. Cool, sunless summers and ild, damp winters are particularly detri-mental. Birds consume many caterpillars and dults, while dragonflies and spiders also take heir toll. Diseases can be particularly rife when opulation densities are high, but the many arasitic flies and wasps that regularly prey on aterpillars probably exert the greatest natural ontrol. Larvae of some species of blues and airstreaks are tended by ants for the honeydew ney secrete, and probably receive some pro-ection from other insects. Natural controls are ecessary and probably do not threaten the ex-stence of butterflies. However, destruction of atural habitats, large-scale spraying to control conomic pests and, possibly, ACID RAIN are man-made hazards that could have far-reach-ng, detrimental effects on Canada's butterfly auna.

Although butterflies are generally harmless to uman interests, a few are pests. Larvae of cab-age white butterflies are a widely distributed est of plants of the cabbage family, while an-ther, accidentally introduced butterfly, the Eu-opean skipper, has become a pest of hayfields. Occasionally, others may become a local nuisance when unusually high population levels develop. Butterflies are useful in plant POLLINATION, in providing food for other creatures, and as indicators of environmental stability. They are a source of scientific and recreational interest, bringing charm and beauty to wherever they live.

BERNARD S. JACKSON

Button, Sir Thomas, explorer (b at St Lythans, Wales; d at Worleton, Eng Apr 1634). He commanded an expedition in 1612 into Hudson Bay looking for Henry HUDSON, confident that the passage to Asia had been found. He wintered near the river he named Nelson, after Robert Nelson, one of the crew who died there. An able navigator, he was commended for gallantry and knighted for his actions against rebels in Scotland.

JAMES MARSH

By, John, lt-col, Royal Engineers (b at Lambeth, Eng and bap 10 Aug 1779; d at Frant, Eng 1 Feb 1836). By was one of the greatest early engineers in Canada. He built the 200-km RIDEAU CANAL (1826-32) from Bytown (named for him, now Ottawa) to Kingston, involving construction of about 50 dams and 47 masonry locks. Without the aid of modern construction equipment, it was completed in 5 summer working seasons. By was born into a family of Thames watermen but was admitted in 1797 to the Royal Military Academy, Woolwich. Commissioned in 1799, he served for 2 years at Plymouth before being sent to Canada in 1802. Here he worked on the first small locks on the St Lawrence R and on the fortifications of Québec. Returning to England late in 1811, he served briefly under Wellington in the Peninsular War but early in 1812 was appointed engineer officer for the Royal Gunpowder Mills. Soon after the victory at Waterloo, munitions requirements being minimal, he was retired, but he was recalled in 1826 to build the Rideau Canal. On returning to England in 1832, despite his superb achievement, he was criticized by the Treasury Board for some allegedly unauthorized expenditures. He died, a broken man, 3 years later.

R.F. LEGGET

Bye-boat (by-boat), a name applied historically to any small inshore fishing craft, usually an open boat carrying 5-10 men, used in Newfoundland in the bye-boat fishery. Bye-boat operators or keepers were a large and significant factor in the Newfoundland cod fishery from the mid-1600s until the beginning of the 1800s. They usually competed with the larger fish merchant firms, although sometimes a merchant would outfit the operator and buy his catch. The bye-boat keeper and the fishing servants he employed travelled to his fishing room in Newfoundland each summer as passengers on a fishing ship. He and his crew would fish for the summer from one or two bye-boats he kept there, usually selling the cured catch to a fishing ship before returning to England in the autumn. A couple of men might be hired to remain in Newfoundland over the winter to protect the boats and room (*see* FISHERIES HISTORY).

ROBERT D. PITT

Byelorussians, like RUSSIANS and UKRAINIANS, are an eastern Slavic people. Byelorussia is now a constituent republic of the USSR, although it existed as a separate country from as early as the 13th century. As the Byelorussian Soviet Socialist Republic (BSSR) it encompasses 207 600 km^2 and has a population of some 10 million. According to one source, 3 Byelorussians settled in Canada in 1817. It has also been argued that some of the POLES who served in Canada with the De Watteville regiment were actually Byelorussians. (Byelorussia was part of Poland from 1569 to 1772, and again from 1921 to 1939).

At the beginning of the 20th century, according to Soviet sources, Byelorussians immigrated to Canada in large numbers. The majority of the immigrants were peasants and were considered, officially, as Russians. After WWI, western Byelorussia was temporarily under Polish rule. It may be assumed that Polish immigrants to Canada included, in 1927, 3500 Byelorussians; in 1928, 3800; in 1929, 5100; and in 1930, 4200.

Among the first Byelorussians to immigrate to Canada after WWII were soldiers from the Polish Second Command who were recruited by Canadian agriculturalists as "agricultural workers." Of the 2800 recruited, 2200 were probably Byelorussians; in 1947 some 800 more Byelorussians arrived in Canada. It can be estimated that Byelorussians comprised 60% of Polish immigrants from 1948 to 1956, and it is probable that as many as 48 000 Byelorussians immigrated between 1946 and 1971. The Byelorussians who immigrated in the postwar period varied in age and in socioeconomic, cultural and political background, and many possessed a sense of national consciousness. It was not until 1971 that Byelorussians were listed in the census. There are today some 100 000 Canadians of Byelorussian origin.

Settlement and Economic Life Byelorussians who arrived in Canada before WWI settled primarily in industrial cities, particularly in northern Ontario, where they worked as labourers. Many immigrants who arrived between the wars settled on the Prairies. In 1927 a group cleared land in Saskatchewan; both they and their children spoke pure Byelorussian.

The postwar immigrants (peasants, labourers, skilled workers, technicians and professionals) enjoyed better economic status and were geographically more mobile. Many Byelorussians are represented in medicine, engineering, broadcasting and academia. By 1981, according to estimates, the majority of Byelorussians were in Ontario, followed by Alberta, BC, Manitoba and Québec.

Religious and Cultural Life The majority of Byelorussians belong to the Roman Catholic or Greek Orthodox churches, but some adhere to the United Church, Anglican and Baptist faiths, among others.

After WWII, nationality-conscious Byelorussians in Canada established various organizations, including the Byelorussian Canadian Alliance (1948) in Toronto, the Byelorussian National Committee (1950) in Winnipeg and the Alliance of Byelorussians (1952) in Montréal, and several monthly newsletters have been published. In 1969 the communal portion of a Byelorussian resort at Lk Manitouwabing, Ont, was opened, and it has become known as a

"Byelorussian village. "Byelorussian Week," first held in 1974, is now a tradition in Toronto.

Reading: John Sadouski, *A History of the Byelorussians in Canada* (1981).

Bylot Island, 11 067 km^2, is nestled into the NE corner of BAFFIN I at the entrance to LANCASTER SOUND. Its southern aspect looks across Pond Inlet and Eclipse Sound; on the W it is divided from Baffin I by the narrow Navy Board Inlet. Bold, rugged coasts, glaciers and a high, mountainous interior have not been conducive to habitation. Inuit from Baffin I have visited seasonally and a trading station operated at Button Pt on the SE corner for several years after 1910, but there are no settlements today. To the E the island overlooks a part of BAFFIN BAY, which was much frequented by European whalers in the 19th and early 20th centuries. It was officially claimed as part of Canada by Capt J.E. BERNIER in 1906. Robert Bylot was a British sea captain who sailed with Henry Hudson and William Baffin early in the 17th century. Today the island is a bird sanctuary. Greater snow geese nest on the SW plain; thick-billed murres and other seabirds on the N and E shores.

Glacier on Bylot Island, NWT, located off northeastern Baffin I (*photo by Stephen J. Krasemann/DRK Photo*)

Byng of Vimy, Julian Hedworth George, Viscount, governer general of Canada, 1921-26 (b at Wrotham Park, Eng 11 Sept 1862; d at Thorpe-le-Soken, Eng 6 June 1935). A British aristocrat and cavalry officer, Byng was appointed to command the Canadian Corps in May 1916. He directed it in the attack on VIMY RIDGE in Apr 1917 and was promoted to command the British 3rd Army. In 1921, the first time the Canadian government was formally consulted about the selection of a governor general, Byng was a prominent nominee. But PM Arthur MEIGHEN preferred someone of civilian experience. Byng was finally chosen because he was willing and available. In Apr 1926 PM Mackenzie KING pronounced Byng the ideal governor; in June, however, Byng refused King's request for a dissolution of parliament, precipitating the KING-BYNG AFFAIR. Byng had acted honestly and (in the view of most constitutional experts) correctly, but he departed from Canada under a shadow. His last major appointment was as chief commissioner of the London Metropolitan Police, 1928-31. Byng's wife Evelyn wrote movingly about Canada in *Up the Stream of Time* (1945). In 1925 she donated the LADY BYNG TROPHY, the National Hockey League's award for sportsmanship combined with excellence.

O.A. COOKE AND NORMAN HILLMER

Julian Hedworth George Byng, Viscount Byng of Vimy governor general of Canada 1921-26. In 1926 Byng refused PM King's request for a dissolution of Parliament and precipitated a constitutional crisis (*courtesy Public Archives of Canada/PA-1356*).

Cabbage (*Brassica oleracea*, Capitata Group), usually biennial VEGETABLE of the Cruciferae family, which is grown as an annual. The cole crops (BROCCOLI, CAULIFLOWER, BRUSSELS SPROUTS, etc) were developed from wild cabbage, native to southern and western Europe. Garden cabbage, the most universally grown cole crop, is popular because of its adaptability, hardy tolerance of low temperatures (young spring cabbage can tolerate temperatures as low as -10°C) and easy growing requirements. In temperate climates, a very large choice of strains enables cabbages to be grown year round. In Canada, however, summer cabbage is consumed immediately after harvesting; late cabbage, picked in autumn, can be stored for several months. Depending on the variety, cabbage heads may be round, flat or conical in shape; red, white or green in colour; and have smooth or wrinkled leaves (Savoy cabbage). Cabbages may be grown from seed (maturing in 90-120 days) or as transplanted seedlings (maturing in 60-90 days). Although 90% water, cabbage is an excellent source of minerals and of vitamins A, B_1, B_2 and C. In 1979 Canadian cabbage production was 130 230 t; the main areas of cultivation are Québec and Ontario. ROGER RUSHDY

Cabinet, "government-of-the-day," political executive that formulates government policies and priorities. It has been described as the "hyphen which joins, a buckle which fastens, the legislative part of the state to the executive part of the state." It is responsible for the introduction and passage of government legislation, the execution and administration of government policies, and the finances of the government. Although its powers are so substantial that some observers refer to "Cabinet dictatorship," for a government institution of such obvious power and potency it has no specific constitutional or statutory basis. In Canada it acts formally as the PRIVY COUNCIL, deriving its legal powers to advise and act in the name of the CROWN from its ability to secure and maintain majority support in the HOUSE OF COMMONS. The governor-in-council is the GOVERNOR GENERAL acting on the advice of the Privy Council (in practice, the Cabinet) through an ORDER-IN-COUNCIL, which has the force of law. Provincial Cabinets are known formally as executive councils and follow the federal model except in certain powers of appointment.

Formed and led by the PRIME MINISTER, the Cabinet comprises members of the legislature invited by the prime minister to head major government departments or ministries of state (*see* CENTRAL AGENCY). With the expansion of government activity Cabinets have increased in size from the original 12 to the 40 members of PM Brian Mulroney's first Cabinet (Sept 1984). Choosing a Cabinet in Canada requires considerable artfulness (if not artistry) on the part of the prime minister, who must try to ensure that it represents the country's regional, linguistic and religious diversity. When a victorious party fails to elect MPs in certain regions, a prime minister often resorts to the Senate to fill out the Cabinet.

Because it has been Canadian practice to include all ministers in the Cabinet, the Cabinet has grown to an unwieldy size, and as a result a secretariat and an elaborate committee system have been developed. The secretariat for full Cabinet and its committees is provided mainly by the PRIVY COUNCIL OFFICE, the staff of coordinating ministries of state and the Treasury Board Secretariat. The TREASURY BOARD itself is a statutory Cabinet committee created by Parliament. (An unusual feature of Cabinet committees in Canada is that senior nonelected public servants participate, although they are excluded from Cabinet meetings proper.) In his short-lived government of 1979, PM Joe CLARK organized an inner Cabinet of approximately 12

ministers whose functions (establishing government priorities and spending limits) were similar to those of PM Trudeau's main Cabinet committee, the Policies and Priorities Committee, created during his first term of office.

All members of Cabinet are bound for life by the Privy Council oath of secrecy, which protects Cabinet deliberations and organization. Opinions publicly expressed by a minister are those of Cabinet, and ministers may disagree publicly with those opinions only after resigning from Cabinet and then must not reveal details of Cabinet discussions or documents. The OFFICIAL SECRETS ACT, which enjoins all Canadians, but particularly public employees, opposition critics and investigating journalists from possessing, distributing and publicizing information deemed injurious to the state, has also been used to protect Cabinet members, who can choose to pose as privy councillors to the Crown rather than as a government responsible to the Commons, from embarrassment. The secrecy surrounding Cabinet business is defended on the grounds that it is necessary for maintaining Cabinet solidarity, without which Cabinet may lose its hold over the legislature and therefore its right to govern. To dominate the legislature, Cabinet can rely as well on its control over the party. Parliamentary government is party government, and prime ministers have substantial legislative patronage at their disposal to ensure party loyalty, including appointment of Cabinet ministers and parliamentary secretaries and of chairmen of legislative committees. In fact, the control exerted by Cabinet over the legislature through the levers of party discipline has contributed to the outcry against Cabinet power. The traditional capacity of the legislature to bring down the government and therefore the Cabinet through a no-confidence vote appears to be losing force, largely because the Cabinet has the power, through its legislative party majority, to prevent such votes, or at worst to refuse to accept their implications or consequences. The dwindling ability of the legislature to hold the executive accountable has had a debilitating effect on the disciplinary impact of the doctrine of collective and ministerial responsibility to the legislature, a doctrine upon which rests the whole notion of RESPONSIBLE GOVERNMENT.

The imbalance between the legislature and the Cabinet is exacerbated by the increasing use of discretionary powers, conferred by the former on the Cabinet collectively or on ministers individually, to legislate by order-in-council or by ministerial order. When added to the Cabinet's traditional role of initiating the budget and ensuring its safe passage (*see* BUDGETARY PROCESS) and its preparation and introduction of all major legislative proposals, this development accounts for the growing belief that Parliament is in decline. Many reforms for improving the legislature's ability to scrutinize Cabinet activities have been proposed. It is because the bureaucratic infrastructure for which ministers are expected to be accountable to the Commons has become so enormous that the doctrine of ministerial responsibility has been discounted by the Cabinet as unreasonable. As a result, the problem of Cabinet dictatorship has been transformed into the larger problem of domination of both Cabinet and legislature by nonelected public servants. Any reforms designed to hold the Cabinet accountable will also have to address this related problem.

In addition to reforms to the Commons COMMITTEES, which may increase the surveillance capacities of the legislature, recent measures, in the name of FREEDOM OF INFORMATION, may alter the imbalance between the Cabinet and the leg-

PM Mulroney's first Cabinet posing with Her Excellency Jeanne Sauvé after the swearing-in ceremony in Sept 1984. Mulroney used the opportunity provided by his sweeping electoral victory to construct a Cabinet that was not only exceptionally large but was representative of regions and linguistic, racial and religious groups, as well as recognizing the increasing role of women in political life (*courtesy United Press Canada*).

islature. To better protect citizen's rights which are endangered by the exercise of discretionary executive powers, the office of OMBUDSMAN or parliamentary commissioner has been widely adopted by the provinces. Whether any remedy can now stem a tide running so strongly in favour of executive domination is doubtful, but responsible Cabinet government will not survive without such efforts. J.E. HODGETTS

Reading: T.A. Hockin, *Government in Canada* (1976).

Cable Television, a technique for transmitting information to and from the home, is revolutionizing many aspects of Canadian COMMUNICATIONS. Although it has been in Canada since 1952 and is technically simple, cable television in the 1980s is transforming Canadian broadcasting and program production, and has far-reaching implications on other aspects of communications as well.

For its first decade, cable TV was only a minor adjunct to the over-the-air television broadcasting system. Primarily a rural phenomenon, cable was concentrated in small communities that lacked a local TV service. Early CATV systems ("community antenna television") consisted of a "head-end" or antenna array placed atop a hill or high tower to trap distant, usually American, signals, and a coaxial cable distribution network to transport these signals to the homes; amplifiers periodically strengthened the signals en route. Even into the mid-1960s the industry remained small and insignificant. By 1964 only 215 000 homes (4% of Canadian households) subscribed.

The industry experienced rapid growth between about 1965 and 1975. Penetration approached 60% of Canadian households and systems were established in all major centres. Two factors help explain cable's popularity in urban communities: the proliferation of high-rise buildings debasing over-the-air reception, and the use of microwave to import distant (US) signals.

By 1982, 4.9 million households subscribed, representing 74.6% of the homes for which cable was available and 59.8% of all Canadian homes. Cable is provided on a local monopoly basis, and in 1982, 441 companies provided cable service; nonetheless, the industry is dominated by 3 multisystem companies — ROGERS CABLESYSTEMS INC, Télécable Videotron Ltée and MACLEAN HUNTER LTD — which together account for 50% of cable subscriptions (*see* MEDIA OWNERSHIP).

Evidently approaching maximum penetration in the mid-1970s, cable companies began to seek new ways of making money. The larger systems expanded capacity from 12 channels to 24 or more with a view to offering additional programming services, such as PAY TELEVISION and specialized channels, for additional fees. Two-way (interactive) capability was also introduced to facilitate nonprogramming services, such as medical alerts, burglar alarms, meter readings, and, prospectively, electronic banking, again at additional fees. Finally, hitherto discrete systems became interconnected by satellite, thereby potentially constituting cable television as a national data TELECOMMUNICATIONS network.

These developments have taken place only under controversy and with bitter disputes. One major obstacle hindering cable's development was the set of restrictions imposed on cable by the telephone industry. The cable industry has always been dependent on telephone companies for access to poles, ducts, easements and rights-of-way; without access to these facilities, few cable systems could even have been constructed. Access was granted, however, only under highly restrictive conditions that were designed to limit service offerings and to neutralize cable's potentially competitive threat. Under the "partial system agreements" offered by the telephone industry, cable companies were precluded from owning coaxial cable; they were required to lease it from the telephone companies after paying for the costs incurred in construction. Moreover, cable companies were prohibited from transmitting signals other than radio or television signals. Frequently proscribed also was all limited network, point-to-point and 2-way communication, which meant that many services, including pay television were excluded. In BELL CANADA ENTERPRISES' territory (Ontario and Québec) these types of restriction were struck down only in 1977 by a decision of the CANADIAN RADIO-TELEVISION AND TELECOMMUNICATIONS COMMISSION (Decision CRTC 77-6) which ordered that cable companies be permitted to own cable, that access charges imposed by Bell be reasonable, and that no restrictions on services be imposed (*see* TELEPHONES).

A second major obstacle slowing cable development was regulatory policy designed to protect over-the-air television broadcasters from a potential financial crisis. Declared to be a component of the broadcasting system by the Broadcasting Act, cable systems (termed "broadcasting receiving undertakings") were placed under the jurisdiction of the newly created CRTC in 1968 (*see* COMMUNICATIONS LAW). Until the late 1970s the commission was most concerned with preventing cable from fragmenting broadcasters' audiences and thereby reducing ADVERTISING revenues to the detriment of the cultural goals set for Canadian broadcasting. In 1969 and 1970, for example, the CRTC announced that cable systems would not be allowed to use microwave to improve the reception of US signals, and that normally only one US commercial and one US noncommercial signal would be authorized for cable rediffusion. Public outcry and the lobbying efforts of the cable industry forced the commission to relent, and in 1971 liberalized policies were announced. First, Canadian signals were to be given priority; paradoxically, this requirement induced many cable systems to expand channel capacity beyond the 12 existing channels in order to carry a full complement of US stations, thereby further fragmenting television audiences. Second, cable systems were "requested" to compensate broadcasters for the use made of their signals; this request was rarely fulfilled, however. Third, cable companies were required to delete US signals during times of program duplication with a Canadian station; however, this obligation served to protect the American content of Canadian stations while it left their Canadian content exposed to the full measure of competition. Finally, while required to offer "community programming," cable companies were nonetheless precluded from selling advertising time and from distributing program material, such as movies, sports and drama, that was competitive with the programming of over-the-air broadcasters (*see* TELEVISION PROGRAMMING).

A new stance toward cable became evident in the early 1980s, signalled first by the CRTC's publication of *The 1980's: A Decade of Diversity: Broadcasting, Satellites and Pay-TV* (1980). Noting that some 35 non-network programming services were then being transmitted on US satellites, the document proclaimed that "a new technological universe . . . [was] already taking shape at a pace that is inexorable." It therefore recommended that cable systems quickly become interconnected by satellites and that pay television and other new programming services be licensed. In 1982 the commission duly licensed several satellite-to-cable pay television services and in 1984 it similarly licensed several specialty channels (music videos, sports, news, etc). These licensing decisions all signal a reversal from the previous protectionist stance of the regulator in favour of established television broadcasters, and an easing of its restrictions on cable television (*see* SATELLITE COMMUNICATIONS).

Cable TV has also been at the centre of continual federal-provincial jurisdictional disputes For example, during the mid-1970s, Québec asserted authority to license all cable undertakings in the province; consequently, cable companies for a time required both federal and provincia licences. In Rimouski the conflict came to a head as different companies were licensed by the 2 governments. In the summer of 1975 the provincial licensee, Cablodistribution de l'Est actually hid its receiving antennae in the surrounding marshlands to prevent it from being confiscated by federal authorities. Subscribers complaining about the resulting disruption in service were told that the antennae, on loan from the provincial government to replace an earlier set already confiscated, would be reconnected as soon as the RCMP left the area. In Québec's view, cable should be under provincia jurisdiction because of its local nature and its impact on language, education and culture (*see* COMMUNICATIONS IN QUÉBEC).

The Prairie governments too have asserted provincial jurisdiction, viewing cable as a telecommunications carrier akin to, and indeed potentially competitive with, provincially owned telephone companies. Exclusive federal jurisdiction was confirmed by the Supreme Cour in 1977, however. By the Radio case of 193. the radio frequency is subject to federal authority; consequently, cable television systems (a "broadcasting receiving undertakings") also fal within federal authority since they make use o radio frequencies.

It is apparent that cable television is transforming Canadian broadcasting. Heretofore the number of entities authorized to broadcast in any locality was limited by spectrum scarcity and by the technical necessity of apportioning radio frequencies geographically. Cable television, however, by using wires instead of spac (ether) permits a much enlarged channel capacity, dramatically increasing the number of competing services. Furthermore, government policy on broadcasting has traditionally centered on the message, using broadcasting as a mean of promoting national unity and safeguarding Canadian culture. These goals, always elusive have become even more problematic as marke forces increase and heighten competition, reducing the ability of govern-ment to legislate or administer performance (*see* BROADCASTING, RADIO AND TELEVISION).

Because of the abundance of channels available on cable and because satellite reception covers a broad area, a reorientation is taking plac in broadcast programming. Instead of being targeted geographically at particular locations, programs are increasingly being targeted at identifiable audiences (eg, the young, the old, womer blacks, professionals). Cable television in conjunction with satellites will, therefore, largel destroy broadcasting as an instrument for Canadian political and cultural sovereignty.

Cable television is also a factor revolutionizing Canadian telecommunications. Hitherto cable and telephone systems were distinct, bot technologically and in the services offered. Al though both industries brought communicatio to the home by wire on a monopoly basis, cabl was one-way for many years while telephon systems were bidirectional. Moreover, telephones possessed full switching capacity an offered point-to-point service, whereas cabl was unswitched, offering only a point-to-mas service. Furthermore, telephone companies wer interconnected nationally by microwave whil cable systems were discrete, local entities. Finally, telephones were optimized at the terminal for one voice channel, while cable systen employed bandwidths of up to several hundre thousand voice channels (50 TV channels). To day, however, telephone and cable systems a converging technologically; consequently the ervices will increasingly overlap as well, at east in the absence of regulatory or collusive arrangements to divide up the markets. Both elephone and cable companies are experimenting with optical fibre (10 KHz bandwidth), which will give enormous capacity at the terminal for both systems. Modern cable systems are bidirectional, and some are experimenting with switched services and techniques; packet switching will probably make introduction of switching quite feasible. Cable is now interconnected nationally through satellite, another development that points to technological convergence.

Inasmuch as cable is transforming broadcasting and converging with telecommunications, it is also causing broadcasting to converge with telecommunications. Cable is thereby placing a severe strain on policy, since the laws, goals and regulations in these hitherto separate areas have been diametrically opposed. Broadcasting policy has historically focused on the messages and their perceived cultural impact, and rarely upon economic or technological issues such as prices, profits, rates of depreciation, and innovative techniques for relaying messages. Licences to transmit were apportioned on the basis of expected contribution to Canadian ocial, political and cultural goals. By contrast, in telecommunications, regulation focused on economic factors and on the means of transmission, attempting to ensure just and reasonable access for senders and receivers of messages, and largely ignoring the nature of the messages or their cultural impact.

It is apparent that such dichotomous policies can no longer be maintained with the convergence of broadcasting and telecommunications. Fundamental policy questions are raised. Should cable continue to be governed by historic broadcasting concerns — the licensing of message originators on the basis of contributions to culture? Or should cable be treated as a common carrier, with price and profit regulation to ensure equitable access by any and all message originators? Should cable companies be required to pay broadcasters for the programming that is at present being rediffused without compensation? Or should program originators pay cable companies access fees for diffusion over cable facilities? Should cable companies be allowed to select (any of) the programming or to integrate vertically into program production (as has been the practice in television broadcasting)? Or should cable companies be precluded from exercising any control whatsoever over the messages they diffuse (the principle of the common carrier)? These are some of the difficult issues facing policy-makers in the 1980s. *See also* COMMUNICATIONS TECHNOLOGY. ROBERT E. BABE

Reading: Robert E. Babe, *Cable Television and Telecommunications in Canada* (1975) and *Canadian Television Broadcasting:* (1979); Babe and C. Winn, *Broadcasting Policy and Copyright Law:* (1984); CRTC, *The 1980's: A Decade of Diversity — Broadcasting, Satellites and Pay-TV* (1980); Dept of Communications, *Towards a New National Broadcasting Policy* (1983); R.B. Woodrow et al, *Conflict over Communications Policy:* (1980); Woodrow and K.B. Woodside, eds, *The Introduction of Pay TV in Canada* (1982).

Cabot, John, Anglo-Italian navigator, explorer (b at Genoa, Italy 1449/50; d probably off the coast of Newfoundland 1498/99). Cabot's voyages of discovery from Bristol, Eng (1497, 1498), were the first recorded landfalls on the N American continent since the Norse voyages. Cabot conceived the idea of reaching Asia by sailing westward across the Atlantic. In 1496 Henry VII authorized him and his 3 sons to search, at their own expense, for unknown lands to the W. Cabot left Bristol on 2 May 1497 with 18 men. On 24 June 1497 he landed somewhere on the N American coast — the actual place of landing most likely being in Labrador, Newfoundland or Cape Breton I. Cabot claimed the

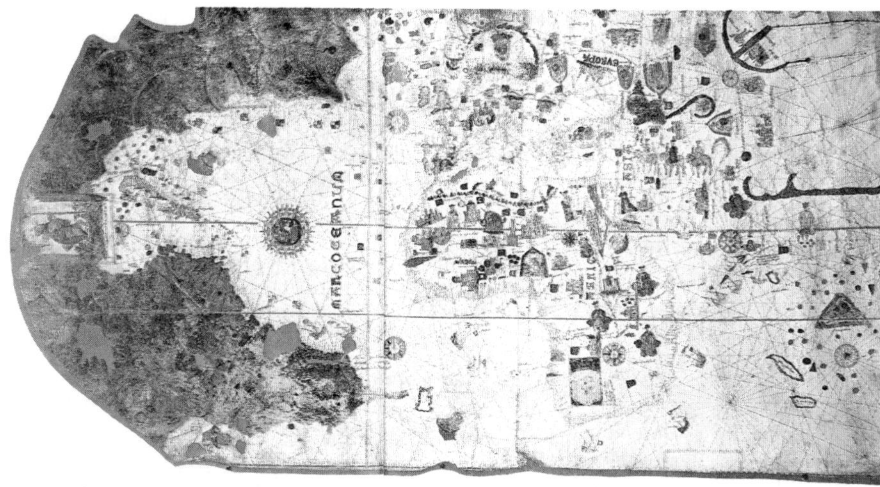

This left portion of La Cosa's world map of 1500/1508 shows the Caribbean area with North America, supposedly explored by John Cabot *(courtesy Public Archives of Canada/NMC-26688)*.

land for England and returned to Bristol, arriving in Aug. Early in 1498 Henry VII authorized a second expedition consisting of 5 ships and 300 men. After landing in Greenland, Cabot sailed southward, probably as far as Chesapeake Bay, but failing to find the rich lands he had envisaged and because supplies were running low he turned back towards England. It appears that Cabot perished on this voyage, though one or more of his ships may have returned to Bristol. Most historians maintain that he was probably lost off the coast of Newfoundland. Because the fact that Cabot had found a new continent soon became known in Europe, Cabot made what has been called "the intellectual discovery of America." His voyages provided the basis for England's claim to N America and led to the opening of the rich NW Atlantic fishery.

JOHN PARSONS

Cabot Strait, the passage between SW Newfoundland and CAPE BRETON ISLAND. Named for explorer John CABOT, it is 110 km wide between Cape Ray, Nfld, and Cape North, NS. The principal oceangoing route to the GULF OF ST LAWRENCE, and hence to much of eastern Canada, it has been of strategic importance in Canadian military and commercial history. Though sometimes hindered by pack ice from the gulf, steamers between CHANNEL-PORT AUX BASQUES and SYDNEY (later NORTH SYDNEY) connected the Newfoundland railway with the Canadian system after 1898. CN Marine ferries now connecting the 2 provinces carry more than 300 000 people across the strait each year. A submarine telegraph cable was laid across Cabot Str in 1856, eventually joining N America and Europe via the transatlantic cable (1866). ROBERT D. PITT

Cactus (Cactaceae), family of PLANTS having fleshy, often spined, stems and branches. Cacti are succulents, ie, they store moisture in spongy tissues. Of an estimated 2000 species, fewer than 50 are cold resistant. Four species are known in Canada: 3 belonging to genus *Opuntia;* one, to genus *Coryphantha.* The most northerly growing cactus in the world, the fragile or little prickly pear *(O. fragilis)* is the smallest Canadian cactus. The easily detached pads (2-4 cm long) are as thick as they are wide (1-2 cm); the small spines (1-2 cm long) are savagely barbed. The species occurs singly or in colonies up to one metre across. The most widespread and adaptable of Canadian cacti, the little prickly pear lives in the most diverse environments: the dry belt and PEACE RIVER areas of BC; WHITESHELL PROVINCIAL PARK, Man (which experiences the coldest Canadian winters); the granite rocks along Mellon Creek near Kaladar, 150 km SW of Ottawa. The common plains prickly pear *(O. polyacantha)* has larger, more typical pads, 5-10 cm long, 4-10 cm wide, 1 cm thick. It is common only in southern Alberta and Saskatchewan. The high concentration on RANGELANDS is thought to result from overgrazing, which thins out the natural grass and leaves behind noxious weeds. Only deer and a few small rodents can eat it without hurting themselves with the sharp, 5 cm long spines. Eastern prickly pear, *O. compressa* (formerly *O. humifusa),* 10-15 cm long, 8-10 cm wide and 1 cm thick, has pads, and has a few long, sharp spines projecting from the top. The rest of the pad is covered with almost invisible, sliverlike barbs. *O. compressa* occurs in large clumps, some over one metre across. It is limited to Essex County, southern Ontario, eg, POINT PELEE NATIONAL PARK. The fragrance-free flowers of Canadian *Opuntias* have vivid yellow, silk-textured, rounded petals and bright red or yellow central filaments.

Coryphantha vivipara, a charming little ball or pincushion, grows as single balls (up to 8 cm diameter) or as a cluster (up to 20 cm) of up to 20 equal-sized balls. Sharp spines (under 1 cm long) surround the ball in tight rosettes. The small flowers (2-3 cm diameter) have pointed, deep magenta petals surrounding the centre of gold-

Ball or pincushion cactus *(Coryphantha vivipara)* in bloom in southern Alberta *(courtesy Elliott and Nicole Bernshaw/Bernshaw Photography)*.

en-yellow filaments. The blooms usually appear in June. The ball cactus is common throughout the southern prairies.

It has been suggested that cacti came to Canada as a result of dispersal of fruits and seeds by rodents and birds. Barbed species could have spread by sticking to migratory animals. The processes by which cold-resistant cacti survive extreme low temperatures are not completely understood; however, they do dehydrate in the fall, thereby concentrating their sap into an antifreezelike solution. Prickly pears become flabby and lie almost flat against the ground. A blanket of protective snow then shields them from the full force of winter. NICOLE BERNSHAW

Caddisfly, small, drab INSECT of order Trichoptera [Gk "hairy wings"]. Adults have long legs and antennae, large, compound eyes, rudimentary mouthparts and 2 pairs of veined, hairy wings. At rest, wings are held rooflike over the body. Almost 600 species are known from Canada; world total may be over 10 000. Larvae are common in most freshwater habitats. Those of the most familiar species live in a portable case of plant fragments or mineral particles held together by silk. They feed principally on leaves. Others spin silken nets, which filter food from water currents, or are free-ranging predators. One to several years are spent as larvae. Larva transforms to adult through a nonfeeding pupal stage, spent in a sealed case in the water. Adults swim to the surface and discard the pupal skin. They are generally nocturnal, with a terrestrial existence lasting a few weeks. G. PRITCHARD

Cadet, Joseph-Michel, butcher, military provisioner (b at Québec City 24 Dec 1719; d at Paris, France 31 Jan 1781). Born of generations of butchers, Cadet worked first for his uncle, a Québec butcher, and became the Crown's purveyor of meat in 1745. Two wars and the increase in the colony's garrisons expanded his trade and opportunities. In 1749 he received a monopoly as beef retailer at Québec and in 1756 became general contractor for military provisions in Canada. His rise owed much to his shrewdness and willingness to take risks. His business expanded and the ships he bought and hired kept the colony supplied until 1759. In 1760 he left for France where he and others were arrested for embezzling government funds. After paying nearly 4 million *livres* "in restitution," he lived as a country gentleman in France. He is regarded as either the greatest profiteer under Intendant BIGOT or a luckless scapegoat for the loss of New France. PETER N. MOOGK

Cadets Public interest in the military training of young Canadians has waxed in time of wars and threat of wars, and waned in peacetime. For more than a century the preparation of young men (and recently, of women) for careers as professional soldiers has been done within the ARMED FORCES, mainly at MILITARY COLLEGES. Less extensive and less specialized training aimed at youth of high school age has been provided mainly through the Canadian cadet organizations. Under the National Defence Act, the Department of National Defence is in partnership with the NAVY LEAGUE, the Army Cadet League, and the Air Cadet League in operating and supporting a movement for youth (both male and female) between 12 and 19. Cadets number approximately 60 000 and are located in over 1000 corps across Canada. Training is conducted at corps headquarters during the school year and at more than 30 DND-supported summer camps. At present about 19 000 cadets participate in cadet training each summer. About 250 cadets take part each year in exchange programs with Britain, the US, and various European countries. N.F. DREISZIGER AND PETER PHELAN

Cadieux, Jean Legendary French Canadian VOYAGEUR of the 18th century who lived in the Ottawa R region. When his cabin was attacked by Indians, he sent his family down the rapids in his canoe and stayed behind to prevent pursuit. The Virgin Mary is supposed to have guided the canoe through the rapids, which were generally portaged. Pursued by the Indians through the forest, Cadieux gradually weakened; he dug his own grave, erected a cross above it and composed a ballad about his misfortune, which he wrote in blood on birchbark; it was found by those who came to look for him. The ballad is well known in French Canadian tradition. NANCY SCHMITZ

Cadieux, Marcel, diplomat (b at Montréal 17 June 1915; d at Pompano Beach, Fla 19 Mar 1981). A tough, astute international lawyer and fierce anticommunist, Cadieux served in the Dept of External Affairs 1941-79. As undersecretary of state 1964-70, Cadieux was an efficient administrator and uncompromising federalist, pressing for a department and a foreign policy that would reflect Canada's bicultural origins. He subsequently was ambassador to Washington 1970-75, headed the Canadian Mission to the EEC 1975-77, and was chief negotiator for Canada-US fisheries and boundary disputes 1977-1979. He wrote an elegant diplomatic primer, *The Canadian Diplomat* (1963). ANNE HILLMER

Cadillac, Antoine Laumet, dit de Lamothe, fur-trader, military officer, founder of Detroit (b at Les Laumets, France 5 Mar 1658; d at Castelsarrasin, France 15 Oct 1730). Cadillac succeeded in promoting himself from obscure origins — he gave himself the noble title de Lamothe Cadillac — to wealth and positions of command. In Acadia *c*1683-91 he served with a privateer, traded and quarrelled with the governor. He moved to Québec in 1691 and was commissioned in the TROUPES DE LA MARINE. One of FRONTENAC's protégé's, he was commandant at Michilimackinac 1693-97, where he successfully pursued the FUR TRADE. With the west closed to trade because of the glut in furs, Cadillac established a settlement at Detroit as a way of preventing English expansion and controlling the trade with the western tribes. There 1701-10, he was removed from command when it became clear that he was attempting to create an empire for himself. He again attempted to enrich himself as governor of Louisiana 1710-17 and was soon at odds with officials there, including BIENVILLE. He left the colony in 1718 and finished his life as governor of Castelsarrasin. Regarded as "sharp," a liar and greedy, he also was an articulate, plausible man with a good deal of charm and undoubted energy. MARY MCDOUGALL MAUDE

Cadmium (Cd), soft, ductile, silvery white metal which melts at 320.9°C and is present in the Earth's crust at 0.1-0.5 parts per million. The most common cadmium MINERAL, greenockite (CdS), is generally found in zinc-bearing ores and is recovered as a by-product during processing. Cadmium is used principally as a protective coating for other metals, eg, for electroplating IRON AND STEEL products to improve appearance and protect against rusting. The second-largest use is in the manufacture of yellow and red pigments. A growing application is in the production of rechargeable nickel-cadmium and silver-cadmium batteries. In 1983 Canada, with a production of 1369 t, was the Western world's third-largest producer of cadmium, following Japan and the US. Cadmium is produced at all 4 Canadian ZINC PLANTS. About 90% of Canadian production is exported, mostly to the US and the UK. M.J. GAUVIN

Cahén, Oscar painter, illustrator (b at Copenhagen, Denmark 8 Feb 1916; d at Oakville, Ont 26 Nov 1956). Trained in Europe, he taught in Prague before escaping the Nazi occupation in 1938. He was interned in England in 1939 and then shipped to Canada in 1940 and interned at Sherbrooke, Qué. After his release in 1942, he worked in Montréal before moving to Toronto in 1944. Cahén gained a major reputation as an illustrator working for such magazines as *Maclean's*, *Chatelaine* and *New Liberty*. In the late 1940s he met Walter Yarwood, Harold TOWN and others involved in avant-garde art in Toronto. Cahén was included in the "Abstracts at Home" exhibition held in 1953 at the Robert Simpson Co, Toronto. He became one of the PAINTERS ELEVEN when the group was formed later that year. Cahén's dark, expressionist paintings of the late 1940s, often on religious subjects, gave way in the early 1950s to brilliantly coloured abstractions. He and his colleagues in Painters Eleven achieved the breakthrough of radical painting in Toronto. DAVID BURNETT

Reading: David Burnett, *Oscar Cahén* (1983).

Larry Cain in action at the 1984 Los Angeles Olympics where he won a gold medal in canoeing (*courtesy Athlete Information Bureau/Service Information-Athlètes*).

Cain, Larry, canoeist (b at Toronto 9 Jan 1963). He finished first in the C-1 canoe over 1000 m (time 4:35.1) and second over 500 m (2:01.7) at the Pan-American Championships in 1980 and in 1981 was the first Canadian canoeist in 4 years to win a World or Olympic event with 2 gold medals at the junior world championships. He competed in numerous international canoeing events through to 1984, in which he finished first in the C-1 1000 m and the C-1 500 m at the Nottinghamshire International Regatta. At the 1984 Los Angeles Olympics he won a gold medal (C-1 500 m, 1:57.01) and a silver (C-1 1000 m, 4:08.67). He was a commerce student at McMaster U at the time of the Olympics. JAMES MARSH

Caiserman-Roth, Ghitta, painter (b at Montréal 2 Mar 1923), outstanding example of the creativity of women artists that has characterized a century of artistic activity in Montréal. Caiserman-Roth's studies in New York led to work characterized by a strong social orientation and expressionist style (*Backyard*, 1948). In the early 1950s she began exploring domestic and studio interiors, self-portraits and portraits of her child and of anonymous models, handling these subjects with quiet and disturbing intensity. Throughout the years certain themes and images have been repeated — the harlequin, the "Flying Wallendas," the deliberate confusion of interior and exterior space, the human figure imprinted on abandoned clothes, lawn chairs, sheets (*Bedscape with Shadow*, 1978). She helped establish the Montréal Artists School and has taught at Sir George Williams U and the Saidye Bronfman Centre. D.F. ANDRUS

Caisse de dépôt et placement du Québec (Québec Deposit and Investment Fund), with head offices in Montréal, is the investor of funds for the QUÉBEC PENSION PLAN. Created in 1965 a a fiduciary institution, the caisse has grown by making substantial investments. It now has a substantial portfolio for the QPP and 13 other public agencies it represents, and there has been concern in some sectors that it is too powerful for a government agency. In 1982, in partnership with others, it took control of NORANDA MINES LIMITED, DOMTAR INC and Gaz Métropolitain Inc, and has large interests in PROVIGO INC, Sogebry Ltd and the Prenor Group Ltd. In 1983 it had sales or operating revenue of $1.8 billion, assets of $18.2 billion (ranking 6th among banks and financial institutions in Canada) and 176 employees. The province of Québec holds 100% of the shares. DEBORAH C. SAWYER

Caisse populaire, established 1900 as a co-operative savings and loans company with nonfixed capital and limited liability in Lévis, Qué, by Alphonse DESJARDINS, a journalist and French-language stenographer in the House of Commons. Desjardins used European savings and loan companies as models for his enterprise. He encouraged the working classes to save and plan for the future and provided the credit they needed for economic recovery. Desjardins also hoped the caisse would contribute to the economic emancipation of French Canadians. The Caisse populaire de Lévis opened on 23 Jan 1901 in Desjardins's own home; 12 people paid a total of $26.40 as first payment of their share in the partnership. The first savings deposit, made on 7 Feb, was for only 5 cents. By 1906, savings amounted to only $9556.53; in the same year, after vigorous lobbying by Desjardins and his friends, the Québec legislature adopted the Act on co-operative credit unions. In 1920, when Desjardins died, 206 caisses populaires had been established, including 23 in Ontario and 9 in French Canadian communities in New England, largely as a result of the clergy's unfailing support of and eager participation in this undertaking. Many caisses were tied to churches through the bond-of-association concept. Desjardins's successors established 10 regional caisses populaires which today form La Fédération de Québec des Unions regionales de Caisses populaires Desjardins, with its head office in Lévis. The fédération provides study, publicity, training, supervision and management services for the financial giant which the caisse populaire movement has become. In 1962 several caisses broke away and formed La Fédération de Montréal. In Dec 1980, the 1566 caisses had assets in excess of $14.7 billion and over 5 million shareholders. Investments include shares of the Provincial Bank of Canada and ownership of La Société de Fiducie du Québec. YVES ROBY

Calder, Frank Arthur, politician, businessman (b at Nass Harbour, BC 3 Aug 1915). Calder, a Nishga, was the first Indian member of a Canadian legislature and second native legislator after Louis RIEL. He graduated from the Anglican Theological Coll, UBC, in 1946 and worked at various times as fish-plant tallyman, trade unionist, machinist and entrepreneur. He served as a British Columbia MLA for 26 years, first with the CCF-NDP and after 1975 with Social Credit. In 1972 he became the first native Canadian Cabinet minister but was dismissed amid controversy in 1973. He was president of the N American Indian Brotherhood in 1944, organizer for the Native Brotherhood of BC, and a founder of the Nishga Tribal Council, now the Nishga Nation (president, 1955-74). Calder's views on Indian economic development, his opposition to the reserve system and his partial endorsement of the 1969 White Paper (*see* NATIVE PEOPLE, GOVERNMENT POLICY) brought him into conflict with others in the Indian movement. His name is widely known through the CALDER CASE, a landmark 1973 Supreme Court decision on Nishga LAND CLAIMS (*see* ABORIGINAL RIGHTS). BENNETT MCCARDLE

Calder Case (1973) reviewed the existence of "aboriginal title" claimed over lands historically occupied by the Nishga Indians of northwestern BC. The Supreme Court of Canada by a majority recognized that aboriginal title could exist in common law, but split 3-3 on its validity, half of them declaring the right was never extinguished by statute or treaty. Justice Pigeon tipped the balance against the Nishga on a procedural point — that permission to sue the BC government had not been obtained from the attorney general. Chief Calder lost his case, but the aboriginal title question was not settled. The decision led to federal willingness to negotiate native LAND CLAIMS. DAVID A. CRUICKSHANK

Calder Trophy is awarded annually to the player chosen by hockey writers as being the most proficient in his first year of competition in the NATIONAL HOCKEY LEAGUE. To be eligible, a player cannot have previously played more than 25 games in any major professional league. It was first presented in 1936 by Frank Calder, NHL President, and was renamed Calder Memorial Trophy after his death in 1943. The first winner was Carl Voss. Among players who have won the trophy and gone on to stardom are Terry SAWCHUK, Bernie GEOFFRION, Frank MAHOVLICH and Bobby ORR. JAMES MARSH

Calgary, second-largest city in Alberta, is situated on the BOW R in the southern part of the province, about 220 km N of the American boundary at the meeting point of the western prairies and mountain foothills. Strategically located on major rail, highway and air corridors, Calgary is an important transportation centre. It is also the financial centre of western Canada and headquarters of Canada's oil and natural-gas industries. With its panoramic backdrop of the Rocky Mountains and historic association with the ranching frontier, Calgary is one of N America's most identifiable cities.

Settlement The earliest indications of human settlement in the Calgary area, dating back some 12 000 years, consist of spearpoints found in ploughed fields E of the city. This period coincided with the end of the last ice age when glaciers from the Canadian SHIELD receded from the valley of the Bow R. The successive cycle of nomadic hunting peoples over the next 10 000 years included at least 3 dominant cultures. The last, around the time of Christ, brought the Blackfoot from the eastern woodlands. Among later arrivals were the Sarcee, who came from the N in the 1700s, and still later the Stoney from the Manitoba area. Archaeological evidence of prehistoric peoples is confined mainly to campsites and bison kills. Fireplaces, storage pits and tipi rings date back over 2000 years. Sites depicting religious customs also exist in the form of fieldstone medicine wheels, cairns and effigies, while a pictograph panel can be seen on the Big Rock near Okotoks, S of Calgary.

The westward movement of the fur trade brought the first Europeans to the area in the late 18th century. David THOMPSON of the North West Co wintered near Calgary (1787), and Peter FIDLER of the Hudson's Bay Co skirted the Calgary region (1792). In the 1860s buffalo hunters from the US appeared in increasing numbers, joined by illicit-whisky traders who erected a network of fortified posts in southern Alberta from which they sold vile alcholic concoctions to the Indians in return for buffalo robes. One such post was located in the Calgary area near the present-day Glenmore Reservoir. The whisky traders' activities in part led to the formation of the NORTH-WEST MOUNTED POLICE by the federal government (1873). Their second post was established at the confluence of the Bow and Elbow rivers in 1875, and was named Fort Calgary in 1876. (The word Calgary, likely of Gaelic origin, may be translated to mean "Bay Farm.") The railway reached Fort Calgary in 1883 and the CPR subsequently laid out its Calgary townsite W of the Elbow and S of the Bow rivers. Calgary was incorporated as the first town in present-day Alberta in 1884, receiving city status in 1893.

Development Calgary's economic growth was closely associated with the development of the livestock industry, and with the city's focal position as the chief transportation centre in Alberta. Before 1906 the open-range cattle industry was dominant and Calgary effected its influence commercially, industrially and socially. The city's first millionaire, Pat BURNS, built up the largest integrated meat business in Canada. The cattle industry, especially after the crippling winter of 1906-07, contributed a volatile element to Calgary's urban development, despite the boosters who continually referred to the city as a thriving cattle town. The opening of southern Alberta to cash-crop farming in the early 1900s produced rapid growth in Calgary, which increased its population by over 1000% from 1901 to 1911. Rails stretching in all directions solidified the city's position as the prime distributing centre for S-central and southern Alberta. After 1912 Calgary's development slowed along with that of rural Alberta, appreciably so after the end of the immigration boom and the onset of WWI.

A third and most crucial element in Calgary's economic development has been the oil and natural-gas industries. Beginning with the first strike in 1914 at TURNER VALLEY, a few km SW of Calgary, local entrepreneurs such as W.S. Herron, A.W. Dingman and R.A. Brown continually promoted Calgary's future as a major oil centre. Alberta's first oil refinery opened in Calgary (1923). Subsequent important discoveries at Turner Valley (1924, 1936) established Calgary's pre-eminence in Canada's oil and natural-gas industries. When the lid was eventually lifted off western Canada's vast oil reserves at LEDUC in 1947, Calgary stood ready to reap the rewards. The city's subsequent phenomenal growth from an urban expression of southern Alberta to a metropolis of international status is a direct offshoot of its economic development. Another aspect of Calgary's development has been a continuation of a longstanding and intense rivalry with Edmonton. The two Alberta cities have competed keenly at every level, and have produced one of Canada's most identifiable urban rivalries.

Cityscape The Bow R valley forms the main topographical feature of the city. Two smaller streams, the Elbow R and Nose Cr, flow through the city into the Bow, creating a configuration of valleys and bluffs. The placement of railways has also affected spatial growth patterns. The main business section is compressed between the Bow R and the CPR main line. Residential development has tended to follow the river valleys, originally along the Elbow, and more recently along the Bow to the NW and SE. Other influencing factors include U of Calgary and the International Airport to the N, and the Glenmore Reservoir, Sarcee Indian Reserve and Fish Creek Prov Pk to the S. Manufacturing districts are located to the E, in the railway suburbs of Ogden, and in zoned areas along the railways. Formal planning began in 1911 when an English town planner, Thomas Mawson, was

Population: 592 743 (1981c; CMA)
Rate of Increase (1971-81): (CMA) 47%
Rank in Canada: Sixth (by CMA)
Date of Incorporation: Town 1884; City 1893
Land Area: 498.9 km²
Elevation: 1048.41 m
Climate: Average daily temp, July 16.5°C, Jan -10.9°C; Yearly precip 437.1 mm; Hours of sunshine 2207 per year

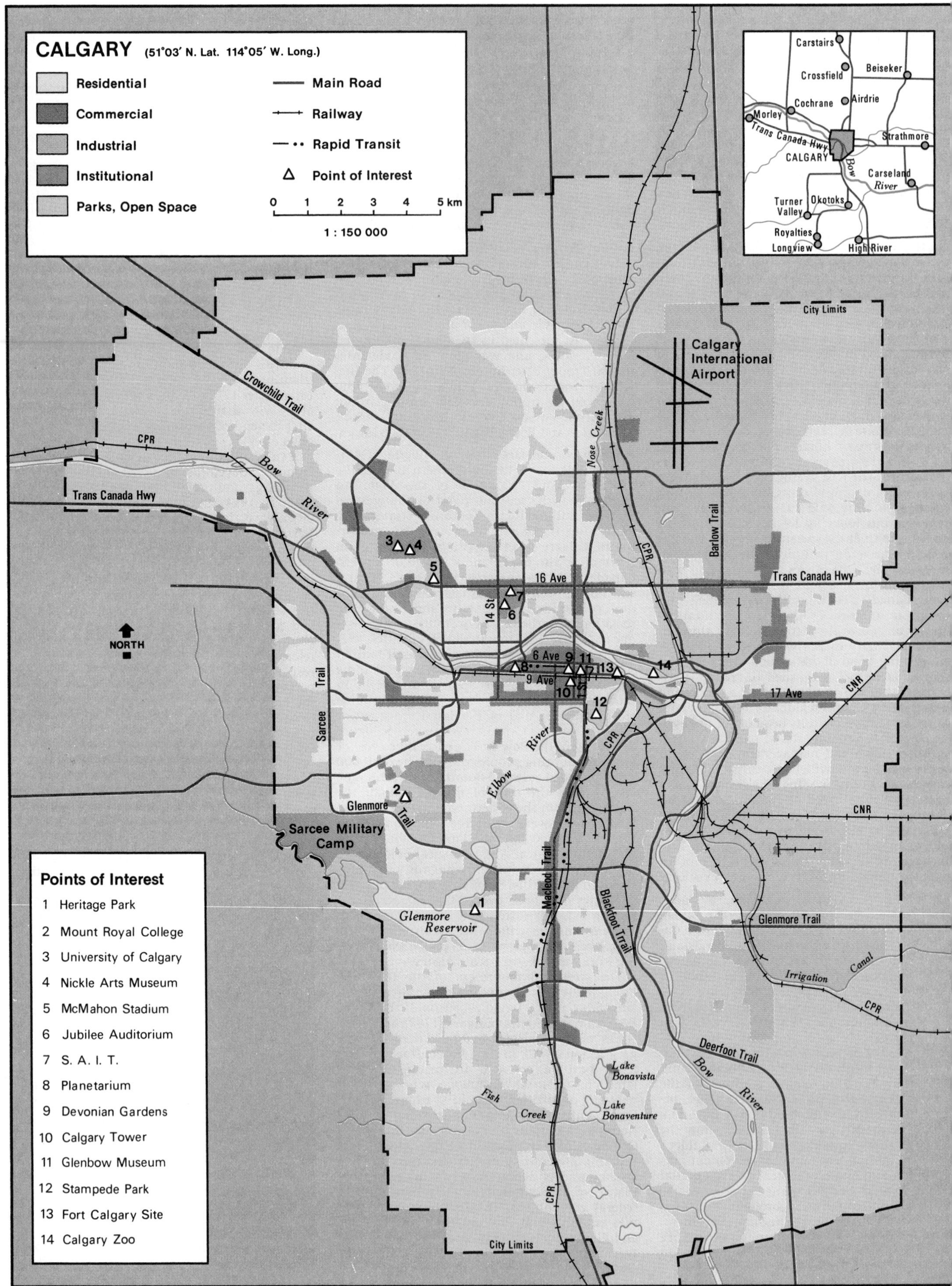

CALGARY (51°03′ N. Lat. 114°05′ W. Long.)
Residential
Commercial
Industrial
Institutional
Parks, Open Space
Main Road
Railway
Rapid Transit
Point of Interest
0 1 2 3 4 5 km
1 : 150 000
Carstairs
Crossfield
Beiseker
Cochrane
Airdrie
Morley
Trans Canada Hwy
CALGARY
Bow
Strathmore
Carseland
River
Turner Valley
Okotoks
Royalties
Longview
High River
City Limits
Calgary International Airport
Crowchild Trail
CPR
Bow River
Trans Canada Hwy
Nose Creek
Barlow Trail
16 Ave
14 St
NORTH
6 Ave
9 Ave
17 Ave
CNR
Sarcee Trail
Elbow River
Glenmore Trail
Sarcee Military Camp
Macleod Trail
Blackfoot Trail
Glenmore Reservoir
Irrigation Canal
Deerfoot Trail
Lake Bonavista
Lake Bonaventure
Fish Creek
Points of Interest
1 Heritage Park
2 Mount Royal College
3 University of Calgary
4 Nickle Arts Museum
5 McMahon Stadium
6 Jubilee Auditorium
7 S. A. I. T.
8 Planetarium
9 Devonian Gardens
10 Calgary Tower
11 Glenbow Museum
12 Stampede Park
13 Fort Calgary Site
14 Calgary Zoo

commissioned to prepare a comprehensive scheme. His extravagant proposals (1914) were never implemented. A zoning bylaw was instituted in 1934 and a city planning department established in 1950. In 1963 the city adopted its first general plan for controlling future development (rev 1970, 1973). The Alberta Planning Act (1977) directed Calgary to adopt a more regional approach to planning.

Population Calgary's population is predominantly Anglo-Saxon (56%, 1970) and Protestant (57.9%, 1970). In 1977 English was the mother tongue of 84% in Calgary, the highest of any large Canadian urban centre. The rapid population growth 1900-11 and post-1947 stemmed from extensive immigration, which in 1980 was estimated at over 75% of the total annual increase. The large migration of young adults has generally kept the city's average age well below the national average. Since WWII Calgary has consistently ranked as one of Canada's fastest-growing cities, and according to current projections it will exceed one million people in 1991.

Population Growth in Calgary 1891-1981

Year	*Population*	*Numerical Change*	*Percent Change*
1891	3 876	—	—
1901	4 398	522	13.5
1911	43 704	39 306	893.7
1921	63 305	19 601	44.8
1931	83 761	20 456	32.3
1941	88 904	5 143	6.1
1951	129 060	40 156	45.2
1961	249 641	120 581	93.4
1971	403 319	153 678	61.6
1981	591 857	188 538	46.7

Economy and Labour Force Calgary's economy has historically been associated with commerce and distribution. Its more recent emergence as a world energy and financial centre is reflected in its third-ranking national position in the location of head offices (40, 1980), including those of NOVA, TRANSCANADA PIPELINES, PETRO-CANADA and DOME. The work force therefore shows a heavy orientation towards the professional, management and commercial sectors. "Blue collar" occupations have traditionally been dominated by the building, railway and, more recently, oil-supply trades. Calgary exceeds the national average in per capita income as well as in the percentage of total population in the work force. Yet, in spite of its recent position as Canada's fastest-growing and most prosperous city, it remains heavily dependent economically on a single, high-risk industry.

Distribution of Industrial Activity* by Industry Grouping within Census Metropolitan Areas, 1980

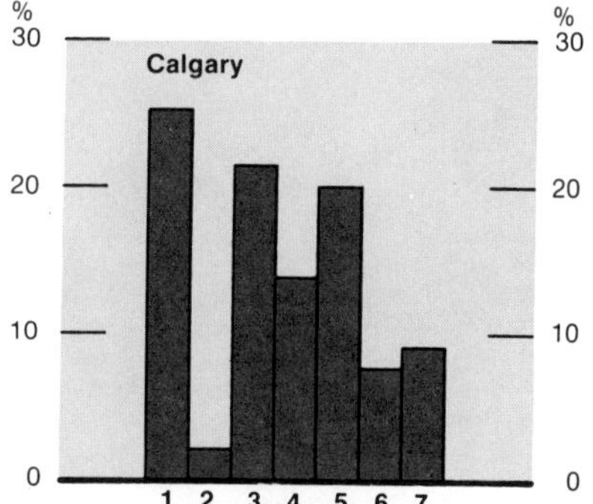

Industry groupings

1. Food and beverage and tobacco products industries
2. Leather, textile, knitting mills and clothing industries
3. Wood, furniture and fixtures, paper and allied and printing, publishing and allied industries
4. Machinery, transportation equipment and electrical products industries
5. Primary metal and metal fabricating industries
6. Rubber and plastic products, petroleum and coal products and chemical products industries
7. Non-metallic mineral products and miscellaneous manufacturing industries.

* Industry activity based on the average of percentage shares of the value shipments of goods of own manufacture, total value added and total number of employees for each of the selected metropolitan areas.

Source: Figure II, Catalogue 31-209, Statistics Canada.

Transportation Calgary is the centre of CPR rail operations in western Canada, with world-class freight classification yards at Alyth and major repair facilities at Ogden. The CNR has container and intermodal services into its Sarcee yards. Calgary's airport, one of the largest in Canada, features a new $130-million terminal (1977). The 8 primary airlines serving Calgary averaged 723 domestic and 133 international flights weekly in 1981. The city's municipal transportation system consists of motor buses supplemented by a recently developed Light Rail Transit (LRT) system.

Aerial view of Calgary, showing the Saddledome in the foreground. The city was established in 1875 as a North-West Mounted Police post at the confluence of the Bow and Elbow rivers (*courtesy City of Calgary/Jim Hall*).

Government and Politics The government of the city has been conducted under powers originally granted by the Northwest Territories and later (1905) by the Government of Alberta, most recently through the Municipal Government Act (1968). Before 1909 civic business was conducted almost entirely by council alone. Since then the system of a council and board of commissioners has been in operation in one form or another. The mayor and council members (representing the city's wards) fill 3-year terms. The board of commissioners consists of the mayor and 4 appointed members. The municipal franchise was reformed to exclude plural voting (1913) and property restrictions (1915). A preferential system of voting was initiated in 1916 and continued until 1958. Since the establishment of a board of public utilities (1916) the provincial government has wielded an ever-tightening control over the scope of local government in Calgary.

Cultural Life Cultural and recreational facilities have reflected Calgary's recent growth. Educationally the city is served by UNIVERSITY OF CALGARY, Mount Royal Community College, Southern Alberta Institute of Technology, Alberta Vocational Centre and the third-largest public-school system in Canada. Major cultural facilities include the GLENBOW MUSEUM, Fort Calgary Interpretive Centre, Calgary Centennial Planetarium and Heritage Park. The new Calgary Centre for the Performing Arts will include the 1800-seat Jack Singer Concert Hall, scheduled to open Sept 1985. while a large performing-arts centre is currently projected for the downtown area. The greatest concentration of enclosed spectator and exhibition facilities is in Stampede Pk, the home of the world-famous CALGARY STAMPEDE. Also the nearby Olympic Saddledome, built in anticipation of the 1988 Winter Olympics, is home to the CALGARY FLAMES of the NHL. The city's other professional sports team is the CALGARY STAMPEDERS of the CFL. Calgary boasts the second-largest zoo in Canada. Fish Creek Prov Pk, one of the world's largest urban parks, is located at the city's southern edge. Another attraction is Devonian Gardens, a 7 ha indoor garden in the heart of the downtown area. MAX L. FORAN

Reading: R.P. Baine, *Calgary; An Urban Study* (1973); B.M. Barr, ed, *Calgary, Metropolitan Structure and Influence* (1975); Max L. Foran, *Calgary: An Illustrated History* (1978); J.W. Grant MacEwan, *Calgary Cavalcade* (1975); Tom Ward, *Cow Town: An Album of Early Calgary* (1975).

Calgary Flames, hockey team. They were originally the Atlanta Flames, part of the 1972 NHL expansion that also involved the New York Islanders. With Edmonton Oilers' Peter Pocklington acting as facilitator, Vancouver's Nelson Skalbania brought the Flames to Calgary and then sold his interest in the team to a group of city businessmen headed by brothers Byron and Daryl Seaman. Under their inaugural and enduring general manager, Cliff Fletcher, the Flames have made the playoffs in all but 2 of their first 12 NHL campaigns, and in the 1983-84 playoffs took the Edmonton Oilers to a dramatic seventh game in the Smythe Division playoffs. In 1983 they occupied the new, 16 700-seat Olympic Saddledome. DEREK DRAGER

Calgary Stampede, whose proper title is Calgary Exhibition and Stampede, is a combined agricultural fair and rodeo. Other presentations such as manufacturing and home and garden exhibitions occur at the same time, as well as Indian displays, an evening stage show and a large midway with sideshows and rides. Every July the Stampede opens with a parade; the rodeo and other events continue for 10 days.

Billed as the "Greatest Outdoor Show on Earth," the world-famous Stampede rodeo began in 1912, instigated by Guy Weadick, an American who had visited Calgary and judged the emerging town to be a prime location for a big rodeo. With the help of H.C. McMullen, Weadick persuaded A.E. Cross, George Lane, A.J. McLean and Patrick BURNS to put up $100 000 financing. The first Stampede was a great success. The parade, combined with the annual Labour Day parade of the Calgary Trade and Labour Council, was enriched by the inclusion of rodeo competitors, the duke and duchess of Connaught and Lady Patricia, and 2000 Indians in full dress — and some 14 000 spectators. Prizes totalling $16 000 were provided for the rodeo events, which were highlighted by an electrifying bronc ride by Tom Three Persons on the famous Cyclone. In spite of its success, the Stampede was not repeated until August 1919 when a "Great Victory Stampede" was held. In 1923 the annual Agricultural Exhibition joined with a stampede with Weadick as Stampede Arena Director. An immediate success, the joint venture has continued to this day. As its fame spread, the Stampede expanded its facilities. Improvements to the grandstand, an ice rink, an exhibits building, which includes 48 sheets of curling ice during winter, and other constructions have increased the variety of Stampede services to the public and visitors.

The rodeo events include the traditional tests of cowboy versus animal, with bronc riding the premier competition. Professional cowboys are the contestants although team rodeo using semipros has been tried to reduce costs. The chuckwagon races — the Rangeland Derby — which began in 1923 have become an outstanding spectator event. The wagons are modifications of the food wagons once used to supply meals to cowboys out on the range during roundup. Each wagon is pulled by 4 horses and accompanied by 4 mounted outriders. The race starts with a tight figure-8 maneuvre in the infield before the wagons burst out onto the horse-racing track for a dash around to the finish. For professional cowboys a Stampede championship is a proud accomplishment. JEAN LEIPER

Reading: F. Kennedy, *The Calgary Stampede* (1964).

Calgary Stampeders, football team. Prior to WWII Calgary was represented in interprovincial competition by such teams as the Tigers, the Canucks, the Altomahs and the Bronks. The Stampeders were formed in 1945, with prewar Regina star Dean Griffing as coach, and 3 years later the club won its first of 4 western championships to date. Coached by Les Lear, they defeated Ottawa in the 1948 GREY CUP game and the celebrations of their accompanying fans gave birth to the annual festival that has surrounded the game ever since. The team played in the national final again the following year but lost to the Montreal Alouettes and waited 19 years for their next Grey Cup appearance. In 1960 the community-owned Stampeders moved into their present home, McMahon Stadium, and in 1968 and 1970 they returned to the Grey Cup, losing to Ottawa and Montreal, respectively, but capturing the championship a year later against the Toronto Argonauts. DEREK DRAGER

Callaghan, Morley Edward, novelist, short-story writer, broadcaster (b at Toronto 22 Feb 1903). Educated at University of Toronto and Osgoode Hall Law School, Callaghan published his first stories in Paris in *This Quarter* (1926) and *Transition* (1927). His first novel, *Strange Fugitive*, was published in 1928. Ezra Pound bought 2 stories for an issue of *Exile*, and by 1929 Callaghan was publishing in *Atlantic Monthly*, *Harper's Bazaar*, *Scribner's* and *The New Yorker*, while also working as a journalist in Toronto and Montréal.

Morley Callaghan. His masterpiece, *The Loved and the Lost*, received the Gov Gen's Award for 1951. His concern for "the little man" has brought his works attention in France, Germany, China and elsewhere, often before their recognition in Canada *(courtesy Macmillan of Canada / Nigel Dickson)*.

The next 2 novels — *It's Never Over* (1930) and *A Broken Journey* (1932) — concern Callaghan's perception of 2 apparently irreconcilable worlds, the self-seeking empirical jungle and the spiritual realm of trust and faith. In *Such Is My Beloved* (1934) the problem is faced directly. The hero, Father Dowling, befriends 2 prostitutes, but is reviled by the world, including his bishop. *They Shall Inherit the Earth* (1935) advances another small step: the hero and heroine reconcile physical and spiritual love. In another fine novel, *More Joy in Heaven* (1937), a reformed bank robber is welcomed by the community as a prodigal son, but pays with his life when he tries to prevent a bank robbery.

From 1937 to 1950 Callaghan was silent, except for *Luke Baldwin's Vow* (1948), a children's story, and *The Varsity Story* (1948), about University of Toronto. Then, in 1951, came *The Loved and the Lost*, perhaps Callaghan's masterpiece. Set in Montréal, it is a moving reprise of his temporal and eternal theme. From this intricately plotted and multilayered novel, Callaghan proceeded to *Morley Callaghan's Stories* (1959) and *The Many Coloured Coat* (1960), another novel set in Montréal, with echoes of the ancient story of Joseph and his brethren; and *A Passion in Rome* (1961), in which secular lovers find their physical-spiritual solution on the occasion of the election and installation of a new pope. In these novels, Callaghan maintains his concern with the meaning of spirit in the temporal world.

If Callaghan published relatively little in the 1950s, he was not idle. In broadcasting, he emerged as a "public" personality. In 1960 American critic Edmund Wilson identified him as "unjustly neglected" and compared him to Chekhov and Turgenev. This pronouncement undoubtedly led to many reprints of Callaghan's works, though he had already been published in France, Germany, Italy, Japan, Sweden and China, where his concern for "the little man" attracted popular taste. His reminiscences of 1929 in *That Summer in Paris* (1963) is one of the finest memoirs in Canadian literature. In 1975 Callaghan published *A Fine and Private Place*, a novel in which a writer is both the hero and victim of a new generation. Then, in *A Time for Judas* (1983), Callaghan turned to the ultimate question of sanctity and human weakness. Judas is perhaps his ultimate image of the temporal-spiritual conflict. Judas, he believed, experienced a "terrible sense of isolation." "Death," said Callaghan, is mysterious, but "You can make out of life whatever you want to make . . . This is your truth."

Recipient of numerous awards and prizes, Callaghan received the 1951 Governor General's Award for *The Loved and the Lost*. Possibly because of his speculations about time and eternity, Canadians have not always been friendly to Callaghan, but in the larger world of literature he remains a classic. HUGO MCPHERSON

Reading: B. Conron, ed, *Morley Callaghan* (1975).

Callière, Louis-Hector de, governor general of New France 1698-1703 (b at Thorigny-sur-Vire, France 12 Nov 1648; d at Québec 26 May 1703). From the Norman nobility and aided by a brother who was private secretary to Louis XIV, Callière impressed his superiors as an able commander at Montréal 1684-98. He was made governor of Canada following FRONTENAC's death. In 1701 he negotiated a peace treaty between the Iroquois and a number of western tribes allied with the French. Although inflexible and rather high-handed, Callière won respect for his leadership during wars with the English and the Iroquois. ALLAN GREER

Callihoo, John, politician, native-rights leader (b at Michel IR, Alta 1882; d at St Albert, Alta 11 Aug 1957). Of Iroquois-Cree extraction and self-educated, he was a freighter and then a farmer, but his leadership capabilities soon made him a rallying point for Indian causes. During the early 1930s he assisted nonstatus relatives in forming a Métis association and in successfully urging the Alberta government to pass the Métis Betterment Act. In 1937 he became president of the League of Alberta Indians and soon gained the nickname of "The Lawyer" from frustrated Indian Dept officials with whom he was often in conflict. In 1939 he reorganized his group as the Indian Assn of Alberta and saw it expand to become a successful province-wide organization. While president he was a delegate to Ottawa and helped to bring about changes in the INDIAN ACT and in provincial legislation affecting Indians. He retired in 1947 but saw the association carry on as one of the most effective native political bodies in Canada. HUGH A. DEMPSEY

Callihoo, Victoria, née Kildaw, author, spokesperson on Métis culture (b at Lac Ste Anne, Alta 1860; d at St Albert, Alta 1966). She participated in buffalo hunts and the establishment of MÉTIS SETTLEMENTS, and with her husband Louis farmed for many years in the Villeneuve district of Alberta. In later life she published several of her reminiscences, mostly dealing with Métis pioneer life, and became established as an authority on Métis culture. Her published works include "Our Buffalo Hunts" (*The Best from Alberta History*, 1981); "Early Life in Lac Ste Anne and St Albert in the Eighteen Seventies" and "Iroquois in Alberta" (*Alberta Historical Review*, summer 1953; spring 1959). HUGH A. DEMPSEY

Callwood, June (Frayne), journalist, civil libertarian (b at Chatham, Ont 2 June 1924). A prominent magazine writer in the 1950s, particularly for *Maclean's*, she became in the 1960s an activist for such social causes as homeless youth and drug addicts. She subsequently fought against censorship, and in 1983 she was a member of the council of Amnesty International in Canada. She has continued writing and besides ghosting the autobiographies of American celebrities, has published various works, including *The Law is Not for Women* (1976) and *Portrait of Canada* (1981).

Calumet, or pipestem, the most potent item of ritual magic in a Plains Indian MEDICINE BUNDLE was also used by many Eastern Woodland groups. Pipes are the medium in which tobacco is transformed into incense that rises to the Almighty, are associated with Thunder, and thereby signify justice, honour and the sacredness of all life (*see* NATIVE PEOPLE, RELIGION). The calumet was used in ceremonies to ratify an alliance, bring needed rain and attest contracts and treaties. There were calumets for commerce and trade, and for social and political purposes. The calumet is sometimes referred to as the peace pipe and war pipe. Descriptions of the calumet may refer to the entire pipe, including bowl and stem, or merely the pipestem. The shaft is long, made of light wood, painted in different colours and adorned with quills, beads, fur and feathers. RENÉ R. GADACZ

Calvert, George, 1st Baron Baltimore, English colonizer (b at Kipling, Eng 1579/80; d at London, Eng 15 Apr 1632). In 1621 he established a colony at FERRYLAND on Newfoundland's Avalon Peninsula, which became, by royal charter (1623), the province of Avalon. Calvert visited the colony personally in 1627 and the next year stayed the winter with his family. He was forced to defend his colony against attacks by French privateers, and also encountered difficulties when the Puritans there resented the Roman Catholic priests and settlers he had brought to Newfoundland. In 1629 Calvert left to seek a grant of land in a more hospitable climate. He obtained, under his son Cecil, what became the colony of Maryland. JOHN PARSONS

Calvinism, Protestant Christian theological system constructed by religious reformer John Calvin (Jean Cauvin, 1509-64) and made more stringent and narrower in focus by his successors. It is considered to have been widely influential in Canadian life. Though educated in law, Calvin published a short manual of religious instruction, *Institutes of the Christian Religion,* in 1536, 2 years after leaving the Roman Catholic Church. Later he enlarged the *Institutes* several times until it became a major theological treatise adopted by most Reformed churches; it also influenced LUTHERAN and ANGLICAN theology. According to Calvin, Scripture gives humankind knowledge of God and of one's duties to God and fellow man. He emphasizes God's sovereignty and humanity's alienation from the Creator because of sinful pride. Since man has lost his free will he cannot avoid sin and is totally dependent on God's love. Salvation (reconciliation) can come only by grace through faith in Christ (receiving God into one's life). Calvin's most controversial teaching concerns election (double predestination): that God has already chosen those to be saved and those to be damned. In this world, however, people achieve fellowship through groups such as the church and the state, which are separate but partners. Although the state's authority comes from God, a bad government may be deposed by society (not the individual) when all other remedies for justice fail.

Calvin, a French citizen, was invited to "reform" the free city of Geneva. With the city council's support his puritanical plans to improve morals and religious life were enforced, but Calvin also enhanced popular control of city politics and created a welfare system for the poor, sick and handicapped. Elsewhere Calvinism was denounced as a revolutionary attack on government and religion, and its followers were persecuted until eventually restricted to Switzerland, the Netherlands, France, Hungary, Britain and some German states. Calvinism was first introduced into Canada by French HUGUENOTS and it later flourished among Scottish, Irish, Dutch and New England settlers. By the end of the Victorian period the PRESBYTERIAN CHURCH was the largest Protestant denomination in Canada, the second-largest Calvinist group being the BAPTISTS.

Before WWI Calvinism was formative in the program of the SOCIAL GOSPEL movement for religiously based social, moral and political improvements to society. More recently it has influenced Canadian support for humanitarian and democratic developments in the Third World. The so-called "Protestant work ethic" has been credited rather inaccurately to Calvinism, as have Canadian puritanical views on sexual matters, sabbatarianism, TEMPERANCE and individualism, all attitudes shared by most Christian denominations during the Victorian era. A late 19th-century revival of European interest in Calvinism influenced Canadian theological thought by the 1930s through the writings of such "neo-orthodox" thinkers as Karl Barth. Canada has also shared in the Dutch branch of this revival, thanks to the postwar immigration of Dutch Calvinists who have sought to establish Christian-controlled schools and Christian trade unions. JOHN S. MOIR

Reading: J.T. McNeill, *The History and Character of Calvinism* (1954).

Cambodians, *see* SOUTHEAST ASIANS.

Cambridge, Ont, City, pop 77 183 (1981c), located 55 km NW of Hamilton, was created 1 Jan 1973 when the communities of GALT, Preston and HESPELER were amalgamated. Prior to 1830 Preston was known as Cambridge Mills, after Cambridge, Eng. The economy is based on diversified manufacturing and there is a campus of Conestoga College of Applied Arts and Technology. The annual Can-Amera, held alternately in Cambridge and Saginaw, Mich, attracts about 2000 amateur athletes. DANIEL FRANCIS

View from the river showing the old post office and warehouses in Cambridge, Ont (*photo ©1984 Hartill Art Associates*).

Cambridge Bay, NWT, UP, pop 815 (1981c), is located on the SE coast of VICTORIA I, 866 air km NE of YELLOWKNIFE. The people of the area are known as the COPPER INUIT because they fashioned implements from native copper and bartered these to other groups. Few Inuit lived year round at the site before the 1950s. Named for the duke of Cambridge (1774-1850), the settlement began to expand with the construction of a loran navigational beacon in 1947 and a DEW Line site in 1955. The economy is still centered around the traditional Inuit activities of hunting and trapping. The community became a NWT government administrative centre in 1981. ANNELIES POOL

Cameron, Alexander Thomas, professor of biochemistry (b at London, Eng 1882; d at Winnipeg 25 Sept 1947). Educated in chemistry at U of Edinburgh, Cameron came to U Man as lecturer of physiology and remained there (except for WWI service in France) until his death. When biochemistry was separated from physiology in 1923, he became head of the new department. His work on the distribution of iodine in plants and animals led to many contributions in the developing field of endocrinology, especially thyroid and parathyroid gland biochemistry. The award of the DSc in 1925 by U of Edinburgh recognized his work on iodine biochemistry. He authored a once widely used textbook of biochemistry and other books. His interest in oceanography, stemming from his research on iodine, culminated in his chairmanship of the Fisheries Research Board of Canada (1934-47). DAVID B. SMITH

Cameron, Thomas Wright Moir, parasitologist, scientist, teacher (b at Glasgow, Scot 29 Apr 1894; d at Silver Spring, Md 1 Jan 1980). Educated at Edinburgh, he came to Canada in 1932 and was director of the Institute of Parasitology of Macdonald Coll 1932-64 and professor of PARASITOLOGY (animal and human) at McGill. He was one of the founders of the *Canadian Journal of Comparative Medicine and Veterinary Science.* Cameron was an excellent lecturer and teacher and guided many students towards postgraduate degrees in parasitology. He published extensively on parasitism in both humans and animals. J.F. FRANK

Cameron, William Maxwell, physical oceanographer (b at Battleford, Sask 24 July 1914). Educated at UBC he was a biologist at the Fisheries Research Board, Pacific Biological Station 1938-41, when he moved to the Meteorological Service as a forecaster at Western Air Command Headquarters, Vancouver. In 1944 he joined the RCN and became involved in antisubmarine warfare research. After WWII he studied under Dr H.U. Sverdrup at the Scripps Institution of Oceanography, U of California. He joined the Defence Research Board of Canada (1949) and played a major role in establishing Canada's first institute of oceanography, at UBC. He carried out extensive arctic research and hydrographic surveys as chief scientist of the Canada/US Joint Beaufort Sea Expeditions 1949-54. He moved to the Dept of Mines and Technical Surveys (later the Dept of Energy, Mines and Resources) 1960 and was director of Marine Sciences Branch 1962-71 when he retired. Cameron's initiative in establishing the BEDFORD INSTITUTE OF OCEANOGRAPHY and his theoretical studies of estuarine circulation and ocean modelling are of international significance. NEIL J. CAMPBELL

Camp, Dalton Kingsley, writer, politician (b at Woodstock, NB 11 Sept 1920). Educated at UNB, Columbia U and London School of Economics, Camp was first engaged in student politics as a Liberal. Disillusioned, he switched to the Conservatives and helped organize Robert STANFIELD's election as premier of NS in 1956. Camp was the PC Party's national president from 1964 to 1969; in that capacity he helped to organize the removal of John DIEFENBAKER as the party's leader. Camp's success in intraparty politics was not matched by personal success in general elections; he was defeated in 1965 and 1968. Thereafter, he advised PC leaders during campaigns, including that of 1984. Camp achieved prominence in advertising and as an author and columnist; his books include his graceful and informative memoirs, *Gentlemen, Players and Politicians* (1970). ROBERT BOTHWELL

Campagnolo, Iona, née Hardy, broadcaster, politician (b at Galiano I, BC 18 Oct 1932). She was raised in Prince Rupert, BC, where she worked as a broadcaster 1965-74. Chairman of the Prince Rupert School Board 1966-72, she was elected alderman for Prince Rupert in 1972. She was Liberal MP for Skeena 1974-79, serving as minister of state for fitness and amateur sport 1976-79. In Nov 1982 Campagnolo was elected president of the Liberal Party of Canada, the first woman to hold that position. She was unsuccessful in her bid for a seat in Vancouver in the 1984 federal election. HARRIET GORHAM

Campbell, Alan Newton, professor of chemistry (b at Halifax, Eng 29 Oct 1899). After receiving a doctorate from King's Coll, London, Campbell became assistant professor of chemistry at U Man in 1930. When he arrived, the department concentrated on teaching, but Campbell began research and founded a research school. He became head of the department in 1945. For 6 years in the 1950s he served on the National Research Council. He retired as head in 1965 but continued teaching until 1969 when he became professor emeritus. Throughout his life he has actively pursued research on the conductance of electrolytic solutions and the thermodynamic properties of solutions. His students, many now eminent chemists, remember him also for his love of literature, music and classical studies. E.M. KARTZMARK

Campbell, Sir Alexander, lawyer, politician (b at Hedon, Eng 9 Mar 1822; d at Toronto 24 May 1892). At age 17, Campbell became John A. MACDONALD's second articled student; he was admitted to the bar in 1843. He practised law initially as Macdonald's partner. Campbell was a successful lawyer and businessman. In 1858 he was elected to the legislative council for Cataraqui district and remained there until 1867 when he was called to the Senate. Campbell held a succession of ministerial posts: commissioner of crown lands (1864-67); postmaster general (1867-73, 1879-80, 1880-81, 1885-87); minister of the interior (1873); receiver general (1878-79); minister of militia (1880); and minister of justice (1881-85). He was leader of the Opposition in the Senate from 1873 to 1878. As a member of the GREAT COALITION (1864-67), Campbell attended the Quebec Conference and was thus a FATHER OF CONFEDERATION. From the 1860s to the 1880s, Campbell was a leader in the Ontario wing of the federal Conservative Party. In 1887 he left the Senate to become lt-gov of Ontario. Campbell was knighted in 1879. DONALD SWAINSON

Campbell, Alexander Bradshaw, lawyer, politician, premier of PEI (b at Summerside, PEI 1 Dec 1933). In 1966 Campbell became one of the youngest (age 33) premiers ever elected. In 1969 his government and Ottawa signed a Comprehensive Development Plan under which large-scale farms, tourism and school consolidation were encouraged; the number of ports designated for government assistance was reduced; and incentives were offered to attract non-resource-based manufacturing. After a decade of substantial expenditure, mounting criticism and few signs of sustained development, Campbell abandoned reform rhetoric and advocated an ecologically balanced, sustainable, CONSERVER SOCIETY. His government also enacted controls over nonresident ownership. In 1978 Campbell was appointed to the PEI Supreme Court. DAVID A. MILNE

Campbell, Sir Archibald, soldier, colonial administrator (b 12 Mar 1769; d in Eng 6 Oct 1843). After a distinguished military career in India, Portugal and Burma he became lt-gov of NB in 1831. Aloof and authoritarian, he was soon at odds with the Reform group in the assembly. Though criticized for not curbing the unpopular commissioner of crown lands, Thomas BAILLIE, he placed him at the head of the Executive Council in 1833. When instructed to surrender the crown revenues to the legislature in return for a moderate civil list and to make his Executive Council more acceptable to the Assembly, he balked and was recalled in 1837. His departure was lamented only by the few officials he had sought to protect. P.A. BUCKNER

Campbell, Douglas Lloyd, politician, premier of Manitoba 1948-58 (b near High Bluff, Man 27 May 1895). D.L. Campbell won election to the Manitoba legislature in 1922 as a Farmers' candidate in Lakeside riding, which he represented for 47 years. In 1936 he was appointed minister of agriculture in the Liberal Progressive government of John BRACKEN, and in Nov 1948 he replaced Bracken's successor, Stuart GARSON, as premier. In coalition with the Conservatives in 1950, his government was re-elected in 1949 and 1953 but defeated by the Conservatives, led by Duff ROBLIN, in 1958. Apart from extending electric service to rural areas and creating the first independent electoral commission in Canada, his government was cautious and thrifty. Succeeded as party leader in 1961 by Gildas Molgat, and retiring in 1969, he continued to denounce big government, bilingualism and deficits. His career exemplifies the transformation of the farmers' protest of the 1920s into a neo-conservative force in western Canada by the 1970s. THOMAS PETERSON

Campbell, Hugh Lester, air marshal (b at Salisbury, NB 13 July 1908). Commissioned in the RCAF in 1931 after gaining an engineering degree from UNB, Campbell was director of training plans at Air Force Headquarters during the formative stages of the BRITISH COMMONWEALTH AIR TRAINING PLAN in 1939-40. He then served in the UK and Middle East before finishing the war as an air vice-marshal and member of the Air Council, Ottawa. Campbell was the first commander of the Canadian Air Division in Europe 1952-55, a period that saw Canada's European air commitment to NATO rise to 12 squadrons. A dynamic leader who did not suffer fools gladly, he became chief of the air staff in 1957, retiring in 1962 when he was appointed a commissioner of the NWT. NORMAN HILLMER

Campbell, Maria, writer (b at Park Valley, Sask 6 Apr 1940). Campbell left school in grade 7. In 1963 she became involved in the human rights movement and, while living in Edmonton, assisted in founding the Women's Halfway House and Women's Emergency Shelter. She began writing because she was upset that so few people knew about historic and contemporary native cultures. She has written a screenplay, several children's books and an autobiography, *Halfbreed* (1973). JON C. STOTT

Campbell, Norman Kenneth, composer, television producer and director (b at Los Angeles, Calif 4 Feb 1924). Campbell, who planned a career in meteorology after his graduation from UBC, composed several songs which brought him to the attention of the CBC while he was learning to be a weatherman on Sable I, Nova Scotia. He became a music producer for radio in Vancouver and moved to Toronto in 1952 to work in television. Long a champion for the presentation of classical ballet on TV, Campbell produced CBC's first full-length ballet, *Swan Lake*, in 1956 and his later productions of *Cinderella* and *Sleeping Beauty* earned him Emmy Awards. Campbell composed the music and collaborated with Donald HARRON in writing the lyrics for the musical version of L.M. MONTGOMERY's *Anne of Green Gables* which opened at the Charlottetown Festival in 1965 and had a successful run in England. In 1972 he composed the music and his wife Elaine wrote the lyrics for *The Wonder of it All*, a musical drama based on the life of Emily CARR. He has also produced Gilbert and Sullivan operettas and opera on TV. His important opera productions include Humperdinck's *Hansel and Gretel* with Maureen FORRESTER in 1970 and Puccini's *La Rondine* with Teresa STRATAS in 1972. *Music East, Music West*, Campbell's filmed account of the Toronto Symphony's historic tour through China, was honoured by the Canadian Music Council in 1978. JAMES DEFELICE

Campbell, Thane Alexander, premier, chief justice of PEI (b at Summerside, PEI 7 July 1895; d at Ottawa 28 Sept 1978). A Rhodes scholar, Campbell became attorney general of PEI in 1930 before being elected to the legislature. He won a seat in 1931 but his party lost power. When the Liberals regained office in 1935, Campbell was renamed attorney general. He assumed the premiership on 14 Jan 1936, serving until 11 May 1943 when he became chief justice. He held that post until 1970 and then was appointed chief commissioner of the Foreign Claims Commission. A companion of the Order of Canada, he also was active in heritage matters. PETER E. RIDER

Campbell, Lord William, naval officer, colonial official (b *c*1730; d at Southampton, Eng 4 Sept 1778). The younger son of a Scottish peer, Campbell rose to captain in the Royal Navy by the end of 1762. In 1764 he was elected to Parliament and in 1766 appointed governor of NS. In office, he attempted unsuccessfully to break the stranglehold of the Halifax merchants on the province, and then shifted to battle financial cutbacks from the mother country. In 1773 he was transferred to the governorship of South Carolina (his wife's native colony), taking up office just in time for the outbreak of the American Revolution. Campbell was critically wounded in a naval action in 1776 off Charleston, SC. J.M. BUMSTED

Campbell, William Bennett, teacher, politician, premier of PEI (b at Montague, PEI 27 Aug 1943). Campbell succeeded Alexander CAMPBELL (no relation) as leader of the Liberal Party and premier of the province in 1978, but his caretaker government was defeated by the PCs in the 1979 election. Campbell entered federal politics, winning the seat left vacant by the death of Cardigan MP Daniel MacDonald in 1980 and subsequently took over MacDonald's portfolio as minister of veterans' affairs. He lost his seat in the 1984 Conservative election sweep. His constituency is considered a bellwether riding in national voting. DAVID A. MILNE

Campbell, William Wilfred, rector, civil servant, novelist, poet (b at Berlin [Kitchener], Canada W 1 June 1858?; d at Ottawa 1 Jan 1918). Although currently less fashionable than the other Confederation poets, Campbell was a versatile, interesting writer, influenced by Burns, the English Romantics, Poe, Emerson, Longfellow, Carlyle and Tennyson. At his best, Campbell controls his influences and expresses his own religious idealism in traditional forms and genres. A lively contributor to the Toronto *Globe* column "At the Mermaid Inn" (1892-93), Campbell wrote 2 prose romances, several closet dramas and, in later years, political poetry and prose setting forth his concept of a "vaster Britain." TRACY WARE

Reading: C.F. Klinck, *Wilfred Campbell* (1942; repr 1977).

Campbell River, BC, District Municipality, pop 15 832 (1981c), area 133 km², inc 1964 replacing former village of Campbell R (inc 1947), is located on the E coast of Vancouver I about halfway between Victoria and Cape Scott at the northern end of the Strait of Georgia. Capt George VANCOUVER of the Royal Navy surveyed the waters here in the early 1790s when the region was inhabited by the Southern KWAKIUTL tribes. By 1900 European settlers, engaged chiefly in logging, had occupied the area, using the estuary of Campbell R as a booming ground. Forest-related industry has continued to dominate the local economy and employment, along with commercial fishing and tourism. Campbell R is famous for the tyee salmon caught in the waters of nearby Discovery Passage. The region has many good fishing lakes and provides numerous outdoor recreation opportunities — all of which have greatly increased tourism over the years. Its strategic location makes Campbell R an increasingly important service centre for northern Vancouver I. ALAN F.J. ARTIBISE

Campbellton, NB, City, pop 9218 (1981c), inc 1958, administrative centre of Restigouche County, is located on the Québec border near the mouth of the RESTIGOUCHE R. The population is primarily English and French speaking (49%/49.6%, 1981c). The site of 16th- and 17th-century French missions and trading posts, it was settled by dispossessed ACADIANS in 1757, though most left with the French defeat in the 1760 naval Battle of the Restigouche. Named Pointe-des-Savages, Pointe-Rochelle and Martin's Point earlier, it received its present name (for Lt-Gov Campbell) after a post-1825 influx of Scots. Its early industries were fishing, shipbuilding and trapping. Lumbering became most important in the late 19th century and remained so until a pulp mill was built at Atholville in 1928. Sugarloaf Mt, 300 m, dominates the skyline and is a park and ski hill. The Restigouche is famous for its ATLANTIC SALMON sportfishing, and Campbellton holds a salmon festival each summer. The Restigouche Gallery is a National Exhibition Centre of Museums Canada.

BURTON GLENDENNING

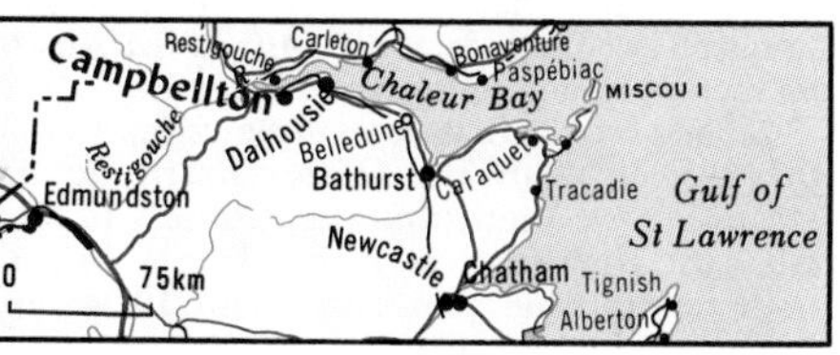

Campeau, Robert, real-estate entrepreneur (b at Sudbury, Ont 3 Aug 1923). In 1949 Campeau began residential construction in Ottawa; in 1953 he incorporated Campeau Construction Co Ltd and in 1969 amalgamated a number of subsidiaries into Campeau Corp Ltd. One of the largest real-estate companies in Canada, Campeau Corp has been operating in the US since 1978. A founding member of the board of governors of Laurentian University, Campeau has been chairman of the finance committee for the Children's Hospital of Eastern Ontario and is a member of the advisory board of Guaranty Trust of Canada. JORGE NIOSI

Camping may be defined as living in a temporary or mobile shelter in the outdoors, whether a lean-to, tent or camper van. For the NATIVE PEOPLES of Canada, camping was usually a way of life in precontact times; for early pioneers, explorers, prospectors, surveyors and trappers, it was often a necessity.

The first recreational campers travelled by canoe, horse transport or on foot, and were limited in mobility by the weight and bulk of the equipment available to them. Military tents of army duck, sheet-iron stoves, folding cots and sheepskin sleeping bags encouraged campers to stay in one spot while they enjoyed HUNTING or SPORTFISHING within close range. In the 1890s the YMCA, followed in later decades by the Boy Scouts, Girl Guides, churches, labour unions and local governments, began sponsoring camps to improve the health and character of the young. The early organized youth camps might have had a few permanent buildings for dining and recreation, but campers generally slept "under canvas." Activities varied from water sports to HIKING and CANOEING, but all stressed the development of self-reliance and life skills. From the 1890s, as well, the CPR publicized camping and climbing in the Rockies. In the early 20th century, the nature and wilderness travel books of Ernest Thompson SETON were read widely, and the GROUP OF SEVEN helped bring an awareness of canoe camping to the Canadian public.

The increasing use of the AUTOMOBILE and expansion of the road network made car camping popular in the 1920s and 1930s. Camping supply houses opened and a variety of camping outfits, trailers and tents were marketed. Several Canadian companies did business in producing camping equipment, including the Peterborough Canoe Co (Ont) and Chestnut Canoes (NB) for wood and canvas canoes, Jones of Vancouver for the Trapper Nelson packboard, Woods of Toronto for tents and sleeping bags, and Coleman for gas stoves and lanterns. Travellers camped by the roadside, and municipal governments began providing free camping grounds, both to attract tourists to their area and to control health standards. Private campgrounds were also established, for which a fee was charged, and which offered increasingly sophisticated facilities such as cabins, electrical and sewage hookups for motorized vehicles, and organized recreation activities. After WWII, as Canadians had more time and money to spend on leisure and as a vast flood of war-surplus equipment hit the market — tents, packs, rucksacks, sleeping bags — there was a tremendous expansion in outdoor camps. Governments released land for campsites in designated areas in national and provincial PARKS and, in 1960, a federal-provincial agreement undertook to develop campgrounds every 160 km along the TRANS-CANADA HWY. These campgrounds had fewer conveniences and lower rates than their private competitors, and proved so popular that authorities had to impose limited stays to allow maximum accessibility to all campers.

In the 1960s the "backpacker boom" hit N America, encouraged by the development of durable, lightweight equipment made from nylon and polyester, dehydrated foods, and a public increasingly concerned with fitness and outdoor skills. Camping became big business, and a number of new Canadian companies (eg, Taiga, Far West, Canadian Mountaineering Equipment) emerged to meet the demand. By 1980, Statistics Canada estimated that 27% of Canadian households owned camping equipment, with 1.3 million households having tents, 323 000 having tent trailers, and 229 000 owning truck campers. There were 3143 tent and trailer campgrounds across the country.

In 1983 the Canadian Camping Assn estimated there were approximately 1500 youth camps in Canada, the majority of which were run by agencies and nonprofit organizations. Camps for special groups, such as the handicapped or children with particular health problems, were becoming more common. Private camps, often begun by teachers in their free summer months as an extension of their educational role, were concentrated mainly in southern Ontario and the Montréal area, parts of Alberta and lower mainland BC; these camps may offer a speciality in canoeing, hiking or similar outdoor skill.

Ironically the greatly increased activities of camping and hiking have had a severe impact on fragile wilderness ecosystems. Much-travelled portage trails have become eroded gullies and camping areas have been denuded of vegetation by scores of people searching for firewood. The result in many national and provincial parks is restriction of entry by a system of permits and a host of regulations about where to camp and the kinds of packaged foods that may be brought in by campers. JAMES MARSH

Campobello Island abuts the border with the US in PASSAMAQUODDY BAY, on the S coast of New Brunswick. Sovereignty over the ruggedly picturesque island was early in dispute, but passed to NB by convention in 1817. The first settlers were imported after 1770 by Capt William Owen, whose family owned most of the island for a century. The name is partly a reference to Lord William Campbell, governor of NS 1766-1773, and partly descriptive of the place. Fishing has been the major activity, though it is most famous as the summer home of American President Franklin Delano Roosevelt. DANIEL FRANCIS

Camrose, Alta, City, pop 12 570 (1981c), inc 1955, located 95 km SE of Edmonton, is the distributing and manufacturing centre for a rich, mixed-farming area. Called Sparling at its inception (1905), Camrose is named for a town in Wales, but the name may also refer to the wild roses that grow along Stoney Cr, which flows through the town. The area was settled in the early 1900s, mostly by Scandinavians, whose influence remains in the Lutheran College and Canadian Lutheran Bible Institute. One of Canada's first ski clubs was formed here in 1911. The area has some light industry and numerous oil wells. There is a local radio station and a weekly newspaper, the *Camrose Canadian*.

ERIC J. HOLMGREN

Camsell, Charles, mining engineer (b at Ft Liard, NWT 8 Feb 1876; d at Ottawa 19 Dec 1958). Son of a Hudson's Bay Co factor, Camsell was appointed geologist with the Geological Survey in 1904, became chief exploration geologist in 1914 and deputy minister of mines in 1920, a post he held until retirement in 1946. Author of many geological papers, Camsell was possibly more important as an organizer, leading his department's methods from the canoe to the aeroplane, initiating laboratory research to complement field exploration, broadening its functions to include publishing and the National Museum (including Indian anthropology and its fossil collections, notably of dinosaurs) and keeping its old esprit de corps alive through the hard times of the Depression. He became a fellow of the Royal Soc of Canada, was a member of the NATIONAL RESEARCH COUNCIL 1921-36 and in 1944 with C.J. MACKENZIE reorganized postwar government science. DONALD J.C. PHILLIPSON

Reading: C. Camsell, *Son of the North* (1954).

Canada, a name derived from the Huron-Iroquois *kanata,* meaning a village or settlement. On 13 Aug 1535, as Jacques CARTIER was nearing Ile d'Anticosti, 2 Indian youths he was bringing back from France informed him that the route to Canada ("chemin de Canada") lay to the S of the island. By Canada they meant the village of Stadacona, on the future site of QUÉBEC CITY. Cartier used the word in that sense, but also referred to "the province of Canada," meaning the area subject to DONNACONA, chief at Stadacona. The name was soon applied to a much larger region. The "Harleian" world map of *c*1547, the first to show the discoveries made on Cartier's second voyage, applied it to an area N of the gulf and river St Lawrence, and by 1550 maps were also placing the name S of the river.

Cartier referred to the St Lawrence as the "rivière de Canada" and the name was in general use until the end of the century. But on 10 Aug 1535 he had given the name St-Laurent to a bay north of Ile d'Anticosti, and the name spread gradually to the gulf and river. In 1603, on his first voyage to Canada, CHAMPLAIN spoke of the river of Canada, but by 1613 he had changed this to St Lawrence. The name Canada was used loosely, even in official correspondence, as a synonym for NEW FRANCE, which included all French possessions; but it was always understood, as Father Pierre Biard pointed out in the Jesuit *Relation* for 1616, that "Canada . . . is not, properly speaking, all this extent of country which they now call New France; but it is only that part, which extends along the banks of the great River Canada, and the Gulf of St. Lawrence." In 1664 François Du Creux, in his work *Historiae Canadensis,* drew the same distinction.

As French explorers and fur traders pushed ever westward and southward, the area to which the name Canada applied increased rapidly, but its extent seems never to have been defined officially. In Mar 1762, after the CONQUEST, Gen Thomas GAGE informed Gen Jeffery AMHERST that the limits between Canada and Louisiana had never been clearly described. He could only state "what were generally believed . . . to have been the Boundaries of Canada & give you my own Opinion." He judged "not only the [Great] Lakes, which are Indisputable, but the whole Course of the Mississippi from its Heads to it's Junction with the Illinois" had been considered by the French to be part of Canada. This may be one reason why Britain temporarily abandoned the name and called the colony the Province of Quebec.

Canada came into its own in 1791 when the CONSTITUTIONAL ACT (or Canada Act) divided Québec, then considerably enlarged, into the provinces of UPPER CANADA and LOWER CANADA. In 1841 they were joined to form the PROVINCE OF CANADA. In 1867 the BRITISH NORTH AMERICA ACT united the Province of Canada (divided into Ontario and Québec) with NS and NB to form "One Dominion under the name of Canada." The new area was relatively small, but it expanded rapidly. The purchase of RUPERT'S LAND in 1870 extended it to the Rocky Mts and the Arctic Ocean; the addition of BC in 1871 created a Canada extending from sea to sea; PEI was added in 1873 and Britain handed over title to the arctic islands in 1880. This gave Canada substantially the present boundaries, except for Labrador and Newfoundland which joined the federation in 1949. In a striking comment, the distinguished American historian S.E. Morison remarked that "never, since the Roman empire, have two local names received such a vast extension as Canada and St. Lawrence." *See also* EXPLORATION; TERRITORIAL EVOLUTION. W. KAYE LAMB

Canada and Australia are large, highly industrialized and urbanized countries with small populations and with standards of living tied to the export of natural-resource products. Both countries achieved independent Dominion status within the British Empire (Canada in 1867, Australia in 1901) as federations of former British colonies, and their parliamentary structures of federal government are comparable. Their economies have depended on substantial IMMIGRATION. Both have experienced economic penetration by foreign investors, with a concomitant sense of cultural threat. Their similar interest in matters related to investment by foreign parties is, nevertheless, subordinate to the maintenance of military alliances with countries that are also their trading partners. In 1941 Robert Menzies became the first Australian prime minister to visit Canada; more recently, Pierre Trudeau's 1970 visit to Australia, the first by a Canadian prime minister, led to greater public recognition of mutual interests and common problems and to increasing contact between the countries, especially in trade and technology. In early 1984 former Gov Gen Edward SCHREYER became Canada's high commissioner to Australia.

Early links between the colonies were sporadic and often accidental. Movement was predominantly from Canada to Australia, with London, Eng, as a common base. James COOK's navigational experience in the Gulf of St Lawrence during the SEVEN YEARS' WAR influenced his appointment to HMS *Endeavour* and led to his 1770 survey of Australia's E coast. The first settlement of Sydney Cove in 1788 included officers with experience in N America, mostly in Halifax. Four of the first 6 governors of New South Wales — John Hunter, Philip King, Lachlan Macquarie and Sir Thomas Brisbane — had served in British North America. A fifth, William Bligh, had been on the NORTHWEST COAST with Cook on the latter's second voyage. Later Australian governors Sir George Gipps, Sir Charles FitzRoy and Sir William Denison continued this pattern. The settlement at Sydney was George VANCOUVER's only link with British officials from 1791 to 1794 when he negotiated with the Spaniards at NOOTKA SOUND and surveyed the Northwest Coast.

Expansion westward in Canada and Australia was effected in large part by companies devoted to exploiting the land's capacity to produce staple commodities: the Australian Agricultural Co and the Van Diemens Land Co produced wool, whereas the NORTH WEST COMPANY and the HUDSON'S BAY COMPANY sought furs. Settlement was conducted in part by COLONIZATION COMPANIES, such as the South Australia Co and the West Australian Co and, in Canada, the BRITISH AMERICAN LAND COMPANY and the CANADA COMPANY. The British settlers' common heritage can be seen in similar PLACE-NAMES, indicating close ancestral ties or the perception by settlers of resemblances between the landscape of the new country and that of the old.

After the Canadian REBELLIONS OF 1837 a number of rebels were sent into exile. Through George Arthur, lieutenant-governor of Upper Canada and previously of Van Diemens Land, 96 followers of William Lyon MACKENZIE were sent to Van Diemens Land [Tasmania]. A monument in Hobart commemorates their pardon and return. Fifty-eight followers of Louis-Joseph PAPINEAU were transported to New South Wales where France Bay, Exile Bay and Canada Bay in Sydney remain as evidence of their presence there before their pardon.

Notable British North Americans moving to Australia included Henry Samuel Chapman and Francis Forbes. Chapman, who in 1833 founded the first daily newspaper in Canada, the *Montreal Daily Advertiser*, supported demands for an elective legislative council as a step towards RESPONSIBLE GOVERNMENT. Subsequently, as a member of the Victoria Legislative Council, he contributed to the evolution of responsible government in Australia (a constitutional gain indebted to Canadian precedents). Forbes, chief justice of Newfoundland 1816-23, became first chief justice of New South Wales, where he served from 1823 to 1837. During the 1850s, British North Americans, including villagers from Barrington, NS, and Carbonear, Nfld, mined gold in what is now Australia. Canadians Alexander Robertson, John Wagner and William Bradley assisted in the extension and reorganization of Cobb & Co coach services, which revolutionized Australian inland transport. Others built slipways and took Maritime timber entrepreneurship to Tasmania. Cape Breton Highlanders followed Rev Norman MCLEOD to Victoria before moving on to New Zealand. Sir William PARRY and Sir John FRANKLIN were natives of England who made important contributions in both BNA and Australia: both were explorers in what is now the Canadian Arctic; Parry was commissioner, Australian Agricultural Co, 1830-34, and Franklin was lieutenant-governor of Van Diemens Land, 1836-43.

Between Canadian Confederation and WWII there was increased contact between the countries, especially after the federation of Australia in 1901. The 2 governments were frequently in touch over matters of education, health, transport, communication, immigration restriction and agriculture. Although the countries competed for immigrants from Britain, some settlers from Australia migrated to the Canadian West, and vice versa. Parallel surges of nationalism were evident as well, and were expressed, for example, in the art of Canada's GROUP OF SEVEN and of the Australian Heidelberg School, a group of Melbourne painters of the late 19th and early 20th centuries. A movement of professionals began between the countries; eg, Alfred SELWYN, director of the Geological Survey of Victoria, in 1869 became director of the GEOLOGICAL SURVEY OF CANADA, and Thomas Griffith TAYLOR, first professor of geography at U of Sydney, became professor of geography at U of Toronto in 1930.

Closer international bonds were established during WWII, as 9600 Australian airmen trained in Canada under the BRITISH COMMONWEALTH AIR TRAINING PLAN. After the war, as the promise of mineral resources and concern for defence motivated both national governments to map their large territories, professional links developed in geodetic survey and topographical mapping (*see* CARTOGRAPHY). Although GEOPOLITICAL priorities influence their foreign policies in different ways, in the 1980s both countries are purchasing the American F-18 fighter aircraft and Australia may purchase Canada's TELIDON information system. Both countries are participating with the US in building and operating Starlab, to be launched on a space shuttle in 1989. Knowledge and experience in high technology, satellite communication, agriculture, transport, land rights and resource development increase mutual contact. Calgary's link with Western Australia is strong: over 25 Canadian-based oil companies have set up joint ventures there. Frequent competition in resource exports includes a British Columbia project, begun in 1983, involving export to Japan of 94 million t of coking coal over 15 years. In 1980 Australia led Canada in coal, iron ore, lead and tungsten production, while Canada led Australia in copper, gold, nickel and zinc.

Canada sent its first agent to New South Wales in 1895. By 1909 the Massey-Harris Co had arranged to sell agricultural machinery to western Australian farmers. Australia established a trade commissioner in Toronto in 1929, reinforcing a long-developing association which has grown recently. Trade missions to Australia from Nova Scotia, Québec, Ontario and Alberta in 1981 were designed specifically to strengthen trade and technology links. Canadian-Australian trade reached Cdn$ 1.5 billion in 1981 operating within the framework of the General Agreement on Tariffs and Trade (GATT) and a 1973 bilateral trade agreement.

Since the 1960s a regular public-service exchange has occurred at the federal level, especially in immigration, and in mapping and personnel-training programs. Higher salaries and landed-immigrant status attracted Australians to Canada in the 1960s. Since then graduate studies and educational exchanges have been continual. Canadian medical and health care systems were prototypes for Australia's Medibank in the 1970s. Canada's diplomatic representation (high commission in Canberra, the Australian capital, and consulates in Sydney, Melbourne and Perth) matches that in W Germany, and is second only to Canadian representation in the US.

Considerable interest in each other's literature is symbolized by the Canada-Australia Literary Award, which was inaugurated in 1976. In journalism, the Canadian Award (est 1975) is allocated for merit in reporting international affairs pertaining to the Pacific region. The formalization of comparative studies, which has been attempted since 1945, was achieved in 198[illegible] with the Canada-Australia Colloquium: Public Policies in Two Federal Countries; with the establishment of a Canadian Visiting Fellowship at Macquarie University; and with the formation of the Australian Association for Canadian Studies. The latter (now the Australian and New Zealand Association for Canadian Studies) has held conferences on theory and practice in comparative studies (1982) and regionalism and national identity (1984). The annual journal *Australian-Canadian Studies* (fd 1983) is published jointly by the faculties of social work at La Trobe U, Melbourne, and U Regina.

Although the national governments have worked in co-operation for many years, and exchanges at the scholarly level are becoming more common, there has been relatively little opportunity for the ordinary citizen of one country to learn about the other. It is to be hoped that this situation will improve as Canada and

Australia continue to increase contact with each other. JOHN ATCHISON

Reading: H. Albinski, *Canadian and Australian Politics in Comparative Perspective* (1973); Bruce Hodgins, *Federalism in Canada and Australia* (1978).

Canada and Britain, *see* COMMONWEALTH; COLONIAL OFFICE; various history articles.

Canada and Its Provinces: A History of the Canadian People and Their Institutions (23 vols, Toronto, 1913-17), ed Adam SHORTT and Arthur G. DOUGHTY, was written by "one hundred associates." *Canada and Its Provinces* was the most comprehensive study of Canadian historical and political development to appear before WWI. The first 6 of its 12 sections deal with Canada's evolution into a Dominion, the next 5 trace the history of the provinces and regions, and the last is a one-volume general index. In its editors' view, the purpose of the work was to prevent "sectionalism" and to promote "a broad national spirit in all parts of the Dominion" as the means to "an enlightened patriotism which vibrates to the sentiment of nationality." Today's reader may find the language dated, but these volumes are still an essential source for Canada's view of itself before 1918. NEIL BESNER

Canada Centre for Inland Waters (CCIW), one of the world's leading WATER-research centres, provides Environment Canada and the federal Dept of Fisheries and Oceans with shared facilities for a range of environmental and marine research and surveys. Established by the federal government in 1967, CCIW occupies a large waterfront site in Burlington, Ont, just inside Hamilton Harbour. CCIW houses the headquarters of Environment Canada's National Water Research Institute, National Water Quality Laboratory, Wastewater Technology Centre and the Ontario Region offices of the Inland Waters Directorate. The 2 Fisheries and Oceans agencies at CCIW are the Great Lakes Fisheries Research Branch and the Bayfield Laboratory for Marine Science and Surveys, which includes the Central Region headquarters of the Canadian Hydrographic Service, one of 3 Canadian centres for nautical-chart production.

Since 1974 CCIW has been the World Health Organization's Collaborating Centre for Ground and Surface Water Quality, responsible for establishing and collecting data from a worldwide network of water-quality monitoring stations, part of the United Nations' Global Environmental Monitoring System (GEMS). Scientists at CCIW play a critical role in developing information for the management of the GREAT LAKES, but are also involved with LAKES, RESERVOIRS and RIVERS across the country, dealing with issues such as ACID RAIN, toxic chemicals, ice jams and shore erosion. ERIC MCGUINNESS

Canada Committee, a British parliamentary committee established 2 May 1828 to settle political disputes which were paralysing representative government in Lower Canada and creating difficulties in Upper Canada. The committee heard the testimony of several notable Canadians and recommended, among other proposals, that the Houses of Assembly should control public revenues in exchange for a permanent Civil List; the Legislative Council (upper house) should be more independent, and should represent the populace as a whole; and the CLERGY RESERVES in UC should be sold, the proceeds to be used to benefit all Protestant denominations. The report was an immense boost to the Reform cause, for its recommendations echoed the demands of reformers in both Canadas. Nevertheless, despite attempts to adopt many of the recommendations, political tension failed to ease and culminated in the REBELLIONS OF 1837. CURTIS FAHEY

Canada Company, brainchild of John GALT, established in late 1824 and chartered in 1825 as a land and COLONIZATION COMPANY in Upper Canada. In 1826 the company purchased from the government about 2.5 million acres (1 million ha) of land for $295 000. Roughly half lay in the Huron Tract (W Ont) and the rest consisted of scattered crown reserves. The payments, spread over 16 years, went directly to the executive branch of the UC government, to the bitter resentment of Reformers in the elected assembly, who also charged that the company failed to provide promised improvements in its structure and treated immigrants dictatorially. After the ACT OF UNION (1841), the company's connection to the Tory elite lessened and, with the implementation of a leasing system, the company operated more effectively and less conspicuously — though settlement would likely have proceeded as quickly without it. Following the sale of its last holdings in the 1950s, it ceased operation. PETER A. BASKERVILLE

Lands in Upper Canada to be disposed of by the Canada Company, from advertising material printed 1832 *(courtesy Public Archives of Canada/C-55033).*

Canada Corn Act, passed in 1843 by the British Parliament and applying to all grains, allowed Canadian wheat to enter the British market at a nominal duty, and flour manufactured in Canada at a proportionate rate. The latter clause was a victory for those seeking to make the St Lawrence a major conduit for American wheat. By removing barriers to Canadian wheat exports imposed by periods of low prices in Britain, the Act encouraged expansion of wheat acreage and flour-milling capacity in Upper Canada. But the Act was short-lived, since Britain was moving towards free trade, and repealed the CORN LAWS in 1846. DOUGLAS MCCALLA

Canada Council In accordance with the recommendation of the Massey Report, on 28 Mar 1957 the House of Commons adopted a bill which officially created the Canada Council. One month later, the Council held its first meeting. According to its mandate as defined by Parliament, the Council was to encourage the study and enjoyment of the arts, humanities and social sciences, as well as the production of related works. From the start, the federal government intended that the Council should have a large measure of autonomy and therefore put aside $50 million in an endowment fund to finance the Council's programs. During its first year the Council had a budget of $1.5 million for the arts, humanities and social sciences.

A board of 21 members operates the Canada Council. Its members are drawn from all 10 provinces and are named by the federal government, as are the director and associate director. The headquarters is in Ottawa. By 1964 the endowment fund was seen to be insufficient, and the government decided to grant enough additional money each year to cover the organization's needs. This grant now accounts for about 85% of the Council's budget. In 1984-85 the Council was to receive $72.5 million before cuts were announced. In 1978 a new organization, the SOCIAL SCIENCES AND HUMANITIES RESEARCH COUNCIL OF CANADA, was established, leaving the Canada Council responsible for the arts.

In order to carry out its enormous mandate, the Council tries to keep in touch with its public. Its employees function simultaneously as bureaucrats, administrators, organizers and cultural travelling salesmen. The Council offers assistance both to individual artists and to artistic organizations and professional associations. Demands on funds exceed the money available, and the Council calls on a number of committees, juries and advisers to help allocate grants. An interdisciplinary consultative committee of artists from every region of the country meets periodically to make recommendations on desirable cultural policies. To date, the Council has defined its mandate broadly. It helps everything from children's theatre to publishing houses, across the whole range of cultural activities. Through its Explorations program, it tries to fill the gaps which precisely defined disciplines cannot accommodate.

The Council celebrated its 25th anniversary in 1982. If its achievements seem prestigious, it is because the foundation of the Council coincided with a Canada-wide cultural revolution. This fortunate coincidence has allowed artists' energies to find expression and the public's thirst for its own culture to be satisfied. NAIM KATTAN

Canada Day, commemorating the creation of the Dominion of Canada, 1 July 1867, is the principal national holiday. As a legal holiday, it is observed on the first Monday in July, and the occasion is marked by formal celebrations across Canada. Canada Day was so named by Parliament on 27 Oct 1982; previous names have been First of July, July the First, Confederation Day and Dominion Day. JOHN ROBERT COLOMBO

Canada Development Corporation, with headquarters in Vancouver, develops and maintains Canadian-controlled and -managed companies in the private sector. Created in 1971 through a special Act of Parliament, the CDC has helped to widen the investment opportunities open to Canadians. Some 35 000 private shareholders have invested in the corporation, and during its first decade CDC was able to acquire diversified assets. Major investments 100% owned by CDC include Canterra Energy Ltd, the fourth-largest Canadian-controlled petroleum company; Kidd Creek Mines Ltd, which mines copper, zinc, silver and other metals; Wordplex International Inc, a word-processing equipment manufacturer; Connaught Laboratories, manufacturing life-sciences products; Polysar Limited, the largest Canadian producer of petrochemical derivatives; Dumex, a pharmaceutical manufacturer; Bio Research Laboratories Ltd, biological testers; and CDC Ventures, which offers venture and expansion capital. In 1983 CDC had sales or operating revenue of $3.8 billion (ranking 14th in Canada), assets of $7.5 billion (ranking 9th) and 20 657 employees. It is 48% owned by the federal government. DEBORAH C. SAWYER

Canada East, *see* PROVINCE OF CANADA.

Canada First, nationalist movement fd 1868 by Ontarians George DENISON, Henry Morgan, Charles MAIR and William FOSTER; and Robert Grant Haliburton, a Nova Scotian living in Ottawa. Inspired by the recently assassinated Thomas D'Arcy MCGEE and viewing CONFEDERATION as a political transaction among elites,

Canada First sought to promote a sense of national purpose and lay the intellectual foundations for Canadian nationality. During the 1869-70 RED RIVER REBELLION the group helped provoke the reaction against Métis, Catholics and French which swept Ontario following Thomas SCOTT's execution. It also campaigned for exclusively British immigration, envisaging a vigorous Anglo-Saxon and Protestant "northern" race that would harness the country's great economic potential. In 1871 the group turned to a less inflammatory expression of its nationalism: Canada's relationship with Britain. The Canada Firsters were dedicated to Canadian independence from the US and to the British connection, but after Britain concluded the 1871 TREATY OF WASHINGTON with the Americans, Canada First placed greater emphasis on Canadian autonomy and self-reliance, though the aim was some form of imperial federation, not separation from Britain.

Between 1872 and 1874 the founders, whose circle had expanded to embrace the "Twelve Apostles," drifted apart geographically. Leadership passed to a Toronto group primarily interested in launching a new political party, the Canadian National Association, which was founded in 1874. Its weekly organ, the *Nation*, had a healthy circulation, and there was speculation that Edward BLAKE, a prominent Liberal, might lead the party. But political action was not in keeping with Canada First's original intentions, and the movement had limited appeal outside Ontario; in fact, the call for reform had blatantly anti-Catholic overtones. The new leaders were divided, and Blake finally entered PM Mackenzie's Liberal government. The political organization quickly collapsed, leaving Canada First with no institutional basis.

Historians have called Canada First the harbinger of 20th-century political developments: third-party challenges, and Canada's complete independence from Britain. But these were not its original goals. Its real heirs were the later imperialists who called for consolidation of the British Empire, as they sought an instrument to protect and advance "superior" Anglo-Saxon values and institutions, and a vehicle for the definition and assertion of Canadian nationhood. Their implicit rejection of French Canadian nationality produced division and conflict rather than unity of purpose.

B.L. VIGOD

Canada-France-Hawaii Telescope, *see* OBSERVATORY.

Canada Goose, *see* GOOSE.

Canada House, a distinctive symbol of Canadian interests in Britain, located in London's bustling Trafalgar Square. After immigration, financial, and trade promotion had been directed for years from rented quarters, the imposing Union Club premises were purchased in 1923, refurbished by the Hon Peter Larkin, high commissioner, with Canadian materials, and opened by George V in 1925. Successive Canadian high commissioners to Britain used its offices until expansion into Sir John A. Macdonald House. Today Canada House is the headquarters in Britain for promoting Canadian culture and information, and a focal point for travelling Canadians. D.M. PAGE

Canada Labour Relations Board, est 1973 under the Canada Labour Code, reports to Parliament through the minister of labour. The federal board administers provisions of the Canada Labour Code concerning COLLECTIVE BARGAINING, conciliation, the declaration of unlawful STRIKES AND LOCKOUTS, the disposition of applications relating to technological change and complaints of unfair practices lodged by workers in industries under federal jurisdiction.

Canada Land Inventory, *see* LAND.

Canada Mortgage and Housing Corporation is the federal CROWN CORPORATION responsible for administering Canada's National Housing Act. CMHC was created in 1946 as the successor to Wartime Housing Corporation, and until 1979 was called Central Mortgage and Housing. Its mandate was to help improve housing and living conditions in Canada. Since 1946 one-half of all housing built in Canada has been assisted through the National Housing Act. CMHC has helped Canadians house themselves through grants, loans and by insuring mortgage monies borrowed from private lenders. Good housing and community design are encouraged through CMHC's research and design programs.

Immediately after CMHC concentrated its activities on providing homes for returning war veterans. During the 1950s housing quality concerns were added to the task of providing for sufficient quantity of housing. Urban renewal programs to redevelop in-ner cities were funded during the 1960s. In the 1970s neighbourhood improvement programs and a residential rehabilitation assistance program encouraged the maintenance and improvement of existing communities. The CMHC is concerned with providing housing for low-income people and meeting the special needs of the elderly and disabled. The corporation administers programs to encourage provinces, cities, nonprofit and co-operative societies to provide housing for Canadians who would otherwise be unable to obtain adequate and affordable shelter. CMHC publishes annual housing statistics, reports the results of housing research and produces the periodical *Habitat*. ANN MCAFEE

Canada Packers Inc, with head offices in Toronto, is the largest Canadian producer of food products. The original company, established in 1927, was Canada Packers Ltd, which acquired the capital stock of Gunns Ltd, The Harris Abattoir Co Ltd, the Canadian Packing Co Ltd and William Davies Co, Inc. In 1932 these operations were consolidated and Canada Packers, Ltd, became an operating company. The present name was adopted in 1979. Today the company produces a full line of food products, processing and distributing meat and poultry products and canning and freezing fruits and vegetables. It also produces and distributes soap, chemical, pharmaceutical, leather, feed and animal health products across Canada. The company has facilities in W Germany, Britain, Australia, Mexico and the US. As of Mar 1983, it had annual sales or operating revenue of $3 billion (ranking 27th in Canada), assets of $558 million (ranking 123rd) and 14 000 employees. Its shares are widely held. DEBORAH C. SAWYER

Canada Pension Plan (CPP), introduced in 1966, is an earnings-related public PENSION plan that transfers incomes from workers to the retired. The current contribution (tax) rate of 3.6% on earnings between the maximum pensionable earnings ($16 500 in 1982) and the basic exemption (about 10% of the maximum) is split equally between employers and employees. Retirement pensions (obtainable from 65 years of age) are 25% of average pensionable earnings, calculated in terms of the wage standards existing at the time of retirement. The CPP also provides survivors' benefits (spouses' pensions, orphans' benefits, lump-sum death benefits) and disability benefits. All payments are indexed to the CONSUMER PRICE INDEX and adjusted annually. The initial CPP contribution rates were designed to produce a pension fund of billions of dollars — money invested in provincial bonds at interest rates tied to rates paid by federal bonds. As the number of those eligible for full pensions increases, benefits threaten to exceed the contribution unless contribution rates are increased. The CPP's financial strength ultimately depends on the contribution rates that workers will accept. If the ratio of the elderly to those of working age increases, so will the cost to workers of public pensions. A. ASIMAKOPULOS

Canada Permanent Mortgage Corporation, with headquarters in Toronto, in 1982 had sales or operating revenue of almost $886 million, assets of $6.4 billion (ranking 9th among banks and financial institutions in Canada) and 4084 employees. Established in 1899, Canada Permanent conducts mortgage, deposit, trust and real-estate services across Canada. GENSTAR owns 99% of the shares. DEBORAH C. SAWYER

Canada Post Corporation, proclaimed a CROWN CORPORATION 16 Oct 1981, replaced the previous Post Office department of the federal government. Canada Post is the largest civilian government organization, administering some 8500 post offices across Canada and employing more than 63 000 people. It handles about 5 billion pieces of mail yearly and its revenues total more than $600 million. Much of the authority is delegated to the 4 regional offices with headquarters in Vancouver, Toronto, Montréal and Halifax. *See* POSTAL SYSTEM.

Canada Safeway Ltd is a food retailer with head offices in Winnipeg. Started as Safeway Stores Ltd in 1929, the company adopted its present name in 1947. At the end of 1982, directly or through its subsidiaries, it operated 294 food retail stores from Ontario to BC and 28 in W Germany. It also operates wholesale grocery warehouses, bakeries, canneries and food-processing plants in Canada. In 1982 it had $3.3 billion in sales or operating revenue (ranking 25th in Canada), assets of $1 billion (ranking 83rd) and 24 231 employees. The company is 100% owned by Safeway Stores, Inc, of Oakland, Calif.

DEBORAH C. SAWYER

Canada Savings Bonds differ from other government bonds in that they can be cashed at any bank for the face value plus accrued interest. They cannot be sold by the original buyer but must be held until cashed or until they mature (usually in 7 years) from the time they were bought. The 1983 bonds offered interest of 9.25% on the first year and at least 7% for the next 6 years. But the interest rate has been as high as 19.5% and as low as 2.75%, the rate on the first issue in 1946. Canada Savings Bonds, which can be bought on payroll deduction plans and which range in denomination from $50 to $5000, grew out of the successful raising of money for the war effort in WWII by Victory Bonds and the sale of War Savings Certificates and stamps, not to traditional investors, but to ordinary citizens and even to school children. From the start there has been a limit on the amount of any one issue any Canadian — they are not sold outside the country — can buy. This limit has been as low as $15 000 and as high as $50 000 (mid-1980s). Canada Savings Bonds are a major source of federal government finance; in mid-1984 the federal government had borrowed about $38 billion from the public in this form, out of a total debt of $142 billion.

D. MCGILLIVRAY

Canada-Soviet Hockey Series, 1972 Soviet teams had totally dominated international hockey for the previous 10 years, but this was the first time they played the best Canadian professionals. The series began amid great anticipation in Canada and the Soviet Union. The victory of the Soviets in the first game, Sept 2 in Montréal, by 7-3, stunned the Canadian players and shocked the Canadian public. The Soviets displayed speed, skill and a haughty disregard for Canadian confidence. The Canadians regrouped in Toronto 2 days later and won 4-1 but the third game in Winnipeg, Sept 6 was a 4-4 tie and Team Canada lost 5-3 in Vancouver, Sept

', amid the jeers of their own fans. In Moscow, Sept 22, the Soviets swept to another victory 5-4, but the Canadians fought back to tie the series with victories on Sept 24 (3-2) and Sept 26 (4-3). The last game, on Sept 28, was watched intently by the largest Canadian TV audience on record. It began with 2 quick Soviet goals, the ejection of a Canadian player, and a long delay as Canadians raged over the officiating. The Soviets led 5-3 at the end of the second period, but Phil ESPOSITO and Yvan Cournoyer tied the game. Paul Henderson scored the most famous goal in hockey history, with only 34 seconds remaining to win the series for Canada. The team played one more match, against Czechoslovakia, winning 2-1, before returning home to an outpouring of pride and relief. On the surface, the series was a dramatic sports event — in retrospect won by determined athletes against the odds. But the series affected Canadians more deeply. Their cherished myth of hockey superiority had been shattered. JAMES MARSH

Paul Henderson's winning goal in the first *Canada-Soviet Hockey Series*, 1972 (*photo by Frank Lennon/Toronto Star*).

Canada Steamship Lines Inc, with head offices in Montréal, began in 1845 as Richelieu Steamboat Co, which was founded by a group of farmers in St-Charles-sur-Richelieu, Qué. Amalgamations resulted in the expansion of the company, and in 1913 Canada Steamship Lines Ltd was incorporated after the merger of several Canadian shipping companies. CSL Ltd became the CSL Group Inc in 1980. Until 1965 the company offered passenger services on the Great Lakes and St Lawrence R. Today, CSL designs, builds and operates freight and bulk-cargo vessels in inland and oceanic waters, runs transportation systems and offers management consulting services in the field of transportation. CSL Inc handles the marine business for CSL Group, which in 1983 had sales or operating revenue of $476.7 million (ranking 149th in Canada), assets of $212.4 million (ranking 214th) and 6000 employees. Passage Holdings Inc owns 50% of CSL shares; Federal Commerce and Navigation Ltd holds the other 50%. DEBORAH C. SAWYER

Canada Studies Foundation, fd 1970, a child of the National History Project (1965-68) financed by Trinity College School in Port Hope, Ont. Perceiving through the project that the study of Canada in schools was itself a divisive force in a diverse and fractious country, A.B. Hodgetts set out to provide opportunities for people from different levels of education and different parts of Canada to work together on Canada Studies project teams across linguistic, cultural and regional barriers. Emphasis on product (school materials about Canada) and process (cross-Canada dialogue) has persisted in various forms.

Walter L. GORDON served as chairman and private-sector fund-raiser for the initial 5 experimental years, with Hodgetts and George S. Tomkins as co-directors of activities; the first year's expenditures were over $500 000. With a solid core of active participants by 1974, the foundation's support was assumed by provincial ministers of education and the federal secretary of state, and by contributions in kind from teachers, schools and local school jurisdictions; the 1975-76 budget was $600 000. Since 1978 direct support has been almost exclusively by the Secretary of State, with yearly expenditures below $300 000. The foundation pioneered new subject matter and new approaches to teaching about Canada. It has published over 65 books and teachers' manuals, stimulated a new market for Canadian textbook publishers, established a network of more than 2000 teachers across the country, distributed a widely read bilingual newsletter (*Contact*) and promoted a structured approach to the study of Canada, as described in *Teaching Canada for the 80's* (1978). *See* CANADIAN STUDIES. PAUL GALLAGHER

Canada-Third World Relations The decolonization of the European empires after WWII produced many "new nations" and revealed how little economic and social development the colonial system had permitted its wards. The problem of the "Third World" and its "underdevelopment" was thus placed firmly on the global agenda. In this postwar context, Canada projected an image of genuine concern for the demands and requirements of the Third World, an image which has struck a responsive chord with many Canadians and with many in the underdeveloped world itself. The allocation by the Canadian government of significant sums for foreign aid — a process marked by the launching of the Colombo Plan (1951) and other regionally focused aid programs; by the founding of the External Aid Office (1960) and its transformation into the CANADIAN INTERNATIONAL DEVELOPMENT AGENCY (CIDA) in 1968 — is the most concrete manifestation of this concern (in 1983-84 CIDA dispensed $1.8 billion in aid to the Third World). The "liberal internationalism" vigorously espoused by Lester B. PEARSON — he followed his prime ministership by presiding over an influential international inquiry into the causes of world poverty — and the support for "North-South dialogue" on development advocated by Pierre TRUDEAU have also been noteworthy.

These initiatives must be put in their proper context, however. Many Third World thinkers and activists have criticized their countries' inheritance of a subordinate and dependent position within the international economic system (termed by them "neo-colonialism") and advocated a radical and structural transformation of the situation, both locally and internationally. In contrast, Canadian policymakers have consistently defended the broad merits of the existing global economy; their goal is primarily one of reform at the margin of the international economic system to allow some amelioration of the condition of the world's poor and to pre-empt more revolutionary demands. Though never quite as extreme as its counterpart in the US, the Canadian government has tended to view radical development strategies proposed by some Third World countries as either unacceptably threatening or as manifestations of an international "communist menace," an interpretation which parallels the American Cold War perspective on the Third World.

There has also been a gap between rhetoric and reality in the Canadian approach. In 1984 the Canadian government pledged to reach an aid target of 0.5% of gross national product by 1985-86 and 0.7% by 1990. Nevertheless, FOREIGN AID has consistently fallen below levels recommended by the UN. Moreover, foreign-aid programs often emphasize the interests of Canadian suppliers and contractors more than the requirements of the recipient countries themselves; simultaneously, there has been a shift in emphasis away from aiding the poorest of the poor countries and towards aiding those larger and wealthier Third World economies which are also the more attractive potential trading partners. This approach also has marked Canada's participation in international forums such as the General Agreement on Trade and Tariffs (GATT), the United Nations Conference on Trade and Development (UNCTAD), the LAW OF THE SEA conferences and the various negotiations directed towards redressing inequities in the realm of INTERNATIONAL TRADE and investment that have emerged around the theme of a "New International Economic Order." In such settings, Canada has frequently found itself taking up a far more intransigent and defensive posture than other western "middle powers" such as the Scandinavian countries.

Canada's own economic difficulties in recent years may partly account for these tendencies, but the very close integration of the Canadian business community into the policymaking process in such spheres has been an important factor as well. Canada's relationship to the less developed areas of the world was structured, long before the post-WWII period, by the expansive role of Canadian-based banks, mining and utility companies. By the turn of this century, this was already true of the links Canada was establishing with the Caribbean and Latin America. Such business interests have continued to be one of the dominant determinants of Canada's relationship with the Third World.

However, Canada's links to the Third World are not monopolized by government and the business community. There is a large network of church-sponsored groups and agencies, voluntary "nongovernmental (aid) organizations" (of the OXFAM type) and more overtly political Third World support groups. A majority of these groups have supported critical views of present workings of the global economy and the causes of underdevelopment, views that are sensitive to the claims of international equity and the legitimacy of revolutionary action in some settings (eg, South Africa). Often critical of Canadian government and business practices in the Third World, such groups have generally not succeeded in determining Canadian policy to any major degree, but they have kept alive a sharp debate on the nature of Canada's links to the Third World, links which are important in the context of greater global integration, continuing worldwide poverty and rising international tensions. JOHN S. SAUL

Canada-US Automotive Products Agreement (Autopact) a conditional free-trade agreement signed by Canada and the US in Jan 1965 to create a single N American market for passenger cars, trucks, buses, tires and automotive parts. In Canada the free trade does not apply to consumer sales; it applies solely to manufacturers who meet certain conditions. Under the agreement, motor-vehicle manufacturers are obliged to maintain the same ratio of production to sales in Canada as existed in the 1964 model year; to maintain Canadian value-added or Canadian content equal to the 1964 model year; and have been required (from 1965 onwards) to increase Canadian value-added by 60% of the growth in the value of passenger cars sold (50% for trucks and 40% for buses). Between 1965 and 1982 Canada had an overall automotive trade deficit of $12.1 billion with the US, with a surplus of about $28 billion in assembled vehicles and a deficit of about $40.5 billion in automotive parts. Canada had overall surpluses in 1970, 1971, 1972 and 1982. In 1983 Canada had a sudden enormous surplus of $3.3 billion. The 2 principal purposes of the Autopact were to lower Canadian production costs through more efficient production of fewer lines of motor vehicles and parts and to lower consumer prices. However, critics note that the industry has remained essentially foreign controlled, and that Canadian subsidiaries are less autonomous than they once were. In addition, they note that the industry spends little on research and development in Canada. Automotive industry employment totalled 70 600 in 1965, reached about 125 000 in 1978 before falling to about 99 000 in 1982. Although the Autopact was initially a Canada-US arrangement, vehicles and parts can come from anywhere in the world provided the criteria for Canadian value-added and the production-to-sale ratio set out in the agreement are met. The Canada-US pact can be terminated at any time by 12 months written notice by either government. DAVID CRANE

Canada West, *see* PROVINCE OF CANADA.

Canadair CL-215, unique amphibious aircraft designed to fight forest fires with water bombing and chemical fire retardants. It can scoop up a load of nearly 6000 litres of water in 10 seconds, while skimming over a body of water and jettison it over a fire in less than 1 second. It first flew Oct 1967, and 65 had been built by 1980. Québec (15), France (15), Spain (17) and Greece (11) have been the main customers.

Canadair CL-215 (*courtesy Canadair*).

Canadair CL-28 Argus, long-range maritime patrol plane built in Canada. Based on the Bristol Britannia, a British passenger aircraft, it carried an operational crew of 15, and was equipped with sophisticated radar and antisubmarine weapons. With a range of over 8100 km, it operated primarily from bases at Greenwood, NS, and Summerside, PEI. The Argus first flew Mar 1957, and a total of 46 were built in 2 versions. It was replaced by the American-built Lockheed Aurora.

Canadair CL-600 Challenger, corporate executive aircraft developed and built in Canada. Exhaustive testing resulted in an advanced wing design, but performance has not lived up to expectations. It carries 30 passengers at a speed of 880 km/h. It first flew Nov 1978, and numerous orders had been received by 1980 from around the world. Later cancellations, the crash of a prototype and the extensive government expenditure made the aircraft controversial.

Canadair Ltd, with head offices in Montréal, is a Canadian aerospace manufacturer. Begun in 1920 as the aircraft division of Canadian Vickers Limited, the company assumed a separate corporate identity in 1944 following reorganization by the Canadian government. In 1947 it was acquired by the Electric Boat Company of Groton, Conn, and the companies then formed the nucleus of General Dynamics Corporation in 1952. In 1976 Canadair became a CROWN CORPORATION under the government's plans for restructuring the Canadian AEROSPACE INDUSTRY.

Since 1944 Canadair has produced over 3900 aircraft for military and commercial purposes, for the Canadian Armed Forces and for export, eg, the CANADAIR CL-28 ARGUS. Its current major project is the CANADAIR CL-600 CHALLENGER executive jet, a new type of business aircraft which made its first flight in 1978, 2 years after the program began. Canadair also produces the CANADAIR CL-215 multipurpose amphibious aircraft, the only one in the world designed specifically for forest firefighting. In 1982 Canadair had sales or operating revenue of $429 million (ranking 160th in Canada), unidentified assets and 5700 employees. The federal government owns 100% of the company and its major infusions of financial support to keep it operating have been controversial. DEBORAH C. SAWYER

Canadarm, name given to the Shuttle Remote Manipulator System (RMS), Canada's contribution to the US Space Shuttle. Canadarm is a complex, 6-degrees of freedom, remotely controlled manipulator used for cargo deployment and retrieval from and to the shuttle's cargo bay. The 15 m manipulator arm functions in a manner similar to that of a human arm and has 6 rotating joints, 2 at its shoulder (yaw, pitch), one at its elbow (pitch) and 3 at its wrist (pitch, yaw, roll). Its snare-type end effector (or hand) is cylindrical; 3 snare wires grasp a post or grapple fixture on the SATELLITE to be captured. The $110 million Canadarm program was largely carried out by Canadian industry, under the direction of the National Aeronautical Establishment, a division of the NATIONAL RESEARCH COUNCIL OF CANADA. The industrial team, led by SPAR AEROSPACE LIMITED, included CAE Electronics Ltd and DSMA Atcon Ltd. Industrial benefits to date include the sale of 3 additional Canadarms to NASA and establishment of an industrial capability in the HIGH-TECHNOLOGY fields of advanced manipulator systems and ROBOTICS.

While the mechanical arm, mounted in the shuttle's cargo bay, is the most visible part, the system also includes hand controllers for ASTRONAUT operation, a display and control panel and a signal processing-interface box. A TV camera

Canadarm (*courtesy National Research Council*).

(or eye), located on the wrist (with an optional second location near its elbow), is part of the shuttle's closed-circuit television system that provides visual cues when an astronaut is performing grappling maneuvers. One of the 5 on-board shuttle COMPUTERS provides the "brain" of the arm. Extensive computer programs enable the arm to be operated automatically or allow the astronaut to operate the arm in several control modes, ranging from complete endpoint control (where the astronaut "flies" the end of the arm) to single-joint operation. The arm also has a contingency back-up mode that can be used to complete missions, if the primary control system fails.

The Canadarm is capable of maneuvering payloads of nearly 30 000 kg mass in space at speeds (depending on the payload mass) of up to 60 cm/s. It must be able to place such payloads in any position, with an accuracy of approximately 5 cm. Each joint is powered by an optically commutated, brushless DC motor, driven by a specially designed servo-power amplifier. To obtain the high joint-output torque needed from the relatively low motor torque available, a high-reduction gearbox with an epicyclic/planet system is used for each joint. Gear ratios range from 1842:1 to 739:1 on different joints. All joints are back-drivable and have zero backlash to maintain positioning accuracy and control.

Demanding stiffness and strength requirements, coupled with volume constraints imposed by the shuttle, have dictated extensive use of the latest AEROSPACE materials (eg, TITANIUM, stainless steel, ultra-high modulus graphite epoxy). The harsh environment necessitated special attention to thermal design and lubrication. The arm is entirely covered with a multilayer insulation system, consisting of alternate layers of goldized kapton, dacron scrim cloth and a beta cloth (fibreglass) outer covering. In extremely cold conditions, thermostatically controlled electric heaters protect critical hardware. Canadarm was designed to have a minimum lifetime of 10 years and to be used for up to 100 missions without maintenance. It weighs under 450 kg and cannot support itself in normal gravity; hence, a complex simulation facility (SIMFAC) had to be developed to verify its operation in space and facilitate astronaut training. On Earth, the assembled arm could only be tested in 2 dimensions by using a special air-bearing cradle, operating on a specially designed flat-floor area.

The arm first flew in Nov 1981 on the second Space Shuttle flight and performed well, exceeding all design goals. It was declared operational one year later, after 3 successful test flights. It has since been used to deploy and retrieve free-flying satellites, deploy the large Long Duration Exposure Facility (LDEF) and played a key role in the mission to retrieve, repair and redeploy the Solar Maximum Satellite, the first satellite repaired in space. GARY LINDBERG

Canada's Food Guide is a daily eating plan designed to help people of all ages choose their food wisely. The Dietary Standard for Canada recommends a daily nutrient intake for Canadians, but because people select food and not nutrients, nutrient recommendations have been translated into food choices. The guide enables many individuals to meet their nutrient needs by following a simple daily food pattern based on 4 food groups, each of which contains a variety of nutrients. Some studies reveal that the pattern will not supply the Recommended Daily Nutrient Intakes (RDNI) for all individuals; women, for instance, may need more iron.

The central principle of Canada's Food Guide is variety. The guide recommends that a specific number of food servings should be chosen every day from the following food groups: milk and milk products (2-4 servings), bread and cereals (3-5 servings), fruits and vegetables (4-5 servings) and meat and alternatives (2 servings).

Each food group offers its own particular pattern of key nutrient strengths. Some people, however, because of allergies or digestive problems, budget limitations, energy requirements (calories), food availability, personal preferences and dislikes, or philosophical or religious beliefs, may not eat a food or foods within a food group. The guide is sufficiently flexible to accommodate these factors.

Both numbers of servings and serving sizes are often expressed in the guide as a range, eg, 4 to 5 servings of fruit and vegetables or 60 to 90 grams of cooked lean meat. Individuals can generally select from within this range the size and number of servings compatible with energy needs and personal preferences. However, with milk and the milk-products group, the recommended number of servings varies because the need for calcium and vitamin D is greater during certain periods of an individual's life.
M.T. CLANDININ

Reading: Health and Welfare Canada, *Canada's Food Guide Handbook; Dietary Standard for Canada* (1975).

Canada's Sports Hall of Fame is Canada's national museum of sport, dedicated to preserving and increasing Canadians' awareness of their sport heritage. Founded in 1955 through the efforts of Harry I. Price, a former assistant athletics commissioner of Ontario, it is located in the centre of Exhibition Place in Toronto, Ont. Its exhibit area covers 557 m^2 and its displays are viewed by an estimated 300 000 people annually. The Hall of Fame maintains a substantial archives of sport, including nearly 35 000 historical photographs. It also publishes a quarterly newsletter and conducts educational programs for school-age children.

The annual election of honoured members draws the most public attention. Chosen by a selection committee of 12, with representatives from every province, men and women are elected to 2 categories, Athletes or Builders. Normally, athletes are only elected after a 3-year waiting period from their retirement from active competition. As of 1983, 311 Canadians have been so honoured. The Hall of Fame is administered by a small staff responsible to a board of governors and also has representatives from coast to coast. It charges no admission fee, being supported by government grants and public and corporate donations. It is open to the general public throughout the year.
J. THOMAS WEST

Reading: D. Fisher and S.F. Wise, *Canada's Sporting Heroes* (1974), published under the auspices of CSHF.

Canadian Advisory Council on the Status of Women (CACSW) was established in 1973 by the federal government on the recommendation of the Royal Commission on the STATUS OF WOMEN. The CACSW advises the federal government on and promotes public awareness of women's concerns. As an autonomous agency, the CACSW reports to Parliament through the minister responsible for the status of women, while retaining the right to publish its views without ministerial consent. The CACSW is composed of 3 full-time officers (a president and 2 vice-presidents), 27 regionally representative part-time members appointed for 3-year terms and an office staff of approximately 30 employees. It has been a leading publisher of research on women and its recommendations have prompted legislative change concerning constitutional reform, pensions, parental benefits, taxation, health care, employment practices, sexual assault, wife battering and human rights.
MARY-JANE LIPKIN

Canadian-American Relations Canada's nationhood is in many ways a by-product of the AMERICAN REVOLUTION, when the victory of the Thirteen Colonies led to the exodus of LOYALIST Americans to BRITISH NORTH AMERICA. Many brought with them a deep distrust of the US and its democratic ways. Many American revolutionaries thought the revolution incomplete while Britain retained any N American outpost. Conflict seemed inevitable, and the Napoleonic Wars spilled over into N America in 1812. The WAR OF 1812 was fought defensively by the British and halfheartedly by the Americans. Both sides welcomed the TREATY OF GHENT, which brought some settlement of outstanding problems between BNA and the US. The RUSH-BAGOT AGREEMENT of 1817 limited the presence of armed vessels on the Great Lakes. The CONVENTION OF 1818 provided for continuation of the boundary from Lake of the Woods to the Rocky Mts. In the East, commissioners appointed under the Treaty of Ghent sorted out boundary problems, except in northern Maine.

In the 1820s and 1830s Upper and Lower Canadians opposed to their governments looked with increasing favour upon American democracy. William Lyon MACKENZIE and Louis-Joseph PAPINEAU sought American support in their REBELLION OF 1837. After his defeat Mackenzie fled to the US, where he fomented border troubles for the following year (*see* HUNTERS' LODGES). A British show of military force and American official unwillingness to support the rebels ended the threats to BNA. In 1842 the ASHBURTON-WEBSTER TREATY settled the NE boundary, but problems west of the Rockies were cleared up in the 1846 OREGON TREATY only after war threatened.

In 1854 fears subsided as BNA and the US were linked by a RECIPROCITY treaty, but they returned suddenly with the AMERICAN CIVIL WAR, 1861-65. Northern Americans resented what they felt was Britain's pro-Southern sympathy. BNA and the US managed to avoid military confrontation, but the end of the war led to new tensions, because it was thought that the North might take revenge against Britain, and because FENIANS were organizing to invade BNA. The Fenian Raids of 1866 failed, but spurred BNA towards CONFEDERATION the following year.

Confederation, the subsequent withdrawal of British garrisons, and conflicts in Europe impelled Britain and Canada to seek settlement of outstanding differences with the Americans in the 1871 TREATY OF WASHINGTON. PM Sir John A. MACDONALD, a member of the British negotiating team, grumbled about the terms, but the treaty was useful to Canada in that the US, through its signature, acknowledged the new nation to its north. Thereafter, Canada's concern about the American military threat diminished rapidly. There were fears of American interference as Canada established sovereignty over the North-West, but by the late 1890s both nations looked back at 3 decades of remarkably little conflict. In 1897-98 a Joint High Commission, reflecting this spirit as well as the Anglo-American desire for rapprochement, sought to remedy remaining discord. On most items the commission was successful, but settlement of the ALASKA BOUNDARY DISPUTE, for which another tribunal was established in 1902, led to Canadian anger, more towards Britain than against the US. It produced a conviction that in the future Canada must rely increasingly on its own resources and less on Britain.

Canada therefore undertook to establish direct institutional links with the US. Best known was the INTERNATIONAL JOINT COMMISSION, established in 1909 to mediate boundary questions. In 1911 PM Wilfrid LAURIER went farther than most Canadians would go when he proposed a reciprocity agreement with the US. In the 1911 election campaign old animosities reappeared, the Conservatives were elected and reciprocity died. Nevertheless, new PM Robert BORDEN quickly reassured the Americans that he wanted to maintain good relations. Borden's action probably eased tensions when Canada entered WORLD WAR I in 1914 while the US remained neutral. When the US finally entered the war in 1917, the 2 countries recognized their common heritage and interests to an unprecedented extent. Immediately after WWI Canadian politicians fancied themselves interpreters between the US and Britain, eg, at the 1921 Imperial Conference, when PM Arthur MEIGHEN dissuaded Britain from renewing the Anglo-Japanese Alliance because it might bring the British Empire into conflict with the US. With PM Mackenzie KING's Liberals in power, there was an ever stronger tendency to emphasize Canada's "North American" character and, by implication, its similarity to the US.

In the 1920s and 1930s Canadians and Americans mingled as never before. Canadian defence plans were altered as planners dismissed the possibility of conflict. Economic and cultural linkages strengthened as suspicion of American influence receded. Canada and the US established legations in 1927 and no longer dealt with each other through British offices. More important was the impact of American popular culture through radio, motion pictures and the automobile. The Canadian government tried to regulate BROADCASTING and FILM but largely failed. Other organizations such as the Roman CATHOLIC Church in Québec tried moral suasion and political pressure to prevent Canadians from partaking of the most frivolous aspects of American culture.

Through the new media, Canadians became familiar with US Pres Franklin Roosevelt. In 1938, as another European war loomed, he publicly promised support if Canada were ever threatened. Roosevelt did co-operate closely after WORLD WAR II erupted in Sept 1939. Although the US remained neutral, Roosevelt and King reached 2 important agreements which formalized the American commitment: the Ogdensburg Agreement (1940) established the PERMANENT JOINT BOARD ON DEFENCE, and the Hyde Park Agreement (1941) united the 2 economies for wartime purposes (*see* LEND-LEASE). Both agreements won widespread popular approval.

Canadians' admiration for the US increased after it joined the war in Dec 1941. Public-opinion polls indicated that many Canadians would have liked to join the US. This new affection frightened King, but Canada retained and even expanded defence and other relations with the US after the war. The COLD WAR with the USSR convinced most Canadians that the US was the bulwark defending common values and security. In Aug 1958 Canada and the US signed a plan for joint air defence (NORAD), and the following year agreed to a Defence Production Sharing Program. Some deplored the growing links. Vincent MASSEY and Walter GORDON headed royal commissions on culture and economic policy which were critical of American influence in Canada. In Parliament the 1956 PIPELINE DEBATE and the debate on the SUEZ CRISIS indicated that some parliamentarians also feared American influence upon Canada's government and its attitudes.

PM John DIEFENBAKER committed Canada to NORAD and the defence-sharing plan and quickly befriended Pres Dwight Eisenhower. Nevertheless, he lamented Canada's increasing distance from Britain and the extent of American cultural and other influence. This feeling became suspicion of the US itself when John Kennedy became president in 1961. The leaders disliked each other, and policy differences grew rapidly. Diefenbaker refused nuclear arms for Canada (*see* BOMARC MISSILE CRISIS) and hesitated to back Kennedy during the 1962 CUBAN MISSILE CRISIS. The Americans openly accused Diefenbaker of failing to carry out commitments. In the 1963 general election Diefenbaker accused the Americans of gross interference, blaming them for his election loss.

Both countries expected better relations when the Liberals assumed power. By 1965, however, relations had deteriorated significantly as PM Lester PEARSON and Canadians found it difficult to give the US the support it demanded during the Vietnam War. By 1967 the Canadian government openly expressed its disagreement with American policies in SE Asia. Canadians generally became less sympathetic to American influence and foreign policy. A nationalist movement demanded that American influence be significantly reduced. The first major nationalist initiatives occurred in cultural affairs, but those most offensive to Americans, such as the National Energy Program, were economic. Although recent Canadian-American relations have not reflected the degree of hostility and suspicion which marked them earlier, neither do they reflect the co-operation of the immediate postwar period. *See also* FRANCO-AMERICANS; ACID RAIN; ENVIRONMENTAL LAW; NATIONALISM.

JOHN ENGLISH

Canadian-American Relations, Economic Economic relations between Canada and the US are of paramount importance to Canada. The US is Canada's most important trading partner (Canada exports 30% of its GROSS NATIONAL PRODUCT and almost 70% of Canadian exports are to the US) and has provided Canada with much of its investment capital and TECHNOLOGY through FOREIGN INVESTMENT, resulting in a high level of US ownership and control of the Canadian ECONOMY. Canada is also the largest export customer of the US (about 10% of US exports go to Canada, and account for more than 60% of Canadian imports, although the trade in manufactured goods between the 2 countries favours the US) as well as a major source of natural resources for US industry (*see* INTERNATIONAL TRADE).

While access to US markets, investment and technology have benefitted Canadians, the resulting commercial arrangements, along with the great disparity in population between the 2 countries, has created serious problems for Canada, including a high level of dependency on and vulnerability to US policies. Recently, US corporate interests have successfully enlisted the support of the US government in widening the Canadian market for US goods and services (eg, banking, data services), in opposing Canadian policies to strengthen Canadian industry (eg, government incentives and grants for Canadian industry, measures to gain Canadian industrial spin-offs for Canadian resource development) and in weakening Canadian measures to control foreign investment (eg, screening of foreign investment, the role of crown corporations, changes to the tax and land regulations to favour Canadian oil and gas companies, and curbs on the role of foreign banks).

The key theme that ran through the first 50 years of Canadian-American economic relations was the issue of free trade. Historically, Canadians opposed to complete free trade have argued that it would entail the eventual loss of political sovereignty, lead to greater integration in economic and industrial policy, and further constrain Canada's ability to adopt independent economic policies. Opponents of free trade have contended that even if the US agreed to free trade, the US Congress would use nontariff barriers to hinder any gains that may accrue to Canadians from such arrangements. Supporters argued that only through free trade, and the consequent unimpeded access to US markets, would Canadian manufacturers be able to become efficient producers with large enough sales volumes to support research and development (*see* INDUSTRIAL RESEARCH AND DEVELOPMENT; INDUSTRIAL STRATEGY).

In 1866 the US abrogated the Reciprocity Treaty of 1854 in angry response to British aid to the Confederate states. Although negotiations leading to the TREATY OF WASHINGTON (1871) failed to restore RECIPROCITY or procure compensation for the damage resulting from FENIAN raids, they did result in US recognition of Canada as a nation in the N American continent. In the 1891 federal election, the Liberals campaigned on a platform of unrestricted free trade, losing by a narrow margin. For its part, the US rebuffed free-trade proposals from Canada and maintained protectionist or high-tariff policies.

Despite the mutual political suspicions, the 2 countries developed from 1875 to 1900 the linkages that determined the pattern for closer economic integration. Americans invested heavily in Canada, establishing "branch plants" and taking over many Canadian-owned enterprises (eg, in 1898 the giant Standard Oil company acquired Canada's largest oil company, Imperial Oil). Trade increased, and business and financial ties were quickly formed, reinforced by transportation, labour and other links. The high-tariff policies of the NATIONAL POLICY attracted enormous amounts of US capital and investment. In 1914, although 72% of nonresident investment in Canada was from the UK, the US supplied twice as much capital for direct investment in mining and manufacturing as the UK. Canadian unions, which burgeoned during this period, were closely affiliated with their US counterparts.

In 1911 President William Howard Taft's administration reversed decades of US protectionism when Taft and PM Wilfrid LAURIER reached an agreement providing for a limited free-trade pact covering tariffs on a significant list of manufactured products. Enabling legislation was passed by the US Congress but was blocked by the Conservative Opposition in Parliament. The Canadian general election of that year was fought largely on the free-trade issue, and Laurier's defeat was partly a result of fears that free trade was the first step to political annexation.

In both the US and Canada the INDUSTRIALIZATION that had begun in the mid-19th century expanded rapidly in the early 20th century. Hundreds of millions of US dollars poured into Canada to create more subsidiaries or branch plants or to take over ownership of promising Canadian companies to serve Canadian and British preferential markets in fast-developing new industries such as motor vehicles, electric appliances, chemicals, machinery and metal processing. With the GREAT DEPRESSION, however, Canadians were made aware of the vulnerable position in which they have been placed by excessive dependence upon the US economy. In 1930 the US Congress passed the Hawley-Smoot Tariff, which raised the duty on US imports to the highest levels in history. Canada responded with new high tariffs of its own while Canadian prime minister R.B. BENNETT pledged to "blast a way" into the world markets and reduce Canadian dependence on the US economy. In 1932 his government hosted the Imperial Economic Conference in Ottawa to revise the system of tariffs within the British Commonwealth and Empire.

Trade relations improved following the passage in the US of the Reciprocal Trade Agreements Act in 1934; Canada and the US began negotiations to lower tariffs and increase trade. In 1935 PM Mackenzie KING concluded the Canada-US trade agreement that had been initiated by the Bennett government. A second and broader Canada-US trade agreement was signed in 1938, leading to further reductions in tariffs. Canadians and Americans collaborated intensively during WWII. In 1940 a meeting between PM King and President Roosevelt near Ogdensburg, NY, led to the creation of the Permanent Joint Board on Defense (PJBD), which also provided the means for close economic and other relations between the 2 countries. Following US entry into the war, the PJBD organized a number of major American-financed activities in Canada, including the ALASKA HIGHWAY and the Canol project, which expanded oil production at Norman Wells, NWT.

Before the official US entry into the war, Canada dramatically expanded its industrial capacity, partly by purchasing vast amounts of machinery and equipment from the US. By early 1941 Canada's foreign exchange reserves of US dollars had plummetted to dangerously low levels and Canada turned to the US for help. King and Roosevelt negotiated the Hyde Park Agreement, which provided for significantly increased US purchases in Canada and allowed British use of US lend-lease funds for American war components imported by Canada for use in British military equipment. Both these measures increased Canadian holdings of US dollars to cover imports from the US.

The postwar demand for consumer goods, the vast influx of immigrants, and the need to convert a wartime industrial machine to civilian needs resulted in a sharp increase in Canadian imports of US consumer goods and industrial machinery. Canada's postwar exports, however, fell sharply. By 1947 Canada was importing twice as much as it was exporting to the US. Because Britain and Europe were devastated by the war and short of foreign exchange, Canada could not, as it had in the past, pay for its US trade deficit from a trade surplus with the rest of the world. By 1950, however, these problems had largely disappeared, and Canada was enjoying an investment boom. In the Cold War atmosphere of the late 1940s and early 1950s, US corporations embarked on a massive program to locate and develop Canadian natural resources, from oil and gas to uranium and nonferrous metals such as copper and iron ore. This program of investment, along with parallel investment in other major industries, helped fuse the Canadian economy even more closely with that of the US. A large and increasing share of Canada's mining, oil and gas and manufacturing industries fell under US corporate ownership and control.

In an attempt to avoid a return to bilateral negotiations with the US, which exposed Canada to the possibility of having to make concessions in one area to obtain US concessions in another, Canadian leaders turned to multilateral arrangements, such as the General Agreement on Tariffs and Trade (GATT) in international economic relations, and the North Atlantic Treaty Organization (*see* NATO) in military relations, believing they offered greater opportunity, through alliances with other countries, to curb the unilateral exercise of power by the US and to reduce the danger of direct Canada-US confrontation.

Nevertheless the process of continental integration continued, with Canada the supplier of raw materials and the US the supplier of industrial capacity and technology. For a number of years the Joint Ministerial Committee on Trade and Economic Affairs, composed of the principal economic Cabinet ministers for each country, met annually to deal with issues such as a US program for the disposal of surplus grains to developing countries, which undercut Canadian commercial grain sales, and the extraterritorial application of US law to US-owned subsidiaries in Canada, which barred exports by these subsidiaries to China, and later Cuba, and which infringed upon Canadian sovereignty.

In 1957 a new Conservative government under John DIEFENBAKER promised to reduce Canada's economic ties to the US. The 1958 ROYAL COMMISSION ON CANADA'S ECONOMIC PROSPECTS warned that Canadians were losing control of their destiny, while other critics voiced concern that Canada's economy was being developed in a distorted manner as a resource supplier for the giant US industrial base. Although in 1965 Canada and the US signed the Autopact agreement, which created, for manufacturers, a conditional free-trade zone for motor vehicle and motor vehicle parts production in Canada, many Canadians had begun to express a desire to reduce foreign ownership and influence in their economy. This desire led to disputes in tax and banking policy and even to diplomatic quarrels over the status of US magazines in Canada. In an attempt to halt the flow of US funds abroad, in 1963 the US government introduced a tax to discourage the outflow of funds, which sparked an immediate crisis in Canadian financial markets, since Canada was highly dependent on access to US capital markets. Canada negotiated an exemption, but only with the understanding that if Canadian borrowing in the US rose above traditional levels the exemption would be reviewed by the US. Canada also had to promise not to increase its foreign-exchange reserves through the proceeds of new US borrowings. Through these constraints, Canada's ability to conduct economic policy was narrowed. In 1968 the US government imposed mandatory guidelines for American multinationals. US subsidiaries were ordered to increase the repatriation of profits from Canada, to carry out more investment in the US than in subsidiaries, and to increase exports for US plants instead of from subsidiaries in Canada or elsewhere. In 1971 President Nixon introduced a series of measures to protect the US balance of payments by imposing a 10% surcharge on those US imports subject to duty. Canada was able to negotiate exemptions to these policies, but the incidents revealed Canada's vulnerability to changes in US policies and led to Canadian efforts to develop a THIRD OPTION designed to increase Canada's economic ties with the rest of the world and reduce its dependence on the US.

ENERGY POLICY became an issue between Canada and the US during the 1970s. In the late 1960s and the early 1970s, Canada was anxious to increase oil and gas sales to the US, but oil sales were restricted by US import quotas. Canada also attempted unsucessfully to persuade the US to build an oil pipeline from Alaska to the US through the Canadian North (*see* MACKENZIE VALLEY PIPELINE). Canadian interest in expanding oil and gas exports to the US had cooled by the mid-1970s, following the 1973-74 OPEC crisis and concern over the adequacy of Canadian oil and gas reserves to meet future Canadian needs. During this period the US reacted angrily to increases in Canadian oil export prices to match world oil prices. Energy reemerged as a source of conflict with Canada's implementation in 1980 of the National Energy Program. One of the NEP's major objectives was that the oil industry be 50% Canadian controlled by 1990. In 1980 the oil and gas industry in Canada accounted for 30% of all nonfinancial industry profits in Canada, and roughly 70% of those profits accrued to foreign-controlled, mainly US, firms. To achieve the Canadianization target, Canada encouraged takeovers by Canadians of foreign-oil subsidiaries, altered the tax system so that government funding of risky oil exploration favoured Canadian companies, and amended land regulations to require 50% Canadian participation in frontier oil and gas fields. The US vigorously protested these various measures. A second NEP objective was to increase the Canadian share of engineering and other services, and of manufactured equipment used in the oil and gas industry projects. US multinationals had relied heavily on the same engineering and other suppliers as their US parents, so that Canadian industry had not benefitted to the extent that it might have from oil and gas development. As a result of US objections, some of these provisions were relaxed.

The broader issue of foreign ownership also affected Canadian-American relations during the 1970s and early 1980s. As a result of widespread concerns in Canada over the regulation of massive US investment in the Canadian economy, the FOREIGN INVESTMENT REVIEW AGENCY (FIRA) was created and began screening new foreign investment plans in 1974. By the early 1980s the US had become a harsh critic of FIRA. The dispute was taken to GATT which in 1983 concluded that, while FIRA was generally acceptable, it should be less vigorous in trying to persuade foreign investors to use Canadian goods and services.

The fundamentals of the Canadian-American economic relationships continue largely unchanged through the 1980s, reflecting the difficulties that any smaller country experiences living alongside a much larger country. While Canadians and Americans share many fundamental values, there are wide differences in economic, cultural and social concerns and policies. The US, for example, champions the cause of free markets and free investment flows, but the Canadian concern is to preserve the capacities of an independent nation. Thus, Canadians are more willing to use government and CROWN CORPORATIONS to develop their own economy and industry to meet Canadian needs. It is hard, as PM Trudeau once remarked, for a mouse to live next to an elephant. From the Canadian perspective, it is critical that the US understands that Canada has legitimate interests and aspirations that are separate from those of the US. In the future, Canada-US economic relations will be tested by a wide array of issues. Discussion of sectoral free-trade agreements are underway, but even without these agreements, tariffs on Canada-US trade will largely disappear during the 1980s as a result of GATT trade agreements. The US need for water may lead to pressures on Canada to supply that resource. Canadian desires for greater Canadian ownership and control of their own economy and US desires for international codes for the free flow of investment dollars and trade in services may generate conflict. US deregulation and changes in technology will have major implications for Canadian airlines, telecommunications services and broadcasting. But there will also be areas of common interest, and the ties that bind will no doubt continue to be stronger than those that divide.

DAVID CRANE

Canadian Association of College and University Libraries, est 1963, is a division of the Canadian Library Assn. As such, CACUL is not a separate entity but does have the authority to act in the name of CLA on matters such as academic status, which are of concern and interest to librarians and libraries in Canadian institutions of higher education. Its annual meeting serves as a forum for discussion of issues and as an informal means of continuing education. A more formal educational program is conducted through a series of workshops offered in conjunction with the annual meeting. Publication is another important activity. The *CACUL Newsletter*, issued 1963-75, was a major scholarly journal in academic librarianship. At present, accounts of CACUL activities appear frequently in *Feliciter* (CLA journal), and some of the workshop proceedings are published as monographs. Membership in CACUL is open to both personal and institutional members and no qualification is required. Its constitutional objective is "to develop high standards of librarianship and to promote these in institutions of post-secondary education." The Community and Technical Libraries Section, a subdivision of CACUL, has been active in producing standards and a directory. SAMUEL ROTHSTEIN

Canadian Banker's Association, a powerful association of Canadian BANKING institutions incorporated in 1900 by an Act of Parliament, empowered to act as an organizing body for bank practice, education and information. A number of the CBA's activities are now carried out by other government or public entities, eg, by the cheque-clearing system is now the responsibility of the Canadian Payments Association. Under the Bank Act revision of 1980, the association still provides representation to the government and the public on behalf of the banking industry. The CBA provides an extensive personnel program and publishes the *Canadian Banker* and the *Institute of Canadian Bankers Review*.

Canadian Bible Society, fd 1904 to publish and distribute biblical scriptures. The British and Foreign Bible Society was founded 1804 in London, Eng, and in 1805 its first overseas publication, the Gospel of John in Mohawk, arrived in Canada. Early NS settlers obtained Bibles from the BFBS, and as early as 1808 collected offerings for its work. Branches sprang up in the Maritimes, and then further west. After some time the formation of a national Bible society was a logical development, and on 14-15 Sept 1904, in Toronto, the BFBS branches in Canada joined together in the Canadian Bible Society. In 1946 a number of national Bible societies formed the United Bible Societies, a world fellowship. The CBS was a charter member. The UBS co-ordinates biblical translation, publication and distribution for 66 societies in 150 countries. The benefits are obvious: competition, duplication and waste have been minimized. The CBS limits itself to the Scriptures only, leaving interpretation to the churches. This ecumenical organization works with all Christian denominations. In 1982 it distributed 11 million Bibles, Testaments, Gospels and Scripture selections in 90 languages in Canada; it provides more than $2.5 million annually for UBS work. The CBS is not in competition with other Canadian organizations. The Gideons, for example, do not undertake translation or production, and often, especially when they need non-English Bibles, they obtain them from the CBS.

The Scriptures are now in some 1800 languages, and annual world distribution by the various societies is 450 million. In the 1980s, demand for the Bible is the greatest in history. Although more Bibles are provided each year, demand in Asia, Africa and Latin America greatly exceeds supply. The CBS, largely financed by the offerings of individuals, has an annual budget of some $7.5 million. It has always been able to attract outstanding Canadians from various professions as its officers.

Canadian Bill of Rights, PM John DIEFENBAKER's pathbreaking but unentrenched 1960 HUMAN RIGHTS charter, applied only to federal law because the requisite provincial consent was not obtained. It recognizes the rights of individuals to life, liberty, personal security and enjoyment (not "possession," which is provincial) of property. Deprivation of these is forbidden "except by due process of law." It protects rights to equality before the law and ensures protection of the law; protects the freedoms of religion, speech, assembly and association, and the press; and legal rights such as the rights to counsel and "fair hearing." Laws are to be construed and applied so as not to detract from these rights and freedoms. One of the bill's weaknesses was that many judges regarded it as a mere interpretative aid without independent vigour. Section 2 provides that Parliament can override the mentioned rights by inserting a "notwithstanding" clause in the applicable statute; this has been done only once, during the 1970 OCTOBER CRISIS. To the extent that it is not superseded by the 1982 CANADIAN CHARTER OF RIGHTS AND FREEDOMS, the bill remains in effect. *See* DRYBONES CASE; LAVELL CASE. W.H. McCONNELL

Canadian Brass quintet was formed in 1970 as the Canadian Brass Ensemble, consisting of Stuart Laughton and William Phillips, trumpets, Graeme Page, french horn, Eugene Watts, trombone, and Charles Daellenbach, tuba. In 1971 the group became Canadian Brass and Ronald Romm replaced Laughton. The following year Fred Mills replaced Phillips. The ensemble then remained unchanged until 1983 when Martin Hackleman replaced Page. Initially members of the Hamilton Philharmonic Orchestra, the group also became artists-in-residence at the BANFF CENTRE SCHOOL OF FINE ARTS. Their first European tour, in 1972 with the Festival Singers, was assisted by the Canadian government and quickly led to a highly successful international career which has included performances at the Paris Festival, Edinburgh Festival and Kennedy Center, tours of China, England, Europe and the USSR, and many international radio and TV appearances. As well as being superb musicians, the members of the quintet have established reputations for onstage hilarity which has a broad appeal for young and old. The Canadian Brass has performed with Canada's major symphony orchestras, and has unearthed several little-known works by major composers. Many Canadian composers have been commissioned and premiered by Canadian Brass. The group's long list of recordings is a clear indication of the breadth of its repertoire, versatility and skill. Canadian Brass plays on a matched set of gold-plated instruments made for it by Renold Schilke. MABEL H. LAINE

Canadian Broadcasting Corporation Created as an independent crown corporation in 1936, the CBC is required by statute to provide comprehensive national radio and TV services to English- and French-speaking Canadians. The CBC also runs the Northern Service, for people living in the Far North; this service provides locally produced programs in English and native languages, and northern-related programs with an Inuktitut soundtrack added, as well as the national network programs. Radio Canada International (formerly the International Service), a shortwave service for listeners overseas, broadcasts in 11 languages around the world. Canadian Armed Forces radio and TV stations in Germany relay certain domestic newscasts and RCI supplies them with taped programs from CBC's English and French networks. As well, the CBC broadcasts the proceedings of the House of Commons via cable. The CBC attempts to provide a broad range of high-quality Canadian and imported programming.

In addition to making extensive use of freelance talent, the CBC has a staff of over 12 000 employees at numerous locations, including its head office in Ottawa, its English network headquarters in Toronto, its French network headquarters in Montréal, and various regional centres across the country. The annual expenditures of the CBC are in excess of $900 million, approximately 20% of which comes from TV advertising revenues (commercials were abandoned on CBC radio in 1975). Despite the unusually high transmission costs involved in operating in 2 languages and reaching a population widely scattered across 6 time zones, the CBC is one of the most efficient public BROADCASTING systems in the world. CBC Radio is available to 99.4% and CBC TV to 99.2% of the population. In the early 1980s the average cost in public funds for all CBC services was about $24 a year per person, or some seven cents a day for each of Canada's 24.3 million people.

The CBC was formed in the midst of the Depression and over the objections of private broadcasting interests. This background partially explains the CBC's reliance upon private-station affiliates, its prolonged underfunding, and the acrimonious criticism to which it has been subjected. Inspired in part by the British Broadcasting Corporation as well as by a trans-Canada network built by the radio department of the CNR, the idea of a publicly owned broadcasting system for Canada appealed initially to those who were worried about the threat to Canadian cultural sovereignty from the flood of American programming. The CBC was first advocated formally by the Royal Commission on Radio Broadcasting set up by the Liberal government of Mackenzie King in Dec 1928. In a report submitted in Sept 1929 the Aird Commission proposed the creation of a national broadcasting company with the status and duties of a public utility and with a source of public funds to develop a service capable of "fostering a national spirit and interpreting national citizenship."

Prepared in a context of economic prosperity and rising national consciousness, the Aird Report was shelved temporarily with the onset of economic depression and the dissolution of the House of Commons in June 1930. This delay enabled some of the more powerful private stations and their principal organization, the Canadian Assn of Broadcasters, to organize a campaign against the Aird Report, the full implementation of which would have eliminated private broadcast ownership. Support for the general principles of the Aird Report was spearheaded by the Canadian Radio League, a private citizens' lobbying group organized by Graham SPRY and Alan PLAUNT. Largely through their perseverance and persuasiveness, the Conservative government of R.B. Bennett introduced the Broadcast Act of 1932 which embraced the philosophy of public ownership in a modified form. The private stations were allowed to continue, but superimposed upon them was the Canadian Radio Broadcasting Commission with a mandate to extend coverage to all settled parts of the country and to provide programs.

For various reasons, including unworkable administrative arrangements, lack of independent funding, political vulnerability and lack of co-operation from some of the private stations, the CRBC failed to live up to expectations. As a result, a new Canadian Broadcasting Act was passed (1936) to create a national organization with a more effective corporate structure and greater operational and financial autonomy. The new Canadian Broadcasting Corporation was to have as its main source of revenue, by law, the proceeds of the licence fee imposed on radio receiving sets. In its early years the CBC established extensive English and French networks, obtaining coverage through stations of its own and through private affiliates. It played a major role in providing wartime information to Canadians. From 1952 it developed a national TV service with stations of its own in some main centres and with newly established private stations as network affiliates in other areas. With the coming of TV, the main source of revenue changed from licence fees to government funding.

From 1936 to 1958, when the Conservative government of John Diefenbaker passed another Broadcasting Act, corporate policy was handled by a board of governors and executive functions were carried out by a general manager and assistant general manager. During this period the CBC was also responsible for regulating the private stations in accordance with the concept of a single national system. Since 1958 the CBC has been headed by a president, appointed by the government for a 7-year period as chief executive officer and chairman of a 15-member board of directors. Also beginning in 1958, the regulatory role previously assumed by the CBC was taken over by the Board of Broadcast Governors. After a decade of conflict between the BBG and the CBC, the Broadcasting Act passed by the Liberal government in 1968 replaced the BBG with the Canadian Radio-Television Commission (*see* CANADIAN RADIO-TELEVISION AND TELECOMMUNICATIONS COMMISSION) and gave the new body greater authority and a clearer mandate.

The CBC has been examined by various royal commissions and parliamentary committees over the years. Except in wartime, it has been able to maintain its political independence. Under the leadership of Davidson DUNTON as full-time chairman of the Board of Governors (1945-57) and of Alphonse Ouimet as general manager and later president (1958-67), the corporation firmly established its credibility as a politically neutral interpreter of the nation's life.

The CBC is the only medium of communication in Canada that attempts to bridge regional and linguistic barriers in the country. It has facilitated mass communication in Canada by allowing the influential few to speak to the many and by enabling Canadians in general to communicate among themselves. This dialogue has been accomplished by a variety of means, including the production of Canadian drama (*see* RADIO DRAMA and TELEVISION DRAMA), the encouragement of Canadian musical talent, the development of special programming for children, the maintenance of an excellent news service, and the sustained commitment to public-affairs programs such as "Farm Radio Forum" and "Citizens' Forum" on radio and "This Hour Has Seven Days" and "The Fifth Estate" on TV.

The CBC has made an incalculable contribution to the social and cultural fabric of Canada. Despite its accomplishments, however, its future is uncertain. The development of cable and satellite systems of transmission, bringing new floods of American programming to Canadian TV sets, the emergence of public broadcasting networks at the provincial level, the CRTC's rejection of the corporation's application for second channels in English and French, the awarding of PAY TELEVISION licences exclusively to private interests, and the marked hostility of the Applebaum-Hébert Commission on the arts have all undermined the ability of the CBC to fulfill its traditional role. The CBC will require broad public support and greater resources to provide a truly Canadian national service in the changing communications environment of today. ROSS EAMAN

Canadian Business, magazine established in 1927, is Canada's leading general interest business monthly magazine. It was owned by the Montreal Chamber of Commerce and published in Montréal, from its inception until 1978 when it was bought by Michael de Pencier, Alexander Ross and Roy MacLaren. MacLaren was later a member of the Trudeau and Turner federal Cabinets. The 1984 circulation of *Canadian Business* was about 95 000, 85 000 of which represent subscriptions and 10 000 newsstand sales. *Canadian Business* covers the gamut of business interests, but it is directed more to executives and small-business readers than to investors and is noted for its profiles of business leaders. The publisher is G. Wallace Wood and the editor is Charles Davies (1984). It is now published at Toronto. D. MCGILLIVRAY

Canadian Business Review, established in 1974, is a quarterly published by The Conference Board of Canada from its headquarters in Ottawa. With a circulation of about 10 000 it fulfills the same role in Canada as the board's US magazine, *Across the Board,* does in that country. S. Scott Hatfield is editor, assisted by an advisory board including James R. Nininger, president of The Conference Board of Canada, and Thomas Maxwell, the chief economist (1984). The *Canadian Business Review* includes pro-and-con discussions of economic questions, but its most distinctive feature is a quarterly survey of economic forecasts of the major Canadian banks and investment houses. The average of these forecasts, published in the review, is usually taken as the consensus view of Canada's economic future in the next year or so. The *Canadian Business Review* accepts no advertising and is funded mainly by the more than 800 associates (members) of The Conference Board of Canada, a list that includes corporations, government departments and labour unions. D. MCGILLIVRAY

Canadian Charter of Rights and Freedoms, the only Charter of Rights entrenched in the Canadian Constitution, came into force on 17 April 1982. According to section 52 of the CONSTITUTION ACT, 1982, every law that is inconsistent with the Constitution is, to the extent of the inconsistency, of no force and effect. The SUPREME COURT OF CANADA in the *Skapinker* case of May 1984, declared unanimously that the Charter" is a part of the Constitution of a nation . . . part of the fabric of Canadian law . . . the supreme law of Canada." It also declared that "the Charter is designed and adopted to guide and serve the Canadian community for a long time . . . with the Constitution Act, 1982, comes a new dimension, a new yardstick of reconciliation between the individual and the community and their respective rights, a dimension which like the balance of the Constitution remains to be interpreted and applied by the court."

The Canadian Charter of Rights and Freedoms was an important issue in the debate concerning the patriation of the Constitution (*see* CONSTITUTION, PATRIATION OF). The majority of the provinces, while not adverse to a Charter of Rights, had other priorities, particularly the enlargement of some of their powers. In Nov 1981 PM P.E. TRUDEAU accepted the Alberta-Vancouver formula of amendment endorsed by 8 provinces, and the provinces accepted the Charter of Rights, but not without imposing the exercise at will of a derogatory clause ("notwithstanding" clause of 33) for certain sectors of the Charter: fundamental rights, legal rights and the equality rights. By invoking the derogatory clause, the provinces (and Parliament) can declare any law exempt from the provisions of sections 2 and 7 to 15 of the Canadian Charter. The compromise resulted in the Canada Act, 1982 and the Constitution Act, 1982 (*see* DISTRIBUTION OF POWERS; CONSTITUTIONAL LAW).

Within the Canadian Constitution, the Charter occupies a central place. The courts, which in the past have ruled on the division of powers and have declared ultra vires statutes that violated such division, will now rule also on whether federal and provincial statutes are compatible with the Charter.

A constitutional Charter of Rights always gives rise to a profound debate between 2 philosophies at the time of its entrenchment in a constitution. The first favours entrenchment, so as to ensure that the courts have the last word in the field of liberties; the second holds that Parliament and the legislatures should have the last word. The general tendency in the constitutions since WWII is in favour of the entrenchment of rights.

The object of a Charter of Rights is to protect the citizen against the STATE, and to protect minorities against parliamentary majorities. The Canadian Charter is comprehensive and covers several fields: fundamental rights, democratic rights, mobility rights, legal rights, equality rights and linguistic rights. The equality between men and women is also expressly protected by a particular section of the Charter. Aboriginal rights and freedoms are not affected.

The Canadian Charter of Rights and Freedoms was not adopted by the House of Commons and the Senate in its original form. More than one amendment was brought to the Oct 1980 version. Several individuals and pressure groups appeared before the Special Joint Committee of the Senate and the House of Commons on the Constitution of Canada. The 1208 submissions and the hearing of 104 witnesses resulted in the April 1981 version, which in the form of a Resolution was passed by both Houses. The April version, after the decision of the Supreme Court on patriation in Sept 1981, was further amended as a result of the 5 Nov, 1981 agreement between the federal authority and 9 provinces. Québec rejected the whole process. Québec has invoked the derogatory clause of s33 of the Charter in respect of all its previous laws dealing with matters related to sections 2 and 7 to 15 of the Canadian Charter; Québec is doing the same since 17 Apr 1982 for its statutes concerning those matters. Article 35 (native rights) was amended, article 28 (sexual equality), article 40 (compensation for education and culture) and article 59 (language rights in Québec) were added in Nov 1981, after the constitutional conference, before the Resolution was finally adopted by the federal Houses and sent to the UK as part of the patriation process. GÉRALD-A. BEAUDOIN

Canadian Coast Guard The CCG was founded as the "Marine Branch" of the Dept of Marine and Fisheries in 1867. In 1936 it came under the jurisdiction of the Dept of Transport, Marine Services, and in 1962 was officially named the Canadian Coast Guard. It currently operates within a total budget of $900 million with 7700 employees. The distinctive red-and-white vessels of the CCG fleet are stationed at the 5 CCG regional offices (Vancouver, Toronto, Québec City, Dartmouth and St John's) as well as at 15 strategically located bases. The fleet consists of 75 major vessels as well as 40 helicopters and fixed-wing aircraft. In addition to the larger ships, there are 70 frontline rescue vessels and hovercraft.

The responsibilities of the CCG under the National Transportation Act and other applicable legislation are icebreaking, search and rescue, aids to navigation and northern resupply. The CCG also has a regulatory responsibility under the Canada Shipping Act with respect to ship inspection and standards. The CCG provides and maintains some 8600 channel buoys and 7500 LIGHTHOUSES and other shore-based navigational aids; 50 coastal radio stations and 15 vessel traffic centres provide navigational hazard and weather advice.

The powerful fleet of ICEBREAKERS aid navigation along the East Coast, across the North and through the Great Lakes-St Lawrence system. In addition to allowing vessels to operate more safely and economically, the icebreaking activity also contributes to flood control and shoreline protection. The 55 permanent and seasonal SAR stations provide year-round search-and-rescue services, staffed by 750 specialists within the CCG assisted by a Coast Guard Auxiliary of volunteers trained in search-and-rescue techniques. Northern resupply activities in the Arctic and along the Mackenzie R ensure the continued existence of remote settlements.

The CCG enforces safety standards and regulations, investigates marine casualties and responds to emergency oil spills. BOATING safety personnel offer courtesy inspections and give safety lectures to thousands of yachters and fishermen every year. *See also* SHIPPING.

Reading: T.E. Appleton, *Usque Ad Mare: A History of the Canadian Coast Guard and Marine Services* (1968).

Canadian Commercial Bank (CCB) became Canada's tenth Schedule A Bank when chartered as Canadian Commercial and Industrial Bank on 30 July 1975. A subsequent name change occurred on 25 Apr 1981. With corporate offices in Edmonton, the bank officially commenced business on 6 July 1976 in Vancouver and Edmonton on initial share capital of $22 million. By Aug 1984 the bank employed nearly 600 and had become international in scope, with 16 deposit and lending offices located across Canada and the western US. Capital had increased to $125 million through public preferred shareholders and private placements by leading pension and institutional funds. Ownership remains 92% Canadian. CCB funds its loan assets in the wholesale and retail markets and provides diverse wholesale lending services to N American corporate clients. Assets in excess of $3 billion and operating revenues in 1983 of $223 million placed it 10th among Canadian Schedule A banks.

Canadian Congress of Labour, fd fall 1940 as a merger of the All-Canadian Congress of Labour and the Canadian section of the Congress of Industrial Organizations. For 16 years the CCL was in the forefront of Canadian union activity and organization. From an initial membership of some 77 000, it had enrolled some 360000 workers by 1956 when it joined with the TRADES AND LABOR CONGRESS to form the CANADIAN LABOUR CONGRESS. Its affiliates included the international INDUSTRIAL UNIONS in Canada: steelworkers, woodworkers, autoworkers, packinghouse workers, clothing workers, miners, electrical workers, and the mine, mill and smelter workers, as well as several large national unions led by the Canadian Brotherhood of Railway Employees. The president of this latter union, Aaron Mosher, also headed the CCL though the real power lay with secretary-treasurer Pat Conroy, a strong nationalist who resigned in 1951 in a dispute with some of the international union leaders.

The CCL was more aggressive than its CRAFT UNION counterpart, the TLC, and organized thousands of unskilled workers most labour experts thought were unorganizable. In 1945 the CCL officially allied itself with the CCF and many of its leaders ran in provincial or federal elections. As well, following WWII, the congress took the lead in expelling influential communist-dominated unions from its ranks. As the voice of Canadian industrial unionism, the CCL played an important role in national political and economic affairs. IRVING ABELLA

Canadian Council of Churches, fd 1944, the national ecumenical fellowship of 12 Canadian churches: Anglican, Armenian Orthodox, Baptist Convention of Ontario and Quebec, Christian Church (Disciples of Christ), Coptic Orthodox, Greek Orthodox, Lutheran Church in America, Presbyterian, Reformed, Quakers, Salvation Army and United Church. The word "ecumenical" comes from the Gk *oikoumene*, "the whole inhabited earth." The purpose of any ecumenical organization is to seek unity for a divided church and to remind Christians that they share Christ's mission of reconciliation, peace, dignity and justice for the whole commu-

Members of the CEF in action. Watercolour *7 a.m., April 22nd, 1915* by A. Nantel (*courtesy Canadian War Museum/NMM/NMC/8629*).

nity. Within individual member churches, local needs and specifically denominational concerns have, in practice, frequently taken precedence over ecumenical efforts, but all CCC members nevertheless maintain a theological commitment to ecumenism. The council works closely with the Roman Catholic Church and other nonmember Christian churches, as well as with communities of other faiths. It participates in Canadian interchurch coalitions for social justice, the Ecumenical Forum of Canada and local councils of churches.

The Canadian Council, which provides an agency for consultation, planning and common action, was founded to co-ordinate the growing number of Canadian co-operative ventures in social service, religious education, evangelization and overseas mission, and to participate in the international ecumenical movement leading to the 1948 formation of the World Council of Churches, in which Canadians were prominently involved. The council communicates and co-operates with other national councils. It works closely with the WCC, though it neither contributes funds to, nor receives financial support from, the World Council. The CCC, with headquarters in Toronto, is governed and supported by its members through a semiannual General Board and Triennial Assembly. Three commissions co-ordinate its work: Canadian Affairs, World Concerns, and Faith and Order. Discussions directed towards the creation of a more comprehensive body, which would include the Roman Catholic and other churches, began in 1975, but no such organization had been formed by 1983. DONALD W. ANDERSON

Canadian Council on Social Development (Counseil canadien de Développement social), fd 1920 as Canadian Council on Child Welfare. It became the Canadian Welfare Council in 1935; in 1970 the organization took on its present name. A voluntary, nonpartisan, Ottawa-based organization that sought to secure clearly defined but limited objectives in social service and welfare, the CWC worked within existing political and economic structures. It initially concerned itself with the needs of children and their mothers, especially war widows. Under its long-time executive director, Charlotte WHITTON, the CWC expanded its work during the GREAT DEPRESSION to deal with the effects of unemployment. The welfare of military service personnel, war workers and their dependants became a major concern after 1939.

Since WWII the council has examined and made recommendations about old-age security, disability and rehabilitation, unemployment insurance, poverty and income security, health services, housing, penal reform, daycare and the education of social workers. More recently, the problems of women and native peoples have increasingly gained its attention. The CCSD, which is funded by all levels of government and through agency memberships and publications sales, has been more effective in co-ordinating the activities of private social service and welfare agencies than in lobbying for legislation involving social change. MICHIEL HORN

Canadian Expeditionary Force, the army raised by Canada for service abroad in WORLD WAR I. In Aug 1914 Canada offered and Britain accepted an expeditionary force whose strength was fixed at first at 25 000. The strength of the first contingent which sailed for England Oct 1914 was in fact over 31 000, many of this number British-born. The size of the mobilized force steadily increased. The 1st Canadian Division went to France early in 1915. A Canadian corps of 2 divisions was formed there later that year, and in 1916 it reached its full strength of 4 divisions. A 5th Division was formed in England, but because of anticipated difficulties in providing reinforcements, it was not sent to the theatre of operations except for its divisional artillery and certain special units. Apart from the Canadian Corps, the CEF included the Canadian Cavalry Brigade, also serving in France, the Canadian Railway Troops, which in addition to working on the Western Front provided a bridging unit for the Middle East, the Canadian Forestry Corps which cut timber in Britain and France, and special units which operated in the Caspian area and in N Russia and E Siberia.

The CEF was maintained by voluntary enlistment until the MILITARY SERVICE ACT of Aug 1917 introduced conscription. In total 619 636 officers and men served in the CEF, of whom 142 588 were enlisted under the Military Service Act; 424 589 served overseas. The peak strength of the CEF at any one point was 388 038 all ranks in July 1918. Total fatal casualties from all causes, 1914-20, were 59 544 all ranks.

During the war Canadian authority over the CEF was steadily strengthened. In the beginning the relationship to the British military authorities was vague. After the Canadian MINISTRY OF OVERSEAS MILITARY FORCES was set up in London in 1916, the force's national nature was fully established. Canadian training in England became entirely a Canadian responsibility. In 1917, for the first time, a Canadian officer, Sir Arthur CURRIE, took command of the Canadian Corps. In 1918 it was formally recognized that while the direction of operations in the field remained the province of the British commander-in-chief, the internal organization and administration of the Canadian force were matters for Canadian authorities. By the end of the war the CEF, which in 1914 had been thought of as a colonial contingent serving under the British Army Act, had become in effect a Canadian national army.

C.P. STACEY

Reading: A. Fortescue Duguid, *Official History of the Canadian Forces in the Great War 1914-1919* (1938); G.W.L. Nicholson, *Canadian Expeditionary Force 1914-1919* (1964); Desmond Morton, *A Peculiar Kind of Politics* (1982).

Canadian Federation for the Humanities, fd Dec 1943 as the Humanities Research Council of Canada. An elected, nongovernmental organization representing 31 academic associations and 60 Canadian universities, CFH is dedicated to promoting scholarship and research in the humanities. Through published reports, surveys and major conferences, it has successfully urged the establishment of a National Library, a federal granting council, increased provincial support for universities, regular sabbatical leave for professors, and the creation of national organizations of university specialists (LEARNED SOCIETIES).

The HRCC was originally funded by American philanthropic foundations. Since the creation of the CANADA COUNCIL in 1957 it has received a majority of its funds from the federal government, and the balance from universities and learned societies. The formation of the SOCIAL SCIENCES AND HUMANITIES RESEARCH COUNCIL in

1978 resulted in HRCC's incorporation as the Canadian Federation for the Humanities. The federation administers programs subsidizing the publication of Canadian scholarly books, financing and co-ordinating the meetings of learned societies, and lobbying governments and granting agencies on behalf of the humanities. VIVIANE F. LAUNAY

Canadian Federation of Labour (National Trades and Labor Congress until 1908), fd 1902 as a solely Canadian body dedicated to national organization. Its founding bodies were the KNIGHTS OF LABOR and the national unions of shoemakers, cigar makers, painters and carpenters, which had been ousted from the TRADES AND LABOR CONGRESS in 1902 after the latter, dominated by the American Federation of Labor, rejected dual unionism by refusing to recognize a national union where an international union existed. This decision created bitter divisions in the Canadian trade-union movement.

The CFL remained weak. At its 1911 conference, for example, only 17 unions were represented, and the delegates were mainly from Québec and the Provincial Workmen's Assn of NS. There were many reasons: its conservatism and attitude toward strikes alienated unionists who might otherwise have been more supportive; it faced fierce opposition from the AFL which regarded dual unionism as anathema; and it concentrated on luring members from rival unions instead of promoting unions among unorganized workers. In 1927 the CFL became a founding member of the All-Canadian Congress of Labour. In 1981, a group of CRAFT UNIONS was suspended by the CANADIAN LABOUR CONGRESS. It united as a new Canadian Federation of Labour on 31 Mar 1982. C.D. CHORNIAWY

Canadian Federation of University Women was founded in 1919 as a Canadian counterpart to and member organization of the International Federation of University Women, and with the aim of emphasizing women's role in social reconstruction and the prevention of war. In 1983 there were 116 University Women's Clubs in Canada, not necessarily associated with a university, with a total membership of 12 400 women graduates representing all ages and academic disciplines. CFUW promotes the involvement of women individually and collectively in professional, economic and political life, and is concerned to encourage women scholars and safeguard the rights of women. Local clubs are involved in community-based and charitable activities, and participate in the federation's work of compiling submissions, briefs and resolutions directed to government task forces and commissions on a wide range of issues of interest to women, including microtechnology, pension reform, education, the environment and peace. SOMER BRODRIBB

Executive meeting of the Canadian Federation of University Women, Winnipeg, 29-30 Aug 1921 *(courtesy Public Archives of Canada/PA-119400)*.

Canadian Fiction Magazine, a literary quarterly devoted to SHORT FICTION. Beginning in 1971 as a student publication at University of British Columbia, this LITERARY MAGAZINE has become an independent journal of national scope. It publishes work by both new and established writers in English, and also has a continuing program of fiction in translation from French and the unofficial languages of Canada. The magazine has published entire issues devoted to individual authors, as well as interviews with writers and a series on "the future of fiction" that encourages discussion about the aesthetics of contemporary fiction. GEOFFREY HANCOCK

Canadian Film Development Corporation (Telefilm Canada) was created by an Act of Parliament in 1967 "to foster and promote the development of a feature film industry in Canada." This crown corporation was originally given $10 million to invest in the FILM industry as a loan fund. Under its first executive director, Michael Spencer, it invested in a number of low-budget English and French films of cultural value. Increasing commercial pressures were brought to bear and by 1973 international co-productions were favoured. In 1978 a new executive director, Michael McCabe, accelerated this process, encouraged the use of foreign stars and, under the advantages of the Capital Cost Allowance, increased total Canadian budgets from about $5 million in 1977 to $150 million in 1979. This commercial orientation of the CFDC was not completely successful as many films remain unreleased. In 1980 André Lamy replaced McCabe, committing himself to a more indigenous industry. PIERS HANDLING

Canadian Football Hall of Fame and Museum, located in Hamilton, Ont, traces the history of Canadian FOOTBALL over the past century and celebrates leading players and builders of the sport. The museum contains a theatre, television monitors, computers programmed to answer questions, and exhibits — notably a series of steel busts of inductees. The GREY CUP and Schenley Trophy are on permanent display. Members of the Hall of Fame are chosen by a committee composed of reporters, editors and sportscasters. The museum was founded in 1962 and housed in its present building in 1972.

Canadian Football League (CFL) began its formal existence in Jan 1958. Previously, it had been known as the Canadian Football Council (CFC), formed in 1956 as a loose merger of the Western Interprovincial Football Union and the Interprovincial Rugby Football Union. Through the CFC, professional FOOTBALL came under its own jurisdiction without outside interference. Ottawa, Hamilton, Toronto and Montréal and the western cities of Winnipeg, Regina, Calgary, Edmonton and Vancouver were represented in the 2 Unions. Present teams in the CFL are HAMILTON TIGER-CATS, OTTAWA ROUGH RIDERS, TORONTO ARGONAUTS, MONTREAL CONCORDES (eastern division); WINNIPEG BLUE BOMBERS, SASKATCHEWAN ROUGHRIDERS, CALGARY STAMPEDERS, EDMONTON ESKIMOS and BRITISH COLUMBIA LIONS (western division). While each club in the eastern division is privately owned and is operated as a business enterprise, the 5 western teams are community owned and are operated as non-profit organizations. Regional as well as east-west rivalries have acted as a catalyst for the growth of the league and of the sport.

Until 1961, teams in the 2 divisions played among traditional rivals, each deciding a winner to meet in the GREY CUP game. By 1981, both divisions were playing 16 games and a fully interlocking schedule. At the end of each division's season, the 3rd- and 2nd-place finishers meet in a semi-final match, the winner playing the 1st-place club for the division championship. The winners meet in the Grey Cup game, traditionally in the last week of Nov, at a site determined 2 years in advance. Each year the league honours outstanding players through the Schenley Awards. League offices are in Toronto. The CFL's commissioners have included G. Sydney Halter (1956-66), Ted Workman, Allan McEachern, Jake GAUDAUR (1968-84) and Douglas H. Mitchell (1984-). FRANK COSENTINO

Canadian Forces in Russia With the collapse of the Russian Empire in 1917, the Allies undertook to support anticommunist White Russian forces if they would, once back in power, resume war on the Eastern Front against Germany and Austria. Acceding to pressure from London, the Canadian government dispatched almost 6000 soldiers to join the Allies in Russia in mid-1918. Although some Canadians died in vicious fighting, most, especially those in Siberia, returned without seeing action. PM BORDEN recognized that Canada had committed a political and military blunder, and Canada would henceforth be more wary of accepting the recommendations of other nations to enter into foreign commitments. ROY MACLAREN

Canadian Forum, fd in 1920, is Canada's oldest continually published political periodical. It originated at University of Toronto as the offshoot of a tiny magazine, *The Rebel,* and its first editorial board intended the new publication to be what its name suggested — a forum of political and cultural ideas. From the start, the *Forum* was avowedly nationalist and progressive, and usually on the left of the spectrum on political and cultural questions.

The *Canadian Forum* has always given ample space to poetry, fiction and the best work of Canadian artists. The *Forum* supported the GROUP OF SEVEN painters. Some of Canada's finest writers, a group that includes A.J.M. SMITH, Frank SCOTT, Irving LAYTON, Dorothy LIVESAY, Earle BIRNEY and

Margaret ATWOOD, began in its pages and have continued to publish there. On the political front, the *Forum* provided a home for Frank UNDERHILL's mordant wit and slashing prose all through the 1930s and 1940s, for Abe Rotstein and Mel Watkins, the leading economic nationalists of the 1960s, and for such well-known and committed intellectuals as Frank Scott, Eugene FORSEY and Ramsay Cook.

The *Forum* was co-operatively owned for most of its history, but for a time in the 1920s and 1930s it was operated by the publisher J.M. Dent and Sons, by Liberals, by Graham SPRY and by the LEAGUE FOR SOCIAL RECONSTRUCTION. Whatever the ownership, however, its editors — including Northrop FRYE, Milton Wilson, Rotstein and Michael Cross — have been remarkably independent. *See also* JOURNALISM; MAGAZINES.

J.L. GRANATSTEIN

Reading: J.L. Granatstein and P. Stevens, eds, *Forum: Canadian Life and Letters 1920-70* (1972).

Canadian Girls in Training (CGIT) was established in 1915 by the YOUNG WOMEN'S CHRISTIAN ASSN and the major Protestant denominations to promote the Christian education of girls aged 12 to 17. Based on the small group whose members planned activities under the leadership of adult women, the program reflected the influence on Canadian Protestantism of progressive education, historical criticism of the Bible, the SOCIAL GOSPEL, and Canadian NATIONALISM. CGIT provided leadership training for many young women. Membership declined after WWII but the organization continued to flourish in numerous congregations. After 1947 the movement was under the direction of the Dept of Christian Education, CANADIAN COUNCIL OF CHURCHES. In 1976 the organization became an independent ecumenical body.

MARGARET E. PRANG

Canadian Government Merchant Marine, *see* SHIPBUILDING.

Canadian Government Railways was the descriptive name of all federally owned railways in Canada from about the 1880s until 1918 when its operations were combined with the recently nationalized CANADIAN NORTHERN RAILWAY; in the following year the CANADIAN NATIONAL RAILWAYS were incorporated to operate both companies. The Canadian Government Railways, entrusted to the CN for operation in 1923, still exists as a component of the CN and has 4 constituents: the Intercolonial, National Transcontinental, Prince Edward Island, and Hudson Bay railways.

In 1867 the government of Canada organized the INTERCOLONIAL RAILWAY to fulfil a Confederation promise of linking the Maritime provinces by rail to Ontario and Québec and assuming ownership of provincially owned railways in NS and NB. In 1879 the Intercolonial purchased the GRAND TRUNK RAILWAY line from Rivière-du-Loup to Point Lévis, opposite Québec City. In 1873, when PEI joined Canada, one condition of union was that the dominion Government assume operation of the expensive island railway system. This network was operated separately from the Intercolonial Railway. Gradually the titles Intercolonial Railway and Prince Edward Island Railway were dropped in favour of the term Canadian Government Railways.

At the turn of the century, the government constructed a new transcontinental railway in conjunction with the Grand Trunk Railway. A Grand Trunk subsidiary, the GRAND TRUNK PACIFIC, completed the western section while the government built the section from Moncton to Winnipeg under the name National Transcontinental Railway. Operation of the National Transcontinental was assumed by Canadian Government Railways in 1915. The final component of Canadian Government Railways was the HUDSON BAY RAILWAY from The Pas to Churchill, Man. This line had been championed by western farmers as an alternative way of exporting grain from western Canada. However, the limited traffic prospects of a Hudson Bay railway deterred private ownership. Consequently, the Canadian Government Railways completed the line in 1929.

C. ANDREAE

Canadian Government Specifications Board, est 1934 under the National Research Council Act as the Government Purchasing Standards Committee, its name was changed in 1948. Answering to the minister of supply and services, its role is to provide voluntary standards for testing, technical practices, and legislation and to support international standardization. It provides standards in both official languages and integrates the efforts of 300 committees and 3000 members representing government, producers, consumers, research agencies, educational institutions and others. It works closely with the Standards Council of Canada and Metric Commission Canada. Its board of directors comprises 8 federal deputy ministers.

Canadian Historical Association, fd 1922 when the Historic Landmarks Assn, est 1907 by the ROYAL SOCIETY, was renamed and reconstituted; incorporated 1970. The CHA is the professional association of all historians in Canada. It is the largest and one of the oldest of the LEARNED SOCIETIES; its membership of some 2500 includes over 400 institutions and 2100 general and student members. The CHA sponsors the National Archival Appraisal Board and acts as an umbrella organization for many local and provincial HISTORICAL SOCIETIES. Through a broad program of publications in both official languages (eg, the CHA *Annual Report* (now *Historical Papers*), published since 1922; and a series of historical booklets published since the early 1950s), awards and annual meetings, the CHA actively encourages historical research, particularly in the history of Canada, and promotes the preservation of the nation's heritage.

JACQUES MONET S.J.

Canadian Historical Review, founded in Toronto in 1920 and published by U of T Press, was the continuation of an earlier Toronto publication dating from 1896. For many years the CHR was edited from the U of T's history department, and many of Canada's most prominent historians, eg, George WRONG, George Brown, G.P. de T. Glazebrook, Donald CREIGHTON, John Saywell, Ramsay Cook and Craig Brown, took turns as editors. At times there was an editorial committee coupled with an advisory board drawn from across Canada. The function of the CHR was to publish articles on Canadian history and events, as well as reviews of important historical works on non-Canadian subjects. Over time, it became more historical and less contemporary, and concentrated its space exclusively on Canadian history, including reviews. Since the 1970s other Canadian historical periodicals have competed with the CHR for articles, but it remains Canada's most prominent historical journal. Circulation in 1983 was 3014.

ROBERT BOTHWELL

Canadian Human Rights Commission, est 1977 by the Canadian Human Rights Act to deal with discriminatory practices. It consists of 2 full-time members, the chief commissioner (Gordon Fairweather, appointed in 1977 to a 5-year term and reappointed in 1982 to a 7-year term) and 3 to 6 other members, and reports to Parliament through the minister of justice. The commission may appoint an investigator to examine a complaint of discrimination and may appoint a conciliator to effect a settlement. One member, designated by the minister of justice, investigates complaints regarding the misuse of information in a federal information bank.

Canadian Imperial Bank of Commerce is a chartered bank with head offices in Toronto. One of CIBC's 2 predecessors was the Bank of Canada (incorporated 1858), which became the Bank of Commerce in 1867. It absorbed smaller banks, beginning with the Gore Bank in 1869 and ending with the Standard Bank of Canada in 1928. CIBC's second predecessor, the Imperial Bank of Canada (incorporated 1875), also absorbed other banks between 1875 and 1956, ending with Barclays Bank (Canada). The present name was adopted in 1961 on the merger of the Bank of Commerce and the Imperial Bank of Canada.

The CIBC provides commercial and personal banking services in over 1600 branches in Canada and operates agencies and branches overseas, including 54 of the latter in the West Indies alone. With changes in the Bank Act during the 1970s, the CIBC, like other Canadian banks, began to promote itself more actively, engaging Canadian entertainer Anne MURRAY as its spokesperson. As of Oct 1983, it had annual sales or operating revenue of $7.4 billion, assets of $68.1 billion (ranking second among banks and financial institutions in Canada) and 33 525 employees.

DEBORAH C. SAWYER

Canadian Institute for Economic Policy, privately funded, independent institute, established in 1979 with a 5-year mandate to study Canadian fiscal, industrial and other public-policy issues. CIEP has published studies critical of the BANK OF CANADA's monetarism and of the extent of FOREIGN INVESTMENT in Canadian industry; its studies of CANADIAN-AMERICAN RELATIONS and the failure of Canada to develop an industrial policy have received wide attention. Former Liberal finance minister, Walter L. GORDON, was chairman and chief benefactor of the institute.

W.F. FORWARD

Canadian Institute of International Affairs (CIIA), an offspring of the British (later Royal) Institute of International Affairs launched in 1928 by such prominent Canadians as Sir Robert BORDEN, Sir Arthur CURRIE, John W. DAFOE, John Nelson and Sir Joseph FLAVELLE. They believed that in coming decades governments would increasingly rely on the support of their citizens in the conduct of world affairs. If Canada was to play an important role, an informed public opinion must be created through the dissemination of information and expert opinion. Branches were established in major cities to host speakers and study the current issues. Its Toronto headquarters initiated research projects and study trips, and published scholarly books and journals on Canadian foreign affairs and international relations. Although it has never been large, its members are found among Canada's leading experts on international affairs in academic, business and government circles.

D.M. PAGE

Canadian International Development Agency (CIDA), formed in 1968 to give prominence to the Canadian government's development assistance to needy nations. Such assistance had begun in 1950 with the COLOMBO PLAN, but the government's mechanism both at home and abroad for co-ordinating the flow of wheat, capital, and technology to the underdeveloped world was inadequate. An External Aid Office, est 1960, managed these diverse activities but it took CIDA's first president, Maurice STRONG, and his successors to define long-term strategies. Disbursements, restricted to countries where they would be of most benefit, became more important than Canadian contributions to multilateral programs administered by the United Nations or the World Bank. Nongovernment projects were also partially funded by CIDA in over 100 countries. Canadian industry provides most of the materials for capital projects, and

Canadian professionals share their skills in engineering, social development, medicine, agriculture and education. Additional emergency relief is available for victims of famines, earthquakes or political disturbances. By 1982 CIDA assistance had risen to about $1 billion.
D.M. PAGE

Canadian Journal of Economics and Political Science was the academic journal of the Canadian Political Science Assn, whose membership originally covered all the social sciences. It was published by University of Toronto Press from 1935 to 1967, when, having earlier spun off a separate journal for sociology and anthropology, it was succeeded by the *Canadian Journal of Economics* and the *Canadian Journal of Political Science*. The *Journal* contained academic articles and book reviews in the fields of economics, political science, geography, sociology and anthropology, although there were few papers or reviews on the last 3 topics. It also contained a Bibliography of Economics which, until the elaboration of the National Library bibliographic services in the mid-1950s, was an essential guide to the subject. Its articles and book reviews, many of them on Canadian topics, were intelligible to the general reader.
IAN M. DRUMMOND

Canadian Labour Congress, a national UNION CENTRAL fd 23 Apr 1956 from the merger of the CANADIAN CONGRESS OF LABOUR and the TRADES AND LABOR CONGRESS OF CANADA. The ONE BIG UNION was absorbed into the CLC, but Québec's Catholic unions chose to remain apart (*see* CONFEDERATION OF NATIONAL TRADE UNIONS). In 1961 CLC and CO-OPERATIVE COMMONWEALTH FEDERATION leaders joined to form the NEW DEMOCRATIC PARTY, a link that has been maintained ever since. In 1983 there were over 2 million trade unionists affiliated with the CLC through 90 international and national unions. The 3 largest are PUBLIC-SERVICE UNIONS; the fourth largest is the United Steelworkers of America. Economic and legislative questions of national importance constitute a major focus of the CLC. Provincial and territorial federations of labour and municipal labour councils co-ordinate comparable programs of CLC affiliates. Every second year some 2500 delegates from affiliated unions convene to set policy for the central body. Between conventions, policy decisions are made by the 38-member executive council. CLC headquarters is in Ottawa.

Canadian Lacrosse Hall of Fame, opened in 1967, is located in New Westminster, BC, a city with a long and illustrious history in both field and box lacrosse. Housed in the Centennial Community Centre, the 15 x 18 m hall contains an outstanding collection of lacrosse sticks, photographs, sweaters, medals and plaques, as well as several trophies, including the Lord Minto Cup, Joseph Lally Trophy and Sir Donald Mann Cup. Bronze plaques list members of the Hall of Fame, in field lacrosse, box lacrosse and builders divisions. The original inductees included lacrosse heroes Lionel CONACHER, Edouard "Newsy" LALONDE and William Fitzgerald, as well as "the Father of Lacrosse," Dr George BEERS.
BARBARA SCHRODT

Canadian League of Composers/La Ligue canadienne de compositeurs was founded in Toronto in 1951 to increase contact between professional composers, to advance common interests, and to stimulate public awareness of Canadian music. Membership has grown from nearly 20 composers in 1951 to over 180 in 1984 and includes composers of concert, film and broadcast music. The league promoted some 40 concerts, mainly of Canadian music, in its first 18 years. Many of these were organized in Montréal and Toronto with the help of 2 concert committees run by nonmembers, the Canadian Music Associates (Ontario) and La Société de musique canadienne (Québec). The league conceived the plan for the CANADIAN MUSIC CENTRE, helped organize the International Conference of Composers at Stratford, Ont, in 1960, and established a scholarship for young composers in 1967. The principal founder and longest-serving president was John WEINZWEIG. By lobbying on behalf of composers' economic and legal interests and by promoting the appreciation of Canadian music at home and abroad, the league has raised the status of the composer in the cultural fabric of Canada and has encouraged individual composers to develop their creativity. The papers of the league are deposited in the NATIONAL LIBRARY OF CANADA.
HELMUT KALLMANN

Reading: Helmut Kallmann et al, eds, *Encyclopedia of Music in Canada* (1981); *The Canada Music Book* 2 (1971).

Canadian Literature (1959-) was the first quarterly concerned entirely with the discussion of Canadian writing. Published by UBC, it was edited by George WOODCOCK 1959-77, and since then by W.H. New. A variety of critical approaches has been encouraged; poets and novelists have been invited to write about their own arts and discuss the works of their fellows. In recent years poems have been published regularly. Many important Canadian critics have appeared in *Canadian Literature*, as have creative writers as varied as Hugh MACLENNAN, Margaret ATWOOD, Irving LAYTON, Timothy FINDLEY, Dorothy LIVESAY, F.R. SCOTT, A.J.M. SMITH, P.K. PAGE and Audrey THOMAS.

Canadian Livestock Feed Board, est 1967 as a crown corporation under the Livestock Feed Assistance Act. It reports to Parliament through the minister of agriculture. Its 3- to 5-member board, appointed by the governor-in-council, is assisted by a 7-member advisory committee which represents livestock feeders in the East and BC. It attempts to stabilize and equalize feed-grain prices in areas outside the designated region of the CANADIAN WHEAT BOARD (BC and E of Thunder Bay). In the East it also makes recommendations for additional storage facilities. The board continually studies and monitors the supply and pricing of feed grain in order to advise the minister and other federal or provincial departments with similar responsibilities. If it finds improper pricing or supply practices, the board may intervene as a buyer or seller. When authorized by the governor-in-council, the board may buy, transport, store and sell feed grains in eastern Canada and BC.

Canadian Manufacturers' Association, founded 1871, incorporated by Act of Parliament 1902, "to promote Canadian industries and to further the interests of Canadian manufacturers and exporters." The CMA operated the forerunner of the present Canadian Trade Commissioner Service, helped create the Board of Railway Commissioners (which became the Board of Transport Commissioners and then the CANADIAN TRANSPORT COMMISSION) and the Canadian National Exhibition, and conducted studies basic to the drafting of Ontario's Workmen's Compensation Act. Member companies comprise more than 80% of manufacturing production in Canada. To be a member, a company must manufacture in Canada and employ at least 5 persons. Most companies (75%) have fewer than 100 employees. The association provides members with information important to the manufacturing industry, and submits its views to all levels of government on matters affecting manufacturers' interests. The CMA employs full-time staff across the country to help members solve problems relating to customs and excise, environmental standards, export and import procedures, energy, labour relations, research and development, taxation, technical standards, telecommunications and transportation. The association is structured nationally, regionally and locally. In addition to its Toronto head office it maintains 7 divisional offices and an Ottawa office.
ROY A. PHILLIPS

Canadian Medical Association, est 1867 by 167 doctors in Québec City. It is a voluntary federation of 10 autonomous provincial medical associations united at the national level and now represents more than 37 000 English- and French-speaking physicians across Canada. Dr Charles TUPPER was its first president.

CMA policies are arrived at after careful study by one of 3 councils, 4 statutory boards, a number of special committees and the board of directors. A final debate on major issues normally follows the General Council (called the "Parliament of Canadian Medicine") comprising over 225 elected physicians. Wholly owned subsidiaries of the association — MD Management Ltd and Lancet Insurance Agency Ltd — operate a number of membership services programs, including a retirement savings plan, investment portfolios and a variety of professional development training programs.

Over 40 organizations representing various fields of medical specialization from sports medicine to neurology and family medicine are affiliated with the CMA. In addition, more than 30 societies, such as the Canadian Cancer Society (founded by the CMA in 1937) are associated members. The *CMA Journal*, published semimonthly, is the association's official publication.
DOUGLAS GEEKIE

Canadian Mediterranean Institute, *see* MEDITERRANEAN ARCHAEOLOGY.

Canadian Museums Association has seen dramatic change since its modest beginnings in 1947. Fewer than 2 dozen members, representing 20 ART GALLERIES AND MUSEUMS, were present at the association's first meeting at the Musée du Québec. The founding members interpreted museums in the broadest sense and aimed to promote the public understanding of the function of museums and the service they could render to research, education and recreation. The young association struggled with problems stemming from its small but diverse membership scattered across great distances. By 1982, following the growth in the number of museums in Canada, the CMA's membership of individuals and institutions had reached 1600.

The association operates a full-time secretariat in Ottawa and offers a variety of services. Members receive *museogramme*, a monthly newsletter, as well as a quarterly journal with news and issues of interest to the museum community. A Museum Documentation Centre (library), open to all members, is maintained in Ottawa and bibliographies and a biennial *Directory of Canadian Museums* are published. A book-sales program offers substantial discounts to members. For professional development, the CMA offers a correspondence course as an introduction to museum philosophy and operations, operates a bursary program to assist museum personnel in upgrading their museological training through workshops, seminars, study tours and internships, and has an individual professional accreditation program. An awards program recognizes special contributions of members to CMA projects or museums. The annual conference provides a forum for information exchange.

The governing body of the CMA is an elected council of 15 members. Standing committees of council are Finance, Government and Public Policy, Research and Editorial, Professional Development and Standards, and Nominations.
ELIZABETH GIGNAC

Canadian Music Centre, founded in 1959, is an arts service organization supporting over 200 of Canada's serious or concert composers. Composers become CMC Associates after being selected by a committee of their peers. The national office and library of the centre are in Toronto; regional centres are in Vancouver, Calgary, Toronto and Montréal. By collecting, freely distributing and promoting the Associates' music, the CMC aims to encourage the study, performance and appreciation of these compositions. It offers the public and music groups both in Canada and overseas information on the Associates, publications on the 7000 scores in its libraries and inexpensive reproductions of the music itself. Centrediscs, the CMC's record label, produces and distributes quality discs of Associates' works performed by Canadian concert artists.

The CMC is funded by 11 Canadian governments — federal, provincial and municipal — and by private composers' organizations, foundations, industries and the donations of its lay members. JOHN A. MILLER

Canadian National Exhibition, world's largest annual exhibition, held in Toronto in late Aug and early Sept. The CNE, or "Ex" as it is popularly called, originated in an agricultural fair that circulated among the towns of Canada West in the 1840s (*see* AGRICULTURAL EXHIBITIONS). In 1878 the city of Toronto leased 20 ha of land on the lakefront as a permanent fairground and held its own exhibition the following year. Called the Toronto Industrial Exhibition, all but one of the 23 wooden buildings — the Crystal Palace — were devoted to agriculture. In 1882 the fairgrounds became the first to be lit by electricity, and Torontonian J.J. Wright introduced the electric railway there in 1883. The Crystal Palace was destroyed by fire in 1906 and replaced by the Horticultural Building and additional imposing structures of brick and stone. The fair was officially renamed the Canadian National Exhibition in 1912.

The CNE continued to grow and to reflect the changes in Canadian society as emphasis shifted from agriculture to industry. By 1912 the fairgrounds covered 141 ha and included one of the finest amusement parks in N America. Elaborate grandstand shows were presented, usually on Canadian themes and, during both world wars, on effort, loyalty and victory. Marathon swims across the lake, such as that of Marilyn BELL, who in 1954 became the first person to swim Lk Ontario, and special events, such as an exhibition of the DIONNE QUINTUPLETS, proved popular. A growing American influence was evident, particularly in the performers selected for the bandshell and grandstand shows. By the 1960s the Ex had evolved into a vast consumer market, displaying the latest automobiles, electrical appliances, computers and the like. The CNE has not been without critics and was cast in a shadow in 1967 by EXPO 67, seeming dull in comparison. Nevertheless, in 1983, 2 528 023 people visited the CNE; along with Ontario Place, the Ex remains part of an extensive recreational development on the revitalized Toronto lakefront. JAMES MARSH

Reading: J. Lorimer, *The Ex: A Picture History of the Canadian National Exhibition* (1973); G. Wall and N. Zalkind, "The Canadian National Exhibition: Mirror of Canadian Society," in G. Wall and J.S. Marsh, eds, *Recreational Land Use* (1982).

Canadian National Railways is the longest railway system in N America, controlling more than 50 000 km of track in Canada and the US. Now called Canadian National, the CROWN CORPORATION's holdings have expanded since the 1920s to include marine operations, hotels, TELECOMMUNICATIONS and resource industries, but the core of CN still lies with its railway system (now called CN Rail), which had its origins in the amalgamation of 5 financially troubled railways during the years 1917-23: the GRAND TRUNK and its subsidiary the GRAND TRUNK PACIFIC; the INTERCOLONIAL; the CANADIAN NORTHERN; and the

Canadian National Railways' steam engine 6218, shown at Brampton, Ont, was the CNR's last operating steam engine (retired 4 July 1971). The diesel was less expensive to operate, and more powerful and flexible (*courtesy Network/Barry Griffiths*).

National Transcontinental. The Grand Trunk was itself an amalgamation of various smaller lines, including the 23.2 km CHAMPLAIN AND ST LAWRENCE RAILROAD (1836) which connected Montréal with boat traffic to Lk Champlain and the port of New York; the GREAT WESTERN RAILWAY linking Niagara, Hamilton and Toronto with Windsor and Sarnia; and the ST LAWRENCE AND ATLANTIC RAILROAD, which gave Montréal access to the year-round port facilities of Portland, Maine. The Grand Trunk became the dominant long-distance railway in central Canada, but its English shareholders would not agree to the expense of building from Québec City to Halifax over Canadian soil, nor to construction westward over the 1600 km of the Laurentian Shield. Those challenges were faced after Confederation by the government-owned Intercolonial from Halifax to Québec City and by the heavily subsidized CANADIAN PACIFIC RAILWAY.

Although Canada by the 1890s was traversed from sea to sea by the CPR, the issues of monopoly in the West and of partisan politics federally led to further transcontinental ventures. The Canadian Northern, founded by William MACKENZIE and Donald MANN, was begun with small Manitoba lines in 1895. In 1903 Sir Wilfrid LAURIER's Liberal government authorized the building of the Grand Trunk Pacific, from Winnipeg west to Prince Rupert, and the National Transcontinental, from Winnipeg east to Québec City, where it would connect with the Intercolonial to Halifax. All of these lines were financed by heavy borrowing and, when WWI diverted the credit of English banks, the debt loads of these railways had to be absorbed through government nationalization.

Completion of government ownership in the early 1920s led to the appointment of Sir Henry THORNTON as CN's first president. Despite an inherited debt of $1.3 billion, gross earnings that barely covered operating expenses, and the difficulty of keeping the government at arm's length, Thornton gradually established annual surpluses while drawing remarkable personal support from among the 99 000 employees of CN. He promoted community service, supporting branch lines and introducing school cars and Red Cross units to serve children and the sick in regions remote from urban centres. Between 1923 and 1932 he was responsible for using CN facilities to develop a network of radio stations, which inaugurated programs such as "Hockey Night in Canada" and led to formation of the CANADIAN BROADCASTING CORPORATION (*see* BROADCASTING, RADIO AND TELEVISION). Unfortunately, partisan politics forced Thornton's resignation in 1932.

Economic depression in the 1930s reduced traffic volume, leading to cuts in wages and dismissal of employees. At the same time, highway and air tavel diverted traffic away from the railway. In 1937, however, under C.D. HOWE as minister of transport, CN organized formation of TRANS-CANADA AIRLINES (now AIR CANADA), and in 1938 the federal government cancelled more than $1 billion of its inherited debt. As a result, before WWII, CN was able to purchase and to finish and service in its own huge shops at Pointe St-Charles, Montréal, a large number of Canadian-built steam locomotives, particularly the 4-8-4 Northern type, which hauled millions of tons of freight and thousands of troops during the war.

In the 1950s and 1960s, CN was modernized under the dynamic presidency of Donald GORDON, who rationalized 80 subsidiary companies down to 30, one of which, CN Marine, operates all ferry service in the Atlantic provinces. Gordon also directed the conversion to diesel locomotives and electronic signalling while adding to CN assets the prestigious Queen Elizabeth Hotel (1958) and a new head office in Montréal.

By the end of the 1970s CN had merged its own system of telecommunications with that of CP, and completed construction in Toronto of the CN TOWER. CN Real Estate has redeveloped company-owned downtown properties in several cities, including the Toronto Convention Centre Complex in 1983-84. In 1981 CN Exploration was formed to develop CN-owned mineral rights in western Canada. On the highway, Canadian National has amalgamated all its trucking subsidiaries into CNX/CN Trucking, their trailers carried over long distances on piggy-back rail cars.

Two problems remain characteristic of CN as a huge crown corporation with profits in 1983 of $260 million. Financially, it has until recently depended on federal subsidies to compensate for statutory freight rates in the long-distance haulage of Prairie grain (*see* CROW'S NEST PASS AGREEMENT). Politically, ownership by the federal government has often influenced high-level appointments with at least as much respect for partisan interest as for "hands off" direction. *See also* RAILWAY HISTORY. ALBERT TUCKER

Reading: J. Schull, *The Great Scot: Biography of Donald Gordon* (1979); G.R. Stevens, *History of the Canadian National Railway* (1973).

Canadian Nature Federation, a national, nongovernmental, charitable CONSERVATION organization, created from the Canadian Audubon Society in 1971. The CNF is aided in its work by a coast-to-coast network of naturalist societies and by its membership in national and international protection groups, including the Committee on the Status of Endangered Wildlife in Canada (COSEWIC), the Canadian Coalition on Acid Rain, the International Union for the Conservation of Nature and Natural Resources (IUCN) and the Arctic International Wildlife Range Society. Through its magazine, *Nature Canada*, and its bookshop, nature sanctuary, nature art scholarship program and conservation directory, the CNF endeavours to foster a greater understanding and appreciation of Canada's wildlife and wilderness heritage. The CNF's environmental action program presents briefs, speeches and reports to government review boards, conferences and environmental pro-ection agencies to ensure that members' concerns are considered when critical decisions affecting the environment are made. This organization is headquartered in Ottawa and is supported by membership fees, bookshop revenues and donations. CHRISTINE VAN ZWAMEN

Canadian Northern Railway was incorporated (1899) as a result of the amalgamation of 2 small Manitoba branch lines. It was built up over the next 20 years by its principal promoters, William MACKENZIE and Donald MANN, to become a 16 093 km transcontinental railway system. The promoters depended heavily on land grants and on the sale of government guaranteed bonds of their company. They built a strong Prairie system, but came to face stiff competition from their transcontinental rivals, the CANADIAN PACIFIC RAILWAY, the GRAND TRUNK RAILWAY and the GRAND TRUNK PACIFIC RAILWAY. To meet that competition, a transcontinental expansion program was undertaken. That expansion, however, proved unprofitable, and severe financial exigencies during WWI repeatedly forced the promoters to seek government assistance. In return for aid given, the federal government ultimately demanded all the shares of the company. Mackenzie and Mann were forced out of the company, which then became one of the first major components of what would soon become the publicly owned CANADIAN NATIONAL RAILWAYS. The corporate identity of the Canadian Northern Ry was retained until 1956, but its existence as an independent company ended with nationalization in 1918. T.D. REGEHR

Reading: T.D. Regehr, *The Canadian Northern Railway* (1976).

Canadian Olympic Hockey Team Prior to the 1964 Winter OLYMPIC GAMES, Canada, represented by club teams, had appeared in 8 Olympic hockey tournaments, winning 5 gold medals, 2 silver medals and one bronze. After the most recent gold (awarded to the Edmonton Mercurys at the 1952 Olympics in Oslo, Norway), it had become increasingly difficult to find clubs that were able to compete effectively for Canada in the Olympics against such countries as the Soviet Union and Czechoslovakia, whose rapidly improving teams were the products of carefully conceived national programs. In 1962 Father David Bauer approached the Canadian Amateur Hockey Association with the concept of a Canadian Olympic hockey team. Born at Kitchener, Ont, in 1925, David Bauer had played for the Oshawa Generals, the 1945 Memorial Cup champions. He was ordained as a Basilian priest in 1954 and continued to be involved in hockey, coaching the St Michael's (Toronto) Majors to the 1961 Memorial Cup championship. In Sept 1963 Father Bauer and a group of university players began training at UBC in Vancouver. This team suffered only 2 narrow defeats, to the Soviet Union and Czechoslovakia, at the 1964 Olympics in Innsbruck, Austria, but placed fourth. In 1965 a permanent national team was established in Winnipeg. Coached by Jackie MacLeod and managed by Father Bauer, it won the bronze medal in the 1968 Olympics at Grenoble, France. As a result of disagreements with the International Ice Hockey Federation over the use of professionals at world championships, Canada withdrew from international amateur hockey entirely and did not send a team to the 1972 and 1976 Winter Olympics. Father Bauer participated in the revival of the Canadian team for the 1980 Olympics at Lake Placid, New York, where they were defeated by the Soviet Union, Finland and Czechoslovakia to finish out of the medals. At Sarajevo, Yugoslavia in 1984, the Canadian team coached by Dave King lost to Sweden in the bronze medal game.
DEREK DRAGER AND GIGI CLOWES

Canadian Opera Co. Canada's leading producer of OPERA, evolved from the Opera Festival of the Royal Conservatory Opera Co. Incorporated in 1950, its name changed from Opera Festival Assn to Company (1954) to COC (1958). Under Herman Geiger-Torel, stage director 1950-56, artistic director 1956-59 and general director 1959-76, the COC forged a strong tradition using Canadian talent and made extensive tours. General director from 1976, Lotfi Mansouri, while building the company's international stature, has introduced the *stagione* system, increased the number of annual productions to seven and augmented the repertoire. Since 1980 through the COC Ensemble, Mansouri has the nucleus of a permanent company ready for a new opera house. GAYNOR G. JONES

Canadian Pacific Railway Completion of a transcontinental railway within 2 years was a condition of British Columbia's entry into Confederation in 1871 (*see* RAILWAY HISTORY). Competition for the lucrative contract for the railway was bitter, and disclosure of methods used by Sir Hugh ALLAN to secure the charter led to the defeat of Sir John A. MACDONALD's government in 1873 (*see* PACIFIC SCANDAL). Macdonald returned to power in 1878 and the contract was finally awarded to interests led by Donald A. SMITH, J.J. Hill and George STEPHEN, and Canadian Pacific Railway was incorporated 15 Feb 1881. The difficulties of construction and demand for early completion of the line ensured generous provisions to the company, including $25 million in cash, 25 million acres (about 10 million ha) of land in a belt along the railway, the cost of surveys totalling $37 million, monopoly over transportation S to the US for 20 years, etc. These terms were loudly denounced by opposing interests at the time and remained contentious with the development of the PRAIRIE WEST. However, in the face of American expansion westward, Macdonald and the federal Conservatives considered completion of the railway a national imperative.

Under the management of W.C. VAN HORNE, construction was rapidly pressed across the plains. Sandford FLEMING had recommended a route through the YELLOWHEAD PASS but a more southerly route through KICKING HORSE PASS was chosen Sept 1882. Construction through the rock and muskeg of the Canadian SHIELD almost equaled in difficulty the ENGINEERING feats of construction through the mountains of BC. The line through to the Pacific coast was completed

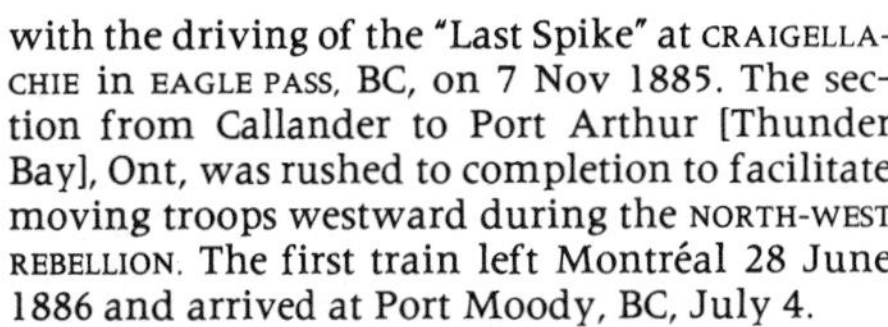

with the driving of the "Last Spike" at CRAIGELLACHIE in EAGLE PASS, BC, on 7 Nov 1885. The section from Callander to Port Arthur [Thunder Bay], Ont, was rushed to completion to facilitate moving troops westward during the NORTH-WEST REBELLION. The first train left Montréal 28 June 1886 and arrived at Port Moody, BC, July 4.

During construction the CPR became involved in the sale and settlement of land (1881), acquisition of the Dominion Express Co (1882) and the acceptance of commercial TELEGRAPH messages (1882). The company provided its own sleeping and dining cars on trains and constructed tourist hotels (eg, at Lake Louise, Alta) and dining halls along the route in the western mountains. This foothold on the tourist industry benefitted the CPR later in its international development of hotels, steamships and airlines (*see* HOTEL; TOURISM).

Following construction, the greatest challenge facing the CPR was to develop business to make the line self-sustaining. Though settlement proceeded rapidly in the wake of the rail lines, population in western Canada was insufficient to sustain the line fully for many years. To increase business, the corporation became very active in promoting trade on the Pacific. Within days of the arrival of the first train on the West Coast in 1886, sailing vessels chartered by the CPR began to arrive from Japan, bringing tea, silk and curios. By 1891 the company had secured a contract from the British government to carry the imperial mails from Hong Kong to Britain via Canada. The result was the purchase of 3 ocean passenger-cargo vessels, forerunners of the present-day fleet (*see* SHIPPING).

By 1900 the mountain hotel system had expanded into the major cities, led by the Hotel Vancouver (1887), Québec's Château Frontenac (1893) and Montréal's Place Viger (1898). Other services expanded simultaneously. A line was opened (1889) across northern Maine from Montréal to Saint John giving the CPR direct access to an all-weather Atlantic port. Attempts to capture traffic from the western American states were made with construction of a line to North Dakota (1893), and control (which remains today) of what is now the Soo Line Railroad Co in the US. Branch lines were greatly extended to feed traffic to the E-W main line. Rapid settlement followed construction of branches to southern Manitoba, from Regina to Prince Albert (1890) and from Calgary N to Strathcona [Edmonton] in 1891. Expansion into the Kootenay mining region of southern BC (1898) involved the acquisition of a railway charter which included a smelter at Trail, BC. This was the nucleus of the CPR's involvement in MINING

Construction of a snowshed through the Rogers Pass on the CPR line in the 1880s (*courtesy Provincial Archives of Alberta/E. Brown Collection*).

and METALLURGY, formalized by the formation of what is now Cominco Ltd (1906), a CP-controlled company. The Pacific fleet was improved and, in 1903, CPR purchased the Beaver Line and opened service in the N Atlantic. In 1914-15, with the purchase of the long-established ALLAN LINE, Canadian Pacific Steamship Services was organized. The widespread expansion of the company, much of it under the presidency of T.G. SHAUGHNESSY (1899-1918), placed a heavy drain on company resources, but continuance of the NATIONAL POLICY, with its substantial tariffs, meant continuing high rates in the West. Attacks on these rates in 1896 had helped to bring about the defeat of the Conservatives. The Liberals reduced rates with the CROW'S NEST PASS AGREEMENT in 1897 and certain grievances were removed by passing of the Manitoba Grain Act in 1900. Finally, charters were granted to the CANADIAN NORTHERN RY and to develop the huge area of northern Prairie left vacant by the CPR.

Consolidation and expansion in the 1920s and the Depression in the 1930s were major challenges, as was competition from CANADIAN NATIONAL RAILWAYS, formed by the government of Canada between 1917 and 1923. The CNR consolidated the failing Grand Trunk Pacific, Canadian Northern, Intercolonial and Canadian Government Railways, and competed with the CPR in hotels, telegraphs, steamships and express services as well as railway services. Despite this massive, government-supported competition, CPR survived as a commercial enterprise. In WWII it provided not only transportation, but also the production in its own main shops of armaments and materiel. During the conflict, much of its merchant fleet was commandeered for military transport purposes, resulting in the loss of 12 vessels.

Canadian Pacific Airlines (now CP Air) was organized in 1942 with the purchase of Grant MCCONACHIE'S Yukon Southern Air Transport and numerous other flying concerns. Under McConachie's leadership after 1949, CPA developed into an international carrier serving the Far East, Australasia, most of S America and several European countries (*see* AVIATION).

Until the late 1950s CP's diverse interests were looked upon as ancillary to the rail system. Beginning at this time, management embraced a policy of full diversification by making each operation fully self-supporting. Thus, operations which had been handled traditionally by specific departments in the railway corporate structure were set up as enterprises in their own right, eg, Marathon Realty Ltd (1963), which took over the administration of real estate other than that required for railway use; CP Hotels Ltd (1965); and CP Oil & Gas Ltd [now PanCanadian Petroleum Ltd] (1958). Concurrently the non-transportation interests were vested in a holding company, now Canadian Pacific Enterprises Ltd, fd 1962, leaving the railway, air, ship and highway transportation fields under the jurisdiction of the parent company. In 1968 a new corporate identity program gave the names CP Rail, CP Ships, CP Transport and CP Air to the various transportation modes. In 1971, to reflect the new and broader orientation of the company, its original name was altered to Canadian Pacific Ltd. In 1967 the communications wing was integrated, along with CN's parallel organization, into a new, jointly owned company known as CNCP Telecommunications Ltd. In 1983 Canadian Pacific Ltd ranked second among Canadian corporations with gross revenue of $12.7 billion, third by assets ($17.6 billion) and first by number of employees (121 000). CP is 75% Canadian owned, with POWER CORPORATION (12%) the major shareholder.

OMER LAVALLÉE

Reading: P. Berton, *The National Dream* (1970) and *The Last Spike* (1971); J.M. Gibbon, *Steel of Empire: The Romantic History of the Canadian Pacific, the Northwest Passage of Today* (1935); H.A. Innis, *A History of The Canadian Pacific Railway* (1923); W. Kaye Lamb, *History of the Canadian Pacific Railway* (1977); J.L. McDougall, *Canadian Pacific: A Brief History* (1968).

CPR train in the Crowsnest Pass, SW Alberta (*courtesy Elliott and Nicole Bernshaw/Bernshaw Photography*).

Canadian Pacific Railway – Chronology

1871	July 20	BC formally admitted to Confederation, with the promise of a railway
1872	April	Sandford Fleming settles on Yellowhead Pass as route through Rockies
	July	Sir Hugh Allan assured by Macdonald that influence will be used to establish him as president of CPR
	Aug 26	Macdonald's telegram to Allan: "I must have another ten thousand"
1873	July	Newspapers publish revelations re "Pacific Scandal"
	Nov 5	Macdonald government resigns
1874	Jan 22	Liberals under A. Mackenzie elected
1875	June 1	Construction begins on main CPR line at Ft William, Ont
1877	Oct 9	*Countess of Dufferin*, first locomotive on prairies, arrives at Winnipeg
1878	Sept 17	Conservatives returned to power
1879	April	A. Onderdonk commences construction at Yale, BC
1881	Feb 16	Canadian Pacific Railway Co incorporated
	Dec 13	W.C. Van Horne arrives in Winnipeg to take up duties as general manager
1882	June 17	Line between Ft William and Selkirk, Man, completed
	July 24	Rogers finds pass through Selkirk Mts
	Aug 23	First train arrives at Regina
1883	Aug 20	Official party arrives in Calgary
1884	Feb 28	CPR Relief Bill passes House
1885	Mar 19	Riel sets up provisional Métis government in Saskatchewan
	Apr 5	First Canadian troops reach Winnipeg
	May 15	Riel surrenders
	May 16	Last rail on Lk Superior line
	June 10	CPR Aid Bill passes House
	July 29	Onderdonk completes line from Port Moody, BC, to Savona's Ferry, BC
	Sept 30	Onderdonk completes line between Savona's Ferry and Eagle Pass, BC
	Nov 7	Last spike driven at Craigellachie, BC

Canadian Permanent Committee on Geographical Names In 1897 Canadian government resource scientists and mapmakers, recognizing a need to standardize geographical naming in Canada, to discourage duplication and to simplify orthography, founded the Geographic Board of Canada. During its early years the board published its decisions in annual reports and sponsored the publication of several studies on the origin and use of geographical names. In 1948, when the board was renamed the Canadian Board on Geographical Names a program to publish the *Gazetteer of Canada* series by province and territory was started. In 1961 the board was reorganized as the Canadian Permanent Committee on Geographical Names to clarify federal and provincial authority regarding the adoption of geographical names. In 1979 the federal government recognized that the provinces have authority to name features in lands under their jurisdiction, while sharing responsibility for naming in federal crown lands in the provinces.

The committee has 21 members, one from each province and 11 other members representing federal mapping agencies, territorial administration, archives and translation services. The committee is supported by 4 advisory committees on undersea feature names, glaciological and alpine nomenclature, toponymy research and names outside Canada. A very active role has been played by the committee in the international standardization of geographical names. The federal Dept of ENERGY, MINES AND RESOURCES provides the committee with its chairman and secretariat. Some provinces (Alberta, Newfoundland, Ontario, Québec and Saskatchewan) have their own boards, which undertake a variety of toponymic studies (*see* PLACE NAMES).

A. RAYBURN

Canadian Press (CP), Canada's principal news agency, is owned co-operatively by 106 daily newspapers and operates as a nonprofit organization. In addition to providing members with a continual supply of domestic and foreign news CP sells its service to private broadcasters through Broadcast News Ltd and provides news to CBC through another subsidiary, Press News Ltd. It also sells a computerized data file to non-media organizations and offers a photo service. CP's output in 1981 was approximately 250 000 words per day. A French-language service was inaugurated in 1951. CP was founded in 1917 partly to provide for an exchange of news among newspapers. Today, two-fifths of its domestic coverage is from member papers, who are obliged to provide swiftly any local news of potential interest to other papers. The remaining Canadian news is written by CP reporters. A news staff of nearly 300 is situated in 14 cities across Canada; the head office is in Toronto. CP maintains bureaus in NY, Washington and London, but most international copy comes from 3 agencies: Associated Press (US), Reuters (England) and Agence France-Presse (France).

PETER JOHANSEN

Canadian Public Policy (*Analyse de politique*) established in 1974 chiefly by the Canadian Economics Association with the co-operation of the Canadian Political Science Association and other scholarly associations. A quarterly journal, it occasionally publishes a fifth issue devoted to some question of public policy. It is funded primarily by subscriptions, but also receives a grant from the Social Sciences and Humanities Research Council of Canada. Its first home was at U of Guelph (where the business office is still housed), but it now has an editorial office at UBC under editor Anthony Scott (1984). *Canadian Public Policy* is an analytical journal that goes beyond the usual academic discussion in scholarly journals to publish articles taking positions on policies of national debate such as the

ROW'S NEST PASS AGREEMENT, casino gambling, the inancing of public pensions and inflation. The ournal solicits articles from academics, administrators, politicians and business officials in the rivate sector. D. McGILLIVRAY

anadian Radio-television and Telecommunications Commission The Broadcasting ct, 1967-68, established the Canadian Radio-elevision Commission to regulate and superise all aspects of the Canadian BROADCASTING ystem. Those functions had been carried out ince 1958 by the Board of Broadcast Governors, nd before that by the Board of Governors of the ANADIAN BROADCASTING CORPORATION. In 1976 arliament transferred to the CRTC jurisdiction ver federally regulated TELECOMMUNICATIONS ompanies, formerly exercised by the Canadian ransport Commission, and changed the name o the Canadian Radio-television and Teleommunications Commission. The CRTC decides on the issuance and renewal of licences for ll broadcasting undertakings, including networks and cable systems. It may attach conditions to licences, and makes regulations respecting BROADCASTING. It may also revoke any icence, except one issued to the CBC. The overnor-in-council may set aside the granting f any licence, or ask that it be reconsidered. The hief function of the Commission in the teleommunications field is in approving rates or olls to be charged to the public by companies ot under provincial jurisdiction. Decisions in his area are also subject to Cabinet review. The egislation provides for a chairman, 2 vicehairmen and 6 other full-time members, all of whom are normally appointed for 7-year terms nd who form the executive committee. There is lso provision for 10 part-time members regularly resident in different parts of the country ut who take an active part in the work of the Commission. The executive committee has ower to make decisions on all broadcast licensing matters except revocations, after consulting with part-time members, and it alone rules on elecommunications matters. The full Commission makes decisions involving the revocation f licences, general broadcasting policies, and egulations and rules of procedure. Public consultation, either through written notice and omment or through public hearings, is a genral practice. In 1982-83, for example, the Commission received 2699 applications, and held 27 ublic hearings across the country. In the same ear it issued 996 decisions in broadcasting natters. Among the important early decisions f the CRTC were a provision for a minimum of Canadian music on the air; rules respecting Canadian content in TV schedules; licensing of hird TV networks in Ontario and Québec; and he wide licensing of cable systems that would arry American programming directly to areas vell beyond the range of US stations.

The staff of some 40 work in a building on the romenade du Portage in Hull, Qué. The organiation is divided into 5 major sectors: secretariat, roadcasting, telecommunications, legal and orporate management. The first chairman was ierre Juneau who held office until he resigned n 1975. Harry BOYLE, a veteran member who vas then vice-chairman, became acting chairnan for a time, and then was appointed to the ffice in Jan 1976 for a term to end the following year. He was succeeded by Pierre Camu who esigned after a 2-year period. In Dec 1979 John MEISEL, a social sciences professor at Queen's, was amed as chairman. He was replaced in Nov 983 by Québec lawyer André Bureau. In 981 the Commission licensed a SATELLITE distribution system to provide radio and TV service o remote and underserved areas. After some ears of study and lengthy public hearings, the Commission licensed 2 national and 6 regional AY-TELEVISION systems in 1982-83. An important telecommunications decision in 1982 permitted the attachment of subscriber-owned terminal equipment to Bell Canada lines.
A. DAVIDSON DUNTON

Pierre Juneau, the first chairman of the CRTC (*photo by Ron Watts/First Light*).

Canadian Ski Marathon In 1967, several hundred cross-country skiers celebrated the Centennial year by skiing 100 miles (160 km) from Montréal to Ottawa. Their 3-day expedition has since evolved into the Canadian Ski Marathon, the largest ski event in N America. The CSM has become a 2-day tour annually attracting almost 5000 skiers from Canada, the US and as many as 10 foreign countries. The course runs from Lachute, Qué, through the forests and farms of the Outaouais region to finish in Ottawa on the Rideau Canal at the climax of the "Winterlude" festival in mid-Feb. Its many categories cater to skiers of all ages and abilities, from 4-year-olds skiing 10 miles (16 km) a day to Gold Coureur de Bois carrying 10 kg packs over the entire distance and camping out overnight. The marathon is organized by a small office staff and some 600 volunteers. MURRAY SHAW

Canadian Studies The use of the phrase "Canadian studies" to designate a distinctive interdisciplinary approach to research and teaching about Canada owes much to the evolution of Canadian NATIONALISM in the 1960s and 1970s. In 1968, inspired by the Centennial celebrations, A.B. Hodgetts published *What Culture? What Heritage?* Hodgetts examined the teaching of Canada in hundreds of schools and concluded, "We are teaching a bland, unrealistic consensus version of our past; a dry-as-dust chronological story of uninterrupted political and economic progress told without the controversy that is an inherent part of history." This analysis was followed in 1969 by a report — *The Struggle for Canadian Universities*, by R. Mathews and J. Steele — on the large numbers of non-Canadians teaching in the country's universities, and in 1972 by a decision of the Association of Universities and Colleges of Canada (AUCC) to commission T.H.B. Symons to "study, report, and make recommendations upon the state of teaching and research in various fields of study relating to Canada." The Symons Report, *To Know Ourselves*, released in 1975, advocated a wide variety of activities in universities and within government agencies, professional associations and private and public organizations. Symons's initial study was followed by changes at all educational levels, by new government programs, and by numerous further studies, commissions and reports. Hodgetts, Symons and others raised issues concerning not only education, but also the BOOK PUBLISHING industry, science and technology, archives, international relations, etc.

The public debate over the concept of a "Canadian identity" had its most dramatic impact on education, however, and contributed to the creation of several new agencies and organizations devoted to the promotion of "Canadian studies." In 1970 the CANADA STUDIES FOUNDATION, an independent, nonprofit organization, was created with the support of the Ontario Institute for Studies in Education to suggest ways of improving the quality of Canadian studies in the country's elementary and secondary schools. Among its many achievements was the publication in 1980 of a design for curriculum entitled *Teaching Canada for the 80's*. At the college level, similar initiatives were undertaken in the early 1970s by the Association of Canadian Community Colleges through a Canadian Studies Project. Funded at first by the Kellogg Foundation and later by the federal government, this project was established to increase the level of Canadian content in COMMUNITY COLLEGE courses and to increase the number of interdisciplinary programs. Through CURRICULUM DEVELOPMENT grants, travel awards for students, faculty and administrators, and through publications and other initiatives, this project achieved considerable success. At the university level, faculty interested in Canadian studies created, in the 1970s, the ASSOCIATION FOR CANADIAN STUDIES, an interdisciplinary organization devoted to encouraging teaching, publication and research about Canada at the postsecondary level through various national and regional programs (by 1984, more than 35 Canadian universities were offering a variety of Canadian studies programs). It also directed some of its programs and publications to the general public, including a newsletter, published quarterly.

In 1981 the International Council for Canadian Studies (ICCS) was formed, partly to provide a means of exchanging information among a growing number of associations abroad. By 1984 its membership included the Association for Canadian Studies (in Canada), the British Association for Canadian Studies, the Association for Canadian Studies in the US, the Association for Canadian Studies in German-Speaking Countries, the Japanese Association for Canadian Studies, the Australian and New Zealand Association for Canadian Studies, the Association of Canadian Studies in Ireland, the French Association for Canadian Studies, the Italian Association for Canadian Studies, and the Nordic Association for Canadian Studies. The ICCS also has affiliate members, eg, Canadian studies centres in Thailand, Belgium and Israel.

Financial support for Canadian studies in Canada and abroad comes from a variety of sources, including membership fees, foundations (private and public), granting agencies, and, most notably, from the federal Department of External Affairs and the Secretary of State. It is also noteworthy that by the time Professor Symons (in collaboration with J.E. Page) published the third and final volume of his report on Canadian studies in 1984, it could be reported that much had happened in the preceding decade, both in the creation or expansion of teaching programs and in the research, publication, collection and preservation of Canadian materials. S. McMULLIN

Canadian Tax Foundation, a nonprofit research and publishing organization that sponsors studies and conferences on taxation and public-finance issues. Founded in 1945 and headquartered in Toronto, it is supported by the Canadian Bar Association and the Canadian Institute of Chartered Accountants. All members of these 2 organizations are also members of the foundation. Corporations and other individuals may also become members. In addition to a wide range of special studies, the foundation publishes annually *The National Finances*, a review of federal spending and revenues, and *The Conference Report*, a collection of the papers delivered at its annual national conference. It also publishes the *Canadian Tax Journal* and *Provincial and Municipal Finances*. DAVID CRANE

Canadian Tire Corporation, Limited, with headquarters in Toronto, is a wholesaler and merchandiser of automotive products. It started in 1922 as the Hamilton Garage and Rubber Company and the present company was incorporated in 1927. Today, Canadian Tire is represented in all provinces, and 91 gas stations operate through a subsidiary. In 1982 the company purchased most of the merchandise and assets of White Stores Inc of Texas. In 1982 it had sales or operating revenue of $1.8 billion (ranking 45th in Canada), assets of $1 billion (ranking 81st) and 5927 employees. The J.W. Billes estate and family own 40%, the Trustee of the Canadian Tire Company Profit Sharing Plan, 12%, and 839 Yonge Main Store Ltd, 10%. DEBORAH C. SAWYER

Canadian Transport Commission, est 19 Sept 1967 pursuant to the National Transportation Act to co-ordinate and harmonize the operation of all carriers engaged in transport, as well as to undertake programs of study and research towards the development of a national TRANSPORTATION policy. It replaces the Board of Transport Commissioners, the Air Transport Board and the Canadian Maritime Commission. The commission reports to the federal minister of transport and has a president, 2 vice-presidents and a maximum of 14 additional members appointed by the governor-in-council. Committees exist for air, rail and commodity pipeline; for extra-provincial transport of the CN-operated bus service in Newfoundland; for reviews and appeals and for consideration of international transport policy. A traffic and tariff branch monitors transport tolls and tariffs under a number of statutes. The commission regulates fares and competition of commercial air carriers and approves their schedule integration. Its 1984-85 budget was $555 million.

Canadian Union of Public Employees, fd 1963 with 86 000 members, a merger of the National Union of Public Employees and the National Union of Public Service Employees. CUPE members are employed mainly in municipal and provincial governments, and in schools, universities, hospitals, nursing homes, electrical utilities, libraries, social service agencies and broadcasting. CUPE's main function has been to bargain collectively for improved working conditions and to press for progressive labour and social legislation. It is Canada's largest labour union with 290 000 members (1983), of whom 44% are women. GILBERT LEVINE

Canadian Unity, Task Force on, est 1976 by the federal government in response to the election of a sovereignty-oriented Québec government. It was co-chaired by Jean-Luc PEPIN, former federal Liberal minister, and John ROBARTS, former Conservative premier of Ontario. Its purpose was to gather opinions about the problems of unity in the country, to publicize efforts being made to solve those problems and to advise the government on how to strengthen national unity. In its report (1979) it recommended that language rights be left to provincial jurisdiction rather than being entrenched in the CONSTITUTION (contrary to federal Liberal government strategy 1969-79); that federal power be reduced; that changes be made in the federal election system (except in economic management) to introduce some proportional representation; that the Senate be replaced with a Council of the Federation appointed by provincial governments; and that the provinces be given power to rule on federal appointments to the Supreme Court of Canada and certain major regulatory bodies. The Québec delegation alone invoked these recommendations during the 1980 constitutional discussions. The accord reached between the federal government and the other 9 provinces (1981) revealed how little influence the task force had had. R. HUDON

Canadian Wheat Board, an AGRICULTURAL MARKETING BOARD charged with orderly marketing of western grains. The CWB is the sole marketing agency for prairie WHEAT, BARLEY and OATS destined for export or for human consumption in Canada. Throughout its history the CWB has been a major agent of government policy for western grains. Temporary forerunners of the board operated from 1917 to 1920. The CWB was established as a voluntary marketing agency for prairie wheat in 1935. Sale of wheat through the board became compulsory in 1943 and, in 1949, CWB powers were extended to include prairie oats and barley. The CWB administers government-guaranteed initial prices paid to producers and operates a system of annual averaging (pooling) of producers' prices. It regulates producers' deliveries of major prairie grains from country elevators to export ports. The board generally does not own or operate physical marketing facilities but uses various GRAIN HANDLING AND MARKETING companies as agents to buy, handle and, sometimes, sell grain on its behalf. The board directly sells export grain; many of its sales are made to state trading agencies of importing countries (as with sales to the USSR and the People's Republic of China). It also sells to international grain companies. Following changes in feed-grain policy in 1974 and 1976, the CWB no longer holds exclusive marketing rights over interprovincial sale of prairie grain fed to animals in Canada, but acts as a residual supplier of feed grains to the domestic market. The CWB is a self-financing CROWN CORPORATION with 3-5 federally appointed commissioners and an 11-member advisory committee elected by prairie grain farmers. Board headquarters are in Winnipeg.
M.M. AND T.S. VEEMAN

Canadian Wildlife Federation, national, non-profit, nongovernmental CONSERVATION organization founded in 1961 and chartered in 1962. CWF was created to promote an understanding of Canada's wildlife resources and ensure that stocks of all species would be preserved for the use and enjoyment of all Canadians. Originally, membership included the 10 provincial wildlife federations; in the early 1970s, individual Canadians were allowed to become direct members. CWF now represents over 528 000 members and supporters across Canada and has a wildlife affiliate in the YT. The federation is affiliated with the International Bird Preservation Society and is a voting member of the International Union for the Conservation of Nature and Natural Resources and the Committee on the Status of Endangered Wildlife in Canada. It is administered by a 40-member voluntary board of directors, elected at each annual convention. Staff, located at CWF offices in Ottawa, carry out policies and directives established by the board. Resource-action programs range from studying long-term environmental implications of development projects to recommending legislative changes to protect wildlife resources and their habitat (including ENDANGERED species and migratory species). The federation conducts public-education campaigns and sponsors research to heighten public awareness. Schoolteachers receive posters, classroom lessons, manuals, etc, during National Wildlife Week and throughout the year. Resource materials, career guidance, scholarships, awards and financial-assistance information are available for students. The federation has received various awards, including the Ernest Thompson Seton Award of the International Association of Fish and Wildlife Agencies, for outstanding contributions to conservation education in Canada. LUBA MYCIO

Canadian Women's Army Corps, est 13 Aug 1941 to answer the Canadian Army's need for manpower and the demand of volunteer women's paramilitary groups to render official uniformed service. Except for nursing sisters, women had not previously been admitted into the Canadian ARMED FORCES. CWAC was separate from and supplementary to the Canadian Militia until 1 Mar 1942, when it became an integral part of the defence forces. CWAC officers thereafter could hold commissions and use military titles and badges. Initially the army needed women in uniform as clerks. All occupations open to CWAC women were noncombatant, although their diversity and number increased to include technical trades. Nonetheless, in 1945 as in 1941, the clerk or secretary in uniform was the typical CWAC. In 1941 basic pay was set at two-thirds that of servicemen of equivalent rank. Trades pay was substantially lower than that for servicemen, and servicewomen could not claim dependants' allowances. These inequalities were cause for complaint from both uniformed and civilian women. In July 1943 the government raised basic pay to four-fifths that of men of the same rank, equalized trades pay and granted allowances for dependent parents and siblings, but not for dependent husbands or children. Although inequalities remained, the services were ahead of most private industry in narrowing the gap between men's and women's pay and benefits.

A 1943 public opinion survey revealed that only 7% of Canadians regarded joining the women's forces as the best way for women to serve Canada's war effort. This attitude accompanied widespread resistance to the breaking down of sexual divisions of labour and authority. Braving the opposition, 21 624 women served in CWAC before its dissolution in 1946. Almost 3000 were stationed in the UK; starting May 1944, select groups of these were dispatched to operational areas in Europe to serve as support staff for Canadian invasion forces. When Germany surrendered in May 1945, the CWAC constituted 2.8% of the total strength of the Canadian Army. Col Margaret Eaton headed the corps Apr 1944-Oct 1945 in the position of Director General, CWAC. Thereafter, this position was gradually downgraded in preparation for the disbanding of the corps. Servicemen as well as women proposed inclusion of women's corps in postwar RESERVE FORCES, but Cabinet did not give approval. Only in 1951, during the KOREAN WAR, was the decision taken to enlist women again in the regular forces.
RUTH ROACH PIERSON

Canadian Women's Press Club was founded in June 1904 in a CPR pullman car when 13 Canadian women journalists were returning home after covering the St Louis World's Fair. The first president was Kathleen (Kit) Blake Coleman of the *Toronto Mail and Empire*, one of the first female war correspondents covering the Spanish-American War. Other early members were Nellie MCCLUNG, Emily MURPHY and Helen MCGILL, who campaigned successfully for women's enfranchisement, had careers in politics and law, and used JOURNALISM as a means of promoting social reform to gain legal rights for women and children.

The CWPC included novelists, short-story writers, newspaper and magazine editors, reporters, playwrights, poets, historians and freelancers in print, radio, television and film. In June 1971 members voted to change the name to the Media Club of Canada, to permit membership by any qualified person active in media communications. The Media Club is an independent national corporation with a head office in Ottawa. DONNA JAMES

Canals and Inland Waterways Canada is unique in having almost 760 000 km² of fresh water within its boundaries. The lakes which make up most of this vast area are interconnected by river systems. The Mackenzie R, draining and area of 1 870 000 km², is the seventh-largest iver system of the world. Better known is the St Lawrence R-Great Lakes Waterway extending halfway across the continent. Using Canada's inland waterways, it is possible to travel on water, by canoe, from tide water near Québec to the Arctic coast in the far northwest, and even across the mountains to the Pacific coast. These 2 great journeys were first made just before the end of the 18th century, and by the same man. Alexander MACKENZIE reached the mouth of the river which now bears his name in 1789, and was the first European to cross the N American continent (to Bella Coola) in 1793. He was one of the almost legendary fur trader-explorers of those days. Banded together in the North West Company, these men, with Indian and Métis guides and translators, pioneered the exploration of the main water routes of the West and the Mid-West. One of the barriers they had to pass was the rough water of the St Mary's R as it leaves Lk Superior. Here the NWC constructed one of the first navigation locks in Canada (1719), a small affair indeed, as were the even earlier tiny locks at rapids in the Soulanges section of the St Lawrence, started by the Royal Engineers (1779) under the direction of Governor Haldimand. With a depth over sills of less than 0.5 m, these primitive locks were the beginnings of Canada's notable group of canals, some still in use in their original form, others enlarged and improved (*see* FUR TRADE ROUTES).

The Lachine Canal, bypassing the rapids on the St Lawrence upstream from Montréal, was the first real canal to be finished, built between 1821 and 1825. Planned by Montréal merchants, it required substantial investment of public funds before completion. The other canals of this early period, the 3 Ottawa R canals (1819-34) and the RIDEAU CANAL (1826-32), were planned and built to provide an alternative military waterway between Montréal and Kingston, following the War of 1812. They were therefore paid for by government, even though they were used for commerce rather than military traffic. The Ottawa R canals were in use until 1961 when they were submerged by the Carillon hydroelectric dam of Hydro Québec. Navigation remains possible via a new lock adjacent to the Carillon powerhouse. The Rideau Canal is still in regular use, essentially as built over 150 years ago. Rapids on the Richelieu R, upstream from St Jean, Qué, were bypassed by the Chambly Canal (1833-43). With a lock at St Ours, near Sorel, vessels had access from the St Lawrence to Lk Champlain and so to the Champlain Canal (US) and the Hudson R. But the narrow locks on the Chambly Canal (only 7.1 m wide) were, and still are, a bottleneck in this international waterway.

Great plans for canals were developed in the Maritime provinces. The Shubenacadie Canal, linking Halifax with the Bay of Fundy, was started in 1826 but completed only in 1861, being lightly used for a mere 10 years. The little St Peter's Canal, linking the Bras d'Or Lakes with the ocean, was built between 1854 and 1869; enlarged, it is still in use. The greatest dream of all, from as early as 1686, was for a canal across the Isthmus of Chignecto. Studied more than any other canal project in Canada, it has not yet been built, although a massive marine railway, as an alternative, was started in 1882, only to be abandoned in 1891 before completion.

All of these early canals, as well as the TRENT CANAL system, which follows old Indian routes through the Kawartha Lakes (1834-1930), were intended to facilitate the movement of small steamboats. The Chambly Canal and the Grenville Canal (one of the Ottawa R canals) were alone in their resemblance to the familiar canals of Europe with towpaths for horse-haulage of barges. In the second half of the 19th century, as the population of Canada became more mobile, and in the absence of improved roads, steamboat services proliferated on all the country's major rivers and lakes. For many years, Sir John A. Macdonald had a cabin reserved on the fine daily boat service between Ottawa and Montréal. Some of the services lasted well into the 20th century. The Montréal-Québec-Saguenay service, for example, stopped in 1965; that on the Mackenzie R still operates, although now with diesel-powered vessels.

Lachine Canal, from *Life of Lord Sydenham* (1843). The Lachine Canal, bypassing the St Lawrence rapids upstream from Montréal, was the first canal built in Canada, 1821-25 (*courtesy Public Archives of Canada/C-5955*).

The greatest success in the improvement of Canada's waterways has been the development of the St Lawrence R into the ST LAWRENCE SEAWAY of today. The Lachine Canal (1825) was the real start, closely followed by the completion in 1829 of the first WELLAND CANAL. Forty small timber locks were required to raise vessels the 100 m from Lk Ontario to Lk Erie, most of them necessary for the steep climb up the Niagara escarpment. Initially built with private funds, the Welland Canal was later taken over by government (as was the Lachine Canal). In effect, all improvements to the waterways of Canada have been publicly financed, and the facilities operated by government. The Welland Canal was rebuilt (1845) with larger locks, now of masonry, as one of the first major operations of the new Board of Works of the United Province of Canada. The Board also completed the several small canals necessary for overcoming the rapids on the St Lawrence between Lk St Louis and Lk Ontario — the Beauharnois (later Soulanges), Cornwall and Williamsburg canals. Only at mid-century was this group of canals complete and in regular use. From 1834 to 1850 the Ottawa R canals and the Rideau Canal, with the rivers they served, constituted the Seaway.

Following Confederation in 1867, inland transportation in Canada was given high priority by the new government. The 1870s and 1880s were years of active canal rebuilding and improvement. The bottleneck locks on the Grenville, the third of the Ottawa R canals, were finally rebuilt; a new Carillon Canal replaced the original canal and the Chute à Blondeau single-lock canal. All the locks on the Lachine and St Lawrence R canals were rebuilt in this period to standard dimensions, each 84 m long and 14 m wide with a depth over sills of 4.2 m (14 feet). The third Welland Canal, a major rebuilding of the second, was finished by 1887. To serve the new St Lawrence system, a fleet of almost 200 stubby, inelegant but efficient freight steamers was gradually developed, achieving fame as "the fourteen-footers" and serving faithfully for 75 years.

After 1909, control of the St Lawrence R came under the INTERNATIONAL JOINT COMMISSION, a Canadian-US tribunal. Discussion of a much enlarged canal system intensified almost immediately. The Ottawa R provided a 483 km shorter route for a seaway to the Great Lakes, but the general election of 1911 put an end to the dream of the Georgian Bay Ship Canal. Construction of the fourth Welland Canal, as part of the alternative St Lawrence route, started in 1913. A wholly Canadian venture, this world-famous canal, with only 8 locks, was officially opened in 1932. Its locks, 260 m long by 24 m wide, enabled a fleet of "upper lakers" to be developed for bulk freight service; they later dictated the size of the St Lawrence Seaway locks when the Seaway was built (1954-59) (*see* LAKE CARRIERS).

Today, the St Lawrence Seaway, incorporating the fourth Welland Canal, is one of the few great ship canals of the world, carrying freight from and to the rest of the world and to and from the heart of the N American continent. The great passenger ship services of earlier years have almost all disappeared, their place now taken (especially on the smaller canals) by ubiquitous private pleasure craft. Once away from these main routes, the lakes and streams remain as one of the delights of Canada. Still used today as they have been for centuries, they illustrate how appropriate the designation "Dominion" is for Canada — "from sea to sea, and from the river unto the ends of the Earth." R.F. LEGGET

Reading: R.F. Legget, *Canals of Canada* (1976).

Cancer is a term describing more than 100 different diseases characterized by the common property of abnormal cell growth. Cancer is the second leading cause of death in Canada. One in 4 Canadians will develop cancer and perhaps 66% of families will experience the DISEASE among close relatives. Slightly more men are cancer victims. At least 50% of those who develop cancer (or some 38 000 individuals) will die from it.

Some cancers (eg, lung cancer) have become more common since the 1940s; some (eg, breast cancer in women) have maintained a steady incidence; and others (eg, cancers of the stomach and uterus, of the bladder and rectum in women) have become less frequent. Lung cancer is the leading cause of death among all cancer patients. Because of SMOKING, its incidence is rising rapidly in young women and may soon exceed that of breast cancer. Cancer of the bowel and rectum is the second leading cause of death from cancer; breast cancer is the third leading cause of cancer deaths and the most common cause in women. In order of mortality rates, other forms of cancers are prostatic, uterine, urologic, oral and pancreatic, followed by leukemia and cancers of the ovary and skin (skin cancer is actually the most common cancer by incidence, but the usual forms are readily treatable and are not fatal).

Causes of Cancer The body is made of billions of different types of cell which normally multiply at a rate just sufficient to compensate for cell losses. When they multiply uncontrollably a tumor (also called a neoplasm) results. There are 3 basic tumor types. *Benign* are those in which cells multiply but remain tightly together; adjacent tissues often develop a fibrous tissue ("capsule") between themselves and the tumor. Benign tumors can be treated successfully by surgery. Malignant tumours can be *locally invasive*, ie, cells spread into adjacent tissues by sending out fingerlike probes. These potentially damaging tumors are often on the skin and can therefore often be treated successfully with surgery or radiation. Malignant *metastatic* tumors are the most devastating, because they "seed" themselves via the blood and other body fluids. These seeds, or metastases, create a new tumor. It was once believed that seeding occurred only when a tumor had reached a certain size, and that if the tumor could be eliminated before it reached this size, it could be cured. Unfortunately, it is now known that metastatic tumors seed long before they are detected.

The basis of malignant transformation remains unknown, but the recent discovery of oncogenes (cancer genes) is an important development in understanding cancer. In their inactive form these widespread genes are part of the normal genetic complement. Their structure has been carefully conserved during EVOLUTION, indicating that they have an important function in aiding the growth of normal cells. They may be activated and transformed by specific viruses, or through minor mutations, by duplication into multiple copies, or by being transported to different chromosomes. Multiple (at least 2) genetic events appear to be needed for transformation (*see* GENETICS; VIRUS).

Although the cause of human cancer cannot yet be explained at the molecular level, epidemiological studies have revealed the practical clinical significance of environmental hazards, social habits and genetic factors. Because of the prolonged period generally required for the development of cancer, it is difficult to analyse the exact roles of such factors, but some 70% to 80% of all human cancers are now thought to be related in some way to environmental factors. Hundreds of chemicals including those used in foods as additives and preservatives have been implicated, as have various drugs and radiation. About 40% of all cancers are thought to be related directly or indirectly to cigarette smoking. Viruses produce cancer in several animal species, including mammals, chickens, fish and frogs, but cause only about 5% of human cancers.

Clinical Manifestations of Cancer Particularly for the more common cancers, early detection and diagnosis are important for cure and prolonged survival. The Papanicolaou (Pap) smear has reduced the incidence and mortality of invasive cervical cancer. The National Cancer Institute of Canada (which along with the Medical Research Council funds cancer research in Canada), in co-operation with cancer agencies across Canada, is studying the effectiveness of screening programs for breast cancer using breast self-examination and mammography (over 90% of new breast cancers are discovered each year by patients). The "7 early warning signals of cancer" (American Cancer Society) are designed to encourage people to seek medical help for the early detection of cancers of the skin, breast, larynx, lung and genitourinary and gastrointestinal tracts. The signals are change in bowel or bladder habits; a sore that does not heal; unusual bleeding or discharge; a thickening or a lump in the breast or elsewhere; indigestion or difficulty in swallowing; obvious change in a wart or mole; and nagging cough or hoarseness. Since cancer can affect any tissue and any bodily part, its clinical manifestations are very diverse and may often be silent for a long period before detection. Examination of tissues or cells by the pathologist remains the essential method of diagnosis.

Principles of Therapy In treating cancer it is assumed that all malignant cells should be destroyed, removed or neutralized. It is not known, however, whether successful treatment must eradicate all malignant cells or merely reduce the cell number to a level where the patient's own defenses can gain control. Five kinds of therapy exist today: surgery, radiotherapy, hormone therapy, chemotherapy and immunotherapy. Because cancer is not one but many different diseases, a combination of therapies is sometimes needed and will differ widely for each type of tumour. For solid tumors, surgery and radiotherapy are used to treat the local disease. Metastatic disease requires a systemic therapy such as chemotherapy (use of anti-cancer drugs) which may be used initially or for secondary treatment. With malignancies involving the blood, chemotherapy may be the initial treatment. Chemotherapy often dramatically reduces the size of the tumor but it is not clear whether it prolongs survival. Over 30 drugs, which may be used singly or in various combinations, exist for the chemical management of cancer. Their mechanisms of action on the cancer cell are varied. Although their selective action is on tumor cells, normal tissues which are rapidly growing may also be damaged, leading to side effects such as reduced circulatory blood cells, loss of hair and bowel upset.

Tumors arising from the breast, prostate and uterine lining may respond to hormonal therapy. Certain hormones (eg, estrogens) may act by binding to specific receptors in the tumor cell. Breast and prostate cancers may be treated by removing sources of circulating hormones that could stimulate or support tumor growth or by the administration of estrogens, androgens, progesterones, or glucocorticoids to suppress tumor growth. The use of immunotherapy as an adjuvant to surgery, chemotherapy and radiotherapy can control only small numbers of cells, and it is still used experimentally. Surgical excision is still the current principal curative therapy, especially for those cancers that can be diagnosed early and removed completely. The surgeon is limited by the location and extent of the tumor rather than by its type.

Ionizing radiations of various types and energies are also used to destroy localized populations of cancer cells. As with surgery, results are best with relatively small tumors detected before they are locally or systemically widespread. The tolerance of adjacent normal tissues limits the amount of radiation that can be given. Although exact mechanisms are undefined, radiation appears to kill cells by interfering with their genetic apparatus through ionization of water molecules. Cobalt irradiation units and more recently computerized linear (electron) accelerators are being used, and research is being conducted on neutrons and atomic particles. Drugs are used to sensitize tumor tissues to radiation. Patients are generally informed of both the benefits and hazards of treatment.

Cancer Services During the past decade cancer services have been organized into regional comprehensive cancer centres in which are integrated the sophisticated technology needed for diagnosis and treatment, educational and consultative resources to surrounding communities, and clinical and basic research programs. In some provinces, including BC, Alberta, Saskatchewan, Manitoba, Ontario and the Maritimes, cancer services are centrally organized and in many provinces registration of cancer patients is mandatory.

Cancer patients are managed largely as outpatients, even in the terminal phase of illness. The early referral of cancer patients for multidisciplinary assessment by specialists is important; often the only chance for cure is the first attempt at treatment.

Psychosocial Aspects of Cancer Much has been written regarding the psychosocial dimensions of terminal cancer, but cancer patients who survive also face severe psychological adjustments to accepting the diagnosis of a chronic and potentially fatal disease. Life with cancer still implies social unacceptability, including fear of painful sufferings, disability, disfigurement, impaired bodily function, and loss of sexual attractiveness and self-esteem. It is commonly believed that once cancer has been diagnosed, a patient is helpless before the relentless onslaught of the disease. This misconception fuels the excessive sense of hopelessness and despair that characterizes the word "cancer." Current research is evolving a biology of host cell resistance to cancer, identifying mechanisms that are similar to those that operate to resist infections. Age, sex, immunity, hormones, nutrition, and psychological and probably other as yet undefined factors appear to influence resistance and help determine favourable or unfavourable outcomes, responses to treatment, and occasionally periods of long remission or even spontaneous regression. L. MARTIN JERRY

Reading: Samuel S. Epstein, *Politics of Cancer* (1978); C.F. McKhann, *The Facts About Cancer* (1981).

Candlefish, *see* SMELT.

CANDU, *see* NUCLEAR POWER PLANTS.

Caniapiscau, Rivière *See* KOKSOAK, RIVIÈRE.

Canniff, William, physician, amateur historian (b at Thurlow, Upper Canada 20 June 1830; d at Belleville, Ont 18 Oct 1910). A noted doctor, medical educator, public-health advocate and Canadian nationalist, Canniff is best known as author of *History of the Settlement of Upper Canada* (1869) and *The Medical Profession in Upper Canada* (1894). Educated in Canada, the US, Great Britain and Europe, he practised surgery in Toronto and Belleville, taught pathology and surgery at Victoria Coll Medical School, and produced the first Canadian textbook in pathology (1866). He was a founding member of the Canadian Medical Assn in 1867 and the Ontario Medical Assn in 1880. He served as the president of the CMA (1880) and as Toronto's first permanent medical health officer (1883-90). As a member of the CANADA FIRST movement in the 1870s and through his historical writings, Canniff expressed his ardent Canadian nationalism.
HEATHER MACDOUGALL

Canning, NS, UP pop 763 (1981c), located 100 km NW of Halifax. Once part of the Acadian district of Minas (Les Mines), in the 1760s Canning was resettled by New Englanders as part of Cornwallis Township. Although it was known as Apple Tree Landing and later as Habitant Corner, the residents changed the name to Canning in 1830 in honour of George Canning, a governor general and prime minister of India. Situated on the Habitant R, Canning was one of the many Bay of Fundy communities to take part in the prosperous shipbuilding era of the mid-19th century. In 1866 a disastrous fire destroyed the business district and several houses standing nearby. Canning was the home of Sir Robert Laird BORDEN, Canada's prime minister during WWI. Because of its location in the Annapolis Valley agricultural region, farming has always been important to the community.
DEBRA MCNABB

Cannington Manor, est 1882 when an Englishman, Capt Edward Michell Pierce, claimed 5 townships 65 km S of Whitewood, NWT (now in SE Saskatchewan), the nearest point on the CPR. Cannington was the name of an English town; "Manor" was added later to avoid confusion with an Ontario town. Knowing little about farming, Pierce nevertheless established an agricultural college for the sons of wealthy Englishmen. The "pups," as his students were known, refused to mingle with Canadian settlers. Three pups built a 26-room house which boasted a ballroom, billiard room and servants quarters. In the mahogany-lined stable each

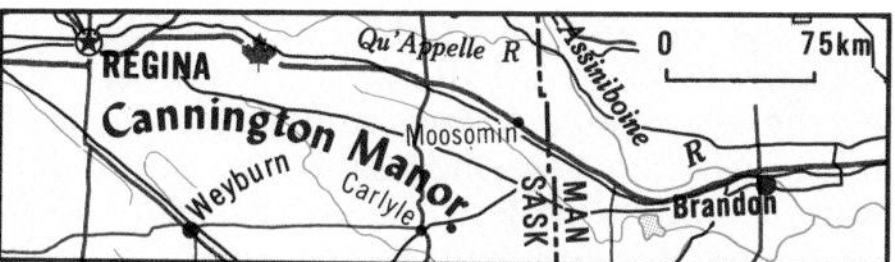

racehorse had a brass nameplate above its stall. By 1890 Cannington Manor included an Anglican church, a flour mill, hotel, smithy, carpentry shop, carriage shop and general store. But the rich English were not serious agriculturalists, playing tennis, cricket and rugby, and spending a week during harvest hunting and playing polo. Failure to adjust to life in Canada quickly brought business and farm bankruptcies. In 1901-02, when a new CPR line bypassed the village, the remaining businesses moved and Cannington Manor gradually disappeared. The site is now a provincial historic park, and a number of the original buildings have been reconstructed. JANE MCCRACKEN

Canoe, Birchbark, principal means of water transportation of the woodlands Indians and the VOYAGEURS. Light and maneuverable, they were perfectly adapted to summer travel through the network of shallow streams, ponds, lakes and swift rivers of the Canadian SHIELD. Canoes were a necessity for the nomadic northern Indians, such as the Montagnais-Naskapi, and were used by the voyageurs in exploiting the fur country. Birchbark was an ideal material, being smooth, hard, light, resilient and waterproof. BIRCH trees were found almost everywhere across Canada, but not always in sufficient number or size - some 8 to 12 trees were required for 1 canoe - and spruce bark had to be substituted in some areas, particularly the western subarctic. The skills required to build the canoes were passed on through generations of master builders. The joints were sewn with white pine roots, which were pulled up, split and boiled by Indian women. The frames were usually of cedar, soaked in water and bent to the shape of the canoe. The seams were made waterproof with spruce or pine resin gathered and applied with a hot stick. As the FUR TRADE grew, the Indians could no longer supply all the canoes needed, and around 1750 the French set up a factory at Trois-Rivières.

The famous *canot du maître,* on which the fur trade depended, was up to 12 m long and carried 6 to 12 crew and a load of 2300 kg over the route from Montréal to Lk Superior. The smaller *canot du nord* carried a crew of 5 or 6 and a cargo of 1360 kg over the smaller lakes, rivers and streams of the Northwest. The canoes were propelled by narrow paddles with quick, continuous strokes, averaging 45 per minute. The *avant* (bowsman) carried a larger paddle for maneuvering in rapids and the *gouvernail* (helmsman) stood in the stern. A canoe could manage 7 to 9 km per hour, and a special express canoe, carrying a large crew and little freight, could achieve up to 140 km in an 18-hour day. Most of inland Canada was first explored in birchbark canoes, and they were used for inland transportation until around 1820 when they began to be replaced by boats. *See* YORK BOATS. JAMES MARSH

Canoeing, an aquatic activity using a small boat, sharp at both ends, paddle-propelled by one or more persons who face the direction in which the craft is heading. There are 2 types of canoe: the open, propelled by a single-blade paddle and known internationally as a "Canadian" or C-boat, and the closed (decked), with a double-blade paddle and known as a kayak or K-boat. Contemporary canoes come in a variety of shapes and materials suited to the variety of water conditions and to recreational or competitive purposes. Most popular is the open canoe used for recreation, hunting and fishing. It is about 5 m long and constructed of wood, canvas, aluminum, fibreglass or plastic. The best-known forms of competitive canoeing are sprint racing, held over 500, 1000 and 10 000 m, with various numbers of paddlers — the only canoe discipline in the Olympic program; "white water" racing with one or 2 paddlers on downriver and slalom courses; and marathon racing over lake and river water and across portages.

Shooting the Rapids, oil painting by Frances Ann Hopkins. The bark canoe was the means of transport of most of the native peoples, and the great *canot du maître* was the means of transport of the fur trade between Montréal and Lake Superior (*courtesy Public Archives of Canada/ C-2774*).

Contemporary canoeing has 2 distinct lines of development. One originated with the native peoples of Canada and continued with the early explorers, fur traders, lumbermen and settlers. Canoeing in open and decked canoes is an indigenous activity of Canadian Indians and Inuit, who designed an amazing variety of water craft, each suited to local materials, the physical environment and tribal customs. Principal classes are the skin boat (KAYAK), the bark boat (particularly the birchbark CANOE) and the log dugout (some up to 15 m long). European explorers, beginning with Jacques CARTIER, readily adopted the light and maneuverable birchbark canoe in place of the heavy, cumbersome rowboats from their ships. In these craft the early explorers and fur traders reached the farthest frontiers of the country. The birchbark canoe was the foundation of a supply route spanning 6500 km from Montréal to the Pacific Ocean and the Mackenzie R, and continued in use for far northern travel to the end of the 19th century. Early settlers along the water routes of central Canada used birchbark canoes for local travel, hunting and fishing. With metal tools they also constructed finely shaped dugout canoes and eventually plank canoes, still fashioned along the lines of the Indian craft. The classic open Canadian canoe — 5 m long, 81 cm beam and 30 cm deep — constructed from cedar planks and elm ribs was developed during the late 1850s along the Otonabee R near Peterborough, Ont. The manufacture of the board-and-batten open canoe, more durable and long lasting than the birch canoe, came in time to serve the needs of middle-class cottagers, hunters and fishermen. During the last 3 decades of the 19th century the canoe from the Peterborough region was exported throughout the world.

The second line of development was strongly influenced by British military personnel stationed in British N America who frequently sponsored competitive aquatic events. Rowing and sailing races were of great interest, but more spectator enthusiasm was generated by Indian canoe races, which were incorporated in regattas from the early 1800s. General boating clubs were started in such places as Kingston, Halifax, Montréal, Peterborough and Toronto. During the 1870s canoe races for gentlemen were added to aquatic events. The formation and the first regatta of the American Canoe Assn at Lake George, NY, in 1880 launched an upsurge in organized canoeing throughout N America. At the ACA's first meet in 1880 Canadian T.H. Wallace from Rice Lake, Ont, won 2 races in his open Rice Lake canoe. In response to the ACA, the Toronto Canoe Club was formed in Dec 1880, and, thereafter, canoe clubs emerged across the country. In 1887 all Canadian clubs banded together as the northern division of the ACA. A national association was founded at Brockville, Ont, in 1900 and that August the first Canadian championships were held there. National championships have been held annually since that time, except during WWI and WWII. In 1924 Canadian and US teams demonstrated canoe racing at the Paris Olympics and an international organization, the IRK, was founded. Since 1936, when canoeing was accepted as an Olympic sport, Canadian paddlers have fared well, especially in the Canadian canoe events. Francis AMYOT won a gold medal in the 1000 m singles in 1936 and Larry CAIN a gold and silver in the C-1 canoe at Los Angeles in 1984.

After WWII, the infusion of Europeans to Canada helped popularize white-water canoeing. A national organization, the Canadian White Water Affiliation, was formed in 1964. In 1967 the first National Slalom and Wild Water Championships were held at the Elora Gorge, Ont. After 1945 professional long-distance paddling was popular in western Canada, Northern Ontario and Québec, but only in April 1980, at Ottawa, was an organization (Canadian Marathon Canoe Racing Assn) established to oversee long-distance racing. The CMCRA held its first national championships in Ottawa in 1981. The Canadian Recreational Canoeing Assn was founded in May 1972, and it works to develop noncompetitive programs to improve paddling skills, instruction and safety in recreational canoeing. C. FRED JOHNSTON

Reading: E.T. Adney and H.I. Chapelle, *The Bark Canoes and Skin Boats of North America* (1964); Bill Durham, *Canoes and Kayaks of Western America* (1960); C.E.S. Franks, *The Canoe and White Water* (1977); Fred Heese, *Canoe Racing* (1979); Bill Mason, *Path of the Paddle* (1980); Wolf Ruck, *Canoeing and Kayaking* (1974).

Canola, common name for the oil, meal and seed of Canadian-developed rape plant varieties with bred-in, superior nutritional qualities. Canola plants are varieties of turnip rape (*Brassica campestris*) and rape (*B. napus*) of the Cruciferae family. TURNIPS (*B. rapa* or, more properly, *B. campestris raifera*) are very closely related;

hence, the name "rape" [from Lat *rapum*, "turnip"]. RUTABAGAS (*B. napus*), CABBAGE and CAULIFLOWER (*B. oleracea*) are also closely related. *B. campestris* originated in the foothills of the Himalayan Mountains; *B. napus* probably originated in the Mediterranean region as the result of natural crosses between *B. campestris* and *B. oleracea* plants.

Rapeseed has been an important source of edible vegetable oil in Asia for almost 4000 years. It was first grown in Canada during WWII as a source of high-quality lubricant for marine engines. After the war, Canadian PLANT-breeding programs, combined with changes in processing techniques, led to a reduction of erucic acid (very high consumption of which has been associated with heart lesions in laboratory animals) and glucosinolates (which cause enlarged thyroids and poor feed conversion in livestock). As a consequence, canola has become established as a major Canadian and European source of cooking oil, margarine, salad dressing and shortening. The meal remaining after oil extraction is a high-protein feed for livestock. Canola is grown on some 2 million ha of the prairies. In future, the winter form, popular in Europe, may be grown in Ontario. About half of Canadian production is processed domestically; the remainder, exported as seed. Sowing and harvesting methods are similar to those of spring CEREALS. *B. napus* canola varieties mature at the same time as wheat and grow 1-1.5 m tall. Although *B. campestris* matures 10-14 days earlier than *B. napus*, less is grown because varieties have a lower potential yield. Flowers have 4 bright yellow petals and, following fertilization by wind or insects, each develops a pod with 15-40 small, round seeds (1.5-2 mm diameter) arranged in 2 rows. Mature seeds contain 40-44% oil and have thin black, brown or yellow seed coats. R.K. DOWNEY

Canso, NS, Town, pop 1255 (1981c), inc 1901, is located on Chedabucto Bay, on the NE shore of mainland NS. Its name derives from the Micmac *Kamsok* ("the place beyond the cliffs"). As early as 1504 the French used Canso as a summer fishing base. During the 1700s the settlement was destroyed several times by natives, French-English conflicts and Revolutionary privateers. Successful settlement did not occur until 1812. Shipbuilding, trading and fishing became major industries. Between 1881 and 1894 transatlantic cables were landed here, making Canso a major communications link between N America and Europe. In 1955 the completion of the Canso Causeway, linking CAPE BRETON I with mainland NS, created one of the finest ice-free harbours in the world. Although its fishing industry is plagued by labour unrest and seasonal unemployment, 20th-century Canso has enjoyed a burst of industrial development.
HEATHER MACDONALD

Canso, Strait of, 27 km long, 3 km wide, 60 m deep, is a deep, narrow channel separating the Nova Scotian mainland and CAPE BRETON I. Formerly this waterway provided free communication between the waters of St Georges Bay in the Gulf of St Lawrence and the Atlantic Ocean. However, in the early 1950s, the Canso Causeway was built to carry rail and highway traffic between the mainland and the Island. The completion of the causeway has created a year-round ice-free port for the major towns along the strait, Port Hawkesbury and Mulgrave, and helped establish the area as an important pulpwood centre. But the closing of the strait has also cut off the supply of gulf-spawned lobster larvae to the Atlantic side. This is thought to be one of the major factors responsible for the precipitous decline of the lobster fishery on the southeastern Atlantic coast since the late 1950s. P.C. SMITH

Cantley, Thomas, businessman, politician (b at New Glasgow, NS 19 Apr 1857; d there 24 Feb 1945). Entering the iron-forging business as a youth when his province was rapidly industrializing, Cantley rose quickly and helped develop a modern steel complex in Pictou County. By 1915 he was president of the Nova Scotia Steel and Coal Corp and a member of the government's Shell Committee, which administered munitions contracts. His firm was the first in Canada to develop steel suitable for shell manufacture, a major contribution. He later served overseas and in 1925 was elected to the House of Commons for Pictou as a Conservative, remaining there until his appointment to the Senate in 1935. P.E. RIDER

Caouette, Joseph David Réal, politician, leader of the Social Credit Party (b at Amos, Abitibi, Qué 26 Sept 1917; d at Ottawa, 16 Dec 1976). Rising in the 1962 general election from virtual obscurity, Réal Caouette became a national political force as leader of the Québec SOCIAL CREDIT movement. Caouette joined the movement in 1939. He was elected to the Commons in a 1946 by-election as a member of the Union des électeurs. Unsuccessful in subsequent efforts to re-enter either the federal or the Québec Houses, Caouette allied his Ralliement des créditistes with the national Social Credit Party in 1961 and ran for the post of national leader. Defeated by Robert THOMPSON, he was appointed Thompson's deputy and Québec's leader. In the 1962 general election, which resulted in a Conservative minority government, 26 of the 30 Social Credit MPs elected were Caouette's followers. Caouette's and Social Credit's appeal in Québec was primarily to voters in rural and small-town ridings, and Caouette's dramatic and exciting oratory, both in person and on his 15-minute TV shows, raised him to the status of a major political figure in Québec. He was a devoted federalist, though many of his economic views, loosely drawn from more orthodox Social Credit positions, represented a radical revolt against large power structures, especially the banks. In September 1963 he broke with Thompson, to become leader of his own Ralliement des créditistes, joined by 12 Québec MPs. His party's strength remained relatively stable in subsequent elections. In 1971 he reunited his Québec national party and became national leader, a post he held until ill health forced him to yield it to André Fortin in 1976. WILLIAM CHRISTIAN

Cap aux Meules, Île du, Qué, 50 km^2, one of the Iles de la MADELEINE (Magdalen Islands) in the middle of the Gulf of ST LAWRENCE, is named after the mountain that supplies the stone used to make grindstones for flour mills. Historically linked to the Magdalens, its inhabitants are French-speaking and of Acadian descent. The sandstone island is round and quite mountainous; Butte du Vent (165 m) is surrounded by undulating plains that were once farmland stretching to the sea. Half the population on the Magdalens is concentrated in 3 main areas: Cap-aux-Meules, Fatima and Étang-du-Nord. Cap aux Meules's industrial and commercial activity includes fish plants, herring smokehouses, fishing ports, a seaport and lobster grounds. A thriving tourist industry has also developed because of the spectacular view from Butte du Vent, the unusual coastal relief, and the sand dunes extending as far as the eye can see. JEAN-MARIE DUBOIS AND PIERRE MAILHOT

Cap-de-la-Madeleine, Qué, City, pop 32 626 (1981c), inc 1923, is located on the N shore of the ST LAWRENCE R at its confluence with the Rivière ST-MAURICE, opposite TROIS-RIVIÈRES. Originally the site of a seigneury (1636) and a Jesuit mission (1640), by 1900 "the Cap" had 300 families who lived from agriculture and lumbering. The arrival of electricity, a railway and a quay set the stage for an industrial boom that began in 1909 with the Grès Falls Co, followed in 1912 by the Wayagamack Pulp and Paper Co (later integrated into Consolidated Corp). Industrialization brought major residential construction. A second development phase began in 1938 with the opening of International Foils Ltd (Reynolds), which still operates. Despite the arrival of Lupel Amiante, a subsidiary of the Cascades Group, industrial activities have slowed since the 1970s and the Cap is increasingly a residential suburb of Trois-Rivières. The sanctuary, Notre-Dame du Cap, built in 1714, is a national pilgrimage site. Construction of the octagonal basilica, renowned for its stained-glass windows, dates from 1974.
CLAUDINE PIERRE-DESCHÊNES

Cap des Rosiers, Anse du [Fr, "cove of the cape of rosebushes"] Named for the many wild rosebushes found there, this steep and shrub-covered promontory is located at the eastern extremity of the GASPÉ Peninsula. A line drawn from the N shore to Cap des Rosiers, according to the PROCLAMATION OF 1763, marks where the ST LAWRENCE R ends and the Gulf of ST LAWRENCE begins. It boasts the highest lighthouse in the Gaspé area (33 m, completed 1858) and borders on the eastern edge of FORILLON NATIONAL PARK (est 1971). A strategic contact point for shipping approaching the St Lawrence R, the cape was named by Samuel de CHAMPLAIN and appears on his map of 1632. It was here, in 1759, that the French first observed the approach of the British fleet sent to capture Québec City. DAVID EVANS

Cape Blomidon lies along the SE shore of the Bay of FUNDY at the mouth of MINAS BASIN, the site of some of the world's highest tides. A provincial park, high on the cape's red sandstone headland, is the home of the legendary GLOOSCAP, powerful man-god leader of the MICMAC, who, as the story goes, scattered agate and amethyst over this region. These semiprecious stones are avidly sought by modern rock hounds. Extending W from the cape is a fingerlike promontory called Cape Split, which divides Minas Channel on the N from Scots Bay and helps to create intense tidal rip currents near the tip. Strong tidal streams are also responsible for the continual erosion of the Blomidon headlands. The name is likely a contraction of the nautical phrase "blow me down." P.C. SMITH

Cape Bonavista, elev 15-30 m, is the bare, rocky extremity of the Bonavista Pen, N of BONAVISTA in eastern Newfoundland. Traditionally the landfall (1497) of John CABOT (who is said to have named it), it was from 1713 to 1783 the southern terminus of the FRENCH SHORE. One of Newfoundland's earliest lighthouses was built here 1843 and declared a provincial historic site in 1970. It was subsequently restored and opened as a museum. ROBERT D. PITT

Cape Breton Highlands National Park (est 1936) stretches across the northern tip of CAPE BRETON I, occupying 950 km^2 of a high plateau covered with bogs and forest and dotted with ponds. Around the seaward edge of the park are 300 m cliffs, sheltered coves and rocky beaches, all under constant attack from the Atlantic Ocean. VEGETATION is varied: hardwood forests of maple, beech and yellow birch contrast with muskeg and heath barrens. Wildlife species include moose, white-tailed deer, black bear, snowshoe hare, bobcat, lynx and, possibly, cougar. Over 230 species of birds have been recorded. MICMAC were living in the area at the time John CABOT is thought to have landed (1494). Portuguese fishermen were the first Europeans to settle, followed by French and Scottish immigrants. Tradition is strong in fishing villages near the park. French is the first language of many residents, while the use of Gaelic eflects a Highland heritage. The 298 km Cabot 'rail, a modern scenic highway, is one way to xperience the park's beauty. LILLIAN STEWART

:ape Breton Island, NS, 10 311 km², a rugged nd irregularly shaped island, approximately 75 km long by 135 km at its widest, is located at he eastern extremity of the Gulf of ST LAWRENCE. ts land mass slopes upward from S to N, culmiating in the massive highlands of its northern ape, the highest elevation in the Atlantic reion. A saltwater lake (the BRAS D'OR) forms the sland's core and has provided the only signifiant access to its interior for purposes of setlement. Divided politically into 4 counties — ape Breton, Inverness, Richmond and Victoria – it is separated from mainland NS by the narow Str of CANSO (bridged by a 2 km causeway in 955), and from neighbouring Newfoundland y the 120 km wide CABOT STR. Its name likely erives from the Basque Cap Breton, a location ear Bayonne, France.

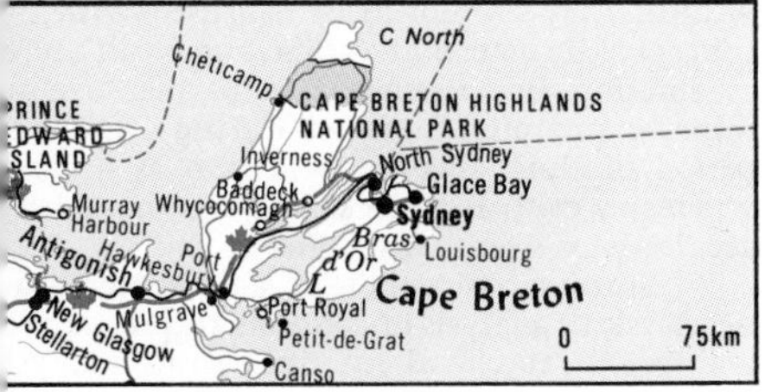

Its population of 70 088 (1981c) is one-fifth of IS's total, but over 70% live in industrialized ape Breton County, which has been steadily eclining in numbers since WWII. Its principal ity is SYDNEY, a large industrial, commercial and dministrative centre, which is surrounded by a roup of declining coal-mining towns, the largst of which is GLACE BAY. More recently, there as been a surge of urbanization in the SE corner f the island, where a substantial oil-refining nd pulp- and paper-making industry has merged at Port Hawkesbury, taking advantage f the large harbour created by construction of e causeway to the mainland.

History The island was probably known to ASQUE fishermen as early as the 15th century nd was sighted and identified by John CABOT 497) and Jacques CARTIER (1534). Claimed by e French as part of Acadia, it remained largely ndeveloped and unsettled, apart from a minor ole as a fur-trading and fishing outpost. When e TREATY OF UTRECHT, 1713, ceded most of Acaia to the British, the French retained Cape Breon, which they renamed Île Royale. Shortly ereafter, they began construction of the fortess of LOUISBOURG at a small harbour along the E coast. For its time, it was the most imposing uropean-style fortress in N America. When ouisbourg and the rest of New France fell to the ritish during the SEVEN YEARS' WAR, the fortress 'as destroyed; the TREATY OF PARIS, 1763 ceded the land and France's remaining possessions in e area to the British.

Joined to NS in 1763, Cape Breton remained rgely undeveloped until 1784, when it was set side as one of several separate jurisdictions for e LOYALIST refugees. The Loyalists, who made ydney the capital of their new colony, were oon overwhelmed by successive waves of Scotsh immigrants. They occupied most of the vailable arable land along the seacoasts and round Bras d'Or Lake, and with a few hundred turning Acadians made up the bulk of the island's largely rural population, which subsisted ostly on farming and the inshore fishery. In 820 the island was returned to the jurisdiction f NS following almost 40 years of tempestuous eparate status.

Economy The emergence of a vital and exansive coal-mining industry from the 1830s on ompletely transformed the island economy. The mines surrounding Sydney harbour attracted the excess population of the already overpopulated rural areas and weighted the island towards the industrial base emerging in Cape Breton County. While the area was the most dynamic growth zone in the Atlantic region up to WWI, its boom was short-lived. When the coal mines were depleted and the steel mill became obsolete, the central Canadian capitalists who had come to dominate the industrial advance abandoned the area for greener fields, leaving the industrial sector to survive on a succession of inadequate subventions from federal and provincial governments. The result was a heritage of industrial decline, labour unrest and a massive out-migration.

Today the island is recovering somewhat. New coal seams are being exploited and the industry has rebounded somewhat from its post-WWII collapse. Smaller industries have taken root to some extent, and the rebirth of the fishery and an expanding pulp and paper industry has combined with the oil refineries and the promise of offshore petroleum resources in pointing to a better future.

Institutions Cape Breton has a proud Scottish heritage that finds expression in lively performing arts and a commitment to maintaining traditional crafts. In addition, there are several important educational and cultural institutions: the University College of Cape Breton in Sydney, the Miners' Memorial Museum in Glace Bay, the Alexander Graham Bell Museum in BADDECK and Fortress Louisbourg (a magnificent reconstruction of the 18th-century site). CAPE BRETON HIGHLANDS NATIONAL PARK preserves the rugged beauty of the island's northern cape, around which curves the scenic Cabot Trail.

D.A. MUISE

Cape Breton Strikes, 1920s After WWI Cape Breton coal and steel industries faced severe difficulties in maintaining central Canadian markets and in surviving the financial mismanagement of a new controlling company, the British Empire Steel Corporation. Meanwhile, the growth of trade unionism among coal miners and steelworkers increased the bargaining power of local workers and limited their employers' freedom of action. Dramatic confrontations resulted, repeatedly bringing provincial police and federal troops into Sydney, Glace Bay and other communities. In 1922 the corporation imposed a one-third wage reduction on the coal miners; in response, the miners reduced production by one-third. In 1924 and 1925 the miners resisted further wage cuts, and the long battle culminated in the shooting of New Waterford coal miner William Davis by company police on 11 June 1925. In 1923 the Sydney steelworkers attempted to gain union recognition; following violence by the provincial police, the coal miners joined in a sympathetic strike which ended in the arrest of 2 union leaders for seditious libel and the temporary suspension of District 26 by the international office of the United Mine Workers of America. Sydney steelworkers reorganized successfully in the 1930s; mindful of the earlier strife, Prem Angus L. Macdonald introduced the NS Trade Union Act (1937), protecting the right to collective bargaining. During the 1920s the coal miners maintained their union and partly protected their economic position. The use of armed forces in labour disputes, a highly unpopular aspect of the Cape Breton strikes, was later virtually abandoned by the federal government. Two Cape Breton leaders, J.B. MCLACHLAN and Silby BARRETT, emerged as figures of national importance in the Canadian labour movement. Despite a legacy of hardship and bitterness, the Cape Breton strikes of the 1920s also marked the growth of strong support for public ownership of the coal and steel industries (achieved in 1967) and a persistent local tradition of working-class consciousness.

DAVID FRANK

Cape Dorset, NWT, UP, pop 784 (1981c), is situated on Dorset I, SW of BAFFIN I, 1891 air km NE of YELLOWKNIFE. The rolling tundra surrounding the community is actually part of the Kingnait Mtn range. It is the entry point to the nesting grounds of the blue goose at the Dewey Soper Bird Sanctuary, NE of the community. While the traditional economy is based on hunting and sealing, many of the majority Inuit population are artists. The famous Dorset printmaking shop is located there. ANNELIES POOL

Cape Kildare extends eastward into the Gulf of St Lawrence, at the northern end of PEI. Named by Samuel Holland in 1765 after James, 20th earl of Kildare, it is part of a series of capes in the area known as the Kildare Capes. The harvesting and sale of IRISH MOSS, a seaweed used as a

Cape Dorset, NWT, home of the famous Dorset printmaking shop and of many Inuit artists (*photo by Sherman Hines/Masterfile*).

stabilizer in food processing, is an important local industry. P.C. SMITH

Cape North is the northern promontory on CAPE BRETON I. Its bald, rocky headland rises abruptly from the shoreline to heights of over 300 m. Nearby Sugarloaf Mtn is thought by some to have been John CABOT's landfall in 1497. The currents around the cape are generally directed out of the Gulf of St Lawrence as part of the Cape Breton Current. However, violent local storms with sustained easterly winds can create opposing flow near the coast and strong current rips. Cape North has long been an important centre for communications. The first undersea telegraph cable from Newfoundland came ashore here in 1856 and the first transatlantic cable was brought to nearby Money Pt in 1872. P.C. SMITH

Cape Race, elev 30-40 m, is the southeastern extremity of Newfoundland's AVALON PENINSULA. Named for its flat-topped (Portuguese, *raso*) cliffs, it has a barren appearance that creates a stark impression for transatlantic passengers arriving in Canada by sea. It is the site of a powerful transmitter for the Loran C navigation system, an important aid to mariners. Icebergs may be seen in the waters off the cape from March to July. In 1977 Cape Race became a national historic site. P.C. SMITH

Cape Sable is the southernmost point of land on CAPE SABLE I, which lies off the southwestern tip of Nova Scotia. It is composed of shifting sand (French, *sable*) dunes up to 9 m high and is nearly joined to the island by a sandy beach transversed by Hawk Channel. Hawk Inlet, on the E side of the channel, dries at low tide. Cape Sable Light, a white octagonal tower on the cape, houses a radar-transponding beacon in addition to a light and foghorn, important navigational aids to mariners in the often fogbound coastal waters. P.C. SMITH

Cape Sable Island is a flat, wooded island off the southwestern tip of Nova Scotia. Connected to the mainland by a causeway on the N side, it shelters the waters of Barrington Bay to the E. There are 2 main settlements on the island, Clark's Harbour on the western side and The Hawk on the southern tip. The primary industry is fishing, with major landings of ground fish (cod, haddock), lobster and scallops. There is also a strong tradition of boatbuilding here: the first Cape Island boat, the familiar craft of Atlantic inshore fishermen, was launched in 1905. In summer the island is often shrouded in fog, produced when warm, moist continental air encounters the unusually cold surface waters off CAPE SABLE. The low sea surface temperatures are caused by intense tidal mixing that blends cold deep water with the warmer surface layer. These conditions also support a highly productive ecosystem and are, in part, responsible for the valuable fisheries. P.C. SMITH

Cape St Mary's, elev 105 m, on Newfoundland's AVALON PENINSULA, is the steep and spectacular terminus of the land separating ST MARY'S BAY and PLACENTIA BAY near rich fishing grounds. The site of a lighthouse since 1860, the cape and an adjacent rock island have been a provincial seabird sanctuary since 1964. It is home to large populations of birds, including one of N America's largest gannet colonies. ROBERT D. PITT

Cape Scott Provincial Park (est 1973, 50 km^2), on the NW tip of VANCOUVER I, BC, includes 64 km of coast, with 23 km of sandy beaches interspersed by rocky headlands. The land rises inland to Mt St Patrick (415 m) and there is a 44 ha body of freshwater, Eric Lk. The park has a rigorous climate with storms and heavy rainfalls; annual precipitation is 375-500 cm. Forests include cedar, pine, hemlock and fir, with a dense undergrowth of salal, salmonberry, huckleberry and fern. Animals include deer, elk, bears, otters, cougars and wolves, with seals, sea lions and gulls along the shore, and migrating Canada geese at Hansen Lagoon. Coastal Indians first occupied and exploited the area. Cape Scott was named in 1786 after David Scott, a Bombay merchant who backed a trading voyage along the coast under Captains Guise and Lowrie. In 1897 and 1910 Danish pioneers made unsuccessful attempts to settle, leaving only place names and abandoned buildings as evidence. Trails provide the only access, the trailhead being reached by public highway and logging road from Port Hardy, some 60 km East. There are few facilities except primitive, often muddy trails that run from the trailhead to Cape Scott, a distance of 27 km. JOHN S. MARSH

Cape Spear, elev 75 m, most easterly point in N America (excluding Greenland), is located 6.7 km SE of the entrance to St John's harbour, Nfld. A rocky, windswept promontory of Precambrian formation, with a thin, sporadic cover of till and bog, it was first named by the Portuguese (*spera*, "hope"). It has been a prime landfall for transatlantic navigators, and since 1836 has been the site of an important lighthouse, continuously in use until 1955, when a modern structure was built. During WWII gun emplacements, now largely demolished, were built on the cape. In 1962 Cape Spear was declared a National Historic Park, and the original lighthouse has been restored to its 1840 condition. MICHAEL STAVELEY

Capilano Review (1972-) is a magazine of literature and the arts, founded at Capilano College, N Vancouver, as an offshoot of the creative-writing program. The magazine publishes poetry, fiction, reviews and also drama. It has made something of a speciality of interviews with writers, and explores those points of contact between the arts offered by experimental movements such as concrete and visual poetry. Most contributors are West Coast Canadian writers, but *Capilano Review* has published many translations of works by foreign experimental writers. GEORGE WOODCOCK

Cape Spear, Nfld, the most easterly point of the N American continent (*photo by Jim Merrithew*).

Capital and Wealth are interrelated concepts in ECONOMICS, and capital is also a component of wealth. They are not to be confused with the concept of income. Both capital and wealth refer to amounts in existence at a particular time rather than amounts created during a specified period of time. Income in a year is a flow whereas wealth is a stock that may have been accumulated over many years.

Within economics there is a mainstream (or neoclassical) analysis of concepts such as capital and wealth, and an alternative, radical analysis (*see* ECONOMICS, RADICAL). The 2 schools of thought define capital differently and disagree as well on questions of growth and distribution. Neoclassical economists isolate 3 kinds of "factors of production": land (natural resources), labour and capital. Capital thus refers to man-made means of production, including machines, factories and public infrastructure such as transportation facilities. Recently, this concept of capital has been expanded to include "human capital," ie, characteristics of the labour force that are "man-made" in the sense that they reflect investments in such things as education and health. Economists carefully distinguish capital from the financial assets (stocks, bonds) that are referred to as capital in everyday parlance.

The concept of wealth includes, in addition to capital, the stock of land and raw materials that was distinguished from capital in the above breakdown of factors of production. Capital, then, is defined as a particular factor of production, and wealth as the value of all means of

Cape St Mary's, Nfld, located on the Avalon Peninsula. The cape and an adjacent rock island became a provincial seabird sanctuary in 1964 (*photo by John deVisser*).

production, resources and accumulated output in an economy.

Neoclassical economists focus on the expansion of capital as a major source of growth. Capital can be used to produce consumer goods or investment (capital) goods. Net investment affects the economy's ability to produce goods in the future by changing the amount and quality of capital goods available. This increases the economy's potential output. Investment opportunities must increase as rapidly as investment in capital goods, or else profit rates will fall and the economy will decline. This expansion of opportunities is the result of technological progress. Growth also results from changes in the quality of capital without absolute increases in net investment; this is referred to as "embodied technical change." Change in the quality of labour provides an additional source of growth. The process of growth increases the wealth of the economy.

Issues of distribution were the major concern of 19th-century economists, but modern neoclassical economists are more concerned with issues of growth. Most capital in a mixed capitalist economy, such as Canada's, is owned privately, although publicly owned companies such as CROWN CORPORATIONS also own capital, and there is such a thing as "social capital," eg, roads. Only a small portion of the population owns physical capital other than houses or shares bought through pensions or insurance funds (these shares represent a portion of the ownership of physical capital); most Canadians own only their own labour. The concentration of capital ownership has tended to increase as the number of firms competing in each industry decreases and as "conglomerate" firms develop. Even though each corporation may be owned by many shareholders rather than a single family, the proportion of the population involved in direct capital ownership is very small. A 1975 study of the 146 private Canadian-owned companies with assets of over $100 million concluded that "of the 136 companies for which we have information, 68% are controlled by individuals, groups of associates or by families." Furthermore, in Canada, more than one-half of the 100 largest industrial firms were foreign owned in the 1980s. Economists do not always agree about how the high concentration of ownership and the high proportion of foreign ownership and FOREIGN INVESTMENT affects output, income and growth in Canada's economy.

Wealth in Canada is also distributed unequally. It has been estimated that the top 10% of Canadian families own 58% and the top 1% own 20% of all net assets. These assets include stocks, business equity, bonds, insurance and pension plans and other financial holdings, real estate, houses, cars and other consumer durables. Inequality of a distribution can be measured by a "Gini ratio," according to which the value of 0 denotes perfect equality (eg, each 10% of the population owns 10% of the wealth) and a value of one denotes extreme inequality (eg, one individual has 100% of the wealth). In 1983 it was estimated that the Gini ratio of wealth distribution in Canada was 0.69 compared to 0.39 for income. Inequality in wealth in Canada is higher than in the US and lower than in the UK. Neoclassical economists do not consider wealth inequality to be a major economic problem. In their analysis, differences in income or wealth primarily reflect differences in individual initiative, ability, risk-taking or luck (*see* INCOME DISTRIBUTION).

Radical economics, which is founded in Marxist economics, examines the source of the "surplus" produced in an economy above and beyond the production needed for subsistence, and the control and distribution of this surplus. The concept of surplus is related to capital and wealth. This analysis focuses on the relations of production rather than simply on the abstract combination of factors necessary to produce a product (*see* MARXISM) eg, who owns the inputs, who controls the production process, who owns the product and who controls any surpluses produced. Because these relations of production affect the process of growth, capital accumulation and the distribution of wealth, in this analysis problems of growth and distribution result from the relations of production in the economy.

To Marx, "capital is, by definition, any value that is increased by surplus value." A merchant exchanges money for commodities which are then sold for more money. An industrialist pays money to buy machines (constant capital) and labour (variable capital), which are used to produce commodities that sell for more than the initial outlay. In both cases capital is used and more capital is created or accumulated; "capital" thus represents control over the means of production and the ability to increase the value of this capital.

This real increase of capital originates in the production process rather than in the realm of market exchange. Socialist economists call this increase "surplus value" and argue that it ultimately derives from labour's ability to produce greater amounts of value than it is paid for, or than it costs workers to live. This production of surplus is common to all societies beyond the bare subsistence level, but the manner in which surplus is extracted and controlled differs in various societies. In Canada, surplus value is created in production by free labour in return for a wage. The surplus then belongs to the owner of capital who has purchased the factors of production, organized production and owns the product. This surplus value is the basis of growth and of the accumulation of capital.

Finally, according to this analysis, the class division between labour and owners of capital is the fundamental inequality in the Canadian economy and the force that defines social, economic and political relations in Canadian society; the distribution of capital and wealth therefore reflects differential economic power rather than differential individual abilities. Economists using this analysis predict increasing concentration of capital in Canada (a prediction consistent with the data on corporate concentration and capital distribution) and uneven growth and recurring economic crises.

Regardless of the analytical interpretations used, the process of growth of capital and wealth in Canada has been both dramatic and uneven, and the distribution of wealth and capital highly unequal. MARTHA MACDONALD

Capital Formation The "capital stock" is one of the basic determinants of an economy's ability to produce income for its members. Composed of equipment, buildings and intermediate goods not themselves directly consumed, the capital stock produces a flow of services which, when combined with labour, yield "value-added," the sum of which is the value of all goods and services produced in the economy. This, in turn, is the NATIONAL INCOME received in the economy. "Capital formation" is simply the enlargement of the capital stock. The higher the rate of capital formation, the more rapid is the growth of the economy's productive capacity and, hence, the more rapid the growth of aggregate income.

Capital formation may be viewed in several ways. First, since part of the capital stock wears out or loses some of its economic potential each year ("depreciation"), provision must be made for its replacement. A certain amount of capital formation must be allocated to depreciation in order for the economy's capital stock to remain constant. Second, after depreciation charges, additions to the capital stock are known as "net investment" or "net capital formation." Third, since capital formation may be financed by both domestic savings and foreign savings, and because Canadians can invest their savings abroad, a distinction is made similar to that found in Canada's national accounts: Gross National Capital Formation (GNCF) measures the flow of real new capital created by Canadians, whereas Gross Domestic Capital Formation (GDCF) measures new capital created in Canada by Canadians and foreigners alike. The aggregate income flows to which these correspond are, respectively, GROSS NATIONAL PRODUCT (GNP) and Gross Domestic Product (GDP); the former is the income received by Canadians from all sources and the latter is the aggregate income received by all individuals from the Canadian domestic economy.

The composition of real capital formation has changed spectacularly in modern history. The important broad categories of investment are construction of both industrial plant and residential buildings; producers' equipment; and inventory adjustment. In a simple trading economy such as early 19th-century Canada, inventories of export goods such as cereal grains and timber constituted a major portion of capital formation alone. As the economy grew in size and took on more industrial characteristics, the importance of inventories declined while the relative importance of construction and producers' equipment increased. Also, more producers' equipment came to be located in the manufacturing sector as agriculture and primary resource harvesting declined in relative importance. In contemporary Canada, construction accounts for about two-thirds of all capital formation, machinery and equipment are about 30% of investment, and inventories are less than 5%. The creation of real capital is financed through the use of savings. Since savings represent a supply of funds that can be loaned, mechanisms evolved to marshal and channel savings to the particular types of capital formation. This process of capital mobilization generally required specialized financial intermediaries (*see* BANKING; INSURANCE; TRUST COMPANY) which of course make a profit from the act of financial arbitrage. *See* BALANCE OF PAYMENTS; CANADA'S ECONOMIC PROSPECTS, ROYAL COMMISSION ON; CANADIAN-AMERICAN ECONOMIC RELATIONS; CAPITAL AND WEALTH; ECONOMICS, RADICAL; FOREIGN INVESTMENT. DONALD G. PATERSON

Reading: K.A.H. Buckley, *Capital Formation in Canada, 1896-1930* (1955); O.J. Firestone, *Canada's Economic Development, 1867-1953* (1958); W.L. Marr and D.G. Paterson, *Canada: An Economic History* (1980).

Capital Punishment Under British law prevailing in Canada until 1859 some 230 offences, including stealing turnips and being found disguised in a forest were punishable by death. By 1865 only MURDER, TREASON and RAPE were capital offences. The drive either to limit or abolish capital punishment began in 1914, when Robert Bickerdike presented a private member's bill calling for its abolition, but the law remained unchanged despite frequent submissions to Parliament. In 1967, a government bill to apply mandatory life imprisonment in all murder cases, except when the victim was an on-duty police officer or prison guard, was passed (by a vote of 105 to 70) for a 5-year trial period. Another trial period was initiated in 1973, supported by a 13-vote majority. By a majority of 6 votes, the House of Commons abolished hanging in 1976 (although under the National Defence Act capital punishment can still be used for cowardice, desertion, unlawful surrender and spying for the enemy). The last execution in Canada occurred in 1962.

Recently there has been a heated public debate over whether capital punishment should be reinstated. Although those in favour claim it is an effective deterrent to homicide, the majority of studies in Western societies conclude that murder rates have remained stable or declined with the decreasing use of capital punishment. Neither abolition nor reintroduction of capital punishment have been shown to affect homicide rates significantly, and there appears to be no difference in the homicide rates of police officers and prison guards for American states that have retained capital punishment compared to those that have abolished it. Widely publicized executions might reduce homicides, but only for brief periods. PAUL GENDREAU

Capote, a hooded greatcoat rather like a parka, usually worn with a sash around the waist, popular with habitants of New France and French Canadian traders and trappers. The word is derived from the French word for "cape." JOHN ROBERT COLOMBO

Capper, Stewart Henbest, architect, educator, army officer (b at London, Eng Dec 1859; d at Cairo, Egypt 8 Jan 1925). He graduated in classics from Edinburgh U 1880 and in 1884 entered the École des beaux-arts, Paris. Returning to Edinburgh 1887, he soon set up his own practice. Through William Peterson, principal of McGill in Montréal, and G. Baldwin Brown, former colleagues at Edinburgh, Capper became the first Macdonald Professor of Architecture at McGill 1896-1903. He initiated practical and theoretical training based on his knowledge of European architecture and encouraged the study of architectural history and the development of national architectural styles. He held a similar position at Victoria U in Manchester until his resignation in 1912 for health reasons. He continued a military career, begun in Montréal, as a major in the Manchester Volunteers, and went to Egypt in 1914. Declared unfit for active duty, he became a military censor because of his extensive knowledge of languages. After demobilization he continued similar work in Cairo. ROBERT LEMIRE

Captain of Militia (*capitaine de milice*), *see* ARMED FORCES.

Caraquet, NB, Town, pop 4315 (1981c), inc 1961, is located 68 km NE of Bathurst. Its houses line the Baie de Caraquet, a rocky section of CHALEUR BAY's southern coast, offering magnificent views of the sea and the GASPÉ PENINSULA. Attracted by the rich fishing grounds, the first French settlers arrived about 1750. ACADIAN refugees, Québec fishermen and English-speaking traders followed, and from 1837-1939, the Jersey-based Robin fishing company dominated the economy. Local industry still depends on the excellent harbour and on fishing and boatbuilding, despite government-subsidized efforts to attract other industries.

A centre of Acadian religion and culture, Caraquet saw riots in 1875 when the government threatened to stop funding the convent school. The Sacré Coeur Coll, operating here 1899-1915, hosted the Acadian Convention of 1905. The Acadian Federation of Caisses Populaires headquarters and the Acadian Museum are in Caraquet, and the Acadian Historical Village is just outside. The Caraquet Festival attracts the best Acadian composers and performers. SHEILA ANDREW

Carbonear, Nfld, Town, pop 5335 (1981c), inc 1948, is located on the W shore of CONCEPTION BAY. The name may come from the Spanish *Carbonera* ("a seller of charcoal"), or the French family name *Carbonnier* or place-name *La Carbonnière*. Near excellent fishing grounds, Carbonear was first fished in the early 1600s and in 1631 Nicholas Guy from the CUPIDS colony was fishing and farming there. It was settled in the late 1600s by English West Country fishermen and Channel Islanders. Nearby Carbonear I was fortified in the 1860s and was the only Newfoundland site to resist French attacks in 1696

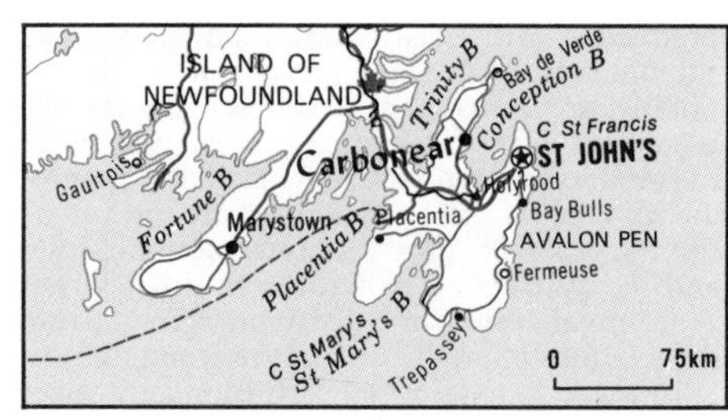

and 1697, although Carbonear itself was razed. The town again fell to the French in 1704 and 1705, and was the object of numerous other attacks by French and American privateers until the early 1800s. With the rise of the seal hunt and the Labrador cod fishery, Carbonear became a major commercial centre in the 1800s. Violent political riots here in the early and mid-1800s led to the dissolution of the Newfoundland Legislature 1840 and the suspension of the constitution. In the 1900s the economy diversified; Carbonear has become a regional service, transportation, government and fish-processing centre. JANET E.M. PITT AND ROBERT D. PITT

Carcross, YT, UP, pop 216 (1981c), is located at the N end of Bennett Lk, 70 km S of Whitehorse. The WHITE PASS AND YUKON RY preempted the townsite in 1898 and made it a stopping point on the line to Whitehorse. Originally Caribou Crossing, the name was changed (1904) to end confusion with places of the same name in Alaska and BC. William C. BOMPAS, who established a boarding school for native children here (1901) is buried at Carcross, as are Kate Carmack, "Skookum" Jim Mason and Tagish Charlie, who were associated with the KLONDIKE gold discovery. H. GUEST

Cardinal, Douglas Joseph, architect (b at Red Deer, Alta 7 Mar 1934). Cardinal was the eldest of 8 children. His father, half Blackfoot, was a provincial wildlife warden and his mother a nurse. Educated at St Joseph's Convent School and at high school in Red Deer, he enroled in the School of Architecture at UBC in 1953 but was asked to withdraw in his second year, partly because his designs were considered too radical and partly because his background was not considered appropriate. After work and travel in Mexico, Cardinal enrolled at U of Texas in 1956, graduating with honours in 1963 and returning to Red Deer to apprentice with Bissell and Holman. His first commission was the round Guloien House at Sylvan Lake, followed by St Mary's Roman Catholic Church at Red Deer, generally considered his masterpiece. Structural calculations for St Mary's complex shape had to be made by computer, and Cardinal later became the first western Canadian architect to convert to electronic drawings. In the 1970s Cardinal produced an erratic but innovative body of work and established his reputation for designing curving brick buildings. In 1983 he was awarded the commission to design the $93-million NATIONAL MUSEUM OF MAN in Hull, Qué, an achievement hinting at future recognition. In the early 1970s, Cardinal studied native religion and became involved in numerous Indian and Métis issues. He is a rare synthesis of native sensibility with Western technology, a Métis thriving in the professional world.

Cardinal, Harold, Indian leader, author (b at High Prairie, Alta 27 Jan 1945). Member of the Sucker Creek Reserve, he became in 1968 the youngest elected president of the Indian Assn of Alberta. During his 9 terms in office 1968-77, he initiated many programs to affirm Indian culture, religion and traditions. He helped draft the "Red Paper" of 1970, titled *Citizens Plus*, and authored 2 strongly critical statements on Canadian Indian policy, *The Unjust Society* (1969) and *The Rebirth of Canada's Indians* (1977). Leaving provincial native politics, he was the first Indian appointed regional director general of Indian affairs in Alberta, where he undertook several innovative reforms. After a controversial 7-month term, he left the public service and subsequently worked as a consultant to Indian bands in northern Alberta. He was elected chief of the Sucker Creek band in 1982-83 and returned to national Indian politics in 1983 when he was appointed vice-chief for the prairie region under the ASSEMBLY OF FIRST NATIONS. IAN A.L. GETTY

Cardston, Alta, Town, pop 3267 (1981c), inc 1901, is located 75 km SW of Lethbridge. It was named for Charles Ora Card (1839-1906), son-in-law of Brigham Young, who led a group of MORMONS to Canada from Utah (1887). He was the first mayor of the town, which grew as agriculture developed. Canada's only Mormon temple, built of white granite on the plan of a Maltese cross, was built in Cardston (1913-23). ERIC J. HOLMGREN

Canada's only Mormon temple, built of white granite, at Cardston, Alta (*photo by Richard Vroom*).

Career Counselling One of the major responsibilities of schools is to prepare students for employment and one of the ways they achieve this is through career counselling. Guidance counsellors are specialized teachers hired by schools to aid students in making educational and personal decisions regarding career opportunities. Counsellors sometimes use guidance courses, which introduce students to issues in the work world, and sometimes administer tests or provide other means of assisting students in matching their skills to job requirements. They may organize work experience for students or provide career-education materials for classroom use. The motivation to provide career counselling developed from early 20th-century educational reforms. Provision for the appointment of guidance counsellors was first made in 1921 in the Ontario Vocational Education Act. The number and role of counsellors gradually increased in all the provinces, but it was not until the 1960s that specialized guidance personnel were well established in Canadian schools.

Vocational guidance has been controversial since its inception. Many have challenged the need for schools to play a vocational, rather than an academic, role. As youth UNEMPLOYMENT has increased, counsellors have been criticized for lacking sufficient information about the job market and for being unable to match students to jobs. Some efforts have been made to shift career counselling to outside the schools, eg, into manpower and labour information centres. As new forms of testing and of work-related curriculum have been introduced, the biases in the materials have been questioned.

The objective of counselling is to increase opportunities for all students to achieve satisfaction and rewards from work, but all students do not have equal access to jobs. Because many jobs require post-secondary degrees, students counselled to discontinue schooling are denied access to employment opportunities. The research evidence reveals that male students, students from higher social-class backgrounds, and students from white, Anglo-Saxon families occupy the better paid, interesting jobs — often because they have better education. Counsellors are more likely to encourage middle-class rather than working-class students to pursue academic work. Girls are often urged to take traditional "women's" courses and jobs, and are discouraged from unconventional career paths or from studying courses in mathematics and sciences.

To overcome these discriminatory practices, new materials, encouraging all students to think carefully about their options and interests, have been developed and career counsellors are being urged to use them.

M. LAZERSON AND JANE GASKELL

Reading: Al Herman, *Guidance in Canadian Schools* (1981).

Careless, James Maurice Stockford, historian (b at Toronto 17 Feb 1919). A graduate of U of T (1940) and Harvard (1950), Careless began his teaching career at U of T as lecturer in history in 1945. The analytical framework he developed for studying the rise of Canadian cities incorporated ideas from the FRONTIER THESIS and the STAPLE THESIS. He is perhaps best known for his elaboration of the METROPOLITAN-HINTERLAND THESIS. He has been honoured for his contributions to historical writing (Tyrrell Medal, 1962; Gov Gen's Award for *Canada: A Story of Challenge*, 1953, and *Brown of the Globe*, 1963), and has contributed to his profession through service on the boards of various historical societies and as mentor to a generation of urban historians. He was elected a fellow of the ROYAL SOCIETY OF CANADA (1962) and appointed University Professor at U of T (1977).

MARGARET E. MCCALLUM

Cariboo Road, running some 650 km along the FRASER RIVER CANYON between Yale and Barkerville, BC, was begun in 1862 to provide a wagon route to the goldfields of the Cariboo region of S-central BC. By 1860 gold returns from the area convinced Governor James DOUGLAS that a system of communication was necessary. A road to the interior would relieve the plight of the miners forced to pay exorbitant rates for supplies and would make the Fraser R the great commercial highway of BC. A contingent of Royal Engineers was brought from Britain to survey the route from Yale, at the head of navigation on the Fraser R, along extremely treacherous terrain to the administrative centre of the Cariboo. The work was begun by the army engineers who completed the 2 most difficult stretches — 10 km from Yale to Boston Bar and 15 km from Cook's Ferry along the Thompson R. Much of the road had to be blasted from solid rock. The rest of the construction was let out to private contractors, and the road was opened in 1864. The TRANS-CANADA HIGHWAY follows much of the route of this early road along the Fraser Canyon.

C.J. TAYLOR

Cariboo Road above Yale, BC, 1867-68. Much of the road had to be blasted from solid rock along the treacherous Fraser Canyon (*courtesy Public Archives of Canada/C-8077*).

Yukon bull caribou (*Rangifer tarandus*) (*photo by Stephen J. Krasemann/DRK Photo*).

Caribou, Canada's symbol of the North, represented on the 25-cent piece, belong to the DEER family (Cervidae). All caribou herds throughout Scandinavia, USSR, Alaska and Canada belong to the species *Rangifer tarandus*. In Canada, one subspecies, *R. t. pearyi*, lives on the arctic islands. A second group, barren-ground caribou, are found N of TREELINE in the NWT in summer, migrating S to northern Sask and Man in winter. The third group, woodland caribou, inhabit mountains and forests from BC to Nfld. Bulls have palmate antlers, as do barren-ground cows; not all woodland cows have antlers. Males use antlers for fighting during the breeding season in Oct, shedding them in early winter. Females shed their antlers at about the time they give birth to a single calf, at the end of May or beginning of June. Newborns weigh 5-9 kg, and follow their dams within an hour of birth. Adult bulls weigh 125-275 kg; females 91-136 kg. Caribou range from forest to tundra habitats, feeding heavily on ground lichens. They also eat mushrooms, leaves and plants, including grasses and sedges. Formerly, biologists believed caribou required lichens and that loss of lichens by fire had caused population declines. It is now recognized that fires are a natural aspect of northern ecosystems and that caribou are adapted to cope with the loss of lichen habitats. Before settlement, some 3-5 million caribou lived in N America; today, there are about one million. Caribou are extinct in NB, NS and large parts of Ont and BC. On the arctic islands, large numbers of Peary caribou starve in some years. Southern woodland caribou are susceptible to brain-worm disease transmitted from white-tail deer, and cannot coexist with high numbers of infected deer. Wolves have been the most constant threat, and much herding and migratory behaviour has evolved to minimize the impact of predation. Wolves often kill enough calves and adults to prevent population increase. If HUNTING is added to these losses, populations commonly decline. Even today, native peoples harvest thousands of caribou, waiting each year for the long line of migrating caribou that trek in single file down trails followed for millennia. In Oct 1984 some 10 000 migrating caribou were drowned attempting to cross the Caniapiscau R.

A.T. BERGERUD

Caribou Inuit, so named because of their almost total reliance on CARIBOU for food, clothing and shelter. During the 19th and early 20th centuries they occupied the barren grounds region to the W of Hudson Bay. The population of some 500 people was divided into 4 regional groups. They differed greatly from other Inuit in their dependence on inland resources, making only occasional visits to the coast to obtain sea mammal products either through hunting or by trading with coastal Inuit. When first studied by anthropologists during the 1920s, they were thought to be a remnant of an ancient way of life that existed before most Inuit groups descended to the coasts and became marine hunters. This view was based on their unique adaptation to the interior, and on the meagre and primitive character of their aboriginal material culture. It has since become apparent that the Caribou Inuit way of life was a recent phenomenon, originating after indirect (and, later, direct) involvement with European traders and whalers. Until the late 18th century, CHIPEWYAN Indians had occupied most of the Barren Grounds area. A few decades later, the Inuit of the W coast of Hudson Bay began to receive firearms which allowed them to hunt caribou more efficiently, and involvement in the FUR TRADE gave them an incentive to move to the interior. The meagreness of their aboriginal material culture came from the fact that, by the time they were studied by anthropologists, they had used and relied upon European technology for over a century.

The social organization of the Caribou Inuit was based on family relationships and partnerships, and families frequently moved from one regional group to another. Religion was based on Shamanism, and most of their language and beliefs were similar to those of other central Arctic INUIT groups. Their seasonal round of activities involved primarily fishing, and hunting caribou during the spring and fall migrations. During the fall hunt, populations gathered at a few good hunting spots and attempted to obtain enough food for the winter, when the majority of the caribou had moved S into the forests. Caribou skin tents were used during the summer months, and snow houses during the winter. The descendants of the Caribou Inuit now occupy the villages of Eskimo Point, Rankin Inlet, Baker Lake and Whale Cove. *See also* NATIVE PEOPLES, ARCTIC.

ROBERT MCGHEE

Carignan, Jean, "Ti-Jean," fiddler (b at Lévis, Qué 7 Dec 1916). The leading exponent of the Celtic tradition in French Canadian fiddling, he played the violin from age 4. He first played on street corners and later with various dance bands in the Montréal area. In 1956 he decided to perform only at concerts and folk festivals in N America and Europe. He premiered in 1976 a concerto written for him by André GAGNON and in 1979 was featured with Yehudi Menuhin on the TV series "The Music of Man." He was awarded the 1977 Prix de Musique Calixa-Lavallée. But the most memorable tribute to this fiddler who combines rare technical expertise with a true passion for music came in 1973 when 400 fiddlers from across N America gathered near Montréal to pay tribute to him.

RICHARD GREEN

Carignan-Salières Regiment, of some 1100 strong, sent from France in June 1665 to curb the devastating attacks of the IROQUOIS on Canadian settlements. By November a chain of forts had been built along the RICHELIEU R, blocking that main invasion route. When peace negotiations proved futile a foolhardy midwinter expedition was mounted: approximately 600 of the troops and 70 Canadians invaded the Mohawk canton in Feb 1666. Some of them were ambushed, but no harm was done to the enemy. Some 60 more of the French perished during the retreat to Canada. In September the regiment again invaded the Mohawk country, found the villages deserted, and burned them and the surrounding cornfields. In July 1667 the Iroquois finally came to terms. The regiment was recalled to France in 1668 but some 400 officers and men chose to settle on seigneuries along the Richelieu R, greatly strengthening the colony's defences, military ethos, and economy. W.J. ECCLES

Carle, Gilles, director, screenwriter (b at Maniwaki, Qué 31 July 1929). A prolific filmmaker, Carle is regarded as one of the most important talents in the Canadian film industry. During the 1940s and 1950s he was a graphic artist. He joined the NFB in 1960 when the French production unit was expanding. In 1965 he made his first feature film, *La Vie heureuse de Léopold Z,* a comedy. When the NFB subsequently rejected several projects, Carle began working independently. Supporting himself by producing TV commercials, he directed 3 feature films in 3 years, *Le Viol d'une jeune fille douce* (1968), *Red* (1969) and *Les Mâles* (1970). These films, combining Carle's commentary on Québec society with scenes of sex and violence, generated a large popular following. In 1972 he produced his greatest commercial success, *La Vraie Nature de Bernadette,* which marked the beginning of his association with actress Carole LAURE. This film earned him recognition in Europe where audiences were captivated by the quality of his direction and fresh approach. His second film with Laure, *La Mort d'un bûcheron* (1973), was also a critical success in Québec and France, although it was not widely distributed in Canada. An immensely skilled director, Carle blends eroticism, romanticism and fantasy to create films as fresh and original as *La Tête de Normande St-Onge* (1976). Despite his popular success in Québec and his international reputation, Carle has had financial difficulties. *L'Ange et la femme* (1977), which he produced himself on a small budget, defied the conventions of commercial cinema and had a mixed reception. In 1980 he tried his hand at musical comedy with *Fantastica.* In the following year, however, his production of *Les Plouffe,* adapted from Roger LEMELIN's TV series, was enthusiastically received, and provided in 1984 a follow-up, *Le Crime d'Ovide Plouffe.* After a dramatized documentary on chess players, *Jouer sa vie* (1982), Carle tackled another Québec literary classic, Louis HÉMON's *Maria Chapdelaine* (1983). PIERRE VÉRONNEAU

Carleton, Guy, 1st Baron Dorchester, army officer, governor of Québec (b at Strabane, Ire 3 Sept 1724; d near Maidenhead, Eng 10 Nov 1808). A colonel at the capture of Québec in 1759, he succeeded James MURRAY as governor in 1768. He advised the passing of the QUEBEC ACT in 1774 and administered it so as to support the Roman Catholic Church and to retain French CIVIL LAW. He overestimated the importance of the seigneurs, however, and was disappointed by Canadian passivity during the AMERICAN REVOLUTION. Though he repelled the American invasion of 1775-76, he was criticized for his slow pursuit of the retreating rebels. He resigned after quarrels with his councillors, especially Chief Justice Peter Livius. In 1782-83 he was commander in chief at New York, which he refused to evacuate until the LOYALIST refugees had been sent to safety. Influenced by William SMITH, he unsuccessfully proposed while in England a single governor general for BNA. He returned to Québec as governor in 1786. Anxious to encourage commerce with the American West, he interpreted the imperial ban on American imports to apply only to seaports. He opposed the division of the Province of Québec into Upper and Lower Canada and the elected assemblies provided for by the CONSTITUTIONAL ACT, 1791, but advised the retention of Montréal in the lower province. Expecting war with the US just before the signing of JAY'S TREATY in 1794, he made and inflammatory speech to Indians and ordered the reoccupation of Fort Miamis (Maumee, Ohio). Given a gentle reprimand, he insisted on resigning. S.R. MEALING

Reading: A.L. Burt, *Guy Carleton, Lord Dorchester, 1724-1808 (1955).*

Guy Carleton, 1st Baron Dorchester. Becoming governor of Québec in 1768, he sought to support the traditional bases of French Canadian society and opposed the elected assemblies provided for in the Constitutional Act, 1791 (*courtesy Public Archives of Canada/C-2833*).

Carleton, Thomas, British army officer, lieutenant-governor of NB (b in Ire *c*1735; d at Ramsgate, Eng 2 Feb 1817), brother of Guy CARLETON, Baron Dorchester. After military service in Europe and America, Carleton was appointed first lieutenant-governor of the newly created colony of New Brunswick on 28 July 1784. He held this position until his death in 1817, although he resided in England from 1803 on. Because of his Anglo-Irish and military background he sympathized with the LOYALIST elite's aspirations. Hence the early development of NB was shaped by Carleton and the Loyalist leaders, with the choice of capital, appointments, religious, political, educational and even economic decisions reflecting this alliance. Carleton had originally hoped his New Brunswick posting would lead to a more substantial military command. Disappointed in this and in the slow growth of the colony, along with an increasingly assertive Assembly-rights party by 1795, Carleton tired of his office. He took a leave of absence, destined to be permanent, in 1803. After 1807 there is little evidence that he played any role in NB affairs and no evidence that he intended to take up residence in the province again. Carleton had many critics during his lifetime and among historical observers but he deserves to be acknowledged as a founding father of NB. WILLIAM G. GODFREY

Carleton Place, Ont, Town, pop 5626 (1981c), inc 1890, located on the Mississippi R, 45 km SW of Ottawa at the junction of 2 CPR lines; it was founded (1818) by William Morphy and his sons. The name is a corruption of Carlton Place, a famous square in Glasgow, Scotland. Lumber mills and manufacturing, especially of textiles and stoves, drew power from nearby falls in the past. Now electronics and tourism dominate the economy. A plaque in Memorial Pk honours native son A. Roy BROWN, WWI flying ace. K.L. MORRISON

Carleton University, Ottawa, Ont, founded in 1942 as Carleton College to provide elementary university courses in the evening for government employees. The return of WWII veterans led to day courses and in 1946 the college acquired a building on First Avenue. Degree programs were established in arts, science, public administration and journalism, although the college did not receive a provincial charter until 1952. Officially it became a university in 1957 and moved to its present site on the Rideau R in 1959. It is governed by a president, a board of governors and a senate. A. Davidson DUNTON presided over the phenomenal growth between 1958 and 1972, with enrolment rising from 1000 to 7000 full-time students. By the end of the 1960s Carleton was offering degrees in engineering, architecture, industrial design and social work. It has faculties of arts, science, social sciences, engineering, and graduate studies, and offers a graduate degree in Canadian studies. The 1970s was a decade of consolidation, with steady growth in enrolment despite financial constraints. Carleton is a publicly supported institution. H. BLAIR NEATBY

Enrolment: Carleton University, 1982-83
(Source: Statistics Canada)

Full-time Undergrad	Full-time Graduate	Part-time Undergrad	Part-time Graduate
8 499	987	4 534	853

Carling, Sir John, brewer, politician (b in London Twp, Upper Canada 23 Jan 1828; d at London, Ont 6 Nov 1911). His father, Thomas C. Carling, a Methodist agricultural labourer, had emigrated from Yorkshire in 1818. At age 21 John joined the brewing and malting business which his father had established in 1843 near Victoria Barracks, London. He inherited the business in 1849 and continued as president, but he left its operation to his brother William and entered politics. He represented London as a Conservative in the assembly of the Province of Canada 1857-67 and in the Ontario Assembly 1867-73. After Confederation, Carling also sat in the House of Commons 1867-74, 1878-91 and 1892-95. He held several Cabinet posts, most notably as postmaster general, under John A. MACDONALD 1882-85, and minister of agriculture 1885-92. In 1893 he was created KCMG; he sat in the Senate 1891-92 and 1896 to his death. The incorporation of the Carling Brewing and Malting Co in 1883 helped to finance his political career. ALBERT TUCKER

Carmacks, YT, UP, pop 256 (1981c), is located on the YUKON R at the mouth of the Nordenskiold R, 175 km downstream from Whitehorse. It was named for George Washington Carmack, who built a cabin at the forks (1893), from which he traded for furs. Carmack found coal at the site and in 1896 was one of 3 prospectors who staked the claim on Bonanza Cr that touched off the KLONDIKE GOLD RUSH. Carmacks grew during the rush as a supply point and fuel stop for riverboats. Now a local improvement district, it remains a service centre for travellers on the Klondike and Campbell highways. H. GUEST

Carman, Albert, Methodist clergyman, teacher (b at Iroquois, Upper Canada 27 June 1833; d at Toronto 3 Nov 1917). Dr Carman was a skilled administrator and preacher, firmly committed to the warm, personal piety of traditional Methodism. Although he had spent 2 decades as a mathematics teacher and school administrator before becoming a clergyman, he opposed those who advocated the "higher criticism" or scientific study of the Bible, charging that they were undermining Christian faith. He was bishop of the Methodist Episcopal Church before the 1883 union of all Canadian Methodist hurches. Though a genial man, he took his personal authority seriously. As general superintendent after union until retirement, he successfully encouraged missions to prairie settlers. His last decade in office was marked by spectacular clashes with more liberal Methodists. He retired in 1915. TOM SINCLAIR-FAULKNER

Carman, Bliss, poet, editor, journalist (b at Fredericton 15 Apr 1861; d at New Canaan, Conn 8 June 1929). Of Puritan New England and LOYALIST descent, he attended University of New Brunswick, and Edinburgh and Harvard Universities. In 1890 he joined the editorial staff of the New York *Independent,* introducing Canadian poets to its readers, and later worked on *Cosmopolitan, Atlantic Monthly, Chap Book* and other literary journals. With *Low Tide on Grand Pré* (1893) and the 3 volumes of "Vagabondia" poems (1894-1900), Carman won international recognition. Some of his best-known work appeared in *The Pipes of Pan* (5 vols, 1902-05). His collected *Poems* (2 vols, 1904) and *Sappho* (1905) contain almost all his best lyrical output.

Carman conducted a syndicated newspaper column, essays from which were reprinted in 3 volumes, notably *The Kinship of Nature* (1903). With Mary Perry King, he collaborated on *The Making of Personality* (1908) and in that year moved to New Canaan. With Mrs King he wrote *Daughters of Dawn* (1913) and *Earth Deities and Other Masques* (1914). Suffering from tuberculosis, he spent many months during 1919 and 1920 in sanitaria. Upon recovery, he embarked on reading and lecture tours of Canada and the US which brought renewed popularity. In 1928 he was awarded the Lorne Pierce Gold Medal by the Royal Society of Canada. Carman's prose works reflect his wide interests but are otherwise undistinguished. As an inveterate letter writer, however, he did develop a lively, epistolary style, and he achieved in his best verse a few finely wrought lyrics of enduring quality.
H.P. GUNDY

Carmichael, Franklin, painter (b at Orillia, Ont 4 May 1890; d at Toronto 24 Oct 1945). A founding member of the GROUP OF SEVEN, Carmichael was active as a painter, industrial designer and teacher. In 1911 he apprenticed with the Toronto commercial-art firm Grip Ltd, where he met several artists who later formed the Group. He studied in Antwerp 1913-14, and then worked as a designer in Toronto, at the same time painting watercolours and oils of northern Ontario landscape. Such paintings as *Jackfish Village* (1926) exhibit elegant compositional structures and lyric charm, gentler in feeling than many paintings by other Group of Seven members. Carmichael was a founding member 1925 and president 1932-34 of the Canadian Society of Painters in Water Colour and a founding member in 1933 of the Canadian Group of Painters. He taught at the Ontario College of Art 1932-45. DOROTHY FARR

Carmichael, James William, shipbuilder-owner, merchant, politician (b at New Glasgow, NS 16 Dec 1819; d there 1 May 1903). Carmichael, son of New Glasgow's founder, James Carmichael, became its most prominent merchant, shipbuilder and shipowner. He supported the transition to manufacturing and in 1882 invested in Canada's first steel company, Nova Scotia Steel. A Liberal and federal MP 1867-71 and 1874-78, Carmichael's strong views against Confederation and in support of free trade brought electoral defeat in 1872, 1878, 1882 and 1896. Appointed to the Senate in 1899, he resigned in 1903. L.D. MCCANN

Reading: J.M. Cameron, *Political Pictonians* (1967).

Carnivorous Plants are flowering PLANTS with leaves adapted for trapping small animals. Pitcher plants (genera *Nepenthes, Sarracenia, Darlingtonia, Cephalotus*) have open, water-filled traps that act as pitfalls for insects attracted by nectar around the rim of the pitchers. In butterworts (*Pinguicula*), sticky leaf surfaces act as flypaper to trap prey; in sundews (*Drosera*), sticky, long-stalked glands serve the same function, then bend inwards to enfold the victim. In aquatic bladderworts (*Utricularia*), each of numerous submerged bladders has a trap door that springs open when trigger hairs around it are touched. The minute animal is then carried inside by the rush of water. Once trapped, the animal is digested by enzyme secretions or decomposed by micro-organisms. Its remains release soluble organic molecules (eg, amino acids) which supplement nutrients in short supply in the plant's habitat. Worldwide, about 500 species have been described and classified; 18 species occur in Canada, among them a single species of PITCHER PLANT (*Sarracenia purpurea*), common to eastern N American bogs. The best-known carnivorous plant, the Venus flytrap, does not occur in Canada. ERICH HABER

Reading: D.E. Schnell, *Carnivorous Plants of the US and Canada,* (1976).

Caroline After the abortive 1837 Upper Canadian REBELLION, its leader, William Lyon MACKENZIE, retreated with some 200 followers to Navy I in the Niagara R. There the *Caroline,* an American-owned ship based in Ft Schlosser, NY, was employed carrying supplies to the rebels. On 29 Dec 1837 a force of UC militia, led by Commander Andrew Drew, Royal Navy, found her moored at Schlosser. A brief encounter ensued, in which one American was killed. The *Caroline,* set ablaze and then adrift, foundered above the falls and sank. The incident exacerbated the already strained relations between Britain and America. J.E. REA

Caron, Sir Joseph-Philippe-René-Adolphe, politician (b at Québec C 24 Dec 1843; d at Montréal 20 Apr 1908). Seminary educated, trained as a lawyer and something of a *bon vivant,* Caron was a Conservative MP, 1873-1900, serving as minister of militia and defence, 1880-92, and postmaster-general, 1892-96. Caron oversaw the expansion of the tiny Canadian permanent force in 1883, but he put his party's political interests over the military reforms urged by the British government. A master of patronage but generally a weak minister, he was surprisingly effective in mobilizing a force to counter the NORTH-WEST REBELLION. Afterwards Caron stood by John A. MACDONALD in his determination to deal harshly with Louis RIEL. Caron was left out of the Cabinet formed in 1896 by Sir Charles TUPPER. NORMAN HILLMER

Carpmael, Charles, meteorologist (b at Streatham Hall, Eng 19 Sept 1846; d in Eng 21 Oct 1894). Carpmael directed the development and extension of the Canadian storm-warning and weather-forecasting services for more than a decade. Following graduation from Cambridge, he came to Canada in 1872 as deputy director of the national meteorological service and succeeded G.T. KINGSTON as director in 1880. Director until 1894, Carpmael expanded the activities of the service in astronomy and became responsible for a national time service in 1883. He was a charter fellow and officer of the RSC and an officer of the Royal Canadian Institute. MORLEY THOMAS

Carr, Emily, painter, writer (b at Victoria 13 Dec 1871; d there 2 Mar 1945). Her English parents had settled in Victoria where her father was a successful businessman. With her brother and 4 older sisters, Emily, a child of independent spirit, grew up in a disciplined, orderly household in the restricted social and intellectual climate of the small, island city. Orphaned in her teens she went in 1891 to study art at California School of Design in San Francisco, pursuing an interest that had little opportunity of serious development in Victoria. On her return home 2½ years later, she set up a studio and started art classes for children. A study trip to England in 1899 did little to advance her art, and a lengthy illness extended the stay into 1904. More significant was a visit to France in 1910, for she returned in the autumn of 1911 with a vigorous, colourful, postimpressionist style of painting that marked the end of her earlier anachronistic English watercolour mode. Back in BC she continued a program begun in 1908 to visit Indian sites, many in remote areas, and paint a record of the vanishing villages, houses and totem poles. By 1913 she had produced a large body of

Emily Carr, *Big Raven* (1931), oil on canvas. Carr's work was deeply influenced by the art of the Northwest Coast Indians (*courtesy Vancouver Art Gallery*).

work on the Indian theme but, unable to live from her art, she built a small apartment house in Victoria for income and spent most of the next 15 dispiriting years in its management.

The period of mature and original production on which her reputation rests commenced when Carr was 57 and was stimulated by a trip to eastern Canada where she was included in a national exhibition, and met Lawren HARRIS and other members of the GROUP OF SEVEN. Their work, friendliness, and encouragement renewed her ambition and brought fresh direction to her art. Slowly, from 1928 on, critical recognition, exposure in exhibitions other than regional; occasional purchases began to diminish her sense of neglect and artistic isolation, though she experienced only the most modest practical success during her lifetime. After 1932, nature themes replaced Indian subjects, and her work became less designed and more freely expressive of the large rhythms of western forests, beaches and skies.

A severe heart attack in 1937 signaled the start of declining health, and she began devoting more time to writing, an activity begun in the 1920s. In 1941 *Klee Wyck* was published and received a Gov Gen's Award. *The Book of Small* was published in 1942, her last year of substantial painting, and *The House of All Sorts* in 1944. *Growing Pains*, *The Heart of a Peacock*, *Pause*, and *Hundreds and Thousands*, her journals, were published posthumously. DORIS SHADBOLT

Reading: Edythe Hembroff-Schleicher, *Emily Carr: The Untold Story* (1978); Doris Shadbolt, *The Art of Emily Carr* (1979); Maria Tippett, *Emily Carr: A Biography* (1979).

Carr, Shirley, union officer (b at Niagara Falls, Ont). In 1960 she became a union activist, serving in several executive positions in Local 133, Canadian Union of Public Employees (CUPE). In 1970 she was instrumental in the formation of a CUPE local representing employees of the Regional Municipality of Niagara and was the local's president until 1974. From 1967 she was an active officer of the Ontario Division of CUPE and at the national level she was elected regional and then general vice-president of the union. She was elected an executive vice-president of the Canadian Labour Congress in 1974. LAUREL SEFTON MACDOWELL

Carrier are an Athapaskan, or DENE, group of about 5000 in north-central BC. Their name (Carrier, *Porteur*) derives from the custom of widows carrying the ashes of a deceased husband in a bag for about a year, at which time a ceremonial distribution of goods released her of the obligation. The Carrier also call themselves Dakelh. There are 3 major subgroupings, based on dialect and culture: Upper Carrier, or Babine, located along Bulkley R and Babine Lk; Central Carrier in the Stuart Lk and Fraser Lk basins; and Lower Carrier in the Blackwater R region.

In the 18th century the Carrier relied upon hunting and fishing. Lower Carrier social organization was based on the extended family, consisting of brothers, their wives and children and married sons' wives and children. Each group (or *sadeku*) was associated with a hunting territory and with fishing sites, but individual ownership of land was not developed. Upper and Central Carrier had matrilineal descent groups (clans). Inheritance of property and use rights was matrilineal for Upper and Central Carrier, and bilateral elsewhere.

Trade and other interaction with Gitksan and BELLA COOLA peoples resulted in Carrier adoption of POTLATCH and ranking systems. Fur-trade posts were established at Ft McLeod (1805), Stuart Lk and Fraser Lk (1806) and at the confluence of the Nechako and Fraser rivers (Ft George, 1808). The Stuart Lk post (Ft St James) was headquarters for the entire New Caledonia fur trading district. The fur trade not only brought technological changes with the influx of European goods, but extensive changes in living patterns and resource allocations as well. After 1860, settlement and mining on the upper Fraser R also broke the relative isolation of the native people in the area. The Oblates established a mission at Ft St James (1873) and pressured the Carrier to end potlatching and other customs. Because of the mission and trading post, Ft St James became an important centre for seasonal gatherings of Carrier from throughout the region. After the completion of a railway in the area (1914), the Carrier became involved in the logging industry as seasonal labourers, though maintaining hunting, trapping and fishing activities — an economic pattern that continues today. Diseases such as smallpox, measles and influenza reduced the Carrier populations, which reached a low point in the late 1920s.

Today the Carrier are divided into 14 administrative bands, each with several small reserves (est in the 1890s). Members of each community are connected by extensive kinship ties, which act as a framework for the inheritance of traplines and the exchange of goods and services. Extensive industrial operations in the region in the past decades have highlighted Carrier dependence on traditional bush resources. DOUGLAS HUDSON

Carrier, Roch, poet, story writer, novelist, playwright, essayist (b in the Beauce, Qué 13 May 1937). After publishing 2 collections of poetry, *Les Jeux incompris* (1956) and *Cherche tes mots, cherche tes pas* (1958), Carrier offered critics *Jolis deuils* (1964), a group of bizarre stories that won him a province of Québec award. *La Guerre, yes sir!* (1968) made his reputation in Québec and abroad. His extraordinary talent as a storyteller was confirmed with *Floralie, où est-tu?* (1969) and *Il est par là le soleil* (1970), which brought back some of the characters from *La Guerre*, as well as themes of war, sexual repression, exploitation of the little guys, French Canadians' distrust of the "Anglais" and the hold of a religion that borders on superstition. This trilogy presents a search for meaning in life and death, a search that permeates all Carrier's work. Carrier has also written a film script, a collection of short stories, a children's story and 2 plays. Individually and collectively, these works bear eloquent witness to Roch Carrier's rich imagination and desire to keep developing his narrative technique and themes, even though he continues to stress certain cherished topics. JACQUES COTNAM

Carrot (*Daucus carota*), cool-climate plant belonging to the Umbelliferae family and grown as a ROOT CROP in Canada. Carrots are biennials, but are grown as annuals. They are native to central Asia and were used as medicinal herbs in Afghanistan before their introduction to Europe in medieval times. Carrots have been improved by selection and hybridization: those destined for processing have large, thick, conical roots; those for the fresh market are rather long and cylindrical. The root is a reservoir for sugars manufactured by the leaves. Leafstalks and leaves, which are used to pull the carrot from the soil during mechanical harvesting, must be protected from leaf diseases. Carrots require 70-100 days to produce a harvest of approximately 30 t/ha for the fresh market and 60 t/ha for the processing industry. Principal INSECT PESTS are weevils and flies; common PLANT DISEASES, *Alternaria* and *Cercospora* blights. Carrots are a source of ascorbic acid and are consumed fresh, cooked or as juice. They are grown in every province; 8000 ha (4000 in Québec alone) are devoted to commercial production. PIERRE SAURIOL

Carse, Margaret Ruth Pringle, dancer, choreographer, teacher, director (b at Edmonton 7 Dec 1916). A woman of courage and optimism, Ruth Carse founded the ALBERTA BALLET CO and nurtured it to professional status. She performed with Boris VOLKOFF's Canadian Ballet and as a member of the Radio City Music Hall's ballet corps in New York C before injury forced her retirement in 1954. She returned to teach in Edmonton and formed small amateur companies. Dance Interlude became the Edmonton Ballet in 1960 and the Alberta Ballet Company in 1966. Carse founded the Alberta Ballet School in 1971 and resigned as director of the company to teach. She has choreographed more than 50 works for TV, opera and musical theatre, and for the Alberta Ballet. MICHAEL CRABB

Carter, Sir Frederick Bowker Terrington politician, judge, prime minister of Newfoundland (b at St John's 12 Feb 1819; d there 1 Mar 1900). Born into one of Newfoundland's most distinguished families, Carter was educated in St John's and in London, Eng, and was called to the Newfoundland Bar in 1842. He was elected to the House of Assembly as a Conservative in 1855. One of leader Hugh HOYLES's most trusted advisers, he became Speaker of the House when the Conservatives won the 1861 election. A Newfoundland representative at the 1864 Québec Conference, Carter returned home a convinced Confederate. Upon Hoyles's retirement (1865), he became prime minister. His government was the first to include both Protestants and Roman Catholics, and thus significantly eased the sectarian tensions that had plagued Newfoundland. Carter's government ran for reelection in 1869 on a platform that promised to bring Newfoundland into Canadian CONFEDERATION and was badly defeated. Although he again became prime minister in 1874, he made no effort to raise the contentious Confederation issue. Carter retired as prime minister in 1878 and was appointed to the Newfoundland Supreme Court. In 1880 he became chief justice. GEOFF BUDDEN

Carter, Sidney Robert, art and antique dealer photographer (b at Toronto 18 Feb 1880; d at Montréal 27 Mar 1956). Carter was an early advocate of pictorialism in PHOTOGRAPHY, and by 1901-02 was exhibiting in London, the US and Canada. In 1904 he became an associate of Alfred Stieglitz's Photo-Secession in New York C, and 3 years later in Montréal he prepared an exhibition promoting pictorialism. Largely between about 1917 and 1928 Carter accepted portrait commissions; his style, however, slowly lost the haunting quality evident in his portrait of Rudyard Kipling (1907), favouring graphic effect and a firmer outline. His photographs from the 1930s are conservative, and he seemed to lose interest in the medium that had won him prominence. LILLY KOLTUN

Carter, Wilfred Arthur Charles, Wilf, singer songwriter (b at Port Hilford, NS 18 Dec 1904). He left the Maritimes in the 1920s and reached Alberta, becoming a cowboy and part-time entertainer. In 1930 he made his radio debut in Calgary. In Montréal, a few years later, he recorded, for RCA Victor, "My Swiss Moonlight Lullaby" and "The Capture of Albert Johnson," which were hits. His popularity grew with subsequent recordings and radio shows on the CBC and on CBS and NBC in the US, where his stage name was "Montana Slim." In 1940 he was seriously hurt in a car crash, and though still able to record, was unable to perform until 1949. Throughout the 1950s Carter's touring show was one of Canada's most popular attractions. In 1983 he was still performing, writing songs and recording for RCA, which that year released a 2-record 50th-anniversary salute to him, one of the fathers of Canadian COUNTRY AND WESTERN MUSIC. RICHARD GREEN

Cartier, Sir George-Étienne, lawyer, railway promoter, politician, prime minister of the Province of Canada (b at St-Antoine, Lower

Sir George-Étienne Cartier, lawyer, railway promoter, and Father of Confederation. His great accomplishment was reconciling French Canadians to Confederation (*courtesy Public Archives of Canada / C-8007*).

Canada 6 Sept 1814; d at London, Eng 20 May 1873). From a wealthy family of grain exporters and millers, and supposedly a descendant of Jacques CARTIER, he was a FATHER OF CONFEDERATION and dominated the politics of Québec for a generation. A graduate of the Sulpician Collège de Montréal and called to the bar in 1835, Cartier joined the radical Fils de la liberté (Sons of Liberty), composed the patriotic song, "O Canada, mon pays, mes amours" — model for the later national anthem — and was secretary of the reorganized ST-JEAN-BAPTISTE SOCIETY in 1843.

In 1837, at St-Denis, Cartier fought bravely alongside Wolfred Nelson and the rebels as they successfully routed Col Charles Gore's Waterloo veterans. After a narrow escape and exile in Vermont, he successfully petitioned in 1838 to return and practise law in Montréal. Specializing in property and railway promotion, Cartier was active in politics and became Louis-Hippolyte LAFONTAINE's campaign manager and right-hand man. With responsible government won, he agreed to run as a Liberal Reformer in Verchères in 1848. He moved to Montréal E in 1861 after the coalition with the Upper Canadian Conservatives, and as Bleu chief, served as co-premier with John A. MACDONALD in the Union parliaments of 1857-58 and 1858-62, in which ministry he set in motion the movement toward CONFEDERATION.

Cartier involved himself heavily in the development of the GRAND TRUNK RY, becoming its solicitor. After his election, despite government assistance to the line he served, he became chairman of the Railway Committee of Parliament. He was a driving force in the early promotion of the CPR, with the goal of making Montréal the terminus of a transcontinental trading network. Rival railway promoters funded his defeat in Montréal E by Amable Jetté of the short-lived Parti national in 1872 and engineered the release in Apr 1873 of election fund raising telegrams — the so-called PACIFIC SCANDAL. Cartier, whose letters had promised Sir Hugh ALLAN the railway contract, was already mortally ill with Bright's disease. He died soon after seeking treatment in London and the CPR languished for almost a decade.

Cartier's accomplishments included ensuring the choice of Ottawa as the national capital and reconciling the majority of French Canada to Confederation on the grounds that it made possible the re-establishment of the old Province of Québec. He negotiated in London for the transfer of the HBC territory of RUPERT'S LAND to the Dominion. While acting PM during Macdonald's illnesses and after personal meetings with provincial delegations, he played the primary role in drafting the Manitoba and British Columbia Acts. He probably met with RIEL, who idolized him, and after passage of the Manitoba Act, sent many of his own handpicked men to administer the new province. A former rebel against the Crown, this great patriot served as Canada's first minister of militia and defence.

ALASTAIR SWEENY

Reading: J. Boyd, *Sir George Étienne Cartier* (1914); Alastair Sweeney, *George-Etienne Cartier* (1976); B. Young, *Sir George-Etienne Cartier* (1981).

Cartier, Jacques, navigator (b at St-Malo, France, between 7 June and 23 Dec 1491; d there 1 Sept 1557). Cartier can be credited with discovering Canada only if one means the small region of Québec called CANADA by the Indians at the time of his 1535 voyage. He was certainly the first to chart the ST LAWRENCE R — discovery of which in 1535 enabled France to occupy the interior of N America. From remarks in the travel accounts credited to him, it would seem that Cartier's career began with voyages to Brazil. He probably accompanied VERRAZZANO to America in 1524 and 1528, and certainly came tc Newfoundland before 1534 since the stated destination of his first official voyage was the "Baie des Châteaux" (Str of Belle Isle), and he sailed there directly.

Charged by François I to look for gold in the New World and a passage to Asia, Cartier arrived at Newfoundland in 1534. Searching for a passage through the continent, he explored the Gulf of ST LAWRENCE and was the first to chart it. He took 2 Iroquois, sons of DONNACONA, back to France and they served as guides for his larger 1535 expedition in the *Grande Hermine, Petite Hermine* and *Émerillon.* On this voyage he discovered the river which was called Rivière du Canada and which was renamed St Lawrence early in the 1600s. He sailed to STADACONA (Québec), where the effect of a severe winter was made more tragic by scurvy. In 1536 he returned to France with some captured Iroquois, including Donnacona. In 1541 Cartier was asked to help establish, under ROBERVAL, the first French colony in America. He built a fort at the western tip of Cap aux Diamants [Cap Rouge] where he wintered. Convinced he had discovered gold and diamonds, he left in 1542 when the colonists and Roberval arrived. In France it was discovered that he had brought back worthless minerals and Cartier retired to his manor at Limoilou.

MARCEL TRUDEL

Reading: Marcel Trudel, *The Beginnings of New France, 1524-1663* (1973).

The N American portion of a 1546 world map by Pierre Desceliers is one of the earliest maps to show Jacques Cartier's exploration of the St Lawrence River. Labrador is at lower left, Mexico is at the upper right (*courtesy John Ryland's Library, Manchester, 11546 / copy in Public Archives of Canada / NMC-40461*).

Cartography, History of Cartography is the art, science and technology of making maps, plans, charts and globes representing the Earth or any celestial body at any scale. Cartographic documents have been used as vehicles of communication by different cultures for many milenia; the earliest map to survive, drawn about 2300 BC on a clay tablet, was found in the Middle East. Centuries before Christ, Greek philosophers and mathematicians such as Pythagoras and Aristotle advanced the concept that the Earth was a sphere, and Eratosthenes (*c*276-196 BC) made a reasonable calculation of the Earth's circumference. In the 2nd century AD Claudius Ptolemy compiled and systematized the geographical knowledge of the day and encouraged the scientific study of geography. He suggested, for example, that maps be drawn strictly to scale (at that time not a common practice), that general world maps should be supplemented with a series of regional maps drawn at appropriate scales, and that maps should be drawn with coordinates.

Ptolemy's works were ignored until early in the 15th century, when an avid interest in the classical period had been revived by the Renaissance. His writings, translated from the Byzantine Greek, were copied in manuscript and later published. In a 1507-08 edition of his *Geographia,* a map showing a portion of eastern Canada appeared, and during the next century the Ptolemaic atlases became a major instrument of the diffusion of geographical knowledge of Canada.

In the following centuries the mapping of Canada evolved with the advance of cartographic techniques around the world and with continued EXPLORATION along the coasts and into the heart of the country. The development of instruments and techniques also changed the nature of the data gathered and the maps produced. The maps of the 16th century were rough and often conjectural; maps of the French period became more accurate in the better-known areas; and after 1800, with the widespread use of the sextant and advanced astronomical techniques for determining longitude (for example, using the marine chronometer), the major gaps in the map of Canada were filled. The 20th century has seen great refinement of mapping skills in Canada. EDWARD H. DAHL

Native Mapmaking

Mapmaking was a widespread and well-developed art among the Indians and Inuit, although this fact has been largely ignored in the history of cartography. Most common were navigational maps, because the more nomadic hunting and gathering bands depended upon effective navigation over great expanses of wilderness. Maps were also drawn to facilitate trade and warfare over long distances. Military maps were used especially by the equestrian plains Indians, whose war parties sometimes ventured into unfamiliar regions of the grasslands.

Inuit and Indian navigational maps were usually drawn on the ground or in the snow. Sketched from memory, these stationary maps were accompanied by verbal descriptions of the country in question. They were thus ephemeral and, in contrast to the European use of maps, required the successful traveller to rely entirely upon memory, a task for which Indians and Inuit were trained from childhood.

When a map was committed to media which affected its size, such as skins or bark, no attempt was made to fill in the entire space. Instead, detail was elaborated only where necessary. Shape was accurately portrayed on most native maps, and in this respect they differ little from modern survey maps. Scale, however, was often measured by the day's journey, and hence varied according to factors affecting travel time. Scale was also varied to exaggerate or clarify significant features for navigation, and in some maps reflected the cartographer's relative familiarity with different areas. Although Europeans frequently found these maps overly simple and often confusing, they were eminently suited to the overriding objective of most native cartography: to accentuate the environmental information salient to successful wilderness navigation.

Native maps were also used as general media of communication and as repositories of cultural life and lore. SHAWNANDITHIT, for example, drew a series of maps to illustrate the history of her tribe in the years leading up to its extinction. Maps also recalled historical events such as battles, and the OJIBWA elaborated charts to record their earlier migrations and past sacred events. Combined with PICTOGRAPHS, maps were used for general communication, most commonly in the form of notices of direction and of trips, and in missives that might properly be called "map letters." Just as native people in these ways communicated crucial geographical information to their fellows, so they afforded the early European explorers, traders and missionaries much of the geographical information that eventually carried them and their supporting enterprises from the Atlantic to the Pacific. D.W. MOODIE

Early Explorers' Mapping

Most 16th-century maps relating to Canada are manuscript compilations, often undated and anonymous, prepared by European cartographers rather than by explorers. Since cartographers had to work with available material, these maps are at times a perplexing mixture of new information and old, copied from unspecified sources. Any review of the sequence in which Canada was first mapped is therefore somewhat conjectural. Until 1974 a map known as the "Vinland Map," acquired by Yale University almost a decade earlier and showing the NE coast of N America, was thought to be the earliest cartographic representation of Canada. It is now generally believed to be a forgery. The earliest known maps of Canada date from about 1502 to 1506. They depict the E coast of Newfoundland as that of an island in the N Atlantic. None of the land between Greenland and the Caribbean was known to Europeans. The most significant early configurations are those known as the "Cantino," "Canerio," "King-Hamy" (in Huntington Library, San Marino, Calif), "Oliveriana" (at Pesaro, Italy) and "Kunstmann II" charts. The earliest of these is probably the "Cantino" chart (*c*1502) which appears to have originated with the voyages of Gaspar CORTE-REAL (1500-01). No maps from John CABOT's voyage (1497) appear to have survived. Some scholars have interpreted the La Cosa chart, dated 1500, as a confused copy of a Cabot map, whereas others have pointed out that it contains information available only as late as 1508. In any case, none of the geographical features of the map that some scholars have interpreted as showing the eastern coast of Canada can be identified in such a way as to achieve scholarly consensus.

The first printed maps to show parts of the New World, such as the Contarini (1506) and Ruysch (1507-08) maps, show the E coast of Newfoundland joined to Greenland as an extension of Asia. These configurations were probably based on the guess that Greenland and Newfoundland were connected (Corte-Real) and were all part of Asia (Cabot). In 1507 a map by Waldseemüller was the first to separate the New World from Asia, a concept that gained popularity during the next decade.

During the 1520s the E and S shores of Newfoundland as well as the E shore of Nova Scotia became better known, and maps of this period portray geographical features less ambiguously than those of the previous 20 years. Better maps, such as the "Miller I" (*c*1516-22), the Pedro Reinel (1516-20) and the map attributed to Diogo Ribeiro (the "Weimar" map, 1527), even hint at openings S and N of Newfoundland where later the Cabot Str and the Str of Belle Isle were explored by Jacques CARTIER. At least some of the features on these maps appear to be based on the exploration of João Alvares FAGUNDES (*c*1519-26). The first maps showing the entire coastline from Florida to Newfoundland were based on the explorations of Esteban Gomez (1525) and Giovanni da VERRAZZANO (1524). Although Gomez had hinted at an opening where the Bay of Fundy should be, all the maps of this period show an unbroken coastline. Later maps, such as the ones by Santa Cruz (1542), Lopo Homem (1554) and Diogo Homem (1558), drawn from data produced in the 1520s, demonstrate that Gomez actually suspected Nova Scotia to be an island, while some Portuguese more or less knew its true configuration.

After Cartier's explorations (1534-42) the entire cartography of Canada underwent revision. None of Cartier's maps have survived. Those believed to be closest to his originals are a chart by John Rotz (1542) depicting the results of Cartier's first voyage (1534), the Desceliers map of 1546 and the "Harleian" world map (*c*1547). The last 2 depict Cartier's explorations to 1536. The outstanding contribution of these maps is that they add the gulf and river of St Lawrence to the shape of N America. A second group of maps, based apparently on French and Portuguese mapping, depicts the St Lawrence along with more realistic shapes for Newfoundland and Nova Scotia. The best example of these maps is one by Vallard (1547). Few printed maps of this period deserve consideration, but one of significance is the famous 1569 world chart by Gerard Mercator which introduced the map projection bearing his name.

Arctic mapping began with Martin FROBISHER's first voyage (1576), although the southern tip of Greenland had appeared on maps since 1502. Frobisher's map of his bay on southeastern Baffin I has survived but, since he did not place his explorations in the context of the rest of N America, cartographers were uncertain where to place it. On the maps of George Best (1578) and Michael Lok (1582) Frobisher's Bay appears as a NORTHWEST PASSAGE across N America. Following the less ambiguous maps that emanated from John DAVIS's voyages (1585-1587), Frobisher's "strait" was moved to the southern tip of Greenland, where it remained through much of the 17th century. Only a few

New information about the Great Lakes not found on Champlain's 1632 map appears on Sanson's map of New France (*courtesy Public Archives of Canada/NMC-21100*).

All of the Great Lakes are finally shown in the 1688 map of Vincenzo Coronelli (*courtesy Public Archives of Canada/NMC-6411*).

artographers made any attempt to link the northern discoveries with those on the St Lawrence and E coast. Probably the best attempt is a world map by Edward Wright printed in 1599.

C.E. HEIDENREICH

Mapping to 1763

Scientific mapping began with Samuel de CHAMPLAIN in 1603. In 1613 he published the first modern-looking map of eastern Canada, combining in it his own explorations with those of Henry HUDSON. By 1616 he had explored and mapped as far W as Georgian Bay. For other areas he used native maps and verbal accounts. His observations were made from compass and latitude readings as well as estimates of distance. Besides his 6 small-scale maps, of which that of 1632 is the most comprehensive, Champlain also produced 23 large-scale maps and picture plans of places between Cape Cod and Montréal.

From the time of Champlain's death in 1635 to the 1670s, the major explorers furnishing geographical information to European cartographers were Jesuit missionaries. By 1649 they had explored the eastern Great Lakes; the maps of Sanson (1650, 1656), and Fathers Bressani (1657) and Du Creux (1660) have survived in printed form. On these the Great Lakes are recognizable for the first time. Further Jesuit mapping led to the first good map of Lk Superior and northern Lk Michigan (1672) by Fathers Allouez and Dablon; the first delineation of the Mississippi R by Father MARQUETTE and Louis JOLLIET (1673); and a series of maps of the Iroquois country in upper New York state by Father Raffeix and others. One of the few non-Jesuit maps of the period was by the Sulpician Galinée, detailing his journey with Dollier from Montréal through the lower Great Lakes to Sault Ste Marie (1670). The necessary observations used to construct all these maps were similar to those used for Champlain's. In 1632 the Jesuits began to observe and, later, to time lunar eclipses to establish longitude W of Paris or Rome.

From the 1670s to the end of the century the mapping of Canada is primarily associated with Jolliet and Jean-Baptiste-Louis Franquelin, of whom the latter was the more talented draftsman. He was Hydrographe du Roy at Québec 1686-97 and 1701-03, teaching hydrography and keeping the maps of NEW FRANCE up to date. The manuscript maps of explorers such as LA SALLE, Jolliet and a number of military surveyors were incorporated in large compilations sent to France, where professional mapmakers had access to them. The chief cartographers to the French court, such as Vincenzo Coronelli and Guillaume Delisle, based their printed maps in part on the information furnished by Franquelin. The maps of Coronelli (1688-89) and Delisle (1703) best sum up the late 17th-century cartography of Canada. The Delisle map also has the distinction of being the first with a fairly modern grid of longitude based on a lunar eclipse recorded at Québec in 1685 by Jean Deshayes.

Large-scale mapping during the 17th century was understandably confined to the St Lawrence R valley. Cadastral mapping (ie, mapping of property boundaries, building locations, etc) commenced with Jean Bourdon's mapping of seigneuries (1641); Bourdon also produced an early plan of Québec (1660). The St Lawrence R was charted by Jolliet and Franquelin (1685), but much more competently by Jean Deshayes (1685-86). Although the printed results of Deshayes's survey (1702) became the standard chart of the river, more accurate surveys were undertaken in the mid-18th century by Testu de la Richardière (1730-41), Gabriel Pellegrin (1734-55) and others. Cadastral maps also continued to be produced during the 18th century, one of the most notable being by Jean-Baptiste Decouagne in 1709. These maps and charts were all constructed by competent surveyors and military engineers using up-to-date instruments and surveying principles.

Increasingly strained relations with England made the activities of the French military engineers more important in the 18th century. The lower Great Lakes frontier was charted with some accuracy by the engineers Gaspard-Joseph CHAUSSEGROS DE LÉRY and his son of the same name. They also prepared maps of Québec and major fortifications from LOUISBOURG to Detroit. On the E Coast one of the first accurate hydrographic surveys was made by Joseph Bernard de Chabert (1750-51). In 1750 he built Canada's first observatory at Louisbourg for astronomical observation and longitude calculation.

While the settled and strategic areas of New France were being charted by trained engineers and surveyors, the interior was still being mapped by amateurs with little training and no instruments more sophisticated than a compass. The first maps of the region W of Lk Superior resulted from the LA VÉRENDRYE expeditions after 1731, while the northern interior of Québec was being mapped by the Jesuit Father Laure. These maps portray a recognizable lake and river sys-

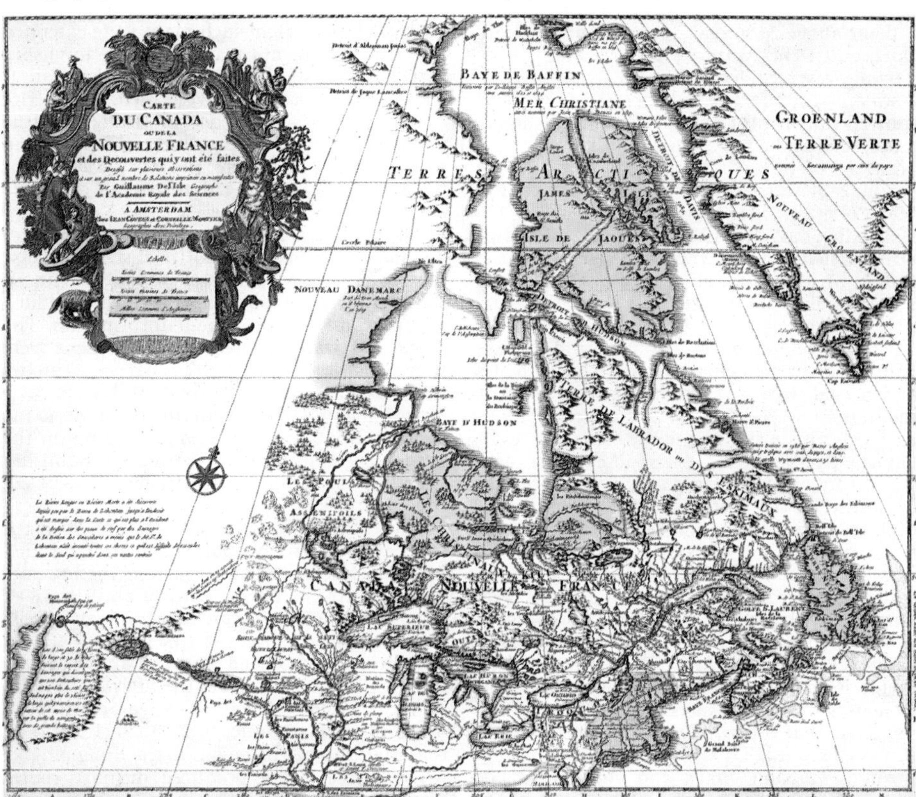

Delisle's 1703 map of New France is the first to depict latitude and longitude more or less correctly (*courtesy Public Archives of Canada/NMC-24722*).

tem based on untrained observations and native information.

Very little 18th-century manuscript mapping found its way to printed maps until Jacques-Nicolas Bellin became chief engineer and geographer of the Dépôt des cartes, plans et journaux of the French MINISTÈRE DE LA MARINE. In 1744 he published 28 maps in Father P.F.X. CHARLEVOIX's combined *Histoire* and *Journal* (1744). These were the first printed maps of Canada based on new material since Delisle's of 40 years earlier. In succeeding years Bellin regularly updated his maps. Another important cartographer, Jean-Baptiste Bourguignon D'Anville, like Bellin had access to original material, and he produced a series of fine maps between 1746 and 1755. Both cartographers published pamphlets explaining their source material and the reliability of their maps.

Primary English mapping of Canada before 1763 was confined entirely to the Arctic and the shores of Hudson Bay. Hudson's 1612 map of the bay's E shore and the straits was quickly replaced by maps of the entire bay by Thomas JAMES (1633) and Luke FOX. John Thornton produced a more accurate chart for the HUDSON'S BAY COMPANY (1685). The HBC did no more mapping until Arthur Dobbs criticized the company for its dismal record in exploration; beginning in 1741, expeditions resulted in a series of excellent charts by Christopher Middleton (1743), John Wigate (1746) and Henry Ellis (1748) as far N as Repulse Bay.

In 1755 the SEVEN YEARS' WAR interrupted mapping activities in New France. The last French map of N America, summarizing the latest geographical information available on Canada before it passed into British hands, was Bellin's "Carte de l'Amérique septentrionale" (1755). It shows that Canada had been mapped, roughly but recognizably, to about 102° W in present-day Manitoba and along the W shore of Hudson Bay to the Arctic Circle. C. E. HEIDENREICH

Explorers' Maps after 1763

Although Québec fell in 1760, the TREATY OF PARIS was not signed until Feb 1763. During the truce the British army under Gen MURRAY made the first detailed survey of this area, from a point above Montréal downstream to below Québec City. The "Murray Map," of which at least 5 hand-drawn copies were made, was drawn at a scale of 2000 feet to the inch (1:24 000) and showed much information of military importance, such as the population of villages and the positions of houses, churches and mills. Two originals of this map are held in the National Map Collection, Ottawa.

Britain's vast colonial empire in N America now stretched from the high Arctic to the Gulf of Mexico. Huge areas were essentially unknown to Europeans, with only sketchily charted coasts and a largely unmapped hinterland. For the development of resources and the expansion of trade, better charts of the harbours and coastal waters and more accurate maps of the interior were required. There were 3 excellent surveyors serving with the British forces in Canada. Samuel HOLLAND and Joseph DESBARRES were army officers; James COOK was the master of a ship in the British fleet. The work was divided among them: Cook was commissioned to chart the island of Newfoundland and the adjacent Labrador coast; Holland, appointed surveyor general of the Northern District of N America (which included all British holdings N of the Potomac R), concentrated on the Gulf of St Lawrence, including Prince Edward and Cape Breton islands and the New England coast; and DesBarres turned his attention to Nova Scotia, which at that time included present-day New Brunswick.

Many valuable maps and charts resulted. Cook's charts were of such high quality that his reputation was assured. DesBarres's major publication was *The Atlantic Neptune*, a navigational atlas of the E coast of N America containing charts at various scales, coastal views, tide tables and sailing directions. He was allowed to publish the *Neptune* privately under his own name, although Holland and Cook had been responsible for some of its charts. Holland's publications concentrated on landward mapping, but of course he used the data produced by the surveys of his colleagues. His map, "A General Map of the Northern British Colonies in America," drawn at 60 miles to the inch (1:3 801 600), is one of the most important of this period.

Meanwhile, other surveyors were carrying out the necessary property surveys so that farmsteads could be established. This work increased greatly after LOYALISTS began arriving in 1783. Settlement in Nova Scotia was handicapped by the lack of a comprehensive land-granting procedure. In the Province of Quebec (which included much of present-day southern Ontario), by contrast, the settlement of the Loyalists was carried out with military efficiency. Gov Gen Frederick HALDIMAND and Holland devised a system, comprising townships and lots, for each settler to get a measured portion of land, surveyed at minimal cost and marked on the ground. An important requirement was the preparation of a map of each township showing the layout of farm lots and the major topographic features.

A second type of 19th-century cartographic survey that equalled the township surveys in importance was the hydrographic survey of the Great Lakes carried out originally by the British Admiralty, but after 1884 by Canadian hydrographers. The work was started in 1815 by Capt William F. Owen and was turned over to Lt Henry BAYFIELD the following year. During the next 40 years Bayfield supervised the surveying of the Great Lakes, the St Lawrence and the Nova Scotia coast, and was personally responsible for the high quality of the charts produced.

Throughout the 19th century and into the 20th, there were hundreds of maps drawn of parts of eastern Canada that were simply compilations and redraftings of the information available from township plans and hydrographic charts. When such maps were extended to cover an area not reached by the township surveyors, the sketch maps of geologists, foresters and even fur traders were used. The "office compiled maps" were poor substitutes for true topographic maps, but they were inexpensive to produce and they were the only large- and medium-scale mapping that Canada could afford.

"County maps" and "county atlases" were very popular. These had a semiofficial status because the basic survey data were supplied without charge to private publishers who then added a certain amount of current information. The roads and trails opened by the settlers were shown, as were stores, mills, wharves, churches and, in many cases, individual houses. The scales ranged from 40 chains to 128 chains to the inch (1:31 680 to 1:101 376) depending on the size of the county. To increase sales the publisher inscribed the name of the owner on each occupied farm lot.

Government agencies also compiled maps from existing survey data. When Holland died in 1801, Joseph Bouchette became acting surveyor general of Lower Canada and, in 1804, surveyor general. He produced 2 remarkable maps of his province, the first in 1815 at 2.66 miles to the inch (1:168 500) and a revised version in 1831 at 2.8 miles to the inch (1:177 400). William MacKay's map of Nova Scotia, published in 1834 at 6 miles to the inch (1:380 160), is a fine example of medium-scale mapping.

The British army produced military route-marching maps and larger-scale "reconnoitring plans" from township surveys by adding details such as the strength of bridges and the billeting capacity of villages. Examples are Col John Oldfield's "Map of the Province of Canada" (1843), drawn at 6 miles to the inch, and "Map of the Principal Communications in Canada West," drawn at 2 miles to the inch (1:126 720) in 1850 under the direction of Maj George Baron de Rottenburg.

During the 1850s Bayfield made another significant contribution to Canadian mapping, instituting telegraph longitude observations at a number of eastern Canadian cities. By using the commercial telegraph companies' lines for the exchange of time signals, he was able to determine very accurately the geographical position of an observatory or a public building in each of the cities. This "known position" was then used to correct the mapping of the surrounding area.

The Western Interior In 1760 the land West of the Great Lakes was poorly mapped. HBC explorers such as Henry KELSEY, Anthony HENDAY and Samuel HEARNE had been sent out on early exploratory journeys, and the La Vérendryes had been able to view only a fraction of the great land. Since none of them could make astronomic observations to fix their positions, they were able to produce only rough sketch maps or route descriptions. In 1778 the HBC hired Philip Turnor, a trained inland surveyor. Turnor mapped the river routes across the company's vast holdings, and trained junior surveyors such as David THOMPSON and Peter FIDLER in the art of field astronomy for position-fixing, and track-surveying for filling in map detail between the "peg points" provided by the astrofixes.

By this time the HBC was in competition with the NORTH WEST COMPANY, which also had surveyors. Shortly after 1780 one of these surveyors, Peter POND, discovered a practical canoe route from the prairie rivers over the height of land into the Athabasca and Mackenzie rivers (*see* PORTAGE LA LOCHE). His 1785 map showing the route led other explorers such as Alexander MACKENZIE and John FRANKLIN into the central Arctic. London map publishers made good use of the information flowing out of the fur-trade lands. By examining the resulting maps in their various editions one can almost see the unfolding of Canada. One in particular stands out: "A Map Exhibiting All the New Discoveries in the Interior Parts of North America," published by Aaron Arrowsmith in 1795 and updated 19 times until after 1850.

In 1857, 2 scientific expeditions, one Canadian and the other British, were sent to the Canadian prairies. The British party under Capt John PALLISER spent 3 years in the West. The Canadian expedition concentrated on the country between Lk Superior and the Red R. Both expeditions gathered topographical and geographical data which were subsequently published on maps and in reports. These were influential in the negotiations preceding the purchase of RUPERT'S LAND.

The West Coast In 1774 Capt Juan PEREZ and his men aboard the Spanish ship *Santiago* were the first Europeans to view the NORTHWEST COAST. Perez had been dispatched there to counter the threat to Spanish sovereignty presented by the Russian expeditions of Bering and Chirikov along the Alaska coastline in 1741. He made several coastal sightings as far N as Dixon Entrance (54° N), but submitted no maps or detailed reports. The following year Spanish hydrographer Juan Francisco de la BODEGA Y QUADRA drew the first chart to show a portion of Canada's West Coast (*see* SPANISH EXPLORATION). James Cook arrived in 1778 to search for the western end of any channel that might connect with the Arctic Ocean, seen 7 years before by Samuel Hearne at the mouth of the Coppermine R, but he found no Northwest Passage.

The sovereignty of the W Coast was to remain in dispute for many years. While diplomatic negotiations were being conducted in Europe during the NOOTKA SOUND CONTROVERSY, both Spain and Britain were allowed to make charts of the coast to support their claims. The British work was done 1791-94 under Capt George VANCOUVER, and the Spanish hydrographers worked under Dionisio Alcalá-Galiano and Cayetano Valdés. There was no animosity between these groups, and on several occasions they exchanged data to improve the work on both sides.

In 1793 Alexander Mackenzie, a NWC explorer, travelled from Lk Athabasca to Pacific tidewater at the mouth of the Bella Coola R. During the next half century fur-trade employees such as Thompson, Simon FRASER, Samuel Black and John McLeod made reconnaissance surveys into what is now central BC, increasing the knowledge of this rugged land and producing, in many cases, significant maps recording the topography of the area. Land surveying began when HBC surveyor Joseph Pemberton arrived in Victoria in 1851. In 1858 he completed a map of Victoria. Gold had been found in the Fraser R, and before the year ended a full-fledged GOLD RUSH was in progress. One section of a detachment of Royal Engineers consisting of 20 surveyors carried out a variety of tasks, including townsite surveys and topographic mapping. By Confederation much of the BC northern interior was still unknown. The coastline had been surveyed, several routes through the mountains to the prairies were known, and military surveyors had mapped small areas in the south.

The Arctic The truly remarkable accomplishments in the Arctic were 2 overland journeys: in 1771 Hearne reached the mouth of the Coppermine R at 67° N, and in 1789 Mackenzie descended the river that today bears his name to tidewater at about 68°N. As well, British navigators still sought the Northwest Passage by sea. Their fascination with this navigational will-o'-the-wisp culminated in the ill-fated FRANKLIN EXPEDITION of 1845. During the ensuing attempts to find Franklin and his men, the searchers undertook further explorations. The resulting maps revealed the outline of Canada's mainland coast and disclosed the positions and shorelines of the major islands lying S of Lancaster and Melville sounds. Admiralty charts compiled from the navigational records of these voyages provided the most reliable geographical information about the region until after WWII. In fact, some of the aeronautical charts of northern Canada used during WWII showed little more than this information. L.M. SEBERT

Official Surveys

Hydrographic Surveys The British North America Act assigned responsibility for safe navigation in Canadian waters to the federal government. This initially involved the erection and maintenance of navigational aids such as lighthouses and buoys. The charting of Canadian waters started in 1883 in GEORGIAN BAY. Canada had hitherto relied on British Admiralty charts for navigation on the East and West coasts, and on the Bayfield charts of the Great Lakes. During the late 19th century, navigation on Georgian Bay became very important in national development: its ports were serving agricultural areas and mining and lumbering industries, and many of these ports were developing industries to supply the westward expansion of railways and the new prairie settlements. Navigation on Georgian Bay was of little interest to the US or Britain, so the Georgian Bay Survey was set up within Canada's Dept of Marine and Fisheries.

In 1891 a party from Georgian Bay was sent to Vancouver to survey Burrard Inlet. This survey was the first undertaken by Canada in salt water. In 1904 the Dept of Marine and Fisheries began officially charting Canadian coastal waters. The Hydrographic Survey Branch was formed, and the Great Lakes Survey amalgamated with a unit in Public Works that had been doing harbour surveys and a unit in Railways and Canals that had been working on the St Lawrence and Ottawa rivers. In 1928 the agency was renamed the Canadian Hydrographic Service (*see* HYDROGRAPHY).

Canada has the longest national coastline in the world, much of it the scene of either active shipping or resource development. The towing in 1981 of a complete barge-mounted ore-concentration plant, 138 m long, from Sorel on the St Lawrence R to Little Cornwallis I in the central Arctic could not have been done if good charts had not been available. The voyage of the US supertanker *Manhattan*, accompanied by Canadian ICEBREAKER *John A. Macdonald*, through the Northwest Passage in 1969 also illustrates the vast responsibility of the Canadian Hydrographic Service.

Cadastral Surveying "Cadastre" is a technical term used in Europe for the registration of land in a given municipal area such as a city or a county. A "cadastral survey" is the measuring, marking and description of parcels of land sufficient for their correct entry into the public land register; or, conversely, the marking on the ground of parcels in accordance with a description in the register. In the latter instance this could be either an original survey or a retracement when the position of the original boundary is not clear. Within provincial boundaries in Canada, land ownership and all fiscal matters pertaining to land are under provincial jurisdiction. The provinces set the rules and procedures for the cadastral surveys of their lands, including the licensing of surveyors. In the Yukon, the NWT and federal lands in the provinces, such as INDIAN RESERVES and national PARKS, the federal government has this responsibility.

An essential part of any cadastral survey is the legal description, which must give the size, shape and location of the parcel being surveyed. It may be in writing, in writing with a plan or entirely on a registered plan. The traditional written description is by "metes and bounds": the parcel's boundary lines are described in succession by stating the direction and length of each line, and by describing the survey markers or natural features that identify the boundary lines on the ground. A registered plan is used when a parcel is being subdivided and a number of lots are being established simultaneously. Such a plan must show the dimensions, boundary line bearings, areas and survey markers of each lot, and each lot must be numbered or otherwise identified. It can then be identified in a deed or other document by plan and lot number and the office where the plan is registered.

In many parts of Canada the original subdivision of crown land was done by township surveys, essential to orderly settlement. Different sizes of townships have been used (eg, Québec's irregularly shaped cantons and Ontario's concession townships), but all were designed to provide rectangular farm lots within a defined rural community. The survey of a township was essentially a subdivision survey, because the plan of the township was registered and the lots (sometimes called sections) were numbered. The description of a whole lot for legal purposes is complete in the identification of the township and the lot within the township. If only part of a lot is in question, a metes and bounds description, or some other method such as fractional parts, must be used (eg, "the north half of Lot 24, Concession II, in the Township of North Burgess"). As cities and towns extend into rural areas, it is common to find a township farm lot being subdivided into a number of city lots.

Urban Mapping All cities and large towns must have maps for tax assessment, the location and planning of public utilities, traffic planning and many other purposes. Most cities have a survey office, but towns generally have a municipal engineer. Both are responsible for the maintenance of survey records and the custody of maps, but the actual mapping is done by contract with Canada's air-survey industry.

Cities use map scales ranging from 1:500 for plans of sewage systems to 1:50 000 for tourist maps showing complete street layouts. Cities are 3-dimensional structures, and the utility mapping must show surface construction underlain by sewers which themselves may be built over power conduits, subways, service tunnels, etc. City maps must be kept up to date; many disastrous delays in municipal works have been caused by unexpected encounters

The 1906 Ottawa sheet, drawn at a scale of one inch to one mile in what came to be known as the National Topographic System (*courtesy Public Archives of Canada/NMC-18372*).

with vital utility lines. Fortunately, most Canadian cities can take pride in the completeness of their maps and survey records.

Boundary Surveys In the "township provinces," the townships are the building blocks of counties and rural and regional municipalities. The district ("land district" in BC) is the equivalent of a county in a sparsely populated wilderness area, and any townships surveyed within its BOUNDARIES form only a small proportion of its total area. Since counties and rural municipalities are composed of townships, their boundaries are surveyed during the opening of the township lines forming their boundaries. District boundaries are rarely surveyed except where they coincide with a provincial or county boundary. Provincial and territorial boundaries, except between Québec and Labrador and between the Yukon and the NWT, have all been surveyed. Canada's international boundary has been surveyed and marked on the ground, and the boundary markers are under continual inspection by the joint US-Canadian INTERNATIONAL BOUNDARY COMMISSION. L.M. SEBERT

Modernization

Because of Canada's size, maps have always been important in the planning and execution of major development projects. The successful settlement of the PRAIRIE WEST between 1872 and the 1930s was the result of good planning, police supervision, and having each farm lot surveyed and marked on the ground before the arrival of most of the homesteaders. Surveyors employed by the Department of the Interior marked on the ground the perimeters of the 6-mile (10 km) square townships and then the sidelines of each of the 36 sections within the township. They also recorded the positions of major topographic features such as rivers, streams, trails and sloughs. From these notes, draftsmen in Ottawa were able to compile the sheets of Canada's first extensive map series, the Three-Mile Sectional Maps of the Canadian Prairies drawn at 3 miles to the inch (1:190 080).

Series mapping provides detailed mapping at medium or large scale, yet the individual sheets are kept to a manageable size. Because the sheet boundaries conform to a predetermined grid, a number of sheets can be joined together to provide a large map of an extensive area such as a drainage basin, a forest-protection area, a county or even a whole province. Ideally a country should first be covered by a large-scale topographic series that displays the complete face of the land, including man-made features, relief, drainage pattern and forest cover. In the early days Canada could afford only the rather simple maps that could be drawn from the field notes sent in by surveyors whose main employment was staking farm lots, not surveying for maps.

The first sheets of the Three-Mile Series appeared in 1892. In all, 134 sheets were published, covering approximately 1.4 million km^2. Each sheet covered 8 townships N-S and from 13 to 15 townships (depending on the latitude) E-W. From 1920 to 1946, 51 of these simple outline maps were converted into true topographic maps through the addition of contours and other details. The series was abandoned in 1956 in favour of the 1:250 000 series (originally drawn at 1:253 440, or 4 miles to the inch) of the National Topographic System (NTS).

Simple straight-line surveys were ideal on the flat prairies, but impractical in the Rocky Mts. When township surveys reached the mountains in 1886, a system was developed using panoramic photographs taken from mountain peaks. A small but important series of mountain maps resulted. The maps themselves were useful, but the technique of mapping from photographs was even more useful because it was adapted to mapping from oblique aerial photographs when these became available after 1925.

The success of the Three-Mile Series encouraged the Dept of the Interior to begin similar medium-scale office-compiled mapping for eastern Canada. The department's chief geographer gathered the information from the many land surveys that had been made and compiled it into maps of a standard design. The maps were published at 2 scales (1:250 000 and 1:500 000), and were known as the Chief Geographer's Series. The first sheet was published in 1904, and by 1948, when work was stopped, 33 sheets at 1:250 000 and 25 at 1:500 000 had been published. For many years they were the most detailed maps available for the settled parts of eastern Canada.

The original Three-Mile Series and the Chief Geographer's Series were not contoured, and because contoured maps were a military requirement, the Dept of Militia and Defence started its own series of true topographic maps in 1904. These were drawn at one mile to the inch (1:63 360), and were modelled on the British Ordnance Survey maps at the same scale. This design, with a few modifications to accommodate the Canadian landscape, proved so successful that it was eventually adopted for the basic topographic mapping of Canada at the 1:50 000 scale.

Since its inception in 1842, the GEOLOGICAL SURVEY OF CANADA had been hampered by the lack of good base maps on which to display the results of field investigations. In many cases geologists had to do their own topographic mapping. This was poor use of geologists, so in 1908 a Topographical Survey Division was formed within the GSC. It was to provide topographic maps that could be used both as bases for geological maps and as general-purpose topographic maps.

In 1920 the Dept of the Interior joined the military and the geologists in the separate production of topographic maps. In 1922 senior officers in the 3 agencies began to unite their efforts into a single topographic system. After study and experimentation, by 1927 what became the NTS had been developed. It was designed as a series of map scales of 1, 2, 4, 8 and 16 miles to the inch. Such a system makes topographic maps available for all requirements, ranging from military and geological use at the one-mile scale to aeronautical chart use at 8 and 16 miles to the inch. In 1950 the basic scales were converted to their metric equivalents of 1:50 000, 1:125 000, 1:250 000, 1:500 000 and 1:1 000 000, and in 1952 a larger scale, 1:25 000, was added to the system for military and urban use. The smallest scale, 1:1 000 000, provides the basic grid that covers the whole country. This grid is quartered successively to provide the sheet boundaries of each larger scale until the largest (1:25 000) is reached. The numbering of each sheet indicates both the scale and the position of the sheet in the grid.

Two NTS scales were subsequently dropped: the 1:125 000 scale because it had few uses that could not be fulfilled by the other scales and the 1:25 000 scale because it competed with provincial programs started in the 1970s at the 1:20 000 scale. The resources previously devoted to these scales are now being used to hasten the completion of the 1:50 000 series. Complete coverage of Canada at this scale will require about 12 922 sheets. At the end of 1983 there were 9309 sheets of the series in print and completion is expected in the mid-1990s. All other active NTS scales have been completed.

By virtue of having their topographic mapping well in hand, Canadians enjoy the availability of a wide range of thematic maps: geological, forestry, pipeline and power transmission, tourist, etc. Many are produced by federal agencies, but the provinces, responsible for the development of their own natural resources, have become active in producing thematic maps. L.M. SEBERT

Mapping Since WWII

WWII can be considered a turning point in Canadian topographic mapping. Before the war topographers used plane tables and sketched out small sections of the terrain which were subsequently joined together into a map. This method was slow, not very accurate and unusable in forested areas. Aerial photographs were used, but in the whole country only one instrument plotted map detail directly from air photos. During the war the staff of Canada's military mapping units became familiar with European photomapping equipment, and they became a postwar source of trained technicians available for the modernization of Canada's mapping agencies. The introduction of photogrammetry (the drawing of maps from aerial photographs) was only one of many technological innovations that have transformed every phase of topographic mapping in Canada.

In remote areas, large tracts of country are normally mapped in a single operation. For example, a block 100 km N-S and 300 km E-W is mapped on 32 sheets (4 rows of 8) in the NTS. Aerial photography is done with certain features predetermined: scale, direction of the flight lines (normally E-W), forward overlap of the photos (normally 60%) and the side overlap of the flight lines (normally 30%). About 850 photos are needed. Overlap is necessary to provide areas on the photos for "tie-points" (points of ground detail selected in the overlapping areas) used to "pin" the photos of the block together. Tie-points are marked by tiny holes drilled in the emulsion on film positives of the air photos, and are measured precisely on a grid co-ordinate system provided for each photo. Each tie-point falls on 3 or more photos, allowing individual photo grids to be combined into a master system covering the whole photogrammetric block. This extension of the grid system is done by computer.

Although photogrammetric techniques have reduced the amount of field surveying required, some surveyed points must still be placed at strategic positions in the photogrammetric block. These are "control points" because they "control" the scale, the orientation, and the position of the lines and symbols on the map. There are 2 types of control points: horizontal (precisely known latitude and longitude) and vertical (precisely known elevation). The horizontal control points must be situated around the perimeter of the photogrammetric block where, in effect, they hold the block in position. It must be remembered that all mapping that covers an appreciable area must be drawn according to the mathematical rules of the chosen map projection. In Canadian topographic mapping this is generally the Universal Transverse Mercator (UTM) projection, which means that the latitude and longitude values of all horizontal control points must be converted to the equivalent grid co-ordinates of the UTM projection. The grid of the photogrammetric block is then adjusted in scale and orientation to fit the UTM grid. This in turn gives UTM-grid values to all the tie-points. The vertical control is set out in lines spaced across the block at right angles to the flight lines. This allows computation of tie-point elevations above sea level.

The overlapping portion of 2 adjoining aerial photographs forms a rectangle that is about half a photo wide and a photo long. A tie-point falls in each corner of this rectangle. Such rectangles are "photogrammetric models" because when viewed through a stereoscopic instrument they appear to be 3-dimensional models of the ground. They are the mapping units of a photogrammetric block. The models are set up, one by one, in photogrammetric plotting instruments, which are adjusted to the known values of the tie-points. The map detail is then traced from the model by the operator, who moves an ptical aiming mark, visible in the eyepiece of ıe instrument, along the roads and streams, round the lakes, etc, of the model. As the aimıg mark moves, a pencil recording every move f the mark moves over a drafting table attached) the plotter. This is the process of drawing the nework of the map. In modern systems the ıovement of the mark is recorded digitally on ıagnetic tapes or discs so that the map can be rawn automatically after the plotting is comlete.

Each phase of the mapping process has its wn instrumentation, almost all of which has een developed since the early 1960s. The most ramatic advances have been made in horizonıl control, which is simply establishing points f known latitude and longitude. The positions f such points were formerly found by meaıring the sides and angles of a series of trianles set out over the surface of the earth. Today it ; more usual to obtain the position directly by sing a Satellite Doppler System (SDS). This in:rument resembles a radio receiver, and is set up ith its antenna at the point to be surveyed. Sigals are received from US Navy navigation satllites which pass through the sky several times aily. The SDS takes the satellite information nd, by measuring the change in frequency of ıese signals as the satellite approaches and dearts, it computes the position of the antenna of ıe set. If readings are taken over 2 days and ompared with readings taken somewhere in ıe region by a second SDS at a previously sureyed station, the location of the new station an be calculated to about ½ m accuracy. The DS is used extensively to establish the fundaıental stations of the Canadian primary horiontal survey net (*see* REMOTE SENSING).

Additional points can be surveyed between oppler stations by using an Inertial Survey Sysem (ISS), consisting of delicate sensors which ecord with remarkable accuracy any moveıent of the set. It can be mounted in a car or helopter, and by starting from a known position ı Doppler station or an older triangulation staon), it measures the vehicle's movement along preselected route, and stopping points where ccurate positions are needed. Such a traverse ; checked by stopping at known positions to onfirm the accuracy of the readings taken long the way. Perimeter control around a phoogrammetric block is greatly facilitated by an SS survey, which is accurate within about 1 m.

Vertical control is traditionally placed by runing lines of levels from bench marks (points f known elevation) to the point where an elvation is needed. In northern Canada this ıethod would be prohibitively slow and exensive. Shortly after WWII a Canadian invenion, the Air Profile Recorder (APR), revoluionized vertical control surveys in wilderness reas. It is a RADAR device that measures vertical istance from an airplane flying at a constant ltitude above the line where elevations are eeded. The absolute value of the survey line is stablished by flying over a lake or broad river f which the elevation is known. The ISS can lso be used to establish elevations, since it reords changes in elevation as well as in direcion. Thus if the ISS starts off from a bench mark can provide accurate elevations along a survey ne, such as the lines of elevations across a phoogrammetric block. An APR elevation is correct vithin 3 to 5 m, whereas an ISS elevation is corect within ½ to 1 m.

Photogrammetric plotters and plotting sysems have undergone improvements over the ast 20 years. The optics now give a sharper view f the model, and the measuring systems allow hoto-grid measurements of control points and ie-points to be made with much greater accuacy. But since the early 1970s the actual plotting of map detail has taken a dramatic step forvard. Lines and symbols of the map are now recorded, not on a manuscript, but on magnetic tapes or discs. This information, including colour coding, can subsequently be read from the tapes or discs by computer-controlled drafting machines that can work rapidly around the clock. The many advantages of such a system include the ease with which the original lines can be drawn and adjusted electronically, as well as the efficiency with which the whole map can be revised when changes in the terrain, made by man and nature, necessitate the drawing of a new edition of the map. *See* GEOGRAPHICAL INFORMATION SYSTEMS. L.M. SEBERT

Reading: W.P. Cumming et al, *The Discovery of North America* (1971) and *The Exploration of North America, 1630-1776* (1974); J.B. Harley and D. Woodward, eds, *History of Cartography* (5 vols projected, 1985-); C.E. Heidenreich, "Mapping the Great Lakes . . . 1603-1700," *Cartographica* 17.3 (1980) and "Mapping the Great Lakes . . . 1700-1760," *Cartographica* 18.3 (1981); G.M. Lewis, "The Indigenous Maps and Mapping of North American Indians," *The Map Collector*, no 9 (1979); N.L. Nicholson and L.M. Sebert, *The Maps of Canada* (1981); D.W. Thomson, *Men and Meridians* (3 vols, 1966-69).

Cartoons The term cartoon originally meant an artist's preliminary sketch for a painting, fresco or tapestry. Although it retains this technical meaning for artists, cartoon now commonly designates a drawing produced to amuse, and perhaps to inform, a mass audience. The cartoonist's art ranges from the comic slapstick of TV cartoons to the social and political satires published in newspapers and magazines. Caricature is a common but not essential element of cartooning, using exaggeration to ridicule a subject, sometimes gently, sometimes with destructive intent. The oldest surviving example of the caricaturist's art may be a sketch of Ikhnaton, drawn in Egypt about 1360 BC. (Or it may be that Ikhnaton really was ugly — the experts still disagree.) Primitive art sometimes verges on caricature. Among the artifacts traditionally produced by the Salish Indians of BC, for instance, are small carvings that bear uncanny resemblance to the little clay effigies of the great French caricaturist of the 19th century, Honoré Daumier.

It was less than 400 years ago that caricature as a consciously developed art first flowered in Italy. Modern political cartooning began at roughly the same time as the political beginnings of CONFEDERATION. With the founding of *Punch and London Charivari* (England, 1841), the satirical magazine became the main vehicle for political cartoons in Europe, and soon after in N America. In the 1890s in Canada and the US, somewhat later in Europe, political cartoons became regular features of daily newspapers. The political cartoon as we know it today, a product of art and journalism, came of age in our own century. More than in many older countries, Canada's image of itself has been shaped by political cartoonists communicating with mass audiences in the years when illustrated magazines and newspapers were at their most influential. Recent decades have seen a "golden age" of political cartooning in Canada, but the future of the art seems to depend on the future of newspapers. Attempts to adapt political cartooning to TV have been unsuccessful so far.

The first recognized and feared cartoonist to work in Canada was Brigadier-General George Townshend, third in command of the British forces that conquered Québec in 1759. The satirical drawings of Townshend already were the talk of London when this witty aristocrat joined General James WOLFE. His caricatures of his commander infuriated Wolfe, who threatened revenge after the siege, but when Wolfe died on the battlefield, it was Townshend who accepted the surrender of the French. For a brief moment of history, the entire colony was at the mercy of an amateur cartoonist.

The start of cartooning as a profession in Canada followed the appearance of *Punch* and other

"Confederation! The Much-Fathered Youngster" by J.W. Bengough (*courtesy Public Archives of Canada / C-78676*).

early comic journals in London. *Punch in Canada*, launched in Montréal (1849) by J.B. Walker, an 18-year-old designer and wood engraver, was the first comic journal to publish political cartoons regularly in Canada. Starting in 1869, political and social cartoons were used extensively in Canada's first illustrated national news magazine, the *Canadian Illustrated News*, and its French-language edition, *L'Opinion publique*. Edward Jump, an itinerant French-born artist who worked for the *Canadian Illustrated News* from 1871 to 1873, was the most accomplished caricaturist in Canada up to that time. J.W. "Johnny" BENGOUGH was the first memorable Canadian cartoonist. Starting his career as a compositor and journalist for the *Whitby Gazette* in Ontario, he was strongly influenced by the work of Thomas Nast, the celebrated US cartoonist whose work appeared in *Harper's Weekly*. Bengough started his own magazine in 1873; for the next 21 years, he was editor and chief illustrator of *Grip*, working under his own name and pseudonymns. His cartoons about Québec, for instance, were done in a "slashing French style" and signed L. Côté, as he later confessed. Bengough once called Sir John A. Macdonald "my chief stock in trade," and his cartoons of Canada's first prime minister are engraved on the memories of Canadians who have seen them. Bengough's cartoons have survived because of their lively portrayal of Canadian politics, but his draftsmanship often was rough, almost childish. The first native-born caricaturist of the first rank to appear in Canada was Henri JULIEN, the son of a Québec printer. Effective but crude cartoons had appeared in French-language comic journals in the 1860s but Julien's experience as an engraver and his technical skill as an artist enabled him to inaugurate a new era in Québec cartooning when his work first started to appear in 1873 in *L'Opinion publique* and the *Canadian Illustrated News*. In 1888, he became chief cartoonist and illustrator for the *Montreal Star*. Among his notable caricatures were the "Bytown Coons" series, which depicted Ottawa politicians as members of a blackface minstrel troupe. Most of the important contemporary Canadian attitudes were sketched in the cartoons of the 19th century; the rivalry between regions and language groups, for instance, and resentment of interference in Canadian affairs, particularly by the US. In Canadian cartoons of the last century, Uncle Sam or Brother Jonathan was often shown as a crafty and disreputable Yankee carpetbagger trying to take advantage of a brawny, virtuous, but naive Jack Canuck.

In the first half of this century, Canadian cartoonists were influenced strongly by British and American models. Cartoonists were prized for "punch" rather than artistic ability. Above all, they were expected to entertain newspaper readers. Among the best in these years were Arch Dale, who started to draw for the Winnipeg *Free Press* in 1913 and produced his last cartoon in 1954; Arthur Racey, who succeeded Julien at the *Montreal Star* in 1899 and remained there for 42 years; and C.W. JEFFERYS, who started in 1900 as a cartoonist with the *Toronto Star* and the *Moon*, a humorous magazine, and went on to become Canada's best-known historical illustrator.

A new style and era of political cartooning in newspapers began in the 1950s when Robert Lapalme reached his peak at *Le Devoir* in Montréal. A self-taught Québec artist who had worked briefly in New York as a free-lance magazine illustrator in the 1930s, LaPalme shocked the readers of *Le Devoir* with vicious, avant-garde drawings of Québec Premier Maurice Duplessis, portraying him as a pimp selling Québec to the Americans or as a corrupt priest attended by his acolyte ministers. LaPalme organized an exhibition of caricatures in Montréal (1963) that developed into the International Salon of Caricature and Cartoon, a permanent museum reputed to be the largest and most important of its kind in the world. Contemporary with LaPalme, Len Norris for more than 30 years has been consistently the funniest cartoonist in the country and among the most popular. Since 1950, when he joined the Vancouver *Sun*, he has delighted Canadians with whimsical, detailed drawings of post-Victorian existence in BC.

Duncan MACPHERSON is generally regarded as the best political cartoonist that Canada has produced. Writing in the *New Yorker* (1964), critic Edmund Wilson credited Macpherson with creating "a phantasmagoria for which the mediocre subjects themselves seem hardly adequate." Within a few months of joining the *Toronto Star* in 1958, Macpherson's caricatures of PM John Diefenbaker brought him wide recognition. He was given a solo exhibition of his work by the Public Archives in Ottawa (1980), where most of his original drawings are stored. Macpherson not only raised the artistic level of cartooning in Canada but forged a new editorial role for himself at the *Star*. He refused to become merely an illustrator of the newspaper's editorials, as his predecessors had been, claiming for himself the freedom enjoyed by columnists who signed their own names to their articles and who often disagreed with the newspaper's editorial writers. This new approach has influenced many Canadian cartoonists since.

Among younger cartoonists, Terry Mosher, working under the name "Aislin" at the *Gazette* in Montréal, has achieved a national reputation that rivals the fame of Macpherson and Norris.

Untitled cartoon by Duncan Macpherson (*courtesy Public Archives of Canada / C-112673 / Toronto Star Syndicate*).

Aislin has won the Canadian National Newspaper Award for Political Cartooning several times, as has Roy Peterson, Norris's successor at the Vancouver *Sun*. In Québec, LaPalme's place has been claimed by Jean-Pierre Girerd, of *La Presse*, who left Algeria in 1961 and arrived in Montréal 3 years later. At present, there are about 25 cartoonists in Canada who support themselves by working for newspapers. Within this group, there is a consensus that rapid political and social changes in Canada, the rise of such charismatic political leaders as Pierre Trudeau and René Lévesque, and the existence of a relatively stable and prosperous newspaper industry, have created unprecedented and unparalleled opportunities for cartoonists. As a result, it is widely believed that the standard of political cartooning in Canada has never been higher. PETER DESBARATS

Reading: Art Gallery of Ontario, *Canadian Cartoon and Caricature* (1969); Peter Desbarats and T. Mosher, *The Hecklers* (1979).

Cartwright, George, soldier, diarist, entrepreneur (b at Marnham, Eng 12 Feb 1739 or 1740; d at Mansfield, Eng 19 May 1819). Cartwright entered the British army at 16, serving in India, Ireland, Minorca and Germany, and in 1769 he went on half pay. His interest in Newfoundland having been aroused by an earlier voyage, he turned Labrador trader, operating coastal posts between Cape Charles and Hamilton Inlet from 1770 to 1786. With his wide-ranging curiosity, Cartwright was a careful student of the native people and natural history of the region. The voluminous *Journal of Transactions and Events, During a Residence of Nearly Sixteen Years on the Coast of Labrador* (3 vols, 1792) is a singular record of his experiences and observations. G.M. STORY

Cartwright, Richard, businessman, officeholder, judge, militia officer, author (b at Albany, NY 2 Feb 1759; d at Montréal, 27 July 1815). A committed LOYALIST, Cartwright was expelled from New York in Oct 1777. After serving until 1780 as secretary for John BUTLER's Rangers based at Niagara, he became a merchant involved in the provisioning trade. By 1785 Cartwright had moved to the Kingston area where he soon became an influential commercial, legal, political and religious leader. Cartwright was, because of his influence on John STRACHAN, a critically important link in the ideological chain that connects the American Loyalist thought of the 1770s with the English-speaking, Upper Canadian Tory conceptual framework of the post-War-of-1812 period. Though Cartwright vigorously opposed, in the early 1790s, many of Lieutenant-Governor SIMCOE's anglophile policies, he had become by 1800 an ardent supporter of the Upper Canadian Conservative status quo. G.A. RAWLYK

Cartwright, Sir Richard John, politician (b at Kingston, Upper Canada 4 Dec 1835; d there 24 Sept 1912). The scion of a rich, powerful, conservative and Loyalist family, he was educated at Trinity College, Dublin, which he attended 1851-56 although he took no degree. Using family money, he became a businessman-investor with extensive interests in finance, transportation, real estate, mining and manufacturing. Cartwright represented various Ontario constituencies in Parliament 1863-1904, then entered the Senate where he remained until he died. Initially a Tory, he broke with Sir John A. MACDONALD in 1869 and was an Independent until 1873 when he joined the Liberal Party. He was a powerful Liberal leader, serving as minister of finance 1873-78 and minister of trade and commerce 1896-1911. From 1887 until after the 1891 general election he was the effective leader of the Ontario wing of the Liberal Party and also led the faction within the party that wanted free trade with the US. He was knighted in 1879. DONALD SWAINSON

Carver, Humphrey Stephen Mumford, architect, community planner, author (b at Birmingham, Eng 29 Nov 1902). Educated in England, he arrived in Canada in 1930. He practised landscape architecture with Carl Borgstrum (1931-37), taught at U of T's School of Architecture (1938-41) and Social Work (1946-48), and pioneered the Regent Park N public-housing project. He was active in the LEAGUE FOR SOCIAL RECONSTRUCTION, outlining in the 1930s the social policy basis for a national housing program. He organized the landmark 1939 Housing Conference and was at the centre of virtually all institutional developments in community planning and housing after 1940. He chaired the Research Committee of Central Mortgage and Housing Corporation (1948-55) and its Advisory Group (1955-67). In his book *Cities in the Suburbs* (1962), Carver advocated that the planning of suburbs be integrated with the wider social community. Under Carver's leadership of the CMHC Advisory Group, Canada's research and programs in housing policy, housing design and community planning attained an international reputation for innovation and progressive development standards. WILLIAM PERKS

Cascade Mountains, BC, are the N end of mountain ranges extending to California, 180-260 km E of the Pacific Ocean. The BC Cascades show a transition from the wet coastal forest of the rugged Skagit Range to the drier interior vegetation of the Okanagan Range and of the ridge E of the Fraser R and S of LYTTON. Eastward they merge with the Thompson Plateau. (There are no active volcanoes in BC as in the US Cascades' Mt St Helens and others.) Near the US border are popular recreation and outdoor areas: Cultus Lk, Skagit Valley, Manning and Cathedral provincial parks. A gold-silver mine opened near HOPE in 1978. PETER GRANT

Casgrain, Henri-Raymond, historian, literary critic (b at Rivière-Ouelle, Qué 16 Dec 1831; d at Québec City 12 Jan 1904). Casgrain was ordained a priest in 1856. After teaching at his former college, Ste-Anne de la Pocatière, he was named vicar at Beauport and then at Notre-Dame de Québec. In Québec City he was a leading figure in the literary movement of 1860, being a founder of its 2 literary magazines, *Les Soirées canadiennes* (1861-65) and *Le Foyer canadien*(1863-66), and author of *Légendes canadiennes* (1861). Casgrain specialized in biography. Despite his poor health and failing eyesight, he published lives of MARIE DE L'INCARNATION (1864), François-Xavier GARNEAU (1866), Philippe-Joseph AUBERT DE GASPÉ (1871), Francis Parkman (1872) and Antoine GÉRIN-LAJOIE (1886), as well as numerous historical studies. His scholarship was sometimes questioned, as was his lack of scruples in copyright matters, but his energy and exuberant style ensured his reputation. A founding fellow of the RSC (1882), he became its president in 1889 and was an honorary doctor of Laval University. DAVID M. HAYNE

Casgrain, Thérèse, née Forget, reformer (b at Montréal 10 July 1896; d there 2 Nov 1981). Best remembered for her leadership of the campaign for women's suffrage in Québec before WWII, she was a leading 20th-century Canadian reformer. Born to a wealthy family, she married Pierre-François Casgrain, Liberal lawyer and politician, and raised 4 children. A founding member of the Provincial Franchise Committee for women's suffrage in 1921, she campaigned ceaselessly for women's rights in Québec and hosted a popular Radio Canada program in the 1930s, "Fémina." During WWII she was one of 2 presidents of the Women's Surveillance Committee for the WARTIME PRICES AND TRADE BOARD. In 1946 she joined the CO-OPERATIVE COMMONWEALTH FEDERATION, becoming provincial leader 1951-57. She worked within the party, strengthening in-

Thérèse Casgrain, who characterized herself as a humanist, campaigned ceaselessly for women's rights in Québec (*courtesy Public Archives of Canada / PA-126768*).

ternational socialist links, and in Québec helped mobilize opposition to Premier DUPLESSIS. In 1961 she founded the Québec branch of the VOICE OF WOMEN to protest the nuclear threat. She was a founder of the League for Human Rights (1960) and of the Fédération des femmes du Québec (1966). In 1970 she was appointed to the Senate. In her autobiography, *A Woman in a Man's World* (1972), she characterized herself as a humanist.
JENNIFER STODDART

Cashin, Peter J., politician, businessman, soldier (b at Cape Broyle, Nfld 8 Mar 1890; d at St John's 21 May 1977). He joined the Nfld Regiment in 1915, served overseas and in Mar 1918 was promoted major in command of the British Machine Gun Corp. After the war he joined the family business. In 1923 he first won election to the Assembly as a Liberal-Labour-Progressive. Crossing to the Liberals in 1925, he was reelected in 1928 and was minister of finance 1928-32. A consistent opponent of the COMMISSION OF GOVERNMENT, Cashin was elected as one of the 3 delegates for St John's W in the National Convention Vote in 1946. Subsequently, he emerged as strongly anti-Confederate and the leader of the RESPONSIBLE GOVERNMENT advocates at the Convention. After Newfoundland joined Canada in 1949, Cashin ran provincially and was elected as an Independent. He was later recruited by the Progressive Conservative Party and served as leader of the PC Opposition until 1953 when he retired from active politics. He was director of civil defence for Newfoundland from 1954 until his retirement in the mid-1960s.
JOHN PARSONS

Reading: Peter Cashin, *My Life and Times, 1890-1919* (1976).

Cassiar Mountains extend from the Yukon Territory 440 km SE to the confluence of the Finlay and Fox rivers in N-central BC. The name is thought to derive from a Nahanni word, *kaska*, or *kasha* ("creek" or "small river"). The Stikine Ranges, with a central ridge of granite, rise to 2760 m. Peaks lower than 2000 m were rounded by glacial action. They have low relief and extensive tundra, owing to the area's severe boreal climate. The Dease R attracted gold prospectors in the 1870s, and mineral exploration continues, especially in the Toodoggone R area, but the mountains remain a remote part of BC. The one community, Cassiar, where an asbestos mine opened in 1952, is company owned. An all-weather highway through the mountains opened in 1972.
PETER GRANT

Casson, Alfred Joseph, painter (b at Toronto 17 May 1898). After study at Hamilton (1913-15) and Toronto (1915-17), A.J. Casson got his first real job in 1919 at a Toronto commercial art firm as Franklin CARMICHAEL's apprentice. Carmichael had the greatest influence on Casson as an artist, taking him sketching and camping, and introducing him to members of the GROUP OF SEVEN, including Lawren HARRIS and J.E.H. MACDONALD. Along with Carmichael and F.H. Bridgen, Casson revived and championed the watercolour medium. In 1926 Casson was invited to join the Group to replace Franz JOHNSTON who had shown only in the group's first exhibition (1920). He also bought his first car and began exploring villages near Toronto. Ontario small towns, such as Elora and Alton, were to become his preferred subjects.

Casson's style always retained what Harris had talked to him about — simplification and the elimination of all nonessentials. This quality in his work culminated in *Country Store* (1945), the start of his so-called period of abstraction. In later years, besides painting, Casson has helped detect forgeries, particularly of Group of Seven works, for the Ontario Provincial Police.
JOAN MURRAY

Reading: Paul Duval, *A.J. Casson* (1980).

Castlegar, BC, City, pop 6902 (1981c), inc (with Kinnaird) 1974, is located on the W bank of the COLUMBIA R at its junction with the Kootenay, midway between Calgary and Vancouver, and about 35 km N of the US border. The Lakes Band of Interior SALISH dominated this vital transportation and fishing site until the mid-18th century. Edgar Dewdney pre-empted the site 1865 while building the Dewdney Trail. A trail linked it with Nelson (43 km NE) in 1889; the first railway followed in 1892. In 1908 DOUKHOBORS took up land in the area, and thrived until 1924 when their spiritual leader, Peter "The Lordly" VERIGIN, was assassinated. Since the 1940s Castlegar has been a bedroom town for Cominco employees, a centre for dam construction workers on the Kootenay and Columbia projects and the Revelstoke Canyon Dam, and a home for pulp-mill employees. BC Timber Pulp Mill and Saw Mill, and Selkirk College, with a variety of university courses and technological training, are important employers. Having excellent transportation facilities, the city is a trade centre with substantial service area.
WILLIAM A. SLOAN

Castors ("Beavers"), a group of ULTRAMONTANE dissident Conservatives, established in 1882. Members opposed Québec Conservative premiers J.A. CHAPLEAU and J.A. MOUSSEAU, whom they accused of ousting them from power in order to ally themselves with the moderate Liberals. The group opposed the government's lax administration, its co-operation with unscrupulous businessmen and its favouring Québec City over Montréal, especially in university matters. François-Xavier-Anselme Trudel gave the group its name by signing the pseudonym "Castor" to his pamphlet, *Le Pays, le parti et le grand homme* (1882). The group lacked structure and remained a fringe group until its demise in the late 19th century.
NIVE VOISINE

Cat The domestic cat, a species of flesh-eating MAMMAL belonging to the family Felidae, order carnivora, is a small, lithe, intelligent, soft-furred animal. About 3.4 million domestic cats inhabit Canada, averaging 1.9 per cat-owning household (just over 1 in every 4 households).

Cat fancy in Canada developed gradually. The first recorded show, a 2-day show with one officiating judge, was held in 1906 in Toronto. Most of the original purebred stock was imported from England. During the war years (1939-45), cat breeding and showing was greatly curtailed. After WWII interest revived and in 1960 the Canadian Cat Association (CCA) was founded. Today, there are active clubs in most major cities and they hold at least one show annually. The Canadian National Cat Club, one of the oldest active clubs, sponsored cat shows at the annual CANADIAN NATIONAL EXHIBITION (CNE). In 1968 CNCC disbanded and sponsorship of CNE was passed to the Royal Canadian Cat Club, an affiliate of CCA. Many clubs in Canada are affiliated with other associations, such as Cat Fanciers Assn (CFA), American Cat Fanciers Assn (ACFA) and American Cat Assn (ACA). Winnipeg's Manitoba Cat Club, the largest and most active club in Canada, averaging approximately 150 members, was organized in 1962 and became affiliated with ACFA.
JOHN M. BODNER

Catfish, small to large, primarily freshwater FISHES of order Siluriformes (about 2000 species worldwide). In southern Canada, 10 species of genera *Ictalurus, Noturus* and *Pylodictis* of the N American family Ictaluridae (40 species in all) are known. They are characterized by having a scaleless body, several pairs of barbels (elongate, fleshy projections around the mouth region), adipose (fatty) dorsal fin in front of the tail, and dorsal and pectoral fin spines that can inflict painful wounds. In some smaller madtoms, the spines have a groove and venom sac. The barbels and much of the skin are covered with taste buds for locating food at night, when catfish are most active. Catfish eat aquatic insects, molluscs, crustaceans, plant material and other fishes. Ictalurid catfish provide parental care, excavating a nest and guarding eggs and young. The reproductive pair engages in a head-to-tail clasping behaviour before deposition of eggs. Most catfish are not used by humans, but the brown bullhead and the channel catfish are fished for sport and commercially in Canada. *See* ENDANGERED ANIMALS.
BRIAN W. COAD

Brown bullhead catfish (*Ictalurus nebulosus*), shown in pond environment with leech, caddisfly larva and mayfly nymph (*artwork by Claire Tremblay*).

Cathcart, Charles Murray, 2nd Earl, general, governor general of BNA (b at Walton, Eng 21 Dec 1783; d at St Leonard's-on-Sea, Eng 16 July 1859). One of Wellington's staff officers in the Napoleonic wars, Cathcart was also an amateur scientist of some reputation. In 1841 he discovered the mineral greenockite, a sulphate of cadmium. He served as commander of British forces in N America, 15 June 1845 to 13 May 1847, and added the responsibility of administrator, 26 Nov 1845 to 24 Apr 1846, and gov gen 24 Apr 1846 to 30 Jan 1847. The highest civil and military executive powers were thus briefly united because of a severe crisis in Anglo-American relations during the Oregon Boundary Dispute. Cathcart was inexperienced in politics but an effective interim governor. He became dispensable with the signing of the Oregon Treaty.
OWEN COOKE AND NORMAN HILLMER

Catherwood, Ethel, track and field athlete (b in Haldimand County, Ont 1909). She is the only Canadian woman ever to win an individual gold medal in Olympic track and field competition. Raised in Saskatoon, she emerged as a high jumper in 1926 when she equalled the Canadian record at a city meet; later that year she broke the world record with a jump of 1.58 m. Followers dubbed her "The Saskatoon Lily" in Toronto, where philanthropist Teddy Oke took her under his wing. At the 1928 Canadian championships in Halifax, she set a new record of 1.6 m. On the final day of the 1928 Amsterdam Olympics, Catherwood cleared 1.59 m in the women's "running high jump" for the gold medal. After a hero's welcome, she turned down motion-picture offers in favour of a business course and piano study; she married and moved to California, never to compete again.

TED BARRIS

Catholic Action Faithful to the Vatican's teachings and following the example of the church in France, elements of the Roman Catholic Church in Québec established Catholic Action groups to associate laymen of various ages and professions with the church's social work, particularly in urban areas. The Association catholique de la jeunesse canadienne-française was founded in 1903-04 by fathers Lionel GROULX and Émile Chartier. Other groups comprised farmers and workers, and the youth movement included Jeunesse ouvrière catholique (JOC), Jeunesse étudiante catholique and Jeunesse rurale catholique, which were formed in the 1930s following the papal encyclical *Urbi Arcano* (1922) and the subsequent formation of JOC groups in Belgium. The influence of these associations, which were criticized by the conservative clergy as being too activist, is difficult to measure. They declined rapidly in the 1950s. *See* CATHOLICISM; SOCIAL DOCTRINE.

RICHARD JONES

Catholic Women's League of Canada, The, with 130 000 members in 1983, represents the largest organized body of Catholic women in Canada. Formed nationally in 1920, the league is committed to the upholding of Christian values and education in the modern world, the understanding and growth of religious freedom, social justice, peace and harmony, and the recognition of the human dignity of all people everywhere. Structured to enable members to make their views known at parish, diocesan and provincial levels, the CWL, through National Council, actively translates the objectives of the organization into statements and briefs to the government on a broad spectrum of concerns.

VALERIE J. FALL

Catholicism [Gk *katholikos*, "general" or "universal"] refers most commonly to that CHRISTIANITY which is in communion with the pope and the Church of Rome, although the modern ecumenical movement sees all Christians as sharing in the church's catholicism, which is derived from the universal headship and reign of Christ. (Many Protestant denominations include the word "catholic" in their creeds, referring thereby to the Christian Church as a whole.) The term is not biblical: St Ignatius of Antioch (d about 110 AD) was the first person known to have referred to the "Catholic Church." St Vincent of Lerins (5th century) later defined the catholic faith as "that which has been believed everywhere, always, and by all." In the church's belief God the creator is father of all, and God the son (Christ) has a universal kingdom, the church. The earliest Christian churches, established amid great linguistic, cultural and ethnic diversity, regarded themselves as constituting one holy, catholic church of Christ.

The Roman Catholic Church recognizes 7 religious acts, or sacraments: baptism, normally of infants; confirmation; the Eucharist (communion), celebrated centrally in the mass (public worship) and offered only to the baptized; confession, which involves the petitioner's penance and absolution by a priest; ordination (admission to one of 7 clerical ranks); marriage; and unction (anointing), normally administered only if the recipient is seriously ill or death is imminent. Government of the church is by a hierarchy of bishops, priests and deacons under the authority of the pope, who is bishop of Rome. The doctrine of apostolic succession holds that the spiritual authority vested in the apostles by Christ has descended in unbroken succession to the present pope, bishops and priests, who possess this authority in varying degrees. All clergy must be males.The church has numerous CHRISTIAN RELIGIOUS COMMUNITIES of both sexes; members commit themselves to chastity, as do priests and bishops of the Western rite.

Since the early centuries of Christianity, Easter, which commemorates Christ's Resurrection, has been the central feast of the liturgical calendar. In the course of time other seasonal and thematic feasts have been added; in contemporary Catholicism, Christmas (feast of the birth of Jesus) and Epiphany (feast of the early manifestations of Christ's divinity) have been highlighted along with Easter as the central feasts of the year (*see* RELIGIOUS FESTIVALS).

Adherents to Eastern rite Catholic churches are not numerous in Canada: the 1981 census shows a total of 190 585 Ukrainian Catholics (the largest Eastern-rite denomination in Canada). The Western-rite, or Roman Catholic, church is much more strongly represented: close to one-half of Canada's population declared itself to be Roman Catholic in 1981. (Census data must be treated with care; identification with the church does not necessarily imply active membership.) This proportion increased from 38.7% in 1921, largely because of IMMIGRATION by great numbers of Roman Catholics. Canada's more than 11.2 million Roman Catholics are unevenly distributed across the country, with 50.0% of them in Québec, 26.6% in Ontario, 14.7% W of Ontario and 8.4% E of Québec.

Roman Catholic Church

Roman Catholicism came to what is now Canada with the first European explorers but was slow to establish itself: whether Jacques CARTIER really was accompanied by chaplains in 1535, it took Samuel de CHAMPLAIN and his pro-settlement propaganda to persuade the French church to plant a branch in the St Lawrence Valley. Circumstances then favoured the missionary spirit that led to a Canadian Catholic church; these included the interest of the papacy and the religious orders in the New World; the end of the religious wars in France; the reforms following the Council of Trent, which regenerated the French church; and the enthusiasm of the devout for missions abroad. Supported by noble benefactors and the French clergy, members of the Récollet order established themselves in Québec in 1615, followed in 1625 by the Jesuits. The missionaries went home to France during the English occupation, 1629-32, but then returned in force (although, by order of Cardinal Richelieu, only the Jesuits were permitted to resume their work).

This young Canadian church was devoted almost entirely to evangelizing the Indians. Without neglecting the increasing number of settlers in NEW FRANCE, the Jesuits (and later the Sulpicians) concentrated on living with the Indians. The accounts of their labours, published in the JESUIT RELATIONS, helped them to hold the interest of Catholics in France. Generous donations funded the Jesuit college (1635); the SILLERY reserve (1637); the Ursuline girls' seminary (1639) run by MARIE DE L'INCARNATION; the HÔTEL-DIEU (1639); and VILLE-MARIE (1642), where the same institutions as those in Québec were established. The church supported the colony and was dominant even in politics, with the Jesuit superior often supplanting the governor.

Everything had changed by the 1650s. In 1648-50 the Iroquois destroyed HURONIA, and with it the Jesuits' most promising mission, STE MARIE AMONG THE HURONS. Thereafter the Jesuits worked in scattered missions among the native peoples, but they had to devote increasing attention to the growing French population. The church received its first prelate in 1659. Though François de LAVAL was only vicar apostolic (ie, acting bishop where no hierarchy exists), he had sufficient jurisdiction to co-ordinate the establishment of the necessary institutions, including the SÉMINAIRE DE QUÉBEC. After New France's reorganization in 1663 as a royal colony, the church had to accept state intervention in joint questions (eg, establishment of parishes) and even in purely religious ones (eg, regulation of religious communities); in return, it could count on state support, which included money. Harmony was sometimes hard to maintain.

Gradually a distinctive Christianity developed. It was homogeneous, for Protestants were allowed into the colony only for brief visits (*see* HUGUENOTS). Most members of the population practised their faith, following the severe Catholicism developed primarily by Mgr de SAINT-VALLIER (*see* JANSENISM). The parish, backbone of religious life, was financially administered by churchwardens (the only elected officials in New France), who were usually influenced by the parish priest. In 1760 Canada had about 100 parishes, most of them run by diocesan clergy (84 members), of whom four-fifths were Canadian-born. The priests were assisted by 30 Sulpicians, 25 Jesuits and 24 Récollets, and over 200 nuns belonging to 6 communities who were responsible for educational and welfare activities. These communities of men and women could offer their services free because the king had granted them lands and financial support. This equilibrium, which characterized church-state relations 1660-1760, was vulnerable to any change in the balance between the forces that composed it.

After the CONQUEST of 1759-60, the Catholic Church of Québec, already weakened by the effects of war, had also to deal with new British — and Protestant — masters. The new authorities were expected to favour the Church of England (*see* ANGLICANISM) and attempt to convert their new Catholic subjects. However, the free exercise of the Catholic rite had been guaranteed in the terms of surrender, though under British limits of toleration, and greater freedom for Roman Catholics soon evolved. Nevertheless, the British interfered in the nomination of bishops and sometimes priests, and required the clergy to communicate certain government documents to their parishioners. The QUEBEC ACT of 1774 further guaranteed free exercise of Roman Catholicism and made it easier for Catholics to enter public office. To protect the newly won freedoms the bishops preached obedience (in varying degrees), led their people in opposition to the American invaders of 1775 and sang hymns of thanksgiving for British victories over the French in the AMERICAN REVOLUTION.

In other parts of present-day Canada, the French church had established missions in the Maritimes by the early 17th century and in Newfoundland by mid-century, but there was soon settlement by nonfrancophone Roman Catholics as well in these areas. Late in the 17th century Irish Catholics began to arrive in Newfoundland, which was under Québec's jurisdiction until 1713; that year France ceded Newfoundland to Britain by the TREATY OF UTRECHT, and ecclesiastical jurisdiction over the island passed to the vicar apostolic of London. In 1796 Newfoundland became a separate diocese under Bishop J.L. O'Donel.

ne dome of St Mary's Ukrainian Catholic Church in orkton displays one of the major religious frescoes of N merica. In the centre, Mary is crowned in Heaven, atnded by the Father, the Son and the Holy Spirit; 157 ngels adorn the perimeter (*photo by John deVisser*).

In the late 18th century significant numbers Scottish Roman Catholics settled on Prince lward Island and in Nova Scotia. For various ersonal, political and ecclesiastical reasons, owever, the church there and in the other ttled parts of present-day Canada, excepting ewfoundland, remained under the jurisdicon of the bishop of Québec until 1817; that ear Nova Scotia was made a separate vicariate postolic under Bishop Edmund Burke. Thereter, new vicariates and dioceses appeared as ttlement spread. The growth of the church in nglophone Canada was spurred especially by e arrival in the 19th century of large numbers Irish immigrants.

Meanwhile, in LOWER CANADA [Québec], by the rly 19th century numerous Catholics, espeally the rising professional class, had disnced themselves from their church. The priests ould not direct the populace as they had done efore, and the people tended to neglect relious practices. Church authorities warded off forts at secular domination, won official recgnition from the bishop and encouraged eduation (including religious vocations), and reved the Catholic faith. But the 323 priests ould not meet the needs of Québec's 500 000 habitants and could no longer count on the ipport of male religious communities, which part from the Sulpicians) had disappeared, or f female ones, which were in difficulties. The arti PATRIOTE (fd 1826), which had mass suport, proposed a liberal program that alarmed e clergy and began a Protestant-style proslytism, primarily around Montréal. The beaguered bishop of Québec won the nominaon of a Montréal auxiliary, Mgr Jean-Jacques artigue, who became bishop of Montréal in 836. Lartigue condemned the REBELLIONS OF 337-38 but, by siding with the government, temorarily alienated himself from his people.

The church was as badly shaken as the rest of ociety by the insurrection's aftereffects, but it vas the first to recover. Under the dynamic new ishop of Montréal, Mgr Ignace BOURGET (inalled in 1840), the clergy assumed increasing ower. Bourget set out to "Christianize" and "reenerate" society, applying the ideas of his preecessor and using the populist sermons of the rench Mgr Charles de Forbin-Janson (*see* EVANELISM) to advantage. Bourget made full use of the religious press, run with passion and skill by laymen; headed fund drives in the city; and made begging trips to Europe. He worked for the people's advancement, allying his church with Rome on liturgy, theological studies and devotions. He supported campaigns for public morality (eg, TEMPERANCE campaigns and the fight against "evil" literature led by the Oeuvre des bons livres and the Cabinets de lecture paroissiaux), ran a social-assistance program for the poor, the sick, the orphaned and the handicapped, and preached social mutual assistance. The Montréal example was followed throughout Québec, though often to a lesser degree.

During the same period a sharp increase in religious vocations led to more and better-served parishes; the number of dioceses (10 in 1900) rose with the birthrate. The priests, now more numerous, often involved themselves in secular activities and seemed to run everything in Québec. Parishes periodically called in specialists (Jesuits, Oblates, Redemptorists, Dominicans and Franciscans) to preach at spiritual-renewal missions. The lay response seemed satisfactory: most were now practising and an elite could even be called devoted.

Catholicism in both English and French Canada was aligned with international Catholicism, whose leadership was becoming progressively more defensive and fearful of postrevolutionary (American and French) Western society. During the early 19th century sectarian violence grew, as demonstrated by the brawling of Irish Catholics with Irish Protestants (*see* ORANGE ORDER) on several occasions in Upper Canada, and by the fighting involved in the so-called SHINERS' WAR of the 1840s. Catholic churchmen saw the social upheaval resulting from INDUSTRIALIZATION and URBANIZATION as the work of the devil, the French Revolution, Freemasonry, socialism and laissez-faire capitalism, and they urged the faithful to return to a stable Christian social order such as that prevailing in the Middle Ages.

One social area in which the church was always active was education. Catholic clergy throughout Canada had been pioneers in early 19th-century education, establishing small local schools with teachers whose primary concern was the moral education of their charges. But toward mid-century the state began to provide schooling, thus moving into an area of social concern that had been a church responsibility for centuries. The first school Act (1841) of the PROVINCE OF CANADA was aimed at the establishment of a Christian but nondenominational school system. However, political realities ensured that Canada East [Québec] soon developed a dual confessional school system (Catholic and Protestant), whereas Canada West [Ontario] allowed the creation of a divided, state-supported school system, one section being nondenominational (public), the other confessional (SEPARATE SCHOOLS). The latter soon became largely Roman Catholic. In subsequent decades other provinces frequently modelled their school systems on that of either Québec or Ontario. As the state took over the schooling of Canadians, therefore, confessional and Catholic schools obtained recognition in law. During the second half of the 19th century, the Canadian Catholic hierarchy was determined to strengthen its Catholic schools, while public school promoters considered that their "public" schools alone should enjoy the support of the state. There ensued lengthy and virulent controversies, such as the NEW BRUNSWICK SCHOOL QUESTION of 1871, the MANITOBA SCHOOLS QUESTION of the 1890s and the NORTH-WEST SCHOOLS QUESTION at the turn of the century; the ONTARIO SCHOOLS QUESTION of 1912-27 was not only a fight between English Protestants and French Catholics, but also the result of a power struggle between French Canadian and Irish Canadian clerics within the church. Other parts of Canada experienced similar quarrels as ethnic groups struggled for church control, but in the process some clerics learned to value diversity and to respect and love one another. Meanwhile, the church had founded numerous denominational institutions of higher learning. A number of Canadian UNIVERSITIES originated in this way, including UNIVERSITY OF OTTAWA and U of St Michael's College (Toronto). In most cases, their administration has passed gradually into secular hands.

As the church increased its influence on society, especially in French Canada, some clergy were tempted by politics. Imbued with ULTRAMONTANE principles, and fearing reforms being suggested by the Liberal Party, the Québec clergy accused that party's supporters of Catholic liberalism and denounced them at election time. In 1871, laymen supported by Bourget and Mgr Louis-François LAFLÈCHE published an election manifesto, the *Programme catholique*, which could have led to religious control of the provincial Conservative Party. The strong reaction of 3 bishops (Archbishop Elzéar-Alexandre TASCHEREAU, Mgr Charles LaRocque and Mgr Jean Langevin) and of politicians doomed the project and made public the split between moderate and intransigent ultramontanists ("Programmists"). In 1875 the groups united in a virulent denunciation of Catholic liberalism; in 1876 the election results in 2 provincial ridings were annulled because of "undue influence" by the clergy. Tension grew between church and state. Rome was consulted, and it sent an apostolic delegate, Mgr George Conroy, to re-establish harmony between the prelates and force them to declare that their condemnation of Catholic liberalism had not been directed against the Liberal Party. Clerical intervention in politics was thereafter more discreet.

During the latter 19th century Québec Catholicism discovered a missionary vocation that persists today. Nuns, priests and brothers first established missions in English Canada (including the present-day Prairie provinces and Northwest Territories) and the US, and then throughout the world. (In 1977, 3375 Québec missionaries — including some laymen — were working abroad in Africa, the Americas, Asia and Oceania, and another 700 were serving in Canada itself.)

The church was active in broader social concerns as well. Various 19th-century sociologists had recognized that new forms of society, with new needs, were being created by growing industrialization and urbanization. Protestants responded to the new "social question" with the SOCIAL GOSPEL movement late in the century. By the 20th century, Québec Catholicism was preoccupied with social concerns. Aware of the problems created by the new technology and the migration to the cities, and challenged by Pope Leo XIII's 1891 encyclical, *Rerum Novarum*, the clergy developed a SOCIAL DOCTRINE to guide the new society. In Québec the Jesuits were particularly active through the École sociale populaire. Their Programme de restauration sociale (fd 1933) was the main inspiration for the political movements ACTION LIBÉRALE NATIONALE, BLOC POPULAIRE CANADIEN and, to a lesser degree, UNION NATIONALE. They supported and directed Catholic trade unions, formed 1907-20, and credit unions, cooperatives and every kind of league, each of which had Roman Catholicism as its main characteristic. Moreover, the church in Québec continued to control education. Secular activities left only about 45% of the clergy for parish duties. This disequilibrium posed few problems, since the province's clergy kept growing: 2091 in 1890, 3263 in 1920, 5000 in 1940 (a ratio of 567, 578, and 539 parishioners to each priest), exclusive of religious communities. The faithful were guided by their priests and in their religious practice emphasized parish missions, pilgrimages and provincial, regional and local conferences. CATHOLIC ACTION helped to form "new" Catholics, whose methods disturbed traditionalists and sometimes led to conflict with clergy.

In Canadian Catholicism's commitment to sociopolitical activity, doctrine and moral teaching were stringent, and political and social involvement was uncompromising. The GREAT DEPRESSION of the 1930s again tested the readiness of Catholics to deal with major social problems. The hard times that gave birth to the CO-OPERATIVE COMMONWEALTH FEDERATION also saw the beginnings of the Catholic ANTIGONISH MOVEMENT. Many Catholic bishops condemned the CCF because it was socialist. True to its tradition the church was generally conservative, supporting the status quo and uneasy with change. But WWII brought with it an increasing awareness of the outside world among Canadian Catholics, and made the church appear to many of them to be too self-sufficient and complacent.

During the century of highly centralized and disciplined Catholicism (1850-1950), while regular worship had become habitual for most Canadian Catholics, it had done so in the form of an increasing number of devotions set in a framework of intense and colourful piety. Devotion to the papacy had intensified after 1850, culminating in 1870 when the dogma of papal infallibility was defined, and successive popes strongly encouraged special devotions, eg, to the Sacred Heart of Jesus, the Virgin Mary or Saint Joseph. The Catholic Church built upon centuries-old customs in nurturing various forms of piety, such as the Rosary, the scapular, adoration of the Blessed Sacrament, and the Forty Hours; pilgrimages became popular, both to the shrines in Europe and the Holy Land and to various shrines in Canada. The crucifix adorned most Canadian Catholic homes, and wayside crosses and shrines were erected in massively Catholic areas. This intense piety would dissipate only after 1960.

Canadian Catholicism emerged from WWII as a church triumphant, as is suggested by the pageantry surrounding the 1947 Marian Congress in Ottawa and the installation ceremonies of Archbishop Paul-Émile LÉGER in Montréal in 1950. But the conservative administrations of Pope Pius XII and US Pres Eisenhower ended in the late 1950s, and the new liberal spirit emerging in the Western world began to affect the church in anglophone Canada. In Québec the changes were more extreme and jarring than they were elsewhere in Canada. WWII and the postwar period were a time of profound transformation for all Québec. Traditional values, even religious ones, were challenged by people wanting an expansion of missionary and community values, an increased lay role in the chuch and a warmer welcome for the positive values of the modern world. Some groups, eg, the Faculté des sciences sociales of U Laval and the Commission sacerdotale d'études sociales, made a new reading of the church's social doctrine and proposed modern solutions to social problems. They were in the forefront of opposition to the Duplessis government during the 1949 ASBESTOS STRIKE and inspired a collective pastoral letter of 1950 which expressed a new sensitivity to labour and to women.

Until 1959, however, Catholicism in Québec still wore the face of a triumphalist, conservative institution. Then the QUIET REVOLUTION of the 1960s forced the church to face some weaknesses. In just a few years, a wind of change produced both the declericalization of society (welfare, health and education passed from church to state control) and the secularization of institutions (eg, Catholic trade unions shed their confessionality to become the CONFEDERATION OF NATIONAL TRADE UNIONS), and associations, social clubs, universities and the state all adopted religious pluralism. At the same time, much of the population ceased practising, and there was a break with traditional morality, especially in sexual matters; a major exodus of members of the clergy and of religious orders; and a sharp drop in religious vocations. The hierarchy and the clergy as a whole seemed overwhelmed, and kept prudent silence.

In 1959 Pope John XXIII announced the convening of an ecumenical council, and the Catholic faith throughout the world began to seek new forms of expression and witness. In Vatican Council II (1962-65) international Catholicism was caught up in a whirlwind of change and challenge that sought to revitalize all areas of Christian concern, from theology to political action, from spirituality to administration, from ecumenism to moral codes. A number of Canadians (eg, Cardinal Léger, theologian Bernard LONERGAN and humanitarian Jean VANIER) emerged as leaders of the *aggiornamento* (modernization movement) in various spheres of activity. The church in Canada could no longer rely on social custom and constraint, as it had done in the past, to ensure church attendance or influence government decision-making. The effects were particularly marked in Québec, where the Quiet Revolution coincided with the church's international renewal. The loosening of these ties to society led to a decade or more of generalized confusion for many Canadian Catholics. Those who had attended mass every Sunday fearing the pain of sin learned the importance of personal responsibility in attendance at worship. Those who saw the cleric as "another Christ" discovered that he was also human. Those who were concerned over sexual sin as "the only sin" discovered the importance of loving God and one's neighbour. Churchmen learned to share some authority and Catholics were called upon to take some responsibility.

One sign of the Catholic renewal was a softening of the teaching on marriage. Before 1960 a Roman Catholic needed special permission to marry a non-Catholic, and the non-Catholic partner needed to agree in writing to the education of his children in the Catholic faith. After Vatican II the church discovered the primacy of conscience and the real Christian faith of many non-Catholic Christians. This led to less stringent disciplinary dictums, many Catholic pastors now acknowledging that the children born of a mixed marriage are best raised in the church of the more committed Christian partner. The ecumenical campaign has been strengthened in the process.

Indeed, Vatican II and the papal documen that followed in its wake constitute a milesto in the history of the Roman Catholic Churc New bridgeheads were established on the shor of a postmodern world whose links with th Christian church had been deteriorating sin the 17th century. The fear of the world th characterized so much of previous spirituali became an open-hearted reaching out towar contemporary humanity. There was greater em phasis on the church as a people of God, and le on the dominant hierarchy; the laity made som advances (although in the early 1980s Canadia women were lobbying for access to the hie archy through women's ordination); Protestan were promoted in the eyes of the Roman Cath lic Church from the rank of heretics to that "separated brethren"; the Third World was give its due as an area of major concern to the churc the scarecrow of socialism became acceptab ideology under certain circumstances; and th treatment reserved for linguistic, cultural ar political minorities was recognized as a val test of the quality of governments.

Forms of worship changed as well after Va ican II, and many of the changes centered on th renewed emphasis on the people as princip constituent of the church. Although comm nion remains the focal point of the mass, pa taking of it is not linked as closely to individu confession as it formerly was. Priests now co duct mass facing the people, and the Latin of th Tridentine rite has given way to vernacular la guages. The practice of preaching and inte pretation of scripture has been revived, and la members of the congregation participate mo fully in the various aspects of the worship se vice. There is also a resurgence of congregation singing and popular hymnology. At the san time, certain features of popular piety (eg, ben dictions, stations of the cross) have virtually di appeared. *See also* CHARISMATIC RENEWAL.

In the wake of Vatican II the Canadian Cath lic church reassessed its attitude toward "othe linguistic and cultural groups. In early Ontar and English Canada, for instance, the leadershi of various Catholic churches had been large French or French Canadian (there was no fra cophone bishop in the Maritimes before 1912 As an English-speaking (largely Irish) hierarch came to the fore in these areas, ethnolinguist polarization developed simultaneously in th ranks of the hierarchy and in Canada generall The result was a Canadian Catholic Church th pretended to be united, but was in fact separate on English-French lines. While Rome preache bilingualism for the Canadian church, Canada bishops indulged in their own peculiar brand ethnocultural warfare.

The new spirit that prevailed after 1960 le Canada's Catholic churchmen to reassess the attitudes. At the centennial of Confederatio (1967) as well as on several other occasions ran ing from the adoption of Québec's charter the French language (1977) to Canada's const tutional debate (to 1982), the bishops of Canad Québec and Ontario issued a series of statemen on the question of minority language rights an the status of French and English in Canada. Fo the first time in a century, the leaders of Ca ada's Catholic Church were constructively com ing to grips with an issue that had long divide them. The Canadian Catholic Church had pra tised bilingualism before Confederation, a po icy that had served it well in evangelizing muc of Canada. It is now returning to such a polic realizing along with others that it is the *sine qu non* of successful policy in Canada. Given th church's numbers and geographic distributio it can contribute immensely to French-Englis understanding in Canada.

The turbulence of the 1960s and 1970s, wit its catastrophic effects on the ecclesiastical in stitution, nevertheless left a solid core: a sign icant number of practicants; a virtually intact network of parishes; an organization of religious communities of men and women who had rethought their objectives; confessional schools and some private colleges; a new plan for parish action and greater lay participation in religious activities. The episcopacy more frequently joined in ECUMENICAL SOCIAL ACTION, taking positions on such topics as BIRTH CONTROL and ABORTION (1977, 1981) and the economic crisis (1982). But it is perhaps at the level of popular religion that the continuity and the hopes are most visible, given (among other things) a new interest in scripture, the continued popularity of pilgrimage and the growth of the Charismatic movement.

The rapidly changing Canadian church experienced in Sept 1984 a climactic event in the visit to Canada of Pope John Paul II. This pilgrim pontiff, who has been seen by more people than all other popes collectively, was the first reigning pope to set foot in Canada. He visited many regions, preaching a gospel of peace, reconciliation and disciplined belief.

NIVE VOISINE AND ROBERT CHOQUETTE

Eastern Rite Catholic Churches

Eastern Catholicism is a federation of particular and semi-autonomous churches in communion with Rome. The history of the Eastern Catholic churches has been a struggle to remain faithful to unity with Rome without Latinization or absorption into the Latin (ie, Western or Roman) rite church, and to preserve particularity — ie, local and cultural autonomy — of both material and formal elements. The material elements are a group of faithful (the people of God); an indigenous hierarchy with apostolic succession; a particular discipline of general norms and canons embodied in liturgical practice; and a spiritual tradition. This tradition entails history, language(s), culture and mentality rooted in a specific world view, connections with particular ethnic communities and a distinct theological orientation; monastic life; religious instruction rooted in the liturgy; and a tradition of religious art imbued with spiritual meaning.

The formal elements of local autonomy consist of recognition (expressed or tacit) of the church's self-governing nature by ecumenical councils and individuals in the church hierarchy, including the pope, and by the faithful themselves; exclusive membership in one's own rite; and the formal exercise of autonomy or particularity.

Eastern and Western Christianity have suffered a long process of drifting apart. In the first 7 centuries of the Christian era, philosophic-minded people began to question their beliefs, especially the mystery of Christ. It took 7 ecumenical councils to resolve such questions to the satisfaction of the church hierarchy. Meanwhile, Monophysites and Nestorians seceded from the unity of the church. Political problems further complicated the matter (eg, in 330 AD Emperor Constantine moved the capital of the Roman Empire from Rome to "New Rome": Byzantium, or Constantinople). For centuries there were rivalries and tensions between the patriarchs of Rome, Constantinople, Alexandria, Antioch and Jerusalem concerning their authority. The church-state relationship was complicated by the "caesaropapism" of the Byzantine emperors and the "papocaesarism" of Pope Leo I and his successors. In 1054 in Constantinople, Patriarch Cerularius and papal representative Cardinal Humbertus de Silva Candida excommunicated each other. In 1204 the knights of the Fourth Crusade sacked Constantinople and established their empire and Latin rite patriarchate. These were the final events that brought about the schism which has lasted to the present time.

The Eastern Catholic churches came into being as a result of a series of reunions with Rome: Maronites in 1181; Italo-Albanians in Sicily and Calabria during the 15th century; Chaldeans in 1553; Ruthenians (Ukrainians and Byelorussians) in 1596; Ethiopians in 1626; Chaldeo-Malabars (St Thomas Christians) in 1699; the Eparchy of Priashiv in 1646; Syrians of Antioch in 1663; Ruthenians of Valachia and Moldavia (today Romanians) in 1697; Melkites in 1724; Armenians in 1742; the Eparchy of Krizhevci in Yugoslavia (Ukrainians, Ruthenians, Croatians, Macedonians and Romanians) in 1777; Bulgarians in 1860; Copts in 1739; and the Syro-Malankarese in 1930.

The Eastern Catholic churches are grouped according to 5 rites, the Alexandrian, Antiochian, Byzantine, Chaldean and Armenian. Eastern rite Catholics in Canada are almost exclusively within the Antiochian, Byzantine and Armenian rites. Ukrainian Catholics, the largest group in Canada, adhere to the Byzantine rite; while in communion with Rome, they share with much of the ORTHODOX CHURCH the Liturgy of St John Chrysostom. The denomination was brought to Canada by UKRAINIAN immigrants around the turn of the century, and the first bishop for Canada was Niceta Budka, appointed by Pope Pius X in 1912. Canadian Ukrainian Catholics are organized in a metropolitian province under the leadership of His Grace Maxim Hermaniuk, Archbishop of Winnipeg and Metropolitan of All Canada; the province is divided into 5 eparchies: Winnipeg, Edmonton, Toronto, Saskatoon and New Westminster. Church statistics show some 229 000 members, although the 1981 Canadian census registered less than 200 000. The faithful, distributed through about 200 parishes, are served by over 260 clergy. Religious orders include Basilian Fathers (OSBM), Redemptorist Fathers (CSsR), Studites, Sisters Servants of Mary Immaculate (SSMI), Missionary Sisters of Christian Charity (MSCC), Basilian Sisters (OSBM), Sisters of St Joseph and Studite nuns. Future priests are educated at the Seminary of the Holy Spirit in Ottawa and at U of Ottawa. The Ukrainian Catholic community has an active press, which publishes the weeklies *Nasha Meta* (Toronto, fd 1948), *Postup-Progress* (bilingual, Winnipeg, 1959), and *Ukrainski Visti* and its English version, *The Ukrainian Record* (Edmonton, 1961); the scholarly theological journal, *Logos;* and the popular religious journals *Redeemer's Voice, Svitlo* and *Beacon.* Two religious presses, the Basilian Press (Toronto) and Redeemer's Voice (Yorkton, Sask), have distinguished themselves through the publication of books and pamphlets.

Slovaks of the Byzantine Rite in Canada are organized in 6 parishes in the Eparchy of Saints Cyril and Methodius (Toronto, est 1980). The approximately 5000 faithful are served by 10 missions and 6 priests under Bishop Michael Rusnak. Their official publication is the monthly journal *Maria.* Armenians in Canada have 2 parishes (Québec and Toronto). The approximately 8000 faithful are served in the Armenian rite by 2 priests and 2 sisters, and are under Bishop Nerses M. Sétian, exarch since 1981 for Armenians in the US and Canada.

The small number of Melkites in Canada, who come from the Middle East, follow the Byzantine rite. They are under Archbishop Michael Hakim, apostolic exarch for the Melkite Greek Catholics in Canada (Outremont, Qué), who was appointed in 1980. Maronites, also from the Middle East but adherents to the Antiochian rite, are under Mgr Elias Shaheen, eparch for Maronite Catholics in Canada (Montréal), who was appointed in 1982. All other Eastern Catholics are under the jurisdiction of the local Latin-rite ordinaries and do not have their own organizational structures. Their numbers are unknown.

PETRO B.T. BILANIUK

Reading: D. Attwater, *Eastern Churches in Communion with Rome,* 2 vols (rev ed 1961-62); Gregory Baum, *Catholics and Canadian Socialism* (1980); J.W. Grant, *The Church in the Canadian Era* (1972); J.S. Moir, *The Church in the British Era* (1972); Nive Voisine, *Histoire de l'Église catholique au Québec (1608-1970)* (1971); H.H. Walsh, *The Church in the French Era* (1966).

Cattail, common name for herbaceous, perennial PLANTS (genus *Typha*) of the cattail family (Typhaceae) which grow in marshes and waterways. The name derives from the cylindrical, brown fruiting spikes. At least 8 species exist worldwide; 2 in Canada (narrow leaved cattail, *T. angustifolia,* and common cattail, *T. latifolia*). Clusters of stiff, ribbonlike leaves, up to 3 m (or more) tall, grow from a thick, horizontal rootstock. The rootstock is a rich source of starch; the succulent, young shoots and green flower spikes are also edible; and the pollen and oil-rich seeds have livestock feed potential. The leaves are tough and pithy, and were used by native peoples to make mats, bags, baskets and clothing. Stems and leaves are suitable for making paper and cloth. Formerly, the cottony fluff attached to fruits was used to stuff bedding. Cattails also provide food and shelter for wildlife. These plants are also called bulrushes, a name which sometimes refers to plants of genus *Scirpus* of the SEDGE family. *See* PLANTS, NATIVE USES.

NANCY J. TURNER

Cauchon, Joseph-Édouard, journalist, politician, businessman (b at Québec C 31 Dec 1816; d in the Qu'Appelle Valley, Sask 23 Feb 1885). On 1 Dec 1842 he launched *Le Journal de Québec,* which he ran until 1862. He was editor until 1875 and used it to promote his political ambitions. He represented Montmagny in the Assembly of the Province of Canada 1844-67 and was mayor of Québec C 1866-68. He was a supporter of the Liberal-Conservatives and was commissioner of crown lands 1855-57, resigning when the government refused to grant land to the North Shore Ry in which he was closely involved. Although earlier opposing political change, he supported CONFEDERATION in 1864 and in 1865 published in French and English a political essay, *The Union of the Provinces of British North America,* promoting the plan. After Confederation, he was elected for Montmorency to both the provincial and federal legislatures. He was initially chosen to be prime minister of Québec but he was unable to put together a government; at his own request he was appointed to the Senate and named Speaker on 2 Nov 1867. In 1872, however, he returned to the Commons as the independent member for Québec-Centre. He switched to the Liberals during the PACIFIC SCANDAL. Argumentative and widely disliked, he had become a liability to PM Alexander MACKENZIE by 1877 and he finished his political career as lieutenant-governor of Manitoba (Oct 1877-Dec 1882), where he continued his business career by speculating in land.

ANDRÉE DÉSILETS

Cauchon, Joseph-Eusèbe-Noulan, engineer, urban planner (b at Québec City 4 Mar 1872; d at Ottawa 28 Oct 1935), son of Joseph-Édouard CAUCHON. While assistant engineer with the Board of Railway Commissioners, Noulan Cauchon completed and publicized a draft plan for Ottawa in 1914; in 1921 he became the first chairman of the Ottawa Town Planning Commission. He advanced such concepts as limited-access expressways, public ownership and leasing of land in a city and its urban fringe, and a hexagonal street plan for residential areas. But the Town Planning Inst of Canada, which he co-founded in 1919, collapsed during the Depression. Ottawa City Council refused to enact his zoning bills, and his recommendations to the parliamentary committee on housing were ignored in the 1935 Dominion Housing Act. During his lifetime Cauchon remained an unheeded prophet, yet after 1945 expressways became common, some governments essayed land banking and the Ottawa master plan of 1948 embodied many of Cauchon's suggestions. WALTER VAN NUS

Caucus, a regular private meeting of all MPs and senators of a political party; a platform for the development of party strategy and an assembly where frustrations with leadership may be aired. Traditionally it does not vote on issues it reviews, but discussion proceeds until the party leader defines a consensus. The governing party uses the caucus to obtain information about how its programs and legislation are being received. Theoretically, discussions, held in camera, can be critical and frank, and can allow backbenchers to express opinions. The Opposition uses its caucus to devise parliamentary strategy to criticize the Government. ROBERT J. JACKSON

Cauliflower (*Brassica oleracea,* Botrytis Group), annual or biennial VEGETABLE of the Cruciferae family, grown in temperate climates for its edible, white, inflorescent head. Originating in Europe and western Asia, cauliflower was probably cultivated well before the 1st century AD. Only the annual variety can be grown in Canada's severe climate. Cauliflower must be grown quickly because its quality can deteriorate in hot temperatures and dryness. From its early development stage, the cauliflower has leaves that cover its flowering head, protecting it from strong sunlight and preserving its whiteness. It is harvested when the head is still very compact. Fresh cauliflower does not keep long but can be frozen for several months. Cauliflower consumption is increasing. In 1979 Canadian production, which is principally located in Ontario, was 33 980 t. ROGER RUSHDY

Cave, roofed-over rock cavity of natural origin, accessible from the surface and large enough for human entry. Caves occur in all kinds of ROCKS and in every geographical region. Lava tube caves, an important minor class, are formed by channelled outflow of molten lava in congealing flows. Sea caves most commonly result from erosion by waves. Most known caves, including the largest, longest and deepest, are created by subsurface WATERS dissolving passageways in soluble rocks, principally limestone. Limestone caves develop along or down natural rock partings, such as joints or bedding planes. Over time, subsurface water may enlarge the diameter of passages in the partings from micrometres to metres or tens of metres. Cave systems comprise interlinked passages and shafts that drain water from upland KARST LANDFORMS to springs at the limestone boundary. In cross section, caves display 3 basic forms: phreatic passages, which are roughly circular and were dissolved by water under pressure filling all the openings; vadose passages, which are roofed canyons carved by ordinary gravitational streams in air-filled openings; breakdown forms, which are seen where parts of the walls or ceilings have fallen.

Valeric Cave, NWT. The natural beauty of caves is enhanced by their secondary mineral deposits, here in the form of stalactites (*photo by Stephen J. Krasemann/DRK Photo*).

Mammoth Cave-Flint Ridge System in Kentucky is the longest known. More than 300 km of interconnected passages are mapped there. Other caves, in Switzerland and the USSR, exceed 100 km. Canada's longest known, Castleguard Cave, BANFF NATIONAL PARK, has 18 km of galleries passing far beneath the COLUMBIA ICEFIELD. Several caves in the Alps, Pyrenees and Mexico have now been explored to a depth of over 1000 m. Arctomys Cave, in the ROCKY MOUNTAINS, is Canada's deepest, at 560 m underground. Many caves contain individual chambers far larger than any constructed by man. Caves trap sediment, flora and fauna, thus preserving natural historic records. Most of our knowledge of human cultural evolution before the last 10 000 years comes from cave dwellings (*see* PREHISTORY). The natural beauty of caves is greatly enhanced by their secondary MINERAL deposits, principally stalactites, stalagmites and flowstones of calcite, a reprecipitate of dissolved limestone. Many varieties of insects, fishes, birds and mammals live in caves, some adapting to the total darkness by losing their eyes and pigmentation. The scientific study of caves is called speleology; "spelunking" is the exploration of caves as a hobby. D.C. FORD

Caven, William, Presbyterian minister, educator (b at Kirkcolm, Scot 26 Dec 1830, d at Toronto 1 Dec 1904). Immigrating to Canada in 1847, Caven studied at United Presbyterian Seminary at London, Canada W, and entered the ministry in 1852. In 1865 he was called to the Chair of Exegetical Theology in Knox College, Toronto, became principal in 1873, and led the college into full affiliation with U of T. He remained as principal until his death.

In 1875, as moderator of the General Assembly of the Canada Presbyterian Church, he was involved in the negotiations which united the Free Church and Kirk in the Presbyterian Church in Canada. Later, he was also a strong advocate of interdenomination Protestant union, in part because of the seeming threat of Roman Catholicism. Caven's ecumenicism in the late 1880s and 1890s must be seen in the context of his strong opposition to the JESUITS' ESTATES ACT of 1888 and to denominational schools in Manitoba in the 1890s. A.B. MCKILLOP

Cavendish, PEI, UP, pop 93 (1981c), is situated 38 km NW of Charlottetown, approximately in the middle of the province's N shore. It was named for Field Marshal Lord Frederick Cavendish, patron of a local landholder. During the summer months the year-round population is submerged by tourists and seasonal residents who flock to PEI National Pk, Canada's second-most-popular such park. Established 1790 by Scottish immigrants, Cavendish was originally a farming community. With the 1930s' establishment of the national park, tourism has become the community's principal employer. It was in Cavendish that novelist and native Lucy Maud MONTGOMERY wrote *Anne of Green Gables.* W.S. KEIZER

Cayuga, when first encountered by Europeans, occupied several villages near the lake bearing their name in NY state. As a member of the IROQUOIS Confederacy, they are represented by 10 chiefs on the confederacy council. During the 17th century, population losses to disease and warfare were offset by large-scale adoption of captives and refugees. War with the Susquehannock to the S led some Cayuga to settle briefly on the N shore of Lk Ontario in the 1660s. For the most part neutral during the French-English conflicts of the 18th century, they fought on the British side during the AMERICAN REVOLUTION. An American army under Gen John Sullivan burned their villages in 1779. After the war, almost half the Cayuga chose to settle in Canada. In population they are second only to the MOHAWK among the peoples of the Six Nations Reserve near Brantford, Ont. Cayuga there number over 2500, but fewer than 400 still speak their native language. *See also* NATIVE PEOPLES, EASTERN WOODLANDS and general articles under NATIVE PEOPLE. THOMAS S. ABLER

Reading: B.G. Trigger, ed, *Handbook of North American Indians,* vol 15: *Northeast* (1978).

Eastern white cedar (*Thuja occidentalis*), with male flowers (dark red) and female flowers (brownish yellow) and cones (*artwork by Claire Tremblay*).

Cedar, in Canada, refers to evergreen CONIFERS (genus *Thuja*) of cypress family (Cupressaceae). They are also called arbor vitae [Lat, "tree of life"]. The true cedars belong to the coniferous genus *Cedrus* (pine family) and are found from the Mediterranean to the Himalayas. Six species of *Thuja* are recognized: 2 in N America; 4 in eastern Asia. Western red cedar (*T. plicata*), found along BC coast and western slopes of Rocky Mts, may attain 60 m in height, 3 m in diameter. Eastern white cedar (*T. occidentalis*), growing to 25 m, occurs in the Great Lakes-St Lawrence forest region. Asiatic species, *T. orientalis,* is often planted as an ORNAMENTAL. Small, scalelike leaves cover flat, spraylike branches. Oval cones are 1-2 cm long. Bracts (modified leaves) and scales (ovule-bearing structures) are fused. POLLINATION occurs in spring; seeds (small, with 2 lateral wings) are shed in fall. Soft, light, aromatic, decay-resistant wood is used for ornament and finishing. West Coast Indians used cedar for totem poles, canoes and lodges. JOHN N. OWENS

Cedar Lake Reservoir, 1353 km^2, 62.5 km long, elev 253 m, is located in W-central Manitoba, N of Lk WINNIPEGOSIS. The lake draws most of its waters from the huge SASKATCHEWAN R drainage basin. Construction of an earthfill dam and 25.6 km of dikes 1961-64 caused lake levels to rise 3.65 m, creating Cedar Lk Reservoir and assuring a mean annual flow of 688 m^3/s at the associated Grand Rapids hydroelectric generating station. R.A. MCGINN

CEGEP, *see* COLLÈGE D'ENSEIGNEMENT GÉNÉRAL ET PROFESSIONNEL.

Celery (*Apium graveolens* var. *dulce*), biennial plant of the Umbelliferae family, widely grown as an annual for its nutritious leafstalks. Rape celery or celeriac (*A. graveolens* var. *rapaceum*) is grown on a more limited basis for its thick, edible root. Celery originated in the Mediterranean basin, was first grown as a medicinal plant, and was possibly first cultivated as a condiment in Italy in the 16th century. Celery has a well-developed root system, a short, fleshy crown (modified stem) and a rosette of leaves. Celery's characteristic taste and odour is produced by volatile oils in its stalk, leaves and seeds. It is rich in ascorbic acid. Preferring a cool climate, celery is sown in spring and transplanted after about 60 days, needing another 90 days to reach maturity. It also requires fertilizer and regular irrigation to produce approximately 90 t/ha. Mechanical harvest is increasing; harvested celery is peeled, measured, chilled in iced water and crated. Principal diseases are *Septoria* blight and black heart. In Canada, about 500 ha are devoted to celery production, mainly in Québec and Ontario. PIERRE SAURIOL

Cement Industry comprises establishments engaged in producing hydraulic cements, ie, cements which set and harden to a stonelike mass by reacting with water. The principal hydraulic cement is portland cement, a finely ground, usually grey, manufactured mineral product. Cement by itself has limited application, but when mixed with water and SAND, gravel, crushed stone or other aggregates, it forms concrete, a rocklike substance that is the most widely used CONSTRUCTION material in Canada and the world. Concrete is used to pave highways, sidewalks and airport runways; in the construction of virtually all types of buildings, bridges, dams, dry docks, harbours, irrigation structures, water resources, sewage disposal systems, piping and storage silos; and in a multitude of other major and minor construction projects, including "do-it-yourself" projects.

Joseph Aspdin, an English mason, is generally credited with the invention of portland cement. In 1824 he obtained a patent for his product, which he named portland cement because it produced a concrete the colour of limestone quarried on the Isle of Portland. The name is used worldwide, with many manufacturers adding their own trade or brand names. Canadian production began in Hull, Qué, in 1889. Before that time portland cement was imported from England in wooden barrels. Plants were soon established at Napanee and Shallow Lake, Ont, and on Montréal Island. The first plant in the western provinces was built in Vancouver in 1893.

Materials used in MANUFACTURING portland cement must contain appropriate proportions of lime, silica alumina and iron components. During manufacture, frequent analyses are made to ensure a uniformly high-quality product. The raw materials are pulverized and mixed in the desired proportions. After blending, the prepared mix is fed into the upper end of a rotary kiln where it is burned or fired at temperatures of 1400-1650°C and changed into portland cement clinker. The clinker is then cooled and pulverized. During this operation, a small amount of GYPSUM is added to regulate the initial chemical reaction of the cement. This pulverized product is finished portland cement, ready for use in making concrete. Different types of portland cement are manufactured in Canada to meet physical and chemical requirements for specific purposes. The Canadian Standards Association provides for 5 types of portland cement for specific purposes, ie, normal, moderate, high early strength, low heat of hydration, and sulphate resisting. Normal portland cement is the type most commonly manufactured; high early strength and sulphate resisting types are usually available. Like moderate and low heat of hydration forms of portland cement, other special cements (masonry, oil well, expansive, regulated set) may not always be readily available from manufacturers because of low demand.

In 1981, 9 Canadian cement companies were operating 22 plants with 48 cement kilns and 2 grinding facilities. Total clinker capacity was 15.9 million t and total cement grinding capacity was 16.8 million t. Grinding capacity was unchanged during the early 1980s, but clinker capacity was higher by nearly 1.8 million t because of major expansion at 3 sites. New preheater/precalciner dry-process kilns, representing the most contemporary technology in the industry, were started up at Mississauga, Ont, and at Exshaw and Edmonton, Alta. With more than one-third of Canada's total cement capacity, Canada Cement Lafarge Ltd is the nation's largest cement company. The second- and third-largest Canadian cement companies, St Lawrence Cement Inc and Genstar Cement Ltd, together account for another third. Moreover, they have other N American affiliates which contribute to the size of the Canadian producers. Canadian cement plants tend to be modern and larger than other N American facilities and rely more heavily on oil and natural gas as kiln fuels. Less than half of Canadian capacity is coal fired, although conversion should continue to increase this proportion. Over 71% of Canadian kiln capacity now uses the dry-process technology that contributed to a reduction in energy consumption of 9-12% per unit of production during the latter half of the 1970s. The Canadian industry is strongly regionalized, with most plants located in high-population areas. High transportation and energy costs strongly influence plant location and economic viability.

Cement consumption in Canada (producers' shipments plus imports less exports) remained relatively stable at near 9 million t annually from 1975 to 1981. At this level, the value of production was estimated at about $735 million. Strong markets for portland cement in western Canada, particularly Alberta, continued through this period, offsetting sluggish Canadian demand in other regions. Since that time, however, western demand has dropped dramatically, particularly in Alberta. Total Canadian consumption dropped to 6 million t during the 1982-84 period. Canada ranks behind 18 other countries in apparent consumption of cement by the leading producers but, ranked per capita, is approximately tenth, with an apparent consumption of 390 kg per capita.

Although individual companies do research on cement production, much experimentation on the use and application of cement and concrete is done through the Canadian Portland Cement Assn, an industry-supported, nonprofit organization, the purpose of which is to improve and extend the uses of cement and concrete through scientific research and engineering fieldwork. The association is active throughout Canada and offers detailed information on concrete use, design and construction. R.A. SERNE

Cemeteries are designated and usually consecrated places in which the dead are deposited. The word comes from the Greek *koimeterion* or the Latin *coemeterium,* meaning "to lie down to rest" or "to sleep." This usage alludes to the Christian belief in resurrection which robbed death and burial of many of their previously perceived terrors, but burial is not only a Christian practice. In Canada, people of all faiths generally locate their dead in a cemetery, whether in a grave or mausoleum or in an urn stored in a special structure, although some people have their cremated remains strewn or stored elsewhere, as in a church's columbarium.

Purpose and Location of Cemeteries Cemeteries are both the accepted places for the dead and for symbols of remembrance, usually gravemarkers. They also serve a psychologically important role for surviving relatives and friends who can visit gravesides. Cemeteries are often located on hill tops or slopes. Drainage is important, but the notion of hill sites as spiritual locations is deeply rooted in Judeo-Christian tradition.

Cemetery operations come under provincial

Gravestone at Cassburn Cemetery, Ont. A great deal of social and demographic information can be gained from early gravestones (*photo by David B. Knight*).

jurisdiction. Cemeteries are owned by private corporations, nonprofit trust companies, churches, synagogues and municipalities. Plots range in price from $200 to over $10 000, with $600-$800 being common. A percentage of plot prices covers perpetual care. The urban land value of cemeteries ranks extremely high, at times even higher than values at the primary intersections in central business districts. Some urban cemeteries preserve open spaces and locations for leisure activities (including bird watching).

Types of Cemeteries Viewed historically, there are several types of burial places. First, undifferentiated, which include burial sites of early explorers and VOYAGEURS along river routes. Remains may be invisible today because of decayed wooden markers or flood-damaged rock piles; some remain, as on the Madawaska R, Ontario. Second, now usually abandoned small family plots dot the agricultural landscape, ranging in size from 5 to perhaps 20 burials. Early farmers who had difficulty reaching community cemeteries buried family members on their farms. The plots became disused and overgrown as children moved away or when farms were sold. Third, some rural activity foci (churches and small villages) have cemeteries serving the surrounding communities. Like small rural schools and churches, many such sites are now rarely used or are abandoned. Fourth, most burials today are in large population centre cemeteries, in towns and cities. Some have grown from small predecessors, others are new; some are relatively small, others are huge; some are surrounded by urban developments, others are peripheral to built-up areas.

Design of Cemeteries Older cemeteries were rectangular in form, reflecting a sense of order also found in town and rural surveying schemes. Most post-1920s cemeteries have meandering crescents and driveways similar to new residential subdivisions. Recent design changes reflect a move from "cemeteries" or "burial grounds" to pleasantly landscaped "memorial parks" and "gardens," a trend that may have resulted from secular attitudes and a need to soften the finality of death. The word "garden" also has special significance for Christians: in Old Testament tradition, man was shut out of the Garden of Eden and cannot return by his volition; in New Testament tradition, Jesus was betrayed in a garden and buried in a garden, so that what man lost by sin and disobedience may now be recovered in a garden by obedience unto death, with Paradise regained. While such religious symbolism is important to many Christians, to most Canadians "garden" cemeteries are simply aesthetically pleasing places for burial. New and some old cemeteries have "gardens of memories" which include mausoleums and columbaria. Holding vaults are seldom used today since excavation technicians — "gravediggers" of old — increasingly use mechanical means to penetrate frozen ground. High-rise mausoleums (some holding 65 000 remains), as found in Japan, Italy and the US, probably will not be built in Canada because of tradition and, especially, investment constraints.

Religious preference leads people to be buried in different cemeteries, eg, Catholic, Jewish, Protestant (of various varieties), interfaith or nondenominational. In the past, people of minority races and of "disapproved" ethnic origins were forced to be buried apart from others. Distributional patterns within cemeteries reflect societal characteristics, eg, socially prominent families clustered in higher priced lots, and national and ethnic-heritage "neighbourhoods."

Grave Markers Stone markers generally indicate graves with, at minimum, names and dates of birth and death inscribed. Markers record past life but also provide a means by which a private family experience with death is made a public one to be shared. In some instances, markers may indicate more about the surviving families' wealth and self-perceived status than about the departed. Some large urban cemetery monuments are extremely grand. Other Canadians shy away from elaborate markers, including the DOUKHOBORS who do not glorify their dead by erecting monuments.

Gravestone styles have changed. In the 18th century stones were severely simple; then Victorian grandeur and fussiness (1880s to early 1900s) gave way to a more severe modern style. Forms have included tablet shapes, obelisks (symbol of eternity), Celtic crosses, scrolls, blocks and pulpits. Heights have decreased through time. Some cemeteries now permit only lawn-height markers that help to create a parklike atmosphere.

Markers may have engraved symbols, including the open Bible, symbolizing the Word through which one gains salvation and revelation; urns, symbolic of the body's death from which rises the soul to heaven; a dove, for the Holy Spirit, peace and Christian constancy and devotion; Star of David, symbolizing Jewish faith; flowers, symbolizing both beauty and brevity of life; grapevines, symbolizing Christ as "the true vine"; carved portraits or photographs embedded in the stone; symbols of fraternal societies. Epitaphs were commonly inscribed on stones in the past but today more than "in memorium" is rare.

Cemeteries as Research Tools Cemeteries are important for tracing genealogy. Other facts can be gained and inferences made about settlement patterns and history of surrounding communities, including ethnic origins, disease and death relationships, attitudes (from epitaphs) about death, societal standing (from relative locations and style of markers) and gravestone styles as reflections of culture change. *See also* FUNERAL PRACTICES.

DAVID B. KNIGHT

Reading: C. Hanks, *Early Ontario Gravestones* (1974); D.B. Knight, *Cemeteries as Living Landscapes* (1982); P.E. Roy, *Les cimetières de Québec* (1941); J. David Wood, "Simulating Pre-Census Population Distribution," *Canadian Geographer* 18 (fall 1974).

Censorship is the exercise of prior governmental control over what can be printed, published, represented or broadcasted. Soon after the invention of the printing press, the English CROWN resorted to various censorship controls. Printing was allowed only under special licences, and this was reinforced by press offences and given a statutory basis with the Licensing Act of 1662. In 1695, when the House of Commons refused to renew the Licensing Act (not so much out of concern for freedom of expression as for a number of reasons related to commercial restrictions, house searches, etc), prior censorship of the press ended, except during wartime. Freedom of the press has since consisted "in laying no previous restraints upon publication, and not in freedom from censure for criminal matter when published."

Censorship can be practised in covert ways, however. One of the earliest attempts to restrict publication was the use of deliberate taxation to inhibit circulation. A Stamp Tax introduced in England in 1712 (and not removed until 1855) required newspapers to affix stamps so that by raising the price of stamps newspaper prices could be raised beyond the purchasing power of all but wealthy readers. Censorship can also be practised through harassment and intimidation. During the "McCarthy era" in the US, the American Supreme Court, in *US* v *Rumely*, warned, "Through the harassment of hearings, investigations, reports, and subpoenas, government will hold a club over speech and over the press." Censorship can also be exercised through the pressure of advertisers and decisions by newspapers themselves, particularly in circumstances where no competitive or alternative source of news is available. R.M. MacIvor, writing after WWII, observed that "one of the major difficulties lies in the extension of large-scale enterprise to the media of opinion. In certain areas modern technology gives an economic advantage to the greater opinion-promulgating units and to the combination of small local units under the control of one syndicate or capitalist owner . . . In consequence the number of independently owned newspapers continually decreases and many editors become the agents of one owner."

The Canadian CRIMINAL CODE makes it an offence to mail "obscene, indecent, immoral or scurrilous" matter (*see* OBSCENITY), and the Post Office Act provides for interruption of such service. Similarly, the Customs Tariff Act prohibits the importation of "treasonable, seditious, immoral or indecent" literature.

The best-known attempts by provinces to impose censorship are the various provincial FILM CENSORSHIP Acts. In *Nova Scotia Board of Censors* v *McNeil* the Supreme Court of Canada held that provincial legislation establishing a board of censors with powers to prohibit the exhibition of films was within the jurisdiction of the provinces, despite the federal jurisdiction in the Criminal Code over determination of what is "obscene."

Other censorship attempts by the provinces have been less successful. Under the 1937 Alberta Press Act, to Ensure the Publication of Accurate News and Information, newspapers would be compelled to disclose the source of their news information and to print government statements to correct previous articles. Three of the 6 Supreme Court justices hearing the case held that the bill was an invasion of liberty of the press and the right of public discussion, which could only be limited by Parliament under its CRIMINAL LAW power. In *Switzman* v *Elbling* (the PADLOCK ACT case), which dealt with the 1937 Québec Act Respecting Communistic Propaganda, under which it was illegal to use a house for the propagation of communism, the Supreme Court declared this was legislation with respect to criminal law and therefore within federal jurisdiction (*see* COMMUNIST PARTY).

Censorship can take many forms. To persons or groups who cannot afford to print newspapers, or to advertise, or who might not be given the opportunity to do so, supervision of the distribution of handbills or posters is a form of censorship. This supervision has been effected through municipal bylaws regulating the use of streets, sidewalks and parks, and requiring the prior approval of the police or some civic official before printed materials can be distributed (*see* SAUMUR V CITY OF QUÉBEC). In *Attorney General of Canada* v *Dupond*, the Supreme Court of Canada held that a city ordinance that prohibited "the holding of any assembly, parade or gathering on the public domain of the City of Montréal for a time-period of 30 days" was valid, being of a "merely local character."

The censorship practised under the OFFICIAL SECRETS ACT (1980) essentially covers 2 distinct, if somewhat similar, activities: spying (*see* INTELLIGENCE GATHERING) and wrongful communication of government information, or leakage (s4.3). The latter provides: "Every person who receives any. . . information, knowing, or having reasonable ground to believe, at the time when he receives it, that the...information is communicated to him in contravention of this Act, is guilty of an offence under this Act unless he proves that the communication to him of the...information was contrary to his desire." Since WWII, this section has been the basis of prosecution only twice. WALTER S. TARNOPOLSKY

Census Metropolitan Area (CMA), a geographical area created by Statistics Canada for the purposes of collecting and organizing data. CMAs define the main labour market of an urbanized core or built-up areas, and have a population of 100 000 or more. They contain municipalities completely or partly inside the urbanized core and other municipalities if 1) at least 40% of the employed work force living in the municipality works in the core, or 2) at least 25% of the employed labour force working in the municipality live in the urbanized core. CMAs may differ from metropolitan areas designated by local governments. They are usually known by the name of the urban area forming their core, eg, Halifax or Winnipeg.

Centaur Theatre Co was founded in 1969 by Maurice Podbrey (current artistic director) and Herbert Auerbach (founding chairman) and has become a prominent English-language theatre in Québec. The Centaur is housed in the Old Exchange Arts Centre in Montréal, originally having one 255-seat theatre, then expanding to a second 440-seat theatre in 1974. Drawing from the energy of the Québec theatre scene, the group has met the challenge of presenting innovative international programming with such authors as Arthur Miller, John Osborne and S African playwright Athol Fugard. It has also placed emphasis on English Canadian authors (David Fennario, John Gray, David French among others), with some experimentation in bilingual productions such as Fennario's *Balconville* and Tom Kempinski's *Brew (Broue)*. The Centaur enjoys continued success, and in 1983 won the Vantage Arts Academy Award for outstanding contribution to Canadian theatre. *See also* THEATRE ENGLISH LANGUAGE. MARILYN BASZCZYNSK

Centennial Year, 1967, was Canada's enthusiastic celebration of the 100th anniversary of CONFEDERATION, 1867. The festivities were launched at midnight on 31 Dec 1966 on Parliament Hill when Prime Minister Lester PEARSON, Secretary of State Judy LAMARSH (the minister responsible for Centennial), Opposition Leader John DIEFENBAKER, and thousands of others participated in a ceremony that culminated in the lighting of the Centennial Flame.

A committee of businessmen, chaired by C.M

ster Pearson lighting the Centennial Flame, Parliament Hill 31 Dec 1966 (*courtesy Public Archives of Canada/ 26964*).

URY, was originally instrumental in convincg Diefenbaker, then prime minister, that Canla's 100th anniversary should be a memorable casion. One of the country's best-known pubcists, John Fisher, "Mr Canada," was appointed ntennial commissioner. Fisher, whose tenure ntinued under Pearson, was ably assisted by eorges E. Gauthier and then by Gilles Bergeron oth associate commissioners).

The year's events fell into 2 categories: those at were monumental and those that were acve. In a desire to leave behind a literally conete memory of the year, the federal and proncial governments financed a wide variety of ilding projects. Each province acquired a cennnial memorial building, and each $1 that as spent on a centennial edifice by a municality was matched by an equal amount from th the federal government and the respective ovincial government. Such largesse encoured the construction of facilities such as librars, art galleries, theatres and sport complexes. ne most lavish concrete monument was the NAONAL ARTS CENTRE in Ottawa, paid for entirely the federal government.

The Centennial Train and Caravans, which aphically depicted Canadian history and the ntributions made by many different cultures, ere visited by over 10 million people. Local stories were compiled and historic sites were stored. The performing arts flourished as Fesval Canada commissioned plays, musicals, eras and ballets. In a lighter vein, there were thtub races, parades and period costume pars. One town even built a landing pad for flyg saucers. As the year progressed, it became evient that the country's most spectacular event, PO 67, was a national and international success.The year ended, as it had begun, on Parliaent Hill. But the Centennial Flame that was iginally to have been extinguished was left ight by popular consent. It was to become a mbol for a year that was not merely signifint in and for itself, but one that marked the nergence of Canada as a mature and selfnfident nation. ROBERT BOTHWELL

ntipede (class Chilopoda), elongate, flattened rrestrial arthropod. The head bears antennae. he adult is composed of 18-180 segments, plus tail-plate. Almost all body segments, except e last, have a pair of appendages totalling, in lults, from 15 (as in the most familiar Canaan species) to 179 pairs. The first pair is moded to form large, poisonous claws; the last air, less strongly modified, has a reproductive nction; others are walking legs. About 2500 ecies are known worldwide, mostly from the opics. About 70 species occur in Canada and laska; a dozen of these have been introduced om Europe. The latter species are largely stern. Some tropical species are very large, one aches nearly 30 cm long. The largest Canadian ecies seldom reaches 8 cm; most familiar cenpedes are less than 2.5 cm long. Centipedes are iefly nocturnal, living under stones, bark, af-litter or in soil. One or 2 species live in creves and under seaweed in marine, intertidal zones. Virtually all centipedes prey on smaller animals (eg, insects) captured with poisonous claws. Some large species may inflict poisonous "bites" on humans if taken unawares, but they are aggressive only toward prey. In Canada, only the introduced house centipede (*Scutigera coleoptrata*) can inflict a painful (not dangerous) nip to humans. The introduced garden or "greenhouse centipede" (*Scutigerella immaculata*), sometimes a horticultural pest, especially in southern Ontario is not a true centipede but belongs to a small, distantly related, noncarnivorous class (Symphyla), with only 2-3 species in Canada. D.K. MCEWAN KEVAN

Central Agency may refer to a departmental central agency in government finance and administration or, generally, to any group whose terms of reference extend across all policy areas. The Department of Finance, for example,is responsible on behalf of all ministers for preparing the budget. The TREASURY BOARD Secretariat (TBS) develops, approves and subsequently monitors the spending plans of departments and agencies. The PUBLIC SERVICE COMMISSION, in conjunction with the TBS, is important in personnel management. The PRIVY COUNCIL OFFICE provides the secretariats for CABINET and its committees, and is involved in wide-ranging liaison, coordinating and advisory functions stemming from its links with the Cabinet and prime minister. More intimately associated with the party and political responsibilities of the prime minister is the PRIME MINISTER'S OFFICE. Recent candidates as central agencies include the ministries of State for Social Development and for Regional Economic Development for their role in coordinating sectors of the budgetary "envelope" into which the total budget is currently divided. The growth of central agencies reflects the increasing size and interrelatedness of government activities; their presence has led to controls that compel regular ("line") departments to provide programs and services effectively and efficiently. J.E. HODGETTS

Central Coast Salish share the same culture but speak 4 distinct languages of the Coast Salish language family. Three of these groups are known by indigenous names: Halkomelem, the largest group, and Squamish bear the names for their respective languages; Nooksack, now entirely in Washington state, is an anglicization of the native name by which other Coast Salish groups knew them. The fourth group, living in both BC and Washington state, has no all-encompassing name for itself and is best known as Straits Salish.

The Central Coast Salish area, with a mild and relatively dry climate, had rich and varied resources. Paramount were tremendous annual runs of salmon which ascended the Fraser and Squamish rivers from May through November. Members of all 4 groups fished the Fraser, but most favourably situated were Halkomelem, who fished with dip nets and large trawl nets towed between CANOES. Straits Salish perfected the reef net, a unique trap set between pairs of canoes at owned locations in the sea where Fraser-bound salmon were known to pass. Most salmon were caught in summer when surplus quantities could be dried on open-air racks.

Large shed-roofed houses were built in villages, from which trips were made to gather seasonal resources. Life centered around the household groups, consisting of extended families with a core or lineage of people linked through male or female lines of descent. Marriage with blood kin was not allowed; thus spouses usually came from different villages and networks of kinship linked people throughout Central Coast Salish territory. Special resource sites and ritual privileges were owned by lineages or kin groups, whose members worked co-operatively under direction of esteemed leaders. There was a class structure with high and low classes as well as slaves. Class position was imprecise, without ranked lineages or titled positions, but people strove to maintain class standing by hard work, selective marriages and proper behaviour.

Summer and autumn were times for potlatches, when people from neighbouring villages were invited to feast and acclaim the hosts' social position (*see* POTLATCH).

Religious activity focused on spirit helpers who conferred personal powers for hunting, doctoring or other human endeavours. These individual powers were celebrated during winter in rituals referred to as spirit dances. Some spirit powers took the form of hereditary cleansing rituals, performed with MASKS, effigies or decorated rattles. Sculptural art found additional expression in tombs, house posts and implements (*see* NORTHWEST COAST INDIAN ART).

The early maritime fur trade, concentrated on the outer coast, did not directly affect Central Coast Salish, whose territory was first explored by Spanish and British ships in the early 1790s. In 1827 the HUDSON'S BAY CO established FT LANGLEY in the centre of Halkomelem territory. In the late 19th century, as settlers were attracted to south Vancouver I and the Fraser Valley, Central Coast Salish territory became the most heavily populated part of BC.

There are now more than 11 000 registered Central Coast Salish listed in 49 bands in BC, and about 2000 tribal members in Washington. Despite great changes of culture, distinctive rituals and religious expression survive, uniting small, dispersed villages and permitting the maintenance of a vigorous sense of Indian identity. *See also* NATIVE PEOPLES, NORTHWEST COAST and general articles under NATIVE PEOPLE. MICHAEL KEW

Reading: H. Barnett, *The Coast Salish of British Columbia* (1975); P. Amoss, *Coast Salish Spirit Dancing* (1978).

Centre de recherche industrielle du Québec (CRIQ) In 1966, 2 bills to establish a scientific advisory agency in Québec were lost when the government changed; CRIQ was finally established as a CROWN CORPORATION in 1969. Until laboratories were completed at Ste-Foy (1975), facilities were rented at Québec City, Sherbrooke and Dorval. That same year, a branch specializing in microelectronics was established in Montréal, and the functions of CRIQ were reassessed to reemphasize its advisory role to small business. It has since served to stimulate development through technical and scientific research and advice. In 1979 the government expanded the centre's role to include provision of advice on licensing requirements and advising or collaborating with business on patenting inventions. CRIQ's aid to business allayed early opposition by the scientific community, but some economists criticized the emphasis on small companies. The centre is headed by a president-director general, with a board of 14, who have been responsible to various government ministries at different stages. CRIQ employs over 310 people. Although much of its advice to small business is free, 61% of CRIQ's income was derived from the industrial sector through contracts and shares of patents. CRIQ is best known for innovations in FURNITURE design and FOOD processing. Co-operative plans are underway with various Québec universities and colleges for research in ROBOTICS (eg, computer-aided design, computer-assisted MANUFACTURING), microelectronics, BIOMASS and BIOTECHNOLOGY. MARTIN K. MCNICHOLL

Ceramics are products made from a nonmetallic mineral compound (especially CLAY) and fired to set the shape. The principal types of ceramic wares are porcelain, which is usually translucent, and earthenware, which is opaque. Both porcelains and earthenware may be glazed or unglazed; unglazed wares are known as biscuit. Unglazed earthenware is porous and needs glazing to make it waterproof.

Canadian-made Ceramics

Earthenware utility pottery has been produced in Canada since the mid-17th century. Utility pottery was the most widely used form of container ware since, being made of local clay, it was inexpensive and readily replaceable. Hand-blown glass, cast or soldered metalwares and barrels or firkins were considerably more expensive and had fewer uses.

Earthenware, produced from indigenous, red firing clays, was formed into various types of vessels. Earthenware production required raw natural clay, which was liquefied, screened to eliminate grit or other intrusions and redried to a more plastic consistency. To assure uniformity between pieces, clay for the wheel was often measured by weight. As the potter produced each vessel on the wheel, it was taken out for air drying to evaporate all possible water (potters had to watch the weather while drying finished pots). Dried pots were stacked into a wood-fired kiln for firing. The process required care, for a kiln load could represent a month's production. Firing was done with dry wood (to minimize effects from smoke) in fireplaces surrounding the kiln. It lasted 2-3 days, after which the kiln temperature was reduced gradually, as the pottery could crack from too-rapid cooling. Pottery was then glazed by dipping in the glaze mixture; for interiors, glaze was poured in, swirled around and poured off. The glazing mixture (usually a lead-oxide and silica mixture in water) was allowed to dry and the pots were again kiln-stacked and refired to fuse the dried glaze. A lower temperature was used than for the initial biscuit firing.

Stoneware was first produced in Canada in 1849 using clays imported from Amboy, New Jersey. In form and fabrication technique, Canadian stoneware was identical to American stoneware of the same period, and many of the early producers had come from American potteries. The expensive New Jersey clay was fired at a temperature of about 1200°C. In Canada it was often "bulked up" with local earthenware clay, which reduced its effective firing temperature to about 850-1000°C. Stoneware clays have a high SILICA content. A Canadian source was not discovered until the late 19th century, when a deposit was located along the Shubenacadie R, NS. The clay was used by the Enfield pottery. The only other source of

Watercooler of salt-glazed stoneware attributed to R.G. Goold, 1864-67 (*courtesy Royal Ontario Museum*).

Red earthenware jug and washbasin, *c*1870 (*courtesy Royal Ontario Museum*).

stoneware clay in Canada is that used by the Medalta Pottery, Medicine Hat, Alta.

Production of stoneware required a more sophisticated TECHNOLOGY than did earthenware. Stoneware, fired at much higher temperatures than earthenware, is a vitrified pottery, ie, waterproof in an unglazed state. Glazing is done by throwing salt into the kiln at maximum firing temperature. The salt (sodium chloride) gasifies; the sodium combines chemically with the silica to form a sodium silicate glaze (ie, a form of glass). The chlorine is either given off as deadly chlorine gas or, if the kiln is cooling, recondenses as hydrochloric acid. Because of its vitrified structure, glazed stoneware is less fragile than red earthenware. The sodium silicate glaze, in chemical combination with the pottery body rather than an overlaid layer as the glazes on earthenware, is insoluble and impervious to acids or alkalis.

Once formed into vessels, stoneware was typically stamped (using printer's type) with either the maker's name or that of a commercial purchaser. The pottery was dried and often decorated, before firing, with designs in cobalt-oxide blue, referred to as powder-blue in potters' glaze recipes. COBALT was the only glazing oxide used for decoration, as it alone could withstand the firing temperatures. The designs ranged from simple brushed-on floral motifs to elaborate incised or glaze-trailed figures or scenes.

Because of its durable body and impervious glaze, stoneware was preferred to cheaper, lead-glazed earthenware for food preparation and storage, especially pickling or salting. However, by the last quarter of the 19th century, a gradual shift of food preparation, from the home to the processing plant, began, and refrigeration, commercial canning and dairy processing began to erode the market for the utility pottery necessary for home processing. In the 1880s, mass-produced, inexpensive GLASS provided the advantage of visible contents and further reduced the pottery market. By the late 1880s the number of pottery operations in Canada was declining and, because of accelerating changes in food preparation and marketing, most potteries closed between 1890 and 1910.

Archaeological investigations of early potteries indicate that firing accidents were common: great quantities of "waster" pottery were discarded. Before the 20th century, potters had little knowledge of the components of their clays and only rudimentary means of measuring kiln temperatures. In small local potteries, an average loss of some 50% of production seems a realistic estimate. Prior to the 20th century, Canadian earthenware pottery followed 4 basic regional forms.

Québec Pottery, the earliest type, was produced from the mid-17th century to the early 20th century. Although the earliest Québec pottery was established in 1655, NEW FRANCE imported French earthenware until 1760. These imports consisted primarily of basic bowls, pitchers and jugs glazed with a green, copper oxide glaze. Québec potters emulated the form but not the colour of French ware. Their pottery usually had a transparent lead-oxide glaze, sometimes over a brown slip coating which covered the pottery body. Québec pottery was not decorated in the 18th century; in the 19th century, a simple American decoration of spatterings of brown slip was adopted.

Maritime Pottery, particularly that of NS and PEI, was basically northern English and Scottish in design derivation. Earthenware was not produced in the Maritimes before the early 19th century and, with rare exceptions, was produced in limited variety. Maritimes earthenware was based on the dense iron-rich clays of the area and fired to a dark red. The interior lining of vessels and the sparse decoration made use of white slip, made of fine white clay from the Magdalen Is. The most common items are crocks and large bowls with deep-red bodies, interiors coated in white slip and transparent lead oxide glazes.

Upper Canada Pottery shows various ethnic influences, the strongest being that of the Pennsylvania GERMANS who had migrated into the region. Ontario Germanic pottery is characterized by a wide variety of forms and shapes and, often, by imaginative and colourful uses of coloured clay slips and different metallic-oxide glazes (eg, copper, iron and manganese, as well as lead). Glaze colour, pattern and variation are infinite, as are vessel forms. Most potters produced primarily basic utility and container vessels, but they also made slipcast wares, molded figures, miniatures, toys, and gift and presentation pieces. The earliest pottery in the region was established in 1794; unlike the situation in Québec and the Maritimes, potteries proliferated because of isolation and the difficulty of receiving British imports.

Generic North American Pottery, eg, slip-cast tablewares, canning vacuum jars and short-term fashions like the "rustic" wares of the 1880s, appeared and became universally popular after regional distinctions began to disappear about 1870. The influence of widespread advertising, and the appearance of mail-order catalogues, very quickly outweighed regional tradition, not only in pottery but in all decorative art forms. The age of the individual craftsman was effectively giving way to the age of the machine and the factory.

Little early pottery is known from W of Ontario because, by the time European settlement began in the late 19th century, the domestic use of handmade earthenware was declining. A pottery was established in Winnipeg in the 1880s. Evidence provided by industrial ARCHAEOLOGY studies indicates that it produced only utility wares. Later, the Medalta Pottery was established at Medicine Hat, producing stoneware from local clay discovered about 1910.

D.B. WEBSTER

British-made Ceramics

After the British CONQUEST, 1760, the ceramic wares most generally used in Canada came from Great Britain. Three factors accounted for this situation: Britain regarded its colonies as natural markets for British goods; developments were occurring in the British pottery industry; and British potters promoted their wares aggressively. Canada came under British rule just as British potters were on the verge of making a determined bid for world prominence. By the mid-19th century, when changes in trade and navigation laws permitted freer entry of foreign goods, the range and variety of British ceramic products was so great and their position so entrenched that Canadians continued to buy them in substantial quantities. In early days, ship captains were recruited to take out samples and make contacts for future sales; Canadian agents were appointed; some potters journeyed to Canada to assess the market; others opened warehouses in cities such as Québec and Toronto. In 1836, William Taylor Copeland, a prominent Staffordshire potter, became the supplier of ceramic wares to HUDSON'S BAY COMPANY posts and shops throughout the Northwest.

Earthenware Although, over the years, everything from pickling pots to ornaments was imported, certain types of British ware predominated in the Canadian market. The first of these popular items was an 18th-century lead-glazed earthenware for the table. Ranging from deep to pale cream in colour, it was called creamware or, after Josiah Wedgwood gained Queen Charlotte's patronage for it in the 1760s, Queensware. Creamware is known to have been used in French Canadian farmhouses, city merchants' homes and government residences.

Early in the 19th century, creamware, its decoration usually hand painted on-glaze, was displaced as the chief tableware by an earthenware of whiter appearance, decorated by a semimechanical process called underglaze transfer printing. The technique involved transferring impressions from engraved copperplates to paper and then to the earthenware. It permitted an endless variety of designs (including Canadian scenes) to be printed on tableware at relatively low cost. The glaze over the decoration protected it and gave it brilliance. Hailed as the coming ware by a Halifax importer in 1811, underglaze transfer-printed earthenware became, and remained, the most widely used tableware in Canada.

Another British development important in the Canadian trade had to do with the earthenware body, as distinct from its decoration. In 1813 Charles James Mason, a Staffordshire potter, patented a tough, high-fired earthenware called ironstone china. Scores of British potters copied Mason's product, marketing it under many names (stone china, opaque china, etc) and offering it painted, printed or plain. Its durability, and the cheapness of the undecorated variety, ensured sales in a pioneer country such as Canada.

Porcelain was never imported in the same quantities as earthenware, although there had always been some supplies of this more expensive ceramic product. In 1793, for example, Worcester porcelain was being offered in Saint John, NB, in exchange for furs if cash was not available. Eighteenth-century English porcelains were apt to be capricious in the kiln. The invention, towards the end of the century, of what is now called English bone china (basically, a composition of china clay, china stone and a high proportion of bone ash) cut kiln losses and ensured wider sales of British porcelain in Canada. By Victorian times, virtually every British porcelain manufacturer had switched to a bone formula.

Victorian times also brought an unprecedented taste for what a Toronto importer called "articles to fill a space and gratify the eye." Of the ceramic ornaments that poured from Britain's potteries into Canadian homes, none had a greater appeal than those in Parian, a porcelain invented in Staffordshire in the 1840s and named after marble from the Greek island, Paros. Its avowed object was to simulate marble. Busts, eg, of Sir John A. MACDONALD and Edward HANLAN (the Toronto oarsman who became world champion in 1880), were produced in Parian.

Canada never developed a pottery industry that seriously challenged imported tablewares or ornaments. As Canadian potters turned out more and more of the common, dark-bodied earthenwares and stonewares for kitchen or storage use, in the second half of the 19th century, imports of these wares dwindled. However, by that time Canada's population was expanding rapidly and the demand for finer wares was increasing in proportion. British potters continued to have a market that saw at least some of their products in every home in Canada.

ELIZABETH COLLARD

Reading: Elizabeth Collard, *Nineteenth-Century Pottery and Porcelain in Canada* (1984).

Ceramics, Contemporary In 1975, 10 000 to 12 000 people were employed full time in crafts in Canada and over 4 million people attended a crafts fair or exhibition. Pottery was estimated, in 1978, to constitute 32% of all craft activity, 9% higher than the next most popular medium, WEAVING. Pottery was relatively more popular in the western provinces.

Before 1950 Canadian ceramists often learned their craft abroad and brought back with them current styles. Thus, their work generally shared the interests of the decorative arts of the time. A lack of focus in Canada led many potters to look to the annual, competitive ceramic National Exhibition in Syracuse, NY, where they repeatedly made a strong showing. Exhibitors included Kjeld and Erica Deichmann from NB, Bailey Leslie from Ontario and Konrad and Krystyna Sadowska from the Ontario College of Art. No typical Canadian style emerged during the period, although excellent individual pieces were created in various idioms. Diversity and growth characterize the post-1950 period. Ceramists added oriental to earlier American and European influences. These 3 influences are to be found in most late Canadian work, mixed and remixed in differing relationships.

The work and writings of British potter Bernard Leach (*A Potter's Book*, 1940) were influential in disseminating technical information and a regard for disciplined experience, mixed with spontaneity and sturdy practicality. Canadian John Reeve, who worked with Leach, left a mark in his brief but influential sojourns on both Canadian coasts and in his workshops across the country. The example of Leach and his followers contrasted with an American antitraditionalist movement, based principally in the art schools, which investigated the abstract possibilities of material and conventional forms. For a time, controversy raged between sculptors (nonfunctional) and the potters (functional). Many ceramic teachers emigrated from the US to Canada in this period. Acceptance of the use of clay for purely artistic purposes led to the proliferation of various low-fire technologies, eg, raku, a free-form, Japanese-derived pottery, and "funk." Canadians such as Wayne Ngan and Walter Dexter are notable exponents of raku. Funk was the most controversial form of nonfunctional clay use in the early 1970s. The work of David Gilhooly, based at York University, became the most notable example. Members of both the functional and nonfunctional schools explored new materials and processes, for example, low-fire glazes (eg, salt glazing), high-temperature processes (eg, wood firing) and, above all, the controlled chances of reduction firing. Ruth Gowdy McKinley was an investigator of the exquisite balance between accident and control.

Canadian tendencies began to be perceptible, epitomized by a restrained interpretation of current international preoccupations. French Canadians, such as Maurice Savoie, Enid Le Gros and Joe Fafard, maintained connections with their heritage. Louise Doucet-Saito and Satashi Saito combined European, pre-Columbian and Oriental interests. Many other Canadians, such as Jack Sures, Les Manning, John Chalke and Robin Hopper (the first Bronfman Award for Excellence recipient) pointed towards a style — cool, well designed, sometimes rich in detail yet severe overall — bearing the mark of its northern origins.

Contemporary ceramic by Robin Hopper (*courtesy Canadian Crafts Council/Robin Hopper*).

Reliable statistics on the economic significance of ceramics are difficult to obtain. In 1978 gross sales of finished goods were estimated at \$1.5-\$3 million. Like any craft, ceramics creates employment in areas where there otherwise might be none, relatively little capital is involved, local materials are used and tourism is attracted. In addition to the revenues derived from sales, these factors comprise the economic significance of ceramics. Ceramics has established itself as a minor but real factor in local and provincial economies.

During the period 1955-75 many organizations designed to give individuals collective strength and services were established, often partly funded by government grants. In many provinces, ceramic organizations parallel, affiliate with or have their functions fulfilled by provincial or territorial umbrella organizations that, in turn, are affiliated with the Canadian Crafts Council. Of the purely ceramic organizations, Ontario Potters Assn (est 1948) is the largest. A national organization called Ceramic Masters was founded in 1975. Earlier, the Canadian Guild of Potters attempted to establish a national focus. The pottery that operated at Rankin Inlet between 1965 and 1976 was probably the only significant example of involvement in clay of Canada's native people. Workshops run by schools and organizations have been very influential in the maturation of ceramics in Canada and have offered the opportunity to view most of the world's major practitioners at work. Formal education in ceramics has occurred entirely as part of the general development in crafts; an APPRENTICESHIP SYSTEM has not existed. Periodicals (except for *Tactile*, which ceased publication in Aug 1976) have been few or foreign in origin and adequate galleries are rare. CHRISTOPHER D. TYLER

Cereal Crops are members of the GRASS family grown for their edible starchy seeds. The important cereal crops produced in Canada are WHEAT, BARLEY, OATS, RYE and CORN; small hectarages of TRITICALE and grain MILLETS are grown. The cool, short growing seasons prevent commercial production of rice and grain sorghum.

Cereal crops may be divided into spring-sown types, which complete their life cycle in one season (summer annuals), and fall-sown types, which require an overwintering period (winter annuals). Among the fall-sown types, winter rye is the most winter hardy, followed by winter triticale and winter wheat, then winter barley; winter oats are least hardy. No winter forms of grain millets or corn exist. Spring-sown cereals are grown in all provinces except Newfoundland. In 1980 approximately 97% of the 11 million ha of wheat, 93% of the 4.8 million ha of barley and 77% of the 1.9 million ha of oats produced were grown in the Prairie provinces. Saskatchewan is the leading producer of spring wheat; Alberta, of barley and oats. Significant quantities of oats and barley are also produced in Ontario and Québec. Over 0.5 million ha of mixed grain (usually oats and barley grown together) are produced, mainly in Ontario. Production of spring rye is negligible. Of almost one million hectares of grain corn produced, about 80% is grown in southern Ontario; smaller hectarages, in Québec and Manitoba. Winter rye can be grown in many areas of Canada but, of the 0.3 million ha, about 90% is produced on the PRAIRIES. Significant winter-wheat production is limited to southern Ontario and southern Alberta. Small hectarages of winter triticale and winter barley are produced in southern Ontario, but winter conditions in Canada are too severe for winter oats.

Wheat, oats, barley, rye and triticale are considered cool-season crops. Their spring forms are normally seeded between mid-Apr and mid-May, completing their life cycles in 80-100 days under Canadian conditions. The winter forms, seeded in Sept, overwinter as seedling plants and mature the following July. The other cereals are warm-season crops. Corn is seeded during the first 3 weeks of May and requires the full growing season to reach maturity. Grain millets may be seeded in May or June and mature in about 90 days. Rye, corn and sorghum are cross-pollinated species; the other cereal crops are self-pollinated.

Corn Grain corn is normally planted in rows 70-90 cm apart, with populations of 50 000-60 000 plants per hectare. Silage corn is more productive at slightly higher populations. Grain corn is harvested (with ear-pickers or picker-sheller combines) when the kernel moisture content is 25-30%. The stalks are left in the field and plowed under. Picked whole-ear corn may be stored outside in slatted cribs, which permit air circulation and low-energy, natural drying. Shelled corn may be dried artificially to 15% moisture content to permit inside storage in open containers, or it may be stored as high-moisture corn without drying, either in airtight containers or in open bins, following treatment with an organic acid to prevent spoilage. Grain yield in corn varies from 5 to 10 tonnes per hectare (t/ha), depending on the length of the growing season, temperature, moisture availability and soil fertility. Whole-plant silage corn yields range from 10 to over 20 t of dry matter per ha.

Small Grain Cereals and millets are seeded in rows 15-20 cm apart, at rates of 60-120 kg of seed per hectare. Small grain cereals are normally harvested with combine threshers, with or without prior cutting and swathing. Moisture content at harvest is usually below 15%, allowing storage of the grain without artificial drying. The remaining straw may be left in the field and incorporated with the soil, or removed and used as feed or bedding for livestock. Grain yields from spring-sown small-grain cereals range from less than 2 t/ha, under dry prairie conditions, to over 4 t/ha, under ideal growing conditions in eastern Canada. Where they survive the winter, fall-sown cereals yield 15-25% more than spring-sown types. Straw yields range from 2 t/ha to 4 t/ha.

Usage

The use made of a cereal crop depends on the chemical composition and quality of its seeds. Over 75% of the spring-wheat crop is used to produce bread flour; much of it is exported for this purpose. Smaller quantities of spring (durum) wheats go into the manufacture of pasta products. Winter wheat is used extensively for cake and pastry flour. All wheats are used to some extent for livestock feed. About 20% of the barley produced in Canada is processed by the malting and BREWING INDUSTRIES, domestic and foreign. Most of the remainder goes for livestock feed. Oats are grown primarily for livestock feed but small quantities are used in oatmeal and other food products. Rye and corn grains are also fed to livestock, although significant quantities are used in the DISTILLING INDUSTRY. Small amounts of corn are milled for starch, oil, syrup and other products. Triticale seed is used mainly for feeding livestock but small quantities are milled for flour. Grain millets are used in N America for animal feed and in the bird-seed industry. In some cases, the entire cereal plant (excluding roots) is used, for example, the entire oat plant, harvested well before the grain is ripe, may be used as hay or silage (feed preserved by the acid-forming action of bacteria); whole-plant corn is also preserved as silage. The total annual value of Canadian cereal crops is estimated at $5.5 billion, ie, about 1.9% of the GROSS NATIONAL PRODUCT.

HAROLD R. KLINCK

CESAR The 1983 Canadian Expedition to Study the Alpha Ridge was possibly the most important scientific expedition ever mounted in Canada. Discovered in 1963, the Alpha Ridge is a submerged mountain chain traversing the Arctic from off ELLESMERE ISLAND to the Siberian Continental Shelf. The range rises 2.7 km above the seafloor, is 200-450 km wide, and is the most westerly of the 3 ranges dividing the Arctic Basin (the others being the Nansen-Gakkel and Lomonosov ridges). The expedition involved over 40 researchers, working from March to May. The cost of the operation ($1.7 million) was defrayed by the federal government, and the expedition's activities were led by Dr Hans Weber of the Earth Physics Branch, Dept of ENERGY, MINES AND RESOURCES. Canadian Armed Forces aircraft transported the 300 000 kg of equipment, which included kitchen and mess structures, dormitory tents, prefabricated plywood buildings for use as offices and laboratories, scientific equipment, food, etc.

The main objective of the multidisciplinary expedition was to carry out a geological survey of the ridge. Researchers, therefore, brought a veritable geotechnical arsenal to bear on the polar ice to gather seismic, gravimetric, bathymetric and other data. They also made observations regarding the origin of the ridge. The question of origin is very important because the answer may determine whether or not Canada has RESOURCE RIGHTS in the region. It is important to determine if the ridge is a genuine oceanic ridge born in a volcanic upheaval, a prolongation of the N American Continental Shelf or a fragment, possibly from the Russian side of the shelf. Under the LAW OF THE SEA countries have exclusive rights to the resources of their continental shelves. If it is found that the ridge is an extension of the continent from Ellesmere I, Canada could lay claim to part of the ridge itself and to 322 km on either side. The issue is the more crucial because, in the Canadian Arctic, the continental shelves offer the best prospects for PETROLEUM EXPLORATION, as is witnessed by soundings in the Beaufort Sea. Much study, analysis of data, and discussion among researchers will be needed to settle the question of origin definitively.

Like its earlier counterpart LOREX (Lomonosov Ridge Experiment, 1979), CESAR ended when the seasonal ice on which the camp was built began to melt. Scientists and the Canadian government are considering building a more permanent station on an ice "island," an ICEBERG that calved from the Ward Hunt ice shelf, off Ellesmere I, in 1982. The island is expected to drift through Canadian and then international waters for the next 3 years, slowly melting.

LUC CHARTRAND

Cetacea, order of MAMMALS consisting of WHALES, DOLPHINS and porpoises. It includes about 80 living species, with worldwide distribution. Highly specialized anatomy and phys-
iology allow cetaceans to maintain a full
aquatic existence while breathing air. Anatomi
cal modifications of modern cetaceans includ
short neck with vertebrae sometimes fused; fu
siform (cigar-shaped) body; body hair generall
absent or reduced to isolated whiskers on th
jaws, chin and rostrum (part of skull in front c
eyes); horizontal caudal (tail) flukes supporte
by cartilage; hindlimbs reduced to small bone
embedded in the flank musculature; and fore
limbs flattened to flippers with bony digits en
closed in a common integument. Most moder
species have a single fin on the back. Immedi
ately below the epidermis is a blubber layer, de
veloped in many modern species to provid
thermal insulation and storage for lipids (fats
The cetacean skull is "telescoped," ie, the bone
of the rostrum extend over and under the brain
case. Except in the sperm whale (*Physeter catc
don*), the external nasal opening is positioned o
the upper rear of the skull and allows quick, ef
ficient breathing at the air-water interface. Con
cealment of genital, mammary and excretor
organs within the body outline contributes t
streamlining. There is no external ear; a pinho
opening leads to a pinched-off ear canal. Never
theless, hearing is well developed; sound plays
key role in communication, navigation and ob
ject detection.

Cetaceans are classified in 3 suborders: Ar
chaeoceti, Mysticeti and Odontoceti. Archae
ocetes, now extinct, were comparatively prim
itive: their skull bones were not telescoped; the
had milk teeth, shed and replaced by permanen
teeth; they had reduced hindlimbs, probabl
protruding externally. They were serpentlik
animals up to 20 m long, with a full battery o
teeth which made them formidable predators
Their descendants are the mysticetes (balee
whales) and odontocetes (toothed whales). Liv
ing mysticetes comprise 3 families, 6 genera an
10 species (in Canada, 3 families, 5 genera, 8 spe
cies); living odontocetes, 7 families, 31 genera
and about 70 species (in Canada, 5 families, 1
genera, about 25 species). Their paired, externa
fleshy nostrils (blowholes) distinguish the mys
ticetes from the odontocetes, which have a sin
gle blowhole. Feeding adaptations also differ
The vestigial teeth of mysticetes are lost befor
birth, and replaced by baleen (whalebone)
hornlike modified skin tissue rooted in and sus
pended from the palate. Baleen consists of many
fibrous tubules packed together to form plates
arranged in a row on either side of the mouth
The ends of the plates become frayed and inter
woven, creating an efficient sieve for trapping
small fish and ZOOPLANKTON. Most odontocete
have undifferentiated, functional teeth. Foo
passes, unchewed, through the esophagus an
into a specialized, multichambered stomach
where digestion occurs. The kidney is divide
into many small lobules or renules (300-300
per side). Cetaceans usually pass normal mam
malian urine, but there is some evidence tha
dolphins can, for short periods, excrete urin
with an unusually high salt concentration.

Most cetaceans are seasonal breeders; the tim
ing of peak breeding varies according to a spe
cies' or population's ecology. Most mysticete
migrate annually between summer feeding
grounds and winter breeding and calving
grounds; some odontocete populations are rela
tively more sedentary. Gestation lasts for a littl
less than one year in most species. Sperm whale
have a 16-month gestation period and in som
other odontocetes it exceeds one year. Cetacea
females rarely carry more than one fetus t
term; energy requirements make it difficult for
female to rear more than one calf in the sam
season. Calves are born tail first and are well de
veloped at birth. Birth and nursing take plac
underwater. Mysticetes wean calves after 7-1
or more months; some odontocetes, much late
at 18 or more months. Thus, except for a fev

naller species, the interbirth interval is at least years.

Maximum swimming speeds range from at east 30 km/h in some porpoises to 37 km/h or aster in the large rorquals (eg, sei whale). iving capabilities vary greatly by species. perm whales and certain beaked whales often ubmerge for over an hour. Cases of entanglement in submarine cables show that sperm whales reach depths of at least 1100 m; other vidence points to even deeper dives. Baleen whales generally do not dive for longer than 0-30 min, although the ice-adapted bowhead *Balaena mysticetus*) is known to dive for over 30 min. Dolphins and porpoises normally surface t intervals of 5-7 min or less.

The only serious, nonhuman predators of etaceans are large SHARKS and killer whales *Orcinus orca*). The latter are known to attack virtually all species of marine mammal, including he blue whale (*Balaenoptera musculus*), the largest etacean. Strong, lasting social cohesion within iller whale pods (extended family units) facilitates group hunting. Odontocetes are observably regarious, and many are thought to have complex social structures. Most mysticetes are hought to be only moderately gregarious, although their long-range communication signals may permit more co-ordinated activity than s evident from casual observation. Only odontocetes have been proven capable of echolocation. The 2 major types of sounds made by etaceans are low-pitched moans, screams, whistles and grunts, probably used for social ommunication, and high-intensity clicks, with requencies ranging up to 200 kHz (about 13 imes the upper frequency of human hearing apability), used for discrimination and navigation. Excellent vision has been demonstrated xperimentally in some small odontocetes; owever, several kinds of freshwater dolphins platanistids) have reduced eyes — Ganges and ndus dolphins (*Platanista gangetica, P. minor*, respectively) are nearly blind. Cetaceans have well-developed taste buds, but chemoreceptor rgans are reduced (Jacobson's organ of mysticetes) or absent (odontocetes).

The many important anatomical differences etween the 2 suborders have been sometimes nterpreted to reflect different terrestrial ancestries. However, an increasingly well-documented FOSSIL record of Archaeoceti shows this roup to be sufficiently diverse to have given ise to both squalodonts (early odontocetes) and gorophiids (early mysticetes). *See* WHALING.

E.D. MITCHELL AND R. REEVES

Reading: D.E. Gaskin, *The Ecology of Whales and Dolphins* 982).

haleur Bay, which lies between the Gaspé eninsula, Qué, and northern New Brunswick, s the largest bay in the Gulf of ST LAWRENCE. t is divided into 2 basins: the outer or eastern asin, with water depths mostly 70-90 m, and he inner or western basin, with depths generally less than 50 m. The RESTIGOUCHE R enters the western end of the bay to produce an estuary oughly 160 km long. In ancient times the western basin and Chaleur Trough to the E were part f the Restigouche Channel, providing a preglacial drainage system for the surrounding area.

Near the mouth of the bay, cold, fresh surface water from the Gaspé Current enters on the N ide, while flow on the S shore is directed outward into the Gulf to create a counterclockwise yre in the surface circulation. The Gaspé water s rich in nutrients and promotes a high and sustained level of primary production throughout he summer months. The bay is a famous fishing ground for salmon and also supports important scallop and clam fisheries. As the name estowed on the bay by Jacques CARTIER suggests, the climate of the bay is unusually warm ompared to adjacent areas of the Gulf, making it a favoured location for summer resorts. Cartier explored the bay in July 1534 and traded for furs with the natives, likely MICMAC. DALHOUSIE, at the mouth of the Restigouche estuary, is a major port for northern NB.

P.C. SMITH

Chalk River, Ont, Village, pop 1010 (1981c), inc 1954, located on Chalk R, a tributary of Ottawa R, 210 km NW of Ottawa. Origin of the name is unknown; it may refer to the colour of the river or to the practice of charring local poplar and alder trees and using them to mark square timbers during the heyday of the logging industry in the 19th century. Prior to WWII, Chalk River was a small bush settlement. In 1944 it was chosen as the site for a heavy-water reactor to produce plutonium from uranium — the first reactor built outside the US. Subsequently the Chalk River Nuclear Laboratories developed into a complex of 5 nuclear reactors owned by Atomic Energy of Canada, Ltd, a crown corporation. Most employees live in nearby Deep River.

DANIEL FRANCIS

Chalk River Nuclear Laboratories, *see* NUCLEAR RESEARCH ESTABLISHMENTS.

Challenger Expedition, the first worldwide oceanographic expedition, voyaged 127 663 km in the Atlantic, Southern, Indian and Pacific oceans between Dec 1872 and May 1876. The voyage of HMS *Challenger*, a 69 m corvette specially modified for research in OCEANOGRAPHY, was intended to investigate the distribution of animals in the deep sea (particularly representatives of ancient groups) and to solve the problem of how the OCEANS circulate. The voyage wasorganized by Charles Wyville Thomson and W.B. Carpenter, with the financial support of the British government and the patronage of the Royal Society. The scientific work of *Challenger* was directed by Thomson aided by a small staff, notably John Murray, a Scot born in Cobourg, Ont, who later completed the 50-volume report of the expedition. *Challenger*'s captain was George S. Nares, later famed for arctic exploration.

The Challenger Expedition provided large amounts of new information about the oceans. Hundreds of previously unknown animal species were described. But although animals were found at the greatest depths sampled (5500 m), showing that the oceans were inhabited at all depths, there were no "living fossils" as Wyville Thomson had expected. Carpenter's hope that the mechanism by which the oceans circulated could be discovered was not realized, although abundant information on the temperature, salinity and specific gravity of seawater was collected during the 3½-year cruise. The composition of seawater was well established by William Dittmar of Glasgow University; and Murray and Alphonse Renard mapped ocean sediments, which proved to be quite different from terrestrial ones. The lengthy reports of the expedition contain information still useful to oceanographers.

Challenger visited Halifax for 10 days in May 1873 before leaving for Africa and S America. Its visit was celebrated by the Nova Scotian Institute of Science and aroused a brief interest in deep-sea animals, particularly on the part of the institute's secretary, Provincial Geologist David Honeyman. A small collection of animals from the voyage is found in the Nova Scotia Museum of Science, and some original volumes of the results are in Dalhousie University Library. The Challenger Expedition's effect on Canadian SCIENCE was short-lived, but the voyage stimulated worldwide explorations by many Western European nations later in the century. *See* SEASHELL.

ERIC L. MILLS

Reading: E. Linklater, *The Voyage of the Challenger* (1972).

Chalmers, Floyd Sherman, editor, publisher, arts patron (b at Chicago, Ill 14 Sept 1898). Brought to Canada by his Canadian father, Chalmers grew up in Orillia, Ont, and Toronto. After WWI service overseas he joined the *Financial Post*, becoming editor in chief at 27. He was president of MACLEAN HUNTER from 1952 to 1964 and then chairman of the board of directors until 1969. He and his wife Jean were volunteers or board members of many cultural organizations and established numerous prizes and awards. In 1964 Chalmers established the Floyd S. Chalmers Foundation to assist young artists and to support innovative projects. It has also commissioned such important compositions as the opera *Louis Riel* by Harry SOMERS. One of his most important contributions was his original sponsorship and ongoing financial support of the manuscript preparation of the ENCYCLOPEDIA OF MUSIC IN CANADA. In 1983 Chalmers completed his autobiography, *Both Sides of the Street*. An Officer of the Order of Canada (1967), he received the Diplôme d'Honneur, honorary degrees, and was chancellor of York U 1968-73. In 1984, through a bequest of $1 million Chalmers and his wife established the Jean A. Chalmers Chair in Canadian Music and the Institute for Canadian Music, at the Faculty of Music, University of Toronto. The first director of the institute and Jean A. Chalmers Professor of Canadian Music was John BECKWITH, composer and teacher.

MABEL H. LAINE

Chamber Music refers to that body of composition for up to about 12 parts in which there is little or no doubling and in which each part is of equal importance. During Canada's formative years, from the 18th century, Haydn, Mozart and Beethoven were establishing the forms and typical groupings of instruments that have become standard, such as the string trio (violin, viola, 'cello), piano trio (violin, 'cello, piano), and especially the string quartet (2 violins, viola, 'cello).

The earliest known activity of classical chamber music performance in Canada, at the opening of the 19th century, centered on Judge Jonathan SEWELL of Québec City, an amateur violinist. Unfortunately, there is little evidence of composition in Canada of chamber music at this time. A contemporary of Sewell's, Joseph QUESNEL from Montréal, is said to have written duos and quartets, although none has survived.

While European composers, from Beethoven to Johannes Brahms, were developing the genre in which both the musical language and the classical forms were much extended, Canadians turned scant attention to the medium until the last quarter of the 19th century. There were a number of marches, dances and character pieces for flute, violin and cornet, with piano accompaniment, but few examples of concert chamber music. Such composers as J.P. CLARKE and Calixa LAVALLÉE supposedly wrote for the genre, but these works too seem not to have survived. One of the earliest extant chamber works is *Fantaisie sonate* (1858) for flute and string quartet by Antoine DESSANE, a Québec City composer, organist and cellist.

From the 1870s several conservatories opened their doors, providing their string, woodwind and brass faculty with the opportunity to form chamber ensembles. Chamber music performance has flourished up to the present day in such teaching institutions. From Québec City's Septuor Haydn (founded in 1871 with string quintet, flute and piano), through several prominent string quartets, including the Toronto String Quartette Club (1884-87), Dubois (1910-38), (Toronto) Conservatory (1929-46), HART HOUSE (1923-45), Parlow (1943-58), ORFORD (fd 1965), Vághy (est in Canada 1968) and PURCELL (fd 1968) string quartets, many of Canada's leading performers have added their expertise to the performance of works by the European masters as well as by Canadian composers.

With the opportunity for performance by the late 19th century, a few composers turned their attention to the genre, including Guillaume COUTURE (*String Quartet*, 1875), W.O. Forsyth (*Quintette*, 1886), Edward Manning (*Trio*, about 1900), Alexis Contant (*Trio*, 1907), and Sir Ernest MACMILLAN (*String Quartet*, 1914). Though these works exhibit a certain cautiousness in expression, lacking elements of current musical ideas from Europe such as in the work of Scriabin, Debussy and Schoenberg, they indicate nevertheless that Canadian composition had reached a high level of craft and expression within its conservative idiom.

A correlation exists between the growth in popularity of the genre among Canadian composers and the growth in experimentation of 20th-century techniques, owing to the flexibility of chamber music as a vehicle for experimentation. The evolution towards greater experimentation began with Rodolphe MATHIEU, whose chromaticism stems from Debussy and early Schönberg and is most apparent in his work from the 1920s (*Quatuor no. 1*, 1920, and *Trio*, 1921). Unfortunately, his work was not well received in Canada.

It was the next generation of composers (those born in the early 20th century) whose experimentation was a more successful attempt to break with the past. John WEINZWEIG, Barbara PENTLAND and Jean PAPINEAU-COUTURE are among the first Canadian composers to have devoted a large part of their output to chamber music. Whether serialism, in the case of Weinzweig and Pentland, or chromaticism generally, in the case of Papineau-Couture, their musical language showed an awareness of current musical thought, which they then imparted to their students. They produced a number of string quartets (Weinzweig and Pentland, 3 each, Papineau-Couture, 2, up to 1983), in addition to Weinzweig's *Woodwind Quintet* (1964) and Papineau-Couture's *Églogues* (1942), with voice, and *Sextuor* (1967). The influence of Bartók and Hindemith is evident in Violet ARCHER's *Trio no. 2* (1957), and Boulez's rigorous serialism is reflected in Serge GARANT's *Offrande I* (1969) and *III* (1971) and *Circuits I & II* (1972) and *III* (1973). Harry SOMERS's 3 string quartets (1943, 1950, 1959) show the influence of his primary teacher, Weinzweig, while his *Twelve Miniatures* (1964), which includes voice, indicates the independent road his style had taken. One of Canada's most widely known composers, R. Murray SCHAFER, contributed much to the genre, including *Requiems for the Party Girl* (1966), which reflects his predilection for vocal lines sung to his own texts, and *String Quartet No. 2* (1976), which shows his interest in the sound environment. Gilles TREMBLAY's interest in timbre is evident in such works as *Champs I* (1965), *II* (*Souffles*, 1968) and *III* (*Vers*, 1969) and *Solstices* (1971). Among the works of younger composers, John Hawkins's *Remembrances* (1969) and Claude Vivier's *Prolifération* (1969) are of particular interest for their incorporation of elements of theatre, which became a prominent preoccupation of many composers in the 1970s. Recent developments such as the influences of minimalism, mysticism and eastern music have also played important roles in the eclectic style of Canadian composition.

The flourishing of chamber music composition would not have been possible without the establishment of ensembles after WWII. Besides the string quartets already mentioned, brass and woodwind ensembles were formed, including the York Winds, the CANADIAN BRASS, and the Montreal Brass Quintet, as well as several ensembles of nontraditional groupings. Perhaps most important for composition in the genre was the establishment of several societies devoted to avant-garde chamber music, including the Société de musique contemporaine du Québec (Montréal), New Music Concerts (Toronto), Array Music (Toronto), and the Vancouver New Music Society. CLIFFORD FORD

Reading: J. Beckwith and K. MacMillan, eds, *Contemporary Canadian Composers* (1975); *Encyclopedia of Music in Canada* (1981); Clifford Ford, *Canada's Music: An Historical Survey* (1982); H. Kallman, *A History of Music in Canada 1534-1914* (1960).

Chamber of Commerce, a nonprofit organization of businessmen and corporations established to promote economic development and collectively represent their concerns to government on public policy. Chambers of commerce, or boards of trade as they are sometimes known, operate at all 3 levels of government — community, provincial and national. The Canadian Chamber of Commerce (est 1929) is a member of the International Chamber of Commerce. The first chamber in N America was founded in Halifax in 1750. Today, there are local chambers of commerce or boards of trade in about 600 communities across Canada, with about 145 000 individual and corporate memberships. The Toronto Board of Trade, with about 15 300 members, is the largest in N America. Community chambers or boards exist principally to promote industrial development or other economic activities such as tourism or resource development, although the larger chambers also conduct salary and other economic surveys for their members. There are 7 provincial chambers of commerce in Canada that date to the early part of this century. The local chambers of New Brunswick, Nova Scotia, PEI and Newfoundland are organized in one body: the Atlantic Provinces Chamber of Commerce. There are also loosely assembled associations in the Yukon and the Northwest Territories. The Canadian chamber's head office was located in Montréal until 1982, when it was moved to Ottawa; it has a full-time president and elected chairman. The chamber has offices in Toronto and Montréal, as well as Ottawa and a full-time staff of about 50. In addition to corporate and community chambers, its membership includes about 80 trade associations. All provincial chamber presidents are on the board of the Canadian Chamber of Commerce. DAVID CRANE

Chamberland, Paul, poet (b at Longueuil, Qué 16 May 1939). Chamberland was the most iconoclastic Québec poet of the 1960s and one of the most innovative essayists of the 1970s. His first collections of poetry, *Genèses* (1962), *Le Pays* (a 1963 collaboration), *Terre Québec* (1964), *L'Afficheur hurle* (1965) and *L'Inavouable* (1968) cried out "the savage need for liberation." He rejected "unidimensional" politics after 1968, and as prophet and mystic he announced the arrival of "the Kingdom" and named the "Agents of the Future" — the Hommenfandieux and Essaimour. It was his time of writing books as manifestos, such as *Éclats de la pierre noire d'où rejaillit ma vie* (1972), *Demain les dieux naîtront* (1974), of the writer-animator of the Fabrike d'ékriture and the contributor to the magazines *Mainmise* and *Hobo-Québec*. Chamberland's books of the 1980s continued to explore the "resolute-ly lucid delirium" of his earlier works: *Terre souveraine* (1980), *Le Courage de la poésie* (1981), *L'Enfant doré* (1981) and *Émergence de l'adultenfant* (1981). *Un Parti pris anthropologique* (1983) is a collection of Chamberland's work published in the magazine *Parti pris*. In 1983 he published *Aléatoire instantané & Midsummer 82* and the essay *Le Recommencement du monde*. RICHARD GIGUÈRE

Chambers, Jack, painter (b at London, Ont 25 Mar 1931; d there 13 Apr 1978). After studying at a technical school in his home town, Chambers spent the years 1953-61 in Europe, travelling and studying at the San Fernando Academia de Bellas Artes in Madrid. He returned to London in 1961. Chambers's paintings through the 1960s contained dreamlike images, combining his immediate personal experience and memory. In 1969, the year he was diagnosed as having leukemia, he published the essay he called "Perceptual Realism," developed on a range of philosophical and theological sources, in particular the French existential phenomenologist Maurice Merleau-Ponty. From that date a striking change took place in his art. The visionary character of his work through the 1960s gave way to an intense and precise representation of reality. Throughout Chambers's artistic life, his work was developed around subjects of great importance to him: his family, his home, the city of London and the surrounding landscape. He expressed a notion of regionalism not based on a nostalgic and sentimental restrictiveness but on a celebration of the reality of living and working in a particular place. He also worked as a filmmaker, producing 8 films between 1964 and 1970.

In 1967, following a dispute with the National Gallery of Canada over reproduction rights, he founded Canadian Artists Representation (CAR) to try to establish fee scales for reproduction rights and rental fees for works in public exhibitions. Under his presidency (1967-7[illegible]) CAR became a national organization with local bodies across the country. DAVID BURNET[illegible]

Chambly, Qué, City, pop 12 190 (1981c), inc 1951, is situated within the south-shore satellite area SE of Montréal. The community fans out around Bassin de Chambly, a widening in the RICHELIEU R. FORT CHAMBLY was erected nearby in 1665 as one of several outposts defending the French colony against Iroquois, and later American, raids. It was named for a soldier who held the first seigneury here. Willet flour and textile mills dominated the Chambly economy 1806-1911. The Chambly Canal, completed 1843, was a key shipping link to the US-Lake CHAMPLAIN region until 1901. Today, shoe, clothing and seasonal canning industries are important employers. PAULA KESTELMA[illegible]

Champagne, Claude, composer, teacher (b at Montréal 27 May 1891; d there 21 Dec 1965). He studied piano and theory with Orpha Deveaux and Romain-Octave Pelletier, and then the violin with Albert Chamberland. Alfred LALIBERTÉ had faith in Champagne's ability as a composer and helped him go to Paris to study (1921-28), where *Hercule et Omphale* and the *Suite canadienne* were created. After returning to Canada, Champagne devoted himself to teaching, composition and administration. Director of musical instruction for Montréal's Catholic School Commission (1934-42), he was also author of 5 volumes of solfeggio for primary-school teachers and taught at McGill 1932-41. As the result of a report he prepared, the Conservatoire de musique du Québec à Montréal was created in 1942 and he became its assistant director. He trained an impressive number of composers, including François BRASSARD, Serge GARANT, Pierre MERCURE, François MOREL, Clermont PÉPIN, Gilles TREMBLAY and Jean VALLERAND. From 1949 to 1965 he was editor in chief for BMI Canada, responsible for the publication of Canadian works. The Canada Council awarded him its medal in 1963 and he was honoured with a "Claude Champagne Year" in 1964, which included a NFB film and a CBC production. French lyricism and Québec folklore themes are important elements in his compositions. HÉLÈNE PLOUFFE

Champigny, Jean Bochart de, chevalier, INTENDANT of New France 1686-1702 (b after 1645; d at Hâvre-de-Grâce, France Dec 1720). A competent and conscientious intendant, Champigny worked to sustain military preparedness during 13 years of war with the the Iroquois nations and the British. He participated in the treaty negotiations with the Iroquois, signed a

Montréal in 1701. Champigny encouraged the cultivation of flax and hemp and the fishing and forestry industries. He instituted reforms in military supply as well as social reforms such as a system of poor relief. After his return to France in 1702, he often acted as an adviser to the minister on Canadian affairs. JEANNETTE LAROUCHE

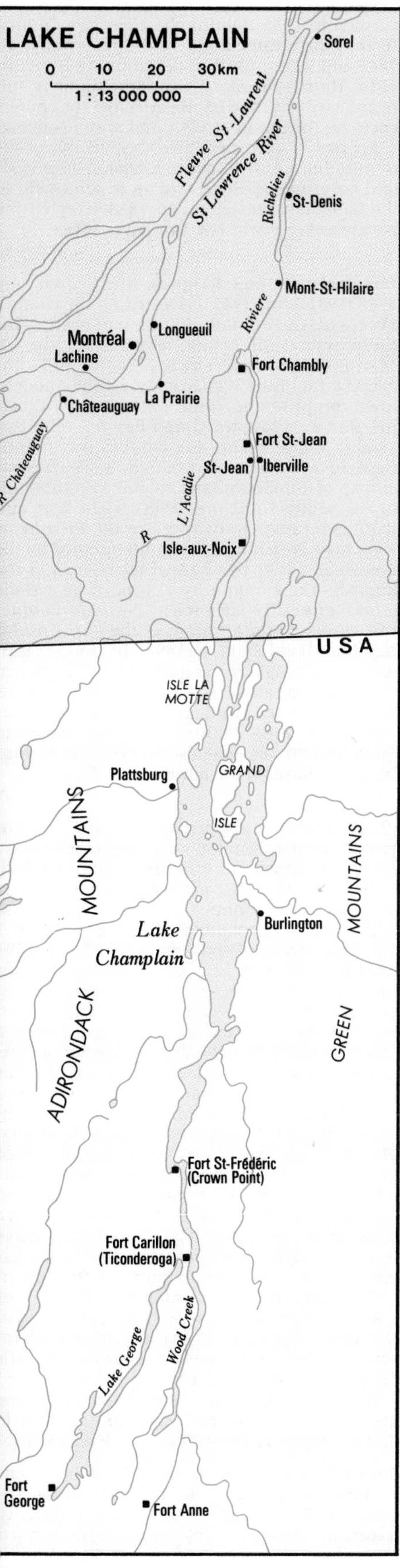

Champlain, Lake, 1269 km^2, of which only the northernmost tip lies in Canada. Together with the RICHELIEU R, which drains the lake northward to the St Lawrence R, Lk Champlain provided a convenient invasion route through the Adirondack and Green Mts, which otherwise isolate the ST LAWRENCE LOWLAND. The lake is long (201 km) and narrow (0.8 to 23 km wide) and interspersed with numerous islands.

The lake route was used by war parties of contesting native groups. Samuel de CHAMPLAIN discovered it (and named it for himself) in 1609 accompanying a Montagnais war party against the Iroquois. Little settlement took place in the area in the time of New France, but French FORTIFICATIONS were established at Ft St-Frédéric (later Crown Point) in 1725-26 and Ft Carillon (later Ft Ticonderoga) in 1755. The British suffered some 2000 casualties in an ill-conceived assault on Carillon (1758), but MONTCALM evacuated the forts and the British pressed northward into Canada (*see* SEVEN YEAR'S WAR). The same invasion route was followed by the Americans during the AMERICAN REVOLUTION and in a British counterattack southward. During the WAR OF 1812 a British strike against the US was thwarted when the British fleet was destroyed at Plattsburg, NY.

In more peaceful times, the lake was used as a transportation route. When frozen it made for fast travel by sleigh in winter. Steamboats were plying the lake by 1810. Canada's first railway, the CHAMPLAIN AND ST LAWRENCE RAILROAD was built to connect Montréal with the lake (1836), which in turn was linked to the Hudson R, providing a connection to New York. JAMES MARSH

Champlain, Samuel de, cartographer, explorer, governor of New France (b at Brouage, France *c*1570; d at Québec City 25 Dec 1635). The major role Champlain played in the St Lawrence R area earned him the title of "Father of New France." There is no authentic portrait of Champlain and little is known about his family background or youth. He may have been baptized a Protestant, but as of 1603 he was a Catholic. He probably made a voyage to the West Indies around 1600; though the account of these voyages, *Brief Discours,* is attributed to him, he himself never referred to it. When his career in Canada began in 1603, on a voyage up the St Lawrence with François Gravé Du Pont, he still had no official position. He published an account of this voyage, the first detailed description of the St Lawrence since Jacques CARTIER's explorations. By this time the Algonquians had taken over the area from the Iroquoians, but nothing in this account suggested a program of colonization at any place in the valley. In 1604 Champlain sailed to Acadia with the Sieur de MONTS, who planned to establish a French colony there. Champlain had no position of command at either of the temporary settlements at the Ste-Croix and PORT-ROYAL (Annapolis Royal, NS). As a cartographer, he was given responsibility for investigating the coast in search of an ideal location for settlement. Twice, in 1605 and 1606, he explored the coastline of what is now New England, going as far S as Cape Cod. Still the leaders of Acadia chose no location. Finally deciding on the St Lawrence instead, de Monts in 1608 sent Champlain to establish a settlement at QUÉBEC, where the fur trade with native peoples in the interior could be controlled more easily.

Champlain established and developed a vast trade network by forming alliances with the Montagnais of the St Lawrence, the nations on the Ottawa R and the Hurons of the Great Lks. This system obliged him to support his allies in their traditional wars against the Iroquois, whose territory was to the S of Lk Ontario; he even had to participate in military campaigns (one in 1609 on Lk Champlain and one in 1615 in Iroquois territory); he spent the winter of 1615-16 in HURONIA. Despite opposition from the various merchant companies that employed him and found it more profitable to be involved only in the fur trade, Champlain vowed to make Québec the centre of a powerful colony. In a 1618 report, he outlined its commercial, industrial and agricultural opportunities. His dream seemed about to come true in 1627 when the COMPAGNIE DES CENT-ASSOCIÉS was founded. But then war broke out and Québec was taken by the KIRKE brothers and occupied by the English 1629-32. Appointed lieutenant by Cardinal Richelieu, Champlain returned in 1633 to Québec, where he had time to see the promising beginnings of the colony he had planned. Paralyzed in the fall of 1635, he died the following Dec. His remains, buried under the Champlain chapel which adjoined Notre-Dame-de-la-Recouvrance, may today lie under Notre-Dame-de-Québec, though they have not been identified. In 1610 he had married a young Protestant woman, Hélène Boullé, who was not yet 12 years old but who brought him a useful dowry. This marriage was to prove disappointing for Champlain. His young wife deserted him, returned reluctantly and was not with him in Canada except 1620-24.

Champlain's 1632 map of New France records his contribution to the geographic knowledge of eastern Canada; the Great Lakes region has begun to appear (*courtesy Public Archives of Canada / NMC-15661*).

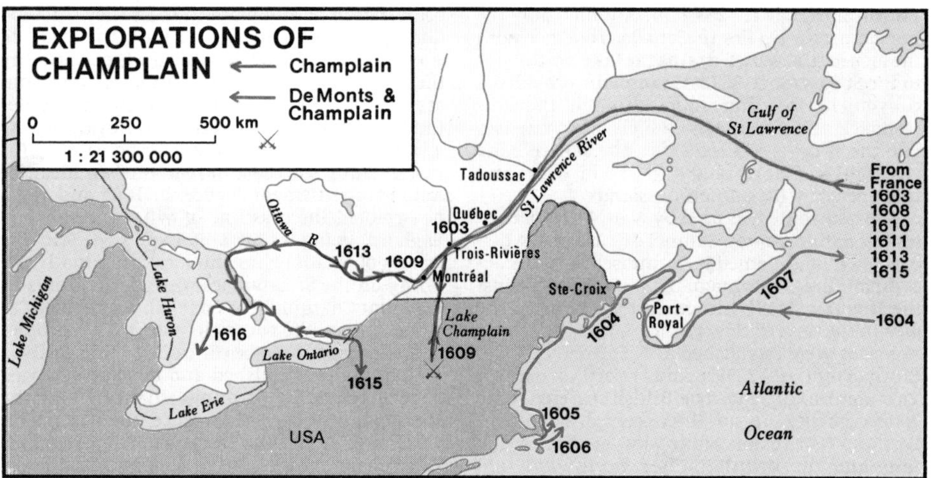

Champlain left behind a considerable body of writing, largely relating to his voyages. The most important editions of his work are the ones prepared by C.H. Laverdière (1870) and the bilingual edition of H.P. Biggar (1922-36). Champlain's works are the only account of the Laurentian colony during the first quarter of the 17th century. As a geographer and "artist" (as a factum states), he illustrated his accounts with numerous maps, of which the most important and the last was that of 1632. It includes a list of place names not on the map as well as previously unpublished explanations and presents everything then known of N. America.

MARCEL TRUDEL

Readings: Marcel Trudel, *Le Comptoir* (1966); S.E. Morison, *Samuel de Champlain* (1972).

Champlain and Saint Lawrence Railroad, Canada's first railway, ran between LA PRAIRIE on the St Lawrence R and St Johns [ST-JEAN] on the Richelieu. In effect, it served as a portage over the most troublesome part of the journey from Montréal to New York, which continued by steamer via Lk Champlain and the Hudson R. Construction began in 1835 with financing from Montréal brewer John MOLSON. The rails consisted of 6" (14 cm)-wide pine timbers joined by iron plates and bolts. Iron straps were then spiked to the upper surface. The railway officially opened 21 July 1836 and began regular operations 25 July. The locomotive, the wood-burning *Dorchester* built in Newcastle Upon Tyne, Eng, could reach up to 48 km/h. The railway was extended to Rouses Point, NY, in 1851 and to St Lambert, Qué, in 1852. In 1857 it amalgamated with the Montreal and New York Railroad (formerly MONTREAL AND LACHINE RAILROAD) under the name Montreal and Champlain Railroad Company. It was leased to the GRAND TRUNK RAILWAY in 1864, and purchased by GTR in 1872. *See also* LOCOMOTIVES AND ROLLING STOCK; RAILWAY HISTORY.

JAMES MARSH

Champlain Sea, a body of brackish water that occupied the depressed land between Québec City and Cornwall, Ont, and extended up the Ottawa R Valley during the late glacial period (*see* GLACIATION). The name was first used by American geologist C.H. Hitchcock in 1906. The relative rise of sea level about 12 800 years ago was as much the result of depression of the land under the weight of glacial ice as of the rise of water level caused by meltwater released from the waning glacier. The Champlain Sea was cold initially, but studies of its INVERTEBRATE fauna indicate that its temperature rose. Its maximum depth, in the centre of the basin, must have been about 200 m. The sea lasted some 2000 years, until approximately 9800 years ago, when the water became too fresh to accommodate marine organisms. The most abundant sediments deposited by the sea, the Leda CLAYS, are mainly rock "flour" incorporated into glacier ice. Their mineralogy principally reflects the composition of the Precambrian rocks from which they are derived, ie, they contain quartz, amphiboles and pyroxenes (*see* GEOLOGICAL REGIONS). Many LANDSLIDES and earthflows have occurred in the clays, sometimes with loss of life and considerable material damage. When disturbed the clays become fluid; therefore, landslides result when a bank is undermined by EROSION, overloaded by a new building or when the clays are disturbed and their internal structure is destroyed. The Champlain Sea area has gradually become an erosional environment. When properly drained, its marine clays constitute the best agricultural land in Québec.

PIERRE LASALLE

Champlain Society, fd 1905 in Toronto to publish new editions of rare books and manuscripts relating to Canada's history. Membership, limited at first to 250, now exceeds 1200. Many early volumes related to New France, including a 6-volume edition of Champlain's works. The society soon became interested in EXPLORATION and the FUR TRADE and published the first dozen volumes prepared by the HUDSON'S BAY RECORD SOCIETY. In recent years, volumes have been devoted to later material, some of a political nature. At the Ontario government's request and expense the society sponsors the Ontario Series, devoted to regional historical records. By its 75th anniversary in 1980 the society had published 79 volumes in all, 56 of them in its own series.

W. KAYE LAMB

Chanak Affair, 1922, PM Mackenzie KING's first major foreign policy test. Britain and Canada signed the Treaty of Sèvres with defeated Turkey after WWI, but the treaty was soon in shreds; by Sept 1922 nationalist forces controlled most of Turkey. British occupation troops were pinned down at Chanak (now Canakkale), a small seaport on the Dardanelles. On Sept 15 Britain sent a telegram calling upon the Dominions to contribute soldiers in a demonstration of the Empire's solidarity against the Turks. The next day the request was made public, a breach of imperial etiquette and political good sense. To make matters worse, King heard from a Toronto *Star* reporter about the developing danger, before he received the official British dispatch. King was noncommittal until Sept 18, when Cabinet agreed that only Parliament could decide such matters. The crisis quickly passed. King's detached attitude gave notice of his desire to disengage Canadian external policy from that of the British. Chanak, however, was not a revolution in Canadian affairs: prime ministers since Macdonald had been reluctant to involve Canada in imperial skirmishes which did not threaten Britain itself.

NORMAN HILLMER

Chandler, Edward Barron, judge, politician (b at Amherst, NS 22 Aug 1800; d at Fredericton 6 Feb 1880). Born into a prominent LOYALIST family, he was admitted to the NB bar in 1823 and appointed judge of probate and clerk of the peace for Westmorland County. In 1827 he was elected to the NB Assemby, where he was regarded as a spokesman of the people and as a cautious reformer, opposed to RESPONSIBLE GOVERNMENT. He was appointed to the Legislative Council in 1836. Joining the Executive Council in 1843, he became leader of the government in 1848 and served until its defeat in the House in 1854. He supported railway development and reciprocity with the US. He attended the conferences on the union of BNA and was a constant supporter of CONFEDERATION, despite his objections to John A. MACDONALD's version of centralized government. He refused an appointment to the Canadian Senate, but in 1878 accepted the position of lt-gov of NB. He died in office.

J.M. BUMSTED

Channel-Port aux Basques, Nfld, Town, pop 5988 (1981c), inc 1945, is located on the Island's SW coast. It is the main western port of entry for the province, the eastern terminal for the CN Marine Gulf Ferry Service to N Sydney, NS, connecting the Trans-Canada Hwy. The modern town comprises the former settlements of Channel, Port aux Basques, Grand Bay E, Grand Bay W and Mouse I. Port aux Basques was named for BASQUE whalers who skirted the southwestern tip of Newfoundland en route to Labrador in the 1500s. Until the 1890s, when Port aux Basques became a railway centre, the settlements were mainly fishing communities settled by the French and later by Channel Islanders and the English. The community expanded as a trade centre, especially later when Port aux Basques was chosen as the terminus of the trans-insular Newfoundland Ry in the 1890s. In 1893 the railway was linked by the gulf steamer service to the Canadian railways. A number of fish plants were built by the 1950s, and one large firm continued to the 1980s. Since incorporation, Channel-Port aux Basques has been the administrative centre for the Burgeo-La Poile region.

JANET E.M. PITT

Chant, Clarence Augustus, professor of astrophysics (b at Hagerman's Corners, Ont 31 May 1865; d at Observatory House, Richmond Hill, Ont 18 Nov 1956). He is often called the "father of Canadian astronomy" because he trained so many young astronomers. Educated at U of T and Harvard, he taught at U of T from 1891 until retirement in 1935. Chant was notable for his early work on X-ray photographs, but especially for his development of Canadian ASTRONOMY. He organized the department at U of T and built up the Royal Astronomical Soc of Canada (established 1890) into one of the world's most successful organizations of its kind. From 1907 through 1956 he edited its *Journal* (published monthly or bimonthly) and its annual *Observer's Handbook* as well as writing many of the articles. He participated in 5 total solar-eclipse expeditions, the most important being the one he led to Australia 1922 to test Einstein's theory of the deflection of starlight by a massive body. Through his efforts the dream of a great observatory near Toronto came to fruition in 1935 when Mrs David Dunlap presented to U of T an observatory with a 74-inch telescope (still the largest optical telescope in Canada). Chant was coauthor of 2 widely used textbooks. His popular *Our Wonderful Universe* (1928, new ed 1940) has been translated into 5 other languages, and he described the early days in *Astronomy in the University of Toronto* (1954).

HELEN S. HOGG

Chant, Donald Alfred, scientist, educator, environmental advocate, businessman (b at Toronto 30 Sept 1928). Chant's early university research at UBC and University of London led him to the forefront of nonchemical pest-control research in Canada, the US and England. A U of T professor of zoology from 1967 with a respected scientific record, Chant was the rare academic who turned his attention to informing the public on environmental issues in the 1970s — pesticides, pollution, wildlife preservation and arctic ecosystems. Eminent, eloquent and outspoken, he was welcomed by the media. In 1980, after 5 years as U of T vice-president and provost and after founding the Joint Guelph-Toronto Centre for Toxicology, Chant accepted a crown appointment to solve one of the complex problems he had helped bring to public debate: the treatment of toxic industrial waste. With Chant as first chairman and president, the Ontario Waste Management Corp will build in 1986 N America's first comprehensive HAZARDOUS WASTE treatment facility. Chant has remained a U of T zoology professor, directing a research program on the use of predators for insect control. TONY BARRETT

Chapais, Jean-Charles, businessman, politician (b at Rivière-Ouelle, Qué 2 Dec 1811; d at Ottawa 17 July 1885). He was a prosperous merchant and dealer in St-Denis de Kamouraska and member for Kamouraska in the Legislative Assembly of the Province of Canada 1851-67. In 1867 he was elected to represent Kamouraska both provincially and federally but lost both seats because of electoral irregularities. Chapais took refuge in Champlain which he won by acclamation. In Jan 1868, while serving as federal minister of agriculture (1867-69) he was appointed to the Senate; he was receiver general 1869-73. Chapais was a FATHER OF CONFEDERATION and one of those politicians who monopolized power in Québec C and Ottawa after the formation of Canada. ANDRÉE DÉSILETS

Chapleau, Sir Joseph-Adolphe, lawyer, journalist, businessman, politician (b at St-Thérèse-de-Blainville, LC 7 Nov 1840; d at Montréal 13 June 1898). He was admitted to the bar in 1861 and taught criminal law at U Laval in Montréal from 1878 to 1885. One of the owners of *Le Colonisateur* 1862-63 and *La Presse* in 1889, he was also a director of the Laurentides and the Pontiac and Pacific railway companies. He was elected to the Québec legislature in 1867, re-elected in 1871, and he was attorney general 1873-74 and provincial secretary 1876-78. He then led the Conservative Party to become premier in 1879. He left provincial politics in 1882, winning a federal by-election in Terrebonne. He was secretary of state until 1892, when he became minister of customs. He became lieutenant-governor of Québec in Nov 1892, retiring 1 Feb 1898. ANDRÉE DÉSILETS

Chapman, John Herbert, physicist, space-scientist, administrator, architect of the Canadian space program (b at London, Ont 28 Aug 1921; d at Vancouver 28 Sept 1979). In Ottawa, he was scientist, superintendent and deputy chief superintendent in the Defence Research Telecommunications Establishment 1949-68 and then assistant deputy minister for research 1968-74 and for the space program 1974-79 in the Dept of Communications.

From 1958-71 Chapman played a key role in initiating and directing the spectacularly successful Alouette/ISIS scientific earth SATELLITE program. With the launch of Alouette 1 in Sept 1962 Canada became the third country to design and build an earth satellite. In 1966 he was appointed chairman of a government study group to examine the upper atmosphere and space programs in Canada. The resulting report was a landmark contribution to space policies and plans in Canada and led to the redirection of Canada's space program from scientific to applications satellites. The formation of Telesat in 1969 and the launching of its first Satellite (Anik A-1) in Nov 1972 made Canada the first country to have a domestic geostationary communications satellite system. He was also the prime mover behind Canada's co-operative program with NASA and the European Space Agency to design, build and demonstrate the Hermes Communications Technology Satellite. Launched in 1976, the Hermes was a forerunner of the direct-to-home TV broadcast satellite. Chapman was a tireless advocate of the Canadian space industry and of the use of space technology to serve the needs of the Canadian people. C.A. FRANKLIN

John Herbert Chapman. He played a key role in directing the Alouette/Isis satellite program and was a tireless advocate of the Canadian space industry (*courtesy National Film Board / Photothèque*).

Reading: J.H. Chapman et al "Upper Atmosphere and Space Programs in Canada," Privy Council Office, Ottawa Feb 1967.

Chaput-Rolland, Solange, writer, editor, broadcaster (b at Montréal 14 May 1919). Chaput-Rolland is a Québecoise federalist, best known in English Canada for her book *Dear Enemies* (1963), a collection of letters exchanged with coauthor Gwethalyn Graham on French-English relations. Her other books include *Mon pays, Québec ou Canada* (1966), *Québec année zéro* (1968) and *Face to Face* (1972) with Gertrude Laing. Chaput-Rolland served on the federal Task Force on CANADIAN UNITY. In 1979 she won a seat for the Liberals in the Québec National Assembly in a by-election, losing it to the PQ in 1981. MARGARET E. MCCALLUM

Char, common name for several species of FISH of genus *Salvelinus* of the SALMON family (Salmonidae). Approximately 11 char species occur worldwide. Five are native to Canada: arctic char (*S. alpinus*), Dolly Varden (*S. malma*), bull trout (*S. confluentus*), brook trout (*S. fontinalis*) and lake trout (*S. namaycush*). Chars are distinguished from other salmonids by light-coloured spots (red, pink, orange, yellow or grey) on their dark backs, and the number of anal fin rays (7-12). They spawn in fresh water in fall: arctic char in lakes or rivers; Dolly Varden, bull trout and brook trout usually in rivers; lake trout primarily in lakes. All char, except lake and bull trouts, have both freshwater and sea-run populations.

Arctic char, the most northern salmonid, has circumpolar distribution. In Canada, it is found in YT, northern NWT, along Hudson Bay, Ungava, Newfoundland and the St Lawrence. It is important to Inuit and northern Indians as a source of food and income, and supports a small sports fishery.

Dolly Varden is restricted to north Pacific Rim countries; in Canada, to southern YT and coastal BC. The species was considered destructive to salmon and TROUT, and a bounty was paid in Alaska. Generally, it is not a popular sport fish where other salmonids are available; however, increasing pressure on all sport fish has prompted a steady increase in its use.

Bull trout has only recently been recognized as a separate species closely related to Dolly Varden. In Canada it occurs in northern and eastern BC and western Alberta.

Brook or speckled trout, naturally ranging eastwards from Ontario, is now distributed throughout all provinces. Until the mid-1900s, it was highly prized as a sport fish, and has been introduced as far afield as New Zealand and the Falkland Is. However, like brown trout, it has been replaced by rainbow trout transplants. It is the smallest char (25-30 cm long) and is often found in small, spring-fed, headwater streams.

Lake trout is the largest char; in 1961 a 46.3 kg fish was taken in Lk Athabasca. It has the widest native range of all salmonids in Canada, including all provinces and territories, and some low-latitude arctic islands, and has been widely transplanted. It is the most valuable char in commercial and sport fisheries; however, catches have declined since the early 1960s.

Splake or wendigo, a fertile hybrid of lake and brook trout has been developed and introduced to many parts of N America, primarily Ontario, where a breeding and stocking program has existed for some time. E.D. LANE

Charbonneau, Robert, journalist, writer (b at Montréal 3 Feb 1911; d at St-Jovite, Qué 26 June 1967). Because of Charbonneau's work, French Canadian literature, particularly the novel, underwent a profound transformation. Considered the leader of the 1940s and postwar generation, he gave literature this new direction through his literary output (particularly his novels and a literary essay), his articles, and his work as an editor (*La Relève*, which became *La Nouvelle Relève*, 1934-48; Éditions de l'Arbre, 1940-48). He was also a founding member of the Académie canadienne-française and president of the Société des écrivains canadiens 1966-67. Because of Charbonneau, Québec literature broke with literary convention and its idealized and stereotyped characters as well as with the literature of France. Charbonneau's creative spirit, critical acumen and originality were recognized in his lifetime. He won the Quebec Literary Competition in 1942, the Prix Duvernay in 1946 and the RSC's Médaille Chauveau in 1965. His works include the essays *Connaissance du personnage* (1944) and *La France et nous* (1947); novels *Ils posséderont la terre* (1941), *Fontile* (1945), *Les Désirs et les jours* (1948), *Aucune créature* (1961), *Chronique de l'âge amer* (1967); and poetry *Petits poèmes retrouvés* (1945).
MADELEINE DUCROCQ-POIRIER

Charbonneau, Yvon, teacher, president of the Centrale de l'enseignement du Québec (CEQ) (b at Mont-Laurier, Qué 11 July 1940). After studying at U de M, Charbonneau taught French and the humanities in Québec and Tunisia 1961-69. His election to the CEQ in 1970 marked the union's abandonment of corporatism as advocated by Roman Catholic social doctrine. Under Charbonneau the CEQ became a genuine union, renouncing its corporate charter, changing its name and opening its ranks to other education workers. The union took a harder line in negotiations with the government and in 1972 formed a common front with other unions. This common front led to the imprisonment of Charbonneau, Louis LABERGE, president of the Fédération des travailleurs du Québec, and Marcel PEPIN, president of the Confédération des syndicats nationaux for urging their members to ignore a no-strike injunction. Defeated as CEQ president in 1978, Charbonneau was kept on as a special adviser and later, director of communications. He resumed presidency of the CEQ in 1982. JACQUES ROUILLARD

Charbonnel, Armand-François-Marie de, Roman Catholic bishop of Toronto (b near Monistrol-sur-Loire, France 1 Dec 1802; d at Crest, France 29 Mar 1891). Of noble birth, Charbonnel entered the priesthood in the Society of St-Sulpice. Coming to N America in 1839, he served as priest in Montréal until 1847. He was consecrated bishop of Toronto in 1850. As bishop, he pressured the Famine Irish laity and politicians to gain separate education for Catholics. The Basilian Fathers, the Christian Brothers and the Sisters of St Joseph were brought to Toronto to assist with education and social work. He established St Michael's College, the House of Providence to shelter the sick, aged and orphaned, and instituted the St Vincent de Paul Soc, the Toronto Savings Bank and other charitable associations. Utilizing his paternal estate, Charbonnel eradicated the diocesan debt, including that of St Michael's Cathedral. He succeeded in having the large diocese of Toronto divided into 3 sees (Toronto, Hamilton, London) in 1856. Living an exemplary life of a beggar among the Irish poor, Charbonnel resigned his see in 1860, entering the Capuchin Order in France and later becoming archbishop of Sozopolis. MURRAY WILLIAM NICOLSON

Charismatic Renewal, a transdenominational Christian movement, theologically diverse and ecumenical, characterizing significant segments of the church in the 1960s and 1970s, and frequently referred to as neo-Pentecostal. The principal similarity with the classical PENTECOSTAL MOVEMENTS is the importance of experiential religion, particularly on experiencing the presence of God, along with appropriate manifestations of the encounter. Like the old Pentecostals, charismatics emphasize the baptism of the Holy Spirit or the reception of the Spirit's power. The external manifestations of that power are charisms (gifts), such as speaking in tongues (glossolalia, or ecstatic speech), healing and prophesying. Although such evidences of the supernatural are not seen as essential to designating someone as spirit-filled, they are nevertheless frequently sought. The experience of the Holy Spirit should not be confused with conversion, but is rather a second "blessing" to be sought by all Christians.

Perhaps the most significant difference from the old Pentecostals is that most charismatics have chosen to stay within existing churches. They form a movement rather than a sectarian group or distinct denomination, although occasionally individual churches with charismatic tendencies may sever ties with a denomination. Charismatics do not share the anti-intellectualism, fundamentalism and dispensational theology of the Pentecostals, nor is the primacy of ecstatic spiritual experience seen as necessarily antithetical to the development of a social conscience.

The movement's distribution among established denominations makes it impossible to obtain meaningful statistics. Since there is no separate organization, there is no formal membership. Nevertheless the renewal has influenced LUTHERAN, PRESBYTERIAN, ANGLICAN, UNITED, MENNONITE, BAPTIST and Roman CATHOLIC churches across the country. Its message appears to be a call to the church to be what it is meant to be: catholic in its commitment to the body of Christ, charismatic in being open to the power of the resurrected Christ, and evangelical in its obedience to mission. Charismatics therefore stress the total work of the church based on the experience of God's power. Although individuals may define themselves as charismatics by speaking in tongues or belonging to identifiable prayer and praise groups, the accent tends to be on participation in the church in order to call the church to its true mission. RONALD NEUFELDT

Reading: Little has been written on the movement in Canada; the following treat it internationally: David Edwin Harrell Jr, *All Things Are Possible* (1975); Richard Quebedeaux, *The New Charismatics* (1976).

Charlebois, Robert, singer, actor, author-composer, guitarist, pianist (b at Montréal 25 June 1945). As well as studying music (6 years of piano), Charlebois studied dramatic arts at the National Theatre School in Montréal from 1962 to 1965. A pioneer among *chansonniers,* both in his use of *joual* and in the theatrical way in which he presented his music, Charlebois received the Prix Félix-Leclerc in 1969 at the Festival du disque with "Lindberg," the same song that in 1968 had won him the grand prize at the Festival international de la chanson française in Spa, Belgium. Another success was "Ordinaire," which took first prize at the International Festival in Sopot, Poland, in 1970. Louise Forestier and Mouffe (Claudine Monfette) have often appeared with him. As an actor, Charlebois appeared in the films, *Un Génie, deux associés, une cloche* and *Entre la mer et l'eau douce.* HÉLÈNE PLOUFFE

Charlesworth, Hector Willoughby, editor, critic, memoirist (b at Hamilton 28 Sept 1872; d at Toronto 30 Dec 1945). He was a Toronto newspaperman and arts commentator, particularly on music and drama, and editor of *Saturday Night* magazine 1926-32, leaving to become first head of Canadian Radio Broadcasting Commission, precursor of the CBC. His autobiography, in 3 volumes, is a splendid source of literary, political, journalistic and theatrical anecdote. Among those only casually acquainted with his work, this honest and productive journalist is best known for having once viciously attacked the GROUP OF SEVEN and also for the uncanny resemblance he bore to Edward VII. DOUG FETHERLING

Charlevoix, Pierre-François-Xavier de, Jesuit historian (b at Saint-Quentin, France 24 or 29 Oct 1682; d at La Flèche, France 1 Feb 1761). Author of the first comprehensive history of NEW FRANCE, Charlevoix taught at the Jesuit Coll at Québec (1709-13) and in 1720 was again in New France, charged with reporting on the boundaries of Acadia and on the existence of the "Western Sea." In 1721-22 he travelled by canoe in the Great Lks basin and down the Mississippi to New Orleans before returning to France. His 2½ years in N America were marked by frustration and illness, but his detailed notes and scientific observations furnished the material for a travel narrative published in 1744 as part of his 3-vol *Histoire et description générale de la Nouvelle-France.* He also published a biography of MARIE DE L'INCARNATION (1724), a history of Christianity in Japan (1715, new ed 1736) and histories of Santo Domingo (1730-31) and Paraguay (1756). Unusually accurate and well documented for their time, Charlevoix's elegantly written histories became erudite obituaries for the French regime in N America and the Jesuit empires in Japan and Paraguay. DAVID M. HAYNE

Charlottetown, capital of Prince Edward Island and seat of the province's middle county of Queens, is situated on a broad harbour opening into the NORTHUMBERLAND STR. Three rivers conjoin there, with the city located on a low-rising point of land between the Hillsborough (East) and North (Yorke) rivers just opposite the harbour's mouth. Some suburban development has also occurred across the Hillsborough at Southport and Bunbury, and between the North and West (Eliot) rivers at Cornwall. Besides its administrative functions, Charlottetown services a considerable agricultural hinterland and is the focus of Island communications. Its favourable climate and nearby beaches have made it a major tourist centre.

Population: 15 282 (1981c); 44 999 (CA)
Rate of Increase (1976-81): (City) -10.4%; (CA) 8.4%
Rank in Canada: Fifty-first (by CA)
Date of Incorporation: 1855
Land Area: 42.8 km²; Greater Charlottetown 256 km²
Elevation: 50 m (Charlottetown Airport)
Climate: Average daily temp, July 18°C, Jan -7°C; Yearly precip 1127.8 mm; Hours of sunshine 1803 per year

History and Development Although the city was incorporated 1855, settlement in the region dates back to 1720, when an expedition sent by the Comte de Saint-Pierre established itself W of the harbour's entrance at a site named Port La Joie. After the assumption of direct control of Île Saint-Jean (the Island's former name) by the French government in 1730, Port La Joie was retained as the administrative centre, even though other Island locales showed more commercial promise. This decision was confirmed by the British when they finally achieved mastery in the region following the capitulation of Louisbourg (1758). Port La Joie, which never had a population much over 100, was renamed Fort Amherst, and its defences were strengthened. In 1768, however, Charles Morris, deputy chief surveyor of Nova Scotia, laid out a new townsite across the harbour, and the community was christened Charlottetown, after Charlotte, wife of King George III. While the area was distant from the lucrative fisheries, it offered excellent transportation corridors to the interior via the rivers and was close to Nova Scotia and a road to Halifax.

The original town plan provided for broad streets on a grid pattern, with the main axis running N from the Hillsborough R, a common for future expansion and a royalty for pasturage and gardening. Sites were designated for a market house, church, courthouse and jail, but it was some time before all of these facilities were provided. Meanwhile, defence works were begun and, after American privateers ransacked the settlement in 1775, strengthened. By then the town's status had been enhanced by a decision of the British government in 1769 to separate the Island, renamed Prince Edward Island in 1798, from Nova Scotia and to make the little community the capital of the new colony. The first governor, Walter Patterson, began establishing essential administrative services, but just as significantly commenced work on roads to more distant parts of the colony. As settlement of agricultural areas progressed, Charlottetown became a market town as well as a communications and administrative centre. These functions remain essential elements in the city's economy.

Throughout the 19th century Charlottetown's population averaged about 9% of the Island's total and grew as the Island grew. Most settlers were of English, Scottish or Irish origin, with a sizable Acadian element and smaller numbers of other ethnic groups, but by 1848 over half of the population were native-born Islanders. When PEI entered Confederation in 1873, Charlottetown was the eleventh-largest city in Canada. Shipbuilding and ship-owning, plus small-scale manufacturing such as tanning, brewing and shoe production, had diversified the economy somewhat. The prosperity, however, was sufficiently limited to ensure thrift in the pro-

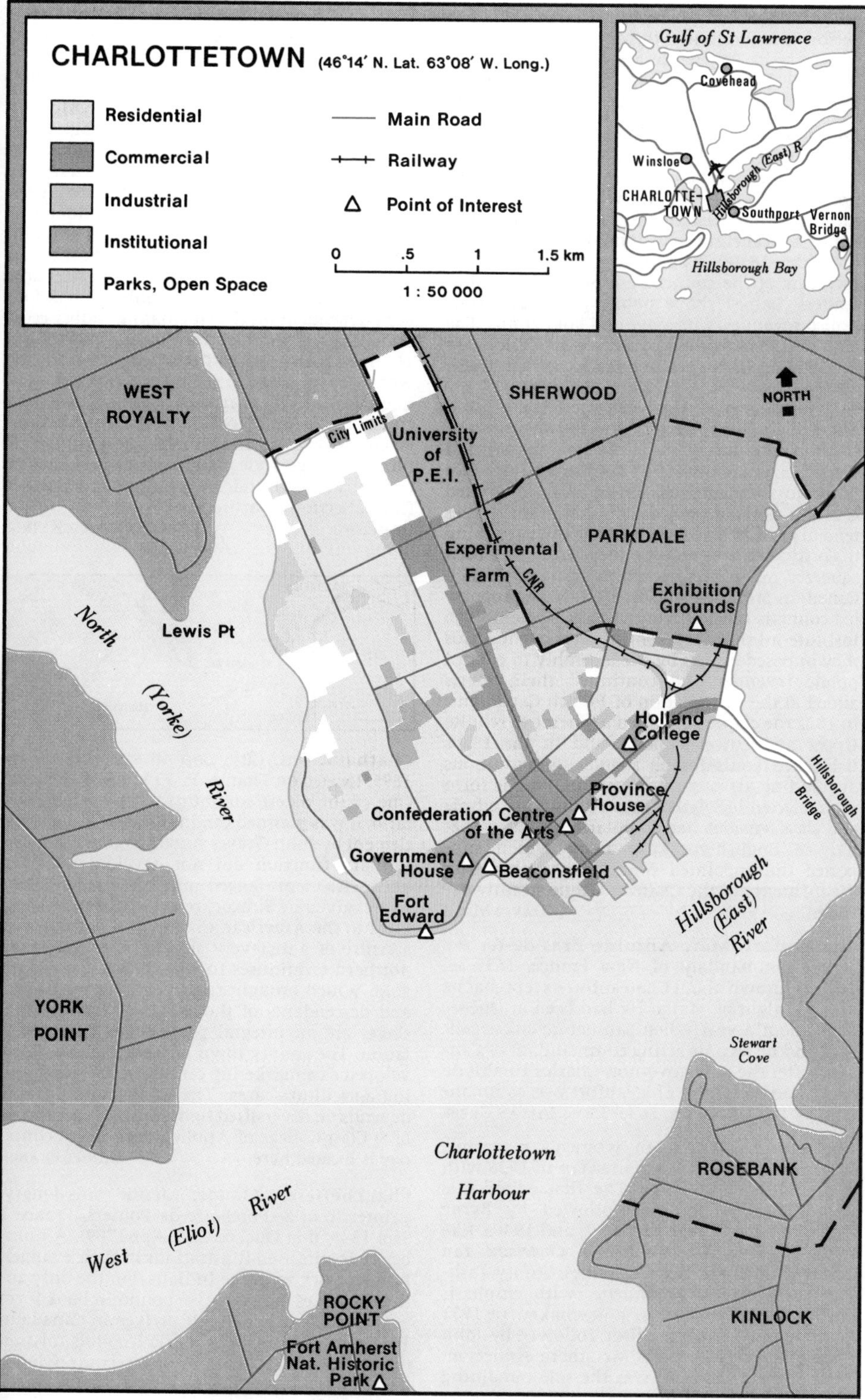

vision of community services. Vigorous opposition to taxes meant that improvements to counter fire and disease tended to follow disasters such as the Great Fire of 1866 or the smallpox epidemic of 1887. Nevertheless, by the end of the century, Charlottetown possessed modern water and sewer services, electric street lighting, proper hospitals and schools and a varied cultural life. Communications links, including coastal steamship service, the railway, and the telephone and telegraph, allowed the city to expand its influence over more distant parts of the Island, although communications difficulties with mainland centres of commerce highlighted Charlottetown's relative isolation.

Economy In the 20th century the population of Charlottetown and its environs has grown steadily as part of the Island's total, but has failed to keep pace with massive urban growth in the rest of Canada. The city's population decreased 10.4% from 1976, but in the same period the metropolitan area population grew by 8.4%. Many 19th-century industries, including shipbuilding, have disappeared. In their stead are plants processing fish, seafood, meat and dairy products and manufacturing knitwear, clothing, farm and marine equipment, metal products and building supplies. Through the port pass outbound agricultural produce and imported petroleum products. While all these activities contribute significantly to the local economy, they have been overshadowed by tourism. First encouraged by the erection of a major railway hotel in 1931, the tourist trade was expanded by motel construction in the 1950s and 1960s and by the completion of an extensive network of paved roads radiating from Charlottetown. In 1964 the Confederation Centre, a large performing-arts and museum complex, was opened to commemorate the CHARLOTTETOWN CONFERENCE of 1864, an event that gave the city the title "The Cradle of Confederation," though largely ignored by the citizens of that era. The centre now houses the very successful Charlottetown Summer Festival of music and light entertainment. A new convention facility has further enhanced the city's tourist appeal. Another recent development has been the transfer of the Dept of Veterans Affairs from Ottawa, a move that brought many newcomers and heightened the significance of the administrative sector.

Cityscape Charlottetown today is a city of contrasts. A market-town atmosphere exists beside extensive cultural facilities, large government offices and 2 institutions of higher education — Holland College, a community college, and UPEI. Expansive suburbs with modern shopping malls are strikingly dissimilar to "Old Charlottetown," which features the classic revival legislature known as Province House, stately old mansions, and refurbished shops and commercial buildings dating from the last century. A new harbour-front complex of homes and offices echoes the old and helps to emphasize the importance of the city's core. Thus, though declining in the order of Canadian municipalities in size, Charlottetown offers a quality of life far richer than its small population would suggest. PETER E. RIDER

Reading: Benjamin Bremmer, *Memories of Long Ago* (1930); A.H. Clark, *Three Centuries and the Island* (1969); A.B. Warburton, *A History of Prince Edward Island* (1923).

Charlottetown Conference, 1-9 Sept 1864 in Charlottetown, PEI, set CONFEDERATION in motion. Maritime union had long been talked of in NS, NB and PEI. In Mar-Apr 1864 all 3 legislatures passed resolutions to have a conference to discuss it. Nothing happened until after the June 1864 constitutional crisis in the PROVINCE OF CANADA, when the Canadians asked to attend the conference to propose a union of all BRITISH NORTH AMERICA. This request rather staggered the Maritime governments, but through the action of NS Lt-Gov Richard MacDonnell the place and date of meeting were selected. At the conference Maritime union was virtually dropped, and the delegates agreed on the outline of a scheme for more general union. It was decided to have a more comprehensive meeting at Québec in Oct. External circumstances, such as the AMERICAN CIVIL WAR, Britain's desire to divest itself of financial and administrative colonial obligations, and the political condition of the Province of Canada, combined to create an ambience at Charlottetown which produced the momentum that was so obvious at the QUÉBEC CONFERENCE and so necessary to carry Confederation. P.B. WAITE

Charlottetown Festival, *see* MUSICAL THEATRE.

Charney, Melvin, architect, artist, educator (b at Montréal 28 Aug 1935). Educated at McGill and Yale, Charney was for some time best known for his Corridart project, a construction commissioned by the 1976 Olympics' Arts and Culture Program, and erected along a 9 km stretch of Sherbrooke St, only to be demolished by the Montréal city fathers on the eve of the opening ceremonies on the grounds that it was obscene. His main works, consisting of experiments with built forms usually constructed of wood, have been exhibited in museums, installed on streets, on select city sites and, more recently, as extensions of the museum buildings themselves (The Museum of Contemporary Art, Chicago, Ill, 1982; Agnes Etherington Art Centre, Kingston, Ont, 1983). Professor of architecture at U de M 1984, Charney has worked successfully apart from the mainstream of traditional architectural activity and distinguished himself on an international scale. SUSAN FORD

Charpentier, Alfred, labour leader (b at Montréal 25 Nov 1888; d at Montréal 13 Nov 1982). Working as a bricklayer 1905-15, he became president of the International Union of Bricklayers in 1911. In 1916 he turned towards the Catholic union movement, which was slowly being created by several clerics led by Fathers Joseph-Papin Archambault and Maxime Fortin during and after WWI. Charpentier's union experience helped define the primary role of Catholic unions as one of defending the professional interests of the workers. Several thousand French Canadian workers belonging to national unions subsequently reorganized themselves as Catholic unions. With their constitution largely written by Charpentier, 80 Catholic unions created the Confédération des travailleurs catholiques du Canada (CTTC) in 1921. Charpentier was its president 1935-46. A tireless advocate of Catholic social thought, he fought for improvements to Québec's antiquated labour legislation and for the creation of a Conseil supérieur du travail and a system of courts to resolve labour disputes. After stepping down in 1946, he wrote extensively on labour issues and published his memoirs, *Cinquante ans d'action ouvrière* (1971). M.D. BEHIELS

Charpentier, Gabriel, composer, poet, artistic adviser (b at Richmond, Qué 13 Sept 1925). Having studied piano with, among others, Jean PAPINEAU-COUTURE, he stayed with the Benedictines at ST-BENOÎT-DU-LAC, where he studied Gregorian chant. He continued his studies in Paris (1947-53), notably with Norbert Dufourcq and Nadia Boulanger. Fascinated by the theatre, for which most of his compositions were intended, Charpentier realized that music written for a theatrical production had to be integral to that production. One of his operas, *Orphée I*, was commissioned for the inauguration of the National Arts Centre in Ottawa (1969). He is a member of the artistic committee for a performing artists' centre in Brussels and a member of the administrative council of the Comus Music Theatre Foundation of Canada, Toronto. He has also been artistic director of the Pro Musica Society (1979-81). HÉLÈNE PLOUFFE

Chartrand, Michel, labour and political activist (b at Outremont, Qué 20 Dec 1913). After a classical education and 2 years as an Oblate monk, he joined the Jeunesses patriotes. After becoming a typographer, he took part in the anti-conscriptionist League for the Defence of Canada and the Bloc populaire canadien. During the 1950s he worked for the Fédération nationale des travailleurs du vêtement and the Syndicat des Métallos, in charge of education. A member and leader of the Parti sociale démocratique (CCF), he helped found the NEW DEMOCRATIC PARTY, but broke with it on the question of Québec's independence. In 1963 he helped found the Parti socialiste du Québec, becoming its first president 1964-65. Critical of Québec's organized labour for its refusal to back a working-class political party, he became an ardent supporter of the PARTI QUÉBÉCOIS. As president of the Conseil central des syndicats nationaux de Montréal 1968-78 he helped advance the rapidly growing movement within organized labour for an independent, socialist Québec. M.D. BEHIELS

Chasse-Galerie French Canadian variant of the Wild Hunt, a legend which interprets strange noises in the air as relating to a hunter condemned to hunt throughout eternity. In Chasse-Galerie, one or several persons together are able, with the help of the devil, to travel in a canoe through the air at tremendous speed. They must take care not to have any blessed object on their person or to pronounce the name of God, lest the canoe crash. The name appears to be derived from the French *chasse*, "hunt"; *galerie*, Sire de Gallery, a condemned hunter. NANCY SCHMITZ

Château Clique, nickname given to the small group of officials, usually members of the anglophone merchant community including John MOLSON and James McGill, who dominated the executive and legislative councils, judiciary and senior bureaucratic positions of LOWER CANADA until the 1830s. Appointed by the governor, members of the councils advised him on local matters, helped shape public policy and controlled revenues, patronage and land grants. The term referred to the governor's residence and the location of government offices, Château St-Louis.

The clique aggressively pursued canal building, the establishment of banking institutions, and the abolition of the SEIGNEURIAL SYSTEM and French CIVIL LAW. By 1810 mercantile influence in the government was limited to the appointed councils, for not only did imperial authorities tend to grant concessions to the French-speaking majority, but anglophone merchants had been squeezed out of the elected assembly by French Canadian professionals. Before 1810 the appointed councils resisted Pierre BÉDARD's attempts to institute ministerial responsibility; in the 1820s they opposed efforts by the assembly to control public revenues and continued their efforts aimed at the assimilation of French Canadians; in 1822 the clique supported a scheme to reunite Upper and Lower Canada; and in the 1830s it blocked Louis-Joseph PAPINEAU's resolutions demanding RESPONSIBLE GOVERNMENT in the form of an elected legislative council. By 1834 ethnic and class tensions had so polarized politics that only 9 English-speaking assemblymen supported the appointed councils, and thereafter the influence of the Château Clique steadily declined. DAVID MILLS

Chateaufort, Marc-Antoine Bras-de-fer de, acting commandant of New France, 1635-36. Little is known about Chateaufort except that he was a Knight of Malta. He had been at Québec only about a year when Samuel de CHAMPLAIN died and he became acting commandant of Canada. After the new governor, Charles Huault de MONTMAGNY arrived, Chateaufort was commandant of Trois-Rivières, 1636-38. ALLAN GREER

Chatelaine, a Canadian women's magazine, was started by MACLEAN HUNTER LTD in 1928 with a circulation of 57 053. The first editor was Anne Elizabeth Wilson, followed by Byrne Hope Sanders. During the 1930s and 1940s, like most N American MAGAZINES, *Chatelaine* ran a heavy content of fiction, recipes, beauty, fashion, child care and etiquette, with emphasis on the role of woman as homemaker. In 1951 Lotta Dempsey became editor, followed by John Clare and, in 1957, Doris McCubbin Anderson. By the 1960s *Chatelaine* was the sole remaining women's magazine in Canada. A dozen other magazines had died owing to the domination of US magazines on newsstands (1961) and over 50% of Canadian advertising dollars flowing into *Time* and *Readers' Digest*. *Chatelaine* survived by responding more rapidly than its US competitors to the concerns of women joining the work force and the beginning of the WOMEN'S MOVEMENT, with articles on equal pay, child abuse, abortion, the poverty of women, as well as traditional service articles geared to the working woman's life. It became the biggest paid-circulation magazine in Canada and in 1976 Bill C-58 effectively stemmed the US competition. Mildred Istona became editor in 1978. Average monthly circulation in 1983 was 1 108 692. *Châtelaine* is a separate French-language magazine, started in 1960 with a circulation of 111 905. Fernande Saint-Martin was editor until 1973. Francine Montpetit was editor in 1984. Average monthly circulation in 1983 was 302 490. DORIS ANDERSON

Chatham, NB, Town, pop 6780 (1981c), inc 1896, is located near the mouth of the MIRAMICHI R. The settlement was named about 1800 by its founder Francis Peabody for William Pitt, earl of Chatham and PM of England. The town's early political and business life was dominated by Joseph Cunard, of the world-famous shipping family (*see* Samuel CUNARD), who controlled most lumbering and shipbuilding interests until his bankruptcy in 1848. Livelihood has long been dependent on the fluctuating timber economy. The removal of the Roman Catholic St Thomas College (est 1910) to Fredericton in 1964 was a severe blow to the area. Since 1941 CFB Chatham and St Margarets nearby have been crucial to the local economy. The only other major employer is Northwood Pulp and Timber, although a large-scale waterfront development is currently (1984) under way. Chatham boasts a fine collection of artifacts at its natural history museum. WILLIAM R. MACKINNON

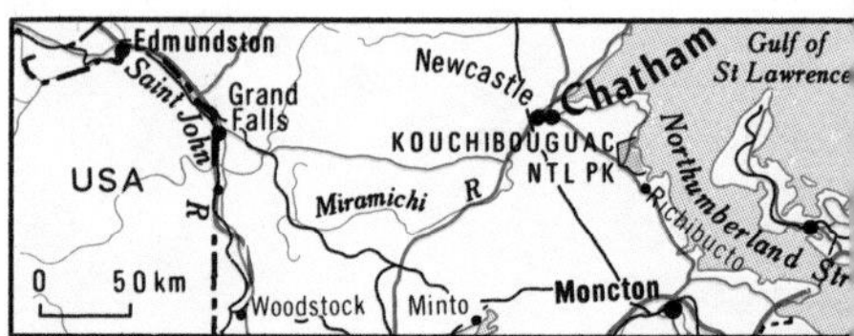

Chatham, Ont, City, pop 40 952 (1981c), inc 1895, located on Thames R, 73 km E of Windsor. One of the oldest communities in western Ontario, it was planned originally as a military settlement by John Graves SIMCOE, lt-gov of UC. The military function did not develop, however and settlement lagged until the 1830s. The name, given by Simcoe, refers to Chatham, Eng. Prior to the American Civil War, Chatham was a centre of antislavery activity and one of the northern terminuses for the UNDERGROUND RAILROAD which brought fugitive slaves to Canada and descendants of thousands of these former slaves are an integral part of the local population. The county town of Kent County, it developed as a marketing centre for the surrounding agricultural area. The local economy now depends on diversified light industry. A campus of St Clair College of Applied Arts and Technology is located here. DANIEL FRANCIS

Chauchetière, Claude, Jesuit missionary, painter (b at St-Porchaire-de-Poitiers, France 7 Sept 1645; d at Québec C 17 Apr 1709). A number of Jesuits used illustrations in their evangelization work with the Indians, but the only authentic pieces to survive — bound in book form — are by Chauchetière. He arrived in Canada in 1677 and went in 1678 to the Iroquois mission of St-François-Xavier at Sault-Ste-Louis [Caughnawaga, Qué]. Most of his time as a missionary was spent in this village of converted Indians. His *Narration annuelle de la Mission du Sault depuis la fondation jusqu'à l'an 1686* relates and illustrates the main events of his mission. The full-length portrait of Kateri TEKAKWITHA in the church at Caughnawaga is attributed to him, even though the chapel in the tableau appears more recent than any he could have known. The work may be an old copy of his painting. FRANÇOIS-MARC GAGNON

Chaudière, Rivière, 193 km long, basin 6603 km^2, located in southern Québec, is named after the waters that "boil" from its falls. The ABENAKI called it *Kikonteku*, meaning "cornfields river." It flows NE from Lac MÉGANTIC to the foot of the Montagnes Frontalières, passes through the rapids of the Appalachian Plateau, and arrives at the lowlands of the St Lawrence R downstream from Ste-Marie, where it flows into the river almost opposite QUÉBEC CITY. It has a 40 m waterfall, "Le Saut de la Chaudière," 6 km from its mouth. The winding river with its pebbly bed is known for its flooding and for the fertile land of its floodplain, Les Beaucerons. As early as 1640, the Abenaki used the Chaudière to travel from Québec City to Maine. In 1776, during the American Revolution, the troops of Col Benedict ARNOLD set out from Boston and used the route for their attack on Québec City.

JEAN-MARIE DUBOIS AND PIERRE MAILHOT

Chaussé, Joseph-Alcide, architect, author (b at St-Sulpice, Qué 7 Jan 1868; d at Montréal 7 Oct 1944). After working in private practice in Montréal, Chaussé was building inspector for the city 1900-18. He wrote articles on fire prevention and handbooks on building laws for Montréal and the province of Québec. Chaussé was the chief promoter of the Royal Architectural Inst of Canada and served as honorary secretary from its formation in 1907 until 1942. Throughout his career he sought the improvement of architectural standards. His most famous work is the Empress Theatre on Sherbrooke St W, a design in the Egyptian manner inspired by the excitement of the discovery of Tutankhamen's tomb in 1922. ROBERT LEMIRE

Chaussegros de Léry, Gaspard-Joseph, military engineer (b at Toulon, France 3 Oct 1682; d at Québec City 23 Mar 1756). After over 10 years' combat service in Europe, Chaussegros de Léry came to Canada in 1716. Subsequently appointed chief military engineer, he served as such until his death in 1756. He was responsible for 40 years for the design and construction of fortifications, town plans and public buildings at Québec and Montréal as well as of such forts as Chambly and Niagara. Through his marriage into a prominent Canadian family, Chaussegros de Léry established a dynasty that distinguished itself in both Canada and France. F.J. THORPE

Chautauqua, a travelling institution begun on Chautauqua Lk, NY, and with Canadian roots in Methodist temperance rallies, which carried education, inspiration and entertainment across N America. John M. Erickson brought the idea from the US to Alberta in 1917. He established Dominion Chautauquas (Canadian Chautauquas after 1926) with headquarters in Calgary, and with the help of his wife, Nola, operated successfully until 1935. They spread a network of tent circuits across Canada from the Pacific into Ontario, edging into Québec, and pushing into the northern fringes of settlement across the prairies.

Chautauqua programs consisted of 4 to 6 days of musical numbers, lectures, dramatic productions and magic or puppet shows. A different performance was presented daily, and performers then moved on to the next town on the circuit. Keeping workers, artists, tents and equipment moving smoothly along the circuits required careful organization and many employees. A total of some 50 young men handled the tents and approximately 80 young women helped organize local committees and directed the operation. These people, mainly university students, developed initiative, self-confidence and skills that gave them an excellent foundation for success in life.

Chautauqua was good family entertainment and the people loved it. To many it provided their only opportunity for a cultural experience. It broadened horizons and brought colour and beauty into many lives. Its end can be attributed to changes in popular taste, the increasing availability of movies and the spread of radio, as well as to an easing of Depression conditions.

SHEILAGH S. JAMESON

Reading: Sheilagh S. Jameson, *Chautauqua in Canada* (1979).

Chauveau, Pierre-Joseph-Olivier, lawyer, politician, premier of Québec, educator (b at Charlesbourg, Lower Canada 30 May 1820; d at Québec 4 Apr 1890). Elected to the Assembly of the Province of Canada in 1844, he later held several Cabinet posts. He resigned from the Assembly in 1855 to become superintendent of education, a post he held until 1867, during which time the 15-member Council of Public Instruction was set up to supervise the school system. Conservatives John A. MACDONALD and George-Étienne CARTIER chose him to become the first premier of Québec, replacing J.E. CAUCHON in 1867, and Chauveau sat in both the provincial and federal houses. He was not a memorable premier and was persuaded to resign in 1873 to sit in the Senate. The following year, however, he unsuccessfully sought re-election to the Commons. In 1878 he began to teach in Laval's law faculty in Montréal and was its dean 1884-90. A man of letters, Chauveau was in demand as a lecturer, wrote extensively on education and other subjects and wrote a novel *Charles Guérin, romàn de moeurs canadiennes* (1853, serialized 1846-47). DANIEL LATOUCHE

Chee Chee, Benjamin, artist (b Kenneth Thomas Benjamin at Temagami, Ont 26 Mar 1944; d at Ottawa 14 Mar 1977). After an unstable youth, Chee Chee, of Ojibwa descent, moved to Montréal in 1965 and was encouraged to develop his love of drawing. His first exhibition, held after his move to Ottawa in 1973, featured colourful abstract compositions of block-stamped geometric motifs. By 1976 his work had dramatically changed to spare, linear representations of birds and animals of great clarity and elegance, animated by a lively sense of humour and movement. Unlike other native artists, Chee Chee denied that his images had symbolic meaning; they were rather "creatures of the present" whose forms expressed aesthetic concerns. At the height of his success, after a renewal of a long-term problem with alcoholism, he committed suicide in an Ottawa jail.

RUTH B. PHILLIPS

Cheese and Cheesemaking World production of cheese in 1982 was 168 million t. In Canada 207 498 t were produced in 1983; per capita consumption was 9.08 kg, consisting of 3.76 kg of Cheddar, 1.22 kg of Cottage and 4.10 kg of other cheeses. Consumption has increased more than threefold since 1950, aided by a wider selection of cheese varieties and better merchandising, transportation, refrigeration and packaging. Cheese, a valuable source of protein, energy, vitamins and minerals, is a useful alternative to meat in the diet: Cheddar, eg, is composed of approximately 26% protein, 33% fat and 36% water; creamed Cottage cheese, 12.5%, 4.5% and 79%, respectively.

Cheese was made for thousands of years as a means of preserving the valuable nutrients of milk. The first cheese was probably made from naturally soured milk, simply by allowing whey to drain from a bag, a procedure that can be used now for Cottage-type cheeses. Eventually, it was found that an enzyme from the fourth stomach of calves, kids or goats could coagulate milk. This enzyme, rennet, has been used for centuries for making most of the cheeses that we know today. Canadian settlers made cheese for their own use or for sale at markets. The first factory in Canada specializing in making cheese from milk from surrounding farms was built by Harvey Farrington in Oxford County, Ont, in 1863. A prototype of the early cheese factory operates at UPPER CANADA VILLAGE, Morrisburg, Ont. Factories proliferated quickly, reaching a peak of 2300 cheese factories and 570 combined cheese and butter factories at the turn of the century; about 10 000 t were exported annually to England at that time. Today, most cheese is made in large, automated factories;

Mammoth cheeses were used for promotion in the 19th century. The largest, weighing 10 t, was made in Perth, Ont, and was displayed at the World's Columbian Exposition in Chicago, 1893 (*courtesy Agriculture Canada*).

the largest was built in 1973 at Notre Dame du Bon Conseil, Qué, making 100 t daily. "Mammoth cheeses" were used for promotion, and aged Canadian cheddar gained a reputation for top quality and fine flavour which it retains today. The largest cheese, the "Canadian Mite," weighed 10 t and was made in Perth, Ont. It was displayed at the World's Columbian Exposition in Chicago in 1893 and then in London, England, where eventually it was cut up and sold.

In cheesemaking, "starter" bacteria are added to milk to grow and convert the milk sugar (lactose) to lactic acid; rennet is added to coagulate the milk. The bacteria and rennet also aid in ripening and development of flavours typical of the variety. The curd is cut and usually cooked to 30-60°C. Whey comes out of the curd and is drained away; the curd is pressed in molds. Salt is added either before pressing or to the surface of the pressed cheese.

Cheese varieties differ because of variations in the making process. Differences in water, fat and salt contents of the cheese result in different firmness and taste. Differences in length and temperature of storage, and type of bacteria, YEAST or MOLD also affect flavour and appearance. For example, the white mold, *Penicillium camemberti* or *P. candidum*, is used for Camembert cheese; the blue-green mold, *P. roqueforti*, is used for Blue cheese. The bacterium *Propionibacterium shermanii* gives the holes in Swiss-type cheeses. Most cheeses are ripened for periods of 2 weeks to 2 years to develop their distinctive flavour; eg, mild Cheddar is 1-2 months old, medium Cheddar, 5-8 months old and aged Cheddar, 10-24 months old. A few cheeses are not ripened and are consumed fresh, eg, Cottage, Cream and Ricotta cheeses. Processed cheese is made by grinding natural cheese, heating it to 70-80°C and cooling; added emulsifiers (eg, citrates, phosphates) give the typical smooth consistency.

Hundreds of varieties of cheese are made around the world. In Canada, 68 varieties were made in 1983, including Cheddar, Mozzarella, Cottage, Pizza, Brick, Ricotta, Brie, Caciocavallo, Camembert, Colby, Cream, Edam, Feta, Furlano, Gouda, Marble, Monterey Jack, Munster, Parmesan, Provolone, Romano, Scamorza, Trecca, Spiced, Swiss and Emmental. One of the earliest cheeses made in Canada by French settlers was "Isle d'Orleans" cheese. Probably Canada's best-known distinctive cheese other than Cheddar is Oka, originally developed and made by monks at the Trappist monastery in Oka, near Montréal. *See* DAIRY INDUSTRY. D.B. EMMONS

Chemical Engineering is the TECHNOLOGY of scaling up to commercial size chemical reactions which have been demonstrated in the laboratory. The SCIENCES of CHEMISTRY, PHYSICS, BIOLOGY and MATHEMATICS underlie the ENGINEERING disciplines brought to bear on the design of safe and profitable chemical plants. An important objective of chemical engineering is to design the chemical reactors and physical processing equipment so that reactions proceed continuously, rather than occurring in batch operations. Because chemical engineers have become so adept at continuous processing, the CHEMICAL INDUSTRIES are skill and capital intensive, the ratio of employees to dollar revenue being low and the proportion of highly skilled employees being high. For the same reason, the chemical industries are quite scale-intensive, ie, the unit price of chemical products depends upon the size of the producing unit and the length of the production run.

The genesis of chemical engineering education in Canada was the formation in 1878 of a diploma program in Analytical and Applied Chemistry in the School of Practical Science, University of Toronto. In 1904 a course in chemical engineering was offered and in 1906 the School of Practical Science became the Faculty of Applied Science and Engineering. Twenty Canadian universities now offer undergraduate and graduate programs in chemical engineering. Details of the special research interests are published annually in the *Directory of Graduate Programs in Chemical Engineering in Canadian Universities.*

Canada's economy is still highly dependent on the RESOURCE industries, ie, FORESTRY, MINING, METALLURGY and ENERGY. The role of chemical engineering in these industries underlines the breadth of the profession. The PULP AND PAPER INDUSTRY involves the separation of lignin from cellulose and the formation, at very high speeds, of sheets which are amenable to a multitude of applications, the most important being in communications. Chemical engineers are involved in every phase: reactors for the digestion process, the behaviour of fibre suspensions, the application of surfactants and coatings, large-scale filtration and drying. Because the paper industry is so energy intensive, striking advances have been made in energy economy. Adhesive development has been crucial to the huge plywood industry.

In the metals industry, the flotation process depends upon knowledge of surface chemistry and the design of machines to exploit this knowledge in the concentration of ores. The revolution in the steel industry, the basic oxygen process, depended upon the development of plants for producing oxygen in tonnage quantities. The hydrometallurgical processes used for COBALT and NICKEL recovery at Sherritt-Gordon depend upon research in reaction rates, diffusion, and heat and mass transfer.

The stability of modern life depends upon a sufficiency of energy and food. Because of the availability of hydroelectricity, Canada has an important world role in electrochemistry for metal refining and for the production of HYDROGEN, as a possible candidate for energy storage and transportation power. The technologies of PETROLEUM processing and of PETROCHEMICAL production (the basis of Canada's PLASTICS-PROCESSING INDUSTRY) are chemical engineering developments which have resulted in refineries throughout Canada and in a concentration of petrochemical industries in Ontario and Alberta. The Canadian NUCLEAR industry involves URANIUM extraction and concentration and the evolution of the CANDU reactor, made possible through extensive chemical engineering in the production of heavy water and purified uranium oxide, and in the transfer of heat under extreme conditions.

Responsibility for the productivity of the FOOD AND BEVERAGE INDUSTRIES is shared among agriculturalists, MECHANICAL ENGINEERS and chemical engineers. The latter have made their contribution through the technology of the fertilizer industry, crucial to the continuity of current patterns of food consumption. In future, provision of protein and carbohydrate will provide a chemical engineering challenge as food processing increasingly employs the techniques of cryogenics, radiation preservation and high-vacuum technology. Here a bridge is forming to the emerging BIOTECHNOLOGIES, with their promising techniques of gene splicing, enzyme technology and new paths to chemical synthesis.

In addition to the foregoing examples, the chemical engineer makes large contributions to PHARMACEUTICAL, paint, TEXTILE, adhesive, health care and environmental technologies, as the bridge between the laboratory and the production-scale plant.

Societies The Canadian Society for Chemical Engineering is the principal technical organization of professional chemical engineers in Canada. It is a constituent society of the Chemical Institute of Canada, with a membership of 2296 in 1982. In the same year, it was estimated that there were 10 000 chemical engineers in Canada. The society publishes the *Canadian Journal of Chemical Engineering* (est 1957) and organizes 2 conferences annually, a chemical engineering exhibition and professional development programs. In 1981, together with the Interamerican Congress of Chemical Engineering, the society hosted the Second World Congress of Chemical Engineering, held in Montréal and attended by 6500 chemical engineers from all over the world.

J.W. HODGINS

Chemical Industries Chemical MANUFACTURING entails the conversion of one material to another by a chemical reaction on a commercial scale. The starting material (feedstock) can be a natural substance or a relatively pure chemical used as an "intermediate" for subsequent upgrading. Hydrocarbons (ie, carbon-containing compounds) separated from natural gas or PETROLEUM are the most commonly used raw materials for PETROCHEMICALS, which range from relatively simple gases (eg, ethylene) to more complex solid compounds (eg, polyethylene). Other "organic" chemicals are also based on hydrogen and carbon and may be derived from COAL, sugar or similar nonpetroleum materials. Coexisting with thousands of organic compounds are inorganic chemicals, ie, chemicals normally obtained by processing various nonpetroleum MINERALS (eg, common SALT, LIMESTONE, POTASH, metallic ores) or atmospheric gases. Such classifications, historically evolved, are less precise than they might be. For example, inorganic nitrogen fertilizers, which embody atmospheric nitrogen in chemical combination, are not generally manufactured without burning natural gas for its hydrogen content.

History in Canada

At the turn of the century, the electrolytic production of chemicals was hailed as one of the modern marvels. Canada, having what then was viewed as 40% of the world's unharnessed HYDROELECTRIC potential, gained a modicum of attention as a home of large-scale chemical plants. Thomas WILLSON, a native of Princeton, Ont, built the first successful electric furnace to make calcium carbide from coke and lime and, in 1896, set up a manufacturing plant at Merritton, close to Niagara hydraulic power. Eight years later, he participated in the establishment of Shawinigan Carbide on the St-Maurice R in Québec. Meanwhile, 2 German chemists discovered that the nitrogen extracted from the atmosphere could be combined with the calcium carbide in a furnace to produce calcium cyanamide. The ability to "fix" atmospheric nitrogen in solid form meant that world AGRICULTURE no longer had to rely so heavily on Chilean sodium-nitrate deposits as the source of nitrogenous fertilizers. The N American licensee chose to exploit this new technology in a plant established on the Canadian side of NIAGARA FALLS. By 1907 the electrochemistry that gave birth to 2 chemical multinationals (Union Carbide and American Cyanamid) had become a prominent part of Canada's nascent chemical-manufacturing industry. Along the Ottawa R, another furnace installation gave the country a local source of elemental phosphorus. William T. Gibbs used the since-depleted phosphate deposits along the Lièvre R in Québec as the raw material. He finally sold the Buckingham plant to a British firm in 1902 because the courts declared he was contravening the latter's patent.

Public awareness of chemical manufacturing rose sharply after 1914, when Canada was suddenly deprived of her main sources of potash, cyanide, dyestuffs and certain PHARMACEUTICALS. One response to the exigencies of war was a concerted effort to commercialize organic syntheses based on acetylene, the flammable gas generated from calcium carbide. Shawinigan Water & Power undertook the task of manufacturing key chemical intermediates (acetaldehyde, acetic acid and acetone) from acetylene in a separate manufacturing facility. Shawinigan was the chemical centre of Canada for the next few generations, producing vinyl resins and plasticizers as well as the organic intermediates. Other chemical firms located near the falls to make hydrogen peroxide, cellulose film, chlorinated solvents, chlorine and caustic soda.

WWII hurried the transition from electricity to OIL AND NATURAL GAS as the wellspring for chemical products. Shawinigan plants played a role in building up a munitions industry in Canada from 1939 to 1945. But this was the era of continuous processing of petroleum-refinery and other hydrocarbon products. Ammonia plants were built with government funds in Calgary, Alta, Trail, BC, and Niagara Falls, Ont, so that the operators could manufacture nitric acid and ammonium nitrate, the latter an effective blasting agent. Other wartime plants emerged, the most ambitious being along the western shore of the St Clair R in Ontatrio. Japanese occupation of the Far East RUBBER plantations prompted the Canadian government to pool the resources of 4 rubber-tire manufacturers, a Michigan styrene producer and a SARNIA petroleum refiner. The crown-owned Polymer Corp (known today as Polysar) was launched as an integrated supplier of several synthetic rubbers.

Once hostilities ceased, the direction of postwar chemical manufacture was dictated by the fact that Sarnia had a network of petrochemical plants. Discovery of oil at LEDUC, Alta, and completion of a PIPELINE from Alberta to Sarnia confirmed the St Clair R area as Canada's "chemical valley" during the next quarter century. A comparable buildup of petrochemical activities took place near Montréal, where a concentration of 6 petroleum refineries at the E end of the island provided an ample supply of both gaseous hydrocarbon by-products and relatively low-cost naphtha. Shawinigan's manufacture of organic chemicals was gradually transferred from the St-Maurice R location to the St Lawrence Valley (particularly Varennes on the S shore), but others in the Montréal complex invested in thermoplastics (polyethylene and polypropylene) manufacturing.

Most of the installations in Montréal and Sarnia were modest by world standards and Canada still was not in a position to compete effectively in export markets. The US Gulf coast states had come to dominate INTERNATIONAL TRADE in petrochemicals (including the major thermoplastics and man-made fibres) because producers there had access to low-cost natural-gas liquids. By the late 1970s, the dramatic rise in world oil prices, coupled with the increase in known natural-gas reserves in western Canada, altered the global economics of petrochemical manufacture. Several rounds of tariff reductions negotiated through the General Agreement on Tariffs and Trade also changed market patterns.

The result has been a pronounced preference by the larger chemical producers for investments predicated on natural-gas or associated liquids surplus to Canada's fuel requirements. Alberta has been home to several petrochemical works ever since the wartime ammonia plants were built. Two Edmonton-area developments of the 1950s presaged this migration to the West, although the construction of several pipelines to central Canada improved the viability of projects centered in Ontario. But the prospect is that Alberta will host most of the new world-scale manufacturing plants and that an increasingly important aspect of the chemical industry in Canada will be the efficient movement of large volumes of synthetic resins, organic intermediates and fertilizer materials to the US and to tidewater points. Chemical manufacturers stepped up capital spending rapidly, beginning in 1976. In the earlier part of that decade, they were collectively investing less than $200 million a year on plants and equipment. By the early 1980s, petrochemical producers alone had committed about $1.2 billion annually. Two large ammonia-based fertilizer projects were also completed during this time. Many projects were conceived when rising world oil prices and specific ENERGY POLICIES within Canada created a favourable climate for these investment decisions. The onset of the recession in 1981 and a downturn in petroleum prices has led to the postponement of several ventures.

The Modern Industry

Chemical manufacturing is a diverse industry. Statistics Canada isolates certain establishments that make only chemicals or primary PLASTICS and, in 1980, their aggregate shipments were about $4.5 billion. If one includes chemical plants that are listed under such industrial categories as petroleum refining, smelting and refining, and miscellaneous chemical specialties, the figure is about $7 billion. In 1982 the value of shipments was at least $9 billion in spite of a recession and, after 1983, chemical manufacturing was expected to become a $10-billion-a-year industry in Canada.

Location of Plants A handful of chemical companies produce a wide range of products, grossing over $1 billion each, but there are dozens of smaller companies as well. Almost 200 separate manufacturing plants in Canada produce at least one chemical for general sale. Most are located in central Canada because of the proximity of large cities, but every province, except PEI, has at least one chemical manufacturing operation. Some are associated with other processing activities: Trail, BC, for example, has for many years produced sulphuric acid, ammonia and fertilizer using the fumes from the zinc and lead smelters.

Ownership The large commodity chemicals can be successfully produced in Canada only with adequate economies of scale. This worldwide trend to higher levels of minimum scale has increased the influence of large multinationals endowed with sizable technological and financial resources and with global marketing skills (*see* FOREIGN INVESTMENT). Several major Canadian-owned corporations, however, have moved into the chemical business because they were already working in related areas. Cominco, NORANDA MINES and Sherritt Gordon Mines branched out into fertilizer manufacture. NOVA Corporation invested in petrochemicals as a corollary to its position in natural gas and associated liquids. Polysar, which had been set up to produce a few key petrochemicals during WWII, evolved almost logically into an international purveyor of synthetic rubbers and polystyrene.

In the late 1970s, various government agencies committed funds to chemical manufacture. The Société générale de financement established Ethylec Inc to participate in the Petromont consortium, operating 2 petrochemical plants in the Montréal area. The Potash Corporation of Saskatchewan acquired several operating potash mines in the province and has been studying the feasibility of investing further in fertilizer manufacturing. PETRO-CANADA is now a vendor of certain aromatic chemicals (benzene, toluene, xylenes) as a result of its purchase of the Petrofina interests in Montréal.

Technology The chemical industry is not built around any single TECHNOLOGY. There are almost as many processes as there are establishments; the same product is often synthesized using different CHEMICAL-ENGINEERING practices. Most processes have originated outside Canada. Yet Canadian chemical producers have consistently spent a significant percentage of gross income on INDUSTRIAL RESEARCH AND DEVELOPMENT. A membership survey by the Canadian Chemical Producers Assn confirmed that chemical companies spend an average of about 1% of sales on R&D ($100 million or more annually); the average for all manufacturing industries was about 0.6% in the 1970s. In 1980 indirect expenditures on technical services, ENGINEERING, production support and other activities (indirectly related to improving technological excellence) came to $77.8 million.

Work Force In 1981 nearly 35 000 people were employed in chemical manufacturing (as distinct from the production of chemical products). About half were in the petrochemical sector, in which average salaries were about $28 000 in 1981. CHEMISTRY and engineering are common disciplines within the chemical industry and educational levels are high. In the petrochemical sector, 2643 employees had a university degree in 1981. Canadian chemical workers do not belong to a single union. In Sarnia, Ont, the most active union is the Energy and Chemical Workers Union; in Windsor, Ont, it is the United Auto Workers. In Montréal the Confederation of National Trade Unions is most prominent. There are independent unions in several locations. Unionization is least evident in newer companies in western Canada.

Energy Consumption Chemical manufacturing uses substantial amounts of ENERGY, accounting for about 5% of Canada's oil and gas consumption. By most standards, the chemical industry is energy intensive, but not more so than certain other industries such as the PULP AND PAPER INDUSTRY or the primary IRON AND STEEL industry. The industry has been striving to use energy more efficiently, if only to be more competitive in world markets. When the oil crisis shocked Canadians into action, the industry committed itself to reduce energy consumption per unit weight of product by 17%, compared with what was used in 1972. By 1985 the reduction should have reached 31% less than in 1972.

Export Status Chemical manufacturing relies heavily on exports. Fertilizers, generally not subject to custom duties, have long been shipped to external markets. In 1981, exports totaled $328 million (excluding potash, which is a mineral rather than a chemical-manufacture product). Exports of other inorganic chemicals in 1981 were worth $411 million; another $122 million in foreign exchange accrued from the sale of organics and specialties outside the country. A more dramatic shift in trading patterns has occurred in petrochemicals. In the past, Canadian chemical companies turned to foreign suppliers for products at the best possible prices, but in the late 1970s the emergence of world-scale petrochemical facilities in Canada shifted the balance of trade toward net export. In 1981 petrochemical exports reached $1.47 billion, $80 million more than imports.

Government Control For many years there was no coherent government policy governing chemical manufacturing. It received about the same general tariff protection as other manufacturing sectors and Petrosar received some indirect federal support when the crown-owned CANADA DEVELOPMENT CORP acted as one of the principals. Ottawa has accepted the concept of 3 petrochemical centres in the country (Montréal, Sarnia and Alberta). The 1980 National Energy Program had a bearing on the fate of these centres in that it established different pricing regimes for petroleum and natural gas. For many years, a significant 10-20% tariff applied to chemicals not manufactured in Canada, but GATT negotiations have eroded this protection. In any event, Canadian export industries and agriculture have had access to duty-free imports through end-use drawbacks or other exemptions from the general tariff policy adopted by successive federal administrations.

Since chemicals are often toxic and have other adverse characteristics, they must be handled carefully during both manufacturing and transport (*see* HAZARDOUS WASTES). Thus, antipollution devices have been introduced into plants and occupational health and safety considerations receive great emphasis (*see* OCCUPATIONAL DISEASE). Adverse effects on the ENVIRONMENT and on the health of specific communities have been documented. MERCURY was released into waterways from certain chloralkali plants until it was shown in the 1970s that this heavy metal was being dissolved and incorporated into food chains. Mercury electrolyzers have since been shut down, fitted with special cleanup devices or replaced with electrolytic cells using a different technology. In other cases the production of chemical products believed to cause environmental problems has been affected. Fluorocarbons, used as aerosol propellants, provide a good example; their production in Canada was reduced after scientific studies indicated that they rise to the stratosphere and may destroy ozone, which protects life on Earth from the sun's ultraviolet radiation. Many aerosol producers now use other propellants.

Associations The chemical industry's commercial interests are most often handled through the Ottawa-based Canadian Chemical Producers' Assn. Many employees of the chemical companies are professional chemical engineers or chemists and are therefore usually members of the Canadian Society for Chemical Engineering (CSCE) or the Chemical Institute of Canada (CIC). CHARLES LAW

Chemistry, the SCIENCE concerned primarily with the structure and properties of matter and with the transformation of one form of matter into another. Now one of the most theoretically and methodologically sophisticated sciences, chemistry had its beginnings in medieval alchemy. Because chemistry studies matter at a basic level, it is concerned with the physical sciences (eg, PHYSICS), the life sciences (eg, BIOCHEMISTRY, MEDICINE) and the earth sciences (eg, GEOLOGY, GEOCHEMISTRY). Not only do chemical studies result in an understanding of all natural processes, they also underpin production of many of the goods essential to daily living, ranging from food and drugs through the many substances used in the visual and plastic arts to heat and electricity. Chemical engineers specialize in the transfer of knowledge from the academic sphere to industry.

History and Training in Canada

Chemistry was first taught in Canada (1720) at the SÉMINAIRE DE QUÉBEC (in 1852, a sponsor of Université Laval). The first Canadian author of a chemistry textbook was J.B. Meilleur whose *Cours abrégé de leçons de chymie* was printed in Montréal in 1833. The first department of chemistry in Canada was established in 1843 at King's College (later University of Toronto); H.H. CROFT was the first full-time professor of chemistry. By 1900 all universities in eastern Canada had chemistry departments, offered honours science degrees and had diversified into chemical physics and organic (ie, carbon-containing compounds) and inorganic chemistry. However, the rate of graduation of chemists was not high. By the end of WWI, a research focus had appeared and universities in the 4 western provinces had chemistry departments. Educational facilities expanded greatly after WWII, a trend that continued into the early 1970s. In later years, honours chemistry courses became more flexible, more interdisciplinary options were introduced and instrumental techniques played a much larger role in laboratory instruction. By the late 1970s and early 1980s, expansions of chemistry departments had stabilized as a result of budget restrictions, as had the number of chemists entering graduate studies. Some schools and faculties were combining facilities and personnel with neighbouring institutions to form chemical-research institutes.

Students are introduced to chemistry primarily at the high-school level. To become practising chemists, students require a university education. University course work involves classroom instruction and laboratory experience. After 3-4 years, the bachelor degree is awarded. Graduates may pursue graduate study or find employment, eg, in product and process control, analysis, science teaching, environmental planning and monitoring, technical sales, market research, scientific writing and management. Those with advanced degrees undertake research and teaching in post-secondary educational institutions or research institutes. The allied subjects of biochemistry and CHEMICAL ENGINEERING are taught in universities; chemical technology in community colleges.

The principles of chemistry are applied in most industries at one time or another because of the need for chemical analysis of raw materials and finished products. Major employers include various industries: CHEMICAL, PULP AND PAPER, metallurgical, FOOD AND BEVERAGES, RUBBER, PLASTICS, PHARMACEUTICALS, PETROLEUM, protective coatings, TEXTILES, explosives and NUCLEAR ENERGY. During WWI the former Shawinigan Chemicals Ltd initiated industrial chemical research in Canada. The company's chemists developed a commercial process to make acetone required for explosives manufacturing. Today, most progressive companies carry out SCIENTIFIC RESEARCH AND DEVELOPMENT. Federal, provincial and a few municipal governments employ chemists in their control laboratories and research institutes.

The federal government's NATIONAL RESEARCH COUNCIL OF CANADA was established in 1916. Laboratory divisions, including a Division of Chemistry, were set up in 1928. One of NRC's scientists, Gerhard HERZBERG, won the Nobel Prize for Chemistry in 1971 for work in SPECTROSCOPY. The 7 provincial research councils conduct major programs in chemical research, the pioneer being the ALBERTA RESEARCH COUNCIL (est 1921). In Canada the universities are the major locations for fundamental chemical research. The earliest noteworthy work was done by physicist Ernest Rutherford and chemist Frederick Soddy at McGill University at the turn of the century. They propounded the general theory of atomic disintegration, which was to earn Rutherford a Nobel Prize for Chemistry in 1908.

Chemistry in Use

The principles of chemistry are at work everyday all around us. In fact, our bodies are miniature chemical factories, producing a myriad of chemicals ranging from digestive acids to such esoteric organic chemicals as norepinephrine in the brain. We use the same principles to extract chemicals and chemical products from their natural environments (ie, the earth we walk on and the air we breathe) and transform them to enhance our daily lives. We mine or quarry the earth for inorganic chemicals (eg, salt, POTASH) and inorganic MINERALS (eg, LIMESTONE, GYPSUM) and nonferrous metallic ores, and for the source of organic (ie, carbon-containing) chemicals, PETROLEUM, natural gas and COAL. Other inorganics are extracted from the air, eg, nitrogen, oxygen, argon and neon. Chemicals are produced by the chemical industries and as by-products of smelting and petroleum refining.

Inorganic Chemicals The general public is largely unaware of the importance of inorganic chemicals to Canada's industrial health. We are all familiar with use of common salt as a condiment in the food industry, in restaurants and in homes. Few know, however, that salt is the starting material for producing chlorine, caustic soda and sodium chlorate. One or other of these chemicals is vital to the production of wood pulp, plastics, pharmaceuticals, disinfectants, PESTICIDES, bleaches, CERAMICS, cosmetics, GLASS, rayon, detergents and aluminum. About 130 years ago, Canada was the world's largest exporter of potassium compounds, leached from wood ashes and used in soapmaking. Today, Canada is again a large exporter of potassium compounds in the form of potash (used in fertilizer) from large deposits in Saskatchewan. Limestone is another important chemical raw material. When heated in kilns, it forms lime, used as a flux to smelt IRON ORE and nonferrous ores, and to make wood-pulp cooking liquor. Until the advent of the PETROCHEMICAL INDUSTRY in Canada during WWII, inorganic limestone had been the basis of Canada's organic chemical industry, centered in Shawinigan, Qué. Limestone and coke from coal were allowed to react to produce calcium carbide, then to produce acetylene, the starting point for a variety of organic chemicals, synthetic resins and plastics. Acetylene was also used in welding. Cyanamide was the precursor of melamine-formaldehyde resins, used in the plastics industry to make tablewares. The cyanamide-based process was discontinued in the 1950s. When calcined, gypsum rock loses its water and can be used to make plaster wallboard or, in powdered form, to make molds for medical or artistic purposes. Gypsum also slows the hardening time of portland CEMENT, which itself is made by heating limestone with clay in large rotary kilns. Ammonia, another useful inorganic, is derived by combining nitrogen with HYDROGEN. Ammonia and its derivatives are used as fertilizers and also to make drugs, cosmetics, detergents, dyes and pesticides.

The metallurgical industries are also major sources of various inorganic chemicals produced as by-products during smelting operations. For example, since the 1920s, SULPHUR and sulphuric acid have been recovered from waste fumes resulting from the smelting of ores in Canada. These fumes continue to be a major source of this important acid, used in a vast number of chemical products and processes ranging from fertilizers and detergents to refining of nonferrous metals and petroleum. The other major source of sulphur is the sour natural gas found in Alberta. Recovery of sulphur from smelter fumes and sour natural gas reduces the ACID RAIN problem in Canada. Large volumes of the industrial gases nitrogen and oxygen are used in welding, food freezing and in medicine. Specialty gases (eg, argon, neon) are used for illuminated signs and for welding where inert atmospheres are required.

Organic Chemicals are created from crude OIL AND NATURAL GAS and, in smaller volume, from animal fats and VEGETABLE OILS. They are important ingredients in many consumer products. Canada's crude-oil deposits led to the start of the petrochemical industry, the products of which include alcohols, antifreeze, plastic resins, solvents, synthetic rubber, synthetic textile fibres and carbon black. Alberta's natural gas is used to produce chemicals such as benzene, toluene and methyl alcohol as well as elemental sulphur. Before the advent of petrochemicals, Canada's IRON AND STEEL INDUSTRY was the sole source for benzene, toluene and other "coal chemicals." With fears of a petroleum shortage, coal recently has become more interesting as a future source of organic chemicals; work on COAL GASIFICATION and liquefaction is underway at several Canadian research centres.

Specialty and Fine Chemicals contrast with "heavy chemicals" sold in tonnage quantities and used in various industrial processes. Specialty chemicals include such items as aerosols, detergents and water-treatment chemicals; flame retardants; food colorants and ingredients; pest-control agents; sanitary chemicals; waxes and polishes. Fine chemicals, including medicinals and pharmaceuticals, are specialized products that were first manufactured in local drugstores as early as the late 19th century. For example, only 4 months after the first use of chloroform in obstetrics in 1847, the chemical was made by an enterprising druggist-chemist in Pictou, NS. During WWI, manufacture of fine chemicals began to assume a substantial volume and Canadian manufacture of acetylsalicylic acid (ie, aspirin) was begun. The manufacture of medicinal chemicals has since grown to include a range of products such as vitamins, hormones, antibiotics, etc. Other fine chemicals made in Canada include synthetic vanillin for flavours; citric acid for food and soft drinks; silver salts and iodines for the photographic industry; stearic acid and metal stearates for paints, lubricants, waterproofers and plastics; disinfectants for soapmakers and householders; silver chemicals for electroplating; cobalt salts to speed drying time of paints; potassium iodide to add to table salt to prevent goitre. It is interesting to note that vanillin in Canada is produced as a by-product of the pulp and paper industry and another by-product, lignin, is used as an ingredient in drilling muds for oil exploration.

In contrast with chemical-products industries that produce chemicals, chemical-process industries use chemicals in making their products. Major examples of these "chemical-user" industries include pulp and paper (using sulphur, acids, alkalis, bleaches, starches, sizes, dyes and pigments); rubber tires and rubber goods (using synthetic rubber, carbon black, fillers, antioxidants, lubricants, antiozonants, detergents); plastics processing (using synthetic resins, carbon black, fillers and colours); textiles (using synthetic fibres, soaps, detergents, dyes). Other areas such as AGRICULTURE AND FOOD use chemical fertilizers, herbicides, fungicides, insecticides and other crop-protection products; sulphur dioxide to produce starch; and corn oil from potatoes and corn.

Chemistry is closely linked with other science and ENGINEERING disciplines, as is shown by the following examples. In Vancouver, BC, the UBC Coal Research Centre was established in 1980. Its activities included coal geology and properties; mining and processing; use in coking, combustion and metallurgical processing; and conversion to gaseous and liquid fuels. The centre is made up of members of the departments of Geological Science, Mining and Mineral Process Engineering, Metallurgical Engineering, Chemical Engineering, MECHANICAL ENGINEERING and Chemistry.

In the 1960s Merck Frosst scientists in Montréal began research on new drugs to control high blood pressure. A team of chemists, drawing on studies of their colleagues in BIOLOGY and pharmacology, began synthesizing new organic chemicals to seek candidates and, by the late 1960s, developed a new chemical entity, called timolol maleate, which appeared to be a most promising new drug. Chemical engineering studies were carried out to develop a commercial production process and the drug was evaluated through PHARMACY research and development.

According to the Canadian Pharmaceutical Manufacturers Assn the process can take as long as 15 years. Timolol maleate passed the federal drug regulatory agency evaluation process in the late 1970s and, in 1984, enjoys a reputation for providing significantly effective therapy in several areas of medicine. Development and production required co-operation among chemists, biologists, toxicologists, pharmacologists, chemical engineers, physicians and pharmacists.

Societies and Journals

Chemical societies first appeared in Canada in 1902 with the McGill Chemical Society, Montréal, and the Canadian section of the Society of Chemical Industry (UK), Toronto. Over 100 people attended the first national conference in Ottawa in 1918, which led to formation of the first national society, the Canadian Institute of Chemistry (1920). This institute amalgamated with other groups in 1945 to form a new national scientific society, the Chemical Institute of Canada. By 1982 the CIC embraced 4500 chemists, 3000 chemical engineers, 1800 chemical technologists and 3000 students in universities and community colleges. Under the CIC umbrella are 2 constituent societies: the Canadian Society for Chemical Engineering (est 1966) and the Canadian Society for Chemical Technology (est 1970). Two separate societies in Ontario and Québec represent the nonscientific interests of chemists in provincial matters. Canadian chemists are also well served professionally by a number of journals. The *Canadian Journal of Research* was founded by the NRC in 1929 to publish original work in all sciences. Later, it was succeeded by several journals serving different disciplines, eg, *Canadian Journal of Chemistry, Canadian Journal of Biochemistry* and *Canadian Journal of Technology*. The latter was transferred to the CIC and CSChE in 1956 and renamed the *Canadian Journal of Chemical Engineering*. There are 2 journals for general chemical news: *Canadian Chemical Processing*, founded in 1917, and *Chemistry in Canada*, founded in 1949 and renamed *Canadian Chemical News* in 1984.

DONALD W. EMMERSON

Chemistry Subdisciplines Early chemistry was principally analytical in nature; only as the body of experimental data increased did the present-day specialties evolve. The principal chemical subdisciplines are analytical, inorganic, organic and physical chemistry.

Analytical Chemistry

Analytical chemistry is the science of recognizing different substances and determining their constituents. Satisfactory methods are available for analysis of most of the major components of a material. The main problems arise in analysing for traces or for particular forms that may be present in a sample. Classical methods such as those using weight and volume (gravimetric and volumetric methods, respectively) are still used in analysis for major components and for standardization; however, measurement techniques have become increasingly sophisticated as desired detection limits continue to be lowered. For example, although all elements in Earth's crust are found in the ocean, only a dozen or so have concentrations above one part per million; most are at the part-per-billion level or less. Methods are being sought for nanogram (10^{-9}) to picogram (10^{-12}) quantities in a wide range of materials. Analysis at these levels requires more sensitive techniques and reduction of background effects; losses and contamination during sampling and storage become highly significant. As a result, considerable attention is being devoted to new preconcentration procedures that selectively concentrate and separate species of interest. Analytical procedures have been developed that use almost all the known chemical and physical properties of both atomic and molecular species. Procedures based on solution reactions, absorption and emission of radiation, thermal properties, optical properties, magnetic-field effects and electroanalytical behaviour are in common use. Computers have become commonplace for automation and handling of data.

Analytical chemistry contributes to daily living through the identification and monitoring of toxic substances in the environment and through the range of laboratory work required in industry (eg, FOOD AND BEVERAGES), the biological sciences (eg, MEDICINE) and the physical sciences (eg, GEOLOGY). Most screening programs and routine quality-control analyses are performed by automated equipment operated by technicians; analytical chemists advise on the selection of equipment, produce and develop new units, and ensure that procedures are scientifically sound.

Many unsolved analytical problems are retarding progress in all branches of science and the need for persons trained in analytical chemistry far exceeds the supply. It is therefore unfortunate that analytical chemistry has been largely neglected in Canada in the 20th century. Before WWII analytical chemistry research was done only at the Universities of Alberta and Toronto. The Science Council of Canada's report, *Chemistry and Chemical Engineering in Canada* (1969), noted that there was a serious lack of university-trained personnel to carry out analytical chemistry research. A report on chemistry research personnel in Canadian universities (*Chemistry in Canada*, Nov 1978) pointed out that, of 25 universities with 15 or more chemists on the academic staff, only 2 (Alberta and Dalhousie) had a presence (group of 5 staff members) in analytical chemistry. Of the older generation of analytical chemists, W.E. HARRIS (U of A) pioneered work in programmed temperature gas chromatography and D.E. Ryan (Dalhousie) established an institute for trace-analysis studies. Important contemporary research includes that of Walter Aue (Dalhousie) on gas chromatography, S. Berman (NATIONAL RESEARCH COUNCIL) on marine analytical chemistry, F.F. Cantwell (U of A) on liquid chromatography and theoretical studies, A. Chatt (Dalhousie) on nuclear analytical chemistry, C.L.Chakrabarti (Carleton) on atomic absorption, Gary Horlick (U of A) on instrumentation, electronics and spectroscopy, D.L. Rabenstein (U of A) on nuclear magnetic resonance, Robert Jervis (University of Toronto), who pioneered Canadian research on identification of very low levels of mercury, J. Page (Queen's) on electro-analytical methods, William Purdy (McGill) on studies in medical analytical chemistry, R. Stephens (Dalhousie) on atomic spectroscopy, magneto-optic and electro-optic behaviour, and J. Van Loon (U of T) on environmental analysis.

D.E. RYAN

Inorganic Chemistry

Inorganic chemistry traditionally was concerned with the behaviour of chemical elements excluding carbon. Compounds based largely on carbon provided the basis for organic chemistry, but the boundary between inorganic and organic chemistry has become blurred. For example, a rapidly expanding field is organometallic chemistry which, being concerned with compounds containing metal atoms bound to one or several carbon atoms, bridges the 2 disciplines. In the early development of chemistry, inorganic chemistry included characterization of elements and the measurement of their physical properties (eg, boiling point, density); however, the main current concern of inorganic chemists is the chemical reactions that elements in combination undergo, and the identification and study of new compounds. In the early 20th century, the development of atomic theory made possible the organization of most information about the more common elements. From 1915 to 1940 inorganic chemistry developed more slowly; however, during WWII it underwent a remarkable renaissance as a result of the need to understand the chemistry of URANIUM and other heavy elements, separate the rare lanthanide elements (atomic numbers 57-71) and determine their chemical behaviour (since these elements are formed in NUCLEAR fission processes), develop fully the chemistry of fluorine (since its high reactivity had previously limited its study), and extend the chemistry of many other elements associated with the development of nuclear weaponry. Facilities at Chalk River, Ont, played a part in those developments and Canadian NUCLEAR RESEARCH ESTABLISHMENTS have continued this research.

In its present form, inorganic chemistry aims to understand the importance of reaction conditions (eg, reaction temperature), and thus find means to prepare new combinations of elements. For example, many inorganic reactions may be greatly modified by the solvent medium; therefore, much research involves inorganic reactions in different solvents, both organic (eg, benzene, alcohol) and inorganic (eg, liquefied ammonia, liquid sulphur dioxide). A second aim is to understand the detailed pathways by which reactions occur; a third, to determine the structure at the atomic level of the products of each reaction. Such structural information allows discussion of the binding forces that hold each molecule together.

In the 1970s and 1980s, considerable emphasis has been placed on aspects of inorganic chemistry related to the solid state and to compounds of the transition metals (eg, COBALT, PLATINUM). Study of solid states has led to preparation of many new materials and to attempts to comprehend the electrical and mechanical properties of solids (an interest stimulated by developments in the ELECTRONICS INDUSTRY). Transition metals form numerous organometallic derivatives, many of which catalyze other chemical reactions, eg, syntheses of important chemical fuels, such as methanol.

Inorganic chemistry is particularly important to Canada's economy because of the significance of MINERAL RESOURCES. The development of Canada's extraction industries (eg, NICKEL, POTASH, LEAD, ZINC, uranium) has involved the application of inorganic chemistry; however, Canada has been a significant contributor to the field mainly since the 1950s. Significant work in the field includes pioneering studies on acids by R.J. Gillespie (McMaster), work on organometallic chemistry by H.C. Clark and W.A.G. Graham, and X-ray diffraction studies of inorganic materials by J. Trotter (University of British Columbia). In 1962 N. Bartlett (UBC) showed that the so-called inert gases (now called noble gases) are not, in fact, inert but are capable of forming stable chemical compounds (eg, xenon tetrafluoride). In 1965 A.D. Allen and C.V. Senoff, at U of T, showed that molecular nitrogen can be bound chemically to a metal atom, thus laying the foundation for much of the present intensive search for alternative economical routes to nitrogen fixation (of enormous significance to Canadian crop production).

H.C. CLARK

Organic Chemistry

The isolation of products from animal and plant fluids and tissues has interested humans since antiquity. Few pure substances were identified before the 19th century. Then, as now, animal and plant products were extremely complex mixtures of largely nonvolatile molecules. Because these substances were derived from living organisms, those involved in investigating them were called organic chemists. The different materials that could be isolated all contained the element carbon. During the 19th century, the inventory grew rapidly of organic compounds that could be isolated in high purity, either directly (as naturally occurring products) or as derivatives (of their thermal or chemical degradation). The carbon content was found to vary greatly among them, and the most common other elements were hydrogen, nitrogen and oxygen. Sulphur and phosphorus also were often present but other elements occurred rarely. As both organic and inorganic (ie, mineral) reagents became available, the theory of organic chemistry developed rapidly. It became apparent that products from natural sources and related new substances could be synthesized from nonliving sources, using increasingly well-understood reaction pathways. These developments made possible an understanding of the molecular structures of organic compounds and their reaction properties.

Complex organic molecules owe their existence to a strong tendency for carbon atoms to share their electrons with other atoms, in strong, direct covalent bonds. This property is the source of the molecular structures that comprise the largest part of dry living matter, and of the over one million man-made synthetic compounds developed over the past century. The chemical manipulation of hydrocarbon molecules, derived mainly from PETROLEUM, has given rise to such indispensable items as synthetic PLASTICS, resins, fibres, RUBBERS, adhesives, paints, detergents, PESTICIDES and explosives. The wide range of prescription drugs of the modern PHARMACEUTICALS INDUSTRY owe their existence to the knowledge and skills of organic chemists. Organic chemistry has also made major contributions to human pleasure, eg, through dyes, colour photography, perfumes, flavours and sweetening agents.

As a result of the continuously increasing and widespread use of its basic principles, organic chemistry in the 20th century has become a mainstay of other scientific disciplines, both within and outside the field of chemistry. Indeed the processing of animal and plant tissues and studies of biological transformations have passed to new disciplines including BIOCHEMISTRY, PHARMACOLOGY, DIETETICS and MOLECULAR BIOLOGY. Nevertheless, although the field has become only marginally concerned with living matter, the term lives on to describe activities that concentrate on the chemistry of carbon-containing compounds. The term "bio-organic chemistry" refers to efforts to use the theory of organic chemistry to imitate living processes. The power of modern synthetic organic chemistry is illustrated by the completion (1973) of the chemical synthesis of vitamin B_{12}. Similar challenges continue to be met in laboratories throughout the world. The technologies behind the space program have also had a revolutionary effect on organic chemistry. In recent decades, developments in COMPUTER SCIENCE, electronics, detectors and materials have placed at the disposal of organic chemists an array of sophisticated instruments for separation, identification and structural analysis of matter. In the case of living matter, such analysis raises moral issues which society, rather than organic chemists, biochemists, geneticists and microbiologists, will have to explore (see BIOETHICS, GENETIC ENGINEERING).

Much notable work in Canada has been carried out on naturally occurring compounds. Perhaps the most significant discovery was that of INSULIN by F.G. BANTING, C.H. BEST, and J.B. COLLIP at U of T (1922). The early work on alkaloids by L.E. MARION and R.H.F. MANSKE at the National Research Council in Ottawa, the first laboratory synthesis of sucrose by R.U. LEMIEUX at the Prairie Regional Laboratory of NRC in Saskatoon (1953) and the brilliant syntheses of many natural products by K. WIESNER at University of New Brunswick, all have received worldwide attention. Gobind KHORANA, who won the Nobel Prize for medicine in 1968 for his work on the genetic code, carried out his early work at the BRITISH COLUMBIA RESEARCH COUNCIL, Vancouver. R.U. LEMIEUX

Physical Chemistry

Physical chemistry begins with the measurement and calculation of the physical properties of atoms and molecules in the gaseous, liquid and solid states (phases). Physical chemists use these results to characterize systems in chemical equilibrium; to study the energy, rate and direction of chemical transformations; and to understand the atomic and molecular structure of matter. In contemporary physical chemistry these goals are met through the study of chemical thermodynamics, SPECTROSCOPY, kinetics and theoretical chemistry.

Chemical Thermodynamics involves the calculation of energy (measured as heat and work) and the evaluation of entropy (degree of randomness). When energy, entropy and chemical potential are known, physical chemists can characterize equilibria in reactions, in solutions and between phases. Electrolysis, the formation of emulsions, the mechanism of transport through membranes and the description of adsorption on surfaces are a few examples of contemporary chemical problems that are treated using thermodynamics and statistical mechanics. The extension of thermodynamic principles to far-from-equilibrium systems (eg, biological systems with their highly ordered structures) has been successfully undertaken by physical chemists.

Spectroscopy The energy of atoms and molecules is available in small packets called quanta, which are characteristic of the energy of electronic, vibrational and rotational motions. Each quantum is associated with a particular wavelength of electromagnetic radiation and appears as a distinct line in a spectrum. Analysis of spectral lines in the visible and ultraviolet range has clarified the electronic structure of atoms and molecules; that of infrared spectra gives bond stretching and bending characteristics and, for simple molecules, bond lengths. X-ray crystallography permits the determination of nuclear positions even in very large molecules.

Chemical Kinetics involves measurement and interpretation of the rates at which molecules, atoms, ions and radicals react to form new products. The effect of pressure, temperature, concentration of reactants and radiation allows kineticists to specify how reactions occur in terms of collisions, transition complexes, intermediates and reaction paths. The study of gas-phase reactions has provided insight about how energy is redistributed as the reaction progresses; indeed the role of the electronic, vibrational and rotational states involved can be examined.

Theoretical Chemistry involves using fundamental principles of PHYSICS and MATHEMATICS to create models for chemical processes. It is best known for its role in explaining chemical bonding. The laws of quantum physics are essential in interpreting and directing spectroscopic measurements. Similar contributions have been made in the evolution of models for kinetic studies, particularly for the redistribution of energy in elementary reactions. With the aid of statistical mechanics, thermodynamic quantities (eg, specific heat) and transport properties (eg, viscosity) have yielded to theoretical interpretation. Computational chemistry began in the 1960s when large-capacity computers became available. Contemporary programs in quantum chemistry not only produce molecular orbitals and electronic energy levels but also provide a wide variety of molecular properties. Complex reaction schemes can be modeled, synthetic spectra can be produced and even properties of fluids can be calculated by computer programs.

Physical chemistry began to take shape in the 1870s when Willard Gibbs' thermodynamics treatise appeared. By the 1890s, electrochemistry was a major preoccupation of physical chemists, especially for industrial applications (*see* METALLURGY), and by the early 1900s physical chemists were deeply involved in the study of radioactivity. The assimilation of results of work in other fields has continued and some ideas (eg, quantum theory) have changed the course of physical chemistry. Other ideas, such as nuclear-magnetic resonance and infrared spectroscopy, were nurtured and perfected by physical chemists and have emerged as essential tools in all chemical subdisciplines.

The past century has seen major Canadian contributions to this development of physical chemistry, from the thermodynamic work of William Lash MILLER in the 1890s to the spectroscopic studies of Gerhard HERZBERG in the 1980s. The electrochemical innovations of T.L. WILLSON (calcium carbide production patent, 1893) and A.E. LeSueur (chlorine production for bleaching paper pulp, 1888) received worldwide application and provided the impetus for Canadian HYDROELECTRIC development and the PULP AND PAPER industries. This early interest in classical thermodynamics was furthered by Andrew GORDON (U of T), who carried out the first calculation of thermodynamic properties of triatomic molecules (1932), by the careful measurements of Otto MAASS on critical phenomena (1930s) and by the phase rule analyses of A.N. CAMPBELL (University of Manitoba, 1930s-1960s). The work of R. Scheissler and J.H. Ross in developing explosives, during WWII, and the more recent development of improved recovery processes for copper-nickel mining and for extraction of BITUMEN from oil sands are examples of Canadian applications of classical thermodynamics to industrial problems. The modern experiments and analysis of S.G. Mason (Pulp and Paper Institute, Montréal) for fluid and particle flow have received worldwide recognition. Studies of radioactivity and atomic and nuclear structures came early to Canada, and the work of physical chemists, such as Ernest RUTHERFORD (on the atom) and Frederick Soddy (radioactivity) at McGill, led to Nobel prizes (in 1908 and 1921, respectively). This interest evolved into contemporary expertise in radiation chemistry (the use of cobalt-60 gamma radiation in cancer therapy was developed first in Canada by Harold JOHNS), to isotope separation (by H.G. THODE) and isotope-labelling techniques in tracer work (by J.W.T. SPINKS) and into the NUCLEAR POWER reactor CANDU. The pioneering contributions of E.W.R. STEACIE (NRC), Carl WINKLER (McGill) and M. Polanyi (U of T) to gas phase and solution kinetics placed Canada in a position to develop a polymer industry (wartime products, such as synthetic rubber, were manufactured at Polysar, Sarnia). This Canadian prominence in free radical chemistry and photochemistry has been carried forward by the conceptual contributions of J. POLANYI (U of T) and by experiments with photosensitized mercury carried out by H.E. GUNNING (U of A). Perhaps the most outstanding contribution of a Canadian to physical chemistry is the work of Herzberg, whose exhaustive investigation of the spectroscopy of small molecules culminated in a Nobel Prize in 1971.

In looking to the future the clearest trend in physical chemistry is the resurgence of interest in the complex chemistry of the ligand and solid phases. Certainly physical chemistry will also turn more and more to the study of biological processes. Computational chemistry must surely continue to expand and with it will come the opportunity to develop and test theoretical models, to do computer experiments. W.G. LAIDLAW

Chenier, Georges, snooker player (b at Hull, Qué 1907; d at Toronto, Ont 16 Nov 1970).

Chenier was the outstanding Canadian snooker player for a generation. He was N American champion 1947-70, even after suffering strokes in 1966 that reduced his stamina and caused partial paralysis. He was a leading challenger for the world championship. In 1950 he briefly held the world record high run with a break of 144. Chenier was also a leading pool player. In the 1963 world championships he became the first to run 150 and out. GRAHAM DUNCAN

Cherry, common name for certain members of genus *Prunus* of the ROSE family, which produce small, fleshy single-stoned FRUITS (drupes). Two species, sweet cherry (*P. avium*) and sour cherry (*P. cerasus*) are grown for fruit. The mahaleb cherry (*P. mahaleb*) is used as a rootstock. Sweet cherries are native to Europe and western Asia; sour cherries, to Asia Minor. Cherry trees are tall, with reddish brown bark, large tapered leaves, white blossoms and black, red or yellow, round or heart-shaped fruit. Sweet cherries are grown in southern BC and southern Ontario, where cultivation hazards are minimal. Sweet cherry trees and fruit buds are sensitive to winter frosts; blossoms, to spring frosts; and the fruit is susceptible to cracking and to rot in rain. Sweet cherry trees are very large and difficult to handle; until recently all cultivars were self-sterile and required selected pollenizers (ie, another plant source of pollen). Lately, self-fertile cultivars (eg, Stella) and dwarf mutants (eg, Compact Lambert, Compact Stella) have been grown. The main sweet cherry cultivars are Lambert, Bing, Van, Hedelfingen; sour cherry, Montmorency. Canadian plantings of cherries total 3000 ha. Cherry fruit is flavourful and rich in minerals, organic acids, riboflavin and niacin. Sweet cherries are consumed mostly fresh; sour cherries, as preserves. In 1980, 9119 t of sweet cherries were produced in Canada with a farm value of $6.3 million; 9992 t of sour cherries, valued at $5.5 million. K.O. LAPINS

Chesapeake During the Napoleonic Wars, Britain insisted on the right to search neutral ships on the high seas for Royal Navy deserters. On 22 June 1807 HMS *Leopard* forcibly took 4 seamen from the American frigate *Chesapeake*. Despite apologizing to the US government and returning the 2 Americans, the British continued to claim the right of inspection. This angered the American public, and the incident contributed to the tension leading to the WAR OF 1812. Britain gained a symbolic victory during the war when HMS *Shannon* captured the *Chesapeake* off Boston on 1 June 1813 and later towed her triumphantly into Halifax harbour. CARL A. CHRISTIE

Chesapeake Affair On 7 Dec 1863, during the AMERICAN CIVIL WAR, 16 Confederates seized American coastal steamer *Chesapeake* off Cape Cod and diverted it to Saint John, NB. After refueling, it moved into Nova Scotian waters, where local residents co-operated with the hijackers. An American naval vessel then seized the ship within British waters, capturing with her 2 Nova Scotians. USS *Dacotah* towed the recaptured steamer into Halifax harbour, where in a melee one of the Nova Scotians escaped. The American vice-consul charged the Haligonians with violation of the ASHBURTON-WEBSTER TREATY. The incident, though ultimately harmless, vividly illustrated the hostility Maritimers felt towards the Northern States. ROBIN W. WINKS

Chess About 20% of adult Canadians play at least one game of chess a year. These games are mostly played for fun in backyards and basements, but for several thousand tournament players chess is a serious game. In 1982 there were 4124 players in Canada who had been "rated" according to their results in tournaments. Organized chess began in Canada in 1844 in Montréal with the establishment of the first chess club. The Canadian Chess Association was established in Hamilton in 1872 for the purpose of organizing Canadian championships. The modern descendant of this organization, the Chess Federation of Canada (CFC), has an office in Ottawa and issues a bimonthly magazine, *Chess Canada Echecs*. The CFC is affiliated with the World Chess Federation (FIDE) and the Canadian champion automatically qualifies for the Interzonals, the international preliminary events to determine world-title challengers.

As of 1982 there have been 61 Canadian Closed championships, played as round robins with entry restricted to provincial champions or top-rated players. Canadian Open championships, open to anyone, have been held since 1956 and usually involve 10 rounds of Swiss pairings in which players with the same scores are matched. The first Canadian Open in 1956 drew a field of 88, including a young Bobby Fischer. Kingston, 1966, was the first Open to draw over 100 players. The record entry was 648 in 1974 at Montréal. The Canadian women's championship was first held in 1975 in Ottawa, with Smilja Vujošević of Toronto winning the title. In 1978 in Vancouver and 1981 in Toronto the finals were won by Nava Shterenberg, a Soviet émigrée residing in Toronto. Junior championships of Canada have been held since 1970, with 12 players since 1978 in round-robin competition.

Canada has 4 women who possess the title of International Woman Master. They are Vujošević, Shterenberg, Angela Day of Toronto and Diane Mongeau of Québec City. On the men's lists Canada has 2 international grandmasters (D.A. ["A6"] YANOFSKY and Duncan SUTTLES) and 15 international masters (Fyodor Bohatirchuk, George Kuprejanov, Paul Vaitonis, Geza Fuster, Laszlo Witt, Leon Piasetski, Bruce Amos, Zvonko Vranešić, Camille Coudari, Lawrence Day, Jean Hébert, Kevin Spraggett, Frank Anderson, Bryon Nickoloff and Igor Ivanov).

Canada has been the site of some important international matches. Montréal was one of the sponsors of the 1894 world championship match where Wilhelm Steinitz lost the title to Emanuel Lasker. Bobby Fischer's path to the world championship included a candidates match in 1971 at Vancouver, where he eliminated Soviet grandmaster Mark Taimanov by winning 6 straight games. Toronto hosted the 1957 world junior championship (won by American Bill Lombardy) and a Grandmaster Invitational was held in Winnipeg in 1967, to celebrate Canada's Centennial. Bent Larsen of Denmark and Klaus Darga of West Germany were joint winners. In 1979 one of the strongest grandmaster events ever held anywhere took place in Montréal. This "Tournament of Stars" was won jointly by world champion Anatoly Karpov and former champion Mikhail Tal.

Canada has competed in the World Team championships (Olympiad) 12 times since 1939, when the Canadian team at Buenos Aires placed 17th among 27 teams. In Olympiads up to 6 players comprise a team, although only 4 boards are played in a match. Canada's 1939 team had 5-time Canadian champion J.S. Morrison on first board and 14-year-old Winnipeg prodigy D.A. Yanofsky on second. Yanofsky was the sensation of the tournament and won the prize for the best percentage on second board. Unfortunately, this Olympiad was interrupted by WWII, and it was not until 1946 at Groningen that Yanofsky had a chance to play in Europe. He had his best individual result there, defeating soon-to-be world champion Mikhail Botvinnik. After the war, a number of chess masters arrived from Eastern Europe, including Fyodor Bohatirchuk from Ukraine, ex-champion of Lithuania Paul Vaitonis and ex-champion of Hungary Geza Fuster. In 1954 Canada competed in the 11th Olympiad at Amsterdam, finishing 14th among 26 teams. Yanofsky played top board followed by Frank Anderson of Toronto, and by Vaitonis and Bohatirchuk. Anderson had been bedridden most of his youth and learned chess during this period. He won the second-board prize at Amsterdam and repeated the feat in the 1958 Olympiad at Munich, where Canada finished 15th among 36 teams. Had Anderson's ill health not kept him from an active chess career, he would have become a grandmaster. At Tel Aviv in 1964 Canada had its best result yet, finishing 12th among 50 countries. The team was Yanofsky, Anderson, Zvonko Vranešić of Toronto, who had defected from a Yugoslavian soccer team in Paris, Elod Macskasy of Vancouver and Laszlo Witt of Montréal (both Hungarian émigrés) and prodigy Duncan Suttles of Vancouver. Yanofsky had his best result ever and received the Grandmaster title. Havana 1966 was a disappointment as Canada missed the finals (finishing 23rd among 52). But Canada rebounded at Lugano 1968, taking 13th among 53 countries, and it did even better at Siegen, 1970, ending 11th among 60 countries. The powerhouse of the 1968 team was Suttles, while in 1970 Vranešić had the best score.

In the late 1960s young Canadians were rising to challenge the immigrant masters. Lawrence Day first appeared on the team in 1968 and Bruce Amos in 1970. In the 1969 Canadian championship, Suttles took the title by a narrow 2½-1½ margin in a playoff with Vranešić. In 1971 Canada played for the first time in the World Student Team championship, held in Puerto Rico, and was very successful, winning the bronze medal and missing the silver by only one-half point. The USSR won with future world champion Karpov on third board. Canada's team was Suttles, Amos, Day, Camille Coudari, Denis Allan and Peter Biyiasas. Biyiasas advanced rapidly, winning the 1972 Closed at Toronto and the 1976 Closed at Calgary. At the 1972 Olympiad at Skopje, Canada was passed in the preliminaries by Sweden and finished a disappointing 19th among 62 countries. Later in the year Suttles became Canada's second grandmaster with a tremendous result at San Antonio. The 1974 Nice Olympiad was Canada's worst result ever, its team finishing 24th among 73 teams, but in 1976 at Haifa Canada rebounded to take 8th placed in a field of only 48 teams (the event was boycotted by the Soviet Bloc). Biyiasas led the Haifa team and picked up the first third of his Grandmaster title. Good results at Lone Pine, 1978, and New York, 1978, confirmed his title just before the 1978 Closed in Toronto, where Jean Hébert of Québec City was the winner. Biyiasas represented Canada in the 1978 Olympiad at Buenos Aires, where he had a prizewinning score on second board, powering the team to a tie for 7th to 11th in a field of 66 countries. In 1979 Biyiasas emigrated to the US.

In 1980 at Malta, Canada finished by sharing 8th to 9th in a record field of 82. The team was Hébert, Day, Yanofsky, Yugoslave émigré Milan Vukadinov, Vranešić and Allan. At Malta Canada also played in the women's Olympiad, finishing 17th to 24th in a field of 42 countries. The team was Nava Shterenberg, Celine Roos (a French émigrée residing in Montréal), Urmila Das (a Czech émigrée residing in Calgary) and Angela Day.

In July 1980 Igor Ivanov took advantage of the Gander stopover on the Havana to Moscow air route to defect to Canada. Within a year the Russian had firmly established himself as Canada's top player. At the 1981 Closed in Montréal he won easily ahead of Kevin Spraggett and Hébert.

In 1981 Suttles became Canada's first postal grandmaster. After an absence of 6 years from over-the-board play, Suttles shared first place with English grandmaster Tony Miles in an international Swiss at Vancouver in 1981. Suttles has an international reputation as one of the pioneers of modern chess strategy, and many of his novel ideas have been adopted by modern masters. Because of Canada's geographical remoteness from the European mainstream of chess theory, Canadians have often adopted openings unusual for their time. N.A. MacLeod, who represented Canada in the great 1889 New York tournament (the de facto Candidates of its day), specialized in what later became known as the Hippopotamus Defence; W.H. Pollack at Hastings 1895 played the Modern Benoni Defence, then quite unexplored. Canadian style in chess involves noncommital preservation of options often connected with a slow development of the pieces. LAWRENCE DAY

Reading: Chess Canada, July/Aug 1972; *Chess Canada Echecs,* July 1977; and B. Kažić, *International Championship Chess* (1974).

Chester, NS, UP, pop 1131 (1981c), 72 km W of Halifax, is situated on a point of land bounded by a harbour, at the N end of MAHONE BAY. In 19th-century NS coastal commerce Chester was important as a site of shipping, shipbuilding, lumbering and fishing. Its sheltered bay, favourable climate and natural beauty encouraged its gradual change to a popular summer retreat. Part of the Municipality of Chester from 1879, the village (first called Shoreham) of Chester was colonized in 1761, when New Englanders arrived and were greeted by about 30 well-established families; 2 sawmills were already in operation. Chester grew little through the 19th century; no direct roadway was built between Halifax and Chester until 1848. Today some light industry is carried on, the summer tourist industry flourishes and most of the labour force is engaged in support or professional services. The village's varied architectural composition includes several 18th-century buildings as well as many from the 19th century; the summer homes reflect this diversity. Cultural and recreational activities include a library, golf club, yacht club, sports complex and puppet theatre. G.B. HALIBURTON

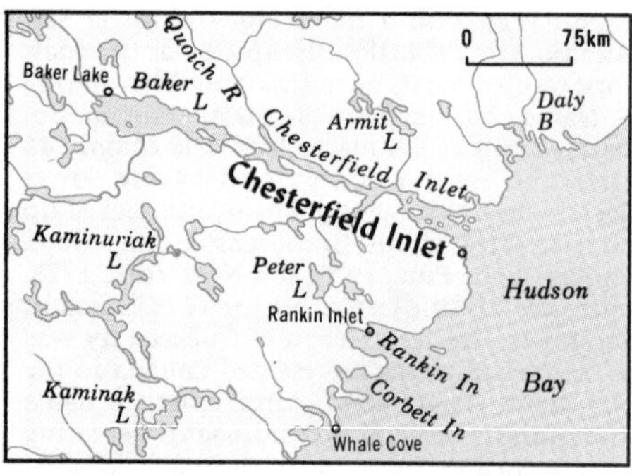

Chesterfield Inlet is a narrow, fjordlike arm of the NW coast of HUDSON BAY that stretches 160 km inland to the THELON R. It marks a physiographic divide along the bay, separating a narrow, rocky coastal plain backing onto a plain and hilly area to the N, from an enormous area of low relief, with poorly developed drainage farther S. Its climate is noteworthy for its windiness, since the inlet is aligned with the prevailing winds from the NW, which are remarkably strong in winter (mean velocity 8.7 m/s, reaching 36 m/s) and constant, blowing on average 20% of the time. The area was first explored 1761-62 by Capt Christopher, an officer in the HBC. The inlet was named for the earl of Chesterfield. DOUG FINLAYSON

Chestnut (*Castanea*), genus of TREES of beech family (Fagaceae). Of 10 known species, one, American chestnut (*C. dentata*), is indigenous to Canada. Its distribution is limited to N of Lk Erie. This species is on the verge of disappearing in N America because of the ravages of a blight

American chestnut (*Castanea dentata*) (*artwork by Claire Tremblay*).

caused by a fungus which appeared at the end of the 19th century. The few surviving trees barely reach 10 m in height; formerly specimens reached more than 30 m in height and 1 m in diameter. Leaves are alternate and spear shaped, with coarsely toothed margins. European sweet chestnut (*C. sativa*) is occasionally planted as an ORNAMENTAL. Horse chestnut (*Aesculus hippocastanum*), also an ornamental, is not related, although it can be mistaken for *Castanea* species. Chestnuts normally grow in sandy or gravelly, well-drained soils. The fruit is edible. The light, soft, decay-resistant wood was once used for posts and poles. ESTELLE LACOURSIÈRE

Chickadee (Paridae), family of BIRDS comprising 43 species of true tits (titmice), of which 6 species occur in Canada. Chickadees are tiny, vocal birds of scrub and forest, with stout, conical bills. Most species have striking black and white head markings; some have a conspicuous crest. Black-capped and boreal chickadees (*Parus atricapillus* and *P. hudsonicus*) are widely distributed in Canada. The black-capped favours deciduous woods and gardens; the boreal prefers coniferous forests. Species with restricted ranges are mountain, Siberian and chestnut-backed chickadees (*P. gambeli, P. cinctus, P. rufescens*, respectively) and tufted titmouse (*P. bicolor*). Chickadees are nonmigratory. They eat insects (especially caterpillars) and spiders in summer, and also seeds in winter. Chickadees often hang upside down to pick prey from undersides of leaves and twigs. Prey are held underfoot and hammered with the bill or beaten on branches. Chickadees nest in natural cavities in trees or stumps, raising one large brood (5-13 young) annually. Males feed their mates during courtship and incubation. The protected nest site allows a long incubation period (17-21 days). Chickadee groups often form a nucleus for mixed-species feeding flocks. Bushtits, formerly included in the Paridae, are now classified as family Aegithalidae. Common bushtit (*Psaltriparus minimus*), a very small, brownish grey bird with stubby bill and long tail, occurs in southwestern BC. JAMES N.M. SMITH

Chicoutimi, Qué, City, pop 60 064 (1981c), inc 1976, is located at the confluence of the Chicoutimi and SAGUENAY rivers between JONQUIÈRE and LA BAIE, 200 km N of Québec City. In the Montagnais language, Chicoutimi means "the end of the deep waters" — a reference to the tides reaching that point.

Regional capital of Saguenay-Lac St-Jean, county seat of Chicoutimi and headquarters of the judicial district of the same name, the city has been a diocesan centre since 1878 and has a major hospital (1884) and a university (Univer-

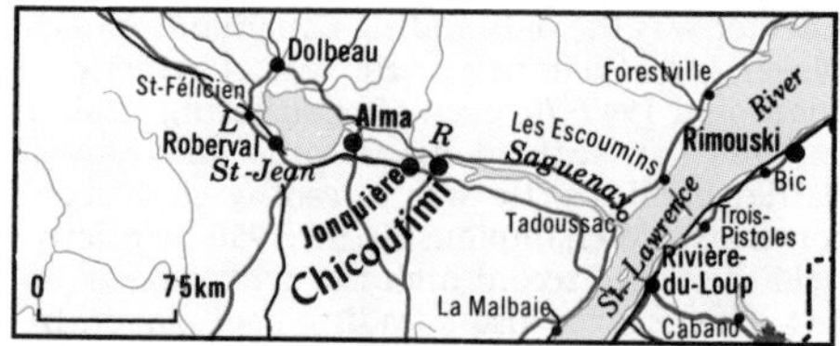

sité du Québec à Chicoutimi, 1969). The present city is the amalgamation of the municipalities of Chicoutimi, Chicoutimi-Nord, Rivière-du-Moulin and the parish of Chicoutimi. It was an important staging point on the route that 17th-century Indian hunters took to sell their furs in Tadoussac, and in 1676 New France authorities built a trading post here. Peter McLeod, Jr, founder of the present city, built sawmills on the du Moulin and Chicoutimi rivers (1842-43), which were acquired by William PRICE in 1852 and operated until the early 20th century. The town's wholesale and retail trade expanded because of its role as a maritime (1875) and railway (1893) terminal. In 1898 the Compagnie de Pulpe de Chicoutimi opened its first pulp mill here, which grew rapidly until the paper industry crisis of the 1920s and the economic collapse of 1929 forced its closure. Prosperity returned with WWII, when many unemployed found work in the Arvida aluminum works. The service sector experienced rapid growth, making Chicoutimi a tertiary centre.

While developing its future, the city remains attached to its past. It houses the Société historique du Saguenay (1934), one of the major private historical societies of N America, and the Musée du Saguenay-Lac St-Jean (1959). As well, the Corporation de la vieille pulperie has restored the remains of the wood-pulp factories, a signi-

Distribution of Industrial Activity* by Industry Grouping within Census Metropolitan Areas, 1980

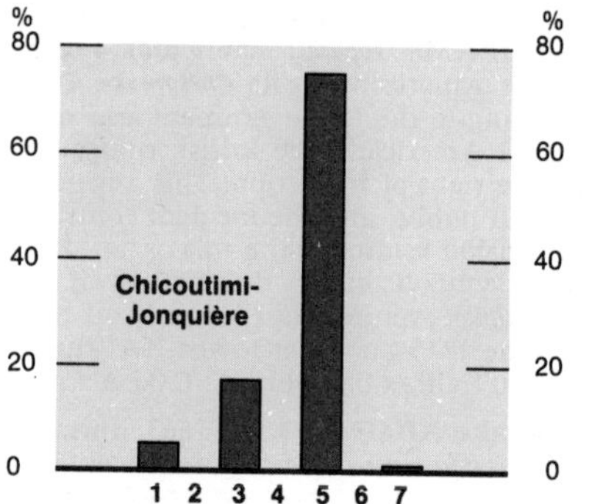

Industry groupings

1. Food and beverage and tobacco products industries
2. Leather, textile, knitting mills and clothing industries
3. Wood, furniture and fixtures, paper and allied and printing, publishing and allied industries
4. Machinery, transportation equipment and electrical products industries
5. Primary metal and metal fabricating industries
6. Rubber and plastic products, petroleum and coal products and chemical products industries
7. Non-metallic mineral products and miscellaneous manufacturing industries.

* Industry activity based on the average of percentage shares of the value shipments of goods of own manufacture, total value added and total number of employees for each of the selected metropolitain areas.

Source: Figure II, Catalogue 31-209, Statistics Canada.

icant item in Canada's industrial heritage. Chicoutimi hosts, each February, the Carnaval-Souvenir which recalls the ancestral days of 100 years ago. Finally the city is departure point for cruises through the majestic fjord of the Saguenay. MARC ST-HILAIRE

Chief Electoral Officer, Office of, est 1920, now operates under the Canada Elections Act. It was designated a department for the purposes of administration. The office ensures that eligible Canadians are able to vote for members of Parliament and that the election-expenses provisions of the Act are respected. The chief electoral officer, who is also responsible for the election process of the councils of the Yukon and NWT, examines the decennial census data and proposes alterations to the electoral boundaries of the provinces and territories. The CEO is appointed by resolution of the House of Commons. *See also* FRANCHISE; ELECTORAL SYSTEMS.

Chignecto Bay, northeastern arm of the Bay of FUNDY. The name comes from an Indian word *sigunikt* that may allude to the great marshlands (*see* TANTRAMAR MARSHES) that lie at the head of Cumberland Basin or to a MICMAC legend. The area around present-day SACKVILLE, NB, was first settled by Acadians in 1671 and by Yorkshire Methodists about 10 years later. The Petitcodiac R flows into the northwestern fork of the bay. A canal across the narrow (27 km) Chignecto Isthmus between the bay and Northumberland Strait was proposed as early as 1686. Henry Ketchum, a Fredericton engineer, built part of a proposed railway across the isthmus in the 1890s and interest in a canal was revived by a feasibility study in 1958. FUNDY NATIONAL PARK is located on the northern (NB) coast of the bay.

Chilcotin live between the Fraser R and the Coast Mts in west-central BC. Their territory includes most of the drainage of the Chilcotin R and the headwaters of several other rivers, and it is thought they may have entered this region from the north in fairly recent times. They speak a Northern Athapaskan or Dene language. In 1983 there were 1809 registered Chilcotin.

The Chilcotin are closely related in language and culture to their CARRIER neighbours to the north. They served as intermediaries in trade between the Homalco and BELLA COOLA on the coast and the Shuswap in the interior, and had limited contact with the Lillooet to the south (*see* SALISH, INTERIOR).

Traditionally the Chilcotin were organized into bands which were more social than political. There were leaders, but the society was basically equalitarian. The Chilcotin were nomadic for most of the year, taking game and fish at traditional hunting and fishing locations. Although they hunted with bow, arrow and spears, much large and small game was taken in traps. In the late summer most families gathered along the rivers to fish the great sockeye salmon runs. In midwinter they moved to sheltered campsites near lakes, where they lived in shed-roofed houses or pit houses covered with bark and earth. Their material culture was well suited to existence under northern forest conditions.

Simon FRASER was the first European to encounter Chilcotin in 1808. The HUDSON'S BAY CO operated an outpost in Chilcotin territory, 1829-44, but the Chilcotin had little contact with whites until the Cariboo GOLD RUSH in 1858. In 1861 a pack-train trail was established through Chilcotin territory and work begun on a railway right-of-way from the coast to the interior. Several labourers were killed in the "Chilcotin Uprising" in 1864, and the 5 Chilcotin responsible were eventually tried and executed.

The Chilcotin have since lived quietly, following traditional ways as much as possible while striving to adjust to the modern world. INDIAN RESERVES became winter bases for the Chilcotin, and many men became cowhands and labourers. A few are small ranchers. By the 1960s game and fisheries resources had declined seriously and non-Indian settlement was making traditional Chilcotin life increasingly more difficult. The various bands have attempted to develop community projects, such as irrigated farming and sawmilling, with very limited success. *See also* NATIVE PEOPLES, SUBARCTIC and general articles under NATIVE PEOPLE. ROBERT LANE

Reading: J. Helm, ed, *Handbook of North American Indians*, vol 6: *Subarctic* (1981).

Child, Arthur James Edward, business executive (b at Guildford, Eng 19 May 1910). He was educated at Queen's, Harvard Business School and U of T. He is credited with saving Burns Foods from bankruptcy and making it into the second-largest meat packer in the country. He became president and chief executive officer of Burns in 1966, owns 25% of the company's shares and is chairman of 5 affiliated companies. He is a founder and chairman of the Canada West Foundation and author of *Economics and Politics in US Banking* (1965).

Child, Philip Albert, writer, academic (b at Hamilton, Ont 19 Jan 1898; d at Toronto 6 Feb 1978). Child's fiction and poetry reflect a period in Canadian literature when traditional forms and subjects were being affected by radical social and cultural change. Novels such as *The Village of Souls* (1933) and *God's Sparrows* (1937) use near-contemporary and historic settings to depict heroes torn between opposing forces. A long poem, *The Victorian House* (1951), deals with the choice between refurbishing a tradition and discarding it. Chancellor's Professor of English Literature at Trinity College, Toronto, Child served as president of the Canadian Authors Assn in 1946. His novel *Mr Ames against Time* (1949) won the Governor General's Award. DENNIS DUFFY

Child Abuse All Canadian provinces have legislation defining a child "in need of protection," but only in Ontario, Manitoba, PEI and NS is child abuse defined by statute. The Ontario Child Welfare Act (1977) defines it as a condition of "physical harm; malnutrition or mental ill health of a degree that if not immediately remedied could seriously impair growth and development or result in permanent injury or death; or sexual molestation." Because child-welfare legislation is under provincial jurisdiction, definitions of abuse and neglect proliferate; some are too broad, others are too narrow or ambiguous. In *Report on Child Protection in Canada*, the author Corinne Robertshaw, claims a child's need for protection may not be reported. Even if it is reported, protection workers may not feel justified in investigating it, or they may believe that although intervention would be beneficial to child and family, the legal basis for it may not exist. Intervention may be opposed by the family and the court may dismiss an application because the situation is not covered under the Act. If definitions of child abuse are too wide, intervention may reflect disapproval of how the parents live and not a child's need of protection, which undermines workers' morale and the confidence of the public in the system's worth and effectiveness.

Battered-child Syndrome is a term coined in the 1960s to characterize the clinical condition of young children who have suffered serious physical abuse, generally from a parent or foster parent. The condition has also been described as "unrecognized trauma" by radiologists, orthopedists, pediatricians and social-service workers.

Although neglect and abuse of children occurred long before the 1960s, it is largely since then that physicians and child-welfare specialists all over the world have come to recognize child abuse as a leading cause of crippling injuries and deaths. Concern about abuse, neglect and the exploitation of Canadian children dates to the 1880s when John Kelso, a Toronto newspaperman, became involved in child-protection work, and it is mainly because of his pioneering efforts that children's aid societies across Canada developed. The name of Mary Van Stolk, however, is most closely associated with recent attempts to focus public and professional attention on child abuse in Canada. She devoted her life to making physicians, educators, social workers, judges, lawyers, politicians, the police and civil servants aware of the urgent need to protect children. In 1972 she estimated that at least 4180 incidents of child abuse occurred in Canada each year, of which 96-140 resulted in death. Her book *The Battered Child in Canada* is still one of the best general texts on child abuse.

Mandatory Reporting Identifying a child as being "in need of protection" is the first vital step in protecting children from abuse, but for the protection to begin the facts must be brought to the attention of the legally responsible agency, usually a children's aid society or the police. Child-welfare legislation in 10 provinces and the territories requires either or both the public and professionals to report the facts. In most provinces, excepting Saskatchewan, Manitoba and Québec, failure to report actual or suspected abuse or neglect is an offence under the law. Reports of sexual assaults against children are increasing rapidly but the legal system is responding slowly. If proposed revisions to the Canada Act, 1982, are passed, however, children (those under 14) will be allowed to testify as sworn witnesses on the basis of understanding what it means to tell the truth.

Incidence Because of the wide variations in definitions and reporting procedures, it is extremely difficult to determine the true incidence of child abuse in Canada. Using 1978 statistics, based on official reports, more than 7329 Canadian children were reported as abused; in the same year well over 145 000 Canadian children were receiving protective or preventive services in their own homes.

Prevention, including family-planning services to reduce the risk of unwanted pregnancies, improved housing, financial and social supports for families with children, and strong social sanctions against all forms of violence, is recognized as being more important and, in the long run, more effective than treating the results of abuse and neglect. *See also* SEXUAL ABUSE OF CHILDREN. CYRIL GREENLAND

Reading: Mary Van Stolk, *The Battered Child in Canada* (1972).

Child Labour Attitudes toward child labour (the regular employment of boys and girls under the age of 15 or 16) have altered dramatically since the late 18th century, when it was generally assumed that from about age 7 children should contribute to the family economy (*see* CHILDHOOD, HISTORY OF). In most cases, this meant assisting parents, but could also entail paid employment outside the home. Such activity might include the acquisition of skills useful in adulthood, possibly even a formal APPRENTICESHIP. Child labour made an important contribution to native Indian culture and to the societies of New France and early English Canada (*see* NATIVE PEOPLE).

During the 19th and early 20th centuries most Canadian children, formerly economic assets, became economic liabilities to their families. Boys' and girls' time was increasingly taken up in securing a formal EDUCATION. By 1911 about 85% of all children 10-12 years old in Canada were in school. Proportions of 13-, 14- and 15-year-olds enrolled stood at 78%, 63% and 42%. The proportion of boys aged 10-14 who were gainfully employed had dropped from 25% in 1891 to 5% in 1911, although that of girls remained steady at 2%. (An important indicator of the decline in child labour is the steady increase in the percentage of children attending school.)

Opportunities for paid employment probably broadened for the minority of children not in school. From the mid-19th century Canada began to undergo INDUSTRIALIZATION and URBANIZATION. As the proportion of urban residents grew from about 17% at Confederation, 1867, to over one-third by 1901 and almost one-half by 1921, new jobs for children became available in Montréal textile mills, Hamilton businesses, Cape Breton and BC mines and small manufacturing enterprises in the Maritimes. While the number of children 10-14 years old employed in agriculture dropped from 62 700 in 1891 to 5400 in 1911, the total otherwise gainfully employed, primarily in business and industry, actually expanded from 13 000 to about 20 000.

Several conditions combined to end child labour in Canada. Many jobs were "dead end": poorly paid, menial positions without any opportunity for advancement. Some positions, such as those of messenger boy and newspaper vendor, did not lead to adult employment. Moreover, most children holding jobs came from working-class backgrounds, and were of special concern to middle-class reformers intent on improving Canadian society. As well as supporting compulsory schooling and measures to combat juvenile delinquency, reformers sought to ban child labour. Although the first provincial legislation regulating child labour in factories and mines had been passed in the 1870s and 1880s, the prohibition of child labour came only in the new century. By 1929 children under 14 had been legally excluded from factory and mine employment in most provinces. Then came the GREAT DEPRESSION, when many adults sought jobs formerly done largely by children. By 1931, 96-97% of children 9-12 years old were in school, with proportions of those 13, 14 and 15 years old having risen dramatically over the previous 2 decades to 93%, 83% and 67%. During WWII many children probably entered the work force, defying school-attendance legislation. Since the war, it has been argued, women came to replace children as part-time contributors to family income.

Child labour did persist into the 20th century in less visible forms. Between Confederation and the mid-1920s about 80 000 British children, most under 14, were brought to Canada by humanitarians wishing to give them a new start away from their working-class backgrounds. Almost all were apprenticed to rural families and in general became child labourers rather than adopted children. Growing sensitivity to their fate led to the prohibition of child immigration in 1925. JEAN BARMAN

Reading: G.S. Kealey, ed, *Canada Investigates Industrialism* (1973); Joy Parr, *Labouring Children* (1980) and ed, *Childhood and Family in Canadian History* (1982); Neil Sutherland, *Children in English Canadian Society* (1976).

Child Welfare in Canada refers to a system of services established by provincial and territorial governments, at times in partnership with private organizations called children's aid societies, to provide services that supplement or substitute for parental care and supervision. Each province now has a well-established system of child welfare services (*see* FAMILY LAW) to prevent or help remedy problems that may result in the neglect, abuse, exploitation or delinquency of children (*see* CHILD ABUSE; JUVENILE DELINQUENCY); to protect and care for homeless, dependent or neglected children; to protect the welfare of children of working mothers; to provide care, including foster care, group homes and residential centres and ADOPTION services for children removed from their homes; and to provide services for single mothers. Child welfare services are primarily concerned with parental behaviour and pay little or no attention to other conditions that may jeopardize a child's development.

Historical Development The tendency of the state to intervene in the care of children is recent. Under the *patria potestas* of Roman law, wide powers of life and death were allotted to the head of the family. These powers were not part of European feudal law systems, although the latter reflected Roman civil law in stressing the family's importance. Under the English COMMON LAW, over several centuries, guardianship, whether by the natural parent or by another guardian, was slowly recognized as including the right of custody, control over a child's education and religious training, consent to his or her marriage, right of chastisement, right of enjoyment of his or her services, etc. Between an Act of 1660 and one of 1886 (Guardianship of Infants Act), mothers were unable to interfere with the father's appointment of a guardian, although they could be designated guardian or coguardian by him. Within a century, however, the mothers enjoyed equal if not superior claims to custody. The Court of Chancery assumed wardship if rights were abused, and the courts gradually, through various Acts, eg, Custody of Children Act (1891), Offenders Against the Person Act (1861), Poor Law Amendment Act (1868), etc, acquired control over abuse of the power of chastisement. If a child died as a consequence of punishment, the charge was for murder or manslaughter, whether the person charged be parent, guardian, teacher or employer.

In Upper and Lower Canada before Confederation, children were primarily the responsibility of the family. Any other assistance came from the church or the local community. Provincial governments provided institutions, eg, jails, reformatories, industrial schools and support to orphanages run by churches and private organizations. They also established a system of indenture whereby a child could be assigned to an employer in exchange for room and board and sometimes wages. At that time most people in Canada lived on farms and family survival relied heavily on the work of children. CHILD LABOUR as a social problem is associated, however, with the rise of industrialism and capitalism. It first appeared with the development of the domestic system, which was replaced by the factory system. In Canada child labour did not become as serious a problem as it did in England or Europe because Canada was predominantly agricultural until well into the 20th century. However, when poverty and destitution, increased by INDUSTRIALIZATION and URBANIZATION, took their toll, little public health or relief was available (*see* SOCIAL SECURITY). Growing numbers of homeless, destitute children in urban centres, greater juvenile crime and changes in child-labour practice pressured governments to respond to the plight of children. At the same time (1870-1925) large numbers of children were brought from Britain to Canada to serve as agricultural labourers and domestic servants, in effect the first large system of foster placement, which often did not serve the best interests of the child.

In the late 1800s the middle- and upper-class men and women who formed the Child Saving Movement sought to rescue children from undesirable circumstances. They blamed the parents of the children for the problem, but at the same time they ideologically reinforced the moral and social value of the family. With the enactment of child protection legislation in various provinces and the establishment and growth of the children's aid societies and child-welfare departments, the state began to regulate and finance a system of child-welfare services. The first Children's Aid Society was established in Toronto in 1891 and the first Child Protection Act was passed in Ontario in 1893. This Act for the Prevention of Cruelty to and Better Protection of Children made the abuse of children an indictable offence for the first time, promoted foster care and children's aid societies, gave the societies guardianship power, and established the office of the superintendent of neglected children. The rapid expansion of services in most provinces over the next 20 years bureaucratized and professionalized the services, greatly influencing the subsequent development of child-welfare services. Changes in child welfare were also affected by changing attitudes toward the participation of children in the labour market. Social workers were hired as the main professional workers in child welfare and they tended to reinforce the earlier approach of focusing on the family and its problems rather than on detrimental social conditions. Simultaneously the increased bureaucratization led to the departmentalization of services (eg, infant care, protection, adoption, child care) and removed decision making farther from the front-line workers. The services developed at the turn of the century focused primarily on child protection and child control; major legislation for the adoption of children was not passed until the 1920s. Earlier child-welfare reformers preferred indenture to adoption, correctly believing it provided more protection for the child because the placement of children in new families was primarily a means of exploiting the child's labour.

Neglect and Abuse Each province's legislation now defines those situations in which state intervention is required to protect a child, eg, those who have been orphaned, deserted, physically or emotionally neglected or abused by the persons who are caring for the child, or whose guardians cannot provide adequate care, or a child whose behaviour is unacceptable to the authorities. Under this legislation the responsibility for investigation and intervention lies with a provincial child-welfare officer or an organization designated for that purpose (eg, a children's aid society). Such offices must investigate any complaint of neglect or abuse and take whatever action is necessary to protect the child. Apparent neglect or abuse of a child can be reported by anyone in the community and in many provinces there is now legislation requiring certain professionals to report any suspected abuse of a child. If the child is removed from the home by the court, the child-welfare authority must arrange appropriate care (usually a temporary placement), and a social worker is assigned to work with the family so that the child can return to the home as soon as possible. Children permanently removed from their homes will usually remain in care until the age of majority, and in most cases the natural parents will be able to maintain contact except where their child is placed for adoption.

In recent years non-ward or voluntary admissions, in which the parents request or agree with the temporary placement of the child, have increased. The child-welfare services provide counselling and supervision for children in their own homes and care of children in alternate settings such as foster homes, group homes and residential settings. The main support services offered to children in their own homes are designed to improve the parents' ability to care for the child and are not concerned with many of the broader social and economic problems that families face. The children of unmarried mothers once represented a large proportion of those admitted to care, and many were subsequently adopted, but this is no longer true and a higher proportion of women are deciding to keep their children.

Alternate Care The child admitted into the

are of a child-welfare authority is usually placed in a foster family recruited by the local child-welfare office or by the children's aid society, and supervised by social-work staff. Foster parents are given considerable responsibility for the daily care of the child placed in their home. The foster-care allowance is the least expensive form of alternate care, utilizing the low-paid income labour of women as substitute mothers. There is difficulty in obtaining adequate foster homes for older children and for those with special needs. Some children are placed in state-financed group homes operated by the child-welfare authority or run privately, where group parents or child-care staff are employed. Some of these group homes simply provide an alternative home setting for a child while others provide specialized treatment for children and youths with special needs. Children are also placed in larger residential centres, some of which provide general custodian child care, while others provide services for children with special needs. The latter, frequently called treatment centres, are usually private and staffed by various professionals but are financed primarily by the state.

Adoption, which transfers rights and responsibilities for the care of a child from the natural parent(s) or the state to another person or persons, is regulated by the Child Welfare Act in each province. Traditionally, children available for adoption were primarily those of unmarried mothers, and abandoned, orphaned, neglected and abused children. Because fewer healthy infants are now available, many older or handicapped children are being adopted. Children are also adopted by the new spouse in many remarriages. Prospective adoptive parents are processed by the child-welfare authority and the child will be placed initially in their home for a probationary period before the final adoption order is granted by the court. In the past there was little contact between the adoptive child and the natural parents, but recently the efforts of adoptive children and their natural parents to locate each other have increased and some provinces have set up systems to facilitate such contacts.

Native Child Welfare Proportionately more native children end up in care than non-native children. There are difficulties finding native foster homes, partly because of the severe poverty many native families endure, both on and off reserve, and partly because of the standards used by non-native, middle-class staff to assess foster homes. Most adopted native children go to non-native homes, losing not only their families but also their culture. Because it is unclear which level of government is responsible for native child welfare, frequently neither government will assume responsibility. No federal legislation concerning native child welfare exists, resulting in less adequate services for native children than for non-native children.

JIM ALBERT

Childhood, History of Biology and the laws and customs of human culture together govern the nature of human childhood. The ways in which biology and culture come together in children change over time; the story of these changes forms the history of childhood. Human infants are born helpless and only gradually learn to care for themselves. In infancy and childhood they are vulnerable to a host of diseases; it is probable that until the 20th century at least one in 7 children born alive in Canada died during the first year. It is also probable that another one in 7 succumbed to disease during the vulnerable years from one to 7.

Children inherit possible patterns of growth from their parents, but these are realized in large part as a function of material conditions. Improved nutrition and living conditions have brought Canada closer than ever before to the optimal conditions for the physical growth of its children. In the mid-19th century, for example, some working-class boys did not reach their relatively short full growth until they were in their mid-20s. Today, Canadian children grow up faster, arrive at puberty earlier, pass through it more quickly, and achieve a greater final size than did any preceding generation.

This early 19th-century portrait of a family shows how children were often perceived as miniature adults, little different from the adults around them *(courtesy McCord Museum/McGill University)*.

Whereas biology makes all childhoods in some way similar, the customs and laws of each society make childhoods very different from each other in different places and in the same place at different times. The first child born in what is now Canada likely was born to people moving eastward along the shore of the Arctic Ocean over 30 000 years ago. Although we know nothing about childhood among these anonymous early settlers we do know something about it among the NATIVE PEOPLES who were their eventual successors. The children of Canada's native peoples had to learn the ways of complex societies. These ways differed from one language group or native nation to another at least as much as child-rearing practices differ between modern nations. An important dimension of native childhood was framed by the ways in which tribes sustained themselves; whether they were primarily hunters like the BLACKFOOT, farmers like the HURON or fishermen like the KWAKIUTL, or whether they lived by a combination of fishing, gathering and hunting, like the MICMAC.

On the central West Coast, for example, Kwakiutl lived in *numaym*, extended households of up to 100 people. Midwives assisted at births. Four days after birth the infant was given its first name, and it spent its first year in a cradle carried by its mother. At about a year the child acquire a new name, and boys had their hair singed and holes pierced in their ears and nose. High-status children were later given other names, owned by the family, which parents saw as appropriate to their developing character. Families marked each new name with a POTLATCH, a gift-giving ceremony. Each *numaym* moved several times a year to one of the 5-7 resource sites owned by the chief. In a society highly conscious of property rights children learned the precise locations of fishing and food-gathering sites and winter village locations. By observation and practice, children gradually mastered some of the skills employed at each site: making wood, stone, bone and metal tools; constructing longhouses, canoes and watertight wooden boxes; preserving and storing food; carving poles and masks; and weaving aprons, capes and blankets. The children of a SHAMAN (medicine man) submitted themselves to rigorous schedules, as they mastered the rituals, spells and dances owned by their families. The children of wealthy and well-born Kwakiutl learned the complex protocol of the potlatch and privately owned songs and dances, and learned to recite their family trees. All children learned the religious notions, mythology and taboos, and the workaday names and winter titles of those in their own *numaym* and neighbouring ones. At puberty, a boy secluded himself and fasted before a ceremony at which he was given a name appropriate to his personal ability. A girl embarked on a complex regimen, governed by taboos and involving seclusion and periods of fasting.

Childhood among native peoples did not repeat itself exactly from generation to generation. When the Blackfoot acquired horses after about 1730, their way of life changed dramatically. Boys in particular had to learn new skills, rituals and taboos associated with caring for horses, and hunting and fighting bareback. Childhood in the various native nations changed again as various groups came into contact with European traders and settlers.

In NEW FRANCE mothers bore their children at home, assisted by a *sage femme* (midwife). Most infants were breast-fed by their mother or a wet nurse until about 14 months. Three or 4 days after birth the parents and godparents took the child to the nearest priest to be baptized. Children began their *enfance* swaddled or tightly bound. They slept in wooden cradles and were given rattles to play with. The average family in New France had 6 children. Some time before they were 7, children were thought to have begun to reason and therefore entered a stage known as *tendre jeunesse*. At about the same time they began to contribute to their family's welfare, at first through such tasks as looking after younger brothers and sisters, frightening birds from ripening crops and herding cows. As they got older their parents added to their responsibilities. In a day that was usually full from daylight to dark, children rose to light the fires in the morning, emptied the chamber pots into the outdoor privy, brought in wood and water, swept floors and cleaned muddy boots. They cleaned stables and tended the stock. They helped seed and weed the garden; and in the late summer and fall they joined the whole family in the arduous task of harvesting. By adolescence most boys and girls had learned the household and farm skills. This competence was reflected in the fact that, theoretically, those who reached puberty (legally 12 for girls and 14 for boys) could be married. In practice, very few youngsters took this step. Growing maturity was recognized by all taking on increased responsibilities, and by boys being enrolled in the militia at 16 and beginning their indentures at about the same time. Although most waited till age 25 for marriage (the mean age of marriage between 1700 and 1730 was 22.4 for women and 26.9 for men), a person became a functional adult in New France at about age 20. The push to maturity was probably hastened by high mortality rates, which ensured that half the adolescents in the colony had only one living parent.

In the late 18th and early 19th centuries childhood among the LOYALISTS and later anglophone settlers was very similar to that described for New France; children were needed and highly valued for the work they did. Since they could be easily fed and clothed from the produce of the household, they were soon an economic asset rather than a liability. Travellers commented that Canadian children of both French and British background tended to be more independent and self-reliant than were their European counterparts.

In the 19th century schooling became a dominant childhood experience. Around 1800 only a small number, mostly boys, had much formal education. By 1900, most children attended publicly supported schools for a few years, and many attended consistently between about 5 and 16 years of age. One reason for this change was that Canadian children became the beneficiaries of new attitudes emerging in western Europe and N America, which saw childhood as a stage of life in which greater protection, sheltering, training and education were necessary. Although this change in attitude affected all children, we see evidence of it first in the care of dependent children. Canadians began to build special institutions to care for orphans and for children whose parents could not care for them. Changing economic conditions accompanied changing attitudes to children. Thus children attended school because maturity and compactness of settlement, improved roads, etc, made it easier for them to meet for schooling; because mature farms could more easily spare youngsters for at least part of the year to go to school; and because parents came to see that education was increasingly useful in a society in which commerce and then industry became important. Parents recognized that, for many jobs, literacy was becoming a practical necessity rather than an ornament.

The growth of cities and industries changed the rhythm of the seasonal cycles of farming, fishing, lumbering and trapping. The home ceased to be the primary place of production. A rising standard of living permitted families to devote more of their incomes to improving the quality of their lives. They moved to larger houses, they ate better food and lengthened the period of time that they kept their children out of the paid workforce. With fathers now away for the customary 60-hour work week, mothers who stayed at home had to assume most of the responsibility for raising the youngsters over this longer period of dependency.

Improved child rearing and child care became public concerns. By the 1920s in anglophone Canada (perhaps a little later in francophone Canada) new social policies and programs had been created for children. Social activists tried first to bolster families who were already doing a reasonable job of raising their youngsters. In their PUBLIC HEALTH work they tried to increase the chances of survival of all children. They strove for an educational system which, in addition to teaching the traditional three Rs, would also prepare girls to be better housekeepers and mothers, and boys to be sober, honest, well-trained and industrious breadwinners and fathers. Reformers tried to improve the physical and social environment of homes and schools, set aside and began to supervise playing-fields and parks, and supported such new organizations as the Boy Scouts and Girl Guides.

The social reformers also tried to help children and families with special problems. So that reluctant families and young people would take advantage of the school system, they pressed for regulation of CHILD LABOUR, compulsory school attendance and the appointment of truant officers. To prevent families from breaking up as a result of the death or incapacitation of the father, they campaigned for WORKERS' COMPENSATION and mothers' pensions. Factory Acts and anti-sweating legislation were introduced to protect the health of working-class mothers and their children, and a few DAY CARE operations were started. At some schools milk or hot lunches were provided, and "fresh air" funds were begun to take poor children and their parents out of their environment once a year.

Social reformers also tried new ways to salvage youngsters whose families would not or could not rear them. They began to question the merits of children staying for long periods of time in the institutions built in the 19th century. Canadians gradually ended the grim practice of "baby farming." They began ADOPTION services to place illegitimate babies in family homes rather than in foundling institutions and to legitimize children whose parents subsequently married. Socially conscious legislators shifted the care of vagrant, orphaned, neglected, dependent, "incorrigible" and delinquent children from institutions to families (*See* JUVENILE DELINQUENCY). They passed the Federal Juvenile Delinquents Act and set up a system of juvenile courts, detention homes, and probation officers to deflect youthful delinquents from crime. Between the 1920s and the 1970s Canadians strove to put all of these programs into effect and to bring them to bear on the lives of all children in the country. *See* CHILD ABUSE; CHILD WELFARE.

NEIL SUTHERLAND

Reading: Joy Parr, ed, *Childhood and Family in Canadian History* (1982); Neil Sutherland, *Children in English-Canadian Society* (1976).

Children's Literature in English, literature for children up to early adolescence, has been written since the mid-19th century. It can be characterized as a literature in which portrayals of life in the new country — confrontations with and adaptations to the landscape and the native peoples, colonizing the territories and then creating and developing a nation — were in search of appropriate vehicles of expression. During the 19th and early 20th centuries the vehicles were generally those fashionable in Great Britain. At the turn of the century the animal story, the first distinctively Canadian genre, appeared. Although animals had been mentioned in earlier literature, the works of Sir Charles G.D. ROBERTS and Ernest Thompson SETON gave the animal story its distinctive form. Seton's highly popular *Wild Animals I Have Known* (1898) influenced Roberts, whose *The Kindred of the Wild* appeared in 1902 and *Red Fox* in 1905. Drawing on their observations of wildlife and their study of Darwinistic theories of natural selection, both writers focused on the lives of superior members of various species. In *Red Fox*, Roberts combined exceptional strength and intelligence in an individual fox, making him the novel's hero. To Seton, the important fact of animal life was death, often at the hands of man and always tragic. Among later wild-animal stories which end with death are Roderick HAIG-BROWN's *Ki-yu: A Story of Panthers* (1934) and Fred Bodsworth's *Last of the Curlews* (1955).

Pets have also provided the focus for many children's books. One of the best-known early children's novels, Margaret Marshall Saunders' *Beautiful Joe* (1894), is the "autobiography" of a "cur" who, having been rescued from a cruel master, lives a long and happy life. Farley MOWAT's *The Dog Who Wouldn't Be* (1957) is the humorous story of Mutt, a pet who "at some early moment of his existence . . . concluded there was no future in being a dog." Sheila Burnford's *The Incredible Journey* (1960) is the account of a 400 km trek across northern Ontario undertaken by 2 dogs and a cat.

The adventure story, a major form of Victorian children's literature, influenced Canadian books in the 19th century and, to a lesser degree the 20th. Emphasizing the goodness of the British Empire, Christianity and physical courage, such British novels as Frederick Marryat's *The Settlers in Canada* (1844) and G.A. Henty's *With Wolfe in Canada* (1886) were immensely popular in Britain and the colonies, and shaped many young Canadians' views of their country. R.M. Ballantyne's firsthand account of the fur trade, *Hudson's Bay* (1848), was followed by his novels *Snowflakes and Sunbeams* (1856) and *Ungava* (1858). The vast landscape, populated by fierce wild animals and heathen savages, was supposedly won for civilization by people such as the young, white heroes and heroines of the novels of these authors.

Of 19th-century stories one of the most interesting is Catharine Parr TRAILL's *The Canadian Crusoes* (1852), which combines a knowledge of the wilderness N of Lk Ontario with elements of the survival story made popular by Daniel Defoe's *Robinson Crusoe*. In addition to describing how the 3 central figures, all teenagers, secure the basic necessities, the book portrays their strong belief in divine protection, and their rescue of a native girl to whom they teach the tenets of Christianity. The popularity of the traditional adventure story during the early 20th century (eg, Seton's *Two Little Savages*, 1906; Alan Sullivan's *Brother Eskimo*, 1921, and *Brother Blackfoot*, 1937) may account for the appearance of many of its traits in such novels as Haig-Brown's *Starbuck Valley Winter* (1943), Mowat's *Lost in the Barrens* (1956) and James HOUSTON's *Frozen Fire* (1977); in each story the male hero grows to maturity, drawing on lessons learned through meeting NATIVE PEOPLES and coping with the harsh wilderness.

There is no self-conscious tradition in Canadian fiction of mythologizing major historical characters and events, as there is in American children's literature. Thus, in historical fiction, Canadian authors cannot relate their narratives with the confidence that their young readers will have a general familiarity with major eras or events. Certain periods of Canadian history, eg, the WAR OF 1812 and the NORTH-WEST REBELLION, seem to be favourites in novels. The former has been treated in Barbara and Heather Bramwell's *Adventure at the Mill* (1963) and John F. Hayes's *Treason at York* (1949); the latter in W.T Cutt's *On the Trail of Long Tom* (1970) and Jan Truss's *A Very Small Rebellion* (1977). The ROYAL CANADIAN MOUNTED POLICE are treated in J.W. Chalmers's *Horseman in Scarlet* (1961), the LOYALISTS' escape to Canada in Mary Alice and John Downie's *Honor Bound* (1971) and the Cariboo gold rush in Christie Harris's *Cariboo Trail* (1957). In *Underground to Canada* (1977), Barbara Smucker describes the dangerous journey to Ontario of 3 slaves who have escaped from a Southern plantation.

Perhaps the most distinguished historical ficɔn for children is found in books dealing with .e native peoples, both before and after Euro- ·an contact. Often these stories centre on the :es of passage, as in Haig-Brown's *The Whale ·ople* (1962) in which a Nootka youth is thrust .to a position of authority after the death of his ther. In Edith Sharp's *Nkwala* (1958), a Salish ɔy searches for a vision to guide him into lulthood. Cliff Faulknor's trilogy, *The White ɪlf* (1965), *The White Peril* (1966) and *The Smoke ɔrse* (1968), is set on the prairies just before and ɪring the arrival of Europeans. Stories dealing ith contacts between native and European cul- .res include J.F. Hayes's *Buckskin Colonist* (1947), ɔris Anderson's *Blood Brothers* (1967) and Har- s's *Forbidden Frontier* (1968).

Writers of biography and historical non- :tion have always had to avoid the pitfalls of ·curate but dry scholarship, and exciting but .accurate fictionalization. Among those bio- .aphies which have avoided the dangers are aig-Brown's *Captain of the Discovery: The Story of ıptain George Vancouver* (1956), Kay Hill's *And To- ɔrrow the Stars: The Story of John Cabot* (1968), ıd Roy DANIELLS's *Alexander Mackenzie and the ɔrth West* (1969). Accurate and lively histories ɪr young readers include Pierre BERTON's *The ɔlden Trail* (1954), T.M. Longstreth's *The Scarlet ɔrce* (1953) and William Toye's *The St. Lawrence* 959). Although native peoples have been sen- tively treated in fiction and in adaptations of ɔlklore, they have not, with the exception of arris's *Raven's Cry* (1966), been the subject of ıajor biographies or histories for children.

Domestic and school stories and the problem ɔvel have not been as popular in Canada as Britain and the US, but there are important ·orks in this area. Ralph Connor (Charles W. ɔRDON), in *Glengarry School Days* (1902), and ellie MCCLUNG, in *Sowing Seeds in Danny* (1908), escribed the lives of young people growing up ı small Canadian towns. Now criticized for ıeir sentimentality and excessive moral ear- estness, these books nonetheless reflect the aily activities, cultural climate and reading stes of the period. L.M. MONTGOMERY's *Anne of reen Gables*, considered by many critics to be the nly classic of Canadian children's literature, ppeared in 1908. Although it too has been crit- ized for its sentimentality, in the lively presen- .tion of an ebullient heroine and the difficult rocess of her socialization it remains one of the ıost widely read Canadian children's books.

In the genre now called social realism 2 im- ɔrtant writers are Jean LITTLE and Kevin Major. ittle, who has a severe visual handicap, has ıronicled the lives of young people with phys- ·al problems, eg, in *Mine for Keeps* (1962), *From ınna* (1972) and *Listen for the Singing* (1977). Ma- ɪr's *Hold Fast* (1978) and *Far From Shore* (1980) eal with troubled adolescent boys who are in ɔnflict with themselves and their Newfound- ınd society. The relationship between native eoples and other Canadians is considered in ɔhn Craig's *No Word for Good-Bye* (1969).

Most of the popular literature read by Cana- ian children has been written in Britain or the S. There are exceptions. Mary Grannan's *Just ſary Stories* (1942) and *Maggie Muggins and Mr. IcGarrity* (1952) are collections of humorous ıntasy stories based on her long-running CBC ıdio series. Two recent authors are also signifi- ınt. In such books as *Murder on the Canadian* 976), *Terror in Winnipeg* (1979) and *The Ghost of ɪınenburg Manor* (1981), Eric Wilson mixes Cana- ian settings and current social problems into ıe adventures of Tom Austen, a boy detective. ɔrdon Korman, who began publishing in his ırly teens, has created humorous stories about ·enagers in *This can't be happening at Macdonald all!* (1978), *Go Jump in the Pool* (1979) and *The ʼar with Mr. Wizzle* (1982).

In the development of Canadian fantasy since ɅWII (*see* POPULAR LITERATURE), many of the best

Pettranella on an ox cart with her parents, from *Pettranella* (1980), text by Betty Waterton, illustrations by Ann Blades (*courtesy Ann Blades and Douglas & McIntyre*).

writers have turned to the wilderness and to the native people's spiritual beliefs, as in Catherine Anthony Clark's fantasies, including *The Golden Pine Cone* (1950), *The Sun Horse* (1951) and *The Diamond Feather* (1962). Christie Harris links modern science and old beliefs in *Secret in the Stlalakum Wild* (1972) and *Sky Man on the Totem Pole?* (1975). Monica Hughes emphasizes the native reverence for both nature and the past in *Beyond the Dark River* (1979). Set in the 21st century after Edmonton has been devastated, presumably by nuclear war, the novel treats the relationship between a young Hutterite and a native healer. Hughes has also written science fiction, including *The Keeper of the Isis Light* (1980), *The Guardian of Isis* (1981) and *The Isis Pedlar* (1982), set on a planet inhabited by fugitives from an overcrowded, polluted Earth, who have degenerated into fearful and superstitious beings. Ruth Nichols has used rugged Canadian landscapes in *A Walk Out of the World* (1969) and *The Marrow of the World* (1972), in both of which children undertake arduous journeys from Earth to the alternate universes in which they were born.

Other works of fantasy include Pierre Berton's *The Secret World of Og* (1961), which portrays the adventures of children who travel down a tunnel found in the floor of their playhouse and enter a strange land. Mordecai RICHLER's *Jacob Two-Two Meets the Hooded Fang* (1975) describes the dream of an insecure child who becomes a hero after he is sent to the children's prison. Janet Lunn's *Double Spell* (1968, published in paperback as *Twin Spell*) and *The Root Cellar* (1981) are time-travel fantasies.

Canadian folktales for children can be divided into European tales adapted by Canadian writers, indigenous folktales of European settlers and reworkings of Indian and Inuit myths, legends and folktales. Two early collections, Cyrus Macmillan's *Canadian Wonder Tales* (1918) and *Canadian Fairy Tales* (1922), contain stories from each of the 3 categories, although most are derived from French Canadian and native tales. The tales reflect early 20th-century tastes, often written in the romantic manner that was popular in late 19th-century England. Legends of the Maritime provinces were collected by Helen CREIGHTON in *Bluenose Ghosts* (1957). Marius Barbeau's *The Golden Phoenix* (tr 1958), is a collection of French Canadian tales, one of which, *The Princess of Tomboso* (1960), was illustrated by Frank Newfeld. Newfeld also adapted and illustrated the Nova Scotia tale *Simon and the Golden Sword* (1976). Traditional European tales retold and illustrated by Canadians include *The Miraculous Hind* (1975) and *Petrouchka* (1980) by Elizabeth Cleaver; *Cinderella* (1969) by Alan Suddon; and *The Twelve Dancing Princesses* by Lunn, illustrated by Lazlo Gal (1979).

The collection of Indian and Inuit oral material began shortly after initial European contact. However, because of the strong Christian emphasis in children's literature well into the 20th century, adaptations of native folktales for children were relatively few. During the late 20th century, in part because of a general increase in awareness of minority cultures, there has been an outpouring of retold native legends. The most significant writers in this trend are Christie Harris and James Houston. Beginning with *Once Upon a Totem* (1963), Harris has written several collections of stories based on the legends of Northwest Coast Indians. Though much longer and containing far greater character development than her sources, the tales reflect her familiarity with the rugged landscape and the cultural beliefs of the peoples. Houston's stories, including *Tikta'liktak* (1965) and *The White Archer* (1967), draw on local legends heard during his 12 years in the Arctic. Other notable collections of native tales are Frances Fraser's retelling of Blackfoot legends in *The Bear Who Stole the Chinook* (1959); Dorothy Reid's *Tales of Nanabozho* (1963), a recasting of Ojibwa myths; and K.L. Hill's *Glooscap and His Magic* (1963), accounts of the Wabanaki hero-god. William Toye has retold and Elizabeth Cleaver illustrated several native tales, including *The Mountain Goats of Temlaham* (1969) and *The Fire Stealer* (1979).

In recent years a growing number of native writers have retold the tales of their own peoples, hoping to preserve elements of a past that is rapidly becoming forgotten. In *Son of Raven, Son of Deer* (1967) George Clutesi has adapted Vancouver Island stories and, in *Tales the Elders Told* (1981) by Basil Johnston, Ojibwa legends are retold. Maria CAMPBELL, in *Little Badger and the Fire Spirit* (1977), has created her own version of a plains *pourquoi* legend.

Although there is a long tradition of Canadian children's fiction, there are few widely known Canadian children's poets or poems. Poetic works written for adults by Thomas D'Arcy MCGEE, Pauline JOHNSON, Bliss CARMAN, Robert SERVICE and others were frequently memorized by children. Two popular anthologies, *The Wind Has Wings* (1968), edited by M.A. Downie and Barbara Robertson, and *All Kinds of Everything* (1973), edited by Louis DUDEK, contained poems by well-known adult Canadian poets. However, it was not until 1974, with the appearance of Dennis Lee's *Alligator Pie* and *Nicholas Knock and Other People*, that a group of poems written specifically for Canadian children achieved a wide audience. The humour and nonsense in these volumes and in Lee's *Garbage Delight* (1977) and *Jelly Belly* (1983) is also characteristic of much other Canadian children's poetry, including Susan Musgrave's *Gullband* (1974), Sue Ann Alderson's *Bonnie McSmithers (You're Driving Me Dithers)* (1974) and Al Pittman's *Down by Jim Long's Stage* (1976).

Because of high production costs and a relatively small market, there have been few picture books published in Canada. However, during the 1970s distinguished picture books appeared, many from Montréal's Tundra Books. Ann Blades's *Mary of Mile 18* (1971) and William KURELEK's *A Prairie Boy's Winter* (1973) and *A Prairie Boy's Summer* (1975) are the best known. Others include Shizuye Takashima's *A Child in Prison Camp* (1971) and Ted Harrison's *Children of the Yukon* (1977). Blades has also written *A Boy of Taché* (1973) and has illustrated several other books, including Michael Macklem's *Jacques the Woodcutter* (1977) and Betty Waterton's *A Salmon for Simon* (1978).

Since the mid-1970s a number of good Canadian plays have been published. In 1975 Rolf

"The bathtub creature wailed, 'Why did you turn that tap?'" From *The Ordinary Bath* (1979), text by Dennis Lee, illustrations by Jon McKee (*courtesy Jon McKee*).

Kalman edited *A Collection of Canadian Plays: Volume 4*, a gathering of 10 dramas for children, including Eric NICOL's "The Clam Made a Face," Carol BOLT's "Cyclone Jack" and Leonard PETERSON's "Billy Bishop & the Red Baron." Native people are the subject of Henry Beissel's *Inook and the Sun* (1974) and Dennis Foon's *The Windigo* (1978).

Although most books bought in Canada are still by English and American authors, Canadian writers are becoming more widely read. This is due in part to the increasing national consciousness manifested since the centennial of Confederation in 1967. However, many reasons for the growth of Canadian children's literature are to be found within the field itself. The CANADA COUNCIL has encouraged writers through a series of grants and the sponsorship of reading tours. In addition a number of LITERARY PRIZES recognizing meritorious works and authors have been established. These include the Canadian Assn of Children's Librarians' Book of the Year for Children (since 1947) and the Amelia Frances Howard-Gibbon Medal for outstanding illustration (1971), the Canada Council Children's Literature Prizes (1975), the Canadian Authors Assn's Award (1963) and the Canadian Booksellers' Assn's Ruth Schwartz Children's Book Award (1975).

In recent years, several SMALL PRESSES have appeared, providing opportunities for small printings of works by lesser-known authors and illustrators. Among these are Tree Frog Press (Edmonton), Breakwater Books (Portugal Cove, Nfld) and Gray's Publishing (Sidney, BC). The 1970s also saw the beginning of the children's magazines *Owl* (1976-) and *Chickadee* (1979-) and of the *Canadian Children's Annual* (1975-).

Serious academic study of Canadian children's literature has also developed since 1967. Sheila Egoff's *The Republic of Childhood* (1967) appeared in its second edition in 1975. The journal *In Review: Canadian Books for Children* was published 1967-82, and *Canadian Children's Literature* began publication in 1975. Canadian books are regularly studied in children's literature classes in Canadian universities, and the Children's Book Center was established in 1976 to publicize Canadian children's books and co-ordinate the annual Children's Book Festival. *See also* FOLKLORE; LITERATURE IN ENGLISH; CHILDREN'S LITERATURE IN FRENCH.

JON C. STOTT

Children's Literature in French does not have a long tradition, and scholarly research in the field is relatively new. If "children's literature" includes books read by children, but not written especially for them, then French Canadian children's literature had its start in the 19th century. One early book popular because of its subject matter was *L'Enfant perdu et retrouvé* (1887) by J.B. Proulx, an adventure story in which 3 kidnapped children are sold as cabin boys. Only the eldest survives to tell of his adventures. Several books devoted to traditional tales and legends were enjoyed by children because of the familiar background and speech patterns (more easily understood than those in the books imported from France), eg, Frederick Marryat's *The Settlers in Canada* (tr *Les Colons du Canada*, 1852), *Contes populaires* (1867) by Paul Stevens, *Légendes canadiennes* (1861) by H.R. CASGRAIN, *Le Tomahawk et l'épée* (1877) by Joseph Marmette, *La Terre paternelle* (1871) by Patrice Lacombe, *Une de perdue, deux de trouvées* (1874) by P.G. Boucher de Boucherville and *Christmas in French Canada* (1899, tr *La Noël au Canada*, 1900) by L.H. FRÉCHETTE. These books were often distributed as school prizes in Québec. The policy to circulate the books in the schools began in 1876 and continued through the early part of the 20th century, in the hope that a sound basis for the development of children's literature could be established.

In 1891 Laure Conan (Félicité ANGERS) published *À l'oeuvre et à l'épreuve*, the romanticized story of Jesuit martyr Charles Garnier, which was popular among young people until the 1950s. Her *L'Oublié* (1900), even more popular, is a historical novel about Lambert Closse who participated in the founding of VILLE-MARIE. Conan wrote numerous articles on Canadian personalities and collected several of them in *Silhouettes canadiennes* (1917). *Contes et légendes* (1915) by Adèle Lacerte was dedicated to Canadian children, for whom, she claimed, no one had previously made a particular effort to write. Four years later, *Récits laurentiens* (1919) by Frère MARIE-VICTORIN (Conrad Kirouac) was published. His *Croquis laurentiens* followed the next year.

In 1920 Arthur Saint-Pierre, managing editor of the magazine *L'Oiseau bleu* (published by the ST-JEAN-BAPTISTE SOCIETY) asked Marie-Claire Daveluy to contribute a pioneer story whose principal characters would be children. Her story about 2 French orphans who settle in New France was serialized in *L'Oiseau bleu*. Published as a book, *Les Aventures de Perrine et de Charlot* (1923), it received the Prix David and became very popular. Although Daveluy also wro modern fairy tales, she is best known for he historical novels on the early French settler Other budding writers of the period, such a Marie-Louise d'Auteuil (*Mémoires d'une sour canadienne*, 1932), contributed to the success c *L'Oiseau bleu*, which ceased publication in 1940.

Others who began to write in the 1920s wer Maxine (pseudonym of M.C.A. Taschereau Fortier) and Eugène Achard. Maxine wrot many fanciful historical novels and short bio graphies, eg, *Le Marin de Saint-Malo, Jacques Cartie* (1946). She is fondly remembered for *Le Petit Pag de Frontenac* (1930), a novel set in 17th-centur New France. Achard, who immigrated to Can ada from France, began his prolific writin career with *Aux quatre coins des routes canadienne* (1921) and ended it with *Sur les sentiers de la Côt Nord* (1960). His books included retellings of tra ditional tales (*L'Oiseau vert et la princesse fortunée* 1956) and biographies (*Les Grands Noms d l'histoire canadienne*, 1940), but are mostly fictio (*Sous les plis du drapeau blanc*, 1935) and collection of modern fairy tales with a Canadian or Québe setting (*Les Contes de la claire fontaine*, 1943 During this period there was an interest in pub lishing natural-science books, which include *L'ABC du petit naturaliste canadien* (9 vols, 1936 by Harry Bernard, *À travers les champs et les boi* by Louis-Jean Gagnon (1931), *Les Confidences d la nature* by Adolphe Brassard (1936), *Nos ani maux domestiques* by Odette Oligny (1933) an *Oiseaux de mon pays* by Alice Duchesnay (1939, The trend was continued in the 1940s b Marcelle Gauvreau who wrote *Plantes curieuses d mon pays* (1943) and Claude Melançon wh wrote several books, including one on Québec' birds (*Charmants voisins*, 1940) and one on Cana dian animals (*Mon alphabet des animaux*, 1944, Besides these 2 books, Melançon wrote his pop ular *Légendes indiennes du Canada* (1967) and othe informational books on a variety of subjects, eg *Mon alphabet des villes du Québec* (1944) and *Le Poissons de nos eaux* (1936).

During WWII there were few children' books available from Europe, and publishers a home attempted to fill the gap. The ever-pop ular genres, fairy tale and legend, were repre sented by Achard's *Les Deux Bossus de l'Îl d'Orléans et autres contes* (1944); Marius Barbeau' *Les Contes du grand-père sept-heures* (12 vols, 1950 53: parts tr in *The Golden Phoenix*, 1958) and *Le Rêves des chasseurs* (1942); and the successful tril ogy of fables and poems *Adagio* (1943), *Allegr* (1944) and *Andante* (1944) by Félix Leclerc. Gu Boulizon (who also immigrated from France and Ambroise Lafortune wrote adventure sto ries in which some of the principal character were Boy Scouts. A typical book by Lafortun (himself a Scout leader) is *Le Secret de la rivièr perdue* (1946). Boulizon's *Prisonniers des caverne* (1950) was rewritten and published in 1979 a *Alexandre et les prisonniers des cavernes*. A few othe notable books published during this period wer Claude Aubrey's *La Vengeance des hommes de bonn volonté* (1944), reprinted twice as *Le Loup de Noël* and Andrée Maillet's *Le Marquiset têtu et le mulo réprobateur* (1944) and her picture book *Ristonta* (1945), illustrated by Robert Lapalme.

Public interest in children's books, however was waning. To remedy the situation, autho Beatrice Clément founded the Association de écrivains pour la jeunesse in 1948 to encourag excellence in writing and to arouse support fo French Canadian children's books. The associ ation lasted only 6 years, but it was active ir creating the children's book firm Édition Jeunesse. It was also largely responsible for per suading established firms such as Fides to re new their commitment to publishing children' books. Children's literature had reached a stag where changes were needed to reflect new socia attitudes and to provide children with mor books that responded to their needs and interests. Although books of the past still brought joy and excitement to countless children, stereotypes of whites and native peoples had developed, and as minor writers entered the field, there evolved a sameness of pattern in the themes and their treatment. Eventually, the literature was marked by lack of originality and often by mediocrity in writing style.

Children's books began to achieve new distinction in the late 1950s, with Paule Daveluy's *L'Été enchanté* (1958; tr *Summer in Ville-Marie,* 1962), Yves Thériault's *Alerte au camp 29* (1959), Claudine Vallerand's (pseudonym "Maman Fonfon") *Chante et joue* (1957) and Monique Corriveau's *Le Secret de Vanille* (1959). Corriveau develops atmosphere that becomes an essential component of the story, as in *Les Saisons de la mer* (1975), about an Irish family in Newfoundland in the 1920s. Another interesting writer of this period is Suzanne Martel, whose *Quatre montréalais en l'an 3000* (1963; repr *Surréal 3000,* 1980; tr *The City Underground,* 1982) shows her lively ability to introduce humour into inventive science fiction novels, which include *Nos amis robots* (1981). Claude Aubry's *Agouhanna* (1974), written in a simple, even poetic, manner, has also worn well. Informational books, eg, *Chevalier du roi; vie de saint Ignace de Loyola* (1956) by Beatrice Clément were not as appealing to young readers as were mysteries and adventures.

A slump occurred in children's literature between 1965 and 1970: books were no longer given as school prizes, and French and Belgian imports increased. Although some excellent books were available, they were poorly promoted. Retail trade declined while textbook publishing increased to meet the demands of the newly laicized educational system. Between 1965 and 1968 only about 70 titles appeared, and in 1969 and 1970, fewer than 10 — a mere trifle compared to the 1000 French titles appearing annually overseas. In the 1970s, efforts were made to revitalize children's literature. The founding of Communication-Jeunesse in Québec in 1971 inspired authors, illustrators, publishers, booksellers, librarians and teachers to work together, and the organization became a key factor in the promotion of children's book publishing.

Several newcomers responded to the need for a specifically Québecois children's literature. Bertrand Gauthier produced inventive, droll stories filled with puns, such as *Hébert Luée* (1980) which, critical of contemporary society without being preachy, is illustrated with colourful, often outlandish, pictures by Marie-Louise Gay. Gay also wrote and illustrated a counting book, *De zéro à minuit* (1981). Ginette Anfousse wrote and illustrated a series of books about a little girl and her toy anteater, all translated into English. The first 2, *La Cachette* (tr *Hide and Seek*) and *Mon ami Pichou* (tr *My Friend Pichou*), were published in 1976. Tibo (Gilles Thibault) created the colour pictures for *Le Tour de l'île* (1980) by Félix Leclerc and excellent black-and-white drawings for *Je te laisse une caresse* and *Mon petit lutin s'endort,* 2 small books of verse by André Cailloux (1976). *Une Fenêtre dans ma tête* (2 vols, 1979) by Raymond Plante, which describes a young child's fantasy world, is illustrated with lively drawings by Roger Paré. A charming fantasy story is *Le Voyage à la recherche du temps* (1981) by Lucie Ledoux, illustrated in black and white by Philippe Béha.

In 1974 Fides inaugurated its series "Du Goéland," whose titles include *Le Garçon au cerf-volant* (1974) by Monique Corriveau, illustrated by Louise Méthé; *Le Ru d'Ikoué* (1977) by Yves Thériault, illustrated by Michelle Poirier; *Le Chat de l'Oratoire* (1978) by Bernadette Renaud, illustrated by Josette Michaud; and *Chansons pour un ordinateur* (1980) by Francine Loranger, illustrated by Laurent Bouchard. Les Editions Héritage, which publishes the magazine *Hibou* (an adaptation of the English-language magazine *Owl*), launched several series of children's books, among them "Pour lire avec toi" (1976), designed for young readers in transition between the picture book and the book for the older reader. Fantasy and reality intermingle in 3 books in this series: *Fend-le-vent et le visiteur mystérieux* (1980) by Serge Wilson, illustrated by Claude Poirier; *Emilie, la baignoire à pattes* (1976) by Bernadette Renaud, illustrated by France Bédard; and *Alfred dans le métro* (1980), written and illustrated by Cécile Gagnon. *La Révolte de la courtepointe* (1979), written by Bernadette Renaud and illustrated by Lucie Ledoux, also combines the real and the fantastic. Another Héritage series includes Suzanne Martel's *Pi-Oui* (1974, tr *Peewee*) and *Contes de mon pays* (1980) by Germain Lemieux. The series "Jeunesse-Pop" by Les Éditions Paulines includes Louis Landry's *Glausgab, créateur du monde* (1981) and *Glausgab, le protecteur* (1981), 2 novels that create a new mythological hero, an Algonquian Indian who lands in France in 1489 and tells his story to the French court.

Young francophone readers have been introduced to good texts from English Canada by Les Éditions Pierre Tisseyre. The works include stories about the art of growing up, eg, *Luke Baldwin's Vow* (tr *La Promesse de Luke Baldwin,* 1980) by Morley CALLAGHAN and *You Can Pick Me Up at Peggy's Cove* (tr *Je t'attends à Peggy's Cove,* 1982) by Brian Doyle; about handicapped children, eg, *Listen for the Singing* (tr *Écoute l'oiseau chantera,* 1980) by Jean Little; about animals, eg, *Owls in the Family* (tr *Deux grands ducs dans la famille,* 1980) by Farley MOWAT; and about Russian Mennonites who settle in Manitoba, *Days of Terror* (tr *Jours de terreur,* 1981) by Barbara Smucker.

Some books offer children a chance to discover authors appreciated by their elders, eg, Gilles VIGNEAULT's *Les Quatre Saisons de Piquot* (1979), illustrated by H.J. Barrett, and *Quelques pas dans l'univers d'Eva* (1981), illustrated by Claude Fleury; Roch CARRIER's *Les Voyageurs de l'arc-en-ciel* (1980), illustrated by François Olivier, and *Les Contes du sommet bleu* (1980), written and illustrated by Claude Jasmin. For older readers Suzanne Martel has written several novels with historical settings, such as *Jeanne, fille du roy* (1974), an adventure story with an authentic 17th-century setting. Martel's stories of Les Montcorbier (*L'Apprentissage d'Arahé* and *Premières armes,* both 1979) and of Menfou Carcajou (*Ville-Marie* and *La Baie du Nord,* 1980) are written for adults, although they appeal to some mature young readers. Another book for older readers is the farcical and fanciful, almost surreal, *La Planète guenille* (1980) by Gilles Rivard and Jean Clouâtre. A series by Éditions Ovale is called "Légendes du Québec," although the stories are not necessarily authentic. It includes *La Grange aux lutins* (1980), adapted by Robert Piette and illustrated by Josée Dombrowski; *La Chasse-galerie* (1980), adapted by Madeleine Chénard and illustrated by France Lebon; and *Les Feux follets* (1981), adapted by Johanne Bussières and illustrated by Josée Dombrowski. There are also mysteries set in Montreal's Museum of Fine Arts (*Le Visiteur du soir,* 1980) by Robert Soulières and in a manor house at the start of the colonial period (*L'Épée arhapal,* 1981) by Daniel Sernine.

Fantasy, humour and wordplay have become increasingly prevalent with such works as *Un Jour d'été à Fleurdepeau* (1981), written by Bertrand Gauthier and illustrated by Daniel Sylvestre; *Crapauds et autres animaux* (1981), a book of original verse by Yvan Adam in collaboration with several other authors and illustrators; *Monsieur Genou* (1981) by Raymond Plante, and *Une Journée dans la vie de Craquelin 1er, roi de soupe-au-lait* (1981) by J.M. Poupart.

In other regions of Canada where francophone communities exist, there are efforts to publish French books for children. Les Éditions d'Acadie in New Brunswick publishes picture books, eg, *Caprice à la campagne* (1982) by Melvin Gallant; Les Éditions des Plaines in Manitoba published *Le Petit Dinosaure d'Alberta* (1980) by Nadine MacKenzie; and Les Éditions Prise de Parole in Ontario has published a beautiful modern version of an Ojibwa legend, *Nanna Bijou, le géant endormi* (1981) by Jocelyne Villeneuve (tr *Nanna Bijou: The Sleeping Giant,* 1981). Other Ontario publishers are presenting French translations of Canadian or foreign titles, eg, *The Paper Bag Princess* (1980) by Robert Munsch (tr *La Princesse à la robe de papier,* 1981) and *Harold Greenhouse to the Rescue,* (1982; tr *Jérôme Lafeuille part à la rescousse,* 1982) by Michael Wilkins.

The momentum engendered by Communication-Jeunesse has supported steady growth in the number and quality of children's books, especially picture books, beginning readers and translations. Illustrators are exploring new techniques, and are making more effective use of design and increasingly integrating their pictures with the text. Two major features of beginners' readers are diversity of themes and excellence of texts, eg, in *Le Bal des chenilles* (1979) by Robert Soulières and *Emilie, la baignoire à pattes* (1976) by Bernadette Renaud. By publishing translations, publishers hope to promote better understanding of the principal Canadian cultures and provide a broader scope of material for readers. Apart from those mentioned above, there are excellent translations published by Les Éditions Héritage, eg, Erik Munsterhjelm's animal story *Canilou* (1979) and James HOUSTON's modern Inuit tale *L'Archer blanc* (1978), both beautifully translated by Maryse Côté. Nonfiction and novels with contemporary settings are still very much needed to provide Canadian children with themes close to home. Nevertheless, impressive strides in the development and promotion of French Canadian children's literature have been made, leading to the spread of that literature to many corners of Canada, and even across international borders. IRENE E. AUBREY

Chilkat Blanket, associated with the northern Tlingit, was traded along the Northwest Coast. The blanket was made of mountain goat wool, spun over a core of cedar-bark string. The men hunted the goat, constructed the frame on which the weaving was done and painted the design board from which the women, who did the weaving, took the design. The design often represents an animal (such as a bear), but reordered and modified through complex principles. Representing the high point of weaving in NORTHWEST COAST INDIAN ART, these blankets are almost always black, white, yellow and blue.
RENÉ R. GADACZ

Chilkoot Pass, elev 1067 m, is situated on the BC-Alaska border. It was used by the Chilkat Coast Indians, expert weavers who traded with the Nahani along the Yukon R to the N and later with HBC employees. In 1883 the US government, unknown to Canada, sent an expedition to the Yukon via the pass to study the terrain and the Indian situation. Irritated by this action, the Canadian government sent William Ogilvie via Chilkoot in 1887 to establish the 141st meridian at the Yukon R. During the KLONDIKE GOLD RUSH, an estimated 20 000 to 30 000 people crossed the pass 1897-98. The NWMP established a post here to stop lawlessness and collect duty. Several tramways were built over the pass to Crater Lk 1897-98, but the trams and pass fell into disuse with construction of the railway over WHITE PASS, completed in 1900. A hiking trail, "Trail of 98," over Chilkoot was rebuilt in the 1960s, complete with shelters, as a joint venture by the Yukon government and US National Pk Service. GLEN BOLES

Chilkoot Trail, alternatively known as the Klondike Gold Rush Trail, is one of the most rugged and demanding long-distance trails in

Canada. It extends approximately 53 km from Skagway, on the Alaska Panhandle, over the Coastal Mt range to Bennett, BC. Historically the trail dates to the 1897-98 KLONDIKE GOLD RUSH, when an estimated 30 000 gold seekers and traders fought their way over the tortuous route, braving a wild terrain, high altitudes and frequent severe weather changes. Today the trail has been somewhat improved and restored by US and Canadian park officials and offers designated campsites and other amenities. However, for the some 2000 people yearly who seek its adventure, it still represents a challenging 4-5 day hike. BART DEEG

Chilliwack, Vancouver rock band, began as The Classics (fl 1964-7), and went through an experimental, psychedelic period (1967-70) as The Collectors before adopting the name and bright melodic style that brought international popularity in the late 1970s. Most popular songs include "Lonesome Mary," "Baby Blue," and "Fly at Night." Singer and guitarist Bill Henderson has been the only constant through many personnel changes. MARK MILLER

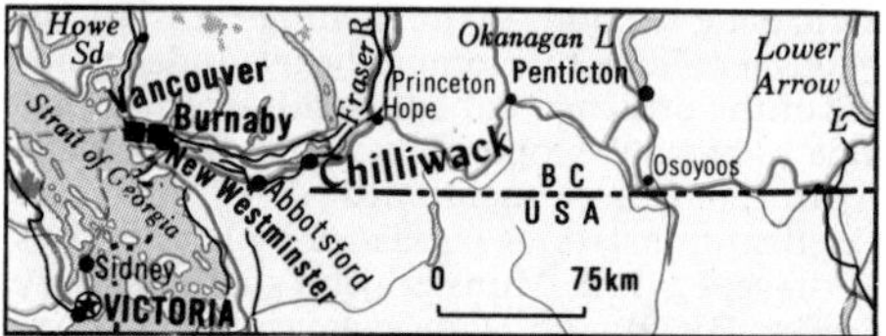

Chilliwack, BC, pop 41 000 (1982e) area 264 km^2, inc as city 1908 and District Municipality 1980, is 100 km E of Vancouver on the S shore of the FRASER R. The name derives from an Indian tribe and likely means "going back up" (ie, home from the Fraser). The district is governed by a mayor and 8 aldermen elected for 2-year terms. Agriculture is the leading resource sector; much of the milk and dairy products consumed in the Lower Mainland originates here. Manufacturing is focused on farm products or inputs and, in the eastern half of the district, on extensive logging. A Canadian Forces base at Vedder Crossing (10 km south) has a large military and civilian payroll. The recreation industry, particularly in the Cultus Lake area to the S, also supports the local economy. Although too far from Vancouver for most commuters, the area's reasonably priced land has prompted considerable residential development. ALAN F.J. ARTIBISE

Chimaera, ratfish, or ghost shark, strange-looking marine FISH belonging to the subclass Holocephali, class Chondrichthyes and thus related to SHARKS and RAYS. There are about 25 species (mostly in the family Chimaeridae), which occur in deep or cool waters of most seas. In Canada, 3 species in 3 genera (*Hydrolagus*, *Harriotta* and *Rhinochimaera*) occur in Atlantic waters and one species (*Hydrolagus colliei*) occurs in Pacific waters. Chimaeras are elongate and scaleless and range from 0.5 to 2.0 m in length. The ventral mouth is overhung by a projecting snout which is sometimes lancelike. At the front of the dorsal fin is a strong spine with a poison gland at its base. The pectoral fins are large and winglike. Males have a clasperlike organ on the front of the head in addition to pelvic claspers. All species deposit eggs, each in an elongate, horny capsule. Chimaeras eat bottom molluscs and crustaceans, crushing them with their strong, grinding teeth. They have no commercial importance. W.B. SCOTT

Unidentified family studio portrait *c*1910, Dong Yee Studio (*courtesy City of Vancouver Archives*).

Chinese immigrants first arrived in Canada from San Francisco in 1858, at the beginning of the Fraser R gold rush in BC. In BARKERVILLE, BC, the first Chinese community in Canada was founded. By 1860 it was estimated that the Chinese population of Vancouver I and BC was about 7000. The first Chinese migrants were young peasants from South China; they were followed, in the 1870s and 1880s, by other young peasants who laboured under appalling conditions to build the CANADIAN PACIFIC RY (*see* IMMIGRANT LABOUR). Chinese communities later spread to other parts of Canada. By 1981, through immigration and natural increase, the Chinese Canadian population was about 300 000.

Origins Both rural poverty and political upheavals have stimulated Chinese emigration. Historically, the majority came from the 4 districts (*sze-yap*) or counties in the Pearl R Delta of Guangdong province, between Canton and Hong Kong. A tradition existed in that locality of seeking opportunity overseas, sending money back to support relatives in China, and eventually returning, if possible.

Migration The major periods of Chinese immigration (from 1858 to 1923 and since 1947) reflected changes in Canadian government IMMIGRATION POLICY. From 1884 Chinese migrants had been obliged to pay an "entry" or "head" tax before being admitted into Canada. By 1900, in response to agitation in BC, the Liberal government increasingly restricted Asian immigration by raising the head tax to $100. After this was greeted with the angry derision of BC politicians, who had demanded it be raised to $500, the government appointed a Royal Commission on Chinese and Japanese Immigration (1902) which concluded that the Asians were "unfit for full citizenship. . . obnoxious to a free community and dangerous to the state." The 1903 session of Parliament passed legislation raising the head tax to $500; the number of Chinese who paid the fee in the first fiscal year dropped from 4719 to 8. Soon afterwards, however, Chinese immigration increased again and on 1 July 1923 (known to the Canadian Chinese as "Humiliation Day") the Chinese Immigration Act was replaced by legislation which virtually suspended Chinese immigration, as it was intended to do. In 1947 the discriminatory legislation was repealed, although restrictions on Chinese immigration were not entirely removed until 1967. Chinese and East Indian Canadians gained the vote federally and provincially in 1947.

Before 1947 Chinese immigration was either arranged by contractors or was individual and voluntary. Typically, and largely as a consequence of the head tax, which made the cost of bringing a wife or aged parents to Canada prohibitive, men came alone and lived as bachelors in Canada. In 1931, out of a total Chinese population of 46 519, only 3648 were women. In the late 1920s it has been estimated that there were only 5 married Chinese women in Calgary and 6 in Edmonton. Since 1947 immigration of families has been the rule. From 1950 onwards, the majority of immigrants have emigrated from Hong Kong (others come from Southeast Asia, South Africa, the West Indies and Peru), often speak English fluently and frequently possess education, financial resources and professional skills. There is some tension between new and old immigrants, but the web of kinship is still strong.

Settlement Patterns Since 1900, Chinese Canadians have chosen to settle in urban areas and are now concentrated in the largest cities. The "Chinatowns" which grew up in the 19th and 20th centuries were originally classical ghettos —overcrowded and squalid— but tended to crumble or change as the migrants experienced some upward social mobility. In Vancouver restrictive covenants prevented the Chinese from buying property outside of the Chinatown area until the 1930s. Until the 1880s almost all Chinese lived in BC, and until the 1940s almost 50% of their population still resided there, but Chinese communities have developed rapidly in other urban centres as well, particularly Toronto; 66% of Chinese Canadians now live in Toronto and Vancouver. Small groups or individual Chinese have also settled in towns across the Prairies, in BC and Ontario and in the Atlantic provinces.

Economic Life When they first arrived in BC the Chinese were involved in various kinds of work. Some were gleaners in the goldfields, often working abandoned claims; others became labourers, cooks, laundrymen, teamsters and merchants, providing auxiliary services to mining communities. In towns and villages many worked as domestic servants. Between 1881 and 1885 more than 15 000 Chinese arrived to work the CPR and during the next 40 years became involved in the rough work of a pioneer industrial economy. Skilled or semiskilled Chinese worked in the BC sawmills and canneries; others became market gardeners or grocers, pedlars, shopkeepers and restaurateurs.

The work of Chinese industrial labourers was often organized on a contract basis. Under the "credit-ticket" system, Chinese lenders in N America or China agreed to pay the travel expenses of a migrant who was then bound to the lender until the debt was repaid, although none of these contracts were legally enforceable in Canada. The other form of contract labour involved Chinese work gangs. At the turn of the century, Chinese cannery bosses were almost invariably hired on a contract basis. They then recruited workers and assumed the financial risk of low production. From the 1880s this practice was employed in railway construction as well.

The Chinese industrial force was characterized by low wages (Chinese workers usually received up to 50% less than white workers for equal work), high levels of transience and a strong work discipline.

The earliest Chinese professionals tended to serve primarily the Chinese community. In BC the Chinese were barred for years from many professions, eg, law, pharmacy and accountancy. The first Chinese Canadian lawyers were called to the bar only in the 1940s, but since then, as discriminatory laws have been repealed and the character of immigration has changed, many more Chinese professionals, serving a mixed clientele, have migrated. Nevertheless, even in the 1980s, Chinese are still heavily involved in service occupations.

Social Life and Community Chinese communities in Canada not only reflected the cultural traditions, particularly the kinship system (based on ancestral descent), the "joss house" or temple and the Chinese theatre, but evolved their own unique N American characteristics as well. For example, it generated its own elite, that of the merchants, and its own "voluntary" associations adapted from models in China to provide personal and community welfare services, social contact, a context for political activity, etc. Typically, rural Chinese who emigrated to Canada had to adapt to urban conditions and these associations helped migrants adjust to a new culture and racial PREJUDICE AND DISCRIMINATION. During the "bachelor" phase, when the men in Chinese communities far outnumbered the women, associations developed to provide services to single men who lived priarily in *fang-k'ou* — formally organized house-olds of Chinese "bachelors" which still exist in e backstreets of Vancouver, Victoria, Toronto ıd Montréal. Certain principles — territory, di-ect, surname — constituted the criteria for embership and recruitment. Older members ho had never married or were too poor to re-rn to China lived in retirement in association ılls.

Bachelor organizations have declined as the ıinese now tend to migrate as families. Associ-ions open to everyone have included, notably, e Kuomintang (KMT) and the Freemasons, aternal-political associations interested in Chi-se and Chinatown politics and community sues. Larger Chinese communities have had, at e apex of their organizational structures, Chi-se Benevolent Associations, which adjudicate sputes with the community and speak for the mmunity to the outside world. None of these ganizations, however, have been effective na-ɔnal voices. More recently, such typically Ca-ıdian organizations as the Lions, Elks and Vet-ans have appeared.

The original Chinese communities were olated from the white culture for several rea-ns. The Chinese tended to see themselves as ojourners," in Canada temporarily to secure me financial security for relatives in China. his mentality was reinforced by legislation Canada that prevented easy immigration of hinese families and that precluded their partic-ation professionally, socially or politically in e dominant society. The white society of BC erceived the Chinese as unassimilable under ıy circumstances, and certain aspects of Chi-ese life in Canada reinforced the racial stereo-pes of the Chinese as a threat to white society. ears of disease, eg, cholera and leprosy, white action to overcrowded living conditions in hinatown, the introduction of opium and con-quently of a drug trade and an obsessive con-rn with Chinese gambling habits, all helped aintain the almost universally held con-iction that the Chinese, as one senator speaking r white residents of BC explained, "are not of ur race and cannot become part of ourselves."

By the 1970s, Chinese society in Canada had een transformed, although traditional, famil-r values are still continued in some respects. or example, the majority of young, working hinese still commit resources to the support of eir parents, and many grandparents live with eir children.

Newspapers are an important form of com-unity expression. Although Chinese-language apers have long been published in Vancouver nd Toronto, they are now in some danger of eing eclipsed by American editions of Hong ong Chinese papers.

Religion and Cultural Life Chinese religion g, ancestor worship) in Canada has commonly een expressed in private but is declining in nportance. The proportion of Christians in the hinese population rose from 10% in 1921 to 0% in 1961. Chinese Christian churches specially the UNITED CHURCH) are an important ɔcal point of family activity and usually the entre of organized social activities for women. he major Chinese festival is the Lunar New ear (February or late January), celebrated in hinatowns with firecrackers and lion and ragon dancers. Other important festive days re "Bright-Clear," a springtime sweeping of raves of ancestors, and "Mid-Autumn," a late ummer occasion for moon watching.

Education Chinese schools date from the 890s. By the 1930s, at their peak, there were 26 f them across the country. They were particu-ırly important during periods in BC when at-empts were made to segregate Chinese children. hinese schools, however, have generally pro-ided supplementary after-school classes in Chi-ese language, history and culture. The Chinese have never been legally prohibited by law from attending universities, even when professional fields were closed to them after graduation. With the growth of family life in the 1950s and the increasing affluence and professional character of the Chinese communities in the 1960s, much larger numbers of Chinese students have sought higher education.

Chinese work gang on the CPR tracks near Summit, BC, 1889. Between 1881 and 1885, more than 15 000 Chinese arrived to work on the CPR (*courtesy Glenbow Archives*).

Politics Until 1950, in Canadian affairs, Chinese depended upon their leaders and other intermediaries who had amiable relations with Canadian politicians, but have since become more active in Canadian politics, particularly for the Liberal Party, probably because of its identification with relaxed immigration regulations. In 1957 Douglas Jung became the first Chinese Canadian MP, and in various places mayors and aldermen of Chinese origin have been elected.

Group Maintenance In large Chinese Canadian communities professionals tend to sponsor cultural exchanges with China, Hong Kong and Taiwan to encourage the linking of cultural maintenance with Chinatown neighborhood preservation, fair presentation of Chinese Canadians in the media and other issues. Canada-based Cantonese opera groups exist and martial arts organizations have flourished. The Hong Kong version of modern Chinese culture is very strongly reflected in Chinese Canadian society.

Language maintenance was essential before 1947, when only jobs in Chinatown, requiring knowledge of Chinese, were open to young Chinese Canadians. More recently, the use of written Chinese is declining. Spoken Chinese ranges from specific, very local dialects to Hong Kong Cantonese.

Chinese New Year, Vancouver. The festival of the Lunar New Year is celebrated with fireworks and lion and dragon dancers (*photo by Gar Lunney/Masterfile*).

From their perspective, the Chinese, with great hardship, completed the CPR, and were then abandoned by those who hired them; only Chinese were forced to pay a humiliating head tax, and only Chinese were excluded from immigration. Chinese Canadian military service for Canada in WWII did help change white attitudes, but traces of nativism against Chinese Canadians still exist, exacerbated by the economic recession and increased immigration.

E.B. WICKBERG

Reading: E.B. Wickberg et al, *From China to Canada* (1982); W. Peter Ward, *White Canada Forever* (1978); Anthony B. Chan, *Gold Mountain* (1983).

Chiniquy, Charles-Paschal-Télesphore, Roman Catholic priest turned Presbyterian minister (b at Kamouraska, LC 30 July 1809; d at Montréal 16 Jan 1899). He travelled throughout Lower Canada 1839-51, preaching temperance, and his fame was such that he was called "Father Matthew of Lower Canada." But he was so arrogant and undisciplined that in 1851 Mgr Ignace BOURGET asked him to leave the diocese. He settled in the parish Ste-Anne-de-Kankakee (Ill) where, in 1856, he was excommunicated by the bishop of Chicago for a grave infraction of ecclesiastical discipline. He then began a new career there, first as founder of the Catholic Christian Church and then as a Presbyterian minister. When he ran into difficulties with the Presbytery of Chicago, he applied in 1863 for admission with his Ste-Anne's congregation to the Synod of the Canada Presbyterian Church and was accepted. The bishops of Québec waged unrelenting war on him, worried by his oratorical talents and endless, outrageous attacks on the Catholic Church. Protestants, for the same reasons, welcomed him enthusiastically. He died after a ministry that had taken him throughout the US, to Europe, Australia and New Zealand. Almost a century later, his career is still highly controversial.

YVES ROBY

Chinook, warm, dry, gusty, westerly WIND experienced in a shallow belt extending some 300-400 km E from the eastern slopes of the Rocky Mts. The wind was named after the Chinook tribe which occupied the mouth of the Columbia R in Oregon, the territory from which the wind seemed to originate. In Canada the highest frequency of chinooks occurs in southern Alberta. Pincher Creek and Calgary receive

Chinook arch, southern Alberta. In winter chinooks, which can raise temperatures by over 25°C in one hour, occur when a cold arctic air mass is replaced at ground level by warm Pacific air (*Elliott and Nicole Bernshaw / Bernshaw Photography*).

an average of 30-35 chinook days each winter. Chinooks occur in summer but are not always noticeable. They can raise air temperature by over 25°C in one hour. In winter they occur when a cold arctic air mass is replaced at ground level by warm Pacific air. When moist Pacific air is lifted over the Rockies, heat is added to it as the water vapour it carries condenses (thereby giving up latent heat) and falls as precipitation. The air then arrives on the eastern slopes as a warm, dry wind (foehn-type wind). The chinook is further warmed by subsidence of the Pacific air down the eastern slopes of the Rockies; descending air is subject to warming at the rate of 1°C per 100 m of height. L.C. NKEMDIRIM

Chipewyan is a term of Cree derivation, meaning "pointed skins," but Chipewyan call themselves DENE or "people." They originally occupied the northern fringe of the boreal forest and adjacent tundra from the Seal R to near the mouth of the Coppermine R. By the 19th century their lands included northern portions of Manitoba, Saskatchewan, Alberta and the southern part of the NWT. The Chipewyan are the most numerous and most widely distributed of the northern Athapaskans. In 1749 the population was estimated at approximately 4000 individuals. Epidemics of European diseases decimated the population, but it has since recovered and in 1970 about 5000 persons were enrolled in Chipewyan bands.

Chipewyan women's costume (*courtesy Provincial Museum of Alberta*).

Chipewyan is a branch of the northeastern Athapaskan language family, closely related to neighbouring DOGRIB and SLAVEY. The CREE, their southern neighbours, are known as *ena*, or "enemy," although peaceful relations were established between 1716 and 1760. The INUIT are known as *hotêl ena*, or "enemies of the flat area," but peace was general by the early 19th century. The YELLOWKNIFE, the northwesternmost group of Chipewyan, were devastated by disease and warfare in the early 19th century. Chipewyan socio-territorial organization was based on hunting the migratory and nomadic herds of Barren Ground caribou. Hunting groups consisted of 2 or more related nuclear families, which joined with other such groups to form larger local and regional bands, coalescing or dispersing with the herds. Leaders had limited authority, which was based upon their ability, wisdom and generosity. Spiritual power was received in dream visions; some men had great powers for curing and some for doing harm.

In 1717 the HUDSON'S BAY CO founded Ft Churchill for the Chipewyan FUR TRADE. In the late 18th century the HBC and NORTH WEST CO established competitive posts in the western hinterland of Hudson Bay and, following the great smallpox epidemic of 1781-82, many Chipewyan began to hunt in the full boreal forest, where fur-bearing animals were more abundant. A few individuals are remembered for their aid to white explorers in the North. Thanadelther, also known as Slave Woman, guided the first English explorer from Cree country into Chipewyan territory in 1715-16. MATONABBEE guided Samuel HEARNE from Churchill to the Coppermine R 1770-72.

In the 1960s the Chipewyan way of life was threatened by a number of government policies that were meant to improve housing, education and health services. In order to receive these services, and the cash payments for family allowance and old-age pensions, many Chipewyan relocated to permanent settlements. The influence of a cash economy and the disruption of social and subsistence patterns often had harmful effects. Many have returned to a traditional relationship with the caribou and their lands. *See also* NATIVE PEOPLES, SUBARCTIC and general articles under NATIVE PEOPLE.

JAMES G.E. SMITH

Reading: J. Helm, ed, *Handbook of North American Indians*, vol 6: *Subarctic* (1981).

Chipman, Ward, lawyer, public servant, politician (b at Marblehead, Mass 30 July 1754; d at Fredericton 9 Feb 1824). A graduate of Harvard College (1770) who assisted the LOYALIST forces during the American Revolution, he helped organize the agitation which led to the creation of NB in 1784. He became the colony's solicitor general, drafted the charter for the city of Saint John, and as clerk of the Crown acted as crown prosecutor in most criminal cases for some 25 years. His law office was a Mecca for students. Chipman's arguments in defence of a black slave in 1800 effectively led to the abolition of slavery in NB. An MLA 1785-95, he was appointed to the Council in 1806 and became a judge of the Supreme Court in 1809. As British agent to 2 commissions established to determine the boundary with Maine, he successfully upheld NB's claim to much of the disputed territory. Before his death he briefly administered the government of the colony. He was arguably the most influential of NB's founding fathers.

P.A. BUCKNER

Chipmunk, diminutive member of the SQUIRREL family belonging to genus *Tamias* or *Eutamias*. *Tamias* is restricted to eastern N America. A single species, eastern chipmunk (*T. striatus*), occurs in the Maritimes and southern Qué, O and Man. *Eutamias* species occur in N Ameri and Eurasia. Four are found in Canada, fro Ont to parts of BC, southern YT and southe NWT: least, yellow pine, Townsend's and re tailed chipmunks (*E. minimus, E. amoenus, townsendii, E. ruficaudus*, respectively). Easte chipmunks weigh about 100 g; *Eutamias* speci are smaller — ranging from 35 g for least chi munk to 85 g for Townsend's chipmunk. Ale sprightly animals, chipmunks run with ta erect. All have 5 dark stripes down the bac eastern chipmunks also have 2 lateral stripes o each side ending at the rump. Chipmunks hibe nate in subterranean nests, feeding on store foodstuffs during frequent arousals. Most *E tamias* species bear one litter (5-6 young) eac summer; eastern chipmunks, 2 (3-4 young Chipmunks are omnivorous, eating seeds, nu invertebrates and occasionally small eggs. The are too scarce to be economically significant bu being diurnal, attractive and almost constant busy, they afford pleasure to all who watc them.

W.A. FULL

Chiriaeff, Ludmilla, née Otzoup-Gorn dancer, choreographer, teacher, director (b Riga, Latvia 10 Jan 1924). As founding direct of Les GRANDS BALLETS CANADIENS, she has helpe establish BALLET in Québec. She trained in Berli and studied ballet with many distinguishe teachers. Choreographer Michael Fokine was family friend and powerful influence on her a tistic development. After WWII, having settle in Switzerland, she danced and choreographe for various companies and directed her ow Ballets des Arts in Geneva 1949-51.

Chiriaeff immigrated to Canada in 1952. Sh opened a school in Montréal and began to ch reograph for the nascent French TV service i Québec. Her new company, the Ballet Chiriaef in which she continued to dance, evolved int Les Grands Ballets Canadiens, of which she r mained artistic director until 1975. She has sinc devoted herself to the company's school Among the many ballets choreographed by Chi riaeff are *Suite Canadienne* (1957), *Cendrillon* (196 and *Pierrot de la lune* (1963).

MICHAEL CRA

Chiropractic is the manipulation of the spina column as a means of curing disease. The wor comes from the Greek *chiro* ("hands") and *pract* ("to practice"). The theory of chiropractic origi nated with D.D. Palmer, who was born in Po Perry (Ont) in 1845. Palmer became a charis matic healer in Iowa and accidentally dis covered chiropractic by adjusting a bump on th neck of his stone-deaf janitor. The janitor's hea ing was restored immediately. Palmer began t look to the spine for solving further healt problems and began to teach his theories an practices. The Palmer College of Chiropract was established and promoted by Palmer's so B.J. Palmer, who continued to research and de velop the new healing art.

Chiropractors employ neither drugs no surgery; they base their treatment on the as sumption that good health requires a proper functioning nervous system, beginning wit the brain and including the spinal cord. Chiro practors believe that, because no part of the bod escapes the dominance of the nervous system spinal biomechanical dysfunction (ie, imprope joint function at a specific point or points in th spinal column) may therefore result in poo health generally — even in areas of the bod that have no obvious connection with the spine The lightest pressure by a vertebra may interrup regular transmission of nerve impulses, pre venting that portion of the body from respond ing fully. A chiropractic spinal adjustment, th application of a precise force to the specific pa of the spinal segment, is thought to correct a ver tebral problem, permitting normal nerve trans mission and recuperative capabilities. Medica ɔctors reject the theory but accept that spinal ljustment treatments are beneficial for some atients.

The Canadian Memorial Chiropractic College ı Toronto offers a 4-year academic program ʼith a prerequisite of 2 years of university eduıtion in a science field with a background in ıemistry and physics. M.L. WHITE

ʼading: B. Inglis, *Fringe Medicine* (1964).

hisholm, George Brock, psychiatrist, medical lministrator (b at Oakville, Ont 18 May 1896; at Victoria 2 Feb 1971). Chisholm enlisted as a rivate in WWI, was commissioned in the field, ʼounded and twice decorated. After the war he ıse to senior ranks in the militia. He graduated ı medicine from U of T in 1924 and after some ears of general practice studied PSYCHIATRY in ıe US and England, practising in Toronto from 934 to 1940. During WWII he became director personnel selection and then director general medical services for the Canadian Army. At ıe end of the war he was appointed federal eputy minister of health and was active in ıany national and international health comıissions. In 1948 he was appointed first director eneral of the World Health Organization, a poıtion he held until 1953.

He received many awards and honours and so his share of criticism for his attacks on suerstitions, myths and methods of indoctriating children. His attack on teaching children believe in Santa Claus received national comıent. Nevertheless, he remained tolerant, wise, alistic and logically persuasive. He was one of ıe first to emphasize the danger of POLLUTION, ʼerpopulation and the nuclear arms race. His ublished works range from pamphlets on ʼmy morale to books on world survival, and ıs last publication (1958) was prophetically tied *Can People Learn to Learn?* J.D.M. GRIFFIN

hitty, Dennis Hubert, zoologist (b at Bristol, ng 18 Sept 1912). Educated at U of T and Oxırd, he studied rodent populations as a research ficer at the Bureau of Animal Population, Oxırd, 1935-61. His pioneering studies on popuıtion fluctuations in small rodents and snowıoe hares culminated in the Chitty Hypothesis population regulation that population owth is stopped by behavioural interactions at lead to the genetic selection of highly agessive animals. Moving, as professor, to UBC ı 1961, Chitty taught ecology and the history ıd philosophy of biology. He was elected to the oyal Soc of Canada in 1969, and he retired om active teaching in 1978 to devote his time ecological research on rodent populations. CHARLES J. KREBS

hokecherry, *see* BERRIES, WILD.

holera, *see* EPIDEMIC.

ıoral Music is performed by groups of sings, called a choir or chorus, in which there is ore than one voice to a part. A group with ıly one voice to a part is called an ensemble. A ıorus, or choir, may consist of all female sings, all male singers, or in a mixed choir a comıation of the two. The voice parts in a mixed ıorus are usually soprano, alto, tenor and bass. ıere is choral music for 8-part (or more) mixed ıoirs where the sections are subdivided into rst and second soprano, first and second alto, rst and second tenor, baritone and bass. The ices with the higher tessitura are designated the term "first." Sometimes a descant (an orımental line usually higher than the soprano) added, most often to the harmony to enhance e sound but not to cover the voices. Choral usic is commonly written on an open score ith one of the staves for each voice part. Choral usic may be written to be performed *a cappella* ıaccompanied) or it may be accompanied by ano, organ, instrumental ensembles of varying combinations or orchestra. The chorus or choir is often combined with solo singers as in operas or oratorios. Choral compositions exist in various styles and forms, often indicated by the term applied to them, such as anthem, hymn, chorale, psalm, motet, cantata, madrigal, mass, passion, requiem, oratorio or all manner of settings of secular texts. The performance of choral music requires that the director develop a unified sound from the singers. This is dependent on correctly produced tone, uniform in quality; good intonation which is dependent on correct tone production; and blend and balance, in turn dependent on intonation and on the number of singers in each voice part.

The first example of choral music known to have been written or arranged in Canada was "Great God Neptune" in the masque *The Theatre of Neptune,* by Marc LESCARBOT, performed at Port-Royal (14 Nov 1606). Extant original writing or arranging of choral music by Canadian composers, in the 250 years following the Lescarbot composition, was published in church music collections, eg, J.P. Clarke's 6 hymn-tunes and 2 anthems in his *Canadian Church Psalmody* (1845). He also composed an 8-part anthem, "Arise, O Lord God, Forget Not the Poor" (1846). J.C. Brauneis wrote a "Mass" (1835), for choir, violin, flute, bass viol, bassoon and organ. Born in Québec City, Brauneis was perhaps the first Canadian to receive additional music education outside Canada. Antoine DESSANE, who came to Canada from France (1849), composed a wealth of church music. Two other composers of the late 19th century were Joseph-Julien Perrault and Jean-Baptiste Labelle. In the first half of the 20th century, Canadian-born composers were among those writing choral music still directed to church performance. Noted for specific choral compositions are Guillaume COUTURE — the oratoria *Jean le Precurseur* (1909) and a setting of the *Requiem Mass*—and William Reed and A.S. VOGT who wrote a number of short choral selections (*see also* RELIGIOUS MUSIC).

Contributions to choral composition by English composers living in Canada were made by Charles A.E. HARRISS, *Daniel before the King* (1890), *Festival Mass* (1901), *A Coronation Mass* (1902); Percival Illsley, a cantata, *Ruth* (1894); Albert Ham, cantatas, *The Solitude of the Passion* (1917) and *Advent Cantata;* and Edward Broome. W.H. Anderson came to Winnipeg (1910) and Alfred Whitehead came to NS (1912), later moving to Montréal. Both were prolific composers of sacred and secular music. Healey WILLAN, a well-established composer when he came to Canada (1913), left a legacy of outstanding choral music and was a strong influence on other composers. Claude CHAMPAGNE of Québec left the same type of influence on the young composers in his province, although he wrote few choral compositions.

By the middle of the 20th century, Canadian composers of choral music were composing for high school and elementary school choruses, secular choruses, as well as church choirs, and a wide variety of choral societies. Catalogues of Canadian choral music, available through the CANADIAN MUSIC CENTRE, list published compositions as well as those available on loan from the CMC libraries. The composers listed in the catalogue who have written major choral works include Jean PAPINEAU-COUTURE, Pierre MERCURE, Roger Matton, Jacques HETU, Claude Vivier, Otto Joachim, Kelsey Jones, Godfrey RIDOUT, Robert FLEMING, Ben Steinberg, Keith Bissell, John BECKWITH, Harry SOMERS, Harry FREEDMAN, Talivaldis Kenins, Oskar MORAWETZ, R. Murray SCHAFER, Clifford Ford, Violet ARCHER, Jean Coulthard and Bernard Naylor. Choral composition, smaller in scope but of equally fine calibre, has been written by Hugh BANCROFT, Milton Barnes, Leslie Bell, Lorne Betts, Wolfgang Bottenberg, Alexander BROTT, Barrie Cabena, F.C. Clarke, Lionel Daunais, Richard Eaton, William France, James Gayfer, Graham George, Irving Glick, Frank Haworth, Derek Healey, Harry Hill, Derek Holman, Richard Johnston, Lothar Klein, Alfred Kunz, Quentin MacLean, Sir Ernest MACMILLAN, Michael Miller, David Ouchterlony, Welford Russell, Robert Turner and Charles Wilson.

It was in churches that choirs were organized and developed. Choirs often sponsored oratorio performances and sometimes concerts of both sacred and secular music. Various kinds of choral societies were formed by the middle of the 19th century. This growing interest in choral music was coupled with an excellence in performance which reached a high standard by the beginning of WWI. This same interest, vigour and excellence was not to resume until early in the 1970s, with a few exceptions such as the TORONTO MENDELSSOHN CHOIR, the FESTIVAL SINGERS and the Bach Choir of Montreal. In the 2 decades beginning in 1950, voluntary church choirs were no longer the main source of choral music. Many schools added choral music to the curriculum, and elementary and secondary schools and university music departments began to develop excellent choral groups. There is a great diversity in the groups that are spread across Canada. Examples are the Toronto Mendelssohn Choir, the Montagnards in Montréal, the Arion Male Voice Choir of Victoria, the Mennonite Children's Choir of Winnipeg, the Armdale Chorus of Halifax, the Montreal Bach Choir; the Elgar Choir of BC, the Tudor Singers of Montreal, the Vancouver Chamber Choir and Pro Coro Canada in Edmonton. The CBC has provided opportunity for choirs to sing in radio competitions as well as on its network programs. By the late 1970s provincial choral federations were being formed culminating in the foundation of the Assn of Canadian Choral Conductors in 1980. ISABELLE MILLS

Reading: Helmut Kallmann, *A History of Music in Canada 1534-1914* (1960).

Choreography The term formerly meant the writing down of dance [Gk *choreia,* "dance"; *graphein,* "to write"], but it now refers to the art of composing dance, and dance notation refers to the writing down of steps. Most dances are created in a workshop through experimentation, as the choreographer invents new combinations of movement to evoke the image he or she is seeking. Dance can complement music, work in opposition to music, or be unaccompanied by music. Dances are inspired from all aspects of life. Black storm clouds inspired Judy Jarvis, of Toronto, to choreograph *Clouds.* Pioneer life in western Canada inspired Lambros Lambrou, Edmonton, to create *Home.* Henry James's novella *Washington Square* inspired James Kudelka, Toronto, to establish, through movement, the characters' relationships. There are 2 national choreography awards in Canada. The Jean A. Chalmers Award in Choreography is administered by the Ontario Arts Council, and the Clifford E. Lee Choreography Award is cosponsored by the Edmonton-based Clifford E. Lee Foundation and the BANFF CENTRE SCHOOL OF FINE ARTS. SUSAN PEDWELL

Chotem, Neil, pianist, composer, conductor, teacher (b at Saskatoon 9 Sept 1920). After the start of a promising career as a piano soloist was interrupted by WWII, Chotem forged a new career in Montréal as performer, conductor and composer. During appearances as soloist and guest conductor in concert hall and recording studio, he often supported fellow Canadian composers, notably in the CBC broadcast "Music from Montréal" (1955-60). Many of Chotem's own compositions are radio and TV scores. His style is conservative yet eclectic, exploring art and popular music, as well as jazz. Since the 1960s he has worked with many Canadian performing artists, including Maureen FORRESTER and Renée CLAUDE. Some of his most acclaimed work has been recorded with the pop group Harmonium (*L'Heptade*). He has taught at McGill and U de M. ANN SCHAU

Chown, Samuel Dwight, Methodist minister (b at Kingston, Canada W 11 Apr 1853; d at Toronto 30 Jan 1933). He was ordained 1879 and served several churches before his appointment 1902 as secretary of the newly created Dept of Temperance and Moral Reform, where he fought for social and political reform. In 1910 he was elected general superintendent of the Methodist Church and led that body into the UNITED CHURCH OF CANADA in 1925. His WWI experiences as chaplain led him to condemn war and actively support the League of Nations. Considered Canada's leading churchman, he continued work for world peace and social improvement after his retirement in 1926. Mount Chown in BC commemorates his contribution to Canada's social development. NEIL SEMPLE

Reading: S.D. Chown, *The Story of Church Union in Canada* (1930).

Chrétien, Joseph-Jacques-Jean, politician (b at Shawinigan, Qué 11 Jan 1934). Educated at Laval, Jean Chrétien practised law 1958-63, and won election to the House of Commons as a Liberal in 1963. He served in PM PEARSON's Cabinet as minister of state and then minister of national revenue; in 1968 he supported Mitchell SHARP for the party leadership. Under PM TRUDEAU, he occupied the portfolios of Indian affairs; treasury board; industry, trade and commerce; finance (the first French Canadian to do so); justice; and energy, mines and resources. A strong and emotional speaker, Chrétien enjoyed considerable popularity both inside and outside Québec. As minister of justice, 1980-82, he directed the federalist forces in the QUÉBEC REFERENDUM of May 1980 and then helped devise and implement the federal government's strategy for the patriation of the CONSTITUTION and the enactment of a charter of rights and freedoms. Using a folksy style in English and French, he was able to create an identification with his audiences. His forceful and engaging speaking style, strong identification with his audiences and skills as a political organizer were amply demonstrated when he ran second to John TURNER in the Liberal leadership campaign in 1984. ROBERT BOTHWELL

Chrétien, Michel, physician, researcher, professor (b at Shawinigan, Qué 26 Mar 1936), brother of Jean CHRÉTIEN. Educated at Montréal, Boston and Berkeley, Chrétien is internationally recognized for his contribution to neuroendocrinology. In 1967 he was the first to propose that pituitary hormones were synthesized from larger precursors. Since then, he has concentrated his research efforts on this hypothesis, which he has proved to be of general application. His work has won him several awards including an honorary PhD from U of Liége (Belgium). Chrétien has spent all his professional career with the Clinical Research Inst of Montréal, of which he became the scientific director in 1984. He is a member of numerous scientific societies and a strong advocate for increased basic medical research in Canada. PHILIPPE CRINE

Christ Church Cathedral, Fredericton, was built 1846-53 to the neo-Gothic plans of British architects Frank Wills and William Butterfield, in collaboration with John Medley, First Anglican bishop of Fredericton. In its cruciform plan, central tower, 3-sided porch and huge west window, it was the first Canadian building to follow closely the ideal of the Ecclesiological Society, a reformist movement of the Anglican Church which sought a return to the architecture of the Middle Ages. The cathedral is distinguished by its nave and side aisles oriented to the choir. Each part of the interior is visible from the exterior and has different roofing. NATHALIE CLERK

Christ Church Cathedral, Fredericton, NB, one of Canada's most impressive churches. It was built 1846-53 according to the ideals of a reformist group in the Anglican Church seeking a return to the architecture of the Middle Ages (*courtesy Parks Canada, Heritage Recording Service*).

Christadelphians, Protestant movement fd 1844 by John Thomas in Richmond, Va. It grew out of the Campbellite movement (originally associated with the CHRISTIAN CHURCH), but its adherents are nontrinitarian, deny the immortal soul doctrine and do not believe in a personal devil. Organization is congregational but there are 2 fellowships: that of the amended, who claim that only those dying in Christ will be resurrected, and that of the unamended, who hold for a universal resurrection. Small *ecclesias* (congregations) of both groups exist throughout Canada. M. JAMES PENTON

Christian Church (Disciples of Christ) in Canada, one of 35 regions of that denomination in N America. The Canadian region, which now has 38 churches and some 5000 members, is unique in that it functions as a national church and has full denominational status at national and international levels, eg, in the World Council of Churches, and in the CANADIAN COUNCIL OF CHURCHES, of which it was a charter member.

The Christian Church, fd 1804 in the US, joined with the Disciples of Christ in 1832. The first Canadian congregation was formed in 1810 near Charlottetown, PEI. Since restructuring, which culminated with publication of the Design in 1978, overall life of the church has been governed by the biennial General Assembly, whose decisions are referred to congregations and other church units for implementation. During non-Assembly years every region has its own convention. Local congregations, autonomously governed by elected boards, appoint voting members for the General Assembly and regional conventions.

Disciples hold nonsectarian views, working to unite all Christians under the restored authority of the New Testament. They are actively involved in social issues and cultural life, nationally and internationally. This participation, like the Disciples' sacramental life, which consists of believers' immersion baptism and weekly celebration of the Lord's Supper, is a response of obedience to the teachings, life and ministry, death and resurrection of Jesus. The Disciples distinguish between clergy and laypersons on functional rather than sacramental ground Congregations are led by elders and deaco who are neither ordained nor appointed for li Lay elders, many of them women, often ta charge of a Lord's Supper celebration. Regio ordain clergy to the ministry of the who church and clergy are granted credentials by t regions. RUSSEL D. LEG

Christian Island, 41 km², situated in the corner of GEORGIAN BAY, at the entrance to Nott wasaga Bay, is 5 km W of the Ontario mainlar (20 km W of MIDLAND, Ont). The entire island an Ojibwa reserve and was originally called Joseph's I. It was renamed by Jesuit mi sionaries who fled there from the mission s MARIE AMONG THE HURONS (5 km SE of Midlan after it was burned to prevent it from fallir into the hands of the Iroquois (1649). Fort S Marie II was built (1649-50) as a tempora refuge until the Jesuits abandoned HURON A plaque marks the site of the second missio Today the island is an attractive summer reso and the handicrafts made by the Ojibwa wome — from sweet grass, birch bark and porcupi quills — have become popular with tourists. DAVID EVA

Christian Religious Communities are grou of religious (ie, men or women who have ch sen to devote their lives to the work of their re pective churches). In Canada, although son religious are within the various communions the ORTHODOX CHURCH, more are Anglican and far the greatest number are Roman Catholic.

Roman Catholic

Religious communities in the Roman Cath lic Church are associations of men or wome approved by ecclesiastical authority as livi out the love of God in a common life marked vows or promises of poverty, chastity and ob dience, according to the particular charism their founder as specified in constitutional do uments. According to their state of life, comm nities may be *clerical*, made up of priests and a pirants to the priesthood; or *lay*, whether of me or women. According to the force of their vow communities may be *orders*, with solemn vow whether of monks or nuns, canons or cano esses regular, of mendicants or of regular cleric *congregations*, with simple vows, to which div sion belong practically all modern foundatio except the *secular institutes*, whose members nc mally take private vows or promises and do n live in community; or *societies of common life*, us ally of priests sharing a common work witho special vows. According to their purpose, th may be *active*, taking on various types of cha itable work; or *contemplative*, given primarily prayer. With respect to ecclesiastical authorit they may be either *of pontifical right*, if the con munity has been approved by the Holy See, or *diocesan right*, if approval has come only fro the bishop of a diocese. All of these varieties a found in Canada.

NEW FRANCE was the place to which the fi religious communities came. Two French Ben dictine priests probably came with Jacques CA TIER on his second voyage (1535-36). The Récc lets began missionary work with the Indians 1615, at the invitation of Samuel de CHAMPLA and in 1625 were joined by the Jesuits; but 1629, with the capture of the colony by t KIRKE brothers, both communities were con pelled to leave. In 1633, after the colony h been returned to France, only the Jesuits we permitted to resume their work. The Jesuit mi sionaries' work among the Huron (*see* HURONIA culminating in the Jesuit martyrdom of t 1640s, was reported in the JESUIT RELATIONS a certainly became the best-known aspect of t colony. In 1657 the Sulpicians, a community priests established in 1642 for the education the diocesan clergy, came to Montréal.

By that time, religious communities of women had also been established. In 1639 two cloistered orders came to Québec: the Augustines de la miséricorde de Jésus, a community from Dieppe, arrived to found the first HÔTEL-DIEU, or hospital; they had just recently adopted the Rule of St Augustine and the cloistered life of canonesses. The Ursulines, led by MARIE DE L'INCARNATION, came on the same ship to open a school for French and Indian girls. The Congrégation des hospitalières de Saint-Joseph was founded that year in France by Jérôme Royer de La Dauversière specifically to establish a hospital in Montréal, but it was unable to come until 1659 to take over the work begun by Jeanne MANCE. In 1658 Marguerite BOURGEOYS, who had come to Montréal 5 years before, gathered the first members of the Congrégation de Notre Dame to begin their work of education. In the 1690s foundations were established by the Augustines for the care of the sick poor in Québec and by the Ursulines for both teaching and care of the sick in Trois-Rivières. In 1737 Marguerite d'YOUVILLE founded the Grey Nuns to assume charge of the General Hospital of Montréal from the Frères Charon, a community of brothers founded for this work in 1694 but in the process of dissolution by 1737.

When the British conquered New France in 1760, there were 3 clerical communities there: Jesuits, Récollets (who had returned in 1670) and Sulpicians, for a total of 79 priests. There were also 7 communities of women, totalling 204 sisters. The British refused to allow the Jesuits and the Récollets to receive new members, but the Sulpicians, who could present themselves as diocesan clergy, were able to carry on. The women's communities, regarded by the British as less dangerous and as offering valuable social services, were allowed to continue. By 1837, although no new foundations had been made, there were over 300 professed sisters.

Meanwhile the structures of the church had been expanding, a process in which religious priests played some part. Capuchins were active in and around Halifax from 1785 to 1827 and a Trappist missionary in Nova Scotia founded a priory at Tracadie in 1815. But it was the establishment of the diocese of Montréal in 1836 that brought a dramatic change.

In 1837 Bishop Lartigue of Montréal invited the Brothers of the Christian Schools (Christian Brothers) to open a school, and by 1850 there were 107 brothers from Québec joined with 17 from France. When Bishop Ignace BOURGET succeeded Lartigue in 1840, developments came even more quickly. In 1841, on a visit to Europe, Bourget approached several French communities. The Oblates of Mary Immaculate, founded in 1816 by Eugène de Mazenod, were looking for a mission outside France. They came to Montréal in 1841 and soon moved on; they were in Ottawa and on James Bay by 1844, and in the following year they went to Red River [Winnipeg] to begin their work in the West. Their Canadian recruitment was slower than that of the Christian Brothers, but between 1841 and 1876 some 151 Oblates came to Canada from France. In 1842 the Jesuits, also at Bourget's invitation, sent 6 priests and 3 lay brothers to Montréal. The Viatorians (fd 1831 by Louis Querbes) hesitated, but in 1847 they sent 5 priests to open a college, school and novitiate in Joliette. Also in 1847 the Congregation of the Holy Cross, under its founder Basile Moreau, sent out a priest, 7 brothers and 4 sisters. For them, as for the Jesuits, this was part of a larger move to the US. Elsewhere, in 1850 Armand de Charbonnel, second bishop of Toronto, brought in the Basilian Fathers (fd 1822 in France).

If the influx of new communities of men in this period was remarkable, still more so was the founding of women's communities. Here too, the influence of Bishop Bourget was strong. In 1844 he approved Émilie Gamelin's founding the Sisters of Providence to care for the poor, and the establishment of the Sisters of the Holy Names of Jesus and Mary by Eulalie Durocher and her companions for the work of teaching. In 1848, to care for unwed mothers and their children, he called on Rosalie Jetté to found the Soeurs de miséricorde. In 1850 he approved the Sisters of Saint Anne, whose task, according to the inspiration of their foundress Marie-Esther Blondin, was to work in the public schools of the countryside. Elsewhere there were similar developments. In English-speaking Canada small contingents of sisters were brought from the US to found new communities. Thus the Sisters of Charity came to Halifax in 1849, the Sisters of Saint Joseph to Toronto in 1851 and to Hamilton in 1852, and the Ursulines to Chatham in the diocese of London in 1860. The Sisters of Providence were established in Kingston in 1861 as an independent foundation from the community of Montréal.

Even in these beginnings a striking difference can be seen in the development of men's and women's communities in Canada. Of some 118 men's communities which have had a presence in Canada, only 10 were founded here and only 4 of these still exist. These 4 are all societies of the common life, devoted mainly to missionary work, and they make up only 4% of the number of Canadian male religious today. On the other hand, of the 229 women's communities that have had a presence in Canada, some 75 were founded in this country, and of these only 6 no longer exist. Of the women in religious communities in Canada today over 70% belong to communities founded here.

The work of religious in education at every level, in care for the sick, the poor, orphans and aged, has been of great importance. Everywhere their schools and hospitals have been among the earliest institutions established. They went to the West and North as missionaries to the Indians and Inuit and, from the early 20th century, to missions overseas as well.

Increased government activity in education, health and welfare has greatly affected the work of religious. In Québec especially, the QUIET REVOLUTION of the 1960s led to the withdrawal of many responsibilities from their hands. The Second Vatican Council brought a profound process of internal renewal in almost all communities, but along with this has gone a crisis of withdrawals by individual members and a drop in vocations (joining by new members). In 1983 the 46 675 Roman Catholic religious in Canada included 5001 priests and seminarians, 4040 brothers and 37 634 sisters. Two-thirds (including 80% of the brothers) are in Québec. These figures show a reduction of 40% since 1967, when there were 78 269 religious in the country. There are fewer now, and they are older. By 1983 half the women religious in Canada were over 65. In men's communities, only 6.4% of professed members were under 35, a proportion which points to problems in the future; women's communities, with only 1.7% under 35, face more immediate problems.

Despite such changes, however, the work of religious remains significant. In 1983 some 8912 were active in education, 3105 in hospitals and 1796 in social work. There were 3042 sisters among the 5908 religious in parochial and diocesan functions, reflecting a recent movement of sisters into this field. Contemplative communities had 870 members, whose principal activity was prayer. The 3473 Canadian religious on missions in Latin America (1409), Africa (1290), Asia (636) and Oceania (138) are not included in the figures for religious in Canada, but their work is an important aspect of the life and work of their communities. *See* CATHOLICISM; CHRISTIANITY; RELIGION; STE MARIE AMONG THE HURONS; SOCIAL SECURITY.

JAMES HANRAHAN

Anglican

Anglican religious orders provide an ordered life of prayer, study and community service, and generally advance the purposes of the whole church. Communities were reestablished in the Church of England during the "catholic revival" sparked by the Oxford Movement in 1833. Monks and nuns live in communities. The basis of their life is the recitation of the daily offices (prayers), and mass. Activities outside the monastic environment range from teaching and the care of the sick to community social work and involvement in conferences.

There are 3 orders for women. The Sisterhood of St John the Divine (SSJD), founded in 1884 by Sister Hannah, is of entirely Canadian origin; in 1984 it had 52 members. The Community of the Sisters of the Church (CSC) was established in England in 1890. It has 15 sisters. The Society of St Margaret (SSM; 3 members), which has American roots, has been working in the diocese of Montréal since 1881.

The 2 communities for men which have been active in Canada are the Order of the Holy Cross (OHC), centered in Toronto, and the Society of St John the Evangelist (SSJE). OHC's 5 members provide alcohol and drug rehabilitation, programs for street people, and counselling. It supports the usual aims of developing and fostering spiritual life within the church. SSJE in Canada, a daughter community of the American congregation in Cambridge, Mass, associated with the Cowley Fathers of Oxford, Eng, was established at Emsdale, Ont, in 1927. In 1984 this small community, at that time in Hamilton, ceased operation; the remaining brothers moved to the mother house in Cambridge. *See* ANGLICANISM.

DONALD ANDREW DODMAN

Reading: Michel Theriault, *The Institutes of Consecrated Life in Canada* ... (1980).

Christianity, a major world religion, and the religion of some 90% of Canadians. Believers hold that the life, death and resurrection of Jesus in the first century AD, as presented in the Bible and in the Christian tradition, are central to their understanding of who they are and how they should live. As the Messiah, or the Christ (Gk *christos*, "the anointed one", or "the one chosen by God"), Jesus was to restore God's creation to the condition intended by its creator, and especially to restore order among God's chosen Jewish people, saving them from the deadly disorder into which sinful behaviour had brought them. Jesus' first followers included some fishermen, a prostitute, a tax collector and a rabbinical student — a diverse group of enthusiasts who scandalized their fellow Jews and puzzled their Greek neighbours. They claimed that Jesus had accomplished his redemptive mission by submitting himself to execution as a state criminal and later rising from the dead. They argued that he was thus revealed to be both human and divine, and they invited all, not just Jews, to join them in living as members of the Church [Gk *kuriakon*, "that which belongs to the Lord"]. Christianity gradually became interwoven with the histories of numerous nations, especially in Europe, and developed its own history, gaining and losing influence in both secular and spiritual worlds and surviving serious schisms within. Today the major divisions of Christianity, all well represented in Canada, are Roman CATHOLICISM (11.2 million adherents, 1981 c), the Eastern ORTHODOX tradition (362 000 adherents) and Protestantism (9.9 million adherents). They have similar calendars of the church year, and all celebrate Christmas and Easter as the major feasts. Sacraments (religious acts regarded as outward signs of spiritual grace) are practised by most groups, although most Protestants view only baptism and communion (Eucharist) as sacramental, whereas the Roman Catholic and Orthodox churches include as sacraments baptism, confirmation (chrismation), Eucharist, penance, extreme unction, holy orders (ordination) and matrimony.

RELIGION is a response to ultimate questions, and it makes ultimate demands. What Christian in Canada can be said to be truly religious? Many Canadians are serious Christians, but although there is certainly a plurality of religious standpoints in modern Canada, there is no general acceptance of pluralism, even within the Christian community itself. All Christians look to the Bible, but Christians live different lives in the light of the Gospel, and Canadian Christians are far from a consensus that all ways are legitimate and worthy. Nor do all Canadian Christians commit themselves to the same degree. If there is disagreement about whether certain Canadians are properly called Christian, there is also dispute about whether Canada itself may be called Christian. Until the mid-20th century, public rhetoric and fundamental laws took it for granted that Canada was a Christian country, but since the 1950s there has been a significant shift away from Christian language in public life to more general affirmations that Canada is a country that recognizes "the supremacy of God," as the CONSTITUTION ACT 1982 puts it. Buddhists and other non-theists chafe at even this mild declaration. But such vague public theism may wither away by the end of the 20th century.

History in Canada VILLE-MARIE, named in honour of Mary, the mother of Jesus, was founded 1642 as a mission station by Roman Catholics caught up in the great 17th-century religious revival in France. The island on which the mission stood had been named Montréal for the Italian home of a cardinal who helped sponsor Cartier's explorations of 1535. (The origin of the name was later ascribed to "Mont Réal" — mountain of the king — in honour of the king of France.) Although one should not romanticize such beginnings, it is true that many early settlers of NEW FRANCE were motivated in part by religious concerns. MARIE DE L'INCARNATION, the Ursuline nun who was a source of civil and spiritual strength to Québec, 1639-72, understood herself as a founder of a "New Church" rather than of a "New France." Later in the 17th century the colony passed effectively into the hands of the king, officially "His Most Christian Majesty." In practice, royal direction proved less Christian than secular.

During the 18th century, both French and British governments took for granted the European tradition that political stability depends in part on the people's allegiance to one church, carefully established as an arm of the royal government. European kings were known as "vicars of Christ" long before the pope assumed that title, and many colonial administrators saw their own role in a religious light. But the notion of an "established church" was difficult to realize in Canada. In the first place, the established churches themselves, Roman Catholic and then Church of England (*see* ANGLICANISM), lacked the financial and human resources to bind together a scattered pioneer society. Secondly, Catholic and Anglican bishops often had agendas differing from those of the politicians. Thirdly, people often turned for inspiration to religious leaders such as mystical revivalist Henry ALLINE, who shunned political involvement. Fourthly, from the common people's personal experience came religious responses and convictions only incidentally related to the rubrics laid down by church leaders, eg, the Acadians' "white mass" (mass without a priest), the curiously pagan healing practices of Scottish Highland settlers, and the home devotions and supernatural tales of French Canadian peasants.

Finally, the consolidation of Canada under the British Crown, effected by the TREATY OF PARIS (1763), created a political entity comprising a highly diverse collection of Christians. To the existing Catholic population of Lower Canada [Québec] were added English-speaking immigrants of all kinds: sundry Protestant dissenters from England, northern Europe and the US, Catholics and Protestants from Ireland, Catholics and PRESBYTERIANS from Scotland. Clergy trained in the home country often accompanied the immigrants and, like the priests of LC, fought to hang on to their flocks and their distinctive traditions. During the early 19th century, independent religious revivals in LC, the Maritimes and Upper Canada (Ontario) greatly strengthened the hands of those churches opposing the feeble efforts of the Anglican establishment to reproduce in Canada the hegemony it had enjoyed in Britain.

By the middle of the 19th century, "public Christianity" was taking shape. Universities, founded by particular churches in order to train indigenous clergy, received public support and began to admit students from all religious backgrounds, even while retaining their peculiar denominational leanings. Public school systems officially committed to producing "Christian citizens" developed; outside Québec they were Protestant for all practical purposes, and English-speaking Catholics struggled to support private schools with little help from government (*see* SEPARATE SCHOOLS). There arose a public rhetoric that was often biblical (eg, Canada was called a "Dominion" because the term is found in Psalm 72:8) and laws pertaining to personal morality reflected popular Christian standards. The public calendar was marked by Christian holidays, particularly Christmas and Easter, and Sunday was traditionally a day of rest.

Within Québec the Catholic majority and Protestant minority came gradually to a workable living arrangement, perhaps because Catholic numbers were balanced by Protestant economic power. Elsewhere, mainstream Protestants such as Anglicans, METHODISTS, Presbyterians, BAPTISTS and CONGREGATIONALISTS came to an accommodation but frequently had acrimonious disputes with the Catholic minority. George-Étienne CARTIER's dream of a Canada stretching from sea to sea with provinces evenly balanced between Protestant and Catholic, as Upper and Lower Canada had been, foundered in the wave of westward migration from Protestant Ontario and the sad results of the RIEL rebellions. French Canadian society adopted a defensively nationalist outlook (*see* FRENCH CANADIAN NATIONALISM), turning inward to consolidate a Catholic homeland while leaving the rest of Canada to more Protestant imaginings.

By mid-19th century both Protestant and Catholic leaders began to realize that they faced a common adversary: cities were beginning to attract more and more Canadians. Small-town parish and congregational organization failed to sink roots in the modern city with its cosmopolitan morality, anonymity, separation of home and workplace, specialization of tasks and complex economy. In response all the churches began to stress the importance of a well-trained, professional clergy and to develop special programs for children — in Québec the clergy gradually replaced lay people teaching in the schools, and elsewhere the SUNDAY SCHOOL movement took hold. The local congregation or parish remained the fundamental unit of organization, but church newspapers and lay organizations based on particular occupational groups or age ranges went beyond the parish. The YMCA, for example, transcended traditional Protestant church boundaries, and the ST JEAN-BAPTISTE SOCIETY transcended traditional Catholic diocesan boundaries. Church buildings became imposing, permanent and expensive structures, funded largely by prosperous church members (*see* RELIGIOUS BUILDING). Working-class Canadians then came to be seen as the object of missionary activity, which was sometimes directed through downtown missions.

The urban threat to traditional Christian ways brought Protestant and Catholic leaders together in support of the Lord's Day Act of 1906 (*see* LORD'S DAY ALLIANCE). Respect for Sunday, the "Lord's Day," was hallowed by custom in rural society, but in urban society it could only be maintained by law. Many of the farthest-reaching modifications to the Act, permitting more amusement and labour on Sunday, occurred during the 2 world wars. The changes were justified as necessary to the success of war efforts "to defend Christian civilization." Some responses to urbanization were even more defensive. For example, the Catholic Church encouraged its people to shun the "Protestant" cities and Protestant New England in order to transform the wilderness of northern Québec into a Catholic, rural civilization. This "colonization movement" was more successful in novels such as *Jean Rivard* and *Maria Chapdelaine* than it was in practice.

But there were often positive and unexpected results from such defensive responses, eg, the efforts of many Christian temperance organizations, Protestant and Catholic, which culminated in Canada-wide PROHIBITION during WWI. After the war the legislation withered away, but meanwhile the Protestants of the WOMAN'S CHRISTIAN TEMPERANCE UNION (WCTU) formed the core of a movement that finally won the vote for women in 1918 (*see* WOMEN'S SUFFRAGE). Protestants often began in the TEMPERANCE MOVEMENT then moved on to broader concerns, ultimately forming part of the SOCIAL GOSPEL movement which spawned Protestant social activists ranging from those who stayed firmly within church structures, eg, Nellie MCCLUNG and novelist C.W. GORDON, to others, eg, J.S. WOODSWORTH and T.C. DOUGLAS, who found the left-wing CO-OPERATIVE COMMONWEALTH FEDERATION less inhibiting. Catholic social activists were more likely than their Protestant counterparts to stay within church-affiliated groups, such as the various CATHOLIC ACTION organizations and the ANTIGONISH MOVEMENT.

By mid-20th century Québec was so highly clericalized that nearly half its Catholic priests were engaged in full-time work outside the traditional parish: teaching, guiding Catholic labour unions (*see* CONFEDERATION OF NATIONAL TRADE UNIONS), administering social services, etc. Catholic lay people had a great respect for the clergy, but they were not puppets of the priesthood, as many Protestants thought. The vitality of anticlerical jokes and songs, and the largely spontaneous generation of popular devotions such as PILGRIMAGE to Brother André's shrine, demonstrated considerable independence from the hierarchy. The lay elites that formed in the worlds of politics and journalism included Henri BOURASSA, Maurice DUPLESSIS and André LAURENDEAU — Catholics who could scarcely be described as "priest ridden."

The Christian communities of the early 20th century suffered many tensions. Among English-speaking Protestants the disputes that arose over the value of the Bible as history and over church involvement in social action sometimes created new institutional divisions (eg, the Baptist schisms of the 1920s and the student divisions of the 1930s leading to the Student Christian Movement and Inter-Varsity Christian Fellowship) and sometimes encouraged solutions that buried the disputes, unresolved, in silence. The Catholic consensus was rarely disturbed, but when it was the results were briefly spectacular (eg, in the ostracism of Jean-Charles HARVEY).

Most Protestant tensions were obscured by a series of movements toward union, starting in the mid-19th century and climaxing in the 1925 foundation of the UNITED CHURCH OF CANADA

Christianity: Affiliation (% of Population) and Participation Rates
(Sources: 1981 census; Reginald W. Bibby, Project CAN80, 1981)

gion	UC	Angl	Luth	Presb	"Conservative"*	Other	Prot Total	RC	Orth
ınada	16	10	3	3	6	1	39	47	2
C	20	14	5	3	7	6	55	20	1
airies	25	9	7	3	7	6	57	30	2
ntario	19	14	3	6	6	4	52	36	2
uébec	2	2	–	1	1	1	7	88	1
tlantic	18	16	1	3	15	1	54	43	–
of affiliates aiming membership	43	45	75	37	52	**	45	46	**
of affiliates tending weekly	19	20	17	19	52	**	24	41	**
of members tending weekly	37	43	23	52	88	**	50	71	**

Consists of Baptist (3%), Mennonite (1%), Pentecostal (1%), Salvation Army (1%)
Insufficient numbers in sample to provide stable percentages
ble compiled by Reginald W. Bibby

sus' call to unity (eg, in John 17:21), coupled ith the practical advantages gained by pooling arce resources in a vast land and with the Ca- ıdian tradition that the churches have a public le, have made this trend toward unity a char- teristic of Canadian church history. It is re- arkable that, although Canada's population is sed on immigration from many different nds and cultures, almost three-quarters of its tizens claim to belong to 3 churches: Roman tholic, United and Anglican. Nevertheless, versity has thrived, largely as a result of the flux of numerous cultural groups and of ideas om outside Canada. Ukrainians, Romanians d others have brought various Orthodox ıurch traditions with them. MENNONITES d others with ANABAPTIST roots immigrated, did LUTHERANS, chiefly from Europe; MORMONS me from the US. JEHOVAH'S WITNESSES and VENTH-DAY ADVENTISTS are well established, and LINESS CHURCHES, such as the SALVATION ARMY, ve a long history in this country. Trans- nominational movements are active as well: the early 20th century, PENTECOSTAL MOVE- ENTS crossed Protestant denominational undaries, and more recently, CHARISMATIC NEWAL has drawn both Protestants and Catho- s. The CHRISTIAN CHURCH (DISCIPLES OF CHRIST), ough considered a denomination, is commit- d to the ultimate unity of all Christians across nominational lines.

In the wake of WWII church leaders were nfident in the strength of the churches: at- ndance at weekly services was high, and the sources that once went into war could now be voted to building the peace. But in the 1960s, urch attendance and vocations to the or- ined ministry fell off sharply, most dra- atically in Québec, but elsewhere as well. In e 1970s it became apparent that conservative ANGELICAL AND FUNDAMENTALIST CHURCHES hose membership made up only a tiny slice of e population as a whole were attracting as any Sunday worshippers as did all the main- eam Protestant giants combined. The reason ay lie in the nature of modern society in hich, generally speaking, public life is secular- ed and religious life has become private. To cularize is to treat something as belonging to e world, rather than to God, and to judge the orth of things according to their usefulness in man activity. For example, the Lord's Day t is regarded as valuable because it gives orkers a weekly rest and therefore increases oductivity, not because it honours God; reli- ous education is good because it produces ell-behaved citizens, not because it cultivates a rson's love of God. Christians have frequently opted purely secular values in the course of fending public Christianity. Virtually every ntemporary Canadian author who writes out the awe and wonder experienced in human life has only scorn for modern churches — an indication, perhaps, that few Canadians expect to find that which is "holy" in the churches.

People have come to think of themselves as "real" or "themselves" only in private. Elsewhere they take on roles dictated by the institution that sustains them: eg, the same person will behave in markedly different ways in school, at work, at a political rally or in a sports arena. Only in the privacy of home does the individual think the real self emerges. Within this private segment of modern life religion has become lodged. The movement of religion into the individual's private life helps to explain why religion in Canadian public life has gradually become secular or has simply eroded, why church attendance is seen to be less and less important, and why private religious practices (eg, watching evangelical TV programs, reading religious paperbacks or magazines) are more widespread than ever in Canadian life. The few public issues seen to be clearly religious are closely tied to this private world of home and family: ABORTION, the use of alcoholic beverages, OBSCENITY, MARRIAGE AND DIVORCE, sex education, etc. People who tell the census taker that they are "Christian" generally want to be married and buried in a church setting, but they often feel no urgent need to take a larger part in the life of the institution with its tradition of public responsibility.

Nevertheless, Christianity remains, its contours constantly changing. The Bible is still the basic reference point for all Christians, though they often differ widely as to how it is to be understood. International Christianity continues to influence what happens in Canada: leaders of the World Council of Churches (1983) and the pope (1984) visit Canada, and Canadians follow their doings through the secular media; most religious broadcasting in Canada originates in the US; candidates for the ministry often journey abroad for their theological education. At the same time, Canadian scholars such as Northrop FRYE, Bernard LONERGAN and Wilfred Cantwell Smith are familiar in Christian circles around the world. The local parish or congregation continues as the basic unit of Christian organization in modern Canada, but the variety of views within congregations is often as significant as are divisions between the denominations to which the congregations belong. The more liberal Christians often find support in the activities of their denominational leaders, particularly those working in central offices, and tend to view the conservatives as too private; the more conservative Christians tend to view the liberals as too secular. Between these groups lies the broad "middle" of church membership, perhaps less intensely involved in the churches' institutional life, but providing stability at the centre.

Co-operation among the churches is channelled through several Canada-wide coalitions devoted to ECUMENICAL SOCIAL ACTION, but members of local congregations often feel alienated from these coalitions with their relatively progressive stances. In addition, public prayer meetings frequently bring Christians together during urban crusades led by travelling EVANGELISTS, or on special occasions such as Good Friday and Remembrance Day with local clerical leadership. The Eucharist (Communion or Lord's Supper, the ritual sharing of bread and wine that commemorates Jesus' crucifixion) is seldom celebrated at such interdenominational gatherings, since the particular ways of celebrating that central and nearly universal rite remain closely linked with denominational identity. But modern Christians in Canada are much more likely than their ancestors were to take part in another denomination's Eucharist, drawn by friendship or marriage to members of that congregation, and there are few clergy who would deny them access. Furthermore, these Christians are now much more likely to be favourably aware of the doctrines and practices of JUDAISM, ISLAM, HINDUISM, BUDDHISM, SIKHISM or the BAHA'I FAITH, and possibly even of NEW RELIGIOUS MOVEMENTS, as practised by other Canadians.

To the extent that Canadian Christians have accepted the secularization of public life and the increasingly private nature of religious life, they have made a working accommodation to the peculiar nature of modern society. But the accommodation is inconsistent with a tradition whose favourite prayer asks, "Thy kingdom come," and takes for granted that a kingdom is no merely private matter. It is also inconsistent with the fundamental nature of religion itself, which aspires to knit everything together into one ultimately meaningful pattern, and which demands that things be holy as well as useful. Therefore it seems likely that Christianity will persist as a useful thing proper to the private lives of many Canadians, but challenged from time to time to be open to that which is holy, and active in that which is public. *See also* BIBLE SCHOOLS; CANADIAN COUNCIL OF CHURCHES; EVANGELICAL FELLOWSHIP OF CANADA; CHRISTIAN RELIGIOUS COMMUNITIES; CANADIAN BIBLE SOCIETY; CALVINISM; MILLENARIANISM; PACIFISM.

TOM SINCLAIR-FAULKNER

Reading: J.W. Grant, *The Church in the Canadian Era* (1972); R.T. Handy, *A History of the Churches in the United States and Canada* (1977); J. Moir, *The Church in the British Era* (1972); Nive Voisine, et al, *Histoire de l'Église catholique au Québec (1608-1970)* (1971); H. H. Walsh, *The Church in the French Era* (1966).

Christie, Loring Cheney, lawyer, diplomat (b at Amherst, NS 21 Jan 1885; d at New York, NY 8 Apr 1941). Educated at Acadia and Harvard, Christie practised law in New York, then worked in the US Department of Justice, serving as acting solicitor general. In 1913 he joined the Canadian Department of External Affairs as its first legal adviser, and was adviser on foreign policy to PMs Borden and Meighen. He helped draft Resolution IX of the 1917 Imperial War Conference, which established a relationship of equality between Great Britain and the Dominions, and he represented Canada at the 1919 Peace Conference. Mistrusted by PM Mackenzie King, Christie resigned from government in 1923 to join a London financial house. Returning to Canada, he worked for Ontario Hydro and Beauharnois Power, then rejoined External Affairs in 1935. An isolationist during the 1930s, Christie resisted efforts to bring Canada into a European war. In 1939 he became Canadian minister to the US. ROBERT BOTHWELL

Chromium (Cr), hard, brittle, silver-white metal (melting point 1875°C), widely known for its use as decorative trim on home appliances and automobiles. Chromium has several industrial uses, the most important being the manufacture of stainless steel, which typically contains about 20% chromium. In its natural MINERAL form (chromite), chromium has heat resistant properties which find application in various types of furnaces. Chromium readily forms various chemical compounds with a wide range of applications, such as pigments and tanning agents. Chromite is the only commercially important ore mineral of chromium. Although chromite has not been produced in Canada since 1949 when small high-grade deposits were mined, there are large low-grade chromite deposits in central Canada which could be exploited in the future. DON LAW-WEST

Chrysler Canada Ltd, with head offices in WINDSOR, Ont, is a major manufacturer and distributor of cars and trucks in Canada. The Chrysler Corporation of Canada was incorporated in 1925 as the successor to Maxwell-Chalmers Motor Company of Canada. In 1929 it completed its passenger car assembly plant outside Windsor, which is the nucleus of the present Chrysler Centre complex, and the same year absorbed Dodge Brothers (Canada), car manufacturers, and Graham Brothers (Canada), truck manufacturers. Since the 1950s, major expansion has occurred as the company established regional parts depots and zone offices and purchased supplier firms to ensure sources of supply. The company adopted its present name in 1963. Chrysler Canada manufactures and distributes Plymouth, Dodge and Chrysler passenger cars and Dodge trucks through over 500 dealerships across Canada. In 1982 it had sales or operating revenue of $3.6 billion (ranking 16th in Canada), assets of $680.4 million (ranking 110th) and 11 176 employees. Foreign ownership of the company stands at 100%, with Chrysler Corp of Detroit holding 90% and Chrysler Overseas 10%. *See* AUTOMOTIVE INDUSTRY. DEBORAH C. SAWYER

CHUM Ltd, controlled by Allan Waters, is one of Canada's largest radio and television broadcasting holding companies. CHUM operates 15 radio stations located in Vancouver; Drumheller, Stettler and Brooks, Alta; Winnipeg; Peterborough, Toronto and Ottawa, Ont; Halifax; and St John's. Its television operations include CJCH-TV in Halifax, CKCW-TV in Moncton-Charlottetown, CKLT-TV in Saint John-Fredericton, CJCB-TV in Sydney, NS, CKVR-TV in Barrie, Ont, and CITY-TV, Canada's second-largest independent television station. Other CHUM interests include "Music by Muzak" franchises for Vancouver, Victoria, Calgary and Ontario; CHUM owns the OTTAWA ROUGH RIDERS football club; a security-systems company; telephone-equipment stores; and is involved with the production of commercials. CHUM's total assets in 1983 were $73.3 million, with revenues of $89 million. PETER S. ANDERSON

Churches, *see* RELIGIOUS BUILDING.

Churchill, Man, UP, pop 1186 (1981c), is located at the mouth of the CHURCHILL R on the SW shore of HUDSON BAY. Although discovered by the Danish explorer Jens MUNK in 1619, the site was not settled until 1685, when the HBC established a post a few kilometres upstream. Named for

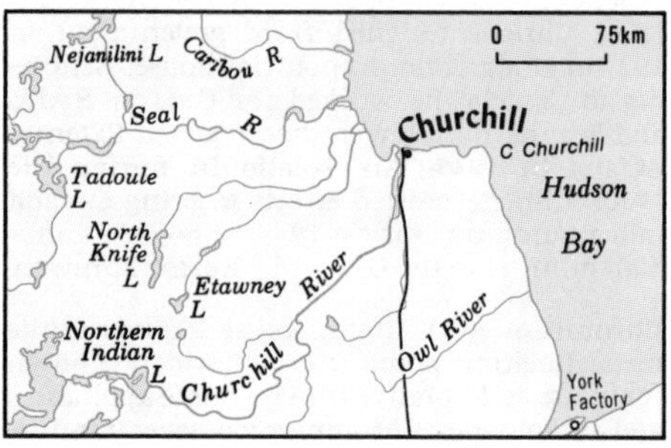

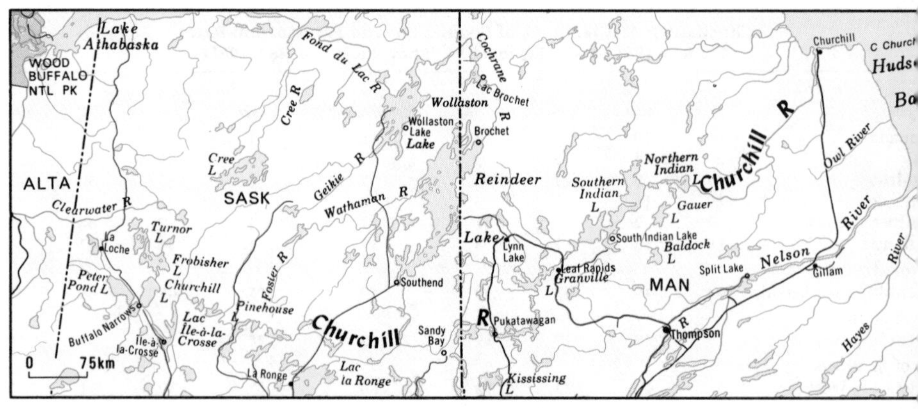

Lord Churchill (later the duke of Marlborough), the post was replaced by another nearer the coast in 1718. This structure was replaced by PRINCE OF WALES'S FORT, on the W bank of the estuary, which remained the centre of the FUR TRADE in the area until it was destroyed by the French in 1782. The HBC reestablished Ft Churchill, which continued its role as a fur-trade post. The present town grew up on the E bank of the river after 1931 when the HUDSON BAY RY terminal and harbour facilities were completed. With WWII, the locality prospered as a northern supply centre and military base and continued as a research station and rocket launching site until the early 1960s, after which the district population declined from its peak of around 6000 as the federal government cut back its operations. Churchill is some 1600 km closer to Europe by sea than is Montréal, but its short 3-month shipping season and shallow waters have restricted its development as an ocean port. Townspeople live in the hope that the harbour and rail facilities will ultimately be upgraded and the shipping season extended; meanwhile the town relies heavily on tourists who visit the area to view the magnificent Inuit museum, the subarctic landscape and wildlife that includes the white beluga whale and the polar bear.

H. JOHN SELWOOD

Churchill, Gordon Minto, lawyer, teacher, politician (b at Coldwater, Ont 8 Nov 1898). One of John DIEFENBAKER's closest Cabinet confidants, Churchill was a knowledgeable and respected parliamentarian who served as Tory House leader in the Diefenbaker era. A veteran of both world wars, he was first elected to the House in 1951. In 1956 he organized and led caucus support for Diefenbaker's leadership bid and was his political adviser during the 1957 election. He was appointed minister of trade and commerce in 1957; in this capacity he led several Commonwealth trade delegations. He moved to the Dept of Veterans Affairs in 1960. After the Feb 1963 Cabinet resignations, Churchill served as defence minister until the election, and was a rallying point for Diefenbaker loyalists in the caucus until 1968. PATRICIA WILLIAMS

Reading: Peter C. Newman, *Renegade in Power: The Diefenbaker Years (1963).*

Churchill Falls, Labrador. The CHURCHILL R drops some 66 m before plummetting 75 m over the falls and a further 158 m through Bowdoin Canyon. The MONTAGNAIS-NASKAPI believed that to look on the awesome falls meant death. John MACLEAN was the first white man to see the falls (1839), but they were largely forgotten until Albert Peter LOW made a scientific excursion to the area in 1894. The massive hydroelectric potential of the falls was realized early on, but it was not until the completion of the QUEBEC, NORTH SHORE AND LABRADOR RY in 1954 and the development of long-distance electric-power transmission technology by HYDRO-QUÉBEC that exploitation became feasible. Complex neg tiations between the governments of Ne foundland and Québec (through which t power would have to pass) were not complet until 1969. The contract provided for the sale 5.2 million kW per year of power to Hydr Québec for 40 years at a price of under 3 mi (three-tenths of one cent) per kWh. Hydr Québec has the option to renew for another years at only 2 mills per kWh.

The project was undertaken by a subsidia of British Newfoundland Development Co (Brinco), and was at the time the largest CIV ENGINEERING project ever undertaken in N Ame ica. Eighty strategically placed dikes pooled t vast waters of the Labrador Plateau in the Smal wood Reservoir (5698 km^2). A massive unde ground powerhouse — until the JAMES BA PROJECT, the largest in the world — was exc vated. The project took 9 years to comple (1966-74), employed more than 30 000 peop and cost $950 million. The first units bega transmitting Dec 1971; the eleventh and fin unit went into service in 1974.

With the dramatic rise in ENERGY costs in t 1980s, Hydro-Québec has reaped huge prof from the resale of the power from Church Falls, and the terms of the contract have been source of acrimony between the governments Newfoundland and Québec. In 1984 the S preme Court of Canada ruled that a proposal Newfoundland to divert water away from t falls was illegal. JAMES MAR

Reading: Philip Smith, *Brinco: The Story of Churchill Fa* (1975).

Churchill River, 1609 km long, issues fro Lac La Loche in NW Saskatchewan and flow SE, E and NE across the lowlands of northe Saskatchewan and Manitoba to Hudson Bay CHURCHILL, Man. Along the course are rapid falls, narrow chutes, long placid stretches smooth water, and — typical of rivers of t Canadian SHIELD — a chain of interconnecte lakes. Largest of these are Peter Pond Lk (7 km^2), Churchill Lk (559 km^2) and Lac Île-à-Crosse (391 km^2) where the river takes in main tributary, the Beaver R (491 km). The riv was travelled by Cree and Chipewyan, and Je MUNK wintered at its mouth 1620. The HBC bui a post, later called PRINCE OF WALES'S FORT, near mouth; it was captured by a French naval exp dition 1782, under Jean-François de Galau comte de Lapérouse, and recaptured by the Bri ish and renamed Ft Churchill, for John Churc ill, duke of Marlborough, governor of the HB 1685-91. The name was later applied to the riv as well; its Indian name had been *Missinipi*, "b river." Joseph FROBISHER of the NWC establish a trade link between the river and the Montré route via the Saskatchewan and Sturgeon We rivers and Frog Portage. River flow is heavy an regular. There are hydroelectric stations at I land Falls and Granville Falls, but much of t river's potential is untapped. JAMES MAR

Churchill River, Labrador, 856 km long (to head of Ashuanipi R), issues from Ashuanipi Lk, drops 75 m over CHURCHILL FALLS, broadens into Winokapau Lk and runs E through a deep glacial gorge past HAPPY VALLEY-GOOSE BAY into Lk Melville, Hamilton Inlet, entering the Atlantic near Rigolet (pop 271). It is the longest river in Labrador and has a DRAINAGE BASIN of 79 800 km² and a mean discharge of 1620 m³/s. The power development at Churchill Falls has backed up the river and created the enormous Smallwood Reservoir. Farther upstream, a hydroelectric plant at the outfall from Menihek Lakes provides power for the former iron-mining town of SCHEFFERVILLE, Qué. With a heavy flow and large drop from the Labrador Plateau, the river has probably the greatest hydroelectric potential of any in N America. Fort Smith (now North West River) was an early HBC post at its mouth. John MCLEAN first reached the river from the interior 1839. It was named for Sir Charles Hamilton, governor of Newfoundland in 1821, but Premier Joseph SMALLWOOD renamed it in honour of Sir Winston Churchill (1965). The change has caused confusion since Canada already had a CHURCHILL R in Manitoba. JAMES MARSH

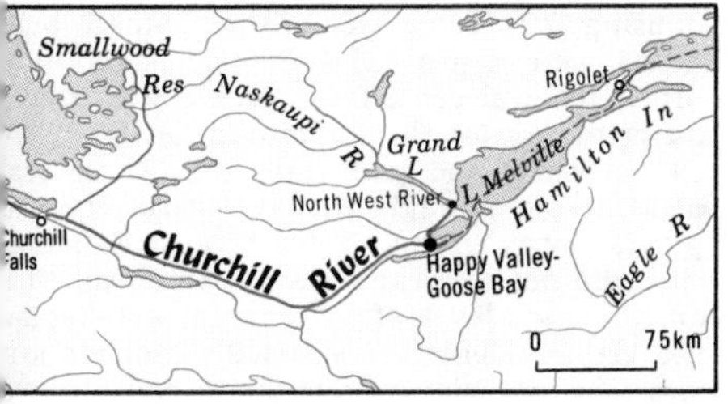

Cinq-Mars, Lionel, plant pathologist, vascular plant systematist (b at St-Coeur-de-Marie, Qué 12 June 1919; d at Québec C 6 Aug 1973). Trained in plant pathology, but interested in the taxonomy of vascular plants, Cinq-Mars initiated and encouraged continued development of floristic studies at Laval. During his early career as a phytopathologist, Cinq-Mars worked on apple diseases. In 1962 he was appointed professor of botany at Laval and remained there until his death. He became conservator of the Herbier Louis-Marie at Laval in 1968 and increased the holdings to over 10 000 specimens. His particular research interests were *Amelanchier* and *Viola*, especially in Québec. Cinq-Mars wrote more than 70 papers in plant pathology, vascular plant systematics and distribution, ornithology and natural history. He also established and edited 2 publications devoted to plant systematics, *Ludoviciana* and *Provanchiera*. His name is commemorated by a species of saskatoon berry, *Amelanchier quintii-martii*. As a charter member and one of the first directors of the Canadian Botanical Assn, he is remembered by the Cinq-Mars Award for the outstanding student paper at the annual meeting. J.R. STEIN

Cisco, *see* WHITEFISH.

Citadel Theatre was founded in 1965 by Joseph H. Shoctor in the Salvation Army Citadel in Edmonton and rapidly outgrew its quarters. In 1975 the theatre was able to move into the striking building which now houses the Shoctor, Rice and Zeidler theatres in the heart of the city. One of Canada's theatrical showcases, it continues to grow and expand, offering the 350 000 patrons who attend each year world-class performances from international stars and directors. At least one major Canadian play is scheduled each season. The Citadel's traveling company, Citadel-On-Wheels/Wings, tours Alberta, the Arctic and the NWT; its in-house Theatre for Young Audiences, the School for the Performing Arts and the International Children's Festival make it one of the more comprehensive theatrical organizations in N America. In 1984 the Maclab, a 700-seat thrust theatre, and the Tucker, a 150-seat open-air amphitheatre, were completed. *See also* THEATRE, ENGLISH LANGUAGE.

Cité libre, magazine fd 1950, bringing together Québec intellectuals who opposed Maurice DUPLESSIS. Inspired by Emmanuel Mounier's philosophic system that took man as its fundamental measure of value, the editorial board, which included Gérard PELLETIER and Pierre Elliott TRUDEAU, assumed that universal man was to be defended from totalitarianism. This abstract philosophy was never translated into concrete social and political objectives. The journal was humanist, progressive and nondoctrinaire — Pierre VADEBONCOEUR and Pierre Vallières rubbed shoulders with Jean Le Moyne and Maurice Blain — and its content demonstrated the unease prevalent in Québec society. Secular and anticlericalist in orientation, *Cité libre* explored religious issues in depth. The journal met intellectual mediocrity and intolerance with a rationalism inspired by the great liberal thinkers. *Cité libre* sometimes took audacious stands on socioeconomic issues, yet never questioned basic social structures: it argued instead for gradual reform. It was antinationalist and, in politics, primarily concerned with the ethical issues of teaching democratic morality and fighting corruption. Its search for new values and an identity was more evident in its first series of issues (1950-59) than in its second (1960-66). In the interval, the QUIET REVOLUTION had begun. *See* LITERARY PERIODICALS IN FRENCH. BENOÎT MELANÇON

Citizen's Arrest originated in Medieval England when there was no police force and it was everyone's duty to assist in chasing criminals. These powers are now set out in the Criminal Code. First, anyone who owns or lawfully possesses property may arrest someone found committing a crime on or in relation to that property, eg, a farmer may arrest someone stealing his tractor. Secondly, anyone may arrest a person found in the act of committing a serious (indictable) offence or escaping from the police after committing a crime. In all cases, the arrested person must be delivered immediately to a police officer. LEE PAIKIN

Citizenship The Citizenship Act does not contain a definition of citizen but states (s5.5) that both native-born and naturalized citizens are equally entitled to all the rights, powers and privileges and subject to all the obligations, duties and liabilities of a citizen, which are governed by numerous provincial and federal laws. In all provinces and in the federal jurisdiction citizens of the age of majority, not infirm of mind and not lawfully incarcerated are guaranteed political rights, including the right to vote and run for office. The Constitution Act, 1982, incorporated these rights.

Before 1947 Canada's Naturalization Acts conferred British citizenship on immigrants. The first Canadian Citizenship Act (1970) was replaced in 1976 by another Citizenship Act which included recognition of the equality of women in citizenship matters and removed the remaining differences between native-born and naturalized citizens. But though the previous law was abolished by the present Citizenship Act, the new Act did not by its terms apply to the past except in very narrow cases. Some persons therefore cannot obtain citizenship although they qualify under the new Act, because they were born under the old Act. It is possible that some of these provisions could be challenged under the new Canadian Charter of Rights and Freedoms, especially where there is discrimination based on sex. All persons born in Canada, except children of foreign diplomats, are now entitled to Canadian citizenship. Children born to Canadians abroad (either parent can be Canadian) are also entitled, but must register their intention of retaining their citizenship or live in or establish a substantial connection with Canada. Children under the age of majority whose parents are entitled to citizenship benefit from their parents' new status if they are included in the application; and children born to a Canadian father after his death are also entitled to citizenship, as are persons who have been permanent residents of Canada for 3 years or more and who fulfill certain conditions (s5.1). The minister of immigration has the discretionary power to grant citizenship to any person in cases of "special and unusual hardship" or to reward services to Canada. This power is almost never used but in a world community that is increasingly conscious of human rights, it could prove very significant.

Under the 1976 Immigration Act (s4) Canadian citizens have the absolute right to enter and live in Canada, as do Canadians under the Indian Act who may or may not be citizens. Permanent residents and convention refugees who are allowed certain rights in Canada are also subject to certain restrictions. Only persons lawfully extradited and children handed over to persons with parental authority who reside outside Canada can be forced to leave Canada. Only Canadian citizens are eligible to obtain Canadian passports, although landed immigrants may be granted a travel document. Many Canadian professional associations, eg, law societies and medical associations, require practitioners of their profession to be citizens.

An application for a grant, retention, renunciation or resumption of citizenship is initially considered by a citizenship judge. Both the minister and the person concerned have a right of appeal to the trial division of the Federal Court. The governor-in-council may refuse an application for citizenship or renunciation of citizenship, but the grounds for the exercise of this power are extremely narrow. Both citizenship and renunciation of citizenship can be revoked if obtained by fraud or misrepresentation. A person who was admitted as a permanent immigrant under false pretensions is deemed to have been given citizenship under false pretensions as well. The annulment is made by the governor-in-council following a report by the minister which can only be made if the person has been notified and given a chance to present his views to the minister or, at the person's option, to the Federal Court.

Citizens residing in Canada may not renounce their citizenship. Those who have ceased to be citizens can resume citizenship under conditions similar to those of immigrants obtaining citizenship, but need only reside in Canada for one year to do so. Canadian citizens can hold any number of citizenships at the same time. Citizens of other Commonwealth countries and Ireland enjoy a special status in Canada, although it has little practical significance today, and Canadian citizens also enjoy a reciprocal special status.

Noncitizens Noncitizens in Canada do not enjoy political rights but generally have all legal rights and are subject to the law in the same way as are citizens. Permanent residents are entitled to work in Canada while visitors usually are not. JULIUS H. GREY

City In Canada "city" is a broad, generic term usually referring to an urbanized area. The size of this area, its economic base, social character and form of local government may be different in each province or territory because MUNICIPAL GOVERNMENT derives its authority from the provincial legislature, and in each province the conditions that must exist before an area may be classified as a city differ. As a result, it is simpler to examine the process of urbanization itself, defined as the generation and spread of characteristic features of urban life. The demographic trend toward urbanization in Canada began well before Confederation and still continues at a rapid pace. By 1981, over 80% of Canadians lived in urban areas, meaning cities, towns, villages or unincorporated settlements with populations greater than 1000 persons, or in built-up fringes of incorporated areas.

Historical Development to 1920 Great empires, with dynamic metropolitan centres such as Paris and London, expanded by establishing colonial outposts. Early Canadian colonial towns were part of this large-scale phenomenon and served as agents of the urban metropolitan centres. Economically, they exploited the colony's staples; culturally, they transmitted the metropolitan-centre style of life to a new frontier; militarily and administratively they were often the means of occupying and holding the colony. The colonial towns were generally entrepôts, collecting staples, eg, fur, fish, minerals or wheat, from the region for shipment to the metropolitan centre, where the final processing was done and from which the manufactured foods were, in turn, distributed. French and British colonial towns preceded the general settlement of a region and constituted an urban frontier, but the growth and prosperity of the colonial towns depended on the potential of their hinterlands. Initially the towns acted as a channel for a region's development and contained a high proportion of the colony's population. Decentralization began as the town's proportion of the total population dropped, even though the towns tended to grow rapidly. The new, smaller, secondary centres developed a degree of autonomy during this second phase because of their isolation in a pre-railway era and because the primary town of the region did not yet have the necessary facilities to dominate all aspects of life in the hinterland. This decentralization process was reversed when colonial towns such as Québec City, Montréal, Toronto and Halifax became major urban centres.

Colonial towns, primarily connected and concerned with the overseas metropolis, lacked significant connections with other colonial towns, even with those of their own region. The beginning of regional and inter-regional connections represented the end of the colonial phase and the beginning of the commercial era, as towns began to produce goods and services not only for themselves but for the entire region. By 1851, the 9 largest cities — MONTRÉAL, QUÉBEC CITY, SAINT JOHN, TORONTO, HALIFAX, HAMILTON, KINGSTON, OTTAWA and LONDON — had developed into dynamic commercial centres and had won considerable hegemony over sizable hinterlands.

The modern Canadian city emerged between 1851 and 1921, although in most respects the changes in the first 30 years after 1851 were relatively minor. Toronto replaced Québec City as Canada's second-largest city (after Montréal), and several manufacturing towns in southern Ontario increased their population to almost 10 000 (GUELPH, ST CATHARINES, BRANTFORD, BELLEVILLE), forming a second tier of cities. By the 1880s, however, Canada's 2 largest cities, Montréal and Toronto, began to outdistance their nearest rivals in importance. Equally dramatic was the rapid growth of western cities, led by WINNIPEG and VANCOUVER, followed by that of 2 other young giants, CALGARY and EDMONTON, developments which signalled the relative decline of Québec City and Kingston in central Canada and of Saint John and Halifax in the Atlantic provinces.

To some extent rapid urban growth and stagnation can be attributed to the aggressiveness of local ELITES. Winnipeg's business elite was crucial to that city's rise to metropolitan status while the local leadership in many Atlantic cities faltered in critical periods, but more important were the vagaries of international markets in staples, and government and corporate decisions. These factors were beyond the control of individual cities. International political events stimulated the growth of Montréal's export trade and Toronto's successful competition with Montréal over the use of American trade routes. The policies of the federal government on tariffs and railways strengthened the growth of manufacturing in central cities and led to a simultaneous weakening of industry in the Maritimes. The CANADIAN PACIFIC RAILWAY decided to run its main line through Winnipeg and created a number of new communities, including Vancouver. Technological change was also important. The conversion from wood and sail to iron and steam undercut a major shipbuilding industry in Québec City and Saint John, and resulted in a shift from an Atlantic to a continental economy.

In their pursuit of metropolitan status, most Canadian cities passed through several stages of development: colonial entrepôt, commercial town, commercial-industrial city and diversified metropolis. Although all cities did not, of course, develop systematically in some deterministic fashion, Canada's urban development can nevertheless be distinguished by particular eras and all cities and towns, regardless of scale, function and regional location, were shaped to a great extent by each era.

The Contemporary City Since 1920, Canadian cities have entered a phase dominated by the technology of the automobile and the truck, an economic orientation away from industry to service functions and to dramatic spatial decentralization of population and activities. City-building, however, is a cumulative process. The pre-1920 city is still the core of the modern, dispersed metropolis. The distinction between modern developments and those of earlier periods is usually very clear and can be identified on any street map. The street systems of urban cores are set out on grids. Surrounding these urban cores are more recent suburban developments with curvilinear street systems. Many of the tensions in contemporary cities derive from the struggle for coexistence between parts of the city built before WWII and those built afterwards. As economic activity has shifted from industry to the service sector, the change has been reflected in building styles as office towers push factories to cheaper land at the urban fringe. Transportation facilities — streets, expressways and public transit lines — are crucial to the functioning of modern cities and often occupy 25% of urban land. Residential housing uses a slightly larger percentage of urban land, followed by industry and office buildings. These land uses represent outward expansion, as the city captures and incorporates more and more farmland, and upward expansion, as the downtown area expands with high-rise buildings that greatly intensify land use for both commercial and residential purposes. (*See* land-use maps accompanying entries on major cities.)

Suburbs The new portion of any city is usually known as the suburb. The suburbs of 1910 in Toronto, Vancouver, Montréal or Halifax are now considered to be part of the central city core and the suburban additions of the 1920s are now integrated into the main area of the city proper. Shortly after 1945, however, the development of suburbs changed significantly. E.P. TAYLOR amassed 2000 acres of farmland on the outskirts of Toronto and developed a new town called Don Mills which, because of its scale, design and distinctive character, changed suburban development. Each of the 4 neighbourhoods into which it was divided centered or focused on a school. The curvilinear road system was used not only to discourage through traffic, but to allow roads to follow the topography. Houses of 1½ storeys were set broadside to the street o a large lot. Residential densities (at 25 units pe ha) were half of standard densities. Land uses i each neighbourhood were deliberately sepa rated. Space was allocated for a shopping centre and single family dwellings were separate from apartment buildings, offices and indus trial space. Don Mills was considered so success ful, both financially and socially, that th model was repeated throughout Canada unti the late 1970s.

Urban Renewal After 1945, urban renewa schemes were attempted by all levels of govern ment (federal, provincial and municipal) to tr to improve the housing conditions in city core (*see* URBAN REFORM). Most politicians and plan ners believed that urban renewal — involvin the expropriation of homes and businesses, th clearing of land and the building of new (ofte public) housing — would revitalize the edges o the downtown and make this housing more ac ceptable to those who were migrating to the sub urbs. Massive urban renewal schemes met wit stiff resistance from the displaced working-clas families. Owners of expropriated property di not receive enough compensation to purchase similar house elsewhere. Tenants complaine that their lives were being uprooted and goo housing was being demolished. Small busi nesses were destroyed. The basic objection t urban renewal came from people who had different idea of their communities from th city planners and politicians did. These resi dents argued strongly that the urban renewa program was wrong-headed because Canadia cities did not have the slums of American citie and that the 3 levels of government were replac ing viable neighbourhoods with concrete jun gles. The struggles over public urban renewa continued until the late 1960s, when after mas sive outcries in Vancouver, Winnipeg and To ronto, the federal government finally agreed t stop funding the public urban renewal pro gram. Since then more modest attempts to revi talize the city have included improved stree lighting, neighbourhood parks, decorative side walks and community centres.

Public authorities were not responsible for a urban renewal. The private development indus try responded to the vastly increased housin needs of young Canadians by building larg apartment buildings, usually where handsom 19th-century houses had been demolished a city councils had approved yet another rezon ing. Neighbourhood groups were formed i reaction to the destruction of neighbourhood and in every Canadian city these groups ha running battles with the developers and Cit Hall (*see* URBAN CITIZEN MOVEMENTS; CITY POLITICS By the mid-1970s, as the apartment boor ended, mainly for economic reasons, citie began developing policies to strengthen down town communities, rather than trying to obli erate them.

Cityscape The image of most Canadian citie is defined by the downtown, where tall offic towers have now replaced smokestacks. Build ings are usually similar in design, reflecting th fact that development companies are among th largest of Canadian-owned corporations. Th natural settings of most Canadian cities are no secondary in importance to the downtown, an in many cases even difficult to identify.

The explosive growth of cities since WWII ha resulted in the destruction of much of Canada urban heritage. Considerable political energ has been spent saving what remains of 19th century buildings from the ravages of the latte half of the 20th century. By the end of the 1970 city officials, developers and the public we ready to admit that more interesting building could be built and more attractive streetscap could be designed, and most cities began to tak steps to improve the downtown areas. The anges have certainly improved an otherwise eak central city, but have done little to make e scale of cities humane again.

City Life Since the introduction of federal vernment multicultural policies in the mid-60s, the social participation by non-English-eaking cultures in Canadian cities has grown. reet signs exist in English, French, Chinese and reek in various cities. Most cities take pride in hnic celebrations and parades, and con-iously try to encourage understanding and -operation among different cultures seeking lf-expression. City residents usually congre-te because of special sports events, although lebrations such as the CALGARY STAMPEDE and e Quebec Winter Carnival have helped de-lop strong community feelings. While vari-s mayors (notably Jean DRAPEAU of Montréal) ave attempted to give their city a strong image, ost such efforts have been interpreted as crass osterism. ALAN F.J. ARTIBISE AND JOHN SEWELL

ading: Alan F.J. Artibise and G. Stelter, eds, *The Cana-n City* (1974).

ty Politics The most obvious difference be-een CITY politics and federal or provincial litics in Canada is the absence of the major litical parties. Although candidates often rely partisan connections when building their ectoral organizations, they generally present emselves to voters as independents. The spec-cle of government and opposition, so familiar Parliament and provincial legislatures, is sually missing in city politics. Instead, city uncils seem to work like the legislatures of the th century, with every member participating the business of government and aligning ith different people on different occasions. On ost issues there is consensus, although this un-rlying agreement among the councillors is ten clouded by heated disputes on particular atters. Since local politicians are free from rty discipline, what surfaces are conflicts of rsonality, ambition, interest and only occa-onally ideology. The complexity and apparent iviality of these conflicts obscure the structure d significance of local politics.

Most of the important conflicts in city politics ncern real property — land and buildings. UNICIPALITIES are primarily responsible for gulating the use of urban land and providing hysical services, eg, streets and sewers. The city uncils obtain most of their own revenues om taxing the land and buildings they are ser-cing and regulating. Legally, the municipa-ties are the creatures of the provinces and are bject to a host of legislative, judicial and ministrative controls; recently, they have be-me heavily dependent on provincial and fed-al financial assistance. They have the most ower and freedom of action in land develop-ent. Traditionally, they have been expected promote development in the interests of onomic growth. Most of the pressure for this as come from business, and businessmen and ofessionals with REAL-ESTATE interests have layed a major role in Canadian city politics. n the other hand, business uses of municipal overnment have always met resistance from tepayers concerned about rising taxes and omeowners worried about the effects of devel-opment on the value of their property and the uality of their lives. The clash between busi-ess and consumer interests is at the heart of city olitics (*see* CITIZEN MOVEMENTS).

This clash became acute at the end of the long onomic boom which followed WWII. Reform oliticians, who identified with consumer in-rests, complained about the effects of rapid rban development that had been encouraged y traditional municipal politicians with close es to local business (*see* URBAN REFORM). In a few ties — notably Winnipeg, Toronto and Ottawa - the New Democratic Party (NDP) has managed to establish itself as the main organization of the left in municipal politics, although generally the reformers have organized themselves into a coalition that is independent of any party. Some, like the Committee of Progressive Electors in Vancouver and the Montréal Citizens' Movement, are in effect municipal parties, but they are loosely organized and weakly disciplined compared to their provincial counterparts. In this respect, the left has followed the example of the right. The most successful local parties have been loose electoral organizations established by conservatives to resist political incursions from the left. The oldest of these, like the Independent Citizens' Election Committee in Winnipeg (1921) and the Civic Non-Partisan Association in Vancouver (1934), originated between the wars. Ironically, one of their aims has been to keep "party politics" out of municipal government.

The only highly disciplined governing party in a Canadian city is the Civic Party of Montréal — the instrument of longtime mayor Jean DRAPEAU. It is unusual for a mayor to dominate a municipal council; power tends to be diffused among council committees, and executive functions are usually divided or assigned to a multimember board on which the mayor has only one vote. Incumbent city councillors normally can rely on their own reputations and organizations in seeking reelection and so remain independent of parties and political leaders. This is especially true of the traditional conservative politicians who hold most of the seats on virtually every municipal council. Reform politicians are perhaps more inclined to accept party discipline, but they are divided on issues of policy and rooted in community organizations with conflicting demands. In fact the concern of contemporary reformers with making city government more sensitive to the demands of people in particular neighbourhoods has contributed to the continuing fragmentation of city politics, in the face of efforts to organize the forces of the left and right.

About half as many voters turn out for municipal elections as for federal and provincial elections, perhaps because of the absence of the major parties, the relative lack of publicity and the seeming unimportance of the issues. Other forms of citizen participation, involving either direct contact between people and their representatives or popular input into public decisions or both, are more feasible and common at the municipal level. For many people, what counts is the sensitivity of councillors to citizen demands between elections. The low rate of voting in municipal elections may actually make politicians more responsive to the demands of small groups or individuals, because margins of victory are smaller. On the other hand, because city politics are focused on a relatively narrow range of issues, people are discouraged from taking part. Until fairly recently, this franchise was based on property qualifications. Recent upheavals in Canadian city politics have yet to broaden its scope sufficiently to encourage the mass commitment desired by proponents of local self-government. WARREN MAGNUSSON

Reading: D.J.H. Higgins, *Urban Canada: Its Government and Politics* (1977, rev 1984); James Lorimer, *A Citizen's Guide to City Politics* (1972); Warren Magnusson and A. Sancton, eds, *City Politics in Canada* (1983).

Civil Code, fundamental legislative enactment which contains a comprehensive and easily understood statement of a nation's private LAW. It is typically found in legal systems whose traditions are traceable to Roman law. In Canada, only Québec has a Civil Code. Unlike an Administrative Code, Criminal Code or Code of Civil Procedure, a Civil Code expounds only on matters of private law, eg, names, domicile, age of majority, filiation, marriage, property, successions, gifts, wills, trusts, contracts, delicts, sale, lease, mandate, partnership pledge and hypothecs. It consolidates the fundamental concepts, rules, principles and ideals of a legal tradition in a clear non-technical style and, as a codification, is intended to be comprehensive in scope. Non-codal private law legislation is to be avoided while judicial decisions are not conceived as setting down the law.

Today Québec has 2 partially overlapping Civil Codes, the 1866 Civil Code of Lower Canada, which contains the bulk of the law, and the 1981 Civil Code of Québec, which covers only certain aspects of family law. The 1866 Code was the fruit of a Codification Commission created in 1857 to consolidate, in a bilingual statement, all civil laws in Lower Canada. For doctrine, the commissioners relied heavily on the works of the great French jurist, Pothier, to a lesser extent on various commentaries on the Code Napoléon and occasionally upon the text of the Louisiana Civil Code. They derived the majority of the Code's provisions from the Custom of Paris, brought to New France in 1663. The Code also includes rules drawn from several French royal ordinances and from the edicts and decisions of the Sovereign Council of New France prior to 1763. Various principles of common law, introduced either by the QUÉBEC ACT of 1774 or by statutes of Lower Canada or the Province of Canada enacted between 1791 and 1866, were also included. For form, the commissioners adopted the model of the 1804 Code Napoléon, the 3 books of which were entitled Of Persons; Of Property and Ownership and its Different Modifications; and Of the Acquisition and Exercise of Rights of Property. To these they appended a fourth, dealing with commercial law. Despite its eclectic sources the Civil Code was a distinctive document closely reflecting the basic values of 19th-century Québec — moral authoritarianism, philosophical individualism and economic liberalism.

Québec society has undergone considerable change but the Code has remained largely unamended, principally because of its status as a reflection of Catholic and francophone culture and as a bulwark against the intrusions of English COMMON LAW. Consequently the Code has lost many of its virtues as a codification. To overcome the growing chasm between the law of the Code and social reality, much non-Codal special legislation was enacted. Judicial interpretations often displaced Code provisions as the definitive statement of law. The language and organization of the Code became outdated. Then, in 1955, the Québec legislature established the Civil Code Revision Office. In 1964, after completing, piecemeal, some of the more urgent reforms, the office embarked upon a comprehensive review of the Code and proposed, in a *Draft Civil Code and Commentaries*, fundamental alterations of many substantive, linguistic and organizational premises of the Code's predecessor. In 1981, a new Civil Code of Québec was promulgated but only certain recommendations relating to family law were enacted. Several other proposals will be considered and implemented over the next few years, so that shortly the 1981 Code will entirely supersede the 1866 Civil Code. R.A. MACDONALD

Civil Defence The problem of protecting civilian populations in wartime grew dramatically with the advent of mass air raids in WWII. Although the threat to N America was negligible, Canada introduced air-raid precautions which provided for active fighter defence, EARLY-WARNING RADAR, blackouts, and rescue and emergency relief organizations. The first peacetime civil defence co-ordinator was appointed Oct 1948 to supervise the work of federal, provincial, and municipal authorities in planning for public air-raid shelters, emergency food and medical supplies, and the evacuation of likely target areas. The development of nuclear weapons and the COLD WAR in the 1950s forced Canadians to consider even more extensive measures. The Diefenbaker government in 1959 transferred responsibility for civil defence to the Emergency Measures Organization (Emergency Planning Canada since 1974) and then assigned all army units in Canada to post-atomic attack evacuation and survival operations. The next year the government launched a campaign in support of home fallout shelters. Public enthusiasm for such programs soon dwindled: costs were prohibitive, and the odds against survival mounted once the superpowers had more than enough missiles and warheads to destroy the world. Today the 3 levels of government maintain attack warning systems, but EPC's mandate has been broadened to give greater emphasis to natural disaster relief. STEPHEN HARRIS

Civil Engineering is that very large field of ENGINEERING concerned with construction of buildings, TRANSPORTATION and sanitation systems, etc; with SOIL mechanics and WATER resources; with CITY planning; and with SURVEYING and mapping.

Before the multiplication of engineering disciplines in the late 19th and early 20th centuries, engineers were either military or civilian. Civilian engineers built nonmilitary structures; those in the military concentrated on fortifications. The early engineers in what is now Canada were almost exclusively military. In NEW FRANCE, military engineers were responsible for surveying, road building and FORTIFICATION, and their work was taken over and further developed by British army engineers after the conquest. Civilian engineers became involved before the turn of the 19th century. For example, while CANAL building began as a military specialty, the first lock on the Sault Ste Marie canal was built in 1797-98 by the NORTH WEST COMPANY. Civil engineers were involved in such projects as the development of STEAMBOATS and RAILWAYS and the construction of roads, public buildings, harbours, etc.

Early engineers received their training as APPRENTICES to established professionals like Samuel KEEFER, who prepared plans for Ottawa's original parliament buildings, his brother, Thomas KEEFER, leading hydraulic engineer of his time, or Sir Casimir GZOWSKI, engineer of the international bridge over the Niagara R. As the extent of Canada's mineral and other resource wealth became apparent, and as the railway boom developed, it became necessary to establish formal training programs to provide critical engineering expertise. The first such courses were offered at King's College (now University of New Brunswick) in 1854; however, the real expansion in training did not begin until the 1870s, when, in the course of 5 years, programs were established at McGill, École polytechnique de Montréal; School of Practical Sciences, Toronto; and Royal Military College, Kingston. The profession has continued to expand since that time; in 1983, 28 universities offered accredited programs in civil engineering.

The Modern Profession

Today, the civil engineer's work tends to be highly specialized, covering every conceivable aspect of the construction of public and private works.

Surveying is the delineation of the position, form, natural or man-made features on a tract of land. Land must be surveyed before building can start, to determine legal boundaries, slopes, potential hazards, etc.

Soil Mechanics or Geotechnical Engineering is the branch of civil engineering which deals with characteristics of the substrate (soil or rock) which influence the suitability of a site for a given form of construction (eg, shear stress on slopes, plasticity of soil, soil seepage) and the peripheral structures needed to make a site safe for a specific structure (eg, foundations, drainage structures). Soil mechanics is important not only to the safe and economical exploitation of familiar environments, but also to successful use of fragile or hostile environments (eg, in Canada, PERMAFROST).

Structural Engineering, closely allied with ARCHITECTURE, deals with the design of buildings. Structural engineers translate architectural designs into precise instructions on building methods, materials, structural configurations (eg, column and beam designs), etc. Innovative buildings, such as Toronto's CN Tower, are lasting monuments not only to the architect's vision, but to the structural engineer's skill.

Materials Engineering Practitioners of this branch set specifications for materials used in the CONSTRUCTION INDUSTRY (eg, asphalt used in road pavements, structural steels) and undertake research to improve such materials (*see* METALLURGY).

Transportation Engineering involves planning, design and construction of all transportation networks, including roads, railways, airports and harbours.

Hydrotechnical or Water Resource Engineering deals with irrigation, drainage, the control of water hazards (eg, FLOODS), harbour and river development for transportation, the improvement of water availability and the protection of structures from attack by water (eg, ocean waves, normal RIVER flow).

Environmental Engineering is concerned with minimizing the environmental impacts of proposed engineering schemes.

Sanitary Engineering, an important part of URBAN AND REGIONAL PLANNING, deals with the design of WATER DISTRIBUTION and WASTE DISPOSAL systems to ensure that people have clean, healthy water to drink and that sewage does not become a POLLUTION hazard.

Before the turn of the century, a civil engineer would have designed many different structures; for example, Samuel Keefer designed not only the parliament buildings, but also a pioneer chain-link suspension bridge in 1836 over the Chaudière Falls, and many other public works. Today, civil engineers must co-operate with specialists from many nonengineering disciplines and engineering subfields to complete a single project. For example, engineers who specialized in urban planning and transportation engineering assist architects and planners in the initial design of a shopping centre. Once the location and size of the centre is determined, a more detailed design is produced. Traffic engineers design entrances and exits and lay out parking lots; structural engineers work with the architect to design the buildings; other engineers design the heating and ventilation, plumbing and electrical systems and join in the design process, to produce a set of engineering drawings and specifications. These are the documents from which the construction engineer estimates the cost of erecting the centre. These drawings and specifications form part of a CONTRACT, specifying the rights and duties of the contractor, the engineer and the owner, drawn up with the aid of lawyers specializing in engineering law.

Training and Societies

Students studying to be civil engineers must complete a 4-5-year university program. Civil engineering programs are periodically reviewed and accredited by the Canadian Accreditation Board of the Canadian Council of Professional Engineers. After graduation the student may be required to write an exam on professional practice to be accepted into a provincial professional engineers association as an engineer in training. Two years later, the trainee may apply for full membership and, based on the recommendations of employers, will be accepted as a professional engineer.

The first engineering society in Canada, t Canadian Society of Civil Engineers, was esta lished in 1887, later becoming the Engineeri Institute of Canada (1918) and now a federati with the Canadian Society for Civil Engineers a member. Civil engineers are also represent by the Canadian Council of Professional E gineers (est 1936), making up about one-quart of its nearly 200 000 members in 1984. FRANK NAV

Civil Law, the system of LAW that evolved fro the Roman law compilations of the Emper Justinian. Today it is found in countries of co tinental Europe as well as their former coloni and, in Canada, in Québec. In many jurisdi tions it is in force in the form of a CIVIL CODE. JOHN E.C. BRIERL

Civil Liberties, generally, freedoms to do ce tain things without restraint from governme ordinarily they also suggest there can be so restraint from private individuals or agenci eg, an individual may publish opinions wit out interference from government, but a new paper or magazine is not obliged to publi them. In this respect civil liberties can be di tinguished from civil rights. Civil rights may protected by legislation prohibiting discrimi ation by public and private officials against pe sons because of their race, colour, creed, sex, re gion or national origin. Civil liberties reflect essentially modern view of man and society b derive as well from older societies, such as tho of Greece and Rome. There is some overla legally, among the terms civil liberties, civ rights, and HUMAN RIGHTS and fundamental fre doms. Traditionally civil liberties included t freedoms of religion, expression (speech ar press), assembly and association. Civil-liberti protection, known as due process of law or t principles of fundamental justice, includes pr hibition of arbitrary arrest, detention, ar search or seizure; the rights to habeas corpu retaining counsel, bail, presumption of inn cence and a fair hearing; and the right not to subjected to torture or to cruel and inhuma treatment or punishment. Until the enactme of the CANADIAN CHARTER OF RIGHTS AND FREEDO fundamental freedoms in Canada were reco nized by common law, court decisions and legi lation. WALTER S. TARNOPOLS

Civil Procedure, the body of LAW concernin the prescribed methods of resolving disput through litigation (*see* CIVIL LAW). "Civil" disti guishes this body of law from CRIMIN PROCEDURE, which concerns the methods of pro ecuting criminal offences. The subject matter civil procedure includes the organization ar jurisdiction of courts competent to dispose civil suits, the conduct of actions from their i stitution through trial and to judgement, th conduct of appellate litigation, and the enforc ment of judgements and judicial orders. The LA OF EVIDENCE, which is germane to civil procedur governs the admissibility and weight of pro adduced in the course of a trial. The study civil procedure also extends to problems such the advisability, cost of and alternatives to li gation, whether litigants are eligible for LEG AID, and the duties of the legal profession in th conduct of litigation. In the same way as rul of COMMERCIAL LAW by their configuration ar soundness affect the course and volume of bus ness, rules of civil procedure affect the admini tration and the quality of civil justice. They d termine, among other important questio when and how citizens can have their "day court."

Legislative Authority Constitutionally, th primary responsibility for the administration justice lies with the provinces and therefo most of the legislation pertaining to civil pr cedure emanates from provincial legislature

However, under a special provision of the CONSTITUTION ACT, 1867, two of Canada's present courts were created by Acts of Parliament: the SUPREME COURT OF CANADA (the highest appellate court in the country), created in 1875, and the FEDERAL COURT, a court created in 1971 for the better administration of federal legislation. The statutes establishing these courts also specify the main features of their procedure.

Sources and History In common-law provinces, the legal rules forming the core of civil procedures are contained in statutes, such as the Judicature Acts, or Rules of Practice, or Rules of Court. These Acts, inspired by English legislation, unified the courts of common law and the courts of equity. They made possible the collection into rules of practice of numerous and technical rules of procedure, most of which had been made by judges on a case by case basis. Today judges still participate in making these rules. In the courts created by Parliament, detailed and often complex rules of practice also regulate most aspects of practice and procedure. In Québec the Code of Civil Procedure, an Act containing over 2000 articles, codifies most of the procedural rules and fulfils a similar function to rules of practice with which it shares many characteristics. Its origins can be traced to the French *Ordonnonce de la Procédure* of 1667. Judicial precedents are another important source of law in civil procedure, primarily in the common-law provinces.

The Process of Civil Litigation Throughout Canada the systems of civil procedure are adversarial in nature, designed to ensure opposing parties access to information necessary for the preparation of their case and to offer them an opportunity to argue against each other in court. Typically, individuals who believe they have suffered an infringement of their rights will consult a lawyer about the costs and risks of a suit. If it is decided to commence an action, the choice of the appropriate court will be the first procedural question considered by the lawyer. The answer depends on the nature of the case, the amount of the claim and on territorial considerations. There are several levels of trial courts in most provinces of Canada (*see* COURTS OF LAW), and within a province some of these courts are subdivided according to the territorial limits of counties or judicial districts. Once the choice is made, the lawyer representing the party who sues (the plaintiff) will attend the office of the court to have issued against the party being sued (the defendant) a document called a petition (or summons, statement of claim, writ of summons). In most cases the writ will be delivered (served) to the defendant in person by a bailiff. The document will inform the defendant of the nature of the claim against him and explain that if he does not appear and defend the action against him, the plaintiff may obtain judgement by default against the defendant. After service, each party in turn will give details of the claim or the defence or rebuttals of the opponent's claim in written pleadings (a statement of claim or declaration, sometimes already served with the original document, a statement of defence, an answer and a reply). The pleadings, served on the other party and filed with the court, will assist the plaintiff and defendant in determining the precise issues between them. The parties will also benefit from several "discovery procedures" (EXAMINATION FOR DISCOVERY, disclosure or discovery of documents, medical examination, etc) designed to facilitate the gathering of relevant information and the joining of issues.

If the parties cannot agree on a settlement out of court, they will proceed to trial. Because of the backlog of cases awaiting trial, months and sometimes years will elapse between the institution of the suit and the actual trial. The trial will take place either before a judge sitting alone or before a judge and a JURY. In Québec all civil trials are heard by judges sitting alone. At the trial each party will be entitled to lead (present) evidence, usually by live witnesses or by papers. Every witness called and examined by a party can be cross-examined by the other party. At this stage of the case, the rules of evidence are crucial. The parties then, through their lawyers, present closing arguments on the facts and the law of the case. The judge commonly renders judgement after preparing written reasons. Where there is a jury, however, the jury delivers a verdict on the issues of fact at the end of the trial and the judge renders judgement accordingly. When the defendant has failed to appear or to defend the action or where the plaintiff has failed to proceed with the action, judgement can be obtained summarily, without a trial. After judgement, the losing party may choose to APPEAL. Depending on the nature of the case and the amount in dispute, he may do so as of right or with the permission (leave) of the court of appeal. There is a court of appeal for each Canadian jurisdiction, provincial or federal. Appellate litigation is usually confined to questions of law. No new evidence is led by the parties, who must rely on a record of the evidence presented at trial. With written arguments ("factums") and later orally, the appellant and the respondent will respectively argue against and in favour of the judgement appealed. The court of appeal may confirm, vary or reverse the trial judgement, or order a new trial. In some cases the party who loses on appeal will bring a second appeal to the Supreme Court of Canada, the judgement of which is not subject to a further appeal. The final judgement in the case (either by an appellate court or by the trial court if no appeal is brought) will dismiss the action, or maintain it in whole or in part. The costs of the action will usually be awarded to the winning party, who will recover them from the losing party. These costs usually amount to a mere fraction of the total expenses. The rules of civil procedure also provide for the compulsory enforcement of judgements in the event that the party against whom judgement was rendered fails to comply with the order of the court. The seizure and sale of property and the garnishment of moneys owed are among the measures available for this purpose. Sometimes a disobedient party may even be jailed.

The Reform and Future of Civil Procedure In the last 20 years efforts have been made in most provinces to modernize and improve the law of civil procedure. A growing concern with the costs and delays of civil litigation and with the poor accessibility of the courts led to the creation and improvement of legal-aid schemes, SMALL CLAIMS COURTS and class-action procedures. During the same period, the need for the simplification and rationalization of civil procedure led to the appearance of reforming bodies in many provinces — some of which extensively revised local rules of practice. Procedural reforms must strike a delicate balance between form and substance. On the one hand, PROCEDURAL LAW should be the servant of SUBSTANTIVE LAW: parties to litigation ought to be heard expeditiously on the merits of their claims and should not be forced into a debate on the manner in which their claims must be presented or heard. On the other hand, a body of procedural rules, the enforcement of which inevitably generates side issues, is essential to the achievement of justice: in a process of adjudication that defines itself as adversarial, what a court decides depends very much on how it is presented with the issues, which in turn depend on how procedural rules assist the parties in preparing their case. YVES-MARIE MORISSETTE

Claire, Lake, 1437 km^2, elev 213 km, max length 63 km, located in NE Alberta in the SE corner of WOOD BUFFALO NATIONAL PARK, is an isolated western extension of Lk ATHABASCA and the largest lake entirely within Alberta. Situated W of Ft Chipewyan (1788), it is fed by the PEACE, Birch and McIvor rivers and drains eastward via Mamawi Lk into Lk Athabasca. Originally one of the deepest lakes in the Athabasca Delta region, it was named Clear Water Lk by Alexander MACKENZIE (1792), and its clarity was remarked upon by David THOMPSON (map of 1814). Over the years it has become shallow through silt accumulation, but still has a commercially profitable goldeye fishery. DAVID EVANS

Clam, common name for any bivalve (hinged shell) MOLLUSC, referring especially to those of economic significance burrowing in beaches or the seafloor. In Canada, numerous species are fished for human consumption. On the West Coast, butter and littleneck clams (*Saxidomus giganteus, Protothaca staminea,* respectively) are most important, but the accidentally introduced Manila clam (*Tapes philippinarum*) is also taken. Recently, an important fishery for the geoduck (*Panope abrupta*, formerly *P. generosa*) has developed. It is the largest clam of the N Pacific, with a body weight up to 5 kg, and a lifespan of up to 150 years. On the East Coast, the soft-shell clam (*Mya arenaria*) and the ocean quahog (*Arctica islandica*) are commercially important. FRANK R. BERNARD

Clan has been used to designate social groups whose members trace descent from either male or female ancestors. For the native people of Canada, the term has been used most often to designate groups based on unilineal descent. This means that a person belongs to the clan of either parent. Examples of matrilineal societies, those tracing descent from a female, are the IROQUOIS, HAIDA and TSIMSHIAN. Clans, named after birds, fish or deer, were important in regulating marriage (usually to forbid marriage with a fellow clan member). Certain rights, privileges and property were also associated with clans, and they functioned as ceremonial units that cut across geographical and even linguistic divisions. RENÉ R. GADACZ

Clancy, Francis Michael, "King," hockey player (b at Ottawa 25 Feb 1903). He joined Ottawa Senators in 1921 where he was a leader and local favourite. He was sold to TORONTO MAPLE LEAFS in 1930-31 for an unprecedented price of $35 000 and 2 players. Though light, his speed and nerve earned him popularity among fans, and his gritty play inspired the successful Leaf clubs of the 1930s. He was an NHL referee, coach of Toronto 1953-56 and later VP of Maple Leaf Gardens. His wit and lively recollections have made him a popular commentator on his sport. JAMES MARSH

Clark, Andrew Hill, historical geographer (b at Fairford, Man 29 Apr 1911; d at Madison, Wisc 21 May 1975). Son of a Baptist medical missionary, Clark was educated at McMaster and U of T where he studied with geographer Griffith TAYLOR and economic historian Harold INNIS. In 1938 he moved to Berkeley to work with cultural geographer Carl Sauer. His doctoral thesis, a study of the colonization of NZ by people, plants and animals, introduced his lifelong interest in the migration of Europeans to mid-latitude environments overseas. Professor of geography at U of Wisc from 1951 until his death, Clark directed a vigorous graduate program, wrote numerous books and articles, and became one of the best-known and most influential geographers of his day. His research focused on the early settlement of Canada, particularly of the Maritimes, whence his people came. With former students and friends scattered throughout Canadian universities, he was a founder of Canadian historical geography. His principal books are *The Invasion of New Zealand by People, Plants, and Animals: The South Island* (1949), *Three Centuries and the Island: A Historical Geography of Settlement and Agriculture in Prince Edward Island, Canada* (1959), and *Acadia: The Geography of Early Nova Scotia to 1760* (1968). COLE HARRIS

Clark, Charles Joseph, Joe, politician, prime minister of Canada (b at High River, Alta 5 June 1939). Clark's father was a newspaper editor. Educated at U of Alberta, he received a BA (and later an MA in political science) and was national Progressive Conservative student president. After working as a director of organization for the Alberta PCs and serving on the Ottawa staffs of Davie FULTON and Robert STANFIELD in the late 1960s, he was elected MP for Rocky Mountain, Alta, in 1972, and has represented Yellowhead, Alta, since 1979. In 1973 he married Maureen McTeer.

Clark emerged from a divided PC convention in Ottawa in 1976 as the surprise winner beneficiary of a mostly "progressive" consensus. In May 1979 the Conservatives won a minority government and he became Canada's sixteenth PM, the youngest ever and first native westerner to hold the office. He believed that he could build public approval by governing as if he had a majority, but he failed to win support from the other parties, especially the NDP, for key parts of his program, eg, the "privatization" of PETRO-CANADA, a mortgage tax credit, and austerity financing, and the government fell that December on a vote of nonconfidence in the House on John CROSBIE'S budget. In the Feb 1980 election Pierre TRUDEAU's Liberals returned to power. As leader of the Opposition 1980-83, Clark delayed the Trudeau constitutional plan in 1981 until judicial review was achieved and federal-provincial compromise was reached (*see* CONSTITUTION, PATRIATION OF). Even though Clark received support at 2 national party meetings and by Jan 1983 his party held a wide Gallup Poll lead, a sizable minority of Conservatives still considered him too "progressive" and an electoral liability. He chose to settle the question of his leadership at a convention, held in June 1983, but lost on the fourth ballot to Brian MULRONEY. After the convention, Clark worked to avoid the divisions that had long plagued the Conservatives and he played a major role in drafting PC policies on international arms control. His unique position in the party, as a still young, bilingual and active former PM who had won the respect of many Canadians, was recognized when he was named secretary of state for external affairs in the Mulroney government. RICHARD CLIPPINGDALE

Joe Clark, 16th prime minister of Canada, 1979-80, and minister of external affairs in the Mulroney Cabinet (1984-), shown at the Conservative Party leadership convention (*photo by John deVisser*).

Clark, Clifford, civil servant (b at Martentown, Ont 18 Apr 1889; d at Chicago 27 Dec 1952). Clark attended Queen's and Harvard before returning to Queen's as a lecturer in 1915, where he helped establish banking and commerce courses. In 1923 he joined the American investment firm of S.W. Strauss as an economic adviser. The Depression ended this career, however, and he returned to Queen's. In 1932 PM R.B. BENNETT made Clark an adviser during the Imperial Economic Conference, and subsequently offered him deputy ministership of the Dept of Finance. Clark helped make Finance a powerful government department by encouraging bright young economists to enter the public service and by taking their advice. Though initially cautious, he began to see an expanded role for the state in economic planning. The man who condemned wage controls at the end of WWI helped implement them in WWII.

As deputy minister, Clark supported the establishment of the BANK OF CANADA and a series of mortgage-assistance measures. During WWII he chaired the Economic Advisory Committee and helped convince PM Mackenzie KING to adopt, among other measures, the 1944 Family Allowance Bill. His ideas and influence made him important in the development of a more active government role in economic planning. DOUG OWRAM

Clark, Howard Charles, chemist, university administrator (b at Auckland, NZ 4 Sept 1929). Educated at U of Auckland and Cambridge, he came to BC in 1957 and rapidly established a reputation for original work in organo-metallic, co-ordination and fluorine chemistry. From 1965 he continued this research as professor of inorganic chemistry at Western, receiving the Noranda Award of the Chemical Institute of Canada, the ScD degree from Cambridge and fellowship in the RSC. He served as head of Western's chemistry department 1967-76, then moved to U of Guelph as VP Academic and professor of chemistry. CHRISTOPHER WILLIS

Clark, Karl Adolf, chemist (b at Georgetown, Ont 20 Oct 1888; d at Saanichton, BC 8 Dec 1966). A pioneer of the hot-water recovery process for extracting oil from tar sands, Clark developed an interest in tar during his first job after leaving university, as chief of the federal Mines Branch's Road Materials Division (1916-20). He then joined the ALBERTA RESEARCH COUNCIL, founded in 1919 by H.M. TORY expressly to apply science to local resources; the ARC functioned in its early years as part of U of A, where Clark worked until retirement (1954). The first tar-sands plants were built in the 1920s but were uneconomic. Clark's process was installed in the first successful plant, Great Canadian Oil Sands (later Suncor Ltd), opened in 1967 at Ft McMurray, Alta, and the later Syncrude plant. *See* BITUMEN. DONALD J.C. PHILLIPSON

Clark, Paraskeva, née Plistik, painter (b at St Petersburg [Leningrad, USSR] 28 Oct 1898). Clark added a bright piquante flavour to the Toronto circle of painters in the 1930s and 1940s, where traces of Cubism learned in Soviet Free Studios (1917-21) contrasted with the prevailing GROUP OF SEVEN, finding more affinity with the Montréal painters. Clark left Russia for Paris with her baby son on the death of her first husband (1923). There she met Canadian Philip Clark whom she married, moving to Toronto in 1931. She continued to paint, revealing Leftist concern in pictures like *Petrouschka* (1937). She developed solid form and an individualistic flair, gradually painting the Canadian scene, as well as flower studies, still life and self-portraits. She is the subject of an NFB film, *Portrait of the Artist as an Old Lady* (1982). ANNE MCDOUGALL

Clark, Samuel Delbert, sociologist (b at Lloydminster, Alta 24 Feb 1910). Trained in history and sociology at U of Sask, London School of Economics, McGill and U of T, he joined the political economy department at U of T in 1938 and became known for studies interpreting Canadian social development as a process of disorganization and reorganization on a series of economic frontiers. His scholarship won him acceptance when Canadian academics were still skeptical of the fledgling discipline of SOCIOLOGY. Under his direction, a series on the SOCIAL CREDIT movement produced 10 monographs by Canadian scholars. In the 1960s his interest shifted to contemporary consequences of economic change, especially suburban living and urban poverty. His publications include *The Canadian Manufacturers Association* (1939), *The Social Development of Canada* (1942), *Church and Sect in Canada* (1948), *Movements of Political Protest in Canada* (1959), *The Developing Canadian Community* (1962, 2nd ed 1968), *The Suburban Society* (1966), *Canadian Society in Historical Perspective* (1976) and *The New Urban Poor* (1978). A former president of the RSC, he became professor emeritus of U of T in 1976 and has since been a visiting professor at universities here and abroad. P.J. GIFFEN

Clarke, Austin Chesterfield, novelist (b at St James, Barbados 26 July 1934). Clarke came to Canada as a student in 1955 and eventually became a journalist in Toronto. After the success of his short stories, published in *The Survivors of the Crossing* (1964), he taught and served as writer in residence in a number of N American universities. He went on to write the humorous yet socially critical trilogy of Caribbean immigrant life in Toronto for which he is best known, *The Meeting Point* (1967), *Storm of Fortune* (1973) and *The Bigger Light* (1975). TERRENCE CRAIG

Clarke, Charles Kirk, psychiatrist, educator (b at Elora, Canada W 16 Feb 1857; d at Toronto 20 Jan 1924). He received his MD from U of T 1879 but had already begun his career in PSYCHIATRY in 1874, serving as clinical assistant to Dr Joseph WORKMAN at the Toronto Asylum. He was assistant superintendent of the Hamilton Asylum 1880-81, of the Rockwood Asylum in Kingston 1881-85, and then superintendent at Rockwood, a position he retained until 1905. He was transferred to the Toronto Asylum that year and resigned in 1911 to accept the superintendency of the Toronto General Hospital. At the same time he served as professor of psychiatry and dean of the Faculty of Medicine at U of T. In 1918 he founded (with Dr C.M. HINCKS) and became first medical director of the Canadian National Committee for Mental Hygiene, later the Canadian Mental Health Assn. The Clarke Insitute of Psychiatry in Toronto is named after him. THOMAS E. BROWN

Reading: C. Greenland, *Charles Kirk Clarke: A Pioneer of Canadian Psychiatry* (1966).

Clarke, Douglas William, conductor, educator, composer (b at Reading, Eng 4 Apr 1893; d at Warwick, Eng 14 Nov 1962). An important influence in Montréal's musical development, and as founder and conductor of the Montreal Orchestra 1930-41, Clarke gave the city its first performances of many symphonic masterworks, including the Canadian premiere of Rachmaninoff's *Variations on a Theme of Paganini*. As dean of McGill's Faculty of Music 1930-55, he established a public concert series that featured lecturers and musicians of world renown. Several of Clarke's compositions — mainly sacred choral works — have been published. BARCLAY MCMILLAN

Clarke, George Johnson, lawyer, editor, premier of NB (b at St Andrews, NB 10 Oct 1857; d at St Stephen, NB 26 Feb 1917). Editor of the *St Croix Courier* and a prominent lawyer in St Stephen, Clarke became Speaker of the NB Legislature in 1909. He became premier in 1914 when ames Kidd FLEMMING was forced to resign over und-raising irregularities. He suffered poor ealth throughout most of his 3-year term and is administration accomplished little of lasting ignificance. ARTHUR T. DOYLE

larke, Henry Joseph, lawyer, politician (b in Donegal, Ire 7 July 1833; d on a train near Medicine Hat, Alta 13 Sept 1889). Admitted to the bar 855, Clarke practised law in Montréal and pent several years in California and El Salador. A bilingual Roman Catholic, Clarke ame to Manitoba in Nov 1870 to assist Lt-Gov Adams G. Archibald in establishing the provinial government. Elected an MLA on 30 Dec 870, he served as Manitoba's first attorney genral from 3 Jan 1871 until 4 July 1874 and elped to found the province's legal system. After returning to California, where he divorced nd remarried, Clarke resumed the practice of aw in Winnipeg in 1877 and acted as counsel or 25 of Riel's followers after the NORTH-WEST EBELLION of 1885. A controversial figure, Clarke nade many enemies but deserves credit for his upport of the Métis. LOVELL C. CLARK

larke, James Paton, composer, conductor, organist, teacher (b at Edinburgh? 1807 or 1808; at Yorkville [Toronto], Ont 27 Aug 1877). An outstanding professional figure in early oronto's musical development, as first conducor of the Toronto Philharmonic Soc, Clarke ave the city its earliest performances of several Mozart and Beethoven symphonies 1847-48. He aught singing, piano and guitar, and was organist of St James' Anglican Cathedral 1848. Clarke composed songs — notably *Lays of the Male Leaf or Songs of Canada* (1853) — and wrote and dited church music. Toronto's King's College ranted him a bachelor of music degree — Canda's first — in 1846. BARCLAY MCMILLAN

lass and Politics Politics is sometimes decribed as the process by which society deternines who gets what, when and how. In other words, POLITICS is defined as a process of alloating scarce resources through the exercise of ower. The electoral process and the competiion among political parties are normally conidered the focus of politics, but there are several ther processes that determine the allocation of esources, the most important of which is the conomic process by which needed or desired oods are produced and distributed. Politics and conomics are interrelated in a number of ways, nd political power cannot be understood withut examining the ways in which economic elations affect its exercise (*see* SOCIAL CLASS).

Because power is divided in a liberal democacy between the private and public sectors, it is helpful for people seeking to change the econmy to organize in both sectors. Therefore, one of the most common political phenomena in liberal democracies throughout the 20th century has been the growth of political parties claiming to represent the interests of a particular class. Workers have also organized themselves into rade UNIONS to exercise influence, primarily in their workplaces but also on the STATE. Moreover, trade unions have often sponsored or otherwise supported political parties that advocate a redistribution of resources. In this way, political conflict in many countries has come to reflect the differing interests of workers and owners, rich and poor, but Canada has always seemed an exception to this general pattern. Elections and parties in Canada do not seem to eflect class divisions. Indeed, neither the LIBERAL PARTY nor the Progressive CONSERVATIVE PARTY make claims to represent any one class; they claim instead to represent all Canadians and to reflect the "national interest." Moreover, these 2 parties have always captured the support of the vast majority of voters. The NEW DEMOCRATIC PARTY (NDP) has never received a majority of the support of the working class, despite the fact it presents itself as a party interested in representing working people.

Considering only the voting patterns in federal elections, it appears that there is very little relation between class and politics in Canada. In recent elections (1980) the NDP has received no more than 20% of the vote. Of those who might be considered "workers", only a minority voted for the NDP, while many more supported the Liberals. There are, however, other manifestations of the relationship between class and politics that can be considered. One consequence of the character of Canadian FEDERALISM is that the politics and parties at the federal and provincial levels of government are often quite different. The experience of the NDP in some provinces — particularly BC, Saskatchewan and Manitoba — has resembled that of social democratic parties in other countries. In Québec, the PARTI QUÉBÉCOIS has advocated economic and social reforms similar to those of social democrats elsewhere. These parties have sometimes won sufficient support from workers, farmers and salaried employees to form a government. Electoral politics in these provinces resemble the traditional relationship between class and politics, where the party of the workers (and their allies) occupies the "left" side of the political spectrum and a party committed to maintaining the economic and social status quo occupies the "right."

That there is, in some circumstances, a strong relationship between class and politics is indicated as well by the history of the organization by farmers of their own political parties, eg, the PROGRESSIVE PARTY (1920s) and the UNITED FARMERS OF ONTARIO and of Saskatchewan and Alberta (1920s and 1930s). The farmers also organized for class action when they provided the backbone of support to the SOCIAL CREDIT party in Alberta and to the Co-operative Commonwealth Federation in the 1930s.

These farmers believed that they were victims of both class and sectional discrimination as a result of the federal government's economic strategy, which they felt was designed to benefit central Canadian manufacturers and the railroads. Throughout the interwar years, Canadian politics did not manifest a traditional social democratic version of class politics but there was a competition for power that nevertheless reflected conflict between classes.

A third manifestation of the relationship between class and politics is the political activity of trade unions. Throughout the 20th century, Canadian LABOUR ORGANIZATIONS had preferred to press their demands through COLLECTIVE BARGAINING and direct negotiations with employers. However, since the mid-1950s and with increasing enthusiasm since the early 1970s, the CANADIAN LABOUR CONGRESS (CLC) has tried to intervene in electoral politics. In 1961 the CLC pledged itself to support the NDP as the official political arm of labour and to encourage its local unions to affiliate with the party. The CLC became a major source of funds for the NDP, and provided personnel for leadership positions within the party. However, this official support for the NDP by the CLC has never translated into solid electoral support, and union members have been only slightly more likely than nonunion workers to vote for the NDP in federal elections since 1962. When collective bargaining and industrial action (eg, STRIKES) have proven insufficient, unions have turned directly to the Cabinet for redress of grievances or to voice their demands. In addition, the tradition of supporting whichever of the major parties seemed the most receptive of unions' goals — a tradition known as "gomperism," after the early leader of the American Federation of Labor, Samuel Gompers — means that those unions not affiliated with the NDP, as well as individual unionists, continue to look to the major parties for representation.

The nature of the relationship between class and politics in Canada has been determined by a number of factors. The first is the relatively late and quite partial commitment of the trade unions to partisan politics. For most of Canada's history as an industrial economy, the trade unions refrained from supporting any party and they confined their demands for reform to those that could be won in negotiations with capital or through influence on the Cabinet. In consequence, people who might have been accustomed to expressing their class identities in politics in the workplace looked to electoral politics for the expression of other identities — those of language or region, for example. Politics came to be defined as a contest over ethnic or regional power, rather than of class struggle for changes in basic economic relationships.

A second reason follows from the important influence of REGIONALISM and FEDERALISM on all aspects of Canadian politics. Because of the great regional variations in production — manufacturing concentrated in Ontario and Québec, wheat farming on the Prairies, oil and gas in the West, fishing on the east and west coasts, etc — the distribution of classes is uneven across the country. Such regional differentiation in the concentration of classes has meant that politics directed against the effects of class relations have often been manifested as regional antagonisms. Thus, although farmers opposed to the NATIONAL POLICY were expressing a class interest, their actions were frequently expressed and interpreted as regional protest. In addition, industrial workers often found that their support of a high tariff and a protected market for goods was not shared by miners and loggers in peripheral provinces. The political strategy of classes therefore divided along lines of region.

Moreover, because either workers or farmers or both in the different regions advocated policies to bring about regional development, they soon found themselves in political alliances with the professionals and small businessmen of their regions whose own class interest depended upon a healthy regional economy in which demand for their goods and services was strong. Therefore, political parties like the Social Credit, the Parti Québécois and even the NDP have become populist parties instead of class parties (*see* POPULISM). Such parties claim to represent all the people of their particular region and promise to protect them against the overwhelming economic and political power of the centre of the country. In this way, class conflicts have been downplayed and regional populist politics have dominated.

The existence of federal institutions, in turn, permitted this regional protest and populism to develop further and be absorbed into the politics of FEDERAL-PROVINCIAL RELATIONS. Provincial parties, especially governing ones, understood that possibilities existed for the mobilization of cross-class coalitions in support of their projects for economic development, projects which the federal government opposed for a variety of reasons. In Québec, for example, when the nationalist movement entered electoral politics via the PQ, it based its strategy on a broadly based, cross-class coalition of opposition to the actions of the federal government. Thus, in several provinces, what might have become protest against the inequalities that had been created between classes by the federal government's development strategies was translated to national or regional populist protest and then to conflict over the division of powers in Canadian federalism. Therefore, despite the fact that there was a visible and important relationship between classes in many aspects of Canadian politics, class conflict disappeared from the electoral agenda. JANE JENSON

Classics, the study of Greek and Roman antiquity, revered for centuries as a quintessential element in a liberal education, gained its foothold in Canada during the 17th century when Latin entered the curriculum of the Jesuit College in Québec. The benevolent "tyranny" of Classics in French-speaking Canada, inaugurated in 1636, ended in 1960 when the collèges classiques ceased being the sole source of the BA degree and when it became acceptable to obtain a BA without Greek or Latin as background study. Elsewhere in Canada, particularly after Confederation, Latin and Greek, tenacious factors in secondary-school class offerings until WWII, were taught along Victorian and Edwardian disciplinarian lines favoured in English and Scottish universities and schools. Literary, historical and philosophical elements were reserved for university programs. Inroads and advances by scientific studies, engineering, medicine, law and business administration, and the effects of technological and social changes during the 1950s, shattered the security of Classics as a discipline. Greek and Latin, one-time haven of university scholarship holders and aspiring intellectuals, damaged by dispiriting teaching founded on grammatical exegesis and prose composition and on literal translation as training in exactitude of expression, were faced with plunging enrolments and accusations of being outmoded and fossilized.

Classicists responded by devising and adopting new methodologies and livelier textbooks to present the ancient languages in the post-Sputnik era. The Cambridge Latin Course in particular won widespread adoption in the 1970s and helped save Latin from extinction in the high schools. Contemporary linguistic theory applied to Latin teaching engendered fresh notions of what a language-learning course should be. In particular, secondary-school students were encouraged to study material that merited both literary and sociological discussion and criticism. Greek, which was moribund or extinct in secondary schools by the 1960s, found renewed life with the McGill University Course, patterned after the successful structuralist Latin courses and employing practices familiar in the language laboratory. Both languages continue to attract registration in the universities, and Latin studies find slender but continuing commitment in secondary schools where administrators countenance small enrolments.

The universities, faced with deteriorating registration in Classics and in combined Honours courses including Latin or Greek, resorted to patterns pronounced successful in the US; courses in translation and in classical civilization or classical studies, introduced tentatively during the 1950s, multiplied rapidly. Nowadays, hundreds of students from different backgrounds and course affiliations attend classes in Greek and Roman drama, epic, biography and historiography, religion and mythology. Mounting interest in MEDITERRANEAN ARCHAEOLOGY and in art history has also helped revive the Classics, and the incorporation of archaeological material into civilization courses has contributed greatly to their popularity. Ancient History, taught under the aegis of either Classics or History departments, supports classical studies in appropriate ways. Classics, by reason of its composite nature, and by choice, has also collaborated with programs in COMPARATIVE LITERATURE, hermeneutics and modern Greek.

Diminishing enrolment in Latin and the demise of secondary-school Greek failed to thwart the development of advanced study in Classics. MA programs exist at most major universities and doctoral studies have been developed at Dalhousie, Laval, McGill, U de Montréal, U of Ottawa, McMaster (Roman Studies), U of Alberta and UBC. The U of Toronto program has the most course offerings and largest enrolment. Degree programs and doctoral dissertations are generally conditioned by the particular scholarly expertise of professors involved and by the universities' research collections. Research and teaching are the primary functions of classicists in universities. Support for their programs derives from federal agencies, university resources and foundations and organizations outside Canada. Prime support comes from the SOCIAL SCIENCES AND HUMANITIES RESEARCH COUNCIL OF CANADA, the Killam Senior Research Fellowship Program, the American Council of Learned Societies, the Institute for Advanced Study at Princeton, NJ, and the Nuffield Foundation (England). Grants-in-aid of publication derive largely from Canadian federal agencies. The quality of teaching and research in the Classics has been recognized not only in national and international awards for excellence, but also in the rich diversity of journals and publishers who by publishing have promoted Canadian classical scholarship.

Several major scholarly projects are in progress: *Lexicon Iconographicum Mythologiae Classicae*, an international iconographical dictionary of classical mythology as depicted in the complete range of art works from the ancient world, and including material in Canadian museums and galleries, with support from the CANADIAN FEDERATION FOR THE HUMANITIES; the Dio Cassius project (U of Calgary); *Catalogus Translationum et Commentariorum* (Pontifical Institute of Mediaeval Studies, Toronto); Vergilian Bibliography (McMaster); and The Collected Works of Erasmus (U of Toronto).

Fresh incentive to classical scholarship and to archaeological and historical study is provided by 3 Mediterranean centres nestling under the aegis of the Canadian Mediterranean Institute since 1980: the Canadian Archaeological Institute at Athens (fd in 1974), the Canadian Academic Centre in Italy (Rome, fd in 1978) and the Canadian Institute in Egypt (Cairo, fd in 1980). These overseas headquarters enjoy amiable and hospitable links with the American Academy in Rome, the British Schools in Athens and Rome, the American School of Classical Studies in Athens and the Vergilian Society in Italy (at Cumae, near Naples).

The Classical Association of Canada (fd in 1946), although an outgrowth of the Ontario Classical Assn, was able to claim national identity by its membership *a mari usque ad mare*. Its annual meetings, in conjunction with those of the Royal Society of Canada and other LEARNED SOCIETIES, cater to anglophone and francophone audiences, and feature colloquia on material and issues of general interest. The association's journal, *Phoenix*, launched 1947, has attained international status as a scholarly quarterly. Canadian classicists have been numbered among presidents, editors and executive members of various international classical organizations. Presidents of the CAC are recognized as vice-presidents of the Classical Association (UK).

The abolition of the Latin requirement at Oxford and Cambridge universities in the 1960s, and the restriction of the use of Latin in the Roman Catholic mass were but visible symbols of the dwindling capital and overstrained credit of the Classics. But new teaching techniques, vigorous research programs and interdisciplinary engagements by classical scholars mark a "Copernican revolution" in the discipline. Degree courses in classical studies for undergraduates who come to university with little or no experience with the classical languages would have been inconceivable to earlier generations. The continuing presence of Classics in the universities indicates that the ability of the Classics to sustain and fortify society in the face of life's problems and predicaments remains durable and intact.

ALEXANDER G. MCKAY

Claude, Renée, stage name of Renée Bélange singer (b at Montréal 3 July 1939). While h early repertoire consisted of French song Claude soon became known for her interpretation of songs by Québec writers such as Jean Pierre Ferland, Stéphane Venne, Clément Desrochers and Luc Plamondon. In 1960 sh made her first appearance on CBC television. I 1968 she was awarded the trophy for best performer in Montréal's Gala des Artistes. Tw years later she performed with the Montrea Symphony Orchestra at Place des Arts. She ha also appeared in the US, France, Belgium Poland, the USSR, Japan, Greece and Venezuel Her biggest hits include "C'est notre fête au jourd'hui," "Le Tour de la terre," "C'est le début d'un temps nouveau" and "Ce soir je fais l'amou avec toi."

HÉLÈNE PLOUFF

Claxton, Brian Brooke, lawyer, politician (b a Montréal, Qué 23 Aug 1898; d at Ottawa, Ont 1 June 1960). He attended Lower Canada Colleg and McGill, graduating with an LLB in 192 the year he began to practise law. During WW he had served overseas with the 10th Siege Battery. He was active in many organizations, including the Canadian Clubs, the Canadian Radio League, the League of Nations Society, an the Canadian Institute of International Affair and he taught insurance law at McGill. Claxto was elected as a Liberal to represent St Lawrence St George in 1940 and was soon appointed parliamentary secretary to PM King. While minister of health and welfare he was responsible fo the introduction of family allowances and a minister of defence he supervised the rebuildin of the Canadian armed forces during and afte the Korean War. He also helped negotiate Newfoundland's entry into Confederation in 194 In 1954 he retired from politics to become general manager of Metropolitan Life and in 195 was appointed first chairman of the Canad Council.

DAVID J. BERCUSO

Clay, common name for complex group of industrial MINERALS, each characterized by different mineralogy, occurrence and uses. All a natural, earthy, fine-grained minerals composed mainly of water-containing aluminum silicates; they may contain iron, alkalis and alkaline earths (*see* SAND AND GRAVEL). The commercial value of clays and of claylike shales depends on proximity to centres where cla products are used, and on physical properties eg, plasticity, strength, shrinkage or heat resistance. Common clays and shales are the principa raw materials available from Canadian deposit for the manufacture of clay products, eg, common and facing brick and structural, partition quarry and drain tiles. Fireclays are used principally for the manufacture of medium- and high-duty firebrick and for crucibles. Know Canadian fireclays are insufficiently refractor (heat resistant) without the addition of som very heat-resistant material, eg, alumina. Stoneware clays are similar to low-grade plastic clay and range from commercially inferior materia through semirefractory to firebrick clays. Stoneware clays are used for sewer pipe, flue liners facing brick, pottery, stoneware crocks and jug and chemical stoneware. Ball clays are extremely heat resistant and are composed mainly o fine-particle kaolinite, quartz, illite and mica However, widespread use of these clays in Canada has been hampered by distance fron markets and lack of proven reserves. Know deposits of china clay (kaolin), a high-quality clay with more alumina and less silica than bal clays, have not been developed in Canada, primarily because of their small size. Almost al clays produced in Canada are used for domestic requirements; however, exports of clay product and refractories were worth about $63.5 millio in 1980.

Common clays and shales are found through

ut Canada, but new deposits with improved drying and firing characteristics are sought. Fireclays occur in the Whitemud Formation of southern Saskatchewan and southeastern Alberta and at Sumas Mtn, BC. In NS some clays at Shubenacadie are sufficiently heat resistant for medium-duty refractories, and clays from Musquodoboit have been used by foundries in the Atlantic provinces. The principal source of stoneware clay in Canada is the Whitemud Formation. Common clays and shales are mined from open pits using modern, surface MINING equipment. Processing involves crushing, screening, extruding and drying. Processing of fireclays and of bentonite (an absorptive clay) is more specialized and may involve calcining, in the former case, and acid activation, in the latter. *See* CHAMPLAIN SEA. G.O. VAGT

Clayton-Thomas, David, pop singer, songwriter (b in Surrey, Eng 13 Sept 1941). An aggressive yet sensitive singer, he was raised in Toronto and led several local bands, including Fabulous Shays and Bossmen, before joining the New York jazz-rock ensemble Blood Sweat and Tears in 1968. He fronted BS&T during its most successful years (1968-72), returned to it in 1974 and assumed leadership in 1976. He sang on its hit recordings of "Spinning Wheel," "Lucretia MacEvil" (his own songs), "You Make Me So Very Happy" and others. Largely a Canadian band in its last incarnation, BS&T broke up in 1980. MARK MILLER

Clear Grits, Upper Canadian Reformers who became discontented with the conservatism of the BALDWIN-LAFONTAINE ministry after 1849. The group was composed of Old Radicals, such as Peter Perry, who attempted to revive the agrarian republicanism of the prerebellion period, and young entrepreneurs such as William McDougall from the Toronto area, who advocated elective institutions, universal manhood suffrage, free trade with the US, secularization of the CLERGY RESERVES, and representation by population to overcome perceived French Canadian domination. As well, they attracted support in rural areas west of Toronto. After the Old Radicals were accommodated in the Hincks-Morin ministry (1851-54), the young Grits fell behind George BROWN, who replaced their republicanism with British liberalism. The Brownite Liberals, advocating REP BY POP and annexation of the North-West, became the dominant party in Canada West by the mid-1850s and formed the basis of the LIBERAL PARTY after Confederation. DAVID MILLS

Clearwater River, 280 km long, rises in Patterson, Forest and Lloyd lakes in NW Saskatchewan, flows SE to Careen Lk and abruptly turns W to join the ATHABASCA R at Fort McMurray, Alta. It has cut spectacular gorges and waterfalls into the sandstone and limestone; the forest along its banks is still wild and is home to moose, deer, bear, wolf, lynx, geese, fox and beaver. The only westward-flowing river between Winnipeg and the Rockies, it was an important link in the FUR-TRADE ROUTE, connected to the CHURCHILL R via Methye Portage. The river is "clear" only in relation to others in the area. JAMES MARSH

Clergy Reserves, one-seventh of the public lands of Upper and Lower Canada, reserved by the 1791 CONSTITUTIONAL ACT for the maintenance of a "Protestant clergy," a phrase intended to apply to the Church of England alone. The reserves excited controversy, especially in UC, although for many years they brought no income since settlers could obtain other lands free. When free land grants ceased in the 1820s, Bishop John STRACHAN decided the C of E should sell rather than lease its lands as it had done since 1819. In 1827, having blocked a transfer to the CANADA COMPANY, he persuaded Britain to authorize sales of one-quarter of the reserves, not to exceed 100 000 acres (40 468 ha) per year.

An increasingly powerful reform movement, including many denominational rivals, opposed Strachan's plans. In 1824 the legislature upheld the claim of the Church of Scotland to a share of the reserves. Later the debate over "co-establishment" of the C of S became an assault on the idea of establishment itself (*see* ANGLICANISM). In 1828 a Select Committee of the Assembly and the CANADA COMMITTEE of the British Commons criticized church establishment and recommended dividing profits from reserves among the Protestant denominations. In 1840 the Assembly accepted a bill dividing half the proceeds between the C of E and the C of S, leaving the remainder to other denominations. Still, by the early 1850s secularization of the reserves was being widely demanded. In late 1854 the MacNab-Morin coalition of UC conservatives and LC reformers passed a bill to transfer reserve-sale proceeds to the Municipalities Funds of UC and LC; to pay present clerical incumbents their stipends for life; and to allow them to cede their life claims to their respective churches, which could commute the total into 6% annuities. Commutation was attacked, but most wished to settle the controversy that had bedevilled religious and political life for 3 decades. The clergy reserves were secularized not because they were obstacles to settlement, but because the policy of church establishment they represented was unacceptable in religiously heterogeneous UC. CURTIS FAHEY

Clermont, Yves Wilfrid, anatomist (b at Montréal 14 Aug 1926). Clermont received a classical French education, but obtained his PhD at McGill Medical School. Less than 3 years after he joined its anatomy department, he became a teaching fellow in histology. He rose to full professorship and, in 1975, became chairman. An outstanding teacher of histology, he is best known as a specialist in male reproduction. Over the years he has clarified the confusing structure of the human testis. Using both the light and electron microscopes with skill, he has described the full sequence of events that give rise to mature sperm cells. CHARLES P. LEBLOND

Clifford, Betsy, alpine skier (b at Old Chelsea, Qué 15 Oct 1953). Practically raised on the slopes of her father's Camp Fortune ski area, she began skiing at age 5. At 12 she was national junior champion and at 13 Canadian senior slalom champion (1967). She became the youngest ever world ski champion with her 1970 victory in the giant slalom championships in Val Gardena, but was most pleased with her silver medal in the 1974 World Downhill Championship. MURRAY SHAW

Climate is often defined as average WEATHER, when weather means the current state of the atmosphere. For the scientist, climates are the result of the exchanges of heat and moisture at the Earth's surface. Here, climate will be used to describe the temperature and moisture conditions of the layer of air near the Earth's surface, ie, the air in which man lives.

Canada is a very large country with many different climates. It extends 4500 km, from 42° N lat (at Pelee I, Lk Erie) to 83° N (the tip of Ellesmere I). Thus, there are great differences in length of day from S to N: in Dec southern Canada receives 8 hours of daylight; Canada's northern tip, none. Latitude is also responsible for the generally westerly air flow in Canada. Southern Canada is often the battle zone between cold air from arctic regions and warm, moist air from the south; hence, airflow is channeled E-W. Latitude is not the only geographic factor significant to climate; position on the continent, especially distance from the OCEANS, also plays a part. Therefore, places with roughly the same latitude, eg, Victoria and Winnipeg, have very different climates since Victoria's climate is modified by the warm Pacific Ocean and Winnipeg's is not.

Temperature is the degree of warmness or coldness. Air temperatures have been measured in some places in southern Canada for over 100 years, but in the Arctic for a much shorter time. Climate statistics are usually expressed as 30-year averages, the most recently published being those for 1951-80. In winter, when northern Canada receives very little solar radiation, temperature differences from N to S are great. The average maximum Jan temperature of Alert, at the tip of Ellesmere I, is -28.1°C, that of Windsor, Ont, -0.7°C, a difference of 27.4°C. In summer the long days in northern Canada result in smaller N-S differences, with maximum temperatures in July of 6.8°C for Alert and 27.8°C for Windsor.

Monthly air temperatures give an indication of the hotness or coldness of a place at a particular time of year, and monthly temperature maps can be drawn for Canada. However, it is also desirable to have a single map which expresses the total amount of heat received by a given place. To express this total, climatologists have formulated an index of potential evapotranspiration (PE), derived from monthly temperatures above 0°C. Potential evapotranspiration is the amount of water that potentially would evaporate and transpire from a vegetated surface; therefore, PE is an index of heat, but expressed in terms of depth of water at the Earth's surface. The high arctic islands, with a PE of under 200 mm, receive very little heat; the warmest areas in southern Ontario, Québec and BC receive 3 times as much. Canada is obviously not a warm country; since tropical areas have an annual PE of over 1500 mm.

The coldness of a place is also of interest, especially in these days of expensive ENERGY, when coldness can be equated with the cost of heating homes. A parameter which summarizes coldness is the heating degree day (HDD), a unit which sums the temperatures below 18°C, the point at which household furnaces must be turned on. Southern Ontario has 4000 HDD annually while the high arctic islands have 12 000 HDD.

Moisture the most important climatic parameter after temperature is precipitation, ie, moisture that falls to the Earth's surface as RAIN, snow, hail, etc. Because of Canada's size, there are great differences in the amounts of precipitation received. Since warm air can hold a great deal more moisture than cold, southern parts of Canada have more precipitation than do northern parts. Because WINDS usually blow from W to E, West Coast areas receive the most precipitation. There are other complicating factors: the N-S trend of the western mountains greatly complicates the precipitation regime there, and the GREAT LAKES in central Canada affect precipitation in that region.

Usually, measurements of average annual precipitation are made where people live; therefore, the precipitation map is most accurate for southern Canada. The isohyets (lines of equal precipitation) are very generalized in mountainous regions and refer to valley conditions; precipitation totals at higher altitudes are not well known. Annual precipitation ranges from 100 mm in the High Arctic to over 1500 mm on the windward side of BC's mountains. Areas of anomalously high precipitation caused by increased winter snowfall appear E of the Great Lakes.

Climatic Regions

Defining climatic regions for any country is difficult; usually, climatologists discuss the various climatic parameters (eg, temperature, precipitation) and conclude by using VEGETATION as

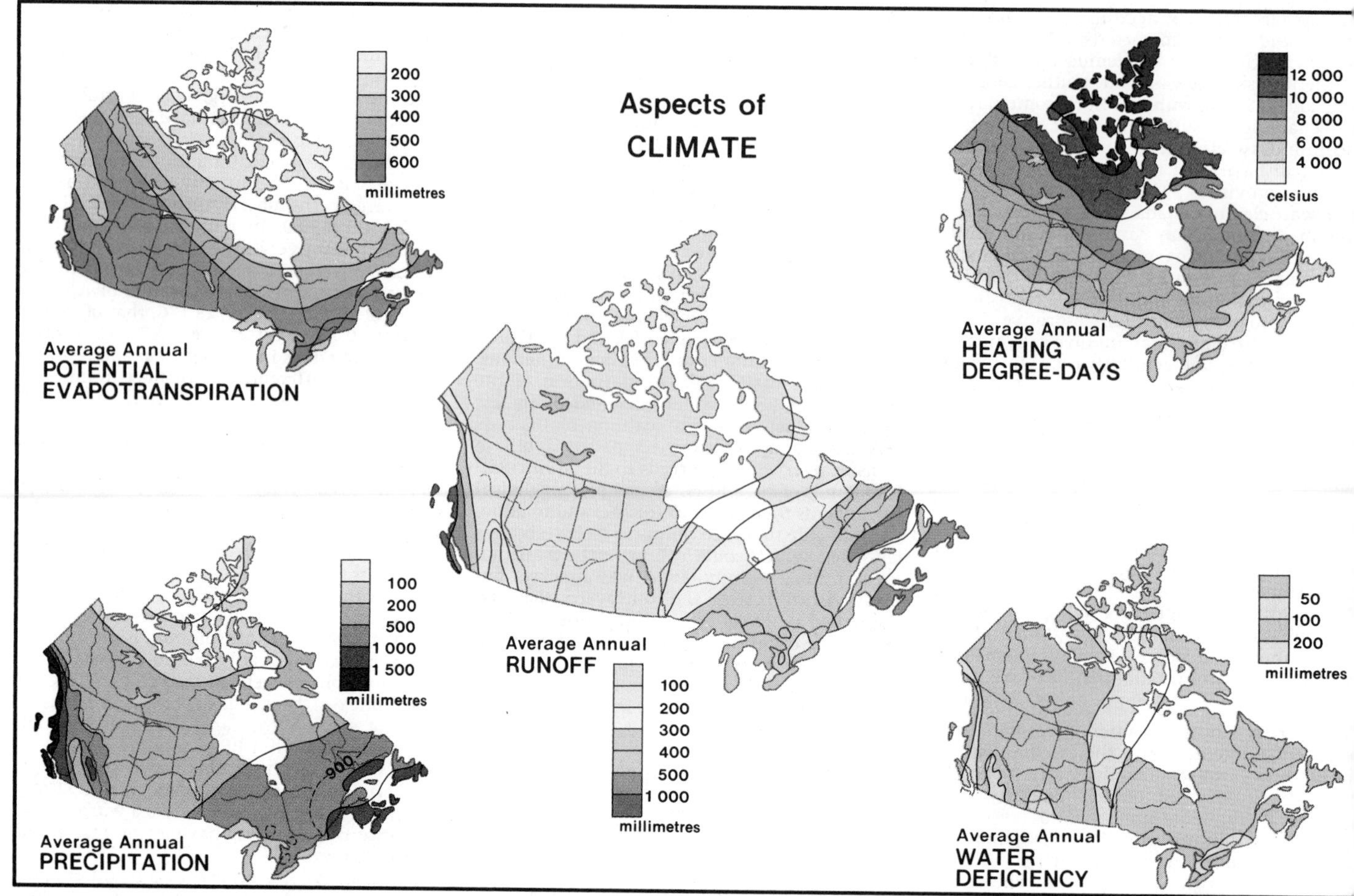

an index. Within a geographical area, climates gradually change from one type to another. There are 5 main climatic regions in the southern populated area of Canada: East Coast, Great Lakes, Prairies, Cordilleran and West Coast. The vast, mostly uninhabited area of northern Canada contains several different climatic regions, but for the present purposes will be subdivided into Arctic and Subarctic. The stations described below are examples of the above regions, with the exception of the Cordilleran. The Cordilleran, or Rocky Mountain, region is a composite of many climatic types. The southern BC valleys have climates that are the driest in Canada, while some of the higher elevations, especially in the YT area, contain permanent ice caps. No one station is typical of its province.

Climate types result from the relationship between monthly potential evapotranspiration and precipitation. By comparing the PE or need for water with the supply for each month, graphs of the water balance can be obtained. In the settled parts of Canada, water need is usually zero during the winter months, rising to an average of 130 mm in July. Only Pacific Coast regions have temperatures high enough to cause a need for water in every month of the year. Monthly precipitation varies widely throughout Canada, and nowhere does it coincide with monthly PE. Most localities receive too much moisture in winter, when the PE is zero, and too little in summer, when maximum need occurs.

East Coast climates are represented by Halifax, NS. Precipitation is fairly uniform throughout the year and only in July does water need exceed supply. The vegetation does not suffer immediately since a moisture reserve is stored in the soil (*see* GROUNDWATER). For most soils the reserve is approximately 100 mm. In Halifax, this reserve is not exhausted before precipitation rises above need and the stored moisture is again built up to its maximum. Thus, for Halifax the actual amount of water loss is almost equal to the potential water loss. After soil moisture has reached its maximum, surface or subsurface runoff occurs; in Halifax, total annual runoff is 773 mm.

Great Lakes Southern Ontario climates are typified by Windsor. Precipitation is rather uniform throughout the year (although less so than at Halifax), but Windsor's summer PE is greater than that of the East Coast, reflecting the higher summer temperatures in the interior of the country. In May PE rises above precipitation; by mid-July, in an average year, the stored soil moisture is exhausted. From then until precipitation is again sufficient to build up the stored soil moisture, vegetation must depend solely on current precipitation. In Windsor this is insufficient and a water deficiency of 86 mm occurs in an average year.

Prairie climates are exemplified by Edmonton. Here, the annual precipitation of 447 mm is inadequate to meet the PE of 555 mm and deficits, averaging 120 mm, are common in the summer months. With low winter precipitation, soil moisture is not always restored to capacity in an average year and water surplus averages only 7 mm (*see* DROUGHT).

Subarctic and Arctic At Inuvik, N of the Arctic Circle, the monthly PE and precipitation resemble those of stations in the Prairies, but the growing season is shorter. Thus, there is a small amount of runoff as well as a deficiency of 100 mm. Alert, in the High Arctic, has a more severe arctic climate, with a growing season of one month and low precipitation. It too experiences water deficiency but has an annual runoff of 76 mm.

West Coast climates are characterized by a winter maximum and summer minimum precipitation regime. Victoria is a typical station. Mean monthly temperatures are usually above 0°C and water is needed in every month. In an average winter, 130 mm of rain falls every month and the PE is only 14 mm; therefore large amounts of runoff occur in winter. In summer, precipitation is least when need is greatest and large water deficiencies occur.

The moisture map shows the distribution of moisture deficiency and runoff in Canada. The lines showing average annual water deficiency indicate the areas where precipitation is inadequate for vegetation needs and moisture is a problem. Even in southern Ontario, deficiencies occur regularly in summer. West Coast and East Coast areas rarely suffer moisture deficiencies. Much of the precipitation that falls in Canada evaporates again into the atmosphere (evapotranspiration); the water that does not evaporate runs off into the RIVERS and LAKES and eventually to the ocean. The lines showing average annual runoff are almost the reverse of those showing average water deficiency. Canada's interior has little or no run-off. Eastern and western areas have large amounts; these are the areas with major HYDROELECTRIC developments.

The above description of Canada's climatic types refers to average conditions; however, climate is very variable. For example, half the time the precipitation is less than the amounts shown and half the time it is greater. Consequently, climate involves more than average weather, and another series of maps showing the "expectation of weather" could be drawn. *See* CLIMATE CHANGE; CLIMATOLOGY; ICE; METEOROLOGY; URBAN EFFECT ON CLIMATE; WEATHER FORECASTING.

MARIE SANDERSON

Reading: F.K. Hare and M.K. Thomas, *Climate Canada* (1979).

Climate and Man Over millions of years, different climates have shaped landforms, laying down carbon deposits, feeding GLACIERS, sustaining RIVERS and producing SOILS. In addition, ere is scarcely one aspect of society that is not fected, in some way, by climate variability. remost, climate provides life's essentials: heat, oisture and light. Climate influences dress, hat we eat, how we feel and behave, the cost heating or cooling our homes and our vacaon plans. By influencing market supply and emand, it can create inflation, financial crises d social unrest, sometimes global in scope. imate can increase personal satisfaction and a matter of great civic pride. It is essential to e production of TREES and CROPS, to the success FISHERIES and the management of WATER reurces. Because it restricts AGRICULTURE, fisheries d FORESTRY to specific geographical areas, cliate has influenced human migration and setement. Through DROUGHT and FLOOD, climate n destroy and debilitate life, damage property d isolate entire communities.

CLIMATE INFORMATION is of enormous econom- worth in such activities as farming, recreion, ENERGY and TRANSPORTATION, providing nswers to such questions as, How much should budgeted for snow removal? Are there sufcient hours of WIND blow to sustain a windiven generator? Which climates are best for eople suffering from asthma or arthritis? Will eaches grow in Kapuskasing or cabbages in Vhitehorse? Is there enough snowfall for a sucessful ski resort? What impact will the effects f carbon-dioxide warming have on the arctic e pack?

Agriculture and Forestry Climate affects manind most closely in farming. Crops that are ecoomically viable in Canada include fruit trees in e Okanagan, wheat and oilseeds on the praiies, corn and grapes in southern Ontario and uébec, and potatoes and grain in the Marimes. Only tropical and equatorial crops canot be grown commercially. To be successful, a armer must minimize risk from climate hazrds by avoiding the risk in the first place or by rotecting against the hazard when it threatens. ll agricultural areas in Canada are subject to rought, frost, winterkill, wind, heavy precipation, HAIL and flooding, and to climatically nfluenced diseases and insect infestations. Crop onation is only one of many ways in which cliate information can influence farming deisions. Seeding, irrigating, spraying, harvesting nd labour and machinery management deend on the application of climate knowledge n agriculture. Post-harvest concerns of storage nd transportation are also sensitive to climatic actors. Livestock performance is affected by emperature, radiation and wind. Climate is no ess a controlling agent in tree production. Forsters seek information on how climate affects he growth and reproduction of FORESTS, and hey use climate data in protecting against hazrds such as drought, excess water, fire, frost, low down and AIR POLLUTION.

Water Resources Precipitation is the source of ll the Earth's fresh water and evaporation is the rimary moisture input into the atmosphere. anada contains no large areas where annual vaporation greatly exceeds precipitation, proucing permanent DESERTS, or where precipitation exceeds evaporation, resulting in frequent flooding. Canada has more usable fresh water than any other country in the world; owever, the water demand is so great that cliate variations are of concern to those involved n securing water supplies. Climatologists work with hydrologists to manage effectively Canda's water resources. On the prairies, farmers nxious about water for irrigation and municpal officials worried about spring flooding egularly seek information about the winter's nowpack. Engineers on the Great Lakes make daily assessments of the basin's water balance in rder to predict lake level changes. In eastern Canada where the export of HYDROELECTRICITY is big business, ELECTRIC UTILITIES count on ample winter precipitation to fill reservoirs. In moist regions with a reliable streamflow, engineers develop schemes for diverting surpluses to water-starved regions.

Energy Consumption Canada consumes more energy per capita than any other nation, the equivalent of 9 t of oil annually. This thirst for energy is caused largely by Canada's vast distances and its climate extremes. About a third of the energy now used in Canada is expended to offset the cold, ICE and snow of winter, and the heat and humidity of summer. In the 1970s and 1980s severe winters and uncertainty of foreign oil supplies focused attention on Canada's vulnerability to climate variations. Further cooling or increased snow would cost the Canadian economy dearly; on the other hand a warming of 2-3°C would decrease winter heating needs by about 15%, the equivalent of 45 million barrels of oil, an annual saving of $1.5 billion. The safe and economic exploitation of energy reserves, be they offshore in the Arctic, high on a mountain slope or inland in the oil sands, demands good climate information. Furthermore, climate-related applications are not restricted to energy exploration and development: electric-power transmission lines are sensitive to icing, LIGHTNING and TORNADOES; and construction and operation of pipelines in PERMAFROST depend on changes of temperature and soil moisture.

Another issue is how much of Canada's energy needs can be met by renewable sources. Passive SOLAR heating could reduce energy bills. Inexhaustible, pollution-free WIND ENERGY, once very popular, could again supply much of the energy needs of small, remote communities.

Building and Construction Architects and builders are often guilty of placing structures suitable for one climate in a very different one, eg, California-style homes in Edmonton. Climate information is useful in determining the orientation of buildings so that there is minimum energy loss and reduced snow drifting, and in designing buildings that have comfortable, healthy, safe and economical indoor climates. Such information can also help in the choice of safe, economical materials that will withstand damage by strong winds, driving rain or frequent freeze-thaw temperature changes. Homeowners can realize greater comfort and reduced energy costs by considering such questions as where to plant trees in order to provide shelter from winter winds and to keep driveways free of snow; what sort of curtains to choose in order to keep out unwanted summer heat; or which wall of the house should contain a large area of glass to let in winter sun.

Transportation Transportation by water, land or air is influenced by climate variability or extremes. Route planning and scheduling and cargo handling and storage all depend upon sound climate information. In marine areas, SEA ICE, poor visibility and storm occurrence are significant problems and affect the design and operation of ships and port facilities. Design must incorporate information about storms, eg, that which sank the Ocean Ranger oil rig off Newfoundland, drowning 84 men (15 Feb 1982), in order to defend against such hazards. Freezing and thawing, precipitation and snow cover are very important to land transportation by road, rail or pipeline. Annual snow removal costs may exceed $1 billion in Canada. Indirect costs are even greater, eg, 1 cm of snow increases vehicular fuel consumption by about 50% and causes average commuter delays of 30 minutes. Air transportation has always been concerned with wind, ceiling, visibility and turbulence, whether for airport siting, timing of favourable takeoffs and landings or en route aircraft operations.

Other Sectors One of the most interesting and challenging areas of modern CLIMATOLOGY deals with the effects of climate on human health. Climate-related health problems include the common cold, hypothermia, hay fever, asthma, frostbite and migraine complaints. Even more common are subtle climate-induced or climate-intensified sickness, fatigue, pain, depression and insomnia, all of which ultimately diminish alertness, learning ability, performance and productivity. Climatic factors are also pervasive in the field of recreation. The economic well-being of vacation areas depends upon the occurrence of expected weather. For example, downhill SKIING is particularly sensitive to the variability of snowfall. The absence of snow generally keeps people from skiing despite snow-making equipment, and a lack of snow between Christmas and New Year's Day can spell disaster for resort operators. Climate information has been used in siting and design of trails and the design of equipment and facilities; in assessment of competing sites for sporting events; and in the scheduling of games and contests. D.W. PHILLIPS

Reading: W.W. Kellogg and R. Schware, *Climate Change and Society* (1981).

Climate Change Climate is average or integrated WEATHER, where weather is defined as the current state of the atmosphere. Climate is often regarded, in fact, as the expectation of future weather. It is specified by average values of the main elements (eg, temperature, humidity) and of their variability, usually over a 30-year period. Climates vary: recent changes show in weather records; longer-term changes can be identified by studies of tree rings, deep-ocean sediments, glacial ICE and the pollen content of lake and bog sediments. These sources show that liquid water has been present at all times throughout the history of the Earth; hence, that the world-average surface-air temperature has always been above 0°C. In fact, this temperature was usually higher than the present 15°C. During the past 30 million years a cooling of the air and the OCEANS has taken place, culminating in repeated glacial episodes during the past 2 million years. The last cold episode peaked about 16 000 BC, when ice sheets covered N America as far S as the Ohio and Missouri valleys and the plateaus of Washington. Parts of the YT, NWT and Alaska, however, escaped GLACIATION.

Canada's climate appears to have rebounded to conditions much like those of today after about 9000 BC. The ice sheets melted slowly, vanishing over Labrador-Ungava and Keewatin about 4000 years ago. FORESTS and PRAIRIES recolonized the country and with them came animals and human populations (*see* BIOGEOGRAPHY). Conditions were warmer than at present until about 2000 BC, then cooled slightly. Since then, the climate has fluctuated without major change. Data from the Northern Hemisphere show that temperatures have varied somewhat in the past century. The 1880s were cold, but temperatures rose about 0.6°C until the late 1930s. A cooling of about 0.4°C ensued but, since 1965, the hemisphere has become slightly warmer. Conditions in Canada were similar, although the warmest conditions here were delayed until the 1950s in some areas. Precipitation has also varied, eg, the 1930s and 1960s had many dry years, especially over the prairies.

In the 1980s few marked trends were visible to indicate what will happen next; however, changes can be expected. For example, carbon dioxide (CO_2) is accumulating in the atmosphere, mainly from the burning of fuels and from forest clearance and soil losses. CO_2 tends to raise surface temperatures, as do various other pollutants (*see* AIR POLLUTION). Although not universally accepted, mathematical modelling suggests that a doubling of CO_2 (possible by mid- or late 21st century) could raise world temperatures by 2-3°C, the effects being strongest in high latitudes, especially in winter. This trend might lead to a longer growing season for Canada (1-3 weeks), earlier spring ice melt and lower soil-moisture availability in the growing season. FORESTRY and farming practices and the use of rivers for generating HYDROELECTRICITY may have to be altered. Navigation may also be affected, as the Arctic Ocean and the channels of the Canadian ARCTIC ARCHIPELAGO should have easier ice conditions. This warming trend should be detectable by 2000 AD. Canada is in an excellent position to monitor the trend and to develop necessary adaptations. Warming may affect sea level, which has risen by 10 cm since 1885, partly because the world's land ice has been melting. A further increase of 40-60 cm may occur by 2050 AD. Part of the antarctic glaciers may break up in the next few centuries, raising sea level by a further 5-6 m. But sudden effects are unlikely: a decrease in SEA ICE will result in heavier snowfall on glaciers, which will tend to offset the melting. *See* PALYNOLOGY.

F.K. HARE

Climate Information Climatological data are measurements of climate elements (eg, rainfall, wind speed) and are obtained hourly, daily and at other time intervals from observers at over 100 000 locations around the world. For many purposes, climatological data are simply information; in other cases, data must be processed or interpreted into values that are meaningful to planners, engineers and other decision makers. For example, temperature data are transformed by fuel companies into indices of fuel consumption (heating degree-days) used to schedule deliveries.

Observing climate has long been a human preoccupation, but the orderly measurement and assembly of climate records is relatively new, made possible by scientific developments of the past few centuries, eg, the invention of the thermometer and barometer in 17th-century Italy and the telegraph in 19th-century US. The telegraph permitted the transmission of weather observations taken simultaneously over large areas (ie, synoptic observations), paving the way for modern WEATHER FORECASTING. More recently, SATELLITES and automatic weather stations have greatly expanded our ability to monitor the Earth's climate and to communicate information. COMPUTERS have enabled climatologists to acquire, record, process and retrieve the millions of pieces of information needed to describe the Earth's climate. Canadian climatological archives alone place at the disposal of all Canadians over 2 billion observations on the country's climate.

Early explorers such as Jacques CARTIER and Henry KELSEY directly or indirectly described aspects of climate in their logbooks and journals. The first regular observations at a specific site in Canada were taken in the 1740s by J.F. GAULTHIER in Montréal. Official observations began in 1839 at a magnetic and meteorological observatory on the grounds of University of Toronto, but the national program awaited the formation of the Meteorological Service of Canada in 1871. This institution was renamed the Atmospheric Environment Service (AES) in 1970. Development of the CPR and western agriculture provided the opportunity and further impetus for the development of a nationwide climate data-gathering system. In 1982, Canada's official climate archives received measurements from 2700 observing sites and held historic records for an additional 2500 locations. Daily measurements of precipitation and temperature are the most commonly taken observations but much fuller programs exist at 330 locations. Hourly observations are taken at 155. These programs allow for the description of rates and types of precipitation, solar radiation, evaporation, brightness of sunshine, soil temperature, snow cover, cloud cover, humidity, wind, etc. In addition, there are upper air observations measuring temperature, humidity and winds at many levels. Measurements of precipitation and temperature are also taken by corporations, provincial governments and private citizens. Attempts are being made to reconstruct historical climate data. Diaries and indirect evidence, eg, tree rings, ice cores and sediment cores, reveal many aspects of climates that existed before settlement, and are being analysed to obtain "proxy" climate data. RADAR and satellite weather observations present new opportunities for gathering data and new challenges in interpreting these data. The radio messages used to create a picture of Canada from a polar-orbiting weather satellite contain 186 million bits of information; a geostationary satellite can produce 7-8 million bits in 30 minutes.

Canada's 2400 voluntary weather observers record information daily and mail their reports monthly to regional offices of the AES. Data from full-time weather stations are transmitted by teletype as are data from remote areas, after being relayed by satellite. Data from upper air stations, satellites, radar and special networks are received on magnetic or punched tape or as charts from recording instruments. On receipt, the data are documented and, when necessary, digitized for processing by computer. The digital archive is maintained on magnetic tapes or other computer-acceptable form. Other parts of the archive contain printed records, summary tabulations on microfiche, maps and pictures of documents on microfilm. As of 1982 the "paper" section of the national climate archive contained over 15 million original observer reports from about 5000 climate stations, as well as serial publications, both dating back to the 19th century. The archive also contains limited data from around the world. Information is published on all official observations, in detailed and summary forms, for periods which include weeks, months, years, decades and 30-year "normal" periods. Data-oriented publications in 1982 included *Climatic Perspectives* (weekly), *Monthly Meteorological Summaries, Monthly Record-Meteorological Observations, Monthly Radiation Summary, Annual Meteorological Summaries, Snow Cover Data, Supplementary Precipitation Data* and Climatic Normals, 1951-80 (for elements such as temperature, precipitation, frost, wind, radiation and degree-days). *See* CLIMATE AND MAN.

G.A. MCKAY

Climatology, a division of METEOROLOGY concerned with the study over extended periods of time of CLIMATE, ie, of both average and extreme WEATHER conditions. Weather may be defined as the current state of the atmosphere, especially its temperature, humidity and movement. The 2 main theoretical branches of climatology are physical climatology, which seeks to understand the principles of mass and ENERGY exchanges between the Earth and its atmosphere, and dynamic climatology, which examines the factors influencing climate according to the laws of PHYSICS. Other divisions include descriptive climatology (climatography); synoptic climatology, which deals with the correlation and analysis of weather observations taken simultaneously at widely distant points; and applied climatology, which makes CLIMATE INFORMATION available to engineers, planners, vacationers, etc (*see* CLIMATE AND MAN). The possibility that man can deliberately or inadvertently influence climate on a large scale is also of interest to climatologists, but remains largely theoretical at present.

Physical Climatology

Physical climatology examines the processes, magnitudes and directions of energy and mass exchanges within the atmosphere at, and immediately below, the Earth's surface. These are in portant in determining all scales of clima from local to global. Solar radiation drives t Earth-atmosphere system, which absorbs abo 65% of the solar radiation that it receives ar emits annually an identical amount of infrar radiation to space. This equilibrium ma change, and with it the world's climate, wi changes in solar emission, sun-Earth distanc reflectivity of the planet, etc. The effect of vari tions in the sun-Earth distance is negligible i the short term, but on geological time scales, o bital variation may have produced substanti radiation changes resulting in ICE AGES. The po tion of the system between 40° N and S is an er ergy source, since radiant energy gains excee losses here; poleward of these latitudes the sy tem is an energy sink, where losses exceed gain WINDS and ocean currents transport energy pol ward to rectify this latitudinal imbalance, ther by preventing systematic warming or coolin The planetary surface also has an annual su plus of energy, since radiant energy gains excee losses; the atmosphere has an energy defici Convective transport of heat from the surfa prevents systematic surface warming and atm spheric cooling.

An energy budget or balance can be drawn u for any volume or surface within the Eart atmosphere system. The radiation balance i this budget is mainly governed by seasonal cor trol of incoming solar radiation and the fractio reflected by the ground. In Canada during wi ter, low solar radiation and high surface refle tivity of snow produce a negative radiation ba ance (with inputs less than outputs) everywher In midsummer, the radiation balance is positiv everywhere because solar radiation is great and snow is less or absent. The midsumme budget is remarkably uniform between the U border and the High Arctic. Long daylight per ods in the North compensate for a weak su which is low in the sky. Mean annual radiatio balance increases gradually from zero in th ARCTIC ARCHIPELAGO to about 17 MJ/m^2/da (megajoules per square metre per day) in south ern Canada.

The magnitudes and seasonal and geogra phical variations of the other energy-budg components are poorly known for Canada. Sen sible and latent heat transfers are the major com ponents, except in spring, when snowmelt use a significant amount of energy (up to 1.25 MJ m^2/day). Sensible heat is the energy of the move ments of the molecules that make up a mas and is perceived as the temperature of the sub stance. Latent heat is the energy required t change the phase of matter, ie, to rearrange th molecules (as from liquid to gas in evaporatin moisture) whether the temperature of the mas changes or not. Latent heat transfer is alway large (about 80-90% of the radiation balanc from open water, wetlands and transpirin vegetation and crops. In drier areas, or as we surfaces become drier, sensible heat transfer be comes more important. Surface modification may radically alter the relative magnitudes o energy-budget components, eg, in many citie replacement of vegetation with concrete an brick has reduced latent energy transfer an increased the transfer of sensible heat. Lan management also has its effects, eg, in dry area irrigation produces moist, cooler oases as a resu of increased latent heat transfer.

J.A. DAVIE

Dynamic Climatology

Dynamic climatology is the study of climat as a branch of physics. The climate system is a physical system governed by reasonably well-known physical laws (fluid dynamics, thermodynamics, radiative transfer, etc). There are 5 major components of the climate system: atmosphere, hydrosphere (ie, OCEANS, LAKES), LAND surface, cryosphere (SEA ICE, permanent ICE CAPS, iow) and biosphere. The global system is inter-lated in many complex ways, and the study of ynamic climatology requires expertise from iany branches of science and data from all arts of the globe.

Some major aspects of the climate system may e appreciated by considering simpler, idealized ystems. A nonrotating Earth with no topogra-hy or oceans would have a climate far differ-nt from that observed. If the atmosphere were ot permitted to move in this idealized case, the esulting climate would not vary with longi-ıde, only with latitude, eg, temperatures would e high at equatorial latitudes, low at poleward ititudes. The resulting temperature structure at ie surface, at various levels in the atmosphere nd at various latitudes could be calculated sing the equations of thermodynamics and adiative transfer. If the atmosphere were al-owed to move on this nonrotating Earth, the varm air in equatorial regions would rise, flow olewards, cool, sink and flow equatorwards nce more, giving rise to a Hadley circulation. he temperature difference from pole to equator rovides the driving force for the motions and vould be reduced as a consequence of the flow. f the planet now began to rotate, the nature of he flow (hence, the climate) would differ re-narkably. A simple Hadley circulation would io longer be found but rather a flow from W to at middle latitudes and a flow from E to W at ower latitudes. Superimposed on this general low would be large ripples and eddies. Without he oceans, winter cold and summer warmth vould be extreme and the coldest and warmest imes of the year would occur at the solstices. If noisture were introduced into the system, as oceans and water vapour in the air, the resulting limate would again change dramatically; hanges would include the appearance of major -W asymmetries in the climate. The oceans iave a profound effect on climate through stor-ge and transport of heat. Topography, ICE and now, etc, add further degrees of complexity to he system.

This complicated, 3-dimensional global sys-em is studied observationally and numerically.)bservational or diagnostic approaches proceed y the collection and study of many millions of bservations of the atmosphere and oceans, not nly at the surface but with height and depth. uch studies attempt to understand how the)hysical system operates and what the domi-iant mechanisms are. They also include at-empts to understand past variations in climate nd to detect and understand variations in the current climate. Numerical models of the cli-nate system attempt to solve the mathematical equations which govern the physical system. These equations are so complex that they must be solved using computers. The more compre-hensive of these general circulation models of the atmosphere, of the oceans, or both, require billions of computations to simulate the climate even approximately. In addition to providing an understanding of the current climate, these models may be used to investigate possible causes of CLIMATE CHANGE.

The climate system has undergone profound changes in the distant past and real, but less ex-treme, variations in historical times. Such changes are caused by natural phenomena (VOL-CANOES, changes in the sun, orbital mechanics of the solar system, etc) and human-induced fac-tors (increased carbon dioxide, deforestation, chlorofluoromethane release, etc). The physics-based investigations of dynamic climatology are designed to shed light on these and other cli-matic questions. As a global system, the climate system must be studied from a global perspec-tive. To this end, the World Meteorological Or-ganization, an agency of the UNITED NATIONS, has established the World Climate Program.

GEORGE J. BOER

Man's Effect on Climate

Human activities can change some aspects of the climate on a local scale. Some changes are deliberate, eg, use of trees or hedges as wind-breaks, to prevent frost hollows or to control snow drifting. Others are incidental, eg, the warming of the downtown cores of expanding cities, or the increase in rainfall downstream from cities caused by increased release of heat and of pollutants which promote condensation (*see* AIR POLLUTION; URBAN EFFECT ON CLIMATE). There is no evidence that human activities have, as yet, had any detectable effect on the large-scale climate. Nevertheless, as the scale of hu-man activities grows, and as the by-products of these activities increase, the potential for large-scale effects on climate becomes very real.

One such by-product is the carbon dioxide (CO_2) produced by the burning of coal, oil and gas to heat homes, operate equipment and generate ELECTRIC POWER. Carbon dioxide existed naturally in the atmosphere long before the In-dustrial Revolution. Since 1880 the levels of CO_2 have increased by about 17%, more than half of that increase coming in the past 20 years. Al-though CO_2 represents less than 1% of the total volume of the atmosphere, it is very important because it interferes with the flow of heat radi-ated from the Earth into space.

Experiments using computer models of cli-mate indicate that, if the volume of atmospheric CO_2 were double its preindustrial level, the aver-age temperature of the air at ground level would increase by about 2-3°C. This would occur only if nothing else was changing the climate and only when the heat content of the atmosphere came into balance with that of the oceans. Such a change would be larger than any climate change in recorded history, and would be ac-companied by much larger regional shifts in cli-mate.

The possibility of deliberately modifying the large-scale climate is intriguing, but cursory examination of the question indicates that energies involved in the climate system are so large that a direct approach would be impos-sible. For example, the energy converted in a single one-hour THUNDERSTORM would supply Canada's entire electrical energy needs for one day. The energy converted in a single low-pres-sure system in one day is 10 000 times greater than that of a thunderstorm. It has taken 2 generations of burning fuels to produce a 17% change in CO_2 levels which has not yet produced any detectable effect. Thus, it is improbable that any direct action could be taken to modify our climates, even if exact methods of doing so were known. One possiblity, however, would be to influence the climate by depositing long-lived dust clouds in the high atmosphere: there is some evidence that volcanoes affect the climate by injecting large amounts of material at high altitudes. It is not known what effects, if any, such a deliberate modification would have on the climate at the surface.

P.E. MERILEES

Reading: J.F. Griffiths and D.M. Driscoll, *Survey of Climatology* (1982).

Clockmaker; or The Sayings and Doings of Sam Slick of Slickville, The, by Thomas Chandler HALIBURTON, originally appeared as newspaper sketches. Sam Slick's colloquial, vernacular, Yankee voice, peddling clocks as well as his views on "human natur," first be-guiled Haligonians in 1835 in Joseph HOWE's newspaper, *The Novascotian*. These sketches were collected and published in Halifax, 1836; Lon-don and Philadelphia, 1837 (first series); Hali-fax, London and Philadelphia, 1838 (second se-ries); and 1840 (third series). In 1923 the 3 series were combined in a single publication (ed Ray Palmer Baker, Toronto). Haliburton found in Sam Slick's Yankee idiom and wit the perfect voice for a running, wryly mocking commen-tary on Nova Scotia's social scene, its political life and its relations with the US and Britain. Be-fore Charles Dickens achieved recognition, Hali-burton was the unrivaled master and most pop-ular writer of comic fiction in English. *The Clockmaker* was translated into German, 1840-42; it has run through almost countless editions to establish Haliburton as one of the founders of N American humour.

NEIL BESNER

Clocks and Watches The manufacture of clocks and watches in Canada may have begun as early as 1700; however, it is generally considered that the practising watch and clock-makers of that time did not make the entire mechanism. The watch or clock originated in England, continental Europe and, later, the US; it came to Canada as an *ebauche* (basic, unfin-ished movement) and was finished by the local horologist, and thus bears his initials or signa-ture, or the stamp of his silversmith. From the beginning, retailers of clocks, and especially watches, were closely associated with silver-smiths and jewellers. The arrangement was logical as the 2 groups were dependent on the same market and required one another's skills. Jean Filiot of Montréal and Thomas Gordon of Halifax were well-known watchmakers of the 18th century.

During the early part of the 19th century the pride of many homes was the grandfather or long-case clock, which would be passed from one generation to the next as a treasured heir-loom. The movements of many of these clocks were imported from continental Europe and England; local merchants then ordered a pine case from the local cabinetmaker. Other clocks came from the US, eg, those of the Twiss broth-ers who operated from Montréal during the early 19th century, specializing in grandfather clocks which came in from the US. Their clocks are now sought by collectors.

Watch and clockmakers were frequently listed as having worked in several places, as they tended to try out several towns before set-tling down. In some cases, the second generation would set up shop in another town as an expan-sion of the family business. After the comple-

Mahogany bracket clock with brass finials, feet and dial, from the late 18th century, Montréal (*courtesy Royal Ontario Museum*).

tion of the Canadian Pacific Railway, there was an extensive migration west, which undoubtedly included horologists to serve the growing population. Members of some communities (eg, the Hutterites) brought with them watches made entirely of wood by their own craftsmen. Wooden movements and cases continued to be made by such craftsmen; however, these artisans did not play an active part in the development of watch and clockmaking technology.

The first large-scale Canadian clock manufacturer on record was the Canada Clock Co of Whitby, Ont, which began production in 1872. The operation later moved to Hamilton, Ont, and continued to produce clocks until 1887. The largest and most successful clock company, that of Arthur Pequegnat, began in 1904 in Berlin (now Kitchener), Ont. Pequegnat's made many models of table, shelf, wall and standing clocks and sold throughout Canada until the company ceased production in 1941. Pequegnat clocks are desirable collectors' items; a nearly complete collection is exhibited at the NATIONAL MUSEUM OF SCIENCE AND TECHNOLOGY in Ottawa.

In 1891 the Canadian Horological Institute was established in Toronto by Henry Playtner of Preston, Ont. This excellent school of watchmaking and repairing produced many fine craftsmen. Playtner's book, *Canadian Horological Institute* (1904), contains a very interesting account of the early days of an apprentice. The school lasted until 1914 when Playtner moved to the US to found the Elgin Watchmakers' College. From time to time "masterpieces" made by graduating students from the institute can be found. They represent a very high grade of horological craftsmanship.

An interesting, although fictional, account of the social aspects of clock marketing in the early 19th century is given by T.C. HALIBURTON in *The Clockmaker; or The Sayings and Doings of Sam Slick of Slickville*, a novel describing the travels of a somewhat disreputable person who sold clocks "door-to-door" in Canada and the US. *See* JEWELLERY AND SILVERWARE INDUSTRY.

CAROL HAYTER AND PAUL LAVOIE

Reading: G.E. Burrows, *Canadian Clocks and Clockmakers* (1973); J.E. Langdon, *Clock and Watchmakers in Canada 1700-1900* (1976).

Closure, procedural provision allowing the Government to curtail debate in the HOUSE OF COMMONS and bring on a vote. A remedy for FILIBUSTERING, it entails 2 different decisions by the House: the vote to apply closure, and then the vote (or votes) on the business being closed. Closure takes 2 days; if the required oral notice is given on a Monday, closure will be moved and the closure vote taken (without debate) after routine proceedings on Tuesday; if the closure motion carries, the rest of that sitting is spent on the business to be closed, which is put to the vote at the end of the sitting. With closure on, the House sits late, with the vote (or votes) coming soon after 1:00 AM. The use of closure is highly controversial. The Opposition cries, "Dictatorship!"; the Government cries, "Filibuster!" Added to the Standing Orders in 1913, the rule was used 18 times before 1982, 4 times during the PIPELINE DEBATE in 1956. It was used to bring on the vote for concurrence in the flag committee report in 1964; and to add 3 new Standing Orders: SO 75A, 75B and 75C (1969), which provide for limitation of debate at each stage of a bill's passage through the House (*see* ALLOTMENT OF TIME).

JOHN B. STEWART

Clothing The colonization of eastern Canada began with the French in the 17th century. For some years, these settlers depended for clothing on what they brought with them. New garb was expensive and the only clothing available was imported, ready-made clothing or garments made locally from imported cloth or, sometimes, from dressed skins. Weaving did not become widespread in the new settlement until early in the 18th century; some local manufacture of fashionable shoes and hats had begun by the late 17th century.

Men's 18th-century clothing. The velvet suit shown was semiformal attire in France and was worn in Montréal in the 1780s. The richly brocaded waistcoat was worn by Barthelemy Gugy, likely in Trois-Rivières, in the 1790s (*courtesy McCord Museum / McGill University*).

Children's clothes, *c*1830-70 (*courtesy Royal Ontario Museum from left to right: Gifts of Miss H.M. Armour, Miss Jean Robertson, Mr Norman MacDonald, and Miss Helen P. Lovesconte. Hats gift of Miss H.M. Armour*).

Fashionable Dress

With the appearance of towns, well-to-do male and female inhabitants dressed in elegant clothing, similar to that worn in France. However, there was a time lag of at least a year between the initiation of a style in Europe and its appearance in Canada, since ships from the continent came only annually. In 17th-century Canada a fashionable male wore a periwig, rich fabrics and elegant lace. Portraits of Jean TALON, the first Intendant of NEW FRANCE, show him stylishly attired in periwig, brocade dressing gown, shirt lavishly trimmed with lace at the wrists and lace cravat. In 1703 Madame Riverin, wife of a member of Québec City's Conseil Souverain, was painted in a stylish dress called a *mantua* and an elegant head-dress known as a *fontange*. Her daughters were dressed similarly and her son was garbed in miniature modish male clothing. Such imitation of adult clothing was customary in children's attire. When the province of UPPER CANADA (present-day Ontario) was created in 1791, the newly formed governing class, as well as the other members of the elite, also attempted to maintain fashionable standards of dress. These standards, like those of English dress, were generally more conservative than the modish styles of Paris.

The first Canadian fashion plate, which appeared in Mar 1831 in the *Montreal Monthly Magazine*, probably was inspired by one in an English publication. With the improvement in overseas communication which took place in the mid-19th century, the time lag between new European fashions and their appearance in Canada was substantially reduced, becoming as short as 3 months.

Everyday Dress

All but the wealthiest settlers wore clothing made in the home, often of cloth spun in the home and woven domestically or by professional local weavers. Styles tended to be conservative and to reflect rural French or, later, English styles. In the mid-19th century, as more ready-made clothing became available, fashion slowly became more accessible to the masses, however, most working-class attire continued to be fashioned at home. Relatively small quantities of this clothing have survived because, as it wore out, it was recycled into QUILTS, RUGS, etc. In 1884 the first mail-order catalogue, the T. EATON COMPANY pamphlet, appeared, making recent styles more accessible to everyone, even in remote rural areas, such as the Prairies. This important development decreased the difference between conservative rural and up-to-date fashionable dress.

Men's Clothing In the early French colonial period, many of the garments worn by ordinary townsmen and male country dwellers (mostly farmers) were similar to those worn in France. In the 17th and 18th centuries these settlers would have worn a variety of garments, sometimes broadly echoing fashionable ones but of a simpler, more utilitarian cut and fabric. During the 19th century similar garments continued to be worn but variety was more limited; everyday clothes were principally reminiscent of fashionable garments. Breeches were replaced by trousers, and waist-length jackets were common. Beginning early in the 19th century, imported manufactured English cloth increasingly replaced homespun in everyday dress.

Certain types of nonfashionable attire for men, during both the French and English colonial periods (and sometimes persisting later), were different from their counterparts on the continent. Everyday clothing had been influenced by Indian garb, eg, the French Canadian's domestically manufactured leather attire, including footwear with a MOCCASIN shape (*bottes* or *souliers sauvages*) and leather or fabric leggings. These garments were especially common among country dwellers and those actively involved in

Frock coat from Upper Canada. Frock coats were worn in rural areas only on Sundays. This example dates from the 1840s. It is of wool and may have been a local product (*courtesy Royal Ontario Museum, Gift of Mr Sidney Holmes*).

This ribbon silk dress was worn by a Toronto bride at her reception in 1859. The dress is completely hand sewn (courtesy Royal Ontario Museum, Gift of Mrs J.D. Murray).

the FUR TRADE (eg, COUREURS DE BOIS). They were adopted as protection against harsh weather and rough countryside. The moccasin-type footwear (mandatory for snowshoes) was used by all HABITANTS. Also of interest were the decorative, high-crowned felt hats, trimmed with ostrich feathers, worn by the VOYAGEURS during the early 19th century. Voyageurs also frequently wore the *ceinture fléchée*, a woollen, finger-woven multicoloured sash with arrowhead motifs. This characteristic French Canadian accessory first appeared generally in the early 19th century and continued to be finger woven in Québec until late in the century. The *ceinture fléchée* was also worn by habitants, used as a trade item in the fur trade and, eventually, adopted for sports and leisure wear by the bourgeoisie, especially with the blanket *capot*. It has undergone a revival recently and is again produced in Québec.

The Québec *capot* (in the 17th century the term generally referred to a cloak and, later, to a greatcoat) developed slowly in response to the harsh winters. Beginning in the second quarter of the 18th century, it could also have a hood. Often, for country wear, it was made from thick grey homespun, *étoffe du pays*. From the 1770s hooded capots were made in Québec from Hudson Bay blankets and became a typical costume for the rural Canadien. They were white, with blue bands from the blanket near the hemline and matching bands near the wrist. They had an upright collar and were closed in front by a series of ribbon ties in red, blue or both colours.

Women's homespun clothing. The green and pink check dress (left) is from Ontario (1860s). The petticoat (right) from Québec would have been worn as a skirt with a bodice or jacket or as a petticoat with a hitched-up skirt (courtesy National Museums of Canada/National Museum of Man).

A coat could be trimmed with ribbon rosettes in the aforementioned colour or colours. This picturesque dress was usually worn with a multicoloured wool sash, a red wool toque (lined in white) or fur cap, leggings (*mitasses*) and *bottes*.

In the 19th century, the blanket capot changed slightly to echo broadly the fashionable greatcoat of the time: buttons and epaulettes were added, ribbon decoration disappeared and different colour combinations in the TEXTILE appeared. During this period, the bourgeois adopted the capot for winter sports and leisure wear, and women began to wear a version of the garment. The attire, especially in white, remains a characteristic one for Québec. Now known as the Hudson Bay coat, it is manufactured in Canada for both sexes. FUR was also important to both men and women for combatting the winter cold. From the mid-19th century on, it was generally worn fur side out, creating a luxurious effect.

Women's Clothing For ordinary and rural wear during the 17th century, and through to the late 19th century in Québec, women generally wore separate tops and skirts. In the 17th century and until the second half of the 18th century, corset bodices (approximately waist length and usually sleeveless), chemises (knee-length undergarments which could function for the working classes as blouses), petticoats (ie, skirts), aprons and caps were worn. This costume resembled attire seen in France and western Europe. With the appearance of handweaving in New France, plain and checked or striped homespuns prevailed. Sometime during the mid-18th century, the corset bodice was replaced by a sleeveless one extending beyond the waist. With its possible stylistic variations, unknown today, it was referred to at the time as a short gown or jacket.

Stylish silk dress worn in Montréal about 1882. The bodice is fitted, lined and boned, and the back section, supported by a bustle, extends into a fishtail (courtesy McCord Museum/McGill University).

As our present century progressed, the dominant development was the gradual change in the supplier of clothing, ie, from the dressmaker to the department store. Yet, for wealthy clients, high-fashion dressmakers continued, for a time, to operate successfully in large cities. Such clients were served in the post-WWII period, in Montréal, through couturiers (ie, stylish, high-quality dressmakers running expensive establishments), who modeled their operations on those of French couture salons. In Canada this type of operation persists, but in a very reduced form. The greatest difference in kinds of clothing in Canada, as elsewhere, relates less to an elite and nonelite mode than to trends towards fashion versus antifashion (attire which makes a point of going contrary to trends) and to an increasingly informal manner of dress.

Tweed suit showing "leg-o'-mutton" sleeve, made in the mid-1890s. As daytime wear, these suits were worn with a high-collared blouse and a bow tie (courtesy Royal Ontario Museum, Gift of Mr Wood).

Ethnic dress of relatively recent immigrants (eg, LITHUANIANS, UKRAINIANS) is generally worn on special occasions and has not blended into the mainstream of Canadian costume. Similarly, the plain, conservative everyday attire of the DOUKHOBORS and MENNONITES has remained quite independent. Religious, legal and academic dress, being of a conservative nature and mostly of medieval derivation, is familiar in Canada. The major development in this area has been the gradual disappearance of religious costume from the streets, especially in Québec, as a result of Vatican II (a gathering of the supreme authority of the Roman Catholic Church in Rome, 1962-65). Most provincial museums display some pioneer clothing, and excellent collections are held at the ROYAL ONTARIO MUSEUM and the NATIONAL MUSEUMS OF CANADA. *See* FASHION DESIGN; UNIFORMS.

JACQUELINE BEAUDOIN-ROSS

Reading: K.B. Brett, *Modesty to Mod: Dress and Undress in Canada, 1780-1967* (1967).

Clothing Industries The Canadian clothing industries consist of companies that make consumer, industrial and institutional apparel. They cut and sew fabrics and knit yarns into garments and finish them for sale. The major subsectors include men's, women's and children's clothing, FUR goods, foundation garments, gloves, hats and caps, hosiery and knitted goods.

Mechanization of clothing manufacture began with the invention of the sewing machine in 1775. Elias Howe obtained patents in the US in 1846. Mass production began during the American Civil War, when large numbers of blue and grey military uniforms were needed to distinguish friend from foe. The increasing sophistication of machines, combined with migration of skilled workers from the US, created a new production industry in Canada. Custom tailors and seamstresses had produced clothing in Canada from the time of Samuel de Champlain, but when volume production methods were developed in the US they were soon adopted in Canada and local craftsmen became entrepreneurial employers. Their factories were located in Montréal, Toronto and Winnipeg, where they could find IMMIGRANT LABOUR and young local women. The first apparel company in Canada that did all cutting and sewing on the premises was the men's fine clothing firm Livingstone and Johnston (est Toronto, 1868), later W.R. Johnston & Co. This company later became a subsidiary of Tip Top Tailors of Toronto, now part of Dylex Ltd, a Toronto-based conglomerate operating Canada wide in both MANUFACTURING and RETAIL.

The union movement in the clothing business dates back to 1911 when the New York-based International Ladies' Garment Workers Union (ILGWU) started a local in Toronto. During the 1920s, as a result of the formation of unions in Toronto, much of the industry moved to Montréal, making that city a major apparel town. This distribution of production still prevails. In 1981 the clothing industry consisted of about 2125 factories, of which more than 1475 were in Québec (Montréal and some 40 neighbouring towns). About 451 were in Ontario, primarily in Toronto, with a few in Kitchener, Hamilton and Waterloo; about 87 in Manitoba, primarily in Winnipeg; 7 in Saskatchewan; 33 in Alberta, primarily in Edmonton; and 60 in BC, primarily in Vancouver. A few are found in the other provinces and territories. Several factories are owned and operated by bands and councils of native people.

Until 1983 there had not been a general strike in the apparel industry for 49 years because the ILGWU preferred mediation or arbitration. Other important unions active today are the Amalgamated Clothing Workers of America (men's clothing), the United Garment Workers of America (women's clothing) and the Allied Clothing and Textile Workers (mixed).

The diversity of clothing required for the Canadian climate gave rise to many sectors: outerwear, pants, suits, blouses and shirts, sleepwear, raincoats, dresses and sportswear, foundation garments and underwear, swim wear, skiwear, leather, fur and knitwear. These are further divided into men's, women's, children's and infants' wear. The many variations in fabric weights and garment styles resulted in the development of more than 1000 different kinds of sewing machine to satisfy the industry's needs.

Canadians spent almost $13 billion on clothing and FOOTWEAR in 1981, not including TEXTILES and knitwear. In 1981 the clothing, knitting and textiles industries employed almost 184 000 people in firms employing 20 or more workers. Thousands more work in smaller plants throughout Québec, Ontario and Manitoba. Almost all Canadian plants employ fewer than 50 people, although 8 have over 1000 workers. In the early 1980s the average hourly wage in the industry was $6.14 but the average in Toronto was closer to $7.00. These averages can be misleading, however, because in Québec apprentices are treated differently in the statistics, but are lumped into the national averages.

The clothing industries are entering a new HIGH-TECHNOLOGY phase. Numerical- and computer-controlled equipment and ROBOTICS are being rapidly introduced into factories. The speed with which factories are modernizing is directly related to the supply of sewing-machine mechanics and technicians who are skilled in servicing the sophisticated equipment. A new program to train technicians has been started at George Brown College, Toronto. Today, alternatives to traditional cutting and sewing methods include LASER or computer-controlled waterjet cutting; computer design and pattern grading (ie, changing the sizes of the pattern); microchip-controlled, multiple-head sewing machines; ultrasonic sewing-machine heads that have no needle or thread, but use high-frequency sound to melt and re-form synthetic fabrics, eg, those used in drapery or plastic raincoats. None of these technologies were initiated in Canada, but various sectors of the industry do suggest improvements through Canadian branches of the sewing-machine manufacturers' association. Unfortunately, Canada's financial contribution to INDUSTRIAL RESEARCH AND DEVELOPMENT in this field is negligible.

The industry in Canada is over 90% Canadian owned, but about 75 American firms and several British companies have subsidiary plants in Canada. Some of the largest from the US are Levi Strauss Canada Inc, H.D. Lee of Canada Ltd, Blue Bell Canada Ltd, Warnaco of Canada Ltd, Cluett Peabody Canada Inc (Arrow Shirts), Lady Manhattan and Kayser-Roth Canada Ltd. S.R. Gent and Corah Ltd have come from England in support of the Marks & Spencer Canada Ltd retail chain. Clothing plants use mostly electricity and are not large energy consumers. Since sewing and cutting machines operate on 110-V circuits with motors rarely larger than 3/4 hp, energy consumption cannot compare with that of heavy industry. In 1981 the Canadian clothing industries produced nearly $4.3 billion in garments, with a work force of 95 850. They captured 80% of the market in dollars but only 60% in garments, not including the textile and knitting industries. The apparent Canadian market was about $5.63 billion. Imports accounted for 21.4%, exports for only 5.7%.

The federal government is under constant pressure to limit imports and reduce quotas; at the same time, it must consider how exporting countries will react to Canadian quotas and exports and how this will affect the BALANCE OF PAYMENTS. Protecting jobs within the country's second-largest employment sector is also a concern (*see* PROTECTIONISM). Consequently the government formed the Canadian Industrial Renewal Board and its apparel section has been given $250 million to assist the clothing industries to become more competitive in world markets, before tariff and other protection is reduced or eliminated under world trade agreements. Canadian clothing companies are expected to compete with Third World countries, but this is very difficult because industrial standards legislation in Canada's producing provinces establishes minimum wages, maximum hours and fringe benefits that are 2-10 times higher than standards in low-wage countries. Consequently, imported clothing, manufactured under conditions that are illegal in Canada, represents a real threat to the future of Canadian companies. The government attempts to control this problem by using a quota system and regulating imports, but $1.2 billion in clothing entered Canada in 1981, compared with exports of $265.4 million.

The textile and clothing industries in Canada rank second to FOOD AND BEVERAGES in the number of employees. Some consider them expendable in a high-technology age. However, some European countries have regretted abandoning this sector and are now trying to restore an industry that is traditionally among the top 5 employers in many industrialized nations. Fo example, the clothing industries also suppor textile mills and retail stores that employ ove 200 000 people.

Sectors of the industry are trying to meet th high-technology challenge with the aid of sophisticated trade associations (eg, the Dress an Sportswear Guilds) and national magazines (eg McLean Hunter's *Style, Canadian Apparel Manufacturer*). Strong training programs have beer developed that offer diploma courses in production and design at various community colleges Holland, PEI; LaSalle, Montréal; George Brown Seneca and Sheridan, Toronto; Red River, Winnipeg; Grant MacEwan, Edmonton; and Capilano, Vancouver. A new degree program in apparel-production management is being offered by Ryerson Polytechnical Institute, Toronto. Continuing education courses are offered at Concordia and McGill universities, Montréal, and University of Manitoba, Winnipeg.

SIDNEY S. SCHIPPER

Cloud, visible suspension in the atmosphere, composed of tiny WATER droplets or ICE crystals from about one to a few hundred micrometres in diameter. Clouds occur when moist air cools to its saturation point as a result of loss of heat through vertical ascent, by radiation, or by mixing with cooler air. In Canada, mean cloud cover (fraction of the sky covered by clouds) varies from about 0.5 on the PRAIRIES to 0.8 or more on the West and East coasts in winter. Clouds are named according to the nature of their motion, their composition and their height in the atmosphere. Two basic varieties are distinguished according to air motion. Heap clouds (cumulus family) result from local convection (overturning) in an unstable atmosphere; layer clouds (stratus family), from slow, widespread, vertical lifting. Nimbus signifies a precipitating cloud; cirrus, a high-level, ice-crystal cloud. A cloud that forms at the surface is called FOG; middle-level clouds (2-7 km above ground) are termed altus. Alone, in combination or with other adjectives, the terms stratus, cumulus, cirrus, nimbus and altus name the most frequently encountered cloud types. Viewed from a satellite, clouds are seen to be organized into bands, clusters and swirling patterns, reflecting large-scale motions of the atmosphere. Satellite images are helpful in WEATHER FORECASTING.

Cloud droplets form on hygroscopic (moisture-retaining) particles, about 0.1-1.0 μm in diameter, called cloud condensation nuclei. Cloud droplet concentrations may reach 1000/cm^3 and a liquid-water concentration of 0.1-10 g/m^3 of air is typical. Cloud droplets grow predominantly by condensation of water vapour when they are small and by collision and coalescence with each other when larger. In clouds with no ice (generally those warmer than -10°C to -15°C), RAIN occurs only if collision and coalescence produce millimetre-size raindrops before the cloud evaporates as a result of warming or mixing with its environment (the warm rain process). In clouds extending above the -15°C level, tiny ice nuclei cause some of the supercooled droplets to freeze. These grow rapidly into ice crystals by vapour deposition, while the nearby unfrozen droplets evaporate. The ice crystals may then aggregate into snowflakes, or grow into snow pellets by sweeping out supercooled cloud droplets as they fall. Depending upon season and cloud vigour, snowflakes and snow pellets may reach the ground intact, may melt and fall as rain, or may continue to grow into hailstones (*see* HAIL). This cold rain process is thought to be predominant in Canada.

Weather modification is an attempt to initiate the cold rain process in clouds deficient in ice crystals by seeding them with dry ice pellets or with silver iodide particles which act as ice nuclei (*see* RAINMAKING). In addition to produc-

Cirrus cloud streaks. The clouds in this picture consist of falling ice crystals stretched out horizontally by the wind shear into long streaks known as mares' tails (*courtesy Arjen Verkaik, Skyart Productions, Islington, Ont*).

Cumulus clouds consist of individual detached elements that grow upwards as a result of convection. They may resemble small domes (fair weather cumulus) or towers with a cauliflower appearance as in this picture (towering cumulus) (*courtesy Arjen Verkaik, Skyart Productions, Islington, Ont*).

Altocumulus clouds. Wind shear has organized the convection (overturning) in this altocumulus layer into a corrugated pattern (*courtesy Arjen Verkaik, Skyart Productions, Islington, Ont*).

Altocumulus clouds. The clouds in the distance are a line of cumulus congestus formed by the merger of several towering cumulus elements. When organized into a line, as here, they often develop into cumulonimbus (*courtesy Arjen Verkaik, Skyart Productions, Islington, Ont*).

ing precipitation, clouds play other important roles in the atmosphere. By reflecting solar radiation, they have a strong influence on the heat balance and, hence, the temperature of the atmosphere. Cumulus cloud formation is important in the vertical mixing of atmospheric properties. Clouds and their precipitation also help cleanse the atmosphere of POLLUTION.

E.P. LOZOWSKI

Clover The "true" clovers (genus *Trifolium*) are herbaceous PLANTS of the PEA family (Leguminosae or Fabaceae) and must be distinguished from bur clovers (*Medicago*) and sweet clovers (*Melilotus*) of the same family. They comprise about 300 species worldwide, occurring naturally in Eurasia (particularly the Mediterranean region), parts of Africa and western N and S America. White clover is found throughout most temperate regions. Some clovers are low and trailing, others grow to 1 m. Small, white, pink or red flowers are borne in dense clusters; leaves are trifoliolate. Nearly 20 European species are grown for FORAGE in America and Australia. In Canada, red clover (*Trifolium pratense*), white or Dutch clover (*T. repens*) and, to a lesser extent, alsike clover (*T. hybridum*) and crimson clover (*T. incarnatum*) are grown. Many short-lived, perennial cultivars of red clover exist. Most clovers are associated with nitrogen-fixing bacteria in the nitrogen cycle.

J.M. GILLETT

Clovis culture was widely distributed throughout most of unglaciated N America, though its duration, including variants, was fairly short (9500-8000 BC). Major sites are located from Arizona to NS, and the culture is characterized by a fluted or grooved lanceolate projectile point or knife called Clovis Fluted, with an accompanying complex of stone tools such as blades, burins, scrapers, knives and drills. Fluting was produced by removal of long flakes from the faces of the point through flaking from the base. The people seem to have hunted mammoths, camels, horses and bison, and presumably also mastodons and some smaller animals. *See also* PREHISTORY.

RENÉ R. GADACZ

Club Moss, perennial, evergreen, coarsely mosslike PLANTS belonging to genus *Lycopodium* of club moss family (Lycopodiaceae). Stems have forked branches, and are often prostrate and covered with scalelike leaves. Leaves are lanceolate to oblong or slender, tapering to linear in shape, entire or minutely toothed. Club mosses show alternation of generations, ie, an asexual phase alternates with a sexual one. Each stage is an independent plant. Reproduction is accomplished by spores produced in spore cases (sporangia) borne on the upper surfaces of modified leaves of plants of the asexual or sporophyte phase. In most Canadian species, leaves are condensed to form a cone. Spores germinate, producing small underground plants (prothallia) on which are borne antheridia, which produce sperm, and archegonia, which produce eggs. Prothallia are the sexual generation. Fertilization of the egg and subsequent development produces the familiar club moss plant, the sporophyte generation. Some species reproduce by gemmae (asexual buds that detach from the parent plant), eg, in Canada, *L. selago*.

This diverse group dates at least to the Devonian period (395-345 million years ago). Tree-sized FOSSIL representatives (eg, *Lepidodendron* and *Sigillaria*) are abundant in coal beds of the Carboniferous period (345-280 million years old). About 100 living species are known. They are most abundant in tropical and subtropical regions, but 13 species occur in Canada, mainly in moist, wooded regions. *L. alpinum* and *L. selago* are alpine and arctic-alpine. Running pine (*L. complanatum* and *L. digitatum*) and ground pine (*L. obscurum*) make good Christmas decorations. The yellow spores were formerly used for coating pills and in medicines; they are also explosive and were used in flash guns.

W.J. CODY

Cluny Earthlodge Village, archaeological site along the N bank of the BOW R in S-central Alberta, consists of a semicircular earth trench about 1 m deep and 2 to 2.5 m wide which, along with a natural terrace edge along one side, encloses an area 129 m long by 90 m wide. Paralleling and from 5 to 8 m inside the trench was a pole palisade. Between the trench and palisade was a spaced series of 10 roughly oval pits, 5 to 6.5 m in diameter and 0.75 to 1 m deep. Research indicates these structures, similar to earthlodge villages found elsewhere in the region, served to fortify the area within for a small group of aboriginal inhabitants probably living in skin TIPIS. Cluny was apparently constructed and briefly occupied in the 1740s by Indian peoples related or ancestral to the historic Crow and Hidatsa. These inhabitants may have fled from their traditional territory along the Missouri R in what is now N and S Dakota to escape the ravages of a smallpox epidemic. *See also* ARCHAEOLOGY.

JOHN H. BRUMLEY

Clutesi, George Charles, artist, author, folklorist (b at Port Alberni, BC 1905), a member of a family of Nootka chiefs of Sheshaht, Vancouver I. His publications and public activities were among the first in the post-WWII period to gain recognition for Indian culture as interpreted by Indians themselves. A fisherman and piledriver for 21 years, Clutesi broke his back in the 1940s. During his convalescence, he began to record, reproduce and teach the stories, songs, dances and art of his people. Emily CARR left him her artists' materials at her death. His books, though conventional in language, are rich in engaging human and technical detail. Clutesi painted one of the murals of the Indians of Canada pavilion at Expo' 67. He is the author of *Son of Raven, Son of Deer: Fables of the Tse-shaht People* (1967) and *Potlatch* (1969).

BENNETT MCCARDLE

CN Tower, Toronto (architects John Andrews, International/Roger Du Toit, and the Webb Zerafa Menkes Housden Partnership; structural engineer R.R. Nicolet, 1973-76) is the world's tallest free-standing structure. Built at a cost of $52 million, it is topped by a sophisticated COMMUNICATIONS antenna for transmission of broadcast and microwave signals. Under the management of CN Hotels, the tower attracts thousands of tourists who ride the glassed-in elevators 342 m to the skypod which houses both wide observation decks and the world's highest revolving restaurant. The hexagonal post-tensioned concrete tower is braced by 3 wings to form a broad "Y" in plan at the ground. The tapering wings rise to 330 m, the concrete tower to 450 m. The Tower is topped by a 100 m steel mast for a total height of 553 m. Of the world's observation and communications towers, the CN Tower is the most elegant.

MICHAEL MCMORDIE

Cnidaria, phylum of multicellular, radically symmetrical INVERTEBRATES (eg, hydroids, JELLYFISH, sea anemones, CORALS) dating to late Precambrian era (630 million years ago). Formerly, phylum Coelenterata included cnidarians and ctenophores (comb jellies). Today, these are considered separate phyla; Coelenterata is used synonymously with Cnidaria. Cnidaria [Gk *knide*, "nettle"] are characterized by their unusual stinging cells. They are found throughout the oceans; relatively few species have colonized fresh water. About 9700 species are known. Two body forms (polyp and medusa) are present, adapted for different life-styles. Polyps are attached to a surface (sessile); medusae, are free-floating (planktonic).

The mouth, facing upward in polyps, downward in medusae, leads into a central gut cavity (coelenteron). The gut lining (gastrodermis) contains cells that secrete digestive enzymes; other cells absorb soluble nutrients. The other tissue layer (epidermis), covering the animal's exterior surface contains the highest concentration of stinging cells (cnidoblasts). They are particularly common on food-capturing surfaces (eg, tentacles). Each cnidoblast houses a flask-shaped nematocyst containing a coiled, hollow thread. The thread turns inside out as it is fired from the capsule by an influx of water which increases pressure inside the capsule. Nematocysts can be used once, then must be replaced. Apparently, a combination of touch and specific chemicals (probably amino acids) released from prey provides discharge stimulus. Many types of nematocysts exist. One type, armed with spines, is capable of penetrating prey and injecting immobilizing toxins. Another, nontoxic type is sticky and wraps around prey, preventing its escape. Others provide adhesion to surfaces and defence from predators. The epidermis also contains muscle and nerve cells and ciliated cells (with hairlike appendages). A true nervous system probably evolved first in Cnidaria. Anemones and corals perceive stimuli by sensory cells scattered throughout the epidermis. Medusae frequently have quite complex sense organs (simple eyes, ocelli; balance organs, statocysts). Between the tissue layers is a sheet of noncellular material (mesoglea) varying in thickness and consistency among species. In medusae, mesoglea is thick, watery and resembles jelly. In polyps, it is thin and resilient because of its high fibrous protein content.

The success of Cnidarians, judged by species diversity and distribution, can probably be attributed to their efficiency as carnivores. Cnidarians usually present a large body area, covered with nematocysts, to the water; small animals are paralyzed and trapped when they touch this surface. Common prey include copepod crustaceans, shrimps, worms and larvae. A few hydroids, anemones and medusae feed on decaying matter, collected by a combination of cilia and mucus. Several species of hydroids, anemones, corals and jellyfish, living in shallow water and receiving a lot of sunlight, harbour symbiotic ALGAE in their gut cells. The algae photosynthesize inside host cells, producing food for the host. In return, host cells provide a stable environment and ready access to nutrients and carbon dioxide. In freshwater hydras, these algae are called zoochlorellae; in marine species, zooxanthellae. Many Cnidarians have complex life cycles in which body form alternates between polyp and medusa. Anemones and corals have no medusa stage. The 3 cnidarian classes are as follows.

Hydrozoa comprises hydroids and their medusae (hydromedusae). About 12 species of freshwater *Hydra* occur in Canadian lakes and streams. *Hydra* species are unusual in having no medusa stage. Hydroids are abundant on Canada's coasts: some 240 hydroid species and 84 hydromedusae species have been identified. Although some hydroids do not release medusae, many undescribed medusae must exist in Canadian waters. This is not surprising, since some are only 4 mm in diameter, with the largest about 12 cm across. Most hydroids have a treelike colonial form that develops by asexual budding of feeding individuals. As the colony grows, buds appear which develop into medusae that are released. Some planktonic hydrozoans, eg, *Velella, Nanomia* and *Physalia* (Portuguese man-of-war) are colonial, containing up to 7 types of individuals forming a co-operative whole. A group of hydrozoan corals, the Hydrocorallina, is common throughout tropical and subtropical seas. A few species which form pink encrustations on rocks in deep water occur in Canadian waters.

Anthozoa includes sea anemones, corals and sea pens. Anemones tend to be solitary. They are the largest cnidarian polyps; some species reach 1 m across the oral disc, eg, *Tealia columbiana* of outer BC coast. Most anemones need a hard surface to attach to; a few species burrow in mud and sand, with tentacles showing above the surface. Several species prefer attaching themselves to snail shells occupied by hermit crabs. Eggs and sperm are released through the mouth; fertilization usually occurs externally. The resulting ciliated larva (planula) eventually settles to the bottom, attaches and transforms into a small polyp. A few anemones brood their young. Like tropical forms, the 65 species of Canadian anemones are often brightly coloured, eg, *Metridium senile* (white), *Anthopleura xanthogrammica* (green), and *Tealia lofotensis* (pink). The only true corals of Canadian waters are solitary, orange cup-corals (eg, *Balanophyllia*). Several species of treelike, horny corals (order Gorgonacea) are found in deep water. Feather-shaped sea pens are common along all Canadian coasts, wherever there is sand in which they can embed their fleshy anchors. Above the anchor is a stem from which numerous, retractable polyps are supported on side arms.

Scyphozoa (true jellyfish) are much larger than hydrozoan jellyfish. They exist throughout the oceans, particularly in coastal areas. Fourteen species commonly occur off Canadian coasts, including the conspicuous, golden orange *Cyanea capillata,* which may reach 1.5 m across. Scyphozoan polyps are small and difficult to find. Normally, a temporary larval form (ephyra) is budded off the polyp by repeated division, so that the polyp resembles a stack of plates. In some species, the medusa develops directly from the polyp; deep oceanic types (eg, *Periphylla*) have no polyp. The medusa stage is sexual, producing eggs or sperm. The planula larva, which develops after fertilization, attaches to a hard surface; from it the polyp phase grows. One group, Stauromedusae, can be found permanently attached to seaweeds by stalks.

A.N. SPENCER

Coady, Moses Michael, "M.M.," priest, teacher (b at North East Margaree, NS 3 Jan 1882; d at Antigonish, NS 28 July 1959). First director of the extension department, St Francis Xavier U, Coady developed a program of ADULT EDUCATION involving economic self-help for the economically depressed Maritimes that by the time of his death had been adopted in many Third World countries. Coady organized the NS Teachers' Union, the United Maritime Fishermen and, as director of extension, launched the ANTIGONISH MOVEMENT. His *Masters of Their Own Destiny* (1939), the story of the movement, is still in print and has been translated into 7 languages. A volume of his speeches, *The Man From Margaree,* was published in 1971. Coady received numerous awards including 3 honorary degrees (Boston, Ottawa, Ohio). In 1959 the Coady International Institute was opened to continue his work in the Third World. DOUGLAS F. CAMPBELL

Coaker, Sir William Ford, union leader, politician (b at St John's 19 Oct 1871; d at Boston 26 Oct 1938). Coaker began organizing the Fishermen's Protective Union during 1908-09. The Roman Catholic Church's hostility confined the union to the largely Protestant NE coast of Newfoundland; nevertheless it had 20 000 members by 1914. From the outset, Coaker had argued that the significant economic, social and political reforms needed to win justice for the working man could only be achieved if the union played a political role. The FPU did well in the 1913 election and joined the 1917 National Government. In 1919 Coaker entered Sir Richard SQUIRES's Cabinet and attempted but failed to impose order and regulation upon a fishing industry dislocated by postwar deflation and long characterized by inefficiency, particularly in marketing.

J.K. HILLER

Coal, combustible SEDIMENTARY ROCK formed from the remains of PLANT life, comprises the world's largest FOSSIL energy resource. It is located primarily in the Northern Hemisphere. Coal is not a uniform substance; rather, it is a wide variety of minerals with different characteristics arising from the nature of its vegetation source and siltation history, and the time and geological forces involved in its formation (including temperature and pressure). Coal is classified according to 4 ranks or classes, each subdivided according to fixed carbon and volatile matter content and heating value. The anthracite class, the most valuable, is blended with bituminous coals to make coke for the IRON AND STEEL INDUSTRY and is also used in the CHEMICAL INDUSTRIES. Bitumous coal, besides its use in steelmaking, is used as thermal coal for ELECTRIC POWER GENERATION. Subbituminous coal supplies thermal-power fuel and steam for industry, and can be used in COAL GASIFICATION and COAL LIQUEFACTION. The lowest grade of coal, lignite, is used for the same purposes as is subbituminous coal. Canada's only known body of anthracite coal was discovered in 1984 in northwestern BC; bituminous coal is found in NS, NB, Alberta and BC; subbituminous, in Alberta; lignite, in Saskatchewan and BC. With its usual perversity nature did not distribute Canada's coal conveniently. In NS, most of it is under the seafloor. In western Canada, which has about 97% of the country's coal, almost all of it is located hundreds of kilometres from either the Pacific tidewater or the slowly growing and potentially larger markets of central Canada.

History in Canada

Coal has been mined in Canada since 1639 when a small mine was opened at Grand Lk, NB. In 1720 French soldiers began to mine at Cow Bay [Cape Breton, NS] to supply the fortress at LOUISBOURG. Cape Breton later supplied coal to Boston and other American ports, and to the militia in Halifax. By 1870, 21 collieries were operating in Cape Breton. These markets disappeared early in this century. Commercial coal mining in New Brunswick began in 1825 and except for some early exports, most of the province's coal production has been used locally. In western Canada, coal was first mined on Vancouver I in 1836 to supply coastal steamboats, a business which lasted until about 50 years ago. The building of the transcontinental railways through Alberta and BC caused coal mines to be developed on the banks of the OLDMAN R near Lethbridge, at Drumheller and Edmonton.

By 1867 coal production had reached an annual total of 3 million t: over 2 million t in NS, most of the balance in western Canada and a small amount in NB. By 1911 western Canada had taken the lead and, despite serious downturns in the 1950s and 1960s, it now produces over 90% of the total. In 1947, the year that OIL AND NATURAL GAS were first produced commercially near Leduc, Alta, coal supplied one-half of Canada's ENERGY needs — Drumheller alone producing 2 million t of coal and employing 2000 men. The rapid conversion of coal's traditional markets to oil and gas caused the coal-mining industry almost to disappear.

Beginning in about 1950, almost all coal used for domestic heating, industrial energy and transportation energy was replaced by PETROLEUM products and natural gas. Coal now supplies less than 10% of Canada's energy needs. In the late 1960s and early 1970s it became clear that the coal-bearing provinces of Alberta, Saskatchewan, NB and NS should rely increasingly on their coal deposits for the production of electricity, and that Ontario should consider adding Canadian sources of coal to the amounts historically supplied by nearby mines in the US. At about the same time, Japan's rapidly growing requirement for coking coal provided the opportunity for the rapid development of metallurgical coal production in BC, Alberta and NS. New mining companies were formed, modern coal-handling facilities were constructed, and a new and very efficient system of unit trains was designed and produced.

Coal stacker-reclaimer at work at Roberts Bank, BC (*courtesy Westshore Terminals Ltd*).

The Modern Industry

The export demand for metallurgical coal has increased to include several other countries, but Canada's share of this demand will be affected by the world economic situation and by the development of competition from the few other metallurgical-coal exporting countries. Some of the factors that are causing a reduction in overall demand for metallurgical coal, such as a depressed world economy and policies of the Organization of Petroleum Exporting Countries, are bringing about a rising offshore demand for thermal coal. In the past dozen or more years these developments have created a Canadian coal industry that is vastly different from its predecessor. Over 400 small producers were in operation in the 1930s; today, Canada has only 10 large producers (plus a very few more under development) and a very small number of minor producers. Although no one is certain of the extent of the resource, Canada has at least 1% of the world's coal resources, and a very high resource and reserve/demand ratio compared to other countries. Estimates are constantly being revised upwards and may rise even more dramatically in the next few decades. Up to 2 trillion t are thought to lie deep under Alberta's plains, and there is serious speculation that one of the world's largest coal deposits lies between Cape Breton and Newfoundland.

The principal coal mines in Canada are located as follows.

Nova Scotia Lingan Mine, No 26 Colliery and the Prince Mine, all run by the Cape Breton Development Corp; Point Aconi Pit, Novaco Ltd; St Rose Mine, Evans Coal Mines Ltd; Drummond Mine, Drummond Coal Co.

New Brunswick Minto/Chipman area pits, NB Coal Ltd.

Saskatchewan Bienfait Mine, Bienfait Coal Co; Boundary Dam Mine, M&S Coal Co; Costello Mine (formerly Klimax Mine), Manalta Coal Ltd; Souris Valley Mine, Utility Valley Mine and Poplar River Mine, all owned by the Saskatchewan Power Corp (with Manalta operating the Utility Mine).

Alberta Montgomery Mine (formerly Roselyn Mine), Manalta Coal Ltd; Vesta Mine, Alberta Power Ltd, with Manalta as operator; Diplomat Mine, Paintearth Mine, Forestburg Collieries Ltd; Highvale Mine, Whitewood Mine, Transalta Utilities Corp, with Manalta as operator; Coal Valley Mine, Luscar Sterco Ltd; Luscar Mine, Cardinal River Coals Ltd; Gregg River Mine, Manalta Coal Ltd; Obed-Marsh Project, Union Oil Company of Canada Ltd; No 1765 Mine and No 1774 Mine, Smoky River Coals Ltd.

British Columbia Corbin Mine, Byron Creek Collieries Ltd; Harmer Surface Mine, Michel Underground Mine and Greenhills Mine, Westar Mining Ltd; Live Creek Mine, Crows Nest Resources Ltd; Fording River Mine, Fording Coal Ltd; Quintette Mine, Denison Mines Ltd and others; Bullmoose Mine, Teck Corp and others.

About 17 million t of coal were exported in 1983, and 14.7 million t were imported; 44.8 million t were produced and 43.7 million t were consumed in Canada. One reason for the apparently anomalous situation of a major coal-producing country importing such a large quantity of coal is that most of Canada's higher-ranking coals are located about 2300 km from the industrial heartland of central Canada, and about 1100 km from the Pacific coast. Transportation costs are high and the steel mills and Ontario Hydro in Ontario have found it advantageous to import their coal supplies from nearby mines in the US. The other major reason is that the international demand for steel has slackened in the last few years, causing the planned expansions of several mines and the opening of a few others to be delayed.

Because of Canada's large size and the location of most of its coals far from large domestic markets in central Canada and from tidewater for export (except in NS and NB), transportation plays a critical role in the national and international coal trade. The 2 major railways that carry western coals to Pacific tidewater also carry potash, sulphur, grain, petrochemicals and forest products, and are approaching their maximum capacity to haul these bulk commodities. Huge capital investments are being made to increase rail capacity, thus enabling the railways to meet projected increases of offshore demand for these products.

Environmental Impact

The production and use of coal creates certain environmental problems. In some countries regulatory processes imposed by governments restrict the expansion and use of coal, developments which are considered essential by the same governments. In fact, there is no way of obtaining and using all the energy needed now and in future without some adverse effects on the environment. What must be done is to make the best possible accommodation between energy, economic and social needs and environmental concerns. In Canada, only relatively small areas in the West are being disturbed at any one time for the purpose of coal mining. Recently, land disturbed annually by operating mines includes 182 ha in mountainous regions of BC, 174 ha in Alberta, and 130 ha in plains areas of Saskatchewan. Using technology now available, coal can be mined, transported and used in most parts of the world in conformity with high standards of health, safety and environmental protection without unacceptable increases in cost.

Industry Organization

Since the beginning of this century, the character and organization of Canada's coal-producing industry has reflected pressures from labour and external circumstances. In the fall of 1906, operators of steam-coal mines in southern Alberta and eastern BC formed the Western Coal Operators' Assn to make districtwide, collective labour and wage agreements. Coal mine employees in the area belonged to District 18 United Mine Workers of America. During WWI a director of coal operations was appointed to deal with labour relations and price adjustments in the absence of collective agreements. As a result, practically all of the larger operating companies in Alberta and eastern BC joined the Western Coal Operators' Assn. This directorate continued in operation until 18 May 1920. On that date, the name of the association was changed to the Western Canada Coal Operators' Association. That association entered into a collective agreement with District 18 United Mine Workers of America.

In 1925 the UMW of A became ineffective in western Canada, as rival labour organizations and various purely local unions designed to deal directly with specific employers were organized. This erosion of collective labour power led to a reduction in membership in the Western Canada Coal Operators' Assn and, in Nov 1925, the remaining members decided to disband it. By 1937 the UMW of A had again succeeded in bringing within its orbit most of the employees at the steam-coal mines and employers were again forced to consider districtwide agreements. As a result, the Western Canada Bituminous Coal Operators Assn was organized and included almost all steam coal operators.

During WWII all concerned concentrated on producing as much coal as possible. At the end of the war, the association included in its 1945 membership almost all thermal coal operators in Alberta and eastern BC. On 27 Sept 1952 the Domestic Coal Operators Assn and the Western Canada Bituminous Coal Operators Assn amalgamated to form the Coal Operators' Assn of Western Canada, with power to deal with any matters affecting the industry as a whole, and exclusive power to make local and general agreements with labour, to settle disputes arising out of the agreements and to act upon legislation, federal or provincial, that might affect the membership.

In Apr 1971 the association became the Coal Association of Canada, which came to abandon its concern with labour and wage agreements and with the administration of welfare and retirement funds. On 24 Dec 1973 the federal government issued letters patent to this new association, with objectives appropriate to a national body representing the coal industry, ie, to project the views of the industry on the international, national and provincial levels, and to coordinate its efforts with those of government in policies effecting coal exploration, development and mining.Today the membership of the association includes all significant coal producers in Canada, mining companies which are seriously engaged in preparing to produce coal, and almost all petroleum companies with sizable coal holdings.

GARNET T. PAGE

Coal Demethanation, process by which methane gas is removed from coal deposits. The principal objective of coal demethanation, since its introduction in 1943, has been to remove the safety hazard that the gas poses to miners; however, methane is the principal component of natural gas and can substitute for it. Methane is generated in coal during coalification, the process in which FOSSIL vegetation is gradually converted from low-rank to high-rank coal. As much as 1400 m^3 of methane is produced per tonne of coal during coalification, but only about 2% is retained in the coal. The highest-recorded gas content of coal in Canada is 21 m^3/t, measured in Canmore, Alta. No estimate has been made of the total coal-gas resource of Canada, but the US Bureau of Mines estimates that as much as 20 trillion m^3 of methane is present in US coal deposits, of which 8.5 trillion m^3 might be recoverable.

A relatively recent coal demethanation technique does not require the presence of a coal mine. The technique can be used to improve mine safety (by removing a major portion of the methane before the coal is mined) as well as to collect methane for use as a fuel. To gain access to the methane, a borehole is usually drilled from the ground surface or boreholes are drilled from a shaft. To start the gas desorbing, the conditions under which the methane is adsorbed on the coal must be changed, so that the coal can retain less gas. This is typically done by reducing the hydrostatic pressure on the coal by removing water. The permeability of coals is typically low; therefore, it is increased by techniques such as fracturing the seam (a technique borrowed from the oil industry). Sufficient pressure is generated in the system to move the methane to the well where it is collected; no suction needs to be applied to the borehole. With no suction applied, there is no air contamination of the methane. Unlike the gas produced in a methane drainage system in a mine, the gas produced by a virgin-coal demethanation system generally contains 95% or more methane. Such a gas has a heat value similar to that of natural gas (37 MJ/m^3) and can be comingled with it. This gas can be used in all applications for which natural gas is used, except for some chemical processes. In 1977 Noval Technologies Ltd (a subsidiary of NOVA, AN ALBERTA CORPORATION) began field experiments in Alberta. A further test program was initiated in Nova Scotia in 1979, in conjunction with PETRO-CANADA. Research indicates that techniques are now sufficiently advanced to make a commercial project feasible. A. KAHIL

Coal Gasification, process by which coal is converted into a FUEL gas rich in HYDROGEN and carbon monoxide. The process was first developed in about 1780 and was widely commercialized by the early 1900s. Before natural gas became widely available in the 1940s, many N American and European cities used a coal gas as a heating and lighting fuel. It was referred to variously as blue gas, producer gas, water gas, town gas or fuel gas. Often using the same low-pressure mains for distribution, natural gas replaced fuel gas in most uses by the 1950s because of its greater heating value and lack of contaminants. Recently, however, there has been renewed interest in coal gasification as a means of replacing or supplementing PETROLEUM resources such as natural gas. In many parts of the world, including Canada, coal resources are so large that fuel gas could become a viable alternative fuel, if natural-gas resources run low. A fuel gas is also produced as a by-product of coal mining, from COAL DEMETHANATION.

A coal-gasification research project is underway at the Canada Centre for Mineral and Energy Technology (CANMET), Bell's Corners, near Ottawa. Researchers at the facility believe that combined-cycle power generation could be in place in Canada by the early 1990s. The system, which would use a turbine fired by syn-gas in combination with a conventional steam turbine (fired by coal, oil or gas), could provide electricity 10% cheaper than that generated by the conventional process. CANMET and the Saskatchewan Power Corp have spent $500 000 to study building such a plant at Shaunavon, Sask. The plant would cost more to build, but savings in electric power costs would more than balance the higher outlay. The ALBERTA RESEARCH COUNCIL has also studied coal-gasification technology, but found that there was little economic incentive to pursue it. *In situ* or underground coal gasification is a recent development. In 1976 an ARC test field showed some promise of advancement in *in situ* technology. Its current work on coal pyrolysis (ie, application of heat to bring about chemical change) indicates that valuable liquid fuels as well as gases could be produced.

R.W. GREGORY

Coal Liquefaction, process by which coal is converted from its solid state into liquid fuels, usually to provide substitutes for PETROLEUM products. Coal liquefaction was first developed in the mid-19th century, but its exploitation was hindered by the relatively low price and wide availability of crude OIL AND NATURAL GAS. In only a few times and places (eg, Germany during WWII, South Africa since the 1960s) have the economics favoured development of coal-liquefaction processes. However, since the oil-price increases of the 1970s and with the growing awareness that conventional supplies are being depleted, there has been renewed interest in producing oil substitutes from the world's relatively abundant coal reserves. Under recent conditions of crude oil price and supply, the production of petroleum substitutes from coal has not been deemed economic in Canada, but it may be reconsidered if cheaper processes are developed or if crude oil prices rise sharply again. The ALBERTA RESEARCH COUNCIL began research into coal liquefaction as early as 1934-35. Since 1980 the council's Coal Research Dept has had a coal-liquefaction program. The department shares facilities at a newly built (1983-84) Coal Research Centre, Devon, Alta, with the Western Regional Laboratories of the federal Dept of Energy, Mines and Resources and the federally and provincially funded Coal Mining Research Centre. A $1-million experimental coal-liquefaction installation has been established at the Canada Centre for Mineral and Energy Technology at Bell's Corners, near Ottawa. SNC, a Montréal engineering firm, is involved in testing the performance of Canadian coals in existing liquefaction processes. Researchers feel that coal-derived liquid fuels could be an economic proposition for Canada before 1995.

Direct liquefaction, in which the coal is first converted into synthesis gas, was developed as a commercial process early in the 20th century. The chemist Friedrich Berguis constructed a pilot plant in Germany in 1922 to liquefy one tonne of coal per day. By 1932, 300 000 t of motor fuel was produced annually from coal in Germany. The direct liquefaction processes used in modern pilot plants are modifications of the original Berguis process. The coal is first ground into particles less than 1 mm in diameter and mixed in equal proportions with petroleum-type solvents, which typically are derived from coal as well. When the mixture is heated to about 475°C in a hydrogen atmosphere at a pressure of about 200 atmospheres, one tonne of coal yields about one-half tonne of liquids and tars. The rate of liquefaction reaction improves as the rank of the coal decreases: lignite gives the fastest reaction; bituminous coal is much slower; the reaction becomes impractically slow as the rank approaches semianthracite.

Indirect liquefaction processes also were developed in oil-short Germany early in the 20th century. In 1913 the chemical manufacturer BASF announced development of a process for producing a variety of organic chemicals. In the early 1920s, Franz Fischer and Hans Tropsch patented a process called Synthol to produce alcohols, aldehydes, fatty acids and other organic chemicals from a synthesis gas of hydrogen and carbon monoxide, which can be produced from coal gasification. This basic form of reaction has become known as the Fischer-Tropsch (F-T) process. Depending on the reaction conditions and the catalyst employed, the process can produce a variety of products with a wide range of molecular weights. This method was used to produce gasoline-type motor fuel during WWII and has been used by South Africa to produce motor fuels and PETROCHEMICAL feedstocks since the 1960s.

More recent versions of the F-T process can produce gasoline, plus a few by-products, from methanol; work is also underway to produce diesel fuel from methanol. The main drawback to the F-T process is that it either produces too many by-products or too much water; research centers on new catalysts to improve its efficiency. For direct liquefaction, the key research objectives have been to lower the operating pressures of the processes and to improve the quality and quantity of the products. The goals have been partially met with some new mixtures of catalysts and changes in operating conditions but no major breakthrough has occurred since WWII. R.W. GREGORY

Coal Mining Although most of Canada's COAL lies at depths of 300 m or more, much of the coal now mined comes from surface mines. Strip mining is used where gently dipping seams lie close to the surface in relatively flat land; open-pit mining, where thick seams come near the surface in mountains or foothills. As the workings in a surface mine reach deeper, the amount of glacial debris and rock (overburden) that must be removed to expose the coal increases. The volume of overburden that must be moved to extract one tonne of coal, the "strip ratio," is an important factor in deciding the depth to which it is economically desirable to continue working. That depth is also influenced by technical considerations which take into account local geological factors and equipment limitations.

In areas suitable for strip mining, the rock strata above the coal bed are, as a rule, tectonically undisturbed (ie, not folded or faulted) and relatively soft; therefore, little, if any, blasting is needed before the dragline can dig the overburden. Overburden materials are deposited in spoil piles in a previously worked-out cut. Strip mining is widely employed in Alberta and Saskatchewan plains areas and in NB, to provide the coal that fuels nearby ("mine mouth") ELECTRIC-POWER GENERATION plants and other industrial installations. After exposure by the dragline, the coal is extracted by electric caterpillar-track shovels or rubber-tired, diesel-driven, front-end loaders, and transferred to bottom-dump trucks which haul it to its destination or to railcars for further transport. In open-pit mines, overburden rock normally requires drilling and blasting before it can be removed by shovels or backhoe excavators and loaded into trucks for disposal in dumps or worked-out pits. Open-pits are always worked down in a series of benches, but where the coal seam has been folded or displaced by a fault, open-pit operations may be severely limited.

In the Rocky Mts and their FOOTHILLS, near-surface coal is mined in the East Kootenay and Peace R coalfields, with mining equipment very similiar to that employed in plains strip mines. Rear-dump trucks are used for hauling blasted overburden and coal. The raw coal is taken to coal processing plants where it is prepared for export as metallurgical or high-grade steam coal. Preparation involves cleaning the coal, ie, removing inorganic rock material to meet market specifications, and normally is accomplished by processes using differences in specific gravity between coal and rock. Rock material is discarded and the cleaned coal is dried before loading into unit trains for transport. Typically the unit trains are composed of about 100 specially designed "gondola" cars, each of which can hold 100 t of coal.

Where the limits of surface mining have been reached or the coal is too deeply buried to be extracted in surface workings, underground mining methods are employed. Vertical shafts or inclined roadways, the latter known as "slopes" or "drifts," are driven into the coal seam or contiguous rock strata. How the seam is thereafter developed, and which of the several alternative mining techniques is used, depends on the geological "envelope" in which the coal lies and is also determined by detailed considerations of development costs, mine life, operating costs and operational flexibility.

In the CAPE BRETON I coalfields, which extend out under the Atlantic Ocean to depths of almost 1000 m and dip at approximately 12°, the shallower coals are only partially extracted. Coal pillars are left in place at predetermined intervals to support the overlying strata and avoid potential breaks from the mine workings through to the seabed. When development has reached sufficient depth, a longwall advance mining technique is employed, in which 200 m long panels are progressively cut, to up to 2 km from the dip slopes. Each panel can yield more than one million tonnes of coal. The coal-cutting machine, a longwall shearer, takes a slice up to one metre wide from the coal face, and a chain conveyor transports the cut coal along the face to a belt conveyor in the main roadway (gate) of the mine. To protect miners from roof falls, hydraulically operated shields and steel roadway arch supports are installed. Holes, drilled into the roof and floor, are connected to pipes to extract methane gas, also called firedamp, which might otherwise constitute an explosion hazard (*see* COAL DEMETHANATION). Water is automatically sprayed wherever coal is being cut or transferred, to eliminate risks of dust explosion and to protect miners against pneumoconiosis (black lung disease). This serious disease, which can result from inhalation of fine dust, used to be the scourge of coal mining operations, but is now virtually stamped out.

In western Canada, adverse economic conditions forced abandonment of older underground mines in the 1950s and early 1960s, but a strong resurgence of the coal industry since the early 1970s has led to numerous new developments, mainly surface mines. Deep coal is also mined, with access by drifts and slopes. Coal seams in the Rockies are often up to 20 m thick and, in many places, have gradients as steep as 60°. In these circumstances, a variety of different mining methods, sometimes specially adapted to local conditions, must be used.

One operation in the CROWSNEST PASS region of southeastern BC has pioneered hydraulic mining for Canadian coal. The thick, pitching seams are cut by a high-pressure jet of water (monitor jet) and the broken coal, after further crushing at the coal face, is transported out of the mine in metal flumes which carry the coal in suspension in water. The water either flows down the mountainside or is pumped, from beneath the mountain, to a plant which recovers the coal and recycles the cleaned water to the monitor jet. The roof over the worked out part of the coal seam (the so-called "gob" area) is allowed to cave in.

In mines near Smoky R, Alta, with coal seams 2.5-7 m thick, caterpillar-track-mounted coal cutters (continuous miners) are used for room-and-pillar mining. In this system, the coal seam and surrounding rock is cut up into roughly 35 m by 25 m pillars which are removed, and the roof is allowed to collapse into the gob as operations retreat from the outer boundary of the working. During development, the rooms are secured against premature collapse by insertion of expanding roof bolts. The continuous miner cuts the coal and loads it into electric, rubber-tired shuttle cars which deliver it to the belt conveying system that takes it to the surface. This procedure has the flexibility needed for mining in disturbed mountain and foothill terrain, but is less productive than longwall retreat mining in which the panels are driven to the far boundary and coal is cut back toward the entrance. It also demands greater skill and judgement of operating personnel.

Although production of underground coal presently represents less than 15% of Canada's total coal output, it is expected that future worldwide coal demand and further advances in mining technology (ie, automation and the introduction of computer-controlled mining operations) will promote increasing dependence on extraction of deep coal. *See also* DISASTERS

N. BERKOWITZ AND N. DUNCAN

Milners coal mine on the N Saskatchewan R near Edmonton, Alta, 1904 (*courtesy Provincial Archives of Alberta/E. Brown Collection*).

Coalition Government includes members of different political parties and normally appears during crises such as war or political breakdown. The fluidity of party lines, the predominance of patronage, and the novelty of RESPONSIBLE GOVERNMENT led to several experimental coalition arrangements in New Brunswick, Nova Scotia and Canada in the 1840s and 1850s. The best known were in 1854 and 1864 (the GREAT COALITION) in the PROVINCE OF CANADA. The former, which united moderate Reformers and Conservatives, was the base for the post-Confederation CONSERVATIVE PARTY. The latter joined CLEAR GRIT Liberals, Conservatives and *bleus* (see PARTI BLEU) to bring about CONFEDERATION, although it had been dissolved by the 1872 election.

The strengthening of party affiliation and the development of the apparatus of a party system since Confederation have made coalitions more difficult to negotiate. At the national level, the only coalition has been Sir Robert Borden's 1917 UNION GOVERNMENT. Faced with strong opposition to CONSCRIPTION and with other major difficulties during WWI, Borden sought to broaden his wartime political base by bringing several conscriptionist Liberals and other public figures into his government. In the Dec 1917 general election, this government won a decisive victory over Sir Wilfrid Laurier's Liberals. The Union coalition did not long survive its triumph: the end of the war brought many Liberals back to their old affiliation while other Unionists supported the new PROGRESSIVE PARTY. With Borden's resignation in 1920, even the pretense of coalition disappeared. The Union government illustrated the dangers of coalition: after 1917, French Canadians associated coalitions with conscription. Indeed, during WWII proposals for coalitions or a "National Government" came from those who also called for a stronger war effort and conscription. Since WWII there have been few proposals for federal coalition governments.

At the provincial level coalitions have occurred in western Canada. Manitoba Liberals and Progressives combined in 1931, and in 1940 all the province's parties joined a nonpartisan administration formed to meet wartime demands. In BC a wartime coalition between the Liberals and Conservatives held off the challenge of the CO-OPERATIVE COMMONWEALTH FEDERATION. The coalition probably benefited the CCF; it certainly damaged the Liberals and Conservatives, soon supplanted by SOCIAL CREDIT. No coalition has been as successful as the "Great Coalition." Politicians have become so wary of the long-term results of coalitions that they are now most reluctant to introduce them. *See also* MINORITY GOVERNMENT.

JOHN ENGLISH

Coast Mountains are an unbroken mountain chain extending from the FRASER R LOWLANDS near Vancouver, BC, 1600 km N into the Yukon Territory. For most of their length they rise abruptly above a coastal strip, facing the Pacific Ocean with rugged slopes and tremendous relief, most extreme where glacial action cuts FJORDS up to 192 km long (one of only 4 such occurrences in the world). Some glaciers remain, notably around Mt WADDINGTON, highest point in the chain. Ice-age volcanic action created such features as Black Tusk in Garibaldi Provincial Park. Westerly winds drop upwards of 440 cm of precipitation a year on some exposed slopes of the mountains, nurturing rapid growth of coniferous forests. The rainiest spots in the mountains are likely the rainiest places in N America. Timber harvested from accessible areas is boomed or barged to tidewater mills. Copper-molybdenum mines operate intermittently in the Stewart area. PETER GRANT

Coastal Landform The fundamental coastal landforms are the beach, a depositional feature, and the cliff, an erosional feature. A beach is an accumulation of wave-worked sediments above and below the waterline along the shore (*see* OCEAN WAVE). Dynamically, it consists of 3 shore-parallel zones: backshore, only rarely affected by ocean waves; foreshore (beachface), continually subject to wave swash and backwash; and the shallow, subaqueous, nearshore (shoreface), where waves approaching from offshore move substantial quantities of sediment on the bottom. The foreshore on some tidal beaches may be hundreds of metres wide; the nearshore zone commonly extends offshore to depths exceeding 10 m. The overall profile of a beach depends on the size of the constituent material, but variations in wave conditions (daily and seasonal) may result in considerable short-term changes. Gravel and cobble beaches are usually steep; sand beaches are flatter and often exhibit a series of intertidal or subtidal bars or ridges. Beaches range from small, curved pocket beaches, contained between rock headlands, to straight, continuous beaches many kilometres long.

A coastal cliff is a steep, often vertical, face produced by wave EROSION of solid rock. The term bluff is often used for similar features developed in unconsolidated materials. The cliff base is frequently undercut by wave quarrying and abrasion, and may be fretted by CAVES. Weathering and slope failure are effective processes on the oversteepened coastal slopes above, and geological factors (eg, rock composition, bedding and jointing) are important controls on the rate of erosion and the form of the cliff. Intertidal shore platforms are developed as the cliffline retreats and these platforms are continually lowered by a combination of abrasion and rock weathering. Rock coastlines exhibiting a wide variety of cliff and shore platform morphologies dominate much of Canada's coastline (*see* PHYSIOGRAPHIC REGIONS). These features and the processes that produce them have been little studied.

Canada's mainland coastline, including the islands of Newfoundland, Cape Breton and PEI, is 71 261 km long and fronts on the North Pacific, Arctic and North Atlantic oceans. If all ISLANDS larger than 129.5 km^2 are included, the saltwater coastline is more than 170 000 km long. There are an additional 3800 km of freshwater coastline along the Great Lakes. The character of any coast depends on a combination of factors, including the relief and GEOLOGY of the land backing the coastline, the availability of coastal sediments and the prevailing wave and tidal conditions (*see* OCEANS; COASTAL WATERS). For example, deep, steep-walled FJORDS, characteristic of mountain coasts that are glaciated or have recently been glaciated, occur in BC and Baffin and Ellesmere islands. Estuaries, often the drowned lower sections of RIVER valleys, are characteristic of lowland coasts; many small estuaries occur in the Atlantic provinces. In NB and PEI, where there is abundant sand in the shore zone, long, narrow spits and barrier beaches have developed across the mouths of the estuaries. The sand is derived from erosion of soft sandstone cliffs and sandy glacial deposits. Where rivers transporting large volumes of sediment reach the coast, DELTAS may develop.

A coastline is continually changing, not only as a result of short-term, readily observable effects of erosion and deposition, but also in the longer term in response to changes in the relative levels of LAND and sea. In the last 2 million years, several major fluctuations in world sea level have occurred as immense volumes of water were alternately stored in and released from the continental ice sheets during the Pleistocene GLACIATIONS. Coastline position has undergone dramatic shifts as a result of these changes. The most recent rise in sea level began about 18 000 years ago. Very rapid initially, it continues today at a very slow rate. This slow, continuing rise is one of the factors causing the erosion and retreat of sandy, depositional shorelines worldwide.

Eroded shoreline at Gabriola I, BC. The energy force of breaking waves can erode the strongest rocks and, along with weathering, can create a wide variety of shapes and forms (*photo by Valerie J. May*).

Large volumes of ice, which accumulated on the continents during periods of glaciation, not only lowered world sea level but also resulted in the depression of the land beneath the ice. With glacial retreat and release of the weight, rock material in and under the Earth's crust adjusted to the decrease in gravitational stress (isostatic rebound). Coastal areas, initially inundated by the rapid rise of sea level during deglaciation, rebounded and beaches and other shoreline features were progressively elevated above the reach of marine action. Much of Canada's coastline was affected, and raised shorelines are characteristic of many areas, most notably the Hudson Bay Lowlands and Queen Elizabeth Is, where coastal evolution over the last 7000 years is dominated by isostatic uplift.

The most important coastal processes are associated with water motions in the nearshore environment caused by TIDES and wind-generated waves. The energy contained in breaking waves can erode the strongest rocks, and the speed of wave-induced, longshore ocean currents in the nearshore zone can transport large quantities of sand along the shore. Tides cause a periodic, usually semidiurnal variation in sea level, thereby influencing the width of the zone in which wave processes are effective. Tidal currents transport mud in suspension and, at narrow inlets and in areas with large tidal ranges, attain sufficient velocities to transport large quantities of sand. The headward reaches of the Bay of FUNDY, with the largest tidal range in the world, are dominated by tidal processes as exemplified in the extensive intertidal sands of the Minas Basin (*see* TIDAL ENERGY). With larger tidal ranges, mud flats and salt marshes become key components of the coastal environment, particularly in protected estuaries and bays. WIND action is significant wherever abundant supplies of sand are available for the development of sand dunes (*see* AEOLIAN LANDFORMS). Salt marshes and dunes illustrate the role of vegetation in the development of coastal depositional landforms. SEA ICE is an important and sometimes overriding factor in zones around the Arctic, Subarctic and parts of the Atlantic coasts of Canada. The presence of sea ice restricts the operation of wave and tidal processes at the shore, and beach morphology may be dominated by the effects of ice push, ice scour and ice rafting (*see* ICEBERG). S.B. MCCANN

Reading: S.B. McCann, ed, *The Coastline of Canada* (1980).

Coastal Marine Flora, *see* VEGETATION REGIONS.

Coastal Waters Canada has one of the longest coastlines of any country in the world (58 509 km excluding islands, 243 797 including all islands). Canadian coastal WATERS support valuable biological resources (eg, FISH, CRUSTACEANS, MOLLUSCS, marine mammals, SEAWEEDS) and are important for TRANSPORTATION, recreation and the MINERAL RESOURCES in the seafloor beneath them. The mountainous West Coast is characterized by deep FJORDS and large offshore ISLANDS which provide shelter for coastal waters (eg, in the Strait of GEORGIA). The moist, mild CLIMATE is influenced by an extension of the Kuroshio Current which moves warm water eastward across the Pacific Ocean (*see* OCEANOGRAPHY). The most important fishes are the 5 species of PACIFIC SALMON, which breed in Canadian rivers but migrate to the sea where they live and grow for several years. For example, after hatching, pink salmon enter the Pacific and swim in the nutrient-rich gyre of the Alaska Current for about a year before returning to the rivers to breed.

North from BC, at the shores of the Artic Ocean, lies the BEAUFORT SEA, into which flows one of Canada's major rivers, the MACKENZIE (*see* DRAINAGE BASINS). The fresh water discharged there forms heavy ICE cover for much of the year. The Beaufort Sea has important PETROLEUM deposits but extraction is rendered very expensive by the need to contend with SEA ICE. Moreover, navigation is hazardous because of numerous submerged mounds of ice and sediment known as PINGOS.

Arctic surface water flows eastward to BAFFIN BAY through the Canadian ARCTIC ARCHIPELAGO. This maze of waterways contains meagre fish resources, but parts of it (eg, LANCASTER SOUND) support large aggregations of SEABIRDS and mammals on which the native peoples have traditionally depended. Care must be taken to protect these RESOURCES during the extraction and

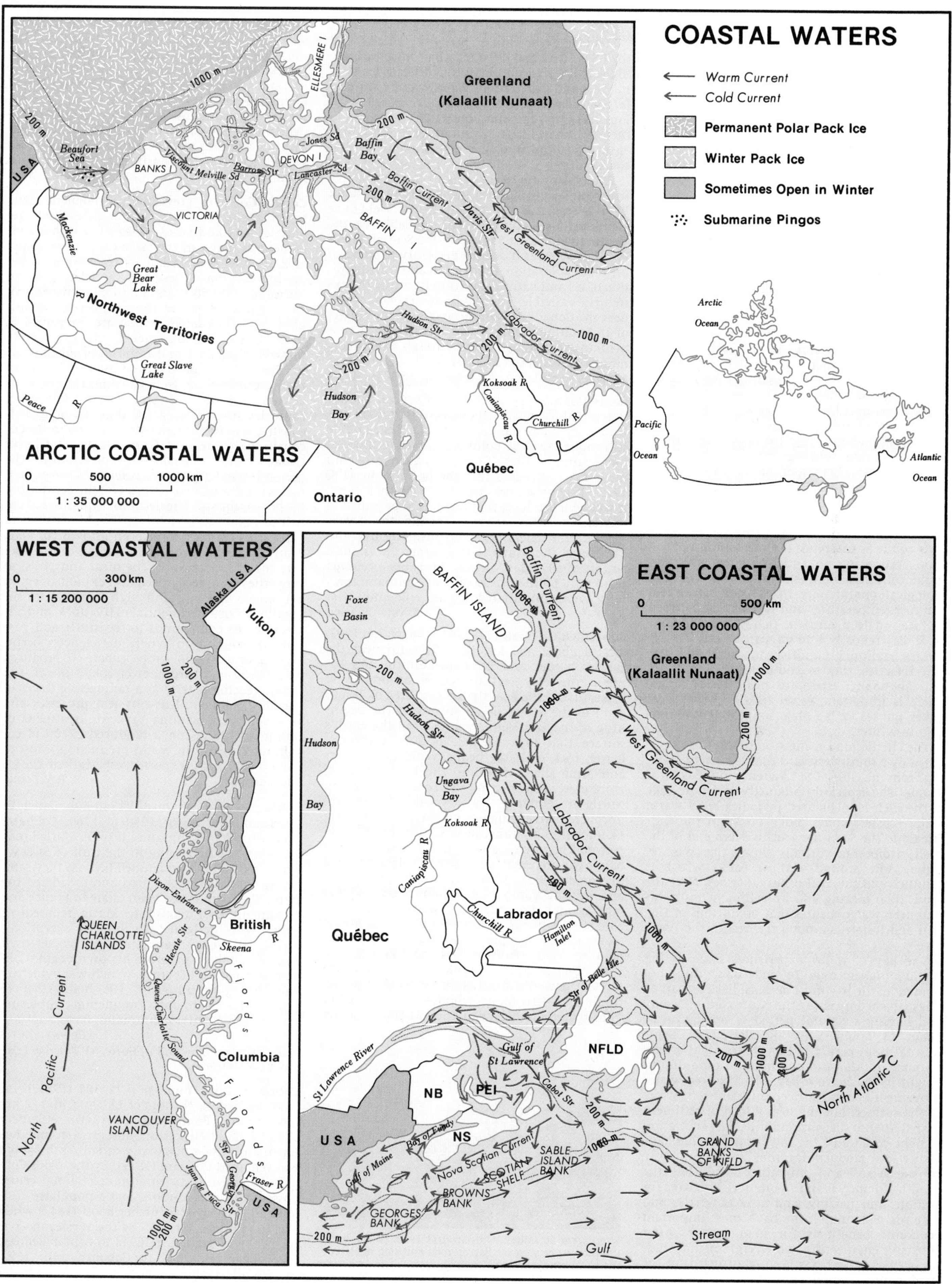
COASTAL WATERS
Warm Current
Cold Current
Permanent Polar Pack Ice
Winter Pack Ice
Sometimes Open in Winter
Submarine Pingos
ARCTIC COASTAL WATERS
0 500 1000 km
1 : 35 000 000
Greenland
(Kalaallit Nunaat)
ELLESMERE I
Beaufort Sea
BANKS I
Viscount Melville Sd
Barrow Str
DEVON I
Jones Sd
Lancaster Sd
Baffin Bay
Baffin Current
Davis Str
West Greenland Current
VICTORIA I
BAFFIN I
Mackenzie R
Great Bear Lake
Northwest Territories
Great Slave Lake
Peace R
Hudson Str
Labrador Current
Hudson Bay
Koksoak R
Caniapiscau R
Churchill R
Québec
Ontario
USA
Arctic Ocean
Pacific Ocean
Atlantic Ocean
WEST COASTAL WATERS
0 300 km
1 : 15 200 000
Alaska USA
Yukon
Dixon Entrance
QUEEN CHARLOTTE ISLANDS
Hecate Str
British Columbia
Skeena R
Queen Charlotte Sound
Fiords
VANCOUVER ISLAND
Str of Georgia
Juan de Fuca Str
Fraser R
USA
North Pacific Current
EAST COASTAL WATERS
0 500 km
1 : 23 000 000
Baffin Current
BAFFIN ISLAND
Foxe Basin
Hudson Str
Hudson Bay
Ungava Bay
Koksoak R
Caniapiscau R
Labrador
Churchill R
Hamilton Inlet
Québec
West Greenland Current
Labrador Current
Str of Belle Isle
Gulf of St Lawrence
St Lawrence River
NFLD
NB
PEI
NS
Cabot Str
Bay of Fundy
Gulf of Maine
Nova Scotian Current
SCOTIAN SHELF
SABLE ISLAND BANK
BROWNS BANK
GEORGES BANK
GRAND BANKS OF NFLD
North Atlantic C
Gulf Stream
USA
200 m
1000 m

transportation of oil and gas. Emerging through Jones and Lancaster sounds, the flow through the archipelago joins the southward-moving Baffin Current. At Hudson Str, large amounts of fresh water (derived primarily from ice melt and river discharge into HUDSON BAY) are injected into the flow which continues S as the Labrador Current. This fresh water stimulates biological productivity in the coastal waters of Labrador, which become progressively more productive from N to S. The seasonal variation in river runoff (peaking in spring when the snow melts) causes seasonal variation in FISHERY productivity all the way to Newfoundland's GRAND BANKS. Hamilton Bank, offshore from HAMILTON INLET on the Labrador Shelf, is an important COD fishing area. In spring, the pack ice off Newfoundland and Labrador is an important breeding ground for harp and hooded SEALS.

The Grand Banks, with almost 250 000 km^2 of water shallower than 200 m, has been known for over 400 years as one of the world's great fishing banks. It is very rich in cod, haddock, redfish, FLATFISH (including halibut), MACKEREL and HERRING. There are substantial oil reserves beneath the seafloor, but their exploitation is made hazardous by the ICEBERGS that drift S in the Labrador Current and by the prevalence of FOG, formed when warm air masses from the S and W encounter cold water from the N.

As the inshore branch of the Labrador Current continues around the S coast of Newfoundland, part of it enters the Gulf of ST LAWRENCE where it joins an inflow from the Str of Belle Isle separating Newfoundland and Labrador. The outflow of the St Lawrence R tends to follow the S shore, producing an anticlockwise circulation in the gulf. Two main factors contribute to high biological productivity in the gulf: its warm summer temperatures and the mixing between surface and deep, nutrient-rich waters. The Gulf of St Lawrence is known particularly for its LOBSTER, scallop, groundfish, mackerel and herring fisheries. WHALES and other mammals are also abundant, especially near the N shore. There is important vessel traffic to the Great Lakes, but sea ice is a major impediment to SHIPPING in winter.

The circulation on the SCOTIAN SHELF is dominated by a southwestward coastal current flowing from the Gulf of St Lawrence to the Gulf of Maine. The especially productive offshore edge of the shelf is influenced periodically by warm water masses which pinch off from the Gulf Stream to the S. At the southwestern end of the shelf, strong tidal currents cause a clockwise residual flow around shallow banks which is conducive to survival of larval fishes. Near the coast, tidal mixing and upwelling of nutrient-rich deep water ensures that production of finfish and losters is among the best in the province.

The Bay of FUNDY experiences some of the world's highest TIDES. To understand this phenomenon, the bay must be considered as part of a system encompassing the entire Gulf of Maine and having a natural period of oscillation of about 13 hours. Since the dominant, semidiurnal tidal period is 12.4 hours, tidal waves resonate in this basin and build to a maximum height in the narrow bay. The vigorous water movement brings the deep, nutrient-rich water to the surface, but the heavy load of sediment stirred up into suspension limits the penetration of light. As a result, the bay's upper reaches have rather low productivity; they are used mainly by SHOREBIRDS and migrating shad, but the mouth of Fundy is an important fishing area for scallops and herring, and attracts whales and seabirds. Potentially, the bay's most important economic benefit is for TIDAL ENERGY. After intensive engineering and environmental studies, a pilot project has been constructed on the Annapolis R and the building of a tidal barrage in the upper reaches of the bay is being considered.

Straddling the border between Canada and the US is GEORGES BANK, which has outstandingly high biological productivity, related to tidal mixing and circulation. Bank waters support large stocks of herring, haddock, cod and scallops and it appears that lobster larvae produced there are carried to the southern part of NS, thus ensuring a continuing replenishment of that stock.

Exploration for hydrocarbons has been active from the Beaufort Sea in the N to Georges Bank in the S (*see* OCEAN INDUSTRIES). The first field to be commercially exploited will probably be the Venture Field, near Sable I on the Scotian Shelf. In all these areas it will be necessary to strive to prevent exploration, production and transportation of oil and natural gas from harming the extremely valuable fisheries. PASSAMAQUODDY BAY, near the Canada/US border, has been the subject of international controversy because of a proposal to route supertankers through a relatively narrow channel in Canadian waters, en route to a refinery in Maine. P.C. SMITH AND K.H. MANN

Coats Island, 5499 km^2, one of several islands that guard the northern entrance to HUDSON BAY. Known originally as Cary's Swan's Nest, a name still applied to its SE point, it received its modern name from William Coats, a sea captain who made many voyages into the bay for the HBC 1727-51. For the most part flat or gently rolling, it was believed by early mariners to be joined to the larger SOUTHAMPTON I. During the 1860s, American whalers began to visit the bay and discovered the straits that separate the islands. Uninhabited today, it was probably occupied seasonally by the SADLERMIUT of Southampton I who were annihilated by an epidemic after 1900. DANIEL FRANCIS

Cobalt, Ont, Town, pop 1759 (1981c), inc 1907, located about 480 km N of Toronto near the Québec border and Lk Timiskaming, lies between the clay belt to the N around New Liskeard and the heavily forested area of Temagami to the S. Extensive mining at the beginning of the 20th century so scarred the earth's surface that today Cobalt is surrounded by barren rock and slag heaps, with deep craters and mine shafts dug into the hills. In 1903, work crews constructing the Temiskaming and Northern Ontario Ry (ONTARIO NORTHLAND) uncovered silver nuggets on the shore of Long Lk (Cobalt Lk), causing a stampede of prospectors. The town, named for the presence of cobalt in the ore, emerged on the W side of the lake to provide goods and services for the prospectors and mining companies which purchased the land around and under the townsite. The ethnic core of Cobalt was of British and French ancestry, but many people — primarily manual labourers — came from central and E Europe.

Its silver production, ranked 4th in the world in 1910, gave the impetus for exploring the Precambrian SHIELD. Many who had apprenticed in Cobalt went on to develop the mineral resources of the N. Similarly, the technique acquired to mill Cobalt's silver ore furthered the nation's scientific and technological skills. Cobalt was thus the cradle of Canadian mining, and its success spurred the growth of neighbouring HAILEYBURY and NEW LISKEARD. The silver began to run out in 1914, and today Cobalt is a depressed region, whose future would seem to depend on the development of tourism. The Cobalt Mining Museum and the annual Miners' Festival attract numerous visitors to the area each summer. DOUG BALDWIN

Street scene in Cobalt, Ont, around 1910. In the background can be seen the barren rock and slag heaps resulting from extensive mining (*courtesy Public Archives of Canada/C-44126*).

Cobalt (Co), hard, greyish white magnetic metal which melts at 1495°C and which closely resembles IRON and NICKEL. Cobalt is a minor constituent of many of the large copper ore bodies of Zaire and Zambia but its recovery as a by-product has made these ores the leading world source for over 50 years. Small quantities of cobalt are also recovered from copper-nickel sulphide ores. The latter, which are the source of most of the world's nickel, are extensively mined in Canada. Small amounts of cobalt occur in the deposits of oxidized nickel found in many countries, eg, New Caledonia, Zaire, Canada and the US. In Morocco and a few other countries small high-grade deposits of nickel-cobalt arsenides furnish significant quantities of cobalt. Arsenide ores from COBALT, Ont, gave Canada world leadership in production for the period 1905-1925. A large potential source of cobalt is the manganese nodules on the ocean floor (*see* OCEAN MINING). The decorative qualities of cobalt compounds, which impart a blue colour to glass and ceramics, have been known for 4000 years. However, it was well into this century before cobalt's remarkable chemical and physical properties were recognized and exploited, eg, in permanent magnets and high-temperature superalloys. Cobalt is essential to livestock, and addition of its compounds to feedstuffs and pastures is widespread where deficiencies occur. The important radioisotope, cobalt-60, produced by neutron bombardment of cobalt metal in a fission reactor, is used as a radioactive tracer in chemical, biological or physical processes and as a source of gamma rays for treatment of cancer. In 1981 Canada produced 2270 t of cobalt, ranking 3rd in world production. Most of Canada's output is exported, especially to the US and Europe. R.S. YOUNG

Cobham, Eric, pirate (*fl* c1740-60). Based in Newfoundland about 1740 to 1760, Cobham, a native of Poole, Eng, and his wife, Maria Lindsay, plundered shipping in the Gulf of St Lawrence, their crimes undetected because they sank nearly every vessel captured and murdered the crews. Cobham retired to an estate in France and was appointed a magistrate. Maria, reputedly a sadist who delighted in bizarre executions, eventually went insane and died by her own hand or Cobham's. Before his own death, Cobham dictated his life story, which was evidently published posthumously. His heirs tried to suppress the book, but a fragmentary copy survives in the Archives nationales, Paris.

EDWARD BUTTS

Reading: Edward Butts and H. Horwood, *Pirates and Outlaws of Canada* (1984).

Cobourg, Ont, Town, pop 11 385 (1981c), inc 1837, located on N shore of Lk Ontario, 112 km E of Toronto. Founded as a LOYALIST settlement 1798 by Eluid Nickerson, Joseph Ash and Asa Burnham, it was originally called Amherst but was renamed Cobourg (1819). By the 1830s Cobourg emerged as an important regional centre possessing a fine harbour and a populated hinterland. It received a further boost (1842) when Victoria College, est 1835 by the Wesleyan Conference, was granted powers to confer degrees; the college remained in Cobourg until 1892. Meanwhile, civic leaders hired a prominent architect, Kivas TULLY, to design an ornate townhall. Victoria Hall, completed 1860, survives as one of the most magnificent mid-Victorian structures in Ontario; a courtroom is a replica of London's Old Bailey. In the 1850s, Cobourg citizens also financed construction of the Cobourg and Peterborough Ry, an ambitious enterprise designed to "capture" the hinterland. But the railway proved a failure, partly because of a tenuous bridge across Rice Lk, almost bankrupting the town in the 1860s. After 1870, the community stabilized, showing little growth until after WWII. Today it contains over 20 industrial firms and is also a tourist centre.

J. PETRYSHYN

Cobourg and Peterborough Railway One of the 2 earliest railway charters granted in Canada, the Cobourg Rail Road Co was incorporated in 1834 to build a railway from COBOURG northward to Peterborough across Rice Lk. The project was shelved until 1846, when it was revived as the Cobourg and Rice Lake Plank Road and Ferry Co. Samuel Gore built his plank road the 17 km to the lake, but it barely survived the first 2 winters. The Cobourg and Peterborough Railway, incorporated 1852, was similarly ill fated. Construction began in 1853 but a cholera epidemic ravaged the German immigrants who had signed on for $1 a day. The Rice Lk bridge — at nearly 5 km long the longest in N America — was largely completed by the end of 1853. It consisted of a long trestle set on piles, with 33 truss spans (24 m each) and a 36 m swing section in the navigation channel. The bridge could not survive the grinding and shifts of winter ice and extensive repairs were required every spring; in 1860 the visiting Prince of Wales was not allowed to cross the bridge for fear it would collapse. The following winter the bridge disintegrated entirely and with it faded Cobourg's hopes of becoming a thriving port. Its citizens had put up over $1 million for their 48 km railway. It was merged with the Marmora ironworks in 1866. The Peterborough to Rice Lk section eventually came under the control of the GRAND TRUNK RAILWAY.

JAMES MARSH

Coburn, Frederick Simpson, painter, illustrator (b at Upper Melbourne, Qué 18 Mar 1871; d there 26 May 1960). Coburn is best known for competent, sympathetic oils of the Québec landscape, usually of a horse and sled heading down a snowy road through a tree-clad valley. European trained, he returned to Montréal in 1896 and began a successful career as an illustrator, notably for 6 books of verse by William Henry DRUMMOND, and for Louis FRÉCHETTE, and Putnam's Sons. Sketching with Maurice CULLEN c1914 turned him back to an early love — drawing horses. His paintings were so much in demand that he never had any on hand for a one-man show.

ANNE MCDOUGALL

Cochrane, Alta, Town, pop 3544 (1981c), inc 1971, is located 35 km NW of Calgary, on the BOW R. It is named for Sen M.H. Cochrane, who founded (1878) the Cochrane Ranch, which was declared a Prov Historic Site 1977. Cochrane became a CPR shipping point for cattle and is still a farming and ranching centre. Recently, it has become a dormitory town for Calgary.

ERIC J. HOLMGREN

Cochrane, Ont, Town, pop 4848 (1981c), inc 1910, located 375 km NW of North Bay. Named after the Hon Francis Cochrane, then Ontario minister of lands, forests and mines, the town was established 1908 at the point where the Temiskaming and Northern Ontario Ry (ONTARIO NORTHLAND) intersected with the National Transcontinental Railway. Destroyed 3 times by fire during its first 8 years, Cochrane grew slowly as a railway-construction and repair centre, and in its early years also attracted a few farmers, lumbermen and merchants. More recently, it has become an important tourist centre, serving as departure point for the Polar Bear Express, Ontario Northland's train excursion to MOOSONEE on James Bay. Its single, largest year-round employer is Cochrane Enterprises Ltd, a plywood and planing mill.

MATT BRAY

Cockburn, Bruce, singer, songwriter (b at Ottawa 27 May 1945). After playing in Ottawa rock bands (The Children, Esquires, Three's A Crowd), he became a folksinger, with a humanist, poetic style combining elements of jazz, rock and reggae, emerging as an international artist by the end of the 1970s. His records include *Sunwheel Dance, In the Falling Dark* and *Dancing in the Dragon's Jaws.* He has written songs in English and French, including "Goin' to the Country," "Musical Friends," "Laughter" and "Prenons la mer"; some have been recorded by other artists (Anne MURRAY, Tom Rush).

MARK MILLER

Cockburn, James, politician, FATHER OF CONFEDERATION (b at Berwick-upon-Tweed, Eng 13 Feb 1819; d at Ottawa 14 Aug 1883). He was educated in Berwick and, after his family immigrated to Canada in 1832, at Upper Canada Coll. After admission to the bar of Upper Canada in 1846, he moved to Cobourg where, with little success, he practised law and participated in various business enterprises. He represented Northumberland W in Parliament 1861-74 and 1878-81. A Conservative after 1863, he was appointed solicitor general in Mar 1864. He retained his place in the GREAT COALITION and attended the QUEBEC CONFERENCE. In 1867 he was demoted and served as Speaker of the House of Commons until 1873. "An inferior man" according to Liberal Alexander MACKENZIE, Cockburn spent his last years in a genteel poverty that was relieved by occasional bits of Tory patronage.

DONALD SWAINSON

Cockroach, swift-running, flattened, oval-shaped INSECT belonging to order Dictyoptera. Although in their native regions they live outdoors, several species are important domestic pests. Of the 3500 species known worldwide most are tropical and subtropical. Only 10 occur in Canada, of which 7 have been introduced through commerce and immigration. Most common are the 5 cm long American cockroach (*Periplaneta americana*), the 2-5 cm Oriental cockroach (*Blatta orientalis*), and the up to 2 cm German cockroach (*Blattella germanica*). The last is the most common urban species. All are general feeders, nocturnal in habit, guided by long antennae while scavenging in kitchens, bathrooms, cellars, restaurants and moist, warm places. Three or 4 species of wood cockroach (*Parcoblatta*) live in leaf litter and debris outdoors in Ontario and western Québec. After mating, the female produces 20-50 eggs that are retained in a leathery case (ootheca) projecting from the genital chamber. In some species, eggs hatch within this chamber, receive nourishment from the mother, and nymphs emerge alive. Nymphs grow slowly, molt as often as 13 times, and mature in 3-12 months. Adults live for several years. Cockroaches not only contaminate and destroy food but also carry disease-causing bacteria and secrete foul-smelling matter. A few have symbiotic protozoa or bacteria in the gut to help them digest wood and other vegetation.

P.W. RIEGERT

Cod, common name for FISHES of class Osteichthyes, order Gadiformes, family Gadidae. This large family contains about 55 species of mostly bottom-living fishes, which, except for the Holarctic, freshwater burbot (*Lota lota*), are found in cool seas. In Canada, 21 species occur in Atlantic waters, 4 in Pacific. The family includes many important food fishes, eg, haddock (genus *Melanogrammus*), pollock (*Pollachius*), Pacific cod (*Gadus macrocephalus*), cusk (*Brosme*), hakes (*Urophycis* and *Antimora*), tomcods (*Microgadus*), whitings (*Merlangus*) and rocklings (*Motella*). Cods have elongate bodies, large heads with strong mouths and long dorsal and anal fins. Most species have a single, fleshy barbel (hair-like projection near the tip of the lower jaw).

The most important Canadian cod, the Atlantic cod (*Gadus morhua*) is heavy bodied, with a large head, 3 dorsal fins, 2 anal fins and an almost square caudal (tail) fin. Scales are small and smooth. The lateral line is pale. It may weigh up to 90 kg but usually averages 3-4 kg. Colour varies from grey or silvery green to brown or red, depending on bottom type and locality. The head and body are covered with many brown to reddish spots. Atlantic cod occurs on both sides of the N Atlantic. Off the N American coast, it ranges from Cape Hatteras to Hudson Str off W Greenland, but reaches greatest abundance off Newfoundland and Labrador. The closely related Pacific cod ranges from central California waters to the Bering Sea.

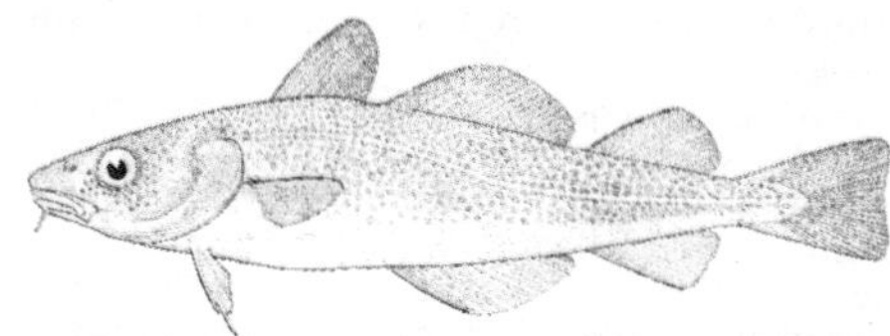

Atlantic cod (*Gadus morhua*), one of the world's leading food fishes, has been caught on the Grand Banks for centuries (*courtesy National Museums of Canada/National Museum of Natural Sciences*).

Spawning usually occurs during cool months, but exact time depends on water temperature and location of spawning grounds. On the GRAND BANKS, spawning occurs Apr-June, and on Nantucket Shoals, Oct-Feb. Atlantic cod are prolific: a 100 cm long female may produce about 5 million buoyant eggs. Hatching time depends on water temperature, and may take several weeks. Young cod grow at different rates in different areas: the colder the temperature, the slower the rate of growth. Young cod eat PLANKTON and bottom creatures, but adults are voracious and feed mainly on other fishes (eg, capelin, herring). Atlantic cod, one of the world's leading food fishes, has been fished on the Grand Banks for centuries. It is caught by vessels from many countries using otter, line or pair trawls, hand lines, jigs, Danish seines, traps and gill nets. The flesh is sold fresh, frozen, salted or smoked. Most of the catch is now frozen, but salted cod, once the most popular form, was esteemed in many countries.

W.B. SCOTT

Cod Liver Oil was in the past a primary source of vitamin A, essential for bone growth, health of skin and mucous membranes, night vision, etc. Today, many other preparations containing vitamin A are available. Before the 1920s, most cod liver oil came from Norwegian COD. In 1924 William Harrison, Ontario sales manager of a Canadian drug company, became interested in a report that liver oil from cod caught off the GRAND BANKS of Newfoundland was a much richer source of vitamin A than the Norwegian oil. In Jan 1925 Harrison and 3 associates, W.A.S. Ayerst, Hugh McPherson and W.J. McKenna, incorporated as Ayerst, McKenna and Harrison Ltd. Letters of patent not only granted the company rights to "produce, manufacture, purchase, sell, import, export chemicals, drugs and medicines of all kinds," but also some rights it never used, eg, "to sell snuff, spices, leaf tobacco, cheroots, shellacs, and crockery."

By Apr 1925 the company had 16 employees and immediately started researching the preparation of liver oil from Newfoundland cod. Its first department of biology consisted of a chicken-wire fence stretched from floor to ceiling. White rats were bought at $5 a head and were fed a normal diet fortified with cod liver oil. The experiment was a success. The white rats visibly thrived on the experimental supplementary diet. For the first time the potency of cod liver oil could be determined, regulated and assured. As soon as the new product became commercially available, Canadian physicians enthusiastically prescribed it; soon it was also sold in the US and worldwide. In 1929 Ayerst introduced the first cod liver oil concentrate in capsule form, under the brand name Alphamettes, a product still available in Canadian pharmacies. ELVIRA STAHL

Cody, Henry John, clergyman, educator (b at Embro, Ont 6 Dec 1868; d at Toronto 27 Apr 1951). Educated at U of T, he was ordained a Church of England priest in 1894. He served at St Paul's Church, Toronto, for 40 years, the last 25 as rector. Appointed a canon of St Alban's Cathedral in 1903 and archdeacon of the diocese of York in 1909, he repeatedly turned down offers of a bishopric from a number of Canadian dioceses.

During WWI Cody became a vocal supporter of PM BORDEN's government in Ottawa and the HEARST government in Toronto, while championing imperialism and a stronger war effort. He joined the Conservative Hearst administration as minister of education in 1918, resigning as MPP on its defeat in 1919. Cody was determined to use the schools in building a postwar society on the traditional foundations of Protestant Christianity, political conservatism and Anglo-Saxon racial superiority. While in office, he strengthened attendance requirements and promoted the cadet movement and patriotism in the schools.

Cody had a long connection with U of T. He was appointed to the provincial royal commission on the university in 1905 and chaired the 1922 commission on university finances. In 1917 he was appointed a member of the university's board of governors, and from 1923 to 1932 served as chairman. He was president of U of T 1932-44 and its chancellor 1944-47.

ROBERT M. STAMP

Cogswell, Fred, poet, editor, translator (b at East Centreville, NB 8 Nov 1917). In 1952 Cogswell joined the English dept at UNB, where he had been educated, and remained there 3 decades. He was long an important figure in maintaining the region's distinctive poetic tradition, both as a teacher and as editor of *The Fiddlehead* 1952-67. He also has national importance as founder and long-time proprietor of Fiddlehead Books, a series of poetry chapbooks especially hospitable to, but by no means limited to, young writers. Cogswell's early interest in Québecois verse, manifest in *One Hundred Poems of Modern Quebec* (1970) and other similar translations, has connected him to a larger movement. His own poetry, best represented in *Immortal Plowman* (1969) and *Pearls* (1983) but available in several selected and collected editions, is characterized by adherence to old conventions, a love of craftsmanship and an unhurried, lightly ironic tone. He is a man of letters in the best sense. DOUG FETHERLING

Cohen, Jacob Laurence, lawyer (b at Manchester, Eng 1898; d at Toronto 24 May 1950). Immigrating with his family to Canada in 1908, Cohen supported his mother and 5 younger children after his father's death in 1911. He attended night school, worked as a law clerk and in 1918 graduated from law school. Associated with the All Canadian Congress of Labour and the Workers' Unity League in the 1920s and 1930s, he turned to labour law and civil liberties, becoming the most influential labour lawyer in Canada. He was the union's counsel in the 1937 OSHAWA STRIKE and in every major labour dispute during WWII. He sat on many conciliation boards and, as a member of the National War Labour Board, supported labour's right to organize and bargain collectively. He was made a KC in 1937. Though disbarred for assault in 1947, he was reinstated by the Law Society in 1950. LAUREL SEFTON MACDOWELL

Cohen, Leonard, poet, novelist, songwriter (b at Montréal 21 Sept 1934). Cohen was one of the most influential and popular 1960s Canadian writers and his songs gained him an international reputation. He came from a wealthy Westmount family, and Montréal's atmosphere is pervasive in his writings, though he has also lived for extended periods in Greece and California. He attended McGill and Columbia but has spent most of his life as a full-time writer and performer. His first book of poetry, *Let us Compare Mythologies,* appeared in 1956. His major creative period was the early to mid-1960s, the highlights being, in poetry, *The Spice-Box of Earth* (1961) and *Flowers for Hitler* (1964), and in fiction, *The Favourite Game* (1963) and *Beautiful Losers* (1966). His first record, *The Songs of Leonard Cohen,* was issued in 1968 and there have been 6 subsequent albums. He won a Governor General's Award (1968) but declined it. His work since 1970 has been sporadic and hesitant: *The Energy of Slaves* (1972) is made up of "anti-poems," rejecting his own stance and stature as a poet; *Death of a Lady's Man* (1978) is diffuse and fragmentary. His recordings, however, have continued to be of a high quality, especially *New Skin for the Old Ceremony* (1974) and *Recent Songs* (1979). Cohen's work has been widely translated; he is especially popular in France and Germany.

Leonard Cohen, one of Canada's most influential and popular poets and songwriters. Although the popular conception of Cohen is of a romantic love poet, his imaginative vision is dark and despairing (*courtesy Ron Watts/First Light*).

Although the popular conception is of Cohen as a romantic love poet — author of the lovely lyrics of *The Spice-Box of Earth* — his imaginative vision is dark and despairing. As a Jew, Cohen has always been acutely aware of the holocaust, and images of the Nazi genocide permeate and condition his work. Poetry, religion, sex, death, beauty and power form an interlocked pattern, heightened by the sensuousness of his language, and also emphasized by a wild, outrageous and black sense of humour. Cohen celebrates the destruction of the self and the abnegation of power. The harshness of this vision reaches its peak in *Beautiful Losers,* itself an extraordinary novel which is by turns historical and surreal, religious and obscene, comic and ecstatic; it remains the most radical (and beautiful) experimental novel ever published in Canada. The songs tend to be gentler, less absolute in their vision. If *Beautiful Losers* is Cohen's masterpiece, perhaps the most concise statement he has ever made of his central vision occurs in the last verse of his song "The Window," from *Recent Songs:*

> Then lay your rose on the fire
> The fire give up to the sun
> The sun give over to splendour
> In the arms of the High Holy One
> For the Holy One dreams of a letter
> Dreams of a letter's death
> Oh bless the continuous stutter
> Of the word being made into flesh

Only Leonard Cohen could conceive of the process of the Word being made Flesh as a stutter — and only Cohen could bless that insight.

STEPHEN SCOBIE

Reading: Stephen Scobie, *Leonard Cohen* (1978).

Cohen, Matt, novelist, short story writer (b at Montréal 30 Dec 1942). Cohen first published as a poet but became known for *Korsoniloff* (1969) and *Johnny Crackle Sings* (1971), 2 experimental novels about youth alienation. Throughout the remainder of the 1970s and into the 1980s, however, he matured as an artist with a number of collections of short stories — later reprinted in *The Expatriate* (1982) — and novels. Most important of the novels are those set in the fictional Salem, Ont: *The Disinherited* (1974), *The Colours of War* (1977), *The Sweet Second Summer of Kitty Malone* (1979), *Flowers of Darkness* (1981) and *The Spanish Doctor* (1984). These works are frequently concerned with a desperate search for roots and are set against a backdrop of rural decay. Those and other works make Cohen one of the most prolific and popular fiction writers of his generation.

Cohen, Morris (Moishe) Abraham, "Two Gun," China hand and soldier of fortune (b at London, Eng 3 Aug 1889; d at Salford, Eng 11 Sept 1970). An unruly youth, Cohen was sent to Canada, to a farm in Saskatchewan where he learned how to handle horses, guns and cards. He moved to Edmonton in 1912 where his skills as a gambler and as a real-estate promoter earned him a small fortune. In frequent contact with the law, Cohen was to change his life after a meeting with Dr Sun Yat-sen, father of the Chinese revolution. Cohen became a member of the Chinese National League and acted as its English-language secretary in Alberta. He represented Chinese interests to all levels of government, attempting, among other things, to combat the growing anti-Asian sentiment. He was invited to China in 1922 to serve as one of Sun Yat-sen's bodyguards and because of his habit of carrying more than one handgun was nicknamed "Two Gun." After Sun's death in 1925 Cohen was granted a pension and the rank of general. He remained close to Chinese politics for the next 2 decades, notably in Canton where he was involved in banking and in arranging arms deals with Western countries. Interned by the Japanese in Hong Kong in 1941, he was later repatriated to Canada. Following the communist victory in 1949, Cohen, persona grata in both Beijing and Taipei, made efforts at reconciliation — all of which failed. A man of great humanity and charm, Cohen in life came very close to matching the legends that flourished around him. BRIAN L. EVANS

Reading: Charles Drage, *The Life and Times of General Two-Gun Cohen* (1954).

Cohen, Samuel Nathan, theatre critic, radio and TV broadcaster (b at Sydney, NS 16 Apr 1923; d at Toronto 26 Mar 1971). As Canada's only "national" theatre critic in the 1960s, travelling across the country for the Toronto *Star*, and as the only serious reviewer of drama in performance in Canada 1946-71, Cohen set the standards for Canadian theatre during its first quarter century of real growth following WWII. He entered Mt Allison U at 16; his erudition and radical editing of the university newspaper fascinated and enraged the authorities. After studying law briefly at U of T, he returned to the Maritimes to edit the mine union paper Glace Bay *Gazette* for 2 years. In the mid-1940s he wrote for communist newspapers in Toronto, began writing play reviews and attracted the attention of Mavor MOORE, who recommended him as a regular theatre critic for CBC Radio. Cohen broke with the effusive praise and uncritical approach that marked current criticism in Canada and forced the country to differentiate between amateur and professional performances for the first time. He enraged Canadians by mercilessly attacking plays, playwrights and performers, while cheering on promising new talents and theatres. Cohen also edited CBC radio scripts and was host of CBC TV's first successful discussion program, "Fighting Words." He was a colourful and controversial personality, both loved and hated for his profound integrity; his untimely death at the age of 47 was a blow to a Canadian theatre just entering its adolescence. The renaissance of alternative theatres and playwrights across Canada in the 1970s owed much to his critical acumen and standards. ALLAN M. GOULD

Coinage Coins are small metal tokens issued, usually by governments, for use as MONEY. A quantity of coins issued at one time, or a series of coins issued under one authority, is called a coinage. Canada's complex political history has meant that Canadian numismatists (coin collectors) have an astonishing variety of coins and coinages to collect and study.

French Regime

The first coins struck for use anywhere in Canada were the famous "GLORIAM REGNI" silver coins of 1670, struck in Paris for use in all French colonies in the New World. Few specimens have been found in Canada; the piece of 15 sols is especially rare. In 1672 the value of these coins was raised by one-third in a vain attempt to keep them in local circulation. None were in use after 1680. In 1717 there was an attempt to produce a COPPER coinage for the French colonies but few were struck because of the poor quality of the available copper. In 1721 and 1722 an issue of copper coins of 9 deniers was struck for all French colonies and a large shipment was sent to Canada. There was considerable resistance to their circulation and, in 1726, most of the coins, which had lain unissued in the treasury at Québec City, were returned to France.

These coinages were inadequate for Canada's needs and French coins were shipped out annually. The treasure recovered from the wreck of the French supply ship *Le Chameau* (lost in a hurricane off Cape Breton I in 1725) was intended to supply the colonial governments at Québec and Louisbourg. The authorities at Québec also issued various kinds of paper money (*see* PLAYING CARD MONEY), eventually far too much of it, and at times had to permit the use of Spanish dollars and their subdivisions.

British Regime

For the first 50 years after the CONQUEST, the British did almost nothing to provide coin, other than sending an occasional shipment of badly worn copper withdrawn from circulation in Britain. GOLD coins consisted of British guineas and, later, sovereigns, some American eagles, French louis d'or, Spanish doubloons (and fractions thereof), and small quantities of Portuguese gold. SILVER coins comprised mostly Spanish coins struck in Mexico and S America, some old French silver circulating in LOWER CANADA, and a sprinkling of English silver elsewhere. American silver appeared after 1815. Copper coins were an insufficient and dwindling supply of battered, worn-out, English and Irish halfpennies dating from the reign of George III, supplemented by locally issued and imported tokens and by small numbers of American cents and various foreign coins. Anything the size of a halfpenny would pass for one in Montréal between 1820 and 1837.

Prince Edward Island During this period, various tokens were in use. Large numbers of lightweight halfpenny tokens circulated from about 1830 till well after 1860. The most numerous were the "SHIPS COLONIES & COMMERCE" halfpennies and tokens inscribed "SUCCESS TO THE FISHERIES" or "SELF GOVERNMENT AND FREE TRADE."

Nova Scotia In 1813 certain Halifax businessmen began importing halfpennies into NS and, by 1816, a great variety was in circulation. The government ordered their withdrawal in 1817. Beginning in 1823, and again in 1824, 1832, 1840 and 1843, the government issued a copper coinage, without authority from England. In 1856 NS issued one of the most beautiful of the Canadian colonial coinages, with the permission of the British government.

New Brunswick An anonymous halfpenny appeared in Saint John about 1830. In 1843 the government issued copper pennies and halfpennies without authority from England. These were followed in 1854 with another coinage, this time issued with the permission of the British authorities.

Lower Canada had the greatest number and variety of tokens in circulation. The Wellington tokens, a series of halfpenny and penny tokens with a bust of the duke of Wellington, appeared about 1814. They were popular and many varieties were issued locally after 1825. In 1825, a halfpenny of Irish design was imported; its popularity resulted in its being imitated in brass and these copies are very plentiful. In 1832 an anonymous halfpenny of English design appeared and was extensively imitated in brass. Then, a Montréal blacksmith began to counterfeit the worn-out English and Irish George III copper and large numbers of these "Blacksmith tokens" circulated. This period ended in 1835 when the banks refused to accept such nondescript copper, except by weight.

The BANK OF MONTREAL circulated sous or halfpennies with a bouquet of heraldic flowers on one side and the value in French on the other. These sous were immediately popular and the government allowed the bank to supply Lower Canada with copper; however, the sous were very soon imitated anonymously. The imitations were accepted because they bore French inscriptions but became too numerous and, once again, the banks had to refuse them, except by weight. To replace them, the government authorized 4 banks, the Bank of Montreal, the Quebec Bank, the City Bank and La Banque du Peuple, to issue copper pennies and halfpennies with the arms of Montréal on one side and a standing HABITANT on the other. These coins arrived in Canada just as the REBELLION OF 1837 began and were issued in 1838.

Lower Canada halfpenny, 1837, obverse (left) and reverse (right) (*courtesy Currency Museum, Bank of Canada/Jas. Zagon*).

New Brunswick halfpenny, 1854, obverse (left) and reverse (right) (*courtesy Currency Museum, Bank of Canada/Jas. Zagon*).

One-penny token, Nova Scotia, 1856, obverse (left) and reverse (right) (*courtesy Currency Museum, Bank of Canada/Jas. Zagon*).

Upper Canada first used local tokens after 1812, when a series of lightweight halfpennies was issued in memory of Sir Isaac BROCK. These coins were superseded after 1825 by a series of tokens with a sloop on one side and various designs (eg, plow, keg, crossed shovels over an anvil) on the other. In 1822 a copper twopenny token was issued by Lesslie & Sons. The firm also issued halfpennies from 1824 to 1830. There were no government issues in UPPER CANADA.

When the 2 Canadas were reunited in 1841, the Bank of Montreal was allowed to coin copper; pennies and halfpennies appeared in 1842. Halfpennies were issued again in 1844. After 1849 the BANK OF UPPER CANADA received the right to coin copper and large issues of pennies and halfpennies appeared in 1850, 1852, 1854 and 1857. The Quebec Bank was allowed to issue pennies and halfpennies in 1852.

There was little need for coinage in the territories controlled by the HUDSON'S BAY COMPANY; the FUR TRADE depended primarily on barter. In colonial BC, very few coins were in circulation. Copper was not used because prices were too high: nothing less than a dime was of any use. Small shipments of English silver and gold were sent to BC in 1861 and these coins, with American coins, were used until after CONFEDERATION. A proposed gold coinage was not made for fear of committing a breach of the Royal Prerogative, although a few patterns were struck.

The decimal system was first adopted by the Province of Canada (southern parts of today's Québec and Ontario) in 1858, based on a dollar equal in value to the American dollar. American silver had become very plentiful and trade with the US made it necessary to adopt a decimal system. NB and NS followed in 1860; Nfld, in 1863; PEI, in 1870. The coinage of the Province of Canada consisted of silver 5-, 10- and 20-cent pieces and bronze cents. NS issued bronze cents and half cents in 1861 and 1864, cents alone in 1862; NB, cents in 1861 and 1864, and silver coins like the Canadian ones in 1862 and 1864; PEI issued a cent in 1871. Newfoundland's coinage began in 1865. All of these coins became legal tender in the Dominion of Canada after the various provinces entered Confederation.

1870 to Present

The first coins of the Dominion of Canada, issued in 1870, were silver 5-, 10-, 25- and 50-cent pieces. Bronze cents were added in 1876. All coins bore on the obverse the head of Queen Victoria. Silver coins bore the value and date in a crowned maple wreath on the reverse; the cent bore the value and date in a circle enclosed by a continuous maple vine. These coins were variously issued till 1901. In 1902 the crowned bust of Edward VII replaced the head of Queen Victoria. In 1911 the crowned bust of George V replaced that of Edward VII.

In 1920 the cent was reduced in size and, in 1922, the 5-cent piece was first coined in NICKEL. In 1942 and 1943 the 5-cent piece was coined in tombac, a copper-zinc alloy (the so-called "blackout" nickel) because of wartime nickel shortages. In 1935 the silver dollar was first coined to commemorate the silver jubilee of the reign of George V. This dollar inaugurated a very popular series of Canadian coins. Except for the war years 1939 to 1944, silver dollars were coined every year until 1967. Special commemorative dollars were struck in 1939 for the royal visit to Canada; in 1949, for the entry of Newfoundland into Confederation; in 1958, for the centenary of the creation of the Crown Colony of British Columbia; in 1964, for the centenary of the CHARLOTTETOWN CONFERENCE and the QUEBEC CONFERENCE; and, in 1967, for the centenary of Confederation.

In 1937 a completely new coinage was introduced after George VI ascended the throne. For the first time each denomination had its own pictorial reverse design. With some modifications, the same designs are on today's coinage. All denominations bore a splendid bare head of George VI. The reverse of the cent shows 2 maple leaves on a common twig; the nickel, a beaver chewing a log on a rock; the dime, a schooner closely resembling the famous *Bluenose;* the quarter, the head of a caribou; the 50-cent piece, the Canadian coat of arms; the dollar, 2 VOYAGEURS in a canoe, with a wooded islet in the background.

There had never been a great need for gold in Canada, as American gold coins supplied domestic needs. Some sovereigns were struck at the Ottawa mint variously from 1908 to 1919. From 1912 to 1914 there was an attractive coinage of gold $5 and $10 pieces. The only other circulating gold coinage in Canada was the Newfoundland issue of $2 pieces, struck variously from 1865 to 1888. Plans to reissue gold coins in 1928 were stopped (*see* GOLD STANDARD). Special issue gold coins were struck in 1967, and annually since 1976, for sale to collectors.

In 1953 a bust of Elizabeth II replaced the head of George VI, and in 1965 was replaced by the portrait now in use, a draped bust of the queen wearing a tiara. In 1967 a special coinage, commemorating the centenary of Confederation, was issued. Each coin bore the bust of the queen on the obverse. The cent featured a dove in flight; the 5-cent piece, a hare; the 10-cent piece, a mackerel; the 25-cent piece, a bobcat; the 50-cent piece, a howling wolf; and the dollar, a Canada goose in flight. The motifs were created by artist Alexander COLVILLE. In the summer of 1967 the silver content of the dime and quarter were reduced from 80% to 50% and production of 50-cent pieces and dollars for general circulation was stopped. In 1968 the regular designs

One-cent decimal coin of Queen Victoria, 1882, obverse (left) and reverse (right) *(courtesy Currency Museum, Bank of Canada / Jas. Zagon).*

Upper Canada halfpenny, 1833, obverse (left) and reverse (right) *(courtesy Currency Museum, Bank of Canada / Jas. Zagon).*

Five-cent decimal coin of George VI, 1937, obverse (left) and reverse (right) *(courtesy Currency Museum, Bank of Canada / Jas. Zagon).*

Sterling silver $10 piece, struck to commemorate the 1976 Montréal Olympics, left (reverse); $100 gold piece, right (reverse) *(courtesy Currency Museum, Bank of Canada / Jas. Zagon).*

were resumed, the dime and quarter being in 50% silver. In Aug 1968 nickel replaced silver entirely for general circulation and a reduced 50-cent piece and dollar were coined in nickel.

Beginning in 1950, special sets of coins for collectors were issued, ie, early strikings from the dies, handled with more care to ensure that they would not be marred. In 1953 the sets were mounted on a white card enclosed in cellophane. From 1961 they were heat-sealed in pliofilm. Silver dollars were also sold separately to collectors until 1965. Nickel dollars were sold separately, in special cases, beginning in 1970. In 1971 commemorative dollars were struck in 50% silver and sold in individual cases. Issued each year since, they commemorate special events. Special sets of sterling silver $5 and $10 pieces were struck from 1973 to 1976 to commemorate the 1976 Olympic Games, held in Montréal. The first gold $100 piece, struck in 1976 for the same event, is the first of a beautiful series of gold coins struck annually.

Canadian Rarities

The rarest Canadian decimal coins are the 50-cent piece of 1921, the 5-cent piece of 1921, the dotted 1936 cent and 10-cent pieces, the 10-cent piece of 1889, the 50-cent piece of 1890 and the 10-cent piece of 1893, with a round-topped 3. Most of the strikings of 1921 were never issued. After remaining in the vaults of the mint for some time, they were melted down. The dotted 1936 coinage was intended to be an extra issued from the 1936 dies to supply Canada's needs, pending the arrival of the 1937 dies. A hole punched into the bottom of the reverse dies produced the dot. Very few specimens are known. The other coins mentioned are rare because the coinages of those years were very small. *See* MINTING. R.C. WILLEY

Colborne, Sir John, 1st Baron Seaton, soldier, colonial administrator (b at Lyndhurst, Eng 16 Feb 1778; d at Torquay, Eng 17 Apr 1863). Colborne entered the British army in 1794 and distinguished himself at Waterloo (1815). From 1821 to 1828 he was lieutenant-governor of Guernsey and on 3 Nov 1828 assumed office as lieutenant-governor of Upper Canada. Colborne vigorously promoted public works and immigration and saw the colony's population increase by 50% between 1830 and 1833. Yet by showing considerable favouritism to the newer immigrants from Britain and diverting public funds in unpopular ways, he contributed to the popular unrest that culminated in the Reform victory in the 1834 election and ultimately in the Upper Canadian REBELLION OF 1837. Early in 1836 Colborne was recalled as lt-gov but placed in command of the British forces in the Canadas. He personally led his troops in suppressing the 1837 insurrection in Lower Canada. He briefly acted as governor general in 1838 and 1839. He crushed the second rebellion which erupted in Lower Canada in Nov 1838 with great severity. In Oct 1839 he returned to Britain and was elevated to the House of Lords, where he spoke against the Act uniting the Canadas. He was lord high commissioner of the Ionian Islands 1843-49 and commander of the forces in Ireland 1855-60. PHILLIP A. BUCKNER

Cold Lake, Alta, Town, pop 2110 (1981c), inc 1955, is located on a lake of the same name, 290 km NE of Edmonton. The Cree named the lake for its deep, cold waters. Settlement commenced in 1910 and increased when a CPR branch line arrived (1928). A Canadian Forces base was established here in WWII and afterwards became a testing range as well as a training base for jet pilots. The base also houses a satellite tracking unit for NORAD. Cold Lake has been a centre of oil exploration and is the proposed site for a huge heavy-oil plant. It is also a popular fishing resort and tourist centre with Saskatchewan's Meadow Lake Prov Pk nearby. ERIC J. HOLMGREN

Cold War, the term applied to cool relations roughly 1947-53, between the Western powers (including Canada and Britain, and led by the US) and communist countries dominated by the USSR. It was precipitated by the reluctance of the US and Britain to accept the extension of Soviet control and communist one-party systems over eastern Europe at the end of WWII. It now seems that each side was irrationally fearful of the other's apparent intentions, although placement of the blame is still disputed. Canada's position was determined by its experience of Russian spying at the end of WWII (the GOUZENKO case); its detestation of the totalitarian Soviet regime; and its economic, cultural and strategic links to the US and Britain. For most of the Cold War both sides were convinced that ordinary diplomatic negotiations were pointless because there was no possibility of agreement on common interest on any important topic. The Cold War eased with the death of the Soviet dictator Joseph Stalin in 1953, and serious diplomatic discussions were then resumed. ROBERT BOTHWELL

Coldwell, Major James William, "M.J.," teacher, politician (b at Seaton, Eng 2 Dec 1888; d at Ottawa 25 Aug 1974). One of the founders of the CO-OPERATIVE COMMONWEALTH FEDERATION, he succeeded J.S. WOODSWORTH as national CC leader, 1942-60. Coldwell came to Canada as a teacher in 1910; he stayed briefly in Alberta and then moved to Regina. He first achieved national prominence as a leader in teachers' organizations, 1924-34. Also a popular alderman in Regina, he developed strong links with socialist labour and farm organizations. When the Great Depression came, he was a natural choice for leader of the new Saskatchewan Farmer-Labour Party in 1932 (which became a part of the CCF) and fought a strenuous campaign in the Saskatchewan general election of 1934, attracting enormous crowds; but the party sent only 5 members to the legislature against 47 Liberals. Himself defeated, Coldwell moved to the national scene.

As MP for Rosetown-Biggar (Sask) 1935-58, he was a polished performer in the House of Commons from the first. He disagreed with Woodsworth (who was a pacifist) on the war in 1939, and Coldwell and the majority of the CCF supported Canada's participation in WWII. His support of collective security was reinforced and he was a member of the Canadian delegation to the founding of the United Nations in 1945. He presided over both the peak of CCF support in the mid-1940s and its slow decline throughout the 1950s, leading the party in 5 general elections. His views seemed to moderate as more of the CCF's social welfare program was implemented by other governments, but he remained convinced of the need for a democratic socialist party. He was named to the Privy Council of Canada in 1964 and made companion of the Order of Canada in 1967. CARL WENAAS

Reading: M.J. Coldwell, *Left Turn, Canada* (1945).

Coles, George, merchant, businessman, politician (b in PEI 20 Sept 1810; d at Charlottetown Royalty, PEI 21 Aug 1875). The son of a farmer, Coles began business as a merchant in 1833. He soon focused on brewing and distilling, although he was also active in other businesses in the Charlottetown area, and became a prominent capitalist in the colony. In 1842 he was elected to the House of Assembly as a Tory. By 1847 he had joined the Reformers, and by 1849 was leader of the struggle for RESPONSIBLE GOVERNMENT. He became the Island's first premier under that system, serving 3 times between 1851 and 1868. His first administration was his most successful, extending the franchise to virtually all adult males, abolishing tuition fees and local taxes for district schools, and enabling the government to purchase large landed estates and sell them to the occupying tenants and squatters. In 1868 Coles left the premiership because of the apparent onset of premature senility. He had been the outstanding Island parliamentarian of his era, dominating the Assembly through his quick native intelligence and thorough familiarity with the issues. IAN ROSS ROBERTSON

Collective Bargaining, a method of jointly determining working conditions, between one or more employers on one side and organized employees on the other. The normal outcome is a collective agreement outlining terms and conditions of employment as well as issues such as union recognition, grievance procedure and special committees. Each side tries to convince the other of the validity of its stand and uses whatever pressure and means of persuasion it can command within a closely prescribed legal framework, which may include recourse to STRIKES, LOCKOUTS and ARBITRATION. In N America a union must be certified as a bargaining unit, ie, prove it has the support of an absolute majority (50% + 1) of the employees before it may represent them in collective bargaining. Government administrative tribunals in all provinces have the power to verify the representative nature of the unions and may call for a vote to determine whether a majority of employees in a specifically defined bargaining unit wish to be represented by a union. In all provinces, an increasing number of aspects of the bargaining process are prescribed by legislation. The federal government has jurisdiction only over federally regulated industries, eg, transportation and broadcasting.

Collective bargaining is essentially a power struggle between 2 mutually dependent parties with very different interests. Historically, management has sought a greater degree of control over the workplace and employees have sought security, as reflected in the issues of wage rates, job security and working conditions. Anything not contrary to law may be written into a collective agreement, which can run 1-3 years. Union achievements at the bargaining table, often the result of a strike, commonly become part of legislation. After an autoworkers' strike in 1947, the basic principle of union recognition was established. Medical insurance in union contracts preceded national medicare, pensions preceded universal pension plans, safeguards against discrimination preceded human rights legislation.

Governments have decided that it is in the public interest to permit and even encourage collective bargaining, and they have legislated the format of the procedures and the requirements for workers who wish to use them. They have also sought to minimize the negative effects of these conflicts by providing the mechanisms of conciliation, or LABOUR MEDIATION, by regulating the use of the right to strike and of the lockout, and by demanding arbitration. The Industrial Disputes Investigations Act (1907), the first such formal intervention, resulted from an Alberta mineworkers' strike. Privy Council Act 1003 (1944), which established certification, bargaining, union recognition and final dispute settlement guidelines, has been a model for most subsequent provincial statutes. When 2 sides fail to reach an agreement, they may turn to a mediator from the Department of Labour to help them reconcile their positions. Some provinces require the 2 sides to submit to arbitration before resorting to a strike or lockout.

Although most unionized employees have a legally recognized right to strike, sometimes precisely defined waiting periods must be observed before a strike or lockout may begin. In numerous cases governments have suspended strikes, and occasionally lockouts. Certain groups, forbidden the right to strike, must submit their dispute to binding arbitration by a tribunal whose decision is final. In some provinces this restriction is imposed on "essential" services, eg, fire and police; in others (Alberta and Ontario) on employees of all crown agencies. The Québec government, upon request, can extend a collective agreement to cover all employers and employees in a given trade and area. The Loi des décrets de convention collective (SRQ 1964, c 143) authorizes the lieutenant-governor-in-council to do this when he thinks an agreement's terms have acquired major significance and importance for a whole trade or industry, the objective being to prevent unfair competition within an industry or trade between employers whose workers are unionized and those whose workers are not, and are therefore usually receiving lower wages. JEAN BOIVIN

Collectivism, a group of ideologies, political, social and religious movements which argue that man is by nature co-operative, not competitive. Collectivism has taken many forms in Canadian history. The settlement process forced people in each stage of colonization to work together at building "bees" and road construction, and at overcoming adversities. The pioneer years were characterized, therefore, as much by mutual aid as by individualism. Intellectually, collectivism has many diverse roots. French Canadians, LOYALISTS and many 19th-century immigrants specifically rejected the 18th-century liberal, individualist philosophy common in the US. As the social evils of INDUSTRIALIZATION and URBANIZATION unfolded in the later 19th century, many Canadians saw the basic problem as an excess of individualism. Early labour movements, farm organizations such as the Grange and Patrons of Industry, church reform groups (*see* SOCIAL GOSPEL) and even professional groups advocated collective protection against the changes of the age.

In politics, collectivist perspectives have been argued most vigorously by a series of SOCIALIST parties since the late 19th century. In the 20th, the NEW DEMOCRATIC PARTY (successor to the CO-OPERATIVE COMMONWEALTH FEDERATION) and the COMMUNIST PARTY have been the main proponents of collectivism. The CO-OPERATIVE MOVEMENT, in its more idealistic institutions, has advocated an economic restructuring of society on a collectivist basis. Many religious and immigrant groups have also established their communities along collectivist lines. These include MENNONITES, HUTTERITES and DOUKHOBORS. English, Scottish and Finnish groups have also developed collectivist communities, particularly on the Prairies and the West Coast. During the 1960s, hundreds of young people organized communal settlements. Though seldom perceived as a major force in Canadian history, collectivism — instinctive or deliberately structured — has been a common response and remedy to contemporary problems. IAN MACPHERSON

Collège d'enseignement général et professionnel (CEGEP) Québec's first COMMUNITY COLLEGES of general and professional training [known in English and French by their acronym, "CEGEP"] opened their doors in 1967. Bill 21, which created the CEGEPs, also established the Commission of Collegiate Instruction within the Superior Council of Education. According to the legislature, this institution of postsecondary, preuniversity education was established to provide interested secondary-school graduates with general training aimed at developing a critical sense and a spirit of analysis, synthesis and creativity, and with specialized training by concentration on studies of a limited number of disciplines or through preparation for a professional career.

The Royal Commission of Inquiry into Education in the Province of Québec (Parent Report) released in the 1960s, proposed the establishment of a level of studies beyond high school, 2 or 3 years in length and complete in itself, and clearly distinct from both secondary schooling and university education. The 2-year course would constitute a preparatory stage for university, and the 3-year course would lead to professional qualifications. These institutions, it was hoped, would raise the average level of scholarship, meet strong demands for education, raise the level of professional studies for technicians by integrating the studies into a multidisciplinary college, and remove from the university level all nonuniversity general or professional training.

The CEGEPs, as free and public institutions, were considered, along with the multidisciplinary secondary schools, to be a major part of the scholastic reforms of the 1960s. These reforms were inspired by the principles of democratization and equality of opportunity, of cultural pluralism and adaptation to the realities of an advanced industrial society.

The number of CEGEPs increased from 5 in 1967 to more than 80 in 1984; 51 are public colleges (6 of them anglophone), 29 are private. In 1984 some 140 000 students were enrolled in CEGEPs, which employ about 8500 teachers. Approximately 40% of students are from the lower socioeconomic levels of society. Each college is administered by a board of administration consisting of teachers, parents, students, government representatives, local community representatives and college administrators.

Québec's CEGEPs offer 6 programs of general university preparation: health sciences, pure sciences, applied sciences, human sciences, administrative sciences, and arts and letters. They also offer 140 programs of professional training within 5 general categories: biological techniques, physical techniques, human techniques, administrative techniques and artistic techniques.

A training program consists of 12 obligatory courses (4 in language and literature, 4 in philosophy and 4 in physical education), 12 hours of concentration in a general-training program or specialization in a professional-training program, and 4 complementary courses. Those who succeed in these studies — most require a 60% average — receive a diploma of collegiate studies (DEC).

During the 1960s and 1970s post-secondary institutions in Québec, as elsewhere, were in ferment, shaken by challenges to authority and to traditional teaching. This ferment, accompanied by the demands of a radical teachers' union, created some dismay in certain parts of Québec's population.

The growth of CEGEPs has been accompanied by a continuing debate about (among other issues) their orientation, administrative structure and main pedagogic thrust. This debate led to the Rocquet Report on the pedagogic regime (1970), the Nadeau Report on student needs (1975), and the White Paper on collegiate training issued by the Québec Ministry of Education in 1980. The Rocquet Report recommended pedagogical changes according to which all students would be obliged to take courses in certain subject areas: mathematics, natural sciences, human sciences (philosophy, language, literature) technology, second language and physical education. In the White Paper the government announced its intention to render obligatory courses in the history and economy of Québec, as well as in philosophy, language, literature and physical education. The government has not yet implemented these changes, but in 1979 certain aspects of Bill 21 were revised and the Council of Colleges was created.

The CEGEPs have maintained their original objectives and distinctive characteristics (generalized access to higher education for all levels of society, a diversified range of programs, the regionalization of educational resources, the establishment of organic ties with local communities and nonscholastic circles) and are now emphasizing the need for the rationalization of the collegiate network, the evaluation of each institution (eg, administrative and pedagogic functioning and results) and an improved response to adult needs. M. CLAUDE LESSARD

Collège dominicain de philosophie et de théologie, Ottawa, was founded 1909 by the Order of Friars Preachers in Canada and recognized as a *studium generale* of the Order. In Mar 1967 it was granted a civil university charter by the province of Ontario, which conferred on the Academic Council the power to grant university degrees in theology and philosophy. There are 3 departments: philosophy, theology (both in Ottawa) and pastoral studies (in Montréal).
G.D. MAILHIOT

Enrolment: Collège dominicain, 1982-83
(Source: Statistics Canada)

Full-time Undergrad	*Full-time Graduate*	*Part-time Undergrad*	*Part-time Graduate*
110	10	406	20

Collegiate, or collegiate institute, is a type of SECONDARY SCHOOL originally required to meet certain minimum standards regarding the number and qualifications of its teachers and its student enrolment in the classics. Within a decade of their introduction in the early 1870s, Ontario's collegiate institutes became markedly less classical, thereby becoming, in effect high schools under another name. In general, the term no longer clearly distinguishes one type of secondary school from another.
WILLARD BREHAUT

Collier, Ronald William, composer (b at Coleman, Alta 3 July 1930). An important participant as composer and trombonist in the Canadian third-stream movement, spearheaded by his teacher Gordon Delamont in Toronto, Collier subsequently wrote for radio, TV and film. His major compositions include *The City* (1960), *Hear Me Talkin' To Ya* (1964), *Carneval* (1969) and *Humber Suite* (1973). His *Aurora Borealis* and *Silent Night, Lonely Night* were recorded in 1967 by Duke Ellington with a Toronto orchestra under Collier's direction; writing collaborations between Collier and Ellington followed. Collier began teaching at Humber Coll, Toronto, in 1974. MARK MILLER

Collingwood, Ont, Town, pop 12 064 (1981c), inc 1858, located on Nottawasaga B at the southern end of GEORGIAN BAY, 55 km NW of Barrie. A battle site where the Huron tried to fight off invading Iroquois 1649-50, it was first settled by Europeans in 1835. The name commemorates Admiral Collingwood, Nelson's second-in-command at the Battle of Trafalgar. The Ontario, Simcoe and Huron Ry, later part of the CNR, arrived 1855. The site of several scenic caves of limestone rock, it has an excellent harbour, surveyed by Sandford FLEMING, and has long been a shipbuilding centre for the Great Lks. Auto parts and home furnishings are also manufactured. It is now a popular winter ski resort and is famous for its Blue Mountain pottery, made from local red clay and originally manufactured after WWII by Jozo Weider, a Czechoslovakian refugee. DANIEL FRANCIS

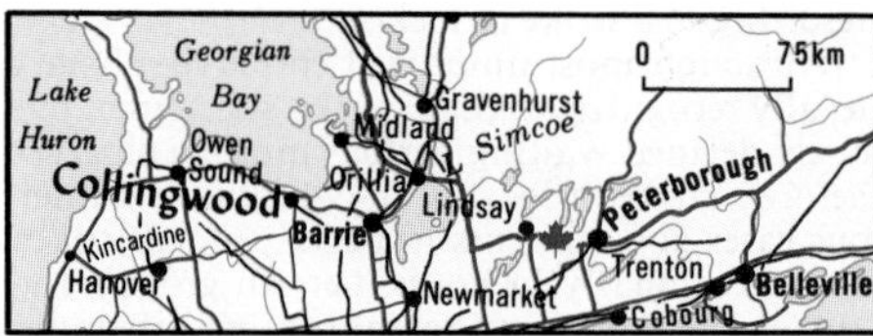

Collins, Enos, merchant, privateer, banker (b at Liverpool, NS 5 Sept 1774; d at Halifax 18 Nov 1871). Enos went to sea as a cabin boy on one of his father's fishing vessels, becoming master of a trading ship before he was 19. He sailed on privateers to the West Indies and in 1811 he bought the *Liverpool Packet,* one of the most famous privateers, which may have captured prizes worth a million dollars in the WAR OF 1812 (*see* PRIVATEERING). He sent ships loaded with provisions to Spain for Wellington's army during the Peninsular War and sold their cargoes at a handsome profit. In Halifax Collins bought ships and cargoes at auction; he stored the cargoes in a stone warehouse on the waterfront, one end of which became the Halifax Banking Company, a private bank nicknamed Collins's Bank, which still stands as part of Historic Properties. A shrewd businessman, he was reputedly "the wealthiest man in the Lower Provinces."
PHYLLIS R. BLAKELEY

Collins, Ralph Edgar, diplomat (b at Kunming, China 23 Nov 1914). An officer in the Dept of External Affairs, 1940-79, known for his brilliance in finding the right words to suit any occasion, Collins rose to be ambassador to S Africa and assistant undersecretary. He was an acknowledged China expert, having served there in WWII, and twice headed External Affairs' Far Eastern Division. Collins was Canada's first ambassador to the People's Republic o[f] China, 1971-72. ANNE HILLME[R]

Collins, Steve, ski jumper (b at Thunder Bay Ont 13 Mar 1964). Trained in Thunder Bay, he burst into international prominence by winning the World Junior 70 m Championship in 1980 and went on to victories in a World Cup meet and an International Ski Flying Championship later the same year. Since that time, he has consistently placed in the top 20 at several World Cup events each year. MURRAY SHAW

Collip, James Bertram, Bert, biochemist, educator, codiscoverer of INSULIN (b at Belleville Ont 20 Nov 1892; d at London, Ont 19 June 1965). Collip received his PhD in biochemistry from U of T in 1916 and embarked on a long and extremely productive career as a medical researcher. In autumn 1921 he was working with J.J.R. MACLEOD in Toronto, during a sabbatical from U of A, when at Frederick BANTING's request Macleod asked him to join the team investigating the internal secretion of the pancreas. Collip's skills as a biochemist proved invaluable in the research, particularly in his Jan 1922 discovery of a method of producing a nontoxic, antidiabetic pancreatic extract. Collip produced the first insulin suitable for use on human beings. Serious quarrelling with Banting, however, as well as difficulties with insulin production in the laboratory, caused Collip to return to Alberta at the end of his sabbatical. With C.H. BEST and Banting he was one of the original patentees of insulin, and in 1923 received from Macleod a one-quarter share of the Nobel Prize money awarded to Banting and Macleod.

James Bertram Collip, biochemist and co-discoverer of insulin in 1922 (*courtesy Public Archives of Canada/C-3775*...)

Collip plunged into endocrinological research and was one of the first to isolate the parathyroid hormone. In 1928 he succeeded A.B. MACALLUM as professor of biochemistry at McGill where for the next decade he and his students were leaders in endocrinology, pioneering in the isolation and study of the ovarian and gonadotrophic hormones. A dominant figure in Canadian wartime medical research, Collip served as dean of medicine at Western 1947-6[1]. A restless, driven man, Collip had been the best scientist on the insulin team, and afterward made the most significant contributions to medical research. He did not court honours and seldom discussed the discovery of insulin. During the 1930s he became a good friend of Banting.
MICHAEL BLISS

Reading: Michael Bliss, *The Discovery of Insulin* (1982).

Collishaw, Raymond, fighter pilot (b at Nanaimo, BC 22 Nov 1893; d at West Vancouver, 2[8] Sept 1976). He was credited with 60 victori[es]

luring WWI, placing him second on the roster of Canadian aces. He remained in the postwar RAF, leading British squadrons to southern Russia and Persia to fight against the "Reds" in 1919. At the beginning of WWII he commanded the RAF forces in Egypt, but his flair was for personal leadership not office work. He was relieved in 1941, served briefly on the staff of Fighter Command in England, and retired with the rank of air vice-marshal in 1943.

BRERETON GREENHOUS

Colombo, John Robert, editor, anthologist, poet (b at Kitchener, Ont 24 Mar 1936). Colombo's career can be broken into 2 phases. The first involves him exclusively as a literary figure, particularly as an exponent and practitioner of "found poetry," with a vaguely European manner and a flair for causing literary activity to happen around him. This aspect became evident when he was at university in the 1950s and continued without challenge for 20 years, when it was joined by Colombo the bibliophile and creator of reference books. At their occasional best, especially *Colombo's Canadian Quotations* (1974) and *Colombo's Canadian References* (1976) and in *Songs of the Indians* (2 vols, 1983), Colombo's compilations are examples of a kind of private-sector scholarship that is as admirable as it is rare. In all, Colombo has published well over 50 books, including translations.

DOUG FETHERLING

Colombo Plan for Co-operative Economic Development in South and Southeast Asia, est following a Jan 1950 meeting of COMMONWEALTH foreign ministers in Colombo, Ceylon (now Sri Lanka), to attack the poverty upon which communist political movements in Asia were thought to feed. Initially confined to the Commonwealth countries of India, Pakistan, Ceylon, Australia, New Zealand, the UK and Canada, its membership soon widened to include most other S and SE Asian countries, along with the US as the largest donor. Specific development projects have always been arranged bilaterally by the governments concerned. Initial Canadian involvement was cautious, with a 1951-52 contribution of only $25 million. Ottawa's participation grew rapidly, however, as its development-assistance programs expanded. India, Pakistan and Ceylon, together more recently with Bangladesh and Indonesia, have been the principal recipients. In 1980-81 Colombo Plan countries received about 38% of Canada's total bilateral aid expenditures of $581.5 million.

DENIS STAIRS

Colonial and Imperial Conferences, 1887-1937, the principal means of high-level consultation between representatives from the United Kingdom, Canada and other self-governing parts of the British Empire-Commonwealth, helping to shape a framework of substantial economic and military co-operation, but consistently rejecting all forms of imperial centralization. Colonial Conferences took place in 1887, 1894, 1897, 1902 and 1907; Imperial Conferences were held in 1911, 1917, 1918, 1921, 1923, 1926, 1930, 1932 and 1937. Twice the conference was held in Ottawa (1894, 1932); all other meetings were in London, Eng. After 1937 the Imperial Conference was replaced by Prime Ministers' Meetings, theoretically without advisers or agendas, designed to produce more informal exchanges among COMMONWEALTH leaders. These met 17 times from 1944-1969. The designation was then changed to "Heads-of-Government Meetings," and these have been held every 2 years since 1971.

NORMAN HILLMER

Colonial Laws Validity Act (An Act to remove Doubts as to the Validity of Colonial Laws) was a British statute passed 29 June 1865 affirming that no law passed by a colonial legislature could be challenged by Britain unless it conflicted with an imperial statute intended to apply to that colony. The Act was passed during the movement toward CONFEDERATION when Britain was relinquishing control to its N American colonies. *See* CONSTITUTIONAL HISTORY.

Colonial Office, a department established by the British government to administer its colonial possessions, including British N America. It established forms of government and the church, appointed governors, approved local laws and made grants for particular purposes. It managed "imperial subjects," such as commerce and shipping, which gradually came under the exclusive control of the self-governing colonies.

Between the 1660s and 1768 British colonies had been governed by a combination of the secretary of state for the Southern Department and the Board of Trade and Plantations, a committee within the Privy Council. In 1768 the American or Colonial Department was established, but this office was abolished in 1782 after the loss of the American colonies. Jurisdiction over the remainder of British possessions was transferred to the home secretary's office until 1801, when colonial administration was moved to the secretary of state for war and the colonies. Colonial affairs expanded and became more important, and in 1825 a permanent undersecretary was appointed to deal with the colonies. This marks the beginning of the Colonial Office, although a separate secretary of state for the colonies was not created until 1854, after the Crimean War began. Further reorganization occurred as the range of powers claimed by the colonies expanded and as relations with these colonies became diplomatic rather than administrative.

A Dominion division within the Colonial Office dealt with the self-governing colonies between 1907 and 1 July 1925, when it became a separate ministry, the secretary of state for Dominion affairs. In 1947 this became the Commonwealth Relations Office, which in 1966 merged with the Colonial Office. Finally, in 1968, Britain combined the responsibility for all its external relations in the single Foreign and Commonwealth Office. *See* COMMONWEALTH.

NANCY BROWN FOULDS

Reading: D.M.L. Farr, *The Colonial Office and Canada 1867-1887* (1955); J. Garner, *The Commonwealth Office 1925-68* (1978); D.M. Young, *The Colonial Office in the Nineteenth Century* (1961).

Colonization Companies, corporations designed to promote and co-ordinate immigration and settlement, employed at various times during Canada's history. Immigration and settlement were vital if the colony, and later the country, were to prosper. Colonization companies usually received blocks of land (eg, Huron Tract, Talbot Settlement) for reduced rates. They usually published brochures attracting potential settlers' attention, arranged for transportation to the block, helped settlers select land, provided (or helped them buy) equipment and seed for the first crop, and assisted with construction of homes. Once a group of settlers was established, the surrounding land would become more desirable to other settlers, and therefore more valuable to the company.

In 1628 the COMPAGNIE DES CENTS-ASSOCIÉS was founded to encourage permanent settlement in New France. It was granted a vast area in return for exclusive fur-trade rights, but was unsuccessful in its goals. The COMPAGNIE DES INDES OCCIDENTALES, fd 1664, assumed control of New France until 1674, when it reverted to the Crown. During the British regime, colonization companies such as the CANADA COMPANY in Upper Canada and the BRITISH AMERICAN LAND COMPANY in Lower Canada were incorporated to promote settlement.

By far the largest government-encouraged scheme, however, was introduced on 23 Dec 1881 when John A. Macdonald's Conservative government, as part of its NATIONAL POLICY, and in an attempt to share responsibility for Western settlement, approved legislation providing for the sale of certain odd-numbered sections of land in the West to any business that demonstrated its goodwill and capabilities, and a sincere interest in promoting settlement. The purchaser was required to locate 2 settlers upon each of the odd- and even-numbered sections of the tract within 5 years, although the Crown maintained exclusive ownership of the even-numbered sections. In return, the company was to receive a rebate of $160 for every newly established, bona fide settler within the colonization tract. Companies were expected to realize profits in proportion to the number of settlers they could induce onto their respective lands. With the maximum rebate, a company could pay as little as $1/acre for the odd-numbered sections. Once its even-numbered sections were fully occupied by HOMESTEADS or pre-emptions, the company could demand $3-15/acre for them.

The government wanted assistance in its DOMINION LANDS POLICY, and it hoped to sell 10 million acres (4.05 million ha) to private colonization corporations, recover $10 million of the $25 million it had pledged to the CANADIAN PACIFIC RAILWAY syndicate, and simultaneously secure the business community's assistance in developing the western frontier. Importunate politicians, church groups and prominent businessmen petitioned the government for land, convinced that the North-West would be invaded by hordes of settlers. Most of their applications were withdrawn when the 1881-82 speculative real-estate boom on the Prairies collapsed. Of 260 applicants, only 27 ratified contracts with the government, and the last of the companies involved was liquidated in 1891. After 1900, colonization companies, operating under the auspices of railway companies or the Dept of Immigration, were much more successful in the West because of the massive influx of settlers and a great demand for land which lasted until WWI. Most of Canada's colonization companies, however, languished; several took no initiative, whereas others were victimized by adverse economic or political conditions, successive crop failures and poor communication with settlers on their tracts.

ANDRÉ N. LALONDE

Columbia Icefield, a mass of ice covering a high plateau between Mt Columbia (3747 m) and Mt Athabasca (3491 m), located between Banff and Jasper national parks, along the BC-Alberta border. Astride the Great Divide, it lies at the geographic and hydrographic apex of N America, at the point from which all land falls away. Called the "mother of rivers," its meltwaters nourish the North SASKATCHEWAN, COLUMBIA, ATHABASCA and FRASER river systems. It contains about 30 distinct glaciers, the largest being

Columbia Icefield, located between Mt Columbia and Mt Athabasca, lies at the geographic and hydrographic apex of N America. It contains 30 distinct glaciers and its meltwaters feed the N Saskatchewan, Columbia, Athabasca and Fraser rivers (*photo by V. Claerhout*).

Saskatchewan and Athabasca. A vestige of the great ice shield that once lay over most of Canada, the Columbia Icefield is the largest accumulation of ice in the Rocky Mtns, covering some 300 km^2 in depths from 100 to 365 m. Tree-ring studies show that the icefield advances and recedes in cycles, the latest advance occurring around 1840. The icefield is a spectacular sight of glistening blue ice, soaring rock peaks and deep ice caverns. At its S face, it drops off into a forested valley dotted with emerald lakes. It is easily reached from the Icefields Parkway, a scenic road connecting Lk Louise and Jasper, and can be climbed to its crest, called Snow Dome, from which it is said waters melt into 3 oceans. JAMES MARSH

Columbia Mountains are a block of mountains 608 km long and 256 km wide that dominate the landscape of southeastern BC. The MONASHEE, SELKIRK and Purcell mountains form parallel lines extending north-south from the US to the ROCKY MOUNTAIN TRENCH. Minerals in the Purcells, between the valley of KOOTENAY LK and the trench, have been exploited since the 1890s, notably silver-bearing lead-zinc ore from Cominco Ltd's huge Sullivan Mine in KIMBERLEY, BC. Alpine areas such as the Bugaboos are increasingly popular for skiing and hiking. To the NW, between the Quesnel-Shuswap Highlands and the trench, are the Cariboo Mtns. They include Bowron Lk and most of Wells Grey Provincial Park, both noted for outstanding scenery and recreation. PETER GRANT

Columbia River, 2000 km long (of which 748 km are in Canada), rises in Columbia Lk (elev 820 m) in SE British Columbia, flows NW in a sharp detour around the Selkirk range and turns S past REVELSTOKE, through Arrow Lk and Lower Arrow Lk, past CASTLEGAR, and across the US border (at elev 390 m). Just N of the border it is joined by the Kootenay R, which also rises in the area of Columbia Lk, loops S into the US and N again into Kootenay Lk, before heading W to join the Columbia. The Columbia continues S across Washington state, but is forced off its natural course by lava flow and glacial debris into a huge curve, called the "Big Bend." At the top of the bend, it is joined by the Okanagan R (314 km), which drains the lakes of the OKANAGAN VALLEY. Just N of the Oregon border it is joined by the Snake R and makes a right-angled turn, flowing W to the Pacific below Portland, Oregon. The Columbia is a long, powerful river, which has cut deep gorges along much of its course, and it commands one of the greatest DRAINAGE BASINS in N America, totalling 155 000 km^2 (including 51 800 km^2 in the US). The average flow at the international boundary is 2800 m^3/s.

Originally called Rio de San Roque by Spanish explorers, it was rediscovered by the Boston trader Capt Robert Gray, who named it after his ship, the *Columbia*. (The river may be unique in being named after a ship.) David THOMPSON of the NWC was the first to explore it from its headwaters to its mouth (1811), but American traders had preceded him overland, and were already at work on Ft Astoria. The HBC later built Ft Vancouver (1824-25) at its mouth, and as the only water route to the interior from the Pacific, the river served as the major transportation artery until the railways came. The Columbia became the de facto boundary between British and American territory, but by the 1840s American immigration to the area was ascendant, and the British agreed to set the border at the 49th parallel. Though its headwaters are in Canada, most of the river's development has been in the US. By the COLUMBIA RIVER TREATY (1961; ratified by Canada 1964), Canada agreed to build 3 storage dams: the Duncan (1967) N of Kootenay Lk, Hugh Keenleyside (1968) on the Columbia, and Mica (1973) N of Revelstoke. The Mica project,

The Columbia River river has cut deep gorges along much of its course and commands one of the greatest drainage basins in N America; illustrated is Columbia Lake at the river's headwaters (*photo by Valerie J. May*).

which began generating 1976-77, produces 1.7 MW, and the total potential of the river is estimated to be 4.0 MW in Canada. The agreement has been controversial because of the environmental disruption of the dams and because the irrigation and hydroelectric power mostly benefit the US. However, Canada shares the power and revenue. Some of the world's largest hydroelectric generators are on the river, eg, at Grand Coulee. The dams have greatly impeded the salmon runs; the Columbia was one of the world's great spawning grounds. JAMES MARSH

Columbia River Treaty, signed by Canada and the US on 17 Jan 1961 after 15 years ofpreliminary investigation by the INTERNATIONAL JOINT COMMISSION and one year (1960) of direct international negotiation; dealt with the co-operative development of the Columbia River. Canada undertook to construct 3 dams for water storage projects in the Canadian portion of the COLUMBIA R basin and to operate them to produce maximum flood control and power downstream. In return, the US would pay Canada $US64.4 million (calculated to be half the worth, in 1961, of the flood protection the US would enjoy over the treaty's 60-year life); it would give Canada title to half the power produced; and would return this power to Canada. The treaty gave the US an option to build a trans-boundary project on the Kootenay R, and gave Canada the right at specified times to divert portions of the Kootenay's flow N into the Columbia.

The treaty did not become effective until 16 Sept 1964, much of the delay resulting from a federal-provincial controversy over BC's 1961 decision to sell the power entitlement in the US. The province prevailed in Jan 1964, when the power benefit for the first 30 years was sold for a lump sum prepayment of $US254.4 million and the treaty was slightly modified by protocol. As the Canadian owner of the resource, BC was heavily involved in the negotiations, and in 1963 and 1964 it assumed Canada's obligations. Its agency, BC Hydro, has constructed all the Canadian treaty projects, and, with an American counterpart, co-ordinates their storage releases to the advantage of both countries. NEIL SWAINSON

Columbine, herbaceous PLANT (genus *Aquilegia*) of buttercup family (Ranunculaceae). The generic name derives from Latin *aquila*, "eagle," common name from Latin *columba*, "dove." Nearly all of the 70 known species are native to the Northern Hemisphere, 5 to Canada. *A. brevistyla* ranges from western Canada to Ontario; *A. flavescens* (yellow columbine), *A. formosa* (Sitka columbine) and *A. jonesii* are native to Rocky Mts. *A. canadensis* (wild columbine) extends east from Saskatchewan. Leaves are divided into 1-3 leaflets, each in 3 parts. The most distinctive feature of the nodding flower is the hornlike spur projecting backwards from each of the 5 petals. Columbines, a popular ORNAMENTAL cultivated for centuries, produce variable forms when grown from seed. Flowers (predominantly blue, lavender, red, yellow, white or a combination) were once used to garnish food and as medicine until overdoses proved fatal. *A. canadensis* was used by N American Indians for intestinal disorders, to sweeten tobacco and as an aphrodisiac. *See* PLANTS, NATIVE USES; POISONOUS PLANTS. ROGER VICK

Columbium (Cb), or niobium, grey, ductile tarnish-resistant and superconductive metal with a melting point of 2468°C. The name niobium (Nb) was officially adopted in 1951 by the International Union of Pure and Applied Chemistry, after 100 years of controversy. In N America many metallurgists and metal dealers still refer to the metal as columbium. Columbium is an important alloy in high-strength low-alloy (HSLA) steels. High-purity columbium products are used in superalloys for the AEROSPACE INDUSTRY and in superconductor magnets for generators. The primary sources of columbium are the minerals pyrochlore and columbite; extensive reserves are found in Brazil, Canada, Nigeria and Zaire. In 1980 Niobec Inc, Canada's sole columbium source, produced 246 t of Cb_2O_5 from a mine in southern Québec, about 12% of the world's output. Several large deposits, mainly in Québec, could be developed in future. *See* MINERAL RESOURCES. D.G. FON[illegible]

Colvile, Eden, governor of Rupert's Land (b 1819; d in Devonshire, Eng 2 Apr 1893), son of the deputy governor of the HUDSON'S BAY CO. Educated at Eton and Trinity Coll, Cambridge, he was sent in 1844 by the London Land Co to manage the seigneury of Beauharnois, LC, apparently without much success. He also represented Beauharnois in the Legislative Assembly of the Province of Canada 1844-47. A pleasant enough patrician with business aspirations, he was made associate governor of Rupert's Land on 3 Jan 1849. Arriving at the RED RIVER COLONY on 11 Aug 1850, he provided a steadying influence in the settlement in a period of increasing racial, social and religious tension. After his departure in the fall of 1852 his connection with the HBC continued and in the 1860s when new interests took over he was one of the few that remained on its London Committee. In 1872 he became deputy governor and was governor from 1880 to 1889. FRITS PANNEKOEK

Colville, Alexander, painter (b at Toronto 24 Aug 1920). He moved with his family to Amherst, NS, in 1929 and studied at Mount Allison (1938-42). On graduating he joined the army and in 1944 was sent to Europe as a war artist. He returned to Canada late in 1945 and worked in Ottawa on paintings based on his European sketches and watercolours until his demobilization in 1946. Colville taught at Mount Allison 1946-63, when he resigned to devote himself to painting. Between 1952 and 1955 the Hewitt Gallery in New York gave Colville his earliest commercial exhibitions. The most substantial Canadian support for his work at this time came from the National Gallery of Canada, which acquired 7 of his paintings in the 1950s.

The 1950 painting *Nude and Dummy* marks the transition from the reportage of Colville's war pictures to a personal creative direction. His subject matter is invariably chosen from his immediate environment: his family, the animals he keeps, the landscape near his home. The representations, however, are never simply a recording of the everyday; they are highly representational reflections of a world which is at once filled with the joyful and the beautiful, the disturbing and the dangerous. Colville has changed his medium a number of times, from oil to tempera to oil and synthetic resin, and after 1963 to acrylic polymer emulsion. He follows a long, careful process for each composition, taking precise measurements and proportioning these to an underlying geometric scheme. He works on only one composition at a time, and since the 1950s has produced only 3 or 4 paintings or serigraphs a year.

In 1966 Colville represented Canada at the Venice Biennale. He was visiting professor at University of California at Santa Cruz in 1967, and in 1971 spent 6 months as a visiting artist in Berlin. He has served on numerous boards and commissions. He designed the Centennial coins, minted in 1967, and the Governor General's Medal, in 1978. He has lived in the small university town of Wolfville, NS, since 1971 and is Chancellor of Acadia. In 1982 he was made a companion of the Order of Canada.

MARILYN BURNETT

Alex Colville, *Hound in Field* (1958), casein tempera on board (*courtesy National Gallery of Canada*).

Come by Chance, Nfld, Town, pop 337 (1981c), inc 1969, is located at the head of PLACENTIA BAY on the Isthmus of Avalon. Originally called Passage Harbour by John GUY in 1612, the name "Comby Chance" was first recorded in 1706 — perhaps in reference to the discovery of the harbour "by chance." Despite the presence of a telegraph station in the early 1900s, the settlement was almost deserted by the late 1930s. It was then chosen as the site of a cottage hospital because of its central location in the TRINITY BAY-Placentia Bay area. Come by Chance gained national importance in the 1970s with the building of a 16 350 m³ per day oil refinery. The \$120-million petroleum complex included two 99 000 m³ crude-oil storage tanks, a CNR spur track, a deep-water oil terminal and the refinery itself, which produced its first oil in Dec 1973. However, after some malfunctions and the loss of its feedstock supply, the refinery went into receivership in 1976. The idle refinery was sold in July 1980 to PETRO-CANADA. JANET E.M. PITT

Comédie-Canadienne, La, was founded by Gratien GÉLINAS in 1958 to foster the production of plays by Canadian authors. After renovating the Radio-City cinema in Montréal, the company presented plays by authors such as Marcel DUBÉ, Jacques Bobet, Jacques Languirand and Gélinas. Seeking a wider audience, the Comédie-Canadienne offered innovations such as an earlier curtain time, a section of inexpensive seats, and acoustic subtitles for translation of plays. By 1961 Gélinas realized that Canadian plays alone could not sustain the 1200-seat theatre house, which was then made available to a variety of stage productions — theatre, dance and song. In the late 1960s an attempt was made to devote 43 weeks each year to Québecois music and theatre, but the company closed down in 1973 and its theatre became the permanent home of the THÉÂTRE DU NOUVEAU MONDE. *See also* THEATRE, FRENCH-LANGUAGE. MARILYN BASZCZYNSKI

Comet, astronomical body orbiting the SUN, which appears for a few weeks as a faint, luminous patch moving slowly, from night to night, relative to the background of stars. The comet may also have a luminous tail pointing away from the sun. In recorded history about 700 comets have been observed well enough to allow an approximate determination of their orbits. Of these comets, about 120 have short periods (3-200 years) and have been observed more than once, so that about 1100 cometary apparitions have been observed in all. The remaining 600 or so long-period comets have been observed only once and their orbital periods are known roughly or not at all. Since a long-period comet is usually observed for only a small fraction of its orbital period, it is customary to represent its orbit by a parabola (an open curve). If the orbit of a comet were truly a parabola or a hyperbola, the comet would not be a permanent member of the solar system but would be passing from interstellar space. However, as far as we know, all comets that have been observed are probably solar-system objects, even if we cannot determine the periods of their orbits.

Upon its discovery (if a new comet) or recovery (if a short-period comet), the comet is assigned a temporary label consisting of the year of discovery plus a letter (a, b, c, etc) indicating the order of discovery (or recovery) in the year. Later, when all orbits have been worked out, it is assigned a permanent label consisting of the year plus a Roman numeral (I, II, III, etc) indicating the order of perihelion passage (ie, point in the orbit nearest the sun). The comet is also named after its discoverer(s). For example, Comet van den Bergh — Comet 1974g-1974XII — discovered by Canadian astronomer Sidney VAN DEN BERGH, was the seventh comet to be discovered and the twelfth to pass through perihelion in 1974. A periodic comet may bear several numerical designations; eg, Comet Halley bears the designations 1835III and 1910II. One astronomer may have several comets named after him, eg, Canadian astronomer Rolf Meier discovered comets 1978f, 1979i and 1980q.

Most comets have rather eccentric orbits, spend most of their time far from both sun and Earth and are invisible, even through large telescopes. When a comet is far from the sun, it is a small, solid object, possibly not more than a few kilometres in diameter. The solid material probably consists partly of frozen volatile substances (eg, water, simple organic compounds) mixed with small particles of nonvolatile stony or metallic dust. The description "dirty ice" is often used.

Only when a comet comes close to the sun and Earth for a brief few weeks near perihelion can the familiar spectacular phenomenon usually associated with comets be seen. The volatile substances evaporate and the organic molecules break up under the influence of sunlight and glow with an eerie fluorescence. Molecular fragments have been identified by analysing the fluorescence spectrographically (*see* SPECTROSCOPY). Some molecular fragments were observed in comets before being observed in any terrestrial laboratory and Canadian scientists have been prominent in subsequent identifications. Two cometary molecules were identified in the Ottawa laboratories of the NATIONAL RESEARCH COUNCIL: C_3 by Alex Douglas and H_2O^+ by Gerhard HERZBERG. Some of a comet's light is sunlight reflected from dust particles released when ice evaporates.

Although there is much variation in pattern, a fully developed comet typically has a head and 2 tails. The head consists of the central nucleus, the small (several-kilometre-sized) body from which gas and dust are evaporating, and the coma, the atmosphere of glowing gas surrounding the nucleus. One tail, known variously as the gas, ion or plasma tail, points directly away from the sun and consists of ionized gases being blown away from the sun. The second tail, the dust tail, is also directed away from the sun, but tends to be rather curved and is amorphous in appearance. Its spectrum (merely reflected sunlight) shows that it consists primarily of tiny solid particles. Because of geometrical circumstances, one tail is often behind the other as seen from Earth, leaving only one apparent.

Most comets are too faint to be seen with the naked eye and not all develop tails. However, occasionally, a large comet passing close to the Earth and sun produces a spectacular sight, eg, during the 1970s the newly discovered Comets Bennett, Kohoutek and West. The most famous comet is Comet Halley. In late 17th-century England, Sir Edmond Halley investigated the orbits of several comets and showed that the bright comets of 1531, 1607 and 1687 were one and the same, occurring at 76-year intervals. Subsequent investigations have shown that Comet Halley has been observed at almost every passage since 240 BC. Last seen in 1910, its next passage will be in Feb 1986; unfortunately, at perihelion it will be on the far side of the sun and invisible from Earth. It should be visible from Canada in late Dec 1985 in the constellation Aquarius before perihelion passage; however, the best views will be from the Southern Hemisphere in Apr 1986, after perihelion passage. JEREMY B. TATUM

Reading: J.C. Brandt and R.D. Chapman, *Introduction to Comets* (1981).

Comfort, Charles Fraser, painter (b at Edinburgh, Scot 22 July 1900). Comfort came to Winnipeg in 1912 and studied art there and at New York C (1922-23) with Robert Henri. His friendship with the GROUP OF SEVEN, his familiarity with the work of Paul Cézanne and other modernists, his interest in the history of art, and his work as a graphic designer in Winnipeg (1914-25) and Toronto (1925-36) were the major influences on his art. The expressive design and dramatic characterization of his large portraits of the 1920s and 1930s are also evident in his later landscapes as well as in his murals for the Toronto Stock Exchange (1937), the first modern interpretation of mural work in Canada. His numerous executive responsibilities in art societies (including president of the Royal Canadian Academy of Arts, 1957-60), and his record as a war artist (1943-46) resulted in his becoming the only artist to be appointed director of the National Gallery of Canada (1960-65). He was made an officer of the Order of Canada in 1972.

CHARLES C. HILL

Commercial Empire of the St. Lawrence, 1760-1850, The, by D.G. CREIGHTON, was published in Toronto, New Haven and London, 1937 (reprinted 1956 as *The Empire of the St. Lawrence)*. Reflecting the new emphasis on socio-economic factors that dominated Canadian historical writing in the 1930s, this masterly and elegantly written work deals with the St Lawrence Valley's influence as a transportation system and a focus of economic activity up to 1849. Creighton argued that the geographic nature of the St Lawrence-Great Lakes system made it a rival of systems such as the Hudson-Mohawk route (NY). The natural advantages of the St Lawrence were, however, offset by political decisions, such as those made in 1783 regarding the international boundary, and by the animosity felt by agriculturally based Québec society toward the entrepreneurial class of Montréal.

Commercial Law, that branch of private law concerned primarily with the supply of goods or services by merchants and other businesses for profit. Textbooks on the subject frequently differ on the range of topics treated in them. Any serious exposition of commercial law, however, will include such topics as sale of goods, bailment and carriage of goods, documents of title and negotiable instruments, banking, the various forms of secured credit, and BANKRUPTCY law.

These topics are often linked through an originating transaction. For example, a seller selling goods to a buyer at a distant location will often have to make arrangements for their shipment; this will involve a contract of carriage (by land or sea and, in overseas shipments, frequently both) with a carrier, who will issue the seller with a bill of lading (a "document of title"), which may be negotiable or non-negotiable. During their transit the goods will also usually be covered by a policy of insurance ("inland" or "marine" insurance) against loss or damage. In commercial transactions, the buyer will almost invariably make payment by means of a negotiable instrument, which in domestic transactions normally consists of a cheque drawn on the buyer's bank in the seller's favour. In international transactions payment will often be arranged through a banker's letter of credit.

If the buyer cannot or does not wish to make immediate payment, the seller may give him a short period of credit. Alternatively the seller may be willing to sell the goods on a "conditional sale" basis, involving an extension of medium- or long-term credit while reserving title until the goods have been paid for; or the buyer may arrange for a loan from a financial institution and give security to the lender to secure repayment of the loan. If the buyer becomes bankrupt before the goods have been paid for, the seller will want to know whether he can recover the goods and, if he cannot, how he will rank with other creditors who have claims against the bankrupt's estate.

In Canada, jurisdiction to regulate commercial transactions is divided between the federal and the provincial governments, so commercial lawyers must be familiar with federal as well as provincial laws. A further complication arises because the commercial law of Québec is derived from the CIVIL CODE of France while the commercial law of the English-speaking provinces is based on English law. At both the provincial and federal levels the relevant rules of many of the principal branches of commercial law have been reduced to statutory form. Thus, all English-speaking provinces have a substantially identical Sale of Goods Act while the Bills of Exchange Act, the Bank Act, the Carriage of Goods by Sea Act and the Bankruptcy Act codify all or a substantial part of the areas of commercial law under federal jurisdiction.

The function of sales law is primarily to determine the rights and duties of the seller and buyer under a contract of sale in which the contract itself does not contain definite provisions. The seller's obligations are generally the more onerous. The seller must not only deliver goods of the right quantity and description and at the agreed time; he must also supply goods that are of "merchantable quality" and reasonably fit for their intended purpose. The oft-quoted maxim *caveat emptor* ("let the buyer beware") has long ceased to represent the Canadian law. If the seller fails to live up to his obligations he may have to compensate the buyers for the losses suffered by them, and these could be very substantial. The buyer's primary obligations under the typical contract of sale are to accept the goods and to pay for them as agreed.

The federal Bills of Exchange Act deals with the following types of payment instrument: bills of exchange, cheques (ie, bills of exchange drawn on a bank or recognized near-bank) and promissory notes. An important function of the Act is to regulate the assignability (ie, negotiability) of rights obtained under one of these instruments and to determine when the transferee of an instrument can obtain better rights to payment than its original holder had. He is then said to be a "holder in due course." Similar principles of negotiability apply to "documents of title," ie, recognized types of documents (such as bills of lading and warehouse receipts) that indicate that the holder of them is entitled to the delivery of goods by the bailee who issued the document in the first place.

Canadian commercial law is changing rapidly in response to a variety of technological and other nonlegal factors. In the sales area, the courts and the legislatures are increasingly having to recognize that the typical retailer is only a conduit for the manufacturer, who produces the goods and creates a market for them through intensive advertising. Therefore, there is strong pressure to hold the manufacturer directly responsible to the ultimate buyer if the goods are defective, even though no contract exists between the parties.

Negotiable-instruments law is deeply affected by the use of electronic systems for the transfer of funds (including the use of automated tellers at the retail level) and the widespread substitution of cheques by CREDIT CARDS. In the foreseeable future debit cards will make a further inroad into the use of cheques, although the "cashless society" is still some distance away. Containerization of cargoes and intermodal methods of transport have radically altered the law of bills of lading and the traditional roles and duties of carriers.

The greatly increased importance of secured credit of all types is also contributing to changes in this branch of commercial law. In particular, 3 provinces (Ontario, Manitoba and Saskatchewan) and the Yukon Territory have now adopted a substantially similar Personal Property Security Act to replace the old provincial Conditional Sales, Chattel Mortgages, and Assignment of Book Debts Acts. The Uniform Law Conference of Canada and the Canadian Bar Association jointly sponsored the Uniform Personal Property Security Act, 1982, and urged its adoption by those provinces that are contemplating modernizing their chattel security law.

JACOB S. ZIEGEL

Commission of Conservation, established 1909 to provide Canadian governments with the most up-to-date scientific advice on the CONSERVATION of human and natural resources. The wastefulness of the common methods of resource exploitation was widely admitted, and the conservation movement was beginning to offer alternative approaches, particularly in the US where the first national commission was struck in 1908. Canada was urged to follow suit, as a step towards a continental conservation policy. This plea won the support of 2 leading Canadian conservationists, Clifford SIFTON and PM Wilfrid LAURIER, by whose government the Canadian commission was created.

Sifton served as the commission's chairman until 1918 and was always its guiding spirit. To Sifton, conservation meant that resources should be used in ways that would generate the greatest benefit for all Canadians. The public interest demanded wise management, but wise management in turn demanded the best understanding of the resource base. The commission was expected to provide this knowledge.

The members of the commission included 3 federal Cabinet ministers, the 9 provincial ministers with responsibility for natural resources and 20 members at large, including a professor from every province with a university. The commission was further organized into working committees which directed a diverse array of research in 7 topical fields: agricultural land, water and water power, fisheries, game and fur bearing animals, forests, minerals, and public health. The results were published in some 200 books, reports and scientific papers that constituted the first large-scale survey of Canadian resources and resource problems. Achievement ı public policy were not as great. Governments were slow to accept the commission's advice, and, as other agencies of the federal government became more active in resource management, the Commission of Conservation came to seem redundant. It was dissolved in 1921. *See* Thomas ADAMS; URBAN AND REGIONAL PLANNING. P.J. SMITH

Commission of Government in Newfoundland was established in response to an extraordinary set of circumstances. The collapse of world trade during the GREAT DEPRESSION of the 1930s was particularly damaging to Newfoundland's economy, which depended on exporting large quantities of fish and forest products. In 1933, following several turbulent years of severe budget deficits and heavy foreign borrowing, the government of PM Frederick ALDERICE asked the British government to establish a royal commission to investigate Newfoundland's financial difficulties. The commission's report blamed both political corruption and international conditions for Newfoundland's predicament, and advocated replacing RESPONSIBLE GOVERNMENT with a "Commission of Government" that would rule until Newfoundland was self-supporting again.

The commission government took office in Feb 1934 and remained in power until Newfoundland became a Canadian province in 1949. It was presided over by a governor who acted on the advice of 6 commissioners appointed by the British government. During its tenure the commission government introduced a number of reforms, including a land resettlement scheme, the reorganization of the civil service and the creation of the Newfoundland Fisheries Board. With the outbreak of WWII in 1939, however, large-scale reconstruction was postponed in favour of a total war effort.

Gradually much of the original goodwill toward the commission government dissipated, and after the war there was increasing agitation for the return of self-government. Consequently, in the first of 2 referendums held in 1948 to decide the island's future, commission government placed a distant third (behind the restoration of responsible government and Confederation), and when Newfoundland entered Confederation on 31 Mar 1949, relatively few Newfoundlanders mourned the passing of the commission government.

DAVID CLARK MACKENZIE

Reading: S.J.R. Noel, *Politics in Newfoundland* (1971); F.W. Rowe, *A History of Newfoundland and Labrador* (1980).

Commissioner for Oaths is any person over 18 years of age commissioned by a lieutenant-governor to administer oaths and take affidavits. Oaths must be taken by the deponent in the presence of a commissioner, who satisfies himself of the signature's authenticity and administers the oath before signing the declaration. Members of Parliament, legislative assemblies, municipal councils, lawyers and many public officials are ex officio commissioners for oaths. K.G. MCSHANE

Committee for an Independent Canada (CIC) was conceived by Walter GORDON, Peter NEWMAN and Abraham Rotstein as a citizens' committee to promote Canadian economic and cultural independence. They recruited Jack MCCLELLAND and Claude RYAN as cochairmen and launched the CIC on 17 Sept 1970. By June 1971 the CIC had 170 000 signatures on a petition to Prime Minister Trudeau demanding limits to FOREIGN INVESTMENT and ownership. Many CIC ideas were eventually incorporated into law, eg, the establishment of the Canadian Development Corporation, PETRO-CANADA and the Foreign Investment Review Agency; controls over land acquisition by nonresidents; tougher rules regarding Canadian content on radio and television; and the elimination of *Time*'s and *Reader's Digest*'s tax privileges.

The CIC's success can be attributed to the skilful use of media and effective persuasion by national chairmen (Edwin Goodman, Mel Hurtig, Robert Page, Dave Treleavan, Bruce Willson and Max Saltsman) and to local leaders who mobilized 10 000 members in 41 chapters. The organization was funded by private gifts, dues and chapter activities. Publications included the monthly *Independencer* and the books *Independence: The Canadian Challenge (1972)* and *Getting It Back* (1974) edited by Abraham Rotstein and Gary Lax. In 1981, the CIC was disbanded, many of its major goals achieved. *See* NATIONALISM; ECONOMIC NATIONALISM. ROGER RICKWOOD

Committees Parliament has many committees which perform functions that cannot be adequately accomplished in debate or question period.

Committee of the Whole (Supply, Ways and Means), chaired by the Deputy Speaker, includes all members of the HOUSE OF COMMONS meeting in its normal chamber. Until 1969 the Commons met as a Committee of the Whole to consider legislation clause by clause after second reading of a bill, a task now delegated to the relevant standing committee (*see* PARLIAMENTARY PROCEDURE). Estimates were also considered in Committee of Supply and many members would like some estimates considered there again, because Committee of the Whole is a public forum attracting great media attention. The Committee of Ways and Means, another version of Committee of the Whole, which dealt with revenue, is now purely symbolic.

Standing Committees The 18 standing committees are the most important parliamentary committees. Usually chaired by government MPs (except for the Committee on Public Accounts), they have 20-30 members, party representation being proportionate to that in the legislature. They include special committees, corresponding roughly in concern to government departments, and other committees dealing with matters such as public accounts, miscellaneous estimates and private bills, procedures and organization, privileges and elections. In Parliament there are also joint standing committees of the House and SENATE. Ministers are not usually standing-committee members although their parliamentary secretaries often are. Membership on committees is temporary and there is frequently a high turnover. Employees of the legislature serve as staff, but there are no personnel for research or for questioning of witnesses as in US congressional committees.

Committees exist primarily to scrutinize government legislation after second reading, including supply and ways-and-means legislation. They usually meet only in the capital city and their witnesses are therefore drawn chiefly from groups who can afford to travel or to maintain permanent representatives there. The committees choose witnesses and decide which recommendations to submit to the legislature, in the form of amendments to bills. If they are reviewing legislation a minister is occasionally the first and last witness, and may review testimony. With supply bills the effectiveness of committees is limited, but the committee can serve as a forum for criticism of government programs and on occasion hold ministers accountable for estimated departmental expenditure. When the Committee on Public Accounts reviews government accounts and the AUDITOR GENERAL reports on them, this attracts important media attention — far more than when the committee submits its own report to the House.

Special committees (sometimes called select committees), eg, the Joint Special Committee on the Constitution, are sometimes established by the House to study specific issues or investigate public opinion on policy decisions. They are sometimes called task forces but should not be confused with government TASK FORCES. Both standing and special committees can be joint committees. The Senate also has standing committees, special committees and a committee of the whole. Their investigations on poverty, aging and science have been noteworthy.

Standing committees are too large and therefore unwieldly, too often partisan and Government controlled; they suffer too many membership changes, are inadequately staffed and cannot choose their own topics of study. In recent years they have overcome some of these weaknesses by creating subcommittees with small, stable membership and expert staff. An example was the Justice Committee's investigation of penitentiaries (1977). In 1982, as a result of reforms adopted for a trial period, the number of members and the number of membership changes on committees were reduced. Committees were given greater discretion to choose subjects for investigation. The Special Committee on Procedure also proposed in 1983 that government legislation be considered by new legislative committees rather than by standing committees.

The increased use of committees has not altered the relationship between Parliament and Government, which disappoints many critics and private MPs. But Parliament's role is not to govern but to examine, criticize and propose alternatives. On the other hand, committees have strengthened Parliament by increasing its ability to examine and publicize its activities.

Provincial Legislatures have committee systems similar to those of the federal government; but generally, partly because of the small size of the legislatures and greater government domination of the legislatures and the committees, they are less useful or active than their federal counterparts. C.E.S. FRANKS

Commodity Inspection and Grading Canada's AGRICULTURE AND FOOD inspection and grading system has 2 major goals: first, it endeavours to provide standards of quality and grades that are readily recognizable and acceptable in domestic and international commodity and food markets; second, it attempts to encourage concern for safety and nutrition in the processing, distribution and retailing of food products. Both of these objectives contribute to consumer protection. Commodity inspection and grading have a long history in Canada. Examples of commodity inspection legislation include the federal Act respecting contagious diseases of animals (1869), the Seed Control Act (1906), hog-grading regulations and grade standards for dressed poultry (1920s), the Canada Agricultural Products Standards Act (1955) and the Meat Inspection Act (1959). The list of federal and provincial government departments and agencies involved is very long, but the following examples illustrate the nature and scope of the system. The most important department, Agriculture Canada, conducts research into animal DISEASE and meat safety and provides technical advisory services on biologics, PESTICIDES, FOOD ADDITIVES, chemical residues on food products, bacteriology and food-borne diseases. The Canadian Grain Commission provides a comprehensive grain grading and inspection service and is responsible for licensing and for regulating grain-grading specifications. The Food and Drug Services Directorate of Health and Welfare Canada is responsible for the surveillance of food and drug quality. J.C. GILSON

Common Law, the system of LAW that evolved from the decisions of the English royal courts of justice since the Norman Conquest (1066). Today the common law, considered more broadly to include statutes as well as decisions, applies in most English-speaking countries, including all Canadian provinces except Québec.

JOHN E.C. BRIERLEY

Commonwealth, a loose, voluntary association of Great Britain and most of its former colonies; 48 independent nations — about one-quarter of the world's population — pledged (according to a 1971 declaration of principles) to consult and co-operate in furthering world peace, social understanding, racial equality and economic development. The Commonwealth Secretariat (est 1965) administers programs of co-operation, arranges meetings and provides specialist services to member countries. The British monarch is head of the Commonwealth, a purely symbolic role.

The roots of the Commonwealth are frequently traced back as far as the DURHAM REPORT (1839) and RESPONSIBLE GOVERNMENT in the 1840s. By 1867 the British North American provinces, as well as other British colonies in Newfoundland, Australia, New Zealand and South Africa, were self-governing with respect to internal affairs. With CONFEDERATION, 1867, Canada became the first federation in the British Empire; its size, economic strength and seniority enabled it to become a leader in the widening of colonial autonomy and the transformation of the empire into a commonwealth of equal nations.

Contingents from all the self-governing colonies freely participated in the SOUTH AFRICAN WAR, 1899-1902. Canada sent only volunteers, and PM Sir Wilfrid LAURIER made it clear at Colonial and Imperial Conferences in 1902, 1907 and 1911 that participation in imperial defence would always be on Canadian terms. In 1914 the king declared war on behalf of the entire empire, but the Dominions (a term applied to Canada in 1867 and used in the first half of this century to describe the empire's other self-governing members) decided individually the nature and extent of their participation. They gave generously: over a million men from the Dominions and 1.5 million from India enlisted in the forces of the empire. There were also huge contributions of food, money and munitions. Although South African nationalists (Afrikaners) and many French Canadians opposed participation in a British war, the unity of the empire in WORLD WAR I was impressive.

Despite the extent of their WWI commitment, the Dominions at first played no part in the making of high policy. But Canadian PM Sir Robert BORDEN was especially critical when the war did not go well. When David Lloyd George became British prime minister in late 1916, he immediately convened an Imperial War Conference and created an Imperial War Cabinet, 2 separate bodies which met in 1917 and 1918. The former was remembered primarily for Resolution IX, which stated that the Dominions were "autonomous nations of an Imperial Commonwealth" with a "right...to an adequate voice in foreign policy and in foreign relations...." This was chiefly an initiative of PM Borden, carried at the conference with the help of Gen J.C. Smuts of South Africa, and marked the first official use of the term "Commonwealth."

The Imperial War Cabinet gave leaders from the Dominions and India an opportunity to be informed, consulted and made to feel a part of the making of high-level policy. A similar body, the British Empire Delegation, was constructed at the Paris Peace Conference. Borden and Australian PM W.M. Hughes also successfully fought for separate Dominion representation at the conference and separate signatures on the TREATY OF VERSAILLES. Constitutionally, however, the empire was still a single unit: Lloyd George's was the signature that counted. The Dominions, now members of the new LEAGUE OF NATIONS, remained ambiguous creatures — part nation, part colony, part imperial colleague.

The war pulled each Dominion in apparently opposite directions: widespread hopes for greater imperial unity clashed with intensified feelings of national pride and distinctiveness which resulted from wartime sacrifice and achievement. Borden, a nationalist who wished to enhance Canada's growing international sta-

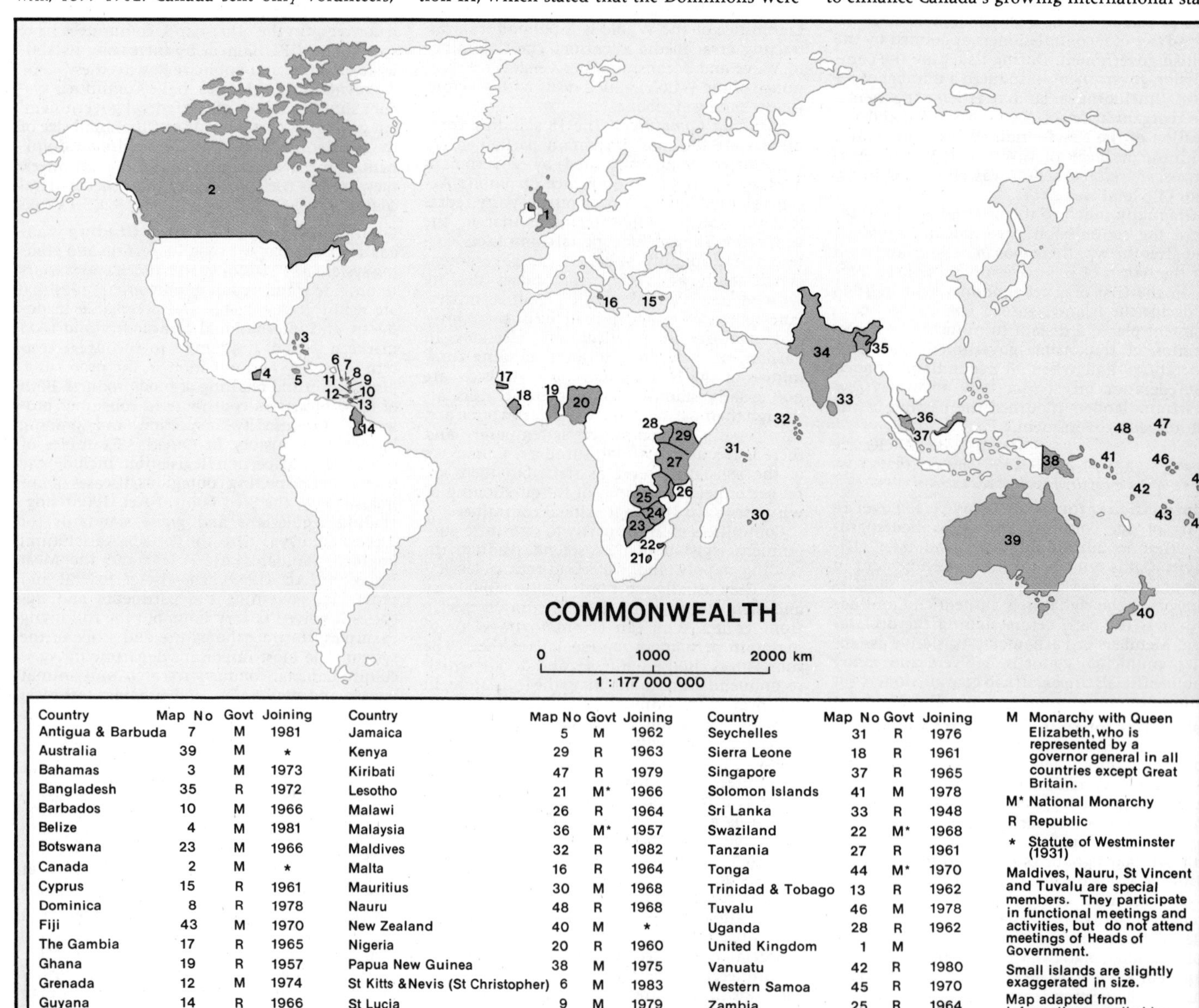

Country	Map No	Govt	Joining	Country	Map No	Govt	Joining	Country	Map No	Govt	Joining
Antigua & Barbuda	7	M	1981	Jamaica	5	M	1962	Seychelles	31	R	1976
Australia	39	M	*	Kenya	29	R	1963	Sierra Leone	18	R	1961
Bahamas	3	M	1973	Kiribati	47	R	1979	Singapore	37	R	1965
Bangladesh	35	R	1972	Lesotho	21	M*	1966	Solomon Islands	41	M	1978
Barbados	10	M	1966	Malawi	26	R	1964	Sri Lanka	33	R	1948
Belize	4	M	1981	Malaysia	36	M*	1957	Swaziland	22	M*	1968
Botswana	23	M	1966	Maldives	32	R	1982	Tanzania	27	R	1961
Canada	2	M	*	Malta	16	R	1964	Tonga	44	M*	1970
Cyprus	15	R	1961	Mauritius	30	M	1968	Trinidad & Tobago	13	R	1962
Dominica	8	R	1978	Nauru	48	R	1968	Tuvalu	46	M	1978
Fiji	43	M	1970	New Zealand	40	M	*	Uganda	28	R	1962
The Gambia	17	R	1965	Nigeria	20	R	1960	United Kingdom	1	M	
Ghana	19	R	1957	Papua New Guinea	38	M	1975	Vanuatu	42	R	1980
Grenada	12	M	1974	St Kitts &Nevis (St Christopher)	6	M	1983	Western Samoa	45	R	1970
Guyana	14	R	1966	St Lucia	9	M	1979	Zambia	25	R	1964
India	34	R	1947	St Vincent	11	M	1979	Zimbabwe	24	R	1980

M Monarchy with Queen Elizabeth, who is represented by a governor general in all countries except Great Britain.

M* National Monarchy

R Republic

* Statute of Westminster (1931)

Maldives, Nauru, St Vincent and Tuvalu are special members. They participate in functional meetings and activities, but do not attend meetings of Heads of Government.

Small islands are slightly exaggerated in size.

Map adapted from information supplied by Commonwealth Secretariat.

as through commitment to a great empire-Commonwealth, tried to reconcile the 2 impulses. He sought a closely knit commonwealth of equal nations that would consult and act together on the big issues of common concern. Resolution IX had called for a postwar conference to readjust constitutional relations along these lines. It was never held.

A nationalism quite different from Borden's took control of the Commonwealth in the 1920s. Canadian PM Mackenzie KING was the heir to Laurier's policy of "no commitments." The CHANAK AFFAIR and the HALIBUT TREATY set the tone, and King was a clear winner at the Imperial Conference of 1923. A trend away from imperial diplomatic unity and towards a devolved, autonomous relationship between Britain and the Dominions was established. King believed that the British connection could be maintained only if it allowed Canadians, particularly the substantial minority of non-British descent, to concentrate on developing a strong N American nation. He was not alone in wishing to emphasize diplomatic autonomy, although the reasons differed. The British had little wish for a co-operative Anglo-Dominion foreign policy that would require the Foreign Office to engage in time-consuming consultation with much smaller powers. South Africa and the Irish Free State, granted Dominion status on the Canadian model in 1921, were even more radical than King in pushing for decentralization.

At the Imperial Conference of 1926, South African PM Gen J.B.M. Hertzog demanded a public declaration that the Dominions were independent states, equal in status to Britain and separately entitled to international recognition. King opposed the word "independent," which might conjure up unhappy visions of the American Revolution in pro-British parts of Canada, but he endorsed the thrust of Hertzog's demand. The conference adopted the BALFOUR REPORT, which led to the passage of the STATUTE OF WESTMINSTER, 1931, establishing the theoretical right of the Dominions to full legislative autonomy.

The Commonwealth of the 1930s was a study in contradiction, a mixture of the national and the imperial, and confusing to outsiders. To some extent Commonwealth countries conducted their own external affairs and managed their own defences. Yet a common head of state, common citizenship and substantial common legislation remained. Association with a vast and apparently powerful empire — then at its greatest extent, covering over 31 million km² — brought the Dominions prestige, prosperity and protection. The OTTAWA AGREEMENTS of 1932, although falling far short of creating the self-sufficient unit some had dreamed about, bound Commonwealth countries tighter in an interlocking series of bilateral trading agreements. There was also substantial military co-operation, of enormous benefit to the Dominions' fledgling ARMED FORCES. Newfoundland, proudly "Britain's oldest colony," had long had responsible government, was represented at Colonial and Imperial Conferences and had fought with distinction in WWI, but financial crisis brought about the return of British rule (*see* COMMISSION OF GOVERNMENT) from 1934 to 1949, at which time it became part of Canada.

Dependence and gratitude did not necessarily lead to commitment, and in peacetime the Dominions were wary of European entanglements. When Britain declared war on Germany in Sept 1939, Australia and New Zealand did not hesitate to become involved in WORLD WAR II. Canada waited one week before Parliament endorsed the King government's decision to fight. South Africans split on the issue and PM Hertzog resigned, but the final response was positive. Only Eire (as the Irish Free State became in 1937) stayed aloof. Immense contributions of men — over 2 million from the 4 Dominions and 2.5 million from India — and material were made. The BRITISH COMMONWEALTH AIR TRAINING PLAN, which trained 131 553 aircrew, was a major Canadian contribution. Such efforts were all the more important and valued because the Dominions alone fought at Britain's side from the first day to the last. But there was no Imperial War Cabinet this time, no Commonwealth consensus on the need to strengthen ties. British power was waning and Dominion confidence was on the rise, weakening traditional links. Britain's subject peoples in Africa and Asia also looked increasingly to themselves for solutions to their problems.

By 1949 the Commonwealth was completely transformed. Eire left in 1948. India, which had been lurching towards responsible government and Dominion status for decades, achieved independence in 1947, although at a price: it was divided on religious grounds into the Dominions of India and Pakistan. Neighbouring Ceylon (now Sri Lanka) and Burma achieved independence in 1947-48, the former obtaining Dominion status and choosing Commonwealth membership. In 1949 India was allowed to remain in the Commonwealth after declaring itself a republic. The British monarch was declared "the symbol of the free association of its member nations, and as such Head of the Commonwealth." The Commonwealth was no longer predominantly white and British; allegiance to a common crown was no longer a prerequisite of membership, and the concept of common citizenship was fading fast.

There were high hopes for the "multiracial" Commonwealth, which many believed could be a force and example for understanding among nations. A bigger grouping, however, was more difficult to keep together, particularly when members were moving more than ever before in different directions, partly in order to develop responses to a COLD WAR world dominated by hostility between the US and USSR. Britain began the long road to eventual membership (1973) in the European Economic Community, to the consternation of much of the older Commonwealth. Canada, Australia and New Zealand looked increasingly to the US as ally and trading partner. India preached the doctrine of nonalignment with either of the superpowers. The SUEZ CRISIS of 1956, over which the Commonwealth was badly split, underlined the decline of Britain's power and gave rise to questions about its judgement and morality in the bargain.

But the Commonwealth did not die. As former British dependencies achieved self-government and took responsibility for their own external relations, it became customary to say that they had "achieved independence," and might or might not "join the Commonwealth" as monarchies or republics. Most did join. The decade after 1957 was one of dramatic growth: virtually all the colonies of British Africa, joined by 4 in the Caribbean, one in Asia and 2 in the Mediterranean, won their independence and became Commonwealth members. So did Bangladesh, on declaring independence from Pakistan in 1971; Pakistan then left the Commonwealth.

The multiracial composition of the postwar Commonwealth has affected both the politics and the policies of the UK. Pressure about its racial policies from Commonwealth colleagues (especially from Canada's PM John DIEFENBAKER) led to the withdrawal of South Africa in 1961. Until well into the 1960s, Britain was led by its Commonwealth connections to maintain an open-door policy towards immigrants from the Asian Commonwealth and the West Indies. When Rhodesia unilaterally declared independence in 1965 to continue white-settler supremacy, Commonwealth states exerted great pressure on Britain to ensure that international recognition would not be granted unless black majority rule was conceded. Only in 1980, when that condition had been satisified, was the state's independence legalized; Rhodesia (as Zimbabwe) became a member of the Commonwealth.

The very idea of such an amorphous institution arouses an easy cynicism in Canada, when it is thought of at all. P.E. TRUDEAU was a cynic when he became prime minister in 1968, but he quickly became a believer. Trudeau played an important role in the 1971 heads-of-government meeting, when the future of the Commonwealth was in question because Britain wished to sell arms to South Africa. Canadian leaders and diplomats have played a prominent role throughout Commonwealth history (Arnold SMITH, for example, was the Commonwealth's first secretary general), not simply in helping to create an international institution, but in keeping it together in moments of stress. One of the Commonwealth's great attractions is that it gives members a forum for making themselves and their views known, and access to an expanding network of economic, social and educational programs — without demanding uniformity of outlook or purpose in return. The COLOMBO PLAN of 1950 was a pioneering effort in development assistance. The Commonwealth Fund for Technical Co-operation (fd 1971) is now the chief means of giving aid to developing countries, Canada providing more than 40% of the budget. The Commonwealth co-operates in ways which would never have been possible in the old days of empire. Today unofficial and official links are in the thousands — from regular meetings of heads of government, and of ministers and officials, to agencies such as the Commonwealth Youth Program, Commonwealth Scholarships and the COMMONWEALTH GAMES. *See* EXTERNAL RELATIONS; CANADA AND AUSTRALIA; FRANCOPHONIE.

NORMAN HILLMER

Reading: Norman Hillmer and P. Wigley, eds, *The First British Commonwealth* (1980); N. Mansergh, *The Commonwealth Experience*, 2 vols (1982); A. Smith, *Stitches in Time* (1981); P. Wigley, *Canada and the Transition to Commonwealth* (1977).

Commonwealth Games Since the first British Empire Games were held at Hamilton, Ont, in Aug 1930, attended by 400 competitors representing 11 countries, Canada has been a leading proponent and participant in this 4-yearly multisport festival. Succeeding Games were held at London (England), 1934; Sydney (Australia), 1938; Auckland (New Zealand), 1950; Vancouver, 1954 and renamed the British Empire and Commonwealth Games; Cardiff (Wales), 1958; Perth (Australia), 1962; Kingston (Jamaica), 1966 and renamed the British Commonwealth Games; Edinburgh (Scotland), 1970; Christchurch (New Zealand), 1974; and Edmonton, 1978 and renamed the Commonwealth Games, by which time nearly 1500 athletes from 46 countries competed. The 1982 Commonwealth Games took place in Brisbane, Australia. The 1986 games are scheduled to be held in Edinburgh, Scotland.

The Commonwealth Games have provided many memorable performances (10 world records were broken at Cardiff in 1958). "The Miracle Mile" at Vancouver, in 1954, when Roger Bannister of Great Britain defeated John Landy of Australia, was one of the most dramatic events in sport history. Canadian athletes have given outstanding performances at several Games — in swimming alone, Phyllis Dewar (1934), Elaine TANNER (1966) and Graham Smith (1978) won 14 gold medals. At the XI Commonwealth Games (1978) in Edmonton, where 10 000 local volunteers assisted in the organization, Canada obtained an unprecedented 45 gold medals, 31 silver and 33 bronze, for a total of 109 (England was nearest with 27 gold and a total of 87). There were 11 sports at these games: athletics (track and field), badminton, boxing, cycling, gymnastics, lawn bowling, shooting, swimming, weightlifting, wrestling and lacrosse (demonstration sport). GERALD REDMOND

Reading: History Committee of the XI Commonwealth Games, *A Historical Record of the Games Leading up to the Commonwealth Games of 1978* (1978); Gerald Redmond, ed, *Edmonton '78: The Official Pictorial Record of the XI Commonwealth Games* (1978).

Communal Properties Act Case *Walter* v *Attorney-General of Alberta* tested the constitutional validity of the Communal Properties Act (1955), which had the effect of restricting the territorial area of communal lands owned by religiously based groups such as the HUTTERITES and the DOUKHOBORS. Although it was argued that the Act dealt with religion and that only Parliament could pass legislation affecting religious freedom, the SUPREME COURT OF CANADA in a unanimous judgement upheld the validity of the statute, saying that it related to land ownership in Alberta and that the province had the constitutional competence to pass legislation dealing with "property in the province" even if it incidentally affected religious matters. The Act was repealed but the case is of historical interest because it tested the validity of what might be considered discriminatory legislation. The case also demonstrates how technical and superficial the Supreme Court of Canada was in protecting fundamental freedoms of Canadians. This may change as a result of the Charter of Rights and Freedoms (*see* HUMAN RIGHTS). M.M. LITMAN

Communauté des biens (community of property), term used in the legal codes of NEW FRANCE and Québec to describe the pooled assets of husband and wife. It began as part of the Coutume de Paris, introduced about 1640 and the sole legal code of the colony after 1664. The codes stipulated that all but the inherited immovable goods (essentially land and annuities) of the partners entered into this arrangement; that within certain limits the husband would be free to manage the communauté according to his lights; and that upon the death of one spouse, the survivor would receive half the communauté — debts and all — and the children the other half. Communauté de biens survived more than 3 centuries of social mutation; only in 1980 did the concept pass out of use. The Québec CIVIL CODE now refers to a *société des acquêts,* or "partnership of acquests." TOM WIEN

Communauté des habitants (Compagnie des habitants), colonial merchants who held the FUR-TRADE monopoly in NEW FRANCE, 1645-63. In principle the COMPAGNIE DES CENT-ASSOCIÉS ceded its monopoly to all inhabitants of the colony, but in practice only a few of the wealthiest benefited. The cost of the monopoly was the equivalent of the colony's administrative expenses plus an annual rent of 1000 livres' weight of beaver skins and the promise to import 20 colonists a year. The communauté was not a success: high interest rates, combined with a lack of experience in commerce, led to serious financial difficulties by 1652. The Conseil de Québec then declared the trade open to all HABITANTS — not the original communauté members alone — and the arrangement continued until its collapse in 1663. TOM WIEN

Communication Studies explore the ways in which information is given meaning by those who produce, distribute and interpret it. Communication studies are a new academic discipline, with departments or programs in 13 universities and many colleges; with 2 journals (*Communication et information,* Laval, and *Canadian Journal of Communication,* St Thomas More College, Saskatoon); with national and Québec associations, and a number of organizations appealing to specialized interests and involving academics, representatives from industry and government and members of the public.

Research may focus on a variety of topics. Mass media, whose influence is significant on all aspects of social, political and economic life, are studied for the content of their programs, the way those programs are produced and the impact of various influences on programming. Media economic structure and the media's role in political life are also topics of research. In addition to mass-media research, communication studies may focus on how particular messages are presented in films, advertisements or school texts; in press statements made during election campaigns; in news reporting and in government documents; or in the way a group meeting or public inquiry is conducted. Any event, text, group action or form of media may be studied from a communication perspective. The purpose of communication analyses is to identify the full range of meanings, intended or not, to see how those meanings are structured into the final message that people receive, and to examine the impact of what is being communicated.

Some of the most important work in communication studies was done by Harold INNIS, the Canadian economic historian who turned his attention to communications in his later works. Innis argued that the way information is disseminated — which physical senses and which technologies are used — influences not only the impact of the message, but also its content and the shape of social life as a whole. Although Innis died (1952) long before the computer or satellite age, his work on ancient writing systems and modern radio enabled him to predict many of the changes that were to occur in a society dependent upon rapid transmission of information. Research in communication studies today draws upon his insights in examining, for example, the impact of literacy and TV on Inuit communities, the relationship between economic and communication development, the impact of new information technologies, and the response of people in less developed countries to the export of mass media and modern technologies from developed countries.

An important aspect of communication studies in Canada is the impact of government policies on mass media, telecommunication services and new technological development. The CANADIAN RADIO-TELEVISION AND TELECOMMUNICATIONS COMMISSION and various departments of communication are of interest, but so too are agencies such as UNESCO, which sponsor research and projects in related areas. Some of these projects are designed to counteract the influence of mass-media programming on indigenous cultures; some research is focused on news and information flows throughout the world or the process of regulation itself. Much research in recent years has looked at the computerized delivery of data as an integral part of the transactions of business and government.

Communication studies developed in the US as an amalgam of engineering, social psychology, advertising or propaganda rhetoric. The focus in the often highly empirical American work is on the dissemination of information — through organizations, in news and by speech. The diffusion of innovations and technology throughout the world is also studied. In Europe, communication studies are more often theoretical and include not only the study of ideology and consciousness but also how theory itself is formed and how theories account for reality. In Canada, communication studies drew their original impulse from the humanities — 2 of the better-known contributors being Marshall MCLUHAN and Northrop FRYE. Canadian communication studies also draw heavily from psychology, sociology, philosophy, political science and economics. This research can be distinguished from the American and European traditions by its synthesis of theoretical and empirical work and by the attention given by many writers to producing recommendations for government policy.

An underlying focus in much Canadian research, and certainly among the active francophone scholars, is cultural experience. Particular attention is given to COMMUNICATION IN QUÉBEC and among regional or native cultures, to problems associated with regional, francophone or national identity; and to centralist and decentralist strains in Canadian social development. Clearly the production, distribution, interpretation and uses of information have great relevance to the study of culture. Cultural studies encompass film, popular music, literature and documents; communication studies, the sister discipline, explore how, when and why these cultural products become significant to some or all members of society. Communication studies may be taught in Canada in conjunction with journalism, business communication, cultural studies and educational or technical media programs. LIORA SALTER

Communications have been the key structural element in Canadian society since the time when canoes slipping down rivers were the connecting links between villages. Communications by water and land made Canadian federation possible; electronic communications today make possible the conduct of business, the political process and the sharing of culture and information. It is no accident that the most renowned commentator on communications in the world this century, Marshall MCLUHAN, was a Canadian. He spent his life in a country obsessed by communications. He was born in Edmonton, then an isolated prairie city connected by the railway, telephone and telegraph to the rest of Canada and the US; and he died in Toronto, the hub of English-language communications in Canada, where at the time of his death more TV channels were available than anywhere else in the world and where the social control of mass communications was a subject of comment in the daily press.

Communications influence all societies, but Canada in particular takes its shape and meaning from communications systems. Since Confederation, Canada has been a landmass much larger than most empires in history; governing its distant settlements and bringing them together in some form of political, social and cultural unity has been primarily a problem of communications management. A communications system is an attempt to offset distance between human beings, whether by railroad, aircraft, telephone or post. The building of the CANADIAN PACIFIC RAILWAY in the 1880s, as part of the political arrangement that created Confederation, was an attempt to counteract the disintegrative effects of Canada's enormous space and to prevent the absorption of western Canada by the US. A similar impulse was behind the building of radio, television, TELEPHONE and TELECOMMUNICATIONS systems. Since 1869 governments have recognized the importance of communications in Canadian life, and communications systems usually have been developed under government sponsorship and always under government control. Since 1932 the federal government has been directly involved in BROADCASTING through the CANADIAN BROADCASTING CORPORATION, first radio and then TV. Since the late 1930s it has had its own filmmaking agency, now the NATIONAL FILM BOARD, which produces and distributes films. Since the 1920s the government has regulated broadcasting and telephone systems; today it is a partner in SATELLITE COMMUNICATIONS. Private business has played an increasingly large role in broadcasting, particularly since the early 1960s. But many communities, especially in the North would not be reached by mass communications without the active participation of the government (*see* COMMUNICATIONS IN THE NORTH).

ADVERTISING is a major component in almost all media and, within the business structure of Canada, consumer advertising is the main role of the media. The media have made the consumer society possible by providing fast, widespread dissemination of information or impressions about products and services. Experience has taught advertisers that TV is one of the most effective ways of selling products. Typically, a TV commercial sets out not to sell a product directly but to surround it with exciting or pleasing images and thereby to insert the product comfortably into the world view of the consumer. Thus, beer on TV is associated with good fellowship, long-distance telephone calls are associated with family feeling, clothing is associated with youth and beauty. A careful study of TV commercials provides a series of clues to the values held by most people at the time when the commercials were made.

The mass media constitute an elaborate and highly sensitive web, stretched over the country, the strands of which are individual NEWSPAPERS, MAGAZINES and radio and TV stations. The people who run these institutions are closely connected and their roles are often interchangeable. A magazine editor may write a book that is serialized in a newspaper, which he discusses at length on radio, and which he then helps to turn into a TV series. The media are also connected by the facts, themes and ideas they convey. Radio listeners will sometimes sense this interdependence when they realize that the news they hear at breakfast is a rewritten version of the news in the morning paper that was prepared the night before. News is a commodity that can be sold. The CANADIAN PRESS, the national newsgathering agency owned cooperatively by the newspapers, sells its service to broadcasters. Through that system, and also informally, news passes freely from one medium to another. A newspaper reporter's story or quotation will be selected by a TV reporter and combined with a fresh comment from a public official to become the basis for another story in another newspaper; a few hours later it may be the subject for a column of comment or a broadcast commentary by another journalist.

McLuhan — who based much of his work on the pioneering media studies of the economist Harold INNIS — believed that media reshape not only our perceptions but our actions. People seeking publicity often create "media events" that lend themselves to coverage by TV and to a lesser extent by newspapers and radio. Campaign tours by political leaders are arranged to provide interesting TV pictures; a visit to a steel plant, for instance, is not only an attempt to solicit the steelworkers' votes but also a way of obtaining precious TV time by putting the candidate against an arresting background. A prime minister's press conference was a small, almost private affair in the years before TV; now it is normally a public performance. The most dramatic event of recent decades in Canada, the OCTOBER CRISIS of 1970 in Montréal, was a media event. The kidnappers set the tone by demanding that their separatist manifesto be read on TV and by regularly communicating with the police through dispatches sent to radio stations. In response, the WAR MEASURES ACT, imposed by the federal government, effectively blacked out the kidnappers' media activities and brought PUBLIC OPINION under the control of the authorities. One political scientist has said that the October Crisis could be seen as a battle for the temporary control of the communications systems in Québec.

Canadians receive most of their news from TV or radio, and, for both owners and journalists, broadcasting has become more profitable than newspaper and BOOK PUBLISHING. Newspapers, having lost much of their advertising revenue to the broadcasters, are increasingly subject to merger or elimination. Nevertheless, they remain at the centre of the communications web in most communities and in both national language groups because they employ more reporters than broadcasting networks and publish more news and comment. Newspapers provide broadcasting with information and a sense of what is important. Newspapers, not broadcasting networks, set the agenda for discussion of public affairs; in particular the GLOBE AND MAIL in English Canada and *Le* DEVOIR in French Canada play this role. Broadcasting, though it has drawn away much of the economic power of the newspapers, has magnified their role as shapers of opinion, a role the newspapers have played since colonial days.

One result of these media interconnections is the development of waves of opinion. A politician may be universally admired in the media one year, reviled the next, and then highly respected a few years later. Just such a series of transformations happened in the public career of Robert STANFIELD between his elevation to the leadership of the Progressive Conservatives in 1967 and his retirement in 1976. Public issues seem to rise and fall in the same way; for instance, ABORTION was held to be a crime in one decade and a human right in the next. In most cases the media reflect what they perceive to be public opinion and public interest, slightly and inevitably distorted by the people who staff the newspapers and broadcasting stations. The communications media sell fashions in thought and are themselves influenced by fashions. A popular broadcaster's intonation may be imitated by hundreds of newscasters, and a style of magazine writing may spread across the continent. There are times when the media seem dedicated to producing a pale sameness. But McLuhan has taught us to look at the technological development of the media for an understanding of their influence, and if we follow that course we see a process repeating itself throughout the communications media, an unexpected process of sophistication and refinement that works against the creation of a homogeneous mass society.

Each medium begins in a fairly basic way, with an attempt to appeal to everyone. The early promoters treat the medium almost as a toy. Later, as the techniques develop and potential audiences are explored by both entrepreneurs and imaginative public servants, it becomes possible to reach smaller, more select audiences and to appeal to specialized tastes. Thus, films began with a few studios in America and Europe trying to gain dominance; later, as the processes became widely available, scores of countries and hundreds of companies developed the ability to make films, often great films. Phonograph records first became popular under the control of a few companies that dictated tastes everywhere; but with the rise of the economical LP record, beginning in 1948, the process of differentiation began and thousands of companies sprang up to serve disparate minority markets. Radio was born as a means of broadcasting popular music and later emerged as a way of conveying sophisticated documentaries, imaginative dramas and music on a specialized level. Something similar has happened to magazines recently: there are now perhaps 10 times as many magazines in Canada as there were in 1960, most of them catering to specialized tastes. In the late 1970s television began to fit into this historic pattern. With the rise of CABLE TELEVISION and PAY TELEVISION, "narrowcasting" (as opposed to broadcasting) became the object of many professionals searching for small, select, dedicated audiences. Only daily newspapers have moved in the opposite direction, growing fewer in number and broader in appeal despite their adoption of advanced techniques such as computerized typesetting. In the early 1980s it seemed that written JOURNALISM might find a new form through videotext systems of interactive TV. With videotext, the consumer calls up a text on a screen (sometimes with still pictures) by switching buttons. The text may be an advertisement, a weather report, an article from an encyclopedia, a news item or anything that can be reduced to words and pictures. This produces a new form of "publishing." Many countries are experimenting with various videotext systems, including TELIDON, the Canadian system created at the Dept of Communications in Ottawa during the 1970s.

As these media developed through the first 80 years of this century, Canada's experience was in some ways identical to that of other countries. Collecting hundreds of Mozart records was no more or less rewarding in Vancouver than in Melbourne or Vienna. But in many other ways Canada is a special case, because Canada exists next door to the most powerful and innovative communications system in the world. American mass culture dominates the Canadian imagination. Most countries regulate imported culture through quotas on FILM and broadcasting, but Canada has set up few barriers and even those have been ineffective. In 1932, when Prime Minister R.B. Bennett introduced legislation that created public broadcasting, he declared in Parliament: "This country must be assured of complete Canadian control of broadcasting from Canadian sources, free from foreign interference or influence. Without such control radio broadcasting can never become a great agency for the communication of matters of national concern and for the diffusion of national thought and ideals, and without such control it can never be the agency by which national consciousness may be fostered and sustained and national unity still further strengthened." Since then, most federal governments and several royal commissions have reaffirmed these views, but with only modest effect. News and public affairs programs on TV have focused the concern of all Canadians on national public issues, but in most other ways our media have lived wanly in the American shadow. As a result, mass communications have been the ground on which some of the most important battles of Canadian sovereignty have been fought. Only occasionally have the forces of national culture been triumphant, as in the creation of French and English TV and radio networks by the CBC or the 1975 legislation which prevented American magazines from establishing Canadian subsidiary editions. One major reason is cost. Canada provides a small market split into 2 language groups: in broadcasting, as with paperback books and magazines and many other fields, Canadians have found it cheaper and more convenient to import what they view or read. Another reason is the ongoing struggle between private and public interests. As a general rule, private interests have encouraged the cultural Americanization of Canada, on the grounds that it is more profitable to resell American films, TV shows and records than to make them in Canada and assume an enormous risk.

The forces representing public interest (the CBC, the federal regulatory agencies and the provincial TV networks) have been sharply divided over the issue of regional interests versus national unity. The latter has implied increasing centralization, a Toronto-dominated system of production, similar to the growing power of federal agencies in Ottawa. Regionalists contend that national media will extinguish the centres of provincial vitality and expression. Centralists argue that Canada's population can support no more than 2 first-class production centres, in Toronto and Montréal, and will be lucky if these cities can produce material good enough to meet foreign competition.

Canadian nationalism became a more powerful force in the 1960s and the 1970s than at any point since the 1920s, and the appreciation and development of national and regional Canadian culture became a public issue. This interest has led to fundamental changes in publishing and the performing arts, but has made no great impression on TV because a more powerful counterforce was at work: cable TV. Bringing American stations to a majority of viewers, cable effectively put Canadian broadcasters in a minority in their own country, pushing Canadian TELEVISION DRAMA and entertainment out to the edge of the country's consciousness. In a period when mass communications in Canada might have flourished, they found themselves more overshadowed than ever. The effect of cable was marked even in Québec. The first 2 decades of TV had tended to strengthen Québec identity by producing a generation of French Canadian TV writers, stars and commentators — the most famous being René LÉVESQUE, a commentator on Radio-Canada in the 1950s who became provincial premier in 1976. But when cable made a broad spectrum of American stations available, French Canadians in considerable numbers began viewing them, and TV presented yet another threat to the survival of the French language (*see* COMMUNICATIONS IN QUÉBEC). In mass communications, every fresh development brings social problems as well as benefits. ROBERT FULFORD

Reading: P. Hindley, G. Martin and J. McNulty, eds, *The Tangled Net* (1977); P. Rutherford, *The Making of the Canadian Media* (1978); B. Singer, ed, *Communications in Canadian Society* (1972).

Communications, Department of, was established by the Department of Communications Act in 1969. The minister is responsible for fostering the orderly operation and development of communications in Canada. The powers and functions of the minister extend to TELECOMMUNICATIONS, national communications policy, BROADCASTING policy, radio and radar research and actions necessary to secure the international rights of Canada in communications. The Space Sector is responsible for SATELLITE COMMUNICATIONS and support of the Canadian space industry. The CANADIAN BROADCASTING CORPORATION, CANADIAN FILM DEVELOPMENT CORPORATION, NATIONAL ARTS CENTRE Corporation, NATIONAL LIBRARY, NATIONAL MUSEUMS OF CANADA, SOCIAL SCIENCES AND HUMANITIES RESEARCH COUNCIL, CANADA COUNCIL, NATIONAL FILM BOARD, the Space Program, Teleglobe Canada, Telesat Canada and the CANADIAN RADIO-TELEVISION AND TELECOMMUNICATIONS COMMISSION report to Parliament through the minister. The department's 1984-85 budget was $266 million.

Communications in Québec What is distinctive about COMMUNICATIONS in Québec is the existence of 2, often competing, media serving different cultures and, above all, the ways in which francophone media have expressed or reinforced the character of French Canada. The development of communications in Québec is associated with an underlying constitutional conflict between Québec City and Ottawa. The government of Québec, basing its position on jurisdiction over language, education and culture, claims complete authority for communications in the province. The scope of the political battle can only be fully understood when viewed in terms of the linguistic and cultural situation of Québec in N America. The evolution of the media is intimately linked with the process of modernization that has been underway in Québec since WWII, particularly the political and cultural upheavals of the 1960s and 1970s. The federal-provincial battle over communications began in 1929, the year in which the Aird Report was published, when the TASCHEREAU government adopted the first "law respecting broadcasting in this province." In 1931 subsequent Québec legislation concerning radio led to court action by the federal government, which won its case before the SUPREME COURT OF CANADA. Québec appealed to the Judicial Committee of the Privy Council in London, which in 1932 confirmed the verdict of the Supreme Court. The reasoning invoked in support of the federal position was based on an interpretation of paragraph 10 of Section 92 of the BNA Act which makes reference to the TELEGRAPH, the only modern method of communication in existence at the time of Confederation. Radio communication was likened to the telegraph in that radio waves could not easily be contained within the borders of a province (*see* BROADCASTING, RADIO AND TELEVISION).

Because the media are major instruments for promoting and broadcasting information, successive Québec governments have claimed responsibility for matters relating to cultural development. In 1945 Maurice DUPLESSIS adopted an "Act authorizing the creation of a provincial broadcasting service," but it was not until 1968 that Radio-Québec was founded. In 1972 the educational network of Radio-Québec offered several hours of programming on cable and in 1975 began broadcasting on UHF.

The JOHNSON government created Québec's Dept of Communications in 1969, and in 1972 the BOURASSA government broadened the mandate of the Régie des services publics (Public Service Board) to "the broadcasting, transmission and reception of sounds, images, signs, signals, data or messages by wire, cable, waves, or any electrical, electronic, magnetic, electromagnetic or optical means." The major issue was control of CABLE TELEVISION broadcasting, as the CRTC and the Régie both claimed authority for granting licences. In 1977 the Supreme Court of Canada ruled in favour of the federal government, granting it exclusive jurisdiction.

The birth of broadcasting in Montréal took place in 1919 with the inauguration of station XWA (later to become CFCF). In 1932 CKAC became the first French-language radio station. The advent of television and its rapid development in the 1950s helped pave the way for the QUIET REVOLUTION, in particular the program "Point de Mire," with host René LÉVESQUE. Francophone NEWSPAPERS, MAGAZINES, novelists and singers also contributed to the revolution (*see* POPULAR MUSIC). The francophone ADVERTISING industry, once little more than a translation service, after 1960 broke free from Anglo control to embrace the French Canadian milieu. The media drew inspiration from and encouraged the creative turmoil that marked all aspects of culture at the end of the Duplessis regime; certain radio and television programs were very successful (*see* RADIO DRAMA, FRENCH-LANGUAGE; RADIO PROGRAMMING; TELEVISION PROGRAMMING). In the early 1970s open-line radio programs became popular to a degree rarely equalled elsewhere. Novels adapted for television — the typical Québec formula for dramatic series — experienced a popularity that has not declined over the years (*see* TELEVISION DRAMA, FRENCH-LANGUAGE). Variety shows involving audience participation were also successful.

In 1983 Québec had 77 AM and 65 FM radio stations and 28 television stations — 13 affiliated with Radio-Canada (French- and English-language CBC), 6 with Télédiffuseurs Associés (TVA), 2 with Radio-Québec, 1 with CTV Television Network Ltd and 6 independent stations. In addition, there were 3 PAY-TELEVISION networks. In 1980 the print medium included 13 dailies, 26 provincial weeklies, 144 regional weeklies and nearly 50 newspapers for various ethnic communities.

Despite constant financing and distribution difficulties, Québec FILM directors have made significant contributions to the development of their art, particularly in what is known as *cinéma-vérité* or *cinéma-direct*. Several others are well known for their research in cinematography (*see also* FILM ANIMATION; FILM, DOCUMENTARY FILM, EXPERIMENTAL).

Since 1960 a series of original experiments have been made in Québec in which the media are used for educational, social and cultural purposes. Québec has earned an international reputation as a testing ground for social communications. In the early 1960s, as part of the work for the Bureau d'aménagement de l'est du Québec (BAEQ) and the Aménagement rural et développement agricole (ARDA), film documentaries were produced for use in group discussions. The NATIONAL FILM BOARD, especially in its "Challenge for Change" ("Société nouvelle") program, was active in Québec and across Canada in the late 1960s and early 1970s. Over the past few years le Groupe de recherches sociales has brought together the pioneers in *cinéma d'intervention* whose circle now includes video groups (*see* VIDEO ART). Their productions are used in various social movements.

In 1967-68 the Québec Dept of Education established a daring educational television pilot (TEVEC) in Saguenay-Lac St-Jean. Its success led to the introduction of an even larger and more ambitious program, Multi-Média, serving a number of regions in the province.

The 1970s saw the birth of several experiments in community media, the first of which was community television, the broadcasting by cable of programs that varied greatly in quantity and quality. Financing, recruitment and organizational problems, as well as battles over ideology, resulted in many of these cable groups closing down after a short period of operation. In addition, the Supreme Court's 1977 decision on cable broadcasting cooled the ardour of the Ministry of Communications and its enthusiasm for giving financial support to these experiments through its community media assistance program.

Community radio started more slowly, but is now growing rapidly. Sixteen such stations are in operation and every year new ones go on the air on the FM band. Less burdensome in financing and cost of operations, they fill gaps in local and regional information. The ARCQ, the association of community radio stations, organized the first world conference on community radio in Montréal in Aug 1983.

Québec is attempting to meet the challenges posed by the development of new COMMUNICATIONS TECHNOLOGY. The multiplication of available television channels is but one symptom of the danger of American cultural influences. The rapid expansion of cable broadcasting, COMPUTERS, OFFICE AUTOMATION systems and telematics requires prompt action on the part of Québecois wishing to develop a domestic software and hardware industry. As in the past, the small size of Québec's domestic market makes this task even more difficult. GAËTAN TREMBLAY

Reading: Government of Québec, *Québec: Mastercraftsman of its own Communications Policy* (1973); J.P. LaFrance and C. Gousse, eds, *La Télévision payante: Jeux et enjeux* (1982); Ministère des Communications, Gouvernement du Québec, *Le Québec et les communications: Un futur simple* (1983).

Communications in the North Communications have played a special role in the NORTH. Terrain, climate and distance made it difficult for northerners to communicate with each other or with southern Canada before the advent of electronic media. In traditional times, INUIT messages were passed through personal contact. Like other native peoples, Inuit had no written language when in the 16th century they encountered literate Europeans.

Early Interaction The early explorers trav-lled in ships and encountered Inuit only by hance. As whalers and traders entered the orth in the 19th century, they brought trade oods and technology which were given to native people in exchange for hunting and trapping. This required Inuit-non-native interacon, but there was little real communication.

In the late 1800s missionaries developed sysms for writing native languages (*see* CREE ALHABET). By 1910 probably 98% of the Inuit in e eastern Arctic could read and write their wn language, but because 3 different systems ere used for writing Inuktitut, the dialect and gional differences among Inuit in Canada ere reinforced. Few books were translated into uktitut, and since most Inuit did not read or rite English they could not participate in the conomic and social changes southern agencies rought to the North. The military and econom significance of the North encouraged the inoduction of electronic media.

Radio and Television Radio reached the North the late 1920s. Messages to and from southern anada no longer had to rely on annual supply nips. By the 1930s, agencies in the North used igh frequency radio for medical emergencies nd business, and broadcast radio kept them in ontact with the South. Because programs were English, early radio did little to encourage ommunication between Inuit and other Caadians. The first Inuit-language broadcast ocurred in 1960 and, by 1972, only 17% of CBC orthern Service shortwave programming was Inuktitut (*see* BROADCASTING, RADIO AND TELESION). Early television service in the North ollowed the same pattern.

In 1967 television programming was introuced to the first of 17 communities in the westrn Arctic through delayed transmission of ideotapes in 4-hour packages. The Telesat anada Act of 1969 supported satellite deelopment in Canada to deliver TELEPHONE and BC television service to remote areas of the ountry, including the North (*see* SATELLITE COMUNICATIONS). Videotape service was extended to e eastern Arctic community of Frobisher Bay 1972. The same year, Canada launched the nik A satellite, which in 1973 began to transit telephone, radio and television services to e North. In 1974 CBC established the Accelerted Coverage Plan to bring broadcasting serices to communities of 500 or more as funds ecame available.

Some Inuit were enthusiastic about television; thers joined Canadians concerned about the mpact this compelling new medium would ave on their language and culture (*see* NATIVE EOPLE, COMMUNICATIONS). The northern videope service did not include native programs. In 972 the NATIONAL FILM BOARD established the rst of 2 film workshops in Baffin I. The Froisher Bay workshop developed into Nunatsiakiut Native Communications Society in 1975. hrough this society, Inuit began to produce rograms for CBC television. Before 1982, howver, CBC carried less than one hour a week of nuktitut programming, none of which could e broadcast live from the North.

It was clear that with electronic media, northrners could more readily communicate with ach other and with the South, but native people ere not benefiting fully from this potential. ew projects encouraged their participation.

Northern Satellite Experiments In 1976 Canda launched the first of 2 experimental satellite rograms to test the uses of new COMMUNICATIONS ECHNOLOGY. Interactive satellites brought teleealth and tele-education to remote northern ommunities. Inuit in northern Québec used the Iermes satellite and the earlier Anik A system o establish an interactive radio network among communities. People in these communities ould telephone their radio stations to have their uestions or comments broadcast over the network. In 1978 the Anik B satellite was launched and was used by Inuit in northern Québec and the NWT for interactive experiments including television broadcasting. In each of these regions the Anik B satellite linked 6 communities to form a small television network. Television was transmitted from only one community in each region, but people in all 6 communities could speak with each other and their messages were broadcast over the network.

These experiments led to the formation of the Inuit Broadcasting Corporation in the summer of 1981. IBC broadcasts several hours of Inuit-language television each week, including "live" northern television programming.

Native initiatives in broadcasting were further encouraged by the 1980 CANADIAN RADIO-TELEVISION AND TELECOMMUNICATIONS COMMISSION report of the Committee on the Extension of Service to Northern and Remote Communities. The report established the first framework for northern communication policy in Canada, and it stressed native participation in northern broadcasting.

Recent Developments The 1980s have brought many new communication services to the North. By 1981 all northern communities had satellite telephone service, and in 1983 the last of 57 Inuit communities received CBC television. All communities receive CBC radio and most have community radio stations through programs sponsored by CBC, by provincial or territorial governments, or by the northern native communications societies. At least 11 Inuit communities have facilities to produce community television and more use CBC equipment for community broadcasting. Broadcasting services other than CBC's are available in the North through Cancom, a package of southern television and radio channels which the CRTC approved in 1981. Many northern communities have receiver dishes and get television programming directly from American satellites, and video playback units are common in northern homes. Indians in the western Arctic and the Yukon have established native broadcasting networks, and in northern Saskatchewan and the Yukon native people have experimented with TELIDON, a new type of interactive technology.

Many native northerners still do not speak or read English. The Northern Native Broadcast Access Program, established in 1983, provides the facilities for native people to receive and send information in their own languages. With northern communication policy and programs, electronic media have brought northerners closer together, have assured their communication with other Canadians, and have encouraged native participation in changes taking place in the North.

GAIL VALASKAKIS

Reading: R. Collins, *A Voice from Afar: The History of Telecommunications in Canada* (1977); "Communications in the Far North: Ten Studies," *Journal of Communications* 27 (autumn 1977); CRTC, "The 1980's: A Decade of Diversity: Broadcasting, Satellite and Pay-TV. Report of the Committee on the Extension of Service to Northern and Remote Communities" (1980); Dept of Communications, Telecommission, Special Study 8(c), *Northern Communications* (1971); N.H.H. Graburn, *Eskimos without Igloos* (1969); P. Pitseolak and D. Eber, *People from our Side* (1975); Gail Valaskakis, "Communication and Control in the Canadian North," in B. Singer, ed, *Communications in Canadian Society* (1983).

Communications Law encompasses not only the actions of the courts in interpreting statutes governing COMMUNICATIONS but also those by federal and provincial authorities that regulate radio, television, CABLE TELEVISION, some telephone companies and some telecommunication services. In contrast with the US, administrative decisions by the agencies are usually the focus of study. Courts have ruled on questions of jurisdiction, on whether, eg, federal or provincial authorities should license particular communication services. Courts have also acted to delimit the scope and powers of regulatory authorities, when licensed operators have contravened regulations, and in several appeals of CRTC decisions.

In 1984 both broadcasting and some TELECOMMUNICATIONS are regulated by the CANADIAN RADIO-TELEVISION AND TELECOMMUNICATIONS COMMISSION, although different legislative mandates govern the CRTC's actions in each sphere of activity. Some services and companies (Telesat Canada) have their own legislative mandates as well.

Broadcasting is defined as any service involving the transmission or reception of programs intended for a general audience and distributed, in part at least, by means of hertzian waves. Thus, although cable television is delivered by wire to homes, it is regulated as broadcasting because the signals delivered were originally broadcast and were received via hertzian waves by the cable company. Cable television is also regulated as broadcasting because broadcasting is regulated as a single system, with the effects of any action taken by a licensee or the agencies considered in terms of the system as a whole. Any new service might not be licensed if, for example, the CRTC believed that it would affect broadcast services negatively or cause serious disruption of existing programming. NEWSPAPERS are not regulated, although broadcast licensing decisions now take into account whether the applicant also owns a daily newspaper serving the same area (*see* MEDIA OWNERSHIP). FILMS are not regulated except by provincial authorities with respect to classification and possible CENSORSHIP of their content.

The mandate and powers of the CRTC, as laid down in the Broadcasting Act (1968), set the framework for the granting of broadcast licences, the supervision of cable rates and changes in ownership or control, and the quality of programming. The CRTC is empowered to "strengthen and enrich the social, cultural and economic fabric of Canada" and to ensure that the broadcasting system is predominantly Canadian. Thus, the CRTC issues, and periodically reviews, Canadian content regulations and, with the support of an order-in-council on ownership first promulgated in 1969, has ensured that the private broadcasting companies are effectively owned and controlled by Canadians.

The CRTC has power to investigate program content to ensure that high standards are met, but has no control over the content of individual programs. Instead, the Act calls for broadcasting to be "varied and comprehensive" and for programming to reflect a diversity of viewpoints. A number of policies are designed to facilitate this diversity, as, for example, the FM policy which calls for only noncompeting FM radio services to be licensed in an area. For many years the CRTC did not license religious stations and currently will only license those that reflect a diversity of religious viewpoints (*see* RADIO PROGRAMMING; TELEVISION PROGRAMMING).

Except in the case of political broadcasts before an election, Canada has no equivalent to an "equal time provision" or "first amendment right" of free speech, although the impact of the Charter of Rights on broadcasting is still to be determined. The CRTC has held several inquiries to ensure that the CBC provides reasonably balanced programming, that controversial issues are covered fairly, that hot-line programmers provide basic information to facilitate informed discussion among their listeners, and that abusive comment is not permitted in the name of free speech. Broadcasters are responsible for their promise of performance and for all the content of their programming. The CRTC may also attach conditions on licences, which are enforceable through the courts.

Individuals who feel wronged may appeal to

the station, network or the CRTC, who may decide to review the situation in a special public hearing or when a licence is being renewed, or simply to act as mediator in a dispute. Broadcast media do not fall under the terms of reference of the federal Human Rights Commission. Rather, the CRTC and the public rely upon persuasion and industry self-regulation to curb abuses and correct problems.

The CRTC is generally master of its own procedures and need not follow courtlike rules or rely on precedents in making decisions. Notice of applications being considered and of policies or new regulations is given in the *Canada Gazette* and, often, in local newspapers or broadcasts. Unless the CRTC specifies otherwise, all information must be made available publicly by the applicant and through the CRTC's regional offices. Public hearings may be scheduled on the merits of a policy or applications. (Public hearings must be scheduled in broadcasting only when consideration is of licence revocation.) Members of the public are invited to intervene, to submit comments in writing and possibly discuss them at a hearing, in support, opposition or simply with regard to any application. Rules of procedure are available from any CRTC office. Groups may also comment on general matters by making a representation to the CRTC, after requesting permission to appear at least 3 days in advance of a hearing.

The CRTC publishes all its decisions, which may be appealed to the federal Cabinet within 60 days. The Cabinet can issue policy directives to the CRTC or request a re-examination of any CRTC decision. Cabinet decisions cannot be appealed and few CRTC decisions have been successfully appealed to the courts to date. However, questions of the CRTC's right to license particular services or facilities are increasingly being addressed by the courts when the CRTC has sought an injunction against an unlicensed operator or service.

Since 1976 the CRTC has regulated some telephone companies (though not, for example, the prairie telephone companies or some in the Maritimes) and telecommunications services offered by those companies or operating interprovincially (*see* TELEPHONES). The Canadian Radio-television and Telecommunications Act incorporates sections of the Railway Act and the National Transportation Act and empowers the CRTC to hold hearings, issue orders, and make regulations. The CRTC must ensure that the rates charged for federally regulated telecommunication services are "just and reasonable" and that any paying user of these services is granted access without discrimination. Telecommunication carriers are not legally responsible for the content of messages carried over their services.

To ensure that the provisions of the Act are met, the CRTC has held a number of special inquiries in telecommunications; eg, the CRTC, examined the methods by which costs are allocated within the operation of major telephone companies, as those costs are reflected in the rates charged for specific services. In general, the CRTC has sought to promote competitive opportunities for new providers of communication services, except for basic SATELLITE and telephone local and long-distance calling facilities. To the extent permitted by its mandate, the CRTC may consider the needs of specially affected groups within the population (eg, the disabled or residents in the North) when making telecommunication decisions.

The minister of communications issues technical construction-operating certificates for both broadcast and telecommunication services, although the CRTC receives comments on the quality of service and may consider them at a regional hearing or when an application for a change in rates is being decided. In telecommunications, public hearings are mandatory and those involved are often represented by legal counsel. Hearings are usually preceded by an exchange of questions ("interrogatories") and demands for information ("particulars"), and informal meetings may be scheduled. All information submitted by the applicants must be made public, unless the CRTC decides it is contrary to the public interest to do so. Participation by the public is welcomed and the CRTC may award costs against an applicant to the intervenors if their intervention is considered substantive in the decision.

Provincial governments regulate telephone companies whose operations are solely within their borders unless the charter of the companies involved specifies otherwise. Most provinces are active in EDUCATIONAL BROADCASTING, usually through an educational broadcasting authority, although educational broadcast stations are provided for but must also be licensed by the CRTC. Provincial governments have been seeking a more active role in communications for many years, through federal-provincial negotiations and agreements, the courts and, in some provinces, by promulgating and implementing legislation to establish regulatory authority over intraprovincial and/or nonbroadcast PAY TELEVISION (*see* COMMUNICATIONS IN QUÉBEC).

History Radio stations have been licensed since 1919, but comprehensive government involvement in broadcasting began with the Canadian Radio Broadcasting Act in 1932. Before that, in 1929, the Aird Commission had recommended that Canada establish a single, national, publicly owned system. The commission was responding to the expansion of American networks into Canada through affiliation with Canadian stations, to reception problems, to the scarcity of available frequencies for Canadian stations, and to charges of influence peddling in licensing. As well, in 1932, the Privy Council awarded the federal government exclusive jurisdiction over broadcasting and a special parliamentary committee recommended that private stations be permitted to continue offering local services. Both the CRBC Act and the Canadian Broadcasting Act passed in 1936 permitted private broadcasting, but after 1936 the Canadian Radio Broadcasting Commission was disbanded and the CBC became both the national service and the regulator of the private sector.

Change came after 2 royal commissions; Massey in 1949 and Fowler reporting in 1957, reiterated the concerns and principles of the Aird Report. In response to growing influence of the private sector and the election of a Conservative government in 1957, the Broadcasting Act in 1958 set up a separate regulatory agency for private stations. It was replaced by the Broadcasting Act of 1968, which brought all stations, public and private, under a single regulatory authority. In both the 1958 and 1968 Acts the public-system needs were granted priority, but, with serious underfunding of the CBC and the development of new services (eg, cable) by an increasingly powerful private sector, public broadcasting, once the cornerstone of Canadian broadcasting, has become one component in a mix of services all regulated by the CRTC.

New technological developments and communication services have thrown communication law and regulation into flux. Problems arise when these new services cannot be classified easily as either broadcasting or telecommunication, as intra- or interprovincial, or as legitimately subject to regulation or not. Pay television, satellite receiving stations ("dishes"), nonprogramming or broadcast-originated services on cable, and new data transmission or information services offered by telephone or cable companies' new interconnections have all been the subject of controversy and of actions by the courts with respect to jurisdiction or the licensing powers of the CRTC. LIORA SALTER

Communications Technology refers to th variety of techniques, tools and methods that a used to facilitate communication. In its larg sense it includes language, gestures, dress, cod of behaviour and religious rituals, as well as a tistic and cultural traditions. It encompasses de velopments such as eye-glasses, hearing aic and artificial limbs which have enhanced th ability of many individuals to communicat and includes smoke and flag signals, pape quill pens and lead pencils, all of which hav profoundly influenced the evolution of soc eties. In technologically advanced countries, th term generally refers more narrowly to thos electronic techniques that have permitted com munication to overcome the constraints of tim and distance.

General Characteristics The TELEGRAPH (183 and telephone (1876) permitted communicatio by wire over long-distances almost instanta neously, a vast improvement over the earlie methods of rail, ship and pony express (*see* TEL PHONES). Communication by the wirele telegraph (1895), shortwave radio (1926) an then more reliable high-frequency microwav radio (1946) overcame the physical constraint c connecting every point by wire or cable. Micro wave provided larger capacity communicatio channels for transmitting television signals, an set the stage for the development of satellit and space communication (1957). Now commu nication signals can be sent around the worl instantaneously.

The thrust of communications technology i recent years has been to expand both the capa bilities and the capacity of the facilities used t communicate. The communication system no can carry different types of messages, includin not only telegraph, voice, and television signal but also facsimile, video and computer data sig nals. Off-air broadcasting has been supple mented by CABLE TELEVISION and direct broadca satellites as well as video cassettes and recorder

Cellular radio is expanding the possibiliti for mobile communication within cities. Tele phone companies are upgrading their voice tele phone systems with digital switching and fibre optics cable to facilitate computer dat processing over telecommunication network with greatly expanded capacity. Some exper predict that by the year 2000 there will be mo data than voice communication on the tele communication system. Cable-television com panies are upgrading their distribution cabl to permit data transfer and even limited voic communication. Business and residential sub scribers may now select from a wide variety c computer communication terminals that can b used to obtain access to computer databanks. I addition, the quality of equipment used t record and transmit visual images (film, tele vision) and sound (music, FM radio) continu to improve at a steady pace, as do the instru ments employed by the artistic community.

Canada always has had a unique associatio with communications technology, perhaps be cause of its relatively small population dis tributed over a vast geographical area. Effectiv COMMUNICATIONS networks were soon recognize as essential to the establishment and mainte nance of Canada as a nation. Alexander Gra ham BELL made the world's first long distanc telephone call in Canada, and telephone system spread from coast to coast. In the 1960s an 1970s, Canada established cable-television sys tems more rapidly than other nations. It was th first to establish a national digital data networ for computer users and a commercial domesti satellite system (*see* SATELLITE, ARTIFICIAL). It ha pioneered in the development of a videotex ter minal, TELIDON, especially designed for COMPUTE COMMUNICATIONS, and in the field of telemedicin — the transmission of computerized images an data for long-distance diagnoses and treatmen

1984 Canada was the only nation employing direct broadcast satellite system (*see* SATELLITE COMMUNICATIONS). The federal government has promoted and subsidized the rapid introduction new communication and information processing technologies, including OFFICE AUTOMATION, as a means of speeding Canada's entry to the INFORMATION SOCIETY.

Institutional Basis It has long been recognized that advanced communication techniques can provide enormous military, political and economic advantages. Information is power, and communication techniques have had an important influence on the distribution of power within societies, as well as the rise and fall of empires, as the studies of Canadian scholar Harold INNIS have shown. The major portion of research and development in communications technology has been financed by the military budgets of the major powers. Current military concerns include data encryption to protect against the interception of signals, techniques for more precise satellite surveillance, communication control over weapons in space, and techniques for jamming enemy communications.

Today, for Canada and other technologically developed nations, communications technology is the cornerstone of an industrial strategy seeking advantage in the competitive world economy. It is hoped that advanced communications technology not only will improve the efficiency of the Canadian economy generally, but also will provide Canada with substantial international sales of communication equipment, services, and management consulting, particularly in developing countries.

The development, application and use of modern communications technology (as well as other technologies) is the result of the expenditure of vast amounts of money on research and development, on the learning of specialized skills, on equipment manufacturing, system installation and operation, and ultimately the marketing of communication services. It reflects major resource allocation decisions, taken by leading government and industrial institutions in Canada and other countries, to give communications technology a high priority and a particular direction.

Promises and Problems for Canada The specific technologies adopted have significant influences on the way many Canadians live and work. Inevitably new opportunities are opened for some Canadians, but traditional ways of doing things are rendered impossible for others. Upgrading the TELECOMMUNICATIONS system to computer standards permits enhanced information service, but the increased costs may force low-income people to disconnect from the system, thereby losing basic telephone service. Computerized information banks provide access to more and better information for government agencies, large corporations and certain professions at a cost they are willing to pay. But with the availability of information banks, the collections and services of public LIBRARIES are already being reduced. Satellites have enabled telemedical services to save the lives of Canadians in the North; but they have also brought an endless flow of southern television that has contributed to the disruption of native life-styles (*see* COMMUNICATIONS IN THE NORTH). The automated office portends efficiency in information processing, but it displaces skilled office workers, creates some dull, monotonous jobs, and for some workers contributes to health problems.

Unfortunately, all the effects of technology cannot be foreseen in advance, and in the competition to obtain the advantages of new technologies, the potential disadvantages and problems of adjustment are too often ignored and sometimes suppressed. It is already apparent that the transition to the information society will not be an easy one. A host of economic, social and political problems will have to be addressed with farsighted policies.

Pioneering in communications technology has been a mixed blessing for Canada. The introduction of cable television and direct broadcast satellite facilities has dramatically expanded the choice of US television programs available to Canadians, but it also has had detrimental financial effects on Canadian television and FILM production and has reduced opportunities for Canadian artistic and cultural expression through its own mass media. Several governmental commissions (most recently the Applebaum-Hébert Commission, 1983) have been created in an attempt to suggest government policies that will overcome these problems (*see* TELEVISION PROGRAMMING).

Similarly, promotion of the computer communications technologies in anticipation of the information society is creating a network of physical facilities over which Canadian information can be transmitted efficiently out of Canada, and Canadians can obtain ready access to information banks outside Canada. Credit, medical and tax information about Canadians is stored in computers outside Canada, as is specialized information about the location and value of Canada's national resources, and many other types of information — some trivial, some crucial.

This compilation has created a series of intergovernmental problems relating to the terms and conditions of trans-border data flow, including the applicability of national laws, rights of access and privacy, as well as implications for the Canadian economy and Canadian sovereignty. Canada has a large and growing balance-of-payments deficit in the communication/information sector ($4.5 billion in 1981). There is some concern that Canadian government policies may be promoting new communications technologies too rapidly and with an imbalanced emphasis on the physical facilities rather than the communication content that is transmitted over them.

Global Implications Historically the distribution of benefits of communications technology throughout the world has been unbalanced. Most modern communications technology requires the use of the radio spectrum, and synchronous satellites require orbital slots 35 900 km over the equator. These are limited public resources, common to all nations. Yet the most desirable frequencies and orbital slots have been taken by the technologically advanced nations on a first come, first served basis. The vast majority of the world's population does not have access to a telephone, and 75% of the world's telephones are found in only 8 of the world's 175 countries. This is a far cry from the "global village" ideal envisioned by Marshall MCLUHAN.

By overcoming the limits of time and space, and expanding enormously the volume and variety of information that can be transmitted and processed, the new communications technologies provide substantial benefits and economies to very large users with substantial budgets for specialized computer communication equipment. The new technologies permit an extension of the bounds of administrative control that is possible and offer increased efficiency in large centralized organization. Perhaps the principal beneficiaries will be transnational corporations, that will be able to expand their scope, enlarge their markets, and transfer financial resources instantaneously around the world. In many countries, especially Third World countries, this development may be seen as a threat to domestic production and employment, to national sovereignty and local cultures. Inasmuch as 25% of the world's adult population (and 95% in some countries) has never had an opportunity to learn to read and write, the most important communications technology for many countries might well be pencil, paper and native language books and teachers.

Communications technology opens new opportunities and inevitably creates new problems. The new techniques have the capability to help in making the world a safer place, in solving political and economic problems, and in permitting a more informed democratic participation in society. Alternatively, they can help create a fragmented and disoriented society of passive observers with access to an endless supply of facts but little knowledge or wisdom, and helplessly vulnerable to instant destruction. The balance will be struck by the political, military, economic and social policies that emanate from the dominant institutions that influence Canadian society and the larger world community.

WILLIAM H. MELODY

Reading: Dept of Communications, "The Future of Communications Technology," Telecommission Study 4(a) (1971); Economic Council of Canada, *The Bottom Line: Technology, Trade and Income Growth* (1983); H.A. Innis, *The Bias of Communication* (1951); B. Maddox, "The Born-Again Technology," *The Economist*, 22 Aug 1981; W.H. Melody, "Development of the Communication and Information Industries: Impact on Social Structures," UNESCO (1983); Ministry of State for Science and Technology, *The Government of Canada's Support for Technology Development* (1983).

Communist Party of Canada was founded in Guelph, Ont, in 1921. Because the War Measures Act was still in force, the party was publicly inaugurated in 1922 in Toronto as the Workers' Party. The Communist Party of Canada (CP) became a legal party in 1924. Banned in 1939 it reformed for a time as the Labour Progressive Party (LPP). The CP was formed from those members of 3 Marxist socialist parties who accepted the strict rules and principles outlined as conditions for membership in the Communist International (CI), especially the one stating that all decisions taken by affiliated parties had to be approved by CI headquarters and that all CI decisions were binding on member units.

Throughout the 1920s and 1930s the police, acting under a Criminal Code amendment (s98), now repealed, against "unlawful associations," harassed the party, broke up meetings, dispersed audiences, raided party offices, confiscated literature and arrested activists. Hundreds of foreign-born suspected communists were deported. After the WINNIPEG GENERAL STRIKE, demands for COLLECTIVE BARGAINING rights were frequently denounced as communist inspired. The PADLOCK ACT (Québec, 1937) gave the provincial attorney general authority to padlock any house and evict the occupants if he believed it was being used to propagate communism.

Many communists became leaders and organizers of important trade unions and were instrumental in creating the Congress of Industrial Organizations (CIO) in Canada. But in 1940 the CIO merged with the All Canadian Congress of Labour to form the CANADIAN CONGRESS OF LABOUR (CCL) and the communists were gradually expelled. During the 1930s the communists were also responsible for initiating the ON TO OTTAWA TREK of the single unemployed, for a Canadian contingent to the Spanish Civil War (MACKENZIE-PAPINEAU BATTALION) and for the Canadian Youth Congress. The communists have elected a number of members to municipal bodies, but only 3 to provincial legislatures (Manitoba, 1936; Ontario, 1943) and one, Fred Rose (later convicted of conspiracy in the GOUZENKO case), to the House of Commons. Since 1954 the party has retained only aldermanic seats (Winnipeg, Vancouver). In the 1950s and 1960s revelations about Stalin, the Soviet Union's imperialist policies and the Sino-Soviet tensions split the party, and many members, including several top leaders, quit over what they considered continued uncritical support for the Soviet Union.

NORMAN PENNER

Community There are 2 basic ideas embedded in the concept of "community." One is concerned with order and consensus and the other with locale. The second report of the Task Force on CANADIAN UNITY (1979) stated that "a community is a group of persons joined together by a consciousness of the characteristics they have in common ... and by a consciousness of the interests they share." Any given human group will exhibit such a consciousness to one degree or another, be it a local sports club, a group of scientists with a special interest, an ethnic group, or an age group. On the other hand, community studies as such usually focus on places — hamlets, villages, towns, cities — as the unit of analysis. Everett Hughes's *French Canada in Transition* (1939), John Bennett's *Northern Plainsmen* (1969) and John Jackson's *Community and Conflict* (1975), to name a few of the many studies of local settings in Canada, all deal with a particular locale. An American sociologist, Jessie Bernard, referred to these 2 concepts of community as "community" and "the community." The first denotes shared values, interests and a common sense of identity; the second denotes places and the activities therein, or locale. Indeed, it has been said that "the term settlement might serve as well as the term community."

Although the 2 concepts are easily distinguished from each other, a problem arises when the latter is defined in terms of the former. If "the community" is defined as shared values, interests and identity, as is often the case, then it would be difficult to find a locale or settlement that conformed to these criteria. Any given locale is as likely as not to exhibit within its boundaries harmony and disharmony, conflict and consensus, order and disorder as various social groupings struggle over resources. The idea of "community" is therefore better retained as an empirical question in relation to particular communities as locale, or to "the community." Westhues and Sinclair's *Village in Crisis* (1974), a study of conflict over development plans in an Ontario town, Gold's *St. Pascal*, a study of changing elites in a Québec town, and Clairmont and Magill's *Africville* (1974), a study of a land development crisis in Halifax, address the issue of conflict within a particular locale — conflicts which are rooted in differing, not common, values and interests.

The tendency to confuse the 2 ways of defining the concept has its origins in earlier sociological studies that stressed the broad historical changes occurring in Western societies as the growth of capitalism and its concomitant processes of rapid urbanization and INDUSTRIALIZATION gradually transformed human relations into commodity relations. The change from person-centered to commodity-centered human relations is part of the transformation of human labour into a commodity to be bought and sold in the marketplace (*see* WORK). This transformation was a classic theme in 19th- and early 20th-century sociology. Exemplary among those who wrote on this theme was Ferdinand Tönnies. His 1887 essay, *Gemeinschaft (Community) and Gesellschaft (Association): A Treatise on Communism and Socialism as Empirical Forms of Culture*, drew attention to this shift in the quality of human relations. Tönnies was writing about communities in the sense of a particular quality of human relations which permeated all activities and social groups, a quality which was disintegrating in the wake of capitalism. The confusion arose when sociologists later reduced this general historical thesis to a definition of communities as settlements, thereby associating a particular quality of human relations, which may or may not be present in any given group, with human settlements as such.

For the most part the confusion has been resolved or, at worst, put aside. Over the past 20 years, Canadian community studies have followed one of 2 routes: network analysis or continuing studies of locale. Regarding the first, the Centre for Urban and Community Studies and the Sociology Department at University of Toronto have developed network analysis into a highly sophisticated tool for describing and understanding human interaction at the local level by analysing the bonds among persons relative to the positions and roles they occupy in particular social settings. Their findings demonstrate that "community" is still very much part of the everyday experiences of people in urban centres.

In the continuing studies of locale, the emphasis is on the fate of particular settlements in relation to the political economy of regions and of Canada as a whole. Patricia Marchak's *Green Gold* (1983) studies the effects of decisions made by multinational corporations in BC's forest industry on the everyday lives of people in 2 resource-based settlements. Carle Zimmerman and Gary Moneo's *The Prairie Community System* (1970) examines different types of western settlements in relation to the overall organization of the West to meet the interests of central Canadian capital.

There is perhaps a third route, one that is as yet underdeveloped but is present in various studies. It is at the local level, in "the community," where most people live out their daily lives — go to school, raise families, work, join associations, attend religious ceremonies — forming networks with others based on common values and interests (communities in the first sense). In the formation of such networks, be they based on friendship, kinship or workplace, there exists a potential for collective action, for mounting resistance and opposition to the overwhelming forces of individualization. This kind of activity, which takes the form of self-determination and self-organization, is not new to Canadian life. Ralph Matthews considers this issue in his study of 3 settlements in Newfoundland, where he found resistance based on "community" to the plans of government policymakers. The potential to oppose the impositions of public and private corporations on local life has been referred to as "emancipatory practices" by Marcel Rioux, a University of Montréal sociologist. "The community" as a base for emancipatory practices is a relatively unexplored route in the field of community studies, but one which may be pursued.

JOHN D. JACKSON

Community College, a non-degree-granting public institution offering vocational or university-transfer studies, or both, of up to 3 years' duration, and programs reflecting the concerns of the community. Community colleges were established in Canada in the 1960s, when it was believed that both formal and informal learning were necessary for economic growth and steady employment.

Canadian community colleges are not an extension of secondary schools, or a dwarf species of UNIVERSITY, or junior colleges. A separate social invention, legitimate in their own right, their goals are responsiveness to community concerns; commitment to excellent teaching; emphasis on student counselling and placement services; open-admissions policy; and low tuition fees. They offer students a curriculum that typically provides vocational and technical programs preparatory to employment in the trades, industry, agriculture or the professions; APPRENTICESHIP training; university parallel courses (in Alberta and BC) providing first- and second-year credits toward a university degree; remedial courses; and programs for personal and community enrichment. To allow for part-time study, courses are offered during evenings and weekends as well as during the day. Most community colleges are located in city centres, but community college courses may be held in places convenient to learners, eg, church basements, community halls or high-rise buildings.

Administration Community colleges in Canada are the creation and ultimately the responsibility of provincial governments. In some provinces, community colleges and universities are included under a department or ministry independent of a general department of education; in others, they are incorporated in a ministry of education. In all provinces except New Brunswick and Manitoba a board of governors or trustees appointed by the provincial government administers the colleges. Boards vary in size, autonomy, range of representation and effectiveness. Some (eg, in Alberta) include a faculty member, a student representative and a representative from the support staff. Boards in Québec are large and tend to be representative of many groups, eg, faculty, students, administrators, noninstructional staff, parents and part-time students. Some provinces use intermediary committees or councils, such as the Ontario Council of Regents, to advise the minister; generally, the committees or commissions function as a "buffer" between the minister and the colleges. They tend to diminish institutional freedom of action and to consolidate control at the provincial level.

Community college boards in Canada have tended to become politicized through the practice of awarding board membership to provincial party faithful. The most effective boards, however, tend to include representatives of labour, low-income groups, and ethnic and other local minorities. The chief executive officers are styled variously as community college president, principal or director-general, and they have greater direct control than their university counterparts. Many early founding presidents were remarkable innovators.

Federal Government Involvement Under the authority of the National Training Act (1982) the federal Canada Employment and Immigration Commission (CEIC) operates adult vocational training programs that support the training and upgrading of workers in a wide variety of occupations. In one sense the national interest in community colleges — reflected in the federal government's efforts to promote the recognition of BILINGUALISM and BICULTURALISM, and its efforts to ensure that artificial barriers will not prevent students in one region from studying elsewhere in Canada — is greater than the aggregate interest of the 10 provinces.

Students of community colleges in Canada reflect a wider range in age, academic competency, career expectation and economic background than students in any other category. Community colleges provide "a second chance" for mature persons to return to the classroom for the purpose of enhancing marketable skills or of preparing for a new vocation. In Québec, Alberta and BC, community colleges attract students headed towards university, as well as those preparing themselves for early employment. Community colleges in Ontario and elsewhere in Canada tend to serve students who will proceed directly to the labour market.

According to Statistics Canada, the 1982-83 full-time enrolment in community colleges (not including institutes of technology or short-term trade programs) was 269 500. Of this number 183 500 students were registered in programs leading directly to careers; the remaining 86 000 were registered in university transfer studies. It is estimated that overall 2 million Canadians participate in college programs.

Teachers Community college teachers are expected to have had field experience in their subject area; ordinarily, they are not researchers. Most belong to a union. In some provinces one civil-service union bargains collectively for all community colleges; in others college unions bargain individually with their respe tive boards. The most militant provincial unions are in Québec.

There are 24 050 community college teachers in Canada (1983-84), 33% of whom are women (twice as many women, proportionately, teach in community colleges as in universities). Sixty-six percent of all community college teachers hold university degrees; the average age of these teachers is 42 and the average salary $32 000.

System Classification There are 4 categories of community college systems in Canada: unitary, binary, ternary and a system used only in Saskatchewan. In the unitary system, the community colleges are the central link in a continuum extending from secondary schools to universities; in the binary system, the community colleges are primarily vocational institutions with virtually no links to universities; in the ternary, the community colleges, universities and institutes of technology operate interdependently; and in the Saskatchewan system, universities and institutes of technology are formal, independent institutions while the community colleges are an informal network of agencies that facilitate learning opportunities for part-time students.

The unitary system operates in Québec. Nowhere in Canada has a community college system been created in such ferment, imagination and daring. The 1961 Royal Commission of Inquiry on Education (Parent Commission) recommended the transformation of the entire existing educational enterprise, including the reconstitution of some 200 postsecondary institutions (*collèges classiques, instituts familiaux* and 5 categories of technological institutes) into one system of colleges. Known as CEGEPs (COLLÈGE D'ENSEIGNEMENT GÉNÉRAL ET PROFESSIONNEL), they link the secondary school to the university. The CEGEPs became "colleges of the community," regardless of whether the community was local or regional, urban or rural, French or English. This dramatic realignment of educational structures and purposes is an astonishing achievement in Canadian education. Québec now has the largest number of colleges — public or "private" — in any province.

Community colleges in Ontario (binary system) were established with extraordinary speed and clever leadership. Provincial legislation establishing the Colleges of Applied Arts and Technology (CAATs) was introduced in 1965. As in Québec, the community college system incorporated existing institutions, but in Ontario the colleges are strictly distinct from universities. CAATs prepare students for employment; many university graduates find that further training in a community college is helpful in seeking employment. There are 22 CAATs situated on 93 campuses with a total enrolment of 116 000 full-time and 685 000 part-time students. Not included in the CAAT system, but performing some of the same services, are 15 colleges, institutes or commissions specializing in such fields as agriculture, horticulture, art and chiropractic.

Binary systems are also found in Manitoba (with 3 colleges) and in the 4 Atlantic provinces. Historical and cultural forces in some Atlantic provinces have combined to favour those colleges developed to serve specific purposes, such as Newfoundland's College of Fisheries, Navigation, Marine Engineering and Electronics; Nova Scotia's Marine Navigation School; and New Brunswick's Maritimes' Forest Ranger School. But in PEI, Holland College is patterned after the Ontario prototype and, indeed, is subtitled a College of Applied Arts and Technology. New Brunswick, strictly speaking, has no community colleges, although it does have a government department of community colleges. The 10 institutions reporting to this department are called "campuses," but they resemble Ontario institutions. Nova Scotia has specialized institutions but no community colleges. Newfoundland has one community college. There is one college each in the NWT and the Yukon.

In the West most community colleges were created outright (on the initiative of communities) and were not fashioned from existing institutions. The post-secondary institutions of Alberta and BC include community colleges, institutes of technology and universities. Most community colleges in BC and Alberta offer the first 2 years of university-level studies, as well as 1-, 2- or 3-year programs in occupation-related study. Students move with relative freedom between community colleges, institutes and universities.

In Alberta there are 10 community colleges, 3 institutes of technology and 4 universities. BC has 15 community colleges, one institute of technology and 3 universities. BC also has a number of special institutions, comparable to community colleges, such as the Pacific Marine Training Institute, Pacific Vocational Institute, the Justice Institute, the Emily Carr College of Art and Design, and the Open Learning Institute. Alberta offers basic training and apprenticeship programs in vocational schools.

The college system in Saskatchewan is both creative and unusual. The combined extension services of the provincial government, the universities, the provincial library and the CO-OPERATIVE MOVEMENT undergird many college programs. Indeed, the present community college system is an outgrowth of this network of organizations and resources. The accent is upon colleges as interstitial institutions, as brokers and agents facilitating exchange arrangements and not upon buildings or full-time instructional staff. The community college principal, the board, organizers and co-ordinators promote formal and informal ADULT EDUCATION by using, wherever possible, the extension services of existing institutions.

There are 15 community colleges in Saskatchewan, 4 institutes of technology and 2 universities. By 1975-76, after 3 years of development, community college programs had become available in 600 different locations. Lakeland College in Lloydminster, located on the border of Saskatchewan and Alberta, is interprovincial. The Saskatchewan Indian Federated College is also unique in Canada.

National Organization Leading educators in the 1960s felt there was enough common interest among colleges across Canada to warrant the creation of a national association. The Association of Canadian Community Colleges was formed in 1970; by 1984, it had 100 institutional members.

Conclusion Canada's financial commitment — provincial and federal — to community colleges is proportionately higher than that of any other advanced industrial society, including the US. Although not united by national policies and overall goals, the network of Canada's community colleges ranks among the most comprehensive in the world. The strengths of the 144 community colleges include their accessibility to all citizens, old and young; and the attention given to the individual student. Their service to communities may be in jeopardy, however, because of increasing provincial centralization of control. The restrictive intervention of provincial governments and the burgeoning bureaucracies within the colleges themselves represent the greatest threat to the continuing and imaginative development of community colleges.

G. CAMPBELL

Comox, BC, Town, pop 6607 (1981c), inc 1967, is located on E coast of Vancouver I, 223 km N of Victoria, overlooking Comox Harbour. The Beaufort Mtn Range and Comox Glacier enhance the town's natural beauty. The adjacent ski slopes of Mt Washington and Forbidden Plateau make it a popular winter sports centre. First inhabited by SALISH Indians, then by Europeans in the early 1860s, Comox slowly became a service centre and shipment point for the Comox Valley. It has recently become the centre of a rich agricultural area, producing potatoes, fruit and dairy products. (The name, of Indian origin, means "abundance.") The area's mild climate has made it popular with retired people. CFB Lazo, 5 km NE, is important for the local economy. There is a ferry service from the Comox peninsula to POWELL RIVER on the mainland.

ALAN F.J. ARTIBISE

Compact Theory of Confederation, *see* CONSTITUTIONAL HISTORY.

Compagnie des Cent-Associés (Compagnie de la Nouvelle France) was founded 29 Apr 1627 (royal approbation 6 May 1628) by Cardinal Richelieu, chief minister of Louis XIII, to establish the French empire in N America; it was granted NEW FRANCE from Florida to the Arctic and from the Atlantic to the unknown West, as well as extensive trading privileges. English rivals captured the company's fleet in 1628 and both the fleet and the colony in 1629; the colony was restored to France in Mar 1632, but the company never recovered. In 1645 it sublet its rights and obligations in Canada to the COMMUNAUTÉ DES HABITANTS; on 24 Feb 1663 the Cent-Associés' grant was revoked and Canada became a royal province.

DALE MIQUELON

Compagnie des Indes occidentales, which replaced the COMPAGNIE DES CENT-ASSOCIÉS, was established in May 1664 by Jean-Baptiste Colbert to drive Dutch traders from French colonies in the West Indies and the Americas, and to emulate Dutch and English commercial success. The company succeeded in the first aim, but failed in the second. It was essentially a state enterprise run by Colbert, and its impressive trade monopoly and SEIGNEURIAL and governmental rights did not attract private capital. In Dec 1674 Colbert dissolved the ailing company and initiated the regime of direct governmental administration of colonies.

DALE MIQUELON

Compagnie du Nord (Compagnie de la Baie du Nord), fd 1682 by Canadian merchants to trade into Hudson Bay by sea. The company upheld French claims on the bay and stabilized, by its trade, NEW FRANCE's Indian alliances N of the Great Lakes. In 1685 the king granted the company a monopoly of the Hudson Bay FUR TRADE, but costly military expeditions against the HUDSON'S BAY COMPANY and ruinous taxation (the *quart*) bankrupted the company. Its monopoly was revoked on 10 Jan 1700 and transferred to the Compagnie de la Colonie.

DALE MIQUELON

Company Town, important in Canada's CAPITAL FORMATION and INDUSTRIALIZATION, urban development and trade-union movement. Few survive in the sense used by sociologist Rex Lucas: "closed communities owned and administered by the industrial employer," with homes, stores and even the church owned by the firm. The decline of the small firm, the enhanced status of trade unions since WWII, and more liberal interpretations of property and civil rights have combined to render the institution largely obsolete. The paternalism of the traditional company town is no longer acceptable to Canadians, but single-industry communities, especially those on the resource frontier from Newfoundland to the Yukon, still bear similarities to earlier company towns.

Company towns emerged during the colonial period, their purpose to ensure a reserve of skilled workers for family-based firms. They were islands of stability in the chaotic pre-industrial labour market. The thrust of industrial revolution between the 1850s and 1890s occurred in cities, not company towns. One exception was the cotton industry, which often created new communities such as Valleyfield, Qué, based on British or American paternalistic principles. Significantly, Valleyfield's cotton workers, many of them women, were among the minority in true factory settings who organized collectively before WWI and used strike and "riot" tactics to advance their claims.

The Canadian company town's development peaked in the post-1890s mining industry. Cape Breton coal communities, Québec asbestos towns and Ontario gold, silver and nickel towns began as company towns. Often the dominant note of social relations was not paternalism, but the hard edge of authoritarianism and naked exploitation. During the 1909-10 strike, members of the United Mine Workers in Cape Breton were thrown out of their homes and locked out of the company stores, where lines of credit formed part of a system of peonage. Clergymen sheltering workers in churches were ordered by the hierarchy to stop. Mine operators in Timmins, Ont, employed "gun thugs" to patrol the town during the 1912-13 gold-mine strike. Only after blood flowed did the provincial government order their removal.

Canadian company towns were generally less violent than their American counterparts, largely because Canadian opinion opposed the use of private armies. But there were exceptions, such as Cape Breton's coal-and-iron police. Once companies lost moral authority, as they almost invariably did, true discipline could be maintained only by force, which politicians often decided not to provide in crises. The Crow's Nest Pass Coal Co at Fernie, BC, for example, failed to evict striking tenants in 1906 because the provincial attorney general heeded local police and maintained a "neutral" stance.

There are examples of attempts to reassert traditional moral authority through "model" community building and social engineering. Coal companies at Brule and Nordegg, Alta, made such attempts during and after WWI. Their position was uniquely favourable, insofar as in NW Alberta companies operated on inalienable crown lands under long-term government leases. The usual challenges to the company town — acquisition of property by individuals, municipal incorporation and incursions by independent merchants — were closed off. But alongside the managers' claims regarding community progress must be placed the long list of residents' petitions and protests. Neither attempt achieved its primary object of avoiding unions and strikes.

Life in the company town could often be fulfilling, but never certain. The fruit of 40 years in Nordegg was destroyed in one day in 1955: Canadian National Railways, increasingly using diesel power, cancelled its Nordegg coal contract, effectively shutting down the mine and consequently the town. It is not the "pluck-me" store or the coal-and-iron police which defines the company town, but the basic economic power wielded over the single-industry community by public and private interests that remain unaccountable for decreeing the life or death of the community. Few may remember that Dominion, NS, is a perpetual monument to long-departed DOSCO, or Cadomin, Alta, to Canada & Dominion Mining, but the phrase "company town" still flourishes in the Canadian language. *See also* RESOURCE TOWN. ALLEN SEAGER

Reading: R.J. Bowles, *Little Communities and Big Industries* (1982); R. Lucas, *Minetown, Milltown, Railtown* (1971).

Comparative Literature is the international or multilingual study of literary history, ie, of broad currents of thought and style and of major schools; of literary genres, forms and modes; of motifs and themes; of the presence of a work of literature, an author, a whole literature or even a country, in another national literature; of authors writing in different languages, but linked with "influences" and typological affinities. Comparative literature includes literary criticism and theory, and sometimes folk or ORAL LITERATURE, as well as the interdisciplinary interrelationships of literature with the other arts and even with other expressions and studies of man, eg, PHILOSOPHY and PSYCHOLOGY. Although present in most countries with established universities and research centres in the humanities, the discipline has been traditionally strong in France, the US and Eastern Europe. It varies from the "orthodox" or "French" school, with its rigorous search for historical evidence of contacts, imitations, translations and influences, to the N American insistence on methodology and theory, to the Eastern European insertion of this approach into the vast study of the history, theory and criticism of world literature.

The term *"littérature comparée"* was probably first used in 1827-28 by the French scholar Villemain and was popularized by the influential critic C.A. Sainte-Beuve. Its rendering in English as "comparative literature" by Matthew Arnold is somewhat misleading, for the discipline is defined less by comparisons (which occur in any inquiry in the humanities) than by studies based on the concept that literature, in addition to being the product of a nation and the expression of a LANGUAGE, is also — like music or painting — a universal human phenomenon. The discipline has been exposed to older methodological trends in scholarship, such as 19th-century positivism and philology, 20th-century history of ideas, Marxism, sociological perspectives and psychoanalysis; and recently it has been inspired increasingly by LINGUISTIC models, eg, in belated manifestations of formalism and particularly by structuralism and communication theory (semiotics).

In Canada, comparative literature became an academic discipline only in the 1960s. Among the academics interested at an early point in comparative literature, the foremost place belongs to Northrop FRYE, who was the first chairman of U of T's Comparative Literature Programme. His various works, including *Anatomy of Criticism* (1957), *The Secular Scripture* (1976) and *The Great Code* (1982), have confirmed him as the prime Canadian literary historian and theoretician. Other senior comparatists include Eugène Joliat (U of T), Zbigniew Folejewski (UBC and U of Ottawa), Edward J.H. Greene (U of A), Victor Graham (U of A and U of T); Paul Zumthor (U de Montréal); Juan Ferraté (U of A); and Lubomír Doležel (U of T). The next generation of comparists is more numerous, and includes such scholars as Mark Angenot, E.D. Blodgett, Roland Bourneuf, Paul Chavy, M.V. Dimić, David Hayne, Linda Hutcheon, Wladimir Krysinski, Eva Kushner, Uri Margolin, Christie McDonald Vance, Patricia Merivale, Clément Moisan, Edward Możejko, Timothy J. Reiss, Hans-George Ruprecht, Stéphane Sarkány, Ingrid Schuster, Philip Stratford, Roman Struc, Ronald Sutherland, Darko Suvin, George Szanto, Mario Valdés, Eugene Vance and Jennifer Waelti-Walters.

Although there was little systematic teaching of comparative literature until the end of the 1960s, Canadian universities granted, between 1921 and 1969, about 125 graduate degrees based on comparative topics; quite a few Canadians studied abroad (mainly in France, Eastern Europe and the US).

The graduate program at U of A, the first in Canada (est 1964), became a full-fledged department in 1969, with both undergraduate and postgraduate instruction. During this period other universities created graduate programs, sharing staff and facilities with English or French and departments of foreign languages. In the early 1980s graduate degrees were offered at Carleton, McGill, U de Montréal, U of T, UBC and U de Sherbrooke; experiments with undergraduate courses have taken place at Windsor, Dalhousie, Mount Saint Vincent, Saint Mary's, Athabasca and Calgary. Some preferences are visible in Canadian schools: eg, literary theory and methodology with an emphasis on structuralism and semiotics at U de Montréal; social theories and literary practice at McGill; theory and methodology with myth criticism, hermeneutics, phenomenology and structuralism at Toronto; methodological pluralism, translation theory and literary history at U of A; and comparative Canadian literature at Sherbrooke. Specialized research centres have been established at Carleton, McGill and Toronto, and a research institute at U of A.

Comparative Literature in Canada, a bilingual newsletter started in 1968, publicizes Canadian programs and theses. It also acts as the "public archives" of the Canadian Comparative Literature Assn (fd 1969). The association, which organizes yearly scholarly meetings, founded the *Canadian Review of Comparative Literature / Revue canadienne de littérature comparée* in 1974, and embarked on a series of books and monographs in 1977 (both edited by Milan V. Dimić). The association and its members have contributed markedly to the professional and scholarly life of the International Comparative Literature Assn, of which a Canadian, Eva Kushner, has been president. Since 1970 Canadian comparatists have participated at most international and many national meetings of the profession and have published widely at home and abroad.

Comparative literature as a discipline in Canada has contributed to the methodological renewal of literary studies in the country and has facilitated research links with international scholarship. Nevertheless, it is financially, administratively and academically still in a precarious position, without a firm basis in the high-school curriculum or in the undergraduate liberal arts education. From the outside it is often perceived as elitist and cosmopolitan, whereas from the inside it appears to its practitioners as today's core of inquiries into literature. There is no doubt, however, that it corresponds to the very multicultural and multi- lingual nature of Canada, and to the character of international scholarship. MILAN V. DIMIĆ

Reading: N.P. Stallknecht and Horst Frenz, eds, *Comparative Literature* (1974); Ulrich Weisstein, *Comparative Literature and Literary Theory* (1973).

Comparative Literature, Canadian The comparative study of the Canadian literatures (which normally means writing in English and French) is of recent origin, the best work dating from the late 1960s. The linguistic situation that obtains in Canada is not unlike that of other countries that practise bilingual policies (eg, Cameroon and Belgium). The problem with language is that it often establishes zones of territoriality, rather than opening lines of communication, and in Canada this situation has profoundly inhibited the comparative study of the country's literatures. Another reason for the slow pace of such studies in Canada is that the normal model for comparative studies has been between, rather than within, nations. Furthermore, since the rise of comparative studies in the 18th century, the assumption has been that the object of COMPARATIVE LITERATURE in general is to unify the literatures of the world and to examine them as part of a harmonious whole. Thus literatures that constitute the culture of a country already unified do not seem to require further unification. Finally the literatures of Canada, until recently, have usually been treated as colonial, and therefore more closely allied to the literature of their respective mother countries. The Official Languages Act, as well as the sense of national unity generated by the CENTENNIAL of Confederation, tended to provide the impetus not only to overcome colonial attitudes, but also to permit an examination of the 2 literatures as significant enough to be studied in their own right. A satisfactory model for comparison, however, has yet to be found. The most frequently cited image is that of the double staircase at the Château de Chambord, proposed over a century ago by P.J.O. CHAUVEAU. The image is apt, for it suggests two cultures that constantly spiral around each other without ever coming into direct contact. The model is most often used by anglophone critics; francophone critics, by contrast, complain of too much contact. Not surprisingly, the majority of scholars who study the Canadian literatures comparatively are anglophone, for it is there that the ideology of comparative studies as conducive to unity is most strongly felt. It is felt, however, with paradoxical delicacy. As Philip Stratford has argued, the Canadian comparatist "must neither unify, nor divide."

The usual method of following, at least implicitly, such an injunction has been to include francophone literature in histories of Canadian literature in a special chapter. Archibald MacMechan's *Headwaters of Canadian Literature* (1924), a pioneering work, only includes francophone literature because it constitutes an exception to "Canadian" literature. That literature also merits a chapter in Lorne PIERCE's *Outline of Canadian Literature* (1927), and the same position is given the writing of Québec in Margaret ATWOOD's widely read *Survival* (1972). Of studies exclusively devoted to probing how two literatures relate, Ronald Sutherland's *Second Image* (1971) must be considered the fundamental point of departure. While confirming that the two literatures cannot be compared as a result of mutual contact, Sutherland argues that on the basis of shared themes they possess sufficient likeness to merit mutual study. The same point is developed in *The New Hero* (1977). Margot Northey's *The Haunted Wilderness* (1976) follows a similar methodology with more attention paid to issues of form. The most significant Québec critic is Clément Moisan, whose first book, *L'Âge de la littérature canadienne* (1969), echoes the pioneering work of Edmond Lareau's *Histoire de la littérature canadienne* (1874); both examine the two cultures from broad, sociological perspectives. Moisan's second book, *Poésie des frontières* (1979; trans *A Poetry of Frontiers*, 1983), follows Sutherland's method in poetry rather than in the novel. The technique is one of "facing-off" thematically similar francophone and anglophone writers. E.D. Blodgett's *Configuration* (1982), more pluralistic in design, endeavours to overcome the impasse of shared francophone and anglophone themes, first, by examining Ukrainian and especially German texts and, second, by employing critical methods more various than thematic analysis.

E.D. BLODGETT

Reading: D.M. Hayne, "Comparative Canadian Literature...," *Canadian Review of Comparative Literature* III.2 (1976); Hayne and A. Sirois, "Preliminary Bibliography of Comparative Canadian Literature," *CRCL* (various issues 1975-83); D.G. Jones *Butterfly on Rock* (1970); A.J.M. Smith, "Introduction," *The Oxford Book of Canadian Verse* (1960); Philip Stratford, ed, *Comparative Canadian Literature*, a special issue of *CRCL* VI.2 (1979).

Competition Policy, legislation used by the federal government to eliminate privately imposed restraints on trade and to encourage competition. The statutory basis of federal competition policy is contained in the Combines Investigation Act. According to the official responsible for enforcing the Act, the director of investigation and research, its purpose is "to assist in maintaining effective competition as a prime stimulus to the achievement of maximum production, distribution and employment in a mixed system of public and private enterprise." The legislation is designed in the interests of economic efficiency and fairness to consumers to eliminate certain practices that restrain trade. The Act applies to all economic activities except those specifically exempted, eg, COLLECTIVE BARGAINING, amateur sports, securities underwriting or activities subject to other legislation, eg, those of banks and industries where price or output or both are regulated by federal or provincial governments. The Act incorporates both criminal offences and civil, reviewable matters. In addition, the director is authorized to intervene in the proceedings of federal regulatory tribunals regarding the maintenance of competition. A Restrictive Trade Practices Commission (RTPC) is responsible for reviewing the evidence and recommending action by the registrar general. An inquiry into alleged offences can be held following an application by 6 adult Canadian citizens, on the initiative of the director or at the direction of the registrar general.

The principal criminal offences are as follows: first, agreements to lessen competition, although only those agreements concerning the supply, manufacture, production, etc, of a product to lessen competition unduly are prohibited. According to recent decisions of the Supreme Court of Canada in the *Aetna Insurance* (1977) and *Atlantic Sugar* (1980) cases, the Crown must apparently show that there was an agreement among the accused and that they intended to lessen competition unduly. Second, being a party to an anti-competitive merger or monopoly is an offence (s33) if competition is likely to be (or has been) lessened to the detriment or against the interest of the public. Monopoly is defined as a situation where one or more persons (usually firms) substantially or completely control a market and have operated or are likely to operate the business to the detriment of the public. Third, suppliers may not attempt to influence upwardly or discourage the reduction of the price at which another person supplies or advertises a product. It is also an offence to refuse to supply anyone because of that person's low-pricing policy or to attempt to induce a supplier to refuse to supply any person because of that person's low-pricing policy. Fourth, it is an offence to discriminate against competitors of a purchaser of an article by granting a price discount or other advantage, eg, advertising allowances, to the purchaser that is not also available to the competitors. It is also illegal to engage in a policy of predatory pricing policies, so that products are sold at lower prices in one area of the country than in others, or to sell at unreasonably low prices where the effect or tendency is to lessen competition substantially or eliminate a competitor. Fifth, all false or misleading advertising and representations are prohibited. Other sections of the Act prohibit double ticketing, "bait-and-switch" advertising, and pyramid and referral-selling schemes.

Civil reviewable matters adjudicated by the RTPC rather than the courts include trade practices which may be anti-competitive in their effects, eg, refusal to sell, consignment selling for the purpose of controlling dealer prices, exclusive dealing, tied selling and market restriction. The majority of inquiries result from complaints by businessmen and consumers. While the director may apply to the RTPC for an order to prohibit the continuation of a civil reviewable trade practice, criminal prosecutions are conducted by the Department of Justice before the courts, although the evidence must be reported to the minister of consumer and corporate affairs.

Between 1889 and 1960 agreements to lessen competition accounted for 81% of the 53 combines cases prosecuted. Between 1960 and 1982 almost 200 combines cases were prosecuted: over half were price-maintenance cases; 40% were conspiracy cases; and the remainder concerned mergers, price discrimination and predatory pricing. Between 1976 and 1982 the conviction rate fell sharply from the 90% rate consistent before the mid-1970s. The Crown has never won a contested merger case (there was one guilty plea) and has won only weak remedies in the few monopoly cases it has prosecuted. For the some 600 cases of misleading advertising between 1977-78 and 1982-83, the conviction rate was about 80%. Although a variety of penalties and remedies are available to the courts, eg, fines, imprisonment, injunctions, tariff reductions and divestiture (in merger or monopoly cases), in most cases a fine, and usually a relatively modest one, is imposed, even though, between 1953 and 1975, the courts could impose an unlimited fine in conspiracy cases. Since 1976 the maximum fine has been $1 million.

Following the Economic Council's report on competition policy (1969), the federal government introduced Bill C-256, which would have entirely replaced the Combines Investigation Act. Business opposition was fierce and effective and the government responded by proposing 2 sets of amendments to the Act. The Stage I amendments, introduced in Nov 1973 but not effective until 1 Jan 1976, brought services under the Act and strengthened the conspiracy, misleading-advertising and price-maintenance provisions. The present civil reviewable matters were enacted then and provision was made for the director to make representations before federal regulatory agencies and to allow private civil actions for damages. In 1977 the government introduced Bills C-42 and C-13, incorporating the Stage II amendments. Neither was enacted, largely because of the opposition of business. The amendments would have moved both the merger and monopoly (extended to include single and joint monopolization) provisions from criminal to civil law to be adjudicated by a special administrative tribunal rather than the courts. In Apr 1981, the minister of consumer and corporate affairs circulated his *Proposals for Amending the Combines Investigation Act: A Framework for Discussion*, comprising a limited set of possible amendments regarding mergers, abuse of dominant position, specialization agreements, systematic delivered pricing and major amendments to the conspiracy section. The weakness of Canadian competition legislation reflects an acceptance of concentrations of power in both private and public sectors; the belief that other forms of government intervention, eg, regulation, direct expenditures and CROWN CORPORATIONS, protect the public's interests; and the political power of PRESSURE GROUPS. Competition legislation needs to be reformed because, in the case of mergers and monopolies, the use of criminal law is unsuitable and virtually ineffective, and because since 1976 several Supreme Court of Canada decisions have severely weakened the law as it applies to mergers, conspiracies and regulated conduct.

W.T. STANBURY

Computer-Assisted Learning (CAL) generally refers to 2 major uses of computers in education and training. The first is often called Computer-Assisted Instruction (CAI) and can be described as "learning through a computer." In CAI, instructional sequence and questions must be preprogrammed. These sequences may be called drill and practice, tutorial, socratic, simulation, gaming, testing and computer-managed instruction (CMI), ie, computer assistance in testing, diagnosing, prescribing, grading and record keeping. The emphasis in CAI is on having students learn new concepts or reinforce previously learned concepts by interacting with a CAI program. Unfortunately, because it takes many hours to develop even one hour of CAI, the cost of producing CAI programs can be expensive. The second major use of CAL is one in which students tend to write their own programs to solve problems; this is described as "learning with computers" or, more simply, using computers as tools. Various programming languages such as LISP, PILOT, APL, BASIC, LOGO and Pascal are being used by students to explore solutions to a variety of problems in a number of different areas.

Until 1977, when fully assembled, low-cost microcomputers became generally available, most CAL activities tended to be centered either in postsecondary institutions or in business and industry. The early uses of CAL in Canada were non-CAI in nature. As programming and problem-solving applications evolved and developed, many universities, colleges and technical institutes established academic computing centres and teaching departments of computing science. In the late 1960s, Ontario school boards took advantage of federal funding to acquire computing equipment and have since established a strong computing program in many Ontario high schools.

One of the first prominent Canadians in this field was Alberta-born K. Iverson. He designed a language called APL (A Programming Language) in 1962, which was later taken over by IBM and is now used worldwide on a wide variety of computers. The UNIVERSITY OF WATERLOO is a leader in the design of student compilers and interpreters. Waterloo's compilers and interpreters run on many varieties of computers and are used widely by students at universities and colleges in many countries.

The first major CAI project in Canada was initiated by Dr Steve Hunka in the Faculty of Education at U of A. An experimental computer-based instructional system, one of about 20 developed by IBM (IBM 1500 System) was installed at the university in 1968. This system was used at U of A for research and development for 12 years and was replaced in 1980 by a Control Data Corporation PLATO System. Other major CAI projects from 1968 to 1969 were at Ontario Institute for Studies in Education (OISE), University of Calgary and the National Research Council (NRC). As a result of the work at these and other CAI centres, 2 major Canadian CAI authoring systems have evolved. Both CAN, which was originally developed at OISE and which is being used in Canada, the US and Europe, and NATAL-74 developed by NRC and Honeywell, run on a number of different computers.

Large-scale CAI materials tend to be produced by development teams, which might include subject-matter experts, instructional designers, instructors, graphic artists, programmers, analysts and technical writers. The time required to develop CAI materials depends on the authoring system, the expertise of the team, and the complexity of the instructional application. Estimates of 100-300 hours of development time being required for each student hour of "on-line instruction" are quite common.

Most CAI programs tend to reinforce previously learned skills by asking questions, analysing the student's responses and presenting summaries of the student's performance; this is evident in many of the commercial mathematics, spelling and language-arts drill and practice programs available for microcomputers. As the programs become more sophisticated (eg, tutorial) students are presented with new material based on both their performance within a lesson and in end-of-unit quizzes. Some CAI courses are quite long (100 hours or more) and are primarily intended to be used without an instructor, whereas others may last only 10 or 15 minutes and are intended to supplement classroom work.

Since 1977, uses of CAL have spread rapidly throughout the Canadian educational system. Almost every provincial department (or ministry) of education has initiated projects to help cope with the rapid increase of computer use in the public school sector. In 1983 Ontario and Québec each announced unique microcomputer hardware specifications and have made funds available for development on various lesson materials for use on these microcomputers. For example, Ontario is providing support to the Canadian Education Microprocessor Corporation (CEMCORP) to develop and manufacture an Ontario-based microcomputer called the Icon, and will also pay 75% of cost of computer systems to school boards if the systems comply with provincial specifications. In addition, the Council of Ministers of Education supports a number of projects concerning the exchange of information in this field.

Although microcomputers have also had a significant impact upon postsecondary institutions, these institutions primarily use mainframe computers and occasionally local area networks to provide CAL to their students. There appears to be more CAL development activity in postsecondary institutions than in the elementary and secondary schools, partly because courses tend to be taught in shorter periods. On the other hand, most Canadian elementary and secondary schools operate on a system in which there is no positive incentive to use instructional techniques to decrease student learning time. This is a major reason for the emphasis upon learning *with* the computer rather than learning *through* the computer. So far, CAI has had little effect on traditional classroom structures and practices, but as computers gain a foothold in the schools the curriculum is being modified to reflect their importance.

Ontario and Québec seem to be making organized attempts at providing hardware and software to educational institutions at reasonable prices. Both provinces are also trying to develop their own software and thereby rely less upon American- or French-produced software. Because most of the commercial software is developed by Americans, some attempts are being made to establish a Canadian "course ware" industry that could provide CAL materials specifically designed for Canadian schools.

E.W. ROMANIUK

Computer-Assisted Mapping, *see* CARTOGRAPHY.

Computer Communications The COMPUTER INDUSTRY grew by developing faster and cheaper methods of processing and storing data. Computer communication occurs when computers are attached to communications lines. Data processing becomes teleprocessing, or data processing at a distance. Teleprocessing has stimulated explosive growth both in the use of computer terminals and in the creation of central data or information banks to which the terminals have access via the TELECOMMUNICATIONS system. Users may have computer terminals anywhere within the range of the telecommunications system — at the office, at home, on the farm. They may obtain access to central computers and databanks located across town or in other countries. One of the earliest users was the airline industry with its computerized reservation systems.

Business and government offices are becoming more automated with increased use of computers (*see* OFFICE AUTOMATION). Even typewriters can be connected to a central computer via telecommunications lines. At home, personal computers and modern TV sets can be used to contact databanks over telephone or CABLE TELEVISION company lines. Computer communication networks may be designed for many different purposes. They can connect a company's plants located around the world. They can provide specialized information to an industry (eg, stock market information for brokers) or a profession (eg, court decisions for lawyers). They can provide specialized information to companies (eg, credit information) and commercial informa tion to consumers (eg, theatre listings in an elec tronic yellow pages). They can provide access t special types of computer processing capabilit for handling voluminous data or highly tech nical scientific calculations. Computer commu nications also can be used to facilitate certai kinds of education and training as well as t provide a source of entertainment via access t computer games.

The extent to which computer communica tion spreads throughout Canadian society wil depend heavily on its costs. All 3 major element of cost — the computer terminal, the informa tion in the databank, and the communication costs — are expected to decline as a result of im proved technology. The costs of transmittin data over the telecommunications system are de clining because new technologies permit greate volumes of data to be transmitted at highe speeds, or more bits of information per second The telecommunications system, which was ini tially designed to provide communication t voice signals in analogue form, is now bein upgraded to provide all types of communicatio — data, voice, facsimile and video — using th digital technique of computers.

New communications switching machines ar really specialized digital computers. Some nev kinds of TELEPHONES have the capabilities o computer terminals. Many new telecommuni cation local-distribution cables contain optica fibre, which has many times the capacity of th older copper wires and is technically much bet ter for digital communications. New long-dis tance systems, including optical fibre, single sideband microwave radio and satellites, can b designed for digital communications. In es sence, the telecommunications system is bein converted into a giant computer.

The costs of this conversion are substantial Telephone companies have indicated a desire t introduce new usage charges for local service be fore 1990, as well as increased monthly flat-rat access charges. Thus the decline in communica tions costs may not continue. The costs may be barrier to the use of computer communicatio services by a high proportion of residential sub scribers, although business use is expected t grow at a high rate.

By providing access to more data, compute communication systems open possibilities fo more informed decision-making and improve efficiency. Businesses will be able to extend thei markets to larger geographical areas. Centralize control by large organizations will be facili tated. But this may lead to a loss of indepen dence for smaller organizations and organ izations outside central areas. The free flow o information over international computer com munication systems may result in important in formation about Canada and Canadians bein kept outside of Canada and of Canadian contro In order to get the full benefits of computer com munication systems, Canadians must have ac cess to these systems and consequently coul become dependent on these systems and th organizations that have dominant control ove them.

If computer communication systems are vul nerable to the theft, misuse, destruction or un authorized manipulation of data, enormou damage can be done (*see* COMPUTERS AND SOCIETY The problem is made especially difficult becaus there is seldom any physical evidence of suc activity. If a file of data is stolen by an unau thorized person, the data is still in the compute databank. Erroneous information in a credit o medical file could ruin reputations or lead t faulty diagnosis of illness. Information gath ered in databanks may invade personal privacy Specialized information may be used by som interests to gain unfair control over others.

Thus, although computer communication sys

ems may provide increased freedom of information for some people, it may result in reduced freedom for others. The successful utilization of computer communication systems will require effective regulations to preserve the rights of individuals, regions and nations. It will require public policies to ensure that the evolving INFORMATION SOCIETY is one that benefits all citizens and not simply a few at the expense of the many. *See also* COMMUNICATIONS TECHNOLOGY.

WILLIAM H. MELODY

Reading: M. Andrieu and S. Serafini, *The Information Revolution and Its Implications for Canada* (1980); R. Cruise O'Brien, ed, *Information, Economics and Power: The North-South Dimension* (1983); S. Nora and A. Minc, *The Computerization of Society* (1980).

Computer Industry, a subcomponent of the ELECTRONICS INDUSTRY that makes use of the same goods and services and relies on the same basic technologies. Goods include hardware and software. Hardware comprises central processors, memories and peripheral devices. Central processors are electronic systems and components capable of performing arithmetic operations at very high speeds. They range in size and complexity from a single semiconductor "chip," which can be held in the hand, to a large cabinet or series of cabinets each the size of a refrigerator. Memories are electronic devices capable of storing large amounts of data and transferring such data at high speed to the central processing unit or to external peripheral devices. The most common peripherals are page printers, keyboards, video display terminals, communications devices and mechanical bulk memory devices (eg, rotating magnetic discs), but modern computers are capable of interacting with almost any electronic device available on the market. Software comprises the programs necessary to make the central processor interact with the memory and the peripheral devices to carry out a specific function or series of functions. Software is usually written by the supplier of the hardware or by firms specializing in such activity and is supplied on a storage medium (eg, magnetic disc, magnetic tape).

Services include hardware maintenance, software consulting and maintenance, and computer service bureaus. Hardware maintenance is the servicing of the computer system after installation. Software consulting and maintenance provides programming expertise (by the original software supplier or a third party) and ensures the continuous upgrading of the software to take advantage of new developments in hardware. Computer service bureaus are firms that sell computing power and services much as common carriers sell COMMUNICATIONS and communications services.

Scope of the Industry In 1985 Canadians are expected to spend about $9 billion on computer goods and services: in-house computing equipment (hardware and software) will cost $2 billion; in-house computer personnel $3 billion; data-transmission services $700 million; services purchased from computer service bureaus $1.8 billion; other goods and services (paper, environmental control systems, etc) $1.5 billion.

The major suppliers of computing equipment are subsidiaries of foreign-owned multinational firms. These subsidiaries import most of the goods they supply, although in recent years a number of small domestic firms have carved out specialty "niches" in this sector for domestic and international markets. The distinction between computers and other devices that perform communications operations and specialized functions (eg, word processing, digital switching) is becoming increasingly blurred. Exports of such specialized systems (including software) by domestic firms, along with exports of subcomponents of computer systems manufactured in Canada by the multinational subsidiaries, have helped alleviate what would otherwise be an enormous trade deficit in this sector. This deficit is estimated to be 90% of total expenditures on equipment, ie, $1.8 billion, plus an additional $180 million (90% of some $200 million of purchases from the computer vendors) and another $200 million spent on imports by other suppliers serving end users.

The heavy foreign domination of the supply sector by multinational corporations has caused several infrastructural problems in the Canadian industry. A 1981 report by Evans Research Corp (Toronto), which compared the economic benefits flowing to Canada in 1980 with those flowing to the home country of the 13 largest foreign computer and communications companies operating in Canada, reached 4 major conclusions. First, if the 13 firms were putting as much investment into Canada, proportionally, as into their own countries, there would be 21 100 more jobs for Canadians in the computer and communications industries. Second, if these firms were putting proportional investment into INDUSTRIAL RESEARCH AND DEVELOPMENT in Canada, 2392 of those jobs would be in R&D — an area vital to Canada's technological future. For firms reporting such expenditures, R&D investment in Canada represented an average of 2% of revenue. This figure compares poorly with the overall proportion of 6% of revenue spent on R&D worldwide. Third, if these firms were manufacturing in Canada on a scale proportional to their manufacturing elsewhere, they would have invested at least $500 million more than the $224 million they already have in property, plants and equipment. The employment so generated would be in addition to the jobs mentioned above. Fourth, if these firms had paid taxes in Canada at a rate proportional to the US rate, the Canadian government would have obtained an additional $49 million, or 30% more than it actually received in 1980.

The $3-billion expenditure on computer personnel is nearly all spent in Canada, as is the $700 million for data-transmission services that goes to the telephone companies and other common carriers. Such carriers, along with the computer service bureaus, acquire hardware and software from the computer suppliers. These expenditures are estimated at about $200 million in 1985. If the 90% ratio of imports to exports exists in this sector, such expenditures will add a further $180 million to the trade deficit. It is in the fourth area of expenditure, purchased computer services, that the Canadian economic contribution is greatest. Canada's service bureaus are among the best in the world. They, along with computer consulting firms, have figured prominently in a number of Canadian firsts in computer technology, particularly in the merger of computer and communications technology.

Computer keyboard and circuit board testing (*courtesy Comterm Inc*).

Canadian Achievements In the mid-1960s, Interprovincial Pipe Line Ltd designed and implemented a network of minicomputers to monitor and control its entire pipeline system linking Edmonton to eastern Canada and the US. This network embodied concepts in software, communications and process control that were at least a decade ahead of their time. The system was conceptualized and designed by a Toronto consulting firm; the hardware was manufactured in Canada by one of the foreign-owned computer suppliers. Other Canadian firsts include the development of what could have been the prototype of the world's first minicomputer at University of Toronto in the late 1950s; invention of a nuclear instrument called a kicksorter, at Atomic Energy of Canada's CHALK RIVER laboratories in the early 1960s, which could also have become a minicomputer with only minor modifications; and creation of a powerful time-sharing computer by Ferranti Packard Ltd of Toronto also in the early 1960s.

Growth Rate The annual growth rate of total expenditure in computer goods and services was as high as 20% during the 1970s, but in recent years it has been closer to 12%. This reduction is not the result of any slowdown in the use of computers: Canada ranks second only to the US in its yearly computer expenditure as a percentage of GROSS NATIONAL PRODUCT. Rather, it reflects a dramatic reduction in computer hardware prices and improved operator and programming efficiencies brought about by more powerful and "user-friendly" software packages.

Research and Development Total Canadian expenditures on computer and communications research and development in Canada in 1985 is expected to be about $300 million, of which about 25% will be spent in government laboratories, 25% in the universities and 50% in the private sector. Of private sector R&D expenditures, about 75% or $100 million will be spent by Canadian-owned firms; in contrast the world's 10 major computer companies are expected to spend over $8 billion. Canadian industrial expenditure will clearly be inadequate for anything other than the creation of very small, specialized niches in the world computer market.

Most of Canada's computer manufacturing and industrial research facilities are located in Ontario: Canadian-owned firms (eg, Gandalf, Mitel, Norpak) are concentrated in the Ottawa area; multinational subsidiaries (eg, IBM) in the Toronto area. The country's major common carriers have their own research facilities and some also have manufacturing facilities. These establishments are dispersed throughout Canada and tend to specialize in computerlike communications control systems and intelligent terminals that incorporate microcomputers.

By 1985, 121 000 computers are expected to be installed in Canada, of which about 80% will be of the microcomputer class. Expenditures on microcomputer hardware and software are expected to grow at 50% per year throughout most of the 1980s, and in 1985 are expected to reach $500 million or about one-third of the total revenue of the hardware-software supply sector. Computers and related devices are expected to change dramatically during the remainder of the 20th century and industries based on computer technology will become extremely important to the economic well-being of Canada. Some experts predict that the computer-communications industry (or, more broadly, the information industry) will rival the transportation industry as a contributor to Canada's gross domestic product by the year 2000. *See* HIGH TECHNOLOGY; MICROCHIPS AND TRANSISTORS; ROBOTICS.

D.J. DOYLE

Computer Science addresses the theory, design and application of information-processing machines. The field is very new: the first successful electronic computer ENIAC (Electronic Numerical Integrator and Computer) was developed in the 1940s at University of Pennsylvania. During the 1950s, 4 main areas of focus emerged. One area concentrated on "hardware," ie, the construction of reliable equipment with faster central-processing units (CPUs), larger memories and more input and output devices, to solve increasingly ambitious problems. Another area covered "software," ie, programming languages, logical techniques and structures needed to direct hardware and organize computational processes. These hardware and software systems rapidly expanded the range of applications, the third area of research and development. The initial applications were in MATHEMATICS, followed by SCIENCE and ENGINEERING, then business, SOCIAL SCIENCE, and eventually almost every field of endeavour. As these 3 areas developed, theorists worked on algorithms (descriptions of how to solve a problem, expressed in a language understood by the computer). This fourth area of study questioned what it meant for an algorithm to be efficient, searched for efficient algorithms in a wide variety of contexts and sought to establish a theory of computation.

During the 1960s, as the body of literature in these areas accumulated, computer science emerged as a distinct discipline separated, in many universities, from mathematics and ELECTRICAL ENGINEERING departments and from the computing service bureaus with which they had been associated. Curricula were drawn up and formal computer-science programs initiated.

Relationship to Other Disciplines Of the 4 areas outlined, only part of one, ie, system software, belongs mainly in computer science and not in the domain of another discipline. Included in system software are such components as operating systems (for starting up and governing program execution, managing memory, recording use of resources, etc); input/output and other utilities (for reading, writing and copying data); monitor and debugging routines (for program development); and compilers and interpreters (for translating statements in a high-level language to the computer's assembly code). Software in general, but system software especially, must be clearly specified, well structured, carefully tested and documented and regularly maintained. The methodology for accomplishing this function is known as software engineering.

Computer science has a special relationship with mathematics, drawing heavily on the formalism of logic, algebraic structures, automata theory and graph theory. Subjects such as numerical analysis and computational complexity belong to both computer science and mathematics. The components of computers (registers, MICROCHIPS, memory devices) are products of electrical engineering. The study of communication systems is central both to electrical engineering and to the subject of computer-systems architecture. Computer and communication technologies appear to be merging as the variety and volume of services based on them grow.

Many disciplines interact with computer science. Together with industrial engineering, computer science addresses systems analysis, process design, modeling and simulation; with linguistics, it shares an interest in language syntax and semantics. The theories and techniques of information storage, retrieval and dissemination are important to both library information science and computing science. With management science, computer science studies data bases, query languages, decision systems and office information systems. through artificial intelligence studies, it shares with PHILOSOPHY an interest in logic, understanding and knowledge formation. With PSYCHOLOGY and neurological science, computer science is concerned with signal processing and the interpretation of sensory perception. Because computers are research tools in so many natural, engineering and biological sciences, control devices in industrial processes and machines central to the conduct of businesses, computer science interacts with many other disciplines.

Computer Science in Canada The work of the first Canadian group addressing the design and use of electronic computers led to the construction of UTEC (University of Toronto Model Electronic Computer) in 1948 and the acquisition of FERUT (Ferranti Computer at U of T) in 1951. Some hardware developments have taken place in Canadian universities, government laboratories (eg, Defence Research Telecommunications Establishment) and industries (Computing Devices of Canada, Ferranti-Packard). However, most computer science research has focused on software, numerical analysis and computer applications, eg, the water-level calculations for the ST LAWRENCE SEAWAY Project, done on FERUT for the Hydro Electric Power Commission of Ontario.

Starting in the 1950s university courses in computer science became available at U of T, McGill, UBC, U of Alberta, Carleton and others, first as extension courses, then as undergraduate and graduate subjects. Much of the impetus for the establishment of university programs came from business and government. The Canadian Conference for Computing and Data Processing, held in 1958, attracted 400 participants and led in the same year to the formation of the Computing and Data Processing Society of Canada (now CIPS, the Canadian Information Processing Society). The WATFOR compiler, developed in the early 1960s by University of Waterloo for fast processing of student jobs, was the first Canadian program product to achieve international distribution. By 1964, computer science courses were being taught at 22 universities and technical schools across the country. Today almost all post-secondary institutions offer computer science programs, and programming courses are given in many high schools. Research laboratories can be found at the universities, the NATIONAL RESEARCH COUNCIL, Northern Telecom, IBM and other computer manufacturers. Many of the large companies using computers are engaged in active research.

C.C. GOTLIEB

Programming Languages

Programming languages are formal notations for expressing algorithms and data so that they can be "understood" by computers. Popular programming languages include Ada, named after Lady Lovelace, Lord Byron's daughter, who worked on Charles Babbage's "analytical engine"; ALGOL, *Algo*rithmic *L*anguage; APL, *A P*rogramming *L*anguage; BASIC, *B*eginner's *A*ll-Purpose *S*ymbolic *I*nstruction *C*ode; COBOL, *Co*mmon *B*usiness-*O*riented *L*anguage; FORTRAN, *For*mula *Tran*slation; GPSS, *G*eneral *P*urpose *S*ystems *S*imulation; LISP, *Lis*t *P*rocessing; Pascal, named after French mathematician Blaise Pascal, who in 1642 developed a calculating machine; SIMULA, *Simu*lation *La*nguage; SNOBOL, *S*tri*n*g-*O*riented Sym*bo*lic *L*anguage; SPSS, *S*tatistical *P*ackage for the *S*ocial *S*ciences. Unlike natural languages (eg, English, French), programming languages must have precise definitions of form (syntax) and meaning (semantics). General-purpose languages are used for problems in many areas; eg, Pascal can be us[ed] for information retrieval, numerical comput[a]tion and system programming. Special-purpo[se] languages are more limited in scope, being d[e]signed for specific application areas. For exam[]ple, GPSS is used for simulation studies.

Programs contain definitions and compute[r] executable statements and expressions. A pr[o]grammer can usually define names of da[ta] objects (variables) and executable objects (su[b]routines, functions) and, in some language[s] types. A type is a set of values together with a[p]propriate operations; for example, a queue [of] integers would have integer sequences as valu[es] and "insert" and "delete" as operations. Stat[e]ments include assignment, input, output an[d] invocation of subroutines, plus ways of co[n]structing sequences of statements, selectin[g] among statements and repeating statements.

Since a computer directly understands ope[r]ations encoded as binary numbers, program[s] can be written in binary. A binary number [is] one expressed using only the numerals 0 and [1]. In this lowest level, called machine language [or] executable code, each instruction and referen[ce] to a data object is a binary number. Assembl[y] languages allow the use of symbolic names f[or] instructions and data; these symbols must b[e] transformed to numbers before the program ca[n] be executed. High-level languages (eg, COBO[L]) allow use of terminology and constructs mo[re] convenient for humans, and require more com[]plex transformations to executable code. Ve[ry] high-level languages allow expression of wh[at] is required, rather than how it is to be compute[d]. For example, in some data-base query languag[es] characteristics of required data are specified, n[ot] ways of finding them in the data base.

Program syntax is usually precisely define[d] using a notation called Backus-Naur For[m] (BNF). The structure of a program is described [in] terms of its components, which in turn are d[e]scribed in terms of their components, and so o[n] until everything has been defined in terms [of] words in the language. This situation is simil[ar] to the way sentences in a natural language a[re] described. Once a machine-language progra[m] exists, it can be improved by being transforme[d] to an equivalent program of fewer or faster in[]structions.

DAVID T. BARNAR[D]

Hardware

When computers were first developed, th[e] physical equipment was referred to as "har[d]ware"; the computer industry soon coined th[e] term "software" to describe the program comp[o]nents executed by the hardware. The hardwa[re] organization of a digital computer, wheth[er] small (microcomputer) or large (mainframe[)] consists of 5 main functional units: control, in[]put, memory, processor and output. Informa[]tion that is read into the memory through th[e] input unit, whether numbers or textual info[r]mation, is encoded into blocks of binary digi[ts] or "bits." Each bit has the value 0 or 1 and com[]mon encoding techniques use a block of 8 bits [(a] "byte") to represent the letters A-Z, digits 0-9 an[d] punctuation marks. The values of individu[al] bits are physically represented by small ele[c]trical voltages and currents, or by the state [of] magnetization of very tiny areas on surfac[es] coated with magnetic material. The form of re[p]resentation depends on whether the informa[]tion is being processed, stored or transmitted b[e]tween functional units.

The numerical calculations or text processin[g] to be done on the input data is specified by a ma[]chine program, stored in the memory as a s[e]quence of simple steps called instructions. Ex[]amples of typical instructions include "add [2] numbers and store the sum in a specific mai[n] memory location; jump to a different section [of] the program, if the value just computed is nega[]tive; send the contents of a particular memo[ry] ocation to an output device for printing." An instruction can usually be encoded in about 30 bits. The electrical networks that fetch individual instructions from the memory and execute them in the processor are composed of many thousands of transistors fabricated in integrated circuits. These circuits are encapsulated in small plastic cases (2-3 cm long, 1 cm wide), each containing up to tens of thousands of transistors. An instruction can be fetched and executed in approximately one-millionth of a second.

Input and Output Units provide communication with the external world (people or electronic or electromechanical devices). Typical input devices are keyboards, which resemble typewriters, graphical tablets that react to pointer positioning or signal converters that transform transducer outputs into binary-coded numbers. Output devices include video displays for characters and graphical shapes, printers for recording output on paper and signal converters that transform binary-coded output values into electrical signals to control motor drives, etc. The magnetic tapes and discs used to store data and programs outside of the processor and memory units are usually classified as input/output devices. They are capable of storing large amounts of data (hundreds of millions of bytes) and constitute the storage media used by business enterprises (eg, insurance companies, banks) for customer records and other business-data files.

Memory Unit Information, which is kept in the memory unit while processing is taking place, is organized into words of a few bytes each. The memory is physically implemented from integrated circuits, each typically containing tens of thousands of bits. The complete memory of a medium-size computer might contain on the order of one million words, which can be moved in or out of the memory at rates of a few million words per second.

Control and Processor Units Control networks, implemented from integrated circuits, are needed to perform the overall sequencing of operations that co-ordinate the activities of all units of the computer. The largest single concentration of controls is associated with the process that performs arithmetic operations on numbers and comparison/searching/sorting operations on text. These controls are needed during processing as well as during the fetch/store operations used to move data between the memory and the processor. Controls are also needed in the circuitry that connects input/output devices to the processor/memory units. In many computer applications, multiple processors and memories must be employed to provide sufficient computing power. Such distributed processing situations lead to the need for synchronization control among the various processors and memories. This area of computer systems design represents the most difficult and challenging task for the hardware designer.

V. CARL HAMACHER

Software

A digital computer stores data and performs various operations on that data (eg, addition, multiplication and comparison). A sequence of operations or instructions (the "program") is also stored in the computer and is interpreted sequentially by the computer's CPU (central-processing unit). A typical instruction might tell the CPU to perform an arithmetic operation using a special place in storage called an accumulator. The collection of operations, and their meaning, is called the computer's native or machine language. Writing a program using machine language is tedious and programs are usually written in a high-level language (eg, FORTRAN, COBOL). A single statement in a high-level language would require hundreds of instructions if written in machine language. Thus a translator (ie, compiler), which generates a machine-language program from the corresponding high-level-language program, is usually required, although some programs can be analysed and executed in one step.

An operating system is a special program that manages the computer system's resources. For example, when several people use the computer simultaneously, they must be prevented from conflicting with one another; there is usually only one processor, and people must be scheduled to use it in turn. An operating system also provides services for the user, such as facilities to input and store data in the computer. These services provide access to sequences of instructions which are required by most programs. The operating system is normally the first program loaded into the computer. Each user communicates with the operating system using a command language to request services. There are hundreds of different operating systems in use, many of them tailored to a specific application area (eg, process control) or to particular, specialized hardware configurations.

A program that addresses a specialized requirement (eg, general ledger accounting) is called an application program. A payroll application program would accept information such as hours worked, and one output might be payroll cheques. Most application programs can be tailored to accommodate various circumstances; some (eg, engineering-design packages and systems for computer-assisted instruction) use special application-oriented languages. Properly designed programs are a good way for most people to use computer systems because they make it unnecessary for users to memorize the details of the computer system. Computer programs are often quite large and can take months or years to prepare. They may be used for years, with changes made to reflect new circumstances. Software methodology provides techniques for writing programs (including structured programming, design and analysis) that are easily understood and modified by other programmers. Some of the tools used are flowcharts, structure diagrams, data-flow diagrams and decision tables.

J.W. GRAHAM

Theoretical Computer Science

Theoretical computer science is the precise (ie, mathematical) study of particular problems and phenomena in computing, including treatment of the inherent limitations of computers, representations of programming languages and program correctness and efficiency. Disciplines in this area are distinguished by their approach and mathematical tools rather than by their subject matter.

Automata Theory is the study of models of computers and their inherent power. Key issues in determining what a computer can do are how much memory it has and how this memory is accessed. Even if time and memory are unlimited, there are tasks that computers cannot do. For example, it can be proved that no computer program can inspect another arbitrary program and determine whether or not it would ever stop running. The unsolvability of this "halting problem" is an important point in computability theory.

Formal Language Theory A program can be thought of as accepting (saying "yes") or rejecting (saying "no"). Hence, we may speak of the set of inputs or language accepted by the program. This formal language theory has been a productive way of studying possible forms and specifications of programming languages, among other computational issues.

Program Correctness Theory The task of writing a correct computer program is difficult; indeed, almost all large programs (including operating systems and compilers) contain errors which can be disastrous. One way to deal with this problem is to develop techniques that offer formal proof that a program does what it is supposed to do, perhaps as part of the process of writing the program. Several approaches have been taken, all based on mathematical logic. A general thread which runs through most approaches is that one must be able to write down assertions that must hold whenever particular lines in the program are to be executed. The theory of program correctness is at the basis of the study of the semantics (meaning) of programs.

Computational Complexity Theory Many problems are best handled by computers because of the large amounts of data involved (eg, income-tax records) or because there are numerous possibilities to explore, even with a moderate amount of data. For instance, to determine the most effective order in which to do 30 jobs, over 10^{32} possible orders could be explored. The fastest computer available today would take 10^8 times the age of the universe to count that high. Therefore, although computers are fast, it is still crucial that efficient methods, or algorithms, be used. The study of the efficiency of algorithms and data organization is a key area of computer science. Consider, for example, a computerized telephone book with a million names and numbers. If the algorithm for finding a number were simply to scan for a given name, a half-million names (on average) would have to be inspected for each search. Instead, a technique known as binary search can be applied. Because the list is sorted by name, the computer can look at the middle element of the name and decide whether to continue the search in the first or second half of the list. Continuing in this way, only about 20 names need be read to complete a search. It can be proved that, for this type of search, this is the best search technique. The study of algorithms has led to many efficient methods, and also to an understanding of why no more efficient method may exist.

J. IAN MUNRO

Reading: Anthony Ralston, ed, *Encyclopedia of Computer Science* (1976, rev 1983).

Computer Systems Applications MATHEMATICS spawned the computer, gave it its name and was its first field of application (ie, in the computation of military ballistic tables). Although many early computers resembled their mechanical predecessors in that they could multiply or divide only by repeated add or subtract functions, their revolutionary speed and precision thrust them quickly into fields involving heavy multiplication. Thus, although computers were later to be emphasized as "information system" devices and applied to logical and sorting problems that did not involve multiplication, literal "computing" dominated the first decade of their use. Two technologies, those of atomic energy and missiles, relied heavily on computation and thus provided the critical demand for ever-better computers. The iterative calculation (ie, repeating to produce a more and more nearly accurate solution) required by atomic PHYSICS remains the principal stimulus to production of the biggest computers. The missile industry, which spawned the space industry, related more to data handling as multitudinous observations had to be processed to derive actual trajectories, to monitor performance via telemetry, and later to enhance REMOTE-SENSING data. The space industry spurred the miniaturization of computers through developments in microelectronic technology. Many observers believe that American space achievements were completely dependent on computers.

Even the earliest computers were useful in constructing mathematical tables; however, when computer processing resorted to fundamentals (ie, ascertaining trigonometric values from formulae, square roots by iterative approximation, etc), the value of such tables quickly diminished. This concentration on basic values stimulated reconsideration and refinement of classical numerical methods (including their use of rounding off) to make use of the power and reduce the limitations of the new tool.

Census tabulation, a field with heavy addition requirements that had influenced developments in punched-card technology, lent itself to computerization, especially in N America where computers were usually tied to card devices. The electronic computing of pay followed, particularly where hourly rates meant extensive multiplication. This step took the computer from the scientific world into that of commerce, and thus from the hands of the science graduate to those of the accountant and eventually the lay user. Computer functions soon moved from payroll into accounts receivable and other financial applications and into inventory control. Speed of processing was the motivator, allowing reduction of the size of inventory and of the delay in receiving payment, and hence decreasing tied-up funds. Energy utilities and insurance companies were among the pioneers in extending the use of computers beyond the payroll function. The addition of video display terminals gave the user immediate access to data. Among the first to capitalize on this now widely used feature were Air Canada (for reservations) and University of Alberta Hospital (for patient data).

Given appropriate sensors, the computer can use its speed and stamina to provide vigilant monitoring (eg, of patients) and elaborate interpretation of events (eg, construction of 3-dimensional images from X-ray data). Given appropriate actuators, a computer can react and hence control events in ways specified by program and human input. Today, computers control PIPELINE flows, NUCLEAR POWER PLANTS, traffic signals, aircraft, refineries, telephone exchanges and, at a smaller scale, machine tools and car engines. Interprovincial Pipe Line Ltd of Edmonton, Alta, ATOMIC ENERGY OF CANADA LTD, and the city of Toronto have been notable pioneers, as has the TRANSCANADA TELEPHONE SYSTEM in its innovative Dataroute and Datapack digital transmission networks. Using early, cumbersome computers, the Canadian navy, with its DATARS Project, pioneered "Command Control" of warships. Small, inexpensive microprocessors today allow computer control to be so unobtrusive as to make the presence of a computer go almost unnoticed. Minuscule energy demands allow computers to be used in a wristwatch or implanted in the human body to control an aberrant heart.

Compared with numbers, textual data is expensive to enter and store (because of its great redundancy), and it lacks the notable profitability of automatic multiplication. While these relative disadvantages cannot be eliminated, vast improvements in hardware economics in the 1970s lessened them and, with improved algorithms (definitions of the means of solving a problem, expressed in a language which the device understands), allowed exploitation of electronic sorting. Textual indexes, notably of scientific literature abstracts, promoted growth in this field in the 1960s. Various forms of text editors have accommodated the computer's own source program material, plus an ever-growing array of documents. The need for speed in the NEWSPAPER industry led to the development of computer programs which took original draft articles and performed all editing and layout, including automatic typesetting. Related software served in the preparation of catalogues, books and, in the special form of word processing, simple correspondence. Tied to laser-beam xerographic printers, the computer has become an information machine, able to produce customized copies as required rather than blind facsimiles in bulk. Computers have become information storehouses, releasing their knowledge to remote callers by means of synthesized speech, data circuits or television images; Canada's TELIDON system is a leading example of this type of application.

The ability to branch (ie, to take alternative paths according to conditions) is an essential computer operation. This characteristic makes the computer a logical device that, for example, can be made to play CHESS. The computer makes choices by trying alternatives: by internally playing several steps down each feasible path and assessing the consequent situations. The computer can use this form of simulation in many practical scenarios (eg, traffic flow, demand/supply economics, patient care) and for modelling, teaching and examination. A refinement allows the computer to remember the consequences of past choices and hence to improve its decision making.

From its rough laboratory beginnings the computer has come to embrace a myriad of applications. This extension has led to the development of various special-purpose computers and to a vast range of power and size, but the trend of application is now towards integration. A single network, if not a single computer, encompasses commercial and scientific applications, secretarial work, message communications and even speech communications. Simultaneously the microcomputer has become a toy, albeit an often useful and educational one, that increasingly absorbs the recreational time and money of Canadians. DONALD FENNA

Computers and Society Computers are the centrepiece of a vast TECHNOLOGY by which goods and services are produced and nations are governed. Because this technology is so pervasive, it has and will continue to have profound effects on individuals and on the conduct of public and private organizations. Many of these impacts are beneficial; others exact a cost. The balance between costs and benefits cannot yet be anticipated for some areas.

Because computers can control other instruments, vast improvements have taken place in activities in which "smart" instruments play an important role. The actions of groups of machines and instruments can be co-ordinated by computers and these machines then function as robots, with uses ranging from the improvement of industrial processes and medical applications to the creation of more destructive instruments of warfare. Computers also influence the structure and functioning of governmental and private organizations. These technological and procedural advances in INDUSTRY, GOVERNMENT, SCIENCE and MEDICINE entail certain social and economic costs. In the past, technological advances have balanced lost employment opportunities by creating jobs through the opening of new fields of endeavour, the exploitation of new opportunities and the satisfaction of new demands. It is still unclear whether such a balance will emerge from labour savings made through computers. The automation of office and bureaucratic procedures will certainly lead to a sharply decreased need for office personnel and managers (*see* OFFICE AUTOMATION). This anticipated decline in white-collar employment is still masked by the need for white-collar workers to computerize the work of the larger organizations that now produce, distribute, provide services or govern. However, once computerization has been completed, white-collar employment will follow the patterns set in industrial work, where there has been a generally lower demand for semiskilled and unskilled labour.

It is in their effect on the management of large organizations that computers have the greatest social impact. Here they are more than machines; they become the focus of a new management technology, which includes not only the physical machine ("hardware") but also program packages, their descriptions and protocols ("software"). Computer technology has also encouraged reorganization of the way public and private bureaucracies conduct their business, the development of new and diverse skills, new organizational units to supply and maintain computer-related services, and new attitudes about what computing is good for and how it may be used efficiently.

Computerization of large organizations has led to centralization and to increasingly hierarchical management structures, in part because vertically organized software for management systems is far less costly than software for distributed data processing, which would support diffusion of authority. The resulting shifts in administrative power in most public and private agencies are not subjected to the judgement of shareholders, voters or elected representatives, although some of these power shifts may significantly influence the future of such agencies.

Because computers support centralized organizational structure, it is becoming more difficult for individual citizens to obtain direct access to decision-making centres, which are often physically and organizationally distant from the individual with a problem. This distance is especially apparent when clients, customers or citizens attempt to correct errors in transactions, obtain necessary exemptions or act in any way that deviates from normal procedures. While computerization decreases the possibility of some errors in transactions between citizens and organizations, it increases the chance of others (eg, through flaws in programs) and simultaneously makes it more difficult to have such errors corrected.

The computerization of organizations may change the pattern of white-collar CRIME, making vandalism and theft take on much more serious proportions than in the past. Vandalism might involve destruction of the records of information systems on which large organizations depend. Opportunities for direct, physical theft are decreased because of the difficulty of gaining access to the financial networks; however, opportunities are available for embezzling very large sums of money by manipulating computer transactions. Other kinds of computer crime include the theft of computer time and the illegal manipulation or accession of confidential computer files.

A great deal of attention has been given to the possible loss of anonymity through the increasing access public and private organizations have to detailed personal records. The files of public and private organizations contain a great deal of information on the activities of individuals. Once these records become machine readable and records from different files can be linked, government and other agencies can obtain information which an individual may not wish them to have, resulting in a "loss of privacy." Some people believe that public agencies engaged in the control of those who abuse the system (eg, welfare cheaters or criminals) may perform their jobs better if they have access to detailed information. Their opponents argue that such agencies might be tempted to obtain records unrelated to their direct operation and thus conduct surveillance of a citizen's personal activities — eg, if Revenue Canada could catch income tax evaders by searching medical, real estate or other records. Of special importance to Canadians is the international flow of information among members of a large network that includes the US, the UK and Commonwealth nations, and Western Europe. Information about the transactions of Canadians flows freely across borders and is made available to authorities in other countries. The possible misuse of this data has not yet been addressed by legislative authorities.

Machine-readable membership lists of persons belonging to various interest groups have proved to be important in the formation of political coalitions (eg, in the US). This type of party coalition may be viewed as counteracting the distribution of powers within a democratic government. The ease with which such coalitions can be formed and manipulated and the effect of this phenomenon on the political process have yet to be seen. In Canada the creation of a national coalition might be valuable in counteracting the REGIONALISM of Canadian politics.

In 1984 personal computers were expected to account for about 10% of the anticipated $8-billion domestic market. In spite of the economic significance of this segment of the computer industry, the personal computer has thus far had a rather minimal impact on society, assuming functions formerly filled by typewriters, adding machines and calculators, and television video games. The personal microcomputer has become a toy that, while useful and educational in some circumstances, is as yet too self-contained to have seriously affected social structures. THEODOR D. STERLING

Comtois, Ulysse, sculptor (b at Granby, Qué 2 Mar 1931). After one year at the École des beaux-arts in Montréal, he took part in 2 important exhibitions: La Matière chante (1954) and Espace 55 (1955). He took 2nd prize for sculpture in the Concours artistiques du Québec (1963), created a mural for the administration pavilion at EXPO '67 in Montréal, and represented Canada at the 1968 Venice Biennale. A professor of art at UQAM 1970-74, he then became professor at Concordia in Montréal. In 1978 the Québec government awarded him the Prix Borduas for his work. In 1982 Montréal's Museum of Contemporary Art and the Musée du Québec held a retrospective of his work. MICHEL CHAMPAGNE

Conacher, Charles William, hockey player (b at Toronto 10 Dec 1909; d there 30 Dec 1967). Playing right wing on Toronto's potent "Kid Line," with Joe Primeau and Harvey "Busher" Jackson, he was known for his rambunctious play and booming shot. He played 12 seasons in the NHL, mostly with TORONTO MAPLE LEAFS, winning the scoring title 1933-34 and 1934-35 and sharing it twice more. He was traded to Detroit 1938 and finished his career with New York Americans. He scored 225 goals, 173 assists in regular season play, adding 17 goals, 18 assists in playoffs. JAMES MARSH

Conacher, Lionel Pretoria, all-round athlete, politician (b at Toronto 24 May 1900; d at Ottawa 26 May 1954). One of 10 children, he grew up in a tough working-class district of Toronto. He got his first taste of sports at Jesse Ketchum School and went on to excel at football, lacrosse, baseball, boxing, wrestling, hockey, and track and field. At age 16 he won the 125-lb wrestling championship of Ontario and in 1920, in his first boxing competition, won the Canadian light-heavyweight championship. The following year he boxed a 3-round exhibition bout with Jack Dempsey, the world heavyweight champion. Conacher's power, stamina and speed (he ran 100 yards in under 10 seconds) were particularly suited to lacrosse and football. He helped Toronto to win the Ontario Lacrosse Assn senior title in 1922. In football he was a ferocious runner and perhaps the best punter in the game. In the 1921 GREY CUP game he led Toronto Argonauts to a 23-0 victory over Edmonton, himself scoring 15 points. He did not learn to skate until age 16, but his aggressive, determined play made him one of the best defencemen in hockey. He turned professional with Pittsburgh in 1925 and played for New York Americans, Chicago Black Hawks and Montreal Maroons (1930-33 and 1934-37). Rugged and ready to brawl (even with his brother Charlie CONACHER), he was NHL first all-star in 1934.

Lionel Conacher, "the Big Train," Canada's finest all-round athlete, shown here in the uniform of the New York Americans (*courtesy Canada's Sports Hall of Fame*).

Conacher entered politics in 1937 and was Liberal MPP for Toronto Bracondale. He was Ontario athletic commissioner and worked to provide recreational facilities in city parks. In 1949 he was elected federal MP for Toronto Trinity. He died of a heart attack after hitting a triple in a charity softball game. Deserving of his nickname "The Big Train," Conacher was the greatest all-round athlete that Canada has produced. JAMES MARSH

Conant, Gordon Daniel, lawyer, Liberal politician, premier of Ontario (b near Oshawa, Ont 11 Jan 1885; d at Oshawa 2 Jan 1953). From 1937 the capable, faithful attorney general in the Ontario government of Mitchell HEPBURN, he inherited the premiership from his leader in Oct 1942. But Hepburn's feud with PM KING was tearing apart Ontario Liberals and his arbitrary choice of successor deepened resentment. Despite a productive legislative session, Conant could not heal the rift and in Apr 1943 he resigned. BARBARA A. MCKENNA

Conception Bay is one of the principal bays of Newfoundland, formed by 2 N-reaching arms of the AVALON PENINSULA. Its name, one of the earliest recorded (1527), commemorates the Feast of the Immaculate Conception. Cape St Francis to the E and Split Point, 32 km NW, mark the mouth of the bay, which stretches 70 km S to Holyrood. Its shoreline, varying from rugged cliffs and fjordlike inlets to gentle sandy beaches and excellent harbours, was the province's earliest settled; its rich marine resources were utilized by Europeans from the early 1500s. In 1610 CUPIDS was the site of the first formal English colony in present-day Canada. The bay has always been Newfoundland's most populous. BELL ISLAND in the E, the bay's largest island, was the location of an important iron-ore mine. ROBERT D. PITT

Conception Bay South, Nfld, Town, pop 10 856 (1981c), inc 1971, is located on the SE shore of CONCEPTION BAY on the AVALON PENINSULA. The town, 32 km long, 5 km wide, comprises a number of smaller former settlements that ring the shoreline: Topsail, Chamberlains, Codner, Long Pond, Manuels, Upper Gullies, Indian Pond and Seal Cove. Most of the constituent settlements were founded by fishermen before 1800. Crops were grown in the areas backing the fishing sites and sold in nearby ST JOHN'S. The area, dotted by numerous ponds and with good seafront beaches, has also been a popular summer resort for St John's residents. Since 1945 most of the labour force has commuted to St John's. Some small-scale fishing and truck farming is still carried on; the local service industry makes up the balance of the community's employment.

JANET E.M. PITT AND ROBERT D. PITT

Concert Halls and Opera Houses When Canada was being settled in the 17th and 18th centuries, buildings for defence, accommodation and religious worship took priority. However, once these essential structures were completed and social order established, inhabitants could consider entertainment. In Québec and the Maritimes early concerts and theatrical presentations took place in what 18th-century newspapers advertised as a concert hall or theatre. In fact, performances generally were located in an assembly room of a hotel or inn, the upper floor of a tavern, or in the local mechanics' hall. During the last 2 decades of the 18th century and especially in the first half of the 19th century, concerts and dramas were regularly presented in Québec City (Thespian Theatre, Marchant's Coffee House, Frank's Tavern), Montréal (Theatre Royal, Dillon's Hotel, Salle de Spectacle), Halifax (British Tavern, Theatre Royal), Saint John (Mallard's Long Room), St John's, Nfld (Globe Tavern), and at the end of the 19th century, Toronto (St Lawrence Hall). Most 18th- and 19th-century structures have not survived fires and demolition. However, some travellers and residents left brief descriptions of these early buildings. For example, William Dyott, a British army lieutenant stationed in Halifax, describes in his diary the first Maritime theatre built for dramas, operas and mixed entertainments: "February (1789) — the officers in garrison fitted up a new theatre. . . . It was as complete a thing for the size as I ever saw. Boxes and a first and second pit." By the mid-19th century, touring performers could find some sort of facility in many towns of central Canada. "Our stay at Hamilton was marked with signal success in a professional light. We played at the Mechanics' Hall — fine one for singing in — well situated and tolerably cheap — 15 dols. a night. . . . We played also at the Templars' Hall, a charming little room well worthy of a trial by any one attempting Entertainments" (Horton Rhys, *A Theatrical Trip for a Wager*, 1861).

With the advent of touring theatrical and musical companies, between 1870 and 1900, a series of opera houses were constructed across Canada. These buildings formed one of the first important Canadian cultural links. With the completion of the railway from east to west, entertainers could travel economically and efficiently. By 1900, Montréal, Ottawa, Kingston, Winnipeg, Vancouver and many smaller cities had completed buildings. Even Dawson City and Barkerville had opera houses — monuments to the extravagance of the gold rush. The name opera house was somewhat misleading because dramas, mixed entertainments of acting and singing, and performances of feats of skill were the most common attractions.

Some early opera houses could seat between 1000 and 2000 people. Toronto's MASSEY HALL, opened in 1894, is the best period example of a concert hall primarily designed for large orchestral and choral performances. However, during the first half of the 20th century few cities had concert halls or opera houses for these specialized purposes. Most of the old so-called opera houses, if they were not destroyed, became movie theatres. Concerts and opera performances usually took place in high-school auditoriums, sports arenas or other makeshift venues. The second half of the 20th century witnessed a growth in the building and restoring of recital halls, opera houses and large multi-purpose performing complexes. PLACE DES ARTS (Montréal), Confederation Centre of the Arts (Charlottetown), NATIONAL ARTS CENTRE (Ottawa), Grand Théâtre de Québec (Québec City), Saskatchewan Centre of the Arts (Regina), Hamilton Place (Hamilton), Orpheum Theatre (Vancouver), Roy Thomson Hall (Toronto), and the companion Jubilee auditoriums (Calgary and Edmonton) are some examples. The 1800-seat Jack singer Hall will open Sept 1985 in Calgary as part of The Calgary Centre for Performing Arts. These structures are the homes for resident orchestras which present concert series to surrounding communities. In addition, concert halls present touring entertainers from N America and abroad, and extensive seasons of varied entertainment.

FREDERICK HALL

Roy Thomson Hall interior, Toronto, Ont, designed by Arthur Erickson (*courtesy Canapress*).

Concession Line, a term used especially in Ontario to refer to the frontages of concessions, or property lots, which if extended would run from one end of a TOWNSHIP to the other. In practice a concession line is likely to be a road with a number ("First Concession," "Concession Road 10," etc). Concession lines are normally spaced at 1.25 mile (2 km) intervals.

JOHN ROBERT COLOMBO

Concordia University, Montréal, was founded 1974 by merger of Sir George Williams University and Loyola College. Loyola, originally the English section of the Jesuit Collège Sainte-Marie (est 1848) had become a separate entity in 1899; SGWU had evolved from the formal educational work of the Montréal YMCA and had received its university charter in 1948. Concordia has 2 campuses, one in downtown Montréal (SGWU) and one in its west end (Loyola). It offers programs in 4 faculties: arts and science, commerce and administration, engineering and computer science, and fine arts. Bachelors' degrees are awarded in administration, arts, commerce, computer science, education, engineering, fine arts and science; undergraduate-level certificate programs are also offered in some areas, and graduate degrees and diploma programs are available in many disciplines. Most undergraduate and graduate programs are open to part-time students, and about half the total student population attends on a part-time basis.

Enrolment: Concordia University, 1982-83
(Source: Statistics Canada)

Full-time Undergrad	*Full-time Graduate*	*Part-time Undergrad*	*Part-time Graduate*
10 346	1 435	11 001	1 782

Condiment Crops grown on a commercial scale in Canada include ONIONS (*Allium cepa*), yellow or white mustard (*Brassica herta*), brown mustard (*B. juncea*), horseradish (*Armoracia rusticana*), dill (*Anethum graveolens*), caraway (*Carum carvi*) and coriander (*Coriandrum sativum*). Basil (*Ocimum basilicum*), fennel (*Foeniculum vulgare*), garlic (*Allium sativum*), MINT (*Mentha piperata, M. spicata*), sage (*Salvia officinalis*) and savory (*Satureja hortensis*) are grown by small cottage industries. The common onion is a herbaceous biennial PLANT with a single large bulb; the numerous cultivars (commercial varieties) differ in size, colour, shape and flavour. Onions are used as seasoning in many foods (eg, sauces, soups, omelettes, meats, pickles). Québec produces 35% of Canada's onions; Ontario, 55%; western Canada, 10%. The approximately 4000 ha planted with onions produce 105 000 t of bulbs (valued at $22 million). Yellow and brown mustards are herbaceous annuals, brown mustard being more pungent. Mustard seed is used to prepare mustard pastes (used in flavouring hot dogs, cheeses, eggs, meats, salad dressing, etc) and as whole seeds (in pickling or boiled with vegetables). Mustards are grown in Manitoba (22%), Saskatchewan (59%) and Alberta (19%) on approximately 75 000 ha. The 81 000 t produced annually is valued at $29.5 million. Canada is the world's leading exporter of mustard seed. Horseradish is a hardy perennial of the mustard family. Its white, fleshy, cylindrical roots are used as table relish with roast beef, raw oysters and fish, in pickling or in sauces or prepared mustards. Horseradish is grown in southern Ontario on approximately 100 ha, which produce 1200 t of fresh roots, valued at $0.75 million. Dill, an annual, is used to flavour soups, sauces and pickled cucumbers. It is grown in Manitoba for the production of dill-weed oil; each year the approximately 400 ha produce 32 000 kg of oil, valued at $0.5 million. Coriander, an annual, is used as whole seed in mixed pickling spice or in ground form in curry powder and flavouring for pastries, sausages and frankfurters. In Canada it is grown on the prairies on approximately 200 ha, which produce 227 t of seed, valued at $0.2 million. Caraway, a biennial, is used to flavour rye bread, cakes, cheese, applesauce, cookies, etc. In Canada it is grown on the prairies on approximately 1000 ha, which yield 57 t of seed, valued at $0.1 million. B.B. CHUBEY

Condominium is a form of tenure that gives the owner clear title and full ownership rights to a specific unit within a building and a shared interest in common areas of the building. Condominiums are run by associations of owners who are responsible for the administration and management of the building and grounds.

In Canada, most provinces introduced condominium or strata-title legislation in the 1960s, though developers began to build condominiums in large numbers only in the mid-1970s. A condominium owner has full ownership rights to the unit. Unit descriptions must define where the dividing line between individual ownership and common property lies. Common property usually includes the land, halls, elevators, heating services, gardens, parking and recreation areas. Individual owners are assessed a fee to cover the cost of common expenses. Owner fees may be related to unit size, or each owner may pay an equal share of the common expenses and have an equal vote at meetings of the condominium corporation.

Condominium is different from co-operative tenure. Condominium owners can renovate or sell their units, and keep any profits from the sale. In a co-operative, the occupant purchases a share in the whole building which must be returned to the co-operative association when the owner moves. In a market co-operative, owners sell their shares; in a nonprofit co-operative, occupants cannot sell their shares. Any form of multiple housing, including row housing and high-rise apartments, can be a condominium. The terms "co-operative" and "condominium" both refer to a type of tenure, not a type of housing. ANN MCAFEE

Confectionery Industry, a MANUFACTURING sector made up of companies primarily involved in processing candies, chocolate and cocoa products, chewing gum and other products such as salted nuts and popcorn. Confectionery manufacturing started to emerge as an important industry in the late 1800s. One of the earliest commercial operations, McCormick's Ltd, was established in London, Ont, in 1857. Robertson Brothers Ltd was in the candy business in Toronto by 1864, and Ganong Brothers Ltd opened in St Stephen, NB, in 1872. In 1873 Moirs Ltd, originally a bakery, commenced candy production in Halifax, NS. Robert Watson Co started in Toronto in 1874, and by 1879 Viau Ltée was in production in Montréal. In Toronto, Patterson Candy Co was established in 1888; the Cowan Co, in 1890. Confectionery production greatly increased in Canada in the early 1900s with the establishment of several major producers, including William Neilson Ltd in Toronto in 1908, Willard's Chocolates Ltd, Toronto, 1914, and Fry-Cadbury Ltd, Montréal, 1920. Walter M. Lowney Co of Montréal and Walter Baker Co of Canada, Toronto, also became established during this period. In these formative years the industry was concentrated in eastern Canada, a situation that prevails today, although in western Canada a number of smaller manufacturers emerged during this period and new companies are still appearing, one of the latest being Hendy's Candies Ltd, which opened in Innisfail, Alta, in 1982. This company sells about $30 million of licorice annually.

Confectionery packaging is controlled by regulations enforced by Consumer and Corporate Affairs Canada. Sanitation and related matters are controlled by the Health Protection Branch of Health and Welfare Canada. The industry is represented by the Confectionery Manufacturers Association of Canada, Toronto.

During the past 2 decades, a considerable amount of plant consolidation has taken place. In 1961 the industry had 194 plants in production. By 1973 the number had been reduced to 112, and in 1982 Statistics Canada reported 110 plants in production: NS had 5; NB, 2; Qué, 33; Ont, 51; Man, 4; Sask, 1; Alta, 2; and BC, 12. As is the case in most other food sectors, the major cause of the reduction has been the steady phasing out of smaller, obsolete production facilities and their replacement with fewer, larger, highly efficient operations.

The confectionery industry is unique among segments of the Canadian FOOD AND BEVERAGE manufacturing system in that it is dependent on foreign supply for 2 of its primary ingredients: sugar and cocoa. Unfortunately, these commodities are subject to rapidly changing prices in spite of accords such as the International Sugar Agreement. This factor, in turn, can seriously affect the industry's sales volumes and profit margins. Any sharp increase in the international price of raw sugarcane or cocoa beans is quickly translated into increased production costs and higher consumer prices; a downturn in production volumes usually follows. Steadily increasing provincial sales taxes are another indirect cost that can have a negative effect on industry sales. However, over the long term, production volumes in most categories have shown slow, steady growth. For example, in 1973 the industry produced 68 895 t of all types of chocolate products, including chocolate bars, boxed chocolates, seasonal novelties and chocolate products sold in bulk and other forms. By 1983 the production of chocolate confectionery had increased to 74 601 t. Similarly, in 1971, 16 772 t of chewing-gum products came off the industry's production lines; by 1983 this amount had increased to 19 871 t. Trends in sugar confectionery, which includes hard candy, pan goods (hard and soft) and similar products, fluctuate. In 1971 the industry produced 49 114 t of sugar confectionery; but in 1983 the volume was 44 556 t. Importation of hard-candy products affects the trend. The UK has always been a major Canadian supplier of high-quality candies, but imports are increasing from S American countries, notably Brazil and Argentina.

In 1982 the industry employed slightly over 9138 people and spent $426 million on materials and supplies. Statistics Canada reported that in 1982 the industry made shipments valued at $922.2 million. ROBERT F. BARRATT

Confederation The Confederation movement followed Newton's first law of motion: all bodies continue in a state of rest or of uniform motion unless compelled by some force to change their state. In the 1860s political union of BRITISH NORTH AMERICA was an idea, the subject of occasional dinner speeches when wine raised a man's sights, softened political asperities, and broadened his horizons. But only in 1864 did it become a serious question in the PROVINCE OF CANADA, and in the Atlantic colonies a great deal of pressure would be necessary to convert romantic ideas of a nation *a mari usque ad mare* into political reality.

As the Province of Canada grew larger and more prosperous and developed politically, socially and industrially, so grew its internal rivalries and difficulties. Whereas the Conservative party believed the 1841 constitution had by no means outlived its usefulness, the Reform party insisted that change was essential. Canada West (Ont), wanting divorce more than Canada East (Qué), could make difficult all ministries that did not conform to its belief in "representation by population." In 1864, after 4 short-lived ministries had fought to stay in power, a COALITION was formed, promising Confederation. The province's problems were to be solved by division of its 2 sections and the union of all BNA. With support from 3 of the province's 4 major political groups, the coalition gave Confederation a driving force that it never lost. Canada West's 2 major political groups were united on the issue; their leaders, John A. MACDONALD and George BROWN, were peculiar partners, but their alliance meant that Confederation proceeded with support from BNA's most populous province. In Canada East, although Confederation was opposed by A.A. DORION'S PARTI ROUGE, it was supported by the dominant political group, the Conservatives under George-Étienne CARTIER, Hector LANGEVIN and A.T. Galt. By 1867 they had the necessary support of the Catholic Church. Confederation was justified by the arguments that French Canadians would get back their provincial identity — the capital of their province would once more be Québec; the anglophone domination of Ottawa feared by French Canadians would be mitigated by the presence of strong French Canadian representation in the federal Cabinet; and Confederation was the least undesirable of the changes proposed. Confederation was in some danger in Canada East, but with the church's support and that of the French Canadian Conservatives, opposition was weak.

The Atlantic colonies of Newfoundland, PEI, NS and NB each had aspirations, but none was as dissatisfied with the status quo as was Canada West. With the exception of Newfoundland, they felt comfortable as they were, and the bulk of the population, especially in NS and PEI, saw no reason to change their constitution just because Canada was finding it had outgrown its own. Even Newfoundland, after economic difficulties in the 1860s had made it susceptible to mainland blandishments, postponed decision in 1865, and in the 1869 Newfoundland general election decisively rejected Confederation. The more prosperous PEI resisted almost from the start. A small, dedicated group of Confederationists made little headway until, early in the 1870s, the railway adventures of successive Island governments forced PEI to seek a solution in the new Dominion. NS was more complicated. Along the axis of the railway that already ran from Halifax to Truro and was to continue to Québec, there was real support for Confederation. The manufacturing and coal-producing areas, Pictou County and to some extent Cape Breton, were also interested. But along the S shore and in the Annapolis Valley — the prosperous world of shipping, shipbuilding, potatoes and apples — Confederation appeared unattractive or even dangerous. Conservative Premier Charles TUPPER, ambitious, aggressive and confident, went ahead with Confederation, convinced that in the long run it would be best for NS, and perhaps also for himself. Fortunately for Confederation, Tupper did not test his electorate: elected in 1863, his government did not need to go to the polls until 1867, after Confederation. Then, too late, it was clear that 65% of Nova Scotians opposed Confederation (*see* REPEAL MOVEMENT). NB supported Confederation only slightly more than any other Atlantic province. In Feb 1865 the anti-Confederate government of A.J. Smith was elected. Confederation could go nowhere until the Smith government collapsed in 1866 and a new pro-Confederate government was brought in, helped by the FENIAN invasions of Apr and June 1866, which badly weakened anti-Confederate positions.

External forces such as the AMERICAN CIVIL WAR and the truculence of American foreign policy (symbolized in the 1866 abrogation of the RECIPROCITY Treaty and 1867 Alaska purchase) made the separate colonies of BNA uneasy about their future. Duty would compel Britain to respond to any military aggression against BNA, as the TRENT AFFAIR showed; but Britain had no taste for it. The best British defence against the US was a BNA federation. Confederation thus had powerful support from London, especially from Colonial Secretary Edward Cardwell. Cardwell instructed his BNA governors, in the strongest language possible, to support Confederation. They did. This policy continued, and under Cardwell's successors the HBC sold RUPERT'S LAND to Canada in 1870, and BC was brought into Confederation in 1871. The only defeat British policy sustained was in Newfoundland in 1869; 80 years later it finally made its contribution to Confederation. *See* CHARLOTTETOWN CONFERENCE; QUEBEC CONFERENCE; LONDON CONFERENCE; CONSTITUTION ACT, 1867; CONSTITUTIONAL HISTORY.

P.B. WAITE

Reading: J.M.S. Careless, *Brown of the Globe* (1963); D.G. Creighton, *The Road to Confederation* (1964) and *John A. Macdonald: The Young Politician* (1952); W.L. Morton, *The Critical Years* (1964); P.B. Waite, *The Confederation Debates in the Province of Canada* (1963) and *The Life and Times of Confederation* (1962).

Confederation of National Trade Unions (CNTU, or Confédération des syndicats nationaux), fd 1921 as Canadian Catholic Confederation of Labour (CCCL) by 2 union groups, the national, nondenominational unions which had emerged in Québec early in the century, and the Catholic unions founded after 1907 by clergy in some Québec dioceses who feared the "socialist" and anticlerical ideas of the international unions. The national unions had refused to join international unions, hoping to establish a truly Canadian movement. With little support from English Canadian workers, their movement, limited almost entirely to Québec, remained very small until merging with the Catholic unions during WWI. The latter promoted good understanding and co-operation between management and workers, but this was quickly seen to be a utopian dream and some new unions witnessed a dramatic decline in membership.

The Catholic unions were reorganized at the end of WWI, stressing protection of members' professional rights and interests. Anxious to unite their forces, they jointly formed the Canadian Catholic Confederation of Labour in 1921 with about 17 600 members. Membership declined during the 1920s but increased again after 1934, especially after WWII (62 690 members in 1946). Support came primarily from the construction, leatherworking, textile and garment industries. After WWII the CCCL's ideology gradually lost its religious nature. Major strikes during the 1950s and opposition from the government of Maurice DUPLESSIS increased union militancy. In 1960 the confederation dropped "Catholic" from its title (it became the Confederation of National Trade Unions) and dropped references to the SOCIAL DOCTRINE of the church from its statement of principles.

The CNTU, radicalized after 1964 by the influx of workers in the public and para-public sectors (*see* PUBLIC-SERVICE UNIONS), gradually became committed to the fight for a new social order. Convinced that the bourgeoisie dominated the state and that workers were inevitably in conflict with this economic power, the leaders argued for the replacement of capitalism by democratic socialism. This ideological swing caused much turmoil within the CNTU. During the 1972 "Common Front" strikes some leaders, including 3 members of the executive committee, left the CNTU to form the Central of Democratic Trade Unions (CDTU). Some 30 000 CNTU members, especially in clothing, textiles, leather and mining industries, joined the breakaway organization.

Since 1964 the CNTU, with its many members in the civil service, hospitals and some education positions, has been at the centre of public sector employees' struggles for better working conditions. In 1972 the CNTU persuaded the Québec Teachers Corporation and the public sector workers of the Québec Federation of Labour to join it in a common front for negotiations with government. Then and in 1976 and 1979, the common front approach won valuable gains in minimum salary, job security and pensions. In 1981 the CNTU consisted of 1400 unions, divided into 9 federations and 22 central councils with a total membership of 210 430. *See* UNION CENTRALS.

JACQUES ROUILLARD

Conference Board of Canada, officially incorporated as AERTC Inc, a nonprofit economic research and analysis institution funded by business, government, unions and universities. Established (1954) as a division of the American National Industrial Conference Board Inc, which was founded (1916) on the belief that many of industrial society's problems could be eased by discussion based on scientifically researched facts, it acquired a separate legal identity in 1981. It publishes quarterly reports on the national and provincial economic outlook, and 2 quarterly surveys, one on business attitudes and investment-spending plans, the other on consumer-spending intentions. It also publishes *Datafacts*, a statistical report on labour markets. Its public affairs division publishes reports on issues such as the responsibilities of corporate directors.

DUNCAN MCDOWALL

Conflict of Interest may be defined as a situation in which politicians and public servants have an actual or potential interest (usually financial) that may influence or appear to influence the conduct of their official duties (*see also* PATRONAGE; CORRUPTION). Even when this conflict is not illegal, it may create doubts or suspicions concerning the integrity or fairness of decisions made by such officials, and over time recurring conflicts may increase the level of distrust and cynicism toward government. In Canada, conflicts of interest have arisen when, for example, the ownership of land by the family of a provincial Cabinet minister could have influenced the minister's decision to approve a new subdivision or influence other officials to do so; when a senator invested money in a firm that subsequently received a lucrative government contract; and when a former federal Cabinet minister had dealings with his department that may have resulted in favouritism in the government's decision to issue a grant to the minister's new company.

Except for bribery and FRAUD, which are covered under the Criminal Code, legislation on broader conflict-of-interest questions is relatively uncommon, 2 notable exceptions being laws in Newfoundland (1973) and in New Brunswick (1978). Guidelines on conflict of interest, like those issued by the federal government for civil servants (1973) and Cabinet ministers (1979), are apparently preferred, but unfortunately tend to be ambiguous. They do not provide sufficient sanctions to deter potential conflicts, or appropriate mechanisms to determine the existence of violations. When charges of conflict of interest fail to provoke disciplinary actions, however, they may cause such acute political embarrassment that a Cabinet minister may feel it necessary to resign to protect the government's integrity, which, although rare, happened in Ontario in 1972.

K. GIBBONS

Congregational Churches, Protestant group arising from Puritanism, organized on the principle that each congregation should be autonomous. Congregations were established among New England settlers in NS from 1751 and later in NB. By 1800, because of the disruptive influence of Henry ALLINE's preaching (as a result of which many congregations became BAPTIST) and because most of the ministers were identified with disloyalty during the AMERICAN REVOLUTION, only 2 churches survived. During the 19th century, receiving its main support up to 1861 from the British Congregational Union, the denomination's strength was among central Canada's urban middle class. With its extension into western Canada after 1879, it developed a strong commitment to missionary work, both at home among German and Swedish immigrants and abroad in Angola. In 1925 the Congregational Union of Canada, fd 1906, consisted of 17 churches in NS and NB, 20 in Québec, 50 in Ontario, 24 (including 14 student fields) in western Canada and 26 Russo-Swedish mission churches, with a combined total of 31 012 members. That year the Union voted 118 to 8 to form part of the UNITED CHURCH OF CANADA.

J.P.B. KENYON

Reading: E.B. Eddy, "The Congregational Tradition," in J.W. Grant (ed), *The Churches and the Canadian Experience* (1963).

Conifers, a large group of cone-bearing TREES and shrubs with about 48 genera and over 500 species, comprise the order Coniferales of the gymnosperms (nonflowering, naked SEED PLANTS). The group contains the oldest (bristlecone pines, over 4000 years old) and largest (redwoods, over 100 m tall) living things. Some 3[illegible] conifers (eg, pine, spruce, hemlock, fir, larch, Douglas fir, cedar, juniper and yew) grow in Canada.

Seeds are borne on the surface of scales that form seed cones which are usually large and woody, occasionally small and fleshy. In some conifers, seeds are borne singly, occasionally with a berrylike covering. All conifers bear pollen in cones. Most conifers are evergreen but some (eg, larch) are deciduous. Leaves usually persist for several years and are needlelike, scalelike or, rarely, broad. A lateral growth zone (cambium) produces large amounts of wood in the stem and root. Wood is soft, consisting primarily of long, hollow cells (tracheids).

Families Conifers are a primitive PLANT group which evolved from ancient gymnosperms. All modern genera originated in the Mesozoic era (280-150 million years ago), and many have persisted relatively unchanged. Eight families are usually recognized. One, Lebachiaceae, is extinct. The oldest living family, Podocarpaceae, with 7 genera and 150 species, occurs in semitropical and southern temperate regions. Araucariaceae (monkey puzzle tree family), a small but ancient family of 2 genera and 40 species, is native to the Southern Hemisphere. Cupressaceae (cypress family) has 18 genera and over 100 species, found primarily in northern

Mature, open cone of Scotch pine (*Pinus sylvestris*), shedding a seed (*courtesy National Museums of Canada/National Museum of Natural Sciences*).

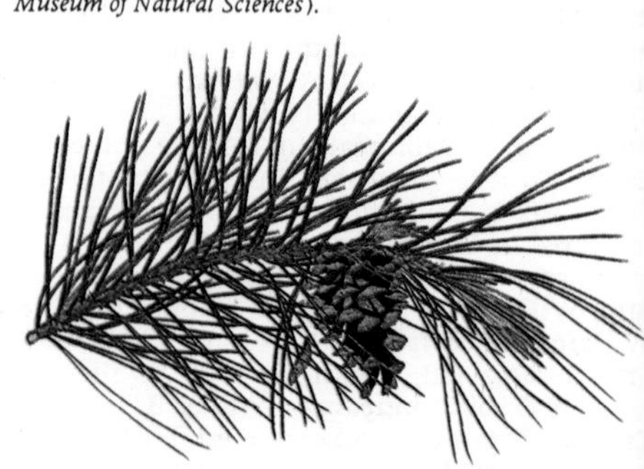

temperate regions. Taxodiaceae (redwood family) is native to northern temperate regions and has 10 genera and about 18 species. Pinaceae (pine family), the largest and most familiar family, containing 10 genera and about 240 species, is restricted primarily to northern temperate regions. Cephalotaxaceae (plum-yew family) consists of one genus and about 5 species, native to China, Japan and Korea. Members of Taxaceae (yew family) are often considered not to be conifers, because they lack seed cones and bear individual seeds enclosed in a berrylike structure (aril).

Structure Mature stems and roots consist primarily of a central core of wood (xylem) produced by cambium (formative or "meristematic" layer). The xylem conducts water and minerals, and also supports the tree. Cambium also forms phloem to the outside, which conducts dissolved food up and down the tree. Outside the phloem, a cork cambium forms outer bark (periderm) that protects the stem and root. Growth rings are prominent in the xylem. Early or springwood consists of tracheids of large diameter; dark, late or summerwood of tracheids of smaller diameter with thicker walls. Some conifer wood contains resin ducts. Conifer leaves are adapted to prevent water loss: the waxy surface (cuticle) is thick and pores (stomata) are recessed. Usually, a single large vein (vascular bundle) and several resin ducts occur in each leaf. Most conifer leaves are arranged spirally, but both leaf arrangement and shape may vary during tree growth.

Reproduction Like other seed plants, conifers show alternation of generations, ie, a sexual stage alternates with an asexual stage. The dominant stage is the asexual sporophyte (spore-producing) generation. The sexual or gametophyte phase is reduced to a one-celled stage retained by and parasitic on the sporophyte. Sporophytes have separate male and female cones (strobili), usually on a single tree. Each cone produces one kind of spore that develops into a gametophyte (reproductive body). Male cones produce thousands of pollen grains (male gametophytes). Pollen may have 2 wings or lack wings entirely. Released in spring, it is carried by wind to a seed cone (female), consisting of a series of modified leaves (bracts), each with a broad, ovule-bearing scale. Bracts and scales may be separate or fused. Each scale usually has 2 ovules. Within each ovule, a female gametophyte develops, containing one to several eggs. Pollen enters the ovule through the micropyle (opening), and germinates, forming a pollen tube that grows into ovule tissue.

The pollen tube reaches a female gametophyte and releases 2 male gametes (sperm) into an egg cell. One sperm fertilizes the egg; the other degenerates. The fertilized egg nucleus divides, ultimately forming a massive embryo. Several eggs in the same ovule may be fertilized, and each may form an embryo (simple polyembryony). In some conifers each fertilized egg forms 4 embryos (cleavage polyembryony). In either case, only one embryo, the most vigorous, normally survives. Conifer embryos develop 2 or many embryonic leaves (cotyledons). The development of the embryo — the new individual of the sporophyte generation — completes the conifer life cycle. The mature ovule (containing female gametophyte and embryo) is a seed. In most conifers, seeds mature in the fall of the same year in which POLLINATION occurs. In others (eg, pine) seeds mature after 2 growing seasons. Most conifer seeds have one or 2 wings. Seed cones open in fall and seeds are wind dispersed. Seeds of most temperate-zone conifers require a chilling period (stratification) before germination. At germination the primary root penetrates soil and branches. The young stem bears cotyledons, but soon forms juvenile leaves and lateral branches.

Uses The FOREST industry is the largest Canadian natural-resource industry, and conifers are its major component. Most lumber and pulp and paper is obtained from conifers, primarily from species of spruce, pine, fir, hemlock and Douglas fir. Conifer wood is classified as softwood, in contrast to the hardwoods of broadleaf trees (eg, maple, oak, birch and ash). Conifers also yield resin (pitch), turpentine and various oils. Tannin, for tanning leather, comes from bark of larches. Juniper "berries" are used for flavouring (eg, gin), and seeds (pine nuts) of some species are edible. Many conifers are used as ORNAMENTALS. Some Canadian conifers (eg, Douglas fir, lodgepole pine and spruce) are planted for timber in Great Britain, New Zealand and many European countries. *See* individual species entries. JOHN N. OWENS

Reading: R.C. Hosie, *Native Trees of Canada* (1979).

Conn Smythe Trophy is awarded annually to the player judged most valuable to his team in the NATIONAL HOCKEY LEAGUE playoffs. The player is selected by hockey writers. The trophy was first presented in 1964 in honour of Conn SMYTHE, former coach, manager and owner of Toronto Maple Leafs. JAMES MARSH

Connaught and Strathearn, Arthur William Patrick Albert, 1st Duke of, governor general of Canada 1911-16 (b at Buckingham Palace 1 May 1850; d at Bagshot Park, Surrey, Eng 16 January 1942). The third and favourite son of Queen Victoria, Prince Arthur was educated privately before attending the Royal Military Academy, Woolwich. He spent a year with the first battalion of the Rifle Brigade in Montréal, where he turned out for a Fenian raid in 1870. After a military career which took him to Egypt, India, Ireland and S Africa, he was made a field marshall in 1902. Disappointed by his failure to succeed the duke of Cambridge as commander in chief of the British army in 1895, as governor general of Canada he took his nominal position as commander in chief of the Canadian Militia more seriously than he ought, particularly during WWI. His advice, opinions and insistence on being consulted about the details of war administration created considerable tension between him and the minister of militia, Sam HUGHES, and stretched his constitutional position and the patience of PM Robert L. BORDEN to the limit. CARMAN MILLER

Connaught Laboratories Limited is a producer of BIOLOGICAL PRODUCTS, including bacterial vaccines (eg, pertussis), toxoids (eg, tetanus), viral vaccines (eg, polio, rabies), hormones (eg, INSULIN), blood fractions (eg, albumin, coagulation factor VIII), diagnostics (eg, for detection of hepatitis B) and veterinary vaccines (eg, rabies, calf scours). The company was established in 1914 in the Department of Hygiene of University of Toronto, largely through the efforts of John G. Fitzgerald, associate professor of hygiene. The laboratories functioned as a financially self-supporting organization and remained an integral part of U of T until 1972.

The first products included a live rabies vaccine and horse antitoxins for diphtheria. In Jan 1922 Frederick G. BANTING and Charles H. BEST demonstrated the effectiveness of insulin against DIABETES. In the same year, Connaught became the first laboratory to introduce insulin commercially. Connaught in the 1980s produced over 95% of the insulin used in Canada. During WWII, Connaught began preparation of fractions of human blood plasma (eg, albumin, immune serum globulin) collected by the Canadian RED CROSS. Clinical use of such fractions has permitted far greater use of each blood donation. Connaught was also one of the early producers of penicillin and, in fact, was the first to prepare the antibiotic in crystalline form. After the war, the tremendous scale of production in other countries and resulting low costs caused Connaught to drop the product. Another major advance was Raymond Parker's discovery, in the late 1940s, of a solution in which monkey kidney cells could be kept growing in glass bottles. This discovery enabled Connaught to prepare a large part of the inactivated polio vaccine (Salk) used in clinical trials in Canada and the US.

In 1972 the Canada Development Corporation (CDC) purchased the laboratories from U of T, changing its name to Connaught Laboratories Ltd. Connaught is a wholly owned subsidiary of CDC Life Sciences, itself a subsidiary of the wholly Canadian-owned CDC. In 1976 Connaught purchased a production facility in Pennsylvania, which mainly produces influenza vaccine. This facility, known as Connaught Laboratories, Inc, provides access to the US market. Connaught has also acquired a major interest in Dominion Biologics of Truro, NS, and has entered into joint ventures in several S American countries to produce vaccines, primarily veterinary, but these activities are not a major investment.

A total of 750 employees work at the Toronto site. Of Connaught's total annual sales of about $50 million, 12-15% is spent on research. Current research is in the areas of improved human vaccines, GENETIC ENGINEERING of hormones, vaccines and blood products, fish vaccines, diabetes prevention and diagnostic test development.
A.A. MAGNIN

Connolly, Harold Joseph, newspaperman, politician, premier of NS (b at Sydney, NS 8 Sept 1901; d at Halifax 17 May 1980). Connolly worked with the Halifax *Chronicle* and was editor of the *Daily Star* when elected a Liberal MLA in 1936. He sat 20 years, first as an assemblyman and after 1941 as a Cabinet minister. Senior minister when Premier Angus L. MACDONALD died in 1954, he became interim Liberal leader and premier. He lost a leadership convention in 1954 when the Protestant delegates apparently united against the only Catholic candidate, the result being a disastrous religious rift within the party. He retired from provincial politics in 1955 to become a member of the Senate, from which he retired in 1979.
J. MURRAY BECK

Connor, Ralph, *see* GORDON, CHARLES WILLIAM.

Connors, "Stompin' Tom," singer-songwriter, guitarist (b at Saint John, NB 3 Feb 1936). He had been singing and writing verses since his childhood in Skinners Pond, PEI, but only began to sing for a living in 1964 when he found himself broke in Timmins, Ont. His success at the Maple Leaf Hotel led to radio and records. His trademark was his pounding foot, first inspired by the need to be heard above the din of a noisy tavern. He was the subject of 2 films, *This is Stompin' Tom* and *Across This Land With Stompin' Tom* (1973). RICHARD GREEN

Conquest (La Conquête), the term used to designate the acquisition of Canada by Great Britain in the SEVEN YEARS' WAR and, by extension, the resulting changed conditions of life experienced by Canada's 60 000 to 70 000 French-speaking inhabitants and numerous Indian tribes. Québec surrendered to British forces following the crucial BATTLE OF THE PLAINS OF ABRAHAM on 13 Sept 1759. Canadian resistance ended a year later with the capitulation of Montréal. By the terms signed 8 Sept 1760, the British guaranteed the Canadian population immunity from deportation or maltreatment; the right to depart for France with all their possessions; continued enjoyment of property rights; the right to carry on the FUR TRADE on an equal basis with the English; and freedom of worship. By the TREATY OF PARIS, 10 Feb 1763, the French colony became a British possession.

After the French Revolution (1789) many Canadians came to see the Conquest as a providential rescue from revolutionary chaos — an idea that was long influential. Later generations, viewing the past through the prism of their own political and constitutional preoccupations, tended to see the Conquest positively — not without reason — as leading to religious toleration and REPRESENTATIVE GOVERNMENT. They were less welcoming of the ethnic dualism that was the inevitable result of the marriage of English government and immigration with an established French colony of settlement. Some modern historians, such as Michel Brunet, have seen the Conquest as a disaster, drawing attention to the monopolization of the higher levels of government and business by English-speaking newcomers as evidence that the Conquest made French Canadians second-class subjects and, ultimately, an ethnic proletariat. Others, such as Fernand Ouellet, downplay harmful effects, pointing to fairly continuous development of economic foundations, of institutions and of culture, little affected by the event. For the native people, the end of Anglo-French hostility meant a fateful decline in their value as allies and warriors, making them increasingly irrelevant to white society.

The Conquest must always remain a subject of debate, interwoven with and inseparable as it is from other influences on Canadian development. Its influence is also visible in the AMERICAN REVOLUTION (which was possible only when the American colonies no longer needed British protection from French forces in N America) and even in the French Revolution, but it is woven into a pattern of bewildering complexity.

DALE MIQUELON

Reading: Dale Miquelon, *Society and Conquest* (1977).

Conroy, Pat, labour leader (b at Baillieston, Scot 1900). Conroy began to work as a miner at 13 and joined the British Mineworkers' Federation. In 1919 he immigrated to Canada, settling in Drumheller, Alta. He worked in the coal mines and joined the United Mine Workers of America. After a tour of the US, he returned to Alberta and from 1922 held several union positions until he became VP of the Western Canadian District 18. In 1940 when the CANADIAN CONGRESS OF LABOUR (CCL) was founded, he became its VP and the next year its full-time secretary-treasurer. In 1949 he helped found the International Confederation of Free Trade Unions. In 1951 he suddenly resigned from the CCL position because of differences with his colleagues on the executive. As a dynamic leader, he wished the Congress to play a larger role. In 1952 he was appointed labour attaché to the Canadian embassy in Washington, a post he held until his retirement in 1972.

LAUREL SEFTON MACDOWELL

Conscription, the compulsory enlistment of citizens for military service. Forms of conscription were adopted by the Canadian government in both world wars.

World War I

By late 1916 the terrible casualties at the front in France and Flanders were beginning to cause reinforcement problems for the Canadian commanders overseas. Recruitment at home was slowing, and the manpower and enlistment system was disorganized. For PM Sir Robert BORDEN, the first necessity was to assist the men in the trenches, and by May 1917, when he returned to Canada from the Imperial War Conference in London and from visits to the trenches, he had decided that compulsory service was necessary. He announced his decision in Parliament on May 18 and then offered a political coalition to Sir Wilfrid LAURIER, the Liberal leader. After consulting his supporters, Laurier refused. Québec would never agree to conscription, he believed, and if he joined the pro-conscription coalition French Canada would be delivered into the hands of Henri BOURASSA and his *nationalistes*. The course was set for collision.

By the fall, after enormous difficulty, Borden had created his UNION GOVERNMENT, and the MILITARY SERVICE ACT became law on 29 Aug 1917. Virtually every French-speaking MP opposed conscription, and almost all the English-speaking MPs supported it. The election of 1917 was as racially divided, and English Canada gave Borden his mandate to put conscription into effect. In Jan 1918 the process of call-ups began, but out of the 401 882 men registered (and despite the lifting of farmers' exemptions in the spring of 1918), only 124 588 were added to the strength of the CANADIAN EXPEDITIONARY FORCE; 24 132 men made it to France by the war's end. As a military measure conscription was a failure; as a political measure it had largely been responsible for the re-election of the Borden government, but it left the Conservative Party with a heavy liability in Québec and in the agricultural West.

J.L. GRANATSTEIN

World War II

As the threat of a new war in Europe became acute, the question of military conscription again caused lively political debate in French Canada. The federal Liberals, sensitive to strong francophone feelings on this issue, repeatedly pledged not to resort to compulsory enlistment for overseas military service. War broke out in Sept 1939, and by the spring of 1940 the government had adopted the NATIONAL RESOURCES MOBILIZATION ACT providing for enlistment for home defence. Registration took place almost without incident, except for the public opposition of Montréal mayor Camillien HOUDE, who was later interned. In 1941, as recruitment slowly progressed, more voices were raised in favour of conscription, first within the Conservative Party and later among English Canadians in general. To appease the supporters of conscription, Prime Minister W.L. Mackenzie KING decided to hold a plebiscite asking Canadians to release the government from its anti-conscription promises. In Québec, the Ligue pour la défense du Canada campaigned for the "no" side, and on 27 Apr 1942, 72.9% of Québec residents voted "no," while in the other provinces the "yes" vote triumphed by 80%. The government then passed Bill 80, authorizing conscription for overseas service if it were deemed necessary. Québec's BLOC POPULAIRE continued to fight against conscription by presenting candidates for the Aug 1944 provincial elections and the June 1945 federal elections.

By the autumn of 1944 J.L. RALSTON, minister of national defence, was convinced of the need for conscription. Unexpectedly high casualties on the front, combined with a large commitment to the RCAF and the RCN, left the Canadian Army short of manpower. King, who had hoped he would not have to invoke Bill 80, replaced Ralston with Gen A.G.L. MCNAUGHTON, a supporter of voluntary service. On Nov 22, however, the prime minister, acknowledging the open proconscriptionist sentiments of many of his anglophone ministers, reversed his decision in an effort to save his government and announced that conscripts would be sent overseas. Even though only 12 908 conscripted soldiers were actually sent abroad, this second conscription crisis again worsened relations between Anglophones and Francophones in Canada, though to a lesser extent than during WWI.

RICHARD JONES

Reading: J.L. Granatstein and J.M. Hitsman, *Broken Promises* (1977).

Conseil du Patronat du Québec is the organization of Québec employers. Founded in 1969 in Montréal where its offices are still located, the CPQ has as its membership 136 organizations representing the employers of 75% of the Québec labour force. The conseil, which has an annual budget of more than $900 000 and has 15 full-time employees, is funded by contributions from about 365 Québec companies. It is unique in Canada in the breadth of its membership and in its contribution to public debate in the province.

D. MCGILLIVRAY

Conservation can be defined as the wise use of RESOURCES for industrial and nonconsumptive purposes (eg, recreation, research), in the spirit of responsible stewardship, to preserve the productivity and diversity of the world's resources. Conservation parallels "environmentalism," but covers a wider spectrum. Conservation traditionally focused on natural resources but the concept has been expanded to include ENERGY, urban spaces, works of art, historical artifacts, heritage buildings, languages and cultures.

Conservation is a matter of trade-offs: deciding how much can be lost to achieve specific gains without losing productive potential and diversity of resources. Many people engaged in RESOURCE USE and management equate conservation exclusively with preservation and environmentalism and feel that its proponents obstruct economic and social progress. Conversely, some preservationists deplore any disturbance of natural conditions, forgetting that disturbances can be natural or man-made and that wildfires and even insect attack can play important roles in plant succession. While "wise use" may at times require unmodified preservation, it usually permits and sometimes requires carefully planned modifications. In fact, both sides have common interests: resource users and managers profit by maintaining resource productivity and a large number of options; and a sound economy, even if based on resource development, is essential if resource renewal, recycling and preservation programs are to be financed.

The modern concept of conservation has evolved since the beginning of the 20th century from a simple hoarding and slow use of resources to attempts to manage resources for sustained yield, minimal waste, recycling, controlling POLLUTION and maintaining the quality of the ENVIRONMENT. Economic growth has been the objective of escalating industrial activity over the past 50 years. The resulting wasteful energy use, diminution of high-grade resources and pollution of LAND, air and WATER have led to the questioning of the desirability of high levels of economic and population growth. People have begun to realize that maximum resource use for maximum economic gain is incompatible with society's long-term objectives. The idea that resource use for optimal sustainable economic gain permits wider social benefits is slowly gaining acceptance (*see* CONSERVER SOCIETY). The desirability of socioeconomic rather than purely economic goals is the subject of considerable debate, and there is a trend toward viewing resources as borrowed from future generations rather than as inherited from the past. Thus, support has grown for ecological reserves, restoration of endangered species and habitats, and careful environmental planning before new developments.

Geographic Factors

Various factors, such as the diversity of rock formations, SOILS, CLIMATE, wildlife, vegetation and people, present special conservation problems. Canada's land area is vast, her human population relatively small, and people with limited funds can do relatively little to preserve and manage extensive resources. Canada encompasses an area of 9.98 million km^2 and has the longest coastline (67 314 km including island coastlines) in the world. The land ascends from sea level on the shores of the Pacific, Atlantic and Arctic OCEANS to MOUNTAINS as high as

950 m in the CORDILLERA. The huge northern plains, E of the Cordillera, contain fertile agricultural soils and immense energy reserves in the form of COAL and PETROLEUM resources. The Canadian SHIELD, a mass of mineral-rich Precambrian rocks, forms the core of central Canada, and GLACIATION has molded the landforms over large areas. The climate of Canada varies from harshly continental (cold dry winters, hot summers) to mildly oceanic; winter temperatures can be well below -40°C, summer days 33°C or more. Average annual temperatures range from -18°C to -12°C in the Arctic Archipelago to 10°C in southwestern BC. Nearly 48% of Canada's land surface is covered by FORESTS, 28% by TUNDRA, 12% by peatland, and about 3% by grassland, each with its own type of wildlife. Freshwater LAKES, covering 7.6% of Canada's surface, account for 15% of the world's total volume of lake water, and Canada has 7.5% of the world's streamflow. The nation's resources extend onto the Continental Shelf, which is known to contain considerable quantities of MINERALS and oil and gas. The lakes, RIVERS and oceans also contain FISH and MAMMALS of considerable economic importance.

Renewable versus Nonrenewable

Renewable and nonrenewable resources require different conservation approaches. To enable ociety to use rather than consume resources, renewable biomes such as forests, tundra and grasslands must be maintained. Such maintenance involves management of the genetic base (vegetation, animals) and the environment (water, air, light, soil) to preserve productivity, genetic diversity and renewal processes. Conservation of nonrenewable resources (eg, minerals, fossil FUELS) requires development of policies to avoid waste (eg, by oil spills, gas flaring), promote wise use and encourage recycling, minimize adverse effects of mineral extraction on renewable resources and develop renewable substitutes. Uses of renewable and nonrenewable resources are interdependent; neither can be exploited or managed in complete isolation. Excessive use ("mining") of renewable resources may transform them into unrenewable losses, as when forest depletion leads to desert formation or an endangered species is hunted to extinction.

Demographic Factors

Canada's great regional disparity in economic development tends to focus attention on the solution of short-term economic problems rather than on the long-term consequences of resource use; hence, resource exploitation often takes priority over wise management and preservation (*see* REGIONAL ECONOMICS). During the past 25 years, Canadians have become more aware of the degradation of the nation's resources and the alarming long-term consequences of this continuing process. The need to conserve resources and develop conservation policies involving ecological, economic, social, ethical, political and legal factors are apparent.

Human Factors

Human activities are responsible for many conservation problems, although natural disturbances also have considerable impact. Technological innovations allow increasingly rapid and efficient harvesting of forests, agricultural crops, wildlife and fish. In forestry, chain saws, mechanical harvesters and on-site tree chippers allow quick and efficient harvest of huge numbers of trees, including stems, branches and leaves. Forest renewal TECHNOLOGY has developed much less rapidly. Forest-harvesting activities, FOREST FIRES, unsuccessful farming attempts and inadequate REFORESTATION have resulted in a backlog of about 16.8 million ha of forest land that has failed to regenerate with commercially useful trees. This problem is even more acute in tropical areas, where forest destruction is threatening the entire ecosystem. Heavy harvesting and processing equipment has been developed for proposed extraction of energy from Canada's peatlands, placing one of the world's major reserves of carbon under threat. Canada's natural grasslands have been nearly depleted through plowing for agriculture.

The development of electronic equipment for locating fish shoals has made fishing more efficient, and the pollution of freshwater lakes by industry has led to serious problems of eutrophication, thereby reducing fish populations and recreational values (*see* WATER POLLUTION). In spite of attempts to restock lakes and rivers, overfishing in many accessible areas has reduced fish populations. Wildlife sustain, at least partially, Canada's native peoples, and provide recreation for hunters as well as considerable revenues. In many cases, wildlife populations are seriously threatened by habitat destruction and easier access to remote areas by snow vehicles and helicopters. Large mammals and easily disturbed species are particularly vulnerable. Migratory herds of CARIBOU in northern Canada are threatened by increasing industrial activity in their main habitats and along MIGRATION routes. These animals have already disappeared from large areas. Visitors to bird colonies may inadvertently reduce nesting success.

Man's activities have provided new habitats, enabling some species to expand into areas where they were formerly scarce or absent. Extensive monoculture cropping practices have resulted in increases of some species (eg, red-winged blackbird) to the extent that they become pests, but have caused a marked decrease in species diversity. Exotic wildlife, vegetation and insects have been introduced to Canada. Some have been harmless or possibly beneficial, but many have had disastrous effects (eg, Dutch elm disease, balsam woolly aphid, winter moth).

SOIL CONSERVATION, the maintenance of soil stability and fertility, is vital if water quality and food, wood, fibre and other crops are to be sustained for future generations. Soil stability has been seriously impaired in some areas (eg, mountainous areas of BC) by forest harvesting, forest road construction and slash burning. Delays in replacing trees after harvesting result in heavy losses of soil nitrogen caused by the accelerated mineralization of soil organic matter. The recent trend toward using high-yielding tree species and shorter rotations involves an inherent risk of accelerating nutrient removal and reducing soil fertility. The massive soil EROSION and desert formation in farmlands of western N America in the 1930s illustrate the consequences of inadequate soil management (*see* DROUGHT; GREAT DEPRESSION). Intensive agricultural practices led to widespread reduction of vital organic matter in agricultural soils. There is evidence that, on Canada's northern Great Plains, as little as 34 years of agricultural cropping has resulted in a loss of 35% of the soil's organic matter and 41% of soil nitrogen. Large areas of fertile agricultural soils are destroyed each year by expansion of cities onto productive farmland. High-grade mineral ores and readily accessible fossil fuels, particularly oil, have been seriously depleted in the last 50 years to meet the increasing demands of an industrial society. Consequently, INDUSTRY must now rely on lower-grade or relatively inaccessible mineral and fossil-fuel resources which are costly to locate, extract, transport and process.

Legislation and Political Activity

Legislation in Canada, with its federal, provincial and municipal levels of government, is complex and traditionally oriented more towards consumptive resource use for economic purposes than to site preservation, but this is gradually changing. In the last 10 years there has been a great deal of conservation legislation (*see* ENVIRONMENTAL LAW). The federal government is responsible for national PARKS and for management and use of large areas of land in the YT and the NWT, as well as for international aspects of control of pollution, migratory birds and import and export of plants and wildlife. Provincial governments are responsible for the use, management and conservation of most of Canada's natural resources. Consequently, conservation measures and associated legislation vary from province to province.

Conservation priorities in Canada have developed in the context of an industrialized nation with a rapidly expanding, mainly urban population, now totalling about 25 million people. Heavy and often conflicting demands are being made on the nation's vast but limited resources. Conservation provides a philosophical and conceptual framework within which resources can be allocated in a manner in keeping with the needs, aspirations and desires of society. J.S. MAINI AND J.A. CARLISLE

Reading: J.S. Maini and J.A. Carlisle, eds, *Conservation in Canada: A Conspectus* (1974).

Conservation of Movable Cultural Property Conservation is the technology by which preservation (one of the 4 classic museum functions: acquisition, preservation, research, presentation) is achieved. Its relatively recent evolution from the ancient art of restoration represents a fundamental reorientation of museology; while the need remains to restore damaged objects as a last resort, conservation seeks to prevent rather than repair deterioration. This development originated with the need of curators and restorers to understand better the nature of the materials in their care; but it was not until the 20th century that major institutions recognized that both the control and the repair of damage depends upon the correct diagnosis of its causes.

The first conservation research laboratory was established at the British Museum in 1919 and was followed by others in the US and Western Europe. In 1950 the International Institute for the Conservation of Historic and Artistic Works (IIC) was founded to disseminate the growing body of conservation knowledge among scientists and restorers, and by 1958 it was able to publish an integrated explanation of the general mechanisms of decay in museum materials. From that time both preventive and remedial techniques advanced rapidly and progressive institutions sought to control the deterioration caused by such environmental factors as temperature, humidity, light, airborne contaminants and biological activity, and by human errors in handling, cleaning, storage, exhibition and transportation. Conservation emerged as a profession based upon the chemistry and physics of materials and of the environment; on biology, history, anthropology, photography, radiography and engineering; and on the history and technology of art and architecture; which in turn influenced all the other disciplines of museology.

Some major institutions in Québec and Ontario had employed restorers intermittently since the 19th century, but by 1970 only the NATIONAL GALLERY OF CANADA (1956), the ROYAL ONTARIO MUSEUM (1956), the National Historic Sites Service (1966), the PUBLIC ARCHIVES OF CANADA (1966) and, in the West, the British Columbia Provincial Museum (1966) had established permanent units specifically devoted to the conservation of their collections. Nationwide, fewer than 20 persons were employed full-time in conservation. In 1971 this small nucleus founded the Canadian Association of Professional Conservators (CAPC) to accredit and register conservators, and the following year a Canadian Group of IIC (IIC-CG) was formed to spread technical and scientific information.

In 1972, as part of its National Cultural Policy, the federal government founded the Canadian Conservation Institute (CCI) to provide conservation treatment, research and training services to all public museums and galleries. In the same year Parks Canada amalgamated its conservation facilities into a single Conservation Division to serve its National Historic Parks and Sites. However, the development of all conservation agencies was severely handicapped during the early 1970s by the absence of training facilities, and later by the deteriorating economic situation.

The first academic credit course in conservation was offered by U Victoria from 1970 to 1977, but it was not until Queen's introduced an MA program in 1974 and Sir Sandford Fleming College at Peterborough introduced its diploma in conservation technology in 1976 that the supply of Canadian-trained conservators was assured. Career-development training became available in 1977, when the CCI commenced its conservation internships.

During the 1970s the BC Provincial Museum earned a national reputation for its advocacy of conservation and for its training and consultation services; in several other provinces facilities developed gradually throughout the decade. The GLENBOW MUSEUM, the Provincial Museum of Alberta, the Northwest Territories Museum, and archives in NB, Ontario, Manitoba, Saskatchewan and BC all established facilities, while in 1979 the Centre de conservation du Québec offered the first provincial government conservation service.

Meanwhile, the unique climatic and geographical challenges of conservation in Canada demanded research and innovation. The CCI developed new techniques ranging from environmental control to the treatment of waterlogged wood and corroded iron, explored the use of light energy as a cleaning tool, analysed artifacts for authentication studies, responded to disasters and provided a nationwide mobile laboratory service. From the TOTEM POLE sites of the West Coast to the arctic islands and the BASQUE settlements of Labrador, conservators of provincial as well as federal agencies devised solutions to problems unknown elsewhere.

By 1980 fewer than 30 of the 1500 provincial custodial agencies employed conservators, and it was evident that financial as well as technical assistance was required. In 1981 the NATIONAL MUSEUMS OF CANADA introduced a Conservation Assistance Programme to provide salary assistance to qualifying institutions wishing to establish new conservation positions, and the CCI's mandate was revised to meet the needs of a less centralized national conservation structure. Despite economic hardship, heritage agencies seized the opportunity to develop conservation capabilities to such effect that, by the end of 1983, the nonfederal conservation work force had doubled. PHILIP R. WARD

Reading: J. Des Gagniers, *La conservation du patrimoine museologique du Québec* (1981); A.M. Lambert, *Conservation in Canadian Museums* (1980); National Museums of Canada, *A National Museums Policy for the 80's* (1981); H.J. Plenderleith and A.E.A. Werner, *The Conservation of Antiquities and Works of Art* (1974, 1st ed 1958); M. Ruggles, "The History of Conservation in Canada: Developments to the Early 1970's," *Journal of the International Institute for Conservation – Canadian Group*; Philip R. Ward, *Keeping the Past Alive* (1974);

Conservatism Few political terms are more widely appropriated (some would say misappropriated) than conservatism. In Canada, those calling themselves conservative range from zealous proponents of free enterprise and limited government to so-called "RED TORIES," who support a significant role for the state in Canada's social and economic life.

Historically, Canadian conservatism was rooted in British Toryism of the preindustrial era. It was reinforced by the influx of United Empire LOYALISTS during and after the American Revolution. While the Loyalists did not comprise a solid Tory phalanx, most were MONARCHISTS who favoured an organic and hierarchical society with a due respect for law and order, ideals generally shared by immigrants from Britain who arrived in the first half of the 19th century. Conservative impulses had also long prevailed among French Canadians as a result of the dominance of the Roman Catholic Church and the determination of a conquered people to preserve their language and culture. Canadian political life was distinguished by an early "Tory touch," in contrast to the liberal republicanism of the US, which many Canadians saw as excessively lawless and POPULIST. Where the American Declaration of Independence espoused the right to "life, liberty and the pursuit of happiness," the BRITISH NORTH AMERICA ACT enshrined the imperatives of "peace, order and good government." Whatever else it may entail, conservatism is based on a respect for lawful authority, tradition and continuity in human affairs. This does not preclude necessary reforms, but conservatives have no use for reforms that are produced by abstract reason and not rooted in communal experience. Most Canadian conservatives, past and present, would agree with Edmund Burke's dictum, "A disposition to preserve, and an ability to improve, taken together, would be my standard of a statesman. Everything else is vulgar in conception, perilous in the execution."

Despite this hostility to rapid change, Canadian conservatism was suffused with liberal strains from the start, with consequent semantic and partisan confusion. The ideas of John Locke (1632-1704), the founder of British empirical philosophy and advocate of civil and religious liberties, are the common heritage of both Canadian conservatives and Canadian liberals. From the time of Sir John A. MACDONALD conservatives have been prepared to change when the need for change was indisputable; however, as historian W.L. MORTON has written, "The essential principles of Canadian conservatism have not changed. It has remained traditional and constitutional, progressive and pragmatic. It has concerned itself with sound administration of existing laws rather than the forming of new laws, and with economic development rather than political reform."

To Canadian conservatives, tradition implied loyalty to the Crown and to British parliamentary procedures. In recent decades the British connection and even the COMMONWEALTH have faded as issues in Canadian politics, and an excess of anglophilia would be a distinct electoral liability. But most Canadian conservatives (as well as many liberals and socialists) still regard parliamentary government under the monarchy as the best means of ensuring individual freedom, cultural diversity and social cohesion. Some Canadian conservatives have also tended to be staunch nationalists, partly because the US, not the UK, has posed the only serious threat to Canadian political, economic and cultural independence, but also because NATIONALISM is based on an appreciation of history and tradition and a conservative sense of a collective entity, dubious values to liberals, who generally respond in an accommodating and continentalist way to the US.

The Canadian conservative tradition has nothing to do with contemporary neo-conservatism, basically an offshoot of laissez-faire liberalism. To the true conservative, human society is an organic entity in which each member has duties as well as rights. For this reason, Canadian conservatives have favoured government initiatives to protect the disadvantaged and to further economic development. Although the Progressive CONSERVATIVE PARTY attracts its share of right-wing ideologues, Conservative governments since Macdonald's have launched social-welfare programs and many public enterprises in areas such as transportation, broadcasting, banking, grain marketing and hydroelectric power.

At its worst, Canadian conservatism has been conformist and authoritarian, insufficiently appreciating Canada's racial and regional diversities. Conservative dedication to peace, order and good government has evoked a popular impression of conservatives (and especially Progressive Conservatives) as a privileged elite — white, Protestant and largely affluent. At its best, however, Canadian conservatism has been compassionate and pragmatic, eschewing ideology in favour of a careful balance between the conflicting claims of social order and individual liberty. CHARLES TAYLOR

Reading: George Grant, *Lament for a Nation: The Defeat of Canadian Nationalism* (1965); Charles Taylor, *Radical Tories: The Conservative Tradition in Canada* (1982).

Conservative Party In 1844 in *Coningsby*, Benjamin Disraeli, future Conservative prime minister of Britain, described CONSERVATISM as "an unhappy cross-breed; the mule of politics that engenders nothing." He wrote this when "Conservative" was first appearing as a party designation, a shift intended to broaden the TORY Party's appeal. In Canada as in Britain, Toryism's mid-19th century anti-democratic values were difficult to maintain when the electoral franchise was continually expanding. The Conservative Party in Canada embraced British Tory traditions, but other strains flowed into it. Indeed, the ancestor of the modern Progressive Conservative Party can be discovered in the 1854 Liberal-Conservative COALITION GOVERNMENT of the PROVINCE OF CANADA. John A. MACDONALD entered the 1854 coalition as a moderate Conservative, and it was he who eventually shaped the Liberal-Conservative Party which was dominant at CONFEDERATION. As Canada's first prime minister, Macdonald constructed a party that emphasized commitment to Confederation and a policy of national economic development. The party's name symbolized Macdonald's own commitment to equilibrium and moderation, to an emphasis on what Canadians held in common, and to an obscuring of those matters where they divided. He managed to combine ULTRAMONTANE Québec Roman Catholics from Québec, Tories, ORANGEMEN and businessmen in all 4 founding provinces. Rejecting "abstract debate," he emphasized personality, patronage and compromise; but by 1872 the many parts of the expanding nation had become too different to patch together. In 1872 he won 103 seats to 97 for the Opposition Liberals. The majority did not hold; in Nov 1873 his government fell.

The PACIFIC SCANDAL which brought down Macdonald's government indicated the problems of his approach. The Pacific railway was essential to his nation-building dream; however, its construction and similar development policies linked the government too closely with private interests which did not always serve the public interest. In opposition Macdonald seems to have become convinced that his party should represent something more than simply support of Canada. By then the party had largely dropped the Liberal-Conservative label in favour of Conservative. In the 1878 election campaign Macdonald committed his party to the NATIONAL POLICY, which emphasized PROTECTIONISM, expansion in the West, and an assertive central government. This appealed to Ontario and Québec manufacturers and to those who feared the US following its rejection of free trade and RECIPROCITY. A strong pro-British message was added, its effectiveness proven by Macdonald's reelection in 1882, 1887 and 1891.

Macdonald complemented the National Poly with shrewd and lavish patronage and a ·illingness to compromise, although compro- ıise evaded him in the case of Louis RIEL after ıe 1885 NORTH-WEST REBELLION. Riel's execution, long with weak leadership among Québec onservatives, led to a decline in support there om 48 seats in 1882 to 30 in 1891. Macdonald's :action to Riel followed logically from his :ntralist perspective, which kept provinces nd local interests in the background. The result ·as that the provinces became increasingly iberal, and supported the provincial rights and of Liberal leader Wilfrid LAURIER. After 1acdonald's death in 1891, his party could not ndure attacks on so many fronts. The Conser- ative governments of John ABBOTT, John HOMPSON, Mackenzie BOWELL and Charles TUPPER ruggled to maintain supremacy, but language nd religious problems (*see* MANITOBA SCHOOLS UESTION) and patronage problems in Québec ·ere great obstacles. The Conservatives lost the 896 election and for many years did not regain ıeir pre-eminence.

Nova Scotia lawyer Robert BORDEN, Conserva- ve leader 1901-20, sought to expand the Mac- onald legacy. He experimented with a Québec eutenant, flirted with American progressivism nd advocated civil service reform and public wnership. He lost the elections of 1904 and 908. To win in 1911 Borden emphasized the ational Policy and the imperial connection, ·inning support in Ontario, BC and part of ıe Maritimes. In Québec the Conservatives al- ed themselves with anti-Laurier *nationalistes* ·ho were seduced by Borden's promise of a ref- rendum on naval assistance to Britain. The onservatives won the election, but the imperi- list-*nationaliste* coalition collapsed. By 1913 *na- onalistes* in his caucus were bitterly disillu- ioned with Borden's siding with the more umerous imperialists. WWI extended Borden's ıandate, but in 1917 an election could be post- oned no longer. The Dec 1917 election was crit- al for Canadian conservatism. To ensure that is CONSCRIPTION policy was upheld, Borden ıade an alliance with conscriptionist Liberals. he resulting UNION GOVERNMENT triumphed, but ıe victory created lasting resentment among rench Canadians and immigrants, especially erman Canadians. Liberals soon deserted the oalition, leaving the Conservative Party with a arrower base than ever before. Moreover, na- ionalization of the Grand Trunk and Canadian Jorthern railways caused the defection of the 1ontréal business community, probably the arty's greatest source of funds.

Arthur MEIGHEN, Borden's successor, immedi- tely tried to shape the remnants of Unionism nto Conservatism. In the 1921 election the Con- ervatives finished third with 50 seats, behind he PROGRESSIVE PARTY with 65 and the Liberals vith 116. Meighen's support of conscription neant the loss of francophone support. In west- rn Canada Progressives identified more readily vith Liberals since they associated Conserva- ives with the despised National Policy. Meighen erved briefly as prime minister in 1926, but a iberal majority soon returned (*see* KING-BYNG FFAIR). Conservatives were too closely linked vith Britain when Canada's Britishness was isappearing. Nor did Meighen manage to adapt he National Policy to postwar economic con- itions.

In 1927 R.B. BENNETT, a wealthy Calgary busi- essman, succeeded him and in 1930 won a ma- ›rity, taking 25 Québec seats. The GREAT DEPRES- ION created the climate for Bennett's victory; it lso assured his defeat 5 years later. Bennett's nitial response to depression was a characteris- ically Conservative attempt to protect industry nd to obtain IMPERIAL PREFERENCE. It did not vork. In 1935 Bennett called for many social re- orms, but these proposals came too late to be onvincing (*see* BENNETT'S NEW DEAL). Many

Campaign poster neatly summarizing the powerful appeal of John A. Macdonald's Conservative Party in the 19th century (*courtesy Public Archives of Canada/C-6536*).

Reformist Conservatives had already left to join the Reconstruction Party founded by former Bennett minister H.H. STEVENS. Moreover, 2 new parties, SOCIAL CREDIT and the CO-OPERATIVE COMMONWEALTH FEDERATION, appealed to areas of English Canada. The 1935 election witnessed the worst Conservative defeat, 40 seats against the Liberals' 173.

Thereafter the Conservatives struggled to rebuild a successful coalition. The enmity of French Canada endured, even though in 1938 the party chose Robert J. Manion, who had opposed conscription, was Catholic and had married a French Canadian. His attempts to conciliate Québec only angered numerous colleagues once WWII began. Party funds were depleted, and party organization had atrophied. In 1940 the Conservatives again won only 40 seats. Manion's defeat turned the party back towards Arthur Meighen, who shunned compromises and to many Conservatives appeared to be the Canadian Churchill. Canada, however, was not Britain, and Meighen lost a Feb 1942 by-election.

Encouraged by Meighen, Manitoba premier John BRACKEN, a Progressive with no Conservative experience, sought and won the 1942 leadership, and the party's name was changed to Progressive Conservative Party. It was attempting to turn left to place itself on the path of wartime reform sentiment. But the CCF and the Liberals were also moving left. In 1944 the Conservatives were caught up again in the proconscription movement. Although the Liberals brought in conscription, the Conservatives' enthusiasm ensured that they would bear the blame. In the 1945 election, they could not even find candidates for most Québec ridings. Elsewhere conscription was largely forgotten when the war ended. The PCs came fourth on the Prairies, behind CCF, Liberals and Social Credit.

The Conservatives were becoming an Ontario party, as indicated by the 1948 choice of Ontario premier George DREW as leader. Drew was unable to escape the Ontario mantle. After 2 disastrous defeats, in 1949 and 1953, the party decided to gamble on John DIEFENBAKER, a westerner, a populist and a remarkable showman. Diefenbaker offered both fiery leadership and a visionary program. He excited Canadians, lulled by 2 decades of Liberal administration. In 1957 he won a minority; in 1958 he astonished Canadians by winning 208 out of 265 seats, including 50 from Québec. For the first time since 1911 the Conservatives were truly a national party.

The Conservative platform appeared to have more substance than it had. Despite strong Québec support, Diefenbaker could not come to terms with Canada's bicultural nature. His policy initiatives seemed eclectic rather than parts of a larger vision. In 1962 Diefenbaker lost his majority, and in 1963 his government collapsed and the Liberals won the subsequent election. Diefenbaker's populism had lost much business support and now lacked urban support generally. French Canada once again shunned the Conservatives. Diefenbaker, however, retained strong support in the West and in pockets elsewhere. His removal as leader in Sept 1967 damaged party unity, and his successor, Nova Scotia Prem Robert STANFIELD, felt the wounds.

Diefenbaker's legacy was strong Conservative support in western Canada. Other successes in the 1960s and 1970s occurred provincially, especially in Ontario, where the Conservatives maintained a regime from 1943 into the 1980s. By 1979 Conservatives governed in Ontario, Manitoba, Alberta, Nova Scotia, Newfoundland, PEI and New Brunswick. But Stanfield was unable to lead the federal party to power, and in Feb 1976 Joe CLARK, an Albertan, became its leader. In May 1979 the Conservatives under Clark formed a minority government, but they were defeated in the House in Dec and lost the Feb 1980 election.

The defeat of the Conservatives in 1980 brought Joe Clark's leadership into question. In 1983 the party rejected Clark and chose the bilingual Quebecer Brian MULRONEY as its leader. Although Mulroney lacked any parliamentary experience, he possessed superb organization skills and a deep knowledge of his native province. The party, so often fractious, united behind the new leader as he faced Pierre TRUDEAU's successor, John TURNER, in the federal election of Sept 1984. Mulroney, backed by a phalanx of provincial premiers and assisted by a Liberal Party which could not decide whether it accepted its heritage, won an overwhelming victory. Despite the party's numerous federal losses since 1963, it had constructed a base from which it could move forward when the Liberal Party stumbled. The Conservative Party may have been the mule of Canadian politics, but it has stood the long haul well. JOHN ENGLISH

Reading: John English, *The Decline of Politics* (1977); H. Macquarrie, *The Conservative Party* (1965); J.R. Williams, *The Conservative Party of Canada: 1920-1949* (1956).

Conserver Society "Canadians as individuals, and their governments, institutions and industries [must] begin the transition from a consumer society preoccupied with resource exploitation to a conserver society engaged in more constructive endeavours." This statement, which includes the first use of the phrase "conserver society," appeared in the SCIENCE COUNCIL OF CANADA report *Natural Resource Policy Issues in Canada*, released in Jan 1973. It was intended to suggest that many environmental problems are symptoms of the larger problems of a society dedicated to turning RESOURCES into garbage as fast as possible in the interests of short-term economic growth; it suggested as well that most environmental problems cannot be resolved until the basic causes are corrected. The Canadian press gave unanticipated attention to the conserver society recommendation when the report was released. Public attention and interest led to a series of studies sponsored by the federal government and others. The use of the term also spread to the US, Australia and New Zealand.

According to the Science Council's brief definition, a conserver society uses 5 principal policy thrusts in making decisions affecting the ENVIRONMENT or its resources: concern for the future; economy of design; diversity, flexibility and responsibility; recognition of total costs; and respect for the biosphere and its capabilities. Ideas included in the concept have been expressed as "doing more with less," "living within the limits to growth," "using technology appropriate to the cultural context and resource base," etc. A conserver society would introduce social and environmental concerns at the very beginning of design, planning and policy formulation processes and would make resource CONSERVATION and social and environmental impact assessments integral components of all projects. In an advanced conserver society, ENVIRONMENTAL LAW would diminish in importance as sound environmental planning and resource conservation became routine.

There have been few significant governmental actions at any level directed at bringing about a conserver society. Canadians still consume more energy, and North Americans produce more garbage per capita, than any other society. However, some progress has been made toward a conserver-society future emphasizing conservation of resources, environmental protection and development of a comfortable, safe society with long-term viability. Areas of significant advancement include improvements in environmental education; establishment of environmental legislation (eg, requirements for environmental impact assessments); increase in skills and knowledge in such areas as environmental and resource management; decreases in the importance of MEGAPROJECTS; changes in corporate attitudes; a relative decline in confrontation and increase in co-operation on environmental issues; and continuing development of the cultural foundations needed to make judgements about environmental issues.

A major difficulty in persuading Canadians of the desirability of a conserver society lies in the persistence of 2 misconceptions about Canada's resources and the economic benefits to be derived from them. The first misconception is that Canada has enormous, even infinite, resources. Confusion still occurs about the difference between our very large land area (about 10 million km^2) and our agricultural land (700 000 km^2 of arable land and about an equal amount of pasture). Until the 1980s government and industry thought that Canada's FOREST resources were so large that there was no pressing need for REFORESTATION. Canadians are frequently told that we have more fresh WATER than any other nation, but are not reminded that our water is spread over a very large area, or that much of it is frozen for part of the year. These misconceptions of abundance have made it difficult to introduce conservation of resources.

The second misconception is derived loosely from economics. It is based on beliefs that resource conservation and RECYCLING are inherently less economical than exploitation of virgin resources; that environmental protection and sound environmental design and planning penalize industry; that all economic growth is good and accelerating economic growth is necessary for the well-being of Canadians; and that there is a direct correlation between energy and resource consumption and the quality of life. Failure to comprehend the dangers of continued population growth and the heightened environmental impact of each citizen in countries with HIGH TECHNOLOGY further slows acceptance of the conserver-society concept.

DIXON THOMPSON

Reading: Science Council of Canada, *Canada as a Conserver Society: Resource Uncertainties and the Need for New Technologies* (1977); L. Soloman, *The Conserver Solution* (1978).

Conspiracy, a difficult legal term to define, implies an agreement between 2 or more persons to commit an unlawful or criminal act, or an act which though lawful in itself becomes unlawful when done by the joint action of the agreeing parties, or for the purpose of using some unlawful means to commit what would otherwise be a lawful act, such as the breaking of a contract. Criminal conspiracy is condemned by the Canadian Criminal Code (s423) but sentences vary according to the intended crime. For example, a conspiracy to commit murder is punishable by 14 years' imprisonment, while a conspiracy to prosecute an innocent person is punishable by 5 or 10 years' imprisonment. A conspiracy to have a woman commit adultery or fornication is punishable by 2 years; the conspirators may also be guilty, in this case, of ABDUCTION. Any conspiracy to achieve an unlawful purpose or a lawful purpose by unlawful means, eg, the use of bribes, is criminal and punishable by 2 years' imprisonment. A mere intention to conspire or to commit an unlawful act is not sufficient to create criminal liability; there must be an actual agreement to act. The Code (s424) expressly provides that a conspiracy in restraint of trade (preventing another from carrying on his trade in a particular way or in a particular area) is not criminal when done by or on behalf of a trade union, which is therefore able to call its members out on strike regardless of any contract of service by which they may be bound, or is able to declare a sympathy strike on behalf of others engaged in a lawful strike.

L.C. GREEN

Constitution, the system of laws and conventions by which a state governs itself; the basic law of a country; the law of laws. A distinction is often made between a formal Constitution, a venerable document formally drawn up that can only be modified through specific procedures, and a material Constitution, a body of dispositions providing for the organization and functioning of the state. Canada's Constitution, though similar to the largely unwritten Constitution of Great Britain, is primarily written, notably the sections on the DISTRIBUTION OF POWERS.

The Royal PROCLAMATION OF 1763, the QUEBEC ACT (1774), the CONSTITUTIONAL ACT (1791) and the ACT OF UNION (1840) which preceded the BRITISH NORTH AMERICA ACT (1867), are all constitutional Acts concerning Canada. The STATUTE OF WESTMINSTE (1931) recognized the independence of Canada the Canada Act, 1982 and the Constitution Ac 1982, patriated the Constitution and gave Canada a Charter of Rights and Freedoms and a general amending formula. Since 17 Apr 1982, th BNA Act has been styled the Constitution Ac 1867, while the Constitution Acts, 1867 to 197 and the Constitution Act, 1982, have been collectively titled the Constitution Acts, 1867 t 1982. The Constitution of Canada also comprise other legislative documents and decrees, includ ing the British Magna Carta (1215), Bill o Rights (1689), Petition of Right (1629) and Ac of Settlement (1701). In its judgement of 28 Sep 1981, the Supreme Court of Canada noted tha the Constitution consists of legislative rules rules of the common law and constitutiona conventions. The first 2 comprise CONSTITUTIONA LAW, the third, while part of the Constitutio and recognized and commented upon by th courts, are not imposed by the courts and are no a source of constitutional law; when they ar flouted the remedy is political, not legal. Th Supreme Court declared that nothing in constitutional law precluded Parliament from pre senting an Address to the British Parliamen requesting amendment to the Constitution o Canada, but that a constitutional conventio nonetheless required that Parliament enjoy substantial support from the provinces before doin so. The Supreme Court provided several exam ples of such conventions. One of the most im portant is that of RESPONSIBLE GOVERNMENT, eg, th Cabinet may only stay in power as long as it en joys the confidence of the House of Commons According to the Supreme Court, "a conventio occupies a position somewhere in between us age or custom on the one hand and a consti tutional law on the other," and its main purpos "is to ensure that the legal framework of th Constitution will be operated in accordanc with the prevailing constitutional values o principles of the period." GÉRALD-A. BEAUDOI

Constitution, Patriation of For 18 lon months — from the May 1980 Québec REFEREN DUM ON SOVEREIGNTY-ASSOCIATION to the signing o the constitutional "accord" between the federa government and 9 provinces in Nov 1981 — th political battle to "patriate" and revise Canada' CONSTITUTION raged furiously, dominating head lines and the political agendas of every govern ment and major institution in the country. Th

The constitution document (*courtesy Public Archives of Canada*).

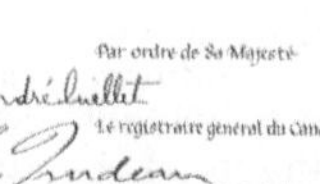

ELIZABETH THE SECOND

BY THE GRACE OF GOD OF THE UNITED KINGDOM, CANADA AND HER OTHER REALMS AND TERRITORIES QUEEN, HEAD OF THE COMMONWEALTH, DEFENDER OF THE FAITH.

TO ALL TO WHOM THESE PRESENTS SHALL COME OR WHOM THE SAME MAY IN ANYWAY CONCERN,

GREETING:

A PROCLAMATION

Attorney General of Canada

WHEREAS in the past certain amendments to the Constitution of Canada have been made by the Parliament of the United Kingdom at the request and with the consent of Canada;
AND WHEREAS it is in accord with the status of Canada as an independent state that Canadians be able to amend their Constitution in Canada in all respects;
AND WHEREAS it is desirable to provide in the Constitution of Canada for the recognition of certain fundamental rights and freedoms and to make other amendments to the Constitution;
AND WHEREAS the Parliament of the United Kingdom has therefore, at the request and with the consent of Canada, enacted the Canada Act, which provides for the patriation and amendment of the Constitution of Canada;
AND WHEREAS section 58 of the Constitution Act, 1982, set out in Schedule B to the Canada Act, provides that the Constitution Act, 1982 shall, subject to section 59 thereof, come into force on a day to be fixed by proclamation issued under the Great Seal of Canada;
NOW KNOW You that We, by and with the advice of Our Privy Council for Canada, do by this Our Proclamation, declare that the Constitution Act, 1982 shall, subject to section 59 thereof, come into force on the Seventeenth day of April, in the Year of Our Lord One Thousand Nine Hundred and Eighty-two.
OF ALL WHICH Our Loving Subjects and all others whom these Presents may concern are hereby required to take notice and to govern themselves accordingly.
IN TESTIMONY WHEREOF We have caused these Our Letters to be made Patent and the Great Seal of Canada to be hereunto affixed.
At Our City of Ottawa, this Seventeenth day of April in the Year of Our Lord One Thousand Nine Hundred and Eighty-two and in the Thirty-first Year of Our Reign.

By Her Majesty's Command

Registrar General of Canada

Prime Minister of Canada

GOD SAVE THE QUEEN

ELIZABETH DEUX

PAR LA GRÂCE DE DIEU REINE DU ROYAUME-UNI, DU CANADA ET DE SES AUTRES ROYAUMES ET TERRITOIRES, CHEF DU COMMONWEALTH, DÉFENSEUR DE LA FOI.

À TOUS CEUX QUE LES PRÉSENTES PEUVENT DE QUELQUE MANIÈRE CONCERNER,

SALUT:

PROCLAMATION

Le procureur général du Canada

CONSIDÉRANT:
qu'à la demande et avec le consentement du Canada, le Parlement du Royaume-Uni a déjà modifié à plusieurs reprises la Constitution du Canada;
qu'en vertu de leur appartenance à un État souverain, les Canadiens se doivent de détenir tout pouvoir de modifier leur Constitution au Canada;
qu'il est souhaitable d'inscrire dans la Constitution du Canada la reconnaissance d'un certain nombre de libertés et de droits fondamentaux et d'y apporter d'autres modifications;
que le Parlement du Royaume-Uni, à la demande et avec le consentement du Canada, a adopté en conséquence la Loi sur le Canada, qui prévoit le rapatriement de la Constitution canadienne et sa modification;
que l'article 58, figurant à l'annexe B de la Loi sur le Canada, stipule que, sous réserve de l'article 59, la Loi constitutionnelle de 1982 entrera en vigueur à une date fixée par proclamation sous le grand sceau du Canada,
NOUS PROCLAMONS, sur l'avis de Notre Conseil privé pour le Canada, que la Loi constitutionnelle de 1982 entrera en vigueur, sous réserve de l'article 59, le dix-septième jour du mois d'avril en l'an de grâce mil neuf cent quatre-vingt-deux.
NOUS DEMANDONS À Nos loyaux sujets et à toute autre personne concernée de prendre acte de la présente proclamation.
EN FOI DE QUOI, Nous avons rendu les présentes lettres patentes et y avons fait apposer le grand sceau du Canada.
Fait en Notre ville d'Ottawa, ce dix-septième jour du mois d'avril en l'an de grâce mil neuf cent quatre-vingt-deux, le trente et unième de Notre règne.

Par ordre de Sa Majesté

Le registraire général du Canada

Le premier ministre du Canada

DIEU PROTÈGE LA REINE

ATRIATION (the term is uniquely Canadian) bat- le of 1980-81 originated in the failings of a half entury of domestic diplomacy and the unex- ected second chance offered to PM Pierre TRU- EAU when the LIBERAL PARTY was swept back to ower in Feb 1980, after 9 months of aborted ory rule. Constitutional reform became one f several major Liberal initiatives and, appar- ntly by accident, the immediate response to the ngoing Québec REFERENDUM campaign, a politi- al fight the federal Liberals had not expected o wage from the seat of power. While Jean HRÉTIEN lobbied against sovereignty-associa- ion in numerous small towns across Québec uring the campaign, Trudeau gave 4 major peeches, promising, "We will immediately take ction to renew the Constitution and we will ot stop until we have done that" — a statement ague enough to defy definition yet inspiring nough to help swing the tide in favour of the ederalist forces. Conceding defeat in the refer- ndum on 20 May 1980, Québec Premier René ÉVESQUE immediately demanded that the PM ulfil his promise. Trudeau quickly despatched hrétien to arrange a meeting with all the pre- niers.

In the weeks before the June 9 meeting Tru- eau assembled a new cadre of aggressive con- titutional advisers and a new set of federal de- nands. The concessions that Ottawa had been repared to make in the failed round of consti- utional talks in 1978 and 1979 were with- rawn; in their place the federal government, or the first time since the failed Victoria Confer- nce in 1971 made significant demands of its wn — for new, centralized powers over the conomy — while at the same time insisting hat the so-called "people's package" of patri- tion and enshrinement of a CANADIAN CHARTER F RIGHTS AND FREEDOMS was not a matter for taw- ry, political trade-offs. The premiers responded ngrily to the change of tactics but nevertheless greed to set in motion a uniquely Canadian vent — a summer constitutional roadshow of ninisters, senior officials and political aides to xplore the 12 agreed-upon agenda items and to eport to a first ministers' conference in early ept.

However, by the time of the Sept 8 first- ninisters' conference (the tenth round of nego- iations to be held since 1927 on the reform of anada's Constitution), the battle lines had al- eady begun to harden. On the eve of the confer- nce, Lévesque quietly circulated to the premiers leaked copy of Ottawa's 64-page, top-secret ne- otiating strategy, known as the Kirby Memo- andum after its chief compiler Michael Kirby, ecretary to the Cabinet for federal-provincial elations. The document was leaked to the press n the second day of the conference, helping to our an already bitter mood of distrust. During 4 ays under hot television lights, the premiers nd the prime minister articulated, occasionally mpressively, widely different visions of Can- da, which were repeated backstage in private neetings. The intractable views of the par- icipants led to the inevitable failure of the con- erence. On Oct 2, following consultations with is caucus and Cabinet, Trudeau announced, ot unexpectedly, that Ottawa would make a nilateral request to the British Parliament. The overnment planned to recall Parliament early nd press the resolution through by Christmas efore significant opposition could be mounted.

The New Democratic Party, under leader Ed- vard BROADBENT, gave tentative approval to the lan, though it split his caucus, essentially along ast-west lines. The federal Conservatives, under esieged leader Joe CLARK, strongly opposed he plan and used every procedural device at heir disposal to halt the resolution. The resolu- ion finally went before the SUPREME COURT OF ANADA in late spring 1981. When the Liberals nvoked CLOSURE to move the resolution into the

Queen Elizabeth II signing the Canadian constitution document, as PM Pierre Elliott Trudeau (left), Michael Pitfield (centre) and Michael Kirby look on, Ottawa, Apr 1982 *(courtesy National Film Board/Photothèque)*.

COMMITTEE stage, a handful of Tories rushed the SPEAKER's chair with fists waving, demanding to be heard.

The Constitution fight offered Clark an explosive issue around which to consolidate his flagging leadership and an opportunity to advance his view of the country as a "community of communities." But his position underscored a rift between the federal Tories and their influential Ontario cousins; Ontario Premier William DAVIS and NB Premier Richard HATFIELD, both Conservatives and the only 2 to attend the aborted Victoria Conference in 1971, supported the prime minister's plan.

The constitutional resolution, with its centrepiece, the Charter, was offered to a special joint parliamentary committee for study, where it was harshly criticized. The first parliamentary committee to have its sittings televised, it was petitioned by 914 individuals and 294 groups. It sat a total of 267 hours over 65 days; and largely because of its deliberations the first charter was significantly redrafted 5 times. The revisions included the incorporation of provisions on aboriginal rights, sexual equality and equal rights for the handicapped. The Conservative Party advocated the entrenchment of "property rights," but the Liberals rejected this proposal because of opposition to it by their allies, the NDP.

The 6 dissident provinces (Québec, Alberta, Manitoba, PEI, Newfoundland and BC) most strongly opposed to the plan united to form a common front. Led largely by the strong-willed premiers of Québec, Alberta (Peter LOUGHEED) and Manitoba (Sterling LYON), they were joined eventually by those of Saskatchewan and Nova Scotia. The group, dubbed the "Gang of Eight," mounted court challenges against the resolution in provincial courts of appeal in Manitoba, Québec and Newfoundland, and launched a public-relations campaign against it both in Canada and Great Britain where they lobbied MPs strenuously. These pressures on the British government led to increased tensions between the 2 governments.

Meanwhile the CONSTITUTIONAL REFERENCE case was weaving a tortuous path through the courts. In Feb 1981 the Manitoba Court of Appeal decided 3-2 in favour of Ottawa. In April the Québec Superior Court of Appeal, in a 4-1 decision, also supported Ottawa. However, just weeks earlier, the 3 justices of the Supreme Court of Newfoundland had unanimously condemned the federal procedure. The Newfoundland judgement was handed down as the Commons was tied in procedural knots by the Conservative opposition and while the 8 dissident premiers were preparing for their own conference to sign an alternative constitutional "Accord," one that would limit the request to Britain to simple patriation with a different amending formula, promoted largely by Premier Lougheed. Trudeau suddenly agreed to submit his resolution to the Supreme Court of Canada for judicial settlement but would not meet the dissident premiers when they arrived in Ottawa 16 April 1981, and he ridiculed their "April Accord" in which Québec's Lévesque had agreed to an amending formula that did not provide a specific veto for his province.

On Sept 28 the court brought down its judgement; it found that Ottawa was legally allowed to make this request of the British Parliament but that the resolution offended the constitutional "conventions" which had developed in Canada over the years, referring to practices which were important but not legally enforceable. The court held by a 7-2 majority that no *legal* limit "to the power of the Houses to pass resolutions" existed. By a 6-3 majority, however, the court also ruled that whenever amendments were proposed that would reduce provincial powers, the presentation of a joint resolution by Ottawa without a "consensus" of the provinces would be a breach of constitutional convention. Although such practice was a matter of convention rather than law, the court argued that such conventions are of great significance. In the words of the court, "Constitutional convention plus constitutional law equals the total constitution of the country." This split decision, interpreted as a messy win for both sides, soon sparked a final round of hurried negotiations and what the prime minister came to call "the one last time" conference of Nov 2.

On the first day of the 4-day conference, the federal side appeared to take the initiative when Premiers Davis and Hatfield offered compromise proposals: Davis to forego Ontario's traditional veto and Hatfield to postpone parts of the Charter of Rights for 2 years. After an opening round of public statements the first ministers and their key lieutenants continued their discussions in a private room on the top floor of the conference centre. The rancour returned on the second day and the formal conference broke up at noon. The Gang of Eight, sequestered in their suite across the street at the Chateau Laurier Hotel, debated a vague compromise plan put together by BC Premier William BENNETT. Eventually, Bennett, Lougheed and NS Premier John BUCHANAN took the scheme to Trudeau who rejected it in an angry confrontation. On the third day Saskatchewan Premier Allan BLAKENEY put forth his own proposal. Manitoba Premier Sterling Lyon was leaving at the end of the day for the campaign trail; Lévesque too planned to leave and accused Blakeney of breaking up the defensive alliance. The Blakeney proposal was given short shrift around the conference table, but an apparently off-the-cuff remark by Trudeau that perhaps only a referendum could resolve the conundrum was unexpectedly well received by Lévesque, to the annoyance of all the other premiers. Nearly all day was devoted to discussing a possible referendum and Trudeau emerged in the afternoon to tell the press somewhat facetiously that there was a new Québec-Ottawa alliance.

Various ministers from the different provinces had been meeting privately in the meantime to discuss other options. Three attorneys general — Chrétien, Saskatchewan's Roy Romanow and Ontario's Roy McMurtry — had traded notes earlier that morning. During the afternoon discussion of referendum procedures, Chrétien and Romanow slipped away to an unused kitchen pantry to continue with their talks. During the so-called "Kitchen Meeting," the scraps of paper exchanged formed the basis, along with similar notions from Newfoundland Premier Brian PECKFORD and Alberta Premier Lougheed, for an eventual compromise. That night, officials from Saskatchewan, BC, Alberta and Newfoundland worked out a one-page compromise, substituting the Alberta amending formula and introducing a *non obstante* clause to limit the effect of the Charter of Rights. All the other participants were informed of their progress, except for Lyon, who was campaigning and Lévesque, who was dining late with his top staff. The next morning the deal was presented to Lévesque at breakfast and formally to the prime minister at the conference table. With some minor adjustments, the deed was done. Lévesque complained bitterly, refused to sign the accord, and tried in vain to press Trudeau to embrace the referendum option.

By Nov 5 the constitutional fight was essentially over. In the next few weeks, native peoples and women's groups lobbied successfully to reinstate certain clauses that had been dropped in the late-night compromise; the resolution was sent to Britain for relatively quick approval and Queen Elizabeth II came to Canada to proclaim the new Constitution Act on Parliament Hill 17 April 1982. On that same day Lévesque left Ottawa prophesying dire consequences for Confederation. "The Canadian Way," he said, mocking the phrase his fellow premiers had used to trumpet their compromise, was "to abandon Québec at the moment of crisis."

ROBERT SHEPPARD

Reading: K. Banting and R. Simeon, *And No One Cheered* (1983); Robert Sheppard and M. Valpy, *The National Deal* (1982).

Constitution Act, 1982

Part 1
Canadian Charter of Rights and Freedoms

Whereas Canada is founded upon principles that recognize the supremacy of God and the rule of law:

Guarantee of Rights and Freedoms

1. The *Canadian Charter of Rights and Freedoms* guarantees the rights and freedoms set out in it subject only to such reasonable limits prescribed by law as can be demonstrably justified in a free and democratic society.

Fundamental Freedoms

2. Everyone has the following fundamental freedoms:
(a) freedom of conscience and religion;
(b) freedom of thought, belief, opinion and expression, including freedom of the press and other media of communication;
(c) freedom of peaceful assembly; and
(d) freedom of association.

Democratic Rights

3. Every citizen of Canada has the right to vote in an election of members of the House of Commons or of a legislative assembly and to be qualified for membership therein.

4. (1) No House of Commons and no legislative assembly shall continue for longer than five years from the date fixed for the return of the writs at a general election of its members.
(2) In time of real or apprehended war, invasion or insurrection, a House of Commons may be continued by Parliament and a legislative assembly may be continued by the legislature beyond five years if such continuation is not opposed by the votes of more than one-third of the members of the House of Commons or the legislative assembly, as the case may be.

5. There shall be a sitting of Parliament and of each legislature at least once every twelve months.

Mobility Rights

6. (1) Every citizen of Canada has the right to enter, remain in and leave Canada.
(2) Every citizen of Canada and every person who has the status of a permanent resident of Canada has the right
(a) to move to and take up residence in any prov ince; and
(b) to pursue the gaining of a livelihood in an province.
(3) The rights specified in subsection (2) are subje to
(a) any laws or practices of general application i force in a province other than those that dis criminate among persons primarily on the basis c province of present or previous residence; and
(b) any laws providing for reasonable residency re quirements as a qualification for the receipt of pub licly provided social services.
(4) Subsections (2) and (3) do not preclude any law program or activity that has as its object the amelio ration in a province of conditions of individuals i that province who are socially or economicall disadvantaged if the rate of employment in tha province is below the rate of employment in Can ada.

Legal Rights

7. Everyone has the right to life, liberty and securit of the person and the right not to be deprive thereof except in accordance with the principles c fundamental justice.

8. Everyone has the right to be secure against unrea sonable search or seizure.

9. Everyone has the right not to be arbitrarily de tained or imprisoned.

10. Everyone has the right on arrest or detention
(a) to be informed promptly of the reasons therefo
(b) to retain and instruct counsel without delay an to be informed of that right; and
(c) to have the validity of the detention determine by way of *habeas corpus* and to be released if the de tention is not lawful.

11. Any person charged with an offence has th right
(a) to be informed without unreasonable delay c the specific offence;
(b) to be tried within a reasonable time;
(c) not to be compelled to be a witness in pro ceedings against that person in respect of the of fence;
(d) to be presumed innocent until proven guilty ac cording to law in a fair and public hearing by an in dependent and impartial tribunal;
(e) not to be denied reasonable bail without jus cause;
(f) except in the case of an offence under militar law tried before a military tribunal, to the benefit c trial by jury where the maximum punishment fo the offence is imprisonment for five years or a mor severe punishment;
(g) not to be found guilty on account of any act c omission unless, at the time of the act or omission, i constituted an offence under Canadian or interna tional law or was criminal according to the genera principles of law recognized by the community c nations;
(h) if finally acquitted of the offence, not to be trie for it again and, if finally found guilty and pun ished for the offence, not to be tried or punished fc it again; and
(i) if found guilty of the offence and if the pun ishment for the offence has been varied between th time of commission and the time of sentencing, t the benefit of the lesser punishment.

12. Everyone has the right not to be subjected to an cruel and unusual treatment or punishment.

13. A witness who testifies in any proceedings ha the right not to have any incriminating evidence s given used to incriminate that witness in any othe proceedings, except in a prosecution for perjury o for the giving of contradictory evidence.

14. A party or witness in any proceedings who doe not understand or speak the language in which th proceedings are conducted or who is deaf has th right to the assistance of an interpreter.

Equality Rights

15. (1) Every individual is equal before and unde the law and has the right to the equal protectio and equal benefit of the law without discrimina tion and, in particular, without discriminatio based on race, national or ethnic origin, colour, reli gion, sex, age or mental or physical disability.
(2) Subsection (1) does not preclude any law, pro gram or activity that has as its object the ameliora tion of conditions of disadvantaged individuals o

roups including those that are disadvantaged be-use of race, national or ethnic origin, colour, reli-ion, sex, age or mental or physical disability.

Official Languages of Canada

. (1) English and French are the official languages Canada and have equality of status and equal ghts and privileges as to their use in all institu-ons of the Parliament and government of Canada.

) English and French are the official languages of ew Brunswick and have equality of status and qual rights and privileges as to their use in all in-itutions of the legislature and government of New runswick.

) Nothing in this Charter limits the authority of arliament or a legislature to advance the equality status or use of English and French.

. (1) Everyone has the right to use English or rench in any debates and other proceedings of Par-ament.

) Everyone has the right to use English or French any debates and other proceedings of the legis-ture of New Brunswick.

. (1) The statutes, records and journals of Parlia-ent shall be printed and published in English and rench and both language versions are equally au-oritative.

) The statutes, records and journals of the legis-ture of New Brunswick shall be printed and pub-shed in English and French and both language ersions are equally authoritative.

. (1) Either English or French may be used by any erson in, or in any pleading in or process issuing om, any court established by Parliament.

) Either English or French may be used by any erson in, or in any pleading in or process issuing om, any court of New Brunswick.

. (1) Any member of the public in Canada has the ght to communicate with, and to receive available rvices from, any head or central office of an insti-tion of the Parliament or government of Canada English or French, and has the same right with spect to any other office of any such institution here

) there is a significant demand for communica-ons with and services from that office in such lan-uage; or

) due to the nature of the office, it is reasonable at communications with and services from that ffice be available in both English and French.

) Any member of the public in New Brunswick as the right to communicate with, and to receive vailable services from, any office of an institution f the legislature or government of New Brunswick English or French.

. Nothing in sections 16 to 20 abrogates or dero-ates from any right, privilege or obligation with spect to the English and French languages, or ei-er of them, that exists or is continued by virtue of ny other provision of the Constitution of Canada.

. Nothing in sections 16 to 20 abrogates or dero-ates from any legal or customary right or privilege cquired or enjoyed either before or after the com-g into force of this Charter with respect to any nguage that is not English or French.

Minority Language Educational Rights

. (1) Citizens of Canada

) whose first language learned and still under-ood is that of the English or French linguistic mi-ority population of the province in which they re-de, or

) who have received their primary school instruc-on in Canada in English or French and reside in a rovince where the language in which they re-ived that instruction is the language of the Eng-sh or French linguistic minority population of the rovince, have the right to have their children rec-ve primary and secondary school instruction in at language in that province.

) Citizens of Canada of whom any child has re-ived or is receiving primary or secondary school struction in English or French in Canada, have e right to have all their children receive primary nd secondary school instruction in the same lan-uage.

) The right of citizens of Canada under subsections) and (2) to have their children receive primary nd secondary school instruction in the language of e English or French linguistic minority popula-on of a province

(a) applies wherever in the province the number of children of citizens who have such a right is suffi-cient to warrant the provision to them out of public funds of minority language instruction; and

(b) includes, where the number of those children so warrants, the right to have them receive that in-struction in minority language educational facili-ties provided out of public funds.

Enforcement

24. (1) Anyone whose rights or freedoms, as guaran-teed by this Charter, have been infringed or denied may apply to a court of competent jurisdiction to obtain such remedy as the court considers appropri-ate and just in the circumstances.

(2) Where, in proceedings under subsection (1), a court concludes that evidence was obtained in a manner that infringed or denied any rights or free-doms guaranteed by this Charter, the evidence shall be excluded if it is established that, having regard to all the circumstances, the admission of it in the pro-ceedings would bring the administration of justice into disrepute.

General

25. The guarantee in this Charter of certain rights and freedoms shall not be construed so as to abro-gate or derogate from any aboriginal, treaty or other rights or freedoms that pertain to the aboriginal peoples of Canada including (a) any rights or free-doms that have been recognized by the Royal Proc-lamation of October 7, 1763; and (b) any rights or freedoms that may be acquired by the aboriginal peoples of Canada by way of land claims settle-ment.

26. The guarantee in this Charter of certain rights and freedoms shall not be construed as denying the existence of any other rights or freedoms that exist in Canada.

27. This Charter shall be interpreted in a manner consistent with the preservation and enhancement of the multicultural heritage of Canadians.

28. Notwithstanding anything in this Charter, the rights and freedoms referred to in it are guaranteed equally to male and female persons.

29. Nothing in this Charter abrogates or derogates from any rights or privileges guaranteed by or un-der the Constitution of Canada in respect of deno-minational, separate or dissentient schools.

30. A reference in this Charter to a province or to the legislative assembly or legislature of a province shall be deemed to include a reference to the Yukon Territory and the Northwest Territories, or to the appropriate legislative authority thereof, as the case may be.

31. Nothing in this Charter extends the legislative powers of any body or authority.

Application of Charter

32. (1) This Charter applies

(a) to the Parliament and government of Canada in respect of all matters within the authority of Parlia-ment including all matters relating to the Yukon Territory and Northwest Territories; and

(b) to the legislature and government of each prov-ince in respect of all matters within the authority of the legislature of each province.

(2) Notwithstanding subsection (1), section 15 shall not have effect until three years after this section comes into force.

33. (1) Parliament or the legislature of a province may expressly declare in an Act of Parliament or of the legislature, as the case may be, that the Act or a provision thereof shall operate notwithstanding a provision included in section 2 or sections 7 to 15 of this Charter.

(2) An Act or a provision of an Act in respect of which a declaration made under this section is in effect shall have such operation as it would have but for the provision of this Charter referred to in the declaration.

(3) A declaration made under subsection (1) shall cease to have effect five years after it comes into force or on such earlier date as may be specified in the declaration.

(4) Parliament or the legislature of a province may re-enact a declaration made under subsection (1).

(5) Subsection (3) applies in respect of a re-enact-ment made under subsection (4).

34. This Part may be cited as the *Canadian Charter of Rights and Freedoms.*

Part II - Rights of the Aboriginal Peoples of Canada

35. (1) The existing aboriginal and treaty rights of the aboriginal peoples of Canada are hereby recog-nized and affirmed.

(2) In this Act, "aboriginal peoples of Canada" in-cludes the Indian, Inuit and Métis peoples of Can-ada.

Part III - Equalization and Regional Disparities

36. (1) Without altering the legislative authority of Parliament or of the provincial legislatures, or the rights of any of them with respect to the exer-cise of their legislative authority, Parliament and the legislatures, together with the government of Canada and the provincial governments, are com-mitted to

(a) promoting equal opportunities for the well-being of Canadians;

(b) furthering economic development to reduce dis-parity in opportunities; and

(c) providing essential public sevices of reasonable quality to all Canadians.

(2) Parliament and the government of Canada are committed to the principle of making equalization payments to ensure that provincial governments have sufficient revenues to provide reasonably comparable levels of public services at reasonably comparable levels of taxation.

Part IV - Constitutional Conference

37. (1) A constitutional conference composed of the Prime Minister of Canada and the first minis-ters of the provinces shall be convened by the Prime Minister of Canada within one year after this Part comes into force.

(2) The conference convened under subsection (1) shall have included in its agenda an item respecting constitutional matters that directly affect the ab-original peoples of Canada, including the identi-fication and definition of the rights of those peoples to be included in the Constitution of Canada, and the Prime Minister of Canada shall invite represen-tatives of those peoples to participate in the discus-sions on that item.

(3) The Prime Minister of Canada shall invite elec-ted representatives of the governments of the Yu-kon Territory and the Northwest Territories to par-ticipate in the discussions on any item on the agenda of the conference convened under sub-section (1) that, in the opinion of the Prime Minis-ter, directly affects the Yukon Territory and the Northwest Territories.

Part V - Procedure for Amending Constitution of Canada

38. (1) An amendment to the Constitution of Can-ada may be made by proclamation issued by the Governor General under the Great Seal of Canada where so authorized by

(a) resolutions of the Senate and House of Com-mons; and

(b) resolutions of the legislative assemblies of at least two-thirds of the provinces that have, in the aggregate, according to the then latest general cen-sus, at least fifty per cent of the population of all the provinces.

(2) An amendment made under subsection (1) that derogates from the legislative powers, the propri-etary rights or any other rights or privileges of the legislature or government of a province shall re-quire a resolution supported by a majority of the members of each of the Senate, the House of Com-mons and the legislative assemblies required under subsection (1).

(3) An amendment referred to in subsection (2) shall not have effect in a province the legislative assem-bly of which has expressed its dissent thereto by res-olution supported by a majority of its members prior to the issue of the proclamation to which the amendment relates unless that legislative assembly, subsequently, by resolution supported by a majority of its members, revokes its dissent and authorizes the amendment.

(4) A resolution of dissent made for the purposes of subsection (3) may be revoked at any time before or after the issue of the proclamation to which it relates.

39. (1) A proclamation shall not be issued under

subsection 38(1) before the expiration of one year from the adoption of the resolution initiating the amendment procedure thereunder, unless the legislative assembly of each province has previously adopted a resolution of assent or dissent.
(2) A proclamation shall not be issued under subsection 38(1) after the expiration of three years from the adoption of the resolution initiating the amendment procedure thereunder.
40. Where an amendment is made under subsection 38(1) that transfers provincial legislative powers relating to education or other cultural matters from provincial legislatures to Parliament, Canada shall provide reasonable compensation to any province to which the amendment does not apply.
41. An amendment to the Constitution of Canada in relation to the following matters may be made by proclamation issued by the Governor General under the Great Seal of Canada only where authorized by resolutions of the Senate and House of Commons and of the legislative assembly of each province:
(a) the office of the Queen, the Governor General and the Lieutenant Governor of a province;
(b) the right of a province to a number of members in the House of Commons not less than the number of Senators by which the province is entitled to be represented at the time this Part comes into force;
(c) subject to section 43, the use of the English or the French language;
(d) the composition of the Supreme Court of Canada; and
(e) an amendment to this Part.
42. (1) An amendment to the Constitution of Canada in relation to the following matters may be made only in accordance with subsection 38(1):
(a) the principle of proportionate representation of the provinces in the House of Commons prescribed by the Constitution of Canada;
(b) the powers of the Senate and the method of selecting Senators;
(c) the number of members by which a province is entitled to be represented in the Senate and the residence qualifications of Senators;
(d) subject to paragraph 41(d), the Supreme Court of Canada;
(e) the extension of existing provinces into the territories; and
(f) notwithstanding any other law or practice, the establishment of new provinces.
(2) Subsections 38(2) to (4) do not apply in respect of amendments in relation to matters referred to in subsection (1).
43. An amendment to the Constitution of Canada in relation to any provision that applies to one or more, but not all, provinces, including
(a) any alteration to boundaries between provinces, and
(b) any amendment to any provision that relates to the use of the English or the French language within a province, may be made by proclamation issued by the Governor General under the Great Seal of Canada only where so authorized by resolutions of the Senate and House of Commons and of the legislative assembly of each province to which the amendment applies.
44. Subject to sections 41 and 42, Parliament may exclusively make laws amending the Constitution of Canada in relation to the executive government of Canada or the Senate and House of Commons.
45. Subject to section 41, the legislature of each province may exclusively make laws amending the constitution of the province.
46. (1) The procedures for amendment under sections 38, 41, 42 and 43 may be initiated either by the Senate or the House of Commons or by the legislative assembly of a province.
(2) A resolution of assent made for the purposes of this Part may be revoked at any time before the issue of a proclamation authorized by it.
47. (1) An amendment to the Constitution of Canada made by proclamation under section 38, 41, 42 or 43 may be made without a resolution of the Senate authorizing the issue of the proclamation if, within one hundred and eighty days after the adoption by the House of Commons of a resolution authorizing its issue, the Senate has not adopted such a resolution and if, at any time after the expiration of that period, the House of Commons again adopts the resolution.
(2) Any period when Parliament is prorogued or dissolved shall not be counted in computing the one hundred and eighty day period referred to in subsection (1).
48. The Queen's Privy Council for Canada shall advise the Governor General to issue a proclamation under this Part forthwith on the adoption of the resolutions required for an amendment made by proclamation under this Part.
49. A constitutional conference composed of the Prime Minister of Canada and the first ministers of the provinces shall be convened by the Prime Minister of Canada within fifteen years after this Part comes into force to review the provisions of this Part.

Part VI - Amendment to the Constitution Act, 1867

50. The *Constitution Act, 1867* (formerly named The *British North America Act, 1867*) is amended by adding thereto, immediately after section 92 thereof, the following heading and section:

"Non-Renewable" Natural Resources, Forestr Resources and Electrical Energy
92A. (1) In each province, the legislature may exclu sively make laws in relation to
(a) exploration for non-renewable natural resource in the province;
(b) development, conservation and management o non-renewable natural resources and forestry re sources in the province, including laws in relatio to the rate of primary production therefrom; and
(c) development, conservation and management o sites and facilities in the province for the generatio and production of electrical energy.
(2) In each province, the legislature may make law in relation to the export from the province to an other part of Canada of the primary productio from non-renewable natural resources and forestr resources in the province and the production fro facilities in the province for the generation of elec trical energy, but such laws may not authorize o provide for discrimination in prices or in supplie exported to another part of Canada.
(3) Nothing in subsection (2) derogates from the au thority of Parliament to enact laws in relation to th

Schedule to the Constitution Act, 1982
Modernization of the Constitution

Item	*Column I* *Act Affected*	*Column II* *Amendment*	*Column III* *New Name*
1.	British North America Act, 1867, 30-31 Vict., c. 3 (U.K.)	(1) Section 1 is repealed and the following substituted therefor: "1. This Act may be cited as the *Constitution Act, 1867*." (2) Section 20 is repealed. (3) Class 1 of section 91 is repealed. (4) Class 1 of section 92 is repealed.	Constitution Act, 1867
2.	An Act to amend and continue the Act 32-33 Victoria chapter 3; and to establish and provide for the Government of the Province of Manitoba, 1870, 33 Vict., c. 3 (Can.)	(1) The long title is repealed and the following substituted therefor: "*Manitoba Act, 1870.*" (2) Section 20 is repealed.	Manitoba Act, 1870
3.	Order of Her Majesty in Council admitting Rupert's Land and the North-Western Territory into the union, dated the 23rd day of June, 1870		Rupert's Land and North-Western Territory Order
4.	Order of Her Majesty in Council admitting British Columbia into the Union, dated the 16th day of May, 1871		British Columbia Terms of Union
5.	British North America Act, 1871, 34-35 Vict., c. 28 (U.K.)	Section 1 is repealed and the following substituted therefor: "1. This Act may be cited as the *Constitution Act, 1871*."	Constitution Act, 1871
6.	Order of Her Majesty in Council admitting Prince Edward Island into the Union, dated the 26th day of June, 1873		Prince Edward Island Terms of Union
7.	Parliament of Canada Act, 1875, 38-39 Vict., c. 38 (U.K.)		Parliament of Canada Act, 1875
8.	Order of Her Majesty in Council admitting all British possessions and Territories in North America and islands adjacent thereto into the Union, dated the 31st day of July, 1880		Adjacent Territories Order
9.	British North America Act, 1886, 49-50 Vict., c. 35 (U.K.)	Section 3 is repealed and the following substituted therefor: "3. This Act may be cited as the *Constitution Act, 1886*."	Constitution Act, 1886
10.	Canada (Ontario Boundary) Act, 1889, 52-53 Vict., c. 28 (U.K.)		Canada (Ontario Boundary) Act, 1889
11.	Canadian Speaker (Appointment of Deputy) Act, 1895, 2nd Sess., 59 Vict., c. 3 (U.K.)	The Act is repealed.	
12.	The Alberta Act, 1905, 4-5 Edw. VII, c. 3 (Can.)		Alberta Act
13.	The Saskatchewan Act, 1905, 4-5 Edw. VII, c. 42 (Can.)		Saskatchewan Act
14.	British North America Act, 1907, 7 Edw. VII, c. 11 (U.K.)	Section 2 is repealed and the following substituted therefor: "2. This Act may be cited as the *Constitution Act, 1907*."	Constitution Act, 1907

Schedule to the Constitution Act, 1982
Modernization of the Constitution

Item	Column I Act Affected	Column II Amendment	Column III New Name
5.	British North America Act, 1915, 5-6 Geo. V, c. 45 (U.K.)	Section 3 is repealed and the following substituted therefor: "3. This Act may be cited as the *Constitution Act, 1915.*"	Constitution Act, 1915
6.	British North America Act, 1930, 20-21 Geo. V, c. 26 (U.K.)	Section 3 is repealed and the following substituted therefor: "3. This Act may be cited as the *Constitution Act, 1930.*"	Constitution Act, 1930
7.	Statute of Westminster, 1931, 22 Geo. V. c. 4 (U.K.)	In so far as they apply to Canada, (a) section 4 is repealed; and (b) subsection 7(1) is repealed	Statute of Westminster, 1931
8.	British North America Act, 1940, 3-4 Geo. VI, c. 36 (U.K.)	Section 2 is repealed and the following substituted therefor: "2. This Act may be cited as the *Constitution Act, 1940.*"	Constitution Act, 1940
9.	British North America Act, 1943, 6-7 Geo. VI, c. 30 (U.K.)	The Act is repealed.	
10.	British North America Act, 1946, 9-10 Geo. VI, c. 63 (U.K.)	The Act is repealed.	
11.	British North America Act, 1949, 12-13 Geo. VI, c. 22 (U.K.)	Section 3 is repealed and the following substituted therefor: "3. This Act may be cited as the *Newfoundland Act.*"	Newfoundland Act
12.	British North America (No. 2) Act 1949, 13 Geo. VI, c. 81 (U.K.)	The Act is repealed.	
13.	British North America Act, 1951, 14-15 Geo. VI, c. 32 (U.K.)	The Act is repealed.	
14.	British North America Act, 1952, 1 Eliz. II, c. 15 (Can.)	The Act is repealed.	
15.	British North America Act, 1960, 9 Eliz. II, c. 2 (U.K.)	Section 2 is repealed and the following substituted therefor: "2. This Act may be cited as the *Constitution Act, 1960.*"	Constitution Act, 1960
16.	British North America Act, 1964, 12-13 Eliz. II, c. 73 (U.K.)	Section 2 is repealed and the following substituted therefor: "2. This Act may be cited as the *Constitution Act, 1964.*"	Constitution Act, 1964
17.	British North America Act, 1965, 14 Eliz. II, C. 4, Part I (Can.)	Section 2 is repealed and the following substituted therefor: "2. This Part may be cited as the *Constitution Act, 1965.*"	Constitution Act, 1965
18.	British North America Act, 1974, 23 Eliz. II, c. 13, Part I (Can.)	Section 3, as amended by 25-26 Eliz. II, c. 28, s. 38(1) (Can.), is repealed and the following substituted therefor: "3. This Part may be cited as the *Constitution Act, 1974.*"	Constitution Act, 1974
19.	British North America Act, 1975, 23-24 Eliz. II, c. 28, Part I (Can.)	Section 3, as amended by 25-26 Eliz. II, c. 28, s. 31 (Can.), is repealed and the following substituted therefor: "3. This Part may be cited as the *Constitution Act (No. 1), 1975.*"	Constitution Act (No. 1), 1975
20.	British North America Act (No. 2), 1975, 23-24 Eliz. II, c. 53 (Can.)	Section 3 is repealed and the following substituted therefor: "3. This Act may be cited as the *Constitution Act (No. 2), 1975.*"	Constitution Act (No. 2), 1975

natters referred to in that subsection and, where such a law of Parliament and a law of a province conflict, the law of Parliament prevails to the extent of the conflict.

(4) In each province, the legislature may make laws in relation to the raising of money by any mode or system of taxation in respect of

(a) non-renewable natural resources and forestry resources in the province and the primary production therefrom, and

(b) sites and facilities in the province for the generation of electrical energy and the production therefrom, whether or not such production is exported in whole or in part from the province, but such laws may not authorize or provide for taxation that differentiates between production exported to another part of Canada and production not exported from the province.

(5) The expression "primary production" has the meaning assigned by the Sixth Schedule.

(6) Nothing in subsections (1) to (5) derogates from any powers or rights that a legislature or government of a province had immediately before the coming into force of this section."

51. The said Act is further amended by adding thereto the following Schedule:

"THE SIXTH SCHEDULE" - Primary Production from *Non-Renewable Natural Resources and Forestry Resources 1.* For the purposes of section 92A of this Act,
(a) production from a non-renewable natural resource is primary production therefrom if
(i) it is in the form in which it exists upon its recovery or severance from its natural state, or
(ii) it is a product resulting from processing or refining the resource, and is not a manufactured product or a product resulting from refining crude oil, refining upgraded heavy crude oil, refining gases or liquids derived from coal or refining a synthetic equivalent of crude oil; and
(b) production from a forestry resource is primary production therefrom if it consists of sawlogs, poles, lumber, wood chips, sawdust or any other primary wood product, or wood pulp, and is not a product manufactured from wood."

Part VII - General

52. (1) The Constitution of Canada is the supreme law of Canada, and any law that is inconsistent with the provisions of the Constitution is, to the extent of the inconsistency, of no force or effect.
(2) The Constitution of Canada includes
(a) the *Canada Act 1982,* including this Act;
(b) the Acts and orders referred to in the schedule; and
(c) any amendment to any Act or order referred to in paragraph (a) or (b).
(3) Amendments to the Constitution of Canada shall be made only in accordance with the authority contained in the Constitution of Canada.

53. (1) The enactments referred to in Column I of the schedule are hereby repealed or amended to the extent indicated in Column II thereof and, unless repealed, shall continue as law in Canada under the names set out in Column III thereof.
(2) Every enactment, except the *Canada Act 1982,* that refers to an enactment referred to in the schedule by the name Column I thereof is hereby amended by substituting for that name the corresponding name in Column III thereof, and any British North America Act not referred to in the schedule may be cited as the *Constitution Act* followed by the year and number, if any, of its enactment.

54. Part IV is repealed on the day that is one year after this Part comes into force and this section may be repealed and this Act renumbered, consequentially upon the repeal of Part IV and this section, by proclamation issued by the Governor General under the Great Seal of Canada.

55. A French version of the portions of the Constitution of Canada referred to in the schedule shall be prepared by the Minister of Justice of Canada as expeditiously as possible and, when any portion thereof sufficient to warrant action being taken has been so prepared, it shall be put forward for enactment by proclamation issued by the Governor General under the Great Seal of Canada pursuant to the procedure then applicable to an amendment of the same provisions of the Constitution of Canada.

56. Where any portion of the Constitution of Canada has been or is enacted in English and French or where a French version of any portion of the Constitution is enacted pursuant to section 55, the English and French versions of that portion of the Constitution are equally authoritative.

57. The English and French versions of this Act are equally authoritative.

58. Subject to section 59, this Act shall come into force on a day to be fixed by proclamation issued by the Queen or the Governor General under the Great Seal of Canada.

59. (1) Paragraph 23(1)(a) shall come into force in respect of Québec on a day to be fixed by proclamation issued by the Queen or the Governor General under the Great Seal of Canada.
(2) A proclamation under subsection (1) shall be issued only where authorized by the legislative assembly or government of Québec.
(3) This section may be repealed on the day paragraph 23(1)(a) comes into force in respect of Québec and this Act amended and renumbered, consequentially upon the repeal of this section, by proclamation issued by the Queen or the Governor General under the Great Seal of Canada.

60. This Act may be cited as the *Constitution Act, 1982* and the Constitution Acts 1867 to 1975 (No. 2) and this Act may be cited together as the *Constitution Acts, 1867 to 1982.*

Constitution Act, 1867, originally the BRITISH NORTH AMERICA ACT, statute enacted 29 Mar 1867 by the British Parliament, providing for CONFEDERATION of the PROVINCE OF CANADA (Ontario and Québec), Nova Scotia and New Brunswick into a federal state with a parliamentary system modelled on that of Britain. RUPERT'S LAND was acquired in 1870, and 6 provinces have been added to the original 4: Manitoba (1870), BC (1871), PEI (1873), Alberta and Saskatchewan (1905), and Newfoundland (1949). The Act does not contain the entire CONSTITUTION of Canada. Complementing its text are British and Canadian statutes having constitutional effect (eg, the Canada Elections Act), and certain unwritten principles known as "the conventions of the constitution." Conventions, such as the power vested in the Crown to dissolve Parliament and call a general election, are usually exercised on the advice of the PRIME MINISTER.

The Act outlines the DISTRIBUTION OF POWERS between the central Parliament (s91, eg, over BANKING, INTEREST, CRIMINAL LAW, the POSTAL SYSTEM and the ARMED FORCES) and the provincial legislatures (s92, eg, over PROPERTY; most contracts and TORTS; local works, undertakings and businesses). Because of the breadth or generality of the legislative powers conferred, occasionally a direct conflict arises between provincial and federal laws regulating the same things (eg, security frauds). By paramountcy, federal law prevails. In the case of concurrent powers, exercisable by both jurisdictions, federal paramountcy prevails in matters involving agriculture and immigration (s95), but provincial in old-age pensions (s94A). Unallocated powers (eg, aeronautics, radio, official languages) go to the federal government rather than to the local units as in the US and Australia. The federal PEACE, ORDER AND GOOD GOVERNMENT power embraces these "residuary" areas and matters falling under "national dimensions" and "emergencies." "National dimensions" signifies that selected matters originally of a local nature and under provincial jurisdiction (eg, day-to-day health care) can, through altered circumstances, such as an epidemic, acquire a new aspect transcending provincial competence and thereby become subject to federal jurisdiction. In wartime virtually all provincial powers may come under central control. In 1976 the SUPREME COURT OF CANADA decided that Parliament also possessed what amounted to a peacetime emergency power to impose national WAGE AND PRICE CONTROLS to combat serious national inflation. Unlike the American constitution, the Constitution Act contains no postulate that all local units are constitutionally equal. The Prairie provinces, for example, unlike the original 4, did not possess their lands and minerals for 25 years after their acquisition of provincial status.

Judicial interpretation has had a substantial effect on the ambit of provincial and federal powers. Until appeals to Britain were abolished in 1949, influential judges on the JUDICIAL COMMITTEE OF THE PRIVY COUNCIL often expansively interpreted provincial powers, such as those over property and civil rights, when they came into conflict with federal powers over peace, order and good government or the regulation of trade and commerce. They sought thereby to offset the excessive centralism they perceived in the BNA Act (eg, the federal veto over any provincial statute in s90) and to preserve a viable federal system. Since 1949 the Supreme Court has pursued a more centralist interpretation. In 1980, the omission of a domestic amending formula in the BNA Act led to a constitutional crisis when PM Trudeau attempted unilaterally to patriate the Constitution, by the "joint address" procedure, without provincial consent. When the Supreme Court decided in Sept 1981 that his proposal was unconstitutional in the conventional sense, he relented, with "patriation" being achieved in Apr 1982 by federal-provincial consensus. *See* CONSTITUTIONAL HISTORY; CONSTITUTIONAL LAW; CONSTITUTION REFERENCE. W.H. MCCONNELL

Constitution Reference (1981), known as Resolution to Amend the Constitution. As a prelude to patriation of the Canadian Constitution, the Supreme Court of Canada was asked to rule upon a resolution asking the Queen to place before the British Parliament a bill that included a Charter of Rights and Freedoms, an amending formula and certain amendments to the Constitution. The majority of the Court found that the resolution could be adopted by the federal Houses and the British Parliament without provincial consent. But the majority of the Court also declared that, according to a constitutional convention, the federal resolution should have "substantial" though not necessarily unanimous provincial consent. Approval by 2 provinces (as was the case) was insufficient. Judged by convention the Resolution was unconstitutional, but because the Court may declare the existence of conventions but may not enforce them, flouting a convention can give rise to a political rather than a juridical remedy.

GÉRALD-A. BEAUDOIN

Constitutional Act, 1791, Act of the British Parliament creating UPPER CANADA and LOWER CANADA. It came into effect on Dec 26, having received royal assent the preceding June. This Act enshrined constitutional changes that were part of that reorganization of BRITISH NORTH AMERICA which, under the pressure of thousands of LOYALISTS seeking refuge after the AMERICAN REVOLUTION, had led to the creation of the provinces of New Brunswick and Cape Breton in 1784. On this earlier model of separation, a constitutional bill was prepared by William Wyndham Grenville to ensure the conditions necessary for the development of British parliamentary institutions in the colonial territory governed by the QUEBEC ACT of 1774. According to its author, the bill's general purpose was to "assimilate" each colony's constitution to that of Britain.

The bill had 4 main objectives: to establish colonial governments that would guarantee the same rights and privileges there as were enjoyed by loyal subjects elsewhere in N America; to ease the burden on the imperial treasury by granting colonial assemblies the right to levy taxes with which to pay for local civil and legal administration; to justify the territorial division of the PROVINCE OF QUEBEC and the creation of separate provincial legislatures; and to maintain and strengthen the bonds of political dependency by remedying acknowledged constitutional weaknesses of previous colonial governments. This involved bolstering the authority and prestige of the governor by making him a true representative of the imperial power, and limiting the powers of the elected colonial assemblies by creating independent legislative councils whose appointed members comprised an aristocratic body modelled on the House of Lords and devoted to the interests of the Crown (*see* CHÂTEAU CLIQUE; FAMILY COMPACT). The Act guaranteed continuity of ownership of lands held under the SEIGNEURIAL SYSTEM in Lower Canada and created the CLERGY RESERVES in Upper Canada.

By giving Upper Canada a provincial constitution and a separate existence, and by favouring British colonization there, Britain took the first steps on the path that led, ultimately, to the creation of the Canadian Confederation. Nevertheless, the Constitutional Act was flawed, and many historians have considered its failure to establish RESPONSIBLE GOVERNMENT and its distribution of financial powers in favour of the appointed councils as factors contributing to the intercultural conflict of the early 19th century (*see* REBELLIONS OF 1837). PIERRE TOUSIGNANT

Constitutional History The CONSTITUTION ACT, 1867 (formerly the BRITISH NORTH AMERICA ACT) with its authoritative division of powers between federal and provincial legislatures, is of central importance in the Canadian CONSTITUTION, but there are other sources of constitutional principles which also apply, among them unwritten custom or convention, and British and Canadian statutes and court decisions. The unwritten convention that in order to remain in power a person appointed PRIME MINISTER or PREMIER should retain the support of the elected branch of the legislature, or that seats on the 9-member SUPREME COURT OF CANADA should be allocated regionally, are nowhere expressed in statutory form. Although not "laws" enforceable in the courts, such principles are of the utmost importance to effective constitutional government. The Supreme Court stated in 1981 (*see* CONSTITUTION, PATRIATION OF) that "constitutiona conventions plus constitutional law equal th total constitution of the country." Since th courts will not enforce conventions, they can b implemented only by the people or the CROWN. A government that violated convention would al most certainly face electoral defeat or, in the ex treme case, revolution.

The Crown, moreover, has the reserve powe to dismiss a premier or prime minister who ha clearly lost the confidence of the elected legis lature and refuses to resign or have an electio called. Such unwritten principles can be mor important than many laws. According to Brit ish and Canadian constitutional theory, settler bring with them to new shores those of thei former laws that are appropriate to local cir cumstances. Such English laws as the Bill o Rights (1689), with its concept of limited consti tutional monarchy, and the Act of Settlemen (1701), with its doctrine of an independent judi ciary, are salient features of the Canadian Con stitution. So too is the Canada Election Act From France is derived Québec's CIVIL LAW sys tem, and combination of the French heritag with the English has resulted in Canada's hav ing 2 official languages. From Britain comes th principle of parliamentary supremacy, mod ified in Canada's federal structure by the divi sion of powers and an entrenched rights Char ter, which were suggested by the classical mode of the US.

Historical Overview Prior to 1663, control o the French colonies in N America was vested i chartered companies which exercised extensiv administrative, lawmaking and judicial pow ers. It is uncertain what system of law was in ef fect. In 1663 France's N American possession came under direct royal rule and the uncodifie Coutume de Paris became the civil law of NEW FRANCE.

In the period of absolute monarchy, Loui XIV acted through Jean-Baptiste Colbert, wh supervised colonial affairs, and his 2 local offi cials, the GOUVERNEUR (governor) and the INTEN DANT. The governor was military commande negotiator with the Indians and emissary t other colonial outposts. The intendant was over seer of civil administration and was responsib for settlement, finance, public order, justice an the building of public works. Although unde royal rule there were no elected representativ institutions, a SOVEREIGN COUNCIL, consisting o the governor, the bishop and 5 other councillor met weekly. From 1663 to 1675 the councillo were nominated jointly by the bishop and gov ernor; thereafter they were chosen by the kin The council dispensed justice swiftly and inex pensively, superintended spending and regu lated the FUR TRADE and other commercial activ ities. Limitations, or "servitudes," exempted civ officials from ecclesiastical discipline; no gov ernment official could be excommunicated fo performing his duties, whatever they might en tail. The church was also powerless to impose i taxes without the consent of the civil autho ities.

During the 18th century France lost its American territories to Britain. By the TREATY O UTRECHT (1713), ACADIA was ceded to Britain, al though France retained control of Île Royal (Cape Breton), Île Saint-Jean (PEI) and part o modern New Brunswick. France interpreted in restrictive sense the grant made under the treat arguing that the Acadians, who lived mostly o the western fringes of the territory, continue under French sovereignty. Caught between riv European powers, the Acadians were expelle by the British in 1755. The French fortress o LOUISBOURG on Cape Breton fell to the British f the last time in 1758, the same year that th Nova Scotia Legislative Assembly (English Ca ada's oldest representative body) was convene in Halifax. When the SEVEN YEARS' WAR ende with the TREATY OF PARIS (1763), the northern Atlantic seaboard, with the sole exception of Saint Pierre and Miquelon, came indisputably under British rule.

In accordance with the Royal PROCLAMATION OF 1763, Gov James MURRAY was to extend English laws and institutions to Québec. He was instructed to govern with the assistance of a council of . An elected assembly was planned but did not appear. Murray's instructions also prescribed a Test Oath for officeholders which, because of its doctrinal content, no Catholic could conscientiously take. This provision would have resulted in all public offices being occupied by English-speaking Protestants, of whom there were only about 200, to the exclusion of nearly 70 000 French-speaking Catholics. Murray interpreted his instructions in such a way that he could govern through a 12-member appointed council. English was the official language, but the government was conducted in French. Catholicism was tolerated; although the British at first refused to allow a bishop to be appointed to the vacant see, they made no difficulties when Jean-Olivier Briand was consecrated bishop in 1766. The Proclamation of 1763 also recognized Indian land title and provided that Indians could relinquish their land only to the Crown and only collectively.

The substitution of British courts and laws in Québec created difficulties. The new Court of King's Bench convened only twice a year, making justice more costly and less expeditious than it had been under the Sovereign Council. With the abolition of the Coutume de Paris, the *censitaires* (tenants) on seigneuries suffered because their rents could be raised arbitrarily according to English law. Because of the Test Oath, no Catholics could practise law in the new Court of King's Bench, although they could practise in some inferior courts.

The QUEBEC ACT (1774) introduced nonrepresentative government by a colonial governor and an appointed council of 17-23 members. The Act was silent on the use of French, but a new oath allowed Roman Catholics to accept office. The council was not empowered to impose taxes, a matter separately dealt with under the Quebec Revenue Act. The SEIGNEURIAL SYSTEM was retained and French civil law was restored, supplemented by English criminal law. Although Gov Sir Guy CARLETON was instructed to introduce English commercial law as well, he did not. The Act was unpopular with Americans because of its toleration of Catholicism and because it extended Québec's SW boundary to the junction of the Mississippi and Ohio rivers, thus impeding American expansion. The Québec Act became one of the "intolerable acts" which prompted Americans to revolt, but many historians feel its concessions helped encourage Québecois support of continued British rule.

The influx of LOYALISTS after 1783 led to the creation in 1784 of the separate colonies New Brunswick and Cape Breton from parts of Nova Scotia. UPPER CANADA [Ontario] was separated from LOWER CANADA [Québec], with the Ottawa R forming the boundary. In Canada, by the CONSTITUTIONAL ACT, 1791, each of the two constitutive provinces was given a bicameral legislature. The nominated executive council was appointed by the governor whose responsibility was to the British COLONIAL OFFICE rather than to the people or their elected representatives. Thus, there was REPRESENTATIVE GOVERNMENT, but without the executive council being responsible to the assembly.

In the early 19th century, the appointment to office of a few intimates of various governors led to charges of government by clique (*see* CHÂTEAU CLIQUE; FAMILY COMPACT; COUNCIL OF TWELVE). In 1837, unsuccessful REBELLIONS broke out in both provinces of Canada. In the MARITIME PROVINCES executive power was enhanced and the assembly weakened by the division of Nova Scotia. Cape Breton, which remained separate until 1820, lacked an assembly altogether and Prince Edward Island, which had possessed its own legislature from 1769 (having been joined briefly to Nova Scotia, 1763-69), was at times in danger of losing it. Newfoundland had an appointed governor and acquired a representative assembly only in 1832.

Gov Gen Lord DURHAM, who came to Canada in 1838 after the recent insurrections, came to regard the French Canadians as unprogressive and lacking a history or culture. He feared that Québec would use any independent political powers it might acquire to frustrate the policies and objectives of the established government. Preferable, he argued, would be the "fusion" of Upper and Lower Canada in a legislative union with a single government dominated by the "more reliable" English-speaking elite. The governor's appointed executive council, moreover, must enjoy the support of a majority in the elected assembly. Under the new system, the responsibility of the council ("Cabinet") would be to the elected assembly and indirectly to the electors, rather than to the Crown. Local policy would be decided at home. Matters of "imperial interest," such as constitutional changes, EXTERNAL RELATIONS, trade and the management of public lands, would remain with Britain.

The DURHAM REPORT marked the watershed between the first and second British empires, as British holdings, including Canada, began to change status from colony to self-governing nation. The ACT OF UNION (1840) established equality of representation between Canada East [Québec] and Canada West [Ontario] in the common legislature (although Canada East was much more populous) in order to ensure the political ascendancy of the "British" element throughout the reconstituted province. After some hesitation, RESPONSIBLE GOVERNMENT was introduced in 1848 in Nova Scotia and the PROVINCE OF CANADA, and was soon in effect throughout BNA. In 1849 Gov Gen Lord ELGIN courageously signed the REBELLION LOSSES BILL on the advice of his ministers, thus affirming the principle of responsible government. Elgin was also instrumental in introducing French as a language of debate in the Canadian legislature, although English was the sole official language.

The equal representation of sections made government of the Province of Canada unwieldy by promoting deadlock. By 1851 the English-speaking population outnumbered the French, and agitation began for "representation by population" instead of sectional parity. With George Brown's Reform Party energetically advocating REP BY POP, and the Conservatives opposing it, a political stalemate lasted from 1858 to 1864. In 1864 the parties formed a GREAT COALITION with the federation of BNA as its object.

The imperial authorities were coincidentally relinquishing control over Canada. Unoccupied Crown lands were surrendered to the provinces, 1840-52; the British submitted to a Canadian tariff imposed on their imported goods in 1858. In 1865, the British Colonial Laws Validity Act affirmed that no colonial law could be challenged unless it was expressly in conflict with an imperial statute intended to apply to the colony. Politicians from Canada East and West, the Maritimes and Newfoundland met at the CHARLOTTETOWN CONFERENCE in 1864 to discuss union. The QUÉBEC CONFERENCE and LONDON CONFERENCE saw further discussion, and CONFEDERATION of the provinces of Canada, Nova Scotia and New Brunswick was achieved on 1 July 1867.

At Confederation, a PARLIAMENT of 2 chambers was established, with seats in the HOUSE OF COMMONS allocated on the basis of population, while each of the existing 3 regions (Ontario, Québec and the Maritime provinces) was given equal representation (24 seats) in the SENATE. In 1915 the 4 western provinces became a full-fledged region with 24 senators, and Newfoundland received 6 in 1949. The Senate was conceived as a guardian of regional or provincial interests, but did not play that role effectively, especially since a federal cabinet, drawn largely from the lower house and appointed on a regional basis, assumed that function.

Historians sometimes debate whether the federal PEACE, ORDER AND GOOD GOVERNMENT power was designed to endow Ottawa with jurisdiction over all matters not defined as exclusively provincial. If it were, federal jurisdiction would probably be enhanced, since the "powers" enumerated in s91 of the British North America Act would be presented merely to illustrate a single broad power embracing everything not given to the provinces. Under the BNA Act those broad matters appropriately treated nationally (eg, defence, post office, trade and commerce, most communications, currency and coinage, weights and measures) were centralized, whereas powers over property, local works and undertakings, municipalities, and most private law matters (eg, contracts and TORTS) went to the provinces. Where a conflict occurs in "concurrent" areas such as agriculture and immigration, or in any subject matter (except old age pensions, where provincial paramountcy obtains), federal law prevails.

Under the Constitution (which contains, as constituent parts, all provincial constitutions), Canadian provinces, which were added or created at various times, are not all treated as equals. Saskatchewan, for example, was precluded in its founding statute from taxing the Canadian Pacific Railway, whereas Québec and Manitoba were required to publish their laws, and allow proceedings in their courts and legislature, in both English and French. The Prairie provinces, unlike the original 4, did not own their natural resources when they entered Confederation, and only received them by transfer from Ottawa in 1930. Federal retention of such assets was defended by Ottawa on the grounds that the resources were needed for railroad building and the settlement of immigrants. The Northwest Territories and the Yukon possess elected legislatures but still do not own their lands or minerals, and they retain a semi-colonial dependency on the federal government.

After Confederation, some provinces advanced the "compact theory," which likened the BNA Act to a treaty that could be changed only by the unanimous consent of Ottawa and the provinces. Opponents of the theory denied its constitutionality, arguing that the final terms of the BNA Act were never ratified, since the Act was not an agreement but a statute of a superior legislature.

With the centralist Macdonald for long at the helm of the national government, premiers Honoré MERCIER of Québec and Oliver MOWAT of Ontario met in Québec City on 20 Oct 1887 with representatives from New Brunswick, Nova Scotia and Manitoba (BC and PEI did not participate) to promote "provincial rights" against an encroaching federal government. The provinces censured the use of the federal power of DISALLOWANCE, which enabled Ottawa arbitrarily to nullify any provincial law; called for appointment of senators by the provinces; and affirmed the right of the provincial Crown to exercise prerogative powers such as the pardoning power over provincial offences. Macdonald chose to portray the "malcontents" as Liberals confronting their Conservative foes in Ottawa for political reasons.

Another sharp confrontation arose when Manitoba, in 1890, purported to make English the only official language in the province, substituting, as well, a single public school system for the former Roman Catholic and Protestant schools. In 1895 JUDICIAL COMMITTEE OF THE PRIVY

COUNCIL agreed that the educational rights of the religious minority had been adversely affected, and thus enabled the minority to appeal to the federal Cabinet for redress. When the Liberals assumed office in 1896, PM Laurier settled the matter by compromise. (In the 1979 *Forest* case, the Supreme Court of Canada held the 1890 Manitoba language law invalid, casting some doubt on the legal validity of 90 years of provincial legislation, and requiring all future laws to be bilingual.) With the proclamation of the WAR MEASURES ACT in both world wars and during the 1970 OCTOBER CRISIS the federal cabinet acquired all legal powers essential to cope with the existing emergencies (whether or not such powers would ordinarily fall under provincial jurisdiction); constitutionally speaking, for the duration of, and in relation to, the emergency, under the Act it is almost as if the constitutional division of powers did not exist.

The early 20th century saw further advances toward full Canadian independence. When WORLD WAR I began in 1914, by constitutional convention Canada was automatically included in the British declaration of war. After WWI, Canada's separate signature at the TREATY OF VERSAILLES and its membership in the LEAGUE OF NATIONS symbolized its developing independence. In 1923 Hon Ernest LAPOINTE signed the HALIBUT TREATY without British participation (as formerly required), despite British objections. In 1926 Gov Gen Lord BYNG's refusal to grant a dissolution of Parliament to PM Mackenzie KING was portrayed by the latter as imperial interference in Canada's domestic affairs, although Byng's refusal was constitutional (*see* KING-BYNG AFFAIR). At the Imperial Conference in the same year, the BALFOUR REPORT described the self-governing Dominions as autonomous and equal communities within the British Empire (*see* COMMONWEALTH). In 1931 the STATUTE OF WESTMINSTER stipulated that the imperial Parliament would no longer legislate for a Dominion unless the latter requested and consented to the law. Other provisions empowered local legislatures to enact laws even if repugnant to the Colonial Laws Validity Act, and allowed Canada to legislate extraterritorially, eg, establishing shipping laws applying to Canadian vessels on the high seas or applying criminal law to Canadian military personnel serving abroad. The statute affirmed (at least according to the provinces) that provincial jurisdiction could not be unilaterally altered by the newly sovereign federal power.

After 1931, in constitutional theory, London was no more central politically than was Ottawa or Canberra, Australia. The Crown, formerly indivisible, now became divided. In 1939 Canada made a separate declaration of war. Treaties between Canadian Indian bands and the British Crown were now deemed to be the concern of the Canadian government. The monarch became king or queen of Canada, with the GOVERNOR GENERAL acceding to all the remaining prerogative powers in 1947. In 1952 Vincent MASSEY became the first native-born governor general; he was succeeded in 1959 by Georges VANIER. Thereafter incumbents from English-and French-speaking Canada alternated.

In 1949 a constitutional amendment enabled Parliament to make amendments solely affecting the federal power (eg, redistribution of seats in the House of Commons), with designated exceptions in sensitive areas (eg, the requirement of holding annual sessions of Parliament). Other indications of sovereignty were the Canadian Citizenship Act (1947) and the adoption of the maple leaf flag in 1965 (*see* FLAG DEBATE).

Between 1934 and 1949 Newfoundland was governed by an appointed COMMISSION OF GOVERNMENT which had full lawmaking powers. After WWII, debate arose about Newfoundland's future. Peter CASHIN, a former Newfoundland finance minister, advocated a return to Dominion status, while Joseph R. SMALLWOOD led the pro-Confederation forces. Some Newfoundlanders supported the retention of commission government. In the second of 2 referenda held in 1948 the Confederation forces prevailed, and in 1949 Newfoundland became Canada's 10th province, with 6 senators and 7 members of Parliament.

Until 1949, when overseas appeals were abolished, the British Privy Council was Canada's ultimate court of appeal, overshadowing Canadian courts. Some important appeals had been made directly from provincial tribunals to Britain without any participation by the Supreme Court of Canada (est 1875). Lords Watson and Haldane, in particular, decentralized the centralist provisions of the BNA Act, demoting the federal peace, order and good government power and expanding provincial jurisdiction over property and civil rights. In 1930 the Judicial Committee of the Privy Council ruled that women were legal "persons" capable of being summoned to the Senate (*see* PERSONS CASE). In 1932 the JCPC granted power over aeronautics and radio to Ottawa. In 1937, however, it eviscerated PM R.B. Bennett's "New Deal" social program (*see* BENNETT'S NEW DEAL), gravely curtailing federal power over such matters. Judicial metaphors such as "living tree" and "watertight compartments" denoted alternate phases of centralist and provincialist interpretation. In 1937 Alberta Prem ABERHART attempted to enact a Social Credit legislative program that invaded federal jurisdiction, particularly the federal power over banking. When the provincial legislation was disallowed a bitter confrontation ensued, but the courts later upheld the federal position.

The Rowell-Sirois Commission, appointed by Mackenzie King's government in 1937, made far-reaching economic recommendations for restructuring the Canadian federation (*see* DOMINION-PROVINCIAL RELATIONS). The commissioners said that Ottawa should have the exclusive right to levy personal and corporate income taxes and succession duties (concurrent fields under the BNA Act). In return, the federal government would assume all provincial debt and certain responsibilities over relief and unemployment insurance (which the court had just consigned to the provinces), and would pay the less affluent provinces a "National Adjustment Grant" enabling them to maintain services at the average national level. Québec's Tremblay Commission (1956), established by Prem Maurice DUPLESSIS, saw this proposal as too centralist, arguing for the principle of "subsidiarity": likening FEDERALISM to a pyramid, he suggested that as many economic functions as possible should be carried out by local organizations at the base (eg, municipalities, co-operatives, churches) with the federal government at the apex performing only those limited economic functions beyond the capacities of local groups. This concept, of course, would powerfully reinforce provincial autonomy.

The Rowell-Sirois Commission's 1940 recommendations were never really implemented, although the EQUALIZATION PAYMENTS to the provinces begun by PM Louis ST. LAURENT after the marked centralization of powers during WWII achieved a similar purpose. In one form or another, federal equalization payments to less wealthy provinces have continued. Although unemployment insurance was centralized by a 1940 amendment, the richer provinces (Ont, Alta, BC) objected to subsidies to the poorer provinces which they would have had to fund. The federal "spending power" was used to fund FAMILY ALLOWANCES and shared-cost programs entered into jointly with the provinces, such as OLD AGE PENSIONS and medicare. These costly social programs placed an enormous strain on all governments in the late 1970s and early 1980s, leading some politicians to question the constitutionality of universal coverage.

An important constitutional development ir 1969 was the OFFICIAL LANGUAGES ACT, whicl declared English and French to be Canada' "official languages," and extended an array o government services in both tongues to all citi zens. The election of the separatist PARTI QUÉBÉ COIS in Québec on 15 Nov 1976 emphasized tha the threat of SEPARATISM was real, but in a refer endum on 20 May 1980 Québec voters rejecte the provincial government's SOVEREIGNTY-ASSO CIATION option by a margin of 60-40%.

PM Pierre E. TRUDEAU supported continue federalism by promising Québec constitutiona renewal in the event of a negative vote. After deadlocked federal-provincial conference, h announced on 2 Oct 1980 that Ottawa propose to entrench unilaterally the core of a new Con stitution embracing a domestic amending for mula and a rights charter (*see* CANADIAN CHARTE OF RIGHTS AND FREEDOMS) which would replac PM DIEFENBAKER'S 1960 CANADIAN BILL OF RIGHTS Trudeau emphasized that an amending formul had eluded federal-provincial negotiators sinc 1927. The controversy in the 1980s ranged Ot tawa and 2 provincial allies, Ontario and Nev Brunswick, against the other 8 provinces. Cen tral to the debate was whether, by convention provincial consent was required before a amendment could be obtained from Britain af fecting provincial rights, privileges or powers In Sept 1981 the Supreme Court held that al though Ottawa had the legal power to present joint address of the Senate and House of Com mons to Westminster seeking an amendment, i was improper, by convention, to do so without "consensus" (undefined, but at least a clear ma jority) of the provinces. Since neither Ottawa no the dissentient provinces had won outright compromise was essential, and all parties excep Québec reached agreement on 5 Nov 1981 Spokesmen for Québec argued that according t the "duality" principle the concurrence of bot English- and French-speaking Canada was re quired for basic constitutional change, and tha the absence of one "national" will constituted veto. All the other parties have denied the exis tence of the "duality" principle in the form as serted by Québec. Left unresolved for futur consideration are such knotty problems as con stitutional revision of the division of power and institutional reform of the Supreme Court the Senate and the Crown. W.H. MCCONNEL

Reading: W.J. Eccles, *France in America* (1972); D. Lindsa Keir, *The Constitutional History of Modern Britain 1485-193* (1966); Arthur R.M. Lower, *Colony to Nation* (1977 W.H. McConnell, *Commentary on the British North Americ Act* (1977); G.F.G. Stanley, *A Short History of the Canadia Constitution* (1969).

Constitutional Law, a branch of public law the body of rules regulating the functioning o the state. According to the patriation decision o the SUPREME COURT OF CANADA (*see also* CONSTITUTION PATRIATION OF) on 28 Sept 1981, the CONSTITUTION the supreme law of Canada, comprises statutor rules and rules of the COMMON LAW (which to gether make up constitutional law), and con ventions (usually unwritten) derived from Brit ish constitutional history which have develope through the political and constitutional exper ience of Canada. The courts, which administe constitutional law, recognize the convention but do not enforce them and the conventions ar not, strictly speaking, part of constitutional law

The primary sources of Canadian consti tutional law are legislative rules. They includ the Constitution Acts, 1867-1982, and other doc uments comprising the Constitution of Canada eg, federal and provincial statutes related to con stitutional matters, orders-in-council, letters pa tent and proclamations. Section 52 of the Consti tution Act, 1982, provides for the Constitutio of Canada to include the Canada Act, 1982, an the Constitution Act, 1982, legislative texts an decrees included in Appendix I of the latter Ac and the modifications to these legislative texts and decrees. According to the preamble of the CONSTITUTION ACT, 1867, the Canadian Constitution is similar in principle to the Constitution of the UK; therefore, Canadians have inherited the Bill of Rights of 1689, the Act of Settlement of 1701 and various other British statutes and charters. Other sources of constitutional law include case law, ie, the interpretation of the Constitution by the courts, which is just as important as the Constitution itself, especially in Canada where statutes are subject to judicial review for their constitutionality. Section 52 of the Constitution Act, 1982, provides that the Constitution overides any incompatible provision of any piece of legislation. The JUDICIAL COMMITTEE OF THE PRIVY COUNCIL has rendered some 120 judgements on the distribution of legislative powers alone; the Supreme Court has handed down even more. Among the more important cases that have affected the Canadian Constitution are the following: in the field of the distribution of powers, the HODGE CASE (local order), FORT FRANCES CASE (emergency power), aeronautics reference (residual power), LABOUR CONVENTIONS REFERENCE (treaties), OFFSHORE MINERAL RIGHTS (resources under the sea), JONES CASE (official languages), DIONNE CASE (cablevision), MONTCALM CONSTRUCTION CASE (labour relations), ANTI-INFLATION ACT REFERENCE (peacetime emergency powers) and CONSTITUTION REFERENCE (patriation); and in the field of civil liberties, the ALBERTA PRESS CASE ACT (freedom of the press), DRYBONES CASE (equality before the law), DUPOND CASE (street manifestations), MILLER AND COCKRIELL CASE (death penalty), MCNEIL CASE (film regulation) and MACKAY CASE (military offences).

The character of the Canadian Constitution reflects Canada's position as a constitutional monarchy (*see* CROWN), a parliamentary democracy and a federation. As a constitutional monarch the Queen, who is SOVEREIGN in Canada, reigns but does not rule. Executive power is effectively wielded by the PRIME MINISTER and the CABINET. The Queen, because of Canada's federal system, is represented at both levels of GOVERNMENT, federally by the GOVERNOR GENERAL and in each province by a federally appointed LIEUTENANT-GOVERNOR. In the Jan 1982 judgement of the Court of Appeal on the *Indians of Alberta*, Lord Denning stated that although in principle the Crown is indivisible, it has become separate and divisible through practice and usage.

The conventional rules of the Canadian Constitution reflect accurately the actual exercise of executive power. For example, although the Crown can refuse to assent to or reserve assent of legislation, under constitutional law this power will not likely be exercised in future. Nowadays it is very unlikely that a governor general or a lieutenant-governor would refuse to give royal assent to a bill duly passed by Parliament or a legislature. Although possible legally, it would constitute in practice a negation of the principle of RESPONSIBLE GOVERNMENT and, as stated by the Supreme Court in the patriation case, it would be contrary to a convention of the Constitution. The Imperial Conference of 1930 ended the governor general's power to reserve a federal bill that had been adopted by Parliament; it also ended the imperial power of DISALLOWANCE in relation to federal bills.

The power of reserve and disallowance of provincial bills is, in the words of Chief Justice LASKIN, "dormant if not entirely dead." The power of disallowance was last used in 1943, and the power of reserve was used as recently as 1961 in Saskatchewan, but the bill was given royal assent by the governor general. The powers of the prime minister and government officials are not unlimited, however. According to the British constitutional expert A.V. Dicey, all officials, from the prime minister to a collector of taxes, are under the same responsibility for any act done without legal justification as every other citizen is, reflecting the principle of the RULE OF LAW, which is also part of Canadian constitutional law (*see* ADMINISTRATIVE LAW).

In Canada the distinction between legislative, executive and judicial powers is not as sharp as it is in the US. Judicial power is separate in Canada, but in the Canadian parliamentary system, although the Cabinet is responsible to the legislative branch of the government, it dominates both the executive and legislative powers. Parliament comprises the Queen, as head of Canada, a SENATE and a HOUSE OF COMMONS. A well-established constitutional convention requires that the government maintain the confidence of the Commons to remain in power. If such confidence is lost, the prime minister must either resign or seek dissolution of Parliament. The government is not responsible to the Senate. On matters of constitutional amendment, the Senate only has a delaying veto of 180 days; otherwise it has the same decision-making powers as the House of Commons, although money bills must originate in the Commons. The concept of parliamentary supremacy, ie, that Parliament's powers are unlimited, originates in British constitutional law. Canada has inherited this concept in its Constitution, but under its federal system the federal and provincial governments are only sovereign within the legislative limits outlined by the Constitution, and their powers are also limited by the CANADIAN CHARTER OF RIGHTS AND FREEDOMS.

In contrast to the American system of government, the Canadian system is a parliamentary democracy in which the offices of head of government (prime minister) and chief of state (Queen of Canada) are distinct; the government is responsible to the elected Commons. In the Canadian system, the legislative and executive branches of the state are not completely separate, since most ministers are members of the elected house. Under the US presidential system, the president is both the chief of state and the head of government; reflecting the American theory of checks and balances among the 3 powers, the executive and legislative branches are more separate than in Canada, and the executive (the president) is not responsible to the Congress. The majority in the Congress does not necessarily belong to the same party as the president. The president is elected for a fixed term of 4 years and may be re-elected once. A president's tenure may be shortened only by death, resignation or impeachment, but even in these cases an election is not held until the term is complete. In Canada the House can be dissolved before the 5-year term; usually it lasts 4 years. In both systems, however, the judicial power is separate, independent and strong. In both countries a charter or bill of rights is entrenched in the Constitution, and a supreme court determines the constitutionality of laws and statutes. Although both countries are democracies, the American republic is based on the principle of popular sovereignty. The preamble to the American Constitution states, "We, the people of the United States." By contrast, the Supreme Court of Canada stated, in its decision to patriate the constitution: "At law, the Government is in office by the pleasure of the Crown although by convention it is there by the will of the people."

Canada has been a federation since 1867. Legislative, executive and judicial powers are divided between the 2 levels of government. The Constitution Act, 1867, lists areas of federal jurisdiction (eg, the POSTAL SYSTEM, CRIMINAL LAW, BANKING, navigation, defence, BANKRUPTCY) and areas of provincial jurisdiction (eg, property and civil rights, municipal institutions). Other articles or sections allocate special powers (eg, education) and concurrent jurisdictions (eg, agriculture and immigration, old-age pensions, supplementary benefits).

Theoretically the distribution of executive power resembles that of legislative power. Judicial power is also distributed in the Constitution Act, 1867. JURISPRUDENCE in constitutional law has established the principle that Parliament and the provincial legislatures may not delegate legislative powers to each other, but that a sovereign authority can delegate powers to a subordinate body which it has created — the classic example being the relationship of the municipality to the provincial legislature. Power can also be delegated from a sovereign body (eg, Parliament or a provincial legislature) to a subordinate body of the other government. For example, Parliament has delegated to provincial commissions the power to issue permits or make regulations in areas of federal jurisdiction, such as extraprovincial motor transport or marketing.

Under the Constitution Act, 1867, the provinces have exclusive jurisdiction over the creation of civil and criminal courts and in the administration of civil and criminal justice, but Parliament has exclusive jurisdiction in respect of criminal law and procedure. Criminal law generally includes matters under criminal jurisprudence contained in legislation promoting public peace, order, security and the protection of health and morality (in certain aspects). The provinces, however, can legislate in regulatory and quasi-criminal matters. Provincial quasi-criminal legislation may be enacted to suppress conditions that may foster the development of crime.

For the administration of federal laws, Parliament may establish ADMINISTRATIVE TRIBUNALS. Parliament has also created a FEDERAL COURT under s101, and under the same section the Supreme Court of Canada was established by statute in 1875. All judges in federal courts are federally appointed, as are those under s96 of the Constitution Act, 1867, of the higher provincial courts. The judges presiding over lower provincial courts are provincially appointed.

The role of the JUDICIARY is of cardinal importance, because the interpretation of the Constitution is as important as the Constitution itself. Courts give life to a Constitution, which must endure, as it cannot be amended as often as a statute can. Courts must favour the evolution of a Constitution. In a federation a supreme court plays a crucial role in the distribution of legislative powers. For example, in the US the Supreme Court centralized the Constitution, but in Canada the Privy Council generally decentralized the Constitution, although the Supreme Court has in certain areas reversed this trend. The courts also play a major role in the interpretation of the Canadian Charter of Rights and Freedoms or, in the US, the Bill of Rights.

EXTERNAL RELATIONS fall under federal jurisdiction because of federal residuary power and royal PREROGATIVE POWERS. Under s132 Parliament and the federal government were given all the desired powers to fulfil, as part of the British Empire, the obligations of Canada or any of its provinces to foreign countries arising from treaties between the Empire and those countries. This section has fallen into disuse since 1931. In the *Labour Convention Reference* (1937) the judiciary established that the central authority could conclude treaties in Canada's name, but that such treaties would not modify internal law (*see* TREATY-MAKING POWER). If a treaty does require a change in internal law, this must be accomplished through the enactment of a statute. The implementation of a treaty must respect the distribution of legislative powers as defined by the Constitution. Parliament implements treaties relating to federal matters; if a treaty relates to provincial matters, the provincial legislatures are responsible for implementing legislation.

In addition to the 10 provinces, Canada has 2 federal territories — the Yukon and the Northwest Territories. Under the Constitution the territories fall under the legislative jurisdiction of Parliament. They have been delegated certain important powers by Parliament. The commissioners of the respective territories are Crown representatives, and the executive exercises substantial power, but the principle of responsible government does not apply because the delegated powers can be modified, extended or withdrawn. Prior to 17 Apr 1982 the territories could have gained provincial status by a simple Act of Parliament. Now, under the Constitution Act, 1982, it is necessary that both federal houses and 7 provinces (with an aggregate of 50% of the country's population) concur in such a move.

FEDERALISM in Canada rests on a trilogy: the DISTRIBUTION OF POWERS; the interpretation of these powers by the courts, who must ensure that the distribution of powers in the Constitution is not violated and that all enacted legislation is constitutional; and the formula for constitutional amendment. The Constitution of 1867 had no general amending formula. Since 1867, the provincial legislatures have had the right to amend their internal constitutions (except where they concerned the role of the lieutenant-governor), but Parliament did not gain the right to amend its internal constitution until 1949. For changes to the most important part of the Constitution it had to address the Parliament at Westminster, which would legislate a constitutional amendment if requested to by both federal houses.

From 1927 to 1981, the federal and provincial governments tried unsuccessfully to agree on an amending formula, suggestions for which have included the Fulton formula, the Fulton-Favreau formula, the Turner-Trudeau formula, and the Alberta-Vancouver formula. Named after E. Davie Fulton, the Fulton Formula provided that the Constitution was to be amendable by federal law, but that no law relating to the legislative powers of a province, the assets of a province, the privileges of a province, the use of the English and French languages, the determination of representation by province in the House of Commons and the amending formula itself, was to go into effect unless it was concurred in by all provinces; that no law affecting other provisions of the Constitution should come into effect unless it was concurred in by the legislatures of at least two-thirds of the provinces, representing at least 50% of the population; that no law in relation to one or more provinces (but not all provinces) should come into effect unless accepted by each province concerned; and that no law in relation to education should come into force unless concurred in by all provinces other than Newfoundland. (A law amending education in that province was not to come into effect except with the consent of that province.) The formula also included the delegation clause, permitting provinces to delegate powers to Parliament, and vice versa.

The Fulton-Favreau Formula of 1964 (named after 2 successive federal ministers of justice, E. Davie Fulton and Guy Favreau) was basically a modification of the Fulton Formula; the federal amending power under s91.1, as revised, and the provincial amending power under s92.1, which had not been covered in 1961, were included in the amending formula of 1964. Both powers were defined with greater accuracy and precision. The delegation clause was retained. This formula was finally rejected by Québec.

The Victoria Charter, 1971, was an agreement reached by Canadian heads of government (with the exception of Québec's Premier Robert Bourassa) concerning constitutional reform. The Turner-Trudeau Formula contained in the Victoria Charter provided that the Constitution could be amended by a resolution of the House of Commons and Senate and by at least a majority of the provinces, which would have included each province with a population of at least 25% of the national population, at least 2 Atlantic provinces, and at least 2 western provinces having a combined population of at least 50% of all western provinces. The delegation clause was dropped. Québec agreed with the Turner-Trudeau Formula but rejected the charter because it proposed paramount power in programs related to social security. Only in 1982 did the British Parliament divest itself of its power of amendment to the Canadian Constitution. By s2 of the Canada Act, 1982 (UK), no Act of Parliament of the UK passed after the Constitution Act, 1982, can extend to Canada as part of its law. The British renounced any legislative role for Canada after 17 Apr 1982. The Constitution Act, 1982, includes a general amending formula under which an amendment requires the agreement of the federal houses and two-thirds of the provinces comprising 50% of the population. A dissenting province may opt out (*see* OPTING OUT) of an amendment concerning a transfer of power from a provincial to a federal jurisdiction, in which case, if the amendment is related to education, or other matters, the province will receive fair financial compensation. If the amendment concerns the composition of the Supreme Court, the role of the monarchy or the amending formula itself, all 11 authorities (the federal government and 10 provinces) must agree on its adoption. On the other hand, some amendments need only the agreement of the federal government and the particular provinces concerned. In principle both Parliament and the provincial legislatures may still amend their internal constitutions. GÉRALD-A. BEAUDOIN

Reading: G. Favreau, *The Amendment of the Constitution of Canada* (1965); P.W. Hogg, *Constitutional Law of Canada (1977).*

Constitutional Problems, Royal Commission of Inquiry on (Tremblay Commission), appointed by the Québec government under chairman Mr Justice Thomas Tremblay to study the distribution of taxes among the federal government, the provinces, the municipalities and the school boards; the "encroachments" of the federal government into the field of direct taxation, especially taxes on revenue, corporations and inheritances; the consequences of these "encroachments" for the legislative and administrative system of Québec and for the collective, family and individual life of its population; and generally the constitutional problems of a fiscal character. The commission's 4-volume report (1956) supported the view that the federal government was a creation of the provinces and that the role of the political regime of 1867 was to establish a framework within which English and French communities could live in a federal state. It called for greater provincial autonomy, proposing that social programs be under provincial jurisdiction. It also proposed major fiscal reforms very different from those recommended by the Royal Commission on DOMINION-PROVINCIAL RELATIONS. The report is considered a classic in-depth analysis of Québec's nationalistic and traditional approach to the federal system.
GÉRALD-A. BEAUDOIN

Construction Industry, Canada's largest industry, executes most of the construction activity in the country. It provides a wide variety of buildings, ranging from houses to skyscrapers and from schools and hospitals to factories and shopping centres, and carries out an equally wide variety of ENGINEERING construction projects, ranging from highways to nuclear-power stations and from dams and dredging to petrochemical plants and PIPELINES. Members of the construction industry put in place most of the capital investment of all other industries, governments, business and individual citizens. Thus, construction is both a production indus try, providing the physical means for shelte and industrial development, and a SERVICE INDU TRY, most work being carried out in response orders and investment decisions of others.

The construction process involves many dif ferent functions from concept to commission ing. On simple undertakings, these function may be performed by one person or organiza tion; on larger, more complex projects they a divided among many specialists. The mai components of the construction process are a follows.

Owners, in most cases, initiate constructio projects, acquire necessary sites and arrange fc project financing. In some instances design c construction activities are performed by th owner or the owner's personnel.

Developers' projects may be developed for sal or lease to others. This procedure is most preva lent in residential and commercial constructio projects (*see* DEVELOPMENT INDUSTRY).

Design team consists of the architect or cor sulting engineer and their specialist subconsu tants who collectively prepare the detailed spec fications and drawings for a project's desig During the construction phase, they are usuall called upon to provide inspection services, inte pret their design documents, prepare necessar modifications and certify completion.

General or prime contractors assume responsi bility for the co-ordination of construction ac tivities and project completion. They may be gen eral building contractors or builders engaged i the construction, alteration or repair of housing commercial, industrial, institutional or far buildings, or the contractors for a wide range c engineering construction projects. The latter in clude transportation facilities (ROADS, BRIDGES AIRPORTS, RAILWAYS, harbours, etc); sewer an water installations; energy projects (gas, petro leum, hydroelectric, thermal and NUCLEAR-POWE PLANTS, etc), transmission lines and pipeline heavy industrial projects; and TELECOMMUNICA TIONS. A firm engaged to fulfil the co-ordinatin role of the prime contractor, without assumin any financial liabilities, does so as a "constru tion manager."

Trade or specialty contractors perform wor related to the various trades, eg, mechanica (plumbing, heating, air conditioning, she metal, etc), electrical, structural steel, concret masonry, carpentry, elevators, roofing, excava tion, piling, flooring, curtain wall, glazing, in sulation, etc, or other specialties such as dem lition. Frequently, such work is executed on subcontract or sub-subcontract basis.

Manufacturers and suppliers. This group in cludes manufacturers, importers, wholesale and retailers engaged in the production an merchandising of thousands of constructio items, ranging from nails to excavating ma chines costing many millions of dollars. It als includes those engaged in supplying energ communication facilities, inspection servic and many other goods and services needed du ing construction.

The Modern Industry After the decrease i construction that occurred during the GREA DEPRESSION, WWII brought about a substanti resurgence in activity in Canada. Noteworth achievements during this period included cor struction of the fully integrated syntheti rubber plant at SARNIA, Ont, and of numerou BRITISH COMMONWEALTH AIR TRAINING PROGRA aerodromes and other installations for th armed services. This rapid increase in the size the overall wartime construction program an the ability of the industry to execute it quickl and efficiently marked the establishment Canada's modern construction industry. Th construction program has continued to expan in physical terms throughout most of the pos war period and there has been a striking in rease in the size and complexity of many individual projects. For example, although HOUSE and apartment building construction had been typically a small-scale operation before the war, the postwar housing "boom" saw the development of "project housing," comprising hundreds of units, of high-rise apartment buildings and complexes and of entire communities.

A new construction market developed in northern Canada with the building of EARLY-WARNING RADAR defence installations, MINING and other RESOURCE developments and transportation facilities. These activities also required a new TECHNOLOGY to meet the challenge of an arctic climate, PERMAFROST and the logistics problems presented by the need to transport men, materials, equipment and supplies hundreds or even thousands of kilometres to isolated job sites, on land or offshore.

In southern Canada the TRANS-CANADA HIGHWAY and the ST LAWRENCE SEAWAY were finally built. Canada has long been famous for its large-scale hydroelectric power projects (eg, CHURCHILL FALLS; JAMES BAY PROJECT); this program was expanded and augmented by thermal and nuclear-power plants. Other energy developments related to PETROLEUM, BITUMEN, natural gas, COAL and alternate energy sources. The preoccupation with energy conservation brought a new importance to "retrofit" work, designed to make existing structures more energy efficient. Perhaps the most striking change wrought by the construction industry in this period was the creation of new skylines in Canada's cities and towns. Rising land values and new construction techniques combined to make high-rise construction viable for many types of building project.

By the early 1980s the total annual construction program in Canada amounted to nearly $60 billion (16% of the GROSS NATIONAL PRODUCT). Construction activity provides some 750 000 person-years of employment for salaried and hourly wage earners. Roughly 7% of people employed in Canada are directly engaged in construction activity. An even greater number are engaged in producing, transporting and merchandising construction materials and equipment.

For many years after the war, the regional breakdown of construction activity showed one-third or more of the total located in Ontario; about one-quarter in Québec; and one-tenth in BC. Toronto and Montréal were the main centres of construction activity, accounting for perhaps 25% of the total. Similarly, there was a quite constant breakdown by main components: residential 30%; other building construction 30%; and engineering construction 40%. Significant shifts became evident in the 1970s in favour of western Canada and of engineering construction. By 1981 the value of Alberta's construction program equaled that of Ontario (both 25%); residential construction's share fell to 25% and that of engineering construction rose to nearly 50%. In 1983 special government programs to stimulate housebuilding activity resulted in the residential sector regaining its previous share but a general decline in housebuilding is predicted for the future. In 1983, $56 billion was spent on construction in Canada: 29.7% ($16.7 billion) for residential construction, 24.8% ($13.9 billion) for nonresidential buildings and 45.5% ($25.5 billion) for engineering construction. The Atlantic provinces accounted for 8.4% of construction ($4.7 billion); Qué, 19.8% ($11.1 billion); Ont, 26.4% ($14.8 billion); Man and Sask, 8% ($4.5 billion); BC, NWT and YT, 16.3% ($9.1 billion). Alberta's share was reduced to 21.4% ($11.8 billion) but still ranked second. Material costs accounted for 38.3% of the total (ie $21.5 billion); labour costs 33.3% ($18.7 billion); other factors 28.4% ($15.9 billion). Construction contractors took 67% of this market ($37.6 billion); others, 33% (18.5 billion).

Over one-third of the total program is financed directly by government departments or agencies at the federal, provincial or municipal level. In addition to construction carried out in Canada, members of the industry have taken on an increasing volume of business in other countries. Nearby regions especially (eg, the US and the Caribbean) have attracted the attention of Canadian developers, manufacturers, designers and contractors. Canadian consulting engineers have developed a substantial overseas market.

Construction Cycles The seasonal and cyclical fluctuations in the volume of construction have a close relationship to the overall business cycle. Therefore, because of the "multiplier effect" of construction activity on other economic sectors, public-works programs are frequently advocated in times of serious unemployment. The effect is enhanced by the optimistic response of those who see the tangible evidence of economic development associated with a construction job. Conversely, when governments deem that the rate of economic development should be slowed down to avoid undue inflation, they often implement cuts in public-works programs, increases in the mortgage interest rates for housing and other measures designed to curb construction.

This use of the construction industry as a regulator of the general economy has tended to accentuate the swings in the construction cycle. This instability is the root cause of the industry's major problems. A detailed study on construction instability was launched under the direction of the ECONOMIC COUNCIL OF CANADA in 1972 and there is a growing appreciation that a more steady growth rate in the construction program would be of general benefit to the industry and the economy as a whole. Progress in implementing policy recommendations to this end has been slow and the industry continues to experience rapid changes in its work load, especially on a sector or regional basis or both.

Associations The construction industry's voluntary organizations are structured along specialized lines related to a trade, product, project type, service or interest and along co-ordinated, industry-wide or sector lines. Employers' associations, professional societies and labour unions are organized and operate on the national, regional or provincial and local levels.

The principal employers' group is the Canadian Construction Assn, which has maintained its head office in Ottawa since its incorporation in 1919. The CCA represents general building and engineering contractors, trade contractors, industrial contractors, manufacturers and suppliers of construction materials and equipment and professional and service firms allied to the industry. Its membership also includes a lengthy list of provincial construction and road-builders' associations, national specialty contractor associations, construction labour-relations associations and local construction associations.

Virtually every major component of the industry has its own national body to deal with its special interests. The Canadian Home Builders Assn is the main spokesman for the residential construction sector. It also has a large number of local branches and provincial councils. The Urban Development Institute and the Canadian Institute of Public Real Estate Companies also represent developers engaged in the residential and commercial fields. Groups representing specialty contractors include the Canadian Institute of Steel Construction, the Pipe Line Contractors Assn of Canada, the Mechanical Contractors Assn of Canada and the Canadian Electrical Contractors Assn. Among the product associations are the Canadian Portland Cement Assn, the Clay Brick Assn of Canada, the Canadian Institute of Plumbing and Heating and the Machinery & Equipment Manufacturers Assn of Canada. The Canadian Assn of Equipment Distributors and provincial lumber dealers' associations are among the leading supplier associations. Construction Specifications Canada is an industry-wide body devoted to the improvement and standardization of construction specifications and related activities. Allied professions (eg, ARCHITECTURE; ENGINEERING) have their own professional organizations.

The traditional nature of many of the building trades and familiarity with the European guild system led to the early establishment of labour unions in the Canadian construction industry. With certain notable exceptions, the building trades unions were organized along craft lines and were affiliated with unions operating in the US or Great Britain. Local construction-employees' groups now operate mainly under charters received from international unions with head offices in the US. They are affiliated with the Building Trades Department of the American Federation of Labour-Congress of Industrial Organizations (AFL-CIO) and with the Canadian Federation of Labour or the Canadian Labour Congress. The Building Trades Department has a Canadian executive board and maintains a Canadian office. Building trades councils, representing these international construction trade unions, operate on district and provincial levels throughout the country.

Of the Canadian-based labour organizations representing construction employees, the largest is the construction branch of the Québec Federation of Labour. Other Québec construction labour groups include the Confederation of National Trade Unions and la Centrale des syndicats démocratiques. The "syndicates" represent the various construction trades. The Christian Labour Assn of Canada (CLAC) and the National Council of Canadian Labour (NCCL) represent a number of local construction-employees' groups in Ontario and BC, respectively.

Advisory committees and joint committees operate at the various levels to achieve closer liaison between the construction industry, governments and other groups. At the national level, the Canadian Joint Committee on Construction Documents and Procedures develops standard forms for construction contracts and guides, relating to various aspects of tendering and contract administration. Other joint committees deal with federal contracting procedures, labour-management relations, construction exports, etc. At the national level, advisory groups include the Construction Industry Development Council (advising the minister of Regional Industrial Expansion), the Associate Committee on the National Building Code of Canada and the Canadian Committee on Building Research (appointed by the NRC).

Training and Education Organized vocational training for construction careers in Canada is carried out under the APPRENTICESHIP SYSTEM. Trades instruction is also available at technical schools and through correspondence courses. Construction-technician courses are commonly given at institutes of technology and special courses are available for supervisory personnel. The increasing complexity of construction operations has led to a substantial increase in the number of professionally trained individuals in supervisory and managerial positions. The Canadian Construction Management Development Institute was established in 1981 to provide a national focus for co-ordinating training courses designed to improve management effectiveness related to on-site construction as provided by universities, community colleges and industry associations. A number of universities have established special centres for building studies and construction engineering. Applied courses for those engaged in real estate, development and property management are available at several universities and community colleges.

S.D.C. CHUTTER

Construction Industry, History The first permanent structures at PORT-ROYAL were erected in 1605 by French artisans using native materials. In 1607 the first water mill in N America was erected nearby (on the L'Equille R) to assist with the grinding of the first locally grown corn. Engineering construction therefore began at the same time as residential construction and agriculture. For almost 200 years, the limited settlements of NEW FRANCE and ACADIA were served by simple wooden structures. Small water mills or windmills provided power. Simple trails had to suffice as ROADS. Masonry construction was used occasionally in the few better houses and some churches, but was mainly confined to military fortifications, such as LOUISBOURG and PRINCE OF WALES'S FORT.

Military engineers constructed the first public works, tiny locks, at the rapids on the Soulanges section of the ST LAWRENCE R. These locks were started in 1779 by a British regiment, the Royal Engineers, for Governor Haldimand. The first major public work to be started in Canada was the Grenville Canal on the Ottawa R begun in 1819 and ready for use in 1834. The canal was built by another British regiment, the Royal Staff Corps, as part of the alternative military route from Montréal to Kingston, Ont, demanded after the WAR OF 1812. The main part of the alternate route was the RIDEAU CANAL, a 200 km waterway from Bytown (Ottawa) to Kingston with 47 locks and 50 dams. It was built by hand in just 5 working seasons (1826-32) by civilian contractors and 2 companies of the Royal Sappers and Miners (UK) working under the direction of the Royal Engineers. It is still used as originally constructed. The construction of the whole canal, but especially that of its great arched dam at Jones Falls, was a stupendous achievement for the time. It was also significant in that all major works were built under contract, employing essentially the same contracting system that is in use today. The Royal Engineers made great contributions to the development of Canada (the CARIBOO ROAD in BC is one of their most remarkable achievements), but as development increased with the coming of RAILWAYS civil (ie, civilian) engineers assumed responsiblity for design and Canadian contractors steadily increased their capability (*see* ENGINEERING).

The great era of railway building began in the 1850s. A leading British contractor worked on the GRAND TRUNK PACIFIC RAILWAY, but Canadian contractors were wholly responsible for building the INTERCOLONIAL RAILWAY (1868-76) from Halifax to Montréal and later the CANADIAN PACIFIC RAILWAY, finished in 1885. The skill of Canadian contractors is shown by the Hoosac Tunnel, Mass (built 1868-74), still the longest railway tunnel E of the Mississippi. The increasing maturity of the profession was indicated by the establishment of builders' associations in Halifax (1862) and Toronto (1867).

The opening in 1860 of the Victoria Bridge across the St Lawrence R at Montréal was a noteworthy event in Canadian construction. Steam pile drivers were used to build the piers; steam-operated rock drills replaced laborious hand drilling; and steam shovels effected great changes in excavation. Mass concrete started to replace masonry, at first as Canadian-made "natural cements," which were replaced before the end of the century by portland CEMENT (also made in Canada). The wrought iron used for the first tubular superstructure of the Victoria Bridge was replaced by structural steel at the turn of the century. Thus the main modern building materials and construction equipment were in use by the turn of the century; further construction advances were in scale rather than in kind, except for the relatively recent switch from steam to internal combustion engines for motive power.

Canal construction inevitably looms large in the history of Canadian construction because of the importance of waterways in the national economy. The fourth WELLAND CANAL, opened in 1932 after a limited start in 1913, with locks of the same size as those of the modern ST LAWRENCE SEAWAY, was another outstanding achievement. The twin-flight locks at Thorold, Ont, have long been world famous. This gigantic structure of mass concrete, with its 6 locks, is almost a kilometre long, yet it was contracted for by one notable Canadian construction firm.

Canadian contractors have introduced major innovations in many fields. Canadian hydroelectric power plants are among the largest in the world and often were built in remote locations where logistics were of supreme importance (*see* CHURCHILL FALLS; JAMES BAY PROJECT). Canadians have made some major innovations in BRIDGE construction and have used special skills in constructing buildings in confined working areas within cities. The Canadian climate has provided its own challenges and winter construction practices in this country are known and respected around the world. Outstanding work has also been done in road construction, often in isolated areas (eg, ALASKA HIGHWAY). At the start of WWII, a unique contribution of the Royal Canadian Engineers was the building of a bypass road in Surrey, England, at a speed previously unknown in the UK. The wheel had turned full circle. *See* ARCHITECTURE; MEGAPROJECTS; URBAN DESIGN.

R.F. LEGGET

Consumer and Corporate Affairs, Department of, was established in 1967 to bring together under one minister the administering of federal policies regulating the marketplace. Responsibilities include consumer affairs; corporations and corporate securities; combines, mergers, monopolies and restraint of trade; bankruptcy and insolvency; patents, copyrights, trademarks and industrial design; and programs designed to promote the interests of Canadian consumers. The Consumer Affairs, Corporate Affairs and Competition Policy bureaus conduct the department's business. The minister, as registrar general of Canada, is the custodian of the Great Seal of Canada, Privy Seal of the governor general and the seals of the administrator and registrar general of Canada. The department is composed of 4 bureaus and 2 functional services: the Bureau of Competition Policy, which includes the RESTRICTIVE TRADE PRACTICES COMMISSION; the Bureau of Consumer Affairs, which is concerned with the fair treatment of consumers in the marketplace; the Bureau of Corporate Affairs, which regulates much of the legal framework in which business operates; and the Bureau of Intellectual Property. Field Operations is responsible for the implementation of programs and the Legal Branch prepares and conducts legal cases. The department's 1984-85 budget was $246 million. *See* COMPETITION POLICY.

Consumer Credit Canadian consumers obtain consumer credit whenever they purchase goods or services on account, or whenever they borrow funds to finance purchases already made. The most common type of consumer credit arrangements involve cash loans, whose purpose is usually to finance retail purchases on instalments. These loans are usually made by financial institutions; about 85% of outstanding consumer credit takes the form of cash loans while the remaining 15% is actually made by retail vendors at the time of a sale. The goods purchased on credit are usually large items such as household furnishings and cars. In addition, cash loans to consolidate existing debts and unpaid balances on CREDIT CARDS constitute important proportions of the total amount of consumer credit. Consumer credit arrangements of this type account for about 25% of all the personal indebtedness in Canada.

Today the dominant suppliers of consumer credit in Canada are the banks, either through instalment loans carried directly on their own books or through the credit-card plans they operate. Mortgage and TRUST COMPANIES also provide consumer credit although they are relatively new entrants to the business and account for a much smaller proportion of the total consumer credit market. CREDIT UNIONS and CAISSES POPULAIRES are also major suppliers of consumer credit, but these institutions deal exclusively with their members and have traditionally offered loans at lower rates than those charged by other financial institutions. Consumer loan and finance companies are financial intermediaries specializing in the provision of both consumer credit and the wholesale financing of consumer durable goods. Some firms of this type, known as acceptance companies, are owned by automobile or other manufacturers. Many large retailers also own and manage finance companies to serve the credit needs of their customers. Finance companies have declined in importance since 1955. At that time, they accounted for over 30% of the consumer credit market; now their share is approximately 7%. Life-insurance companies also provide consumer credit by means of policy loans — loans to policyholders secured by the cash value of life-insurance policies.

Apart from credit unions and caisses populaires and some mutually owned life insurance companies, the suppliers of consumer credit are profit-oriented firms. These lenders will extend credit, if it is profitable, to any class of client, but are reluctant to extend credit to clients whom they regard as presenting either a low potential for profit or a higher than normal risk. Consequently, disadvantaged minorities sometimes find it difficult to obtain consumer credit because lenders regard these borrowers either as less profitable or more risky. Because credit unions and caisses populaires are co-operative organizations founded on a self-help principle, they will sometimes extend consumer credit in situations where the other lenders are unwilling. Also, within limits defined in their policies, life-insurance policy loans are made at the sole discretion of policyholders.

The principal advantage of credit is that it allows consumers to purchase and use an item before they have the funds to pay for it completely. Through consumer credit, goods or services can be obtained with someone elses's money for a price, ie, INTEREST. Borrowers determine the size of monthly payments by choosing the terms of the loan. A second advantage of using consumer credit is that responsible borrowers have the opportunity to establish a good credit rating, making it easier for them to obtain credit for future dealings. The principal disadvantage of consumer credit is that some persons are tempted to borrow more than their earning power allows them to repay readily, with the result that they can become so heavily indebted that they have difficulty in meeting the instalment payments on their loans.

WILLIAM T. CANNON AND EDWIN H. NEAVE

Consumer Law, that branch of law concerned with the supply of goods and services in the most comprehensive sense for the personal use or consumption of individuals and their families. It differs from COMMERCIAL LAW in that in commercial transactions, the participants engage in such transactions for the purpose of profit or otherwise in the course of a business. Consumer law is barely 25 years old. Its growth reflects the tremendous changes in life-style and in the products and services offered in the modern marketplace since WWII. Some of the important factors contributing to the rise of consumerism are the transition in N America from an agrarian to a predominantly urban way of life, mass production and the proliferation of ew and often very complex products, a more ffluent society with greater discretionary in- omes, and the phenomenal growth of con- umer credit.

Concerns about the vulnerability of con- umers are not new; significant traces of it are ound in the Bible (in the condemnation of sury, for example) and throughout medieval nd modern European history. In Canada, both ne Interest Act and the Food and Drugs Act, to ive 2 important examples, originated in 9th-century concerns. Consumer problems to- ay are more numerous and complex than those aced by consumers before WWII, and in most ases cannot be solved by an individual without overnmental or other outside assistance.

At the federal and provincial levels, de- artments or ministries of consumer affairs and onsumer-protection bureaus were rapidly stablished from about 1965 onwards. The fed- ral Department of CONSUMER AND CORPORATE AF- AIRS was established in 1967. The institutional hanges have been accompanied by the adopt- on of much new consumer-protection legis- ation and the revision of older legislation. Gen- rally speaking, existing legislation is designed o promote one or more of the following objec- ives.

Protection Against Dangerous Products ederal examples of this type of legislation in- lude the Food and Drugs Act, the Hazardous roducts Act, the Motor Vehicle Safety Act and he Motor Vehicle Tire Safety Act. Consumer rotection is achieved by a variety of means, uch as prohibiting the sale of dangerous, un- afe or adulterated products, limiting sales to rescribed outlets and on prescription, or by set- ng standards of safety and purity.

Protection Against Fraudulent and Deceptive ractices The federal Weights and Measures Act s an early example of this type of legislation. Iore recent examples include the Combines In- estigation Act with its important provisions oncerning misleading advertising. From 1974 nwards a substantial number of the provinces lso adopted "trade practices" or "business prac- ices" Acts with the same objectives but employ- ng different enforcement techniques.

Protection Against Unconscionable Contracts Iany modern contracts are standardized and ften contain harsh or unreasonable terms, of whose existence the average consumers are un- ware and which they would be powerless to hange even if they knew they were there (*see* ONTRACT LAW). Legislation directed against this nd related types of abuse include the pre- iously mentioned trade practice Acts, as well as warranty provisions in the provincial onsumer-protection Acts and Part V of the fed- ral Bills of Exchange Act. The latter provisions eal with the use of negotiable instruments in onsumer credit sales.

Better Access to Information Modern con- umers are not always given sufficient informa- ion to make an informed choice between com- eting products or services, or else the nformation is presented in a confusing form. he "truth in lending" provisions in the provin- ial consumer-protection Acts and the federal anking Act are designed to provide the needed nformation in consumer-credit contracts. Im- ortant disclosure requirements with similar bjectives are found in the federal Consumer ackaging and Labelling Act and the Textile La- elling Act.

Improved Sources of Advice and Access to onflict Resolution Agencies Provincial con- umer-protection bureaus have been created to rovide general advice on consumer problems nd to receive complaints. Community legal ervice clinics (now found in large cities across anada) and, to a lesser extent, provincial legal id plans provide legal advice and other forms f assistance to those who cannot afford a private lawyer. At the judicial level the jurisdiction of the SMALL CLAIMS COURTS has been substantially increased with respect to the size of claims; also noteworthy are the important procedural innovations introduced in the Québec Access to Justice Act of 1971 and the Class Actions Act (the first in Canada) adopted in 1978.

This description of postwar legislative developments may leave the impression that the modern Canadian consumer is well protected. The appearance is unfortunately misleading, and the picture is not as encouraging as a recitation of the legislation may suggest. The principal difficulty is that much of the legislation is only weakly enforced or not enforced at all. Some of the legislation is also poorly drafted. Most of the provincial consumer-protection agencies have always suffered from inadequate funding; since the early 1980s the inadequacy has become chronic and both the federal and provincial governments have eliminated or reduced important programs altogether.

This anticlimax to the postwar period of intense legislative activity is explained by some critics on the ground that much of the legislation was never really needed or that, in some cases, it went too far. A more persuasive explanation is that consumers are not politically a cohesive group and cannot match other interest groups in effectiveness, particularly during periods of economic adversity. JACOB S. ZIEGEL

Consumer Price Index, a monthly measure of changes in the retail prices of goods and services purchased by Canadians in communities of 30 000 or more across the country. The index is based on the shopping "basket" of 375 goods and services (excluding commodities for personal benefit, eg, education or health care, which are financed by government) that, in 1967, families of 2-6 people with annual incomes of $4000-$6000 would buy. The index is "weighted," emphasizing price changes in food and housing. The CPI is published monthly for Canada and for 15 major cities, using 1971 as a base year (1971=100). The base year changes about every 10 years. The CPI in Canada has risen dramatically but erratically since WWII — 50% from 1945 to 1951; 50% from 1951 to 1971; 137% from 1971 to 1981. Generally, the CPI is used in cost-of-living allowance clauses and in indexing of income taxes and social-security benefits.

Consumer Standards are documents describing acceptable characteristics or usage for products, materials and services used by individual consumers. They may specify dimensional, performance or safety requirements for household products. In Canada, standards are published by specialized private and government organizations grouped in the National Standards System, co-ordinated by the Standards Council of Canada. Standardization begins when public needs are recognized and involves field and laboratory research. The detailed work of writing a consumer standard is performed by volunteers representing a balance of all groups having an interest in the particular product, material or service. Such standards are known as consensus standards, as their final acceptance depends on substantial agreement among the participants. Standards are usually applied voluntarily. If governments pass laws making usage mandatory, they often simply refer to consensus standards, rather than specifying detailed technical requirements. The development of a consumer standard is one of the most difficult tasks of standardization. Part of the difficulty is identifying precisely the purpose of a standard for a particular product. For example, except for those regulating safety of operation, no Canadian standard yet exists for television sets because of the difficulty of agreeing on the requirements that the standard should cover.

Consumer groups (eg, the CONSUMERS' ASSOCIATION OF CANADA) are actively involved in the standardization process. Consumer representatives have been participating in standards-writing groups or committees since the 1950s. Standardization professionals generally agree on the necessity of having adequate consumer representation during the preparation of standards affecting consumer products. Because of the somewhat limited role consumer representatives have had in standards-writing committees, and because of consumers' ever-growing demands to be more involved in the standards-writing process, consumer advisory panels have been set up. Each panel consists of 30-40 individuals who meet regularly to study, comment and make recommendations regarding a particular consumer standard. Through the Standards Council of Canada, consumer representatives also participate in international standardization work. They are represented on the Committee on Consumer Policy (COPOLCO), a committee of the International Organization for Standardization (ISO).

In Canada one of the better-known series of consumer standards pertains to children's clothing sizes, prepared by the then Canadian Government Specifications Board (CGSB, now Canadian General Standards Board) at the request of the Consumers' Association of Canada. This series demanded one of the most exhaustive technical investigations ever carried out in Canada prior to the publication of a consumer standard. Research culminated in 1969 with the publication of 75 CGSB standards specifying "Canada Standards Sizes" for children's clothing. Use of these standards is entirely voluntary but the benefits are clear: they help reduce buyer frustration, facilitate ordering by mail or telephone and reduce the need to return clothing because of poor fit.

Many other far-reaching consumer standards are legislated by government. Legislation regulating WEIGHTS AND MEASURES has been in effect since 1872, when reference was made to British standards. Today's law stipulates that "all units of measurement in Canada shall be determined on the basis of the International System of Units determined by the General Conference on Weights and Measures," although provisions are made for use of the imperial system (*see* METRIC CONVERSION). The Packaging and Labelling Act specifies that packages for food and nonfood products intended for consumption must carry a label showing the name, nature, volume and weight of the product along with the name and address of the manufacturer. Federal departments of health and welfare, agriculture and CONSUMER AND CORPORATE AFFAIRS share responsibilities in administering food standards and FOOD LEGISLATION. Agriculture Canada is responsible for enforcing government standards affecting the quality and condition of agricultural food products and the wholesomeness of meats and meat products (*see* VETERINARY MEDICINE). Meats are graded into different classes, thereby indicating that standards have been met. Health and Welfare Canada is chiefly concerned with enforcing standards specifying the composition and wholesomeness of nonagricultural foods and food products. It also administers the Food and Drug Act and Regulations, which set minimum standards for various products. The Act is intended to protect the public against health hazards and fraud in the sale and use of foods, drugs, cosmetics and medical devices (*see* SAFETY STANDARDS). Among other things, this exhaustive Act prohibits the sale of foods, drugs or cosmetics manufactured under unsanitary conditions; of any article of food that contains any poisonous or harmful substance; of drugs that do not perform according to prescribed standards; and of cosmetics that may cause injury to health. The Dept of Consumer and Corporate

Affairs is responsible for investigating economic fraud concerning food and for administering the packaging, labelling and advertising of food products. R.L. HENNESSY

Consumers' Association of Canada (CAC), a voluntary, nonsectarian, nonprofit, nongovernmental organization known until 1962 as the Canadian Association of Consumers. The CAC was formally est in 1947 as the outgrowth of successful efforts of the federal Wartime Prices and Trade Board to enlist (1941) 56 various women's organizations to monitor prices in aid of wartime rationing. In 1961 the association expanded its membership to include men.

CAC volunteers serve their communities across Canada in over 70 local organizations affiliated with provincial organizations which are in turn affiliated with CAC National.

The CAC has helped achieve change in many areas, including the ban on use of DDT and other long-life pesticides; banning of diethylstilbestrol in animal feeding; removal of federal tax on prescription drugs; development and use of safety closure for drugs; passage of the Packaging and Labelling Act; establishment of the Food Prices Review Board; many regulations under the Hazardous Products Act; lowered speed limits; safety standards for school buses; nonsmoking areas in public conveyances; warnings on tobacco products; elimination of sales tax on building materials; and decreases in proposed telephone rate increases.

With a budget of over $3 million, CAC is funded mostly from membership fees and sales of its magazine *Canadian Consumer*. Some government funding is also received. MARILYN LISTER

Contact (1952-54) was a mimeographed "little magazine" of poetry, the third journal founded by Toronto poet Raymond SOUSTER. Its predecessors were *Direction* (1943-46) and *Enterprise* (1948). It came into existence as an alternative to John SUTHERLAND'S NORTHERN REVIEW, which assumed a traditional direction after Sutherland's conversion to Roman Catholicism; Souster, with his close associates Louis DUDEK and Irving LAYTON, felt that a more experimental magazine was needed. *Contact* was open to young Canadian writers, but also published American and European poets such as Charles Olson, Robert Creeley, Denise Levertov and Jean Cocteau. *Contact*'s influence was carried on by Contact Press (1952-67), in which Layton and Dudek collaborated with Souster. The press's first publication, *Cerberus*, was a book jointly written by Souster, Layton and Dudek.
GEORGE WOODCOCK

Contemporary Arts Society was formed Jan 1939 to promote public awareness of modern art in Montréal. Membership was open to all artists of "non-academic tendencies," and the initial 25 members included Paul-Émile BORDUAS, Fritz BRANDTNER, Stanley COSGROVE, Louis MUHLSTOCK, Goodridge ROBERTS, Jori Smith and Philip SURREY. John LYMAN, a prominent Montréal painter and critic, was the society's founder and first president. In May 1939 the CAS began to admit nonartist associate members, many of whom were francophone art teachers, critics and collectors. This transformation from an essentially anglophone group continued in 1943 when Alfred PELLAN and Borduas were allowed to bring their young followers into the society as exhibiting but nonvoting junior artists. These new members included Marcel BARBEAU, Léon Bellefleur, Pierre GAUVREAU, Fernand LEDUC and Jean-Paul RIOPELLE.

Lyman did not conceive of the CAS as an exhibiting organization, but many members realized that by banding together it would be easier to get exhibition space and to lobby for attention at the conservative Art Assn of Montréal (now the Montréal Museum of Fine Arts). In May 1939 the Society sponsored "Art of Our Day," a survey of modern European art in Montréal collections. In Dec it held the first annual members' show at a commercial gallery in the city, though many subsequent shows were hung in the Art Assn itself. Most of the early anglophone members of the CAS could be broadly described as French-influenced post-impressionists. Roberts was one of the most respected painters within this group, but as Borduas and Pellan rose to prominence in the early 1940s, the society's exhibitions were increasingly dominated by abstraction. Borduas's personal influence also grew steadily, to the vexation of some conservative anglophone members and Pellan's circle of admirers. Although the CAS was a dynamic and forward-looking artists' organization in Canada during the 1940s, it received little attention outside of Montréal. Jack HUMPHREY and Miller BRITTAIN from Saint John were the only non-Québec artists to join. The National Gallery of Canada, which played an important role in promoting the GROUP OF SEVEN, gave it no support.

By 1945 the CAS included virtually every innovative and ambitious painter in Montréal. The size, diversity and growing divisions within the society made it increasingly difficult to govern or direct. In an effort to save the organization in 1948, Borduas was elected president, but he was met by a storm of protest from members who considered him too radical (he was circulating draft copies of REFUS GLOBAL at the time). Sensing he would be unable to govern, Borduas resigned from the presidency and the CAS the day after his election. Shortly thereafter, Pellan and several of his supporters left. Lyman's coalition of artists must be considered a success; many artists found mutual support and encouragement in the society, and through its lectures, exhibitions and lobbying, it greatly increased public awareness of modern art in Montréal. *See also* PAINTING. CHRISTOPHER VARLEY

Reading: D. Burnett and M. Schiff, *Contemporary Canadian Art* (1983); J. Russell Harper, *Painting in Canada* (1977); D. Reid, *A Concise History of Canadian Painting* (1973); Christopher Varley, *Contemporary Arts Society* (1980).

Contemporary Verse (1940-52), poetry magazine founded by Alan Crawley in N Vancouver. It appeared when there were few literary magazines of any kind in Canada. Because Crawley was blind and all work submitted had to be read to him, editing was difficult, but he maintained a high standard while admitting a wide variety of poets; all he asked was that their work be "serious in thought and expression and contemporary in theme, treatment and technique." The writings of more than 120 poets were printed; contributors included leading figures of that vital, formative time in Canadian writing, but also new poets, some of whom later became distinguished. After 39 issues Crawley felt *Contemporary Verse* had fulfilled its role. More than 20 years after *Contemporary Verse*'s termination, *CV/II* was founded in 1975 as its successor; Dorothy LIVESAY, who had helped Crawley with *Contemporary Verse*, was one of its founders.
GEORGE WOODCOCK

Continental Bank of Canada, with head offices in Toronto, began operations as a subsidiary of a finance company, IAC Limited (fd 1925 as Industrial Acceptance Corp Ltd). In 1981 it absorbed IAC and was chartered as a bank. In 1984 it had 55 branches and had plans to add 58 more, all offering full commercial and personal banking services in Canada and abroad. In Oct 1982 the company had sales or operating revenue of almost $543 million, assets of $4.1 million (ranking 15th among banks and financial institutions in Canada) and 1858 employees. Carena-Bancorp Holdings Ltd owns 19.3% of the shares. DEBORAH C. SAWYER

Continental Divide, is the line following the height of land that separates areas drained b rivers that flow to opposite sides of the N Ame ican continent. In Canada, the water flowing i rivers eventually reaches the sea in either th Arctic, Atlantic or Pacific oceans. The lir dividing rivers flowing W to the Pacific fro drainage to the Arctic and Atlantic is easiest visualize, since it lies along the main ranges the ROCKY MTS. Often it is convenient to use suc natural boundaries for human organization an the ALBERTA-BRITISH COLUMBIA border follows th Divide for a considerable distance, as does th border between the YUKON and NORTHWEST TERR TORIES. The Divide running across the interior Canada is low and less obvious. This line star from a point somewhere in the COLUMBIA IC FIELD of the Rockies from which the 3 axes of th Continental Divide diverge. It follows a lir through southern Alberta and SASKATCHEWAN, of which drainage flows to the Arctic throug the PEACE, ATHABASCA and MACKENZIE rivers, or HUDSON BAY by the N and S SASKATCHEWAN an NELSON rivers. Rivers S of this line are part of th Missouri-Mississippi system. The divide swin into the US south of the RED R which flows into MANITOBA. The divide continues into Car ada, separating drainage going N and that ente ing the GREAT LAKES-ST LAWRENCE R basin. Alon the much-eroded SHIELD in QUÉBEC and Labrad the divide is indistinct, permitting the diversio and transfer of water from rivers north of th divide to south-flowing rivers, as developed i the JAMES BAY PROJECT. Although the divide used as the Québec-Labrador border, the low re lief along which the line is presumed to li makes it hard to demarcate on the ground (s LABRADOR BOUNDARY DISPUTE). DOUG FINLAYSO

Continentalism is a term used to describe th theory of closer ties (eg, in the form of close trade links, energy sharing or common wate use policies) with the US. An impressive numbe of the crucial turning points in Canadian politi cal history have pitted the forces of NATIONALISM against those of continentalism. Washington abrogation in 1866 of the RECIPROCITY Treaty c 1854 deprived Canadians of the considerable ac cess they had enjoyed to the US market, and s contributed to the BNA colonies' decision to fed erate in order to solve their economic problem The celebrated NATIONAL POLICY of 1879 was Si John A. MACDONALD's response to his failure achieve his preferred policy, a free-trade ar rangement with the US. When the governmer of Sir Wilfrid LAURIER proposed signing a free trade treaty with the US, it was decisively de feated in the 1911 election by the Conservative who exploited anti-American nationalism.

Much of Canadian development can be see as the product of a dynamic interaction betwee forces pressing for national autonomy and thos pushing for continental integration. Althoug the extreme form of Canadian continentalism advocates outright political absorption of Can ada by the US, such positions have been argue only by fringe elements since the ANNEXATIO movement died out as a significant politica force in the 19th century. The best articulatio of current continentalist thinking is in the writ ings of Canadian mainstream economists wh have identified a goal and a program concern ing Canada's relationship with the US. The goa is maximum continental integration. "I believ that closer integration of the two economies int one continental economy would be beneficial t both countries, and would involve no loss o any Canadian nationalist objectives worth pur suing," wrote the late Harry Johnson, Canada' pre-eminent economist, in 1965. The progran consists essentially of opposition to policies tha put obstacles in the way of FOREIGN INVESTMEN and strong advocacy of tariff reduction to th point of achieving continental free trade.

Unrestricted free trade is another importan

omponent of continentalism: "A totally free trade situation has to be seen as the best answer to Canada's industrial concerns," since "in a single step our living standards would be raised permanently to a new level," the ECONOMIC COUNCIL OF CANADA suggested in 1975.

Strong hostility to nationalism is a third characteristic of continentalism. Nationalism complicates CANADIAN-AMERICAN RELATIONS, in the opinion of the Canadian-American Committee, an active lobby for American and Canadian conglomerates. "With economic nationalism once again increasing in Western Europe and in other parts of the world, Canada and the United States can ill afford to indulge in measures which involve sacrificing the benefits of economic interdependence," the CAC wrote in 1971. Interdependence, the operative concept, is the natural economic state with which governmental policy should not interfere. A key mechanism for ensuring interdependence is the maintenance of a common market for capital without regard for which country controls the dominant corporations.

Continentalism is not merely an economic phenomenon. Culturally, the dissemination of American values in Canada through the mass media plays a powerful role in instilling American values and attitudes in the Canadian psyche. Canada's integration into US defence planning and the American military industrial complex was institutionalized by the North American Air Defence command (NORAD) of 1958 and the Defence Production Sharing Arrangement of 1959.

The politics of continentalism is a complex product of the interactions of the American and Canadian governments, corporate interests, public opinion and political parties. Following the 1971 blow to N American harmony provoked by Pres Richard Nixon's drastic program of PROTECTIONISM, Ottawa responded with a series of nationalist measures designed to protect Canadian interests, eg, the FOREIGN INVESTMENT REVIEW AGENCY, the CANADA DEVELOPMENT CORPORATION and PETRO-CANADA. The unveiling of the ambitious National Energy Program in 1980 represented the farthest point to which the nationalism of the Trudeau period went (*see* ENERGY POLICY). By the mid-1980s, reactions to these policies by both American and Canadian interests had returned the Canadian pendulum back toward continentalism to a point at which one of the Trudeau government's principal legacies was a process of active negotiations with the US aimed at establishing more sectoral free-trade agreements on the lines of the 1965 CANADA-US AUTOMOTIVE PRODUCTS AGREEMENT.

Trudeau's successor, John TURNER, a corporate lawyer with close American connections, represented the Liberal Party's return to its continentalist roots. What appears politically more surprising is the shift of the Conservatives during the 1970s from the nationalist position, last espoused by John DIEFENBAKER, to one that is even more continentalist than that of the Liberals. Conservative PM Brian MULRONEY and his senior Cabinet members have adopted continentalist positions favouring foreign investment, N American free trade and American foreign-policy positions.

While it has been subjected to far less academic analysis than its opposing ideology, nationalism, continentalism must be recognized as a force that continues to have a powerful impact on Canada's POLITICAL ECONOMY. *See also* ECONOMICS.

STEPHEN CLARKSON

Contraception, *see* BIRTH CONTROL.

Contract Law A contract is a legally binding agreement between 2 or more persons for a particular purpose. In general, contracts are always formed on the same pattern. A person offers to give another person something (eg, to deliver an item in return for a certain price); to provide a service (eg, to work for a certain salary); or to refrain from doing something (eg, not to compete for a certain time in return for compensation). If the offer is accepted, the contract is then valid in principle. A contract is, above all, an instrument for the economic exchange of goods and services. The most common types of contracts are the contract of sale, whereby a person acquires the ownership of property in return for payment of a certain price; lease and hire of services, whereby a person offers his services to another in return for remuneration; and lease and hire of things, whereby a person is temporarily granted the enjoyment of property (eg, an apartment), in return for a price (rent).

Unlike other agreements, a contract is considered to be a binding promise; if one of the parties fails or refuses to fulfill its promise, eg, to pay the agreed price, to provide the rented space, or pay the employee's salary, without a valid reason recognized by law, the party suffering the consequence of this breach of promise may call upon the courts either to force the defaulting party to carry out its promise (specific performance) or to demand compensation in the form of damages. Québec CIVIL LAW and Canadian COMMON LAW follow similar rules in this regard: a contract legally entered into represents a legal bond between the parties. Parties are free to contract whenever and for whatever reason they wish. The only limits to absolute contractual freedom are certain restrictions imposed by legislation and by accepted ethics. Contracts contrary to a statutory law such as the Canadian CRIMINAL CODE are null and void. The same is true for a contract, eg, a work contract for a professional killer or a prostitute, that goes against accepted ethics. CIVIL CODE regulations governing contracts in Québec are derived mainly from French civil law which is in turn derived from Roman law. These rules are written and codified in sections of the Québec Civil Code. In other provinces, regulations governing contracts are based on the jurisprudence of British common law. Many provinces, however, have adopted laws codifying the rules of certain contracts, particularly sales contracts. Although Canada's 2 major legal systems differ in certain respects, in contract law the practical solutions they provide are very similar.

Conditions To be valid and therefore legally binding, 5 conditions must be met. The first is the mutual consent of both parties. No one can be held to a promise involuntarily made. When consent is given by error, under physical or moral duress, or as a result of fraudulent practices, the contract may be declared null and void at the request of the innocent party. The second is contractual capacity — the ability to keep the promise one has made. A young child, a person suffering from a serious mental disorder and sometimes even a minor are all considered incapable of contracting. The third condition is that the contract should have a purpose; it must concern a specific and agreed-upon good or service. The fourth condition is "lawful cause" in civil law and "consideration" in common law. In this area technical differences arise between the 2 legal systems. Briefly, however, according to this fourth condition, the promise made must be serious and each promise made by one of the parties must find a corresponding, but not necessarily equivalent or equal, promise made by the other party. Thus a person may legally sell goods at a price that does not represent their actual market value. The fifth condition, which is not required in all cases, is the adherence in certain cases to formalities provided by law. In general, this condition holds for contracts that may have enormous consequences for the parties, or those that must be made public.

Sanctions Parties to a valid contract are always bound to carry out their promise. If they do not, the other party is free to go to court to force them to do so. At times, the court may order the defaulting party to do exactly what he has promised. Civil law provides more readily for the forced execution of promises than common law, in which specific performance is still an exception to the rule (*see* TORTS; DELICTS). Sometimes the courts award financial compensation in the form of damages equal in value to the loss suffered and profits lost as a result of the breach of promise, but this loss and profit must be directly related to the unfulfilled promise. Furthermore, the courts award only damages equal to those benefits that the parties might reasonably have expected to receive at the time the agreement was concluded.

Increasingly, provincial and federal legislatures are acting to protect citizens against certain contractual abuses. CONSUMER LAW, in which rules and standards are imposed to suppress FRAUD, avoid forced sales and protect the consumer against dishonest practices, is an example of this type of action. JEAN-LOUIS BAUDOUIN

Convey, John, metallurgist (b at Craghead, Eng 29 Mar 1910). Having immigrated to Alberta in 1929, he later moved to Ontario, where he earned a PhD in atomic physics at U of T in 1940. After service in the navy during WWII and a spell of teaching at U of T, he went to Ottawa in 1948 to become chief metallurgist at the federal government's Mines Branch, later renamed the Canadian Centre for Mineral and Energy Technology. He served as director 1951-73, and it was under his leadership that the extensive laboratories became an important scientific base for national research into mining, metallurgy and energy resources. A man of wide interests and a talented raconteur and public speaker, he received many honours, including the Blaylock Medal of the Canadian Institute of Mining and Metallurgy and fellowship in the American Soc for Metals, before his retirement from the public service in 1974.

W.M. WILLIAMS

Cook, James, explorer (b near Marton, Eng 27 Oct 1728; d at Kealakekua Bay, Sandwich I [Hawaii] 14 Feb 1779). The greatest navigator of his era, he served as master of the *Pembroke* at the siege of LOUISBOURG (1758) during the SEVEN YEARS' WAR. He charted part of Gaspé and helped prepare the map that enabled James WOLFE's armada to navigate the St Lawrence R. He was a painstaking surveyor, and was chiefly responsible 1763-67 for mapping the intricate and treacherous coast of Newfoundland, which England acquired at the end of the war; he had charted part of its E shore in 1762, including St John's harbour. Cook revolutionized Europe's knowledge of the S Pacific in his great circumnavigations 1768-71 and 1772-75. In July 1776 he began a third voyage, to search for a NORTHWEST PASSAGE. He sailed E across the Pacific and anchored in NOOTKA SOUND, on Vancouver I (29 Mar 1778). His men repaired his ships and carried on a lucrative trade with the Nootka for otter pelts. He departed 26 Apr 1778 and sailed into Bering Str in search of the passage, retreating in the face of a wall of ice. He was killed in the Sandwich I in an altercation with the local people. Cook was not the first to explore the NORTHWEST COAST, but he and his men were the first to reveal its attractions, particularly the FUR TRADE. Among those who followed was George VANCOUVER, who had sailed with Cook on his second and third voyages. JAMES MARSH

Reading: J.C. Beaglehole, *The Life of Captain James Cook* (1974).

Cook, William Harrison, chemist (b at Alnwick, Eng 2 Sept 1903). Living on a remote Alberta homestead from age 8, Cook began his formal education at agricultural school at 17 — which led to U of A and Stanford (PhD 1931).

From 1924 he assisted Robert NEWTON's research on drying damp wheat, joined the NATIONAL RESEARCH COUNCIL staff under Newton in 1932 and succeeded him as director of biology in 1941. A natural engineer, Cook worked as a young scientist on constant-condition chambers (refrigerated greenhouses to simulate prairie farming conditions). This led to unusual war work such as the overnight conversion of freighters into refrigerated food ships. After 1945 he reorganized the NRC's food research laboratories and personally solved the structure of polysaccharide proteins in carrageenin, a seaweed used by the food industry. After nominal retirement in 1968 he continued to work as executive director of the NRC and director general of Canadian participation in the International Biological Program until 1976. He then wrote 2 books, *My Fifty Years with NRC, 1924-1974* and a memoir of his cowboy youth. DONALD J.C. PHILLIPSON

Cookbooks, *see* POPULAR LITERATURE; CUISINE.

Co-operative Commonwealth Federation (CCF), fd 1932 in Calgary as a political coalition of progressive, socialist and labour forces anxious to establish a political vehicle capable of bringing about economic reforms to improve the circumstances of those suffering the effects of the GREAT DEPRESSION. The main impetus for the formation of the new party came from farmers' organizations (including the UNITED FARMERS OF ALBERTA, which governed that province), a handful of academics in the LEAGUE FOR SOCIAL RECONSTRUCTION (LSR) and a GINGER GROUP of MPs in Ottawa allied with both farmer and trade-union organizations.

In 1933 the party met in Regina, where it chose J.S. WOODSWORTH as its first president. Woodsworth, an MP since 1921, was the acknowledged leader of the party both inside and outside Parliament. The party also adopted the Regina Manifesto, which set out its goals, including that of creating a mixed economy through the NATIONALIZATION of key industries and that of establishing a WELFARE STATE with universal pensions, health and welfare insurance, children's allowances, unemployment insurance, workers' compensation and similar programs.

The CCF quickly established itself in Canadian political life, electing members to Parliament and to several provincial legislatures. In 1935, 7 CCF MPs were returned and the party captured 8.9% of the popular vote. In 1940, 8 MPs were returned on 8.5% of the popular vote. At the beginning of WWII the CCF was split between supporters of Woodsworth's uncompromising pacifism and supporters of Canada's entry into the conflict. M.J. COLDWELL, who succeeded Woodsworth as leader during this period, favoured Canada's participation, and under his moderate guidance the party began to flourish electorally. It won the critical York South by-election in Feb 1942, in the process preventing the Conservative leader, former PM Arthur MEIGHEN, from entering the Commons; topped a Sept 1943 national Gallup poll; came second in that year's Ontario elections; and, under the leadership of T.C. DOUGLAS, took office in Saskatchewan in 1944. In the 1945 federal election the CCF returned 28 MPs, garnering 15.6% of the popular vote.

Although the CCF was well established, it gradually declined in popular appeal after the war. A socialist party, it was accused of being associated with communism, and during COLD WAR tension this image was damaging. An attempt in 1956 to soften the party's image by replacing the Regina Manifesto with a new, moderate document, the Winnipeg Declaration, could not reverse the trend, and in 1958 the party suffered a disastrous defeat: only 8 MPs were elected with a mere 9.5% of the popular vote. Both Coldwell and Deputy Leader Stanley Knowles, were personally defeated.

Following this debacle an arrangement was negotiated by David LEWIS between the CCF and the CANADIAN LABOUR CONGRESS. The CLC, urged by Lewis to save democratic socialism in Canada, agreed to enter a formal alliance with the CCF to create a new party. In 1961 the CCF entered a new phase, and emerged from a founding convention as the NEW DEMOCRATIC PARTY. Although the CCF had never held power nationally, the adoption of many of its ideas by ruling parties contributed greatly to the development of the Canadian welfare state. J.T. MORLEY

Reading: W.D. Young, *The Anatomy of a Party* (1969).

Coot, aquatic BIRD of the RAIL family. Ten species occur worldwide; only the American coot (*Fulica americana*) is found in N America. Although a marsh dweller, the coot is conspicuous because, except when molting, it swims, dives and feeds in open water rather than confining itself to dense marsh thickets. Its lobed toes are an adaptation to aquatic life. Its pugnacious behaviour helps ensure biological success. This white-billed, slaty black, chickenlike bird bobs its head as it swims, picking bits of vegetation and animal life from the surface, occasionally diving for food. Coots, often called mud hens, breed in pothole marshes and sloughs of southern Canada and as far N as Great Slave Lk. Coots lay 8-12 light brown eggs, speckled with dark brown, on a floating platform of marsh plants. Young are black with startling, orange-red heads and shoulders. Coots migrate in the evening and at night, wintering on lakes, brackish water and estuaries on the southern and eastern US coast. E. KUYT

Copper (Cu), tough, soft, ductile, reddish metal which melts at 1083°C. Only SILVER is a better thermal and electrical conductor. Copper slowly forms a greenish surface, called patina, in moist air. Copper is sometimes found in the native state, eg, near Lk Superior, but more commonly occurs in sulphide MINERALS (chalcopyrite, bornite, covelite, chalcocite), in tetrahedrite, enargite, cuprite, azurite, malachite, chrysocolla and others. It is readily extracted and easily worked. Chalcopyrite and, to a much lesser extent, bornite are the minerals most commonly found in Canadian copper mines. Copper ores often provide significant quantities of gold, silver, nickel, molybdenum, selenium and tellurium.

In Canada native copper, from the Coppermine R area of the NWT and from the southern shore of Lk Superior, was used by native peoples to manufacture weapons and tools. Commercial production began at the Bruce Mine, E of SAULT STE MARIE, Ont, which was discovered 1846. Mines were later developed in Québec's Eastern Townships and in the Precambrian SHIELD. In the 1960s the large copper ore bodies of the CORDILLERA were discovered and developed. Canada ranks after the USSR, the US and Chile in world mine production. About 55% of copper concentrate from Canadian mines is converted to copper metal (99% pure) at smelters in Québec, Ontario and Manitoba. Refined copper is produced in Montréal (the world's largest copper refinery) and in TIMMINS and SUDBURY, Ont. BC is the leading mine producer; much BC copper is shipped as mineral concentrate to Japan for smelting and refining.

Copper was one of the first metals used by man; alloyed with tin it was widely used for weapons and tools during the Bronze Age. About half of today's copper consumption is for electrical uses, eg, electrical and telecommunications wire and cable, and electric motors. Other major uses are in industrial machinery, heat exchangers (such as refrigerators), turbines, locomotives and plumbing. Copper is alloyed with zinc to make brass, with tin and zinc for bronze and with zinc and nickel for German silver. Other significant uses are in copper chemicals, munitions, coinage and jewellery. Copper-nickel alloys have been developed for use in marine and desalination equipment. D. CRANSTON

Copper Inuit, so named because of their extensive use of artifacts made from the native copper deposits of the region, aboriginally occupied BANKS and VICTORIA islands and the adjacent mainland region of the central Canadian Arctic. In the early 20th century, they numbered about 800 people, divided into numerous regional bands averaging about 50. Several bands would combine during the winter when engaged in hunting seals. At this season they lived in large snow-house communities on the sea ice, moving to new areas as the local seal population was hunted out. In the spring these communities broke up and the bands moved to specific areas on the coasts, from whence they travelled into the interior in search of caribou, musk oxen and fish. Throughout the summer they moved about the interior within defined territories, in small groups of one or a few families, living in skin tents. Caribou hunting was intensified in late summer, and people began to gather at points along the coast where the women prepared winter clothing.

Social organization was based on kinship and on various types of formal partnership, and affiliation between individuals tended to be more a matter of personal choice than is usually found among other INUIT groups. Religion was based on shamanism, with the SHAMAN charged primarily with curing the sick and providing good hunting. Religion, language and most other aspects of the culture were similar to those of other central arctic Inuit groups, of whom the Copper Inuit were the most westerly.

Archaeology indicates that the Copper Inuit are descended from a group of THULE-culture

Co-operative Commonwealth Federation (CCF), founding meeting at Calgary, Alta, 1932. Among those present was J.S. Woodsworth (1st row, third from right) (*courtesy Public Archives of Canada/C-29313*).

eople who moved into the area shortly after 000 AD, and adapted their maritime way of life o seal and caribou resources. During the cooler limate of the Little Ice Age of the 17th to 19th enturies, these people abandoned the permanent winter houses and other elements of their Thule ancestors. Greater nomadism and increasing exposure and involvement with imported uropean technology gave rise to the distinctive ulture of the historic Copper Inuit. Regular European contact began during the early 20th entury, involving the Copper Inuit in a trapping economy. Most now live in the villages of achs Harbour, Holman, Coppermine, Bathurst nlet and Cambridge Bay. *See also* NATIVE PEOPLES: ARCTIC. ROBERT MCGHEE

eading: Diamond Jenness, *The People of the Twilight* 1959).

oppermine, NWT, UP, pop 809 (1981c), is situted W of the mouth of the COPPERMINE R on the nainland Arctic coast, 563 air km N of YELLOWKNIFE. The way of life for the INUIT living around his semipermanent fishing and sealing camp hanged in 1916, when a trading post was estabished at the site. As more services became available, the COPPER INUIT began to settle permanently. In the late 1970s, oil and gas exploration n the BEAUFORT SEA has provided some economic iversity to this community, where the residents till subsist on hunting, sealing and craftwork. ANNELIES POOL

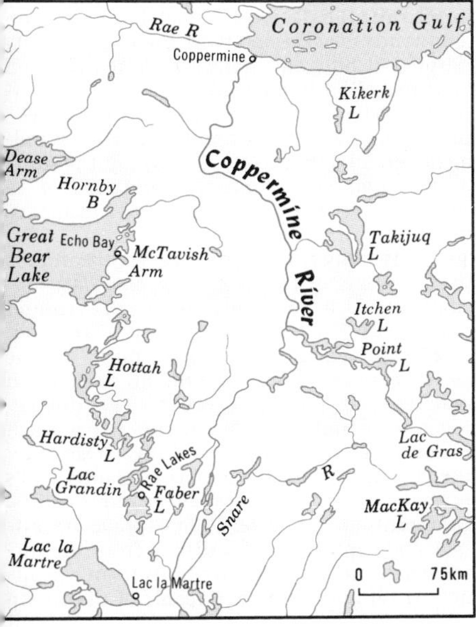

Coppermine River, 845 km long, rises in the Barren Lands of the NWT in Lac de Gras, flows NW through Point and Itchen lakes to Coronaion Gulf on the Arctic Ocean. At Bloody Falls, 16 km S of the ocean, a series of rapids tumble hrough a narrow gorge of volcanic rock. The valley floor lies some 150-200 m below the surounding plateau. Samuel HEARNE named the alls in 1771 after witnessing the killing of a party of Inuit by his Chipewyan guides. Sir John FRANKLIN and George BACK travelled the iver 50 years later. The river is named for the OPPER INUIT. JAMES MARSH

Coppers, pieces of copper hammered into the hape of a shield, were among the most valued tems at Northwest Coast potlatches. They were ften decorated with crests and designs. Each opper had a name, and its POTLATCH history etermined its value. Among the KWAKIUTL, copers increased in value each time they changed ands. In the late 19th and early 20th centuries, Hudson's Bay Co blankets were used to purchase hem, and some coppers were worth thousands of these blankets. Coppers were sometimes broen and thrown into the sea or a fire as signs of the owner's wealth and status, but more frequent was their transfer between families at the time of marriage. RENÉ R. GADACZ

Copperware, usually of sheet COPPER, hand formed and soldered, was in common use for cooking vessels from the late 18th century. Most copperware of this period was imported from England or continental Europe, although so much has been imported in recent times by dealers that it is impossible to identify Canadian contexts. Canadian sheet-metal workers who produced copperware in the early part of the 19th century did not mark their work. Most existing Canadian copperware dates from the manufacturing period, from 1880 to the 1930s. Cooking pots, measures and teakettles are found marked by McClary, GSW (General Steel Wares) and various other makers. Manufactured copperware was being produced in Canada as late as the middle 1930s. The metal was subject to tarnishing and contained corrosive salts that were toxic if mixed with food; therefore, use of copperware began to decline rapidly in the 1890s with the introduction of ALUMINUM cookware. By 1897 Sears Roebuck listed only copper teakettles and washtubs; as of 1901, the T. EATON COMPANY of Toronto no longer offered polished copperwares at all. D.B. WEBSTER

Copway, George, or Kahgegagahbowh, meaning "He Who Stands Forever," Mississauga (Ojibwa) translator, Methodist minister, lecturer, author (b near present-day Trenton, Ont 1818; d at Oka, Lake of Two Mountains, Qué Jan 1869). At age 12 Copway converted to METHODISM, and later became an ordained minister. He helped translate into Ojibwa the Acts of the Apostles and the Gospel of St Luke. But when 2 Upper Canadian Indian bands accused him of embezzling their funds, the Methodists expelled him. In late 1846 Copway left for the US, where he became a successful lecturer and author. Between 1847 and 1851 he published 3 books: his autobiography, a history of the Ojibwa and an account of his European travels in 1850. He edited the weekly *Copway's American Indian* for several months in New York. Immediately before his death in 1869, he converted to Roman Catholicism. DONALD B. SMITH

Copyright Law is included in what is commonly known as the law of intellectual and industrial property. This branch of law also includes PATENTS, TRADE MARKS and the law of industrial designs. In Canada, the CONSTITUTION ACT, 1867, gives exclusive jurisdiction over the law of copyright to the federal government. The current Copyright Act was enacted by Parliament in 1921.

Copyright is the right of an author to prevent unauthorized copying or use by others. Because section 4(1) of the Copyright Act provides that copyright subsists in every "original literary, dramatic, musical and artistic work," copyright protection applies to books, poetry, plays, motion pictures, songs, phonograph records, paintings, drawings, sculptures and photographs. However, not every literary, dramatic, musical or artistic work is protected. A work must be "original" in the sense that it must not be a copy itself. Secondly, the work must be in fixed or written form capable of identification. Finally, for copyright to subsist in Canada the author must, at the date of creation, be a subject or citizen of a Commonwealth country or a foreign country that either is a member of an international agreement of which Canada is also a member or has arrived at an international agreement with Canada.

The specific rights underlying copyright that arise automatically with the creation of an original work are enumerated in section 3(1) of the Copyright Act. The most important rights include the right "to produce or reproduce the

Copper kettle marked "Made by W.J. Clouston NFLD," Newfoundland 1930 (*courtesy Royal Ontario Museum*).

work or any substantial part thereof in any material form whatever," "to perform the work or any substantial part thereof in public" and, "if the work is unpublished, to publish the work or any substantial part thereof." These rights continue, in most cases, for the life of the author and a period of 50 years after his or her death.

Section 12(1) of the Copyright Act provides that the author of the work is the first owner of the copyright. However, if a work is created by an employee in the course of employment, the employer is the first owner of the copyright. Owners can sell or assign their rights in return for a lump-sum payment or a royalty.

Any person who, without the consent of the copyright owner, does anything that only the copyright owner has the right to do or who sells, rents, distributes, exhibits by way of trade in public or imports into Canada any work that infringes copyright or, for private profit, permits a theatre to be used for a public performance without the owner's consent, has broken the law of copyright. However, where the similarity of the work and the alleged copy arises from mere coincidence or from resort to the same source, copyright has not been infringed upon. Further, under section 17 of the Copyright Act, "fair dealing with any work for the purposes of private study, research, criticism, review or newspaper summary" does not constitute infringement.

Particulars of a copyright work and its owner, as well as assignments and licences, may be registered at the Copyright Office in the Department of Consumer and Corporate Affairs in Ottawa.

Canada has signed 2 major international copyright agreements: the 1928 Rome revision of the Berne Convention and the 1952 Universal Copyright Convention. The Berne Convention provides for automatic reciprocal copyright protection in Canada and other member countries. The Universal Copyright Convention, the only major international copyright agreement signed by the US, also provides for reciprocal copyright protection in Canada and member countries, but only upon compliance with certain formalities. The US and Canada also have a reciprocal arrangement.

Membership in the Berne Convention has an important bearing on the importation of foreign editions of Canadian books. Under the Copyright Act (s17), copyright in a work is infringed by a person who imports into Canada any work that infringes copyright. Indeed, under section 27 of the Act, the copyright owner can appeal to customs officials to bar importation of such copies into Canada. However, section 28 allows the importation of foreign editions of books by Canadian authors if those books have been printed in Great Britain or in a foreign country adhering to the Berne Convention. Unfortunately, there may be practical impediments to the protection guaranteed by the Copyright Act. For example, it may be difficult for customs officials to determine which books, among a large number imported into Canada from the US, are editions of a "Canadian" book.

New technology constantly challenges the law of copyright. In the 1950s a Canadian court held that the distribution of film telecasts by CABLE TELEVISION to individual subscribers at home does not constitute infringement of copyright in the film telecasts. In the US the practice of sound recording at home is not considered to be copyright infringement of the sound production; and the US Supreme Court ruled in 1984 that audio-video recording at home is not copyright infringement. Under Canadian law, both such practices would most likely be considered infringements of copyright. However, it is almost impossible in both cases for the copyright owners to detect infringement and enforce their rights. Similarly, reprography, the technology of reproduction that includes photocopying, is an infringement of copyright in literary work; however, the difficult problems of detection again arise. Computer software is more challenging; even if it is accepted that copyright protection can extend to software, which is not conventionally regarded as a literary work, there may be major problems in proving infringement when a copy is, for example, merely "reproduced" by storage in the memory of a computer.

In 1984 the Liberal government issued a white paper, *From Gutenberg to Telidon*, on revision of copyright law. The proposed revisions would do away with the registration system, protect special works such as computer programs and data bases, choreography, photography and films, and introduce statutory minimum damages and criminal sanctions to improve enforcement of the law. BRIAN A. CRANE

Reading: A.G. Blomquist and Chin Lim, *Copyright, Competition and Canadian Culture* (1981); P. Burn, *Guide to Patent, Trademark, Copyright Law in Canada* (1977); J. Palmer and R. Reesendes, *Copyright and the Computer* (1982).

Coquitlam, BC, District Municipality, pop 61 077 (1981c), inc 1891, is located on the N bank of the FRASER R between Burnaby and New Westminster (W) and Pitt Meadows (E). The name derives from a Salish tribal name meaning "small red salmon." NE Coquitlam includes the lower slopes of Mts Coquitlam, Eagle and Burk — with peaks up to 1600 m high. The district is mainly residential but has some large industries, including extraction (primarily gravel), wood products, wholesaling and warehousing, and transportation and trucking. There are 29 developed parks (about 765 ha) within the district, including Mundy Park (about 200 ha). French Canadians arrived from Québec 1909-10 to work in the logging trades at Fraser Mills, and Maillardville remains the largest French-speaking community in BC.

The district council consists of 6 aldermen and a mayor elected at large. The Town Centre area, in the NE section, is one of 4 such proposed areas in the Greater Vancouver Regional Dist. About one-third complete, it is expected to accommodate 27 000 residents. To the north, the province plans to develop the Westwood Plateau region for about 17 000 residents. ALAN F.J. ARTIBISE

Coral, common name for various small, sessile, usually colonial, marine INVERTEBRATES of phylum CNIDARIA. The individual coral animal (polyp) secretes a cup-shaped exoskeleton around its saclike body. The mouth is surrounded by tentacles covered with specialized poison cells (nematocysts), used to immobilize prey. Colonial corals reproduce by budding and, in tropical areas, may form massive coral reefs composed of skeletal material. The cold, often turbid, Canadian waters support no coral reefs. There are, however, numerous solitary stony corals, none larger than 10 cm, in all Canadian oceans. Colonial forms develop in the soft corals (subclass Octocorallia). Some of these, the huge sea fans, grow slowly off Canadian coasts. In the deep waters off BC they reach 2 m high. V. TUNNICLIFFE

Cordillera [Span, "mountains"], term normally applied to groups of MOUNTAIN RANGES. Sierra [Span, "sawtooth"] is applied to individual ranges, eg, Sierra Nevada. In English, cordillera refers to a major MOUNTAIN system and includes the plateaus, valleys and plains enclosed by the mountains. The various mountain ranges and plateaus of eastern N America are sometimes collectively referred to as the Eastern Cordillera. The name Western Cordillera is commonly applied to all mountains and intermontane plateaus of the western part of the continent. *See* GEOLOGICAL REGIONS; PHYSIOGRAPHIC REGIONS; VEGETATION REGIONS. J.M. RYDER

Coriander, *see* CONDIMENT CROPS.

Cormack, William Eppes (Epps), merchant, explorer, naturalist (b at St John's 5 May 1796; d at New Westminster, BC 30 Apr 1868). During 2 expeditions to the Newfoundland interior he made important contributions to knowledge about the island's geography and collected information about the BEOTHUK Indians. Educated in Scotland, Cormack returned to St John's early in 1822 to run his family's business interests. A keen naturalist and explorer, he crossed Newfoundland on foot that year with an Indian guide, the first white man to do so. His account of the expedition is a classic of Newfoundland literature. Host for several years of SHAWNANDITHIT, Cormack founded the Beothic Institution in 1827 in a fruitless attempt to locate survivors of this tribe. He left Newfoundland about 1830, eventually settling in BC. DANIEL FRANCIS

Cormier, Ernest, architect, engineer (b at Montréal 5 Dec 1885; d there 1 Jan 1980). A dominant figure in Québec ARCHITECTURE in the 20th century, Cormier is notable for his quest for high-quality building appropriate to its physical and historical context. Influenced by the École des beaux-arts in Paris where he studied 1908-14 (Grand Prix de Rome, 1914), Cormier made many trips to France and incorporated into his projects the major trends in contemporary European architecture. The Palais de Justice, Montréal (1920), reflected Cormier's interest in art deco, as did his own house (1418 av des Pins, Montréal) built 1930-31. The UNIVERSITÉ DE MONTRÉAL (1924-50), his major work, incorporates both the ornamental art-deco style and the more refined international style which he later favoured, and illustrates the complementary balance between Cormier's engineering knowledge and architectural talents. ODILE HÉNAULT

Ernest Cormier (right), dominant figure in 20th-century Québec architecture, whose major work, Université de Montréal, incorporates both the ornamental art-deco style and the international style. He is shown here receiving the Order of Canada from Gov Gen Jules Léger (*courtesy Canapress*).

Great cormorant (*artwork by Crosby*).

Cormorant (Phalacrocoracidae), family of predominantly black BIRDS with hooked, laterally compressed bills and naked, coloured skin on the throat. Highly adapted to an aquatic environment (eg, all toes are connected by a web), cormorants are awkward on land. When standing or perching they assume an upright posture. Twenty-eight species occur worldwide; 4 in Canada, 3 restricted to marine environments. The great cormorant (*Phalacrocorax carbo*, 2.4-5.3 kg) breeds along the Gulf of St Lawrence and the East Coast. Brandt's cormorant (*P. penicillatus*) inhabits brackish to nearshore waters around Vancouver I. The pelagic cormorant (*P. pelagicus*, 1.6-2.7 kg), Canada's smallest, most marine species, nests on cliffs along the BC coast, often wintering on the open ocean. The double-crested cormorant (*P. auritus*) occurs across much of southern Canada, inhabiting freshwater lakes, brackish waters and marine islands. Nests are on the ground or in trees, on islands or cliffs. Cormorants are fish eaters. They forage gregariously and capture prey by diving from the surface. Frequently, swimming birds form a semicircle, driving their prey. Capable of diving up to 37 m, cormorants perhaps use wings as well as feet for underwater propulsion. They are susceptible to disturbance when nesting. Cormorants have been persecuted for presumed depletion of economic fish stocks, although they subsist mainly on coarse fish. Double-crested cormorant populations, greatly affected by habitat loss caused in part by the drought of the 1930s, have increased in recent years. PHILIP H.R. STEPNEY

Corn, Field (*Zea mays*), spring-sown annual belonging to the GRASS family (Gramineae). Native to N America, Indian corn, or maize, has diverged so radically from its ancestral species that these forerunners cannot be identified with certainty. Maize is the tallest of the CEREAL CROPS (reaching over 4 m in height). The single, thick stalk is pithy and jointed; leaves are large. Each plant bears both male and female flowers: male flowers in a tassel at the top of the stalk, female flowers in a cluster (cob) enclosed in a leafy husk at the stalk joint. Corn silks, projecting beyond the husk, pick up pollen, which grows down the silk to reach the egg cell. Field corn has become a major commercial crop in Canada only during the last 3 decades. Before 1960 most f the corn produced was used on the farm, primarily as fodder. World grain-corn production eached an all-time high of nearly 438 million t n 1981: 48% was produced in the US; about .5%, in Canada. Between 1977 and 1982, Canadian production of grain corn increased 50% (4.2 nillion t-6.3 million t). Maize is produced in almost all provinces; SW Ontario, the leading region, had 800 000 ha planted in 1981. Corn is elatively easy to grow, but the profit margin vas low in the early 1980s.

"Corn breeding" was practised by native peoles and farmers before 1900. Scientific corn reeding, which depends on GENETICS and STATISTICS, was initiated in universities and RESEARCH STATIONS across N America by 1920, but has come o be largely the responsibility of seed companies. A company may have 10-15 research stations from Texas to Ontario, employing a large umber of scientists and technicians, making p to a few million controlled pollinations and esting untold millions of plants each year. Breeders attempt to build up genetic resistance to LANT DISEASES and to breed for maximum yield. Corn represents humanity's greatest plant breeding achievement: 50 years ago, yields averaged nder 75 bushels/ha (2727 L); now, yields of 350 ushels/ha (12 726 L) are often attained. Similarly, 50 years ago, 100% of the corn crop was sed for food or feed. Today, although over 10% f the 12 000 different items sold in a modern upermarket derive directly from corn, less than 0% of the total crop goes into the food system; he remainder constitutes the raw material for a ast array of industrial products, eg, paper, inulation. D.B. WALDEN

Corn, Sweet (*Zea mays* var. *saccharata* or *rugosa*), annual VEGETABLE of the GRASS family. Sweet orn is the result of a gene mutation (in dent orn), which appeared in the US early in the 9th century. The genetic change prevents sugar n the kernels from being converted into starch; ence, the sweet taste. Otherwise, sweet corn is dentical to field corn. In Canada and the US, weet corn is an important vegetable, eaten fresh on the cob) or stored canned or frozen (on or off he cob). Sweet corn requires at least 10°C for ermination; its growth is progressively better p to 35°C. Sweet corn requires 60-100 days to each maturity, depending on cultivar and locality. The newest hybrids have been bred for dditional sugar and for slower conversion of ugar into starch (to prolong the period of high uality). Hybrids make it possible to grow sweet orn in regions where the temperatures at harvest time would be otherwise too high. Harvesting is done by hand for the fresh market, by mechanical harvesters for the canning industry. ROGER BEDARD

Corn Laws, 1794-1846, set duties on grain imports into Britain to protect British agriculture rom outside competition. (In Britain, "corn" is he name for CEREAL CROPS.) By the 1820s, increased food demands in Britain led to revisions iving preference (lower duties) to colonial over oreign imports, thereby promoting an imperial rain supply. Preferential rates offset the costs of ransatlantic transport for BNA grain and built p a major colonial stake in wheat exporting. hifts in the level of duties primarily to suit British harvests and prices could still trouble his commerce; yet in general it rose steadily, particularly after the CANADA CORN ACT was passed in 1843. Then in 1846 Britain repealed the Corn Laws as part of a movement towards free rade. The consequent loss of preferential duties eemed a hard blow to the Canadian grain trade; ut it recovered in the prosperous 1850s. Moreover, the lifting of imperial economic controls lso brought relief from political controls, and hus imperial recognition of RESPONSIBLE GOVERNMENT in BNA. J.M.S. CARELESS

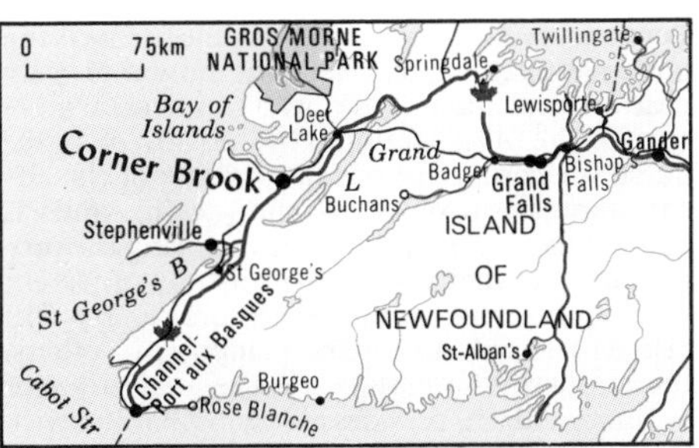

Corner Brook, Nfld, City, pop 24 339 (1981c), inc 1955, is located on Humber Arm of the Bay of Islands on Newfoundland's W coast. The province's second-largest city, it is the amalgamation of 5 towns: Curling, Corner Brook West and East, Townsite and Humbermouth. Fishing, farming and lumbering attracted settlers to this hilly, heavily wooded area on fjordlike Humber Arm, which culminates in a deep-water port open 9 months a year to oceangoing vessels. Curling, formerly Birchy Cove, was settled first and by 1864 Corner Brook had a sawmill. The subsequent growth of Corner Brook and Curling sparked the Newfoundland government's interest in its potential industrial development, and in 1923 the Newfoundland Power and Paper Co, in association with the British Armstrong, Whitworth and Co, was formed. By 1925 the company had constructed a wholly company-owned and planned townsite, a large pulp and newsprint paper mill, and a power plant at nearby DEER LAKE. In 1938 the mill became the property of the British Bowater-Lloyd firm. The Bowater pulp and paper mill, which in 1984 employed 2000 in the mill and another 5000 loggers in the woods, made Corner Brook one of the most prosperous cities in Atlantic Canada, but the announcement that the company was leaving Newfoundland at the end of 1984 left the city's future in grave doubt.

After Confederation (1949), a gypsum plant, a construction company, a cement plant and 3 fish plants were built, attracting new residents and leading to haphazard growth of the area beyond the townsite until amalgamation under one municipal government in 1955. The modern city of Corner Brook has attracted many other facilities, including Sir Wilfred Grenfell College (1975), the western branch of MEMORIAL UNIVERSITY. JANET E.M. PITT AND ROBERT D. PITT

Corner Brook, Nfld, looking E from Crow Head, with the Bowater pulp and paper mill in the foreground. The mill, one of the world's largest, began production in 1925 and the announcement in 1984 that it would close left the city's future in doubt (*photo by John de Visser / Masterfile*).

Cornwall, Ont, City, pop 46 144 (1981c), inc 1945, seat of the counties of Stormont, Dundas and Glengarry, is located on the ST LAWRENCE R, 110 km SW of Montréal. Founded in 1784 as a LOYALIST settlement by veterans of Sir John JOHNSON's regiment, it was called New Johnstown and renamed Cornwall for the Prince of Wales (also duke of Cornwall) by the 1790s. A regional administrative centre, it was also an important transshipment point until completion of the upper St Lawrence canals in the 1840s and the GRAND TRUNK RY in 1856. In the 1870s and 1880s several textile and paper mills located here, revitalizing the community and drawing a large French-speaking work force from Québec. Today about half of Cornwall's inhabitants are of French origin. Domtar Fine Papers is the main employer, augmented by petrochemical and textile industries. Construction of the ST LAWRENCE SEAWAY and of a hydroelectric generating station in the late 1950s brought temporary prosperity. The city is now trying to widen its industrial base and develop as a tourism centre. Cornwall has a campus of St Lawrence Coll of Applied Arts and Sciences and a satellite campus of U of Ottawa. It has the second-oldest courthouse in the province (1833) and a restored "Regency Cottage" museum, "Inverarden" (1816). ROBERT J. BURNS

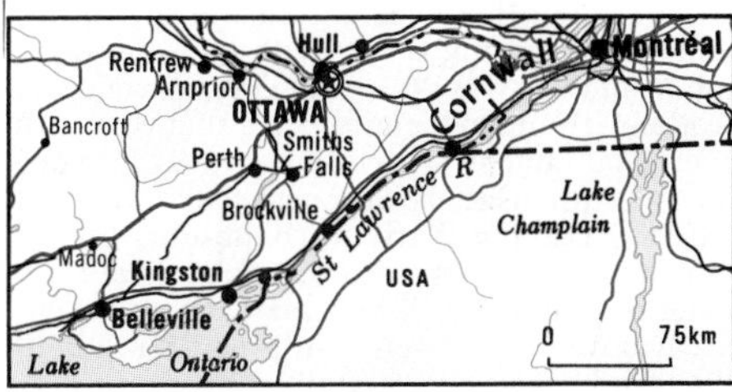

Cornwall, James Kennedy, known as "Peace River Jim," "Apostle of the North," "Lord of the Athabasca," adventurer, businessman, politician, soldier (b at Brantford, Ont 29 Oct 1869; d at Calgary 20 Nov 1955). For 60 years Cornwall was the northland's most effective ambassador. By the time he arrived in Alberta in 1896, he had crisscrossed the Atlantic and hiked across Europe, Russia and Asia. In 1897 he settled at Athabasca Landing where he founded several businesses, including the Northern Transportation Co. He was Liberal MLA for Peace River, 1908-12. Cornwall served overseas in WWI as lt-col of the 218th Battalion of the CEF, a railway unit he founded and financed. He was awarded the Croix de Guerre by the French and the DSO by King George V. He was the champion promoter of his beloved north country, and through his efforts capital was raised, telegraph lines and railways built and settlement encouraged. J.B. CZYPIONKA

Cornwall Island, 2258 km², located in the northern ARCTIC ARCHIPELAGO, some 100 km W of Ellesmere I. It is generally low, rising to a 375-m summit towards the W. It was discovered in 1852 by Sir Edward Belcher and named North Cornwall. JAMES MARSH

Cornwallis, CFB, Naval Training Centre, 489 personnel (Dec 1983), is located at Deep Brook, NS, on the Fundy Shore, 17 km E of DIGBY. Established 1942, it became the site of naval training 1943. In 1951 the first regular-force female training began here. Designated a CFB in 1966, the base covers 250 ha and is essentially a self-contained town with its own post office, bank, hospital, gymnasium, theatre, library and weekly newspaper. The training centre for all English-speaking recruits, it takes semitrained personnel from basic-training establishments and turns out practised seamen with sea experience, able to operate and maintain complicated naval equipment. JANICE MILTON AND JEAN PETERSON

Edward Cornwallis, founder of Halifax (1749), governor of Nova Scotia and later of Gibraltar (*courtesy Public Archives of Canada/C-11070*).

Cornwallis, Edward, soldier, administrator (b at London, Eng 22 Feb 1712/13; d at Gibraltar 14 Jan 1776). He served 17 years in the British army until retiring (1748) with the rank of lt-col. In 1749 he was appointed governor of Nova Scotia. Arriving in the summer of that year with over 2000 English settlers, Cornwallis founded the new townsite of Chebucto (later renamed HALIFAX). Leaving a thriving community behind him, Cornwallis returned to England in 1752. After resuming a military career, he was eventually given the governorship of Gibraltar in 1762, and held this post until his death.
DAVID EVANS

Cornwallis Island, 6996 km^2, located between Bathurst I and Devon I in the ARCTIC ARCHIPELAGO. It is separated from Somerset I to the S by Barrow Str. The island is generally flat, though there are prominent (400 m) cliffs along the E coast. The land surface is strewn with rock debris, cemented by PERMAFROST. Traces of ancient INUIT camps are common along the S coast. It was discovered by Sir William PARRY in 1819 and named for Sir William Cornwallis. An airstrip was established at Resolute on the S coast in 1947 — it is now the major communications centre of the Arctic Archipelago and a weather station and transshipment point to stations on the icebound outer islands. JAMES MARSH

Coronach, Sask, Town, pop 1032 (1981c), inc 1978, is located 15 km N of the international boundary and 145 km SW of REGINA. The community was created in 1927 when the CPR branch line for S-central Saskatchewan began servicing the site. It was named for a horse that had won the Epsom Derby, and developed as a small service centre for the farmers and ranchers of the area. The village's decline was arrested during the mid-1970s by Saskatchewan Power Corp plans to build the Poplar River Dam, a thermal-power generating plant and a strip coal-mining operation. DON HERPERGER

Coronation Gulf, a broad indentation in the arctic shore of the NWT, roughly the shape of the S coast of VICTORIA I, which lies directly N. The gulf receives the COPPERMINE R, Tree R, Rae R and others and merges with BATHURST INLET to the E. The small settlement of Coppermine lies at the mouth of the Coppermine R. The gulf was named by Sir John FRANKLIN in 1821, in honour of the coronation of King George IV. The environment and native culture of the area were studied by R.M. Anderson and Diamond JENNESS in 1916, as part of the Canadian Arctic Expedition. JAMES MARSH

Coroner, public servant responsible for carrying out investigations to determine how and why deaths other than those by natural causes occurred. The investigation is in the form of an inquest; the coroner listens to evidence of the circumstances surrounding the death, and is entitled to question all witnesses during the proceedings. Inquests are governed by different rules in different provinces. In some a jury will also be selected to hear the evidence; in others, the coroner, who may be a judge, magistrate or ordinary citizen, presides alone. B. WINDWICK

Corporate Concentration, Royal Commission on (Bryce Commission), appointed in Apr 1975 under R.B. Bryce, in response to POWER CORPORATION OF CANADA'S bid to take control of ARGUS CORPORATION, to study and report upon "the nature and role of major concentrations of corporate power in Canada; the economic and social implications for the public interest of such concentrations; and whether safeguards exist or may be required to protect the public interest in the presence of such concentrations." The resignation of Bryce, due to illness (1977), as chairman greatly influenced the commission's conclusions, summarized as, "While we have recommended a number of improvements (in public policy), we conclude that no radical changes in the laws governing corporate activity are necessary at this time to protect the public interest." No significant changes in competition policy legislation have been passed. *See* PRESSURE GROUPS. THOMAS K. SHOYAMA

Corporation Law is a term used to describe the immense and varied body of law concerning corporations. In Canada the phrase "corporation law" is generally synonymous with "company law." (In England, corporation law is invariably referred to as "company law"; in the US, as "corporation law.") Modern Canadian law in this area is a combination of English and American law with some purely Canadian innovations. Throughout the remainder of this article the phrase "corporation law" and the word "corporation" will be used, and unless the text draws a particular distinction, these terms will include "company law" and "company."

A corporation is considered a separate legal person, ie, it has the legal status to enter into contracts, to sue and to be sued and to do everything that a natural person can do with a few exceptions that are obvious and some that are not so obvious. For example, a corporation cannot swear an affidavit because it has no conscience to bind it, from which fact probably derives the phrase "the soulless corporation." A corporation can be convicted of a crime under the CRIMINAL CODE or any of the vast number of other regulatory statutes, but only if the penalizing section provides for a fine in lieu of imprisonment. When a statute in Canada uses the word "person" it includes a corporation; when a statute uses the word "individual" it generally refers only to natural persons.

The corporate form of conducting any particular activity has 4 main advantages. First, the corporation continues to exist until it is liquidated or dissolved; the death of a shareholder, even if there is only one shareholder, does not affect the life of the corporation. In law, this is referred to as the right of perpetual succession. Second, because the corporation is a separate juristic personality apart from its shareholders, any liability it incurs in carrying on its activities redounds to the corporation alone; the shareholders or members are not responsible for the corporation's debts unless they have personally guaranteed their payment. In law this concept is referred to as "limited liability." Third, the corporation provides a mechanism for the accumulation of blocks of capital with which large projects can be financed and developed. The public can participate in these projects through the ownership of shares. Fourth, for both large and particularly small corporations the structure provides a unique and convenient method of financing day-to-day operations through the mechanism of the "floating charge debenture." A partnership, unless the partnership agreement is carefully drawn, or a sole proprietorship have neither of the first 2 advantages and neither the sole properietorship nor the partnership, no matter how carefully drawn the partnership agreement, have the last 2 advantages.

The structure of a corporation consists of the shareholders or members, the directors and the officers. The directors are responsible for the management of the corporation, for the appointment of the officers and for broad policy decisions. The officers are responsible for the day-to-day operation of the corporation's business. Ultimate power rests with the voting shareholders or members who, in theory, can at least elect a new and different board of directors. In the one-person corporation all of these functions may be carried on by the single shareholder and director who is also the president of the organization.

The bewildering array of corporate forms in modern Canadian society can be divided by function into 3 main categories: municipal corporations, nonprofit (or charitable) corporations, and commercial corporations (including some CROWN CORPORATIONS).

Municipal Corporations include cities, towns, villages, COUNTIES and municipal districts, each of which is governed by an elected board (*see* MUNICIPAL GOVERNMENT). Municipal corporations have all of the features of any other corporation except shares. They are separate legal persons having perpetual succession and their liabilities are the liabilities of the corporation, not the residents of the area. The Crown in the right of Canada and in the right of each province is a corporation and has the same attributes, although many statutes exempt the Crown or its servants from being sued.

Charitable Corporations Medieval charitable corporations, created by crown charter or as part of the medieval church, predate commercial corporations. The early universities of Oxford and Cambridge were created by crown grant. Hospitals and almshouses were separate entities under various orders or dioceses of the church. Following the Reformation and Henry VIII's confiscation of church property, charity became a secular activity. While the Crown occasionally granted charters for charitable organizations, charitable activity was overwhelmingly accomplished through the mechanism of the charitable trust. It was not until approximately 100 years ago that English company law made any provision for nonprofit corporations by means of special provisions in the Companies Act of England.

Nonprofit or charitable corporations, despite their nomenclature, can make a profit, but any profit must be used to further an activity that is charitable or beneficial to the community. For example, a symphony society that profits from an auction must use those profits to support the orchestra and may not distribute them among members of the society.

Since Confederation, 1867, Québec's CIVIL CODE has differed from the CIVIL LAW of the remaining 9 common-law provinces, although each regime has influenced the other. The laws governing the formation and the conduct of nonprofit corporations testify to the different attitudes prevailing in various provinces. Alberta permits incorporation under either a Societies Act or a Companies Act, and Saskatchewan does the same under the Not-for-Profit Corporations Act. Manitoba, Ontario, New Brunswick, Newfoundland, Québec and the federal jurisdiction of Canada have no General Societies Act. Incorporation must be achieved, as in England, under special sections of each respective Corporation Act. In BC, Nova Scotia and PEI, incorporation can only be accomplished under the provisions of a General Societies Act.

The Income Tax Act imposes different rules for their own classification of nonprofit corporations. A corporation whose objects are charitable (the legal definition of "charitable" is neither simple nor precise but organizations such as the Red Cross, various health societies or foundations and cultural societies fall in this category) or for whom special provision is made in the Income Tax Act, is exempt from income tax and may issue receipts that are deductable from the donor's income tax if the organization has been approved and issued a number by the minister of finance. Before the minister will issue a number he must be satisfied that the corporation falls within the exempt classification, that its constitution prohibits any distribution of assets or profits to the members during the life of the organization, and that upon liquidation or dissolution any funds left over following payment of all creditors will not be distributed among the members but will be donated to another charitable corporation whose objects are most similar to those of the dissolved corporation. Mutual benefit corporations (eg, trade associations, clubs organized for various sports) are exempt from tax on their income but cannot issue deductible receipts. They need only to provide for an exempt object and a prohibition against distribution during their existence. Upon dissolution they may distribute any remaining surplus to their members. A golf club, for example, is not taxable on the dues that it receives from members to operate the golf course; it is, however, taxable on any income from investments or from any profit it earns in renting out facilities for meetings or receptions.

There are, in addition to the commercial and nonprofit corporations, a wide variety of specialized corporations in each province. All provinces provide for the incorporation of co-operatives. All provinces have enacted CONDOMINIUM laws and all, except Québec, provide for condominium corporations whose shareholders are the unit holders in the building. Each province has a number of specialized nonprofit corporations Acts. For example, Alberta provides for agricultural societies under the Agricultural Societies Act, for the ownership of church lands under the Religious Societies Lands Act, and for ownership of cemeteries under the Cemetery Companies Act.

Over and above all of these are the corporations incorporated by private Act of the legislature of each province, the vast majority of which are nonprofit corporations. They run the spectrum from private clubs to hospital boards and hospitals operated by various religious orders, and include incorporated charitable trusts, FOUNDATIONS and some religions and educational organizations.

Commercial Corporations, which may vary in size from the corner store to national corporations such as Alcan or the even larger multinational corporation, constitute by far the majority of corporations in Canada. They are created with the intention of engaging in business, of making a profit and of distributing that profit among their shareholders.

Before 1970, Canadian corporation law, with one main exception, was based on English company law. English company law embraces both pure company law and that area of law referred to in N America as securities law. Securities legislation in Canada, as distinct from corporation law has, since its inception, relied more on the model of American law and the concepts developed by the US securities Exchange Commission. Canada differs from the US in that it has no federal securities Act. On the other hand Canada, unlike the US, provides for federally incorporated corporations.

Under the Constitution Act, 1867, the provinces were given the power to incorporate companies with provincial objects. The Act contains no reference to the power of the federal government to incorporate or regulate companies, but the power to do so has generally been conceded as implicit under S91(2), the trade and commerce section, or as part of the implicit jurisdiction of any sovereign state to grant incorporation.

Before 1970 there were 2 basic forms used by the various jurisdictions in Canada for the creation of companies. Both derived from English law. The first is by a grant of letters patent from the Crown as represented by the particular provincial government. This form is the direct descendant of the great monopolistic Crown charter companies of the 16th and 17th centuries in England, eg, "The Governor and Company of Adventurers Trading into Hudsons Bay," (HUDSON'S BAY CO), whose charter was granted by Charles II in 1670. Three hundred years later it became a Canadian corporation under the jurisdiction of the Canada Corporations Act. Whether or not a Crown will grant letters patent for a particular corporation is still, in theory though seldom in practice, entirely dependent on the Crown's discretion. Until 1970 Manitoba, Ontario, Québec, PEI, New Brunswick and the federal government used this form. Once incorporated under this form the incorporators prepare bylaws to govern the internal management of the corporation.

The second form of incorporation is by registration of memorandum and articles of association, and so long as the documents are properly prepared incorporation is a matter of right. This form derives from the English Companies Act of 1862 which in turn derived from an earlier form known as the Deed of Settlement Company, basically a use of the TRUST devised by English lawyers. Under this system the incorporators prepare a memorandum of association setting out the name of the company, the objects for which it is to be incorporated, and the proposed capitalization of the company. They also prepare articles of association which set out procedural rules for the calling of meetings of shareholders and directors, the procedure to be followed at these meetings, and such other matters as the ingenuity of legal draftsman can devise. Alberta and Saskatchewan used this form until recently. BC, Nova Scotia and Newfoundland still do. The provisions of the memorandum and articles of association are deemed to represent a contract among all of the shareholders and as such the provisions are enforceable by any one or more shareholders as a party to the contract.

The 1970s saw a wave of law reform in corporation law in Canada. In 1970 Ontario enacted the Ontario Business Corporations Act modeled primarily on the corporate law of New York state together with some concepts taken from the US Uniform Commercial Code. The form of incorporation may be described as a halfway house between the letters patent form and the articles and memorandum form. Under this system the corporation is created by one or more incorporators filing a statutory form called "articles of incorporation," together with a notice of registered office and a notice of directors, with the Registrar of Corporations. Following the issuance of a certificate of incorporation by the registrar, the corporation comes into existence. The directors named in the notice of directors then hold an organizational meeting, issue the shares of the corporation and adopt bylaws to govern procedural matters and internal management. In 1975 the federal government enacted the Canada Business Corporations Act, a modified form of which has now been enacted in Alberta, Saskatchewan, Manitoba and New Brunswick.

Commercial corporations are either private or nondistributing corporations, or public or distributing corporations. The private or nondistributing corporation has a limited number of shareholders, restricts the transferability of its shares and is prohibited from soliciting public purchase of its securities. Unless such a corporation is a subsidiary of a public or distributing corporation, it does not come under the jurisdiction of the provincial securities acts. American law generally refers to such corporations as "close corporations"; English law tends to use the phrase "incorporated partnership."

Public or distributing corporations can have an unlimited number of shareholders whose shares are freely transferable and are usually traded on a stock exchange. It actively solicits the public to buy its securities and is subject to regulation by the Securities Act of each province in which its securities are traded, and by the regulations of each stock exchange upon which its stock is traded.

Basically, corporation law attempts to balance 2 conflicting interests; the external conflict between the corporation and its creditors or others with whom the corporation has dealings, and the internal conflict between the majority or control group of shareholders and the minority group. Corporation law does not by itself attempt to deal with the duties and responsibilities of a manufacturing corporation to produce a safe usable product nor does it deal with such matters as POLLUTION or SAFETY STANDARDS in the work place of the employees. All of these and similar matters are the subject of separate legislation.

Given the fact that the corporation is a separate person in law and that the shareholders are not personally liable for the corporation's debts, the questions arise of how employees and creditors who supply goods or services to the corporation can ensure that they will be paid, and how lenders who have financed the corporation's operations can ensure that their loan will be repaid. Practice or legislation has sought to protect employees and lenders; normal trade creditors who supply goods or services to creditors are more or less left to their own devices to protect themselves as best they can and in the event of BANKRUPTCY of the corporation usually end up the last in line, receiving very little, if any, of their claim.

Originally, the expectation was that the fund to which all of the creditors could look to payment was the basic capital of the company raised through the issue of shares. Historically, and except for the modern business corporations Acts in Canada, this amount was called "paid-up capital." Under the modern corporations status it is referred to as "stated capital." No dividend can be paid out of this sum; dividends can only be paid out of profits. There is no minimum amount that a private or nondistributing corporation must raise as stated capital before it commences business. The paid-in or stated capital may amount to no more than $10 and in some cases even less. Slightly over 97% of the companies incorporated in Alberta fall within this class and the percentage does not vary greatly from province to province. The original concept of the fund has therefore become almost totally meaningless for the vast majority of corporations. Historically, a British or Canadian corporation could not buy back its own shares, because by doing so it would reduce its capital. However, the ability to do so has long been part of American corporation law and the modern Canadian Acts all make provision, subject to certain safeguards, for the repurchase by a corporation of its own shares.

A share in a corporation confers 3 basic rights,

although all may not be included in any one class of shares. These rights are the right to vote at a meeting of the shareholders, a right to share in the profits of the corporation by the receipt of dividends, and the right to receive a share of the capital of the corporation upon its liquidation or dissolution. If there is only one class of shares these rights are equal among all shareholders. They may however be divided among different classes of shares, and this division can be very complex, depending upon the particular purpose for which each class of share is issued and the ingenuity of the lawyer who drafted the provisions regarding the rights, privileges and restrictions attaching to each class. Shares that confer some preference in payment of dividends or upon repayment of capital upon liquidation or dissolution are generally referred to a preference shares or preferred shares. Shares that carry a right to vote and a right to share in the assets of a corporation remaining after payment of all creditors and preferred shares upon liquidation or dissolution, are referred to as common or equity shares.

Generally only the large public or distributing corporations have a substantial amount of share capital. Institutional lenders therefore protect themselves by taking additional forms of security when lending money to the private or non-distributing corporations that have no large share capital base. This additional security will almost invariably include a personal guarantee by the shareholders and directors that they will repay the loan if the corporation does not, a general assignment of the corporation's accounts receivable, and a mortgage on any real property owned by the corporation together with an assignment of loss payable under a policy of fire insurance insuring the real property. If the corporation's success depends on the efforts of the principals, the lender will often insist that the corporation take out a policy of life insurance on the life of the principals with an assignment of the proceeds to the lender in the event of the death of one or any of them.

Over and above all of these forms of additional security is the "floating charge debenture" granted by the corporation in favor of the lender. It is a unique and expeditious form of security that is available only to corporations. From the time it is granted and registered it creates an equitable charge over all of the corporation's assets but the corporation can still deal with its assets in the normal day-to-day course of its business. The debenture contains a provision that in the event of default in payment of the loan or in other circumstances that create an event of default, the lender can appoint a receiver who will take control and management of the corporation and can sell off whatever assets he chooses in order to repay the debt. A floating charge debenture has been described as a great black cloud hanging over the assets of the corporation that crystallizes into hail when the receiver is appointed. Receivership does not preclude bankruptcy proceedings, which may be commenced by any other creditor. Employees are given a priority for wage claims under the provisions of the various labour Acts in each province and under federal bankruptcy legislation. Over and above this they have the right to sue the directors for up to 6 months wages if they have been unable to collect what is due to them from the corporation.

The most intractable practical problem facing any person desiring to incorporate a corporation today is the problem of obtaining clearance for the name of the proposed corporation. A corporate name must be unique and distinct from the name of all other existing corporations in the province of incorporation and may not conflict with the name of a federally incorporated company. If the organizers plan to carry on business in more than one province they must be sure that the name will not conflict with that of a corporation existing in that other province. In addition there are a large number of prohibitions on corporate names. Words such as "government," "university" or "bank" may not be used as part of an ordinary corporation name, nor may any name that is obscene in the opinion of the registrar of corporations. Obtaining clearance for the name of a proposed incorporation can involve long and substantial delays. It is for this reason and to enable speedy incorporation that every Canadian jurisdiction now permits the incorporation of number companies with the addition of the name of the province or, in the case of a federal corporation, the word "Canada" (*see also* TRADE MARK).

Until the 1950s, the lot of minority shareholders was not a happy one. A group that controlled over 50% of the voting shares had the power to elect themselves as directors of the corporation. The concept of the directors' fiduciary duty did evolve in the courts but it was a limited concept and often of not much avail. A director must act in good faith when exercising the powers of his office, but there is no similar duty upon him to act in good faith when he is voting as a shareholder at a shareholders' meeting. It is a breach of the directors' fiduciary duty if they issue more shares in the company to themselves to obtain or regain voting control. A director who found himself in a conflict of interest situation acted at his peril, because he could be held accountable for any profit he might make in such circumstances. These shadowy controls over the conduct of directors were often defeated by the principle of ratification, ie, directors holding voting control of a corporation could convene a meeting of the shareholders at any time and ratify any questionable acts they had done. Courts were loathe to interfere and to substitute their judgement for that of the corporation's controllers unless they could be shown that the conduct in question amounted to fraud.

Modern corporate law seeks to protect the interest of minority shareholders by 3 divergent but interlocking concepts. The first is to define more precisely the directors' duties and liabilities within the corporate statute; the second is to give minority shareholders specific remedies and easy access to the courts to redress their grievances; and the third has been described as "the glaring searchlight" of full disclosure.

Under the modern corporation statutes a director has a statutory duty to act with the highest good faith in his relations to the corporation, with diligence and with a reasonable degree of skill and prudence. Directors are personally liable if they vote for the declaration of a dividend or for other matters affecting the capital of the corporation and the corporation is unable to meet the statutory requirement for the proposed action. Directors are liable if they use information not generally known to the public to profit from the sale or purchase of the corporations shares, an activity known as "insider trading."

Minority shareholders have the right to dissent from any fundamental change in the constitution of the corporation, such as an amalgamation or the alteration of the share structure. They can also compel the corporation to buy back their shares at fair value. A shareholder can apply to the court for an order that an investigation be conducted of the corporation's affairs and has the right to apply to the court for leave to commence or defend an action in the name of the corporation in the event that the directors have failed to do so because of a personal interest in the matter. Finally, minority shareholders have the broad general right to commence an action against the corporation and its directors if they feel that the conduct of the latter has been oppressive or unfairly prejudicial to the shareholders' interests.

These remedies are not of much use to shareholders who do not know what is going on. The primary source of information about the affairs of a large corporation is the annual report, which must contain the audited financial statements with their accompanying notes. ACCOUNTING has been described as an art, not a science; the format of presentation of financial statements has now been generally standardized in Canada to comply with the recommendations set out in the handbook of the Canadian Institute of Chartered Accountants. The auditor of a corporation has been called the watchdog of the shareholder. To supervise the auditor's work, to act as a channel of communication between the auditor and the directors and management, and to ensure the independence of the auditor, distributing corporations must now have an audit committee of the directors, the majority of whom cannot be full-time employees of the corporation.

Notice of the annual meeting of the shareholders of any distributing corporation must include an annual report and a proxy circular containing information about the corporation and the proposed slate of directors. A copy of the information circular must be filed with the securities commission in each province in which the corporation has distributed its securities. Directors and officers must notify the provincial securities commission in writing of any purchase or sale of shares of their corporation within 10 days of the purchase or sale. In the event of any proposed major change in the corporation, the directors must include an information circular along with the notice of the meeting of the shareholders convened to approve the change. The circular must contain sufficient information to enable a reasonably intelligent shareholder to assess the proposed changes and to determine whether it is or is not in his interest. Full disclosure is presumed, therefore, to have a dual effect: it gives the shareholders the information they may need to commence some remedial action, and it encourages directors not to do anything that they would not wish to be disclosed. G. FIELD

Corporatism was originally a 19th-century doctrine which arose in reaction to the competition and class conflict of capitalist society. In opposition to the trend towards both mass suffrage and independent trade unionism, it promoted a form of functional representation — everyone would be organized into vocational or industrial associations integrated with the state through representation and administration. The contention was that if these groups (especially capital and labour) could be imbued with a sense of mutual rights and obligations, such as presumably united the medieval estates, a stable order based on "organic unity" could be established. Although the notion of industrial parliaments was commonly raised in liberal democracies after WWI, the only states that explicitly adopted a corporative form of representation were the fascist regimes of Italy, Germany, Spain, Portugal, Vichy France and various S American dictatorships. In all these cases, corporatist structures were primarily a decorative facade for authoritarian rule, state repression of independent trade unionism being the main motive and consequence. Given this experience, corporatist ideology has not been popular in Western liberal democratic societies, but it has become increasingly common for social scientists to discern that certain political arrangements have developed within these frameworks which in operative premise and institutional form bear resemblance to the functional-representation notions of corporatism. This has been particularly true in many W European countries, where the central trade-union and business federations have joined government representatives in national economic and incomes policy planning. These arrangements conform to the concept of the Keynesian welfare state, in which governments seek to stem inflationary tendencies in the economy and encourage productivity. Central to all such arrangements has been the effort to persuade unions to accept national wage-restraint policies in exchange for representation in economic decision making.

Corporatism is now seen as either a new economic system, successor to capitalism, where the state controls and directs a highly concentrated, but still privately owned economy; or a new form of state, where the important representation, decision making and administration take place not in the parties, parliaments and ministerial bureaucracies, but in the tripartite structures where business, labour and governments are joined; or a new form of interest-group politics, where instead of the competitive, lobbying activities of many pressure groups, there is a monopoly of access to the state by one group from each sector of society, with the state exercising reciprocal influence over the groups. While each of these scenarios captures some aspects of modern corporatist developments, they are all too expansive and grandiose. Corporatist structures may take supplemental parliamentary forms in certain countries, but they have hardly become the centre of the liberal democratic state. They have been confined primarily to the relations among big business, organized labour and government. Above all, corporatist arrangements do not challenge capitalism as the economic system of these societies. Important key investment decisions, although influenced by the state partly through corporatist structures, remain with private corporations. Indeed, far from emerging as the new dominant institutions, corporatist structures have displayed an inherent instability, reflecting the asymmetry of the relative power of capital and labour and the tendency of trade unions to withdraw their co-operation in wage-restraint policies when members insist that their leaders represent their demands rather than act as junior partners in managing the modern capitalist economy.

Corporatist ideologies were popular in Canada in the first half of this century. The Québec Catholic Church was heavily influenced by corporatist doctrine and this had a direct impact on French Canadian trade unionism, through the Confédération des travailleurs catholiques du Canada (CTCC), and on political parties such as the UNION NATIONALE. Corporatist influences were also at work in the doctrine of "group government" espoused by the Prairie Farmers' parties between the wars. Mackenzie KING explicitly espoused a corporatist ideology in his book *Industry and Humanity* (1918). However, political and economic conditions have not been propitious for corporatist developments; both the decentralized nature of the movement and the absence of a governing social-democratic party at the national level have been critical in precluding them. Additionally, the heavy pro-business bias of the Canadian state and the difficulty of planning an economy as open as Canada's to FOREIGN INVESTMENT led the state, even in the post-1945 era, to rely much more on unemployment and on legislative restriction of the right to strike than on the incorporation of union leaders into national decision making. Various attempts, ranging from the establishment of the Economic Council of Canada to the discussions with business and labour around prices and incomes policy in 1969-70 and 1975-78, were made in the 1960s and 1970s to create national corporatist structures, but these developments have either remained exceedingly minor or have come to nothing because business and unions have refused to engage in the necessary compromises to institutionalize corporatism. The government itself, while increasingly vocal in calling for voluntary co-operation between capital and labour in restraining inflation, has tended to impose statutory wage controls and restrictions on the right to strike rather than create a groundwork for integrating the union leadership into economic decision-making structures. While particular examples of corporatism exist in federal and provincial labour-relations boards, in various government-sponsored "quality of working life" programs and in occasional task forces on economic development, they are modest. LEO PANITCH

Reading: R. Schultz, et al, eds, *The Canadian Political Process* (1979).

Corriveau, Marie-Josephte, murderess (b at St-Vallier, Qué 14 May 1733; d at Québec City 18 Apr 1763). She was hanged for killing her second husband with an axe and her body was displayed in an iron cage at Pointe-Lévy. The gruesome episode left an impression locally and tales of LA CORRIVEAU'S ghost terrified settlers around Québec in the late 18th and early 19th centuries. Descriptions appear in AUBERT DE GASPÉ'S, *Les Anciens Canadiens* (1863) and William KIRBY'S, *The Golden Dog* (1877). JAMES MARSH

Corruption Political corruption may be defined as behaviour by public officials, elected or appointed, which violates social or legal norms regarding what is or is not legitimate private gain at public expense. For example, the direct profiting by an official or his family from the use of his official position to secure contracts for the family business is a violation of social and, increasingly, of legal norms, although these norms may change. Political corruption exists in a variety of forms from that which is almost universally condemned to behaviour widely held to be corrupt but about which members of the public or political decision makers disagree, and behaviour that may be mildly corrupt for many but which is widely tolerated. Some might argue that behaviour in the latter category is not corrupt but socially acceptable, even though it may not be actively encouraged. However, generally this behaviour is considered ethically dubious but too difficult to uproot.

CONFLICT OF INTEREST is a form of political corruption which is quickly becoming universally condemned. Although all corruption constitutes a type of conflict of interest, the term refers to corruption arising from the conflict between the actions of an individual officeholder and the public interest. Certain forms of conflict of interest are illegal in Newfoundland (since 1973) and NB (since 1978). In other jurisdictions, conflict of interest, although not illegal, may violate guidelines and be penalized by resignation from office or temporary suspension. Guidelines, however, lack the force of law, and their implementation often rests on the goodwill and fairness of the government rather than upon the independent judiciary.

Vote buying, illegal and proscribed by the Canada Elections Act, is a form of corruption which is almost universally condemned, although some campaign workers and candidates may feel it is simply a pragmatic form of campaigning. As recently as 1975, the then premier of NS admitted publicly that it was still practised in his province. Other illicit electoral practices, eg, forging of ballot papers, voting twice or impersonating another voter, are also proscribed by the Act. Bribery, by which an official is offered, and may even accept, money or other valuable considerations in exchange for doing or not doing what he is expected to do in fulfilment of his official duties, is almost universally condemned as corrupt. Bribery is apparently less common in Canada than in countries where public servants and politicians are poorly paid. Illegal under the Criminal Code, it carries a maximum sentence of 14 years in prison for the official, the person guilty of bribing the official, or both. Graft is much like bribery except that the official initiates the exchange, and demands money or other considerations from the public in return for carrying out (or not carrying out) his official duty. Bribery and graft both fall under the same section of the Criminal Code and it is sometimes difficult to distinguish between them, even analytically. For example, Prime Minister John A. MACDONALD was directly implicated in the 1872 PACIFIC SCANDAL when he was charged by the Opposition spokesman and by newspapers with accepting $10 000 in return for his support in Parliament of a group bidding for the railway contract. The evidence took the form of one of the most famous telegrams in Canadian history; on 26 Aug 1872, Macdonald wired railway lawyer and politician J.C. ABBOTT, "I must have another ten thousand." Bribery and graft are also occasionally linked with government licensing or government contracts. Robert Summers, forestry minister for the BC government (1958), became the first Cabinet minister in the Commonwealth to be jailed for corruption in office when he was convicted of accepting bribes.

Influence peddling, which occurs when someone, not necessarily a government official, offers to use his presumed influence over other officials to secure a benefit for another in exchange for a reward, is a somewhat grey form of corruption, not because there is disagreement on the principle, but because it is difficult to decide, in practice, what is legitimate influence. Attempts to influence Parliament by means of a petition, or by appearing before a legislative committee during a hearing are examples of legitimate tactics, as is an attempt to influence Parliament or a city council by a public demonstration, although this is usually more controversial (*see* PRESSURE GROUPS). But if a Cabinet minister were to promote mining legislation that would benefit an old friend's company or taxation policies that would help a manufacturer who was also a friend, there would be cause for concern; even if the minister does not benefit personally. These are examples of the "old-boy" network, where political decisions are made not for personal profit but to benefit those who share the same social and economic values as the minister. The study of ELITE politics is frequently concerned with political decisions that are based on the needs and desires of political, administrative and economic elites. Nevertheless, convictions have occurred under section 110 of the Criminal Code, despite the rather subtle nature of the offences. In May 1983, 2 prominent Nova Scotians were convicted of influence peddling and fined $25 000 each. One was a senator in danger of losing his seat. A third individual had been fined $75 000 in the same case one year earlier. The 3 men were prosecuted for charging a fee from distillers in exchange for their influence in securing the distiller's products a place on government liquor-store shelves.

Corrupt campaign financing provides an excellent illustration of changing social and legal norms. Prior to recent federal and provincial statutory innovations, there was no consensus about the degree of corruption involved in excessive campaign contributions and spending. With laws such as Alberta's Election Finances and Contributions Disclosures Act of 1977, which made certain contributions illegal, this has changed. For example, contributions of more than $10 000 to any single political party by an individual, group or company may result in a fine of up to $10 000. The purpose of such laws is to avoid the possibility that wealthy contributors to party campaigns might buy political favours in return. No one would suggest, however, that the laws are foolproof (*see* PARTY FINANCING).

PATRONAGE and nepotism are frequently, but

not universally, condemned as corrupt. Patronage, the practice of hiring and promoting civil servants and other government officials on the basis of their party affiliation rather than merit or ability to do the job, is common in Canada. Patronage can become a major political issue, as it did during the 1984 federal election. During June and July 1984, outgoing PM Pierre Trudeau and incoming PM John Turner appointed at least 225 people, the vast majority of whom were said to be Liberal Party supporters, to senior level government positions as senators, judges, ambassadors, commission members, crown corporation executives and civil servants. Some of these appointments created a great deal of public criticism as an abuse of public office, and at least one member of Trudeau's Cabinet publicly criticized Trudeau for ignoring competence in some of the appointments. Interestingly, Turner's Progressive Conservative opponent, Brian Mulroney, was also criticized for indicating that he too would engage in such activities if he were in a position to do so. Nepotism refers to the hiring and promoting of relatives or friends who are not necessarily qualified. These terms are also applied to the letting of government contracts for the same reasons. Patronage has been defended as a method for ensuring the vitality of the Canadian party system by providing sufficient incentive to recruit prospective party members and even possible candidates for public office. For example, a defeated candidate may, if his party is victorious, be appointed to a government post as a reward for running, but it may be asked whether this is a proper use of public money. A second rationale for patronage is that unless new governments can replace civil servants and other government officials, the permanent administrative personnel may effectively block new programs. This rationale is more difficult to criticize. Critics do argue that patronage is inefficient because employees are not chosen on the basis of their ability to perform a task, and unfair because it discriminates against those who do not support the right party. The debate over this issue has continued since the 1830s, the time of Jacksonian democracy in the US, when patronage became a popular political tool. In Canada, in the 1970s and 1980s, 2 successive Manitoba governments attacked each other with repeated allegations of patronage. The federal and all provincial governments have established PUBLIC SERVICE commissions designed to preclude the practice of patronage or nepotism, but they have not been completely effective because governing parties often consider government jobs the spoils of electoral wars and their followers often demand jobs as a just reward. In recent years, patronage has apparently declined for the lower level civil-service positions but increased for the higher levels.

Finally, pork-barrelling, the offer of a public-works project to a constituency in exchange for its electoral support, is frequently decried by journalists, academics and reform-minded politicians, but continues unabated. Opponents condemn it because rational planning and national or provincial priorities are overridden for local voter support, eg, a road is built in a constituency not because it is needed but as a reward for voting the "right" way. Others claim it is the duty of those who represent constituencies to look after their interests and that all parties dispense such rewards. Examples of pork-barrelling are rampant at almost every election and it is not likely to become illegal, since it would be extremely difficult to decide fairly which campaign promises were pork-barrelling and which were not.

Causes of Corruption Political corruption, according to functional theories, arises in response to societal needs. For example, it has been argued that political machines practise certain forms of corruption in order to provide necessary social services or to provide a less impersonal form of government. Unfortunately, this does not explain why corruption is the only response or why it continues long after the need has evaporated. Another explanation is that corruption is a consequence of greed and the desire for power. Many forms of corruption provide new and illicit avenues to wealth for public officials willing to use them, an explanation frequently advanced to explain corruption in developing nations, where civil servants are comparatively much less well paid than in developed nations. The desire for power, on the other hand, explains why individuals and parties, some of whom are capable of much higher earnings outside government, are still willing to pursue public office through corrupt means. The notion that power is the cause of corruption is frequently noted in political science literature. According to the theory of patron-client relations, corruption is an exchange mechanism which frequently reflects the unequal distribution of wealth and power in society; the relatively powerless can exchange votes or campaign work for something else. Other theories contend that corruption is a persistent but necessary feature of capitalist economics, but this does not account for the chronic corruption in noncapitalist systems, although it can be argued that in these societies power is also unequally distributed.

The consequences of corruption are somewhat clearer and are most noticeable perhaps in the increase in public cynicism and distrust of government and politicians, which may lead to alienation from the political system and a resulting decline in the legitimacy of the state. Corruption creates a major problem for public policy, because public money is being diverted to satisfy the needs of a few. It also affects a nation's image abroad. Canadian governments, relatively virtuous by international standards, are still troubled by corruption despite new legislation and regulations which attempt to control it. Ultimately it is up to the public, however, to demand honest and less self-serving government officials. KENNETH M. GIBBONS

Reading: Kenneth M. Gibbons and Donald C. Rowat, *Political Corruption in Canada* (1976).

Corte-Real, Gaspar, explorer (b 1450?; d 1501). A native of the Azores, he initiated Portuguese claims in the N Atlantic. It is thought that he reached Greenland and worked his way S to Newfoundland in 1500, and that he returned in 1501 with 3 caravels and explored the Labrador coast and Hamilton Inlet. Two of the vessels returned with native captives, but his vessel disappeared. His brother Miguel searched for him the following year but was lost as well. A third brother was refused permission to follow.

JAMES MARSH

Corvée, required labour. Labour demanded of HABITANTS in NEW FRANCE by seigneurs in addition to rent or for pasture rights was illegal and was suppressed by the INTENDANTS. As militiamen, all habitants were required to work on roads, bridges, fortifications and transport; this enforcement of labour was legal and of indeterminate duration and, though resented, it continued after the French regime. By mid-19th century the term had come to mean voluntary help from the community for building a church, erecting a barn, etc. DALE MIQUELON

Cosgrove, Stanley Morel, painter (b at Montréal 23 Dec 1911). Of Irish and French Canadian descent, Cosgrove studied at Montréal's École des beaux-arts and at the Art Assn of Montréal under Charles Maillard and Edwin HOLGATE. With a provincial scholarship in 1939, he pursued his studies in New York C and Mexico. He returned to Montréal in 1944 and taught decorative composition, painting and fresco painting at the École. In 1953 he was awarded a one-year Canadian government fellowship to study in France. Since 1958 he has devoted himself to his own work, participating in numerous group and solo exhibitions. Cosgrove, a member of the Royal Canadian Academy of Arts (1951), is a superb draftsman and fine colourist. His landscapes, still lifes, figures and portraits are characterized by a subtle combination of form and colour. JULES BAZIN

Reading: Jules Bazin, *Cosgrove* (1980).

Cosmology, the branch of ASTRONOMY that studies the cosmos, ie, the universe (in the astronomical sense): its origin, evolution, structure, etc. Since cosmological experiments cannot be performed in a laboratory, the interpretation of observational data is often in dispute. Canadian work has tended to focus on obtaining and interpreting observational data. Although speculation about the universe has occurred since the earliest civilizations, modern cosmology dates from 1917, when Albert Einstein applied his newly developed General Theory of Relativity to produce a geometrical model of the universe. Most cosmological models are now based on General Relativity, the best existing theory of gravity. Such models predict that the expansion of the universe (first observed in the 1920s) began with an explosive origin, a "Big Bang," 10-18 billion years ago.

Modern cosmological theory is predicated on the Cosmological Principle, which assumes that the universe is homogeneous and isotropic (ie, distribution of matter and motion is the same in all directions). In 1922 A. Friedmann, a Russian mathematician, proposed 3 models of the universe: "open," in which the universe expands without limit; "closed," in which the universe expands to a finite size and recollapses; and "flat," in which the universe expands without limit but the rate of expansion of its parts tends towards zero in the infinite future. Significant work in this area is being done by Paul Hickson at University of British Columbia.

American astronomers Edwin Hubble and M.L. Humason, as a result of studies of the spectral lines of galaxies, noted that the galaxies are moving away from each other at great speeds and that the universe is therefore expanding. The Hubble Constant (H_0) relates the radial velocity of a GALAXY to its distance from Earth. Sidney VAN DEN BERGH of the Dominion Astrophysical Observatory, Victoria, and others in the US suggest that the value of the Hubble Constant is in the range 75-100 km per second per megaparsec; Allan Sandage (Mt Wilson Observatory, California) and his colleagues favour 50-60 km/s/Mpc. The age of the universe, ie, the time since the Big Bang, is inversely proportional to Hubble's Constant.

The lumpy structure of the universe, galaxies and clusters of galaxies has become an important area of theoretical research, since simple cosmological models assume a homogeneous distribution of matter. Canadian work in this area includes that of Charles Dyer and Robert Roeder (University of Toronto) on deviations from the "classical" Hubble Law; Charles Hellaby and Kayll Lake (Queen's University) on possibilities of galaxy formation; and Paul Wesson (University of Alberta) on clusters of galaxies.

ROBERT ROEDER

Reading: J. Silk, *The Big Bang* (1980).

Costain, Thomas Bertram, editor, novelist (b at Brantford, Ont 8 May 1885; d at New York, NY 8 Oct 1965). Costain worked as an editor and reporter with several newspapers and magazines and was editor of *Maclean's* from 1914 until 1920 when he emigrated to the US to be associate editor of *Saturday Evening Post*. From 1934 to 1936 he was a story editor at Twentieth-Century Fox, returning to publishing as adviry editor at Doubleday in 1939. His writing reer began in 1942 with publication of *For My eat Folly*, a best-seller. His fast-paced historical ction was extremely popular and sold in the illions. The *Black Rose* (1945) sold over 2 million copies. His novels with Canadian settings re *High Towers* (1949), dealing with the LE OYNE family of New France; and *Son of a Hunred Kings* (1950). He also wrote a history of New ance, *The White and the Gold*. DAVID EVANS

ottnam, Deborah, née How, teacher, poet at Grassy Island, Canso, NS 1728; d at Windr, NS 31 Dec 1806). Polished and literarily clined, Cottnam met the vicissitudes of the ench-English wars and the American evolution with an initiative rare in 18thntury women and established a high standard f female private education in the Maritimes. fter the fall of Canso (1744), Cottnam and her mily were again displaced in the mid-1770s hen their Tory sympathies forced them to flee om Salem, Mass. From 1777 to 1786 Cottnam rected an academy for women in Halifax, oving to Saint John from 1786 to 1793, where e continued to instruct the daughters of the YALIST elite. Her 405 ha settlement in NS was ne of the largest granted to a Loyalist woman nd she retired to Windsor after 1793 with a overnment pension. A classical poet (pseudnym "Portia"), she was an inspiration for her eat-granddaughter, poet Griselda Tonge. GWENDOLYN DAVIES

ouchiching Conference is the usual name for e annual conference held at Geneva Park on ake Couchiching, near Orillia, Ont, by the anadian Institute on Public Affairs (fd in 1932 y the YMCA National Council as an edutional body for the critical discussion of naonal and international issues). The confernces, ordinarily held in August, quickly ecame a gathering place for those interested in e intelligent discussion of Canadian concerns. uring the GREAT DEPRESSION the focus was on ch issues as social reform, the state of the onomy and the darkening world scene, and uring WWII much attention was paid to construction planning. In 1947 the possibility f a military alliance of N Atlantic nations (later ATO) was made public. More recently, Couchhing's topics have ranged widely through polics and international affairs, technology and ther subjects. J.L. GRANATSTEIN

oudres, Île aux, 30 km², 11 km long, 4.3 km ide, 92 m high, is situated 60 km downstream om Québec City in the ST LAWRENCE R estuary. he island consists of 2 Appalachian ridges ined by an embankment. Their rocky upream end forms the coves of L'Eglise and du avre. A broad sandbank surrounds the island. arth tremors are frequent. In 1535 Jacques ARTIER named the island in recognition of its any hazel trees *(coudriers)*. The island was iven as a fief to Etienne de Lessard in 1677, en to the SÉMINAIRE DE QUÉBEC in 1687, and reeived its first colonists around 1720. In 1759 it rovided moorage to the Durell flotilla. Fishing r porpoise took place here. SERGE OCCHIETTI

ougar, puma or mountain lion (*Felis concolor*, amily Felidae), is the most gracile of the New Vorld wild CATS. It has long legs and tail and a mall head. Colour varies from grizzled grey or ght brown to cinnamon or reddish brown; nderparts are dull white. The backs of the ears nd the last 5-8 cm of the tail are black. Cougars re swift, skilful, solitary hunters that run own their prey. They hunt wapiti, deer, hares nd other small game. Their range was northern C, across southern Alberta, Saskatchewan, Onario and Québec to NB and NS, as well as S merica — in fact, wherever their chief prey, eer, was present. Because they were believed to take domestic stock, they have been exterminated in settled N America, but populations still survive in forested mountainous regions. Females breed at 2-3 years and at any time of the year, although 2 kittens (1-6) are usually born in the spring, after 90-97 days gestation. Newborn kittens are spotted and weigh 250-500 g. At 3 months, after weaning, the mother teaches them to climb trees and hunt. Cougars may purr, hiss, growl or scream. C.S. CHURCHER

Cougar (*Felis concolor*), the most gracile of the American wild cats, found in forested areas across Canada. They are taught to climb trees and hunt at 3 months (*photo by Lyn Hancock*).

Coughlan, Laurence, missionary (b at Drummersnave, Ire; d in London, Eng 1784?). Ordained a Church of England priest in 1765, Coughlan sailed to Newfoundland in 1766 under the auspices of the Society for the Propagation of the Gospel. A Methodist in doctrine and discipline, his evangelical labours in the Harbour Grace area were the origin of METHODISM in Newfoundland. He aroused great hostility during his mission, partly because of his abrasive tongue. In 1773, Coughlan left Conception Bay because of ill health. He returned to Great Britain and 3 years later published *An Account of the Work of God in Newfoundland*. J. ROGERS

Coughtry, Graham, painter (b at St-Lambert, Qué 8 June 1931). Coughtry studied at the Ontario Coll of Art 1949-53. His first exhibition was with Michael SNOW at Hart House, U of T, in 1955, and his first one-man show was held the following year at Avrom Isaacs's Greenwich Gallery in Toronto. He became, along with Snow, Joyce WIELAND, Dennis BURTON, Gordon RAYNER, John MEREDITH and others, part of the "Isaacs Group," artists joined by the radicalism of their art and by their interests in dadaism and jazz. Coughtry became a member of the Artists' Jazz Band formed about 1962. Coughtry's work is almost exclusively concerned with the abstracted human figure and is characterized by rich colour and powerful impasto surfaces. Through his teaching at the ONTARIO COLLEGE OF ART, the New School of Art and York, and by the example of his work, he has had a substantial influence on a younger generation of painters in Toronto. DAVID BURNETT

Reading: B. Hale, *Graham Coughtry Retrospective* (1976).

Coulter, John William, writer (b at Belfast, Ire 12 Feb 1888; d at Toronto 1 Dec 1980). Coulter is best known for his historical trilogy *Riel* (1950), *The Crime of Louis Riel* (1968) and *The Trial of Louis Riel* (1968). Most of his other plays are on Irish subjects. Among them, *The House in the Quiet Glen* (1937) won the Dominion Drama Festival Bessborough Trophy and *The Drums Are Out* was premiered at the Abbey Theatre, Dublin, Ire, in 1948. With composer Healey WILLAN he created the first 2 operas commissioned and broadcast by the CBC: *Transit through Fire* (1942) and *Deirdre of the Sorrows* (1944). His nondramatic works include a biography of Winston Churchill and a record of his courtship, *Prelude to a Marriage* (1979). ROTA HERZBERG LISTER

Council of Ministers of Education, Canada (CMEC), modeled on the West German Kultursministerkonferenz, was established in 1967 to provide a collective provincial voice on educational matters to federal government offices and agencies and to facilitate interprovincial consultation and co-operation. One of the council's outstanding accomplishments was that of co-ordinating the OECD review of national policies for education in Canada, which was completed in 1975. It has also administered federally supported official-languages programs in the provinces, the preparation of the metric style manual, and a guide for the equivalency assessment of transfer students. Its concerns include multi-media school programs, computer education, curriculum surveys and the preparation of reports on manpower research. Since 1977 the CMEC has increased its efforts to conduct conferences with representatives of nongovernmental national educational organizations, such as those representing secondlanguage teachers, school trustees, teachers, colleges and university associations.

The council also provides for representation at international meetings, such as those of UNESCO and OECD, and arranges for the hosting of visiting international scholars. The council has no constitutional powers; although council decisions are not binding on any minister of education, decisions of the council generally reflect consensus positions of the provinces. There is unfortunately a continuing turnover in council membership because of the relatively brief tenure of provincial education ministers. JOHN J. BERGEN

Council of Twelve, est 1719 in Nova Scotia to advise the governor, deliberate on bills in the legislature's upper house, and act as a civil court of appeal. Councillors were appointed by the governor and served for life. Until the 1750s the council was dominated by military officers.

After the introduction of REPRESENTATIVE GOVERNMENT in 1758 the council, now including a growing Halifax merchant elite, began to perform both executive and legislative functions, controlling local patronage and land grants and ensuring Halifax's domination over the colony. LOYALISTS were added after Sir John Wentworth, a Loyalist, became governor in 1792. By 1830 the Council consisted of an anglophone, Anglican merchant elite linked by family connection, and including Bishop John Inglis, R.J. UNIACKE and Samual CUNARD.

Growing opposition to the Council's domination came from the middle class, non-Anglicans and a number of young professionals, including Joseph HOWE. In 1836 Howe was elected to the Assembly and demanded an elected council. In 1837 the old council was divided into an appointed legislative council of 19 members and an executive council of 12 which remained dominated by the old elite. The agitation for RESPONSIBLE GOVERNMENT continued, however, and by the 1840s the power of the Halifax elite was broken and its bastion, the legislative council, had collapsed. The executive became the focus of political conflict as reformers continued the struggle until 1848, when responsible government was granted. DAVID MILLS

Countertrade, *see* BARTER.

Country and Western Music roots lie in the British folk tradition, particularly as preserved in the rural mountain areas of the southern US. Pop music, black music and the demands of commercial recording and radio have also influenced C and W music. The Maritimes, parts of Ontario and BC shared a strong folk tradition similar to that of the Appalachian region, and country music found ready acceptance in Canada. Country music was first popularized by fiddlers such as Don MESSER and George Wade, who started their careers on radio in the late 1920s. Canadian Victor Record Co signed Wilf CARTER in 1932, and his success prompted Victor to sign Wade (1933), Hank SNOW (1936) and Hank LaRiviere (1941). Carter, Snow, and later Earl Heywood started a unique style of country music that uses a lower, less nasal-sounding voice with clearer enunciation and fewer of the blues-like slurs and high whining sounds that dominate much American country music. Canadian singers have continued to rely more on the traditional ballad and story songs than on the "cheating" and barroom songs often preferred in the US.

The Great Depression, WWII, a more mobile population, the success of the "singing cowboy" movies, the number of US radio stations with access to Canada, the increasing number of pop adaptations in country music, and national radio shows and tours all increased the popularity of country music throughout the 1930s, 1940s and into the 1950s. Canadian artists have been hampered by the sparse population and the regional nature of the country. Until the mid-1950s country artists relied on live radio shows, extensive regional touring in clubs, and barn-dances and local TV appearances to earn a living. With a shortage of places to perform and the absence of good recording studios many artists, including Ray Griff, Stu Phillips, Lucille Starr and Ronnie Prophet, followed the lead of Hank Snow and moved to the US.

In the 1960s the instrumentation and singing style on country records became more pop oriented. Artists such as Anne MURRAY, R. Harlan Smith and Shirley Eikhardt received airplay on commercial radio. Rock music began to reflect more of its country origins and country music began to use more of a rock beat and to have more explicit lyrics. People like the Good Brothers, Danny Hooper and Colleen Peterson then gained a wider audience. The urban folk boom of the 1960s fostered artists such as Ian and Sylvia Tyson, Gordon LIGHTFOOT, Murray MCLAUCHLAN and Bob Ruzicka, who have both a strong urban and a strong country appeal. The folk-music boom also introduced bluegrass, the jazz of country music, and traditional Canadian fiddle music to a much larger audience, bringing national recognition to Jean CARIGNAN, Graham Townsend, Vic Mullen and others.

Canadian-content regulations for commercial radio in 1970 gave valuable airplay to artists such as Dick Damron, Stompin' Tom CONNORS, Carroll BAKER, Gary BUCK, Dallas Harms and the Family Brown. More radio stations were licensed and more began to program for specialized markets. In 1960 there was one radio station, CFCW in Alberta, featuring country music entirely. By 1982 more than 52 stations programmed some country music during their broadcast day. A corresponding increase in the number of TV stations led to a demand for syndicated TV programs. The Academy of Country Music Entertainment (formed 1975) has sponsored an annual country-music week in different cities across Canada. Country Music Week and the Big Country Awards have brought artists and industry people together and have become major events in the promotion and development of country music. RICHARD GREEN

County is the principal division of land subordinate to the province in Nova Scotia, PEI, New Brunswick, Québec and Ontario. Counties were first established in these provinces, after the English model, for a variety of purposes, principally property registration, local judicial courts, local MUNICIPAL ADMINISTRATION and provincial electoral districts. In PEI, New Brunswick and Québec, the historic county structure is now used only in property description, with the remaining functions being administered through reorganized provincial and municipal structures. In Nova Scotia the county remains a rural administrative unit, with some of the counties divided into districts for municipal purposes. Ontario has retained many of its counties as municipal and judicial units, with some of them united for these purposes although maintaining separate registry offices. Wellington represents the typical county structure in Ontario. There are 22 municipalities united in the county: one city, 4 towns, 5 villages and 12 TOWNSHIPS. The county's functions embrace a variety of services including roads, building inspection and social services, SCHOOL BOARDS and senior-citizen homes. Ontario, north of Muskoka and Algonquin Provincial Park, is organized into districts for judicial and administrative purposes. Québec completely reorganized its municipal county administration in 1979, resulting in new units known as "regional county municipalities" (MRC). The 71 former municipal counties are now components of the 94 new MRCs, 2 urban communities and one regional community. Within this new municipal structure are over 1500 cities, towns, villages and other rural municipalities. The only western province using the county structure is Alberta, where 30 municipal counties and 18 municipal districts have a variety of administrative and educational functions. In BC the word county is used in terms of the county court divisions. Elsewhere in Canada the land division comparable to "county" is usually called a district or rural municipality. ALAN RAYBURN

Reading: C.R. Tindal, *Local Government in Canada* (1979).

Courcelle, Daniel de Rémy de, governor of New France 1665-72 (b in France 1626; d there 24 Oct 1698). Courcelle, a nobleman and a military officer, arrived at Québec "breathing nothing but war" and determined to defeat the powerful Iroquois Confederacy. In the winter of 1666, he led an ill-fated expedition into the Mohawk country, losing many men to cold and hunger but failing to engage the enemy. A second attack later that year established the Frenc for the first time as the principal power in th Great Lakes area. In civil matters, Courcel quarrelled frequently with the INTENDANT, Jea TALON. ALLAN GREE

Coureurs de bois, itinerant, unlicensed fu traders of NEW FRANCE, known as "wood-run ners" to the English on Hudson Bay and "bush lopers" to the Anglo-Dutch of Albany (NY). Fe French colonists had ventured W of the Ottaw R until the mid-1660s, when a sudden drop i the price of beaver, the arrival of some 3000 in dentured servants and soldiers, and peace wit the Iroquois made the change both necessar and feasible. By 1680, despite repeated prohi bitions from the church and colonial author ities, some 500 coureurs de bois were in the L Superior country attempting to outdistance th Indian middlemen. As a result, fewer Indian brought furs to trade at Montréal and Trois Rivières, inducing colonial merchants to hi some coureurs de bois in order to remain i business. Licensing was eventually introduce by the authorities to control the seasonal exodu into the hinterland. Thus professional, "respect able" VOYAGEURS, usually associated with partic ular interior posts, came into being. Renegad traders persisted, becoming the primary bearer of the designation "coureur de bois" after th emergence of New Orleans as an alternative fo cus of the trade in the 18th century. The inde pendent coureurs de bois played a key role in th European exploration of the continent and i establishing trading contacts with the Indians. TOM WIE

Coureurs des côtes, itinerant traders of 18th century rural French Canada, who emerged i significant numbers when LOUISBOURG and th West Indies began to furnish an irregular mar ket for the colony's surplus wheat. Since th countryside was not populous enough to sup port periodic markets, the travelling agent of export merchants increased in number, con stituting formidable competition for sedentar merchants both in the towns and in the *côte* (one of the merchants referred to the itineran buyers as "strolling imps"). Yet presumably th peasants, at least those who were not tied b debt to a resident merchant, appreciated th agents, who offered higher prices and, in man cases, cash advances as well. TOM WIE

Courtenay, BC, City, pop 8992 (1981c), inc 1915 is located on the E coast of Vancouver I, 219 kn by road N of Victoria. The city is situated on narrow plain, with mountains to the W risin to 1830 m. Nearby Forbidden Plateau was onc feared by Indians because of legends of hairy gi ants. An abundance of fish, game and berrie brought a large Comox Indian community t the area. The first white explorers were Spanis navigators in 1791. Rear-Adm George Willian Courtenay (RN) surveyed the area 1846-49. A HBC store was established in the 1850s an white settlement began in the 1860s. Regina Pidcock, who owned the site and built a mil and Nova Scotian Joseph McPhee, who starte the first store and later bought most of Pidcock land, helped develop the community. Comple tion of a road from Victoria 1910 and the arriva 4 years later of the Esquimalt and Nanaimo R spurred Courtenay's growth. Immigration fron England, Scotland and the Maritimes followe WWI.

Courtenay has become a service centre for th surrounding fishing, logging and farming re gion of 35 000 people. CFB Comox and tourisn are also important economic features of thi region. An annual event of increasing im portance is the 9-day winter carnival, which at tracts many visitors to the region's excellen skiing facilities. A special summer attraction i the Courtenay Youth Music Centre, known throughout N America as Canada's summer community of musicians. ALAN F.J. ARTIBISE

Courts of Law The Constitution Act, 1867, provides for provincial superior courts of general jurisdiction to be established by the provinces, with federally appointed judges. These courts are charged with administering all laws in force in Canada, whether enacted by Parliament, provincial legislatures or municipalities. This essentially unitary aspect of Canadian courts is fundamental to the Canadian judicial system. The provinces constitute, maintain and organize superior, county and district courts, of both civil and criminal jurisdiction, and the federal government appoints the judges (*see* JUDICIARY) and pays their salaries. The remaining provincial courts are courts of inferior jurisdiction whose presiding officers are appointed by the province in which they sit. In addition, section 101 of the Act gives Parliament power to "provide for the Constitution, Maintenance and Organization of a General Court of Appeal for Canada, and for the establishment of any additional Courts for the better Administration of the Laws of Canada." All of the courts constituted and appointed solely by the federal government owe their existence to this power. Finally, all courts, except those in Québec, enforce the common LAW. In Québec the source of the civil or noncriminal law is the CIVIL LAW.

Federally Constituted Courts

The Supreme Court of Canada was established in 1875 by the SUPREME COURT Act as a general court of appeal for Canada. The court comprises 9 judges, appointed by the governor-in-council, 3 of whom must come from the Bench or Bar of Québec. The composition of the court can now only be amended by resolutions of Parliament and each province. An amendment relating to the court in other respects can, however, be effected with a parliamentary resolution concurred in by the legislatures of two-thirds of the provinces comprising at least 50% of the population of all of the provinces. The court has, since 1949, been the ultimate court of appeal for Canada. Prior to 1949 the final appellate tribunal was the JUDICIAL COMMITTEE OF THE PRIVY COUNCIL. In 1975, the role and function of the court changed again when the automatic right to appeal to it in civil matters, previously based on a purely monetary criterion, was abolished. Appeals may now only be taken to the Supreme Court with leave of the Supreme Court or of the lower court whose decision is being challenged. There remains a right of appeal in criminal cases in circumstances where one judge of a provincial court of appeal has dissented on a question of law, where an acquittal of an indictable offence by the trial court has been set aside by the court of appeal or where the accused has been found not guilty by reason of insanity.

In civil matters, the court now only hears cases which, in its opinion or in the opinion of the court of appeal, are of importance to the country as a whole or involve some important question of law; these include a large number of cases involving the constitutional validity of federal or provincial statutes and the authority for decisions of government officials and tribunals. Fewer cases involving purely private law issues now are heard by the court. The court must also adjudicate upon questions referred to it by the governor-in-council or appeals from questions referred to provincial courts of appeal by the executive governments of the provinces. These cases, known as references, almost always deal with the constitutional validity of legislation, proposed or existing. References are peculiar to the Canadian legal system. They enable governments to know, expeditiously, whether legislation on which their actions depend is lawful.

The Federal Court of Canada was established by Parliament in 1971. Prior to that time, its predecessor, the Exchequer Court of Canada, established by parliamentary statute, existed principally to judge claims by or against the federal government or matters relating to maritime law (*see* LAW OF THE SEA), COPYRIGHT, patent and trademark law and federal taxation statutes. The FEDERAL COURT of Canada has the same jurisdiction, but also has a supervisory jurisdiction in relation to decisions of tribunals and inferior bodies established by federal law. It is divided into a Trial Division and a Court of Appeal. Generally, matters originate in the Trial Division, but some appeals from, and some actions to set aside decisions of inferior tribunals proceed directly to the Federal Court of Appeal. An appeal lies from the Court of Appeal to the Supreme Court of Canada with leave of either court. The main office of the court is in Ottawa but it regularly sits throughout Canada according to the circumstances of the action and to suit the convenience of the parties. In 1983 several new positions were added to its Trial Division because of its increasing case load.

Other Federal Courts The Court Martial Appeal Court, established under the National Defence Act, is composed of judges of the Federal Court and provincial superior courts named by the governor-in-council. The Court Martial Appeal Court hears appeals from decisions of the service tribunals of the Canadian ARMED FORCES and its decisions can be appealed to the Supreme Court of Canada in a procedure similar to appeals in ordinary criminal matters. The Tax Court of Canada was created in 1983 as a continuation of the Tax Review Board. This court hears and determines appeals on matters arising under the various statutes relating to taxation, eg, the Income Tax Act. Its decisions are subject to review by the Federal Court.

Because they conduct some judicial and quasi-judicial functions, certain federal administrative boards and tribunals are designated courts of record. These include the CANADIAN TRANSPORT COMMISSION, the NATIONAL ENERGY BOARD and the Tariff Board. The decisions of such boards are subject to review by the Federal Court (*see* ADMINISTRATIVE TRIBUNALS).

Courts Established by the Provinces or Territories

Superior Courts Provincial and territorial superior courts can hear and determine any civil cause of action brought before them, with the exception of suits within the exclusive jurisdiction of courts established by Parliament. In criminal matters, superior courts have jurisdiction to hear trials of any serious offences and have exclusive jurisdiction to hear cases involving particularly serious crimes, such as murder, treason and piracy. For a number of other crimes, eg, serious sexual assault, manslaughter and attempted murder, accused persons can demand that their trial be heard by a superior court.

In every province except Alberta JURIES are mandatory in criminal trials for charges over which superior courts have exclusive jurisdiction, and a jury can be demanded by either the prosecution or the accused in every other trial of an indictable offence over which the superior court has jurisdiction. Twelve persons comprise juries in criminal cases, except in the Yukon and NWT, where there are 6 jury members. The constitution of juries for civil cases is now rare. It can be requested by either side when permitted by provincial law, and it is within the discretion of the trial court whether to allow the request. Civil juries have 6 members. In all trials in which a judge and jury are involved, it is the judge's duty to determine questions of law and instruct the jury and the jury's duty to determine the questions of fact.

Superior courts are usually divided into trial and appeal divisions. The appellate division is, in most provinces, called the Court of Appeal; it hears appeals from the trial division and lower courts and its decisions can, subject to certain restrictions, be appealed to the Supreme Court of Canada. In most provinces the Court of Appeal has no original jurisdiction; all cases come to it as appeals from the trial division or from lower courts, the principal exception being the reference procedure whereby the provincial Cabinet may refer questions to the Court of Appeal.

In Newfoundland, NS, Ontario and BC, where the amount of money involved in a civil action surpasses the limit for SMALL-CLAIMS COURT (and is less than a specified amount), county or district courts have jurisdiction to hear civil trials. The trial division of the superior court hears all other civil trials in those provinces and all civil trials in other provinces, without regard to monetary limit. Similarly, in criminal cases in all provinces except Newfoundland, NS, Ontario, BC and Québec, the trial division will hear all trials of indictable offences except those where the accused has elected to be tried by a magistrate or where the offence is one over which the magistrate has absolute jurisdiction. The superior-court trial division is referred to as the Court of Queen's Bench in NB, Manitoba, Saskatchewan and Alberta. In Newfoundland and BC it is called the Supreme Court of the province. Nova Scotia's is entitled the Supreme Court of Nova Scotia Trial Division; Québec's, the Superior Court of Québec. In Ontario the trial division is called the High Court of Justice, which for the purposes of reviewing the actions of administrative tribunals is constituted as the Divisional Court. PEI is unique in that its Supreme Court is the only court (other than provincial criminal courts) in the province, the General Division of which fulfils the function of other provinces' superior trial courts. The Territorial Court of the Yukon exercises superior-court jurisdiction in the YT; in the NWT it is the Supreme Court of the NWT.

County or District Courts At one time all provinces had a system of county or district courts with local jurisdiction within the provinces to hear criminal trials of serious offences not within the exclusive jurisdiction of a superior court or the absolute jurisdiction of a magistrate, and civil cases involving specified amounts of money. Only Newfoundland, NS, Ontario and BC have retained these courts. Newfoundland has no maximum monetary jurisdiction in its district courts, but the maximum amount which can be at issue in county or district courts in each of the other provinces is $50 000, $15 000 and $25 000, respectively. As well as civil and criminal trials, these courts hear appeals from magistrates' or provincial judges' courts in less serious criminal cases. In all other provinces the jurisdiction of county and district courts now belongs to the superior courts.

Provincial or Magistrates' Courts All provinces have courts staffed by judges appointed by the province to deal with lesser criminal matters, including trials of minor or summary conviction offences, trials of serious (indictable) offences where the accused elects to be so tried and preliminary inquiries of indictable offences — a procedure whereby the MAGISTRATE determines whether there is sufficient evidence against the accused to warrant a trial. Although the Criminal Code refers to these judges as magistrates, most provinces have now renamed these courts provincial courts and describe the presiding officers as provincial judges or provincial-court judges. In some provinces, eg, Newfoundland, Ontario and Manitoba, the provincial court (criminal division) handles the matters assigned to magistrates under the Criminal Code, while other divisions handle small claims and such matters as FAMILY LAW. In Québec, similar functions are performed by the Courts of the Sessions of the Peace, and in some cities, by municipal courts. The YT still has a magistrate's court, but the NWT Territorial Court now performs these functions. Most provinces also have a court, presided over by justices of the peace, for minor offences, such as infractions of the provincial and municipal laws. In Québec, this is referred to as the Court of Justices of the Peace, in Ontario, as the Provincial Offences Court.

Family Court While divorces and their results fall under the jurisdiction of a superior court, family courts, which are provincially constituted and appointed, are responsible for custody of and access to children, support obligations and adoption. In most provinces the family court is part of the provincial court. In PEI the provincial court only deals with criminal matters and there is a Family Division of the Supreme Court. In Saskatchewan and in parts of Newfoundland and Ontario, the Unified Family Court, with judges appointed jointly by the federal and provincial governments, can adjudicate all family-law matters, including divorce and division of property.

Juvenile Court Children charged with offences contrary to federal, provincial or municipal laws appear before juvenile court. By 1985 everyone under 18 charged with an offence will come under the jurisdiction of juvenile or youth courts (*see* JUVENILE DELINQUENCY). In most provinces such cases are heard by the family division of the provincial court. In PEI it is the Family Division of the Supreme Court, in Québec the Social Welfare Court, and in Saskatchewan the Unified Family Court that has jurisdiction.

Small-Claims Court is responsible for civil cases involving sums less than a set amount. In Québec this limit is $10 000, but in the other provinces it is $1000, $2000 or $3000. Most provinces have a small-claims or civil division of the provincial court to hear these cases. There are some variations, eg, in Halifax the municipal court can hear cases of less than $500.

Probate or Surrogate Court, established in most provinces and usually presided over by judges of county or superior courts, adjudicates matters involving estates of deceased persons.

P.K. DOODY AND T.B. SMITH

Coutts, James Allan, politician (b at High River, Alta 16 May 1938). Educated at U of A and Harvard, Coutts took an interest in politics at university. After being defeated as a Liberal candidate in 1962, he worked as PM PEARSON's appointments secretary 1963-66. After a period as a private consultant, Coutts returned to Ottawa in 1975 as Pierre TRUDEAU's principal secretary 1975-81. He ran unsuccessfully for Parliament in a by-election in 1981 and in the 1984 general election. Coutts was identified with the reform wing of the Liberal Party and was known for his interest in social-welfare causes.

ROBERT BOTHWELL

Coutume de Paris, the customary law of the *Prévoté et Vicomté de Paris* (written 1510; revised 1580), was a code of law first introduced to NEW FRANCE by the COMPAGNIE DES CENT-ASSOCIÉS in 1627. In 1664, under the royal Act creating the COMPAGNIE DES INDES OCCIDENTALES, it officially became the colony's only legal code. *See* CIVIL CODE.

Couture, Guillaume, teacher, choirmaster, composer (b at Montréal 23 Oct 1851; d there 15 Jan 1915), grandfather of Jean PAPINEAU-COUTURE. One of Canada's music pioneers, Couture studied in Paris with Romain Bussine and Théodore Dubois and in 1875 his *Rêverie* opus 2 was performed in concert, along with works by Duparc, Fauré and Franck. On his return to Montréal that year, he began teaching and also became a music critic for *La Minerve*. Léo-Paul MORIN and Rodolphe PLAMONDON were among his pupils. Renowned for his teaching skill, Couture returned to Paris in 1876 and became choirmaster at Ste-Clotilde church with organists César Franck and Charles Bordes. Late in 1877 he returned to Canada and in 1894 founded and directed the Montréal Symphony Orchestra. Between 1907 and 1909 he composed his major work, the oratorio *Jean le Précurseur*.

HÉLÈNE PLOUFFE

Couture, Joseph-Alphonse, veterinarian (b at Ste-Claire, Qué 15 Dec 1850; d at Québec C 12 Mar 1922). He served in the Canadian militia 1866-68 against the FENIANS and then in the Papal ZOUAVES in Italy, 1868-70. Bilingual, he entered the anglophone Montreal Veterinary College in 1870 and was granted a veterinary degree from McGill in 1873, becoming one of Canada's first francophone veterinarians. He lectured and gave demonstrations in animal anatomy to French-speaking students at Montreal Veterinary Coll 1876-78. Posted to Québec C as a federal veterinary inspector in 1878, he was superintendent of the Animal Quarantine Station at Lévis 1879-1922. He organized this major gateway for purebred livestock imported into Canada to prevent the introduction of epidemic infectious diseases and protect exports of Canadian live animals and animal products. Couture produced the first Canadian textbook on breeding and livestock diseases in 1882. A gifted communicator, he wrote in agricultural journals and spoke at farmer's meetings to support and defend Canadian livestock breeds. Under the pseudonym of Jérôme Aubry he also contributed fiery columns on current religious and socio-political issues of the early 1900s in *La Vérité*, an influential weekly owned by Jules-Paul TARDIVEL.

LOUIS-PHILIPPE PHANEUF

Covington, Arthur Edwin, radio scientist, astronomer (b at Regina, Sask 21 Sept 1913). In 1946 near Ottawa, Covington made the first radio astronomical observations in Canada using surplus equipment from the wartime development of radar at the National Research Council Laboratories. His discovery, during the partial solar eclipse on 23 Nov of that year, that microwave emission was by far weaker from the bright undisturbed surface of the sun than from dark, relatively cooler sunspots was startling. His subsequent pioneering observations on the variability and polarization of sunspot-associated microwave emission stimulated study of how the solar corona is energized above sunspots. In Feb 1947 Covington inaugurated at NRC daily measurements of the total flux from the entire solar surface. The program, which he supervised for 31 years, now provides the longest accurate record of solar radio emission anywhere, precise data often supplanting the sunspot numbers traditionally used as an index of solar activity.

V. GAIZAUSKAS

Cowan, Gary, golfer (b at Kitchener, Ont 28 Oct 1938). One of Canada's finest amateur golfers, Cowan learned his craft under teaching professional Lloyd Tucker in Kitchener. He represented Canada in many international competitions, including the World Amateur and Commonwealth team matches. He was the only Canadian to win 2 US Amateur championships (1966, 1971). He won the 1961 Canadian Amateur championship and between 1964 and 1984 took 9 Ontario Amateurs. He resisted the temptation to turn professional.

LORNE RUBENSTEIN

Cowan, Ian McTaggart, conservationist, educator (b at Edinburgh, Scot 25 June 1910). An outstanding advocate of WILDLIFE MANAGEMENT based on sound research, he has had a distinguished research and teaching career. His field studies in the Rocky Mts in the late 1930s and 1940s, suggesting protection for wolverines and decrying the destruction of grizzlies, were an early call for recognition of the ecological role of predators. There are many prominent ecologists among his graduate students. His research travels, especially in western and northern Canada, have contributed to ornithology and mammalogy, notably through his distributional works on BC birds and mammals. After a career as professor (1945-75) and head of zoology, and dean of arts and science and of graduate studies (1964-75) at UBC, he became chancellor of U of Victoria 1979. He has served on numerous advisory committees, was elected honorary life member and fellow of several learned societies, and has received a Medal of Service, Order of Canada.

MARTIN K. MCNICHOLL

Cowansville, Qué, Town, pop 12 240 (1981c), inc 1931, is located on the S fork of the Yamaska R in the EASTERN TOWNSHIPS of Québec. Named after Peter Cowan, its first postmaster and storekeeper, it was originally settled by LOYALISTS from the US. Its present population is predominantly French Canadian, with a substantial English Canadian presence. Cowansville was an agricultural and textile centre until 1940, when it underwent industrial diversification. Situated about 20 km from the US border and 85 km SE of Montréal, it has attracted several large companies based in the northern states and Ontario. Major industrial employers include producers of consumer and industrial textiles and plastics, printed paper, skis and hockey sticks. Smaller firms supply the construction and transportation sectors of the province. Social services — including the Institut de Cowansville, a federal penitentiary—employ a large professional work force. The town's preserved Victorian architecture and proximity to Mt Brome are tourist attractions.

PAULA KESTELMAN

Cox, George Albertus, financier, philanthropist, senator (b at Colborne, Upper Canada 7 May 1840; d at Toronto 16 Jan 1914). A telegraph operator, Cox became prominent in Peterborough, Ont, as mayor, TEMPERANCE leader and president of the Midland Ry and the Central Loan and Savings Co. In 1888 he moved to Toronto and by 1900 had become one of Canada's most influential businessmen as president of the Bank of Commerce and the Canada Life Assurance Co and founder, president, VP or director of over 40 other firms. Although colleagues found his individualistic business methods and efforts to create a family dynasty inappropriate, Cox symbolized Toronto's aggressive challenge to Montréal's financial leadership in the prewar period. In 1896 Sir Wilfrid LAURIER appointed him to the Senate. A Methodist, Cox helped many needy individuals and contributed generously to that church, Toronto General Hospital and U of Toronto.

JOSEPH LINDSEY

Coyne, James Elliott, banker, businessman (b at Winnipeg 17 July 1910). Coyne became the highly controversial governor of the BANK OF CANADA in 1955 after 17 years with the bank. He warned against the dangers of FOREIGN INVESTMENT and spoke out on economic matters despite the divergence of his views from government policy. His outspokenness caused friction with the DIEFENBAKER government, which already distrusted him because of his close links with prominent Liberals. Ultimately, Coyne's refusal to adopt the government's expansionist MONETARY POLICY irritated not only Finance Minister Donald FLEMING but many leading economists, who signed an open letter calling for his resignation. Coyne initially refused but, confronted with a bill firing him, he stepped down 13 July 1961.

JOHN ENGLISH

Coyote (*Canis latrans*, family Canidae), often called prairie wolf or brush wolf, is inter-

Coyote (*Canis latrans*) is found in Canada's prairies and in open mixed hardwood and coniferous habitats (*photo by Stephen J. Krasemann / DRK Photo*).

mediate in size between WOLF and FOX. It resembles a lightly built German shepherd dog with erect, pointed ears, pointed muzzle, flat forehead, bushy tail (usually held rather low), and coat of long, grey, russet or yellowish brown hair. Coyotes are restricted to the N American prairies and to open mixed hardwood and coniferous habitats. In Canada they are found in BC, YT and western NWT, Alta, central and southern Sask and Man, E to the Maritimes. Coyotes usually breed in Feb; litters of 5-7 pups (maximum 19) are born 60-63 days later (Apr-early May) in a den. Breeding begins at one year, and coyotes mate for life. They co-operate in hunting, denning and raising young. Coyotes can howl, singly or in unison, and reply to howls of other coyotes, wolves or dogs, even car horns or sirens. They are primarily carnivorous, preying chiefly on rabbits and rodents, but also consume insects and fruits. They are considered, mistakenly, a threat to livestock. C.S. CHURCHER

Crab, common name for 2 groups of decapod ("ten-footed") CRUSTACEANS. The Anomura, including hermit, mole and lithoid crabs, have relatively normal abdomens. In true crabs, infraorder Brachyura, including genera *Cancer* and *Carcinus*, the abdomen is greatly reduced in size and flexed beneath the thorax. Worldwide there are 4500 species inhabiting marine, freshwater and terrestrial environments. Crabs comprise one of the largest groups of the subphylum Crustacea; as individuals, they are among the largest of arthropods. Giant Japanese and Australian spider crabs, larger in size than the largest lobsters but weighing somewhat less, may have a claw span of over 3 m and weigh up to 14 kg. In Canada, crabs are found in marine deepwater, intertidal and estuarine environments on both coasts. Some, eg, East Coast snow or queen crab (*Chionoecetes opilio*) and West Coast Dungeness crab (*Cancer magister*), are of considerable economic value. *See* CRUSTACEAN RESOURCES.
D.E. AIKEN

Crab Apple (genus *Malus*), deciduous tree that differs from the orchard APPLE in bearing smaller, often acid, fruits. It is grown for its special ORNAMENTAL attributes (eg, tree form, showy blossoms, colour of fruit) and climatic adaptability. The fruits are valued for their superior jelly-making properties and as preserves. The numerous ancestral wild species probably include *M. sylvestris, M. prunifolia* and *M. pumila*. Considerable efforts have been made in Canada to improve hardiness with *M. baccata*, the Siberian crab apple, as a major source for hardiness. Recently, a number of species have been used as sources of disease resistance; *M. floribunda*, the Japanese flowering crab, has been a major source for resistance to apple scab (*Venturia inaequalis*). Several local forms of *M. fusca* have been collected at University of British Columbia, Vancouver. A.D. CROWE

Cradle Board, or papoose carrier, served (and in some areas still serves) as home to an Indian infant. Securely bound to the thin rectangular board, the baby could be carried on its mother's back or placed out of the way while she worked. The design of the board prevented injury to the child even if the board were to fall over (in many types a hoop or bow at the top of the cradle board served to protect the infant's head). The exact form varied from group to group across the continent, but almost invariably considerable energy was spent decorating the cradle board and its fittings. RENÉ R. GADACZ

Craft Unionism, a form of labour organization developed to promote and defend the interests of skilled workers (variously known as artisans, mechanics, craftsmen and tradesmen). Craft skills have always involved both manual dexterity and conceptual abilities; their value and scarcity have given such workers considerable power in the workplace. Craft unions sought to maintain that power by controlling training, regulating the work process, and insisting that only members should practise any particular trade. Pride and independence bred a spirit of solidarity and led to Canada's first labour movement.

A full-fledged guild system protecting traditional crafts on the British and European model never developed in BNA. Men were generally expected to serve lengthy apprenticeships before becoming fully qualified practitioners or journeymen. Craft unions first appeared early in the 19th century when some journeymen began to recognize their common interests. By the 1830s journeymen shipwrights, printers, tailors, stonecutters, carpenters and others had formed unions and even launched a few strikes for higher wages and improved working conditions. Many of these unions also established mutual-benefit funds to help their members cope with sickness, accident or death.

The first craft unions united skilled workers in single communities but, beginning in the 1850s, craftsmen began to affiliate with larger organizations. At first, British workers established local branches of the unions they had left behind, like the Amalgamated Society of Engineers or the Amalgamated Society of Carpenters and Joiners. But skilled workers in Canada increasingly linked their local unions to such new American craft unions as the Iron Molders' Union and the National Typographical Union, which were organizing workers across the continent — a development that reflected the growing tendency of workers to "tramp" around N America in search of work. This "international unionism" was intended to establish common standards of employment across the continent.

When Canada's INDUSTRIALIZATION began after 1850, many employers attempted to erode craft skills by subdividing tasks among less-skilled workers and by introducing new machinery. By WWI these changes had brought mass production and "scientific" management. Craftsmen used their unions to resist any changes they believed would disrupt work routines, lower wages or threaten unemployment. For the practice of each craft the unions developed much tighter rules and regulations, which employers were expected to accept as a condition of hiring skilled workmen. These new rules governed such matters as apprenticeship, daily workload, hours of labour and tools of the trade.

Many employers resisted these restrictions on their unbridled control, and craft unionists fought hundreds of bitter strikes in the half century before 1920. Craftsmen were often the most vigorous and articulate critics of industrialization, which they believed was degrading the worker and his job. By the 1920s industrialists had driven craft unions out of most workplaces and had transformed work processes so thoroughly that they no longer relied on many scarce handicraft skills. Only in the printing and construction industries did craft unionism survive with any vitality.

Craft unions had a long history of uniting across occupational lines to form labour councils in individual communities, at the national level in the TRADES AND LABOR CONGRESS of Canada, and across the continent in the American Federation of Labor. Craftsmen became uneasy, however, about the rise of INDUSTRIAL UNIONISM, which would unite all workers in a single industry regardless of skill and might dilute the skilled workers' power. In 1919 they opposed the ONE BIG UNION, which promoted the new form of industrial organization, and in the 1930s set themselves against the American-based Congress of Industrial Organizations. In 1939 the TLC succumbed to AFL pressure and ousted CIO unions from its ranks. Some craft unions (eg, machinists' and carpenters' unions) nonetheless broadened their membership base gradually to include workers in mass production and related industries.

In 1956 craft and industrial unionists reunited in the new CANADIAN LABOUR CONGRESS. The friction did not disappear, however, and during the 1970s disputes over craft-union jurisdictions and autonomy of Canadian unions from international headquarters prompted several construction unions to withhold their CLC dues. Suspended in 1981, the following year these craft unions formed a new national organization, the CANADIAN FEDERATION OF LABOUR. Thus craft unionism once again had a distinct identity. *See* WORKING-CLASS HISTORY. CRAIG HERON

Reading: Eugene Forsey, *Trade Unions in Canada, 1812-1902* (1982); Desmond Morton with Terry Copp, *Working People* (1980); Bryan D. Palmer, *Working-Class Experience* (1983); H. Clare Pentland, *Labour and Capital in Canada, 1650-1860* (1981).

Crafts An accurate and useful definition of contemporary crafts is unattainable, partly because the concepts underlying crafts are changing and partly because the word is used in 2 different senses. The root meaning [Ger *kraft*, "strength"] is the skillful application of force, yet, in ordinary speech, the words "art" and "craft" are sometimes used interchangeably to mean a highly skilled occupation, as in the art of cookery or the craft of poetry. As a term for objects, crafts is largely a 20th-century usage; in the 19th century such artifacts were called applied, decorative or ornamental arts, terms which usually meant utilitarian objects that were a pleasure to the senses and showed high skill in execution. Unfortunately the Victorians' love of excessive decoration brought the decorative arts and their producers into disrepute. It was not always so: many of the greatest artists of the Renaissance were trained as goldsmiths and applied their skills equally well to the design of tapestries, goblets, stage sets and more.

By the beginning of the 20th century, crafts had become "handicrafts," ie, products of cottage or home industry. This definition still applies in the Third World where crafts are still a matter of tradition, handed down from parent to child. Side by side with the large demand for utilitarian objects (eg, baskets, pots, boxes) there has always existed a luxury market, ie, objects required for religious or ceremonial purposes or used by the wealthy. This division still exists everywhere. In Europe, N America and Australasia the luxury market often involves objects of "art," ie, unique objects serving a purely aesthetic function, which are made in traditional craft media (eg, clay, fibres, wood, GLASS, metal, LEATHER).

Contemporary Crafts in Canada The 1950s and 1960s saw an upsurge in the number of people producing crafts for a livelihood. In part, this growth was an extension of the self-sufficiency movement of those years. However, the trend (called voluntary simplicity) continues today, partly as a result of high UNEMPLOYMENT. Concurrently the number of hobbyists and "do-it-yourselfers" has increased. Various surveys in Canada indicate that over 1.5 million people spend more than 7 hours per week on a craft; about 12 000 earn their living from making and selling craft items. The retail value of domestically produced crafts in Canada is about $300 million per year. The market for well-made, well-designed things, which express the individuality of the purchaser as well as the producer, has also expanded.

In Canada most raw materials used in crafts (eg, cotton, silk, jute) are imported; the growing of hemp (the source of marijuana and hashish) was banned half a century ago. Recently, concern has arisen about the use of materials from ENDANGERED species (eg, various skins, ivory) but most craft materials are still the traditional ones. Newer substances have given rise to health concerns: craftspeople and hobbyists have unknowingly been put at risk by using solvents, varnishes, glazes, pigments, plastics and additives that have been found to be dangerous. However, craftwork also has considerable therapeutic value. Occupational therapists have long recognized the value of handiwork in rehabilitation and millions of people all over the world simply derive satisfaction and pleasure from working with their hands.

Traditionally, crafts were taught by APPRENTICESHIP or by transmission of skills from parents to children. Various new movements in education led to the use of traditional craft materials (eg, clay) in primary education, but as a means of self-expression, not to instill basic training in the medium. Formal education in craft techniques hardly existed in Canada before the boom in the construction of COMMUNITY COLLEGES in the late 1960s. For example, in Ontario a school of crafts and design was founded and attached to Sheridan College, although the school was residential and intended to teach crafts and design to all Ontario students. There is also considerable demand for evening classes and summer courses teaching the basic skills. In times of economic hardship, schools of crafts and design that are not autonomous are finding their programs being cut and suspended, sometimes whole departments, and, in one case in BC, an entire college.

Modern communications have largely destroyed the distinctive provincial or regional craft styles that once prevailed in Canada. Québec and Newfoundland probably have the greatest claim to distinction, as certain traditional styles have not yet been widely copied, eg, *ceinture fleché* weaving and hooked rugs, respectively. Some provinces have established a particular name, eg, Nova Scotia is well known in Canada and the US for QUILTING. But CERAMICS are extensively produced in every province, WEAVING and surface printing are taught everywhere and there is little distinction between one region and another. Even less common crafts (eg, glassblowing) still share an international style. In Canada as a whole, the most advanced work internationally is probably being done in glass and leather, but these media are not the prerogative of any particular province, although Québec and Ontario, being the largest provinces, also have the greatest number of craftspeople.

Associations Because the basic skills of many crafts are quickly learned, many amateurs attempt to sell what they make. The consequences are an undercutting of the professional market and a deterioration of standards. Craft organizations have long played an important role (in Canada as long ago as 1658) in maintaining standards of quality in design and production. In 1902, in part as a result of the general interest in handicrafts aroused by the Art Nouveau movement, the Women's Art Association succeeded in setting up a shop in Montréal. The group was chartered in 1906 as the Canadian Handicrafts Guild (later renamed the Canadian Guild of Crafts). The objectives of the guild are to encourage, revive and develop crafts; to aid craftsmen in marketing; to undertake, and participate in, exhibitions; to provide craft instruction; and to educate the public in the value of crafts and good handiwork. At the request of Sir Wilfred GRENFELL the guild set up craft centres in Labrador. In Newfoundland, the Outport Nursing Committee (fd in 1920) established a service whereby local women could help pay for nursing and medical care by knitting and weaving goods which were later sold. The trademark for the goods produced later became "NONIA" to reflect the group's new name (Newfoundland Outport Nurses' Industrial Assn).

From its beginning, the guild was interested in native crafts. In 1930 they held a major exhibition of Inuit work in Montréal. In 1933, they formed an Indian Committee to help renew INDIAN ARTS; in 1940, they were asked to include INUIT ART as well. In 1948-49 they appointed James HOUSTON as their representative in the Arctic and it was largely his work that led to a renaissance of Inuit art.

Every province and territory has a major craft organization and there is one national body, the Canadian Crafts Council. If these organizations are still devoted to the aims that stimulated the Canadian Handicrafts Guild in 1906, it is not because they have failed to learn from history but rather because the problems of that time are still with us today. PETER H. WEINRICH

Reading: U. Abrahamson, *Crafts Canada: The Useful Arts* (1974); J. Flanders, *The Craftsman's Way: Canadian Expression* (1981); H. Gordon Green, *A Heritage of Canadian Handicrafts* (1967).

Craig, Sir James Henry, officer, colonial administrator (b at Gibraltar 1748; d at London, Eng 12 Jan 1812). Governor of LOWER CANADA from 1807 to 1811, Craig tried to influence the elections of 1809 and 1810, imprisoning without trial leaders of the Parti canadien in Mar 1810 in what has been called a "reign of terror." Craig, his senior administrators and leading British merchants advocated a variety of ways to eradicate what they viewed as the menaces of democracy and FRENCH CANADIAN NATIONALISM, suggesting union of the Canadas or replacing the Assembly by a primarily British and aristocratic council, abolishing the seigneurial regime, encouraging immigration from Great Britain and the US, church submission to royal prerogative and control of education. Thus they heightened French Canadian nationalism. Under the threat of war between England and the US, Craig strengthened ties with the Indians and reinforced the fortifications of Québec City and the surrounding district. JEAN-PIERRE WALLOT

Craigellachie, BC, located at the W entrance to EAGLE PASS, was the place where Donald SMITH drove the symbolic "last spike" in a ceremony marking the completion of the CANADIAN PACIFIC RY, 7 Nov 1885. It was named for a rocky crag in Morayshire, Scotland, where Smith grew up.

Craigflower Manor and Schoolhouse was built in 1856 by the Puget's Sound Agricultural Co, a subsidiary of the HUDSON'S BAY COMPANY. The manor was to house the manager of Craigflower Farm, developed to provide fresh farm produce to the nearby Hudson's Bay post at Ft Victoria and to form the basis of a permanent agricultural settlement in the area. Craigflower Schoolhouse was built in 1855 to encourage settlers into the community. Both buildings are modest 2-storey wood-frame structures. The combination of classical and Gothic details on the manor was an unusual design feature, but the basic design of both buildings, with their compact rectangular plans and regularly spaced windows, was typical of vernacular building within a British classical tradition. Craigflower Manor and Schoolhouse are owned by the province of BC and have been restored. JANET WRIGHT

Craigie, John Hubert, plant pathologist (b at Merigomish, NS 8 Dec 1887). Craigie discovered the sexual process in rust diseases of wheat. After military service (1914-20), Craigie joined the Dominion Rust Research Laboratory at Winnipeg in 1925 as its specialist in plant diseases. The laboratory was created that year to apply science to crop epidemics that threatened the whole prairie economy, based as it was on Marquis wheat. Earlier scientists assumed that wheat rust (named for its visible red spores) was a single disease that could be controlled by a single chemical or by breeding a naturally rust resistant wheat. By 1916 it was discovered that rust comprised a whole family of diseases which affected different wheat varieties differently. In 1927 Craigie made a fundamental discovery, that the rust organism reproduced sexually. It could hybridize — and thus produce new strains of the disease — every season. This breakthrough provided the intellectual basis for research that continues to this day. Wheat crops have to be monitored constantly to detect new strains of rust as early as possible and the task of breeding new wheats that resist new rusts is never ending (*see* C.H. GOULDEN). Craigie received many honours and awards for his discovery, notably fellowship in the Royal Soc of London. He was director of the Rust Laboratory 1928-4[illegible] and subsequently Dominion botanist in Ottawa. DONALD J.C. PHILLIPSON

Cramp, John Mockett, Baptist minister, writer, educator (b at St Peter's, Isle of Thanet, Eng 25 July 1796; d Wolfville, NS 6 Dec 1881). Although a well-known writer and theologian, Cramp made his important contribution in higher education. After an unsuccessful period at the Canada Baptist Coll, Montréal, Cramp wa[illegible] ppointed president of Acadia Coll, Wolfville. le was president 1850-53 and 1860-69, principal of its theological institute 1853-69, and chairman of faculty" 1856-60. Over these years, e built that small Baptist college into a flourishing institution. He taught a vast array of ourses, established an endowment fund, increased the number of students and professors ignificantly, and still found time for writing, diting and preaching. More than anyone else, ramp shaped the early development of ACADIA NIVERSITY, at a time when most institutions of igher learning in the Maritimes were experiencing severe difficulties. In the process he influenced several generations of Baptist ministers, educators and leaders. BARRY M. MOODY

ranberry, *see* BERRIES, CULTIVATED; BERRIES, WILD.

ranbrook, BC, City, pop 15 915 (1981c), lies ear the western edge of the ROCKY MTN TRENCH, n the Kootenay region, 870 km E of Vancouver. ocated at the apex of 3 large valleys, the Elk to he E, the Central and the Valley of Moyie to the V, it is scenically situated between prominent At Baker (7244 m) and Cranbrook Mtn (6711 m) n the S and W and the massive Kootenay anges to the E. It lies near the prehistoric population centre of the Upper KOOTENAY Indians. he city site was known by Indians and early uropeans as Joseph's Prairie. James Baker, an arly settler, named his lands Cranbrook Farm fter his English birthplace. Railway development in the late 1890s and lumbering at earby Lumberton were the impetus for Cranbrook's growth. Cattle raising developed also to erve railroad construction workers. It later became a CPR divisional point as shops, roundouse and accommodations were centered there. he first urban centre of the region, Cranbrook oday is East Kootenay's main service and commercial centre. Recent expansion of coal mining nd the forest industry has increased its role in varehousing and distribution. To some extent it s integrated commercially with the city of KIMERLEY, 26 km to the N. WILLIAM A. SLOAN

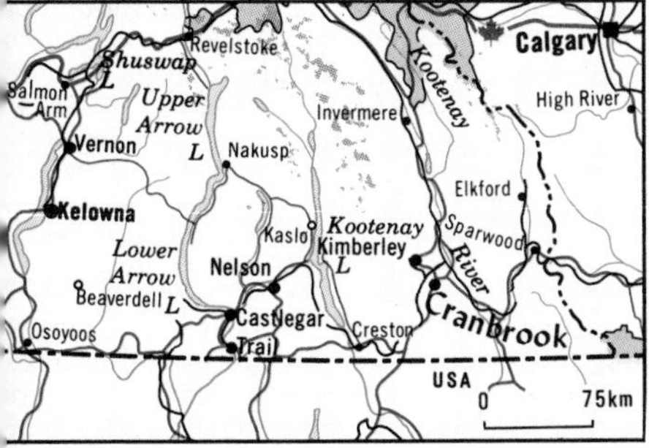

rane (Gruidae), family of large, long-necked IRDS with sturdy bills and long, powerful legs. hey nest in marshes, bogs, sedge meadows and pland tundra. Of the 14 species found worldwide, at least 5 have become rare, partly because f loss of nesting habitat. In Canada, 2 species ccur: sandhill crane (*Grus canadensis*) is common, although the greater sandhill subspecies is onsidered threatened in BC; WHOOPING CRANE *G. americana*) is endangered. The sandhill crane ests as far N as Banks and Devon islands. Nests re large mounds of dry plant material. Usually 2 brown or buff eggs with dark brown or purplish spots and blotches are laid, hatching after bout 30 days. Parents share incubation. During MIGRATION, sandhill cranes favour uplands and agricultural areas and may be seen in spectacular concentrations in south-central Saskatchewan, where they feed in grainfields. arge numbers winter in southern US and Mexico. Limited hunting is allowed in portions of Saskatchewan and in several states of the US. Cranes may live as long as 20 years. E. KUYT

Crawford, Isabella Valancy, author, poet (b at Dublin, Ire 25 Dec 1850; d at Toronto, 12 Feb 1887). The daughter of a rather unsuccessful physician, Crawford emigrated with her family to Canada (1857?) and lived in a succession of Ontario settlements before moving to Peterborough in 1869. There she began to write and publish the poems and stories that became her family's chief source of income following her father's death in 1875. To further her writing career, she moved with her family to Toronto, where they lived in a succession of boarding houses (1883-87). During this productive period she contributed numerous serialized novels and novellas to New York and Toronto publications and wrote much popular verse. The one book of poetry published during her lifetime, *Old Spookses' Pass, Malcolm's Katie, and other poems* (1884), was privately printed and sold few copies, and it was only with J.W. Garvin's *The Collected Poems of Isabella Valancy Crawford* (1905) and Katherine Hale's *Isabella Valancy Crawford* (1923) that she began to be recognized as a serious writer. In the early 1970s renewed interest in Crawford resulted in the publication of forgotten manuscripts and critical articles. Her long narrative poems have received particular attention, but generally she is admired for her unique response to a distinctly Canadian landscape. C.J. TAYLOR

Crawley, Frank Radford, "Budge," film producer (b at Ottawa 14 Nov 1911). Through his company Crawley Films, he has produced hundreds of films over his 40-year career. His vitality and enthusiasm combined with his enterprising nature enabled him to turn his filmmaking hobby into a career. *Île d'Orléans* (1938), a film he made on his honeymoon, won the Hiram Percy Maxim Award for best amateur film 1939. With the outbreak of war there was a pressing need for training films; John GRIERSON hired Crawley's fledging company to make many of them. After the war Crawley Films survived by making films for government and corporate sponsors. *The Loon's Necklace* (1948) won Film of the Year honours at the first Canadian Film Awards, 1949. *Newfoundland Scene* (1950), *The Power Within* (1953), *The Legend of the Raven* (1958) and *The Entertainers* (1967) were all award winners. In the late 1950s Crawley moved his company into TV production and developed an animation studio. Crawley's interest increasingly turned to feature films. *Amanita Pestilens* (1963) was quickly followed by the acclaimed *The Luck of Ginger Coffey* (1964). Crawley also produced the popular *The Rowdyman* (1972), starring Gordon PINSENT. His best-known film, *The Man Who Skied Down Everest* (1976), won an Academy Award for feature-length documentary. PIERS HANDLING

Crayfish, moderately sized freshwater CRUSTACEAN of order Decapoda, similar in appearance to the American LOBSTER. The term is also applied occasionally to marine spiny lobsters, although there have been attempts to discourage this usage. In southern US, the preferred spelling is "crawfish." Crayfish are the *écrevisses* of French

Crayfish (*Orconectes sp.*) shown in pond environment with caddisfly larva and oligochaete (*artwork by Claire Tremblay*).

cuisine. Freshwater crayfish, found on all continents except Africa, number about 300 species worldwide. Distribution spans both hemispheres except for a narrow tropical belt approximately 15-20° on either side of the equator. In Canada, there are 11 species in 2 distinct subfamilies separated by the Rocky Mts. The Pacific watershed of BC contains 2 subspecies of *Pacifastacus lenisculus*. East of the Rockies, there are 9 species in 2 genera: *Orconectes* and *Cambarus*. They are found from Alberta (*Orconectes virilis*) to NB (*Cambarus bartonii*), but the most diverse population appears to be in Ontario, where all 9 species have been recorded. D.E. AIKEN

Credit Bureau provides a credit profile of consumers based on the latter's repayment record of outstanding debts. A credit bureau monitors, with constantly updated information provided by credit card and other lenders, not only whether consumers repay loans but whether they do so regularly and on time. Credit bureaus, unlike investigative agencies, do not assemble information on the life-style or character of individuals, or determine whether or not an individual is credit worthy; that is decided by lenders. Credit bureaus merely provide information to help lenders make decisions. Many of Canada's early credit bureaus were organized by merchants in the 1920s as a more efficient means of maintaining information on the credit history of individuals than the prevailing practice of contacting each other to conduct a credit check. There are about 147 credit bureaus in Canada. A national association, the Associated Credit Bureaus of Canada (est 1939) is based in Toronto. There are also provincial associations. The activities of credit bureaus fall under provincial jurisdiction; legislation in each province allows individuals to know the contents of their credit files and requires credit-granting bodies to advise individuals seeking a loan, a credit card or other financing, that their credit history will be checked. DAVID CRANE

Credit Card, a card authorizing the holder to make purchases on credit. Cards are issued by department stores, banks, credit-card companies, airlines, car-rental agencies, gasoline companies or other businesses. Billings are usually monthly, and interest is generally charged only on the balance outstanding at the end of 30 days or less. Credit-card companies and banks issuing cards usually charge businesses a percentage of the bill as a handling charge, and charge the card user a fee. Payments by credit card are settled between banks and participating institutions through a system administered by the Canadian Payments Association. According to a special 1980 study, by 1978 about 42 million credit cards had been issued in Canada by 35 institutions, but only 5%-7% of total consumer debt resulted from credit-card use because most Canadians pay off the balance owing within the interest-free period. With the computerization of banking operations, however, a client's bank balance will probably be debited instantaneously for the amount of purchases, and if clients wish to postpone payment they will likely incur a true debt. HENRI-PAUL ROUSSEAU

Credit Unions, financial co-operatives that provide deposit, chequing and lending services to the member owners. Owned locally and operated under provincial jurisdiction, they jointly own provincial central organizations. Robert Owen began a consumer co-operative among unemployed weavers of Rochdale, England, in 1844, and co-operative principles for buying and selling were applied to borrowing and lending in an experiment in Germany. The original credit unions were not only mutual self-help societies but a strong moral and spiritual force.

The first successful credit union in Canada, a CAISSE POPULAIRE, was started at Lévis, Qué, in

1900 by Alphonse DESJARDINS. Attempts in the 1920s to establish credit unions in English-speaking areas in Ontario and the West did not succeed. In the 1930s the organizers of the ANTIGONISH MOVEMENT associated themselves with the (American) Credit Union National Association and established a credit union in Broad Cove (1932). Credit unions grew rapidly in Atlantic Canada during the GREAT DEPRESSION, and by the early 1940s they were being established across English Canada. The CCF government in Saskatchewan specifically encouraged their formation. To facilitate the exchange of savings and to help local credit unions become more efficient, credit-union leaders in all the English-speaking provinces organized provincial centrals (called co-operative credit societies or credit-union leagues), which distinguished them in name if not in substance from caisses populaires. In 1953 some of the centrals, along with other nonfinancial co-operatives, organized the Canadian Co-operative Credit Society, a national organization used primarily to transfer funds among the centrals. During the 1950s and 1960s credit unions, which are generally smaller than caisses populaires, grew rapidly, largely through using member savings to provide mortgages and short-term loans. They are able to compete effectively with banks because of low administrative costs, inexpensive premises, and convenient service hours. In the same period, they gradually acquired the legal right to offer most of the financial services, such as chequing, provided by banks. In many areas, particularly on the Prairies and in BC, anyone in a geographic area could join — not just members of a specific trades union or of specific professional or church organizations. Growth continued through to the early 1980s, largely because of the demand for mortgages (caisses populaires have, on the other hand, reduced the proportion of their funds invested in securities and mortgages). In 1982, credit unions in English Canada served over 4.5 million members and had more than $19 billion in assets. Vancouver City Savings Credit Union had more than 75 000 members and $1 billion in assets; several others had over $100 million in assets. IAN MACPHERSON

Créditistes, Québec party involved in federal politics. For nearly 2 decades before its 1958 formation into a political party, the Ralliement des créditistes had operated a mass sociopolitical movement known as the Union des électeurs. With Réal CAOUETTE as their fiery leader, Créditistes burst upon Canadian politics in the 1962 federal election, capturing 26 seats and 26% of the popular vote in Québec. With a handful of western SOCIAL CREDIT members of Parliament, the party held the balance of power in the House of Commons for several years. The party's ideology reflected the traditional right-of-centre attitudes of Québec's rural and small urban population, and embraced Maj C.H. Douglas's monetary-reform ideas. Despite Caouette's spirited leadership, the Créditistes gradually declined after 1962 and disappeared entirely soon after his death in 1976. MICHAEL STEIN

Reading: Michael Stein, *The Dynamics of Right-wing Protest* (1973).

Cree The tribal name originated from a group of Indians near James Bay, recorded by the French as *Kiristinon* and later contracted to Cri, spelled Cree in English. Most Cree use this name only when speaking or writing in English, and have other, more localized names for themselves. Cree live in areas from Alberta to Québec, a geographic distribution larger than that of any other native group in Canada. The major divisions of environment and dialect are the Plains Cree (Alberta and Saskatchewan), Woods Cree (Saskatchewan and Manitoba) and Swampy Cree (Manitoba, Ontario and Québec). Their population in the 1600s is estimated to have been 30 000 and in 1980 was roughly 60 000, with many more not registered under the INDIAN ACT.

Cree Indians from Big Bear's band trading furs inside Fort Pitt, Sask, just before the North-West Rebellion, 1885 (*courtesy Public Archives of Canada/C-14154*).

The Cree language belongs to the Algonquian language family, and the people historically had relations with other Algonquian-speaking tribes, most directly with the MONTAGNAIS-NASKAPI, ALGONQUIN and OJIBWA. For perhaps 7000 years the ancestors of the Cree were thinly spread over much of the woodland area that they still occupy. Following contact with the HUDSON'S BAY CO, some Cree moved westward to trap in the new territories. Those who remained on the plains became the Plains Cree. During the late 1700s and the 1800s, they changed with rapid, dramatic success from trappers and hunters of the forest to HORSE-mounted warriors and BISON hunters. Smallpox, destruction of the bison herds, and INDIAN TREATIES brought the Plains Cree and other "horse-culture" tribes to ruin by the 1880s. Obliged to live on INDIAN RESERVES, they existed by farming, ranching and casual labour, yet the majority preserved their native language and religion.

During this time, many Cree remained in the boreal forest and the tundra area to the north, where a remarkably stable culture persisted. In aboriginal times their living came from hunting moose, caribou, smaller game, geese, ducks and fish, which they preserved by drying over fire. They travelled by CANOE in summer and by SNOWSHOES and TOBOGGAN in winter, living in conical or dome-shaped lodges, clothed in animal skins and making tools from wood, bone, hide and stone. Later, they traded meat, furs and other goods in exchange for metal tools, twin[e] and European goods.

Cree bridle trim (*courtesy National Museums of Canada/National Museum of Man/S75-602*).

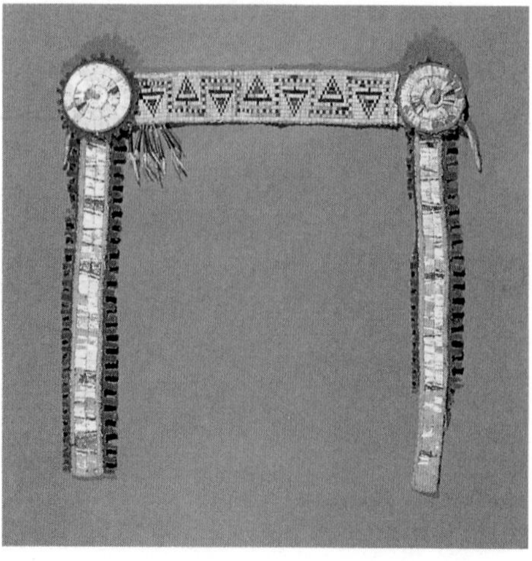

The Cree lived in small BANDS or huntin[g] groups for most of the year, and gathered int[o] larger groups in the summer for socializing, ex[-] changes and ceremonies. Religious life wa[s] based on belief in animal and other spiri[ts] which revealed themselves in dreams. Peopl[e] tried to show respect for each other by an idea[l] ethic of noninterference, in which each individ[-] ual was responsible for his actions and the con[-] sequences of his actions. Leaders in group hunts raids and trading were granted authority in di[-] recting such tasks, but otherwise the ideal was t[o] lead by means of exemplary action and discree[t] suggestion.

The European traders were new authority fig[-] ures, but only while the Cree were at tradin[g] posts, since few white men went into the bush For many years the traders depended on the In[-] dians for fresh meat. Gradually an increasin[g] number of Cree remained near the posts, hunt[-] ing and doing odd jobs and becoming involve[d] in the church, schools and nursing stations. To[-] day, many Cree are townsmen for much of th[e] year; others have migrated to cities, though of[-] ten for only a temporary stay. Self-governmen[t] and economic development are major contem[-] porary goals. *See also* NATIVE PEOPLES, PLAINS; NA[-] TIVE PEOPLES, SUBARCTIC and general articles unde[r] NATIVE PEOPLE. RICHARD J. PRESTO[N]

Reading: D. Ahenakew, *Voices of the Plains Cree* (1977); J. Helm, ed, *Handbook of North American Indians*, vol 6: *Sub[-] arctic* (1981); D. Mandelbaum, *The Plains Cree* (1979).

Cree Lake, 1435 km², elev 487 m, max length 8[?] km, max width 57 km, located in northern Sas[-] katchewan W of REINDEER LK and S of Lk ATH[-] ABASCA, is the fourth-largest lake in Saskatche[-] wan. Containing many islands, one of whic[h] has the settlement of Cree Lake, it drains in [a] northerly direction into the Lk Athabasca sys[-] tem, via Cree R and Black Lk, and eventuall[y] into the DUBAWNT R. A trading post was estab[-] lished there as early as the 1870s, and the presen[t] name (from a French corruption — *Kristeneau* — of an Indian name of unknown origin) wa[s] suggested by J.C. Sproule, a geologist with th[e] Dept of Mines and Resources. DAVID EVAN[S]

Cree Syllabics The CREE language is tradition[-] ally written not in the Roman alphabet but i[n] syllabics, symbols representing a combinatio[n] of consonant and vowel. This system is appro[-] priate for Cree because the language is syllabic i[n] its structure, ie, words are composed o[f] consonant-vowel, consonant-vowel sequences Syllabics work less well for the Athapaskan an[d] Inuktitut (Inuit) languages, for which they wer[e] later adapted.

Syllabics are widely known among Canadia[n] Cree, especially older people who learned th[e] system in mission schools (*see* NATIVE PEOPLE, EDU[-]

ᐅᐱᖕᒑᒥ

ᐅᐱᓐᖕᒑᒥ ᖄᖅᑲᐃᒃ ᑳᖕᒐᓅᖅᑎᐊᖅ
ᐱᐅᔫᐳᖅ.
ᑕᑯᓄᖕᒐ ᑕᑯᔭᖅᖃᐱᑦ ᑕᑯᓂᐊᖅᑐᑎᑦ
ᓄᑖᒍᓕᖅᑐᒥᒃ ᓄᓇᒥᒃ. ᐃᒪᖅ
ᑰᑎᓪᓗᒍ ᓱᖅᑯᔩᓪᓗ ᐅᒥᐊᖅᑐᓐᖑᖃᖅᑐᑦ.
ᓈᓚᒃᓗᒋᑦ ... ᓈᓚᒃᓗᒋᑦ ... ᓈᓚᒃᓗᒋᑦ.
ᖁᐊᓄᐊᑦ ᓂᓪᓕᐊᔪᑦ.
ᐱᖅᑯᖅᑐᐃᑦ ᑎᐱᖕᒋᑦ ᓇᐃᓂᐊᖅᓗᒋᑦ
ᓇᐃᒋᐊᖅᖃᐱᑦ.
ᑕᐃᒫᒃ ᐱᖃᑦᑕᖅᐳᑦ ᐅᐱᓐᖕᒑᒥ.

yllabic version of a poem about winter's exodus (*from* nuktitut, *May 1972*).

ATION). Moreover, syllabics are currently taught n many reserve schools. Although Cree usually onsider the syllabic alphabet to be uniquely In-lian (as opposed to the white man's alphabet), it vas actually devised by the Rev James EVANS at Norway House, Man, in 1840. He had designed similar alphabet for Ojibwa, a closely related anguage, in 1836. Evans produced considerable rinted material in syllabics, largely hymnals nd prayer books.

Evans's system has been modified slightly to dapt to local dialect variation and to increase ts phonetic accuracy (correspondence of sound o alphabet symbol). Nine geometric forms, each ssociated with a consonant (m, p, k, n, y, s, ch, , ø), are rotated through 4 geometric positions representing the vowels a, i, e, o) to produce 36 yllabic characters. A system of final diacritics llows for syllables of consonant-vowel-con-onant structure and for diphthongs (which are are in Cree). A diacritic is also used for /h/.

The system provides a consistent and reliable rthography for Cree and shows no signs of dy-ng out. Rather, it is closely associated with Cree ultural identity. *See also* NATIVE PEOPLE, LAN-UAGES. REGNA DARNELL

eading: Regna Darnell and A.L. Vanek, "The Psycho-ogical Reality of Cree Syllabics" in Regna Darnell, ed, *anadian Languages in their Social Context* (1973); N. Ship-ey, *The James Evans Story* (1966).

reelman, Lyle, nursing administrator (b at Jpper Stewiacke, NS 14 Aug 1908). A school-eacher before becoming a nurse, Creelman graduated from Columbia U, where she special-zed in nursing administration. She began her areer as a public-health administrator in Van-ouver. Immediately after WWII she was ap-ointed chief nurse for the UN relief and reha-ilitation administration in British-occupied Germany. Returning to Canada, she helped arry out an intensive study of public-health ractice. In 1949 she joined the World Health Organization, eventually becoming chief nurs-ng officer, a position which involved her in ursing all over the world. DANIEL FRANCIS

reeper (family Certhiidae), small, brown-acked BIRD with stiff tail and thin, downward-urved bill. Of the 5 species known worldwide, nly brown creeper (*Certhia americana*) is native, ound throughout southern Canada. Creepers orage in a distinctive way, alighting low on a ree trunk, spiralling upwards and probing in revices for insects and spiders. They nest in revices, often behind loose bark, laying 5-7 ggs. Creepers are common in Canada, but are asily overlooked because of their inconspicu-ous habits and colour. In winter they often asso-iate with other birds in mixed-species feeding locks. JAMES N.M. SMITH

Creighton, Donald Grant, historian (b at Toronto 15 July 1902; d at Brooklin, Ont 19 Dec 1979). Creighton studied at Victoria College, U of T, and Balliol College, Oxford. In 1927 he was hired as a lecturer in U of T's Dept of History, becoming professor in 1945, chairman 1954-59 and professor emeritus in 1971. The first of his many books, *The Commercial Empire of the St Lawrence* (1937), established him as the foremost English Canadian historian of his generation. Under the influence of Harold INNIS, Creighton adopted as a first principle the idea of the St Lawrence as the basis of a transcontinental economic and political system: the LAURENTIAN THESIS. He was also committed to history as a literary art, and his 2-volume biography of John A. MACDONALD won the Gov Gen's Award (1952, 1955). As a nationalist with a centralist bias, Creighton in later years spoke out against the threats of continentalism and regionalism. His histories became increasingly didactic and he frequently turned to journalism, where unfortunately his views were open to caricature and exploitation. M. BROOK TAYLOR

Reading: Carl Berger, *The Writing of Canadian History* (1976).

Donald Grant Creighton, a historian committed to history as a literary art. His increasingly didactic works warned against the threats of continentalism and regionalism (*courtesy Public Archives of Canada/PA-123984/Robert Lansdale*).

Creighton, Mary Helen, song collector, folklorist, writer (b at Dartmouth, NS 5 Sept 1899). A pioneer collector of FOLK MUSIC of the Maritimes, Creighton first travelled throughout NS, often on foot, with a melodeon in a wheelbarrow, listening to and transcribing the songs she heard. Short-term teaching jobs provided minimal finances, but she gradually received academic recognition and won 3 Rockefeller Foundation fellowships. After collecting for the Library of Congress she joined the National Museum of Canada and remained for 20 years, ultimately bringing to light over 4000 songs in English, French, Gaelic, Micmac and German. Creighton lectured throughout N America, helped to organize folk choirs, and assisted in CBC presentations of folk music. She is a member of the Order of Canada, has received 5 honorary doctorates and the Canadian Music Council Medal. MABEL H. LAINE

Reading: Helen Creighton, *Bluenose Ghosts* (1957); *Bluenose Magic* (1968) and *A Life in Folklore* (1975).

Crémazie, Octave, bap Claude-Joseph-Olivier, poet, bookseller (b at Québec, Lower Canada 16 Apr 1827; d at Le Havre, France 16 Jan 1879). Known as the father of French Canadian poetry, Crémazie on finishing his studies in 1844 was one of those French Canadians determined to preserve their identity within the United Province of Canada through economic and cultural development. He opened a French bookstore in Québec City, which prospered. He was a founder at Québec of the traditionalist INSTITUT CANADIEN and was its president 1857-58. But it was his poetry which made him famous. His nostalgic evocation of the happiness that preceded the Conquest and the miseries that followed roused his compatriots' fervour. "Le vieux soldat canadien" (1855) and *Le Drapeau de Carillon* (1858) were enthusiastically received and won Crémazie his title as "national bard." He tackled other lyrical subjects as his range of interests broadened, and seemed destined to play a major role in the 1860s literary movement. But after his bookstore's 1862 bankruptcy he fled to France and abandoned poetry. His writings consist of his youthful poetry, his correspondence and a "Journal du siège de Paris." His letters to Henri-Raymond CASGRAIN offer pertinent thoughts on poetry and criticism and his own literary beliefs. Crémazie loved romanticism; realism and fantasy attracted him. This poet who celebrated the glories of his ancestors received extraordinary posthumous acclaim himself. ODETTE CONDEMINE

Crerar, Henry Duncan Graham, army officer (b at Hamilton, Ont 28 Apr 1888; d at Ottawa 1 Apr 1965). A graduate of RMC he was commissioned into the artillery in 1910 and was counter battery staff officer of the Canadian Corps at the end of WWI. Between the wars he held various staff appointments and attended the British Staff College and the Imperial Defence College. He became chief of the general staff in 1940 and must bear much of the responsibility for the dispatch of Canadian troops to HONG KONG in Nov 1941. A month later Crerar was appointed to command of 1 Canadian Corps in the UK; he took that formation to Italy in Nov 1943. He was brought back to England to lead the First Canadian Army in the invasion of France. Promoted full general on 21 Nov 1944, he commanded the field army throughout the NW Europe campaign. He retired in Oct 1946. Although Crerar was an excellent staff officer, he was a mediocre commander, and Field Marshal Montgomery, under whose command First Canadian Army served, had little confidence in him. BRERETON GREENHOUS

Crerar, Thomas Alexander, businessman, politician (b at Molesworth, Ont 17 June 1876; d at Victoria 11 Apr 1975). He taught school, farmed and managed a Farmers' Elevator Co-op in Manitoba. President-manager of the Grain Growers' Grain Co (United Grain Growers), Winnipeg 1907-30, he was a Mill-Gladstonian Liberal and agrarian-reform activist, endorsing the Single Tax and Free Trade and farmers' economic ventures, though sceptical of the wheat pools of the 1920s. Appointed minister of agriculture and privy councillor in the UNION GOVERNMENT in 1917, he resigned in 1919 when agrarian discontent heightened. He reluctantly accepted the formation of a farmers' party and became leader of the PROGRESSIVE PARTY in 1920. Though the Progressives won 65 seats in the 1921 election, Crerar refused official opposition status, hoping for an accommodation with the Liberals. Unable to achieve it, he resigned in 1922, and the Progressives fragmented. Leaving politics in 1925, he resurfaced as minister of railways and canals in 1929 in PM KING's Cabinet. Defeated in 1930, he returned with the Liberals in 1935 as minister of mines and resources. In 1945 he was appointed to the Senate; he resigned in 1966. His business connections were maintained by various directorships, and he was the first politician to be named companion of the Order of Canada (1974). F.J.K. GRIEZIC

Creston, BC, Town, pop 4190 (1981c), inc 1924, is located on the edge of a fertile floodplain near the outlet of the Kootenay R into Kootenay Lk, 760 km E of Vancouver and 10 km SW of Cranbrook. Creston was the home of the prehistoric Lower KOOTENAY band. David THOMPSON travelled the area 1808. The first dikes, built in 1893, were washed out by the great flood of 1894. In 1928-30 the federal government began reclaiming bottomlands on a vast scale (eventually 8100 ha), and the cash-crop area swelled to 18 210 ha. In 1974 a large vegetable-processing plant was built. After agriculture, the most important activities are the forest industries and tourism. The Creston Valley Wildlife Management Area, extending S from Lk Kootenay to the US border, is a stopover point for thousands of migrating waterfowl in spring and fall. WILLIAM A. SLOAN

Cricket Over 2000 species of true crickets (superfamily Grylloidea) are known worldwide. Closely related species include the long-horned grasshoppers, basement-inhabiting camel crickets and katydids. These species resemble GRASSHOPPERS with long antennae. All belong to order Grylloptera, with 96 representatives in Canada. Crickets are frequently wingless. All have hind legs fitted for leaping. Their front wings, when present, lie flat on the back; the ovipositor is needlelike or spear-shaped. Most species are nocturnal and feed on plant and animal matter. Eggs are laid singly in the ground, or in twigs by some species. These eggs overwinter, producing one generation annually in northern areas. Crops and gardens can be severely damaged by black field crickets (genus *Gryllus*), which can also invade dwellings in autumn. Twigs and berry canes are damaged by pale green tree crickets (*Oecanthus*). The chirping songs of true crickets, often high-pitched, pulsating or buzzing, are very familiar. P.W. RIEGERT

Cricket is a game played with a ball and solid wood bat by 2 sides of 11 players on a grassy field centering on 2 wickets, each defended in turn by a batsman. The name may come from the Saxon word *cryce* or the French word *criquet*, both meaning stick. It was probably the first of the major games played in Canada, being popular among the garrisons in the late 18th century. An early contest between the 68th Regiment and the Montreal Cricket Club was reported in 1829. The first regular club formed was probably the St John's Cricket Club (1828).

The first international match in cricket history took place between teams from Canada and the US in Toronto in 1844. Some 5000 spectators watched a Canadian team win. The match began a series that has continued, with interruptions, and is likely the oldest of its kind in the world. On the Canadian side was G.A. Barber, of Upper Canada College, sometimes called the "Father of Canadian Cricket." The game was nurtured in other private schools as well, and in 1847 UCC defeated a provincial team. In 1858, *The Canadian Cricketer's Guide* noted 81 matches played the previous season. The first visit by a team from another continent for sports competition came in 1859, when an English team played in Montréal and Hamilton. (Canadian teams fielded 22 players against England's 11.) International matches continued with visits by English teams (which included the famous Dr W.G. Grace) in 1868 and 1872 and a West Indian side in 1886. A Canadian team toured England in 1887, obtaining the creditable record of 5 wins, 5 losses and 9 draws. Aided by the patronage of the governor general, Lord Lansdowne, by advertising, reporting and the spread of railways, the game was nationwide by the 1890s, and a Canadian Cricket Assn was formed in 1892. However, cricket's earlier claim to be Canada's national sport did not survive the growth of curling and lacrosse.

By 1911-12, when the John Ross Robertson Trophy was first offered for the national championship, there were leagues and associations across Canada. Participation declined in the 1920s but was revived in 1932 by a tour of an Australian team, featuring the famous Don Bradman. In 1936, a strong Canadian team toured England and defeated Marleybone Cricket Club (the traditional name of the English national side) at Lords. The first interprovincial tournament for the Hiram Walker Trophy took place in 1947. The sport was well served by the untiring administrative efforts of Donald King during the 1960s and 1970s, when teams from several countries toured Canada. A highlight was the victory of eastern Canada over the Australians in 1975. Increased sponsorship, expert foreign coaches and a national coaching scheme, and the promising play of Rick Stevens and Glenroy Sealey, along with Canada's first entry into the 1979 World Cup competition, have all combined to raise the status of cricket in Canada. Its popularity may never match it pedigree in Canadian sport history or rival tha of some other sports, but cricket has endure and its status now transcends its former "pioneering" or "ethnic" labels. GERALD REDMON

Reading: R. Bowen, *Cricket: A History of its Growth and Development throughout the World* (1970); *Canadian Cricketer* magazine; J. Hall and R. McCulloch, *Sixty Years of Canadian Cricket* (1895).

Cricket at Trinity College School, Port Hope, Ont. The sport was probably the first of the major games played in Canada (*photo by John deVisser*).

Crime, in modern civilized societies, can be defined officially as acts or omissions prohibite by law and punishable by sanctions. Althoug crime is sometimes viewed broadly as the equivalent of antisocial, immoral and sinful behaviour or as a violation of any important grou standard, no act is legally a crime unless prohibited by law. Conceptions of crime var widely from culture to culture; only treaso (disloyalty to the group) and incest are condemned virtually universally, but were not always treated as crimes. Societies tend to prohibi acts they fear will harm their structure, eg heresy is labelled criminal by theocracies an other states where civil and religious codes o behaviour are not clearly distinguished fro each other; totalitarian regimes make politica dissent criminal and capitalist societies proliferate statutes to protect private property (*se* PROPERTY LAW). Even within one culture the definition of crime will vary over time. Adultery fornication, PROSTITUTION, HOMOSEXUALITY an other disapproved forms of sexual activit sometimes fall under the CRIMINAL CODE of various contemporary societies and sometimes d not. The killing of a human being, a crime in al civilized societies, may in primitive societies b considered a private matter to be settled withi kin groups. On the other hand, if crime is defined as violation of criminal codes enforced b the state, it cannot be said to exist in societie where political and legal institutions are no codified, and where conduct is largely controlled by customs and standards shared by al members. Generally, in primitive societies infractions of social norms are treated as privat wrongs rather than crimes, there is less concer with the state of mind or intention of the offender (*see* MENS REA) and guilt is usually collectively assessed. The criminal codes of moder nations, however, are complicated, growin bodies of written rules.

History of Crime The earliest comprehensiv laws extant, the Babylonian Code of Hammurabi (1900 BC), are apparently based on retribution, eg, "an eye for eye, a tooth for a tooth," bu most early laws allow compensation of th value of an eye or a tooth or any other thing, including life. All codes reflect social class differences. Under Mosaic law the 10 commandment have no punishment attached as such but sever punishment is threatened for the breaking of al kinds of rules, many of them ritual in nature Their application, however, was limited b rules of procedure and evidence which were almost insurmountable as far as establishing crime was concerned. The Greeks too allowe compensation; the word "punishment" in Gree meant *harm money*. After Solon, in the 6th century BC, all Athenian citizens had the righ to initiate prosecutions. In Rome, civil la developed rapidly into a coherent system bu CRIMINAL LAW remained largely a matter of loca custom.

In medieval England, crime was not at firs distinguished from what are now known a civil wrongs (tort) and even killing could b compensated by "werglit" (man-money). Onl the body of the King was excepted, and this exception is now the rule as "the King's peace" an a crime is still charged as having been committed against the Crown. A distinctive body c criminal law developed only after the Norma conquest. Under the influence of Christianity concepts such as guilt ("guilt" derives from geld money paid for a fine) and sentence (first used in conjunction with excommunication) entered the law. Torture was used for extracting confessions and punishments were harsh but their application varied. Criminal prohibitions were increasingly used as a means of social control, as they are now.

In Canada offences are set out in the CRIMINAL CODE, numerous other federal statutes, provincial statutes and municipal bylaws. The Law Reform Commission of Canada has estimated there are about 40 000 offences, not counting those in municipal bylaws, for which Canadian citizens can be prosecuted. Ignorance of these offences is no defence. In addition, most of the more recent offences are ones of "strict liability," meaning commission of the act (*actus reus*) alone constitutes guilt without necessary proof of a mental element such as intent, recklessness or negligence (*see* TORTS).

Measurement and Statistics Information about crime is generally derived from official agencies. Additional information is supplied by research projects and surveys, eg, those on self-reported crimes, victim surveys and special offence groups, that attempt to shed light on the "dark" or unreported crime figures. Even violent crimes, eg, assaults between family members are rarely reported, and it is difficult to establish whether incidents such as wife beating or CHILD ABUSE are increasing or whether they are more frequently detected, reported and prosecuted. Serious problems have plagued national data collection and processing. As a result, the Canadian Centre for Justice Statistics (Juristat) was established in 1981, and is beginning to yield more reliable and useful data, although a consistent national reporting system will still take years to develop. Many provinces have now begun to develop their own data systems.

Crime statistics have to be viewed with reservation. While the national figure for offences reported to the police was about 2.5 million in 1980, charges laid in Ontario alone during the same period were reported to be almost 4 million. Statistics based on offences, offenders or charges yield very different counts. Figures also change in the process from complaint to conviction. Nevertheless, crime figures are constantly quoted. Increases in crime are widely publicized but little notice is taken of decreases. For example, violent crimes have constantly increased, but the most serious and most reliably measured crime, HOMICIDE, has tended to decrease in Canada.

Causes and Explanations of Crime Contemporary literature on causes of crime is linked with literature in anthropology, psychiatry, social psychology and sociology. CRIMINOLOGISTS have studied how people become criminals and the relation of crime rates to culture and social organization. Little systematic theoretical research on crime was conducted until the 20th century; before that this subject was generally treated by theologians, physicians and reformers. During the past 100 years crime has been blamed on the biological constitution and heredity of offenders, their psychological makeup, and social conditions. It has also been seen as an expression of political power. Offenders are a selected group identified by official agencies, but many other people actually commit crimes. Also, crime involves so many different situations and acts that it is difficult to generalize. The definition of crime is not static but contextual, eg, the overrepresentation of native people in Canadian prisons reveals more about cultural differences and social deprivation than about criminal behaviour as such. The 2 territories have consistently a much higher crime rate and rate of imprisonment than any of the provinces.

It is now generally agreed that what is defined and measured as crime reflects the values

Actual Number of Criminal Code Offences[1] with Actual and Percentage Change: Canada, 1977 and 1981
(Source: *Juristat*, vol 2, no 5, Aug 1982)

Offences	*1977*	*1981*	*Actual Change*	*Percent Change*
Violent crime (offences against the person):				
– Homicide	707	647	-60	-8.5
– Attempted murder	684	900	216	31.6
– Kidnapping	536	782	246	45.9
– Sexual offences	10 932	13 313	2 381	21.8
– Assault – Not indecent	103 931	121 077	17 146	16.5
Total	116 790	136 719	19 929	17.1
Property crime:				
a Offences against rights of property (Type "A"):				
– Robbery	19 491	26 292	6 801	34.9
– Breaking and entering	270 659	367 250	96 591	35.7
– Motor vehicle theft	84 252	96 229	11 977	14.2
– Theft	600 821	828 122	227 301	37.8
– Possession of stolen goods	18 433	25 599	7 166	38.9
– Fraud	85 523	112 327	26 804	31.3
Total	1 079 179	1 455 819	376 640	34.9
b Willful and forbidden acts in respect of certain property (Type "B"):				
– Arson	7 569	9 613	2 044	27.0
– Willful damage – Private	214 387	294 972	80 585	37.6
– Willful damage – Public	34 862	35 138	276	0.8
Total	256 818	339 723	82 905	32.3
Total[2]	1 335 997	1 795 542	459 545	34.4
Other Crime:				
a Offences against public order and disorderly conduct:				
– Prostitution	2 843	1 551	-1 292	-45.4
– Gaming and betting	3 487	2 527	-960	-27.5
– Public morals	1 161	950	-211	-18.2
– Indecent acts	9 396	10 837	1 441	15.3
– Disturbing the peace	43 802	43 591	-211	-0.5
– Trespass at night	9 338	11 623	2 285	24.5
Total	70 027	71 079	1 052	1.5
b Offences against the administration of law and justice:				
– Obstructing public peace officer	4 916	6 354	1 438	29.3
– Escaping custody	2 393	2 541	148	6.2
– Prisoner unlawfully at large	2 402	2 530	128	5.3
– Bail violations	29 729	29 534	-195	-0.7
Total	39 440	40 959	1 519	3.9
c Offensive weapon offences:				
– Explosives	366	513	147	40.2
– Prohibited weapons	1 524	2 709	1 185	77.8
– Restricted weapons	2 008	2 047	39	1.9
– Other offensive weapons	9 534	12 437	2 903	30.4
Total	13 432	17 706	4 274	31.8
d Other Criminal Code offences:				
Total	78 334	106 221	27 887	35.6
Total Other crime:	199 233	233 965	34 732	17.3
Criminal Code offences:				
Total	1 654 020	2 168 226	514 206	31.1

Note: 1981 statistics are preliminary and subject to revision.

[1] The offence classification format developed for this release parallels more closely the format employed in the Criminal Code than does the major offence categories of the traditional format. It should not, however, be considered to be a replacement for the traditional format.

[2] The classification of property crime into these 2 categories is similar to the format used in the Criminal Code. Offences categorized as Type "A" crime generally relate to the illegal acquisition and possession of property. Type "B" crime refers to those offences which involve primarily the destruction of property.

and judgements of a society. Changes in crime patterns express social stresses, social change and uncertainties. One of the recent crime waves, the use of prohibited drugs, is a case in point (*see* DRUG USE, NON-MEDICAL).

Classification of Offences Offences and offenders can be classified in many ways. The most common, but not necessarily the most helpful, are groupings of charges according to the various statutes, eg, Criminal Code offences, which include offences against the person (now more frequently referred to as offences of violence, although actual violence may or may not have occurred), offences against property, sex offences and others. Property offences are by far the most common in criminal statistics although, judging from the business of the courts, offences involving motor vehicles are even more common and no less serious, as there is more loss of life, limb and property damage caused by motor vehicles than by traditional street crimes. Social scientists now classify criminal activity according to the discernible behaviour systems of those who practise it (although such classification does not necessarily correlate with crime statistics): violent personal crime, eg, murder, rape, child molesting; occasional property crime, eg, shoplifting, cheque forgery; occupational crime (*see* WHITE-COLLAR CRIME); political crime, eg, treason, sedition, espionage; public-order crime, eg, drunkenness, vagrancy, gambling, drug addiction; conventional crime, eg, ROBBERY, larceny; ORGANIZED CRIME, eg, racketeering; and professional crime, eg, confidence games, forgery, counterfeiting.

General offence classifications, however, tell us little about when and where crime occurs and who is involved. It is often assumed that violence takes place mainly in public places and is committed by strangers, but the opposite is true. With an offence such as theft, which is classified by whether the value of the stolen article(s) was under or over $200, there is no way of knowing whether the thief picked pockets, shoplifted, stole cars or from cars, or was involved in corporate or white-collar crimes. Almost every legitimate activity has its criminal counterpart and there are "grey" areas in between which are often the most profitable (*see* UNDERGROUND ECONOMY). It is important that the bewildering variety of crimes be appreciated if we are to avoid simplistic solutions — the greatest problem with anti-crime measures.

Control of Crime "Keeping the peace" has become the "war against crime." Veritable armies of LAW ENFORCEMENT and correctional officers have grown phenomenally since the 1960s, not only in manpower but in programs and technical sophistication. For example, in 1981 there were over 60 000 POLICE and 21 000 correctional personnel in Canada. Expenditures for correctional services (*see* PRISON) alone were $845 million in 1980-81, a 24% increase over 1978-79. Official expenditures for social defence in Canada are now between $2 and $3 billion annually. The private security industry is larger in many places than the official police force. More attention is paid to housing design, street lighting and security installations, measures that unfortunately also encourage the creation of a fortress mentality.

Punishment, however, is still the basic response to crime. The threat of punishment is supposed to deter the population from committing crime (general deterrence) and accordingly the imposition of punishment is supposed to deter offenders (specific deterrence). There is no conclusive evidence that punishment does deter crime, a fact recognized long before actual studies threw doubts on its effectiveness. Measures such as penitence, work, education and treatment have also been discredited as deterrents. Crime is now seen predominantly as a social and political problem, but class differences and POVERTY cannot be solved by anti-crime agencies. The growing recognition that crime is an expression of human conflict is reflected in new approaches to its solution which attempt at least to reduce the vicious circles of accusation, conviction and punishment. Demands are being made to decriminalize certain forms of behaviour, especially victimless crimes. Diversion programs are being instituted to provide alternative options for offenders (*see* PROBATION AND PAROLE). The basis of victim assistance and compensation programs is that the victim, and not the state, is the hurt party. In sentencing, more stress is laid on restitution and community service orders to try and make offenders responsible for their acts. It is now recognized that even large expenditures on crime control are not likely to reduce crime substantially, and communities and citizens have to recognize their responsibility in crime control. J.W. MOHR

Criminal Code, a federal statute enacted by Parliament pursuant to the CONSTITUTION ACT, 1867, giving to the federal government exclusive jurisdiction to legislate criminal offences in Canada, other offences being incorporated into other federal statutes. The Code not only defines types of conduct that constitute criminal offences, it also establishes the kind and degree of punishment that may be imposed when an individual is convicted of an offence and the procedures to be followed throughout the criminal process (*see* CRIMINAL PROCEDURE).

Based on a proposed codification of English CRIMINAL LAW, the Code was enacted in 1892. It has never been fundamentally revised, although there were consolidations in 1906, 1927 and 1953. The 1953 consolidation was an attempt to reorganize, clarify and reconcile internal inconsistencies. More significantly, perhaps, this consolidation abolished all COMMON-LAW offences (ie, those created by case law rather than by a statute) while preserving common-law defences, justifications and excuses.

Amendments to the Code have been made almost yearly, to keep abreast of technological, social and economic changes in society (eg, amendments regarding theft of telecommunications and the hijacking of aircraft, and those concerning CAPITAL PUNISHMENT, sexual offences, attempted SUICIDE, and ABORTION).

The first portion of the Code consists of enactments of general principles followed by Parts (several sections each) creating offences against the person, offences against property, currency offences and conspiracies. The rest of the Code is concerned with procedure and punishments. It is estimated that 33% of the Criminal Code deals with criminal law procedure and the remaining 66% with criminal law offences and sentencing options available to judges.

The Code has been severely criticized, however, for failing to reflect the attitudes of the majority of Canadians. The federal Department of Justice is currently conducting a review of the Code. The task is to produce a Criminal Code that reflects the essential aims and principles of criminal law in the context of modern Canadian society. A preliminary document entitled *The Criminal Law in Canadian Society* has set forth the major philosophical premise for the review, emphasizing that the criminal law should clearly define criminal conduct and should be used only when other forms of social control are inadequate. It also emphasized that a criminal code must reflect the values and principles set out in the CANADIAN CHARTER OF RIGHTS AND FREEDOMS. It is expected that a major revision of the Code that will, it is hoped, reflect statutory needs of modern Canadian society in the area of criminal law and procedure will be completed shortly. A. PRINGLE

Criminal Investigation involves the investigation of violations of CRIMINAL LAW. In a criminal investigation, the state is responsible for the expense of investigating a case and presenting it in court. This responsibility includes ensuring that all witnesses (prosecution and defence alike) appear at the trial. The victim (if there is one) of the criminal act is considered a witness; the complainant can be compelled to testify in almost all cases. It is the state that decides whether a matter will proceed through the COURTS, and in making this determination it is not bound by the wishes of the victim or complainant. In contrast, in civil court, the person who considers himself wronged must launch the action, secure his own witnesses, serve all processes and be responsible for the costs of the hearing. The 2 processes differ also in the type of penalty handed down. In a criminal matter, convicted individuals either serve a term of imprisonment or pay a fine to the state; in the civil process, there can be no imprisonment and the disputants may be ordered to pay to the offended party certain sums of money.

Constitutionally, the federal government is responsible for legislating in all areas that relate to criminal matters, while the various provinces are responsible for legislating in the areas of POLICING and the administration of justice within their boundaries. Each province has passed a Police Act to meet these responsibilities.

Types of Crime Historically, all CRIMES have devolved either from a trespass against a person or a trespass against a person's property. Today the distinction is less clear because of the growth of numerous so-called victimless crimes. The particular crime being investigated will, to a large degree, dictate the course that an investigation will follow. For example, some crimes are planned and deliberate while others happen spontaneously; some are motivated by revenge, gain, pride or greed; some are committed by people suffering psychological abnormalities.

Evidence A criminal investigation is conducted to identify, gather and preserve evidence. Almost anything can constitute evidence, according to the particular circumstances of a case. The legal definition of evidence, "all means by which a fact may be proved or disproved in a court of law," is of necessity very broad (*see* LAW OF EVIDENCE). Evidence must be factual or based upon factual grounds; opinion evidence is sometimes admissible, usually with the prerequisite that it is an opinion given by an expert on a specific matter. Evidence can also be categorized by the forms it takes (eg, real, documentary or testimonial) and the purpose it serves. Real evidence includes physical objects that are either used in the commission of a crime, are found at the scene of a crime, or will in some way help to prove or disprove evidence that is relevant to a crime. Documentary evidence is any type of document entered as evidence. Testimonial evidence is that given by witnesses under oath at a trial. All evidence will eventually become testimonial because a witness will be required t explain the relevance of a real object or a docu ment. Historically, it was relevance that de termined whether evidence was admissible, bu with the entrenchment of the CANADIAN CHARTE OF RIGHTS AND FREEDOMS admissibility also de pends on how the evidence was gathered. A present the law does not prescribe any pro cedural rules for the conduct of investigation Some indirect regulation has been provided by rule of evidence, according to which a statemer by a suspect will only be admitted as evidenc if a prosecutor can prove the statement wa not induced by fear or hope held out to the sus pect by an authority, ie, if the statement wa "voluntary." Nothing in the law requires tha the police issue a warning about the rights of suspect to remain silent before he or she is inter rogated. Nor does the law oblige the police t prepare a thorough and reliable record of an in terrogation, although both these issues are ad dressed in a recent working paper by the Law Reform Commission of Canada. If, in a judge' view, a suspect's rights have been violated in th process of gathering evidence, the admission c such evidence must be disallowed.

Evidence is also categorized by purpose: dire and circumstantial. Direct evidence denotes tes timony of eyewitnesses to the actual crime. Ci cumstantial evidence supports one of the ci cumstances that forms part of the overall pictur of the crime. For example, B is poisoned and die and there are no witnesses to the murder, but th investigation reveals that A was being black mailed by B, that A purchased an amount of th same type of poison found in the victim's bod and that A's vehicle was seen in the area of B' home on the night of the murder. None of thes facts, in isolation, would be sufficient to convi A of the murder, but their cumulative effe might be sufficient.

Ingredients of Crimes All crimes have essen tial "ingredients," each of which must be prove beyond any reasonable doubt before an individ ual can be convicted. For example, the crime c possession of stolen property is composed of essential ingredients: that the property wa stolen by someone; that the accused had pos session of it; that the accused knew that some one had stolen it; and that the identity of the ac cused is known. The investigator must be awar of the ingredients of a crime before an investi gation commences so that he or she can gathe evidence to support each one.

Investigation of a Crime A criminal investi gation is a search for facts and informatio which can be supplied by witnesses, articles c documents. A criminal investigation may b initiated when a peace officer witnesses th crime or when it is reported, in which case a officer will be dispatched to investigate. Th type and severity of the crime will dictate th rank of the investigating peace officer.

When a crime (regardless of its nature) i reported to the police, a constable will almos always be the first peace officer to respond. De pending upon the crime and the circumstance upon his arrival at the scene of the crime, th constable may do no more than protect the scen to preserve it in its original state; or may arrest suspect and conduct the entire investigatio himself. A constable is trained to attend to vari ous tasks in a specific order: care for any perso in need; arrest the suspect; identify and loca witnesses; and secure whatever physical evi dence is available at the scene. For example, if call is received concerning a robbery of a corne grocery store and if the constable arrives in tim to see the culprit fleeing the store and manage to catch him, and if the culprit is still in pos session of the stolen money, the circumstance are such that there is no need for specialized as sistance from detectives or officers; there i abundant direct and circumstantial evidence.

In another sitution, a constable may be dis-atched to a stabbing in a restaurant. Upon his rrival, he finds the victim dead. The assailant as fled but 2 people witnessed the stabbing. The onstable will order all doors to the restaurant ocked, will ensure that nothing is disturbed, nd will call for specialized help immediately. Ie will endeavour to keep the witnesses at the cene until the homicide detectives and identi-ication officers arrive. He will also summon his mmediate supervisor. Upon the arrival of the etectives, the constable will be relegated to the ole of assistant.

Detectives are trained to investigate crimes, uch as homicide, sex crimes, fraud and arson, which may require protracted work or special-zed knowledge. Where possible, detectives will eek from the victim(s) an exact description of he culprit, with emphasis on unique identi-ying marks such as scars, tattoos or deformities, nd will want to know about weapons used, noney or property stolen, mode and direction of light, and any accessories who might have been nvolved. In many crimes, the culprit is ac-uainted with the victim; in others, the know-edge possessed by the culprit, eg, the place where the money is hidden in a restaurant, is nown only to a few. If the culprit is identified t this stage, all efforts will be made to appre-end him, leaving him less time to create an al-bi or dispose of the property or weapons.

Witnesses are critical to the successful appre-ension of a criminal, but individuals cannot be ompelled to help police or to provide them with information about a crime. However, if witnesses have been identified, they can be com-elled to testify in court, although the pros-cution generally tries to discover, before calling hem to the stand, what they will say.

Physical evidence (eg, anything transferred rom the victim or the scene to the assailant; nything transferred from the assailant to the ictim or the scene), opportunity and motive are lso crucial to a criminal investigation. An ex-erienced detective will seek to understand the ulprit's method of operation ("MO"); he will lso want to know who is in or out of prison at hat time and who has used similar MO's in the ast.

Some crimes are insoluble without the help of nformants. An informant is often a member of he criminal strata of society who may sell in-ormation or who may owe a favour to a partic-lar peace officer. Informants, however, include nyone who can provide information; de-ectives will therefore often try to cultivate riendships with taxi drivers, hotel desk clerks, partment-building managers, etc.

Many police departments in Canada have ad-ertised call-in telephone numbers whereby eople who wish to remain anonymous can rovide information about crimes in return for ash. For example, the TIPS operation of the Ed-nonton police is funded by the business com-unity but manned by police personnel. Each veek, they re-enact an unsolved crime and air it n local television and solicit telephone calls vith information. Most informants are reluc-nt to testify at trial and generally will not be ompelled to do so unless to prove the accused nnocent.

Preservation of Evidence Investigators must ecord and preserve evidence to ensure that it is vailable at trial and to prove that the articles roduced at trial are those that were seized at the me of the investigation. For example, in a nar-otics trial, if continuity of possession by the in-estigator cannot be proved, the defence could llege that between the investigation and the ial there was a switch of substance, creating a asonable doubt about what exactly was taken om the accused. It is critical that any victims' r witnesses' statements be written down as on after the incident as possible, so that people may refresh their memories from these recorded statements prior to testifying. The investigator also records an account of the investigation as soon as possible.

Investigative Aids Criminal investigation has been greatly influenced by technological developments in fields such as forensic science and pathology. For example, in *R* v *Workman and Huculak,* the 2 accused were convicted of murder, although the body of the deceased was never found. There was sufficient circumstantial evidence, much of it of a medical nature, to prove that not only had the deceased been murdered, but that he was murdered by the 2 accused. Technology used in criminal investigation includes breathalyzers, polygraphs, listening devices and surveillance cameras.

Identification Officers Most police departments have Identification Sections staffed by personnel (often civilian) trained in the various methods of evidence gathering, eg, fingerprints and photography. Generally, these specialists are called upon by an investigator either when there are no good witnesses and the investigator has been unable to find sufficient evidence, or if the crime is serious. It has been estimated that latent evidence, eg, fingerprints or other identifying evidence, can be found at the scene of the crime in 50% of cases.

Search Warrants, as a general rule, will be issued by a judge if reasonable grounds exist to believe that the described articles will be found in a described place involving a particular crime. Search warrants empower police to enter private dwellings or other places for the purpose of searching for the articles named in the warrants. In some instances, searches of persons found on the premises are allowed. If evidence is found, it may be seized and held until the trial date.

Conclusion It can be said that successful criminal investigators are fashioned not so much by training and education as by personal traits, eg, qualities such as curiosity, intuition, patience, affability and the ability to judge people's characters and to analyse evidence. The successful investigator may find that these qualities, rather than technical or legal skills learned in training, are crucial to criminal investigation. CHRIS BRAIDEN

Reading: M. Campbell, *A Century of Crime* (1970); R. Ericson, *Making Crime* (1981); Law Reform Commission of Canada, *Police Powers* (1983).

Criminal Law, in its widest sense, includes substantive criminal law, the operation of penal institutions, CRIMINAL PROCEDURE and evidence, and POLICE investigations (*see* CRIMINAL INVESTIGATION). More precisely, the term refers to substantive criminal law — a body of law that prohibits certain kinds of conduct, making particular acts or omissions unlawful and imposing sanctions. In general, the prohibitions contained in criminal offences are concerned with protecting the public at large and the "social values" of society. These values include the preservation of morality (through such laws as the OBSCENITY and PROSTITUTION offences); protection of the person (eg, murder and assault offences); protection of property (eg, theft and fraud offences); preservation of the public peace (eg, incitement to RIOT and causing a disturbance); and preservation of the STATE (eg, TREASON offences).

Underlying all the theories explaining the purpose of criminal law is the basic premise that criminal law is a means by which society reaffirms its values and denounces violators. A change in values entails a change in the types of conduct society wishes to prohibit. Recent amendments to the CRIMINAL CODE in areas such as sexual offences, ABORTION, and punishment for murder, demonstrate that Canadian criminal laws develop, at least to some extent, in response to changing social values. Criminal law has also changed in response to technical advances, eg, recent amendments to the Criminal Code concerning theft of telecommunications, CREDIT CARD fraud and provisions regulating the use of wiretap surveillance.

The sources of substantive criminal law in Canada are limited. Most offences are created by the Criminal Code, which prohibits conviction of an offence at COMMON LAW (except for the offence of contempt of court). Criminal offences are also contained in other related federal statutes, such as the Narcotic Control Act, the Food and Drug Act, and the Young Offenders Act.

A number of federal offences and offences under provincial statutes (eg, liquor and highway control offences) and municipal bylaws (eg, parking tickets, pet control) are not criminal offences in the true sense, but are generally processed through the courts in the same general manner as criminal offences. These offences are often called "regulatory offences."

Origin of Criminal Law

According to the CONSTITUTION ACT, 1867, Parliament was granted legislative jurisdiction with respect to "the criminal law, except for the Constitution of the Courts of Criminal Jurisdiction, but including the Procedure in Criminal Matters." This particular constitutional provision gives the federal government power to pass laws concerning criminal law and procedure. The provinces can pass legislation dealing with subjects in which the provinces have constitutional power and can enforce these laws (under s92 of the Constitution Act, 1867) by imposing "punishment by fine, penalty, or imprisonment." It is therefore possible to have "provincial offences" enacted by the province, but if these offences conflict with a parliamentary statute passed under the federal government's criminal-law power, the federal law is generally paramount. The provinces were also granted legislative competence concerning "the administration of justice in the Province, including the Constitution, Maintenance and Organization of Provincial Courts, both of Civil and of Criminal Jurisdiction." Therefore, POLICING, appointment of prosecutors, administration of the COURTS and appointment of lower-court judges are provincial responsibilities. The appointment of county and supreme court judges is a federal responsibility under s96 of the Constitution Act (*see* JUDICIARY).

Criminal law and procedures are subject to provisions of the CANADIAN CHARTER OF RIGHTS AND FREEDOMS. The charter is part of the Constitution of Canada. The CONSTITUTION ACT, 1982, holds that "the Constitution of Canada is the Supreme Law of Canada, and any law that is inconsistent with the provisions of the Constitution is, to the extent of the inconsistency, of no force and effect." The courts must therefore measure all legislation, including the Criminal Code and related statutes, against the charter's provisions. The charter may directly affect criminal-law procedure and may have an impact on the definition of certain crimes and the resulting punishment.

It is a cardinal principle of Canadian criminal law that there can be no crime or punishment except in accordance with fixed, predetermined LAW. To this end, the courts have concluded that a criminal prohibition must be in existence at the time of the alleged crime and that the offence created by such prohibition must be clearly ascertainable. If the provision providing for the criminal offence is ambiguous, then it will be interpreted by the courts in favour of the accused.

The application of the criminal law by police, prosecutors, judges and juries depends very much upon the facts of each case. Courts seek to apply the law consistently. Judges, when determining the law applicable to a case, are influenced greatly by previous court decisions, ie, "precedents" involving similar situations. The fact that judges tend to follow precedents creates consistency in the interpretation of the statutory law and helps to indicate how the law will be interpreted in the future. An appeal system exists in the criminal courts not only to correct injustices but also to avoid inconsistencies in the application of the law itself. Previous legal precedents, upon which the judge hearing the case feels bound, can be overruled by higher courts if it can be demonstrated that the precedent is either wrongly decided or out of date.

There are many legal wrongs that are not crimes. These wrongs fall in the field of CIVIL LAW and are the basis of private law suits. A civil action is a private legal proceeding brought to court by one person against another. A civil court can compensate the aggrieved party by providing monetary damages or, in some cases, can cause the defendant to rectify the wrong caused. In criminal law a crime is a wrong against the community as a whole rather than against the individual victim; a criminal prosecution is launched by the state and the victim is merely a voluntary (and sometimes reluctant) witness for the prosecution.

Constituents of a Crime

A crime may be divided into 2 elements: the prohibited conduct or act (*actus reas*) and the required mental element (MENS REA). Generally, before an act can become a crime it must fall precisely within the definition of the offence. It may be an act of omission as well as commission. It is a general rule that individuals cannot be found guilty of an offence for only hoping or thinking that they had committed it.

Mens rea ("guilty mind") is a difficult concept. It is not defined in the Criminal Code and in Canada, depending upon the particular offence, the prosecution may be required to prove a state of mind that may include either intention (the most common state of mind required to be proven in criminal cases), advertent negligence, knowledge, recklessness, willful blindness or more specific states of mind contemplated by such words as "maliciously or fraudulently." Nevertheless, there is still an overriding principle in the criminal law that there is no criminal responsibility unless the guilty mind required by the offence can be proven. Most criminal trials are in fact contested on the basis of whether the accused had the requisite state of mind rather than whether he actually performed the prohibited act. This state of mind has to be proven with the same certainty as the other ingredients of a crime, and the prosecution must therefore present a clear picture of what was in the individual's mind at the time the offence was committed. In order to ease this difficulty, the common law generally recognizes the commonsense notion that a person can be said to have intended the natural and probable consequences of his acts. Furthermore, some criminal law statutes create or recognize a presumption or inference regarding the required mental element.

In regulatory offences, the law distinguishes 3 different forms of the mental element. If the legislation uses words such as "wilfully" or "intentionally," the legislature is presumed to have intended that the mental element required is an intent to commit the prohibited act. For the second class of regulatory offences, eg, those relating to PUBLIC HEALTH, highway traffic, ENVIRONMENTAL LAW, and safety in the workplace, it is only necessary that the accused knows that his acts or omissions may result in the offence being committed. The final category of regulatory offences (strict liability offences) requires no mental element whatsoever and there is consequently no necessity of proving any fault on the part of the accused; the Crown need only prove the prohibited act.

Defences

Both the Criminal Code and the COMMON LAW recognize a number of defences to criminal charges.

Defence of Capacity In certain cases individuals will be found not guilty, even though the prohibited act and the intention to commit this act are proven, because the individuals are deemed incapable by law of committing the offence in question. For example, any child under the age of 7 years cannot commit a criminal offence, and children between the ages of 7 and 14 are conditionally exempted. As well, there may be persons whom the law deems physically incapable of committing certain offences. For example, under the Criminal Code, a boy under 14 is deemed incapable of committing sexual assault or related offences. Practically speaking, any boy or girl under the age of 18 must be tried in the juvenile courts under the Young Offenders Act unless he or she is ordered to stand trial in the adult court by a juvenile court judge (*see* JUVENILE JUSTICE SYSTEM). Insane persons are also considered to be incapable of committing criminal offences. Section 16 of the Criminal Code presumes that everyone is sane but permits defendants to establish that they were insane at the time of the commission of an offence. If insanity is established, then the person is found to be not guilty by reason of insanity and is detained indeterminately for treatment until a government-appointed board of review determines that the individual may return to society. An individual cannot be found guilty of a crime if he or she is unfit to stand trial because of mental illness. These individuals are held in hospitals until they recover sufficiently to understand the legal proceedings against them.

Defences that Negate Proof of the Prohibited Act To prove that someone has committed a prohibited act, it must be demonstrated that the act or omission was consciously and voluntarily committed. For example, a person who commits an offence while sleepwalking is not guilty of the charge. Offences in this category include accident, duress (ie, a person has been compelled to commit an offence because his, or his family's, life or safety have been threatened), and automatism, which may be generally defined as involuntary, unconscious behaviour where the physical movements are performed without volition or without exercise of the will (eg, a person, as a result of an external blow to the head, commits a prohibited act while in an unconscious or semiconscious state).

Defences that Negate Proof of Mens Rea In most "true" criminal offences, the Crown must prove that, before committing the act, the accused actually intended to achieve the unlawful consequence or realized that there was a possibility that the unlawful consequence might come about as a result of the action. The law recognizes that certain factors raise a reasonable doubt that the person intended to achieve the unlawful consequence. The defences usually mentioned in this context include intoxication (which is commonly used to reduce a murder charge to the lesser offence of manslaughter), honest mistake of fact, and, in some very limited circumstances, mistake of law. However, in the vast majority of factual situations, ignorance of the law provides no defence.

Defences of Excuse or Justification With these defences the law recognizes human frailty and weaknesses and will hold that the accused was either justified in committing the unlawful act or is at least partially excused for the conduct. Examples of defences of justification are self-defence and defence of property. Defences of excuse include obedience to authority (eg, a soldier who believes he is simply obeying lawful orders), provocation (which only applies in murder cases and involves a killing committed in the heat of passion, which has been caused suddenly by a wrongful act or insult sufficient t deprive an ordinary person of his self-control, and entrapment (in which the person has committed the offence under pressure to do so by police authorities).

Under Canadian law, criminal responsibilit may be placed on parties other than the actua perpetrator. Persons who aid, assist or counse the commission of an offence can be foun guilty of the same offence as the actual perpetrator. Also, attempting or conspiring to commit a crime or counselling an offence that is nc actually committed are all criminal offences However, courts have held that mere preparation to commit a crime is not sufficient to constitute an attempt.

In any criminal trial, one of the most important principles of all is the presumption o innocence. According to this principle, th Crown must prove the guilt of the accused, an it is not for the accused to establish innocence Furthermore, the Crown must establish guil beyond a reasonable doubt. This principle ha been enshrined in the Charter and is considere by many to be one of the most important pro tections for the individual against the state.

Sanctions

If an individual is convicted of a criminal offence, the presiding judge must impose a sentence. In Canada, judges have a great deal of discretion in sentencing. There are few mandator minimum sentences and the maximum sentences given in the Criminal Code are generall set quite high. A judge may choose an absolut discharge, conditional discharge, probation, suspended sentence, fines or imprisonment.

In determining an appropriate sentence judges must consider a multitude of factors an remind themselves that each sentencing i unique because the individual characteristics o each crime and offender are never the same Some of the more important factors that the take into consideration when imposing sentenc are the degree of premeditation, whether the accused has a previous criminal record, the gravit of the crime committed, the degree of participation of the offender in the crime, the incidenc of this particular crime in the jurisdiction, pas sentences imposed for the same or similar offences, and the age, life-style and personality c the offender. A. PRINGL

Criminal Procedure is an integral but distinc part of CRIMINAL LAW in Canada. It is distinc from the substance of criminal law in that i does not define the type of conduct that constitutes a criminal offence or establishes punishment, but rather determines by whom an in what circumstances prosecutions against ac cused offenders may be initiated, conducted, terminated and appealed. Criminal procedure i a set of rules according to which the substantiv law is administered. The principal objective c criminal law procedure is to ensure a just dis position of the issues being tried by the cour which ultimately result in a determination c guilt or innocence and the resulting sentence i the accused is convicted. Determination of thes issues is made in accord with those principle that Canadians have accepted as reflecting th proper balance between the value of protectio of society and the value of individual freedor (*see* LAW AND SOCIETY).

Criminal procedure commences long befor an accused person appears in court, as detaile laws cover how police may investigate a crim (*see* CRIMINAL INVESTIGATION). For example, the are many procedural rules in the CRIMINAL COD or in the COMMON LAW that define how an when police may interrogate witnesses or sus pects, search persons and places, arrest suspect seize evidence, and use telephone wiretap Criminal procedure then sets out the rules as t how a charge is laid, when accused persons wi obtain bail, and in what court they will eventually have their trial. The actual court process is set in motion by the swearing of an Information (popularly known as a charge) before a justice of the peace or MAGISTRATE. An Information is an allegation by a citizen (usually a police officer) that reasonable and probable grounds exist to believe another person (the accused) has committed a crime.

All offences in Canada may be classified as indictable (the more serious) or summary conviction (the less serious). Some offences may, at the discretion of the Crown, be prosecuted either by indictment or by summary conviction. The trial of summary conviction offences is either before a magistrate or a justice of the peace, and generally carry a maximum punishment of $500.00 or 6 months in PRISON. Summary conviction proceedings generally have a limitation period of 6 months from the date of the offence.

Procedure with respect to indictable offences is more complicated and varies from province to province. Depending upon the type of indictable offence, the Criminal Code will determine whether the trial can be heard by a magistrate, a high-court judge (county, district, supreme or Queen's bench judges appointed by the federal government), or a court composed of a judge and JURY. Generally, when an accused is going to have a trial by a high-court judge or a court composed of a judge and jury, he has the right to a preliminary hearing. There are several procedural provisions in the Criminal Code that deal with how the preliminary hearing should be conducted and what rights the accused has at this stage of the criminal prosecution. The preliminary hearing is held by a magistrate and the Crown prosecutor presents the witnesses that he will rely upon at the trial. The public is allowed to attend a preliminary hearing, but often the press are not able to report the evidence heard. The issue at the preliminary hearing is not to determine innocence or guilt, but whether there is sufficient evidence to justify a trial. If it is decided sufficient evidence exists, the accused will be committed to stand trial in the higher court by the magistrate. There is no specific time limitation regarding when the accused must be charged with an indictable offence, although the CANADIAN CHARTER OF RIGHTS AND FREEDOMS indicates that an accused must have a trial within a reasonable time. The maximum punishment for each indictable offence is set out in the Criminal Code and varies from offence to offence. Whether an accused is charged with a summary conviction offence or an indictable offence, he is eventually called upon to indicate in open court whether he pleads guilty or not guilty. If the plea is not guilty, the case will proceed to trial; if guilty, then a sentencing will take place before the judge who received the plea. There are several procedural rules as to how guilty pleas may be entered and how a judge may sentence an accused. In all criminal cases, both the accused and the Crown may have statutory rights of appeal against the determination of guilt or innocence, as well as sentence. Once again, there are many procedural rules governing appeals.

There are different theories concerning the best method of achieving a balance between the control of crime and the protection of individual rights. In Canada, England and the US, an adversarial or accusatorial system is used, in contrast to the inquisitorial system practised in France. Canadian procedural rules are therefore designed to support the adversarial system in which the proceeding is a dispute between the state or Crown and the defendant or accused. As has been indicated above, the parties appear before an independent arbitrator, either a judge or jury, who must determine the guilt or innocence of the alleged offender. Both parties are responsible for gathering and presenting evidence. The arbitrator is expected to play a relatively passive role, maintaining an impression of independence and impartiality, and ensuring that the rules of procedure are observed. In contrast, the inquisitorial system is a judicial inquiry. The responsibility for investigating and bringing out the facts rests upon the decision maker. The parties' roles are relatively restricted to ensuring that their interests are properly handled during the trial.

The adversarial system and the procedural rules that comprise that system unquestionably favour the accused to a greater degree than does the inquisitorial system. The Crown generally has the burden of adducing evidence to prove the guilt of the accused, who is almost always entitled to a presumption of innocence until the Crown has proven otherwise beyond a reasonable doubt. With very few exceptions, the accused is not required to give evidence and the court must acquit him if the Crown has not proven its case. The accused may still be actively involved in the trial, as he (or his counsel) is closely involved in the process through such techniques as the cross-examination of crown witnesses. On conclusion of the Crown's case, the accused may elect to call his own witnesses and testify himself. This is very different from the inquisitorial system in which the accused is generally subjected, without election on his part, to extensive questioning, but is otherwise inactive in the process.

Nevertheless, certain principles are common to both systems, including the requirements that trials be public, that determinations be based on evidence presented in open court, and that the accused is presumed innocent until proven guilty. However, even though both systems may be based on the same principles, there are differences in the manner in which these principles are applied.

The Constitution Act, 1867, gave the federal government jurisdiction to legislate with respect to "the criminal law, except the constitution of Courts of criminal jurisdiction, but including the procedure in criminal matters." Pursuant to this authority, Parliament has incorporated most Canadian procedural rules in the Criminal Code. Related statutes, such as the Narcotic Control Act, also include their own specific procedures, and in fact most federal statutes will contain at least some procedural rules. Some procedure has been established through case law (judicial decisions) and some are the result of local, provincial or national practice.

A very important development in Canadian criminal procedure (as in most, if not all, areas of criminal law) is the inclusion of the Canadian Charter of Rights and Freedoms into the Constitution Act, 1982. Although the Charter does not set out any procedural rules, it does provide many of the principles that procedural rules must follow. Legislative procedures, eg, the reverse onus requirement (in which the accused must prove his innocence) under the possession for the purpose of trafficking offence found in the Narcotic Control Act, have been struck down as contrary to the Charter. Judicial interpretation of procedural rules has also been affected by the Charter. A. PRINGLE

Criminology is a subfield of SOCIOLOGY. At the beginning of the 20th century criminology was primarily limited to trying to explain the behaviour of those who committed crimes. Since then criminologists have examined as well the characteristics of societies, the clash between cultural values, family characteristics, and a variety of social factors. Studies of prisons initially focused on individual inmates, but by the 1930s the "culture" of inmate society was being studied. Criminal behaviour is now viewed as something integral to a complex society, rather than as something inherent in individuals. Recently, criminologists have studied the POLICE, the courts, and other aspects of the social-control system, and WHITE-COLLAR CRIMES and crimes without victims, eg, DRUG USE and PROSTITUTION.

The Université de Montréal established the first School of Criminology in Canada in 1960. In 1984 the school had approximately 20 professors and 400 students, and offered 60 courses in criminology. The approach is interdisciplinary and includes academic programs leading to BA, MA and PhD degrees. While much of the work is theoretical, some courses provide training for workers in the field, eg, correctional services. In 1970 an International Centre for Comparative Criminology was also established at U de M.

The Centre of Criminology at University of Toronto was established initially (1963) as a research organization. Although much early research was oriented towards law, the centre later reflected the influence of informal links with the Clarke Institute of Psychiatry. The centre has conducted research on the police, the courts and other agencies of control in Canada.

Criminology at University of Alberta is under the auspices of the Department of Sociology. By the early 1970s, 1000 students were enrolled in 5 courses of introductory criminology; and 1000 others in deviance courses, advanced criminology and graduate seminars. An American-trained criminologist, Gwynn Nettler, influenced criminology in Canada by supervising doctoral dissertations of many professors who are now teaching criminology. His textbook, *Explaining Crime*, has been popular both in the US and in Canada. The Centre for Criminological Research at U of A was established in 1977 and currently sponsors seminars, research and other activities.

The Department of Criminology at University of Ottawa was created in 1967 to offer an MA program. The interdisciplinary program in both French and English stresses applied criminology. With no criminology courses or professors in 1973, the Department of Criminology at Simon Fraser University grew to 20 members by 1979. Extensive financial support from the BC government made this possible. An MA program is in place and a PhD program is being planned. The Human Justice Program established at the University of Regina in 1977, with a grant from the federal SOLICITOR GENERAL, offers an undergraduate degree in criminal justice, conducts contract research within Saskatchewan and has established a Prairie Justice Research Consortium.

Other criminology programs have been developed at Carleton University, University of Manitoba and University of Windsor. A police administration program has been introduced at St Mary's University in Halifax and the Atlantic Institute of Criminology was established at Dalhousie University.

Criminologists in Canada may approach their field from different perspectives. According to traditional theories the source of deviant behaviour is located in factors such as personality, family structures, CULTURE, social disorganization and differences in opportunity (*see* SOCIAL MOBILITY). Those who embrace these theories argue that rules for living are shared by all and that it is therefore the behaviour of those who violate the rules that deserves attention. Other criminologists hold that deviant behaviour cannot be studied apart from particular historical forms of political and economic organization and that it is important to study the powerful groups in society and the way they exert control over others (*see* SOCIAL CLASS).

Regardless of the theory employed, there is little evidence that Canadian criminologists have had much impact on legislation or on the criminal justice system. For example, although criminological research suggests that laws regarding marijuana are unrealistically harsh; that the numbers of inmates incarcerated and the length of time they serve does little to reduce crime; that the preponderance of persons from lower socioeconomic groups in prison creates cynicism about social justice; and that the offences of those in higher socioeconomic brackets are much more damaging to society than those committed by persons in lower socioeconomic brackets, this research has not influenced government policy.

When political pressures do lead to new legislation, the research that is compatible with the winds of political change may be acknowledged. For example, changes in policy regarding wife beating and CHILD ABUSE which are politically important may be based on or may reflect criminological research in the area. But generally such research has virtually no impact on reform, at least in the short term.

The training of criminologists in Canada reflects 2 distinct perspectives. U de M, Simon Fraser, and U of O offer programs that emphasize specialization in criminology, but at U of A and U of T less course work in criminology itself and more background in the more established social sciences is offered.

The Social Sciences and Humanities Research Council supports criminological research. The ministry of the solicitor-general of Canada focuses on applied research related to policy issues and provides specific research contracts and sustaining grants to 7 university centres. These sustaining grants, called contribution grants, are unique and provide modest but flexible funding for research training and small-scale research.

Canadian criminologists participate in organizations representing the social sciences and the law in Canada, the US and internationally. These include the American Society of Criminology, the Society for the Study of Social Problems, and the Law and Society Association. Canadian criminologists may also be involved with the Canadian Association for the Prevention of Crime (formerly the Canadian Criminal Justice Assn). The biennual congress emphasizes corrections and prevention, but the *Canadian Journal of Criminology*, produced by the Association, is mainly research oriented. The Canadian Association for Criminological Research is a small organization which tends to hold meetings with the larger congresses.

JIM HACKLER

Croatians The first Croatians to arrive in Canada may have been 2 sailors from Dalmatia serving as crew on the voyages of Jacques CARTIER (1542-43) and a miner who accompanied Samuel de CHAMPLAIN (1605-06). Later, Croatians served in Austrian military units sent by the French government to help defend NEW FRANCE (1758-59) and were involved in the early salmon fisheries of BC, the Cariboo gold rush of the 1860s and the Yukon gold rush of the late 1890s. Over the main period of migration, which spans the 20th century, approximately 75 000 Croatians have immigrated to Canada.

Origins Calculating numbers of Croatian immigrants has been difficult because Croatia has since the 10th and 11th centuries been variously a part of the Hungarian dynasty, the Holy Roman Empire, the Austro-Hungarian Empire (to WWI), the Kingdom of the Serbs, Croats and Slovenes (1918-29), the Kingdom of Yugoslavia (1929-41) and the Independent State of Croatia (1941-45); since 1945, it has constituted one of the republics of the Socialist Federal Republic of Yugoslavia. Croatians were classified with Austrians and Hungarians before 1918, and as Yugoslavs after the formal establishment of Yugoslavia in 1929. It has been estimated that 65% of the emigrants from what is now Yugoslavia have been Croatian. Because only 32 210 of the Croatians and their descendants now in Canada identified themselves in the 1981 census as Croatian by mother tongue, it is assumed that many in the second and third generation classified themselves as English Canadians or were described by census takers as Yugoslav.

The Croatians were predominantly Roman Catholic peasants in the 19th and early 20th centuries, particularly those from the inland regions of Slavonia, Zumberak and Zagorje. The population of the Croatian littoral (Istria, Primorje and Dalmatia) on the Adriatic was somewhat more diverse, comprising some people of Muslim faith and a social mix of traders, sailors, fishermen, woodsmen and herders. Most of the immigration to Canada has been from this coastal region inland to the capital of Zagreb.

Migration and Settlement The first group of migrants were called "kolumbusari" (those who came with Columbus). Prior to WWI, about 4000 Croatians immigrated to Canada. Between 1928 and 1939 some 12 000 arrived. The third major group of post-WWII immigrants came in a wave of over 100 000 emigrants from Yugoslavia, the majority of whom were from Croatia. The main motive for immigration has been the search for a better life, but in the 1920s and after WWII many Croatians emigrated in protest against political conditions in their homeland. Many recent immigrants have been from an urban and professional class from the larger Croatian towns and cities, eg, Zagreb, Rijeka, Karlovac, Split and Zadar.

Of the 29 Croatian settlements established before WWI, 14 were in BC. Other Croatians settled in Saskatchewan, Alberta and northern and southern Ontario. During the 1920s some 171 settlements were established in the mining towns and mill towns across Canada's mining, forest and agricultural frontier and in Windsor, Toronto and Montréal. The postwar immigrants have largely settled in major cities, particularly Toronto and Montréal. The majority of postwar foreign-born immigrants were part of the industrial labour force, while the majority of the Canadian-born have been employed in the professional, clerical and service sectors of the economy.

Social Life and Community For the first and second group of immigrants, group life centered about kinship circles reminiscent of the familial and communal peasant *zadruga*. Fraternal and self-help organizations, eg, the American-based Croatian Fraternal Union, which opened its first Canadian lodge in Nanaimo in 1903 and which had 10 000 members by 1971, were established. Other networks were sponsored by political parties such as the Croatian Peasant Party of the 1920s, which founded the Croatian Peasant Society in 1930. Other social, cultural and political activities were promoted by the Communist Party and by the monarchist Yugoslav organizations in the 1930s. Since the war, organizations have proliferated, eg, the United Croats of Canada, the Federation of Croatian Societies in Canada and the Croatian Cultural Societies. More recently, Croatian folklore and dance groups have enjoyed prominence in the multicultural folklore festivals of urban ethnic communities.

Religion and Cultural Life and Education The Roman Catholic Church, while unable to serve the isolated frontier communities of the 1920s and 1930s, has played a prominent role in Croatian Canadian life since 1950, the year the first Croatian Catholic parish was established in Windsor. Currently there are parishes and churches in all of the major urban communities, in addition to the community halls and cultural centres sponsored by political and fraternal organizations. Croatians have also enjoyed an active ethnic press, broadly representative of political factions from far left to right. *Hrvastki Glas* (*The Croatian Voice*), est 1929 and sponsored by the Croatian Peasant Society, and the Communist Party's *Borba* (*The Struggle*), est 1930, are both still published, the latter more recently as *Jedinstvo* (Unity) and then as *Naše Novine* (*Our News*). Other nationalist newspapers include *Naš Put* (*Our Way*), *Hrvatski Put* (*The Croatian Way*) and *Nezavisna Država Hrvatska* (*The Independent State of Croatia*). Several writers have also emerged from the emigré community, such as the poet Alan Horić, who won recognition for his works *L'Aube assassiné* and *Blessure au flanc du ciel*. Others in the fields of ballet, classical music and the fine arts have also won acclaim. Chess and soccer are very popular among postwar immigrants. Croatian chess clubs have won at least 2 provincial chess championships and the Metros-Croatia soccer team (now the Toronto Blizzard) won the N American Soccer League Championship in 1976.

The Croatian language was maintained by the family until the 1950s, when informal extracurricular schools were organized by community leaders and organizations. In the 1970s a network of Croatian-language schools established in the US spread into Canada, and a few courses on Croatian language and culture at the university level have been introduced as well. Language skills and cultural traditions have been somewhat lost through assimilation, particularly in the small isolated communities of the 1920s and 1930s, but because of the more recent and greater concentration of Croatians in large cities, cultural maintenance has been more consciously pursued by community leaders.

A.W. RASPORICH

Reading: A.W. Rasporich, *For a Better Life: A History of the Croatians in Canada* (1982); N. Paveskovic, "Croatians in Canada," in *Slavs in Canada* (1968).

Crocus, Prairie, *see* ANEMONE.

Croft, Henry Holmes, educator, scientist (b at London, Eng 6 Mar 1820; d near San Diego, Tex 1 Mar 1883). For 37 years Croft was professor of chemistry (the first) at U of T and its antecedent King's College. His special interests included toxicology and forensic science, which led to his frequent service as a consultant and expert witness in the courts. He also supplied scientific advice to the early refiners of Ontario petroleum. Having a keen interest in biology, Croft contributed to the formation and activities of the Entomological Soc of Canada. Inspired to disseminate scientific knowledge, he participated actively in the work of the Mechanics' Institute and the Canadian Institute (now Royal Canadian Institute) in Toronto.

W.A.E. MCBRYDE

Croix de Saint Louis The Ordre royal et militaire de Saint Louis, fd 1693, was the only military order awarded in NEW FRANCE. The insignia, which had to be returned to the king when the owner died, was a golden cross edged with golden fleurs-de-lis, with 8 points enameled in white. Commanders of the order wore it on a sash and chevaliers wore it on a small red ribbon. To qualify one had to be an officer in the regular army and serve the king of France. In Canada Louis-Hector de CALLIÈRE (1694) was the first to receive the decoration; Louis de Buade de FRONTENAC received it in 1697. The first Canadian chevalier was Pierre Le Moyne d'IBERVILLE (1699). By 1760 some 145 men had been decorated in Canada. The Croix de Saint Louis rapidly lost its value in France because it was too easily obtained, but in Canada it was rare and retained its value. *See* HONOURS; DECORATIONS.

Croke, John Bernard, soldier (b at Little Bay, Nfld 18 May 1892; d near Amiens, France 9 Aug 1918). At an early age, Croke moved with his family to Glace Bay, NS, where he later worked in the coal mines. During WWI he served with the 13th Infantry Batt, Quebec Reg, CEF, and was recognized and honoured for valour, 8 Aug 1918, during the opening stage of the BATTLE OF AMIENS. Croke was the posthumous recipient of the first Victoria Cross awarded a Newfoundlander. Single-handedly, he bombed a machine gun nest and captured the crew and gun. Despite a severe wound, he rejoined his platoon and led a charge into a trench line, capturing 3 guns and the garrison. Again he was severely wounded, and died shortly after. JOHN PARSONS

Croll, David Arnold, lawyer, politician (b at Moscow, Russia 12 Mar 1900). Elected a Liberal MLA in 1934, he became a Cabinet minister but resigned in Apr 1937 over Prem HEPBURN's opposition to industrial unionism. Croll served in the Canadian Army 1939-45 and was MP for Toronto-Spadina 1945-55. Appointed to the Senate in 1955, he was responsible for several studies on poverty and aging. ROBERT BOTHWELL

Crombie, David, teacher, politician (b at Toronto 24 Apr 1936). Educated at Western and U of T, he was appointed lecturer in political science and urban affairs at Ryerson Polytechnical Inst. From 1966 to 1971, Crombie was director of student affairs at Ryerson. A central figure in the civic reform movment of the late 1960s in Toronto, Crombie was a cofounder of the short-lived Civic Action Party (CIVAC). He was unsuccessful in aldermanic elections for 1966, but sat for Ward 11, 1970-72. In 1973 he won the mayoralty, following a well-orchestrated personal campaign. Crombie's success within City Hall and increasing public popularity made the "Tiny Perfect Mayor" unbeatable at the polls; he was easily re-elected in 1975 and 1977. In Aug 1978 he resigned as mayor and won the federal by-election in Rosedale riding for the Progressive Conservatives. He held the seat for the PCs in the general elections of 1979, 1980 and 1984 in spite of strong challenges and was minister of health and welfare in the Joe CLARK government and minister of Indian and northern affairs in the MULRONEY Cabinet in 1984. VICTOR RUSSELL

Cronenberg, David, filmmaker (b at Toronto 15 Mar 1943). Cronenberg studied literature at U of T and while there made several short films. His first 2 feature films, *Stereo* (1969) and *Crimes of the Future* (1970), were abstract and ironic commentaries on contemporary life. *Shivers* (1976) launched his career as an original and inventive writer and director of horror and science-fiction films. In *Rabid* (1977), *The Brood* (1979), *Scanners* (1981) and *Videodrome* (1983), Cronenberg explored large philosophical questions, demonstrating that even within the constraints of commercial genres a personal vision could be conveyed. Cronenberg has made films for the CBC. His feature *The Dead Zone* (1983) marked his emergence as a filmmaker of international status. PIERS HANDLING

Cronyn, Hume, actor, director (b at London, Ont 18 July 1911). He is a skilled farceur and character player who often teamed with his wife Jessica Tandy. Educated at Ridley Coll, St Catharines, Ont, and McGill, Hume was an active amateur before training in Austria and New York. His professional career began in 1931 in Washington, DC, and from 1934 on he established his Broadway reputation in productions of *Three Men on a Horse, High Tor, Room Service* and *The Three Sisters*. He won his first "Tony" Award opposite Tandy in *The Four-poster* (1951-53). They were also together in *A Day by the Sea* (1955), the London production of *Big Fish, Little Fish* (1962), the inaugural season of the Guthrie Theatre in Minneapolis (1963), *A Delicate Balance* (1966), *Happy Days* (1972), and *The Merchant of Venice* as well as *A Midsummer Night's Dream* (1976) and *The Gin Game* (1978) at Canada's STRATFORD FESTIVAL. The pair toured the USSR with *The Gin Game* in 1979-80. His famous stage roles have included Polonius (Tony Award 1964), Shylock, Richard III, Willy Loman in *Death of a Salesman*, and *Hadrian VII*, the latter again for Stratford. DAVID GARDNER

Crop Insurance An all-risk crop-insurance program is available to Canadian farmers under the authority of the federal Crop Insurance Act (1959) and through concurrent and complementary legislation enacted by each province. This federal-provincial cost-shared program is designed to stabilize farm income by minimizing, at the individual farm level, the detrimental effects of crop losses caused by uncontrollable natural hazards. The federal government contributes financially to federally approved, provincially administered crop-insurance plans through Agriculture Canada. The provinces also contribute to the program, and the remaining funds come from annual insurance premiums paid by the more than 100 000 farmers who participate in the program voluntarily. Most major commercial crops in Canada are now insurable under the program. The major natural hazards covered include frost, HAIL, DROUGHT, excessive rainfall, FLOODING, INSECT PEST damage, plant disease and WIND damage. When crop yields fall below some actuarially determined level, the insured farmer is given an indemnity payment to make up the difference. J.C. GILSON

Crop Research may be defined as activity directed to making the growing and marketing of commercial crops more efficient and profitable. Hence, crop research may comprise any or all of the following: PLANT breeding, plant physiology and BIOCHEMISTRY, crop protection studies, cultural management studies, storage methods research, and processing and products studies. The importance of plant breeding in the adaptation of crop plants to Canadian conditions is treated in a separate article. Well-known successes include Marquis WHEAT, TRITICALE and CANOLA.

Canadian plant physiologists and biochemists have contributed to both on-farm research and basic research conducted under carefully controlled conditions at the laboratories of the NATIONAL RESEARCH COUNCIL, research stations and the universities. Important work has been done in tissue culture, WEED control, host-parasite relationships and PESTICIDE research.

Tissue Culture is the growing of complete plants from individual cells or small groups of cells. Since many new plants can be produced from a small amount of starting material, this method promises to provide, economically, clonal material (ie, material in which all individuals are genetically identical). Clonal blueberry plants have been produced by tissue culture at the Kentville, NS, research station.

Weed-Control Research by Agriculture Canada researchers has centered at Regina but other station and university laboratories have also contributed.

Host-parasite Relationships Canadian research into the relationship between the wheat plant and the stem rust organism began in earnest in 1950-51. M. Shaw's laboratory at the University of Saskatchewan, Saskatoon, was very productive, with many graduate students joining in research. The Winnipeg research station still retains an active program. Although some progress was made in the use of chemicals to control stem rust, the main importance of this research was in a better understanding of the physiological and biochemical interactions of the rust FUNGUS with the wheat plant.

Spraying seed potatoes, St Quentin, NB *(photo by Richard Vroom)*.

Other noteworthy achievements include the outstanding work on the physiology and biochemistry of lignin (a substance related to cellulose), fungal by-products and edible SEAWEEDS at the NRC laboratories at Ottawa, Saskatoon and Halifax, respectively; and the pioneering work in GENETIC ENGINEERING done by O. Gamborg at NRC's Prairie Regional Laboratory in the 1960s and 1970s.

Although weed competition, INSECTS, fungi and bacteria were serious problems from the beginning of agricultural practice in Canada, weed-control chemicals, broad-spectrum organic insecticides and fungicides did not become available until after WWII. Most new pesticides were discovered outside Canada and Canadian research dealing with such chemicals has centered on determining the proper amounts to use and the most effective means and time for application. The notable exception to the above restriction is a program on the chemical basis of the activity of many of the pesticides currently in use, carried on at Agriculture Canada's Research Institute at London, Ont.

The preferred means of protecting plants against diseases and insects is to find or produce resistant varieties. Excellent research to this end has been accomplished in Canada, eg, plant breeders have consistently been able to provide new varieties of hard red spring wheat resistant to stem rust and oat varieties resistant to crown rust. Resistance to wheat stem sawfly has been incorporated into winter wheat. In the control of wheat stem rust, the campaign to eradicate barberry plants, the parasite's alternative host, was as important as the development of resistant wheat varieties. Similarly, the campaign to eradicate buckthorn, the alternate host of oat crown rust, was important in crown rust control. In eastern Canada, the removal of wild apple trees has been a key in the fight against the apple maggot.

The integrated method of pest control involves using the smallest possible amount of chemicals and encouraging natural predators to assist in insect control. The method received its impetus from the increased cost of pesticides, the development of plant and insect resistance to chemicals and the uneasiness of the general public about the use of toxic substances in food production. A.D. Pickett of the Kentville, NS, research station was a leader in the development of the method (*see* INSECT, BENEFICIAL).

When large-scale agriculture was introduced to Canada, the thrust was to clear all unwanted trees, plants or sod from the SOIL so that monoculture (cultivation of one type of plant) could be practised. After the disastrous loss of topsoil during DROUGHT years in western Canada and similar losses during excessively wet years in denuded rolling land elsewhere, the trend has been towards the use of more responsible AGRICULTURAL SOIL PRACTICES. Attempts have been made to control wind EROSION by maintaining sufficient straw in or on the soil and by avoiding exposure of finely divided soil to wind action (*see* SOIL CONSERVATION). To minimize disturbance of soil, no-till methods have been developed for many crops: the annual crop may be seeded into rye or clover which are then removed by chemical weed control before the annual crop has sprouted. The practice of grassing down apple and pear orchards once they approach bearing age also helps protect soil from washing or blowing away. Perhaps the most significant addition to Canadian soil management has been the promotion of the liming of the acidic soils of eastern Canada. Once soil acidity has been substantially reduced, plants can use added nutrients more effectively. The NS government subsidizes the cost of lime used for agricultural purposes.

In N America grains (ie, corn), fruits (eg, cranberries) and vegetables (eg, beans, squash) were stored for winter use before the arrival of Europeans. The settlers introduced other fruits (eg, apples, pears) and vegetables (eg, potatoes, cabbage, celery, turnips, onions, carrots) which required new methods of long-term storage. The first storages were of a type known as common, air or ventilated storage. Many are still in use in Canada because, after fall harvest, ambient nighttime temperatures usually are suitable for preserving potatoes, dry onions, cabbage and mature carrots. Earlier storages were underground but the modern trend is to locate most of the building above ground and use automatic control of louvres and fans to draw in cool, outside air when required. A few cool stores used ice to lower temperatures inside a storage room. For many years after ice-cooled stores were abandoned, ice was used to cool railway cars carrying perishable products. Mechanically refrigerated storage was a major advance, allowing many fruits and vegetables to be maintained for up to 6 months in good condition. Fruits and vegetables not adapted to long-term storage could benefit from refrigeration for short terms, allowing orderly marketing. Canadian government and university research laboratories have made noteworthy advances in the science of food storage; the more recent improvements are described below.

Jacketed Storage rooms are built so that cooling air circulates around the room in a sealed envelope, instead of through the room as in conventional ventilated storage. Jacketed storage is especially effective for maintaining high relative humidities and is used for storing carrots, cabbage and celery.

Controlled-atmosphere Storage is a system for holding produce in an atmosphere that differs substantially from air in the proportion of nitrogen, oxygen or carbon dioxide present. The research has been done mainly at Agriculture Canada laboratories at Kentville (NS), Ottawa and Summerland (BC), at NRC laboratories at Ottawa and at University of Guelph. Over a period of many years, valuable information about the optimum conditions for storing fruits and vegetables has been passed along to commercial interests. The term "controlled atmosphere storage," first suggested by W.P. Phillips of Agriculture Canada, is now used around the world.

Low-pressure Storage involves holding products in a partial vacuum, with controlled oxygen levels. The system is still largely experimental, although prototype vans are available. Pioneering work in the use of LPS for fruits and vegetables has been conducted at the University of Guelph.

Ultra-low-oxygen Storage is the most successful development in McIntosh apple marketing since controlled-atmosphere storage began. It reduces oxygen from 5% to a range of 0.5-1.5% and also lowers carbon dioxide levels. The altered composition of the atmosphere slows the ripening process; thus, the system allows marketing over a year after harvest, with little loss of original flavour and texture. Canadian experiments on ultra-low-oxygen storage began in Kentville in 1976, following initial work conducted in the UK.

In 1982, raw agricultural products produced in Canada were valued at nearly $20 billion. Processing adds greatly to the final value and provides thousands of jobs. The food and beverage industries have been very innovative in creating new products (eg, new breakfast cereals). In addition, the provincial research laboratories at Vineland, Ont, and the federal laboratories at Summerland and Kentville have searched for new means of processing fruits and vegetables, mainly with a view to reducing costs. For example, the steam blancher developed at Kentville to replace hot-water treatment saves energy as well as conserving the vitamin content by using a shorter blanching period. Another example is the rotated can method (roll cooker) of heat-processing tinned fruit, developed at Summerland to provide more rapid and effective heat treatment and, thus, preserve the product's quality.

The Canadian wine industry improved rapidly following WWII with the influx of European wine-making experts and hybrid grapes from France. The research stations at Summerland and Kentville have been active in testing newly introduced grape varieties because of the desire to maintain and expand wine-making facilities in BC and NS. Government research has also assisted the maple sugar industry by testing pilot plant models of a method of concentration known as reverse osmosis. In reverse osmosis a liquid under pressure is restrained by a membrane through which water molecules will pass but the molecule to be concentrated (eg, the sugar in maple sap) will not.

The Kentville research station acquired a small flexible-retortable-pouch processor from France in 1977. The laminated plastic and foil pouches are able to withstand heat and pressure in cooking and to resist puncture during commercial handling. The advantages of processing food products in the pouch include transportation and storage savings on empty and filled containers, energy conservation during processing and better nutritional, flavour and textural properties. The new container is likely to replace cans and bottles. Finally, by-products of the agricultural industry are being studied as possible raw products for single-cell-protein production, at first for animal feed, but eventually for human consumption.

In 1982 Agriculture Canada's Research Branch maintained 44 research establishments (*see* agricultural research and development). Other research at the federal level is carried out by the NRC and Environment Canada. At the provincial level, research is undertaken by the BC Ministry of Agriculture and the british columbia research council; Alberta Agriculture and alberta research council; the Crop Development Centre, Saskatoon, and the saskatchewan research council; the Manitoba Dept of Agriculture and the manitoba research council; the Ontario Ministry of Agriculture and Food; Agriculture Québec; the NS Dept of Agriculture and Marketing and the nova scotia research foundation corporation; and the NB Dept of Agriculture and Rural Development. Various industrial corporations support research, eg, Monsanto Canada Ltd and United Oilseed Products Ltd. Most of the major universities and agricultural colleges also have research programs, as do some technical schools.

F.R. Forsyth

Crops are plant species grown for human or animal consumption or for special purposes (eg, flax, tobacco). In Canada, most major crops grown are used for food and feed. Crops can be classified in several ways. By growth habit they are annual, biennial or perennial, depending on whether they complete their life cycle in one or 2 years, or persist for over 2 years. The special term "winter annuals" is used for crops that are planted and germinate in fall, overwinter in a dormant state, renew growth in spring and are harvested in July or Aug. A more useful classification of crops, based on the general trade use, divides them into cereal crops, forages, oilseeds, orchard crops, berries, vegetables and special crops. Cereals are plants grown for the mature seeds they produce (eg, wheat, oats, barley, rye, corn). Forage crops are grown for animal fodder. They may be harvested and stored until used, or grazed as a pasture or range crop (eg, grasses such as timothy and bromegrass, legumes such as clover and alfalfa). When cereal crops (especially corn) are harvested as whole plants, chopped and fed to animals, the crop is classed as a forage or fodder crop. Oilseed crops are grown for their oil-bearing seeds (eg, soybeans, sunflowers, flax, canola). Orchard crops are edible fruits or nuts (eg, apples, peaches, pears, walnuts). Berries are small, fleshy fruits grown on a vine or small shrub (eg, strawberries, raspberries, currants, blueberries, grapes). Vegetables are herbaceous plants of which all or a part is eaten, raw or cooked (eg, carrots, onions, tomatoes, lettuce). potatoes are classed as a trade vegetable but also considered a field crop when hectarages are large. The term "special crops" designates crops that do not fit neatly into other categories (eg, tobacco, buckwheat) or vegetable crops traded in a manner different from the normal one, such as peas, beans or lentils, which are raised as field crops and sold like grain through the elevator system.

Canadian Constraints While the total land area of Canada is nearly one billion hectares, only about 45 million ha (5%) is improved farmland. An additional 24 million ha of rangeland and wild pasture, mostly in the Prairie provinces and BC, is used by ranchers. The northern sections of the prairies and the northern clay belt of Ontario and Québec include some 15 million ha that could be used for agricultural production, but the soils are marginally developed and a very short growing season makes the potential much less than that of the land now farmed. The most productive land is the 40 million ha in crop and summer fallow. Summer fallowing, the practice of leaving land unplanted to a crop, is a moisture-conserving measure, forming part of the sequence of crop rotation on the prairies. About 75% of Canada's farmland is located in the Prairie provinces of Alberta, Saskatchewan and Manitoba; about 10%, in Ontario; the remainder, in the other provinces.

Canada lies in the North Temperate Zone; all its prairie farmland is N of the 49th parallel of latitude. Productive farming, therefore, depends upon crops that ripen early, if they are spring sown, or are winter hardy, if they are winter annuals, biennial or perennial. Unlike many producers in tropical and subtropical areas where 2 or more crops per year are possible, Canadians can rely on only one crop. The vastness of Canada and the variations in climate preclude accuracy in any general statement but, with the exception of the lower mainland of BC and southern Ontario (where less hardy crops survive), crop growth, other than for forage or for range, is secure only from May to Sept. Victoria Day, around 24 May, is a safe date for gardeners from coast to coast to transplant ornamental and garden plants that have been started in greenhouses. Late spring frosts may occur after that date, but the probability is not great. Early fall frosts occur in Sept; thus, the frost-free period is 100-120 days. Canadian summers are usually quite warm, with temperatures often reaching over 30°C. These temperatures, coupled with adequate sunshine, make crop growth rapid. However, as the climate is continental, much of the farmland of Canada (especially the Prairie provinces) suffers from lack of moisture. Some grain crops are produced with as little as 375 mm of rain, but the moisture usually comes when needed for fast summer growth. Some 400 000 ha of land in southern Alberta and central Saskatchewan are irrigated.

Canada's soils developed under regimes of varying amounts of rainfall and are dependent upon the inherent properties of the material from which they formed; thus, they may be either alkaline or acidic. In general, western soils are alkaline; eastern ones, acidic. Acid soils can be limed to alter the acidity, but the practice is costly and must be done annually. Liming is subsidized by some provincial governments. In eastern Canada, higher water tables and poor rainage reduce the capacity of soils to produce ome crops. In spring, flooding can occur in ome areas of all parts of Canada.

When settlers first opened up the country, nany different crops were grown on each farm o provide subsistence. The practice is still folowed in some remote regions or on isolated arms but, in general, crop production has been pecialized to provide economic returns. As land rices increase, greater returns per hectare are eeded, and producers have had to specialize. The choice of a crop is dictated by geographic egion, latitude and moisture; therefore, there is strong regional bias in the production of most rops. Most wheat, oats, barley, rye, flax, canola, nustard and sunflowers are grown on the praiies. Wheat and summer fallow occupy about ne-third of the total hectarage. Soybeans, toacco and beans are grown mostly in Ontario; odder and grain corn, in Ontario and Québec; ruit, in BC, Ontario and NS. Potatoes are grown n all provinces; sugar BEETS, in Manitoba and Québec and, under irrigation, in Alberta.

Handling In 1981 there were over 318 000 arms in Canada. The size of individual farms aries greatly: by census definition, farms can be s small as one acre with produce of only $250, r they can be extensive, highly capitalized oldings with sales in the thousands of dollars. The latter group comprises only about 20% of all roducers but accounts for over 70% of total arm production. A wide variety of crops can be rown in all regions of Canada, and the handling of crops will vary with the size of the farm nd the type of production carried out. The maor producers of cereal crops, oilseeds and some pecial crops aim their production for cash sales. The standard practice for such crops in the Praiie provinces is for farmers to have on-farm torage for a quantity of produce and to deliver he remainder to grain elevators, where it is raded, stored or shipped to terminal elevators or sale domestically or abroad. The price is stablished by grade and quantity. Grading facors include purity of type, soundness, maturity nd test weight. Because weather at harvest can reatly affect the quality of grain crops, grades btained by farmers will vary by year, district nd cultivar (commercial variety) grown. In Ontario, where quantities of winter wheat, soyeans, corn and field beans are grown, there is ery little farm storage, and producers rely on eed and grain companies to purchase quantities f produce harvested in fall. Many farmers proluce cereal and forage crops for their own use s feed for livestock. Some farmers produce hay or cash sales; most, for home use. Other forage rops make up pasture and rangeland used for attle production.

Many Canadian gardeners produce a mixture f vegetables, berries or orchard crops for their wn use. With more extensive holdings, some ff-farm sales are made, eg, "U-pick" strawerries or roadside stands for fruits and vegetales. A subsistence farmer normally plans to ive off his farm but may supplement his income with some off-farm sales. Market-garden perations grow vegetables for local markets or hipment into large urban areas. Orchard crops, otatoes, tobacco, sugar beets and vegetables rown for off-farm sales are marketed through pecial systems. Canada is a net exporter of agricultural products, the chief exports being grains nd oilseeds. Our chief imports are fruits, vegeables and specialty items (eg, sugar). The pattern of net exports has long been a part of Canada's normal trade pattern and will likely emain so. J.W. MORRISON

Crosbie, John Carnell, lawyer, politican (b at St John's 30 Jan 1931). He was elected to the St John's City Council in Nov 1965 and appointed deputy mayor on 1 Jan 1966. He resigned that July to join the Cabinet of Liberal Premier Joey SMALLWOOD and won election to the Assembly in Sept. In 1969 he unsuccessfully challenged Smallwood in a party leadership convention. He joined the Progressive Conservatives led by Frank MOORES in June 1971 and his support helped Moores win the 1972 election. Crosbie held several senior Cabinet portfolios and was the main advocate of the government's policy of greater local control and management of Newfoundland's resources. Elected to the House of Commons in 1976, he was minister of finance in the brief 1979 minority government of Joe CLARK, which on 14 Dec lost a nonconfidence vote when Crosbie's budget was defeated. In 1983 he contested the leadership of the PC Party, finishing third behind Brian MULRONEY; he was appointed minister of justice in the new Conservative government in 1984.
MELVIN BAKER

Crosbie, Sir John Chalker, merchant, politician (b at Brigus, Nfld 11 Sept 1876; d at St John's 5 Oct 1932). An aggressive and energetic entrepreneur he created a fortune (which he lost) and started the Crosbie dynasty, which continues to flourish. Crosbie founded Crosbie and Co in 1900 and by 1920 was one of the leading fish exporters in Newfoundland. He entered politics as MHA for Bay de Verde in 1908. He was minister of shipping 1918-19 and minister of finance and customs under PM MONROE from 1924 until 1928, when he retired from politics.
KEITH MATTHEWS

Cross, Alfred Ernest, rancher, brewer (b at Montréal 26 June 1861; d there 10 Mar 1932). A graduate of Ontario Agricultural Coll and Montréal Veterinary Coll, Cross came to Calgary in 1884 as veterinarian and assistant manager of the British-American Horse Ranch Co. In 1885 he started his own ranch, the A7, becoming one of the West's most prominent cattlemen and one of the "Big Four" founders of the CALGARY STAMPEDE. In 1892 he founded the Calgary Brewing and Malting Co and in 1899 he was elected Conservative MLA for the NWT. DAVID H. BREEN

Reading: David H. Breen, *The Canadian Prairie West* (1983).

Cross-Country Skiing From its origins over 5000 years ago in Scandinavia up to the early 1900s, SKIING was mainly a form of winter transport. Although a few daring athletes intentionally challenged their skills by SKI JUMPING or racing down hills, most of the early ski pioneers simply toured "cross country" over relatively flat routes. In 1905, for example, the Montreal Ski Club built on a long-established snowshoe club tradition by introducing largely social ski tours into the LAURENTIANS.

In the early 1900s, most skiers carried a single pole and wore long (2.5 to 4 m), wide (over 80 mm), unlaminated wooden skis that were so heavy (several kg each) and awkwardly fastened that skiers usually removed them and carried them up steep hills. In 1915 the Norwegian Thorleaf Haug invented screw-on steel toe-plates which eliminated the need to carve slots through the middle of the skis to hold toe-straps. This made skis much stronger and permitted the adoption of shorter (under 2.5 m), narrower (less than 60 mm) and lighter (under 1 kg each) skis. Used with a pair of bamboo poles, such skis remained the standard for all forms of skiing for the next 20 years.

In order to ski efficiently over a variety of snow types, ski-base preparation became an inconvenient but highly aromatic art. Pine tar was carefully heated into the bases and then covered with various complex and often secret "dopes." In the West, where there were long steep slopes to be climbed, stronger grip was obtained by fastening sealskin under the skis, with the hairs pointed backward.

In 1927 the CPR introduced Laurentian ski trains, which led to the wide use of an extensive trail network blazed by "Jackrabbit" JOHANNSEN and the resorts opened by early developers such as Louis Cochand and the Wheeler brothers. By 1935 similar developments were to be found all across N America, where skiers enthusiastically adopted the use of ski lifts, from the rope tow, invented in Shawbridge, Qué, in 1932, to the chairlift, introduced into Canada at Mont Tremblant in 1938. Skis were quickly adapted for use on large hills through the introduction of steel edges for stability on ice (about 1930) and cable bindings that held the heels down for greater control. Within a decade, cross-country skiing became a sport requiring special equipment, and practised by only a small core of devotees.

During the 1970s people caught up in the FITNESS boom or rebelling against the expense and congestion of alpine skiing took up cross country in great numbers. The CANADIAN SKI MARATHON, eg, grew from 400 to over 4000 participants during that decade and scores of other tours and races for the general public sprang up across the country. Although Canadian national cross-country championships have been held since 1921, only with the last few years has increased interest in the sport produced internationally competitive athletes such as Sharon and Shirley Firth and Pierre Harvey.

During the 1970s and 1980s, technological innovation has changed the sport. Synthetic materials have allowed manufacture of extremely light, strong skies and poles. New boot-binding systems improve control at high speeds. Since the new skis glide much faster, skating and double poling techniques have assumed increased importance. Waxing remains an obscure art, but is the subject of intense scientific study and constant improvement.

Despite the increasing cost and sophistication of the competitive sport, cross-country skiing remains extremely popular with its almost 4 million Canadian participants. More than half of them set forth at least once a week to rediscover the age-old joys of the sport. MURRAY SHAW

Crow (Corvidae), large family of BIRDS that includes JAYS, MAGPIES and nutcrackers as well as crows and RAVENS. The family is thought to have originated during the middle Miocene period (12-15 million years ago) in the Old World. Jays are believed to be the most primitive Corvidae. From this group, magpies and, later, ravens and typical crows evolved. At present, 103 species of Corvidae are recognized. Crows, largest members of the order Passeriformes (perching birds), range in length from 17.5 to 70 cm. The typical crow (genus *Corvus*) is either wholly black (including bill and legs) or black with white, grey and brown. Of the 3 species of *Corvus* native to Canada, only the northwestern crow (*C. caurinus*) has a limited range. It inhabits the coast and islands of BC, where it forages along shores, beaches and tidal flats. The highly adaptable American crow (*C. brachyrhynchos*) occupies many habitats and feeds on both animal and vegetable matter. It breeds from north-central BC to Newfoundland. Similarly, the common raven (*C. corax*) is found in most of Canada. Both northwestern and American crows tend to forage in open areas, but prefer wooded regions for nesting and roosting. The northwestern crow nests mainly in coniferous trees; the American crow, in deciduous and coniferous trees and, occasionally, in low bushes. The male American crow helps incubate the clutches of 4-6 eggs. The crow family represents one of the most advanced stages of avian evolution, showing, for example, a highly developed intelligence and complex social organization. In places, crows have proven more harmful than helpful to humans, since, although they kill a large number of insects, they also damage CROPS, particularly corn. They also prey on eggs and young of many desirable birds. LORRAINE G. D'AGINCOURT

Crowfoot, head chief of the Blackfoot, 1887 (*courtesy* Glenbow Archives).

Crowfoot, Blackfoot chief (b near Belly R, Alta *c*1830; d near Blackfoot Crossing, Alta 25 Apr 1890). Born a BLOOD, he grew up among the BLACKFOOT. As a teenager, he showed great bravery in a battle by advancing and striking a painted TIPI in the hostile Crow camp. For this deed he was given an ancestor's name, *Isapomuxika*, meaning "Crow Indian's Big Foot," shortened by interpreters to Crowfoot. He went to war 19 times and was wounded 6 times. His most heroic deed was to attack and kill a grizzly bear with a lance in sight of the whole camp. Shortly after, in 1865, he became chief of the Big Pipes band, and in 1870 became one of the 3 head chiefs of the tribe.

Crowfoot was perceptive, farseeing and a diplomat. He established good relations with fur traders and peace with the CREE. He adopted a Cree named POUNDMAKER, who became a leader of his own people, and rescued missionary Albert LACOMBE during a Cree raid. In 1874 Crowfoot welcomed the NWMP when they came W to stamp out the whiskey trade. He was recognized as an ally and was given a prominent role in Treaty No 7 negotiations in 1877.

After the Blackfoot settled on their reserve in 1881, Crowfoot became disillusioned with the Canadian government, but he refused to allow his people to join the 1885 RIEL Rebellion, less out of loyalty to the government than from the belief that it was a losing fight. Sick during his last decade, he constantly mourned the loss of his children, of whom only one blind son and 3 daughters reached maturity. HUGH A. DEMPSEY

Reading: Hugh A. Dempsey, *Crowfoot* (1972).

Crown, the collectivity of executive powers exercised, in a monarchy, by or in the name of the SOVEREIGN. These powers flow from the historic rights and privileges known as Crown or PREROGATIVE POWERS of the English Crown. In Canada, a monarchy since its founding, the FATHERS OF CONFEDERATION created a parliamentary democracy through a unique partnership between a federal STATE and a monarchy. Through the Crown, power is held in a nonpartisan office. Federally the Crown is represented by the GOVERNOR GENERAL and provincially by the LIEUTENANT-GOVERNORS, although both are federal offices. The statutory responsibilities of Crown representatives are outlined in the CONSTITUTION ACT, 1867, and delineated further in the Letters Patent (1947), which allow the gov gen to exercise royal prerogatives at his discretion. *See* ADMINISTRATIVE LAW. JACQUES MONET, SJ

Crown Attorney Criminal prosecutions are the responsibility of the ATTORNEYS GENERAL but are normally conducted by their agents, crown attorneys, who prepare and conduct prosecutions of all indictable offences. In criminal proceedings, the prosecuting counsel is frequently referred to as the Crown, short for crown attorney. K.G. MCSHANE

Crown Corporation, wholly owned federal or provincial organization, structured like private or independent enterprises. Established to carry out regulatory, advisory, administrative, financial or other services or to provide goods and services, crown corporations generally enjoy greater freedom from direct political control than do government departments. Although the 1951 federal Financial Administration Act (FAA) declared that crown corporations are "ultimately accountable, through a minister, to Parliament, for the conduct of (their) affairs," they are not subject to budgetary systems or direct control of a minister in the same way as government departments. Indeed, one AUDITOR GENERAL has claimed that parliamentary scrutiny is sporadic to nonexistent. Parliament has also established crown corporations that are not subject to the FAA and not accountable to Parliament. In 1982 crown corporations spent $30 billion and employed 263 000 Canadians.

The first crown corporation, the Board of Works, was established in 1841 to construct a canal system in the Province of Canada. Crown corporations such as CANADIAN NATIONAL RAILWAYS, PETRO-CANADA and several provincial hydro firms now rank among Canada's largest enterprises. They have been created by various governments, including NDP, Liberal, Progressive Conservative and Social Credit governments. The establishment of important crown corporations in the fields of transportation (AIR CANADA, CNR, ST LAWRENCE SEAWAY) and communications (CANADIAN BROADCASTING CORPORATION) attests to the unwillingness or inability of private firms to provide important services in a vast, sparsely populated country, rather than to a preference for PUBLIC OWNERSHIP. Since WWII other federal crown corporations have emerged as important providers of loans and related financial services to farmers (Farm Credit Corporation), small businesses (Federal Business Development Bank) and exporters (Export Development Corporation), interests whose needs were not always met by private financial institutions. The federal government also owns and operates coal mines (Cape Breton Development Corp), aircraft plants (Canadair Ltd, de Havilland Aircraft of Canada Ltd) and an armaments factory (Canadian Arsenals Ltd).

Provincial crown corporations are also significant, although differences exist in their roles, economic importance and administration. For example, CCF and NDP governments in Saskatchewan have traditionally relied heavily on crown corporations, while the number of crown corporations in Québec has only increased significantly over the past 20 years. In most provinces crown corporations are responsible for the generation and transmission of electricity and the retail distribution of liquor. In the Prairie provinces, telephone service is usually provided by crown corporations (*see* UTILITIES). Recently, provincial crown corporations as diverse as the Potash Corp of Saskatchewan, the Sydney Steel Corp of NS and provincial energy companies in Saskatchewan, Ontario and Québec have been formed. In BC, Saskatchewan, Manitoba and Québec, crown corporations sell automobile insurance, while the Alberta, BC and Ontario governments own railroads.

It is often advanced in defence of crown corporations that the managerial freedom from constant government intervention and legislative oversight that they enjoy ensures the flexibility necessary for the successful administration of governments' commercial activities. In Canada, however, crown corporations have not solved the problem of reconciling their autonomy with legitimate political direction and parliamentary scrutiny.

The FAA categorizes most federal crown corporations according to 3 distinct "schedules." Departmental crown corporations, responsible for "administrative, supervisory or regulatory services of a governmental nature," include the Atomic Energy Control Board and the ECONOMIC COUNCIL OF CANADA, which enjoy no greater freedom from political control than do departments since the TREASURY BOARD must examine and approve their budgetary estimates. Because departmental corporations are not normally engaged in commercial activities, their crown-corporation status is questioned by critics. Agency crown corporations, eg, Atomic Energy of Canada Ltd, Crown Assets Disposal Corp and the NATIONAL HARBOURS BOARD, are involved in the "management of trading or service operations on a quasi-commercial basis" or the "management of procurement, construction or disposal activities." Proprietary crown corporations which are responsible for "the management of commercial and industrial operations involving the production of or dealing in goods and the supply of services," enjoy greater independence than corporations in the other schedules. Theoretically, proprietary corporations are financially independent of Parliament, but some are not. Like agency corporations, they are legally liable for their actions. They include such large and frequently controversial firms as Air Canada, CNR and Petro-Canada.

Schedules provide a woefully inaccurate measure of the number and importance of federal government corporations. First, many important crown corporations, eg, the BANK OF CANADA and the CANADIAN WHEAT BOARD, have never been included. Second, since the FAA, the number of crown corporations has increased, but not all new corporations or subsidiaries of existing firms have been incorporated into the schedules. Finally, the schedules ignore various mixed ownership corporations, wherein government and private ownership are combined, eg, the Canada Development Corp and Telesat Canada which are not counted as crown corporations because they have other shareholders.

Because crown corporations may depend heavily on direct government support and may frequently exert important economic and political pressure, their freedom cannot be absolute. Controls over their operations are imposed to ensure they pursue their mandates and contribute to the achievement of governments' broader goals. As crown corporations grow in size, number and economic significance, the development of appropriate political control has become a controversial problem. The CABINET exercises the most important controls. The statutes creating crown corporations normally outline the corporations' goals, roles and mandates. The FAA attempts to provide a framework for their financial control and accountability, and requires agency and proprietary corporations to submit annual capital budgets to the responsible minister, the minister of finance and the president of the Treasury Board. The budgets need the approval of these 3 ministers, Cabinet and ultimately Parliament. Agency corporations must also submit operating budgets for approval to the responsible minister and the president of the Treasury Board. However, both the government and crown corporations have complained about the budgetary review process suggesting it be reformed. Cabinet also controls the appointments, remuneration and dismissal of crown corporations' boards of directors and senior officers. Theoretically, boards of directors provide the key link between the government and corporate management, but their effectiveness may be undermined by a lack of precise definitions of the powers, duties and responsibilities of boards, political PATRONAGE in the selection of board members and, finally, the federal government's unorthodox and controversial practice of appointing senior civil servants to the boards. Ineffective boards may not be able to withstand government intervention. The Acts of some federal crown corporations, notably Petro-Canada, empower the Cabinet and sometimes the minister responsible to issue directives allowing the government to order a crown corporation to implement particular government policies. Directives have been used rarely and the wisdom of extending the directive power to all crown corporations has been questioned. Whether crown corporations should be compensated by the government for the costs incurred in implementing directives is also debated.

Parliament passes the legislation establishing federal crown corporations and must approve any subsequent amendments. It approves the tabled budgets of crown corporations and any government-requested appropriations to cover operating deficits. Parliament also reviews the annual reports of crown corporations, queries ministers during question period and discusses corporate performance with ministers and senior management in the forum of parliamentary committees. In federal politics, however, no standing committee specializes in the scrutiny of crown corporations, although such committees operate in BC and Saskatchewan. Recent reform proposals have not emphasized a greater role for Parliament in the administration of crown corporations.

The formal controls on crown corporations are buttressed by a range of informal processes and influences. In fact, the relationships between governments and crown corporations, like most political relationships, are sometimes fractious and often characterized by bargaining, negotiations and compromise. Widespread debate during the 1970s over the behaviour, effectiveness and roles of crown corporations was inspired by the view that the scope and economic importance of crown corporations had clearly outdistanced the federal government's capacity to control them. The FAA appeared antiquated. Many observed that major crown corporations, particularly the CNR, had escaped political control. The auditor general severely criticized the financial management of crown corporations, and controversy developed over the activities of Atomic Energy of Canada Ltd and Air Canada. The federal Liberal government responded in 1977 with a major report on the control and accountability of crown corporations, but so far no new legislation has been passed. The 1979 Conservative government under PM Clark tabled a major bill on the subject, but was defeated before the legislation was passed. Clark's promise to "privatize" Petro-Canada and other crown corporations raised basic questions about the effectiveness and purpose of government firms. The administration of provincial crown corporations in BC, Manitoba and Québec has also been controversial.

Should crown corporations use the same criteria as private firms in making decisions? What balance should they strike between commercial considerations and the accomplishment of political and social goals? What ground rules should govern competition between public and private enterprise? (*See* COMPETITION POLICY.) The expanding role of crown corporations, especially Petro-Canada, in the resource industries has raised the last problem to new prominence. Some private firms have argued that crown corporations enjoy advantages which render any resulting competition unfair. Finally, balancing corporate autonomy, government control and legislative supervision will become more difficult as crown corporations expand and assume new roles.
ALLAN TUPPER

Reading: M. Gordon, *Government in Business* (1981); Allan Tupper and G.B. Doern, eds, *Public Corporations and Public Policy in Canada* (1981).

Crow's Nest Pass Agreement In the 1890s, when rich mineral deposits were discovered in the Kootenay region of southern BC, American developers began to move into the region and extend rail lines northward from their transcontinentals. The CANADIAN PACIFIC RAILWAY, determined to retain control of southwestern Canada, asked the federal government for assistance to extend its own line over the CROWSNEST PASS into BC. At the same time, Prairie farmers were complaining about high freight rates charged by the CPR, and further federal assistance to that company would be unpopular unless something was done about the freight rates.

The Crow's Nest Pass Agreement, dated 6 Sept 1897, was an agreement between the CPR and the Canadian government. The CPR was given a cash subsidy of $3.3 million and title to pass into BC, in exchange for reducing, in perpetuity, eastbound rates on grain and flour and westbound ones on a specified list of "settlers' effects" (total rate reduction about 15%). The CPR obtained access to the valuable mining and smelting activities in the BC interior, and the government was able to allay western concerns over national transportation policies. The rate reduction coincided almost exactly with the beginning of the settlement boom, and quickly became enshrined in the public mind as a key part of the economic strategy of the day.

The suspension of the agreement in response to wartime inflation created consternation among western farmers. The CPR resisted attempts by the Board of Railway Commissioners to reimpose the terms after 1922, and there followed a period of complicated political and legal maneuvering. in 1925 the 1897 rates on grain and flour traffic were reinstated, applicable to all such traffic on all rail lines to Ft William, and the "settlers' effects" provision was canceled. This solution was not satisfactory to anyone, and further negotiations produced in 1927 the agreement that the rates would be applied to all the company's lines but only on grain and unprocessed grain products.

The "Crow rate" pays only a fraction of what it now costs to transport grain, and there has been a lengthy search for a more equitable rate. For farmers the Crow rate has been an important factor in reducing costs enough to attract and keep export markets. But the railways have been unable to afford the improvements and expansion to their lines made necessary by increased traffic and demanded by farmers. After much heated discussion and disagreement by government, railway, farmers and farmers' organizations, the Western Grain Transportation Act was passed 17 Nov 1983 (effective 1 Jan 84); it replaces the Crow and allows grain-shipping costs to increase gradually, but never to exceed 10% of the world price for grain. The federal government pays the rest of grain-transportation costs, estimated to be $660 million annually by 1988. The railways agreed to spend $16.5 billion on new equipment and expansion of service by 1992.
T.D. REGEHR AND KEN NORRIE

Crowsnest Pass, elev 1357 m, is situated in the ROCKY MTNS, on the BC-Alberta border, 40 km N of the US border. The area was explored extensively by the PALLISER EXPEDITION 1857-60. In 1882 G.M. DAWSON of the Dominion Geological Survey did exploratory work for a Crow's Nest Pass Ry (built 1898 as part of the CPR system). The most southerly of the important railway passes crossing the continental divide, the pass is also crossed by Hwy No 3 and a pipeline. The surrounding area, dotted with towns and villages, is famous for its coal production.
GLEN BOLES

CRTC, *see* CANADIAN RADIO-TELEVISION AND TELECOMMUNICATIONS COMMISSION.

Cruikshank, William, painter (b at Broughty Ferry, Scot 25 Dec 1848; d at Kansas C, Mo 19 May 1922). A reclusive eccentric, Cruikshank was most influential as an art instructor in Toronto in the late 19th and early 20th centuries. He arrived in Canada in 1856 but studied in London and Paris (1864 or 1868 to about 1873). He worked as an illustrator for various London periodicals and in New York 1873-76 for *Scribner's* and *St. Nicholas Magazine.* In 1876 he returned to Toronto as an illustrator and art teacher. His best works were drawings in black and white, but he was capable of producing fine paintings, such as his portrait *Anne Cruikshank.*
DOROTHY FARR

Downtown Coleman, in SW Alberta, one of the old coal-mining towns of the Crowsnest Pass. Visible are the coal piles behind the town and the coaltipple in the middle of the town (*courtesy Elliott and Nicole Bernshaw / Bernshaw Photography*).

Crum, George, conductor (b at Providence, RI 26 Oct 1926). A student at Toronto's Royal Conservatory of Music, Crum made his professional debut as a pianist at age 16 and soon joined the faculty of the Conservatory's OPERA department. In 1951 he became the first conductor and music director of the NATIONAL BALLET OF CANADA, building its orchestra and repertoire while conducting operas throughout Canada and the US, leading Prom concerts in Toronto and conducting for the CBC. With the National Ballet, Crum conducted award-winning performances of *Cinderella* and *The Sleeping Beauty* (Emmys in 1970 and 1973) and of *Romeo and Juliet* (Prix René Barthélemy, 1966); in 1972 he won the Celia Award. He retired from the National Ballet in 1984. PENELOPE DOOB

Crump, Norris Roy, railway executive (b at Revelstoke, BC 30 July 1904). Born into a railway family, Crump began with the CANADIAN PACIFIC RAILWAY as a labourer in 1920, taking time off to study science at Purdue U. He graduated in 1929 and in 1936 received a master's degree. Crump was especially interested in the new diesel electric engines and it was becoming clear that the railway would have to confront "dieselization." Crump was promoted through the CPR's engineering departments and, as a senior executive, was responsible for the transcontinental flagship train, the "Canadian." He became president in 1955 and chairman in 1961. Under him Canadian ownership of company stock rose from 15% in 1955 to 55% in 1965 and 63% in 1972. In 1962 Crump diversified the company by forming Canadian Pacific Investments to handle nontransport investments. He retired as president in 1964 and as chairman in 1972. ROBERT BOTHWELL

Crustacean, shelled INVERTEBRATE with segmented body and limbs at some stage of its life, an exoskeleton and 2 pairs of antennae. The exoskeleton, a protective and supportive framework located outside the body, is periodically molted to allow for growth. Crustaceans, with over 31 300 living species, comprise a subphylum of the phylum Arthropoda. They occupy terrestrial and fresh and saltwater habitats, and range in size from the Japanese spider crab, with a 3.65 m claw-span, to microscopic WATER FLEAS. The well-known SHRIMP, CRAB and LOBSTER belong to the Malacostraca, one of 8 classes. Various reductions and fusions notwithstanding, the crustacean body is essentially composed of a head with 5 pairs of appendages, and a trunk with numerous segments and appendages. The Cephalocarida, first discovered near New York (1955), are reminiscent of the primitive crustacean condition: many segments and trunk limbs are very similar, one after another (serial homology). Diversification and specialization of the appendages has occurred through evolutionary time: the modern crab bears little superficial resemblance to the BARNACLE.

The filter-feeding habit is common and many bottom-dwelling forms are detritus feeders. Anterior appendages (often 7 pairs) catch and handle food. In some Malacostracans, food maceration is aided by chitinous (horny) teeth in the muscular stomach. Gas exchange takes place in gills attached to the bases of the trunk appendages. A copper-based respiratory pigment in some crustaceans causes blue-tinged blood. Sexes are separate in some species; others change sexes in mid-life, are hermaphroditic, or are born pregnant (making males unnecessary most of the time). Many brood their eggs until larvae emerge. Numerous molts follow while the larva is free swimming. The presence of a rigid exoskeleton necessitates a molting process initiated by hormones, following which the naked crustacean rapidly swells with water. The outer cuticle (tough covering) hardens again while the animal remains in hiding.

Ancestral crustaceans were probably swimmers. Through appendage modification, walking, crawling, burrowing, sessile and parasitic life-styles have also been adopted. The ZOOPLANKTON link in the ocean's food chain is composed primarily of tiny crustaceans. Many of Canada's great WHALES, the fin, grey, sei, blue and humpback, feed almost exclusively on these small animals. Some crustaceans are common pests (eg, terrestrial amphipods in greenhouses, isopods boring into wood and barnacles fouling ships); however, the group makes a major contribution to Canadian FISHERIES. A brief discussion of the 8 crustacean classes follows. V. TUNNICLIFFE

Cephalocarida, tiny (2-4 mm long), hermaphroditic, shrimplike crustaceans; 9 species and 4 genera are known. Inadequate collection probably accounts for absence of Canadian records. The body consists of a shield-shaped head, elongated thorax and abdomen. The head has 5 pairs of appendages; the thorax, 8 segments, each possessing a similar pair of legs, the last pair reduced or absent; the abdomen, 11 ringlike, limbless body segments (somites) and an anal segment bearing a pair of appendages (uropods). These most primitive living crustaceans inhabit soft, muddy bottoms, silty sands or algal beds and occur in the Atlantic and Pacific oceans between 40° N and S latitudes, usually from intertidal zones to 300 m depths. C.T. SHIH

Branchiopoda, crustacean class comprising 3 orders: Anostraca (fairy shrimps), Notostraca (tadpole shrimps) and Diplostraca (clam shrimps and water fleas). Branchiopods are nearly all restricted to fresh water. Although most are microscopic, they represent an important element in the planktonic food chain. The name derives from structures on the legs that function as gills; the multiple appendages are used for swimming and filter feeding. Branchiopods are characteristic of waters that frequently dry or freeze. Many branchiopods are parthenogenetic (males are rare; females are born pregnant). Thus, they can quickly take advantage of the reconstitution of their habitat. Most branchiopods are pale and transparent; hemoglobin in the body gives some a rosy colour. V. TUNNICLIFFE

Ostracoda, seed shrimp, are microscopic, bean-shaped, bivalved crustaceans living at the bottom of fresh or marine bodies of water. Over 2000 living species have been described worldwide; about 150 freshwater species and many more marine forms are known from Canada. Habitats range from temporary pools in semiarid southern Saskatchewan to large lakes and streams transcontinentally, including the Arctic. Ostracodes molt about 8 times before adulthood; shells lack growth lines. Ostracodes serve as food for bottom-dwelling fish. They are important indicators of habitat changes. Their FOSSIL record is continuous and contains the largest number of fossil species (about 10 000) among crustaceans. L.D. DELORME

Mystacocarida, small class of minute crustaceans, usually less than 0.5 mm long. The elongated, cylindrical body is divided into head, bearing 5 pairs of appendages, and eleven-segmented trunk. Each of the first 5 trunk segments bears a pair of appendages. The telson possesses a pair of clawlike tail branches. Sexes are separate. These marine, benthic animals live between fine sand grains in intertidal and subtidal zones of the Atlantic and SW Indian oceans. There are 10 known species in 2 genera. Inadequate collection probably accounts for absence of Canadian records. C.T. SHIH

Copepoda, small crustaceans, from 0.1-300 mm long (usually 0.5-5.0 mm), some free-living, others parasitic during part of their lives. The body is divided into cephalothorax, bearing up to 11 pairs of appendages, and limbless abdomen. Parasitic copepods may deviate from the basic form. Copepods inhabit all aquatic environments (including the High Arctic), from deep oceans to temporary freshwater ponds, and may be PLANKTONIC, benthic or periphytonic (livsymbionts with other marine invertebrates (symbionts with other marine invertebrates. Parasitic species attach themselves externally or internally to fishes, marine mammals and marine invertebrates. About 8000 species are known. In Canada the most common species belong to the following genera: *Calanus, Oithona* (marine); *Diaptomus, Cyclops* (freshwater); and *Caligus* (parasitic). C.T. SHIH

Branchiura, fish lice, are crustaceans with a depressed body (up to 3 cm long) divided into head, 4-segmented thorax and unsegmented abdomen. A shield-shaped carapace covers head and part of thorax. The head and its 5 pairs of appendages are adapted for locomotion. Each thoracic segment bears a pair of legs modified to form a grasping organ in the male. The reduced, fin-shaped abdomen bears a pair of minute tail branches. Sexes are separate. Fertilized eggs are laid on hard substrata. Young hatch as modified larvae or juveniles and soon attach to a host. Branchiura are external parasites of marine and freshwater fishes, but frequently leave the host to swim or crawl. About 130 species and 4 genera are known. Ten species of genus *Argulus* are recorded from Canadian Atlantic and Pacific coastal waters and freshwater lakes. C.T. SHIH

Cirripedia, group of crustaceans with over 900 species, including sessile and parasitic forms. They live from intertidal zones to the deep sea. Familiarly known as barnacles, most cirripedes cement themselves to hard surfaces and secrete protective calcareous plates. A goose barnacle has its plates perched on a flexible stalk. Fine setae (bristles) filter out food particles from water currents generated by leg movements. Parasitic barnacles can be found on organisms ranging from jellyfish to whales. There are at least 20 species of acorn and goose barnacles on the rocks of Canada's West Coast. One species grows to 15 cm. V. TUNNICLIFFE

Malacostraca Ancestral malacostracans lived in the oceans some 200 million years before DINOSAURS roamed the earth. Today, they constitute nearly 75% of all crustacean species, and include lobsters, crabs, CRAYFISH and shrimp, some of the largest and most economically valuable invertebrate species. Most are still found in the marine environment, although a significant number of species have become established in fresh water, and the pill bugs (wood lice) are a fairly large terrestrial group. A typical malacostracan has stalked eyes, 19 segments plus a telson (18 according to some experts, who do not consider the antennules to be associated with a true segment), a cylindrical body in which the thorax is partially fused with the head and covered with a carapace, and one or more pairs of anterior thoracic appendages modified for handling food. However, the malacostracans are a diverse group, with as many exceptions to this basic plan as followers of it. In 2 of the largest orders, the Isopoda and Amphipoda, there is no carapace and the eyes are sessile (immovable) rather than stalked. In the isopods the body is generally flattened from back to belly (dorsoventrally); in the amphipods it is more commonly compressed laterally. Variations on the generalized plan seem limited only by the numbers of species and the variety of ecological niches occupied.

The various classification systems divide Malacostraca into 10-12 orders, of which only 4 have freshwater representatives in N America. Two-thirds of all malacostracans are in 3 major orders: Isopoda, Amphipoda and Decapoda. The remainder are mainly small, little-known species, but many are important parts of aquatic food chains for economically valuable animals. Mysids (opossum shrimp) are almost exclusively marine, but in the Great Lakes a freshwater mysid occasionally constitutes 80% of the diet of trout. Another lesser-known group, the pelagic euphausiids (krill) often occur in large numbers in the marine environment; some species form a major part of the diet of large whales. It has been estimated that a blue whale can consume 2-3 t of euphausiids in a single feeding. The euphausiids are also unusual in being bioluminescent, ie, capable of producing their own light from organs (photophores) located at several points on the body.

The order Isopoda includes some 4000 species, most of which are marine and have dorsoventrally flattened bodies, sessile eyes and no carapace. The order also includes parasitic forms, freshwater species and the only large group of terrestrial crustaceans, the pill bugs, sow bugs or wood lice. The name pill bug comes from the animal's tendency to roll into a pill-shaped sphere for protection from physical danger or dehydration. The various species of pill bugs can be found beneath stones, matted vegetation and fallen trees, where they feed on algae, moss, bark and decaying organic matter.

The order Amphipoda comprises about 3600 species, typically with sessile eyes, no carapace and a humpbacked, laterally compressed body. Most are marine but there are a significant number of freshwater species, and even a few that might be considered terrestrial. Although some live in the ocean depths, amphipods are most common in shallow water and in the intertidal zone, where they are known as sandhoppers or beach fleas. In the freshwater habitat they serve as transmitters of acanthocephalan parasites (intestinal worms) of ducks, and as an important food for aquatic birds and fish.

The order Decapoda contains 8500 species, including the shrimp, crayfish, crabs and lobsters, and is by far the largest crustacean group. Most decapods are marine, but crayfish, some shrimp and a few other species are found in fresh water. In decapods, the first 3 pairs of thoracic appendages are modified as maxillipeds for the handling of food, leaving 5 pairs as walking legs (hence the name Decapoda, "ten feet"). Decapoda are divided into 2 major groups: the Natantia (swimmers), encompassing the shrimp; and the Reptantia (crawlers), including lobsters, crayfish and crabs. Decapods are among the most interesting invertebrates and, as a group, are certainly the most economically valuable in Canada. D.E. AIKEN

Reading: R.D. Barnes, *Invertebrate Zoology* (1980).

Crustacean Resources In Canada, all crustacean species with significant economic value are in the order Decapoda. The decapods constitute a major portion of the dollar value of various Canadian FISHERIES, and in some areas, particularly in the East, the local economy is almost completely dependent on them. The American lobster (*Homarus americanus*) is the most valuable of these resources. Freshly caught LOBSTER may be shipped live immediately to points in N America, Europe and Asia, or held in pounds until demand and price are more favourable. A much smaller percentage is cooked and canned. Some areas in the Gulf of St Lawrence have special fisheries for "canner" lobsters, which are slightly smaller than the "market" sizes shipped live. In 1983, almost 28 000 t were landed along the Atlantic coast, valued at over $142 million — more than twice the combined value of the CRAB and SHRIMP industries. On the East Coast, snow or queen crab (*Chionoecetes opilio*) is the most valuable crab species (over $53 million), a distinction that goes to Dungeness crab (*Cancer magister*) on the West Coast (nearly $3 million in 1983). In BC waters the principal commercial species is the prawn (*Pandalus platyceros*) which, with the smooth pink shrimp (*Pandalus jordani*), was worth about $4 million in 1983, considerably less than the nearly $19 million commanded by *Pandalus borealis* on the East Coast. Because of the seasonality and unpredictability of traditional fishing, AQUACULTURE of valuable species is an attractive prospect. Of all decapods in Canada with potential for culture, the American lobster has received the most attention. Most of the technological and biological problems have been overcome, but high costs of rearing from egg to market size remain a constraint. D.E. AIKEN

Crysler's Farm, site of a battle fought 11 Nov 1813 between 4000 American troops and a combined force of about 800 British regulars, Canadian militia and a few of His Majesty's Indian allies. The location was along the upper St Lawrence R near present-day Morrisburg, Ont. Led by Lt-Col Joseph Wanton Morrison of the 89th Regiment of Foot and elements of the 49th Foot, the British won a resounding victory over the American invasion force, which was attempting to capture Montréal and thus isolate UPPER CANADA. This was one of the decisive battles of the WAR OF 1812. A monument commemorating the Battle of Crysler's Farm is at UPPER CANADA VILLAGE. ROBERT S. ALLEN

Cuban Missile Crisis began 22 Oct 1962. Following intelligence reports that the USSR was installing ballistic missiles in Cuba capable of hitting US and Canadian targets, Pres John Kennedy announced an American naval blockade of the island, threatening further action if preparation of the sites continued. The issue for the Canadian government, informed of Kennedy's intentions only 1½ hours in advance, was whether to comply with an American request to move Canadian forces to an alert status known as "Defcon 3." With the approval of Minister of National Defence Douglas Harkness, the units concerned quietly did so, but formal authorization was delayed while Cabinet debated, Oct 23-24. Harkness argued that the nature of the crisis, combined with existing arrangements for defence co-operation, made the alert necessary. Fearing a Canadian alert would provoke the USSR, believing the Americans' Cuban policy to be generally unbalanced, angered by the lack of advance consultation and concerned about implications for Canadian policy on nuclear weapons, PM John Diefenbaker and Secretary of State for External Affairs Howard Green were reluctant to acquiesce. About half the ministers were undecided, but, as Soviet ships approached the quarantine zone later in the week, the Harkness position gained support. On Oct 24 Diefenbaker authorized the alert, and the decision was announced Oct 25 in the Commons.

The hesitant Canadian response reflected in part the desire of the prime minister and others to preserve the independence of Canadian foreign policy and to maintain a balanced posture in crisis conditions. The delay, however, was widely criticized, and contributed to a growing perception of indecisiveness in the Diefenbaker government. It also exacerbated already difficult relations with the Kennedy administration and fuelled further controversy over nuclear weapons. The crisis itself ended Oct 27-28 when Soviet Premier Nikita Khrushchev agreed to dismantle the missiles. DENIS STAIRS

Cuckoo (Cuculidae), family of BIRDS with 125-127 species, including common cuckoo, anis, couas, coucals and roadrunners, distributed almost worldwide. Cuckoos are long and slim with long tails, longish wings and stout to long, usually slightly downcurved bills. Legs are short except in ground-dwelling species with zygodactylous feet (2 toes forward, 2 back). The loud, unmusical call of the commonest European species gives the family its name. A false belief that cuckoos call only before rain accounts for a colloquial name, rain crow. Several species are brood parasites, laying their eggs in nests of other birds. The hosts raise the young cuckoos, often at the expense of their own young. Most cuckoos establish exclusive breeding territories, but the tropical anis build large communal nests in which each pair occupies a compartment. Two species occur in Canada, the black-billed cuckoo (*Coccyzus erythropthalmus*) breeding from the Maritimes to central Alberta, and the yellow-billed cuckoo (*C. americanus*) primarily in SE Ontario and adjacent Québec, with smaller populations in southwest NB and S coastal BC, rarely also in Manitoba. They are similar in appearance: plain brown above, white below. Both species lay 2-5 eggs in frail nests in trees of open woodland, with both species incubating, although both occasionally lay eggs in other birds' nests, including each others'. Larger species eat lizards, snakes and occasionally birds, but most are insectivorous. The fondness of the 2 Canadian species for tent caterpillars makes them economically valuable.

MARTIN K. MCNICHOLL

Cucumber (*Cucumis sativus*), herbaceous annual VEGETABLE of the Cucurbitaceae family. Only 3 wild plants belonging to this family occur in Canada, the most common being the climbing cucumber, a distant relative of the cultivated cucumber. Cultivated in China 3000 years ago, the cucumber spread to Europe in the 14th century. Christopher Columbus introduced it to Haiti. Generally, each plant bears both male and female flowers; however, female and seedless varieties also exist. The cucumber develops long stems with tendrils. Some plants have small, short fruits called gherkins; others produce long fruit, either American (field) type or European (greenhouse) type. Cucumber is usually sown in fields but can be cultivated out of season in GREENHOUSES. Few insects attack cucumbers and modern strains are becoming increasingly disease resistant. Although low in vitamins and minerals, cucumbers are rich in water and have practically no calories. More than 3500 ha are cultivated in Canada, over 1000 ha in Québec alone. ROGER DOUCET

Cuisine Throughout recorded history, foodstuffs and methods of preparation have been transplanted from one region or country to another; thus the cultural heritage of every country is reflected in its cuisine. While such factors as Canada's climate, available food resources, customs and economic and social development are important, the adaptation of recipes and foodstuffs from many lands has created enormous variety in Canadian cuisine.

Although Canada has benefited from the "foodways" of its native people and its settlers for many years, EXPO '67 brought the culinary influence of many nations into sharper focus for millions of Canadians. This broader appreciation and knowledge has been strengthened by the rapid growth in international travel and the recent huge increase in the amount and variety of imported foodstuffs available. Rapid transportation, fast freezing and other forms of food preservation, and vastly improved distribution systems have brought various foodstuffs from across the country and abroad within reach of most Canadians, and have virtually eliminated the seasonal unavailability of most products. As a result, Canada has left behind a large part of its pioneer gastronomic past. Great efforts are being made by governments, FOOD AND BEVERAGE INDUSTRIES, the food services industry and private citizens to develop Canada's food potential. In all parts of the country, attention is being paid to excellence of food and drink.

Provincial Specialties

The wide variety of Canadian-grown foodstuffs, augmented by imported products and enriched by the foodways of newcomers from many lands, has resulted in a rich mosaic of food and cookery.

British Columbia is noted for the quality and variety of its FISH and shellfish, its rich market gardens and its orchards. SHRIMP, CRAB, SALMON, black COD and halibut, lamb from Saltspring I and FRUIT and VEGETABLES from the Okanagan (including several varieties of grape for wine making) are complemented by fine cheddar cheeses from Armstrong. Typical dishes include crab bouchées, baked salmon, halibut, black cod seethed in milk, roast lamb, fresh fruit and cheese plates, and apple dumplings.

Alberta is world famous for its BEEF and WHEAT. Its lamb, pork and turkey are achieving popularity, along with buffalo (ie, BISON) when available. Other excellent foods are elk, partridge, pheasant, MUSHROOMS, chokecherries, honey and a large variety of cheeses. Typical dishes include beefsteaks, beef stew, buffalo steaks, and roast turkey, beef, pork and lamb.

Saskatchewan Most of southern Saskatchewan is divided into large farms producing wheat, OATS, BARLEY, RYE, CANOLA and other grains. The northern half provides WHITEFISH, TROUT, PICKEREL, antelope and many wild BERRIES, including the unique saskatoon berry and the pin cherry, both delicious in pies and preserves. The province is on the main MIGRATION paths of birds, including the Canada GOOSE, partridge, prairie chicken and small mallard DUCK. Typical dishes include roast turkey, baked partridge, Canada goose or prairie chicken, roast or boiled corn on the cob, saskatoon berry pie, bannock, baked lake trout and broiled pickerel.

Manitoba also produces wheat and other grains and shares the abundance of migratory birds with Saskatchewan. It is noted for smoked Winnipeg goldeye, WILD RICE, honey, whitefish, pike, caviar, white-tailed deer, red CABBAGE and various berries, including the wild cranberry. Typical dishes are wild rice accompanying meats, wild and domestic fowl or fish, roast wild duck, baked stuffed whitefish and Manitoba caviar with sour cream, Winnipeg goldeye and hot biscuits with honey.

Ontario produces many kinds of food. Its orchards supply a variety of fruit; its vineyards produce grapes for the growing WINE INDUSTRY; its market gardens produce a multitude of other vegetables. Three-quarters of a million lakes provide whitefish, lake trout, pike and smelt. Ontario is world famous as the source of fine cheeses, such as those of English, French, Dutch, Danish and Swiss origin. It is a hunter's paradise, with pheasant and other GAME BIRDS in abundance. Typical dishes are roasted cheese canapes, smelts baked in wine, roast pheasant, turnip scallop, macaroni mousse, pumpkin pie, plus the myriad of foreign dishes brought by various ethnic groups over the years.

Québec The long culinary history of Québec is based on pork, MAPLE SUGAR, specialty cheeses, wild game, partridge, domestic ducklings and special varieties of APPLES and MELONS. These foods are augmented by an abundance of fish from Québec's many rivers and lakes. Traditional dishes include pea soup, onion soup, pork chops with maple sugar, tourtière, cretons, sugar pie, Montréal melon with Oka or Ermite cheese, and pâté de foie gras.

New Brunswick has delicious seafoods, excellent POTATOES, and an edible young ostrich fern called the FIDDLEHEAD. Its salmon, OYSTERS, LOBSTER, clams and shad are famous. Less well-known is a type of dried SEAWEED, called dulse, which is eaten locally as a snack. Fine lamb is grown on New Brunswick's salt marshes, and its blueberries, strawberries, rhubarb and mushrooms are excellent. Typical dishes are shad amandine, broiled Restigouche salmon, blueberry crisp, baked beans, clam chowder, boiled or steamed fiddleheads and roast lamb.

Prince Edward Island produces the finest seed potatoes in the world, oysters, lobsters and mackerel, and excellent cheeses and other DAIRY products. Traditional dishes are Malpeque oyster bisque, soused mackerel, potato pancakes and fried smelts.

Nova Scotia enjoys both saltwater and freshwater fishes, apples, cranberries, strawberries, dike mushrooms, maple syrup and dairy products. Its Digby scallops are internationally known, as are its TUNA and swordfish. Traditional dishes include oyster stew, fried Digby scallops, clam chowder, fish chowder, Lunenburg sausage, blueberry grunt, Cape Breton oatcakes, solomon gundy, Mahone Bay steamed brown bread and fried Gaspereau herring.

Newfoundland, home of the cod, enjoys this fish in many forms, along with lobster, seal and squid. Salt pork and beef are popular, along with dandelion greens, turnips and turnip tops, cabbage, potatoes and carrots. Partridgeberries, marshberries and squashberries are found, as are the unique, amber-coloured bakeapple berry, rich in vitamin C. Traditional dishes are baked cod cheeks and tongues, seal-flipper pie, cod roe, fish stew and the boiled dinner featuring salt beef or salt pork.

Yukon Territory has moose, wild blueberries and arctic grayling.

Northwest Territories is the home of arctic char, caribou, ptarmigan and various wild berries.

These regional specialties would be complemented by the standard dishes that are readily available in most parts of Canada, excellent baked goods and dairy products, and the large number of ethnic dishes available in Canadian cities and towns. Canadian foods and beverages are enjoying increasing international acclaim. Canadian beef, ham, bacon and cheeses are world renowned. Canada's blended rye whiskies, beers and a few wines have won prestigious awards.

Research, Development and Quality

The federal and provincial governments devote many millions of dollars annually to research and development designed to improve the quality and availability of grain, fruits, vegetables, animals, poultry and fish for use in Canada and for export. Over 2000 inspectors in all parts of Canada administer the National Sanitation Code, to ensure the highest standards of freshness and quality and to maintain food-product integrity and consumer health (*see* COMMODITY INSPECTION AND GRADING). Considerable research is done by governments, producers' organizations and professional chefs into methods of food preparation that will maximize the nutrition and appeal of all foodstuffs.

Professional Chefs

Basic education and training in nutrition and food preparation has been generally available in the school system for decades, along with the scientific study of nutrition and DIETETICS at some universities and colleges. Professionally trained commercial and institutional chefs from Europe brought a high level of expertise to central Canada and contributed to the development of professional training in Québec and Ontario. By the late 1950s formal professional training in food preparation and service had begun in western Canada, centered largely in post-secondary institutes of technology. Canada has only recently begun to produce a significant number of Canadian-trained chefs. The profession is now well established, and each major city has a local academy of chefs. These academies, together with provincial organizations, form the Canadian Federation of Chefs de Cuisine. This organization plays an active role internationally as a member of the World Federation of Cooks' Societies, which held its world meeting in Banff, Alta, in 1974 and which had a Canadian as president 1982-84. Canadian chefs continue to rank among the world's best, consistently winning top honours at the World Culinary Olympics, held every 4 years. A 5-member Team Canada, captained by Henri Dane of Vancouver, won the 16th annual World Culinary Olympics in Frankfurt, West Germany, in Oct 1984. More than 40 Canadian chefs took part, winning 24 golds.

Food Service Establishments

Canadian hotels and restaurants are making concerted efforts to improve the quality of dining out. Many are active members of the Canadian Restaurant and Foodservices Association and its provincial constituent associations. These associations provide leadership and on-the-job training in many facets of the industry, including effective short courses in hygiene and sanitation in food preparation and service. Canada's food industry now has the highest standards of hygiene and sanitation in the world. In 1984 the industry is expected to employ about 625 000 people directly; many thousands more are involved in growing and handling the food it serves.

Dining Out

With the availability of international travel, the increasing sophistication of Canadian taste, the availability of more European chefs and the professional training of large numbers of Canadians in food-preparation services, Canadians have increasingly dined out over the past 20 years. Canadian cities now afford the diner a choice of many kinds of food, from fast or take-out foods (eg, hamburgers, hotdogs, submarine sandwiches, pizzas, fried chicken, Cantonese dishes) to the most sophisticated examples of French and Italian cuisine. Other restaurants offer the best foods of many other eastern and western European, Far Eastern and N American cultures.

Gastronomic Societies

Samuel de CHAMPLAIN established l'ORDRE DE BON TEMPS, an association devoted in part to the ceremonious presentation of meals, at Port-Royal 1606-07. Societies dedicated to the advancement of good cooking continue to flourish in Canada. The world's oldest gastronomic society, la Confrérie de la chaîne des rôtisseurs, is represented in Canada, as is the International Wine and Food Society, les Amis d'Escoffier, l'Ordre mondial des gourmets, the American, German and Italian wine clubs, the several Commanderies de Bordeau and the Opimian Society. These societies and others are growing in popular appeal, supplemented by numerous small local groups.

Cookbooks and the Media

In 1831 James Macfarlane of Kingston published *The Cook Not Mad; or Rational Cookery*, Canada's first cookbook. Later in the century appeared *The Canadian Home Cook Book* (1877) and *Mrs. Clarke's Cookery Book* (1883), revised in 1899 under the name *The Comfort Cook Book*. Mrs James MacDonald's *The Cook's True Friend* appeared in the same year. Early in the 20th century, locally published cookbooks began to appear, such as *Culinary Landmarks, or Half Hours with Sault Ste Marie Housewives* (1905). Specialty publications by makers of flour, baking powder, yeast and other basic ingredients were also published.

Landmarks in Canada's more recent cookbook history are Kate Aitken's national collection of 1950, *Helen Gougeons's Good Food* (1958) and *The Encyclopedia of Canadian Cookery* (1970). The most comprehensive collection of the recipes of many lands as used in Canada was published as *Fare Exchange*, by Dorothy Allen-Gray in 1963, and an equally comprehensive collection of recipes from northern Canada, the *Northern Cookbook*, was published in 1967 by Eleanor A. Ellis, with the support of the Department of Indian Affairs and Northern Development. The 1972 publication *Indian Recipes*, by Bernard Assiniwi, adapts an excellent Canada-wide collection of centuries-old native Indian recipes to modern life.

During the past decade Canadian publishers ave produced a multitude of local, region-l, specialty and beautifully illustrated "coffee able" Canadian books about food and wine. dna Staebler's *Food That Really Schmecks* (1968) is n example of a popular regional cookbook. ehane Benoît, besides popularizing Québecois ishes such as sugar pie, has produced general ookbooks, eg, *Enjoying the Art of Canadian Cooking* 1974) and the *Complete Heritage of Canadian Cook-ng* (1976). Paralleling this outpouring of infor-nation, Agriculture Canada has tested recipes nd produced hundreds of cookbooks for fish, neat, poultry, vegetables, fruits, berries, etc, all ased on products that are most enjoyable, least ostly and most nutritious. Various provincial overnments also publish works of this kind. n many homes, several basic cookbooks are upplemented by an abundance of recipes and uidance found in newspapers, family maga-ines, specialty magazines and television pro-rams. GARNET T. PAGE

ullen, Maurice Galbraith, painter (b at St ohn's 6 June 1866; d at Chambly, Qué 28 Mar 934). Cullen moved to Montréal with his fam-ly in 1870. There he began his art training as a culptor at the Conseil des Arts et Manufactures nd with sculptor Louis-Philippe HÉBERT. Like ther artists of his generation, he went to Paris or additional training. He arrived there in 1889 nd decided to become a painter; he attended the cole des beaux-arts, studying, like Paul PEEL, vith Jean-Léon Gérôme, then with Élie Delau-ay. By 1895, when Cullen returned to Montréal, he had darkened the tonality of the impressionist style learned abroad. In time he became the true interpreter of Montréal's cityscape, particularly of night or dusk scenes, invariably with shimmering lights. He was also one of Canada's great painters of snow. Like his colleague and friend James Wilson MORRICE, Cullen was a major figure in Canadian art. His gift was that of a romantic — an ability to capture light and mood. Some of his work was influenced by William Blair Bruce, whom Cullen often visited in Gréz 1892-94. Cullen in turn influenced many by teaching for years at the Art Assn of Montréal. He showed in the first exhibition of the Canadian Art Club, an advanced group of the period, and was made a member in 1910. A.Y. Jackson said of Cullen, "To us he was a hero." JOAN MURRAY

Old Houses, Montreal (c1908) by Maurice Cullen, oil on canvas. In his impressionist style, Cullen was the true interpreter of Montréal's cityscape and one of Canada's great painters of snow (*courtesy The Montreal Museum of Fine Arts*).

Cultural Dualism is both a term that describes some characteristics of Canadian society and, in many people's view, an ideology according to which the social and political systems of Canada should be organized. It is based on the historical fact that Canada was colonized by both the French and the English, and that both groups are therefore the "founding peoples" of Canada. This fact is used to justify the privileges accorded these 2 groups in comparison to those accorded other ethnic groups, and to justify the equality of the 2 groups.

Although the notion of cultural dualism has been translated into legislation and into policies of schooling, religion, language and the institutional rights of provinces, its origins are difficult to determine. Some legislation, eg, constitutional laws of Canada, can be interpreted as a defence of cultural dualism. For example, the 1774 QUEBEC ACT legally recognized the Catholic religion, the seigneurial system and French CIVIL LAW in Québec. The 1841 Act of Union recognized that the 2 colonizing groups coexisted, and the CONSTITUTION ACT, 1867, formalized some of the principles of cultural dualism. First, it determined the powers of the federal state and of the provinces (thus recognizing some of the specificities of Québec, where French Canadians formed the majority); second, legislation in regard to civil law was confirmed; third, in education, a provincial domain, a clause allowed for public funds to subsidize confessional schools and protected religious minorities in Québec. Ironically, this clause was demanded by Québec English Protestants who feared they would be outnumbered and overpowered by French Catholics in Québec. French Catholics in the rest of Canada later attempted, with little success, to use the same clause to defend themselves against similar fears with regard to English Canadians. Under recent Québec language legislation (BILL 22 and BILL 101), children of some groups, particularly immigrants, have been obliged to attend French schools, but the legislation has not altered the denominational structure of education in Montréal or the public funding of private, religious or ethnic schools in Québec.

It has often been said that Canada was created as a state by mercantile capitalists and railway owners who needed a central administration from which to settle and exploit the country. Others, especially many French Canadians, believed that CONFEDERATION was a step towards a new state, one independent of England. It was understood that the 2 founding groups were to coexist, but the rights and privileges of Catholic French Canadians outside Québec were either not specified or were denied and ignored (*see*

NEW BRUNSWICK SCHOOL QUESTION; ONTARIO SCHOOLS QUESTION; MANITOBA SCHOOLS QUESTION). Catholic schools (often French) were not subsidized by public funds; French was forbidden in the public schools (as were all languages other than English), and a general assimilation into the "Anglo-Saxon," "British" or Anglo-Canadian world was seen as the only future for both French Canadians and immigrants.

In the 1960s, the Royal Commission on BILINGUALISM AND BICULTURALISM brought to light some of the difficulties encountered by French speakers and other groups in Canada. In 1969 the OFFICIAL LANGUAGES ACT made Canada, at least symbolically, an officially bilingual country and measures were taken to allow for service in French in the federal administration. In 1971 the government adopted the policy of MULTICULTURALISM in a bilingual framework. Finally the CONSTITUTION ACT, 1982, affirmed some of the principles of cultural dualism; the CANADIAN CHARTER OF RIGHTS AND FREEDOMS stresses the right to equality and forbids discrimination. French and English are described as "the official languages of Canada" with equality in status in all parliamentary institutions and in the government of Canada. The Charter also protects the rights of French and English minorities to be educated in their own languages, and for minority schools to be funded by public funds, and confirms that it does not modify "any rights or privileges guaranteed by or under the Constitution of Canada in respect of denominational, separate or dissentient schools." French and English are also the official languages of New Brunswick, the only officially bilingual province.

There have been various interpretations of how the ideology of cultural dualism should actually manifest itself. It has been argued that French and English should be equally represented by bilingual public servants at all levels of the federal system (or that every federal government unit should have 2 components, one French, one English), and that there should be equality of opportunity at all levels of society, eg, political, economic, educational and social.

Many French Canadians believe that cultural dualism recognizes their specificity and their rights, while others believe that it has never been applied in practice and that Canada, originally a British colony, is now a US colony. Part of the French Canadian population has also been in favour of a unilingual Québec, as a "refuge" for Francophones, and some believe that Québec should secede from Confederation. But cultural dualism has been opposed most vociferously by English-speaking groups. Many British colonialists wanted Canada to be a primarily English-speaking, Anglo-Saxon dependency of Britain. Today, several groups (particularly, but not exclusively in the West) consider that Canada should be unilingually English and that CANADIAN-AMERICAN RELATIONS should be fostered because of a common general culture and because of the economic power of the US.

Other groups have very much resented the ideology of cultural dualism, believing that it excludes them from Canadian life. The native people stress that they were the first inhabitants of Canada, and that the French and English have eliminated them from the political and social life of the country. Ethnic groups who have immigrated during the last 2 centuries believe that cultural dualism effectively excludes them as well from social and political life. On the other hand, many French Canadians do not support the policy of multiculturalism, because they consider that it does not recognize their special status. MICHEL LAFERRIÈRE

Culture, a term used by social scientists, is also widely used in popular speech. It apparently arose first in the Old French of the Middle Ages to indicate a religious cult, or religious worship or ceremony. The verb *culturer* meant "working the soil." In the 17th century, people referred to the "wheat culture," "legume culture," and, by analogy, to the "culture of letters" and "culture of sciences." In the 18th century the word was used alone to mean "formation of the spirit." Eighteenth-century German philosophers and historians borrowed the term from the French, but *Kultur*, as it was written, had for the Germans both social and historical dimensions. Some writers used it to mean progress, the improvement of the human spirit, a step towards the perfection of humanity. Others used it to mean "civilization," that is, the refinement of mores, customs and knowledge. For German (and some French) authors of the day, the terms "culture" and "civilization" referred to the progress of Reason, that is, of science, knowledge and a new moral conscience liberated from religions and mythologies.

It was in English, however, that the term "culture" took on the modern meaning (culture signifying "husbandry" appeared in English as early as 1420). Anthropologists used the term to denote the mores, customs and beliefs of the "primitive" people they were studying. By the early 20th century, culture had become a central concept of the SOCIAL SCIENCES; it is a term now used in all the social sciences and in all languages. The technical use of the term in ANTHROPOLOGY was introduced by the English anthropologist E.B. Tylor (1871): "Culture or civilization, taken in its wide enthnographic sense, is that complex whole which includes knowledge, belief, art, law, morals, custom and any other capabilities and habits acquired by man as a member of society."

In *Culture: A Critical Review of Concepts and Definitions* (1952) A.L. Kroeber and C. Kluckhohn analysed 160 English definitions of culture used by anthropologists, sociologists, psychologists, psychiatrists and others, and classified them according to their principal emphasis. Drawing on all these definitions and on others more recent, culture may be defined as an ensemble, formalized in varying degrees, of ways of thinking, feeling and behaving which once learned give people a particular and distinct collectivity.

Canadian Culture Given the diversity of Canadian society it is easier to describe Canadian culture as a group of cultures interrelated with and juxtaposed to the 2 dominant cultural groups.

It is not surprising, given its size, that Canada should have several regional subcultures (*see* REGIONALISM). No exhaustive study has yet been made of these subcultures, yet it is possible to assert that West Coast Canadians have a different way of thinking and a different spirit from central or East Coast Canadians. Canadians who live on the Prairies are distinct from those in Ontario, as are Quebeckers or Newfoundlanders. Further divisions exist within the subcultures: northern Ontarians distinguish themselves from southern ones; Quebeckers in Abitibi, the Beauce or Lac St-Jean are different from those in Montréal or Québec City. Differences in spirit, ways of thinking and attitude exist between Edmonton and Calgary, Victoria and Vancouver, Montréal and Québec City.

But the expression "Canadian mosaic" refers to the ethnic and cultural diversity of the country. Four constituent cultural groupings are usually distinguished in Canada. The first 2 are the cultures of the "founding peoples," the Anglo-Saxon culture and French culture (*see* ETHNIC AND RACE RELATIONS). The former subdivides into cultures of different origin — ENGLISH, SCOTS, IRISH, WELSH. French culture is more homogenous. Though French Canadians originally emigrated from different provinces of France, under the French regime they quickly merged into one "Canadian" culture, although those French Canadians living in Ontario or Manitoba are qui different from those in Québec (*see* FRENCH IN TH WEST).

With the exception of the native peoples, th remaining non-British and non-French cultur groups comprise all the other ethnic groups th have immigrated to Canada since the beginnin of the 19th century. The vitality of these cultur communities has grown in recent years. Th composite of cultural groups includes cultur from Europe, the Near East, Asia, Central an S America, and Africa. The members of thes communities usually adopt English as the working language and finally as their moth tongue, but many still speak their former na tional language and teach it to their children (*se* LANGUAGE IN USE) and many devotedly maintai the customs and traditions of the old countr Canadian television and (especially) radio offe programs in a wide variety of languages.

The fourth Canadian cultural group consis of the native peoples. This group includes man subdivisions. When the first Europeans arrive in N America at least 6 cultural groups appa ently inhabited what is now Canada. Each o these cultural and linguistic groups contained certain number of tribes. These differences sti exist to some extent; the greatest distinguishin factor among native peoples now is the degree t which they maintain ancestral ways or have in tegrated into the structures and adopted the cu ture of industrial society. The MÉTIS and mixe blood are the most highly integrated into urba and industrial life, but they have always fough and still fight for the preservation and recog nition of their own cultural identity and fo political rights (*see* NATIVE-WHITE RELATIONS an various entries under NATIVE PEOPLE).

Cultural Conflicts Canada has experience many cultural conflicts. In the 17th century, th French vainly tried to convert the Indians to non-nomadic, Christian and French way of life After the British Conquest (1759-60) of NE FRANCE, the conflict between the English an French moved from the military to the politica battlefield. Many British colonists, merchant and administrators thought it simpler to angli cize the 70 000 French colonists and to impos on them British political, legal and religious in stitutions rather than to live peacefully wit them. Nevertheless, the 2 groups have had t accept coexistence. The coexistence has, how ever, suffered many stumbling blocks; eg, th battles are still being fought for the recognitio of French outside Québec and of English insid Québec (*see* FRANCOPHONE-ANGLOPHONE RELATIONS).

In the 20th century, and particularly sinc WWII, the massive arrival of new cultural mi norities has posed other problems. Sociologist have identified the various forms that charac terize the relations of the English and French t cultural minorities as assimilation, integratio and accommodation (*see* MULTICULTURALISM). I Canada there has been a certain amount of as similation of native people and of French Cana dians (outside Québec) into the dominant anglo phone culture. Other cultural communities hav been both assimilated and integrated. On thei arrival in Québec, members of these commu nities choose for themselves or their childre one of Canada's 2 official languages. Simulta neously, many have fought to have the cultur of their countries of origin recognized as constit uent elements of the Canadian mosaic.

Finally, the reality of both conflict and com plementarity has led each cultural group withi the Canadian ensemble to seek out some form o accommodation. GUY ROCHE

Cumberland, BC, Village, pop 1947 (1981c), in as town 1898 but reclassified as village 1958, i located on E coast of Vancouver I about 6 km S of Courtenay and 100 km NW of Nanaimo Robert Dunsmuir became involved in COA

mining here in the 1880s and by 1891 a townsite was planned. In 1898 it was named after Cumberland, Eng. At its height the town had a population of 10 000 and its "Chinatown" was the largest N of San Francisco. From the 1940s on the community declined rapidly and logging replaced mining as the main industry. Agriculture has also developed in the region, and Cumberland has become a resort community.
ALAN F.J. ARTIBISE

Cumberland, Frederick William, engineer, architect, railway manager, legislator (b at London, Eng 10 Apr 1821; d at Toronto 5 August 1881). Educated in England and Ireland, Cumberland served as an assistant engineer under the great Isambard Brunel on docks and railways in England, giving him not only a solid engineering background but also a special touch in design. He arrived in Toronto in 1847 and, after the city suffered its first great fire in Aug 1849, he won the competition for the rebuilding of St James' Cathedral. But his engineering training became known and he was appointed engineer for the first railway in Upper Canada; he selected Sandford FLEMING as one of his assistants. His architectural practice grew concurrently. In partnership he designed UNIVERSITY COLLEGE, Toronto, but his main task was the building of the Northern Ry, of which he was made general manager in 1858. A man of many parts, he was elected a member of the first Ontario legislature in 1867 and of the House of Commons in 1871.
R.F. LEGGET

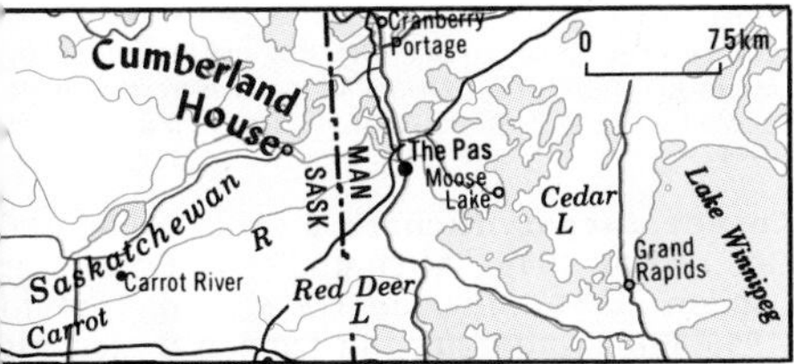

Cumberland House, Sask, UP, the oldest continuously occupied site in Saskatchewan and the first inland post built by the HUDSON'S BAY COMPANY. The site, at the SE corner of Cumberland Lk on the route from Hudson Bay to the Saskatchewan R and Churchill R fur-trading areas, was selected in 1774 by Samuel HEARNE after competitors began to intercept furs from the area's Indians. The construction of Cumberland House in 1774 marked a change in HBC policy, which had hitherto expected Indians to bring their furs to the bay posts to trade. It also marked the beginning of intense rivalry between the HBC and Montréal traders, later the NORTH WEST COMPANY, which lasted until 1821. Cumberland House became less important to the FUR TRADE in the mid-19th century when more direct trade routes to the interior were developed. The HBC still operates a trading post at Cumberland House. The post was named after Prince Rupert, duke of Cumberland.

Cumberland Sound is a major inlet, 300 km long, with an average width of 65 km, in the E coast of BAFFIN I. Its steep sides rise over 2125 m to glacier-covered uplands. Past continental glaciation, followed by modification of the upland margins by local alpine glaciation, has created a shoreline deeply indented with FJORDS. Outwash deposits at the head of fjords during deglaciation have been elevated as raised deltas and are markedly terraced. The head of the sound is backed by a hilly lowland with valleys leading to interior plains. The structural alignment and parallel sides of Cumberland Sound suggest its origin was through large-scale faulting.
DOUG FINLAYSON

Cunard, Joseph, businessman, politician (b at Halifax 1799; d at Liverpool, Eng 16 Jan 1865), brother of Samuel CUNARD. He left Halifax around 1820 and established a branch of his father's firm at Chatham, NB, where he was soon involved in lumbering, milling and shipbuilding. In 1832 he was described as one of the wealthiest men in the province. He expanded into Kent and Gloucester counties and became involved in a bitter rivalry with Alexander Rankin, head of the largest commercial firm in northern NB. Having entered politics in 1828 as an MLA, he was appointed to the Legislative Council 1833 and sat on the Executive Council 1838-46. His bankruptcy in 1847 left hundreds out of work. He moved to Liverpool where he entered the commission business, purchasing supplies for colonial merchants and selling their ships and lumber.
WILLIAM A. SPRAY

Cunard, Sir Samuel, merchant, shipowner (b at Halifax 21 Nov 1787; d at London, Eng 28 Apr 1865). Cunard joined his father in the timber business and with interests that expanded into whaling, lumber, coal and iron as well as shipping, he amassed a large personal fortune by the 1830s. His shipping activities largely encompassed SAILING SHIPS although he had some experience in early steam navigation as a shareholder in the wooden paddle wheeler, the ROYAL WILLIAM, which in 1833 made an historic crossing of the Atlantic, mainly under steam power. Among his business interests, Cunard was a founder of the Halifax Banking Company in 1825 along with Enos COLLINS. A Tory supporter, he was a member of the COUNCIL OF TWELVE 1830-38 and of the NS Executive Council 1838-40, although he was active in council meetings only for the first 3 years.

In 1839 he submitted a bid to the British government to undertake a regular mail service, by steamship, across the N Atlantic from Liverpool to Halifax, Québec and Boston, for £55 000 annually for 10 years. The bid was successful and in the same year Cunard, with associates in Glasgow and Liverpool, established the British and North American Royal Mail Steam Packet Company, the ancestor of the Cunard Line. The first Cunard sailing was made in May 1840, but the paddle steamer *Britannia* began regular mail service by steam that July by crossing from Liverpool to Halifax and Boston in 14 days and 8 hours. Although Cunard had severe financial difficulties in his NS and NB businesses in the early 1840s, his shipping operation, well-managed and technically innovative, prospered. It relied on iron ships after 1855 and on screws rather than paddles by the early 1860s. It was forced, by stiff competition from the US, to drop Halifax as a regular port of call and send its vessels directly to New York. There were no Cunard sailings to Canada until just before WWI but thereafter service was maintained from Montréal until air transportation brought about the demise of N Atlantic ocean passenger service.

Cunard moved to England to supervise his shipping interests, was made a baronet in 1859 for the services of his vessels in the Crimean War and died in London. He left an estate estimated by some at £350 000, by others at considerably more. He was the largest of PEI's absentee land proprietors by 1860 (*see* LAND QUESTION, PEI), and his holdings there were sold in 1866 for some $258 000.
D.M.L. FARR

Cunard Company, conceived and built by the Haligonian shipowner and entrepreneur Samuel CUNARD. With several British partners Cunard formed the British and North American Royal Mail Steam Packet Company in 1839, winning the British government contract and subsidy to carry mail to Canada and the US. Cunard and his Scots engineer Robert Napier built 4 side-wheelers for the N American service; the first, the *Britannia*, left Liverpool 4 July 1840 and arrived at Halifax 12 days later. Thus was established a regular fast steam packet service which eventually led to the decline of N American shipping and the disappearance of transatlantic commercial sailing ships. In 1867 Cunard ships ceased making regular stops at Halifax. The Cunard group became a public company in 1878, adopting the name Cunard Steamship Company Limited. It ultimately absorbed Canadian Northern Steamships Ltd and its competitor, the White Star Line. Cunard dominated the Atlantic passenger trade with liners such as the *Lusitania* and *Mauretania*, and later the legendary *Queen* ships (including the still-active *Queen Elizabeth 2*), almost to the end of the era of the superliners. *See* SHIP BUILDING; SHIPPING, MARITIME.
PETER HOPWOOD

Reading: F.E. Hyde, *Cunard and the North Atlantic 1840-1973* (1975).

Cupids, Nfld, Town, pop 706 (1981c), inc 1965, is located in SW CONCEPTION B on the AVALON PENINSULA. Originally known as Cupers Cove (1612), and later as Cuperts, Coopers and Copers Cove (possibly variants of an English surname), it was the site of the Sea Forest Plantation, established by John GUY in Aug 1610, the first attempted colonization by the LONDON AND BRISTOL CO and one of the earliest English settlements in the New World. The colony, governed by Guy under the terms of the company's first charter, was effectively the seat of the first attempt to colonize Newfoundland, and the site of the earliest known English birth in Newfoundland (27 Mar 1613). Between 1621 and 1631 the formal colony collapsed, although the site was later used by migratory fishermen and had evolved as a year-round site by the early 1700s. A prosperous inshore cod fishery and the annual seal hunt were the main sources of employment in the settlement. Today the fishing community is the site of numerous plaques and monuments commemorating its history. In 1978 archaeologists excavated a sawpit, a cesspit, 2 building sites and a possible palisade and wharf believed to correspond roughly to descriptions of the site left by Guy.
ROBERT D. PITT

Reading: G.T. Cell, *English Enterprise in Newfoundland 1577-1660* (1969).

Curley, Tagak, Inuk politician, administrator (b at Coral Harbour, NWT 1944). A strong advocate of Inuit concerns, Tagak Curley was a founding member and first president of the INUIT TAPIRISAT OF CANADA (1971). From 1979 to 1983 he was president of Nunasi Corp, an Inuit development corporation responsible for the investment of the proceeds of future Inuit LAND CLAIMS settlements. Tagak Curley was first elected to the NWT Assembly in 1979, representing Keewatin S. During this period he led the Inuit "shadow" caucus, which formed the largest single block of votes within the legislature. In 1983 he was re-elected for the newly renamed riding of Aivilik. He was appointed to the NWT Executive Council in 1984.
HARRIET GORHAM

Curling, sport in which 2 teams of 4 players each send stones over an ice surface toward a target circle in an attempt to place nearest the centre. Although there is some artistic and etymological evidence from the 16th century in the Low Countries of Europe for a similar ice game, most authorities agree that curling as we know it today was codified in Scotland and exported from there in organized form. Certainly the origins and early evolution of this sport in Canada were owed to a consistent, enthusiastic and ubiquitous Scottish presence. Undoubtedly, too, curling has thrived to a prodigious and unparalleled extent here. Factors contributing to its contemporary popularity in Canada include the climate and geography, the traditions of the game, certain technological advances and the active patronage of influential persons (many of them Scottish). From their influential position in Canadian society, many Scots were comfortably

Curling on the Kaministikwia River, *c*1893. Curling was played informally in Canada before 1800 and grew rapidly in the late 19th century, aided by Canada's long, cold winters and abundant ice (*courtesy Ontario Archives*).

situated to indulge in and to promote the traditions of their native land, including curling.

Some historians have suggested, without documentation, that curling began on the N American continent among Scottish soldiers during the Seven Years' War of 1756-63. Curling certainly occurred informally before 1800, until a group of Scots who were identified chiefly with the fur trade formed the Montreal Curling Club in 1807, described as the first sports club in Canada. Other Scots formed clubs in Kingston (1820), Québec (1821) and Halifax (1824-25). These pioneering enthusiasts experimented with "stones" made of iron or maple, besides importing them from Scotland. But by 1839, when more clubs had been formed, locally made granite curling stones were being advertised in Toronto at $8 a pair. A year later the first book on curling in Canada was published — James Bicket's *The Canadian Curler's Manual*. Inter-city matches began in 1835, inter-provincial ones in 1858, and in 1865 the first international bonspiel was held between American and Canadian clubs at Buffalo, NY. Much of this progress was aided by the long, cold winters and the availability of innumerable lakes and rivers, ensuring abundant and safe ice on which to enjoy curling. Indeed, these conditions surpassed even those in Scotland, an unusual occurrence for a transplanted sport. As the sport's most comprehensive historian, Scottish Reverend John Kerr, wrote of these winters in 1904: "They make Canada the Eldorado of the curler." But often it was too cold to participate outdoors, and the solution for curling fanatics was to take their sport indoors; it is possible that members of the Montreal Curling Club did this first in 1837. The neighbouring Thistle Club constructed an enclosed rink 7 years later. By 1859 Toronto had its first indoor facility, and soon indoor curling rinks became common across Canada. During the 1880s and 1890s, until ice-hockey arenas were created, they were being gratefully used by many fledgling ice-hockey teams. Looking back in 1911, George Bryce wrote: "Almost every railway town in Western Canada early in its history erects a commodious building, which is flooded on the interior ground floor and forms an ice sheet which lasts, with some addition, for 3 or 4 months." By this time, Winnipeg was the acknowledged curling centre of Canada. In 1950 it had more curling clubs than Montréal and Toronto combined; and Manitoba had more clubs than Ontario and Québec. The Flin Flon club was the largest in the world, with over 50 rinks.

Despite the dominating Scottish influence, other nationalities participated from an early date. Because a Canadian-born curler, William Reynolds, had won the Denham Medal in 1843, a Toronto newspaper claimed: "Curling may now be considered in this Province a Canadian rather than a Scottish game." Similar sentiments were expressed in Québec in 1861 when a French Canadian (Benjamin Rousseau) won a gold medal in curling competition. And the progress of non-Scottish teams (often called "barbarians") against Scottish-born teams was keenly reported. Perhaps on occasion the native-born were motivated towards success against the socially superior and influential Scots. But sporting rivalries were usually well controlled by the etiquette and code of conduct expected of curlers and the democratic traditions associated with the sport.

Since the earl of DALHOUSIE was reported as a member of the Quebec City Curling Club in 1828, the sport has never lacked for famous figures within its ranks. Naturally, many of these powerful men — such as Sir John A. Macdonald, Lord Aberdeen and Lord Strathcona — were Scots pursuing an ethnic interest. The viceregal support of the governors general was especially significant. Lord DUFFERIN (1872-78) was an ardent exponent and had a rink built at his own expense at his official residence, Rideau Hall. In 1880 he instituted the Governor General's Prize, one of Canada's coveted curling trophies. His successors, Lorne, Lansdowne, Aberdeen and Minto, also sponsored the sport, adding to its prestige. Another stimulus to the sport was provided when at last a Scottish curling team toured Canada (1902-3), captained by Reverend Kerr. The team played matches in 11 cities from Halifax to Winnipeg, then visited 6 American cities. The Scots lost more matches than they won and returned home tremendously impressed with the status and progress of curling in the Dominion. When a Canadian team first toured Scotland in 1908, it won 23 of 26 matches, including 3 international contests for the Strathcona Cup.

The copious quantities of whiskey said to be consumed at bonspiels apparently delayed the participation of women in curling, but in 1894 the first ladies' curling club was formed in Montréal. Before 1900 there were several women's clubs in eastern and western Canada and curling was soon established as a sport for both sexes and almost all ages.

A Dominion championship competition was inaugurated in 1927, sponsored by the W.D Macdonald Co for a trophy known as the Macdonald Brier Tankard. The Dominion Curling Assn (renamed the Canadian Curling Assn in 1968) was formed in 1935. During the 1940s, outdoor curling with cement-filled jam tins became a craze across the Prairies; the first "Carspiel" was held at Mipawin, Sask, in 1947, with 4 Hudson sedans valued at $2200 each as prizes, and in 1949, Ken WATSON of Manitoba became the first curler to win "The Brier" 3 times. Ten years later Ernie RICHARDSON formed the famous Richardson Rink from Stoughton, Sask, which went on to win 4 Briers in 5 years, together with many other titles, trophies and "cash bonspiels." Also in 1959, Scotch Cup competition began between Canada and Scotland, which grew to a world championship among 10 nations. This was superseded by the Air Canada Silver Broom trophy as the emblem of the world curling championship in 1968, when Canada won the first of 5 successive victories. In recent years, such Canadian successes have been harder to come by as the calibre of curling competition from the US and European nations has improved. Yet Canada remains the major home of the sport by any criteria, with Scottish bagpipes heard at any one of hundreds of bonspiels across the country as the most obvious symbolic reminder of its illustrious heritage.

GERALD REDMOND

Reading: W.A. Creelman, *Curling: Past and Present* (1950); Gerald Redmond, *The Sporting Scots of Nineteenth-Century Canada* (1982); D.B. Smith, *Curling: An Illustrated History* (1981).

Curnoe, Gregory Richard, artist (b at London, Ont 19 Nov 1936). After studies in Ontario at London (1954-56), Doon (1956) and Toronto (1956-60), Curnoe settled in London to start his career as a painter. He has since made the chronicle of his life there the source of all his works as a painter, as well as a writer in *20 Cents Magazine* and as a musician, with the Nihilist Spasm Band.

Curnoe's friends, family and surroundings have been the subject of countless paintings, watercolours, drawings and prints — the most important of these being the encyclopedic *The View of Victoria Hospital Second Series (10 February 1969-10 March 1971)*, the 194 drawings illustrating David McFadden's *The Great Canadian Sonnet* (1970), the watercolour *Homage to Van Dongen No 1 (Sheila)* (1979-80) and the silk screen on Plexiglas, *Mariposa T.T.* (1978-79). In 1981 Curnoe had a major retrospective at the National Gallery of Canada; important work of his is also at the Art Gallery of Ontario and the London Regional Art Gallery.

PIERRE THÉBERGE

Reading: Pierre Théberge, *Greg Curnoe* (1982).

Currant, *see* BERRIES, WILD.

Curriculum Development can be defined as the systematic planning of what is taught and learned in schools as reflected in courses of study and the school programs that are embodied in official documents and made mandatory by provincial and territorial departments of education. Typically, programs are accompanied by textbooks for pupils and curriculum "guides" for teachers. Textbooks have often constituted the content of the curriculum, thus giving publishers a powerful role in curriculum development which they still retain.

Although "curriculum" as a term seems to have been rarely used in Canada before Confederation, the Jesuit *Ratio Studiorum* ("plan of studies"), arguably the most systematic course of study ever devised, was introduced in New France in the 1630s. This established a classical tradition based on centralized control and ensured that the Canadian curriculum would develop in an international context.

Early French Canadian education was expected to "render children good servants of the King . . . and of God." Later in Nova Scotia and Upper Canada, anglophone education had similar goals, expressed in the teaching of Judeo-Christian morality and British patriotism. As a result, when education came under provincial jurisdiction after Confederation, the curriculum was based on common conservative social values. As such, it served, (and still serves), an imperative of cultural survival that resulted from the efforts of various groups in the Canadian mosaic to maintain their distinctive identities through the agency of the school. Political, linguistic and religious conflicts in Canada have often arisen from the objectives, content and materials of the school curriculum.

Prior to 1840 schooling in Canada was an informal and intermittent experience, not yet sharply separated from work. It took place in a parent- and church-controlled "system" aimed at teaching basic literacy and religious precepts. In New France, a formal curriculum was available to only an elite minority who were trained for religious and other high-status vocations. Following the British Conquest in 1759-60, church-controlled schooling in Québec was a primary agent of cultural survival and remained so until 1964, serving to maintain the French language and the Catholic religion.

In anglophone Canada, survival was linked to fears of Americanization. American textbooks, widely used in Canada, described the US population as "the most free and enlightened under heaven." Fears were exacerbated, especially in Upper Canada, by the arrival during the 1840s of the "famine IRISH" and other dispossessed immigrants. School promoters such as Egerton RYERSON, the founding father of Canadian curriculum development, saw state-controlled schooling as the primary means of assimilating these "alien" elements. Over the next half-century school promoters elsewhere in Canada followed Ryerson's lead by establishing administrative structures that enabled them to sort children into classes and grades, to create a trained, hierarchically organized teaching force, and to devise a common curriculum for a whole province. This curriculum was implemented through uniform textbooks and policed through inspection and examinations in a system that ensured that all children were taught to believe, to think and to behave in the same way (*see also* EDUCATION, HISTORY OF).

Over several decades following 1900, this system produced a *de facto* national curriculum across anglophone Canada. Curriculum change occurred by accretion during a period of urbanization and industrialization as traditional education was called into question in all Western nations. Herbert Spencer's question, "What knowledge is of most worth?" posed earlier in England, became an international rallying cry for a more systematic, deliberate process of curriculum development to meet pressing social needs. In Canada, typically cautious adaptation took the form of the "New Education" whereby such innovations as KINDERGARTEN, manual training, domestic science (HOME ECONOMICS), agriculture and "nature study," temperance and health education, PHYSICAL EDUCATION and commercial education were introduced with mixed success. Nevertheless, the schools were given credit for the sharp decline in illiteracy by the 1920s. They were a prime agent of assimilation of the huge numbers of non-English-speaking "new Canadians" who thronged into the eastern cities and the Prairies. Anglo-Saxon values infused the curriculum; bilingual education in all "second languages", including French, was virtually eliminated.

During the interwar years further progressive (mainly American) ideas were adopted including new notions of scientific testing, mental health and administrative structures based on business management models, while the cultural content of the anglophone curriculum remained British. However, serious deficiencies in Canadian schooling were revealed during WWII and various studies during the 1940s proposed new efforts to broaden the curriculum and keep pupils in school. Postwar affluence, the BABY BOOM and unprecedented public demands led to an expansion of schooling at the same time that conservative criticism of the supposed excesses of progressive education created a shift to a more subject-centered curriculum (*see* SCHOOL SYSTEM). This shift had been reinforced by 1960 as Canadians followed their American neighbours in demanding a more rigorous curriculum, especially in science and mathematics, in order to "catch up with the Russians." This was to be achieved by teaching the "structure" (basic concepts) of each subject by means of inquiry "discovery" methods, which ironically owed much to the despised progressive theories. These ideas gained cautious approval in Canada where, typically, a lack of resources forced curriculum developers to rely on British and American innovations.

After 1965 a new permissiveness in the school curriculum was manifested by a relaxation of centralized control, fragmentation of courses of study, and a new child-centered thrust in elementary education. New knowledge, new demands for more practical schooling, a larger and more diverse school population and new tensions in society resulting from a breakdown of the old social consensus and from a questioning of traditional values led to demands for innovation. With renewed fears of Americanization, with the rise of Québec separatism, and in response to the demands of the native peoples and other minority groups for equality, curriculum developers moved to establish bilingual, multicultural and native studies programs, while also seeking to counter RACISM and sexism through more balanced and accurate treatment of minorities and women in textbooks. Special curricula were designed for the estimated 1 million exceptional children (*see* EDUCATION, SPECIAL). Ontario's master list of approved classroom materials increased from 61 titles (1950) to 1648 (1972). New advocacy groups included not only liberal proponents of "values education" but conservative advocates of "values schools." The latter group demanded the inclusion of traditional Christian beliefs, the censorship of curriculum materials, and stricter discipline. Other advocacy groups — federal agencies, human rights, environmental and consumer organizations, foundations, labour and business groups and others who saw the school as a proselytizing agency — directed a steady stream of teaching materials at classrooms. What was most striking about the efforts of all those who sought to influence the curriculum was their immense faith in the power of schooling to redress social and economic inequities.

As the curriculum development process became apparently more open, policymakers were frequently forced to respond in an *ad hoc* fashion to broad but often fleeting public concerns. Sometimes demands led to immediate action for which teachers, in the absence of adequate support, training and materials, were often ill-prepared. The result was that curriculum development was less rational than it appeared to be. By 1980 ministries of education were reverting to centralization as demands for "accountability" led to a restoration, in most provinces, of previously abandoned province-wide testing. This new interest in "evaluation" was accompanied by a concern for curriculum "implementation," as developers sought to ensure that programs were taught as prescribed. Implementation was promoted by "guidelines" in the form of detailed suggestions that tacitly acknowledged the teacher's central role in curriculum change.

These and other trends revealed a new interest in "scientific" curriculum development, entailing precise statements of "objectives" and the assessment of pupil "behaviours" measured by skill performance in the traditional "three r's." This emphasis on the "basics" belied the lack of consensus on what constituted basics and on the extent to which emphasis on them had declined in schools. Ironically, in 1976 a unique external study of Canadian education by the Paris-based Organization for Economic Cooperation and Development (OECD) praised the remarkable growth and the high standards of schooling in Canada but criticized the limited place in curricula of such "frills" as music and art.

Demands for greater uniformity of curricula across Canada ignored the fact that a considerable degree of communality in goals, subject matter, textbooks and teaching methods already existed. By 1980 the interprovincial Council of Ministers of Education (CMEC) was consciously attempting to align curricula across Canada more closely. After 1960 Québec and Newfoundland, by creating their first truly public high-school systems, by adopting "scientific" ideas of school administration and by modernizing their programs, brought their curricula into line with those of other provinces. The increased availability of resources and facilities across Canada reduced educational disparities between rural and urban areas and between have and have-not provinces, with the result that curricula were enriched everywhere. Students shared more common learning experiences even as those experiences became more diverse. In this respect, their school lives paralleled the general social life of Canadians, whose life-styles had become at once more homogeneous and more diverse and culturally enriched since 1950. National studies of science teaching, the educational work of many national organizations and growing university-based research indicated, that despite provincial differences, the concept of a Canadian curriculum was very much alive. Although controversy over curriculum revealed sharp differences among Canadians regarding what knowledge was of most worth, it also obscured the fact that in accommodating, however imperfectly, conflicting demands, the schools were reflecting a new social consensus based on a new ethic of respect for cultural diversity. G.S. TOMKINS

Reading: A. Chaiton and N. McDonald, eds, *Canadian Schools and Canadian Identity* (1976); H.A. Stevenson and J.D. Wilson, eds, *Precepts, Policy and Process* (1977).

Currie, Sir Arthur William (changed from Curry in 1887), soldier, educator (b at Strathroy, Ont 5 Dec 1875; d at Montréal, Qué 30 Nov 1933). He was the first Canadian appointed commander of the Canadian Corps during WWI. He began the war with no professional military experience but several years of service in the Canadian Militia. He was appointed commander of the 2nd Canadian Infantry Brigade on 29 Sept 1914, commander of the 1st Canadian Division on 13 Sept 1915 and commander of the Canadian Corps on 9 June 1917. He participated in all major actions of the Canadian forces during the war but is best known for his planning and leadership during the last 100 days, beginning 8 Aug and lasting until 11 Nov 1918, perhaps the most successful of all Allied offensives during the war. Criticism of this campaign by Sir Sam HUGHES in Parliament resulted in postwar controversy and a libel action in 1928 which completely vindicated Currie. British wartime PM Lloyd George called him a "brilliant military commander," and PM BORDEN said he was

Gen Arthur William Currie, first Canadian appointed commander of the Canadian Corps during WWI; 1917 photo (*courtesy Public Archives of Canada / PA-1370*).

"the ablest Corps Commander in the British forces."

Currie served as inspector general of the militia forces in Canada, 23 Aug 1919 — 30 July 1920, and in Aug 1920 became principal and vice-chancellor of McGill, a position he held until his death. Without benefit of post-secondary education himself, he was extraordinarily successful as a university administrator, and at a time of particular importance in McGill's development. A.M.J. HYATT

Reading: H.M. Urquhart, *Arthur Currie* (1950).

Currie, Walter, teacher, administrator (b at Chatham, Ont 1 Oct 1922). He was among the earliest activists in Indian educational reform during the period after WWII. A nonstatus Indian born of Potawatomi and Ojibwa parents, Currie was a schoolteacher in Kitchener and principal in Toronto (1953-68) before becoming assistant superintendent for supervision with the Ontario Dept of Education with responsibility for native and northern schools (1968-71). He was concurrently president of the Indian-Eskimo Assn and first chairman of the Toronto Indian Friendship Centre (1969-71). He was first chairman of Trent's Dept of Native Studies (1971-75) and one of the first 2 members of Ontario's Human Rights Commission (1972-74). He has advocated improving standards of government-funded Indian schools and fitting them more closely to native needs. BENNETT MCCARDLE

Photographer Walter Curtin's outstanding photojournalism is evident in his photo of drama teacher Dora Mavor Moore visiting a class of young students at the New Play Society school, Toronto, Dec 1957 (*courtesy Public Archives of Canada / PA-137084 / Walter Curtin*).

Curtin, Walter Anthony, photographer (b in Vienna, Austria 16 Aug 1911). Curtin turned to photography in 1946, setting up his own shop in London (1948). Economic recession in Britain prompted Curtin to immigrate to Canada (1952), where he became an outstanding photojournalist, using a fast-handling rangefinder camera. His photo essays have appeared in *Life*, *Time*, *Maclean's* and *Saturday Night*. A member of the Royal Canadian Academy, Curtin has been honoured with medals, certificates of merit and other awards, such as the Max Sauer Memorial Award (1957) from the Art Directors Club, Montréal. LOUISE ABBOTT

Curtis, Wilfred Austin, air marshal (b at Havelock, Ont 21 Aug 1893; d at Nassau, Bahamas 7 Aug 1977). As chief of the air staff 1947-53, Curtis presided over unprecedented peacetime growth in the RCAF. He flew with the Royal Naval Air Service on the Western Front 1917-18, being credited with downing 13 enemy aircraft. In the interwar years, he had his own insurance business while helping to start the Toronto Flying Club and assisting as a RCAF reservist. He was called back to active service in 1939 and was deputy air officer commanding, RCAF Overseas Headquarters in London 1941-44. He became a member of the Air Council in 1944 and then succeeded Robert LECKIE as chief of the air staff. His appointment, after only 8 years of full-time RCAF service, was controversial. Astute and businesslike, he successfully pushed for the acquisition of the AVRO CF-100 and other modern aircraft. Upon his retirement he became vice-chairman of A.V. Roe (Canada) Ltd and subsequently of Hawker Siddeley (Canada) Ltd. Understandably, he lamented the cancellation of the AVRO ARROW. He was one of the founders of York U in Toronto and was its first chancellor. NORMAN HILLMER

CUSO (formerly Canadian University Services Overseas), a private organization involved in international development, founded 6 June 1961 by representatives of 21 universities and 22 organizations from across Canada with overseas interests. CUSO has remained independent of government control, although with 90% of its funding coming from the CANADIAN INTERNATIONAL DEVELOPMENT AGENCY, it meets Canadian foreign policy goals.

In its first 20 years, CUSO and its francophone equivalent SUCO (Service universitaire canadien outre-mer) placed some 8000 volunteers in 65 countries. The annual number overseas peaked at 1000 in the late 1960s, and has averaged about 700 since then. Persons interested in becoming involved with CUSO are interviewed to determine whether they have the ability to adjust to serving overseas and the qualifications or work experience to meet the needs of the host countries. Canadian volunteers ("co-operants") become employees of host governments or local agencies, not of Canada. Successful candidates are hired on local terms for 2 years. Conditions are not rigid: supplements can be provided where local salaries are low, and terms can extend beyond 2 years. Since the 1970s CUSO has funded overseas projects and supported development education work designed to increase Canadians' awareness of their relation to the underdeveloped world. Because of its base of returned co-operants, CUSO is in a unique position to assist community groups across Canada in developing awareness and action programs. Another part of CUSO's work is the funding of projects overseas in the areas of health, education, agriculture, community development and appropriate technology. These projects, aimed at helping local people to help themselves, often complement closely the work of CUSO co-operants. RICHARD STUART

Customs and Excise, taxes on goods, are one of the world's oldest sources of government revenue. Customs duties are applied on imported products while excise duties and taxes generally apply on goods of domestic manufacture, notably liquor and tobacco. The word "customs" derives from custom, a habit.

Customs and excise have played a vital role in Canada's development. They were at the centre of the dispute, especially in Nova Scotia, between Crown and legislature for the right to impose and dispose of customs duties; they were the key element in the NATIONAL POLICY which endured for nearly a century; and they were central to the achievement of national independence through government use of tariff negotiations with other countries.

Customs duties were already here when the Europeans brought rum and religion to N America: some Indian tribes exacted tribute from members of other tribes passing through their territories. The French regime helped to support NEW FRANCE through an export duty on furs and did not rely on import duties until its dying years. The British did not use customs as much for revenue as for enforcement of their NAVIGATION ACTS, which required that British goods move in British ships. After Britain turned to free trade in the 1840s, customs and excise in Canada became almost exclusively a revenue producer until after Confederation.

When BNA representatives met in 1865, they discussed a "common commercial policy." Until then their only common policy had been for each to tax the manufactured goods of the others as readily as those of other nations. In 1867 responsibility for the tariff was given to the national government. The Province of Canada's Customs Act of 1866 was adopted, and in 1868 the average tariff was set at 15%, a compromise between protectionist Canada's 20% and free-trading Nova Scotia's and New Brunswick's 10-12%. A higher tariff to nourish and protect domestic manufacture was not introduced until 1879 under PM Sir John A. MACDONALD. By 1883, annual revenue had risen to $23.2 million. Until WWI, when income and sales taxes were first imposed in Canada, customs and excise revenue comprised about 75% of the federal government's revenue.

In the Province of Canada (1841-67) customs was administered by the Finance Dept. Customs and Inland Revenue, established in 1867 as separate ministries, were united in 1918 and in 1921 became Customs and Excise. In 1925, income tax collection was moved from Finance to Customs and Excise, resulting in another name change, to National Revenue, in 1927. The unofficial motto of Customs and Excise was "The Revenue [always spelled with a capital R] must be protected." Early collectors had to swear on the Bible before a judge 4 times a year that they had turned in all of their quarterly collections. On the Klondike Trail in 1897, the customs officer set up a tent beside Tagish Lake and waded out to the passing prospectors' boats to collect duty on any American goods. Sometimes the revenue was not properly protected. During PROHIBITION, the golden age of liquor SMUGGLING and bootlegging, a 1926 customs scandal temporarily brought down the government (*see* KING-BYNG AFFAIR).

A political battle has long raged in Canada between protectionists and free traders. In 1854 Canada and the US signed a RECIPROCITY treaty (free trade in 50 items). The US abrogated the agreement in 1866, and it was not until 1935 that the 2 countries extended most-favoured-nation treatment to each other in tariff matters. During that time, Canadian voters were occasionally presented with the clear issue of protection versus free trade and every time free trade lost. High tariff walls were not breached until after WWII through the 1947 General Agreement on Tariffs and Trade. By the 1980s the tariff, with some major exceptions, was generally at the level it held at Confederation. Even the British trade preference, established in 1769, had vanished.

Most customs work used to be conducted at seaports and on the 8893 km frontier with the US. But rail, motor and plane travel has changed that. A staff of some 10 000 operates 650 Customs and Excise locations in Canada, 140 of them on the border, some so remote (eg, Little Gold Creek, YT) that they are abandoned in winter. The cost of collecting the revenue is less than 2% of collections which, in 1983-84, amounted to $16.6 billion. The Finance Dept sets taxing laws, including the tariff, while Customs and Excise administers them. These include narcotics, pornographic materials, firearms, diseased plants and "dumped" foreign goods that injure Canadian industry and employment.

DAVE MCINTOSH

Reading: G. Blake, *Customs Administration in Canada* (1957); Dave McIntosh, *The Collectors* (1985).

Cuttlefish, decapod ("ten-footed") MOLLUSC of class Cephalopoda. Cuttlefish comprise over 100 species in genera *Sepia* and *Spirula*. They are characterized by porous, calcareous, internal shells, best known as cuttlebones, which are given caged birds as a source of lime salts. The pores are gas filled to adjust the animal's buoyancy, and even dead shells float. The closest Canadian relatives are 4 species of small *Rossia* of the same order, Sepioidea, but lacking cuttlebones. Cuttlefish have oval bodies up to 60 cm long and look rather like flattened SQUID. Thousands of nervously controlled chromatophores (pigment-bearing cells) give them capabilities for camouflage and pattern formation, eg, mating males display a revolving zebra-stripe pattern unequalled in nature. To escape predators, they darken, eject a gelatinous, cuttlefish-shaped, dark brown ink-blob decoy, turn pale instantly and swim away. Sepia ink, derived from and named for the organism, has been used as an artist's medium.

R.K. O'DOR

Jocelyn Lovell was virtually unbeatable in cycling in Canada during the 1970s and won gold medals in the Commonwealth and Pan-American Games. His career ended tragically in a traffic accident in which he was completely paralysed (*courtesy Ron Watts / First Light*).

Cycling Bicycle racing comprises many events, from short-distance sprints on banked velodromes to road races covering distances of 30 to 3000 km. Although there is no reliable information on when the first bicycle reached Canada, the Toronto *Globe* of 6 Mar 1869 reports on a "Grand Riding Academy" with pupils instructed in the art of velocipede riding. The first "high wheel" was imported in 1876 by A.T. Lane. The mayor of Montréal was so impressed that he proclaimed a half-day holiday for the citizens to see Lane ride through the city. The Montreal Bicycle Club, the first in Canada, was formed in 1876. The Canadian Wheelmen's Assn, later renamed the Canadian Cycling Assn, was formed at St Thomas, Ont, in Sept 1882 to protect cyclists' rights, promote bicycling and control championships. It was a founding member of the Union cycliste internationale, the world governing body now listing 120 affiliations. The association launched a campaign to improve roads, a struggle that involved them in political activity at many levels, and produced a series of travel guides and road maps — the first of their kind in Canada. Bicycle ownership significantly affected the social mores of the day. It allowed the owner to travel farther, to socialize with greater ease, especially at the parks and places where cyclists congregated, and in the case of women, to travel unchaperoned. Mainly a Sunday activity, it suffered the wrath of many ministers of the church who attacked this freedom as a pastime of the devil, referring in particular to its adverse affect on women. They were further incensed by the "rational dress" adopted by those daring women who refused to cycle in the voluminous ankle-length dresses then considered the appropriate costume. Despite persistent harassment, women continued to cycle.

The 1880s and 1890s were boom years. Racing on outdoor tracks attracted large crowds and produced many notable performers. The Dunlop Trophy Race, instituted in 1894, ran for 33 years and attracted the leading Canadian and American competitors. The World Cycling Championships were held in Montréal in 1899, and in 1912 the first Canadian 6-day race was held at the Arena Gardens, Toronto. In the 1920s and 1930s, the 6-day race was a regular promotion throughout N America and lucrative contracts drew the best amateurs to the professional ranks, the most famous being W.J. "Torchy" PEDEN of Vancouver, who amassed a total of 38 wins, a record unbeaten until 1966.

Early in 1900, the arrival of the automobile diverted public interest from cycling with a consequent drop in attendance at meetings and membership of the CWA. Much of the enthusiasm generated by cycling was transferred to AUTOMOBILE RACING, and innovations which appeared first on bicycles found their way to the automobile. Popularity waned, although competitors and crowds continued to be attracted to 6-day races. The cycling boom of the 1960s revived interest. Road racing, always strong in Québec, grew apace with the introduction of "tours" modelled on the Tour de France. In 1974 Montréal once again hosted the World Cycling Championships, attended by over 1000 riders and officials, amateurs and professionals. During the 1970s, Jocelyn Lovell of Toronto was virtually unbeatable in Canada. He won gold medals in Commonwealth and Pan-American Games and a silver in the 1978 World Championships. Lovell's career ended tragically when he was seriously injured in a collision with a truck near Toronto in 1983; he was completely paralysed. Gordon Singleton of St Catharines, Ont, emerged as a world class sprinter, placing 2nd in the 1979 World Amateur Championships and in the 1981 World Professional Sprint Championships. Women's cycling was in the ascendant with Karen Strong-Hearth, of St Catharines, winning a bronze medal in the 1976 World Championships and sweeping the women's events at the 1976 Canadian Cycling Championships.

In the 1984 Olympic Games, Canadian competitive cycling achieved world recognition when Canada won its first 2 silver medals. Curt Harnett of Thunder Bay, Ont, captured the silver in the 1000 m time trial; and Stephen Bauer of Fenwick, Ont, narrowly missed taking the gold medal in the 190 km road race. Bauer then turned professional and, one month later, went on to win the bronze medal in the 250 km World Professional Road Race Championships.

KENNETH V. SMITH

Cypress, in Canada, common name for white cedars or false cypresses, evergreen CONIFERS of genus *Chamaecyparis* of the cypress family (Cupressaceae). Six species are recognized: one in western Canada, 2 in the US and 3 in eastern Asia, Japan and Taiwan. Alaska or yellow cypress (*C. nootkatensis*) occurs in a narrow band from Alaska, along the BC coast and in the Cascade Mts into northern California. It is medium-sized, up to 30 m in height and 1.5 m in diameter. Leaves are small and scalelike; cones are round (1-cm diameter), bracts (modified leaves) and scales (ovule-bearing structures) are fused. POLLINATION occurs in spring. The seeds are small with 2 lateral wings. They complete their development and are shed in the fall of the second year after pollination. The wood is light, hard, strong and decay resistant. True cypresses belong to the genus *Taxodium*, not native to Canada.

JOHN N. OWENS

Nootka cypress (*Chamaecyparis nootkatensis*), with young cones (top), female flowers and older cones (right) and male flowers (*artwork by Claire Tremblay*).

Cypress Hills, about 2500 km^2, are situated in southeastern Alberta and southwestern Saskatchewan. With a maximum elevation of over 1460 m, they rise 600 m above the surrounding prairies, forming the highest point in mainland Canada between the Rocky Mts and Labrador. Their name probably derives from an early French Canadian explorers' term, *montagne de cyprès*, used to describe their pine-covered character. The word *cyprès* (cypress) was widely, though erroneously, used in reference to Canadian pine forests. The area is identified as the Cypress Hills on the Palliser map of 1857-60 (*see* PALLISER EXPEDITION). It was a centre of whisky trade in the 1860s, and in 1873 a gang of American wolf hunters massacred 36 Assiniboine there. Outraged by the incident, PM John A. MACDONALD established the North-West Mounted Police, who built FORT WALSH (1875) near the site of the massacre.

The hills form a rolling plateaulike upland with lodgepole pine, white spruce, balsam poplar and aspen forests above the drier grass and shrub-covered lower slopes. The area is a humid island in the semiarid prairies, with many varieties of plants and animals representative of the Rocky Mts, over 200 km to the W. Some 200 bird species have been sighted here. Capped by a layer of stream-laid gravels up to 100 m thick (the Oligocene-aged Cypress Hills formation) derived from the Rockies, the Cypress Hills are an erosional remnant of a once-extensive higher-level plains surface that was largely removed by stream action during later Tertiary and early Quaternary times (*see* GEOLOGICAL HISTORY). The hills were high enough to have been one of the few areas in Canada not completely ice-covered during the Wisconsin glaciation. Their higher portions projected through the ice as NUNATAKS. Wind-blown loess, in places over 2 m thick, was deposited during this period. Cypress Hills Provincial Pk contains evidence of human habitation dating back over 7000 years.

The Cypress Hills form a rolling plateaulike upland amid the prairie (*courtesy Alberta Recreation and Parks*).

IAN A. CAMPBELL

Reading: J.B. Bird, *The Natural Landscapes of Canada* (1972).

Cypress Hills Provincial Park, comprising 182 km^2 of the CYPRESS HILLS, consists of 2 blocks located some 30 km S and SW of Maple Creek, Sask. The forested N slopes, largely burned in 1886, have now recovered; the dominant species are white spruce and lodgepole pine. On the drier plateau are PRAIRIE grasslands interspersed with stands of poplar and shrubby cinquefoil. Animals finding sanctuary in the hills include the white-tailed and mule deer, moose, wapiti, pronghorn, porcupine, coyote, skunk, ground squirrel and sharp-tailed grouse. The small lakes and rivers around the hills support beaver and fish (eg, trout, perch). Historically, the plains Indians occupied the area, leaving behind many artifacts, including tipi rings. In 1875 the NORTH-WEST MOUNTED POLICE built a fort and trading post, FORT WALSH, in the area. Gradually, the hills were surrounded by farm settlements and exploited for their timber, water and grazing resources. Their recreational appeal was also recognized and parts of the hills in Saskatchewan and Alberta were designated as provincial parks.

JOHN S. MARSH

Cyr, Louis, strongman (b at St-Cyprien-de-Napierville, Canada E 10 Oct 1863; d at St-Jean-de-Matha, Qué 10 Nov 1912). Cyr's family moved to Massachusetts and as a young man he was a lumberjack in New England before returning to Montréal in 1882 to take a job as a policeman. Though not unusually tall, Cyr weighed as much as 165 kg and was immensely strong. In days when feats of strongmen aroused intense interest, Cyr became a legend. There was no formal sport of WEIGHTLIFTING; competitions were held as challenge matches, and at these he was never defeated. He won the "weightlifting" championship of N America in 1885 and the "world championship" in 1892. Most of his feats were public demonstrations that drew great crowds, including royalty. He was fêted in London, Eng, where on 19 Jan 1889 he lifted in succession a 250 kg weight with one finger, 1860 kg on his back, and 124 kg above his head with one hand. He proudly returned to Canada with one of the marquis of Queensberry's horses after winning a bet that he could hold 2 driving horses to a standstill, one tied to each of his massive arms. In 1895 in Boston he lifted on his back a platform holding 18 fat men, weighing 1967 kg — believed the heaviest weight ever lifted by a man. From 1894 to 1899 he toured with Ringling Brothers and Barnum and Bailey circuses and he later opened a tavern in Montréal.

JAMES MARSH

Czechs It is generally recognized that the Czechs and SLOVAKS comprise one ethnic group composed of 2 closely connected but still distinct Slavic units. Until the 19th century they shared a common literary language, that of the 16th-century Czech translation of the scriptures, the Králice Bible. The spoken languages are still very similar.

In 1771 a lay religious community, the Moravian Brethren (which had emerged in Saxony in 1727 as a continuation of the old Hussite Fellowship of Brethren) arrived in Labrador to do missionary and social work among the Inuit. Not long afterwards a group of Moravian Brethren from the US led by David ZEISBERGER founded Fairfield, commonly known as MORAVIANTOWN, on the Thames R near present-day Thamesville, Ont. The colony was razed during the WAR OF 1812, but the mission, rebuilt across the river, continued until 1903.

Czech immigration into Canada started in the mid-1880s in response to Sir Clifford SIFTON's wide-ranging program of settlement and development of the Canadian West (*see also* IMMIGRATION POLICY). The first recorded Czech immigrants settled in Kolin, Sask, in 1884. In Alberta Czechs founded Prague; in Manitoba Moravian Brethren settled in the Mennonite community. The early immigrants, farmers, miners, artisans and labourers came for economic reasons. After 1921, when the US introduced a quota system for immigration, many Czechs emigrated to Canada instead. The 1921 Census reported 8840 people of Czech origin in Canada; this figure jumped to 30 401 (1931), 42 912 (1941) and 57 840 (1971). Emigration increased 1938-39 as a result of German occupation; and rose again in 1948 with the establishment of a communist regime and in 1968 because of the Soviet invasion. In 1981 there were 67 695 persons of Czech and Slovak origin in Canada.

The Czechs and Slovaks have as a rule had little difficulty integrating themselves into Canadian life, but they have also been rather successful in maintaining their cultural heritage. Their first newspaper, the *Slovenské Slovo* (*Slovak Word*), started publication in the coal-mining town of Blairmore, Alta, in 1910. There are now several publications. A national association, the Czechoslovak National Alliance (est 1939 in Toronto), promotes Czech and Slovak cultural and educational activities and is also active in the social field. Politically, it supports the Council of Free Czechoslovakia, a group advocating the re-establishment of a democratic Czechoslovakia. Another Czech social and cultural organization is the Sokol ("Falcon") movement, patterned on an athletic and patriotic organization founded in the Czech lands in the 19th century. Although the majority of Czechs are Roman Catholic, it was not until larger Czech and Slovak communities were founded that Czech-language parishes were built. There are also numerous Baptist congregations.

Czechs and Slovaks have made important contributions to Canadian economic development and Canadian cultural life. Well-known names include Thomas BATA, head of the worldwide Bata shoe-manufacturing and retailing enterprise; Stephen Roman, pioneer of uranium mining in Canada; the Koerner brothers, leaders in BC's lumber industry; Oskar Morawetz, composer; Peter C. NEWMAN, author; the poet and novelist Pavel Javor; and writer Josef ŠKVORECKÝ.

JOHN GELLNER

Reading: John Gellner and J. Smerek, *The Czechs and Slovaks in Canada* (1968); J.M. Kirschbaum, *Slovaks in Canada* (1967).

Da Roza, Gustavo Uriel, architect (b at Hong Kong 24 Feb 1933). Of Chinese and Portuguese descent and one of the best-known architects practising in Winnipeg since WWII, da Roza received his architectural education in Asia. In 1958 he joined U of Calif, Berkeley, and in 1960 came to Winnipeg and University of Manitoba. While da Roza's principal commissions have been houses, a significant recent work is the Winnipeg Art Gallery (1971). As an educator, visiting critic and member of competition juries, da Roza has greatly influenced Canadian architecture. WILLIAM P. THOMPSON

Dafoe, Allan Roy, physician (b at Madoc, Ont 29 Mar 1883; d at North Bay, Ont 2 June 1943). A shy recluse with an indifferent academic record, he achieved worldwide fame for his successful delivery on 28 May 1934 of the DIONNE QUINTUPLETS. Dafoe's commonsense approach, together with the advice of his brother William, a Toronto gynecologist, kept the babies alive. Placed in charge of their welfare (over the protests of their father, Oliva Dionne), Dafoe became a public figure, portrayed on films and radio by Hollywood actor Jean Hersholt. Created OBE, 1935, he was author of *Dr. Dafoe's Guidebook for Mothers* (1936) and *How To Raise Your Baby* (1941). PIERRE BERTON

Dafoe, John Wesley, journalist, liberal reformer (b at Combermere, Canada W 8 Mar 1866; d at Winnipeg 9 Jan 1944). As editor of the Manitoba, later Winnipeg *Free Press* from 1901 until his death, he was one of the most influential Canadian journalists in history, continuing the editor-as-public-man tradition of Joseph HOWE, W.L. MACKENZIE and others. Born and reared a Conservative, he shifted to liberalism in 1885-1900, when he worked variously in Ottawa (as premier editor of the *Journal*) and Montréal. A great admirer of LAURIER and his policies, he viewed the LIBERAL PARTY as the best means of social progress and greater national autonomy, but was not slavish in his devotion. He endorsed Sir Robert BORDEN for his nationalism and later, briefly, the PROGRESSIVE PARTY for its concern with agriculture. A man of the centre, he always denounced extremes of the left and right, represented in his view by the CCF and Social Credit, respectively. He wrote several books, including *Laurier: A Study in Canadian Politics* (1922) and *Canada: An American Nation* (1935). Dafoe also founded an editorial dynasty. His son Edwin (1894-1981) became editor of the *Free Press*, and 2 nephews are now prominent in the newspaper field in western Canada.

Reading: R. Cook, *The Politics of John W. Dafoe and the Free Press* (1963).

Dr A.R. Dafoe, shown with the Dionne quintuplets. He was placed in charge of the girls' welfare and became a well-known public figure portrayed in radio and films (courtesy Public Archives of Canada/PA-26034).

Dagger, Francis telephone expert (b at Liverpool, Eng 3 June 1865; d at Unionville, Ont 21 June 1945). He was an active participant in the movement for public ownership of Canadian telephones, and his efforts are reflected today in government ownership of telephone systems in the Prairies. After gaining experience with privately owned telephone companies in England 1881-99, he moved to Canada, joining the Bell Telephone Co for 11 months. By 1900 he was agitating for municipal ownership of telephones by Toronto. Retained by the federal government to report on telephones in Canada and England (1903), Dagger was then appointed technical adviser to the Select Committee on Telephone Systems, chaired by Sir William MULOCK (1905). He was hired both by Manitoba (1905) and Saskatchewan (1907) as a telephone expert to facilitate provincial takeover of Bell's operations in these provinces. He served as supervisor of telephone systems for the Ontario Railway and Municipal Board from 1910 until his retirement in 1931. ROBERT E. BABE

Dair, Carl, typographer, typographic designer, teacher, writer (b at Welland, Ont 14 Feb 1912; d on flight from New York C to Toronto 28 Sept 1967). Dair became interested in typesetting as a child and by age 18 was doing advertising and layouts for the *Stratford Beacon-Herald*. Throughout the Depression he worked at jobs related to typesetting and printing. He moved to Montréal and opened a design studio in 1947. He also began to teach design and typography and to write on typographic design and its relationship to commerce, art and communication. There followed 10 years of commercial design, teaching and writing in Montréal and Toronto, during which he built an international reputation. In 1956 he was awarded an RSC fellowship to study type design and manufacture in Holland, where he began to design the typeface he called Cartier. He continued to work on this intermittently until 1967, when he published the *First Proof of Cartier Roman and Italic*, the first typeface for text composition designed in Canada. It is now widely used and appears to have achieved the status of an identifiable national type. Through his writing and teaching over 3 decades, he inspired a generation of graphic designers, not only with standards of excellence in design but with something of his personal philosophy which saw "inspired typography" as an important "means of visual communication." Among his many publications is *Design with Type* (1952; 2nd ed 1967), now a standard text on the subject. LAURIE LEWIS

Dairy Farming Dairy cattle (family Bovidae, genus *Bos*) are breeds of cattle raised for their ability to produce large quantities of high butterfat-content milk. In 1983 Canada had some 2.4 million milk cows and dairy heifers (1.7 million lactating cows), about 72% in Ontario and Québec. Between 1951 and 1981, the number of dairy farms declined from 451 000 to 67 890. At the same time, herd size and production per cow increased; hence, production output has been maintained. About 65% of the milk produced is processed into butter, cheese (primarily cheddar) and skim milk powder; the remainder is consumed in liquid form. Canadian dairy products for domestic consumption or export must meet stringent quality regulations imposed by Agriculture Canada and Health and Welfare Canada (*see* FOOD LEGISLATION).

Per capita consumption of milk, pure cream, butter and evaporated milk has gradually decreased, although consumption of products such as specialty cheeses and yogurt has increased. Milk marketing boards ensure stable, orderly production and marketing of milk, thus benefiting producer and consumer. Producers can plan in advance, adopting modern animal-management, ANIMAL-BREEDING and financial techniques; consumers are provided with a range of dairy products at stable prices year-round.

The Canadian DAIRY INDUSTRY uses 7 breeds of cattle: Ayrshire, Guernsey, Holstein-Friesian, Jersey and Shorthorn. These dairy breeds are distinguished from BEEF CATTLE by their triangular, elongated, tall body form. In addition to their physical and performance characteristics, all breeds have distinctive behavioural traits. For example, heavy breeds (eg, Holstein, Brown Swiss) are quite calm and easy to manage.

Holstein-Friesian Cattle, which originated in Holland and were introduced to Canada in 1881, today comprise over 85% of Canadian dairy cattle. The breed is characterized by its colour (shiny black on a white background), large size and exceptional milk production. Mature bulls weigh up to 1090 kg; mature cows, up to 635 kg. A mature cow annually produces an average of 6500 kg of 3.7% butterfat, 3.1% protein milk.

Ayrshire Cattle originated in Scotland's Ayr county and were introduced to Canada around 1821. The coat is light or dark red and white in varying proportions. Roughly one-half of Canada's Ayrshires are found in Québec. Bulls weigh up to 910 kg; cows, 570 kg. A cow annually produces about 5000 kg of 4.0% butterfat, 3.3% protein milk.

Jersey Cattle originated on Jersey I and were brought to Montréal in 1868. Jerseys are a fawn colour, except along the spine, around the muzzle and on the inside of the legs, where they are a paler shade. Bulls are darker than cows and some strains produce offspring with white markings. Bulls weigh up to 725 kg; cows, 500 kg. Each cow produces about 4200 kg of milk annually.

Guernsey Cattle, like Jerseys, were produced from Breton and Norman breeds. Developed on Guernsey I, they were brought to Canada in 1876. Guernseys are comparable in size to Ayrshires and are a buff colour, with distinctive white spots. A mature cow produces about 4700 kg of 4.9% butterfat, 3.6% protein milk annually.

Canadian Cattle were developed in Québec from cows imported from Britanny and Normandy, the first, by Jacques CARTIER around 1541. This breed is limited almost entirely to Québec. It is black or brown, although the back, muzzle and udder or scrotum are generally paler (sometimes yellow). Bulls weigh up to 770 kg; cows, 545 kg. A cow annually produces about 3800 kg of 4.4% butterfat, 3.6% protein milk.

Shorthorn Cattle originated in England and were first imported in 1832. They are considered a dual-purpose (milk and beef) breed; in Canada, all strains are registered in the same herd book. Shorthorns are red, white, roan or a mixture of red and white. Bulls weigh up to 1045 kg; cows, 770 kg. Cows annually produce about 4250 kg of 3.8% butterfat milk.

Brown Swiss Cattle originated in Asia, were developed in several European countries, particularly Switzerland, and were brought to Canada in 1888. These cattle mate well with beef breeds. Bulls weigh up to 1135 kg; cows, 635 kg. Mature cows will annually produce about 5900 kg of 4.0% butterfat, 3.5% protein milk.

New developments in animal reproduction will have a further impact. Embryo transfer is already practised commercially; the best dairy cattle are superovulated (forced to produce exceptional numbers of eggs at one time) and impregnated with the semen from exceptional bulls; embryo freezing and cloning of embryonic tissues are also practised. Canada has achieved an international reputation for the quality of its dairy cattle and now exports bull semen as well as livestock. In 1983, 17 756 registered Holsteins were exported to 20 countries; semen was exported to 40 countries. Embryo freezing will facilitate our international cattle trade, and sperm and embryo sexing also offer enormous potential. Rapid developments in BIOTECHNOLOGY will make it possible to increase productivity still further, through production of vaccines, hormones and certain nutrients. For example, a growth hormone injected into a lactating cow increases milk production without changing food consumption.

Feed represents over half of the cost of milk production: in high-performance herds, nutrition and food management are the factors promoting highest production. Cattle are ruminants, ie, they have a 4-compartment stomach in which bacteria and protozoa break down fibrous plant material into usable nutrients. A high-performance dairy cow annually consumes roughly 75% of its nutrients as fibre-rich grasses. The Canadian climate imposes difficult conditions on feed production and storage, and optimal use of grasses is a challenge. Milk production is increasing in all regions suitable for livestock feed production.

Increased productivity has resulted in higher frequency of mammary, digestive and reproductive disorders. Infertility and sterility are the 2 major reasons for culling dairy cattle. The causes of these disorders are complex and a great deal of research is conducted into reproduction problems and mammary disorders. Detecting when the cow is in season continues to be a major concern for producers. It is reported that roughly 50% of N American cattle suffer from various forms of mastitis (an infection of the mammary gland). GASTON J. ST-LAURENT

Dairy Industry Canada's dairy-products industry is made up of companies that process raw milk and cream. Primary products include pasteurized, packaged fluid milk and cream; cheese (natural, process, paste, spreads, curds); condensed, evaporated or powdered milk or cream; creamery butter, butter oil and whey butter; ice cream, ice-cream mix and ice-cream novelties; and frozen desserts (eg, sherbets, ices).

The first dairy product consumed by humans was fluid milk. While the cow is the major milk producer today, the milk of other mammals (eg, buffalo, reindeer, goat) is widely consumed in some parts of the world. Unquestionably, the first "processed" dairy product made from fluid milk was cheese. It was standard fare in ancient Egypt, Greece and Rome and was frequently used as field rations by ancient armies. In Europe, cheesemaking industries were run in monasteries, which produced varieties still made today. In Canada the popular Oka cheese was developed in a Québec monastery. Canada's modern, highly sophisticated, multi-billion-dollar dairy-processing industry began in the early 1600s, when French settlers brought in dairy cattle. For the next 250 years, dairy production remained a farm or cottage industry. As towns and villages were established, fluid milk, butter and cheese were provided by local farmers, a situation that did not change until the 1850s. The modern factory method of cheesemaking was introduced by Jesse Williams, who built the first cheese factory in Rome, NY, in 1851. The first cheese factories in Canada were built in Oxford County, Ont, in 1864 and at Dunham, Qué, in 1865. About 20 years later, the factory method of cheese production was introduced to Scotland where it was called the Canadian cheesemaking system.

By 1873 there were about 200 cheese factories in Canada. In 1873 a group of farmers established the first creamery in Canada at Athelston, Qué, but it survived for only about 10 weeks. Another creamery, started in Helena, Qué, in the same year, remained in production for about 11 years before being converted to a cheese factory. The first Canadian company to produce condensed milk was established in Truro, NS, in 1883. Dried milk powder was manufactured for the first time by a company started in Brownsville, Ont, in 1904. In 1900 modern large-scale milk distribution began in Toronto, Montréal and Ottawa; in 1927 homogenized milk was sold in Oshawa, a N American first.

As is the case in a number of other Canadian FOOD AND BEVERAGE processing sectors, the dairy industry has experienced a substantial decrease in numbers of factories. Improvements in road and rail delivery systems, packaging methods and processing techniques permitted dairies to increase dramatically the distribution range of even their most perishable product, pasteurized fluid milk. Consequently, large, modern, centrally located production facilities have been constructed and many small, regional dairy companies phased out. In 1961 there were 1710 dairies; by 1982, 402. Retail distribution of most dairy products has also changed significantl In the 1940s and 1950s many dairy produc were delivered door-to-door; today, consume buy most dairy products directly from a grocer store and home delivery has virtually disap peared.

Major changes have also occurred in the pack aging of pasteurized fluid-milk products. Unt fairly recently, most fluid dairy products wer in returnable glass containers; now most are i plastic, heat-sealed bags or in rigid containe made from paper laminated with plastic film Both packaging types have significantly in creased the shelf life of liquid dairy product The latest development in milk packaging is th so-called "aseptic" (sterile) packaging. A total sterile container is filled with fully sterile mil and sealed in a sterile environment before goin to an outside carton-handling line. Fluid dair products so processed are shelf stable at roon temperatures for 6 months or more. The fir Canadian aseptically packaged fluid milk wa produced by a Montréal dairy in the mid-1960 After a slow start, aseptic packaging facilitie were established in most provinces.

The Canadian dairy MANUFACTURING industr is highly regulated (*see* FOOD LEGISLATION). It mus comply with regulations set by the dairy divi sion of Agriculture Canada, by the Health Pro tection Branch of Health and Welfare Canad by Consumer and Corporate Affairs Canada an by provincial counterpart agencies. The dairy processing sector is represented by the Nationa Dairy Council of Canada in Ottawa. In 198 there were 402 dairy manufacturing operation in Canada: Nfld had 6; PEI, 13; NS, 16; NB, 1 Qué, 107; Ont, 155; Man, 26; Sask, 15; Alta, 3 and BC, 24. In 1973, with 646 plants in pro duction, the industry had shipments valued a nearly $1.7 billion. Materials and supplies tha year cost $1.3 billion; fuel and electricity cost were $24.3 million; and the industry employe 27 819 people. In 1982 industry sales had in creased to almost $5.5 billion. Materials an supplies costs increased to $4.2 billion; fuel an electricity costs increased to $94.5 million. Em ployment had declined to 25 796, undoubtedl as a result of changing distribution patterns. ROBERT F. BARRAT

Dakota (Sioux) Archaeological evidence indi cates that the Dakota occupied what is nov western Ontario and eastern Manitoba prior t 1200 AD, and western Manitoba and easter Saskatchewan prior to 900 AD. These popula tions later withdrew to the drainage basins o the Red, Mississippi and Rainy rivers, wher they were located when first contacted by Pierr RADISSON in 1649. By then the Siouan-speakin Dakota population had divided into 3 groups Farthest E, along the Mississippi R and its trib utaries, dwelt the Dakota (Santee Sioux), wh practised horticulture, occupied semipermanen villages, harvested WILD RICE as a food staple an hunted buffalo (*see* BUFFALO HUNT). Between th Mississippi and the lower Missouri R were th Nakota (Yanktonai Sioux), speakers of the sam dialect of Dakota as is spoken by the ASSINIBOIN and STONEY of Canada. This population wintere along the wooded tributaries of the Mississipp and summered on the plains, hunting big game Farthest W, along the Missouri R, lived th Lakota (Teton Sioux), who were wholly mobil and largely dependent upon the buffalo. Eve though different in many respects, all wer politically united and referred to themselve collectively as *Dakota* (Nakota, Lakota) or "th allies."

After acquiring the HORSE in the early 1700s the Dakota expanded their territory from th Mississippi R to the Yellowstone R, and fron the Platte R to the Qu'Appelle R. HUDSON'S BAY CO records from Ft Qu'Appelle to Rainy Lake Hous (Ft Frances, Ont) commonly mention the Dakot

A Sioux (Dakota), oil on canvas by Paul Kane (*courtesy Royal Ontario Museum*).

occupying that territory from the late 1700s. During the WAR OF 1812, the Dakota pledged their alliance to Britain, in return for oaths of perpetual obligation. This alliance was betrayed at the TREATY OF GHENT (1814), when Britain abandoned her Indian allies as a term of peace. The Dakota then drew closer to their lands in the US; however, though land use in Canada decreased, the northern territory was never abandoned.

The western expansion of the Americans ended Dakota territorial sovereignty when, in 1862, the US military, after the Minnesota Troubles, drove some of the eastern population into Canada, where they have since taken up reserve lands in Manitoba and Saskatchewan. A few Lakota, including SITTING BULL, moved into southern Saskatchewan following the Battle of the Little Big Horn (1876). The Dakota have since been treated as political refugees by Canadian governments. They were never admitted to treaty, as were all other Plains Indian populations, and were expected to make their own future in Canada (*see* INDIAN TREATIES). The Dakota became commercial farmers, producers of specialty crops, woodworkers, cattle ranchers, small-scale resource exploiters and labourers, traditions that are carried on today. In 1982 the Dakota in Canada numbered about 2500 and occupied 7689 ha of land on 9 INDIAN RESERVES. *See also* NATIVE PEOPLE: PLAINS and general articles under NATIVE PEOPLE. PETER DOUGLAS ELIAS

Reading: G. MacEwan, *Sitting Bull: The Years in Canada* (1973); R.W. Meyer, *History of the Santee Sioux* (1967).

Dalhousie, NB, Town, pop 4958 (1981c), inc 1905, shire town of Restigouche County, is located on NB's north shore, at the mouth of the Restigouche R. The population is primarily English and French speaking (51.6%/47.8%, 1981c). Founded 1826 and named for Gov Gen the earl of Dalhousie, it developed as a shipbuilding and lumbering centre. Lumbering lost its preeminence in 1930 with the opening of the NBIP paper mill. Chemical plants constitute the other major industry. The town is a year-round seaport and site of a NBEPC 300 MW thermoelectric generating station. The Chaleur Area History Museum has displays on pioneer life and early industries. BURTON GLENDENNING

Dalhousie, George Ramsay, 9th Earl of, soldier, administrator, governor-in-chief of Canada (b 23 Oct 1770; d at Dalhousie Castle, Scot 21 Mar 1838). He joined the British army in 1788 and saw service in both Spain and France 1812-14. After fighting at the battle of Waterloo, he began a career in administration. In 1816 he was appointed lt-gov of Nova Scotia and, after the sudden death of the duke of RICHMOND, became governor-in-chief of Canada. Known for his authoritarian views, Dalhousie clashed with the French Canadian majority led by Louis-Joseph PAPINEAU. He was recalled in 1828, and a British parliamentary committee was formed to deal with the Canadian situation. During his tenure he founded Dalhousie College (later DALHOUSIE UNIVERSITY) in 1818 and the Québec Literary and Historical Society. After leaving Canada, he was appointed commander in chief of the forces in India (1829-32). DAVID EVANS

Dalhousie Review, fd 1921 at DALHOUSIE UNIVERSITY as "A Canadian Journal of Literature and Opinion," is one of those academic quarterlies that have largely taken the place in Canada of the journals of affairs that flourish in Britain and the US. The first editor, H.L. Stewart, declared, "we avow a nationalism that is not prejudice and a provincialism that is not narrowness." The *Review* has sustained this ideal, representing faithfully the intellectual life of the Maritimes while remaining open to scholars from elsewhere. *Dalhousie Review* also publishes the work of fiction writers and poets, many of them, like W.K. Valgardson, early in their careers. A large section is devoted to reviews of recent books, and current affairs receive attention as well. GEORGE WOODCOCK

Dalhousie University, Halifax, was founded in 1818 by Lt-Gov George Ramsay, 9th earl of DALHOUSIE. Dalhousie envisaged a liberal, nondenominational college, based on the educational standards of Edinburgh U and offering a progressive alternative to the Anglican UNIVERSITY OF KING'S COLLEGE at Windsor, NS. The institution's initial funding came from customs duties collected at Castine, Maine, during the British occupation, 1814-15. Its auspicious beginnings were soon marred by governmental indifference and sectarian rivalry. Both the colonial establishment and the college's board of governors were unenthusiastic, favouring instead the precedence of King's College. Religious guidelines excluded all but ANGLICANS from King's and, during the early years, effectively restricted faculty appointments at Dalhousie to Presbyterians. As a result, various denominational colleges were established throughout Nova Scotia, seriously impeding the growth of higher education for some 50 years. Attempts to unite with King's College failed in 1824 and 1832, with the Windsor group fearing a dilution of their Anglican exclusivity and Oxford standards. (Affiliation did not occur until 1923, when circumstances dictated that King's adopt a more pragmatic educational approach.) Dalhousie languished until 1838, when Thomas MCCULLOCH became the first president. University status was granted in 1841 but, after McCulloch's death in 1843, the institution again declined and in 1848 was reorganized as a high school. In 1863 Dalhousie was reconstituted as a university, primarily through co-operative Presbyterian efforts to improve higher education. The Presbyterians' willingness to renounce denominational control opened the way for expansion, and progress since then has been continuous.

An early emphasis on mathematics and the classics shifted to modern scientific studies, introduced during the latter 19th century. A medical faculty began in 1868, women were admitted in 1881, and the law school — the first to teach common law in the British Empire — was founded in 1883. Since 1879 the university has been financially assisted by such benefactors as George Munro, Sir William YOUNG and Dorothy Killam, enabling continuous expansion of both the curriculum and the physical plant. In 1887 Dalhousie moved from its original downtown location to Forrest Hall, now part of a 24 ha campus. Today, Dalhousie provides over 90 degree and diploma programs in arts and science, administrative studies, the health professions, dentistry, law, medicine and graduate work. The university is an integral part of the community and is world renowned for law, medical research and ocean studies. LOIS KERNAGHAN

Dallaire, Jean-Philippe, painter, illustrator, professor (b at Hull, Qué 9 June 1916; d at Vence, France 27 Nov 1965). Raised in a working-class family of 15, he started drawing at age 11. Though he registered in various art classes, he was mostly self-taught. In Oct 1938, with the support of a Québec government grant, Dallaire went to Paris where he attended the Atelier d'art sacré, the Lhote studio and worked in his Montmartre studio. He became familiar with the work of Picasso and the surrealists and met Alfred PELLAN. Under the German Occupation (1940-44) he was prisoner at St-Denis. He taught painting at the École des beaux-arts in Québec City 1946-52, worked for the NATIONAL FILM BOARD in Ottawa 1952-57, mostly illustrating animated films, then lived and painted in Montréal 1957-59. In 1959 he went to Europe to stay. His accidental death in 1965 terminated a brilliant career. Dallaire's works show varied stylistic influences and are always recognized by their draftmanship and spontaneity in subject and use of colour. MICHEL VINCENT CHEFF

Dally, Frederick, professional portrait and landscape photographer (b at Southwark, Eng 29 July 1838; d at Wolverhampton, Eng 28 July 1914). Educated at Christ's Hospital, London, Dally arrived in Victoria at the height of the Cariboo gold rush in 1862. He began business as a general merchant, but in 1866 turned to photography. Prominent citizens, public buildings, local scenes and special events were all his subjects. In and around Victoria, he recorded the presence of the colonial government and the Royal Navy. A keen observer and amateur anthropologist, Dally photographed the coast and interior tribes and also collected Indian artifacts. Best known are his 1867-68 photographs of the CARIBOO ROAD and of the creeks and claims of the goldfields; many of these views were later used to produce engravings for the pictorial press. In Sept 1870 Dally sold his stock-in-trade and left Victoria. After studying at the Philadelphia Dental Coll, he returned to England to work in dental surgery. JOAN M. SCHWARTZ

Daly, Kathleen Frances, painter (b at Napanee, Ont 28 May 1898). Daly studied in Toronto, Paris and New York. She travelled annually, 1924-30, on sketching trips to Europe. Her accomplished sense of line and rhythm, although closely associated with the work of the GROUP OF SEVEN, reveals an underlying confidence in her own stylistic interpretation and use of colour. She married George Pepper in 1929 and they worked out of the Studio Building, Toronto, 1934-35. They painted together in all parts of Canada, and over 25 years (1930-56) she showed work in all the major Canadian exhibitions, as well as in London, Eng. ERIK J. PETERS

Daly, Thomas Cullen, filmmaker, film producer (b at Toronto 25 Apr 1918). Daly has been a key figure at the NATIONAL FILM BOARD since its inception. His influence on the NFB aesthetic has been considerable. After graduating from U of T, he went directly to the NFB in 1940, assisting Stuart Legg in the editing of *The World in Action* series. He was in charge of the famed Unit B 1950-64 and responsible for such classic films as *Corral* (1954), *City of Gold* (1957), *Universe* (1960) and *Lonely Boy* (1962), as well as the multi-screen *Labyrinth*, produced for EXPO 67. Since that time, he has produced numerous NFB films. PIERS HANDLING

Damselfly, thin-bodied, carnivorous INSECT with 2 pairs of long, membranous, narrow-based wings. Damselflies belong to order Odonata [Gk "toothed," referring to mouthparts], suborder Zygoptera. There are over 2800 known species worldwide, most in the tropics, 51 in Canada. Adults are brightly coloured, generally about 3 cm long, with mobile heads and large compound eyes. Larvae are aquatic, usually dark in colour, and characterized by 3 flat tail appendages, probably serving as gills. Larvae shoot out a peculiarly modified, toothed mouthpart (labium) to capture small aquatic insects and worms; adults sweep up small, flying insects with their legs. Adults usually occur near water. Eggs are placed in aquatic plants. Although some species may spend over 3 years as larvae, larval stages of Canadian species usually last only one year. Transformation to adult occurs after larva leaves the water. Adults live for a few weeks. *See* DRAGONFLY. G. PRITCHARD

Danby, Kenneth Edison, painter (b at Sault Ste Marie, Ont 6 Mar 1940). Ken Danby was at Toronto's Ontario College of Art 1958-60 and studied with J.W.G. MACDONALD. He began as an abstract painter, though a visit to an exhibition of Andrew Wyeth's work at Buffalo, NY, in 1962 confirmed his disenchantment with abstraction. He turned to painting carefully posed, snapshotlike views, often of rural Ontario seen in a strong light. Danby is best known for his study of anonymous sports figures: subjects from everyday life, which at the same time reveal his rare gift of creating unforgettable visual images. In *At the Crease* (1972) the masked ice-hockey goalie recalls knights of an earlier day; for many, the painting has become something of a national symbol. JOAN MURRAY

Dance Education refers to education or training that leads to dancing, as opposed to "dance in education," which is limited to dance in elementary, secondary and post-secondary schools, where dance is considered to be a useful tool for physical and personality development. The distinction is not always clear. Some universities claim, for instance, that whether or not students emerge as dancers, they should be given the same intensity of training as a dancer would be given; and conservatories are beginning to offer courses in dance notation, anatomy, music, and other related subjects not previously thought to be essential to dance training.

Dance, and consequently dance education, grew dramatically in Canada during the 1960s and 1970s. Dance as a performing art gained a large supportive audience, and thousands of young people now enrol in studios hoping to become professional dancers. Many more take dance classes for enjoyment or physical exercise. Ballroom dancing remains popular and franchised ballroom studios are still found in most Canadian cities. Ethnic, folk, and square dancing are encouraged through dance clubs and festivals of dance across the country. It was also during the 1960s and 1970s that the scope of dance expanded in educational institutions. Previously, university dance was limited to physical-education departments, with little emphasis on dance as an arts discipline. Taking the lead from the US, degree-granting programs have now been established in several Canadian universities, offering programs in dance notation, composition, analysis, history, criticism, pedagogy, and performance. YORK UNIVERSITY was the first to offer all these options, with an additional study stream in dance therapy. Its dance department was the first in the world to offer a graduate degree (MFA) in dance history and criticism. The UNIVERSITY OF WATERLOO offers BSc and BA degrees in dance, with a wide range of subject possibilities, including kinetic and psychological dance research. SIMON FRASER UNIVERSITY grants a major degree to dancers and choreographers within an interdisciplinary framework. The UNIVERSITÉ DU QUÉBEC À MONTRÉAL awards a baccalaureate in dance, concentrating on the training of teachers for primary and secondary levels of education. CONCORDIA UNIVERSITY emphasizes training in modern dance technique, leading to performance and choreography with a BA degree. Diplomas in dance are awarded at George Brown College/Lois Smith School of Dance, Ryerson Theatre Canadian College of Dance (both in Toronto), and Grant MacEwan Community College in Edmonton. The Université de Montréal has a certificate program.

Dance in education is another important stream of dance study within Canadian universities. The Canadian Association of Health, Physical Education and Recreation (CAHPER), Dance Portfolio, has campaigned for the introduction of dance into primary and secondary schools. CAHPER is modeled after its American counterpart, AAHPER, but is influenced by the teachings of Rudolf von Laban, who introduced dance into English schools shortly after WWII. The Dance and Child Conference, held in Edmonton in 1978, was a landmark contribution from this organization.

Almost every community in Canada has a studio where children and young adults may study ballet, tap, baton, jazz, ballroom and modern dance. But studio dance teaching has always existed without comprehensive controls on teaching standards. No licence is required to open a studio. The national Canadian Dance Teachers Association sets specific criteria for its own membership. The Dance in Canada Association, formed in 1973 to serve all aspects of professional dance, gives priority to teaching and serves the large constituency of dance teachers through its information services.

Before the formation of Canada's 3 major ballet companies, excellent teachers in Canada helped provide the base for what has become a ballet tradition. Gerald Crevier and Elizabeth Leese of Montréal; Mildred Wickson, Bettina Byers and Boris VOLKOFF of Toronto; and June Roper and Mara McBirney in Vancouver trained dancers who joined the original companies of Les GRANDS BALLET CANADIENS, the NATIONAL BALLET OF CANADA and the ROYAL WINNIPEG BALLET. As these companies grew it was necessary to provide professional schools to ensure consistently well-trained dancers suitable to the repertory of each company. The NATIONAL BALLET SCHOOL, which has a resident day school, funded by govt agencies and staffed by excellent teachers, has produced a number of very successful dancers for the National Ballet and for other companies throughout the world. Les Grands Ballets Canadiens provides an excellent training program through l'École supérieure de danse, and the professional program of the Royal Winnipeg Ballet produces well-trained dance personnel. Professional schools have also recently attached to modern-dance companies in Canada. The largest and first of these is the school of the TORONTO DANCE THEATRE. Others are affiliated with the ANNA WYMAN DANCE THEATRE, WINNIPEG'S CONTEMPORARY DANCERS and Le GROUPE DE LA PLACE ROYALE. There is also a school attached to Les BALLETS JAZZ DE MONTRÉAL, with satellite schools in Québec City and Toronto.

There are also professional schools not aligned with a specific company. The BANFF CENTRE SCHOOL OF FINE ARTS is a stimulating meeting ground for dancers and choreographers during summer months. The Canadian College of Dance is a teacher-training school emphasizing the Royal Academy of Dance syllabus and has been a part of the RYERSON POLYTECHNICAL INSTITUTE in Toronto for many years. The Lois SMITH School of Dance joined George Brown College in Toronto to offer a 2-year professional curriculum. The National Choreographic Seminars brought choreographers, composers, musicians and dancers to creative heights in 1978 at York University and at the Banff Centre in 1980. Summer sessions held annually at SFU and York attract professionals, mostly modern dancers, interested in intensive work in technique and dance composition.

Dance education has grown phenomenally, but a healthy future will depend on the development of choreographers, which has not kept stride with the increase of dance activity in Canada, as well as on more effective dance teaching in primary and secondary schools. Many educators are working to establish dance as an accepted study within schools, but little has been accomplished beyond the occasional inclusion of dance as a recreational activity in physical-education programs. A recognition of dance for its aesthetic and cultural potential within schools will ensure an informed, discriminating dance public for the future. GRANT STRATE

Dance History Dance has always been an integral part of Canadian Indian and Inuit life, giving ritual expression to the social and religious aspects of culture. A rich and complex dance heritage existed in Canada long before the arrival of the first explorers. The earliest written record of dancing in Canada is found in the diaries of explorer Jacques Cartier, who wrote in 1534 of being approached, near the mouth of the St Lawrence River, by 7 canoes bearing "wild men . . . dancing and making many signs of joy and mirth." Explorers and settlers who followed him made frequent reference to Indian dance in their journals. However, the indigenous dance forms of Canada have had little influence on the country's theatre-dance traditions. Theatre dance has existed in Canada for more than 300 years, but the significant influences on its development have been largely external and closely linked with the influences most affecting the development of Canadian society as a whole: colonization by 2 invading cultures; the inhibiting force in Québec of a conservative church; massive immigration, particularly from Europe in the middle 19th and early 20th centuries; and, in the 20th century, the pervasive cultural influence of the US. However, the history of professional theatre dance in Canada dates from as recently as the 1930s, and 50 years later there still is not an identifiably Canadian dance character. Like the country itself, Canadian dance is a mosaic of diverse traditions and influences.

The earliest imported dance influences were French. A masque, probably containing dance, was mounted in the harbour at PORT-ROYAL in 1606. Forty years later the Jesuit fathers were reporting the performance of a kind of ballet at the marriage of a soldier in Québec City, and the following Feb a ballet was given at the warehouse of the Compagnie des Cent-Associés. Ballet at this time was far closer to pageantry, blending movement with singing and acting, than to classical dance as it is known today. Audiences would have seen little intricate technical display or elevation. However, ballet technique and content evolved steadily throughout the 18th and early 19th centuries, and Canada was exposed to a variety of itinerant troupes, generally offering dance as a divertissement alongside plays. John Durang, one of the earliest professional dancers in the US, appeared with a circus company in Montréal and Québec City in the winter of 1797-98; comedy ballets were regularly given in Halifax in the same period; Jean Dauberval's *La Fille mal gardée*, first performed in Bordeaux in 1789, was seen in Canada for the first time in Québec City in 1816; the famous French dancer Mme Celeste (Keppler) visited Québec City and Montréal several times in the 1820s and 1830s; and in 1847 a highlight of the entertainment year in Canada East seems to have been a tour by the Petites Danseuses Viennoises, a troupe of 48 dancing children

Canada continued to provide a fertile touring ground for foreign dancers in the late 19th and early 20th centuries. Loie Fuller performed her famous *Fire Dance* at the Vancouver Opera House in 1896; Anna Pavlova toured the country regularly from 1910; Ruth St Denis and Ted Shawn were frequent visitors between 1914 and 1924; the Diaghilev Ballet Russe company, with Vaslav Nijinsky, made its only Canadian appearance in Vancouver in 1917. Later, Martha Graham, Doris Humphrey and other pioneers of American modern dance made frequent tours; in the 1930s the itinerant Ballets Russes companies paid regular visits. Despite this frequent exposure to much of the best and most innovative theatre dance then available, professional dance in Canada was slow to develop, and until as late as the 1950s it was necessary for Canadians wishing to make a career in dancing to leave the country to do so.

The groundwork for professionalism in Canadian dance was laid in the 1930s by a handful of immigrant teachers, most of them women. In Vancouver, June Roper, from Rosebud, Texas, combined the theatrical flair of her Hollywood teacher, Ernest Belcher, and her experience as a star of supported adagio in Europe and the US to become, in the late 1930s, what *Dancemagazine* was later to call "North America's greatest starmaker." Over a 5-year period beginning late in 1934, she turned out over 60 dancers for the world's major professional companies, 8 of them for the Ballets Russes. In Ottawa at about the same time, the Boston-born Gwendolyn Osborne was doing the same thing on a smaller scale. Since this was a period in which Russian dance had captured the public imagination, many of the Canadians who went to the senior companies adopted Russianized names. Roper students Rosemary Deveson and Patricia Meyers, for instance, became, respectively, Natasha Sobinova and Alexandra Denisova; Osborne student Betty Lowe became Ludmilla Lvova.

Boris VOLKOFF, born Boris Baskakoff in Tula, Russia, arrived in Toronto in 1930 from the US after a career as a character dancer in Russia and the Far East. He found work as a dancer and ballet master for live divertissements presented between films at a city movie theatre, and rapidly established himself as a teacher and choreographer. Among his pupils was young Mildred Herman, later to become, as Melissa Hayden, a star of the New York City Ballet. Volkoff's work as a choreographer of ice ballets for the Toronto Skating Club in the early 1930s first brought him to Canada in the noncompetitive dance section of the Berlin Olympiad. Three years later, in May 1939, he launched the Volkoff Canadian Ballet. It was Canada's first company by a matter of weeks. The following month, the group that was to become the ROYAL WINNIPEG BALLET gave its first performance. The Winnipeg company was the creation of 2 immigrant English dance teachers, Gweneth LLOYD and Betty FARRALLY. Two of its first members were David Adams, later to become a soloist of Britain's Royal Ballet, and Paddy Stone, later to become a prominent variety choreographer in London. From the start, the company's founders opted to keep its membership small, dancing a repertoire designed to appeal to a broad audience.

The year 1948 was an important one in the development of dance in Canada. In Winnipeg, the Canadian Ballet Festival movement was launched; and in Montréal, REFUS GLOBAL was published. The festival was conceived by RWB manager David Yeddeau and Boris Volkoff as a means to give dancers in Canada a sense of what was happening in their art elsewhere in the country. The first festival was held in Winnipeg, and brought together 3 companies: the Winnipeg ballet, Volkoff's company, and a Montréal modern-dance group led by the Polish-German immigrant Ruth Sorel. The following year, 10 companies met in Toronto. Over the 6 years of the movement's existence, the festivals became so popular, and so effective as vehicles of communication for the dance community, that Anatole Chujoy, editor of the NY publication *Dance News*, urged the adoption of the idea in the US, giving direct rise to the powerful and extensive regional ballet movement of today.

La Dance Ronde / Circular Dance of the Canadians by George Heriot, coloured aquatint (*courtesy Public Archives of Canada / C-251*).

Refus Global was the title of a manifesto of cultural rebellion published in 1948 by a group of Québecois artists of various disciplines clustered around the automatiste painter Paul-Émile BORDUAS. The manifesto demanded an end to social, religious, and political restrictions on art in Québec. Its significance for dance lies in its influence on the thinking and artistic attitudes of 3 women who were to help shape modern dance in Québec: Françoise Sullivan (who both signed and contributed to the manifesto), Jeanne Renaud and Françoise Riopelle (both connected with the Borduas group). Sullivan spent several years in the late 1940s and early 1950s as a choreographer, turned to sculpture and painting, and returned to choreography in the late 1970s, establishing a company of her own and passing on the surrealist influence to a new generation of Québec choreographers. In 1962, Renaud and Riopelle, after each spending several years in Paris, founded a Montréal-based modern-dance group that, in 1966, under Renaud and Peter Boneham, a dancer from New York, became Le GROUPE DE LA PLACE ROYALE, a company that developed a reputation as one of the country's most audacious dance experimenters and a nursery of new dance thinking in Canada.

The success of the RWB in the late 1940s, and the first visit to Canada by the highly regarded Sadler's Wells company from London in 1949, convinced a group of Toronto dance enthusiasts that Toronto should have a professional company of its own. Acting on the advice of Sadler's Wells founder-director Ninette de Valois, the Torontonians invited the young English dancer-choreographer Celia FRANCA to observe the standard of Canadian dance at the 1950 festival, in Montréal. She was impressed by the enthusiasm she saw, returned to Canada the following year and, in the fall of 1951, launched the NATIONAL BALLET OF CANADA. From the start its structure and philosophy differed from those of the RWB; Franca set out to create a major ballet company in the European opera-house style, dancing a repertoire rooted firmly in the staples of the 19th-century classical ballet repertoire. Among the company's founder-members were David Adams and his wife Lois SMITH, who would become Canada's first nationally famous ballerina; Grant STRATE, who would later become immensely influential in the field of Canadian dance education; and Brian MACDONALD, whose active international career as a choreographer and artistic director would begin in 1953, following the abrupt curtailment of his dancing career because of an accident.

Canada's third major ballet company, Les GRANDS BALLETS CANADIENS, owes its origins to the launching of the French Canadian TV branch of the CBC in Montréal (1952). Ludmilla CHIRIAEFF, born into a Russian literary family in Riga, Latvia (1924), and raised in Berlin, arrived in Montréal with her family as an immigrant in 1952, after a dancing careeer in which she had performed with the de Basil Ballet Russe company and with various companies in Germany and Switzerland. She immediately found work choreographing short ballets for the French TV station's first music producer, Pierre Mercure (*see* DANCE ON TELEVISION AND FILM). Soon she had created Les Ballets Chiriaeff, a performing ensemble that appeared many times on TV. The company gave its first live performance in 1954, and after an enormous success with a Chiriaeff version of *Les Noces* (music: Stravinsky) at the Montréal Festival (1956) changed its name in 1958 to Les Grands Ballets Canadiens and concentrated on live performance. Like the early Lloyd works in Winnipeg, the ballets made for the Montréal company in its early years were carefully tailored to show the company to its best effect and to appeal to diverse audiences.

The launching of TV in Canada was one of the earliest responses of government to the Massey Commission (NATIONAL DEVELOPMENT IN THE ARTS, LETTERS AND SCIENCES), which had been appointed in 1949 and reported in 1951. A far more significant recommendation of the commission, for all the performing arts, was the establishment of the CANADA COUNCIL (1957). Implicit in its creation was a recognition, at the federal level, of the responsibility of government to provide state patronage of the arts, to establish and affirm a particularly Canadian culture, built from Canadian talents. All 3 of the ballet companies received grants in the council's first year — $100 000 to the National Ballet of Canada, $20 000 to the RWB and $10 000 to LGBC, out of a total for all the arts of $749 000. In the 1980-81 season, the council gave $5.6 million to dance alone, a 43-fold growth over 23 years and a reflection of the phenomenal explosion of dance activity that took place in the late 1960s and early 1970s.

It was an explosion fostered in part by the very availability of funding for the arts. But it was also fostered by the new social climate of Canada. The 1960s, a time of social and intellectual liberalization in much of the Western world, had broken the tight bond between modern Canada and its prim past. The art form of the body attracted new audiences, new practitioners and new acceptability. At the same time, audiences broadened their receptiveness and increased their anticipation. Choreographers found a new freedom to create works in which form was content; the non-literal and the abstract won a slowly widening respect. These changes were not limited to Canada, but their impact was particularly strong in Canada because so little had gone before. In the area of modern dance, in particular, the 1960s and 1970s was a period of remarkable blossoming. A series of modern-dance festivals was held in Toronto in the early 1960s, and by 1965 modern-dance companies existed in Winnipeg (Rachel Browne's WINNIPEG'S CONTEMPORARY DANCERS) and Vancouver (the PAULA ROSS DANCE CO). The beginnings of the TORONTO DANCE THEATRE, regarded today as one of the foremost modern-dance companies in Canada and the principal Canadian repository of the Martha Graham technique and tradition, can be traced to the return to Canada (1967) of Patricia BEATTY, a Torontonian who had studied in the US with Graham and danced with Pearl Lang. She founded the New Dance Group of Canada, which in 1968 was absorbed into the newly formed TDT. She joined 2 other Graham disciples, the Canadian David EARLE and the former Graham company member Peter RANDAZZO, an American, as co-director.

Lavish spending by govt on the Centennial and Expo celebrations of 1967 gave an added boost to dance, as politicans realized the value of the arts in creating a national image. Federal make-work programs in the early 1970s gave further stimulus to the emergence of new, young dance-makers. Art of all forms flourished; it was a period of unparalleled growth and prosperity for Canada's performing-arts community. In this period new modern-dance companies came to prominence, including ANNA WYMAN DANCE THEATRE, Regina Modern Dance Works, and a little later, the DANNY GROSSMAN DANCE CO; and Les BALLETS JAZZ DE MONTRÉAL, a lively hybrid, first made its mark. Alongside this burgeoning modern-dance scene, Canada's 3 senior ballet companies also experienced a period of unprecedented expansion and success. The Royal Winnipeg Ballet won medals in Paris and audience enthusiasm in the USSR; Les Grands Ballets Canadiens caught the pulse of the youth generation with Fernand Nault's setting of the rock opera *Tommy;* the National Ballet of Canada celebrated its coming-of-age by performing to great acclaim in London, Franca's hometown, and, a little later, acquired both Rudolf Nureyev (as a regular guest) and a sumptuous new Nureyev mounting of *The Sleeping Beauty*.

Inevitably, this growth, much of which had been stimulated by Canada Council funding, strained the council's resources, and as the world economy began to lose its buoyancy in the middle 1970s, economic cutbacks meant the council was unable to keep pace with the growth it had helped to foster. In dance, the economic crisis split the community into 2 clear camps — those with adequate federal funding (the 3 major ballet companies, 4 modern-dance companies, and the National Ballet School) and those without. In the late 1970s, conditions became tense. The Dance in Canada Assn, which had been created (1973) as a point of contact and a lobbying force for the Canadian dance community, had, by 1977, become the spokesman of the under-privileged groups, voicing outspoken criticism of the council's policies and priorities. Partly in protest against this, partly out of a desire to create a voice for professional dance, the 8 "senior" organizations broke away from DICA to form the Canadian Assn of Professional Dance Organizations. DICA, which has by far the largest membership, is the grassroots service organization for the broad Canadian dance community, open to performers, educators, writers and others with dance interests; it produces a quarterly magazine, *Dance in Canada,* a monthly newsletter and performance calendar, and it organizes annual national conferences. CAPDO concerns itself with the major professional companies, and in 1981 staged a gala showcase of its members' work (subsequently filmed by the NFB) at the NATIONAL ARTS CENTRE in Ottawa.

In the late 1970s and early 1980s, the most marked phenomenon of Canadian dance was the emergence of independent CHOREOGRAPHY, owing partly to new financial pressures, partly to the desire of young creators to make dance outside the confines of a company, and partly to the influence of the New York modernist movement. Some choreographers, Judith Marcuse, Linda Rabin, Margie Gillis, and Jennifer Mascall, have tried to make their way alone; some, such as members of the Toronto Independent Dance Enterprise or Terminal City Dance Research (Vancouver), formed themselves into loose, exploratory ensembles. In Québec, where the liberating influences of the 1970s were accentuated by a politico-cultural revolution uniquely French Canadian, the experimentalism of the early 1980s had an enormous vitality, as young choreographers such as Paul-André Fortier, Edouard Lock, and Daniel Leveillé tested the limits of their new freedoms of subject, style and approach.

The education of dancers and of choreographers began to take on a new significance at this time. Dance schools of varying quality have existed in Canada since at least the 18th century, but only since the establishment of the senior ballet companies in the 1950s was the training of professional dancers given serious attention. Even after the country's 3 companies had become established, it was still common for Canadian dancers of exceptional talent to go abroad. Lynn SEYMOUR and Jennifer Penney both left BC for distinguished careers with the Royal Ballet in London; Wayne Eagling, of Montréal, did the same; and Reid Anderson, from New Westminster, BC, became a principal dancer with the Stuttgart Ballet. However, the development of professional dance schools (*see* DANCE EDUCATION) and the sudden expansion of interest and activity in dance in the 1970s lessened this trend.

The preeminent institution for ballet training in Canada is the NATIONAL BALLET SCHOOL, which has won international recognition for the thoroughness of its training and the quality of the dancers it produces. Graduates have frequently won awards in international competition: most notable have been Karen KAIN (silver prizewinner, women's solo, Moscow, 1973), her partner Frank AUGUSTYN (together they won first prize for the pas de deux the same year) and Kevin Pugh (silver medal, Moscow, 1981). Other important ballet training programs are attached to the Royal Winnipeg Ballet. One of its most distinguished graduates is Evelyn HART, who won the women's solo gold medal at the Varna competition in 1980. Les Grands Ballets Canadiens produced Sylvie Kinal-Chevalier, winner of the silver medal at Varna (1976) at the age of 17.

Though Canadian dancers have made considerable impact abroad, Canadian choreographers have made little impact internationally, and their development was given little serious attention until the late 1970s. In ballet, the emphasis on imported work and (in the case of the National Ballet of Canada) on remounted classics of the 19th century provided a clear reflection of the early tastes of the Canadian audience. The market for the home-made has never been large, and the reluctance of those in charge of the major companies to devote large amounts of time, space, and money to the development of choreographic talent is understandable. Without that commitment, however, it will be impossible for Canadian dance to establish itself as anything more than a branch plant, albeit a diverse one of the choreographic creativity of other cultures.

Arnold SPOHR, who took control of the RWB in 1958 and directed it to international glories, was responsible for encouraging the early work of a number of choreographers, particularly Brian MACDONALD and Norbert VESAK. Les Grands Ballets Canadiens later came to give extensive regular display to the work of Macdonald and, to a lesser extent, other Canadian choreographers (primarily Fernand NAULT). The National Ballet of Canada has always had a policy of encouraging its own (in the company's first decade both David Adams and Grant Strate were given a number of opportunities to choreograph), and in the late 1970s an interesting group of choreographers (Ann Ditchburn, James Kudelka and Constantin PATSALAS) began to emerge from the company's sporadically held choreographic workshops. Even so, the lack of opportunity for young choreographers to learn their craft and experiment with technique within the country's major companies is a recurring complaint. It was not until the institution of the dance program at York University in the early 1970s and Grant Strate's introduction of the National Choreographic Seminars at York (1978) and at the BANFF CENTRE SCHOOL OF FINE ARTS (1980), that there was any concentrated or responsible attempt to develop Canada's indigenous choreographic talent. Giving extra stimulus to the emergence of new creators are 2 national choreographic awards, presented annually by the Chalmers Foundation (Toronto), and the Clifford E. Lee Foundation (Calgary), and both the Canada Council and the Ontario Arts Council make regular grant awards to underwrite developing choreographers.

By the beginning of the 1980s, it was clear that the years of adolescence and startling growth in Canadian dance were over, and that a period of steady, unspectacular maturing had begun.

MAX WYMAN

Dance, Modern Unlike classical dance, with its adherence to academic principles of movement developed through past centuries, modern dance stresses individual expression and personal style. Canadian modern dance has derived from 2 powerful influences, European and American. Between 1940 and the birth of TORONTO DANCE THEATRE (1968), virtually all modern dance in Canada owed its origin to Central and Eastern European traditions, particularly the work of Rudolf von Laban. A wide diversity of personalities worked within this idiom, but von Laban and his pupils shared a view of dance as an enriching and ennobling art form.

Elizabeth Leese was the first of several exiles from Europe's political turmoil to bring this seriousness of purpose to the Canadian dance scene. A former soloist with Trudi Schoop, Leese joined Boris VOLKOFF'S Toronto-based ballet company in 1939 and then, in the early 1940s, moved to Montréal to open her own school. In 1944, a pupil and dancer of Mary Wigman's, Ruth Sorel, also established a school in Montréal. Leese and Sorel played important roles in the early years of the annual Canadian Ballet Festival (1948-54), which brought together dancers and choreographers from across the country. They created a vibrant atmosphere in Montréal in which a second generation of modrn dancers could grow. Over 20 years after the rrival of Leese and Sorel in Montréal, Jeanne enaud and ex-ballet dancer Peter Boneham ounded le GROUPE DE LA PLACE ROYALE. Le Groupe, vhich has made its home in Ottawa since 1977, eeps alive a fiercely cerebral approach to modrn dance. The European tradition continues in Iontréal in the work of Dansepartout, Pointpienu and especially 1981 Chalmers Award inner Paul-André FORTIER, whose *Fin* created a ance counterpart to Samuel Beckett's nihilistic lays.

The European influence also dominated early nodern dance in Toronto a decade after the eginnings in Montréal. Its major practitioners, ianca Rogge and Yone Kvietys, were both astern European refugees, and with a former upil of Leese's, Nancy Lima Dent, they mouned Canada's first modern-dance festivals (1960-2). Among Rogge's pupils was Judy Jarvis, vho studied in Germany with Mary Wigman. n her return she established the Judy Jarvis ance and Theatre Co, which, throughout the 970s, presented the spare and haunting vision f human existence that was Wigman's trade-ıark. Another pupil was Kathryn Brown, now irector of Toronto's Pavlychenko Studios. Yone vietys, a less flamboyant figure than Rogge, ave classes to Donald Himes, Susan MacPheron, and David EARLE, and so could be called an ndirect progenitor of Toronto Dance Theatre.

The TDT heralded the appearance of the more ersonal expression of American modern dance, vhich places less emphasis on formal training. achel Browne, a former soloist with the ROYAL VINNIPEG BALLET left that company in 1964, and y the mid-1970s, had created the highly skilled nd versatile company, WINNIPEG'S CONTEMPORARY ANCERS. WCD has helped develop the careers of reelance choreographers Anna Blewchamp and udith Marcuse, both of whom are trained in lassical and modern dance. Marcuse, the only horeographer to win both the Chalmers (1976) nd the Lee (1979) choreographic awards, uses he talents of dancers from a wide variety of ance backgrounds. Blewchamp's years of trainng in the Graham technique are obvious in uch works as *Arrival of All Time.* In the late 940s, Nancy Lima Dent studied with Graham nd others in New York, returning to Toronto, vhere her work showed until the early 1960s. atricia BEATTY, another dancer in the Graham radition, created the New Dance Group of Canda, which gave its first Toronto concert in Dec 967. On that program was a dance called *Fragnents* by guest choreographer Peter RANDAZZO, a ancer with the Graham company in New York; ancing in *Fragments* as well as in *Momentum* vas Torontonian David Earle, who had just pent 4 years at the Graham school and a year vith the José Limon company. The following December, under the artistic direction of Beatty, Randazzo, and Earle, TDT gave its first concert.

Anna Wyman, who came to Canada in 1967, egan her career as a classical ballet dancer, later aking up the study and teaching of modern ance. The ANNA WYMAN DANCE THEATRE is now successful, Vancouver-based company. PAULA oss, also in Vancouver, was one of the first inividuals to establish a modern-dance company n Canada. Her work, influenced by both jazz nd ballet, contains a strong emotional element, ncompromising personal statement, and coninuing experimentation with modern movenent styles. Maria Formolo's Regina Modern Dance Works company attempted to formulate n accessible and conservative dance style that vould enable it to draw and hold audiences in a ity relatively unexposed to modern dance. Ultinately the company was reduced to 2 (Formolo nd Keith Urban), and in the spring of 1982 the uo left Regina to re-establish themselves in Ednonton.

The first graduates of the dance department at York U were inspired by the teachings of some of the most avant-garde New York artists. In a sense, 40 years of American dance history was being compressed into less than 10 in Toronto. Only 6 years after TDT made its debut, 2 former National Ballet dancers, Lawrence and Miriam Adams, opened 15 Dance Lab, whose programs represented a cross-section of contemporary dance forms, from minimalism to trance-dancing to contact improvisation. Grant McDaniel joined WCD; Peggy Smith Baker and Patricia Miner joined and later co-directed Dancemakers, a group founded in 1974 by two York students, Nancy Radler and Andréa Ciel Smith. Over the years, Dancemakers has cultivated an eclectic repertoire featuring the dances of choreographers such as Anna Blewchamp, Paula Ravitz (co-director with Denise Fujiwara of Toronto Independent Dance Enterprise) and Karen Rimmer, of Vancouver's experimental Terminal City Dance. As guest artist with TDT (1973-78), DANNY GROSSMAN also contributed several works to the repertoire before creating his own company.

The American influence was felt most keenly in Toronto, although it spread to other centres. Toronto-born Jennifer Mascall, a former participant in New Yorker Douglas Dunn's postmodernist experiments, took her interest in improvisation to Vancouver, where Iris Garland had been exposing her students at Simon Fraser to the work of a wide range of American modernist choreographers and where Helen Goodwin had been doing the same thing on a smaller scale at University of British Columbia. The Graham tradition turned up in Calgary with Elaine Bowman, formerly with TDT, at Dancers Studio West; in Edmonton with Brian Webb, who had studied extensively with Graham's first male partner, Erick Hawkins; and in Halifax with Jeanne Robinson, another former member of TDT who created Nova Dance Theatre. The influence of José Limon is expressed in the work of Linda Rabin, a Montréal dancer, teacher and choreographer. Postmodernism is represented in Montréal by artists such as minimalist Marie Chouinard, as well as Édouard Lock, whose gangling, loose-limbed, punk-influenced style of dance owes something to New York mentor Pooh Kay.

Much interesting work is being done independently of American ties; notably in Montréal where, since 1976, there has been an upsurge in dance activity. A new generation of dancers and choreographers has struck off along very distinctive, very personal paths without a self-conscious need to defend any theory or school. Artists such as Christopher House and Phyllis White of Toronto Dance Theatre; Daniel Leveillé, Édouard Lock, Paula Ravitz; independent artists such as Murray Darroch, Susan Cash, Holly Small (Toronto), Santa Aloi, Judith Marcuse, and Jennifer Mascall (Vancouver), Tedd Robinson and Stephanie Ballard (WCD), and Karen Rimmer at Terminal City are exploring a wide variety of modern idioms, many of them overlapping with other media. It is evident that Canadian modern dance is finding its own identity. GRAHAM JACKSON

Dance of the Happy Shades (Toronto, 1968), Alice MUNRO's first book of stories, established her as one of Canada's most accomplished contemporary writers. Her preferred settings, always painstakingly realized, are recognizably southwestern Ontarian; her themes include the gaps in communication within families and the pressures exerted by memory and the past. Munro's powerful realism, her precision of style and her eye for revelatory detail place her stories among the finest being written in English today. *Dance of the Happy Shades* was translated into French as *Danse des ombres* (Montréal, 1979).

NEIL BESNER

Dance on Television and Film offers an unsurpassed degree of public exposure to dance. Although the small two-dimensional image lacks the impact and viewer involvement of a live performance, television and film can offer visions impossible to duplicate on the theatrical stage. Recently, video has begun to play an important role on a smaller local level, offering the opportunity to risk experimentation and to document lesser-known artists and dance companies.

Dance first became a regular feature on television in Québec in the 1950s, under the direction of producer-composer Pierre MERCURE, in series such as "L'Heure du concert." Les Grands Ballets Chiriaeff (later Les Grands Ballets Canadiens) appeared on TV more than 300 times between 1952 and 1958. CBC Television was 2 years old when the NATIONAL BALLET OF CANADA made its TV debut, and series such as "Musicamera," "Festival" and "Spectrum" have helped secure a place for dance on TV.

The 2 great innovators were producer-director Norman Campbell and Norman MCLAREN, who is best known for his film features created for the NATIONAL FILM BOARD. Campbell successfully combined dance and TV with smooth and mobile camerawork, well-placed close-ups and imaginative use of special effects. His 1965 *Romeo and Juliet,* featuring Earl Kraul and Veronica TENNANT, won the Prix Rene Barthelemy for artistic excellence at the International Television Festival of Monte Carlo. His 1970 Emmy-winning *Cinderella* (1968) used slow motion and trick photography to enhance the ethereal qualities of the fairies. Unlike these ballets, which were recorded in slightly remodelled studios, Rudolf Nureyev's Emmy-winning *The Sleeping Beauty* (1972) was a stage performance recorded by 6 cameras. Norman McLaren has experimented boldly with the dancing figure. His remarkable *Pas de Deux* (1968) displayed dancers Margaret Mercier and Vincent Warren of Les Grands Ballets Canadiens in "memory images" — individual frames were exposed up to 11 times and overlapped. The dancers, dressed in white and lit from behind as silhouettes, were filmed against a black backdrop. In his *Ballet Adagio* (1971) McLaren filmed and projected the dancers 4 times more slowly than normal.

Other stage dances impressively mounted by CBC include James Kudelka's *A Party* (1978); the 1982 presentation of Agnes de Mille's *Fall River Legend* (1980) with the ROYAL WINNIPEG BALLET; Anne Ditchburn's *Mad Shadows* (1979); an energetic dance through Canada's native and pioneer roots by Les FEUX FOLLETS and choreographed by Alan LUND; and Campbell's two *Swan Lakes,* 1961 and 1965. Two particularly important works in the development of dance on TV were *Dancin' Man* (1980) by dancer-choreographer Jeff Hyslop and director-producer Bernard Picard, and Brian Macdonald's *Catulli Carmina* (1981), a CBC story ballet.

Among the many film documentaries are Grant Munro's *Tour en l'air,* a 1973 study of David and Anne-Marie Holmes; *Gala,* the NFB's film of the historic 1981 Canadian Dance Spectacular at Ottawa's National Arts Centre, which gathered 8 of Canada's top professional companies; *For the Love of Dance,* an NFB film about the daily activities of those 8 companies; *Young and Just Beginning — Pierre,* a sentimental 1979 study of a young boy entering the National Ballet School; Norman Campbell's *The Looking Glass People,* a 1962 behind-the-scenes look at the National Ballet; and a 1965 CFTO special, *Inside the National Ballet.* The works of modern-dance companies, such as Entre-Six and the DANNY GROSSMAN DANCE COMPANY, receive a more documentary approach from the CBC. An inspired exception was a modern *L'Oiseau de Feu* by Hugo Romero, filmed in 1981 and produced for Radio Canada with dancers Claudia Moore, Louis

Robitaille and Jean-Marc Lebeau and incorporating animation and electronic effects. It was awarded an International Emmy. CBC Vancouver director Keith Christie has made 2 nationally aired programs on the ANNA WYMAN DANCE THEATRE, *Klee Wyck: A Ballet for Emily* (1975) and *Anna in Graz* (1974). PAT KAISER

Dandelion [Fr, *dent-de-lion*, "lion's tooth"], perennial, herbaceous PLANT of family Compositae or Asteraceae. Over 1000 species have been named. Because dandelions reproduce without fertilization, innumerable variants have arisen. Common dandelion (*Taraxacum officinale*) has many names including blowball, faceclock, dumble-dor (Newfoundland) and pissenlit (Quebec). Each mature flowerhead produces approximately 180 wind-dispersed, seedlike achenes. Preferring moist, grassy places and disturbed sites, dandelions occur from sea level to subalpine elevations. This European native has become a tenacious farm and garden WEED. However, its golden yellow flowers provide nectar for innumerable pollinating insects; its achenes, food for many birds. Much of the plant is edible. Leaves are high in vitamin A, iron, phosphorus, calcium and potassium, and are among the best sources of copper known. Valued for its medicinal properties, the dandelion has been used to stimulate the kidneys and to combat liver disorders, weak digestion, anemia and eczema. BERNARD S. JACKSON

Danes The first Danish contact with Canada resulted from the voyage of Captain Jens MUNK, who had been dispatched by King Christian IV of Denmark in the early 17th century to find the NORTHWEST PASSAGE. On 7 Sept 1619 Munk landed at the mouth of the Churchill R, named it Munk's Bay and claimed the land for the Danish king, calling it "Nova Dania" — New Denmark.

For many years thereafter, individual Danes, mainly sailors, migrated to N America. There are early accounts of Danes working as trappers in Canada but few traces of their experiences. In the 1860s, however, Danes in large numbers joined the massive European migration to N America. The 1961 census enumerated 85 473 Canadian residents of Danish origin, although by 1971 the number had declined to 75 725.

Migration and Settlement Danes emigrated to Canada in 3 distinct periods. From 1870 to WWI, of 20 000 Danish immigrants, some migrated directly from Denmark and others from the US. There was a large increase in the population of Denmark in the 19th century (as there was in all of Europe) and many Danes preferred to seek better opportunities overseas. Political and religious events also inspired many Danes to migrate.

Danes have been the only Scandinavian group to settle in large numbers in the Maritimes. In 1872 several hundred Danish immigrants from Denmark settled in a region of Victoria County between the St John and Salmon rivers and named it New Denmark. For about 25 years cheesemaking, operated on a co-operative basis, transformed New Denmark into a promising dairy district until cheesemaking gave way to a thriving potato-growing and distributing system.

In 1893 some Danes settled also in London, Ont, and at Pass Lake near Thunder Bay. Most of the first Danish settlers on the Canadian prairies arrived via the American midwest and northwest. Danish settlers played a major role in the founding of a number of communities on the prairies, eg, Dickson, Standard and Dalum (Alta); Alida and Redvers (Sask); and Ostenfeld (Man).

A second period of Danish migration (about 20 000 immigrants) to Canada occurred in the 1920s. While some settled in rural areas, a sizable number sought work in Canada's urban-industrial centres, mainly in Ontario and BC. Most of the Danes arriving in this period were able to adapt readily to conditions in the Canadian cities. With the GREAT DEPRESSION, however, many returned to Denmark.

Between 1951 and 1960, thousands of Danes, including many professionals and highly skilled workers, attracted to Canada by the postwar economic opportunities, emigrated. The 1961 census enumerated more than double the number of Canadians of Danish origin to that listed in the 1951 census. Most headed directly for the cities of BC, Alberta and Ontario. According to the 1971 census, these 3 provinces each had about 20 000 inhabitants of Danish origin. Many postwar Danish immigrants have returned to Denmark.

Social and Cultural Life Most of the Danish Canadian cultural activities in Canada have been at the local community level; there has been no national network to co-ordinate the activities of Danish clubs. Danish Lutheran congregations, direct offshoots of congregations established in the US, played a major role in the small Danish communities of the prairies. Most of these Danish Canadian congregations were affiliated with the United Danish Synod, which eventually became a part of the American Lutheran Church in 1960. All have lost their original Danish-language identity. Danish immigrants arriving after WWII have established a number of Danish Lutheran congregations that are not affiliated with any N American Lutheran synod but maintain direct ties with the state Evangelical Lutheran Church of Denmark.

Because early Danish communities were small, scattered and few in number, a Danish-language periodical established as a spokesman for the Danish community over time has never existed. Several small Danish-language periodicals, however, have been founded in Canada to serve regional and religious needs but most of these have been short-lived.

Danish Canadians have established a number of organizations to serve their social and cultural interests, eg, choirs, sports clubs, mutual benefit societies, Danish-language instruction and various kinds of social events.

Group Maintenance Although Danes have lived in Canada for over a century, their group identity is not as strong as other ethnic grou[ps] of the same size. Many of the early Danis[h] immigrants to the prairies, and their childre[n] had lived in the US and generally acculturat[ed] into the N American way of life before arrivi[ng] in Canada.

The Danish immigrants that arrived in t[he] 1920s did not add a sufficient concentration [of] numbers that would sustain Danish-langua[ge] culture in a region for more than one gene[r]ation. By the 1950s, most of the early Danis[h] Canadian churches and clubs were conducti[ng] their activities exclusively in English. The 195[0s] immigrants, who established a number of ne[w] Danish churches and clubs for their religio[us] and social needs, were able to assimilate readil[y] into Canadian society. LENNARD SILLANPA[A]

Reading: F.M. Paulsen, *Danish Settlements on the Canadi[an] Prairies* (1974).

Daniells, Roy, professor, poet, critic (b at Lo[n]don, Eng 6 Apr 1902; d at Vancouver 13 A[pr] 1979). Educated at UBC and U of T, Daniel[ls] taught for most of his career at UBC, retiring [in] 1974. He was one of the editors of the *Litera[ry] History of Canada* (1965), and he wrote numero[us] insightful articles on a wide range of Canadia[n] poetry and fiction. His major critical work w[as] on Milton (1963). His 2 books of poetry, *Deep[er] Into the Forest* (1948) and *The Chequered Sha[de]* (1963), show his mastery of the sonnet form an[d] his sophisticated technical skills. NEIL BESNE[R]

Danny Grossman Dance Company, a Toro[n]to-based modern dance troup founded (197[5]) by Danny GROSSMAN, had grown from 2 mem[]bers to a company of 8 by 1982. The compa[ny] became fully professional in 1978 and sin[ce] 1979 has made annual tours to the US an[d] Europe. Most works performed by the compa[ny] are choreographed by Grossman. One of h[is] better known pieces is *Higher*, choreograph[ed] (1975) to music by Ray Charles, and original[ly] performed by Grossman and Judith Hendin. [In] 1978, Danny Grossman was awarded the Jea[n] A. Chalmers Award in Choreography.
SUSAN PEDWE[LL]

Danny Grossman Dance Company, a contempora[ry] dance group formed in 1975, is known for its humo[r] and virtuosity (*courtesy of company*).

Dansereau, Mireille, filmmaker (b at Montréal 19 Sept 1943). Dansereau directed the first dramatic feature film made by a woman in Québec, *La Vie rêvée* (1972). After studying at U de M, she obtained an MA in film and TV in London, Eng, where *Compromise* (1968) won first prize at the 1969 National Student Film Festival. Returning to Québec she helped form the Association coopérative des productions audio-visuelles, which produced *La Vie rêvée*. She worked for the NFB, directing 2 feature documentaries, *J'me marie, j'me marie pas* (1973) and *Famille et variations* (1977). She returned to the private sector to make *L'Arrache Coeur* (1979), a bleak, uncompromising examination of a marriage in crisis. PIERS HANDLING

Dansereau, Pierre, ecologist, educator (b at Montréal 5 Oct 1911). Educated at the Institut agricole d'Oka, Qué, and at Geneva (DSc 1939), Dansereau worked at the Montréal Botanical Garden 1939-50 and taught at the U of Michigan for 5 years before becoming dean of science at the U de M in 1955. He was professor of botany and geography at Columbia U 1961-68 and joined UQAM as professor of ecology in 1971. Dansereau's 1957 book *Biogeography, an Ecological Perspective* won him an international reputation, and he later popularized his theme in the influential CBC Massey lectures "Inscape and Landscape" (1972). He transmitted important scientific and humane values to his students and sought to combine the strengths of technical scholarship in English with the broader emphases of the French tradition, notably Teilhard de Chardin's concept of mind as part of the continuum of evolution. He was awarded the MOLSON PRIZE in 1975. *See* BIOGEOGRAPHY. DONALD J.C. PHILLIPSON

Dark Harbour, located on the W side of GRAND MANAN I, NB, is the only suitable haven for fishing craft along the island's western shore, which is dominated by high cliffs. It is relatively isolated from the communities on the more hospitable eastern side facing the Bay of Fundy. In the 1840s Dark Harbour's potential as a natural deep-water port was recognized by marine surveyors, along with its commercial viability as a fishing centre; but except for sporadic seasonal fishing stations, it drew little attention until the close of the 19th century. A sizable smoked-fish operation was established on a natural break wall of Dark Harbour in the 1890s, and though lobster and herring fisheries have been an integral part of its history, the worldwide reputation of Dark Harbour rests on the presence along its rocky shoreline of dulse, a popular edible seaweed. Still relatively unpopulated, Dark Harbour offers a unique landscape and has become a popular draw to tourists because of its natural beauty. ROGER P. NASON

Darter, *see* PERCH.

Dartmouth Lakes are 25 separate lakes located within the city of Dartmouth, NS, across the harbour from HALIFAX. Formed by Pleistocene glaciation about 15 000 years ago, they range in area from 1 to 140 ha.

Long before British settlement of Halifax in 1749, the principal lakes (Banook, Micmac and Charles) had been used for thousands of years by the seminomadic MICMAC as part of a trans-province canoe route from Chebucto (Halifax) to Cobequid (head of the Bay of Fundy). The same 3 lakes formed a critical part of the ill-fated Shubenacadie Canal, constructed 1826-61 but abandoned 1870 because of railroad competition. Sections of the canal and deteriorating locks remain today. The lakes have been a water supply since settlement. Prior to 1950 an ice-cutting industry flourished and icehouses were common along the shores. The lakes have played an important recreational role for over a century. In the 19th century, residents from Halifax crossed the harbour by ferry to take part in skating, hockey, curling and iceboating. Dartmouth's Starr Manufacturing Co was world famous for its innovative metal skates. Around the turn of the century, canoeing and rowing became popular and regattas were started by newly formed boat clubs. Five boat clubs are active today and Lk Banook is the site of many regional, national and international competitive paddling events. Swimming, waterskiing and cross-country skiing, fishing and sailing have also become popular activities in more recent years.

Despite extensive urbanization in the city during the past 30 years, the Dartmouth Lks are relatively clean, and pollution only occasionally interferes with recreational use. Recognizing the tremendous value of the lakes to all residents, the city gives high priority to lake protection, and is assisted in this task by a unique volunteer organization known as the Dartmouth Lakes Advisory Board. D.C. GORDON

Daubigny, Victor-Theodule, veterinarian (b at Crillon; district of Beauvais, France 29 Feb 1836; d at Terrebonne, Qué 11 Dec 1908). Emigrating from France as a widower with a 7-year-old son, he landed at Montréal in 1872. He studied law and had been a notary at St-Denis near Paris. He farmed at Lachenaie, Qué, married, and at age 40 entered the Montreal Veterinary Coll, where he was a particularly brilliant student, graduating 3 years later. From 1880 to 1885 he supervised the college's French section and built a private practice. In 1885, with teaching colleague Orphyr Bruneau, he founded the School of Veterinary Medicine of Montreal and the next year joined with a group of surgeons to create a French veterinary school of Montréal, which they affiliated with the Montréal branch of Laval. In 1894 this school absorbed the other French veterinary schools in Montréal and Québec. A distinguished administrator, Daubigny remained director of the School of Comparative Medicine and Veterinary Science until his death. LOUIS-PHILIPPE PHANEUF

Daudelin, Charles, sculptor (b at Granby, Qué 1 Oct 1920). He worked in Beaugrand's studio 1939-41, went to the École du Meuble in Montréal, made 2 stays in New York (1943, 1948), working with Fernand Léger and Henri Laurens. He taught at the École des beaux-arts in Montréal until 1967. The recipient of first prizes in the Concours artistiques du Québec for painting (1946) and sculpture (1964), Daudelin has created important pieces for the National Arts Centre (Ottawa), Palais de Justice (Montréal), parliamentary fountain in Charlottetown and the Church of St-Thomas d'Aquin in St-Lambert. He also created the reredos in the Sacred Heart Chapel of Montréal's Église Notre-Dame and the visual conceptualization of Montréal's Mont-Royal metro station. Daudelin has made marionettes, created stage sets and illustrated several books. His work is held in private and public collections at home and abroad. He received the Lynch-Staunton Award from the Canada Council (1972) and the Prix Philippe-Hébert from the St-Jean-Baptiste Society of Montréal (1981). MICHEL CHAMPAGNE

Dauphin, Man, Town, pop 8971 (1981c), inc 1910, is located in SW Manitoba, 310 km by road NW of Winnipeg, on the Vermilion R. It is a prosperous supply, distribution and transportation centre, serving a rich agricultural region stretching from the Saskatchewan border E to Lks Manitoba and Winnipeg and N to Swan R. It is also a government administration centre and has an active tourist trade. LA VÉRENDRYE first visited the area in the 1730s and gave the name Dauphin, for the eldest son of the king of France, to a post in the area (1741). Settlers from Ontario arrived in the 1880s, and the villages of Old Dauphin and Gartmore developed near

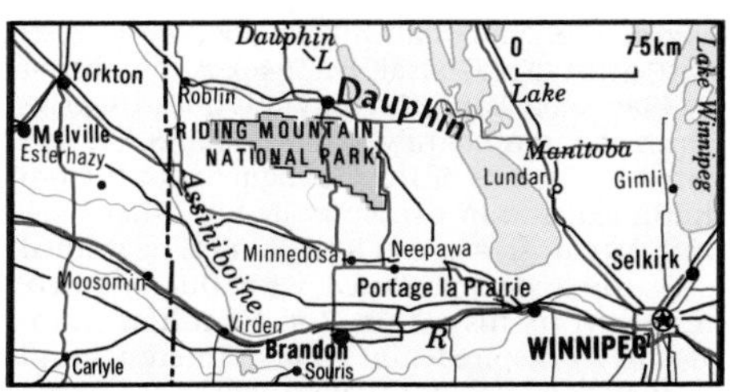

the present townsite, which was established after the arrival of the Lk Manitoba Ry (1896). UKRAINIANS set up one of their earliest rural settlements in the area (1896-98) and still maintain a strong sense of their cultural past. Dauphin initiated Canada's annual National Ukrainian Festival in the early 1960s. The local government consists of a mayor and 4 councillors. Directly S of Dauphin is RIDING MTN NATIONAL PARK, and to the NW, Duck Mtn National Forest and Park. ALAN F.J. ARTIBISE

Davaugour, Pierre Dubois, Baron, governor of New France 1661-63 (d fighting the Turks on the border of Croatia 24 July 1664). Davaugour was the last governor to serve the COMPAGNIE DES CENT-ASSOCIÉS. He was enthusiastic about Canada's potential but insisted on the need for massive reinforcements to protect it from the Iroquois. When he removed restrictions on the brandy trade with the Indians, Davaugour became embroiled in bitter disputes with Bishop LAVAL and with MAISONNEUVE, the governor of Montréal, which led to his recall. ALLAN GREER

Davey, Frank, poet, critic, editor (b at Vancouver 19 Apr 1940). As a 1960s UBC student, Davey was a founding editor of the controversial poetry newsletter *Tish*. Since 1970 he has taught at York U in Toronto, and is the editor of *Open Letter*, the most important Canadian magazine for critical discussion of avant-garde literary works and theories. Davey has argued strongly against the thematic basis of much Canadian criticism and in favour of a more formalist approach. Through his work with Coach House Press, Davey has been in the forefront of the application of computer technology to small-press publishing. He has published 14 volumes of poetry; much of his best work is collected in *The Arches: Selected Poems* (1980). He has also published numerous articles on Canadian literature and several critical studies. Davey's poetry reveals a strong mistrust of metaphor: he bases his work on a direct emotional presentation of both public and private events. STEPHEN SCOBIE

Davey, Keith, politician (b at Toronto 21 Apr 1926). After graduating from U of T's Victoria Coll, Davey worked in radio and held a number of positions in the Toronto area Liberal Party. After Liberal defeats in the 1957 and 1958 general elections, Davey organized a small group, known as "Cell 13," to rejuvenate the party in Ontario. In 1961 Davey became the Liberal's national campaign director and helped to devise the strategy that defeated the Conservatives in 1963. His advice was less successful in 1965, when the Liberals sought a parliamentary majority. Made a senator by PM PEARSON in 1966, Davey chaired a Senate investigation of Canadian mass media. Following the Liberal Party's near-defeat in 1972, Davey was summoned by PM TRUDEAU to guide the party's electoral fortunes and was rewarded by a successful election in 1974. Although the Liberals were defeated in 1979, Davey returned the Liberals to power in 1980 as their national campaign cochairman and was brought back to try to revitalize John TURNER's flagging campaign in 1984. Despite the Liberal debacle in that election, his record as a political organizer is unmatched in Canadian history for both longevity and success. ROBERT BOTHWELL

David, Joe, Nuu-chah-nulth (Nootka or West-coast) artist (b at Opitsat, BC 1946). A member of the Clayoquot Band, Joe David is a leading figure in modern NORTHWEST COAST INDIAN ART. Inspired by the arts of the Clayoquot people from childhood, and in particular by his father Hyacinth David, Sr, a carver and painter, he studied in Seattle and apprenticed with Duane Pasco. In later years his cousin Ron Hamilton (Hupquatchew) inspired him to take interest in all aspects of his culture. David's works are found in international public and private collections, including the National Museum of Man. Noted for his innovative silkscreen drum design prints he is also much sought after as a mask maker.
CAROL SHEEHAN

David Dunlap Observatory, *see* OBSERVATORY.

Davidialuk, Alasua Amittuq, Inuk artist (b on a small island near Povungnituk, Qué *c*1910; d on an emergency evacuation flight near Povungnituk 1 Aug 1976). An indifferent hunter, he lived in poverty until he gained recognition as a folk artist near mid-life. Only then could he afford the hunter's indispensable dog team (and later snowmobile). Davidialuk entranced his countrymen with spellbinding "true stories" — legends, myths and his own inventions. These he later translated into stone carvings, prints and drawings, now collected because of their ingenuous revelations of a cultural mystique. His last creative outpouring suggests a precognitive need to broadcast his personal view of Inuit history and morals.
M.M. CRAIG

Davidson, Florence Edenshaw, or Jadał *g'egeôngaá*, "Story Maid," Haida elder, artist (b at Masset, Queen Charlotte Is, BC 1895), daughter of Charlie EDENSHAW. She began weaving Haida-style baskets and sewing ceremonial button blankets as a girl, but she put such works aside with marriage to Robert Davidson, Sr, and the subsequent birth of 13 children. In 1952 she began making button and appliqué blankets again, and since then she has made over 50, as well as traditional spruce-root and cedar-bark hats. She has willingly shared her knowledge of traditional Haida ways, and thus has been a key figure in the resurgence of Haida culture. Her son Claude Davidson and grandsons Robert DAVIDSON and Reggie are all accomplished artists.
CAROL SHEEHAN

Davidson, Joe, labour leader (b at Shotts, Scot 1915). Always political, he described himself as an evolutionary socialist "with the proviso that evolution needed a shove at every opportunity." He came to Canada in 1957 and worked in iron foundries in Hamilton and Dundas, Ont, before he became a mail sorter in Toronto and a shop steward in the Canadian Postal Employees Assn (CPEA), transformed into the Canadian Union of Postal Workers (CUPW) in 1965. During the 1965 strike, he was active on the Toronto strike committee. He was elected president of the Toronto local 1967, became VP of CUPW in 1968 and was president 1974-77. His presidency encompassed 2 national postal strikes and dozens of smaller skirmishes over automation. He became the media's choice as the most hated man in Canada. In 1983 he retired.
LAUREL SEFTON MACDOWELL

Reading: Joe Davidson and J. Deverall, *Joe Davidson* (1978).

Davidson, Robert Charles, Haida artist (b at Hydaburg, Alaska 4 Nov 1946). Master carver, printmaker and jeweller, Robert Davidson is greatgrandson and heir to the legacy of Charlie EDENSHAW. Robert first learned carving from his grandfather. In 1966 he apprenticed to Bill REID and the next year followed him to the Vancouver School of Art. While a student, Davidson became an able instructor at the Gitenmaax School of Northwest Coast Indian Art at KSAN, Hazelton, BC. He secured a grant to carve the 12 m Bear Mother pole, erected in Masset in 1969, the first TOTEM POLE to be raised in living memory of the Masset elders. Ever maturing and innovative, he has expanded the boundaries of Northwest Coast image and design in increasingly complex and unconventional serigraphs. Davidson's 3 monumental totem poles erected in 1984 in the Maclean Hunter Building, Toronto, reflect the artist's deep personal commitment to innovative art, and to the evolving culture of the Haida people.
CAROL SHEEHAN

Davie, Alexander Edmund Batson, lawyer, politician, premier of BC (b at Wells, Eng 24 Nov 1847; d at Victoria 1 Aug 1889). He immigrated to Vancouver I in 1862 and was the first person to receive a complete legal education there, being called to the bar in 1873. He was clerk of the BC legislature 1872-74 and was elected in Cariboo, 1875, with the patronage of Premier WALKEM, but he gravitated to the Opposition. In 1877 he accepted office in the government of A.C. ELLIOTT but was defeated in the resulting by-election. Elected for Lillooet, 1882, he became attorney general in the new SMITHE government and supervised an extensive revision of the province's statutes. Davie succeeded Smithe as premier (1887) but soon fell ill and died in office.
H. KEITH RALSTON

Davie, Theodore, lawyer, judge, politician, premier of BC (b at Brixton, Eng 22 Mar 1852; d at Victoria 7 Mar 1898). The brother of A.E.B. DAVIE, he was called to the bar in 1877 and elected to the BC legislature in 1882. In 1889, when John ROBSON became premier, he was chosen attorney general and in 1892 succeeded Robson as premier. In 1895 he resigned to become chief justice of BC. Davie was one of a succession of premiers who embodied the dominance of Victoria and Vancouver I in the political and economic life of late 19th-century BC. During his premiership a loan bill for new Parliament Buildings "anchored" the capital in Victoria.
H. KEITH RALSTON AND MAIRI DONALDSON

Davies, Sir Louis Henry, lawyer, politician, judge, premier of PEI (b at Charlottetown 4 May 1845; d at Ottawa 1 May 1924). Member of a family prominent in local business and politics, Davies was educated at Prince of Wales College, Charlottetown, before studying law in London. Upon returning to PEI he was active in politics and won a by-election to the Assembly in Nov 1872. An outstanding public speaker, he became PEI's youngest premier in 1876 as leader of a coalition committed to resolving the school question. In 1877 his government passed the Public Schools Act, making attendance compulsory and the educational system nonsectarian. Despite the Act's success, the coalition disintegrated and in 1879 left office. Davies was elected in 1882 to the House of Commons, where he was a leading member of the Liberal caucus. He became Wilfrid LAURIER's minister of marine and fisheries in 1896, and was knighted in 1897. He left the Cabinet in 1901 for the Supreme Court of Canada, remaining a member until his death. He was appointed chief justice in 1918.
IAN ROSS ROBERTSON

Davies, Robertson William, writer, journalist, professor (b at Thamesville, Ont 28 Aug 1913). Davies is acknowledged as an outstanding essayist and brilliant novelist. Third son of Senator William Rupert Davies, Robertson Davies participated in stage productions as a child and developed a lifelong interest in drama. He attended Upper Canada Coll 1926-32 and went on to Queen's 1932-35 as a special student not working towards a degree. At Balliol Coll, Oxford, he received the BLit in 1938. His thesis, *Shakespeare's Boy Actors*, appeared in 1939, a year in which he pursued an acting career outside London. He spent 1940 playing minor roles and doing literary work for the director at the Old Vic Repertory Company in London. That year he married Brenda Mathews, a girl he had met at Oxford, who was then working as stage manager for the theatre. Davies returned to Canada in 1940 as literary editor of *Saturday Night*. Two years later, he became editor of the Peterborough *Examiner*, a position that afforded him unlimited material for many characters and situations which appeared in his novels and plays. While editing this paper 1940-55, and when he was publisher 1955-65, Davies published 18 books, produced several of his own plays and wrote numerous articles for various journals.

Robertson Davies, outstanding essayist and author of the Deptford Trilogy: *Fifth Business*, *The Manticore* and *World of Wonders* (photo by Peter Paterson).

Davies moved from the theory of acting outlined in *Shakespeare for Young Players* (1947) to the writing of plays with *Eros at Breakfast*, a one-act play which won the 1948 Dominion Drama Festival Award for best Canadian play. *Eros at Breakfast and Other Plays* and award-winning *Fortune, My Foe* were published in 1949; *At My Heart's Core*, a 3-act play based on the Strickland sisters, appeared in 1950. Meanwhile, Davies collected some of his humorous essays (written under the pseudonym Samuel Marchbanks) from the *Examiner* in *The Diary of Samuel Marchbanks* (1947), *The Table Talk of Samuel Marchbanks* (1949) and *Samuel Marchbanks' Almanack* (1967).

In 1960 Davies joined Trinity Coll at University of Toronto, where he taught literature courses for the next 21 years. The next year he published a collection of essays on literature, *A Voice from the Attic*, and was awarded the Lorne Pierce Medal for his literary achievements. In 1963 he became master of Massey Coll, the university's new graduate college. By 1967 he was made an RSC fellow, and soon began receiving honorary degrees from many Canadian universities. Some of his best essays and speeches appeared later in *One Half of Robertson Davies*, *The Enthusiasm of Robertson Davies* and *The Well-Tempered Critic*. In them, Davies explored his many esoteric interests with characteristic wit.

Davies found his metier neither in drama nor in occasional humorous essays, but in fiction. His first 3 novels, later known as the Salterton trilogy, were *Tempest-Tost* (1951), *Leaven of Malice* (1954), which won the Stephen Leacock Medal for Humour, and *A Mixture of Frailties* (1958). These novels explored the difficulty of sustaining a cultural life in Canada. During the 1950s he played a major role in launching the STRATFORD FESTIVAL, serving on the board of governors and publishing with director Sir Tyrone Guthrie (1953-55). He also continued to produce plays, none of which ranked with his novels.

In 1970 Davies drew on Jungian psychology . preoccupation which replaced his earlier ıterest in Freud) to produce his best novel to ate, *Fifth Business*. The novel casts characters in ɔles that roughly correspond to Jungian arche- pes to show Davies's belief that things of the ɔirit are more important than worldly con- rns. He built on the success of *Fifth Business* 'ith two sequel novels (the 3 later known as he Deptford Trilogy): *The Manticore* (1972), a ovel cast in the form of Jungian psycho- nalysis which won the Gov Gen's Award for ction, and *World of Wonders* (1975). A seventh ovel satirizing academic life, *The Rebel Angels* 981), appeared at the close of Davies's aca- emic career. In 1983 Davies published *The Mir- r of Nature*, an examination of 19th-century elodrama. ELSPETH CAMERON

ading: Elspeth Buitenhuis [Cameron], *Robertson Davies* 972); P. Morley, *Robertson Davies* (1977).

avin, Nicholas Flood, lawyer, journalist, olitician (b at Kilfinane, Ire 13 Jan 1843; d at Vinnipeg 18 Oct 1901). First MP for Assiniboia ', Davin was known as the voice of the North- Vest. Davin was a parliamentary and war ɔrrespondent in England before arriving in oronto in 1872, where he wrote for the *Globe* nd the *Mail*. Although a fully qualified lawyer, avin practised little law. The highlight of his gal career was his 1880 defence of George Ben- ett, who murdered George BROWN.

A chance visit to the West in 1882 determined is future. He founded (1883) and edited the egina *Leader*, the first newspaper in Assiniboia; ıe paper carried his detailed reports of the 1885 ial of Louis RIEL. A spell-binding speaker and onservative MP for Assiniboia W, 1887-1900, avin tried to gain provincial status for the ter- tory, economic and property advantages for e new settlers, and even the franchise for omen, but he never achieved his ambition to e a Cabinet minister. A mercurial personality, e became depressed by the decline of his politi- al and personal fortunes and shot himself dur- ıg a visit to Winnipeg. He wrote *The Irishman in anada* (1877), as well as poetry and an unpub- shed novel. LEE GIBSON

avis, John, also spelled Davys, explorer (b ear Dartmouth, Eng 1550?; d near Singapore 27 ec 1605). In a 1585 voyage in search of the ORTHWEST PASSAGE, he rediscovered Greenland nd found the strait later named for him. He ailed again in 1586, and on a third voyage 587) skirted Hudson Str and Frobisher Bay and ntered the Labrador fjord that bears his name. ater, he discovered the Falkland Is and served s a pilot on Dutch vessels in the South Seas. He vas killed by Japanese pirates near Singapore. avis was a brilliant navigator and keen ob- erver, and was the inventor of the backstaff, a evice for determining latitude. JAMES MARSH

avis, Robert Atkinson, businessman, poli- cian, premier of Manitoba 1874-78 (b at Duds- ell, Qué 9 Mar 1841; d at Phoenix, Ariz 7 Jan 903). Davis came to Winnipeg in May 1870 and ought a downtown hotel, which he named avis House. Elected an MLA in Apr 1874, avis was appointed provincial treasurer that uly and succeeded Marc GIRARD as premier on Dec 1874. Davis emphasized economy and etrenchment, negotiated better financial terms 'ith Ottawa, and abolished the Legislative ouncil. Davis retired from politics after re- gning the premiership 15 Oct 1878, sold his roperty in Winnipeg, and removed to Chicago vhere he became a wealthy businessman. LOVELL C. CLARK

avis, Victor, swimmer (b at Guelph, Ont 10 eb 1964). He won the 100 m and 200 m breast- troke events at the Canada-USSR-W Germany Meet in July 1981, set a world record for the 200 n breaststroke at the world championships in

Victor Davis in action at the 1984 Los Angeles Olympics at which he won a gold medal (*courtesy Athlete Information Bureau / Service Information — Athlètes*).

Ecuador, Aug 1982, and won a gold medal and set a Commonwealth record at the 1982 Australia COMMONWEALTH GAMES in the 200 m breaststroke. He was incapacitated in 1983 by mononucleosis but at the 1984 Los Angeles Olympics won a gold medal in the 200 m breaststroke (world record, time 2:13.34) and silver medals in the 100 m breaststroke and 4x100 m medley relay. Davis is known for his fiercely competitive approach to swimming. JAMES MARSH

Davis, William Grenville lawyer, politician (b at Brampton, Ont 30 July 1929). Premier of Ontario since 1971, Davis is leader of one of the most successful political parties in any democracy. He is a product of small-town Ontario. Brampton is now merely a bedroom suburb of Toronto, but when the future premier was born it was a separate, small community where people took their politics seriously. Educated in the local schools, Davis went to U of T (BA, 1951) and Osgoode Law School. He was called to the bar in 1955 and 4 years later won election as Conservative MPP for Brampton. In 1962 Premier John ROBARTS gave the novice the political "hot potato" of the Dept of Education, and as minister Davis presided over the most extraordinary period of change since Egerton RYERSON's day. Universities such as TRENT and BROCK were created. Rural schools were consolidated, forcing students to be bused long distances twice each day. And a new attitude, that schools should be co-operative not competitive, took root in public schools. Over this frenetic change, the calm, unflappable Davis presided, and by 1971 education in the province had been transformed.

Davis was the beneficiary of this process. He had begun to build a national reputation — in

As minister of education, William Davis presided over extraordinary growth and change in Ontario's education system. He became premier in 1971 and, still unchallenged, announced his resignation in Oct 1984 (*courtesy Canapress*).

1967 he was policy chairman at the Conservatives' national convention — and he seemed the logical heir to Robarts. At a convention in Feb 1971 Davis won the leadership on the fourth ballot, and the new premier, still only 42, came to power with a progressive (if rather undefined) image. This was crystallized 4 months later when Davis forced a halt to the Spadina Expressway, a roadway cutting through downtown Toronto, which had been vigorously opposed by young urban professionals. That startling decision became almost typical. His moderate government was capable of rapid change, not least the decision in 1984 to give full financial support to SEPARATE SCHOOLS beginning in 1985.

Davis's calm style (and the "Big Blue Machine") won each election, as his government's moderate reformism struck a responsive chord with the electorate. His record was good, but there were flaws. Education was allowed to starve from the mid-1970s as the public mood and economic situation altered, and despite his support of PM TRUDEAU in the negotiations leading to the CONSTITUTION ACT, 1982, Davis was unwilling to give Ontario's half million Francophones official bilingual status, although characteristically he had put the infrastructure in place. Although in 1984 he and his party were unchallenged, Davis surprisingly announced his resignation on 8 Oct 1984. J.L. GRANATSTEIN

Davis Strait, situated between BAFFIN I and Greenland, is the entrance to BAFFIN BAY from the N Atlantic. It is a large stretch of water over 950 km across at its greatest width and never less than 300 km wide. At the narrowest point, its submarine topography consists of an undersea ridge, a continuation of the mid-Labrador ridge, extending from the coast of Baffin I to Greenland. The shallowest waters in the strait are found along this sill, from 350 to 550 m deep, before plunging down to abyssal basins on either side. Some of the greatest depths in the eastern Arctic are reached here (3660 m) in the southern end of the strait. The surface waters are strongly affected by counterclockwise-flowing currents. Along the W side, an outflow of cold water from the Arctic Basin moves S, at flow velocities of 8-20 km/day, to feed the Labrador current. On the E side the W Greenland countercurrent brings warmer water N. Ice conditions reflect this flow regime, with heavy ice movement and icebergs along the western shore, contrasting sharply with more open water along the Greenland side. The strait was first explored by John DAVIS, leader of 3 voyages 1585-87 organized by merchants of London, Eng. DOUG FINLAYSON

d'Avray, Joseph Marshall de Brett Maréchal, 2nd Baron, educator, journalist (b at London, Eng 30 Nov 1811; d at Fredericton 26 Nov 1871). Educated at the French royal court, Marshall d'Avray (as he preferred to be known) established a normal school on Mauritius prior to his arrival in NB in 1848. As first master of the Fredericton Normal School (1848-50) and later as superintendent of education (1854-58), d'Avray was frequently involved in political turmoil and debate. In 1854, as editor of the Fredericton *Headquarters*, he seized every opportunity to satirize opponents of his progressive views on teacher training, compulsory assessment and a "rounded" liberal education. From 1852 until his death, d'Avray was professor of modern languages at King's College (which became UNB in 1859). Removed from office as superintendent for "political reasons" in 1858, the Baron devoted the remainder of his life to teaching, leaving an indelible mark on his students. WILLIAM B. HAMILTON

Dawes, Norman James, brewer, corporate director (b at Lachine, Qué 13 July 1874; d at

Montréal 14 Apr 1967). Son of James P. Dawes, a third-generation Montréal brewer, he was educated at McGill and the US Brewers' Academy and entered the family brewing business in 1894. In 1909 he joined his father in forming National Breweries, the largest brewing merger in Canada to that date, involving 14 Québec companies. As managing director of National Breweries 1922-26 and president 1926-52, Dawes was one of the most powerful brewing figures in Canada. He remained chairman when National was bought by Canadian Breweries in 1952. ALBERT TUCKER

Reading: M. Denison, *The Barley and the Stream* (1955).

Dawson, YT, City, pop 697 (1981c), inc 1902, is located on the E bank of the YUKON R at the mouth of the Klondike R, 530 km N of Whitehorse. The Klondike was originally a salmon stream, and each summer the Indians dried their catch on the flat where it joined the Yukon. In Aug 1896 Joseph Ladue, a trader and prospector, staked the flat as a townsite, in anticipation of a rush into the KLONDIKE valley. The town was named after G.M. DAWSON, director of the GEOLOGICAL SURVEY OF CANADA and leader of the expedition that explored the region in 1887. Although Dawson became the Yukon capital in 1898, it lacked municipal institutions until after the turn of the century.

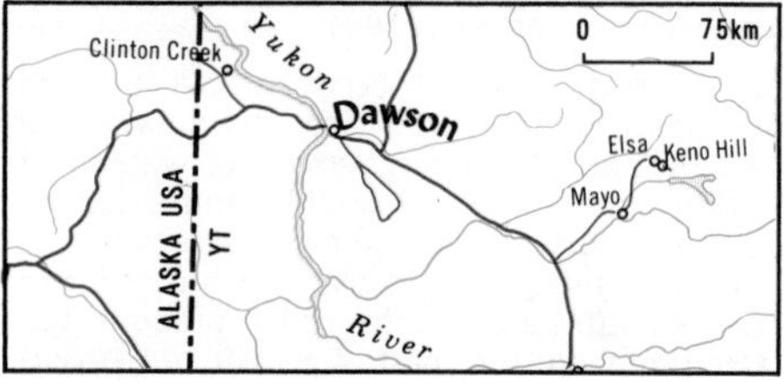

Economy At the axis of 2 transportation corridors, Dawson grew quickly as the transshipment point for men and materials destined for the Klondike goldfields. As a port, it developed service industries for the people who disembarked, and it became the mercantile and distribution centre of the Yukon. At the height of the gold rush in the summer of 1898, Dawson's population rose to 16 000. It declined throughout the following decade, however, and the introduction of sophisticated mining technology slowly drove people from its hinterland, thus reducing the need for its services. WWI curtailed mining activity, and the next 20 years saw little development in the Klondike. Dawson experienced some growth when the mining industry expanded in the 1930s, but WWII disrupted gold production again. The ALASKA HWY enabled Whitehorse to supersede Dawson as the commercial and administrative centre of the territory, and the capital was transferred S in 1951. The opening of the Klondike Hwy in the same period put an end to commercial traffic on the Yukon R and rendered Dawson's port facilities obsolete. Another blow came in 1966, when the Yukon Consolidated Gold Corp shut down its last dredge in the Klondike valley. Since then, tourism has been the major industry for Dawson's permanent residents.

Dawson, YT, nestles on the flats at the junction of the Klondike and Yukon rivers. It was founded as a transshipment point for men bound for the Klondike goldfields (*photo by Richard Harrington*).

Townscape In 1960 the federal government initiated a long-term program to maintain Dawson as a national historic site. The Klondike Visitors Assn produces a theatrical revue at the restored Palace Grand Theatre each summer and operates Diamond Tooth Gertie's Gambling Casino in the old Arctic Brotherhood Hall. People from throughout the Yukon flock to Dawson to celebrate Discovery Day, a territorial holiday commemorating George Carmack's discovery of gold on 17 Aug 1896. H. GUEST

Reading: H.J. Woodside, "Dawson As It Is," *Canadian Magazine*, Sept 1901; Pierre Berton, *Klondike* (1958).

Dawson, George Mercer, geologist (b at Pictou, NS 1 Aug 1849; d at Ottawa 2 Mar 1901), son of J.W. DAWSON. He studied at McGill, then at the Royal School of Mines, London. His superior mental and observational powers became widely known from his work as a geologist and botanist to the International Boundary Commission, which surveyed the 49TH PARALLEL from Lk of the Woods to the Rockies 1873-75. He accurately reported on the geology, mineral resources, agriculture and climate, including locust invasions, of the western plains. In 1875 he joined the GEOLOGICAL SURVEY OF CANADA. His survey of BC strongly influenced government decisions on the proposed route of the CANADIAN PACIFIC RY. A charter ROYAL SOCIETY OF CANADA member (1882), Dawson by 1883 was assistant director of the GSC. In 1887 he surveyed the Alaska boundary at the Yukon R and investigated gold discoveries there. In 1892 he became British commissioner on Bering Sea natural resources and in 1896, a member of the Ethnological Survey of Canada. He was also GSC director 1895-1901.

Dawson's brilliance in systematic mapping provided a sound basis for understanding the geology and mineral resources of much of northern and western Canada, and offered reliable guidance to mining, ranching, agricultural and lumbering industries. He also encouraged investigation and development of western coal and petroleum resources. SUZANNE ZELLER

Reading: Morris Zaslow, *Reading the Rocks* (1975).

Dawson, Sir John William, geologist, principal of McGill (b at Pictou, NS 13 Oct 1820; d at Montréal 19 Nov 1899). The first Canadian-born scientist of worldwide reputation, Dawson personally created most of the 19th-century foundations of the 20th-century Canadian scientific community.

Educated in Pictou, NS, and Edinburgh, Scot, as a geologist, then the most advanced branch of applied science, Dawson became superintendent of education for NS in 1850 and principal of McGill in 1855. Over the next 38 years, he built McGill into one of the world's leading universities; he taught 20 hours a week, published 20 books, formed the ROYAL SOCIETY OF CANADA, became the only individual ever to preside over both the American and the British Assns for the Advancement of Science, and was knighted in 1884 for his public services. His son, G.M. DAWSON, was director of the GEOLOGICAL SURVEY OF CANADA.

Principal Dawson's career spanned the transformation of science from a fixed curriculum of "natural philosophy" to an array of professional disciplines focused on research. Like his predecessors, he wrote on subjects from farming to philanthropy, but he also earned a solid reputation as a geologist, equally at home on a cliff chipping out samples, or in his study, synthesizing and interpreting the processes of geological time. He was the leading expert of his day on early FOSSIL PLANTS and took special pride in his identification as a coral of Eozoon canadense, the oldest nonplant fossil known: always controversial, it was not for another 50 years that Eozoon was shown to be a rare crystal formation rather than a living animal.

Sir John William Dawson (*courtesy Public Archives of Canada/C-49822*).

As well as a modernist in science and education (eg, admitting women to McGill), Dawson was a devout Christian and the leading anti-Darwinist of the late Victorian period. As a geologist, he knew the Earth was very old (100 million years and perhaps older); but he could not see, from his direct knowledge of the fossil evidence, that new species had actually evolved out of earlier ones. Many of his books were technical criticisms of Darwinism and attempts to reconcile up-to-date science with the Christian scriptural tradition. Since the theory of EVOLUTION lacked any mechanical explanation until the science of GENETICS appeared in the 20th century, Dawson's being wrong does not diminish his historical importance. The remoteness of Canada and McGill's newness did not prevent Dawson's leading one faction in the greatest scientific controversy of his day. His international reputation added strength to his mission to establish in Canada the institutions of up-to-date science: higher degrees, lifelong research and publication of research results. DONALD J.C. PHILLIPSON

Reading: W.R. Shea, "Introduction" to J.W. Dawson, *Modern Ideas of Evolution* (repr 1977).

Dawson, Robert McGregor, political scientist (b at Bridgewater, NS 1 Mar 1895; d there 16 July 1958). He was a graduate of Dalhousie, Harvard and London School of Economics, and taught at Dalhousie, Rutgers and U Sask before going to U of T in 1937. He wrote major studies on the Canadian civil service, the constitution and on Dominion status, and his textbook, *The Government of Canada,* first published in 1947, was the standard introduction to the subject for a generation of students. Many of his graduate students became prominent academics and public servants. He demanded high standards of scholarship and literary style, but with colleagues and students his arguments were leavened by a vital enthusiasm and a sense of humour. He left U of T in 1951 to write the official biography of Mackenzie KING, but completed only the first volume before his death. H.B. NEATBY

awson, Simon James, surveyor, engineer, gislator (b at Redhaven, Scot 1820; d at Ottawa 0 Nov 1902). After immigrating to Canada, awson was engaged initially on surveys in uébec but by Apr 1858 was surveying the ough country between Lk Superior and the Red . In 1868 he was asked to construct the line of ommunication proposed in his 1859 report of at survey. Work on what came to be known as e Dawson Route, which involved the use of kes and portage trails, was well advanced hen, in 1870, he was ordered to assist in transorting the Red River Military Expedition along e still incomplete "road." The route remained use until the opening of the CPR. Dawson as elected to the Ontario legislature in 1874 nd to the House of Commons in 1878, where e served until 1891. R.F. LEGGET

awson, William Bell, surveyor, engineer, ivil servant (b at Pictou, NS 2 May 1854; d at lontréal 21 May 1944). Son of Sir John William DAWSON, he studied at McGill and the École es Ponts et Chaussées, Paris, France. After orking several years as a surveyor and enineer, he joined the CANADIAN PACIFIC RY in 1884 nd was involved in the arbitration between the anadian government and the railway over the uality of construction of the western sections of he railway in BC. He is best known for his work s engineer and superintendent of the Tidal urvey, Canadian Dept of Marine and Fisheries, 893-1924. Technically difficult and performed nder arduous conditions, the work resulted in ide tables for all the principal harbours of Canda, invaluable for the fishing, lumber and coal ndustries. A member of the Royal Society of anada, in retirement he devoted much time to riting articles on the relationships between eligion and science. M.J. KEEN

awson Creek, BC, City, pop 11 373 (1981c), nc 1958, is located on the BC-Alberta border, bout 400 km NE of Prince George and 570 km W of Edmonton. It is the regional centre for ortheastern BC. The region's economy is based n agriculture, forestry and mineral exploration nd development. The construction of the BC y, the massive Peace R hydroelectric project nd, most recently, mineral exploitation near umbler Ridge have produced rapid expansion ver the past 30 years. Dawson Creek's mile 0" on the ALASKA HWY has made tourism imortant, as all traffic over the highway must ass through the city. The area also boasts exellent hunting and fishing opportunities for portsmen. As the terminus of the Pacific Great Western and Northern Alberta railways, the city s an important grain-shipping centre. Its atractions include the Northern Alberta Ry Park nd Museum, Alberta Wheat Pool Elevator and everal campsites and rivers close to the city. ALAN F.J. ARTIBISE

ay, James, equestrian (b at Thornhill, Ont 7 uly 1946). A specialist in show jumping, Day vas a member — with James ELDER and homas GAYFORD — of the gold-medal Canadian eam at the 1968 Mexico City Olympics. Day irst entered international competition in 1964, winning the N American junior jumping championship; in 1966 he was senior champion. He won the individual jumping event at the Pan-American Games in Winnipeg and was on the team that won the Grand Prix events at the N American jumping championship and Royal Horse Show (1969) and the world championships (1970). Day also represented Canada in the 1972 and 1976 Olympics. BARBARA SCHRODT

Day Care The licensed or approved care of young children, for all or part of the day, outside the children's own home. The 2 most common types of day care are centre care and family day care. The latter refers to the care of children (between a few weeks of age to about 12 years old) in private homes that have been assessed and are supervised by a social agency or governmental staff. The older children are cared for in after-school programs during their out-of-school hours. Major types of day care include private commercial; private nonprofit; and those under municipal welfare services.

The federal government, through the provisions of the Canada Assistance Plan, shares in the cost to provinces and municipalities of providing day care to families who are in need, or who may fall into this category if they do not receive the service. Health and Welfare Canada also provides consultation services on day care to the provinces and the public and operates a National Day Care Information Centre.

Because day care falls under provincial jurisdiction, the provinces are responsible for the licensing procedures, the establishment of standards, and the basic design of the day-care system. Day-care programs across Canada share some similarities, particularly regarding standards regulating health and safety, child-staff ratios and staff training; but there are some significant differences, because of differing provincial philosophies and perspectives. For example, Saskatchewan will only license day-care centres that are operated as parent co-operatives, while in Alberta about 65% of day-care centres are operated as commercial ventures. Ontario and Alberta are the only provinces where municipally owned and operated day-care centres exist, although they are not numerous. Some provinces will provide a partial subsidy to everyone using the service regardless of family income, while others restrict subsidization to families who pass a needs or income test.

Although some day-care centres date to WWII and before, the majority have been established since 1972 in direct response to the increasing number of working mothers with preschool children. In 1971 there were only 17 400 full-time day-care spaces in Canada; by March 1983 there were approximately 140 000 spaces. For working mothers in 1973, however, less than 2% of their children under 2 years of age and 7% of those aged 2-6 were in licensed or approved day-care spaces. By 1982 the percentages had increased to 5% and 14%, respectively; so although day-care spaces have increased sevenfold since 1973, the percentage of preschool children being served by day care has only doubled. Infant day care is the least developed service, partly because it is so costly.

The cost of day-care services is directly related to almost all of the current day-care issues. Day-care staff, generally underpaid, are faced with the dilemma that because day care is so labour intensive (representing about 70-80% of day-care costs), an increase in salaries places its cost beyond the means of many low-income and middle-income earners. The challenge is to find ways of making day care accessible and affordable to all who require it. HOWARD CLIFFORD

De Cosmos, Amor, newspaper editor, politician, premier of BC (b William Alexander Smith at Windsor, NS 20 Aug 1825; d at Victoria, BC 4 July 1897). Smith left his job in a Halifax wholesale warehouse in 1851 to make his way to the California goldfields. A keen amateur photographer, when he reached the Pacific he set up a studio instead of digging for gold. Settling in Mud Springs, soon renamed El Dorado, Smith followed the town's example. In 1854, the California Senate passed a bill naming him Amor de Cosmos; the name, he said, "tells what I love most . . . order, beauty, the world, the universe." When news of gold on the FRASER R reached California in 1858, De Cosmos trekked northward, but stayed in Victoria and founded the *British Colonist*. Highly critical of Governor James DOUGLAS, De Cosmos began a political career as well. He served in the Legislative Assembly of Vancouver I 1863-66, and in the Legislative Council of BC 1867-71. De Cosmos promoted CONFEDERATION with Canada, but organized a "Confederation League" to get RESPONSIBLE GOVERNMENT in the "Terms of Union." When both were achieved (1871), he was elected to the new provincial Legislature as well as the House of Commons. From 1872 to 1874 he was both premier of BC and a federal MP. He proved as mediocre in power as he had been brilliant in opposition, and his career ended in 1882, when Victoria voters rejected him for advocating Canadian independence. His last years were marked by growing eccentricity and finally, in 1895, madness. GEORGE WOODCOCK

Reading: G. Woodcock, *Amor de Cosmos* (1975).

Amor De Cosmos, 1874, eccentric politician who promoted Confederation in BC. He was both premier of BC and a federal MP (*courtesy Public Archives of Canada / PA-25397*).

de Cotret, Robert-René, politician (b at Ottawa 20 Feb 1944). After an MBA at McGill and a doctorate in business economics at U of Mich, de Cotret served as a staff member of the President's Council of Economic Advisers in the US, 1970-71, and as an adviser to the Dept of Finance 1971-72. From 1972 to 1978 he was a director and then president of the CONFERENCE BOARD OF CANADA. He was elected Conservative MP for Ottawa Centre in a 1978 by-election, immediately becoming a trusted economic adviser of Opposition leader Joe CLARK. He was defeated in the 1979 election but was appointed senator so that he could serve in Clark's Cabinet as minister of industry, trade and commerce. He resigned from the Senate to run unsuccessfully in the 1980 election. He was VP of the National Bank of Canada to 1984, when he regained a seat in the Commons and, as president of the Treasury Board and member of all the spending committees, was one of the most powerful members of the MULRONEY Cabinet. NORMAN HILLMER

de Havilland Aircraft of Canada Limited, with head offices in Toronto, is an aircraft manufacturer. Incorporated in Ontario in 1929, the company manufactures the DE HAVILLAND OTTER (now Twin Otter), the Buffalo (a military plane) and the DE HAVILLAND DASH 7 aircraft. During the 1970s the company experienced difficulty when commuter airlines did not create the high demand for Dash 7s that de Havilland had expected. In 1974 the federal government purchased the company from its British owners, Hawker Siddeley Aviation, and invested in research and development. But it was not until 1978, as airlines began facing deregulation in the US and higher fuel costs, that sales of the Dash 7 started to climb. De Havilland then launched plans for yet another medium-sized, short-takeoff-and-landing (STOL) craft, the Dash 8, which would fill a gap in the short-haul market. De Havilland's aircraft are used worldwide, with approximately 85% of the company's production exported to 87 countries. The company also does a considerable business in the manufacture of spare parts. As of May 1982, it had annual sales or operating revenue of $450 million (ranking 154th in Canada), assets of $492 million (ranking 132nd) and 4980 employees. The Canadian government owns 100% of the shares.

DEBORAH C. SAWYER

The de Havilland Beaver, outstanding STOL aircraft used worldwide (*courtesy de Havilland Aircraft of Canada Ltd*).

de Havilland Beaver, DHC-2, successor to the NOORDUYN NORSEMAN as the all-purpose bush plane of the Canadian North. Its specifications were based on results of a questionnaire circulated by "Punch" DICKINS, and it first flew 16 Aug 1947. Generous power and a special wing/flap system designed by R.D. Hiscocks gave it excellent STOL capabilities; it could take off in 181 m. Carrying a pilot, 6 passengers and heavy loads, it saw service in both polar regions, African deserts and airfields high in the Andes. Service in Antarctica was so valuable that a lake, glacier and island were named after it. By 1965, some 1600 were operating in 63 countries, with the biggest customer being the US Army. There are 6 in museums, including one, the prototype, CF-FHB, in the National Aviation Museum, Ottawa.

JAMES MARSH

de Havilland Caribou, DHC-4, twin-engined STOL aircraft, capable of taking off in only 220 m. It was characterized by the sharp upward angle of the rear fuselage, providing access for large loads. It first flew July 1958, and was used mostly in a military role. In 1965, it was replaced by the similar but larger DHC-5 Buffalo, which was the first aircraft of its size to execute the steep takeoff and descent required for city-centre STOL operation.

JAMES MARSH

de Havilland Dash 7, DHC-7, STOL aircraft designed for efficient transport from city centres. It first flew Mar 1975 after a long development costing $120 million, four-fifths of which was paid by the federal government. Its outstanding STOL performance comes from highly specialized wings; it can take off in 747 m and seats 50 people. Its turbine engines and slowly revolving propellers make it the world's quietest airliner. It first went into operation in Colorado, later from Yellowknife to northern communities. By 1980, 28 had been delivered and orders or options taken for another 119. The CANADIAN COAST GUARD uses the Dash 7 for monitoring offshore pollution and the 200-mile limit.

JAMES MARSH

The de Havilland Otter, versatile STOL aircraft whic[h] has provided dependable transport in the Canadia[n] North since the 1950s (*courtesy de Havilland Aircraft of Canada Ltd*).

de Havilland Otter, DHC-3, versatile bush aircraft with STOL capabilities designed to operate on wheels, floats or skis in extreme conditions. It first flew Dec 1951 and provided dependable transport in the Canadian North, Greenland, Norway, Antarctica, Nepal, China and numerous other countries. The Canadian forces used it for search and rescue, and commercial airlines for feedliner routes and air taxi. The Twin Otter, DHC-6, which first flew 1965, is powered by 2 Canadian-made Pratt and Whitney PT6 turbine engines. It was used for the first city-centre air service, from Ottawa to Montréal, July 1974.

JAMES MARSH

De Koninck, Charles, philosopher (b at Thourout, Belgium 29 July 1906; d at Rome, Italy 13 Feb 1965). When he arrived at Québec's Laval U, a graduate of Louvain U, Thomism was the established doctrine of PHILOSOPHY in Québec. Director of Laval's philosophy faculty 1939-56, he determined the course of philosophy there and in much of French Canada through his numerous publications and his connections with the Catholic Church.

De Koninck's work, more than 150 papers and books, was devoted mainly to the philosophy of science. He published also in the philosophy of religion and metaphysics. Because of his willingness to write in both English and French he became well known in English Canada and in the US, where he lectured frequently. His popular book *The Hollow Universe* (1960), published after a series of lectures at McMaster in Hamilton, attempted to reconcile philosophy, science and religion. De Koninck argued that, divorced from concrete experience, the scientific world was an empty shell. A controversial philosopher, he was influential for many years.

ELIZABETH A. TROTT

De la Roche, Mazo, writer (b at Newmarket, Ont 15 Jan 1879; d at Toronto 12 July 1961). Among the most prolific and widely read of Canadian authors, she wrote 23 novels, more than 50 short stories, 13 plays and many other works. Her Jalna novels have sold 9 million copies in 193 English- and 92 foreign-language editions. Mazo de la Roche began writing short stories before WWI and published 2 novels in the 1920s before winning international recognition with the publication of *Jalna* in 1927. Thi[s] story of an Ontario family named Whiteoak an[d] its home Jalna won the *Atlantic Monthly* awar[d] for the best novel of that year. Sequels depicte[d] other episodes in the history of the Whiteoaks *Young Renny* (1935) was several months on th[e] New York *Herald* bestseller list. A play based o[n] the Jalna stories was a hit in London, New Yor[k] and Toronto and inspired a Hollywood film. Her books continued to sell well after WWII (2[?] of her books were still in print in 1960), although her novels of the 1950s do not compar[e] well with her earlier work. In 1972 the CB[C] produced a TV series based on the Jalna stories.

Although still a best-selling author, Mazo d[e] la Roche was not taken seriously by critics afte[r] WWII. Her later works too closely resemble[d] formula romances and succumbed to sentimentality. This later criticism has been unfairly extended to the full body of her work, includin[g] her earlier novels, which are distinguished b[y] well-defined characters, good dialogue and subtle imagery. Thus, one of the greatest of 20th century Canadian writers is also one of the mos[t] underrated.

C.J. TAYLO[R]

Reading: R. Hambleton, *Mazo de la Roche of Jalna* (1966[);] D. Livesay, "Mazo de la Roche," in M.Q. Innis, ed, *Th[e] Clear Spirit* (1966).

De Meurons, Swiss infantry regiment raise[d] 1781; transferred 1795 to the British army. I[t] served in India until Oct 1806, then moved t[o] England, and was sent to Lower Canada in Au[g] 1813. There it saw limited service in the WAR O[F] 1812 under Sir George PREVOST during the Plattsburg campaign of Sept 1814. Remaining in th[e] Canadas, it was disbanded in July 1816, mor[e] than half of the 640 other ranks electing to sta[y] as settlers. Some were immediately recruited b[y] Lord SELKIRK for his expedition to the RED RIVE[R] COLONY. In 1821 some former officers helpe[d] recruit Swiss settlers for Red River.

STUART R.J. SUTHERLAN[D]

De Mille, James, professor, novelist (b at Sain[t] John 23 Aug 1833; d at Halifax 28 Jan 1880). H[e] spent most of his life teaching history, rhetori[c] and literature at Dalhousie in Halifax. His reputation, however, rested on his writing; he wa[s] one of N America's most popular novelists o[f] the late 19th century. He wrote historical romances, novels of manners and adventure wit[h] nternational settings, and tales of mystery and ensation. In addition, he produced 2 notable eries of books for boys, in which he avoided nuch of the trite moralizing found in such works during this period. THOMAS B. VINCENT

de Pédery-Hunt, Dora, sculptor (b at Budapest, Hungary 16 Nov 1913). Dora de Pédery-Hunt ompleted her studies in sculpture and design in Budapest in 1943 and immigrated to Canada in 1948. Her first solo show of medals and small sculptures in Toronto established her reputation as a sensitive representational artist endowed with superb technical skills. She was instrumental in introducing the ancient art of medal sculpture to Canada and is the Canadian representative of the Fédération internationale de la médaille. A cast bronze medal she created for the Canada Council in 1961 and her design for the Canadian Olympic gold coin in 1976 are among her public commissions. CLARA HARGITTAY

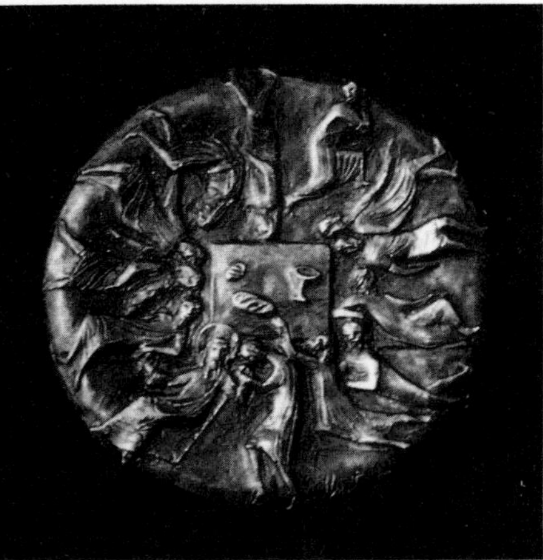

Dora de Pédery-Hunt, *The Last Supper* (1979), bronze, 92 mm in diameter (*courtesy Dora de Pédery-Hunt / photo Elizabeth Frey*).

De Sola, Alexander Abraham, clergyman, professor, author, publisher (b at London, Eng 18 Sept 1825; d at New York, NY 5 June 1882). During his ministry to Montréal's Sephardic Jewish Congregation, Shearith Israel (1847-82), De Sola organized its educational, benevolent and fraternal life; taught Hebrew, rabbinical literature, oriental literature, Spanish and philology at McGill; and played an active part in the city's literary and scientific life. A prolific author, editor and translator, concerned chiefly with the contemporary debate on religion and science, De Sola's own writings included studies on Jewish history, cosmography and medicine. In 1858 McGill made him an honorary doctor of laws, the first Jewish minister to receive this honour in England or N America; in 1872 he became the first British subject to open the US House of Representatives with prayer, a privilege that brought him wide acclaim. CARMAN MILLER

Deafness, *see* AUDITORY IMPAIRMENT.

Dean River, 241 km long, world-famous steelhead and salmon-fishing stream, rises in the Fraser Plateau of west-central BC, flows NW and W through the COAST MOUNTAINS and empties near the head of Dean Channel. The name was given by Capt George VANCOUVER in 1793, the same year Alexander MACKENZIE paddled the upper Dean R in his overland journey to the Pacific Ocean. PETER GRANT

Dease, Peter Warren, fur trader, arctic explorer (b at Mackinac I, Mich 1 Jan 1788; d at Montréal 17 Jan 1863). From age 13 he was engaged in the FUR TRADE, first with the XY Co, then the NORTH WEST CO and finally the HUDSON'S BAY CO. He served principally in the Athabasca and Mackenzie districts, though he was in charge of the New Caledonia trade 1831-35. Dease assisted Sir John FRANKLIN on his second land expedition to the Arctic. Between 1837 and 1839 Dease and Thomas Simpson made 3 expeditions along the arctic coast, leaving only a small part of the NORTHWEST PASSAGE unsurveyed. Dease retired to a farm near Montréal in 1841. DANIEL FRANCIS

Death For centuries the law has accepted the cessation of heartbeat and respiration as the determination of death, but now the heart can be removed, the breathing stopped and blood pumped by machines without preventing the individual's resumption of lucid consciousness. The Manitoba legislature, in its Vital Statistics Act (1975), has provided the only statutory definition of death in Canada: "For all purposes within the legislative competence of the Legislature of Manitoba the death of a person takes place at the time at which irreversible cessation of all that person's brain function occurs." In 1981 the Law Reform Commission of Canada recommended that Parliament enact this provision in the Interpretation Act: "For all purposes within the jurisdiction of the Parliament of Canada, a person is dead when an irreversible cessation of all that person's brain functions has occurred." Rules relating to the registration of death vary from province to province, but generally, when death occurs an appropriate person, eg, a relative, must complete an official form for the district registrar. At the same time a certificate of the cause of death must be completed and sent to the district registrar either by a doctor or, in suspicious circumstances, by a coroner. Morticians need certificates in order to bury a body. FRANCIS C. MULDOON

Death and Dying Death, the irreversible cessation of life, has always intrigued and frightened mankind. Every known culture has attempted to provide an explanation of its meaning; like birth or marriage it is universally considered an event of social significance, amplified by ritual and supported by institutions. Death has been studied by anthropologists, sociologists, philosophers, psychologists and biologists who have tried to understand its cultural, social or individual meanings. Death is also a matter of legal and political concern — the Law Reform Commission of Canada has published several working papers on euthanasia, cessation of treatment, the definition of death and related matters, while Health and Welfare Canada has published analyses and guidelines for establishing standards for hospital-based palliative care. Answers to problems caused by death have been addressed by RELIGION, PHILOSOPHY and political ideology. (*See*, for example, BUDDHISM; CATHOLICISM; MORMON CHURCH.)

Prior to the Industrial Revolution, mortality rates in Canada were high, extremely variable and dependent upon crop conditions, weather, EPIDEMICS, etc. The crude death rate (number of deaths per 1000 people per year) has declined from 22-25 deaths in the mid-1800s to 11.8 in 1923 to just 7.1 in 1979, while at the same time the infant death rate (deaths during the first year) has decreased dramatically, by 65% between 1951 and 1976 (*see* POPULATION). Life expectancy at birth now exceeds 70 years for males and 77 years for females. Age-specific mortality rates for the native population are higher than those for the Canadian population in almost all age categories; as a result, life expectancy at birth for the native population is about 10 years less than for the population as a whole. Women have lower death rates than men at all ages and have actually increased their life-span advantage over men in the past several decades. Today, a woman who reaches the age of 65 has a 50% chance of living an additional 18 years, while a 65-year-old man has a similar chance of living another 14 years. Women also have a 1-in-6 chance of being predeceased by their first child, if it is a son. About 73% of all deaths are of people over the age of 60, and death at an earlier age is frequently considered tragic. Health and Welfare Canada treats deaths occurring before the age of 70 as premature. Today it is difficult to appreciate that children a century ago could reasonably expect to be orphaned before reaching maturity, or that parents might expect to lose one or several children before the children reached adulthood.

Causes of death have also changed dramatically since 1867. Deaths from infectious diseases have declined, while those from chronic diseases, especially cardiovascular diseases (50% of all deaths), have increased. About 20% of deaths are caused by neoplasms (cancer), and about 1 in 10 is caused by accident, poisoning or violence. Pneumonia used to be called "the old man's friend" because it brought a swift and relatively painless death to the elderly, but today it accounts for less than 30% of deaths.

Social institutions have generally evolved to facilitate life and prevent death. Some social scientists have postulated that death in societies with low mortality rates poses a greater threat to the personality than it does in societies with high mortality rates because such societies tend to proscribe social solutions to the problems of mortality. Studies of attitudes toward death have revealed the importance to the dying individual of a secure environment and close family ties. The fact that dying is now usually the termination of a long, chronic illness, most likely in advanced age, affects not only how people think about death and about their own dying, but the type of care provided to dying persons. The great majority of nonaccidental deaths occur in hospitals, but nursing homes have also become an important place where people, especially women, die. As a result, death is less familiar in the experience of most people and dying largely a process managed by health-care professionals. Since the late 1960s, the increasingly technological nature of hospital death has aroused concern. A hospital is perceived as a cold and indifferent setting where existence is often prolonged by technology long after the individual has ceased to enjoy quality of life and where the needs of the dying person and his or her relatives or friends are less important than the smooth functioning of the hospital bureaucracy. Dr Cicely Saunders in England, Dr Elizabeth Kübler-Ross in the US and Dr Balfour Mount of the Royal Victoria Hospital in Montréal have pioneered palliative-care services or "hospice" units which specialize in caring for the terminally ill. St Christopher's Hospice in England, established by Dr Saunders, is a freestanding, 62-bed unit. Today, smaller units based within hospital settings are more common; often these are linked to community-based home-care services because, although palliative care began as an attempt to humanize dying in hospitals, it has increasingly emphasized community-based care and the use of nonprofessional volunteers. These services share a commitment to providing high-quality care, including an emphasis on adequate pain control; to ensuring emotional support to patients who realize they are dying; to allowing the staff to develop an emotional commitment to the patients; and to recognizing a concern for the relatives and others close to the patients. Some programs also provide counselling and support for staff. Hospice units, some integrated into hospitals, and palliative-care programs, which support the dying and those who care for them, have spread rapidly in Canada. In Toronto, the Palliative Care Foundation conducted a survey (1981) which identified 109 palliative-care groups, organizations, programs or centres of activity in Canada, ranging from hospital-based programs and hospices to professional groups such as the Toronto Palliative Care Working Group.

Within the past 15 years research and teaching about death and dying, particularly from social-science and health-care perspectives, has burgeoned in N America, perhaps because through science and technology we have gained much more control over the timing of death and are now confronted with the dilemma of determining to what extent and with what measures dying should be shortened or prolonged (*see* MEDICAL ETHICS). In 1969 there were about 6 university-level courses on death and dying, one of which was taught at the University of Calgary. Today there are hundreds of such courses, as well as numerous in-service and continuing-education courses in health care. Curricula for such courses vary widely but may include attention to changing causes of death, clinical help for the dying, psychological impact of death and dying on those of various ages who are dying and on those around them, the processes of bereavement and grief, and ethical issues, eg, euthanasia and clinical decision making. Many courses also focus on philosophical or literary treatments of death and dying. In 1969, the journal *Omega*, a major research journal in the area, was founded. *Essence: Issues in the Study of Aging, Dying and Death*, a York University journal, has published international research. In the area of palliative care alone, a small subsection of the death and dying literature, more than 12 000 references have been found in 29 computerized bibliographic data bases covering the past 10 years.

Fear of death is the subject of extensive current psychological and sociological research. The anticipation of personal death apparently initiates preparatory processes in which people try to put their affairs in order and to make sense of their impending death and of their lives. Fear and other attitudes toward death appear to vary by age, ie, anticipated remaining years of life; education levels; and belief systems. The fear of death can be mediated by a sense of continuity, eg, through biology, through works that will survive the creator, through a belief in a deep relationship with nature, etc.

Counsellors claim that compassion, honesty and reassurance help the seriously ill adapt to the approach of death. Dying persons are often abandoned, psychologically, by family, friends and doctors. Dr Kübler-Ross has claimed that psychological distress diminishes if the patient is not alone and is able to express feelings and concerns, but her theories that dying patients experience a predictable 5-stage sequence of adjustment after learning of their condition, although held by many health-care practitioners, are rejected by most reputable scholars in this field. Bereavement is now perceived as a normal psychological and physiological reaction to death. Grief can be characterized by somatic distress, guilt, hostility, change in patterns of conduct, etc. In Western societies, individuals, after the initial shock, are typically left to grieve alone. There is no conclusive evidence that religious belief helps to alleviate bereavement.

The new character of death is associated with changes in the way it is experienced; eg, usually it follows a lengthy, chronic illness and occurs late in life. In modern Canadian society it is in many respects hidden, especially from the young, as few people die at home. Formal ritual to mark its occurrence has also changed. Mourning dress is now rare in Canada except among some ethnic communities, and FUNERAL PRACTICES are becoming less ornate, frequently reflecting the wishes and prior arrangements of the deceased. *See* CEMETERIES.

VICTOR W. MARSHALL

Reading: C. Charmaz, *The Social Reality of Death* (1980); Victor W. Marshall, *Last Chapters* (1980); R. Kastenbaum and R. Aisenberg, *The Psychology of Death* (1972); J. Fruehling, ed, *Sourcebook on Death and Dying* (1982).

Debassige, Blake Randolph, artist (b at West Bay, Ont 22 June 1956). A leading member of the "second generation" of Ojibwa artists influenced by MORRISSEAU, Debassige has broadened the stylistic and thematic range of this school. In his teens he was deeply influenced by the legend painter Isidore Wadow and by a close study of rock art. From these sources he has developed a "visual language" to express both personal experiences and traditional values of continuing relevance. Debassige married the Cree painter Shirley CheeChoo in 1978.

RUTH B. PHILLIPS

Reading: E. McLuhan and T. Hill, *Norval Morriseau and the Emergence of the Image Makers* (1984).7

Debert, archaeological site located in north-central NS. It is the earliest dated archaeological site found in eastern Canada. Radiocarbon dating places its age at about 10 600 years. Among the many stone implements are distinctive fluted, lanceolate spearpoints of a type ultimately derived from the CLOVIS Big-Game Hunting tradition of western N America. Similar assemblages found at sites in the eastern US suggest a rapid spread of early man into the Maritimes region. Many of the stone tools found at Debert relate to hunting and butchering activities. Although no bone remains were preserved, it is believed that the site served as a hunting encampment, strategically located to intercept herds of Woodland caribou then abundant in the region. Paleoecological data indicate a forest-tundra environment prevailing at the time of site habitation. *See also* ARCHAEOLOGY.

DAVID L. KEENLYSIDE

Decentralization, in federal countries, occurs when there is a substantial sharing of power, authority, financial resources and political support among federal, provincial and local GOVERNMENTS. The less concentrated these resources in the central government, the more decentralized the system. Decentralization may also mean a process of shifting power from the federal to provincial governments. It is often said that the provinces' strength may make Canada the world's most decentralized federal country, and that Canada has resisted economic and social forces which increased centralization elsewhere (*see* FEDERALISM). Decentralization also means power-sharing among any set of units; centralization within the federal or provincial governments can be gauged by assessing power in Cabinet as compared to that in legislatures, judiciaries or other bodies.

RICHARD SIMEON

Decorations for Bravery Three decorations for bravery were instituted in 1972 to serve as a public expression of respect and admiration for persons who perform selfless acts of courage. The scale of awards reflects the degree of peril faced by the recipients.

The Cross of Valour, at the head of Canada's system of HONOURS, takes precedence before all orders and other decorations except the VICTORIA CROSS and GEORGE CROSS. It is a gold cross of 4 equal limbs, the obverse enamelled red with, at its centre, a maple leaf surrounded by a laurel wreath. On the reverse is the royal crown and cypher with the words "Valour-Vaillance." The decoration is worn at the neck on a red ribbon. The Star of Courage is a 4-pointed silver star with a maple leaf encircled by a laurel wreath at the centre and, on the reverse, the word "Courage." The ribbon is red with 2 blue stripes. The Medal of Bravery is a circular silver medal with a maple leaf centered within a laurel wreath on the obverse and the words "Bravery-Bravoure" on the reverse. The ribbon is red with 3 blue stripes. Recipients of bravery decorations are entitled to have the relevant letters placed after their names: CV, SC or MB.

Awards are made by the governor general with the advice and assistance of the Canadian Decorations Advisory Committee and the investigative resources of the police services.

CARL LOCHNAN

Distinguished Flying Cross (obverse), decoration established 1918. Struck in England (silver, 55 mm), it was designed by E. Carter Preston (*courtesy Public Archives of Canada*).

Deer (Cervidae), family of antlered, hoofed ruminants containing about 40 species worldwide (5 in Canada including white-tailed and mule deer, CARIBOU, MOOSE, WAPITI). Deer are large-brained and adaptable. Antlers are found in males of all Canadian species, and in most female caribou. They consist of bone and grow rapidly (4 months in moose), and are shed annually. Velvet (hairy skin, well supplied with nerves and blood vessels) covers and nourishes the growing antlers. In autumn, when antlers are fully grown, the velvet dies and is rubbed off and males are ready to mate. Antlers are used as weapons against rival males and predators and as display organs to intimidate rivals and lure females. Increase in antler size, symmetry and complexity varies with age, health and diet. Deer began their evolutionary radiation as small-bodied, antlerless, tropical herbivores. For 30 million years they evolved slowly. As they invaded open parkland habitats and harsher climates, increases occurred in body size, antler size and complexity, and coat coloration and ornamentation. This evolution resulted in grotesque giants in subarctic, subalpine and glacial environments, eg, the extinct Irish elk (Old World), and the moose (New World). Both could exceed 600 kg in weight. The Alaska bull moose may carry antlers exceeding 30 kg and 2 m in spread; those of Irish elk exceeded 38 kg and 3 m.

The 2 most common deer in Canada, white-tailed and mule deer, are closely related species of genus *Odocoileus*. Both occur in many subspecies including dwarf island forms. A Eurasian species, fallow deer (*Cervus dama*), has been successfully introduced to James I, BC. Fossils of white-tailed deer (*O. virginianus*) predate the Ice Age; the mule deer (*O. hemionus*) originated more recently. Its most primitive subspecies, black-tailed deer (*O. h. columbianus*), lives along the Pacific coastline from Alaska to California. Mule deer, characteristic of the mountains and foothills of western N America, sometimes occur as far E as Manitoba. White-tailed deer occur across southern Canada and as far N as the Peace R, Alta. If protected, both species thrive around human settlements; white-tails, being very secretive, may thrive with little protection. Both are

White-tailed deer fawn. White-tailed deer (*O. virginianus*) are dispersed widely across Canada and live secretly in cities where green belts or large parks provide cover (*photo by V. Claerhout*).

adapted to feed on soft vegetation; however, they have different antipredator strategies. Mule deer throw obstacles in the path of pursuing predators; white-tails combine hiding with rapid getaway over unobstructed ground. Both can be gregarious on open terrain, secretive in dense forests. Females may become territorial when raising young; black-tailed deer may cluster into group territories. At northern latitudes, mating occurs in late Nov and early Dec; fawns are born in June. Males guard one female at a time and do not advertise their whereabouts to rivals. Both species have long sparring ceremonies, but few fights occur. Deer are economically significant mainly as game animals, although the reindeer is domesticated and the velveted antler has been used for pharmaceutical purposes. Deer have been widely introduced as game and park animals. They generally respond well to adequate habitat and protection from excessive HUNTING: moose have spread widely in Eurasia and N America; in America, white-tailed and mule deer have dispersed widely and live secretly in cities where green belts or large parks provide food and cover. In Canada, the caribou is economically and culturally significant to native people; moose and white-tailed deer have provided meat for many rural families. White-tails are the most important big-game animals in N America today.

VALERIUS GEIST

Deer Island abuts the border with the US at the entrance to PASSAMAQUODDY BAY on the S coast of New Brunswick. Long in dispute with the US, sovereignty over the island passed to NB in 1817. The name is probably descriptive. Fishing is the most important economic activity. The island is the site of the world's 3 largest lobster pounds, natural inlets converted by fences and nets into corrals where lobsters are held while waiting shipment to market. The 2 largest communities are Fairhaven and Leonardville. Ferry service connects with Letete, NB, and Eastport, Maine.

DANIEL FRANCIS

Deer Lake, Nfld, Town, pop 4348 (1981c), inc 1950, is located at the N end of Deer Lk in western Newfoundland. The eastern shore of the lake was settled 1867 by a Cape Breton I family who began an operation to cut pine trees. The site was named Nicholsville and expanded with the building of the railway in the 1880s and 1890s. In 1923 Deer Lake was selected as the site of a power plant to support a pulp and paper mill at nearby CORNER BROOK. In 1957 the federal government built a large airstrip here. This, with the railway and highway connections to Bay of Islands, Humber Valley, Great Northern Pen and Baie Verte Pen, has made Deer Lk one of the main pulpwood, service and transportation centres of Newfoundland.

JANET E.M. PITT AND ROBERT D. PITT

Deer Mouse (*Peromyscus maniculatus*), typical MOUSE with moderately long tail, large ears, prominent eyes and pointed nose well supplied with tactile hairs. Upperparts are grey or brown, depending on age and subspecies; underside, white. Even the tail is two-toned. Deer mice occur in forests and grasslands throughout Canada, excluding Newfoundland, and down the Mackenzie Valley beyond the Arctic Circle. They are strongly nocturnal. In winter, northern deer mice (*P. m. borealis*) undergo bouts of light torpor, lasting for up to several days, in which body temperature may fall several degrees, but they do not actually hibernate. Deer mice breed only in summer. Females of northern populations never have more than 2 litters (of about 5 young). In southern Canada, females produce more, smaller litters; some may become sexually mature in the season of their birth. A few animals are known to have survived 2 winters. Deer mice may destroy stored food, but otherwise are of little direct economic importance. They provide food for carnivorous birds and mammals. The large, pale-grey Cascade deer mouse (*P. oreas*) of the Coast Range of BC may represent a distinct species.

W.A. FULLER

Defamation law protects an individual's reputation and good name. Libel can include defamatory written words, pictures, statues, films and even conduct; whereas slander is a defamatory spoken word. A claimant must prove the defamation, that it referred to the claimant and that it was communicated to a third person. Sometimes a defamatory statement can be made if it is not malicious, but this is a qualified privilege. Fair comment protects any opinion fairly made on public-interest matters. For a defendant, truth is a complete defence; if someone is liable, compensatory and punitive damages may be demanded. The court may also restrain further publication of the defamation. Debates or discussions within certain forums, eg, Parliament, are absolutely protected against charges of defamation.

LEWIS N. KLAR

Defence, *see* ARMED FORCES; CANADIAN-AMERICAN RELATIONS; EXTERNAL RELATIONS; NATO; NORAD; NATIONAL DEFENCE, DEPARTMENT OF.

Defence Counsel, lawyer who advises accused (defendants in civil cases) and presents their case to the court, ensuring that clients have a fair trial. If a client is convicted, the defence counsel speaks in respect of sentence.

K.G. MCSHANE

Defence Research, initiation and development of weapons or technologies likely to be useful in national defence, is a comparatively recent phenomenon in Canada. Although there were some rudimentary efforts at developing new defence technologies during WWI, it was only with WWII that the Canadian government began to pay attention to innovations in equipment and techniques. Various research establishments were set up to investigate problems as diverse as ordnance, ballistics, radar, winter warfare, chemical warfare and aviation medicine (*see* ARMAMENTS).

At the end of the war, at the insistence of Chief of the General Staff Gen Charles FOULKES, Canada's defence research programs were consolidated and preserved as much as limited funds would allow. It was obvious that certain limitations obtained: only a few projects could be pursued at any time; research had to be co-ordinated with that of Canada's principal allies, Britain and the US, and the research program should be integrated as far as possible into other research enterprises. It was decided that the best means of securing a relatively independent and prestigious research enterprise was to set up a Defence Research Board under the Department of NATIONAL DEFENCE. In addition to members and staff of the board in Canada, liaison officers were appointed to work in London and Washington, and later also in Paris.

The work of the DRB has been extremely varied. Attention has been given to relatively conventional subjects such as explosives and propellants, but also to missile development (on a modest scale compared to the US or the USSR), northern or arctic research, and telecommunications, including research into exploring the ionosphere. At the Suffield Experimental Station at Ralston, Alta, chemical and other highly classified work has been carried on since WWII. In co-operation with the navy the DRB developed new antisubmarine technologies, such as the Variable Depth SONAR, and helped to adapt helicopters for antisubmarine work. The DRB also contributed heavily to siting and developing the EARLY-WARNING RADAR of the 1950s across the Canadian north (*see* NORAD). More broadly, Canadian defence research has contributed technological expertise to Canadian industry, although there is some dispute as to whether the DRB is the appropriate organization to help guide industrial development. Defence research also presents the possibility of aiding in arms control as well as weapons research, but whether such a linkage will prove successful is not certain.

ROBERT BOTHWELL

Deiter, Walter, politician, businessman (b at Peepeekesis Indian Reserve, Sask 31 May 1916). Deiter was active in the development of Indian political organizations in the 1960s. His first political position was as president of the Regina Indian and Métis Friendship Centre (1962-67). As chief of the newly reactivated Federation of Saskatchewan Indians (1967-68), he helped establish the National Indian Brotherhood (*see* ASSEMBLY OF FIRST NATIONS) and became its first president (1968-70). During his tenure the NIB became a working national organization and helped to oppose the 1969 White Paper (*see* NATIVE PEOPLE, GOVERNMENT POLICY). Deiter maintained a relatively conservative stand on such matters as Indian-government relations, education and community development. Opposition from local and more radical factions of the Indian movement led to his defeat by George MANUEL in 1970. Since that time he has worked with various Indian organizations in Saskatchewan and is a senator of the Federation of Saskatchewan Indian Nations. BENNETT McCARDLE

Dekanahwideh, "the Heavenly Messenger," reputed founder of the Five Nations Confederacy. He was said to have been born among the HURON of a virgin mother, destined to bring peace and power to his people. His first miracle was building a stone canoe, in which he travelled to the Onandaga, where he made his first convert — Hiawatha. He spoke his message of peace among the warring Mohawk, Oneida, Cayuga and Seneca. His power in defying death and darkening the sun converted sceptics; a Great Peace was achieved and the Confederacy of the Five (later Six) Nations was born. Dekanahwideh planted a great white pine, the Tree of Peace, appointed 50 chiefs and slipped into the Great Lks in his stone canoe, promising to return if the peace were threatened. This majestic narrative fostered unity among the fiercely independent IROQUOIS, and homage is still paid to his memory among the Six Nations people. JAMES MARSH

Delict, in Québec CIVIL LAW, is a civil wrong other than a breach of contract. The law of delicts covers approximately the same field as that of TORTS in COMMON LAW. Strictly speaking, a distinction should be made between delicts, ie, intentionally committed wrongs, and quasi-delicts, ie, unintentionally or negligently committed wrongs, although with some minor exceptions, the practical consequences of both are identical. The purpose of the law is not to punish but to provide compensation for damages (material and moral), compensation aimed at putting injured parties back into the situation they enjoyed before the delict or quasi-delict was committed. In a number of isolated instances Québec law now awards punitive or exemplary damages as well, particularly for wrongs committed under Article 49 of the Québec Human Rights Charter and Article 272 of the Consumer Protection Act.

The Québec law of delicts is part of the law of obligations. Traditionally, delicts did not govern breach of contract, but recently Québec courts and the SUPREME COURT OF CANADA have allowed plaintiffs to sue in delict even if there exists a contractual agreement with the defendant. Examples of delictual liabilities include those arising from traffic accidents, destruction of or damage to property, nuisance, medical and other professional MALPRACTICES, DEFAMATION and the manufacturing and distribution of defective or dangerous products.

The Québec law of delicts originated in the Napoleonic Code and the works of the French jurist Domat. Both the French and the Québec laws of delicts contain one general delictual principle and a number of subsidiary special rules. In that sense French and Québec law differ from both traditional Roman and traditional common law, which know a system of different nominate torts or delicts, each with its own rules and fields of application.

The Napoleonic Code and the Québec CIVIL CODE are extremely concise in their treatment of delicts, but although their basic notions are identical, drafting and substantive differences do exist. In both France and Québec JURISPRUDENCE (in the civil-law sense of case law) is extremely important to the law of delicts precisely because the codes' treatment of the subject matter is so concise and often very general. The law of delicts cannot be understood unless the text of the code is read in conjunction with the court cases that interpret and elaborate upon it. In Québec, common law has considerably influenced the cases governed by the law of delicts.

The fundamental principles and concepts of the Québec law of delicts are contained in Articles 1053-1056 of the Civil Code. Article 1053 states, "Every person capable of discerning right from wrong is responsible for the damage caused by his own fault to another, whether by positive act, imprudence, neglect or want of skill." On the basis of this provision, of case law and of doctrine, 4 characteristics of a delict or quasi-delict can be identified: fault, imputability, damage and causality. First, the wrongdoer must be at fault. Fault is an objective criterion; it can consist of commission, eg, acting contrary to the standard of a reasonable person in similar circumstances, or of omission, eg, failure to act where the reasonable person would be under a legal duty to do so. Second, the wrongdoer must be imputable, ie, able to discern right from wrong. Imputability is a subjective criterion. Young children (generally under 6 years of age) and insane persons, for instance, are held unable to discern right from wrong. Third, the wrongdoer must cause damage. Damage may be material (injury, property damage, loss of profit) or immaterial (harm to reputation, pain and suffering, loss of enjoyment of life). Fourth, the fault must have caused the damage. Québec case law does not adhere to any particular causation theory, but generally the courts say that the fault must have been the determining cause of the damage. There is no compensation for so-called indirect or ricochet damage. Once a delict has been established, the victim is entitled to obtain payment of damages from the wrongdoer. Sometimes the victim can also obtain a court injunction against the wrongdoer under the provisions of the Code of CIVIL PROCEDURE.

Article 1053 covers liability for one's personal acts. Articles 1054 and 1055 deal with liability for the acts of others and liability for things under one's care. Article 1054 (s2-7) makes parents liable for the damage caused by their minor children; tutors for damage caused by their pupils; guardians for damage caused by insane persons under their care; teachers for damage caused by their students; and employers for damage caused by their employees. The main difference between Articles 1053 and 1054 (s2-7) is that generally the wrongdoer's fault under Article 1053 must be proven by the victim, but the fault of the responsible persons under article 1054 is legally presumed. They can exculpate themselves by proving absence of fault, eg, having adequately fulfilled their duties of supervision or upbringing or both. However, an employer's fault is irrefutably presumed; if an employee has through his fault caused damage during employment, the employer is automatically liable. Liability for things under one's care is based on Articles 1054(s1) and 1055. Owners and users of animals are liable for damage done by such animals unless they can prove the occurrence of a fortuitous event. The same applies to owners of buildings for total or partial ruin of a building due to construction defects or want of repairs. For things other than animals and buildings, there is a legal presumption that the guardian of a thing is responsible for damage caused by the autonomous act of the thing, although the guardian can rebut the presumption by proving absence of fault.

Although generally both direct and indirect victims (eg, relatives of the victim, or his employer) may sue for damages in delict, under Article 1056, which originated in the English Lord Campbell's Act, in death actions only the spouse, parents and children of the deceased victim are considered indirect victims.

Recently, delictual rules have also surfaced outside the Civil Code in special statutes. Besides the Human Rights Charter and the Consumer Protection Act, relevant statutes include the Automobile Insurance Act and the Crime Victims Compensation Act. Furthermore, a revision of the code articles on delicts has been proposed by the Civil Code Revision Office in its 1977 Draft Civil Code. P. HAANAPPEL

Reading: M. Lancelin, *Théorie du droit des obligations* (1975); J. Pineau, Théorie des obligations (1979).

Delta, BC, District Municipality, pop 74 692 (1981c), area 17 600 ha, inc as the Corporation of Delta 1879, is located in the southern part of Greater VANCOUVER — S of the Fraser R, W of the muncipality of Surrey and touching the US border. Its 3 main communities are North Delta, Ladner and South Delta. Most of the district, as its name implies, is low-lying delta land, and much is farmland designated "agricultural reserve" by the province. By the early 1900s the community supported 40 businesses, but with the shift of marine traffic from the Lower Fraser to Burrard Inlet and the newly emerging port of Vancouver, Delta's importance declined and it became a rural farming area with limited fishing activity. The opening of Boundary Bay Air Force Station in 1941 significantly increased Ladner's population. Postwar growth was first felt in N Delta as the Vancouver metropolitan area spread S of the Fraser. Completion of the Massey Tunnel under the Fraser in 1959 increased suburban growth. Recent features of Delta's economy include developing industrial areas such as Annacis and Tilbury Is and River Port. Completion of a ferry terminal in 1960 on Roberts Bank in S Delta was followed by construction of the Roberts Bank Superport. The communities of Beach Grove, Boundary B and Tsawwassen offer beaches and other recreational facilities for tourists. Distinctive features and attractions include the recently opened Deas I Regional Park, the Delta Museum and Archives, the Reifel Bird Sanctuary and Roberts Point. The muncipality remains largely a suburban community. ALAN F.J. ARTIBISE

Delta, deposit of sediment accumulating at the mouth of a river. By-products of continental EROSION, deltas form when rivers flow into standing bodies of water (eg, lakes, oceans) rapidly depositing their load of alluvial material (eg, gravel, sand, silt and clay). Deposition results from a loss of transporting capacity caused by deceleration of the current. Deltas vary enormously in scale and complexity, ranging from small lacustrine deltas with lobate shape and tripartite structure (topset, foreset and bottomset) to large, composite birdfoot deltas formed along ocean shorelines. The shape of large deltas, many of which have persisted over long periods of time, is controlled by stream HYDROLOGY, the nature of transported sediment, wave and tidal dynamics, sea-level changes, crustal movements and basin and coastline configuration. Depending on density differences between the sediment-laden river water and the lake or ocean water, the inflowing water may move down the prodelta slope as a gravity underflow (ie, below the surface), spread out over the surface of the standing body of water, or otherwise mix with it as an interflow. The kind of movement has a bearing on the mechanism of growth. Strong tidal currents and high WAVE ENERGY, which tend to disperse sediment, militate against delta formation. Large deltas (eg, Mississippi) are traversed by a network of distributory channels, and delta growth is accompanied by development of a low-lying delta plain associated with different depositional environments, eg, distributary, levee, backswamp and marsh (*see* SWAMP). Superposition of depositional environments over time may produce a favourable habitat for oil and gas accumulation, eg, the MACKENZIE RIVER delta region, NWT. Because of their rich soils, water supply and transportation access, deltas in temperate and tropical climates have played an important role in the history of civilization. However,

FLOOD control, land reclamation and channel maintenance have posed problems for inhabitants. In Canada the Mackenzie and Fraser river deltas are outstanding examples of this RIVER LANDFORM. ALAN V. JOPLING

Delta (1957-66), poetry magazine established in Montréal by Louis DUDEK. Its 26 issues appeared irregularly. Dudek encouraged experimental POETRY and occasionally published essays of his own; these reflected his conviction that poetry should have clear relevance to its time and particularly to social issues. *Delta* strongly projected its editor's personality and spoke especially to those who shared his modernist views.
GEORGE WOODCOCK

Demasduwit, Shendoreth, Waunathoake, or Mary March, one of the last of the BEOTHUKS (b 1796; d at Bay of Exploits, Nfld 8 Jan 1820). An expedition sent to Red Indian Lk in Mar 1819 to recover stolen articles and establish friendly contact with the dwindling Beothuk tribe captured Demasduwit and killed her husband Nonosbawsut. Demasduwit was taken to Twillingate and put in the care of Anglican missionary John Leigh, who recorded from her a Beothuk vocabulary. She was later brought to St John's and an unsuccessful effort made to return her to her own tribe. Demasduwit succumbed to pulmonary consumption and her body was returned to Red Indian Lk in Feb 1820 by a party led by British naval officer David Buchan. In 1828 W.E. CORMACK saw her body, placed side by side with that of Nonosbawsut, in an elevated sepulchre erected by the last survivors of her people. G.M. STORY

Demers, Jérôme, priest, vicar general, architect, teacher (b at St-Nicolas, Qué 1 Aug 1774; d at Québec City, Canada E 17 May 1853). Demers taught literature, philosophy, architecture and science for over 50 years at the Séminaire de Québec and was also superior and bursar of the community. In 1835 he published *Institutiones philosophicae ad usum studiosae juventutis,* his course notes made over 30 years of teaching and the first Canadian PHILOSOPHY textbook. A master in communicating his knowledge and in stimulating appreciation of difficult philosophical problems and discoveries in physics and astronomy, Demers also respected his students and treated them with kindness and understanding. He took charge of building the new churches needed in the diocese and drew up plans for others and for the Collège de Nicolet. His advice was also sought by politicians, such as his former pupil Louis-Joseph PAPINEAU.
CLAUDE GALARNEAU

Demographic Data Collection As civilization has developed, so have systems of counting and record keeping. Periodic population counts have been an essential activity of human societies throughout history, but modern industrialized nations are more dependent upon detailed knowledge of their populations than ever before. Representation in government, generation of revenue, mobilization of manpower and effective economic and social planning require information about population characteristics, eg, numbers, distribution, education, language spoken, labour-force status and occupation, age, sex and marital status.

Historically, demographic data have been acquired by total enumerations (census), which are basically inventories of defined populations within specified areas at particular periods of time; continuing registers which maintain a complete record of individuals throughout their lifetime; registration systems which record births, deaths and marriages by place of occurrence; and sample surveys that are used to collect data on part of the population (which are used to represent the whole). Census and registration systems were used as early as 1000 BC by the Chinese. Sporadic local and national censuses were relatively common prior to the 18th century, and by the mid-19th century most European countries were taking censuses of one kind or another. The first continuing periodic census was established by Sweden in 1749, and in 1787 the new American Constitution established the basis for the regular US decennial census. Canada did not commence its series of regular censuses until 1851 (provided for in the Statistical Act of 1848), but since then has conducted a census every 10 years. In 1886 it established a quinquennial census of the Prairie provinces, which was expanded to include the rest of Canada in 1956.

Early Data Collection in Canada The first modern population census was conducted in N America in 1666 by order of Louis XIV. The names, ages, occupations, conjugal condition and relationship of persons to the head of the family in which they lived were obtained for all persons then residing in NEW FRANCE. This was followed by the first agricultural census in 1667 of cattle, sheep and farmland under cultivation. Over the next 100 years no less than 45 complete or partial censuses were taken in New France, and during the latter part of the French regime as many as 78 complete or partial censuses were taken in ACADIA, Terre-Neuve [Newfoundland], Île Royal [Cape Breton] and Île St-Jean [PEI].

When the British assumed control in 1763, both the quality and quantity of censuses declined. Only 3 (1765, 1784, 1790) were taken of LOWER CANADA before the end of the century. UPPER CANADA had an annual census from 1824 to 1844. They were less frequent in Nova Scotia and New Brunswick, but censuses of Assiniboine and Red River District were taken, on average, every 3 years between 1814 and 1856. The Statistical Act of 1848 provided for the census of 1851-82 and the 1861 census, and reaffirmed the principle of a regular decennial census for Canada. The results of all censuses during more than 2 centuries preceding Confederation were made available in Volume IV of the 1871 Census of Canada.

Vital statistics on baptisms, burials and marriages within the French Catholic population were kept by ecclesiastical authorities from the beginning of the 17th century. The system of keeping vital statistics was extended to British North America and continued until it was replaced by provincial registration systems run by civil authorities.

Data Collection Activities Since Confederation According to the BRITISH NORTH AMERICA ACT, 1867, representation in the federal House of Commons was to be based on population. The Dominion was responsible for censuses and statistics and provision was made for the registration of births and deaths in the provinces. In 1870 an Act provided for the census of 1871. Its provisions were later extended to the territory beyond the original 4 provinces and to any territory that might be added. An Act of 1879, provided for the census of 1881 and the "collection, abstraction, tabulation and publication of vital, agricultural, commercial, criminal and other statistics."

Continuing demand for population data led to the establishment of a permanent Census and Statistics Office in 1905 under the Ministry of Agriculture. Following recommendations of a review commission in 1912, the Office of Dominion Statistician was created in 1915. The Dominion Bureau of Statistics was created and given the mandate in 1918 to "collect, abstract, compile and publish statistical information relative to the commercial, industrial, social, economic and general activities of the people." It was also instructed to "establish a system of coordination with provincial governments in order that statistics collected by provinces could be processed for inclusion in national summaries." The Dominion Bureau of Statistics was renamed STATISTICS CANADA in 1971.

Dominion censuses collected data on births and deaths prior to the 1911 census, but a Dominion-Provincial Conference on Vital Statistics in 1918 shifted the responsibility for collecting vital statistics to the provinces. Since 1921, according to legislation in every province except Québec and Newfoundland, the registration of births, stillbirths, marriages and deaths is compulsory. Québec entered the national registration system in 1926 and Newfoundland in 1949, when it joined Confederation. A nationwide conference in 1920 established nationwide statistics on education and shortly after arrangements were made with the Department of Immigration for securing more comprehensive data on the characteristics of immigrants that would be comparable to data collected during the regular decennial censuses. Canada's WWII mobilization effort and a review of its statistical activities in 1943 led to the establishment of a Research and Development Division and a sampling organization within the bureau. The former compiled a new series of economic statistics that have provided the basic statistical background for financial and fiscal policy in postwar Canada. The work of the sampling group led to a 1948 amendment of the Statistics Act authorizing the collection of statistics using more efficient sampling techniques. LABOUR-FORCE data from the census are now supplemented and updated through monthly labour-force surveys.

Scope of Demographic Data Collection Prior to 1851, censuses collected only names of heads of households and the total number of persons in each household, or in some cases reported only aggregate numbers without names. Most included censuses of agriculture, eg, livestock as well as population. Between 1871 and 1911, census coverage expanded considerably. Census schedules included questions on age, sex, marital status, religion, origin, birthplace, occupation, literacy and an assortment of infirmities. Information was also collected on housing, agricultural products, implements and livestock, as well as on industrial establishments, forest and mineral products, shipping and fisheries, and public institutions, eg, schools and churches.

Since 1921 the decennial census has been primarily a population and agriculture census, but censuses of RETAIL TRADE and WHOLESALE TRADE and services have also been taken since that time. In 1941 a sample survey of housing was included in the census and in 1961 additional questions of fertility, internal migration and income of persons not living on farms were asked of respondents selected in the 20% sample of households for the housing census. In the 1971 census, only one household out of every 3 was asked all of the population and housing questions. In the census of 1981, most persons answered a basic questionnaire of only 12 questions on age, sex, marital status, language and housing. The data on housing expenses, education, ethnic origin, migration, income, employment and occupation were only obtained from every fifth household.

Many of the same questions have been included in every census since Confederation; some have changed over the years while new ones have been added and others dropped in response to altered social and economic conditions. Because of more efficient collecting and processing techniques and the use of sampling, an increase in the number of questions included in the census has been possible. Increasing population and more complex census operations have also contributed dramatically to costs which increased from $250 thousand for the 1891 census to $15 million for the 1971 census. The cost of the 1981 census was $143.4 million (1983 dollars).

Improvements in Data Collecting and Processing Mechanical tabulation was first used in 1911 to increase the efficiency and accuracy of data processing, and unique innovations of tabulating equipment were introduced in both 1931 and 1941. The 1951 census employed "mark-sense" documents and the new IBM 101 (ESM) "electronic statistical machine." This was followed in 1961 by the use of an optical document reader that directly transferred information from the census schedules to magnetic computer tapes for processing by high-speed computers. Through improved computer technology, not only were large amounts of data more ably and speedily processed, but many sources of human error were eliminated.

Errors of coverage, concept, definition, reporting and enumerating are all potential errors of census taking. Experience and tests have shown that the largest source of error has been enumerator fallibility. The role of the enumerator was minimized in 1971 and again in 1981 when mail questionnaires and self-enumeration forms were introduced for most of the population. The estimated undercount for the 1971 census was just under 2% compared to an undercount of between 2.5% and 3.0% in 1961. The accuracy of coverage tends to vary between regions and various subgroups within the population. Young, mobile adults were undercounted by 5%. Divorced persons tend to be more easily missed than persons of other marital statuses, as were those who rented or lived in mobile homes.

Response errors also vary according to the kind and difficulty of the questions asked. In tests the greatest errors have been found in responses to questions about mother tongue, language use, ethnic origin and employment status. Inability to obtain answers varies according to the type of respondent as well as the type of question. Mathematical techniques have been devised for correcting certain types of errors in population aggregates, eg, misstatements of age, techniques for imputing information have been devised for estimating missing data on the basis of known correlations of individual and family characteristics.

In the final analysis, the quality of population data is directly related to the degree of literacy and educational attainment levels of the population, the willingness of individuals to co-operate, their confidence in government, and the efficiency and dedication of those involved in the collection, processing and dissemination of data. The need for demographic and vital statistics is expected to increase. Technological, economic and social change creates new demands for accurate, consistent, comparable and timely statistics. Computer technology will undoubtedly continue to improve the quantity and accessibility of census and vital statistics.

WARREN E. KALBACH

Reading: Warren E. Kalbach and W.W. McVey Jr, *Demographic Bases of Canadian Society* (1979); Statistics Canada, *1981 Census Dictionary*.

Demography, the study of changes affecting human population, is concerned with the overall POPULATION, the immediate phenomena that alter it as a whole (births, deaths, migrations), or changes in its composition (sex, age, marital status, language, religion, education, income, etc). A population is usually defined as a group of individuals living in a particular area. However, studies are often conducted on subpopulations, eg, ethnic groups, the school-age population or the working population. This is the "narrow" concept of demography. Over the past 300 years, demographers have developed an impressive battery of methods for analysing all these phenomena and the ways in which they relate to one another. This set of facts, relationships and methods constitutes the heart of demography. When confined to this core area, demography is virtually the study of renewable resources in the mathematical sense of the term, and can also be applied to animal or plant populations.

Most demographers, however, devote themselves to studies that go beyond this core, eg, by questioning why purely demographic phenomena (fertility, mortality, nuptiality, age structure) vary and what social consequences may result from these variations. The resulting studies cover a large number of disciplines, in particular sociology, economics, history, psychology and biology.

Strictly speaking, demography has no subdisciplines. Two types of demographic studies may, however, be defined: those confined to narrow demography (some of these studies use rather sophisticated mathematical models), and those concerned with relationships between purely demographic and social (or sometimes biological) phenomena.

Evolution of Demography in Canada Demography, a very empirical discipline, draws upon few theoretical models and many statistical findings. These findings were mostly supplied by censuses and vital statistics (ie, statistical information on births, marriages and deaths). In Canada, as in other industrialized countries, these information sources once constituted the very basis of demography (*see* DEMOGRAPHIC DATA COLLECTION).

With the 1871 census, a few elementary analyses of a historical nature were performed, but it was not until 60 years later that the Dominion Bureau of Statistics, the predecessor of Statistics Canada, once again began to conduct demographic analyses of its data. The 1931 census contained 10 very detailed monographs published in 2 volumes. There were 2 census monographs in 1941, none in 1951, 8 in 1961 and about 10 in 1971. The authors were primarily university researchers. Since 1961 more limited studies, always linked to censuses, have been conducted on various aspects of Canada's population. Since 1974 Statistics Canada has from time to time published population forecasts for all of Canada and for every province. Statistics Canada employs many, but certainly not all, demographers. The contributions of a few independent researchers are noteworthy, including *Histoire de la population canadienne-française*, the work of journalist Georges Langlois. During the 1950s several researchers, including 2 Canadian demographers who now work in American universities, Nathan Keyfitz and Norman B. Ryder, began to produce work in demography.

It was not until the 1960s that groups of professors specializing in population research and training students in demography established a few Canadian university programs designed specifically for this discipline. There is only one real department of demography (at Université de Montréal), but at University of Alberta and University of Western Ontario, groups of professors, researchers and students interested mainly in population studies work within departments of sociology. Demography is also taught at a number of other universities, where there is no formal program. Outside of universities, most researchers in demography are employed in departments and certain para-public agencies of the federal and Québec governments.

Scope of Application In examining the work of the 200-300 Canadian demographers, it will be found that "applied" demographic studies relate mainly to the forecasting of housing, health and education needs, and services to the elderly; client forecasts concerning certain major public services; and the development of policies relating to economic planning, birth control, social welfare, manpower, immigration, language and the preservation of cultural minority groups. However, certain studies, eg, population forecasts, which are helpful to all sorts of users, and some research conducted in universities which is oriented toward knowledge of the past and problems of Third World countries, are not as precisely defined.

Institutions In Canada there are 2 demography associations and a national federation. Founded in 1971, the Association des démographes du Québec has a membership of approximately 140 francophone demographers. It publishes the *Cahiers québécois de démographie* 3 times a year. The English counterpart is the Canadian Population Society, fd in 1974. It has approximately 110 members and publishes the annual journal, *Canadian Studies in Population*. The Federation of Canadian Demographers links the 2 associations.

JACQUES HENRIPIN

Dene Nation (prior to 1978 the Indian Brotherhood of the Northwest Territories) is the political organization that represents the Dene, or northern Athapaskan-speaking peoples and their descendants, of the Mackenzie R valley and the barren grounds in the NWT. It has its headquarters in Yellowknife.

Incorporated in 1970, the organization evolved in response to long-standing concerns over the written terms found in the federal government's version of Treaties 8 and 11 signed with the Dene in 1899-1900 and 1921-22 respectively. This concern led, soon after incorporation, to the filing of a caveat (or legal warning to third parties) respecting continued Dene interests in lands described in these treaties. This caveat (the so-called *Paulette* caveat) was challenged, but in 1973 Mr Justice W. Morrow of the Supreme Court of the NWT found that certain native rights continued to exist. Although this judgement was subsequently overturned by the Appeal Court on technical grounds, it led the federal government to accept that further negotiations on the Dene interests were necessary (*see* LAND CLAIMS).

The Dene Nation consistently held that ABORIGINAL RIGHTS, negotiations were essentially over the establishment of a political relationship between the Dene and the Canadian state: a view that was underscored by the wording on self-determination in the Dene Declaration (1975), in the Preamble to a Proposed Agreement-in-Principle (1976), and evidence led at the Berger hearings on a proposed MACKENZIE VALLEY PIPELINE (1975-77). Incompatibility between this position and that of the federal government of the time, to the effect that the nego-

Dene woman stands beside her home and smokehouse (*courtesy Nortext*).

tations were to deal with nonpolitical matters alone, stalled progress on claims until 1981. Since then, progress on resolving the non-political matters respecting the claim has been considerable, although no final agreement has been reached as of 1984.

The Dene Nation is also engaged in programs concerning Dene health, education, community development, legal issues, land and resource development, and communications. The first president of the Dene Nation was Mona Jacobs of Ft Smith, NWT. Subsequently, Roy Daniells, Richard Nerysoo, Georges Erasmus and Stephen Kakfwi have held the senior executive position. *See also* NATIVE PEOPLE, POLITICAL ORGANIZATION AND ACTIVISM. MICHAEL I. ASCH

Reading: R. Fumoleau, *As Long as This Land Shall Last* (1977); M. Watkins, *Dene Nation: The Colony Within* (1977).

Denison, Flora MacDonald, née Merrill, feminist, journalist, busineswoman (b in N Hastings County, Ont 20? Feb 1867; d at Toronto 23 May 1921). Denison, who combined running a successful Toronto dressmaking business with a writing career, was active in the suffrage movement in Toronto from 1906. President of the Canadian Suffrage Assn 1911-14, she was forced to resign because of her support for the English militant suffragettes. Denison was also active in the Canadian Whitmanite movement and as a Theosophist. Her views on religion, marriage, birth control and social class, expressed through her regular 1909-13 column in the *Toronto Sunday World,* were more radical than those of most Canadian suffragists. DEBORAH GORHAM

Denison, Francis Napier, weather forecaster, engineer, scientist (b at Toronto, Canada W 19 Apr 1866; d at Victoria 24 June 1946). An innovative scientist, Denison was known to thousands of Victorians as "our weatherman." Educated at Upper Canada Coll, he joined the Meteorological Service in 1882 and subsequently was appointed assistant observer at the Toronto Observatory (1884). He was transferred to Victoria as weather forecaster/observer in 1898. In Victoria, Denison became one of the best-known meteorological scientists in N America. His many contributions ranged from studies of weather cycles to research on seismic disturbances. Coincidentally, he developed several ingenious instruments to aid in daily weather prediction. He retired with honours in 1936, but even in retirement produced a seismograph, intended for use in mines as a safety device, and also a dust remover for hospital cabinets. J.R. MATHIESON

Denison, George Taylor (3rd), lawyer, magistrate, soldier, author (b at Toronto 31 Aug 1839; d there 6 June 1925). The descendant of LOYALISTS, he enjoyed an international reputation as a military historian and analyst, foreseeing the tactical advantages of rapidly deployed mobilized infantry in modern warfare. As Toronto's senior police magistrate 1877-1921, he meted out justice in such a colourful fashion that his court became a tourist attraction. Commanding the Governor General's Body Guard, a cavalry troop established and supported by his family, he saw action in the 1866 FENIAN raid and during the 1885 NORTH-WEST REBELLION. Denison was an active supporter of the Confederacy's operations in Canada during the American Civil War. Afterward, he was a founder of the CANADA FIRST movement (1871) and party (1874). As the most vocal Canadian spokesman for the idea of imperial unity 1880-1910, Denison portrayed the US as the chief threat to Canadian nationhood, and reasoned that a federation of the British Empire, with Canada as an equal partner, would provide the security, prestige and power essential to national greatness. DAVID P. GAGAN

Reading: David P. Gagan, *The Denison Family of Toronto* (1974).

Denison, Merrill, playwright, journalist, writer, historian (b at Detroit, Mich 23 June 1893; d at San Diego, Calif 13 June 1975). English Canada's first important 20th-century playwright, he emerged from the Canadian Little Theatre movement in the 1920s. His satire *Brothers in Arms,* produced in 1921 at Hart House Theatre, U of T, became one of the most frequently produced English Canadian plays. Denison's literary reputation as a playwright of realistic dramas and satirical comedies is largely based on his 1923 anthology *The Unheroic North,* which contains his most important naturalistic social problem play, *Marsh Hay,* not produced until 1974. *Henry Hudson and Other Plays* (1931) was the first Canadian radio play anthology published. Denison also authored the novel *Klondike Mike* (1943) and corporate histories for Massey-Harris, Molson's, Ontario Hydro and the Bank of Montreal. ANTON WAGNER

Dennis, Agnes, née Miller, teacher, feminist (b at Truro, NS 11 Apr 1859; d at Halifax 21 Apr 1947). Dennis succeeded Edith ARCHIBALD as president of the VICTORIAN ORDER OF NURSES, 1901-46, and of the Halifax Council of Women 1906-20. She mobilized women in WWI for the RED CROSS, of which she was provincial president 1914-20. They produced medical supplies, organized hospitals, looked after prisoners of war overseas, and sought to enter the jobs left by soldiers recruited for overseas service. Dennis also helped co-ordinate relief efforts for victims of the 1917 HALIFAX EXPLOSION. Her determined but self-effacing style of leadership proved highly effective in building and winning recognition for women's organizations. On the death of her husband, Senator William Dennis, in 1920, she became president of the Halifax *Herald* Ltd. She had 10 children. ERNIE FORBES

Denny, Sir Cecil Edward, 6th baronet of Tralee Castle, police officer, Indian agent, author (b in Hampshire, Eng 14 Dec 1850; d at Edmonton 24 Aug 1928). Denny is best known as the author of 2 colourful accounts of life with the NWMP — *The Riders of the Plains: A Reminiscence of the Early and Exciting Days in the North West* (1905) and *The Law Marches West* (1939). He joined the force in 1874 and served principally in the Whoop Up country. Although able, he was undisciplined, and he resigned following a scandal involving a woman. He served as Indian agent at FT WALSH and in Treaty 7, but resigned from the latter position following disputes with his superiors. He served as a special Indian agent during the NORTH-WEST REBELLION. Subsequently, he ranched and worked as police scout, packer, guide and fire ranger until 1922 when he was appointed archivist of Alberta. A.B. MCCULLOUGH

Denonville, Jacques-René de Brisay, Marquis de, governor general of New France, 1685-89 (b at Denonville, France 10 Dec 1637; d there 22 Sept 1710). He arrived at Québec 1 Aug 1685 at a dangerous point in the colony's conflict with the IROQUOIS and English. Taking the initiative, he sent de TROYES overland to attack English posts on James Bay (1686), and in 1687 led a destructive foray against the Seneca. The colony remained vulnerable, and the Iroquois launched a major attack on LACHINE 5 Aug 1689, forcing Denonville to abandon FT FRONTENAC. Denonville was deeply concerned about social and health conditions in the colony, attempted to curb abuses in the fur trade, and established a navigation school at Québec to train pilots. He sailed from Québec Nov 1689. JAMES MARSH

Dent, John Charles, journalist, historian (b at Kendal, Eng 8 Nov 1841; d at Toronto 27 Sept 1888). After a newspaper career abroad and in Toronto he became a free-lance writer. His most successful book was the illustrated 4-vol *Canadian Portrait Gallery* (1880-81); he wrote 185 of its 204 sketches. In *The Last Forty Years: Canada since the Union of 1841* (2 vols, 1881) and the more partisan *Story of the Upper Canadian Rebellion* (2 vols, 1885) he sided with moderate reformers. John King, W.L. MACKENZIE's son-in-law, attacked him in *The Other Side of the "Story"* (1886). Later, however, Dent thought that RESPONSIBLE GOVERNMENT had made Canadian politics corrupt. A convinced free trader and lifelong admirer of John Bright, he insisted on economy and probity in government. In addition to history he wrote fiction, much of which was published posthumously. S.R. MEALING

Dentistry is the art of the treatment of teeth and their supporting tissues. The Egyptians, in their papyri dating back to 3500 BC, described dental and gingival ("of the gums") maladies and their management, and evidence of teeth restoration has been found in Egyptian mummies. Documents from the Hebrews, Chinese, Greeks and Romans all refer to aspects of dentistry. In more recent times, the Frenchman Pierre Fauchard (1678-1761) author of the first classic treatise on dentistry, *Le Chirurgien dentiste* (1728), has been recognized as the founder of modern scientific dentistry. He was responsible for the separation of the science and art of dentistry from general medicine and surgery.

In N America, physicians and barber surgeons accompanied colonists to America. Although several people advertised that they could extract and replace teeth, they were not trained dentists. They included an ivory turner and umbrella maker, a wigmaker and hairdresser, and Paul Revere, a silversmith. During this colonial period dentistry in N America lagged far behind the advances being made in Europe. In the early 1800s "dentists" with some skills acquired through apprenticeship immigrated to Canada from the US. They included a Mr Hume, who advertised his profession in Halifax in the *Acadian Reporter* in 1814; and a Mr L.S. Parmly, who practised in Montréal in 1815 and published the first Canadian book on dentistry, *The Summum Bonum,* and who called himself a dentist and "medical electrician."

On 3 Jan 1867, 9 dentists met in Toronto to form the Ontario Dental Association, and in 1868 the Royal College of Dental Surgeons of Ontario was established. Also in that year, *The Canada Journal of Dental Science* began publication. After several attempts from 1867 to 1870 to establish a school, the first dental college in Canada was founded, in Toronto, in 1875 by the Royal College of Dental Surgeons of Ontario; it consisted of 2 full-time staff, 5 part-time staff and 11 students. Over the next 100 years dental schools were incorporated into Canadian universities. In 1888 the Royal College of Dental Surgeons of Ontario became affiliated with University of Toronto and the university agreed to confer the degree of Doctor of Dental Surgery upon students completing the prescribed course of study. The first examination was held after 4 months instruction, in 1889; 25 candidates were successful. These were the first doctorate degrees conferred on dental graduates outside the US.

McGill U Dental School dates from 1905, but its origins can be traced to 1892 when the Association of Dental Surgeons of the Province of Québec was founded in Montréal. A French-speaking school was established at Université de Montréal in 1905. A fourth dental school was opened in 1908 as part of Dalhousie U. In western Canada, the first dental school was not established until 1923, when a 4-year program was introduced at U of Alberta; it was followed by one at U of Manitoba (1958) and at UBC (1964). Three further dental schools were introduced during the 1960s and 1970s: at U of Western Ontario (1966), U of Saskatchewan (1968), and Laval (1971). Some 11 500 dentists were practising in Canada in 1981.

During the 20th century, dentistry evolved from a profession based on empirical methods, through one based on mechanics, to one based on sound research methodology supported by both basic science and clinical research. In 1983, at the annual meeting of the International Association of Dental Research, over 1200 research presentations were given.

Specialization in dentistry in N America began during the early 20th century. W.G. Beers of Montréal (1843-1900) confined his practice to exodontia (oral surgery) and is considered to be the first specialist in dentistry in Canada. The main specialties that subsequently developed were exodontia, periodontia and orthodontia. Several societies and graduate programs related to specializations were established; after many controversial years the Royal College of Dentists of Canada was created in 1964 by federal statute to promote high standards of specialization, to determine qualifications, to establish training programs in Canadian dental schools, and to provide the recognition and designation of dentists who possessed special qualifications. This legislation was supported by all the provincial dental licensing boards, which are responsible for the licensing of dentists and the practice of dentistry in each province.

With the development of the profession of dentistry, it was proposed that a profession of auxiliary dental workers might be established, but the issue was hotly debated. In 1947 the Ontario laws governing dentistry were amended to cover dental hygienists. The first Canadian dental training school for dental hygienists was opened at the Toronto dental school in 1951, and by the mid-1960s most schools and provinces offered similar training programs. Dental hygienists are employed in private dental offices and dental public-health programs, and recently their duties have been extended in several provinces. Saskatchewan has instituted a program, based on the New Zealand Dental Nurse system, whereby certain operative procedures on children can be undertaken.

Dental mechanics, responsible for the manufacture of dental appliances for dentists, have been allowed in some provinces to work directly with the public to provide dentures. Dental assistants work closely with dentists in the chairside provision of dental care to patients.

Canada has a lower percentage of women dentists than many other countries. The first Canadian woman to graduate from a dental college was Mrs Caroline Louisa Josephine Wells, who completed her training at the Royal College of Dental Surgeons of Ontario in 1893.

Dental associations have been established in each province, but the national spokesman is the Canadian Dental Association. One of the association's objectives has been to ensure that dentistry is considered an autonomous healing art, ie, not part of medicine and therefore not covered by medicare programs. In many countries dental care falls under government health-care programs, but in Canada only selected groups, eg, children and the elderly, have benefitted from subsidization for dental expenses, and then only in some provinces.

J.A. Hargreaves

Reading: D.W. Gullett, *A History of Dentistry in Canada* (1971).

Denys, Nicolas, trader, colonial promoter (b at Tours, France 1598; d 1688). A young La Rochelle merchant, Denys sailed for Acadia in 1632 with Isaac de RAZILLY, and spent the next 40 years trying to develop the colony. Many of his ventures were unsuccessful, and he suffered heavy losses from such commercial failures as his fishing establishments at Port Rossignol (Liverpool, NS) in the 1630s and on Cape Breton I in the 1650s. Other enterprises provoked conflicts with rival traders and he made a powerful enemy of colonial governor Charles de MENOU D'AULNAY. In 1653 he acquired territory on the Gulf of St Lawrence from Canso to the Gaspé, including Cape Breton and the other gulf islands, with rights to land and government. Plans to bring settlers were never fulfilled, but he continued trading. About 1670, leaving his headquarters at Nipisiguit (Bathurst, NB) to his son Richard, Denys returned to France and turned to writing. His *Description and Natural History of the Coasts of North America* (1672; repr, ed W.F. Ganong, 1908) is a vivid account of Acadia and a reminder that Denys, despite many reverses, promoted French colonial development there for 4 decades.

John G. Reid

Deputy Minister, generally an officer of the public service appointed as managerial and administrative head of a department or ministry of the federal or provincial governments. A deputy minister is the official primarily responsible for the co-ordination and flow of policy and program advice and technical analysis to the minister or CABINET and for management of the department and program implementation. The appointment of deputy ministers, based in statute law and customary practice, is federally the prime minister's responsibility and provincially that of the premier, although at the provincial level ministers may exercise greater influence in the selection. Because tradition and convention have established that they should be politically nonpartisan in their work, deputy ministers are entitled to continue in office even with a change of government, although in recent years there have been demands for the politicization of such ORDER-IN-COUNCIL appointees, after the American model.

Thomas K. Shoyama

Derick, Carrie Matilda, natural scientist (b at Clarenceville, Qué 14 Jan 1862; d at Montréal 10 Nov 1941). A brilliant student at McGill (BA 1890, MA 1896), she also studied at Harvard, the Marine Biological Laboratory at Woods Hole, Mass, the Royal Coll of Science in London and University of Bonn, Germany. She was appointed demonstrator in BOTANY at McGill in 1891 — first woman on McGill's academic staff; in 1912 she became professor of morphological botany — the first woman in Canada to be made a full professor. Her courses introduced the teaching of GENETICS at McGill. A social activist, she championed such causes as compulsory school attendance, care for abnormal children, industrial and technical education, women's rights and birth control.

Margaret Gillett

Reading: Margaret Gillett, *We Walked Very Warily: a History of Women at McGill* (1981).

Carrie Matilda Derick, the first woman in Canada to be made a full professor (*courtesy Margaret Gillet*).

Dernière Heure et la première, La (1973) a theoretical essay by Pierre VADEBONCOEUR arguing that the French Canadian people have paradoxically been excluded from history in their successful pursuit of "la survivance": entrenched language rights and a thriving culture are no substitute for genuine political power, the power of sovereignty. Focusing on the liberal philosophy of FEDERALISM articulated by the CITÉ LIBRE group in the 1950s and 1960s, Vadeboncoeur claims that Pierre TRUDEAU's view of Québec nationalism was merely an extension of traditional 19th-century nationalism, a palliative measure. According to Vadeboncoeur, only the neo-nationalism of the sovereignty movement, implicitly socialist, addresses the cultural and economic deprivation of the inner exile, a colonized being. "Intuitively" substituting a vision of universally recognized self-determination for the technocrat's "sterile" obsession with statistics, Vadeboncoeur aims to delineate the points of continuity and departure between traditional and radical nationalism. Vadeboncoeur's cultural depth, clarity of style and intellectual sophistication preclude any simplistic summary of his ideas and loyalties.

Michèle Lacombe

Des Groseilliers, Médard Chouart, explorer, fur trader (bap at Charly-sur-Marne, France 31 July 1618; d at New France 1696?). A man of courage who valued personal freedom and initiative, Des Groseilliers opened Lks Michigan and Superior to the fur trade and Jesuit missionaries. Resentful of perceived injustices at the hands of French officials, he joined the English and with Pierre-Esprit RADISSON helped found the HUDSON'S BAY CO. Des Groseilliers probably came to Canada in 1641. In 1645-46 he worked for the Jesuits at Ste Marie in Huronia. The IROQUOIS WARS (1648-53) cut the St Lawrence colonies off from their fur suppliers, but a peace made with the Iroquois early in 1654 and the arrival of a contingent of Ottawa-Huron gave Des Groseilliers the opportunity to explore W of Lk Huron. He left 6 Aug 1654 and returned Aug 1656 with 250 natives in 50 canoes from the Green Bay (Wis) area and the southwestern shore of Lk Superior, bearing a fortune in furs. During this trip he learned of the rich fur country N and NW of Lk Superior which, he was told, was only 7 days by canoe from Hudson Bay. In Aug 1659 Des Groseilliers, this time accompanied by his brother-in-law Radisson, undertook a second voyage to the S shore of Lk Superior to Chequamegon, Mille Lacs area of Wisconsin, and in the spring of 1660, to the N shore of Lk Superior near Pigeon R. Upon their return to Trois-Rivières on 24 Aug 1660, with 60 canoes and another fortune in furs, they were arrested for illegal trading and their furs confiscated. Further frustrations with French officials took the pair to Boston in 1662 to solicit English help in a venture directly to Hudson Bay.

After an abortive New England expedition Des Groseilliers was persuaded to take his plans to England (1665). Three years later, a successful voyage in the NONSUCH led to the founding of the HBC on 2 May 1670. Over the next 5 years he was busy setting up company posts on James Bay. Persuaded by Father Albanel to rejoin the French, he returned to Canada in 1676. In 1682 he entered the COMPAGNIE DU NORD and built a French post at the mouth of the Hayes R. English complaints of the destruction of their posts by Des Groseilliers and his companions as well as evasion of the French tax on furs again led him into trouble. After pleading his case in Paris (1684) he returned to New France and seems to have retired.

C.E. Heidenreich

Des Sauvages, ou, Voyage de Samuel Champlain (1603) records CHAMPLAIN's first voyage to Canada as François Gravé Du Pont's guest aboard *La Bonne Renommée,* searching for the

NORTHWEST PASSAGE. The 1603 summer voyage took them up the St Lawrence to the present location of Montréal; Champlain describes the Gaspé coast, the Saguenay R and the Lachine Rapids. Cast as a diary, his first book of travels relates conversations with MICMAC and MONTAGNAIS, and includes useful impressions of the climate and topography. Gravé du Pont took a Micmac family back to France, and Champlain contributed to the European fascination with the Indian by recounting Indian legends and customs and telling of his attempt to convert natives to Christianity. *Des Sauvages* is included in the first Canadian edition of Champlain's complete works (*Oeuvres de Champlain*, 6 vols, 1870) and the standard CHAMPLAIN SOCIETY edition (1922-35). A facsimile of *Des Sauvages* appeared in 1978. MICHÈLE LACOMBE

Desbarats, Georges-Édouard, publisher, inventor of halftone photographic printing (b at Québec City 5 Apr 1838; d at Ottawa 18 Feb 1893). Desbarats briefly succeeded his father (d 1864) as queen's printer in Ottawa (a post held by his family since 1799), but resigned in 1869 to found the weekly *Canadian Illustrated News*. This was the first periodical in the world to carry halftone photographs, rather than engravings prepared by artists, using a process invented by Desbarats and his engraver, William Leggo. The two went to New York in 1873 to found the *Daily Graphic*, the first daily paper to use photographic illustrations. *Canadian Illustrated News* appeared weekly 1869-83. Other Canadian periodicals created by Desbarats included the *Dominion Illustrated*, *Canadian Patent Office Record* and *Mechanic's Magazine*. DONALD J.C. PHILLIPSON

DesBarres, Joseph Frederick Wallet, military engineer, surveyor, governor of Cape Breton and of PEI (b probably at Basle, Switz Nov 1722; d at Halifax 27 Oct 1824). At age 31 he emigrated to Britain and attended the Royal Military Coll, Woolwich. In 1756 he was posted to N America as a lieutenant in the Royal American Regiment and saw action at LOUISBOURG in 1758, Québec in 1759 and in the expedition against the French at St John's, Nfld, in 1762. His skill in surveying and mapping had been noted, and in 1763 he was employed by the Admiralty to prepare charts of the coastline and offshore waters of NS, at the same time James COOK was working in Newfoundland and Samuel HOLLAND in the Gulf of St Lawrence and New England. In 1777 DesBarres published the first version of his navigational atlas, *Atlantic Neptune*, containing his charts and sketches from the previous 10 years along with some adaptations of Holland's work. The final version was published in 1781. In 1784, DesBarres embarked on a new career when he was appointed first lieutenant-governor of Cape Breton, and in 1785 he laid out the settlement that would become SYDNEY. He left the island in 1787. In May 1804 he became governor of PEI. He was finally recalled at age 90.

DesBarres possessed an abrasive personality. He was impatient and quarrelsome, but no one has ever denied his splendid talents and energy. L.M. SEBERT

Reading: G.N.D. Evans, *Uncommon Obdurate: The Several Public Careers of J.F.W. DesBarres* (1969).

Deschamps, Yvon, actor, comedian (b at Montréal 1935). He left school early and worked at Radio-Canada as a messenger. He took private drama lessons from several individuals, including Paul Buissonneau, who offered him work in 1959 as an actor at the Roulotte, hired him as an assistant in 1963 and cofounded the Théâtre de Quat'sous with him in 1964. Deschamps played his first roles at the Théâtre universitaire canadien with Paul Hébert in 1958-59. In 1959 he also made his first TV appearançe, on CBC. He appeared at La Poudrière and L'Égrégore in 1960 and, as of 1961, at Claude LÉVEILLÉE concerts. He appeared in his first revues in 1963 and in his first film, *Délivrez-nous du mal*, in 1964. But Deschamps is above all known for his satirical, political monologues, which he began to perform in 1967 in restaurants and clubs like the Boîte à Clémence. He became famous especially after his participation in *L'Osstidcho*, a revue that also brought Louise Forestier and Robert CHARLEBOIS into the limelight. Some of Deschamps's monologue performances have played to full houses for months at a time in Montréal's largest concert halls. ANDRÉ G. BOURASSA

Yvon Deschamps is famous for his satirical, political monologues (*courtesy Canapress*).

Deserontyon, John, "Captain John," Mohawk chief (b in the Mohawk Valley, NY 1740s; d at Bay of Quinte, Upper Canada 7 Jan 1811). As a young man Deserontyon aided the British in the SEVEN YEARS' WAR and later during the 1763 PONTIAC uprising. When the American Revolution broke out, by which time he had become a chief, he again sided with his old allies. With Joseph BRANT he participated in the Battle of Oriskany (1777), and on his own and organized raids into enemy territory. After the American victory Deserontyon and Brant were angered to learn that the 1783 peace treaty made no provision for restoration of the Mohawks' ancestral lands in NY, and they heatedly made their position known to Gov HALDIMAND in Montréal. Eventually they were obliged to accept the situation and settled their followers on lands granted elsewhere. Brant opted for a "retreat" in the Grand R valley and urged Deserontyon to join him there in a unified community, but Deserontyon preferred a Bay of Quinte site far removed from the victorious "Yankees," and where he could manage his own affairs. With government assistance Deserontyon built a church and a schoolhouse for his followers, most of whom were Christians. At times, his leadership proved controversial, and quarrels and factionalism disrupted the closing years of his life. The modern town of Deseronto, Ont, was named for him. CHARLES M. JOHNSTON

Desert, region in which evaporation greatly exceeds precipitation, resulting in a water deficiency which only a few life forms can endure. Precipitation is under 200 mm annually, coming at very irregular intervals. Deserts cover 20% of the Earth's surface. Tropical deserts occur between 15° and 35° N and S latitudes in regions in which dry air masses allow intense solar radiation to reach the ground surface. Mid-latitude deserts are located in the centres of large continental masses, far beyond the reach of moisture-bearing oceanic air masses. Desert landforms are diverse, consisting of mountains and plains. The mountains have characteristic, angular forms and end abruptly at the edge of plains, where they are replaced by gently inclined, eroded bedrock surfaces (pediments). Desert regions have internal drainage, where runoff waters are directly evaporated. Ephemeral streams carry the runoff in channels called *wadis* (N Africa) or *arroyos* (western US). The centre of desert basins may be occupied by a dry, flat area (playa) which occasionally receives runoff carrying fine silts and clays. Rarely, a playa lake may form, lasting only a few days. Relatively small portions of desert regions (20%) are occupied by sand dunes, which may be transverse, barchane, longitudinal (seif), star or dome shaped (*see* AEOLIAN LANDFORMS). Canada has no true deserts, only regions that exhibit some desertlike features, eg, the sandy expanse S of Lk Athabasca, which lies within a forested region with a humid CLIMATE. It formed on raised, coarse-grained, glacial deltaic deposits which retain insufficient surface moisture to allow vegetation to become established. Smaller areas in the Canadian Arctic, lacking vegetation and being exposed to strong winds, exhibit a desert-like appearance. In the driest parts of the prairies (eg, N and S of the CYPRESS HILLS) and the most southerly parts of the Fraser, Thompson, Nicola, Similkameen, Okanagan and Kootenay river valleys, precipitation can be as low as 250-300 mm and vegetation is of the semiarid type (eg, sagebrush, rabbitbrush). P.P. DAVID

Design, *see* FASHION DESIGN; GRAPHIC DESIGN; INDUSTRIAL DESIGN; INTERIOR DESIGN; LANDSCAPE ARCHITECTURE; PRINT INDUSTRY; STAGE AND COSTUME DESIGN; URBAN DESIGN.

Desjardins, Alphonse, journalist, Parliamentary reporter, founder of the CAISSE POPULAIRE (b at Lévis, Canada E Nov 1854; d there 31 Oct 1920). Desjardins was 46 and French-language reporter for Hansard when on 6 Dec 1900 he founded the first Caisse populaire, or people's bank, in Lévis. In promoting the doctrine of cooperation, Desjardins's goals were to fight usury, improve the lot of the working classes, bring economic liberation to French Canadians and slow their exodus to the US. The Caisse populaire was the fruit of 3 years' study, discussion and assiduous correspondence with the great advocates of mutualism and economic cooperation in Québec and Europe. His was an original synthesis, a true "plum pudding" composed of foreign elements but adapted to local conditions. Desjardins was responsible for everything. He ran the Caisse in Lévis, saw to the establishment of 205 other Caisses in Québec, the rest of Canada and the US and, with solid support from the clergy, assured their success.

After 1916, illness forced him to abandon the taxing work of promotion and expansion. He devoted the last 4 years of his life to considering how to protect and guarantee the survival of his life's work. Death prevented him from realizing his plans for a federation of Caisse populaire centrale. His success won Desjardins an international reputation. Honours and requests poured in from all over Europe, the US, Latin America and even from New Zealand. He acknowledged that the custom, which caught on after 1913, of calling the new institutions "Caisses populaires Dejardins" gave him the most pleasure of all. YVES ROBY

Deskaheh, also known as **Levi General,** Cayuga chief and speaker of the Six Nations Hereditary Council (b on the Six Nations Reserve near Brantford, Ont 1873; d at the Tuscarora Reservation, NY 25 June 1925). A member of the Longhouse religion, Deskaheh insisted that the Six Nations retain their languages and distinctive culture. When the Canadian government tried in 1923 to unseat the Six Nations Hereditary Council and to institute an elected one, Deskaheh acted immediately. He worked to obtain international recognition of the Six Nations as a sovereign Indian nation ruled by a hereditary council of chiefs. Travelling on a passport issued by the Council he went to the League of Nations in Geneva, Switz. But the League's secretariat refused to allow him to address the assembly, arguing that Canada had jurisdiction over the Six Nations. Exhausted, Deskaheh became ill shortly after returning to N America and died from pneumonia. Six months before his death the Canadian government ended the Confederacy's administrative functions on the Reserve and organized a vote for an elected council. Both councils exist in 1984, but only the elected body is recognized by the state. DONALD B. SMITH

Deslongchamps, Pierre, chemist, educator (b at St-Lin, Qué 8 May 1938). He is an international leader in the field of organic synthesis and his work on the stereo-electronic effects operative in many organic processes is widely acclaimed. After studies at Université de Montréal (BSc 1959) and UNB (PhD 1964), he became assistant professor at U de M in 1966 and the next year moved to U de Sherbrooke, where he was promoted professor of chemistry in 1972. Well-spoken in both national languages, he is a polished and popular lecturer and a stimulating teacher. His synthesis of the complex insecticide ryanodine stands as a landmark achievement in the field of organic synthesis. He was elected to the Royal Society of Canada in 1974 and in the same year awarded the E.W.R. STEACIE prize by the National Research Council. Twice honoured by the Assn canadienne-française pour l'avancement des sciences (Médaille Vincent, Médaille Pariseau), he won the Merck, Sharp and Dohme Award of the Chemical Institute of Canada in 1976. In 1983 he was elected to the Royal Soc (London). W.A. AYER

Desmarais, Paul, financier (b at Sudbury, Ont 4 Jan 1927). After studying at U of O and McGill, Desmarais worked for Courtois, Fredette et Cie, a Montréal accounting firm, 1945-51; he then returned to Sudbury to run his father's bus company. In 1961 he gained control of Provincial Transport, a sizable passenger-transport company. In 1965 he bought his first conglomerate, Trans-Canada Corp Fund, through which he gained control of the major French-language newspaper *La Presse* (Montréal), the major francophone radio station CKAC, a large assurance company (Imperial Life, Toronto) and several other daily and weekly newspapers. In 1968 he took control of Power Corp of Canada; one of the major conglomerates in Canada, Power Corp now includes the principal mutual fund in Canada (Investors Group), one of the largest trust funds (Montreal Trust), the fourth-largest paper company in the country (Consolidated-Bathurst), the second-largest life-assurance company (Great-West Life, Winnipeg) and several other Canadian and European firms. In 1983 Desmarais sat on the boards of 18 companies other than Power Corp. JORGE NIOSI

Desmarteau, Étienne, strongman (b at Boucherville, Qué 4 Feb 1873; d at Montréal 29 Oct 1905). A Montréal policeman, Desmarteau excelled in tug-of-war and weight-throwing events and was the first Canadian to win an Olympic gold medal. He won the world heavyweight and the junior world hammer-throwing championships in 1902, captured the gold medal in the 56-lb throw at the 1904 St Louis Olympics and set 2 56-lb world records in 1905, but died of typhoid fever later that year. In 1972, Montréal dedicated a park to his memory. JEAN R. DUPERREAULT

DesRochers, Alfred, journalist, translator, poet, critic (b at Saint-Elie d'Orford, Qué 5 Aug 1901; d at Montréal 12 Oct 1978). As a poet and critic DesRochers was an important figure in Québec literature between the wars. *L'Offrande aux vierges folles* (1928) and, in particular, *À l'ombre de l'Orford* (1929, Prix David 1932) reveal an innovative poet who went beyond the regionalism and land-based themes of his time. Inspired by French romanticism and the vastness of N America, DesRochers adopted a realistic viewpoint as well as the verse and structures of traditional versification. *Paragraphes* (1931) is the work of an original critic who greatly influenced 1930s poets. Two other collections of his poetry appeared in the 1960s, *Le Retour de Titus* (1963) and *Elégies pour l'épouse en-allée* (1967). In *Oeuvres poétiques* (1977), Romain Légaré included with DesRochers's published collections important poems that had appeared in magazines and newspapers. RICHARD GIGUÈRE

Desrosiers, Léo-Paul, writer, civil servant (b at Berthier-en-Haut, Qué 11 Apr 1896; d at Montréal 20 Apr 1967). Desrosiers, who lifted the genre of historical novel to a new level, is the least appreciated and most retiring writer of his generation. He came from a peasant family whose ancestors were among the first colonists of the St Lawrence Valley. After classical studies at the Séminaire de Joliette, he was influenced by the nationalism of Henri BOURASSA and Lionel GROULX. He was successively parliamentary correspondent in Ottawa for Le DEVOIR, editor of *Hansard* and chief librarian of the Montréal Municipal Library; he was a member of the Société des dix, the Royal Society of Canada and the Académie canadienne-française. Desrosiers's interest in history inspired biographies as well as his best novels. His greatest contribution to literature was without doubt *Les Engagés du Grand Portage* (1938), set in the fur-trade years of the early 19th century. His *L'Ampoule d'or* (1951), deserves rereading for the sobriety and poetry of its narration.
RÉJEAN BEAUDOIN

Desrosiers, Robert Guy, dancer, choreographer, director (b at Montréal 10 Oct 1953). A brilliant dancer in his own right, Desrosiers has assumed national prominence as a choreographer of startling imagination and originality. He graduated from the NATIONAL BALLET SCHOOL in 1971 and danced briefly with the NATIONAL BALLET OF CANADA before continuing to dance and train in France, England and the US. He was never able to settle long in any one company, but instead began to develop his own choreographic ideas which found full expression in the creation of his own Robert Desrosiers Dance Co in 1980. MICHAEL CRABB

Dessailliant, *dit* **Richeterre, Michel,** painter (fl 1701-23). A victim of France's mercantile policy, he was not able to settle permanently in New France and practise his art. This fact is regrettable since the only work that may be attributed to him with certainty, the portrait of Mère Louise Soumane, *dite* de Saint-August (1708), shows great skill and sensitivity. Archival documents record that he did other portraits, but there is no proof that he painted the ex-votos now in Ste-Anne-de-Beaupré that are attributed to him. FRANÇOIS-MARC GAGNON

Dessane, Antoine, organist, pianist, cellist, teacher, composer (b at Forcalquier, near Aix-en-Provence, France 10 Dec 1826; d at Québec City 8 June 1873). Founder of the choral Société musicale Ste-Cécile (1869), Antoine Dessane was an active member of several Québec music clubs. He received his musical education from his older brother and his father until he enrolled in the Paris Conservatory at age 10. Life was difficult for artists after the 1848 Revolution, and Dessane accepted a position as organist at Notre-Dame Basilica in Québec C (1849-60). He was subsequently an organist in New York, but returned to Québec C in 1869, this time to a position at St-Roch Church. Many of his works — over 50 sacred and secular pieces — reflect his adopted country; they include *La Québecoise* and *Souvenir de Kamouraska*. HÉLÈNE PLOUFFE

Désy, Jean, diplomat (b at Montréal 8 Jan 1893; d at Paris, France 19 Dec 1960). Educated at Laval and the Sorbonne, the highly intelligent Désy was called to the Québec bar in 1915 and taught history and law at U de M, 1919-25. He joined the Dept of External Affairs in 1925, the year it came under the direction of O.D. SKELTON. Along with Laurent Beaudry and Pierre Dupuy, he was one of the pioneering Francophones in the department; like Dupuy, he avoided Ottawa, preferring to serve abroad. As minister to Belgium and the Netherlands, 1939-40, Désy was among the first career diplomats to head a Canadian post in a foreign country. Ambassadorships in Brazil, Italy and finally France followed. NORMAN HILLMER

Detroit River, 52 km long, flows S from Lk ST CLAIR to the W end of Lake ERIE, forming part of the boundary between Ontario and Michigan. Detroit, Mich, and WINDSOR, Ont, dominate its shores. Part of the ST LAWRENCE SEAWAY, it is heavily used by commercial traffic. The largest islands are Michigan's Belle I, a park, and Grosse I, site of an American naval base, and Ontario's Fighting I. The name comes from the French for strait or narrows. DANIEL FRANCIS

Deutsch, John James, educator, public servant (b at Quinton, Sask 26 Feb 1911; d at Kingston, Ont 18 Mar 1976). He was educated at Queen's (B Com), and spent over half his life in the federal public service: as a member of the research department of the Bank of Canada 1936-42 although often on loan to government departments and especially the Rowell-Sirois Royal Commission; as special assistant in External Affairs 1942-44; as director of the International Economic Relations Division of the Dept of Finance 1946-53; as secretary of the Treasury Board 1954-56; and finally, as first chairman of the Economic Council of Canada 1963-6. In addition, he was a member of several other royal commissions, commissions of inquiry and advisory commissions or committees. As an educator, he was head of the dept of economics at UBC 1956-59; vice-principal administration and professor of economics at Queen's, 1959-63; principal designate 1967 and principal and vice-chancellor of Queen's, 1968-74; professor of economics, Queen's 1967 to his death. He was co-author or coeditor of 3 books and author of many articles. His incisiveness of mind and his warm personality were the source of his great achievements as public servant and educator. A companion of the Order of Canada he received 17 honorary degrees. M.C. URQUHART

Deux Nations ("two nations"), a theory developed in Québec when the 1960 election of the LESAGE government led to a new, secular, provincial nationalism (*see* QUIET REVOLUTION). Québec politicians began to speak of Québec as a "nation." During the 1968 federal election campaign, the Progressive Conservative Party, on the advice of Québec businessman Marcel Faribault, hesitantly embraced the concept. To Conservative leader Robert STANFIELD, "nation" had meaning only in "a sociological sense," but to Faribault and others the meaning was much broader. The policy won few votes for the Conservatives, and afterwards "deux nations" had meaning only for academics and historians.
JOHN ENGLISH

Development Industry Developers build and own all types of urban property, from high-rise apartments to industrial buildings and shopping centres. The typical developer organizes new projects, finds a site, obtains financing and city-hall approvals, organizes architects, engineers and contractors to build the building, and locates tenants or buyers. Projects such as suburban houses are built to sell. Others are built to own, with tenants' rents covering expenses and slowly paying off the mortgage.

Though most developers think of themselves as individualists opposed to government regulation, the land-development industry is in fact the creation of postwar industrial development policy. Ottawa set out to foster large construction companies that would provide employment while needed housing and other facilities were being built. A crown corporation, CANADA MORTGAGE AND HOUSING CORPORATION, was established to provide the necessary support. Ottawa helped ensure the availability of the necessary investment capital through financial institutions and investors, and provided the industry with special tax concessions so that developers paid little or no tax on their profits.

After 1945 entrepreneurs in every city saw opportunities in suburban house-building. Some entrepreneurs realized that land development was more profitable than construction. In the 1950s other entrepreneurs saw the potential of high-rise apartments. By the 1960s and 1970s developers were producing many commercial and retail projects along with housing.

The postwar city the developers built was a radical departure from the past. Five building types are particularly important: high-rise apartments, towering 15, 20 or 25 storeys above their surroundings in the central city and in the suburbs; new suburbs, featuring a new style of house on a larger lot, on streets laid out in a circular pattern rather than on the rectangular grid (the prototype was Don Mills, built next to Toronto in the 1950s by industrialist-promoter E.P. TAYLOR); suburban industrial parks, with single-storey buildings on large lots serviced by road rather than rail; downtown office-commercial complexes, combining huge amounts of office space with some shopping (the prototype was Montréal's PLACE VILLE MARIE, built by US developer William Zeckendorf in the 1950s, *see* URBAN DESIGN); shopping centres, where a developer-owner provides all the retail facilities for a community under one roof, renting space mainly to chain retailers (the prototype was Vancouver's Park Royal, built by the Guinness brewing family).

Developers of these projects are often embroiled in controversy. Local citizen groups may resist because of expected harmful results. In the early 1970s developers were criticized for being too powerful. Citizen-oriented politicians challenged, often successfully, pro-developer aldermen. In the mid-1970s the industry was criticized for the rapidly increasing prices of the housing it produced. The focus was on land, because serviced building lots were selling at prices that had no relationship to the developers' costs. Some analysts suggested that the few large firms supplying a major share of serviced lots were taking advantage of their market power. Others argued that the high prices and profits resulted not from the developers' actions but from artificial regulation on the supply of land, imposed by planners and municipalities (*see* ZONING). In 1980 the market reached a postwar peak when an ordinary 3-bedroom house in suburban Vancouver cost more than twice as much as the same house in suburban Montréal. Montréal was unusual in that building lots were produced by hundreds of small developers.

During Canada's urban boom, land-development companies grew quickly. More than a dozen firms with assets of $100 million or more had emerged, partly from internal expansion, partly from takeovers. Some were entrepreneur-owned; others were owned by Canadian and foreign investors. One industry leader was Cadillac-Fairview Corporation Ltd (assets $3.1 billion, 1983), the result of a merger between a Toronto-based entrepreneur-owned firm and a Montréal-based company owned by one branch of the Bronfman family. Another was Olympia & York Developments Ltd, a private company owned by the Reichmann family of Toronto. Other leading firms had roots in different cities: Jack Poole's Daon Developments in Vancouver (assets $1.9 billion, 1983); Ralph Scurfield's Nu-West (assets $1.986 billion, 1980) in Calgary; Robert Campeau's Campeau Corporation (assets $1.8 billion, 1983) in Ottawa.

As the boom slowed in the late 1970s many Canadian developers expanded into the US. The deep recession and high interest rates of 1980 only worsened their problems. Some firms had difficulty paying interest on money borrowed to finance this American expansion and had to sell valuable assets to generate cash. The same high interest rates caused the demand for housing to collapse in Canada.

As an industry, land development is a remarkable example of what can happen when entrepreneurs are combined with profit opportunities and large amounts of investment capital. Canadian financial institutions and other lenders provided $14 billion for real-estate financing in the 1960s, and $90 billion in the 1970s. The developers earned very substantial profits, and paid little or no corporate tax owing to federal concessions. They provided much-needed accommodation in Canada's cities, though the standard building forms they used came to be questioned on social, economic and ecological grounds. The investment of capital in urban real estate does not significantly add to an economy's productive capacity. The Canadian funds invested in property could have gone to other, more productive uses — a stronger, more independent Canadian manufacturing sector, for instance. Instead, they fueled a real-estate price boom and overexpansion by the developers. The development industry has been successful in some ways, but there are many questions about how appropriate the industry has been for Canada, and how viable are the projects built by this industry. JAMES LORIMER

Reading: R.W. Collier, *Contemporary Cathedrals: Large-Scale Developments in Canadian Cities* (1974); Federal-Provincial Task Force on the Supply and Price of Serviced Residential Land, *Down to Earth,* 2 vols (1978); James Lorimer, *The Developers* (1978) and *The City Book* (1976); James Lorimer and C. MacGregor, eds, *After the Developers* (1981); L.B. Smith and M. Walker, eds, *Public Property? The Habitat Debate Continued* (1977); P. Spurr, *Land and Urban Development* (1976).

Deville, Édouard-Gaston, surveyor (b at La Charité sur Noire, Nièvre, France 21 Feb 1849; d at Ottawa 21 Sept 1924). Educated at the naval school at Brest, Deville served in the French Navy and was in charge of their hydrographic surveys throughout the world. In 1875 he retired and came to Canada, becoming inspector of surveys in Québec. In 1881 he was appointed inspector of Dominion Land Surveys and in 1885 surveyor general of Canada. He experimented with photography in surveying in mountainous areas and in 1889 published *Photographic Surveying.* Regarded as the father of photogrammetry in Canada, he supervised many major surveys in Canada. ERIC J. HOLMGREN

Devine, Donald Grant, agricultural economist, teacher, farmer, premier of Saskatchewan (b at Regina 5 July 1944). Raised on a farm near Lake Valley, Sask, Devine attended U of Sask (BSc 1967), Ohio State (PhD 1976). While continuing to farm near Moose Jaw he taught agricultural economics at U of Sask 1976-79. Though defeated in Nutana in 1978, he was elected leader of the Saskatchewan PC Party in Nov 1979. Defeated again in a by-election in Estevan in 1980 he was elected there in 1982 when he led his party to an overwhelming victory, bringing it to power in Saskatchewan for the first time since 1929. He was sworn in as premier on 8 May 1982. D.H. BOCKING

Devoir, Le, Montréal NEWSPAPER started by Henri BOURASSA in 1910 as a pan-Canadian nationalist, pro-French Canadian, pro-Catholic, anti-British but independent newspaper. Its editors and publishers were Bourassa (1910-32), Georges Pelletier (1932-47), Gérard FILION (1947-63), Claude RYAN (1963-77), Michel Roy (interim editor, 1978-81) and Jean-Louis Roy (1981-). From 1958 to 1968 André LAURENDEAU was the chief editorial writer. Daily circulation was 12 529 in 1910, 20 112 in 1940, 48 284 in 1965, and 27 714 in 1976. In 1984 *Le Devoir* had an estimated circulation of 30 000-35 000.

Le Devoir was well known as a newspaper of opinion. It campaigned against CONSCRIPTION in 1917 and 1942 and opposed Maurice DUPLESSIS and the patronage system. In the 1970s it remained federalist but continued to be a pan-Canadian and French Canadian nationalist paper. Its international coverage was excellent, based on the *Agence France Presse* (AFP) and *Le Monde,* but, in an attempt to increase its audience in the early 1980s, it expanded its economic and leisure content to the detriment of foreign news. ANDRÉ DONNEUR AND ONNIG BEYLERIAN

Devon Island is the second-largest island (55 247 km^2) among the QUEEN ELIZABETH ISLANDS, NWT. The island was first sighted by William Baffin in 1616 and was named North Devon by W.E. PARRY for Devon, Eng. Its eastern third is covered with an ice cap with a maximum thickness of 500-700 m. The rocks are very old, consisting of Precambrian, Cambrian and Ordovician in the E and Ordovician and Silurian siltstones and shales in the W. Because most of the island is a plateau, 300-500 m in elevation, it is a barren landscape, dominated by frost-shattered rocks and nearly devoid of plants and animals. The mean annual temperature averages about -16°C.

The Truelove Lowland area of the island has diverse vegetation and wildlife, an abundance of soil water in the summer owing to blocked drainage, and greater precipitation and higher summer temperatures (4° to 8°C), with more clear days than other parts of the island. The ground is snow free for only 45-50 days each summer. The poorly drained lowlands are characterized by a sedge-moss tundra in which MUSKOXEN graze year round. Most of the living organisms in this system (98.9%) are plants, with the remainder being herbivores and carnivores, soil bacteria, fungi and INVERTEBRATES that decompose the organic matter. The peaty soils are cold and wet all summer and have low levels of available nutrients. The island's raised beach ridges of coarse gravels and sands have higher summer air and soil temperatures and drier soils than elsewhere on the island. This system is characterized by a cushion plant (polar semi-desert) vegetation on which collared LEMMING feed year-round. Of the living mass in this system, 98.7% are plants.

On both the beach ridges and wet sedge meadows, the soil invertebrates (worms, protozoa, midge and fly larvae, and collembola) are more productive and consume more organic matter (4.73%) than do the lemming, waterfowl and large muskox. Clearly the tiny insects and other soil organisms are more important in the functioning of this system than are the 15-25 muskoxen that graze in summer and 60-125 that graze in winter in this small oasis in the High Arctic. Because of the island's short growing

season (40-55 days) and low daily summer temperatures (2° to 8°C), plants and animals grow slowly and have a long life cycle. Many invertebrates that take from a few weeks to 1 or 2 years to complete their life cycle in temperate regions require 2-9 years at these latitudes. While the same basic ecosystem components are found in a Saskatchewan grassland or an Ontario hardwood or coniferous forest as those that occur in the High Arctic, the diversity of species, rates of organismic growth and levels of ecosystem production are much reduced, owing to the limited solar-energy input into these cold and nutrient-deficient systems near the top of the world.
LAWRENCE BLISS

Devonshire, Victor Christian William Cavendish, 9th Duke of, governor general of Canada 1916-21 (b at London, Eng 31 May 1868; d at Chatsworth House, Devonshire, Eng 6 May 1938). The youngest member in the British House of Commons in 1891, he remained there until 1908, when he succeeded to the dukedom. Retiring, deliberate and a pedestrian speaker, he was easy to underestimate as governor general. But he travelled widely, was politically helpful and the soul of constitutional propriety. There were none of the problems there had been with his predecessor, the duke of CONNAUGHT. As one of Britain's great landowners, he took a particular interest in Canadian agriculture. After returning home, he served briefly as secretary of state for the colonies. His wife was the daughter of the marquess of LANSDOWNE, governor general in the 1880s. Their son-in-law, Harold Macmillan, provides an affectionate portrait of Devonshire in the first volume of his memoirs, *Winds of Change* (1966). NORMAN HILLMER

Dewar, Phyllis, swimmer (b at Moose Jaw, Sask 5 Mar 1916; d at Toronto, 8 Apr 1961). Spurred from age 4 by a strong competitive instinct, Dewar was the best swimmer on the prairies by age 17. She became Canada's aquatic darling at the 1934 British Empire Games by winning gold medals in the 100- and 400-yd freestyle, the 300-yd medley and the 400-yd relay, and was crowned Canada's female athlete of the year. Weakened by flu, she performed poorly in the 1936 Berlin Olympics but regained top form to win another gold medal in the 1938 British Empire Games. After her husband's death in a 1954 car accident, the mother of 4 young children grew despondent; her health failed, and she died at 45. BOB FERGUSON

Dewdney, Edgar, surveyor, politician (b in Devonshire, Eng 1835; d at Victoria 8 Aug 1916). Dewdney came to BC in 1859 and built the Dewdney Trail. In 1870 he was elected to the Legislative Council of BC as member for Kootenay. He was elected to Parliament as Conservative member for Yale, BC, in 1872, 1874 and 1878. He was Indian commissioner for the North-West Territories 1879-88 and lieutenant-governor of the North-West Territories (1881 to 88). In 1888 and 1891 he was re-elected to the House of Commons as member for Assiniboia East. He was created privy councillor in 1888 and until 1892 was minister of the interior and superintendent general of Indian affairs. He was lt-gov of BC 1892-97, after which he retired from public life to become a mining broker and financial agent in Victoria. ERIC J. HOLMGREN

DeWolf, Harry George, naval officer (b at Bedford, NS 26 Jun 1903). Joining the navy in 1918, DeWolf took command of the destroyer *St Laurent* in 1939, and following brief service off France returned to Canada, eventually becoming director of plans in Ottawa in 1942. In 1943 he assumed command of HMCS HAIDA and saw action in the Atlantic and Arctic oceans and, in particular, the English Channel, for which he received a DSO and a DSC. An exceptionally clear thinker, DeWolf held a series of posts afloat and ashore between 1944 and 1955 and was appointed chief of the naval staff in Jan 1956. He retired in 1960. MARC MILNER

Dexter, Alexander Grant, journalist (b at St Andrews, Man 3 Feb 1896; d at Winnipeg 12 Dec 1961). Grant Dexter was the archetypal Canadian political reporter of the 1940s, a splendid journalist with access to the best governmental sources. After attending Brandon College, in 1912 he joined the *Manitoba Free Press*, where, with time out for war service, he was schooled in Liberal journalism by J.W. DAFOE. After serving in various posts, in 1938 he became Ottawa correspondent. Through links to T.A. CRERAR, in particular, and to key bureaucrats, Dexter learned of government decisions more quickly than most, and his coverage of politics was informed by this inside knowledge. Although he was editor of the *Free Press* 1948-54, he is remembered for his reportage and through his fine collection of papers at Queen's U.
J.L. GRANATSTEIN

Dextraze, Jacques Alfred, "Ja Dex," soldier (b at Montréal, 15 Aug 1919). He served during WWII in Iceland, England, France, Germany and the Netherlands and was promoted from private to lt-col commanding the Fusiliers Mount-Royal. In the Korean War he commanded the 2nd Battalion, Royal 22e Régiment. Commandant of the Royal Canadian Infantry School at Camp Borden and commander, Camp Valcartier, he was chief of general staff in charge of UN operations in the Congo in 1963. In 1972 he was promoted general and became chief of defence staff. In 1977 he retired from the CAF to become chairman of the board of directors of CN. JEAN PARISEAU

Deyglun, Henry, playwright (b at Paris, France 1903; d 1971). As a young man he joined the Théâtre du Vieux-Colombier, under Jacques Copeau, and went with the company to New York, where it remained 1917-19 at the request of Clemenceau. In 1920 Deyglun moved to Montréal, where he married actress Reine Leborgne, known as Mimi d'Estée, and joined the Barry-Duquesne company. Given the Québec public's lack of interest in the poetry of Baudelaire, Rimbaud and Verlaine, which he was trying to present, he opted for melodrama. With 20 or so radio soap operas (broadcast daily 1938-47) and about 30 radio plays broadcast on CKAC, CBF and CKVL, he became one of the most prolific authors of melodrama. Starting in 1929, he published 2 dramas for radio, 4 novels and 5 plays. He was cofounder of the Théâtre Stella, which chose one of his plays, *Gens de chez nous*, for its 1937 tour of Europe (Nancy, Lyons and Brussels). He founded a small theatre, Théâtre du Lazarre, where Gilles Pelletier made his debut. Interviewed widely on the history of Québec theatre and left a manuscript on the subject, now in the Public Archives of Canada.
ANDRÉ G. BOURASSA

Diabetes Mellitus is a disease complex resulting from relative or absolute INSULIN deficiency, that may also be associated with altered effectiveness of insulin. The cardinal manifestation is high blood glucose concentration, which reflects carbohydrate metabolic disturbances, but protein and fat derangements are also present. Diabetes, which causes a disease of blood vessels in the eye, is the most frequent cause of blindness. Because of complications arising from diabetes, it is also ranked as the third most important cause of death in Canada. Acute complications of diabetes arise from excessively high or low blood glucose concentrations which may result from severe (and usually prolonged) insulin deficiency or (usually acute) insulin excess during treatment. Chronic complications include small and large blood vessel disease and damage to the nervous system.

Diabetes mellitus has been known for millennia. The familial nature of the disease has also been recognized for a long time, but the genetic determinants are still controversial. The characteristics and causes of a patient's illness may differ according to the type of diabetes. Effective treatment for diabetes became available only after the discovery and isolation of insulin for which F.G. BANTING and associates were awarded a Nobel prize.

It has been estimated that 1 million Canadians have diabetes; 50% of them may be undiagnosed. No age group is immune, but people between the ages of 15 and 64 are the most prone to diabetes. The chances of developing diabetes double with every 20% of excess body weight.

The characteristics and causes of a patient's illness may differ according to the type of diabetes. Type I is insulin-dependent diabetes mellitus (IDDM). Patients with IDDM are unable to secrete insulin. The illness usually begins abruptly with frequent urination, excessive thirst, weight loss and fatigue, and it may progress to an extreme imbalance between severe insulin deficiency and an excess of insulin-opposing hormones. A genetic susceptibility to viral infection may be one of the mechanisms causing IDDM. Type II is non-insulin-dependent diabetes mellitus (NIDDM). While NIDDM patients retain some insulin secretion their blood glucose regulation is disturbed and they may exhibit other metabolic abnormalities The majority of patients with NIDDM are diagnosed in adulthood. Obesity is common in patients with NIDDM. Secondary diabetes mellitus is present in patients in whom other health problems, eg, diseases of the pancreas or overactive states of other hormone-producing glands such as the adrenals or pituitary, have caused interference with insulin secretion or impairment of the actions of insulin. A special category of patients have gestational diabetes. This occurs especially during the latter 3 months of pregnancy in women with normal carbohydrate metabolism before pregnancy. The majority return to a non-diabetic state after delivery.

Treatment of diabetes, designed to correct as closely as possible metabolic abnormalities, invariably includes a special diet and frequently the use of insulin or oral antidiabetic drugs. It is estimated that 50% of diabetics are treated by diet alone; 24% by oral hypoglycemic agents, and 26% by insulin injection. Because exercise can lower diabetic blood glucose levels, activity must be considered as part of the treatment. The insulin treatment is intended to make up for the insulin deficiency. Usually insulin must be injected beneath the skin, because digestive enzymes make it unavailable from the gastrointestinal tract if taken by mouth. Once insulin has been injected, its course of action is determined by the type of insulin (rapid or prolonged) and its dosage. Oral antidiabetic drugs (principally sulfonylureas), which promote insulin secretion, may have other effects as well The safety of these drugs in diabetic (Type II) management has been questioned on the basis of large-scale but controversial studies in some of which cardiovascular problems (heart attacks and strokes) were reported to be more frequent among oral antidiabetic drug users than among those treated with either diet alone or with insulin. G.D. MOLNAR

Reading: J. Biermann and B. Tookey, *The Diabetic's Book* (1979); L.J. Laulor and H. Kadison, *Diabetes Explained* (1976).

Diamond, Abel Joseph, architect, planner (b at Piet Retief, S Africa 8 Sept 1932). Educated at U of Capetown, Oxford, and U of Penn, Diamond came to Toronto in 1964, worked in partnership with Barton MYERS between 1969 and 1974, and has been in private practice since 1975. One of his concerns has been to provide alternatives to high-rise housing, eg, his Hydro Block in Toronto, and the use of existing buildings for new purposes. Diamond's work is characterized by a diversity in scale from office interiors to downtown revitalization plans. His buildings include Innis Coll, U of T. SUSAN FORD

Diamond, Billy, politician (b at Rupert House, Qué 17 May 1949). A leading figure in Indian politics of the James Bay region of Québec, Diamond was born and raised in the Cree community of Rupert House, becoming band manager there in the 1960s and chief of the band, 1970-76. As founding member and grand chief of the Grand Council of the Cree of Québec (1974-84) he was a prime mover and signator of the JAMES BAY AGREEMENT on behalf of his people, and chairman of the Cree Regional Authority (1975-) which administers the implementation of the agreement in relation to land, economic development and social services. He has also been involved in a wide variety of local services (eg, as chairman of the James Bay Cree school board from 1976 and president of Air Creebec from 1980) and political activities, notably as representative of the Québec Cree in constitutional talks after 1981. BENNETT MCCARDLE

Diamonds of Canada, mined by Jacques CARTIER's men at the mouth of Rivière du Cap-Rouge in 1541. Cartier's "treasure" proved to be worthless quartz. The episode is remembered in the name of Québec's Cap aux Diamants and in the French saying, "As false as Canadian diamonds."

Dickens, Francis Jeffrey, NWMP inspector (b at London, Eng 15 Jan 1844; d at Moline, Ill 11 June 1886), third son of Charles Dickens. In 1864, after numerous unsuccessful career starts, Dickens joined the Bengal Mounted Police in India. He returned to England in 1871 and eventually obtained a commission in the NWMP in 1874. His unspectacular career was marked by recklessness, laziness and heavy drinking. He retired in 1886 and died shortly thereafter. Dickens can be blamed for worsening relations between the Blackfoot and the NWMP and for the growing antipathy of the officer cadre toward Englishmen. DAVID EVANS

Dickie, Donalda James, educator, author (b at Hespeler, Ont 5 Oct 1883; d 1972). Educated at Queen's, Columbia, Oxford and Toronto, Dickie was influential in Alberta education as a normal school instructor, curriculum reviser and textbook author. She advocated the "Enterprise," a progressive educational approach to teaching the elementary school curriculum. By offering courses at the normal schools, writing a reference book, *The Enterprise in Theory and Practice* (1940), and publishing a variety of textbooks that incorporated progressive philosophy, she passed her ideas on to the next generation of teachers and children. Besides textbooks in composition, reading, geography and history, she also wrote many children's stories, receiving the Governor General's Award for juvenile literature in 1950. NANCY M. SHEEHAN

Dickie, Lloyd Merlin, marine ecologist (b at Canning, NS 6 Mar 1926). After studying at Acadia, Yale and Toronto, Dickie became founding director, Marine Ecology Laboratory, BEDFORD INSTITUTE OF OCEANOGRAPHY, NS, in 1965, establishing it as a major centre for the study of marine production systems for the Fisheries Research Board of Canada. He was chairman of the Department of Oceanography at Dalhousie from 1974 to 1977 and since 1978 has been senior research scientist at the Marine Ecology Laboratory. Dickie has an international reputation for his work on marine production systems, including fisheries bioenergetics, genetics, acoustics, theory of search, species interactions and population demography. He is also well known as a teacher and has been appointed to various academic, governmental and international agencies concerned with fisheries and biological OCEANOGRAPHY. S.R. KERR

Dickins, Clennell Haggerston, "Punch," aviation pioneer (b at Portage la Prairie, Man 12 Jan 1899). Dickens grew up and was educated in Edmonton, Alta. He was awarded the Distinguished Flying Cross for gallantry in the Royal Flying Corps in WWI. He joined Western Canadian Airways in 1927 and dramatized the value of the bush plane, flying vast distances across northern Canada. He piloted the first aircraft on the prairie airmail circuit and flew the first prospectors into the Great Bear Lk area. Operations manager of FERRY COMMAND in WWII, he managed 6 BRITISH COMMONWEALTH AIR TRAINING PLAN schools. He joined de Havilland Aircraft as director in 1947, and developed a successful worldwide sales organization. He was awarded the MCKEE TROPHY in 1928 and was named an officer of the Order of the British Empire in 1936 and officer of the ORDER OF CANADA in 1968. JAMES MARSH

"Punch" Dickins, aviation pioneer who dramatized the value of the bush plane, flying vast distances across northern Canada *(courtesy Public Archives of Canada/C-57671)*.

Dictionary, a reference book that explains items listed in alphabetical order; in Canada, for example, there are *The Dictionary of Canadian Quotations and Phrases,* by Robert M. Hamilton and Dorothy Shields (1979), and the multivolume DICTIONARY OF CANADIAN BIOGRAPHY (1966-). Normally, however, the word "dictionary" refers to a book that lists the words of a language alphabetically and shows the spelling and meaning of each, along with such other information (eg, pronunciation, part of speech, examples of use, derived forms, origin and history) as the editors choose. From time to time "lexicon" has been used as a synonym for "dictionary," but it is now used mainly to refer to all the words in a language, as in "No dictionary covers the whole lexicon of English." Even so, a person who compiles dictionaries is still called a "lexicographer," and dictionary-making is called "lexicography."

The earliest dictionaries of English, beginning with Robert Cawdrey's *A Table Alphabeticall. . .* (1604), gave explanations of "hard words." The first book that sought to be a complete dictionary of English was Nathaniel Bailey's *Universal Etymological English Dictionary* (1721), which was a starting point for Samuel Johnson's *A Dictionary of the English Language* (1755). This in turn formed the basis for the 10-volume *Oxford English Dictionary* (1884-1928). The 12-volume 1933 reprint with *Supplement* contains over 400 000 definitions. The updated *Supplement to the Oxford English Dictionary* (ed R.W. Burchfield) is being published in 4 volumes (1972-) and includes many items from the US, Australia, Canada and other English-speaking countries. In 1984 U of Waterloo became involved in a project to place the OED on a computer data base in order to make it easy to update and accessible on-line. Among the best-known dictionaries of the French language are the *Dictionnaire de l'Académie Française* (first published in 1694), the Littré *Dictionnaire de la langue française* (5 vols, 1863-72) and the *Dictionnaire alphabétique et analogique de la langue française* (7 vols, 1965) by Paul Robert.

Dictionaries used in English-speaking Canada have too often been either British or American, few of them showing Canadian terms or even Canadian variant spellings and pronunciations. But even some dictionaries published in Canada have had little Canadian content. As early as 1937 there appeared *The Winston Dictionary for Canadian Schools,* which was simply an American work with a few Canadian additions and alterations. In recent years the desire of school authorities to purchase books of Canadian origin and manufacture has resulted in several publishers producing "Canadian" volumes that are reprintings of American dictionaries with some Canadian entries incorporated.

In the 1960s Gage Publishing produced the *Dictionary of Canadian English* series, 3 graded books covering the needs of students from Grade 3 or 4 through senior high school. These books were based on the American Thorndike-Barnhart series, but the text was thoroughly revised for Canadian use. The dictionaries are frequently updated and now exist in revised editions as the *Canadian Junior Dictionary* (1977), the *Canadian Intermediate Dictionary* (1979) and the *Gage Canadian Dictionary* (1983; now a general-use desk dictionary).

Also fully edited for Canadian students was *The Winston Dictionary of Canadian English,* of which only the *Intermediate Edition* (1969) and the *Elementary Edition* (1975) were published, both edited by T.M. Paikeday and based on American models. They have not been kept up to date. *Funk and Wagnalls Standard College Dictionary, Canadian Edition* (1973), published by Fitzhenry and Whiteside, has since 1976 been revised and published independently of its American parent.

Distinct from these are dictionaries on historical principles, based on the tradition of the OED, which give dated citations to illustrate each meaning of every entry word. Such is *A Dictionary of Canadianisms on Historical Principles* (1967), published as part of the Dictionary of Canadian English program and prepared for the Lexicographical Centre for Canadian English by editors Walter S. Avis, Charles Crate, Patrick Drysdale, Douglas Leechman and M.H. Scargill. It presents over 10 000 words that originated in Canada, have meanings peculiar to Canada or have special significance in Canada. A shorter version, *A Concise Dictionary of Canadianisms,* was published in 1972. In the same historical tradition is the *Dictionary of Newfoundland English* (1982), edited by G.M. Story, W.J. Kirwin and J.D.A. Widdowson, which uses authenticated oral evidence as well as citations from Newfoundland literature and folklore. Rich material exists for other regional dictionaries if the personnel and the funds can be found to prepare them.

Another scholarly project in the OED tradition is the *Dictionary of Old English,* which is being prepared under the auspices of the Centre for Medieval Studies, U of Toronto, with an international group of advisers. This project is interesting for its use of the computer in collating and editing material. The data base, from which entry words and citations are being drawn, consists of every word of every known text in Old English.

Speakers of Canadian French started in the late 19th century to produce dictionaries showing how their variety of French differed from the standard form of France. The first was *Dictionnaire canadien-français* by Sylva Clapin (1894), and in 1930 La Société du parler français au Canada published *Glossaire du parler français au Canada.* Louis-Alexandre Bélisle compiled and published *Dictionnaire général de la langue française au Canada* (1957), a significant work of scholarship which was revised in 1974 and then republished as *Dictionnaire nord-américain de la langue française* (1979). Several recent books have concentrated on the distinctiveness of current Québec French, often admitting variant forms and expressions, such as anglicisms and vulgarisms, that are frowned upon by traditionalists. An example is Léandre Bergeron's *Dictionnaire de la langue québécoise* (1980), which has been translated into English as *The Québécois Dictionary* (1982). Canadian Francophones, like Anglophones, have suffered from having a Canadian label placed on imported dictionaries that have been reprinted with little or no revision (eg, *Dictionnaire Beauchemin canadien,* 1968). But French Canadians will soon enjoy their own dictionary on historical principles, *Trésor de la langue française au Québec,* which is being prepared at U Laval.

A bilingual dictionary, *The Canadian Dictionary/Dictionnaire canadien* (ed Jean-Paul Vinay, 1962), is being revised and expanded under the Canadian Bilingual Dictionary Project at U of Victoria. Such dictionaries are not limited to French and English: interest in the cultures of Canada's native peoples has resulted in the publication of a number of bilingual dictionaries of indigenous languages, such as Anne Anderson's *Cree Dictionary in the "y" Dialect* (1975). *See* NATIVE PEOPLE, LANGUAGES.

Indigenous Canadian dictionaries have helped to define a Canadian identity and have provided valuable sources of reference for writers and scholars; lexicographers, for their part, have benefited from the surge of Canadian writing since the 1960s. The original research on which the dictionaries of the 1960s and 1970s were based is now over 20 years old, but the small size of the Canadian market makes it difficult for publishers to undertake a new the production of original dictionaries. No Canadian publisher has produced a college dictionary or a mass-market paperback dictionary from scratch, and only one English Canadian publisher maintains a dictionary department. Although the use of computers for editing, revision and typesetting is now making lexicography more efficient, outside funding will undoubtedly be needed to initiate new projects.

PATRICK DRYSDALE

Reading: Walter S. Avis, "Introduction," *A Dictionary of Canadianisms* (1967) and "Canadian English," in *Gage Canadian Dictionary* (1983); Angus Cameron and Roberta Frank, *A Plan for the Dictionary of Old English* (1973); Patrick Drysdale, "Aspects of Canadian Lexicography," in *Papers on Lexicography in Honor of Warren N. Cordell* (1979).

Dictionary of Canadian Biography/Dictionnaire biographique du Canada is a multivolume, comprehensive reference work on the lives of people who have contributed to Canada's history in every field of endeavour. The volumes are arranged according to the death dates of subjects, so that each one gives a full picture of a period in Canadian history. Contributions to the DCB/DBC, which are based on the best scholarship and documentary sources available, are written by a wide variety of specialists. They are painstakingly edited and checked for accuracy by teams of editors in Toronto and Québec, who have worked under the direction of general editors George Brown (1959-63), David Hayne (1965-69) and Francess Halpenny (1969-) and, in Québec, directeurs généraux adjoints Marcel Trudel (1961-65), André Vachon (1965-71) and Jean Hamelin (1973-).

The project began with the bequest of Toronto businessman James Nicholson, who left most of his estate to U of Toronto for the preparation of a Canadian biographical reference work on the model of Britain's *Dictionary of National Biography.* Work began at U of T Press in 1959 on the English edition, and in 1961 a French edition was announced by Les Presses de l'université Laval. By 1984, 8 of the 12 volumes planned for the period 1000-1900, each containing 500-600 biographies, had been published in both languages; the question of how best to deal with the 20th century had not yet been resolved. Since the mid-1960s the project has received additional funding from government sources; this practice was regularized through major operating gran[t] from the CANADA COUNCIL (1957-80) and th[e] SOCIAL SCIENCES AND HUMANITIES RESEARCH COUNCI[L] (1980-85).

JAMES A. OGILV[IE]

John Diefenbaker in the House of Commons, 26 Mar 1973 (*courtesy Canapress*).

Diefenbaker, John George, lawyer, politician[,] prime minister (b at Neustadt, Ont 18 Sept 1895 d at Ottawa 16 Aug 1979). Well known as a de[-]fence lawyer before his election to Parliament[,] Canada's 13th prime minister was an eloquen[t] spokesman for "nonestablishment" Canada bot[h] as a lawyer and as a politician. He developed [a] distinctive speaking style that allowed him t[o] talk directly to his audience; his speeches wer[e] both inspiring and popular.

He moved to the Fort Carlton region of th[e] North-West Territories with his family in 190[?] and attended schools in several prairie commu[-]nities before moving to Saskatoon in 1910. H[e] saw and was profoundly influenced by th[e] transition of Saskatchewan from a frontier to [a] modern society. He attended U of Sask and, afte[r] serving in the army in WWI, completed his la[w] degree and articles and was called to the Sas[-]katchewan Bar in 1919. His first law office wa[s] in Wakaw, Sask, but the larger northern centre of Prince Albert attracted him and he moved there in 1924.

Diefenbaker's path to the prime minister's office was long. He ran federally for Prince Albert in 1925 and 1926; provincially in 1929 and 1938; and for mayor of Prince Albert in 1933. He lost each time. Despite a growing reputation as an able defence lawyer (named KC, 1929), he held firmly to the belief that his future lay in politics. He was given some encouragement when he became leader of the Saskatchewan Conservative Party in 1936, only to preside over the party's defeat in the 1938 election when they won no seats. He continued to preach his own brand of Conservative politics, visiting many Saskatchewan communities with his wife, Edna Mae Brower, building party organization and exhorting his colleagues to "keep the faith."

In June 1939 Diefenbaker was nominated for the federal riding of Lake Centre and in Mar 1940 he was elected an MP. The skills he had refined during his legal career served him well on the Opposition back benches. He gained a reputation as an astute questioner of government actions, a reputation that went far beyond the boundaries of his constituency. He was re-elected for Lake Centre in 1945 and 1949 but, when redistribution radically altered his constituency, he almost quit politics. His highly successful legal career could easily fill his time (he had defended Atherton in the "Canoe River" case), and he had not yet recovered from the death of his wife in Feb 1951. Diefenbaker's friends in Prince Albert persuaded him to let his name stand as the PC candidate for Prince Albert in the 1953 election. The campaign and its slogan, "Not a partisan cry, but a national need," captured the imagination of Prince Albert voters and Diefenbaker was elected. That same year he married Olive Freeman Palmer, who gave up her own highly successful career in the Ontario Dept of Education. Olive Diefenbaker was closely associated with her husband's political career for the rest of her life. In 1956 Diefenbaker was chosen to succeed George DREW who resigned as leader of the PC Party. In 1957 Diefenbaker led his party to an upset victory over the Liberals, who were led by Louis ST. LAURENT, and formed the first Tory government since that of R.B. BENNETT. Backed by a Cabinet that included Davie FULTON, Donald FLEMING, George HEES, G.R. PEARKES, Douglas HARKNESS, Ellen FAIRCLOUGH, Léon Balcer and Gordon CHURCHILL, Diefenbaker consolidated his position in Mar 1958 when the electorate returned his government with 208 seats — the highest number held by a single party in Canada to that time.

The Diefenbaker era featured the personality and the style of the "man from Prince Albert"; many things now taken for granted were initiated during his administration. Wheat sales to China and agricultural reform revitalized western agriculture. His determination to guarantee certain rights for all led to the CANADIAN BILL OF RIGHTS and to granting the federal franchise to Canada's native peoples; James GLADSTONE, a Blood from Alberta, was appointed to the Senate. Under the philosophical umbrella of "social justice" many programs were restructured to provide aid to those in need. The "northern vision" that figured so prominently in rhetoric of the 1957 and 1958 elections increased public awareness of the Far North and led to some economic development. A tour of the COMMONWEALTH in 1958 reinforced Diefenbaker's strong feelings about the value of that organization and other international bodies. It also helped to define his role as a supporter of the nonwhite Commonwealth; he played a key role in the 1961 antiapartheid statement that contributed to South Africa leaving the Commonwealth.

During the 1962 election, the Liberals were able to exploit the crisis in the economy (the Canadian dollar had dropped to 92.5¢ US), the debate over nuclear weapons on Canadian soil (with charges against Diefenbaker of anti-Americanism) as well as the controversial 1959 cancellation of the AVRO ARROW; the PC government was reduced to a minority. The 1963 election returned the Liberals to power, but Diefenbaker, travelling the country by train, almost won the election for his party. It was possibly the most spectacular one-man political campaign in Canadian history. In the period following that election, Diefenbaker delighted in questioning PM PEARSON's government to such an extent that the House's business slowed considerably. He argued vigorously against Pearson's proposal for a new Canadian flag (*see* FLAG DEBATE) and led the attack on the Liberals during the scandals of 1965.

Despite the recent electoral setbacks and a party deeply split over the question of his continuing leadership, Diefenbaker refused to resign and put up a spirited defence at the 1967 LEADERSHIP CONVENTION, which chose Robert STANFIELD as the new leader. Diefenbaker remained in politics, however, and won a seat for the thirteenth time in May 1979. His state funeral in Ottawa, the final train journey across Canada, and his burial in Saskatoon beside the Right Honourable John G. Diefenbaker Centre at U of Sask — all planned by himself — is pageantry that few Canadians who witnessed it will forget.
PATRICIA WILLIAMS

Readings: John Diefenbaker, *One Canada*, 3 vols (1975-77); P. Newman, *Renegade in Power* (1963); P. Stursberg, *Diefenbaker*, 2 vols (1975-76).

Diefenbaker Lake, a man-made reservoir lake S of Saskatoon, Sask. It was formed by the construction of 2 dams that created a widening in the S SASKATCHEWAN R as part of the S Saskatchewan R Development Project, inaugurated 1958. The reservoir has a live storage capacity of about 4 billion m^3 of water that feeds a hydroelectric power plant and an irrigation project. It contributes to the water supply of Saskatoon and is a popular water recreation area. It was named in 1967 for John DIEFENBAKER, the first Saskatchewan resident to become prime minister of Canada; the larger of the 2 dams is named for J.G. GARDINER, Diefenbaker's arch-opponent.
DANIEL FRANCIS

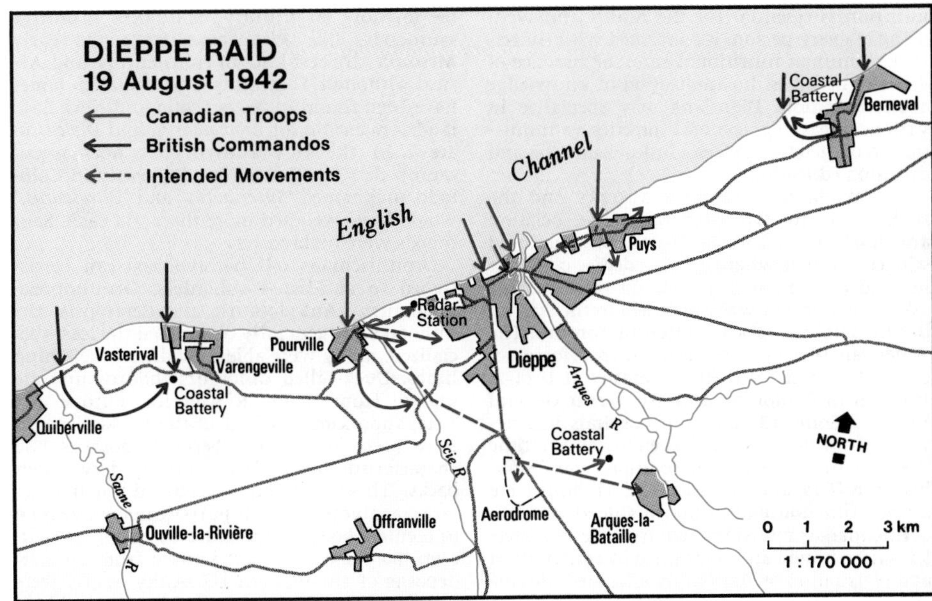

Dieppe The raid across the English Channel (Operation *Jubilee*, 19 Aug 1942) on Dieppe, a small port on the French coast between Le Havre and Boulogne, was planned as a "reconnaissance in force" to test the defences of Hitler's continental fortress and the capability of the Western Allies to launch large-scale amphibious assaults against his *Festung Europa* (Fortress Europe). It was a major disaster; only the battle-hardened British commandos assigned to subdue the coast artillery batteries near Varengeville and Berneval enjoyed some success. Troops of the 2nd Canadian Infantry Division under Maj-Gen J.M. Roberts, landing on the Dieppe esplanade at Puys, 1.6 km east, and Pourville, 3 km west, failed to achieve any of their objectives. The raid lasted only 9 hours, but among nearly 5000 Canadian soldiers involved more than 900 were killed and 1300 taken prisoner — more prisoners than the army lost in the 11 months of the 1944-45 NW Europe campaign. Two Canadians received the VICTORIA CROSS. In the air battle the Allies lost 106 aircraft and 81 airmen, the RCAF 13 machines and 10 pilots. German casualties were light, although they could ill afford the loss of 48 aircraft. For the Allies, the raid did provide valuable experience for subsequent amphibious assaults in N Africa, Italy and, most notably, NORMANDY on 6 June 1944.

Although it has been suggested that the Germans had prior knowledge of the raid, there is much evidence to the contrary. The enemy was alert but not forewarned, and failure was primarily caused by poor and overly complex planning, inadequate training, insufficient fire support, and the employment of troops undergoing their baptism of fire. BRERETON GREENHOUS

Diesing, Freda, or Kant-wus, meaning "the wake of the great whale as it travels through the water"; Skil-kew-wat, "the trail where the supernatural woman walks in the moss"; and Wee-gwe-daast, "greatest princess," Haida artist (b at Prince Rupert, BC 1925). A noted carver and printmaker, Freda Diesing is one of the few women of the 20th century to carve TOTEM POLES. Descended from a long line of Haida artists, she studied at the Vancouver School of Art and later at the Gitanmaax School of Northwest Coast Indian Art at KSAN with Robert DAVIDSON, Tony and Henry HUNT, Bill Holm and Duane Pasco. Later, she devoted more time to teaching and dancing; she is also a board member of the Indian Arts and Craft Society of BC. Her works are found in many private and public collections, notably the National Museum of Man.

Dietetics Diet (from the Greek *diaita*, meaning "mode of life") has been implicated in the cause, cure and prevention of disease from earliest recorded history. The profession of dietetics, which is based on the philosophy that optimal nutrition is essential for the health and well-being of every person, is concerned with the science of human nutritional care; the practice of dietetics involves the application of knowledge about nutrition. Dietitians may specialize in various areas, eg, general practice, administration of dietetic services, clinical nutrition and nutrition education.

In Canada the origin of dietetics and the founding of the Canadian Dietetic Association are closely related to the history of household science at U of T where the first degree course of its kind was initiated in 1902. In 1908 the first qualified dietitian was appointed to the staff of the Hospital for Sick Children in Toronto. The American Dietetic Association then offered accredited courses for dietetic training at U of A Hospital in Edmonton and Vancouver General Hospital. Some 12 Canadian hospitals had developed similar training programs by the time the Canadian Dietetic Assocation was established in 1935, and provincial associations were already functioning in Ontario, Québec and BC.

In Canada professional competence in dietetics is determined and warranted by certification and registration by nationally affiliated provincial associations. Universities in all provinces now offer academic programs in dietetics but, in addition, to be a qualified dietitian one must serve an approved internship or have equivalent experience. M.T. CLANDININ

Reading: M. Long and E. Upton, eds, *The Dietetic Profession in Canada* (1983).

Digby, NS, Town, pop 2558 (1981c), inc 1890, is located on the W side of the Annapolis Basin in western NS. Referred to as *Oositookum* ("ear") by the Micmac, it was called Conway by some early New England settlers, and was later named for Admiral Robert Digby, commander of the HMS *Atlanta,* which had conveyed LOYALISTS to the area in 1783. By the 1790s Digby was exporting lumber, fish and some farm produce. At the end of the 19th century, Digby and nearby Smiths Cove had been established as tourist resort areas. Today a major seaport, Digby is noted for having one of the world's largest SCALLOP fleets. It is a centre for distribution, shipping, fishing and general commerce. A ferry makes 3 trips daily to Saint John, NB. JEAN PETERSON

Dill, *see* HERBS.

Dimakopoulos, Dimitri, architect, urban designer (b at Athens, Greece 14 Sept 1929). He came to Canada in 1948 to study architecture at McGill, and in 1957, with Fred LEBENSOLD, became a founding member of Arcop Associates, an acclaimed architectural firm with great influence upon contemporary Canadian design development. The firm has won numerous prizes in design competitions across Canada. The present partnership designed the UNIVERSITÉ DU QUÉBEC campus in Montréal and the provincial courthouse in Québec City, and other works in Greece, Italy, Saudi Arabia, Hong Kong and Algeria. NORBERT SCHOENAUER

Dinosaur [Gk *deinos sauros,* "terrible lizard"] term used for 2 orders of large REPTILES, Saurischia (lizard-hipped) and Ornithischia (bird-hipped), that dominated Earth during the Mesozoic era (225-65 million years ago). The 2 lineages probably evolved independently from the same ancestral stock as did pterosaurs (flying reptiles) and crocodiles. Saurischians can be subdivided into 2 major types: theropods (beast-footed) and sauropods (lizard-footed). Theropods, dominant carnivores of the Mesozoic, were bipedal and include some of the smallest (eg, genus *Compsognathus,* less than 3 kg) and largest known dinosaurs. Typical forms, *Albertosaurus* and *Tyrannosaurus,* have been found in Alberta, Montana and S Dakota. Although dinosaurs are legendary for their small brains, some smaller theropods had relatively large brains, comparable to those of primitive MAMMALS. Primitive sauropods, like *Plateosaurus* from the early Mesozoic, are best known from Europe and Africa, although footprints and isolated bones have been found in Nova Scotia and New England. *Apatosaurus,* or *Brontosaurus,* and *Diplodocus* are 2 of the best known, but not largest, sauropods. Two forms found recently in Colorado, nicknamed *"Supersaurus"* and *"Ultrasaurus,"* would have weighed more than 50 t each. Sauropods were herbivorous.

Ornithischians (all herbivorous) can be assigned to at least 4 suborders: Ornithopoda, Stegosauria, Ankylosauria and Ceratopsia. Ornithopods are generally considered the least specialized; many were able to walk on their hind limbs. Duck-billed dinosaurs (hadrosaurs) are known from N and S America, Europe and Asia; approximately half of the known species have been found in Alberta. Stegosaurs had characteristic bony plates running down their backs. These may have protected them from large carnivores, or their purpose may have been to regulate body temperature by acting as radiators. Stegosaurs are best known from Jurassic deposits of the western US. Ankylosaurs were armoured dinosaurs, protected by thousands of bony plates covering the top of the head and body, even the eyelids and cheeks of some species. *Panoplosaurus, Euoplocephalus* and *Ankylosaurus* once lived in western Canada. Horned dinosaurs (ceratopsians) were one of the most successful groups. More than 10 genera, including *Triceratops, Centrosaurus* and *Styracosaurus,* are known from Alberta alone. Enormous diversity of form occurred in the horns projecting from over the nose and eyes, and in the frill extending backwards over the neck.

Even the earliest dinosaurs must have been well-adapted to their environment. From their first appearance early in the Mesozoic, they rapidly evolved into many different forms, and competed so successfully with the mammallike reptiles that they became the dominant land animals. Mammals did not rise to prominence until almost 150 million years later, after dinosaurs became extinct. The success of dinosaurs has long been a source of wonder. It has only been since the 1970s that reasons for this success have been seriously examined. A breakthrough came when scientists realized that it might be more appropriate to compare dinosaurs with mammals and birds than with living reptiles. Debate continues on whether or not dinosaurs were warm-blooded; however, it is now generally accepted that they were not simply oversized crocodiles in their physiology, ecology, behaviour and other adaptations. Detailed examination of dinosaur bone cells shows that dinosaur bone is much closer to that of mammals and birds than to that of living reptiles. A great deal of other evidence, including limb structure and the presence of sophisticated feeding and breathing adaptations, has been used to support the hypothesis that dinosaurs were warm-blooded. However, most paleontologists feel that the evidence is inconclusive. Despite their popularity, dinosaurs are still relatively poorly known.

Although size range of dinosaurs is enormous, most species were over 100 kg at maturity. Because they hatched from eggs, baby dinosaurs would have been relatively small. Dinosaur eggs have been found at numerous localities worldwide, and more than half a dozen eggshell sites are now known in Alberta alone. Sauropod eggs, from France and Mongolia, have diameters of less than 20 cm, and eggs of most other dinosaurs are much smaller. The sauropod hatchling would have been less than 2 m long. Because dinosaurs could grow throughout their lives, this hatchling might have increased its size more than 15 times during its lifetime. Baby dinosaurs are rare. Perhaps they never made up a significant portion of the population, or, as seems more likely, these tasty little morsels would simply have been eaten whole when caught by predators. Occasionally, the bones of baby hadrosaurs and ceratopsians are found in Alberta, and footprints of baby hadrosaurs have been identified in BC's Peace River Canyon. A spectacular site at which about 75% of dinosaurs recovered are juveniles was found in Montana. Eighteen baby hadrosaurs were recovered from one nest alone. The fact that these babies had hatched several months before they died suggests that the juveniles were gregarious animals and that there may have been some form of parental care.

Study of dinosaurian anatomy has long been a fascinating subject because of its diversity. For example, hadrosaurs were born with relatively flat heads, but forms such as *Lambeosaurus* developed characteristic bony crests on the head as they increased in size. Crest size differed in males and females. Diversity of shape and size of hadrosaurian crests has been a source of speculation since the discovery of the first hooded form, but the key to their function lies in the pronounced development of crest, which came only at sexual maturity. It appears probable that crests were little more than display structures recognized visually for mating, protection of territory, dominance display, etc. A space inside the crest, connected to nasal passages, probably served as a resonating chamber. As each species had a crest (hence resonating chamber) of a different shape, each would have made different sounds, allowing members of the same species to recognize one another.

Most of our understanding of the ecology of late Mesozoic terrestrial faunas and floras is derived from DINOSAUR PROVINCIAL PARK, Alta, because of numerous specimens and other data collected there. In many ways, the world of dinosaurs was not as exotic as most people imagine. The environment superficially resembled that of Florida. Dinosaurs were greatly outnumbered by insects, fish, turtles, lizards, snakes, crocodilians and other animals, which were no larger than their living relatives and, in many cases, indistinguishable from them. Small mammals, including relatives of the modern opposum, would have been seen scurrying through the undergrowth, and BIRDS would have occupied many of the niches they do today. Our understanding of dinosaurian ecology is constantly being refined. Fragmentary specimens that would have been ignored before now provide information on previously unknown animals. Species have been identified in Alberta that were once known only from Mongolia, and scientists now realize that many of the differences between Asian and N American forms were related to differences in environment, not to simple geographic separation.

It is becoming apparent that dinosaurs were capable of more complex behavioural patterns than modern reptile species. Trackways can be particularly useful in showing what animals were doing when alive. Herding behaviour can be implied for hadrosaurian dinosaurs because of trackways found in Peace River Canyon. At one canyon site, parallel trackways show a herd of 17 hadrosaurs walking in the same direction. At one point, 4 animals were walking so closely together that, when one lurched sideways, it bumped its neighbour, initiating a chain reaction that affected all 4. Other trackways in the canyon suggest that juveniles stayed together after hatching. They may not have joined more mature herds until almost half-grown.

Bonebeds are accumulations of bones from many individuals concentrated by natural processes into a single area. A river in flood, for example, might pick up bones of animals that died along its banks, and deposit them in a quiet backwater or pool. In most cases, it is impossible to know which bones came from which individuals, although types of animals can be identified. There are probably thousands of Cretaceous bonebeds in western Canada, study of which is producing important anatomical, ecological and behavioural data. A small percentage of these bonebeds is dominated by single species of ceratopsian (eg, *Centrosaurus, Styracosaurus, Pachyrhinosaurus* and *Triceratops*). Some sites appear to represent mass deaths of herds, which seem to have occurred periodically, over a period of at least 10 million years.

A major question concerning dinosaurs is why they became extinct at the end of the Mesozoic (65 million years ago). Dinosaurs were not the only animals affected. Some evidence suggests that perhaps as many as 75% of all known types of animal species (INVERTEBRATES, AMPHIBIANS, reptiles, mammals) may have become extinct at the same time. PLANTS, on the other hand, seem to have had relatively few problems in crossing the boundary into the Cenozoic era (Age of Mammals). Innumerable theories have been proposed to explain the extinctions. They range from climatic changes and collapse of ecosystems to a collision between Earth and an asteroid. Two related questions are critical if the answer is ever to be found. Did the extinctions take place gradually over a period of several million years, or were they catastrophic? Did the extinctions occur worldwide at the same time on land and sea, or did dinosaurs live in some parts of the world for millions of years after they became extinct in N America? Paleontologists, geologists, physicists and even astronomers are working together to answer these questions. Whatever the cause, it is remarkable that animals as diverse, adaptable and successful as the dinosaurs could have died out completely. Completely, that is, with exception of their descendants — the birds. PHILIP J. CURRIE

Reading: W. Stout, et al, *The Dinosaurs* (1981).

Dinosaur Hunting in Western Canada Dinosaurs were unknown to science until 1824, when FOSSIL teeth and bones were discovered in the late Jurassic and early Cretaceous rocks of southern England. Since then, their remains have been found on all continents and in rocks 200 million to 64 million years old. Most early discoveries were made in artificial excavations, eg, rock quarries or coal mines. With the opening of western N America to geological exploration, large areas were found where natural erosion had removed soil and rock, making possible the deliberate search for, and organized collection of, fossil skeletons. One such area is the Red Deer R valley in Alberta, the so-called BADLANDS. Here DINOSAUR hunting has been carried on for 100 years, at first intermittently and amateurishly, later by organized expeditions of experienced collectors. Dinosaur fossils are irreplaceable. Every province has legislation to prevent indiscriminate removal of these historical resources, eg, collectors in the badlands must have the written permission of Alberta's minister of culture.

Collecting dinosaur fossils in the field involves 2 distinct phases, discovery and excavation. No modern technique has yet superseded the old-fashioned method of prospecting, ie, just looking. This requires keen, experienced eyes and strong, nimble legs. The dinosaur hunter carries a digging tool, usually a light pick, which serves in making exploratory excavations and is useful in climbing steep slopes. A typical prospecting party might consist of 3 persons. Each would concentrate on a particular level of the exposure. In the Red Deer R badlands, exposures are mostly intricate ravines, often with clifflike sides. Keeping as much as possible to his own level, the fossil hunter works his way along these slopes, up one side of the ravine and down the other. It is important that rock surfaces be examined thoroughly but, often, a steep interval forces the hunter to detour up or down, then climb back to his original level. The work is strenuous and tiring, but the fossil hunter is kept alert by the thought that just ahead may be the discovery of the year.

There is no way of detecting fossil bone unless it is exposed. It is brittle and easily broken and, as natural erosion proceeds, pieces fall off and are strewn down slopes and erosion channels. These are the fossil prospector's "float," and he follows their lead to where they either give out or reveal bones still in place and projecting from rock surfaces. Fossil bone is usually easy to recognize from its smooth outer surface or, in broken specimens, its layered or honeycombed interior structure. Complete bones are recognizable by their form and their unique sheen, which is most easily recognized in bright sunshine.

The importance of the find must be tested by carefully uncovering the bone, using the pick or a hand tool like an awl, with a whisk broom to clear away debris. If the bone looks promising, the second phase of collecting begins: the uncovering of bones for wrapping and removal. A kind of quarry is made by excavating overlying rock layers. The steeper the slope on which the find occurs, the higher the excavation must be to obtain a flat working surface over the bones. The basic principle in uncovering specimens is to expose only as much bone as is needed to determine extent and orientation in the rock. The excavation would follow the bones, with minimum exposure, laying bare a floor of rock with patches of bone showing through. From the time of discovery, fossil bone must be protected from further disintegration. Exposed surfaces are hardened and cracks sealed by applying thin, liquid cement, which penetrates well and sets quickly.

After the area occupied by the bones has been delineated by a floor, a trench is dug around the perimeter to a depth well below the bone-bearing level. This trench is expanded as an undercut, as far beneath the bone-bearing layer as hand tools and the stability of the matrix will allow. Excess rock from the upper surface may be removed at this time. Depending on the hardness of the rock, the tools may be scrapers or hand-held chisels. Small pneumatic or electric chisels may be used where suitable. Debris is brushed or shovelled away, and all exposed bone thoroughly impregnated with cement. When the cement is dry, rice paper or facial tissue is placed over the exposed bone and wetted down with brush or spray. This serves to separate bone and plaster wrapping.

Burlap is cut into long strips about 12 cm wide, and liquid plaster is prepared. One strip of burlap at a time is rolled into the liquid to impregnate the fabric and form an easily handled roll. The plaster-soaked burlap is unrolled across the rock and bone surface, patted and squeezed to form a close contact. The strips are continued over the edge of the rock and tucked into the undercut. Successive strips of plaster-burlap are applied, each overlapping the preceding strip by about 2.5 cm, until the entire block or section has been bandaged. When the plaster bandage has hardened, possibly overnight, the block of matrix and bone is undercut more deeply, until the remaining pedestal is small enough to crack across with careful prying. The block is then turned over. The unwrapped lower surface, if sufficiently strong and not too large, will remain intact. When the block is turned over, excess rock may be removed, as with the upper side. Exposed bone is cemented and covered with paper, and the protruding edges of the upper bandage are trimmed flush with the matrix. Then the plaster bandage is applied to the inverted underside, with edges firmly lapped over the upper bandage. If the specimen is too large to be bandaged and transported in one block, it is divided into sections, each of which is bandaged separately. When each section has hardened and dried, it is labeled, and moved to the packing area. Sometimes this is difficult, owing to the inaccessibility of the quarry. In earlier years a small wooden sled (stone boat) was used, the section being roped to the sled and the load dragged out by a team of horses. Today, 4-wheel-drive vehicles and power winches have made movement somewhat easier, and helicopters have been used, in Saskatchewan and Alberta, to retrieve large specimens.

Early collectors had only man or horse power for quarry excavation and transportation of bandaged blocks. Automobiles were introduced to the Alberta fossil fields in 1921, and motor transport has improved progressively. Motor-driven jack hammers speed up excavation. Dy-

Dinosaur Provincial Park, Alta, est 1955, located in the badlands and prairie along the Red Deer R. The park has been declared a UNESCO World Heritage Site for its valuable fossil record (*courtesy J.A. Walper / Alberta Recreation and Parks*).

namite may be used to loosen overburden or break up hard rock layers. House trailers have replaced tents, and camp kitchen facilities now include naphtha stoves and propane refrigerators. But success in dinosaur hunting still depends on walking and climbing, on the ability to recognize a find from a few fragments and on knowing what to do about it. *See* PALEONTOLOGY.

L.S. RUSSELL

Reading: L.S. Russell, *Dinosaur Hunting in Western Canada* (1966).

Dinosaur Provincial Park (est 1955, 90 km^2) encompasses BADLANDS and PRAIRIE along the RED DEER RIVER in SE Alberta. The badlands, named because the land is not arable, possess an exotic beauty and contain layers of sandstone and mudstone deposited by rivers almost 75 million years ago. The sediments were carried by prehistoric rivers to the Mowry Sea, which covered the great plains region of N America. Each layer of sediment contains characteristic FOSSIL plant and animal species of the epoch in which it was transported. The HOODOOS, gullies, etc, characteristic of the region, were formed as a result of EROSION processes following the last ICE AGE. Vegetation is sparse and desertlike (eg, CACTUS). The fossilized remains of DINOSAURS and other REPTILES, AMPHIBIANS, BIRDS and primitive MAMMALS are abundant, allowing scientists a detailed glimpse into a chapter of Earth's history. No other area of comparable size has produced such a diverse record of dinosaurs and their contemporaries. Bus tours and hikes are organized in summer and certain areas are restricted. The park has been declared a UNESCO World Heritage Site.

PHILIP J. CURRIE

Dion, Gérard, priest, sociologist, professor (b at Ste-Cécile de Frontenac, Qué 5 Dec 1912). After receiving his BA at the Collège de Lévis in 1935, Dion completed a degree in theology at Laval in 1939 and was ordained a priest. He continued his studies at Laval and in 1943 joined Laval's faculty of social sciences, becoming assistant director of the newly established department of industrial relations in 1946; he was director in 1957-63. He also edited *Relations industrielles/Industrial Relations*. During the late 1940s and early 1950s he was an active member of the Commission sacerdotales d'études sociales, a committee of clerics established in 1948 to advise the Québec Assembly of Bishops on the numerous socioeconomic problems facing Québec society after WWII. Of particular concern were the roles to be adopted by the Confédération des travailleurs catholiques du Canada and the Association professionnelle des industriels. During the 1950s he and his colleague Father Louis O'Neill became public figures when they published a scathing indictment of Québec politics entitled *L'immoralité politique dans la province de Québec*. Father Dion published extensively on labour relations, especially on the evolution of the Catholic labour movement in the 1940s and 1950s and its role in the development of a healthy industrial democracy and a modern Québecois society.

M.D. BEHIELS

Dion, Joseph Francis, political organizer, teacher (b near Onion Lake, Sask 2 July 1888; d at Bonnyville, Alta 21 Dec 1960). Dion was central to the shaping of today's Prairie native political organizations. Born to a status-Indian family of Kehiwin's Band on the Alberta-Saskatchewan border — followers and relatives of BIG BEAR — Dion as an adult abandoned Indian status and became a farmer (1903) and teacher on the Kehiwin reserve (1916-40). In the 1930s he worked with Jim BRADY and Malcolm NORRIS to found what are now the Métis Assn of Alberta (1932; president, 1932-58) and the Indian Assn of Alberta (1944). Serving in the executives of Indian, Métis and Catholic Church organizations, he travelled, lectured, recorded living traditions (published as *My Tribe the Crees*, 1979) and managed a Métis dance troupe. A relatively conservative reformer, Dion promoted the idea of native self-help through local agricultural development and the preservation of traditional culture.

BENNETT MCCARDLE

Dionne, Charles-Eusèbe, ornithologist (b at St-Denis de Kamouraska, Qué 11 July 1845; d Québec City 25 Jan 1925). The model of the self-taught man, Dionne was one of the most respected naturalists of French Canada. At 16, he became a servant at the Séminaire de Québec, where he distinguished himself by his intelligence and thirst for knowledge. Having been successively a laboratory assistant in the Faculty of Medicine at Laval U and assistant librarian, in 1882 he became curator of the zoology museum there. Under his direction, the museum rapidly became one of the richest and best organized in Québec. Dionne was a master taxidermist and the college's major source of natural-history specimens. In correspondence with ornithologists around the world and as member of the American Ornithologists' Union and several other learned societies, Dionne did much to popularize natural history in Canada with his articles in *Naturaliste canadien* and many books.

RAYMOND DUCHESNE

Dionne Case (1978), known as Re Public Service Board et al, Dionne et al, and Attorney General of Canada et al. When François Dionne, a cable-system operator, challenged the Québec Public Service Board's competence to give licences, the Supreme Court of Canada found that Parliament had exclusive jurisdiction over the regulation of the technical aspects of CABLE TELEVISION stations and over their programming if it involves the interception of television signals and their rebroadcast to subscribers of a cable-television company. Nevertheless, according to the minority opinion of 3 judges, a cable system is different from radio broadcasting (a federal matter), just as a navigation company is different from navigation, because distribution by cable can be limited to a defined territory and a cable-broadcasting company operating within a single province would therefore fall within provincial jurisdiction.

GÉRALD-A. BEAUDOIN

Dionne Quintuplets Annette, Emilie, Yvonne, Cecile and Marie aroused worldwide attention after their birth at Corbeil, Ont, to Oliva and Elzire Dionne on 24 May 1934. A sport on the human species (only 2 previous cases are on record), they were the only quintuplets to survive for more than a few days. This miracle, plus their baby cuteness, the poverty of their French Canadian parents and the controversy over their guardianship, made them the sensation of the 1930s. Fearing private exploitation, the Ontario government removed them from their parents and placed them in a specially built hospital under the care of Dr Allan Roy DAFOE, who had delivered them. Oliva Dionne fought a 9-year battle to regain them. In the interval, they became the country's biggest tourist attraction and a $500 million asset to the province. Three million people trekked to "Quintland" to watch the babies at play behind a one-way screen. Hollywood fictionalized their story in 3 movies. Dozens of commercial endorsements swelled their trust fund to nearly $1 million. But the reunion with the family in Nov 1943 was not successful. Eventually the quintuplets moved to Montréal. Three, Annette, Cecile and Marie, took husbands but the marriages failed. Annette, an epileptic, entered a convent and died in Aug 1954 during a seizure. The 4 survivors told their own, often bitter story in *We Were Five*, published in 1963. Marie, the weakest, died in Feb 1970. The remaining 3 shared the final instalment of the much depleted trust fund in 1979.

PIERRE BERTON

Diorama, museum exhibit which creates the illusion of a natural or historic scene. Typically mounted animals and preserved plants blend imperceptibly into a realistic background painting, simulating a natural habitat (the name habitat group is sometimes used). Miniature dioramas recreate natural or historic scenes on a reduced scale. Dioramas are expensive to produce, but effectively convey atmosphere as well as information and are rightly popular with museum visitors. Large dioramas are produced by artists, taxidermists and modellers, using traditional materials and new plastics. Some new dioramas are being created using computerized enlargements of smaller paintings. American taxidermist Carl Akeley created the first modern diorama in 1889. His first Canadian imitator, Lester Lynne Snyder, created dioramas at the ROYAL ONTARIO MUSEUM from 1919. Today, dioramas in major museums showcase the work of fine nature artists. The Nova Scotia Museum shows groups by Azor Vienneau. Ontario features Terry Shortt's world landscapes at the ROM, and representative scenes by Hugh Monahan, Clarence Tillenius and others at the NATIONAL MUSEUMS OF CANADA. At the Manitoba Museum of Man and Nature, Tillenius's spectacular *Red River Hunt* is complemented by several large ecological dioramas. The Saskatchewan Museum of Natural History devotes a floor to dioramas, mainly by Fred Lahrman and Robert Symons. The Provincial Museum of Alberta features a large gallery of groups (some of unusual depth), largely by Ralph Carson and Ludo Bogaert. The BC Provincial Museum presents, among others, a spectacular walk-through diorama of coastal forest and beach.

DAVID SPALDING

Dipper (Cinclidae), family comprising 4 species of BIRDS known colloquially as water ouzel. The American dipper (*Cinclus mexicanus*) occurs along mountain streams from Alaska to Panama, rarely straying into Saskatchewan. Dippers are plain, chunky and wrenlike, with short wings and tails and slender, straight bills. They dive and swim well. Both sexes sing all year. The territorial grey-black American species moves downstream in winter only where streams freeze. Dippers bob up and down on their long legs (hence their name), blinking their white eyelids as they fly into and out of water, hunting aquatic insects and sometimes fish. They are usually monogamous, occasionally polygynous. The female incubates the 4-5 eggs; both sexes care for young after they leave the nest. Nests usually domed and made of moss, are above water, often behind waterfalls or on bridges, occasionally in artificial boxes or swallows' nests.

MARTIN K. MCNICHOLL

Disability, according to the World Health Organization's (WHO) International Classification of Impairments, Disabilities and Handicaps, is the temporary, prolonged or permanent reduction or absence of the ability to perform certain commonplace activities or roles: impairment, which produces this disability, is an abnormality in an organ or in the physical or mental functions of the body; and handicap refers to the social and environmental consequences of an individual's impairment and his inability to assume his social roles. These 3 notions are interrelated, disability being the direct and inevitable consequence of an anatomical, physiological or mental impairment of the individual's daily functions; a handicap is the sociocultural consequence, in the sense that it leaves a negative impression and stigmatizes the person who is different.

According to *Obstacles*, the 1981 report of the Special Committee on the Disabled and Handicapped, over 2 million Canadians are physically or mentally disabled. WHO maintains that, worldwide (1980), one in 10 adults suffers rom some kind of chronic disability. The estimated prevalence of disability varies because ategories of impairment and degrees of disability are not always calculated in the same vay from one study to the next. The 1981 Canadian census did not contain a section on disabilities, but Statistics Canada will probably include some questions on this subject in 1986. At present, the most reliable data for Canada are included in the 1981 Canada Health survey, which learly distinguishes between short-term disability, calculated on the basis of days of inactivity, and long-term disability, which involves prolonged or chronic restriction in one or several activities.

The WHO definitions do not entirely resolve he problem of identifying those who suffer rom a disability and thus from a handicap-producing impairment. Current death rates resulting from heart disease, cancer, arthritic problems (*see* ARTHRITIS) and the rapid AGING of he Canadian population, together with accompanying degenerative illnesses, are producing a new and complex situation in which growing numbers of Canadians are impaired for at least a few years of their lives.

Scientific literature generally distinguishes between muscular-skeletal, sensory, organic, mental and psychic impairments. Muscular, skeletal and motor impairments are usually the result of the way we live (stress, lack of exercise, etc) and threaten every Canadian in the forms of, first, encephalopathies, or brain diseases produced in about 80% of cases by sudden cerebrovascular disturbances in adults (usually aged 50 years or more) and resulting in paralysis; second, myelopathies, or diseases of the spinal cord, which are caused generally by accidents and frequently result in permanent paraplegia or quadriplegia among young adults between the years of 15 and 40; third, arthropathies, or diseases of the joints resulting from arthritic or rheumatic illnesses, the incidence of which increases among Canadians over 40; fourth, myopathies, or diseases of the muscles, which are either acquired (poliomyelitis) or congenital (muscular dystrophy). To the brain and spinal cord impairments can be added hereditary diseases of the central nervous system, eg, ataxias (inco-ordination of voluntary movements) or contracted diseases such as multiple sclerosis and Parkinson's disease, whose symptoms are well known but whose causes are not. Finally, there are amputations, usually the result of an accident or of an evolutive disease such as diabetes. Results of the 1981 Health Canada survey reveal an increase in motor impairments among Canadians; restriction of activities is generally caused by pains in parts of the body and joints, heart disease, arthritis and lesions.

Sensory impairments are visual, auditory or communicative. According to the 1981 Health Canada survey 45% of Canadians wear glasses, and another 4% complain of sight problems. However, only those whose central vision is equal to or less than 20/200 for the better eye with corrective lenses and those whose peripheral vision is 20/100 or less are considered legally blind (*see* BLINDNESS AND VISUAL IMPAIRMENT). There are also degrees of AUDITORY IMPAIRMENT. Health Canada estimates that over 200 000 Canadians are profoundly deaf (but less than 1% wear a hearing aid) and an additional 1.8 million suffer hearing problems. There is a major distinction between congenital deafness, which in most cases delays a child's growth in every respect, and deafness that occurs later as a result of working conditions or age. Speech and language impairments vary in nature and severity. They generally accompany congenital deafness, but also occur in severely brain-damaged victims of sudden cerebrovascular disturbances.

Organic impairments do not always lead to a significant restriction of activities, although some have a real stigma attached to them. The organic diseases of cancer, diabetes, epilepsy, cystic fibrosis, emphysema, obesity, etc, may be the result, again, of how we live.

All mental impairments cannot be classified because not enough is yet known of them, and what happens in the life of the embryo to produce a permanently impaired person still remains a mystery. Mongolism, or Down's Syndrome, is the most frequent and best-understood type of mental retardation (about 1 birth in 600 and almost 10% of cases of mental retardation). However, only 33% of severely mentally retarded people are accurately diagnosed. Chromosome disorders, metabolic disturbances and severe neurological problems explain some cases of mental retardation, but increasingly infection and toxic agents (mainly mercury and lead) are being linked with the abnormal development of the fetus. People with IQs under 70 are generally included in the mentally retarded category, but most of them are only slightly impaired. The Canadian Association for the Mentally Retarded estimates that about 3% of Canadians suffer from some degree of mental retardation. The deteriorating quality of the environment may also play a large part in this high rate.

In Canada, severe psychic problems are generally judged by the disability they cause and the stigma attached to those suffering from them. There is a danger, however, in the resulting temptation to pass legislation making it easy to place people in protected environments and of encouraging the institutionalization of "insanity." Although all major mental problems have disabling consequences for individuals, they should not be considered as psychopathological impairments that are to the mind what spinal diseases are to the body.

Attitudes Towards Impaired People People with noticeable impairments are labelled different or "deviant." Following the work of Irving Goffman, deviance has been interpreted as divergence from the dominant norms that vary from society to society. Stigmatization has been defined as the social process of identifying an undesirable difference in an individual and of disqualifying the individual with that deviance. Victimization is the process by which the stigmatized individuals interiorize the very norms that disqualify them, thus contributing to their own stigmatization. This is the complex process within which attitudes towards the disabled and programs designed to change other people's negative attitudes must be understood. Some 60 research studies clearly established the relationship between attitudes towards the disabled and variables such as categories of impairment, the setting in which the interaction occurs, and socio-personal data on the disabled and nondisabled groups. These studies have generally confirmed not only that people do have negative attitudes towards disabled persons, but that it is difficult to specify what exactly could be considered a positive attitude. These studies also reveal that negative attitudes can be altered when disabled persons are encountered in a day-to-day context, but that in these same circumstances the desire to help disabled persons diminishes and assistance may be viewed as springing more from a negative than a positive attitude. Most of the people taking part in the studies were intensely anxious in the presence of a disabled person and their avoidance increased with the visual severity of the handicap. A number of observations reveal that children react more positively to physical than to other impairments.

According to researchers who have studied methods of changing negative attitudes, professionals who are supposedly helping the disabled to readapt may be among those most guilty of stigmatization. The evidence of one study suggests that the programs that succeed in fostering positive attitudes are those in which equal status exists between the subjects (same age or professional category); those that reduce the discomfort of the nondisabled person; and those that include meetings with disabled people who do not behave according to stereotypical patterns. The failure of most programs to change social attitudes illustrates how deeply rooted — psychologically, socially and culturally — are negative behaviour and stigmatizing attitudes.

Rehabilitation Philosophies The new "normalization" philosophies that have been recently advanced by groups of disabled persons take exception to the marginalization noted above. Normalization implies that the disabled should be able to live as similarly as possible to the nondisabled. The Autonomous Living Movement is more particularly concerned with battling for rights and emphasizes that such rights will not be attained until the disabled, like any other minority group, demand them. The battle will probably be long because employers are less inclined to hire disabled people than any other group, believing it to be less expensive to hire nondisabled people. Twenty years ago, the creation of large specialized institutions such as residential centres, specialized schools and sheltered workshops represented Canada's most progressive solution to the problems posed by most disabled persons. In the early 1970s, society began to accept the philosophy of normalization and recognition of the rights of the disabled. In the past 10 years, personalized services have been established and integration and direct political activity by disabled groups have increased, all of which is beginning to change the nature of the services offered to these people. However, these advances are not very significant considering that 70% to 95% of provincial budgets in 1982 were still allocated to covering the cost of direct services in rehabilitation institutions cut off from society, and that few resources were used for personalized and integrated services. Genuine changes appear to be coming more from disabled groups themselves, which are organizing ongoing, self-help groups, or from politically militant action groups. It is no longer a question of adapting behaviour to the dominant social norms, but of challenging the definitions established by those who are "normal" and demanding the right to be different.

Theoretically, it seems obvious that rehabilitation must occur in a context that is as similar as possible to that of the nondisabled and that it must include medical and physiotherapeutic features. Despite this emphasis on the rehabilitative process, the importance of early detection of impairment and prevention must not be ignored. GILLES BIBEAU

Disallowance The CONSTITUTION ACT 1867 provides that any ACT of a provincial legislature must be promptly sent to the GOVERNOR GENERAL and that the governor general-in-council (federal CABINET) may disallow any such Act (wipe it off the statute book) within 1 year. Every province except PEI and Newfoundland has had provincial Acts disallowed (the combined total being 112), for a variety of reasons: they were considered unconstitutional, "contrary to Dominion policy" or "Dominion interest," or "contrary to reason, justice and natural equity." The last disallowance was in 1943. EUGENE A. FORSEY

Disarmament Since the 19th century, world powers have conferred in peacetime about disarmament, believing that to avoid war, weapons should be reduced in number or eliminated. A new era in warfare began when bombing of cities and industry through WORLD WAR II climaxed with the atomic bombing of Hiroshima and Nagasaki, Japan. Many political and scientific leaders began to put disarmament at the head of problems to be solved in order for humanity to have a better future.

Negotiations to prevent nuclear war began in 1946, usually under the auspices of the UN. In 1959 Nikita Khrushchev proposed in the UN General Assembly that the nations should commit themselves to complete disarmament. Although this was not achieved by several subsequent UN disarmament committees, some measure of "arms control" was reached — eg, the 1963 partial ban on testing nuclear weapons and the 1968 Non-Proliferation Treaty. Meanwhile, since the race to build intercontinental missiles continued, the superpowers in 1969 decided to hold strategic arms limitation talks by themselves. A treaty, SALT I, came into force in 1972. A second treaty, SALT II, was rejected by the US Senate.

NATO fears that the Warsaw Treaty nations (the USSR and its eastern European allies) have superiority in conventional weapons (guns, tanks, attack aircraft), which would allow them to invade western Europe, sweeping aside the defending conventional forces. Until the 1970s the US was believed to have superiority in intercontinental aircraft and missiles so that it could deter any conventional attack by the threat of nuclear destruction, which it could visit on the USSR and its allies without incurring corresponding damage. However, with a change through the 1970s in the balance of intercontinental armaments, the theory of graduated response was evolved. An invasion by conventional forces would be met by limited response with nuclear weapons of theatre range, the threat of escalation causing the combatants to cease hostilities.

Because Canada helped produce the atomic bomb, it has participated in disarmament talks since the beginning, advocating mutually balanced, verifiable disarmament. But Canada's freedom of expression has been limited by the need for solidarity within NATO. The government's concerns, apparently shared by an increasing number of Canadians in the 1980s, include global destruction, the strategic implications of a nuclear war between the superpowers (because of Canada's geographical location) and damage to delicate environments such as the Arctic, Great Lakes and coasts, caused by the testing of nuclear weapons or war. International conferences on arms control are to continue, but it seems clear that no useful results can be expected unless the superpowers resume negotiations on SALT or START (Strategic Arms Reduction Talks). See ARMAMENTS; PACIFISM; WOMEN'S INTERNATIONAL LEAGUE FOR PEACE AND FREEDOM; PEACE MOVEMENT. E.L.M. BURNS

Disasters Catastrophic accidents or natural disasters may be spectacular or tragic, but seldom have great historical significance. In the spring of 1914 Canada's worst mining and marine calamities and Newfoundland's worst sealing disasters did not affect the world as much as did a single assassination in Sarajevo. Nevertheless, catastrophic events even with few fatalities may have historic implications, aside from the personal tragedies suffered by the victims, their families and communities. A gold-mine disaster in Moose River, NS, 12-23 Apr 1936, involved only 3 trapped men, 2 of whom survived; but firsthand accounts by the Canadian Broadcasting Corp broke new ground in radio news reporting. In addition, studies of numerous major accidents have led to improvements in the safety of equipment and work practices.

Rockfalls and Avalanches The Lower Town in Québec City has been the site of major rockfalls. On 17 May 1841, boulders from Cap Diamant demolished 8 houses and killed 32 people but did not deter building in dangerous areas. On 19 Sept 1889 a massive ROCKSLIDE smashed much of Champlain St, killing 45; the disaster would have been worse if many families had not been absent, attending 2 wakes. The most disastrous rockfall in Canadian history was the FRANK SLIDE of 29 Apr 1903, which claimed at least 70 lives in Frank, NWT [Alberta].

Snowslides have always been a threat in the Rockies. Just before midnight on 5 Mar 1910, an AVALANCHE at Bear Creek in the ROGERS PASS engulfed a work crew that had been clearing snow from an earlier slide across the CPR main line. One man survived; 62 were killed.

On 4 May 1971, during a prolonged rainstorm, a 213 m hole appeared in the mud and clay of St-Jean-Vianney, Qué. The crater swallowed 36 homes, several cars and a bus, and claimed 31 lives.

Aviation The first death involving an airplane in Canada was at Victoria, BC, on 6 Aug 1913, when American barnstormer John M. Bryant was killed in the crash of his Curtiss seaplane. In subsequent fatal accidents the small load capacities of the aircraft minimized the number of deaths, but when aircraft became larger, and their commercial use more common, crashes assumed horrendous proportions. Canada's first major air disaster occurred on 25 Aug 1928 when a Ford Trimotor flew into Puget Sd in bad weather; 7 persons were killed. The worst commercial airline accident in Canada or involving Canadian aircraft was at Ste-Thérèse-de-Blainville, Qué, on 29 Nov 1963, when a TCA DC-8F crashed 4 minutes after takeoff from Montréal International (Dorval) Airport, killing all 118 persons aboard. The cause of the crash was never satisfactorily explained. At Toronto on 5 July 1970 an Air Canada DC-8 made a heavy landing, bounced and lost one starboard engine. In the pilot's attempt to take off and land again the other starboard engine fell off and the aircraft crashed, killing all 109 persons aboard. A number of other commercial airline crashes have occurred, several of them claiming dozens of lives each. They have involved faulty aircraft, collisions between aircraft, collisions with ground vehicles and undetermined causes.

Some disasters are notable for reasons other than casualty figures. The crash of a Pan-Arctic Oils Lockheed Electra (Rea Point, NWT, 30 Oct 1974) was the worst accident involving a non-commercial aircraft; 32 of the 34 persons aboard were lost. Twenty-three persons were killed on 9 Sept 1949 when a Québec Airways DC-3 was sabotaged with a bomb and exploded and crashed near St-Joachim, Qué. J.A. Guay and 2 accom plices were convicted and hanged. The wors crash in the history of the RCAF, apart from ca sualties sustained overseas, occurred on 19 Oc 1943 when a Liberator bomber crashed near St Donat, Qué, killing 24; many of those aboar were on leave. The wreckage was not locate until June 1946.

Bridges The QUÉBEC BRIDGE was involved in major accidents during construction. On 29 Au 1907, 75 workmen were killed, and on 11 Sep 1916, 13 men died. Of the several bridges tha have been built to cross the harbour of Victoria BC, at Point Ellice, a metal, 4-span structur built in 1885 was too weak for tramlines tha were later built across it. On 26 May 1896, dur ing celebrations for the queen's birthday, on span fell out, taking a loaded streetcar with it Fifty-five persons died in this, the worst street car accident in N American history. On 1 June 1958, during construction of Vancouver' present Second Narrows Bridge, one span col lapsed into Burrard Inlet, taking 18 men to thei deaths. It was later concluded that design error had been committed by 2 engineers who wer among the dead.

Coal Mining involves deep tunnels, soft rock dust, explosives and vulnerable ventilation sys tems. Major coal-mine disasters have occurred a various times across the country. The first wa probably at Westville, Pictou County, NS, on 1 May 1873 after a fire broke out at the coal face As workers were leaving and a squad of fire fighters entering, an explosion ripped through the tunnels; secondary explosions trapped many rescuers. The mine was sealed to starve the fir of oxygen, and 2 years passed before the las of 60 bodies were recovered. The men left 3 widows and 80 children.

The worst coal-mine disaster was on 19 June 1914 at Hillcrest, Alta. It is believed that a fall of rock struck a spark, setting off dust explosions that crippled the ventilating fans and burned away half the oxygen in the mine. A total of 18 men died, leaving 130 widows and about 40 children.

In the SPRINGHILL, NS, mines alone, from 1881 to 1969, 424 persons lost their lives. On 21 Feb

Coal mining has been one of Canada's most dangerous occupations. Shown below is the mass grave for the victims of the 1914 coal-mine explosion — the worst in Canadian history — at Hillcrest, Alta (*courtesy Elliott and Nicole Bernshaw/Bernshaw Photography*).

891, 125 miners were killed in an explosion. On 1 Nov 1956 an accident killing 39 men was notable for the rescue of 88 trapped survivors. On 23 Oct 1958, after the collapse of a tunnel in which 75 men died, 18 were rescued from levels as deep as 3960 m — the deepest rescues ever conducted in Canada. The other 185 died in 167 separate accidents. *See* MINING SAFETY.

Earthquakes Although parts of central and Atlantic Canada have been shaken by earth tremors, the only one causing extensive loss of life was centered on the Gulf of St Lawrence on 18 Nov 1929. A 4.6 m tidal wave struck Newfoundland's Burin Peninsula, sweeping away houses, boats and fish stages. Damage was estimated at $1 million; 27 people died.

Epidemics Before modern immunization programs and vaccines practically eliminated EPIDEMICS in Canada, thousands of deaths resulted from outbreaks of smallpox, cholera, typhus, INFLUENZA and other contagious diseases. In 1953 polio affected more than 8000 Canadians, killing 481; the next year, with Salk vaccine coming into use, the death toll fell to 157. Such progress has sometimes been difficult; compulsory vaccination for smallpox was bitterly opposed in Montréal until an 1885 outbreak claimed 5864 lives and made vaccination respectable.

Fires and Explosions The most deadly structural fire in what is now Canada consumed the Knights of Columbus hostel in St John's, Nfld, on 12 Dec 1942. An arsonist set fire to the building when it was packed with military personnel and their companions. The hostel was a firetrap: doors opened inward, exits were restricted and there was no emergency lighting system. Within 5 minutes, 99 persons had been burned to death and 100 seriously injured. The main fire station was only 180 metres away, but the building was doomed before the engines arrived.

The burning of the cruise ship NORONIC in Toronto Harbour, on the night of 17 Sept 1949, claimed 118 lives. The blaze, apparently due to spontaneous combustion in a closet, broke out at 2:30 AM when passengers were asleep and fewer than 20 crewmen were aboard; it was well advanced before discovery. Contributing factors included the absence of automatic alarms, a lack of direction by officers and panic.

On 9 Jan 1927 a small fire broke out in the Laurier Palace Theatre, Montréal. Firemen arrived within 2 minutes and the blaze was extinguished in 10, but in the panic to escape an overcrowded building, many children piled up at the bases of stairways; 12 were crushed to death and 64 were asphyxiated. The most deadly fire in recent years occurred at Chapais, Qué (31 Dec 1979), when a man playing with a lighter in a social club set a fire that killed 44 persons.

Several major forest fires have destroyed large stands of timber and taken many lives. The Miramichi fire, which began 5 Oct 1825 after a dry summer, devastated some 15 500 km^2 north of NB's MIRAMICHI R, and destroyed Douglastown and NEWCASTLE. Estimates of the death toll run from 200 to 500. The area's TIMBER TRADE was crippled for many years, but the fire actually spurred development of logging elsewhere in British North America.

Northern Ontario has been struck by several disastrous forest fires. The worst, the Matheson fire, resulted from small blazes started by lightning and locomotive sparks which combined into a firestorm on 29 July 1916. A wall of flames struck Cochrane, Matheson and environs, burning both towns and killing at least 228.

Many cities have had disastrous fires, particularly in the 19th century when crowded, flammable buildings were concentrated, and before the advent of modern watermains, pumps and professional fire brigades. In St John's, Nfld, 3 fires (12 Feb 1816, 7 Nov 1817 and 21 Nov 1817) drove 2600 people (of a total population of 10 000) from their homes. Another fire, on 9 June 1846, levelled most of what was still a tinderbox. The city was rebuilt with more stone and firebreaks. Nevertheless, on 8-9 July 1892 a windswept blaze destroyed the city again. Québec City had 2 fires, 28 May and 28 June 1845, which killed at least 23 and left 15 000-18 000 homeless. The old walled section and lower town were spared, but the surviving city was smaller than that captured by James Wolfe 86 years before. The city was rebuilt with more stone and wider streets. However, to save money the city skimped on fire-fighting equipment and in 1866 reduced the size of the fire brigade. On 14 Oct 1866 a fire pushed by high winds took 5 lives, burned over 2000 homes and left 18 000-20 000 homeless. Again, the walled city and lower town were spared. Saint John, NB, had major fires in 1837 and 1839. In spite of tighter building bylaws, a fire on 20 June 1877 destroyed two-thirds of the city, leaving 15 000 homeless.

The HALIFAX EXPLOSION of 6 Dec 1917 probably ranks as Canada's most famous disaster and, epidemics aside, the worst single one in our history. Property damage exceeded $35 million and over 1600 persons were killed.

Highway The worst single-vehicle accident in Canada (and the worst bus disaster in Canada or the US) occurred near Eastman, Qué, on 4 Aug 1978. The brakes of a chartered bus failed and it plunged into Lac d'Argent, killing 41 physically or mentally handicapped persons. This toll was more than double that of Canada's worst previous accident, that of 31 July 1953, when a bus plunged into a canal near Morrisburg, Ont, drowning 20.

Marine The earliest shipwreck may have involved John CABOT, who disappeared in 1498 on his second voyage; or Gaspar CORTE-REAL, who vanished in 1501 on a voyage to Newfoundland; or an anonymous BASQUE whaler. The wreck of the *Delight*, one of Sir Humphrey GILBERT's ships, on Sable I (29 Aug 1583), when at least 85 men were drowned, is the first identifiable marine disaster. On 23 Aug 1711 a British fleet under Rear Adm Sir Hovenden Walker, sailing to attack Québec, blundered onto the rocks of Île-aux-Oeufs. The 19 warships and 41 other ships carried over 11 000 men; 7 transports and a supply ship were lost with as many as 950 men. Poor charts, rugged and sparsely inhabited coastlines and inadequate marine aids (fog signals, lighthouses, lifesaving stations) combined to take a terrible toll of ships, which frequently lacked lifeboat capacity for all aboard. As with air disasters, the casualty figures were often relatively low simply because the carriers had limited space.

Three Canadian marine disasters are particularly noteworthy. On 29 May 1914, on her first night out on a voyage from Québec, the EMPRESS OF IRELAND, owned by the Canadian Pacific Steamship Co, was sailing in scattered fog near Father Point [Rimouski], Qué. She was struck broadside by the loaded Norwegian collier *Storstad*, which opened a large hole in the liner's hull. The *Empress* filled rapidly and passengers were trapped. Only 14 minutes elapsed from impact to sinking. Of 1057 passengers and 420 crew, 1014 died.

On 20 Mar 1873 the *Atlantic*, owned by White Star Line, sailed from Liverpool to New York with 811 passengers, 4 officers and a crew of 141. Its coal was consumed faster than was anticipated, and on Mar 31 the captain decided to make for Halifax. At 3:15 AM, Apr 1, the ship blundered onto Meagher's Rock (Prospect, NS) and listed so sharply that those below deck were trapped; many who reached the deck were washed overboard. In spite of heroic rescue efforts by crewmen and local inhabitants, 534 men and one child died.

On 23 Oct 1918, sailing in a snowstorm from Skagway, Alaska, to Vancouver, the *Princess Sophia*, CP Steamships, ran onto Vanderbilt Reef, Lynn Canal. Smaller craft approached, but heavy seas prevented them from rescuing passengers. Two days of pounding by waves finally broke the ship's hull; on Oct 25 the ship sank with the loss of all 343 aboard.

Some wrecks have attained notoriety for particularly dramatic, tragic or unusual aspects. The *Montreal* (715-ton paddle steamer) burned near Québec on 26 June 1857 with the loss of 253. The crew was scandalously slow responding to the report of fire; the ship had caught fire on at least 3 previous occasions. On 24 May 1881, the overloaded *Victoria* (27-ton paddle steamer) capsized in the Thames R near London, Ont. In spite of relatively shallow water, 182 perished. The tragic sinking of the oil rig *Ocean Ranger*, 265 km east of Newfoundland on 15 Feb 1982, was Canada's first disaster with this type of vessel; 84 men were lost.

Both fishing and sealing off the Atlantic coast have claimed many lives over the years. As recently as 20 June 1959 the fishing fleet of Escuminac, NB, was hit by a massive storm that sank 22 boats and drowned 35 men. It is estimated that between 1810 and 1870 the Newfoundland seal fishery lost some 400 vessels and 1000 men in the ice floes. Although most mishaps involved relatively few lives, the failure of the *Newfoundland* to recover her sealers during a storm, 31 Mar-2 Apr 1914, caused 77 to perish; and the sealer *Southern Cross* vanished with 173 aboard.

Railways The first major rail tragedy was on 27 Oct 1854 at Baptiste Creek, 24 km west of Chatham, Ont. In predawn darkness and fog a gravel train on the Great Western Ry's main line was hit by an express that was 7 hours late. The accident killed 52 persons and seriously injured 48 more. The worst wreck occurred at St-Hilaire, Canada E, at 1:10 AM, 29 June 1864. A Grand Trunk train with 458 passengers was unable to stop for an open swing bridge over the Richelieu R. The train piled up in a massive wreck on the barges passing through; there were 99 deaths and over 100 injuries. The worst level-crossing accident in Canada was at Louisville, Qué, on 15 Aug 1936, when a truck carrying 43 men from a political meeting was hit by a freight; 22 died.

Storms and Floods The RED R in southern Manitoba floods regularly. In May 1950 a flood inundated many valley towns and one-sixth of WINNIPEG; more than 100 000 persons had to be evacuated. The worst aspects of such floods have been alleviated by the construction of floodways to carry off spring overflow.

A tornado struck the core of Regina on 30 June 1912, killing 28 persons and causing $6 million in damages. The worst inland storm was Hurricane Hazel, which struck southern and central Ontario on 15 Oct 1954 and dumped over 100 mm of rain on Toronto in 12 hours. There were 83 deaths, most of them in the Toronto area, and extensive property damage.

HUGH A. HALLIDAY

Discovery, famous ship belonging to the East India Company, which first sailed into the Arctic under the command of George Weymouth in 1602. The same ship was used by Henry HUDSON to explore Hudson Bay in 1610. Hudson was cut adrift, but his ship and 8 of his mutinous crew survived the passage home. James COOK and George VANCOUVER sailed different ships of the same name.

JAMES MARSH

Disease can be defined as an unhealthy condition of body or mind. Many diseases are exacerbated by malnutrition and infection (which are often the consequence of poverty, ignorance, bad sanitation, polluted water, contaminated food) and are influenced by, among other factors, geography, climate and excessive population growth. Modern man, who has created a physical and social environment often inimical to his health, is vulnerable as well to a wide range of GENETIC DISEASES and conditions that may affect the whole body or parts of the body. These congenital diseases and conditions include clubfeet, heart defects, various deformities of the nervous system, Down's syndrome (characterized by distinctive physical appearance and mental defect) and many biochemical defects and anomalies.

In Canada in the early 1980s the average age at death of males and females was 61.5 years and 67 years, respectively. The leading causes of death in Canada are HEART DISEASE, CANCER, accidents, pneumonia and INFLUENZA, DIABETES MELLITUS and cirrhosis of the liver. Infectious diseases, which killed between 25-33% of Canada's population in 1861, now rarely cause death. *See also* SEXUALLY TRANSMITTED DISEASE; ALCOHOLISM; MENTAL HEALTH; NATIVE PEOPLE, HEALTH.

Distance Learning commonly refers to learning that takes place in a situation where teacher and student are physically separated. The terms "distance education" and "open education" are often used interchangeably, although the latter also indicates that the standards for entry are "open," which may not be true for all distance-education institutions.

Distance education is not new, but it has only recently become the subject of academic interest. In 1969 the Open University was founded in the UK. Established by Harold Wilson's Labour government it is committed, like distance-education programs everywhere, to democratizing education by making it accessible to people unable or unwilling to attend traditional institutions. In the past 16 years, post-secondary distance-learning institutes, all patterned to some degree on Britain's Open University, have sprung up throughout the world. Distance educators in both industrialized and nonindustrialized nations share a belief in the power of education to help individuals realize their own potential and to help them contribute more productively to the economy. They are also united by the awareness that among traditional educators and the general public, distance education, perhaps particularly at the post-secondary level, is considered second-rate. This opinion stems partly from unreliable correspondence schools, partly from the belief that there is no valid substitute for face-to-face interaction between student and teacher, and partly from the lack of entrance requirements. Distance educators, in reaction to these negative opinions, avoid the term "correspondence" in favour of "distance" and "open." They argue that they meet and often surpass the rigorous standards of conventional universities by presenting uniform courses and by strictly regulating controls over examinations; that students receive support through tutors who are often more accessible than most professors are; and that students are encouraged to improve their writing skills and realistically plan their education with the help of the universities' counselling staff. At the twelfth conference of the International Council for Correspondence Education held in Vancouver in June 1982, the most intensely debated motion was one to change the council's name to the International Council for Distance Education, a motion passed by a vote of 500-50.

Distance learning has proven suitable to the needs of both industrialized and Third World nations. In the former, it is increasingly useful for continuing education (in Canada, distance-education programs have reached native people in rural areas, prisoners, the handicapped, etc); in the Third World, it is gaining favour as an economical means of raising the levels of LITERACY and of teaching skills to people who are under enormous pressure to industrialize.

In Canada, all 10 provinces have correspondence programs, most of which are run by the correspondence branch of the Department of Education. These programs, which serve individuals wishing to complete the provincial public-school curriculum, account for the majority of enrolments in distance education, and most of those enrolled are adults. The Alberta Correspondence School, founded in 1923, now serves some 28 000 students.

Several private companies and business and professional associations run their own continuing-education divisions, which develop programs for the professional upgrading of their employees or members. In most cases this involves specific vocational and professional courses rather than academic subjects. Where academic subjects are required, associations usually involve a university in the program. For example, ATHABASCA UNIVERSITY and the Law Society of Alberta jointly produced a distance-education course, "Accounting in a Law Office," which Athabasca offers to students identified by the society. At University of Alberta, the Faculty of Extension develops and delivers distance-education courses for local government administrators throughout the province. Inaugurated 25 years ago, the Local Government Studies Certificate program has an advisory committee representing the university, 3 government departments and several municipal associations.

Although several colleges and institutes of technology have developed excellent distance-learning materials, generally these institutions tend to be more interested in increasing access to education through adult extension programs. The increasing involvement of universities, however, is reflected in the establishment of departments or faculties of extension on most Canadian campuses. Many of these faculties, which have developed steadily since the 1960s, have shifted their emphasis from offering evening courses on campus to offering correspondence credit courses. Although no postgraduate-level distance-education programs are yet available in Canada as they are in countries such as England and Australia, nearly 25 universities now offer distance-learning programs leading to undergraduate degrees and 3 Canadian institutions serve distance students exclusively at the university level: the Télé-université in Québec (est 1972); Athabasca University in Alberta (est 1972); and the Open Learning Institute of BC (est 1978). These 3 institutions are distinguished by their emphasis on services to students and on course design. Until recently, university correspondence courses consisted of elaborated lecture notes mailed to students. Interaction between teacher and student was restricted to the marking of assignments and exams. These 3 institutions, however, offer much more extensive assistance, ranging from teleconferencing (telephone tutoring to remote learning centres, which are equipped with video playback machines, computer terminals, etc) to group tutorials and seminars. The augmented services reflect the recognition that distance learning is a lonely activity and that the motivation traditionally supplied through personal contact with the instructor in the classroom is not available; course materials must therefore be carefully designed to alleviate some of the impersonal aspects of what has been called "the most industrialized form of education." Courses are designed by editors and instructional designers, working with the course author.

While correspondence courses in the past consisted entirely of printed materials, there is a growing use of educational technology, eg, radio, television, teleconferencing, audio cassettes and, most recently, computers. In Alberta, for example, University of Calgary and Athabasca University have successfully conducted experiments in teleconferencing with TELIDON, Canada's computer-graphics innovation, and th Alberta Correspondence School has used Telido to teach a course in mechanics. The private sec tor has also made advances in the area of com puterized instruction, eg, a videodisc progran was launched by General Motors throughout N America. JOHN R. THOMPSO

Reading: J.S. Daniel, M.A. Stroud and John R. Thomp son, eds, *Learning at a Distance* (1982).

Distant Early Warning (DEW) Line, *see* EAR LY-WARNING RADAR.

Distilling Industry, that part of the FOOD AN BEVERAGE INDUSTRIES engaged in clarifying, fla vouring, blending and aging alcohol to mak potable spirits (eg, brandies, grain spirits, rum and establishments which manufacture ethy alcohol, whether or not used in potable spirits Manufacturers of methyl, butyl or isopropy alcohol are considered part of the CHEMICAL IN DUSTRIES. The Canadian distilling industry is world-class multinational INDUSTRY; in fact, th 2 companies ranked largest in the world (SEA GRAM and HIRAM WALKER) are Canadian. Canadian distilled spirits products are internationally renowned for quality and consistency.

In 1982 Canada's 33 distilleries employe over 2600 production workers and were responsible for over 10 000 jobs in the supplyin industries. In 1983 Canadians consumed approximately 140 million litres of domesticall distilled beverages. This amount was substantially less than the 1980 total of 160 million litres, and the decrease can be attributed to th general economic recession and to higher taxe on alcoholic beverages. In 1982 whisky accounted for two-thirds of the total domestic production of 807 million litres. The distilling industry is one of Canada's largest exporters o finished goods: 45% of domestic production i exported each year.

Distillers annually purchase over $300 million worth of Canadian grain (the raw materia used in making spirits) and manufacture goods (eg, GLASS bottles, caps, other packagin materials). Part of the stillage or refuse from grain distilleries has been turned into useful byproducts, eg, supplements in cattle, poultry and hog feeds.

History

The earliest settlers in NEW FRANCE imported their alcoholic beverages from France, usually (because of high transportation costs) high-proof brandies and liqueurs. The first distillery in what is now Canada was probably established by Intendant Jean TALON: there is evidence that the brewery he ordered built in 166 contained a still. As West Indian rums becam available relatively cheaply, there was little incentive for settlers to establish a domestic distilling industry until the latter half of the 18th century, when heavy shipping duties began t make West Indian rum prohibitively expensive. Thus, the first recorded distillery was established at Québec City in 1769 to produce rum from imported molasses. After the arrival of the LOYALISTS, whisky from grain began to be produced throughout the grain-growing areas. A that time, millers received a tithe (one-tenth) of all the grain they milled in payment. Some operators turned their surplus into whisky, which was usually easily sold in the neighbourhood and enjoyed the added advantage of being cheaper to transport than grain or flour. Canadian spirits were in demand in the US at least as early as 1861. Some millers abandoned the FLOUR MILLING industry and, by 1840, over 200 distilleries were operating in Upper and Lower Canada. Some of the leading distillers began operations in this early period; eg, Hiram Walker established his enterprise in 1858.

Distillers played a vital part in WWI, since alcohol was a necessary product for various war materials. Every distiller contributed to the war

The Seagram Museum, interior display showing early copper still *(courtesy ©Hartill Art Associates)*.

ffort and one entire plant was converted to the manufacture of acetone, a component of the smokeless explosive cordite. The wartime need for alcohol led to the adoption of prohibition in all provinces except Québec (which, in 1919, enacted laws prohibiting sale of distilled spirits but permitting that of wine and beer). Prohibition was repealed at different dates in the different provinces, between 1921 and 1930. PEI was the exception, retaining prohibition until 1948. Liquor rationing was common in many areas during WWII, largely because alcohol was again required for wartime purposes. In 1942 all Canadian distilleries began production of war alcohol and, from 1943 to 1945, produced 68 million litres of high-proof alcohol annually.

Even before its development into an industry proper, distilling had been under government regulation. For example, John Graves SIMCOE, first lieutenant-governor of UPPER CANADA, issued 51 still licences during his first year in office. Shortly after the turn of the 19th century, the first government distillery inspectors were appointed and, in 1846, a law was enacted regarding strength requirements. The federal government's power to pass laws relating to the import or manufacture of liquors in Canada was established under the CONSTITUTION ACT, 1867; the same Act gave the provinces control of the retail liquor trade. The Canadian government enacted its first "adulteration of food" legislation in 1874, prompted by the quantity of adulterated liquor being sold. Common additives were salt, tobacco, opium, Indian hemp, copper sulphate and salts of lead or zinc. The Food and Drugs Act, passed in 1954 and now administered by Health and Welfare Canada, includes careful definitions of standards for all types of spirits and specifies packaging and labelling requirements. The department maintains a staff of inspectors to ensure the observance of the regulations (*see* FOOD LEGISLATION; REGULATORY PROCESS). Also, the excise division of Revenue Canada has specially trained officers to carry out the rigid regulations governing distillers and their products in every phase of the distilling, bottling and packaging operations. The offices and equipment they use are provided by the distillers and located on their premises. A label marked, for example, "distilled," "blended," "bottled in bond," "under Canadian Government supervision," guarantees that the regulations have been carried out.

Duties were levied on alcoholic beverages imported into Canada from earliest colonial times; however, the first tax (one shilling and 3 pence per gallon) was imposed on Canadian-produced spirits in 1794. Today's excise duty stands at $9.649 per litre of pure alcohol. To this is added a 12% sales tax on the duty-paid value of the goods. After each province repealed PROHIBITION, it introduced government-controlled liquor stores. Today distillers may sell only to provincial and territorial liquor boards which, in turn, sell distilled spirits products in government-run retail stores. The federal and provincial governments now extract over $2 billion of direct taxes from distilled spirits products with an FOB (free on board) value of approximately $400 million. KAY KENDALL

Distribution of Powers, the legislative competences of the federal and provincial orders of government as outlined in the CONSTITUTION ACT, 1867, and interpreted by the JUDICIAL COMMITTEE OF THE PRIVY COUNCIL until 1949, and from then by the SUPREME COURT OF CANADA. The distribution of executive power is theoretically similar to the distribution of legislative power; judicial power is also divided to some extent, although most of it belongs to the federal government. The Constitution Act, 1867 (s91), grants broad powers to the federal government to legislate for "Peace, Order and good Government in Canada in relation to all Matters not coming within the classes of subjects by this Act assigned exclusively to the Legislatures of the Provinces." The Fathers of Confederation took as their guiding principle that jurisdiction over matters of national interest would be given to Parliament and those of particular interest to the provinces. Because Québec was governed by a CIVIL CODE, the provinces were granted jurisdiction over property and civil rights and Québec was excluded from section 94, which allowed for the possible standardization of private law for the provinces. Parliament was also given greater residuary jurisdiction than were the provincial legislatures. Areas of federal jurisdiction include trade and commerce, direct and indirect taxation, currency, the postal service, census taking and statistics, national defence, the federal civil service, navigation, fisheries, banking, copyright, Indians and Indian reserves, naturalization, marriage and divorce, criminal law, penitentiaries and interprovincial works and undertakings. By constitutional amendment, Parliament gained exclusive jurisdiction over unemployment insurance in 1940.

In 1949, by amendment (s91.1) to the Constitution Act, Parliament was granted the power to amend the Constitution of Canada except in matters affecting provincial jurisdictions and privileges. In a 1949 decision on the Senate, the Supreme Court of Canada restricted the interpretation of the expression "Constitution of Canada" by stating that this expression in s91.1 referred to the internal federal Constitution and not to the Constitution of all Canada. For example, Parliament could not abolish the Senate because it represents the provinces and is not exclusively a federal concern. The Constitution Act, 1982, repealed s91.1. Section 44 of the Act states that, subject to sections 41 and 42, "Parliament may exclusively make laws amending the Constitution of Canada in relation to the executive government of Canada or the Senate and House of Commons." The provinces have had the right to amend their internal constitutions (except as regards the office of the lieutenant-governor) since 1867. Through jurisprudence, federal residuary power has come to include (partly or wholly) the incorporation of businesses with federal objectives, aeronautics, radio, television, nuclear energy, responsibility for the national capital, offshore mineral rights along the BC coast, official languages within the federal sphere, citizenship, foreign affairs and the control of drugs. Again, through jurisprudence, the introductory clause to s91 now includes emergency powers in peace and war.

Provincial legislatures have jurisdiction, among other things, over their internal constitutions, direct taxation for provincial purposes, municipalities, school boards, hospitals, property and civil rights (their largest area of competence), administration of civil and criminal justice, penalties for infraction of provincial statutes, prisons, celebration of marriage, provincial civil service, local works and corporations with provincial objectives. The courts have restrictively interpreted federal power over commerce and liberally interpreted provincial power over property and civil rights. There are 4 concurrent jurisdictions: agriculture, immigration (s95), old-age pensions and supplementary benefits (s94A). In the case of dispute, federal legislation will prevail for areas under s95 and provincial legislation for those under s94A. Education is allocated to the provinces (s93), but is subject to certain religious guarantees. The conditional and supplementary powers allocated in s93 to Parliament have fallen into disuse. Even though each level of government is restricted to its own legislative sphere, frequently one or another has assumed responsibilities which did not clearly belong to it. The provinces, through a legal fiction recognized by the courts, have converted some originally indirect taxes, eg, sales and purchase taxes, into direct ones. The power to spend money remains an extremely vague and contentious area. Parliament assumes that it may do so where it does not necessarily have the power to enact legislation; such spending is well received by the provinces when it applies to EQUALIZATION PAYMENTS, but less so when it infringes on provincial fields such as health, social security and education.

Under the Constitution Act, 1982, the principle of equalization is enshrined (s36), but it is unclear how it can be implemented. Provincial jurisdiction over natural resources was enlarged, in 1982, to include concurrent power in interprovincial commerce and extraterritorial marketing (though with federal paramountcy). The provinces have also been granted power of indirect taxation of their natural resources (*see also* INTERGOVERNMENTAL FINANCE). The history of Canadian FEDERALISM is basically an account of disputes over the distribution of powers. From the 1880s until the 1930s federal powers waned relatively, largely because the Judicial Committee of the Privy Council ignored the centralist intentions of many (but not all) of its creators and favoured provincial autonomy in its interpretation of the Constitution Act, 1867; the Supreme Court of Canada, on the other hand, has in its judgements tended generally to strengthen the legislative powers of the federal government in some areas. Despite several conferences between the provinces and the federal government there have been few amendments to the division of powers. *See also* CONSTITUTIONAL LAW.

GÉRALD-A. BEAUDOIN

Diving, the sport of plunging into water from a platform, can be traced back to 400 BC through pictures on Egyptian and Roman vases. Plain diving was practised from cliffs to the oceans during the 8th to 10th centuries by Vikings in Sweden and later in the 1770s by Indians in Acapulco, Mexico. Between 1800 and 1820 a new form developed in Germany and Sweden. Acrobatic gymnastics over water was the beginning of the fancy diving known today. Competitive diving began in the 1880s in Germany and in 1904 became an Olympic event, but it did not commence until the 1920s in Canada, under the auspices of the Canadian Amateur Swimming Assn. In 1969 Vaughn L. Baird incorporated the Canadian Amateur Diving Assn as a member of the Aquatic Federation of Canada, a development largely responsible for the continued growth of the sport, which is now practised in 9 provinces. Competitive diving is separated into men's and women's springboard and platform events. Competitors perform a set number of dives, each of which is marked on a scale of one to 10 by a panel of 5 or 7 judges, leading to a final total score.

Alfie Phillips was the first nationally recognized Canadian diver, winning 10 straight national championships 1926-35 and finishing seventh in both the 1928 and 1932 Olympics. During the 1940s and 1950s, George Athans, Bill Patrick and Irene MacDonald competed internationally for Canada. Macdonald won a bronze medal in the springboard event at the 1956 Melbourne Olympics and finished sixth at Rome in 1960. Beverley Boys won 4 Commonwealth gold medals in diving and was seventh in the 1968 Olympics and fifth in 1972 in the springboard and fourth in 1968 in the platform. Cindy Shatto was fifth in the platform event at the 1976 Montréal Olympics. The crowning achievement of Canadian competitive diving was Sylvie BERNIER's gold medal in 1984 in Los Angeles.

JANICE WATERS AND MARK LOWRY

Beverley Boys, who won 4 Commonwealth gold medals in diving (*courtesy Canada's Sports Hall of Fame*).

Diving, Underwater Probably the first large-scale diving efforts, beginning at least 6500 years ago, were directed to acquiring pearls and mother-of-pearl and involved divers trained from childhood for lung capacity and endurance. The first underwater mechanical devices, eg, wooden diving bells, were constructed as early as 332 BC and underwent significant modification even before the 19th century. The first workable diving suit was developed by Augustus Siebe of England about 1839. This waterproof suit had a detachable helmet connected to the surface by a hose through which air was pumped. This kind of tethered suit remained the only practicable diving dress until 1943, when 2 Frenchmen, renowned underwater explorer Jacques-Yves Cousteau and engineer Émile Gagnan, adapted a previously developed breathing apparatus to underwater use. Their improvement was named the "aqualung," or *s*elf-*c*ontained *u*nderwater *b*reathing *a*pparatus (SCUBA).

Commercial Diving Diving equipment is being continuously improved in response to demands from the offshore PETROLEUM EXPLORATION industry for diver support to ever greater depths. In some deepwater work the dexterity of a diver is not required or the cost of diver compression and decompression is prohibitive. A pressure-resistant diving suit (one atmosphere suit), developed in Britain, allows a diver to work to depths of 460 m and return to the surface with none of the usual problems associated with breathing high-pressure gases. These suits are massive and awkward; lighter, more versatile versions are being developed by Can-Dive Services, a prominent Canadian diving contractor (*see* OCEAN INDUSTRIES; SUBMERSIBLES).

Recreational Diving Diving for recreation is popular along Canada's coasts and waterways. Equipment providing the reliability and freedom needed by sport divers was developed a century later than the first standard commercial equipment. Recreational equipment has evolved steadily to the point where divers now employ higher pressure air cylinders, single-hose regulators for easier breathing and drysuits for greater warmth. Submersible diving computers, developed first in Canada by Kybertec International Inc, give continuous digital readouts of depth, time, air consumption and decompression status.

Sport divers are trained by certified instructors who are registered with training agencies. The largest agency in Canada, the National Association of Underwater Instructors (NAUI), incorporated in 1971, has headquarters at Etobicoke, Ont. The Association of Canadian Underwater Councils (ACUC) has an office in Markham, Ont. The Professional Association of Diving Instructors (PADI) maintains an office in Victoria, BC. Other agencies providing instruction in Canada are the National Association of Skin Diving Schools, Scuba Schools International and the Confédération mondiale des activités subaquatiques. Diving councils and clubs are active throughout Canada and local diving retailers have information on these groups. The Ontario Underwater Council (OUC), the world's largest noncertified association of divers, celebrated 25 years of operation in 1983. This group holds an internationally recognized divers' show in Toronto every spring.

Scientific Diving Scientists in such fields as ARCHAEOLOGY, BIOLOGY, CHEMISTRY, GEOLOGY, marine ecology, OCEANOGRAPHY and PHYSICS use diving to make observations and gather data. Incorporated in 1984, the Canadian Association for Underwater Science was established to promote interest in underwater studies and to advance the techniques and safety of diving. Canadian scientists and technicians are gaining world recognition for underwater studies carried out in challenging circumstances. Canadian arctic oil development prompted increased research and technological advances in areas such as oil and ice interaction.

Various federal departments and agencies such as Environment Canada, the Environment Protection Service, Fisheries and Oceans, and Energy, Mines and Resources use divers in scientific research. Such divers may install and recover recording instruments; help maintain study platforms, canals and locks; collect bottom samples, water samples, fish or invertebrates for analysis; make surveillance dives in environmentally sensitive areas. One Parks Canada group has logged thousands of diving hours locating and excavating historic underwater sites. Noteworthy are the *San Juan*, a BASQUE whaling galleon sunk in RED BAY, Lab, in 1565, the *Machault*, one of 3 French supply ships sunk in Baie des Chaleurs in 1763. The American WAR OF 1812 frigates, *Hamilton* and *Scourge*, and the BREADALBANE, an arctic expedition supply ship sunk in the NORTHWEST PASSAGE in 1853, are being investigated by privately funded groups under observation by Parks Canada. Parks Canada maintains a support system that includes a 150 ton research barge equipped with low-pressure compressors to supply airlifts, generators to supply underwater lights, a recompression chamber, and offices and workshop facilities. The ROYAL ONTARIO MUSEUM used divers to recover artifacts found along the voyageur fur-trading routes and, in 1971, commissioned the search for the *Hamilton* and *Scourge*. Canada is becoming an internationally recognized leader in underwater archaeology as a result of these enterprises.

Military Diving The work of military divers ranges from being clearance divers on board government vessels to performing classified defence tasks. The Defence and Civil Institute of Environmental Medicine (DCIEM) is a multidisciplinary laboratory of the Dept of National Defence. It provides for testing and development of personal diving equipment, training of military personnel and research and development into the problems associated with human underwater operations.

VALERIE I. MACDONALD

Reading: Reg Vallintine, *Divers and Diving* (1981).

Dixon Entrance is a strait between the QUEEN CHARLOTTE ISLANDS, on the N coast of BC, and Prince of Wales and Dall islands in Alaska. About 65 km wide, it connects the Pacific Ocean with HECATE STR and the inside coastal passages. It was named for George Dixon, whose exploration of the BC coast in the 1780s helped to initiate the maritime FUR TRADE.

DANIEL FRANCIS

Dobsonfly, large, soft-bodied, freshwater INSECT of order Megaloptera, family Corydalidae; smaller forms are called fishflies. Dobsonflies have 2 pairs of veined membranous wings, chewing mouthparts, long, many-segmented antennae and 3 simple eyes. Dobsonflies are primarily nocturnal; closely related ALDERFLIES are smaller and diurnal. Dobsonflies deposit 2000-3000 dark brown eggs in rows forming large masses on objects near rapidly flowing water. Larvae hatch in 10-14 days, make their way into water and usually settle under stones or other debris. While adults do not feed and are short-lived, larvae are predaceous and take 2-3 years to develop. Fully grown larvae leave the water to pupate in a cell in soil, moss, under stones, etc. Adults, appearing in early summer, are feeble fliers usually found near water. Six species occur in Canada: *Corydalis cornutus*, with wingspread of about 125 mm, is perhaps the best-known eastern species. Males have hornlike mandibles often 25 mm long. Larvae and adults are food for many fish and bait for anglers, particularly larvae of *C. cornutus* (sometimes called hellgrammite).

J.E.H. MARTIN

Dock, herbaceous PLANT of genus *Rumex*, family Polygonaceae (BUCKWHEAT); most docks are pe ennial. Some species are called sorrels. About 50 species occur worldwide; of 22 in Canada, bout half are native. In the Northern Hemiphere, most docks are common WEEDS. The reenish flowers, at the top of the plant, turn redish brown at maturity. The seeds are smooth, rown and 3-sided. Curled dock (*R. crispus*), one f the 5 most widely distributed plants in the vorld, is a troublesome weed in disturbed land n all provinces. Its long, narrow leaves have rumpled, wavy margins. Broad-leaved dock (*R. btusifolius*) occurs in damper, partly shaded sites n eastern Canada and BC. Across the prairies, ield dock (*R. pseudonatronatus*) is more common han curled dock. Sheep sorrel (*R. acetosella*) ocurs on impoverished lands in all provinces. his slender plant, 15-30 cm high, has sour, cid-tasting leaves, each with 2 basal lobes on a ong stalk. The larger, "narrow-leaved" garden orrel (*R. triangulivalvis*) is abundant along the ower St Lawrence. Leaves of sorrel species can e eaten like spinach. Indians valued leaves nd taproots for medicinal properties. *See* PLANTS, ATIVE USES. PAUL B. CAVERS

ocumentary Film, *see* FILM, DOCUMENTARY.

og (*Canis familiaris*), carnivorous MAMMAL, robably the first domesticated animal. Many eparate domestications occurred in different laces beginning 10 000 to 20 000 years ago. The ain progenitor was the WOLF; the jackal may lso have contributed. In N America, local dog tocks may have derived in part from the COYOTE. hese wild species can interbreed with dogs and roduce fertile progeny. Despite persistent folk tories, hybridization between dogs and foxes is ot successful and foxes cannot be considered ncestral to any dog breed.

Dogs were kept by native peoples throughout anada in the centuries before European exloration and settlement. They had various uses: or transportation and draft work, hunting, lothing materials and sometimes human food. nuit dogs are still used to pull sleds and carry ackpacks, in SEALING and to provide protection rom polar bears. Canadian Plains Indians reied on dogs for transportation (eg, by dog traois) until they acquired horses in the early 700s; their breeds are now extinct. On the West oast, the Salish kept a small, woolly type of og, using the hair for weaving; it became exinct by about 1860. Dogs were also important in eligion; the White Dog Festival, observed by ome eastern tribes, required the sacrifice of dogs f a special breed. Dogs have been an important omestic animal wherever people have settled. Iundreds of distinctive breeds developed over he centuries, partly through regional isolation nd partly through conscious selection by huans. Several hundred breeds are currently amed and recognized by various kennel clubs; ome, eg, Poodles, German Shepherd Dogs and rish Setters, have worldwide distribution. The anadian Kennel Club (CKC), which maintains egistration records for Canadian purebred dogs, fficially recognizes 143 breeds. Several other reeds are present but are not formally regisered. The recognized breeds are classified into roups generally indicating the purpose for vhich they were developed: sporting dogs, ounds, working dogs, terriers, toys and nonporting dogs. A seventh category, miscellaeous, is for breeds which are in the process of chieving full recognition.

Canadian Breeds

Five of the breeds recognized by the CKC can e claimed to be uniquely Canadian: the Tahltan ear Dog, the Canadian Eskimo Dog, the Nova cotia Duck Tolling Retriever, the Newfoundand and the Labrador Retriever. The last 2 have anadian names, but owe most of their developent to breeders in Great Britain and Europe.

Tahltan Bear Dog, kept by the Tahltan Indians of northwestern BC, was a small dog, probably of the Spitz family, with a foxy head and erect bat ears. Its distinctive, medium-length tail was carried erect and ended in a wide brush. Most were white with black patches. They were used for hunting bear and lynx. The breed was recognized by the CKC in 1940, but only 9 dogs were ever registered. There are none left in Tahltan country, and those that were registered have long since died. Breeders continue to search for survivors, without much hope of success.

Canadian Eskimo Dog When SNOWMOBILES were introduced to the Arctic, the need for sled dogs rapidly diminished. It soon became evident that the Eskimo dogs which had been kept by people of the Thule culture for 1100-2000 years were facing extinction. The breed had been recognized by the CKC but registered stock had not persisted. The Eskimo Dog Research Foundation was formed to reestablish the breed. A few dogs of the original type were obtained from remote Inuit camps in Boothia Pen, Melville Pen and Baffin I. They were taken to Yellowknife to form the nucleus of a breeding colony. This stock has now been accepted for registration by the CKC under the revised name "Canadian Eskimo Dog." Many have been returned to the Inuit. They are intermediate in speed and strength to the Siberian Husky and Alaskan Malamute. They are sled and backpack dogs and are useful in hunting.

Nova Scotia Duck Tolling Retriever, a small breed familiar to Canadians, is almost unknown in other countries. To "toll" means to entice game to approach by arousing curiosity. A tolling dog is trained to play along the shoreline, attracting inquisitive ducks to swim within gunshot range; the dog is then sent into the water to retrieve the birds. In the late 19th century, a breed with these characteristics was developed in Yarmouth County, NS. Several breeds and crosses were used in its development. The dogs are rather foxlike in colour and activity and are intermediate in size and conformation to spaniels and retrievers.

Newfoundlands may have originated in dogs kept by native peoples, or may be traced to dogs brought by the Vikings about 1000 AD. There probably was later admixture with dogs brought to the island by Basque and Portuguese fishing fleets. British visitors were attracted to the big black dogs and took some of them back to England, where they became very popular. The heavy, long-coated dogs are excellent swimmers and are renowned as family companions and guardians. A black and white variety was depicted by Sir Edwin Landseer in his famous painting *A Distinguished Member of the Humane Society* and the variety has since become known as the Landseer.

Labrador Retriever These dogs, probably from the same stock as the Newfoundland, were shaped into a distinctive breed by the English nobility, who selected them for smaller size, finer bone and a short coat. Other sporting breeds were crossed into the stock. The breed is one of the best gundogs in existence and has been found suitable as a "seeing-eye" dog. Most are black but other colours (yellow, chocolate and cream) have become popular.

Most dogs in Canada are kept as pets. Many purebred dogs provide recreation and employment for people participating in competitive events governed by the CKC. Such competitions include conformation shows, obedience trials, field trials for hounds and sporting breeds, tracking tests and the new spectator sports, lure coursing and scent hurdle racing. Sportsmen use various specially bred and trained breeds for hunting upland GAME BIRDS, WATERFOWL and small mammals. Greyhounds and wolfhounds are used in western Canada to hunt coyotes and wolves.

Many kinds of dogs actively work for man. Sled dogs are useful in the North. Border Collies retain their superiority for sheepherding, and the Komondor breed is being used experimentally in western Canada to guard flocks. Australian Cattle Dogs, formerly known as Queensland Heelers, are gaining popularity with Canadian cattlemen for driving livestock. The German Shepherd Dog, Doberman Pinscher and Bouvier des Flandres are widely used in police and military work and as guard dogs. *Schutzhund* (protection dog) training is increasing in Canada. It involves intensive schooling in obedience, tracking and defense. The most remarkable dogs are those trained to guide the blind; several hundred, all from training schools in the US, are at work in Canada helping their blind owners to lead more normal lives. Several breeds are used, including German Shepherd Dogs, Labrador Retrievers, Boxers and Collies.

R.D. CRAWFORD

Canadian dog breeds: Eskimo Dog (upper left); Nova Scotia Duck Tolling Retriever (lower left); Tahltan Bear Dog (centre); Newfoundland (upper right) and Labrador Retriever (lower right) *(artwork by L. Shaw)*.

Dogrib Their name for themselves is *Doné*, meaning "the People." They fall within the broader designation of DENE, tribes of the widespread Athapaskan language family. To distinguish themselves from their Dene neighbours — CHIPEWYAN, SLAVEY, BEARLAKE and HARE — they have come to identify themselves as "dog's rib," although the epithet derives from a Cree term for Athapaskan speakers. Dogrib lands lie E of the Mackenzie R between Great Slave Lk and Great Bear Lk in the NWT. From a population of about 800 (mid-19th century), the Dogrib numbered some 1700 by 1970, and the population continues to increase.

From aboriginal times to the present, Dogrib have hunted the barren-ground CARIBOU in the boreal forest during winter and followed them to the edge of the barrens in spring, where they meet them again in the fall. Moose and hare of the forest, and fish, are also important food resources. Extended kinship ties have allowed easy movement of families from one BAND group to another. In earlier times, supernatural powers gained through the aid of animal-spiritual beings were experienced by many persons. Hunting prowess coupled with generous concern for the well-being of the group, wisdom, oratorical skills and "medicine" power led to authority and leadership.

Dogrib began to be drawn into the FUR TRADE around the beginning of the 19th century. However, Ft Rae (1852), on the North Arm of Great Slave Lk, was the first trading post established on their lands. Roman Catholic missionaries began the conversion of Dogrib in 1859. In the early 19th century, Dogrib were intimidated and attacked by Yellowknife. In 1823 the massacre by Dogrib of Long Leg's Yellowknife band broke the threat. Dogrib oral tradition tells that, a few years later, the Dogrib Edzo and a few companions met the great Yellowknife leader, Akaitcho, and his band, and by medicine power and oratorical force brought a lasting peace.

The establishment of day schools at all Dogrib settlements (late 1950s) has facilitated access to advanced schooling and preparation for non-traditional occupations. Ft Rae has been transformed into a year-round settlement (Rae-Edzo complex) for hundreds of Dogrib. Other, smaller settlements include Detah, near the city of Yellowknife, and hamlets at Lac la Martre, Rae Lakes and Snare Lk. In the isolated hamlets the traditional reliance on hunting, fishing and fur trapping remains vital. *See also* NATIVE PEOPLES: SUBARCTIC and general entries under NATIVE PEOPLE.

JUNE HELM

Reading: June Helm, ed, *Handbook of North American Indians*, vol 6: *Subarctic* (1981).

Dogwood (Cornaceae), family of perennial herbaceous PLANTS, TREES and shrubs, represented in N America by about 15 members of genus *Cornus*. The genus comprises approximately 45 species, found mainly in N temperate regions. Of the 10 species native to Canada, 2 are herbaceous, the most familiar and smallest species be-

Ten species of dogwood are native to Canada. The Pacific or western flowering dogwood (*Cornus nuttallii*) was chosen in 1956 as the floral emblem of BC (*photo by Mary W. Ferguson*).

Western flowering dogwood (*Cornus nuttallii*), with flowers and fruits (*artwork by Claire Tremblay*).

ing Canadian dogwood or bunchberry (*C. canadensis*). It is very common in the boreal forest, but also occurs across southern Canada. This species has 4-6 large, white bracts resembling petals, which attract insects to the dense flowerhead composed of small, greenish flowers. Its red fruit is edible. Most dogwoods are shrubs or small trees; however, Pacific or western flowering dogwood (*C. nuttallii*), the PROVINCIAL FLORAL EMBLEM of BC since 1956, grows to 25 m. It flowers Apr-May, before the leaves appear; flowers form a head supported by 4-6 white or pinkish bracts measuring 10-12 cm across. This tree, which prefers shade, is covered with bunches of red fruit and brilliantly coloured foliage in autumn. The very hard wood can be used to make small items (eg, mallet heads, piano keys). Several dogwood shrubs are popular ORNAMENTALS, growing easily in well-drained soil.

CÉLINE ARSENEAULT

Doherty, Charles Joseph, lawyer, educator, judge, politician (b at Montréal 11 May 1855; d there 28 July 1931). Educated at McGill, he later taught civil and international law there for many years while practising law. He served as a judge of the Quebec Superior Court 1891-1906. He entered federal politics and was an MP 1908-21 and minister of justice and attorney general 1911-21 in the administrations of PMs BORDEN and MEIGHEN. Doherty was Canadian representative at the Versailles Peace Conference 1918-19 and Canadian delegate to the League of Nations 1920-22. He is credited with initiating the Canadian Bar Assn in 1912 and was its firs honorary president in 1914. He was appointe to the Imperial Privy Council in 1921.

JOHN E.C. BRIERLE

Dolbeau, Qué, Town, pop 8762 (1981c), in 1927, is located at the confluence of the Mis tassini and Mistassibi rivers (Lac SAINT-JEAN) opposite the city of MISTASSINI. Named after Jea Dolbeau, a priest who served the Montagnai mission at Tadoussac, Dolbeau was born whe the Lake St John Pulp & Paper Co, an America firm later bought out by the Canadian compan Domtar, decided to build a paper mill on th Rivière Mistassibi. The factory owners also buil a city to house their employees, making Dolbea a company town whose charter, modelled o that of Arvida, contained some deviations fron the Québec law for cities and towns. Afte WWII, Dolbeau became the major service centre including a hospital (1955) for the area N o Lac Saint-Jean. It is also home to one of the fev astronomic OBSERVATORIES in the province, an the site each July of a province-wide wester festival.

MARC ST-HILAIR

Dollar-a-Year Man, a term used during WWI to describe those business executives who wer brought to Ottawa to work in government largely in the Department of MUNITIONS AND SUP PLY and in the WARTIME PRICES AND TRADE BOARI Their salaries were paid by their companies while Ottawa provided living expenses.

J.L. GRANATSTEI

Dollard Des Ormeaux, Adam, soldier (b i France 1635; d at Long Sault May 1660). In lat

Apr 1660, 17 Frenchmen with Dollard in command left Montréal to ambush Iroquois hunters returning by the Ottawa R. They were joined by 44 Hurons and Algonquins. At the foot of Long Sault rapids, they were soon discovered by the advance guard of 300 Iroquois. The allies took refuge in a derelict enclosure, where they were besieged for a week while the Iroquois summoned reinforcements. The Hurons deserted, water failed and when a gunpowder keg exploded within the palisade, the defenders were overwhelmed. Nine survived to be ritually tortured and eaten. Nineteenth-century historians converted the battle into a religious and nationalistic epic in which zealous Roman Catholics deliberately sacrificed themselves to fend off an attack on New France. Revenge, trophies and captives were the traditional goals of Iroquoian warfare and the Iroquois probably went home well satisifed. PETER N. MOOGK

Dollier de Casson, François, explorer, superior of the Sulpicians in New France (1671-74, 1678-1701), seigneur of Montréal, vicar general, historian (b in the château of Casson-sur-l'Erdre in Lower Brittany 1636; d at Montréal 27 Sept 1701). After 3 years' military service, Dollier joined the Sulpicians in Paris and was sent to Canada in 1666. He became military chaplain and then parish priest at Trois-Rivières, and in 1669 he undertook a missionary trip south of the Great Lakes. In 1670 he was named superior of the Sulpicians and seigneur of Montréal. He devoted himself to organizing the city, constructing a church and completing his *Histoire du Montréal*, an important document in French Canada's historiography. Respected for his humanity, energy and understanding of the colony's problems, he competently fulfilled his religious duties and tried to improve education in Montréal. After 1680 he helped with the Lachine Canal project, and established a conciliatory climate for relations between the colony's civil and religious authorities. JACQUES MATHIEU

Dolphin and Porpoise, common names for small, toothed MAMMALS of the order CETACEA which also includes WHALES. They are known from all oceans and many major river systems. In N America dolphins, with long snouts, are distinguished from porpoises, with blunt heads, but the terms are sometimes applied interchangeably to many small toothed whales, including members of the families Delphinidae, Phocoenidae, Stenidae and Platanistidae. Five species are common in Canada. Harbour porpoise (*Phocoena phocoena*) is especially abundant in the lower Bay of Fundy and parts of the Gulf of St Lawrence. This, one of the smallest Northern Hemisphere cetaceans, has a relatively high metabolic rate and a short life span (about 13 years). Unlike some dolphins and porpoises, it does not live in large social aggregations, nor does it normally engage in aerial displays. Dall porpoise (*Phocoenoides dalli*), native to the N Pacific, occurs along the BC coast. Its colour pattern is reminiscent of the killer whale (*Orcinus orca*) which, at 9.5 m and 8000 kg, is the largest delphinid. Three species of temperate-region dolphins occur in Canadian waters; all are gregarious and sometimes acrobatic. White-beaked dolphins (*Lagenorhynchus albirostris*) and Atlantic white-sided dolphins (*L. acutus*), both endemic to the N Atlantic, have overlapping ranges between Cape Cod and Davis Str. Their N Pacific relative is the Pacific white-sided dolphin (*L. obliquidens*). The bottlenose dolphin (*Tursiops truncatus*), popular in animal exhibits, generally does not range into Canadian waters. Most captive specimens come from Florida or the Gulf of Mexico region. R. REEVES AND E.D. MITCHELL

Dome Petroleum Limited is a Canadian energy company with head offices in Calgary. Started in 1950 as Dome Exploration (Western) Ltd, the company adopted its present name in 1958 and grew by making acquisitions in the energy industry. Most famous was the 1981 acquisition of Hudson's Bay Oil and Gas Company Limited: Dome acquired a 52.9% interest through its wholly owned subsidiary, Dome Energy Limited. However, with increasing debts from past takeovers and a changed economic situation, Dome made history in 1982-83 by receiving substantial loans from 4 Canadian chartered banks and by having the federal government intervene in its affairs. The company's activities are divided between 2 entities: Dome Petroleum explores for, develops, produces and markets crude oil, natural gas and natural gas liquids in Canada and the US, and HBOG handles natural resource exploration and development. The company explores mainly in western Canada, the Beaufort Sea and the arctic islands. In 1983 it had sales or operating revenue of $2.6 billion (ranking 30th in Canada), assets of $8.2 billion (ranking 8th) and 6500 employees. Foreign ownership of the company stands at 42% with the major Canadian shareholder, Dome Mines Ltd, holding 26%. DEBORAH C. SAWYER

Domestic Service, a predominantly female occupation, was the most common paid employment for Canadian women before 1900: in 1891 there were nearly 80 000 women servants in Canada. With the expansion in the 20th century of factory, office and shopwork for women, the proportion of the female work force in domestic service decreased (from 41% in 1891 to 18% in 1921). The decline was most pronounced after WWII and was accompanied by an increase in shifts from live-in to live-out and part-time work. Most live-in domestics were young women who did general work in one- or 2-servant households; a small minority had specialized positions as part of a large staff.

In service in an urban Ontario household, *c* 1898. Most live-in domestics were young women who did general work in a one- or two-servant household. The 13-year-old shown here left in 1906 to train as a nurse (*courtesy Barnardo Photo Library*).

Employers hired domestic servants to confirm middle-class status as well as to obtain needed help. The private employment conditions and general devaluation of housework made domestic service unpopular. Objections to low social status, unregulated hours, isolation and lack of independence remained unchanged over time. A shortage of Canadian domestic servants led to the employment of immigrant women from Britain, Scandinavia, central Europe and, after WWII, the West Indies and the Philippines. In the 19th and early 20th centuries, British child-emigration societies as well as Canadian orphanages placed girls in service (*see* CHILD LABOUR). The policy of welcoming immigrant domestics as permanent residents and future wives changed in the 1970s, when the government introduced temporary employment visas which allowed domestics to stay in Canada only for a limited period and only on condition that they retain domestic employment.

The vulnerability of immigrants augmented the difficulty of improving conditions for workers in isolated, usually temporary, employment. The domestic-science movement in the early 20th century unsuccessfully tried to professionalize domestic service by raising standards. Early domestic-servant organizations in Vancouver and Toronto were short-lived, but beginning in the 1970s union activity has achieved immigration reform and some legislative control of employment standards. MARILYN BARBER

Reading: B.D. Palmer, *Working-Class Experience* (1983).

Domestic Utensils may be classified into those used in the preparation of food and those employed in the cleaning of clothing and household furnishings. For many years after the settlement of Canada, household utensils were made by local craftsmen and BLACKSMITHS. By the middle of the 19th century more sophisticated devices were in use, most of them imported from Britain or the US.

Kitchen Utensils Much of the preparation of food (eg, peeling and slicing of vegetables, cutting of meat) was done with simple knives. Sausages were popular because they could be preserved, but it was necessary that the sausage meat be well minced and thoroughly mixed with the spices and seasoning that provided flavour and preservation. Cutting and mixing could be done in a wooden bowl, using a knife with the handle behind the blade rather than at one end. Patented chopping knives appeared late in the 19th century, with multiple or removable blades.

Mechanical devices for chopping or grinding meat and vegetables were imported from about 1860. These implements were hollow iron cylinders containing rotary shafts with teeth. By the end of the century, they had evolved into the familiar food grinder, in which a screwlike revolving shaft cut the meat and forced it through a perforated end plate, with or without cutting edges. A grinder of this type, identical with those still in use, was patented in Canada by L.T. Snow in 1897.

The ground sausage meat was usually wrapped in cloth bags and stored in a cool place until needed. Settlers of GERMAN origin preferred to make sausages in the familiar "links" by forcing the ground meat into a case (length of washed intestine) with a "sausage gun," ie, a metal cylinder with a narrow spout at one end and a wooden plunger at the other. More elaborate stuffers used a piston and lever; some were of wood and were made locally, but cast-iron stuffers appeared about 1850, with either a lever or a screw for applying pressure. The full case was tied at intervals into the sausage links.

Slicers were used with vegetables, most commonly with cabbage used for sauerkraut. A shredding board, with a diagonal slot over which was mounted a cutting blade, was used. The cabbage head was pushed down the board, and slices were cut off by the knife and fell through the slot into a pan. Plastic slicers of this design are still in use.

Apples were widely available in 19th century Canada and were commonly preserved as dried slices. This method of preservation required paring, ie, removal of the skin. Paring could be done by hand with a sharp knife, although this technique was slow and semi-mechanical parers came into use at an early stage. Such implements might consist of a fork (on which the apple was impaled) turned by a handle or pulley. The knife edge was held against the revolving apple. By 1803 an apple parer with a knife mounted on an arm with a universal joint had appeared. Parers of this type were being made and used in Canada about 1840. Beginning about 1849 a host of mechanical metal parers appeared in the US and were soon in use in Canada. The cutting blade was attached to a threaded shaft or a set of gears, which caused the tool to travel across the surface of the apple as it was rotated by a hand crank. These utensils were later elaborated with the addition of a coring attachment and an arm to push off the pared apple.

Until about 1830 cooking was almost always done in an open fireplace. One of the problems was providing stability for the cooking utensils. Pots for stews or tea water had curved handles by which they were suspended from a swinging bar called a crane. A more reliable means of support was the trivet, an iron ring large enough to hold the pot and having 3 vertical legs that could be set in the fire. The trivet could be combined with the frying pan or skillet by attaching legs directly to the pan bottom; this combination was called a spider. Cooking pots were also made with permanently attached legs.

Meat could be cooked on a grill, an arrangement of parallel iron bars, spaced close enough to support the meat but far enough apart to provide exposure to the flames. In some grills, the bars were little troughs along which juices from the cooking meat could flow to a collecting cup at one end of the grill. Grills were usually supported on their own 4 legs. Roasting meat over the open fire was usually done on a spit, a horizontally mounted iron rod, which was thrust through the meat and supported on each side of the fire. The spit had to be turned to ensure uniform cooking; hence, the rod projected at one end beyond the heat of the fire, terminating in a handle or a pulley wheel. Meat could also be roasted by being suspended over the fire on a hook from the crane. To ensure uniform cooking a clock jack, ie, a powerful clockwork motor housed in a brass cylinder, might be used. Meat suspended below the jack was rotated back and forth automatically.

Introduction of the cooking stove in the 1830s fundamentally changed culinary techniques and utensils. Pots, pans and skillets now had a solid base on which to rest. Degree of heat could be controlled by the position of the vessel on the stove top. If open flames were required, the lid could be removed from one of the pot holes and the vessel placed directly over the fire. The skillet without legs, renamed the frying pan, needed only a solid handle. Handles were made for lifting rather than for suspension. Grills and toasters could be placed directly over an open hole. Kettles were adapted by having the perimeter of the base recessed, to fit into the pot-hole.

The most fundamental change was the replacement of the fireplace oven by the stove oven. To heat the former, a fire had to be built in the oven, then removed, and the food introduced. The stove oven derived its heat directly from the firebox, which allowed for shorter cooking time and better temperature control. Cakes, pies and biscuits could be baked as well as bread; special baking pans and plates came into use. Roasting of meat could also be done in the oven, in large covered roasting pans.

In early years cooked food was usually served on plates of PEWTER, an alloy of lead and tin. Pewter, as preserved today, has the dull grey tarnish of time, but in the days of its use it was kept highly polished by scouring with wood ashes. Pewter spoons were cast in iron molds. Knives and forks were of steel, with firmly attached wooden handles. Table knives were wiped on an abrasive scouring brick (a block of baked clay) to keep them free of rust or tarnish.

Laundry Utensils The change from fireplace to stove also altered the methods and utensils used in washing clothes. The large amounts of wash water needed could be heated on the stove in a washboiler, ie, an oval tub of sheet metal with a removable lid. The soiled clothes and the soap were dropped into the boiling water and stirred with a wooden stick or tongs. The actual washing was done on a low table in a circular tub, usually made of sheet metal but possibly of the lower half of a barrel. The traditional washboard was used, a corrugated surface on which the wet clothes were rubbed vigorously. After washing, the clothes were rinsed in clear water in the same tub.

Such scrubbing was one of the more tiring operations in laundering clothes. It was easier to use a plunger, an inverted sheet-metal funnel at the end of a wooden rod. Working this plunger up and down in the sumberged clothes forced the hot soapy water into and out of the fabric. Improved plungers, eg, the double model, were patented in the 1880s. An ingenious version was invented in 1890 by Isaac Shupe of Newmarket, Ont. In Shupe's plunger the conical head was extended upward as a tube, which contained a spring-loaded piston with a valve. Soap was placed in the tube and, when the plunger was pushed down, the valve closed and water was squeezed through the clothes. On the upstroke the valve opened, releasing soap.

More elaborate washing devices combined a tub and manipulator, eg, a swinging set of slats, as in the Raulston (Ont) patent of 1884, or a reciprocating rotary agitator, as in the Cadran (Qué) patent of 1885. The latter arrangement has been retained in the modern automatic washer.

Before drying, washed clothes were wrung out, ie, squeezed free of excess water. Early in the 19th century, the old method of twisting by hand was replaced by the use of a set of rollers between which the saturated clothes were squeezed. These wringers persisted well into the time of the electric washing machine.

Ironing underwent an interesting development during the 19th century. In the fireplace era, the irons could not be heated directly without soiling the contact surface; therefore, they were hollow, with a removable core that could be heated separately and then placed inside the iron. Irons heated on a stove top could be solid, but this raised the problem of a handle too hot to hold. The difficulty was resolved in 1871 by Mrs Florence Potts of Iowa, who had already invented the double-pointed iron. The handle of the Potts iron was of wood, semicircular in shape, with a metal device at the base which could be latched or released on the top of the iron by lifting a small knob. Potts irons were manufactured in various Canadian foundries. Other irons with detachable handles were patented in the late 19th century, but the Potts iron outlasted them all.

L.S. RUSSELL

Dominion refers to Dominion of Canada (BRITISH NORTH AMERICA ACT preamble), to the federal government or Parliament, and to Canada's status in relation to the imperial government. The FATHERS OF CONFEDERATION wanted to call the new nation the Kingdom of Canada, but the British government, fearing the sensitivity of Americans to references to the Crown and anxious not to antagonize them after the American Civil War, insisted the Fathers find another title. Sir Leonard TILLEY suggested "dominion": "He shall have dominion also from sea to sea, and from the river unto the ends of the earth" (Psalm 72). The Fathers said it was intended to give dignity to the federation, and as a tribute to the monarchical principle. Under the CONSTITUTION ACT, 1982, "Dominion" remains Canada's official title.

EUGENE A. FORSEY

Dominion Arsenal, the first government cartridge and shell factory and proofing facility, est 1882 at Québec to provide the Canadian Militia with ammunition. A second arsenal was built in LINDSAY, Ont, during WWI, and other plants were built or converted to small arms and artillery-shell production during WWII by the Department of MUNITIONS AND SUPPLY. In Sept 1945 these were brought together as Canadian Arsenals Limited, a crown corporation now reporting to the Department of Supply and Services. The only plant still operated by Canadian Arsenals in 1982 was at Le Gardeur, Qué.

STEPHEN HARRIS

Dominion Astrophysical Observatory, *see* OBSERVATORY.

Dominion Drama Festival, *see* LITTLE THEATRE MOVEMENT.

Dominion Foundries & Steel, Limited (Dofasco) Dominion Foundries was established in Hamilton, Ont, to provide castings for the railways. After its establishment in 1912, as much as 75 t of castings were shipped every day to locomotive and freight-car manufacturers. In the early 1950s, Dofasco became a fully integrated steel producer and pioneered the use of basic oxygen steelmaking in N America. This process revolutionized steelmaking by producing a batch of steel in less than one hour, compared to over 6 hours in an open-hearth furnace. Dofasco's Hamilton Works currently has 4 blast furnaces, 2 BOSF (basic oxygen steelmaking furnaces) shops, and extensive steel rolling and finishing facilities. Its annual steelmaking capacity of about 4 million t makes Dofasco Canada's second-largest steelmaker. Dofasco produces mainly steel sheet for the AUTOMOTIVE INDUSTRY. It is also a leader in producing new steel products for the Canadian market and was the first domestic producer of steel plate and continuously galvanized (ie, zinc-coated) steel. In 1983 Dofasco had sales or operating revenue of $1.6 billion (ranking 52nd in Canada), assets of $2.2 billion and 11 400 employees. *See* IRON AND STEEL INDUSTRIES.

JOHN G. PEACEY

Dominion Lands Policy When the Canadian government acquired RUPERT'S LAND from the Hudson's Bay Co and granted provincial status to Manitoba in 1870, it intended to use western natural resources and lands to promote WESTERN SETTLEMENT and RAILWAY construction. Specific HOMESTEAD policies were devised to encourage settlers intending to establish themselves. The Dominion Lands Act of 1872, modelled on American homestead legislation, provided the legal authority under which lands were to be given to intending settlers in return for the payment of a small $10 fee and the performance of specified settlement duties, eg, building a habitable residence and cultivating a certain area annually. A simple, effective survey system divided the arable prairie lands into square townships, each comprising 36 sections of 640 cres (259 ha), with the basic homestead comprising one 160-acre (64.75 ha) quarter section. Two sections in each township were reserved for the support of education, and a variety of grazing, haying and quarrying leases were available or lands not yet claimed for homesteading.

The Pacific railway, regarded as a national necessity, was to be financed through an elaborate system of land subsidies. Since it could not be completed without additional cash subsidies, the federal government also provided for the sale of Dominion lands at reduced prices to various COLONIZATION COMPANIES to provide the needed funds. In the 3 decades after 1870, settlement on the prairies was slow, but early in the 20th century it advanced rapidly. Prairie politicians regarded federal control over western Dominion lands and resources as an unfair intrusion into areas clearly given to provincial jurisdiction in the BRITISH NORTH AMERICA ACT. Negotiations undertaken to transfer control of the remaining western lands and resources to the provincial governments were completed in 1930. Thus ended the 60-year existence of Dominion lands. *See* PRAIRIE WEST. T.D. REGEHR

Reading: C. Martin, *"Dominion Lands" Policy* (1938).

Dominion-Provincial Relations, Royal Commission on (Rowell-Sirois Report) A landmark in the development of Canadian FEDERALISM, the commission was established (1937) unilaterally by the federal government to reexamine "the economic and financial basis of Confederation and the distribution of legislative powers in the light of the economic and social developments of the last 70 years." Commonly named after its successive chairmen, N.W. Rowell and Joseph Sirois, the 3-volume report (1940) recommended a transfer of functions and a shifting of TAXATION power to the federal government and the creation of grants to the provinces to equalize provincial tax revenues, a principle enshrined in the 1982 constitution. The federal government was to assume responsibility for unemployment insurance and contributory pensions, and to assume full control of personal and corporate income taxes and succession duties, while taking responsibility for provincial debts. A program of National Adjustment Grants was to make payments to poorer provinces. On the grounds of administrative complexity, provincial autonomy and the need for legislative accountability, the commission rejected greater use of the shared-cost programs, which were to become a central device of postwar "co-operative federalism." WWII and opposition by some provinces prevented the adoption of many recommendations; others were introduced piecemeal (*see* CONSTITUTIONAL PROBLEMS). RICHARD SIMEON

Dominion Radio Astrophysical Observatory, *see* OBSERVATORY.

Dominion Stores Limited/Les Supermarchés Dominion Ltée, with head offices in Toronto, is a Canadian food distributor and merchandiser incorporated in 1919. The company adopted its present name in 1976. Dominion grew by various acquisitions until 1983, when it acquired ARGUS CORPORATION's share of Standard Broadcasting Corporation. That year Argus Corporation increased its holdings in Dominion to 40%, and a government investigation of trading activities resulted. Dominion operates 390 grocery stores in 7 provinces (all its assets in Québec were sold in 1981) and, through subsidiaries, also operates convenience stores, delicatessens, drugstores and gas bars. In 1983 it had sales or operating revenue of $2.4 billion (ranking 34th in Canada), assets of $1.2 billion (ranking 76th) and 21 399 employees. Argus Corporation and its associated companies hold 45% of the shares and foreign ownership stands at 1%.
DEBORAH C. SAWYER

Domtar Inc is a Canadian manufacturer of paper products with headquarters in Montréal. Founded in 1929 as the Dominion Tar and Chemical Company Ltd to acquire the assets of a former business of the same name, the company became Domtar Ltd in 1965 and adopted its present name in 1977. It operates through 4 main groups — pulp and paper, construction, chemicals and packaging — producing a wide variety of products ranging from fine papers, envelopes and newsprints to construction materials, salts and special chemicals, and kraft papers and corrugated containers. Domtar operates 82 plants in Canada, the US and the UK. In 1983 it had sales or operating revenue of $1.8 billion (ranking 47th in Canada), assets of $1.3 billion (ranking 67th) and 15 151 employees. The CAISSE DE DÉPÔT ET PLACEMENT DU QUÉBEC holds 24% of the shares and DoFor Inc 21%; foreign ownership stands at 7%. DEBORAH C. SAWYER

Donalda, Pauline, stage name of Pauline Lightstone, soprano, teacher, administrator (b at Montréal 5 Mar 1882; d there 22 Oct 1970). Known for her contribution to lyrical art in Montréal, she was a pupil of Clara Lichtenstein and travelled to Paris on a grant from arts patron Lord STRATHCONA. With Massenet's help she made her debut in Nice in 1904. Later she performed at Covent Garden, sang with Caruso and, in 1906, made her professional Canadian debut at the Montreal Arena. She pursued her career in New York, at the Opéra-Comique in Paris and in Russia. In 1922 she devoted herself entirely to teaching. She settled in Montréal in 1937, where she founded the Opera Guild in 1942. HÉLÈNE PLOUFFE

Donnacona, St Lawrence Iroquois leader (d in France probably in 1539). Headman of the village of STADACONA [near Québec C] during Jacques CARTIER's voyages of 1534-36, Donnacona attempted to establish an alliance with the French but was reluctant to assist Cartier to reach HOCHELAGA [Montréal]. In 1535 the French learned through him of a cure for scurvy, made from white cedar. Cartier took Donnacona and 9 other Iroquois to France to be received by the king. There Donnacona's tales of the riches of the kingdom of the Saguenay ensured support for Cartier's third voyage. None of the captives returned home, which embittered Cartier's relations with the people of Stadacona.
HARRIET GORHAM

Donnellys, The Early in the morning of 4 Feb 1880, a party of armed men brutally murdered James Donnelly, a farmer living near the village of LUCAN, Ont, his wife Johannah, his sons Thomas and John, and his niece Bridget Donnelly. Two eyewitnesses, 11-year-old Johnny O'Connor, and James Donnelly's eldest son, William, claimed to have identified 6 of the murderers, who were subsequently brought to trial in nearby London. The case aroused international interest as it became known that the killings were the result of a factional feud originating in County Tipperary, Ire. In Canada, over the preceding 3 decades, the vendetta had claimed a heavy toll in lives and property. There were 2 trials of the accused men. At the first, in Sept 1880, the jury disagreed. A second jury, in Jan 1881, returned a directed verdict of "not guilty." A century later the case continues to excite interest and controversy. More than 100 factual and fictional accounts have appeared in recent years, the best known being T.P. Kelley, *The Black Donnellys* (1954); Orlo Miller, *The Donnellys Must Die* (1962); Ray Fazakas, *The Donnelly Album* (1977); and playwright James Reaney's *The Donnellys: A Trilogy* (1983). ORLO MILLER

Doric Club, fd 1836 in Montréal, a paramilitary political association of young anglophone Tories. It replaced an earlier organization which, because of its armed contribution to political tensions in Montréal in the 1830s, was disbanded by Gov Gosford. A violent clash between the Doric Club and the patriote organization, the FILS DE LA LIBERTÉ, on 6 Dec 1837 was a prelude to the REBELLIONS OF 1837-38. The Doric Club dissolved when many of its members were recruited by Gen Colbourne to fight the rebels.

Dorion, Sir Antoine-Aimé, lawyer, politican, judge (b at Ste-Anne-de-la-Pérade, LC 17 Jan 1818; d at Montréal 31 May 1891). A member of the Assembly of the PROVINCE OF CANADA 1854-61 and 1861-67, Dorion became a well-known PARTI ROUGE leader in the 1850s, praising American political institutions, supporting liberal ideas, promoting tariff reform and colonization of virgin lands, and attacking financial and business interests as well as certain aspects of the Roman Catholic Church's presence in society. In 1858, CLEAR GRIT leader George BROWN formed a short-lived government with Dorion as leader for Canada E. He was also attorney general (Canada E) in the John Sandfield MACDONALD-Dorion ministry of 1863-64. Vigorously opposed to the CONFEDERATION project, however, he refused to adhere to the GREAT COALITION of 1864 that united Brown and the Clear Grits from Canada W with the Conservatives from both halves of the province. In Nov 1864, following the QUEBEC CONFERENCE, he denounced the projected federation as a disguised legislative union that would accord virtually no autonomy to the provinces even in matters of local concern. He also insisted that the people should be consulted, since it was their interest and prosperity that were clearly at stake. For the next 2 years Dorion led Lower Canadian opposition to the proposals.

Following Confederation, Dorion sat in the House of Commons until 1874 and was briefly minister of justice and attorney general in the Liberal government of Alexander MACKENZIE. In 1874 he was named chief justice of the Court of Queen's Bench of Québec. RICHARD A. JONES

Dorion, Jean-Baptiste-Éric, journalist, politician, pioneer settler (b at Ste-Anne-de-la-Pérade, LC 17 Sept 1826; d at L'Avenir, Canada E 1 Nov 1866), brother of A.A. DORION. From a family that strongly supported liberal principles, he defended liberalism with such passion that his political adversaries nicknamed him "enfant terrible." On 17 Dec 1844, he helped found the INSTITUT CANADIEN in Montréal; with George Batchelor, he established the newspaper *L'Avenir*, the first edition of which appeared on 16 July 1847. Dorion used these 2 forums to express his views which became so radical after 1848 on issues such as the separation of church and state, nondenominational education and annexation of Canada by the US that in Nov 1852 the opposition to his demands obliged him to stop publishing *L'Avenir*. He withdrew to a community near Drummondville which he called L'Avenir where he was elected MP for Drummond-Arthabaska in 1854 and 1861. He argued at length on the disadvantages of CONFEDERATION in his newspaper *Le Défricheur*, which he founded in 1862. PHILIPPE SYLVAIN

Dorset Culture, 500 BC-1500 AD, is known archaeologically from most coastal regions of arctic Canada. The Dorset people were descended from Paleoeskimos of the PRE-DORSET CULTURE. Compared to their ancestors, the Dorset people had a more successful economy and lived in more permanent houses built of snow and turf, heated with soapstone oil lamps. They may also have used dogsleds and KAYAKS. They lived primarily by hunting sea mammals and were capable of taking animals as large as walrus and narwhal. About 500 BC they moved down the Labrador coast and occupied the island of Newfoundland for about 1000 years. About 1000 AD they were displaced from most arctic regions by an invasion of THULE Inuit from Alaska, but they continued to live in northern Québec and Labrador until approximately 1500 AD. *See also* PREHISTORY. ROBERT MCGHEE

Reading: Robert McGhee, *Canadian Arctic Prehistory* (1978).

Double Hook, The, by Sheila WATSON (Toronto, 1959), is described by some as Canada's first modern novel. *The Double Hook* departs from traditional plot, character development, form and style to tell a poetic tale of human suffering and redemption that is at once fabular, allegorical and symbolic. When James Potter kills his mother in the opening scene, he sets in motion the Potter family's struggle against fear — symbolized most dramatically by the figure of Coyote — and with various forms of withdrawal from community into isolation. James must discover "That when you fish for glory you catch the darkness too. That if you hook twice the glory you hook twice the fear." His return to his isolated community in the Rockies after first fleeing to town represents the rebirth of hope and the confrontation with fear which might knit the Potters into a human community. Watson weaves Christian myth, native legend and natural symbol into a profound prose poem. *The Double Hook* has been translated into French, as *Sous l'oeil de coyote* (Montréal, 1976), and Swedish. NEIL BESNER

Double Majority, *see* MACDONALD, JOHN SANDFIELD.

Double Shuffle After the George-Étienne CARTIER-John A. MACDONALD ministry in the PROVINCE OF CANADA was forced to resign on 29 July 1858, a Reform ministry was formed under George BROWN and A.A. DORION. Under parliamentary rules, newly appointed ministers were obliged to resign their seats and face a by-election; but this rule did not apply to a minister who resigned one office and took another within a month. When the Reform ministry fell on Aug 4 and Gov Gen Sir Edmund HEAD called upon Cartier and Macdonald to form a second government, each minister took a new portfolio on Aug 6 and resumed his former office on Aug 7. The notorious "double shuffle" allowed the Macdonald-Cartier ministry to retain power without facing by-elections. DAVID MILLS

Dougall, Lily, novelist, religious writer (b at Montréal 16 Apr 1858; d at Cumnor, Eng 9 Oct 1923). In 1880 she went to Britain, deciding on permanent residence there in 1900. Her first story was published in 1889. Her first novel, *Beggars All* (1891), received critical and popular acclaim, as did *What Necessity Knows* (1893), one of 4 novels set in Canada. Her novels are carefully structured, with unusual plot twists, lively dialogue and flashes of humour. The characters usually face moral and ethical dilemmas. Dougall turned to religious writing with the anonymous essay *Pro Christo et Ecclesia* (1900), the first of 8 books on religious and theological topics. Farsighted in her views, she was concerned with the relationship between physical, psychological and spiritual health, and stressed Christianity's responsibility to adapt to new knowledge and to take a stand on contemporary issues. LORRAINE MCMULLEN

Doughty, Sir Arthur George, historian, archivist (b at Maidenhead, Eng 22 Mar 1860; d at Ottawa 1 Dec 1936). He immigrated to Canada in 1886 and worked in business before becoming a drama critic in Montréal and joining the Québec public service in 1897. A cultured man, who illuminated books and composed a libretto for an opera, he moved from being joint librarian of the Legislative Library at Québec to Dominion Archivist in 1904. Under his direction the PUBLIC ARCHIVES OF CANADA expanded enormously. He had an uncanny ability to persuade people to donate materials and established a network in Europe that paid off with the acquisition of the papers of Lord DURHAM among others. He began a collaboration with Adam Shortt that produced the valuable sourcebook *Documents Relating to the Constitutional History of Canada: 1759-1791* (1907) and CANADA AND ITS PROVINCES (23 vols, 1913-17). DAVID EVANS

Douglas, Alice Vibert, astronomer (b at Montréal 1894). Douglas received her doctorate from McGill in 1926. During WWI she was engaged in war work in England and then studied at the Cambridge Observatory and the Cavendish Laboratory 1921-23. On the McGill faculty until 1939, she became dean of women and later professor of astronomy at Queen's. Because of her interest in the history of astronomy and her personal knowledge of the man, she was asked to write the biography of Arthur Stanley Eddington. Published in 1956, it is still the only biography of this outstanding astronomer. An MBE (1918), Douglas was president of the Royal Astronomical Soc of Canada 1943-45 and of the International Federation of University Women 1947-50, and received honorary doctorates from McGill, Queen's and Queensland universities. A.H. BATTEN

Douglas, David, botanist (b at Scone near Perth, Scotland 25 July 1799; d in Hawaii 12 July 1835). Douglas became an apprentice gardener at age 11; at 20 he moved to the Botanic Gardens, Glasgow, and at 23 became a collector for the Horticultural Society of London in N America. He collected in Canada: near Amherstburg, Upper Canada, in 1823; along the Columbia, Saskatchewan and Hayes rivers to Hudson Bay in 1827; and along the Okanagan and Fraser rivers beyond Fort George [Prince George] in 1833. Douglas was the first white man known to have climbed Mt Brown in the Canadian Rockies. He described nearly 200 new species of plants and introduced more plants (254) to Europe from N America than any other man. About 50 plant species and one genus, *Douglasia,* are named for him, in addition to the DOUGLAS FIR, "the most important tree in the American lumber trade." He died when he accidentally fell into a pit used to trap wild bullocks and was trampled. C. STUART HOUSTON

Douglas, Sir Howard, soldier, author, colonial administrator (b at Gosport, Eng 23 Jan 1776; d at Tunbridge Wells, Eng 9 Nov 1861). The son of a naval officer, Douglas finished military academy in time to see action in the French Revolutionary and Napoleonic wars in Canada, Spain and Holland. Promoted major gen in 1821, he became lieutenant-governor and commander in chief of New Brunswick serving from 27 Mar 1823 to 19 Feb 1831. During those preradical years he ruled effectively, becoming the "most popular" of all imperial governors. He oversaw administrative, military and cultural changes in a period of rapid growth. As would be expected of an author and fellow of the Royal Society, his major achievement was in the improvement of King's College (UNB), of which he was chancellor. The Douglas Gold Medal is still awarded annually at UNB. Militarily the troubled New Brunswick-Maine border led him to encourage an active local militia, which numbered over 15 000 by 1831. He was less successful in his battles over the civil list and with crown lands commissioner Thomas BAILLIE. Douglas returned to England in 1831 as a strong supporter of the British N American colonies and their preferences in the British marketplace. CARL M. WALLACE

Douglas, James, surgeon (b at Brechin, Scot 20 May 1800; d at New York C, NY 14 Apr 1886). Admitted to the Edinburgh School of Medicine after a 5-year apprenticeship with Dr Thomas Law in Penrith, Eng, Douglas was admitted to the Edinburgh College of Surgeons in 1819 and to the London College of Surgeons in 1820. After practising in India, he came to Québec C in 1826 and around 1837 was given charge of the Marine and Emigrant Hospital, practising and teaching there. In 1845 he acquired the first Québec asylum for the mentally ill, the Centre hospitalier Robert Giffard at Beauport. Because of respiratory problems, he spent winters in Italy, Palestine or Egypt and in 1875 moved to Phoenixville, Pa. He is buried at Mount Hermon Cemetery, Sillery, Qué. The mental asylum of Verdun is now called the Douglas Hospital. SYLVIO LEBLOND

James Douglas acquired the first Québec asylum for the mentally ill in Verdun, now named for him.

Douglas, Sir James, fur trader, governor of Vancouver I, 1851-63, and of BC, 1858-64 (b at Demerara, British Guiana 15? Aug 1803; d at Victoria 2 Aug 1877). A resourceful, energetic and intelligent man, Douglas helped the HUDSON'S BAY CO become a trading monopoly in the N Pacific. As colonial governor he initiated British rule W of the Rocky Mts, and as the founder of settlement, trade and industry, he is remembered as "the Father of BC."

A "Scotch West Indian," Douglas was the son of "a free coloured woman" and a Scottish mer-

Sir James Douglas, governor of Vancouver I, 1851-63, and first governor of British Columbia, 1858-64 (*courtesy Public Archives of Canada / PA-61930*).

chant. He was taken to Lanark for schooling when he was 12. At age 16 he was apprenticed to the NORTH WEST CO, and entered the HBC's employ on the merger of the 2 companies in 1821. In 1826, while attached to Ft St James in the New Caledonia district, Douglas accompanied Chief Factor William Connolly on the first annual fur brigade to Ft Vancouver. On 27 Apr 1828, after the custom of the country, he married Amelia, Connolly's part-Indian daughter, confirming the marriage in 1837 by Church of England rites.

George SIMPSON, governor of Rupert's Land, who met Douglas at Ft St James in 1828, described him as "a stout, powerful active man of good conduct and respectable abilities," but one who became "furiously violent when aroused," a tendency which brought Douglas into conflicts with the CARRIER Indians and caused Connolly to obtain his transfer in 1830 to Ft Vancouver to serve under John MCLOUGHLIN. There Douglas became chief trader in 1835 and chief factor in 1839.

In 1842 Douglas accompanied Simpson to Alaska to negotiate with the Russian American Co. In 1843 Douglas began constructing Ft Victoria on the southern tip of Vancouver I to replace the northern coastal forts. Anticipating the eventual withdrawal of the HBC from Ft Vancouver after the British accepted the FORTY-NINTH PARALLEL as boundary in 1846, he had a new brigade trail blazed on British territory from New Caledonia to Ft Langley on the lower Fraser R. Ft Victoria, where the furs from the interior were transshipped, became the main Pacific depot in 1849. The fear of American expansion northward caused Britain on 13 Jan 1849 to lease Vancouver I to the HBC for 10 years. Douglas, the supervisor of the fur trade since 1845, was appointed HBC agent on the island.

The British government selected for governor Richard Blanshard, a barrister willing to serve without salary. Blanshard arrived at Ft Victoria in Mar 1850 to find his residence not completed. Remaining on shipboard, he sailed northward. Blanshard was shocked by the HBC's harsh discipline of striking miners at the Ft Rupert mine and accepted local fears of an Indian attack. Douglas would brook no interference with his Indian policy which now was based on mutual confidence. Blanshard soon resigned and departed in Aug 1851.

Without pleasure or satisfaction, Douglas learned on Oct 30 that he had been chosen Blanshard's successor. His worries were great; it would be difficult to reconcile the conflicting interests of governor and company official; the only revenue available for public buildings, schools, a church and road was from liquor licences; and qualified men were in such short supply that he appointed his own brother-in-law, newly arrived from Demerara, as chief justice of the Supreme Court.

Blanshard had appointed a Legislative Council in 1851 and in 1856 Douglas was instructed to establish an Assembly for the island. He was opposed to universal suffrage and believed that people really wanted "the ruling classes" to make their decisions. Property qualifications for the franchise and for membership in the Assembly were set so high that only a few landowners could qualify.

The first evidence of impending change on the Pacific seaboard came on Sunday 25 Apr 1858 when a boatload of boisterous miners from California, the first wave of 25 000 newcomers, arrived on their way to search for gold on the Fraser sandbars. Douglas had taken the precaution of claiming the land and the minerals for the Crown. Now he began to license the miners and, to stem an invasion, to stop foreign vessels entering the river. For this action, which seemed designed to protect the HBC monopoly, he was reprimanded.

With the gold discovery, Britain decided to cancel the special privileges granted the HBC until Mar 1859. A new colony on the mainland was created by parliamentary Act. Douglas was offered the governorship on condition that he sever his fur-trade connections. He would be given extensive political power since it seemed unwise to experiment with self-government among men "so wild, so miscellaneous, and perhaps so transitory." In Nov 1858, no longer a fur trader, and the rights of his old company W of the mountains having been extinguished, Douglas, who was still governor of Vancouver I, was inaugurated at Ft Langley by Chief Justice M.B. BEGBIE as governor of BC.

Douglas expected that a location near Ft Langley would be chosen for the colony's capital. But for military reasons Col Richard Clement Moody, RE, in Jan 1859 selected a steep, heavily timbered site (New Westminster) on the N bank of the Fraser. Douglas was concerned about the cost involved in laying it out. He also preferred Victoria as an administrative centre and as his place of residence. His visits to New Westminster were rare, and despite the grant of municipal self-government in 1860, the citizens demanded a resident governor and political reform.

As governor of BC, Douglas was chiefly concerned with the welfare of the miners. He relied on his gold commissioners to lay out reserves for the Indians and thus eliminate the threat of warfare, to record mining and land claims, and to adjudicate mining disputes. For the gold colony he devised a land policy which included mineral and pre-emption rights. His water legislation met the needs of the miners who employed rockers and flumes.

During the winter of 1858 he had used voluntary labour to make a pack trail to the mining area above the Fraser gorge. By 1862 he was planning to finance by loans (about which London was not fully informed) a wagon road 640 km long following the Fraser to distant Cariboo where gold nuggets had been found (*see* CARIBOO ROAD). It was extended in 1865 to Barkerville, an ebullient mining community.

Perhaps because of sensitivity over his, and his wife's, background, Douglas had developed a singularly aloof manner. Some of his old friends complained about his pomposity. New associates complained about his despotism. New Westminster merchants complained about having to pay customs duties. The effect was cumulative. Douglas's term as governor of Vancouver I was up in 1863; since BC was about to be given a more liberal type of government, it seemed to London an opportune time to retire him. Praise for his work and his talents and the award of a KCB softened the blow. MARGARET A. ORMSBY

Reading: D. Blakey Smith, *James Douglas* (1971); Margaret A. Ormsby, *British Columbia: a History* (rev ed, 1971).

Douglas, Thomas Clement, Tommy, Baptist minister, politician, premier of Saskatchewan (b at Falkirk, Scot 20 Oct 1904). Douglas led the first socialist government elected in Canada and is recognized as the father of socialized medicine. He also helped establish democratic socialism in the mainstream of Canadian politics. His proudly working-class and religious family provided a strong background for both his politics and his faith. His family settled in Canada in 1919 in Winnipeg and Douglas witnessed the WINNIPEG GENERAL STRIKE of that year. Leaving school at the age of 14, Douglas began a printer's apprenticeship. He became involved in church work and in 1924 decided to enter the ministry. He was at Brandon Coll for 6 years, and it was here that he was exposed to the SOCIAL GOSPEL, a belief that Christianity was above all a social religion, concerned as much with improving this world as with the life hereafter.

When Douglas moved to Weyburn, Sask, following his ordination in 1930, he found much suffering, for that province had been especially hard hit by economic depression and drought. Douglas soon became involved in ministering to people's physical and spiritual needs, while he pursued further academic studies in Christian ethics. These studies, along with his experience of the GREAT DEPRESSION, led him to conclude that political action was necessary to alleviate the suffering. In 1931 he established a local association of the Independent Labour Party, and 2 years later he attended the founding convention of the new, avowedly socialist CO-OPERATIVE COMMONWEALTH FEDERATION (CCF). Douglas ran unsuccessfully in the 1934 Saskatchewan election. He was then convinced by friends that he should be a CCF candidate in the federal election of 1935. This time he was successful, partly because he had learned to exploit a special talent — the ability to make people laugh. WWII further convinced Douglas that the socialist case was valid. Although he heard it repeatedly argued in Parliament that money could not be found to put people to work, money was forthcoming to finance a war. During his first 2 terms in Parliament, Douglas earned a reputation as a skilful and witty debater. He claimed as his constituency the underprivileged and exploited, and he took unpopular stands in defence of civil liberties.

As CCF premier of Saskatchewan 1944-61, Tommy Douglas was leader of the first socialist government elected in N America and the father of socialized medicine in Canada (*courtesy Public Archives of Canada/C-36219*).

In 1944 Douglas resigned his federal seat to contest the Saskatchewan general election. As premier of the province for the next 17 years, he became a symbol of what the socialist alternative promised. His government was innovative and efficient, and pioneered many programs that would later be implemented by others, notably in the field of social services. Douglas resigned as premier in 1961 to lead the federal NEW DEMOCRATIC PARTY (NDP), created as a formal alliance between the CCF and organized labour. Douglas was the new party's obvious choice, primarily because of his success in Saskatchewan, but also because he was universally regarded as the left's most eloquent spokesman. He was able to inspire and motivate party workers and he could also explain democratic socialism in moral, ethical and religious terms. Despite these qualifications, Douglas was defeated in the federal election of 1962, largely because of the backlash against the Saskatchewan government's introduction of Medicare, which had culminated in a long and bitter strike by the province's doctors. Winning a seat in a by-election, Douglas went on to serve as leader of the NDP until 1971, when he became his party's energy critic until his retirement in 1979.

Though Douglas did not realize his dream of a socialist Canada, he and his colleagues had considerable influence on government. Programs such as Medicare, a Canada-wide pension plan and bargaining rights for civil servants were first advocated by Douglas and his party, and these are now more or less firmly in place and universally accepted in Canada. L.D. LOVICK

Reading: T.C. Douglas, *The Making of a Socialist*, ed, L.H. Thomas (1982); Doris Shackleton, *Tommy Douglas* (1975).

Douglas Fir (*Pseudotsuga menziesii*), evergreen CONIFER of PINE family (Pinaceae). Six species of *Pseudotsuga* ("false hemlock") are recognized: 2 in western N America; 4 in China, Taiwan and Japan. Only *P. menziesii* occurs in Canada, along the West Coast, E into the Rocky Mts and extending S to central Mexico. A coastal variety (var *menziesii*) may attain heights of 100 m and diameters of 2 m; an interior variety (var *glauca*) is smaller. The leaves are evergreen, needlelike and 2-3 cm long. The cones are 5-10 cm long, have rounded scales and distinct, three-pronged bracts (modified leaves). POLLINATION occurs in early spring; seeds are shed in late summer or fall. Douglas fir resembles true firs, hemlocks and spruces but is most closely related to the LARCH. One of the most important timber species in N America, it is now planted in many regions of Europe. *See* David DOUGLAS. JOHN N. OWENS

Doukhobors, a sect of Russian dissenters, many of whom now live in western Canada. Since they arose as a peasant group in southern Russia, with orally transmitted teachings and traditions, their origin is obscure. Their doctrines appear to have been at least partially derived from those of a 17th-century renegade preacher, Danilo Filipov, who dissented radically from the ORTHODOX CHURCH. The Doukhobors rejected church liturgy, believing that God dwells in each man and not in a church; they rejected secular governments; and they preached PACIFISM. They replaced the Bible with orally transmitted psalms and hymns, which they called the Living Book; these are sung to this day at the *sobranyas* (gatherings which serve as both religious services and community meetings). Doukhobors revere their chosen leaders, whom they regard as especially inspired by God.

During the late 18th century the group was persecuted for its heresy and pacifism. In 1785 an Orthodox archbishop called them Doukhobors, or "Spirit-Wrestlers." It was intended to mean "Wrestlers against the Holy Spirit," but the group adopted it, interpreting it as "Wrestlers for and with the Spirit." Under Tsar Alexander I persecution lapsed, and in 1802 the Doukhobors were gathered in settlements in the Crimea, which was then a frontier region. Forty years later, under the less sympathetic Nicholas I, they were resettled among the fierce tribesmen of the recently conquered Caucasus. There they overcame initial difficulties and eventually prospered, particularly under their woman leader Lukeria Kalmikova.

Lukeria died in 1886, and the ensuing struggle for leadership split the sect. Peter Verigin emerged as the majority leader, but was immediately arrested and sent into exile. From afar Verigin was nevertheless able to exhort his followers to reaffirm their ideals. Persecuted again, many of the Doukhobors were allowed to emigrate to Canada, assisted by novelist Leo Tolstoy and British and American QUAKERS. More than 7400 sailed in 1898-99 and settled in what was to become Saskatchewan, where they lived as a community. Verigin joined them there in 1902.

Initially, Doukhobors were permitted to register for individual homesteads but to live communally, and they received concessions regarding education and military service. Frank Oliver, who succeeded Clifford Sifton as minister of the interior in 1905, interpreted the Dominion Lands Act more strictly. When Doukhobors refused to swear an oath of allegiance — a condition for the final granting of homestead titles — their homestead entries were cancelled. In 1908 Verigin led most of his followers to southern BC, where he bought land and established a self-contained community of 6000. Some Doukhobors split off to their own farms and became Independents. A tiny splinter, the radical Sons of Freedom (fd in 1902 in Saskatchewan), burnt several schools in a dispute with BC over education. Many in this group were later imprisoned for nude protest parades. During the 1930s the effects of the Depression, internal disenchantment and mismanagement, combined with the incendiarism of fanatics and the unsympathetic policies of finance companies and government, ruined the community, which had been one of the largest and most complex undertakings in communal living in N American history. In 1939 foreclosure took place and the land passed to the BC government, from which individual Doukhobors bought it back in the 1960s. After much Sons of Freedom unrest in the 1950s and 1960s, fanatical activism died down. Members of the various Doukhobor groupings still struggle to forestall the effects of encroaching assimilation. Descendants of the original Doukhobor settlers now number approximately 30 000 across Canada, with about half of that number remaining active in the culture, maintaining their religious customs, Russian language and pacifism. The majority group, known as the Orthodox Doukhobors, or Union of Spiritual Communities of Christ (USCC), has been most successful in integrating into the Canadian multicultural mosaic. The USCC is headed by Peter Verigin's great-grandson John J. Verigin. GEORGE WOODCOCK

Reading: George Woodcock and Ivan Avakumovic, *The Doukhobors* (1977).

Doutre, Joseph, lawyer, editor, writer (b at Beauharnois, Lower Canada 11 Mar 1825; d at Montréal, 3 Feb 1886). As the editor of *L'Avenir* and charter member of the *Institut Canadien* of Montréal, Doutre had a career in law and politics as an early liberal that has obscured his literary reputation until recently. He is known primarily as the author of the romantic novel *Les Fiancés de 1812* (1844), and his significance as a novelist has been obscured by the tradition of the *roman du terroir*, a genre which developed in reaction to novels such as *Les Fiancés*. Part of the novel's importance lies in its effort to adapt the works of the French novelist Eugène Sue to Canadian fiction, and part in its preface, which at-

Douglas fir (*Pseudotsuga menziesii*), with male flowers (bottom left), female flowers (top left) and cones (*artwork by Claire Tremblay*).

tacks the contemporary audience for its indifference to Canadian literature. Since the novel attacks religious intolerance, it was predictably condemned as immoral. Valued now largely because of the author's commentary on contemporary society, the novel is rare in its refusal of the official ideologies of the day. E.D. BLODGETT

Dove, name applied to certain species of the PIGEON family, especially to those of smaller size. No scientific distinction exists between doves and pigeons, and the names are interchangeable; eg, *Columba livia* is commonly known as domestic pigeon, rock dove or rock pigeon. W. EARL GODFREY

Downey, Richard Keith, scientist, plant breeder (b at Saskatoon 26 Jan 1927). Educated at U of Sask and Cornell, he has been employed at Agriculture Canada research stations at Lethbridge, Alta, 1951-57, and Saskatoon from 1957. Since 1958 he has been principal research scientist in charge of oilseed crop breeding at Saskatoon. Downey initiated and carried out a plan to transform rapeseed into an edible oilseed crop of superior quality. His most outstanding work to the present is the development of low-erucic-acid and low-glucosinolate rapeseed, now designated in the world trade as CANOLA. He has delineated the scientific basis of his work in numerous scientific journals, books and articles, and his work has stimulated quality plant breeding worldwide by showing how an old common species can be transformed into a high-quality crop. J.E.R. GREENSHIELDS

Downs, Barry Vance, architect (b at Vancouver 19 June 1930). After graduating in architecture from U of Washington, Seattle, in 1954, Downs worked for THOMPSON BERWICK PRATT AND PARTNERS in Vancouver before joining Fred Thornton Hollingsworth in partnership from 1963 to 1967. After 2 years of independent practice, he formed Downs/Archambault Architects with Richard B. Archambault in 1969.

Examples of the firm's work are the North Vancouver Civic Centre and Britannia Community Services Centre, Vancouver; Lester Pearson College of the Pacific, Pedder Bay, Vancouver I (in collaboration with Ron THOM), 1977; and a rich variety of houses and housing developments. Downs is a leading exponent of the thoughtful, low-key, mostly undecorated but carefully detailed architecture characteristic of the Canadian West Coast and the American northwest. His materials and colours are direct and unadorned, and his buildings, informally organized, low and economical, harmonize with the existing setting. MICHAEL MCMORDIE

Doyle, John Christopher businessman, industrialist (b at Chicago, Ill 1915). The flamboyant and controversial chairman of the Executive Committee of Canadian Javelin Ltd, he was resident in Panama in 1984 and engaged in legal battles in the Canadian courts. Doyle came to Canada as a coal salesman and, after serving with the US Corps of Engineers in WWII, acquired Javelin Foundry and Machine Works in Québec in 1949, reorganizing it as Canadian Javelin Ltd. Javelin became involved in mineral and forestry development in Newfoundland and Labrador in the 1950s and 1960s and expanded to control, through subsidiaries, natural resources in Saskatchewan, Québec, Arizona and El Salvador. Convicted by a Connecticut court in 1965 of Securities Exchange Commission violations, Doyle left the US for Canada. In 1973 he was charged in a St John's court with breach of trust and fraud but relocated to Panama.

Doyle, Richard J., "Dic," newspaper editor (b at Toronto 10 Mar 1923). Reared at Chatham, Ont, he worked on the *Daily News* there following RCAF service during WWII. He soon joined the Toronto GLOBE AND MAIL as a reporter, becoming editor of the *Globe Magazine* (1957) and managing editor of the daily (1959). Editor of the *Globe* 1963-83, he was Canada's most influential newspaper editor and the one most respected by working journalists. He was renowned for his love of good prose, feisty independence and peculiar ability to match apparently unlikely personnel to particular jobs. He has continued as a columnist for the paper.

Dragonfly, a carnivorous insect of the order Odonata; 143 species exist in Canada, including the ten-spot dragonfly (*photo by Mary W. Ferguson*).

Dragonfly, common name for robust, carnivorous INSECTS of order Odonata [Gk, "toothed," referring to mouthparts]. Name may include closely related DAMSELFLIES (suborder Zygoptera), but properly refers only to members of suborder Anisoptera. About 2800 species of anisopterids are known worldwide, 143 from Canada. Dragonflies have large, compound eyes, well-developed mouthparts, and 2 pairs of membranous wings, with hindwings wider at the base than forewings. Larvae are aquatic, but lack tail gills. They obtain oxygen by taking water into the hindgut; rapid expulsion of this water allows them to propel themselves. Eggs are usually deposited in water or in aquatic vegetation. Larval life may last 1-3 years or more. The transformation from drab, aquatic larva to brightly coloured, aerodynamically adept, terrestrial adult is dramatic. Larvae and adults may feed partly on mosquitoes; adults may prey on bees. G. PRITCHARD

Drainage Basin, area of land that contributes the water it receives as precipitation (except for losses through evaporation, transpiration from plants, incorporation into the SOIL or GROUNDWATER, etc) to a RIVER or network of rivers. Drainage basins are defined by topographical features, called drainage divides, which determine the direction of flow of water. Canada has 6 major drainage basins.

Arctic Drainage

This region of 3.58 million km^2 receives streamflow from the northern two thirds of Alberta, northern BC, northern Saskatchewan, the YT and the NWT, including the arctic islands. The estimated average annual discharge rate is 15 500 m^3/s. The largest river of the region is the MACKENZIE. Its watershed, 1.87 million km^2 comprises about 50% of the arctic drainage area, about 20% of Canada's area and 60% of the drainage water of the arctic region. The most important tributaries, the PEACE, ATHABASCA, LIARD and SOUTH NAHANNI rivers, all rise on the eastern slopes of the Rocky Mts. The Mackenzie has an average discharge of 9700 m^3/s into the Beaufort Sea. The annual streamflow is equivalent to a mean depth on the watershed of 170 mm. The longest flow route is 4241 km, from the head of the Finlay R in northern BC via the Peace R, Lk Athabasca, Great Slave Lk and the Mackenzie R to its mouth. This length exceeds by over 1000 km that of any other Canadian river system. The Mackenzie's peak flow occurs in June; otherwise it is quite uniform from May to Sept, when 70% of the annual discharge occurs. This uniformity is attributable to the influence of the relatively flat barren lands E of the river and to the many lakes, the largest of which, GREAT BEAR and GREAT SLAVE, each cover about 30 000 km^2.

ICE is significant to the HYDROLOGY of the region and much of the terrain is underlain by PERMAFROST. Lakes and rivers are open from about 15 June to 1 Nov in the more northerly part of the Mackenzie Basin, less in the arctic islands. The Mackenzie River Valley has been the subject of intensive technical, social and cultural studies during the 1970s because of concern over the potential impact of proposed petroleum PIPELINES. The delicate ecological balance existing between native people and their natural environment has given rise to many questions about the effects of TRANSPORTATION corridors in the valley.

Pacific Drainage

The 1.08 million km^2 Cordilleran region, W of the continental divide and extending from the international border at the boundary of Alberta and BC into the YT near the Mackenzie Delta, sheds water into the Pacific Ocean at an average rate of 21 200 m^3/s. This rate is equivalent to an annual depth of 620 mm over the area, the largest hypothetical average depth of any hydrologic region of Canada. The high average discharge is attributable to the large amounts of precipitation received at higher elevations of the Rockies and coastal mountain ranges, caused by moist air masses moving off the Pacific Ocean. Stream water supply is, however, highly variable. In the dry interior valleys the equivalent annual depth of runoff is 100 mm or less; in the coastal zone 3200 mm.

The 1300 km FRASER R flows through spectacular canyons and rich agricultural land to

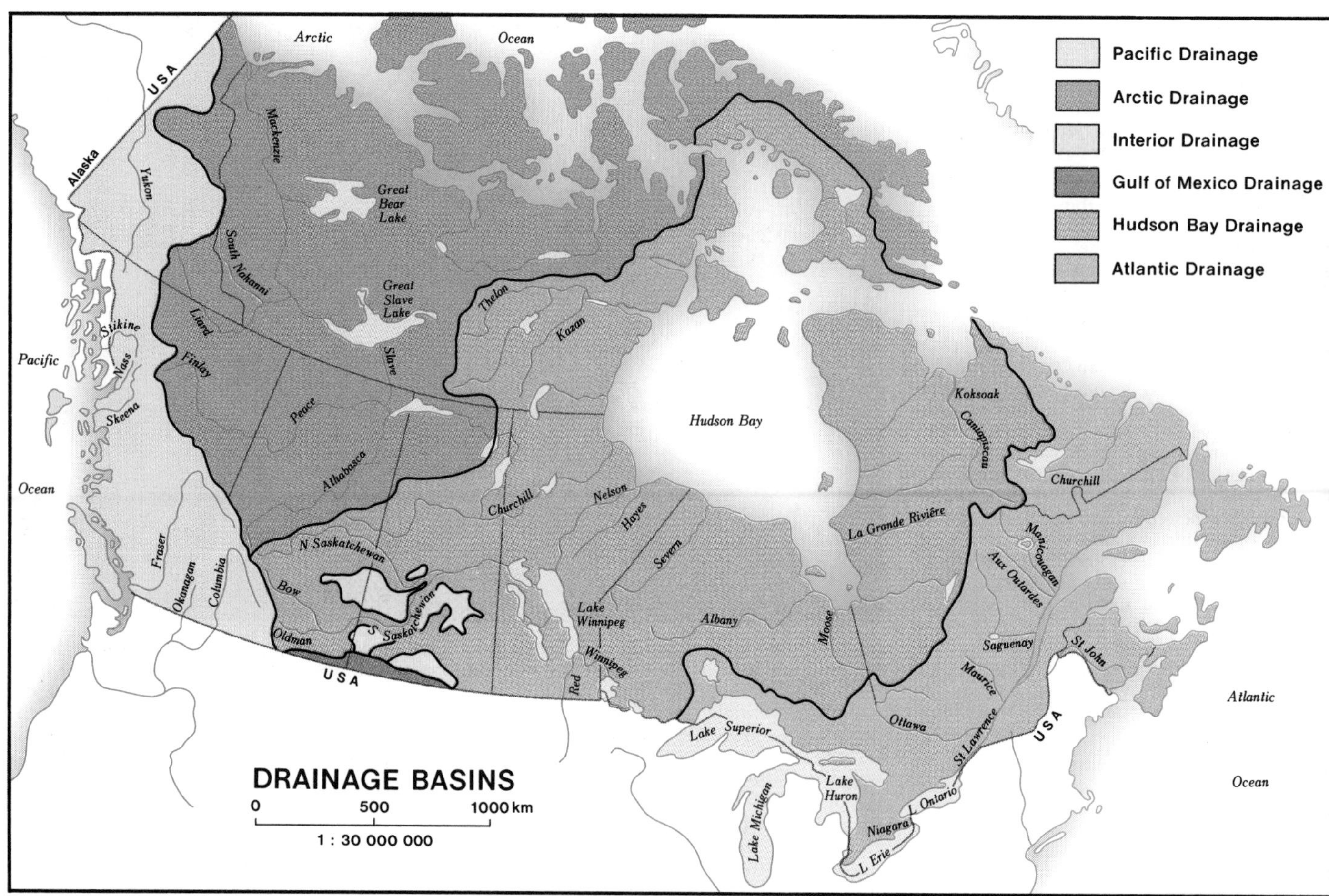

provide drainage to 220 000 km^2 of interior BC. The mean discharge rate is about 3500 m^3/s. Highest flows are experienced in June; lowest in March. The risk of flooding in the Fraser's lower reaches has been a matter of concern for some years.

The COLUMBIA R system in southeastern BC has an average flow at the international boundary of 2800 m^3/s. A portion of this flow originates from 50 000 km^2 of drainage area in the US. Three large RESERVOIRS in the Columbia system provide significant FLOOD-control benefits to the US and will ultimately allow installation of 4000 MW of hydroelectric-generating capacity in Canada (*see* BC HYDRO). The Okanagan R, which flows to join the Columbia S of the international boundary, is of great benefit to fruit growers in the semiarid valleys.

Coastal rivers, including the Fraser, swarm with SALMON during the season when they return inland to their spawning grounds. The other large rivers, the SKEENA, NASS and STIKINE, discharge a combined average of 3800 m^3/s into the Pacific. The Yukon, with a drainage area of 800 000 km^2, has an average discharge of 2300 m^3/s where it crosses into Alaska. Only a small fraction of the potential hydroelectric-generating capacity has been installed on any of these streams. In addition to the benefits to fisheries and agriculture and for HYDROELECTRICITY, the waters of the Pacific drainage provide a valuable resource to the LUMBER, PULP AND PAPER and mineral processing industries and to municipalities.

Western Hudson Bay and Mississippi Drainage

This region of 2.64 million km^2 includes all of Manitoba, most of Saskatchewan, the southern third of Alberta, most of the District of Keewatin, a part of Ontario W of Lk Superior and about 150 000 km^2 immediately S of the international boundary. A 27 500 km^2 zone of southern Saskatchewan and southeastern Alberta drains into the Mississippi Basin and thence to the Gulf of Mexico. The major rivers discharging into western HUDSON BAY are the HAYES, NELSON, CHURCHILL, KAZAN and THELON. The estimated mean rate of discharge for the region is about 9400 m^3/s.

The most important drainage basin is the 1 million km^2 drained by the Saskatchewan-Nelson river system. The BOW, OLDMAN and North and South SASKATCHEWAN RIVERS rise on the eastern slopes of the Rockies and flow E for 1900 km through the central plains. Extensive tracts in the plains region drain into interior depressions (sloughs). Sloughs have no outlet to the principal streams which enter a chain of lakes in south-central Manitoba. Here the flow is joined with that of the RED R flowing in from the S and the WINNIPEG R from the E. The latter carries drainage from southeastern Manitoba, the Lake of the Woods region of Ontario, and Minnesota. The flow discharges from Lk Winnipeg (24 000 km^2) into Hudson Bay via the Nelson R.

The mean flow of the Nelson at its outlet is 2370 m^3/s, equivalent to a mean depth of about 125 mm annually over the watershed. The principal source areas of streamflow for the Nelson are the eastern slopes of the Rockies and the lake area of Manitoba, northwestern Ontario and the adjacent states. The latter region contributes over 50% of the total annual discharge. The several large lakes and hundreds of smaller ones, totalling over 50 000 km^2 in area, regulate the Nelson's flow, so that the mean flow rate in any month is seldom 30% greater or less than the annual average. Highest discharge occurs in July; lowest flows in Jan-Mar. The Nelson and Churchill rivers are sites of large hydroelectric-power generating facilities with significant potential for further development.

The North and South Saskatchewan river system is important to agriculture since it flows through a region of fertile soils, limited in their productivity by uncertain rainfall. The water supply from the Bow, Oldman, North and South Saskatchewan rivers and their tributaries is vital to cities, towns and industries of Alberta and Saskatchewan. The high variability of local tributary flow has necessitated construction of many dams to provide carry-over storage from years of abundant flow to years of low discharge.

South and East Hudson Bay Drainage

This region includes most of northern Ontario and western and northern Québec, an area of about 1.4 million km^2. There are at least 15 individual watersheds of 30 000 km^2 or more in area. The largest of these are the SEVERN, draining into Hudson Bay, ALBANY (134 000 km^2), MOOSE (108 000 km^2); LA GRANDE RIVIÈRE (98 000 km^2) flowing into JAMES BAY; and KOKSOAK (133 000 km^2) draining into UNGAVA BAY. The region, part of the Canadian Shield, consists of massive ancient crystalline rocks. As a result of GLACIATION there are large areas of lakes, ponds and swamps. In some parts as much as 15% of the drainage area is covered by fresh water. The many lakes result in fairly uniform rates of river flow throughout the year. The waters are generally of good quality and very little influenced by human activities.

Although the rivers and lakes are ice covered annually for 6 months, water continues to flow under the ice. The lowest flows occur in Mar for the more southerly streams, Apr for those draining into Ungava Bay. The time of highest discharge is late May or June, following the breakup of the ice cover in mid-May. About 45% of the total annual flow occurs May-July, except for streams draining into Ungava Bay, where about 60% of the annual flow occurs

June-Aug. The average annual rate of flow of all streams draining into Hudson, James and Ungava bays is estimated at 20 000 m^3/s, which is equivalent to a mean annual water depth of 450 mm over the entire region and represents about 60% of precipitation received. There is considerable hydroelectric potential in the region. The JAMES BAY PROJECT is one of the largest in the world. The average flow in La Grande Rivière is to be increased from 1700-3300 m^3/s and the eventual generating capacity will be 10 000 MW, 20% of 1982 Canadian capacity for hydro-power generation (*see* HYDRO-QUÉBEC).

Great Lakes-St Lawrence Drainage

This basin, with an area of 1 million km^2 above Montréal, is dominated by the GREAT LAKES, covering 245 000 km^2. About one half the basin is Canadian, Lake Michigan is wholly within the US; the international boundary passes through Lakes Superior, Huron, Erie, Ontario and St Clair. Most of the land drainage from the Canadian portion is from the Canadian Shield; the ST LAWRENCE LOWLANDS make a small contribution. The lowlands include peninsular Ontario, bounded by Georgian Bay, Lakes Huron, St Clair, Erie and Ontario and the fringes of the St Lawrence R. The Great Lakes-St Lawrence system provides an important navigable waterway of over 2000 km from the city of Montréal to the head of Lk Superior (*see* ST LAWRENCE SEAWAY).

Most streams in the lowlands are less than 300 km long. They are important for industry, agriculture and urban water supply, and provide recreational opportunities for the region's urban population. The intensive land use in the southern parts of the basin, coupled with variability of the glacial deposits, results in high variability of seasonal flows, localized flooding, periodic low summer flows and impaired WATER quality.

The average flow in the NIAGARA R at Queenston, between Lakes Erie and Ontario, is 5760 m^3/s. By the time the St Lawrence R reaches Cornwall, downstream of the Great Lakes, the average flow is 6430 m^3/s. After the river is joined by the OTTAWA R at Montréal and by other tributaries, its average flow is 9800 m^3/s, equivalent to an annual average depth of 300 mm over the entire basin. The St Lawrence Basin is the most southerly in Canada. This factor, coupled with the lakes' relatively large areas of open water, results in significant evaporation losses. Streamflow is reduced to about 25-30% of received precipitation. Nevertheless, the large lakes maintain a steady rate of flow throughout the year, and from one year to the next.

Atlantic Drainage

The region includes that part of Canada draining to the St Lawrence R (from Montréal eastward), the Gulf of ST LAWRENCE and the Atlantic ocean. It includes all of Nfld, NS, NB, PEI and part of Qué, an area of 1 million km^2.

The drainage from the north shore of the St Lawrence and Labrador is largely from the Canadian Shield, where 10-15% of the area is in freshwater lakes. The balance of the area is part of the Appalachian Region, consisting of a mixture of crystalline and sedimentary rocks, with thin surficial materials. The rivers are short and drainage is well developed as a result of long periods of erosion. About 9% of Newfoundland and 5% of NS are in lakes. There are few lakes in NB and PEI.

The largest watersheds discharging into the St Lawrence R are the Manicouagan (45 000 km^2) and the Saguenay (88 000 km^2). The Churchill R in Labrador drains 79 800 km^2 and discharges directly to the Atlantic Ocean. The SAINT JOHN R, in NB, draining 55 400 km^2, discharges into the Bay of FUNDY. Most of the large rivers of the basin have extensive hydroelectric installations.

The total discharge of the watersheds in the basin averages 21 000 m^3/s, ie, an equivalent annual depth of 650 mm of water, or about 50% of the annual precipitation. The annual rate of runoff per-unit area is lowest (17 L/s/km^2) for the St Maurice R in the most westerly part of the region; highest (45 L/s/km^2) in southwestern Newfoundland.

The minimum daily rates of runoff from the larger watersheds range from 3 L/s/km^2 for the Churchill R to 1 L/s/km^2 for the Aux Outardes R. Many smaller streams dry up completely for a short period during summer or as a result of ice formation in winter. Local problems of water-quality impairment are encountered in regions of intensive agricultural, forestry or industrial activity. *See* GEOLOGICAL REGIONS; PHYSIOGRAPHIC REGIONS.

H.D. AYERS

Drake, Sir Francis, one of history's great seamen and adventurers (b near Tavistock, Eng 1540?; d off Panama 28 Jan 1596). He likely sighted VANCOUVER I on his voyage around the world (1577-80). After plundering Spanish ships off Mexico, Drake tried to find a polar route back to England; the supposition that he sailed N to Vancouver I is based on a study of the winds and currents of the northwestern Pacific.

JAMES MARSH

Drake, Theodore George Gustavus Harwood, physician, historian, collector (b at Webbwood, Ont 16 Sept 1891; d at Toronto 28 Oct 1959). Drake graduated from U of T in 1914. He was a co-developer of the infant food Pablum and Sunwheat Biscuits, and the royalties of these products were given to the Hospital for Sick Children (Toronto). He was awarded the OBE after WWII for designing nutrition levels for RCAF meals and prisoner-of-war parcels. Drake wrote extensively on the history of pediatrics and was the author of many scientific articles. His collection of some 5000 antiques of pediatric interest, from Ancient Greece and Egypt to 19th-century Europe, was donated to the Museum of the History of Medicine, Academy of Medicine, Toronto, in 1960.

WILHELMINA M. DRAKE

Drama in English Drama is a literary genre in which texts are written generally for the ostensible purpose of theatrical performance, but dramatic literature includes much writing that has never been performed and much that, despite its form, is not intended to appear on stage. Canadian drama in English has gone through a process of evolution, affected by the colonial experience, the rise of nationalism and many other forces.

The naturally small amount of early Canadian drama in English is shaped largely by foreign modes, as in the case of Lt Adam Allan's *The New Gentle Shepherd* (1798), which is Allan Ramsay's *The Gentle Shepherd* (1725), a pastoral drama in Scottish dialect, "reduced to English." Seventeenth-century English heroic tragedies, such as John Dryden's *The Conquest of Granada* (1670, 1671), were the obvious antecedents for George Cocking's verse drama *The Conquest of Canada* (1766), in which Gen WOLFE leads his greatly outnumbered British soldiers to victory. Even Robert Rogers's *Ponteach* (1766), a sometimes-engaging verse drama depicting the defeat of the noble savage, PONTIAC, by evil European invaders, is Canadian only in that its American-born author resided briefly in Canada. The anonymous "Acadius," extant as a 2-act extract in the *Nova Scotia Gazette and the Weekly Chronicle* (1774), dramatizes a wealthy Boston merchant's extramarital activities and his black servants' attempts to cope with their exploitation.

The 19th Century The common impression that poetic drama was the 19th century's dominant dramatic genre can be challenged, as more plays are found in prose. Authors with literary pretensions did, however, write poetic dramas and "dramatic sketches" not intended for the stage, many of which were published in the *Literary Garland*. The anonymous "The Queen's Oak" (1850), which treats in conventional verse Elizabeth Woodville's meeting with Edward IV, is typical. Eliza Lanesford Cushing is the most notable of the *Garland* contributors; among her 10 plays is "The Fatal Ring" (1840), about a virtuous countess seduced by an alluring, womanizing king. The uneven quality of its blank verse and its moral tone are evident also in Cushing's biblical drama, "Esther" (*Lady's Book*, vols 16-17, 1838). One of the first plays printed in monograph, Charles HEAVYSEGE's *Saul* (1857), gained respect from John A. MACDONALD and Henry Wadsworth Longfellow, among others, but, like Heavysege's *Count Filippo* (1859), this bulky, sententious piece has fallen into deserved obscurity. Thomas Bush's sprawling *Santiago* (1866), one of the most ambitious poetic dramas of the age, suffers from obscure allusions, passages of incomprehensible blank verse and melodramatic excess.

The end of the century saw poetic dramatists using indigenous subjects with greater frequency, but the quality of their expression improved only slightly. *Tecumseh* (1886) displays Charles MAIR's minor poetic talent and his fervent patriotism. Sarah Anne Curzon, whose poetic talent was more limited than Mair's, also follows a patriotic bent in *Laura Secord* (1887). John Hunter-Duvar in *De Roberval* (1888) tries to dramatize too many themes suggested by Sieur de ROBERVAL's adventures in early Canada. Foreign and indigenous elements often came together in poetic drama, a fact well illustrated by the range of William Wilfred CAMPBELL's works; eg, "Daulac" (1908) presents DOLLARD DES ORMEAUX's brave defence at the Long Sault, whereas "Mordred" (1895) centres melodramatic intrigue on King Arthur's bastard son. As is characteristic of the genre, Campbell's 5 plays suffer from ponderous "Shakespearean" verse and weighty philosophy which render them impractical to stage.

The practice of publishing political or social satire in newspapers created a lively topical drama early in the century, as illustrated by "The Charrivarri" (*The Scribbler* vols 3-4, 1823) by Samuel Hull Wilcocke (pseudonym Lewis Luke MacCulloh), "The Triumph of Intrigue" (anon, *New Brunswick Courier* 1833) and the "Provincial Drama Called the Family Compact" (*British Colonist*, 1839), attributed to Hugh Scobie (pseudonym Chrononhotonthologos). Similarly biting sketches, such as William Henry Fuller's "The Unspecific Scandal" (*Canadian Illustrated News* 1874), which deals with the PACIFIC SCANDAL, and Curzon's "The Sweet Girl Graduate" (*Grip-Sack* 1882), which exposes sexual discrimination against women at University of Toronto, continued to appear to the end of the century. Topical satire appeared in monographs by mid-century. *The Female Consistory of Brockville* (1856) allowed its anonymous author, "Caroli Candidus," to attack hypocrisy in the Brockville Presbytery. "Sam Scribble" wrote both *Dolorsolatio* (1856), a burlesque in which Federation is the answer to Grandpapa Canada's *dolors*, and *King of the Beavers* (1865), in which FENIANS conspire to attack Beaverland. *The Fair Grit* (1876) by Nicholas Flood DAVIN is an enjoyable satire on party politics.

Government figures played a significant role in the development of Canadian drama. In Ottawa, Lady Dufferin organized dramatic entertainments between 1872 and 1878 in the theatre in the governor general's residence, Rideau Hall. Frederick A. Dixon, author of the comic operetta, *The Maire of St. Brieux* (1875?), was one playwright whose work she encouraged. Dixon's *A Masque Entitled "Canada's Welcome"* (1879), which chronicled pioneer settlement in the Canadian wilderness, was presented for the Marquess of Lorne and Princess Louise at Ottawa's Grand Opera House in 1879.

Musical dramas also were important entertainment in the 19th century. *Leo, the Royal Cadet* (1889) by George Frederick Cameron (music by Oscar Telgmann) centres on Nellie's love for Leo, an army cadet who becomes a hero fighting the Zulus. *Nina* (1880s) by Thomas Herbert Chesnut is a "nautical comic operetta" influenced by Gilbert and Sullivan. Musical parodies and burlesques prevailed, the most famous being William Henry Fuller's *H.M.S. Parliament* (1880), which borrowed from *H.M.S. Pinafore.* Jean Newton McIlwraith showed more originality exploring Canadian identity in the context of the ANNEXATION issue in her comic *Ptarmigan* (1895, music by J.E.P. Aldous).

The century produced plays in a number of other genres. Catharine Nina Merritt's prose history *When George the Third Was King* (1897) celebrates LOYALISTS who settled in Canada. Stage melodramas are represented by pieces like John Louis Carleton's *More Sinned Against than Sinning* (1882), a meaningless formula play which became an annual treat in Saint John, NB. Like Harry Lindley's inferior *Chick* (1893) or W.P. Wood's sketchy scenario *Minnie Trail* (1871), these melodramas suffer from the genre's weaknesses without having its strengths.

The 20th Century Poetic dramas, such as the Rev Robert Norwood's *The Witch of Endor* (1916), continued to be written in the 20th century, as did melodramas and light comedies by W.A. Tremayne and others. *The Man Who Went* (1918), a wartime spy thriller, is typical of Tremayne's formulaic plays for the American commercial stage. Children's plays and scripts for educational, temperance or religious purposes were prevalent during the early 20th century, as were humorous dramatic sketches, eg, adaptations from Dickens, and Stephen LEACOCK's burlesques of outdated theatrical modes. After WWI Canadians wrote in the environment of the amateur movement that grew up across the country. In *Canadian Plays from Hart House Theatre* (2 vols, 1926-27) editor Vincent MASSEY gives us examples in various genres of this "little theatre" activity, including 3 short, ironic comedies, "Balm," "Brothers in Arms" and "The Weather Breeder" by Merrill Denison, the first significant playwright of the century. His "Marsh Hay," a 4-act, realistic drama published in *The Unheroic North* (1923), treats important rural Canadian themes.

One-act plays in a variety of styles became the predominant form of the time. Poet Marjorie Pickthall's evocative verse drama, "The Woodcarver's Wife" (*University Magazine* 1920) was performed at Hart House, University of Toronto. *One Act Plays by Canadian Authors* (1926) collects 19 plays, of which only "Come True" and "Low Life" bear mention, those chiefly because they are by Mazo DE LA ROCHE; they antedate *Whiteoaks* (1936), the conventional drama, adapted from her novel, which ran for over 2 years in London, Eng, before the war. In the mid-1930s, Samuel French (Canada) Ltd launched a Canadian Playwrights Series offering a range of one-act plays, including Martha Allan's *Summer Solstice* (1935), shaped by G.B. Shaw's *Heartbreak House;* Lillian Thomas's amusing *Jim Barber's Spite Fence* (1936); and *The Lampshade,* an English murder story by W.S. Milne. In his 4 *Plays of the Pacific Coast* (1935), A.M.D. Fairbairn dramatizes West Coast Indian stories; the Québec legend of Rose's dance with the devil is rendered into rhyming couplets in E.W. Devlin's *Rose Latulippe* (1935). The hardships of the GREAT DEPRESSION inspired Eric Harris's domestic drama *Twenty Five Cents* (Toronto 1936).

The Depression also led to numerous "Worker's Plays." Dorothy LIVESAY, whose "Joe Derry" (*Masses* 1933) is a narrated pantomime, was the most famous author involved; *Eight Men Speak* (1934) by Oscar Ryan, E. Cecil-Smith, H. Francis and Mildred Goldberg was the most notable play, although for historical rather than dramatic reasons. Aside from "Worker's Plays," the most daring experiment was Herman Voaden's "symphonic expressionism." His ballet-music-dramas were reputedly compelling on stage, but now are dated, their image-laden language stilted. If a single one-act play of the period stands out, it is Gwen RINGWOOD's "Still Stands the House" (*Carolina Playbook* 1938), a moving, realistic portrayal of spiritual starvation and suppression in hard times on the Prairies. Len Peterson's radio play, *Burlap Bags* (1946, pub 1972), also bears citing for its portrayal of an alienated, absurd postwar world.

The leading playwright of the late 1940s and early 1950s was Robertson DAVIES, who dramatized in a witty, often eloquent style his satirical view of philistine Canadians. His early plays received amateur productions, but *A Jig for the Gypsy* (1954) and *Hunting Stuart* (1955, pub 1972) were staged by Toronto's professional Crest Theatre. The 1950s saw the establishment of modern Canadian professional theatre, highlighted by the founding of the Stratford Festival. From the 1930s radio had aided the professional evolution by employing playwrights. Among them was Lister Sinclair, author of "The Blood is Strong" (*A Play on Words* 1948), who emerged in the late 1940s as a prolific radio dramatist. W.O. MITCHELL, in "The Devil's Instrument" (1949, pub 1973), showed a prairie Hutterite youth rebelling against his religion; in "The Black Bonspiel of Wullie MacCrimmon" (1951, pub 1966) Mitchell humorously pitted Wullie against the Devil, an avid curler. Earle BIRNEY wrote "Trial of a City" (1952), an inventive, witty indictment of Vancouver. *Teach me How to Cry* (1955), Patricia Joudry's sentimental study of small-town prejudice, was first a radio play, then won the 1959 Dominion Drama Festival Best Play award before going to New York and London, and finally becoming a movie. In the manner of Dylan Thomas's *Under Milk Wood,* John REEVES fashioned *A Beach of Strangers* (1961), hitting out at Canadian puritanism. John COULTER, whose 1930s plays were popular with amateur groups, also wrote for the radio, then used a Canadian hero in the episodic and moving *Riel* (1962). Coulter's last dramatic work was *François Bigot* (1978), also a history play. The late 1960s saw an unprecedented increase in the quantity and quality of drama, a trend which continued through the 1970s. In 1967 George RYGA's *The Ecstasy of Rita Joe* (1970) made an emotionally provocative statement on Indian-white relations; this was followed in 1969 by Ryga's controversial "hippie" play, "Grass and Wild Strawberries" (1971). John Herbert's prison drama, *Fortune and Men's Eyes* (1965) graphically depicts intellectual and sexual oppression. British Columbia playwright Beverly SIMONS used absurdist techniques in *Crabdance* (1969) to present the plight of middle-aged Sadie Goldman trapped by the stress of modern life.

In the early 1970s, small professional theatres dedicated to new Canadian plays sprang up across the country. Some relied on scripts of a traditional nature. In *Leaving Home* (1972) and its sequel, *Of the Fields, Lately* (1973), David French used the conventions of realism to explore the psychological tensions within a Newfoundland family forced to move to Toronto. His *Jitters* (1980) is a more sophisticated comedy of manners satirizing Canadian theatre. Joining French in ushering in a muscular Canadian realism was David Freeman, whose *Creeps* (1972) is a searing revelation of life among the physically or psychologically handicapped. Freeman's subsequent plays have not been as successful as *Creeps,* but were also part of the early 1970s' realism, which included French's poolroom drama, *One Crack Out* (1975), William Fruet's "Wedding in White" (1973) and Mary Humphry Baldridge's *The Photographic Moment* (1974). Using less realistic conventions, Herschel Hardin's Inuit drama, "Esker Mike and his Wife Agiluk" (*TDR,* 1969), received attention, as did Carol BOLT's documentary satire *Buffalo Jump* (1972), about the ON TO OTTAWA TREK, and her episodic portrait of anarchist, feminist Emma Goldman, *Red Emma* (1974). Bolt's more recent psychological thriller, *One Night Stand* (1977), with its melodramatic ending, and her lightweight satire, *Escape Entertainment* (1982), suggest that she has allowed popular appeal to replace depth of insight as a dramatic value.

In Newfoundland, Michael Cook wrote "Colour the Flesh the Colour of Dust" (1972), "The Gayden Chronicles" (*CTR* 13, 1977) and "On the Rim of the Curve" (1977), this last about the demise of the BEOTHUK Indians. These somewhat Brechtian dramas use incidents from Canadian history to comment on modern social and political injustices, and head a list of large-scale history plays including Stewart Boston's "Counsellor Extraordinary" (1971), Michael Bawtree's *The Last of the Tsars* (1973), James Nichol's *Sainte-Marie Among the Hurons* (1977) and Ron Chudley's *After Abraham* (1978). Cook's shorter plays, "Quiller" (1975) and "Tiln" (1975), and his 2-act plays, "The Head, Guts and Sound Bone Dance" (*CTR* 1, 1974) and *Jacob's Wake* (1975), take a philosophical attitude to modern Newfoundland life.

In Western Canada, *Walsh* (1972), an episodic treatment of the NWMP officer's anguish over the injustice he helped perpetrate on Sitting Bull, was the first of 5 major plays establishing Sharon Pollock's reputation. Since *Walsh,* she has written *The Komagata Maru Incident* (1978), which uses a circus atmosphere to comment on Canada's handling of a 1914 shipload of SIKH immigrants; "One Tiger to a Hill" (1981), depicting the complex tensions in a prison hostage taking, and "Blood Relations" (1981), a skillful handling of the Lizzie Borden tale. "Generations" (1981) is Pollock's only play in a wholly realistic mode; the others demonstrate an imaginative restructuring of reality that forces the audience to concentrate on issues inherent in the actual events portrayed.

"Collective creation" is a term coined to describe the working process of many theatres in the early 1970s in preparing performance pieces, often "documentary dramas" improvised around a specific topic or theme. Among the best of the genre are scripts such as *The Farm Show* (1976) by Toronto's Theatre Passe Muraille and "Paper Wheat" (*CTR* 17, 1978) by Saskatoon's 25TH STREET THEATRE. They gain strength from imaginative staging rather than deep insight into the topic; hence, they yield little to traditional modes of dramatic analysis. Often the collective process involves a playwright, as in the very popular "1837: The Farmers' Revolt" (*CTR* 6, 1975), which Rick Salutin scripted with Theatre Passe Muraille. Salutin's equally famous *Les Canadiens* (1977), written "with an assist from Ken Dryden," uses the rapid changes of time, place and action, the character doubling and vignette structure associated with collective works, but provides more analysis of its topic: social and political life in Québec. Rex Deverall scripted "No I Hard" (1978) from a collective creation process, but he is the playwright of *Boiler Room Suite* (1978), where 2 old winos find joy in each other's company, and *Black Powder* (1982), his documentary drama about the 1931 Estevan riots. Even English Canada's most acclaimed dramatist, James REANEY, has often exercised his manifest genius through improvisational collaboration with acting companies. Over the years, following amateur first productions of his more conventional early plays, Reaney has evolved a mythopoeic drama based on fragmented plots and resonant thematic imagery that echoes between rich dialogue and the stage action, characters or objects. His Donnelly trilogy ("Sticks and Stones," *CTR* 2, 1974; *St. Nicholas Hotel* 1976; *Handcuffs* 1977) has been called the strongest drama yet written in English Canada.

Experimental work by many other playwrights has challenged the boundaries of traditional English Canadian theatre. Québec dramas in translation, notably the multilayered, symbolic plays of Michel TREMBLAY, have helped extend conventional modes. The many successful productions of Michael ONDAATJE's *The Collected Works of Billy the Kid*, which he adapted for the stage from his brilliant poetic narrative (1970), created a dramatic form by juxtaposing short scenes in prose and verse. Rich imagery, in the manner of Reaney's Donnelly plays, transforms the chronicle of Billy the Kid into myth. In the early 1970s, Lawrence Russell used surrealistic techniques in the short pieces in *Penetration* (1972) and *The Mystery of the Pig Killer's Daughter* (1975). Michael Hollingsworth dabbled with bizarre events in *Clear Light* (1973) and *Strawberry Fields* (1973). "Mathematics" (1973), 190 seconds without dialogue during which 6 groups of carefully selected objects are thrown one by one upon the stage, indicates the ephemeral, yet daring experiments of Hrant Alianak. His "Western" (1973) finds a gunslinger and 2 beautiful women in humorous dialogue consisting of the titles and names of stars from western movies while they wait for the cavalry to rescue them from 500 attacking Indians. Ken Gass, the author of the cartoonlike, anti-fascist *Hurrah for Johnny Canuck!* (1975), raised controversy with his *Winter Offensive* (1978) in which Adolf Eichmann's wife hosts a kinky sex party for Nazi officials. Bryan Wade's *Blitzkrieg* (1974) about Hitler and Eva Braun, and many of his earlier shorter plays (eg, *Lifeguard* 1973 and "Alias" 1974), have imaginative unconventional qualities, but have not been followed by anything substantial. A talking dog and exploding croquet mallets make Larry Fineberg's *Hope* (1972) slightly unusual, but his other work is mainstream. His undistinguished adaptation of Constance Beresford-Howe's novel *Eve* (1977) was performed at the Stratford Festival, as was his dull rendition of Euripides' *Medea* (1978). George Walker's *Zastrozzi* (1977), *Theatre of the Film Noir* (1981) and *Science and Madness* (1982) abound in entertaining theatricality, usually in the service of making fun of traditional dramatic modes, but when they move beyond simple parody, his plays flounder intellectually. One of the most innovative scripts in recent years is John Krizanc's "Tamara" (unpublished), which won a Dora Mavor Moore Award in 1981. Its "environmental theatre" form allowed audience members to follow a chosen character through the large, old house in which it was staged. No individual saw all the 1920s' political and amorous action unravelling simultaneously in the many rooms, but playgoers gained enjoyment piecing the strands together from chats with others after the show.

There was special attention focused on women in the theatre during the 1970s and after. The plays of Sharon Pollock and Carol Bolt pursue feminist themes, and Margaret Hollingsworth has entered the forefront of Canadian dramatists. Her full-length *Ever Loving* (1981) traces the lives of 3 war brides who come to Canada to live with their husbands. *Ever Loving* joins "The Apple in the Eye" (1977), *Mother Country* (1978), "Operators" and *Bushed* (1973) in illustrating Hollingsworth's skill at creating lively human characters and scenes loaded with humour and tension. Erika Ritter demonstrates a rapierlike wit and a perceptive reading of life in *Automatic Pilot* (1980), her most significant play to date, but too often allows an easy laugh to deflect us from probing the relationships among her characters.

The period since the mid-1970s has produced many talented writers who have as yet only one or 2 considerable plays, eg, Timothy FINDLEY and his resonant *Can You See Me Yet?* (1977) and American-born Sheldon Rosen with *Ned and Jack* (1979). David Fennario has written what may be the most "Canadian" of plays, *Balconville* (1980), a bilingual slice of life comically revealing the oppression of French and English slum dwellers in Montréal. Tom Walmsley's handling of sex and violence in *Something Red* (1978), *The Jones Boy* (1978) and *The Workingman* (1976) is forceful and graphically realistic, if sometimes overdone. In *Waiting for the Parade* (1980), John Murrell creates nostalgia to link vignettes of 5 women living out WWII in Calgary. His earlier *Memoir* (1978) lacks truly dramatic action but is a theatrical vehicle for the actress playing the aged Sarah Bernhardt.

Most of the recent plays mentioned combine box-office appeal with enough substance to engage the mind, but a current trend has also seen the proliferation of situation comedies like Allan Stratton's *Nurse Jane Goes to Hawaii* (1981) and Alden Nowlan and Walter Learning's *The Incredible Murder of Cardinal Tosca* (1978). In fairness, one must note Stratton's subtle, thoughtful *Rexy* (1981) and Nowlan-Learning's engrossing history play, *The Dollar Woman* (1981). Financial restraint has also fostered one-person shows seemingly beyond count. Pierre Trudeau's notorious marriage and the novelty of Linda Griffiths playing all three roles in *Maggie and Pierre* (1980), which she wrote with Paul Thompson, made this play exceedingly popular despite a very thin script. John Gray's *Billy Bishop Goes to War* (1981) has been equally popular and combines the solo performer with another recent trend towards musical theatre. Gray has also written "18 Wheels" (unpublished) and *Rock and Roll* (*CTR* 35, 1975), 2 small-cast musicals. This form has been used well by Ken Mitchell in his "trucker's *Othello*," *Cruel Tears* (1976). Contemporary Canadian drama is highly promising, in part because of the high quality of first major works by a new group of young dramatists which includes Judith Thompson, Frank Moher, Charles Tidler, Anne Chislett, Lawrence Jeffery and Gordon Pengilly. RICHARD PLANT

Reading: G. Anthony, ed, *Stage Voices* (1978); J. Ball and R. Plant, eds, *A Bibliography of Canadian Theatre History 1583-1975* (1976) and *Supplement 1975-1976* (1979); D. Rubin and A. Crenmer-Byng, eds, *Canada's Playwrights* (1980); A. Wagner, ed, *The Brock Bibliography of Published Canadian Plays in English 1766-1978* (1980); R. Wallace and C. Zimmerman, eds, *The Work* (1982). In addition, informative articles appear regularly in the journals *Canadian Theatre Review* (1974-), *Canadian Drama/L'Art dramatique canadien* (1975-) and *Theatre History in Canada/Histoire du théâtre au Canada* (1980-).

Drama in French Québec drama is often said to have started in 1948, even though Gratien GÉLINAS's 1948 play *Tit-Coq* had been preceded by other popular works. One was the melodrama by Léon Petitjean and Henri Rollin, *Aurore, l'enfant martyre*, which made all Québec weep from 1920 to 1950. Québec theatre did not begin with Tit-Coq, successor to Gélinas's earlier character, Fridolin, another beloved child of the stage, whose heyday was 1938-46. But the theatre was limited for the first half of the 20th century to burlesque and reviews (many of them imported), to melodrama and the eclectic repertoire of the Compagnons de Saint-Laurent; it became a "national" theatre with the Gélinas play. It was only after this "baptism" that Québec professionals and amateurs busied themselves with this new and beloved child martyr, the Québec theatre. Even so, theatre had been part of the cultural expression of French Canada since the early days of the colony.

The first dramatic presentation was *Théâtre de Neptune en la Nouvelle France* by Marc LESCARBOT in 1606. This author, living in the young overseas French society of the day, had written a few rhymes "to serve our history as well as to show that we live joyfully." This first dramatic fantasy sought to express the cultural health of a newly transplanted population. But such diversions soon came up against the Canadian clergy who, through condemnations and threats of reprisal, long managed to keep the dramatic expression of the country both subdued and sporadic in nature. In 1789, for example, Montréal's Théâtre de la société and its leader Joseph QUESNEL fought with the clergy because they wished to present, among other pieces, the "first Canadian opera," Quesnel's *Colas et Colinette*. But clerical threats ensured that, until the early 20th century, the bishops, often through the lower clergy, firmly controlled public morality which (in their eyes) was being dangerously threatened by an already unduly liberal theatrical expression.

The clergy's clear and sustained opposition was not aimed solely at theatre: the clergy rejected all cultural activities outside the religious context as rebellious by definition. Yet despite clerical vigilance, during the 18th and 19th centuries it was possible to see a number of dramatic presentations, either local amateur productions or plays mounted by touring groups of American, French and English actors. Montréal and Québec City were then part of the "American circuit."

Drama began to appear more and more regularly in Montréal after 1825, when the Théâtre royal (Molson Theatre) was founded. Whether English or French, theatre always found part of its public among the Francophones, including some of the most respected members of the religious flock.

It took a long time for women, who traditionally supported the clergy in its self-appointed role as social educator, to find a place in Québec theatre as spectators, actors or characters. It was not until the 20th century that theatre made room for feminist expression, not until 1970-80 that plays such as France Theoret's *La Nef des sorcières*, (1976), Denise Boucher's *Les fées ont soif* (1978) and the sustained and consistent work of the Théâtre expérimental des femmes (TEF) gave Québec women their own dramatic voice. Finally, thanks to scripts by authors like Marie Laberge and Jovette Marchessault, we now have believable characters, full of female aspirations and capable of expressing themselves. After long exclusion, the female voice and feminism have won a special place in Québec drama.

The post-1948 theatre faced a double challenge until 1965. It had to create both the habit of theatre-going and a body of plays reflecting Québec experience. The Compagnons de Saint-Laurent (1937-52) and other less enduring troupes such as Pierre Dagenais's L'Équipe (1943-48) and the Compagnie du masque of Charlotte Boisjoli and Fernand Doré (1946-51) were followed by other groups in the 1950s which through their professionalism gave a certain institutional status to Québec theatre. The development of a Québec repertoire was not their major concern, but they created the structures which made its growth possible. The companies they founded — the THÉÂTRE DU RIDEAU VERT (1949), the THÉÂTRE DU NOUVEAU MONDE (1951), Théâtre-Club (1954-64) and the Théâtre de Quat'Sous (1955) — mainly offered boulevard and classical (foreign) theatre. They marked a new approach to theatrical reality and an explosion of styles and challenges, even though they did not manage to develop a recognizably Québecois dramaturgy. The early plays by Marcel DUBÉ showed the viability of a distinctive Québec dramaturgy, but it was only in the 1960s, in the atmosphere of the QUIET REVOLUTION, that people felt an urgent need to see their own reality, their hopes and their setbacks, on stage. The occasional previous efforts to mount Québec plays had seldom drawn large audiences and had won more suspicion than praise.

These first steps in the 1950s to institutionalize the theatre were matched by the birth of more avant-garde companies which devoted themselves to the development and establishment of theatre in Québec. By 1949, the Troupe des Treize at Université Laval, founded by Jacques Duchesne in Québec City, was already sparking theatrical activity in the capital. This was the age of the "théâtres de poche" which generally lasted only a short time, eg, l'Anjou (1954), founded by Paul Hébert, and l'Amphitryon (1955), by Patrick Anderson. Alongside these brave but doomed efforts, some other, largely amateur, groups managed to make contact with a faithful theatre-going public. These troupes — les Apprentis-Sorciers (1956), led by Jean-Guy Sabourin; l'Estoc (1957), by Jean-Louis Tremblay in Québec City; and l'Egrégore (1959), founded by Françoise Berd and Claude Préfontaine — brought the European avant-garde to Québec spectators. Another such group was Saltimbanques, born of a split within the Apprentis-Sorciers and led, after 1962, by Rodrigue Mathieu. In 1963 Jacques Duchesne founded the Théâtre de la Place Ville-Marie, whose repertoire expanded to include Québec plays as well.

Although there were many companies and much theatre, there were few authors, scripts, institutions and structures to support the activity. In the early 1960s European plays still dominated Québec boards, but steps were being taken to create support structures for the infant dramaturgy. In 1958 Gratien Gélinas had bought the old Gaiety Theatre and founded the Comédie-Canadienne, whose very name signalled its intentions. The Théâtre du Gesù, taken over in 1961 by Gilles Marsolais and several others, played an educational role with the student public by transforming itself in 1964 into the Nouvelle Compagnie théâtrale. By 1963 the Jeunes Comédiens of the Théâtre du nouveau monde were touring Québec schools. But the establishment of a solid theatrical apparatus outpaced both the repertoire and the public's readiness to be educated.

Official theatre schools were established to fill the gaps in Québec drama: in 1954 Jan Doat set up the Conservatoire d'art dramatique which in 1962 came under the ministry of cultural affairs; in 1960 Jean Gascon founded the National Theatre School; in 1958 Guy Beaulne founded the Association canadienne du théâtre d'amateurs (ACTA) which in 1972 became the Association québécoise du jeune théâtre (AQJT). But the catalyst for the modern growth of Québec drama was undoubtedly the founding of the Centre d'essai des auteurs dramatiques (CEAD) in 1965. Through its readings and round-table discussions, the CEAD gave young authors a chance to receive critiques on their early efforts and provided them with opportunities to meet the public and other writers and to escape their isolation into a collective theatrical experience. Two good examples of the vitality of this period are the readings of Michel TREMBLAY's *Les Belles-Soeurs* (1968) and Yves Sauvageau's *Wouf Wouf* (1969) — both of them major works of the new Québec dramaturgy.

Also in 1965, Pierre LAPORTE, minister of cultural affairs, created the Commission de la pièce canadienne, whose mandate was to establish an official repertoire of original Canadian plays. The project ended 2 years later. This was also a time when numerous arts centres were built (eg, Montréal's Place des Arts, Québec's Grand Théâtre). Despite a lack of comprehensive planning by government, the times encouraged the emergence of original plays.

It is easy enough to list the few authors and companies of the pre-1965 days; it grows successively harder thereafter. There was an average of 80 new Québec plays (including those for radio and television) per year, 1965-73; the average rose to 100 after 1975. This abundance grew out of the potential of 1965. From the beginning, CEAD had fostered the work of such authors as Michel Tremblay, Robert Gurik, Antonine MAILLET, Michel Garneau and Yves Sauvageau. Françoise LORANGER and Claude Levac travelled a more political path. The vogue for collective creation which emerged in 1969 signalled an awareness of a new social and cultural reality. The collective voice — often fleeting, often vulgar — became part of the general questioning of traditional values and the vehicles which articulated them. This movement was not limited to Québec, but there it fitted perfectly with the sociopolitical currents of the Quiet Revolution: a political awakening with an independence orientation, the affirmation of a Québec language (JOUAL), anticlericalism, etc. This challenge to the idea of the sacred single author and script was led by Maurice Demers's Théâtre d'environnement intégral (1968), by Jean-Claude Germain's Théâtre du même nom (1969) at Théâtre d'aujourd'hui, the Grand Cirque ordinaire (1969) and Théâtre Euh! (1970) in Québec City. Each company, according to its own ethical and aesthetic criteria, set about developing new theatrical forms in an effort to reach spectators in their own lives and reality.

This period of intense activity was followed by a period of near stagnation. Both the Grand Cirque ordinaire (1977) and Théâtre Euh! (1978) disappeared. Collective creation flagged. The lack of real policy, of adaptable playhouses and adequate financial backing, plus a general decline in public enthusiasm for culture, caused some discouragement. But in the late 1970s and early 1980s, new regional companies began to appear (eg, Théâtre Parminou, Victoriaville; Théâtre les Gens d'en bas, Rimouski; le Théâtre du sang neuf, Sherbrooke) and urban groups, drawing on different aesthetic and political currents, are now beginning to renew the Québec theatrical landscape (eg, La Commune à Marie and Théâtre de la Bordée in Québec; l'Eskabel, le Mime omnibus, le Nouveau Théâtre expérimental, Productions Germaine Larose, Groupe de la veillée, Carbone 14, Troupe les Pichous, la Rallonge, Théâtre de quartier and others in Montréal). Many companies now specialize in the long-neglected area of children's theatre, eg, Théâtre carrousel, Centre le gyroscope, le Théâtre petit à petit. They have an increasing number of good texts to perform. Women's theatre has grown rapidly since 1976 and has become part of the theatre of protest which had previously been limited to political theatre or collective creation.

The supporters of collective creation and those of single-author scripts have now reached a modus vivendi. Whether the result of spontaneous creativity or the occasional commission, new scripts use and honour this double reality of the process of dramatic creation. A number of young authors have now produced solid, socially relevant works that receive both critical and popular success. These playwrights include Réjean DUCHARME, Serge Mercier, Jeanne-Mance Delisle, Marie Laberge, Pierre K. Malouf, Elizabeth Bourget, Serge Sirois, René-Daniel Dubois and Normand Chaurette.

Québec theatre since 1976 has been enriched by new forms of expression, apprenticeship, investigation and analysis. Theatrical publishing is so abundant as to suggest a certain lack of discrimination. Québec publishers offer an alluring range of theatrical collections. Theatre programs and departments in the universities and theatre options in the community colleges make theatre and production more accessible than ever. Two magazines devoted exclusively to the theatre — *Jeu* (1976) and *La Grande Réplique* (1977, renamed *Pratiques théâtrales* in 1981) — also help spread appreciation of the theatre.

The economic crisis of recent years has led to the creation of new theatrical forms: the one-person show, café theatre, reviews, cabaret, improvisation, etc. The popularity of the Ligue nationale d'improvisation (LNI) and of plays such as *Broue* and *Pied de poule* remind us of the escapist theatre that appealed to earlier generations in times of economic and social crisis. At the same time, Québec theatre is increasingly recognized elsewhere, as is shown by some European tours (eg, the LNI tours, 1981-83; the CEAD tour of 1982) and by European productions of Québec scripts such as Tremblay's *Les Belles-Soeurs*, 1973, and Jean-Pierre Ronfard's *Vie et mort du Roi boiteux*, 1982).

Improved stagecraft has become important to dramatists in recent years, and has made possible the appearance of script/productions such as Ronfard's *Vie et mort du Roi boiteux* — which is, read or seen, the most significant and daring show in recent years. The script, a cycle of 6 plays, is in the form of separate tableaus, drawing on such diverse inspirations as the Bible, Shakespeare, oriental culture, world geography and the levels of Québec language. It has not broken entirely with the review tradition, though it respects more classical rules of composition. Ronfard and his colleagues at the (Nouveau) Théâtre expérimental de Montréal have been consistently exploring possibilities since 1975. Their accumulated research and sense of fantasy have resulted in a very accessible show willing to draw from any source that meets its needs.

Between 1948's *Tit-Coq* and 1982's *Vie et mort du Roi boiteux* the antihero, central character of Québec dramaturgy, has bestowed upon himself an enormous territory whose size befits his excesses and his ambitions. During the 1970s this territory seems to have been integrated or at least associated with the search for independence. Now it appears to have opened itself culturally so that it is no longer confined by the geographic boundaries of Québec itself. Since its first theatrical venture in 1606, but especially with the appearance of Tit-Coq the bastard and Richard the cripple, Québec has been creating its own national dramaturgy so as to make its theatre its own. LORRAINE CAMERLAIN AND PIERRE LAVOIE

Theatre of Intervention

In the early 1970s there emerged in Québec a theatre movement that was a distant heir to the European *agitprop* and *proletkult*, and was closely related to contemporary troupes such as the San Francisco Mime Troupe and El Teatro Campesino and to progressive black American theatre. Political theatre emerged in Québec in the aftermath of the Quiet Revolution, and was to some extent heralded by the journal PARTI PRIS (1963-68) and the FLQ movement. In 1971, 2 articles from Théâtre Euh! (1970-78), the real founder of the movement, set forth the major issues on which cultural and political establishments were being challenged. Members of this group denounced the alienation or "colonization" of the Québecois and argued that theatre should be given back to the people. The group also attacked elitist forms of theatre, which it contrasted with the theatrical practice of group, or collective, creation, perceiving the latter as nonauthoritarian and capable of associating new content with popular forms (songs, monologues, farce and satire) in the tradition of street theatre.

The advocates of committed theatre met with a variety of disappointments in their militant effort to reach "the voiceless," partly because they lacked sufficient knowledge of the working class and also because their sociopolitical objectives were too radical for a time when nationalist sentiments left little room for class-related issues. With its *Manifeste pour un théâtre au service du peuple* (1975), the major part of the movement broke away from the *Association qué-*

écoise du jeune théâtre, despite the fact that the association had been a supportive, dynamic component of the new theatre. Consequently the thrust of political theatre slowed down: a number of groups, among them the Théâtre Euh!, disappeared, swept away by their leftist ideology. Militant theatre groups were unable to revitalize, enrich and give depth to their themes because of their growing isolation and lack of resources.

However, less radical or less impatient groups took over and became more directly involved by using themes that were more community-based than communist-inspired. The actresses of the Théâtre des Cuisines (1973-81), for example, concentrated on feminist consciousness-raising work, while other (sometimes amateur) groups dealt with such issues as day-care, senior citizens, drug abuse, poverty, the competitive nature of schooling and juvenile delinquency.

Another characteristic of this second wave of interventionist theatre is that it stresses the principle of presenting plays in the very settings it is trying to reach. Théâtre Parminou (1973) and Théâtre de quartier (1975), for example, allied themselves with unions and citizens' groups. Group production remains the main vehicle of intervention troupes, although some occasionally appoint a dramatist or, like Théâtre du 1er mai (1972) and Gens d'en bas (1973), produce foreign plays by such authors as Bertolt Brecht and Dario Fo whom they consider relevant to their interests. Lately there have also been efforts, influenced by Augusto Boal (Théâtre de l'opprimé, France), to present "invisible theatre," "forum theatre" and "instant theatre."

The aesthetic dimension of this theatre, which is usually circumstantial and produced with a small budget, is not left out. For example, recent productions of the Théâtre à l'ouvrage (1978-83) have used increasingly diversified stage language, a fact that suggests a trend toward stricter and more effective theatre, particularly when plays are designed for long runs and a broadly based public. In the early 1980s, after almost 15 years of experimentation, about half a dozen intervention-theatre troupes operated with fairly large regular casts. GILBERT DAVID

Reading: Jean Béraud, *350 ans de théâtre au Canada français* (1958); Jean-Cléo Godin and Laurent Mailhot, *Le Théâtre québécois*, 2 vols (1970, 1980).

Drapeau, Jean, lawyer, politician, mayor of Montréal (b at Montréal 18 Feb 1916). A leader of great political longevity, Drapeau presided over the gentle decline of Montréal as Canada's leading metropolis — but he gave the city its greatest moments: EXPO 67, which drew 50 million visitors and the 1976 Summer OLYMPIC GAMES.

A protégé of Abbé Lionel GROULX, Drapeau was a nationalist candidate in a 1942 federal by-election and in the 1944 provincial election. He lost both campaigns, but his reputation grew when he supported the union during the 1949 ASBESTOS STRIKE and then led a public inquiry into police corruption. When Montréal's mayor Camillien HOUDE retired, Drapeau swept to power in the 28 Oct 1954 election. Rightfully sensing that Drapeau had larger ambitions, Québec premier Maurice DUPLESSIS smashed the Drapeau-led Civil Action League in the 1957 election. Three years later, after Duplessis's death, Drapeau purged many of his old allies, formed a private political club, the Montréal Civic Party, and returned as mayor in the 1960 election. Drapeau kept his election promises to build a subway and to preserve Montréal's old quarter. He ignored or skirted issues such as environmental pollution, low-cost housing and the flight of head offices from the city, but in 1969, he single-handedly brought in a major league baseball team, the MONTREAL EXPOS. He declared these achievements monuments to *La Survivance*, the survival of French Canadians. But, despite the nationalism of his youth, he stayed neutral during the 1980 REFERENDUM on Québec independence. A master of circumlocution and charm, Drapeau demonstrated ruthlessness in the civic election held during the 1970 OCTOBER CRISIS. Drapeau labelled the opposition a terrorist front and used the WAR MEASURES ACT to jail his principal opponent. On Oct 25 Drapeau's private party won all 52 council seats and 92.5% of the mayoralty vote. His power enabled him to ram through his plan for the massive concrete structures of the Olympics, which embodied his *politique de grandeur*. Budgeted at $310 million, the final cost was $1.3 billion, not counting an unfinished Olympic stadium tower. A public enquiry, the Malouf Commission, charged that the mayor "must assume the greater part of the blame" for allowing inflated costs and rampant corruption, but Drapeau was personally untouched and, in 1978, won another mandate.

By 1984 Drapeau's reign spanned 8 Québec premiers and 7 Canadian prime ministers and he had won the respect of international leaders as diverse as de Gaulle and the British royal family. Over the decades he received many appeals to run in provincial or federal politics — but he sensed Montréal was his best platform and there he remained. BRIAN MCKENNA

Reading: Brian McKenna and Susan Purcell, *Drapeau* (1980).

Drapell, Joseph, artist (b at Humpolec, Czech 13 Mar 1940), one of the most important abstract painters in the generation after PAINTERS ELEVEN. He immigrated to Halifax 1966 and studied at the Cranbrook Academy (Bloomfield Hills, Mich) 1968-70, where he met visiting artist Jack BUSH and American critic Clement Greenberg. He moved to Toronto and, inspired by Georgian Bay and influenced by Morris Louis, developed his own technique of applying paint with a broad spreading device attached to a movable support (1972-74). The resultant "Great Spirit" pictures rank among the most successful of all Canadian efforts to find spiritual values in the land. His abstract 1977 "Red" paintings found little interest in Canada until the Boston Museum purchased one in 1979. KEN CARPENTER

Draper, William Henry, politician, judge (b at London, Eng 11 Mar 1801; d at Toronto 3 Nov 1877). Draper was instrumental in founding the Conservative Party and was the first colonial politican to be styled "premier." Brought into politics as a young lawyer in 1836 by John Beverley ROBINSON, Draper strove to turn the old FAMILY COMPACT into a modern Conservative Party with wide appeal through accepting a measure of RESPONSIBLE GOVERNMENT, through educational and sectarian reforms and through forming an alliance with the French Canadians. He attained his greatest power, as attorney general, during the administrations of Sir Charles METCALFE and Lord CATHCART. Although forced out of office by the right wing of his own party in 1847, Draper later saw most of his political ideas fulfilled by his former follower, John A. MACDONALD. Appointed to the judiciary in 1847, Draper eventually became chief justice of the Court of Error and Appeal in Ontario in 1869. GEORGE METCALF

Reading: George Metcalf, "William Henry Draper," in J.M.S. Careless, ed, *The Pre Confederation Premiers* (1980).

Drawing may be an autonomous art form or a preparatory step in establishing the design of another work of art. Though drawing is defined by its linear quality and has nothing to do with the medium used, the principal drawing media are ink, pastel, charcoal, metal point, graphite pencil, conté crayon and chalk. The history of drawing in Canada is marked by blank areas, periods when artists produced few drawings or when "working drawings" were regarded as mere notations for compositions in other art forms. Not until late in the 19th century were collectors or exhibition bodies interested in drawings as finished works of art. By the 20th century the situation had changed and drawings were more appreciated by the public.

Drawings that belong to the period of early exploration, to CARTOGRAPHY and to developments in NEW FRANCE were carried out by Europeans exclusively and were closely tied to European stylistic traditions: fact, fantasy and contrivance are not easy to distinguish in such drawings (*see also* PAINTING). Changes in approach are visible by the 18th century when precision became important, as, eg, in the noble drawings of buildings in Québec City by Charles Bécart de Granville and the panoramic view of Louisbourg (1731) by Étienne Verier. In contrast to the French colonial period, when engineering drawings and draughtsmen's plans for FORTIFICATIONS and buildings were produced, the English colonial period generated a wealth of pen and ink or watercolour views, by travellers, military men and their dependents, which record exploration, military and naval campaigns, immigration and settlement. During the SEVEN YEARS' WAR, several British officers made sketches of the siege of Québec City (1759) and the ruins after the battle; Wolfe's aide-de-camp, Hervey Smyth, showed troops scaling the Heights of Abraham and naval vessels operating in the St Lawrence. Many historic Québec buildings are known only through the detailed drawings executed by Richard Short. In the peace that followed, officers trained at the Woolwich Military Academy in England made accurate drawings of fortifications and the scenic landscape, many of which were later engraved and reproduced in popular travel books (*see* TOPOGRAPHIC PAINTERS). In their westward travels after 1845, Paul KANE and William HIND made hundreds of on-the-spot pencil, ink and watercolour sketches — portraits, landscapes, artifact and figure studies. Art in Québec in the same period was mainly religious painting and sculpture, but some preparatory drawings of church murals by artists such as François BAILLAIRGÉ have survived. The other mainstay of Québec art was portraiture and many lovely drawings by the leading artists (Antoine PLAMONDON, François Beaucourt and Louis DULONGPRÉ) were made for those people who could not afford oil portraits.

As well-trained artists emigrated to Canada and native-born artists increasingly spent a period in study abroad, Canadian art became exposed to influences from France, Holland, Germany and the US. The artists' societies of the period, particularly the Royal Canadian Academy (fd 1880) did little to encourage drawing as an art form, which probably explains the dearth of finished drawings in the last 2 decades of the century (*see* ARTISTS' ORGANIZATIONS). Drawings tended to be regarded by many artists solely as preparation for paintings, and thus good drawings often remained hidden in sketchbooks. Yet these preliminary sketches often possess a spontaneity absent in the worked-over exhibition pieces of the academicians. The sketchbooks of

Tales Over the Camp Fire (1862) by W.G.R. Hind, pencil and grey wash (*courtesy Public Archives of Canada/C-33722*).

Robert HARRIS and William RAPHAEL, for example, contain vivid studies of figures later incorporated in well-known paintings, while Lucius O'BRIEN, John A. FRASER and T. Mower MARTIN made quick and sometimes detailed drawings of the Rockies and the West during the CPR-sponsored excursions in the 1880s and 1890s. Homer WATSON, Horatio WALKER and Marc-Aurèle de Foy SUZOR-COTÉ made lush and beautiful drawings in chalk, graphite and charcoal of peasants in the rural landscape, the subject of their often prolific and popular paintings. While the drawings of James Wilson MORRICE, Maurice CULLEN and Clarence GAGNON show some of the elusive touch of French Impressionism, these artists were interested primarily in colour and light and their few surviving sketches are essentially notations for future paintings. Morrice, however, was a brilliant draughtsman and, in his hundreds of tiny oil sketches, the under drawing is often visible beneath a thin surface of paint. Ozias LEDUC was perhaps the most prolific draughtsman, creating detailed pencil or charcoal drawings of compositions and figures, some of which were intended for church murals and paintings; his study for *L'Enfant au pain* (1892-99) is remarkably close to the finished painting in the National Gallery.

The Canadian artists who studied in London, Paris or Philadelphia in the late 19th century — William BRYMNER, George REID, Paul PEEL, Sidney Strickland Tully — were well trained in "correct" drawing, first from plaster casts, then in life classes (*see* ART EDUCATION). They perpetuated the practice of preliminary sketches for paintings; however, a drawing, such as Reid's *Hattie* (1880), was obviously intended as a finished work.

At the end of the 19th century the bulk of Canadian drawing was done for the utilitarian purpose of periodical illustration. The Toronto Art Students' League (1886-1904), a society of artists dedicated to the art of drawing, took as its motto "Nulla Dies Sine Linea" ("No day without a drawing"). The members, some of whom were former students at the Ontario School of Art (now ONTARIO COLLEGE OF ART), worked in print shops and engraving firms and included Charles MacDonald Manly, Robert Holmes, Frederick Henry Brigden, William CRUIKSHANK and Charles William JEFFERYS. This group of artists met for study and sketching trips and published a calendar illustrated with pen-and-ink drawings between 1892 and 1904; Jefferys, fascinated with historical themes, produced *The Picture Gallery of Canadian History*. Another well-known illustrator was Henri JULIEN, who contributed vigorous figure drawings and caricatures to journals in Montréal and abroad. Some prominent painters also supplemented their income by illustration, as when Lucius O'Brien, Henry SANDHAM and John Fraser contributed drawings to *Picturesque Canada* (1882).

The drawings of F.H. Varley, such as *Catherine* (charcoal on paper) show the brilliant skill of the artist in many media (*courtesy Art Gallery of Greater Victoria/Gift of Harold Mortimer-Lamb/Photograph Trevor Mills*).

Although members of the GROUP OF SEVEN made rapid and skilful sketches in pencil, ink or oil wherever they travelled across Canada, most of their drawings were working plans for paintings, never intended to be displayed in public. The sketchbooks that survive, however, are a creative shorthand to their more famous paintings - notations that isolate the images most characteristic of the landscape they wished to portray. A.Y. JACKSON, Arthur LISMER and F.H. VARLEY were the most able and prolific in the medium, though Varley surpassed the others in talent, sensibility and range. His drawings, whether landscapes, portraits of women, or sketches done on site during his period as an official war artist, show brilliant skill. Lismer, a superb and quick draughtsman and caricaturist, created a large gallery of irreverent portraits of his friends. The drawings of Lawren HARRIS, never an end in themselves, reflect his progression from streetscape to landscape to abstraction, and are often linked to his philosophy of art. Lionel LeMoine FITZGERALD was only briefly a member of the Group, but drawing was ideally suited to his subtle art. Whether his subject was still life, nudes or the landscape, he was concerned to set form against form, edge against edge, fine line against stippled areas, in an orchestrated, delicate design in space; he produced a large body of ephemeral drawings, often in coloured pencil or chalk.

While David MILNE produced little that can be called drawing in the strictest sense, his watercolours and drypoint etchings reveal his command over basic drawing techniques. His paintings are such triumphs of economy and linear strength that they might be seen as drawings in oil. His contemporary, Emily CARR, produced a large number of charcoal and oil drawings on paper, which were often done on the spot. These drawings reveal her powerful expressionist vision of the forest and her basic respect for Indian life and, in their rapid, broad, economic yet almost calligraphic strokes and scumbles, they capture the essence of her understanding of West Coast living and her awe before a totem pole.

Goodridge ROBERTS occupies a secure position among Canadian landscape painters, but his restrained and sometimes sombre brush drawings are reminiscent of Chinese ink drawings in their balance and subtlety. John LYMAN, in works such as *Dancing Nude*, took a new approach to drawing, based on ideas put forward by the French artist Matisse, in which the vitality of the line took precedence over the depiction of the model. In the next decade, the AUTOMATISTES brought spontaneous, unpremeditated, nonobjective art to Québec. As their leader, Paul-Émile BORDUAS went on to produce a series of powerful abstract drawings that forecast the major developments in his brilliant progress in abstract art. Alfred PELLAN, who returned to Montréal in 1940 from Paris, set up a rival movement. His drawings and paintings are imbued with Surrealist imagery.

In 1954 a group of nonobjective painters in Toronto, inspired more by Abstract Expressionism in New York than their contemporaries in Montréal, formed PAINTERS ELEVEN as a means of exhibiting their work. Oscar CAHÉN made many drawings incorporating Abstract Expressionist and Surrealist elements, but the most talented and prolific figurative draughtsman was Harold TOWN, who continues to create thoroughly independent series of drawings.

After the 1960s the number of artists working in drawing expanded considerably. Their variety of styles usually reflect their work in other media. Alex COLVILLE, Christopher PRATT and Jack CHAMBERS are known as "realists" whose drawings show a high degree of technical skill, if not vitality and spontaneity. Ernest LINDNER produces microscopically detailed drawings of

End and Beginning (1973) by Ernest Lindner, pen and ink (*courtesy National Gallery of Canada/Ernest Lindner*).

trees in decay as potent metaphors of death and renewal. There are drawings by Christiane PFLUG, imbued with haunting, sombre imagery; vibrant, mixed-media abstracts by Gordon RAYNER; subtle, textural abstracts by Betty GOODWIN; figure studies by Robert Markle and Graham COUGHTRY; harsh, monumental drawings by John Scott; domestic interiors by Mary PRATT; and landscape sketches by Ann KIPLING, Dorothy KNOWLES, Takao TANABE and Gordon A. SMITH.

Drawing is, and always will be, a 2-dimensional form of art, even if used on modern devices such as the COMPUTER screen. Drawing will continue to change in style, technique and media; but its content will capture the more personal, often private, reactions of artists to the world around, not unlike a tenuous melody which awaits orchestration.

Reading: M. Allodi, *Canadian Watercolours and Drawings in the Royal Ontario Museum*, 2 vols (1974); P. Duval, *Canadian Drawings and Prints* (1952) and *Group of Seven Drawings* (1965); *Harold Town Drawings*, Introduction and text by R. Fulford (1969); P. Krauz, *Drawing: A Canadian Survey, 1977-82* (1983); J. Morris, *100 Years of Canadian Drawings* (1980); D. Shadbolt, *The Art of Emily Carr* (1979).

Dresden, Ont, Town, pop 2550 (1981c), inc 1881, located in SW Ontario on Sydenham R, 80 km S of Sarnia. It was named after the German city. In 1841 Rev Josiah HENSON, a former slave from the US, helped to establish the British American Institute, a vocational school and refuge for fugitive slaves. Henson is reputed to have been the model for Uncle Tom in Harriet Beecher Stowe's *Uncle Tom's Cabin* (1852). His 2-storey house, built around 1842, is now part of the Uncle Tom's Cabin Museum in Dresden. The town has an economy based on diversified light industry, mainly food processing, and serves the surrounding rural area. DANIEL FRANCIS

Drew, George Alexander, lawyer, politician, premier of Ontario (b at Guelph, Ont 7 May 1894; d at Toronto 4 Jan 1973). After recovering from a serious wound suffered in WWI, he attended Osgoode Hall. Called to the bar 1920, he practised law in Guelph, of which he was mayor 1925. He was made master of the Ontario Supreme Court 1929 and became first chairman of the Ontario Securities Commission 1931. An ardent Conservative, he was elected leader of the Ontario party 1938, and led it to victory 1943. He served as both premier and minister of education, and founded the dynasty that ruled Ontario into the 1980s. In 1948 he entered national politics as party leader, but he failed in 2 elections to mount an effective challenge to the Liberal administration. He resigned as leader 1956 and was appointed Canadian high commissioner to London, Eng, 1957 — the last distinction in a noteworthy public career. Eloquent, combative and patrician in bearing, Drew was never wholly at ease in the hurly-burly of democratic politics. His opponents labelled him reactionary, a reputation largely belied by his record as premier. ROGER GRAHAM

Reading: Jonathan Manthorpe, *The Power & the Tories* (1974).

Drought is the condition of critically low water supply caused by persistently below-normal precipitation. Drought begins with decreased SOIL moisture and surface and underground WATER supplies, and leads to decreased PLANT growth and restrictions in the use of surface and underground water supplies for domestic, municipal, agricultural and industrial purposes. Drought temporarily disturbs the ecological regime, creating conditions favourable to the spread of certain INSECT PESTS and plant and animal diseases. Drought-tolerant plants tend to displace conventional vegetation, and wild and domestic animals put stress on the reduced vegetation, thereby adversely affecting future plant growth. Drought also creates conditions favourable to FOREST FIRES. There is no universally accepted definition of drought; definitions depend on how people are affected. Therefore, criteria may include factors such as precipitation, stream flow, lake levels, groundwater levels, soil moisture, crop yields and economic hardship.

Droughts have occurred throughout the world for millions of years. Prehistoric droughts can be inferred from evidence left in tree rings, LAKE and OCEAN sediments and ICE cores from GLACIERS. Evidence is also available from ancient writings and diaries. Recent major droughts have affected the Great Plains of N America in the 1930s; the Sahel, a semiarid region between Ethiopia and Senegal, in the 1970s; Great Britain in 1975-76; and California in 1976-77.

Meteorological Drought is measured by the deficiency in precipitation compared to the normal precipitation received. Evaluation of such a drought requires consideration of factors such as total precipitation over a given period (week, month, year) and length of time between and timing of significant RAINS.

Agricultural Drought is caused by meteorological drought, but its severity is increased by high evapotranspiration losses. The practice of summer fallowing lessens the severity of an agricultural drought by carrying over soil moisture from the previous year (*see* AGRICULTURAL SOIL PRACTICES). In areas where irrigation water is available and stored water supplies ample, a meteorological drought may not lead to an agricultural drought.

Hydrological Drought is measured by the decrease in available water supply in flowing streams and in surface and underground storage. Hydrological drought is primarily caused by a deficiency in precipitation and further intensified by high evaporation, but nonmeteorological factors such as demand for water, availability of surface-storage RESERVOIRS and development of wells to use underground storage affect its impact.

Weather and Drought

Atmospheric circulation usually provides a progression of low- and high-pressure systems across a region. Low-pressure systems usually produce general rains and trigger the formation of convective storms, which result in locally heavy thundershowers. Occasionally a situation known as blocking develops when a high-pressure system becomes anchored over a region, causing storm-producing low-pressure systems to be steered well to the S or N. Such blocking can prevent normal rainfall for weeks, months or even years. Drought of regional or subcontinental proportions can strike anywhere on Earth, although the mechanism described above is limited mainly to temperate latitudes, in which much of Canada is located. The cause of blocking is not yet understood; therefore efforts to provide long-range drought predictions have been unsuccessful. Research includes COMPUTER modelling of the atmosphere, studies of drought cycles, identification of physical predictors such as solar activity or sea-surface temperature anomalies, and the search for matching weather patterns or analogies from the past (*see* METEOROLOGY).

Canadian Droughts

Written accounts of past droughts (in newspaper articles and diaries of settlers and explorers) refer to major droughts during the 1800s on the prairies. A more recent major drought was recorded for the region in the 1930s. Local droughts of shorter duration have occurred since the 1930s in parts of Canada, especially in the prairies (1940s, early 1960s, late 1970s) and in Ontario (1963). In Canada the effects of droughts have been felt most severely in areas where agricultural activities allow little margin of safety in the water supply. One such area was identified by explorer Capt John PALLISER as a result of his field work (1857-60). The dry area (later referred to as the Palliser Triangle) is an irregularly shaped area roughly defined by lines joining Cartwright, Man; Lloydminster, Sask; and Calgary and Cardston, Alta. Annual precipitation averages 38 cm, compared to 80 cm at Toronto and 140 cm at Vancouver and Halifax.

The drought of the 1930s is of special importance because of its areal extent and severity, and because of the government policies, programs and farming practices that resulted. The drought began in 1929 and continued, with some respites, until midsummer of 1937. Some 7.3 million ha, one-quarter of the arable land in Canada, was affected. Severe wind EROSION of the topsoil compounded the effects of the drought. Many farms were abandoned and farm families moved elsewhere (*see* AGRICULTURE HISTORY; GREAT DEPRESSION).

The drought of the 1930s brought into being federal and provincial government agencies to develop and manage drought-alleviation programs, the most notable being the creation of the PRAIRIE FARM REHABILITATION ADMINISTRATION by an Act of Parliament in 1935. The PFRA was established to help prairie farmers cope with drought by providing financial and technical assistance in the building of water-storage reservoirs such as dugouts and small dams. Submarginal farming lands were taken over by PFRA, regrassed and turned into community pastures. The farmers were assisted in moving to more suitable areas, including areas on which farm IRRIGATION was being practised. The Dominion experimental farm system was expanded to provide research and advice to farmers on cropping and cultivation practices more suitable to drought conditions. The federal Indian Head Tree Nursery provided trees, free of charge, to prairie farmers for shelterbelts to control soil drifting and to trap snow. New tillage machines were developed which disturbed the soil as little as possible and therefore decreased soil susceptibility to wind erosion. Alleviation programs developed during the 1930s have been modified and expanded on the basis of experience gained during subsequent dry periods. Agencies of the governments of Alberta, Saskatchewan and Manitoba developed programs, alone and in combination with federal agencies, to provide facilities enabling overland pumping of water to fill small reservoirs, cattle-feed assistance and wells and irrigation projects.

Future Droughts

Based on recorded and inferred evidence, droughts have been a recurring phenomenon. Unless there is a drastic change in CLIMATE, droughts will continue to occur with essentially the same frequency. The difficulty of forecasting the timing, extent and severity should not deter the development of contingency plans. In many areas of Canada water uses for agricultural, municipal and industrial purposes are rapidly reaching the limits of natural supplies. Thus there is always the possibility that a severe drought could cause a serious disturbance to the Canadian economy. Study and planning could alleviate many of the hardships of a drought. One necessary prerequisite in planning for future droughts is the gathering of information. Precipitation, stream-flow and water-level data, gathered by Environment Canada at some 2700 climatological stations and 2500 hydrometric stations across the country, are supplemented by information collected by provincial agencies. Statistical analyses can be made to determine long-term average conditions, the possible start of a drought and the severity of an ongoing drought. Mechanisms to alleviate drought hardships can then be activated. H. HILL

Reading: N. J. Rosenberg, *North American Droughts* (1978).

Drug Use, Non-medical Although drug use generally refers to the nonmedical use of psychotropic (mind-affecting) drugs, eg, cannabis (marijuana and hashish), opiate narcotics (eg, heroin and morphine), amphetamines, cocaine, hallucinogens (eg, LSD, psilocybin and mescaline) and volatile solvents (including certain fast-drying glues, fingernail-polish removers and petroleum products), most drug-related problems in Canada derive from use of alcohol and tobacco. While some of these drugs have legitimate medical uses, their social use is generally considered potentially physically or psychologically harmful. The volatile solvents are readily available, but the importation, production, sale and in most cases possession of the other drugs are criminally prohibited — except for very narrow medical functions.

Prior to this century, the use of psychotropic drugs was not considered a serious social problem and was not a criminal offence — even though more Canadians were dependent on opiates at the turn of the century than at any time before or since. Canada's decision in 1908 to prohibit under criminal law the importation, manufacture and sale of opium (it was the first Western nation to do so) was inspired more, as were related statutes, by racial prejudice (particularly against Asians) and moralistic fervour than by any scientific knowledge. Until the 1960s, addiction to opiates, particularly heroin, was the greatest social concern. While other nations, such as the UK, experimented with medical management and maintenance programs, Canada relied almost exclusively on increasingly punitive applications of the criminal law. As a result of zealous law-enforcement efforts and the elimination of licit sources of supply or avenues of therapeutic assistance, most narcotics dependents were forced into subcultural ghettos, where they became the kind involved in crime just as advocates of the criminal-law solution had always maintained they were. The situation has not changed. For at least 30 years they have represented the stereotypical horrors of drug abuse in the public imagination. In reality the plight of most heroin dependants derives very little if at all from the chemical properties of the drug. It is the official response to this problem which forces dependents to commit property crimes to purchase drugs at prices grossly inflated by stringent international and domestic enforcement.

In the 1960s concern about heroin was eclipsed by that about the consumption of cannabis, amphetamines and hallucinogens. The use of many of the hallucinogens, especially LSD, was relatively new, but small groups had been inconspicuously indulging in many of these drugs in most Canadian urban centres for at least a decade before the public noticed. While Parliament had incorporated most of these drugs into existing criminal statutes (and added the newer ones as soon as their chemical composition could be identified), the sudden public and media attention was undoubtedly caused by the ostentatious use of these drugs by middle-class youths who affected an apparently alien lifestyle associated with the hippie movement. Unlike heroin dependents, a largely invisible presence, marijuana, hashish and LSD users were increasingly vocal about their indulgences. Many openly championed what they perceived to be the beneficial attributes of recreational drug use and crusaded for legislative reform. By 1969 the number of persons charged with cannabis offences, almost negligible at the beginning of that decade, had risen to 5000, and by 1977 the annual figure had swollen to a relatively constant 50 000.

In 1969 the federal government appointed a royal commission to investigate the problem of the NON-MEDICAL USE OF DRUGS. In a series of internationally respected reports published over 4 years, the commission recommended, among other things, a gradual withdrawal of the use of the criminal law against nonmedical users of drugs, the repeal of the offence of possession of cannabis, a general reduction of penalties for all other cannabis offences and no increase in the penalties for other drug offences, and for opiate dependents an emphasis on treatment and medical management rather than criminal sanctions. Although none of these recommendations have been implemented in Canada, they did contribute to the decriminalization of cannabis use and possession in several American states. The commission also helped Canadians to consider drug use in a more rational perspective.

While more Canadians experiment with nonmedical drug use each year, the incidence of regular use has generally stabilized since the mid-1970s. Over 5 million Canadians have tried marijuana at least once during their lives and about 2½ million have done so during each of the past several years. This use, like all drug consumption for nonmedical purposes, tends to be concentrated among adolescents and adults under 30 years of age. National survey data for 1981 indicate that most current marijuana users are regular but relatively infrequent consumers; of the some 2.4 million Canadians who used marijuana at some time during the month prior to being surveyed, only 500 000 were weekly users, and only 120 000 used it daily.

There has been no national canvassing of the nonmedical use of other drugs since the commission's 1970 surveys, although provincial surveys of high-school students have tended to indicate relatively constant levels of use among Canadian adolescents over the past decade. Of Ontario high-school students surveyed (1981), only about 5% used hallucinogens, 2% cocaine and 1% glue or heroin more frequently than twice a year. A 1982 BC high-school survey produced roughly similar results, suggesting that, apart from cannabis, the nonmedical use of drugs is a generally infrequent phenomenon indulged in by a very small proportion of the adolescent population. Cocaine use has probably increased significantly among Canadian adults over the past decade, but its cost and occasionally adverse effects are likely to prevent its use from reaching levels of marijuana and hashish use. Heroin use is the most difficult form of drug consumption to measure reliably. The dependent population is chiefly concentrated in BC; nationally about 10 000 to 15 000 people are dependent.

In 1983 the RCMP estimated that Canadians spent 8.5 billion dollars on illegal drugs. Apart from some insignificant hallucinogen manufacturing, a small amount of low-grade marijuana cultivation and the diversion of pharmaceuticals from their licit channels of distribution, Canada is not a source for illicit drugs. Only 5-10% of the drugs imported into Canada each year are intercepted. International efforts to stem the drug trade have proven equally ineffective but have contributed to a continual inflation of the price of drugs without any apparent abatement of demand. Financially the drug trade has become the most attractive and corruptive criminal enterprise in the world.

Some policymakers have recommended a strategy specifically directed at the health and safety hazards associated with each drug, including alcohol and tobacco, based on a scientific appraisal of drug-related risks. The perennial national debates about cannabis reform and heroin maintenance are 2 examples of this reorientation. MELVYN GREEN

Drumheller, Alta, City, pop 6508 (1981c), inc 1930, is located on the RED DEER R in southern Alberta, 136 km NE of Calgary, and lies at the head of the famed 48 km "Dinosaur Trail" of the Al-

Horsethief Canyon, near Drumheller, Alta (*photo by Richard Vroom*).

erta BADLANDS. Shortly after ranchers first settled there (1897), the townsite was bought by Col Samuel Drumheller (1910). He started COAL MINING operations (at sites around the townsite) in 1911, and the first post office was named after him. The railway arrived in 1912, and in quick succession Drumheller became a village (1913) and a town (1916). Today, although coal mining has all but disappeared from the city's economy, the Drumheller Exhibition and Stampede (held each July), the Red Deer River valley fossil remains, the Drumheller Dinosaur Fossil Museum, and Prehistoric Park still attract many tourists yearly. In June of 1985 the Alberta government opened the Tyrrell Museum of Paleontology. The museum exhibits include 50 complete DINOSAUR skeletons (the largest display of complete dinosaur skeletons in the world) and the skulls and parts of many other animals.
DAVID EVANS

Drumlin, smooth, half egg-shaped or ellipsoidal hill which formed beneath Quaternary GLACIERS. Drumlins [Gaelic *druim*, "hill"] were first described in Ireland. They lie parallel to the direction of ice movement, the blunt (stoss) end facing up-glacier, the lee sloping down-glacier. Drumlins may be up to 50 m high and several kilometres long, with an average length/width ratio of 2 or 3 to 1. Highly elongated drumlins are often called drumlinoids. Drumlins occur in broad fields or swarms, up-glacier from major end MORAINES in Europe and N America. Swarms of several thousands occur in NS, southern Ontario and the Thelon Plain of Keewatin, NWT; smaller groups, in most other provinces. Drumlins are usually composed of layers of till (rock debris deposited by a glacier), frequently clay rich, in which the pebbles are oriented subparallel to drumlin elongation and the direction of ice flow. Some drumlins have cores of stratified sand, boulders or bedrock. Rock drumlins are rock outcrops smoothed by ice to a drumlin shape. Scientists are not certain how drumlins originated. The popular "dilatancy" theory postulates that drumlins were initiated beneath ice of a critical thickness, down-glacier from high basal pressure zones and up-glacier from moraine deposition, where till became dilatant (ie, expanded), forming hummocks. Other hypotheses suggest that subglacial crevasses, frost heave, helical ice motion or water loss from saturated till initiated hummocks. All theories hold that the hummocks were subsequently enlarged by layers of till which were plastered on and streamlined by the ice sliding over. *See* GLACIATION.
R.J. ROGERSON

Drummond, Sir Gordon, soldier, administrator (b at Québec City 27 Sept 1771; d at London, Eng 10 Oct 1854). He joined the British army in 1789 and rose rapidly from ensign to lt-gen. Drummond saw action during the French Revolutionary Wars and returned to Canada in 1808. After a 2-year absence in Britain, he became second-in-command to Sir George PREVOST in 1813. During the WAR OF 1812, Drummond gained a qualified victory at Lundy's Lane 25 July 1814, but then undertook an unsuccessful siege of Ft Erie Aug-Oct. He was administrator of Upper Canada in 1813-15 and of Lower Canada in 1815-16. Created KB in 1815, he returned to England in 1816 and was promoted general in 1825.
DAVID EVANS

Drummond, Robert, labour leader (b at Greenock, Scot 9 Oct 1840; d at New Glasgow, NS 26 Dec 1925). Drummond helped organize one of Canada's first coal miners' unions, the Provincial Workmen's Assn of NS in 1879 and was its grand secretary 1879-98. Appointed to the NS Legislative Council by Prem W.S. FIELDING in 1891, he advised the government on the coal trade until retiring in 1924. He founded, edited and published the PWA's *Trades Journal*. Under Drummond, the union grew to include some 2000 members and fought several strikes, and he increasingly emphasized lobbying for legislative reform, for example, the arbitration bill that became law in 1889. He resigned in 1898 after the American Knights of Labor raided PWA locals and the union was almost destroyed. Drummond then began publishing the *Maritime Mining Record*. He also wrote *Minerals and Mining, Nova Scotia* (1918).
SHARON REILLY

Drummond, Thomas, botanist, (b in Scot *c*1780; d at Havana, Cuba early Mar 1835). Assistant naturalist to John RICHARDSON on the second expedition led by Sir John FRANKLIN, Drummond did not accompany Richardson to the Arctic but instead botanized at Cumberland House on the Saskatchewan R, 1825, in the Rocky Mts near Jasper, 1826, and at Carlton House, 1827. In the mountains alone, Drummond collected 1500 specimens of plants, 150 birds and 500 mammals, some new to science. He had a narrow escape from the jaws of a grizzly bear, and once went 7 days without food. In 1828 he became curator of the botanical garden in Belfast and from 1830 to 1834 made important collections in the southern US, especially Texas. A number of plants, including those of the genus *Drummondia*, and the yellow mountain aven, *Dryas drummondii*, bear his name.
C. STUART HOUSTON

Drummond, William Henry, poet (b at Mohill, County Leitrim, Ire 13 Apr 1854; d at Cobalt, Ont 6 Apr 1907). Drummond arrived in Canada with his parents in 1864. He studied at Bishop's and practised as a general physician in Montréal and Brome County, Qué. Attracted by the folkways of rural Québec, he began writing narrative verse in the English idiom of the French Canadian farmer. His first book of poetry, *The Habitant* (1897), was extremely successful, establishing for him a reputation as a writer of dialect verse that has faded since his death.
C.J. TAYLOR

Drummondville, Qué, City, pop 36 567 (1981c), inc 1875, is located on the Rivière ST-FRANÇOIS in the Piedmont Appalachians, 100 km NE of Montréal. The town was founded in 1815 and named in honour of the then governor general, Sir Gordon DRUMMOND. The Abenaki called the site "the big waterway." Originally settled by English soldiers and French settlers who had to clear land to survive, it became a focal point for people crossing the river at the foot of the falls. Potash was the town's first economic activity. Later, Confederation brought industrialization: sawmills, tanneries, forges, the railway, a hydroelectric plant and a cement factory. In 1915, during WWI, a firm manufacturing "smokeless gunpowder" opened and transformed the town's economy. However, real development began with the establishment of the textile industry in 1918. Drummondville now has a diversified industrial park, Park des Voltigeurs, a "Village Québécois d'Antan" and is host to an international folklore festival.
JEAN-MARIE DUBOIS AND PIERRE MAILHOT

Drury, Charles Mills, "Bud," public servant, politician (b at Montréal 17 May 1912). During WWII Drury attained the rank of brigadier, and then was chief of the UN Relief and Rehabilitation Administration in Poland. After a brief stint in External Affairs, Drury was deputy minister of national defence 1948-55. He spent 1955-62 in private business, but in 1962 entered politics as a Liberal. Elected MP for St Antoine-Westmount, he joined the 1963 PEARSON Cabinet. He held various posts in both the Pearson and TRUDEAU governments, including president of the treasury board. He left the Cabinet in 1977 and the House of Commons in 1978, subsequently becoming chairman of the National Capital Commission.
ROBERT BOTHWELL

Drury, Ernest Charles, farmer, politician, writer, local historian, premier of Ontario 1919-1923 (b at Crown Hill, Ont 22 Jan 1878; d at Barrie, Ont 17 Feb 1968). A son of Charles Drury, Ontario's first minister of agriculture, and a graduate of Ontario Agricultural Coll, Drury was active in the farm movement, serving as secretary of the Canadian Council of Agriculture and master of the Dominion Grange and Farmers' Alliance. He was a cofounder and first president of the UNITED FARMERS OF ONTARIO, formed in 1914 to promote agrarian interests in the province. After WWI the UFO became a political force, but Drury was not a candidate when it challenged the Conservative government in the Ontario general election of 1919. With the support of labour it won enough seats to form a government, and it called on Drury to lead it. He became the province's eighth premier and won a seat in Halton in Feb 1920. His administration was noted for important social legislation and for the strict enforcement of the Ontario Temperance Act. Following the defeat of his government in 1923 Drury retired from provincial politics and ventured unsuccessfully into the federal field as an independent Liberal. In 1934 he was appointed sheriff and registrar of Simcoe County and devoted considerable time to writing on public affairs and preparing local histories: *Forts of Folly* (1932), an attack on the tariff, and *All for a Beaver Hat* (1959), a history of early Simcoe County. His memoirs, *Farmer Premier*, were published shortly before his death.
CHARLES M. JOHNSTON

Dry Fishery, that portion of the Newfoundland cod fishery in which the split and cleaned product was salted and dried on shore before being transported and sold. Compared with the GREEN FISHERY, the dry fishery required less salt but more time curing on land — on fishing "flakes" or beaches — near the fishing grounds. The dry fishery, particularly popular with early English fishermen who had limited access to salt, required the use of the land and eventually promoted settlement. Because of its dependence on the land, it tended to be a more localized nearshore fishery in areas where the weather was suitable for drying fish. The fishing gounds were within easy reach of the home base (*see* FISHERIES HISTORY).
ROBERT D. PITT

Drybones Case (1970) In *R.* v *Drybones* the Supreme Court of Canada, in a divided judgement called by certain persons the decision of the century, rendered inoperative a provision of the Indian Act, basing its judgement on the "equality before the law" clause of the Canadian Bill of Rights. The court ruled that if a federal statute cannot be reasonably interpreted and applied without abolishing, limiting or infringing upon one of the rights or liberties recognized in the Bill of Rights, it is inoperative unless Parliament expressly declares that it is to apply notwithstanding the Bill of Rights. The court concluded that J. Drybones, who had been found drunk off reserve land in a lobby of a Yellowknife hotel, had been punished because of his race under a law whose scope and penalty differs from that governing other Canadians.

GÉRALD-A. BEAUDOIN

Dubawnt Lake, 3833 km^2, elev 236 m, is situated on the border of Mackenzie and Keewatin districts, NWT, 350 km S of the Arctic Circle. Within the Precambrian SHIELD, the lake has irregular shorelines and numerous islands. It is drained northward by DUBAWNT R into ABERDEEN LK, then eastward by THELON R into HUDSON BAY. Its water is clear and deep. Lake trout, lake and round whitefish and arctic grayling are common in the lake. The surrounding slopes consist of glacial till, festooned by the abandoned beaches of a proglacial lake up to 73 m above the present water level. The vegetation is low arctic tundra with heath and lichens, although scattered groves of stunted spruce occur at the south end. The lake is on the migration route of the Kaminuriak caribou herd, consisting of over 100 000 animals. Muskoxen occur in the area, especially to the W, within the Thelon Game Sanctuary. Wolves, foxes and grizzly bears are the main predators. The lake is at the contact point between the Chipewyan and inland Inuit, but there are no permanent settlements here. The lake was discovered by Samuel HEARNE in 1770, but remained virtually unknown until explored by J.B. TYRRELL in 1893. S.C. ZOLTAI

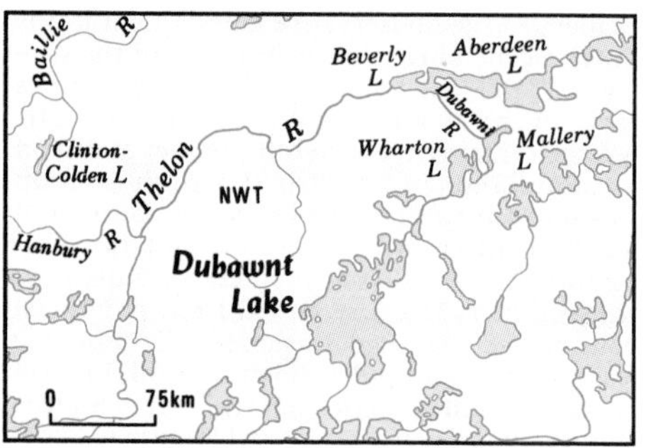

Dubawnt River, 842 km long, rises in a web of lakes in the NWT, 120 km NE of Lk Athabasca, flows NE, gathering the waters of Wholdaia, Boyd, Barlow, Nicholson, Dubawnt, Wharton and Marjorie lakes, and turns abruptly NW to join the THELON R at Beverly Lk. The Thelon flows on to James Bay. The river was discovered by Samuel HEARNE 1770 and traversed by Joseph B. TYRELL in 1893. DUBAWNT LK, icebound most of the summer, is just N of the treeline in the Barren Lands. The name Dubawnt is a corruption of an Indian word. JAMES MARSH

Dubé, Marcel, writer (b at Montréal 3 Jan 1930). In 1950 Dubé helped found a troupe called La Jeune Scène. The 1951 production of *Le Bal triste* at L'Ermitage in Montréal was the first of a collection that is the most extensive, significant and representative body of Québec and Canadian plays of the 1950s and first half of the 1960s. Other plays of his, such as *De l'autre côté du mur* (1952) and *Zone* (1953), have won many awards and distinctions. Dubé's usual theme is the tragedy of human destiny. Dubé lived in France 1953-55. NFB scenarist, journalist, producer and author for both stage and TV, Dubé has received many grants and won the St-Jean-Baptiste Society's Prix Morin (1966) and Québec's Prix David (1973) for his work as a whole.

PIERRE LAVOIE

Ducharme, Réjean, novelist, playwright, scriptwriter, songwriter (b at St-Félix-de-Valois, Qué 13 Aug 1942). Ducharme was one of the first Québec novelists to be published in France. A prolific writer, he is also one of the most original and innovative authors of French Canada. His first novel, published in 1966 at the height of the QUIET REVOLUTION, won a Governor General's Award. This book, like the next 2, caused an uproar known as the "Ducharme Affair." His works (7 novels, 4 plays, 2 film scenarios) are marked by unfettered imagination, a characteristic language style approaching "verbal frenzy," anti-heroes and heroines searching for freedom, and unexpected, hilarious plot developments. The counterpoint to this game-playing and carefree side of his writing are themes of love and death, the conflicts of child/adult, nature/culture, affirmation/negation, portrayed with lucidity and insight. Although Ducharme's works deal with universal themes such as religion and marriage, they are rooted in Québec and America. Two of his plays are parodies, but the other 2 and his film scripts present situations and characters similar to those in his novels. He has also written words for several songs by Robert CHARLEBOIS. RENÉE LEDUC-PARK

Duchesneau de La Doussinière et d'Ambault, Jacques, chevalier, INTENDANT of New France 1675-82 (d at Ambrant, France 1696). Despite his experience and the high hopes of his protector, the French minister Colbert, Duchesneau did not live up to his illustrious predecessor, Jean TALON, largely because of his difficult relations with Governor FRONTENAC. Duchesneau denounced the illegal trafficking of many of the COUREURS DE BOIS and suggested that the governor's attitude was so permissive as to smack of desire for personal gain. When he backed Bishop LAVAL in his fight against the sale of alcohol to the Amerindians, Frontenac accused him of being the clergy's tool. The 2 antagonists were recalled to France simultaneously: their disputes had injured the colony and angered the minister. FRANCE BEAUREGARD

There are 29 breeding species of ducks in Canada, including the mallard shown above *(Amas platyrhynchos)* *(photo by Tim Fitzharris)*.

Duck, WATERFOWL with short legs, webbed feet and narrow, pointed wings. A few island species are flightless but most are strong fliers and migratory (*see* MIGRATION). Ducks, geese and swans comprise a family (Anatidae) with 142 to 148 living or recently extinct species. Ducks have worldwide distribution, except for polar regions. Canada's 29 breeding species belong to 4 tribes in one subfamily; 8 other species from this subfamily have occurred in Canada, as have one species of whistling duck and the Labrador duck (*Camptorhynchus labradorius*), last seen in 1878.

Bills of mergansers are long and tubular with deeply toothed edges. All other ducks have a flat, wide bill with fine serrations. The bill is swollen into a spoon shape in northern shovelers (*Anas clypeata*). Male breeding and winter plumage is distinct from that of females and post-breeding males. Plumage is often highly coloured in males, especially in the wood duck (*Aix sponsa*). An unusual feature of ducks is that all primaries (flight feathers) are moulted together, making the birds temporarily flightless. Legs of dabbling ducks are centrally placed, allowing easy takeoff and walking; those of diving ducks are placed far back, aiding in diving but impeding walking and necessitating "pattering" along the water surface prior to takeoff.

Most ducks are gregarious, gathering in large feeding, moulting and wintering flocks. At early stages of nesting, males in several species are territorial, but pair bonds are temporary and females undertake all incubation and care of young. Female Barrow's goldeneye (*Buchephala islandica*) are also territorial. Nests of most species are of grasses and on the ground, often under shrubbery and usually near water. Wood duck, common goldeneye (*Buchephala clangula*), bufflehead (*B. albeola*) and hooded merganser (*Lophodytes cucullatus*) nest in holes in trees; common and red-breasted mergansers (*Mergus merganser* and *M. serrator*, respectively) often nest in crevices underground. Mallards (*Anas platyrhynchos*) sometimes nest in trees or inside buildings. Several marsh-dwelling species have floating nests. The blackheaded duck (*Heteronetta atricapilla*) of S America always lays its eggs in nests of other species; such brood parasitism is frequent but less developed in redhead ducks (*Aythya*

Wood duck (*Aix sponsa*) male shown in its highly coloured plumage (*photo by Stephen J. Krasemann/DRK Photo*).

mericana) and infrequent in ruddy ducks (*Oxyura jamaicensis*). Clutches are usually large, 4-16 eggs in Canadian species. Downy young are active at hatching, swimming within hours. Hens guard and brood ducklings but do not feed them.

Ducks nest in aquatic habitats ranging from marshes and tundra ponds to fast-flowing mountain streams and large lakes across Canada. Dabbling ducks are most common on the prairies; seaducks range far into the Arctic. The American black duck (*Anas rubripes*) is centered in the Maritimes and Québec; most other species are widespread or primarily western. Barrow's goldeneye and harlequin ducks (*Histrionicus histrionicus*) breed in disjunct populations on both coasts. The cinnamon teal (*Anas cyanoptera*), primarily of interior BC and extreme SW Alberta, has the most localized range in Canada. Most species gather along the coasts and Great Lakes in winter or fly S. Thermally maintained RESERVOIRS have resulted in increasing numbers of wintering ducks, even on the prairies. Two Eurasian species, Eurasian wigeon (*Anas penelope*) and tufted duck (*Aythya fuligula*), are increasingly wintering in coastal BC.

Mallards and Muscovy ducks (*Cairina moschata*) are widely domesticated for food; the common eider (*Somateria mollisima*) is semi-domesticated in Iceland for down. Most ducks eat a mixture of vegetation and invertebrates; several dabblers sometimes feed on grain crops. Mergansers eat mostly fish. Ducks are a favourite object of HUNTING. *See* GAME BIRD.

MARTIN K. MCNICHOLL

Duck Lake, some 50 km SW of Prince Albert, Sask, scene of the outbreak of the 1885 NORTH-WEST REBELLION. On Mar 26 a small party of NORTH-WEST MOUNTED POLICE rode from Ft Carlton towards Duck Lake for supplies, but were fired upon and turned back. To assert police authority, 56 Mounties and 43 Prince Albert settlers, led by Supt L.N.F. Crozier, rode for Duck Lake. When again intercepted by Métis and Indians strategically settled in the surrounding woods, Crozier attempted to negotiate with their commander, Gabriel DUMONT. A shot was heard, and the police fired. Well-hidden snipers fired back. When the police retreated, Louis RIEL prevented any further attacks. Duck Lake gave Riel an important victory; Dumont lost 5 men, while Crozier lost 12 dead and 11 wounded. A cairn now marks the battle site. WALTER HILDEBRANDT

Dudek, Louis, poet, critic, professor (b at Montréal 6 Feb 1918). Born to Polish parents who had emigrated in 1917, Dudek graduated in English and history from McGill in 1939, and then studied at Columbia in NY for 8 years. In 1943 he became editor for First Statement magazine; he continued to contribute to it and its successor *Northern Review* during several years in the US. He began teaching at McGill in 1951 and, as part of an effort to create alternate means of publication for Canadian poets, helped found Contact Press in 1952. Although an established university professor, Dudek is relentlessly anti-academic in his approach to writing and studying poetry. He has always shown an interest in the international avant-garde and has preferred socially aware, realistic writing. He has published 9 volumes of poetry since 1946 as well as a number of book-length meditative poems that marked the beginning of widespread experiment with this form in Canada. MARLENE ALT

Duel, formal armed combat between 2 people in the presence of witnesses, to settle differences or a point of honour. Duels were recorded in NEW FRANCE as early as 1646; the last known duel in what is now Canada occurred in 1873 at St John's, Nfld (a hilarious shoot-out for which the seconds had loaded the pistols with blanks). Duels in the French regime were fought exclusively with swords; after the Conquest almost all were with pistols. Most incidents ended without injury, but there were some fatal encounters: at least 9 died in New France, 2 in Lower Canada, 5 in Upper Canada, 2 each in Nova Scotia and New Brunswick and 1 in Newfoundland. The last fatal duel occurred 22 May 1838 at Verdun, Lower Canada, when Robert Sweeny shot and killed Henry Warde for sending a love letter to Mrs Sweeny.

Several famous Canadians fought duels: James DOUGLAS duelled at Ile-à-la-Crosse in 1820 during a fur-trade dispute; Joseph HOWE fought in 1840 to prove his courage and gain the opportunity to decline further challenges; George-Étienne CARTIER duelled in 1848 to prove his courage at the Battle of St Denis; and in 1849 John A. MACDONALD had to be prevented from fighting a political opponent.

Duels were fought in a variety of places: in locked rooms, in open fields or across tables. Causes also varied, and were often trivial. In 1800 at York [Toronto], John Small shot and killed John White after the latter spread gossip that Mrs Small was the former mistress of an English lord. A quarrel over card-game winnings led to a fatal duel in St John's, Nfld, in Mar 1826. Sharp political disputes in Lower Canada resulted in a spate of challenges and meetings, 1834-37.

Authorities considered duelling a crime, and to kill in a duel was tantamount to murder. However, the laws were irregularly enforced. In New France, several duellists were imprisoned, banished or executed; even the bodies of men killed in duels were desecrated. Under English rule, juries consistently refused to convict duellists if they felt that the encounters had somehow been conducted fairly and honourably.

HUGH A. HALLIDAY

Duff, Sir Lyman Poore, chief justice of Canada 1933-44 (b at Meaford, Ont 7 Jan 1865; d at Ottawa 26 Apr 1955). Educated and called to the bar in Ontario, he moved to Victoria in 1894 where he soon established himself as a skilled and busy counsel. After 2 years on the BC Supreme Court he went to the Supreme Court of Canada in 1906 where he served for nearly 38 years. He was the leading figure on the court while Canada was making the transition from an agrarian society to a modern industrial state. In constitutional law his decisions were, and still are, pre-eminent. Perhaps his greatest contribution to Canadian nationhood was his decision in 1940 upholding the power of the Dominion Government to abolish appeals to the Privy Council in London unilaterally; he thereby established a wholly indigenous court system. DAVID RICARDO WILLIAMS

Reading: David Ricardo Williams, *Duff: A Life in the Law* (1984).

Duff, Wilson, anthropologist, museologist (b at Vancouver 1925; d there 8 Aug 1976). Duff's entire professional career centered on the study of the Northwest Coast Indians. Educated at UBC (BA 1949) and U of Washington (MA 1951), Duff was curator of anthropology at the BC Provincial Museum 1950-65. He then moved to Vancouver to teach and do research at UBC's dept of anthropology and sociology and the Museum of Anthropology. He was a founding member of the BC Museums Assn, chaired the provincial government's Archaeological Sites Advisory Board (1960-66), and served on the province's Indian Advisory Committee (1963-76). He is perhaps best known for his work in helping preserve the last remaining TOTEM POLES from Kitwancool and the abandoned villages of the Queen Charlotte Is in the 1950s. Later in life, his interests changed from the empirically oriented ethnography reflected in such publications as *The Indian History of British Columbia*, vol 1 (1964) and *Arts of the Raven: Masterworks by the Northwest Coast Indians* (1967) to an analysis of the visual logic in Northwest Coast art forms, reflected in the catalogue *Images Stone: B.C.* (1975).

CAROL SHEEHAN

Dufferin and Ava, Frederick Temple Blackwood, 1st Marquess of, governor general of Canada 1872-78, viceroy of India 1884-88 (b at Florence, Italy 21 June 1826; d at Clandeboye, Ire 12 Feb 1902). Frederick Temple was educated at Eton and Christ Church, Oxford, but did not graduate. He served as lord-in-waiting to Queen Victoria 1849-52 and again 1854-58. Dufferin sat in the Lords as a Liberal and in 1868 entered Gladstone's ministry as chancellor of the duchy of Lancaster. He came to Canada in 1872 as governor general. Although initially he possessed an exalted view of his powers, this polished, articulate diplomat displayed great tact and judgement during the PACIFIC SCANDAL that forced John A. MACDONALD to resign and brought Alexander MACKENZIE in as prime minister. Dufferin's attempts to reconcile BC to CONFEDERATION annoyed the Mackenzie government. He supported the Supreme Court of Canada Bill, however, and his amnesty to those in the RED RIVER REBELLION saved the government considerable embarrassment. The first governor general to make the QUÉBEC CITADEL a vice-regal residence, Dufferin persuaded the city fathers to save the old French walls from destruction: Dufferin Terrace was named in his honour. After leaving Canada Dufferin was British ambassador to Russia, Turkey, Italy and France.

CARMAN MILLER

Dufresne, Guy, playwright, scriptwriter (b at Montréal 17 Apr 1915). He studied at the Jesuit colleges of Ste-Marie and Jean-de-Brébeuf (BA 1939). Health problems caused him to abandon his studies and settle in Frelighsburg, Qué, to raise apples. Dufresne wrote for radio, TV and theatre; his scripts made him famous, either for the quality of his historic and ethnographic research (as in *Le Ciel par-dessus les toits*, 1947-55; *Cap-aux-sorciers* 1955-58; and *Les Forges de St-Maurice*, 1972-76), or for his sensitive psychological analyses. The son and brother of physicians, he provided the public with his well-crafted observations about the hospital milieu in a TV series entitled *Septième-nord* (1963-67), which appeared well before most American series on this subject. He was awarded the Prix Anik in 1978 for his play *Johanne et ses vieux*. In 1980 he became visiting professor of drama at UQAM. He has published 5 plays and a remarkable TV adaptation of the John Steinbeck novel *Of Mice and Men*.

ANDRÉ G. BOURASSA

Duggan, Alphonsus Gregory, labour leader (b at Holyrood, Nfld 21 Sept 1884; d at Grand Falls, Nfld 26 July 1970). In 1913 Duggan helped organize Local 63 of the International Pulp, Sulphite and Papermill Workers Union and became its first president. He believed that social justice for the working class could best be achieved by means of one Newfoundland body for all unions. He organized the Newfoundland Trades and Labor Council in 1937, becoming its first president. In 1939 the council became the Newfoundland Federation of Labor, and Duggan became president emeritus. That same year King George VI made him a Member of the British Empire. Duggan was also active in the Grand Falls co-operative movement and was the first president of the Newfoundland Co-operative Union (1950). BILL GILLESPIE AND MELVIN BAKER

Duguay, Rodolphe, artist, engraver (b at Nicolet, Qué 1891; d there 1973). Duguay's work expresses a profound religious message based on goodness, innocence, purity and suffering, all of which are captured in his country scenes. From a poor, rural environment, he began his studies at Montréal's Monument National only in 1911, and became familiar with the tradition established in French Canada by artists such as Joseph SAINT-CHARLES, Alfred LALIBERTÉ and Ozias LEDUC, as well as SUZOR-CÔTÉ with whom he studied 1918-20. From 1920 until 1927, he stayed in Paris, travelled around Europe, studied at the Académie Julian and learned in 1925 the techniques of wood engraving. It was in this medium that he achieved his most original expression, illustrating the texts of his wife, Jeanne L'Archevêque-Duguay (*Écrin*, 1934; *Cantilènes*, 1936; *Offrande*, 1942), as well as those of many other writers, including Clément Marchand (*Courrier des villages*, 1941). Encouraged by Bishop Albert Tessier he began the publication in 1935 of several series of wood engravings that made his work more widely known. His *Carnets intimes*, covering his activities in Europe, were published in 1978. Two exhibitions at the National Gallery of Canada (1975) and the Musée du Québec (1977) showed his engravings and paintings as part of the slow movement toward modern art expression in Québec.

LAURIER LACROIX

Duley, Margaret Iris, writer (b at St John's 27 Sept 1894; d there 22 Mar 1968). Duley won international recognition with 4 novels: *The Eyes of the Gull* (1936), *Cold Pastoral* (1939), *Highway to Valour* (1941) and *Novelty on Earth* (1942). *The Caribou Hut* (1949), a brief history of a St John's hostel during WWII, is a local classic. Duley's work is regional. She depicts vividly the seasons, landscapes, folk customs, moody waters and winds of Newfoundland. Outport characters are unsophisticated and idiomatic, city characters cerebral and witty. The novels focus on the female psyche. Male protagonists are usually less courageous and less intellectual than the fine-grained heroines. Duley's ideas mark her as feminist in advance of her place and time. A poetic prose style, skillful use of animals and children and a ghoulish humour enhance her books.

ALISON FEDER

Dulhut, Daniel Greysolon, COUREUR DE BOIS, fur trader, explorer (b at St-Germain-Laval, France *c*1639; d at Montréal 25 Feb 1710). Dulhut helped extend the French trading empire around the Upper Great Lakes (*see* FUR TRADE). After military service in France, Dulhut immigrated to NEW FRANCE in 1675. In 1678-79 with a small party he travelled to the country of the Sioux (headwaters of the Mississippi) where he formally claimed the area for France, persuaded the Sioux [DAKOTA] and their neighbours to accept a tentative peace agreement, and began a profitable trade in furs. He returned to Montréal in 1681. In 1683 he was commissioned by Gov LA BARRE to return to the Lk Superior area, and he spent the next 3 years there trading and working to keep peace among the Indians. Stationed at Michilimackinac, he built posts at Lk Nipigon and at Kaministiquia on Lk Superior to facilitate the trade, as well as one at Detroit. Dulhut took part in the campaigns of the IROQUOIS WARS in 1687, 1689 and 1696, when he was left in command at Ft Frontenac.

MARY MCDOUGALL MAUDE

Dumaresq, James Charles Philip, architect (b at Sydney, NS 18 Dec 1840; d at Halifax 20 Dec 1906). Educated at Acadia, Dumaresq began a practice 1870 that eventually extended throughout the Maritime provinces, Newfoundland, Ontario and Québec and from the eastern US to the W Indies. His work includes the Forrest Building at Dalhousie, the Pinehill Library in Halifax, St Mary's Girls' School in Halifax and, most important, the Legislative Buildings in Fredericton. GRANT WANZEL AND KAREN KALLWEIT

Dumbells One of several Canadian Army concert parties in France during WWI, the Dumbells were performers drawn from the Third Division who entertained front-line soldiers with collectively conceived skits about army life, popular songs and "torch" songs by Ross "Marjorie" Hamilton. They also played 4 weeks at various locations in London in 1918. Amalgamated with other top army performers in 1918-19, and reformed as civilians, the Dumbells, managed by "Capt" Merton Plunkett, undertook 12 cross-country tours in vaudeville revues between 1919 and 1932, including 12 weeks at the Ambassador, New York, with *Biff, Bing, Bang* in 1921. Members included Hamilton, Al Plunkett, "Red" Newman, Jack Ayre and Jack McLaren.

PATRICK B. O'NEILL

Dumoine, Rivière, 129 km long, rises in Lac Dumoine in SW Québec and flows off the S edge of the LAURENTIAN HIGHLANDS through a series of waterfalls, wild rapids and long chutes into the OTTAWA R. It was an important route in the early fur trade, being used by the Huron to avoid tolls charged by the Allumette or Iroquois raids on southerly routes. Later, superb white pines were floated down the river, and decayed log chutes are still visible. Still in a wild state, the Dumoine is a popular canoe route. JAMES MARSH

Dumont, Gabriel, Métis leader (b at Red River Dec 1837; d near Batoche, Sask 19 May 1906). Gabriel Dumont, son of Métis hunter Isidore Dumont and grandson of French Canadian voyageur Jean-Baptiste Dumont, was brought up to the free prairie life of the age before government entered the West. Though he could not read or write, he knew 6 languages; he was a good shot with bow and rifle, a splendid horseman and canoeist and an unrivalled guide. Dumont was introduced early to plains warfare when, aged 13, he took part at Grand Coteau in the defence of a Métis encampment against a large Sioux war party. Yet in 1862, with his father, he concluded a treaty between the Métis and the Sioux, and later one with the Blackfoot, that helped ensure pacification of the Canadian prairie. Dumont's skill as a buffalo hunter led to his election at 25 as permanent chief of the Métis hunters on the Saskatchewan. Until the virtual elimination of the buffalo he led the Métis on the hunt; the last time was in 1881.

As adjutant general of the Métis army during the 1885 North-West Rebellion, Gabriel Dumont showed himself to be a remarkable guerrilla leader (*courtesy Glenbow Archives*).

Dumont took no direct part in the Red River rising of 1870, though he made an offer — rejected by Louis RIEL — to bring Métis to resist WOLSELEY'S expeditionary force. He recognized that great changes were coming to the prairie, with the decline of the buffalo and spread of Canadian influence. In 1873 he became president of the commune of St Laurent, the first local government between Manitoba and the Rockies. Modelled on the organization of the buffalo hunt, the commune tried to establish a system of landholding, since Dumont recognized that when hunting ended, his people would have to turn to farming. In 1875 the commune confronted the newly arrived NWMP and the attempt at local government ended; concern over land did not, however, for government surveyors and land speculators began to flood the West and Dumont led the Métis in agitating for recognition of their rights. When the campaign made no progress, Dumont was one of the delegates who sought Louis Riel's assistance. Negotiations with the government foundered, and when Riel declared a provisional government at Batoche, Dumont became "adjutant general" in charge of the tiny Métis army of 300 men. During the subsequent NORTH-WEST REBELLION he was a remarkable guerrilla leader. He won the first battle against the NWMP at DUCK LK in Mar 1885; he halted Gen Middleton's army at Fish Creek on 23 Apr. But Riel did not allow Dumont to continue his successful guerrilla campaign, and Batoche was besieged and captured, despite the resistance Dumont organized, on 12 May. Hearing Riel had surrendered, Dumont fled to the US. He plotted to rescue Riel, but the latter was too carefully guarded; following Riel's execution Dumont joined Buffalo Bill's Wild West Show as a crack marksman. After the amnesty for rebels, he returned to Canada in 1888 and to Batoche in 1893. He hunted and traded a little, and dictated 2 vivid oral memoirs of the rebellion. He died suddenly of heart failure in 1906. Gabriel Dumont was a man of great chivalry, superbly adapted to the pre-settlement prairie life; in the world that followed, his skills lost their relevance, and so his qualities of intelligence and personality were ultimately wasted.

GEORGE WOODCOCK

Dumouchel, Albert, printmaker, teacher (b at Bellerive, Qué 15 Apr 1916; d at Montréal 11 Jan 1971). He studied etching and lithography in Paris. In Montréal in 1945, he participated in the "cadavres exquis" experiments with Léon Bellefleur, Jean BENOÎT, Jean Léonard, Mimi Parent and Alfred PELLAN, and, in 1947 and 1949, published 2 famous issues of *Les Ateliers d'arts graphiques*, the review of Montréal's École des arts graphiques. In 1948 he joined the free-art "Prisme d'yeux" group and contributed to the first publications of Roland GIGUÈRE's Éditions Erta. Between 1949 and 1954, his lithographs illustrated Giguère's *Faire naître*, *Les Nuits abat-jour* and *Les Armes blanches*. Giguère interested Dumouchel in the Cobra movement, and his work appeared in the *Revue internationale de l'art expérimental - Cobra* (1954), and in *Phases de l'art contemporain* (1955), the review published by poet and surrealist critic, Édouard Jaguer. His work as an art teacher at the École arts graphic and École des beaux-arts in Montréal until his death influenced several generations of artists. The Montréal Musée d'art contemporain held an exhibition of his engravings in 1974.

ANDRÉ G. BOURASSA

Dunbar, Isobel Moira, public servant, ICE research scientist (b at Edinburgh, Scot 3 Feb 1918). In 1947 Moira Dunbar, an Oxford graduate, immigrated to Canada after 7 years in professional theatre. She joined the Arctic Section of the Defence Research Board at a period when scientific work in the North was opening up.

Collaborating with K.R. Greenaway, she produced the standard work *Arctic Canada from the Air* (1956), which led to her interest in ARCTIC EXPLORATION. She later specialized in SEA-ICE research, particularly the climatological aspects, and was the first woman to be taken on summer cruises in Canadian government icebreakers. Observations on these cruises and on reconnaissance flights over the arctic islands led to analytical studies of ice conditions and work on the standardization of ice terminology. She was active in evaluating remote sensors for collecting ice data and pioneered sideways-looking RADAR for airborne reconnaissance. She also visited the USSR and Finland in 1964 to look into icebreaking practices, worked as ice adviser on the hovercraft trials, 1966-69, and observed the cruise of the *Manhattan* in 1969 to test supertankers in ice. Author of many scientific articles, she received the Massey Medal in 1972.
DIANA ROWLEY

Dunbar, Maxwell John, oceanographer (b at Edinburgh, Scot 19 Sept 1914). Dunbar received his BA and MA from Oxford and his PhD from McGill. He was acting Canadian consul to Greenland between 1941 and 1946 and joined the McGill faculty in 1945. He is a fellow of the RSC, the Arctic Inst of N America, the Royal Geographical Soc and the Linnean Soc of London. Active in research in ARCTIC OCEANOGRAPHY all his professional life, he has published numerous works on marine biology in Canadian arctic waters. During the 1930s and 1940s he participated in numerous expeditions to Greenland and the Canadian Arctic. Emeritus professor in the Institute of Oceanography at McGill in 1984, Dunbar was professor of zoology and director of the Marine Sciences Centre. He was responsible for the training of a large group of oceanographers at work in the Canadian North.
JOHN B. LEWIS

Duncan, BC, City, pop 4228 (1981c), inc 1912, is located on Vancouver I midway between Victoria and Nanaimo, in the Cowichan Valley, surrounded by scenic, rugged mountains. The area was first inhabited by the Cowichan ("Land Warmed by the Sun") Indian nation, encompassing all the independent bands in the valley. The colonial government did not allow white settlement in the area until 1862, and although there were 18 200 ha of good agricultural land available, growth was slow until the valley was reached by the Esquimalt and Nanaimo Ry in 1886. William Duncan, a farmer, led a petition for a station, which was built on his land. His son, Kenneth, was the city's first mayor. Duncan became the service centre for the valley's main industries, lumbering and agriculture. A mining boom in the region 1889-1909 increased population and prosperity. More recently, Duncan's mild climate has attracted retired people.
ALAN F.J. ARTIBISE

Duncan, Douglas Moerdyke, art dealer (b at Kalamazoo, Mich 1902; d at Toronto 26 June 1968). Educated at U of T, Duncan lived in Paris 1925-28 where he studied fine bookbinding. He returned to Toronto in 1928 to establish himself as a bookbinder, earning a reputation as a skilled craftsman. He founded the Picture Loan Soc in 1936 with others and became sole sponsor and director, a position he held until his death. During this time Duncan was responsible for the first exhibitions of many distinguished artists, among them Carl SCHAEFER, Will OGILVIE, Kazuo NAKAMURA. Many artists left the Picture Loan Soc because of its limited space and the difficulty of acquiring a financial accounting from Duncan. Nevertheless, he must be considered a significant force in the art market in the 1930s to 1950s, and as a confidant and adviser to the rich was able to sustain the career of David MILNE, among others.
HAROLD B. TOWN

Duncan, James Stuart, businessman (b at Paris 2 May 1893). Duncan joined Massey-Harris in Berlin, Germany, in 1909 and transferred to Canada in 1911. He served in the British army in WWI, returning to Massey-Harris afterwards. He was appointed general manager in 1936 and president in 1941, a position he held until 1956. In 1940 Duncan declined PM Mackenzie KING's invitation to join his Cabinet, but agreed to serve as acting deputy minister of national defence for air. His work proved invaluable and was instrumental in the success of the BRITISH COMMONWEALTH AIR TRAINING PLAN. At the end of the war Duncan returned to Massey-Harris to find that the company was being reorganized out from under him. He left the firm in 1956 and later wrote a number of books, including his autobiography, *Not a One-Way Street* (1971).
ROBERT BOTHWELL

Duncan, Norman, journalist, writer, professor (b in Oxford County, Ont 2 July 1871; d at Buffalo, NY 18 Oct 1916). Remembered today for his fiction, Duncan was also a successful journalist and travel writer. He was raised in small-town Ontario and reflects in his writing his love of different places and cultures. After working for the *New York Evening Post* (1897-1900), he travelled as a *McClure's Magazine* correspondent to Newfoundland and Labrador, where he met Sir Wilfred GRENFELL and gathered materials for his fictional best-sellers, *Doctor Luke of the Labrador* (1904) and *The Cruise of the Shining Light* (1907). Of over 20 published volumes (short stories, novels, travel pieces), a number are suitable for younger readers, particularly the Billy Topsail series. After 1900 he lived primarily in the US, writing about his travels and teaching in universities.
MARY RUBIO

Duncan, Sara Jeannette, journalist, novelist (b at Brantford, Canada W 22 Dec 1861; d at Ashstead, Eng 22 July 1922). Duncan's notable career as a journalist in the 1880s testifies to her determination and ability. The first woman employed full time by the Toronto *Globe* 1886-87, she also worked for the Montreal *Star* 1887-88. In the fall of 1888, Duncan embarked upon a round-the-world tour which resulted in her first novel *A Social Departure* (1890). While in Calcutta, Duncan met her future husband, Everard Cotes. After her marriage, Duncan lived in India for the next 25 years, subsequently moving to England. Only 2 of Duncan's 22 books have Canada as their focus. *The Imperialist* (1904) is a brilliant study of a small Ontario town in which an idealistic young man is thwarted in politics and love. *Cousin Cinderella* (1908) deals with the disillusionment that a similarly idealistic Canadian brother and sister experience in English aristocratic circles. One of the most penetrating observers of Canadian society in her time, Duncan combined shrewd analysis with a vivid, personal style.
THOMAS E. TAUSKY

Duncombe, Charles, doctor, politician, rebel (b at Stratford, Conn 28 July 1792; d at Hicksville, Calif 1 Oct 1867). Duncombe came to Upper Canada in 1819, finally settling in Burford Twp where he had a large medical practice. Elected to the assembly in 1830 as an independent, he gradually aligned himself with the Reformers, becoming a leading radical spokesman on social issues by the mid-1830s. He travelled to England to protest the corrupt election of 1836 but was disillusioned by the British government's disinterest. This blow and personal tragedy caused him to withdraw from politics until word came of the Toronto rising of 1837. In response, Duncombe hurriedly organized his area to fight, but the arrival of government forces caused him to disperse his forces and flee to the US. *See* REBELLIONS OF 1837.
RONALD STAGG

Reading: C. Read, *The Rising in Western Upper Canada* (1982).

Dundas Island, 166 km^2, largest of 5 islands (the others being Zayas, Baron, Dunira and Melville) comprising the Dundas Islands Marine Area, is situated off the BC coast NW of PRINCE RUPERT and between Dixon Entrance and the W side of Chatham Sound. Only 10 km S of the Alaska boundary, Dundas I is characterized by a rugged terrain and the 464 km Mt Henry in the S end. Believing that the group consisted of a single island, Capt George VANCOUVER named it in honour of Treasurer of the Navy Henry Dundas in 1793.
DAVID EVANS

Dunkin, Christopher, lawyer, politician, judge (b at Walworth, Eng 25 Sept 1812; d at Knowlton, Qué 6 Jan 1881). Admitted to the bar in 1846, he gained renown defending the legal rights of the seigneurs in 1854. He was a Québec MLA 1858-71 and MP 1867-71, provincial treasurer 1867 to 69 and federal minister of agriculture 1869 to 71. A philosophical conservative, known for the pro-temperance Dunkin Act of 1864, he represented English Protestant and Eastern Townships interests in Québec and Ottawa. He was a brilliantly lucid opponent of CONFEDERATION in 1865.
PIERRE CORBEIL

Dunlap, Clarence Rupert, "Larry," air marshal (b at Sydney Mines, NS 1 Jan 1908). As a youngster in Cape Breton, Dunlap's imagination was fired by a nearby seaplane base and by memories of Baddeck, where the SILVER DART had flown. He joined the RCAF in 1928, specializing in aerial photography and then in air armament. Posted overseas in 1942, he commanded No 331 Wing in 1943, carrying out operations from Tunisia. He was the first RCAF officer to command a British operational bomber wing: his No 139 Wing participated in daylight raids from England against V-1 launching sites in Germany 1943-44, and Dunlap himself flew 35 operational sorties. A trim, competent, principled officer with a pleasant personality, he rose steadily after the war, serving as commandant, National Defence Coll 1951-54, and vice-chief of the air staff 1954-58, before becoming chief of the air staff 1962-64, and deputy commander in chief of NORAD 1964-67. He retired in 1968.
NORMAN HILLMER

Dunlap, David Alexander, lawyer, mine executive (b at Pembroke, Canada W 13 Oct 1863; d near Toronto 29 Oct 1924). Dunlap was a lawyer in Mattawa when he and his associates, Henry and Noah TIMMINS and the McMartin brothers, acquired the LaRose silver mine near COBALT, Ont. They also acquired properties in the Porcupine district that formed the basis of Hollinger Consolidated Gold Mines Ltd, of which Dunlap was secretary treasurer 1911-19, and VP and treasurer 1919-24. A Liberal and Methodist, Dunlap was honorary treasurer of the Social Services Council of Ontario and the Missionary Soc of the Methodist Church, trustee of the Art Gallery of Toronto (later Art Gallery of Ontario) and the Toronto General Hospital, and member of the Board of Regents of Victoria U. He bequeathed $250 000 to Victoria U and $100 000 to University of Toronto — to which his family presented the David Dunlap Observatory in 1931.
J. LINDSEY

Dunlop, William "Tiger," journalist, politician (b at Greenock, Scot 1792; d at Lachine, Canada E 1848). Dunlop was one of the most colourful figures of the 1820s and 1830s in UPPER CANADA. He first came to Canada in 1813 as a military physician, but a few years later went to India, where he edited a Bombay newspaper, and then back to England. In 1826 he re-emerged as a bureaucrat of the CANADA COMPANY, resigning some years later, after charging the company with neglect of settlers' rights. But while still in its employ he wrote *Statistical Sketches of Upper Canada* (1832) to try to lure more immigrants. He also wrote *Recollections of the American War,*

1812-14. *Two and Twenty Years Ago* (1859), a novel about the 1837 uprising, has sometimes been attributed to him as well. At the time of his death, he was superintendent of the Lachine Canal. He has often caught the sustained attention of Canadian historians and there are several biographies. DOUG FETHERLING

Dunn, Alexander Roberts, army officer (b at York, Upper Canada 15 Sept 1833; d near Senufe, Abyssinia 25 Jan 1868). Dunn was the first Canadian recipient of the Victoria Cross, won as a lieutenant in the 11th (Prince Albert's Own) Regiment of Hussars at the charge of the Light Brigade at Balaklava in 1856. He helped to organize the 100th (Prince of Wales' Royal Canadian) Regiment of Foot, a British unit raised in Canada, and later became its commanding officer in Gibraltar. He was killed on an expedition to Abyssinia when his hunting rifle accidentally discharged. O.A. COOKE

Dunn, Sir James Hamet, financier, industrialist (b at Bathurst, NB 29 Oct 1874; d at St Andrews, NB 1 Jan 1956). Dunn attended Dalhousie Law School 1895-98 and, after stints as a lawyer in Edmonton and Montréal, turned to investment banking. From the Montréal Stock Exchange, he graduated to the city of London in 1905 and prospered in the arbitrage trade and in underwriting Canadian utilities and industries. In 1921 he was knighted for wartime services. In 1935 he gained control of the bankrupt Algoma Steel Corp, Sault Ste Marie, Ont. As president and sole owner, and assisted by his friend C.D. HOWE, Dunn oversaw Algoma's emergence as a profitable company. DUNCAN MCDOWALL

Dunn, William Lawrence, Willie, or Roha'tiio, meaning "his voice is beautiful," musician, filmmaker (b at Montréal 14 Aug 1941). A folk musician of Micmac-Scottish origin, he served in the army 1960-63 (UN Congo medal) before joining the Newport, RI, folk-music festival. Since then he has developed his own quietly powerful style. He has made 6 albums in Canada, the US and Germany, and worked in the Company of Young Canadians with Ernie Benedict at the National Film Board. There he made the *Ballad of Crowfoot* (1968) and *The Other Side of the Ledger* (1972) with Martin Defalco. He has written and performed music for film and radio and has published several poems and song texts. ROY WRIGHT

Dunning, Charles Avery, businessman, politician, premier of Saskatchewan (b at Croft, Eng 31 July 1885; d at Montréal 2 Oct 1958). General manager of the Saskatchewan Co-operative Elevator Company, Dunning entered provincial politics in 1916 when opposition to both national parties was spreading. He remained loyal to the Liberal Party, however, and his adroit political maneuvering as premier 1922-26 saved it from defeat. Dunning was elected MP in 1926, serving as minister of railways and canals and then minister of finance under Mackenzie KING, 1926-30 and 1935-39. Ill health forced his retirement in 1939 and he returned to business. He was named chancellor of Queen's University in 1940. J. WILLIAM BRENNAN

Reading: J. William Brennan, "C.A. Dunning, 1916-1930," in J.E. Foster, ed, *The Developing West* (1983).

Dunsmuir, James, industrialist, politician, premier of BC (b at Ft Vancouver, Wash 8 July 1851; d at Cowichan, BC 6 June 1920), son of Robert DUNSMUIR. Main heir to his family's coal fortune and spokesman for capital over labour, Dunsmuir dominated BC's economy until 1900. From 1876 to 1910 he managed the family coal operations on Vancouver I, increasing annual output tenfold by opening new fields and improving mining methods. He invested widely in transport, agriculture, manufacturing and other resource industries. Dunsmuir withstood all attempts at unionizing his operations, becoming labour's chief target in western Canada. In 1905 he sold the Esquimalt and Nanaimo Ry to the CPR and in 1910 his collieries to William MACKENZIE and Donald MANN for $10 million.

Dunsmuir was elected MPP for Yale in 1898; he was premier of BC from 1900 to 1902, leading a Conservative administration concerned chiefly with oriental immigration, railway construction and BC's position within Confederation. A less prestigious figure would have had problems redistributing the legislature to reflect the now dominant mainland, and a more partisan politician would have remained longer in office. Dunsmuir disliked politics and served more from a sense of public duty than a desire for power. He reluctantly agreed in 1906 to be the province's lt-gov, but resigned in 1909, relieved to be free to enjoy his lands and yacht. DANIEL T. GALLACHER

Reading: S. Jackman, *Portraits of the Premiers* (1969); M.A. Ormsby, *British Columbia* (1964); M. Robin, *The Rush for Spoils* (1972).

Dunsmuir, Robert, industrialist, politician (b at Hurlford, Scot 31 Aug 1825; d at Victoria 12 Apr 1889). Dunsmuir was best known as the coal king of BC. He came to Vancouver I in 1851 and worked as a coal miner for the HBC. After discovering a rich coal seam N of NANAIMO, he established his own mine and his own company town at Wellington. His disregard for safety, and his employment of cheap oriental labour and disallowance of unions made him unpopular with labour. Dunsmuir sat on Nanaimo's first school board and was elected MLA for Nanaimo in 1882 and 1886. In 1883 Dunsmuir and his son James DUNSMUIR contracted to build the Esquimalt and Nanaimo Ry, payment for which included $750 000 and about one-quarter of the land on Vancouver I. In 1888 he became president of the Executive Council of BC. Dunsmuir retired in Victoria, where his elaborate mansion, Craigdarroch Castle, was unfinished at his death. DAVID R. ELLIOTT

Craigdarroch Castle, Victoria, BC, built in 1889 by Robert Dunsmuir at a cost of $650 000. It is now the home of the Victoria Conservatory of Music (*photo by Richard Harrington*).

Dunton, Arnold Davidson, public servant, educator (b at Montréal 4 July 1912). He was educated at Lower Canada College, Montréal, and at universities in Canada, France, Britain and Germany. He worked as a reporter on the Montréal *Star* 1935-37 and as associate editor 1937-38 and was editor of the Montréal *Standard* in 1938. He joined the WARTIME INFORMATION BOARD in 1942 and was general manager 1944-45. In late 1945, at age 33, he was appointed the first full-time chairman of the CANADIAN BROADCASTING CORPORATION. Throughout the controversies that arose over the funding and regulation of the new medium of television, Dunton was a persuasive defender of the corporation's independence and a strong advocate of the need to fund publicly a television system that would be of great national benefit. Shortly after the CBC completed its network from coast to coast in July 1958 he resigned and became president of CARLETON UNIVERSITY. Dunton was widely commended for the tact and intelligence with which he had overseen the development of the CBC. He was appointed co-chairman of the Royal Commission on BILINGUALISM AND BICULTURALISM in 1963, which has profoundly influenced federal government language policies. He stepped down as Carleton's president 1972 and was director of the Institute of Canadian Studies at Carleton 1973-78 and fellow of the Institute 1978- . He is a companion of the Order of Canada.

Duplessis, Maurice Le Noblet, prime minister and attorney general of Québec, 1936-39 and 1944-59 (b at Trois-Rivières, Qué 20 Apr 1890; d at Schefferville, Qué 7 Sept 1959). Duplessis's father, Nérée Le Noblet Duplessis, was a fervently Catholic and Conservative MLA for Trois-Rivières, 1886-1900, and an unsuccessful federal Conservative candidate before being named a superior court judge by Sir Robert L. BORDEN in 1915. Duplessis's mother was of part Scottish and Irish descent. After studying at Collège Notre-Dame in Montréal (where he became something of a protégé of Brother André) and the Séminaire de Trois-Rivières, he graduated from Laval's Montréal law faculty in 1913, spending WWI in the local militia. He developed a successful popular law practice in Trois-Rivières, was narrowly defeated there in the 1923 provincial election, but won the first of 9 consecutive elections there in 1927.

He helped mayor Camillien HOUDE of Montréal ease out Arthur Sauvé as leader of the provincial Conservatives in 1929 and Duplessis deposed Houde after the electoral débâcle of 1931. Confirmed as leader in 1933, Duplessis wooed disgruntled reform Liberals and Nationalists who had become disillusioned with the arch-conservative government of Louis-Alexandre TASCHEREAU, and had formed a movement styled ACTION LIBÉRALE NATIONALE, and 2 weeks before the 1935 election united with them to form the UNION NATIONALE, with the rather unworldly Paul GOUIN as ostensible coleader. Taschereau was returned in 1935 but Duplessis forced him out in June 1936 with a sensational performance before the Public Accounts Committee exposing corruption and profligacy in the regime, accompanied by a filibuster in the Assembly. He also dispensed with Gouin and outmaneuvred his other Action libérale nationale allies, defeated the hapless Joseph-Adélard GODBOUT, and won a landslide victory in Aug 1936, ending 39 years of Liberal rule.

Duplessis's first term was a disappointment. Except for his successful farm credit scheme, his Fair Wages Commission (effectively minimum wages) and provisions for destitute mothers and the blind, there was little significant legislation. The administration was prodigal. Duplessis himself lived riotously (he was a lusty and somewhat alcoholic bachelor in these times, and never did marry), and he blundered disastrously in Sept 1939 by calling a snap election on the issue of participation in the war effort. The Québec federal ministers, including Ernest LAPOINTE, Arthur Cardin and C.G. POWER, threatened to resign, leaving Québec defenceless against a conscriptionist English Canada, if Duplessis were re-elected, and pledged that they would prevent CONSCRIPTION if Duplessis were defeated.

Though he was personally re-elected, his government lost badly to Godbout. In opposition Duplessis's health collapsed, and, after months in hospital in 1941-42 fighting pneumonia and diabetes, he never drank again, campaigned strenuously for 2 years, and was narrowly re-elected in 1944 over Godbout, the nationalist BLOC POPULAIRE CANADIEN led by André LAURENDEAU and Jean DRAPEAU and supported by Henri BOURASSA. The Union nationale was re-elected in

948, 1952 and 1956 and successfully intervened in other elections, especially the defeat of Mayor Drapeau in Montréal in 1957 and the election of 50 DIEFENBAKER Conservatives in Québec in 1958. His 15-year second term saw Duplessis assert the authority of the Québec state over that of the Church; wrestle part of the concurrent jurisdiction over direct taxes back from the federal government after WWII; and introduce social legislation, including Canada's most generous minimum wage and home ownership assistance Acts. His government produced enormous public works, highway, hospital, school and university construction projects and ambitious hydroelectric power schemes, extending electrification throughout rural Québec.

Maurice Duplessis, almost universally known as "Le Chef" in recognition of his strong though controversial leadership of Québec; 1930s photo *(courtesy Public Archives of Canada / C-9338)*.

Duplessis became equally known for dealing harshly with striking unions, especially at Noranda, ASBESTOS, Louiseville and Murdochville; and for disdaining most contemporary concepts of civil liberties, particularly in litigation over the anticommunist PADLOCK ACT, overruled by the Supreme Court of Canada in 1957, and the RONCARELLI case in which Duplessis was personally ordered to pay damages of $46 132 by the Supreme Court in 1959. Apart from his jurisdictional gains, Duplessis presented a number of symbolic nationalist measures, such as the adoption of the Québec flag. Duplessis developed a very powerful political machine. The patronage system reached legendary proportions, yet Duplessis presided over a period of unprecedented prosperity, economic growth and investment in which Québec was for the first time by almost any social or economic yardstick gaining on Ontario.

A modernizer except in political methodology, Duplessis perfected the techniques of the past in exalting the Québec state to an unprecedented position of strength in relation to the church, the federal government and the Anglo-Saxon Montréal business establishment. His system depended upon employing the clergy at bargain wages to do what was really secular work in schools and hospitals, while reducing the episcopate to financial dependence; reducing taxes, balancing budgets and persuading the conservatives and nationalists to vote together (for "Autonomy" as he called it). His system crumbled after his death with the demise of his successors, Paul SAUVE and Daniel JOHNSON and the triumph of the QUIET REVOLUTION Maurice Duplessis was an enigmatic and picturesque character, the public demagogue at some variance with his urbane, elegant and witty private personality. For much of his career he was almost universally known as "le Chef" in recognition of his strong, though controversial leadership of Québec. CONRAD M. BLACK

Dupond Case (1978) In a case testing the scope of provincial interest in the area of public order, the Supreme Court ruled as valid a Montréal ordinance forbidding for 30 days any public assembly, parade or riotous gathering, on the grounds that it was a case, as in the HODGE CASE, of local public order in the province, and therefore authorized by the Constitution Act, 1867 (s92). The legislative measures were preventive and not punitive. A majority of the judges held that fundamental liberties fall under the concurrent legislative jurisdiction of the 2 orders of government. The holding of assemblies, parades or riots in the public domain falls within either federal or provincial jurisdiction, depending on the aspect in question. GÉRALD-A. BEAUDOIN

Dupuy, Claude-Thomas, lawyer, intendant of NEW FRANCE 1725-28 (b at Paris, France 10 Dec 1678; d near Rennes, France 15 Sept 1738). From a bourgeois family Dupuy became a layer in the *parlement* of Paris and in 1720 purchased the office of *maître des requêtes*. In 1725 he was appointed INTENDANT of New France and he took up the position in Sept 1726. Stubborn inflexible, and pre-occupied by his status, by late 1726 he had already begun the quarrels with Governor BEAUHARNOIS that continued until his departure. Dupuy was recalled in 1728 when his precipitate actions in challenging the colony's ecclesiastical authorities over Bishop SAINT-VALLIER's death and funeral became known in France. MARY MCDOUGALL MAUDE

Dupuy, Michel, diplomat (b at Paris, Fr 11 Jan 1930). A specialist in economics and the law, with an Oxford BA and a Paris doctorate, Dupuy spent a year in the Privy Council Office before entering the Dept of External Affairs in 1955. Small, neat, exuding charm, he served in Washington, Brussels and Ottawa, becoming assistant undersecretary of external affairs in 1971. He was highly successful as president of CANADIAN INTERNATIONAL DEVELOPMENT AGENCY, 1977 to 80, succeeding the controversial Paul Gérin-Lajoie, and a quietly effective ambassador to the United Nations, 1980-81. As ambassador to Paris since 1981, he has emphasized trade and investment. NORMAN HILLMER

Dupuy, Pierre, diplomat (b at Montréal 9 July 1896; d at Cannes, France 21 May 1969). An intelligent, personable lawyer, he entered the Dept of External Affairs in 1922 as secretary to Philippe ROY in Paris. Coming to prominence in WWII, Dupuy travelled on several missions between London and Pétain's Vichy government in France, 1940-42. Charles RITCHIE wrote of him in his diaries: "From being a dim little diplomat he has become an international figure — the only Canadian except for the Prime Minister whose name is known in Paris and Berlin political circles and in the inner circle of London." Both Canadian and British governments, however, thought him too trusting and talkative. Dupuy was ambassador to Italy, 1952-58, and to France, 1958-63, before become commissioner-general of EXPO 67. NORMAN HILLMER

Duquesne, Ange Duquesne de Menneville, Marquis, naval officer, governor general of NEW FRANCE 1752-55 (b at Toulon, France *c*1700; d at Antony, France 17 Sept 1778). He joined the navy as a boy and saw action in the WAR OF THE AUSTRIAN SUCCESSION. Former governor LA GALISSONIERE put his name forward to succeed LA JONQUIERE in New France in 1752. Duquesne was instructed to secure the Ohio Valley where French sovereignty was being threatened by English traders, and to this end in 1753-54 he sent an expedition south under Paul Marin de La Malgue to establish a series of forts. A second expedition in 1754 completed the occupation of the area with the building of Fort Duquesne [Pittsburgh, Pa]. MARY MCDOUGALL MAUDE

Durham, John George Lambton, 1st Earl of, politician, diplomat, colonial administator (b at London, Eng 12 Apr 1792; d at Cowes, Eng 28 July 1840). Scion of a wealthy Northumberland family, Durham was educated at Eton, briefly held an army commission, was elected to the Commons in 1813 and raised to the Lords in 1828. Affiliated with the liberal wing of the Whig party, "Radical Jack" was lord privy seal in 1830 in the Cabinet of his father-in-law, Lord Grey, and played a significant part in drafting the Great Reform Bill of 1832. He was a difficult colleague and, suffering from poor health, he resigned in 1833 but was ambassador to Russia 1835-37.

Primarily to appease the radicals, PM Lord Melbourne persuaded him to become governor general and high commissioner to British N America with responsibility for preparing a report on the Canadian REBELLIONS OF 1837. In May 1838 Durham landed in LOWER CANADA. His administration was warmly endorsed by the English minority in Lower Canada, the moderate reformers in Upper Canada, the American government, as well as the authorities at home. But when the British government refused to sanction an illegal ordinance exiling a handful of political prisoners to Bermuda, Durham resigned and in Nov 1838 returned to England where in Jan 1839 he completed his famous *Report on the Affairs of British North America.* The union of the Canadas that he recommended was adopted but the British government refused to implement RESPONSIBLE GOVERNMENT (a term for which Durham denied paternity) until 1847-1849 when it was formally conceded in Canada by Durham's son-in-law Lord ELGIN. Recent historiography tends to be more critical of Durham's behaviour and skeptical of his accomplishments, but he remains pre-eminent among the founders of the modern COMMONWEALTH. PHILLIP A. BUCKNER

Durham Report After the REBELLIONS OF 1837 in Upper and Lower Canada a known reformer, John George Lambton, the earl of DURHAM, was appointed governor general to investigate colonial grievances. He resigned after 5 months and returned to Britain. His *Report on the Affairs of British North America,* published in Feb 1839, proposed such reforms as the creation of municipal governments and a supreme court, and resolution of the LAND QUESTION in Prince Edward Island.

Durham's 2 main recommendations emerged from an analysis of the causes of the rebellions. He criticized the defective constitutional system in Upper Canada where power was monopolized by "a petty, corrupt, insolent Tory clique" (*see* FAMILY COMPACT). His solution was RESPONSIBLE GOVERNMENT, a system in which the executive would be drawn from the majority party in the Assembly. It would stimulate colonial expansion, strengthen the imperial connection and minimize American influences. In Lower Canada, Durham found "two nations warring in the bosom of a single state. . . ." To ensure harmony and progress, he recommended assimilating the French Canadians through a legislative union of the Canadas in which an English-speaking majority would dominate.

Durham's Report was condemned by Upper Canada's Tory elite, but Reformers in UC and NS hailed the idea of responsible government. Montréal Tories supported union largely because of the economic benefits; French Canadians were opposed to it and reaffirmed their determination to defend their nationality. The British government accepted the recommendation for a union of the Canadas and was prepared to accept a limited form of responsible government (implemented by Lord SYDENHAM after the union of 1841); Durham's division of powers between imperial and colonial responsibilities was rejected. Although full responsible government was not granted until 1847, the Durham Report is generally regarded as important in developing Canadian autonomy and in forming the Canadian nation.

DAVID MILLS

Reading: J.M.S. Careless, *The Union of the Canadas (1967)*; G.M. Craig, ed, *Lord Durham's Report* (1963); Chester New, *Lord Durham's Mission to Canada* (1963); J.M. Ward, *Colonial Self-Government* (1976).

Durkin, Douglas Leader, author (b at Parry Sound, Ont 9 July 1884, d at Seattle, Wash 4 June 1967). Raised to be a missionary, Durkin instead developed a literary interest and an appreciation for a profane lifestyle. A sense of justice and belief in spiritual redemption were retained, though, and these sentiments are found in his early publications, written during WWI while he was a lecturer at Brandon Coll and University of Manitoba. In 1921 Durkin moved to the US, abandoning his family and career, and completed *The Magpie*, a novel focusing on postwar unrest in Winnipeg. He was joined in 1923 by Martha Ostenso, and the 2 collaborated on *Wild Geese*, published under her name in 1925. Thereafter Durkin issued only one novel under his own name, producing short pieces and working with Ostenso on various novels. Although long neglected by scholars and the public, Durkin's work is of enduring quality.

P.E. RIDER

Durnan, William Arnold, hockey player (b at Toronto 22 Jan 1915; d there 31 Oct 1972). He was the greatest goaltender of his day. Tall but quick, he had a rare ability to catch and block shots with either hand. He joined MONTREAL CANADIENS in 1943, age 29, and in only 7 seasons won the VEZINA TROPHY 6 times. Among his amazing records was a period of 309 min 21 sec (over 5 games) in which he did not allow a goal. His career record was 2.35 goals allowed per game and 34 shutouts in regular season play, and 2.20 goals per game and 2 shutouts in playoffs. He was a victim of the pressures of his profession, suffering from nausea and insomnia, and he quit abruptly during the playoffs in 1950.

JAMES MARSH

Dutch Although the Dutch arrived in N America in the 17th century, it was not until the American Revolution that an indeterminate number of Dutch American LOYALISTS entered the British N American colonies. Already considerably anglicized, this group was quickly assimilated into the welter of immigrants who flooded into the colonies after 1815. Because of economic pressures, emigration from the Netherlands grew rapidly at mid-century and in the following decades, but it was directed to the rapidly developing American frontier. When cheap arable land became scarce in the US, the Dutch and Dutch Americans turned to the Canadian "Last Best West." Since that time, approximately 200 000 immigrants of Dutch origin have settled in Canada; and today, numbering about 400 000, they comprise the sixth-largest ethnic group. The Dutch quickly adopted Canadian culture and traditions, and have been assimilated almost to the point almost of invisibility.

Migration and Settlement The Dutch have settled in Canada in 3 main periods. During the first, 1890 to 1914, Dutch immigrants joined the migration to the Canadian West to take up homestead lands, helping to open the PRAIRIES and establishing ethnic settlements such as New Nijverdal (now Monarch, Alta), Neerlandia (Alta) and Edam (Sask). The majority of the immigrants were scattered across the West either as farmhands or farm owners. Some concentrations did occur, however, particularly in and around Calgary, Edmonton and Winnipeg. Indeed, Winnipeg probably had the largest Dutch community in Canada prior to WWI. The second period of immigration developed in the 1920s. Cheap, accessible arable land was in shorter supply, but the demand for farm, construction and industrial labour was high, particularly after 1925. Dutch immigrants spread across Canada to take up these opportunities, particularly in Ontario and the western provinces. During this period significant concentrations of Dutch immigrants settled in southern and southwestern Ontario, especially in Toronto. It is estimated that between 1890 and 1930 approximately 25 000 Dutch or Dutch American immigrants entered Canada. The GREAT DEPRESSION and WWII curtailed Dutch immigration until 1947, when 150 000 new immigrants fled from a war-devastated and economically ruined homeland. Initially the immigrants, as in the past, were agriculturalists, but by the mid-1950s they included many skilled and professional workers. Ontario became a particularly important destination, followed by Alberta, BC and the Maritimes. By the late 1960s these Dutch immigrants were well settled in all provinces, but particularly Ontario and the urban areas of the western provinces. These communities served as beacons of welcome for other Dutch immigrants.

Social and Cultural Life The majority of Dutch immigrants have been of lower- or lower-middle-class and working-class origin. This common background has meant that social stratification within the community has not been a serious problem. Religion, however, has cut broad divisions across the Dutch Canadian community. While Dutch Roman Catholics formed the largest single religious entity, they have been outnumbered by the combined population of Dutch Protestant groups, many of whom have continued their religious traditions in Canada. The majority of Dutch Canadian Catholics and Protestants belong to "Canadian" churches and thus the only visible Dutch entity on the Canadian religious scene is the Dutch Calvinist or "reformed" tradition.

The various churches unanimously encouraged integration and the adoption of those things Canadian that were not antithetical to social or religious practices. As a result, the Dutch language has largely been discarded, as have "old country" practices that could have blocked the attainment of economic security. This fact, combined with a strong work ethic and minimal past involvement in the cultural life of the native land, has meant that "ethnicity" has only a very personal, familiar or religious connotation to the Dutch, all of which helps to explain why Dutch Canadian clubs represents no more than a minority of the Dutch community. Only recently have the children of immigrants begun to examine the history of their parents' migration and struggle, and to give their discoveries academic or literary form.

Group Maintenance The Dutch in Canada have until recently expressed little interest in maintaining or continuing their cultural traditions, the major exception being the Dutch Calvinists who have sought to make their religious ideas relevant to Canadian society by involving themselves in "Christian" schools. The rate of assimilation has been high and in most Canadian-born Dutch it is almost complete. While family ties remain strong, intermarriage with other Canadians is not regarded as a problem by the majority. The Dutch church, the Dutch Credit Union and the Dutch Canadian clubs, representing only a minority of Dutch Canadians, are the only remaining visible landmarks of an ethnic culture which is rapidly and willingly disappearing into the Canadian multicultural state.

HERMAN GANZEVOORT

Reading: K. DeJong, *Cauliflower Crown* (1973); Herman Ganzevoort and M. Bockelman, *Dutch Immigration to North America* (1983); T.E. Hofman, *The Strength of Their Years* (1983).

Dye, Cecil Henry, "Babe," hockey player (b at Hamilton, Ont 13 May 1898; d 2 Jan 1962). His learning the skills of hockey from his mother on a backyard rink in Toronto became part of hockey lore. He joined Toronto St Pats in 1919, and in a brief, meteoric career led the NHL in scoring 4 times (1920-21, 1921-22, 1922-23 and 1924-25), scoring 5 goals in a game twice, 38 goals in 29 games 1924-25 and a total of 200 goals in 271 games. He played for Chicago 1926-28, for New York Americans 1928-29 and 6 games for Toronto Maple Leafs 1930-31.

JAMES MARSH

Dyonnet, Edmond, painter, teacher (b at Crest, France 25 June 1859; d at Montréal 6 July 1954). Dyonnet studied in Turin with Gilardi and in Naples with Morelli. He came to Canada with his parents 1875. By 1891 he was teaching art and he was elected associate of the Royal Canadian Academy of Arts in 1893 and academician in 1903, also serving as the Academy's secretary 1910-49. A professor at and director of the design school at the Board of Arts and Manufacturers in Montréal for 31 years, he also taught at the École polytechnique in Montréal 1907-22. Dyonnet helped found Montréal's École des beaux-arts in 1922 and was a professor there until 1924. He taught at McGill 1920-36. In 1910 France made him an officer of the Académie. He won silver medals at the exhibitions in Buffalo (1910) and in St Louis, Mo (1904). In 1968 U of Ottawa published his *Mémoires d'un artiste canadien*.

MICHEL CHAMPAGNE

Dysart, A. Allison, lawyer, politician, judge, premier of NB (b at Cocagne, NB 22 Mar 1880; d at Moncton, NB 8 Dec 1962). Educated at Ont Agricultural Coll, St Joseph's U and Dalhousie, he practised law in Buctouche. He was elected MLA in 1917 for Kent County, was Speaker 1921-25 and minister of lands and mines 1925. Following the Liberal defeat, Dysart succeeded P.J. VENIOT in 1926 as leader of the Opposition. In 1935 he led his party to victory, defeating every member of the Cabinet of L.P.D. TILLEY. His government introduced the first Landlord and Tenants Act 1938, modernized the Labour Relations Act and worked to restore economic health following the Depression. Re-elected in 1939, Dysart resigned in 1940 as premier to become county court judge for Kent and Westmorland. He retired in 1957.

DELLA M.M. STANLEY

Eagle (family Accipitridae), large BIRD OF PREY with exceptionally keen vision, long, powerful wings, hooked bill and strong feet with sharp curved talons. They are fierce predators, spotting their animal prey as they soar or from their perches, and then swooping to kill. The more than 50 species of eagles are found on all continents and are divided into 4 major groups: the mainly tropical snake eagles and harpy eagles, not found in Canada; fish eagles, represented in Canada by the bald eagle (*Haliaeetus leucocephalus*); and booted eagles, including the golden eagle (*Aquila chrysaetos*), which breeds in mountain regions of western and northwestern Canada. Bald and golden eagles are immediately recognizable by their large size and 1.8 m wingspan. As adults, the 2 are easily distinguished: the bald eagle has a white head (not truly bald) and tail, contrasting with the solid brown of the golden eagle, and the golden eagle has legs feathered to the talons. Bald and golden eagles nest in treetops or cliff ledges. Nests are made of sticks lined with grasses, weeds, etc. Because nests can be used for years, they can become enormous. Usually, 2 eggs are laid (range 1-3). Golden eagles incubate eggs for 43 days; bald eagles, 35 days. Young are down covered and remain helpless in the nest for 50-100 days. The feathers of an eagle were of great symbolic value to the Plains Indians, signifying bravery or holding the power of spirits. R.W. FYFE

Eagle Pass, elev about 550 m, provides a corridor through the Gold Range in the MONASHEE MTS between Shuswap Lk and the Columbia R, 2 km SW of Revelstoke, BC. In 1865 Walter Moberly, BC's assistant surveyor general, set out to explore the interior for possible railway passes through the mountain barrier E of Shuswap Lk, and discovered and named the pass after he had shot up a nest of eagles that flew away through it. Eagle Pass was chosen as the CANADIAN PACIFIC RY route through the Monashees; here the western railway portion from Port Moody met the eastern rail crews, and on 7 Nov 1885 the last spike was driven at CRAIGELLACHIE, W of the pass. The Trans-Canada Hwy also traverses the pass. GLEN BOLES

Eagleson, Robert Alan, lawyer (b at St Catharines, Ont 24 Apr 1933). In 1966, as hockey's first player agent, he negotiated Bobby ORR's first contract with the Boston Bruins, a $70-thousand deal that made the 18-year-old rookie

the highest-paid player in professional hockey. Eagleson ultimately built a practice with 150 athlete clients. He was dedicated to the idea of N American professionals playing Europe's best hockey teams, and his work was important to the success of the 1972 CANADA-SOVIET HOCKEY SERIES. He has remained the most important figure in the organization of hockey matches between European teams and the NHL. He was the organizer for the 1976, 1981 and 1984 Canada Cup tournaments, and is the chief negotiator for Hockey Canada. He is also the executive director of the NHL Players Assn and maintains an active law practice. J. THOMAS WEST

Earle, David, dancer, choreographer (b at Toronto 17 Sept 1939). He trained in Toronto at the NATIONAL BALLET SCHOOL and studied in New York with Martha Graham. After a season in the José Limón Dance Company, he helped set up the London Contemporary Dance Theatre (Eng). In 1968 he returned to Toronto as co-director with Peter RANDAZZO and Patricia BEATTY of the TORONTO DANCE THEATRE. His dances are highly theatrical, reflecting perhaps his years with the Toronto Children's Players, and very lyrical. He has also shown an interest in the rituals of ancient cultures. His most popular work remains the *Baroque Suite*, a tribute to his late mentor, José Limón. GRAHAM JACKSON

Early-Warning Radar Air-defence RADAR stations were first established in Canada along the Atlantic and Pacific coasts in 1942, but were dismantled following the defeat of Germany and Japan in 1945. Although the USSR's military

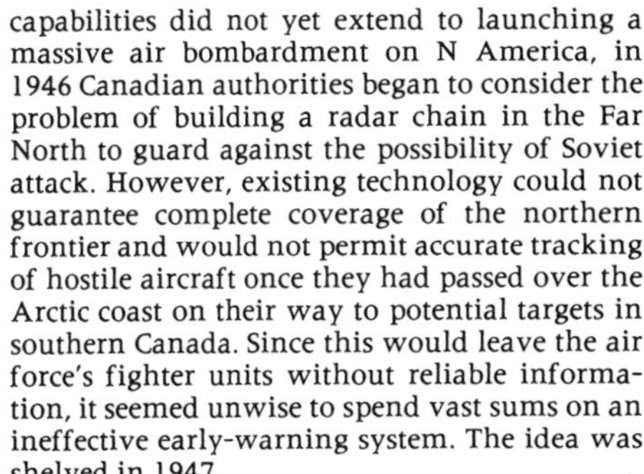

capabilities did not yet extend to launching a massive air bombardment on N America, in 1946 Canadian authorities began to consider the problem of building a radar chain in the Far North to guard against the possibility of Soviet attack. However, existing technology could not guarantee complete coverage of the northern frontier and would not permit accurate tracking of hostile aircraft once they had passed over the Arctic coast on their way to potential targets in southern Canada. Since this would leave the air force's fighter units without reliable information, it seemed unwise to spend vast sums on an ineffective early-warning system. The idea was shelved in 1947.

Conditions had changed by 1949. The USSR had developed its own atomic bomb and was in the process of creating a long-range bomber force. This, coupled with increased East-West tensions in Europe, convinced the Canadian government that it should construct a radar line, this time farther south, to provide early warning of an attack. The US decided to build a similar chain on its northern border that same year. Joint discussion eventually led to a co-operative effort, the Pinetree Line. Completed in 1954 for $450 million (of which Canada paid $150 million), it was a network of 33 stations running from Vancouver I through Alberta, northern Ontario and Québec to the Labrador coast. Eleven stations were financed and manned by Canada, and a further 5 were staffed by Canadians but paid for by the US.

Interest in improving N American radar coverage grew as the USSR upgraded its bomber force in the early 1950s. In Feb 1953 Defence Minister Brooke Claxton discussed the construction of an arctic chain with the Eisenhower administration, but no decisions were made. When the Soviets exploded their first hydrogen (thermonuclear) bomb in Aug 1953 the question became more urgent. Instead of an arctic chain, however, Canadian defence-research scientists recommended the construction of a mostly unmanned radar warning system (the McGill Fence) at 55° N to complement Pinetree. Louis St. Laurent's government accepted the advice in June 1954 and proceeded with this all-Canadian Mid-Canada Line project because technology was available in Canada, the line was cheaper than an arctic chain, and the plan avoided the troublesome issue of American presence on Canadian soil. Ninety-eight Mid-Canada stations were built by 1957 at a total cost of $250 million.

The idea of an arctic early-warning chain was not dropped. In June 1954 the Canada-US Military Studies Group — a bilateral advisory body under the aegis of the PERMANENT JOINT BOARD ON DEFENCE — urged that such a network be built because the USSR could outflank both the Pinetree and Mid-Canada lines. Under pressure from the US, and receiving similar advice from the RCAF, the federal government ultimately accepted the need for a radar chain in the Far North, and in Nov 1954 Canada and the US agreed to the construction of the Distant Early Warning (DEW) Line along the Arctic coast from Alaska to Baffin I. The US would bear the full cost of construction but had to employ Canadian firms and native labour. Canada also retained ownership of the sites located in Canada, and the major stations would be commanded by Canadians. Stretching 8046 km (5944 in Canada), the 22-station DEW Line was completed in 1957 after a massive construction engineering job that employed over 25 000 people. Such extensive co-operation between Canada and the US to solve the common problem of N American air defence was an important first step in the creation of the bilateral North American Air Defence Command (NORAD) in 1958, which integrated all Canadian air-defence radars and fighter forces.

The importance of these radar lines decreased

The bald eagle (*Haliaeetus leucocephalus*) is immediately recognizable by its large size, white (not bald) head and tail, and broad wingspan (*photo by Tim Fitzharris*).

substantially almost as soon as they were completed. Intercontinental and submarine-launched missiles, against which all 3 early-warning lines were useless, began to replace the manned bomber as the main Soviet threat in the early 1960s and a Ballistic Missile Early Warning System (BMEWS) was constructed in Alaska and Greenland. Satellites and BMEWS took over as the primary attack early-warning system. As a result the Mid-Canada Line was phased out of service in 1965. By 1983, 21 modernized DEW Line stations remained in operation in Canada to maintain sovereignty over the country's airspace and to detect any Soviet aircraft that might undertake a bombing raid on N America in conjunction with or following a missile attack. Twenty-four Pinetree stations also remained in operation at the end of 1983, but the US was threatening to withdraw its financial support for the maintenance of this line.

STEPHEN HARRIS

Earnscliffe, built in 1857 for Thomas MacKinnon, a successful businessman, was one of Ottawa's most impressive mansions of the mid-19th century. Designed in a Gothic revival style, its asymmetrical plan, medieval window moldings, and multi-gabled roof accented by an ornately carved bargeboard provide an unusually elaborate interpretation of this style. Its picturesque quality is enhanced by its spectacular site on top of the limestone cliffs overlooking the Ottawa R. Earnscliffe has seen a succession of distinguished residents. Between 1871 and 1891 it was the home of Sir John A. MACDONALD, and since 1930 it has served as the official residence of the British high commissioner to Canada.

JANET WRIGHT

Earthquake, vibratory motion generated in the Earth by the rupture of subterranean ROCK subjected to elastic stresses greater than its breaking strength. The rupture gives rise to seismic waves which propagate outward from its initiation point or focus. Immediately above the focus at the surface, the epicentral region experiences the strongest shaking. At greater distances, the seismic ground motion is detectable only by sensitive instruments (eg, seismographs). There are many measures of an earthquake's size, the most commonly used being that devised by Charles Richter in 1935. Recognizing the need to quantify earthquake size, Richter created a scale (calibrated against seismograph records) that takes into account the attenuation of seismic waves with distance from the earthquake focus. On the Richter magnitude scale (M), earthquakes below M2 are generally not felt, even when occurring at shallow depth. Shallow M5 events cause damage only when the epicentral region supports structures built on loose soils or unconsolidated sediments. M6 earthquakes in populated areas frequently cause considerable damage. The great earthquakes of this century have had magnitudes of about 8.5. Approximately 100 earthquakes each year are of M6 strength or greater; fortunately, most occur offshore or in unpopulated areas.

The severity of surface ground shaking at a particular distance from the source is described by its intensity at that location. The Modified Mercalli Intensity Scale, used in N America to quantify the degree of surface effects, ranges from MMI (barely perceptible ground motion) to MMXII (total destruction). MMVI is the threshold of damage. The depth of an earthquake focus varies from near surface to 700 km. Most continental earthquakes occur in the crust at depths less than 40 km. Deep-focus earthquakes (below 300 km) are restricted to parts of very active seismic belts.

In Canada earthquakes occur in the CORDILLERA, along the West Coast and offshore, in the Yukon and the High Arctic, in eastern Canada and along the eastern seaboard. Elsewhere in Canada, earthquakes are rare and of small magnitude. In the Cordillera, moderate earthquakes occur in the crust at minor to moderate levels of activity throughout, in a generally compressive regime. A large earthquake (M7) occurred in the vicinity of Hope, BC, or farther S in northern Washington State, in 1872. This is the largest known event in the region; all others have been M6 or less.

Along the West Coast and beneath Vancouver I and the Str of Georgia, earthquakes are the product of active plate subduction (*see* PLATE TECTONICS; GEOLOGICAL HISTORY). The small Juan de Fuca Plate is at present being thrust beneath the Olympic Mts and southern Vancouver I. The result is a zone of earthquakes beneath Puget Sound at depths of 70-100 km, overlain by a zone of shallower, generally smaller events. The regime extends N to Canadian territory and the southern Str of Georgia. The smaller Explorer Plate is no longer being thrust beneath northern Vancouver I; thus the junction of the 2 plates is a shear zone marked in the offshore by the Nootka Fault and extending deep beneath the islands. The shallower crust is occasionally subjected to large earthquakes (eg, the M7 event on Vancouver I near Courtenay, 1946), presumably in response to the shearing stresses below.

Offshore, a transform-spreading ridge system separates the Explorer and Juan de Fuca plates from the Pacific Plate. None of the many earthquakes occurring there each year is felt onshore. Further N the transform system intersects the Continental Shelf and extends N along the shelf as a transcurrent fault. Canada's greatest known earthquakes have occurred along this feature. In 1949 a 200 km long segment of the fault ruptured in an M8 earthquake that caused chandeliers to sway in Jasper. The thrusting of the Pacific Plate beneath Alaska generates many severe (M8) earthquakes that may affect Canadian territory. The Good Friday, 1964, M8.6 earthquake generated a TSUNAMI or seismic sea wave that caused considerable damage in Port Alberni, Vancouver I.

There are active seismic zones in the Richardson and Mackenzie mountains, YT, and a relatively limited seismic zone in the Beaufort Sea. Numerous earthquake zones occur in the arctic islands, one extending S through the Boothia Pen, across the mouth of Hudson Bay and northern Québec to the Labrador Sea. Baffin Bay was the site of an M7 earthquake in 1933. An event of similar magnitude occurred in the Laurentian Channel S of Newfoundland in 1929, generating a tsunami that caused considerable damage and drowned 27 people on the Burin Pen.

In eastern Canada seismicity is diffuse throughout the northern Appalachians, the series of M5 events in the Miramichi region of NB in 1982 being the most recent example. More concentrated zones occur at the mouth of the St Lawrence, in the St Lawrence Valley near La Malbaie in Charlevoix County, and in western Québec. The Charlevoix zone is the site of most of the larger events in eastern Canada. One of the largest occurred in 1534-35 between the voyages of Jacques CARTIER, and was reported to him by the Indians of the area on his return. More recently, an M7 earthquake in 1925 was felt throughout eastern Canada and the northeastern US. In the western Québec zone, damaging earthquakes have occurred at Témiscaming (1935) and Cornwall (1944). Both events were approximately M6.

Earthquakes in Canada are monitored by the National Seismograph Network operated by the Earth Physics Branch, Dept of Energy, Mines and Resources. Approximately 80 seismographs are distributed from St John's to Vancouver I and from Alert in the High Arctic to the Niagara Pen. The network is capable of detecting all earthquakes greater than M3.5 anywhere in Canada and those greater than M2 in more densely populated regions. Approximately 300 events greater than M3 are located annually. Probability estimates of seismic ground motion resulting from Canadian earthquakes are incorporated into the National Building Code of Canada; structures designed in compliance with its provisions can resist moderate earthquakes without significant damage and major earthquakes without collapse.

MICHAEL J. BERRY

Reading: Bruce A. Bolt, *Earthquakes: A Primer* (1978).

Earthworm, segmented worm of phylum ANNELIDA, class Oligochaeta. The class comprises some 14 families, including Lumbricidae to which the common earthworm (*Lumbricus terrestris*) belongs. Canadian species are all of familiar backyard size. Aquatic relatives may be microscopic; some Australian and Brazilian species may reach 3 m long and weigh 500 g. Earthworms are vital as soil mixers. Darwin estimated that 63 000 earthworms can shift, annually, 7.5-18 t of soil per acre (0.4 ha). In fact, there may be up to 32 million specimens per hectare in some places. Worms eat plant pieces and some animal remains in soil. They are reared and harvested for fishing bait (eg, night crawlers) and classroom specimens. Although hermaphroditic (of both sexes simultaneously), worms mate inside a mucus sheath secreted by the saddle-shaped thickening (clitellum) on the body of mature earthworms. The mucus sheath binds mating pairs and produces the egg-containing cocoon. Eggs and sperm fuse in the sheath, and fertilized eggs develop in the cocoons until tiny earthworms hatch. Many species are capable of self-fertilization, or eggs may develop without being fertilized. Very little work has been done on Canadian earthworms; only 19 species are recorded, 18 of which are primarily European, and one, *Bismastos parvus*, primarily N American. There are more than 150 related aquatic species. The ICE AGES are thought to have destroyed native earthworms wherever glaciers covered land; hence, all species in Canada are probably introduced (from Europe, often by humans) or reintroduced from southern US. Earthworms are separated from other oligochaetes by a combination of characteristics, including 8 setae per segment; multicellular clitellum; small eggs without yolks; 2 pairs of testes and one pair of ovaries; male pores opening behind female; and relatively large size compared to aquatic species.

R.O. BRINKHURST

East India Company, trading company chartered 1600 by Elizabeth I of England with a monopoly over the Eastern Hemisphere. Schemes for promoting the British FUR TRADE between the Pacific coast and China, including those of Alexander Dalrymple and Alexander MACKENZIE necessitated inclusion of the EIC, whose privileges deterred such commerce. With the exception of the period 1814-16, when the EIC licensed NORTH WEST COMPANY ships to carry furs to China, its monopoly forced the NWC to use American ships for its Canton trade. The EIC's monopoly ended by 1833, and the company was dissolved in 1874.

JEAN MORRISON

Eastern Temperate Forests, *see* VEGETATION REGIONS.

Eastern Townships Region located in S-central Québec, between Montréal and Québec City. The townships extend from GRANBY to Lac MÉGANTIC and from DRUMMONDVILLE to the US border. The first inhabitants were the ABENAKI, who used the region for hunting and fishing. The only settlement during the French regime was a trading post at Grandes-Fourches [SHERBROOKE]. Early in the English regime (from 1760), the area was called Buckinghamshire. Shortly after the American Revolution a large number of English LOYALISTS left the US for Canada and settled on 259 km^2 in southern Québec. In 1791 the British government granted them land in the form of townships. The 93 townships formed thereafter became known as the "Eastern Townships" (as opposed to the "Western Townships" of Upper Canada, now Ontario). The English-speaking settlers were mainly American, English and Irish, but after 1840 a wave of French colonization swept into the region, and by 1871 Francophones constituted the majority in most of the townships.

Equipped with an excellent road system since 1815, the region underwent considerable growth following construction of the GRAND TRUNK RY, which linked Montréal and Portland, Maine. The road and rail networks encouraged the exploitation and development of natural resources such as timber, asbestos, granite, copper and limestone. Hydroelectric power generated by the numerous waterfalls of the Rivière ST-FRANÇOIS and its tributaries resulted in the establishment of sawmills and flour mills, and the development of textile plants, foundries and the pulp and paper industry. The 20th century brought heavy industry to Sherbrooke, and the town gradually became the "Queen of the Eastern Townships." The snowmobile industry flourished in Valcourt after its foundation by J. Armand BOMBARDIER, and asbestos mines in THETFORD-MINES and ASBESTOS produce close to 35% of the world's asbestos. University research and the arrival of high technology in the field of microprocessors have resulted in the establishment of a microelectronics industry. The region's lively, bicultural nature is reflected in its 2 universities — U Sherbrooke (francophone), and Bishop's (anglophone) in LENNOXVILLE. One of the region's curiosities is its round barns, designed — because of the legend that "the devil hides in the corners of barns" — to protect their owners from the devil. The MAGOG-Orford area has become a major international tourist centre.

JEAN-MARIE DUBOIS AND PIERRE MAILHOT

Eastmain (or East Main) refers to the E shore of Hudson Bay, although in the 1680s the term was restricted to the vicinity of the EASTMAIN R. The corresponding reference to the W shore of Hudson Bay is the Westmain (West Main). Both terms were used in the early FUR TRADE when the region was well travelled by trappers and traders.

JOHN ROBERT COLOMBO

Eastmain, Rivière, 760 km long, rises in the central part of Québec on the side of a low drainage divide from which streams flow W to JAMES BAY. Since the 46 000 km^2 drainage basin of the river is situated in an area of heavy snowfall, the resulting mean discharge of the river is an impressive 895 m^3/s. The river encounters a sharp break of slope coming off the Canadian SHIELD peneplain as it meets the narrow coastal plain of James Bay, and in its final 65 km descends 125 m in a series of rapids and falls that have considerable potential as sites for hydro development.

DOUG FINLAYSON

Easton, Peter, pirate (*fl* 1602-15). He was a privateer in Elizabeth I's navy who lost his commission on the accession of James I in 1603 and turned to piracy. He looted shipping in the English Channel until 1610, when he withdrew rather than fight Sir Henry MAINWARING. He arrived in Newfoundland in 1610, built a fort at HARBOUR GRACE, and for several years plundered fishing fleets and settlements and recruited Newfoundland sailors into his private navy. He destroyed a BASQUE fleet intent upon capturing Harbour Grace attacked Spanish shipping in the Caribbean, raided Puerto Rico, and captured the Spanish plate fleet in 1614. Pardoned by King James, Easton abandoned his Newfoundland base and settled in Savoy. He bought a castle at Villefranche, became "Marquis of Savoy," and lived the rest of his life in luxury. There is a monument to this Newfoundland folk hero at Harbour Grace.

EDWARD BUTTS

Eaton, Cyrus Stephen, financier, philanthropist (b at Pugwash, NS 27 Dec 1883; d at Cleveland, Ohio 9 May 1979). Educated at McMaster, Eaton moved to the US in 1900. He became involved in public utilities and after 1925 in steel, eventually forming Republic Steel. He also had investments in Canada, including Steep Rock Iron Ore. In 1950 Eaton and C.D. HOWE quarreled over administration of the company. They became estranged and Eaton later helped Howe's political opponents in Port Arthur [Thunder Bay]. Eaton became best known for his sponsorship of a series of conferences at his birthplace, the Pugwash conferences, at which he attempted to bring together scientists and public figures from East and West to foster international conciliation. For his efforts he received the Lenin Peace Prize in 1960.

ROBERT BOTHWELL

Eaton, Frederik Stefan, merchant (b at Toronto 26 June 1938), great-grandson of Timothy EATON and grandson of John Craig EATON; president of the T. Eaton Co. At the conclusion of his university education in 1962, Eaton, following family tradition, gained on-the-job experience within the organization in numerous capacities in both Canada and England. Since 1977 he has presided over the continued expansion and consolidation of his great-grandfather's business and assisted in the development of Toronto's EATON CENTRE. In 1983 the company had 107 stores across Canada employing 35 000.

JOY L. SANTINK

Eaton, Sir John Craig, merchant, philanthropist (b at Toronto 28 Apr 1876; d there 30 Mar 1922). Third son of Timothy EATON, he worked in numerous capacities within the T. Eaton Co before becoming president 1907. Recognizing the opportunities for development in the West, he was largely responsible for establishing the Eaton store in Winnipeg 1905. He also opened buying offices in Great Britain, the US, Europe and the Orient. By 1919 he had established Saturday holidays and evening closing at 5 PM in his stores, factories and mail-order offices. The Eaton Boys and Girls clubs also provided educational and recreational facilities for company employees. Eaton employees on active war service continued to receive full pay for the duration of WWI — ultimately more than $2 million. He was knighted in 1915 for his philanthropic activities.

JOY L. SANTINK

Eaton, John David, merchant (b at Toronto 4 Oct 1909; d there 4 Aug 1973), second son of Sir John Craig EATON. He left Cambridge at age 21 to begin his apprenticeship with the T. EATON CO LTD in the men's wear dept of the Toronto store. He learned the firm's various operations, became a director in 1934, a VP in 1937, and president in 1942. During his presidency the business expanded in the North and West, and contributory medical insurance and a retirement plan for employees was introduced. Eaton personally contributed $50 million to the latter when it began in 1948, fuelling speculation that he was the richest man in the country. A shy man, he lived quietly. He was reported to regard his failure to complete the EATON CENTRE, first announced in 1965, as his greatest disappointment.

Eaton, Timothy, merchant, founder of Canada's largest privately owned department store, the T. Eaton Co (b near Ballymena, Ire 1834; d at Toronto 31 Jan 1907). After apprenticing in a general store in Ireland, Eaton followed 2 older brothers to Canada 1854 and worked for a time at a store in UC. In 1856 with his brother James, he opened a small store in the Huron Tract at Kirkton, which they moved in 1860 to St Mary's, near Stratford. Convinced that change was in the air, Eaton in 1869 opened his own

Timothy Eaton introduced Canadians to the idea of cash sales and a fixed price for goods. He built his small store into a thriving department store network employing over 9000 people at the time of his death in 1907 (*courtesy Archives / Eaton's of Canada Ltd*).

store at 178 Yonge St, Toronto, and introduced Canadians to the idea of cash sales and one fixed price, in contrast to the older credit, bargain and barter method. He displayed a sympathetic attitude towards his employees, having by the late 1880s instituted evening closing at 6 PM and the summer Saturday afternoon holiday. He also vastly improved their working environment by creating light, airy work places. The introduction of the Eaton catalogue 1884 gave Canadians, particularly those in pioneer farming communities, access to a variety of merchandise. At his death in 1907 at age 72, Eaton employed over 9000 people in his Toronto and Winnipeg stores, in factories in Toronto, Oshawa, Hamilton and Montréal and in buying offices in London, Eng, and Paris.

JOY L. SANTINK

Reading: J.W. Ferry, *A History of the Department Store* (1960); G.G. Nasmith, *Timothy Eaton* (1923); J.E. Middleton, *The Municipality of Toronto* I (1923).

Eaton, Wyatt, portrait, genre and landscape painter, illustrator (b at Philipsburg, Qué 6 May 1849; d at Newport, RI 7 June 1896). Eaton left Canada for New York around 1867 and studied at the National Academy of Design, and then for 5 years under Joseph Oriel Eaton. He went to London, then Paris where he studied at the École des beaux-arts (1872-76) and became a disciple of Millet and several other Barbizon painters. On his return to New York (1876), he taught at the Cooper Union and executed a series of pen-and-ink portraits of American poets for *Century Magazine*. In France again, 1883-84, he painted his most famous canvas, *Harvest Field*. His portraits of George STEPHEN (Lord Mount Stephen), Sir Donald SMITH and William VAN HORNE, painted in Montréal, 1892-93, were so well received that orders for portraits of Sir William DAWSON, William C. MACDONALD and others followed. His last working days were spent in Ottawa. He was founding member and president of the American Art Assn (later Soc of American Artists), and founding member of the Soc of Canadian Artists (1867).

ROBERT STACEY

Eaton Centre, Toronto (designed by the ZEIDLER Partnership and Bregman and Hamann, phase 1 opening in 1977, phase 2 in 1979) is the epitome of those vast multistorey interior "atrium" spaces for which Canadian ARCHITECTURE became known internationally in the 1970s. The Centre comprises a new T. EATON CO department store, 2 new office buildings and a 274 m glass-covered shopping galleria flanked by 3 levels of shops and restaurants and 4 levels of parking. The architecture plays with the simple technological themes of traditional modern design, unadorned concrete and steel structure, metal pipe handrails, transparent and mirror glass, together with the decoration provided by plants and fountains, shop signs and banners to create a lively and varied gathering place that is well integrated with the existing downtown.

MICHAEL MCMORDIE

Eau Claire, Lac à l', 1383 km^2, elev 241 m, max length 68 km, is located in northwestern Québec about 133 km E of the SE shore of Hudson Bay. Probably formed by the impact of a meteorite, the lake drains W via the Clearwater R into Lac GUILLAUME-DELISLE (Richmond Gulf). After joining with the flow from the Rivière de Troyes, it empties into Hudson Bay. The lake's name is purely representative, and it is often called Clearwater Lk. DAVID EVANS

Eayrs, James George, political scientist, educator (b at London, Eng 13 Oct 1926). Educated at U of T, Columbia and London School of Economics, Eayrs is Eric Dennis Memorial Professor of Political Science and Government at Dalhousie. He taught at U of T 1952-80 and was editor of *International Journal*, 1959-84. He is a superb stylist and influential pioneer in the study of 20th-century Canadian foreign and defence policy, and his major scholarly publications include *The Art of the Possible* (1961) and *In Defence of Canada* (5 vols to date, 1964-83). Eayrs's reputation outside the university world rests upon his controversial journalism and public commentary on Canadian and international affairs, selections of which are collected in *Northern Approaches* (1961), *Minutes of the Sixties* (1968) and *Greenpeace and her Enemies* (1973). His early journalism displays a pro-NATO, Cold War liberal sympathetic to the US. The 1960s and 1970s saw him an opponent of NATO, an advocate of Canadian neutrality and harshly critical of diplomats and diplomacy. He received the MOLSON PRIZE in 1984. NORMAN HILLMER

Echinodermata [Gk, "spiny skin"], phylum of exclusively marine INVERTEBRATE animals. The 6000 known species occur from shores to greatest depths of all oceans. None are found in fresh water; very few are capable of coping with diluted seawater of estuaries. The name is derived from the characteristic internal skeleton of calcium carbonate formed into numerous small, bony structures (ossicles). Ossicles are embedded in the skin, often giving it a rough or spiny texture. There are 5 classes of living echinoderms: crinoids (sea lilies and feather stars); asteroids (STARFISH); ophiuroids (brittle stars); echinoids (SEA URCHINS, etc); and holothuroids (sea cucumbers). Echinoderms have been well preserved as FOSSILS; all existing classes and several others now extinct were present in the Ordovician (500 million years ago). They may have originated in the Precambrian (over 600 million years ago).

Living classes differ principally in body plan. All show radial symmetry (symmetry about an axis) but there are many variations. In general, the axis of symmetry runs between the oral and aboral surfaces (sides bearing mouth and anus, respectively). Crinoids, asteroids and ophiuroids are basically star shaped; the axis of symmetry is vertical. In asteroids and ophiuroids, the oral surface is usually directed downwards, in crinoids, upwards. Sea urchins are spherical, with the oral surface downwards. Holothuroids are sausage shaped and, typically, lie on one side; oral and aboral surfaces are at either end. Fundamentally, echinoderms are composed of 5 radially arranged parts. This configuration, most apparent in the star-shaped asteroids and ophiuroids, also occurs in echinoids and holothuroids, which typically have body parts in some multiple of 5.

Another characteristic is the water-vascular system, an arrangement of tubes and canals employing hydrostatic pressure to operate tube feet. Water within ampullae (small sacs resembling medicine-dropper bulbs) is squeezed out by muscular contraction, causing the tube feet to elongate. Contraction of muscles in the tube feet walls causes retraction of feet and return of water to the ampullae. Tube feet usually occur in rows radiating out from the oral surface. They function in locomotion, feeding and respiration.

Crinoids are the oldest and most primitive living class of echinoderms. Their common name, sea lilies, derives from the fact that some species are attached to the sea bottom by a stalk. Long, feathery arms surrounding the mouth give appearance of a lilylike flower. Crinoids that have lost this sessile lifestyle and no longer have a stalk are commonly called feather stars. Crinoids usually feed on suspended particles that fall on their oral surface. Some feather stars swim by thrashing arms up and down. In a comical, unco-ordinated manner, they can lift themselves off the bottom and avoid predators.

Asteroids (starfish or sea stars) are common seashore animals. Starfish are voracious carnivores. Those that feed on clams and mussels pull open the hinged shell with their tube feet, evert their stomach into the slightly gaping MOLLUSC and secrete digestive juices that dissolve the victim in its shell. The remarkable regenerative powers of starfish enable them to regrow a lost body part. For most species, only a piece of central disc need be present for missing parts to grow back.

Ophiuroids (brittle stars) are named for their habit of casting off arms when threatened. The arms are not really brittle; the ophiuroid is using one of its remarkable capacities, autotomy or self-cutting. The ability to regrow missing parts is exceptionally well developed in ophiuroids. They are usually filter feeders, using tube feet to catch particles suspended in seawater.

Echinoids include sea urchins, sand dollars and heart urchins. Ossicles of the body wall have fused into a rigid, solid, internal skeleton (test). All members of the class have external surfaces covered with spines. In sand dollars, these are reduced to a fine, feltlike covering. The elaborate chewing apparatus just inside the mouth is called Aristotle's lantern, a name that originated with Aristotle, who thought the structure resembled lanterns of the day.

Holothuroids are called sea cucumbers because of their elongate bodies and habit of lying on their side. They frequently have numerous branched tentacles surrounding the mouth which serve to filter food. Other forms lack tentacles and sweep the bottom like vacuum cleaners, extracting nutrition from bottom sediments. In many parts of Asia holothuroids are considered a delicacy and are extensively fished.

Many echinoderms reproduce by releasing eggs and sperm into seawater, where fertilization occurs. The embryo develops into a small planktonic or swimming larva. Larvae of each class have their own characteristic forms and names. They differ dramatically from adult forms. Larvae may drift and feed in the PLANKTON for many weeks before they finally settle and metamorphose into adults. Each class contains many species that have a specialized brood pouch within the mother and, therefore, do not form larvae. There are also some species that reproduce asexually by dividing their bodies in half and regrowing missing parts. R.D. BURKE

Eckhardt-Gramatté, Sophie-Carmen, "Sonia," née Friedman, composer, pianist, violinist, teacher (b at Moscow? 6 Jan 1899; d at Stuttgart, West Germany 2 Dec 1974). Although most of her professional career was spent in Europe, she became a strong force in Canadian music from the time of her arrival in 1953 (with her husband, Dr Ferdinand Eckhardt, who had become director of the Winnipeg Art Gallery) until her death. As an 11-year-old prodigy she gave recitals on the violin and piano in Paris, Geneva and Berlin, and by age 13 had several small pieces published in Paris. Her concert career peaked in 1929 with performances in America where she was championed by Leopold Stokowski. She next concentrated on composition, her style gradually evolving through the conservative influence of her instructor, Max Trapp, and through her 1939 move from Berlin to Vienna (neoclassicism and a modest bow to serialism). Works written in Canada show an increasing emphasis on intervallic relationships (Bartok), metric organization and "basic note groups" (Webern). Many were commissioned: *Woodwind Quintet, Piano Trio, Duo Concertante* for cello and piano, *String Quartet No. 3, Symphony-Concerto* for piano and orchestra and the *Manitoba Symphony*. Her name is memorialized in the Eckhardt-Gramatté National Competition for the Performance of Canadian Music held annually at Brandon, Man. LORNE WATSON

ECOLOG, acoustic instrumentation system developed at the BEDFORD INSTITUTE OF OCEANOGRAPHY, Dartmouth, NS, for research on and survey of fish populations. A dual-beam, vertical echo sounder is towed from a ship, transmitting sound and receiving echoes at a frequency of 50 kHz (echoes from swim bladders of fish are strongest in the 30-120 kHz range). Echoes are received simultaneously on narrow- and wide-beam transducers (ie, ACOUSTIC transmitters). Echo signals are digitized and recorded on magnetic tape. Computer programs on board ship, or later in the laboratory, give position, depth, number and size of fish encountered, allowing estimates of local abundance. L.M. DICKIE

Economic Council of Canada, est 1963 to assess medium- and long-term prospects of the economy; to consider ways of strengthening Canada's international financial and trade position; to study the effects of economic growth and technical change on employment and income; to explore policies to foster regional development; and to study means of increasing Canadian participation in the ownership, control and management of industries in Canada. A federally funded crown corporation, it reports directly to the prime minister. It maintains a large staff in Ottawa and publishes not only its own consensus recommendations but research projects of individual economists as well.

WILLIAM F. FORWARD

Economic Forecasting is a projection or estimation of the future economic or technological performance of a country, group of countries, firm, industry or community. Economic forecasts, which may be short-, medium- or long-term, are published by banks, investment dealers, the CONFERENCE BOARD and economic-research organizations. The ECONOMIC COUNCIL OF CANADA publishes forecasts (also called, in this instance, 5-to-10-year economic and social goals), as do some provincial governments. Twice a year the Organization for Economic Co-operation and Development publishes forecasts, including those for individual members such as Canada.

The financial community pays close attention to forecasts. Companies, eg, manufacturing businesses, use them to help plan for employment, production, inventories and costs. Large utilities such as telephone companies, electric power suppliers and pipelines depend upon longer-term economic forecasts for help in planning the construction of new facilities.

Forecasters rely on various techniques, including an analysis of leading indicators (ie, statistical information on certain factors, such as steel production, which provide advance warning of changes in economic activity) and econometric computer models. In these models forecasters attempt to create mathematically, through equations, a picture of how the economy (or market, industry, etc) functions. These equations may identify relationships such as those between prices and wages, or between consumer spending and investment or production. Forecasts are very rarely completely correct, and are often quite wrong, but the growing speed of computer processing may improve their accuracy.

W. EMPEY

Economic History, the study of the evolution of the economy and economic institutions. The subject grew out of history and economics in the 19th century and arrived in Canada when an English economic historian was appointed professor of political economy in Toronto (1888). It uses material and ideas from economics, history, geography and political science, supplying information to these subjects; it must not be confused with the history of economic ideas or with the interpretation of general history using economic forces. Distinctive contributions to Canada's economic history came in the 1920s and 1930s both from economists such as H.A. INNIS and from historians such as D.G. CREIGHTON, who stressed the importance of what they called "staple products" — fur, fish, timber, wheat, metals — whose markets were abroad. Emphasizing the importance of Canada's distinctive geography — the Canadian SHIELD and the Great Lakes-St Lawrence system — they traced interactions between geography, resources, foreign markets and the inflow of people and funds from abroad. They treated regional growth in relation to the staple products. More recent approaches have supplemented the old with modern economics and statistics. Work has been done in areas, including WORKING-CLASS HISTORY, urban growth, BUSINESS HISTORY and the industrial development of central Canada, that fitted rather poorly into the STAPLE THESIS. Meanwhile, historical geographers produce invaluable material on settlement patterns and on the growth of towns, while regional studies, which staple theorists treated as components of nation-building, have become routes to regional self-confidence, especially in Québec and Atlantic Canada. Marxist scholars share business and labour history and other fields with scholars whose ideologies are very different.

Although the following sections describe Canadian economic history by region, the country is historically a single economic unit. The FUR TRADE first created a single transcontinental trading economy; since Confederation, 1867, labour and finance have moved freely among the regions. The improvement of transportation — the railways between 1867 and 1915 (see RAILWAY HISTORY), and the highway and PIPELINE systems after 1945 — has helped. The provinces have become important markets and suppliers for one another, so that an investment boom in one region such as the Prairie West could create a nationwide boom, while a slump in Ontario manufacturing becomes a nationwide slump.

Central Canada

Most of the native peoples lived by hunting and gathering; only among the Iroquoian groups (HURON, PETUN, NEUTRAL) was agriculture established. Furbearing animals were trapped to provide clothing, and silver and copper were used to make ornaments. Trading among native groups, for a wide variety of items, was common, but there does not seem to have been any specialized merchant class. In the 16th century French and British traders began to buy furs, for which they offered iron tools, weapons and alcohol, all of which the Indians valued highly. The result was profound economic and cultural changes among the NATIVE PEOPLES, who were to play a critical role in the early fur trade.

Permanent European settlers first came to Canada to exploit the FISHERY and the fur trade. Until the end of the 17th century, because the climate and soil were not encouraging, agricultural progress was slow (*see* AGRICULTURE HISTORY). Like the French, English-speaking merchants engaged in the fur trade; after the CONQUEST (1759-60), when many British businessmen began to control a large portion of the fur trade from Montréal, they also quickly extended their interests throughout commerce and finance. The population grew through natural increase and through immigration from Britain. By the 1820s the good agricultural land in the St Lawrence Valley had almost all been taken up. After the NORTH WEST COMPANY merged with the HUDSON'S BAY COMPANY in 1821 the transcontinental fur trade was no longer managed from Montréal. But by that time Upper and Lower Canada had developed an immense trade in timber, which went first to Britain and then, after mid-century, to the US and domestic buyers (*see* TIMBER TRADE HISTORY).

Until the 1780s there was no significant European population in present-day Ontario, although its waterways were used by the fur traders. Settlement began with the arrival of the United Empire LOYALISTS, British and American settlers, and British troops and officials. Forest land was gradually cleared, and export trades in WHEAT, POTASH and timber developed. A few roads and CANALS were built, of which the most important were the WELLAND CANAL and St Lawrence R canals. By 1867 most good land in the province had been claimed, although not all of it was under cultivation.

At the Conquest, present-day Québec contained 3 towns, Montréal, Québec and Trois-Rivières. Ontario contained none. Thereafter, towns appeared along with settlement and with the development of commerce and government. But even in 1871, much of central Canada's industry, including the 2 great industries, milling and lumbering, was dispersed through the countryside or in small villages. After Confederation, however, rapid INDUSTRIALIZATION and URBANIZATION occurred in both provinces, so that by 1911 half of Ontario's population lived in cities and towns.

From 1870 to 1900 some established industries such as tailoring and shoemaking were becoming factory activities, and provincial governments began to regulate working conditions. MINIMUM WAGE legislation came much later: Ontario adopted it partially in the 1920s. Some unions had begun in the 1830s, and in the 1880s, with the rise and decline of the American-based KNIGHTS OF LABOR, union activity increased. But relative to the nonfarm work force, union membership remained small until the 1940s, when federal and provincial protection was extended to unions.

Central Canada's industrial advance was especially rapid between 1896 and 1914, when the whole nation experienced investment and export booms. After 1900 a few industries such as carriage-making and blacksmithing declined. But new industries appeared: electrical equipment and chemicals in the 1890s, cars and aluminum after 1900, pulp and paper 1890-1914, radio and home appliances in the 1920s and aircraft in the 1940s. After 1890 cheap HYDROELECTRIC power helped accelerate industrial change, as did both world wars and nuclear power in the 1970s (at least in Ontario). In both provinces labour was drawn from natural population increase and immigration.

There were cyclical downturns in the mid-1870s, the early 1890s, the early 1920s and especially between 1929 and 1933; the GREAT DEPRESSION lasted until the war began. Thereafter, economic expansion continued substantially uninterrupted until another cyclical downturn 1981-82 (*see* BUSINESS CYCLES).

Because so many of the newer industries were concentrated in Ontario, during the 1920s Québec's economic advance was less spectacular; although it shared fully in the development of pulp, paper and nonferrous metals, it took no part in the AUTOMOTIVE INDUSTRY, and little part in the ELECTRICAL APPLIANCE INDUSTRIES. Also, because a higher proportion of Québec industries were low-productivity activities which could not pay high wages, Ontario workers earned more on the average than did Québec workers. After 1945, and especially after the 1960s, these gaps closed. General Motors built a plant outside Montréal. Both federal and provincial authorities spent lavishly to attract factories into Québec; indeed, the Québec government owned plants in such industries as steel-making and auto assembly. Québec's birth rate became the lowest in Canada, and average REAL WAGES rose. Although the national financial centre had shifted from Montréal to Toronto by the beginning of WWII, Québec's financial system became more sophisticated and more francophone in its attitudes. In the 1970s and early 1980s, as anglophone business and professional people left a province in which they no longer felt at home, there was increasing scope for francophone expertise. Much more serious than the uncertainty among investors were the troubles of Québec's established textile and clothing industries, increasingly threatened by cheaper goods from the Third World. The federal authorities provided advice, new kinds of PROTECTIONISM and adjustment finance. Furthermore, thanks to the presence of Northern Telecom, CANADAIR and BOMBARDIER, by 1980 Québec was an important player in the game of "high-tech industry."

Agriculture in central Canada began as a battle against forest and climate, passed through an export phase, and by 1900 depended chiefly on the local urban markets which it was not able to supply fully. Around 1800 the farmers of the lower St Lawrence produced an exportable grain surplus, but for most of the 19th century Québec residents depended on grain from Ontario. In turn, for most of the century Ontario regularly exported grain not only to Québec, but overseas. However, after 1880, as Ontario's population rose while its wheat acreage declined, the province gradually imported more wheat from western Canada while increasing its output of oats and other fodder crops. Both Ontario and Québec, between 1871 and 1914, specialized increasingly in meat and DAIRY products. From the 1860s until the 20th century, much cheese, butter and Ontario bacon was sold abroad; thereafter, more of these goods were consumed within central Canada. After WORLD WAR I, with the decline of the horse and the concomitant fall in oats acreage, the shift to other fodder crops became even more pronounced and some land began to fall out of cultivation. Meanwhile, city growth encroached on farmland.

From Confederation to 1929, spasmodic efforts were made to extend the frontier of agricultural settlement in Ontario and Québec. These efforts were not very successful, but by 1929 there were pockets of farmland around Lac SAINT-JEAN, the Ontario Clay Belt, Rainy River and Thunder Bay. More important for northern development were mining, pulp and paper. These activities scattered small communities throughout northern Ontario and Québec between 1886 (when the Sudbury NICKEL deposits were first exploited) and 1929.

By 1867 the great cities of central Canada were Montréal and Toronto. The former began as a port and commercial centre. By mid-19th century it was a place of industry, and by 1900 it was producing large amounts of clothing and textile products, electrical equipment, railway rolling stock and many light industrial products. It was also an important financial centre. Toronto, after a slow and inauspicious beginning, developed after 1867 on similar lines, much of its early prosperity being based on Great Lakes shipping. By 1900 both cities had energetic banks and insurance companies and active stock exchanges. Both cities had begun to attract immigrants from central Europe and Italy. It was largely natural increase and migration from Britain that built the cities of central Canada between Confederation and 1914, or even 1939. Indeed, before 1900 many Québecois and Ontarians went to the US, where prospects were better: the nation was not managing to retain the natural increase of its own population (*see* FRANCO-AMERICANS). However, between 1900 and 1929, and again after 1939, the economic prospects were so much better that emigration was no longer a problem. Really large-scale immigration from Italy and southern Europe occurred only after WWII.

In Québec and Ontario, as elsewhere in Canada, urbanization and industrialization were assisted by the thrift and diligence of the population, whose members were also willing to borrow funds and skills from abroad and, at least until the 1970s, to receive immigrants during times of prosperity. Educational arrangements helped, first by providing for general literacy; next, by arranging for higher liberal and professional education; and then, starting in the 1870s, by offering various sorts of specialized secondary and tertiary technological studies in, for example, ENGINEERING and agriculture.

By 1982 both economies had become very urbanized, and the "service" industries and occupations were much more important than manufacturing, which in turn was more important than agriculture, forestry or mining. The earnings from the service industries helped to balance central Canada's accounts with the rest of the country, a process to which the sale of manufactures also contributed. This pattern of regional specialization had established itself between Confederation and 1900; Ontario and Québec industrialization was not created at the expense of other regions. Most of the 2 provinces' markets have always been in central Canada because that is where most Canadians live. Also, since the 19th century there have been export markets for many Québec and Ontario manufactures — cheese, sawn lumber, cars, agricultural implements, pulp and paper, refined nickel and aluminum. Developments elsewhere in Canada, especially in the West, helped accelerate central Canada's industrialization, but they did not cause it. Economic evolution had been similar on the southern side of the Great Lakes, where there is a similar pool of raw materials, capital, labour and skills. Indeed, because on the Canadian side there was more hydroelectric potential, plus nickel, gold, silver, uranium and plenty of pulpwood, in some respects circumstances were more favourable. Since 1858-59 Canada's tariff has protected manufacturing industries, but locational advantages, not the tariff itself, ensured that most of that protected manufacturing would locate in central Canada.

Atlantic Canada

Although there was some early fur trading, serious economic development in the Atlantic provinces really began with the sea fisheries, whose markets were in Europe and later in the West Indies. Much of the 16th-century fishing was conducted from British and European bases. Settlement was slow, especially in Newfoundland. On the mainland some francophone settlers arrived during the 17th century (*see* ACADIA), and some anglophone migrants from Britain and New England in the 18th, but the European population was small until the arrival of the Loyalists. Early in the 19th century Scots settled on Cape Breton. But settlement remained sparse, partly because there was little good agricultural land. Prosperity came from the fisheries, forests and maritime carrying trades. Colonial lumber enjoyed preferential treatment in Britain (*see* TIMBER DUTIES), while the carrying trades served the whole Atlantic basin. By mid-19th century lumber preferences ended and, in shipping, iron and steam began to edge out wood and sail. Cape Breton coal found a market in Boston; other favourable developments were hard to find. Although there were efforts at manufacturing, local markets were small and communications among the colonies were bad. The INTERCOLONIAL RAILWAY to Canada created some new markets for local industry, but the line did not eliminate the locational disadvantages. When the Dominion tariff was raised in 1879 (*see* NATIONAL POLICY) many Maritime capitalists built factories, only to find that markets were smaller than they had expected and that new managerial skills were needed. Nor could Maritime coal compete in Ontario with Pennsylvania coal. Bankruptcies and takeovers were numerous. However, iron and steel production in Nova Scotia was stimulated by the tariff, the Dominion's iron and steel bounties and the post-1900 railway-building boom. By 1900 Halifax had become a local financial centre whose capitalists were raising money not only for local industry, but for utilities in Latin America. But Maritime banks tended to fail, merge or move their executive offices to central Canada (*see* BANK OF NOVA SCOTIA; ROYAL BANK).

During the 19th century Newfoundland acquired a settled population largely by immigration from Britain. The rest of the region attracted few migrants, at least after 1867, and the population grew slowly: much of the natural increase flowed to the US or to other Canadian regions.

The 1920s and 1930s were unhappy decades in the Atlantic region. The iron, steel, coal and machinery industries were in chronic difficulty and, like the fishery, they suffered severely in the Great Depression. Nor did new manufacturers make much headway, in spite of continuing federal subsidies for rail transport. The few rays of hope included new pulp and paper plants and new protected markets for apples and lumber in Britain. WWII brought hectic prosperity to those communities which served the naval and air bases, and after 1945 the situation improved. New hydroelectric plants and new governmental initiatives attracted new industry, but these programs had some successes and many failures. More useful to economic growth, perhaps, was the new army base in New Brunswick. By 1983 offshore oil had been discovered in commercial quantities, and there were good prospects for natural gas. But the old heavy industries and the fisheries were in chronic trouble, and by 1983 were kept alive by government subsidy (under various names) and government ownership. It was largely on this basis that Atlantic cities grew.

Western Canada

Economic development in western Canada began with the fur trade. By the end of the 18th century the traders' activities on the prairies had produced a small population of MÉTIS who, like the Indians, depended on the trade. Fur-trade posts were scattered throughout the region, and on Vancouver I, the city of Victoria began as an HBC trading post.

Settled agriculture began in 1812 with Lord Selkirk's RED RIVER COLONY. However, the building of the CANADIAN PACIFIC RAILWAY in the 1880s gave Manitoba a wheat economy. Winnipeg became a centre for commerce and railways, and soon acquired a few factories. In the late 1890s, as world prices rose, transport costs fell, methods of dryland farming improved, and more appropriate varieties of wheat became available, the prospects for development brightened. Until 1929 the Prairie provinces enjoyed an immense expansion of the wheat economy, onto which was grafted, before 1914, a very much larger rail system, a network of cities and towns, coal mining and RANCHING. By 1914 the frontier of settlement had been pushed well toward the northwest, attracting migrants from many lands. The result was a regional economy which depended almost entirely upon the world price of a single crop, and on local yields, both of which fluctuated greatly. There was little diversification except in Alberta, which began to produce small quantities of oil and gas.

BC's economic evolution before 1929 was very different. There was little agricultural land, and most farm products were locally consumed. There were few European residents except fur traders until the Cariboo GOLD RUSH of the 1850s. After the gold was gone, coal mining on Vancouver I was no substitute, and until well after Confederation the population grew very slowly. However, with the construction of the CPR and that of the CANADIAN NORTHERN RAILWAY and GRAND TRUNK PACIFIC RAILWAY between 1900 and 1914, much more rapid development and urbanization occurred. Important activities were lumbering, the fisheries and copper, silver, coal and base metal mining in the south. Ranching and fruit-growing were also established. Some industries, especially shipbuilding and repairing, were set up, and the great smelter at TRAIL came into operation in 1920. With regular transpacific sailings to the Far East and Australasia, Vancouver became an important port, not only for the province's own goods but for prairie grain. After the Panama Canal opened in 1914, trade with Britain became faster and much cheaper. Coastal shipping also developed, partly to serve the lumber trade. Thanks to urban growth, there was rapid development of hydroelectricity. There was very large immigration not only from elsewhere in Canada but from Britain and Asia. Oriental immigration was much feared and rigidly controlled, although a small Oriental community did develop.

From 1914 to the late 1940s, especially during the Great Depression, conditions were often difficult. All 4 provinces felt themselves to be the victims of Canada's tariff policy, which raised the price of the manufactured goods that came from elsewhere, but did nothing for the price of the primary products and simple processed goods which they had to sell. Prairie drought, adverse price movements and foreign protective tendencies, as in the 1920-22 recession and the slump of 1929-33, were serious matters. Ottawa provided relief money, protected the provincial governments from bankruptcy, and tried through trade negotiations to improve the conditions for western exports (*see* OTTAWA AGREEMENTS). After the collapse of the co-operative wheat pools in 1929-30, Ottawa also supported the marketing of prairie wheat, although until the middle of WWII the farmers could market their wheat through private channels if they wished. Wartime prosperity helped western farmers pay off their debts. In BC, meanwhile, co-operative marketing increased for such goods as apples and peaches. But new manufacturing plants were slow to appear. By 1939 a Ford assembly plant near Vancouver supplied export markets in India and the Pacific, but when these markets vanished after 1939 the plant vanished too. WWII saw a rapid development of shipbuilding and aircraft construction on the West Coast, but after the war these industries dwindled or vanished.

The years after 1945 saw new resource-based development, rapid urbanization and dramatic increases in standards of living. The most striking new projects were in oil, gas, pipeline-building and potash, which transformed the economies of Alberta and Saskatchewan. BC began to produce oil and gas; BC and Manitoba acquired immense new hydroelectric plants, and aluminum smelting began at KITIMAT, BC, in 1951. There were new export markets, as oil and gas moved to Ontario and the US and BC coal and lumber products moved to Japan. Prairie wheat, which gradually lost its old markets in Britain and Europe, eventually found new markets in communist countries and the Third World. Federal policy was helpful: Ottawa began to make EQUALIZATION PAYMENTS to Manitoba and Saskatchewan, and it provided a protected Ontario market for expensive Alberta oil 1960-73, although thereafter it held oil prices below world levels. It also reduced or removed many tariffs. Lumbering, pulp and paper expanded, and most of the time did well because of the N American construction and communication booms. In 1967 the exploitation of Alberta's tar sands (*see* BITUMEN) began. By 1984 Alberta had developed a petrochemical industry and Manitoba was producing buses and light aircraft. Yet the western provinces remained heavily dependent on the export of a few primary products and on the investment activity which the primary industries could generate. The West remained "development-minded" as it had been between 1896 and 1914.

In 1867 Canada's economy was smaller and more agrarian than it was by the early 1980s. By then most Canadians had become city dwellers, and the majority of workers were in white-collar jobs, generally in the service-producing industries. Disparities in earnings, living standards and ways of life had been much reduced, especially after 1945. Nevertheless the various regional economies were still very different. Manufacturing remained largely a matter for Ontario and Québec, while the 4 western provinces still generated immense surpluses of natural products. In the Atlantic provinces, living standards remained comparatively low and prospects were much less bright. Partly for this reason, interregional subsidies have become deeply entrenched in Canada's way of life.

IAN M. DRUMMOND

Reading: W.T. Easterbrook and Hugh Aitken, *Canadian Economic History* (1956); W.L. Marr and D.G. Paterson, *Canada: An Economic History* (1980); R. Pomfret, *The Economic Development of Canada* (1981).

Economic Nationalism, in Canada, is a movement aimed at achieving greater control by Canadians of their own economy. In recent years it arose in response to the high degree of foreign (especially American) control of the Canadian economy. Two separate strands of economic nationalism can be distinguished. The first, protectionism in trade — the establishment of a system of tariffs to favour domestic production of goods and discourage imports — dates at least to the NATIONAL POLICY of 1879. The policy was partly intended to encourage the creation of an industrial base in Canada by protecting so-called "infant industries" against the competition of larger and more established firms abroad. The second, which is concerned with the ownership of Canadian businesses by foreigners, is largely a post-WWII phenomenon, although some foreign direct investment did exist prior to 1940 as a classic 1936 study, *Canadian-American Industry,* revealed.

The rapid increase of foreign ownership in the Canadian economy after WWII was linked to the rise of the MULTINATIONAL CORPORATION. Various multinationals realized they could bypass tariff restrictions by building and operating their own branch plants (or subsidiaries) inside Canada. As these foreign-owned corporations proliferated, economic nationalists became concerned with the special problems created by this type of investment, particularly the truncated (stunted and distorted) pattern of economic development. Such investment also tended to shift control over economic decision making outside Canada to the head offices of these foreign corporations. Economic nationalists began to demand legislation to monitor the activities and to restrain the growth of foreign ownership in the Canadian economy.

Anti-nationalists generally responded to both stands of economic nationalism by emphasizing the benefits of a "free and unhampered" trade with all nations and the doctrine of economics known as the law of comparative advantage, according to which economic growth will be maximized when government restraint, eg, tariffs on trade flows, is minimized and all countries specialize in the goods they produce best and trade freely with each other. Although this argument is only relevant to trade protectionism, it was extended to cover foreign direct investment — foreign-owned firms would succeed in establishing themselves in Canada only to the extent that they could produce their goods more cheaply than local firms, thus benefitting Canadian consumers and the Canadian economy; therefore foreign investment ought to be freely permitted for the same reason as "free trade." This argument depends implicitly upon the assumption of a competitive economic environment with free markets where flexible prices prevail for both flows of goods and of capital. It is this very assumption that economic nationalists questioned by indicating the peculiar economic and political features of the extension of multinationals and of the American presence in the Canadian economy.

The concerns of economic nationalists were articulated in a series of 4 government-sponsored reports drawn up over the past several decades. The first, on Canada's Economic Prospects (1957-58), known as the Gordon Commission after its chairman, Walter L. GORDON, was established in response to the growing tide of foreign ownership in the Canadian economy, estimated at that time to be about 40%. The Gordon report was moderate; it noted the growth of foreign direct investment, concluded that perhaps "legitimate Canadian interests" were being compromised in the process, and recommended that Canadians be permitted at least part ownership in foreign-owned subsidiaries operating in Canada.

The governments of that period did not pay much attention to the report. Throughout the early 1960s it was the anti-nationalists, best represented by Professor Harry Johnson, who dominated the debate. Johnson argued that nationalism "has been diverting Canada into a narrow and garbage-cluttered cul-de-sac" and that economic nationalism was an emotional reaction founded upon selfish, middle-class interests. Canada and Canadian workers in particular, he argued, would benefit by the removal of all restrictions to trade and foreign direct investment, for nothing would raise the level of economic activity and boost incomes more rapidly.

However, a new current of economic nationalism emerged in the 1960s, best exemplified by some of the essays published by the University League for Social Reform in *Nationalism in Canada* (1966). The book was followed by 3 more government-sponsored reports in the late 1960s and early 1970s which described various problems created by foreign-owned subsidiaries operating in Canada. For example, Canadian branch plants generally did not conduct research and development and lacked the facilities to do so. They also lacked full-fledged marketing and purchasing departments because these functions would often be managed by the parent firm in the US or Europe. Consequently, Canadian initiatives in developing new technology and in the design and marketing of products were retarded. Because the companies were directed from abroad, Canadian managers and management were not able to develop to their full potential. A dependence on various US capabilities was slowly being built into the structure of Canadian industry, leaving it less able to adapt to change and international competition. There were other problems also, including the lack of Canadian directors on the boards of foreign-owned subsidiaries, and the tendency of branch plants to purchase their production inputs from the parent firm's suppliers abroad, thereby reducing the number of orders for Canadian companies. The ability of the head office to establish prices for both inputs and outputs ("transfer prices") of their subsidiaries made it possible to maintain balance sheets to reduce taxes payable to the Canadian government.

Extraterritoriality — the tendency of the American government to assert legal jurisdiction over the branch plants of US-based firms operating in other countries — is a major political problem. Under the Foreign Assets Control Regulations (Trading with the Enemy Act), the Sherman Act and Section 7 of the Clayton Anti-Trust Act, the American government retained for itself the primary jurisdiction in deciding with which countries its foreign subsidiaries could or could not trade, when they might or might not discuss mergers and various other functions. Canadian sovereignty in this regard has been compromised, for despite various negotiated administrative accommodations the US has successfully retained primary jurisdiction over its subsidiaries abroad.

In response to these various problems, a number of policies were recommended in 3 government studies. The Watkins Task Force, in its 1968 report FOREIGN OWNERSHIP AND THE STRUCTURE OF CANADIAN INVESTMENT, recommended the creation of a special agency to co-ordinate government policies and programs dealing with multinational corporations. One of its tasks would be the gathering of more information on their activities in Canada, enabling the government to better monitor their behaviour. The Wahn Report, published in 1970 (*The Eleventh Report of the Standing Committee on External Affairs and National Defence Respecting Canada-U.S. Relations*), reiterated this recommendation, suggested that Canadians attempt to secure 51% ownership in foreign firms, and recommended, as the Watkins Report had done, stringent laws to countervail American extraterritorial jurisdiction. These laws would effectively make it illegal for corporations operating in Canada to refuse legitimate export orders from any country, regardless of the nature of that country's diplomatic relations with the US. It also proposed that future takeovers of Canadian businesses by foreign-owned firms require the consent of a control bureau such as the one outlined by the Watkins Report. And finally certain "key sectors" of the economy would be identified, "where no further takeovers would be allowed." The 1972 *Foreign Direct Investment in Canada,* known as the Gray Report after its chairman, Herb GRAY, again recommended the creation of a "screening agency," but also specified the particular areas that should be considered in the decision to permit or forbid a foreign direct investment proposal. For example, a foreign firm contemplating the purchase or erection of a plant in Canada might be questioned regarding the need for its particular products (would it only duplicate products already available in Canada?), the nature of the technology to be employed in comparison with technology available in Canada, employment possibilities, its plans for research and development and product innovation in Canada, plans for purchasing materials, components and services in Canada.

On the basis of these reports, nationalist sentiment crystallized in Canada in various ways in the 1970s. Several organizations and lobby groups arose, eg, the COMMITTEE FOR AN INDEPENDENT CANADA (CIC), which was formed in 1970. Its members, from a broad array of professions and geographic locations and from all 3 major political parties, wanted to involve concerned citizens in a campaign to influence governments across Canada to adopt the "legislative policies that will significantly diminish the influence presently exerted by outside powers . . . on Canadian life." The CIC produced a number of books on economic nationalism and provided an important forum for nationalist policy proposals.

As a result of recommendations in the Watkins, Wahn and Gray reports, the FOREIGN INVESTMENT REVIEW AGENCY (FIRA), was established in 1974 to review all proposals for foreign takeovers of existing businesses or the creation of new foreign-owned businesses in Canada, for the purpose of ensuring maximum benefits to Canadians from these enterprises. FIRA was structured very closely upon the recommendations of the Gray Report, and Herb Gray became its first chairman. However, because Canadian and foreign businesses complained that FIRA's lengthy review procedures effectively impeded new foreign direct investment, its procedures were revised in 1982. The shorter and less complicated "small business" review procedure now applies to all proposals involving businesses with less than $5 million in gross assets and less than 200 employees (in contrast with the previous ceiling of $2 million and 100 employees).

The National Energy Program (NEP), established by the Liberal government in 1980, also emerged from the movement for economic nationalism. It was created to guarantee the security of Canada's energy supply (in particular, to end Canadian dependence on world oil and gas supplies) and to provide Canadians with the opportunity to increase their ownership of the energy industry. The original goal was 50% ownership of Canadian oil and gas production by 1990. With the revenues from a new tax imposed upon all oil and gas producers in Canada the government has funded the Petroleum Incentives Program, under which monies are redistributed to Canadian companies investing in the energy industry. Canadian control of the energy sector increased from 22.3% to 33.1% in the first 2 years.

The NEP was heavily censured by critics of the former Liberal government, who claimed that the purchase of foreign assets under the NEP was made at inflated prices and extremely high interest rates. They also asserted that the NEP financially crippled Canadian energy companies by overextending their investment capabilities and is itself nothing more than a gigantic "revenue grab" on the part of the federal government. Advocates of the program concede that bad luck and high interest rates have dogged the NEP, but insist the program itself was necessary in order to allow Canadians to share in the enormous profits of tens of billions of dollars that would otherwise have flowed almost exclusively into foreign hands.

Economic nationalism, it is important to realize, can best be understood in the broader context of Canadian dependence on the US. In entertainment, publishing, magazines, education, defence, the media, etc, American influences have threatened to become overwhelming, adding impetus to the arguments of economic nationalists who understood themselves to be fighting for the survival of a Canadian way of life. What was seen by anti-nationalists as self-interested protectionism prompted by vested interests at the expense of the economic welfare of the Canadian public as a whole could better be regarded as a countermovement for the protection of Canadian society. ABRAHAM ROTSTEIN

Reading: H.G.J. Aiken, *American Capital and Canadian Resources* (1961); H.G. Johnson, *The Canadian Quandary* (1963, repr 1970); *Foreign Ownership and the Structure of Canadian Industry* (1968); *Foreign Direct Investment in Canada* (1972); H. Marshall, F. Southhard, Jr, and K.W. Taylor, *Canadian-American Industry: A Study in International Investment* (1936, repr 1976); P. Resnick, *Independence: The Canadian Challenge* (1972); Royal Commission on Canada's Economic Prospects, *Final Report* (1975).

Economic Regulation, a form of government intervention designed to influence the behaviour of firms and individuals in the private sector. Other forms include public expenditures, taxes, government ownership, loans and loan guarantees, tax expenditures, equity interests in private companies and moral suasion. Defined as the "imposition of rules by a government, backed by the use of penalties, that are intended specifically to modify the economic behavior of individuals and firms in the private sector," regulation in general is aimed at narrowing choices in certain areas, including prices (airline fares, minimum wages, certain agricultural products, telephone rates), supply (broadcasting licences, occupational licensing, agricultural production quotas, pipeline certificates "of public convenience and necessity"), rate of return (public utilities, pipelines), disclosure of information (securities prospectuses, content labelling), methods of production (effluent standards, worker health and safety standards), standards for products or services (safety of children's toys, quality or purity of food products, Canadian-content requirements in broadcasting) and conditions of service (requirements to act as a common carrier or not to discriminate in hiring or selling goods and services).

Governments use economic regulation to improve the efficiency with which society's resources are allocated, to alter the distribution of income and to achieve broad social or cultural goals. Improving economic efficiency may involve the regulation of monopolies, which by restricting output and raising prices may restrict the production of the socially optimal amount of goods or services. Regulation may be used in situations in which costs are not paid by those responsible, eg, the social costs of extensive pollution caused by private firms. Because of interdependencies in the utilization of collectively owned resources, government management is necessary to prevent the over exploitation of fish, whales and forests; the reduction of pressure of oil and gas wells so the total amount recovered may be less than what is economically feasible under single ownership; and overcrowding of the broadcasting spectrum.

Government also imposes regulations to alter the distribution of income partly to prevent monopoly profits and certain kinds of price discrimination, which were the justification offered for the regulation of both the railroads in the 19th century and of UTILITIES early in the 20th century. Regulation was an attempt to prevent unjust discrimination and to ensure that consumers were charged "fair and reasonable" rates, terms still used in regulatory statutes. Regulation may also be used to reduce the speed of economic change and the redistribution of income through administrative processes, a justification based on the notion that the public is generally averse to risk and that the marketplace, with its sometimes abrupt changes, unfairly distributes income. Finally, regulation may be used to confer benefits on certain customers at the expense of others (cross-subsidization).

Regulation has been used extensively in Canada in the pursuit of social and cultural goals, including nation building through the provision of transportation infrastructure (*see* TRANSPORTATION POLICY) and the promotion of national unity and cultural identification (broadcasting and Canadian-content regulations; *see* CANADIAN RADIO-TELEVISION AND TELECOMMUNICATIONS COMMISSION). There have also been attempts to increase domestic ownership of business enterprises by restricting foreign ownership in certain sectors, eg, broadcasting and banking (*see* ECONOMIC NATIONALISM). Direct and social regulation are conventionally distinguished from each other. Through the former, the price structure (rates, tariffs, fees, etc), the conditions of entry and exit or the level of output are altered. A specific regime of direct regulation is confined to a single industry, although quite a number of industries are subject to direct regulation, eg, airlines, railroads, telecommunications, certain agricultural products, pipelines, taxicabs (in some cities) and broadcasting. Social regulation, on the other hand, is usually concerned with methods of production, attributes of a product or service, or disclosure of information. It typically affects a wide range of industries although its impact on different industries will vary enormously. It includes government rule making on environmental protection, health and safety, fairness (human rights, protection against fraud, deception or inaccuracy), culture (content, language), land use and building codes. Both the federal and provincial government exercise significant regulatory responsibilities with respect to environmental protection, natural resources, the marketing of farm products, occupational health and safety, human rights, consumer protection, human health protection, employment standards and financial institutions.

The amount of government regulation has been measured in a variety of ways. For example, the Economic Council's researchers have estimated that in Canada 29% of Gross Domestic Product at factor costs was subject to direct regulation in 1978. The comparable figure for the US was 26%, although these measures do not reflect the stringency of the controls, which varies enormously. It has been estimated that federal government expenditures in 1977-78 on regulation amounted to only 1.6% of total budgetary expenditures. Employees involved in regulatory activity in federal departments and agencies accounted for 6% of total federal employment. None of these regulatory expenditures, however, indicates the vastly larger indirect effects of regulation on private-sector activity.

In the 1970s, federal regulation increased in both Canada and the US. Of the 140 federal economic regulatory statutes enacted in Canada at the end of 1978, 25 were enacted between 1970 and 1978. An additional 11 had been passed earlier but were reenacted in the 1970s. More new federal regulatory statutes were passed in that period than were passed between 1940 and 1969. The new statutes were enacted primarily in the areas of environmental protection, health and safety, and consumer protection. In 1978 the Economic Council concluded that 1608 provincial regulatory statutes existed, 262 of which had been enacted since 1970.

Two different kinds of efforts to reform regulation in Canada have been underway for at least 5 years. The first consists of studies, conducted largely by the federal government or its agencies, focusing on the REGULATORY PROCESS, eg those conducted for the LAW REFORM COMMISSION, the Institute for Research on Public Policy, the ONTARIO ECONOMIC COUNCIL, the Economic Council of Canada and the Canadian Consumer Council. Official inquiries include those of the Ontario Professional Organizations Committee and Commission on Freedom of Information and Individual Privacy; the Regulation Reference of the Economic Council of Canada; the Parliamentary Task Force on Regulatory Reform (Peterson Committee); and the Royal Commission on Financial Management and Accountability (the Lambert Commission). Generally, all the studies have recommended the requirement of an *ex ante* review of proposed regulations using cost benefit analysis, earlier and more extensive consultation, the establishment of a regulatory agenda, the institutionalization of periodic *ex post* review of existing regulatory programs, the replacement of appeals to Cabinet by government policy directives, clearer definition of regulatory mandates in statutes and regulation, closer scrutiny of proposed new regulations and evaluation of existing ones by the legislature, and the improvement of the access and funding of public-interest groups. The second kind of effort, which has been largely independent of the first, consists of a series of decisions by regulatory agencies or changes in government policy which have liberalized direct regulation in airlines, telecommunications, banking and the brokerage industry.

The loosening of regulatory constraints and the increase of competition in the airline industry was accomplished first by a series of steps between 1977 and 1979 to remove the capacity restrictions on CP Air, allowing them to compete more effectively with Air Canada; second, under the 1978 Air Canada Act, the crown corporation became subject to the same statutory provisions and regulations as other carriers until 1959 Air Canada had a monopoly on all transcontinental traffic); third, beginning in 1973, but particularly in the late 1970s, regulations governing both international and domestic charter flights were seriously altered, resulting in an increase in the range of services offered, a reduction of the various "fences," eg, advance-booking periods, length of stay, etc, and an enormous growth in low-cost discretionary travel; fourth, beginning in 1978 the Canadian Transport Commission permitted Canadian airlines to introduce a variety of discount fares. Following hearings requested by the minister of transport, the CTC decided in mid-1984 to give airlines more freedom in setting fares, and to reduce (but not eliminate) the restrictions on entry by new carriers and existing carriers into new routes.

Regulatory and policy decisions that have resulted in a loosening of regulatory restrictions and increased competition in the telecommunications industry stemmed from technological change. For example, technology has undermined the natural-monopoly rationale for government regulation of the telephone industry. In the 1970s the CRTC began to distinguish between the monopoly provision of transmission services from the supply of terminal equipment, eg, the basic black telephone, data terminals, etc. Following the terminal attachment decisions concerning Bell Canada and BC Tel in the early 1980s, subscribers were able to own their own terminal equipment. As a result, there has been a high degree of competition for the supply and maintenance of such equipment. Increased competition has also been greatly facilitated by the CRTC's decision in May 1979 regarding system interconnection. Customers of CNCP Telecommunications can now enjoy dial access to CNCP's data networks and private-line services. While CNCP cannot offer direct competition with unit-toll, voice long-distance or WATS services, it does offer strong competition for data transmission, private lines and telex services. The greatest barrier to increased competition for long-distance voice transmission is the extensive cross-subsidization of local exchange services by high long-distance rates. In Oct 1984, the CRTC began hearings to determine whether competition should be permitted in unit-toll, voice long-distance service as is the case in the US.

The new Bank Act (1980) appears to liberalize BANKING regulation further. It is easier to establish a new bank, and existing financial institutions can be converted into banks. Foreign banks are now permitted to enter the industry but are limited collectively to 8% of total domestic banking assets, a figure they have now attained and have lobbied successfully to double. By mid-1984 more than 60 foreign banks had been chartered and many argue they will increase competition in various aspects of commercial lending and export business. The effect of these and other regulatory requirements will be to raise the new entrants' costs and make them less competitive in lending to small and medium-size businesses, where more competition is needed. Other changes in the new Bank Act seem to encourage competition in other aspects of banking.

In general, Canada has experienced much less regulatory reform (including deregulation) in the area of direct regulation than has occured in the US since 1975. W.T. STANBURY

Reading: Economic Council of Canada, *Reforming Regulations* (1981); W.T. Stanbury and F. Thompson, *Regulatory Reform in Canada* (1982).

Economics involves the study of 3 interrelated issues: the allocation of RESOURCES used for the satisfaction of human wants; the INCOME DISTRIBUTION among individuals and groups; and the determination of the level of national output and employment. Economists investigate these issues from either the perspective of microeconomics, an analysis of the behaviour of the individual units in the national economy, including business firms, workers and consumers; or of macroeconomics, the study of the larger aggregates in the economy, such as total investment and consumption, the average levels of INTEREST rates and price indexes, and total employment and UNEMPLOYMENT.

Economic research consists primarily of the formulation of theories that seek to explain observable events, such as variations in Canadian exports of pulp and paper or Canadian purchases of computers, and the testing of theories by comparison of their implications or predictions with actual events. Theories and tests may be either formal and mathematical, or informal and based on nonmathematical discourse. The formulation and testing of both kinds of theories in Canada has been greatly aided by the growth of a reliable body of national statistical data on economic phenomena which followed the founding of the Dominion Bureau of Statistics in 1918.

The trend of economic research over the past 50 years has been toward reliance on increasingly sophisticated mathematical models and formal statistical tests, to the despair of some critics in the profession who argue that the discipline tends to ignore or distort human behaviour and institutional complexity, which are not easily amenable to such analysis. Mathematical models often focus on the concept of equilibrium, a situation in which producers and consumers of a good are assumed to be maximizing their incomes and utility subject to their initial wealth and to market prices, and have in the course of their trading found a consistent or equilibrium price that maintains the outputs and purchases of all parties. The models allow comparisons of equilibrium positions after a change in a particular parameter; for example, with a formal mathematical model of production in the plastics industry, the impact of a substantial increase in the price of oil on equilibrium output, employment and oil consumption in the industry can be determined, on the assumption that the industry seeks to minimize its costs of production.

Such "state" equilibrium analysis has often been criticized for its lack of attention to the dynamic elements of adjustment to changes such as resource discovery, population change, technical innovation, managerial initiative and investment undertaken when future market conditions are uncertain. Critics also charge that such an analysis does not deal adequately with either sustained long-term national growth or the so-called BUSINESS CYCLE of successive peaks and troughs in macroeconomic variables. Among the critics are the post-Keynesian economists (*see* KEYNESIAN ECONOMICS), who stress the dynamic analysis and emphasis on uncertainty in the work of John Maynard Keynes, a British economist who founded modern macroeconomics with his book, *The General Theory of Employment, Interest, and Money* (1936). Other critics of formal mathematical equilibrium models stress the role of politics and institutions in economic affairs, often focusing on the inequality and dependency among persons, groups and nations which they see as characteristic of advanced industrial societies. There are many such schools of thought, including MARXISM, institutionalism, POLITICAL ECONOMY and radical economics (*see* ECONOMICS, RADICAL). For years many economics programs at Canadian universities were formally associated with POLITICAL SCIENCE in departments of political economy or economics and politics. To the dismay of many institutionalist economists, most of such joint departments have by now been formally split.

Econometrics, the branch of economics that deals with statistical tests of economic theories, has become an essential part of economic analysis over the past 2 decades, through its use in evaluating alternative policy decisions and theoretical models. Econometrics has been subject to criticism in recent years, primarily for the unfortunate practice of presenting statistical results from nonexperimental data as definitive, when in fact they are at best suggestive. There is concern about the advancement of economics as a scientific discipline, because statistical tests are often inadequate for distinguishing among competing theories.

Canadian economics and economists are in constant interaction with economics and economists in the UK, Europe, the US and elsewhere, and it is thus no more possible to define a "Canadian" economics today than it would be to define a Canadian chemistry. Nonetheless the practice of economics in Canada has been strongly influenced by the distinctive demography and geography of the country — its large land base and relatively small population, and its proximity to a country with a national economy 10 times larger than its own. Professional economists generally specialize in one or more fields of the discipline and Canadian economists have been particularly drawn to fields such as the economics of INTERNATIONAL TRADE and investment, resource economics and transportation economics. However, there is important work being done in Canada in all major fields of economics, including ECONOMIC HISTORY, economic growth of underdeveloped economies, mathematical economics, industrial organization, labour economics, money and BANKING, public finance, urban and REGIONAL ECONOMICS and econometrics.

Until the 1920s most writing on economics in Canada was done by government officials, businessmen and citizens in other occupations concerned with certain issues of public policy, eg, the best methods of settlement on new lands, the relative advantages of free trade and tariff protection, and government control of currency and banking. Of the many pioneers of economics in Canada, 3 names stand out: Adam Shortt and W.A. Mackintosh, both of Queen's University, and Harold INNIS of U of T. Shortt, appointed lecturer in political economy at Queen's, edited several volumes of documents on currency, finance and constitutional issues in Canada, and organized the remarkable 22-volume study, *Canada and its Provinces* (1913-17), containing a wealth of material on Canadian economic development and public policy. W.A. Mackintosh edited volumes on western settlement and historical statistics but is best known as the author of *The Economic Background of Dominion-Provincial Relations* (1939), a classic economic history of post-Confederation Canada written as a background study for the Rowell-Sirois Royal Commission. In 1930 Innis published *The Fur Trade in Canada: An Introduction to Canadian Economic History,* a masterly survey of the importance of the trade in beaver furs in the 17th and 18th centuries and its decline in the face of the expanding settlement. His subsequent volume *The Cod Fisheries* (1940) and *Empire and Communications* (1950) and his many essays established him as Canada's most influential economic historian. Innis emphasized the role of staple exports — such as fur, fish, timber and wheat — in Canada's economic, political and social development, establishing what came to be known as the STAPLE THESIS.

International trade and investment has long been an important area of research for Canadian economists. This area was surveyed in 1924 by Jacob Viner, a Montréal-born economist who taught at University of Chicago and Princeton University, in his classic volume, *Canada's Balance of International Indebtedness, 1900-1913.* Canada's foremost trade economist was Harry G. Johnson, author of *The Canadian Quandary* (1977), who also wrote scores of articles on the pure theory of international trade, the BALANCE OF PAYMENTS and Canadian economic policy with regard to international trade and investment. Johnson, who published over 500 scientific papers and 19 books from 1947 to 1977, also made important contributions to macroeconomics, particularly in the areas of domestic and international monetary economics. Johnson's outspoken commitment to free trade and the free movement of international investment was not without its critics among Canadian nationalists, including Abraham Rotstein and Mel Watkins of U of T, who argued that Canadian economic dependence on the US necessarily implied political and cultural dependence and led ultimately to a lowering of the Canadian standard of living.

Economic research in French Canada in the 20th century has been centered at École des hautes études commerciales (HEC), founded in Montréal in 1970; Université de Montréal, which began its École des sciences sociales in 1921; and Université Laval, whose Faculté des sciences sociales was founded in 1938. HEC began publication of an economics journal, *L'Actualité économique,* in 1925, 10 years before the inauguration of the *Canadian Journal of Economics and Political Science* in 1935, and 4 decades before that of the *Canadian Journal of Economics* in 1968. Leading French Canadian economists from 1900 to 1945 included Robert Errol Bouchette, a civil servant, and Édouard Montpetit of HEC, who both wrote on the importance to French Canadian development of a knowledge of economics and participation in business affairs; Henry Laureys of HEC, who wrote on Canadian exports; and E. Minville, who wrote on social aspects of economic development in Québec. Important research after 1945 included that of Maurice LAMONTAGNE and Albert Faucher, whose 1953 paper on the "History of Industrial Development" in Québec explained the province's lag in industrialization in terms of geographical and technological factors, rather than cultural differences, an analysis developed at length in Faucher's *Québec en Amérique au XIXe siècle* (1973); that of André Raynauld, who wrote a classic study of *Croissance et structure économiques de la province du Québec* (1961); and that of Roger Dehem, who published widely in the field of economic theory.

There has been a virtual explosion of economic research in Canada over the last 2 decades, fueled by a rapid expansion of graduate programs and a seemingly insatiable demand in the public and private sectors.

Harold Adams Innis *(courtesy Public Archives of Canada/ C-3407).*

A taste of the wide variety of topics treated by Canadian economists is reflected in the annual Harold A. Innis Memorial Lecture, an invited public address by a distinguished economist to the Canadian Economics Association, which meets each spring. The lecture is published in the November issue of the *Canadian Journal of Economics* and generally contains an excellent bibliography of Canadian and foreign research on the topic in question. In 1980 the Innis Lecture was delivered by Thomas Courchene of U of Western Ontario. In "Towards a Protected Society: the Politicization of Economic Life," Courchene analysed the growth of government legislation designed to increase economic security for individuals and groups, with particular reference to the generally poor economic conditions after 1973 and to competition among governments in Canada's federal system. He concluded with an appeal to his fellow economists to educate the general public better about the workings of the market mechanism, and to incorporate more real-world, nonmarket institutions in their economic theorizing. In 1981 John Helliwell of UBC discussed "Canadian Energy Policy," arguing that raising Canadian energy prices to world levels would result in relatively large gains in economic efficiency and relatively small increases in inflation. Using a formal econometric model, he showed the impact of higher oil prices on inflation, potential output and economic rents, with special attention to the way in which interprovincial revenue sharing could produce a more equitable distribution among the regions of the benefits of higher oil prices. The 1982 Innis Lecture, by Samuel Hollander of U of T, dealt with the rise, led by William Jevons and Léon Walras, of marginalist economics in the 1870s in Europe, and its relation to the work of earlier British economists such as David Ricardo and John Stuart Mill. Against the widespread notion of a "marginalist revolution," Hollander argues there was substantial continuity in economic theory during the 19th century. In 1983 Anthony Scott of UBC lectured on "Property Rights and Property Wrongs," focusing on the role of property rights to land in the use and management of such resources as ground and inland water supplies, fisheries, forests and oil pools (*see* RESOURCE RIGHTS). Scott argues that common-law rights, as defined by intermittent litigation, must sometimes be modified or replaced by government legislation or regulation to ensure efficient resource use. The 1984 Innis Lecture, by John Whalley of Western, concerned the issue of tax incidence, the study of who actually pays a given tax; for example the burden of an increase in the corporate-profits tax may be borne by the corporation's shareholders, or passed on in higher prices to the consumers of the corporation's products. Whalley reviews the different theoretical and statistical approaches used in estimating tax incidence, and concludes that while economists have many useful things to say on the topic, the complexity of modern economic institutions results in a great deal of uncertainty about who ultimately pays a given tax.

Unemployment and Inflation Perhaps the major reason for the growth of economics as a field of study over the past 2 decades has been its increasing importance in public-policy formation in areas such as TAXATION, income security, resource development, and federal-provincial financial relations. The issues of unemployment and inflation illustrate the interaction between economics and public policy.

The Canadian economy in the 1970s was plagued by STAGFLATION, ie, sharp increases in unemployment and inflation, and a sustained slowdown in the rate of growth of real output and productivity. Both problems led to a remarkable volume of theoretical and applied work in Canada. The most disconcerting aspect of the increases in unemployment and inflation was their temporal coincidence. Economists were accustomed to thinking of unemployment and inflation as alternative evils to be avoided. It was not easy to explain the concurrent increase in both problems during the 1970s, or suggest how government policy should respond to the new economic development.

The dominant view of inflation and unemployment until the mid-1970s was summarized in the "Phillips Curve," which showed a negative relation between inflation and unemployment, with more of one implying less of the other. Periods of high unemployment in Canada, such as the 1930s, and the recession years of 1958 to 1962, tended to have low inflation while inflation tended to accelerate in boom years with low unemployment, as in the period 1947 to 1951 and in the late 1960s. Much of the statistical work by Canadian economists was devoted to estimating the coefficients of the Phillips Curve, with a view to understanding how much inflation was necessary to lower the unemployment rate by one percent. The Phillips Curve literature in Canada is reviewed in S.F. Kaliski, *The Trade-off Between Inflation and Unemployment: Some Explorations of the Recent Evidence for Canada* (1972); among the best-known estimates in the 1960s were those of R.G. Bodkin et al in *Price Stability and High Employment: The Options for Canadian Economic Policy* (1966).

In the 1970s the simple trade-off between unemployment and inflation implied in the Phillips Curve broke down; the unemployment rate rose from 4.5% in 1968 to 5.5% in 1973, 8.4% in 1978 and 7.6% in 1981; the annual inflation rate for the Consumer Price Index in Canada for these same 4 years rose from 4.0% to 7.6%, 8.9% and 12.5%. Economists differed greatly in their interpretation of these new trends. The Keynesians tended to focus on particular institutional and demographic events to explain the inflation of the 1970s, with special emphasis on the sharp increases in oil and other commodity prices in 1973-74 and 1979-80. They stressed the danger of fighting such inflation with restrictive MONETARY POLICY and FISCAL POLICY, which would result in unacceptable increases in the UNEMPLOYMENT rate. Unemployment had risen in part because of the large increases in the LABOUR FORCE as the BABY BOOM generation entered the LABOUR MARKET, and as the participation of WOMEN IN THE LABOUR FORCE increased in an unprecedented manner. Some Keynesians therefore argued fo reimposition in the 1980s of the federal government's WAGE AND PRICE CONTROLS of 1975 to 1978, which they credited with slowing the inflation caused by the oil price shock of 1973-74. The Keynesian case is set out in Clarence Barber and John McCallum, *Unemployment and Inflation: The Canadian Experience* (1980).

Monetarist economists had a very different view of inflation and unemployment, as explained in a volume by Thomas J. Courchene, *Money, Inflation, and the Bank of Canada* (1976). The monetarists argued that inflation was caused by excessive expansion of the Canadian MONEY supply by the BANK OF CANADA, and that the Bank should be charged with responsibility for fighting inflation by reducing the rate of growth of the money supply. In 1975 the governor of the Bank of Canada, Gerald BOUEY, announced the adoption of monetarist principles in future bank policy, which would be directed at a gradual reduction in the growth of the money supply until inflation was eliminated. This was easier said than done: the annual rate of growth of the money supply (defined here as currency and demand chequing deposits) was reduced from 13.8% in 1975 to 8.0% in 1976, but then increased to 10% in 1978. From Nov 1981 to Nov 1982, the money supply actually fell by 6.2% as the economy dove into the worst recession since the 1930s. By Oct 1982 the money supply was no higher than its level of 2 years earlier, but then it rebounded, growing by 13.3% to Sept 1983, when Bouey announced that the monetarist experiment was over.

The severe recession of 1981-82 reduced inflation to an annual rate of about 5%, but at the cost of an unemployment rate of over 11% in 1982, 1983 and 1984. Government and private agencies forecast high unemployment to the end of the 1980s and beyond. Canadian economists were divided as to how much stimulation the government should apply to the economy in order to bring the unemployment rate down. The divisions reflected not only different evaluations of the real costs of unemployment and inflation, but also great uncertainty about the possible trade-offs between the 2 policy goals of high employment and stable prices.

Government policy, as reflected in the federal budgets of April 1983 and Feb 1984, eschewed strong stimulation of the economy. High interest rates in the US constrained Canadian monetary policy in the early 1980s because monetary expansion would weaken the value of the Canadian dollar, whose value in US funds fell from 94¢ in 1977, to 83¢ in 1981, to 76¢ in the summer of 1984. The high budget deficits of the early 1980s undoubtedly inhibited federal economic policies; sustained inflation and recession had both increased the deficit. The most effective methods for controlling inflation and reducing unemployment will remain one of the central areas of economic research in Canada over the next decade, as economists revise their theories and hone their statistical tests in order to achieve a better understanding of how to improve Canada's macroeconomic performance.

The generally poor economic performance of industrial economies over the past decade has been a sobering experience for economists in Canada and elsewhere. The increasing sophistication in mathematics and statistics that has marked the discipline over the past 2 decades has not been associated with better control over the economy. Yet this humbling experience may in the end be a positive one if it induces economists to expend more energy and creativity in the revision of their models and policy proposals. Economics should continue to flourish as a field of study in Canada over the next decade, both in pure research and in response to demands for applied work from the public and private sectors.

PAUL DAVENPORT

Economics, Radical The word "radical" popularly denotes a sharp departure from conventional, orthodox interpretations of reality. The term "radical economics" is used to label the work and ideas of those (usually political economists) who take a so-called left-wing perspective on the discipline of ECONOMICS, on the development and operation of capitalist and other economies, and on institutions of power and control. There are, and have always been, orthodox and radical streams of economic thought. The specific contents of orthodoxy and radicalism shift from one generation to another as new problems arise in the economy. There have also always been variants of orthodoxy and of radicalism. The presence of so many contending schools of thought produces a persistent tension within economics that mirrors, within the sphere of ideas, persistent conflicts between economic classes and groups in the real world.

During periods of economic stability, eg, the 1950s and early 1960s, a wide consensus develops around the prevailing orthodoxy and radical economics is relegated to the fringe, but when existing economic arrangements fail to generate the kind of economic growth that ensures widespread prosperity and relative harmony among SOCIAL CLASSES, and when prevailing economic theories and conventional government economic policy fail to explain or solve the persistence of social and economic problems, consensus among economists breaks down. Some economists will search for an alternative economic analysis. Such a process of disillusion and reconstruction occurred in Canada in the mid-1970s with the beginning of the most severe economic crisis since the GREAT DEPRESSION. Economic thought shifted abruptly to both the right (eg, in the form of MONETARISM) and to the left (eg, in the form of MARXISM).

Modern radicalism originated with Karl Marx, author of *Capital*, but a wide variety of economic theories and policies, viewed as radical in their time, have also been developed, and some have been absorbed into orthodox economic thought and adopted by governments.

Orthodox Economics holds that the substance, manner and distribution of production are determined by individual preferences, technology and personal endowments, ie, consumers determine what is produced, technology prescribes how goods are made, transported and exchanged, and endowments of talent, skills and material wealth determine to whom goods are distributed. The economy cannot be changed unless these foundations are changed, but none of these foundations can be changed without violating what orthodox economists regard as "human nature" and "natural liberty." Because orthodox economists argue that disturbing INCOME DISTRIBUTION would destroy incentives (based on the assumption that all human effort is closely related to material reward); that technology is irremediably determined by science or history; and that ignoring consumer preferences violates freedom, they reject any role for the STATE that disturbs this "natural" economic order.

In 1848 John Stuart Mill, an orthodox but liberal and reform-minded critic, wrote in *Principles of Political Economy* that, while "laws of production" were "natural" and universal, those of distribution were "partly of human institution" and subject to alteration by legislation. Income redistribution via TAXATION was not perceived as a violation of any natural law and a progressive tax structure was gradually accepted by economic orthodoxy. Canada introduced such a system in 1917. In the wake of the Great Depression, John Maynard Keynes, in *General Theory of Employment, Interest and Money* (1936), demonstrated that left to itself the mature capitalist economy tends to break down and stagnate, a process that was not, contrary to orthodox thought, self-correcting. Keynes advocated state regulation of the overall level of economic activity by means of what he called "socialization of investment," but he was satisfied to leave the composition of that output to the free market. By the end of WWII a modified version of his thought was being adopted and many governments accepted responsibility for maintaining high levels of output and employment. In Canada KEYNESIAN ECONOMICS was accepted in the highest levels of the civil service, and in the 1945 White Paper on EMPLOYMENT AND INCOME, the federal government pledged to maintain economic stability. In practice, this involved varying the money supply and size of government deficits and surpluses to moderate the business cycle as well as introducing UNEMPLOYMENT INSURANCE and WELFARE STATE measures to stabilize incomes. In 1958 traditional theories were further challenged in *The Affluent Society* by John Kenneth GALBRAITH, who wrote that consumer tastes are shaped by advertising, packaging and frequent style changes, and that the corporate sector rather than the sovereign consumer is to be held responsible for production priorities, including frivolous, wasteful and ecologically unsound consumption patterns. In particular, the massive effort devoted to advertising inevitably produces a bias in favour of private consumption as opposed to collective, community services. The result is private affluence on the one hand and public squalor on the other; as a corrective, Galbraith advocated greater state expenditures on social services and public infrastructures.

Generally, liberal critics of traditional economics have demonstrated that the free-market system can only function ideally if unrealistic circumstances exist, ie, perfect competition between large numbers of powerless buyers and sellers in the market for goods and services and for labour and capital; perfect mobility of human and physical resources; and perfect information on all alternatives available to buyers and sellers. The violation of even one condition may distort the system and justify extensive state intervention, including regulation and subsidization. These critiques have formed the basis for modified versions of traditional economics which in turn have provided the theoretical basis for the mixed ECONOMY.

From 1945 to 1970 a broad consensus developed among economists around the "neoclassical" synthesis, which in Canada was founded materially on the export of resources to the US. Resource extraction was largely financed by US-based MULTINATIONAL CORPORATIONS. The creation of US-owned branch plants in manufacturing and the resulting economic structure and economic growth was large enough to generate high profits and rising wages and to finance the welfare state and other state expenditures.

The consensus (1945-70) over the economy was shared by the major political parties and by labour and capital. The NEW DEMOCRATIC PARTY and the affiliated trade-union movement accepted the basic economic institutions of the capitalist economy and the profit system, while emphasizing the need to pursue full employment policies, control giant corporations more stringently and expand the welfare state. Their demands embody in policy form what may be considered the "left wing" of the consensus (*see* SOCIAL DEMOCRACY). The LIBERAL PARTY, responsible for introducing modified versions of many of the social democratic reforms demanded by the labour movement and popularized by the NDP, has tended to occupy the centre of the spectrum.

The consensus among supporters of orthodox economics and its variations broke down in the 1970s and 1980s. Traditional orthodoxy was resurrected and refined under the name of monetarism and adopted, in various degrees, by the federal and provincial governments. Another response has taken the form of post-Keynesian economics, which advocates, among other things, state supervision of wages and state guidance and subsidization of private investment. Both responses reveal that the size of government has little to do with "left" or "right" economic policy. The responses represent alternative policy options for meeting the economic crisis, the one calling for a dismantling of state regulation and a return to the free market, the other for the expansion of state regulation and assistance for private industry.

Radical Economics According to this school of thought, the process of production — ie, producers and their skills, materials and tools; the general level of technology; and the social relations among people in production — governs the economy and influences the shape and role of other institutions, eg, the family, state, education. Radical economics is concerned with how economic surplus (margin of output beyond that required for the maintenance of direct producers and the replacement of outworn capital equipment) is used and to whose benefit. Under capitalism, workers surrender, for wages, all rights of ownership to the product they produce and agree to submit to the control of the capitalist or his representative during the production process. A surplus or profit is extracted when the capitalist pockets the difference between what is paid to the workers and the value of the things produced. The surplus supports the capitalist but is also used to increase the productive capacity of the economy from which more surplus can be extracted. In capitalist economies labour is necessarily treated as a commodity, from which stems many of the fundamental conflicts in industry, eg, because improvement in wages and conditions of work cut into profits, employers will naturally resist pressures for improving the workers' lot. Workers' jobs are always at the mercy of changing economic and technological circumstances; if the demand for goods and services slumps, or if new technology lessens the costs of production, workers will find themselves unemployed. Radical economists contend that mainstream thought, which has minutely analysed the laws of supply and demand, ignores the sphere of production. It leaves out of account the fact that once the ownership of the major means of production is confined to a small class of owners, the freedom of most workers is restricted to choosing from among those means of livelihood that do not require possession of land or capital. Workers can only gain a livelihood by selling their labour power on whatever terms and under whatever conditions they can negotiate, individually or collectively.

In disagreement with J.S. Mill and the reform school, radical economists believe modifying the distribution of income through welfare, UNEMPLOYMENT INSURANCE and tax reforms is heavily constrained by the capitalist system's need for an incentives structure that does not interfere with the LABOUR MARKET, nor discourage private investment. While accepting Galbraith's critique of the mainstream assertion of consumer sovereignty, they reject his belief that the consumers' subordinate role results from the gullibility of consumers or the power of advertising. Radical economists also reject the liberal and social-democratic theory of a pluralistic society where power is distributed among different groups, with the state acting as arbitrator in cases of disagreement, arguing instead that because the prosperity of the nation ultimately depends on the willingness of capital to produce, the state cannot develop policies that severely impinge on their profits. In short, radicals believe that within a capitalist economy based on private ownership of the means of production the possibility of reform is necessarily limited, even if a benevolent state wants to introduce progressive measures.

Radical economists dispute the alleged efficiency of the capitalist economy. They see it as a highly wasteful system, laying off large numbers of workers and idling capital equipment during long stretches of stagnation and depression and unable to tap the reservoir of creative abilities of an alienated, indifferent workforce. Economic democracy at the workplace is the radicals' alternative to private enterprise.

While orthodox economists are viewed as working for the stabilization or reform of capitalism, radical economists work for the establishment of a new society that includes public ownership of all large enterprises; the elimination of production for profit; economy-wide planning to eliminate unemployment; and an egalitarian redistribution of income and wealth. However, the lessons of Soviet-style communism have convinced most radicals that changing the economic system cannot simply mean nationalizing industry and imposing centralized planning. It must involve worker control at the point of production and community control over investment decisions: which goods and services are produced, in what amounts and in what locations. The most widely embraced vision of contemporary western Marxism is best expressed by the solidarity principle: keeping economic differences to a minimum while recognizing the variability in aptitude, tastes and psychological temperament among individuals. Individuals advance as part of the general economic advancement rather than in competition one with the other, with the winnings of the few trickling down to meet the needs of the many. The difference between the radical and the orthodox vision of the good society stems from their divergent views of human nature. The rock upon which most orthodox thinking rests is that human beings are "naturally" acquisitive and motivated primarily by self-gain. Radicals insist that human values and behaviour are socially determined and that survival and sustenance in capitalist societies require that people heed their own self-interest. Implicit in the radical vision is the belief that with a democratic and egalitarian social structure devoid of class domination, human values and human behaviour can evolve towards a greater social consciousness and communal identity.

Introduced to Canada by small socialist groups early in the 20th century, the radical perspective has never informed the politics of any major Canadian party. It has always been part of the perspective of the Canadian working class and elements of it are apparent in the women's movement, the ecology movement and the churches, eg, it was reflected in the *Ethical Reflections on the Economic Crisis* produced by the Canadian Conference of Catholic Bishops in 1983. The radical system of analysis has also made important inroads into various academic disciplines, including sociology, economics, political science, history and anthropology. In Canada political economists who utilize a radical analysis include, among many others, N. Penner, L. Johnson, L. Panitch, C.B. MacPherson, P. Phillips, B. Palmer, G. Kealey, D. Smith, M. Lebovitz, D. Vallancourt, R. Whitaker, C. Cuneo, D. Drache, K. Levitt, T. Naylor, I. Parker, H.C. Pentland, S. Ryerson and M. Watkins.

In the deep social and economic crisis following WWI, workers in many countries were radicalized in their ideas. One of the results of this radicalization, the WINNIPEG GENERAL STRIKE, was a unique event in Canadian history. The process was repeated in the Depression which inspired radical movements, hunger marches, organization of the unemployed and new trade unions of the unskilled and semiskilled workers. Radical ideas were again reborn as a resu of the economic crisis which began in t mid-1970s. CY GONI

Reading: I. Adams et al, *The Real Poverty Report* (1971); \ Clement, *Class, Power and Property* (1983); Clement ar D. Drache, *A Practical Guide to Canadian Political Econon* (1978); Cy Gonick, *Out of Work* (1978).

Ecumenical Social Action Church life i Canada since the late 1960s has been characte ized by a reawakening of the SOCIAL GOSPEL pa sion for justice and a new level of co-operatio between Protestants and Roman CATHOLICS. Fo lowing the Second Vatican Council (1962-65 Roman Catholics joined the Religion-Labo Council and the Women's Inter-Church Counc and worked more closely with the CANADIA COUNCIL OF CHURCHES. New organizations such the National Committee on the Church and I dustrial Society, the Inter-Church Consultati Committee on Development and Relief, and number of jointly sponsored groups, were d signed to facilitate Protestant-Catholic collab ration. The war against domestic poverty pr vided an initial focus for ecumenical soci action. The 1968 national conference, "Christia Conscience and Poverty," led to the creation the Coalition for Development. This ambitio attempt to co-ordinate the antipoverty struggl of a wide range of organizations did not su vive, but the desire to work together remaine strong.

International emergencies such as the Biafra and Bangladesh crises of the late 1960s and earl 1970s, and the growing gap between rich an poor nations, heightened the churches' desire co-ordinate relief and development activitie The Inter-Church Campaign Committee pr duces shared materials for each denomination annual appeal for relief and developme funds; Ten Days for World Development c ordinates a development education progran and CAFEA (Church Action for Emergency Ai and ICFID (the Inter-Church Fund for Inte national Development) co-ordinate emergen assistance and administer jointly sponsored d velopment projects.

The churches' responses to domestic an Third World poverty reflected the social gosp conviction that justice, not charity, was r quired. The need for carefully targeted researc was recognized as a starting point for combinir compassion for victims with a sophisticated u derstanding of existing policies. For exampl the experience of church observers at UNCTA (United Nations Conference on Trade and D velopment) III (the poor nations' organizatio strengthened the conviction that the church should examine Canada's role as a member the rich nations' club — the General Agreeme on Tariffs and Trade (GATT). The GATT-F Project was created to help the churches to more effective gadflies in criticizing Canada trade and aid policies.

Other specialized groups created in respon to different issues include the Taskforce c Churches and Corporate Responsibility, Proje North (native rights and northern develo ment), the Inter-Church Committee on Huma Rights in Latin America, the Church Council c Justice and Corrections, Project Ploughshar (defence policy and DISARMAMENT) and the Inte Church Committee for Refugees. Each group h a small specialized staff and an administrati committee consisting of denominational repr sentatives. PLURA (named after its Presb terian, Lutheran, United, Roman Catholic ar Anglican sponsors) works through region committees to assist local antipoverty organiz tions.

Although participation in such activities h generally been more strongly supported l denominational headquarters than by ordina church members, these organizational innov tions have nevertheless been accompanied by a developing tradition of ecumenical social thought. The central conviction that the transformation of unjust social structures is an integral part of mission and ministry has been expressed in various documents. Statements typical of the ecumenical consensus can be found in briefs to the federal government, such as "Development Demands Justice" (1973), "Justice Demands Action" (1976), the "Inter-Church Brief on Economic Outlook" (1978) and the "Statement of Canadian Church Leaders on Canada's Nuclear Weapons Policies" (1982).

ROGER HUTCHINSON

Eddy, Ezra Butler, manufacturer (b near Bristol, Vt 22 Aug 1827; d at Hull, Qué 12 Feb 1906). Part of the influx of American manufacturers to the Ottawa Valley in the 1850s, Eddy moved his small friction-match factory from Burlington, Vt, to Hull in 1851 and developed markets from Winnipeg to Halifax. Overcoming a series of disastrous fires, notably in 1883 and 1900, Eddy expanded, modernized and diversified to produce a wide range of wood and paper products. At his death his business was estimated to be worth more than $4 million. Elected mayor of Hull 6 times, he represented Ottawa County in the Québec Assembly 1871-75. An opponent of "racialism," he supported Catholic and Protestant institutions alike. A vocal promoter of the British Empire, he was buried in Bristol, beneath the impressive monument which he had built in his honour.

RICHARD REID

Edenshaw, Charlie, or Chief Idinsaw, Tahaygen, "Noise in the Housepit," and N ngkwigetklals, "They Gave Ten Potlatches for Him," Haida chief, artist (b at Skidegate, Queen Charlotte Is, BC *c*1839; d there 1920). Charlie Edenshaw was among the first professional Haida artists and is noted for his flawless execution of dynamic flowing forms in an otherwise strict and disciplined art tradition. Much of his early life was spent in the Northwestern villages of Kiusta and Yatze, and in 1882 his Eagle clan moved to Masset. He was tutored in Haida traditions by his uncle, the chief of the Stastas Eagles, Albert Edward Edenshaw. Charlie Edenshaw frequently met museum anthropologists and collectors at Masset and Prince Rupert. His contributions to world art are therefore not only marked by exquisite works in gold, silver, ivory, argillite and wood, but are found in the recording and documentation of Haida language and culture. Art historians and anthropologists continue to study his vast corpus of works.

CAROL SHEEHAN

Edith Cavell, Mount, elev 3363 m, highest mountain in the environs of JASPER, Alta, is situated W of the ATHABASCA R, 24 km S of Jasper. A prominent landmark, it was called "La Montagne de la Grande Traverse" by voyageurs during the days when ATHABASCA PASS was used as a fur-trade route across the Rockies. It was named in 1916 after the English matron of the Red Cross Hospital in Brussels. Its first ascent was made in 1915. Mountaineers consider the N face to be one of the great climbs in N America.

GLEN BOLES

Edmonton, capital of Alberta and largest city in the province (by CMA), is located on the N SASKATCHEWAN R, near the geographical centre of the province. Commonly known as the "Gateway to the North," it is strategically situated on an economic divide between the highly productive farmlands of central Alberta and a vast, resource-rich northern hinterland.

Settlement Edmonton's valley setting, with its abundance of water, timber and wildlife, has attracted settlement for several thousand years. The archaeological record is scanty, but in 1976 a large campsite containing stone tools from the Middle Prehistoric period (between 3000 and 500 BC) was discovered on a high bluff overlooking the N Saskatchewan R, likely a place where bands of seminomadic hunters and gatherers met regularly. Europeans began to penetrate the western plains in the 18th century, and Anthony HENDAY may have wintered at the site of Edmonton in 1754. Settlement followed in 1795, when the Hudson's Bay Company and the North West Company built the first in a series of fortified trading posts. After the 2 companies merged (1821), Fort Edmonton became the dominant centre of the western fur trade. The fort was reputedly named for Edmonton, now part of London, Eng, the birthplace of a clerk of the HBC. In 1830 the fort was rebuilt for the last time, on the present site of the Alberta legislature building. It gradually fell into disuse after the HBC surrendered its rights to RUPERT'S LAND (1869).

Development Permanent settlement outside the fort did not begin until the 1870s, and even then was slow to develop. The construction of the CPR through Calgary (1883) did not help. A branch railway came N in 1891, but it terminated at Strathcona, on the S bank of the N Saskatchewan R. Edmonton did not receive its own transcontinental connection (Canadian Northern Ry) until 1905, by which time it was the designated capital of the newly created province of Alberta and the natural service centre for a huge agricultural region then coming under intensive development. With Strathcona, Edmonton entered a frantic boom period. When the 2 cities amalgamated (1912), their combined population was over 40 000 and may have reached 70 000 soon after, only to drop to 50 000 in WWI. For the next 25 years Edmonton's fortunes were closely linked with those of its agricultural hinterland. It grew in the good times, stagnated or declined in the bad. By 1941 it was still a small city (92 409), only the ninth largest in Canada, confined to a local role, with an economy built around wholesale trade, transportation and the processing of agricultural produce, notably meat packing.

During WWII Edmonton began a sustained period of growth and assumed a distinctive new character: first as a strategic centre for northern military operations, including the construction

Population: 532 246 (1981c); 657 057 (CMA)
Rate of Increase (1971-81): (CMA) 32.5%
Rank in Canada: Fifth (by CMA)
Date of Incorporation: Town 1892; City 1904
Land Area: 679.5 km²
Elevation: 665 m
Climate: Average daily temp, July 17.4°C, Jan -15.0°C; Yearly precip 466.1 mm; Hours of sunshine 2247 per year

of the ALASKA HIGHWAY, and later as a servicing and processing centre for the petroleum industry. It has since become the major location of oil refining and the petrochemical industry in western Canada, and has risen to unimagined prominence, politically as well as economically. Edmonton's modern development, together with that of Calgary, has completely overshadowed Winnipeg, the historic commercial centre of the prairie region. Today, Edmonton and Calgary compete more with each other for industrial investment and related services. Edmonton also has to compete more directly with Vancouver, as it tries to expand its influence in Pacific Rim countries while Vancouver intrudes upon Edmonton's traditional sphere of influence in the Mackenzie Valley and western Arctic.

Cityscape In the process of growth, the city of 1941 has been engulfed. The central area, in particular, has been rebuilt continuously since the 1950s. A few noteworthy buildings have survived, and several have been restored to fashionable use, but they are dwarfed by the clustered towers that now dominate the Edmonton skyline. Only a few older buildings on open riverbank sites (the Legislature Building, Government House and the Macdonald Hotel) have retained some prominence. The river valley, which is Edmonton's outstanding natural feature, has had a profound influence. It is both a barrier, crossed by many bridges, and a magnificent amenity. High-rise apartments and elite residential areas compete along both banks for views of the river, and parks, golf courses and woodland trails stretch through the valley. Modern architecture, typified in the descending terraces of the convention centre, complements the valley setting. Downstream (NE) to Fort Saskatchewan and beyond, the valley has developed over the past 30 years into the largest industrial complex in Alberta. Fort Saskatchewan's industrial base makes it unusual; most of

Aerial view of Edmonton. The Convention Centre, built into the bank of the North Saskatchewan R, is seen in the foreground (*courtesy Edmonton Economic Development Authority*).

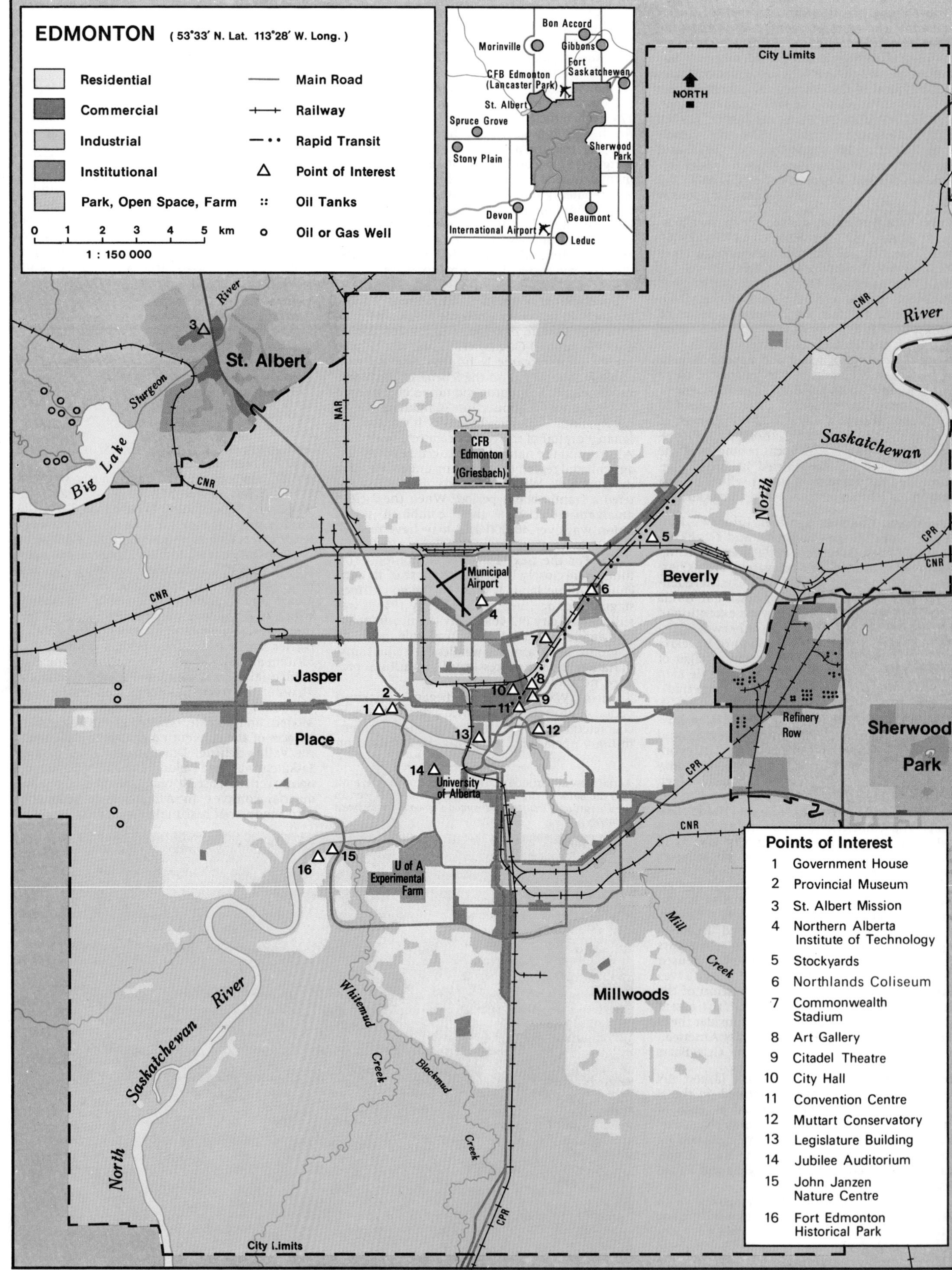

EDMONTON (53°33′ N. Lat. 113°28′ W. Long.)
Residential
Commercial
Industrial
Institutional
Park, Open Space, Farm
Main Road
Railway
Rapid Transit
Point of Interest
Oil Tanks
Oil or Gas Well
0 1 2 3 4 5 km
1 : 150 000
Bon Accord
Morinville
Gibbons
Fort Saskatchewan
CFB Edmonton (Lancaster Park)
St. Albert
Spruce Grove
Stony Plain
Sherwood Park
Devon
Beaumont
International Airport
Leduc
City Limits
NORTH
St. Albert
Sturgeon River
Big Lake
CNR
NAR
CFB Edmonton (Griesbach)
Municipal Airport
Beverly
Jasper Place
University of Alberta
U of A Experimental Farm
Refinery Row
Sherwood Park
North Saskatchewan River
Mill Creek
Millwoods
Whitemud Creek
Blackmud Creek
CPR
City Limits
Points of Interest
1 Government House
2 Provincial Museum
3 St. Albert Mission
4 Northern Alberta Institute of Technology
5 Stockyards
6 Northlands Coliseum
7 Commonwealth Stadium
8 Art Gallery
9 Citadel Theatre
10 City Hall
11 Convention Centre
12 Muttart Conservatory
13 Legislature Building
14 Jubilee Auditorium
15 John Janzen Nature Centre
16 Fort Edmonton Historical Park

Edmonton's other satellites are bedroom communities for people working throughout the widespread metropolitan region. Metropolitan development came with postwar growth, and led in 1950 to the establishment of the first regional planning organization in Canada. A city planning department was created at the same time, and has been especially successful in keeping control over Edmonton's expansion. Development has been well regulated, though Edmonton has not been spared the problems of urban sprawl that beset other Canadian cities. In 1941 the city's territory covered 110 km^2; at the beginning of 1982 it had reached 700 km^2, making it the largest major Canadian city in area. Unfortunately, Edmonton's area includes some of Alberta's richest farmland.

Population Since the 1940s Edmonton has consistently been one of the 2 or 3 fastest-growing cities in Canada. Until about 1961, natural increase was high, but migration was the chief factor in the city's growth, as rural-urban migration from within Alberta and migration from Europe were both at a peak. Over the next decade, foreign migration dropped sharply and natural increase became more important, a fact reflected in the youthfulness of Edmonton's population. The pattern changed again in the 1970s, as birthrates fell and migration increased, though the majority of migrants now came from other Canadian provinces. Between 1941 and 1983, Edmonton's population increased sevenfold, and its boundaries have also been extended many times to accommodate anticipated growth.

Economy and Labour Force Edmonton's booming economy and normally low unemployment were extremely attractive to entrepreneurs and investors. Because of the high pace of development, the construction and service industries until 1982-83 continued to prosper; the latter have accounted for the greatest increases in Edmonton's employment base since 1951. Traditional trade and transportation functions continue to be represented strongly, but the effect of the petroleum industry on employment is not easy to gauge because exploration and production generate relatively few jobs directly in Edmonton. The refining and manufacturing of petrochemical products are not labour intensive either. Like all facets of the oil and natural-gas industries, they generate growth in all other sectors of Edmonton's economy, but Edmonton does not have large numbers of industry-related office jobs in the way Calgary has, and it has comparatively few head offices of petroleum firms. Edmonton's employment is based more on government and administration.

Transportation Since the 1830s Edmonton has been a major hub in the transportation network of western Canada. As a modern rail centre, it occupies a key position in the transcontinental freight system of the CNR, and has strong links to the CP Rail system as well. It also dominates the transmission system for petroleum products of all kinds, a pattern that arose from the proximity of the Leduc, Redwater and Pembina oil fields, where exploitation began. LEDUC is also the location of the Edmonton International Airport, opened in 1957. It caters to main-line service to Canadian, American and European cities; the original airport, near the city centre, handles northern traffic and regular flights to Calgary. In intra-urban transportation, Edmonton was the first medium-sized Canadian city to construct a Light Rail Transit (LRT) system (1978).

Government and Politics Until 1984 Edmonton had a council-commission board form of MUNICIPAL GOVERNMENT, with each council serving a 3-year term. The commission board has now been replaced by an executive committee. The mayor is elected at large, while 12 councilors represent 6 wards. Although most stand as

The Hub, combined student residence and shopping mall on University of Alberta campus, Edmonton (*photo by Wilhelm Schmidt / Masterfile*).

Independents, the nomination of party slates of candidates is gaining popularity and possible electoral reforms are frequently debated. So too are relations between city council and the only other elected bodies in Edmonton, the public (Protestant) and separate (Catholic) school boards. Half the annual property tax is raised for the school systems, yet city council has no control over the school boards' levies. Relations with the provincial government are typically ambivalent. Pleas for more financial assistance and a share of natural-resource revenues are tempered by the awareness that existing grants-in-aid, although generous, reduce the council's freedom of action. Indeed the principle of local autonomy is held to be so important for all municipalities in the Edmonton area that the province has so far rejected the implementation of REGIONAL GOVERNMENT or the unification of the metropolitan area under Edmonton's jurisdiction, despite the conflicts arising from the city's expansion. Instead, in 1982, the province proposed to create a regional service authority for the metropolitan communities, and reorganized the regional planning system to give stronger representation to Edmonton.

Cultural Life The Edmonton Symphony Society, Edmonton Opera Assn and Citadel Theatre are 3 of the largest performing-arts organizations in Canada, but they are merely the most visible elements in a prolific arts scene in Edmonton. There are musical and theatrical performances for every taste, and numerous talented painters, potters, actors, directors, writers, poets, filmmakers and artists are based in the city. In Aug 1984 the Fringe Theatre Event, a 9-day showcase for local and regional performing artists, attracted over 30 000 people, making it the largest annual festival of its kind in Canada. The many different ethnic groups also contribute a lively folk culture, and artistic and ethnic festivals are increasingly popular. The chief facilities for artistic performances and displays are the Jubilee Auditorium, the Edmonton Art Gallery, the Edmonton Public Library, the Citadel Theatre and UNIVERSITY OF ALBERTA, founded in 1907 and now one of Canada's leading universities. Other major educational institutions are the Northern Alberta Institute of Technology and Grant MacEwan Community College. (ATHABASCA U was moved to Athabasca in 1984.) These are complemented by a range of popular facilities, including the Provincial Museum and Archives, Strathcona Science Pk, Muttart Conservatory, John Janzen Nature Centre, Fort Edmonton Historical Pk and the Space Sciences Centre. In sports Edmonton holds 3 professional franchises, the EDMONTON ESKIMOS of the CFL, the EDMONTON OILERS of the NHL and the Trappers of the Pacific Coast Baseball League. The main facilities are Commonwealth Stadium (built for the 1978 COMMONWEALTH GAMES and expanded to 60 000 seats for the WORLD UNIVERSITY GAMES 1983), the Kinsmen

Distribution of Industrial Activity* by Industry Grouping within Census Metropolitan Areas, 1980

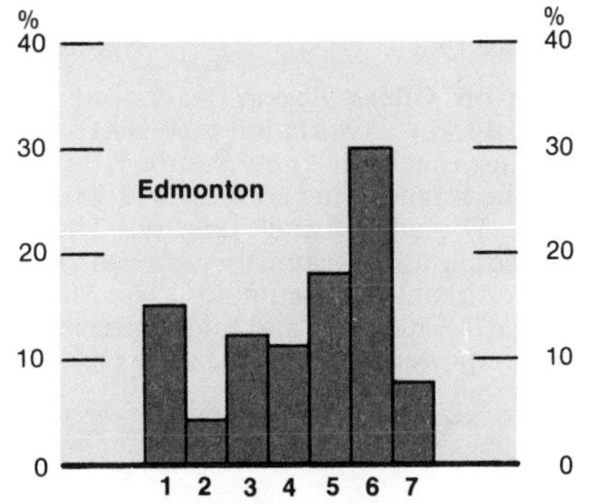

Industry groupings

1. Food and beverage and tobacco products industries
2. Leather, textile, knitting mills and clothing industries
3. Wood, furniture and fixtures, paper and allied and printing, publishing and allied industries
4. Machinery, transportation equipment and electrical products industries
5. Primary metal and metal fabricating industries
6. Rubber and plastic products, petroleum and coal products and chemical products industries
7. Non-metallic mineral products and miscellaneous manufacturing industries.

* Industry activity based on the average of percentage shares of the value shipments of goods of own manufacture, total value added and total number of employees for each of the selected metropolitain areas.

Source: Figure II, Catalogue 31-209, Statistics Canada.

Aquatic Centre (also built for the Commonwealth Games) and the Edmonton Northlands complex of hockey arena, racetrack and exhibition space. P.J. SMITH

Reading: J.G. MacGregor, *Edmonton: A History* (1967); P.J. Smith, ed, *Edmonton: The Emerging Metropolitan Pattern* (1978).

Edmonton Eskimos, FOOTBALL team. They began play in 1910 and participated in the first 2 East-West GREY CUP games, losing to Toronto in 1921 and Queen's University the following year. The Eskimos competed on and off throughout the 1920s and 1930s and were reborn as a publicly owned enterprise in 1948, after which they recorded more Grey Cup appearances and victories than any other team in Canadian football's modern era. In 1952 they lost to Toronto in the Dominion final, but 2 years later, led by Jackie PARKER, Johnny Bright and Normie KWONG, they defeated Montreal Alouettes in 3 straight Grey Cups (1954, 1955, 1956). The remnants of this fine squad lost to Ottawa in the 1960 Grey Cup and the club faded during the ensuing decade. Coach Ray Jauch helped return the Eskimos to power in the early 1970s, winning 3 straight Western Conference titles (1973, 1974, 1975) and one Grey Cup (1975). Under his successor, Hugh Campbell, the Eskimos made the 1978 move into Commonwealth Stadium (eventually expanded to hold over 60 000) and became one of the great dynasties of Canadian sport, winning a Western Conference title for each year of Campbell's tenure (1977-82) and an unprecedented 5 consecutive Grey Cups (1978-82). DEREK DRAGER

Edmonton Grads The Commercial Graduates Basketball Club was the formal name of the team, coached by Percy PAGE, based at McDougall Commercial High School in Edmonton. Beginning as a high-school team, the Grads ruled women's BASKETBALL from 1915 to 1940, winning 93% of their games and 49 out of a possible 51 domestic titles. They did not lose a series in the Underwood International Championships, winning 23 times. After losing the first N American Championship series (1933), the Grads came back to win the next 3 (1934, 1935, 1936). In 1924 they played 6 games in conjunction with the Women's Olympics and also in Paris at the invitation of Fédération Sportive Feminine Internationale, who declared the Grads world champions. In 1928 they won the French and European championships and they played 9 games in conjunction with the Berlin Olympics (1936). In their 3 European tours the Grads won all 24 games they played. At the time of their retirement, the Grads held 108 titles at local, provincial, western, national, international and world levels.

During the Grads' 25-year career, there were only 48 players listed in the official game reports. Allowing for an original core of 5 players, the average turnover was fewer than 2 players a year. All but 2 of these came from the school at which Page taught. The Grads' competitive success was accompanied by the respect they earned in Canada and abroad. Edmontonians regarded them proudly as representatives of the city, while eastern sportswriters hailed them as a national institution. Perhaps the finest compliment came from the inventor of basketball, Dr James NAISMITH, who called them "the finest basketball team that ever stepped out on a floor." CATHY MACDONALD

Edmonton Grads, photo taken in 1923 after the Grads won the Underwood International Trophy (*courtesy Provincial Archives of Alberta / A-11413*).

Edmonton Journal was founded as the *Evening Journal* on 11 Nov 1903. The first issue of 1000 was produced on a hand-fed press and marked Edmonton's first telegraphic news service. In 1984 the *Edmonton Journal* was the largest-circulation daily (circulation 162 364; Fri 207 726; Sun 136 188 — these figures fluctuate sharply from quarter to quarter) between Vancouver and Toronto, operating 27 full-colour press units. These computerized, automated Goss Metroliners place the NEWSPAPER in the forefront of printing technology (*see* PRINT INDUSTRY). In 1984 the *Journal* became the first Canadian newspaper to employ direct satellite links in transmission of colour photographs. A controlling interest was acquired by William SOUTHAM and Sons in 1912; subsequently the *Journal* became a division of SOUTHAM INC. In 1938 the *Journal* was awarded a special Pulitzer Award, the first ever bestowed outside the US, and has won several national awards and citations for its coverage of human-rights issues. The newspaper has always maintained a strong interest in northern affairs, and is the only major Canadian newspaper with a permanent bureau in the NWT. The *Journal* has been politically independent since 1909. STEPHEN HUME

Edmonton Oilers, HOCKEY team. One of the World Hockey Association's (WHA) original franchises, they were known as the Alberta Oilers in the league's first season (1972-73), representing Edmonton and Calgary. Thereafter solely Edmonton's team, they moved into the new Northlands Coliseum in 1974 (since expanded to 17 308 seats) and into respectability as a hockey power in 1978 when the club's third owner, Peter Pocklington, acquired Wayne GRETZKY from erstwhile partner Nelson Skalbania. After losing to the WINNIPEG JETS in the last WHA championship series (1979), they joined the NHL's Smythe Division and became the most rapidly successful expansion franchise in league history. Under coach, general manager and president Glen Sather, they captured the STANLEY CUP in only their fifth NHL season. In their first 5 NHL campaigns they finished at the head of the Smythe Division 3 times. DEREK DRAGER

Edmonton Symphony Orchestra, the successor to several previous orchestras in the city, was established in 1952 under conductor Lee Hepner. Thomas Rolston served as acting conductor 1960-64, until Brian Priestman became conductor and music director. He was succeeded by Lawrence Leonard in 1968, Pierre HÉTU in 1973 and Uri Mayer in 1981. In addition to its subscription series and special concerts, the ESO performs for the ALBERTA BALLET COMPANY and Edmonton Opera Assn productions. It regularly travels to other centres in Alberta and has toured to the Yukon, the NWT and BC. BARBARA NOVAK

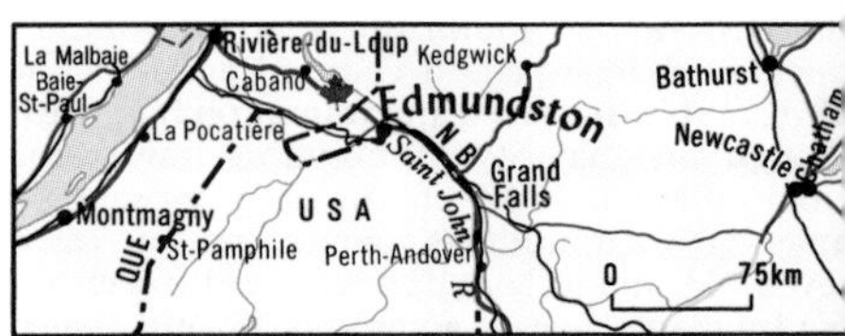

Edmundston, NB, City, pop 12 044 (1981c), inc 1952, is nestled on the eastern bank of the SAINT JOHN R, opposite Madawaska, Maine, and 285 km above FREDERICTON. Initially called Little Falls (as contrasted with GRAND FALLS, 57 km downriver), it was renamed in 1848 in honour of Lt-Gov Sir Edmund Head. It was first settled as early as 1790 by ACADIANS who relocated from St Anne's Point (Fredericton) at the time of the LOYALIST influx. During the 19th century the community's population was supplemented by small numbers of English-speaking immigrants and a protracted immigration of French-speaking settlers from Québec. For many years now, Edmundston has been the ski resort for much of western NB and the centre of francophone awareness, as embodied in the mythical "république du Madawaska." Since establishing a division in Edmundston in 1911 Fraser Inc has expanded from a sawmill operation to a pulp mill and has grown to be the city's primary employer. Collège St-Louis, an affiliate of U DE MONCTON, is situated here. FRED FARRELL

Edson, Alta, Town, pop 5835 (1981c), inc 1911 distribution centre for a mining, timber and oil area 200 km due W of Edmonton. Named for Edson J. Chamberlain, president of the GRAND TRUNK RY 1912-17, it was founded (1910) as a divisional point, some 100 km from the mountains. It served as a point of departure to the PEACE RIVER country, via a trail to GRANDE PRAIRIE until 1916. ERIC J. HOLMGREN

Edson, Aaron Allan, landscape painter (b at Standbridge, Qué 18 Dec 1846; d at Glen-Sutton Qué 1 May 1888). His first teacher (around 1863) was likely Robert Duncanson, an American artist living in Montréal, and later he studied in London, Eng. A founding member of the Soc of Canadian Artists, he exhibited in their first exhibition (1868). By the 1870s he was considered one of Canada's foremost landscape painters. He lived in Cernay-la-Ville, France, in the early 1880s, becoming a student of Barbizon painter Léon Pelouse, and in London in 1886-87. In 1887 he settled in the Eastern Townships, Qué. His early paintings (eg, *Sheep in Landscape*, 1869) show a quietude of mood, a strong interest in

the effect of light and observation of detail, and warm, rich colour. His later work (*The Coming Storm, Lake Memphremagog*, 1880) is more dramatic. His best Canadian work synthesizes the influence of current American, British and French painting in a distinctive personal style.
JOYCE ZEMANS

Education, Alternate Philosophical roots of "alternate education," in the broadest sense, derive from 2 related but conflicting educational traditions. One is the modern progressive tradition represented by American philosopher John Dewey and his followers in the US, by the post-WWI New Schools Movement in Great Britain, by the Steiner (Waldorf) schools on the European continent and, more recently, by the Hall-Dennis (Committee on Aims and Objectives of Education) and Worth (Commission on Educational Planning) reports for Ontario and Alberta, respectively. This tradition stresses both the need to accommodate curriculum and teaching to the stages of child development and the gradual integration of the child into adult society through planned experiential learning. Education is also viewed as a major vehicle for social reform and the broad dissemination of democratic principles and practices. The second tradition is strongly libertarian, stressing the rights of parents and children to make their own educational and life choices. Writers in this tradition, eg, A.S. Neill in Great Britain and John Holt in the US, uphold the individual freedom and innate goodness of the child against institutional and social conformity and the corrupting influences of modern society. Some writers, eg, Ivan Illich in *Deschooling Society* have attacked conventional schooling and compulsory education as ethnocentric, paternalistic, bureaucratic, etc. Independent "free" schools which flowered in Canada and the US in the middle and late 1960s (and soon disappeared) were rooted in this libertarian tradition.

While both traditions share certain attitudes, eg, accommodation of individual needs and interests and a critical stance toward modern corporate society, the progressive tradition leans toward intervention and careful planning of the child's educational experiences and activities while the libertarian tradition stresses non-interference with "natural" growth and learning processes and the importance of personal choice and freedom in educational matters. Both traditions intermingled in Canada in the open-education movement in public elementary education in the late 1960s and in the alternative schools which emerged in the 1970s.

The term "alternative school" first came into general usage in Canada with the establishment in the early 1970s of several small elementary and secondary schools, mainly initiated by parents, students and teachers under the jurisdiction of public boards of education in major urban centres from Montréal and Toronto to Vancouver and Victoria. The term "alternative" was adopted partly to distinguish these schools from the independent, parent-student-teacher-run "free" schools which preceded them (and from which some of them actually evolved) and to emphasize the board's commitment to options within the public system.

With the increasing stress on educational pluralism and choice in the 1970s the alternative-school label was adopted by many newer independent private schools which wished to identify themselves as alternatives to "mainstream" public education (which generally refers to neighbourhood elementary schools, collegiates, vocational and technical high schools and comprehensive SECONDARY SCHOOLS within the regular public-school system). These included denominational schools (eg, the Christian Schools), new university preparatory schools, remedial learning centres and elementary schools rooted in the progressive tradition. Simultaneously, political pressures within public systems to provide for the "special" learning needs of students who were doing poorly in or dropping out of regular schools persuaded more SCHOOL BOARDS to establish alternative programs, eg, re-entry and work-study programs for high-school dropouts, community-oriented outreach programs and independent study programs for bright, self-motivated secondary students. In the early 1980s attention shifted to special schools and programs for the academically gifted and artistically talented as well as to programs linking schooling with the work place ("co-operative education").

The alternative label has now become so widely and loosely applied to so many diverse educational programs that it is quickly losing educational meaning. In the private education sector the label has been applied to or appropriated by religious day schools, "special education" schools, schools with a linguistic emphasis, French immersion schools, schools with a unique program structure (eg, Montessori, Steiner/Waldorf) and to more traditional preparatory schools and colleges. In the public sector most alternative schools serve adolescents and young adults, offering independent study programs for capable, self-directed, university-bound students, basic-skills programs for students with academic deficiencies, mini-high schools with a mixture of conventional and nonconventional courses and schools with an arts focus. Along with these alternatives to high school, a growing number of parent-teacher co-operative elementary alternative schools have emerged, mainly organized along the lines of the family-grouped, activity-based British Infant Schools which served as a model for the open-education movement in Canada and the US. This development is most prominent in Toronto, where many parents who have been involved in co-operative, preschool day-care programs have initiated primary-school projects to continue the co-operative tradition. Teacher-initiated senior public schools offering a variety of small, individualized programs for early adolescents are another prominent part of the alternative school network in Toronto.

Since new alternative schools are opening each year and definitions of what an alternative school is vary from place to place, it is very difficult to estimate the number of such schools currently operating under public school boards in urban centres across Canada. It is likely, however, that the total exceeds 100. More alternative schools are being established even though many regular schools are being closed because of declining enrolments, perhaps because alternative schools (and alternate education) seem to appeal to different educational constituencies in different ways and for different reasons. For some adolescents and young adults they provide an escape from the large, seemingly impersonal, modern comprehensive high school. They offer smaller classes, closer and more informal relations with teachers and greater flexibility (though not necessarily variety) in course selection and timetabling. Alternative high-school classes generally meet once or twice a week, leaving students time to pursue individual interests and hobbies, to undertake intensive training in the arts or athletics or to hold regular jobs. Finally, alternative schools provide a change of pace in the final year for capable and motivated university-oriented students. Resembling the liberal arts college more than the high school in style and format, they ease the transition from the highly programmed high school to the more loosely structured pace of university student life.

The attraction for many teachers to alternative secondary schools is much the same, with a stress on the opportunities to develop courses around their own interests and to work with a larger proportion of bright, motivated students than is usually the case in a regular high school. Moreover, because most of these schools are too small to be assigned an on-site, full-time principal, teachers enjoy more autonomy and more involvement in policy decisions and the governance and administration of the school than in most high schools.

For parents, particularly those with younger children, co-operatively governed elementary-school alternative programs provide not only a choice of program philosophies but also opportunities to be involved more closely with the schooling of their children. Parents in these programs may sit on various internal governance committees, assist in the classroom, serve as resource people in the program and have direct access to the teachers. Co-operative/alternative elementary schools have also pioneered the extension of early childhood education through all-day kindergarten programs and the provision of after-school day-care programs for children of working parents (especially single mothers). As well, the Canadian Alliance of Home Schooling estimates that 1000 families in Canada have chosen to educate their children at home; the parents usually work out the home curriculums with the local school board.

Whether or not parents take advantage of all these opportunities, many, along with the teachers, have come to develop a feeling of ownership about their schools. In this sense the expanding network of co-operatively run new elementary alternatives may be viewed as a renaissance of the spirit of the small community school in the face of a general trend toward increased centralization and bureaucratization in school systems. In addition, for those parents and teachers who remain committed to the ideals and principles of progressive, open education in the face of the "back to basics" movement, these alternative schools represent islands of progressivism in a sea of conservatism.

Alternative schools have also benefited from heightened political and media criticism of mainstream education and from fears of shrinking funds (and jobs) on the part of those who have a strong stake in the protection of existing resources in the education sector. Rightly or wrongly many parents have come to believe that mainstream schools are not providing their children with adequate preparation for either post-secondary education or work, or both. While some turn to private, independent schools with established academic reputations, others place their hopes on their ability to influence the programs of these newer tax-supported alternatives. While board administrators have generally been wary of the autonomy and community control of public alternatives, they have also come to see them as helping to maintain the system by providing for students with "special" needs.

Clearly, judged by curriculum, pedagogy and, in the case of elementary alternatives, even size, the differences are not great between alternative and traditional schools. Teachers in public alternative schools are drawn by and large from the same universities and teacher-training programs as teachers in traditional schools, and most teach in traditional schools before moving to an alternative school. Basic curriculum and materials are similar in both types of alternative schools. Pedagogical practices probably vary more from teacher to teacher than from school to school. With declining enrolments even some mainstream elementary schools have shrunk to the size of alternative schools. At the secondary level in particular, stiffer university admission requirements and a general trend toward curriculum standardization threatens to reduce even further any curriculum differences between mainstream and alternative schools.

What seems to differentiate many alternative schools from the others is the sense of ownership, autonomy and control that teachers, parents and students enjoy in relation to the system. The receptivity of many school boards to the concept of alternative schools provides unprecedented opportunities for teachers and parents to collaborate in developing and operating educational programs that embody their own ideals and aspirations rather than those of a distant bureaucracy. At the same time there is a clear move to assert and maintain stronger administrative control over alternative schools. In such a long-term struggle between democratic localism and bureaucratic professionalism the outcome is difficult to predict. If present trends continue alternate education may well be incorporated under an expanding "special education" network within school systems. In a more optimistic scenario, alternative schools might serve as forerunners of a more decentralized, pluralistic, community-based education system.

MALCOLM LEVIN

Education, Early-Childhood, embraces a variety of group care and education programs for young children (primarily 2-8 years old) and some services for parents. The traditional focus on DAY-CARE, NURSERY-SCHOOL and KINDERGARTEN programs has expanded recently to include attention to the needs of infants and school-aged children in primary grades, but programs designed for children in the 2-to-8 age range still outnumber those for older and younger children. Various types of day-care and nursery programs are designed for the care and education needs of preschool children. Although different kinds of day care exist, there is increasing demand for the kind of group program associated with a centre. In schools, kindergarten and the early primary grades are considered within the purview of early-childhood education. For some Canadian children, entry to kindergarten or first grade represents the first organized early-education experience.

Although, depending on the age and experience of the children involved, programs may emphasize either the care or education of the child at a particular time, all early-childhood education is guided by concern for the individual child and by an awareness of the need to nurture all aspects of his or her development. Early-education practice reflects the thinking of Johann Pestolazzi (1746-1829), the renowned Swiss educator whose concern for and work with young orphan children is generally acknowledged as responsible for the birth of early-childhood education. The influence of European educators, such as Friedrich Froebel, Maria Montessori and Margaret McMillarn is obvious in N American and European early-childhood education. The Montessori schools in Canada are a concrete example, but the more widespread and enduring impact of these educators is reflected in classroom practices based on their beliefs about child development and their respect for a child's individuality. In the latter part of the 20th century, early-childhood education has been strongly influenced by Swiss psychologist Jean Piaget's theories. Piaget's studies of children's thinking, in particular, have stimulated a wave of research exploring children's intellectual development, resulting in many innovations in early-childhood programs.

There is controversy over what constitutes the best educational experience for the young child, although generally the goals and purposes of this experience are in less dispute than the means by which they are to be achieved. For example, the extent to which the teacher, or any adult, should intervene in a child's learning is debatable, particularly when intervention takes the form of direct instruction in teacher-directed lessons. A second, related question, concerns the desirability of a prespecified learning objective. Sometimes this controversy is described as the "play" versus "instruction" approach to learning. At issue are conflicting beliefs about when children can and should direct their own learning. Much of the debate concerns school programs for children in the 5-to-8 age range, but it has spilled over into preschool programs as well.

Compensatory education for preschool children, developed principally in the US with extensive government funding, was intended to meet the needs of socially and economically disadvantaged children. Some programs designed by groups of educational researchers and developers challenged the long-standing early-childhood education emphasis on social and emotional development and emphasized intellectual development. The conflict between the more traditional and the experimental programs and the effect of these programs on the children became part of the general discussion about the means and ends of the preschool experience. This discussion, in Canada, has centered around "at risk" children, ie, those who because of one or more factors in their background may face some difficulties in school achievement or social adjustment, or both.

In Canada, some of the questions related to special needs are associated with the needs of second-language learners and of children identified as having particular learning or developmental needs. Children of parents who have recently immigrated to Canada frequently enter kindergarten or first grade with little or no facility in English or French. Opinions differ regarding the best approach to developing the child's competence with the language of the school. The identification of other special needs and capabilities at the time the child enters school is the objective of the early-identification procedures adopted by many school boards. Again, there are different views regarding the best means of identifying existing and potential problems and of meeting the needs that are identified. The early-identification movement is concerned with identifying physical, social, emotional and learning problems (actual or potential) in preschool and early-primary children. Screening procedures have been designed for this purpose and some follow-up in response to the identified needs of individual children is encouraged.

Perhaps the greatest influence on early-childhood education in Canada today has been the philosophy and practice of the British infant and primary schools. Frequently referred to as "informal" or "open" education, this approach is viewed by many as the embodiment of the "child-centered" philosophy. Attempts to implement "informal" education in Canada and the US have been directed, in particular, to kindergarten and primary-grade programs. In Ontario alone, almost 400 open-area schools were constructed between 1967 and 1972. Even where the open areas were not provided, water tables, "junk" boxes and other materials used in British classrooms appeared in Canadian classrooms. Multi-age grouping practised in Britain was also tried in Canada.

Other developments within the field of education and society have also influenced the scope and direction of early-childhood education. For many years the study of child development and early-education practice were dominated by the child developmentalists, who resisted direct intervention by teachers in children's learning. However, since the 1960s scholars and researchers in other disciplines and professions have turned their attention to the study of children and the early-education setting. In Canada today a number of university departments of education and psychology are engaged in research exploring dimensions of child development and learning, and dimensions and outcomes of early-childhood practice. The research of linguists, eg, has provided new understanding of the development of and relationship between language and thought. These findings have generated new discussions about the teacher's role in language development.

Changing ways of life and other social change have also affected early education because of changing needs and demands for child care and education. The increasing number of working women, many of whom are mothers of young children, has resulted in a demand for increased day-care facilities. In Canada this demand and the related issue of day-care funding have attracted the attention of many interest groups and policymakers, and the role of the school in providing day-care needs has become a subject of debate.

Perhaps the greatest challenge to early-childhood practitioners and researchers today is finding a way to determine whether early-childhood education achieves its objectives. Developing valid and reliable measures to assess program effectiveness, or even to define the criteria of effectiveness, has been difficult because some early-childhood educators are reluctant to support formal evaluation of program effects on children. This reluctance seems to stem from concern that any formal assessment of children promotes a kind of child evaluation that is antithetical to the notion of respecting individual differences. However, advances in research design and methodology and an awareness of the need to support claims with evidence have combined to support a growing body of research in the field. This research increasingly demonstrates concern with long-term as well as immediate effects of early-childhood programs, and with determining relationships between different types of programs and different learning development outcomes.

ELLEN M. REGAN

Reading: A. Biemiller, "Early Childhood Education," *Canadian Research in Education* (1982); S.J. Braun and E.P. Edwards, *History and Theory of Early Childhood Education* (1972); E.D. Evans, *Contemporary Influences in Early Childhood Education* (1975); L.M. Logan and V.G. Logan, *Educating Young Children* (1974).

Education, Higher, usually refers to education and training in universities, colleges and institutes of technology or art. What would now be called higher education was first organized by the churches in the 17th century (*see* EDUCATION HISTORY), but it was not until 1789 that the first church-sponsored UNIVERSITY, University of King's College (NS), was chartered in Canada. In 1829 MCGILL UNIVERSITY (founded in 1821) became the first private nondenominational university to receive a charter. The establishment of provincial universities began with UNIVERSITY OF TORONTO in 1850. There are 3 federal government foundations, all military colleges, of which the first, the ROYAL MILITARY COLLEGE OF CANADA, was founded in 1876. Of Canada's approximately 70 universities, 6 use French as the language of instruction, 6 use both French and English, and the rest use English. The universities' chief functions are teaching, research and community service. Programs of study leading to bachelor, master and doctoral degrees are offered in the arts and sciences and in the professions. The universities undertake most of the country's basic and some of its applied research. Community service includes the provision of opportunities for study in nondegree programs of both general and professional interest.

Until the mid-1960s, post-secondary vocational education was provided by a variety of specialized institutions. At that time, systems of colleges were introduced, mostly by provincial governments. In some cases the colleges absorbed former institutions of post-secondary education (PSE). There are now nearly 200 such nonuniversity institutions, most teaching in English, some in French and a few in both, and they are called by a variety of names — college, COMMUNITY COLLEGE, regional college, college of applied arts and technology, COLLÈGE D'ENSEIGNEMENT GÉNÉRAL ET PROFESSIONNEL (CEGEP), institute of technology, etc. These colleges offer programs leading to diplomas rather than degrees. Some provide academic education for transfer to university, some provide vocational training, chiefly at the technician level, while others offer both academic and vocational programs. The colleges are not expected to undertake research, but do provide a wealth of community services.

Enrolment in PSE has risen steadily since WWII and the participation rate (total of full-time students in PSE as a percentage of the population 18-24 years old) is now close to 20%. Students in university and nonuniversity institutions are about equal in numbers; about 50% attend full-time, 50% part-time. According to the 1981 census, of the population over 19 years of age, 9% had a degree and 12% had another postsecondary qualification.

PSE is funded primarily by governments (approximately 84%), tuition fees (8%) and other sources (8%). Both the provincial and federal governments contribute, but in the context of overall federal-provincial fiscal arrangements the federal share is being constantly renegotiated (*see also* EDUCATIONAL OPPORTUNITY).

Recurrent issues in higher education include who should be served; what mix of general and specialized courses should be offered by universities and colleges; how good teaching can be assured; what the desirable balance is between teaching and research; how costs should be shared by the student and society; what the respective roles and responsibilities of institutions and governments should be; and whether aims and outcomes are commensurate.

EDWARD SHEFFIELD

Reading: Robin S. Harris, *A History of Higher Education in Canada, 1663-1960* (1976); Edward Sheffield, et al, *Systems of Higher Education: Canada* (1982).

Education, History of The history of education is a central theme in Canada's social, economic and political development. In NEW FRANCE, education was usually an informal process in which skills and values were passed from one generation to the next by parents, relatives and older siblings. Three hundred years later, informal learning has become an adjunct to extensive systems of formal schooling. The growth of schooling in Canada reflects a transformation in the nature of social organization, which has become increasingly based on institutional structures.

During the French regime in Canada, the process of learning was integrated into everyday life. While the French government supported the responsibility of the Catholic Church for schooling, the FAMILY was the basic unit of social organization and the main context within which almost all learning took place. In the labour-intensive economy of the 17th and 18th centuries, families relied on the economic contributions of their children, who were actively engaged in productive activity. Children learned skills such as gardening, spinning and land clearing from other family members. Young males were trained for various trades through an APPRENTICESHIP system. Similarly, because the population was small and dispersed, it was the family that undertook religious instruction and, in some cases, instruction in reading and writing. In certain areas, parish priests established *petites écoles* in which they taught catechism and other subjects. However, the majority of the population in New France, particularly in the rural areas, could not read and write.

In the towns of New France, formal education was more important for a variety of purposes. The Jesuits, Récollects, Ursulines, the Congregation of Notre Dame and other religious orders provided elementary instruction in catechism, reading, writing and arithmetic. More advanced instruction was available for young men who might become priests or enter the professions. By the mid-17th century, a course in classical studies, grammar and theology was available at the college founded by the Jesuits in 1635. In the 1660s Bishop LAVAL founded the SÉMINAIRE DE QUÉBEC, which later became UNIVERSITÉ LAVAL. Formal instruction for females was quite limited and usually did not extend beyond religious instruction and skills such as needlework. However, girls who lived in the countryside may have been better educated than boys as a result of the efforts of the sisters of the Congregation of Notre Dame, who established schools in rural areas as well as in towns, and travelled as itinerant teachers.

Kindergarten was meant to promote spontaneous learning through song and play but came to be seen as a bridge between home and school (*courtesy Ontario Archives*).

While only a minority of colonists in New France received instruction in an institutional setting, Catholic missionaries played an important role in formal education. The Recollects hoped to undermine the traditional culture and belief systems of the native people by educating the young boys and girls in the Catholic religion and in French customs. The Jesuits, who also embarked on an ambitious program to "francisize" the native people, compiled translations of the native tongues and established various schools. Other groups, such as the Ursulines, focused their educational efforts on native girls. However, the Catholic Church's missionary efforts met with minimal success and the educational programs had little impact on the society of native people, in which learning continued to be viewed as an ongoing part of everyday activity (*see* NATIVE PEOPLE, EDUCATION).

During the 18th and early 19th centuries, the family remained the unrivalled setting for education; few children in what was then British N America received formal instruction either from tutors or in schools. The pattern began to change during this period, however, as the British government looked to education as a way of promoting cultural identification with Protestantism, the English language and British customs.

In the years after the Conquest of 1759-60, the British authorities were exceedingly concerned about the strong French Canadian presence in the colony, and they tried repeatedly to assist in the establishment of schools that were outside the control of religious authorities. These efforts were undermined by the Catholic Church and, more importantly, by the disinterest of local communities, in which education was associated more with households than classrooms. However, the concept of schooling as an agent of cultural change became more widespread among social leaders during the 19th century, especially as American influence and IRISH immigration added to concern about the cultural complexion of British N America. In these years, politicians, churchmen and educators debated questions of educational financing, control and participation, and as early as the 1840s the structure of the modern SCHOOL SYSTEMS can clearly be discerned in an emerging official consensus.

The consensus involved a fundamental redefinition of the content and structure of education, eg, formal education became a public responsibility under secular rather than religious control. Schools were promoted as components of educational systems rather than as products of single communities. In most regions, the financing of schools became compulsory and attendance by all children (and not just the more affluent) was encouraged. One of the major promoters of these developments was Egerton RYERSON, who as a Methodist minister in UPPER CANADA began a long career of educational leadership when he took up the cause of nondenominational schooling in the late 1820s. The position of assistant superintendent to which he was appointed in 1844, had been created by the School Act of 1841, which was intended to provide for a uniform school system for the United Province of Canada. However, the Act did not effectively resolve the complicated issue of control, administration and finance, and Ryerson sought possible solutions in the US and Europe. During 1844 and 1845 he visited more than 20 countries and was particularly impressed by teaching methods in Prussia, by textbook use in Ireland, and by educational administration in New York and Massachusetts. The recommendations for legislative change included in his 1846 report were based partly on his impressions of education in these countries. These recommendations were incorporated into the Common School Acts of 1846 and 1850 and refined in the 1871 Act to Improve the Common and Grammar Schools. This legislation was not only the foundation for the contemporary Ontario school system, but served as the model for school Acts in most other regions of Canada.

Ryerson and other school promoters such as Alexander Forrester in NS and John Jessop in BC sought to establish a system of universal tax-supported elementary education based on Christian morality. Ideally the administration of this system would blend centralized control and local responsibility. In most cases, property taxes would finance the new institutions to guarantee free access to all children. Teachers would be trained and certified and pupils would be provided with standardized textbooks. Fulfilment of these ambitions depended upon a complex array of circumstances. To begin with, school promoters had to convince property owners that they should pay taxes to support the schooling not only of their own children but also, and most importantly, of poorer children. To do so, educators argued that schooling had become necessary as a result of widespread political, social and economic changes. The association of formal education with social purpose was potent in the mid-19th century; school promoters believed that common schooling not only provided an opportunity for general social improvement but that it would serve as an antidote to social instability. Canadian leaders interpreted the REBELLIONS OF 1837 as a sign that the future political stability of their society depended upon achieving a new consensus on the importance of social order and the moral value of self-regulation.

At the same time, economic changes were transforming the family, especially the position of women and children. Until around 1920, Canada was a predominantly rural society, but throughout the 19th century rapid commercial and manufacturing development spurred the growth of major cities in which productive activity moved out of the home and into centralized workplaces (*see* WORK). This transition redefined production as employment. Women and children were most affected, because the emerging wage-labour economy generally offered job opportunities only to men. Older children and unmarried women were employed in sectors such as the TEXTILE INDUSTRY, but by the mid-1800s the number of these potential workers greatly exceeded the number of jobs available for them. Social leaders viewed the dislocation of children from productive activity with concern, fearing that cities such as Toronto and Hamilton might be threatened by the appearance on the streets of numerous idle children from working-class families. These children were generally considered by educators to be ignorant, criminally inclined and in need of social training. In the mid-19th century, therefore, school promoters argued that public systems could respond to the emerging political, social and economic dimensions of a new Canadian society, and that "free" schools would create social harmony by providing a common experience for children of disparate socioeconomic groups. Of course, common schooling was not intended to alter the actual social structure but to preserve it by shaping the behaviour and attitudes of what were perceived as certain potentially disruptive groups, eg, immigrants and the poor. The role of education was to engender a "proper" appreciation (and acceptance) of one's place in society and to promote shared values and customs, thereby ensuring social stability. School promoters considered taxation a small price to pay for these benefits, and although some ratepayers in communities as disparate as Toronto and Victoria did oppose the taxation, the promise of education was sufficiently attractive to encourage support at the local level.

The rapid construction of school systems during the mid-19th century resulted not only from official promotion of public schooling but also from the willingness of parents to send their children to school. Even before compulsory attendance legislation was enacted in the late 19th century, most children between the ages of 7 and 12 attended school at least several months each year. Children from affluent families attended regularly and stayed in school until they were older, while children from poorer families only attended irregularly because other demands were more pressing. Official motivation for promoting school construction and local motivation for sending children to school have been distinct from each other, therefore the history of education since the 19th century has been one of conflict and controversy.

Educational development since Ryerson's day has been characterized by an increase in the years of formal attendance at school. SECONDARY SCHOOLS became commonplace in cities. By 1921 many Canadian children registered at school until age 16, while a smaller percentage continued to higher levels. However, social position continued to influence attendance patterns. Children from working-class families received far less schooling than those from more affluent backgrounds. In addition, children in rural areas had less EDUCATIONAL OPPORTUNITY than their counterparts in cities, where population density encouraged the construction of high schools and UNIVERSITIES. The development of public school systems in the 19th century was marked by the standardization of textbooks, teacher training, classroom organization and curriculum. Children were viewed as clay to be molded in desired forms, but over time a view of children as inherently distinct with varying levels of potential (ie, seedlings that had to be cultivated according to their individual natures) came to prevail. The changing view of children contributed to the growth of new educational programs (especially at the secondary level) designed to accommodate the differing abilities and potential of different students. Most importantly, technical and vocational courses were developed for students who were deemed unsuitable for further academic study. Not surprisingly, the criteria for assigning children to various courses reflected cultural and social prejudices more than intellectual assessments. Measures such as IQ tests, developed by the 1920s, revealed unintentionally more about the school administrators than the students, but they were nevertheless used to place different students in different courses of study after the elementary years. This approach has been constantly revised during the 20th century, especially after WWII, when the expansion of post-secondary institutions provided a new way of sorting different students into different programs. In these years, educational debate focused on the content of the appropriate curriculum for various age groups (*see* CURRICULUM DEVELOPMENT). Questions of administration, financing, teacher training and other structural features of school systems have tended to follow the general pattern established during the 19th century.

A great deal of educational conflict and controversy has involved religion and language. The establishment of schools brought local practice under official scrutiny and forced communities to conform to prescribed standards of formal instruction which did not accord with the reality of a diverse society. For example, religious groups did not always agree on the desirability of nondenominational Christian curricula, and their protests led to the growth of parallel Catholic and Protestant school systems in Québec, the provision for SEPARATE SCHOOLS in provinces such as Ontario, and a completely denominationally based school system in Newfoundland. These developments were legally guaranteed by the Constitution Act, 1867, which not only assigned education to the provinces but also enshrined the continued legitimacy of denominational schools that were in place in the provinces at the time that they joined Confederation.

Canada's educational history has been marked by constant conflict over minority-lan-

Manual Training Room, OAAC, Ottawa 1901 (*courtesy Public Archives of Canada / PA-28236*).

guage education. Most controversies have involved Francophones outside Québec, but recently the language question has affected Québec Anglophones and has also concerned heritage language instruction to children of immigrant groups (*see* SECOND-LANGUAGE INSTRUCTION). These conflicts reflect the fact that within the general expansion of standardized public schooling, there have been competing educational visions among both policymakers and parents.

Similarly, within the concept of a standard education, there was a sharp distinction between males and females. The ideal public schoolhouse included separate entrances, classrooms and recess areas for boys and for girls. In addition, the redefinition of the family as less of an economic unit of production than an association based on emotional attachment was accompanied by the idea that girls should be educated for household responsibility while boys should be trained as breadwinners. By the late 19th century, girls attended HOME ECONOMICS programs to learn cooking and cleaning skills while boys, especially from working-class families, learned manual skills related to factory production. The idealization of women as wives and mothers, as well as the relative paucity of other employment opportunities for females, contributed to the feminization of the elementary-school teaching force. While the proper sphere for women was considered the home, young single women came to be viewed as ideal teachers for younger children who could benefit from their supposedly inherent nurturing qualities. Women teachers were poorly paid and were supervised by male officials who saw themselves as the real educators. Even in the later 20th century, many of the earlier patterns remain unchanged. The history of education has therefore been quite different for males and females.

Formal education also had different implications for Canadians of non-European ancestry. The ambitions of educators to encourage the assimilation of native peoples continued unchanged after the time of New France. In the 19th and 20th centuries, boarding schools were a major strategy for separating native children from their own people, but this approach only served to confuse the children culturally and damage them psychologically. Recently, there have been attempts by official educators to collaborate with native peoples in developing educational programs that respect cultural identity, but thus far the political, social and economic context of NATIVE-WHITE RELATIONS has worked against effective educational collaboration.

Similarly the history of Canadian education includes the establishment in the 19th century of separate schools for BLACKS in Ontario and Nova Scotia and special regulations for Asians in BC (*see* CHINESE; JAPANESE; SOUTHEAST ASIANS). Such discrimination is no longer official policy in Canada, but more subtle and informal racism is still apparent in some educational programs and textbooks.

Conclusion The history of education in Canada, as in other Western countries, has involved the growth of formal instruction funded by taxes and supervised by the state. This growth resulted from concern about cultural, moral and political behaviour, from the emergence of a wage-labour economy, from changing concepts of childhood and the family, and from the general reorganization of society into institutions. By the late 20th century, schooling has become part of an institutional network which includes hospitals, businesses, prisons and welfare agencies. Various groups have experienced this development in different ways, sometimes by official design and sometimes by their own choice. As a result, there are many histories of Canadian education and important distinctions within the general trends. CHAD GAFFIELD

Education, Special, is remedial education designed to help children and young adults who are exceptional in some way as a result of low intelligence, visual or auditory impairment or specific learning difficulties or problems. Remedial techniques may include the use of special schools or classes, individual instruction, and specifically designed programs in reading, language or other areas. Up to 40% of youngsters may at some time require special educational help, but as a field, special education is particularly concerned with the 10-15% of the population who suffer major or chronic handicaps (*see* DISABILITIES).

The behaviour of exceptional children varies, but one of the more common characteristics associated with a handicap is instability of behaviour, eg, the motivation to learn may increase or decrease markedly from day to day or even during the course of a day. Teachers, psychologists, social workers and medical practitioners frequently collaborate as an interdisciplinary team, assessing the problems of exceptional children and designing programs suited to the children's individual needs.

Categories of Exceptional Persons The largest group of exceptional persons consists of those who have below average intelligence and below average social and educational attainment. The majority suffer mild handicaps, but they may be afflicted with physical handicaps as well, although multiple handicaps are most common among persons with a severe intelligence handicap. Children who are mildly or moderately handicapped frequently attend special classes, but others study at regular schools. Some severely handicapped children may also attend special schools.

There is a large group of persons who have seemingly normal cognitive ability and physique but have difficulty learning to read, spell, etc. Specific techniques and specialized learning centres have been designed to help alleviate these problems. Learning centres may be run by a school board or private agency. Sometimes they are attached to universities such as the learning centre at McGill University, which was started by Dr S. Rabinovitch. Generally, they provide assessment of learning problems and intensive individualized or small-group (3-5 persons) instruction. Children usually attend 2 or 3 times per week. The centre staff sometimes support and advise the child's regular teacher.

Visual and hearing impairments are less common handicaps. The majority of those so impaired enjoy partial sight or hearing and often attend special classes using technological aids such as opticon and loop induction. An opticon, used by persons with very restricted vision, magnifies the size of print; with the loop system, designed to aid those with auditory difficulties, a wire around the classroom passes amplified signals to hearing aids.

Physical handicaps include problems of the motor system and diseases such as diabetes. Many people with physical or sensory handicaps exhibit average or above average intelligence and many attend regular schools.

Educational Services In many cases the severity of a child's handicap decreases over time through the use of remedial techniques and because of changes in personal or social circumstances. For example, with adulthood different demands are made upon exceptional individuals and there may as well be a change in the perception of what constitutes "normality." Skills learned in school (eg, reading, mathematics) are not necessarily of major importance in certain occupations of the work force. Frequently, intelligence increases substantially during late adolescence and early adult years.

Provincial governments have recently revised curricula for exceptional children. Special education now involves not just remediation of basic school subjects, but emphasizes social education, eg, the development of basic language and self-help skills, and may include vocational preparation and training. Day-to-day skills used in a home (eg, meal preparation, cleaning) and skills used in leisure activities, which include not only skills learned through participation in sports but those involved in choosing and planning leisure activities at home, are also taught as part of special education and are considered very important to adult adjustment. Development of this approach has already begun to change the concept of the sheltered workshop. Although special schools and special classes are provided for exceptional children, these children are integrated, wherever possible, into regular classes and remedial education is provided. Exceptional learners may be integrated with their age group for some subjects but not for others.

Assessment of Exceptional Children Assessment procedures involving diagnostic and attainment tests are used to ascertain if a child is suffering serious difficulties with hearing or visual impairment, with levels of motor attainment, education (reading or math) or cognitive ability. Intelligence tests have been used frequently for administrative purposes and have resulted in the unjustified segregation of children. Tests of social adaptation, to assess levels of social, vocational and home-living skills, have been developed recently. Staff, parents and sometimes the child discuss goals and procedures and progress. Ideally an individual program plan (sometimes called Individual Education Plan) is developed to achieve very specific goals, eg, what the child needs to learn, in what sequence he or she will do so, which techniques of special education will be used to assist the child, who the teacher will be, and where the child will be taught.

The process of "normalization," which is designed to assist a handicapped person to develop as normal a way of life as possible, took root in Canada in the early 1970s. The Canadian Association for the Mentally Retarded played an important part in this development. A requirement for compulsory education in other countries during the mid-1970s led to the development of the individual program plan which is now a required procedure within many Canadian educational institutions. During the early 19th century, some medical facilities were provided for handicapped children, but educational institutions gradually assumed greater responsibility for their welfare. Until the 1970s, handicapped children were isolated in special schools, often run by private agencies; others were sent to institutions or remained at home. With the development of the Individual Education Plan, the labelling has waned, and there has been some recognition that standardized performance tests are of limited help in assessing and developing educational procedures for such children. Denis Stott of Guelph University has played an important role in the development of curriculum material in special education and in the change of concepts in this area. At the provincial level, pioneers in this field include Dr Christine Meikle from Alberta, who began a school and training centre for mentally handicapped children and initiated the internationally recognized Vocational and Rehabilitation Research Institute in Calgary. John Dolan promoted developments in Saskatchewan, notably the Alvin Buckwold Centre.

Professional Education Many universities provide courses in special education; BEd degrees often include majors in special education, and such studies can be pursued at the graduate level. In a number of Canadian universities, student teachers are now required to take a course in special education because all teachers will become involved with handicapped persons as the process of integration accelerates. Beyond the school system, Canada has developed, through the National Institute on Mental Retardation under Allan Roeher, the internationally recognized National Manpower model, which provides for the training of rehabilitation practitioners through diploma programs in community colleges and calls for education beyond this level — at undergraduate and graduate levels in universities. The community-college diploma courses have been in place since the early 1970s in many provinces.

Future of Special Education Regular class teachers generally know too little about learning difficulties and the common behavioural signs of handicapped children. Exceptional children require considerable structure in learning processes. Reading kits using specialized techniques, and social and allied programs have been developed. Computer-assisted instruction increasingly helps physically handicapped people who can use modified terminals. Microcomputers can be used to teach a range of verbal and nonverbal skills in a structured manner. Reading, math and social-skill training are among the programs available on computers.

Agencies that provide services to exceptional persons include the Council for Exceptional Children, Canadian National Institute for the Blind, Canadian Rehabilitation Council for the Disabled, National Institute on Mental Retardation, and Institut national canadien-français pour la déficience mentale. ROY I. BROWN

Education, Technical, combines education and training in preparing persons for gainful employment in occupations that require an understanding of applied scientific principles. Education fosters the development of the whole person without regard to practical applications, while training focuses on transmitting certain practical skills. The terms "vocational education" and "technical education" are often used interchangeably, but vocational education may refer to preparation for nontechnical work or it may describe a series of learning activities that concentrate on narrow training and have little value beyond the immediate application. Technical education, on the other hand, incorporates both training and educational components, although the emphasis on each will vary according to subject matter. Students who enrol in technical-education courses handle materials and tools, gain a degree of technological literacy (in a society that depends almost totally upon technology for material needs), and develop skills for utilitarian or recreational purposes. The standard of living in Canada is tied to the ability of its population to compete with other industrial nations in the international market. There is a growing awareness in Canada that technical and engineering education of a high quality must be available to produce graduates for industry and for governmental agencies.

History The beginnings of formal technical education in Canada can be traced to 1668 when church authorities opened trade schools in Québec City and St-Joachim. At these schools, not only were sculpture and painting taught both as trades and as arts, but basic instruction was given in cabinetmaking, carpentry, masonry, roofing, shoemaking and tailoring. By 1700, Jesuit colleges in Québec City and Montréal were training pilots, ships' captains, explorers and surveyors by instruction in mathematics, surveying and hydrography. Significant developments in technical education did not occur, however, until the latter half of the 19th century, and even then growth was slow and unsteady, partly because immigration provided much of the skilled labour (a pattern that has persisted until very recently) and because of APPRENTICESHIP programs. Some of the early developments across Canada included the establishment of a Mechanics' Institute in St John's in 1839 and another in Victoria in 1864; and the founding of the Halifax Marine School in 1872, the Ontario Society of Artists' School (later the Ontario College of Art) in 1876, 13 trade schools in Québec in 1880, industrial schools for Indians in Saskatchewan and Alberta in 1884, and a manual training centre in Manitoba in 1900.

Role of Governments Involvement by provincial governments in technical education increased in the early part of this century when legislation covering matters such as authorization, financial grants and supervision was passed. Various other schools were founded, eg, a technical school in Montréal (1907), and the Nova Scotia Technical College (1907) and Agricultural College (1905). The Ontario Industrial Education Act (1911) led to the construction of several technical and commercial high schools within the decade. Several other events also reflected the role of provincial governments. A royal commission to enquire into the state of vocational education was created in Manitoba (1910); an amendment to the Secondary Education Act (1911), which initiated manual training, was passed in Saskatchewan; the Alberta School of Agriculture was established (1913); and BC's Department of Education extended manual training to high schools (1909).

The federal government became active in this area in 1910 when it set up the Royal Commission on Industrial Training and Technical Education. Since then, 18 major federal government Acts and agreements have been passed; each has provided funds for use by provincial authorities in the development of a wide range of technical or vocational training.

During the first half of this century, 2 of these Acts were particularly important. The first was the Technical Education Act (1919-29), under which the Dominion agreed to share up to 50% of provincial expenditures for technical education, resulting in federal grants of $10 million over a 10-year period. The second was the Youth Training Act (1939), out of which the War Emergency Training Program (1940-46) was developed as a special schedule. This provided technical training to both skilled and semiskilled levels for individuals in war industries and in the armed services. Nearly $24 million was expended under this program, and more than 300 000 persons received training.

By far the most influential of government actions was the Technical and Vocational Training Assistance Act of 1960. Under this legislation, the federal government helped the provinces undertake the construction of new vocational high schools, institutes of technology, and adult-training centres. Under the stimulus of this Act, projects valued at over $2 billion were approved within a decade, providing nearly 600 000 new student places.

Although the term "technical education" does not extend to degree programs offered by universities, it does encompass the COMMUNITY COLLEGES and institutes of technology. These post-secondary institutions emerged in considerable numbers during the 1960s, although a few, such as the prestigious Ryerson Institute of Technology (*see* RYERSON POLYTECHNICAL INSTITUTE) in Toronto, had been established soon after WWII.

Courses Offered The range of technical subjects covered in Canadian secondary schools, post-secondary institutes and industry, is extensive. From the first years of secondary school to technological courses at community colleges, the emphasis shifts from manual operations to intellectual comprehension as the content becomes more complex and theoretical. Courses in basic electricity are expanded into computer electronics or industrial power circuits; simple woodworking evolves into building construction, drafting into machine design or architectural planning, and machining operations into automated, programmed sequences.

Until recently, technical courses were taken almost exclusively by males, but an increasing number of females now enrol in high-school technical courses and in technology programs at the post-secondary level. Another trend is toward "co-operative education," whereby students are employed part-time in work situations under the supervision of employers and school staff. D.E. LONEY

Education Organization The wide diversity in organizational structures in Canadian schools and post-secondary institutions largely reflects the fact that Canada has never had a co-ordinated EDUCATION POLICY and is not likely to have one in the future. Co-ordinated action in education has been frustrated by the vast differences in economic, cultural and demographic conditions among various regions in Canada. While each province has attempted to develop its own educational organization, the federal government has also introduced many policies that influence provincial structures (*see* SCHOOL SYSTEMS). There are 6 main legal bases for education in Canada: the CONSTITUTION ACT, 1867; the stipulations related to the admittance of other provinces to Confederation after 1867; provincial legislation; provincial department of education regulations; rules set by post-secondary institutions and local school boards; and court precedents and quasi-judicial decisions.

Types of Organization Elementary and secondary schools in Canada are under public, federal or private control. Publicly controlled schools in all provinces are run by local SCHOOL BOARDS that operate under provincial jurisdiction and are supported either by local taxation or provincial grants, or by both. This includes publicly supported Protestant and Roman Catholic SEPARATE SCHOOLS in some provinces. Education in local school districts is a provincial-local arrangement that allows some local adaptation to provincially set curriculum. Nearly 95% of the almost 5 million pupils enroled in all schools (1982-83) were enrolled in public schools.

Federal schools are operated by the federal government. The Department of Indian Affairs and Northern Development is responsible for Indian education in all provinces except Newfoundland (*see* NATIVE PEOPLE, EDUCATION). Federal schools generally follow the curriculum of the province in which they are located. The Department of National Defence operates a handful of schools in Canada and overseas for the children of Canadian servicemen. The overseas schools generally follow the curriculum of Ontario, whereas those in Canada follow the curriculum guidelines for public schools of the province in which they are located.

The term PRIVATE SCHOOLS generally describes schools that are not under the direct control of either the federal or provincial governments, although some provinces do provide some financial support. Religious organizations or other groups are directly responsible for the administration of these schools, which nevertheless usually operate within the guidelines determined by provincial departments of education. In 1981-82 private schools represented 4% of total enrolment, an increase of 2% in 10 years.

At the local level, the provinces are divided into public school districts that are typically governed by elected boards of trustees and administered by superintendents and their staffs. These local districts implement provincial educational policy; evaluate and promote students; employ, transfer and dismiss teachers and administrators; develop some local curricula; select texts; and raise supplementary funds through local property taxation (which is usually incorporated without review into municipal tax levies). They also assume responsibility for functions, such as CURRICULUM DEVELOPMENT, which may be decentralized by provincial governments. Several western provinces allow locally developed courses to be counted towards high-school graduation credits.

There are degree-granting post-secondary institutions (eg, universities, and liberal-arts colleges with degree-granting authority) and non-degree-granting institutions (eg, COMMUNITY COLLEGES, the one remaining teachers' college in Nova Scotia, and hospital NURSING schools). An extensive number of non-degree-granting organizations (eg, labour unions, libraries, churches, private companies, museums) are involved in providing ADULT EDUCATION.

Post-secondary institutions are organized differently in the various provinces. In some provinces, for example, public school boards are actively involved in delivering courses, while in others they are represented on the boards of colleges.

By 1982 full-time enrolment in undergraduate programs in colleges and universities had reached 693 300. The enrolment rate, ie, full-time enrolment, in post-secondary institutions as a proportion of the 18-24 age group, rose from 10% in 1960 to almost 25% by the early 1980s. The size and variety of the post-secondary system also increased during the 1960s and 1970s. New professional schools were created within the universities and there was an increase in graduate programs. By 1981-82, 34% of post-secondary learners were enrolled in community colleges; 22% in universities; 11% in programs run by high schools; 7% in programs at work; 4% in informal settings; and 22% in other learning situations.

Provincial Systems of Education Because the Constitution Act, 1867, made the provinces responsible for education, 12 autonomous education systems have developed in the 10 provinces and 2 territories. Each province has at least one minister of education, who is an elected member of the legislature (or, in Québec, the National Assembly). Each minister has one or more deputy ministers, appointed civil servants who administer their departments and advise the minister on policy. The minister and the department of education establish curricula, certify staff, approve textbooks, authorize capital developments and allocate the majority of operating funds to local school districts.

The typical provincial financing scheme is the foundation program, whereby a province guarantees a basic level of support for each public-school child and provides the difference between the funds raised by local school districts and the foundation level of support. A variety of special grant mechanisms to meet the special needs of particular school districts and pupils supplement this scheme.

The proportional contribution of local municipalities varies. For example, in 1980-81, no municipal dollars were raised in PEI or New Brunswick, but Manitoba municipalities contributed 30.9% of elementary-secondary school expenditures. The 2 territories received 57% of their expenditures from the federal government, which in total supplied between 6.3% to 14% of expenditures to various provinces.

Pluralism in school organization is most marked in the treatment of religious schools. Each province has developed its own solution to the issue of state-supported sectarian (usually Roman Catholic) schools. The pre-Confederation arrangement in Ontario led to the recognition of elementary separate schools organized as part of the public school system. In 1984 Premier William Davis announced that his government would extend funding of separate schools to grade 13. Saskatchewan and Alberta followed the same arrangement in 1905 when they became provinces (Alberta also has separate high schools). Québec's dual system (Catholic and Protestant) has been administered by a department of education since 1964. Unofficial local arrangements for public support to Catholic schools evolved in New Brunswick, Nova Scotia and PEI, although no legal provisions for sectarian schools existed when these provinces joined Confederation. Manitoba rejected legal and political attempts to re-establish state support for Roman Catholic schools in the 1890s (*see* MANITOBA SCHOOLS QUESTION), but by the 1960s modest state assistance was extended to them as well as to private schools. BC has a single public-school system but has provided tax support to private schools since 1977. The Terms of Union under which Newfoundland entered Confederation in 1949, guaranteed an exceptional denominational system, which has 3 types of school boards divided among several Christian groups.

The difference among the 12 education systems in Canada is also reflected in the establishment of different levels of schooling. New Brunswick does not support kindergartens in the elementary schools. The elementary level spans only the first 6 grades in 6 of the provinces and in the NWT. Other provinces include seventh or eighth grade in their elementary divisions. Secondary education (high school), covers 3 to 5 grades and is subdivided into junior high schools, senior high schools, or junior-senior high schools. Grade 12 is the highest grade in most provinces, but in Newfoundland and Québec it is grade 11, and in Ontario it is grade 13.

The institutional bases of post-secondary education have been brought increasingly under provincial authority. The development of college systems under close provincial control has been the most significant change in post-secondary education since the mid-1960s. Most universities, with few exceptions, operate under provincial charters. Until 1960 the majority of universities were considered private institutions and were not fully integrated with the provincial systems of education. Then provincially supported universities were established in Manitoba, PEI, Ontario, Québec, New Brunswick, Alberta and BC. Government review of university expenditures became more stringent, although in many cases it was conducted by an intermediate buffer authority such as a grants council. The Maritime Provinces Higher Education Commission plans and co-ordinates higher education systems and advises the 3 provincial governments. All provinces are increasingly exerting their authority in the overall planning, development and programming of universities.

The Federal Role Canada has no national ministry of education, nor even a co-ordinating body within the federal government. The federal government intervenes in education through a variety of programs operated by a multitude of departments and agencies. Although the most visible programs are sponsored by the Canada Employment and Immigration Commission and the Department of the Secretary of State, the federal presence in education is also manifest through the educational work of agencies such as the National Film Board and the Canadian Broadcasting Corporation.

Education is no longer what it was in 1867: the simplest of government services, easily administered and financed locally. The federal government has had to act to meet many national educational demands, financial and otherwise. The incursion of the federal government into a constitutional area where it had no legal jurisdictional powers commenced with very modest federal agricultural grants in 1912 to provinces and agricultural institutions and continued through the Technical Education Act of 1919, which provided grants to the provinces for upgrading vocational, technical, and industrial education. Powerful forces — the state of the economic system regional financial disparities, national unity — compelled a re-examination of the federal stance by the 1960s. Two programs in particular, one respecting vocational training (the Technical-Vocational Training Act, 1960) and the other official language instruction (OFFICIAL LANGUAGES ACT, 1970) effectively restructured these aspects of education in provincial schools and led to the growth of vocational education (some provinces built comprehensive high schools incorporating academic and vocational courses) and the growth of SECOND-LANGUAGE INSTRUCTION.

The federal role in post-secondary education expanded after WWII. By 1981 federal educational expenditures had reached $5.7 billion, of which more than $5 billion went towards post-secondary education. Under the 1960 Technical and Vocational Training Act, the 1967 Adult Occupational Training Act and the 1982 National Training Act, Parliament authorized the payment of allowances to individuals selected by the federal government to take occupational training. The Canada Student Loan Act (1964) authorized the federal government to subsidize bank loans to full-time students (Québec operates its own program) and the Fiscal Arrangements Act (1967, revised 1977) authorized federal unconditional grants to the provinces to defray 50% of the operating costs of post-secondary education (*see* STUDENTS, FINANCIAL AID TO).

The COUNCIL OF MINISTERS OF EDUCATION, CANADA (CMEC), which has operated at the national level since 1967 (on an interprovincial rather than a federal basis), sees itself as the official channel for decisions affecting Canada-wide educational policy. A small staff co-ordinates and supports committees on research related to reviewing federal legislation and financing and interprovincial co-ordination on concerns such as educational media and statistics.

An Assessment One of the most illuminating evaluations of Canadian education was made in the 1976 Report on Education in Canada by the Organization for Economic Cooperation and Development (OECD). Its declaration that "Canadian education policy may be one of the least 'politicized' in the world" explains the absence of a broad public dialogue about ends and means in education. The OECD Report concludes that "reforms in education are almost totally pragmatic, or so generally conceived and relying so heavily on United States, British, and French models, more or less adapted to Canadian conditions, that the opportunity for conflict is, for all practical purposes, excluded."

This absence of open political controversy helps maintain the status quo. The report also noted the dominance of unplanned development in education which can be traced largely to the inadequate funding of educational research. As a result, shifts in education often occur in response to public and political pressures rather than to well-researched systematic policy. In the 1960s, school organizations responded to the winds of change with "continuous progress" plans, vocational education, community colleges, more course options, "alternative" schools, decentralization and faculty power. The 1970s and 1980s saw a shift back to a more subject-oriented regime, centralization of power and "back to the basics" programs. It is doubtful that these shifts did much to relieve the problems of Canadian educators identified by the OECD examiners concerning the poor treatment of the arts and the educational handicaps of underprivileged groups. In addition, it may well be that the greater centralization of decision making in government bureaucracies, the priorities of government and demographic trends are all likely to generate increased uncertainty in respect to the organization (and implicity of the goals) of education in Canada. LIONEL ORLIKOW

Education Policy in each province is meant to develop the personal capacities of individuals, but also to impart skills useful to society, to induce conformity to community values and generally to encourage socialization. The tension between these aims has resulted in controversies over various aspects of the structure of EDUCATION systems, including curriculum (especially concerning sensitive subjects, eg, religious instruction or sex education); rights of ethnic, linguistic and religious minorities; the extent and forms of public financial support at the local, provincial and federal levels; and the related question of government control relative to the rights of pupils or students, parents and teachers.

Historically education was essentially a local and private matter (*see* EDUCATION HISTORY), undertaken largely at the initiative of parents and clergy. Colonial and later provincial governments legislated a general framework within which municipalities and religious or charitable institutions might establish and operate schools, especially where local taxes provided a public subsidy. The law ensured general public access to tax-supported schools even where these were confessional or sectarian. Provincial governments also licensed teachers and approved textbooks mainly to ensure that public funds would not be expended on schooling that catered only to a particular religious denomination. In some places special provision was made for religious and, implicitly, for linguistic minorities by establishing sectarian or "dissentient" schools. An attempt was made to offer constitutional protection for minority education rights in the BRITISH NORTH AMERICA ACT and in the Acts creating Manitoba (1870), Saskatchewan (1905) and Alberta (1905). Canadian education history is marked by controversies over separate schools in one province after another: NB, 1871; Manitoba, 1891-96; Alberta and Saskatchewan, 1905; Ontario, 1912; Québec, 1969-82. In every case constitutionally enshrined education rights were ineffective in protecting minorities increasingly concerned with questions of language and religion. In recent years, however, minority language instruction in several provinces has become far more widespread, and under the CONSTITUTION ACT, 1982, language rights (in English or French) in education were guaranteed where numbers warrant. Although the courts can enforce these rights, it remains to be seen how extensive they will become in practice; a particular problem may arise with Québec, which in 1974 and 1977 passed laws restricting access to English-language schools.

The protection of minority rights is the most visible feature of education policy, historically and currently; but of equal and perhaps even more fundamental importance has been the extension of the government's role in supporting and controlling educational institutions. The provincial governments, and in some respects also the federal government, feel responsible for ensuring universal access to high-quality instruction. From the age of 5 to about 16, school attendance is compulsory. Increasing attendance rates and the average number of years spent in school are major policy goals. Correspondingly, the control by provincial departments of education over local school boards has increased. The trend towards larger, eg, county, SCHOOL BOARDS and the extension of government control over some private but state-supported educational institutions (most universities in Ontario and eastwards, and several schools in Québec) also reflect centralization. The extension of the state's role has been the most far-reaching of the changes in Canadian education policies over the past century and has transformed the machinery for implementing education policy.

Policy Formation and Implementation In each province locally elected school boards are legally responsible for providing free and public schooling up to but not including the college or university level. The school system is typically divided into a primary level and a secondary level. Some programs of instruction terminate at grades 9 or 10, but most continue to grades 11, 12 or (in Ontario) 13. The BNA Act assigned education "in and for each province" exclusively to the provincial legislatures, except for the never-used federal power of remedial legislation if the rights of religious minorities were being disregarded. Provincial jurisdiction is jealously guarded, and there is considerable variation among the provinces in the structure of education systems. Overall policy is normally set by provincial departments of education. Departmental regulations or ministerial directives prescribe the basic components of the curriculum (*see* CURRICULUM DEVELOPMENT) as well as the range of courses that may be offered at the option of local boards or individual schools. The provincial government also approves instructional materials, establishes qualifications for teachers, specifies the rights of parents and students (eg, in the case of handicapped or gifted children), and sets expenditure ceilings on a per-student basis. Within the fairly narrow limits set by provincial regulations and financial constraints, the trustees elected to county or district boards exercise discretion over curriculum, the hiring, placement and remuneration of teachers, the location of schools and the range of programs offered by each. The degree of centralization in the system varies in each province.

The extension of provincial government control has not always been achieved without controversy. The most wrenching conflict occurred in Québec, where prior to the reforms of the 1960s most students going on to university attended private — mainly church-sponsored and -administered — "classical colleges." It was widely felt the state's role in education should consist mainly of providing financial support for a system of schooling (both public and private institutions) controlled in all important respects by the Roman Catholic Church. In policy-making structures the supervision of the school system was in practice the responsibility of 2 advisory committees, one Catholic (effectively the council of bishops) and the other Protestant, which was actually nonsectarian and served the entire English-language population of the province except for the Anglo-Catholics. By the late 1950s the Catholic system's deficiencies had become obvious, partly from the very low percentage of youth who obtained secondary schooling and partly from the curriculum's weakness in scientific and technical subjects. The plans of Paul GÉRIN-LAJOIE, minister of youth in the newly elected government of Jean LESAGE, to create a Ministry of Education (1964) and to modernize the system was strongly opposed by many traditional leaders of Québec society, who rightly perceived that the transformation of the education system would transform the entire society, and by much of the rural and lower-income population who would have to finance a system which they believed benefited primarily the aspiring urban middle class. Many rural dwellers also resented having to send their children to distant regional comprehensive schools. Successive governments nevertheless succeeded in remaking the system from kindergarten to university, revamping the curriculum and creating a network of comprehensive secondary schools and post-secondary institutions, or COLLÈGES D'ENSEIGNEMENT GÉNÉRAL ET PROFESSIONEL (CÉGEPs).

The controversial changes in Québec, which still generate bitter public disputes because fundamental reforms are still under way, are in some way similar to those experienced elsewhere in Canada at an earlier period and over a longer time. Nonetheless the Québec situation was and is unique; because of the minority position of the francophones within Canada and because of the former economic dominance of the anglophones, a linguistic and religious minority within the province, Québec has a special interest in preserving full control over the educational system at all levels.

Provincial autonomy in education has recently been challenged by the federal government. At the primary and secondary levels its interest has been limited to the extension of minority-language education through bilingualism grants. However, since WWII it has initiated manpower-training programs and has also attempted to broaden access to and rates of participation in post-secondary education. Over the past 30 years Ottawa has actively pursued all these policy aims through a variety of direct-expenditure programs (student aid, purchase of retraining services from vocational colleges, and from 1951 to 1967 direct grants to universities) and conditional grants to the provinces — a cash subsidy for which provinces are eligible if they adopt policies that meet certain conditions specified in federal legislation. At present the federal government transfers some $2 billion to the provinces annually, nominally for post-secondary education but in fact without conditions. There has also been since 1977 a transfer of a portion of the income tax, enabling provinces to swell revenues by an amount almost as large as the cash transfer (*see* INTERGOVERNMENTAL FINANCE). These sums, the cash transfer and the value of the tax points, grow each year at a rate faster than provincial spending. The provinces now finance a decreasing proportion of post-secondary education costs from their own revenue, which the federal government has stated flatly it does not like. It has hinted it will intervene more directly in post-secondary education in the future if the provinces do not support colleges and universities more generously and otherwise act to further national objectives in post-secondary education.

Critique of Education Policies Policies in any area must be evaluated according to their objectives. With education policy, individual and community preferences vary considerably. In matters of curriculum it is argued that pupils or students should be allowed to study what they choose at their own pace, while others demand a return to basics and a less liberal classroom atmosphere. Some critics urge respect for linguistic and religious particularities, while others insist that the building and preservation of community requires a common educational experience for the young, according to norms established by the majority. A single issue — whether education is primarily for the development of the individual's personal capacities or for molding character and imparting skills so that people become useful and well-adjusted social beings — underlies these disagreements; it is also at the root of controversies over the extent of public support for education (particularly at the post-secondary level), the importance of private institutions and the degree of government control over the system. There is, however, widespread agreement that the largest possible number of young people should complete a high-school program and that access to post-secondary education ought not to be restricted by the finances of individuals or their families. Internationally, Canada is second only to the US in rates of educational attainment (number of years of formal schooling commonly achieved). Within Canada, Québec now has the highest rates; otherwise, they tend to rise from E to W, probably because of varying community values and expectations and of differences in educational philosophy and practice.

Access to post-secondary education is commonly discussed as if it were primarily a ques-

tion of financial means (*see* EDUCATIONAL OPPORTUNITY). This factor is undeniably important; its recognition in government policy explains the continuing decline in the proportion of university operating costs borne by fees. In 1950 the average was 50%; in 1980 it was about 5%. Grants and loans are now far more generous and available than in the past; each province (except Québec) administers the federally funded Canada Student Loans Plan and supplements it with its own grants and loans. In most cases the restrictions on access to post-secondary education are now probably traceable to other than financial factors, eg, the program a student takes at the secondary level and whether he or she completes it. Here family background and the encouragement given or withheld by teachers at the primary and secondary levels are probably crucial.
PETER M. LESLIE

Educational Broadcasting refers to TELEVISION PROGRAMMING and RADIO PROGRAMMING providing or related to courses of study. The term "educational" is also applied at times to other programs that are particularly enlightening, informative or stimulating. Educational broadcasting can be received in the home or in an educational institution. Learning by yourself, in the home, is often called "distance education" and broadcasting is only one of several media that can be used to provide the course contents. Films, videotape recording and playback facilities, computer communications, and videodisc recordings are used to supplement written materials and the teacher's work.

Educational programming on radio has had a long, interesting history in Canada going back to the late 1920s. The University of Alberta was probably the first educational institution to get a radio-broadcasting licence in Canada (CKUA in 1927). Since then, many universities and colleges have become broadcasting licensees. Some stations are owned by the institutions themselves and others are owned and operated by student societies or associations. The most active in producing and broadcasting educational radio programs has been the CANADIAN BROADCASTING CORPORATION (CBC). From its start (1936), the CBC has used radio in original and innovative ways. Aside from the programs for preschool and school-age children, the CBC has received international recognition for its "National Farm Radio Forum" (1941-53). These programs discussed major issues and topics of interest to a farming community and were designed to be heard by adults in voluntarily organized listening groups, which would hold their own discussions after the program. Because of the "Forum's" great success, a similar program, called "Citizen's Forum" (1943-52), was established for a broader audience. However, "Citizen's Forum" was considered less successful because there were fewer listening groups and interests were too diffuse to be easily focused. The "Farm Forum" idea has been copied widely in developing countries since the 1950s as an excellent method for distributing information to rural people isolated from modern sources of agricultural knowledge and for encouraging people to exchange information and ideas among themselves.

The CBC's traditions in educational programming on radio are still carried on today although to a lesser extent. When TV services were introduced, the demands on CBC resources increased. It was impossible to engage in the more costly TV production on the same scale as had been possible for radio. The CBC's position as national broadcaster of educational programs has always been complicated because the CBC is a federal CROWN CORPORATION and education is a provincial responsibility. So, all CBC instructional programs for schools have been produced and aired under arrangements whereby the provincial educational departments would be responsible for the content of a program though CBC produced the program and transmitted it to the audience. At present, the COUNCIL OF MINISTERS OF EDUCATION works with the CBC to develop programming plans and to work out cost-sharing arrangements. In addition to the broadcasts for each province alone, some programs are shared by several provinces. Programs produced by the CBC for countrywide distribution are called Canadian Schools Broadcasts and Canadian Schools Telecasts.

Scene from the popular children's program "The Polka Dot Door" (*courtesy TVOntario*).

Some provinces indicated in the 1960s that they wanted educational TV facilities of their own. In metropolitan areas such as Toronto, local school boards began producing TV programming and using CABLE TV channels to reach viewers at home and in schools. Furthermore, several provinces, particularly Ontario, indicated that they wanted to control their own educational TV programs. A satisfactory agreement was reached in 1969 when it was decided that a province could establish a specially incorporated provincial educational authority that would hold any broadcasting licences issued. Each such authority depends entirely on funds voted by the provincial legislature to pay for its broadcasting service. The Québec Broadcasting Bureau (Radio Québec) was first established in 1969 and revised in 1972 to meet the new licensing requirements for educational broadcasting. The Ontario Educational Communications Authority (OECA) was set up in 1970 to provide educational programs for all ages; this authority is called TV Ontario, or TVO. The Ontario and Québec authorities each hold licences for several TV stations. Both provinces will be able to reach more people when new transmitters or satellite distribution systems can be set up. In Alberta, the Alberta Educational Communications Corp (ACCESS) was set up (1973) to carry out the educational broadcasting goals of the Alberta Educational Communications Authority. ACCESS now operates the radio station CKUA, which has become the basis for a province-wide radio service. ACCESS also engages in TV production to provide programs through cable TV systems, satellite distribution and some private TV stations. In BC, another approach was taken when the Knowledge Network of the West Communications Authority (KNOW) was established (1980). KNOW does not engage in program production but provides a communications distribution system for all universities and colleges in the province who wish to use it. KNOW uses a satellite linkage from the Vancouver area to Anik B, which then beams the signal throughout the province to cable TV systems for distribution. Much of the programming schedule distributed by KNOW is produced outside the province, principally by OECA, the Open University in Britain, and some American sources. Saskatchewan set up an Educational Communications Corp (SaskMedia) in 1974 to distribute educational materials. So far, the corporation has not sought broadcasting licences, preferring to rely on circulation of audio-visual materials directly to schools and other institutions. There have been discussions about the development of a nationwide educational TV network using the existing authorities' resources, with contributions from the others of programs or funding. The Agency for Tele-Education in Canada (ATEC), made up of representatives from Radio Québec, OECA, ACCESS, KNOW and SaskMedia, has put forward proposals for such a network that would be received by most Canadians.
JEAN MCNULTY

Educational Foundations and Endowments The *Canadian Directory of Foundations and Granting Agencies* lists 595 agencies that exist primarily to disburse funds. Within the directory's subcategory of "Education," only 14 FOUNDATIONS and endowments (terms used interchangeably) are listed. Of these 14 the oldest, McLean, was established in 1945, and most of the others were established between 1960 and 1975. On the basis of 1981 data, this group was responsible for grants of approximately $20 million annually, ranging from $60 000 (Lepage) to over $6 million (Hospital for Sick Children). A number of the endowments are in fact limited to projects either in medicine or in areas related to medicine. None of the 14 foundations is either exclusively or even primarily concerned with education itself.

On the other hand, a number of Canadian foundations and endowments not listed under "Education" do support work in this field. Most of these funds were established after WWII. Some of the better known include Atkinson, Donner Canadian, Bronfman Family, Laidlaw, McConnell and Max Bell. These funds represent median annual disbursements of over $2 million whereas the corresponding figure for the first group is less than $1 million. In addition, there are agencies, such as the Canadian Education Association and the Canada Studies Foundation, that provide some funding for research and program development. In relation to the annual Canadian public investment in education of $10 billion, the effective contribution of Canadian endowments and foundations is marginal at best.

Several of the Canadian educational foundations and endowments (eg, Labatt, McDonald Stewart, Jackman, McConnell) are general purpose in scope; much more common (at least with regard to education) are endowments for specialization. For example, Max Bell is likely to be focused on health care and medicine; Bronfman on learning disabilities; Canada's North on native people and heritage projects; Foster on mental retardation; and Donner on law reform and Canadian foreign policy. Moreover, even when published guidelines are general in nature, funds are frequently disbursed for particular purposes. There is at least one fund that specifies the eligibility of broad areas of education research but which in fact supports university-based research only in medicine. Individuals and institutions who are in search of funding support need to develop a very detailed knowledge of the particular preferences of each fund.
BERNARD J. SHAPIRO

Educational Opportunity Education has been seen in modern industrial societies, as the way to provide equality of opportunity. Education, it is argued, can provide this opportunity because it prepares young people for jobs in a continually changing world and allows the most able to develop their talents and to rise to the top. Inequalities in a society can be justified if everyone has a chance to acquire the rewards that the society has to offer. One of the goals of education since the early 1960s in Canada as well as in the rest of the Western world has been to eliminate barriers that are based on race, ethnicity, sex and social class.

Although equality of opportunity has always been seen as a reason for the expansion of education, economic and social reasons have been equally important. In Upper Canada, Egerton RYERSON, the first superintendent of education, lauded education as "the most effectual preventative of pauperism and its natural companions, misery and crime." In the 19th century, the goal of educational reformers was not access to higher education but the provision of free, universal, compulsory, elementary education (*see* EDUCATION, HISTORY OF). This goal was strenuously opposed by those who were not prepared to have their taxes used for the benefit of other people's children and by those who resisted the intervention of the state in the lives of families.

By the 1960s, the new goal, accessibility to UNIVERSITY for all who wished it and were able to benefit from it, was endorsed by the 1948 Universal Declaration of Human Rights adopted by the UN General Assembly with the qualification: "Higher education shall be made equally accessible to all on the basis of merit." In the 1960s the expansion of education was promoted as being essential in order to provide a postindustrial society with the skills it would require.

In Canada, until the 1960s, there were few educational opportunities for high-school students (only 4% went on to university). During the 1960s, however, post-secondary education expanded enormously. COMMUNITY COLLEGES were established, existing universities were expanded, and new ones created. Full-time enrollments to all post-secondary institutions increased by 214% in a decade. Simultaneously, expenditures increased. These expenditures and the economic crisis of the 1970s and 1980s led to a questioning of the educational system and the policy of accessibility on which it was based.

In the 1960s, however, post-secondary education was seen as a panacea for personal, social and economic ills. To widen accessibility, student assistance plans were implemented in all provinces (*see* STUDENTS, FINANCIAL AID TO). The federal government's involvement began with aid to veterans after both world wars. The Dominion-Provincial Student Aid Program (1939) was supplanted by the Canada Student Loans Plan (CSLP) in 1964. Under the CSLP the federal government assumed responsibility for providing guaranteed loans to all students who demonstrated need. The provinces were to administer the program under jointly agreed criteria. All provinces and territories, except Québec, which provides its own program, participated. Provincial governments supplemented the Canada Student Loans with loans, grants and bursaries.

Both the idea that education could ensure equality of opportunity and the belief that the postindustrial world would require an upgrading of the labour force were later challenged. In *The Rise of the Meritocracy* (1970), author Michael Young predicted that in a society based on meritocracy ruthless competition and rigorous selection would create an upper class of masters and an under class of drones. Others have questioned the idea that a just society can emerge based on equality of opportunity. In *Labour and Monopoly Capital*, Harry Braverman argued that in a technologically advanced society there would be a degrading of the labour force; a relatively few highly trained workers would be necessary, and the mass of workers would require fewer skills.

Others have argued that the society that develops as a result of the expansion of higher education is one in which credentials, rather than job requirements or a person's inherent skills and ability, determine accessibility to occupations. This argument is based on evidence that the increasing educational requirements for jobs are not a result of the increasing complexity of jobs; rather, they are caused by employers using educational credentials as screening devices.

Finally, there are critics who believe that the educational system does not provide opportunities for equality but perpetuates the inequalities that already exist, and that one way that it does so is by "streaming" students from different socioeconomic backgrounds into different programs (*see also* SOCIAL CLASS). Moreover, these critics claim that attitude and personality are more important than intelligence and ability in determining who is "successful" in school.

Canadian society has not found easy answers to these questions, but general support still exists for the belief that it is profoundly unfair to limit opportunities for higher education to those who through their socialization in privileged families can best meet rigid selection procedures.

MARION PORTER

Reading: H. Braverman, *Labor and Monopoly Capital* (1974); John Porter, "Education, Equality and the Just Society," in John Porter, *The Measure of Canadian Society* (1979); Porter, Marion Porter and B.R. Blishen, *Stations and Callings* (1982).

Edwards, Henrietta Louise, née Muir, women's rights activist, reformer (b at Montréal 18 Dec 1849; d at Ft Macleod, Alta 10 Nov 1931). Of a wealthy family, Edwards early evinced feminist sympathies; in 1875 she founded the Working Girls' Assn to provide vocational training and edited a journal, *Women's Work in Canada*. She helped Lady ABERDEEN found the National Council of Women (1893) and also helped found the Victorian Order of Nurses. One of Alberta's "Famous Five" in the PERSONS CASE and a supporter of divorce on equal grounds, prison reform and mother's allowances, she aimed to expand women's rights in the political and especially the legal sphere. She wrote *The Legal Status of Women in Alberta* (1921) and pressed for the 1917 Dower Act. ELIANE LESLAU SILVERMAN

Henrietta Louise Edwards, an early women's rights activist (*courtesy Glenbow Archives*).

Edwards, Robert Chambers, "Bob," newspaper publisher (b at Edinburgh, Scot 12 Sept 1864; d at Calgary 14 Nov 1922). Related to the Chambers publishing family, he emigrated to western Canada in 1894; in 1897 he launched the *Wetaskiwin Free Lance*, forerunner of the Calgary *Eye-Opener*, an itinerant newspaper first published in High River in 1902 that gained a reputation for originality and wit. Lampooning society and political personalities, the *Eye-Opener* was the target of legal actions that included one on behalf of Prem A.L. SIFTON. The *Eye-Opener* called the 3 biggest liars in Alberta "Robert Edwards, Gentleman; Hon A.L. Sifton (premier); and Bob Edwards, Editor of the Eye-Opener." The suit was dropped when Edwards filed a similar action on behalf of Robert Edwards, Gentleman, and Bob Edwards, Editor. An alcoholic, usually in debt, Edwards moved to Toronto in 1909, then to Montréal, Port Arthur, Ont, and Winnipeg, returning to Calgary in 1911. Unconventional to the end, he supported PROHIBITION in the referendum of 1916, then won election as an Independent in the 1921 provincial elections. He was able to attend only one sitting before his death. His reputation was such that police in dress uniform were his pallbearers, and today his status as a maverick publisher has become a western legend.

JOHN PATRICK GILLESE

Bob Edwards, *c* 1910. His wit and his lampooning of society and political personalities landed him with several legal suits but gained him an unmatched reputation as a maverick journalist (*courtesy Provincial Archives of Alberta/H. Pollard Coll*).

Edwards, William Cameron, industrialist, politician (b in Clarence Twp, Russell County, Canada W 7 May 1844; d at Ottawa 17 Sept 1921). Edwards entered the lumbering business in Thurso but moved to Rockland in 1868 and founded W.C. Edwards and Co, building large sawmills at Rockland and New Edinburgh. A noted stockbreeder and agriculturalist, he represented Russell in Parliament 1887-1903, when he was appointed to the Senate. He accompanied PM Wilfrid LAURIER to Queen Victoria's Diamond Jubilee in 1897 and King Edward's coronation in 1902. Edwards was president of Canada Cement and the Russell Agricultural Soc, and director of many companies, including the Canadian Bank of Commerce, Canada Central Railway, Canadian Forestry Association and the Central Canada Exhibition. In 1920 he helped organize a $60-million merger involving Riordon Pulp and Paper Co. RICHARD REID

Eel, snakelike FISH of class Osteichthyes, order Anguilliformes (or Apodes). There are about 20 families, 130 genera and 600 species, including moray, conger, snake and snipe eels. Except for the freshwater family Anguillidae, they are marine, abounding in shallow waters of tropical and subtropical seas. Some inhabit deep seas. There are 11 species in 11 genera in Canadian Atlantic waters, including deep- and shallow-water forms; 4 species in 4 genera of deep-water forms occur in Canadian Pacific waters. The American eel (*Anguilla rostrata*) occurs widely in eastern Canadian fresh waters. Eels, typically, are elongated, round in cross section at the front and laterally compressed toward the back. They lack pelvic fins; the dorsal and anal fins are usually continuous with the tail fin. Most species lack scales. Eels are predaceous and tend to be nocturnal. The American and European eels are catadromous, ie, spend their lives in fresh water, returning to the ocean (the Atlantic, near the West Indies) to spawn and die. Larvae take one year to reach the N American coast and probably 3 years to reach the European coast. Spawning behaviour and exact place and time of spawning are subjects of continuing research. These eels are highly regarded as food, especially when smoked. W.B. SCOTT

Eenoolooapik, "Bobbie", Inuk traveller, guide (b Qimisuk, Cumberland Sound, NWT 1820?; d at Cumberland Sound 1847), brother of TOOKOOLITO. He travelled to Britain in 1839 with whaling captain William Penny, who had hoped to establish a wintering base for whalers in Cumberland Sd. Penny's plan was rejected, but Eenoolooapik's friendliness and sense of humour endeared him to the British, who followed newspaper reports of his activities. In 1840, after helping Penny enter Cumberland Sd, he returned to his birthplace where he married and lived as a hunter and trader. Not long after his death, wintering in Cumberland Sd became common practice among whalers, and thus the knowledge Eenoolooapik provided to his European friends served to accelerate the colonization of his homeland. JOHN BENNETT

Eggplant (*Solanum melongena* var. *esculentum*), or aubergine, perennial herbaceous PLANT of the NIGHTSHADE family. The genus contains about 1500 tropical and temperate climate species; one wild and 5 cultivated species occur in Canada. Native to SW Asia, eggplant was derived from a wild species with egg-shaped fruits. Plants are either bushy or upright, 45-100 cm tall; flowers (2-4 cm across) are purple and usually occur singly. Fruits (20-25 cm long) are a glossy purplish black with a green calyx. A long-season crop, eggplants require a greenhouse or hotbed start of 9-10 weeks and reach maturity 55-80 days after transplanting. INSECT PESTS are fleas and Colorado potato beetles; plant diseases, *Verticillium* and bacterial wilts. Eggplants are comparable to TOMATOES in nutrition, but have better shelf life. Eggplants are a low-hectarage commercial crop in Canada but are grown in gardens across the country. V.W. NUTTALL

Elbow, Sask, Village, pop 313 (1981c), inc 1909, is situated midway between SASKATOON and MOOSE JAW. It received its name because of a configuration of the S Saskatchewan R, on which it sits. While the village of Elbow dates only from the early years of this century, the general location had been so designated for more than 100 years. The first known use of the term "elbow" is found in the journal of John Macdonald of Garth, a fur trader of the NWC, who wrote, "There is an elbow in the river parallel to that of the north branch, a most beautiful place." The first settlers appear to have been ranchers. By 1903 settlers were taking up homesteads near Elbow, and by the end of the decade lands in the elbow were extensively occupied. The CANADIAN PACIFIC RWY, which arrived in 1908, has accounted for the continued existence of Elbow. DON HERPERGER

Elder, shrub of genus *Sambucus*, family Caprifoliaceae (honeysuckle). Elders grow up to 3 m high and spread to form thickets. About 20 species are known worldwide; 3 are native to Canada. The leaves are large, opposite and pinnate with 5-11 leaflets. They are usually hairy underneath. Several stems arise from one root. The pithy-cored stems are sometimes hollowed out and used for peashooters and whistles; however, the roots, stems and leaves are poisonous. Their emetic and purgative properties were used in European and N American folk medicine. The small, cream-coloured flowers are borne in dense clusters. They are edible and are used to flavour beverages. The juicy, berrylike fruits are blue, black or red, depending on species. The fruits of blue- and black-fruited species are seedy, and not very palatable when raw, but make excellent wine, jelly and pie, alone or combined with other fruits. *See* PLANTS, NATIVE USES. NANCY J. TURNER

Elder, James, equestrian (b at Toronto, Ont 27 July 1934). An illustrious international equestrian for over a quarter-century, Elder was a member of the bronze-medal Canadian team in the 3-day event at the 1956 Melbourne Olympics and of the winning 1959 Pan-American Games team. With the Canadian show-jumping team since 1952 — for several years as captain — he formed a trio with James DAY and Thomas GAYFORD that brought Canadian equestrians to the fore in the late 1960s. Their victories included the Grand Prix at the 1968 Mexico City Olympics, the World Championships (1970) and the Pan-American Games (1971). Elder represented Canada in the 1972, 1976 and 1984 Olympics, and was on the winning teams at the Olympic Games alternate Nation's Cup in Rotterdam (1980) and at the CSIO Nation's Cup in Sydney, Australia (1982). He was individual international champion at the Royal Horse Show 3 times. BARBARA SCHRODT

Elder, Richard Bruce, filmmaker, critic (b at Hawkesbury, Ont 12 June 1947). Internationally recognized for his avant-garde films and his writing on film and computer technology, Elder studied cinema at Ryerson and the University Film Study Centre after graduating from U of T with an MA 1970. His *Barbara is a Vision of Loveliness* won the 1976 Canadian Film Award for best experimental film and his autobiographical *The Art of Worldly Wisdom* (1979) was named Best Independent Experimental Film by the Los Angeles Critics Circle. Elder's recent works — *1857: Fool's Gold* (1980), *Illuminated Texts* (1982) — are characterized by their incorporation of written texts and their use of computer-generated optical printing and sound. SETH FELDMAN

Election Expenses Act, which came into effect on 1 Aug 1974, made important changes to federal ELECTION and income tax laws. The new laws provided that a certain proportion of an individual's contribution to a federal registered political party or a federal election candidate could be deducted from payable federal income tax. Some provinces have now made similar provisions for their own elections. The new legislation also limited the amount of money that could be spent in an election campaign (*see* ELECTORAL SYSTEMS). The amount that a registered party can spend is limited to a total based on the number of electors in each district where it is running candidates. Individual candidates' election expenses are also limited by the number of names on the list of electors in their district. After an election, candidates and parties must file audited reports detailing expenses incurred and contributions received. Candidates who receive at least 15% of the votes cast in their district are entitled to a partial reimbursement of their expenses. TERENCE QUALTER

Elections Canadian elections are held under a process which reflects well-understood principles and is an integral part of the country's political culture. Despite the varying regional differences that often appear in election results, the process itself is national; the same basic rules are in force from coast to coast. The first few federal elections were held under disparate provincial laws, but in the 1870s the first national election provisions were enacted, laying the foundations for the present system. Seats are shared first among the provinces, and then constituency boundaries are drawn by commissions established under federal law. Between elections, by-elections can be held to fill vacancies in the HOUSE OF COMMONS; one of the duties of the Chief Electoral Officer is to keep the whole system under continual review, with improvements constantly in mind. The apparent stability of the process can be misleading. A political party can poll more votes than a rival but lose an election, as the CONSERVATIVE PARTY did in 1896. A party can win almost identical shares of the popular vote in consecutive elections but lose the first disastrously and score a triumph in the second, as the LIBERAL PARTY did in 1930 and 1935. A party can be weak nationally but, if its support is concentrated in one area, may elect several members, as the SOCIAL CREDIT PARTY did in Alberta through several elections beginning in 1940. A party can have a stable national support but, if votes for it are scattered across the country, its share of victories in any election may lag far behind its share of the vote, as the CO-OPERATIVE COMMONWEALTH FEDERATION (CCF) and its successor, the NEW DEMOCRATIC PARTY (NDP), have experienced.

The unbalanced nature of many election results can be attributed chiefly to the single-member constituency system (*see* ELECTORAL SYSTEM), in which a candidate need poll only one vote more than the runner-up to win the seat no matter how many votes the other candidates amass, and to the federal distribution of the seats in the House of Commons. The distribution not only makes it easier for a party concentrating in one area to win seats there, but the disproportionate size of Ontario and Québec (which between them have always had more than half the seats in the Commons) permits a party to do reasonably well in either of them without necessarily winning many seats. The classic case is that of the federal Conservative party in Québec prior to the 1984 election, but since the 1950s the Liberals have had similar difficulties in the West. A relatively new factor, the extent of whose influence on election results is as yet unknown, is the combined use of television and advertising agencies in campaign strategies.

National elections can occur for several reasons. A House of Commons ceases to exist 5 years after the writs for the last election are returned, and an election may be necessary because the existing Commons has constitutionally expired, as happened in 1896 and (almost) in 1935, and might have happened in 1916 if the CONSTITUTION had not been temporarily amended to prolong the life of the Parliament chosen in 1911. A PRIME MINISTER has the power to advise the dissolution of Parliament when he considers it wise or expedient, and elections have been held as close together as 1872 and 1874, 1925 and 1926, 1957 and 1958, and 1962 and 1963. A change of prime minister may bring on an election; eg, when Pierre TRUDEAU became prime minister in 1968, one of his first official acts was to advise the dissolution of Parliament. The defeat of a government in the House of Commons may precipitate an election (1926, 1963 and 1979): if the government loses the ensuing election, it is replaced; if it wins, it simply continues in office. While elections and changes in either prime minister or the government as a whole may be related to each other, there is no necessary connection between elections and changes in the executive. The Conservatives won in 1872, but their leader, Sir John A. MACDONALD, resigned in 1873 because he was convinced he had lost the support of too many of his own party members in the Commons to carry on; the next election, called by his Liberal successor, Alexander MACKENZIE, was in 1874. Macdonald, who died after the election of 1891, was followed by 4 consecutive Conservative prime ministers, one of whom also died in office, but there was no election until 1896. In 1925 the Conservatives won more seats than the Liberals, but remained in opposition. In 1926 the Conservative leader, Arthur MEIGHEN, did become prime minister without an election, but when he called an election in that year and lost it, he also lost the prime ministership. Sometimes there is a connection between an election and executive changes, and sometimes there is not.

All the prime ministers mentioned above were party leaders, and the election system relies wholly on parties (*see* PARTY SYSTEM); Parliament provides through elaborate laws for the holding of elections, but the laws do not require anybody to come forth to hold one. Each party assumes that function in its own interests, providing candidates, planning and financing the campaigns, selecting the issues over which each election is fought, and providing the leader who, each party hopes, will become prime minister or at least leader of the Opposition (*see* LEADERSHIP CONVENTION). While it is not impossible for independents to get elected to Parliament, it is unusual; the parties, in effect, provide candidates for each election. They use an elaborate and closely regulated administrative machine provided by the state, but in so doing privately raise and spend large amounts of money. The amounts, and the purposes on which the money can be spent, are now also regulated (*see* ELECTION EXPENSES ACT) but the limits on both parties and candidates are generous. The law of elections also provides for reimbursement of candidates for certain legitimate expenses (provided they win a prescribed share of the vote), so that serious aspirants to Parliament need not be deterred from running solely for financial reasons.

Each general election is unique, for while the basic principles on which elections are conducted have varied remarkably little since the beginning, the personnel involved and the issues fought over are never entirely the same. Some elections are fought mainly on one clear-cut issue: eg, in 1911, the governing Liberals favoured a comprehensive reciprocal trade agreement with the US; the Conservatives opposed it and won. In 1917 the Conservatives favoured CONSCRIPTION for overseas service, and the issue so deeply divided the Liberals in Opposition that they could not mount a united campaign either for or against it; the leader, LAURIER, opposed conscription, and while the issue in 1917 reduced Liberal strength in Parliament to its lowest ebb since CONFEDERATION, the Conservatives thereafter found Québec all but closed to them. If a Government has been long in power, as the Conservatives were under Macdonald to 1891 and the Liberals were under KING and ST. LAURENT to 1957, its record is invariably an issue in each election.

Rising prosperity is generally good for a governing party, as the Liberals showed after 1896 and 1945, and its opposite, depression, can haunt a party for decades, as the Conservatives found after 1935. Modern electronics has created new kinds of issues, since the parties' credibility on television, and in particular the leaders' images, have become factors in attracting and repelling voters. In a manner that successful former electioneers such as Macdonald, Laurier, BORDEN and King might find difficult to approve, a modern election produces a series of selling campaigns in which each leader and party is packaged as enticingly as possible for marketing. In a modern election an individual party leader may become an issue.

Few Canadian elections have been fought on issues as fundamental as free trade versus protectionism, monarchy versus republicanism, or democracy versus authoritarianism, although there have been elections in which basic issues have been important. The 1911 election, for example, created heated arguments over Canada's relations with the US, and that of 1926 was exploited by King to challenge Canada's relationship with the UK in a way that soon altered the relationship. But the raising of fundamental principles as election issues in Canada is not often attractive to political parties because of 2 considerations that are also fundamental. Quite apart from the difficulties of making abstract principles comprehensible as useful material in election campaigns, the Canadian electorate is so varied that a basic issue can provoke vastly different and even opposing responses in different parts of the country. The clearest single historical example is the question of whether Canadians should be conscripted to fight in wars abroad: in 1917 the Government gave one answer, and the party chiefly responsible for it suffered electorally for decades; in WWII the Government believed that a yes or no answer at the national level was not possible and produced a slogan that is a Canadian model of its kind, "Conscription if necessary, but not necessarily conscription."

The diversity of the country produces the other basic consideration; any party hoping to find electoral success in Canada has to have a broad appeal, and the result is that the parties rarely differ deeply on fundamental issues. All parties successful in elections contain individuals of enormously varied opinions, but during elections the parties generally present a united front which does not encourage the expression of the extremes of opinion within the party. All the parties agree on the retention of the monarch, of Parliament, of the party system and of free elections. All are committed to a broad range of health and welfare policies and to a mixture of public and private enterprise. All recognize that foreign investment in Canada can have undesirable effects but that it is necessary. No "extreme" party in Canada has ever, in fact, successfully used elections to produce a regular contingent of members of Parliament. *See* ELECTORAL BEHAVIOUR. NORMAN WARD

Electoral Behaviour Nearly 11.5 million Canadians (76% of those eligible) went to the polls in May 1979 to elect a new Progressive CONSERVATIVE government headed by Joe CLARK. Almost as many returned 9 months later to defeat Clark's government and return Pierre TRUDEAU'S LIBERALS to power. At a time when participation in ELECTIONS has been declining in many countries, voting turnout in Canada has remained high. It compares very favourably with the 54% turnout in the 1980 US presidential election. While a sharp swing from one party to another seemed unusual in the 1979 and 1980 federal elections, volatile political trends are fairly commonplace in Canada. John DIEFENBAKER swept to power with a record majority in 1958 but was ousted by the Liberals under Lester PEARSON only 5 years later. The sudden rise and fall of provincial political movements such as the SOCIAL CREDIT PARTY or the PARTI QUÉBÉCOIS provides further evidence of the Canadian electorate's capacity for sudden and sometimes dramatic political change.

The results of federal elections are not always clear and decisive. Canadians have elected MINORITY GOVERNMENTS in 6 of the last 10 federal elections, partly because no single political party consistently enjoys the support of a majority of all voters. It has been especially difficult for one party to obtain a majority in recent years because political trends in one part of the country are not always reflected in others. In the 1979 federal election the Liberals lost ground in most of the country but managed to improve their position in Québec by enough to deny the victorious Conservatives a majority of seats. In spite of Clark's efforts to establish a base for his party in Québec, the Conservatives' showing in that province slipped further in the next election. The Liberals were unable to win any seats in 3 of the 4 western provinces in the 1980 federal election in spite of their strong performance in eastern and central Canada. This regionalization of Canadian politics made government of a large and diverse country difficult and elections unpredictable. However, the massive electoral sweep by the Conservatives under Brian MULRONEY in 1984, including 58 seats in Québec, changed the situation dramatically.

While most Canadians identify themselves at least nominally with one of the 4 main political parties, these ties are not as durable as they tend to be in some European countries where the political parties reflect strong social class or religious feelings. An observer comparing Canada to the US, the UK and Australia a few years ago said that Canada had a form of "pure non-class politics." Feelings about class, religion or ethnic ties are capable of explaining no more than about 10% of the behaviour of Canadians in elections (*see* CLASS AND POLITICS). In this century the Liberal Party has tended to enjoy greater support among Roman Catholics and among people of French ancestry, partly because of its persistent strength in Québec (until 1984), but its support among these groups extends beyond provincial boundaries, as the election of a Liberal member for the St Boniface riding in Manitoba in the 1980 federal election demonstrates. The Conservatives, although strong in the West, have been losing ground in recent years among younger voters in all parts of the country. The NEW DEMOCRATIC PARTY has sought to consolidate its position with organized labour, but in spite of this affiliation its support is only slightly better among voters who are members of trade unions than among those who are not. Short-term factors — eg, particular political issues or people's feelings about individual political leaders, factors more vulnerable to change from one election to another or from one region to another — have much more to do with voting behaviour. The principal issues in the 1979 election were inflation, the performance of the economy and national unity, of particular concern with regard to Québec; but in 1980, the election campaign focused more heavily on the federal budget on which the Clark government had been defeated in Parliament, energy pricing issues and the general question of leadership. PM Trudeau's personal popularity declined significantly in the 1972 and 1979 federal elections but rebounded in 1974 and 1980. Former PM Clark, whose political popularity never equalled Trudeau's, found his leadership a major issue during and after the 1980 election and lost his party's leadership at a convention in 1983. With Trudeau replaced by John TURNER as Liberal leader, new Conservative leader Mulroney was able to focus the campaign on a rash of Liberal patronage appointments and the need to end the long Liberal rule.

Because Canada is a federal political system, both national and regional or provincial feelings sometimes affect the behaviour of voters in elections. Some Canadians feel more strongly about the politics of their own province or region and some provinces have party systems quite different from those at the federal level. The Social Credit Party, which has held power provincially in BC and Alberta, has never been a significant political force in Ontario or the Maritimes. The NDP is a small third party in much of the East but a strong contender for power in 3 of the 4 western provinces. The Liberals have been extraordinarily successful in Québec but increasingly weak in the West and at the provincial level in many other parts of the country. At the time of their victory in the 1980 federal election, they did not hold power in any of the 10 provincial governments.

These patterns of behaviour in elections are characteristic of Canada's decentralized political system and are not likely to change soon. Younger generations of Canadians behave very similarly in electoral matters to their elders — they too have their preferences for one party or an-ther but are quite willing to change them in esponse to a new problem or issue, or to support new political leader. LAWRENCE LEDUC

lectoral Systems, methods of choosing gov-rnment representatives. The Canadian federal LECTION system is governed by the Canada Elec-ons Act, which is amended from time to time. he provinces have election systems governed y provincial election acts and very similar to he federal system, but they are all slightly dif-erent from each other in important details. Fed-ral election practices are not to be taken as an ccurate guide to provincial elections. The Cana-ian election process is extremely complicated; he rules apply to most people most of the time, ut in every case there are exceptions and special ircumstances.

Voting Until 1917, in Canada, only men were llowed to vote, and even then only those with considerable amount of property (*see* HUMAN IGHTS and FRANCHISE). Now any Canadian citi-en at least 18 years old and living in Canada an vote, but the voter's name must appear on n official list of voters. In urban areas, enumer-tors go from door to door some weeks before an lection, gathering a list of people entitled to ote. In rural areas the strictness of the rules is elaxed a little; eg, the enumerator may compile ists from visits, personal knowledge of people n the area, information from neighbours, etc. Also, in rural areas those not on the list may vote if another qualified voter will vouch for hem. The enumeration procedure is one reason or the length of Canadian federal election cam-aigns (normally about 60 days). It takes a great eal of time to appoint and instruct enumer-tors, to visit every resident in Canada and to ollect, check and print a list of names. The al-ernative — a permanent voters' list — has many advantages, but is extremely expensive to naintain. With a maximum interval of 5 years, federal election may be called at any time, argely at the discretion of the PRIME MINISTER.

Candidates With some exceptions, and after complying with certain legal requirements, any voter may also be a candidate, but the only can-didates who have any real chance of being elect-ed are those who have a party label; most candi-dates are judged by their party affiliation rather than their personal qualifications. Since 1972 the candidate's party has appeared following his or her name on the ballot paper, and this has made it even more difficult for an independent candidate to win more than a few hundred votes. However, the procedures by which the parties nominate their candidates are de-termined by the parties themselves, and are not subject to election laws (*see* ELECTION EXPENSES ACT).

Example 1		Example 2	
Candidate	*No. of Votes*	*Candidate*	*No. of Votes*
A	37 400 (91%)	A	7 999 (26%)
B	1 965	B	7 940
C	1 583	C	7 662
D	182	D	7 121

Constituencies Canada is divided into single-member constituencies — increased from 282 in 1976 to 310 after 1982 (*see* REDISTRIBUTION). Voters can vote only in the constituency in which they have been enumerated and for one of the candi-dates running in that constituency. The constit-uencies are divided into a number of polling divisions, each with about 250 electors. Voters must cast their ballots in the polling division where their names are registered. Certain catego-ries of voters, required to be away from their constituencies (sometimes called "ridings") on election day may vote by proxy; that is to say, they may arrange for another elector in their home constituency to vote on their behalf.

Voting System Some parts of the world have very complicated voting systems but Canada's, known as the plurality system, is very simple. In any constituency the voter casts a single vote and the candidate with the greatest number of votes is elected. This can produce some strange results; while the winning candidate in a constit-uency contested by only two candidates must have a majority of the votes cast, a candidate in another constituency, contested by several can-didates, might be elected even though a substan-tial majority of the electors voted against him. Far more often than not a Canadian government will be elected with a majority of seats and con-siderably less than a majority of votes. A further consequence of this political arithmetic is a re-gional concentration of political party represen-tation. A party may appear strong in one region and weak in another, due only to a disparity in number of seats far greater than the actual dis-tribution of the popular vote. There are many alternative voting systems, but none is perfect. Any of the defects of the present Canadian sys-tem could be corrected, but not without creating new, and perhaps even more serious problems.

Election Administration The actual operation of a federal election is under the overall author-ity of a Chief Electoral Officer; authority in each constituency is vested in a permanent Returning Officer. Voting in a federal election is on the same day across the country, with the hours of voting extensive enough to give all who want to vote a reasonable opportunity to do so. Those who have reason to suppose they will not be able to vote on the day of the general election may vote in special advance polls a few days be-fore. To prevent voters from being influenced on the main polling day, the ballots from the advance polls are not counted until the polls close on election day. Candidates or their repre-sentatives may be present in the polling divi-sions to witness the votes being cast and to en-sure the honesty of the count. The results of an election decide not only who the representatives will be, but which party will form the govern-ment. If a party wins a majority of the seats in the House of Commons, it wins the election. The leader of the winning party will then be ap-pointed prime minister and will in turn appoint some fellow party members to the CABINET, which is the effective Government of Canada.

Electoral Fraud Electoral fraud techniques include "ballot stuffing" (multiple voting at one election); "telegraphing" (impersonating a legiti-mate voter); "treating" (bribing voters); "false enumeration" (excluding opposing partisans from voters' lists); "padding" the voters' lists (enumerating fictitious voters) and physical in-timidation. Fortunately, chicanery, being costly, is rare, and it is also unnecessary for incumbent parties, which are in the best position to practise it. Ballot stuffing has been more common in provincial than in federal elections. As a result of false enumeration, babies have been listed as potential voters and thousands of voters left off lists. Such irregularities have been successfully prosecuted in various elections. East of Ontario bribing voters was once not uncommon; during the 1940s women were provided with nylons, men with alcohol and both sexes with small sums of money. With today's standard of living, bribery is too expensive and not as reliable. If it happens, voters are now bribed not to vote at all, to reduce the risk of a wrong vote. Mal-apportionment and gerrymandering are more creative, effective and not necessarily illegal means of obtaining seats. The former consists primarily of overrepresenting certain regions; the latter is the redrawing of constituency boundaries. In the elections of 1872, 1882 and 1892 the Conservatives made shameless use of gerrymandering. As a result of the Electoral Boundaries Commissions Act (1964) the practice has become almost extinct. Malapportionment favours parties with a rural support base, be-cause rural population is usually overrepresen-ted. Federally malapportionment is less com-mon, because delays in redistribution are not as easily tolerated. TERENCE QUALTER

Electric Power Electricity is a property of the atomic structure of matter, and is manifested as attraction between 2 oppositely charged bodies or repulsion between 2 similarly charged bodies. Subatomic particles may have a positive charge (proton), a neutral charge (neutron) or a nega-tive charge (electron). Electrons are mobile and can be activated to create electric currents if a low resistance path (conductor) is provided. These currents provide a clean, controllable, ver-satile ENERGY commodity, which has been largely responsible for profound changes in the quality of life of all Canadians, reducing, for ex-ample, drudgery in homes, farms and factories. Some uncontrolled forms (eg, LIGHTNING) occur in nature. The widespread availability of cheap electric energy (notably HYDROELECTRICITY), made possible by large, integrated power systems, has given rise to major industrial developments across Canada. Canadian industries such as alu-minum, PULP AND PAPER, IRON AND STEEL and chemicals consume large amounts of electricity.

Gravitational energy, SOLAR ENERGY and its de-rivatives (eg, COAL, PETROLEUM, BIOMASS, WIND), TIDAL ENERGY, NUCLEAR ENERGY, etc, are primary energy sources. In contrast, electricity is usually regarded as a secondary energy source, since it must be generated by the conversion of grav-itational (falling water), chemical (fossil fuels) or nuclear energy. Conversion typically requires 3 units of input energy (eg, burning coal or fall-ing water) to produce one unit of electricity; the other 2 units are wasted as low-quality heat.

History The generic inventions that gave birth to ELECTRIC-POWER GENERATION were the wa-ter wheel (used in Roman times to grind corn), the steam engine and the dynamo or electric generator. The harnessing of water power in the 19th century, notably to drive textile mills, corn mills and woodworking and metal-shaping machinery, was largely responsible for Canada's emer-gence as an industrial nation (*see* TECHNOL-OGY). With the development during the 1870s of reliable electric generators of adequate capacity, it was logical to generate electricity based on hy-dro power as well as on wood- and coal-fuelled steam engines. The product was used originally

Energy Conversion Processes

Source	*Processes*	*Conversions*	*Characteristics*
Gravity	falling water rotates water turbine cou-pled to elec-tric generator	gravita-tional to mechani-cal to electrical	renewable; can maintain 24 hour/day oper-ation, also valu-able for provid-ing peak power; very efficient
Fossil fuels	heat of combustion powers steam turbine, die-sel engine, gas turbine or internal combustion engine cou-pled to elec-tric generator	chemical to high-quality thermal to me-chanical to elec-trical	nonrenewable; high-cost fuel; used primarily for peaking power; com-paratively low efficiency; po-tential for POLLUTION
Nuclear-fission fuels	fission of uranium-235 atoms creates heat to power steam turbine cou-pled to elec-tric generator	nuclear to high-quality thermal to me-chanical to elec-trical	nonrenewable, but virtually ex-tendable indefi-nitely; low cost fuel; 24 hour/day operation; comparatively low efficiency; safety and envi-ronmental concerns

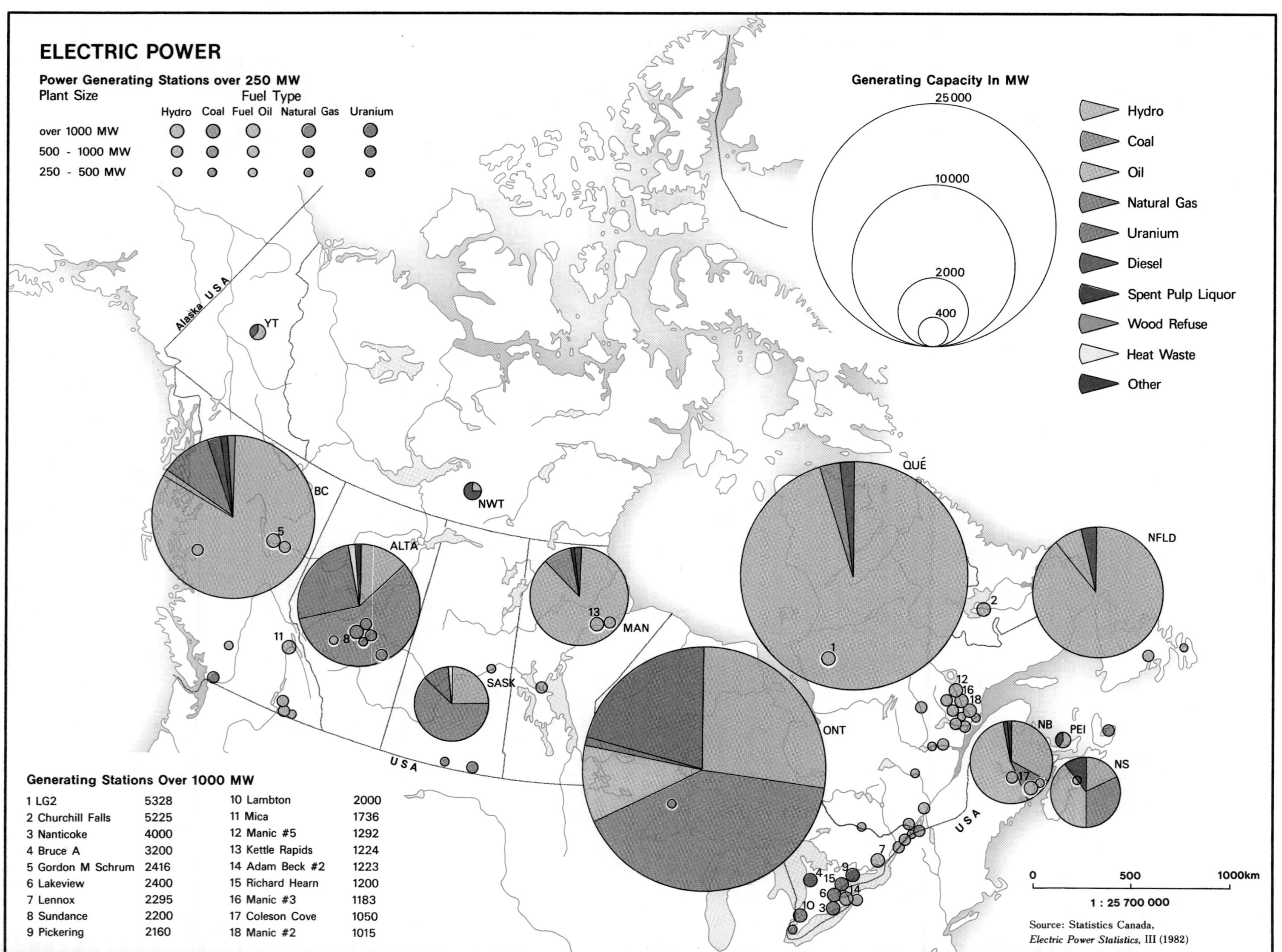
ELECTRIC POWER
Power Generating Stations over 250 MW
Plant Size
Fuel Type
Hydro Coal Fuel Oil Natural Gas Uranium
over 1000 MW
500 - 1000 MW
250 - 500 MW
Generating Capacity In MW
25 000
10 000
2000
400
Hydro
Coal
Oil
Natural Gas
Uranium
Diesel
Spent Pulp Liquor
Wood Refuse
Heat Waste
Other
Alaska U S A
YT
BC
NWT
ALTA
SASK
MAN
ONT
QUÉ
NFLD
NB
PEI
NS
U S A
U S A
Generating Stations Over 1000 MW
1 LG2 5328
2 Churchill Falls 5225
3 Nanticoke 4000
4 Bruce A 3200
5 Gordon M Schrum 2416
6 Lakeview 2400
7 Lennox 2295
8 Sundance 2200
9 Pickering 2160
10 Lambton 2000
11 Mica 1736
12 Manic #5 1292
13 Kettle Rapids 1224
14 Adam Beck #2 1223
15 Richard Hearn 1200
16 Manic #3 1183
17 Coleson Cove 1050
18 Manic #2 1015
0 500 1000km
1 : 25 700 000
Source: Statistics Canada,
Electric Power Statistics, III (1982)

for electric lighting and later for the host of applications that characterize contemporary society. In 1881 a 1.86-kW steam-driven electric generator was installed in downtown Toronto and the first skating rink was lit by arc lamps. Electric arc lights were installed at the CANADIAN NATIONAL EXHIBITION in 1882 and in 1883 street lighting was installed in Toronto and Montréal. In 1884 the Ottawa Parliament Buildings and University of Ottawa were lighted electrically with generators powered by steam engines. All the streets of Ottawa were electrically lighted in 1885; it was the first city in the world to achieve this distinction. Several other Canadian cities were supplied with electric power in varying degrees before the year 1900. For example, the Royal Electric Co was established in Montréal in 1884; Québec City and Sherbrooke were provided with electric power in 1895 and 1896, respectively. But the harnessing of NIAGARA FALLS and the transmission of electric power to local communities in 1903 heralded the real dawn of the age of electric power in Canada. Subsequently, in 1910, the Ontario Hydro Electric Commission, one of the world's first integrated public ELECTRIC UTILITIES, completed the first 115 000-volt bulk electric-power transmission lines to supply several municipalities in SW Ontario. This major achievement placed Canada in the forefront of electric-power pioneering nations.

The first Canadian thermal-electric (coal-burning) power station with an installed capacity of 1 million kW was put in service in 1951 in Toronto. Canada's first NUCLEAR-POWER PLANT, at Rolphton, Ont, first delivered power to the grid in 1962. It was based on the Canadian Deuterium Uranium reactor (CANDU) subsequently used in Ontario's Pickering and Bruce generating stations, which have proved the world's most reliable commercial nuclear plants.

Capacity and Consumption From 1900 to 1981 the installed generating capacity in Canada has increased from 130 to 83 309 MW, an average annual growth rate of over 7%. During 1981, the total consumption of electric energy in Canada was 342 749 million kWh The average power demand was 39 127 MW; the peak demand, 62 847 MW. The overall load factor (average/peak x 100) was 62.2%. The generation reserve (available generating capacity minus peak-power demand) was 20 462 MW or 24.5% of total capacity. This magnitude of generation reserve is essential for the maintenance of acceptable system-reliability levels during scheduled maintenance or forced outages of generating units. Industrial users consumed 36% of the generated electric energy; the commercial sector, 26%; domestic and farm customers, 24%. Losses, mostly in transmission lines and transformers, account for the remaining 14%.

Type of Generation	*Generating Capacity (MW)*
hydroelectric	49 216
fossil-fueled thermal	28 493
nuclear-fueled thermal	5 600
Total	83 309

Government Regulations Under Canada's CONSTITUTION, electricity production falls within provincial jurisdiction. Because of the importance of electricity to Canadian life, it is understandable that most provinces and territories have created publicly owned electric-power commissions to provide electricity at the lowest possible cost, a high level of reliability and with minimal environmental impact. Privately owned electric utilities have also been established in most provinces; in Alberta and Newfoundland, private ownership predominates. To ensure the regulation and orderly growth of the electric-power utilities, each province has passed legislation which sets out mandates and standards and establishes regulatory boards con-

Electrical-Generating Capacity, Production, Consumption

(Source: E. W. Humphrys based on material from the Dept of Energy, Mines and Resources, 1981)

	Installed Capacity				*Production*				*Consumption*		
	Total		*Hydro*		*Total*		*Hydro*		*Total*	*Source*	
	MW	*%*	*MW*	*%*	*MWH*	*%*	*MWH*	*%*	*MWH*	*Hyd %*	*Other %*
Nfld	6 961[1]	8.4	6 210	89	44 665	11.8	44 212	99	8 626	95	5-oil[2]
PEI	118	0.1	0	0	31	0.1	0	0	514	0	6-oil[3] 94-imp(NB)
NS	2 029	2.4	360	18	6 569	1.7	1 167	18	6 761	17	80-coal/oil 3-imp(NB)
NB	2 795	3.4	900	32	8 936	2.4	3 830	43	8 789	44	56-coal/oil
Qué	21 955	26.4	20 771	95	102 905	27.2	102 730	99.8	120 489	85	15-hydro imp(Nfld)
Ont	25 987	31.2	7 145	27.5	110 039	29.1	37 335	34	106 717	35	30-coal 35-nuclear
Man	4 142	5.0	3 641	88	18 431	4.9	17 899	97	13 502	96	4-coal/oil
Sask	2 340	2.8	579	25	9 674	2.6	3 097	32	9 896	31	60-coal/oil 9-imp(Man)
Alta	6 182	7.4	718	11.6	24 497	6.5	2 035	8	24 405	8	75-coal 17-gas
BC	10 525	12.6	8 785	84	51 005	13.5	49 408	97	43 175	97	2-oil 1-gas
YT	94	0.1	58	62	392	0.1	290	74	392	74	26-oil
NWT	180	0.2	47	26	480	0.1	250	61	480	61	39-oil
Canada	83 308	100.0	49 214	59	377 622[4]	100.0	262 253	69	343 748[4]	76	13-conv th

[1] Includes the 5225 MW Churchill Falls hydro station; most of its output is exported to Qué

[2] Imp(NB) = imported from NB, etc; 5-oil = 5% produced by oil-fired generation; conv th = conventional thermal generation

[3] In 1981 there were net exports from Nfld to Qué; NB to NS and the US; Qué to NB, Ont and the US; Ont to the US; Man to Ont, Sask and the US; BC to Alta and the US

[4] Production exceeds consumption by exports to the US (33 875 MWh) from NB, Qué, Ont, Man and BC

cerned with setting rates, emission standards and safety standards in connection with the generation, transmission and distribution of electricity. Some aspects of electric-power regulation are undertaken by the federal government. Of primary importance is the licensing of CANDU-based steam-generating units — the responsibility of the Atomic Energy Control Board (AECB). Before issuing a licence, the board assesses reactor safety, health and environmental factors relating to radioactive discharges, and the handling of spent nuclear fuel. The AECB also develops codes and standards for the mining and milling of uranium ores. The export of uranium and nuclear materials in general is controlled by the federal government. Several of Canada's provincial power networks are interconnected across provincial and international boundaries to ensure optimal reliability and to reduce costs. Export of energy is regulated by the NATIONAL ENERGY BOARD (NEB), a federal agency.

Research and Development The Canadian electric-power industry has pioneered many significant developments in nuclear power, the design of electric-power stations and the production of generators, transformers, transmission lines and energy-conservation systems. Major research programs are conducted by HYDRO-QUÉBEC, ONTARIO HYDRO and the national laboratories of Atomic Energy of Canada Ltd and the NATIONAL RESEARCH COUNCIL. Some research areas deserving special mention include the safety, reliability and efficiency of nuclear-power stations; the management and storage of spent nuclear fuel; the environmental impacts of burning coal (eg, ACID RAIN) and methods of minimizing them (eg, SO_2 "scrubbers"); the design of ultra-high-voltage transmission lines; the development of renewable sources of energy for electric-power generation and small-scale hydroelectric plants. The total national research and development budget for electric-power related projects exceeds $100 million annually.

ARTHUR PORTER

Reading: Canadian Enerdata, *Canadian Energy Trends* (May 1983).

Electric-Power Generation In Canada the 2 basic methods of producing ELECTRIC POWER are hydroelectric generation, based on the energy contained in flowing water, and thermal generation, based on the production of steam. Thermal generation may be conventional, using COAL and PETROLEUM products, or nuclear, using URANIUM in thermonuclear fission (*see* NUCLEAR ENERGY). Canada is abundantly supplied with most of the resources from which electric power can be generated, and Canadians are among the world's highest per capita producers and consumers of electricity. Canada's installed electrical generating capacity in 1980 was 81.6 gigawatts (GW = 10^9 watts): 59% derived from HYDROELECTRICITY, 18% from coal, 10% from oil, 7% from nuclear sources, 5.5% from natural gas, and 0.5% from other sources. Installed capacity is the amount of power that could be generated at a given instant if all power plants were working simultaneously at full capacity. Actual production depends on the amount of time particular generators are running and on load (appliances, motors, etc) placed on the system. ELECTRIC UTILITIES build 10-25% extra capacity into their systems, above the expected maximum load, to serve as backup during emergencies and maintenance shutdowns. In 1980, actual production in Canada averaged 38.7 GW; the total produced was 339 terawatt hours (TWh = 10^9 kilowatt hours). Of actual production, 68% was hydroelectric, 15% coal, 10% nuclear, 4% oil and 3% gas. The difference between the various sources' shares of capacity and production (ie, a higher proportional production from hydro and nuclear, lower from fossil fuels) reflects the economics of electric-power generation, and the pressures placed by CONSERVATION concerns on petroleum-based thermal development.

Hydroelectric Generation converts the energy of Canada's RIVERS into electrical energy for industrial, commercial and residential use. Building a dam to retain water requires a large capital investment, but the method has several major advantages, being nonpolluting, based on a renewable resource and requiring no expensive fuels. Canada's principal hydroelectric generating stations are LG-2, on the La Grande R, Qué,

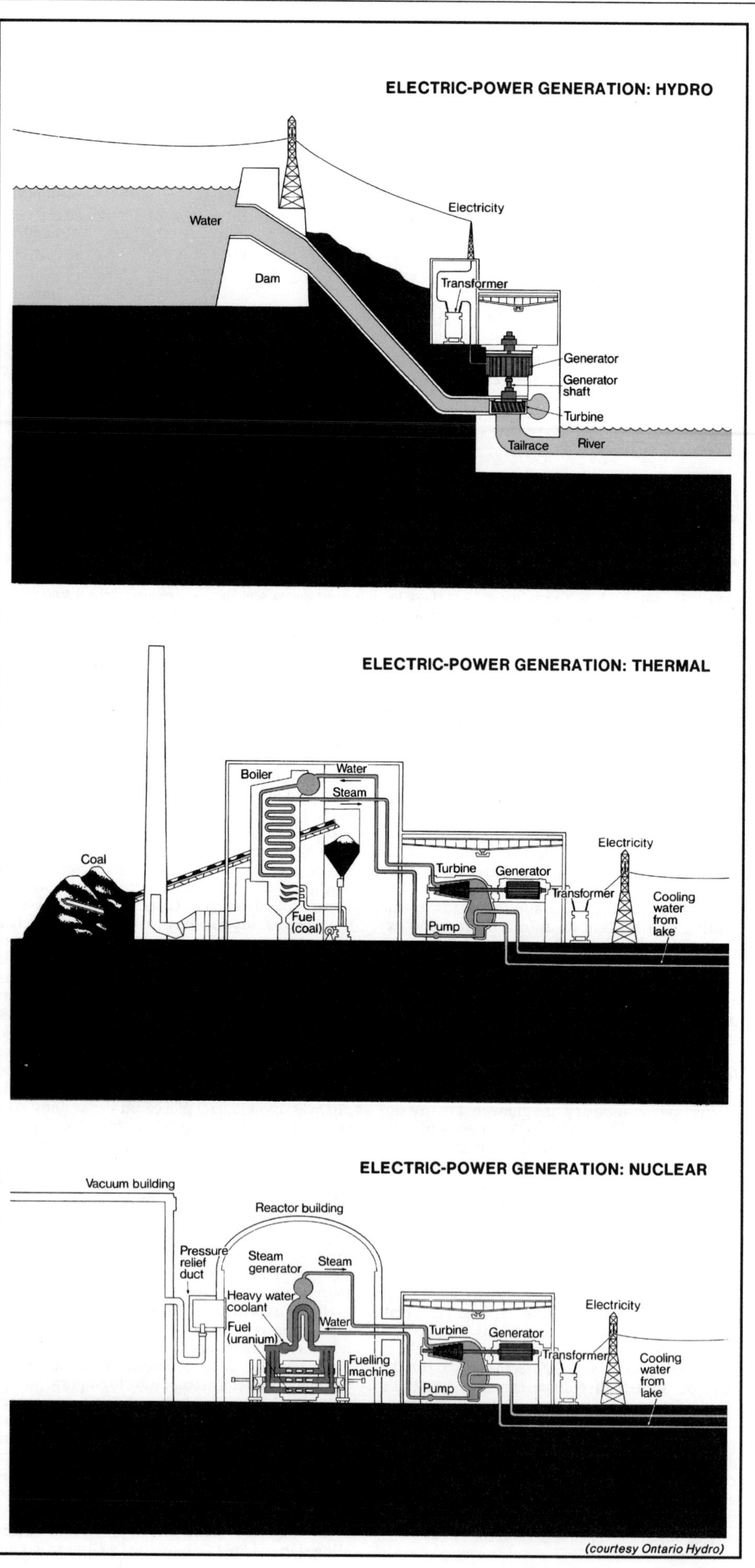

(courtesy Ontario Hydro)

5328 MW; Churchill Falls, on the Churchill R, Lab, 5225 MW; and Gordon M. Shrum, on the Peace R, BC, 2091 MW. LG-4, also on the La Grande R, will rank fourth in 1985 with 2074 MW. Others are listed on the map.

Thermal Generation uses the heat energy of fossil fuels or uranium to produce steam to drive a steam turbine which is coupled to a generator. In addition to its fuel requirements, a thermal plant must have a supply of water to cool and condense the exhaust steam from the turbine so that it can be reused in the steam cycle. Conventional thermal plants have relatively low capital costs but high operating costs. Their disadvantages include pollution from exhaust gases (*see* ACID RAIN; AIR POLLUTION) and low efficiency. Efficiency is limited by the Carnot cycle of a heat engine, which effectively means that less than 40% of the heat energy of the fuel is converted into electricity, the remainder being lost as waste heat. Several research projects are exploring ways to use this waste heat for agriculture, AQUACULTURE or industrial purposes. Canada's principal coal-fired generating stations are Nanticoke, Ont, 4000 MW; Lakeview, Ont, 2430 MW; Lambton, Ont, 2030 MW; and Sundance, Alta, 1725 MW. The largest natural gas-fired facility is Richard L. Hearn, Ont, 1230 MW. Oil-fired facilities include Lennox, Ont, 2295 MW; Wesleyville, Ont, 2000 MW.

A NUCLEAR POWER PLANT is a thermal plant in that steam is produced by a nuclear reaction and used to drive a conventional steam turbine. However, the economics are quite different since the capital cost of the plant is high and the construction time longer than for a conventional thermal plant. The complexity of the plant also adds to the operating cost. Such expenses are offset by the low cost of fuel and the absence of atmospheric pollution, factors that make nuclear generation using the Canadian CANDU system economically attractive in parts of Canada, notably Ontario and the Maritimes. Concern about the long-term storage of the spent radioactive fuel remains (*see* NUCLEAR SAFETY). Canada's principal nuclear generating stations are Bruce, Ont, 6400 MW (1983); Pickering, Ont, 4320 MW; and Darlington, Ont, 3000 MW (1984).

Unlike most other forms of energy, electricity cannot be stored economically in large quantities. Instead, the energy is stored in fuel stockpiles or in water held above hydroelectric dams, and power is produced on demand. The demand on a typical power system varies significantly with time of day, season and general economic activity; hence, the number of generators and the load on each must be varied. To meet this varying demand, 2 types of generating plant are required, for base-load generation and for peaking generation. The base load is the continuous minimum demand; the peak load is the maximum demand. Thermal plants are more suited to base-load operations because they take a long time to warm up and bring on line, and they operate most efficiently at a constant load. Nuclear plants have an added base-load advantage in that their capital cost is high, and their fuel cost low; hence, they are most economical when run at a high, constant load. Hydro plants can be designed as either peaking plants or base-load plants, depending on the ratio of electrical capacity to water flow and water-storage capacity. If a hydro plant is operated parallel with a thermal plant, the hydro plant is typically used for peak loads, as it can be brought on line quickly. Gas turbines are also well suited to peaking generation since they start up quickly and have low capital cost and high fuel costs.

The location of electric-generating plants is always a compromise between the location of the population to be served and the location of the energy resource to be tapped: the longer the transmission line to the service area, the higher the effective cost of the plant. Hydroelectric sites require a stable base for a dam and geographic features that minimize the necessary size of the dam and control structures; the effects of flooding above the dam must also be considered. For thermal plants, the availability of cooling water is a crucial consideration. Proximity to a fuel source or cheap transportation is a major factor in choosing a location for coal-fired plants; electricity is cheaper to transport than is coal. The safety concerns of neighbouring populations can influence the siting of nuclear plants.

The mix of electric-generating sources varies considerably across Canada. In 1980, hydroelectricity provided most electricity in Newfoundland, Québec, Manitoba, BC and the YT; coal, in NS, Saskatchewan and Alberta; and oil, in NB, PEI and the NWT. Nuclear power provided about 28% of Ontario's electricity production, ranking a close third after hydro and coal. Nuclear generation began in NB in 1983. Many alternative means of electric-power generation are under active study. These include TIDAL ENERGY, WIND ENERGY, photovoltaic SOLAR ENERGY, ocean thermal energy, WAVE ENERGY, GEOTHERMAL ENERGY, magnetohydrodynamic generators, NUCLEAR FUSION energy, low-head and small-scale hydroelectric dams, and thermal plants burning BIOMASS and PEAT. Cogeneration, the production of both heat and electricity, can substantially improve the economics of thermal stations. Two of the alternatives, vertical-axis windmills and tidal power, are being used in small-scale trials at present, but it will be some years before they offer a significant alternative to the resources now in use. Canada is also participating in nuclear fusion research to a limited extent, although it will be at least several decades before fusion is available to generate electricity commercially. M.M.C. COLLINS

Electric Utilities are private or government organizations involved in the production, transmission, distribution, marketing and sale to consumers of ELECTRIC POWER. Canadian electric UTILITIES account for approximately 90% of the total production of electrical energy in Canada; the remaining 10% is produced by industrial establishments for their own use, chiefly in the MINING, metal- processing and PULP AND PAPER industries. In 1981 about 90% of the utilities' production was consumed in Canada, the remainder being exported to the US.

The electrical-utility industry started in the 1880s as a multitude of privately owned enterprises which supplied electrical ENERGY in specific communities or regions. Many also provided other services such as gas distribution and street railways. As the use of electricity increased, many of the original companies were absorbed by larger, investor-owned corporations. In most instances, nonelectrical energy activities were split off, eg, street railways were taken over by municipalities. Early in this century, the concept of PUBLIC OWNERSHIP of the electrical-utility business emerged, beginning with municipal ownership of electrical generation or distribution within a particular community. A very significant development was the creation of a provincially owned utility, ONTARIO HYDRO, in 1906.

Increasing demand for adequate supply of electrical energy at roughly uniform rates created a trend towards provincial ownership of the industry in most provinces. Provincial government takeover of municipally and investor-owned electric utilities accelerated after WWII. Provincial ownership was intended to provide electricity at lower cost to consumers, as a result of such factors as provincial guarantee of capital debt, co-ordinated planning and absence of profit-taking and income-tax burden. By the 1980s, Canada's electrical-utility industry was characterized by a mix of investor, municipal and provincial ownership. Except in Alberta and PEI, provincial bodies play the dominant role in generating capacity, transmission network and assets. These bodies are BC Hydro and Power Authority (BC HYDRO); Saskatchewan Power Corporation (SPC); Manitoba Hydro-Electric Board (Manitoba Hydro); Ontario Hydro-Electric Commission (Ontario Hydro); HYDRO-QUÉBEC; New Brunswick Electric Power Commission (NB Power); Nova Scotia Power Corp (NS Power); and Newfoundland and Labrador Hydro.

A federal CROWN CORPORATION, Northern Canada Power Commission (NCPC), is the principal generating and transmitting utility distributing electrical energy in 2 communities in YT and most communities in NWT. In YT, an investor-owned utility operates several diesel generating stations supplying isolated communities, and purchases power from NCPC to augment its supply for distribution within the Whitehorse area. In NWT, NCPC supplies an investor-owned distributing company serving the Yellowknife area, and another investor-owned utility supplies 3 communities with diesel-generated power. Investor-owned utilities dominate in Alberta and PEI, and play a minor but significant role in BC, Ontario and Newfoundland. Municipal ownership is a minor element in BC, Québec and PEI, but is very significant in Alberta, Manitoba and Ontario. In Ontario, distribution and some generation in urban municipalities is provided by over 320 municipal hydroelectric commissions, most of which purchase supply from Ontario Hydro in a quasi co-operative arrangement. These commissions are autonomous with respect to the parent municipality, but are subject to a degree of regulation by Ontario Hydro, especially in respect to tariffs.

Two investor-owned utilities are responsible for generation and transmission of about 80% of the power consumed in Alberta. Distribution in major urban centres is by municipal utilities, and 2 of these produce the remaining 20% of the provincial consumption. Planning and operations are co-ordinated by an Electric Utility Planning Council which includes representatives of the municipally and investor-owned utilities and the provincial government. In 1981 the Alberta government became an active participant in the province's electrical-utility industry by establishing the Alberta Electrical Marketing Agency. This agency will purchase power from the utilities, set a province-wide wholesale rate and resell to the various utilities for distribution to consumers, with the intent of equalizing rates across the province.

While the electrical-utility industry is structured on a provincial basis, electric-power transmission interconnections for interchange of supply have been established between all adjacent provinces, except between Saskatchewan and Alberta. Interconnections with US utilities have been developed by NB Power, Hydro-Québec, Ontario Hydro, Manitoba Hydro, SPC and BC Hydro. These cross-border connections are primarily for export of electricity from Canada, but they also permit some imports when needed. Electrical-energy exports and export facilities are licensed by the NATIONAL ENERGY BOARD (NEB).

An important component of the electrical-utility industry is the Canadian Electrical Association (CEA, est 1891). All major investor-owned and provincially owned utilities, and some municipal utilities, are corporate members of the association, and many manufacturers of electrical equipment have nonvoting membership status. The CEA co-ordinates the exchange of general and technical information, and provides a liaison with the provincial and federal governments. It also sponsors and co-ordinates research which supplements activities of the 4 utilities that have research divisions: Hydro-Québec, Ontario Hydro, SPC and BC Hydro.

Because investor-owned utilities are profit oriented and operate in a monopolistic environment, their rate structures are generally subject to review and regulation by public authorities. Formerly, publicly owned utilities were generally autonomous in setting rates within guidelines requiring them to provide service at cost, in some instances, subject to approval by the parent government. Recently, a trend has developed toward having public boards examine the rate structures of the publicly owned utilities, but final jurisdiction remains with the government concerned. A development in this area was the 1981 decision by the government of Québec to depart from the service-at-cost principle in favour of a rate-setting philosophy tied to government policy. The rates now reflect energy CONSERVATION objectives and the cost of other forms of energy; any profits above a specified minimum level accrue to the government as dividends. E.W. HUMPHRYS

Electrical Appliances Industry The dominant activity of the electrical appliance industry in Canada is the design, manufacture and sale of major household appliances. The core products (ie, those with very high saturation levels, approaching the category of necessities) are refrigerators, ranges, automatic washers and dryers. Other major appliances include dishwashers, freezers, microwave ovens and room air conditioners. Manufacturing takes place entirely in Ontario and Québec.

History in Canada The major appliance industry is a postwar phenomenon with its roots in the American consumer-products boom of the 1950s. All major-appliance products originated in the US and initially reached Canada as imports. Brands such as Kelvinator, Frigidaire, Philco, General Electric (GE) and Westinghouse became household words in Canada. Because of high Canadian import tariffs, most US manufacturers found it more economical to produce major appliances in Canada once the Canadian sales volume had climbed to permit reasonable economies of scale. The result was an industry dominated by high levels of foreign ownership, although the tariffs permitted a number of Canadian entrepreneurs to operate profitably as small regional manufacturers.

Among the most successful Canadian entrepreneurs were W.C. Wood and Ralph Barford, both of whom developed major appliance companies that have survived the ups and downs of the industry and the deep recession of 1982. Wood survived by specializing in a single product (freezers) and exporting to the US. By 1984 Wood was the largest and most modern freezer manufacturer in Canada. Mainly by acquiring existing small businesses (eg, McClary, Easy, Moffat), Barford put together the only Canadian-owned, full-line appliance company (GSW Inc). The Moffat acquisition, probably Barford's largest, brought GSW into the big 6 full-line appliance makers. The other 5, all foreign controlled, were Admiral, GE, Inglis, White and Westinghouse.

As early as the mid-1970s, the federal government had begun to urge the industry to consolidate to achieve greater economies of scale and become more competitive. An opportunity for consolidation arose in 1975 when White agreed to purchase the major appliance division of Westinghouse in the US. The Canadian assets were contingently part of the agreement; however, Canada's FOREIGN INVESTMENT REVIEW AGENCY (FIRA) intervened to block the sale in Canada. If it had gone through, White-Westinghouse would have had the scale potential to put pressure on the other 4 full-line competitors, particularly GSW. Barford, in an attempt to protect GSW's position, negotiated a merger with Canadian General Electric (CGE), each firm contributing its major appliance activities to a joint venture called Camco. Camco then proceeded to purchase the Canadian major appliance division of Westinghouse, and because GSW held 50% of the voting shares of Camco, the purchase was exempted from FIRA procedures. By 1976 there were only 4 full-line competitors: Admiral, Camco, Inglis and White. The number was reduced to 3 in 1982 when Inglis, with some government assistance, bought out ailing Admiral.

Economic Performance Although industry exports had increased and imports declined (largely because of weakness in the Canada dollar), a trade deficit in major appliances still prevailed in 1982, which was the worst year the industry had faced in over a decade as sales declined by 20%. A recovery began in 1983 and continued at a somewhat slower pace in 1984. Microwave ovens represent the only bright spot in the industry. Sales of microwaves had climbed steadily since 1976, when 65 000 units were sold, to 1982, when sales reached 252 000 units. Unit sales of appliances as a whole, however, had been in decline since 1978. The decline was caused by high saturation levels of core products and low replacement buying. For example, the same proportion of Canadian households (over 99%) owned a refrigerator in 1980 as in 1976. Saturation levels for electric ranges (87%) and automatic washers (76%) had not grown either. Clothes dryers had grown modestly from 55% in 1976 to 63% in 1980.

Beyond the core products, saturation levels varied. Freezers reached 51% in 1980, but room air conditioners had reached only 11%. With the newer products, Canadian saturation levels were still catching up with those in the US. Dishwashers reached 26% in Canada in 1979, compared to 43% in the US. By 1982 the Canadian figure was 33%. A similar pattern arose with microwaves: in 1982 US saturation was around 27%; Japanese, 31%; and Canadian, 10%.

The Modern Industry in Canada

Since import tariffs were scheduled to drop in the early 1980s to 12.5% by 1987, industry participants realized that more INDUSTRIAL RESEARCH AND DEVELOPMENT would be needed for the industry to prosper under international competition. By 1984 the US could not ship core products to Canada below Canadian costs. This situation is unlikely to change by 1987, unless there is a radical change in the EXCHANGE RATE between Canada and the US. In 1984 the imports that were still coming in were mainly from US firms that produced and marketed premium products above normal prices. Canada's exports were concentrated in refrigerators and freezers. In 1981 they reached 156 000 units, valued at $36 million, but declined in 1982 to 98 000 units valued at $29 million. International trade in newer products was governed less by cost than by innovation. Products such as dishwashers and microwaves were imported because the design and development were done abroad. They were manufactured in Canada only when the sales volume was high enough to make it economical. Industry sources estimated in 1983 that Canadian production costs were 15-20% higher than US costs in core products and 30-40% higher in new products, assuming parity between the Canadian and US dollars.

All of the surviving full-line manufacturers expect to expand employment in both Ontario and Québec. Camco, now 51% owned by CGE, will compete largely through the Hotpoint, GE and Moffat brand names, and will manufacture part of the Beaumark line for the Bay and Simpsons. Inglis, 43% owned by Whirlpool, will compete with the Admiral, Inglis and Whirlpool names and will manufacture the Kenmore line for Sears. White, almost wholly owned by White US, will compete with the White-Westinghouse, Kelvinator and Frigidaire names and will manufacture much of the Viking line for Eatons and certain models in the Beaumark line.

Associations The Canadian work force in the industry is represented by several unions, including the United Electrical Workers (UEW). Employment in the industry has declined from 11 888 in 1976 to 6902 in 1981, partly because of reduced output but largely as a result of improved efficiency. Canadian wage rates in the major-appliance industry, on average, were higher than those in the US in the mid-1970s, but the relative decline in the Canadian dollar had reversed this situation by the early 1980s. By 1984 both countries were facing strong competition from manufacturers in the Far East and Latin America in low-cost component parts. The industry was represented by the Canadian Appliance Manufacturer's Assn which, in turn, was a section of the Electrical and Electronic Manfacturers' Assn of Canada, with head offices in Toronto.

HAROLD CROOKELL

Electrical Engineering, discipline in the ENGINEERING profession which deals with the application of electricity to serve the needs of society. Electrical engineers are involved in a wide range of activities, from designing and manufacturing computer and COMMUNICATION systems, to planning and overseeing the operation of large ELECTRIC-POWER stations. The field is expanding rapidly and, over the past decade, many universities have modified their programs to provide a degree of specialization. Upon graduation, many electrical engineers form their own companies to manufacture electrically based products or to provide consulting services. Others are employed in salaried positions and become involved in research, design, manufacture, sales or maintenance of electrical equipment.

One of the earliest programs in electrical engineering was established at McGill University in 1891. In 1907 University of New Brunswick had 3 professors offering courses in electrical engineering. Since that time enrolments have increased in universities across Canada to a level of 6675 in 1982. The curriculum is regulated by the Canadian Council of Professional Engineers, with periodic reviews made at each university by the Canadian Accreditation Board. Technical societies such as the Institute of Electrical and Electronics Engineers sponsor conferences and meetings, in Canada and the US, for the exchange of technical information. Other organizations, eg, the Canadian Electrical Assn, which is funded by many Canadian ELECTRIC UTILITIES, organize technical conferences and provide funds for research projects related to the electric power industry.

K.E. BOLLINGER

Electroacoustic Music is composed, performed or reproduced with the aid of electronic technology, excluding instrumental and vocal music heard via loudspeakers. The term includes tape, electronic and computer music, each with its own techniques. Tape music includes any composition created with magnetic tape using prerecorded or electronic sounds that have been modified and assembled through techniques of mixing, splicing, speed changes, tape reversal, tape loops, tape echo and feedback, as well as electronic modifications. Electronic music refers to compositions produced with sounds generated electronically by oscillators and modified with filters, modulators or other equipment. Early work in electronic music occurred after WWII in Europe and N America, although many electric musical instruments (the Theremin, Ondes Martenot and Hammond organ) were invented earlier in the century. Since the 1960s electronic music has become associated with commercially produced sound synthesizers, which are groupings of sound-generating and -modifying units using the principle of voltage control to determine the sound parameters. Live electronics refers to musical performance with any combination of synthesizers and associated equipment, whereas studio composition involves mixing all materials on to tape for later playback. Computer music is the application of digital technology to musical activity, such as computer-assisted composition, digital sound synthesis and, most recently, live performance with digital synthesizers. Computer music differs from other forms by using programs or software to control the process, and by representing sound as a series of numbers called samples. Digital technology is being integrated into all aspects of music and audio engineering, including digital recording and signal processing. Some early computer-music systems in Canada were developed by Ken Pulfer of the National Research Council in 1969, Gustav Ciamaga and William Buxton at the U of T, and Barry Truax at Simon Fraser U.

Electroacoustic techniques are used for both commercial and artistic types of music, the former usually associated with multi-track recording studios, and the latter with university and private studios as well as national radio networks in Europe. The first Canadian studios were established at U of T (1959) by Myron Schaeffer and at McGill (1964) by Istvan Anhalt, and now are found in almost every university music faculty. Hugh LE CAINE of the NRC was the most significant pioneer of electronic music in Canada through his design and construction of many specialized devices for composers and performers, including the first synthesizer, the Sackbut, in 1945. Today, electroacoustic music, despite the public's lack of familiarity with its artistic forms, is an important aspect of musical life.

BARRY D. TRUAX

Electronics Industry The Canadian electronics industry consists of more than 700 firms that manufacture HIGH-TECHNOLOGY products such as advanced telephones, COMPUTER SYSTEMS, word processors and other electronic office systems, televisions and radios, communications SATELLITES and other TELECOMMUNICATIONS systems and electronic control and monitoring devices used in many industrial and scientific applications. In 1982 industry shipments were valued at over $5.55 billion, divided among 4 subsectors: COMMUNICATIONS and components, 54% ($3 billion); office machines and computers, 21% ($1.17 billion); instrumentation, 18% ($98[illegible] million); consumer electronics, 7% ($398 million). The apparent domestic market (shipments plus imports minus exports) was $8.82 billion in 1982.

Despite some strengths, notably in telecommunications, Canada has traditionally been a net importer of electronic goods, mostly from the US and Japan. The trade deficit grew steadily, by an alarming 292%, between 1973 ($85[illegible] million) and 1981 ($3.33 billion). In 1982 this deficit dropped marginally to $3.27 billion with office machines and computers accounting for more than half ($1.68 billion). In fact, between 1973 and 1983, all 4 major subsectors were in deficit. The only bright light was provided by telephone-apparatus commodities which produced a 1982 surplus of over $33[illegible] million. Exports of these commodities increased by a third ($116 million) over the previous year. However, the continuing serious deficits in this industry, coupled with the growing importance of electronics to a nation's economic health and international competitiveness, have caused grave concern about Canada's ability to maintain its status as a technologically advanced industrialized nation.

It is difficult for Canada to compete with the US and Japan in major areas of electronics research and development (R & D); in the early 1980s, for example, the US and Japan started a cutthroat multi-billion-dollar competition to develop the most advanced computer technologies; that race is simply out of Canada's league. The preferred Canadian strategy has been to find "niches" (specialized subsections of the market) and to move into them before anyone else, in the hope of establishing momentum and a lasting reputation. In part, this strategy is dictated by the fact that, by world standards, Canadian electronics firms are comparatively small (most have sales of under $1 million). Northern Telecom Ltd, which makes advanced telecommunications devices, is the largest, with 1983 revenues of over $3 billion.

In 1983 the electronics industry employed about 67 000 people, down from the 1982 total of 82 000, which was the highest for the decade 1973-83. The industry is "knowledge intensive"; ie, it is the largest employer of technically and scientifically trained people in Canada and accounts for about a quarter of all industrial R & D in Canada, more than any other industry. This amount represents about 4-5% of sales spent on R & D, compared with about 1% for other industries.

There is a high degree of FOREIGN INVESTMENT in Canada's electronics industry. Although about 80% of Canadian electronics firms are Canadian owned, they account for less than half the industry's sales (less than 20%, if Northern's sales are excluded). Nearly three-quarters of the 100 largest firms are foreign owned, a degree of foreign ownership virtually unparalleled in other industrialized countries. In mid-1983, Evans Research Corp reported that only 2 of the top 10 computer companies in Canada were Canadian owned, 20 of the top 50.

Most of Canada's electronics output comes from firms located in Ontario and Québec, mostly in large cities, which provide the necessary technological support structure and skilled workers. Perhaps the greatest concentration occurs in Kanata, a community outside Ottawa that has been dubbed "Silicon Valley North." Montréal and Toronto also have concentrations of high-tech electronics firms. Some of the most prominent companies that produce the range of technologies included in this industry sector are described below.

Northern Telecom Ltd, Mississauga, Ont, a public company which is controlled by BELL CANADA ENTERPRISES INC, is Canada's largest telecommunications/electronics firm, specializing mainly in sophisticated telephone and telephone-switching technology. In 1983 its sales exceeded $3.2 billion; it employed about 38 000 people worldwide (nearly 20 450 in Canada); and it had about a 70% share of the Canadian market for the products it makes. Northern produces a very wide range of telecommunications products, including business communications systems (data-switching networks, electronic telephone systems, electronic private-branch-exchange telephone systems); electronic office equipment (a wide variety of voice and data terminals, including the Displayphone, a combination telephone and desktop computer terminal); several types of telephones (rotary dial, push-tone, coin-operated, electronic, etc) and related equipment (headsets, hands-free speaker units); a wide range of telecommunications wire and cable products; several telephone-switching systems; telecommunications test equipment; power equipment; and voice- and data-transmission systems. The last category includes fibre-optics technology, which involves transmitting information (eg, a telephone conversation) as light signals through ultra-thin fibres made of extremely pure glass. Northern and its research arm, Bell-Northern Research Ltd of Ottawa, have spent about $45 million on fibre-optic R & D; by mid-1983, there were some 10 000 miles of fibre cable in operation in Ontario and Québec.

Overall, Northern spent about $315 million on R & D in 1983, up about 30% from $241.4 million the previous year. The company does a great deal of research on semiconductors (microelectronic chips). It is among the world's top 10 users of semiconductors and is one of very few Canadian companies able to design and fabricate custom MICROCHIPS. Northern's products are used in about 90 countries by telephone companies, businesses, governments and educational and military institutions. It has a large number of offices or plants in Canada, the US, England, Switzerland, Singapore, Ireland, France, Malaysia and Brazil. By mid-1983 US revenues accounted for 55% of the total (up from 47% in 1982); Canadian revenues contributed 34% (down from 42% in 1982); and international business accounted for the remainder.

Spar Aerospace Ltd, Toronto, is a company engaged in the design, development, manufacturing and servicing of systems and products for the AEROSPACE, AVIATION, communications and defence industries. It was founded in 1968 and employs 2000 people. It has one of the largest staffs of highly qualified scientific and technical workers in private industry in Canada. Spar's sales in 1983 totalled over $214 million, 42% from exports. Spar is famous as the developer of the CANADARM, the remote manipulator system used on the US Space Shuttle. The Canadian government paid $110 million for development of the first arm, which was given to the US National Aeronautics and Space Administration (NASA) and flown on a shuttle flight for the first time in 1983. Spar subsequently received a $74-million contract from NASA to build 3 more arms, which were delivered between 1982 and 1984. The company has been studying the potential uses of remote-manipulator technology in such industrial applications on Earth as underwater or nuclear-reactor work. Spar is also a major supplier, both in Canada and internationally, of satellite communications systems (including satellites and subsystems); it produces components and systems for satellite-earth receiving stations. It has also developed remote heat-sensing technology for detecting ships, missiles and aircraft for defence and navigation purposes.

AES Data Ltd is a Montréal firm that designs, manufactures and distributes OFFICE AUTOMATION equipment, ranging from stand-alone desk-top word-processing machines to sophisticated shared-logic, multiple work-station systems. The company, which was established in 1974, had sales of about $188 million in 1982. It employs more than 2000 people worldwide. Its products are sold in more than 55 countries.

Canadian Astronautics Ltd, Ottawa, does R&D in aerospace, electronics and computers. Its products include satellite-ground receiving stations and other equipment for receiving satellite signals; space-hardware subsystems (eg, high-reliability batteries, deployable antennas); space-related computer software; airborne RADAR; electronic warfare systems; scientific and engineering minicomputers and microcomputers and various instruments. The company had sales of about $8 million in 1982.

Gandalf Data Ltd, Nepean, Ont, specializes in data-transmission technologies, including private automatic computer exchanges, mobile computer terminals and various communications modems for linking computers together using telephone or cable lines. The company has sold over 400 000 devices to telephone companies, educational institutions, government departments and industries around the world. Perhaps its most well-known product is a computerized receiving device for taxi drivers. A major product is PACXnet, a sophisticated, intelligent "switching" system that connects many different computers, computer terminals and switching networks, allowing users access to electronic mail, information data banks and other electronic services. In its fiscal year ending July 1983, it had sales of about $60 million. Its 1983 R & D budget was about $8 million. About 70% of its products are sold outside Canada; 40-50% of the devices produced in Canada are exported. The company has subsidiaries in the US, England and Switzerland and it has distribution agreements in 20 countries. It employs about 900 people worldwide.

Lumonics Inc is an Ottawa firm that develops and manufactures industrial and scientific LASERS and laser systems. Founded in 1970, it is now the third-largest company in the world specializing in lasers. It has subsidiaries in the US and England; 95% of its sales are outside Canada. By mid-1983, annual sales were running about $24 million. The company's products include Lasermark, a high-speed, noncontact laser-marking system used to put product codes on packaged foods, beverages, toiletries, drugs and other supermarket products. Other laser products are used in industry for cutting, welding and drilling.

Mitel Corp of Kanata, Ont, is an international manufacturer of telecommunications products and semiconductor devices. The company had sales of $225 million in 1983 and employed 5000 people at 60 plants and offices in Canada, the US, England, Ireland, Europe, Africa, Hong Kong, New Zealand and Japan. Major products include microchip-controlled telephone switching systems for office use, earth-terminal switching devices for satellite systems, special telephone handsets and a successful IBM-compatible personal computer called Hyperion. Mitel is also one of the few Canadian companies designing and manufacturing advanced microelectronic circuits, including the latest generation of VLSI (very large-scale integration) chips.

CAE Electronics Ltd, Montréal, a wholly owned subsidiary of CAE Industries Ltd, Toronto, is a major designer and manufacturer of commercial digital flight simulators for civilian and military aircraft and helicopters (devices used primarily for pilot training). The company makes simulators for major aircraft manufactured by Boeing, Airbus, Lockheed and McDonnell Douglas; customers include major international airlines such as British Airways, KLM, Swissair, United Airlines and Air Canada. CAE also makes control-room simulators for training nuclear-power plant operators, as well as supervisory control and data acquisition systems for nuclear and fossil-fuel power stations, electric substations and oil and gas pipelines. The company also makes a computerized data processing and display system for use in air-traffic control and it was one of the companies that contributed to development of the CANADARM, the remote manipulator system for the US Space Shuttle. This division employs about 1700 people, more than 600 of which are scientists, engineers and technicians. CAE Electronics GmbH is a West German division of the company that provides maintenance and service for military flight simulators and various commercial and military communications and electronic systems throughout Europe. This division also designs and manufactures communications equipment for worldwide telecommunications services. About 300 Europeans are employed.

NORPAK Corp, Kanata, founded in 1975, develops and markets a wide range of colour-graphics computer-display terminals and associated computer hardware. The company was the major developer of Canada's TELIDON videotex system. Videotex is a computerized, interactive (2-way) system for the electronic delivery of text and graphics information to special Telidon-receiving terminals or personal computers for use in homes or offices. NORPAK's products include the Telidon Information Provider System (the terminals used to create and edit Telidon text and graphics information); the MK IV Videotex Decoder (the receiving terminal that displays the information and a number key pad and keyboard that allow the user to request the information desired); and an Electronic Projection System (a decoder with added memory so that it can call up already stored information, either from its own memory storage or from a remote computer data base). The company also makes similar teletex equipment. Unlike 2-way videotex, teletex involves a one-way broadcast of information to a receiving set, eg, by regular or cable TV. NORPAK also makes products for use in education and computer-aided design and in electronic warfare, command and control and training applications. It is developing a videotex military information handling system. The company has several facilities in Canada and the US. In 1981 Noranda Mines, through its wholly owned subsidary Maclaren Power and Paper, acquired a substantial interest in NORPAK.

Electrohome Ltd, Kitchener, Ont, is one of the oldest firms in Canada belonging to the electronics sector. It was incorporated in 1933, but predecessor companies date back to 1907. The company had sales of $142.1 million in 1983 and a work force of 2100. In the early 1970s its main product was TV sets; later it concentrated its electronics capabilities in industrial markets, specializing in video display units. Products include monitors for computer terminals and personal computers, electronic games and medical and industrial control equipment; Telidon terminals; systems and electronic circuit boards for satellite receiving stations.

SED Systems Inc, Saskatoon, Sask, makes a variety of products for the aerospace, communications and instrumentation and control markets in Canada, the US, Europe and Australia. It had sales of $13 million in the fiscal year 1981-82 and employs about 300 people. Aerospace products include satellite ground-station control facilities; satellite-systems test equipment; defence electronics and support; payloads (scientific instrument packages) for the Space Shuttle and Rockets. It also operates an earth station, receiving data from the Landsat earth-resources REMOTE-SENSING satellite. Communications products include equipment for transmitting and receiving a wide range of signals via satellite; transportable satellite-earth receiving stations; mobile test facilities; automatic telephone dialers. Instrumentation and control systems include farm monitoring systems for tractors, seeders, sprayers, grain loss and combines that provide farmers with instant information on all farming operations; sprayer-control systems; storage tank and bin monitors; and control systems used in industry.

The Ontario Centre for Microelectronics is an Ontario government CROWN CORPORATION set up in 1982 to provide technical expertise and assistance, advice and information for industry in the field of microelectronics. The centre offers consulting services, feasibility studies, training programs and information services. It also contracts to design integrated electronic circuits. The purpose of the centre is to help small- and medium-sized companies exploit the latest advances in microelectronic technology. The Ontario government has also set up 2 other centres that focus on electronics technologies: one, in Cambridge, Ont, specializes in CAD/CAM (computer-aided design and computer-aided MANUFACTURING); the other, in Peterborough, specializes in ROBOTICS.

In 1982 the federal government also helped to establish a number of microelectronic centres across Canada, in collaboration with provincial governments. An example is the Alberta Microelectronic Centre, based at University of Alberta, Edmonton. This nonprofit centre was designed to help Alberta businesses learn about and apply new electronic technologies — to increase productivity and international competitiveness. The centre will offer laboratory facilities, machine shops, computers, CAD/CAM systems and other equipment to industry in return for fees and will conduct research on microelectronic applications in collaboration with industry and university researchers.

Many of Canada's top electronics firms belong to the Canadian Advanced Technology Association (CATA), based in Ottawa, which had about 118 members in 1983. Corporate members of CATA must be Canadian controlled (ie, 51% or more of common stock must be held in Canada by Canadians or landed immigrants resident in Canada), and the companies must be engaged in research, development or manufacturing of advanced-technology products or services.

Industrial trade associations and technical societies whose members belong to the electronics sector include the Electrical and Electronic Manufacturers' Association of Canada, Air Industries Association of Canada, Canadian Society for Electrical Engineering, Canadian Information Processing Society and Institute of Electrical and Electronic Engineers. *See* COMPUTER INDUSTRY; ELECTRICAL ENGINEERING; SATELLITE COMMUNICATIONS; SPACE TECHNOLOGY. LYDIA DOTTO

Elgin, James Bruce, 8th Earl of, governor general of Canada 1846-54 (b at London, Eng 20 July 1811; d at Dharmsala, India 20 Nov 1863). As a student at Eton and Oxford, Elgin displayed the brilliance that sparked his later reputation as an inspired orator, cultured humanist and judicious administrator. Appointed as governor of Jamaica in 1842, Elgin was named governor general of Canada in 1846 and arrived in Montréal on 30 Jan 1847. The Colonial Office had previously resisted the concession of RESPONSIBLE GOVERNMENT as demanded by Canadian Reformers, but Elgin and the new Colonial Secretary, Earl Grey, believed it offered the best way to settle Canadian political strife. When the Draper-Viger administration lost the election of 1848 to a Reform majority, Elgin commissioned Louis-Hippolyte LAFONTAINE to form the first truly responsible government. The new administration passed the REBELLION LOSSES BILL in 1849, evoking vehement Tory opposition. When Elgin gave the bill his assent he was attacked by angry mobs and the Parliament buildings in Montréal were burned. Elgin weathered this crisis without compromise, ensuring that responsible government would prevail. Elgin is also noted for the diplomatic finesse with which he secured ratification by the US Senate of the RECIPROCITY treaty in 1854, a measure much desired by Canadians at the time as an antidote to economic stagnation.

After leaving Canada in 1854, Elgin was special commissioner to China 1857-59 and 1860-61. In between these appointments he served as postmaster general in the Palmerston Cabinet. In 1862 he was appointed viceroy to India.

JACQUES MONET, SJ

Reading: J.M.S. Careless, *The Union of the Canadas* (1972); Jacques Monet, sj *The Last Cannon Shot* (1969).

Elites, used in an everyday sense, refers to those who are best at any given activity, eg, top athletes, artists, or soldiers. More precisely, elites are those who hold the uppermost decision-making positions in any powerful activity organized in a definite hierarchy; those who occupy these positions are powerful by virtue of the positions they hold, not necessarily because they are "the best." To examine elites it is necessary first to locate the most powerful activities within society; second, to identify the uppermost or decision-making positions within these activities; and finally to specify the characteristics of the people holding these positions.

Power may be defined as the ability to mobilize resources, including people, money, military strength, opinions and goods or services. At a given time, the military, politicians, religious leaders or economic leaders may be the most powerful group in a society. To determine which activity or activities are most powerful the organization of a society must be understood. According to the materialist perspective, no matter what institution is the most powerful, a society reproduces itself through the production of a means of living (food, clothing, shelter) and therefore the economy is always a fundamental activity, whether organized by religious, political, military or business leaders. Those who control the economy are a powerful elite within any modern society. To determine which are the uppermost positions within the most powerful activities, it is necessary to examine how these activities are organized, eg, the church, labour unions, the military, corporations or the state. In government, for example, PRIME MINISTERS OR PREMIERS and their CABINETS occupy the most powerful positions; in corporations it is the executive (chairman of the board and president) and board of directors; in the military, generals; in labour, the executive positions within unions and labour centrals; in the church, archbishops.

"Uppermost positions" refers to 2 phenomena, both related to the idea of hierarchy. In the corporate world, corporations such as the Royal Bank of Canada (22 times the size of General Motors, Canada) are very large while others, eg, the BANK OF BRITISH COLUMBIA, are relatively small. The most powerful banks can be identified by their assets or profits. The uppermost banks ("dominant corporations") clearly stand above the others. In Canada's case these include the ROYAL BANK OF CANADA, the CANADIAN IMPERIAL BANK OF COMMERCE, the BANK OF MONTREAL, the BANK OF NOVA SCOTIA and the TORONTO DOMINION BANK. Among themselves these 5 banks control over 90% of the assets, income and profits of all banks in Canada. The Toronto Dominion Bank (which alone is almost 2.5 times the size of Canada's top 4 oil companies combined) is the smallest of the 5 dominants, but has twice the assets of its closest rival, the NATIONAL BANK OF CANADA. These dominant corporations are the power bases for the economic elite.

The next hierarchy is reflected in the internal structure of the corporation. Those in the uppermost positions, eg, executive and directors, determine the corporation's direction. In the case of the banks, the executive and board of directors establish policy, review the performance of management and approve or disapprove large loans or investments. The elite of Canadian BANKING are the executive and directors of the 5 dominant banks. Frequently one person holds more than one position. In the case of the banks, however, a director of one bank cannot sit on the board of another bank in Canada, although he or she may sit on the boards of other corporations. There are 11 dominant life-insurance companies in Canada and directors of the 5 banks hold 41% of the highest positions of power in these 11 companies, and 28% of the top positions in the dominant banks are held by people who occupy the same positions in one of the dominant life-insurance companies.

Among the 113 dominant corporations (each controlling many other corporations or subsidiaries) that command the economy in Canada are 1848 interlocked positions, called interlocking directorships, 56% of which are interlocked with important positions on American corporations.

Economic Elite The more elites tend to

resemble one another as particular social types and are distinguishable from the society in general, the more it can be concluded that access to an elite is exclusive and biased in favour of certain social types. Of all the elites in Canada, the economic elite is the most exclusive. It is overwhelmingly male; only 8 of its 798 members (or 1%) are women. People of British origins comprise about 87% of the economic elite but only 45% of the entire population; in contrast French Canadians comprise only 8% of this elite but 29% of the population. Of the "non-charter" (neither French nor British) ethnic groups, only Jewish Canadians surpass their proportion of the population (4% of the elite and 1% of the population), while all other ethnic groups are seriously underrepresented (1% of the elite but 25% of the population). Region of birth is also a factor; those born in Ontario and those currently resident in Ontario have a disproportionate chance of entering the economic elite, reflecting Ontario's traditional position as the centre of the Canadian economy and location for most head offices of major financial, transportation and manufacturing companies. At least 41% of the members of the economic elite characteristically attend private schools, eg, Upper Canada College. The parents of the economic elite could afford such luxuries because they were themselves from privileged positions in society (*see* SOCIAL MOBILITY). Only about 1% of the society can be classified as upper class, but in 1972, 61% of the elite had these class origins; 33% came from the middle class, compared to about 15% of the population and 6% from the working class, which accounts for about 85% of the population. Over the past 20 years the social-class origins of the elite have become more exclusive. John PORTER's classic study, *The Vertical Mosaic*, revealed that 50% of the economic elite in 1951 had upper-class origins, 32% had middle-class origins and 18% were of working-class origins.

Media Elite The elite of the mass media, which controls the major private media complexes in Canada, is similar to the economic elite. Nearly 50% of its members are also members of the economic elite, the 2 overlapping to such an extent that together they can be categorized as the "corporate elite." The media elite tend to be even more upper class in origin than the economic elite, have a slightly higher proportion of women (4%) and slightly higher proportion of French Canadians (13%).

State Elite Members of the state elite share some common features with the corporate elite, but there are important differences. In *The State Elite*, an update of Porter's work, Dennis Olsen divides the state elite into political, bureaucratic and judicial elites. The first comprises the prime ministers, premiers and federal and provincial Cabinet members holding the top posts in the largest provinces (Québec, Ontario, Alberta and BC). Women, again, are seriously underrepresented, accounting for only 2% of these office holders between 1961 and 1973. French Canadian representation in the political elite is greater than it is in the corporate elite; between 1961 and 1973 it rose to 25% from 22% between 1940 and 1960. Only 8% of noncharter ethnic groups are represented. Individuals with British origins comprise 68% of the political elite, which, like all the state elites, is overwhelmingly middle class in its origins (69%). The upper class is still overrepresented, nevertheless (22%), and the working class underrepresented (9%). The bureaucratic elite, eg, deputy ministers and assistant deputy ministers or their equivalents in government departments, crown corporations, regulatory boards and commissions at the federal level and in the 4 largest provinces, are overwhelmingly middle class in their origins (75%) with fewer from the upper class (10%). Only 2% are women. Ethnically it resembles the political elite, and the number of French Canadians in the federal bureaucracy has now increased from 13% in 1953 to 24% in 1973. The judicial elite, eg, the justices of the Supreme Court and the chief justices of the federal and provincial courts, are drawn overwhelmingly from the 2 charter groups and are almost all male and somewhat more upper middle class in origin than the other state elites.

Labour and Religious Elites Although Porter attempted to identify labour, intellectual and religious elites in Canada, none of these have been studied as intensively as state or corporate elites and it is difficult to argue that they wield the same degree of power. Labour is not organized in the same hierarchical way as the corporate and state worlds. The Canadian Labour Congress, the main labour central in Canada, cannot direct its constituent members in binding ways and the member unions and locals enjoy considerable autonomy. Moreover, only about 33% of Canada's labour force is organized into unions. Porter's survey of labour leaders in the early 1950s revealed that they are more representative of a variety of ethnic groups and more representative of the working class. Porter attempted to identify intellectual leaders in Canada by examining members of the Royal Society of Canada, but this is an honorific organization with no decision-making power of its own. While religion has had an important place historically in Canada's power structure, its influence is clearly waning. The power structure of the dominant churches, particularly Roman Catholic and Anglican, and the uppermost positions, eg, archbishops and bishops, can be identified, but the extent of their power relative to other societal elites is doubtful.

The most powerful elites, those that command the greatest resources in Canada today, are the corporate and state elites. Studies have demonstrated that entrance to these elites is strongly affected by social-class origins, region of birth and residence, ethnic origins and gender; the most powerful decision-making positions in Canada are therefore held by people who do not represent a cross section of Canadians.

WALLACE CLEMENT

Reading: Wallace Clement, *The Canadian Corporate Elite: An Analysis of Economic Power* (1975); Dennis Olsen, *The State Elite* (1980).

Elk, *see* WAPITI.

Elk Island National Park (est 1913) is a 194 km² sanctuary of rolling woodlands and meadows dotted with lakes, bogs and ponds, 48 km W of Edmonton. Preserved within the PARK's fenced boundary is a remnant of Alberta's Beaver Hills. Frequent fires have created a mosaic of aspen and mixed-wood forests, meadows and wetlands, which provide ideal habitat for wildlife, including moose, elk, mule deer, some 450 bison, various smaller mammals and over 200 species of birds. In presettlement days, Cree inhabited the park area, trading beaver pelts and harvesting plains bison. Europeans settled in the late 1800s in anticipation of railway construction. Advertisements for homesteading properties brought large ethnic populations westward, and the Ukrainian influence remains strong in the area. Semiserviced camping facilities are available in the park, as are canoeing, swimming, golf, cross-country skiing and hiking.

LILLIAN STEWART

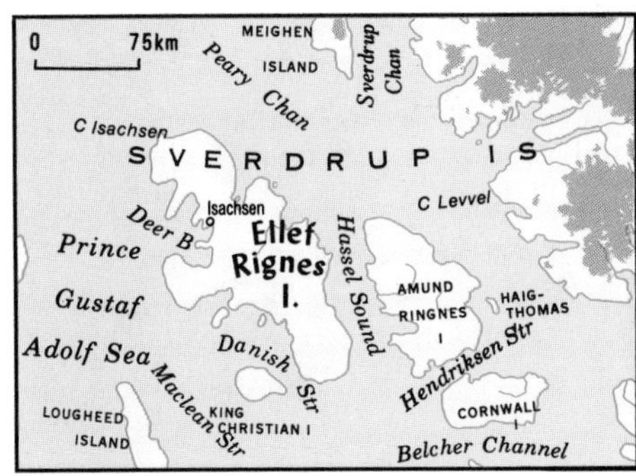

Ellef Ringnes Island, 11 295 km², is part of the SVERDRUP group that borders the Arctic Ocean. Most of the island consists of great thicknesses of sedimentary rock, except for an occurrence of the arctic coastal plain in the NW corner. The island's topography reflects these structural and lithological controls, and is characterized by broad lowlands and dissected uplands. Domal structures, like the 250 m high Isachsen Dome, are the most striking feature of the landscape. Despite generally arid conditions the surface becomes saturated in summer, owing to an active layer derived from water-retentive shale, underlain by impermeable PERMAFROST.

DOUGLAS FINLAYSON

Ellesmere Island, 196 236 km², third-largest island in Canada and most northerly island in the ARCTIC ARCHIPELAGO. It is separated from Greenland by Kane Basin and Kennedy Channel, which is a mere 30 km wide in places, and from Devon I to the S by Jones Sound. Cape Columbia (88°07′ N lat) is Canada's most northerly point of land. The entire island is deeply incised by fjords, and the N coast is extended by ice shelves — aprons of sea ice which are fused to the shore. The N is dominated by the Grant Land

Elk Island National Park, Alta, est 1913, a 194 km² sanctuary for moose, elk, mule deer, bison and over 200 species of birds (*courtesy Parks Canada / R.D. Muir*).

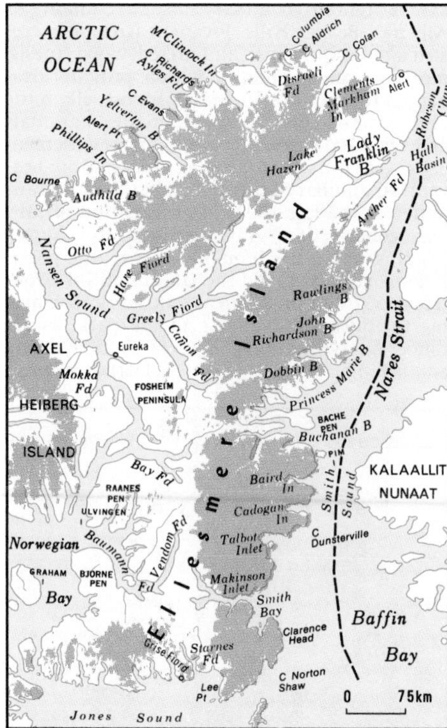

Mts, a jagged chain of sedimentary rocks, shrouded in ice nearly 2000 m thick — remnants of the last ice age, some 100 000 years old. Rock spires project through the ice; Barbeau Peak (2616 m) is the highest mountain in eastern N America. The land descends southward to Hazen Plateau, dominated by Lk Hazen — the largest lake in the polar region. In central Ellesmere, mountains of the Central Ellesmere Fold Belt rise to 2000 m.

Ellesmere is distinguished by spectacular landscape and an exceptional and fragile environment. Small herds of MUSKOXEN are dispersed across Hazen Plateau, along with the remnants of a CARIBOU herd decimated by Peary in 1900. There are numerous species of birds and several other land mammals, but coastal SEA ICE discourages sea mammals. Though the climate is extreme, a peculiar "thermal oasis" at Lk Hazen produces surprisingly warm summers. The frost-free period at Tanquary Fjord averages 50-60 days. Ellesmere is a true polar desert, with only 2.5 cm of precipitation annually in some places. Vegetation is consequently sparse.

One of the most remote places on Earth, Ellesmere I has experienced little human activity. However, archaeological evidence shows that the fjords of Hazen Plateau were occupied some 4000 years ago. Excavations of THULE-culture winter houses in Bache Pen, dating from 1250-1350 AD, have uncovered numerous Norse artifacts. The island was sighted by William BAFFIN 1616, but was not explored until the 19th century. John Ross discovered parts of the coastline 1818 and the island was named during the Inglefield expedition of 1852 for the earl of Ellesmere. Sir George Nares carried out extensive observations in 1875. As part of the First International Polar Year activities, an American group led by A.W. Greely explored widely in N Ellesmere in 1881 from a base on Discovery Harbour. The expedition ended tragically when supply ships failed to arrive, and only 7 of 26 men survived. Much of the exploration was incidental to the search for the North Pole. In 1903-04 the Canadian government was moved to send A.P. LOW to the area to demonstrate Canadian sovereignty; he placed a cairn at the farthest "northing" and installed a flag. A research camp was established at Lk Hazen during the International Geophysical Year (1957-58), and today there are stations at Craig Harbour and Alexandra Fjord. Grise Fjord is an important native community. Joint Canadian-US stations are maintained at Eureka and Alert — the northernmost station in the Canadian Arctic (82°31′ N lat). JAMES MARSH

Ellesmere Island Archaeological Sites were occupied about 4200 years ago by hunting bands believed to have originated from NE Asia and Alaska. Remains of seasonal hunting camps have been found in northern interior valleys and on raised marine terraces along the south and northeast coast. Artifacts include small, finely made stone tools of the Arctic Small Tool tradition and artistic carvings from the late DORSET period. Around 1000 AD the THULE culture Inuit, direct ancestors of all the present-day INUIT, arrived from the Bering Sea and replaced the Dorset population. The remains of their settlements are found along the coastlines of fjords and islands advantageous to hunting sea mammals, including large bowhead whales. Contact with Norsemen seems to have occurred around 1250 AD in the Smith Sound region. Ellesmere I was abandoned by the Inuit sometime during the Little Ice Age, between 1650 to 1850 AD. PETER SCHLEDERMANN

Ellice, Edward, fur trader, merchant, politician (b at London, Eng 23 or 27 Sept 1783; d near Glengarry, Scot 17 Sept 1863). He was the son of a prominent London merchant and was educated at Marischall College, Aberdeen, before being sent to Canada where he assisted in 1804 in the merger of the XY COMPANY and NORTH WEST COMPANY. As a NWC partner, Ellice (always known as "Bear") was active in the pamphlet warfare with Lord SELKIRK, and he was a major party in the negotiations for unification of the NWC and HBC completed in 1821. For years thereafter he was involved in litigation over the claims against the NWC. From 1818 on Ellice almost continuously, until his death, represented Coventry in the House of Commons, and after the Whigs took office in 1830 he held several cabinet posts 1830-34. With large landholdings in Canada, including the seigneury of Beauharnois, Ellice followed developments there closely and behind the scenes he had great influence on British policy. J.M. BUMSTED

Elliot Lake, Ont, Town, pop 16 723 (1981c), is located 140 km W of SUDBURY. Elliot Lake formally came into existence in 1955, only 2 years after the famous "backdoor staking bee" of J.J HIRSHHORN had alerted the mining world to the area's URANIUM potential. Stimulated by the American military demand for uranium, Elliot Lake boomed 1956-63. By 1959 a dozen mining companies were in operation and nearly 25 000 people resided in the carefully laid out government-planned community. The American government's decision that year not to renew its contracts was a devastating blow. By 1965 Elliot Lake's population had dwindled to 6600, and by 1970 only Denison Mines and Rio Algoma were in operation. In the later 1960s and 1970s the uranium industry was revived by the advent of nuclear-generated electrical power in Canada, Japan and West Germany. The fortunes of the "Uranium Capital of the World" rebounded slowly until the early 1980s, when long-range sales to ONTARIO HYDRO stimulated a second spectacular surge in growth. MATT BRAY

Elliott, Andrew Charles, lawyer, judge, politician, premier of BC (b in Ire *c*1828; d at San Francisco, Calif 9 Apr 1889). A barrister of Lincoln's Inn, London, Elliott held several judicial and administrative posts in colonial British Columbia, was a member of the Legislative Council (1865-66) and in 1875 was elected to the provincial legislature, replacing William SMITHE as leader of the Opposition. On the defeat of G.B WALKEM's government (1876) he became premier, but he was no match for Walkem, who attacked his attempts at conciliation in the Pacific Railway dispute with Ottawa. Heavy tax increases and the end of Victoria's hopes of being the transcontinental terminus caused Elliott to lose his seat in the electoral defeat of his government (1878). H. KEITH RALSTON

Elliott, George Alexander, economist, professor, civil servant (b at Napier, Ont 22 July 1901). A man whose imagination, exactitude and humanity inspired his students, Elliott made important contributions to economic theory in articles in learned journals while professor at U of Alberta 1929-46 and U of Toronto 1946-57. References to his work still appear in scientific literature. Turning his attention to Canadian trade policy, he published *Tariff Procedures and Trade Practices* in 1954 and was ap-

Ellesmere Island, NWT, 3rd-largest island in Canada and one of the most remote places on Earth. The Northern Mts are shown *(photo by John Foster/Masterfile).*

ointed to the Tariff Board of Canada from 1957 to 1971. He was elected to the RSC in 1947 and president of the Canadian Political Science Assn in 1957, he was awarded an LLD by Queen's in 1965. H.C. EASTMAN

Elliott, Kenneth Allan Caldwell, biochemist-neurochemist (b at Kimberley, S Africa 24 Aug 1903). A founder of the study of the brain's chemistry, Allan Elliott was the first person officially titled neurochemist at the Montreal Neurological Institute (1944). He was the first director of the Donner Lab of Experimental Neurochemistry (MNI) and then chairman of the Dept of Biochemistry at McGill and Gilman Cheney Professor of Biochemistry. Elliott did original research on brain swelling following trauma, inhibitory and excitatory neurotransmitters, and the biochemistry of epilepsy as well as careful analysis for the chemical composition of the fluid that bathes the brain. His careful chemical analysis of the cerebrospinal fluid led to "Elliott's solution," which is in standard use by neurosurgeons. Elliott has written over 140 publications and was senior editor of 2 editions of *Neurochemistry*. After retirement from McGill he joined CUSO and taught biochemistry to medical students in Enugu, Nigeria. He was the first Norman Bethune Exchange Professor from McGill to the Chinese Medical College, Peking. LEONHARD S. WOLFE

White elm (*Ulmus americana*), with fruit (*artwork by Claire Tremblay*).

Elm (*Ulmus*), genus of TREES of elm family (Ulmaceae), found only in temperate regions of the Northern Hemisphere. Twenty-five species occur worldwide; 3 are native to Canada. White elm occurs as far W as central Saskatchewan; rock and slippery elms are restricted to parts of extreme SW Ontario and SE Québec. Elms, especially white or American elm, may reach imposing heights and are characterized by an umbrella-shaped crown. Leaves are simple, short stalked, oval (slightly asymmetrical at base) and veined, and have teeth of 2 sizes along the margin. They alternate along the twig. The flat, winged fruit develops in very early spring. Elms can grow in various habitats but are usually found in wet, fertile ones (eg, alluvial flats). The very hard wood is used for specialized items, eg, hockey sticks, and for piano bodies, caskets and furniture. Elms are often planted as ORNAMENTALS but many have died recently from Dutch elm disease. ESTELLE LACOURSIÈRE

Elmira, Ontario, UP, pop 7063 (1981c), is located about 17 km NW of KITCHENER. Founded on the banks of the Canagigueh R, it was part of the original Six Nations Reserve and a stopping point on the Canada Co's Guelph-Goderich Road. Its first settlers were English and Irish, then predominantly German from the 1850s. It has been a supply centre for Kitchener's agricultural hinterland. Elmira achieved town status in 1923, but disappeared as a legal corporation with the inauguration of Waterloo Regional Government. KEN MCLAUGHLIN

Elora, Ontario, pop 2666 (1981c), inc 1858, is a picturesque village at the junction of the Grand and Irvine rivers; the sheer beauty of the junction rivals NIAGARA FALLS. Elora was founded 1832 by Capt William Gilkison of Irvine, Scotland, and named after *Ellora*, his brother's East Indian merchantman. Gilkison, a cousin of John GALT, the Canada Co promoter, was impressed by the magnificence of the limestone gorge. Development ceased in the 1870s but there remained a magnificent unspoiled array of 19th-century Ontario architecture in brick and stone to complement the natural landscape. KEN MCLAUGHLIN

Eloul, Kosso, sculptor (b at Mourom, USSR 22 Jan 1920). Eloul's art training started in Tel Aviv in 1938 and continued in 1939 at the Art Institute of Chicago, where he studied with Frank Lloyd Wright, and at the Chicago School of Design with Laszlo Moholy-Nagy. After service in WWII and the War of Independence in Palestine, he returned to his art in 1948. In 1959 he represented Israel at the 29th Venice Biennale. After the First Sculpture Symposium in Yugoslavia in 1961 he set up a similar event in the Negev Desert in 1962; his lifelong involvement with international SCULPTURE conferences began then. He settled permanently in Toronto in 1969 and was the moving force behind the 10th Sculpture Conference held there in 1978. Eloul's characteristic monumental sculptures grace the public spaces of many Canadian cities. His gleaming rectangles of highly polished aluminum or stainless steel are balanced precariously at unusual angles, testing and probing the laws of gravity. Although usually described as minimalist, their inherent energy and restless potential for movement transcend the contemplative minimalist sensibility. CLARA HARGITTAY

Kosso Eloul, *Innercity Gate* (1978) stelcoloy, TD Centre, Toronto (*courtesy Kosso Eloul*).

Emblems of Canada At CONFEDERATION in 1867 no armorial bearings were assigned to the new Dominion of Canada. In 1868 the original provinces, Nova Scotia, New Brunswick, Québec and Ontario, received arms by a royal warrant that also provided for a great seal of Canada, a shield bearing the quartered arms of the 4 provinces. Although not intended as arms of federal authority, the shield came to be considered the arms of the Dominion. As additional provinces entered Confederation, armorial bearings assigned to them were added to the federal shield, creating an unsatisfactory aggregation. A Canadian committee appointed in 1919 had decided within a year on the basic elements of a new design, which was forwarded to the College of Arms in London, Eng, for its consideration. On 21 Nov 1921 King George V, by royal proclamation, assigned armorial bearings for Canada.

The blazon (heraldic description) of Canada's arms is as follows: Tierced in fesse: the first and second divisions containing the quarterly coat following, namely, 1st, gules, three lions passant guardant in pale or; 2nd, or, a lion rampant within a double tressure fleury-counter-fleury gules; 3rd, azure, a harp or stringed argent; 4th, azure, three fleurs-de-lis or; and the third division argent three maple leaves conjoined on one stem proper. Upon the royal helm mantled argent doubled gules a wreath of the colours surmounted by a lion passant guardant or imperially crowned proper and holding in the dexter

The Armorial Bearings of Canada (*courtesy Picture Division, Public Archives of Canada / artwork by Karen E. Bailey*).

paw a maple leaf gules nerved or; the whole ensigned with St Edward's Crown. *Supporters:* on the dexter a lion rampant or holding a lance argent, point or, flying therefrom to the dexter the Union flag; and on the sinister an unicorn argent armed, crined and unguled or, gorged with a coronet composed of crosses patée and fleurs-de-lis a chain affixed thereto reflexed of the last, and holding a like lance flying therefrom to the sinister a banner azure charged with three fleurs-de-lis or. (For a guide to the specialized vocabulary used here, *see* EMBLEMS, PROVINCIAL AND TERRITORIAL; HERALDRY.)

The design is traditional, with the shield displaying the arms of England, Scotland, Ireland and France to symbolize the nation's founding races. Underneath the 4 quarters, on a white field, is a sprig of 3 maple leaves to indicate the new nation of many peoples. Originally green, in 1957 the leaves officially became red, a common autumnal colour, and thus were in accord with Canada's national colours, red and white. The crest and the shield's supporters are strikingly similar to the royal arms of Great Britain. The motto A MARI USQUE AD MARE ("From sea to sea") is from Psalm 72, "He shall have dominio also from sea to sea, and from the river unto th ends of the earth" (King James Version).

Canada's flag (*PAC / Karen E. Bailey*).

Flag

The red and white flag featuring a stylize maple leaf was proclaimed Canada's nationa flag by Queen Elizabeth II on 15 Feb 1965. I adoption was the culmination of many years c discussion, hundreds of designs and the heate FLAG DEBATE in Parliament. Its blazon is "Gule on a Canadian pale argent a maple leaf of th first." The proportions of the flag are 2 by lengt and one by width, with a white square in th centre the width of the flag.

Before 1965 Canada did not have an officia flag. During the French regime the flag flow was the royal banner of France, "Azure, thre fleurs-de-lis or, arranged two and one." Th golden lilies symbolized the Holy Trinity. Afte the CONQUEST in 1760 the flags most commonl flown were Great Britain's Union Flag (Unio Jack) and the Canadian Red Ensign. The latte was the flag of the British merchant marin red, with the Union Jack in the canton (ie, nea the staff). In 1892 the British ADMIRALTY autho rized its use, with the addition of a shield fo Canada in the fly, on vessels registered in Can ada. In 1924 a Canadian order-in-council de creed that the flag could be flown over Canadia government buildings abroad. The Red Ensig was later carried by Canadian athletes at th Olympics and by Canadian troops in WWII. I 1945 another order-in-council approved the fly ing of the flag over federal buildings withi Canada. To many Canadians the Red Ensig was the national flag, and this led to intens feeling when Parliament proposed to replace i with a new design.

Emblems

Beaver The BEAVER, most significant of th fur-bearing animals sought in the FUR TRAD was identified early as an emblem suitable t represent portions of the vast territories that i the 19th century became Canada. In 1621 Kin James I granted Nova Scotia to Sir William Al exander. In 1633 when Alexander became ea of Stirling and Viscount Canada, his new arm featured a beaver to symbolize his fiefdom i the New World.

From 1678 the HUDSON'S BAY COMPANY (char tered 1670) possessed an armorial seal charge with 4 beavers and separated into compartment formed by a St George's cross. About the sam time Gov Frontenac of NEW FRANCE suggested th beaver as a suitable emblem for the colony, bu arms were never authorized. In 1690, to com memorate Frontenac's successful defence of th QUÉBEC CITADEL against the naval attack by Si William Phips, the Kebeca Liberata MEDAL wa struck. It bore a representation of France as seated woman, and of Canada as a beaver at he feet.

The use of the beaver as a Canadian emblem declined in the second half of the 19th century perhaps because Montréal ceased to be a majo fur entrepôt. The animal's emblematic im portance was revived by Sir Sandford FLEMIN when he designed Canada's first postage stam the 1851 threepenny beaver. Today the beave noted for its industry and perseverance, qual ities considered suitable for a nation to emulate decorates the reverse of the Canadian 5-cen coin.

Maple Leaf Along the St Lawrence the leaf c the indigenous common MAPLE, with its dis tinctive shape and beautiful autumnal col ouring, seems to have been considered as an em blem by 1700. When the first ST-JEAN-BAPTIST SOCIETY was founded in 1834, the maple leaf wa made its emblem. In Toronto the 1848 issue c Rev John McCaul's literary annual, *Maple Lea* referred to the leaf as the chosen emblem of Can ada. In 1860 the leaf was incorporated into th adge of the 100th Regiment (Royal Canadians), nd that year the leaves were used extensively n decorations for the Prince of Wales's visit. In 867 Alexander Muir composed "The Maple eaf," a song which for decades was regarded as national hymn. By royal warrant on 26 May 868 the designs of arms granted to Québec and)ntario each incorporated a sprig of 3 maple eaves. The maple leaf was the badge of the ANADIAN EXPEDITIONARY FORCE in WWI. When ational armorial bearings were assigned in 921, a sprig of leaves was an important feature, nd in 1965 it became the dominant element in he new national flag. BRUCE PEEL

eading: Conrad Swan, *Canada: Symbols of Sovereignty* 1977); Canada, Secretary of State, *The Arms, Flags and mblems of Canada* (1981).

mblems, Provincial and Territorial Each Canadian province and territory has, at some oint, chosen or been granted formal emblems o symbolize such things as its history, its flora nd fauna, its geographical setting, and ultimately its existence as a sovereign entity. These mblems are coats of arms, flags and PROVINCIAL LORAL EMBLEMS, and sometimes a tartan or an nimal or mineral. Coats of arms are properly escribed in the formal language of HERALDRY, which, among English speakers, is a vocabulary erived from Norman French with borrowings rom Latin and other languages. Since their descriptions are in words, the emblems may vary n their visual execution from artist to artist, but he basic elements must always appear in correct elation to one another. The following glossary s intended as an aid to interpretation of the heraldic description both here and in EMBLEMS OF ANADA.

Glossary *addorsed:* back to back; *argent:* silver; *zure:* blue; *bar:* narrow horizontal stripe; *barulet:* narrow bar; *base:* horizontal band occupying bottom third of shield (also called "champagne"); *bezant:* gold roundel; *billety:* strewn with illets (upright, oblong figures); *charged:* bearing heraldic figure; *chief:* horizontal band occupying top third of shield; *crined:* referring to colour f mane, hair or beard; *cross patée:* cross with expanding arms; *dexter:* right side as seen from behind shield, hence viewer's left; *fesse:* horizontal and occupying centre third of shield; *field:* ackground; *fleury-counter-fleury:* with fleurs-de-is placed alternately in opposite directions; *fructed:* bearing fruit, *garb:* sheaf of grain; *gorged:* encircled round the neck; *guardant:* with head urned to face viewer; *gules:* red; *haurient* (of fish r sea animal): vertical, with head upwards; *elm:* helmet; *langued:* referring to tincture of ongue; *mantle:* cloth hanging from helmet; *of the irst, last,* etc: of the first, last, etc, tincture mentioned in the description; *or:* gold; *pale:* vertical and occupying centre third of shield; *pallet:* 2 or nore narrow vertical stripes; *passant:* walking; *ile:* wedge-shaped figure with point downward; *proper:* in normal colours; *rampant:* with ne hind paw on ground, the other three raised, ail erect; *reflexed:* looped; *roundel:* circular shape; *able:* black; *sinister:* left side as seen from behind hield, hence viewer's right; *slipped:* torn from tock or branch; *statant:* standing; *tierced:* in 3 arts of different colours; *tinctures:* colours and netals, the metals are argent and or; *tressure:* arrow band bordering shield, often double; *nguled:* referring to colour of hoofs, nails, laws; *vair:* bell-like shapes, white and blue; *vert:* reen.

Alberta

Coat of Arms was granted by King Edward VII, 30 May 1907. The crest and supporters were anted 1980. *Arms:* Azure, in front of a range of now mountains proper, a range of hills vert, in ase a wheatfield surmounted by a prairie both lso proper, on a chief argent, a St George's Cross. *Crest:* Upon a helm with wreath argent and gules, a beaver couchant upholding on its back the royal crown, both proper. *Supporters:* On the dexter side, a lion or armed and langued gules, and, on the sinister side, a pronghorn antelope (*antilocapra americana*) proper; the compartment comprising a grassy mount with the floral emblem of the province of Alberta growing therefrom proper. *Motto:* "Fortis et liber" (Strong and Free).

Flag consists of a royal ultramarine blue field bearing in the centre the provincial arms. It was approved by Queen Elizabeth II on 1 May 1968 and proclaimed on June 1. The proportions are 2 by length and one by width. The arms are in length seven-elevenths of the flag's width.

British Columbia

Coat of Arms was granted by King Edward VII, 31 Mar 1906. Crest and supporters have become part of the provincial achievement through usage. *Arms:* Argent, three bars wavy azure, issuant from the base a demi-sun in splendour proper, on a chief, the Union Device charged in the centre point with an antique crown or. *Crest:* Upon an imperial crown proper, a lion statant guardant imperially crowned, all or. *Supporters:* On the dexter side, a wapiti stag, proper. On the sinister side, a ram of the *"ovis montana."* *Motto:* "Splendor sine occasu" (Splendour without diminishment).

Flag The royal warrant of 1906 authorized the use of the arms for the provincial flag. This was put into effect by a provincial order-in-council, 20 June 1960. The proportions are 5 by length and 3 by width.

Manitoba

Coat of Arms was granted by King Edward VII, 10 May 1905. *Arms:* Vert, on a rock, a buffalo statant proper, on a chief argent, the Cross of St George.

Flag The Red Ensign, bearing in the fly the provincial arms, received royal approval 11 May 1965 and was proclaimed 12 May 1966. The proportions are 2 by length and one by width.

New Brunswick

Coat of Arms was granted by Queen Victoria, 26 May 1868. The royal crown and the motto were added by order-in-council in 1966. *Arms:* Or, on waves, a lymphad, or ancient galley, with oars in action proper, on a chief gules, a lion passant guardant or. *Motto:* "Spem reduxit" (Hope was restored).

Flag The royal warrant of 1868 authorized the use of the arms for the provincial flag. This was put into effect by provincial proclamation, 24 Feb 1963. The proportions are 4 by length and 2½ by width. The red portion with the lion occupies one-third of the surface.

Newfoundland

Coat of Arms was granted by King Charles I, 1 Jan 1637. *Arms:* Gules, a cross argent, in the first and fourth quarters, a lion passant guardant crowned or; in the second and third quarters, an unicorn passant of the second, armed, maned and unguled of the third, and gorged with a crown, thereto a chain affixed passing between the forelegs and reflected over his back, of the last. *Mantling:* Gules doubled argent. *Crest:* On a wreath or and gules an elk passant proper. *Supporters:* Two savages of the clime armed and apparelled according to their guise when they go to war. *Motto:* "Quaerite prime regnum dei" (Seek ye first the Kingdom of God).

Flag Adopted by the provincial legislature, 28 May 1980. The flag is white. In the portion near the staff 4 right-angle triangles, all separated by the field, are arranged in pairs to form rectangular patterns horizontally. In the fly, a gold arrow bordered red between 2 red right-angle triangles, completely voided in their centre, point away from the staff.

Northwest Territories

Coat of Arms was authorized and approved by Queen Elizabeth II, 24 Feb 1956. *Arms:* Per bend wavy gules and vert billety or, in sinister chief, the mask of an arctic fox argent, on a chief indented also argent, a barrulet wavy azure. *Crest:* On a wreath argent and gules, a compass rose proper between two narwhals haurient and addorsed or.

Flag The flag adopted by the territorial council, 1 Jan 1969, is divided vertically in the proportions: one blue (near staff), two white (middle), one blue (fly). The white square displays in its centre the arms of the Northwest Territories.

Nova Scotia

Coat of Arms was first granted by King Charles I in 1625. It was reinstated by King George V, 19 Jan 1929, to supersede the coat of arms granted 26 May 1868. *Arms:* Argent, a Cross of St Andrew azure charged with an escutcheon of the Royal Arms of Scotland. *Crest:* On a wreath of the colours, a branch of laurel and a thistle issuing from two hands conjoined, the one being armed and the other naked, all proper. *Supporters:* On the dexter side, an unicorn argent armed, crined and unguled or, and crowned with the imperial crown proper, and gorged with a coronet composed of crosses patée and fleurs-de-lis a chain affixed thereto passing through the forelegs and reflexed over the back, or. And on the sinister side, a savage holding in the exterior hand an arrow, proper. *Motto:* "Munit haec et altera vincit" (One defends and the other conquers).

Flag The royal warrant of 1929 authorized the use of the arms for the provincial flag.

Ontario

Coat of Arms The arms were granted by Queen Victoria, 26 May 1868; the crest, supporters and motto were granted by King Edward VII, 27 Feb 1909. *Arms:* Vert, a sprig of three leaves of maple slipped or, on a chief argent, the Cross of St George. *Crest:* On a wreath of the colours, a bear passant sable. *Supporters:* On the dexter side, a moose, and on the sinister side a Canadian deer both proper. *Motto:* "Ut incepit fidelis sic permanet" (Loyal it began, loyal it remains).

Flag The Red Ensign bearing in the fly the provincial arms received royal approval as the provincial flag, 14 Apr 1965, and was proclaimed on May 21. The proportions are 2 by length and one by width.

Prince Edward Island

Coat of Arms was granted by King Edward VII, 30 May 1905. *Arms:* Argent, on an island vert, to the sinister an oak tree fructed, to the dexter thereof three oak saplings sprouting all proper, on a chief gules, a lion passant guardant or. *Motto:* "Parva sub ingenti" (The small under the protection of the great).

Flag The 1905 warrant authorized the use of the provincial arms for the flag. On 24 Mar 1964 the province adopted a design bearing the arms within a red and white border. The proportions are 6' (183 cm) by length and 4' (122 cm) by width including the border, which is 3" (7.6 cm) wide. The alternating strips of the border are each 10" (25 cm) long.

Québec

Coat of Arms was authorized by a provincial order-in-council on 9 Dec 1939. These arms resemble those granted by Queen Victoria in 1868 except that the upper portion bears 3 gold fleurs-de-lis on a blue field instead of 2 blue fleurs-de-lis on a gold field. The same order-in-council approved the use of the royal crown above the shield. The motto, adopted 1883, was suggested by Eugène Taché, architect of the "palais législatif." *Arms:* Tierced in fesse: 1, azure, three fleurs-de-lis or; 2, gules, a lion passant guardant or; 3, or, a sprig of three leaves of sugar maple

Arms of Alberta (*PAC/Karen E. Bailey*).

Arms of British Columbia (*PAC/Karen E. Bailey*).

Arms of Manitoba (*PAC/Karen E. Bailey*).

Arms of New Brunswick (*New Brunswick Information*).

Arms of Newfoundland (*PAC/Karen E. Bailey*).

Arms of Northwest Territories (*PAC/Karen E. Bailey*).

Arms of Nova Scotia (*PAC/Karen E. Bailey*).

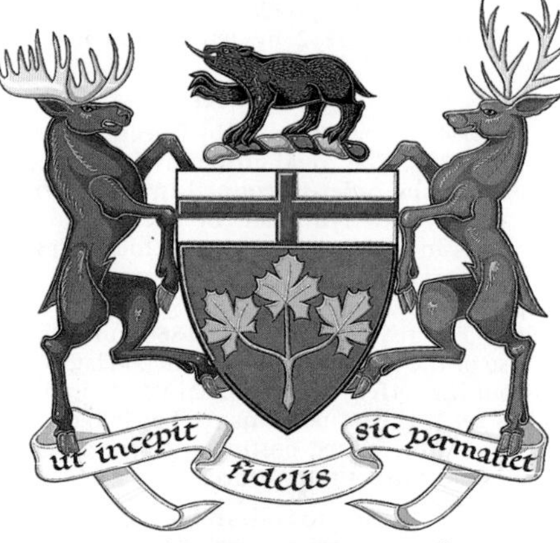

Arms of Ontario (*PAC/Karen E. Bailey*).

Arms of Prince Edward Island (*PAC/Karen E. Bailey*)

Arms of Québec (*PAC/Karen E. Bailey*).

Arms of Saskatchewan (*PAC/Karen E. Bailey*).

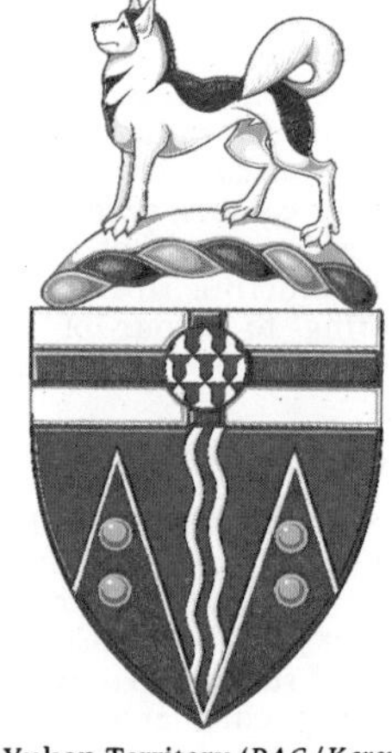

Arms of Yukon Territory (*PAC/Karen E. Bailey*).

'ert veined of the field. *Motto:* "Je me souviens" (remember), in letters azure within a scroll ar-ent edged azure.

Flag Adopted 21 Jan 1948 by an order-in-ouncil and by an Act assented to 9 Mar 1950, he fleurdelisé flag is described as "Azure a cross etween four fleurs-de-lis argent." The propor-ions are 6 units by length, 4 by width, and the rms of the cross are one unit wide.

Saskatchewan

Coat of Arms was granted by King Edward 'II, 25 Aug 1906. *Arms:* Vert, three garbs in fesse r, on a chief of the last, a lion passant guardant ules.

Flag Saskatchewan's flag was officially ded-cated 22 Sept 1969. It is divided horizontally, reen above and yellow below. On the green ortion near the staff are the provincial arms. In he fly over both tinctures is the provincial flo-al emblem.

Yukon

Coat of Arms was authorized by Queen Eliza-eth II on 24 Feb 1956. *Arms:* Azure, on a pallet vavy argent a like pallet of the field, issuant rom base two piles reversed gules edged also ar-ent each charged with two bezants in pale, on a hief argent, a cross gules surmounted of a oundel vair. *Crest:* On a wreath or and gules, a usky dog standing on a mount of snow proper.

Flag The flag, adopted by the territorial ouncil in 1967, is divided vertically in equal arts: green (near the staff), white (middle), blue fly). On the white field above a wreath of fire-veed are the arms of the Yukon with the crest.

AUGUSTE VACHON

'eading: A.B. Beddoe, *Beddoe's Canadian Heraldry* (1981); Canada, Secretary of State, The Arms, Flags and Em-lems of Canada (1981); C. Swan, *Canada: Symbols of Sov-reignty* (1977).

Emerson, Man, Town, pop 762 (1981c), inc 879, 96 km S of Winnipeg, is the province's nain port of entry on the international bound-ry. When settlement began in 1874, the area al-eady had a varied historical heritage — as the ite of fur-trade rivalries; a link in the move-nent of people and goods between St Paul, Ainn, and Manitoba; and the site of an 1871 ENIAN raid and of Ft Dufferin, staging area of he newly formed NORTH-WEST MOUNTED POLICE 1874). Two Wisconsin businessmen sought to nake Emerson a railway centre and gateway to he Northwest. The town did become a trade entre for the border region. A population and uilding boom occurred 1880-82 based on ef-orts to establish a new railway, then to draw he CPR to the town. Both schemes failed and Emerson was bankrupt by 1884. The province ntervened to restore stable government. Em-rson today is a local service centre for a thriving gricultural region (cereal grains and special rops). The federal border station is a major em-loyer.

D.M. LYON

'eading: J. McClelland and D. Lewis, eds, *Emerson 875-1975: A Centennial History* (1975).

Emerson, John Norman, professor, archae-logist (b at Toronto 13 Mar 1917; d there 18 Nov 978). As a Huron-Iroquois specialist, he was he first in Canada to establish a training pro-ram for Canadian archaeologists. Educated at U f T and Chicago, and supervisor of archae-logical studies at U of T for 30 years, Emerson vas a humanitarian teacher and a socially ninded scientist. He firmly believed in the learn by doing" philosophy of teaching. His rodigious excavations at nearly 50 sites helped xpose numerous students and the general pub-ic to Ontario archaeology. He founded the mod-rn Ontario Archaeological Soc, and helped es-ablish the Canadian Archaeological Assn in 968.

W.C. NOBLE

Emery, John, bobsledder (b at Montréal 4 Jan 1932). Infected by brother Vic EMERY's enthusiasm for the sport, John teamed with Vic, Doug Anakin and Peter Kirby to provide Canada with a 1964 Innsbruck Olympics gold medal in a sport few Canadians dared attempt because of cost and inadequate training facilities.

BOB FERGUSON

Emery, Victor, Vic, bobsledder (b at Montréal 28 June 1933). Sailing and skiing were his first loves, but Emery became captivated with BOBSLEDDING and luge while watching the 1956 Cortina Olympic Games. He assembled a crew, including his brother John EMERY, that won startling gold-medal victories at the 1964 Innsbruck Olympics and 1965 world championships.

BOB FERGUSON

Emigration, the act of leaving a place of residence or country to live elsewhere. Of the 4 major components of Canadian population growth (births, deaths, immigration and emigration), emigration is the most statistically uncertain. Canada does not maintain an exit-visa register. Intercensal estimates of emigration measured by collecting data from the US and UK and combining them with a figure of 48 000 (the annual estimate for emigration to all other countries in the world) are published annually by Statistics Canada. Emigration from Canada between 1851 and 1971 was as volatile as immigration, especially since, during the period of early settlement, Canada was a way station for immigrants travelling to the US. Early estimates of emigration, which vary from 170 000 (1851-61) to 1 089 000 (1911-21), were based on the population census conducted every 10 years from 1851 to 1951 (the 1851 and 1861 data are aggregates of separate censuses for Canada E, Canada W, NS and NB). Since 1951 a national census has been taken every 5 years.

Demographers use 2 methods in making emigration assumptions when projecting Canadian population growth. The standard technique is to derive an absolute number (based on annual data for Canadian migration to the US and UK, plus an additional 48 000) and to hold it constant over time; eg, with the most recent population projections, Statistics Canada assumed that 75 000 emigrants would leave Canada per year until the end of the century. A second method is to assume emigration as a certain percentage of gross immigration. In 1975 a Special Joint Committee of Parliament on IMMIGRATION POLICY indicated that future emigration from Canada could be estimated as one-third of gross immigration. However, the use of immigration statistics creates problems, eg, the difficulty of distinguishing between nationality, country of birth and country of last residence. Immigration data usually record only the last residence. The US provides comprehensive data on the numbers and characteristics of non-US citizens migrating there from Canada, but because it does not record the return of its noncitizens it is impossible to distinguish between "quasi-migrants" and "semi-permanent migrants." With this qualification, it can be said that in the period 1973-79 Canada received about 120 000 immigrants from the US and lost about 109 000 emigrants to the US. Many of the emigrants were highly skilled, eg, engineers, doctors, surgeons, graduate nurses, systems analysts, tool and die workers, machinists, electricians, mechanics and repairmen, pipefitters, plumbers, etc. In this period, emigration of physicians and surgeons from Canada to the US was almost 90% of the number of physicians and surgeons who immigrated to Canada from all countries; among graduate nurses the figure was 40%. This trend continued during 1977-79, when there was a similar increase among all occupational groups, eg, engineers 30%, systems analyists 25%, carpenters 22%. But as was mentioned above, emigration assessments are statistically uncertain. Early results from the 1981 census suggest that the figures for 1976-81 may have been overestimated by between 10 000 and 15 000. Statistics Canada is reviewing the efficacy of its methodology and is examining new approaches, including the possible use of taxation or family-allowance data, or both.

Aside form the quality of the data, the interpretation of statistics is also problematic. The loss of 11 skilled Canadians will have 121 times the impact on Canada as would that of one skilled American leaving the US, although the exchange (11 Canadians for one American) may seem equivalent in view of the population figures. The degree of emigration from Canada to the US is also problematic, though it is estimated to represent 25% of all emigration from Canada. Although there is fairly reliable evidence to suggest that in a few occupations (eg, medicine) the US receives most Canadian emigrants, anecdotal evidence (sporadic reports from industry, etc) suggests that there is a much wider global dispersal of those with other critical skills.

Various theories have been developed to explain the relationship between economic development and the movement of people. Britain was once the world's largest exporter of capital, technical skills and unskilled labour to the developing countries overseas, but now it is questionable whether the international flow of human capital is still an economic blessing to the sending as well as the receiving countries. It is now determined by growth in the most developed sector; skilled labour emigrates out of rather than into underdeveloped regions, a reversal of the pattern in the 19th century. The market for highly skilled individuals is much wider than it has been in the past. Canada is an example of a nation which, because of expanding industrialization, is able to provide increasing numbers of positions for highly qualified manpower; yet Canada has exported large numbers of skilled people to the US, a more advanced industrial nation, while at the same time importing manpower from abroad. Thus Canada still tends to act as a way station between the US and the world. *See also* IMMIGRATION; POPULATION.

CHRIS TAYLOR

Emmerson, Henry Robert, lawyer, businessman, premier of NB (b at Maugerville, NB 25 Sept 1853; d at Dorchester, NB 9 July 1914). A successful businessman and lawyer, Emmerson was an MLA 1888-90, a legislative councillor 1891-92 and MLA 1892-1900 (during which he was commissioner of public works). In the years 1897 to 1900 he was premier of NB and held the post of attorney general. Emmerson was elected MP in 1900 and became minister of railways and canals in Sir Wilfrid LAURIER's Cabinet 1904-07. In that capacity he played an important role in the development of railway terminals, docks and canals. Forced to resign over a scandal in his private life, he continued to sit in the House of Commons until his death.

ARTHUR T. DOYLE

Empire Day, observed annually on the school day preceding the May 24 holiday for Queen Victoria's birthday, was the most important patriotic rite for children in English-speaking Canada during the half century following its first observance 23 May 1899. The idea originated with Clementina Fessenden of Hamilton, and was publicized across the country by George Ross, Ontario education minister. Empire Day celebrations were associated with IMPERIALISM, militarism and immigrant assimilation. After an initial decline in the 1930s, the celebrations were rejuvenated by WWII. In later years various provinces renamed the day Commonwealth or Citizenship Day.

ROBERT M. STAMP

Employment and Income, White Paper on, described the government's immediate post-war fiscal and economic policies. Presented to Parliament in 1945 by the Hon C.D. HOWE, minister of reconstruction, it outlined the government's intention to adopt Keynesian economic policies to maintain a high level of employment and income. Deficits would be incurred and national debt increased when unemployment threatened, but would be balanced by surpluses in periods of prosperity. A major shift in policy, the White Paper introduced the period of greatest prosperity in Canadian history and helped set the style of federal-provincial relations for 15 years. C.E.S. FRANKS

Employment Law generally refers, in Canada, to the law governing the relationship of an individual employee to an employer, as distinguished from LABOUR LAW, the law of unionized COLLECTIVE-BARGAINING relationships. Employment law includes both the common, or judge-made, law of "master and servant," which is concerned mainly with wrongful dismissal, and a complex mass of statute law dealing with minimum labour standards, human rights, occupational health and safety, workers' compensation, etc. With some important exceptions, unionized employees are also protected by the statutory part of employment law, although they are seldom concerned with minimum standards because their collective agreements almost always establish higher levels of wages and benefits. Other statutes, such as those regarding human rights, wage-payment protection, occupational health and safety, workers' compensation, pension and unemployment-insurance laws, do concern them.

The law of wrongful dismissal in all provinces except Québec is largely inherited from England, but Canadian courts now rarely refer to English case law. The equivalent Québec law is based on the French Civil Code. Generally an employee cannot be dismissed without cause unless he or she has been given due notice or pay in lieu thereof, but outside of these conditions the law of wrongful dismissal provides no protection against firing. What constitutes cause and how much notice is "due" notice have been the subjects of countless court cases. The essence of cause for dismissal is usually an employee's failure to fulfill an obligation, within the scope of the job, to obey the employer's lawful directions. The period of notice to which the employee is entitled depends, first, on any agreement or understanding with the employer arising from the practice of the industry or the particular workplace. For example, in some industries or types of jobs, layoffs are a matter of course. In others, in the absence of employee misconduct, employment is assumed to be long term, and in that case an employer's economic difficulties will not justify dismissal without due notice. Where there is no agreement or understanding, the length of the notice to which the employee is entitled depends on the character or status of the employment, the employee's length of service and age and the availability of similar employment. Some minimum periods of notice are tied directly to the way wages are paid; eg, if payment is made every week, a week's notice may be all that is required. In the majority of jurisdictions, the minimum protection is only available to employees who have been employed for a specified period of time, usually 3 months. A wrongfully dismissed employee can sue in the ordinary courts and will be awarded money damages equal to the pay he or she would have received if proper notice had been given, but the employee is under a duty to mitigate the damages; ie, any money earned at a new job or which could have been earned if a reasonable effort had been made to find a new job will be deducted. Because of court costs, wrongful dismissal cases usually involve executive-level employees. Unionized employees working under collective agreements cannot sue for wrongful dismissal. They must go through their grievance procedures and finally to ARBITRATION. This may be preferable because arbitrators, unlike the courts, order employers to put employees who are found to have been dismissed without just cause back on the job. Moreover, grievance arbitration normally costs the employee nothing.

Master and servant law may be thought of as the "old" employment law and the statute law as the "new" employment law, although there has been statutory regulation of the terms and conditions of employment since the Middle Ages. The earliest regulation of employment was largely for the benefit of employers, but since the 1900s, Factory Acts legislation, however inadequate, has existed to protect employees.

Whether or not a person is subject to any employment law depends on whether he or she is in fact the employee of an employer. There are a surprising number of cases where legally it is unclear whether people are employees or independent contractors. For example, taxi drivers or truckers may do work for only one company but not be considered employees by the law. The courts, or the administrators of labour legislation, will ask whether the driver, or any other person who claims to be an employee, owns the equipment or tools of the trade, stands to make a profit or take a loss and, most important, whether he or she is subject to control not only regarding what will be done on the job but how it will be done.

In each province and in the federal jurisdiction the Labour Standards Code or its equivalent regulates minimum wages, hours of work, overtime, the mode and interval of wage payments, wage statements, daily rest, weekly rest, statutory holidays, vacations and vacation pay, time off to vote, maternity leave and equal pay for men and women. In some jurisdictions the equal-pay law is found in the human rights code, which prohibits discrimination based on sex, race, religion, ethnic or national origin and a variety of other grounds that differ somewhat from province to province. In every province and as part of the federal government's Canada Labour Code there are statutory provisions that buttress the law of wrongful dismissal by setting minimum periods of notice to be given employees prior to their termination. The Canada Labour Code, applicable to employees in industries under federal constitutional jurisdiction, eg, banks, also provides that employees who have been employed for more than one year are entitled to reinstatement if they are found by special adjudicators to have been dismissed without just cause. Many other statutes, eg, corporations legislation and debt-collection legislation can be considered part of employment law, as can legislation governing various aspects of public employment, eg, the civil service and public-school teaching.

Through the 1970s the individual-employer relationship in Canada became increasingly regulated, exemplified by the changes in the Canada Labour Code which gave wrongfully dismissed employees the right to claim reinstatement through a special low-cost administrative procedure. Judges became increasingly generous in the damages they awarded to wrongfully dismissed executives, to the point where a year's pay became quite common — a measure of damages far in excess of that normally given by American courts. With the adverse economic climate of the early 1980s, however, the momentum for greater employee protection appears to have been lost, and the question is whether economic pressure will result in the recall of protections already gained. INNIS CHRISTIE

Empress of Ireland, Canadian Pacific ocean-going passenger ship that sank in the St Lawrence R near Rimouski, Qué 29 May 1914. She was rammed in dense fog by the Norwegian collier *Storstad,* severed amidships, and sank in only 14 minutes; 1014 passengers and crew died while 465 managed to abandon ship. Bodies recovered from the *Empress* were gathered in the village of Ste-Luce and buried near Métis-sur-Mer, where a monument stands to their memory. Capt Anderson of the *Storstad* was later held responsible for the disaster. JAMES MARS[H]

Encyclopedia, a written work containing numerous entries, usually in alphabetical arrangement, attempting to cover all branches of knowledge or all aspects of one subject. The late Latin word is a misconstruction based on the Greek expression for "complete education." Various efforts were made in ancient times to encompass all knowledge in a single work. The first modern encyclopedia, with broad coverage and elaborate cross-referencing, was the *Cyclopaedia* (London, 1728) edited by Ephraim Chambers. With Denis Diderot's *Encyclopédie* (Paris, vol 1, 1751) the encyclopedia reached a point of literary excellence and social influence. The greatest English-language encyclopedia, *Encyclopaedia Britannica,* was first issued in 1768 in 3 volumes, and by the scholarly 11th edition of 1910-11 it had grown to 29 volumes and 43 million words.

The first attempt to produce an encyclopedic work entirely on Canada was *Canada: An Encyclopaedia of the Country* (5 vols, Toronto, 1898-99) edited by J. Castell HOPKINS. More comprehensive was *The Encyclopedia of Canada* (6 vols, Toronto, 1935-37), edited by W.S. WALLACE, which was arranged alphabetically and included numerous biographies and descriptions of places. A supplementary volume on Newfoundland compiled by Robert Blackburn, was published in 1949. The encyclopedia was sold to the Grolier Society, an American publisher, and provided the core of *Encyclopedia Canadiana* (10 vols, Toronto, 1958), edited by John ROBBINS.

Attempts have been made to compile encyclopedic works on aspects of Canada. Sir Arthur DOUGHTY and L.J. BURPEE compiled the *Index and Dictionary of Canadian History* (1911) as a companion to the Makers of Canada series, and Doughty and Adam Shortt edited the 23-volume *Canada and Its Provinces* (1914-17). *The Oxford Companion to Canadian History and Literature,* by Norah Story, was published in 1967, and a supplement edited by William Toye appeared in 1970. A new *Oxford Companion to Canadian Literature,* edited by Toye, was published in 1983. The ENCYCLOPEDIA OF MUSIC IN CANADA was published in 1981 after [.] years' research and production. A recent attempt to produce a modern encyclopedia of a province is the *Encyclopedia of Newfoundland and Labrador* edited by Joseph SMALLWOOD (vol 1, 1981). JAMES MARS[H]

Encyclopedia of Music in Canada, edited by Helmut KALLMANN, Gilles Potvin and Kenneth Winters and comprising over 3100 articles and 500 illustrations, was the first music encyclopedia published in Canada. Entries include biographies and histories of organizations involved with any facet of music in Canada. National topics such as Inuit music, piano building and awards, and regional topics such as education, instrument collections and folk music ar[e] treated, as are music activities in Canadian cities and Canada's relations in music with other countries. Bibliographies, discographies, lists of compositions, filmographies and cross references to other articles are included, and 15 000 index entries locate subjects which ar[e] mentioned in articles.

Prompted initially in 1971 by Floyd S. CHALMERS, preparation began in 1973. With the editors, a peak staff of 23, aided by consultants, processed original articles from 400 writer[s]

Equal attention was paid to all areas of music. Information was gathered from records of individuals and organizations, from personal interviews and from research of related documents. *EMC* was published in English by U of T Press (1981) and in French by Editions Fides (1983). Procedures for continuous editorial revision have been established. MABEL H. LAINE

Endangered Animals ANIMAL species already extinct (extc) or extirpated (extp) from Canada include swift fox (extp), great auk (extc, 1844), Labrador duck (extc, 1878), passenger pigeon (extc, 1914), timber rattlesnake (extp, 1941), paddlefish (extp, 1800s) and blue walleye (extc, 1960s). A number of other animal species are on the brink of extinction. The endangered species listed at present by the Committee on the Status of Endangered Wildlife in Canada (COSEWIC) follow.

Listed in the table are those species judged by COSEWIC, up to June 1982, to be endangered (as opposed to threatened, rare or other). Their status may be changed, and new species will be added to the list. The status of the following species, for example, is under consideration: woodland caribou, Rocky Mountain wolf, Queen Charlotte weasel, Gaspé shrew; spotted owl, Cooper's hawk; blue racer, island watersnake; aurora char, pugnose shiner, pugnose minnow, Banff dace, Campbell sucker, black redhorse, brindled madtom and blackstripe top minnow.

A considerable number of other animals have been classified as threatened or rare in Canada. The problem deserves serious attention, especially if viewed as a sign of the general deterioration of the natural ENVIRONMENT. Factors affecting the quality of the environment and leading to a steady loss of habitat include decrease in FOREST cover (cutting exceeds reforestation in most provinces); lack of natural VEGETATION to control EROSION on stream banks and woodlots on many farms; AIR POLLUTION by acid and other toxic substances; and WATER POLLUTION by industry, individuals and municipalities.

The major factors involved in the disappearance or endangering of Canadian species have been exploitation (hunting, fishing, gathering of eggs or young), destruction of habitat and pollution. Study of case histories is instructive. The sea otter was exploited on the W Coast by hunters who sold as many as 1200 pelts per year during the 1700s and 1800s. By 1900, sea otters were on the verge of extinction; the last documented sighting in BC was in 1929. An international treaty (1911) gave protection, and by the late 1960s the Alaskan population had grown to about 30 000. Transplants to BC (1969-72) were successful and 70 individuals were sighted in 1977.

The introduction of mammalian predators onto Langara I reduced the population of ancient murrelets and of the peregrine falcon which fed on them. Many populations of peregrines were decimated by DDT, which, when metabolized to DDE reduces calcium in eggshells, causing them to break.

The greater prairie chicken originally occurred in Alberta, Saskatchewan, Manitoba and Ontario. The species occupied large blocks of ungrazed or lightly grazed grasslands where preferred habitat included native bluestem and Indian grass, wild rye, switch grass and sand dropseed. The birds flourished amid the small-scale farming activities of the early 1900s, but when vast amounts of native prairie grassland were converted to cultivated crops and cattle grazing, the habitat was destroyed. The greater prairie chicken has been extirpated from all provinces except Saskatchewan, where there were 15 reports, some of which might not have been valid, between 1965 and 1977. The recently created GRASSLANDS NATIONAL PARK, Sask, is sufficiently large and protected, and might permit re-establishment of this species.

The leatherback turtle is a large (up to 680 kg), unique, mainly tropical, open-sea species. Sparse sightings have occurred in the Atlantic Ocean north to Nain, Lab, and along the BC coast to Cordova, Alaska. Estimates place world population at 30 000-40 000, but up to 20-30% of some populations are killed annually. The world population is believed to be declining and endangered. The exact significance of Canadian records is uncertain. The turtles may be migrants or strays, but appear to be vigorous and to feed in Canadian waters, where only adults are seen. Although adults are occasionally tangled in fishing gear or harpooned as curiosities in Canadian waters, most mortality takes place in tropical waters, where eggs are collected for human consumption. Responsibility for conservation measures must be taken there. Thus, in some cases, protection of species occurring in Canada may require international co-operation.

The habitat of the Vancouver Island marmot is threatened by logging and disturbed by skiers (*photo by Tim Fitzharris*).

Immature male peregrine falcon (*courtesy Alberta Fish and Wildlife Division*).

The Acadian whitefish was discovered as a distinct species only in 1967. When discovered, it was already being threatened by a dam blocking its upstream spawning migration from the sea. The dam was provided with an inadequate fish ladder. Recently, ACID RAIN, originating in the US and Ontario, has decimated Atlantic salmon in southern NS and has probably had the same effect on Acadian whitefish. Scarcely anything is known of the whitefish's life history. The species may be vanishing, a victim of our desire to save pennies on power bills.

The brindled madtom is a tiny, spotted catfish reaching 87 mm at most in Canadian waters. It inhabits rivers, streams and lakes, where it is most active at night. It once occurred in tributaries of L Erie, the Niagara and Sydenham rivers of southern Ontario. The parents share nest-building activities and guarding of young. Madtoms guard themselves with a sharp, pectoral-fin spine which could sting a would-be predator. The species was last reported in Canada in 1976, although suitable habitats and localities known to support the species have been searched. Because of the madtom's size and habitats, it is difficult to be certain whether population levels are exceedingly low or whether the species has already been extirpated in Canadian waters.

The shorthead sculpin was discovered in Canadian waters in 1957, in the lower 24 km of the tiny Flathead R drainage of BC, between elevations of 1000-1400 m. Sculpins are most abundant on gravel or stony bottoms that are not heavily sedimented and have summer temperatures up to 13-17°C. They reach 100 mm in length, may lay up to 690 eggs, probably on underside of rocks, and feed on insects and small fish. A proposal to develop surface coal mines in the Flathead Basin for export of coal to Japan, and to redirect the flow of Howell Creek, a Flathead tributary, may threaten the species. Sedimentation, acidification or modification of flow and temperature regimes could be harmful.

While it is obvious that protection from overhunting is needed to save a species from extinction, it is less apparent that many subtle features of the habitat may also have to be protected. Habitat requirements for a fish might include stream spawning grounds, nursery area for feeding of fry in a lake, unobstructed river for migration to sea, estuarine and offshore feeding grounds for young and adults and, again, an unobstructed river for return to spawning ground. The spawning ground itself may require clear, oxygenated water, free of pollutants, running at the correct velocity, and gravel of a certain size, free of both organic and inorganic sediments. The gravel bed will have to be within a certain temperature range, neither too warm nor freezing, and never exposed by dropping water levels. Stream-bank trees, often removed by common logging and farming practices, are important to stream life. Summer temperatures, runoff from snowmelt and rain, and bank soil erosion are moderated by trees, bushes and herbaceous plants. Leaf fall into streams is an important food-energy component of the ecological network. Leaves are fed on by bacteria and single-celled animals, that in turn are eaten by insects and other invertebrates which serve as food for birds and fishes. A species habitat is complex and small changes may make it unsuitable. If a single habitat requirement is unavailable, a species may not survive. Terrestrial habitats are equally vulnerable; salt licks, summer and winter ranges, and undisturbed calving grounds may be necessary for certain ungulates inhabiting them. Slow degeneration of the environment may be more dangerous to survival of a species, as it is less apt to be noticed and corrected than are dramatic spills of pollutants. The gradual buildup of pollutants may have catastrophic effects. It took several years before DDT began significantly to thin eggshells of falcons.

Species	*Causes of Decline or Threat*
Mammals	
Vancouver Island marmot *(Marmota vancouverensis)*	habitat threatened by logging and disturbed by skiers
right whale *(Balaena glacialis)*	hunting, oil spills and pollution (feed on plankton near surface)
bowhead whale *(Balaena mysticetus)*	hunting
sea otter (*Enhydra lutris)*	extirpated by hunting in Canada in 1929; transplants into BC waters from Alaska survive
eastern cougar *(Felis concolor couguar)*	habitat conflict with humans; low prey density
wood bison *(Bison bison athabascae)*	hunting decimated species; hybridization threatens pure stock
Birds	
peregrine falcon *(Falco peregrinus anatum)*	DDT (DDE) caused thinning of shells; taking of young and hunting
greater prairie chicken *(Tympanuchus cupido)*	habitat lost to crops and cattle; extirpated in 3 of 4 provinces
whooping crane *(Grus americana)*	hunting, disruption of breeding, and habitat destruction 1879-1900; increasing: 21 in 1941, 76 in 1977
Eskimo curlew *(Numenius borealis)*	excessive shooting caused decline to point where it was thought to be extinct; a few survive
Reptiles	
leatherback turtle *(Dermochelys coriacea)*	use of eggs by humans
Fishes	
Acadian whitefish *(Coregonus canadensis)*	dams, poaching and now acid rain threaten the species

The advance of acid rain, clear-cutting of forests and drainage of wetlands clearly portend serious ecological (and economic) consequences if they are not reversed.

Several organizations are engaged in study and management of rare and endangered species. The NATIONAL MUSEUM OF NATURAL SCIENCES, Ottawa, has for many years evaluated the status of Canada's fauna and flora, although it has never been given special resources for this task. The Canadian Wildlife Service has had a role in managing and studying Canada's migratory birds; Dept of Fisheries and Oceans in managing and studying fishes and sea mammals. Canada is a signatory to the Convention on International Trade in Endangered Species (CITES), which regulates trade in these species or their by-products. Provinces and territories have mandates in WILDLIFE CONSERVATION AND MANAGEMENT. The Committee on the Status of Endangered Wildlife in Canada is an organization of specialists from federal, provincial and territorial governments and national, private conservation organizations. It decides which plant or animal species (the future of which is in doubt in Canada) is in what category (rare, threatened, endangered, extirpated or extinct). COSEWIC provides status reports, but it is up to the appropriate management agency to correct adverse factors. A number of other organizations are active in protection of Canadian species and the environment; they include the World Wildlife Fund (Canada), Toronto; Canadian Wildlife Federation, Ottawa; and Save Our Streams, Don Mills, Ont.

To protect now-endangered species, we must remove immediate threats to their existence, and ensure that their habitat requirements are met. This may require natural-history preserves, public education, protective legislation, enforcement and other measures such as artificial breeding. Individuals and industries are coming to realize that many wastes do not disappear when dumped into air, earth or water, but spread through the biosphere; that we will have to consider the environmental effects of each of society's requirements (eg, energy, transportation, sewage disposal, wetlands and leisure time); and that the habitat of choice of mankind includes nature as well as asphalt.

D.E. McALLISTER

Endangered Plants are those in imminent danger of extinction. The International Union for Conservation of Nature and Natural Resources (IUCN) recognizes 4 stages in endangerment: rare, vulnerable, endangered and extinct. A PLANT may be endangered locally, nationally or throughout its range. The yellow LADY'S SLIPPER (*Cypripedium calceolus*), familiar in many parts of Canada, is probably Britain's rarest plant, with only 3 or 4 individuals surviving in the wild. The lost Franklinia (*Franklinia alatamaha*), named for Benjamin Franklin, is extinct in the wild but survives in cultivation.

Extinction, a natural process that has occurred throughout earth's history, takes place when an organism is unable to adapt to a changing environment or to compete with better-adapted species. In recent times humans have become the major threat to the survival of many plants. Technological developments in industrial nations and increasing pressure for agricultural land in developing countries can cause rapid environmental changes that threaten the survival of thousands of plants. Because destruction of habitat is now the principal cause of endangerment, habitat protection is the only effective way to save plants from extinction. Growing a plant in a BOTANICAL GARDEN is no substitute for maintaining it in its wild habitat. Botanical gardens can, however, be useful in providing a reservoir of material to restock wild populations of endangered plants.

Cypripedium candidum — the white lady's slipper orchid which is now rare throughout its range of distribution (*courtesy J.K. Morton*).

Legislation protecting rare plants in Canada is fragmentary and of limited effect. As a natural resource, plants are a provincial rather than a federal responsibility; hence, each province must enact its own endangered-species legislation. However, the federal government, as a signatory of the Convention on International Trade in Endangered Species, 1973 (CITES), can provide protection for some plants (eg, all cacti, orchids and other plants traded across international boundaries). GINSENG (*Panax quinquefolius*), of the deciduous forests of eastern and central Canada, is one such plant. The roots are harvested and sold for their reputed medicinal properties. Most of Canada's flora falls outside these regulations. Several provinces have endangered-species legislation; however, as yet, very few plants are protected by it, although protection could be extended to other species with sufficient pressure from botanists and the public. More effective protection comes from national and provincial PARKS, and through some local conservation authorities and natural-history societies. National parks provide the most stringent, effective and lasting protection for Canadian flora. Many are situated in areas where rare plants occur, and part of the mandate of Parks Canada is to ensure the protection for all time of rare plants and their habitats. The effectiveness of provincial parks and conservation authorities in protecting endangered species varies considerably. Many place greater emphasis on exploiting the natural environment for human enjoyment than on protecting habitats or rare plants; furthermore, any protection provided can be overridden without reference to Parliament. Rare plants can also be protected if environmental assessments and impact studies are required before major development work can begin. In Canada, however, the impact of this type of legislation has been minimal. The presence of a few rare plants usually is not sufficient to persuade those in power that development should be stopped or moved elsewhere. Canada has a long way to go to provide effective legislation protecting rare plants.

Canada's flora includes about 3300 native species of vascular plants, of which an estimated 500 are endangered. Lists of rare plants for each

Isopyrum savilei — a small anemonelike herb found in the Queen Charlotte Islands *(courtesy J.K. Morton).*

province are being published by the NATIONAL MUSEUMS OF CANADA. Ontario's list contains over 600 species; Alberta's, over 300. These lists do not apply to Canada as a whole, since many species rare in one province are common in another. Rare or potentially endangered plants can be divided into 3 groups: endemic species that occur only in Canada or in restricted areas straddling the borders; plants of widespread occurrence that have become so rare throughout their range that they are in danger of extinction; and plants of widespread occurrence that are only endangered in the Canadian part of their range.

Canadian endemic plants tend to be concentrated in several centres. Important centres from W to E are the region straddling the Alaska-YT border — endemics include an anemone (*Anemone multiceps*), 2 fleabanes (*Erigeron mexiae* and *E. muini*) and a rare chickweed (*Stellaria alaskana*); the Queen Charlotte Is — a ragwort (*Senecio newcombei*), an avens (*Geum schofieldii*) and an isopyrum (*Isopyrum savilei);* sand dunes on the S shore of Lk Athabasca — a chickweed (*Stellaria arenicola*), several dwarf willows and sea thrift (*Armeria maritima*); the shores of the Great Lakes — 2 thistles (*Cirsium pitcheri* and *C. pumilum*), an iris (*Iris lacustris*), Houghton's goldenrod (*Solidago houghtonii*) and an alpine sunflower (*Hymenoxys acaulis* var. *glabra*); the Gulf of St Lawrence (eg, the mountains of the Gaspé Pen, Mingan I and Ile d'Anticosti and the limestone and serpentine tablelands of Newfoundland) — a sandwort (*Arenaria marcescens*), a gentian (*Gentianella crinita victorinii*), 2 roses and several willows.

Iris lacustris — a dwarf iris endemic to the Great Lakes region *(courtesy J.K. Morton).*

In Canada, several species occur that are now so rare and restricted that their continued survival is endangered. Their rarity is usually caused by destruction of natural habitats. For example, the small white lady's slipper orchid (*Cypripedium candidum*), which recently became the first plant to be protected under Ontario law, now occurs only in 3 small colonies in SW Ontario and in several isolated stations in the US.

The main threats to Canada's flora are to those plants that reach the northern limit of their range in southern Canada. Unfortunately, population density is high and agriculture and industry are concentrated in this region. Little now remains of the deciduous forests that once covered southern Ontario and Québec, but these forests support a large and very special assemblage of plants found nowhere else in Canada. Most are now rare; some are on the verge of extinction; a few are extinct. Many trees are included in the list: magnolia (*Magnolia acuminata*), pignut hickory (*Carya glabra*), pitch pine (*Pinus rigida*), black walnut (*Juglans nigra*) and no less than 6 oaks. Associated with them are many herbaceous plants, shrubs and climbers, including the beautiful trumpet flower (*Campsis radicans*), the redbud (*Cercis canadensis*, extinct in Canada) and the medicinally important goldenseal (*Hydrastis canadensis*). Most survive in small woodlots or conservation areas, fragments of the continuous forest that covered this region before European settlement. Similar problems exist in other provinces. In NS and NB, many plants characteristic of the Atlantic seaboard and the eastern forests are threatened by cottage developments, agriculture, forestry and dam construction. These include the Canada lily (*Lilium canadense*), an iris (*Iris prismatica*) and the redroot (*Lachnanthes tinctoria*). On the prairies, almost all the natural grassland has succumbed to the plough or is heavily grazed. Many prairie plants now survive precariously along roadsides and railway tracks, where they escape the pressures of agriculture but are threatened by herbicides. Examples include legumes such as *Astragalus purshii* and *Bahia oppositifolia*, prairie parsley (*Lomatium orientale*) and ironweed (*Vernonia fasciculata*). The western mountains have their own unique assemblage of alpine flowers. Many species, although common in the US, reach their northern limit here and are rare. Examples include the western white trillium (*Trillium ovatum*), a lowly sandwort (*Arenaria nuttallii*) and the very beautiful Townsendia daisy (*Townsendia condensata*).

Why protect plants from extinction? Why not let nature take its course and allow the plants to die out? There are many reasons, including aesthetic ones. Plants afford pleasure and relaxation to many people, and provide a source of inspiration in most art forms: painting, photography, poetry and prose. All life, as well as the quality of life, depends on plants, yet only about 30 kinds have been exploited to form the world's major food crops (eg, rice, wheat, corn, potatoes). The potential for producing new crops and for improving existing ones is unlimited, but this depends on using the genetic diversity found in wild plants. Plants vary depending on where they grow; eg, northern populations often differ genetically from southern ones. Each has become adapted to the habitat and climate in which it grows. For the continued survival of a species, it is essential that the diversity of its gene pool be maintained so that it can adapt to the continual small changes in environment, shifts in climate, changing pressures from predators, disease, competition, etc. For this reason, we must protect those plants that reach the limits of their range in Canada, even though they may be abundant in the US. In addition, agriculturalists must be concerned to protect wild ancestors of cultivated plants and to ensure the survival of others that may be potential new crops, new horticultural varieties or new sources of useful products.

Plants have been a major source of medicines since prehistoric times. Modern research is discovering an apparently unlimited source of new chemicals in wild plants, many of which can form the basis for new drugs or other products important to human well-being and development. Cortisones were originally developed from wild yams (*Dioscorea*), and recently an obscure bush in the semidesert of Arizona, the jojoba bean (*Simmondsia chinensis*), has been found to be a potential commercial source of an oil for car transmissions, similar to that obtained from the endangered sperm whale. Recent work in Canada and Britain indicates that an effective treatment for eczema may have been found in evening primroses (*Oenothera*). The potential for economic and material benefit is unlimited, for we have barely begun to exploit the wealth of useful products contained in wild plants. At this early stage, we cannot afford to let plants become extinct for, once lost, a species can never be recreated. JOHN MORTON

Endicott, James, missionary, clergyman (b in Devonshire, Eng 8 May 1865; d at Toronto 9 Mar 1954). Coming to Canada at age 17, he served Methodist home missions until he returned to school at Wesley Coll, Winnipeg, and was ordained in 1893. That same year, he went to Sichuan, China, and was active in church publishing and education at Chengdu. He returned to Canada in 1910 and from 1913 to 1937 headed the Foreign Missions Board of the Methodist and, after 1925, of the United Church of Canada. He was the second moderator of the UNITED CHURCH 1926-28 and explained the new church to missionaries in the field. A respected preacher and pamphleteer, Endicott worked for world peace and especially for aid to the Third World. He condemned Chiang Kai-shek's government of China and served on the World Peace Council. He led in explaining the needs of the Orient to Canadians. NEIL SEMPLE

Endive, or escarole (*Cichorium endivia*), herbaceous biennial VEGETABLE belonging to the Compositae family. In continental Europe the term is used to refer to the closely related species *C. intybus*, CHICORY (Belgian or French endive). Endive is cultivated much like LETTUCE, although it is sometimes blanched (ie, bleached by excluding sunlight) before harvest to reduce its bitter taste. The curly leaves may be served raw in salad or cooked. Commercially, endive is a summer or GREENHOUSE crop; it is also grown in home gardens. ADRIANA A. DAVIES

Energy embraces all motion and radiation in the universe, including all the forces that act on matter. Although the term is used interchangeably with the word "power," there is a distinction, energy being the capacity to do work, and power, the amount of work performed. Power is measured in watts (W) and refers to the force available at any given instant. Energy is measured in joules (J) or watt hours (1 Wh = 360 J) and refers to the amount of force applied over a period of time. Potential energy is that resulting from the position of one body relative to another; kinetic energy is that manifested by bodies in motion.

Another categorization of energy, commonly used by economists, refers to primary, secondary and tertiary energy. Primary energy is recovered from natural RESOURCES such as solar radiation, falling WATER, WIND, COAL, PETROLEUM products and URANIUM. It is consumed by primary energy industries such as ELECTRIC-POWER generating stations and oil refineries. A significant portion is lost in storage, processing and transportation before primary energy is delivered to consumers as secondary energy. Further energy is lost through the inefficiencies of conversion devices (cars, appliances, heaters, etc) that turn the secondary energy into useful work. The amount of useful work actually obtained is the tertiary energy.

Primary energy resources are frequently described as renewable or nonrenewable. Renewable energy resources include geothermal heat, falling water, tidal forces, wind action, solar input, vegetable and animal matter, and ocean thermal gradients. Nonrenewable resources include hydrocarbon materials such as natural gas, crude oil, BITUMEN and coal, as well as isotopes from which energy may be extracted through nuclear fission or NUCLEAR FUSION. The extraction of primary energy resources and their use, either direct or after conversion to secondary forms, have resulted in the evolution of sophisticated technologies and systems during the 20th century. There have been rapid developments in resource exploitation, MINING, refining, machine design and operation, PIPELINE transportation, electric-power transmission and energy marketing. Since 1900 world annual energy consumption has increased more than tenfold. The expected large growth in future world population would mean that continued increase in per capita energy demand would double the world's energy requirement again between 1980 and 2000. Human ingenuity would be taxed to meet such a supply challenge.

Nonrenewable resources now provide the bulk of purchased secondary energy. In 1980 some 92% of the consumption of commercially provided energy, totalling 280 exajoules (EJ = 10^{18}J), came from crude oil, coal and natural gas. The balance was produced in hydroelectric and NUCLEAR POWER PLANTS. An estimated 30 EJ of additional energy was derived from noncommercial renewable sources such as wood wastes and animal refuse (BIOMASS ENERGY), SOLAR ENERGY, wind action and geothermal steam (*see* WIND ENERGY, GEOTHERMAL ENERGY). Renewable energy forms are particularly important to those developing areas of the world where crude oil and natural gas are neither indigenous nor affordable, and where sophisticated systems of power generation, transmission and distribution have not yet been introduced. In many such areas, population pressure is leading to an

Distribution of Energy Consumption in Various Sectors of the Economy, by Type, 1976 and 1982

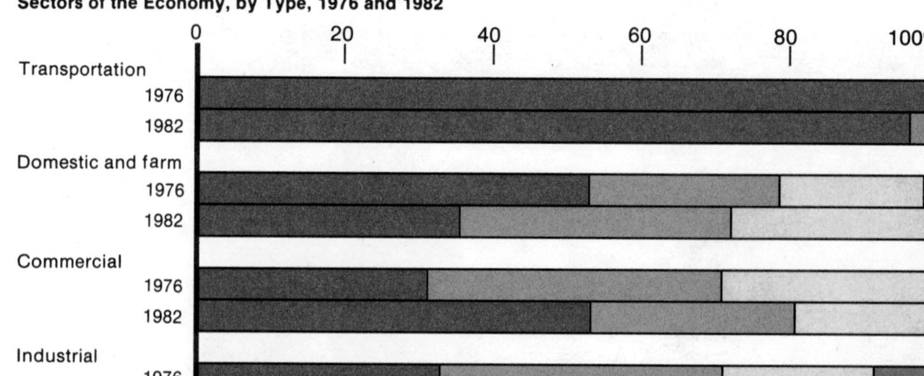

Source: 57-203, Quarterly Report on Energy Supply-demand in Canada.

increased demand for energy and other resources and consequently to a rapid denudation of the world's forested tropical and subtropical zones. Concern is growing therefore about serious future climatic and ecological changes that may be precipitated on a worldwide scale, as a result of the existing, often rapacious, exploitation of the forests.

In the past 40 years, world dependence on crude oil as an energy source has grown remarkably, so that now nearly half of all primary energy is provided by oil. A peak in production may already have been reached in 1979, with an output of 10.5 million m³/day. By 1981 production had dropped to 9.4 million m³/day. The decrease was partly caused by a glut of oil which developed following a twofold price increase imposed in 1979-80 by a 13-member group of major producers, the Organization of Petroleum Exporting Countries (OPEC). Another factor affecting the decrease was the increased cost of developing replacement reserves for those being consumed so rapidly; at the end of 1981, proved reserves were only some 30 times the 1981 consumption rate. Many analysts have concluded that serious worldwide depletion of both crude oil and natural gas will have occurred by about the middle of the next century. By then the world population may have more than doubled.

Hence, even assuming that judicious use and conservation of energy supplies will be pursued in the coming decades, it appears that increased reliance must be placed on coal, nuclear power and renewable energy sources. Unfortunately the development of each of these is likely to be impeded. The mining, transportation and combustion of coal impose severe environmental hazards which could restrict the industry's growth rate. Not the least of the concerns is that burning vast quantities of coal would cause a significant increase in the carbon-dioxide content of the Earth's atmosphere, and this might have a serious effect on the world's climate.

The direct environmental damage resulting from the installation and operation of nuclear power plants is much less severe. In fact, many technical experts consider nuclear power to be the most benign of all energy sources available for future long-term use. Antinuclear activists, however, have campaigned against that energy option on the basis of perceived hazards of low-level radiation effects, nuclear accidents and the proliferation of nuclear weapons (*see* NUCLEAR SAFETY).

The development of renewable energy resources has been curtailed by economic constraints. Meaningful sources of geothermal steam, for example, are few in number, and many of these are located far from large consumer centres. Similar limitations apply to the relatively small number of large hydroelectric sites remaining to be developed. Perhaps the most promising future prospect for renewable resource development is in the utilization of solar energy for direct use in heating, for conversion to hydrocarbons or for generation of electricity. Many technical and economic challenges remain to be overcome, however, before solar energy can successfully compete with the traditional nonrenewable energy sources. Most industrialized countries are not expected to become self-sufficient in long-term energy supplies because of the paucity of indigenous sources. Canada is an exception. It has a large landmass, a relatively small population and a profusion of proven and potential resources that include crude oil, natural gas, oil sands, coal, undeveloped hydroelectric sites, large uranium deposits and a highly sophisticated nuclear technology (*see* NUCLEAR RESEARCH ESTABLISHMENTS). The federal-provincial sharing of responsibility for resource control, ownership and taxation imposes barriers to efficient development, but the plethora of resource wealth may be large enough to overcome such man-made obstacles.
O.J.C. RUNNALLS

Reading: Energy, Mines and Resources, *Current Energy Statistics* (1982); National Energy Board of Canada, *Canadian Energy Supply and Demand, 1980-2000* (June 1981); W. Sassin, "Energy," *Scientific American* (Sept 1980).

Energy, Mines and Resources, Department of, est in 1966 by the federal Government Organization Act. Some of the department's components have long histories. The Department of Mines, created in 1907, was reorganized as the Department of Mines and Resources in 1936. The Department of Mines and Technical Surveys was formed in 1949. In 1966 the department took on a new and important role of energy development. The main objective of EMR is to enhance the discovery, development and use of Canada's mineral and energy resources through national policies based on research, data collection and social and economic analyses. The Energy Sector is responsible for the development and implementation of a national ENERGY POLICY. The Mineral Policy Sector performs a similar role for nonrenewable resources, supporting appropriate exploration, development and movement of minerals. A Science and Technology Section includes the GEOLOGICAL SURVEY OF CANADA (fd 1842), a Canada centre for REMOTE SENSING, the Polar Continental Shelf Project and the Surveys and Mapping Branch, which is responsible for topographical mapping, aeronautical charting and the National Atlas of Canada. An Explosives Branch controls the production and handling of explosives in Canada. ATOMIC ENERGY OF CANADA LTD, Eldorado Nuclear Ltd, the NATIONAL ENERGY BOARD, Uranium Canada Ltd and PETRO-CANADA report to Parliament through the minister. The department's 1984-85 budget was $3 billion.

Energy, Royal Commission on (Borden Commission), established (1957) by the government of John DIEFENBAKER, under chairman Henry Borden, the president of Brazilian Traction, Light, Heat and Power Corp, to investigate "a number of questions relating to sources of energy." The most important issue before the commission was the demand by the Alberta independent oil producers to find a market for their crude oil by building a pipeline from Edmonton to Montréal. Their opponents, the large, international oil companies, found it more profitable to use imported oil in their Montréal refineries. Probably the most influential individual at the hearings was Walter J. Levy, a New York oil consultant, who proposed that the pipeline not be built and that Alberta oil be exported to the US while Montréal continued to be supplied from abroad. In its reports (1958 and 1959), the commission accepted this recommendation, called the National Oil Policy (NOP), thereby securing the market west of the Ottawa Valley for the western oil producers. The NATIONAL ENERGY BOARD, proposed by the commission to administer the policy, was established by Parliament in 1959. The NOP, established in 1961, remained in effect until the events of the 1970s precipitated dramatic changes in ENERGY POLICY. ED SHAFFER

Energy in Society Energy plays a unique and critical role in the world; no activity of any kind (no "work") can take place without the movement or conversion of energy. Energy use in society is a flow that begins with a source (eg, COAL, URANIUM, PETROLEUM, the SUN), passes through several intermediate processes for refinement or conversion to a different form (eg, electricity, diesel oil, methane), finally reaching a home, vehicle or industrial plant where it is introduced into a consuming device (eg, furnace, motor). In between are imports, exports and losses of various kinds, including the energy needed to operate the energy system itself. The final consumer does not want energy as such, but only the services it can provide: services that are not measured in litres or joules but in warmth, motion, sound, etc. Although higher-income countries, provinces and individuals tend to use more energy, energy use does not necessarily indicate standard of living; efficient energy use produces more services (ie, wealth) from a given amount of resources.

Two thermodynamic laws govern all aspects of energy use. The first states that a given system will always contain the same amount of energy: we can "use" energy but cannot really "consume" it. The second states that every time some quantity of energy is used its quality declines: what we consume is the ability to get useful work from energy. Hence, it is essential that we keep track of both the quantity and quality of the energy we use. Quantity is measured in familiar units, such as litres (L) of oil, kilowatt-hours (kWh) of electricity and tonnes (t) of coal, all of which can be converted to one standard unit of energy content, the joule (J). Quality is more difficult to measure: scientific measures of the ability to do work exist, but for many purposes it is sufficient to define higher-quality energy as being hotter or denser (ie, containing much energy in a small volume, eg, gasoline) or more versatile (eg, electricity). People are generally willing to pay more for high-quality energy. Energy CONSERVATION involves not only saving quantities of energy but also ensuring that high-quality forms are used only when truly needed. Thus, while dense fuels are most useful for TRANSPORTATION and electricity is most appropriate for lighting, ELECTRONICS and motors, heating buildings involves raising temperatures by relatively small amounts and needs only a low-quality energy source.

Energy use is characterized by the efficiency with which the energy is consumed. There are 3 ways to measure efficiency. First-law efficiency indicates how much energy is being used compared with the service provided (eg, L of gasoline per 100 km of car travel). Calculations using this measure suggest that the Canadian economy may be 40% efficient. A second measure, second-law efficiency, relates the energy used to obtain a service with the theoretical minimum needed under ideal conditions. Estimates suggest that in these terms the economy is less than 10% efficient (as low as 1-2% if materials use and recycling are considered). The third measure of efficiency, cost effectiveness, relates economic resources being used to energy services obtained, and is needed for decisions in which energy must be balanced against other economic activities (eg, adding more insulation versus buying more fuel to warm a building).

Causes of Energy Use

Four sets of factors determine how much energy is used in a society. First are the demographic and geographic factors: other things being equal, the greater the population, the bigger the area and the colder the CLIMATE, the more energy will be used. Thus Canada's relatively small, dispersed population requires a lot of transportation. Canada is colder than most countries, although new building techniques make this factor less important.

The second set of factors is economic. While there is no direct relationship between national income and energy use, higher-income countries with more INDUSTRY tend to use more energy than poorer, less-industrialized ones. Moreover, in Canada industry is concentrated in the primary sectors (PULP AND PAPER, smelting and refining, AGRICULTURE) which tend to use more energy per dollar of output than do MANUFACTURING or service industries. Energy use also reflects availability and cost of energy resources. Historically, Canada and the US have had an abundance of relatively low-cost energy available and, hence, have used it extensively. Most other countries have had less available energy and, as it has been more expensive, have used it more moderately. Consumers, private and industrial, use less energy as its price goes up. This effect, called the price elasticity of demand, has been estimated statistically to lie between -0.5 and about -1.2, ie, for each 10% increase in energy price, use will drop by 5-12%.

The third set of factors is technological. Until the 1970s, when all energy prices began to rise, little attention was paid to the technology of energy use. The American automobile was one example of this neglect, but others abounded in the CONSTRUCTION INDUSTRY and in industry in general. With the rise in prices, many old techniques were reintroduced and research into new ones began (*see* SCIENTIFIC RESEARCH AND DEVELOPMENT). For example, Canadians have become world leaders in constructing energy-efficient buildings. Typical single-family homes built around 1973 require about 175 gigajoules (GJ = 10^9 J, roughly the energy content of 4500 L of heating oil) for heating each year. Many homes being built today use 50 GJ annually; the most cost-efficient ones (modeled on the Saskatchewan Conservation House) need only 15 GJ. In 1973 typical high-rise office buildings required 600 kWh per m^2 per year for operation; many being built today have cut this to 200 kWh, and the Gulf Canada Square tower in Calgary requires only 125 kWh.

The fourth set of factors involves life-styles: how people choose to live, what they buy, the use they make of their purchases, etc. For example, people who choose to live in smaller houses or in apartments, buy smaller cars or use them less, and buy goods in returnable or recyclable containers use less energy. N American life-styles have tended to go in the opposite direction, towards "conspicuous consumption," although some trends seem to be changing.

Measurement of Energy Use

Energy use is a flow which may be measured at various stages. The most useful results are obtained from measurement at the point of purchase by the final consumer. This measurement is called secondary energy consumption to distinguish it from primary energy consumption (an almost meaningless statistic of "use," measured at the point of production) and tertiary consumption (a useful but difficult to standardize measurement of the amount of energy that actually keeps us warm or reaches the drive-wheels of a vehicle).

Statistics on secondary energy use typically are divided according to the form of energy used (eg, gasoline, electricity) and the sector in which it is used (eg, residential, commercial, industrial, transportation). A separate sector may be designated for energy supply, to cover the energy consumed or lost in energy production, conversion, transportation and transmission. In recent years this sector has accounted for 20% as much energy as has secondary use. In addition, statistics on energy use should be (but seldom are) broken down according to the use made of the energy: heating and cooling (including all space and water heating plus low-temperature process heat), higher-temperature process heat (used only in industry), electricity specific (uses that truly depend upon the properties of electricity, eg, electronics, lighting, electroprocessing and stationary motors) and liquid fuels (for portable uses, primarily transportation and mobile equipment). This breakdown takes account of quality and shows, for example, that most Canadian energy requirements are for heat at various temperatures (55% of total use, 70% of industrial use) and that electricity-specific uses represent little more than 12% of the total.

Energy data must also be adjusted to allow for nonenergy products (eg, plastics, fertilizers, construction materials, lubricants) that are produced from energy raw materials. For oil and gas, the adjustment is small (perhaps 5% of total output in 1980), but half of the coal used in Canada (and all of that exported) is used as coking coal in smelters and blast furnaces. Another problem involves the energy that does not pass through an organized market. Statistics usually report only usage of commercial energy; therefore, energy use in rural areas of Canada and less-developed parts of the world tends to be understated. Thus the use of wood as a residential fuel never actually fell to the low levels shown in statistics; much of that used came from woodlots or from local sales that were not accounted for in the statistics.

A statistical problem particularly important to Canada involves ELECTRIC POWER, a form of energy that can be manufactured from very different sources (eg, falling water, burning coal or controlled nuclear reactions), each with its own rate of conversion (the difference between the energy content of the source input and that of the electricity output). The best approach for production of energy-use statistics is to ignore the source of the electricity and convert directly from electrical output to joules (3.6 MJ per kWh). However, in most international and some Canadian statistics, electricity is converted to energy units expressed as the amount of coal or oil that would be needed to produce it, which, for thermodynamic reasons, is about 3 times as large. This practice leads to the calculation that 35% of Canada's energy is used in the form of electricity, when the correct figure is about 17%.

Secondary Energy Use in 1980

Total secondary energy use in Canada in 1980 was about 6.4 exajoules (EJ = 10^{18}J). Ontario and Québec account for about three-fifths of this use. The levels of energy use per capita in these 2 provinces are about equal, but Ontario is well below Québec and most other provinces in energy use per dollar of provincial product (because Ontario has relatively more light manufacturing compared with primary industries). Other provincial variations follow mainly from geographic and economic differences. Less energy is used for heating in BC than elsewhere, but more is used in the forest industry. The Atlantic provinces are the lowest per-capita users of energy; the Prairie provinces are highest. This gap reflects differences in both incomes and energy prices.

Residential Uses Energy is used in the residential sector for space and water heating and for lighting and appliances. The sector accounts for 21% of total secondary use in Canada. Space and water heating (88% of residential energy) are simple services that can be provided by almost any energy form; lighting and appliances (12%) generally require electricity. Coal and wood, which used to provide much residential heating, have declined to 2% in favour of oil (46% but declining), natural gas (38%) and electricity (14%). It is hard to separate residential and agricultural uses, and many statistics combine them, although agriculture is really an industry. Nationally, energy use on farms accounts for 3% of secondary energy use, 9-12% on the prairies. The major use is in liquid fuel for trucks, tractors, etc.

Commercial Uses account for 12% of Canadian energy use, including energy for offices, schools, hospitals, stores, hotels and most government activities. Despite this diversity, about three-quarters of commercial energy is used for heating and cooling buildings and for water heating. Energy for this sector is increasingly supplied by natural gas and electricity or by electricity alone.

Industrial Uses The industrial sector, including primary industries, manufacturing and construction, accounts for more energy than any other sector (37% of the total), and most projections show this share growing to one-half. In contrast to other sectors, industry uses energy of all qualities and forms. Over two-thirds of industrial energy is used as heat, some 25% for temperatures above 260°C. Energy forms are divided among oil products (36%), natural gas (28%) and electricity (21%). The industrial sector is the only significant user of coal and wood as fuel (8% each).

Three subsectors (pulp and paper, chemicals and primary metals) account for over one-half of all industrial energy; the addition of 4 additional subsectors (FOOD AND BEVERAGE, MINING, industrial minerals and construction) brings this share to nearly 75%. The subsectors vary widely in the forms of energy used: the CHEMICALS and PETROCHEMICALS industries use large volumes of oil and gas as fuel and also as inputs to produce plastics and other nonenergy products; the ALUMINUM industry is a particularly heavy user of electricity; the FOREST industries have become major users of what were once waste wood products (thus simultaneously cutting POLLUTION). Three subsectors (PULP AND PAPER, chemicals and primary metals) account for 65% of all high-temperature heat. Many industries do not use any heat above 100°C.

Transportation Uses Transportation accounts for more energy use in Canada than in most other countries: 28% of total use and, more significantly, half of oil use. Automobiles and light trucks account for 53% of transportation use (14% of Canada's total energy use); larger trucks take 27% and buses 5%; therefore, road modes use a total of 85%. The remaining sectors — air, marine and rail — follow in declining order (although in some provinces the positions vary; eg, in Newfoundland marine rises to second place). About half of transportation energy is used within urban areas, the remainder between cities. The transportation sector is unique in depending almost exclusively on one form of energy, liquid fuel (primarily gasoline, diesel oil and aviation turbo fuel), derived from one source, oil; a tiny fraction is electricity, used for public transit. The sector also depends on such nonenergy, petroleum-based products as asphalt and lube oil.

The International Dimension

World energy use in 1980 was about 315 EJ, or an average of about 60 GJ per capita. Variations around the average are large; industrial countries typically use 150-200 GJ per capita (260 in Canada), Third World countries 20-25 GJ per capita. Canada, with about 0.4% of the world's population, accounts for 2% of world energy use. It is often said that we consume more energy per capita or per dollar of GROSS NATIONAL PRODUCT (GNP) than any other country. Strictly speaking such statements are incorrect. International statistics tend to make Canada appear more energy intensive than it really is. For example, the manner in which international electricity data are compiled causes overstatement of Canada's energy use and production. In addition, because primary industry is so important in Canada, we export a lot of energy in the form of raw or semifinished goods. Our nonenergy exports contain about 25% more energy per dollar of trade than do our imports. This "embodied" energy should in principle be counted against the country where the steel, paper or aluminum is used. Nevertheless, after all adjustments and allowances have been made, Canada remains one of the world's most energy-intensive nations.

Changes in Energy Use

With growth in population, economy and income, Canadians have used more and more energy. Before WWII secondary energy use was climbing at about 3% per year, but during the era of cheap energy after the war the annual growth rate climbed to 5% and higher. Such growth, which would have been impossible to maintain for long, ended quickly with the energy crisis of 1973. Since then the rate has fallen, partly because of slower economic growth, mostly because we have become more efficient. Between 1974 and 1980 energy use grew by an average of only 2.3% annually, and the rate of growth is still falling. Oil use has barely grown at all because fear of shortage enhanced the effects of higher prices.

Projections of future energy use abound, but one thing is striking: the projections are falling. A 1973 report of the federal Dept of ENERGY, MINES AND RESOURCES expected 4.5% annual growth; a 1976 report envisioned 3.7%; the 1980 National Energy Program projected 1.9%. The decline reflects mainly our growing awareness of energy efficiency. Since 1970 the energy required to produce a dollar of GNP in Canada has fallen by 7% and the decline is continuing. Federal policy has dictated that average fuel consumption of new cars must be halved between 1975 and 1985 (to 8.5 L per 100 km). The AUTOMOTIVE INDUSTRY has stated that this target will probably be exceeded. Industry has planned to cut its energy use by 25% per unit of output by 1985; thereafter continued annual gains of about 1% are likely. Throughout the economy there is growing attention to end-use technology, to ways to use waste products and waste heat as sources of energy, and to techniques such as cascading and cogeneration in which the same quantity of energy is used for a series of services as it gradually declines in quality (eg, first for generation of electricity, then for high-temperature process heat, finally for space heating).

Even the lowest official projections may be too high. Analyses that begin not with energy production, as do conventional energy studies, but with end-use demand for energy services show that future energy use could be lower still. These studies have come to be called "soft energy" studies because of their emphasis on smaller scale, decentralized and environmentally less destructive means of providing energy. They show that cost effectiveness alone makes zero energy growth an economically feasible goal. Soft-energy studies have been prepared for most industrial nations of the world, including Canada, and for Third World countries (for which some energy growth is essential). They allow for population and economic growth and reasonable time for investment in energy-efficient structures, equipment and vehicles. Even without life-style changes, it is apparent that soft-energy paths offer the prospect of a world that is more efficient economically and also environmentally, socially and politically more stable. Neither global climate nor local land use would be threatened and the availability of energy for lower-income regions and countries would be enhanced.

Canada's rate of energy use will be determined, in part, by physical laws and, in part, by technology, but to a far greater extent it will be determined by individual choices and government policies. The limits to energy production and use are set by physics and geology, but those limits are wide; within them the rates actually achieved are mainly determined by politics and economics — in a word, by values. As values change, conservation plays a greater and greater role in ENERGY POLICY. DAVID B. BROOKS

Reading: Robert Bott et al, *Life After Oil: A Renewable Energy Strategy for Canada* (1983); David B. Brooks, *Zero Energy Growth for Canada* (1981).

Energy Policy comprises government measures concerned with the production, transportation and use of energy commodities. Governments may adopt energy policies to meet goals such as economic growth, the distribution of income, industrial diversification and the protection of the ENVIRONMENT. Since the large jump in energy prices in the early 1970s, governments around the world have played an increasingly active role in energy policy.

Although Canada appears to be generously endowed with major forms of ENERGY, eg, COAL, OIL AND NATURAL GAS, URANIUM and HYDROELECTRICITY, and although its production of certain fuels has occasionally exceeded domestic requirements, it has never been entirely self-sufficient in energy. Historically, Canada has been dependent on energy imports largely because of the great distances separating indigenous sources of supply from markets. It is therefore primarily as a result of geography, rather than geology, that questions concerning the importation, export and particularly the transportation of energy have preoccupied energy policymakers.

The attempt to reconcile diverse economic interests in overcoming the transportation challenge has been a central theme of Canadian energy policy. These interests have traditionally pitted energy producers — whether of Nova Scotia coal before WWI, of Nova Scotia and Alberta coal between the 2 wars, or Alberta oil and gas since WWI — against energy consumers, the majority of whom live in Ontario and Québec.

A second major determinant of Canadian energy policy derives from Canada's system of government. As a result of the constitutional DISTRIBUTION OF POWERS, strong powers over resource management (*see* RESOURCE RIGHTS) are vested in both levels of government. Section 109 of the CONSTITUTION ACT, 1867, grants the provinces control over all the natural resources within their territory. A province also has the right to levy direct taxes (royalties) on these resources. The federal government, however, enjoys broad taxation powers and has jurisdiction over all aspects of interprovincial and international trade. The federal government also has the constitutional power to void provincial legislation and to assume control over provincial works "for the general advantage of Canada," although neither power has been invoked in the last 40 years.

Because this division of power gives the 2 levels of government overlapping responsibilities, Canadian energy policy has often been the product of federal-provincial bargaining. The bargaining can become acrimonious when the federal government and the producing provinces diverge in their views, as they did for most of the 1970s and early 1980s (Canada is perhaps unique in encompassing in a single country the interests that globally divide energy producers and consumers).

The influence exerted by the US constitutes a third major element that has shaped Canadian energy policy. Over the years, the US has both supplied and bought energy from Canada; Canadian-American energy trade exceeded $11 billion in 1982. The US has also represented an important source of investment capital and has consequently played a large role in the development of Canada's oil and gas resources.

Canadian Energy Policy to 1973 After Confederation, 1867, Canadian energy policy was designed to promote the greater use of domestic coal reserves by the imposition of a tariff on American imports. This tariff was part of the 1879 NATIONAL POLICY. Nevertheless, Canadian coal rarely comprised more than 50% of the domestic market. Ontario, the largest consumer, was (and still is) supplied by Pennsylvania mines, while Nova Scotia and Alberta producers supplied the eastern and western provinces, respectively. Following WWI, as a result of the increased penetration of American imports and growing concerns about energy security, new policies (including the subsidy of transportation costs) were introduced to protect the Canadian coal industry. These policies had limited success in relieving the industry's chronic productive overcapacity, a problem that was aggravated by the discovery of oil in 1947 at Leduc, Alta. After WWII, government policy was aimed at sustaining coal communities. The importance of coal as a dominant source of energy declined (which deeply affected New Brunswick and Nova Scotia) until Canadian domestic consumption rose between the mid-1960s and late 1970s by some 150%. The US has increased its coal consumption as well, and the expanded use of coal in both countries has contributed to environmental problems, particularly that of acid rain. In Canada there is a growing advocacy of a national policy on coal, and some Alberta coal producers have demanded that they supply central Canada, partly because Alberta coal contains 8 times less sulphur (the main ingredient of acid rain) than American coal. However, as in the 1920s, the counterargument that Alberta coal is too expensive has been made.

Oil and Gas Although oil was being produced in southern Ontario as early as 1857, reserves and domestic consumption were small. The modern oil era was triggered by the 1947 strike in Leduc and by several subsequent oil and gas finds in the 3 western provinces. Coincidentally, demand for oil in Canada and internationally had increased rapidly as a result of the war and the subsequent economic boom.

The overriding objective of Canadian energy policy for the next 20 years was to stimulate the growth of the domestic PETROLEUM INDUSTRIES. As a result, major oil and gas PIPELINES were built from the producing provinces to markets in both Canada and the US, encouraging investment and promoting exports.

From the beginning, the US played a large role in the development of Canada's oil and gas reserves, not only because the industry was largely American owned, but because of the distribution of Canada's petroleum resources. Economic efficiency dictated that Alberta supply the markets closest to itself, ie, the American Pacific Northwest and Midwest, while eastern Canada continued to rely on American imports. When pipelines were finally built from the western provinces to domestic markets, the western provinces exported part of the throughput to amortize the costs of transporting oil over these considerable distances. As a result of Canada's reliance on the export of oil and gas, first to serve its own energy needs and then to spur the growth of the oil industry, an increasing share of domestic oil and gas production was dedicated to the American market. This share peaked in 1971 when Canada exported to the US 57% of its oil production and 47% of its gas production.

The oil industry's rapid growth in the 1950s, the controversy surrounding the construction of Canada's first 2 major gas pipelines (the 1956 Trans Canada PIPELINE DEBATE contributed to the electoral defeat of the Liberal government the following year), and an acknowledgement that the government's information concerning energy matters was inadequate, led in 1957 to the creation of the Borden Commission (*see* ENERGY, ROYAL COMMISSION ON) to study Canadian energy policy. The commission's recommendations resulted in the creation of the NATIONAL ENERGY BOARD (1959) to regulate the interprovincial pipelines and the interprovincial marketing of energy resources, and to advise the federal government on energy matters. The commission also championed the establishment of a national oil policy (NOP) to shelter the Canadian oil industry against imports of cheaper foreign oil. This policy, introduced in 1961, established a protected market for domestic oil W of the Ottawa Valley, which freed the industry from foreign competition, while the 5 eastern provinces continued to rely on imports. The NOP remained the cornerstone of Canadian energy policy for the next decade.

The 1960s were a period of consolidation; no new major policy initiatives were launched until the early 1970s. Canadian oil and gas consumption grew steadily, prices were stable, and the country's hydrocarbon potential appeared virtually unlimited. This uneventful decade made the adjustment to the energy crisis of the early 1970s traumatic.

Hydroelectrical and Nuclear Policy The public sector has played an important role in the development of Canada's electricity resources since the early 1900s, when the Hydro-Electric Power Commission of Ontario was created. Today, every province except Alberta and PEI manages its own power utility. The federal government's involvement in hydroelectricity, however, has historically been limited, partly because electricity-generating sources are more evenly distributed across the country and the interprovincial trade in electricity has therefore been on a smaller scale. Nevertheless, in 1907 Parliament passed the Electricity and Fluid Exportation Act to regulate the export of electricity and natural gas, a function that was transferred to the National Energy Board in 1959. In 1963 the federal government announced a National Power Policy (the basic tenets of which still endure) to encourage the development of power resources, the greater interconnection of provincial transmission systems and the export of surplus power to the US.

Hydropower in the 1980s provided fully 70% of Canada's electricity needs. Expansion of hydroelectrical power presents significant difficulties, as most remaining potential hydro sites are far from centres of population and long-distance transmission lines are costly to build. The building of dams can also cause severe environmental damage.

The federal government was deeply involved in the development of NUCLEAR ENERGY, largely as a result of its expropriation in 1944 (for military reasons) of Canada's only (at the time) uranium mine. The government strengthened its control over uranium resources in 1946 with the passage of the Atomic Energy Control Act, which transferred jurisdiction over uranium from provincial to federal authorities and regulated the production and uses of uranium in Canada. Two important federal crown corporations are involved in atomic energy: ATOMIC ENERGY OF CANADA (AECL) and Eldorado Nuclear. The former is responsible for nuclear research; the latter for the mining and refining of uranium.

Canada's nuclear energy program was born in 1953 when feasibility studies on the CANDU reactor design were initiated. Although the first commercial CANDU reactor began operations only in 1971 in Pickering, Ont, by 1980 nuclear energy accounted for 38% of Ontario's electricity consumption. In 1985 there were NUCLEAR POWER PLANTS in Ontario, Québec and New Brunswick.

Canadian Energy Policy after OPEC Canada, like most industrialized countries, was unprepared for the consequences of the fourfold increase in international oil prices and the partial oil embargo imposed by the Arab members of the Organization of Petroleum Exporting Countries (OPEC) in the wake of the 1973 Middle East war. Canadian energy policy entered a decade of unprecedented turmoil as a result of the fight between the western provinces and the federal government for control over growing energy revenues and over the issue of whether domestic oil and gas prices should track world levels.

Some of the federal government's initiatives between 1973 and 1974 provoked forceful provincial reaction. In March 1973 Ottawa moved to control the export of oil when a rapid jump in shipments to the US threatened to disrupt domestic supplies. Then, in Sept, Ottawa froze the domestic price of oil for 6 months and imposed an export tax on oil to ensure fair returns from US sales and to help subsidize eastern Canadians dependent on oil imports. Interpreting these actions as federal intrusions into their traditional areas of responsibility, the western provinces retaliated through new legislation that purported to control the production, regulation, marketing and pricing of their resources. Included were new royalty schemes designed to capture a larger share of revenues. Alberta also created the Alberta Petroleum Marketing Commission, with broad powers over the production, pricing and provincial marketing of oil. The federal government responded by amending the Income Tax Act to disallow the deductibility of provincial royalties from corporate income tax, and by enacting the Petroleum Administration Act, under which Ottawa assumed broader powers to control oil and gas pricing in Canada.

In Dec 1973, as part of its response to the "energy crisis," the federal government announced the creation of PETRO-CANADA — to boost oil and gas exploration in the North and offshore, to assist in the development of the tar sands (*see* BITU-

Sources of Canadian Energy Consumption
(Source: Statistics Canada)

Forecast (percentages)

	1920	*1930*	*1940*	*1950*	*1960*	*1970*	*1980*	*1990*	*2000*
Petroleum	7	15	20	33	54	55	51	40	36
Natural Gas	–	2	3	3	13	18	21	27	29
Coal and Coke	75	63	58	49	17	12	12	14	14
Hydroelectricity*	1	4	7	7	11	9	10	11	11
Nuclear Electricity*	–	–	–	–	–	–	2	4	6
Others	17	16	12	8	5	6	4	4	4
Total	100	100	100	100	100	100	100	100	100
Consumption (petajoules)	1 204	1 492	1 681	2 546	3 350	5 997	8 019	8 971	11 767

* Converted at 3.6 MJ/kWh

MEN) and to secure reliable oil imports. By the 1980s Petro-Canada had become one of Canada's largest petroleum companies. As the federal government's "window on industry," it has acted both as a source of information to the government about oil and gas and served as a policy instrument, eg, in increasing frontier drilling.

Between 1973 and 1978, the price of oil and natural gas in Canada rose quickly through agreements reached between the federal government and the producing provinces, but did not reach world levels. By mid-1978 the gap between domestic and international prices had closed to less than $3 per barrel. In the wake of the 1979 Iranian Revolution, however, world prices increased by 150% and the federal government renounced its intention of ensuring eventual parity between domestic and world prices. This left Canadian prices far below international ones and created difficult strains between Alberta and the federal government.

The 1980 National Energy Program The 1979 increase in world oil prices aggravated some of the problems Canada already faced. First, it represented a large transfer of wealth from consumers to producers. In Canada this wealth transfer had 2 significant dimensions: a large interregional transfer of wealth from Ontario and Québec (which together accounted for 58% of domestic oil consumption in 1980) to Alberta (which produced 86% of Canada's oil), and an international transfer of wealth from Canada to the US as a result of the high level of American ownership of the oil and gas industry (*see* FOREIGN INVESTMENT).

Second, the rapid increase in international prices made it difficult for the federal government to manage the national economy. It aggravated inflation and strained the EQUALIZATION PAYMENTS system. It contributed to the federal deficit as well, because the federal government continued to subsidize oil imports to maintain a uniform domestic price across the country. The increase in the world oil price, however, also represented an opportunity to achieve a higher level of oil self-sufficiency through the development of high-cost oil in the frontier and increased synthetic production from the tar sands.

In 1980 the federal government introduced the National Energy Program (NEP). Its objectives were to increase Canadian ownership of the oil industry, to achieve oil self-sufficiency and gain a greater share of energy revenues. Although all 3 objectives were controversial to some degree, the third aroused the most debate because it raised the concerns of the producing provinces and the oil industry that "their" revenues would be reduced if the federal government increased its share. The means chosen to advance the NEP's objectives also proved contentious because they represented an unprecedented degree of federal intervention and were imposed without prior consultation with industry or with the producing provinces. For example, to "Canadianize" the industry, the federal government introduced a tax to fund acquisitions by Petro-Canada and favoured Canadian-owned companies when distributing exploration grants. In addition, the federal government continued to hold domestic oil prices below international ones. Finally, to achieve oil self-sufficiency, the government sponsored expensive frontier exploration and instituted a system of grants to encourage consumers to conserve energy and switch to alternative fuels.

Previously, energy policy had reflected the assumption that demand can only rise and that new supplies must therefore be developed continually. But the the NEP's recognition that the solution to a "shortfall" in energy lay in controlling both demand and supply was an innovation. Although a number of conservation and "off-oil" programs have been eliminated since the NEP came into being, the emphasis on encouraging conservation remains.

Coming after 2 years of unsuccessful negotiations with Alberta, however, the NEP precipitated an intense confrontation between the province and the federal government. Alberta cut back its oil production and withheld approval of 2 large tar-sand and heavy-oil projects, and challenged in court the legality of the proposed federal tax on gas exports. As energy producers, Saskatchewan and BC also denounced the NEP without, however, retaliating directly against the federal government. An understanding between Alberta and Ottawa was only reached when the federal government substantially altered the NEP's pricing and taxation provisions to bring domestic prices closer to world levels. Although this agreement put an end to the political conflict, it failed to produce renewed stability in energy policy. The 1983 drop in world oil prices, the fall in gas exports to the US, and the recession forced adjustments to the NEP and to provincial fiscal regimes, and at the same time forced a deferral in the achievement of some of the NEP's objectives.

Conclusion Oil and gas will continue to fill a large share of Canadian energy requirements into the next century, although oil's importance is already declining. The depletion of western conventional reserves will force Canada to become dependent on oil from the tar sands, on heavy oils, and on arctic and offshore oils. These sources of oil will be more expensive to find, will in some instances pose new environmental risks, and will often require the development of new technology.

The election of a Conservative government in 1984 led to further changes in the NEP. Although the increase in domestic oil prices, the reduction in consumer programs and the elimination of the 25% crown share, or "back in," were all significant departures, they did not alter the 3 fundamental objectives that have underlain federal energy policy since the 1970s; energy security, Canadianization and the equitable sharing of revenues.

The rising cost of energy — oil, gas, electricity — has already led to a greater emphasis on conservation and to a search for alternative sources of energy, particularly liquid fuels and renewable forms of energy, such as SOLAR ENERGY, WIND ENERGY and BIOMASS ENERGY. These and other forms may eventually replace much contemporary oil and gas uses, although hydrocarbons are likely to remain important in transportation fuels and as components of petrochemical products.
FRANÇOIS BREGHA

Reading: Canada, Department of Energy, Mines and Resources, *The National Energy Program* (1980); B. Doern and G. Toner, *The NEP and the Politics of Energy* (1984); J. McDougall, *Fuels and the National Policy* (1982).

Enfranchisement is the most common of the legal processes by which Indians lose their INDIAN status under the INDIAN ACT. The term is now used both for those who give up their status by choice, and for the much larger number of Indian women who lose status automatically upon marriage to Indian men (*see* Jeannette LAVELL). Only the former are entitled to take with them a share of band reserve lands and funds, but both groups lose their treaty and statutory rights as Indians, and their right to live in the reserve community. The right to vote, often confused with "enfranchisement" in the technical sense discussed here, was only one of the supposed advantages of loss of status before Indians acquired the federal vote in 1960. From its first enactment in 1857 up to at least the 1960s, voluntary enfranchisement was the cornerstone of Canadian Indian policy (*see* NATIVE PEOPLE, GOVERNMENT POLICY). By enfranchising, a person was supposed to be consenting to abandon Indian identity and communal society (with its artificial legal disabilities) in order to merge with the "free," individualistic and non-Indian majority. There have in fact been relatively few such enfranchisements over the years; a law to force enfranchisement of Indians whom the government thought should be removed from band lists (in force 1920-22, 1933-51) was unpopular and a failure. The idea of enfranchisement, along with the Indian status laws generally, are rejected by most Indian political groups today.
BENNETT MCCARDLE

Reading: DIAND, *The Historical Development of the Indian Act* (1978), *Indian Acts and Amendments 1868-1950* and *Contemporary Indian Legislation, 1951-1978* (1981).

Engel, Marian, née Passmore, writer (b in Toronto 24 May 1933). Engel grew up in Galt, Sarnia and Hamilton, Ont. Educated at McMaster, McGill and Aix-en-Provence, France, she has taught in the US, Canada and Cyprus. She is widely known and respected, particularly because of her Gov Gen Award-winning novel, *Bear* (1976). She has also been influential in the movement to enable Canadian writers to deal collectively with publishers and other institutions. She was the first chairman of the Writers' Union of Canada (1973-74). In her novels and stories, Engel writes with wit and grace about the everyday lives of contemporary people, especially women. Among her 6 novels are *No Clouds of Glory* (1968), *Monodromos* (1974) and *Lunatic Villas* (1981). She has also written 2 juvenile books and a collection of short stories called *Inside the Easter Egg* (1975).
JEAN WILSON

Engineering, in its broadest sense, is any activity which applies scientific and mathematical knowledge to the solution of material problems. The modern profession of engineering is involved with designing, building and manufacturing most of the devices, systems and structures which characterize technical civilization. Engineering touches virtually every human activity in industrial society, from COMPUTERS, SPACE vehicles, LASERS and SATELLITE COMMUNICATIONS to buildings, ROADS, harbours, sewage systems, food packaging and paper manufacturing. To some extent, the history of engineering is the history of humanity's progress in using tools and observations on the nature of matter to overcome physical limitations and to modify, harness and control the natural environment. Highly organized, complex engineering works were a prominent feature of many of the civilizations of antiquity, where abundant technical skill developed in the design and construction of fortifications, monuments, roads, aqueducts, irrigation networks and other installations, some of which are still in use.

History in Canada

The early history of engineering in Canada is largely that of the military engineers of France, and later Britain, who undertook the work of mapping, surveying, road building and military fortification. Initial progress was slow in NEW FRANCE, hindered by limited manpower and funds and by the difficulty of communications but, by 1735, Montréal and Québec City were joined by road and a number of accurate maps and surveys had been made (*see* CARTOGRAPHY).

After the CONQUEST, British engineers expanded this work producing, under colonial Surveyor General Samuel Holland, many maps and surveys which provided a basis for future progress. As early as 1781, Capt Twiss of the British Army had built a CANAL with a set of locks to bypass the rapids of the St Lawrence at Côteau du Lac. In the first half of the 19th century, canals were seen as the solution to the colony's defence and TRANSPORTATION needs. By 1800, locks were completed at Sault Ste Marie, between Lakes Superior and Huron, followed by the WELLAND CANAL, between Lakes Ontario and Erie (completed in 1828) and the RIDEAU CANAL, between Ottawa and Kingston (completed in 1832).

Canadians were quick to realize the potential of steam power in transportation. The ACCOMMODATION, the first steamboat built entirely in N America, was commissioned by John MOLSON, in 1809, for the Québec City to Montréal route. By 1819, seven STEAMBOATS were running between the 2 cities. Steamboats increased travel comfort and greatly reduced travel time; however, their use was limited by the availability of waterways and attention shifted to another application of steam power, the RAILWAY. Railway construction was advocated for military, economic and political purposes. The ensuing railway boom produced many lines and thousands of miles of track after 1850, culminating in the completion of the CANADIAN PACIFIC RAILWAY in 1885. The driving force behind this accomplishment was Canada's legendary engineer, Sir Sandford FLEMING, who also contributed to the international TIME system now used throughout the world.

Other prominent engineers of the time were Samuel KEEFER, designer of the PARLIAMENT BUILDINGS in Ottawa and active in canal and railway construction, and Sir Casimir GZOWSKI, who engineered many roads, harbours, canals and BRIDGES, including the International Bridge across the Niagara R. Frederick GISBORNE pioneered in the field of telegraphy, contributing to the laying of transatlantic cables between Ireland and Newfoundland in 1858 and 1866.

INDUSTRIALIZATION and the growth of urban populations intensified the problems of disease, POLLUTION and fire in Canadian cities of the late 19th century. Engineers responded to these problems by proposing rational measures such as sewage control, waterworks, BUILDING CODES and materials testing. The idea of publicly sponsored development of essential services also found expression in the creation of a publicly owned UTILITY for ELECTRIC-POWER GENERATION and distribution in Ontario, championed by Sir Adam BECK early in the 20th century (*see* ONTARIO HYDRO). With industrial growth and the problems of pollution and uncontrolled RESOURCE exploitation, engineers began to consider resource supply management: the CONSERVATION movement was born.

The Modern Profession

The engineering profession is the result of 2 important developments which took place in Europe during the 18th and 19th centuries: the Industrial Revolution and the increasing reliability of SCIENCE. As the industrial production of factories surpassed the output of craftsmen and artisans, both the scope of engineering and the demand for engineering skills greatly increased. Science became the principal means of technical advance, allowing engineers to predict the behaviour of materials and natural forces with increasing accuracy. Engineering schools were founded around the world during this time; specialized engineering disciplines began to develop and the stage was set for an explosion of technical knowledge in the 20th century.

Estimates suggest that the volume of scientific and technical knowledge now doubles every 20 years or less. Since no one person can possibly be familiar with all knowledge relevant to a given field, today's engineer most commonly works as part of an engineering team, with scientists, technologists, technicians and other specialists. Thus, in addition to training in MATHEMATICS, PHYSICS, systems analysis, CHEMISTRY and other sciences required by a particular engineering discipline, engineers require good communications skills to be effective in a team context. As most engineering requires compromise between the competing demands of economy, performance, compatibility with existing systems, environmental concerns and other factors, engineers also require good judgment, creativity and diplomacy to achieve the best use of limited materials, energy and human resources.

While the rapid pace of technical development continues to produce new areas of engineering specialization, most of these new fields are related to one or more of the principal branches, which include agricultural engineering, CHEMICAL ENGINEERING, CIVIL ENGINEERING, MECHANICAL ENGINEERING, MINERAL AND MINING ENGINEERING, and SURVEYING, as well as the fields discussed briefly below.

Bioengineering involves the use and control of biological systems, through the application of engineering methods in fields such as human engineering, biochemical engineering, medical engineering and environmental engineering. Human engineering concerns the optimal integration of tools, procedures and environments to human dimensions and performance criteria. Medical engineering produces TECHNOLOGY for use in MEDICINE, including diagnostic devices, monitoring and life-support systems such as pacemakers and artificial organs, and tools such as surgical instruments (*see* MEDICAL DEVICES INDUSTRY). Biochemical engineering uses the processes and physical properties of living organisms in applications such as the production of chemicals and drugs (*see* BIOLOGICAL PRODUCT; BIOTECHNOLOGY; GENETIC ENGINEERING; PHARMACEUTICALS INDUSTRY). Bioengineers usually complete advanced study in a related life-science discipline.

Naval Architecture concerns the design of oceangoing vessels and includes both an understanding of the physical influence of the sea and the ability to conceive designs integrating the piping, electrical circuits, structural members and other subcomponents into a compact and functional whole (*see* SUBMERSIBLES).

Marine Engineering concentrates on the technical aspects of SHIPBUILDING, eg, establishing design specifications and installing and testing shipboard machinery.

Industrial Engineering is the field dealing with the effective management of manpower, machinery and materials in the industrial production environment. Using systems analysis, queuing theory (ie, the study of waiting-line processes), STATISTICS and other mathematics-based disciplines, the industrial engineer may assume direction of such industrial functions as plant design, materials handling, automation and INDUSTRIAL QUALITY CONTROL, and implement the use of computers and data-processing procedures in the production cycle (*see* ROBOTICS).

Aeronautical Engineering deals with the design, construction, testing and maintenance of aircraft and their components and may include many specialized areas related to AERODYNAMICS, materials, propulsion and the myriad problems related to flight.

Metallurgical and Materials Engineering is concerned with the extraction, alloying, shaping and fabrication of metals and related materials. The practitioner is well-versed in chemistry and physics, with a strong emphasis on thermodynamics, high-temperature and solution chemistry and electrochemistry, the principles of solidification, phase transormations in the solid state, corrosion and deformation, and is familiar with an extensive range of chemical, optical and microanalytical techniques and physical testing methods. Thus, there is very little professional distinction between the metallurgical engineer and the metallurgist.

Nuclear Engineering is broadly concerned with discovering practical applications for nuclear physics in the areas of medicine, nondestructive testing, NUCLEAR-POWER generation and weaponry.

Petroleum engineering Natural or artificial forces may cause fluids to be stored or to move within structures or traps in the porous rocks of the Earth's crust. Petroleum engineering is concerned with locating and delineating such traps (reservoirs), determining the nature and quantity of the fluids they contain and the orderly and economic exploitation of such fluids. Another concern is the injection of fluids into reservoirs to store or dispose of them, or to use them to remove the reservoir's original contents. Discovery, production, transportation, processing and marketing of petroleum and petroleum products requires the interaction of many specialists during road building and the preparation of well sites and production, pumping and treatment facilities, PIPELINES, etc.

Engineers may also be classified according to the work they do. Thus, for example, the design engineer creates the plans and specifications for a particular job, drawing plans and details of each part, indicating how the parts fit together and preparing specifications of the materials to be used and performance standards to be maintained. Design may be in satellites, heart-lung machines, offshore drilling rigs, etc. The CONSTRUCTION engineer supervises building, working from detailed plans. In industrial processes the research engineer performs applied science and engineering research on processes and products. The development engineer develops products based on scientific and engineering research. The operating engineer manages industrial operations and production facilities. The production engineer works to find the most economical way of transforming raw materials into finished products. The service engineer supervises the installation or repair of equipment delivered to a client.

Relationship With Other Sciences

Engineering calls upon knowledge from all the disciplines of science in combinations which reflect the engineer's specialization and the nature of a given project. Mathematics, physics and their applications in the materials sciences are fundamental to the study and practice of engineering. While computers and computerized design aids have reduced the burden of performing extensive calculations, skill in advanced mathematical procedures remains essential for engineering work. Depending on the area of specialization, an engineer may require advanced study of one or more related disciplines, eg, physics, chemistry, GEOLOGY, OCEANOGRAPHY, BIOLOGY and medicine. Engineering training in Canada also involves study of the humanities and SOCIAL SCIENCES; ECONOMICS and SOCIOLOGY help the engineer evaluate the impact of new technologies and assess the socioeconomic dimensions of technological problems. BUSINESS MANAGEMENT studies can be invaluable assets to the financial and management aspects of engineering.

Engineering generalists are concerned with integrating the work of specialists from the engineering and scientific communities, a role which demands wide general knowledge of engineering and the sciences. Many problems require an engineer to use knowledge outside the scope of formal engineering training. This factor, combined with rapidly changing technology, leads most engineers to continue to study throughout their careers.

Training

In the first half of the 19th century, Canadian engineers were trained as apprentices in the offices of established professionals, such as Keefer or Gzowski. In 1854 the first engineering school in Canada was established at King's College (now UNIVERSITY OF NEW BRUNSWICK). Other applied science courses were established by the 1870s at McGill and l'École polytechnique de Montréal and at the School of Practical Sciences (now part of University of Toronto). Engineering education has continued to grow in Canada throughout the 20th century. One of the most significant areas of development, in which Canada is a world leader, has been in petroleum engineering. The U of Alberta, Edmonton, established the first petroleum engineering degree program in Canada in 1948 and continues to offer BSc, MSc and PhD degrees. In 1983, 28 Canadian institutions offered 167 accredited engineering programs, monitored by the engineering profession through the Canadian Accreditation Board, a committee of the Canadian Council of Professional Engineers, and certified to meet minimum quality standards for entry into the profession. University graduates normally undergo a 2-year APPRENTICESHIP, before being registered with the provincial engineering association as a Professional Engineer (PEng). Prospective engineers who lack the necessary educational requirements may become registered by passing exams offered by the associations.

Engineering Organizations

Canada's engineering organizations fulfil several different roles: some regulate and administer the profession; others facilitate an interchange of technical ideas between engineers working in the same field or exchanges between engineers and other groups within society or with engineers in other countries; still others are concerned with advancing the purposes of an engineering occupation or industrial sector. The engineering profession is regulated by provincial legislation, administered through the 10 provincial and 2 territorial engineering associations. The Canadian Council of Professional Engineers was organized in 1936 to co-ordinate the activities of the provincial associations. Its membership of nearly 120 000 represents about 95% of Canadian engineers. Civil, electrical and mechanical engineers each make up about 25% of the Council's membership; chemical engineers, 10%; others, including mining and petroleum engineers, 15%. The Council's activities include monitoring (accrediting) university engineering undergraduate education and providing statistics on engineering manpower. The first association of practising engineers in Canada was the Canadian Society of Civil Engineers, formed in 1887, which became the Engineering Institute of Canada in 1918. It now represents approximately 8000 Canadian professional engineers. Other engineering organizations are the Canadian Society for Chemical Engineering, the Canadian Institute of Mining and Metallurgy, the Association of Consulting Engineers of Canada and the Institute of Electrical and Electronics Engineers.

Engineering Law

The professional engineer's conduct is governed by a code of ethics which determines professional duties to the public, the employer, the client, other engineers and to the profession. In addition, the extensive financial and public safety responsibilities of engineering require professional engineers to be aware of the law relevant to practice.

Contracts, primarily covered by COMMON LAW (CIVIL LAW in Québec), are usually written documents stating terms and conditions of a purchase or agreement, but may be considered to exist without writing. Engineers routinely contract for goods and services where a failure to live up to the terms of the CONTRACT (eg, late delivery) may involve extensive financial loss and result in lawsuits for damages.

Specifications determine the required characteristics of contracted goods and are important in determining the warranty obligations of the manufacturer or seller and in settling lawsuits resulting from damages or injury in the event of product failure.

Corporate Law The CORPORATION is normally recognized as a legal entity separate from its holders, whose personal liability for its indebtedness is limited. Corporate liability is an important consideration for the engineer embarking on a career in private practice.

Industrial (or Intellectual) Property Industrial property rights are covered by PATENTS, COPYRIGHTS and TRADE MARKS. Patents and copyrights are means of protecting original creative ideas; trademarks offer rights to an original trade name. Patents are granted to a new invention meeting certain conditions, giving the patent holder a monopoly of rights to the invention for a specified period. Copyrights cover every original literary, dramatic, musical and artistic work and generally refer to the sole right to reproduce the work or any part of it. Of special interest to engineers are provisions of the copyright act dealing with engineering drawings, which preclude a client from reproducing or repeating the design without permission from the engineer who produced the drawing.

Safety The professional engineer is responsible for the health and safety of people who may be affected by his or her work and may be held liable for injuries resulting from failure to perform to a reasonable level of competence.

CLAUDE LAJEUNESSE

Englehart, Jacob Lewis, industrialist (b at Cleveland, Ohio 2 Nov 1847; d at Toronto 6 Apr 1921). In 1869, at age 19, he established Englehart and Co, one of the most successful producers in the Petrolia, Ont, fields, where the world's first commercial oil production had begun in 1857. Englehart started by acquiring the remains of a refinery, used to distill kerosene from crude oil, which had been destroyed by fire. He was one of 16 operators at Petrolia who merged their interests in 1870 to form Imperial Oil, which in turn was soon exporting kerosene around the world. Englehart was a major shareholder and VP of Imperial. Unable to raise capital for expansion elsewhere, Imperial in 1898 turned to John Rockefeller's Standard Oil Co, which purchased controlling interest. In 1905 Englehart was appointed chairman of the board of the Temiskaming and Northern Ontario Ry (ONTARIO NORTHLAND), which he administered with outstanding success for 15 years.

EARLE GRAY

Reading: Earle Gray, *The Great Canadian Oil Patch* (1970).

English The English were among the first Europeans to reach Canadian shores and waters after the Norse seafarers of the 10th and 11th centuries. English mariners probably fished in Canadian waters even before John CABOT's voyage of 1497; Dr John Dee, Queen Elizabeth I's astrologer who was interested in the discovery of the NORTHWEST PASSAGE, found evidence to suggest that 2 Bristol merchants — Thorne and Eliot — may have reached Newfoundland *c*1494. British merchants financed several voyages at the beginning of the 16th century, and as early as 1527 the harbour of ST JOHN'S became a rendezvous site for fishing vessels. When Sir Humphrey GILBERT arrived to claim the land for Queen Elizabeth I in 1583 he found a makeshift town to serve the Devon fishermen already there. In 1610 John Guy, also of Bristol, founded the well-known English settlement at Cupars Cove, later known as CUPIDS, and from this point onwards settlement continued, people from the English West Country outnumbering the Irish immigrants 2 to 1. To this day Newfoundland remains, by descent, the most English province of Canada.

Another early direction of English penetration was through the Northwest Passage to Hudson Bay. Some of the famous Elizabethan captains went in search of the passage, including Martin FROBISHER, who received an Inuit arrow in his rump at Frobisher Bay in 1577. In 1610 Henry HUDSON entered the inland sea now called Hudson Bay. In 1670 the foundation of the HUDSON'S BAY COMPANY brought an influx of English traders and employees, largely recruited from the urban unemployed. Englishmen based in the company's forts on the bay conducted pioneer explorations of the West and the North, including Henry KELSEY's 1690 travels in the Canadian prairies, Anthony HENDAY's sighting of the Rockies in 1754 and Samuel HEARNE's epic journey down the Coppermine R to the Arctic Sea in 1771-72.

Origins People of English descent came to Canada either directly from England or indirectly through the American colonies. In the first case their motives were largely economic. In the early 19th century, many working people were unemployed, and among the upper and middle classes, younger sons and discharged officers emigrated because they were unable to keep up appearances at home. In the later period of the settlement of the PRAIRIE WEST, many English immigrants were attracted to Canada by the offer of free land. The motives of those of English descent who emigrated from the US were largely political, for most of them were LOYALISTS, although it is true that many English-Americans emigrated to Upper Canada and later to the Prairies because of the farming opportunities. Apart from the special connection between Newfoundland and the western counties of Devon and Dorset, no part of England can be singled out as having contributed particularly to the Canadian population; immigrants have come from all parts of the country, and from urban as well as rural areas.

Migration Because England was the imperial centre and by definition the "old country" of English Canada, many of the English, at least until 1867, came in official capacities as public servants and soldiers who on release from service remained in the country. For example, almost all the officials in BC, when it entered Confederation in 1871 were English or Anglo-Irish. Migration in the broader sense began on the mainland with the foundation of HALIFAX in 1749. Two-thirds of its early population of 3000 were Englishmen based there as a counterbalance to the French force at LOUISBOURG. With the capture of Louisbourg in 1758 and of Québec in 1759 and with the Treaty of Paris, 1763, New France became another British colony. Shortly afterwards, in the 1760s, New England farmers of English descent began to settle around the Bay of Fundy on former Acadian lands, and in the early 1770s a group of Yorkshiremen put down roots in northern Nova Scotia. Then, at the end of the American War of Independence, the Loyalists came northward and carved out in 1784 the province of New Brunswick, whose population — apart from the returning Acadians — has remained largely English in descent.

Some of the Loyalists travelled to the region which in 1791 became Upper Canada. Here they were joined after the Napoleonic Wars by a considerable influx of English from England suffering the effects of high unemployment and depressed wages. By 1819 one-half of the British subjects who sailed for British N America were English from the British Isles. Many of these emigrated in various ways with official encouragement or assistance. The imperial authorities hoped to reproduce, at least partially, the English graded social system in Canada, and for this reason they encouraged ex-officers and other members of the gentry with generous grants of land, hoping to establish a kind of aristocracy. Speculative companies such as the CANADA COMPANY were given large tracts of land (over 1 million acres) on condition that they bring in suitable settlers from England. At the bottom of the scale were the schemes by which English parishes unloaded into Canada the paupers who were victims of crop failures and economic recession and who reached Canada with no means and none of the skills they needed in a pioneer environment. By 1851 this wave of immigration had settled down, and after a considerable inflow into the US some 93 000 people actually born in England remained in Upper Canada, constituting about one-tenth of the population. They were almost matched in number by the Scottish born (90 000) and greatly outnumbered by the 227 000 Irish born.

There were at least 3 other great waves of English immigration. After Confederation, children from private homes, industrial schools and poor-law schools were given free passage to Canada, where they became wards of various societies. Between 1867 and 1914 more than 60 000 British children, the majority of them English, were settled across Canada (*see* CHILD LABOUR). Between 1890 and 1914, in response to the opening of the Prairie provinces, there was another large influx of English settlers. In 1901 they numbered less than 10 000, but in 1906, 3 years after an immigration office was established in central London, 65 000 immigrants arrived in Canada and in 1913 the number peaked at 113 004. Although the British government, under the Empire Settlement Act (1922), helped 130 000 British immigrants settle in Canada after WWI, the number of English immigrants did not rise significantly until after WWII. In 1947 over 7000 English, many of them trained industrial workers, artisans and technicians, emigrated to Canada; in 1957 the number rose to 75 546 and in 1967 it was 43 000.

Over the years, despite immigration, the proportion of Canadians of English descent has declined slightly. In 1871 those of English descent numbered 706 369 out of a total population of 3 485 761; in 1931, 2 741 419 out of 10 376 786. By 1981 Statistics Canada did not distinguish "English" from "British" immigrants.

Settlement Patterns Proportionately the most heavy English settlement has been in Newfoundland, BC, the Maritime provinces, and later in Ontario. In Québec the English are found mainly in enclaves in Montréal and the Eastern Townships. But wherever they have settled, except in Québec, they have tended to become assimilated quickly into the local community, largely because they have not had to learn a new language and have encountered little prejudice. Outbursts of anglophobia have been rare enough for such manifestations as the "Englishmen Need Not Apply" job notices of the early 1900s to have passed into Prairie legend as historic curiosities. Popular resentment against the English (as indeed against immigrants generally) was most acute during periods of economic crisis. During the depression of the early 1900s the government dealt as harshly with the English as with other immigrants; of nearly 1800 persons deported in 1908, 1100 were returned to the British Isles. The few cases of all-English agrarian settlements have usually existed because their members shared the same class attitudes or the same opinions rather than because they shared "Englishness." An example of the former was the colony of English gentlemen founded at CANNINGTON MANOR in Saskatchewan in 1882; one of the latter was the Barr Colony (*see* BARR COLONISTS) on the Alberta-Saskatchewan border.

Mrs Corbett and family from Surrey, England, coming to meet her husband at Québec around the year 1911 (*courtesy Public Archives of Canada / PA-10150*).

Economic Life The English entered into every level of Canadian life. They have been prominent in government and have shared the control of Canadian business with the SCOTS not only in the English-speaking parts of Canada but also in Montréal (*see* ELITES; BUSINESS ELITES). The Canadian armed forces were created and have largely been staffed by officers of English descent.

The first waves of English immigration contributed greatly to the farming population in the rural areas and to the skilled artisan population in the towns, but after WWII many English immigrants were professionals, technicians or individuals concerned in various ways with the arts. English immigrants have made important contributions to many Canadian institutions, including the NFB, the CBC, the Canada Council, the National Ballet and the Stratford Festival.

Social and Cultural Life The English, perhaps because they are so widely and evenly spread across Canada and because they consider themselves a founding race, have tended to be less self-defensively clannish than other groups. The family unit facilitated and promoted their ethnic identity. The ratio of male to female English prior to WWI was 5:3 while for other groups it was 5:1. The largest and most important English cultural society was the Sons of England, which in 1913 had 40 000 Canadian members. Lodges formed across Canada were usually led by affluent Englishmen, professionals, clergymen and former military officers who had joined local elites. The most important vehicle for maintaining traditions was the social evening "At home," which was modelled on the English music hall. On these occasions the Sons were expected to thrill to jingoistic songs, weep at evocations of England, savour warm, dark ale and revert to regional dialects. As a mutual benefit society, the Sons organized receptions for newcomers, provided medical services and paid unemployment and disability benefits.

The English were often perceived by other ethnic groups as xenophobic and industrious. English ethnicity could be asserted productively in Canada, because it provided not only status but a competitive advantage in securing employment. Companies such as T. Eaton Company were so partial to English workers that they imported them from London to work in their factories, and the CPR used the union which had organized metal-trade workers in Britain as a supplier of labour.

Unlike the Scottish and Irish groups, the English pay scant attention to national days; only in Newfoundland is St George's Day celebrated seriously. They maintain few organizations to nurture group ties, and as the generations have passed and the class accents of England have dissolved into Canadian speech, the divisions of the homeland's sharply stratified society have blurred. If the descendants of the English in Canada are now vertically divided, it is more by wealth than by birth. The snobbish English enclaves of Westmount and Victoria are almost as obsolete as that uniquely English institution, the once numerous corps of remittance men — feckless sons of wealthy families paid to stay in Canada. Many of the remittance men died during WWI; the rest finally vanished when currency restrictions ended their English subsidies during WWII.

A number of Canadian institutions — some of them very important — have been profoundly influenced by English models and are still largely supported by Canadians of English stock. Representative institutions and the traditions of the British and English COMMON LAW are among the most important inheritances Canada has received from Great Britain. The parliamentary system, under which the Cabinet, which rules the country, is responsible to Parliament, is an extension of the British Cabinet system to colonial government, embodied in the British North America Act of 1867. In the realm of LAW, the civil law in 9 of Canada's provinces (the exception is Québec where French CIVIL LAW is maintained) is based largely on English common law; the system of courts follows the English model closely.

Another institution is the exclusive club frequented by businessmen and professionals which exists in all Canadian cities and is modelled directly on the clubs of London's West End; many of them still, like their English counterparts, exclude women and some have only recently abandoned policies of racial exclusion. These are inherited from a transformed English class system now based less on descent than on fortune. The PRIVATE SCHOOL, of which Upper Canada College is the best example, is based on the English public school. The English maintain private schools in Canada not to preserve their culture but to maintain, in a changed form, their traditional class system.

The Anglican Church, formerly the Church of England in Canada, is perhaps the largest of the distinctively English institutions, transplanted almost unchanged from the homeland (*see* ANGLICANISM). About 50% of Canadians of English descent adhere to it; the rest belong to the United Church and some smaller Protestant sects, with a relatively small minority being Roman Catholics.

The RCMP, as the North-West Mounted Police, was originally modelled closely on British light cavalry units. Institutions such as the RED CROSS, the Boy Scouts and the GIRL GUIDES were also brought from England.

Finally, English workingmen brought to Canada their own traditions of trade unions and social democracy. Canadian labour unions as they exist today are a hybrid of American and English forms, but their militancy is Anglo-Scottish in character. Politically, Canada is distinct in N America because, unlike the US, it has a viable party (the NEW DEMOCRATIC PARTY, previously the CO-OPERATIVE COMMONWEALTH FEDERATION) dedicated to democratic socialism, which was founded and built mainly by English, Welsh and Scots reared in the traditions of the British Independent Labour Party and later of the Labour Party. To this day the NDP operates more like an Anglo-Scottish party than an American one, and its structure — of constituency branches combined with labour unions — reflects that of the Labour Party in Britain.

English cultural activities have permeated Canada, largely through the dominance of the English language outside Québec and NW New Brunswick. This is true especially in literature. The influence of English traditions and English models has inevitably been profound, and it is only within the present generation that a distinctive English Canadian literature has really emerged. Yet there has never been a distinctive literature of Englishmen writing to preserve or portray English culture in Canada, as there has been one of, for example, Icelanders writing to preserve an Icelandic culture. Again, the English person's sense of being part of the dominant culture precludes particularism; immigrant writers from England have quickly found their places in the Canadian setting and in helping to form a Canadian literature an English tradition has been freely modified to its N American milieu.

GEORGE WOODCOCK

English Language Although English was used in Canada before the 19th century, there were neither enough speakers nor enough significant features in the language for it to be regarded as anything other than British English. However, between 1825 and 1846 more than half a million immigrants came to Canada directly from Britain, and by 1871 over 2 million people in Canada listed the British Isles as their land of origin. These new Canadians brought with them the kind of English that they had learned from their parents, and it bore little similarity to what is now often called Standard British English, or simply Standard English. Since the 14th century the regional dialect used in London, the centre of British government, and in nearby Oxford and Cambridge universities, had become associated with British educated and upper-class speakers. However, very few people spoke it. It was not until 1880 that education became compulsory in England; and it is unlikely that most British immigrants to Canada in the early 19th century had received much schooling or had had any opportunity to acquire a form of British English associated with educated or upper-class people. Those who were educated often objected to the English they heard in Canada, as did Susanna MOODIE in *Roughing It in the Bush* (1852) and Rev A.C. Geikie in *The Canadian Journal* (1857). The kind of English introduced to Canada in the early 19th century was by no means standard. It was spoken English, often typical of the region from which the speakers came, such as Ireland, Yorkshire or Devon. When people move to a new land isolated from their homeland, two things happen to their language: first, it escapes the direct influences of changes in grammar or pronunciation that take place in the parent language; and second, it undergoes great changes in vocabulary in order to allow its users to accommodate their speech to their new circumstances. In Canada one rarely hears, for example, "clerk" pronounced to rhyme with "dark." Acceptable late-18th-century British pronunciation rhymed "clerk" with "lurk," "caught" with "cot," and "aunt" with "ant," and those pronunciations are the ones immigrants brought with them. In some instances, more than one pronunciation of a word came to Canada. This is true of the common ways of saying "schedule": one with an initial *sk* sound and one with *sh*, both acceptable in British English until the mid-19th century. The former pronunciation has been reinforced in Canada by American influence; but it did not, in fact, reach Canada from the US: the source for both countries was pre-19th-century British English. Similarly, although the pronunciation of "new" to rhyme with "do" rather than with "few," as in British English, is often regarded as due to American influence in Canada, that is not the case. Until the late 19th century both pronunciations were current in British English, and immigrants brought both with them.

Grammatical differences between British and Canadian English are very few, since the major changes that were to affect the grammatical structure of English had taken place in Britain well before the periods of heavy emigration to Canada. The grammatical differences that exist are minor ones, concerning choices in the use of prepositions and verbs, which late 18th-century British English had not yet decided. Both "dived" and "dove" are heard as the past tense of "dive" in Canada, but the latter no longer has currency in British English. Two verbs heard occasionally in every Canadian province date from the Old English period (approximately 6th-12th centuries AD): "snuck" and "clumb" for "sneaked" and "climbed." Since the 19th century both verbs have become parts of British regional dialects, but they are not dialect usage in Canada, although "snuck" is often regarded as a rather amusing past tense of "sneak." Of the three prepositions used after "sick" in "sick to," "sick at" and "sick in" the stomach, British English has largely dropped "to," which survives in Canada as majority usage. Standard British English no longer uses the phrasal prepositions "back of" and "in back of," but Canadian English preserves both. In 18th-century British English the omission of the infinitive ("to go" or "to come") in "wants out" and "wants in" was frequent, but it is now rarely heard except in Scotland; Canadian English preserves this feature.

It is in vocabulary that the English language in Canada has undergone the greatest change, largely because of the settlers' need for new words to describe new things. Vocabulary may be increased in predictable ways: words are borrowed from other languages; existing words are given new meanings; new compounds are created; people and places give their names to things with which they are associated. Canadian English has used all those ways.

Borrowings from the Canadian Indians include *moose, muskeg, caribou* and *chipmunk;* and from the Inuit, *parka, mukluk, kayak, umiak* and *igloo.* From Inuit also comes *tupek,* the skin tent that is the Inuit equivalent of the Indians' *wigwam* or *tepee* (TIPI).

It was from French Canadians that the English and Scots fur traders learned to navigate the rivers of the new land. From the French Canadian VOYAGEUR the English learned about the problem of *rapids* (the turbulent sections of a river), and how to avoid them by lifting the canoe from the water and making a PORTAGE. Canadian Indians showed the travellers how to prepare PEMMICAN (meat prepared with fat), and how to make *watap* (the roots of trees used as thread in repairing damaged canoes). From the Canadian French, the British learned about the *travois,* an A-shaped frame devised by the Indians that allowed a dog or a horse to carry a heavy load by trailing the legs of the frame on the ground, with the load fastened low on the frame.

In addition to borrowing words, English the world over has always followed the practice of giving new meanings to existing words. Thus, in N America, "section" gained a new meaning during the settlement of the West: one square mile (640 acres, or 259 ha). With the Canadian movement towards representative government, the British word "riding," borrowed centuries ago from Scandinavian (meaning "a third"), and used to refer to administrative areas in English counties, came into general Canadian usage to refer to an electoral district. In the gold camps of the Cariboo, "hurdy gurdy," an old name for a barrel organ, was used to refer to dance hostesses because their music was provided by that instrument.

The English language in Canada has also followed the practice of the parent language of creating new compounds from existing words. Thus, "sour" and "dough" become "sourdough," a name for both a fermenting dough used as a starter in baking bread and the gold seekers who used such dough on their travels. From the French *la crosse* ("hooked stick") comes "lacrosse," the name used for the game that Algonquian Indians called *baggataway* ("playing ball"). To combat the lampreys in the Great Lakes, Canadian biologists developed a hybrid fish by crossing the speckled trout with the lake trout and named the hybrid "splake" by compounding elements of "speckled" and "lake."

Since the Renaissance, English has drawn freely on Latin and Greek to create new words, especially in medicine. That tradition was followed in Canada when the drug developed to control diabetes was named *insulin* (Lat *insula,* "island"). "Kerosene" was coined from Gk *keros* ("wax") by Dr Abraham GESNER, a 19th-century scientist in the Maritimes who developed a process for extracting coal oil.

The British named *sherry* after its place of origin (Xeres, or Jerez, Sp) and called policemen *bobbies* after Robert (Bobby) Peel. A similar naming practice has occasionally been used in Canada. The *malpeque oyster* carries the name of the bay in Prince Edward Island where it originates. The *malemute,* a dog made popular by Robert SERVICE, is named after the Inuit people of that name who first bred it. A BOMBARDIER in Canada is not a soldier but a tracked snow vehicle, developed by Armand Bombardier of Québec. From Digby, NS, comes the *Digby chicken,* a variety of smoked herring; and from Labrador comes the *Labrador* dog.

Until the end of the 14th century, Standard English was no more standard than any other regional dialect of British English, but from that time until the mid-20th century it was held as the ideal to which speakers of regional dialects should aspire. Canadian English, on the other hand, has never elevated any one form of regional speech to a position of prestige. The federal government is in Ottawa; but Ottawa English is not held up as a model of the best speech. However, a form of Canadian English, the language stripped of its regional features, is used by English-speaking Canadians across the country. Although Canadian English does not have the regional dialects of British English, French or German that have developed over the centuries, it does have marked differences in speech among the various regions. Newfoundland is the most obvious example, with its undertones of Irish and the regional speech of southwestern England. What is often called the Ottawa Valley twang reminds one that thousands of Irish immigrants settled there in the 1840s. In general, local dialect boundaries in English-speaking Canada may be considered to be Newfoundland, the Maritimes, eastern Ontario, western Ontario, the Prairies and British Columbia (the most "British" region in Canada). M.H. SCARGILL

Reading: J.K. Chambers (ed), *Canadian English* (1975); R.E. McConnell, *Our Own Voice* (1979); M.M. Orkin, *Speaking Canadian English* (1970); M.H. Scargill, *A Short History of Canadian English* (1977).

Ense, Donald Orion Henry, artist, illustrator, poet (b at Mindemoya, Manitoulin I, Ont 17 May 1953). An early member of the Manitoulin group of native painters, he found his theme in the teachings of the Anishnabec (Ojibwa) and genre paintings of reserve life. His style reflects the 2-dimensionality of the pictographic native style plus some postimpressionistic influences; he paints in a simplifed realistic manner with black form line and areas filled in flat colour. He has great narrative ability and is an excellent illustrator. MARY E. SOUTHCOTT

Entomology is the branch of ZOOLOGY dealing with INSECTS, although which organisms are included is open to interpretation. Probably, those animals covered by the Gk word *entomon* ("cut up, segmented") are appropriately considered insects, ie, the arthropods, but CRUSTACEANS (except for a few terrestrial species) and a few small, marine arthropod groups, such as sea spiders and horseshoe crabs, are generally excluded. Entomologists study the following groups: Insecta; Myriapoda (eg, MILLIPEDES, CENTIPEDES); and Arachnida (eg, SCORPIONS, SPIDERS, MITES). Hence, entomology embraces the study of the majority of known species of organisms. Entomology has made contributions to almost all life sciences, from ecology and taxonomy to GENETICS, nuclear biology and medicine. The science comprises many subdisciplines including, among its more theoretical aspects, insect morphology, taxonomy, ecology, ethology, physiology and biochemistry. Agricultural, forest, medical and veterinary entomology (aimed at pest and disease control) and related branches (eg, environmental and POLLINATION biology and quarantine services) are among its applied aspects. Ethnoentomology studies the role of insects in human culture.

In Canada, entomology began as an applied discipline. In 1856, the Bureau of Agriculture for Upper and Lower Canada offered prizes for essays on various pests of wheat. The winners were amateurs; in fact, many early contributions were made by amateurs, eg, H.H. CROFT, first president of the Entomological Society of Canada (est 1863), was professor of chemistry at King's College (University of Toronto). In 1884, James FLETCHER became the first Dominion Entomologist. He was transferred, in 1887, to the newly created Dominion Experimental Farm, Ottawa. In 1914, the Division of Entomology, Experimental Farms Branch, became a branch of the Dept of Agriculture — the Entomological Service, now part of the Biosystematics Research Institute.

Largely because of increased public awareness of the numbers of insects, the destruction a small percentage of them do to crops and other products, and the distress caused by their transmission of diseases to humans and livestock, the demand for professional entomologists has increased enormously in the last 100 years. This demand, particularly in government, necessitated the establishment of university-level schools of entomology. In Canada independent university departments of entomology are found at Macdonald College, McGill, which until the end of the 1950s was responsible for training half of Canada's professional entomologists, U of Manitoba, and U of Alberta. The Dept of Environmental Biology, U of Guelph, successor to what was virtually a fourth independent department, also remains predominantly entomologically oriented. Several other Canadian universities have departments of zoology or biology, with strong entomological leanings (and often traditions), offering excellent education and research facilities. These include the following universities: British Columbia, Simon Fraser, Saskatchewan, Toronto, McMaster, Carleton, Montréal, Laval, New Brunswick and Memorial. Some entomological research is carried on at most other Canadian universities. Most professional entomologists are employed by the federal government in the departments of Agriculture and Environment (especially the Forestry Service of Environment Canada). Both have research laboratories and advisory services across the country. Provincial governments employ entomologists in similar capacities, and the larger municipalities engage a few. Various industries have staff entomologists and, of course, universities and museums hire some. Entomologists may also become schoolteachers or work with private firms undertaking environmental studies. Many are associated with government and international organizations and exchange programs that deal with entomological or other biological problems.

The principal entomological collections in Canada are those at Agriculture Canada, Ottawa (Canadian National Insect Collection); McGill (Macdonald Campus, Lyman Entomological Museum and Research Laboratory); U of T (Royal Ontario Museum); and those associated with departments of entomology at the universities of Alta and Man, and the Dept of Zoology, UBC. The first 3 are of international importance. Insect collections are also held in provincial museums, notably at Halifax and Victoria. Canadian entomological societies are Entomological Soc of Canada (the oldest national Canadian scientific society); the Acadian Entomological Soc (serving the Atlantic Provs and northern New England); La Société Entomologique du Québec; entomological societies of Ont, Man, Sask, Alta and BC; and a few amateur, local societies. La Société de Protection des Plantes du Québec is largely oriented to entomology, and Canadian Soc of Zoologists has a very large entomological contingent. D.K. MCEWAN KEVAN

Environment, the physical, social and psychological milieu in which we exist, which affects us and is in turn affected by us. Throughout its 4-billion-year history, profound changes have occurred in the geological and ecological systems of planet Earth. As long as human populations remained small and communities were part of local ecosystems, most changes took place slowly and seemingly without major disturbances in the global system. However, the geometric increase in the human population and the extensive INDUSTRIALIZATION of the last 200 years have placed stresses on the complex processes that maintain the stability of the biosphere (the relatively thin but highly complex layer on and above the surface of the planet, consisting of the atmosphere, water, minerals and organisms). Disturbances in one part of the biosphere do not necessarily remain localized but can affect its composition and stability elsewhere (*see* BIOGEOGRAPHY). Thus the burning of fossil fuels in the Northern Hemisphere has increased the carbon-dioxide content of the AIR over the South Pole. Sulphur compounds produced by industrial activity in the UK and continental Europe have caused a marked decline in the biological productivity of LAKES in Sweden; while deleterious changes in lakes in Ontario are attributable to pollutants from the US and from Ontario itself (*see* ACID RAIN; ENDANGERED ANIMALS).

The growth of ENVIRONMENTAL AND CONSERVATION MOVEMENTS originated in the 19th century in the initiatives of private individuals and groups largely concerned with the despoliation of their immediate surroundings. Increasing knowledge and sophistication in analysis has broadened this largely middle-class preoccupation with the more visible aspects of POLLUTION to include concerns about RESOURCE shortages, impacts on human mental and physical health (eg, contamination of food, indoor AIR POLLUTION), aesthetics and appropriate land-use policies. In the 1950s, an early worker in the area of creating systems for assessing the degree of environmental degradation was the Canadian environmentalist Pierre DANSEREAU. He created a model of the ecosystem, the "Ball of Arrows," which attempted to show the intricate web of relationships among its living and nonliving components.

A rational conservation strategy requires adequate knowledge of processes governing interactions within and between highly complex ecosystems; a knowledge of the sources of damage (types and nature of pollutants) and of the technology available for counteracting their effects; promotion of economic policies that accept that development and conservation programs should be linked and that "diseconomies" that reduce the quality of the environment should be minimized; and development of legal and administrative structures that designate standards and ensure their maintenance. Canadian zoologist and systems analyst C.S. Holling and his co-workers have used computer models to deal with these issues.

Global Perspectives

Environmental problems require international co-operation because many cross international boundaries; the benefits of work done must be maximized by sharing experiences to avoid duplication of effort (particularly in developing countries); and the establishment of "pollution havens" must be prevented.

Over the last 2 decades, considerable progress has been made towards achieving a global strategy for the maintenance of the health of the biosphere. Concern for the environment received international recognition through the 1972 UNITED NATIONS Conference on the Human Environment, held in Stockholm. The conference, under the chairmanship of Maurice STRONG, provided an international forum for discussion of global environmental problems by government and nongovernment personnel. A major result of the conference was establishment of the UN Environment Programme (UNEP), which now funds and co-ordinates many studies concerned with conservation. Governments are also linked through other specialist bodies of the UN (eg, Food and Agriculture Organization, World Health Organization and, especially, United Nations Educational, Scientific and Cultural Organization). Many of these programs are carried out co-operatively, facilitated by UNEP. UNE-

Pond environment. A national conservation strategy requires knowledge of the process governing interaction within and between highly complex ecosystems (*artwork by Claire Tremblay*).

SCO is responsible for environmental matters and promotes education programs about the processes operating in the biosphere. These programs involve governmental organizations and nongovernmental bodies, eg, the International Council of Scientific Unions (ICSU) and International Union for the Conservation of Nature and Natural Resources (IUCN). UNESCO receives financial help from the World Bank and the UN Interim Fund for Science and Technology for Development. The following UNESCO programs are concerned with the environment.

Man and the Biosphere Programme (MAB) Planned in 1973-75, largely as a successor to the International Biological Programme (IBP, 1967-72), this program in 1983 involved 95 countries. Priority is now given to studies in the humid tropics, arid zones and urban systems. A network of biosphere reserves is being developed to promote conservation of important natural systems and to ensure preservation of genetic material. Over 200 reserves in 50 countries have already been named. More than 3000 sites have been surveyed in Canada.

International Geological Correlation Programme (IGCP)was concerned with developing knowledge of the processes governing the evolution of the Earth's crust, with special emphasis on the rational use of MINERAL and ENERGY resources.

International Hydrological Programme (IHP) The first 6-year phase has been completed and a second phase is underway. The major aim is to advance understanding of hydrologic processes and their interactions with human activities (*see* HYDROLOGY). The World Meteorological Organization is closely associated with many parts of this program (*see* METEOROLOGY).

The publication in March 1980 of the World Conservation Strategy was a major step towards the development of a unified approach to conservation of the biosphere. The document, prepared by IUCN, commissioned by UNEP and financially supported by the World Wildlife Fund, represents a compromise statement of conservation priorities among organizations with very different viewpoints. It aims to stimulate a global approach to the management of living resources and provide guidelines to the policymakers and their advisers, conservationists and development agencies. Government acceptance and implementation of the strategy would ensure maintenance of essential ecological processes and life-support systems; of genetic diversity in important animals, plants and microorganisms; and of renewable resources (species and ecosystems) at levels which will permit their use and guarantee their continued existence.

Canadian Scene

The increasing power of the TECHNOLOGY available for manipulation of the environment and its resources has produced in Canada a complete turnaround in attitudes towards the natural environment. In Canada's early development the wilderness was considered something to be fought, although it provided apparently unlimited resources. Exploited at a small-to-modest scale, those resources provided wealth without severe repercussions other than the extermination of several wildlife species (eg, passenger pigeon, Plains grizzly). Increasingly powerful and large-scale technologies started to overwhelm parts of the environment to the point where the resource base and human well-being were sometimes threatened. Under these circumstances, wilderness is now perceived as a valuable and dwindling resource to be respected and protected.

The actors in the environment drama can be divided into 4 overlapping groups: the general public and special-interest groups, industry, governments and academia. Public interest in and concern about environmental issues have been increasing since the late 1960s, but have not yet been translated into action. The special-interest groups have been largely responsible for raising and maintaining public interest. Most environmental organizations have become increasingly knowledgeable and skilled, and now depend less on vociferous protest and more on quiet discussion and hard work. A small minority has come to advocate violence in pursuit of its aims, eg, bombing power facilities in BC or threatening to ram SEALING vessels on the East Coast. Industrial representatives who still maintain that environmental protection infringes on free enterprise and is too expensive have become a small minority. Legal requirements, the importance of public image and the discovery that environmentally acceptable planning and operations can be cost-effective have caused industry, with exceptions, to become increasingly inclined to incorporate sound environmental planning into its developments.

In the early 1970s the federal and all provincial governments passed legislation regarding environmental issues (*see* ENVIRONMENTAL AGENCIES;). In most jurisdictions, experience and increasing knowledge have led to amendments in the legislation and changes in its application (*see* ENVIRONMENTAL LAW). In education, courses, programs, textbooks and other resource materials have greatly improved. New environment units within universities have established credibility with their academic colleagues, industry and government. Consequently, graduates with greatly improved skills and knowledge can move quickly to resolve problems rather than having to learn on the job, as was often the case in the past. The most important remaining transition is in development of the will and ability to anticipate and avoid environmental problems rather than simply reacting to them as they arise. This development will be accomplished through monitoring and evaluating new and existing projects and products. It will also be essential to move social and environmental concerns to the beginning of research and development, design and planning processes rather than having them tacked on at the end.

DIXON THOMPSON

Reading: Pierre Dansereau, *Harmony and Disorder in the Canadian Environment* (1975).

Environmental Agencies In Canada environmental problems may require action by governments at 4 levels: international, national, provincial and municipal. At the international level, activities include protection of WHALES, control of ACID RAIN, and the work of the INTERNATIONAL JOINT COMMISSION on water-quality questions. At the other 3 levels of government, powers and responsiblities are divided, but the divisions are frequently ambiguous and uncertain. A great deal of co-operation and co-ordination is required. With 3 levels of government, different departments at each level and sometimes numerous legislative requirements for each department or agency, industries seeking approval for projects face a maze of legislation which is costly and time consuming. At the federal and provincial levels, some governments are attempting to reduce costs without reducing standards by moving to a "single window" approval process in which one government agency would be responsible for co-ordinating all requirements for proposed projects.

In addition to the agencies listed in the table, legislation or responsibility for various environmental issues often rests in such other government departments as agriculture, culture, health, fish and wildlife, transportation, housing and municipal affairs and recreation, as well as other agencies and tribunals. Jurisdiction is frequently transferred from one agency to another, or may involve interdepartmental or intergovernmental agencies. *See* ENVIRONMENTAL LAW.

DIXON THOMPSON

Canadian Federal and Provincial Environmental Agencies[1]

Jurisdiction	*Authority*	*Legislation*
Canada	Dept of the Environment	Government Organization Act, 1970
	Canadian Environment Advisory Council	Cabinet decision (1972)
BC	Ministry of Environment	Dept of the Environment Act, 1975
	Pollution Control Board	Pollution Control Act, 1967
	Environment and Land Use Committee	Environment and Land Use Act, 1971
Alta	Dept of the Environment	Dept of the Environment Act, 1971
	Environment Council of Alberta[2]	Environment Council Act, 1977
	Energy Resources Conservation Board[3]	Energy Resources Conservation Act, 1971
Sask	Dept of the Environment	Dept of the Environment Act, 1972
	Environment Advisory Council	Dept of the Environment Act, 1972 (1973)
Man	Environmental Management Division, Dept of Mines, Natural Resources and Environment	Clean Environment Act, 1971
	Manitoba Environmental Council	Clean Environment Act, 1972
	Clean Environment Commission	Clean Environment Act, 1968 (1972)
Ont	Ministry of the Environment	Environment Protection Act, 1971 (1972)
	Environmental Assessment Board	Environmental Assessment Act, 1975 (1976)
Qué	Affairs Municipales et de l'Environnement	Environment Quality Act, 1972 (1974)
	Conseil Consultatif de l'Environnement	Environment Quality Act, 1972, amended La Loi 69, 1978 (1973)
NB	Dept of the Environment	Clean Environment Act, 1972
	Environment Council of New Brunswick	Ecological Reserves Act, 1976[4]
NS	Dept of the Environment	Environment Protection Act, 1973
	Environmental Control Council	Environment Protection Act, 1973
PEI	Dept of Environment	Environment Protection Act, 1975
Nfld	Dept of Consumer Affairs & Environment	Dept of Consumer Affairs & Environment Act, 1973
	Environment Quality Advisory Commission	Dept of Consumer Affairs & Environment Act, 1973 (not yet in effect)
YT	No formal agency	
NWT	Environmental Protection Service	Environmental Protection Ordinance, 1973
	Science Advisory Board	Science Advisory Board Ordinance, 1975 (1976)

[1] Unless otherwise stated, the year of establishment is the year of passage of the establishing legislation.

[2] Supersedes Environment Conservation Authority, est 1970.

[3] Supersedes Oil and Gas Conservation Board.

[4] Supersedes Clean Environment Act, 1972.

Environmental and Conservation Movements Probably the first conservationists in Canada were the native peoples, the Indians and Inuit. After all, for centuries they lived off the land with little apparent destruction. Such practices as clearing areas or driving game by lighting fires would have affected forests, but there is little evidence that such activities caused any long-term damage. Furthermore, Indian bands and Inuit family groups often moved their settlements to new areas for better HUNTING, allowing the regions left to grow back and repopulate with wildlife. Hence there was no need for concern about CONSERVATION problems before the first permanent European settlement in the 17th century. In Canada since that time, attitudes towards the conservation of nature and natural RESOURCES have developed in 5 overlapping but distinct periods.

The first period, from about 1680 to 1860, has been called the "Tree Reserves Period." In this period the French and English tried to ensure a steady supply of ship timber. During the second, the "Land Reserves Period" (1625-1895), land was reserved by church and state for schools, universities and railways (*see* CLERGY RESERVES). Sales of land and land taxes were the only sources of wealth for governments. The first Canadian naturalist club was established in Ontario in this period (1863). A wide variety of PARKS, forest reserves, BIRD SANCTUARIES and wildlife preserves were created during the third period, the "Resource Reserve Period" (1880-present). Emphasis was placed on using wildlife wisely, rather than merely preserving or protecting it. During the fourth period, called the "Recreation Reserves Period" (1885-present), recreation facilities such as parks, HISTORIC SITES and fish and game reserves were established, especially near urban areas. The "Nature and Wilderness Reserves Period" dates from about 1960, when Canadians began to see value in setting aside areas of wild country, simply because of their wildness. Emphasis is less on resource use or recreation than on retaining areas where only the forces of nature are allowed to shape the environment.

The first Canadians to study the natural environment were probably the amateurs (doctors, diviners, etc) who began to catalogue the natural history of the country (eg, flora, fauna, rocks, fossils) and laid the bases of the sciences of BIOLOGY, BOTANY, GEOLOGY, PALEONTOLOGY and ZOOLOGY in Canada. The view they took of nature and the environment was shaped initially by European art and scientific traditions. European experiences of FORESTRY and game preserves also had an effect. Writers such as Jean Jacques Rousseau, William Wordsworth and Lord Byron influenced Canadians, as did the writings of Grey Owl (A.S. BELANEY), Englishman who settled in Canada. American thinkers had an even greater effect. These included the eminent ornithologist John James Audubon, who visited Canada in the 1830s, and the writers James Fenimore Cooper, Ralph Waldo Emerson and Henry David Thoreau. The American conservationists John Muir, the founder of the Sierra Club (1892), and Gifford Pinchot, who with President Theodore Roosevelt launched the American conservation movement in the early 1900s, were also significant.

Americans were generally ahead of Canadians in concern for the conservation of resources. This concern probably resulted from more extensive settlement in the US, which demonstrated the harm that civilization could do. In Canada a pioneer mentality of "unlimited" forests, lakes and wildlife persisted longer. The development of national parks clearly illustrates the difference between early American and Canadian conservation action. The first N American national park was Yellowstone created in the US in 1872. From the beginning, such parks were intended to protect scenic attractions. In Canada the first national parks were established in the Rocky Mts (Banff in 1885, Yoho and Glacier in 1886), but their purpose was economic: to produce revenue from forest reserves and tourist travel. Parks were not conceived as wilderness preserves at this stage. In 1916 the US passed the National Park Service Act, which stated that parks were to be "unimpaired for the enjoyment of future generations." This wording was not used in the Canadian National Parks Act until 1930. In this respect, 1930 is a kind of turning point in Canadian conservation thought.

In the area of wildlife conservation, however, Canada did react to some emergency situations quite early. The first bird sanctuary was created in Saskatchewan in 1887. By 1889 the plains BISON had been reduced from about 60 million to less than 2000 animals. In 1907 and 1909 the government purchased about 700 bison and placed them in national parks. Between 1910 and 1920, 3 areas were set aside as reserves for ANTELOPE in Alberta and Saskatchewan; these were later abolished as unnecessary. In 1911 Canada formally established a parks branch; James Harkin was appointed dominion parks commissioner. Harkin, probably the first leading Canadian to argue for protection of wilderness for its own sake, was deeply influenced by the American conservation movement. Canada's first significant international conservation effort was a treaty with the US, signed in 1918, for the protection of migratory birds.

Until 1945 conservation in Canada focused on establishing national and provincial parks in remote areas. After WWII emphasis was on park expansion for recreational purposes. National and provincial park systems grew slowly during this period. The 1960s marked a different era for conservation and the environmental movement in Canada. Conservationist attitudes were no longer restricted primarily to naturalist groups. A growing number of Canadians became concerned not only about using resources wisely, but also about the effects of human activity on the environment. During the 1960s, concern about POLLUTION became a major public issue. Specialized groups such as the Society for the Promotion of Environmental Conservation (in the West), Pollution Probe (in the East) and the Ecology Action Centre (in the Maritimes) were born. Such groups were led by scientists such as Donald CHANT, who was deeply concerned about issues such as air and WATER POLLUTION, HAZARDOUS WASTES and the careless use of PESTICIDES documented by American conservationist Rachel Carson in her 1962 book *Silent Spring*. Preservation of the natural environment had come to be seen as more than a question of recreation or preserving scenic beauty, but as being important to human survival.

The nature conservation movement received a boost from the environmental interest of the 1960s. The National Provincial Parks Association of Canada was established in 1963, the Sierra Club in Canada in 1970 and, in 1971, the Canadian Audubon Society and several of its affiliates established the Canadian Nature Federation, a national assembly of naturalist groups from across the country. Scientific biological associations and groups traditionally less active in conservation issues, such as game and fish associations, also increased their emphasis on environmental issues.

During this period, the concern for nature conservation centered on preserving wilderness and protecting unique areas or ecosystems as ecological reserves. Each province experienced a burst in the growth of local groups focusing on local conservation and environmental issues, and provincial naturalist and conservation federations became increasingly active and vocal. In a single decade, federal and provincial governments established ministries or departments of the environment, environmental protection Acts and environmental assessment legislation. Acts to protect endangered species, such as that passed in Ontario in 1971, were unique in the world because they sought to protect rare or endangered species of all plants and animals (including insects). In 1978 the intergovernmental Committee on the Status of Endangered Wildlife in Canada began to define a national list of species at risk.

In 1972 the UNITED NATIONS convened in Stockholm an international Conference on the Human Environment. Canada was well represented and, as a result, Canadian conservation concern became increasingly international through participation in agencies such as the Convention on International Trade in Endangered Species and the International Union for the Conservation of Nature and Natural Resources. Environmental concerns are now seen in a global context as awareness grows that all people depend on clean air and water and healthy ecosystems. MONTE HUMMEL

Reading: J. Foster, *Working for Wildlife: The Beginning of Preservation in Canada* (1978); J.I. Nicol, *The National Parks Movement in Canada* (1969).

Environmental Law is a relatively new field the boundaries of which are still vague. Some would include URBAN AND REGIONAL PLANNING laws in environmental law; others would limit the field to legislation designed to protect the natural environment. The latter definition is used here.

Constitutional Jurisdiction

In Canada the power to pass laws relating to the environment is divided between federal and provincial governments. The Constitution gives the federal government power to pass laws relating to FISHERIES, SHIPPING, interprovincial trade and commerce and CRIMINAL LAW. The federal residuary power to pass general legislation for the "Peace, Order, and Good Government of Canada" might also justify environmental legislation. Federal legislation enacted under these powers includes the Oil Pollution Prevention Regulations (under the Canada Shipping Act), the Arctic Waters Pollution Prevention Act, the Canada Water Act, the Clean Air Act, the Environmental Contaminants Act and the Fisheries Act.

Provincial powers cover all matters of a local nature and property and civil rights within the province. These powers give the provinces ample authority to pass most kinds of environmental laws. Provincial governments also "own" most natural RESOURCES. Provincial provisions for exploitation of these resources may include measures intended to protect the environment. Most provinces have now passed legislation concerning WATER and AIR POLLUTION. Provincial legislation also includes most WILDLIFE CONSERVATION AND MANAGEMENT regulations, creation of ecological reserves and wilderness areas, and environmental controls in FORESTRY and MINING. Migratory bird regulations, however, are administered federally, in co-operation with the US and Mexico. Other wildlife regulations increasingly involve interprovincial arrangements.

The Common Law

Historically, the LAW left private individuals to solve what are now considered pollution problems by negotiation or, if that failed, by suing one another in the COMMON-LAW courts. Judges developed 2 key principles for dealing with these problems. The first TORT of significance to environmental law is the nuisance action, which dates back to the early common law, long before Confederation. Any landowner has the right to sue another who injures him by creating a "nuisance," defined as a use of land that causes physical injury to neighbouring land or substantially and unreasonably interferes with the use and enjoyment of neighbouring lands. The second kind of tort, a specialized form of the first, arises from the principle established in the leading case *Rylands* v *Fletcher*, decided by the British House of Lords in 1866. It holds that people who bring dangerous substances onto their land and allow them to escape are strictly liable for resulting damages. For example, if your neighbour uses herbicides that escape and damage your gardens or crops, your neighbour will be liable to you for the damage, regardless of precautions taken. These 2 kinds of actions (nuisance actions and actions based on *Rylands* v *Fletcher*) are still the key legal means by which private persons may bring POLLUTION problems before the courts.

The torts discussed above do not provide an effective means of pollution control. Air pollution in your neighbourhood is probably caused by several factories. In order to sue one of them, you would be required to identify injuries that it caused and to prove that the specific factory caused them. Such proof would be very difficult to establish in most cases. Moreover, you would be able to sue only for the actual economic injury suffered, probably a small amount. Since the cost of a lawsuit is very high, suing the company under either of the torts outlined above would be economically foolish.

Since the late 1960s and early 1970s, Parliament and the provincial legislatures have passed numerous laws intended to protect the natural environment. One legal reference book, for example, contains 6 volumes devoted exclusively to federal and provincial legislation relating to the environment. It catalogues 132 separate statutes and numerous regulations passed under each of them, with over 364 separate enactments listed (*see* ENVIRONMENTAL AGENCIES). Obviously, regulating environmental quality is complex.

Water-Pollution Control

A key law in Canada pertaining to water pollution is the federal Fisheries Act, which prohibits discharge or deposition of substances harmful to fish if that discharge or deposition can contaminate waters where fish might be found. The term "fish" is used broadly to include all marine animals and eggs. Steep penalties are provided (in 1983, $50 000 for the first offence and $100 000 for any subsequent offence); each day on which the violation continues is considered a separate offence. Court decisions hold firms convicted in violation of this Act as strictly liable, ie, guilty regardless of intention. However, a firm will not be found guilty if it establishes "due diligence," ie, that it took reasonable steps to avoid causing the pollution. These provisions play a leading role in Canadian environmental law because of vigorous enforcement by the Environmental Protection Service of the federal Department of the environment. The Fisheries Act also gives certain regulatory powers to the federal Cabinet, which may pass regulations establishing standards with respect to certain industries. After standards have been established for a particular industry, any firm violating them is subject to the penalties outlined above. Standards have been established for the following industries: chlorine manufacturers, PETROLEUM refineries, PULP AND PAPER mills and metal-mining and finishing plants.

Other federal laws also concern water pollution. The Canada Water Act was intended to establish a basic framework for federal and provincial co-operation on water quality management. Instead the federal government has relied on the Fisheries Act and the provinces have relied on their own laws. Informal co-operation between officials of both levels of government seems to work well; consequently the Canada Water Act has been little needed. The federal International Boundary Waters Treaty Act implements a treaty between the US and Canada (entered into by Great Britain on behalf of Canada). The treaty established the INTERNATIONAL JOINT COMMISSION, which is empowered to report on water quality issues referred to it by the 2 nations. The IJC has been instrumental in establishing water quality standards and cleanup programs in the Great Lakes Basin. Water quality in the Territories is regulated under the federal Northern Inland Waters Act, which establishes territorial water boards and a licensing system for the use and diversion of water. It also controls disposal of waste in or near water. The Canada Shipping Act prohibits discharge of certain pollutants, notably oil, by ships operating in Canadian waters and includes elaborate safety standards (*see* HAZARDOUS WASTES). The Arctic Waters Pollution Prevention Act accomplishes the same objective for the Arctic. The Ocean Dumping Control Act regulates disposal of waste at sea.

All provinces have passed legislation regulating water pollution. Some follow an approach similar to the federal Fisheries Act. For example, Ontario prohibits discharge of contaminants that would impair water quality in the province. The minister responsible for the environment may order firms to clean up environmental pollution that they have caused. Some provinces, such as BC, use a licensing or permit approach to pollution control; ie, firms may not discharge any contaminants until they have received a permit from the appropriate agency. The firm must outline the system of pollution control that it intends to use. Officials base a permit decision on a comparison of the application with established environmental standards or guidelines. The permit sets limits to what the company may discharge, and usually specifies the kind of pollution-control equipment the company must use.

Air Pollution Control

The federal government has elected to play a leading role in development of standards for air pollution. The key legislation is the Clean Air Act. Its most important provisions allow the federal government to establish "ambient air quality objectives" or goals with respect to air pollution. The objectives specify "desirable" levels of concentration for most significant air contaminants. In themselves, these objectives have no legal effect, ie, it is not illegal to create pollution in excess of that allowed by the objectives. However, the federal objectives have been incorporated into most provincial schemes. When a company applies to provincial agencies for a permit to discharge contaminants to the air, most agencies check to ensure that federal objectives will not be exceeded.

Other sections of the Clean Air Act allow federal authorities to set legal standards of maximum allowable concentrations of certain air contaminants. This power is limited to situations where emission of substances (eg, arsenic, MERCURY, vinyl chloride) creates a significant danger to health or results in the violation of an international treaty.

Provincial air pollution control measures are similar to water pollution control schemes. A company planning to build a plant that will emit contaminants into the air must get a permit before beginning construction. Additional permits are required before the plant can begin operation. Air pollution standards or guidelines are set by provincial authorities, usually based on the federal objectives. Most provincial authorities also have the power to issue control orders to prevent significant air pollution.

Ecotoxicity and Impact Assessment

Long-term ecotoxicity also presents governments with difficult problems. More than 100 000 chemicals are now in commercial use, with over 300 new chemicals produced each year. Most have never been tested, and we know little about them, but inevitably they end up in the environment. Many are both toxic and persistent (ie, do not break down quickly) and build up in food chains. The challenge for government is to detect and regulate dangerous chemicals before they become a problem.

PESTICIDES and herbicides are regulated federally under the Pest Control Products Act. Basically, the Act imposes control over the manufacturing, importing, labelling and distribution of these products. Other toxic substances are regulated under the federal Environmental Contaminants Act, which allows the government to designate substances that are likely to pose a significant danger to the environment. The government may prohibit anyone from releasing these chemicals into the environment. In addition, the Act establishes a kind of early-warning system with respect to new chemical compounds. It requires anyone who manufactures or imports more than 500 kg of a chemical compound to report this to the minister of the environment. The report is made only once, when the chemical is first manufactured or imported, but it informs government of the new chemical and thus allows government to consider whether it should be regulated.

Environmental impact assessment is another tool that government uses to prevent or reduce environmental problems. An environmental impact assessment is usually required when a company plans to build a new mine, dam or other facility that is likely to have significant impact on the environment. The legal source of this requirement varies. Some provinces have statutes providing for environmental impact assessments. The federal Parliament has not passed a law requiring such assessments, but a Cabinet directive requires assessments before approval can be given to projects that come under federal regulatory control.

Environmental law has made great strides in the last decade, but many challenges remain. ACID RAIN, ecotoxicity and the transportation and disposal of hazardous wastes are among the unsolved problems. The development of offshore resources and the NORTH will require new legal approaches (*see* OCEAN INDUSTRIES). A number of aspects of private ownership versus public access to major developments need to be clarified. Few areas of the law are completely static; however, environmental law will probably continue to change with unusual rapidity as governments try new solutions to environmental problems created by development and new technologies (*see* MEGAPROJECTS). It will continue to offer a challenge for judges, lawmakers and lawyers. ROBERT T. FRANSON

Reading: D. Estrin and J. Swaigen, *Environment on Trial* (1978); Science Council of Canada, *Policies and Poisons* (1977).

Epidemic, a contagious disease that is prevalent in the the population at a given time. Although Canada has little overcrowding and benefits from alternating hot and cold seasons, it has not escaped the devastation of epidemic outbreaks. There are 2 main reasons: first, overcrowded ships linking America to Europe favoured the development of contagious disease, and ignorance of their causes and modes of transmission helped spread them into port cities; secondly, since native peoples had not experienced these diseases, they had no natural defences (*see* NATIVE PEOPLE, HEALTH).

Epidemics have a great social impact, preoccupying and disrupting whole communities and making severe demands on the abilities of individuals and their societies to cope with crisis. Epidemics also spur the development of control and prophylactic measures. Research has led to the development of medicines to control measles, mumps and numerous other contagious diseases. A polio outbreak in 1953 killed 481 Canadians and affected many more, but the following year, with Salk vaccine coming into general use, the death toll dropped to 157.

Smallpox The Indian population in contact with Europeans suffered sporadically after about 1616 from contagious diseases such as smallpox. The first epidemic manifestations appeared in 1635. In 1702-03 smallpox claimed 3000 lives in Québec City and undoubtedly as many among the Indians. (All numbers referring to victims in early Canada are approximate.) By 1736 smallpox had reached the western part of present-day Manitoba, affecting the Sioux (DAKOTA) and the Assiniboine. It flared up again in Québec, Montréal, Niagara and New England in 1755-57 and appeared in 1780 among Hudson Bay Indians. By 1783 it had reached the Indians of the West, killing much of the population. That year 1100 Québec City inhabitants died in a smallpox outbreak. By the end of the century, inoculation (the introduction beneath the skin of smallpox pus) had become a popular preventative method in Europe. Soon after, vaccination — more effective and less dangerous — appeared in N America.

In 1814 smallpox appeared in Halifax and Dartmouth, where the black population suffered greatly; in 1823 it erupted in Sault Ste Marie. Several times between 1830 and 1854 ships anchored at Québec reintroduced this terrible scourge. Montréal was also hit, especially in 1872-85. In 1885 vaccination became obligatory, but doctors disagreed over whether vaccination itself spread the disease. Many doctors were inept at vaccination, and their techniques caused severe reactions. The terrified population of Montréal refused to be vaccinated. On 18 Sept 1885 a riot broke out. The disease's death toll of 3164 finally sobered Montréalers into obeying the authorities. Smallpox thereafter remained endemic (ie, restricted in its distribution). The isolation of victims, obligatory vaccination and improved sanitation prevented further epidemics in that province. Epidemics killed dozens in Winnipeg in 1882, in BC in 1892, in Galt in 1902 and in Windsor in 1924. Of all the provinces, Québec has suffered most from smallpox.

Typhus first appeared in Canada in 1659; in 1685, 20 of 300 victims died. It may have struck again in 1718, and from 1740 to 1759 Québec suffered 9 epidemics, some perhaps of typhus. In 1746, of 3150 French soldiers sent to retake Port-Royal, 2400 died of typhus. The disease killed more than one-third of the region's MICMAC. Halifax was hit by a typhus epidemic which left 800 of the city's 1100 inhabitants dead. The disease spread throughout Nova Scotia and to Newfoundland and New Brunswick.

1847 was "the year of the typhus," when 9293 British immigrants died during the Atlantic crossing. Another 10 037 died at GROSSE-ÎLE, the quarantine station in the St Lawrence R below Québec, or in the hospitals of Québec, Montréal, Kingston and Toronto. Monuments commemorate 5424 dead on Grosse-Île, 3862 in Montréal, and those who died at sea, at CAP DES ROSIERS on the Gaspé coast. Two thousand died at Saint John, NB. The Canadian government requested that there be no more diseased emigrants sent to Canada.

Cholera In 1831 Asian cholera devastated Europe, and the Canadian government feared its introduction by European immigrants. New regulations forbade visits to ships in port. A sanitation committee was set up, quarantine laws were strengthened, and Grosse-Île was placed under military command. However, one boat was permitted to leave the quarantine station. On 9 June 1832, the day after its arrival in Québec, the first case of cholera appeared there. One week later, 259 people were ill. The epidemic ended in Sept, having caused 3451 deaths in Québec and almost 2000 in Montréal. Cholera also spread to Upper Canada. Over 6000 people died in all. Two years later, Irish immigrants reintroduced cholera at Québec. 913 died in Montréal, 342 in Upper Canada and others in the Maritimes.

In 1849 cholera came into Canada from the US through Kingston, killing hundreds. It struck again in 1851, 1852 and 1854. That year an epidemic in Saint John was soon checked. In all British North America, over 5000 people died in 1854. Sporadic outbreaks continued into the 1880s.

Influenza Some epidemics in early Canada were of INFLUENZA, and influenza was sometimes epidemic at the same time as was typhus or another disease. William OSLER listed 4 influenza epidemics in the 19th century: 1830-32, 1836-37, 1847-48 and 1889-90, each lasting 6-8 weeks. Mortality was low, about 1 in 1000, except during the last one, when pulmonary complications killed many victims. A serious epidemic (Spanish Flu) affected many parts of the world after WWI. By the end of 1919 Québec had registered 530 704 cases, 13 880 fatal. There were an estimated 300 000 cases in Ontario and 8705 deaths. In New Brunswick the flu caused 1394 deaths; in Saskatchewan, 3906. The mortality rate was lower in Alberta and British Columbia. The epidemic faded in 1921 and finally disappeared within the next 2 years. Since then scientific discoveries have rendered infectious diseases less deadly. Recent influenza epidemics, for example, have caused much sickness but few deaths.

MARCEL CADOTTE

Epp, Arthur Jacob, Jake, politician (b at St Boniface, Man 1 Sept 1939). The son of a Mennonite preacher, Epp graduated from U of Man in 1961 and then taught high school for 11 years in Steinbach, Man, where he was a town councillor 1970-72. Elected to the House of Commons for Provencher in 1972, he was minister of Indian affairs and northern development in the CLARK government 1979-80. Quiet and respected by his colleagues, Epp was Clark's most trusted parliamentary ally in the leadership battles that followed the election defeat of 1980, and he was prominent in opposing the TRUDEAU government's plan to patriate the constitution unilaterally. PM Brian MULRONEY named Epp minister of health and welfare and chairman of the Cabinet committee on social development in 1984.

NORMAN HILLMER

Equal Rights Association for the Province of Ontario (ERA) est June 1889 in Toronto, was in response to Québec's JESUITS' ESTATES ACT. The ERA criticized alleged Catholic interference in politics and politicians' subservience to the Roman Catholic Church. At first it agitated for disallowance of the Estates Act, and later, at the behest of Tory MP D'Alton MCCARTHY, extended its attack to include Catholic separate schools and French-language schooling in the North-West Territories and Manitoba as well as Ontario. This extension, coming on the eve of the 1890 Ontario election, alienated many Liberals, including ERA president Rev William Caven. The ERA won only one seat in Ontario, but the movement forced both political parties to adopt parts of its program. Weakened by the election, the ERA was spent by the 1891 federal contest, although McCarthy's rhetoric contributed to the acrimony of the developing MANITOBA SCHOOLS QUESTION. Some members later supported the Protestant Protective Association. J.R. MILLER

Equalization Payments are payments that the federal government makes to the poorer provinces. The monies come from Ottawa's general revenues and are unconditional transfers that can be spent as the recipient provinces please (*see also* TRANSFER PAYMENT). Their purpose is to reduce the horizontal imbalance among the provinces.

In general, 2 kinds of fiscal imbalance can arise in a federation — vertical and horizontal. The former is an imbalance between the 2 levels of government, federal and provincial. For instance, there is vertical imbalance when the responsibilities of the provinces are disproportionately large compared with their share of revenues. Such an imbalance can be remedied by a transfer of responsibilities to the federal government (eg, family allowances and UNEMPLOYMENT INSURANCE) or by a transfer of revenues from Ottawa to the provinces. By contrast, horizontal imbalance is a fiscal imbalance among the provinces themselves — the fact that some provinces have more sources of revenue and are therefore richer than other provinces. in this case, equalization payments help adjust the balance. The Constitution Act, 1982, states: "Parliament and the Government of Canada are committed to the principle of making equalization payments to ensure that provincial governments have sufficient revenues to provide reasonably comparable levels of public services and reasonably comparable levels of taxation."

The concept of equalization can be traced to the statutory subsidies in the CONSTITUTION ACT 1867 and more recently to the National Adjustment Grants recommended by the Royal Commission on DOMINION-PROVINCIAL RELATIONS as part of an overall reorganization of federal-provincial financial arrangements (*see also* INTERGOVERNMENTAL FINANCE; FEDERAL-PROVINCIAL RELATIONS). The first formal equalization program was introduced in 1957. The transfers were designed to ensure that per-capita revenues of all provinces from shared taxes (*see* TAXATION) — personal income taxes, corporate income taxes and succession duties — matched those of the wealthiest provinces, at that time BC and Ontario. In the first of the required 5-year revisions, the level up to which these transfers were equalized became the all-province average, rather than matching the wealthiest 2 provinces. As compensation, the recipient provinces were also guaranteed revenues equal to 50% of the all-province per-capita average of resource revenues. Throughout this time equalization payments rose, largely because the federal government transferred increasing proportions of the personal income tax to the provinces; from 10% in 1957 to 24% by 1967.

The comprehensive nature of the current equalization program dates from 1967. In effect, most of the categories of revenues collected by the provinces were equalized to the national average level. With one major exception (energy) and with some modifications, eg, increasing the number of revenue sources included, the system remained unchanged until 1982. Canada's equalization program became the most comprehensive and most generous in the world.

However, problems began to develop in 1973 with the increase in world energy prices. Maintaining full equalization of energy revenues and increasing domestic energy prices would have meant a tripling of total equalization flows and the inclusion of Ontario as a recipient province. Temporary steps were adopted to reduce the impact of energy on the system and in the 1977 revision only 50% of resource revenues could be calculated in the formula. In spite of this modification, Ontario still qualified for equalization payments over the 1977-82 period and was retroactively excluded from receiving payments by what has come to be known as the "personal income override," ie, essentially, no province whose per capita income exceeds the national average level is eligible for equalization.

In the 1982 version of the program provinces are eligible to receive sufficient equalization to raise their revenues from all provincial and local revenue sources to a level that is calculated by applying national average tax rates to the average per-capita tax bases of 5 designated provinces (Ontario, Québec, Saskatchewan, Manitoba and BC). As a result, Ontario will no longer qualify for payments and energy revenues will have less impact on equalization flows, chiefly because Alberta is not one of the 5 provinces.

Row 1 of the Table presents the values for equalization payments for the fiscal year 1981-1982. Québec receives more than 50% of the $4.162 billion total but on a per-capita basis its payments are actually the lowest ($361). Row 3 presents an index of the horizontal fiscal imbalance across the provinces. PEI has access to only 55% of the all-province revenue-raising capacity and about 25% of Alberta's capacity. Row 4 demonstrates how the equalization system restores horizontal balance. Except for the 3 westernmost provinces, the fiscal capacities of the provinces are now fairly uniform. This is even more the case once all federal transfers are included (row 5). Interestingly enough, Ontario has the lowest fiscal capacity of all provinces.

The 1982 system will undoubtedly be revised again. For example, if there are major changes in the financing of health care, university education or welfare, these changes will have to be incorporated into the equalization program, because the formal equalization program is only one of the instruments that can be used to ameliorate horizontal imbalance in the federation. Moreover, the continuing debate about whether equalization payments are too large, thereby inhibiting economic adjustment, or too small, thereby encouraging too much migration into the rich provinces, is likely to continue. While the philosophy underlying the program is rather clear, there is no obvious way to implement it, largely because there is no accepted definition of what constitutes "reasonably comparable public services" or "reasonably comparable tax rates." T.J. COURCHENE

Equalization and Provincial Revenues 1981/82:
(Source: Ontario Budget, 1982)

	Nfld	*PEI*	*NS*	*NB*	*Qué*	*Ont*	*Man*	*Sask*	*Alta*	*BC*	*Total*
Equalization ($ million)	427	103	509	414	2 320	–a	387	–	–	–	4 162
Equalization ($ per capita)	750	840	600	596	361	–a	376	–	–	–	176
Own source revenues (% of all-province revenue raising) b (Index)	59	55	66	66	78	94	79	112	217	111	100
Own source revenues plus equalization b (Index)	83	83	84	84	86	88	88	105	203	104	100
Own source revenues plus all transfers b (Index)	90	96	89	92	90	87	90	106	186	102	100

Note: a Ontario is excluded by the personal income override.
According to the formula, it would qualify as a recipient province for this year.
b per capita.

Equestrian Sports Today's major equestrian sports have developed principally from the 17th- and 18th-century activities of academic horsemanship, the fox hunt and the steeplechase, although the use of horses in competitions dates back at least to the ancient Olympic Games.

The first modern Olympic equestrian events, held in Paris in 1900, consisted of show jumping, the long jump and the high jump. Dressage and the three-day event were included with show jumping in Stockholm in 1912. The three-day event tests the all-round ability of horse and rider, and consists of dressage, endurance tests and show jumping, each on a separate day. These 3 disciplines have been an integral part of the summer Olympics since that time. Dressage (from the French term for the training of horses) consists of a series of movements of varying difficulty that test the harmonious development of the physique and ability of a horse. (Individual and team competitions at the Olympics feature the Grand Prix test, the most accomplished form of dressage.) In show jumping, horse and rider jump a set course of obstacles. Nation's Cups, which include the Olympics, are premier invitational international competitions for jumpers. Women have long been active in equestrian competition, but were not admitted to the Olympics until 1952; this is one of the few Olympic activities where women and men compete in the same events. Equestrian sports are also included in the Pan-American Games.

The international governing body, Fédération Equestre Internationale (FEI), was founded in 1921.

Equestrian activities have been part of Canada's sporting scene since the early 1800s. The Montreal Fox Hunt was established in the late 1820s, and the first steeplechase race in British N America was held in Montréal in 1840. By 1873 women were active participants in hunts. A hunters' and jumpers' stake was part of a Toronto hunt meeting in 1875, and by the late 1880s competitions in hunting and jumping classes were included in the programs of agricultural fairs across Canada. The first Dominion equestrian championships took place in Toronto in 1895, with several events for both men and women. The Royal Agricultural Winter Fair, held in Toronto every Nov since 1922, signalled the emergence of the Royal Horse Show, Canada's premier international equestrian event.

Equestrian sport in Canada is controlled by the Canadian Equestrian Federation (CEF), formed in 1977 from the National Equestrian Federation of Canada (sport) and the Canadian Horse Shows Assn (industry). CEF membership includes all 10 provincial associations and several affiliated ones. Horse shows in Canada are licensed by the CEF; in 1982 there were 450 recognized shows. The Canadian Equestrian Team is a semiautonomous committee of the CEF, responsible for the selection of Canada's international representatives in dressage, show jumping and the three-day event.

Canadian equestrians began making international appearances as early as 1909, when a team of jumpers entered the Military Tournament in the International Horse Show at Olympia, London. Canadian Army teams continued to compete abroad after WWI; Maj R.S. Timmis became the first Canadian to win an international contest, at the Toronto Coliseum (1923). In 1926, the first official Canadian jumping team entered the Royal Winter Fair and competed in Boston and London. The military monopoly of Canadian teams continued until the early 1950s, when reduced cavalry units and a broadened equestrian base resulted in an increase in civilian participants. Canada's first Olympic equestrian team (Helsinki, 1952) had a majority of civilian members. At the 1956 Olympic equestrian events, held in Stockholm, the Canadian three-day team (Brian Herbinson, John Rumble, and James ELDER) captured 3rd place. Canadian 3-day eventers have also performed well at the Pan-American Games, winning the team gold and individual bronze medals (Norman Elder) in 1959; the individual silver (Elder) in 1967; the team gold and individual silver (Clint Banbury) in 1971; and the team silver in 1975.

International competition in dressage has attracted Canadians since the early 1950s. In 1953, Dorinda Hall-Holland won the first FEI international jumping class event held at the Royal Horse Show. Christilot Hanson (now Bolyen), earned the distinction of membership on 4 consecutive Olympic teams. In 1972, she became the first Canadian to place in the top 12 international individual dressage riders, when she was 9th in the Olympics; in 1976, she was 7th. In Pan-American Games competition, she won gold medals in 1971 and 1975. In team dressage, Hanson, Cynthia Neale and Zoltan Sztehlo won the gold medal at the 1971 Pan-American Games; in 1975, Hanson-Bolyen teamed with Barbara Stracey and Lorraine Stubbs to place 2nd at the Games; and the Canadian team was 5th at the 1976 Montréal Olympics.

Canadian equestrians have garnered their highest honours in show jumping. In 1967, James DAY won the individual event at the Pan-American Games and the jumping team placed 3rd. On the final day of the 1968 Mexico City Olympics, James Day, James Elder and Thomas GAYFORD thrilled Canada by winning the team Grand Prix event. This same team won the N American Grand Prix and Royal Horse Show events in 1969, and the World Championship at La Baule, France, in 1970. 1971 saw Canadian jumpers win at the Pan-American Games (Terrance Millar, bronze), NY National Horse Show and Royal Horse Show. The 1972 Olympic team placed 6th; James Day was 4th in the individual event. Barbara Simpson Kerr placed 3rd in the Ladies World Show Jumping Championships in 1974, and the Canadian team won the Pan-American bronze medal in 1975. A highlight of the 1976 Olympics was Michel Vaillancourt's silver medal performance in individual jumping. The 1978 world championship 3-day event was won by Canada in Lexington, Kentucky. With the equestrian boycott of the 1980 Moscow Olympics, the designated alternative competition was the Nation's Cup in Rotterdam. Canadian jumpers won the team event and Ian Millar was the individual winner. Canadians were also successful in the 1980 Washington International Horse Show pair relay test; the NY National Horse Show Cavcotte Challenge (1980) and speed class (1981); and the Nation's Cup in Sydney, Australia (1982). Mario Deslauriers won the jumping World Cup in Sweden in 1984. An important development in Canadian show jumping was the construction, in 1975, of the show-jumping complex at Spruce Meadows, S of Calgary. The finest outdoor competition site in N America, it is ranked among the best in the world, and has brought a much-needed practice and competition facility to western Canada.

BARBARA SCHRODT

Erasmus, Georges, politician (b at Fort Rae, NWT 8 Aug 1948). Erasmus has been a central figure in NWT Indian territorial politics of the 1970s and 1980s (*see* NATIVE PEOPLE; LAND CLAIMS). After a period with the Company of Young Canadians he moved into native politics, becoming president of the DENE NATION (1976-83) and continuing as an active member of NWT and national native organizations thereafter.

BENNETT MCCARDLE

Erasmus, Peter, interpreter (b at Red River Colony [Man] 27 June 1833; d at Whitefish Lk, Alta 28 May 1931). Of Danish-Cree parentage, he studied to become an Anglican clergyman, but was drawn to the free life farther west. In 1855 he agreed to serve as interpreter for a Methodist missionary in the Ft Edmonton region and in 1858-59 he was interpreter and guide for the PALLISER EXPEDITION, working mainly with James HECTOR. Returning to the Methodists, he helped build a mission at Smoky Lk and then worked for 3 years with G.M. and J.C. MCDOUGALL. In 1865 he became a free trader, trapper and hunter around Whitefish Lk. Having acted as an interpreter for Treaty No 6 at Forts Carlton and Pitt in 1876, he was employed by the Indian Dept, off and on, for the rest of his life. A man of great influence, he encouraged the Saddle Lk Indians to remain loyal during the NORTH-WEST REBELLION of 1885. His autobiography *Buffalo Days and Nights* was published in 1976.

HUGH A. DEMPSEY

Eric the Red, Eirikr Thorvaldsson, explorer (*fl* 985). According to the *Saga of Eric the Red,* he spent 3 years of outlawry exploring the coast of Greenland and in 985 AD established 2 settlements there. Eric's son LEIF ERICSSON was likely the first European to set foot in N America.

JAMES MARSH

Erickson, Man, Village, pop 540 (1981c), inc 1953, is located 18 km S of RIDING MTN NATIONAL PARK and 73 km N of Brandon. Swedish and Norwegian immigrants were among the first settlers in the region, taking up homesteads in the Otter Lk/Rolling R area on a reserve called New Scandinavia, est 1885 as part of a campaign to attract Scandinavian immigrants to Canada. The nearest railway was 30 km away, and extensive clearing was required before farming could begin. But the timber, soil, grazing, water and fishing resources were promising. A disastrous fire and internal dissension hampered progress. Government assistance, a sawmill operation, and railway and road construction work saved the village. In 1908 it was named after Albert Erickson, its first postmaster. Today it is a local service centre for grain, dairy and mixed farms in a region that is also noted for its recreation and a rainbow trout research program.

D.M. LYON

Erickson, Arthur Charles, architect (b at Vancouver 14 June 1924). Erickson studied at UBC and McGill and completed his architectural training in 1950. Army service took him to Asia, and after graduation he travelled in Europe and the Middle East. In partnership with Geoffrey Massey he began private practice in Vancouver in 1953; their success in the design competition for SFU in 1963 brought them international attention. A series of major commissions followed, including theme buildings at EXPO 67 in Montréal; the MacMillan Bloedel office tower in Vancouver in 1969; the Canadian Pavilion, Expo 70, Osaka, Japan; U of Lethbridge, 1971; the Museum of Anthropology at UBC 1971-77; the provincial government offices and courthouse (and Vancouver Art Gallery) complex, begun in 1973; the Bank of Canada, Ottawa, 1980; and Roy Thomson Hall, Toronto, 1982. Erickson has also received numerous commissions from Middle Eastern countries, the US and S America, and was chosen architect for the new Canadian embassy in Washington, DC.

Perhaps the first Canadian architect to be widely known by the international public, he has gained high popular regard by his ability to create places of great drama with apparently simple means. A consistent theme through many of his buildings is the simple frame to create a welcoming and sheltering portal, a motif found in West Coast Indian building. Such restricted means, and muted colours, are used in his best buildings to create a sense of occasion, and places that are striking in themselves as objects in the landscape. If there is a weakness it is an emphasis on the grand gesture, unsupported by details that extend the conception of the building on close experience and prolonged acquaintance. Nonetheless, Erickson's work is among the most accomplished and satisfying of any recent Canadian architecture.

MICHAEL MCMORDIE

Arthur Erickson, Vancouver architect, shown here with a photo of Toronto's Roy Thomson Hall, which he designed (*courtesy Canapress*).

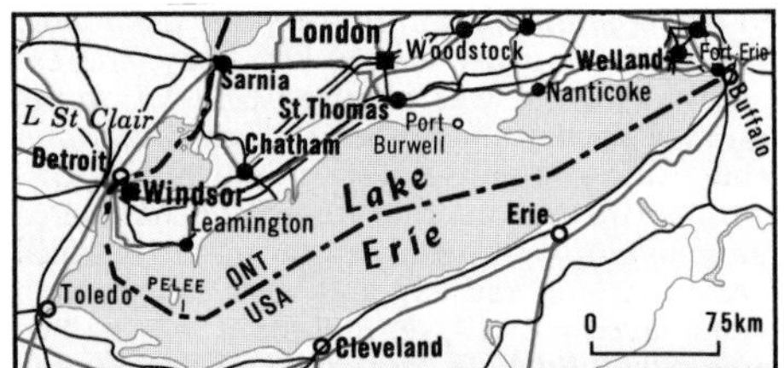

Erie, Lake, 25 700 km², of which 12 800 km² lie in Canada, elev 173.3 m; maximum dimensions are 388 km long, 92 km wide and 64 m deep. The shallowest of the 5 GREAT LAKES, it receives most of its waters from Lk HURON via the DETROIT R. Other major inflowing streams are the Maumee and Cuyahoga rivers in Ohio, and the Grand R in Ontario. The lake outflows through the NIAGARA R at FORT ERIE, falling almost 100 m at NIAGARA FALLS, and thence into Lk ONTARIO, and is joined to Lk Ontario by the WELLAND CANAL. The lake drainage basin measures 58 800 km² in area, and is home to over 15 million people in Canada and the US, making it the most densely populated of all the Great Lakes basins. Buffalo, NY; Erie, Pa; Toledo and Cleveland, Ohio, are large, heavily industrialized cities on the US side. The Canadian shore is relatively unpopulated, with NANTICOKE the only sizable community. Industrial and municipal wastes have polluted the lake and rendered the lower waters devoid of oxygen during summer.

Lk Erie is the southernmost of the Great Lks (lat similar to northern California), and this, combined with its relatively shallow depth and large nutrient inflows from the urban areas and intensively cultivated farmlands making up its watershed, contributes to a high level of biological productivity. Despite pollution and LAMPREY infestations, the lake supports the largest commercial fishery in the Great Lks, yielding more than 20 000 t annually, consisting mainly of yellow perch. Warm summers, excellent beaches and well-preserved coastal marshes make Erie a favourite rendezvous for summer recreationists and wildlife enthusiasts (*see* POINT PELEE NATIONAL PARK). Bird-watchers flock to these areas to take advantage of the lake's position on the major migration routes. Although Erie freezes over most winters, it remains an important part of the ST LAWRENCE SEAWAY system.

Like most of the other Great Lks, Erie occupies a glacier-deepened river drainage system, in which the less resistant shales and limestones of the Paleozoic rock column were differentially eroded to create the huge elongated depressions in which the lakes formed. These Pleistocene glaciers, hundreds of metres thick, periodically occupied much of the basin and left behind extensive deposits of clay and silt, which now comprise much of the rapidly eroding shoreline. More resistant dolomites form the shoreline only in the extreme eastern and western portions of the lake.

The N shore was frequented intermittently by NEUTRAL Indians, who lived around the Niagara Peninsula and along the Niagara Escarpment. Louis JOLLIET was likely the first European to sight the lake (1669). The decisive naval battle at PUT-IN-BAY was fought on the lake during the War of 1812. Called Lac du Chat by the French explorers, the lake came to be called after the Erie, an Iroquoian tribe inhabiting the S shore.

J.P. COAKLEY AND M.N. CHARLTON

Ermine, *see* WEASEL.

Erosion is the collective result of all processes that pick up and transport material at or very close to the Earth's surface. The main erosional agents are water, WIND, ICE and gravity, each of which acts in several ways.

Water erosion, the most complex form, encompasses rain splash, unconcentrated surface erosion by sheetwash or rill wash, channel erosion in rivers or in gullies flowing only during storms, erosion by water flowing through surface materials, and erosion in the shallow zone of lakes and oceans by tides, currents and wave action. Rain splash is rather specialized and is effective only on agricultural fields and exposed loose materials; otherwise, water erosion can be classified as chemical or physical. Chemical erosion occurs primarily when material is dissolved and transported by water. It depends on such factors as water chemistry, surface materials and temperature. Most commonly its effects are hidden, but up to 70% of the load carried by many rivers is in solution. Where the surface is formed of soluble rocks such as limestone, KARST LANDFORMS develop. In Canada excellent examples occur in the Nahanni region, YT, and in many parts of the Rocky Mts.

Physical water erosion occurs when moving water achieves sufficient velocity to pick up or move loose particles or to pry fragments loose from SOIL or bedrock. In some rivers this is continual, but in many perennial streams and in gully erosion, sheetwash and rilling, such velocities occur only during rainstorms or snowmelt; therefore, erosion is closely controlled by patterns of storm activity. This is also true in lakes and oceans, but the key factor in these cases is wind force, which generates severe wave action. Water erosion rates differ greatly with location, depending on the mixture of processes and on the nature of surface materials. Available data on sediment loads in Canadian rivers show a range from below 2 to over 400 tonnes/km²/year. If equally distributed, the upper rate (found in north central BC) would correspond to a surface lowering of approximately 0.1 mm/year. The actual rate of surface lowering in most parts of Canada is much lower, but in some highly erodible areas, such as the Alberta BADLANDS, measurements have shown surface lowering rates as high as 4 mm/year.

Wind erosion acts in essentially the same manner as does physical water erosion but, because air is less dense than water, higher wind velocities are required to effect erosion. Theoretically, almost any material is vulnerable but, in practice, wind speed is rarely high enough to move material larger than sand grains, and these only if dry and unbound by vegetation. Significant wind erosion is, therefore, confined almost entirely to coastal areas, to glacial outwash plains and agricultural fields, where vegetation is minimal. The most severe wind erosion recorded in Canada occurred in the southern Prairies during the prolonged DROUGHT of the 1930s. Vulnerable soils were disturbed by tillage and blown in immense clouds, creating the "Dust Bowl." Erosion was sporadic and varied but surface lowering of 0.5 m in one storm was not uncommon.

Ice Erosion As ice moves over the surface or is constricted through valleys it can pluck protruding or loose material away from adjacent surfaces and transport it on or in the GLACIER. This matter joins with material falling onto the glacier and into crevasses to form an englacial MORAINE, which makes the ice an extremely effective abrasive agent capable of planing off surfaces and scouring out valleys. Valley or alpine glaciers tend to increase local relief by scouring valleys while adjacent peaks protrude above the ice. Continental glaciers spreading over the complete surface tend to reduce relief. Most of Canada was covered by ice during the Pleistocene epoch (2.5 million-10 thousand years ago) and excellent examples of both effects are found in many areas. Although glacial erosion now occurs only in the Cordillera and the Arctic, residual features formed during the Pleistocene still dominate most landscapes.

Gravity is an important erosional agent because it acts continually on all sloping surfaces. Gravitational stress at any location does not vary, but the resistance of surface materials does alter, particularly in response to moisture changes. Many of the most dramatic movements tend, therefore, to follow prolonged periods of wet weather. By definition, material can only be moved relatively short distances to the base of the original slope, but very large amounts of material can be moved in a few minutes. Among the classic examples of major gravitational erosion in Canada are the FRANK SLIDE, Alta (1903), the Hope Slide, BC (1965), and numerous quick clay slides in the old marine deposits of the CHAMPLAIN SEA in the St Lawrence Valley (*see* LANDSLIDE).

R.B. BRYAN

Escarpment, steep or vertical cliff which usually extends over a considerable distance. The most common type of escarpment occurs where more resistant strata form a cap rock over easily eroded rocks. As EROSION takes place, the lower rock erodes more rapidly so that the cliff remains very steep. In the NIAGARA ESCARPMENT, which continues over some 645 km from Tobermory, Ont, to New York state, the resistant cap rock, formed by the Lockport Dolomite, overlies several weaker shale and sandstone beds. Some escarpments are formed by tectonic activity (ie, deformational movements of the Earth's crust or volcanism), particularly uplift along fault lines, and are distinguished as fault scarps. An excellent example is in the Aspy Valley of northern Cape Breton I, NS. The angle of the fault scarp is controlled by the inclination of the fault plane and is often more gentle than that of the classic escarpment formed by strata of differing resistance. The latter can vary, however, from the flat, vertically sided feature, eg, the Niagara Escarpment, to a cuesta (with a steep scarp face and gentle dip face), or to a hogback ridge in which both faces are equally inclined. *See* PLATE TECTONICS.

R.B. BRYAN

Esker, narrow, sinuous ridge of gravel and sand emplaced during glacial retreat by the deposition of sediments from meltwater streams flowing in tunnels on, through or, most frequently, under glacial ice. Eskers were deposited in segments, each ending in a delta formed in a proglacial lake (ie, a lake formed beside the margin of a GLACIER). As the wall of ice melted, esker sediments collapsed to the angle of repose (ie, the steepest slope at which loose material will stand, about 30°). The sides are generally covered by finer, proglacial lake sediments. Eskers may run for tens of kilometres and are generally 1-2 km wide. The sediments may reach 50 m deep in depressions. Sediment grain size varies from sand to coarse gravel, suggesting that meltwater in the ice tunnel was under high pressure. One of the world's best areas to observe eskers is the mining region of NW Québec, where many eskers, generally aligned N-S, were emplaced during the last deglaciation. Eskers do not generally survive from one GLACIATION to another. They are features of a deglaciation phase and are usually destroyed when ice readvances over them. Their orientation is affected by various factors, but generally they are roughly parallel to the ice flow and the general slope of the subglacial topography. However, as they have been reported to cross divides between valleys, meltwater pressure may also play a role in their orientation. Eskers form good, confined aquifers (water-bearing strata) when covered by fine, impermeable sediments. Esker sediments can be used to locate ore deposits upstream from the ore-indicator-bearing esker bed (*see* PROSPECTING).

PIERRE LASALLE

Eskimo, a group of N American aborigines, forming part of the Eskimoan linguistic stock. They inhabit the coasts and islands of arctic N America, from eastern Greenland and Labrador to western Alaska and Siberia. The name "Eskimo" is said to come from the Abenaki word

Esquimantsic, or from *Ashkimequ*, the Chippewa equivalent, signifying "eaters of raw flesh." The Eskimo of arctic Canada call themselves INUIT, meaning "people." They constitute a distinct physical type, whose language, Inuktitut, and customs are relatively homogeneous throughout the arctic and subarctic zones. Ethnological groups can be distinguished on the basis of territory and are recognized by the Inuit. *See also* NATIVE PEOPLES, ARCTIC. RENÉ R. GADACZ

Eskimo Lakes, 880 km², lie along the southern edge of the Tuktoyaktuk Pen, NWT, and drain into Liverpool Bay on the Beaufort Sea. They are tidal lakes, with tide heights averaging 2 m, and occupy a fault zone separating geological blocks. The lakes are almost partitioned into several separate water bodies by bow-shaped, nearly parallel, ridgelike peninsulas that project across them from N and S shores. These relic ice-pushed ridges narrow the lakes to less than 50 m in places and are highest at the inland end of the lakes, reaching heights of 30 m. Inland the lakes are shallow (10 m) and flat bottomed, deepening towards the outlet to 66 m with uneven lake beds. DOUG FINLAYSON

Eskimo Point, NWT, UP, pop 1022 (1981c), is located on the W coast of HUDSON BAY, 1086 air km E of YELLOWKNIFE. The site was a summer camp for the inland Pallirmiut INUIT of S Keewatin until the 1900s. It acquired permanent settlement status when an HBC trading post and a Roman Catholic mission were built in the early 1920s. Today the community is one of the major settlements of the eastern Arctic. It is known for its Inuit Cultural Institute, which was established to preserve and encourage Inuit culture. The community has the largest number of independent local entrepreneurs in the Keewatin. ANNELIES POOL

Esposito, Philip Anthony, hockey player (b at Sault Ste Marie, Ont 20 Feb 1942). He began his NHL career in 1963 with the Chicago Black Hawks and was traded to the Boston Bruins in 1967. He and Bobby ORR led the Bruins to STANLEY CUP victories in 1970 and 1972, but his best season was 1970-71 when he scored 76 goals, a record that stood until Wayne GRETZKY's 92-goal performance of 1981-82. Although not a fast or graceful skater, Esposito's large and immovable presence in front of the opposition net and his ability to score from all angles won him the ART ROSS TROPHY 5 times (1969, 1971-74), and the HART TROPHY in 1969 and 1974. He was the inspirational leader of Team Canada during the dramatic CANADA-SOVIET HOCKEY SERIES of 1972. He was traded to the New York Rangers in 1975 and retired in 1982, second only to Gordie HOWE in both goals (717) and points (1590) on the all-time NHL scoring list. DEREK DRAGER

Esquimalt, BC, District Municipality, pop 15 870, area 1000 ha, inc 1912, is located on the SE coast of VANCOUVER I adjacent to VICTORIA. It is the most established residential area of Metropolitan Victoria and its excellent harbour has made it an important Pacific coast naval establishment. It is governed by a mayor and 6 aldermen, and shares some responsibilities with the Capital Regional Dist. SALISH Indians first occupied the site ("a place gradually shoaling"). James DOUGLAS surveyed the harbour 1843, and later purchased land in the area from the Indians for the HBC. Esquimalt's quiet development was shattered by the GOLD RUSH of the late 1850s. By the 1880s rapid growth was occurring through the building of Royal Navy dry docks, the construction of the Esquimalt to Nanaimo railway, and the founding of a military base at Work Point.

Of the region's original economic supports, agriculture and the military, only the latter has remained important. A large Canadian Forces Base in Esquimalt and shipyards, dry docks and attendant enterprises are prominent in the economy. Several structures inside or adjacent to the naval dockyard have been listed as heritage buildings. St Paul's Anglican Church (1866) contains relics and plaques covering over a century of naval history. Some of Esquimalt's pleasant residential neighbourhoods make effective use of the community's extensive waterfront with its bays and beaches. ALAN F.J. ARTIBISE

Reading: F.V. Longstaff, *Esquimalt Naval Base: A History of its Work and Defences* (1941); A.C. Wurtele, *Esquimalt, 1912-1962* (1962).

Essay in English An essay is a brief, discursive piece of prose which develops a single theme from a personal point of view, following the prototype established by French essayist Michel de Montaigne (1533-92). The earliest Canadian resemblance to this form emerged during the 19th century in the Maritimes, where the primary intention of writers such as Joseph HOWE and George STEWART was usually descriptive or hortatory. JOURNALISM has always provided the greatest stimulus to the essay in Canada. In *The Week* (Toronto, 1883-96) appeared articles discussing current political or religious questions. Those by Goldwin SMITH or his private secretary Theodore A. Haultain, though polished, have less in common with the traditional form than the unpretentious and intimate "Saunterings" of Sara Jeannette DUNCAN. Yet the only contributor who really deserves the title "essayist" is Archibald MacMechan. His collections, *The Porter of Bagdad, and Other Fantasies (1901)* and *The Life of a Little College, and Other Papers* (1914), contain whimsical reveries, written in a simple and restrained style, recreating an innocent era of nature and art reminiscent of essays by Victorian writers John Ruskin and Matthew Arnold, whom he admired.

Physician Sir William OSLER, concerned that his medical students might miss "those gentler influences which make life worth living," enunciated in *Aequanimitas* (1904) with clarity and elegant aphorism the need to harmonize the humanities and sciences. Bliss CARMAN's *The Kinship of Nature* (1904), although graceful and lyrical, treats his recurring didactic theme of self-betterment and personal harmony. Sir Andrew MACPHAIL, a medical professor at McGill University and editor of *The* UNIVERSITY MAGAZINE, published *Essays in Puritanism* (1905), *Essays in Politics* (1909) and *Essays in Fallacy* (1910), which are distinguished by their pungency and winsome vigour. Of less literary interest are the moralizing articles of journalist Thomas O'Hagan, which originally appeared in the *Catholic Register* and were published as *Chats by the Fireside* (1911).

In Pastures Green (1915), *The Red Cow and her Friends* (1919) and *Around Home* (1925) are collections of another journalist, Peter McArthur, from his farm column in the Toronto *Globe*. His unpretentious, humorous and often rambling depiction of Ontario pastoral life reflects the freshness and earthiness of the countryside. The simple pleasures of natural settings were also celebrated by Toronto lawyer William Hume Blake, who describes angling in the Laurentians in *Brown Waters, and Other Sketches* (1915), *In a Fishing Country* (1922) and *A Fisherman's Creed* (1923). Contemplative and engaging, he represents the challenges of fishing and the hospitality and skill of the Québecois guides as epitomizing the virtues of the good life.

Essays and Literary Studies (1916) by Stephen LEACOCK, although primarily humorous, sometimes present serious themes. Deceptively simple in structure and highly individual in their point of view, his satiric pieces reflect the advance made by the essay form in Canada since its early didactic and descriptive precursors.

The *Canadian Forum* (fd 1920) encouraged the journalistic essay. Perhaps its most eloquent contributor was scholar Douglas Bush, who displayed a gift for witty phrasing and apt allusion, along with a genial irreverence for some of his colleagues' preoccupation with a national literature and identity. W.D. Woodhead and John D. Robins wrote in a similarly whimsical vein but with more overt humour. The essays of other contributors such as Barker FAIRLEY, Margaret Fairley, John Macnaughton, Frederick Philip GROVE, E.K. Broadus, B.K. Sandwell, Frank UNDERHILL and A.J.M. SMITH treated art, the humanities, criticism, contemporary poetry, education and socialist politics with an academic rather than familiar tone.

That the critical spirit continued to dominate the form is indicated in the title of Malcolm ROSS's anthology covering much of this period, *Our Sense of Identity* (1954). William Arthur Deacon, for example, moved from the diversified whimsy and brisk humour of *Pens and Pirates* (1923) to the frankly critical *My Vision of Canada* (1933). Lucid and scholarly essays on people, books and ideas were also being published by Maurice Hutton, John Charles Robertson and Gilbert Norwood, professors at University of Toronto.

Less detached and contemplative are the collections of newspaper feature writers, yet many of these in their use of description, anecdote, reminiscence and humour approach the timeless quality of the essay. Noteworthy among them are *One Thing After Another* (1948) by C.B. Pyper and *From Our Town* (1959) by Jack Scott. The most widely read columnists were the humorists. The sketches of Peter Donovan from *Saturday Night* were collected in *Imperfectly Proper* (1920). Newton MacTavish of *Canadian Magazine* published *Thrown In* (1923), recollections of a rural childhood which are amplified in the posthumous *Newton MacTavish's Canada* (1965). In 1959 *The Best of Gregory Clark* was culled from his entertaining personal anecdotes in *Weekend Magazine*. Eric Patrick NICOL has recorded refreshingly satirical anecdotes, some of which were collected from columns in the Vancouver *Province*, in illustrated books including *The Roving I* (1950) and *Canada Cancelled Because of Lack of Interest* (1977). Common sense, tolerance and gentle amusement at human foibles permeate the style of these journalists.

A significant journalistic theme of the period was the return to nature. Cecil Francis Lloyd describes its attraction in *Sunlight and Shadow* (1928). His *Malvern Essays* (1930), modelled after Montaigne's, express a wistful if weary acceptance of "The Burden of Existence" in an easy, graceful style. More in the tradition of American writer Henry David Thoreau were Harry Lutz Symons in *Friendship* (1943) and *Canadian Forum* contributors and academics E.K. Broadus (*Saturday and Sunday*, 1935) and John D. Robins (*The Incomplete Anglers*, 1943). Roderick HAIG-BROWN, a fisherman in the Waltonian tradition, describes in exact detail outdoor delights and their value for the individual in *A River Never Sleeps* (1946) and *Measure of the Year* (1950). His *Fisherman's Spring* (1951), *Fisherman's Winter* (1954) and *Fisherman's Summer* (1959) as well as his posthumous *Writings and Reflections* (1982) provide in a thoughtful, quiet tone a pattern of civilized life. Kenneth McNeil Wells collected into 4 books a series of articles from the Toronto *Telegram* chronicling life at *The Owl Pen* (1947) farm, which was *Up Medonte Way* (1951), and was particularly successful in transcribing Ontario rustic idiom.

Various writers used the essay to increase the awareness or appreciation of the "average reader." B.K. Sandwell, editor of *Saturday Night*, employs Swiftian irony in *The Privacity Agent and Other Modest Proposals* (1928) to contrast the 20th century with happier past eras and a utopia where reason, common sense and justice prevail. F.P. Grove in *Over Prairie Trails* (1922) describes natural scenery with cosmic implications, tracing changing moods and emotions during 7 journeys over one Manitoba road. His *The Turn of the Year* (1923) is more forbidding and less personal. Morley CALLAGHAN, in monthly commentaries for *New World* magazine (1940-48) and pieces in *Saturday Night, Maclean's* and other journals, dealt with topical themes from an imaginative point of view. In *Cross Country* (1949) Hugh MACLENNAN treats the Canadian character in a cultivated style marked by personal memories and biases. His *Thirty & Three* (1954), *Scotchman's Return* (1960) and *The Other Side of Hugh MacLennan* (1978) attempt to define and reconcile transition with the world around him.

Novelist, dramatist and editor Robertson DAVIES ignores the "average reader" as being incapable of understanding "good talk." In *Diary* (1947) and *Table Talk* (1949) are portrayed the tastes and opinions of the fictional Samuel Marchbanks, who like Dr Samuel Johnson "loved tea, conversation and pretty women, and had not much patience with fools." *A Voice from the Attic* (1960) pursues the theme that reading as a private, individual art is the mark of the cultivated mind and the central activity of the good life; and *Samuel Marchbanks' Almanack* (1967) continues Davies's witty and critical examination of Canadian society. Somewhat different from the development traced here are the essays of arctic explorer Vilhjalmur STEFANSSON. The logical and even philosophical structure of his pieces in *Adventures in Error* (1936) conceals an ironical exploration of man's mental processes which affirms that "errors" of the human imagination are true and that human desires, even when self-deceptive, are important.

Northrop FRYE has maintained the tradition of the scholarly essayists in volumes such as *The Educated Imagination* (1963), *The Modern Century* (1967), *The Bush Garden* (1971) and *Spiritus mundi* (1976). In muscular and witty prose he provocatively explores literature, education and other aspects of contemporary society. George WOODCOCK, a less academic but wider ranging "man of letters," displays an easy competence in the essay form in such books as *The World of Canadian Writing* (1980). Established writers of fiction have always found the genre challenging. In *Hunting Tigers Under Glass* (1968), *Shovelling Trouble* (1972) and *The Great Comic Book Heroes* (1978) Mordecai RICHLER expatiates in a sceptical and often disparaging tone on such themes as the Jewish experience, "Why I write" and the changing national scene. Hugh HOOD, in *The Governor's Bridge is Closed* (1973), expresses with clarity and good humour his cheerful belief in Canadian life and culture. Margaret LAURENCE collected in *Heart of a Stranger* (1976) pieces published between 1964 and 1975. Like Gabrielle ROY's essays in *The Fragile Lights of Earth* (1982), a translation from the French covering the period 1942-70, they are perceptive insights into the writer's world and social history.

Running to Paradise (1962) by Kildare Dobbs (although largely autobiographical reminiscence), *Reading the Time* (1968) and *Pride and Fall* (1981) are marked by a versatile style befitting the wide range of topics treated. Norman Ward in *Mice in the Beer* (1960) and *The Fully Processed Cheese* (1964) displays an attitude of tolerance and amusement toward topical themes and toward his academic colleagues. The posthumous collection of contributions by Ralph ALLEN to the *Toronto Star* and *Maclean's* entitled *The Man from Oxbow* (1967) contains a number of balanced and relaxed pieces. *Crisis at the Victory Burlesk* (1968) is a collecton of Robert FULFORD's early journalism, which is less reflective than his regular essays in *Saturday Night*. The waspish miscellanies of Richard Needham, originally published in the *Globe and Mail*, have appeared in several collections, including *Needham's Inferno* (1966) and *The Wit & Wisdom of Richard Needham* (1977). Columnist Allan Fotheringham has collected a number of his acerbic, irreverent political essays in *Malice in Blunderland* (1982). Another exemplar of *persona* journalism is Harry Bruce, whose collection of *Toronto Star* columns, *The Short Happy Walks of Max MacPherson* (1968), combines history and description in a chatty fashion.

Neurosurgeon Wilder PENFIELD, emulating his mentor Osler, in *The Second Career* (1964) and *Second Thoughts* (1970) reflects engagingly on the need for "eternal vigilance and resolute action" in a changing world. Economist John Kenneth GALBRAITH gives an ironic and acerbic account of his boyhood in *The Scotch* (1964), and presents the viewpoint of a perceptive and versatile diplomat in *A Contemporary Guide to Economics, Peace, and Laughter* (1971).

Folksy and nostalgic memories of rural simplicity form H. Gordon Green's central theme in a number of books, including *A Time to Pass Over* (1962) and *With My Sock Feet on the Oven Door* (1975). Harry J. BOYLE exploits the same vein, beginning with *Mostly in Clover* (1961) and continuing through *Memories of a Catholic Boyhood* (1973). Another rambling variation of the pastoral mode is *The Battle of Mole Run and Other Offenses* (1967) by Howard T. Mitchell. A more enduring presentation of farm life is *Western Windows* (1967) by Bruce HUTCHISON. In *The Far Side of the Street* (1976) his informal essays cover 50 years of change in Canadian life.

In a provocative exploration of semantic and kinetic aspects of language, *The Medium is the Massage* (1967), Marshall MCLUHAN developed a type of *essai concret*, involving a mosaic of verbal and visual, spatial and durational material, in what he called a "collide-oscope of interface situations" without linear sequence. His unique technique has been assimilated rather than imitated by other writers.

During the second half of the 20th century the Canadian essay continues to be influenced chiefly by journalism, although television's slickness has made it difficult for the columnist to maintain freshness. The increased tempo and pragmatic urgency of technological life have militated against undogmatic attention to theme and easy discursiveness, which survive mainly in reminiscences of more relaxed eras.

See SHORT FICTION; LITERATURE IN ENGLISH.

A.B. CONRON

Essay in French The hallmark of the French Canadian essay is that it is both personal (or subjective) and creative. The essay stands apart from any writing that claims to offer an objective explanation of reality or explores a preordained, objective truth that is assumed to be valid for any time and place. The essayist is not at the service of the truth, a cause or a class: he proclaims and defends his own irreducible sincerity and recognizes that, while his experience and the account he gives of it are subjective, they may still serve as a model to others. The essay may range from popular to scholarly treatment of a subject. The writer may just as easily deal with a scientific subject as with a theological, literary or political one, and his tone may be polemical or discursive. The literary quality of an essay, as of any other genre, rests in the quality of the writing, in the capacity of the author to interpret the world about him, to reconstruct it and awaken in the reader as much admiration and wonder for the interpretation as for the reality being interpreted. ANDRÉ GIROUARD

Pamphlets and Polemics

Philosophical and political essays, pamphlets, manifestos and polemic exchanges are all arguably forms of the essay. When placed in their original contexts, they afford excellent opportunities to observe sociopolitical and cultural phenomena of their eras. Polemical texts and pamphlets are not always self-evidently critical in nature, and they are made all the more effective when the author's indignation is camouflaged. A complete polemic structure is to be found as an undercurrent in accounts of early voyages, in private and administrative correspondence and in the writings of religious orders in NEW FRANCE. Generally addressed to authorities in the mother country, these texts crystallize metropolitan antagonisms around Canadian situations. They contain a double contradiction, expressing the New World in the linguistic and cultural codes of the mother country, which is itself replete with antagonisms such as those between Récollets and Jesuits or, at another level, proponents of evangelization and champions of exploitation.

The texts of Cartier, Champlain, Lescarbot, Biard and Sagard, and the JESUIT RELATIONS (*see* EXPLORATION AND TRAVEL LITERATURE IN FRENCH), should be read in the context of the actual conditions in which they were written (literary strategies, thinly veiled battles to obtain local credit, privilege and power). So, too, should one read the protests of Canadian naval personnel against French officers during the SEVEN YEARS WAR. Essays of protest continued to be written after the Conquest, and pamphlets regarding the GUIBORD AFFAIR (1869-74) and the battle between Mgr BOURGET and the INSTITUT CANADIEN carried the genre into the late 19th century. Parliamentary battles in the Canadas gave scope to the pamphleteer and essayist as well: oratorical jousts were taken up and exaggerated in the polemics between francophone and anglophone newspapers (eg, in the *Anti-Gallic Letters*).

Striking examples of the use of polemical essays in political settings include exchanges during the MANITOBA SCHOOLS QUESTION (1890-96), the anticommunist campaigns of the 1930s (*Pamphlets de Valdombre*, 1936-43) and the CONSCRIPTION debates during the 2 world wars. In 1960 Jean-Paul Desbiens, in *Les* INSOLENCES DU FRÈRE UNTEL, and Gilles Leclerc, in *Journal d'un inquisiteur*, took up the language debate and other matters with vehemence. The authors offer pragmatic commentary on current events, using this as a device to discredit the targets of their scorn, hoping thus to alter the attitudes of the reading public. Since the QUIET REVOLUTION there has been an explosion of polemical writings about independence, unionism and native people by leftist individuals, groups and magazines. In the early 1980s feminism held the limelight, with its radical challenge to all the institutions that have traditionally excluded women.

BERNARD ANDRÈS

Political Essay

Political essays may be distinguished from other works in the fields of history, sociology and political science as the products of a more personal and untrammelled quest. Memoirs, reminiscences, notebooks, diaries and autobiographical fragments all overlap partially and unevenly with the political essay. Among the best political memoirs in French are the 3 volumes by Georges-Émile LAPALME, the leader of the Québec Liberal Party who was caught between Prem Maurice DUPLESSIS and PM Louis ST. LAURENT. He makes some lucid comments on the subject of the limits of political action.

The major political or ideological essays of the 19th century were not the work of orators or public figures (Papineau, Mercier, Laurier) but the discussions and chronicles of some leading journalists (Étienne PARENT, Arthur BUIES). *L'Avenir du peuple canadien-français* (1896), by sociologist Edmond de Nevers, was a cultural and deeply political essay, a mixture of idealism, pessimism and prophecy. In the 20th century as well, the best political essays have been the work of a few well-educated journalists (Olivar Asselin, Jules Fournier, André LAURENDEAU) and nationalist historians (Lionel GROULX, Michel Brunet). They raised (or revived) the question of

Québec's relations with London and Paris and with English Canadians; they were as concerned about war and conscription as about elections.

The birth of political magazines free from party affiliation — CITÉ LIBRE (1950-66) and PARTI PRIS (1963-68) — led to a proliferation of the political essay. The collection of articles, studies and testimonials about the ASBESTOS STRIKE, *La Grève de l'amiante* (1956), which appeared with a comprehensive introduction by Pierre Elliott TRUDEAU, was the prototype for numerous other collections. Many were the products of conferences, such as that held in Cerisy-la-Salle, France (*Le Canada au seuil du siècle de l'abondance*, 1969), which had brought together Francophones of every persuasion. Independentists produced manifestos, declarations and testimonies, but also a few essays of a more structured nature, such as *Le Colonialisme au Québec* (1966) by André d'Allemagne. A Marxist-tinged theory of decolonization, inspired by the experiences and rhetoric of the Third World, marked a number of the essays published at the beginning of the Quiet Revolution, in particular NÈGRES BLANCS D'AMÉRIQUE (1968) by Pierre Vallières. Neofederalists (most of them in the group around Trudeau and Gérard Pelletier) began countering the arguments of the fervent neo-nationalists. They seemed to be calmer and more staid than their antagonists, but they were just as lively in their use of history and statistics. True essays were rare: the writers slid easily from a constitutional treatise or thesis to a circumstantial or journalistic approach.

Some of the meatiest and most thought-provoking essays written since the late 1960s are *Le Canada français après deux siècles de patience* (1967) by political scientist Gérard Bergeron; *La Dernière Heure et la première* (1970) by Pierre Vadeboncoeur, trade unionist turned writer; *La Question du Québec* (1971) by sociologist Marcel Rioux; and *Le Développement des idéologies au Québec* (1977) by political scientist Denis Monière. The most trenchant political essays are perhaps to be found in certain novels (eg, those of Hubert Aquin and Jacques FERRON).

Québec political essayists have been obsessed since the mid-1960s by the state and the constitution. The essay must now move beyond partisanship and dogma to a new definition of the central issue: the division of powers is not solely a Québec-Ottawa dispute; it is also an issue for Montréal and its suburbs, the regions of Québec, women, ethnic and marginal groups. The political essay looks outward as well: in 1982, *Le* DEVOIR carried articles by political scientist Paul Painchaud and editorial writer Lise Bissonnette which offered new perspectives on the subject of Québec's international role. LAURENT MAILHOT

Literary Essay

Unlike literary criticism, which necessarily passes judgment on the work under study, the literary essay freely considers the written work, offering nondefinitive, personal comments on its aesthetic value. The literary essay first appeared in newspapers and magazines of the mid-19th century as well as in papers presented in literary circles, at the Institut canadien and in reading groups. These first stirrings prepared the way for true literary essayists, journalists Étienne Parent and Napoléon Aubin, Abbé Henri-Raymond CASGRAIN, Octave CRÉMAZIE, Arthur Buies and a few others who were prompted by religious and moral concerns to deal with aesthetic questions.

The literary essay developed strongly in Québec in the early 20th century, thanks to Laval professor Camille ROY, who explored the "nationalization" of Canadian literature in some 30 essays. He was followed by Olivier Maurault and Émile Chartier of U de Montréal, the major voices of nationalism, who concentrated on the land, the parish, the family, religion, customs and ancestral traditions; and by the next wave, regionalists associated with the journals *Le Pays laurentien*, *La Revue nationale* and L'ACTION FRANÇAISE (later *L'Action canadienne-française* and then *L'Action nationale*). The "Parisianists" ("exotics"), who followed modern French thought in their subjects and writings and often sharply disagreed with the first group, included Paul Morin, Marcel Dugas, Jean Charbonneau, Robert de Roquebrune, Olivar Asselin, Victor Barbeau and his *Cahiers de Turc* (1921-22; 1926-27), and the people associated with *Le* NIGOG, *Cahiers des Jeunes-Canada* and *La* RELÈVE. Happily, the often vigorous disagreements led to an affirmation of a French Canadian literature that was autonomous yet always strongly influenced by France.

With this ideological battle behind them, writers could finally pay serious attention to the different genres of expression. From 1940 to 1960 the literary essay was particularly important. The many publications included writings about Canadian as well as French authors; general studies of French Canadian literature by Roger Duhamel, Benoît Lacroix and Séraphin Marion; specialized studies of THEATRE by Léopold Houlé and Jean Béraud, poetry by Jeanne Crouzet and the novel by Dostaler O'Leary; and histories of literature by Samuel Baillargeon, Berthelot Brunet and Auguste Viatte.

The proliferation of literary essays has been boosted, since the Quiet Revolution, by the development of the teaching of Québec literature (*see* LITERATURE IN FRENCH, SCHOLARSHIP AND TEACHING). Analyses of literature and of literary movements (the historical novel, the novel of the soil, literary nationalism, *Parti pris*, the AUTOMATISTES, surrealism) were accompanied by many essays dealing with literary genres: the novel (Gérard Bessette, Yves Dostaler, Paul Gay, Maurice Lemire, Gilles Marcotte, Mireille Servais-Maquoi, Henri Tuchmaïer); theatre (Michel Belair, Beaudoin Burger, Jacques Cotnam, Martial Dassylva, Jan Doat, Jean-Cléo Godin and Laurent Mailhot, Chantal Hébert, G.E. Rinfret); poetry (Paul Gay, Philippe Haeck, Jeanne d'Arc Lortie, Axel Maugey); and the literary essay (Jean Terrasse). There were treatments of subject-matter (mothers, winter, etc), a host of monographs on French Canadian writers, general studies of Québec literature (Guy Laflèche, Gilles Marcotte, Jean Ménard, Guy Robert) and histories of literature (Pierre de Grandpré, Laurent Mailhot, Gérard Tougas). There are also collective literary essays, such as the *Archives des lettres canadiennes*, and anthologies, including *L'Anthologie de la littérature québécoise* (directed by Gilles Marcotte) and the *Dictionnaire des oeuvres littéraires du Québec* (directed by Maurice Lemire) — both brilliant works, although their contents tend to be literary criticism rather than essays. Only rarely do Québec essayists study broad issues the way Europeans do. Finally, most Québec literary essays are aimed at students, professors and researchers in both foreign and Québec colleges and universities, though they are occasionally intended to reach a larger public. *See* LITERATURE IN FRENCH: CRITICISM AND THEORY; LITERARY PERIODICALS IN FRENCH. GILLES DORION

Esson, James, photographer (b at Preston [Cambridge, Ont] 10 Aug 1853; d at Toronto 1933). He learned PHOTOGRAPHY from his father and in 1875 established his own business. At age 30, he built a large, 3-storey brick "atelier" — purportedly the most elegant, complete and costly establishment in the country. A familiar name in art circles throughout Ontario, Esson attracted patrons of social and political prominence, including the marquess of LORNE and Princess Louise. He is probably best remembered for his hundreds of photographs of Ontario towns, Canadian and American scenery, and a variety of still-life subjects taken around 1880 for viewing through a stereoscope. JOAN M. SCHWARTZ

Estate, all property owned by an individual. From 1958 to 1972 Parliament levied an estate tax on all property left when people died (see TAXATION). More technically, an estate refers to ownership of an interest in land. As a result of the feudal system imposed on England by William the Conqueror in 1066, all land in Canada's common-law provinces is still owned by the CROWN.

Strictly speaking, an individual does not own land but an estate "in land." The largest and most common estate is a "fee simple absolute" (grant of an estate on land to a person or his heirs absolutely). Another freehold estate (an interest in land of indefinite duration) in land is a "life estate." Owner of the fee simple can divide part of the full estate by creating a life estate in A, who now has a freehold estate determinable by A's own death; if the owner dies before A, the freehold estate reverts to his estate only after A's death. If A conveyed his life estate in the land to B, B would acquire a life estate not measured by B's own life but measured by A's. The owner of a fee simple may also lease the land. The leasehold is an estate in land entitling the tenant to exclusive possession for the term of the lease. Other land interests, eg, easements, licences and restrictive covenants, are not classified as estates (see PROPERTY LAW).

Québec civil law does not have a doctrine of estates. In the modern civil law, ownership of property is absolute and means having all the rights of disposition, management and enjoyment. GORDON BALE

Esterhazy, Sask, Town, pop 3065 (1981c), inc 1957, is located in E-central Saskatchewan, 65 km SE of Yorkton. It is named after Count Paul Esterhazy, who founded a colony of Hungarian families S of the future townsite in 1886. The Kirkella branch of the CPR reached the area in 1902 and the community served the mixed farming area surrounding it. Potash was discovered in the 1950s and the "world's largest potash mine" went into production in 1962. The town was developed as an agricultural and mining centre. DON HERPERGER

Estevan, Sask, City, pop 9174 (1981c), inc 1957, is located on the SOURIS R, 210 km SE of Regina and 16 km N of the US border. The townsite was surveyed in 1892 where the Soo Line of the CPR crossed the river, and grew steadily from that date, largely because of its dual role as a trading and energy centre. The large lignite-coal deposits in the area were quickly recognized as a valuable source of fuel for the treeless plains, and coal mining developed rapidly. It has remained significant and the construction of the coal-fueled Boundary Dam generating station of the Saskatchewan Power Corp during the late 1950s confirmed the city's position as the "energy capital" of Saskatchewan. Oil was discovered in the 1950s and the oil industry plays an important role in the local and provincial economy. DON HERPERGER

Estonians belong to the Finno-Ugrian (and not the Indo-European) language group. From 1900 to 1944, fewer than 3000 Estonians immigrated to Canada. Of the 72 000 Estonian political refugees who had fled their home country in 1944 for Sweden and Germany, nearly 14 000 immigrated to Canada between 1946 and 1955. Between 1947 and 1949, 1600 of them crossed the Atlantic in 9-12 m "Viking" boats that they had bought in Sweden. Since 1960 almost no Estonians have immigrated. In the census of 1971, 18 810 Canadians (0.07% of the population) were reported to be of Estonian ethnic origin.

Migration and Settlement A few small Estonian farming communities emerged in southern Alberta during the first half of the century, but most prewar Estonian immigrants settled in urban areas. The postwar immigrants settled in industrial cities, especially in Toronto, where, since 1960, more than 50% of all Estonians in Canada have lived. Other sizable Estonian communities are found in Montréal, Vancouver and Hamilton.

Social and Cultural Life Because of their professional and occupational skills, Estonian immigrants did not encounter serious adjustment problems, although few were able to maintain their former professions. At present Canadians of Estonian origin are among the ethnic groups with the highest average incomes. The Estonians have contributed particularly to the development of amateur sports (volleyball, skiing, modern rhythmic gymnastics) and, particularly in Toronto and Vancouver, to architecture and the construction industry.

Group Maintenance Since the 1950s the Estonians have maintained an elaborate structure of ethnic organizations, especially in Toronto. They continue to co-operate closely with similar communities of the Estonian diaspora in the US, Sweden, Australia, England and West Germany. Every fourth year these communities organize a well-attended, week-long Estonian World Festival that rotates among Canada (Toronto), the US and Sweden. The Estonian communities abroad continue to maintain strong choir singing, theatre, folk dancing, amateur sports and scouting traditions. However, because Estonians have been well assimilated into Canadian society, only in Toronto do a significant number of second- and third-generation Estonians use Estonian as their home language. K. AUN

Reading: K. Aun, *The Political Refugees: Estonians in Canada* (1985).

Estrogen, female sex hormone produced primarily in the ovaries. Estrogen-deficiency diseases include menstrual dysfunction and various menopausal and postmenopausal health problems, eg, osteoporosis (loss and thinning of skeletal bone). In 1885 the French physiologist Claude Bernard discovered that, in addition to external excretions, many of the body's glands produce internal secretions which may affect all or specific body organs. In 1906 investigators discovered that the ovaries secrete a hormone that produces the phenomenon of estrus (hence, estrogen). Other researchers explored further the action of estrogen. At McGill University, J.B. COLLIP, D.L. Thomson and J.S.L. Browne studied placental and ovarian hormones and, in 1930, published 3 papers in the *Canadian Medical Assn Journal* describing isolation of the estrogen complex in pure form from a human placenta. They named this natural compound Emmenin. In collaboration with the McGill investigators and with the approval of McGill's biochemistry department, Ayerst, McKenna and Harrison in Montréal manufactured Emmenin, the first orally active, female sex hormone available for clinical use.

In 1938 another group of researchers published data describing the isolation of estrogens from pregnant mares' urine. Drs Stanley Cook and Gordon Grant, of Ayerst, decided to investigate this estrogenic complex as a possible source of an orally active product. On 17 Jan 1939 the first gallon of pregnant mares' urine was processed at Ayerst. During the following years, Ayerst researchers determined the biologic and metabolic effects of the various estrogenic components of the new compound, which they named Premarin. When Premarin became available for general clinical use (1941), physicians recognized its powerful metabolic and therapeutic effects. Ayerst still processes Premarin at its estrogen-extraction plant in Manitoba, depending on prairie farmers to deliver urine from thousands of pregnant mares. The finished product is exported all over the world. *See* BIOLOGICAL PRODUCTS. ELVIRA STAHL

Éthier-Blais, Jean, professor, writer, literary critic (b at Sturgeon Falls, Ont 15 Nov 1925). Professor of French literature at McGill since 1962, Éthier-Blais regularly contributed literary criticism to *Le Devoir* from 1961. Some of these articles were published in *Signets* (3 vol, 1967, 1973). His original works include poems, stories, essays and novels (*Mater Europa*, 1968, and *Les Pays étrangers*, 1982). Éthier-Blais handles the universal themes of love and death, but always through the perspective of his personal experience and the cultural situation of French Canadians. He became a member of the French Canadian Academy in 1971; in 1983 the St-Jean-Baptiste Society of Montréal awarded him its prestigious Prix Duvernay. NICOLE BOURBONNAIS

Ethnic and Race Relations Canadian society can be described, at one level, as a complex network of relations among ethnic groups which occupy unequal economic, political and social positions in Canadian society. Within this complexity 3 main axes of ethnic differentiation are identifiable: the relationship between natives and non-natives, between English and French and between the colonizing (or "charter") groups and other immigrants and their descendants. These distinctions are relevant not only to the private experiences of individuals but also to public issues, eg, aboriginal rights and land claims; linguistic rights; particular government powers; IMMIGRATION POLICY; PREJUDICE AND DISCRIMINATION; and MULTICULTURALISM. Although interrelated, these issues pertain to different matters largely because they concern different groups. For example, the controversy over language between English and French differs from that between other ethnolinguistic groups (eg, Ukrainians, Italians, Greeks) and the English-speaking or French-speaking communities because the *official* languages of Canada are English and French.

The relations among ethnic groups cannot be considered apart from the class structure, ie, the access to and control of a society's resources and the functioning of rules and practices that benefit or exclude particular groups. Inequality among groups can result from several factors, including the circumstances of their arrival in Canada; their visibility; their internal economic, political and social organization; the direct or indirect support received from other groups or countries; and whether improvements in material conditions of life are achieved primarily through individual mobility or through the growth of the group's institutions (which in turn depends on the nature and extent of the historical relations with the dominant ethnic groups).

Power and control are almost invariably linked to the ethnic origin of those in authority, and those in authority will almost invariably tend to protect and extend their power. The denial of access to power and control to other groups, and the institutional and bureaucratic barriers designed to preclude or defuse attempts by such groups to act politically have nearly all been "ethnically inspired." The disadvantaged may attempt to change the existing rules, but their chances of success depend on the very factors which brought about inequality. As a result, improvements in the situation of disadvantaged minorities are frequently very slow (*see* ELITES).

Natives and Canadian Society The relationship between native peoples and the rest of Canadian society is characterized first by "marginality." Native Indians and Inuit are largely excluded from competition for power and constitute, in effect, a castelike minority in society. Following the pattern of paternalism and condescension which has characterized the treatment of native peoples by the dominant groups, the affairs of Indian bands have been administered by a government bureaucracy, which until recently was staffed almost entirely by non-Indians.

The settlement and expansion of English and French societies led to the displacement and control of the native populations, manifest in successive Indian Acts and treaties, and the establishment of the Indian affairs bureaucracy. Total control of Indian lands was given first (1850) to the Commission of Indian Lands and then, through the BRITISH NORTH AMERICA ACT, to the federal government. Through INDIAN TREATIES, from 1850 to 1921, large tracts of land in central and western Canada were surrendered in exchange for reserve lands, money and promises of social assistance. The INDIAN ACT of 1876 and its subsequent modifications created dependence. The Act defines which Indians, according to their native ancestry, are to be considered "status Indians." Status Indians include those registered in 1874, their closest descendants in the male line, and their wives and children. They may or may not live on reserves.

Although the situation of off-reserve status Indians, non-status Indians, Métis, Inuit and reserve Indians may differ somewhat, all are deeply affected by the dominant society's ideology of superiority and inferiority. Immigrant groups, on the other hand, do not necessarily seek equality with the dominant group but improvements in their condition relative to the condition of people in their homeland. Although they may have to accept inferior occupations when they arrive in Canada, the situation is perceived as temporary. Native minorities, however, have no "homeland" condition against which they can gauge their present situation, as the very basis of their identity and heritage has largely been destroyed.

The symbols of a common culture can be used to help strengthen group solidarity against continuing discrimination and to provide an avenue for individuals to establish identity. The formation of native organizations, including Pan-Indian national associations whose primary objective is the defence of Indian interests in land, may restore both objective and subjective equality to native peoples. However, in their efforts at social, economic and political organization, native people will have to overcome the legacy of marginality and dependence. They will also have to transcend the numerous cleavages within the native population arising from different cultural and linguistic backgrounds, from the division of status Indians into some 510 bands, and the division of status from non-status Indians.

Francophone-Anglophone Relations can be characterized as a competition between 2 colonial powers. Since the Conquest of 1760 up to the more recent conflict over LANGUAGE POLICY, the 2 groups have struggled, unequally, for the control of cultural, economic and political institutions.

The competition between the English and French societies has always been manifested in the struggle over the control of government institutions. The Québec Act of 1774, the 1791 Constitutional Act, the Act of Union of 1840, the BNA Act and its modifications and the 1982 patriation of the Constitution have all been concerned with the DISTRIBUTION OF POWERS and the symbolic recognition of the language and culture of both groups. The issues of job distribution and control of economic institutions have been reflected in conflicts over immigration policy, family allowances, and language of education and work. The competition is unequal, however, largely because of differences in population and wealth, because of the Conquest and its implications, the British influence in the shaping of Canadian society and government institutions and the anglophone character of N American society.

Immigrants and Canadian Society By 1981 Canadians of British descent accounted for less than 44% (from 60.6% in 1871) and those of French descent less than 28% of the Canadian population. Other ethnic groups accounted for some 27%. The decrease in British representation, however, did not lead to a concomitant decrease in their control of the economy or of the political system or to a change in the status of Canada as a "white" society. Other European immigrants do not share equality with the charter groups. John PORTER in *The Vertical Mosaic* argued that the crucial fact of Canadian life was the "exclusion of minority groups from the main loci of decision making within the corporate sector of the economy" (*see* BUSINESS ELITES). In politics the composition of federal Cabinets since 1867 has reflected only the struggle to balance English and French interests. The decision by certain groups, eg, FINNS and UKRAINIANS and other central and eastern European immigrants, to become engaged in radical political activities has reflected their decision to challenge what has been called "the notion of Canadian society on the one hand and the existence of ethnic groups as something independent of the society on the other."

Conflicts between immigrant and charter groups are a result of unequal access to employment and education, and unequal security and social respect. Several groups have been the victims of systematic exploitation, discrimination and social exclusion, but their situation has largely improved as a result of their own individual and collective efforts, and because of legislation and economic prosperity.

For the first generation of immigrants the structure of social networks and organizations is formed largely for adaptive purposes, ie, to advance or defend shared interests and to provide social support. The structure tends to weaken in succeeding generations if the group has achieved some measure of economic advancement and assimilation. On the other hand the rediscovery of ethnic roots by later generations is a response to the atomization of mass society and the competition among groups. In times of crisis, symbols such as shared language, food, music, etc, may seem more attractive than the abstract notion of brotherhood with strangers with whom only class structure is shared.

Visible Minorities One of the most controversial issues in anthropological and sociological literature is whether there exists a conceptual distinction between ethnicity and race. Third World immigrants and other visible minorities who can be distinguished by skin colour are stigmatized as "outsiders" regardless of how long they or their families have been settled in Canada.

RACISM in Canada has not been well documented except in historical studies of immigration policy. In fact Canadians manifest in exemplary fashion an ostrichlike approach to the problem, although studies reveal that suspicion and ethnocentrism are in reality as alive in Canada as anywhere else (*see also* BLACKS; JAPANESE; CHINESE; JEWS). Members of visible minorities in Canada, unlike those in the US, have tended not to demand affirmative action or quota systems, but have concentrated on acquiring professional qualifications.

The Relationship of Ethnic Groups to Anglophone and Francophone Cultures raises the question of how certain manifestations of individual and collective ethnicity (if they are to exist) are to be recognized and incorporated into Canadian society and how social institutions are to be modified to accommodate and recognize various cultural traditions. The danger of attempts by governments to answer these questions by instituting multiculturalism programs and policies is that "folklorism" may be glorified at the expense of genuine cultural pluralism. Unless the political and economic structures are altered to reflect more clearly the composition of Canadian society, the celebration of multiculturalism may advance the depoliticization of Canadian ethnicity and contribute to the illusion that all ethnic groups enjoy equality simply because their cultures are officially declared to be deserving of equal recognition.

Ethnic Languages There have been several distinct periods of IMMIGRATION into Canada by groups of non-British or non-French origin. By 1901, only slightly less than 10% of the total population consisted of members of ethnic minority groups (primarily European, but also a significant number of Chinese who came to Canada to work on the railway). The early 20th century saw a spectacular increase in European immigration, particularly from Ukraine and Germany. This period was also marked by the appearance of substantial numbers of Serbo-Croatian and Greek immigrants, as well as smaller groups from countries as diverse as Lebanon, Romania and Turkey. During WWI immigration was insignificant, but the period between the wars brought a new wave — again mostly from Europe. Immigration virtually stopped once more during WWII, but the postwar period brought a steady stream of newcomers, over half a million of them from Italy. In this later period significant numbers of non-European immigrants arrived, particularly Asians. Since 1979 Canada has accepted thousands of Indo-Chinese REFUGEES through both government and private sponsorship. Today Canadians of non-British, non-French origins represent more than 35 different ethnic groups and constitute more than 30% of the country's total population.

Although immigrants are free to settle where they choose, a disproportionate number live in Ontario. The Royal Commission on BILINGUALISM AND BICULTURALISM reported that in 1961 almost 42% of Toronto residents were born outside the country. Fully 47% of the population of the Prairie provinces, 35% of the population of BC and 29% of Ontario's population is comprised of immigrants of other than British or French origin (1981c).

These statistics do not reflect the number of Canadians who have declared a non-official language as a mother tongue. According to the 1981 census, just over 3 million of the 8 million ethnic population learned a language other than English or French in childhood, and of these over 1.5 million now use an OFFICIAL LANGUAGE in the home. They understand the first language but use it infrequently. These individuals have integrated into Canadian society.

The Royal Commission on Bilingualism and Biculturalism states that *integration* "does not imply the loss of an individual's identity and original characteristics or of his original language and culture." *Assimilation*, on the other hand, is "almost total absorption into another linguistic and cultural group. An assimilated individual gives up his cultural identity and may even ... change his name." It was the impression of the commission that immigrants of non-British, non-French origin clearly preferred integration to assimilation. Obviously, the maintenance of a mother tongue together with mastery of an official language is indicative of integration; however, loss of the mother tongue by an ethnic community does not necessarily imply total assimilation. A variety of factors such as RELIGION, folk traditions, race, marriage outside the community, geographic concentration, size of the group, its economic strength and the ratio of foreign-born to native-born individuals within it all interact in determining the degree of assimilation undergone in a given group.

Certain ethnic groups have maintained strong linguistic and cultural ties with their places of origin, as well as developing new ethnic-Canadian, integrated cultures here. The Ukrainians in western Canada are a case in point. It has been suggested that a principal factor in their retention of the Ukrainian language was their settlement in rural areas. The combination of isolation and a fierce pride in the culture of the homeland resulted in the development of very strong Ukrainian communities which survived and flourished when Canada underwent mass URBANIZATION. The unique set of circumstances faced by the first Ukrainian immigrants upon their arrival had a major impact on their successful integration. Other groups, under different circumstances, have been assimilated to a greater extent (eg, Scandinavians).

Ethnic origin	*Region of settlement*
German (1 142 365)	Ont, Alta, Bc, Sask
Italian (747 970)	Ont, Qué, BC
Ukrainian (529 615)	Alta, Ont, Man, Sask
Dutch (408 240)	Ont, BC, Alta
Chinese (289 245)	Ont, BC
Scandinavian (282 795)	BC, Alta, Sask

A powerful force that leads to both integration and assimilation is the desire for identification with the prestige (majority) group: the anglophone community in English Canada and the francophone community in Québec. This is particularly evident in the children of various ethnic groups. The desire for identification pervades all aspects of their behaviour: play, mode of dress, recreation, food, values and language. Linguistic identification means speaking the official language grammatically, without accent. It ensures that the individual will be recognized and accepted as one of the prestige group. The desire to identify with the majority is so strong that it entails the rejection of everything that could delay this identification, including one's mother tongue. The process often takes place against the will of parents who wish their children to maintain the language and culture of origin. Identification with peers is usually stronger than the influence of the family; however, if other cultural factors (eg, a strong religious influence, as is present in most Canadian Jewish communities) contribute to ethnic identity, the child can integrate successfully without assimilating completely. The educational systems across Canada have recently provided for increased opportunity for ethnic groups to maintain their mother tongues. The number of immersion programs in other than official languages (*see* SECOND LANGUAGE INSTRUCTION) is on the rise; in the early 1980s the Edmonton Public School Board, for example, offered immersion schooling in Arabic, Mandarin, Hebrew, Ukrainian and German.

It is inevitable that many ethnic groups settling in Canada should undergo linguistic assimilation; what is remarkable is the revival of interest in the languages of origin and the ongoing integration into Canadian society of cultural traditions that originated elsewhere. *See also* ETHNIC LITERATURE; LANGUAGES IN USE.

BERNARD SAINT-JACQUES

Reading: W.H. Coons et al, eds, *The Individual, Language and Society in Canada* (1977); H. Giles, ed, *Language, Ethnicity and Intergroup Relations* (1977); H. Giles and Bernard Saint-Jacques, eds, *Language and Ethnic Relations* (1979); Stanley Lieberson, *Language and Ethnic Relations in Canada* (1970); Bernard Saint-Jacques, "The Languages of Immigrants" in J.K. Chambers, ed, *The Languages of Canada* (1979).

Ethnic Literature In Canadian English, the term "ethnic" has been used to designate those immigrants who do not belong to Canada's founding European cultures: the Catholic French and the Protestant Anglo-Celtic. It also embraces the aboriginal inhabitants of Canada, the native Indian and Inuit who have stood distant and often alienated from Canadian society. Literature by ethnic writers or about ethnic experience has generally been regarded as outside the literary mainstream and has often been overlooked by scholars. The expression "Canadian ethnic literature" is itself complex, dependent on combinations of such variables as the writer's ethnic identity, the language of writing or translation and the literary expression of ethnic themes. To be fair, a definition of Canadian ethnic literature must be comprehensive and include émigré writing, both in the nonofficial languages and in translation; literature by writers who perceive themselves as belonging to an ethnic minority and write from this perspective (usually in English or French); and works that deal with immigrant or ethnic experience but are not necessarily written by a member of the group portrayed.

The relationship between ethnic literature and mainstream writing is very much in flux. The latter is increasingly defined in the light of Canada's ethnic diversity. This can be seen in reevaluations of the separate Irish, Scots and Welsh traditions in mainstream writing; the recognition in English Canadian letters of Jewish writers; the increasing thematic significance of ethnicity in the works of contemporary writers; and the growing numbers of authors of ethnic descent who are making their mark on Canadian literature. The work of second and later generations of ethnic writers such as George RYGA, W.D. Valgardson, Rudy WIEBE, Andrew Suknaski and Pier Giorgio Di Cicco is permeating the mainstream sensibility; the work of émigré writers such as George Faludy, Josef Škvorecký, Waclaw Iwaniuk and Robert Zend is becoming increasingly available in translation; and the work of new immigrants such as Kristjana Gunnars, Pablo Urbanyi and Cyril Dabydeen is becoming accessible as it receives critical acclaim.

Canadian literature was born of the colonial mentality of early immigrants from the British Isles and France. The earliest form of ethnic bias may be seen marginally in the period 1841-55, which is described by Carl F. Klinck in *Literary History of Canada* (2nd ed 1976) as that of "genteel colonialism." The period's prominent English-language writers desired to be English and aristocratic in every sense, not only in life-style but in language. Thus some objected to "uncivilized" Irish and Scottish pronunciations invading Canadian speech patterns. Susanna MOODIE expressed a more blatant prejudice against the Irish in ROUGHING IT IN THE BUSH (1852), calling the Irish "savages" without "common decency." Although British Canadian writers like Moodie may sometimes have perpetuated Old-World prejudices against the "ethnic" Irish and Scots, the Anglo-Celtic community remained fundamentally united as a social and literary force.

A more deeply significant ethnic subject of early English Canadian literature was one who, ironically, most deserves not to be considered foreign: the native Indian. Yet no other group has been as persistently portrayed as "the other" in the white man's literary world as have Indians, nor has any other "ethnic" group registered as strongly on the consciousness of writers. Whether the fictional Indian was depicted as the barbaric antagonist or the noble savage — in such early works as John RICHARDSON's gothic novel, WACOUSTA (1832), and the romantic poetry of Charles MAIR, Charles SANGSTER and Duncan Campbell SCOTT — he became a projection of the imaginative needs of colonial culture. Even in late 20th-century works where the Indian is sympathetically drawn, he remains the "other" and thus a touchstone for white culture. In works such as George Ryga's *The Ecstasy of Rita Joe* (1970) and W.O. MITCHELL's *The Vanishing Point* (1973), the Indian is a fitting vehicle through which to express dissent from white society. Nonetheless, contemporary writers such as Mitchell and Margaret LAURENCE portray with some realism, and a great deal of sympathy, the condition and status of the modern Indian and the Métis. Several writers, particularly in the West, have created fiction and poetry in which aboriginal mythology and perspectives shape literary forms or contribute to the definition of the artist, his contemporary characters and his region. These writers include John NEWLOVE, Dale Zieroth, Andy Suknaski, George BOWERING, Sheila WATSON, Robert KROETSCH, Susan Musgrave, Leonard COHEN, Margaret ATWOOD and Marian ENGEL. Rudy Wiebe has made honest attempts to realize the Indian's point of view in his historical novels *The Temptations of Big Bear* (1973) and *The Scorched-Wood People* (1977).

If the legacy of British colonialism meant the literary interpretation of the Indian through the view of whites, it also meant that other ethnic groups were dimly seen. English Canadian literature, if it treated the ethnic as a subject at all, demonstrated less interest in ethnic character than in assimilation. This is true of the work of Presbyterian minister Charles W. GORDON (pseudonym Ralph Connor) in the novel *The Foreigner* (1909), in which the protagonist, Kalmar Kalman, a "Slav," lives in the "foreign colony" of North Winnipeg of 1884. Ascribing to Kalman the stereotyped "Slavic" traits of exotic features and primitive passions, Connor "Canadianizes" and "civilizes" his hero by having him adopt the religion and moral values of the Anglo-Saxon Protestant.

The pressure to assimilate necessarily affected the ethnic person's view of himself and his people. A crisis of identity is particularly evident in those second-generation, English-speaking ethnic writers who write of themselves in relation to their immigrant parents, eg, Ukrainian Canadian Vera Lysenko, in *Yellow Boots* (1954), and Hungarian Canadian John Marlyn, in *Under the Ribs of Death* (1957). In more recent literature, the second-generation ethnic writer may express similar dislocation but does so with less shame and with a new authority and pride in ethnic roots, at the same time often protesting against racial discrimination or unfair treatment of ethnic minorities. Joy KOGAWA, for example, vindicates her Japanese Canadian people in *Obasan* (1981). Immigrant writers, too, can write with self-confidence about injustice. Bharati Mukherjee, an accomplished writer born in Calcutta, writes bitterly but with self-esteem of her unsatisfactory life in Canada, as both an Indian woman and an ethnic writer; Guyana-born Cyril Dabydeen records the hard ironies of being a black immigrant in Canada, without relinquishing his self-respect. Assimilation continues to be problematic also for the characters in ethnic literature, but their authors are making increasingly bold pleas for equal rights and opportunities.

Inuit Literature The Inuit did not develop a written language; Christian missionaries introduced written Inuktitut early in the 18th century. Consequently the first Inuktitut literature consisted of translations of the Bible and other religious materials, to which secular classics were soon added. The first major scholarly sources of traditional Inuit poetry are *Expedition — the Danish Ethnographical Expedition to Arctic North America, 1921-24* (1928-45, 1976), by Knud Rasmussen, and *Songs of the Copper Eskimos* (1925), collected by Helen Roberts and Diamond JENNESS. Among southern Canadians there has been a growing interest in Inuit literature. Drawing on the pioneering work of Rasmussen, Roberts and Jenness, others such as John Robert COLOMBO (*Poems of the Inuit,* 1981) have collected traditional Inuit literature.

Contemporary Inuit literature, published in both Inuktitut and English, includes important diaries and autobiographies, such as *Sketches of Labrador Life* (1980), by Lydia Campbell. *People for Our Side* (1975), by Dorothy Eber and Peter PITSEOLAK, depicts, often humorously, recent Inuit culture, shaped by contact with the N American mainstream. Modern Inuit culture is depicted in darker tones by Anthony Apakark Thrasher in *Thrasher: Skid Row Eskimo* (1976). Recently a number of Inuktitut-English journals, such as *Inuit Today,* have published the work of contemporary Inuit writers. Both traditional and contemporary Inuit literature are included in Robin Gedalof's *An Annotated Bibliography of Canadian Inuit Literature* (1979).

Indian Literature Indian literature in Canada is rooted in the oral tradition of storytelling and includes all types of traditional narratives, such as myths, legends, fairy tales, animal stories and fables (*see* ORAL LITERATURE). Such narratives have proven to be fascinating to white culture, beginning in the 17th century when Jesuit missionaries first recorded Huron and Algonquian tales in the JESUIT RELATIONS, and continuing into the 19th and 20th centuries when scores of anthropologists, folklorists and sociologists studied various tribes and recorded their FOLKLORE. Thus, there is a wealth of transcribed Indian legends and myths. However, written translation has unavoidably lessened both the nuances and the oral impact of the narratives; the imposition of Christian value systems has altered aboriginal meanings; the tendency of folklorists to place Indian folklore in a European context of storytelling has often led to distorted interpretations; and the many Indian tales that deal, often humorously, with the body processes, because they have been unacceptable to white morality, have been left out of anthologies. As a result of the early influence of white contact, a purely aboriginal tradition of Indian narrative is difficult to trace. Moreover, because the Indians are not a homogenous cultural or linguistic group, the mythology as expressed in their narratives is vast and complex. Indian storytelling also allowed the storyteller to invent and alter narratives as he pleased; thus there can be many variants of a story, although certain motifs and narrative patterns appear to be common (eg, the trickster figure as the source of creation).

Contemporary native authors are finding their own voice. Their writing includes rhetorical and political works, such as Harold CARDINAL's *The Rebirth of Canada's Indians* (1977) and Duke Redbird's *We Are Metis* (1980); retrospectives of the Indian way of life, such as *Potlatch* (1969) by George CLUTESI of the Northwest Coast Indians, *These Mountains Are Our Sacred Places* (1977) by Chief John SNOW of the Stoney and *The Ways of My Grandmothers* (1980) by Beverly Hungry Wolf of the Blood Tribe; autobiographies, biographies and memoirs such as Anahareo's *Devil in Deerskins* (1972); and creative literature including poetry, legend and drama, such as Norval MORRISSEAU's Ojibwa *Legends of My People* (1965) and Chief Dan GEORGE's poetic volume *My Heart Soars* (1974). A milestone in the recognition of Indian literature was the publication of the anthology *I Am an Indian* (1969), edited by non-Indian Kent Gooderham.

Acadian Literature ACADIA first referred to the French Atlantic-seaboard colonies in the New World. In 1755, during the SEVEN YEARS' WAR, British authorities stripped the Acadians of their lands and rights and deported many of them. Some returned when French-English hostilities abated. The Acadian story first found sympathetic literary expression in T.C. HALIBURTON's *An Historical and Statistical Account of Nova Scotia* (1829), which influenced American poet Henry Wadsworth Longfellow to write EVANGELINE (1847), a narrative poem of the expulsion. This romantic tale received international attention and inspired mainstream writers, such as Charles G.D. ROBERTS, to write fictional romances of Acadian history and induced Acadian writers themselves to express an Acadian consciousness.

The theme of cultural survival is synonymous with Acadian literature, which often celebrates a lost past, extols Acadian traditions and language and protests past and present treatment. Since the publication of Napoléon Landry's *Poèmes de mon pays* (1949), Acadian literature has flourished; its impetus has come, in part, from the example of cultural nationalism in Québec, from the election in 1960 of the first Acadian premier of New Brunswick, L.J. ROBICHAUD, from the establishment in 1972 of the first publishing house in Acadia, les Éditions d'Acadie, and from the national and international recognition of Acadian writer Antonine MAILLET for such works as *Pointe-aux-Coques* (1958) and *La Sagouine* (1972). Notable modern Acadian writers include poets Ronald Després (*Silences à nourrir de sang*, 1958) and Raymond LeBlanc (*Cri de terre*, 1973).

Irish, Scottish and Welsh Literature Some Scottish Irish from largely Protestant Ulster immigrated in the mid-18th century, as did SCOTS from Scotland. By the end of the century Scots were immigrating in droves, followed by many IRISH in the first decades of the 19th century and scores more with the potato famine of 1846-47. The greatest WELSH immigration coincided with economic depressions in Wales in the 19th and early 20th centuries. These groups were integrated into the culture around them and their literature has been considered mainstream. Thomas D'Arcy MCGEE, for example, attempted to foster a national spirit in Canada through such works as his *Canadian Ballads* (1858), which were based on Irish ballad forms. Scotsman Alexander MCLACHLAN was a popular poet who wrote such "Canadian" works as *The Emigrant, and Other Poems* (1861) in the tradition of Robert Burns. Much scholarship remains to be done in assessing the nature of Irish and Scottish immigrant literature and in tracing the Irish and Scottish literary heritage from the colonial period until the present day, when such contemporary writers as Brian MOORE, Morley CALLAGHAN, Alice MUNRO and Margaret Laurence continue to demonstrate an Irish or Scottish sensibility.

Many early Scottish settlers were Scottish Gaels (Highlanders) who brought with them to settlements in the Maritimes, Manitoba and parts of Ontario the Gaelic language and the ancient, oral, bardic tradition of songs, folktales and epic narratives. Gaelic poets, such as pioneer bards John McLean (who came to Nova Scotia in 1819) and Rev Duncan Black Blair, have had little effect on mainstream literature, but their poetry has remained intact and is of interest to those who know the language, as Margaret MacDonell's translated edition, *The Emigrant Experience* (1982), bears witness.

Later Arrivals Other immigrants who came later and settled primarily in the West brought literary traditions, both oral and written. One early group was the ICELANDERS, who came to Canada in the mid-1870s fleeing volcanic eruptions in their homeland. Despite their small numbers, they produced a notable body of literature in Canada. In Manitoba the new settlers quickly established newspapers, which became vehicles for lively debate as well as for creative writing. A number of writers, exemplified by Thorsteinn Thorsteinsson and Sigurbjorn Johannson, wrote poetry and stories in their native language but about the Canadian immigrant experience. The literary achievement of one pioneer, Stephan STEPHANSSON, was particularly remarkable. Though he was largely unknown to Canadians until recently, Stephansson received the title of poet laureate of Iceland on the strength of poems he composed in Canada. He profoundly revitalized the Icelandic language and tradition in which he wrote, while addressing the Canadian experience with insight and a freshness of imagery that are not altogether lost even in translations of his lyric poetry. The pioneers were followed by a generation of writers who, though continuing to write in Icelandic and out of an essentially Icelandic tradition, addressed Canadian experience. Notable among them are Guttormur Guttormsson and Einar Pall Jonsson. Jonsson's well-known poem "The Laundress" captures the sense of loss engendered by assimilation. Like the work of numerous early ethnic writers, that of Stephansson, Guttormsson and Jonsson first became available to English-speaking Canadians through the efforts of Watson Kirkconnell, an English professor who translated and compiled collections of poetry in languages other than English and French, most notably his 1935 *Canadian Overtones*. Kirkconnell also wrote the "Publications in Other Languages" section of UNIVERSITY OF TORONTO QUARTERLY from 1935 to 1966.

Caught between the remnants of the immigrant culture and the evolving mainstream, the ethnic writer of the second or third generation typically becomes a "mediator" between cultures. Icelandic Canadian writer Laura Goodman Salverson, in her romantic novel *The Viking Heart* (1923), tells the story of her people through fictional characters who gradually commit themselves to Canada and find acceptance here. In her more realistic autobiography, *Confessions of an Immigrant's Daughter* (1939), she explores with some frankness the problems the immigrant family faces. Some contemporary writers of Icelandic background, eg, W.D. Valgardson and recent immigrant Kristjana Gunnars, still explore Icelandic characters and themes. Valgardson's collections of short stories, *Bloodflowers* (1973), *God is Not a Fish Inspector* (1975) and *Red Dust* (1978), his book of poetry, *In the Gutting Shed* (1976), and his novel, *Gentle Sinners* (1980), present with stark clarity a dark vision of the interface between ethnicity and the post-modern world. In her poetry, particularly *The Settlement Poems* (1980), and in her book of short stories, *The Axe's Edge* (1983), Gunnars attempts to merge historical research and poetic, almost mystical, vision to provide a narrative vehicle for Icelandic Canadian experience.

Other Scandinavians have been present in Canadian literature as well, either as writers or as characters. Norwegian-born Martha Ostenso contributed to the emergence of realism in Canada through her prairie novel, *Wild Geese* (1925), which portrays an authoritarian farmer's impact on his wife and children. German immigrant Frederick Philip GROVE brought naturalism to his treatment of Scandinavian immigrant characters in *Settlers of the Marsh* (1925), and Anglo-Canadian writer Nellie MCCLUNG presented a Finnish immigrant as her main character in *Painted Fires* (1925). Danish-Norwegian writer Aksel Sandemose spent several years in the Maritimes and the western provinces, and ultimately wrote several novels dealing with the Canadian immigrant experience; perhaps the most notable is *Ross Dane* (1928), which is well known in Scandinavia.

Many Ukrainians came to Canada from eastern Europe after 1896, and they have produced a significant body of literature in Canada. Its evolution has been distinctive and complex, because of the Ukrainians' large numbers, their pioneer status in western Canada, their continuing immigration in significant numbers after WWII and the unique political history of their homeland. Combined, these factors have fostered a vital émigré tradition that finds its ultimate raison d'être in the belief of many Ukrainian writers and intellectuals that Ukrainian is a legitimate Canadian language (albeit not an offical one) and that the Ukrainian literary tradition can continue to develop in Canada (*see* UKRAINIAN WRITING).

A natural offshoot of this tradition has been writing in English by authors of Ukrainian background. The writer best exemplifying the second-generation apologist's stance is Vera Lysenko, whose novel *Yellow Boots* tells the story of second-generation character Lili Landash, who assimilates into Anglo-Canadian culture through education and intermarriage. Other writers have been less willing to glorify the shedding of ethnic culture. George Ryga, for example, who does not directly fictionalize his own experience as the son of Ukrainian immigrants, nevertheless portrays ethnic characters from the inside while looking at Canadian society from the outsider's perspective, as in his play *The Ecstasy of Rita Joe* (1970) or his novels *Hungry Hills* (1963) and *Ballad of a Stonepicker* (1966). Andrew Suknaski, in *Wood Mountain Poems* (1976) and *The Land They Gave Away* (1982) attempts to create and give earthy expression to a personal mythology that embraces ethnicity and fuses it with Canadian experience.

GERMANS, Canada's third-largest ethnic group, settled in Canada as early as the 1750s and continue to do so. German Canadians have produced a significant body of literature, though it is difficult to generalize about it since the group is remarkably diverse. It includes, for example, Catholics and various ANABAPTIST sects (eg, MENNONITES) and secular immigrants from postwar Germany. In addition, Germans have settled throughout the country, though there are concentrations in Nova Scotia and Ontario and in the Prairie provinces. Their linguistic heritage is complex, including both High and Low German and a variety of dialects (*see* GERMAN WRITING).

Jewish writing is perhaps the most impressive of Canada's ethnic literatures, despite the relatively small number of JEWS in Canada. Shaped by successive waves of immigration that began in the early 1890s, Jewish writing reflects a variety of cultural and linguistic influences. Most of the early immigrants spoke Yiddish; consequently, though some writers chose to write in Hebrew, Jewish Canadian literature before WWII was written primarily in Yiddish. Jewish writers, principally those born in Canada, have also written in English. A.M. KLEIN, Irving LAYTON, Miriam WADDINGTON, Eli MANDEL and Mordecai RICHLER, as well as Fredelle Maynard, Morley Turgov and others, have so skillfully articulated Jewish experience in Canada that it has penetrated the mainstream sensibility, earning Jewish writing a major place in modern Canadian literature. Regardless of the language in which it is written, Jewish literature in Canada characteristically reflects an international vision, a minority sensibility and the profound influence of the WWII Holocaust (*see* JEWISH WRITING).

A number of the other small European groups in Canada, most notably HUNGARIANS, CZECHS and ITALIANS, have also produced substantial bodies of literature; as well, significant works have appeared in Estonian, Latvian, Lithuanian, Slovak, Croatian, Romanian, Russian and Spanish. Although the presence in Canada of a number of these groups dates back to the turn of the century, their literary activity has been most notable since WWII. Postwar European immigrants, often fleeing political upheaval in their own countries, were generally educated, urban people, and included writers and intellectuals who revitalized the cultural life of the group in Canada. Toronto, which attracted a majority of postwar European immigrants, has become the major centre of émigré writing.

Hungarians came to Canada during the early waves of immigration primarily as farmers and miners. They produced some literature, such as the epic poem written in the early 1900s by John Szatmari in which he describes his immigrant experiences, and the 1919 collection of poetry by Hungarian Canadians, *Mezel Virágok* (*Prairie Flowers*). But the Hungarian Canadians' most substantial literary achievement has been since

WWII, as a result of the coming of age of second and subsequent generation writers such as John Marlyn, and in the work of postwar émigré writers, particularly those who fled Hungary after the uprising of 1956. Many Hungarian émigré writers, particularly the older ones such as poets Ferenc Fay, Tamas Tuz, Robert Zend and George Faludy, continue to write in Hungarian, whereas younger writers such as George Jonas write in English (although some, such as Gyorgy Vitez and Kemenes Gefin, also write in Hungarian). As Hungarian Canadian scholar John Miska points out, the Hungarian writer often wishes to be a "champion of freedom," and this "self-imposed crusading function" is reflected in the nationalistic, "heroic-emotional" tone of Hungarian Canadian poetry. A number of these writers also deal with Canadian subjects, exploring the tensions of émigré marginality. In 1969, Hungarian Canadian writers formed an association which has published several anthologies in Hungarian and one in English translation, *The Sound of Time* (1974).

POLES have also had a literary presence in Canada. In his epic novel *Three Generations* (1973), Melchior Wánkowicz, who immigrated to Canada in 1950, depicts the life of early Polish immigrants. The most notable second-generation writer of Polish descent is poet and literary scholar Louis DUDEK, whose achievements are very much a part of the mainstream. The postwar period brought to Canada writers such as poet Waclaw Iwaniuk. In his *Ciemny Czas* (1968; tr *Dark Times,* 1979) and most recently in his *Evenings on Lake Ontario* (1981) Iwaniuk explores, in tightly controlled verse and from both European and N American perspectives, the condition of contemporary man, but idealizes neither the Old World nor the New.

Postwar émigré writers from other European countries explore similar themes. Czech Canadian Josef ŠKVORECKÝ was already a known literary figure before he immigrated to Canada following the Soviet invasion of Czechoslovakia in 1968. He has published a number of books in Canada that have been translated into English, such as his novella, *The Bass Saxophone* (1977) and *The Story of an Engineer of Human Souls* (1984). Although Škvorecký's work has political overtones, it is preoccupied with the universal themes of the individual's fate in history and the importance of art. Also noteworthy as a postwar émigré who writes about WWII and its political aftermath is Estonian Arved Viirlaid, who came to Canada in 1954.

Postwar immigration also revitalized ITALIAN WRITING in Canada, and literary activity among Italians has burgeoned, particularly since 1970. As with other groups, this growth follows as the result of an infusion of immigrants and increasing educational levels and affluence in Canada, but, unlike Hungarians, Czechs and others displaced by the war and subsequent political events, the Italians are not political expatriates. Most have come to find a better material life, and the old country remains at least partially accessible to them. Consequently, Italian Canadian writers, who most often write in English or French, are not preoccupied with European politics or a sense of exile. Rather, in the works of contemporary authors Frank Paci, Giorgio Di Cicco, Mary Di Michele and Alexandre Amprimoz, there is an attempt to balance material and spiritual values as the authors explore the price their parents, often labourers, paid for success in Canada. Their writing, which expresses a cosmopolitan sensibility, explores the contrasts and connections between Italy and Canada, often fusing the authors' Italian and Canadian identities. Italians in Canada can also claim the "protean literary force," John Robert COLOMBO, whose translations and anthologies have been crucial to bringing the work of ethnic writers into the mainstream of Canadian literature.

Asian Canadian literature also came of age during the 1970s. Although CHINESE and JAPANESE Canadians have lived in Canada for over a century, the earlier waves of immigrants produced little significant literature. This is true for a variety of reasons, not the least being the discrimination and hard labour they faced. However, some literature from early immigrants does exist, such as the poetry of Japanese-born Takeo Nakano, who came to Canada in 1920. He published a number of poems, many in the traditional Japanese 31-syllable *tanka,* such as "My Hands" (which appears in English translation in Colombo's *The Poets of Canada,* 1978). *Maple,* an anthology of *tanka* poems by Nakano and other first-generation Japanese Canadians, was published in 1975. Nakano also wrote of his WWII INTERNMENT experience in *Within the Barbed Wire Fence* (1980). The Chinese Canadian immigrant experience has been addressed by Charlie Jang, though his work has not yet been translated into English. In the 1970s, influenced by FRENCH CANADIAN NATIONALISM and by the Asian cultural revival that occurred in the US in the mid- and late 1960s in the wake of the black power movement, a number of young writers began to write about the Asian Canadian experience. These new writers, such as Roy Kiyooka, Paul Yee and Kevin Irie, are preoccupied with the question of their identity as they articulate the experience of growing up as N Americans, albeit often with a second-class status, while being regarded as culturally "other" by the predominantly white society. Asian Canadian writers, perhaps most notably Joy Kogawa, are examining their roots, thus bringing the missing perspective to the standard interpretations of events. In addition, these writers often reject assimilation. Their work has appeared in the journals *Asianadian* and *Rikka* as well as in an issue of *West Coast Review* (1981).

Recent Arrivals Since the 1970s ethnic literature has proliferated remarkably, largely because of the increased diversity of recent immigrants. Responding to the liberalization of Canada's immigration law in 1967, immigrants, most of them well educated and many of them members of visible minorities, have come from all parts of the globe. Just as they have changed and enriched Canadian society generally, they have also brought new dimensions to Canadian literature. Now, in addition to *belles lettres* in the traditional European nonofficial languages, ethnic literature includes such work in languages previously considered exotic to Canadian culture. Moreover, in bringing a Third World perspective to their writing, the new immigrant writers have extended the landscape of Canadian literature, enriched its forms and broadened its concerns.

For example, working in several languages, including Punjabi, Urdu and English, contemporary SOUTH ASIAN writers in Canada, such as Urdu poets Shaheen, Irfana Azia and Abdul Qavi Zia; Pakistani short-story writer M. Athar Tahir; Indian short-story writer Rohintin Mistry and novelist Reshard Gool; and Sri Lankan poet Rienzi Crusz depict in various ways the sharp contrasts between South Asian and Canadian life. Many of these writers publish in the *Toronto South Asian Review.*

West Indian writers in Canada also explore the tensions between "have" and "have-not" nations, and the racial and cultural hostilities that are the residue of British colonialism, as well as the problems faced by the visible immigrants in Canada. Perhaps the most distinguished is Austin Clarke, whose impressive body of fiction is set in both Barbados and Toronto, and includes a trilogy that in portraying West Indian immigrants reveals a deep undercurrent of racism in Canadian society. Younger West Indian writer, Cyril Dabydeen, explores similar themes in both poetry and prose.

Recent Canadian ethnic literature also in cludes the work of South American writers, th most substantial being that of the Chilean With the exception of Ludwig Zeller, perha the best known of the Chilean writers throug his iconoclastic poetry collected in *In the Countr of the Antipodes* (1979), most are political RE UGEES, either having been forced to flee or hav ing chosen to leave Chile following the 197 coup d'état. Most, in the early 1980s, we relatively young, and went to Ontario, whe they continued to write in Spanish. Amon them are Jorge Etcheverry, Erik Martínez an Naín Nómez, members of an avant-garde poetr movement known in Chile as the "Santiag School." Their sophisticated poetry, which draw on both European and Chilean traditions of su realism, is both political and personal. Thoug they are preoccupied with Chile, the émigr also address Canadian experience, as do Gonza Millan, Manuel Aránguiz, Claudio Durán, Ra món Sepúlveda and José Leandro Urbina. A anthology, *Chilean Literature in Canada,* was pub lished in 1982. The S American voice also in cludes the work of Argentinian writer Pab Urbanyi, who came to Canada in 1977 and ha since published a novel, *The Nowhere Idea* (1982 which comments on Canadian life.

Before 1970, for English-speaking Canadian access to and information about ethnic writin in nonofficial languages were very limite Kirkconnell's pioneering translations, colle tions and bibliographic work stood practicall alone. In the 1970s and 1980s, partially as a re sult of the federal government's 1971 announce ment of a policy of MULTICULTURALISM, sever significant translations and anthologies of eth nic literature have been published, includin *Volvox* (1971) and 2 translation issues of *Canadia Fiction Magazine* (1976, 1980), as well as a num ber of anthologies representative of particula groups. Scholarship in the field has also proli erated. The most ambitious bibliographic effo to date is John Miska's *Ethnic and Native Canadia Literature 1850-1979* (1980).

Conclusion The profile of Canadian ethni literature is currently being strengthened bot within and without the country. Canadian eth nic writers today are receiving internationa acclaim: in the early 1980s, Jewish Canadia Irving Layton was nominated for the Nob Prize; Japanese Canadian Joy Kogawa won international awards, including the America Book Award for *Obasan;* and Czech Canadia Josef Škvorecký was awarded the Newsta Prize for *The Bass Saxophone,* an honour which generally considered a prerequisite for the Nob Prize. These authors are celebrated for their ar but theirs is also a contribution to the histor of the Canadian mosaic.

TAMARA J. PALMER AND BEVERLY J. RASPORIC

Ethnic Studies are concerned with the stud of peoples who may share common cultural ori gins and physical traits. The study of intergrou relations embraces a wide range of discipline eg, history, the social sciences, education and th humanities. The development of ethnic studi has reflected developments in Canadian societ in government policy and in the various ac demic disciplines.

While Canadian society has always bee ethnically heterogeneous, the interest in ethni studies began in the 1920s. The concept of th cultural "mosaic," developed in the 1920s, wa later criticized by John PORTER as being a strat fied or VERTICAL MOSAIC. The emergence of th concept of cultural pluralism, or MULTICULTURA ISM, in the 1960s and 1970s was sparked by th growth of "visible minorities" in Canada and b increased intergroup conflict. In the 1970s th federal government proclaimed a policy multiculturalism within a bilingual framewor and a new Citizenship Act. Several province also proclaimed policies of multiculturalism. Since 1972, a number of federal programs have initiated or encouraged ethnic studies. Provincial departments of education have increased opportunities to study not only mother tongues and cultural origins, but also ethnic diversity as a dimension of Canadian society.

It was only with the "ethnic revival" in the US, the expansion of Canadian universities, the advent of non-British and non-French scholars, and the development of multiculturalism policy that ethnic studies' research and publication have burgeoned, especially since the 1960s, with the journal *Canadian Ethnic Studies*.

Ethnic studies have tended to develop unevenly. In particular, studies have often concentrated on changes in ethnic groups that have apparently resulted from "assimilation," or adjustment. These studies have ignored other changes. They have also tended to deal with single groups, to be descriptive rather than analytical and interpretive, and to deal with European groups rather than the "visible minorities," except for studies of attitudes, which have focused on the latter (*see* ETHNIC AND RACE RELATIONS). JEAN BURNET

Reading: H. Palmer, ed, *Immigration and the Rise of Multiculturalism* (1975).

Ritual Head (1976), bronze by Sorel Etrog (*courtesy Sorel Etrog/Gallery Moos*).

Etrog, Sorel, sculptor, writer, philosopher (b at Iaşi, Romania 29 Aug 1933). After a turbulent and traumatic childhood, Etrog began his formal art training in Tel Aviv after his family immigrated to Israel. A chance meeting with Toronto collector Samuel J. Zacks resulted in a solo show in Toronto in 1959, and Etrog moved to that city in 1963. His reputation as an intense, dynamic sculptor was quickly established and in 1966 he was chosen as one of the 3 artists representing Canada at the Venice Biennale. Etrog has important private and public commissions to his credit, some of which, such as *Ritual Head* (Calgary, 1976), are monumental in scale. Crafted predominantly in bronze and more recently in rolled sheet metal, Etrog's sculptures are reminiscent of the structures of the human body or of the massive bolts and hinges of heavy machinery, always suggesting a latent potential for movement. CLARA HARGITTAY

Evangelical and Fundamentalist Movements include Protestant Christian denominations and subgroups, nondenominational and paradenominational organizations whose designation indicates their differentiation from "liberal" or "modernist" religious, social and cultural currents, and identifies them with Christian currents which are measured against standards believed to be based on the Bible. Evangelical, the broader category, has the longer and richer history. A derivative of the Gk *euangelion* ("good news," or "gospel"), "evangelical" is a virtual equivalent of "Christian." Throughout Christian history, however, it has been used by certain groups to differentiate themselves from those considered less true to the Christian gospel. Accordingly, LUTHERANS claimed to be evangelical in contrast to Roman CATHOLICS, METHODISTS to ANGLICANS, low church Anglicans to their high church brethren, and the more revivalist BAPTISTS and Methodists on the American frontier to the more liturgical Anglicans and Lutherans. Hence, the term lacks precision historically and even today some Christians resist the co-opting of the term by a particular Protestant movement.

Evangelicalism, in current usage, is shaped by the fundamentalist-modernist controversy. Believing that liberals were abandoning the Christian essence in accommodating to the modern era's evolving ideology, conservatives in most Protestant denominations fought back in the late 19th and early 20th centuries. The Baptists bore the brunt of the battle in Canada. MCMASTER UNIVERSITY, still Baptist in the 1920s, became the centre of the controversy when Thomas Todhunter SHIELDS, pastor of Toronto's Jarvis Street Baptist Church, accused the board of harbouring a modernist professor of divinity. Shields's refusal to compromise led to his congregation's censure by the Baptist Convention of Ontario and Québec in 1926. In turn, he organized the Union of Regular Baptist Churches with 70 churches and its own college; URBC members were expelled from the BCOQ in 1928. Other dissenters formed the Fellowship of Independent Baptist Churches, which in 1953 united with URBC to form the Fellowship of Evangelical Baptist Churches. Lesser conflicts, eg, one surrounding Brandon College (now BRANDON U), similarly caused schisms that, in turn, added to this new alliance of evangelical Baptists.

Outside Baptist circles the controversy (which reached its zenith in 1925 with the Scopes "monkey" trial in the US), seemed upstaged in Canada by the union that year of more liberal denominations in the UNITED CHURCH OF CANADA. Some fundamentalist PRESBYTERIANS refused to join, considering United Church theology too liberal. Yet resistance to the "liberalization" of major Protestant churches was also redrawing the denominational map in Canada, if only gradually. Conservative movements and denominations, some arising in the 19th century, continue to show disproportionate growth even into the 1980s. The various HOLINESS and PENTECOSTAL groups shared in the fundamentalist cause and are partners in the larger evangelical movement.

Several more strictly fundamentalist or evangelical denominations can be noted as representative. Plymouth Brethren (Christian Brethren) separated from the Church of England in the 1820s to regain certain emphases of primitive Christianity. Their renowned leader John Nelson Darby travelled extensively in Ontario in mid-century, drawing Baptists and Presbyterians among others to his unique "dispensationalist" reading of the Bible. His premillennialism, a conviction that Christ's second coming would precede the millennium (*see* MILLENARIANISM), undergirded a long series of late-19th-century international "prophetic" Bible conferences, several of them in Niagara-on-the-Lake, Ont. The fundamentalist movement drew ideology, leadership and organization from these conferences, but most of Darby's disciples did not follow him into the Brethren churches. Nonetheless, Brethren assemblies, of some 8 varieties according to degrees of exclusivism, were established in Canada and are growing today. Regent College, an interdenominational evangelical graduate theological school in Vancouver, owes much to the Christian Brethren.

Christian and Missionary Alliance, centered in Nyack, NY, where the denomination established one of the first BIBLE SCHOOLS, was founded in the 1880s by former Canadian Presbyterian minister A.B. Simpson. Emphasizing conversion, holy living and missionary endeavours, the CMA became a classical evangelical denomination. This church operates the Canadian Bible College and Seminary in Regina. With a theology much like the CMA's, the Missionary Church arose from the 1969 union of the United Missionary Church and the Missionary Church Association, which originated in several late-19th-century MENNONITE divisions. The new body, emphasizing mission work, has Bible colleges in Kitchener, Ont, and Didsbury, Alta. Another example is the Associated Gospel Churches of Canada, organized in 1925 in Ontario to serve fundamentalists leaving other denominations. Their belief in premillennialism, an inerrant Scripture, holy living, and sectlike separation from the world was typically fundamentalist. This group has 105 churches in Canada today.

By the 1940s numerous Evangelicals sought to distance themselves from the strident militancy, rigorous separatism, anti-intellectualism and premillennial primacy identified with fundamentalism, and claimed the label evangelical. In the US, the National Association of Evangelicals, fd 1942, embraced the likes of evangelist Billy Graham, theologian Carl F.H. Henry, the journal *Christianity Today* and Fuller Theological Seminary. The Evangelical Fellowship of Canada followed in 1964. Adherents affirm the full authority of Scripture in matters of faith and conduct; the necessity of personal faith in Jesus as saviour; and the urgency of converting the sinful. Fundamentalists saw this movement as a betrayal and in Canada formed the Canadian Council of Evangelical Protestant Churches in 1953, parallel to the American Council of Christian Churches, to emphasize premillennialism and strict separation from all liberalism. On the other hand, the 1960s and 1970s produced young evangelicals more open to biblical HIGHER CRITICISM and critical of the identification with conservative and even reactionary politics common in the US.

Already in the 1930s Canadian fundamentalism had proved much less reactionary politically than the American parallel. The dispensationalist founder of the Calgary Prophetic Bible Institute and preacher on the *Back to the Bible Hour*, William ABERHART, and his lieutenant, Ernest MANNING, combined belief in the imminent end of the world with a populist mixture of social reform and small-time capitalism, known as SOCIAL CREDIT, to lead Alberta out of the GREAT DEPRESSION. With Aberhart, Canadian evangelicalism rarely embraced socialism, identified as it was with SOCIAL GOSPEL, but neither did it identify Christianity with raw anticommunism. Even the recent Renaissance Canada movement — directed against secular humanism in family, school and government — and the television show *100 Huntley Street* are restrained versions of their US counterparts and exemplify Canadian moderation.

Fundamentalist separatism and internecine conflicts between various types of fundamentalism and evangelicalism obscure their impact on society. Yet these movements must not be underestimated: nondenominational fundamentalist and evangelical Bible schools, colleges and seminaries teach theology to increasingly more students each year than all mainline Protestant and Catholic schools combined. Besides, evangelically oriented renewal movements are growing even in such denominations as the United Church. Fundamentalism and evangelicalism are very much a part of modern Canada.
RODNEY J. SAWATSKY

Evangelical Fellowship of Canada, a national church agency, organized in 1964 to foster co-operation among evangelical (conservative) Christian denominations and individuals. With headquarters in Willowdale, Ont, the group includes 17 denominations and many interchurch service agencies. The largest member denomination is Pentecostal Assemblies of Canada, with about 1000 congregations. Others are smaller evangelical denominations, such as the SALVATION ARMY, Mennonite Brethren Church, The Christian Reformed Church, and Christian and Missionary Alliance churches. The member denominations have a constituency of about 750 000, and the individual members are evangelicals who are members of mainline denominations or of other denominations not aligned with EFC. Members of all Protestant denominations are on the general council, and 3 of its presidents have been ministers of mainline Protestant denominations.

Previous attempts to organize Canada's estimated 1-2 million evangelicals have been frustrated by their preference for independent initiative. EFC seeks to promote renewal among the churches and to serve as a forum for interaction and stimulation. It also represents an evangelical voice to the media, government and the general public. A full-time executive director and 3 commissions (World Wide Mission and Evangelism, Social Action and Christian Education) implement its program. A quarterly, *Faith Alive* (formerly *Thrust*), is the official EFC publication. *See* EVANGELICAL AND FUNDAMENTALIST MOVEMENT. LESLIE K. TARR

Evangeline: A Tale of Acadie (Boston, 1847), a poem by American poet Henry Wadsworth Longfellow. In 1841 he had heard the story of young lovers parted by the deportation of the ACADIANS, to be reunited only at the end of their lives. His imagination was the main source for his poem, but he used the work of Abbé Raynal (a contributor to Diderot's *Encyclopédie*) and of T.C. HALIBURTON to provide background material. The poem quickly gained worldwide popularity. Its first translation into French in N America was by Pamphile Le May in 1865, but 1851 had already seen its translation into German and Polish, and in 1853 a French translation was published in London. For Longfellow the story was "the best illustration of the faithfulness and constancy of women that I have ever heard of or read." But for many Acadians, especially those of the elite at the turn of the 19th century, it was the true story of their ancestors, "those simple Acadian farmers" who "Dwelt in the love of God and of man. Alike were they free from/Fear, that reigns with the tyrant, and envy, the vice of republics." To them it was the poetic distillation of their history, the true legend of their past. N.E.S. GRIFFITHS

Reading: Naomi Griffiths, "Longfellow's *Evangeline*...," *Acadiensis* II (1982).

Evangelism [Gk *euangelion*, "good news," or "gospel"] is the attempt to win new converts, or to revive existing commitments, to Christ, usually through fervent preaching. The term has been used since the Reformation to identify the proselytizing activities of Protestants who believed in divine grace through faith and the supreme authority of the "gospel." It is currently applied to those who lay special stress on personal conversion, as in the "born-again" movement.

The history of evangelism in Canada can be traced to Henry ALLINE, who in 1779 launched the GREAT AWAKENING movement among the scattered settlers of Nova Scotia. During the 1830s and 1840s, Mgr de Forbin-Janson, bishop of Nancy, France, and other charismatic preachers mounted a Roman Catholic revival to combat the active Protestant evangelists. By the 1860s Anglicans, Roman Catholics and Methodists were all vying for converts in Upper and Lower Canada.

Most Methodist preachers were self-educated natives of Upper Canada who conducted informal services at camp meetings. Ralph HORNER, a Methodist minister, introduced the use of the large tent in 1886. He laid claim to "cyclones of power," which were capable of converting the most stubborn sinner in an instant. Expelled from the Methodist Church, he founded the Holiness Movement Church in 1897 and the Standard Church of America in 1916 (*see* HOLINESS CHURCHES).

The SALVATION ARMY tried tents but soon abandoned them in favour of street services, which municipal authorities tried to suppress. Angry mobs attacked the street-corner evangelists, and both Montréal and Québec were scenes of mass arrests. Nonetheless, the Army's popularity spread rapidly through Canadian urban centres. Numerous Methodist ministers switched to the more evangelically minded Salvation Army. In an attempt to counteract this movement the Methodists supported the efforts of Hugh T. Crossley and John E. Hunter, who toured Ontario and the West in 1887-89. These evangelists formed the Gospel Band movement, out of which evolved the Epworth League. Anglicans, for their part, organized the Church Army.

Since about 1880 American evangelists have had a profound effect on Canadian religious life. Usually unconnected with any church, often unordained, they made their appeals to regular church followers. One, Dwight L. Moody, held gigantic rallies in Toronto, where in 1884 his Christian convention attracted half the adult population of the city. Two years later Georgia evangelists Sam Jones and Sam Small held a 3-week campaign in Toronto, outstripping Moody in attendance and in the enthusiasm of their audiences.

Although most evangelicals maintained that transformation of society could come about only through the conversion of individuals, there was a growing trend to become more involved in Canadian social and political issues (*see* SOCIAL GOSPEL). As the evangelical movements became more established and urbanized, their early political radicalism changed to conservatism. This was true in 19th-century Upper Canada, where Methodist leader Egerton RYERSON led his following away from the REFORM MOVEMENT and thus contributed to Tory victories. In 20th-century Alberta, William ABERHART's Prophetic Bible Institute provided the basis for the formation of the SOCIAL CREDIT party. His successor, Ernest MANNING, was once referred to as the "unofficial pope to Canada's evangelicals." The movements tended to serve those largely ignored by the larger and wealthier church bodies.

A Pentecostal revival in England in 1907 led several Canadian Anglican clergymen to identify with the movement. One who became prominent in the PENTECOSTAL MOVEMENT in western Canada was J.E. Purdie, who later became principal of Western Bible College, Winnipeg (this is now Central Pentecostal College, Saskatoon).

American evangelists found in Canada fertile ground for successful revivalist campaigns and evangelical rallies. The best known and most widely accepted was Billy Graham, whose appearance in Canada in the mid-1950s was welcomed not only by crowds of eager worshippers but by most local churches, which saw him as a means of renewing their members' Christian commitment. Canadian churches launched their own campaigns in the 1950s, principally that of Charles TEMPLETON, a Toronto-born evangelist who conducted several cross-country missions for the UNITED CHURCH. Graham's Canadian brother-in-law, Leighton Ford, headed revival crusades in the 1960s.

Ken Campbell, a Canadian Baptist from near Milton, Ont, who in the 1970s conducted numerous annual crusades across the country, is head of Renaissance International. This is a political pressure group organized in 1974 to lobby on issues of morality, particularly against permissive education and homosexuality.

Electronic Evangelism The advent of radio gave the evangelists a powerful tool to spread their gospel. Aberhart, one of the most popular radio evangelists, began a series of "prophetic lectures" from a Calgary theatre in 1925. In his broadcasts he mingled prophecies on political and economic events with premillennial theology (*see* MILLENARIANISM). During the Depression years these economic ideas became popular, and he soon built a large political as well as religious following. He became premier of Alberta in 1935.

In 1925, the newly formed United Church started its own radio station (VOWR: "Voice of Wesley Radio") in Newfoundland. By 1928 various churches operated stations. In Vancouver the United and Presbyterian churches and the International Bible Students Assn (an organization of the JEHOVAH'S WITNESSES) all had stations. The latter also had stations in Edmonton and Saskatoon. Another Edmonton station belonged to the Christian and Missionary Alliance. In Toronto, CJYC was operated by Universal Radio of Canada, which was later revealed to be the International Bible Students Assn. In 1928, because of complaints concerning the "unpatriotic and abusive" nature of CJYC, the Canadian government closed it down. The ensuing controversy contributed to the movement toward greater government control of BROADCASTING.

One of the most popular evangelists in N America was Canadian Aimee Semple MCPHERSON. For 20 years, until her death in 1944, she attracted large audiences at her $1.5 million Angelus Temple in California and through her own radio stations. She also started a BIBLE SCHOOL and a magazine, wrote several books and spread her gospel through some 200 missions. She founded the International Church of the Foursquare Gospel (fundamentalist, perfectionist, adventist and charismatic).

With the coming of network television the "electronic evangelists" from the US were able to reach all of Canada with appeals for converts and money. In 1984 about 60 syndicated American religious television programs were available in Canada. Purchase of religious air time in Canada and the US totaled over $600 million annually. Canada has about a dozen television evangelists, most prominent among them David Mainse of Toronto, whose program *100 Huntley Street* is broadcast daily over the Global Television network and numerous independent Canadian and American stations. In the early 1980s many of Canada's mainline churches joined Mainse to apply to the CRTC for permission to form an all-religious cable television network in Canada; the application was presented in Nov 1984. The major denominations, faced with declining membership, now see television as a means to spread the Gospel and achieve conversion as did the tent meetings and revival missions of the past. *See* EVANGELICAL AND FUNDAMENTALIST MOVEMENTS. ROY BONISTEEL

Reading: S.D. Clark, *Church and Sect in Canada* (1948).

Evans, James, Methodist minister, linguist, creator of Cree syllabic writing (b at Kingston-upon-Hull, Eng 18 Jan 1801; d at Kelby, Eng 23 Nov 1846). Ordained in 1833, Evans served in various missions in Upper Canada, learning Ojibwa and translating and printing various texts. In 1840 he was appointed superintendent of the British Wesleyan mission to the Hudson's Bay Territories and stationed at NORWAY HOUSE. He established a thriving mission at Rossville and his experience enabled him to create the

Cree syllabic form of writing. He again translated and printed materials and travelled extensively. His life and work were shortened by ill health, by increasing conflict with the HBC and by his accidental shooting of a man in 1844. In 1845 HBC Governor George SIMPSON requested Evans's removal. The Wesleyan Society invited Evans to London to discuss this request, as well as charges of immorality against him, but he died before the investigation was completed. *See* CREE SYLLABICS. GERALD M. HUTCHINSON

Evans, Thomas Dixon Byron, soldier (b at Hamilton, Ont 22 Mar 1860; d at Battle Creek, Mich 23 Aug 1908). The outstanding Canadian soldier of his generation, he joined the 43rd (Ottawa and Carleton) Rifles in 1880, and was promoted captain and adjutant in 1884. After serving with the Midland Battalion in the NORTH-WEST REBELLION (1885) he joined the Permanent Force in 1888, serving with the infantry, mounted rifles and cavalry, and commanding the Canadian cavalry contingent sent to England for Queen Victoria's Diamond Jubilee (1897). He was promoted lieutenant-colonel to command the YUKON FIELD FORCE in 1898, and commanded the 2nd Battalion, 1st Canadian Mounted Rifles, in S Africa (1900) and the 2nd Canadian Mounted Rifles (1901-02). In 1907 he was appointed District Officer Commanding at Winnipeg but the following summer he fell suddenly ill and died. BRERETON GREENHOUS

Evans, William, journalist, agronomist (b at Carana, Ire 22 Nov 1786; d at Côte St-Paul, Canada E 1 Feb 1857). Evans immigrated to Lower Canada in 1819 and settled on a farm in Côte St-Paul near Montréal. His first work, *A Treatise on the Theory and Practice of Agriculture in Canada,* was published in 1835 and translated into French a year later. An agricultural pioneer, Evans published other books and agricultural journals, including the first agricultural journal to be published in French (1844), trying by writing and example to change and reform traditional farming techniques. JEAN-CLAUDE ROBERT

Everson, Ronald Gilmour, poet (b at Oshawa, Ont 18 Nov 1903). Educated at U of T and Osgoode Hall, Everson practised law before moving into public relations. His poetic career began in the 1920s, though his poems have appeared in book form only since the late 1950s. He cofounded the publishing company Delta Books in Montréal, where he has spent most of his life. Most of his poems are concise and direct responses to his environment and personal situation, his later work turning darker and more plaintive. A gathering of his poetry is found in *Selected Poems 1920-1970* (1970). PETER STEVENS

Evolution Modern understanding of evolution began in 1859 with publication of Charles Darwin's *On The Origin of Species by Means of Natural Selection.* In this revolutionary work, Darwin presented an extensive catalogue of evidence to show that all living creatures have descended from ancestors unlike themselves. He also proposed a dynamic, natural mechanism, which he called "natural selection," to explain "descent with modification." The theory of natural selection was developed independently by A.R. Wallace at the same time, and the 2 explanations were presented jointly to the Linnaean Society of London (1858). Throughout the next decades, biologists such as T.H. Huxley improved the theory, defended it from attack by antievolutionists, publicized it and contributed further evidence to it. Three outstanding sources of evidence are discussed below.

Fossil Record Creatures have not always been of the same kinds as they are today. Fossil evidence shows that there has been a unique succession of life forms, progressing from simple to complex, and involving groups replacing other groups which, once extinct, never originate again. Fossils in older rocks are less like living organisms than are fossils in younger rocks; and groups recognized as being distantly related can be seen to be more and more alike, the farther back their fossil ancestors are traced. At local exposures of undisturbed SEDIMENTARY ROCK strata, geologically older fossils occur at lower horizons (layers) and younger fossils at higher (eg, at the BURGESS SHALE, BC, and the dinosaur BADLANDS, Alta). Some successions allow direct observation of evolutionary change through time, ie, of species giving rise to new and different species directly, through intermediate generations.

Comparative Anatomy and Embryology Organisms of different species show resemblances in anatomy and embryonic development that are inexplicable unless the species are descended from a single ancestral species, different from any descendant. For example, the forelimbs of bats, moles, horses and humans are superficially very different, and function in different ways in accordance with their varying designs. Yet the underlying anatomy and development of forelimb bones, muscles, nerves and blood vessels are the same in all. The differences are only in proportions: forelimb anatomy in each group has been modified, from an original pattern in ancestral mammals, to meet diverse adaptive needs in the descendants.

Biogeography Organisms are distributed geographically according to their relationships, not according to their ecological role; hence similar environments, if widely separated, do not necessarily support similar species. For example, most native Australian mammals are MARSUPIALS (they do not develop placentae, young incubate in external pouches), but marsupials do not occur in Africa or SE Asia, which have climates similar to that of Australia. Nothing in the climate or geography of Australia suggests that pouches would be especially advantageous there. The diversity of Australian marsupials results from their descent with modification from a primitive, opossumlike ancestor that entered Australia from S America at least 50 million years ago. When land connections between continents were severed, Australian marsupials evolved in isolation, filling niches occupied elsewhere by placental mammals. Marsupials were prevented from dispersing to Africa and Asia by ocean barriers surrounding the island continent.

How does evolution happen? Darwin realized, and contemporary evolutionary BIOLOGY confirms, that natural selection is the major mechanism governing evolutionary change. Because organisms vary, no 2 members of a species (the basic evolutionary unit) are identical. Many variations can be passed, by genetic inheritance, from parent to offspring. Population size of any organism is limited by the resources of the environment and, in each generation, more offspring are produced than can survive and reproduce. Some individuals in each generation will survive longer and will produce more offspring than others. If enhanced survival and reproduction are caused by heritable variations, offspring that have inherited the favourable variations will also survive longer and reproduce more. Consequently, unless the environment changes to make a favourable variation neutral or disadvantageous, individuals carrying the variation will make up an increasingly high proportion of the species, ie, evolutionary change will occur. It will tend inevitably towards the accumulation of favourable changes. Selection of the variants will be brought about by environmental factors (physical and biological) acting directly on individual organisms (ie, selection is not random). If variations do not occur to meet changing environmental demands, fewer individuals survive and reproduce and ultimately the species will become extinct. Selection was once thought to be either "natural," leading to the longer reproductive life of the organism, or "sexual," leading to the easier attraction of mates. Physical characteristics, eg, antler size or feather coloration, and some genetically patterned behaviours, were thought to have resulted from sexual selection. Sexual selection is now considered simply as natural selection.

In recent years, particularly in N America, both fact and mechanism of evolution have come under attack by some Christian groups espousing "Creationism," the belief that earth and its creatures were miraculously created, as is, only 6000 years ago. Creationist beliefs make no contribution to the scientific explanation of adaptation in plants and animals or of the history and diversity of life; therefore, they lack credibility in the scientific community. *See* ANIMAL; INVERTEBRATE; SOCIAL DARWINISM; VERTEBRATE. RICHARD C. FOX

Reading: S.J. Gould, *Ever Since Darwin* (1977).

Ewart, John Skirving, lawyer, publicist (b at Toronto 11 Aug 1849; d at Ottawa 21 Feb 1933). Educated at Upper Canada College and Osgoode Hall, Toronto, Ewart moved to Winnipeg to practise law in 1882. He was counsel for the French-speaking minority in the MANITOBA SCHOOLS dispute, 1890-96. He settled in Ottawa in 1904 to facilitate his many appearances before the Supreme Court of Canada and the Judicial Committee of the Privy Council, London. He wrote a series of essays urging Canadian constitutional independence, as well as other works on law, Canadian constitutional development and the diplomatic origins of WWI. D.M.L. FARR

Ewen, William Paterson, painter (b at Montréal 7 Apr 1925). Studying at McGill and the Art Assn of Montréal's School of Art and Design in the late 1940s, Ewen was attracted to abstract art through the AUTOMATISTE and PLASTICIEN movements. In 1968 he moved to London, Ont, where painting on gouged plywood sheets led to his return to figuration and a new subject, meteorological phenomena. Included in numerous Canadian group shows, he has had 2 retrospective exhibitions and in 1982 represented Canada at the Venice Biennale. Through his intentionally awkward drawing, emotionally charged images and exceptional handling of materials, he has revitalized Canadian landscape painting. SANDRA PAIKOWSKY

Ewing, Walter Hamilton, trapshooter (b at Montréal 11 Feb 1878; fl 1908). The records of the Amateur Athletic Union of Canada claim incorrectly that Ewing won a gold medal at the 1900 Paris Olympics. There is scant evidence of Ewing's career, though indications are that he was one of Canada's best marksmen at the turn of the century. Even as a member of the 1908 Olympic team, he competed in relative obscurity as media attention was focused on the Canadian runner, Tom LONGBOAT. Despite having to adjust to a more difficult style of shooting — British rules for the sport were used — Ewing proved himself the most consistent competitor. He had a score of 72 points out of 80 for the 3-day event, 12 more than his nearest competitor, and won the gold medal. J. THOMAS WEST

Examination for Discovery is a legal proceeding, also known as examination on discovery, which enables a party to a civil action to examine another person orally and before trial. This proceeding assists the examining party in preparing for trial by compelling the disclosure of relevant facts and by bringing to a focus the issues in dispute. Examination for discovery also serves as a means of obtaining admissions from an adverse party and of evaluating the evidence in his hands; finally, it may, as a side effect, open avenues for out-of-court settlements. The transcript of the examination does not gen-

erally form part of the evidence on which the court will decide the case, but at trial the examining party may introduce any part of the transcript into the record or may use the transcript to point to contradictions or variations between a witness's testimony in court and prior statements made by the same witness on discovery.
See also LAW OF EVIDENCE. YVES-MARIE MORISSETTE

Exchange Rates are rates at which nations' currencies are exchanged, or the price of one currency as opposed to another. Almost every country now uses the American dollar (US$) as the standard against which to measure the value of their own currency. As the majority of Canada's international trade and financial transactions are with the US, the value of the Canadian dollar (Cdn$) in relation to the US$ is of prime importance to Canada.

The dollar became the official monetary unit of the Province of Canada on 1 Jan 1858 and the official currency of Canada after Confederation. Its "spot" or current market value has approximated the US$ until the former's recent decline, the significant exception being during the US Civil War when the Cdn$ rose to US$1.45. From 1879 to 1914 Canadian and US currencies were defined by fixed and equal units of gold. Following WWI, except for the brief period between 1926 and 1929, the Cdn$ has been either pegged at a particular value in relation to the US$ (1962-70) or allowed to fluctuate according to international demand and supply. From 1952 and 1962 and since 1970, the Cdn$ has fluctuated or "floated." During these periods the BANK OF CANADA has bought and sold foreign exchange to smooth out daily fluctuations in the rate. It has also raised or lowered Canadian interest rates, relative to those in the US, to encourage or discourage funds flowing into Canada that increase or decrease the value of the Cdn$.

The exchange rate of the Cdn$ is influenced by several factors besides direct government policy. Good grain harvests, new resource developments, improved labour productivity and prosperous business conditions abroad all help to stimulate exports and put upward pressure on the dollar's foreign worth. An increase in either foreign investment in Canada or foreign tourists visiting Canada has a similar effect. Conversely the opposite of these forces places downward pressure on the dollar's external value. Concurrently the dollar's worth abroad affects the international competitiveness of Canadian products, especially manufactured goods. If increased capital inflows cause the value of the Cdn$ to rise, Canada's manufacturing industry could be adversely affected because foreign products would be cheaper. BRUCE WILKINSON

Experimental Farm, *see* RESEARCH STATIONS.

Exploits River, 246 km long, the longest river in Newfoundland. Its tributaries, the Lloyds and Victoria rivers, rise in the SW corner of the Island and flow NW into Red Indian Lk (250 km^2). The Exploits begins at the NE outlet of the lake, where a dam regulates its flow. The river valley is flat and the river wide and shallow. At GRAND FALLS, the river turns NE and empties into the Bay of Exploits on NOTRE DAME BAY. It is dammed at numerous points and harnessed for hydroelectric power, notably at Grand Falls and Bishop's Falls. The origin of the name, which appeared as early as James COOK's charts of 1774, is unknown. In 1810-11 an expedition led by David Buchan travelled up the river on snowshoes, encountering a camp of BEOTHUK at Red Indian Lk. JAMES MARSH

Exploration Until well into the 16th century, Europe's knowledge of the nearest part of America, its eastern extremity at Newfoundland, was misty and uncertain. Stimulated by the thought that, even with primitive vessels and navigation, the northern crossing to that region could be made in the summer by island hopping via the Faroes, Iceland and Greenland, scholars have debated "prior discovery." Claims have been made for the sighting of some part of Canada's Atlantic coastline by the Irish monk St Brendan in the 6th century, and more credibly for the landing of NORSE adventurers and settlers in the late 10th and early 11th centuries. Archaeological excavations at L'ANSE AUX MEADOWS near the northern tip of Newfoundland have lent substance to the ambiguous evidence in the sagas. These show that the earliest landfall was probably made by BJARNI HERJOLFSSON in 985 or 986, and that about 1000 LEIF ERICSSON landed in the first of a series of expeditions culminating in the establishment of a short-lived Norse settlement. But the sagas are far from clear as to precise locations, and the crucial question of the identity of the Norse seafarers' "Vinland" has never been definitely resolved. Further, if we judge exploration to involve not only discovery but also recording and placing for posterity lands hitherto unknown, then it should be noted that the Norse saga evidence was lost to sight until the end of the 16th century. When Europeans again approached NE America in the late 15th century, they were likely unaware of the routes and discoveries of their predecessors.

A leap forward of 500 years might be expected to produce firmer evidence of voyages attempted and discoveries made. On the contrary, such documents as exist for the half century before the 1520s are fragmentary and obscure. There has been speculation that seamen from Bristol reached Newfoundland, or thereabouts, as early as the 1480s, thus predating Columbus's voyage of 1492. But the only hard evidence points to John CABOT's English expedition of 1497 as the first known voyage to mainland N America in the new era of overseas discovery. Cabot probably coasted the shores of Maine, NS, Newfoundland and Labrador; certainly he saw enough to organize a more ambitious but totally disastrous venture the next year. Equally difficult to pinpoint is the activity in that area of the Portuguese CORTE-REAL family 1500-03; and a rumoured expedition in about 1508-09 by John Cabot's son, Sebastian, may simply have been a hoax. Maps of the period show the rudimentary and hesitant outline of a coast stretching from the Spanish discoveries around the Carolinas NE to the cod fisheries; but there was as yet no realization that Newfoundland was an island, nor any clear idea as to the nature of the coastline between the area of Spanish knowledge and the fishing banks 3000 km N where the English, Portuguese and Bretons were active. Although Giovanni da VERRAZZANO sailed from N Carolina to Newfoundland in 1524 in French service, he stayed too far from shore to sight the strait separating Cape Breton from Newfoundland, and so remained ignorant of the Gulf of St Lawrence.

This major discovery fell to the Breton, Jacques CARTIER, who in 3 voyages in 1534, 1535-36 and 1541-42 (this last for colonization, rather than discovery) began to give recognizable shape to eastern Canada. On his first voyage he entered and explored the Gulf of St Lawrence by way of the Str of Belle Isle. On his second he followed the St Lawrence to the Indian townships of Stadacona [Québec] and Hochelaga [Montréal]. At the latter spot, 1600 km into the continent, Cartier's native informants insisted that the river, now broken by rapids, stretched 3 months' travel to the W. For the first time, Europeans were given some idea of the vastness of the continent in northern latitudes. On his return voyage Cartier discovered Cabot Str between Cape Breton and Newfoundland: he had now navigated both northern and southern entrances into the gulf, and had shown Newfoundland to be insular. The achievement was remarkable. Cartier had discovered the great river which, with its tributaries, was to enable the French to explore and dominate much of the NE of the continent in the 17th century. He also discovered the Canadian winter, for in 1535-36, frozen in at Stadacona, he lost almost a quarter of his men through cold and scurvy. The very extent of Cartier's explorations showed a close, if increasingly uneasy, relationship with the native inhabitants of the St Lawrence Valley. The IROQUOIS, so important in Canada's history, now enter the journals and the consciousness of the French. Cartier had not found the "great quantity of gold, and other precious things" mentioned in his instructions; but to the gulf's teeming fisheries he added the mainland's furs to tempt Europe's commercial acquisitiveness; and if he had not reached the Pacific and so, like Cabot and Verrazzano, failed in that obsessive quest, he had at least found a route pointing straight west.

For the remainder of the century there was no significant advance. The French and other Europeans continued to exploit the FISHERIES and the FUR TRADE, but after Cartier the limits of French enterprise stopped at TADOUSSAC. New explorations, which began in the 1570s, were far to the N (*see* ARCTIC EXPLORATION) where the English, in particular, made repeated attempts along the icebound shores of the eastern Arctic to find a water route to the Pacific. Martin FROBISHER, John DAVIS, William BAFFIN and Henry HUDSON were among the long list of explorers who sought a NORTHWEST PASSAGE in vain. One effect of the search was that it opened up to European view, and eventual English domination, the great inland sea of Hudson Bay, which was explored by a series of expeditions culminating in those of Luke FOXE (1631) and Thomas JAMES (1631-32).

An alternative entry into the continent was essential if the English were to challenge the French, for in the early 17th century the activities of Samuel de CHAMPLAIN confirmed and extended Cartier's claims. The century began with a new departure: in 1600 the first European trading post in Canada was established at Tadoussac. In 1603 Champlain followed Cartier's old route to Hochelaga, and also explored more of the Saguenay and Richelieu rivers. The next year he landed in ACADIA, where he explored the Bay of Fundy and established PORT-ROYAL Habitation [Annapolis Royal]. By 1607 the French had mapped the Atlantic coastline from Cape Breton to Cape Cod (Cap Blanc). Champlain's writings and his last great map of 1632 show the extent of his achievement: the opening up of the difficult country N of the St Lawrence by way of the Saguenay and St Maurice rivers, the crucial discovery of the route from the St Lawrence to the Hudson R by way of Lk Champlain, the exploration of much of the Acadian coastline, and above all the indications of the Great Lakes, based on European exploration and native accounts.

For the explorations of the 40 years following Champlain's death in 1635, the JESUIT RELATIONS provide a unique source. The missionaries' first concern was to record the life and, they hoped the conversion of the Indians, but their travel brought them a close knowledge of the land itself; and in the *Relations* there is telling detail of its rivers and forests, swamps and portages, its harsh winters and brief, insect-ridden summers. For the first time, perhaps, the Canadian environment took shape and form for European readers. From their mission stations in HURONIA the Jesuits in the 1640s pushed westward to Sault Ste Marie and founded a post at VILLE MARIE [Montréal] where the Ottawa R offered a new route to the W. Dominating the Jesuit reports now were Indian and then missionary descriptions of Lk Superior, thought by some to be the gateway to the Pacific. Other French group prospected new portage routes that linked Lk Superior, Georgian Bay and Lk Ontario, reache

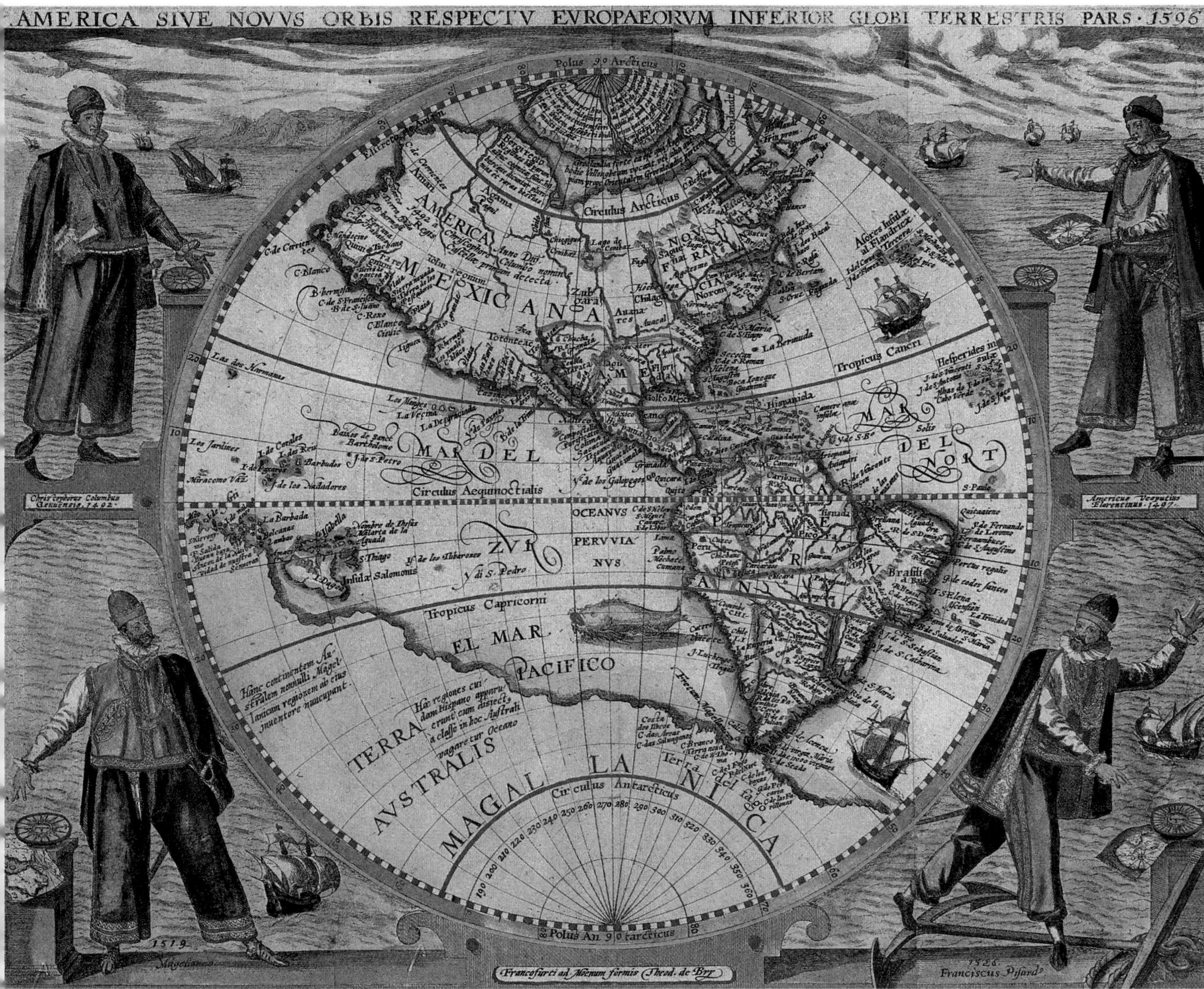

T. de Bry's 1596 map of North and South America gives an impression of the state of geographical knowledge a century after the voyages of Columbus *(courtesy Public Archives of Canada/NMC 8589)*.

the Niagara R from Lk Ontario and wintered (in 1669-70) on Lk Erie. The information from these scattered sources was brought together and given graphic form in the impressive 1672 Jesuit map of the Great Lakes. In the *Relations* we catch glimpses of the COUREURS DE BOIS, the rough outriders of French expansion and discovery, pushing westward in search of furs. The importance of the Indians as guides and helpers emerges clearly in the French accounts. Although the Indians lacked European surveying techniques (*see* CARTOGRAPHY), it was Indian knowledge of the terrain ahead, its peoples and animal life, and the ability to act as interpreters and mediators, that opened the way to the French advance. At least as valuable as direct native assistance to the European was observing and imitating Indian methods of travel, the birchbark canoe in summer and the snowshoe in winter.

One of the most authentic and vivid accounts of life among the HURON and Mohawk in the mid-17th century comes from the narrative of Pierre-Esprit RADISSON, whose explorations with Médard Chouart des GROSEILLIERS, if often obscure in location and direction, were to have profound commercial significance. In their wanderings, which may have taken them as far as Lk Superior, they learned that many prime furs brought down to the French came from the CREE, who lived near "the Bay of the North Sea" (Hudson Bay). Groseilliers and Radisson were convinced that the most direct route for these furs was not the long canoe journey to the St Lawrence and Montréal, but the shorter way N to Hudson Bay, and then to Europe by ship. By 1670 this idea resulted, not in French exploitation of the scheme, but in the establishment of the HUDSON'S BAY COMPANY. It marked the beginning of a 150-year rivalry between the St Lawrence and the Hudson Bay approaches to the fur country, which in the end would take the competing traders, and with them the course of exploration, to the Pacific coast. Although the French in the 1670s finally managed to cross the height of land from the St Lawrence to James Bay by way of the Saguenay R and Lk MISTASSINI, that tortuous route could never compete with Hudson Str. By the 1690s the new company not only had posts on the shores of James Bay, but had established YORK FACTORY at the mouths of the Nelson and Hayes rivers — waterways which led deep into the western interior.

As yet the HBC showed little interest in inland exploration, but in 1690 to 1692 one of its servants, Henry KELSEY, made a remarkable journey. Travelling with the Cree, he reached the Saskatchewan R, a busy waterway of the Indian trade, and from there the great plains, thick with herds of buffalo, and with an Indian population that included Siouan-speaking Assiniboine and Algonquian-speaking BLACKFOOT. To the N the prairie broke into wooded areas where moose, deer and beaver were plentiful — a lush region compared to the immediate hinterland of York Factory. The key to Kelsey's achievement was his ability to speak Cree, and to live and travel with the Indians. He was the first European to reach the Saskatchewan R and the Canadian prairies, the first to leave a description of the grizzly bear and bison. His journey disappeared into an obscurity from which it was not rescued until the 20th century, and long afterwards the only English interior explorations of any note from Hudson Bay were the ventures of William Stuart (1715-16) and Richard Norton (1717-18) northwestward among the CHIPEWYAN. On the canoe routes west from Superior the French took the lead. In 1688 Jacques de Noyon reached Rainy Lk, and the next year possibly Lake of the Woods; on these journeys he heard garbled reports of the Winnipeg R and Lk Winnipeg. Here the westward movement halted until the TREATY OF UTRECHT (1713) ended the prolonged Anglo-French wars in N America.

Dominating French concepts of the "upper country" was the conviction that not far to the west lay the MER DE L'OUEST, envisaged as a N American Mediterranean, connected to the Pacific by a strait (perhaps that alleged to have been discovered on the Pacific coast by Juan de FUCA in 1592), and linked on its other shore with the rivers and lakes along which the French were advancing. The belief distorted all views of western Canada's geography because it could not coexist with a range of mountains running N-S; no indication of the Rockies appears on maps until late in the 18th century. To search for this western sea, and to find new fur areas, was the task of the last great French explorers, the LA VÉRENDRYE family. Much of their exploration took place in what is now the US, but toward the end of the father's life he turned back to the N. In 1739 one son, the Chevalier, reached the Forks of the Saskatchewan R, and in the absence of contemporary knowledge of Kelsey's route must be accounted the effective European discoverer of the river. He reported a great range of mountains far to the W, but geographers obsessed by inland seas, westward-flowing rivers and a nearby Pacific could not assimilate them. More important was that French posts were being built in a steady westward progression — on or near Rainy Lk, Lk Winnipeg, Cedar Lk, and finally, in 1753, Ft St-Louis near the Forks.

Even though the French seemed poised to capture the northwestern fur trade, the HBC was slow to react. Attempts by the ADMIRALTY, by private groups and, rather unenthusiastically, by the company, to find a strait on the west coast of Hudson Bay to the South Sea — the traditional English concept of the NW Passage — had petered out by the late 1740s, but in the following decade the company began to move in different directions. Efforts were made to survey the bleak shores of the Labrador-Québec peninsula with coastal expeditions along the "East Main" of Hudson Bay, and of more far-reaching significance were probes deep inland from York Factory, of which Anthony HENDAY's in 1754-55 was the most spectacular. His method of travelling and his objectives were much the same as Kelsey's. Living with an Indian woman, Henday followed the Cree along their canoe route from York to the lower Saskatchewan R, across the South Branch and the North Branch, to the great buffalo herds of the plains and the horsed Atsina Indians. At his farthest W, somewhere near modern Innisfail, Alta, Henday should have been within sight of the Rocky Mts. It is a puzzle that his journals nowhere specifically mention the great mountain range; as with the La Vérendryes' slightly earlier ventures, conclusive evidence of the first European sighting of the Canadian Rockies is missing.

The SEVEN YEARS' WAR and the CONQUEST affected expansion and exploration. The campaign against Québec in 1759 produced the next year a superb published chart of the St Lawrence by James COOK and other naval surveyors. This work, combined with Cook's subsequent hydrographic surveys around Newfoundland, set a new standard, and brought a new precision to Europe's knowledge of the region. Far to the W the conquest led to the abandonment by the French of the interior posts; but the pause was brief. Within 10 years the posts had been reoccupied by "pedlars" from Montréal, thrustful, energetic traders supported by British and American capital, and using many of the French canoemen and interpreters. Once more the HBC reacted, if slowly, by sending its servants to and beyond the Saskatchewan R, notably Matthew Cocking in 1772-73, and in 1774 the company established its first inland post at CUMBERLAND HOUSE, 100 km beyond The Pas (Man). In command was Samuel HEARNE, newly returned from an impressive overland journey from Ft Churchill down the Coppermine R with a Chipewyan band to the shores of the Arctic Ocean, becoming on 17 July 1771 the first European to sight the continent's northern coastline. Although Hearne's single observation of latitude (71°54′ N) was almost 4° too far N, it established approximately the continent's northern extent, and pushed future searches for a saltwater passage into the icy maze of the ARCTIC ARCHIPELAGO.

Hearne apart, the most extensive explorations were being carried out by NORTH WEST COMPANY traders. The commercial struggle had begun which was to take the rival companies westward into Athabasca, across the Rockies and finally to the Pacific. As the traders battled westward, naval expeditions from Europe were also heading for the unknown NORTHWEST COAST. Vitus Bering's Russian expedition of 1741 had made several landfalls along the Alaskan coast, but there was no southern approach until the 1770s. In 1774 and 1775 Spanish expeditions from Mexico coasted northwards towards Alaska (*see* SPANISH EXPLORATION), and in 1778 Cook made his more comprehensive, but still incomplete, survey northward from NOOTKA SOUND to Bering Str. The approximate outline and location of the coast were at last established, in the same decade as Hearne had reached the polar shore, but neither the British nor their predecessors had determined whether the stretches of coastline glimpsed through mist and rain were islands or mainland. And on the major problem of how far N the Rockies extended, these seaborne expeditions provided no help.

Also in 1778, the NWC, in the person of Peter POND, moved decisively westward. Using Grand Portage at the western end of Lk Superior rather than Montréal as a supply base, Pond tracked NW across the height of land at the Methye Portage and into the Athabasca region. He had crossed the watershed separating the Hudson Bay and Arctic Ocean drainage basins, opened a magnificent new fur-producing region, and taken European enterprises nearer the mountains and the Pacific. By placing Lk Athabasca 1100 km too far W, Pond greatly underestimated its distance from the Pacific, and he made the same error when he discovered Great Slave Lk, from where he suggested a river ran into Cook's R [Cook Inlet, Alaska] on the NW Coast. Lacking formal surveying skills, Pond was one of the last of the old explorers, men tough in body and mind, but often unable to represent accurately in map form where they had been or what they had seen. In 1789 Alexander MACKENZIE followed Pond's river out of Great Slave Lk, only to discover that it led to the Arctic Ocean, not the Pacific. He reinforced the foreboding lesson of Hearne's arctic journey, pointing out that permanent ice virtually ended all hopes of a navigable NW passage. In 1793 Mackenzie again sought a route to the Pacific. From Lk Athabasca he followed the Peace R into the Rockies, crossed the continental divide, followed the turbulent Fraser R down the western slopes, and finally reached the coast by way of the Bella Coola R.

With this magnificent journey Mackenzie became the first European to cross the Canadian Rockies, but the difficulty of his route meant that the discovery had little commercial importance. Coastal and overland exploration were now working together to define the features of the Northwest, for the spot where Mackenzie reached the Pacific coast in July 1793 had been mapped 7 weeks earlier by George VANCOUVER's British naval expedition, in its middle season of a 3-year survey of the coast. Spanish survey expeditions were also on the coast, as were a number of trading vessels; but it was Vancouver's meticulous survey, published in 1798, which formed the definitive record of that intricate shoreline. For the first time the outline of modern Canada was emerging on the maps — most notably on those of Aaron Arrowsmith, who had access to the surveys of the British Admiralty, the HBC and the NWC, and whose maps of N America from 1795 onwards traced the accelerating pace of exploration across the continent.

The overland expeditions had spun thin lines of knowledge across the plains, through the mountains and down to the Pacific and Arctic oceans. After Mackenzie, Duncan MCGILLIVRAY crossed the Rockies by White Man's Pass in 1801, although he stopped well short of the sea; in 1808 Simon FRASER followed the river which was to bear his name down to tidal waters; and in 1811 David THOMPSON made the crucial commercial discovery when he traced the Columbia R down to its Pacific outlet (by then, he found, in American hands). But away from these trails, all was uncertainty, ignorance and rumour; and on both sides of the mountains serious if sporadic exploration continued. While NWC men made the more dramatic journeys, the HBC had since the late 1770s trained and used explorers of considerable technical ability — Phillip Turnor, Thompson, Peter FIDLER — who with the aid of Indian guides mapped the fur-country waterways with a care and accuracy previously unknown. Thompson, in particular, was a prodigious traveller; switching to the NWC, he had by the turn of the century carried out extensive surveys along both the N and S Saskatchewan rivers, in Athabasca, along the Churchill R and around Lesser Slave Lk. It was estimated that he travelled 80 000 km on his surveys, on foot, on horseback and by canoe.

After the union of the rival companies in 1821 the enlarged HBC continued filling in the blank spaces on the maps. With settlement confined to the Atlantic colonies, the St Lawrence Valley, Upper Canada and RED RIVER, the fur trade still provided the main motivation and resources for exploration, opening up new fur regions, or finding better routes in existing areas of exploitation. In the frontier areas of the fur trade such as the Mackenzie Valley and, across the mountains, NEW CALEDONIA, exploration of the waterways continued. Across terrain rugged even by the rigorous standards of the fur trade, Samuel BLACK, John McLeod and Robert Campbell followed rivers on both flanks of the northern Rockies — the upper reaches of the Peace, the Liard flowing into the Mackenzie, the Pelly and Lewes rivers leading into the Yukon, and the Stikine which reached the sea in Alaska. In the E, similar commercial motives led James Clouston, William Hendry and John MCLEAN to make the first crossings of the inhospitable Labrador-Québec peninsula, until then inviolate.

Far to the N the British government and the HBC joined forces in tracing the polar shoreline. The Admiralty sent seaborne expeditions into the Arctic after the Napoleonic Wars in search of the Northwest Passage, while fur traders helped John FRANKLIN's land journeys across the barrens to Hearne's Coppermine R, from which he explored E and W along the coast 1819-22 and 1825-27. From 1837 to 1839 the HBC's Peter DEASE and Thomas Simpson made long sweeps along the polar shoreline from Point Barrow in the W to Rae Str in the E. From 1846 onwards John RAE, one of the most self-sufficient explorers of the North, whose techniques for travel and survival owed much to the INUIT, criss-crossed the huge area bounded by Great Bear Lk, the Boothia Peninsula and the NW coast of Hudson Bay in a series of arduous journeys that soon became directed towards the search for the missing Franklin Expedition.

These explorations were for the most part taking place on or even beyond the margins of profitable fur-trading areas, but slowly the trade was losing its predominance. In the S, interest in settlement overtook the claims of the fur trade, and for this different sorts of surveys were needed. The prospects for agriculture, settlement, telegraph lines and railways became major concerns. It is in this context that the mid-century surveys of S.J. DAWSON, H.Y. HIND and above all, Capt John PALLISER must be seen. They were less explorations of wholly unknown territory than efforts to determine the productive resources of a land previously viewed through the narrow vision of the fur traders. Exploration in the conventional sense remained to be done, particularly in the Arctic; but by the mid-19th century most of the main geographical features of Canada were known and mapped.

GLYNDWR WILLIAMS

Reading: J.B. Brebner, *The Exploration of North America 1492-1806* (1964); W.P. Cumming et al, *The Discovery of North America* (1971) and *The Exploration of North America 1630-1776* (1974); Bernard DeVoto, *Westward the Course of Empire* (1953); S.E. Morison, *The European Discovery of America* (1971); D.B. Quinn, *England and the Discovery of America 1481-1620* (1973).

Exploration and Travel Literature in English Although innocent of literary ambition, the accounts of primary geographical EXPLORATION in Canada are not without literary interest, for they constitute the foundation upon which much of our imaginative literature is built. These documents record the first European images of the Canadian landscape and articulate the experience of entering into it. The Canadian context is not all: the narrators deal with the same universal themes of quest, journey and initiation as are found in the works of Homer and Melville. The importance of exploration writing to modern poetry and prose has gained recognition since the 1960s. The narratives of Alexander MACKENZIE and David THOMPSON have been edited by scholars with literary backgrounds, and Canadian anthologies have begun to include excerpts from the writings of Jacques CARTIER, Alexander HENRY, Samuel HEARNE and others. The notion that the origins of Canadian literature lie almost wholly in the creative efforts of a handful of 19th-century immigrants is beginning to make way for other views.

The initial survey of the land occurred on 3 fronts: overland from Montréal and Hudson Bay, largely motivated by the FUR TRADE's search for profits; through the arctic islands, spurred by the quest for a NORTHWEST PASSAGE; and up the Pacific coast, where British, Spanish, American and Russian mariners rapidly reduced the sea-otter population. The fur industry produced many accounts of interest only to the geographer or historian; yet curiously this profit-oriented enterprise also spawned writing of considerably greater literary significance than did the somewhat less materialistic search for the Northwest Passage. One reason for this may be that the fur trade tolerated personal idiosyncrasies so long as they did not hinder profits. Several fur-trade narratives — particularly Hearne's *Journey from Prince of Wales's Fort in Hudson's Bay to the Northern Ocean* (1975) and Thompson's unfinished *Travels* (ed Richard Glover, 1962) — rise to the level of literature through their success in conveying the author's personality and palpable narrative presence. Hearne's horror at his own powerlessness as he watches his Indian companions slaughter a camp of Eskimos, for example, becomes our horror, not by virtue of the event itself, but through the emotional intensity of observing with the explorer's own eyes. Numerous other fur-trade documents, such as Mackenzie's *Voyages from Montreal* (1801), Alexander Henry the Elder's *Travels and Adventures* (1809) and Alexander Ross's satiric *The Fur Hunters of the Far West* (1855), achieve literary significance to the extent that they create a convincing narrative point of view, presenting models for later writers to draw upon.

The same is true of the writing about the Northwest Passage. *The Strange and Dangerous Voyage of Captain Thomas James* (1633) has intrinsic merit in its vivid description of a winter in the Arctic. James's expedition was privately financed; like the fur traders, he had the freedom to create a firm narrator's perspective. However, even though the imaginative and dramatic potential of the search is immense, that potential remains dormant in all but a few accounts, a situation arising because the narratives fail to create individual human voices through which experience can be communicated. Most of this failure in 19th-century accounts can be attributed to the influence of the British ADMIRALTY, the agency which dominated ARCTIC EXPLORATION between 1818 and 1859. The Admiralty expected of and nurtured in its officers an objective and impersonal sensibility, one that served naval interests well, but limited the subjective dimension of literature. John Ross's *A Voyage of Discovery* (1819), W. E. PARRY's *Journal of a Voyage for the Discovery of a Northwest Passage* (1821) and Robert MCCLURE's *The Discovery of the North-West Passage* (1856) all suffer from this restriction. Johann Miertsching, a Moravian missionary aboard McClure's ship as interpreter, kept an evocative and powerful journal that McClure apparently tried, but failed, to suppress. The author's compassion and sensitivity to the human suffering on the nearly disastrous journey of 1850 to 1854 are freely expressed, a freedom from naval restrictions granted by Miertsching's civilian status.

There are other literary dimensions to these records: some accounts became catalysts for imaginative works, and Northwest Passage accounts, when read together, have the flavour of epic. The intrinsic value of an isolated piece, however, depends very much on the image we receive of the man behind the journal or narrative.

RICHARD C. DAVIS

Travel Literature

Hundreds of travel books on Canada have been published in the last 2 centuries, packed with cultures and climate, people and places. Long subtitles specify their scope, eg, George Head's *Forest Scenes and Incidents in the Wilds of North America; being a Diary of a winter's route from Halifax to the Canadas, and during four months' residence in the woods on the borders of Lakes Huron and Simcoe* (1829). Most titles are shortened here.

Earliest English reports, in Richard Hakluyt's *Divers Voyages* (1582) and *The Principall Navigations* (1589; 1598-1600), and Samuel Purchas's *Hakluytus Posthumus* (1625), mostly described rocky shorelines; but late 17th- and early 18th-century French travellers Louis HENNEPIN, L. A. de LAHONTAN and P.F.X. de CHARLEVOIX, and the Swede Pehr KALM moved inland to describe Québec life. French Canadian culture retained dominant interest for British writers from Isaac Weld, *Travels Through the States of North America and the Provinces of Upper and Lower Canada* (1799), George HERIOT, *Travels Through the Canadas* (1807) and John Lambert, *Travels* (1810 — beautifully illustrated in aquatint), to William Teeling, *England's French Dominion* (1932). American writers who also relished the quaint Old World flavour of convent and citadel included John Ogden (*A Tour*, 1799), H.D. Thoreau (*A Yankee in Canada*, 1866), Walt Whitman (*Diary in Canada*, 1904), Anson Gard (*The Last West*, 1906) and Dorothy Duncan (*Here's to Canada*, 1941). Some American travellers also felt the charm of the Maritimes, eg, John Cozzens in *Acadia* (1859); and later the attractions of the northern frontier, eg, Warburton Pike (*Through the Subarctic Forest*, 1896).

To British tourists the American presence in Canada was puzzling. Those Britons who tucked a Canadian tour into a visit to America in order to test the difference between colonial and republican life included Basil Hall (*Travels*, 1829), Frederick Marryat (*A Diary in America*, 1839), Charles Dickens (*American Notes*, 1842), Anthony Trollope (*North America*, 1862) and Basil Newman (*American Journey*, 1943).

Military men reported on garrison life as a distinctive imperial feature. Gentlemanly sports, flirtations, road building and marches added verve to Col Richard Levinge's *Echoes from the Backwoods* (1846), George Warburton's *Hochelaga* (1846), Col J.E. Alexander's *L'Acadie* (1849) and Sir Richard Bonnycastle's *The Canadas in 1841* (1842) and *Canada and the Canadians* (1846). Lt Francis Duncan described *Our Garrisons in the West* (1864). Anywhere in Canada, "a face yet burned by the suns of India, encircled in a fur cap," might appear to "a friend from China or Aldershot." Officers and other British gentlemen wrote often about sporting pleasures, eg, Capt F. Tolfrey's *The Sportsman in Canada* (1845), Campbell Hardy's *Sporting Adventures in the New World* (1855) and P.E. Doolittle's *Wheel Outings in Canada* (1895).

Other observers described the alternate culture — or lack of it — outside the garrisons, in backwoods settlements. Sour reports on narrow, isolated lives appear in John Howison's *Sketches of Upper Canada* (1821) and Isaac Fidler's *Observations on Professions, Literature, Manners, and Emigration* (1833). The unglamorous life of pioneers is described by E.A. Talbot in *Five Years' Residence* (1824), which parodies the colonizer's glowing accounts of the trip upriver to Ontario; disillusionment is tinged with bitterness in comparable later reports, such as W.H.P. Jarvis's *The Letters of a Remittance Man* (1908), N.P.R. Noel's *Blanket-Stiff* (1912) and E.F.G. Fripp's *The Outcasts of Canada* (1932). But some settlers' stories strike a happier note of acceptance of this strange, ungenteel life: Samuel Strickland's *Twenty-Seven Years in Canada West* presents advice for prospective British immigrants, and A.J. Church edited the letters of his 2 young sons in the cheery *Making a Start in Canada* (1889).

Canadian women appear in all these reports, as pretty French Canadian "muffins" or as indomitable ladies in the lonely bush. Some women, temporarily based in Canada, contributed excellent books on their travels: Anna Jameson, *Winter Studies and Summer Rambles in Canada* (1838), Lady Monck, *My Canadian Leaves* (1873), Lady Dufferin, *My Canadian Journal, 1872-78* (1891), Lady Aberdeen, *Through Canada With a Kodak* (1893), Marion Cran, *A Woman in Canada* (1910), Georgina Binnie-Clark, *A Summer on the Canadian Prairie* (1910) and Eva Hasell, *Across the Prairie* (1922). Other ladies, birds of passage, also published their impressions, among them Isabella Bishop (1856) and the duchess of Somerset (1890). They were particularly aware of the environment — winter cold, mosquitoes, autumn colours and wild flowers — although they also comment on social conditions. John Mactaggart in *Three Years in Canada* (1829) and John Bigsby in *The Shoe and Canoe* (1850) give an equally vivid sense of harsh conditions and varied terrain.

Travel books add to our sense of life in the Canadian art world: Horton Rhys in *A Theatrical Tour for a Wager!* (1861) and Peggy Webling in *Peggy* (1924) give inside glimpses of touring life on provincial stages; T.R. Richman in *Short Notes* (1886) recounts discussions with fellow architects; and Marion Cran spends a chapter on Canadian art and artists.

In *Wanderings of an Artist* (1859) Paul KANE combines glimpses of the artist's life with notes on his dominant subject, the Canadian Indian. Other travellers emphasized the Indian peoples as well. Sir George SIMPSON in *An Overland Journey Around the World* (1847) begins with an account of the great treaty gatherings; L. Oliphant in *Minnesota and the Far West* (1855) and J.G. Colmer in *Across Canadian Prairies* (1894) extend the story to the Plains Indians; S.P. Day in *English America* (1864) updates the Manitoulin gatherings; and *B.C. 1887* (1888) by J.A. Lees and W.J. Clutterbuck adds an effective mix of comic and sympathetic vignettes of West Coast Indians to its many other excellences. Travellers generalize from very selective experience, but the travel books are the best, and for many decades the only, reports on contact between NATIVE PEOPLES and other Canadians. In this as in many other ways, W.F. Butler's *The Great Lone Land* (1872) is a most important document.

In the later 19th century the journey across the prairies to, and sometimes through, the Rocky Mts became increasingly popular. British visitors included the earl of Southesk, who published a record of his travels of 1859-60 in *Saskatchewan and the Rocky Mountains* (1875), and Viscount Milton and W.B. Cheadle, whose *Northwest Passage by Land* (1865) gives a good picture of the prairies. Fraser Rae reported on his travels from *Newfoundland to Manitoba* (1876), and in 1884 Gov Gen the marquess of Lorne published *Canadian Pictures*. Canadians too began to write travel books in increasing numbers; G.M. Grant (*Ocean to Ocean*, 1873) and Charles Horetzky (*Canada on the Pacific*, 1874) both recorded their experiences on the difficult overland journey. Sir Sandford Fleming, surveyor and chief engineer for the Canadian Pacific Railway, wrote about his travels in *England and Canada* (1884). The opening of the CPR in 1885 made transcontinental travel very much faster and easier, and travel books proliferated. The new style of travel was reflected in Edward Roper's *By Track and Trail* (1891) and Douglas Sladen's *On the Cars and Off* (1895). Twentieth-century accounts of the transcontinental tour include Bruce Hutchison's *The Unknown Country* (1942) and Eugene Cloutier's *Le Canada sans passeport* (2 vols, 1967; tr *No Passport*, 1968), a Québecois account tinged with tension over biculturalism.

Even the great West, however, could not supplant Niagara Falls as the showpiece of Canadian travel books. Most tourists would agree with George Warburton: "The sight was precisely what I expected — the sensations it caused, totally different." Of all Niagara pieces, the most exciting is perhaps Charles Lyell's in *Travels in North America* (1845): this geologist expanded his theory of fossil life as he explored the escarpment, then topped his fine description of the falls with the report of a ride northwards, presenting a vision of great land terraces circling upward from the Great Lakes to the Ontario northlands.

Air travel has ended the slow experience of distance, the passage through changing regions, the encounters by the way that were once the staple of Canadian travel books. Few travellers keep travel diaries, and fewer publish them. But through their long history, travel books, by both creating and clarifying our image, at home and abroad, have helped make Canada.

Elizabeth Waterston

Reading: G. Warkentin, "Exploration Literature," and Elizabeth Waterston, "Travel Literature," in W. Toye, ed, *The Oxford Companion to Canadian Literature* (1983); various articles in C. F. Klinck, ed, *Literary History of Canada* (2nd ed, 1976), vols 1 and 2.

Exploration and Travel Literature in French Travel accounts, in their dual capacity as documentation and literature, were the founding texts of Québec culture. The early narratives offer eyewitness accounts of how a small group of Europeans established settlements in N America. For the years 1534-1634 in particular, they are our richest sources for the reconstruction of both the period's mentality and its events. As literature, they established subjects that later writers picked up: nomadic life in the open spaces, the St Lawrence R, the seasons and the process of settling a country. The accounts of travels in New France fall into 3 somewhat overlapping categories: the investigations and explorations reported by Jacques Cartier and Samuel de Champlain; the more encyclopedic accounts written by Gabriel Sagard, Nicolas Denys and the Jesuits; and the critical analyses of Louis Hennepin and Baron de Lahontan.

Cartier studied the St Lawrence R, offered the first overall view of the Montréal region and attempted to develop a comprehensive profile of the Indian. Champlain left the waterways behind, penetrated the land and its villages, formed alliances and waged war. Sagard, whose descriptive narrative is predominantly ethnological in approach, takes a narrow but perceptive look at the Huron, pores over the details of their daily life, and attempts to draw conclusions about their sexual, religious, dietary and political practices. The Jesuits, on the other hand, in their comprehensive 60-year inquiry recorded in the Jesuit Relations, produced a more fragmented but also more systematic study. Their knowledge was informed by a mixture of mysticism and militant evangelism and a vision of the world as a vast theatre where God and Satan fight a bitter, unending battle, in this case through the "savages." Finally, Lahontan, in his *Nouveaux Voyages*, *Mémoires* and *Dialogues*, sought not so much to record new knowledge about the new land as to challenge the nature of what was already known. Whereas P.F.X. de Charlevoix had presented N American history as a coherent, comprehensible whole, Lahontan argued that because it was forever changing, it could have no lasting meaning.

The travel account, a complex genre, is both a description of individual experiences and a means through which existing general knowledge can be disputed or expanded. Yet how can the author convey the uniqueness of his own adventures when, in many cases, others have travelled his route before him? It is not enough to stress exotic and curious events and places; they must be dramatized, ordered and put into an appropriate context for the understanding of the reader. This explains the numerous dissertations on climate and on the Indians' origins and religion; the many charts and drawings of N American Indians and of *septentrional* (northern) and *méridional* (southern) plants and animals; and, finally, the long descriptions of certain phenomena — for Lahontan, the beaver; for Hennepin, Niagara Falls; for the Jesuits and Marie de l'Incarnation, the earthquake of 1663, war, hunting, and the elaborate Huron marriage rituals and Festival of the Dead.

From 1760 on, travel accounts fall into 3 main categories. Reports written by the voyageurs, traders and explorers comprise the first of these groups. Although relatively few first-hand narratives are extant, 20th-century Canadian and American scholars have brought to light interesting accounts written between 1779 and 1810 by Joseph-François Perrault, Jean-Baptiste Perrault, Charles Le Raye, Jean-Baptiste Trudeau, Pierre-Antoine Tabeau, François-Antoine Larocque and Gabriel Franchère.

A second category, which flourished in the first half of the 19th century, consists of missionary reports replete with observations on Indian and Métis life. *Les Missions* by Frs Modeste Demers and François-Norbert Blanchet and descriptions of the Pacific coast region by Frs Jean-Baptiste Brouillet and Jean-Baptiste Bolduc are typical of such accounts. By the 1880s French Canadian missionary orders (*see* Christian Religious Communities) were sending their members out to labour in the far corners of the British Empire, Latin America, French Africa, Japan and China, and reports of their travels were published in a plethora of mission-oriented periodicals.

The third and by far the largest category of travel literature produced since the end of the French regime belongs to the golden age of transatlantic luxury tourism, from the mid-19th century to the early 1960s. More than 70 accounts of travel to the "Old World" were published between 1815 and 1914. France is described in 46 of these, Italy (especially Rome) in 38 and England in 20. Tourists and pilgrims also visited the Holy Land, Algeria, Egypt, Spain and Greece. All these narratives provide valuable insights into the mentality of the clerical and intellectual elite of Québec at the time. Accounts still recognized for their literary merit include Mgr J.O. Plessis's *Journal d'un voyage en Europe . . . 1819-1820*; François-Xavier Garneau's *Voyage en Angleterre et en France [1831-33]* (1854-55); and a variety of accounts by Adolphe-Basile Routhier, Honoré Beaugrand, Narcisse-Henri-Edouard Faucher de Saint-Maurice, Jules-Paul Tardivel, Fr Léon Provancher, Fr Jean-Baptiste Proulx and Fr Henri Cimon. Quality declined after 1914, but there were exceptions to the general banality, eg, the writings of Henri Bourassa, Jean Bruchési, Charles-Joseph Magnan, Dr Jules Dorion, Germaine Bernier (*Impressions*, 1954) and Alain Grandbois (*Visages du monde*). Eugène Cloutier also wrote a series of fine personal travel reports (*En Suède*, 1970; *À Cuba*, 1971; *Au Chili*, 1972, etc).

Travel writers also wrote about trips through Québec, Canada, the US and even Africa. Arthur Buies was clearly the best of those writing on Québec. Others wrote of specific historical events such as the War of 1812; the Rebellions of 1837-38 (seen through the eyes of political exiles who described their adventures as deportees in Bermuda and Australia); the California gold rush; the expedition to Mexico (Faucher de Saint-Maurice); the experiences of the pontifical Zouaves; the North-West campaign of 1885; the Klondike Gold Rush; and the 2 world wars.

In sum, travel accounts in French were at their richest — from every point of view — during the French regime. Thereafter, the adventurous missionary and colonial expeditions, with all their suspense, sense of purpose and excitement of discovery, were followed by relatively uneventful tourist excursions. In the 19th century autobiography and the novel supplanted travel literature as expressions of personal adventure. Finally, by the 1960s, as a result of mass tourism and the competition of mass media, this genre had virtually disappeared from French Canadian literature.

P. Savard and R. Ouellet

Reading: J. Hare, *Les Canadiens français aux quatre coins du monde* (1964); Maurice Lemire, ed, *Dictionnaire des oeuvres littéraires du Québec*, vols I-IV (1978-84); G. Rousseau, *L'Image des États Unis . . .* (1981).

Expo 67 (the Canadian Universal and International Exhibition) was held in Montréal from 28 April to 27 October 1967. It was the first first-category exhibition in the Americas and the first since the Brussels World Fair of 1958. Conservative senator Mark Drouin, on his return from Brussels, suggested that a universal exhibition would be a fitting way to celebrate Canada's Centennial Year. Application was made to the International Bureau of Exhibitions, but the Soviet Union, which was celebrating its 50th anniversary in 1967, was granted the right. When the Soviets withdrew because of the prohibitive costs, Canada, spurred on by the tireless lobbying of Montréal mayor Jean Drapeau, reapplied. On 13 Nov 1962 Canada's proposal was accepted. A corporation to supervise organization and construction was established, and in Sept 1963 Pierre Dupuy was appointed commissioner general, Robert Shaw was made deputy commissioner, Col Edward Churchill was placed in charge of construction and P. de Gaspé Beaubien was placed in charge of operations.

Although not obvious initially, a monumental task had been undertaken. With 3 governments participating (Canada, Québec and Montréal), the power struggles and wrangling were at times overwhelming. Canada's interminable winters and problems associated with creating an island landfill site in the St Lawrence combined to form a widespread belief just 42 months before the opening that losses should be cut and Expo abandoned. Despite the poten tial hazards, however, Expo was completed on time and was a resounding success.

The fair's theme was Man and His World (Terre des Hommes); it was subdivided into 4 categories — Man the Explorer, Man the Creator, Man the Producer and Man in the Community. Each was a theme pavilion or a complex of pavilions, and these themes appeared in many of the national exhibits.

Over 60 nations and a multitude of states, cities, provinces, international organizations and private companies participated. The approaches taken by some of the world's greatest architects in designing the pavilions were varied and frequently breathtaking. Arthur ERICKSON's pyramidal Man in His Community was built from hexagonal frames of Douglas fir; the German pavilion, a 15-storey, multi-peaked tent of plastic, indicated how concept and materials might radically alter the design of buildings such as auditoriums; and Buckminster Fuller's geodesic dome for the US became the prototype for a new trend in construction. The interiors of the pavilions also varied greatly. Some presented prosaic displays of consumer goods and machinery while others imaginatively depicted their history and cultural traditions. Montréal architect Moshe SAFDIE's revolutionary Habitat '67 was a graphic demonstration that by industrializing the building process, there are better and cheaper ways to house people. Expo also witnessed the development of new approaches to viewing film. The multi-screen technique was omnipresent, transforming everyday sights and sounds into more vital images.

More than 50 million visitors attended the fair. They came from all corners of the globe and from all parts of Canada to participate in what was eventually lauded as the best world's fair ever.

Reading: R. Fulford, *This Was Expo* (1968).

External Affairs, Department of After CONFEDERATION in 1867, British diplomats continued to handle Canada's boundary disputes and treaty negotiations with other countries. In 1909 PM Sir Wilfrid Laurier created the Dept of External Affairs. Under a distinguished civil servant, Sir Joseph POPE and a handful of clerks, the department functioned as an archive, issued passports to Canadians travelling abroad, provided the focus for liaison with the British COLONIAL OFFICE and a foreign consular core, and handled routine relations with the US. Diplomacy, however, remained largely in the hands of the prime minister. Transformation to a proper foreign office began in the mid-1920s under PM Mackenzie King and his undersecretary of state for external affairs, O.D. SKELTON. As Canada acquired more autonomy within the COMMONWEALTH, it needed its own diplomatic representatives abroad. A foreign service was established and, between 1925 and 1929, Canadian posts opened in Geneva, Washington, Paris and Tokyo. During and after WWII, additional posts were opened and Canada emerged as a MIDDLE POWER. With the department as their headquarters, Canadian diplomats played important roles in creating the UNITED NATIONS, NATO and various PEACEKEEPING forces.

The department's headquarters in the Lester B. Pearson Building on Ottawa's Sussex Drive co-ordinates activities of 117 posts in 75 countries. The department provides policy guidance to other government departments and agencies; plans and interprets the international impact of domestic decisions; ensures international representation of Canadian interests through its ambassadors, high commissioners and consuls; negotiates international agreements; fosters an awareness and understanding of Canada abroad; and provides assistance and guidance to Canadians travelling and working abroad. Since 1982 a restructuring and integration of government departments has brought international trade, export promotion, immigration policy and development assistance under the department's control. D.M. PAGE

External Relations To a great extent, the history of Canada's external relations is the history of the development of a British colony into an independent nation within the COMMONWEALTH. Colonial foreign relations were normally controlled by the mother country. In the case of BRITISH NORTH AMERICA, foreign relations largely meant relations with the neighbouring US. The implicit understanding was that the metropolis controlled relations with foreign states, and that as a corollary it had the obligation to defend the colony. This assumption did not lose all its force until well into the 20th century.

Concession of RESPONSIBLE GOVERNMENT to the N American colonies in the late 1840s did not alter this situation. The colonies that united in CONFEDERATION were essentially self-governing in internal affairs. Nevertheless, the BRITISH NORTH AMERICA ACT which effected the union said nothing about external relations. It was assumed that those relations were virtually the exclusive concern of the UK. The authorities conducting Canada's business with the US were the GOVERNOR GENERAL, the British minister in Washington and the foreign secretary in London. The governor general consulted his Canadian ministers and transmitted their views to London; but final authority rested with the British.

The Canadian government acquired influence over the relationship only gradually. An important landmark was the TREATY OF WASHINGTON in 1871, which liquidated dangerous issues between Britain and the US left over from the AMERICAN CIVIL WAR. The British government nominated as one of its 5 negotiators PM Sir John A. MACDONALD. This recognized both Canada's growing status and her concern with the issues; but Macdonald was present as a British plenipotentiary, not as a representative of his country. To a large extent the negotiation was triangular: Macdonald had serious disagreements with his British associates, particularly over the Atlantic fisheries. Although unhappy over this aspect of the treaty, he signed it; and the treaty was in fact advantageous to Canada, simply because it restored friendly relations between the British Empire and the US.

In 1874 the Liberal government of Alexander MACKENZIE prevailed on Britain to accredit George BROWN (along with the British minister in Washington) to seek a RECIPROCITY treaty similar to that of 1854, which the US had terminated in 1866. Macdonald and his colleagues had tried for this in 1871, without success. Brown failed likewise. Macdonald, on returning to power in Sept 1878, enacted the NATIONAL POLICY. Tariff reciprocity with the US continued to be a Canadian goal, but successive American administrations gave no encouragement. Trade policy remained Canada's most persistent problem with the US, with fishery troubles a close second. In 1880, with Britain's reluctant consent, Sir Alexander Galt was appointed Canadian high commissioner in London. In 1882 a *commissaire général* was appointed in Paris; he doubled as a representative of Québec until 1912. He had no diplomatic status. No further development of Canadian representation abroad took place until after WWI.

In the latter part of Queen Victoria's reign, British anti-imperialism (reflected in the withdrawal of British garrisons from central Canada in 1870-71) had given place to its opposite. In Canada, IMPERIALISM gave an outlet to growing NATIONALISM and the desire to play an expanding part in the world. When British Gen C.G. Gordon was cut off in Khartoum in 1884, there was considerable demand in Canada for a contingent to go to the Sudan. Macdonald deliberately damped this down. But when Britain sought to raise at its own expense a body of Canadian voyageurs to help a rescue expedition surmount the cataracts of the Nile (*see* NILE EXPEDITION), no objection was made.

The beginning of the SOUTH AFRICAN WAR in 1899 raised more serious questions. Sir Wilfrid LAURIER's Liberals were now in power in Canada. Québec, the citadel of Laurier's political authority, was largely unmoved by the imperial enthusiasm of other provinces. On the question of contributing a contingent, Cabinet was deeply divided. Ultimately, Laurier was forced by the majority to send a battalion of volunteers. Further contingents followed, and in spite of Laurier's disclaimers when attacked by his Québec compatriots (notably Henri BOURASSA), it was clear that a precedent had been set.

Relations with the US continued to turn largely on commercial policy. In 1888 the Liberals had adopted "Unrestricted Reciprocity"; on it they fought and lost the election of 1891, Macdonald's last. Thereafter, the Liberals abandoned unrestricted reciprocity, and, death having removed Macdonald from the scene in 1891, were elected, headed by Laurier, in 1896. Laurier's government would come to grief, in due course, over reciprocity, but meanwhile he had to confront the ALASKA BOUNDARY DISPUTE, the last great boundary dispute between Canada and the US. This old controversy acquired new importance during the KLONDIKE GOLD RUSH. The handling of the question by US Pres Theodore Roosevelt aroused bitter resentment in Canada, as did the behaviour of British representative Lord Alverstone, who, when the tribunal on the matter met in 1903, voted with the Americans. Nevertheless, as with the Treaty of Washington, this settlement served Canada's paramount interest by removing an obstacle to friendly relations between the empire and the US.

Canada's relationship with the empire found a focus in the series of COLONIAL AND IMPERIAL CONFERENCES, the first of which was held in London in 1887. During Lord Salisbury's Conservative government (1895-1902), the colonial secretary was the energetic Joseph Chamberlain, who envisaged an empire more organized and centralized than the informal affair that had grown up. In Laurier he met a determined defender of the status quo. Sir Wilfrid regularly declared that Canada was well satisfied with things as they were and had no demands to make; it had its autonomy and, he more than hinted, intended to keep it. After the turn of the century, the menace presented by the growing German navy led to demands both in Canada and in Britain for some Canadian naval assistance. Sir Wilfrid's ultimate response was not a contribution to the Royal Navy, but an autonomous Canadian navy, provided for by the NAVAL SERVICE ACT of 1910.

The general election of 1911 turned to an unprecedented extent on questions of external policy. Any naval policy was unpopular in Québec. Robert Laird BORDEN, the Conservative leader, argued that no permanent policy should be adopted until approved by the people; meanwhile there should be a contribution to the RN. His campaign played down the naval issue; but the Naval Service Act did Laurier much harm in Québec. Elsewhere the paramount issue was reciprocity with the US. The agricultural West had been pressing for freer trade, and there was similar agitation in the US. The result had been the 1911 reciprocity agreement which provided for free trade in a wide range of agricultural products and a limited number of manufactured goods. Violent nationalistic opposition developed against this measure; manufacturers assailed it as a menace to Canadian industry, and it was claimed that it would open the door to political union. Laurier lost the election, and Borden became prime minister.

The predominantly British province of Ontario now succeeded Québec as the main seat of the government's political power, and external policy reflected this fact. Borden was as much of a nationalist as Laurier, though his nationalism found different expression. Where Laurier had sought to stand aside from imperial entanglements, and had asserted no claim to influence in the imperial system, Borden was prepared to participate but attempted to exact a price. In England in 1912 he told British statesmen that Canadians would now expect "a voice" in the formation of imperial policy. When later that year he proposed that Canada should contribute 3 battleships to the RN, he clearly expected a quid pro quo in the form of such influence. Britain's Liberal government was loath to commit itself; and the Canadian Senate rejected Borden's naval bill.

Everything changed with the outbreak of WORLD WAR I. Canada was united behind the decision of Borden's government to give full support to Britain, and to dispatch a CANADIAN EXPEDITIONARY FORCE. There was now a stronger argument than ever before for a Canadian "voice" in the making of policy; but British PM Lord Asquith still had nothing to offer. In Dec 1916 Asquith fell and David Lloyd George became prime minister. Lloyd George realized that the Dominions could not be expected to continue making sacrifices without being called to Britain's councils. He therefore summoned an Imperial War Cabinet and an Imperial War Conference, which first met in Mar 1917, and between them discussed both the conduct of the war and imperial matters generally. In Apr 1917 the conference passed Resolution IX, largely Borden's work, which placed on record the opinion that any postwar readjustment of constitutional relations "should be based upon a full recognition of the Dominions as autonomous nations of an Imperial Commonwealth," and should give the Dominions and India "an adequate voice in foreign policy." There was a second series of sessions of the Imperial War Cabinet and War Conference in 1918, in which Borden was active; and in 1919 the Imperial War Cabinet in effect became the British Empire Delegation to the Paris Peace Conference. Largely as a result of Borden's insistence, the dominions were accorded what amounted to dual representation at the conference: as nations in their own right, along with other small Allied nations, and as units of the British Empire. In both capacities Canada signed the TREATY OF VERSAILLES and became a member of the LEAGUE OF NATIONS, whose covenant was part of the treaty. Thus the country acquired a new international status, won by its soldiers on the battlefield and confirmed by its statesmen's pertinacity at the conference table.

A small department of EXTERNAL AFFAIRS had been instituted by statute in 1909, principally to ensure the businesslike conduct of the country's external concerns. In 1912 an amendment made the prime minister also secretary of state for external affairs — an arrangement that lasted until 1946. For many years the department's most important official was Loring C. CHRISTIE, appointed by Borden in 1913 with the title of legal adviser. He was Borden's confidential assistant at the Imperial War Cabinet and the Peace Conference, and a major contributor to the national achievements of the period. When in July 1920 Borden retired and Arthur MEIGHEN became prime minister, Christie remained as Meighen's trusted adviser.

Meighen represented Canada at the Imperial Conference of 1921. This conference proceeded on the general assumption that it was desirable that the empire should pursue a common foreign policy arrived at by consultation. Difficulties arose, however, over the renewal of the Anglo-Japanese alliance. Meighen, influenced by Christie, argued that the alliance constituted a serious obstacle to amicable relations with the US, so vital to the empire and particularly to Canada; whereas Australia regarded the alliance as important to her security. A disastrous break was avoided by Lloyd George's diplomatic tactics; at the subsequent Washington Conference of 1922 (attended by Borden and Christie), the alliance was abandoned, to be replaced by a 4-power treaty was signed by Britain, the US, Japan and France, who agreed to respect one another's rights and possessions in the Pacific. This conference was the last important occasion when a British Empire delegation functioned as a unit at an international negotiation.

In the Dec 1921 general election Meighen was defeated by Mackenzie KING's Liberals. Although external policy was not an ostensible issue, in fact 1921 marks a reversal even more striking than that of 1911. The Liberals took every one of Québec's 65 seats in the Commons, and it was inevitable that King's policies should be tailored accordingly. In 1921 Québec was strongly isolationist; the war and CONSCRIPTION had left deep marks. The result was the abandonment of unified diplomacy in partnership with the other countries of what was now increasingly being called the Commonwealth, and the substitution of separate national policy. At Paris, Canada had been recognized both as a member country of the British Empire and as a separate nation; King's policies consistently emphasized the latter aspect at the expense of the former. Symbolically, Christie was frozen out of the Dept of External Affairs in 1923. His successor as the prime minister's confidential adviser was O.D. SKELTON, who became undersecretary in 1925 and held that appointment until his death in 1941.

Skelton was not the deviser of King's policies, which were well developed before Skelton joined him, nor were their opinions exactly the same. Skelton has been called anti-British, not without reason, whereas King would have wholly repudiated that label. King was an admirer of British institutions and practices, and always considered that in another world war Canada would have to stand by Britain. But King and Skelton entirely agreed in rejecting a common foreign policy for the Commonwealth and maintaining that in normal conditions Canada and the UK should pursue their own national policies. At the Imperial Conference of 1923 King made it clear to Britain that he had no intention of maintaining Borden's policies. In his memoranda for King, Skelton gave no recognition to the nationalistic aspect of the Canadian Conservative proceedings of 1911 to 1921, and even avoided mention of Resolution IX of the Imperial War Conference; he represented those events as, in effect, a centralizing British plot. The CHANAK AFFAIR of 1922, with its bungled British request for a Canadian expeditionary force, had provided only too convincing a background for King's attitude. And he had given a striking example of his view of policy when in Mar 1923 he insisted that the HALIBUT TREATY with the US be signed by Canada alone, without the traditional participation of the British ambassador. He was delighted when the Imperial Conference accepted this procedure as normal. He was unaware that the British Foreign Office was as hostile as he to the idea of an imperial policy formed in consultation with the Dominions; to the Foreign Office such consultation was merely a trammel on British freedom of action.

Under King, Canada achieved separate diplomatic representation in Washington. An arrangement for this had in fact been made in Borden's time, but no action had been taken. In 1926 Vincent MASSEY became the first Canadian minister to the US. Legations were opened in France in 1928 and Japan in 1929. Early in 1939 missions were established in Belgium and the Netherlands (served by the same minister); this was the extent of Canadian representation abroad before WWII.

Canada's relations with the League of Nations began at Paris in 1919 with an effort to weaken Article 10 of the Covenant, which bound members to defend the territorial integrity and independence of all other members. Successive Canadian governments continued to fight against this article (especially unpopular in Québec) until 1923, when a resolution leaving to each member the decision as to how far it was bound to use force in fulfilment of Article 10 failed of the necessary unanimous support in the Assembly by one vote. In 1927 Canada was elected to a nonpermanent seat on the League Council, with the reluctant assent of King, who feared unnecessary commitments and complications.

The Imperial Conference of 1926 resulted in a formal widening of Dominion autonomy. South Africa insisted on a definition of Britain's relation with the Dominions. The result was the BALFOUR REPORT, which led to the 1931 STATUTE OF WESTMINSTER giving the Dominions complete legislative independence so far as they desired it. In Canada's case this stopped short only of the right to amend its own constitution, the core of which was found in the 1867 BNA Act. This reservation was the result of pressure from Ontario and Québec. It ceased to be operative only as a result of the CONSTITUTION ACT, 1982. The word "independence" is not found in the Statute of Westminster, largely because King would not hear of it in the discussions of 1926; but Canada's independence may be said to date from that statute (11 Dec 1931).

By this time the GREAT DEPRESSION had brought the Conservatives, led by R.B. BENNETT, to power in the 28 July 1930 election. Bennett, motivated by the desperate state of the economy, raised the tariff, primarily as retaliation against the US's new Hawley-Smoot tariff, though British preferential rates were also raised. At the Imperial Conference of 1930 he made a dramatic gesture, inviting the delegates to a special economic conference at Ottawa, and proposing, not a general reduction of imperial rates, but a 10% increase in rates levied against countries outside the Commonwealth. British politicians saw how little the offer was worth; nevertheless, the Imperial Economic Conference finally met at Ottawa in 1932 (*see* OTTAWA AGREEMENTS) amid hopes that something might be done to alleviate the depression. Bennett, theoretically an imperialist, was in fact an economic nationalist of the first order. The Anglo-Canadian trade agreement made at the conference contained some concessions on both sides. But the achievement was much less than optimists had hoped, and there was ill will between British and Canadian negotiators. Relations between the 2 countries were at a low ebb.

As the general election of 1935 approached, the world situation was threatening. Hitler had come to power in Germany in 1933, Japan was engaged in aggression against China, and Italy was preparing to attack Ethiopia. The League of Nations' effort to restrain Italy led to apprehension of an Anglo-Italian war. The Bennett government showed itself prepared to support sanctions against Italy, but after the election of 14 Oct 1935 returned the Liberals to power, PM King adopted a policy of economic conciliation, putting an end to a trade war with Japan and (more important) reaching a trade agreement with the US — an object Bennett had lately pursued without success. King's cautious policy as the danger of war in Europe grew (*see* MUNICH CRISIS), much criticized as pusillanimous, was to be justified by the fact that Canada entered WWII a united country.

After WORLD WAR II King still pursued a cautious and generally isolationist policy, apprehensive of the growing American influence in Canadian affairs, hostile as ever to imperial centralization, and tending to resist the increasing involvement of Canada in world affairs. Nevertheless the movement seemed irresistible. By 1947 Canada had 36 missions abroad, and in 1946 the office of secretary of state for external affairs was finally separated from that of prime minister, the first secretary of state under the new regime being Louis ST. LAURENT. King's own retirement from politics in Nov 1948 was the end of an era.

O.D. Skelton's best legacy to the Dept of External Affairs had been the group of able civil servants he recruited beginning in 1927, notably L.B. PEARSON, Norman ROBERTSON and Hume WRONG. The professional standard established by these men and their colleagues was a great asset to a country beginning to make its way in diplomacy. Robertson became undersecretary in 1941, succeeding Skelton, and Pearson succeeded Robertson in 1946. When St. Laurent was about to become prime minister, Pearson entered Cabinet as secretary of state for external affairs.

After King's retirement, Canadian external policy took a rather bolder tone. Tendencies to assume commitments had already appeared, notably in Canada's actions at the founding conference of the UNITED NATIONS in 1945. When faith in the UN's effectiveness was undermined by the COLD WAR between the Soviet Union and the West, Canada not only accepted but even advocated the idea of a western regional union for collective defence, and signed the North Atlantic Treaty in 1949. As a result, Canadian military units were sent to Europe in 1951 to serve under the North Atlantic Treaty Organization (NATO). During the same period the Canadian government (somewhat reluctantly) dispatched a brigade group to fight under UN command in the KOREAN WAR. These commitments led to large increases in Canada's ARMED FORCES.

Joining NATO marked a turning point in Canadian policy. Traditionally, Canada had been loath to accept commitments either to Britain or the US individually; it was easier to accept commitments to an organization of which both were members, the more so as they too were abandoning isolationist positions. These new attitudes reflected the experience of WWII and the traumatic effect of the advent of atomic weapons. At the same time it was becoming clear that the war had greatly weakened Britain's world position; that confrontation between the superpowers, the capitalist US and the communist USSR, was now the dominant fact of the international situation (*see* MIDDLE POWER); and that relations with the American neighbour eclipsed all other Canadian external problems.

As Britain gave up her imperial obligations, the Commonwealth became increasingly multiracial, a development that the Canadian government encouraged. The new polity was severely strained in 1956 by the SUEZ CRISIS, when Britain and France made a military attack on Egypt following Egyptian nationalization of the Suez Canal Co. The UN, including the US, condemned the aggression, which was also strongly reprobated by the nonwhite Commonwealth countries. It was a classic example of the difficulty in which a serious Anglo-American dispute places Canada. Canada abstained from voting on a resolution demanding a cease-fire and Anglo-French withdrawal, but proposed an international PEACEKEEPING force to supervise the cessation of hostilities. The Commonwealth stayed together, and L.B. Pearson received the Nobel Peace Prize for his peace initiatives. Canada was at the height of her diplomatic influence.

An electoral upset on 10 June 1957 brought the Progressive Conservatives under John DIEFENBAKER to power. During his period in power, until 1963, foreign relations turned largely on the military connection with the US. At the very beginning, accepting a proposal that had been before their predecessors, the new government associated Canada with the US in the North American Air Defence Command (NORAD). Diefenbaker's personal relations with Pres John F. Kennedy (1961-63) were poor (*see* CUBAN MISSILE CRISIS), and there was trouble over whether or not Canada should accept nuclear weapons (*see* BOMARC MISSILE CRISIS). Early in 1963 Pearson, now Opposition leader, reversing his earlier stand, advocated accepting them in order to carry out obligations to the US. Diefenbaker's vacillations led to resignations from his Cabinet, and finally to the government's defeat.

Under Pearson, leader of the new minority government, CANADIAN-AMERICAN RELATIONS were less acerbic than under Diefenbaker, but US participation in the Vietnam War contributed to poisoning them. A positive development of 1965 was the so-called Autopact providing for free trade between the 2 countries in motor cars and parts, one result of which was that large numbers of cars were produced in Canada for sale in the US. The large lines of Canadian policy changed little under Pearson, who had done so much to lay them down. The lesson the generation that had fought WWII had drawn from its experience — that security could be best ensured by the Western nations being united and strong — was still accepted.

With Pearson's retirement in 1968 and his replacement by Pierre TRUDEAU, there was a change of atmosphere. Trudeau was not, like Pearson, a member of the Ottawa establishment, and he had played no part in the war. The PRIME MINISTER'S OFFICE became more important and the Dept of External Affairs less influential. In 1969 there was a drastic reduction in the armed forces and a considerable reduction in the foreign service. The cut in military strength certainly contributed to a decline in Canadian diplomatic influence, though this had already been in progress as the result of the postwar recovery of France and West Germany. In 1970 a series of government pamphlets entitled *Foreign Policy for Canadians* defined Canada's goals: to "foster economic growth, safeguard sovereignty and independence, work for peace and security, promote social justice, enhance the quality of life, [and] ensure a harmonious natural environment." These high-sounding phrases seemed to traditional diplomatists hardly a practicable basis for foreign policy, and some feared that, taken with the measures of 1969, they were harbingers of a new isolationism.

Economic relations with the US provided the worst problems of the Trudeau era. There was considerable popular anti-Americanism, sparked by resentment of growing US investment and therefore control in Canada (though this FOREIGN INVESTMENT had been welcomed in earlier times) and by continuing dislike of the Vietnam adventure, which terminated only in 1973. Energy problems following a crisis caused by the Organization of Petroleum Exporting Countries (OPEC) in 1973-74 were a violent irritant, particularly in view of the domination of the Canadian oil market by American companies. In the autumn of 1980 the Trudeau government announced the National Energy Program, one objective of which was at least 50% Canadian ownership of oil and gas production by 1990. This almost coincided with the election of US Pres Ronald Reagan, and to his conservative Republican administration the NEP, much hated by the US oil companies, was an object of hostility. So was another Trudeau institution, the FOREIGN INVESTMENT REVIEW AGENCY, established 1974 to monitor foreign investment in Canada.

During the last generation the pattern of Canadian external trade has been transformed. Before WWII Canada had 2 great trading partners, Britain and the US. Exports to Britain exceeded imports; with the US the situation was the reverse. After the war, Canada's British market never wholly revived. In recent years Japan has been Canada's second-largest trading partner, and in imports Venezuela, from which Canada takes large quantities of oil, stood ahead of Britain in 1983. Canada has recently sold great quantities of wheat to China and the USSR. The US dominates the Canadian trading scene as never before: over 75% of all Canada's trade is with that country. Canadian commercial policy has been influenced in the direction of freer trade by adherence to the General Agreement on Tariffs and Trade (GATT), first drawn up in 1947 and modified several times since.

C.P. STACEY

Reading: Canadian Annual Review of Politics and Public Affairs (1960, continuing); *Documents on Canadian External Relations* (1967, continuing); James Eayrs, *In Defence of Canada*, 5 vols (1964-83); G.P. de T. Glazebrook, *A History of Canadian External Relations*, 2 vols (rev ed, 1966); C.P. Stacey, *Canada and the Age of Conflict*, 2 vols (1977-81).

Eyre, *Sky Terrace* (1971-72), acrylic and oil on canvas (*courtesy Robert McLaughlin Gallery, Oshawa*).

Eyre, Ivan Kenneth, painter (b at Tulleymet, Sask 15 Apr 1935). Eyre has often been described as a neo-realist because of his detailed imaginary landscapes, and as a surrealist because of his works that rely on the juxtaposition of apparently incongruous forms and objects. He regards himself as an abstractionist, in the sense of taking given forms and arranging them in new structures that imaginatively project thoughts in a language of symbolic form.

Raised on the Saskatchewan prairie and in the suburbs of Saskatoon, Eyre developed a perception that enabled him to see the aesthetic content of natural scenes. After studying sporadically under Ernest LINDNER and Eli BORNSTEIN, he began art training in 1953 at the University of Manitoba School of Art. In 1959 he joined the faculty and has taught there ever since. His studies of the old European and Japanese masters gave him a broad perspective, and when he began to develop his individual style in 1961, through concentrated drawing, followed by painting, he stayed aloof from the changing novelties of the art scene. His first show was in 1962, and since then he has exhibited in Canada, Germany and the US. A major retrospective was held at the Robert McLaughlin Gallery, Oshawa, in 1980. Eyre is also a fine draftsman, sculptor and printmaker. In all his work, with its remarkable virtuosity, he seeks to interpret the human condition, man's relationship to reality. For him, form, like words, must have a meaning beyond itself.

GEORGE WOODCOCK

Faba Bean, or broad bean (*Vicia faba* or *Faba vulgaris*), legume family member, which is not a true bean but a VETCH. It originated in Eurasia, and archaeological evidence indicates that it was known to various ancient Western civilizations. The faba bean has a high protein content (25%) and has played a key role in human nutrition, being used in the green, immature state (as a shelled green VEGETABLE) or dried and stored for future use. A cool-season plant, the faba bean does not thrive where summers are hot and dry. Black APHIDS constitute its principal pest. Plant height varies among the half dozen or so cultivars (commercial varieties), with a range of 59-118 cm. Leaves are pinnately compound (ie, featherlike) and turn blackish with age. Flowers are white with wings marked by a large black spot.

The main cultivar is Broad Windsor, of English origin. Selections have been made resulting in varying plant size and heat resistance. Seeded in spring (mid-May), the bean matures in 65-85 days, depending on location and cultivar. Broad beans for home consumption may be produced in most garden areas across Canada. Commercial production in Canada began in 1972; by 1980, 23 000 ha were cultivated, but hectarage decreased in 1981 as a result of limitations in the export market. Faba beans are grown as a silage crop and as a vegetable; there is increasing interest in smaller-seeded types for use as a source of vegetable oil. CROP RESEARCH is concentrated at Morden, Man, and Lethbridge, Alta. *See* OILSEED CROPS. I.L. NONNECKE

Fackenheim, Emil Ludwig, philosopher, theologian (b at Halle, Germany 22 June 1916). Educated at U of Halle, and ordained a rabbi in 1939, he fled Germany after a short imprisonment in a concentration camp. He studied at U of Aberdeen and then at U of T (PhD, 1945) where he taught 1948-84. Profoundly affected by the anti-Semitism and genocide of the Nazi era, he developed, from interests in 19th- and 20th-century European thought, particularly on questions of religion and history, a Jewish response to the Holocaust and to Western culture in general. He discusses God's presence in history and maintains that, since Auschwitz, there is a divine command to the Jews to survive and to struggle for justice. Fackenheim's writings include *Metaphysics and Historicity* (1961), *Quest for Past and Future* (1968), *The Religious Dimension in Hegel's Thought* (1968), *God's Presence in History* (1970), *The Jewish Return into History* (1978). THOMAS MATHIEN

Fafard, Joseph, sculptor (b at Ste Marthe, Sask 2 Sept 1942). He began his career making kinetic sculpture but soon after his appointment at U of Sask in Regina in 1968 he turned to satirical plaster portraits of his colleagues and people in the art world. He started working in ceramic around 1972, broadening his range of subjects to respond to the life and the people of his community. Through his ceramic portraits of people and animals in the FOLK ART tradition, he has gained considerable recognition across the country. In 1984 his work *The Pasture*, comprising 7 bronze cows with varying patinas, was commissioned for one tower of the Toronto-Dominion Centre, Toronto. MARILYN BURNETT

Fagundes, João Alvares, explorer (fl 1521). In 1520 he explored the coast S and W of Cape Race, Nfld, and perhaps entered the St Lawrence R. He may have sighted St Pierre and Miquelon, Cape Breton I and Sable I. Fagundes may have established a Portuguese colony but no trace has been found. JAMES MARSH

Fairclough, Ellen Louks, politician (b at Hamilton, Ont 28 Jan 1905). A chartered accountant by profession, she became secretary of state and Canada's first woman federal Cabinet minister in the 1957 DIEFENBAKER government. Owner of a Hamilton accounting firm, she was a member

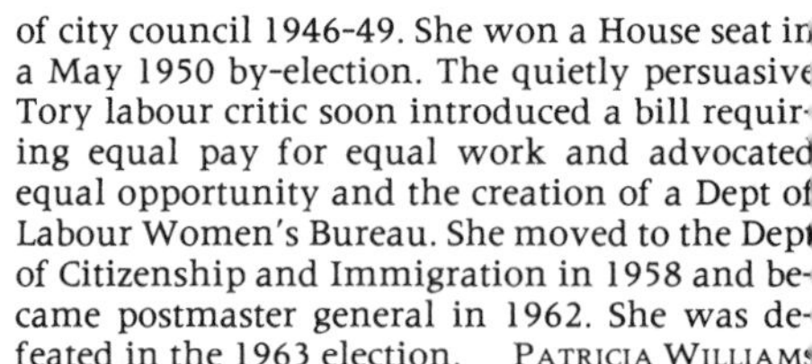

of city council 1946-49. She won a House seat in a May 1950 by-election. The quietly persuasive Tory labour critic soon introduced a bill requiring equal pay for equal work and advocated equal opportunity and the creation of a Dept of Labour Women's Bureau. She moved to the Dept of Citizenship and Immigration in 1958 and became postmaster general in 1962. She was defeated in the 1963 election. PATRICIA WILLIAMS

Fairley, Barker, scholar, literary and art critic, painter (b at Barnsley, Eng 21 May 1887). One of the foremost German scholars of the century and author of 2 epoch-making books on Goethe (*Goethe as Revealed in His Poetry*, 1932; *A Study of Goethe*, 1947), Fairley was cofounder of the CANADIAN FORUM, friend and promoter of the GROUP OF SEVEN. His wide-ranging opinions on art and literature were always expressed in a provocative and felicitous prose style that appealed to the general reader. After graduating from U of Leeds, he began his academic career at U of Jena (1907-10) and was then invited to join the newly founded U of A in Edmonton (1910-15). From 1915 until his retirement in 1957 (except 1932-36) he taught at University Coll, U of T. In retirement he devoted considerable time to his painting (see his 1981 book, *Portraits*) and enjoyed increasing recognition as a painter of portraits, landscapes and still lifes. Although first and foremost a scholar of German literature, he wrote articles and books on many writers and was instrumental, chiefly through his columns in *Canadian Forum*, in focusing public attention on Canadian art in general and on the Group of Seven in particular. RODNEY SYMINGTON

Fairn, Leslie Raymond, architect (b at Waterville, NS 26 June 1875; d at Halifax 13 Aug 1971). Fairn attended Acadia, studied architecture in Boston, Mass, and apprenticed with Edward Elliot, architect of the Halifax City Hall. In 1904 he began a career that lasted 65 years. His commissions include county courthouses at Kentville, NS (1903); Digby, NS (1908-10); and Newcastle, NB (1912-13); Killam Library, Dalhousie; and Memorial Library and Grace Maternity Hospital in Halifax. A fellow of the Royal Soc of Arts and the Royal Architectural Inst of Canada, he was also one of the founders of the NS Assn of Architects.
GRANT WANZEL AND KAREN KALLWEIT

Joe Fafard, artist known for his droll figures and cows; shown here with his self-portrait in clay (*courtesy Canapress*).

Ellen Fairclough was Canada's first woman federal Cabinet minister (*courtesy Public Archives of Canada PA-129249/Duncan Cameron*).

Fairweather, Eugene Rathbone, theologian, ecumenist (b at Ottawa 2 Nov 1920). An ordained priest of the Anglican Church of Canada, Fairweather has been a member of the theological faculty of Trinity Coll, U of T, since 1944. He was appointed dean of divinity in 1983. He is known as a Thomist, intensely interested in ecumenical conversations, particularly with the Roman Catholic Church. He served on the Anglican-Roman Catholic International Commission, for which he received the Cross of the Order of St Augustine's of Canterbury in 1981. He has been a member of the Canadian and World Council of Churches' Commissions on Faith and Order and was a delegated observer at Vatican II. He is a member of the Board of Patrons of the Ecumenical Institute for Advanced Theological Research, Tantur, Jerusalem. Fairweather assisted in the founding of the *Canadian Journal of Theology* and was subsequently its editor (1960-70). He has worked to promote ecumenical co-operation in theological education in the university. WILLIAM O. FENNELL

Faith, Percy, conductor, arranger, composer (b at Toronto 7 Apr 1908; d at Los Angeles 9 Feb 1976). After injury to his hands interrupted an early career as a concert pianist, he turned to composition and arranging. Faith joined CRBC Toronto in 1933 as conductor-arranger for a series of programs. One of these, "Music by Faith" (1938-40), also gained him popularity in the US. As a result Faith joined NBC radio as music director of the "Carnation Contented Hour" 1940-47. He quickly became one of the best-known arrangers in the US, working for Columbia Records until his death. Faith's many recordings include his own film scores and popular songs and choruses. ANN SCHAU

Falcon (family Falconidae), small- to medium-sized predatory bird noted for swiftness in flight. Falcons range in size from sparrow-sized (falconet of SE Asia) to raven-sized (powerful, arctic-dwelling gyrfalcon). Falcons tend to have more distinctive plumages than most other BIRDS OF PREY, frequently having striking facial patterns or contrasting markings. They are characterized by large, dark brown eyes, a hooked beak with a toothlike projection on the mandible and a small tubercle in the centre of each nostril. Most have very distinctive, long, pointed wings and a long tail. Female falcons are noticeably larger than males. Because of their speed, many species have long been prized by falconers, who train them to hunt. Gyrfalcons and PEREGRINE FALCONS have become status symbols for falconers worldwide. Five falcon species breed in Canada. The brightly coloured, robin-sized American kestrel (*Falco sparverius*) is relatively common and, except in winter, may be seen perched or hovering along roadsides from coast to coast. The more elusive merlin (*F. columbarius*) also occurs across the country. Recently, merlins have become more common in urban areas in western Canada. The crow-sized, sandy-coloured prairie falcon (*F. mexicanus*) is restricted to grasslands and, although fairly abundant, is seen only in very specific habitats in the Prairie provinces or in some interior valleys of BC. The peregrine falcon (*F. peregrinus*), similar in size to the prairie falcon, formerly bred wherever suitable nesting habitat and prey were found. The gyrfalcon (*F. rusticolus*) of the Canadian Arctic feeds mainly on ptarmigan and arctic hare. Although its population fluctuates in relation to prey, it has not been affected to any great extent by pesticides or other pollutants. R.W. FYFE

Falcon, Pierre, poet and troubadour, magistrate (b at Elbow Ft [near Swan R, Man] 4 June 1793; d at Grantown, now St-François-Xavier, Man 26 Oct 1876). Of Cree and French parentage he was the son of an NWC employee. Sent to Montréal for education, he returned to the Northwest and became a clerk with the NWC and worked for the HBC 1821-25. He then moved to Grantown, on the White Horse Plain, where he farmed and later became magistrate.

Throughout his life, he spontaneously composed poems or songs about any stirring event, and they were sung by voyageurs across the country. The ballad "La Chanson de la Grenouillère," for example, was occasioned by the SEVEN OAKS INCIDENT. His songs that survived are found in M.A. MacLeod, *Songs of Old Manitoba* (1960). Falcon Lk on the Manitoba-Ontario border was named in his memory. MARGARET CHARTRAND

Falconer, Sir Robert Alexander, clergyman, scholar, educator (b at Charlottetown 10 Feb 1867; d at Toronto 4 Nov 1943). Falconer spent much of his youth in Trinidad, where his Presbyterian clergyman father had been posted. He was educated at London and Edinburgh universities, concentrating on classics and philosophy, and pursued postgraduate work at Leipzig, Berlin and Marburg, Germany. In 1892 he was ordained a minister in the Presbyterian Church in Canada and took up a lectureship in New Testament Greek at Pine Hill College, Halifax. Becoming a professor there in 1895, he was appointed principal in 1904.

Falconer is most important, however, for his 25-year tenure as president of UNIVERSITY OF TORONTO (1907-32). A royal commission appointed to investigate all aspects of the university had found administrative chaos and low morale. It recommended a complete constitutional reorganization and implicitly a new president in 1906. To the surprise of many, the 40-year-old Falconer was asked to replace James LOUDON. Much of Falconer's time and energy for the next 2 decades was given to executing the recommendations of the 1906 commission. He inherited a collection of colleges; he left behind him an integrated university that led the country in industrial and scientific, as well as humanistic, research.

An unemotional and cerebral scholar, Falconer was much in demand as a public speaker, particularly on the importance of maintaining the British imperial connection, the nurturing of "idealism in national character" (the title of his 1920 collection of wartime addresses), and the integrity and place of the humanities in an increasingly scientific and practical university environment. Active in the Presbyterian Church in Canada, Falconer was one of those who sought to bring his denomination into union with Canada's Methodists and Congregationalists in the 1920s. Such was his reputation within the Empire that in 1929 Edinburgh U broke with tradition to offer him its principalship, a position he declined. A.B. MCKILLOP

Falher, Alta, Town, pop 1102 (1981c), inc 1955, is located 60 km S of the town of Peace River. It is named for Rev C. Falher, OMI, who brought the first French Canadian settlers to the area 1912. In 1916 the Edmonton, Dunvegan and BC Ry arrived, and Falher grew as a distribution centre for a prosperous cereal grain and CANOLA growing area. Some 35 000 beehives in the region produce more than 2 million kg of honey. ERIC J. HOLMGREN

Falk, Gathie, artist (b at Alexander, Man 31 Jan 1928). A multimedia artist with a strong national reputation, Falk began a successful artistic career in 1965 when she left teaching to study art. In 1967 she abandoned formal studies at UBC to become a self-supporting artist and in 1968 her Home Environment show at the Douglas Gallery, Vancouver, established her reputation. From 1968 to 1977 her many exhibitions were counterpointed by her work as a performance artist. After 1974 she turned to drawing, watercolour and oil-painted images in an impressionist vein. Her works are owned by major public galleries and in 1985 the Vancouver Art Gallery staged a retrospective. ANN ROSENBERG

Fallon, Michael Francis, Roman Catholic bishop (b at Kingston, Canada W 17 May 1867; d at London, Ont 22 Feb 1931). After graduating from the U of Ottawa 1889, he entered the Congregation of the Oblates of Mary Immaculate, and after studies in Holland and Rome was ordained a priest in 1894. He was professor of English, then vice-rector of the U of O before becoming pastor of parishes in Ottawa 1888-1901 and Buffalo, NY, 1901-09, where he became an American citizen. Made provincial superior of his order, he was appointed bishop of London, Ont, in Dec 1909. He became the leader of Ontario's Irish Catholics who were endeavouring to keep Franco-Ontarians "in their place," that is, trying to prevent the acceptance of bilingual schooling. During his more than 20 years as bishop, Fallon stood at the centre of the ethnolinguistic fighting in Ontario during the ONTARIO SCHOOLS QUESTION 1912-27. He died a hero to many Irish Catholics but a demon to Franco-Ontarians. ROBERT CHOQUETTE

Reading: Robert Choquette, *Language and Religion* (1975).

Falls, Robert Hilborn, naval officer (b at Welland, Ont 29 Apr 1924). Falls joined the RCAF in late 1942 and trained as a pilot. He transferred to the navy after WWII, moving through a series of naval flying and command responsibilities (including HMCS BONAVENTURE) to senior management positions at headquarters and a period as commander of the Canadian Flotilla Atlantic. Vice-chief of the defence staff 1974-77, he became the first naval officer to serve as chief of the defence staff 1977-80. He was the first Canadian to be chairman of the NATO Military Committee, the alliance's senior military authority, 1980-83. He caused controversy with farewell remarks in 1983 suggesting that NATO might have more nuclear weapons in Europe than necessary. NORMAN HILLMER

False Face Society Among the IROQUOIS there were several curing societies. The best known is the False Face Society, whose rituals were accomplished through MASKS carved on living trees and then removed for further finishing. Curing, the restoration of well-being for the community and health for the individual, was a vital part of native religious practice. Much of the ritual in curing ceremonies consisted of specialized songs and dances. The mythological base of the origins of the curing society was important in the continuity of the culture. Relations with the supernatural world were through individual experiences (visions) or group activities (tribal ceremonies). *See also* NATIVE PEOPLE, RELIGION; SHAMAN. RENÉ R. GADACZ

Family There is no such thing as the "Canadian" family. Membership in a family, the activities of those members in and out of the household, and the relationship among members varies with economic conditions and also with regions, historical periods, SOCIAL CLASS and ethnicity. Yet most people eat, sleep, work, procreate, recuperate, learn, love, laugh, cry and die within what most would agree is a family. While the variations are in many ways endless, there is usually a dominant pattern, one that is more common than others in each region and time.

Before the arrival of the Europeans, family patterns among Canada's native peoples were enormously varied, as were the subsequent interpretations of those patterns by scholars. While some of the many societies and language groups functioned as nomadic hunting bands, others had complex organizations for agriculture, fishing and hunting. Family structures reflected the varying economic conditions.

Agricultural societies frequently engaged in the co-operative production and preparation of food, and provided collective child care and other "family activities." Women did much of the farming and men often lived with their wives' relatives ("matrilocal residence") after marriage. Among fishing communities on the Pacific coast, on the other hand, separation of property was often practised, there were greater social differences within the group, women moved in with their husbands' relatives ("patrilocal residence") and the men fished. There was a division of labour by age and sex, but the specific tasks assigned to each group were different from society to society. In many of these families, women exercised a considerable amount of power as well as contributing directly to the survival of the group. What are often considered modern trends — premarital sex, adoption of children, divorce and trial marriages — were not uncommon among the native people, particularly in seminomadic societies.

With the arrival of the Europeans, economic conditions and family structures altered, but the variety remained. The organization of rival fur-trading companies led to the formation of different family relationships between whites and Indians. The temporary stations of the NORTH WEST COMPANY often permitted only short-term liaisons, the Indian women being left to tend their MÉTIS offspring. The HUDSON'S BAY COMPANY, however, had permanent posts and allowed or encouraged relatively stable relationships to develop, at least with regard to officers of the company. What today would be called common-law marriages were frequently established, and some of the children — but rarely the wives — were taken back to England when the officers returned home. These practices, and the introduction of private property, disrupted family patterns within Indian societies, discouraged co-operative production, and created single-parent households.

Meanwhile, in the central and eastern regions of the country, Europeans were establishing more settled agricultural communities and, along with them, different kinds of families. Patterns from the Old World were adapted to the new economic, social and physical conditions. While from the beginning of NEW FRANCE some people survived by working for the government, for the fur-trading companies, for the church, or as independent artisans, an increasingly dominant group produced most of what they needed for survival by working the land. Women, men and children laboured together to grow or to make the necessities of life. Men held most of the legal power in these families, but the mutual economic dependency that existed in most households contributed to the women's strength. The scarcity of women, combined with the fact that their work was essential to household survival and that — except for a career as a nun or work as a domestic — marriage offered practically the sole means of support, meant that almost all women married. As a result of the high casualties of war, disease, accidents and death in childbirth, few marriages lasted long. Unlike the custom in France, widows and widowers did not wait long to remarry; consequently, many households contained children from 2 or more marriages. Women born in Canada married early, especially if their families were poor, but those who immigrated were often prevented from marrying at a younger age by long contracts for domestic service. These early marriages, the need for labourers in agricultural communities, the high proportion of children dying at birth or in their early years, the lack of contraception (*see* BIRTH CONTROL) and the religious proscription against it, all contributed to the high birthrates, especially among those families working the land (*see* MARRIAGE AND DIVORCE).

Although remarriage was strongly encouraged, religious beliefs and the desire for legitimate children to inherit the property in these settled communities accounted for the strong sanctions against premarital and extramarital sex, especially for women. Marriages were frequently arranged, for the wealthier to ensure the protection of their property, and for the poorer to ensure their own survival.

The British, and many of the other European settlers who came later, brought with them a firm belief in private property and self-reliance, but those who worked the land formed families that were similar in many ways to those of New France. The household was the place where the majority of goods and services were produced. Therefore, for most people — even those earning wages — home and workplace were one. Households were large, including as they often did an average of 4 or 5 children, hired help, single relatives and paying boarders. Few contained grandparents because most people did not live to be elderly and because many children left at an early age. In these early agricultural communities, the differences in family assets and resources tended to be small because almost everyone worked the land for a living.

Labour was divided by sex and age. Women centered their activities around the house, performing highly skilled and visible tasks such as baking bread, preserving food, and making soap, candles and clothes. In addition to bearing primary responsibility for teaching children to read and write and for the family's health care, women also frequently tended the vegetable gardens and the small animals, looked after the milking, and worked in the fields at sowing and harvest times. Men tended the larger animals, constructed furniture and buildings, slaughtered animals, felled and chopped trees, and planted and harvested the fields. Children worked alongside their parents, carrying out the more menial tasks and learning the skills necessary for survival. While this meant that men were actively involved in child rearing, infants were primarily cared for by women, older children and the hired help. And while women sometimes did "men's work," men rarely did any "women's work" other than looking after older children. In English common law, men were the decision makers, although women and children had some basis for power, because they contributed in obvious and visible ways to the maintenance of the household.

The physical distances between many of these households meant that entertainment was mainly a family affair. Even in more populated areas, social gatherings tended to involve the entire family, allowing the parents to supervise many of their children's contacts with others. In these households, the selection of marriage partners was less likely to be arranged formally. The idea of romantic love was gaining a certain popularity, but economic and family considerations were still the most important factors in most decisions to marry, and marriages, particularly among the wealthier families, usually required parental approval.

Although most Canadians lived in rural areas until after the turn of this century, some people worked for wages from the earliest years of settlement. Both women and men frequently began life in Canada by working for someone else, often as servants or on farms, in shops, in hotels and, somewhat later, in factories, but only men held jobs in the army and in the government. At first, readily accessible land meant that there was a way out of this work and a large proportion of men married and left the paid labour force to establish their own farms. When good land was no longer available and when new TECHNOLOGY reduced the need for workers in the fields and forest, it was primarily men who were cut off from the means of directly producing for their needs and who thus had to work for others.

A large number of single women, and women whose husbands were dead or disabled, did work for pay, but for the overwhelming majority of women, marriage meant the end of such labour. Until well into this century, most women could still contribute directly to the family's survival by growing, preserving and preparing food, making clothes and baking bread. Many also generated cash income by selling their produce, by sewing clothes, and by taking in laundry and boarders. As job possibilities expanded in the labour force, many single women rejected domestic labour in favour of the somewhat greater freedom and pay associated with other work. The decline in domestic servants coincided with changing household technology, a technology that made it increasingly possible for one married woman to do the work alone.

Some children worked in factories and shops, or as hired help on farms or in other households, although from the 17th century on, the government restricted CHILD LABOUR. The application of these laws, combined with the declining need for labour and the increasing need for a literate labour force (which contributed to the introduction of compulsory schooling), meant that from the latter part of the 19th century, the number of employed young children dwindled. The need for children's labour in the household also decreased as fewer goods and services were produced in the household. Children became economic liabilities rather than economic assets. This, along with better health care, which meant that more children survived, contributed to declining birthrates.

These changes, which started in central Canada, gradually spread to the western and eastern parts of the country. Increasingly, families were distinguished from each other by social and class differences. Wealthier farmers and industrialists were able to send their children away to PRIVATE SCHOOLS long before compulsory schooling was introduced, and some households could afford to pay servants long after DOMESTIC SERVICE disappeared from the majority of homes.

It was not until the early part of the 20th century that what came to be called the "traditional" family — mother at home, father in the labour force, children at school and no other hired help or related individuals — appeared as the dominant family form in Canada. Although it has lasted only some 50 years, this kind of family structure has come to be popularly regarded as ideal.

Today the majority of married women (just over 3 million) are working or are actively looking for work in the labour force. Even mothers with very young children are returning to their paid jobs after the birth of their babies, although the overwhelming majority of small children are still looked after mainly by their parents and other relatives. Fewer and fewer women can contribute directly to family maintenance by earning money or making goods at home. This, combined with the fact that the expenses of a family can often be met only through 2 incomes, means that most married women have sought paid employment because their families need the income.

The legalization and increasing accessibility of contraceptive devices have helped to lower birthrates, as have rising prices. Most families now have only one or 2 children and are having them closer together. These children are staying in school and often in the home longer especially with current unemployment rates These declining birthrates and increasing education levels have in turn contributed to women's rising labour-force participation rates That most women now keep their paid jobs after marriage and childbirth may also help explain why bridegrooms are younger now; fewer men have to anticipate being the sole income earners in the household.

As more and more women have entered the labour force, they have demanded fairer marital and PROPERTY LAWS. While earning wages has probably increased women's power in some areas, low wages, part-time jobs and segregation into poorly paid occupations reinforces and is reinforced by their continued responsibility for household chores and child care. Rising unemployment rates may also, in some households, severely threaten male authority.

Such changes contribute to tension in families, which not infrequently erupts in violence directed against women and children. Domestic violence is not new and it is difficult to tell how much it may have increased over time. It is clear, however, that because of the nuclear family structure, there are few individuals to witness or stop the violent acts, or to support the victims.

Divorce is certainly more common in Canada now than in the past, particularly since the advent of the 1968 Divorce Act. Divorces are easier and less humiliating to obtain. People are living longer, making "happily ever after" much longer than it ever was before. One out of 4 couples can anticipate being divorced at least once. Rising divorce rates and the increase in legal separations and in the number of unmarried women having babies mean that the number of single-parent households is growing. This does not necessarily mean, however, that there is now a higher proportion of households in which children are living without both their biological parents, because high death rates in early Canada ensured that this situation was common in the past.

The growing participation of women in the labour force has helped many families to maintain their standard of living, but it has not prevented some families from living in POVERTY. Although estimates vary (depending on how poverty is defined), in 1983 approximately 15% of all Canadian families were living at or below the poverty line (*see* INCOME DISTRIBUTION). The majority of these households contain 2 parents and 50% of poor families have a "head" who is in the labour force. However, low wages for women and women's child care responsibilities help explain why female-headed households have a very high poverty rate. Women's greater life expectancy, their low wages, lack of private pensions and disrupted employment patterns also explain why the majority of the elderly poor are widows. At the other end of the scale, families in the top 20% of income brackets collect almost twice their share of total family income. It is these households that are most likely to contain a married couple (at least one of whom generally has a university degree) who live in a major city, own a home and a car. Women in these families (which are the most likely to conform to the popular but distorted image of the family) generally do not work in the labour force.

Conclusion Most Canadians today marry and stay married to the same person throughout life. The majority of men marry in their mid-twenties. The brides — a couple of years younger — usually share with their husbands a similar education and a similar ethnic and religious background. Most of these couples have children. Moreover, most children are born and raised in 2-parent households. The children are usually born to women who are in their mid- to late twenties. Since most women complete their child bearing within a short period of time, the children are separated from each other by only a few years. While there is little information available on the sexual practices and attitudes of these families, the numbers and spacing of children clearly indicates that most couples are practising some form of birth control. Most do not beat their children and most wives escape physical assault. Although most women now hold paid jobs for much of their lives and although there have been some important moves towards greater equality in the household, women still do most of the HOUSEWORK. These are dominant patterns, but the important variations on these patterns must be kept in mind. The number of unmarried couples living together has certainly increased, although this is not an entirely new phenomenon. Perhaps the only really new family form is the older couple whose children have grown and left home.

PAT ARMSTRONG

Reading: Pat Armstrong and Hugh Armstrong, *The Double Ghetto: Canadian Women and Their Segregated Work* (1978); J. Brown, *Strangers in Blood* (1980); M. Eichler, *Families in Canada* (1983); F. Elkin, *The Family in Canada* (1964); M. Kronby, *Canadian Family Law* (1983); M. Luxton, *More Than a Labour of Love* (1980); J. Parr, ed, *Childhood and Family in Canadian History* (1982); A. Prentice and S. Houston, eds, *Family, School and Society in Nineteenth Century Canada* (1975); D. Ross, *The Canadian Fact Book on Poverty* (1983); S.M. Trofimenkoff and A. Prentice, *The Neglected Majority* (1977).

Family Allowance, a monthly allowance paid to families with children to help cover the costs of child maintenance. Canada's first universal welfare program, it was introduced by the federal government in 1944. Under it, all families were paid a monthly sum on behalf of children under 16 who were attending school. Critics called it a waste of taxpayers' money, claiming the "baby bonus" would encourage poor families to procreate. Some suggested the money should be distributed by way of services to needy families instead. Supporters of family allowances argued that the service approach was paternalistic and that money distributed to mothers on behalf of their children would enhance the autonomy of families. Furthermore, because studies counted family size a significant cause of poverty, family allowances would ensure a basic income for families with children. Their universality was defended on the grounds that the administrative costs involved in determining who was poor would be substantial. In fact, family allowances did not result in an increase in the birthrate, which has steadily declined since the mid-1950s. In 1973 a new Family Allowances Act increased allowances from an average of between $6 and $7 to $20, which is paid to all dependent children, under age 18, of Canadian citizens or landed immigrants. The allowances, indexed to the cost of living, are taxable. In the fiscal year 1982-83 on behalf of 6.7 million children (Mar 1982) approximately $2.2 billion was redistributed. Québec and PEI pay a provincial supplement to federal family allowances.

DENNIS GUEST

Reading: Dennis Guest, *The Emergence of Social Security in Canada* (1980).

Family Compact, disparaging epithet applied by contemporaries to the small group of officials who dominated the executive and legislative councils, senior bureacratic positions and the judiciary of UPPER CANADA until the 1830s. The group emerged after John Graves SIMCOE, UC's first lieutenant-governor, attempted to create a local aristocracy by appointing his LOYALIST friends to government posts and granting them land. The next generation, including John Beverley ROBINSON, was supplemented by Britons, including John STRACHAN, who arrived before 1812 and were drawn into the governing TORY elite. The compact, centered at York [Toronto], was linked by family, patronage and shared political and social beliefs to the professional and mercantile upper middle class. It was sustained by conservative groups throughout the province — professionals, officials and retired military officers. The compact gave vitality to the political ideology that shaped Upper Canada: drawing upon Loyalist beliefs, the Tories envisaged the development of a society strengthened by the imperial connection and hostile to the US. It idealized British institutions such as a balanced constitution, a hierarchical society and an established church.

By the 1830s the compact was losing influence. Its exclusiveness provoked opponents to seek to reform the political system, and helped provoke the discontent that led to the REBELLION OF 1837. The rebellion was easily crushed, but the victorious Family Compact Tories in the government were soon squeezed out of politics by a new group of moderates who accepted the legitimacy of political opposition and the development of a PARTY SYSTEM.

DAVID MILLS

Family Court, the common name of courts established by provincial statutes to administer FAMILY LAW. Judges are appointed by the provincial government. Although the 3 main consequences of the breakup of a marriage or common-law relationship — custody of and access to children; support obligations among spouses, parents and children; and division of property — fall under family law, provincially appointed judges cannot adjudicate on property division or divorce and its consequences — matters which must be heard by a superior court. Family courts do deal, however, with adoption and juvenile delinquency. Most provinces have a family division of their provincial court; Québec's is the Social Welfare Court, PEI's is the Family Division of the Supreme Court of PEI. Judges of unified family courts in Saskatchewan and parts of Newfoundland and Ontario are appointed by both the federal and provincial governments and can thus deal with all aspects of family law. *See also* COURTS OF LAW.

P.K. DOODY

Family Law governs relations between spouses and between parents and children, as well as covering some other areas. In family law some matters, such as MARRIAGE AND DIVORCE (including custody and maintenance arising on divorce), are under federal jurisdiction; but most matters (including adoption, matrimonial property disputes, and custody and maintenance unrelated to divorce) are governed by provincial laws that vary widely from province to province. However, even within areas of provincial jurisdiction, certain matters, eg, occupation of the family home, can only be dealt with by judges appointed under s96 of the Constitution Act (*see* JUDICIARY). There is a growing trend in Canada towards the creation of unified family courts in which all family law matters, whether federal or provincial, could be dealt with before one judge.

Family Law in Common-Law Provinces

Marriage The licensing and formalities of a valid marriage ceremony are governed by provincial law, but Parliament has jurisdiction over marriage, eg, the age at which individuals may marry, the laws forbidding marriage between certain persons, and divorce.

Annulment makes a marriage legally void, retroactively, on the grounds that it was never fully legal owing to some disqualification. A marriage may be annulled if the parties are within the prohibited degrees (of consanguinity or through marriage), if one or another is or was under age (unless the consent of both parents had been granted), or as a result of bigamy, a defective marriage ceremony, duress, mental incapacity, or the failure to consummate the marriage because of the physical or mental inability of one of the parties. Annulments granted by church authorities, unlike legal annulments, have no effect in secular law.

Separation is a legally recognized parting by spouses or the agreed cessation of cohabitation. It can be cited as grounds for divorce.

Divorce is the legal termination of a valid

marriage. Until the federal Divorce Act of 1968, divorce was governed by pre-Confederation provincial statutes. In Newfoundland and Québec, where no divorce legislation existed, divorces could only be obtained through a private Act of Parliament. The 1968 Divorce Act provides that if the petitioner is domiciled in Canada and either party has been ordinarily resident for one year in the province in which the divorce is sought, the provincial supreme court can hear the case. Grounds for divorce include fault grounds, eg, adultery, mental or physical cruelty, homosexual conduct, imprisonment of the respondent for a certain period of time, or gross addiction to alcohol or narcotics (as defined under the Narcotic Control Act) for at least 3 years; and breakdown grounds, eg, separation for 3 years or, if the deserting spouse wishes to petition for divorce, desertion for 5 years. Over 90% of divorces are undefended and are usually granted after a short hearing. A divorce is granted in 2 parts but only the decree absolute entitles the parties to remarry. In 1969, 26 093 divorces were granted; in 1982, 70 436. In 1984 the federal government introduced a bill intending to make a one-year separation the only ground for divorce. Parties could initiate proceedings before they had been separated for a year but no decree could be issued prior to the parties having lived separate and apart for one year. The bill died on the order paper.

Maintenance can fall under federal law in connection with divorce, and under provincial law otherwise. Spouses, parents, children (who may have to support dependent parents) and guardians of children all have a legal obligation to support dependents. Increasingly, spouses are expected to become self-supporting where this is possible. The means and resources of the parties are important factors in establishing the amount of maintenance, as is their tax status, because the payer of periodical maintenance (but not lump sum maintenance) can deduct it from taxable income. Wives may have to support their husbands and children, and in some provinces common-law relationships may result in support obligations. Maintenance orders made under the Divorce Act are effective throughout Canada upon registration, but the enforcement of orders made under provincial laws, when spouses live in different provinces, depends upon the more cumbersome Reciprocal Enforcement of Maintenance legislation. Canada has not adopted a "parent locator" system, such as that in the US, although some provinces allow applicants to search provincial motor vehicle or health records in an attempt to locate missing spouses. Frequently a man who has remarried and acquired new dependents is unable to support both families and the law is unclear about which family has priority regarding financial resources.

Matrimonial Property Under old COMMON LAW, a husband acquired the right to own or manage his wife's property. The one recompense allowed the wife was a "dower," ie, a life interest in the freehold property the husband owned when he died (*see* PROPERTY LAW). Married women had limited contractual capacity except as agents for their husbands. In the 1890s, married women's property Acts introduced into all Canadian provinces the concept of separation of property. This gave wives contractual and tortious rights and responsibilities, though in several provinces actions between husband and wife in TORT are still forbidden. Giving women power to acquire property, however, did not alter the fact that employment opportunities for women were restricted and that most property was paid for by husbands and bought in the husband's name. A wife obtained no property ownership for her work of looking after the home and rearing the children, although she did obtain a measure of protection in her occupation of the matrimonial home under Homestead Acts in the West and, to a lesser extent, Dower Acts in the East. The traditional rules required that for a wife to own property it must be bought in her name or she must have made some direct contribution to its purchase, so cases arose like the MURDOCH CASE, in which the wife obtained no rights of ownership in what she thought were family assets. The harshness of this rule led all of the provinces to amend their legislation to give married women a fairer share in the division of the family's assets (*see* HUMAN RIGHTS), though the court has a discretion to vary the proportions according to certain criteria, eg, the date and manner of acquisition of assets, whether there is an agreement between the spouses about the property, etc. Frequently the Acts distinguish between family and other assets. In *Leatherdale* v *Leatherdale*, however, the Supreme Court of Canada upheld an Ontario court judgement that a wife has no right to an equal sharing of the shares that the husband has acquired under a scheme available to employees. Spouses who contribute to the business assets of their partner are entitled to compensation.

Recent case law developments suggest that common-law spouses who contribute money, or money's worth, to property purchased in their partner's name may acquire an interest in the property (*Pettkus* v *Becker*, 1980). This is important, because common-law spouses are not usually covered by the matrimonial property laws. These systems have been revised but they generally operate to give a wife ownership rights in property acquired after marriage, which has meant that spouses have not had the almost complete freedom of testation that was once available under common law (*see also* SUCCESSION).

Custody refers to the legal rights of parents regarding possession of children. Once a marriage has broken down these rights are not usually shared (joint custody) without both parents' consent, since the courts, particularly after a 1979 Ontario Court of Appeal decision are generally reluctant to look favourably on joint custody. Custody and rights of visitation are increasingly seen as a parental privilege rather than a right. There is no law requiring that the custody of young children be granted to mothers. Where both parents are working full-time, fathers are increasingly winning custody. The courts do operate, however, on certain premises of common sense, eg, their unwillingness to disturb a satisfactory status quo and their reluctance to separate siblings. In some provinces separate representation of children is permitted. Third parties, such as aunts or uncles, can also seek custody of a child.

Illegitimacy Historically the illegitimate child was "filius nullius" or the "son of no man." References to children in wills were usually taken as referring only to legitimate children, but the harshness of this rule has been gradually eroded. Illegitimate children in several provinces have rights of intestate succession against their mothers, or the right to ask for proper provision from their parents' estate under dependents' relief legislation. The obligation to support illegitimate children has been imposed on both parents under provincial maintenance legislation and the distinction between legitimate and illegitimate children in Ontario was abolished under the Children's Law Reform Act (1977). Similar legislation has recently been passed in Manitoba. The procedure for establishing paternity is called filiation; blood tests may be used to prove or contest such allegations. In custody cases between unwed parents there seems to be a residual preference for the mother.

Where spouses cannot have children of their own they may seek medical help. Artificial insemination of the mother by the husband generally produces no legal problems for a child born in consequence, but a child born as a result of insemination by semen from a donor might well be illegitimate or have a right to maintenance against the donor, though in many cases the presumption of legitimacy, unless rebutted by blood tests, would presume the husband of the mother to be the father of the child. Only in Québec is a husband who consents to the insemination of his wife the legal father of the child; any attempt to establish a link between the donor and the child is barred.

In the case of in vitro fertilization and embryo tranfers, an ovum is retrieved from the mother-to-be by laparoscopy and fertilized in a culture medium with sperm from the father before reintroduction into the womb of the gestational mother. If the mother who provides the ovum and the gestational mother are different persons, questions can arise about who is legally the mother of the resultant child. Problems can also arise about additional ova which are fertilized but not reintroduced into the gestational mother. If such ova are allowed to develop and are subjected to research before disposal, their status, and whether their disposal is an offence, is unclear.

If a woman agrees to have a child by artificial insemination by the husband of an infertile wife, the current view is that the agreement is probably not legally enforceable and that payments to secure the surrender of the mother's rights of custody may constitute an offence under provincial adoption Acts. The father of such a child could, however, rely on his own rights as biological father to retain his child if the mother was prepared to surrender it to him, but his wife would have no legal ties to the child in the absence of adoption. A. BISSETT-JOHNSON

Family Law, Québec

Québec family law is largely of French origin, but because marriage and divorce are within federal jurisdiction, there is a strong common-law influence. Moreover, because Québec law has been revised drastically by legislation in the last 20 years, differences in family law between Québec and the rest of Canada are not as strong as they once were. Traditionally the Québec Civil Code consecrated a notion of "paternal authority," which made the husband the head of the family and gave him considerable powers over his wife and children. This notion was recently applied by the court of appeal in *Cheyne* v *Cheyne* (1977), but the decision has since been repealed and the revised Civil Code (1982) insists on absolute equality of spouses.

Other aspects of Québec family law have also changed drastically. Traditional Québec family law was heavily influenced by the church. Divorce was utterly prohibited; separation and annulment of marriage were difficult to obtain. Women could be deprived of their part of community property as punishment for adultery. Illegitimate children were subject to various discriminatory rules and even adopted children were denied full equality. All of this has now changed and has been replaced by modern, liberal provisions. One aspect of the new Québec law has been questioned, however, and that is the marked tendency to delegate discretion to courts instead of to individuals. For example, a minor who wishes to marry will, in the future, ask the court and not his parents for permission. Given the usual court delays and appeal procedures, this could be a long and cumbersome process.

Marriage Marriage law in Québec reflects principles similar to those underlying marriage law in other provinces, ie, it is strictly monogamous, requires capacity and consent of both parties and must include a ceremony, either civil or religious. Marriages that do not conform to the rules may be annulled.

Separation and Divorce Separation can now be obtained in Québec with a minimum of formality. It does not break the marriage tie. Divorce is obtained under federal law. Québec adopted fairly liberal divorce provisions in the 1982 Code but these articles have not been proclaimed because they are not constitutional.

Children The 1982 Code abolished the concept of illegitimacy. Adoption is included in the Civil Code and creates the same relationship as birth. It is illegal to trade in children or to accept payment for a private adoption and presumably any contract to have a child and give it up to someone would be void, unenforceable and unlawful. Parents and children owe each other support even when the child has reached majority, although both parties must strive to be as independent as possible.

Matrimonial Property Québec law has kept the civilian concept of matrimonial regime, ie, the system of sharing or separating property between spouses. Couples are free under the Marriage Act to choose one of 3 regimes and to change it. The most common regimes are separation of property and partnership of acquests. If no regime is chosen by marriage contract, the couple is presumed to have selected partnership of acquests. Under this system, each partner keeps the property he or she had at the time of marriage and each administers his own property after marriage. However, when the marriage or the regime end, the property acquired after marriage (with some exceptions, such as inheritance) is divided equally between the parties.

Marriage contracts must be drafted by a notary. In addition to the choice of regimes, contracts often contain gifts from one spouse to the other, either while both spouses are alive or in contemplation of death. Such gifts are enforceable notwithstanding a subsequent will. In case of divorce or separation, the court may reduce or eliminate the gifts and it appears that those contracted in contemplation of death lapse automatically since the 1982 change of law.

Since 1982 the Civil Code has protected the spouse's interest in the matrimonial home and the furniture. In the case of a home owned by one spouse, the other spouse's rights are not protected unless a "declaration of matrimonial domicile" is registered at the appropriate registry office. One spouse is not entitled to dispose of furniture garnishing the matrimonial domicile without the other spouse's consent; however, purchases for value in good faith are protected. There is at present insufficient jurisprudence to judge what constitutes "good faith" in these circumstances.

Procedure The Québec Civil Code and Code of Civil Procedure have been amended to provide remedies suitable for family law. The most controversial features include provision for separate representation of children and for adoption and return of children. In December 1983 a new set of rules for the recognition of foreign adoptions came into effect and as a result it is very difficult for Quebeckers to adopt foreign children, even with the consent of the foreign authorities.

The most debated issue has been the new law under which all family law trials take place behind closed doors. Lawyers have protested vigorously but the validity of the law has yet to be contested. The law has also provided that, in reporting cases, the names of the parties not be published. JULIUS GREY

Family Studies Because marriage and the family are so important to the lives of many people, the study of the family attracts individuals from different disciplines. Basic to most approaches is a knowledge about how families exist — their composition, duration, economic behaviour, etc. This descriptive task, mainly the responsibility of STATISTICS CANADA, is complex. Definitions change (eg, that of a head of a household) over time, and the information Statistics Canada can gather is limited. Nevertheless, through its periodic censuses, correlated with vital statistics (births, deaths, marriages, divorces) registered by the provinces, Statistics Canada maintains an extensive body of information about Canadian family life. In addition, many limited or special studies, eg, those on consumer spending or sickness and health care, contribute to our knowledge of the family. However, no comprehensive guide to all the information gathered by governments exists.

Following the 1968 changes of laws regarding divorce, the number and rate of marriage breakups increased dramatically. Forty percent of marriages are now dissolved in divorce. Marriage and remarriage rates are also very high, creating concern about divorce and its impact on children, and concern as well about the new, "blended" families. In family studies, an increasingly popular approach is to study marriage and the family as relationships regulated by law and social policy. In recent years the federal government and most provinces have set up law reform commissions to examine how laws affect family relationships and how they might be changed to reflect and shape current realities. No general analyses or interpretations have yet been published, though M. Eichler's *Families in Canada Today* is a long step in this direction. Sociologists and anthropologists have studied how people live within families and how the family is linked to other social institutions. Many particular aspects of marriage and family life in various communities or groups have been documented, eg, in *The Canadian Family* and *The Canadian Family in Comparative Perspective*. Families are intimately involved in and affected by local, regional and national economies, and by changing ideologies about the status of women, the rights of children, the dissolution of marriage, etc. The Vanier Institute of the Family in Ottawa has been active in documenting and publicizing some of these aspects and changes.

Many psychologists and other social scientists have studied the family as the matrix within which adults exist and children are socialized; their work has been mainly academic, though their conclusions have been applied in school programs, parent effectiveness training programs, etc. Family-life education is taught in many school curriculums; although it is frequently a euphemism for sex education, the current trend is to expand the subject to include homemaking, child rearing and interpersonal skills. Family studies are offered as a course or specialization in colleges and universities; they have developed from what was earlier known as home economics or household science and have broadened to include many courses on household skills, consumer behaviour, interpersonal skills, etc, although critics of these courses argue that the image of the family in school and college courses is biased, is inherently conservative and idealized, and does not reflect the experience of most people.

The recognition that it is within families that much individual and interpersonal pathology develops has spurred a new "science" of family diagnosis and family treatment, which is applied in SOCIAL WORK, psychology, psychiatry and family medicine, although there is as yet no national organization in Canada specifically devoted to this type of study and practice. *See also* MARRIAGE AND DIVORCE. NORMAN BELL

Reading: M. Baker, ed, *The Family: Changing Trends in Canada* (1984); M. Eichler, *Families in Canada Today* (1973); K. Ishwaran, *The Canadian Family* (rev 1976); L. Larson, *The Canadian Family in Comparative Perspective* (1976); R. Pike and E. Zureik, eds, *Socialization and Values in Canadian Society*, 2 vols (1975).

Fantasy Fiction, *see* POPULAR LITERATURE.

Farm Credit Corporation, a federal crown agency set up in 1959 under the Farm Credit Act to develop efficient farm businesses through the use of long-term mortgage credit. The FCC succeeded the Canadian Farm Loan Board, which had been in operation since 1929. Corporation headquarters are in Ottawa with regional offices in each province except NS, PEI and Newfoundland, which are served by the NB office. The corporation's board is composed of 7 members appointed by the federal minister of agriculture. Regional appeal boards hear appeals from farmers not satisfied with FCC decisions on loan applications. A national advisory committee, with members appointed by the minister of agriculture, advises the minister or corporation on lending policies and practices. The FCC may borrow from the Consolidated Revenue Fund or may raise funds in private money markets. The corporation provides standard loans and phase-in loans. Standard loans may be made of up to 100% of the appraised farm value to a maximum dollar ceiling set by the corporation. Phase-in loans aid beginning farmers under 35 years of age, permitting them to phase into farming over a 5-year period. Either type may be used to acquire farmland, modernize or erect buildings and purchase equipment and livestock. The corporation also administers the Farm Syndicate Credit Act, under which 3 or more farmers may apply co-operatively for a loan to purchase equipment or erect buildings. This type of loan reduces production costs by encouraging joint ownership and use of machinery and equipment. J.C. GILSON

Farm Drainage Drainage problems are caused by an excess of water at the SOIL surface or in the root zone. Drainage work is carried out to improve the root-zone environment for crop growth, improve conditions for cultivation, planting and harvesting, allow earlier spring planting for better use of the short Canadian growing season, and convey salts out of soil in areas where salinity is a problem. The problem of excess water and inadequate drainage is obvious wherever pondings remain after rainfall or snowmelt. A less obvious problem exists when the root zone is saturated but no water is present on the surface. Most crops prefer moist, unsaturated soil, with over 6% of the volume filled with air. Air space allows roots to respire, grow and obtain nutrients from greater depth.

Land drainage work began in Canada more than 200 years ago. As the population increased in the 19th century, the limitations of Canada's CLIMATE and soils became obvious. Eastern Canada and the coastal valleys of BC had a cool, moist climate; frequently, there was more rain than needed. Much of the higher land, which had adequate natural drainage, lacked fertility, or was stony or had a shallow soil which suffered from DROUGHT; flatter lands and river valleys usually had greater food-production potential after drainage work was carried out. Before 1900 some rivers and streams were deepened to provide better outlets. Ditches were dug by human and animal power to improve field drainage. Dikes were constructed to protect lands from high TIDES around the Bay of FUNDY and along the S shore of the ST LAWRENCE R estuary. The construction of additional drainage ditches and cleaning of former ditches has continued through the 20th century to allow increased food production and to improve marginal land to replace farmland lost to expanding cities. Steam shovels, employed on the larger drainage jobs from 1870 to 1930, have been replaced by diesel shovels and draglines. Since 1970 most channel excavation has been done by high-capacity hydraulic backhoes. Approximately 1000 km of main ditches are dug annually in Canada.

Subsurface drainage by means of tiles, stones and wooden drains was introduced in the mid-19th century. The work was done by hand. The prospect for increased subsurface drainage came with the introduction of wheel-type ditching machines in 1907. The power and speed of new trenching machines have increased steadily since 1945. Drain-laying plows, pulled by bulldozers, were introduced in 1968. Since 1971, LASER grade-control systems have improved the accuracy and speed of trenchers and drain-laying plows. The installation of subsurface drains to intercept seepage from farm IRRIGATION canals and help reduce soil salinity in Alberta and Saskatchewan proceeded after field experiments conducted before 1970. Construction of drainage systems to reduce waterlogging and salinity is accelerating now, as the need is great.

Canadian drainage engineers, contractors and drainage material manufacturers have made rapid advances in drainage technology in the past 20 years, as subsurface drainage installations have increased from 22 000 km to more than 100 000 km per year. This technology has made it possible for a construction crew of 5 persons to install 7000 m of pipe per day in 1983, compared with 800 m per day in 1968. Less than one-third of the farmland that needs subsurface drains to achieve its crop production potential has had drains installed. R.S. BROUGHTON

Farm Law In Canada over 99% of farm businesses are family operations; these operations involve about one million people. The total capital value of Canadian farms in 1981 was $130 billion; the average capital value per farm was $409 000; and, on average, farm real estate was worth over $375/ha. Because of the economic and social importance of the family farm and the dramatic increase in farm bankruptcies in the 1980s, farm groups have emphasized the importance of establishing the farm business on a sound legal footing, both to protect individual farmers and to maintain the family farm as a viable unit. Because of its special social and economic problems, the rigid marketing structures that surround it and the high risks attached to it, farming requires a more sophisticated approach to legal matters than do many other businesses. Regulations relating to marketing vary according to the product, the part of the country in which it is produced, the intended market (eg, domestic or export), etc. A general outline can be drawn, however, of business arrangements and taxation rulings affecting farm businesses.

The 2 broad areas of business relationship are the connection between the owner and his business and that between the owner, his estate and his family. These kinds of relationship have special implications in farming because the farm family is the major source of farm labour and management. Business arrangements between fathers and children are the most frequently encountered in farming, and each party has problems that must be resolved. The father has accumulated substantial, usually nonliquid assets (ie, land, buildings, machinery, inventories of grain and livestock), and wishes to make an adequate arrangement to assure the continuance of the child or children in the farm business, while maintaining some control of business management and income. Finally, he desires to assure succession of the business to the child, but wishes to be paid for the capital he transfers to the child and to provide income and capital for his wife and for beneficiaries not involved in the business. The child desires an adequate income, means of acquiring a controlling capital interest in the farm and eventual, guaranteed succession.

Both parties must consider certain areas of mutual interest, eg, evaluation and ownership of assets, amount of time each shall contribute to the enterprise, apportionment of income now and in future, regular transfer of capital from father to child (by gift, purchase or both), agreements regulating purchase and sale of shares in the farm, and the means by which other children may acquire interest in the business.

The farmer considering his farm as an estate is faced with the problem of how to divide control of his business. Related questions include continuity of management, the effect of his death on the availability of business credit and funds for the purchase of his business by his children, and the need to make funds available for executors to pay debts and taxes and provide an income for dependants. A properly thought-out estate plan will do much to establish credit, create acceptable collateral, provide retirement funds, prevent the sale of assets at distress prices, establish the value of the business and achieve continuity in business activity. In most instances, funding for the purchase by the son from the father is secured by mortgage financing from a bank, the FARM CREDIT CORPORATION or a provincial government credit association. Any outstanding balance owed to the father is secured by additional financing which ranks second to the aforementioned mortgage obligation. Accordingly, the father's equity, on which he relies to support himself and his wife during retirement, is at risk and, in difficult times, is often obliterated. It is therefore essential that other methods be sought to secure protection for the father.

The farm business involving 2 or more people can be carried on by 2 major methods, the partnership (general or limited) and the limited corporation, each with its own advantages and disadvantages. In certain instances a combination may be warranted.

The Farm Partnership

A partnership is the relation between persons carrying on a business in common with a view to profit. It is not a legal entity; all rights and obligations accrue to the individuals in the partnership. Each partner is regarded as the agent of the other and is capable of making the other liable. The relationship between the partners is separately liable for all debts and obligations incurred by the partnership. A general partnership consists of 2 or more general partners who are jointly and severally liable for the firm's debts, not only to the extent of their investment in the partnership but, if this investment is insufficient to satisfy the creditors, to the extent that their private property is required for this purpose. Each partner has a right of indemnity against the other. A limited partnership consists of one or more general partners and one or more limited partners. A limited partner is liable for the firm's debts only to the extent of his investment, but his liabilities increase to those of a general partner if he allows his name to appear in the firm's name and if he publicly helps conduct the business. To be considered a limited partner, one must be so designated in a declaration filed with the government. A limited partnership must be registered and all partners are considered general partners until so registered.

Capital contributions from the different partners may vary, as is often the case in family farm partnerships. In some such cases the partner with the higher capital investment may be paid interest on such excess by the partnership. Such interest is charged as an expense to the partnership; therefore the partner is, in effect, paying part of his own interest. In other instances the partner contributing least capital may contribute most labour. These positions are sometimes equated so that profits are divided equally. Alternatively, excess labour may be compensated by payment of a wage, leaving the rate of return of profit related to the amount of capital contribution. The cost of labour is charged to the partnership and the partner being paid for his labour contributes personally to his own wage.

The division of income from a farm partnership is often difficult. The father needs cash to support and educate other members of the family; the child may also have a growing family and may require a maximum amount of income. In such a case, capital acquisition must either be limited or have payment amortized over a long period to make the maximum amount of cash available. At the same time the goal may have to be towards the immediate expansion of the farm unit. Thus, there may be a most difficult conflict between the capital needs for expansion and the immediate need for cash. To resolve such a conflict the first necessity is to determine whether the existing farm unit can support the partners and, if not, what can be done to alter it to allow it to do so. The various factors that must be taken into account in the division of income are the amount required by each party for family spending, contributions to labour, management or capital made by each party, and a formula that relates the minimum wage to be earned by each partner, plus a division of surplus, to the growth of the business. The arrangement chosen must be flexible and must recognize the changing needs of each partner.

The Farm Corporation

A corporation is a legal person with the capacity (subject to the Corporations Act), rights, powers and privileges of a natural person. It is an advantageous form of business association because it gives potential income tax advantages, accommodates the many variations of business relationships, can be a vehicle for estate planning, and its liability is usually limited to the assets it owns. Finally, a corporation has an identity distinct from that of its shareholders and potentially can exist forever. Thus it offers opportunities for investment and management decisions that are largely independent of an individual owner or partner. An individual invests in a corporation by purchasing shares. Shares are allotted for amounts fixed by the directors, and such values, determined at the time of issue, become the paid-up or "stated" capital of those shares. There may be more than one class of shares, each carrying different rights and restrictions. The directors should determine the nature and attributes of the shares to be issued by considering the nature of the business the corporation will carry on, the relationship between the persons who will be shareholders and the method of securing the repayment of any monies owed by the corporation.

A farmer considering incorporation must consider various aspects of CORPORATION LAW as they will affect his business. For example, the appointment of directors and the rules governing voting (including the definition of a quorum) will influence who has managing control over farm-business decisions. Similarly, regulations established within the corporation to govern purchase and sale of shares will affect how shares in the farm may be traded within the family or to persons outside the family corporation. The means of repayment to a retiring shareholder or to the estate of a deceased shareholder can influence the continued economic health of the farm corporation. In this connection the importance of insurance on the lives of the principals should be emphasized.

The corporation offers certain advantages to the farm business. For example, a farmer may incorporate his farm business by selling assets to a corporation owned by himself or by members of his family without incurring tax liability. Such a sale must comply with Section 85 of the Income Tax Act. Further, a corporation lends itself particularly well to the estate plan. Provided it is adequately established, it can freeze the value of the farmer's estate so that all future growth will go to those persons he wishes to benefit. It allows the farmer to give nonvoting participating shares during his lifetime without affecting his control of the corporation, its assets or its income. It permits the farmer to give his heirs specific interests in such proportions as he desires, immediately and in the future. It allows for the maintenance of control by the farmer's executors beyond his death to maintain the farm's value, carry on business and protect the farmer's wife and dependants. Finally, it allows a farmer to complete arrangements with those of his children who wish to operate the farm, so that they share in the income and continued growth of the assets, obtain eventual control and thus stay with the business.

Taxation

The Income Tax Act generally requires that business income must be computed on an accrual basis. However, if the taxpayer chooses, income from a farming or fishing business can be computed on a cash basis. Thus a farmer may include only amounts actually received in that year and deduct amounts actually paid in that year.

Livestock herds are now treated as ordinary inventory. Livestock acquisition costs, deducted from income on a cash basis, may result in the farmer realizing a loss for the year. Losses may only be carried forward and applied against income for 5 years. To allow a farmer to use these losses without having to reduce his herd to generate income against which the losses could be charged, the Act permits a farmer in each year to include as income any amount up to the fair market value of his livestock at the end of that year (the amount claimed in the previous year being deducted the following year). Thus livestock acquisition costs can be carried forward indefinitely for deduction against actual future income.

Restricted Farm Loss TAXATION law distinguishes 3 categories of farmers. Farmers who are in the "business" of farming can fully deduct all losses incurred in farming. Those persons who farm as a sideline with a reasonable expectation of profit can deduct losses to a maximum of $5000 per year, the balance (ie, restricted farm losses) being carried forward. Persons who farm for enjoyment (ie, as a hobby) are not entitled to any deductions.

Transfer of Farm Property To preserve the family farm, the Income Tax Act contains certain provisions that allow a farmer to transfer farm property to his spouse or children on a tax-deferred (rollover) basis. Included in the type of property that may be transferred are farm property, shares in a family farm corporation and an interest in a family farm partnership. In each case the property must be used by the taxpayer, his spouse or his child in the business of farming. *See* AGRICULTURAL ECONOMICS; FAMILY LAW; PROPERTY LAW. Y.M. HENTELEFF AND M.S. PALAY

Farm Silo, storage structure for silages and high-moisture grains used for livestock feeds. Silos are a common fixture in livestock and mixed-farming operations across Canada. Silage is formed by microbial fermentation of plant material under anaerobic (oxygen-free) or near-anaerobic conditions. Whole-plant CORN silage (30-35% dry matter) is made by chopping the entire plant finely (1-2 cm); haylage is silage composed of wilted GRASS or ALFALFA dried to 35-50% dry matter. High-moisture grains (eg, whole shelled, ground shelled and ground ear corns and BARLEY) go through the same fermentation process as silage. Under normal conditions, silage-producing microbial fermentation produces lactic and acetic acids until acidity is such that growth of all microorganisms stops (after 2-3 weeks). With well-ensiled material in anaerobic storage, the quality and palatability of the feed is maintained until the material is exposed to oxygen, which causes silage to deteriorate quickly. Silos are of bunker or tower type. The bottom-unloading tower silo allows a greater degree of automation but is somewhat more expensive to build. Bunker silos are the cheapest but allow little automation and have the greatest feed loss by oxidation.

Typical farm in Huron County, Ont. Silos, such as the one shown here, are common in mixed farming operations across Canada (*photo ©1984 Hartill Art Associates*).

Bunker Silos are paved areas surrounded on 3 sides by concrete or 3-5 m high timber walls. Forage is dumped within the walled area, compacted and covered with polyethylene sheets weighed down with old tires. Unloading is by front-end loader or by allowing cattle to feed directly from the exposed face of the silage.

Tower Silos are 15-30 m high, cylindrical, concrete or steel structures, usually closed with a domed roof. Forage is blown into the top via a pipe mounted on the silo's side. Special unloading equipment is mounted inside. Top-unloading silos have a rotating scraper that sweeps silage through openings in the wall into a chute mounted on the side. Silage falls into a feeding cart, or onto a conveyor belt for distribution to livestock. Bottom-unloading silos have a screw-type unloader, which moves silage into a central hopper from which it is conveyed further by belt or screw conveyor. J.C. JOFRIET

Farnham, Qué, Town, pop 6476 (1981c), inc 1876, is located about 65 km E of Montréal on the Yamaska R, at the boundary between the plain of Montréal and the Eastern Townships. The township of Farnham West was settled in the early 19th century by colonists from northern New England, mainly Vermont. A little later, Francophones migrated from regions around the Richelieu and Yamaska rivers (Rouville and St-Hyacinthe counties). Farnham West was incorporated as a village 1862. Francophones have long been in the majority and now represent over 90% of the population. Between 1860 and 1900, Farnham made remarkable progress as a railway centre, thanks to its geographic position and competition among railway promoters. In the 1880s South Eastern Rail established its main office and facilities for rolling-stock maintenance in Farnham. South Eastern was later absorbed by the CPR and the town became a major stop on the CPR route along the lower St Lawrence through Maine. In

CPR station at Farnham, Qué, 1901. The town was a major stop on the CPR route along the lower St Lawrence (*courtesy Canadian Pacific Corporate Archives*).

the early 20th century the CPR employed about 500 men from Farnham (pop 3114, 1901c) in maintenance and repair workshops, in the manufacture of rolling-stock parts and on the trains themselves. These activities diminished in the following decades, however. The growth of road transportation and removal of several regional railway lines after 1930 tended to limit Farnham's development. In addition, it had to compete with neighbouring centres such as Saint-Jean and Granby.

In the 1940s the presence of a large military base nearby spurred development. Railway employees once again formed a large segment of the town's population. Farnham's industries have included sugar-beet refining and wood, clothing and rubber manufacturing. Today the main industries are textiles, linoleum and carpets. JOHANNE LEDOUX

Farnon, Robert Joseph, composer, arranger, conductor (b at Toronto 24 July 1917). A successful purveyor of good, light music, he is considered one of the most influential film composers of his generation in Europe and N America. Farnon became trumpeter in several 1930s Toronto dance bands and in the Canadian Radio Broadcasting Commission's orchestras of Percy FAITH and Geoffrey WADDINGTON. He was a member of CBC Radio's "Happy Gang" 1937-43. After serving overseas during WWII as musical director of the Army Show, Farnon settled permanently in Great Britain and built a solid reputation as orchestral conductor, arranger and composer through a series of BBC radio programs and recordings for Chappell and Co Mood Music. His arrangements have been recorded by such well-known performers as Vera Lynn, Lena Horne and Frank Sinatra. As well as numerous film scores, Farnon's own compositions include the popular suite *Canadian Impressions* and *Rhapsody* for violin and orchestra (recorded by Steven STARYK). ANN SCHAU

Faro, YT, Town, pop 1652 (1981c), is located 6 km N of the Campbell Hwy, 200 km by air NE of Whitehorse. The Cyprus Anvil Mines Co built the town in 1969 to house employees of its open-pit lead and zinc mine. Ravaged by a forest fire in its first year, it was quickly rebuilt and became the territory's second-largest community. The mine was Canada's largest producer of LEAD, and its exports became a mainstay of the Yukon economy in the 1970s. Faro's name is derived from a game of chance, popular in Klondike saloons, in which the cards bore a stylized portrait of an Egyptian pharaoh. H. GUEST

Farquharson, Donald, politician, premier of PEI (b at Mermaid, PEI 27 July 1834; d at Charlottetown 26 June 1903). A teacher by training, Farquharson subsequently entered the wholesale and shipping business and in 1876 won election to the PEI Assembly as a Liberal. He was a member of the government in 1878-79 and from 1891 to 27 Dec 1901, serving as premier after 1 Aug 1898. He resigned to contest Queens W successfully in a federal by-election for the Commons 15 Jan 1902. PETER E. RIDER

Farquharson, Ray Fletcher, physician, medical educator (b at Claude, Ont 4 Aug 1897; d at Ottawa 1 June 1965). Farquharson was Sir John and Lady Eaton Professor of Medicine, U of T (1947-60), and first chairman of the Medical Research Council (Canada) in 1960, and held the position until his sudden death during a council meeting. Farquharson did significant research in pernicious anaemia, Simmond's disease, anorexia nervosa and hyperparathyroidism. He was an excellent teacher and an outstanding consultant, much revered by his patients for his warm and sympathetic personality. He was consultant to the RCAF during WWII and president of the Royal Coll of Physicians and Surgeons of Canada (1945-47). ROBERT B. KERR

Farrally, Betty, née Hey, dancer, teacher, ballet director (b at Bradford, Eng 5 May 1915). As cofounder of the ROYAL WINNIPEG BALLET and later through her teaching, Farrally, renowned for her vivacity and energy, has become one of the most respected figures in Canadian BALLET. Following completion of dance studies in England, she immigrated to Canada with her former teacher Gweneth LLOYD in 1938. She was instrumental in helping Lloyd establish the Winnipeg Ballet (Royal Winnipeg Ballet) and, following her colleague's move to Toronto in 1950, remained artistic director until 1957 when she founded a new school in Kelowna, BC. Farrally was also longtime co-head and continues as an artistic adviser of the Banff Centre's summer dance program. MICHAEL CRABB

Fascism is a term often loosely used to describe military dictatorships and extreme right-wing governments and organizations (or individuals) known to be violently either anticommunist or violently anti-Semitic, or both. These are often important elements within fascism (as are the institutionalization of sexual repression and strong antifemale, antihomosexual and pro-family biases), but the term should be more precisely confined to those mass movements and political parties that originated in the capitalist economies of Europe in the late 19th and early 20th centuries, culminating in Mussolini's Italy and Hitler's Germany. (Fascism existed but was not terribly influential in Britain, the US and Canada [mainly Québec] during the 1930s.) It is characterized by a hatred for liberalism, socialism, democracy and the parliamentary system; by extreme and aggressive nationalism and hostility to other nations and races; by a glorification of power, violence and war; by dreams of conquest and expansion; by a hankering after a supposedly glorious past; by paramilitary associations; by the myth of the "leader" to whom superhuman qualities are attributed; and by the creation of a convenient scapegoat — usually JEWS — for all social, national and economic ills.

Fascist movements became prominent after WWI among the losing nations that had suffered humiliating defeats, lost large territories and faced harsh terms of peace. Reconquest of old colonies and territories and restoration of prewar positions in the world was a major theme of all fascist movements. Fascism attracted not only the military, but those who had lost their traditional place in society and were frightened of the future, particularly the lower-middle classes. Essential to the rise of fascism was the devastating economic crisis that threw millions out of work and threatened the economic security of many more millions, but other conditions were important as well: a capitalist class fearful of powerful working-class organization and of strong communist and socialist parties who seemed on the verge of taking power, and the existence of weak and ever-changing minority governments in countries where parliamentary institutions and liberal democratic social values were poorly developed and where leadership was widely discredited by indecision, paralysis, and corruption.

Once in power, fascist parties banned all opposition parties, independent trade unions and strikes, eliminated the independent press, established one-party states and reorganized industry along corporatist lines. In practice, CORPORATISM severly curtailed the rights of workers while emphasizing and protecting the rights of employers. Fascism ceased to be a powerful force with the defeat of the Axis powers of WWII and the long wave of postwar prosperity, but elements of fascism flourish in some underdeveloped Third World countries and survive in some fully developed capitalist countries. In Canada fascist elements are evident in organizations such as the KU KLUX KLAN. C. GONICK

Fashion Design is the creation of styles for wearing apparel that will satisfy more than the physical needs of men, women and children for protection against the elements and for modesty. It is characterized by seasonal changes that often reflect social, political, historical and economic influences. Canada's contribution to international fashion dates back to the 16th century when French explorers returned to Europe with luxurious beaver pelts. For centuries, Canada struggled to become self-reliant in satisfying its clothing needs. Pioneer settlers not only produced fabrics and clothing, but fashioned the necessary tools by hand, importing the first machines from England and Scotland after 1846. Increased immigration brought skilled tailors from Europe, who became the basis for the apparel industry. Today, this industry, including textiles and knitting, is the second largest employer in Canada, with retail sales of $7.3 billion.

In the past, most designers and manufacturers depended on Europe and the US for inspiration. However, Elen Henderson was known internationally by 1949, as was John Warden by 1963. The international Association of Clothing Designers (men's fine clothing) has had Toronto and Montréal chapters since before 1929. The 1967 Centennial celebration inspired the fashion industry to enhance its own identity. Fashion/Canada, a crown corporation, was set up by the government to promote Canadian fashion and designers during the formative years, 1968-71, and it became a major force in design. Fashion designers turned their attention to furs and made impressive inroads into export markets. Designers established, with Fashion/Canada's help, the Fashion Designers Association of Canada in 1974. Among the founders were internationally acclaimed designers Leo Chevalier, John Warden, Michel Robichaud and Hugh Garber of Montréal and Alfred Sung, Elen Henderson, Claire Haddad and Pat McDonaugh of Toronto. Chevalier has received both the Designer of the Year Award and the Merit Award of Québec as well as the Order of Canada. Haddad is the country's top designer of ladies' lounge and sleep wear, and enjoys both national and international recognition. She was the first Canadian to receive the coveted Coty Award, the top fashion award in the US, and holds the Order of Canada and 6 Eedee Awards (Ontario government awards for fashion). Robichaud ap-

A page from *Simpson's Catalogue* shows the fashion range of the 1920s (*courtesy Public Archives of Canada/C-49409*).

prenticed with foremost French designers before returning to Montréal to open his own boutique and design ready-to-wear clothing. Henderson is internationally known as a designer of children's clothes. She received the Eedee Award for 6 consecutive years and designed the uniform of the Canadian Girl Guides and Brownies. Gabriel Levy and Albert Shu are famous Canadian fashion designers working in Vancouver.

There are annual incentives for young and aspiring designers offered by government and industry. Nine universities, 22 community colleges and 28 private and technical schools offer fashion design courses and programs across Canada; these vary from 1 to 4 years in duration. Some of their graduates, such as Linda Lundstrom and Wayne Clarke, are internationally known designers today.

S. SCHIPPER, C. GONZALES AND E. SHANNON

Fathers of Confederation No one has adequately defined a Father of CONFEDERATION. Some definitions include the delegates from the RED RIVER COLONY who created Manitoba in 1870, and those who came to Ottawa to bring in Newfoundland in 1949. The conventional meaning includes all who represented colonies of BRITISH NORTH AMERICA at the CHARLOTTETOWN CONFERENCE and the QUÉBEC CONFERENCE (1864), or the LONDON CONFERENCE (1866-67).

Charlottetown Conference Province of Canada: George Brown, Alexander Campbell, George-Étienne Cartier, Alexander Galt, Hector Langevin, John A. Macdonald, William McDougall, Thomas D'Arcy McGee; NB: E.B. Chandler, J.H. Gray, J.M. Johnson, W.H. Steeves, Samuel L. Tilley; NS: Adams G. Archibald, R.B. Dickey, W.A. Henry, Jonathan McCully, Charles Tupper; PEI: George Coles, J.H. Gray, A.A. Macdonald, Edward Palmer, W.H. Pope.

Québec Conference Those named above were joined by, for Canada, J.C. Chapais, James Cockburn, Oliver Mowat, Sir Étienne P. Taché; for NB, Charles Fisher, Peter Mitchell; for PEI, T.H. Haviland, Edward Whelan; and for Nfld, F.B.T. Carter, Ambrose Shea.

London Conference Some of the above did not attend, and there were 3 new delegates: for Canada, W.P. Howland; for NS, J.W. Ritchie; and for NB, R.D. Wilmot. P.B. WAITE

Reading: G.P. Browne, ed, *Documents on the Confederation of British North America* (1969); P.B. Waite, *The Life and Times of Confederation, 1864-1867* (1962).

Fauna, *see* ANIMAL.

Fauquier, John Emilius, air-force officer (b at Ottawa 19 Mar 1909; d at Toronto 3 Apr 1981). Educated at Ashbury College, Fauquier, a commercial pilot, joined the RCAF in 1939, eventually commanding 405 (Pathfinder) Squadron, RCAF, and from Dec 1944, 617 (Dambuster) Squadron, RAF. He was awarded the DFC for gallantry and the DSO for his "skillful and courageous example" over Peenemunde and Berlin, Aug 1943. He received a bar to his DSO Jan 1944 and at the war's end became the only Canadian airman to be awarded a second bar, for his "brilliant leadership, undoubted skill and iron determination." He also received the Croix de Guerre avec palme and was made Chevalier de la Légion d'Honneur. He returned to private business and in 1973 was named to the Aviation Hall of Fame. JEAN PARISEAU

Fauteux, André, sculptor (b at Dunnville, Ont 15 Mar 1946). He received his basic art education at Central Technical School in Toronto and worked with Anthony Caro (York U, 1974-75). Fauteux is known for the elegant, controlled line of drawing that characterizes his abstract sculptures. Profoundly influenced by the minimalist paintings of Kenneth Noland, Fauteux has successfully dealt with and transformed Noland's painterly concerns to his sculptures. The carefully articulated thin outlines enclose the volume of each work, but the flatness of the steel, the convergence of verticals and horizontals at sharp, dramatic angles, and the surrounding negative space defy the mass and weight of the sculptures. Fauteux's approach uses the interaction of geometric shapes as a point of departure in the building of a sculptural form. CLARA HARGITTAY

Favreau, Guy, lawyer, politician (b at Montréal 20 May 1917; d there 11 July 1967). Favreau was a prominent Montréal lawyer who was elected to the House of Commons in the 1963 election. A member of the "new guard" of Québec Liberals, Favreau quickly rose to prominence under PM Lester PEARSON's patronage. His first appointment on 22 Apr 1963 was as minister of citizenship and immigration. On 3 Feb 1964 Pearson appointed Favreau minister of justice and attorney general as well as Liberal House leader. In Apr 1964 Favreau also became Québec Liberal Party leader. The tasks were too much for him. Press criticism of Favreau intensified as a result of the Lucien RIVARD scandal. The Dorion Commission criticized Favreau's handling of the scandal, and on 29 June 1965 he resigned as justice minister. On 7 July 1965 Pearson, in a controversial move, appointed Favreau president of the Privy Council. His political reputation was tarnished beyond repair. He faded quickly from public view, his health failed, and in 1967 this tragic figure died. JOHN ENGLISH

Reading: Peter Newman, *The Distemper of Our Times* (1968).

Favro, Murray, artist (b at Huntsville, Ont 24 Dec 1940). Favro began his career painting brightly coloured works on masonite. Around 1965 he abandoned painting for other-than-art interests — guitars, machines, airplanes, experiments with film images and inventions. A Canada Council Arts Bursary in 1970 allowed him to devote himself to his art. That year he developed his first successful "projected reconstruction," in which images on a slide are projected onto their wooden, white, life-sized counterparts, giving them colour, detail and identity. He later produced modified inventions (*Windmill Electric Generator*, 1975-76; *Perpetual Motion Machine*, 1976-77), evolved inventions (*Propeller Engine*, 1978), and material, three-dimensional renderings of airplanes (*Flying Flea*, 1976-77 and *Sabre Jet, 55% Size* 1979-83).

Favro's work deals in a unique way with the nature of perception, reality and art itself, as well as with the insistent presence of the machine environment. His art has its own language of form — a vocabulary of constituent properties, a grammar of particular functions. It has a touch presence, a poetic logic and an integrity of being.

Reading: Marie L. Fleming, *Murray Favro: A Retrospective* (1983); P. Smith and P. Theberge, *Boucherville, Montreal, Toronto, London* (1975).

Fear, Alfred Henry, "Cap," football player (b at Old Sailbury, Eng 11 June 1901; d at St Catharines, Ont 12 Feb 1978). He played with the Toronto Argonauts (1919-26, 1 Grey Cup) and Hamilton Tigers (1927-32, 3 Grey Cups) as an outside wing in an era when, with no forward pass, this position was noted for defensive tackling. He was also an accomplished hockey player in the Toronto Mercantile League, was runner up for the N American welterweight boxing title and, as a member of the Toronto Argonaut Rowing Club, won victories at the Royal Canadian Henley Regatta. But it was on the football field where the square-jawed, stocky Fear became famous for his "bone-crunching" tackling. FRANK COSENTINO

Feast of the Dead, held by the HURON whenever a large village shifted location, every 10-15 years. The bodies of all those who had not died violent deaths were removed from their temporary tombs and buried in a common ossuary — a deep pit lined with beaver robes. The ceremony expressed the great affection the Huron held for their dead relatives and exercised a powerful reinforcement of the alliances among the tribes and villages. The final burial was believed to release the souls of the dead and allow them to travel westward to the land where Iouskeha and Aataentsic lived. *See* NATIVE PEOPLE, RELIGION. JAMES MARSH

Federal Court of Canada, est 1971 to replace the Exchequer Court, enjoys jurisdiction chiefly over matters involving the federal government, eg, lawsuits against it and supervision of actions by federal government bodies and officials. The Federal Court is also the only court in Canada with jurisdiction over certain specialized areas, eg, maritime law, patent and copyright law, although in some specialized areas it shares concurrent jurisdiction with provincial superior courts. The court is divided into the Federal Court of Appeal and the Federal Court, Trial Division. The Trial Division hears lawsuits and initial applications to review some types of governmental actions; the Court of Appeal hears appeals from the Trial Division and supervises the formal decisions of government tribunals. Decisions of the Court of Appeal can be appealed, with leave, to the SUPREME COURT OF CANADA. The Federal Court's main office is in Ottawa, but it sits throughout the country. The number of judges was expanded in 1983 from 14 to 21 (*see* JUDICIARY). PETER K. DOODY

Federal Government popularly refers to the national or dominion level of GOVERNMENT and in its most general sense includes the executive, legislative and judicial branches, along with the numerous departments and agencies comprising the administrative branch. The 3 principles regulating the powers of the various components of government and the relationships between them are inherited from Britain: parliamentary supremacy, meaning that the SENATE and HOUSE OF COMMONS acting in conjunction with the CROWN possess constitutional plenary powers to legislate; the fusion of executive and legislative instruments, eg, as opposed to the American principle of separation of powers; and the RULE OF LAW, applied and maintained by an independent JUDICIARY. The relationship between the legislature and the CABINET is held in equilibrium by the doctrine of individual and collective ministerial responsibility to the legislature. If the executive can maintain the confidence of the legislature, it can continue to govern. If not, a Cabinet must resign or seek dissolution of the legislature and call an ELECTION.

A more precise definition of federal government focuses on the term "federal." A federal government is distinct from a unitary government, eg, that of Britain. In the latter, there is only one seat of ultimate authority. In a federal government, there are 2 independent seats of authority. Parliament and the provinces are each assigned certain powers and jurisdictional terrain. In practice, this subdivision modifies the principle of parliamentary supremacy; each separate level of government is supreme as long as it does not trespass on the preserve of the other. The umpire for resolving jurisdictional disputes is the SUPREME COURT. *See also* FEDERALISM; DISTRIBUTION OF POWERS. J.E. HODGETTS

Federal-Provincial Relations, the complex network of relationships between Canada's federal and 10 provincial governments that take place at many different levels, from informal day-to-day contacts between bureaucrats to more formal meetings of senior officials and ministers. The apex of the process is the First Ministers' Conference, which brings together, usually

The Nov 1978 First Ministers' Conference, at the National Conference Centre in Ottawa (*courtesy National Film Board/Photothèque*).

in the glare of national publicity at the National Conference Centre in Ottawa, the prime minister and provincial premiers, along with their ministers and advisers. In the 1950s and 1960s the term "co-operative" or "administrative" federalism was used to denote the extensive network of interdependence between governments, which was reflected in negotiations over revenue sharing, the development of shared-cost or conditional grant programs and the widespread overlapping of responsibilities and activities. In the 1960s and 1970s "competitive federalism" described the increasing tendency for intergovernmental relations to become more conflict ridden as governments pursued divergent policy goals and expressed rival views about the nature of CONFEDERATION. "Executive federalism" refers to the central participants in federal-provincial relations — senior officials and Cabinet ministers. "Federal-provincial diplomacy" indicates that while both orders of government serve the same people, relations among them are often much like negotiations among governments internationally.

Federal-provincial relations (which are not mentioned in the Constitution) arise from the expanding interdependence of federal and provincial governments. Central and provincial government activities are intertwined in a pattern of shared responsibilities, divided authority and joint funding in most areas of public policy. Many of the concerns of contemporary government cut across jurisdictional boundaries because, in response both to its own objectives and to public demand, each level of government has often "intruded" into the other's sphere, frequently with mutual consent, sometimes with considerable disagreement (*see* INTERGOVERNMENTAL FINANCE). For example, Ottawa provides many of the funds for provincial welfare schemes, and provinces increasingly seek to influence federal policies in areas like transportation and foreign trade. Political factors have increased the salience of federal-provincial relations and the frequent acrimony that characterizes them. The regional concentration of support for all major political parties, combined with other features of the parliamentary system, has made it difficult for the federal government to claim national support and to bridge and accommodate divergent regional interests (*see also* REGIONAL ECONOMICS. Because provinces participating in intergovernmental discussions are frequently able to claim that they are the legitimate spokesmen for regional interests that feel underrepresented in Ottawa, federal-provincial relations have come to play a central role in regional accommodation well beyond simple policy coordination.

Federal-provincial relations are pervasive and take place in many arenas. An incomplete estimate lists 158 federal-provincial bodies which met 335 times in 1977 (more than 5 times the number in 1957), of which 39 were at the ministerial level and 296 at the level of officials. In the same year, 30 interprovincial bodies met 37 times. These meetings cover all fields of government activity, with an emphasis on constitutional and economic matters. A catalogue of federal-provincial programs and activities for 1982-83, prepared by the federal government, lists 316 activities, ranging from major programs, eg, equalization payments and medicare, to the "Canada/British Columbia Sturgeon Bank Management" agreement; it also reflects the breadth of intergovernmental relations. A similar inventory by Alberta lists 110 federal-provincial programs operating in the provinces. Most governments have established special ministries or agencies to manage their intergovernmental relationships.

The most important federal-provincial mechanism is the First Ministers' Conference. It has no constitutional status, regular schedule of meetings or formal rules for decision making. The conference is chaired by the prime minister and the agenda is usually negotiated. The conferences have become major public events, and are often televised. However, many sessions are held in camera and much of the work is conducted in back-room meetings among ministers and officials. Meetings have tended to focus on specific issues, most recently on the Constitution, economic policy and fiscal federalism.

For some the First Ministers' Conference is primarily an opportunity for governments to debate, discuss and seek to influence each other. For others, it is or should be a decision-making body, reaching agreements that would be binding on all, as in the constitutional "accord" of Nov 1981. Increasingly the conference has become the arena for expressing highly divergent views. The provinces generally argue for a greater voice in national decision making and Ottawa usually asserts the prerogatives of the national government. As the capacity of governments to reach agreement through negotiation has declined, there has been greater recourse to the courts to resolve basic issues, although court judgements are often a signal for further rounds of negotiation.

Below the First Ministers' Conferences, and often reporting to them, are a variety of ministerial conferences. Some are called on an ad hoc basis, eg, the Continuing Committee of Ministers on the Constitution 1979-81. Others, such as the annual meetings of finance ministers to co-ordinate budgetary plans and discuss fiscal arrangements, are held regularly. Several parallel committees of officials exist, the most important of which is the Continuing Committee on Economic and Fiscal Matters, est 1955. The success of such committees in achieving policy harmonization varies widely. Many federal-provincial meetings are provided with common organizational and secretarial services through an intergovernmental body, the Canadian Intergovernmental Conference Secretariat, which has no policy, research or advisory role.

Most analyses of intergovernmental relationships focus on the collective meetings of all 11 governments, but interprovincial relationships are becoming more important. Annual meetings of provincial premiers have been held since 1960, not only in an attempt to harmonize policy in areas of common interest, but also to develop common provincial positions on matters of contention with Ottawa. However, on many issues the interests of the provinces diverge and conflict, depending on the political orientation of their leaders and their economic and social circumstances. There are also 2 regional groupings of provinces, the Prairie Provinces Economic Council and the Council of Maritime Premiers, which hold regular meetings to resolve interprovincial issues and develop common positions. The latter has a professional secretariat and operates a number of joint programs for the region. In addition, provinces have established several interprovincial ministerial bodies, such as the COUNCIL OF MINISTERS OF EDUCATION and the Canadian Council of Resource Ministers.

Many federal-provincial contacts involve Ottawa and one or more individual provinces. For example, the negotiations on ENERGY POLICY in the 1970s were conducted primarily between Ottawa and the oil-producing provinces. Less dramatic consultation takes place on a host of other economic development, social and cultural issues.

Despite many successes in building a flexible system of revenue sharing and EQUALIZATION PAYMENTS and the building of the WELFARE STATE, the machinery and processes of intergovernmental relations have been widely criticized. For example, the high level of conflict in recent years has led many observers to argue that far from being an arena within which major political differences can be compromised, the First Ministers' Conference has instead become a forum for heightening them. It is also argued more generally that the process has frequently led not to co-operation between governments but to long delays and contradiction and duplication between federal and provincial programs. Federal critics argue that "set piece" conferences give provincial premiers an opportunity to attack "the feds" without having to take responsibility, and blur responsibility by inviting provinces to influence national policies. As a result, since 1980, the federal government has sought to minimize the frequency and visibility of such conferences and to act alone or bilaterally, wherever possible. Conversely, others argue that the federal government must recognize that it cannot act alone, that effective national policies must involve the collaboration of both orders of government and that its programs in individual provinces must be developed in co-operation with provincial authorities. The process has also been criticized for secrecy and for its concentration on the financial, political and bureaucratic concerns of rival governments, which may reduce public participation in policy discussion. The process also obscures the issue of governmental accountability, making it difficult to judge which government is responsible for what.

Such criticisms have resulted in many reform proposals. Some observers feel the need for intergovernmental discussion could be reduced by "disentanglement" — clarifying responsibilities of each government. Others argue that, whatever its faults, the process is indispensable and should be conducted more regularly, and that the First Ministers' Conference should be given constitutional status, requiring meetings at least annually and perhaps providing a secretariat with research and advisory roles. Some proposals call for a federal-provincial council or for replacement of the SENATE with a body of provincial delegates on the model of the German Bundesrat. Other reforms are designed to allow greater legislative scrutiny and more public access.

Much of the increased conflict of the 1970s and early 1980s was the product of a combination of especially divisive forces: Québec nationalism, the energy debate, the regional imbalance in party support, the conflicting views of federalism expressed by the prime minister and a number of premiers, and the focus on constitutional questions. By 1984 the conditions may have been propitious for a more co-operative relationship for the future, as old issues were removed from the agenda and new concerns for economic growth and for social goals cutting across regional interests came to the fore. The election of a Progressive Conservative government in Sept 1984, with support from all sections of the country, may also reduce tensions and alter the dynamic of federal-provincial relations, at least in the short run. On the other hand, each government will necessarily continue to serve different constituencies with different needs. RICHARD SIMEON

Reading: Richard Simeon, *Confrontation and Collaboration — Intergovernmental Relations in Canada Today* (1979); D.V. Smiley, *Canada in Question: Federalism in the Seventies* (1980); G. Stevenson, *Unfulfilled Union: Canadian Federalism and National Unity* (1979).

Federalism is a type of political system in which legislative power is divided between a central or federal legislature and state or provincial legislatures. The FEDERAL GOVERNMENT has jurisdiction over the entire national territory and population; the PROVINCIAL GOVERNMENT has jurisdiction only over particular portions of territory and population. Both levels of government derive their authority from a written CONSTITUTION. In a centralized federation the powers of provincial governments are relatively narrow; in a decentralized federation the provincial sphere of authority is wider. Federalism is distinguished from unitary government, in which subnational institutions derive their authority from the central government and are therefore subordinate to it, and also from various forms of association, such as economic communities or military alliances, whose members retain sovereign powers and can withdraw from the arrangement at will. A true federation, in the modern sense, means a STATE in which the component units are not sovereign and cannot legally secede (*see* CONSTITUTIONAL LAW).

Although imaginative efforts have been made to trace the history of federalism back into antiquity, the US Constitution (1787) is the earliest example of a modern federal constitution. The possibility of establishing a federal union among the remaining British colonies of N America was considered sporadically early in the 19th century, and more seriously from 1857 onwards. Negotiations among political leaders from the PROVINCE OF CANADA, NB and NS resulted in the Imperial Parliament's adoption of the BRITISH NORTH AMERICA ACT, which united those 3 colonies into a federal state in 1867. CONFEDERATION marks the beginning of Canadian federalism. Unification was desired, particularly by commercial interests, as a means of facilitating economic growth, territorial expansion and military defence. Retention of existing governments and boundaries, however, was desired by many influential people for a variety of reasons. French Canadians, a majority only in Québec, were unwilling to place all powers in the hands of a central government where they would be a minority. Federalism was therefore a necessary compromise. PM John A. MACDONALD was not enthusiastic about federalism and would have preferred a unitary state. Moreover, the AMERICAN CIVIL WAR had contributed to a belief that powerful provincial governments would be a source of instability. For these reasons the Canadian Constitution, of which Macdonald was the principal author, includes features incompatible with a strict theory of federalism. The lieutenant-governor of each province, who is appointed by the central government, can prevent provincial legislation from taking effect until the central government has approved it. The central government can also disallow any provincial statute within a year of its adoption (*see* DISALLOWANCE). Parliament can adopt legislation concerning education within a province to protect the rights of certain religious minorities and can also declare that "works and undertakings" within a province fall under its jurisdiction, regardless of the normal DISTRIBUTION OF POWERS. The BNA Act, because of these unitary features, has been described as quasi-federal rather than strictly federal, but the quasi-federal powers have fallen into disuse.

Although Canadian politicians have a reputation for being uninterested in political theory, they have actually articulated a variety of different concepts of Canadian federalism. Differences of opinion over federalism have been sharper in Canada over a longer period than in most federations, and no consensus has ever been achieved regarding the appropriate relationship between the 2 levels of government, either in theory or in practice. National and provincial politicians tend to espouse different views, and these have become associated with partisan conflict when one party has held office at the national level for a long period while enjoying less success at the provincial level. Macdonald's quasi-federal concept was associated with the CONSERVATIVE PARTY until about 1900, when the generation of politicians that had been involved in drafting the BNA Act ceased to be influential in that party. It has had little support during this century, although a centralist view of federalism, emphasizing the importance of a strong and active central government, continues to enjoy considerable support. Modern centralists do not normally favour using the quasi-federal powers of disallowance and reservation. Instead, they argue for a broad interpretation of Parliament's legislative powers and believe that the central government should be permitted to make policy in its areas of jurisdiction without consulting the provincial governments. They also believe that the central government should have access to a predominant share of revenue from taxation and that it should be entitled to make conditional grants to provincial governments even in relation to matters not strictly within its jurisdiction.

A centralist view of federalism, with certain qualifications, was expressed in the 1939 report of the Royal Commission on DOMINION-PROVINCIAL RELATIONS (the Rowell-Sirois Commission). Since then, centralist ideas about federalism have been influential in the LIBERAL PARTY. The NEW DEMOCRATIC PARTY also tends towards a centralist position. Politicians and political thinkers who have articulated a centralist concept of federalism include Louis ST. LAURENT, F.R. SCOTT, Eugene FORSEY, David LEWIS, Bora LASKIN and Pierre Elliott TRUDEAU. Macdonald's view that the provincial governments should be subordinated to the central government was controversial from the outset, and in the early 1880s a Québec judge, T.J.J. Loranger, wrote that the central government had been created by the provincial governments and that no increase in the central government's powers, and indeed no substantial change in the Constitution, was permissible without the unanimous consent of the provincial governments. This view became known as the COMPACT THEORY OF CONFEDERATION and has continued to be popular with provincial leaders, eg, Peter LOUGHEED of Alberta. The emphasis on the importance of provincial autonomy has been influential since 1939 in the Progressive Conservative Party, in the SOCIAL CREDIT Party and in all parties at the provincial level in Québec. Supporters of the anticentralist view believe that the functions of the central government should be limited to those that the provincial governments cannot perform for themselves, and that its control over revenue should be restricted accordingly. They also argue, particularly in recent years, that the central government should consult the provincial governments before initiating major policies. An eloquent statement of the anticentralist view was the 1956 report of the Québec Royal Commission on CONSTITUTIONAL PROBLEMS and a more recent expression may be found in the 1979 report of the task force on CANADIAN UNITY.

Canadian federalism, in practice, has fluctuated between the extremes of centralization and DECENTRALIZATION in response to a variety of political, economic and social circumstances. Macdonald's preference for a highly centralized regime seems to have triumphed for a few years after Confederation, but by the time he died, in 1891, the provincial governments were becoming as powerful as their US counterparts, if not more so. Provincial control over natural resources facilitated the development of largely self-contained provincial economies, and the concentration of secondary manufacturing in Ontario made its government particularly important and influential. Deteriorating relations between francophone and anglophone Canadians undermined Macdonald's Conservative Party and increased anticentralist sentiment in Québec. Centralization revived temporarily during WWI and immediately after, when the central government levied an income tax for the first time in 1917, imposed military conscription and exercised an unprecedented control over the economy. These tendencies were largely reversed after 1921, and the GREAT DEPRESSION demonstrated that the central government lacked the power to deal effectively with a severe economic crisis. Efforts were made to ensure that centralization during WWII would have more lasting effects than it had had during WWI. The central government monopolized personal income tax from 1941 until 1954, and constitutional amendments gave Parliament the power to establish UNEMPLOYMENT INSURANCE and universal PENSIONS in 1940 and 1951 respectively. Interpretation of the BNA Act by the JUDICIAL COMMITTEE OF THE PRIVY COUNCIL, considered favourable to provincial autonomy, was terminated in 1949. During the postwar period, extensive conditional grants were introduced to encourage provincial spending on health and welfare and federal grants were also given direct to universities.

A shift of power towards the provincial governments, however, became evident after 1960, when a dynamic and interventionist Québec government, headed by Jean LESAGE, emerged as an effective opponent of centralization. Other contributing factors included the growing importance of provincial natural resources, the decline of the old commercial and financial elite based in Montréal, economic integration between Canada and the US, and the development of a more competitive party system at the national level after the defeat of St Laurent's Liberal government in 1957. Between 1960 and 1980 these circumstances led to a substantial increase in the provincial share of TAXATION and PUBLIC EXPENDITURE. Grants to universities were replaced by subsidies to the provinces. By OPTING OUT of certain conditional grant programs, Québec received unconditional grants in return and established its own contributory pension plan, although the central government established one for residents of other provinces. Conferences between the PM and provincial premiers became more frequent, a phenomenon described as "executive federalism." Provincial governments began to intervene more aggressively in provincial economies as they challenged the right of the central government to make economic policy without their collaboration or consent. Provincial relations with foreign governments also became significant. The dramatic increase in Alberta's petroleum revenues after 1972 imposed severe strains on the federal system. In Québec the emergence of a major political party dedicated to seeking independence for that province, the PARTI QUÉBÉCOIS, suggested that the survival of Canadian federalism could not be taken for granted.

Formal changes in a country's constitution usually follow, rather than precede, informal shifts in economic and political power. The trend away from centralization in Canadian federalism was underway by 1960, and demands for a formal transfer of constitutional authority towards the provincial level of government became widespread in Québec shortly afterwards. Other provinces, with the partial exception of Ontario, had little interest in constitutional change at that time; this encouraged the idea of "special status," whereby only Québec would receive additional powers. After 1972, increasing natural-resource revenues caused a number of other provincial governments to demand additional powers in a revised constitution, Alberta being the most militant. In response to these pressures, the central government convened a number of intergovernmental conferences on constitutional change between 1968 and 1981, although it insisted that a charter of individual rights and the restructuring of national institutions be discussed in addition to the distribution of legislative powers. A related problem was the absence of an amending formula in the BNA Act. The constitutional negotiations included efforts to devise such a formula as a necessary prelude to "patriating" the Constitution, a matter that had been sporadically and inconclusively discussed as far back as 1927. In 1980 the Trudeau government attempted to patriate the Constitution with an amending formula that would require the support of Ontario, Québec, 2 western provinces and 2 Atlantic provinces for any subsequent change, and simultaneously to entrench a CANADIAN CHARTER OF RIGHTS AND FREEDOMS in the Constitution. This initiative, which followed the breakdown of negotiations over the distribution of powers, was opposed by 8 provincial governments, and was ruled unconstitutional, although not strictly illegal, by the Supreme Court of Canada. Further negotiations led to qualifications in the charter of rights and replacement of the original amending formula by one that requires the approval of 7 provinces comprising at least half of Canada's population, but permits dissenting provinces to exempt themselves from the application of amendments that would reduce their powers. These took effect on 17 Apr 1982.

The future evolution of Canadian federalism is difficult to predict because it will depend on economic and political developments throughout Canada and the world. The new amending formula is conducive to further decentralization since it makes it easier for provincial governments to increase their formal powers and it allows dissident provinces to exempt themselves from amendments that would increase the powers of the central government. On the other hand, the deteriorating international situation may produce effective demands for greater centralization, as happened between 1929 and 1945. Patriation of the Constitution has brought Canada no closer to achieving consensus on the direction in which federalism should evolve. Supporters of greater provincial autonomy emphasize the diversity of provincial interests and argue that a more stable and legitimate political order would result if the distribution of power between the 2 levels of government was adjusted to accord with what they view as the socioeconomic realities. On the other hand, those who support the retention or enlargement of the central government's powers argue that decentralization contributes to the appearance of diverse provincial interests and ignores the significant common interests of Canadians that can only be expressed through a strong central government. They also argue that excessive decentralization weakens Canada's economy and its influence in the world. It is unlikely that these differences of opinion will be resolved soon. GARTH STEVENSON

Reading: D.V. Smiley, *Canada in Question: Federalism in the Seventies* (1980); Garth Stevenson, *Unfulfilled Union: Canadian Federalism and National Unity* (1979).

Federated Women's Institutes of Canada is the national organization that co-ordinates the activities of the provincial Women's Institutes. The first institute was founded in 1897 in Stoney Creek, Ont, by Adelaide HOODLESS and by 1913 institutes were established in all the provinces. In 1919 provincial representatives met in Winnipeg to form the FWIC and a national office was established in Ottawa in 1958. The motto "For Home and Country" reflects FWIC aims: to promote an appreciation of rural living, develop informed citizens through the study of national and international issues (particularly those affecting women and children), and initiate national programs to achieve common goals. Each provincial organization is represented on the board of directors, which meets annually; new executives are elected at triennial conventions. Reflecting the urbanization of Canadian society, FWIC membership has slowly declined; in 1982 there were 47 177 members. JEAN E. DRYDEN

Reading: A. Walker, E.M. Collins and M. McIntyre Hood, *Fifty Years of Achievement* (1948).

Federation of Medical Women of Canada was founded in Ottawa in 1924 and held its first annual meeting in Victoria in 1926. Membership numbers 600, comprised of practising physicians and medical students from across the country. The federation is an independent member of the Medical Women's International Assn and has been affiliated with the CANADIAN MEDICAL ASSN since 1964. The objects of the federation are the promotion of interests of medical women, the aid and encouragement of women medical students at all levels, and establishment and administration of scholarship and loan funds. The major scholarship fund is named for Dr Maude ABBOTT, a founding member. JANICE DICKIN MCGINNIS

Feild, Edward, bishop (b at Worcester, Eng 7 June 1801; d at Hamilton, Bermuda 8 June 1876). Ordained in the Church of England in 1827, Feild displayed organizational ability and his arrangements became known as the "Feild System." Offered the see of Newfoundland in 1844, he faced unusual difficulty and was embroiled in strife for the greater part of his episcopacy. By temperament an uncompromising rigorist and extremist, he battled local politicians, Roman Catholics, Methodists, and Evangelicals of his own church to build a strong, independent Anglican church with a distinctly high-church tone. Newfoundlanders in time gave this man of iron will not only respect but also appreciation and affection. Feild served Newfoundland with extreme devotion, personal humility and kindliness, visiting his people, scattered along a rugged shore of some 5000 km, in the church ship *Hawk*. J. ROGERS

Feldbrill, Victor, conductor (b at Toronto 4 Apr 1924). A versatile conductor with an international reputation, Feldbrill is widely known for his enthusiastic promotion of Canadian music and for his support of young musicians. Following his TORONTO SYMPHONY conducting debut at age 18, he was active as a violinist and guest conductor and was conductor of the Winnipeg Symphony Orchestra 1958-68. Since 1968 he has been associated with U of T as lecturer and conductor. With the Toronto Symphony he was director of youth programming (1968-78), resident conductor (1973-77) and music director and conductor of its youth orchestra (1974-78). He has been a frequent director of the National Youth Orchestra summer workshops. All Feldbrill's concerts include at least one Canadian work. BARCLAY MCMILLAN

Fencing, or duelling with a sword according to established rules, was practised in ancient times as a pastime as well as in war. Skilful swordplay with light weapons developed in the 14th century when gunpowder made heavy armour obsolete. As DUELS were outlawed, fencers refined their skills into the elegant art of fencing. The organized sport of fencing emerged at the end of the 19th century as a contest in which the number of hits are counted to determine the winner of a bout. Fencing was included in the first Olympic Games in 1896. Fencers today compete in categories determined by the type of sword used. The foil is light and flexible; the épée is as long as the foil, but heavier and less flexible; and the sabre is a cut-and-thrust weapon. The target area of the body varies with the type of sword. Women usually compete in only the foil event. Electrical scoring machines, first developed in the 1930s, are used to record hits in foil and épée bouts; foil fencers wear an electrically conductive jacket over the target area. With protective masks, gloves and jackets, there is little danger in the sport, which demands subtle tactics, poise, speed and balance.

In Canada, fencing schools were well attended in the late 18th and early 19th centuries, and the sport began to flourish in the late 19th. The Toronto Fencing Club and a women's fencing club at Toronto's University College were formed in 1895. During the next decade, fencing clubs were established in eastern universities, and in 1902 the first Canadian championships were held. The 1930s saw further development, and after WWII immigration from Europe brought distinguished fencers and masters to Canada. Fencing is organized by the Canadian Fencing Assn. Canadian fencers, both men and women, have competed in the Olympic Games since 1932, but have been most successful in the Commonwealth and Pan-American Games. Several silver and bronze medals have been won at the Commonwealth Games, and in 1954 the men's sabre team won the gold medal. At the Pan-American Games, Canadian fencers have won a number of bronze medals; silver medals were won by the women's foil teams in 1975 and 1979. BARBARA SCHRODT

Fenerty, Charles, inventor (b at Upper Sackville, NS Jan 1821; d at Lower Sackville 10 June 1892). Concerned about the difficulty a local paper mill was having in obtaining an adequate supply of rags to make quality paper, Fenerty succeeded in producing paper from wood pulp as early as 1841. Fenerty's inspiration has been variously attributed to a thorough study of spruce fibres, influenced by the reports of Titus SMITH concerning its possible usefulness, or to his observation of how wasps made a form of paper from vegetable fibres; but most likely it came from perceiving that the fibrous matter formed by the constant friction of wood upon wood in the moving parts of sawmills could be used to make paper. Fenerty neglected to publicize his discovery until 1844, by which time others had patented papermaking processes based on wood fibre. TERRENCE M. PUNCH

Fenians, members of a movement initiated in 1857 by Irish-Americans to secure Irish independence from Britain. Its titular chief, James Stephens, organized an underground movement in Ireland with the aid of funds collected by his American deputy, John O'Mahony. The American wing emerged as a powerful force, and by the end of 1865 the Fenians had nearly $500 000, and about 10 000 AMERICAN CIVIL WAR veterans organized in military clubs. At this time they split into 2 factions, one led by O'Mahony, favouring an uprising in Ireland, and another led by William Roberts, intent on invading Canada. A small group of Canadian Fenians was headed initially by Michael Murphy of Toronto. When it was obvious that there was to be no immediate uprising in Ireland, O'Mahony launched a raid against the New Brunswick frontier in Apr 1866. The raid collapsed and its only lasting consequence was to turn opinion in the Maritimes in favour of CONFEDERATION. The Roberts wing crossed the Niagara frontier on 1 June, defeated Canadian militiamen at Ridgeway, and withdrew. A second group crossed the Québec frontier at Missisquoi Bay on 7 June, and remained 48 hours. After the failure of an Irish uprising in 1867, the movement fragmented. Yet a Fenian apparently assassinated Thomas D'Arcy MCGEE in 1868, and in 1870 the faction led by "General" John O'Neill launched 2 small raids over the Québec frontier. Fenianism added a page to Irish folklore and helped to unite Canadians by providing an external threat during the period of Confederation.
HEREWARD SENIOR

Ferguson, George Howard, lawyer, Conservative politician, premier of Ontario 1923-30 (b at Kemptville, Ont 18 June 1870; d at Toronto 21 Feb 1946). He personified Ontario in the 1920s: a mix of 19th-century values and 20th-century ambitions. As premier at the climax of industrialization's first great wave, he set a style of government that prevails still. Confident that industry, protected by the tariff, and development of natural resources would provide work and wealth for all, his government tried to create the climate and facilities conducive to private investment in Ontario's forests, mines and factories. Yet his administration did not permit untrammelled exploitation; measures to conserve and regulate were instituted. Action to meet the social problems of industrialization was slow and parsimonious, yet at times innovative, designed to extend educational and medical services to all regions and groups. He lifted some of the restrictions placed on Ontario's bilingual schools by the infamous Regulation 17 (1912), his earlier answer to mounting FRENCH CANADIAN NATIONALISM and a factor in national disunity during WWI. A master of brokerage politics, he maintained harmony among the classes and regions comprising Ontario.
BARBARA A. MCKENNA

Reading: Peter Oliver, *G. Howard Ferguson* (1977).

Ferguson, George Victor, newspaper editor (b at Cupar, Scot 20 Apr 1897; d at Montréal 26 Jan 1977). One of John W. DAFOE's newspaper "pupils" and a distinguished journalist in his own right, Ferguson was educated at U of A and Oxford, where he was a Rhodes Scholar. He served in WWI as a private soldier and joined the *Manitoba Free Press* in 1925, rising to managing editor under Dafoe in 1933. Like Dafoe he took a strong nationalist view and sought to understand the roots of Canadian unity. In 1944, when Dafoe died, Ferguson became executive editor of the *Free Press*, but soon after, left for Montréal, where he served as editor in chief of the *Montreal Star* and where his editorials on French-English relations were important reading. Ordinarily Liberal in politics, Ferguson, much like Dafoe, had the capacity to take issue with his party, and he was positively exultant when the Conservatives won power under DIEFENBAKER in 1957. J.L. GRANATSTEIN

Ferguson, Ivan Graeme, film director, executive (b at Toronto 7 Oct 1929). He was a summer student at the National Film Board, 1950, and then made a number of films in the US before returning to Canada in 1970. He formed his own company (now Imax Systems Corp) which developed the multiscreen system that was used at Ontario Place and other locations. His multiscreen films include *North of Superior* (1971) and *Snow Job* (1974). In 1984 an IMAX/OMNIMAX camera was flown aboard US space shuttle flights, taking footage due for release in 1985.
GAYLE BONISH

Ferguson, John Bright, "Fergie," chemist, professor (b at Londesborough, Ont 2 Nov 1889; d at Toronto 7 Jan 1963). Associate professor of physical chemistry at University of Toronto 1920-48, he also spent 7 years with the Geophysical Laboratory in the Carnegie Institute, Washington, DC, where he solved problems in the manufacturing of optical glass for the War Industry Board; and a short time with Western Electric Co, New York C. During WWII he and his students undertook a number of studies for the Canadian Army, including the development of a method for testing activated charcoals for use in respirators. He was the author of over 100 scientific papers. HARRY SHEFFER

Ferguson, Maynard, jazz trumpeter (b at Verdun, Qué 4 May 1928). Renowned in jazz for his exhibitionistic, high-note trumpet style, Ferguson worked in Montréal until 1948 with Stan Wood and Johnny Holmes, and with his own band. Thereafter based in the US, he was featured in the bands of Boyd Raeburn, Jimmy Dorsey, Charlie Barnet and, from 1950 to 1953, Stan Kenton. In 1956 he formed the first of a succession of big bands which, by the 1970s, had taken up a brash, rock-oriented music, showcasing Ferguson's remarkable range. He recorded 45 albums under his own name, 1954-82, and had a hit recording with *Gonna Fly Now*, the theme from the US film *Rocky*. MARK MILLER

Ferguson, Robert, businessman (b at Logierait, Scot 17 Apr 1768; d at Campbellton, NB 10 Aug 1851). He came to the RESTIGOUCHE R in 1796 and was soon the most prominent merchant and largest landowner in the region. He farmed, built ships and exported timber and fish to Europe, his large house and store becoming the business centre of the Restigouche. In 1826 he began selling lots in what became the town of CAMPBELLTON. Along with Hugh Munro, he controlled the trade of northern NB until his authority was challenged with the arrival of Irish immigrants in the late 1820s. He was in part responsible for the creation of Restigouche County in 1837. One of the commissioners for laying out the first highway between NB and Lower Canada, he was active in the agricultural society, in the militia and as a magistrate. He was referred to as "the founder and father of Restigouche." WILLIAM A. SPRAY

Cinnamon fern (*Osmunda cinnamomea*) with two cinnamon-coloured fertile spore-bearing leaves (*courtesy National Museum of Natural Sciences.*)

Fern, common name for a diverse group (division Polypodiophyta) of usually perennial, spore-producing PLANTS with divided, evergreen or deciduous leaves (fronds) arising from slender, horizontal rhizomes (underground stems) or stout, ascending rootstalks. Tropical and subtropical tree ferns may grow several metres high. Related treelike species, dating to Devonian (395-345 million years ago) and reaching highest development in Carboniferous period (345-280 million years ago), comprised some of the vegetation forming coal beds (*see* FOSSILS). Recent advances in knowledge have necessitated taxonomic realignments: 21 families encompassing 308 genera (each containing 1-200 or more species) are now recognized; 11 families, 31 genera and 97 species have been recorded for Canada.

Ferns show alternation of generations, ie, a sexual stage (gametophyte) alternates with an asexual, spore-producing stage (sporophyte). Each stage is an independent plant. Spores are produced in spore cases, which may be naked on a leafless branch, as in primitive *Ophioglossum* and *Botrychium;* arranged in clusters (sori) on the backs or margins of sometimes drastically modified leaflets (pinnae), as in several families, eg, Polypodiaceae, Schizaeaceae; or in fruiting bodies (sporocarps), as in *Azolla* and *Marsilea.* Spores germinate to form tiny, often heart-shaped plants (prothallia) that bear antheridia (structures producing sperm) and archegonia (structures producing eggs). The prothallia are the gametophyte generation. Fertilization of the egg, and subsequent development, produces the familiar fern plant, the sporophyte generation, and completes the life cycle. Many ferns also reproduce vegetatively (eg, by buds on roots or fronds).

Most ferns are tropical or subtropical; *Woodsia ilvensis, W. alpina, W. glabella, Cystopteris fragilis* and *Dryopteris fragrans* grow in Canada's arctic islands. Ferns are usually terrestrial; some, like *Polypodium glycyrrhiza* of coastal BC, are partly or wholly epiphytic (growing on other plants); others, like *Marsilea* and *Azolla,* are aquatic, the latter free floating. Habitats are usually moist.

Sporedots on the underside of a fern leaf (*courtesy National Museum of Natural Sciences/G.L. Christie*).

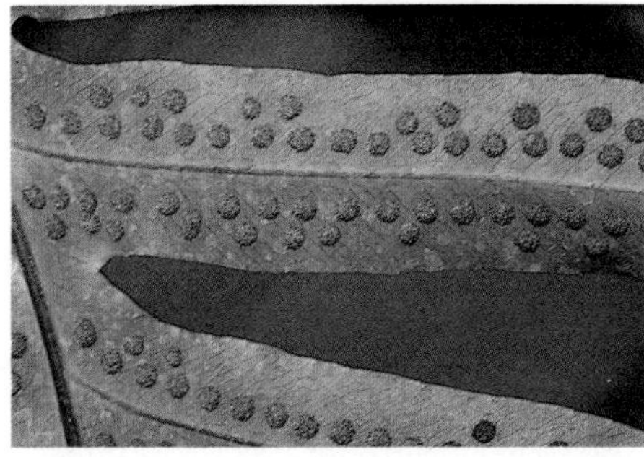

Most Canadian ferns grow in wooded regions, but bracken (*Pteridium aquilinum*) and hay-scented fern (*Dennstaedtia punctilobula*) thrive in open areas. Species of *Pellaea,* with leatherlike blades, grow in dry crevices of cliffs.

Most Canadian ferns have relatively wide distribution. Some are restricted in range: curly grass, *Schizaea pusilla,* grows in *Sphagnum* moss or wet depressions in NS and Newfoundland; netted chain fern, *Woodwardia areolata,* in southern NS; hart's tongue fern, *Phyllitis scolopendrium,* is associated with the limestone of Niagara Escarpment; polypody, *Polypodium scouleri,* grows along the BC coast, often in reach of salt spray; filmy fern, *Mecodium wrightii,* forms mats on shaded cliff faces and tree bases from the Alaska Panhandle to Vancouver I.

Ferns have little economic value, but many are beautiful. Edible FIDDLEHEADS or ostrich fern, *Matteuccia struthiopteris,* are gathered commercially in NB; this species is also used in foundation plantings. Boston fern, *Nephrolepis exaltata* var *bostoniensis,* is a common houseplant. Some woodland ferns are excellent for cool, moist, shaded gardens. Bracken, sometimes eaten as a green, has been shown to be carcinogenic in rats and responsible for livestock diseases; therefore, is not recommended for human consumption.

W.J. CODY

Reading: W.J. Cody and D.M. Britton, *Ferns and Fern Allies of Canada* (1984).

Fernandes, João, explorer (fl 1486-1505). A Portuguese of the Azores, he probably sailed with John CABOT in 1498 as pilot. He may also have taken part in the voyages of CORTE-REAL. Fernandes was a landowner, or *labrador* in Portuguese, and it is said that the coast from Greenland to Newfoundland (thought to be contiguous) was named for him. JAMES MARSH

Fernie, BC, City, pop 5444 (1981c), inc 1904, lies in the broad valley of the Elk R, between prominent mountain ranges, about 35 km N of its junction with the Kootenay R. It is 970 km E of Vancouver. Originally called Coal Creek, the city was later named for William FERNIE. It was founded in 1898 with the construction of the Crow's Nest Pass Ry. Wiped out by fire in 1908, it was rebuilt in impressive fashion. Referred to in its early years as the "Pittsburgh of the West," it became the centre for the region's coal mines, particularly Coal Creek Mines. At the end of WWI, 4500 people resided there. A recession followed that was prolonged by the switch from coal to oil on American railroads and intensified by the Great Depression. The first coal was shipped to Japanese steelmakers in 1970 and Fernie's economy today is dependent on coal mining developments in the Elk Valley. Snow Valley Ski Area is a popular attraction for local people and tourists from Alberta.

WILLIAM A. SLOAN

Fernie, William, prospector, miner, entrepreneur (b at Kimbolton, Eng 2 Apr 1837; d at Victoria 15 May 1921). After travelling through Australasia and S America, he came to Vancouver I in 1860 but soon moved to the Kootenay district where he worked as a miner, cattle rancher and in various provincial government posts, including that of gold commissioner 1873-82. In the summer of 1887, with his brother Peter, Fernie discovered coal while laying a trail through the CROWSNEST PASS. He became an original director of the Crow's Nest Pass Coal Co, promoter of the BC Southern Railway and founder of the BC city that bears his name. A bachelor, he retired to Victoria in 1906 where he was noted for his beautiful Oak Bay home and his philanthropy. PATRICIA E. ROY

Ferrer Maldonado, Lorenzo, apocryphal navigator, adventurer (b in Spain; d 1625). In 1601 he submitted to King Philip III of Spain a document about his purported 1588 voyage through the NORTHWEST PASSAGE from E to W. His descriptions bear little semblance to reality, though his account received some support from geographers. In 1791 the Spanish government diverted Alejandro MALASPINA's expedition to search the NORTHWEST COAST at 60° N lat for the passage's entrance. CHRISTON I. ARCHER

Ferret, Black-footed (*Mustela nigripes*), large WEASEL, probably extinct in Canada and almost so in the US. It is mink-sized, long, slender and short-legged. Males reach about 53 cm in length; females, 10% less. They are sandy buff in colour, with face, neck, legs and tail tip dark-brown or black, and white on face, throat and underparts. The black-footed ferret was a prairie animal usually associated with PRAIRIE DOG towns, but ranged beyond them in southern Alberta and Saskatchewan. Food was prairie dogs, ground squirrels and other small mammals. In the US, it was virtually extirpated as a result of the prairie dog eradication program. Nothing is known of its reproductive biology. The last specimen taken in Canada was captured in 1937. The European ferret (*M. putorius*) has been introduced.

IAN MCTAGGART COWAN

Ferries are vessels that carry passengers and vehicles across a body of water, such as a lake, river or harbour, on a regular schedule. Simple ferries have operated across rivers and lakes for centuries. The earliest ferries were skiffs or rafts, rowed by oars, or towed by men or horses using ropes. The modern car ferry employs the roll-on, roll-off (RO-RO) method of loading and unloading vehicles through bow and stern doors. The distinction between ferries and other vessels has become less clear during the past decade. The RO-RO method is used in many oceangoing cargo vessels, while ferries are being built larger and are being used on longer routes, necessitating the provision of staterooms and other passenger facilities similar to those provided on cruise ships and passenger liners.

In addition to car, truck and train ferries, there are also passenger-only ferries that generally operate over very short distances such as across harbours (eg, Vancouver and Halifax). New marine technologies have increased the speed and efficiency of ferries. The *Abegweit,* a CN Marine ferry, has icebreaking capacity and is fitted with an air-bubbler system that eases the vessel through the ice by lubricating the sides with air. Hydrofoils, hovercraft and catamarans are all surface-effect ships that attempt to maximize speed by reducing the friction between water and hull. Hovercraft can attain speeds of 60 knots; hydrofoils and catamarans can attain 45 knots; whereas large, conventional car ferries generally operate at less than 22 knots.

Operators of large ferries around the world include Sealink (operating between Britain, Ireland and Europe), Danish State Rail, Hong Kong and Yaumati Ferry Co, Washington State Ferries and the British Columbia Ferry Corporation. The largest ferries carry over 2000 passengers and up to 700 vehicles on 3 car decks. To berth these large new ferries most major ferry terminals are now equipped with ramps that enable vehicles to be loaded and unloaded from 2 decks simultaneously. The BC Ferry Corporation operates some of the busiest terminals in the world. It also has the 4 largest double-ended ferries in the world. The *Queen of Cowichan, Queen of Coquitlam, Queen of Surrey* and *Queen of Oak Bay* carry 1500 passengers, plus 360 cars on 3 decks, and travel at up to 22 knots. The term double-ended refers to the propellers at each end, which alleviate the necessity of turning the ferry around and backing into a dock. Because of the variety of services provided in Atlantic Canada, the CN Marine fleet includes vessels ranging from 30 m high-speed craft to a 148 m ship capable of carrying 39 railway freight cars; from vessels that take a dozen passengers with a load of cargo to others capable of carrying 1100 people, their automobiles, trucks and tractor trailers. Some vessels operate between 15 main terminals and others between 100 Newfoundland and Labrador outports, many of which have no other transportation link with the outside world.

In Canada there are also dozens of small ferries operating across rivers and lakes, for example, those plying Toronto Harbour to Centre I, or the service on Georgian Bay from Tobermory to Manitoulin I. Over the past 20 or 30 years, many of these small ferries have been replaced by bridges. The major ferry systems in the country, however, are saltwater operations. CN Marine, owned by the federal government, operates 18 ships on routes between Newfoundland, PEI, NS, NB and Maine. The Société des traversiers du Québec, owned by the province of Québec, operates 9 vessels on 6 routes across the St Lawrence R. The BC Ferry Corporation, owned by the province of BC, operates 25 vessels on 13 routes along the BC coast. The BC Ministry of Transportation and Highways operates a separate fleet of 11 ferries on 11 routes serving small coastal islands (in addition to a few remaining inland ferries on rivers and lakes). Each of these government-owned ferry operators is financed in a different manner. In BC, the Ministry of Transportation and Highways does not separate the costs of highways from ferries. The BC Ferry Corporation is a provincial crown corporation that receives a small federal subsidy (because one of its routes is an extension of the Trans-Canada Highway to Vancouver I), but the bulk of its subsidization comes from the provincial government. In Québec, the government ferries are a separate organization subsidized by the provincial government. CN Marine receives its entire subsidy from the federal government because it provides a transport link between provinces.

LEONARD ROUECHE

Ferron, Jacques, doctor, writer (b at Louiseville, Qué 20 Jan 1921). His father was a Liberal Party organizer, and Ferron was early attracted to political opposition. His earliest works, published in the late 1940s in Montréal newspapers and directed against the DUPLESSIS regime, carried the profoundly humanist and socialist stamp that helped earn him a reputation as the Voltaire of Québec letters.

His commitment to socialist principles, partly due to his first wife's affiliation with the Communist Party, was expressed in his involvement with left-wing magazines (*Situations, La Revue socialiste, Parti pris*) and in his political campaign as a candidate for the Co-operative Commonwealth Federation (CCF) in the 1958 federal election. He was later approached by the Rassemblement pour l'indépendance nationale and was an RIN candidate in the 1966 provincial election. Meanwhile, in 1963 he and friends founded the RHINOCEROS PARTY, which turned its main weapon, irony, on the increasingly dominant power of the federal government.

A remarkable and prolific stylist, Jacques Ferron has tackled the full range of literary genres. He has written some 20 plays, none frequently performed. Some are traditional intimist works (*L'Ogre, La Sortie*); others are theoretical reflections on drama as a genre (*Le Coeur d'une mère*); some are strongly nationalistic (*Les Grands Soleils, La Tête du roi*). Ferron has used his experience as a physician in poor neighbourhoods as subject matter for most of his stories and novels. His narrative works all denounce the social and cultural alienation of the Québecois. These works mix memories with allusions to current events, thereby creating a new fiction that is peopled by both historical characters and imaginary beings, that sometimes takes on mythological dimensions (*Le Ciel de Québec, Papa Boss, Le Saint-Elias*), or puts the common people at the centre of the fictional universe (*Les Roses sauvages,*

La Chaise du maréchal-Ferrant), or is autobiographical (*Les Confitures de coings, L'Amélanchier*).

An observant and lucid chronicler, Ferron demonstrates his historical knowledge in a genre he has rescued from oblivion: the satirical chronicle (*Historiettes, Du fond de mon arrière-cuisine, Escarmouches*). He has written more than 1000 of these pieces, in almost sloganeering style, skilfully bringing irony and sarcasm to bear on Québec's political, social and literary life. Ferron has won several literary awards: the Gov Gen's Award in 1962 for *Contes du pays incertain;* the France-Québec in 1972 for *Les Roses sauvages;* the prix Duvernay also in 1972; and the Prix David in 1977. PIERRE CANTIN

Ferron, Marcelle, artist (b at Louiseville, Qué 20 Jan 1924). She was an active participant in Les AUTOMATISTES, led by Paul-Émile BORDUAS, and has pursued an innovative artistic career, where her work in stained glass is noteworthy. After studying at the École du meuble in Montréal and the École des beaux-arts in Québec City, Ferron became part of Les Automatistes, signing that association's polemical manifesto *Refus global.* Her nonfigurative paintings were hung in all the major Automatiste exhibitions. She lived in Paris 1953-66 and continued to show in avant-garde exhibitions, including the 1961 São Paulo Biennial where she won the silver medal. The paintings of this dynamic artist became progressively more forceful. Vibrant colours and larger, fluid forms dominated the canvas. After 1964 her interest in light was effectively translated into a new medium — stained glass — examples of which can be seen in the Champ-de-Mars and Vendôme metro stations in Montréal. Ferron is represented in Canadian and foreign collections, including the Montréal Museum of Fine Arts. ANN DAVIS

Ferry Command was established early in WWII to improve aircraft deliveries to Britain from US factories, since surface shipping was too slow and the ships themselves were needed for other cargoes. Against the British Air Ministry's advice, Lord Beaverbrook (Maxwell AITKEN), the Canadian-born minister of aircraft production, asked Sir Edward BEATTY of CPR to assemble an organization to fly new multiengined aircraft across the Atlantic. A handful of experienced transatlantic flyers from British Overseas Airways Corporation worked with servicemen and civilians of virtually every Allied nation from headquarters in Montréal. At the time transatlantic flight was in its infancy, yet knowledgeable observers who believed such a scheme to be impossible were proved wrong. The CP Air Services Department, established in July of 1940, and its successors, Royal Air Force Ferry Command and No 45 Group of RAF Transport Command, eventually delivered over 9000 warplanes, losing only about 100, and also paved the way for mass postwar transatlantic air travel. CARL A. CHRISTIE

Ferryland, Nfld, Community, pop 795 (1981c), inc 1971, is located 60 km S of St John's on the shores of a picturesque harbour dominated by a large lighthouse. The name Ferryland is probably derived from the French (*forillon*) or Portuguese (*farelhao*) for "steep rock" or "reef," and was first noted on maps as early as 1529. A seasonal fishing station for migratory European fishing ships in the 1600s, Ferryland was founded in 1621 as the capital of the English colony of Avalon by George Calvert, first Lord Baltimore. In 1638 it was forcibly possessed by David KIRKE and it remained in the immediate Kirke family until 1708, despite claims by Calvert's heirs. The fishing settlement was fortified from Baltimore's time, and was further fortified 1743, 1746, 1776 and 1812 during periods of Anglo-French and Anglo-American conflict. The predominantly English colony received a great influx of Irish fishing servants in the 1700s. In the 1800s it was a major supply and fishing centre controlled by local and St John's merchants. Modern Ferryland is a fishing community that continues to be a regional services and administrative centre.
JANET E.M. PITT AND ROBERT D. PITT

Fertility, *see* POPULATION.

Fessenden, Reginald Aubrey, radio inventor (b at Milton-Est, Canada E 6 Oct 1866; d at Hamilton, Bermuda 22 July 1932). After attending Bishop's University, Fessenden joined Thomas Edison's laboratory in 1886 and later worked for Westinghouse, the US Weather Service and 2 American universities, making several fundamental discoveries in radio, including the superheterodyne principle, the basis of all modern broadcasting. In 1902 Fessenden formed his own company. In 1906 he achieved 2-way voice transmission by radio between Machrihanish, Scot, and Brant Rock, Mass (Marconi had sent radio signals from England to Newfoundland in 1901, but only one way and in Morse code). On Christmas Eve 1906 Fessenden made the first public broadcast of music and voice. In 1910 he lost control of his company and thereafter lived in relative seclusion, although continuing his research. Many of his patents were widely adopted (without his consent) during WWI, and in 1928, in recognition of his contributions to radio technology, the US Radio Trust paid him $2.5 million. DONALD J.C. PHILLIPSON

Reading: Ormond Raby, *Radio's First Voice* (1970).

Festival Lennoxville opened in 1972 at BISHOP'S UNIVERSITY in the Eastern Townships of Québec. Drama department chairman David Rittenhouse and director William Davis founded it to present new productions of outstanding Canadian plays staged earlier by other theatres across the country. Their first season included Ann Henry's *Lulu Street,* George RYGA's *Captives of the Faceless Drummer,* and Mavor Moore's *The Ottawa Man.* Robertson Davies's *A Jig for the Gypsy* and *Hunting Stuart,* Lister Sinclair's *The Blood is Strong* and Ted Allan's *The Secret of the World* were 4 older plays revived. Plays by Michael Cook, Sharon Pollock, Betty Lambert, David Freeman, Herschel Hardin and Michel TREMBLAY were presented. Richard Ouzounian, artistic director from 1978 to 1980, had to adopt a more commercial version of the original policy, selecting more musicals and comedies to attract larger audiences and increase revenue. Festival Lennoxville cancelled its 1981 season to reduce its deficit and to give new artistic director Scott Swan time to plan. However, in spite of Swan's effort to design a repertoire that would appeal to both anglophone and francophone audiences, Festival Lennoxville closed permanently after a truncated 1982 season. ROSS STUART

Festival Singers of Canada Founded in 1954 by Elmer ISELER as the Festival Singers of Toronto, the chorus reached professional status in 1968 when it became the core of the TORONTO MENDELSSOHN CHOIR. Early concerts brought the 25 singers recognition and, expanded to 36 voices, the choir performed regularly on the CBC and soon won international acclaim. A 1967 performance in the White House, Washington, DC, was the beginning of tours which, in 1971, 1972 and 1977, took the choir to Britain, France, Germany, Austria, Yugoslavia and the USSR. Further concerts were performed in the US in 1972, 1976 and 1977, western Canada in 1974 and 1977 and eastern Canada in 1975. The repertoire included music of all periods and styles, with emphasis on Canadian choral music. The Festival Singers commissioned and premiered compositions by Canadian composers, bringing an artistry to the performance that earned the selections a place in universal choral literature. Recordings made by the choir reflected this varied repertoire. In 1978 Giles Bryant succeeded Iseler as director, one year before the chorus suspended activities. ISABELLE MARGARET MILLS

Festivals began in antiquity as religious and ritual observance of the seasons, often including sacred community meals or feasts. Today, festivals are held to commemorate, celebrate or reenact events and seasons. Close to 200 major and numerous minor festivals are held in Canada each year. These celebrations have both indigenous and borrowed sources. Long before European contact, the native people marked seasonal changes with religious festivals. Among the OJIBWA there were 2 thanksgiving celebrations, one in spring at the rising of the sap to give thanks for deliverance from winter, and one in fall at harvest time. On the NW Coast there were potlatches (ceremonial feasts marked by lavish gift giving), and among the Plains Indians, POWWOWS are still held as social events to maintain and promote their culture. Religious observances marked festivals imported from Europe in the 17th century. From the earliest days of colonization, French-speaking settlers celebrated, on June 24, the Fête St Jean-Baptiste, a Christian overlay to earlier pagan celebrations of the summer solstice.

Since the climate strongly shapes the Canadian way of life, it is not surprising to find these ancient threads of seasonal celebration in festivals held today. The awakening of nature after the winter provides the focus for several spring festivals. In NS, there is the annual Annapolis Valley Apple Blossom Festival, in Ontario's fruit belt the Niagara Falls Blossom Festival, featuring horticultural exhibits and the Blossom Festival Parade, and in the Okanagan Valley of BC the Creston Blossom Festival. Other spring events are the maple syrup festivals held in April in Ontario, NS and Québec. There are 32 held in southern Ontario alone, and in Plessisville, Qué, the Maple Syrup Festival is held in the heart of Québec's maple sugar belt. Here numerous sugaring-off parties celebrate the process of converting maple syrup into sugar. Tied to history as much as the season, is the week-long Festival of Spring (Tulip Festival) held in Ottawa each year. To express her thanks to Canadians for their hospitality during her war exile, Queen Juliana of the Netherlands gave 10 000 tulip bulbs to the city. The royal family of Holland and the tulip producers continue to send 25 000 bulbs each year which bloom as an annual reminder.

The warm weather lingers briefly in Canada and more festivals are held in summer than in any other season. Food is the focus of many: potatoes, strawberries, salmon and shrimp, blueberries, oysters and trout are all feted where they are grown or harvested. In mid-July, the NS Pictou Lobster Carnival marks the end of the lobster-fishing season, with fishermen's boat races a reminder of the traditional way of letting off steam after gruelling weeks at sea. Outdoor seafood suppers add to the festivities. In late July in Altona, Manitoba, there is the annual Sunflower Festival highlighting agriculture, with displays of sunflower seeds and also Mennonite cooking. In August, at L'Anse Amour in Labrador, the annual Bakeapple Festival celebrates the tasty bakeapple berry, with food, dancing and storytelling. Pine Days in Pine Point, NWT, in mid-June, has a more unusual focus. During a 2-day celebration, residents and visitors celebrate the longest day of the year in the land of the midnight sun, with horseshoe tournaments and canoe jousting.

By fall, there are fewer seasonal festivals. These are held in recognition of the coming hard winter months, and in thanksgiving for the harvests. In the European tradition, Oktoberfests are held in many communities, particularly in areas where German immigrants have settled. One notable event is the Kitchener-Waterloo

Oktoberfest in Ontario, attracting many students to a last fling before hard studying begins. And in Rimouski, Qué, the Fall Festival focuses on the relationship between man and the land. Survival skills are emphasized with a pheasant hunt and clay pigeon shooting contest.

As a relief from winter, several festivals, usually beginning in late January and lasting through April in northernmost latitudes, ease the notorious "cabin fever." Most famous is the Québec Winter Carnival, a pre-Lenten celebration which first ran from 1894 to 1900 and was revived during the 1950s. The symbol of the carnival is a talking snowman, "Bonhomme Carnaval," who holds court in an ice palace and comes out to celebrate with the crowds. Ottawa holds the 10-day Winterlude festival along the Rideau Canal, the world's longest (7.8 km) skating rink. In Whitehorse, YT, a Sourdough Rendezvous features dogsled and snowshoe races (and more modern competition between snowmobiles), contests for flour-packing, and 1898 costumes and beards. The namesake food, first eaten in the north by prospectors, is featured at sourdough hotcake breakfasts. Most festivals in the Far North test survival skills, such as tea-making and animal-skinning under frigid conditions: these are featured activities at gatherings such as the Hay River, NWT, Ookpik Carnival and Yellowknife's Caribou Carnival.

As nature was tamed and European civilization took root, Canadians began to look back and started celebrating the events that formed the country. St John's Day Celebrations in Newfoundland commemorate the day (24 June 1497) when John Cabot first sailed into the quiet water off the coast of Newfoundland. Loyalist Days in Saint John, NB, commemorates the arrival (1783) of 4200 United Empire Loyalists, fleeing the aftermath of the American Revolution. The Festival of the Townships, an anglophone celebration in Sherbrooke, Qué, reaches back to that town's founding, by Loyalists, in 1796. On PEI, Charlottetown Natal Day, in June, honours both the birth of the city (1835) and the fact that Charlottetown is the birthplace of Canada, as the setting for meetings of the FATHERS OF CONFEDERATION. In Ontario in August, Simcoe Day honours the first governor of what was then Upper Canada, as well as the beginnings of the province in the 1790s. The opening of the Canadian West is celebrated with events such as Winnipeg's Red River Exhibition in June, Saskatoon's Pioneer Days in July, and Edmonton's Klondike Days, looking back to the late 1890s when prospectors surged north from the city in search of gold. In the Yukon, the Discovery Days, held in August, commemorate the 1896 founding of Dawson City on the last frontier.

Another mark of Canadian development is MULTICULTURALISM, which has fostered the growth of many ethnic and multicultural festivals celebrating heritage and ancestry. Appropriately, Canada's original peoples celebrate with various Indian Days festivities held across Canada. In Ontario, the Brantford Six Nations Indian Pageant in August features crafts and theatre based on native history. The Opasquia Indian Days in The Pas, Man, is organized by residents of the Opasquia reserve to spotlight native woodland games, traditional foods, crafts and canoe races. In the NWT the unique Northern Games are celebrated each year, roving from town to town, with Inuit and Dene sports, dances, drumming, competitions and displays. The Fête Acadienne in PEI celebrates French settlement on Île St-Jean (as PEI was first called) in 1663. The distinctive nature of Acadian culture is illustrated in festivities including Acadian drama, song, fiddling and step-dancing contests. New Brunswick's Brayon inhabitants celebrate in late July with the Foire Brayonne, founded in 1979 to showcase Brayon folksinging and culture. In Manitoba in June there is the Fête Franco-Manitobaine, celebrating the French presence in Manitoba, dating from the late 1700s. Folk concerts in the traditional boîte-à-chanson style, French Canadian dancing and food are part of the entertainment. In Québec, there are events such as Sherbrooke's Festival des cantons and Québec City's annual Festival d'été, a 2-week celebration of Québecois and international culture.

Other groups who helped to build Canada also pay tribute to their ancestral heritage. In NS, descendants of Scottish settlers celebrate throughout the summer. In Pugwash, the Gathering of the Clans with caber tossing and drum and pipe-band contests is the first event of the season, followed by the Antigonish Highland Games in July and the Festival of Tartans in New Glasgow in Aug. Often these events draw visits from Old World Scots as well as Scottish performing groups on tour. The influence of Ukrainian settlers was felt most on the Prairies, and in Dauphin, Man, Canada's fifth-largest ethnic group hosts Canada's National Ukrainian Festival. At Gimli, Man, where a self-governing New Iceland flourished 1878-87, the Icelandic Festival or Islendingadagurinn is held each year with parades, songs and poetry.

The newest entrants on the festival calendar are the multicultural festivals: Toronto's Caravan, Winnipeg's Folklorama, Regina's Mosaic and Edmonton's Heritage Days. All gather together and share the food, culture and spirit of the various ethnic groups. The Canadian Heritage Festival is an annual amateur folkloric performing arts event co-sponsored by the federal government and the host province. Heritage Festivals are often held in conjunction with other major events (Olympic Games, Qué, 1976; Saskatchewan's 75th Anniversary, 1980; Newfoundland's 400th Anniversary in 1983) and highlight the concept of cultural pluralism.

Other aspects of culture (art, music, theatre and film) have come to be celebrated in Canada as well. Festivals such as the Guelph Spring Festival in Ontario focus on music; the Banff Festival of the Arts in Alberta encompasses music, theatre and art. Individual styles of music are also celebrated: Toronto's Mariposa Folk Festival, the Winnipeg Folk Festival and the International Jazz Festival or Jazz City in Edmonton are 3 examples. Other festivals focus on styles and eras of music: baroque, classical and religious music are the themes of several smaller gatherings held in Ontario each summer. Canadian theatre festivals have also grown up over the years in cottage country, finding ready audiences among vacationers from the cities. Others are long-established traditions drawing international audiences: the STRATFORD FESTIVAL in Ontario, founded in 1953, and the SHAW FESTIVAL, at Niagara-on-the-Lake, established in 1962, both balance Canadian and international works. All summer long, the Charlottetown Festival celebrates theatre (*see* MUSICAL THEATRE), and in St John's, the Summer Festival is a well-known mecca for theatre lovers. Film has also attracted followers and is now fêted: the World Film Festival in Montréal each August, and Toronto's Festival of Festivals in September feature new international and Canadian films as well as retrospectives of genres, performers and directors.

Other festival celebrations range from the CANADIAN NATIONAL EXHIBITION in Toronto, the world's oldest permanent exhibition, to the CALGARY STAMPEDE (July), calling itself the Greatest Outdoor Show on Earth with 10 days of World Cup Rodeo and chuckwagon races; and from Vancouver Island's All Sooke Day in July, celebrating pioneering woodsmen with log rolling, tree chopping, high rigging and axe throwing, to Yellowknife's Annual Midnight Golf Tournament, another commemoration of the longest day of the year. Whatever the season, the day, the occasion or the people, Canadians show with their festivals that they have much to celebrate. *See also* FOLK FESTIVALS. DEBORAH C. SAWYER

Feux Follets, Les, begun as an amateur folk ensemble in the 1950s, turned professional in 1964. Its repertoire, at the insistence of founding director Michel Cartier, was inspired by indigenous native lore and historical events. In 1972 the troupe became associated with the Charlottetown Festival under artistic director Alan LUND. Feux follets, meaning "dancing fire" or "fireflies," was recognized for its lavish costumes, stage sets and special effects. It has not presented public performances since 1975.
CAROL BISHOP

Fiddlehead, The, LITERARY MAGAZINE fd 1945 at Fredericton, NB, by A.G. BAILEY as a mimeographed in-house organ of the Bliss Carman Poetry Society. Prominent in the magazine's early years were Bailey, Elizabeth BREWSTER, Fred COGSWELL, Frances Firth, Donald Gammon (the first editor), Robert Gibbs, Desmond PACEY, Robert Richards and A. Robert Rogers. During its early years the magazine reflected strongly both the poetic techniques of T.S. Eliot and W.B. Yeats and those masters' desire to fuse the present with the traditional past through the use of myth and symbol.

In 1952, to fill a publishing vacuum among Canadian magazines, *The Fiddlehead* was converted to an international magazine of poetry and was issued in a printed format. Between 1952 and 1966, under Cogswell, it became a quarterly, added a book-review section, undertook to publish prose fiction and established a reputation for eclecticism. In 1967 the magazine became officially the property of University of New Brunswick; editorial and managerial duties were subdivided among individuals connected with the university and, after a brief flirtation with monthly publication, the magazine continued as a quarterly with an expanded and improved format. During its long history, *The Fiddlehead* has published many writers who afterwards became famous. FRED COGSWELL

Fiddlehead Greens (*Matteuccia struthiopteris*), edible PLANT of the FERN family (Polypodiaceae) that is considered a delicacy in parts of Canada. The new leaves are tightly coiled and look like violin-tuning heads (hence name). The shoot

Fiddlehead greens (*Matteuccia struthiopteris*) grow in alluvial lands alongside streams across Canada. They are harvested commercially for a few weeks around the beginning of May (*photo by Bill Ivy*).

and main axis uncoil upwards; the lateral parts, outwards. This perennial fern, also called ostrich fern, sends up a ring of leaves from a circular, brownish rootstock. It should not be confused with the bracken fern, which is carcinogenic and sends up a single leaf from below ground. Fiddleheads are most popular in the Maritimes. The MALISEET Indians in NB, with a long tradition of harvesting this delicacy, considered it medicine as well as food. In BC it remains part of the diet of coastal Indians. Ostrich fern grows in moist, rich soil (bottomlands, SWAMPS) and in alluvial areas alongside streams across Canada. The fern propagates through spores released from under the leaves, or through the rootstock, which spreads numerous underground runners. The growing season is restricted to a few weeks around the beginning of May. Fiddleheads are best harvested when young shoots are 10-20 cm high, leaving 2 or 3 leaves so that the clump will not be weakened. Commercial demand far exceeds supply because the fern has not yet been successfully cultivated on a large scale. It is sold frozen out of season. Fiddleheads are eaten raw or, more commonly, cooked. Raw fiddleheads contain the enzyme thiaminase which attacks vitamin B when ingested in sufficient quantities; therefore, caution is recommended. NICOLE BERNSHAW

Fidler, Peter, fur trader, mapmaker, explorer (b at Bolsover, Eng 16 Aug 1769; d at Fort Dauphin [Man] 17 Dec 1822). Long obscured by his contemporary, David THOMPSON, Fidler has come to be recognized for his contribution to the mapping of western Canada. Fidler joined the HUDSON'S BAY CO as a labourer in 1788 and was appointed chief surveyor and mapmaker in 1796. His surveys took him to Lk Athabasca and Great Slave Lk (1790-92), the foothills of the Rockies (1792-93), northern Manitoba (1793-95) and the Assiniboine R (1795-96). After 3 years as a trader at YORK FACTORY and on the Saskatchewan R, he was sent to spearhead competition against the NORTH WEST CO on the Beaver R (1799-1800), S Saskatchewan R (1800-02) and Lk Athabasca (1802-06). Two years completing surveys around Lk Winnipeg and REINDEER LK were followed by 3 difficult ones competing against the NWC on the Churchill R. After leave in England he served the company in the Red R area until his death; his last job as a surveyor was to lay out river lots for the RED RIVER COLONY. JOHN S. NICKS

Field Hockey is a stick-and-ball goal game of 11 players per team, with many of its rules patterned after soccer. A noncontact game, its distinctive features are a stick, of which only one side can be used to play the ball, and an obstruction rule that prohibits a player from turning between the ball and a nearby opponent. The game's origins are lost in antiquity. As an organized team sport, it developed in England, the first club being formed sometime before 1861. Women in the British Isles started playing the game late in the 19th century, and it spread throughout the world, played as much by women as by men.

In Canada, field hockey is generally restricted to spring, summer and early autumn seasons, except in southwestern BC, where it can be played year-round. It is principally a girls' sport in schools, but is played by both men and women in adult leagues across the country. In 1980, there were approximately 2500 adult players in Canada. The modern form of field hockey was first played in BC; in 1896, the first recorded match in Canada was played by Vancouver girls, and the Vancouver Ladies Club was formed. Men were also playing at the turn of the century in Vancouver and Victoria, and a Vancouver league was in existence in 1902. The first women's organization in Canada was formed in Vancouver in 1927. During the first half of the 20th century, field hockey was played on Vancouver I and in the Vancouver area, and contests were recorded with teams from California and Australia in the 1930s.

After WWII, the immigration of players to Canada from all parts of the British Commonwealth influenced the establishment of field hockey across the country, and by 1959 the game was being played in the Maritimes, Ontario and Alberta. The Canadian (men's) Field Hockey Assn was founded in 1961; the Canadian Women's FHA a year later. International contests have increased markedly since the 1950s. The Canadian women's team participated in the women's international tournament for the first time in 1956, and in 1979 Canada hosted 18 countries in Vancouver for that world event; Canada placed 9th. The 1978 Canadian team was the first to enter the Women's World Cup, placing 5th. The men's team first qualified for the Olympic Games in 1964 and the World Cup in 1977. They have also participated in the Pan-American Games, placing 4th in 1967, 3rd in 1971, 2nd in 1975 and 1979, and 1st in 1983. BARBARA SCHRODT

Fielding, William Stevens, journalist, politician, premier of NS (b at Halifax 24 Nov 1848; d at Ottawa 23 June 1929). He rose from clerk to managing editor of Halifax's *Morning Chronicle* by 1874 and retained that post until he became premier in 1884. Concerned with the province's precarious economic condition and the refusal of federal assistance, he led his Liberal Party to victory in 1886, pledged to withdrawal from Confederation. When he failed in his pledge, he attempted to rescue the province's economy by developing its coal resources. In 1896 he resigned as premier to become the minister of finance and receiver general in LAURIER's government. Apart from lowering the tariff against British goods (called the Fielding, or imperial preferential, tariff), Fielding retained the high tariff policy of his Conservative predecessors. In 1910 he negotiated a reciprocity agreement with the US, but when it was opposed in Parliament an election was called for Sept 1911. Fielding and his party were defeated, and he accepted the editorship of Montréal's *Daily Telegraph*. Seen as Laurier's successor, Fielding's support of CONSCRIPTION cost him the leadership of his party in 1919, when Mackenzie KING won by 38 votes on the third ballot. After King became PM in 1921, Fielding resumed his position as minister of finance for 4 years. CARMAN MILLER

Fields, John Charles, mathematician (b at Hamilton, Canada W 14 May 1863; d at Toronto 9 Aug 1932). Educated at U of T and Johns Hopkins U, Fields taught mathematics for 4 years in Pennsylvania, then continued his studies at Paris, Gottigen and Berlin. On his return to Toronto (1902), he was appointed a lecturer in the mathematics dept at U of T, becoming Research Professor of Mathematics in 1923. Fields was an ardent campaigner for both business and state support for scientific research, taking his message to the Canadian Manufacturers' Assn and Boards of Trade. He was active in the creation of the School of Graduate Studies at U of T, the NATIONAL RESEARCH COUNCIL and the ONTARIO RESEARCH FOUNDATION. Fields was instrumental in arranging the first postwar meeting of the International Congress of Mathematicians (1924), at which he presided. With funds left from organizing the meeting, he attempted to establish a mathematics prize to be awarded at Congress meetings, held every 4 years. The Fields Medal, named in his honour, was first awarded in 1932. Fields was elected a fellow of the Royal Soc of Canada (1909), of London (1913) and to honorary membership in nearly all of the world's mathematical societies, including the Academy of Sciences, USSR. He was president of the Royal Canadian Institute, 1919-25. MARGARET E. MCCALLUM

Fife, David, farmer, wheat breeder (b at Kincardine, Scot 1805; d near Peterborough, Ont 9 Jan 1877). Fife immigrated to Otonabee, Upper Canada, with his parents in 1820. In 1842 he planted seeds of wheat obtained by a friend in Scotland from Danzig [Gdansk, Poland]. All but one plant perished over the winter and most of the survivor was eaten by a cow, but the remaining seeds, later identified as Galician, produced plants of better rust resistance, threshing quality, yield and flour than previously available. At first distributed locally the strain was used widely after 1848, becoming the leading one in Ontario by 1851 and virtually replacing all others there by 1860. The strain, eventually known as Red Fife, was also popular in the US and was introduced into Manitoba about 1870, ranking as the leading variety there from 1882 to 1909. Red Fife served as the male parent of the Marquis strain which proved more frost tolerant and even less susceptible to rusts, allowing wheat farming in Manitoba to spread farther west and north. MARTIN K. MCNICHOLL

Fifth Business, novel by Robertson DAVIES (New York and Toronto, 1970; London, 1971). The first of 3 novels called the Deptford Trilogy opens with Percy Staunton throwing a snowball at Dunstable Ramsay but hitting the pregnant Mary Dempster, causing the premature birth of Paul. These characters' fates intertwine for the rest of their lives. When Dunstable is gravely injured in WWI, he associates an apparition of a saintly figure with Mary Dempster. Ramsay returns to Canada, becomes a historian and hagiographer (a writer of the lives of saints) and tells the story of his self-discovery, which occurred through encounters with an unusual cast of characters. As he discovers he is "fifth business" (ie, an actor in a secondary role, but one who is nevertheless essential to the development of a drama), Ramsay gains deep insight into the mysterious relations between myth and history, spirit and flesh, fiction, fact and faith. *Fifth Business* has been translated into French, as *Cinquième emploi* (Montréal, 1975), and Polish. NEIL BESNER

Figure Skating is a sport for solo and pair skaters, in which style and technical skill are tested. Competition is conducted in single skating for men and women, pairs skating and ice dancing. Single skaters are judged in school figures, a short program with prescribed elements of free skating, and an original program of free skating. Pairs perform in compulsory and free-skating sections. Ice dancers demonstrate skill in compulsory dances and free dance, with no jumps, spins or lifts above the waist, and partners separate only to change positions. International competition in figure skating is organized by the International Skating Union, founded in 1892. The most important championships are the Olympic Games, and the world and European championships. The N American championships (last held in 1963) were also a top-ranked event. Among the important international invitational competions is Skate Canada, first staged in 1973. In world championships and Olympic Games, the number of entries are determined by previous results, with a maximum of 3 entries allowed per nation for each event.

Figure skating, in which prescribed patterns or figures are etched on the ice with precision, began to evolve after 1742, when the Edinburgh Skating Club was established. In the 1880s the centre of the activity became St Moritz, Switzerland, where skaters from Great Britain developed more figures and established a graduated system of figure tests. Meanwhile, free skating was being promoted by the "Viennese" school, a more theatrical approach that incorporated elements of dance with jumps and spins. Jackson Haines, an American ballet master, introduced music to the ice in the 1860s, producing the style that became free skating. Organized ice dancing dates from the 1880s in Vienna, and the waltz was danced on ice in Halifax as early as 1885. The first official world championship in figure skating for men was held in St Petersburg, Russia, in 1896. Separate women's championships began in 1906, with pairs starting 2 years later. World ice-dancing championships date from 1952.

In Canada, what was then called "fancy" skating began to develop a strong following in the 1860s, in part inspired by Haines, who toured eastern and central Canada in 1864. Exhibitions were staged at the opening of new rinks, and gala balls and carnivals were frequently held at the Victoria Rink in Montréal. F. Perkins, of Toronto, was the leading skater of this period and won the Gold Medal of Canada in 1867. That same year, the Montréal Skating Club offered a championship cup for amateurs, "open to the world." The most important Canadian figure skater in the late 1800s was Louis RUBENSTEIN, who won the unofficial world championship in St Petersburg in 1890. He also won the US amateur title in 1885 and 1889. George Meagher of Montréal won an open competition in 1891 that was claimed as the world championship. Figure skating grew in popularity during the next decades, and in 1903 the Minto prizes were presented by Governor General Lord MINTO and his wife to encourage the development of skilful performance in figures.

In 1914, figure skating was recognized as a separate sport, distinct from speed skating, with the formation of the Figure Skating Department of Canada as a section of the Amateur Skating Assn of Canada. Louis Rubenstein was the first president, and the membership consisted of the Minto Skating Club of Ottawa and the Earl Grey Skating Club of Montréal. In 1939, the department became the Canadian Figure Skating Assn, which became autonomous in 1951 with direct affiliation to the International Skating Union. Although figure skating had been included in the Olympic Games since 1908, Canadians did not participate until 1924, when the first Winter Olympic Games were held in Chamonix, France. Cecil Smith and Melville Rogers were Canada's first participants. Cecil Smith was also the first woman to represent Canada in any Olympic event, and when she placed 2nd in the 1930 women's world championship, she became the first Canadian woman to earn a top position in international figure-skating competition. In 1932, the world championships were held in Canada for the first time (in Montréal), and the Canadian skaters, Montgomery WILSON and Constance Wilson-Samuel, placed 2nd and 3rd, respectively, in their singles events. That same year, Wilson won the bronze medal in the Olympic Games at Lake Placid; as Canadian men's champion, he has been unequalled, winning that title 8 times between 1929 and 1939.

After WWII, Barbara Ann SCOTT of Ottawa established Canada as an important figure-skating nation. She won her first Canadian title in 1944 at age 15, and was such an excellent skater that in 1947 she became world champion in her first attempt at overseas competition. In 1948 she won the Canadian, US, N American, European and world championships as well as the Olympic gold medal. In 1948, the Olympic bronze medal win by Suzanne Morrow and Wallace Diestelmeyer began an era of outstanding pairs combinations from Canada. Frances Dafoe and Norris Bowden won the world championship in 1954 and 1955, and placed 2nd in the 1956 Olympics. Barbara WAGNER and Robert PAUL won their first of 4 consecutive pairs world titles in 1957; in 1960 they became the first non-European pair to win the Olympic title. Maria and Otto Jelinek followed with a 1962 world championship win, and Debbie Wilkes and Guy Revell placed 3rd in the 1964 Olympics. In the

World gold medallist pair, Barbara Underhill and Paul Martini, Ottawa, 1984 (*photo by Jim Merrithew*).

late 1970s, Canadian junior pairs made excellent showings in the world junior championships. Outstanding Canadian single men skaters include Donald JACKSON who placed 3rd in the 1960 Olympics and won the 1962 world championships, and Donald MCPHERSON who won the 1963 world title. The 1970s were dominated by the innovative skater Toller Cranston, Canadian champion from 1971 to 1976. He won the free-skating segment of the world championship 4 times and was awarded the bronze medal in the 1976 Olympics. A number of women skaters have also gained international recognition. Wendy Griner placed 2nd in the 1962 world championships, the same year that a young Petra BURKA demonstrated her potential by executing a triple salchow — the first by a woman in competition. Burka placed 3rd in the 1964 Olympics, and next year won the world championship. In the early 1970s, after overcoming stress fractures in both legs, Karen MAGNUSSEN placed 2nd in the 1972 Olympics and won the 1973 world title.

The CFSA, the association responsible for amateur figure skating in Canada, is the largest of its kind in the world. From 2 clubs in 1914, it grew to a membership of 360 in 1967, and of 1190 in 1979. There were 160 000 skaters registered with affiliated clubs in 1979. The CFSA National Skating Test program operates 8 tests, from preliminary to gold. In 1977, a system was introduced to separate test and competitive skaters, and the program is used to determine the eligibility of skaters for novice events, the first stage of competition. Only skaters registered with a CFSA affiliated club may try official tests. The CFSA also operates courses for amateur and professional coaches. BARBARA SCHRODT

Reading: Nigel Brown, *Ice Skating: A History* (1959).

Filibuster, the use of delaying tactics by the Opposition in a parliamentary body. Filibusterers speak as often and as long as possible, raising many points of privilege and order to prevent votes they expect to lose. Their aim is to kill the Government's bill or motion, create the impression that chaos reigns, or cause an election — possibly all three. The length of a filibuster, or even whether one has occurred, is a matter of opinion. Generally accepted examples of filibusters in Parliament include the CPR bill, 1881; the Manitoba remedial bill, 1896; the reciprocity bill, 1911; the naval bill, 1913; the PIPELINE DEBATE, 1956; and the FLAG DEBATE, 1964. The CLOSURE rule was introduced to end the naval bill filibuster (*see* ALLOTMENT OF TIME).
JOHN B. STEWART

Filion, Gérard, publisher (b on Île Verte, Qué 18 Aug 1909). Educated at Laval and Montréal's École des hautes études commerciales, he became editor of *Terre de chez nous* in 1935, and then secretary general of the Union des cultivateurs catholiques, the journal's proprietor. Appointed publisher in 1947 of *Le Devoir*, French Canada's most renowned independent daily, Filion was able, with his editorial staff headed by close friend André LAURENDEAU, to make the paper the most vocal critic of Québec's Union Nationale government during the 1950s. Championing the modernization of Québec society at all levels, he helped redefine traditional FRENCH CANADIAN NATIONALISM by demanding the creation of an activist, interventionist Québec state to help the nascent French Canadian bourgeoisie gain control over Québec's economy through a range of state corporations. In the 1960s he promoted the modernization and secularization of education as a member of Québec's Royal Commission on Education, was VP and director general of the Société générale de financement du Québec, and headed several of Québec's new state corporations. MICHAEL D. BEHIELS

Filion, Hervé, harness-racing trainer and driver (b at Angers, Qué 1 Feb 1940). Filion was the 6th child of a harness-racing family and drove his first race at age 12. Adept, aggressive and horse-wise, he became a leading driver at Ottawa's Connaught Park Raceway when only 17. He soon was a popular idol on Québec, Ontario and northern NY tracks. Ten times from 1968 to 1978 Filion was the leading N American driver. With over 1½ times the wins of his nearest competitor, he leads all drivers in life purse earnings. He is a member of the US Hall of Fame of the Trotter and the Canadian Horse Racing and Sports Halls of Fame, was named French-speaking athlete of the world, won the LOU MARSH TROPHY as outstanding Canadian sportsman. MARGARET NEAL

Filipinos The Philippines is an archipelago of 7083 islands off the Asian mainland with a population of about 50.9 million, some 80% of whom are Roman Catholics, 14% Protestant and

2% Muslims. Filipinos belong to the Indo-Malay group that spread out from the southern tip of Asia to settle as far as Polynesia in the South Pacific. The Philippines was a colony of Spain from 1564 to 1898, when it was ceded to the US following the Spanish-American War. Americans governed the country until 1941, when it was lost to Japan in WWII. It was subsequently retaken by the Americans and granted independence on 4 July 1946.

Overpopulation and economic and political difficulties have inspired emigration. Compulsory mass public education has produced a highly skilled and educated people.

Filipinos were first reported as a separate listing in Canadian immigration statistics in 1965, when 1467 entered Canada, nearly twice the number admitted in the previous 2 decades. The new emphasis in Canada's IMMIGRATION POLICY on Canada's own labour needs enabled the skilled and well-trained Filipinos to enter Canada in large numbers. By 1982 about 85 000 Filipino citizens, generally young (20 to 34 years), predominantly female, well-educated, Roman Catholic and proficient in English, had entered Canada.

A 1972 survey of Canadian Filipinos revealed that some 85% of immigrants held at least a BA degree. Their intended occupations were in health, manufacturing and in the mechanical, sales, service and clerical categories. However, as parents and dependent minors joined the original migrants, the percentage of college graduates among the new arrivals decreased significantly.

Filipinos usually settle in metropolitan areas, but not in ethnic enclaves. Because of their relatively high education and good incomes they have tended to become integrated into suburban communities. Over the past 20 years, more than 50% of all Filipino immigrants have settled in Ontario; about 40 000 have chosen Metro Toronto. Other provinces in which they have settled are Manitoba, BC and Alberta.

Social and Cultural Life The Roman Catholic Church serves as the centre of much Filipino social interaction outside the home. Religious holidays are celebrated with traditional rites featuring native songs and special foods and decorations. Most Filipino clubs and associations, which include the Filipino-Canada Association and regional associations affiliated with the United Council of Filipino Associations, participate in festivals and civic celebrations.

ELEANOR R. LAQUIAN

Filles du Roi, women of marriageable age who were shipped (the term is appropriate) to NEW FRANCE under royal auspices, 1663-73. As private interests preferred to send male indentured servants, the French state and religious communities had to rectify the imbalance of the sexes in the colonies. In Canada's case, although women began crossing in the 1630s, only the approximately 800 who disembarked during the first 11 years of royal government are commonly referred to as the *filles du roi*. Equipped with a trousseau and in some cases a small dowry, almost all found husbands quickly. Some were Parisian beggars and orphans; others were recruited from the La Rochelle and Rouen areas of France. Administrators' reports suggest that many of the urban born were ill prepared for the arduous life of the Canadian peasant.

THOMAS WIEN

Film A nation is rich in proportion to the pride it takes in its image of itself, an image that can be created most persuasively in our cinemas and on our TV screens. If an iconographical study were made of Canadian films of the 1960s and 1970s, whether French or English, certain images would recur. There would be many shots of landscapes depicting the vastness and beauty of the land. There would be the recurring presence of winter and streets clogged with snow, and there would be Canadian beer. Does this ubiquitous presence of beer in films suggest that Canada is a nation of drinkers? Does it suggest that the national cinema depicts the people living on the fringes of society, people from the regions, people out of work, more than it does the secure middle class? Or does it express a kind of pride that in this country, where so many industries are controlled by foreign interests, Canadians at least drink Canadian beer? Any of these images can help us to see our cinema as our own, but because Canada is considered part of the American domestic market, Canadian films have no guaranteed access to our theatres and only intermittent access to our TV screens. When Canadian films appear, they are generally compared with the more familiar American product. Like our dollar, films often are considered inferior rather than different. Most Canadians do not see Canadian films. Children are brought up with American TV and graduate to American movies shown on Canadian screens. Except for the occasional short film from the NATIONAL FILM BOARD, there is scant exposure to Canadian films in schools. Even in the post-secondary institutions that have ambitious film departments — UBC, York, Ryerson, Concordia, UQAM — there is no effort to base production training on a thorough knowledge of Canadian achievement. Yet there is an achievement; even if, for most people, it remains invisible. From *Back to God's Country* (1919) to *Les Fleurs sauvages* (1982), Canadian films have been shot mostly on location, using the local terrain less as decorative backdrop than as one of the protagonists. Films have been structured at such a pace that we are allowed to look at, feel and even at times to think about what we are experiencing. In classic Canadian films, we are seldom driven along by an identification with larger-than-life characters or held firmly in the grip of suspenseful narrative. There are fewer jolts-per-minute than in most American films, and since Canadian films are often about families or groups of people (*Mon Oncle Antoine* or *Who Has Seen the Wind*), there are no outstanding heroes and no international stars.

Canadian cinema is not a fantasy cinema, or a cinema of escape. Repeatedly, it is an observational cinema. Characters are placed within their milieu and the films seem to ask why the characters behave as they do. Frequently the protagonists seem trapped, yet judgements are seldom made. The characters in *Between Friends, Paperback Hero, Entre la mer et l'eau douce, The Rowdyman*, or even in *Les Bons Débarras* rarely understand their own dilemmas. Since the films do not move inexorably towards a resolution, a sense of understanding is withheld from the audience as well. Canadian scripts are often inconclusive, reflecting the uncertainties of the world. There is the sense of an inner, private journey as in some of our finest novels (Margaret ATWOOD's *Surfacing* or Marion ENGEL's *Bear*). Films such as *Goin' Down the Road, Isabel, The Hard Part Begins* and *Les Maudits sauvages* all depict a feeling of isolation, a movement through a hostile or unknown world. Canadian films seldom provide the easy comfort that is possible when personalities are depicted whose characteristics are familiar enough to lend themselves to satire. This is why Canadian films are so serious, especially films made at the NFB or the CBC. We do not know ourselves well enough to satirize.

Since 1977, advantageous tax incentives have created a flurry of filmmaking activity, much of it a limp imitation of American films. In a bid to gain access to US screens, Canadian locations have been disguised and the Canadian identity denied. Toronto has been passed off as Houston, and Montréal has had to stand in for New York. Though an industry might be created through these deceptions, such an industry would be culturally as important to Canadians as General Motors or Imperial Oil. For Canadian cinema to survive and be important, the cultural integrity of the films of the 1960s and early 1970s must be combined with the production skills that have been developed in the late 1970s and early 1980s. If large-scale productions can be made successfully, so much the better, but small-scale productions are also needed to give a stronger sense of Canadian identity. Perhaps in this way, as the Australian experience has demonstrated, Canadian films will be of increasing interest to the rest of the world.

PETER HARCOURT

Film History

The first Canadian films were produced in the fall of 1897, a year after the first public exhibition of motion pictures on 21 July 1896 in Ottawa. They were made by James Freer, a Manitoba farmer, and depicted life on the Prairies. In 1898-99, the Canadian Pacific Railway showed them throughout the UK to promote immigration. They were so successful that the federal government sponsored a second tour by Freer in 1902 and the CPR began directly financing production of immigration films. The CPR hired a British company to bring together a group of filmmakers, known as the Bioscope Co of Canada, to produce *Living Canada*, a series of 35 films depicting Canadian life, plus one 15-min drama (the first in Canada): *"Hiawatha," the Messiah of the Ojibway* (1903). Their successful release led to similar sponsorship by other railway companies and by the federal and provincial governments. In 1910, the CPR hired the Edison Co to produce 13 story films, to dramatize the special virtues of settling in the West. These promotional films are characteristic of most Canadian production through 1912: financed by Canadians but made by non-Canadians to sell Canada or Canadian products abroad. The few Canadians (such as Ernest OUIMET in Montréal, Henry Winter in Newfoundland and James Scott in Toronto) who initiated their own production made only newsreels or travelogues. Meanwhile, American film companies were beginning to use Canada as the setting for story films that featured villainous French Canadian lumberjacks, Métis, gold prospectors and noble Mounties.

After 1912, film companies in several Canadian cities began producing fiction as well as factual films. In Halifax, Canadian Bioscope Co made the first Canadian feature, EVANGELINE (1913), based on the Longfellow poem about the expulsion of the Acadians. It was a critical and financial success. The company made several other less successful films before folding in 1915. The British American Film Co of Montréal, one of several short-lived companies in that city, produced *The Battle of the Long Sault* (1913). In Toronto, the Conness Till Film Co made several comedy and adventure films (1914-15), and in Windsor the All Red Feature Co produced *The War Pigeon* (1914), a drama of the War of 1812.

The growth of Canadian nationalism around WWI promoted Canadian production and other aspects of the industry. The first widely released Canadian newsreels appeared, feature film production expanded as did the Canadian-owned Allen Theatres chain and associated distribution companies, and motion picture bureaus were established by the Ontario government (1917) and the federal government (1923). This optimistic period of expansion was led by such producers as George Brownridge, principal promoter of studios at Trenton, Ont, and producer of 3 features including *The Great Shadow* (1919); Ernest Ouimet, producer, exhibitor and distributor who had also opened the world's first luxury movie theatre in Montréal in 1907; Blaine Irish, head of Filmcraft Industries, producer of the feature *Satan's Paradise* (1922) and of 2 successful theatrical short film series; Ben Norrish, first head of the Canadian Government Motion Picture Bureau and later head of Associated Screen

News; Charles and Len Roos, producers, directors and cameramen of many films including the feature *Self Defence* (1916); and A.D. "Cowboy" Kean, cameraman and producer since 1912. The most successful producer was Ernest SHIPMAN, who had already established his reputation as a promoter in the US when he returned to Canada in 1919 with his author/actress wife, Nell Shipman, to produce *Back to God's Country* in Calgary. This romantic adventure story of an embattled heroine triumphing over villainy was released worldwide and returned a 300% profit to its Calgary backers. During the next 3 years Shipman established companies in several Canadian cities and made 6 more features based on Canadian novels and filmed not in studios, as was then common, but on location. Though these films — eg, *God's Crucible* (1920), *Cameron of the Royal Mounted* (1921), *The Man from Glengarry* (1922), and *The Rapids* (1922) — were not as profitable as his first, they were not failures. Only his last film, *Blue Water* (1923), made in NB, was a disaster. Shipman left Canada and died in 1931 in relative obscurity.

Shipman's departure also marked the end of a minor boom in Canadian production that had begun during WWI. Only 2 features were in production in 1923 (there had been 9 in 1922) and even the production of short films showed a sharp decline. But the number of Hollywood films with Canadian plots increased markedly. At this same time Canadian box-office receipts began to be included under domestic receipts for the US, and distribution companies and theatres came under direct Hollywood control. The takeover of the Allen Theatres chain (1923) by Famous Players Canadian Corp gave Famous Players control of the Canadian exhibition market. European film industries also faced the threat of Hollywood domination in the 1920s, but most governments moved quickly to protect their domestic industries by controlling ownership of exhibition and distribution companies, or by stimulating national production. Canada took no comparable action. Throughout the 1920s, production in Canada was mainly restricted to inserts for American newsreels, sponsored short films, and documentaries produced by government motion picture bureaus and a handful of private companies.

There was one brief resurgence in 1927 when private investors contributed $500 000 to produce *Carry on Sergeant!*, a drama about Canadians in WWI written and directed by British author and cartoonist Bruce Bairnsfather. Though well received by critics, it died within weeks of its release. Apart from the work of Associated Screen News and government production (which also suffered funding cutbacks during the Depression), the Canadian film industry in the 1930s became virtually a branch plant of Hollywood. Feature production was restricted to the making of "quota quickies" for the British market under a British law requiring that a certain number of British or Commonwealth films be shown in British theatres. "Quota" companies, legally Canadian but financed by Hollywood, were established in Calgary, Montréal and Toronto, but the most active was Central Films of Victoria, BC, which produced 12 films from 1935 to 1937. Several of these low-budget adventure films were not even set in Canada and none can be considered Canadian in a cultural sense. Even this level of production ended in 1938 when the British excluded Commonwealth production from protection, mainly because of the way the Canadian government had allowed Hollywood to circumvent the intent of the original law. The only memorable feature of this period is *The Viking*, a dramatic depiction of the hazardous life of Newfoundland's seal hunters, produced in Newfoundland in 1930-31 by the American Varick Frissell (and, technically, not a Canadian production). It is a key example of what was to become a characteristic Canadian genre: documentary dramas and films blending fiction and non-fiction, often rich in a sense of place and connotation, which explore the relationship between people and their environment. This approach emerged early in Canadian film and distinguished many later Canadian features.

But in the 1930s this approach was scarcely evident. The commercial industry had died, the Ontario Motion Picture Bureau had been closed down, and even the federal Motion Picture Bureau had lapsed into sterility. Only in the work of a few individuals (especially Bill Oliver in Alberta and Albert Tessier in Québec) and at Associated Screen News (founded 1920, active until 1958) was there any continuing sense of creative vitality. Though this Montréal company's mainstay was newsreels and sponsored films, it did produce 2 widely released short film series: *Kinograms* in the 1920s and the *Canadian Cameo* series from 1932 to 1953. Supervised and usually directed by Gordon SPARLING, these films showed flair and imagination, and were almost the only film representation of Canada either at home or abroad. This arid scene began to change in the late 1930s. New film companies were established, Odeon Theatres emerged to compete with Famous Players, and John GRIERSON wrote a report (1938) that led to the creation of the NFB. PETER MORRIS

Film in English Canada

The history of English Canadian cinema has been one of sporadic achievement accomplished in isolation against great odds. It has existed within a hostile environment where access to capital for production, the marketplace for distribution, and theatres for exhibition have been extremely difficult. It has largely been a concurrent history of a struggle against an entertainment monopoly (Hollywood), which has a vested interest in delaying its development, and a search for an audience that is still largely unaware of an indigenous industry. The lack of production can only be understood against this economic backdrop, where the major distribution and exhibition outlets have been owned and controlled by foreigners. Without access to the marketplace, any industry will remain underdeveloped.

Before the outbreak of war in 1939, Canadian film production was almost nonexistent. The war changed all this, owing entirely to the establishment of the NFB, which naturally began to train and develop Canadian filmmakers. The NFB acted as a kind of film school and it was only natural that with time these people would restlessly turn their energies to the more complex form offered by the fiction-feature film, which commanded the greatest popular attention. There is evidence that in the immediate postwar period this was beginning to happen. However, these visions remained unrealized for 2 decades as Hollywood moved ruthlessly and efficiently to protect its interests. The problem was complex and involved the Hollywood hegemony in Canada. After the war Canada, like many other countries, experienced a balance of payments problem with the US. The government restricted imports on a large number of goods in 1947. Money made on films was also discussed, and there were rumours that some kind of quota system would be conceived to force Hollywood to invest part of its box-office profits in Canada. This never happened. Instead, an arrangement was made and formalized into the Canadian Co-operation Project. In return for the uninterrupted flow of dollars out of Canada, the American film lobby attempted to boost tourism to Canada, by (among other things) placing Canadian references in American films. The nationalistic lobbying on behalf of Canadians was successfully defeated, and the chance to create a pool of capital by taxing US dollars was lost. The NFB, which had lobbied for fiscal restrictions on Hollywood money, was also thwarted. This episode is important because it helps to understand the 20 years after the war, in which there was virtually no production in Canada.

Only one English Canadian feature film was made outside Québec in the 1940s, *Bush Pilot* (1946), an imitation of Hollywood's *Captains of the Clouds* (1942). A half-dozen or so English feature films were made in the 1950s. Tyrone Guthrie, who was instrumental in establishing the theatre at Stratford, Ont, directed a production of Sophocles's *Oedipus Rex* (1956), the only film to this date that has used the resources of Stratford. A young Canadian, Sidney Furie, directed 2 films of considerable promise, dealing with young people in rebellion against society. Both *A Dangerous Age* (1957) and *A Cool Sound from Hell* (1959) attracted international critical attention, especially in Britain; but the neglect the films suffered in Canada persuaded Furie to emigrate to Britain in 1960, and he has never returned to Canada to direct. Furie is typical of the emigration of talent from Canada at this time.

The 1960s started in much the same way as the previous decade had ended, with insipid and pedestrian films occasionally appearing, one of which employed the fashionable 3-D process, *The Mask* (1961). However, times were about to change and a new optimism was apparent. Ottawa filmmaker and producer F.R. "Budge" CRAWLEY turned his limitless energies towards features and produced *Amanita Pestilens* (1963) and the gritty story of an immigrant, *The Luck of Ginger Coffey* (1964). The NFB, although primarily focusing on documentary films, produced 2 features in the early 1960s that were a harbinger of things to come. *Drylanders* (1963) turned to history for its subject matter, and the seminal *Nobody Waved Good-bye* (1964), directed by Don OWEN, followed the problems of 2 teenagers in contemporary Toronto. Production also began to flourish in other ways. The aesthetic advances made by the French "New Wave" of filmmakers led to a more "personalist" cinema and development of the cheap mobile 16 mm camera allowed more access to a medium that had hitherto been the preserve of few. A wave of low-budget feature production swept Canada, much of it from university campuses. The first film, made by Larry Kent while studying at UBC, created the most controversy. The sex scenes in his *The Bitter Ash* (1963) turned it into an overnight sensation. Kent went on to direct 2 more features on the West Coast before moving east. Many other student features were made, some by one-time directors, others by people who continued to work in the industry. Films such as *Winter Kept Us Warm* (1965), *Slow Run* (1968), *The Columbus of Sex* (1969), *The Plastic Mile* (1968) and *Great Coups of History* (1968) were all low-budget films of some interest. An important figure was David CRONENBERG, who made 2 experimental, futuristic films as a student before turning his talents to commercial production. The emerging filmmakers of the 1960s, both English and French, looked to government to protect their fledgling interests. In 1967 the federal government took a significant step by creating the CANADIAN FILM DEVELOPMENT CORPORATION, funded with $10 million to develop a feature film industry that would last. The CFDC was only to concern itself with production, and not with commercial distribution or exhibition.

At first the CFDC gave money to some of the student filmmakers. Many of the subsequent films were artistic and commercial failures. A few attempts to imitate American models of filmmaking were supported, but with a similar lack of success. However, 2 films indicated future directions. In 1967 Paul ALMOND, without CFDC money, directed *Isabel*, a story set in the Gaspé starring Geneviève BUJOLD. In 1970, To-

Photo from the film *The Rowdyman*, with Gordon Pinsent (left) and American actor Will Geer (*courtesy National Film Board/Photothèque*).

ronto filmmaker Don SHEBIB appeared with the landmark *Goin' Down the Road* (1970), an artistic and commercial success that received national distribution and attracted large audiences. Both films were unmistakably Canadian, using regional landscapes and characters with sensitivity. They spawned a number of films such as *Paperback Hero* (1973), *The Hard Part Begins* (1973), *Wedding in White* (1972), *The Only Thing You Know* (1971), *Montreal Main* (1973) and *The Rowdyman* (1971). The first fiction feature made by a woman, *Madeleine Is . . .* (1971), was made on the West Coast during this vibrant period. Most of these films were made on modest budgets; none of them were major commercial successes. The CFDC was pressured to raise the visibility of the material it was funding, either by legislating the marketplace so the distribution and exhibition of Canadian films would be guaranteed, or by employing foreign talent in conjunction with Canadians. In 1973 a voluntary quota on Canadian films was negotiated with the 2 theatre chains. The quota was not successful, but it was the furthest the federal government would go. Instead, foreign stars and directors were used with increasing regularity, a number of them employed on co-productions. The government did act decisively to provide financial incentives for investment in the domestic film industry through tax benefits and the Capital Cost Allowance program, which resulted in a massive increase in the amount invested in Canadian production. This policy shift marked a new aggressiveness within the industry, and within government agencies responsible for film. Priorities shifted from the low-budget, cultural film to high-budget, commercial projects. At the CFDC a shift in management was made (1978) to reflect the new orientation. The emphasis was placed on film as an industry, not as an art form. Producers, not directors, were given priority.

Initially the use of foreign talent was fortuitous, producing 2 films of high quality that went on to become commercial hits: *The Apprenticeship of Duddy Kravitz* (1974) and *Lies My Father Told Me* (1975). These years also saw the success of thrillers such as *Black Christmas* (1974), horror films such as *The Parasite Murders* (1975) and the rock film *Janis* (1974). The NFB produced the occasional feature as well, eg, *Why Rock the Boat?* (1974) and *One Man* (1977), continuing a practice begun a decade before. Unfortunately fewer low-budget films with a sense of place and Canadian identity were being made. The string of international co-productions and films using international stars in trite commercial vehicles, littering the second half of the 1970s, was an almost complete disaster. Co-productions such as *Ragtime Summer* (1976), *Cathy's Curse* (1977), *Welcome to Blood City* (1977), *It Rained All Night the Day I Left* (1979) and many others went unseen. Canadian films using foreign stars in films such as *Echoes of a Summer* (1975), *Angela* (1977), *Starship Invasions* (1977), *Agency* (1979), *Tanya's Island* (1979), *Mr. Patman* (1979) and many more suffered a similar fate. These films were artistic as well as financial disasters.

Though the majority of Canadian films in the late 1970s suffered from identity crises, a few exceptional films emerged from this commercial period. *Why Shoot the Teacher* (1976) and *Who Has Seen the Wind* (1977), both adapted from Canadian novels, retained their integrity and did well at the box office. *Murder by Decree* (1978) was a co-production made with flair and style. *The Silent Partner* (1978) and *The Changeling* (1979) used foreign stars and did well commercially. David Cronenberg's horror films *Rabid* (1976), *The Brood* (1979) and *Scanners* (1980) established his reputation at home and abroad. Ivan Reitman had a financial success with *Meatballs* (1979) and the animated fantasy *Heavy Metal* (1981). As attrition depleted the number of opportunists attracted solely by the financial benefits of the film industry; those producers who had something to contribute began to prosper. The CFDC again underwent changes designed to establish more of an equilibrium between commercial and cultural imperatives.

The culturally viable film had all but disappeared, but some brave and intelligent works continued to be made. *The Far Shore* (1976), *Skip Tracer* (1977), *The Rubber Gun* (1977), *Outrageous!* (1976), *Aerial View* (1979) and *Alligator Shoes* (1981) were all made in the gritty tradition of *Goin' Down the Road*. Regional co-operatives sprinkled across the country began to train young filmmakers who remain committed to the concept of a cultural cinema. Nevertheless, the English Canadian film remains a fragile and precarious adventure. The past 15 years are dotted with occasional successes and a fair share of mistakes. Access to the marketplace is still not guaranteed and capital is difficult to raise. The tension between film as industry and film as art is still being debated by those who define and affect policy. The lessons of the past few years are being absorbed, in the hope that policies can be developed to promote a healthy industry.

PIERS HANDLING

Film in Québec

In 1939, when the Canadian government founded the NFB, Québec films consisted of the work of a few enthusiastic amateurs, most of them priests, such as Maurice PROULX and Albert TESSIER. These works today, in addition to their undeniable cinematic qualities, contribute valuable ethnographic documentation. The early filmmakers found a natural outlet in the Service ciné-photographie, founded in 1942 by the Québec government. Its mandate was to meet certain propaganda and educational needs, but it was ill equipped to do so with a minimum of staff, and working only in 16 mm. The NFB did not have these constraints, but in the early years it was primarily an anglophone organization. Dubbed versions of English-language films were made for Québec, and little thought was given to French-language production. Under the circumstances, Vincent Paquette, Jean Palardy and a few others did heroic work. After the war they were joined by Roger Blais, Raymond Garçeau and Bernard Devlin. A francophone team took shape and encouraged the emergence of Québec filmmaking within the NFB. In its infancy it was not always differentiated from anglophone production, and sometimes even produced in English. It achieved its best results when reacting to some specific event: *Les Reportages* was a noteworthy series that began offering biweekly newsreels in French in Sept 1941.

After WWII there was a period of active feature film production in Québec. The war caused a scarcity of French-language films, and sent some French filmmakers into exile in Québec. As a result, feature filmmaking awakened in 1944 with *Le Père Chopin*. This film helped create a new, vertically integrated (from production to exhibition) industry, with international contacts and religious support (financial and ideological). Other Québecois were eager to produce films, hoping to recoup their expenses on the local market and find distribution abroad. In 1947 Québec-Productions brought out *Whispering City/La Forteresse*, in English and French versions. This psychological thriller did not achieve the commercial success for which the producers had hoped. The US film industry at the time was in poor shape, and QP had to modify its aspirations and be content with local markets. The company therefore drew on the highly popular subject matter of RADIO DRAMAS for its next 3 films (1949-50). Another company, Renaissance, wanted to make Catholic films and finally brought one out in 1949. Both companies tried to break out of the strictly domestic market by arranging co-productions with French companies but these efforts failed, and they reverted to Québec themes. Their relative success did inspire several other, smaller outfits to produce a total of 7 feature films, 2 of them in English and most of them adapted from theatrical dramas. Paradoxically, 2 of these became the most famous of the era: *La Petite Aurore l'enfant martyre* (1951) by J.Y. Bigras, the story of a child tortured to death by a stepmother destined to be hanged, and *Tit-Coq* (1953) by G. GÉLINAS, the drama of an illegitimate orphan whose fiancée was persuaded to marry another man while Tit-Coq was overseas during the war. In 1954, after 19 films, the feature-film industry collapsed. Television dealt a fatal blow to an industry made vulnerable by its mediocrity. Today, the quality of these films is not important, but they have great value as social documents. In the 1940s and 1950s, Québec changed from a traditional, agricultural society to an urban one. The films seem to defend the traditional social order, especially the role of the clergy, but a closer look reveals the contrary. The characters and themes of these films, despite the negative impressions of Québec society that they evoke, depict a society in transition, a society in which the traditional Catholic values were being questioned, and thus contradict the surface message of the plot.

Throughout the next decade, feature films and private production were virtually nonexistent, although a few semiprofessionals produced work for the Québec government. Thus, the only place where Québec film survived was within the NFB. A number of brilliant filmmakers joined the NFB during the 1950s: L. Portugais, M. BRAULT, G. GROULX, C. JUTRA and others. They, and the NFB "old-timers," finally had opportunities worthy of their talents. This explosion was the result of 3 developments. First, the NFB moved from Ottawa to Montréal (1956), which meant that Québec filmmakers could live and work in Québec. Second, in 1957 public attention focused on francophone filmmakers who were not being given the same opportunities as their anglophone colleagues; the result was that French and English productions were separated administratively and financially, leading ultimately to the creation of a distinct francophone service. Third, TV demanded large amounts of material; this meant that both popular entertainment and artistic innovation received as much support as did films for government departments and educational institutions (eg, 39 films in the *Passe-Partout* series, 1955-57; 26 dramatic episodes of *Panoramique*, 1957-59, a landmark for Québec fictional cinema; *Temps présent*, late 1950s and early 1960s). Filmmakers were also pushing the technological limitations, trying to improve their equipment and its capacity to capture natural sound and images while mobile on location. In 1958 Brault and Groulx produced *Les Raquetteurs*, which was important technologically as a key step in the development of direct cinema and socially as a statement of the nation's awakening.

The period was one of profound social change. Duplessis died in 1959; the Liberals came to power in 1960 and the QUIET REVOLUTION began. French Canadians became Québecois, and film met the need to give expression to the change. *Les Raquetteurs* went beyond picturesque scenes to stress membership in a national community. The early 1960s accelerated the development of Québec cinema, both within and outside the NFB. People such as Brault, Pierre PERRAULT, Jutra, P. Patry and F. Dansereau were eager to try new directions. In 1963, a new era began with 2 categories (documentary and fiction) and two films: *Pour la suite du monde*, by Perrault and Brault; *À tout prendre*, by Jutra. The first, through its technique and the importance it gave to the spoken word, marked another major step in the development of direct cinema. The second was an example of films being produced by nationalistic filmmakers throughout the world and was a personal statement by Jutra. Groulx's *Le Chat dans le sac* (1964) was one of the best films to that time about petit-bourgeois youth. J.P. LEFEBVRE, a prolific filmmaker, brought out *Le Révolutionnaire* (1965), a fable/commentary on society. Gilles CARLE, who had been with the NFB since 1961, was working on his first feature, a comedy, *La Vie heureuse de Léopold Z* (1965). Coopératio, a private company, tried to get the film industry moving again. Its director, P. Patry, made *Trouble-fête* in 1964 and then, in the space of just over a year, 3 more films. Others also tried feature films, working privately or for the NFB or the Québec government (A. LAMOTHE, D. ARCAND, R. Lavoie, A.C. POIRIER, J. GODBOUT, B. Gosselin, G. Dufaux, C. Perron, J.C. Labrecque and others). Ferment and change were occurring in all aspects of the arts, and film forms evolved to meet the needs of the filmmakers. Direct cinema in all its variations, auteur films (documentary or docudrama) and every genre of commercial film were attempted.

Perrault dominated direct filmmaking of these years with his saga of the people of Île aux Coudres. With his cameramen Brault and Gosselin, he wanted not only to observe and record the awakening of the Québec nation, but to play a part in that awakening as well. Yet direct cinema was not limited to nationalistic subjects. Some producers wanted to use the techniques for social action films. A number of these efforts took place within the framework of the NFB program Société nouvelle (francophone equivalent of Challenge for Change), which made its début in 1968 with *St-Jérôme* by F. Dansereau and lasted more than a decade. Others at the NFB concentrated on workers, eg, Denys Arcand, whose extraordinary *On est au coton* (1970) was the victim of political censorship for 7 years. Others (including Dansereau and, most notably, A. Lamothe) left the NFB in order to work more freely. Lamothe's *Le Mépris n'aura qu'un temps* (1970) gave us an economic, social and political analysis that film had not previously offered. Between Perrault's approach and that of the activist films arose many other forms of direct cinema, united only by their technique and their methods. This kind of film moved steadily to the forefront. Another significant figure in the late 1960s and early 1970s was Labrecque, particularly with his *La Visite du général de Gaulle au Québec* (1967) and *La Nuit de la poésie* (1970).

But the movement began to falter at the beginning of the 1970s, partly because some of its practitioners (Labrecque, Gosselin and, especially, Brault and Groulx) were attracted by the possibilities of fiction film. Brault made his first solo feature film in 1967, *Entre la mer et l'eau douce*, which showed the marks of his long apprenticeship as a cameraman/producer. In 1974, with *Les Ordres*, Brault once again put documentary skills at the service of fiction and, with his reconstruction of Québec under the War Measures Act in 1970, made the perfect synthesis of the flexibility, improvisation and attention to detail of direct cinema with the dramatic progression and structured narrative of fiction. Groulx went exactly the opposite way, in both style and content. He offered a clear personal statement for discussion and criticism. Three features illustrate his methodology, *Où êtes-vous donc?* (1969), *Entre tu et vous* (1969) and *24 Heures ou plus* (1972). His films integrated documentary and fiction at the editing stage, a technique in which he still leads.

Fiction moved away from direct cinema and won new adherents for a second reason. In 1967, the CFDC was born, and with it, avenues of financing. That same year D. HÉROUX brought out *Valérie*, Quebec's first erotic film and commercial success. These 2 factors opened the way for commercial filmmaking and explain the 1970s production boom. Québec had its various waves — erotic films (including C. Fournier's box-office hit *Deux femmes en or*, 1970), subtle comedies and thrillers. But this boom in commercial films soon ran into trouble, made even worse by foreign control of the key sectors of distribution. Some commercial films surmounted the problems of quality versus commercial viability. Gilles Carle, essentially a storyteller, knew how to lace his films with humour and sex, ideology and social colour, showmanship and stars, making them much more interesting than most of the others in his field. With his fifth feature, *La Vraie Nature de Bernadette* (1972), Carle won lasting international acclaim.

Others also knew how to combine quality with commercial success. The best known is probably Denys Arcand, whose *Réjeanne Padovani* (1973) and *Gina* (1974) blended social observation and colour with perfect artistic harmony; or Claude Jutra, who won acclaim for his NFB film *Mon Oncle Antoine* (1971), one of the finest Québec films ever made. Unfortunately, he did not have the same commercial success with *Kamouraska* (1973), a period film based on the celebrated novel, and an expensive co-production. A number of other NFB producers (M. Carrière, C. Perron, J. Godbout, etc) made films that could scarcely be distinguished from private ones. The trailblazer of this kind was J. BEAUDIN's tender and simple period film, *J.A. Martin, photographe* (1976).

J.P. Lefebvre dominated the field of the more personal statement for 15 years, with 18 very important features to his credit. His work evolved from 2 fundamental approaches to filmmaking: the first, social, concrete, reflective and critical; the second, abstract, symbolic and intimate. Jacques LEDUC, who concentrated on non-dramatic moments of daily life and the state of the soul, belonged to that same generation. Leduc's work, marginal yet high profile, belonged both to the school of direct cinema (*On est loin du soleil*, 1970) and to fiction (*Chronique de la vie quotidienne*, 1973-78).

A group of women filmmakers within the NFB produced *En tant que femmes* (1973-74), a series of films, some direct and some fictional, about issues that concerned women. Women had very recently found their voice in Québec film with the appearance of the first feature made by a woman in Québec (*De Mère en fille*, by A.C. POIRIER, 1968), followed in 1972 by the first feature privately made by a woman, *La Vie rêvée*, by M. DANSEREAU. The NFB series encouraged film production by women. Dansereau now has several films to her credit, as does Poirier (including the famous *Mourir à tue-tête*, 1979, about the psychological, social and political implications of rape). Filmmakers such as L. Carré, P. Baillargeon and M. Lanctôt explored new and unexpected paths in fiction. Direct films moved onto uncharted ground (eg, sexism, domestic work, the couple, violence) with the work of L. Guilbeault, H. Girard, D. Létourneau, T. Rached and others. The work done was much more important than its numerical output would indicate, and was a sign of awakening, renewal and dynamism.

Another kind of dynamism in the 1970s originated with young producers who concentrated more on individual, even marginal, problems than on social ones. Some excelled in film for children (A. Melançon); others went happily from fiction to direct (J. Chabot and R. Frappier). Some were more traditional, more narrative, one of the best being F. MANKIEWICZ (*Les Bons Débarras*, 1980). Three names dominated the ironical fringe: M.A. FORCIER (4 features, including *Bar salon*, 1973), J.G. Noel (3 features, including *Ti-cul Tougas*, 1976) and P. Harel. These filmmakers had in common that several of their films were produced or co-produced by the Association coopérative de productions audio-visuelles, which receives funding from the INSTITUT QUÉBECOIS DU CINEMA (IQC) for shorts and first films. This production by young people assures Québec film a vitality and creativity that otherwise would be lacking — especially in fiction, since this field has been dominated for some years by large established companies. An exception to this is the astonishing *Les Plouffe* (1981) by G. Carle, in which historical authenticity is matched by emotional accuracy.

In the late 1970s and early 1980s, direct films have once again become the best part of Québec cinema. This is primarily because of the work of the veterans: Perrault, with his 2 major film cycles on Abitibi and the MONTAGNAIS-NASKAPI (including the *Pays de la terre sans arbre ou le Mouchouânipi*, 1980); Gosselin, Brault and a few others with films that mix ethnology, pop culture and nationalism; M. Moreau's pedagogic and ideological films; A. Lamothe's 2 social and political series about Indian life and culture (*Carcajou . . . et le péril blanc*, 1973-76; *Innu asi*, 1979-80); and G. Dufaux, a director/cameraman of sensitivity and humanity whose subjects have included everything from old age to education to China.

As the 1980s began, Québec film was again in crisis. The number of private productions was declining dangerously; even the NFB faced cutbacks. Filmmakers with high hopes for the 1975 Loi sur le cinéma were disillusioned. The IQC's 5-year plan also closed down some possibilities. The CFDC was interested in a profitable, commercial film industry based on international markets, and this is not always compatible with filmmakers' definitions of a national film industry. Fewer productions, money problems, higher costs, unemployment for competent producers, technicians and artists, and huge international-content productions are elements of current Québec filmmaking. Much of the direct filmmaking is based on co-operation of the private sector with the IQC and TV (Radio-Québec or Radio-Canada). Feature co-productions are being made by the NFB, private industry, the IQC, the CFDC and TV. Since the crisis in Québec film is not primarily one of creativity or quality, but of production, this multiple participation may provide the means for continuing growth. PIERRE VÉRONNEAU

Reading: Peter Morris, *Embattled Shadows, A History of Canadian Cinema 1895-1939* (1978); Pierre Véronneau and Piers Handling, eds, *Self Portrait: Essays on the Canadian and Québec Cinemas* (1980).

Film, Documentary The genre is virtually synonymous with the NATIONAL FILM BOARD, but earlier work preceded this development. In the first decade of the century, companies such as Canadian Pacific and Massey-Harris used film for promotional purposes. The federal government established its own agency, mainly as a result of its involvement with film in WWI. From this evolved the Canadian Government Motion Picture Bureau in 1923, which for a brief time in the 1920s led the world in using film to spread information. The bureau's most notable film was *Lest We Forget* (1935), a documentary history of the Canadian effort in WWI, compiled from newsreels, graphics and reenacted scenes. Another successful documentary was *The Royal Visit* (1939), a record of the Royal Tour of that year. In the 1930s Associated Screen News, a private film company in Montréal, produced many films and series, such as *Canadian Cameo*, for theatrical release. Gordon SPARLING spent most of his career at ASN, and *Rhapsody in Two Languages* (1934) remains a classic prewar documentary. In Québec, a number of priests, most notably Maurice Proulx and Albert Tessier, shot films extolling the land and Catholic virtues, documents of a life-style that has now disappeared.

With the arrival of John GRIERSON, who was responsible for creating the NFB in 1939, the documentary began to flourish. The coming of war meant that Canada needed propaganda films, and series such as *Canada Carries On* and *The World in Action* reached audiences of millions. Grierson also promoted films that dealt with ethnic groups, Indians, social problems and Canadian art. The arrival of peace in 1945 signalled a new direction for the NFB. By the early 1950s a group of young NFB filmmakers, part of Unit B, began to produce a unique body of work based on the Canadian experience. *Corral* (1954), *City of Gold* (1957) and *Lonely Boy* (1961) dealt with issues of the past and the present in a quiet, delicate fashion. The *Candid Eye* series, made for TV, examined socially relevant issues in *The Days Before Christmas* (1958) and *The Back-Breaking Leaf* (1959). Unit B produced much of its work for TV in the period 1952-58 before the CBC developed its own capability.

In 1956 the NFB moved from Ottawa to Montréal and this provided a great incentive to French Canadian production. The French Unit made socially active films of commitment and contestation. In direct cinema, which relies on portable, lightweight 16 mm cameras and magnetic sound-recording equipment, the director does not preplan, but allows events to dictate the direction of the finished film. This direct cinema movement produced classics in Québec such as *Les Raquetteurs* (1958) and *La Lutte* (1961). The feature documentary *Pour la suite du monde* (1963) captured the vanishing life-style of islanders in the St Lawrence. Its directors, Pierre PERRAULT and Michel BRAULT, went on to make outstanding contributions to the Québec documentary film. By the late 1960s the material emerging from French production at the NFB took on a more political bias and some films were banned. Meanwhile, in the rest of the NFB the objective documentary still flourished. Donald BRITTAIN rose to the fore with *Memorandum* (1965) and followed this with numerous finely crafted films, many of which employed archival footage. Other filmmakers produced excellent work of a diverse nature at this time: Don OWEN, Robin Spry and Tony Ianzelo, to mention a few. More personal statements were made by people such as Derek May and Michael Rubbo, whose film on Vietnam, *Sad Song of Yellow Skin* (1971), won the prestigious Robert Flaherty Award.

In the private sector, Allan KING gained international repute with his *cinéma-vérité* films, *Warrendale* (1967) and *A Married Couple* (1969). King formed his own company to produce documentaries before moving on to direct fiction features. F.R. "Budge" CRAWLEY, an Ottawa filmmaker who formed his own company (1938), won an Oscar for *The Man Who Skied Down Everest* (1974), the pinnacle of a long, distinguished career that also included *The Loon's Necklace* (1948). Harry Rasky achieved prominence with his portraits of famous people: Marc Chagall, Will and Ariel Durant, Leonard COHEN, Arthur Miller and Anne Frank.

The NFB began to revitalize itself in the 1970s through a new program entitled "Challenge for Change," which had an overt social and political function. This program produced some of Canada's finest documentaries. Another fortuitous development resulted from the "Challenge for Change" program: the establishment (1974) of a women's studio at the NFB. Studio D has produced a number of fine works on a variety of problems, from a woman's perspective. Its most controversial effort has been its film on pornography, *Not a Love Story* (1981). Québec women filmmakers have had an illustrious history at the NFB. Anne-Claire POIRIER has made feature documentaries, her film on rape, *Mourir à tue-tête*, garnering many accolades. Women have contributed a number of highly interesting films in the private sector: *Les Servantes du Bon Dieu* (1979), *D'abord menagères* (1978) and *P4W — Prison for Women* (1981).

Regional filmmakers began to make their own distinctive contributions: on the West Coast Phil Borsos with his film *Nails* (1979); on the Prairies, Tom Radford, *China Mission* (1980) and Anne Wheeler, *War Story* (1982); Michael Scott, *For Gentlemen Only* (1976) and Bob Lower, *Something Hidden* (1981) from Winnipeg; Kent Martin, *Empty Harbours, Empty Dreams* (1979) from Halifax; and Sturla Gunnarsson and Steve Lucas, *After the Axe* (1981) from Toronto. Another Toronto filmmaker, Jessi Nishihata, examined issues in the West surrounding the MACKENZIE VALLEY PIPELINE with *The Inquiry Film*. Québec began to reassert its documentary prowess in the late 1970s and made films about its music (*Le Son des français d'Amérique* series, 1973-77), Indians (*Carcajou et le péril blanc* series, 1973-76), its heritage (*La Belle Ouvrage* series, 1977-80), deprived people (*Les Exclus* series, 1978) and daily life (*Chronique de la vie quotidienne* series 1973-78). In addition to the upsurge in regional filmmaking, both English and French filmmakers have visited China and recorded their experiences in films such as *Images de Chine* (1974), *North China Commune* (1979) and *Guî Dao* (1980). Outside of the NFB, autonomous studios or filmmaking co-operatives were producing films in Halifax, Toronto, Winnipeg, Edmonton and Vancouver. French-language studios operate in Moncton, Toronto and Winnipeg.

The documentary idea has unique significance in Canadian art, and most especially for Canadian cinema. Indeed, the realist tradition dominates even our fictional cinema. Perhaps its roots can be traced to a number of sources. This distrust of the "imaginary" and the irrational could arise out of a utilitarian philosophy that provides the cornerstone for our educational and social system. Others feel that the documentary form has been rooted in a need to comprehend the alien and hostile landscape that surrounds us. Grierson's philosophy, which had a great influence on documentary film in Canada, was essentially educative and informative. He wanted to bridge the gap between people by showing them how others lived. This pragmatic approach found its natural form in the factual or documentary film. PIERS HANDLING

Film, Experimental Even though the avant-garde has produced some of Canada's most accomplished films, it has been involved in the medium a comparatively short time. Film artists in Germany, France, the US and the Soviet Union began making experimental films in the 1920s. Although political censorship brought the movement to an end in the Soviet Union permanently, and in Germany for a time, artists in France and the US continued to produce experimental films throughout the 1930s and 1940s. During the 1950s and 1960s, especially in the US, production accelerated as artists attempted to reformulate the cinema according to modernist ideals. In Canada, except for Norman MCLAREN, an animator, there was almost no experimental filmmaking until the mid-1960s. There are 2 major reasons for this delayed development. Traditionally Canada has lacked the political and intellectual interest in the arts that accompanies the growth of an avant-garde, and Canadian artists have retained a longstanding dedication to representation and documentation — not only through documentary films but through depictions of landscape and of social life in painting, poetry and fiction. The artistic doctrine that dominated experimental film until the mid-1960s and was known as modernism was largely committed to abstraction. There were a few filmmakers who made experimental films, for example, Burton Rubenstein (*The Hyacinth Child Bedtime Story*, 1966), Peter Rowe (*Buffalo Airport Visions*, 1967) and John Hofsess (*The Palace of Pleasure*, 1966 and *The Columbus of Sex*, 1969). However, none of these established a career in experimental filmmaking.

Not until the development in the late 1960s of postmodernism, with its greater concern with representation and its interest in photography, did avant-garde filmmaking became widespread in Canada. Given Canada's commitment to representational art, it is not surprising that a Canadian, Michael SNOW, became one of the key innovators within postmodernist forms of cinema, and that several other Canadians (Joyce WIELAND, Jack CHAMBERS, David RIMMER and Bruce ELDER) have also made significant contributions. Many of Snow's films attempt to reconcile the demands of photographic representation with the material and formal interests of the modernist tradition. His film ↔ (1967) suggests how abstraction, depiction and construction, haptic space and optical space, illusionistic devices and devices revealing the work's material construction can be brought into a balanced, integrated form. Jack Chambers, like Snow, worked in painting before making films. In his films *Mosaic* (1966), *Hart of London* (1970) and *CCCI* (1971), Chambers developed structures to convey his ideas about light, mind and nature, and the qualities of photographic images.

In the work of Canadian avant-garde filmmakers, there are several forms that have found special importance; all are based on characteristics of the photographic image. One is the landscape film exemplified in such films as Snow's *La Région centrale* (1971); Wieland's *Reason over Passion* (1969); Rimmer's *Real Italian Pizza* (1971) and *Canadian Pacific I* (1974) and *II* (1975); and Chambers's *Circle* (1968). None of these works is a simple or straightforward representation of a landscape: all explore the capacity of the photographic and cinematographic image to represent nature, meta-nature or the relation of self to nature. The second form is the diary film which chronicles the daily life of the filmmaker. Here the subject explored is usually the affinity of the photographic and filmic image for the ordinary matter of everyday life and the manner in which a photograph converts natural matter into art. Examples are Judy Steed's *Hearts in Harmony* (1973), Rich Hancox's *Home for Christmas* (1978) and Elder's *The Art of Worldly Wisdom* (1980). The final form depends on the use of theme and variations in a structure. The different variations are generated by optical printing, a process that enables the filmmaker to rephotograph an already existent film image. In such works, the cinematic image becomes the subject of the film. Filmmakers who have done work in this form include Rimmer (*Surfacing on the Thames*, 1970, *Watching for the Queen*, 1973), Al RAZUTIS (*98.3KHZ Bridge at Electrical Storm*, 1973; *Lumière's Train*, 1980) and Elder (*1857: Fool's Gold*, 1981). Canadian experimental films, like Canadian documentaries and animation films, enjoy an international reputation.

Film Animation Canada commands worldwide respect for work in film animation. This reputation has been built over the last 40 years and is largely, though not entirely, based on the work of Norman MCLAREN and the films produced by the NATIONAL FILM BOARD. Some Canadian pioneers in animation were Walter Swaffield, Harold Peberdy and Bert Cob; however, the first animated films, all predating 1920, have disappeared. In the 1920s a Toronto painter and illustrator, Bryant Fryer, began work on the first of a series of animated films entitled *Shadow Laughs;* only 2 films in the series of 12 were completed, both in 1927. Six years later he embarked on a new series, *Shadowettes*, producing 3 films using the silhouette technique made famous in Germany by Lotte Reiniger. Shortly afterwards, Fryer was forced to suspend his activities, and he moved into commercial production. These early attempts were all necessarily sporadic and unconnected. With the founding of the NFB (1939), conditions were established that would guarantee continuity of production, free from commercial pressures. Shortly after John GRIERSON was appointed to head the NFB, he asked his friend and former colleague, the gentle Scotsman, Norman McLaren, to join him in Canada. McLaren was put in charge of the fledgling animation department to produce short propaganda messages for the war effort. McLaren's effervescent imagination was applied to this task immediately. He also began to recruit young artists from across Canada to assist him, thereby laying the foundation for the future success of the animation department. With a minimum of means, animators such as George Dunning, Grant Munro and René Jodoin produced films of charm and vitality.

After WWII McLaren turned his attention towards more personal projects, leaving a legacy that is legendary. His technical innovations in animation, for instance, drawing directly on film and eliminating the need for a camera, were revolutionary. His pixillation techniques of animating live actors were also extraordinarily imaginative. Both *Neighbors* (1952) and *A Chairy Tale* (1957) were made this way, the former winning him an Academy Award. McLaren dazzled audiences around the world with his colourful, innovative films, reaching millions of people. In the 1960s he became fascinated with dance and broke new ground with the beautiful *Pas de deux* (1967), a black-and-white visual poem using multiple exposures.

While McLaren was quietly absorbed in his own work, a generation of animators began to develop their own techniques in the 1950s. Colin Low's *The Romance of Transportation in Canada* (1952) was only one of many interesting efforts, but it signalled the arrival of Canadian animation. By this time Robert Verrall, Wolf Koenig and Sidney Goldsmith had joined the animation section at the NFB to make their own singular contributions. The move of the NFB to Montréal in 1956 stimulated French animators Bernard Longpré, Yvon Mallette, Pierre Moretti and Pierre HÉBERT. The styles were as numerous as the animators. Some became interested in using computers, others used charcoal, watercolours, photographs and the pin screen. By the late 1960s animation production had split along linguistic lines, but with no deterioration in quality; diversity was rampant. Don Arioli used his acerbic wit to amuse; Co HOEDEMAN created fantastic creatures out of sand in *The Sand Castle* (1977); Caroline Leaf used watercolour and ink on glass in *The Street* (1976); Ishu Patel employed thousands of beads in *Bead Game* (1977); Laurent Coderre utilized painstaking cutout animation in *Zikkaron* (1971); and Bernard Longpré and André Leduc returned to pixillation with *Monsieur Pointu* (1975). The NFB's stress on regional production in the 1970s resulted in many entertaining efforts from Vancouver, Winnipeg and Halifax. The board has won prizes worldwide for its animated films and 3 of its films have won the coveted Oscar: *Neighbors, The Sand Castle* and *Special Delivery* (1977). Filmmakers in the private sector were making equally intriguing films. Crawley Films had established an animation studio very early in its history and the award-winning *The Loon's Necklace* (1948), which recounts an old Indian legend, is still in active distribution. In the 1960s Crawley began to produce animation for American TV, notably *The Tales of the Wizard of Oz* (1962), *Return to Oz* (1963).

In the 1950s, Jim McKay and George Dunning left the NFB to found Graphic Associates, and after Dunning's departure in 1955, under its new name Film Design Ltd, it has continued production to the present. Al Guest formed his own company in the same year and at one time it was the third largest of its type in the world. Guest now runs Rainbow Animation. On the West Coast, the self-educated Al Sens opened his own studio and continues to make films. *The See Hear Talk Think Dream and Act Film* (1965) combines live action and animation into one of his best pieces. Gerald Potterton, another ex-NFB animator, formed his own company in Montréal (1968); it produced many films of note, among them the feature-length *Tiki Tiki* (1970-71), before its demise in the mid-1970s. Potterton recently returned to the spotlight by directing Canada's most expensive animated feature film, *Heavy Metal* (1981), which became a box-office success. Many animators and production companies shared in this effort. Interestingly, there had been an animated feature made in Canada as early as 1955, *Le Village enchanté*, directed by Marcel and Réal Racicot, which drew on Québec folk legends. Another independent animator is John Straiton, an advertising executive who works in animation in his spare time. *Portrait of Lydia* (1964) uses a succession of sexual images and symbols, and *Eurynome* (1970) is a technical wonder employing plasticene. Straiton's films have won numerous awards. Canada's unique and innovative animated films continue to elicit the respect of critics and the public everywhere.

PIERS HANDLING

Film Censorship has existed in Canada for almost as long as films have been shown. CENSORSHIP takes a variety of forms: customs official may forbid entry to pornographic films, cities may ban films within their municipal limits and provincial attorneys general may lay criminal charges. Production houses, especially governmental agencies, practise self-censorship. The NATIONAL FILM BOARD has demonstrated this a number of times, most notably in 1972 when on political grounds the presiding government film commissioner banned several Québec films made by the French unit.

Censorship is a provincial responsibility. With the exception of PEI and Newfoundland, each province has its own censorship, supervisory or classification board. Between 1911 and 1913, 5 provinces passed censorship laws and then established boards to apply them. In Québec where censorship was seen as an extension of family rights and responsibilities, the emphasis was placed on protecting children from corruption. Western provinces took the same approach and added an element of anti-Americanism. For about 50 years, censorship boards have had almost unchallenged control over the fate of films. Reasons for banning a film or demanding certain cuts are extremely diverse and vary from province to province. In the post-WWII years, censorship was justified on the grounds of protecting the public interest against outrages to morality. In Québec everything that ran counter to church teaching and morality was forbidden, but this censorship began to be criticized and, paradoxically, Québec became the most liberal province. In 1963, following a commission of inquiry, Québec established a classification policy, and in 1967 the censorship board became the supervisory board. The following year, Manitoba substituted classification for censorship. In 1976, the Superior Court of NS ruled that censorship was not under provincial jurisdiction. Five provinces appealed this ruling and won its reversal in the Supreme Court of Canada. Their powers reaffirmed, the provinces continue to impose 10 different sets of cinematic standards. A modest form of liberalization has triumphed lately — except in Ontario which, since 1975, has become the stronghold of conservatism and the object of protests and anticensorship movements. Canadian censorship, subject to institutional, political, police and religious interference, remains a matter of provincial control and continuing controversy. PIERRE VÉRONNEAU

Reading: Malcolm Dean, *Censored! Only in Canada* (1981).

Film Festivals, Prizes The first major film festival in Canada was started in Montréal (1960) and it included a competitive section for Canadian films. In the mid-1960s Vancouver started its own festival, and both Ottawa and Stratford hosted a number of events in the early and mid-1970s. None of these events has survived. In 1976 the first Festival of Festivals was held in Toronto and it has continued to be a success. In the same year Ottawa began the biennial, competitive International Animated Film Festival, and a year later the World Film Festival, a competitive festival that awards the Grand Prix of the Americas, started in Montréal. In 1979 the Banff International Television Festival of films was inaugurated as a competitive event. The oldest film festival, which still runs biennially, was begun in 1950 as a documentary film festival in Yorkton, Sask. The Yorkton International Film Festival has expanded to include all short films; its major prize is the Golden Sheaf. Other competitive festivals include the Banff Festival of Mountain Films, the Canadian International

Amateur Film Festival, the Super 8 Film Festival and the Canadian Student Film Festival. Important noncompetitive events are Canadian Images Film Festival, a celebration of Canadian cinema, Montréal's Festival international du nouveau cinéma de Montréal and the Grierson Film Seminar.

In 1948 the first Canadian Film Awards were organized; they became an annual occurrence. By 1979 the Academy of Canadian Cinema was established to continue this work, and it gives Genie awards as symbols of film excellence in a range of categories. The Canadian Motion Picture Distributors Assn awards the Golden Reel Award to the top-earning film of each year. Another major prize of importance, given by the Québec critics' organization, is the Prix de la critique québécoise. The Alberta Motion Picture Industries Assn presents a number of prizes at its annual Alberta Film and Television Awards, begun in 1974. PIERS HANDLING

Fils de la Liberté, an association of 700-800 young PATRIOTES fd 5 Sept 1837 in Montréal. Inspired by the ideals of the American Revolution, the Fils de la Liberté published a manifesto on Oct 4 which proclaimed their belief in the right of a people to choose its own government and of a colony to become independent. André Ouimet led the civil and political arm of the movement, while Thomas Storrow Brown looked after its military wing. On 6 Nov 1837 the Fils de la Liberté clashed violently with the members of the anglophone DORIC CLUB in Montréal. The association died with the outbreak of the REBELLION OF 1837. FERNANDE ROY

Finance, Department of, was formally created by statute in 1869, inheriting its title, structure and personnel from the tiny finance department of the pre-Confederation Province of Canada. Originally, its primary function was bookkeeping: administering the collecting and spending of public monies, and servicing the national debt. During WWI the federal government borrowed from taxed individual Canadians directly for the first time (through Victory Loans and income taxes), which complicated but did not fundamentally alter the department's task.The Great Depression and WWII transformed the department into a hive of national economic managers. For the first time, university-trained economists, such as Clifford Clark, W.A. Mackintosh, R.B. Bryce, and Ken Eaton, occupied senior offices. Massive expansion of the economy during the war (Gross National Product doubled and total annual federal spending increased to 10 times that of the 1939 figure) led to an expansion of the influence of the department and, more generally, of the federal government as a whole. Financial structure was changed permanently in WWII with the introduction of measures such as UNEMPLOYMENT INSURANCE (1941) and FAMILY ALLOWANCES (1944). More significantly, in 1939 departmental officials developed a new approach to the federal budget. Instead of simply attempting to balance expenditures with revenues — the prewar practice — they began to use taxing powers and spending policies to influence economic development in general. Management of the economy, especially through its FISCAL POLICIES, remains the most important function of today's department. The Anti-Dumping Tribunal, BANK OF CANADA and AUDITOR GENERAL report to the minister of finance. DAVID FRANSEN

Finance Act, Aug 1914, emergency measure ending Canada's GOLD STANDARD and giving the Department of Finance new powers. The same name applied to a 1923 measure continuing these new powers while providing for the return to the gold standard on 1 July 1926, and for its suspension in certain emergencies. Before 1914 each bank had issued its own paper currency while the federal government issued Dominion notes in exchange for gold, or vice versa. Thus when gold flowed in, the Dominion would issue more paper money; chartered bank notes were convertible into gold or Dominion notes. After 1914 the government could issue new Dominion notes without gold backing to finance the war effort and to lend to the chartered banks at their request. This arrangement continued until 1935 when the BANK OF CANADA was formed; it meant that the chartered banks could never be short of cash, because they could always borrow newly printed Dominion notes, whose quantity was no longer related to the amount of gold in Ottawa's vaults. Thus the note issue was unlikely to be proportionate to the gold, although from 1 July 1926 Dominion notes were convertible into gold, at a fixed price, as they were before 1914. In late 1928 gold did run short, and the emergency provisions of the 1923 Act were invoked. *See* EXCHANGE RATES. IAN DRUMMOND

Financial Post, a magazine founded by John Bayne MACLEAN, who also founded MACLEAN'S magazine. Intended to provide reliable investment information, especially to the Toronto business community, the *Financial Post* published its first issue on 12 Jan 1907. A weekly, it is now published at 777 Bay Street, Toronto, by Maclean Hunter Ltd. Its circulation is about 197 000. The editor is Neville J. Nankivell and the publisher is James K. Warrillow (1984). The *Financial Post* reflects orthodox Canadian business opinion but has no political affiliation. It leans slightly towards Canadian nationalist positions. D. MCGILLIVRAY

Financial Times The *Financial Times* of Canada is a weekly tabloid-sized business newspaper, first published as the *Montreal Financial Times* on 21 June 1912. It was purchased in 1961 by Southam-MacLean Publications Limited, a subsidiary of the Southam Company Limited, now Southam Inc. The headquarters of Financial Times were in Montréal until 1 July 1975 when it was moved to Toronto where it is published at 920 Yonge Street. Noted editors of the past include Bernard Keble Sandwell, later editor of *Saturday Night,* and Michael Barkway. David Tafler is now publisher and Terence Corcoran is executive editor (1984). The viewpoint of *Financial Times* is orthodox business, leaning towards free-market economics. D. MCGILLIVRAY

Finch, common name for one of the largest BIRD families, Fringillidae, which occurs worldwide (excluding Australia). It includes some GROSBEAKS, crossbills, Hawaiian honey creepers, redpolls, siskins and birds specifically named finches. In Canada, about 14 species are known, ranging in length from the redpolls (*Acanthis hornemanni, A. flammea*), pine siskin (*Spinus pinus*) and American goldfinch (*S. tristis*), as small as 11 cm, to the pine grosbeak (*Pinicola enucleator*), up to 25 cm. Although a diverse group, all members of the family have a stout, conical bill with a cutting edge angling sharply near its base. This makes it ideal for crushing seeds, principal food of most finches; insects are also eaten. Bill dimensions vary considerably: grosbeaks and cardinals have large, deep bills; goldfinches and siskins have relatively slender bills; the mandibles of crossbills overlap. Both plumage and song show tremendous variability. Males have bright and often strikingly patterned plumages, and most species have elaborate, tuneful songs.

In northern Canada, most species raise only one brood annually. As the summer is longer in southern Canada, most species attempt to raise 2 broods. Generally, the female alone incubates eggs. Both sexes contribute food to young in the nest (nestlings) and after they have left the nest but cannot fend for themselves (fledglings). Sometimes, a male will take over feeding fledglings of the first brood, while the female constructs a second nest and lays another clutch of eggs.

In southern Canada, a few species are resident, eg, house finches (*Carpodacus mexicanus*) in southern BC. Some species perform altitudinal MIGRATIONS: gray-crowned rosy finch (*Leucosticte tephrocotis*) nests at the summit of mountains in Alta, BC and YT, but winters in lowlands and foothills of western Canada. Southern Canada is a wintering area for species nesting in northern Canada, eg, redpolls, crossbills (*Loxia curvirostra* and *L. leucoptera*) and pine grosbeaks, but numbers vary considerably from year to year, depending on food availability farther north. Only a very few hardy species can survive winters in northern Canada; eg, at Churchill, Man, only hoary redpolls attempt to overwinter and even they are not found in some winters. RICHARD W. KNAPTON

Findley, Timothy, writer, actor (b at Toronto 30 Oct 1930). For years a successful actor (charter member, Stratford Shakespearean Festival 1953; original Edinburgh Festival cast of Thornton Wilder's *The Matchmaker* 1954), Findley published his first novel, *The Last of the Crazy People,* in 1967 and the second, *The Butterfly Plague,* in

About 14 species of finch are known in Canada, including the common redpoll (*Acanthis hornemanni*), which nests in northern Canada and winters in southern Canada (*photo by Bill Ivy*).

1969. *The Wars* (1977) won a Gov Gen's Award and an international reputation for the author, which *Famous Last Words* (1981) enhanced. A play, *Can You See Me Yet?*, was performed at the National Arts Centre, Ottawa, in 1976. He has also written TV scripts, including *The National Dream* (1974) and *The Whiteoaks of Jalna* (1971-72). *The Wars* depicts the experiences of a young Ontario man during WWI, and *Famous Last Words* deals with the life of a fictional international man of letters during and before WWII. The former is an intense, single-minded vision, the latter a densely populated panorama of a society in decay. Despite their differences, both novels display wit and invention, and a fascination with memory and perception. Public and private histories alike are recounted through the use of scraps, fragments, diaries and manuscripts as narrative devices. DENNIS DUFFY

Finn, Henry James William, expatriate actor, playwright (b at Sydney, NS 17 June 1787; d 13 Jan 1840). Taken to New York as a child, he travelled to London, eventually acting small parts at Haymarket Theatre 1811-12. He returned to America in 1815 and he appeared in New York, Philadelphia and Boston, playing Hamlet, Richard III and Othello. With his triumphant Aquecheek in *Twelfth Night* (1824), he eschewed tragedy for farce, becoming a comic favourite. He managed Boston's Federal St and Tremont theatres 1825-30 and wrote about 9 plays, *Montgomery; or, the Falls of Montmorency* (1825) and *Removing the Deposits* (1835) being best known. He died aboard a burning steamship on the way to his summer home on Rhode I. DAVID GARDNER

Finns The first Finnish migrants to arrive in N America were part of a group of settlers who established the colony of New Sweden along the banks of the Delaware R between 1641 and 1655 (*see* SWEDES). The total number of settlers was small and was soon assimilated into the American mainstream. Between 1835 and 1865, several hundred Finns settled in Alaska (which at that time was a part of Russia) and many moved down the coast to BC. Some early Finnish immigrants to Ontario worked on the construction of the first WELLAND CANAL, which was completed in 1829. The 1981 census listed 52 315 residents of Finnish origin in Canada.

Origins Finland was part of Sweden until 1808 when it was ceded to the Russia Empire. In Dec 1917 the Finnish Parliament declared its independence from Russia; there followed a bitter civil war in 1918, in which the conservative White Guard defeated the Red Guard workers. Finns had been migrating to N America in large numbers prior to WWI and continued to do so in the first decade of Finnish independence, primarily for economic reasons. A large population explosion in rural areas coincided with a lack of available farmland, forcing many rural inhabitants to look elsewhere. The overseas migration was mainly from the provinces of Vaasa, Oulu and Turku-Pori in southeastern Finland, and later from Helsinki. Other factors encouraging immigration included religious freedom and a desire to escape compulsory military service in the Russian army.

Migration and Settlement Until 1914, most Finnish emigrants went to the US, although a small minority came directly to Canada and others came to Canada via the US during periods when the Canadian economy was attractive. Canada became the main destination of emigrants from Finland in the 1920s when the US established entry quotas. Landless groups, with no economic prospects in their homeland, made up the largest proportion of overseas emigrants.

Finns again migrated to Canada in large numbers (20 000) between 1950 and 1960, seeking better economic opportunities than were available in postwar Finland. These Finns were generally from urban areas, were better skilled and educated, and were more willing to settle in the urban areas of Canada than pre-1930 Finnish immigrants. Since 1960, with the expansion of the Finnish economy, few Finns have immigrated to Canada.

Ontario and BC have traditionally attracted the largest numbers of Finnish immigrants. The 1981 census lists 33 395 Finnish Canadians in Ontario (63.8% of the national total) and 10 810 in BC (20.7%). Finns settled as pioneers in Thunder Bay, Sault Ste Marie, Sudbury, Kirkland Lake and Timmins, Ont. Before WWI some Finns settled in Toronto and their population there increased after WWII. Small Finnish communities were also established in Windsor, Hamilton and St Catharines, Ont, in the 1950s. There has been an active Finnish community in Montréal since the 1920s, but few settled elsewhere in Québec. Some small rural Finnish communities were established in Alberta and Saskatchewan.

Economic Life Many of the first Finnish settlers worked on the construction of the CPR. Later, jobs were found in mining and lumbering. Many of these early Finnish immigrants worked in industry and then settled on small farms outside these urban centres. This was particularly the pattern in northern Ontario. Many single women arrived in Canada to work in DOMESTIC SERVICE.

It was not until after WWII that children of Finnish farmers left the farms for jobs in industry. Finnish immigrants arriving in Canada in the 1950s settled immediately in the urban centres, where some established businesses and moved into the professions.

Social Life and Community Finns established temperance societies, sports clubs, churches, and clubs for dances, drama, choirs, bands, and folk dancing, to meet their community and cultural needs. Many of the Finns of the pre-1930 period were of working age and spoke only Finnish; consequently, there was a very real need for these social activities and a close bond linked the members. Today a number of senior citizens' homes for Finnish Canadians are being established.

The Finnish Organization of Canada, est 1911 (originally the Finnish Socialist Organization of Canada), is the oldest Canadian nationwide cultural organization for Finns. The prolabour activism of some of its leaders in the 1920s and 1930s occasionally brought it into confrontation with the Canadian authorities and caused some dissension within the Finnish community itself. Today the few remaining FOC locals provide activities for their members, who are mainly senior citizens.

In 1940, a number of Lutheran churches and non-FOC clubs organized the first of the Finnish Grand Festivals that was held to raise funds for Finland during WWII. These festivals, featuring track and field, gymnastics, folk dancing, choirs, drama, and a wide range of social activities, have continued as an annual summer event. The Finnish Canadian Cultural Federation (with some 40 member groups) was founded in 1971 to undertake the activities of the Grand Festival and to serve as a nationwide organization to promote Finnish culture.

Religion and Cultural Life Most of the Finns in Canada are Lutherans, although only a minority participate actively in the Lutheran churches. Finnish Lutheran congregations have been established in Montréal, Toronto, Timmins, Sudbury, Sault Ste Marie, Thunder Bay and Vancouver. Some Finns support the United Church, others the Finnish Pentecostal Church, which has a number of active Finnish-language congregations, primarily in Ontario.

Several significant Finnish-language newspapers were founded in Canada, eg, the independent *Vapaa Sana* (1931), published in Toronto, the leftist *Vapaus* published in Sudbury from 1917 to 1975; and the independent *Canadian Uutiset* published in Thunder Bay since 1915. However, since few Finnish immigrants have arrived in Canada since 1960, the readership of the Finnish-language press in Canada will probably decline.

Education The children of Finnish immigrants adapted readily to the Canadian educational system, but the GREAT DEPRESSION prevented many from moving up the social scale. The children of many of the earlier Finnish immigrants who settled in the rural areas of northern Ontario retained the Finnish language and customs. In the 1970s, as a result of a growing cultural consciousness and support from government agencies, a number of Finnish-language schools were established.

Politics Many Finns played a leading role in the Canadian labour movement and in the establishment of co-operatives; during the 1930s some FOC leaders were prosecuted by the authorities for supporting communism. A large number of Finns within the FOC at this time opposed this activism and broke away.

Electoral data indicates that, for many years, a large number of Finns in northern Ontario supported the CO-OPERATIVE COMMONWEALTH FEDERATION in elections. Today the political support of the Finnish Canadian voter tends to be based on social status rather than on any ethnic factors. Each of the 3 main political parties has nominated Finnish Canadians in recent federal and provincial elections. In 1980, Judy Erola, a descendant of one of the original Finnish settlers of Sudbury, was named to the federal Liberal Cabinet. LENNARD SILLANPAA

Balsam fir (*Abies balsamea*), with male cones (left) and female cones (right) (*artwork by Claire Tremblay*).

Fir, Scandinavian for "pine," designates the "true" firs, ie, evergreen CONIFERS (genus *Abies*) of pine family (Pinaceae). About 50 species occur worldwide, all in the Northern Hemisphere; 4 are native to Canada. Balsam fir (*A. balsamea*) occurs from Alberta to the Atlantic provinces. Alpine fir (*A. lasiocarpa*) grows at high elevations in the West, from Alaska to Mexico. Pacific silver fir (*A. amabilis*) and grand fir (*A. grandis*) grow along the BC, Washington and Oregon coasts. Three introduced species (white, shasta and Spanish firs) are planted as ORNAMENTALS. Firs are stately trees with single, straight trunks and narrow, pyramidal crowns. Branches are regularly whorled; leaves are flat and needlelike. Cones are erect and usually restricted to upper branches. POLLINATION occurs in spring; seeds are mature in fall. The bracts (modified leaves) and scales (ovule-bearing structures) are shed from the cone axis with the winged seeds. The relatively light, soft, weak wood is used extensively for pulp, paper and lumber. JOHN N. OWENS

Firearm It is not known exactly when or where firearms were invented, but cannons that could fire a ball of stone or iron were sufficiently well developed to be used in the siege of Trent (1278). Firearms are mentioned frequently in literature, but the earliest datable illustration yet found dates to 1326. Most early guns were muzzle loading; ie, the powder was put into the breech from the muzzle and a ball was put on top of it. A red-hot wire was used to ignite a small "train" of powder leading, through a vent at the breech, to the main charge. The burning powder produced a tremendous amount of gas, which propelled the ball out of the barrel and towards the target.

The early development of firearms was very slow. "Hand cannons" light enough to be carried by one man were produced but the method of firing did not change for about 100 years. About 1400 a mechanical device, consisting of a lighted wick of twisted hemp that could be drawn by means of a lever into a pan at the breech, was invented. The result was the first self-contained small arm, the matchlock musket. When Sir Humphrey GILBERT landed in Newfoundland in 1583, his ship was armed with cannon and some of his men carried matchlock muskets.

In the late 15th century a wheellock mechanism, which used a stone (iron pyrite) rubbed against a revolving steel wheel to produce a spark, was invented in Italy. The spark ignited the priming powder to discharge the gun. News of this improvement moved slowly through Europe. The device was expensive and, although it was made in large quantities for hunting by the nobility, it did not become a "general issue" military arm. When Pierre du Gua de MONTS and Samuel de CHAMPLAIN were outfitting their expeditions to inhabit Canada, they brought with them cannons and matchlock muskets. By 1619 there were also at least 2 of the expensive wheel locks in the habitation at Québec, along with 3 small cannons and 6 breech-loading swivel guns.

About the time Champlain was establishing Québec (1608), a French gunsmith of the Le Bourgeoys family was perfecting an inexpensive, efficient lock mechanism. The flintlock, as it was known, positioned a piece of flint in the jaws of a vice or "cock" powered by a strong "V" spring. When the trigger was pulled, the cock fell forward; the flint struck a steel plate (battery); the sparks produced fell into a small pan of priming powder, and this igniting the main charge. The flintlock rapidly became the most common and best form of firearm available. It was rapidly adopted by the settlers of America and quickly found its way into the hands of the Indians. Gunsmiths and gunmakers in Canada copied designs originating in France or England and supplied a small portion of the local requirement, although most guns were imported by the trading companies or merchants.

In the 200 years which followed Le Bourgeoys's invention, many improvements were made to the flintlock, but it remained fundamentally unchanged until its replacement in the first half of the 19th century. In 1807 Alexander Forsyth, a Scottish clergyman, patented a lock that used a small amount of fulminate to ignite the main charge. This development quickly led to the invention of the percussion cap (about 1818), the separate primed paper or metallic cartridge (about 1821) and the self-contained cartridge (about 1826). Canadian gunmakers quickly adopted these innovations and developed improvements of their own. The first guns yet found that are known to have been made in Canada date from the 1830s. William Gurd of York [Toronto] made guns having locks converted from flintlocks. The markings on the pistols and rifles made by J. Woods of Brantford indicate that he was the proprietor of a "Rifle Factory" prior to 1840.

The greatest difficulty in perfecting a breech-loading gun was preventing the escape of gas through the breech. This problem was resolved by invention of a thin-walled metallic cartridge that expanded to produce a seal and then contracted, after the gas had left the barrel, to allow removal of the cartridge case. Development of the cartridge took place mainly in the US, Britain and France. Dudley Booth of Ottawa invented an unsuccessful breech loader and its cartridge in 1867, and several other Canadians obtained patents for breech-loading guns in the period 1850-80. A few of these obtained some local acceptance, but none achieved national recognition.

Most of the firearms used in Canada were imported from England or the US: fine shotguns from Britain, rifles from the US, pistols and revolvers from both countries. Arms having serial numbers under 100, by all major US makers, have been found in Canada. In 1866 Smith and Wesson, the large revolver manufacturers of Springfield, Mass, first advertised in the Oshawa, Ont, *Vindicator*.

Military weapons were supplied in large quantities from England. Canada was usually used as a proving ground for cold-weather trials of most new weapons, and many were not produced because of the experience gained. The first shipment of Snider-Enfield breech-loading rifles was sent to Canada in 1866, when threats of a FENIAN invasion from the US were prevalent. Smaller quantities of American-made weapons were purchased for Canadian militia use. In 1855-56, 800 Colt Navy Model-1851 revolvers were purchased for the militia cavalry of Upper and Lower Canada. These are easily recognized by the company markings and numbers on the grips. In the 1860s a quantity of Spencer repeating rifles and carbines was purchased along with those of other manufacturers. In 1885 the NORTH-WEST MOUNTED POLICE placed the first of many orders for Winchester Model 1876 carbines. In the same year the Colt Repeating Arms Co lent Canada 2 Gatling guns, under the command of A.L. Howard of the Connecticut National Guard, for use in the NORTH-WEST REBELLION. Howard remained in Canada to establish the Dominion Cartridge Co at Brownsburg, Qué.

At the same time, Canadian gunmakers were supplying fine-quality target rifles to the militia and sporting rifles to farmers, hunters and sportsmen. The skills of some gunmakers were as good as any in the world, and the accuracy of their rifles was equal to that of the finest English makers. James Paris Lee came to Canada as a youngster from Scotland and was educated in Galt [Cambridge, Ont]. He was trained as a jeweller and set up business in Chatham (Canada W) in 1850. Lee later moved to Janesville, Wis, where he developed a number of firearm designs, one of which was the bolt-action rifle, which later became the basis of the Lee-Enfield rifle, manufactured for Commonwealth troops until 1950. The Lee-Enfield rifle was used by Canadian troops through 2 world wars.

About 1900, Sir Charles Ross, the designer of a bolt-action rifle, which was being made for him in the US, moved to Canada and interested the Canadian government in his design. A factory was established at Québec City, and the first shipment of Canadian-made Ross rifles was turned over to the government in 1905. The Ross went through many variations until it was replaced by the Lee-Enfield rifle during WWI.

Beginning in the mid-1860s, the demand for custom-made guns was slowly replaced by that for machine-made repeating rifles, most of which could be more economically made in the US. Nevertheless a few excellent gunmakers have continued to work in Canada. Although very few of them have made much money, they have continued a tradition by making fine rifles to meet the requirements of Canadian sportsmen.
S. JAMES GOODING

Fireweed, common name for *Epilobium angustifolium*, a member of a genus of herbaceous or shrubby PLANTS of the evening primrose family (Onagraceae). Roughly 160 species of *Epilobium* (willow herbs) are found throughout temperate regions; 12 are native to Canada. Willow herbs have alternate or opposed leaves, and regular or slightly irregular flowers. The calyx forms a 4-part tube; the flower has 4 petals. Eight stamens surround the compound ovary; the fruit is a long, narrow capsule. Seeds are numerous and tufted at the top. The Yukon Territory adopted fireweed as its floral emblem in 1957. The flowers are arranged in an elongated cluster, situated terminally on a stem 50-200 cm long with alternate, spear-shaped leaves. The large purple, magenta or occasionally white flowers blossom from the bottom up. This species propagates quickly after forest fires (hence the name). Because it tends to overrun the area where it grows, fireweed should be grown in dry, poorish soil. It may be grown from seeds, shoots or root cuttings. *See* PROVINCIAL FLORAL EMBLEMS.
CÉLINE ARSENEAULT

First Canadian Army was an army of some 170 000 men organized in 2 corps (5 divisions and 2 armoured brigades) formed overseas in 1942 under Lt-Gen A.G.L. MCNAUGHTON. McNaughton's aim was to keep the Canadian Army together to lead the cross-channel assault on NW Europe; instead, the Canadian government dispatched I Canadian Corps from McNaughton's command to serve in the Italian campaign in 1943 so that Canadian troops could see action. Because the existence of an identifiably Canadian army was important at home, Allied formations were added to First Canadian Army to keep it up to strength. Accordingly, when First Canadian Army (now commanded by Lt-Gen H.D.G. CRERAR) went into battle on the left flank in France, Belgium, and Holland, clearing the Channel coast after the NORMANDY INVASION, it had more Allied than Canadian troops. The balance was redressed in Mar 1945 following the Rhineland campaign, when the Canadians in Italy rejoined First Canadian Army for the LIBERATION OF HOLLAND. *See* WORLD WAR II.
STEPHEN HARRIS

First Ministers' Conference, *see* FEDERAL-PROVINCIAL RELATIONS.

Fiscal Policy, the use of government taxing and spending powers to achieve economic goals especially full employment, growth, stable prices, and alleviation of sharp fluctuations in the business cycle. The total expenditures by individuals and government, plus what foreigners buy from Canada and minus what Canadians spend on foreign goods, come back to individuals, businesses and government as wages, profits and other forms of income and tax revenues. If private expenditures fall, government might prevent total demand for goods and services and so total income from falling by increasing expenditure or reducing taxes. When a government's revenues exceed its expenditures (a surplus) the economy tends to contract. If expenditures exceed revenues (a deficit), incomes, output and employment will tend to expand and prices to rise.

Neither fiscal policy nor the combination of fiscal and MONETARY POLICIES has stabilized the Canadian economy. Economic growth has been very poor since the 1970s; unemployment has been high and inflation rose until 1981. Canada's international payments position has worsened and the deficits of the federal and some provincial governments have reached record highs. There has been a loss of confidence in government's ability to manage the economy, and controversy about proper policy directions is greater than it has been since the 1930s.

Government of Canada Revenues and Expenditures, National Accounts Basis

	1980-81	1981-82	1982-83	1983-84	1984-85	1985-86
			(Millions$)			
Revenues:						
Direct taxes, persons	24 530	29 965	34 045	40 770	45 800	50 985
Direct taxes, corporations	8 390	10 945	15 060	17 350	19 370	21 925
Direct taxes, nonresidents	923	980	1 065	1 155	1 265	1 375
Indirect taxes	13 302	20 495	22 290	23 900	25 420	26 990
Other current transfers from persons	20	25	25	25	25	25
Investment income	4 873	5 900	6 845	7 690	8 710	9 615
Capital consumption allowances	800	895	1 000	1 105	1 225	1 350
Total	52 847	69 205	80 330	91 995	101 815	112 265
Expenditures:						
Current goods and services	14 336	16 130	18 050	20 190	22 415	24 860
Transfer payments to persons	17 245	19 875	22 740	25 425	28 745	31 580
Subsidies	5 547	7 950	9 575	10 875	11 620	12 735
Capital assistance	655	1 335	2 435	3 145	3 515	3 890
Current transfers to nonresidents	778	900	1 250	1 400	1 600	1 850
Public Debt interest	10 499	14 535	16 575	17 830	19 135	20 095
Transfers to other levels of government	12 876	14 770	15 120	16 795	18 950	20 840
Gross capital formation	775	1 070	1 145	1 275	1 365	1 445
Total	62 711	76 565	86 890	96 935	107 345	117 295
Surplus or deficit (-)	-9 864	-7 360	-6 560	-4 490	-5 530	-5 030

The BUDGETARY PROCESS itself has been improved through a new expenditure-management system (1979) and the budget consultation process reformed to include the appointment of a committee of outside experts to examine proposed tax changes. Co-ordination of fiscal policy changes between the federal and provincial governments continues to be somewhat weak although federal and provincial finance ministers have met regularly. But even when policy direction seemed clear to many economists, governments have been restricted in their actions or in their explanations of budgets by public opinion.

PETER M. CORNELL

Fish, member of a large, heterogeneous group of VERTEBRATES, living in a wide variety of aquatic habitats. There are slightly more species of fish than of all other vertebrates combined. They include jawless species (Agnatha), such as hagfishes and lampreys, and species with jaws (Pisces). The vast majority of the latter are fishes with cartilaginous skeletons (Chondrichthyes), eg, sharks and rays, or with bony skeletons (Osteichthyes), eg, salmon, perch and flatfishes. The term "fish" is used by some ichthyologists (zoologists studying them) in a more restricted sense than that used here. Some would include only forms with jaws. A few would include only the Osteichthyes, the largest and most diverse class of vertebrates. As the term is used here, fishes may be defined as cold-blooded vertebrates with gills throughout life, and limbs, if any, in the shape of fins. Most have scales and paired fins; however, many unrelated groups lack scales (eg, lampreys, bullhead catfishes), or one or both of the paired fins (eg, lampreys, eels, sand lances).

Body Covering Sharks and rays have placoid scales resembling tiny teeth. Most species of bony fishes with scales have either cycloid scales (smooth bordered) or ctenoid scales (rough bordered). Teleosts, the largest and most evolutionarily advanced group of bony fishes, display both forms of true scale: cycloid scales characterize relatively primitive teleosts (eg, salmon, minnows); ctenoid scales characterize advanced teleosts (eg, perch, sunfishes). Generally, fishes with cycloid scales have pelvic fins in the midportion of their bodies and lack spines in the fins; those with ctenoid scales have pelvic fins beneath the pectoral fin and have spines in some of their fins. Although frequently used to tell a fish's age, scales are not always reliable; certain bones in the head may be more accurate.

Buoyancy and Respiration Most bony fishes possess a swim or air bladder which helps them attain neutral buoyancy in water. Many bottom fishes lack the bladder, enabling them to stay on the bottom, even in relatively fast streams, with minimum energy expenditure. Some species (eg, longnose dace) can change bladder volume over relatively short periods of time, increasing it when in a lake, decreasing it in a river. Although a few fishes have lungs or other organs for breathing air, all fishes possess gills. In Canada, fishes are virtually always confined to water for respiration, but elsewhere there are species that can breathe in the atmosphere and even make short journeys onto land.

Form and Colour Fishes exhibit a wide variety of shapes, sizes and colours. They range from highly elongate, almost stringlike, to globular in form. They can look like a lumpy rock, a leaf or a snake. Most have a tapering, variably compressed body with smooth contours, a torpedo-like shape exemplified by trout. Fishes range in size from a whale shark, exceeding 15 m, to a tiny, 8 mm goby. In Canadian waters, the smallest fishes (eg, some minnows, darters, sculpins) may not exceed 10 cm; those over 3 m include Atlantic sturgeon and bluefin tuna; several may even exceed 5 m (eg, white sturgeon and thresher, white and basking sharks). Fishes are highly variable in colour. In the tropics, many brilliantly coloured freshwater and marine fishes occur, but those in Canadian waters, as in other northern areas, are generally drab. There are some exceptions, however, and males of several species can develop bright colours at spawning time (eg, arctic char, sockeye salmon, northern redbelly dace, longnose sucker, some darters). There tends to be more variation in colour among populations of the same species of northern freshwater fishes than among tropical fishes. The marked colour variations of rainbow trout or northern pike have convinced some anglers that there are different species of these fishes in different localities.

Nutrition Fish consume a wide variety of foods. Northern fishes have more generalized feeding habits than do tropical fishes, tending to eat what is available. Most species are carnivorous; some are herbivorous, usually consuming ALGAE. The latter tend to have longer intestines. Many species are primarily bottom feeders (eg, sturgeons, suckers); others feed on PLANKTON in open water (eg, herring, cisco). Piscivorous fishes (eg, northern pike) feed primarily on other fishes. Insects and crustaceans are generally the most important diet items for nonpiscivorous, freshwater species in Canadian waters. The lamprey is the only parasitic northern fish; adults of many species feed on the blood of other fishes.

Reproduction Reproductive habits vary greatly. Chondrichthyes have internal fertilization; most Osteichthyes have external fertilization. In Canadian waters, most Osteichthyes have distinct spawning seasons. Eggs laid in fresh water by fall-spawning fish generally hatch in spring; those laid in summer hatch in a few days or weeks. Some (eg, sticklebacks, sunfish) build nests in which eggs are deposited and sometimes guarded. Herring and cod abandon their eggs after spawning. Individuals of most species can spawn for several years but lampreys and Pacific salmon spawn once and die. Many species migrate great distances to reach spawning grounds. One of the longest migrations is made by chinook salmon, which swim, without feeding, for about 2800 km up the Yukon R.

Habitat In both marine and fresh water, various species can be characterized as bottom dwelling (benthic, these are the "groundfishes" of commercial FISHERIES) or open water (ie, pelagic in oceans, limnetic in lakes). Littoral zone fishes are inshore and, in the oceans, may occur in tide pools. In the Arctic Ocean and High Arctic lakes, fish may spend most of their lives under ice. There the marine waters can be superchilled, colder than -1°C.

Freshwater habitats of fishes are diverse, including hot springs, cold torrential mountain streams, deep lakes and saline waters. In the Cave and Basin Hot Springs drainage system near Banff, Alta, a form of longnose dace, normally found in cold lakes and streams, lives in temperatures up to 26°C and in close proximity to introduced, tropical aquarium fishes (eg, sailfin molly and mosquito-fish, which live in temperatures of up to 30°C and give birth to live young). In WOOD BUFFALO NATIONAL PARK, fishes live in sinkhole lakes, formed by the surface collapsing through dissolved-out bedrock. In some cases, they got to the small ponds by underground channels.

Evolution Fishes probably evolved from descendants of ECHINODERMS and in turn gave rise to AMPHIBIANS. Their origin dates back to about 500 million years ago. In Canada, there is an extensive FOSSIL record of fishes, including Agnatha, Chondrichthyes and Osteichthyes. Placoderms and acanthodians are 2 other large groups known only from the fossil record.

Canada has a diverse fauna of living species, including representatives of all classes. This fauna is rich in numbers of individuals, but not in numbers of species, especially when the vast amount of freshwater lakes and rivers and the extensive coastline are considered. There are about 22 000 recognized species of living fishes worldwide, in about 450 families; almost 40% of the species live in fresh water. D.E. McAllister, National Museum of Natural Science, Ottawa, has recently calculated numbers of native species in Canadian waters at about 950, in 190 families. Of this number, about 760 are confined to marine waters (Pacific, Arctic and Atlantic oceans). Several species are diadromous, ie, spend part of their life in the ocean and part in fresh water. Of these, some (Pacific salmon, many lampreys) are anadromous, spawning in fresh water, while the American eel of the Atlantic coast is catadromous, spawning in the ocean. The native species confined to fresh water (about 190) occur in drainages of the Pacific, Arctic, Hudson Bay, Atlantic and Gulf of Mexico. The Great Lakes and southern Ontario have the greatest number of species; YT, NWT, Alberta and Saskatchewan have relatively few, considering their area and extent of water.

The ICE AGES had a profound effect on Canada's fish fauna. Differences in species numbers across Canada can be explained by glacial events. Until about 15 000 years ago, most of Canada was covered by ice. A reinvasion of fishes occurred from ice-free areas (refugia), with most of our modern freshwater fish coming from the Mississippi-Missouri refugium. Most of British Columbia's species came from the Columbian R refugium; in other areas of Canada, the Yukon R and Atlantic coast refugia were important. As the ice sheet melted, species could cross from one DRAINAGE BASIN to another, eg, from the Columbia R to the Fraser R. Only fishes with some salt tolerance could reach offshore areas (eg, Newfoundland, Vancouver I).

More new species of fishes are described each year around the world than of any other vertebrate group. It is unlikely that many species new to science will be found in Canadian waters (although range extensions may continue to be found). Few species appear to be confined to Canadian waters. A species of whitefish (*Coregonus canadensis*), confined to part of NS, has been described, but its existence may be threatened by ACID RAIN. Although biologists in provincial and federal government agencies, universities and consulting companies are involved in fish studies, many gaps remain in our knowledge. Collecting trips often reveal a species not previously recorded in a particular province or even in Canada, particularly off the Pacific coast. The observant fisherman, interested in identifying his catch, can provide valuable distributional records. Important gaps also exist in our knowledge of the life history of many commercially important species (eg, very little is known about habitats of larval herring and lake whitefish). *See also:* ATLANTIC SALMON; BASS; CATFISH; CHAR; CHIMAERA; COD; EEL; FLATFISH; GAR; GRAYLING; HAGFISH; HERRING; LAMPREY; MACKEREL; MINNOW; MUSKELLUNGE; PACIFIC SALMON; PERCH; PICKEREL; PIKE; RAY; SALMON; SCORPION FISH; SCULPIN; SHARK; SMELT; SPORTFISHING; STICKLEBACK; STURGEON; SUCKER; TROUT; TUNA; WHITEFISH. JOSEPH S. NELSON

Reading: J.L. Hart, *Pacific Fishes of Canada* (1973); A.H. Leim and W.B. Scott, *Fishes of the Atlantic Coast of Canada* (1966); W.B. Scott and E.J. Crossman, *Freshwater Fishes of Canada* (1973).

Fish Classification There is no single, accepted classification system for fishes, and there are more disagreements among ichthyologists about the interrelationships of fishes than exist among other vertebrate systematists about their groups. This results, in part, from our relatively poor knowledge but also from differing approaches to classification, which are not necessarily the result of differing views on evolutionary relationships. Many ichthyologists have adopted a relatively new method, cladistics, that classifies strictly according to the recency of common descent. Others use the more conventional approach, evolutionary or synthetic systematics, where the inferred amount of divergence among groups is considered, as is the history of their evolutionary relationships (phylogeny). These perspectives can result in markedly different classifications. For example, in a cladistic system, HAGFISHES probably would be placed in a category separate from LAMPREYS and other vertebrates because, relative to hagfishes, lampreys are thought to share a common genealogical branching point with all other vertebrates. Systematists using the evolutionary approach could express the relationship in several ways but would tend to place hagfishes and lampreys in the single category of jawless fishes, separate from all jawed vertebrates, although recognizing that they are very distantly related. Cladists may use terms in ways that differ significantly from classical usage: eg, cladists would include all evolutionary derivatives of Osteichthyes within that category and, therefore, would consider the tetrapods (including mammals) as Osteichthyes. Differences may also exist among classification systems depending on whether the worker is a "lumper" or a "splitter." A lumper constructs a classification with categories containing more groups than that of a splitter. There are no rules for the amount of difference necessary to designate various categories. A lumper recognizes one family for salmon, whitefish and grayling; a splitter, 2 or 3 families. JOSEPH S. NELSON

Fish Creek, some 65 km SW of Prince Albert, Sask, scene of battle, 24 Apr 1885, during the NORTH-WEST REBELLION. As half of Maj-Gen Frederick MIDDLETON's forces moved towards BATOCHE, they were attacked by Métis and Indians entrenched along the high banks of Fish Creek. Gabriel DUMONT, Métis commander, had hoped to surprise the Canadian soldiers as they crossed the stream. The element of surprise was lost, however, when Middleton's men discovered still-fresh campfires near the crossing. After several hours of fighting, the battle ended in a stalemate. Dumont's men sensed a moral victory: they had resisted an enemy armed with artillery and inflicted significant injury. Of Middleton's 350 men, 55 casualties included 6 dead. The Métis and Indians lost 4 men and left behind over 50 dying horses. A cairn now marks the site. WALTER HILDEBRANDT

Fisher (*Martes pennanti*), cat-sized MARTEN with relatively short legs, long tapering tail, and feet clawed for climbing. Its heavy pelage includes a dense grey underfur overlain by brown, silver-banded guard hairs. Females have finer, more lustrous fur than males. Males may reach 100 cm in length and 7 kg in weight; females seldom exceed 90 cm and 2.7 kg. Fishers are a forest species, formerly distributed from coast to coast, N to lat 65°. They were exterminated S of the St Lawrence R, but have been reintroduced to NS and NB. Food is mainly hares, squirrels and mice, but porcupines are regularly killed and other species, as available. Fishers are generally solitary except for the female and her young. Mating is polygamous, during Mar-Apr. The gestation period is about 350 days because of delayed implantation. The young (1-4) are born in Mar. Sexual maturity is reached in 2 years. Fishers are among the most valuable Canadian furbearing animals but are not abundant and only 6000-9000 furs are marketed annually. *See* FUR TRAPPING. IAN MCTAGGART COWAN

Fisher, Charles, lawyer, politician, judge, premier of NB (b at Fredericton 15 Aug or 16 Sept 1808; d there 8 Dec 1880). He led the first RESPONSIBLE GOVERNMENT in NB (1854-1861) and was the leading constitutional lawyer of his day. He was educated at King's College (UNB) and was elected to the Assembly in 1837. A somewhat tardy convert to responsible government because he considered Newbrunswickers "too loyal and too ignorant" to reject the the ruling clique, he served on the compact Council 1848-50 before leading the Opposition to power as attorney general in 1854. His Cabinet, perhaps the province's most talented, then implemented its administrative, electoral and educational reforms. Ousted by S.L. TILLEY as premier in 1861 over a crown land scandal, Fisher later joined with Tilley as a FATHER OF CONFEDERATION at the QUEBEC CONFERENCE and LONDON CONFERENCE. Elected to the Canadian House of Commons in 1867, Fisher resigned when he was appointed a judge of New Brunswick's Supreme Court (3 Oct 1868) where he served conscientiously. CARL M. WALLACE

Fisher, Gordon Neil, publisher (b at Montréal 9 Dec 1928). Fisher is president of Southam Inc, one of the largest newspaper chains in Canada. He attended Lower Canada Coll, Trinity Coll School and McGill, where he studied engineering. At Southam, as president and director, he has played an important role in keeping the firm's interests diversified into radio, TV, print and other areas. J.L. GRANATSTEIN

Fisher, Hugh, canoeist (b in New Zealand 1 Oct 1955). He finished first in the K-2 500 m and K-4 500 m events at the 1976 national championships and was 1979 and 1980 outrigger world champion. He missed the 1981 season because of injury but had a second-place finish (K-2 1000 m, time 3:37.45) at the 1982 world championships, a third-place finish at the 1983 world championships (K-2 500 m, 1:49.58) and a second (K-2 500 m) and third (K-2 1000 m) at the Brandenburg Regatta in 1984. With Alwyn MORRIS he won a gold medal in the K-2 1000 m (3:24.22) and bronze in the K-2 500 m (1:35.41) at the 1984 Los Angeles Olympics. He was in 1984 a medical student at UBC. JAMES MARSH

Hugh Fisher and Alwyn Morris in action at the 1984 Los Angeles Olympics, at which they won a gold medal (*courtesy Athlete Information Bureau/Service Information-Athlètes*).

Fisheries In 1980 Canada's commercial fisheries contributed slightly over $1 billion to the national economy (less than 1% of the value of all commodity-producing industries). However, in some regions, the industry is pre-eminent. In the Atlantic provinces, it contributed $655.3 million in 1980, over 12% of the value of all commodity-producing industries in the region. Along the Atlantic coast, about 1000 communities are mostly or wholly dependent upon the fisheries. Lesser numbers of such communities are found on the Pacific coast and around the lakes of the interior. Most are hamlets with less than 500 people, but the industry also supports larger urban centres in all 3 regions. The fisheries of BC, NS and Newfoundland are of greatest significance. BC's is usually the leader in value of production. In the Atlantic provinces, Newfoundland leads in volume and NS in value of production; together they account for 80% of Atlantic output. The fisheries also have a strong regional impact through links with suppliers of goods and services, especially the SHIPBUILDING industry but also ancillary shipyards, chandlers, etc. These links, plus the interaction between fishermen's households and the local community, mean that economic changes in the fishing industry are transmitted and multiplied through the general economy; for example, in NS a 1% change in fishery production causes a 1.4% change in total provincial income.

The industry has many part-time fishermen: half of the fishermen registered in the Atlantic region, two-thirds of those in the Pacific region and three-quarters of those in the central region receive their main income from sources other than fishing. Some of these people depend on fishing to augment other income; others participate because of culture or family tradition and are often strongly attached to their identity as fishermen.

Those who claim fishing as their principal source of income derive about 65% of total income from it. In the Pacific and central regions, the balance comes mainly from nonfishing activities; in the Atlantic region the major income supplement is unemployment insurance benefits to which self-employed fishermen (owner/operators) and crewmen are entitled. In all regions, the typical net annual income from all sources is $5000-10 000 (fishermen in the Pacific region are near the top of the range; those in the central region near the bottom; those in the Atlantic region in the middle). The evidence suggests that most fishing enterprises at present are incapable not only of generating surplus revenue for capital accumulation and investment but even of providing adequate personal incomes.

Herring fishing on Deer Island, NB, using weirs and seines (*courtesy New Brunswick Tourism*).

Resource Base Fishery resources are classified as finfish (including major marine species and all commonly used freshwater species) and shellfish (CRUSTACEANS and MOLLUSCS). Aquatic mammals and SEAWEEDS also are considered fishery resources. Marine species are classified as littoral or inshore (found within the 50-60 fathom contour adjacent to the coastline); demersal (dwelling near the seafloor, chiefly on offshore banks); and pelagic (found near the surface on the open sea). Littoral stocks include crustaceans (LOBSTER and certain CRAB species) and molluscs (most CLAM species and OYSTERS). Major demersal stocks include some crustaceans (crabs), a mollusc (SCALLOP) and a great variety of finfish (eg, COD, FLATFISHES, rockfishes). The important pelagic species are all finfish (eg, HERRING, TUNA), except for one mollusc, the common SQUID.

Certain species — eg, redfish (ocean perch), which combine demersal and pelagic features — elude this classification. Others, particularly the anadromous species that swim upstream to spawn (eg, SALMONS), must be classified separately. Because of their dependence on watershed and estuarine habitats, anadromous species are, along with the relatively immobile littoral species, most vulnerable to environmental damage. Demersal species and the larger or predator pelagic species are relatively long lived and subject to low natural mortality. Stocks tend to be relatively stable, eg, the year-to-year variation in the Atlantic cod catch averages about 10%, compared with about a 30% variation in the PACIFIC SALMON catch. The smaller or forage pelagic species feed on PLANKTON and, being located at a low trophic level, generally occur in relative abundance. Because of high mortality in the younger stages, these stocks fluctuate widely, some (eg, common squid) in the short term and others (eg, some herring stocks) over the long term. A fish community as a whole has far greater stability than the many individual species it contains.

Stocks of most pelagic species have a regular seasonal north-south MIGRATION pattern, sometimes over long distances. Some of these species, as well as anadromous and certain demersal species, also exhibit a seasonal inshore-offshore migration. The presence inshore of these stocks and of sedentary littoral stocks provides the basis for various small-boat fisheries. Operations on the offshore fishing grounds are based on schools (ie, feeding and spawning concentrations of demersal and pelagic stocks) and involve larger craft.

Canada has abundant fishery resources on the Atlantic and Pacific coasts and in inland waters but, while renewable, they are limited and exhaustible. Stock restoration and enhancement projections indicate that, even with full use of all available species stocks, the total yield or nominal catch is unlikely to exceed 2.5 million t annually, ie, somewhat less than twice the present level. This amount would be only 3.5% of the annual world catch, which appears to have reached a limit at 70-75 million t.

Resource Harvesting A peculiarity of fishery resources is that typically they are common property, ie, under the "rule of capture," and fish in a wild stock become the private property of a fishing enterprise only when caught and removed from the water. Each such enterprise therefore tries to maximize its share of a harvest limited by nature or regulation. The results are large fleets, high production costs, increased wastage and spoilage, and idle periods for vessels and handling/processing facilities. Because of mounting pressure to circumvent and subvert CONSERVATION measures, fish stocks are jeopardized.

Most Canadian enterprises are individually owned and operated; partnerships are common in some fisheries and there are influential producers' co-operatives on both coasts and in the inland fisheries. Native bands run communal enterprises in certain areas. Vertical integration (ie, ownership by corporations involved in fish processing) is predominant in the Atlantic trawling and scallop-dragging fleets and, although declining in importance, still occurs in the Pacific purse-seining fleet and elsewhere. Remuneration is generally made on the basis of shares in the proceeds of the catch. Typically the owner receives a fixed percentage as the "boat's" share and deductions are made to cover certain expenses and, in larger operations, officers' bonuses; the balance is then divided equally among the crew. Sharing ("lay") formulae vary with the scale of the operation; the owner's share in the Pacific purse-seining fleet is about 35%; in the Atlantic trawler fleet, 60%. With the unionization of crews, such arrangements are subject to bargaining and modification (eg, to provide a basic rate of pay, regardless of the success of the trip).

A distinction is often made between small-scale and large-scale (ie, industrial) fishing enterprises, usually called "inshore" and "offshore," respectively. Inshore craft, defined for administrative purposes as those under 25 gross tons, account for 95% of all vessels in the Canadian fleets but only 35% of the tonnage. The distinction, however, is an oversimplification: vessels of all sizes, except perhaps the smallest, fish the same grounds. More significant is the distinction between vessels with year-round versus seasonal operating capability and between those capable of versatile operation versus enforced specialization.

Nearly 95% of the Canadian fish harvest is converted to food products: 70-75% is fresh chilled or frozen; 15%, cured; 5%, canned; about 1%, roe. About 98% of the total is handled by the fish-processing industry, which doubles the value of the fish caught. Advanced processing (eg, canning, curing, filleting/freezing, etc) predominates in the industry. This is because of the need for storage (in view of the seasonal peaking of raw-material supplies) and because the products must be transported over long distances; it is also a response to the increasing use of "convenience" foods.

Processing companies range from small, usually specialized firms to large, integrated ones supplying a wide range of products. In the Pacific region, consolidation of operations around the major coastal centres has been accompanied by a massive concentration of ownership through mergers and acquisitions. In 1980 the 4 largest firms produced 60-65% of the regional output of frozen salmon and about 80% of canned salmon and herring roe. The central region is dominated in the West by the FFMC, which handles about half the region's production, and in the Great Lakes area by a private firm. Concentration has also occurred in the Atlantic region where about 60% of the regional output of groundfish products comes from the 4 largest firms (40% from the catch of their own fleets). With the Canadian Saltfish Corp, a crown trading company, these firms account for possibly 80-90% of the export trade in groundfish products. In the Atlantic region, this concentration has not been associated with consolidation of processing activity. On the contrary, as the traditional cottage industry declined, plant processing dispersed to replace it. In 1983 some 440 coastal communities had processing facilities, most of them being independently owned, but many also belonging to integrated companies and co-operatives. More critical, perhaps, is the fact that redundance in processing capacity causes an obsession with throughput and leads to counterproductive competition for raw material.

Marketing Although a significant part of total fish production is handled in the marketplace by specialized dealers, brokers and export/import houses, most is marketed by processing companies and co-operatives. Substantial quantities of some products (eg, canned salmon, frozen groundfish) are prepared for export under labels of foreign buyers. The Canadian market absorbs about one-third of the annual production, the proportion varying among products from virtually zero to 100%. Canned salmon probably is the major product for which the domestic market is the more important outlet; conversely, only 20% of Atlantic groundfish is consumed in Canada. When domestic sources are deficient, some products (eg, canned and frozen shrimp and tuna) are supplemented with imports (valued at $353.5 million in 1980), of which two-thirds are from the US.

The Canadian fish trade has always been strongly export oriented and is likely to remain so. By the end of the 1970s, Canada had become the world's foremost fish-exporting nation. But, by 1980, Canada commanded only a 7% share of international fish trade, about $1.1 billion (US) in a $15-billion (US) international market. Canadian exports go to many countries but are highly concentrated in the US, which takes 50-55% of the total, including most of the freshwater fish, chilled and frozen Atlantic groundfish, and lobster and scallops; western Europe (especially the European Economic Community) takes about one-quarter; Japan takes less than 10%. The EEC is the most important market for canned salmon and frozen herring; Japan is the major market for frozen salmon and almost an exclusive market for herring roe. Cured fish, chiefly salted and dried codfish, is exported mainly to Mediterranean and Caribbean countries; canned herring products are exported worldwide.

Institutional Aspects The 2 large fishermen's unions at present, in BC and Newfoundland, comprise fish-plant workers and some vessel owners as well as crewmen — groups with partially conflicting economic interests. Otherwise, fishermen on the Pacific coast, in inland waters and on the Atlantic coast outside Newfoundland are generally organized into associations based on a particular fishery, gear type or other special interest. In the Maritimes, many of these associations are linked by an umbrella federation. Unlike unions, which negotiate with buyers, mainly over fish prices, associations tend to represent members to the government on matters of fishery regulation. In addition, fishermen's co-operatives which embrace processing and marketing as well as fish-harvesting operations operate in BC, Saskatchewan, Québec and the Maritimes. Co-operatives and private firms in the processing and marketing divisions of commercial fisheries support associations representing the interests of those divisions. These associations, organized provincially, are federated in the Fisheries Council of Canada in Ottawa, the principal channel of communication between the industry and the federal government.

The federal government has exclusive jurisdiction over fishing operations and over interprovincial and export trade in fishery products. The port market and fish handling and processing come under provincial jurisdiction. Subject to federal approval of regulations, management authority has been delegated to Ontario and the Prairie provinces for commercial freshwater fisheries and to Québec for littoral marine fisheries. All provincial governments and various federal agencies are active in fishery development activities; co-ordination of policy is sought, with mixed success, through a number of formal and *ad hoc* arrangements. The federal powers are exercised through the Department of Fisheries and Oceans and through certain special agencies which report directly to the minister of fisheries. The national headquarters are in Ottawa; regional administrative headquarters are located in Vancouver, Winnipeg, Moncton, NB; Halifax and St John's. There are major research stations and laboratories at Nanaimo, BC; Winnipeg; Burlington, Ont; St Andrew's, NB; Dartmouth, NS; and St John's.

The basic statute administered by DFO is the Fisheries Act, under which regulations are made for fishery management, including the patrol of coastal waters, the protection of fish life in streams, etc. The Coastal Fisheries Protection Act empowers the government to control the conduct of foreign fishing vessels in Canadian ports and territorial waters, and the Fish Inspection Act provides for control of the quality of fishery products. Assistance programs and intervention in industrial trade and development fall under a group of statutes, eg, the Fisheries Development Act, the Fisheries Prices Support Act, the Freshwater Fish Marketing Act and the Canadian Saltfish Act. *See also* SEALING; WHALING.

W.C. MACKENZIE AND J. GOUGH

Fisheries History Canada's Atlantic fishery was the attraction that drew the first Europeans to the northern half of N America. Economist Harold INNIS and others have argued that the fishery encouraged the growth of the British, French and Dutch empires partly because of its value as a "nursery for seamen," but more because fishing, shipbuilding, shipping and trading economically reinforced one another. The fishery also encouraged the development of the N American colonies, and it still sustains large coastal and inland regions. The fishing industry has been complex, contradictory and varied, with a "boom and bust" economic nature. Its independent participants, who have traditionally faced hazards and hardships in the pursuit of the trade, in the 20th century have formed powerful unions and other organizations to protect themselves against loss and to lobby governments for improved conditions in the industry.

Beginnings: 1500-1750 Europeans, including the ENGLISH, French, SPANISH, PORTUGUESE and BASQUES, began fishing off Newfoundland in the 16th century. The plentiful, easy-to-catch COD was the most valuable commodity: dried or salted, it could be transported long distances and would keep for several months. Fleets of fishing boats were numerous, for they required little capital investment. Fishermen arrived in the spring and stayed until about September. They fished directly from the boats using hooks and lines.

By the late 16th century the English and French were the chief rivals. The English fishery, operated primarily by West Countrymen, was concentrated in semipermanent fishing stations in protected harbours on Newfoundland's SE coast. The captain of the first ship to arrive at a harbour became the FISHING ADMIRAL and governed the station. Fish were caught close to shore from small boats brought from England. The day's catch was unloaded directly onto a "stage" (wharf), where the fish were cleaned, split and lightly salted. They were then dried on "flakes" (open tables that allowed maximum circulation of air). This shore-based DRY FISHERY resulted in a "hard-cure" cod suitable for trade to distant markets, and it became the basis for England's territorial claims to Newfoundland.

By contrast, French fishermen from widely scattered ports fished off the GRAND BANKS and other banks (productive, relatively shallow areas off the coast). They had access to more salt than the English, and most French fishermen processed the catch aboard their ships. This GREEN FISHERY yielded a shorter-lived product more suited to home use than distance travel, but it allowed French fishermen to get the fish to markets faster than the English, and they could return to the banks more than once in a season. PLACENTIA, Nfld, served as French headquarters until the TREATY OF UTRECHT in 1713,

Drawing of a 16th-century Newfoundland fishing ship. The cod were so plentiful that they could be hauled in with baskets (*courtesy Public Archives of Canada/C-92348*).

when French territorial claims to Newfoundland and mainland Nova Scotia were lost. The French fishery then became dispersed, with fishermen using Cape Breton and temporary fishing stations on Newfoundland's N and W coast. Cape Breton was lost through the TREATY OF PARIS, 1763, but French fishermen were allowed continued use of Newfoundland's W coast (*see* FRENCH SHORE).

Meanwhile, a British fishery had developed in the Maritimes. Although SALMON received increasing attention, cod still dominated. In all Atlantic areas, settlers fished in small open boats from shore using single lines with hooks, like the Europeans. Some European fishing vessels gradually began to bring passengers who fished from small boats (*see* BYE-BOAT) and might return or might settle; some took aboard fish cured by settlers (who were called PLANTERS in Newfoundland). Some ships only brought trade goods and took away salt fish. By mid-18th century, the WHALE fishery around Newfoundland and the WALRUS fishery at the Magdalen Is had practically disappeared.

1750-1867 From the second half of the 18th century, a great schooner fleet developed in the Atlantic fishery. Schooners (fore-and-aft rigged vessels such as the BLUENOSE), in search of cod, halibut and haddock on banks, carried dories; fishermen would set out in these rowboats and bring fish back for splitting and salting on board the schooners. In Newfoundland a large schooner fleet fished the banks and the Labrador coast. LIVEYERS were permanent residents, "floaters" moved along the coast, and "stationers" set up fishing stations where they could cure fish ashore. Conception Bay schooners also developed a large SEAL fishery which became important in Newfoundland's growth.

The AMERICAN REVOLUTION and the Napoleonic Wars increased British dependence on northwestern Atlantic fish and lumber. The mutually reinforcing fisheries, lumbering and trade, all related to wooden vessels, brought vigour to the Atlantic economy, so that even today the period is considered a golden age. But most fishermen appear to have been poor: most operated small shore boats rather than schooners, and many, especially in the southern areas, alternated between fishing and the shipping trade. Southwestern Nova Scotia and New Brunswick's Bay of Fundy shore began to lead the Atlantic fishery. The region had a good lumber and trading base, a long ice-free fishing season, an abundance of fish, a good mix of species, a short coastline allowing some concentration of enterprise, nearby markets, and nearby alternative employment in the US. Although small enterprises dominated the southern areas, elsewhere large fish-curing and schooner-owning firms, such as St John's firms and the Robin interests in the Gulf of St Lawrence, controlled much of the fishery. In Newfoundland, smaller-scale local merchants and schooner owners made some gains.

New methods emerged in the 19th century. For example, fishermen had used the beach seine, which required points of land to help in the encirclement of fish with nets. The new purse seine, developed by American fishermen, operated in open water by surrounding surface-schooling fish with a net hanging down from a line of corks. The fishermen then tightened a purse line at the bottom of the net to enclose the fish in what looked like a floating bowl. As well, French fishermen started using bultows (now "longlines"), which were long "groundlines" anchored near or on the bottom with many short sections of hook and line. Instead of a single hook on the line, as before, hundreds could be used.

During this period the presence of American and French fleets fishing off the Maritimes and Newfoundland led to numerous incidents, as colonial authorities laboured to keep foreign vessels outside the 3-mile limit. By the CONVENTION OF 1818 New England fishermen could generally use BNA waters only for shelter and repair, and to purchase supplies. But Americans could fish within 3 miles along parts of the Gulf of St Lawrence, western Newfoundland and Labrador shores, and could cure fish in some unsettled areas along these shores. Between 1854 and 1866 a RECIPROCITY treaty with the US allowed fishermen from each jurisdiction to fish within the other's territorial waters and provided some measure of free trade. The end of reciprocity coincided with some economic distress among Nova Scotia and Newfoundland fishermen.

Confederation to WWI After Confederation in 1867, Canadian politicians attempted to turn from a commercial-marine economy and to develop a continental economy. Maritime leaders tried to take advantage of new opportunities in railways and manufacturing, and made little effort to preserve the self-reinforcing lumbering-fishing-exporting marine economy. By WWI only fishing remained a major employer. But the dispersion of its facilities along the coastline — attributable to a harvesting technology requiring proximity to the resources and a curing technique (drying on flakes) needing enormous spaces — persisted, and since WWI the fishery has never been able to support its scattered communities properly.

The growing urban and industrial economy of the late 19th century brought changes to the fishery. Steel vessels with greater reliability, safety and size began to displace wooden trading vessels. In Newfoundland's seal fishery, steamers replaced sail by the 1860s. From about 1870 to 1900, improved canning technology encouraged the creation of the lobster and Bay of Fundy sardine industries. Although salted groundfish (white-fleshed species such as cod, halibut and haddock which feed near the ocean bottom) continued to dominate the industry, American fishermen began to sell fresh fish. Fast schooners enabled them to get groundfish from GEORGES BANK and other banks near Nova Scotia onto the market before the fish spoiled. Schooners from LUNENBURG, NS, followed the Americans from Labrador to the Grand and other banks, and gradually other Canadian vessels did so also. Newfoundland schooners, despite some Grand Banks fishing, continued to depend on the Labrador saltfish fishery, and the codtrap (a net enclosure) largely replaced the hook-and-line technique.

Elsewhere in Canada, Ontario fisheries in the 19th century had fresh-fish markets nearby and depended less on salting and canning. Persistent fishing trends in the Great Lakes led to the depletion of desirable species, which allowed less valuable ones to take over. As well, environmental changes resulting from increased population caused the disappearance of ATLANTIC SALMON from Lk Ontario. In the West, the early lake fishery was dominated by companies that rented small boats to fishermen, who were often Indians. A strong winter fishery, in which nets were set below the ice, developed as well.

On the Pacific coast, salted and dried fish had been used by Indians, fur traders and miners. After the 1870s numerous salmon canneries were built. Canning technology and settlement patterns gave the BC industry a more concentrated character than that of the Atlantic, because even in isolated places the industry depended on bringing together many plant workers and many boats to take advantage of the seasonal migrations of PACIFIC SALMON. Railways provided transport to larger markets for the growing salmon industry and, later, for the halibut fishery. Increased bait requirements encouraged the herring fishery.

Conflicts primarily with the US over fisheries continued to test and strengthen Canadian sovereignty. Between 1871 and 1885 the TREATY OF WASHINGTON settled some fisheries disputes and slightly boosted the fishing industry. Conflicts in the 1880s between Americans and Canadians sealing on the Bering Sea were settled by international tribunal in 1893 (*see* BERING SEA DISPUTE). Colonial authorities established bounties (subsidies) or regulations to encourage fishing; some (eg, Newfoundland's BAIT ACTS) were in response to heavy subsidies provided by the French fishery on the NW Atlantic. Newfoundland won more respect from the US and Canada, and more independence from Britain, through its stubborn and partly successful efforts to govern foreign fishing (*see* BOND-BLAINE TREATY).

At Confederation the federal government was given authority over the fisheries. In the Province of Canada early legislation had included a system of licensing largely designed to protect private ownership of salmon-fishing stands. The emphasis after Confederation was on conservation, and the 1868 Fisheries Act provided for licensing on a much broader scale. Various royal commissions provided the rationale for regulatory action, and the resulting restrictions have usually been applied to fishing seasons, fish and catch size, equipment (eg, the purse seine was banned for many years from the Atlantic fishery) and, in BC, the number of boats and plants. The original Fisheries Act also contained provisions to outlaw the introduction to the water of substances deleterious to fish. These provisions, and the Act's clauses on licensing, remain the pillars of Canadian fishery management. Despite frequent difficulties in the industry, Canadian fishery management is among the best in the world.

The Canadian Fisheries Service was established after Confederation, and over the next half-century the Dept of Marine and Fisheries developed an extensive hatchery program (*see* AQUACULTURE). Although fishery authorities claimed excellent results, by the mid-1930s the program's success was minimal and most hatcheries were closed. Scientific research commenced in 1898 when the federal government established the first of several fisheries biological and technical stations. The Biological Board of Canada (later the Fisheries Research Board) was independent until the early 1970s, when the federal fisheries department took over research.

WWI interrupted fish supplies to Europe and made manpower scarce. A brief postwar period of prosperity, plus the need of veterans for employment, ended "limited entry" (licence limitation), which had been applied in the BC salmon fishery since 1889. The federal government also abandoned the system, established before the war, of transport subsidies for fish. Finally, decisions by Britain's JUDICIAL COMMITTEE OF THE PRIVY COUNCIL in this period and the 1920s weakened the federal government's authority over the fisheries relative to that of the provinces.

Boom and Depression: 1919-39 The GREAT DEPRESSION started early in the Atlantic fisheries. After WWI, while Newfoundland and Gulf of St Lawrence fisheries were served largely by superannuated fishing craft from Nova Scotia, European fleets used trawlers (large vessels that drag conical nets along the bottom), which were more reliable than either the hook-and-line fishery or the seasonal codtrap fishery. In the 1920s, after losing some of its market to European suppliers, Newfoundland competed more strongly in the West Indies markets traditionally supplied by the Maritimes, causing prices to decline. Some Maritime companies acquired trawlers, and small-boat fishermen believed that some of this price drop was a consequence. As overseas competition damaged salt-fish markets for Newfoundland and Canadian producers, New England fishermen and processors developed the filleting and quick-freezing processes and were able to sell packaged fresh or frozen fillets, instead of whole fish, to a wider market.

Increasing economic difficulties brought about a 1927 royal commission, whose findings had 2 main effects. First, the trawler fleet was reduced to only 3 or 4 vessels during the 1930s. This restriction, combined with decreased markets and investment capital, extended an existing technological lag and retarded development for many years; and, although the Lunenburg fleet in particular began winter-fishing for the fresh-fish market, the restriction also blocked the growth of a fresh and fresh-frozen fishery and of a year-round fishery. Second, the commission prompted the federal government to help set up fishermen's co-operatives (*see* CO-OPERATIVE MOVEMENT), leading to the creation of the United Maritimes Fishermen's Co-operative and the Québec United Fishermen.

Fishermen, wearing traditional oilskin jackets, pants and sou'wester hats, catching cod on the Grand Banks *(courtesy Wilfred L. Eisnor/Knickle's Studio).*

Fisherman hauling trawl into dory. The rubber rings on their hands are nippers to protect the hands (*courtesy Wilfred L. Eisnor/Knickle's Studio*).

In Newfoundland a remarkable fishermen's movement had begun before WWI when William COAKER built the Fishermen's Protective Union into a powerful industrial and political force. Coaker's attempts to reform fishery marketing failed, and the FPU faded away during the 1930s.

In the inland fisheries, overfishing and overcrowding, lack of organization and weak marketing created an unstable, low-income fishery. Governments tried various schemes of amelioration, including lake and boat quotas and fleet limitations, but without thorough and effective application.

BC fishermen weathered the Depression better than their Atlantic counterparts. The salmon industry, with roughly 100 plants at the beginning of the century, began to consolidate in the late 1920s (as it did again in the 1950s and the late 1970s). In 1923 the HALIBUT TREATY with the US regulated the Pacific halibut fishery. The pilchard (California sardine) fishery, developed in the late 1920s and the 1930s, suited the purse seine and the "reduction" fishery, which reduced fish flesh and bones into fertilizer or fish meal. The pilchard fishery boomed in the 1930s but failed in the 1940s when the resource declined. BC fishermen continued to organize more than Atlantic fishermen, and their organizations have been influential for decades. One, the Prince Rupert Fishermen's Co-operative Assn, took hold in the 1930s and became one of the world's most successful fishermen's co-operatives; in the early 1980s it dominated the northern BC fishery.

Federal fisheries management showed little vigour or innovation. In 1922 the federal government allowed Québec to manage its own fixed-gear fisheries, and in 1930 it turned over fishery management to the Prairie provinces and separated the Dept of Fisheries from the Dept of Marine. It also set up a Salt Fish Board to regulate and subsidize exporters. Newfoundland exporters remained weak; exports were finally regulated 2 decades after Coaker's attempt.

The Age of "Productivity": 1940-67 WWII brought increased prosperity and productivity through a high demand for fish and a new technology (radios, radar, sonar) which fishing fleets rapidly adopted. The fishing industry began to emphasize development. A special example of this occurred when Saskatchewan's CCF government enacted a series of interventionist measures, eventually producing a system of producer co-operatives. The federal government extended increasingly generous subsidies to help build both vessels and plants, chiefly for groundfish. It set up the Fisheries Prices Support Board (1947), extended UNEMPLOYMENT INSURANCE to self-employed fishermen and extended a loan program and vessel-insurance program to fishermen. On the Atlantic coast provincial loan boards offered advantageous interest rates to fishermen, allowing them to modernize their fleets.

Development in the Atlantic region came as refrigeration in transportation and storage facilities, stores and homes led to increased demand for frozen fish. The federal government had withdrawn the ban on purse seining in the 1930s, and now ended the ban on groundfish trawlers. In the groundfish industry, which rapidly switched to frozen-fish production, a few vertically integrated companies (fishing, processing and marketing) began to dominate; they have since extended partial dominance into lobster, SCALLOP and HERRING fisheries.

Government explorations and demonstrations of techniques helped open a number of fisheries, all of them — except the Great Lakes smelt fishery — on the Atlantic: redfish, flounders and other flatfish, sea scallops, crab and shrimp. In the 1940s and 1950s Bay of Fundy fishermen built up a purse-seine herring fishery. In the 1960s the federal government encouraged purse seining on the Atlantic, despite the overfishing of herring stocks on the Pacific coast; purse-seining was banned there 1967-72. Atlantic provincial governments helped get more boats and plants into the herring fishery. The result has been a series of unresolved crises stemming from overfishing and overcapacity.

Before the war, a main problem had been too little capacity to catch fish; after the war, the problem was too great a capacity. The Canadian fleet of vessels 50 t and over multiplied its capacity fivefold from 1959 to 1974, and the groundfish catch actually fell as both domestic and foreign fleets added pressure. Overexpansion of the fleet depleted stocks and drove down average incomes. The International Commission for the Northwest Atlantic Fisheries, est 1949, gathered comprehensive data on fish abundance and location and established mild restrictions, but it lacked the power of enforcement and the political will to take effective measures. In Atlantic Canada scientists seemed carried away by the stress on development, and few voices in government warned of the consequences of overfishing.

By contrast, federal fisheries officials in BC developed a superb corps of salmon managers who kept stocks fairly stable despite increasing pressure from the fishing fleet and from the encroachment of urban-industrial society on fish habitats. The department led public opinion in a struggle that held back potential damage to salmon stocks from hydroelectric dams. BC fishermen's organizations such as the United Fishermen and Allied Workers Union and processor organizations more actively influenced fishery management. Although a few major Atlantic processing companies developed a powerful fleet of 150 or more large trawlers, in BC vessel ownership by processors decreased. The BC fleet became more independent and the salmon-canning industry increasingly consolidated.

Conservation and Economics: 1968-80s The expansionist trend brought on a number of crises and semicollapses in the Canadian fishery. When the BC herring fishery reopened in 1972, a new and rich Japanese market for herring roe helped to fuel investment. By that time, the federal government had limited entry by fishermen into the herring and salmon fleet; and fleet limitation, while increasing incomes, made more money available for investment. By the early 1980s, overinvestment had thwarted the intent of licence limitation: increased fishing power endangered the stocks and the fishermen's profit margins. A commission of inquiry in 1982 recommended further fleet reduction and a system of licence fees and landing taxes that would remove windfall profits and dampen the boom-and-bust pattern.

In 1974-75 the Atlantic groundfish industry faced depleted stocks and high fuel and other costs; poor markets threatened major companies with bankruptcy. The federal government authorized some $200 million in special aid and undertook other measures. It extended Canadian fishing limits to 200 nautical miles (370 km) on 1 Jan 1977 (*see* LAW OF THE SEA). Licence limitation had been established in 1967 for the Atlantic lobster fishery, and gradually from 1973 for all other major fisheries on the Atlantic and Pacific coasts. The federal Dept of Fisheries and Oceans (as it became in 1979) tried to take a more comprehensive approach to management and imposed tight quotas and other conservation measures on Atlantic groundfish stocks. As well, between 1974 and 1982, fisheries min-

The modern dragger *Cape Brier* operates out of Lunenburg, NS (*courtesy Wilfred L. Eisnor/Knickle's Studio*).

ister Roméo LeBlanc encouraged organization of fishermen. Incomes generally increased, and Canada became the world's leading fish exporter.

Excessive optimism after 1977 brought overinvestment (especially in plants, despite federal advice to the contrary) and a near-collapse of major Atlantic groundfish companies. The fisheries are common property, and each fisherman tries to carve out the biggest possible share of the catch. This naturally leads to a race for the biggest and best vessels. In 1982 the federal Task Force on Atlantic Fisheries recommended "boat quotas," a system that would entitle each licensed fisherman to a portion of the total catch and would reduce the perceived need to upgrade equipment uneconomically. The federal government also promised to impose stricter rules on fish quality and encouraged some co-operation in marketing.

Tension has increased between Atlantic processing companies, traditionally the main influence on government, and newly powerful fishermen's organizations such as the Newfoundland Fisherman, Food and Allied Workers' Union and the Maritime Fishermen's Union. Fishermen's organizations have suggested that government should force the major vertically-integrated groundfish producers to relinquish their trawler fleets, which supply 30-40% of Atlantic groundfish, so that independent fishermen would control the supply. Processing companies have been sensitive to suggestions of further government intervention, especially after federal and provincial governments created 2 crown corporations in the late 1960s: the Canadian Saltfish Corp, which has a monopoly on marketing salt fish from Newfoundland and parts of Québec, and the Freshwater Fish Marketing Corp, which has a monopoly on selling fish in interprovincial and export trade in the Prairie provinces, the Northwest Territories and parts of northwestern Ontario.

Private enterprise has worked in places such as BC and the SW Nova Scotia-Bay of Fundy area, where more favourable conditions allow fishermen and processors alike to display a great deal of independence. Elsewhere — especially in Newfoundland — more difficult conditions have created an industry that has alternated between expressions of independence and requests for government help. Fishermen often resent regulations affecting their own vessels, yet ask the government to regulate vessels using different methods or coming from different areas. Management and understanding of the fishery by fishermen, processors and government officials have advanced in recent years, but the built-in conflicts of a private-enterprise yet common-property industry (with fishing under federal jurisdiction and processing under provincial jurisdiction) continue to foster tensions.

Notwithstanding its difficulties, the fishing industry now has increasingly good chances for stability and prosperity because of the 200-mile limit, the greater understanding by all parties and the new approach that tries to tailor production capacity to the size of the resource and to get the maximum value per fish. Despite the turmoil and crises that have beset the fisheries, the fish keep coming in, the boats keep fishing and communities generally stay alive. JOSEPH GOUGH

Reading: Canada, *Navigating Troubled Waters* (1983); Joseph E. Forester and Anne D. Forester, *Fishing: BC's Commercial Fishing History* (1975); C. Grant Head, *Eighteenth Century Newfoundland* (1976); H.A. Innis, *The Cod Fisheries* (2nd ed, 1954).

Fisheries Policy The management and development of fishing is a significant area of public policy. Federal jurisdiction over Canada's coastal and inland fisheries dates to the CONSTITUTION ACT, 1867, and a federal fisheries administration has existed, either as a separate department or as a branch of another department or ministry, since that time. In 1979 the federal government established the Department of Fisheries and Oceans (DFO). However, the provinces are responsible for certain areas of fisheries jurisdiction, including fish processing and the training of fishermen.

The challenge of fisheries policy is to preserve fish stocks while maximizing economic benefit to the people involved in the industry, to the communities that depend on it, and to the nation as a whole. The fishing industry is complex and difficult to administer, made up as it is of many different and often conflicting interest groups.

Some of the difficulties stem from the "common property" nature of the resource. There is no arrangement for proprietary tenure over fish, which tends to result in a "free-for-all" race for limited fish stocks. The first priority of fishery policy is to maintain and if possible expand the resource by annually setting an overall quota or Total Allowable Catch (TAC) for discretely identifiable species stock. This procedure is applied particularly in the management of demersal (groundfish) and pelagic (open-sea) fisheries. In other fisheries, different approaches are used, eg, an optimal necessary "escapement" (salmon) and a minimum legal size (lobster), etc. The federal government has also pursued a policy of limited entry into the fishing industry and of restricted licences to fish certain species. Recently, there has been a trend in federal policy toward the introduction of quasi-property rights or enterprise allocations, whereby each fishing enterprise is given its own individual quota. Proponents of this approach believe it will help solve the problem of overinvestment and self-defeating competition associated with the common-property resource.

Fish stocks were severely depleted during the 1960s and early 1970s as a result of overfishing off Canadian coasts by foreign factory freezer-trawler fleets. Following a series of multinational negotiations, a new fisheries management regime came into effect in 1977 when Canada's jurisdiction was extended to 200 nautical miles (370 km). The federal government then moved to reverse the decline in fish stocks by gradually reducing foreign fishing within the 200-mile limit while increasing Canada's own effort. The subsequent growth of the important northern cod stock off Labrador has been one of the success stories in fisheries management, although by 1983-84 this growth appeared to have slowed.

Some fish stocks that are important to Canada's fishing industry remain outside the 200-mile management zone. Organizations set up to protect stocks in international waters include the Northwest Atlantic Fisheries Organization (NAFO) and the International North Pacific Fisheries Commission (INPFC). Problems can still arise between individual countries. In the early 1980s, for instance, Canada charged Spain (which had not then signed the NAFO treaty) with overfishing just outside the 200-mile limit in the area known as the Tail of the Grand Banks. This led to some curtailment of trade between the 2 nations. The jurisdictional boundary around the French-owned islands of SAINT PIERRE AND MIQUELON off the S coast of Newfoundland is still disputed between Canada and France. There are also lingering disputes with the US over salmon, fishing rights on the Pacific coast and over ownership of GEORGES BANK, S of Nova Scotia. (In 1984 the latter case was being argued before the international court in the Hague.)

In the early 1980s the Atlantic and to a lesser extent the Pacific fishing industries found themselves in deep economic trouble. On both coasts, it was charged that there were "too many boats chasing too few fish." With the introduction of the 200-mile limit, fishermen and processors had been encouraged to overexpand their operations in anticipation of a boom that never materialized. Many went heavily into debt, only to be hit with extremely high interest rates that coincided with a periodic slump in the world market. In response, the federal government created 2 royal commissions (under Peter Pearse and Michael Kirby, respectively) to study the Pacific and Atlantic fisheries. The policy issues on each coast are different. On the West Coast, the most important issues are conservation, rationalization of effort, reduction of fleet size, and market stabilization. On the East Coast, the main issues involve the upgrading of the quality and therefore of the market value of fish products (particularly cod and herring); the development of markets for abundant, underutilized species, eg, hake, mackerel, herring, alewife; some reduction in numbers of fishermen; improved and stabilized income for fishermen; and the creation of a proper and stable balance between inshore, nearshore and offshore fleets and effort.

The recommendations produced by the 2 commissions were and remain controversial. On the West Coast, the DFO met resistance from fishermen in its efforts to implement the Pearce Commission's plan to reduce the fishing fleet drastically through a system of royalties and buy backs. The Pearse Commission Report suggested that a government-appointed board should offer compensation to holders of fishing licences for voluntarily giving up their licences, thus reducing the total number of fishermen involved in the salmon and roe herring fisheries. The report proposed that the cost of such a program should be shared between government and the remaining holders of fishing licences, who would supposedly benefit from the fleet reduction by increasing their individual catches. According to this plan, revenue would be derived from fishermen themselves in the form of royalties, which would be a fixed percentage of the value of fish landings.

On the East Coast, a "restructuring" process was set in motion, involving the infusion of public money to refinance 5 major offshore fishing companies that were virtually bankrupt. Out of this restructuring emerged 2 new "super-companies," one based in Newfoundland and the other in Nova Scotia. The Newfoundland-based company is owned by the federal and provincial governments, while the Nova Scotia-based company remains in private hands. The restructuring deals were sharply criticized, particularly because nothing substantial was done to assist independent fishermen who were caught in a financial squeeze as a result of steep increases in operating costs.

Just what role government should play in the fishing industry is a question that underlies much of the debate on restructuring and indeed on fishery policy in general. Fish-plant owners in particular still subscribe to a private enterprise philosophy, but critics charge that private enterprise has repeatedly been responsible for the crises in the fishery industry, crises that have necessitated government intervention.

Under the Fisheries Prices Support Act, in force since the 1940s, government programs have helped shield primary producers from periodic fluctuations in international commodity markets, and many argue that such programs should be expanded. The Norwegians, who are among Canada's leading competitors in the fish trade, have similar programs for their fishermen. In 1969 the Canadian government established the Freshwater Fish Marketing Corp (FFMC), a crown trading corporation modeled on the Wheat Board, to control the export of freshwater fish and fish products from the Prairie provinces, the NWT and northern Ontario. The traditional salt-fish trade to Mediterranean and Caribbean countries has declined in Canada because of undisciplined marketing by a multitude of small exporters and because of effective competition from Norway and Iceland. In 1970, in response to an initiative from the Newfoundland government, the federal government established the Canadian Saltfish Corporation (CSC), modeled on the FFMC but with a slightly different mandate. It handles the export (and interprovincial trade) in dried salt codfish and similar products originating in Newfoundland, Labrador and the lower North Shore of Québec. Both the FFMC and the CSC are joint federal-provincial companies.

Role of Unions While more government involvement in fish marketing is generally opposed by processors it is supported by most unions representing Canadian fishermen and fish-plant workers. Increasing numbers of fishermen and plant workers have banded together into unions and other organizations to protect their interests in dealing with fish companies and governments. Unions bargain directly with fish companies to establish fish prices and plant wages, and lobby with governments for fishing policies they favour.

An early example of unionization in Newfoundland was the founding of the Fishermen's Protective Union by William COAKER in 1908. This was a social and political movement aimed at breaking the old credit or "truck" system which kept fishermen in a condition of semi-serfdom. A fisherman never saw any cash throughout the year; instead the merchant supplied him on credit with staple goods such as flour and molasses. At the end of the season the merchant took the fisherman's cured fish, calculating its worth at a price set not by fishermen but by traders. In this way fishermen were kept permanently in debt and completely dependent on the merchant. Coaker attempted to assure the fishermen some financial independence by creating a shareholding company that operated cash stores which supplied staple goods at non-inflated prices. Coaker's movement declined after 1919 when as minister of fisheries in a coalition government he tried unsuccessfully to introduce certain reforms in fisheries policy, including co-ordination of salt-fish exporting.

On the West Coast, the chief union in the fishing industry is the United Fishermen and Allied Workers Union, which was founded in 1945 and remains an effective bargaining agent for fishermen and shoreworkers. In BC, however, there is no provincial legislation giving independent fishermen the formal right to collective bargaining. The first province to pass collective bargaining legislation for fishermen was Newfoundland, which did so in 1971 as a result of political pressure from the newly formed Newfoundland Fishermen, Food and Allied Workers Union (NFFAWU). New Brunswick fishermen obtained collective bargaining rights in 1982, but Nova Scotia and PEI still have no collective bargaining legislation for self-employed fishermen. The NFFAWU, representing some 28 000 inshore fishermen, offshore trawlermen and plant workers in Newfoundland and Nova Scotia, is now Canada's largest fishing-industry union. It is affiliated to the United Food and Commercial Workers International Union, which also has several other fishing industry locals across Canada. The NFFAWU has played a major role in increasing fish prices and wages, influencing public policy and introducing social benefits, such as workers' compensation, for fishermen. Unions influence government policy through representation on various committees that advise the federal government on establishing quotas for different species, eg, the NFFAWU has representatives on the Atlantic Groundfish Advisory Commmittee (AGAC). When fishermen and processor's organizations mount conflicting lobbies to influence policy, fishermen sometimes prevail. For example, government policy allows "over-the-side sales" (which are opposed by processors) whereby self-employed fishermen who are unable to sell their catch to a fish plant may sell directly to foreign factory ships. When fishing-industry unions perceive that government policy favours the interests of the fish companies, their last resort may be an attempt to mobilize their membership at the ballot box, eg, in 1984 they mounted the "Unity '84" campaign against Ottawa's restructuring policy, which involved 7 different fishing-industry unions in the Atlantic provinces. RICHARD CASHIN

Reading: Harold A. Innis, *The Cod Fisheries: The History of an International Economy* (1940; 1978).

Fisherman Lake, archaeological site located in the foothills of the Mackenzie Mts, in the extreme SW corner of the NWT. Archaeological work since 1952 has exposed a long and problematic history of human occupation extending from the early Holocene until historic times. Of the 154 sites found and evaluated, 10 have been excavated. The earliest occupations are poorly represented and difficult to interpret, but by at least 6000 or 5000 BC the area may have been inhabited by a Northern Cordilleran/Plano culture moving north in the wake of optimal climatic conditions. These people may have been bison hunters, although no bone remains have been preserved. About 4000 BC new people entered the area from Alaska and the Yukon, characterized by a distinctive stone technology based on tiny stone blades ("microblades"). Eventually, many of the more distinctive aspects of this technology disappeared, but these people may be the ancestors of the SLAVEY who inhabit Fisherman Lake to the present day. *See also* ARCHAEOLOGY; PREHISTORY. DAVID A. MORRISON

Fishing, Ice Ice provides a seasonal platform for fishing by netting, spearing and angling. Net, spear and hook were in use in northern Europe and N America, winter and summer, long before the dawn of history.

Netting Nets are used by people fishing commercially, or requiring regular supplies of fish for feeding families or dog teams, or supplying fox or mink ranches. They are easiest to set before ice is thick. A line must be stretched 50 m or more under the ice. A series of holes is cut in the ice and a line is passed from one to the next, often by means of a long, straight pole. The line is then used to pull through a rope which, in turn, is used to extend the net, floats and weights beneath the ice. Another method uses a prairie ice jigger, a sledlike, wooden device that slides along the underside of the ice. The jigger is launched under the ice, towing a rope. When the rope is pulled, a lever is raised; when the rope is released, the lever springs back in such a way that it pushes against the ice and jerks the jigger forward. It can be traced by watching through clear ice, or by listening through snow-covered ice. When the appropriate length of rope has been drawn out, the jigger is retrieved through another hole, cut over it. The net is retrieved from the opposite direction when the catch is removed. Nets must be deployed well below the bottom surface of ice, or floats may become frozen-in. A rope or net header embedded in the new ice that forms in the hole is almost certain to be cut when the hole is reopened; therefore, headers are best held down by poles extending well into the water.

Spearing Fish spearing may date from the Paleolithic. N American natives often were accomplished fish spearers, eg, Inuit speared lake trout and arctic char through ice. The fish spear (kakivak) of the eastern Arctic had a central prong to transfix fish and lateral, reverse prongs to hold them. Bone, antler or ivory decoys were dangled to attract cruising fish into range. In Canada, the fish spear is prohibited, except for taking eels wintering in estuaries in the Atlantic provinces, and for game fishing in Québec.

Angling Hooks were derived from earlier devices, eg, gorges, which date from Paleolithic times and were designed to be swallowed by animals. Bright metal and enamelled lures have largely replaced baited tackle designed to be swallowed by fish. Ice angling is a widespread Canadian pastime: from Labrador to Okanagan Valley, from Lancaster Sound to Lk St Clair. Catches range from perch and pike to Greenland shark on the fast ice off Pond Inlet, inconnu on a quiet channel of the Mackenzie Delta, pickerel in Bay of Quinte, smelt in Lk Erie, poulamons at Ste Anne de la Pérade, and brook trout in Halifax County ponds. Most Canadians have access to waters inhabited by more than one of the following: lake whitefish, yellow perch, pickerel (walleye), ling (burbot), northern pike and rainbow trout. A.H. MACPHERSON

Fishing Admiral, a position of authority claimed by the first fishing ship's captain to enter each Newfoundland harbour every year, although in some harbours in the 1500s each ship's captain may have taken a turn during the fishing season. The practice was in effect by the late 1500s and continued to some extent until

Ice fishing near Tuktoyaktuk, NWT (*photo by Karl-Heinz Raach*).

the late 1700s. Their authority confirmed by a British charter in 1633, the fishing admirals, in addition to having the choice location in their harbour, were responsible for enforcing British regulations and law. Together with the second and third captains to enter the harbour — the vice admiral and rear admiral — the fishing admiral administered the earliest form of "government" in Newfoundland. Since they were simply ships' captains, the justice they dispensed was often wanting, and many accounts of abuses appeared in the historical records (*see* FISHERIES HISTORY). ROBERT D. PITT

Fishing Islands, an archipelago of about 15 islets in Lk HURON (scattered in an area of 10 km²), lie off the W coast of the BRUCE PENINSULA in western Ontario between Chiefs Pt and Pike Bay. The archipelago is named for the teeming shoals of fish that were once caught there.
DAVID EVANS

Fitness Broadly defined, fitness is a state of physical, mental and social well-being. Concern for becoming and staying fit is increasingly important to Canadians. Interest is reflected in all age groups, but involvement in physical activity by people 60 years of age and over has increased 3 times faster than that of younger people over the past few years. One consequence of the interest in fitness has been a renewed effort to implement daily PHYSICAL EDUCATION in Canadian schools.

Canada Fitness Survey

In the Canada Fitness Survey (1981), which involved nearly 12 000 households in 80 urban and rural communities across Canada, 16 000 people, ages 7 to 69 years participated in a fitness test, and 22 000 people completed a questionnaire about their physical activity and life-style. The results of the survey provided a comprehensive picture of fitness in Canada.

Physical Activity Patterns According to the survey, 11.5 million Canadians (56% of those aged 10 and over) are physically active in their leisure time; walking is a favourite activity, followed by bicycling, swimming, jogging and gardening. Jogging is the first choice of activities people wish to begin, and there would be 15 million new participants in all activities if there were no barriers holding them back. Active Canadians are more likely to be young, and to be westerners, managers and professionals, single and better educated. They are equally likely to be male or female. The survey also found that active Canadians score higher on all measures of health and emotional well-being; that strength and muscular endurance decline rapidly after age 25; that females are more supple than males, but suppleness in both sexes declines precipitously after age 25. Based on the survey results, an estimated 46% of Canadians would achieve a recommended level of cardiovascular (aerobic) fitness, 33% would reach the minimal level of fitness and the remaining 20% of Canadians would be assessed as unfit. Males are fitter than females and the young are generally fitter than the old. The findings are somewhat biased as an ever-increasing number of Canadians over the age of 40 were screened out of the testing for medical reasons. Seventy eight percent of persons in the survey placed "regular physical activity" in the top 5 components of a healthy life, behind such basic components as adequate sleep and nutrition. Lack of time and the distance to facilities were the major barriers to participation in such activity.

International Comparisons

In 1972 PARTICIPaction introduced the famous comparison between the 60-year-old Swede and the 30-year-old Canadian in a 15-second television commercial. The idea that a 60-year-old Swede was fitter than a 30-year-old Canadian captured the nation's imagination. In fact, only when Sweden and other countries undertake a survey as comprehensive as the Canada Fitness Survey of 1981 can true comparisons be made; nevertheless, the advertisement was effective.

Canadian researchers are well recognized in the international fitness community. In particular, Dr Roy Sheppard of U of T is an internationally renowned scholar in the field.

Federal and Provincial Fitness Programs

The fitness movement of the 1970s and 1980s was generated partly through the efforts of the federal and provincial governments. Fitness Canada, the federal government agency with a mandate to "encourage, promote and develop increased participation of physical activity leading towards fitness for all Canadians," has created a number of national programs and resources and has undertaken co-operative work with national agencies in the physical activity and health field. Fitness Canada was formed in 1979 from the Fitness and Recreation branches of the Fitness and Amateur Sports Directorate. PARTICIPaction, an independent nonprofit communications company funded by Fitness Canada, is a unique and successful model for encouraging Canadians to become involved in regular physical activity. Recently, Fitness Canada has sponsored National Physical Activity Week, demonstration employee-fitness programs, a national conference on Fitness in the Third Age (60 plus) and the development of a national volunteer leadership program.

Every provincial government in Canada through departments of recreation, youth, culture, tourism or health promote fitness through physical activity. The organization of each program varies, ranging from the large Kino Québec network with over 100 community offices to the typical agency in a smaller province in which a small core of professionals work with voluntary agencies across the province.

Voluntary Fitness Agencies and Organizations in Canada work in the fields of fitness, SPORT, and recreation. More than a million Canadians are actively involved in these organizations as coaches, board members, officials and helpers and many millions more are involved as participants. Some of the voluntary organizations, such as running clubs, serve one community; others, such as those created for organized sport, sponsor community clubs across the country and are organized into provincial chapters and a national organization to govern the sport nationally and internationally. In the field of fitness development, the YMCA and the YWCA have been among the most influential organizations.

Commercial Fitness Centres The private sector has responded to the new interest in fitness by developing many new fitness facilities, often in conjunction with a racquet club. Standard qualifications for fitness leaders and those conducting fitness testing are being developed. Good program leaders should have completed a recognized training program from the provincial agency, the YMCA or YWCA, or a university or national association such as the Canadian Association for Sport Sciences.
P. EDWARDS AND J. HAUSER

FitzGerald, Lionel LeMoine, painter (b at Winnipeg 17 Mar 1890; d there 7 Aug 1956). FitzGerald spent almost his whole life in Winnipeg painting, drawing, and sketching quiet contemplative scenes. He trained in Winnipeg, Pittsburgh and NY. He was principal of the Winnipeg School of Art 1929-47, and exhibited with the GROUP OF SEVEN in 1930, but remained a loner. From a decorative and impressionistic style FitzGerald moved to a pointillist technique. *Williamson's Garage* (1927), *Doc Snider's House* (1931) and *Farm Yard* (1931) illustrated the fine texture he built up, using dry paint, tiny brush strokes, bleached tones and subtle colour. *The Pool* (1934) explores geometric relationships. In *Jar* (1938) he uses glistening daubs of paint to illuminate the jar from within.

In the 1940s FitzGerald turned to coloured chalks, pen and ink, sometimes oil on a palette knife. After his death a set of self-portraits and drawings of the nude were found, unusual for the shy painter. He painted the apple in all media and was stimulated by visits to the West

Doc Snider's House (1931), oil on canvas, is one of Lionel LeMoine FitzGerald's masterpieces *(courtesy National Gallery of Canada/gift of Dr P.D. Ross, 1932).*

Coast. Retired in 1949, he painted *From an Upstairs Window* in 1951, one of his best works. On a trip to BC he met Lawren HARRIS and afterwards did pen and ink studies with thousands of tiny dots and dashes shaping the forms. *Still Life with Hat* (1955) creates his characteristically mysterious world, made with weightless cross-hatching. By *Autumn Sonata* (1954) and *Abstract in Blue and Gold* (1955), FitzGerald became totally abstract. The surface rhythms give way to a smooth brushstroke. His entire body of work is distinguished by a painstaking, original way of handling brush, pen, pencil, crayon or paint brush to get his own look and texture.

ANNE MCDOUGALL

Fitzpatrick, Sir Charles, minister of justice, chief justice of Canada (b at Québec City, Canada E 19 Dec 1853; d there 17 June 1942). After studying law at Laval, he was called to the bar 1876. Fitzpatrick quickly made a name as a criminal lawyer and acted as chief counsel for Louis RIEL in 1885, and for Honoré MERCIER after his dismissal from office in 1892. Fitzpatrick sat as a Liberal in the Legislative Assembly of Québec 1890-96 and the House of Commons 1896-1906, and served as solicitor general 1896 and minister of justice 1902 during the LAURIER administration. He resigned in 1906 to become chief justice of Canada. Upon retirement, he was lt-gov of Québec 1918-23.

DAVID EVANS

Fjord, long, narrow bay formed by glacial erosion of river valleys during the ICE AGES and consisting of one or more basins separated by sills. Fjords occur on the coasts of BC and eastern Canada, Alaska, Chile, New Zealand, Greenland and Norway. In cross section they are U-shaped, often with a flat bottom. The fjords of the Pacific coast are 3-400 km long, 0.6-15 km wide, and 20-500 m in average depth. Sill depths range from a few metres to 500 m below the water surface. The water in fjords comes from 2 sources: the ocean supplies salt water, which being dense fills most of the fjord basin; rivers provide lighter fresh water, which forms a layer on top of the salt water. The rivers flowing into fjords are fed by rainfall draining from their watersheds and, in summer, by meltwater from mountain snowfields and glaciers. Glacial meltwater usually carries finely ground rock (rock flour), which gives it a milky appearance. Most of this material is deposited to form the flat bottom typical of many fjords.

In oceanographic terminology, fjords are estuaries, ie, semienclosed bodies of water in which seawater is measurably diluted by fresh water from land drainage. As there is a continual supply of river water, usually at the landward end of the fjord, the upper layer (a few metres thick) flows toward the sea, picking up some salt water from below en route and carrying it out to sea. An inflow of salt water from the ocean balances this export. The combination of surface-layer outflow of low-salinity water and deeper inflow of more saline ocean water is known as an estuarine circulation. It serves to exchange or ventilate the basin water. If the outer sill is very shallow, projecting up into the outflowing upper layer, this ventilation is hindered. In this case the basin water stagnates and most or all of its dissolved oxygen is used up by bacterial processes; therefore, fish may be unable to live in it. In some shallow-silled fjords stagnation may persist for years; in others there is an annual cycle in which inflow of deeper salt water occurs seasonally when dense water upwells outside the mouth of the fjord. The degree of ventilation of a fjord basin is important when experts considering whether or not it may be permissible to discharge industrial effluent or mine tailings into it. Of the many fjords that have been investigated, only a small minority exhibit marked stagnation.

Most of the fjords on the West Coast have been

The great Pangnirtung Fjord, on the SE coast of Baffin I, NWT (*courtesy Parks Canada/Prairie Region*).

studied. In particular the seasonal variations of water properties in Bute Inlet have been observed for over 30 years, and intensive studies in Knight Inlet since 1977 have revealed many features of subsurface motions and internal waves. On the East Coast, fewer fjords have been investigated, but the physics, chemistry and geology of Saguenay Fjord, 100 km long and 275 m deep, off the north shore of the St Lawrence estuary, have been investigated in some detail (*see* SAGUENAY R).

G.L. PICKARD

Flag Debate The form Canada's flag should take was debated from Confederation until 1964. Canada's official flag from 1867 was Britain's Union Flag, although the Red Ensign with the Canadian badge was occasionally flown. After WWI an upsurge of NATIONALISM resulted in King George V's granting Canada, on 21 Nov 1921, a coat of arms with red and white as official colours. In 1925 PM Mackenzie KING appointed a committee to investigate possible designs, but it did not report. Almost annual debate in the House of Commons failed to settle the issue, which rested on whether a Canadian flag should be free of colonial symbolism. In 1946 another committee presented a design with the red ensign bearing both the Union Flag and a maple leaf, but it was not adopted.

In 1963 PM Lester PEARSON, with Liberal MP and heraldic assistant John Matheson, promoted a flag with 3 maple leaves on a white centre square with blue bars on each side. DIEFENBAKER's Conservatives generally favoured a red ensign which honoured the British and French traditions, whereas the NDP preferred a design similar to Pearson's with only one maple leaf. Debate in the House opened 15 June 1964, and it was prolonged and rancorous. On Sept 10 Pearson appointed a special committee, which developed and then proposed a suggestion from George F.G. STANLEY: a flag closely similar to that of the ROYAL MILITARY COLLEGE with a red maple leaf instead of the college crest in the centre. Parliamentary debate on this recommendation continued until CLOSURE was imposed; on 15 Dec 1964 the proposal was accepted by 163 votes to 78. Senate approval followed Dec 17. On 28 Jan 1965 Queen Elizabeth proclaimed that, effective 15 Feb 1965, Canada's flag would be red, with the proportions 2 by length and one by width, containing in its centre a white square the width of the flag, bearing a single red maple leaf. Under average wind conditions the leaf should resemble the 23-point sugar maple leaf. *See* HERALDRY; EMBLEMS OF CANADA.

JOHN ROSS MATHESON

Reading: John Ross Matheson, *Canada's Flag* (1980); G.F.G. Stanley, *The Story of Canada's Flag* (1965).

Flatfish, common name for bottom-living, primarily marine FISHES, of class Osteichthyes, order Pleuronectiformes (Heterosomata). Among the flatfishes are some of the most valuable food fishes, eg, halibut, plaice, flounder, turbot and sole. About 520 species in 6 families inhabit Continental Shelf waters of world oceans, but a few occur in deep seas and some ascend rivers. Most occur in temperate and tropical seas but some penetrate the Arctic. In Canada, 34 species in 25 genera and 3 families occur in coastal waters: 21 species in the Pacific and 13 in the Atlantic. The family Pleuronectidae, the right-eyed flounders, with 26 species (including halibut, genus *Hippoglossus*, and plaice, genus *Hippoglossoides*), is best represented in Canadian waters. The other families are the Bothidae (left-eyed flounders, eg, sand dabs, genus *Citharichthys*) and the Cynoglossidae (tonguefishes).

The loss of bilateral symmetry sets the flatfishes apart from all others. Newly hatched flatfishes swim upright and are symmetrical, but a few days after hatching, one eye begins to migrate across the skull and eventually both eyes are on one side. The dorsal fin grows forward onto the head. Changes in jaw structure, pelvic fins and anatomy also occur. Finally, young flatfish drop to the bottom to lie eyed side uppermost, blind side on the bottom. The left eye migrates in some species; the right in others.

Starry flounder (*Platichthys stellatus*). The loss of bilateral symmetry sets the flat fishes apart from all others. With both eyes on one side, the flatfish lies blind side on the bottom (*courtesy National Museums of Canada/National Museum of Natural Sciences*).

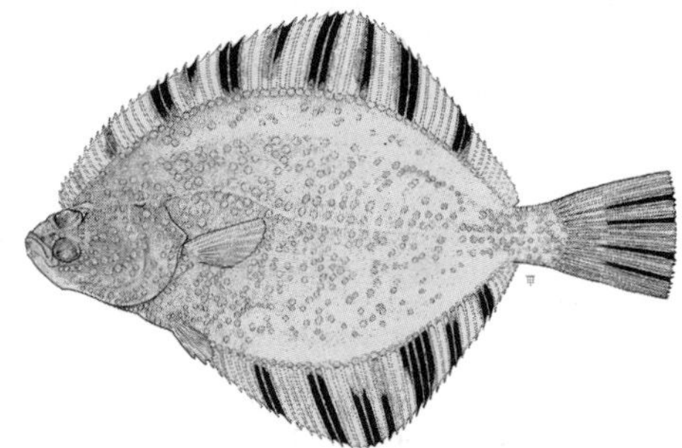

Flatfish with both eyes on the right side are said to be right-eyed (dextral); those with both eyes on the left side are left-eyed (sinistral). The eyed side is pigmented; the blind side is usually white. Some flatfishes have a highly developed ability to vary body colouring to match the ocean bottom. Most flatfishes are small (30-38 cm long) but the halibuts may attain lengths of 267 cm and weights up to 316 kg. The mouth is usually small (except in halibut). The lower jaw is prominent in most species but in true soles (found in European waters) the rounded snout projects beyond the mouth. Dorsal and anal fins are usually soft rayed and long. Flatfishes are carnivorous, eating various fishes, crustaceans and bottom-dwelling invertebrates. They are caught mainly by otter trawl, Danish seines or longlines; some are angled. In Canada, Atlantic and Pacific halibut (*H. hippoglossus* and *H. stenolepsis*, respectively) are the most highly esteemed flatfishes and command the highest price on both domestic and foreign markets. The smaller flatfishes, known locally as flounder, sole, yellowtail, dab, witch or plaice, are marketed as fresh or frozen fillets under the name sole.
W.B. SCOTT

Flatworm (Platyhelminthes), phylum of soft, bilaterally symmetrical INVERTEBRATES. Flatworms vary in shape from leaflike to ribbonlike; size ranges from microscopic to over 15 m long (some parasitic forms). Flatworms have an identifiable "head," sometimes highly modified as an attachment organ in parasitic forms. A body cavity is lacking; internal organs are suspended in a spongy matrix (parenchyma). Flatworms lack circulatory and respiratory systems, but have well-developed reproductive and excretory ones. A simple alimentary tract (gut) occurs in most forms, but is absent in tapeworms and one group of free-living flatworms (Acoela). With few exceptions among the flukes, the gut has only a ventral-surface opening, often close to the front end, serving both as mouth and anus. Most flatworms are hermaphroditic; however, cross-fertilization between 2 individuals is the rule. Flatworms occur worldwide. Most of the roughly 15 000 known species are parasitic. Probably thousands of species occur in Canada, but only a fraction have been discovered, eg, 200-250 free-living species and 400-450 species of fish parasites. Platyhel minthes are subdivided into 5 classes: Turbellaria, Temnocephalida, Monogenea, Trematoda and Cestoidea. Some zoologists include Temnocephalida in Turbellaria.

Nemertea (proboscis or ribbon worms) resemble flatworms, but have a tubular, muscular organ (proboscis) that can be turned inside out, for capturing food. They differ also in having a circulatory system, an anus and separate sexes. They are mainly free-living, littoral, marine organisms; some live in fresh water or moist terrestrial areas; a few are commensals of invertebrates. Length ranges from under 1 mm to several metres. Often they are brightly coloured. About 500 species are known. L. MARGOLIS

Flavelle, Sir Joseph Wesley, meat packer, financier, philanthropist (b at Peterborough, Canada W 15 Feb 1858; d at Palm Beach, Fla 7 Mar 1939). Inspired by Methodism's demand for personal holiness, self-denial and careful stewardship, Flavelle rose from humble origins to become one of Canada's most able, respected and influential businessmen, as president of the British Empire's largest pork packer, William Davies Co of Toronto, and as chairman of the Bank of Commerce, the National Trust Co and Simpsons Ltd. Successful in business, he devoted much of his wealth and energy after 1900 to charities, needy individuals and public service. He played a major role in the affairs of U of Toronto, the Methodist Church, the Toronto General Hospital and the CNR. Chairman of the Imperial Munitions Board in WWI, Flavelle converted a scandal-ridden and inefficient industry into a vast, well-organized operation and received a baronetcy in 1917 — the last resident citizen of Canada to receive a hereditary title. Shortly thereafter, he and the William Davies Co were accused of profiteering from the wartime bacon business and, though an inquiry exonerated him, the episode sullied his reputation.
JOSEPH LINDSEY

Reading: M. Bliss, *A Canadian Millionaire* (1978).

Flax (*Linum usitatissimum*), annual PLANT belonging to the family of the same name (Linaceae). Flax is sown and harvested much like a spring CEREAL CROP and matures at the same time as WHEAT. The flowers have 5 petals (usually blue but sometimes white) and produce a boll (fruit capsule) with up to 10 small, flattened, ovate seeds, 2-6 mm in diameter. Mature seeds contain approximately 40% oil, 25% protein. The seed coat is usually brown but some varieties are yellow. Although the place of origin of flax is unknown, it was cultivated in ancient Egypt, where its stem fibres were used to produce linen cloth. Oil crushed from the seed (linseed oil) was initially a by-product of linen-fibre production but, with the Industrial Revolution, it came into demand as an industrial drying oil (eg, in paints, steelworks and oilcloths). By the 20th century, flax was grown primarily for oil. In Europe, one type is produced for linen fibre, used in producing linen cloth, and for industrial purposes where toughness under water and in corrosive conditions is required.

In Canada, flax is produced only as an industrial OILSEED CROP and is grown annually on over 600 000 ha in western Canada. Average yield is 870 kg/ha. Some seed is crushed in Canada for the domestic paint industry, but most is exported to the US, Europe and Japan. The meal, which remains after crushing, is used as a protein supplement in animal feeds. Flax straw can be processed to produce fine paper, used primarily as cigarette paper since it is clean burning and tasteless. The fibres are also used in paper money and give it toughness. G.G. ROWLAND

Flea, very small, wingless, laterally flattened INSECT of order Siphonaptera. Of the 180 species and subspecies indigenous to Canada, 23 are PARASITES of birds, the remainder being mammal parasites. Six species, introduced from Europe or Asia, are common parasites of humans and domestic animals. Worldwide, the flea fauna is much larger, but incompletely documented. Adult fleas are highly specialized: their tough, bristly integument (outer covering) helps adapt them to existence as external parasites of warm-blooded hosts. Ancestors originated in Asia and evolved, primarily, as temporary parasites of small mammals. The life cycle begins with an egg, laid in fur or feathers, which drops to the host's nest or the ground. The larva is nonparasitic, feeding on organic debris. It develops into a pupa, enclosed in a cocoon. Both stages are sedentary. Adult fleas can leap 200 times their own length. Fleas are most numerous in dry climates, being as much as 4 times as numerous in BC and Alberta as in Québec and the Maritimes. Their habits of feeding on blood and occupying filthy places make fleas potential transmitters of disease, particularly bubonic or sylvatic plague. W.O. HAUFE

Fleming, Archibald Lang, Church of England bishop of the Arctic 1933-49 (b at Greenock, Scot 8 Sept 1883; d at Toronto 17 May 1953). In 1906 he went to Canada to train at Wycliffe Coll, Toronto, and in 1909 he established a mission at Lk Habour, Baffin I, where he stayed until 1916. For his crossing of Foxe Pen on his return, he was made a member of the Royal Geographic Soc. Until his first appointment as archdeacon of the Arctic in 1927, he served first as financial secretary and chaplain to Wycliffe College and then as rector of Old Stone Church, Saint John, NB. His incredible travels as bishop of the Arctic earned him the title "The Flying Bishop." He was author of *The History of St. John's Church, Saint John, New Brunswick* (1925) and *Archibald the Arctic* (1956). FRITS PANNEKOEK

Fleming, Donald Methuen, lawyer, politician (b at Exeter, Ont 23 May 1905). Minister of finance in the DIEFENBAKER government, Fleming is best remembered for his dispute with Bank of Canada Governor James COYNE. Elected to the House in 1945 he contested the Tory leadership in 1948, 1956 and 1967. In May 1956, during the PIPELINE DEBATE, Fleming was ruled out of order in asking a question — incorrectly as history has shown — and expelled from the House by the Speaker. A highly publicized debate with Coyne over monetary and fiscal policy overshadowed his hard work when finance minister. In 1962 he became minister of justice and apart from a brief flirtation with the leadership in 1967, he resigned from public life in 1963.
PATRICIA WILLIAMS

Fleming, May Agnes, née Early, novelist (b at Saint John 15 Nov 1840; d at Brooklyn, NY 24 Mar 1880). She began publishing while still a schoolgirl, her early stories appearing in New York and Boston, Mass, as well as local papers. By the time she moved to Brooklyn, around 1875, she was an established writer. Her novels were serialized in New York and London before being published in book form. Prolific and highly paid, she combined in her fiction elements of romance and gothic mystery and introduced into her later work a private detective. Her best novels are enlivened by fast-moving plots, brisk dialogue and flashes of humour.
LORRAINE MCMULLEN

Fleming, Robert James Berkeley, composer, educator (b at Prince Albert, Sask 12 Nov 1921; d at Ottawa 28 Nov 1976). One of the most prolific Canadian composers of his generation, Fleming won an international reputation through his work at the National Film Board as a staff composer 1946-58 and music director 1958-70. Some 250 film scores are complemented by his large output of music for other performance media — ballet, orchestra, chamber ensemble, band, organ, piano and voice. His ballet, *Shadow on the Prairie* (1952), and the song cycle *The Confession Stone*, composed for Maureen FORRESTER in 1966, both recorded, are representative of the appealing blend of traditional and 20th-century techniques typical of Fleming's style. A devout churchman, Fleming served several parishes as organist-choirmaster. A number of his hymns, carols and settings of the Anglican Eucharist have been published. From 1970 until his death, Fleming taught at Carleton U. BARCLAY MCMILLAN

Fleming, Sir Sandford, civil engineer (b at Kirkcaldy, Scot 7 Jan 1827; d at Halifax 22 July 1915). He was Canada's foremost railway surveyor and construction engineer of the 19th century and a distinguished inventor and scientist. He came to Canada in 1845 and, after studying science and engineering in both Scotland and Canada, joined the engineering staff of the Ontario, Simcoe and Huron Ry, becoming engineer in chief of the successor Northern Ry in 1857. In 1863 the Canadian government appointed him chief surveyor of the first portion of a proposed railway from Québec City to Halifax and Saint John. Subsequently built as the INTERCOLONIAL RY, Fleming was its chief engineer. In 1871 he was appointed engineer of the proposed new Canadian railway from Montréal to the Pacific Coast. He was in charge of the major surveys across the

Sir Sandford Fleming was Canada's foremost railway surveyor and construction engineer. He was also instrumental in the adoption of standard time, and he designed the first Canadian postage stamp (*courtesy Public Archives of Canada/C-14128*).

prairies and through the Rocky Mts. He proposed constructing the railway along a northerly route through Edmonton and the YELLOWHEAD PASS and then turning S to Burrard Inlet on the Pacific. Although his specific recommendations regarding the route were not followed, his extensive survey work of various routes, including the KICKING HORSE PASS through which the Canadian Pacific main line was built, greatly facilitated Canadian railway construction. In the early years of the 20th century the CANADIAN NORTHERN RY was built along the survey route advocated by Fleming.

Fleming retired from the CPR when the Canadian government turned the project over to a private syndicate in 1880, but he continued to do consultative railway work. He also turned his attention to other projects. He was a strong advocate of a telecommunications cable from Canada to Australia, which he believed would become a vital communications link of the British Empire. The Pacific Cable was successfully laid in 1902. He was also interested in the development of a satisfactory world system of keeping time. The railway had made obsolete the old system where every major centre set its clocks according to local astronomical conditions. Fleming advocated the adoption of a standard or mean time and hourly variations from that according to established time zones. He was instrumental in convening an International Prime Meridian Conference in Washington in 1884 at which the system of international standard time — still in use today — was adopted. Fleming also designed the first Canadian postage stamp, the 3-penny beaver, issued in 1851. He was created a CMG in 1877 and a KCMG in 1897. T.D. REGEHR

Flemming, Hugh John, lumberman, politician, premier of NB (b at Peel, NB 5 Jan 1899; d at Fredericton 16 Oct 1982). Elected in 1921 as a municipal councillor for Carleton, Flemming became Conservative MLA for Carleton in 1944. In 1951 he was selected Conservative leader; he led the party to victory in 1952, ending 17 years of Liberal government. He served as premier 1952-60, minister of public works and minister of municipal affairs and modernized NB's hydroelectric system through construction of the Beechwood complex. His government was defeated over hospital taxes. Named federal minister of forestry in 1960 by PM Diefenbaker, he sat for Royal. In 1962 he was elected MP for Victoria-Carleton and appointed minister of national revenue. He continued as MP until 1972 and served on the Atlantic Development Board. DELLA M.M. STANLEY

Flemming, James Kidd, businessman, premier of NB (b at Woodstock, NB 27 Apr 1868; d there 10 Feb 1927). Flemming served as provincial secretary and receiver general before becoming premier in 1911. Three years later he was forced to resign after a royal commission found him guilty of fund-raising irregularities. In 1925 and again the following year he ran for the House of Commons and won resounding victories. He is remembered more for his oratorical ability and colourful personality than for his legislative accomplishments. ARTHUR T. DOYLE

Fletcher, James, entomologist, botanist (b at Ashe, Eng 28 Mar 1852; d at Montréal 8 Nov 1908). Fletcher had been a bank clerk and library assistant, without formal training in biology before his appointment as Canada's first Dominion entomologist and botanist in 1876. He became a recognized specialist on moth, butterfly and weed identification. Through correspondence, he determined the types and number of insect pests in Canada and the damage they caused. The San José Scale Act of 1898, permitting import restrictions and fumigation of insect-infested material and the first federal legislation pertaining to insects, was enacted under his direction. He pressed for government entomological research, instructed the public in practical insect and weed control, established an insect-identification service and founded the Canadian National Collection of insects. The annual reports (1886-1908) and numerous bulletins of the federal Dept of Agriculture and many scientific papers illustrate his achievements. P.W. RIEGERT

Reading: P.W. Riegert, *From Arsenic to DDT: A History of Entomology in Western Canada* (1980).

Flett, John A., trade-union organizer, carpenter (b at Hamilton, Canada W 1860; d there 19 Mar 1941). Flett began a long distinguished labour career in his local carpenters' union. By the end of the 1890s he had filled several important posts in the Hamilton labour movement and was emerging as a leader within the fledgling Trades and Labor Congress of Canada (TLC), where he was an early and outspoken advocate of independent political action for labour. In 1900 the American Federation of Labor (AFL) chose him as its Canadian organizer and Flett travelled across the country adding new recruits. At its 1902 convention the TLC decided to consolidate international unionism in Canada by expelling any "dual unions" which were competing in the same field with AFL affiliates. That meeting also confirmed its commitment to the continental connection by choosing Flett as its president. He remained AFL organizer for Canada until 1925. CRAIG HERON

Fleur-de-lis, *see* LILY.

Flin Flon, Man, City, pop 7894 in Man, 367 in Sask (1981c), inc 1970, is situated along the Manitoba-Saskatchewan border, 870 km NW of Winnipeg. The Saskatchewan part of Flin Flon is jointly administered by the 2 provinces. Despite the discovery of extensive mineral deposits at the site in 1915, it was more than a decade before production occurred. Construction of a railway link with The Pas (1928), development of a power source at Island Falls on the Churchill R (1929) and successful extraction processes facilitated development, as did the involvement of H.P. Whitney of New York, who by 1927 had formed Hudson Bay Mining and Smelting Co Ltd. By 1930 production began at what became Canada's largest zinc refinery and third-largest copper smelter. Many families left the Prairies during the 1930s for Flin Flon, determined to make new lives for themselves. Flin Flon is still dependent on mining. In recent years HBMS has established satellite mines in the region, including a new concentrator at Snow Lake, a community to the E. The city has a trade population of 15 000 and is a tourism/recreation centre.

Flin Flon, named after the fictional character Josiah *Flin*abbatey *Flon*atin, developed initially in an unplanned manner near the mine and plant. Costs of materials and the rocky terrain led to construction of small houses and businesses with minimal amenities. Redevelopment and newer residential areas have improved the townscape. The city hosts an annual Trout Festival in July, and is known for its production of fine hockey talent. D.M. LYON

Reading: V. Hedman et al, *Flin Flon* (1974).

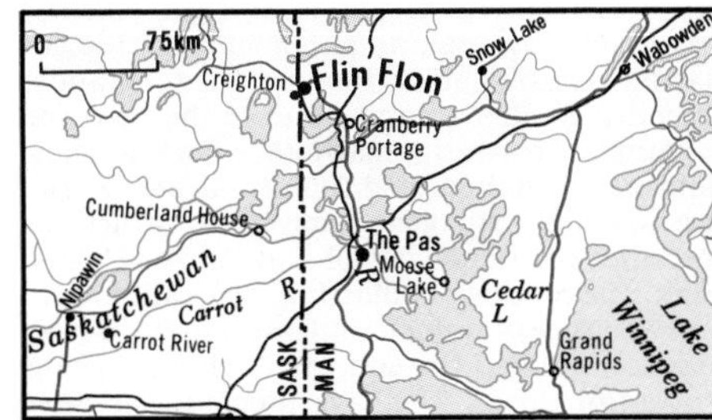

Floods and Flood Control Floods are the result of naturally occurring variations in the height of rivers, lakes and oceans. Flood damage occurs when people knowingly or unknowingly locate their activities, buildings and other property within range of the variations that occur above "normal" levels. There are 2 definitions of a flood: the hydrological definition, ie, when water levels exceed their "normal" range (flood stage); and the economic definition, when damage begins (flood damage stage).

The main cause of riverine flooding is excessive runoff following heavy RAINS. Runoff is augmented by snowmelt in early spring; for much of Canada spring is the peak flood season. Floods can also be caused by ice jams, when upstream water is blocked by accumulations of ice downstream, and by heavy convectional storms in summer. Similar high-water problems occur on lakes. Damage to shoreline facilities is not uncommon on the Great Lakes and occurs occasionally on most other lakes (eg, Lk Winnipeg). Coastal flooding may be caused when seasonally high tides are augmented by storm activity, or when a tsunami, generated by EARTHQUAKES, is driven ashore. This phenomenon occurs occasionally on the West Coast. Coastal flooding related to hurricanes sometimes occurs in Atlantic Canada.

One of Canada's most difficult flood problems is on the RED R in Manitoba. Snowmelt waters from the US flow N through a wide, flat plain, and severe flooding sometimes creates havoc in many small communities as well as in Winnipeg. Major floods occurred in Winnipeg in 1950 and 1966. To alleviate the danger to the city a major flood diversion channel has been constructed. Major floods also occur in the lower FRASER R valley, S of Vancouver. In 1948, 16 000 people were evacuated from their homes, and damage was estimated at over $20 million (1948 dollars). In 1954 heavy rains associated with the passage of Hurricane Hazel caused flooding on the Don and Humber rivers in Toronto and resulted in 81 deaths and high damages. Damaging floods have also occurred at Red Deer, Alta (Red Deer R); Swift Current and Moose Jaw, Sask; Fredericton (Saint John R); along the Châteauguay, Richelieu, Yamaska, St François and Chaudière rivers, Qué; and at many other localities in Canada.

Flood Control A traditional approach to flooding has been to attempt to control high flows by construction of dams, dikes and diversion channels. While there are no accurate statistics on national flood damage, some evidence suggests that such engineering works have not prevented a rise in nationwide damages. In many regions, urban and suburban developments for housing, industry and commercial activities have been located on floodplains. When floods occur they cause more damage than in the past because more property lies in the path of floodwaters.

In an attempt to reverse this trend the federal government invited the provinces to join in a co-ordinated program to tackle the increasing toll of flood damages in a more comprehensive way. A flood-damage reduction program was announced in 1975, its main element being the preparation of flood risk maps to identify hazard areas. Provincial and municipal policies, regulations, bylaws and public information activities are based on such maps. The program is intended to alert communities to the need for a comprehensive approach to reducing flood damage, including flood forecasting and warning systems, emergency measures, structural measures for flood control and land-use planning. The concept of adjusting the location, pattern and type of human settlement to flood hazard has replaced the concept of simply trying to control floods. The new program has been well received by most provinces and is being carried out under federal-provincial agreements. *See* DISASTERS. IAN BURTON

Floras and Botanical Journals A published "flora" may be defined loosely as a comprehensive, itemized description of the PLANTS of a specific geographical region. Usually more than a mere list, it should involve an analytical description, discussing habitats and distribution and citing previous authorities. This definition would not apply to travelogues, natural histories, botanical art books or popular manuals, of which there were several in Canada by the late 19th century. Before this time, floras dealing with the area now comprising Canada were published elsewhere and written by botanical explorers and by sedentary scholars who identified specimens received from colonial residents, travellers and professional collectors.

Until the 19th century the only published floras containing predominantly Canadian plants were those of Jacques Phillippe Cornut in 1635 (*Canadensium Plantarum Historia*) and Pierre-François-Xavier de CHARLEVOIX in 1744 (*Histoire et description générale de la Nouvelle France*). The manuscripts of Canadian flora known to have been started in the 18th century by Michel SARRAZIN, Jean-François GAULTHIER and Pehr KALM were not published. Early in the 19th century, André MICHAUX and Frederick PURSH included more than 400 Canadian locales in their northern American floras, and Bachelot de la Pylaie wrote a modest flora of Newfoundland, but never completed the expected sequel. In 1815 Pursh began collecting for a Canadian flora but he died in Montréal in 1820, shortly after his collection was destroyed by fire.

The era of the itinerant botanical visitor or absentee scholar reached its climax in Canada with William Jackson Hooker, who amassed the collections of explorers, collectors and residents from coast to coast for his monumental *Flora Boreali Americana* (1833-40). Among his contributors in Québec was a small group of botanizers, including Harriet and William Sheppard, who were encouraged by Pursh, and who also sent specimens to John Torrey and Asa Gray for their *Flora of North America* (1838-43). Sheppard, a lumber merchant, did not confine his communications to foreign professionals. In 1829 Canada's first scholarly journal, the *Transactions of the Literary and Historical Society of Quebec*, contained Sheppard's identifications and popular descriptions of Charlevoix's plants and in 1831 and 1837 his articles titled "Notes on some of the plants of Lower Canada." Although intended for local amateurs, this pioneer work gave Linnaean classification and synonyms, translated Pursh's Latin descriptive specifications and elaborated on habitats, uses and points of interest.

Botanical articles including plant lists were carried in *The Canadian Journal* (1852) in Toronto, *The Canadian Naturalist and Geologist* (1856) in Montréal, the short-lived *Annals of the Botanical Society of Canada* (1860) in Kingston and the *Proceedings and Transactions of the Nova Scotian Institute of Science* (1863) in Halifax. Their pages frequently announced intentions to compile regional or national floras, but none were published. Credit for the first extensive flora by a Canadian belongs to another Québec amateur, Abbé Léon PROVANCHER, whose 2-volume *Flore Canadienne* appeared in 1862. Because he openly borrowed numerous illustrations from 2 books by the influential Asa Gray, this flora was seldom cited by contemporary botanists; subsequently, Provancher successfully shifted his scientific efforts to entomology, much of it published in his *Naturaliste Canadien* (est 1868).

Later regional periodicals, such as the *Transactions of the Ottawa Field-Naturalists' Club* (est 1880) and the *Bulletin of the Natural History Society of New Brunswick* (est 1882) carried detailed local floras as well as botanical notes. The more professional Canadian botanists, such as George LAWSON in Halifax, continued to publish articles of high quality abroad or in the *Transactions of the Royal Society of Canada* (est 1882). Throughout this period, abbreviated floras were appended to many botanical textbooks and manuals published in Canada, and lists of plants from remote regions were included in the reports of the GEOLOGICAL SURVEY by such indefatigable field men as Robert BELL and John MACOUN.

The ultimate in historic Canadian floras, the first that could compare favourably with the best from abroad, was the *Catalogue of Canadian Plants*, compiled by Macoun and published in 7 parts (1883-1902). Despite its thousands of species, some with descriptions, synonyms, habitats, locales and authorities, Macoun modestly considered it only preliminary to a "Flora of Canada", which would have to await the 20th century. Nonetheless, Canadian botanical description could be considered to have come of age after a painful adolescence marked by catastrophic losses, disappointed hopes and deplorable neglect. This slow maturation deserves recognition as pioneering scholarship under adverse conditions. J.M. NEELIN

Reading: M.A. Downie and M. Hamilton, *'and some brought flowers': Plants in a New World* (1980).

Florenceville, NB, Village, pop 709 (1981c), inc 1966, is situated 146 km up the SAINT JOHN R from Fredericton. The initial wave of LOYALIST settlers was augmented by 19th-century immigrants to form the basis of Florenceville's population. (It was so named in 1855 by Lt-Gov L.A. Wilmot in honour of Crimean War heroine Florence Nightingale.) The community's initial growth flourished on the W bank of the Saint John R, but the completion of a bridge in 1884 and a spectacular fire in 1911 shifted the centre of commerce activity to the E bank. In the 20th century Florenceville's development has been synonymous with the development of a small dealer in potatoes and other agricultural products into an international frozen-food industry. FRED FARRELL

Flounder, *see* FLATFISH.

Flour Milling is the process of grinding grain into flour or meal. Canada's flour milling industry comprises mills which produce flour and other products for use in baked goods, pasta and other food products. By-products of the milling process, such as bran, shorts (fine bran) and wheat germ, are used mainly in the production of animal feeds, but small quantities of bran and wheat germ are also required for human consumption. Flour milling predates agricultural production; its evolution from a tedious manual chore to a highly automated, efficient and exact industrial process reflects many social changes and significant technological developments.

In N America, in precontact times, native people hand-ground corn and other substances (eg, acorns) into flour used in porridge, flat cakes, etc. By the middle of the 16th century, the first European settlers had arrived in NEW FRANCE, bringing with them their flour milling TECHNOLOGY. The first water-powered mill commenced operation in 1607 at PORT-ROYAL. Many of the early wind and water-driven mills have been preserved and may be seen in Ontario, Québec and the Maritimes. Pairs of circular millstones were used for grinding the grain. The best millstones, made of burr, a hard silicate found in France's Seine River Valley, were constructed in segments, cemented together and bound with heavy iron bands. Both milling faces of the stones were grooved. The miller's skill lay in maintaining the grinding faces of the stones, since the precision of the millstone dressing determined the fineness of the grist. Stones were dressed with a chisel-faced hammer, called a "mill-bill." A flour miller also required a "true-steel" (ie, a straightedge used to test the evenness of the millstones), a bar scale for weighing and a slate for tallying the incoming grain and the outgoing grist.

For most of history, flour milling has been a very manpower-intensive operation with grain, ground stocks in process and finished products requiring handling at every stage. The 18th century saw a growth of scientific ideas which brought significant changes to the process. Vertical and horizontal conveying of grain and ground materials by mechanical means (achieved by 1785) halved the manpower requirements in a mill and transformed flour milling into a completely mechanized continuous-process industry. Flour milling was one of the earliest applications of the steam engine. James Watt used one to drive a mill which he built in London, UK, in 1786. The mill used 6 pairs of millstones and, before its destruction by fire in 1791, was enlarged to 20 pairs, driven by 2 steam engines. In the latter part of the 19th century, Canadian millers were quick to replace millstones with steel rolls and to adopt the "Gradual Reduction System," a milling method developed in Hungary, which proved to be much more efficient with the use of steel rolls. The method involves milling in stages, the gound stock at each stage being sifted to remove the product and classify the remaining stocks for futher gradual reduction. Many more-or-less successful variations have appeared throughout the past century.

The construction of a railway linking the prairie grain-producing region with the Great Lakes markedly influenced Canada's milling industry, permitting western Canadian wheat to be shipped to the eastern seaboard ports for export and to the mills in eastern Canada for processing. The railway was extended to the western seaboard by 1885. Canadian wheat was already known for its excellent milling and breadmaking qualities and, as domestic and export demands increased, wheat production in the Prairies expanded to meet it. By 1900, annual flour exports exceeded 80 000 t. The first decades of the 20th century were a period of competition and rationalization in the industry. The number of mills decreased from 2550 in 1891 to 801 in 1922. The industry was affected by the GREAT DEPRESSION of the 1930s, but expanded during WWII. Since that time, the industry has been futher rationalized and modernized as flour exports have fallen and most trading partners have developed domestic milling industries.

Modern flour mills are very highly automated and some parts of the process are easily adapted to computer control. Automation, improvements in transportation and declining trade have led to a further reduction of the number of mills in operation. As of June, 1984, Canada had 36 flour mills: Ont had 17; Qué, 5; Alta, Man and Sask, 4 each; BC and NS, one each. Total milling capacity, over 11 000 t of wheat ground per day, produces slightly over 8500 t of flour. The industry employs over 5000 people and has an annual payroll of over $81 million.

White flour for the Canadian market is enriched in accordance with regulations outlined in the Food and Drugs Act (*see* FOOD LEGISLATION). Other optional additives are used to meet customer specifications; however, the kinds and quantities of each FOOD ADDITIVE are also controlled through the Food and Drugs Act and a system of inspection ensures adherence to all regulations.

The Canadian National Millers Association is a national trade association representing virtually 100% of Canada's millers. The CNMA was founded 29 Oct 1920 and its permanent office is in Ottawa. Most of the information distributed from the CNMA national office is of a technical nature (eg, relating to contracts, traffic considerations, statistical details, metrication). In the recent past the CNMA has made representations on numerous government policies and acted on the industry's behalf in a successful appeal to the Supreme Court of Canada. The CNMA maintains ongoing contact with officials from various departments and agencies, including the CANADIAN WHEAT BOARD and the Dept of Regional Economic Expansion. Each year CNMA executives negotiate Canada's yearly sale of flour to Russia for export to Cuba. The most recent contract was for 260 000 t, a significant percentage of the industry's overall production.

PAUL W. BRENNAN

Flowers, Cultivated Flowers are cultivated by both commercial growers and hobbyists. In Canada, most commercial production is carried out under glass or plastic, with rare exceptions (eg, gladiolus, baby's breath, Shasta daisy). Commercial GREENHOUSE production is a year-round enterprise with crops such as carnation, ROSE and chrysanthemum, but is seasonally oriented with crops such as poinsettia (Christmas) and Bermuda lily (Easter). Houseplants (eg, cyclamen, cineraria, pelargonium, African violet) are produced in many commercial greenhouses but the volume is not large, relative to the previously mentioned crops. In 1980 the commercial flower and VEGETABLE industry in Canada had 4 million m^2 under glass or plastic; the sales of flowers in the same year amounted to approximately $185 million.

For those who grow flowers for sheer enjoyment, the culture of perennial flowers appears to offer the greatest satisfaction. Regional, national and international societies exist to promote interest in and improvement of special kinds of flowers, eg, lily, dahlia, peony and gladiolus. A brochure titled *Canadian Specialist Plant Societies*, compiled by T.J. Cole of the Ottawa Research Station, Agriculture Canada, lists 47 societies catering to the interests of the growers of 17 plant specialties. Public interest is also fostered by participation in flower shows sponsored by local societies.

Flowers in great variety may be seen in all parts of Canada, from the time the last snow disappears until the first killing frost of autumn. The earliest flowers, the small flowering bulbs (eg, crocus, puschkinia, chionodoxa, scilla), are followed by the larger narcissus and tulip. In many parts of Canada the primrose (*Primula*) and its relative the cortusa have become very popular spring flowers. Low cushion plants (eg, phlox, aubretia, arabis) also provide colour at this time of year.

In summer, gardeners will generally opt for the use of annual flowers only, or for a combination of long-blooming perennials with annuals. The first option limits the gardener to a constant, unchanging array of colour from the time the plants reach full bloom in late June (in most parts of Canada) until they are killed by autumn frost. The second option provides the grower with greater variety by employing the more ephemeral perennials in key positions, with annual flowers being supplementary. The perennials most commonly used are Shasta daisy, peony, oriental poppy, lythrum, hollyhock, anthemis, day lily, monkshood and delphinium. The most common annuals used are snapdragon, petunia, aster, verbena, bush balsam and marigold.

The sources of information for the amateur flower grower are abundant. The popular literature is immense, and the information is generally of universal acceptibility. Commercial growers are also generally well supported by specialists employed by Agriculture Canada (eg, at RESEARCH STATIONS across the country), provincial departments of agriculture, and horticulture departments in some colleges and universities. *See* BOTANICAL GARDENS. R.H. KNOWLES

Reading: Reader's Digest, *Illustrated Guide to Gardening in Canada* (1979).

Fluke, *see* FLATWORM.

Fly, term commonly applied to many actively flying INSECTS; restricted by scientists to two-winged flies of order Diptera. This order includes BLACK FLIES, blow flies, bot flies, crane flies, deer flies, face flies, flesh flies, gnats, horn flies, horse flies, house flies, MIDGES, MOSQUITOES, no-see-ums, stable flies and warble flies. Four-winged "flies," eg, ALDERFLIES, BUTTERFLIES, CADDISFLIES, DAMSELFLIES, DRAGONFLIES, LACEWINGS, MAYFLIES, SAWFLIES, scorpionflies, snakeflies, STONEFLIES and whiteflies, are not true flies. About 100 000 species of Diptera have been described worldwide; the actual number may be double that. Over 7000 species have been reported in Canada, a figure also estimated to represent only half the species present. Flies range in size from 1 mm to 5.5 cm. Their relative abundance in the insect fauna increases northwards; in the most severe arctic localities, they outnumber all other winged insects, both as species and individuals. The most obvious characteristic distinguishing true flies from other insects is the modification of the hind wings into knob-shaped, gyroscopic organs (halteres), essential for maintaining balance in flight. They allow flies to perform outstanding feats of aerobatics (eg, landing upside-down on ceilings).

Adult flies have sucking or piercing mouthparts and lack mandibles with which other insects bite food. The term "biting flies" is incorrect, since all such flies (eg, horse flies, mosquitoes, etc) pierce skin with a stabbing action. It is thought that adult flies were, primitively, predators of other insects, using their mouthparts to pierce prey's integument (body covering), and that the habit of sucking VERTEBRATE blood evolved from this. Many modern flies, including voracious predators like robber flies and dance flies, still attack only other insects. Most predatory flies feed on carbohydrates, eg, honeydew and nectar, as well as animal prey. Some flies have abandoned predation and use pollen (hover flies) or decaying material (house flies) as their protein source. Adult warble and bot flies do not feed, relying on fat reserves accumulated in larval stage.

Dipteran larvae are legless. Most are maggots living concealed within a moist substrate, but some hoverflies have free-living larvae, which prey on APHIDS. Specialized swimming larvae have evolved in mosquitoes and related groups of nonbiting midges. Most fly larvae feed on microorganisms or decaying matter. A few are predatory or parasitic: larvae of marsh flies (sciomyzids) kill snails; those of horse flies (tabanids), robber flies (asilids) and dance flies (empidids) prey on other insect larvae; those of tachinids (parasitic flies) are specialized internal parasites, important in biological control of INSECT PESTS. Although few groups of flies have evolved exclusively plant-eating larvae (notably fruit flies, gall midges and leaf-mining flies), those that have are unusually diverse and actively evolving. Among aquatic larvae, those of nonbiting midges form a major part of the invertebrate biomass in Canadian waters.

Flies are holometabolous insects, ie, they pass through a nonfeeding pupal stage before becoming adult. In higher flies, the pupa is enclosed in an outer shell (puparium) which gives added protection against drying, drowning, etc. The earliest described fossil Diptera date from Upper Triassic (170 million years ago). More advanced Diptera probably did not appear until late Cretaceous, but dating is uncertain. Western Canadian amber from the Cretaceous (about 80 million years ago) is a promising source of fossil Diptera. The enlarged salivary glands of many Diptera contain giant chromosomes convenient for GENETIC studies. This trait, and their willingness to breed in bottles make *Drosophila* a popular experimental animal. G.C.D. GRIFFITHS

Reading: G.C.D. Griffiths, ed, *Flies of the Nearctic Region* (1980).

Flycatcher, Tyrant (Tyrannidae), large, diverse New World family of BIRDS. The name flycatcher also refers to some members of Old World family Muscicapidae and to some other birds. Of the 367 known species of Tyrannidae, 16 regularly breed in Canada (10 called flycatchers, 2 kingbirds, 2 pewees, 2 phoebes); 7 others stray here. Tyrannidae range from robin to warbler size. Many are dull olive green; some are strikingly coloured. All feed by capturing a flying insect and returning to a perch to eat it. They are the only representatives in Canada of the suboscine perching birds (ie, those without true songs), and their loud, abrupt calls are the easiest means of distinguishing many species in the field. Canadian Tyrannidae are present May-Sept, when insects are available. Great crested flycatcher (*Myiarchus crinitus*) of eastern broad-leaved woodlands and olive-sided flycatcher (*Contopus borealis*) of coniferous forests across Canada are large compared with species of genus *Empidonax*. Yellow-bellied flycatcher (*E. flaviventris*) of northern spruce forests, least flycatcher (*E. minimus*) of broad-leaved stands and alder flycatcher (*E. alnorum*) of alder and willow thickets are widespread from Newfoundland to northern BC. Three others (*E. oberholseri, E. hammondii*, and *E. difficilis*) occur only in the West, and 2 southern species (*E. virescens, E. traillii*) breed only a short distance N of US border. The kingbirds are large, pugnacious flycatchers. Eastern kingbirds (*Tyrannus tyrannus*) breed from NWT to NS; western kingbirds (*T. verticalis*) are found in the southern prairies and southern BC. Pewees are little larger than *Empidonax* flycatchers. Eastern wood pewees (*Contopus virens*) breed in southern Canada from Man to NS. Western wood pewees (*C. sordidulus*) are found from SW Man to southern YT, including coastal BC. Phoebes are bluebird sized. Eastern phoebes (*Sayornis phoebe*) are found from southeastern YT across southern Ontario and SW Québec to NB. Say's phoebe (*S. saya*) breeds in the NWT, YT, BC, Alberta and southern Saskatchewan. A.J. ERSKINE

Flynn, Edmund James, premier of Québec (b at Percé, Canada E 16 Nov 1847; d at Québec C 7 June 1927). A meticulous politician, he proved a highly competent minister of natural resources, but when asked to succeed Premier TAILLON, he was unable to breathe life into the moribund Conservative Party. He served as premier from May 1896 to May 1897. His party was defeated in the elections of 1897, 1900 and 1904, thereby ushering in a Liberal regime that was to last until the 1936 election of Maurice DUPLESSIS.

DANIEL LATOUCHE

Fog, concentration of atmospheric particles (usually minute water droplets or ICE crystals) of sufficient density to reduce visibility. For practical purposes, in Canada, a reduction of visibility to 1000-9600 m is arbitrarily called mist; reduction to under 1000 m is called fog. In contrast, haze is a condition where such dry atmospheric particles as dust, ocean salt, natural oils from forest vegetation or forest-fire smoke are present in sufficient quantity to obscure vision. Near or downwind from industrial centres, combustion products such as smoke, soot, sulphuric and nitric oxides can combine with and acidify fog (*see* ACID RAIN). The major centres in Canada that experience most fog are St. John's, Nfld, with fog reported on an average of 126 days per year; Halifax, NS, with 74; Vancouver, BC, with 62. Penticton, BC, receives least fog, an average of 4 days per year.

Radiation fog forms most commonly as moist air is cooled below its dew point, ie, the critical temperature at which air can no longer hold all its water vapour. A dense fog develops if the liquid water droplets or ice crystals formed by condensation are trapped and concentrated in a shallow layer near the ground by a temperature inversion (in which temperature increases with height rather than decreasing with height as is usual). Such special meteorological conditions arise quite frequently. For example, in Canada's coastal regions the cool Pacific and Atlantic Ocean waters chill warm, moist air masses moving over them, especially in spring and early summer, causing huge banks of persistent fog (called advection fog). Inland fog is commonly caused by the cooling of the lower atmosphere through the radiation of heat into space on cloudless nights. In early morning (particularly in autumn), dense fog banks form and persist until dissipated by the heat of the sun. Weather satellite pictures show that this drying out process proceeds inwards from the outer edges of the fog bank. Warm fronts of weather systems also cause fog when the cool air below the frontal surface becomes saturated by rain falling into it from the warmer air above. This type usually persists until swept away by drier air.

Occasionally, freezing fogs form (mainly of the radiation and frontal types) when liquid water droplets exist at temperatures a little below freezing. Such droplets are said to be supercooled and freeze into beautiful fringes of hoar frost on wires, trees and other objects. In the depths of Canada's arctic winters, the air is so bitterly cold that it can hold very little water vapour. When cooled further, what little vapour there is condenses into a fog of tiny, sparkling ice crystals rather than liquid droplets. Any extra moisture placed into the atmosphere (eg, by vehicle exhaust) also expands into an immediate ice-crystal fog. Arctic sea smoke, another type of winter fog, is formed when air, made warm and moist by contact with open water, rises through convection and condensation takes place immediately. MICHAEL J. NEWARK

Fogo Island, 260 km^2, 15 km off Newfoundland's NE coast, was named *fuego*, "fire," by the Portuguese. The irregularly shaped island, heavily forested in the S, lies on shallow Fogo Shelf, which attracts salmon, cod and other species. Until the late 1700s Fogo was a summer home of the BEOTHUK. European fishermen visited its waters from the early 1500s and settlement began at Fogo Harbour (now Fogo), an outpost of Poole and Dorset businesses, in the early 1700s. The island, connected by ferry with Carmanville across Hamilton Sound, now supports 10 settlements though it once had 26. In the 1960s attempts to resettle Fogo I were countered by a movement towards rural development, aided by the NATIONAL FILM BOARD, whose short documentaries helped to unite residents, crossing traditional social, cultural and religious lines. The "Fogo Process," the interactive use of film and videotape to foster community awareness and identity, is now used for the same purpose in underdeveloped countries. In Fogo, resettlement was abandoned, a fishermen's co-operative founded, educational facilities integrated, and a near-shore, long-liner fishery developed.

JANET E.M. PITT

Folk Art embraces a wide range of artistic works, a mixture of naivety and sophistication, cultural tradition and individual innovation. Although varied definitions abound, folk art in general falls into 2 categories: cultural and individual. Cultural art has an ethnic basis (French, English, German, Polish, Ukrainian), tends to be conservative, and reflects the common ethos in a community; individual art is innovative, the expression of a unique if sometimes eccentric personality. Whether they are paintings, sculptures, carvings or objects embellished with pictorial and decorative motifs, all folk-art products have popular appeal. The people who fashioned them intended them to interest the ordinary citizens who were their neighbours, friends and acquaintances. Traditionally, folk art sprang from a desire to make human and meaningful the daily round of work and home life, and thus reflected the cultural and regional diversity in Canada. Contemporary folk art, often shut off from traditional sources and responding to the demand by museums and collectors for "goods," is an art of individual and aesthetic expression, employing new techniques and responding to influences in modern society. While traditional folk art is usually anonymous, recent artists are known and specialize in particular media and styles.

Folk art mirrors the basic ideas and customs that regulate life-styles, and may be based in religion, patriotic affection for king and country, satisfaction with daily living or appreciation for nature. Folk art is sometimes described as "primitive," for the artists are untrained, work by instinct and deal in a simple way with the basic truths as known to ordinary people.

Folk art based on religious belief has flourished in Canada from the days of early European settlement and embraces a sense of continuity and tradition. Visitors to 18th- and 19th-century Catholic Québec described the pious decorative mottoes, the religious paintings depicting old themes, and the cocks on church steeples, which reminded parishioners of St Peter's in Rome. They had been painted or fashioned by simple, devout people who lacked artistic training but who had in common a great desire to express their inner artistic sensibilities. A significant form of early religious folk art, copied from France, was the VOTIVE PAINTING that illustrated miraculous happenings such as escape from impending shipwreck through the intervention of Ste-Anne (collection of Ste-Anne-de-Beaupré, Québec). The sculptured figures of the Holy Family and favourite saints that adorned many churches inspired the carving of more primitive copies for private religious devotion. Wayside crosses throughout Québec were erected at many crossroads and the crucified Christ who hung on some of them was often carved by a local worker. Such carvings sometimes rose to the level of the finest folk art. An example originating in the Gaspé Peninsula and now in the Montreal Museum of Fine Arts is a massive, simple, austere, Christ figure, with dignified simple planes; it does not strive for the realism of high art. Local people carved nativity figures for the Christmas crib, painted pictures of the lamb on banners that were carried in religious processions, or carved sugar molds with biblical motifs. All these artifacts were reminders of religious teachings and emphasized the importance of religious life in an agreeable way. In Charlevoix County during the 1930s and 1940s a group of local artists pictured well-known themes, some of them religious, such as the wise men visiting a local home and mingling informally with the family at Christmas.

Polish cut-out depicting a peacock and a flower (*courtesy National Museums of Canada/National Museum of Man/82-331*).

The carving of explorer Marco Polo graced the stern of the famous NB clipper of the same name (*courtesy New Brunswick Museum*).

The religious art of Protestant provinces in Canada seems less obvious because they did not allow representations of God. Yet wall memorials to departed relatives or SAMPLERS embroidered in Nova Scotia during the early 1800s demonstrate deep religious piety. Protestant ORANGE ORDER lodges carried painted banners with religious symbols in their street processions, and many Protestant homes had little paintings of King Billy on his white horse. Religious banners hung in Sharon Temple, built by a Protestant group N of Toronto. A century ago Anna WEBER, a Mennonite, painted motifs in Waterloo County, Ont, that symbolized nature as described in the "Songs of Solomon." Early TOMBSTONES in local cemeteries almost everywhere in Canada are often overlooked as folk art. One such stone in Ontario recalls graphically how a pioneer was killed by a falling tree when clearing the primeval forest. An 18th-century Halifax tombstone shows Ezekiel blowing his trumpet on Judgement Day, and nearby another stone pictures Adam and Eve flanking the serpent encircling an apple tree. Another example of religious folk art is the "corn dolly" artistically woven from the last sheaf of the harvest and sometimes thrown into the fire to propitiate the gods, which harks back to superstitions in England during the Druid age.

Loyalty to country, racial origin and religion have been common themes of the folk artist in Canada, whether British, French, German, Italian, Mennonite, Ukrainian, Doukhobor or Polish. Battle memorials in the form of descriptive paintings or soldiers carved in full uniform are numerous, and patriotic mothers hooked pictures of tanks and flags on mats during both world wars. LOYALIST immigrants to Canada left no doubt of their continuing British sympathies; they erected a signboard on which was painted the head of George III in front of the King's Head Inn at Burlington, Ont. A local carver fashioned a statue of General WOLFE that stood in a niche at a Québec street corner for many years. Lutheran immigrants from the Palatine region of Germany who settled along the upper St Lawrence in 1784 fashioned a weather vane in the form of a swan because the Swan of St Lothair had been a traditional symbol in their homeland. It declared their ancestry. Inn and trade signs in English and French towns were like a popular picture gallery which fascinated the people, and in imitation similar signs were painted in Canada. Traditional designs for clothes and decorations used in Europe were continued in the New World. Ukrainian Easter eggs are an ancient and sophisticated folk art with religious and symbolic significance. The tradition of hand-lettered and decorated documents, books and miscellaneous items was brought by Mennonite immigrants to Ontario between the 1780s and 1830s (*see* GERMANIC FRAKTUR AND CALLIGRAPHY). Gradually, Canadian loyalties and heroes developed. John A. MACDONALD was featured on a sampler in the 1880s, and designs incorporated maple leaves, beavers and Mounties on any number of objects. Other occupational figures, particularly the cowboy and the pioneer settler, were favourite motifs in folk art.

These Good Old Thrashing Days by Jan Wyers, oil on fabric (*courtesy Norman Mackenzie Art Gallery, Regina*).

When sailing ships were links with distant places, up to the early 20th century, much distinctive folk art relating to the sea was produced, particularly in the schooner and lighthouse motifs on the eastern seaboard (*see* SCULPTURE). Crews had an affection for their ships and named vessels in honour of celebrated naval heroes such as Admiral Nelson, or after more personal associations, such as the "Mary W." Craftsmen in the shipyards of Québec City, Saint John, Digby or Summerside carved figureheads of buxom women or a tall admiral to illustrate the name. A notable carving graced the clipper MARCO POLO, which had been built near Saint John and made record-breaking voyages to the Orient. Sailors on distant voyages passed long hours in a myriad of activities; some made models or paintings of their ship to be displayed at home, often with intricate riggings; others carved trinket boxes or whalebone ivory, engraving the polished surfaces with pictures of unicorns, polar bears, or tokens of endearment for absent loved ones.

Similarly, much Canadian folk art relates to farming, which played a major role in national life. Agriculture in Ontario and Québec reached a peak of visible prosperity in the later 19th century when vast BARNS were constructed, many of them crowned by decorative metal and wooden weather vanes fashioned as horses, cows or sheep. Progressive farmers of the day exhibited their finest livestock at country fairs or provincial exhibitions in Toronto, Québec City and Fredericton and artist/craftsmen such as J.W. Swift of Toronto were commissioned to paint the best stock in watercolour or oil. Some farmers still hang hand-painted signs depicting their particular herd type at the entrance to their property. Dutch immigrant Jan Wyers has produced some of the country's finest popular paintings of the last half century, especially of farm life, and William Panko, a western artist of the 1940s who knew nothing about perspective, painted scenes that reveal a direct joy in the fresh outdoors. On the self-sufficient farm, where a variety of tasks were performed in the fields and in the home, many useful objects were fashioned in an attractive shape and with fine, meaningful ornamentation. Hand tools, trivets, molds, and combs used in spinning were often examples of high craftsmanship (*see* LEATHERWORKING). Wooden butter stamps served as a trademark and as proof of the farmer's aesthetic sensibility. Rural women recycled textile fibres into decorative hooked RUGS and QUILTS whose blocks of colour and design rival fine contemporary nonobjective painting. They embroidered pillowcases, table linen and handkerchiefs with pictorial tokens of love. Whittlers in the family created models of family pets and dancing dolls, and carved wall shelves and cabinets, rocking horses and TOYS for the children (*see* FURNITURE, COUNTRY). More sophisticated sculptors turned out elaborate decoys for the hunting season, painted to depict every detail of the species. Wooden chests served as travelling trunks and as storage boxes in the home.

With increasing industrialization, many craftsmen turned their skills to creating miniatures of a passing rural life, recording the skills, amusements and tales of the past in tangible form for the next generation. Other carvers depicted the new technology, in steam engines that worked and intricate models of prairie farm machinery.

Folk art does not have to be useful, or based on culture or tradition. It may be purely whimsical, rooted in the particular imagination of the artist. Garden ornaments, birdhouses, shadowboxes and figurines may be exotic, erotic, humorous or fanciful, though always direct and spontaneous in their "folksiness." The sculptor J.B. Côté of Québec once carved a wooden figure, a gaunt, gangling youth who sang in the choir and had about him the air of a young "man-about-town" but who was trussed or strangled by his starched Sunday collar. His attractive human qualities gave him immediate popular appeal and, like all successful folk art, enlivened the life of ordinary people around him. *See also* FOLK DANCE; FOLKLORE and FOLK MUSIC.

J. RUSSELL HARPER

Reading: M. Bird, *Canadian Folk Art* (1983) and *Ontario Fraktur* (1977); P. Crépeau et al, *From the Heart: Folk Art in Canada* (1983); J. Russell Harper, *A People's Art* (1974).

Folk Dance exists on a variety of levels and folk dancers think of it in many ways. A definition includes several key elements. Folk dance is vernacular in that it is characteristic of a particular time and place and relates to a popular rather than an elite aspect of a culture. Folk dance belongs to the "little" tradition within the "great" tradition of a society since it is primarily an oral or customary tradition, unwritten and unofficial. "Survival" folk dances are those that serve an integral function within a community; "revival" folk dances lack this stature and are performed by a select group of people who dance for various personal reasons.

One result of an oral, as opposed to a written, tradition is that people see, hear and perform differently; therefore they transmit the material in a variety of ways. With folk dance, no particular version of a dance is the definitive one. If variants do not exist, then a dance was undoubtedly passed on in a nontraditional way, perhaps by written official sources or by a group that zealously guarded the "purity" of the dance. Although documents that record the historical development of folk dance are scarce, some researchers believe that many dance forms grew from religious rituals. Each culture area has experienced its own evolution, although some areas have had more contact with external influences than others.

Social dance, although not usually considered so, is an important form of folk dance and exists at several levels. Dance studios teach the "right" way, but in practice people invent, simplify and change the order, thereby creating variants in dances such as the waltz, cha-cha, disco or jitterbug. Social dance is part of the "little" tradition in a culture, and is vernacular. At its most sophisticated, social dancing can be executed as a performance. In the western European tradition, social dance is performed in couples and its usual function is courtship, a valuable ritual. Most social dances enjoy a short but intense popularity, which then declines. Some, however, possess an unusual longevity: the waltz, polka, square dance and longways forms and the minuet of the 18th and 19th centuries are good examples. Not as popular as it was in past periods, social dancing is still considered a convenient and acceptable way to meet people. Companies, clubs, university groups, high schools and community centres host social dance events regularly.

In Canada, with the exception of social dancing, there is little activity on the level of survival folk dancing. As there are few studies in folk dance, it is difficult to determine precisely the amount of survival dancing. However, it is found among relatively isolated (geographically or psychologically) communities, such as the native peoples, and the francophone and Hassidic cultures. Urban-based minority groups, such as Indian, Chinese, Italian, Portuguese, Ukrainian, Macedonian, Greek, Polish, German, Armenian, Irish, Latin-American and West Indian, might have retained some of the dances which are unique to their regional origins. But as the first- and second-generation immigrants die off, the third and subsequent generations tend to assimilate into mainstream society, and with them go the dances which were once an important part of their social, occupational or religious spheres.

Revival dances are more frequent and more visible. They are especially noticeable among groups who have strong feelings for their ethnic roots. One way to preserve, express and perpetuate this sentiment is to perform "national" or "ethnic" dances. Dances may be acquired either when older group members recall dances from the past, or when an outside expert is summoned to teach the dance. The dances are then "set" for the group, who enjoy dancing them on suitable occasions.

Another area of activity is "international" folk dancing, performed by people who seek not cultural identity, but the enjoyment of dances from many countries. A large proportion of the dances are from the Balkans, for line dances with intricate footwork seem to hold the greatest attraction. Again the dances are "set" by an expert, and as such are indicative of only one of the possible variants which may be found in the native milieu.

A third type of revival dancing involves the groups whose goal is to execute the dances "perfectly," eg, square-dance clubs. Here participants casually perform for each other, although some groups have costumes for more formal, presentational occasions. Another type of group whose emphasis is on perfection is the theatrical folk-dance troupe. Choreography, costumes and lighting designs combine to create a particular effect. Dances are presented in a highly theatrical manner and sometimes several dances are combined into one. The labelling of this material as "folk dance" is misleading, since it is "set" and variants are not encouraged. A better designation might be "folk-inspired" or "folk-derived" dance, labels which might help audiences to discriminate between theatrical presentations and survival folk dancing. In spite of these limitations, perfection-oriented groups express a vernacular form of dance within the "little" traditions of society, and this can be classified as folk dance.

The French Canadian dance tradition is a good example of a culture with both survival and revival forms. In Québec, folk dances are those based on square and longways formations, on sung-circle dances, and on the percussive, rhythmic pattering of the feet called step dancing or *gigue*. Many of these dances have an elite and noble history, such as the complex quadrille of Île d'Orléans. Simpler square dances and others like the longways *la contredanse* and *le brandy* were probably a result of British or American influences. All these styles have emerged as folk dances, complete with variants and a paucity of documentation verifying their form and existence.

The *gigue* is traditionally passed down from parent (usually father) to child. Though its origins are not certain, it seems likely that it derives from the Irish jig. Because the *gigue* has always been an oral dance form, contemporary manifestations clearly demonstrate the process of a folk tradition — a vibrant dance form where structural and stylistic variants abound. Sung-circle dances, which were once popular with adults, have now mostly passed into the children's repertoire. A couple of adult *rondes* have been documented in isolated communities and from time to time they are resurrected at workshops. Some of these dances represent part of the rich store of culture brought from France in the 17th century.

Survival dance in Québec usually revolves around the home *veillée*, where dancing is one of many activities such as gossiping, eating, card playing and music. Dancing serves as a catalyst to socialization, an important aspect of individual and community development. Today, as a result of television, smaller families and a rejection of "old-fashioned" ways, many "dancing families" no longer dance. There is, however, an active revival movement. The workshops sponsored by the Féderation des loisirs-danse du Québec emphasize learning the dances and having fun. In Québec City, Les Danseries offers weekly lessons in pedagogy, calling for dances, and fiddle and accordion playing. The performance troupe has been a popular entertainment spectacle in Québec for many years. In the 1950s les Folkloristes du Québec were the first to theatricalize, in that they wore period costumes. Later, troupes such as les Feux follets, les Danseurs du St-Laurent, les Gens de mon pays and the present les Sortilèges performed to enthusiastic audiences.

In English Canadian folk dance, the square dance is the most widely disseminated dance, popular from Newfoundland to BC. However, recent growth of the step-dance contest, especially in Ontario, has catapulted this form into the limelight. Step dancing in this context is an interesting mixture: it is both a vehicle for performance and as such must be routinized, and it is a dance in a constant state of evolution. Younger contestants usually take lessons from experts, or learn from within the family. Only the "old timers" purport to dance in a traditional or old-fashioned style, while the others appear to have some of the exhibitionistic tap-dance influence. Nontraditional taps are worn on the shoes in order to accentuate the sound. The music remains within the folk genre — a certain amount each of hornpipe, jig and reel. Only the tempo has increased as a result of the performance/contest situation where competitors feel speed is important.

Native peoples' dance is often connected with important rituals, and thus cannot properly be considered folk. Dances of lesser consequence, however, can be shared with other tribes or with non-Indians. The most visible occasion for folk dancing is the pan-Indian POWWOW, where prizes are won by dance competitors and there is dancing for noncontestants. The BLOOD of Alberta, for example, present 2 types of dances at powwows: collective solo dances such as the Sioux Dance, Grass Dance and War Dance, and Couples Ring Dances, such as the Owl Dance. Another opportunity to do powwow dancing is at the annual SUN DANCE, where many of the younger participants are unfamiliar with ritual dancing. Pan-Indian powwow dancing limits the attention given to specific tribal dances, but promotes identification with general Indian culture.

Non-native folk dances are also popular among some tribes. Square dances are probably the most pervasive; they have been reported among the Blood INDIANS as Spi-ye-Buska/ Mexican Dance and among the HARE at Fort Good Hope. The Hare also enjoyed the two-step, waltz, jive and Scots reel.

Across Canada then, there are many types of folk-dance activities. Dancing is usually associated with an ethnic community and often parents encourage children to participate in folk dance as a means of learning about and identifying with their cultural heritage. However, elementary school children in general are obliged to learn squares or other types of folk dance, depending on their teachers' expertise. Carefully graded record and book sets are available to interested educators. The children usually perform these dances in a cultural void, considering them tedious and unimportant.

Organizations, clubs and societies cater to the revival in folk dancing. A recent publication, *People's Folk Dance Directory*, has compiled an extensive list of folk-dance places, teachers and societies for both the US and Canada. Though useful as a general guide, the directory is far from comprehensive since many groups are not even mentioned.

Along with regularly scheduled folk-dance classes, special events such as folk festivals and ethnic celebrations are open to folk-dance enthusiasts. Some of the more easily identified festivals include the Irish *feis*, Scottish highland-dancing contests, May Day festivities (often involving English Morris-dance teams), Québec winter carnival, Caribana and Israeli Independence Day. Other events, such as Caravan in Toronto, Man and his World in Montréal, and Folk Fest in BC, are multicultural in scope and provide an opportunity to watch and participate in the activities of a variety of cultures.

The university campus is often a major force in the folk-dance community, sponsoring clubs that are usually open to all. Academically, faculty and students at U Laval (Québec) and Memorial U (Newfoundland) have researched dance in their regions, and dance departments at York and Waterloo have also contributed to folk-dance studies.

Several umbrella-type organizations both prepare folk-dance events and act as a storehouse and information centre on activities in the area. The Canadian Folk Arts Council has branches throughout Canada, with head offices in Toronto and Montréal that have documentation centres. The Ontario Folkdance Assn publishes *Ontario Folkdancer*, a magazine/newsletter that includes notices of events across Canada and in parts of the US. In Montréal the Fédération des loisirs-danse du Québec organizes soirées and weekend workshops, houses archival material and publishes the folk journal *La Jarnigoine*. *See also* FOLK MUSIC. ELLEN SHIFRIN

Reading: A. Brodsky et al, eds, *Stones, Bones and Skins: Ritual and Shamanic Art* (1977); C. Carpenter, *Many Voices: A Study of Folklore Activities in Canada* (1979); G. Emmerson, *A Social History of Scottish Dance* (1972); B. Everett, *Canadian Square Dances* (nd) and *Traditional Canadian Dances* (1967); H.S. Hara, *The Hare Indians and their World* (1980); G. Kurath, *Dance and Song Rituals of the Six Nations Reserve* (1968); L. Melamed, *All Join Hands: Connecting People Through Folk Dance* (1977); R.L. Séguin, *Les Divertissements en Nouvelle-France* (1968); R. Witmer, *The Musical Life of the Blood Indians* (1982).

Folk Festivals The 1984 Canadian Folk Music Bulletin listed 132 major and minor summer festivals in every province. More than half of them were in Ontario, and another one-third in the Maritimes. Hundreds of old-time fiddling contests also take place throughout Canada in summer and fall. These festivals resulted from the widespread popularity of traditional music in the 1950s and 1960s. Early festivals such as Miramichi (1958-) in NB were devoted to preserving the authentic FOLK MUSIC of local performers who rarely appeared outside of their rural communities. As interest in folk music continued and festivals grew, urban "revival" performers who learned their music from books and records became popular. At the peak of the folk-music revival in the mid-1960s, urban folksingers were composing their own songs and music on folk models. Singer-songwriters such as Stan Rogers were featured at all major festivals.

A handful of Canadian festivals have attained international recognition and draw both performers and listeners from all parts of Canada as well as the US and Europe. Best known of these is the Mariposa Folk Festival, founded in 1961. It began modestly in Orillia, Ont, but by 1968, when it moved to TORONTO ISLAND, it was the largest festival in N America, capable of attracting international performers such as Joni MITCHELL, Joan Baez, IAN AND SYLVIA Tyson and Gordon LIGHTFOOT. Mariposa's use of multiple workshop and concert stages and its development of separate craft, children's and other specialty areas became the model for other major festivals.

The Winnipeg Folk Festival, now the largest, began in July 1974. It offers a wide variety of music, song, dance and stories from all over the continent. Urban singer-songwriters are popular but traditional music is still featured. Folk festivals are scheduled in August in Vancouver (1979-) and Edmonton (1980-). These festivals draw 10 000 — 20 000 people of all ages and backgrounds. Dozens of workshops are offered during the days and concerts take place at night.

Many of the small Maritime festivals still feature traditional performers rather than the more popular urban folksingers. Other festivals throughout Canada offer a mixture of traditional and contemporary material. Ontario, for example, offers dozens of medium-sized festivals such as the Owen Sound Summer Folk Festival in August and the Toronto Festival of Storytelling in February. KAY F. STONE

Folk Music, Anglo-Canadian Folk music is the music of ordinary people: songs and tunes that are passed on from one to another by ear rather than by print and thus acquire variations. They are sung or played for pleasure rather than for profit, and usually the composer is unknown. The largest number of Anglo-Canadian folk songs came to this country with the early settlers from Britain and Ireland and were passed from generation to generation over the last 300 years. They include 77 of the *English and Scottish Popular Ballads* catalogued by Francis James Child and several hundred of the later broadside ballads, as well as lullabies, love songs, sea shanties and music-hall songs.

Newfoundland is particularly rich in the ancient supernatural ballads that are rare elsewhere in N America. The most popular ballad in Canada, as throughout the English-speaking world, is "the little Scotch song of Barbry Allen" which delighted Samuel Pepys in 1666: over 60 different versions of it have turned up across the country. Other popular titles include "Lady Isabel and the Elf Knight," "Little Musgrave and Lady Barnard," "Lord Randall," "The Cruel Mother," "The Gypsy Laddie," "The Sweet Trinity" and "The Farmer's Curst Wife."

Even more numerous than the Child ballads are the later broadside ballads (printed on single sheets known as "broadsides"). Some 240 of the 290 that G. Malcolm Laws, Jr, catalogued in *American Balladry from British Broadsides* were sung in Canada, and many more have turned up since his guide appeared. Most of these are romantic tales of family opposition to lovers, of lovers' disguises and tricks, or of faithful and unfaithful lovers. The most popular of all plots was that of the broken ring or returned lover which has been told and retold in dozens of different ballads.

Fewer songs were composed in Canada than were imported from the British Isles, and nearly all the native Canadian songs borrowed their tunes from Old World sources. Most of our native Anglo-Canadian songs were inspired by the occupations of the early settlers, the 2 largest groups springing from men who earned their living on the sea or in the woods. Nova Scotia and Newfoundland are noted for sea shanties, songs of whaling, sealing and fishing, and ballads about disasters at sea. In New Brunswick and Ontario most of the native songs came from the lumber camps, some telling of the winter's work, others describing tragic accidents in the woods or on the rivers, and still others relating the shantyboys' experiences when they left the camps in spring. Smaller numbers of songs came from sailors on the Great Lakes, miners in Cape Breton and BC, and homesteaders and cowboys on the Prairies. Western Canada produced few Anglo-Canadian songs, but some American songs found their way across the border. Canadians adopted or adapted some pioneer American ditties like "The Little Old Sod Shanty" and "Bury Me Not on the Lone Prairie." The most widespread Prairie song, known variously as "Prairie Land," "Alberta Land," or "Saskatchewan," was a localized form of American verses based on "Beulah Land."

Other native songs reflect outstanding events in our history. The BATTLE OF THE PLAINS OF ABRAHAM inspired the earliest known Anglo-Canadian ballad, "Brave Wolfe" or "Bold Wolfe." The WAR OF 1812 produced such lively songs as "Come All You Bold Canadians" and "The *Chesapeake* and the *Shannon*." Other ballads recall the REBELLION OF 1837-38 and the FENIAN RAIDS of 1866, and CONFEDERATION inspired some anti-Confederation songs in Newfoundland.

Besides the occupational and historical songs, there are various accounts of local happenings: murders, disasters, celebrations, or other newsworthy incidents. Ballads tell of the J.R. Birchall murder, the Miramichi fire, the HALIFAX EXPLOSION, and the Springhill mine disasters, and ditties like "The Kelligrews Soiree" and "The Feller from Fortune" immortalize lively Newfoundland parties.

The most notable characteristic of the native Anglo-Canadian songs is their predominantly Irish quality, which is evident not only in Newfoundland but also in the Maritimes and Ontario. Both sea ballads and lumbering songs fall into the typical "come-all-ye" pattern and nearly all are set to Irish tunes.

Traditional folksingers always sang unaccompanied until very recently, and "mouth music" or lilting was sometimes used to accompany dancing. The fiddle was by far the most popular folk instrument, followed by the accordion and tin whistle. The most common fiddle tunes were Scottish and Irish, and some were composed by local fiddlers.

Anglo-Canadian collectors have concentrated on folk songs to a far greater extent than on any other type of FOLKLORE. There are over 20 major books of folk songs and very few devoted to any other single genre. The pioneer collectors were W. Roy Mackenzie in Nova Scotia and Elizabeth Greenleaf in Newfoundland, followed by Helen Creighton and Kenneth Peacock. Edith Fowke has collected in Ontario and P.J. Thomas in BC. An American, Edward D. Ives, has produced 3 important books dealing with Maritime singer-composers. EDITH FOWKE

Reading: Canadian Folk Music Journal (1973-); H. Creighton, *Songs and Ballads from Nova Scotia* (1932); Edith Fowke, *The Penguin Book of Canadian Folk Songs* (1973); Fowke and Alan Mills, *Singing our History: Canada's Story in Song* (1984); Fowke and R. Johnston, *Folk Songs of Canada, I and II* (1954; 1967).

Folk Music, Franco-Canadian French colonists brought their customs, way of life and music with them to the shores of the St Lawrence. From the Conquest, 1759-60, until well into the 20th century these French communities, mostly rural, persisted in a linguistic and cultural isolation that helped maintain the vitality and strength of their traditional culture.

French Canadian instrumental music is derived from several sources. Unfettered by the linguistic constraints affecting song, it has benefited from its contact with Celtic music and the music of France and the British Isles. While retaining some characteristics of the country of origin, French Canadian folk music has become freer and more lyrical, and has adapted to the rigours of the country and the Latin temperament of its inhabitants. It is essentially functional music, meant to accompany dances such as quadrilles, the cotillion, the jig (a solo demonstration of skill) and various *rondes* and *jeux dansés* (*see* FOLK DANCE).

The violin (fiddle), the most common instrument in French Canadian folk music, dates back to New France. Joseph Allard, Jean Carignan and Jos Bouchard established reputations as masters of the fiddle. The harmonica came from Germany, via the US, in 1866 and quickly became popular. In 1892 the diatonic accordion also arrived from Germany and became a favourite instrument among French Canadians. Two of its best-known interpreters in Québec were Alfred Montmarquette and Philippe Bruneau. The jew's harp and simple percussion instruments such as spoons, bones and feet are also characteristic of the traditional music of French Canada.

Folk Songs seem to have come from the people, the peasant classes, and were passed down, generation by generation, through oral tradition, renewing and transforming along the way. The songs have basic, straightforward verses, rudimentary metre and simple vocabulary. Some French Canadian folk songs derive from a medieval French tradition brought over by the early colonists; they exist today as an old form of folkloric repertory, richer than anything now found in France. Other songs are of more recent composition with rough and imitative lyrics. Expressed as lament or satire, these songs reflect the social conditions of the French Canadian community: the life of the VOYAGEURS, the lumber camps, disasters and misfortunes, and political and communal life. Acadia has long been a rich source of this form of music.

Research on folk songs, which began in France in 1853, had an impact in Canada. In 1863 Hubert LaRue published an article entitled "Les chansons populaires et historique du Canada" in *Le Foyer canadien.* He persuaded Ernest GAGNON to collect and transcribe tunes for some of the lyrics he had collected. Two years later Gagnon published a work entitled *Chansons populaires du Canada,* with melodies and abundant commentary. In 1916 Marius BARBEAU, an anthropologist with the National Museum of Canada, began collecting folk songs. His collection of over 10 000 songs is preserved in the Canadian Centre for Folk Culture Studies in Ottawa. His major books on traditional songs are *Romancero du Canada* (1937), *Jongleur Songs of Old Quebec* (1962), *Le Rossignol y chante* (1962), and *En roulant ma boule* (1982). In 1944 Luc Lacourcière founded the Archives de folklore at Laval. Conrad Laforte began classifying folk songs in 1954 and between 1977 and 1983 published 5 of his 6 volumes of *Catalogue de la chanson folklorique française.* From 1942 to 1983 Anselme Chiasson published *Chansons d'Acadie* in 6 volumes; he is also one of the founders of the Centre d'Etudes acadiennes at U Moncton. Another collector of note is Germain Lemieux at the Centre franco-ontarien de folklore at U de Sudbury. *See also* FOLKLORE.

DONALD DESCHÊNES

Reading: M. Béland, *Chansons de voyageurs, coureurs de bois et forestiers* (1982); M. and R. Harcourt, *Chansons folkloriques françaises au Canada* (1956); C. Laforte, *Poétique de la chanson traditionelle française* (1976); J.P. Joyal, "Le processus de composition dans la musique instrumentale du Québec," *Canadian Folk Music Journal* 8 (1980); L. Ornstein, "Instrumental Folk Music of Quebec," *Canadian Folk Music Journal* 10 (1982).

Folklore was first introduced as a term in England in 1846 and today refers to information, wisdom and human expression that is passed on, usually anonymously, from generation to generation or transmitted and circulated as traditional cultural behaviour. Folkloric materials can be found anywhere and in any form, although past scholarship has favoured verbal folklore or oral literature — folk songs, folktales, epic, myth, legend, folk drama, riddles, proverbs, sayings and a variety of verses. Nonverbal folklore includes material culture such as folk architecture, folk art and crafts, dance, music, custom, ritual and belief, traditional folkways and amusements.

To become folklore, a song, story, custom or belief must go through a process of "folklorization" and meet the criteria and approval of the receiving community. During this filtering process, the item may undergo one or more revisions before it definitely enters into the community's cultural heritage. Along with general recognition and appreciation, anonymity and variation are also features that characterize the folkloric process; thus, jokes come in many versions, folk songs in many variations and Easter eggs with different designs. Folk life is another general term that is sometimes used interchangeably with folklore, popular culture and folk tradition, although each has its own history and bias.

The main purposes of folklore are to instruct, support, entertain, and express communal and individual artistic taste and creativity. Modern scholarship has shown that folklore is an important aspect of all cultures because it helps people to comprehend and cope with their social and natural environment. The myths of Canada's Indian and Inuit peoples exemplify how large bodies of folklore in many parts of the world depend on nature (eg, the seasons and the cycle of life itself) to provide a meaningful framework for their folkloric traditions (*see* INUIT MYTH AND LEGEND).

Guyasdomo D'Sonogua (1912), watercolour by Emily Carr (*courtesy Provincial Archives of British Columbia*).

Folklore continues to be important in industrialized societies, where the growth of literacy has spawned various forms of "paper folklore" ranging from chain letters to photocopied office jokes. These and other forms of the new urban folklore provide safety valves by helping to dissipate hostilities (eg, ethnic-joke cycles) and by offering the individual and the group a sense of identity.

The urge to see and experience something out of the ordinary partly accounts for the periodic revival of interest in ethnic folklore and folk traditions, as illustrated by the popularity of Toronto's "Caravan," Winnipeg's "Folklorama," Edmonton's "Heritage Festival" and similar events. New interest in folklore focuses on sensory, nonlingual phenomena: the taste and smell of unusual foods, the moving colour and visual excitement of the ethnic FOLK DANCE, the detail of FOLK ART and handiwork, and the unique acoustic appeal of folk song and FOLK MUSIC. These manifestations of folklore thrive in modern settings, as shown by the popular annual Winnipeg Folk Festival. Sophisticated marketing techniques produce a highly compressed showcase of talent, ranging from contemporary folksingers to demonstrations of traditional weaving.

The trained folklorist sees a continuity from the winged deities of classical mythology to N America's "Superman." Folklore is able to bridge old and new by selecting and reinterpreting elements from the past in order to meet present needs.

Canadian Folklore Geography and a diverse linguistic and ethnocultural composition prohibit a concise description of Canadian folklore. Most books structure folklore in chronological fashion, with 4 main bodies of lore reflecting the traditions of Canada's main population groups: aboriginal (native Indian and Inuit), French Canadian, Anglo-Canadian (English, Irish, Scottish, Welsh), and other ethnic groups. Various factors favoured the preservation and development of folklore throughout the country: the prevalence of a rural population (at least until after WWII), a high percentage of illiteracy among certain groups in earlier times, and the use of folklore to foster local and national self-consciousness. French Canada, for instance, enjoyed a "golden age" of oral literature lasting into the 20th century. This was largely a result of French colonial policy, which did not allow the establishment of a press in New France, and later of the policies of English authorities, who consistently used English to introduce that language and Protestantism. The lack of publication in French and the scarcity of French schools helped to maintain a culture rooted in folklore. Early French Canadian writers incorporated many traditional customs and legends into their works and fostered the recognition and admiration of the folk heritage. French Canada's rich contact with the native population and Anglo-Canada's predilection for life by and on the sea helped to differentiate further the bodies of lore from one another. Since the 19th century the intermittent waves of immigrants and refugees from all parts of the world have greatly expanded the bounds of Canadian folklore by introducing new elements.

Canadian folklore has always been influenced by the US as well as other countries, and vice versa (eg, the impact of the Canadian wilderness and the Mountie hero on the imagination of Americans). Elsewhere abroad, the exodus of native sons and daughters to Canada, and their early experiences as immigrants in this country, have stimulated the production of entire cycles of songs and stories about immigrating to Canada, cycles which in turn enter into the folklore of the original countries.

Travel notes and reports of 17th-century explorers, traders and missionaries are the earliest records of Canadian folklore. The first conscious efforts at recording and publishing folklore appear in the 19th century in French Canada. The search for a national identity and the corresponding reaction against foreign influences in Canadian life and letters provoked, after WWII, a renewed interest in the national past and popular tradition. Folklore recordings and publications in folklore, partly in its genuine form, partly reshaped, began to appear in increasing numbers. The initiation of 2 especially important serial publications, *Les Archives de folklore* (published by Laval U since 1946) and the Mercury Series (published by the Canadian Centre for Folk Culture Studies at the National Museum of Man in Ottawa since 1972), enriched scholarly research. Centennial celebrations in 1967 stimulated further interest in folklore and emphasized the attractiveness of the nation's folklore heritage. As the country became more urbanized, transitional forms emerged. TV and other mass-communication media have played an important role in this process, although their impact on Canadian folklore has not yet been fully researched or evaluated.

All categories and types of folklore appear in Canada, but their distribution varies from culture to culture. Efforts to identify this lore properly and to assess and characterize the nature of distribution are frustrated by the lack of suitable, comparative data. The particularly rich and multiform development of folklore among Canada's native peoples is largely explained by the delayed impact of European influence. This situation has long attracted the attention of scholars and enthusiasts whose collections and studies of native lore tended to focus on spoken narrative and ritual activities. The SUN DANCE and ceremonies associated with the medicine man (SHAMAN) and native healing practices (eg, the SHAKING TENT ritual) are among the best documented. The myths of Indian and Inuit populations are unique and significant aspects of Canada's folklore. These often tell about the theft of light and fire, and feature a culture hero who secures various things for his people. Such creation and hero myths include the RAVEN and THUNDERBIRD cycles of the West Coast and the NANABOZO stories of the Algonquian, which form 2 of the most extensive bodies of native Indian myth. Sacred legends, incorporating elements from tribal history, and to a lesser extent fables or wonder tales, are important parts of both Inuit and Indian folklore (*see* NATIVE PEOPLE, RELIGION).

Sung and spoken narrative is the major focus in French Canadian folklore, which includes, in addition to that of Québec, the folklore of Acadian communities in the Maritimes and of French communities in northern Ontario and parts of western Canada. The impact of Roman Catholicism is especially pronounced in many religious legends about the saints of the Middle Ages, miraculous healings and rescues, the creation and the flood. This body of folktale also features international tales of magic, many of which have been traced to pre-Christian sources. Their plots illustrate the features of typical wonder tales: repetition by threes, an emphasis on trials and quests, the triumph of the youngest son, magic objects and supernatural helpers, marvellous transformations and happy endings. In addition to an active inventory of jokes, anecdotes and circular formula tales, the traditional narrative folklore also includes many local legends reflecting life-styles associated with such traditional occupations as farming, hunting, fishing and lumbering. Common subjects include hidden treasures, will-o'-the-wisps, flying canoes, werewolves, sorcerers and encounters with the devil. Prominent personages in the French Canadian narrative tradition are the popular hero-figure Ti-Jean (Little John), a fabulous hunter named Dalbec, and Jean CADIEUX, a voyageur whose tragic death is the subject of the earliest, distinctly French Canadian folk song (*see also* ORAL LITERATURE IN FRENCH).

Anglo-Canadian folklore has not attracted attention equal to that given aboriginal and French Canadian folklore. This has resulted in comparatively few study materials, although much folkloric data can be culled from local histories and related sources (*see* ORAL LITERATURE). Many varieties of folk songs have been well documented, especially those that pertain to children, lumbermen and seamen, including an important category of shipwreck songs from the East Coast and the Great Lakes. Few examples of international tales of magic have been found among Anglo-Canadians, although jokes and anecdotes are widespread and include popular tall tales and ethnic jokes, of which the "Newfie" jokes are especially common. There are some collections of superstitions and supernatural tales, mainly from Nova Scotia. An active Dept of Folklore at Memorial U of Newfoundland in St John's provides the best documentation of Anglo-Canadian folklore. Especially important are MUMMING, riddles and other forms of folklore that are traced, recorded and studied in Newfoundland, although poorly documented elsewhere in Canada. Square-dance calls, children's autograph verses and legends about the SASQUATCH, OGOPOGO and related monsters of western Canada are also collected. The material folk culture of Anglo-Canadians attracted much interest as a consequence of the 1967 Centennial celebrations. A profusion of attractive coffee-table picture books and albums appeared, devoted to the documentation of Canadian houses, BARNS, LOG HOUSES, fences, churches, LIGHTHOUSES, outhouses, as well as FURNITURE, pottery, QUILTS and hooked RUGS. The reports of the activities of English poltergeists on Canadian soil show the continued influence of "Old Country" folklore. The large number of popular urban tales, in the form of migratory belief legends transmitted by teenagers and bearing such motifs as "Baby-sitter mistakes child for turkey," "Girlfriend's legs cut off" and "The grandfather's liver," reveals the strong impact on Anglo-Canadian folklore of new folkloric patterns from the US.

Canada's folklore composite in the second half of the 20th century has its roots in over 70 different traditions from around the world (*see* MULTICULTURALISM). Preliminary studies show, for example, the existence of a considerable body of folk beliefs and practices associated with folk medicine of the Pennsylvania Germans of southern Ontario; a sizable and varied body of lore among Ukrainians on the Prairies; Old-World narrative patterns among Icelanders in Manitoba and Yiddish-speaking Jews of Montréal. In addition to these groups, folklore studies relating to other ethnic communities in Canada have also appeared among Canadian Poles, Norwegians, Koreans, Danes, Hungarians, Swedes, blacks, Italians, Greeks, Chinese, Doukhobors, Gypsies, Romanians and Finns. In the 1960s, ethnic FOLK FESTIVALS became an especially productive phenomenon from coast to coast and attracted attention to Canada's rich heritage of folk traditions.

Folklore Studies Undergraduate and graduate degree programs in folklore are offered in French (since 1944) at Laval in Québec City and in English (since 1962) at Memorial in St John's, Nfld. Instrumental in organizing and heading these programs in early years were Luc Lacourcière at Laval and Herbert Halpert at Memorial. Both Laval's Archives de folklore and Memorial's MUNFLA (Memorial U of Newfoundland Folklore and Language Archive) have amassed archival materials relating to the folklore of their respective provinces. Other universities offering courses in Canadian folklore include Moncton, Québec at Trois-Rivières, York, Laurentian, Winnipeg, Manitoba, Saskatchewan, Calgary and Alberta. The Dept of Folklore at Laurentian U in Sudbury, founded by Germain Lemieux, has an extensive collection of Franco-Ontario folklore materials, and the Centre for the Documentation of Traditional Culture at Trois-Rivières, founded in 1970 by Robert-Lionel Séguin and Maurice Carrier, is important for its photographic and documentary archival materials relating to Québec material culture. The country's leading folklore-research centre is the Canadian Centre for Folk Culture Studies, a unit of the National Museum of Man in Ottawa. The centre is important for its holdings relating to French Canada, West Coast and Huron Indians and the country's minority ethnic groups. In 1964 the Canadian Folk Arts Council was established under government sponsorship and, with its network of affiliated councils, serves as the rallying point for the nation's numerous amateur and semiamateur folk performing groups. The council maintains its head offices in Toronto and Montréal and publishes a quarterly magazine, *Troubadour*. Other national organizations are the Canadian Folk Music Society (est 1957) and the Folklore Studies Assn of Canada (est 1975).

The major pioneering figure in Canadian folklore research in the 20th century is Charles Marius BARBEAU, many of whose publications appeared under the auspices of the National Museum. However, no distinctly Canadian approach has been developed for the study of folklore, and almost all major folklorists in Canada have received much of their formal academic training abroad. By 1980 the country's 3 major folklore study centres had unofficially assumed separate but occasionally overlapping responsibilities for French Canadian folklore (Laval), Anglo-Canadian folklore (Memorial) and minority-language ethnic groups (Ottawa). The most important bibliography in Canadian folklore is the joint compilation of Edith FOWKE and Carole Henderson Carpenter, *A Bibliography of Canadian Folklore in English* (1981). General works include Carpenter's monograph, *Many Voices: A Study of Folklore Activities in Canada and Their Role in Canadian Culture* (1979); K.S. Goldstein's *Canadian Folklore Perspectives* (1978); the only autobiography written by a prominent folklorist, Helen Creighton's *A Life in Folklore* (1975); Magnus Einarsson's multicultural photo-study, *Everyman's Heritage: An Album of Canadian Folk Life* (National Museums, 1978); and Edith Fowke's pioneering anthology, *Folklore of Canada* (1976). In 1972 the journal *Ethnomusicology* (vol 16, no 2), edited by Israel J. Katz, devoted a special issue to Canada. Regional collections include *Folklore of Nova Scotia* by Mary L. Fraser, *Folklore from Nova Scotia* by Arthur Huff Fauset, *Folklore of Lunenburg County, Nova Scotia* by Helen Creighton, *Christmas Mumming in Newfoundland* edited by H. Halpert and G.M. Story and *Folklore of Waterloo County, Ontario* by W.J. Wintemberg. Among the varied publications on French Canadian folklore, the series *Les Archives de folklore* is internationally significant, as are the many works of C. Marius Barbeau.

Books by Leonard Bloomfield on the Cree, by Franz BOAS on Northwest Coast Indians and by Barbeau on the Huron and West Coast Indians hold special interest in folklore studies of Canada's native peoples. Other researchers include Marie-Françoise Guédon, Diamond JENNESS, Gertrude P. Kurath and Paul Radin. The special issue of *Canadian Ethnic Studies* 7 (1975, ed Robert B. Klymasz) on *Ethnic Folklore in Canada* is particularly valuable for folklore of ethnic groups. The

National Museum of Man's Canadian Centre for Folk Culture Studies in Ottawa has also released a number of relevant reports in its Mercury Series of publications. In addition to *Les Archives de folklore* and *Troubadour*, 4 other folklore periodicals have been active since the 1970s: *Bulletin of the Folklore Studies Association of Canada* (1976–), *Canadian Folk Music Journal* (1973–), *Canadian Folklore Canadien* (1979–) and *Culture and Tradition* (Memorial and Laval, 1976–).

The field of children's lore in Canada has attracted the attention of such researchers as Barbara Cass-Beggs, Edith Fowke and Kay Stone. Notable publications include a compilation by Peter B. Michalyshyn, *Tic-Tac-Togetherness: A Collection of Intercultural Games for Children* (1979). Study kits and exhibits prepared by several museums across the country alert developers of educational curricula of the richness of Canada's folk heritage. *Oracle*, a bulletin published by the National Musuem of Man, is also useful for teachers.

Nonprint materials relating to Canadian folklore include several works produced by or available through the National Film Board. Folk arts and crafts are well represented by 3 films, *Maud Lewis*, *In Praise of Hands* and *Inventors of Thingumajigs*. Three other films, *Pen-Hi Grad*, *Wedding Day* and *Pleasure Faire*, provide an insight into folk festivals, celebrations and rituals. Folk religion is well documented in the NFB's film *The Hutterites* (*see* HUTTERITES), and in another film about the DOUKHOBORS and their *Living Book*. *The Sunny Munchy Crunchy Natural Food Shop* shows, in humorous fashion, the impact of traditional recipes and ingredients on modern eating habits. *The Songs of Chris Cobb* documents folk singing in a Newfoundland outport, and *Hinchinbrook Diary* and *Bekevar Jubilee* depict the general folklore complex of a particular community. *Canadians Can Dance* reveals the array of current Canadian folk-dance styles and traditions.

Of the many sound recordings produced over the years, the following are of special importance: *Canadian Folk Songs* (ed C. Marius Barbeau and released as vol 8 in the Columbia World Library of Folk and Primitive Music); over 20 titles on the Folkways label; and *Canadian Folk Songs: A Centennial Collection*, 9 records featuring innovative performers (RCA Victor, 1967).

ROBERT B. KLYMASZ

Food Additives Consumers normally consider that the term "food additive" refers to almost all substances, primarily chemical in nature, added to foods during production, manufacture, packaging or storage. However, as defined under the Canadian Food and Drug Regulations, a "food additive" means any substance, including any source of radiation, the use of which results or may reasonably be expected to result in it or its by-products becoming a part of or affecting the characteristics of food. Based on this definition, the term does not encompass materials such as salt, sugar and starch used as ingredients of food or commonly sold as food products. Certain other substances are excluded from the definition because they fall into categories covered separately under the Food and Drug Regulations and are thus subject to other controls. These ingredients include vitamins, mineral nutrients, amino acids, spices, seasonings and flavouring preparations, as well as agricultural chemicals, food-packaging materials and veterinary drugs.

Food additives are controlled by means of a positive listing system of permitted substances. If an additive is not on this list, it may not be used in a food offered for sale in Canada. The permitted list names the additive and lists the foods in which it may be used and the levels of use. The list encompasses some 375 substances classified into 14 tables based on the function of the additives. Food additives perform a variety of functions in food manufacture. For each function a number of different additives are permitted, to allow manufacturers the choice necessitated by variations in food properties, processing variations and market availability of the additive.

The function of additives and their exact mode of action is complex; however, for the functions noted, the additives do what is implied in the table title. For example, certain food products (eg, salt, dried-powder mixes) tend to absorb moisture from the atmosphere, which causes them to clump or cake. Anticaking agents prevent this from occurring and allow the food product to remain free running. Similarly, firming agents maintain the texture of a number of processed foods, such as fruits and vegetables, which would otherwise go soft as a result of heat treatment during processing. Dough conditioners modify the strength of flour, improve the handling properties of dough and reduce mixing time, resulting in better texture and volume in bakery products. Colouring agents are added to foods to give them an appetizing and attractive appearance. Emulsifying, gelling, stabilizing and thickening agents modify texture and impart a desired consistency to foods. Such agents may also be used to help keep suspended food particles from separating and settling to the bottom (eg, the chocolate in chocolate milk) and to modify the consistency of products (eg, frozen desserts).

Because food technology is forever changing and new foods are constantly under development, there is a continual demand for new food additives. In Canada, for a new substance to be added to the listing of permitted additives, a submission of information is required, the format of which is outlined under the Food and Drug Regulations. This submission must include a description of the food additive, its method of manufacture, chemical and physical properties, composition and specifications. The submission must also include data establishing that the additive will have the intended effect and detailed reports of tests made to establish the safety of the additive under the conditions of use recommended.

Additives may be removed from the positive list of substances based upon evidence of possible hazard to the consumer. Examples of substances which are no longer permitted in Canada are nitrogen trichloride (bleaching agent in flour), cobaltous chloride (foam-stabilizing agent in beer), benzyl violet (colour in foods) and saccharin (sweetener in dietetic foods). Food additives have been and continue to be a controversial subject. Although it would be possible to produce and manufacture some foods without using these substances, many of the products currently available would not be possible without them, particularly convenience "ready-to-serve" products and foodstuffs requiring preservation.

S.W. GUNNER

Food and Beverage Industries Food and beverage processing or MANUFACTURING is one of Canada's major secondary industries and a vital component of the nation's overall AGRIBUSINESS system. In 1981 the industry had 4683 plants in production and the value of shipments was $31.84 billion. It spent nearly $22 billion on materials and supplies.

For statistical purposes, the total agribusiness system can be broken down into 5 sectors: agriculture (and fisheries); food and beverage processing; wholesale trade; retail trade; and institutional feeding (restaurants, etc). Statistics Canada figures indicate that, in 1981, agribusiness employed 1.6 million people or 13.4% of Canada's labour force. Agriculture is the largest employer, with 481 275 people. It is interesting to note that, despite significant improvements in agricultural production, this figure has remained almost unchanged since 1971. In contrast, employment in the restaurant business expanded by an astounding 133% during the same period, from about 200 000 in 1971 to 470 680 a decade later. The third-largest sector, manufacturing, has a work force of 306 080, followed by retail with 275 515 and wholesale with 61 905. In some provinces, employment exceeds the 13.4% national figure: in Sask 26% of the labour force is engaged in agribusiness, in PEI 25%, in Nfld 19%, in Man 17%, in NB 15.8%, in NS 14.6% and in Alta 13.9%. Only Qué (12.5%), Ont (12.2%) and BC (11.6%) fall below the national average.

The food and beverage industries consist of 17 sectors: MEAT-PROCESSING INDUSTRY, with 550 plants in operation in 1981; poultry-processing industry, 90; fish products industry, 390; DAIRY INDUSTRY, 456; CONFECTIONERY INDUSTRY, 109; SUGAR INDUSTRY, 13; FRUIT AND VEGETABLE INDUSTRY, 232; BAKING INDUSTRY, 1487; biscuit industry, 33; miscellaneous food industries, 315; VEGETABLE OIL INDUSTRY, 11; feed industries, 612; flour and breakfast cereal industry, 50; SOFT-DRINK INDUSTRY, 238; DISTILLING INDUSTRY, 33; BREWING INDUSTRY, 41; WINE INDUSTRY, 33. This industrial complex is one of the world's most modern and efficient food and beverage production systems. Statistics Canada data show that, in 1982, Canadians spent only 16.4% of personal disposable income on food and nonalcoholic beverages consumed at or away from home; in 1981, 16.9%; in 1971, 18.3%. The proportions of personal income for food and beverage purchases at stores for home consumption suggest a similar trend: from 14.3% in 1971 to 12.4% in 1982. Food purchases in restaurants has averaged about 4% of disposable income between 1971 and 1981. The US is the only country in which the cost of eating is lower (16.1% in 1981); other developed countries spend considerably more, eg, France, 18.9%, Switzerland, 19.9%, West Germany, 23.7%, Japan, 24.8%, Italy, 29.1%, and Greece, 35.6%. It has been estimated that consumers in most Soviet Bloc countries spend more than 35% of income on food and beverages.

In contrast, Canadian food and beverage industries have among the lowest levels of profitability of all Canadian industries. There has been a steady decline in recent years. In 1982 after-tax profit per dollar of sales was 1.74%, a sharp drop from 2.25% in 1980 and 2.63% in 1978. Despite low profits, the food and beverage industries continue to invest heavily in building new plants, expanding and modernizing existing facilities and purchasing newer, more efficient process and packaging systems.

Paradoxically, food- and beverage-processing companies are high-risk operations in environmental terms because of the wastes they produce. Unlike industrial wastes polluted with toxic chemicals, effluents from food operations are a problem because of their high nutritional value. If such wastes are released untreated to surface waters, a rapid and unacceptable growth of ALGAE and bacteria may occur. In the case of algae, such development depletes the oxygen supply, destroying fish populations. As a result, Environment Canada strictly enforces a set of effluent guidelines for every type of food- and beverage-processing operation; several provinces have even more demanding food-industry waste guidelines. The food and beverage industries are among the most highly regulated industries in Canada, affected by regulations administered by several federal and provincial departments (*see* FOOD LEGISLATION).

Technology The industry employs the most modern processing and packaging techniques. For example, thermal processing of foods and beverages in cans, glass and other forms of rigid packaging permits products to be stored at room temperature for several years without deterioration in product flavour or nutritional quality. Other methods of food preservation used in Canada include freezing, freeze-drying, drying, pasteurization, pickling and fermentation. Canadian companies are often leaders in N America in introducing new processing and packaging methods. A recent example is the use of the retortable pouch (the so-called soft tin can) for the production of shelf-stable products. Aseptic packaging of milk and fruit juices in laminated (paper and plastic) containers, a technique developed in Europe, first appeared in Canada in 1965 and was well established by the early 1980s. One other sophisticated processing technique, food irradiation, is not currently used in N America, although Canadian researchers at ATOMIC ENERGY OF CANADA LTD have been prime movers in developing this completely safe approach to food preservation. In 1984 there were over 130 irradiation installations in the world, more than 80% developed and built by AECL. Most of the systems are used to produce sterile medical and drug supplies and packaging materials, but at least 13 are used for food preservation. In 1983 the Health Protection Branch initiated a proposal that irradiation be reclassified as a food-processing method, rather than as an additive as at present.

Associations Most sectors of the food and beverage industries are represented by a national association, often supported by provincial counterparts. A major function of these associations is to gain industry consensus on issues affecting their sector and to consult with governments on these problems. They also act as information clearing houses. ROBERT F. BARRATT

Food Legislation Legislation designed to prevent the sale of unsafe or unwholesome food represents one of the oldest forms of governmental or societal intervention in the AGRICULTURE AND FOOD system. One of the earliest references to food adulteration is found in the English Assize of Bread Act, which dates back to about the year 1200 during the reign of King John. This statute began as an economic measure relating to the quantity of bread which bakers were obliged to offer for sale. During the 13th century it was expanded to include ale, fish, meat and various other food commodities. Over the years the statute evolved to include quality of the food because it made little sense to purchase a certain quantity of food only to find that it had been watered down or was so unsafe or unwholesome as to be unusable. In 1860 the English Parliament enacted a landmark broad food law, not designed to control specific items but rather aimed at preventing adulteration of all food and drink. This law was amended in 1872 and again in 1875.

In Canada in the latter half of the 19th century, developments were influenced by English initiatives. While certain food laws were in force before Confederation (1867), the first federal legislation dealing with adulteration of food was enacted in 1874. It is interesting to note that the US did not pass similar legislation until 1906, although before that time various commodity-oriented statutes were in existence which contained elements relating to adulteration and food safety. The 1874 law received its impetus from the large quantities of grossly adulterated liquor being consumed. Parliament was besieged with requests to do something about the situation. In response, early legislators took the position that liquor *per se* should not be banned, only adulterated or unsafe liquor. Hence, on 1 Jan 1875 an Act to Prevent the Adulteration of Food, Drink and Drugs came into effect. This statute included a penalty of a $100 fine and a month in jail, with or without hard labour, for any manufacturer of liquor adulterating his product with substances such as salt, copper sulphate, opium, tobacco, Indian hemp or salts of lead and zinc. The second offence carried a $400 fine and 3 months in jail. The 1875 Act has been amended and altered many times over the years, and in 1920 it was superseded by the Food and Drugs Act. The most recent revision came into effect in 1954 and is currently in force.

The Food and Drugs Act is considered to be a consumer statute and is intended to protect consumers from health hazards and fraud in the sale and use of food, drugs, cosmetics and medical devices. The Act finds its constitutional authority in that section of the CONSTITUTION ACT, 1982, dealing with criminal law. Its enforcement is one of the responsibilities of the federal minister of national health and welfare. Unlike legislation enforced by the federal ministers of agriculture and fisheries, it is not and never was intended to assist producers, manufacturers or retailers in preparing or marketing foods. Sections 4, 5 and 7 of the Food and Drugs Act are very important because they cover, in a very general way, all major aspects of safety and fraud associated with the sale and consumption of food. Section 4 deals with product safety, integrity and freedom from adulteration. Section 5 deals primarily with aspects of economic fraud and section 7 with production, manufacturing and storage of food under unsanitary conditions.

Section 25 provides authority for writing and passage of regulations for carrying out the purposes and provisions of the Act. It is through the use of these regulations that specific control is exercised. For example, division 16 of the regulations lists, in table form, some 340 permitted FOOD ADDITIVES. If a substance does not appear in one of the tables of division 16, it may not be used as a food additive. Regulations prescribing maximum permissible levels for the occurrence of PESTICIDES and other agricultural chemicals in foods are also tabled on a similar "positive listing" basis. When a substance is found to be toxic and required to be severely restricted or prohibited in the food supply, a "negative listing" principle may be used. This device has been used in section B.01.046 of the regulations to restrict severely or prohibit the presence of some 16 substances with demonstrated toxicity by declaring them to be adulterants.

In addition to the "positive" and "negative" listing techniques, certain specific regulations have been established to prohibit the presence of pathogenic SALMONELLA bacteria in susceptible products, including chocolate, processed eggs and frogs' legs. Regulations have also been used as a means of standardizing or providing a legal identity to foods or groups of foods considered basic to the Canadian diet (eg, dairy products, meat products, grain and bakery products, fats and oils). More recently, regulations have also been established to ensure nutritional adequacy of certain foods considered critical in the diets of certain individuals or groups of individuals. For example, stringent compositional and nutrient requirements have been established for infant formula products which serve as the sole source of nutrition during the first few months of life.

The Food and Drugs Act and Regulations may be considered as the basic federal statute dealing with food safety and nutrition in Canada, but there are many other pieces of legislation that have an impact on the sale of foods at both the federal and provincial levels. For example, departments of agriculture and fisheries at both federal and provincial levels have legislation used for control and marketing of specific commodities. These statutes often deal with product identity and quality in relation to grade standards. The Pest Control Products Act and Regulations are of particular interest, in that the federal minister of agriculture is responsible for registering pesticides for use in Canada, while the minister of national health and welfare acts as principal health adviser in evaluating the safety of pesticide residues and establishing maximum safe limits for these residues in food. Federal and provincial departments of the environment have, in recent years, established regulations respecting discharge into the environment of certain toxic substances which could ultimately contaminate the food chain. All provincial jurisdictions also have public-health Acts and regulations which provide the medical officer at the city, regional, county or municipal level with considerable authority in regulating food-manufacturing and food-service establishments. Regulation of food safety must continue to be a dynamic process reflecting both technological and societal change. In this way, Canadian consumers will continue to enjoy one of the safest food supplies in the world. *See* COMMODITY INSPECTION AND GRADING; CONSUMER STANDARDS. B.L. SMITH

Food Poisoning includes intoxication and infection resulting from consumption of foods contaminated by toxins (poisons) produced by specific micro-organisms, or the presence of infectious micro-organisms, heavy-metal contaminants (eg, copper) or natural toxins. Food poisonings are generally characterized by gastrointestinal disorders and occasionally result in death. In Canada, approximately 1000 outbreaks, involving 5000-6000 cases, are reported annually. This figure probably represents 1% of actual cases. Most cases go unreported or are attributed to "24-hour flu." Most outbreaks in Canada are associated with meats and poultry, the principal cause being severe mishandling of food, especially improper cooling and inadequate reheating.

Staphylococcal ("staph") food intoxication is most common. It is caused by a heat-stable toxin produced by some strains of *Staphylococcus aureus* bacteria. Symptoms, including cramps, nausea, vomiting and diarrhea, begin in 1-6 hours and last for 24 hours. Of growing concern is salmonellosis, *Salmonella* food infection, especially associated with poultry and egg products but also with many other foods, from spices to chocolate candy. Symptoms, including cramps, chills, vomiting, diarrhea and fever, begin in 8-24 hours and last 2-3 days or longer. Infected persons often become asymptomatic carriers of SALMONELLA. In the aged, infirm or infants, salmonellosis can result in death. A few outbreaks, involving many cases, of *Clostridium perfringens*, ie, perfringens poisoning or "institutional" food poisoning, occur annually. Symptoms are mild, including abdominal cramps and diarrhea. Food contaminated with *C. botulinum* may contain a neurotoxin that causes the rare but severe form of food poisoning, BOTULISM. Food poisonings associated with *Escherichia coli*, *Yersinia enterocolitica* and other bacteria are uncommon in Canada. Heavy metals account for less than 1% of outbreaks. During the 1970s, *Campylobacter jejuni* was identified as a major cause of human gastroenteritis. *Campylobacter* are frequently found in poultry meat, but thus far outbreaks of campylobacterosis from foods have only been associated with unpasteurized milk and untreated water supplies. Each year outbreaks of trichinosis, ie, infestation by the parasite *Trichinella spiralis*, occur from ingestion of undercooked meats, especially pork, and wild game such as bear meat. MICHAEL E. STILES

Football For many years, the term football described the practice of kicking an object, usually a round ball, and directing it into a designated goal area. It was not until 1823, a traditional myth says, that William Webb Ellis, a student at the British Public School of Rugby, picked up the ball and ran, contrary to the game's conventions. Others naturally took after him to bring him down. A code of rules evolved and the "Rugby game" was taken and played wherever the school's graduates were placed. Thus did RUGBY make its way to Canada, brought by the various immigrants, civil servants, clergy and military personnel who had a Rugby educational background.

By the 1870s a hybrid form of the Rugby game was being played in Montréal among the garrison personnel, citizens and McGill U. In 1874, McGill was invited to Cambridge, Mass, to play a game of "football" with Harvard. It was only upon arrival that the McGill team found that Harvard played a version of the kicking (soccer) game. To solve the dilemma, 2 games were played, each under the other's rules, and thus was the McGill version introduced into the US. Harvard took immediately to the new game and sent to England for the current rugby rules. Within a year of their receipt, Harvard had persuaded other eastern US teams (known as the Ivy League) to adopt the game. Although rugby featured spontaneity of play, the Americans soon made the style of play more organized and subject to planning and design. For example, where rugby called for the ball to be put into play by a scrum, with possession going to whoever won the ball from the scrum, the Americans introduced a "snap back" system and a certain number of attempts to gain a set amount of yardage or give up possession. The continual evolution and development of the American game served to influence the Canadian, more so as British influence waned in Canada.

The present sport of Canadian football closely resembles the American, with some significant differences: the Canadian playing field is much larger (9 m longer, 6 m wider and with end zones 13 m deeper); the Canadian game allows 12 players per side, compared to 11 in the US, and allows much more movement of players before the ball is put into play; only 3 downs, compared to 4 in the US, are allowed for the offensive team to make 10 yards and retain control of the ball; the team receiving a punt must run it back — there is no option to call the ball dead by a "fair catch"; any member of the offensive backfield may be in motion prior to the snap of the ball. Other minor differences exist, eg, there is a 1-yard restraining area between offensive and defensive lines. Partisans of the Canadian version claim it is more exciting and unpredictable than American football.

Football is played at most Canadian universities and its acceptance at high schools has given it advantages over other team sports, such as baseball. There is some regional variation in the rules among Canadian leagues, but the scoring is the same: 6 points for a touchdown (for carrying the ball across the opponent's goal line), 3 for a field goal (placement kick between the goalposts), 2 for a safety touch (tackling a ballcarrier who by his own momentum has entered his own end zone), 1 for a conversion of the touchdown (some leagues allow for 2) and a single point when the ball is kicked through the end zone and out of play or when the ball is downed in the end zone after a punt (formerly called a "rouge") or a missed field goal. These points for kicking are unique to Canadian football.

In Canadian football's formative years, various regional sports governing bodies were responsible for declaring a champion as well as setting the rules and regulations among member teams. The Québec Rugby Football Union (QRFU) and Canadian Rugby Football Union (CRU) were formed in 1882; the Ontario Rugby Football Union (ORFU) in 1883; the Canadian Intercollegiate Rugby Football Union (CIRFU) in 1898; and the Interprovincial Rugby Football Union (IRFU) in 1907. The Western Canada Rugby Football Union, encompassing unions from Man, Sask and Alta, was formed in 1911. Each union declared a champion, except for the Canadian, which was to provide a "Dominion Championship" arrangement. Gradually, the prestige associated with the CRU's Dominion title led to more uniformity in rules. The GREY CUP game, first played in 1909, symbolized henceforth the Canadian championship. The first game was played between the University of Toronto, representing the CIRFU, and the Toronto Parkdale Canoe Club (ORFU); U of T won 26-6.

Western teams competed for the trophy for the first time in 1921. The game between the EDMONTON ESKIMOS and the TORONTO ARGONAUTS was won by Toronto 23-0. Nevertheless, there was no question that the best football was being played by the university teams during the early years of the Grey Cup. Under Harry Griffith, who was classified as an "honorary coach" (in those days a paid professional coach was not acceptable in a sporting milieu governed by the rules and conventions of amateur sport), and with players such as Smirle "Big Train" Lawson and Hughie Gall, consecutive titles (1909, 1910 and 1911) were won by the U of T team. McGill, coached by Frank Shaughnessy, whose hiring as a "professional coach," the first for such a purpose, created much controversy, was perhaps the best team from 1912 to 1919, but they refused to take time from their studies to pursue the Grey Cup. During 1922, 1923 and 1924, Queen's won 3 consecutive Grey Cups led by Harry "Red" Batstone and Frank "Pep" Leadley. An indication of the strength of the Queen's team coached by Bill Hughes was evident in the score of the 1923 game. Queen's defeated the WCRFU Regina Roughriders by a score of 54-0 !

From 1925 on, the Intercollegiate Union gave way to the stronger city-based teams and unions. Football began to attract large numbers of spectators and teams sought ways to make the game more pleasing to the public. Clubs set out to attract proficient players, and amateurism lost its control. In 1931, when the forward pass was approved for all Canadian leagues (it had long been part of the US game) the Montréal Amateur Athletic Assn, known as the "Winged Wheelers," imported Warren Stevens from Syracuse U to play quarterback. The team's success in winning the Grey Cup sparked a more intense search for American talent, especially by western teams, to augment the players on whom they could draw with their smaller population base. Winnipeg's general manager, Joe Ryan, was able to sign 9 Americans for the 1935 season for $7500. The move paid off handsomely as Winnipeg defeated the Hamilton Tigers 18-12, the first Grey Cup victory for a western team. It also heightened the conflict between the CRU and the leagues competing for the Grey Cup. The CRU was interested in maintaining at least a facade of amateurism, while the leagues wanted to field the best teams possible. The friction would continue until 1956 when the CRU was controlled by the leagues representing the 9 strongest teams in Canada. An ORFU team from Sarnia had gained similar success because of sponsorship by an oil firm. The "Imperials," as they were known, were able to augment local talent with players such as "Bummer" Stirling, Norm Perry and the giant Orm Beach. They were the 1936 Grey Cup champions.

In an effort to stem the influx of American "imports," the CRU sought to impose a residence rule. It soon became obvious, however, that the member clubs and leagues were not as adamant. The Grey Cup was gaining prestige and acceptance with the public. With the end of WWII and the resumption of the various leagues, the 1946 CRU meeting stipulated that each team could play with 5 American imports. Some teams, notably the Toronto Argonauts, preferred to play with an all-Canadian lineup. The Argos did so until 1950 and in the process won 3 consecutive Grey Cup championships under coach Teddy Morris (1945, 1946 and 1947). The 1948 Grey Cup game, won by Calgary 12-7 over Ottawa, was a catalyst in several ways. To be sure, the excitement generated by the westerners turned the final into a national celebration. But just as importantly for the development of football, the 1948 game marked an escalation in the quality of player attracted to play in Canada. Previously, many clubs got much of their import talent from among those with American college football experience. The American Football Conference's disbanding meant that many players would be available to the Canadian game.

It soon became obvious that the smaller centres of the ORFU (Toronto Balmy Beach, Kitchener, Sarnia and Brantford) could not compete. In fact, they seemed to be a hindrance to the Western Interprovincial Football Union (1936) and the eastern teams, known as the "Big Four." The 1954 game between Edmonton and Kitchener (actually a "farm team" for the Eskimos) represented the last time the ORFU was scheduled into the Grey Cup play-downs. By 1956, the Canadian Football Council was formed, becoming the CANADIAN FOOTBALL LEAGUE (CFL) in 1958. The professional league was now in charge of its own operations and proceeded to modify the game according to its perceived needs. The CRU remained in existence but was effectively controlled by the CFL. In 1966, the CRU turned the trusteeship of the Grey Cup over to the CFL and changed its name to the Canadian Amateur Football Assn (CAFA).

The CFL, in the meantime, increased rosters (34 in 1982), allowed unlimited blocking, introduced a "taxi squad" (players who could practise in order to play in emergency situations) and allowed 15 imports. A controversial regulation, known as "the designated import rule," that permitted 2 imports designated as quarterbacks to play at any time effectively curtailed the development of Canadians at this position after its passage in 1970. Since most head coaches and general managers of the 9 CFL teams have been Americans, it is natural that graduates of the American colleges are sought for the critical quarterback position, rather than Canadians with potential who need time to develop. Indeed, since the CFL teams are controlled by Americans, it is not surprising that there is pressure to make Canadian football more akin to the American game because it is the style of play most familiar to the coaches and many players. Because of this some critics say that the football played in the CFL is becoming less and less an expression of Canadian culture. Although Canadians, such as Russ JACKSON, have excelled at the quarterback position, most of the key players on CFL teams are American. It could be said that Canadian football is a game played by Americans for a Canadian championship represented by an Englishman's cup. The play-off system continues to admit 6 of 9 teams to post-season play and every team has won the Grey Cup since the mid-1950s. During the 1970s a superb Edmonton team dominated Canadian football, winning an unprecedented 5 consecutive Grey Cups between 1978 and 1982.

Intercollegiate football has developed independently under its own governing body, the Canadian Intercollegiate Athletic Union (CIAU). The last representative of the CIAU to challenge for the Grey Cup was the 1932 U of T team. Once the CIAU decided to bypass this challenge, regional unions became the focal point of the growing number of universities. In Nov 1959 the first Canadian college championship game was played at Toronto's Varsity Stadium. The Western Ontario Mustangs defeated the UBC Thunderbirds 33-7 to win the Sir Winston Churchill Trophy, an original sculpture entitled "Onslaught," by R. Tait MCKENZIE. Not until 1965, however, was the college championship played regularly. That year, Governor General Georges VANIER lent his name to a trophy, the Vanier Cup, to be contested in an annual College Bowl. For the first 2 years, it was an invitational event, but in 1967 it was declared the national championship of the CIAU. Semi-finals are played in the Maritimes and western Canada to determine the 2 finalists. The 4 regions eligible are the Western Intercollegiate Football League (WIFL), the Ontario Universities Athletic Assn (OUAA), the Ontario-Québec Intercollegiate Football Conference (OQIFC) and the Atlantic Universities Athletic Assn (AUAA).

Since 1966, the CAFA has concerned itself with the game as played outside the CFL and educational institutions. It organizes national championships as well as recreational "touch" football for those who want to enjoy the throwing, kicking, running and catching aspects of the game. The CANADIAN FOOTBALL HALL OF FAME was opened in Hamilton in Nov 1972.

FRANK COSENTINO

Reading: Frank Cosentino, *Canadian Football: The Grey Cup Years* (1969); G. Currie, *One Hundred Years of Canadian Football* (1968); J. Sullivan, *The Grey Cup Story* (1974).

Foothills, a region of rolling, undulating or hilly terrain lying between an area of plains and a MOUNTAIN RANGE. Generally, foothills are regarded as a transitional relief form combining some of the elements of a lower-elevation, flat landscape with those of mountainous topography, but without extensive or extreme portions of either. Physiographically, the foothills are regarded as part of the mountains. The French word *piedmont* ["at the foot of the mountain"] is sometimes used to describe an area within which foothills lie. In northern Italy the region of Piemonte is a hilly area lying between the wide, flat valley of the River Po and the Italian Alps. In Canada, the foothills of the ROCKY MOUNTAINS occupy an area between the Rockies and the Alberta plains and associated lowlands of northeastern BC. Covering about 60 000 km^2, this region extends from the Canada-US border northwestward, a distance of some 1100 km, to the Peace R region of BC, and averages about 50 km in width. Summit elevations in the foothills average approximately 1800 m; the plains area to the E and the mountains to the W average about 1200 m and 2500 m, respectively. Most of the foothills of the Rockies consist of folded and faulted Mesozoic and Cretaceous sedimentary ROCKS that were deformed by mountain-building forces (the Columbian and Laramide Orogenies) that occurred during Cretaceous and early Tertiary times (140-65 million years ago). The foothills were extensively glaciated during the Quaternary. In the last major ice advance, the Wisconsin, the mountain (Cordilleran) glaciers and the Continental Ice Sheet merged and covered some areas of the foothills while other areas, especially in the S, remained ice free (*see* GLACIATION).

I.A. CAMPBELL

Footwear Industry, sector of Canada's MANUFACTURING industries that produces footwear to meet various needs, including specialized industrial footwear, functional footwear, cold-weather footwear, slippers, and dress, casual and athletic shoes for men, women and children.

History The footwear industry is one of the oldest in Canada, second only to the fur industry. The name of the first person in Canada to cobble a pair of shoes has not been recorded, but François Bissot of Lévis, Qué, built the first tannery in 1651. Bissot was assisted by Jean TALON, who advanced the sum of 3268 livres from the royal coffers. The shoe-hungry settlers of New France contributed another 1500 livres. The first Canadian census (1667) revealed that 20 shoemakers served a population of 3915 inhabitants. The industry was required not only to look after the needs of the colony but also to equip a regiment of soldiers. Like cobblers all over the world, Canadian shoemakers used an awl, a curved knife, a needle and a wooden last. They set up shop in their own homes, employing 4 or 5 workers.

Toward the middle of the 19th century, the introduction of machinery revolutionized the production of footwear. The sewing machine was adapted for stitching footwear components. Other devices were developed for cutting, cementing, nailing and vulcanizing parts of the shoe. Eventually, what had been a cottage craft became a sophisticated, highly mechanized factory industry. The 1871 census reported 4191 footwear-manufacturing establishments in Canada. Most were small shops which also did shoe repairs. With the advent of mechanized shoemaking equipment, many of these small manufacturers were forced out of business by the high capital cost of machinery and plant construction.

The Modern Industry Consolidation has also marked the modern industry. In 1950 the 292 footwear factories in Canada produced 33.9 million pairs of shoes, valued at $111 million. The industry employed 20 785 workers. In 1983 there were 142 factories which employed 16 000 persons and produced 39.1 million pairs of footwear valued at $683 million. The industry is concentrated in Montréal, Québec City, Toronto and the Kitchener-Cambridge area. About 90% of the firms are Canadian owned. Successful Canadian shoe manufacturers include Bastien Brothers Inc, St-Émile, Qué, who produce winter boots for the N American market; Bootlegger Inc, Montréal, producers of women's and men's casual and dress winter boots; Greb Industries, producers of Bauer skates, Hush Puppies and Kodiak work and hiking boots; Kaufman Footwear, Kitchener, Ont, producers of waterproof footwear, safety and hiking boots; Susan Shoe Industries Ltd, Hamilton, Ont, producers of Cougar casual footwear; and Tender Tootsies Ltd, Canada's most successful and largest maker of popular-priced women's footwear, using man-made materials. Bata Ltd, Don Mills, Ont, is the world headquarters of the Bata Shoe Organization, the largest shoe marketing and manufacturing enterprise in the world (100 companies in 95 countries).

In 1968 shoe production reached a peak of 52.9 million pairs, falling to 39.1 million pairs in 1983, a drop caused chiefly by the influx of footwear imported from low-wage countries in which average earnings are one-tenth those of a Canadian shoe factory worker. Until the early 1960s, imports were not significant in the Canadian market, but they soared from 6.8 million pairs in 1972 to 57 million pairs in 1983, the latter figure representing 62.1% of the apparent Canadian market for footwear that year. Imports from Asia took over most of the low-price ranges; those from Europe captured much of the market for fashion footwear. The deterioration in the Canadian share of the domestic market caused shoe manufacturers to seek the protection of the federal government against the flood of imports. The industry maintains that the current market share, less than 50%, threatens the survival not only of the Canadian footwear industry but also of related industries (eg, the leather industry) and many suppliers. In response to the shoe manufacturers' briefs, the government convened the Anti-Dumping Tribunal in 1977 and again in 1980. In both cases the tribunal found that imports were indeed causing serious injury to the Canadian industry. As a result the government imposed quotas on all footwear coming into Canada, rolling back import levels to 80% of average imports for the 3 previous years. The quotas have been extended until Mar 1986 and, under their protection, the industry will continue to introduce automation and electronic technology, and undertake restructuring programs to help it meet foreign competition. The Canadian industry is also developing export markets and increasing specialization in winter footwear, for which it has already gained a world reputation for excellence.

Although wages have more than doubled in the past decade, they have remained below those for other manufacturing industries. Of every dollar received by manufacturers from footwear sales, half pays for materials and a quarter for labour. The remaining 25% covers administration costs and profits. *See* APPRENTICESHIP; Thomas J. BATA; LEATHERWORKING.

FRANCES KELLEY

Forage Crops are PLANTS grown primarily for livestock feed and are consumed either as hay, silage or green feed, or grazed by animals. The 2 major forage plant groups are legumes and GRASSES.

Legumes All legumes have seed pods and are able to fix nitrogen in their root nodules. Of the 2 commercial ALFALFA species, *Medicago sativa* has been Canada's most valuable forage, producing high yields for hay or silage; *M. falcata* has provided cultivars that succeed under low-moisture PRAIRIE conditions. Red CLOVER (*Trifolium pratense*), a biennial, succeeds better under imperfect drainage than does alfalfa; it is widely grown in Canada, where sufficient rainfall occurs. Alsike clover (*T. hybridum*) has characteristics similar to those of red clover and is grown in mixtures with grasses. White cover (*T. repens*), used in mixtures with grasses for pasture and hay, grows along the ground and has numerous runners. Bird's-foot trefoil (*Lotus corniculatus*) has yellow flowers; its persistent habit of growth makes it valuable for long-term pasture. Sweet clover (genus *Melilotus*) is a tall biennial, most widely grown in western Canada for hay or silage. FABA BEANS, field PEAS and various VETCHES have been used as green feed or hay.

Grasses Grasses have played an important role because of their diversity and ability to grow under a wide range of SOIL and CLIMATE conditions. Timothy (*Phleum pratense*), the most widely grown grass outside dry parts of the Prairie region, grows best on heavy soils with high moisture-retaining capacity. Orchard grass (*Dactylis glomerata*) has a deep, fibrous root system, adapted to open, drier soil types, and responds to fertilizers and irrigation. Bromegrass (*Bromus inermis*), well adapted to open dry soils, has been grown in mixtures with alfalfa in drier areas of eastern Canada and on the Prairies. Reed canary grass (*Phalaris arundinaceae*), native to N America, grows in clumps which spread rapidly by stout, creeping rootstalks and does best under high-moisture conditions. Kentucky bluegrass (*Poa pratensis*) is widely distributed, especially in cool humid areas, where it provides natural pasture in uncultivated areas. Crested wheatgrass (genus *Agropyron*) was introduced from western Siberia. A bunchgrass with a dense, deep root system, it produces leaves from mid-Apr to late June and is adapted to prairie conditions. Intermediate wheatgrass (*A. intermedium*), with a deep root system, is adapted to dry prairie conditions, is easy to establish and provides palatable pasture. Russian wild ryegrass (*Elymus junceus*) is drought and cold tolerant, has a high protein content and is palatable in autumn.

Cultivation In 1981 there were 4.4 million ha of improved pasture and 5.1 million ha of forage crops in Canada. Cultivation practices vary with climatic zone but, in general, forage crops are established in spring, on fully ploughed land, and are seeded using grain drills, with oats or barley as nurse crops. Recent developments on dairy farms have resulted in direct seeding of alfalfa and grass mixtures; a hay harvest is taken in the first year. In areas where corn silage provides high-energy (ie, high-carbohydrate) feed, alfalfa and alfalfa-grass mixtures provide the high-protein feed, and many farms grow both. Timothy-alfalfa is used on well-drained, heavy soils that have a high moisture-retaining capacity. In imperfect drainage situations, red clover and alsike are mixed with timothy for hay or silage. In the northern clay belt of Ontario and Québec, red clover, alsike and timothy are used to provide hay or silage in support of a cow-calf system. In eastern Québec and the Maritimes, timothy represents over 80% of the forage produced; it is established with oats as a nurse crop. In western Canada, crested wheatgrass is widely used and alfalfa-bromegrass dominates the irrigated regions of Alberta and Saskatchewan for hay and silage. Brome-alfalfa is widely used for hay in Manitoba and on drier soils in Ontario and Québec. In BC, alfalfa, red clover, orchard grass and perennial ryegrass are top forage species.

Variations in soil type, fertilization practices, intensity of farming systems and climatic zones make it difficult to estimate yields. For example, under favourable conditions, timothy may yield 9 t of dry matter per hectare; if moisture is restricted and summer temperatures are high, yields would be only one-third as great. Thus, in southern Ontario yields of timothy approach 12 700 kg/ha; in northern Ontario, 6500 kg/ha. In the prairies, crested wheatgrass and bromegrass would yield 3700 kg/ha under conditions prevailing in central Saskatchewan. The contribution of forage crops to the GROSS NATIONAL PRODUCT would parallel closely the value of dairy products, beef and sheep, as over 85% of the feed used on the farm comes from forages, hay, silage or grazing hectarages. W.R. CHILDERS

Forcier, Marc-André, director (b at Montréal 19 July 1947). His first feature film, a small-scale production called *Le Retour de l'Immaculée Conception* (1971), revealed his original approach to cinema. He developed his style by creating a world composed of eccentric characters who apparently reject the values of the society in which they live but who nonetheless are deeply rooted in that society. Forcier explored that world in *Bar salon* (1973); the film that established his reputation, *L'Eau chaude, l'eau frette* (1976); and the extraordinary *Au clair de la lune* (1982).

PIERRE VÉRONNEAU

Ford, Robert Arthur Douglas, diplomat, poet (b at Ottawa 8 Jan 1915). Ford joined the Dept of External Affairs in 1940 and in 1946 was second secretary in the Canadian embassy in Moscow, where he spent much of his career in various positions, culminating in his tenure as ambassador (1964-80). Other postings have included Yugoslavia and the United Arab Republic. Ford is the author of 4 collections of verse, including translations — *A Window on the North* (1956), *The Solitary City* (1969) and *Holes in Space* (1979). All are distinguished by a clinical despair and a precision of language and form. Ford might be said to be, like Lester PEARSON or Charles RITCHIE, in the humanistic tradition of Canadian diplomacy that is now, alas, obsolete. *Needle in the Eye: Poems New and Old* (1983) is his most recent publication. DOUG FETHERLING

Ford Motor Company of Canada, Limited, with head offices in Oakville, Ont, is a major manufacturer and distributor of automobiles in Canada. First incorporated in Ontario in 1904, the Canadian company was reincorporated in 1911. In the 1960s, following implementation of the CANADA-US AUTOMOTIVE PRODUCTS AGREEMENT, Ford's manufacturing and assembly operations were modified to permit longer production runs of fewer products. The company manufactures automotive safety glass and, in partnership with Essex Manufacturing (formed in 1978), engines and casts. Automobile and truck assembly operations are located in Oakville. The company also imports vehicles from its US parent. In 1983, it had sales or operating revenue of $8.6 billion (ranking 5th in Canada), assets of $2.1 billion (ranking 37th) and 33 500 employees. Total foreign ownership of the company stands at 90%, with Ford Motor Company of Dearborn, Mich, holding 89%. *See* AUTOMOTIVE INDUSTRY. DEBORAH C. SAWYER

Foreign Aid The modern concept of foreign aid — assistance from rich, industrialized countries to poorer, developing countries — has its roots in post-WWII RECONSTRUCTION. The success of the Marshall Plan in channelling resources from the US to war-torn Europe convinced Western leaders that a similar transfer of resources to newly independent countries in Asia and Africa would likewise lead to rapid development. Canada's aid program began in this period of prevailing optimism. In 1950 Canada joined the COLOMBO PLAN to support the recently independent COMMONWEALTH countries of Asia. During the next 2 decades Canada's program grew steadily, expanding to include the Commonwealth Caribbean (1958), Commonwealth Africa (1960) and francophone Africa (1961). In 1970 the program was extended to Latin America.

The foundations for Canada's program for the 1970s were laid in the mid-1960s, when the government undertook to raise levels of aid drastically. In 1968, 3 significant events occurred: first, the CANADIAN INTERNATIONAL DEVELOPMENT AGENCY was created to administer Canada's aid efforts; second, Pierre Trudeau, a man with an abiding interest in international development, became prime minister; and third, former PM L.B. Pearson formed an international commission to examine the results of 20 years' development assistance and to propose policies for improvement. The commission's report, *Partners in Development*, called for each donor country to provide foreign aid equal to 0.70% of its GROSS NATIONAL PRODUCT. Canada accepted this target in 1970 and repeatedly reaffirmed its commitment, but by 1982 had achieved only 0.42%. Still, in 1982 Canada distributed over $1 billion of aid through various channels and covering a vast array of activities. Direct country-to-country (bilateral) aid accounts for almost half of all Canadian aid, supporting over 90 countries. Most bilateral aid is concentrated on about 30 countries, with India, Pakistan, Bangladesh and Sri Lanka — 4 of Canada's first recipients — still receiving about one-third. Bilateral aid is normally provided not in cash, but in Canadian goods and services, including wheat and flour, railway locomotives and parts, equipment for hydroelectric generation and transmission, fertilizer, seeds and farm implements, and Canadian personnel to serve as advisers or instructors.

Multilateral aid, generally in cash, flows from Canada to many international organizations, which undertake their own activities. Most notable are the World Bank and other multilateral development banks, and the specialized agencies of the UNITED NATIONS. These multilateral institutions account for over one third of Canada's foreign aid. The balance supports the International Development Research Centre — a public corporation founded in 1970 to fund research on the needs of developing countries — and Canadian nongovernmental organizations in developing countries. Each year over 200 such organizations, most of which also raise funds through private donations, receive matching support from the Canadian government as well as from some provincial governments.

There are few precedents for one state or people accepting some continuing responsibility for the improvement of other states and peoples, without demanding repayment in wealth or power. The very newness of the phenomenon makes it complex and controversial. There is still no completely shared view in donor countries about what aid should do, or how best to do it. Some people still adhere to the ideological or strategic view that the West should aid developing countries in order to maintain friendly relations and dissuade them from aligning themselves with the competing Soviet bloc. Other people view underdevelopment in Third World countries as a product of exploitation by advanced countries, and see generous aid as a kind of reparation. The prevailing motivation for Canadian foreign aid, as revealed in public-opinion surveys and in the statements of political leaders, is a humanitarian concern for the many millions of people who are obviously far poorer than most Canadians. Disparities in living standards are so great and so far beyond the control of poor people that many Canadians now view the obligation to help as one of basic justice rather than of charity. Humanitarianism, however, is never the only motive, particularly for government-to-government aid. When the Canadian government allocates official development assistance, it is also influenced somewhat by commercial interests (developing sales and future markets for Canadian products) and by political interests (the desire to build or maintain good relations with the recipient government).

Even when the primary motive is humanitarianism, there are tensions between the need for short-term assistance to relieve hardship and longer-term help to enable poor people eventually to become more self-sufficient. The latter approach has become more widely accepted, especially with the emphasis since the mid-1970s on "basic human needs" development. But it is proving frustratingly difficult to achieve quick or impressive results with this kind of aid. Many experts are convinced that existing power structures in many developing countries are themselves a major obstacle to improvements for poor people, and that official aid often reinforces these structures, rather than making them more responsive. Observers who are sceptical of government intervention in economic life also raise doubts about the potential effectiveness of official aid, which by necessity is channelled through recipient governments. In most developing countries, aid is a small part of total investment and is concentrated in areas where the private sector can rarely take a leading role. Nevertheless, foreign aid is a small but important component in the development process. Its success depends on both the domestic efforts of the developing countries and the whole range of other links between developed and developing countries. BERNARD WOOD AND ROGER EHRHARDT

Reading: Canada, *Strategy for International Development Co-operation 1975-1980* (1975); K. Spicer, *A Samaritan State?* (1966).

Foreign Investment in Canada is both direct (made to control enterprises) and portfolio (made only for the interest or dividends paid or the possible capital gain to be achieved). Foreigners control a substantial fraction of the Canadian economy and are paid huge sums every year in the form of interest and dividends. In 1979 foreign-controlled firms owned 28.5% of the total assets of nonfinancial industries and were especially prominent because of their size; of the country's 100 leading enterprises exactly half were foreign controlled.

Foreign control of the Canadian economy peaked in the early 1970s. In certain MANUFACTURING industries, notably automobiles, tobacco, paper, chemicals and electrical products, Canadian-controlled companies were practically nonexistent. Oil and gas mining and petroleum refining were also largely foreign controlled. By 1978 about 80% of foreign direct investment was American, over 50% of which was by a relatively small number of multinational giants;

the UK was responsible for under 10% and all other countries for 10%. This large foreign presence in the economy, quite unparalleled in other parts of the world, has deep historical roots. Beginning in the mid-19th century, when Canada was still a British colony, British investors readily supplied capital needed for development. Until WWI, British capital largely financed the construction of railways and cities.

Meanwhile, the US was building a national economy which would surpass that of any European country. The railway network linking the US made mammoth industrial plants feasible and profitable. For some of these giants it became desirable to operate in distant branch establishments, closer to natural resources or where local markets might be more economically served; and railway, telegraph and later telephone made it possible to exercise effective control over operations far away from headquarters. As US natural resources became depleted, American industrial firms sought supplies elsewhere. The first Canadian resource upon which Americans drew heavily was timber, especially that of Québec and Ontario. American lumbermen came to Canada and built large mills to process lumber for sale in the US. These were not branches of US firms, however. The men who established and owned them eventually became Canadians. The first significant branch plants were newsprint mills, built by US papermakers. They would have preferred simply to buy logs to feed their mills in the US, but provincial governments, anxious to secure jobs and economic development, refused to permit the export of logs from forest lands that they controlled, insisting that US companies build local mills. By 1929 Canada accounted for about 65% of world exports of newsprint; 90% of it went to the US.

The discovery of valuable minerals (gold, nickel, zinc and other nonferrous metals) created a MINING industry in which US and some British capital soon played a commanding role. Gold, found in river bars and surface deposits, was extracted first by individuals using cheap and simple methods and then by large-scale, capital-intensive methods. Established US mining firms set up branches to carry on this type of activity, furnishing skill, capital and experience. From the beginning, base-metal deposits were exploited chiefly by companies established and controlled by US mining corporations. After WWI, US firms in other industries began to operate branches in Canada on a large scale. Manufacturing companies set up branch plants to serve the Canadian market, thereby avoiding high freight costs and import duties. Also, US-owned branch plants were able to take advantage of exports to Commonwealth countries, under a system of preferential tariff rates. New variety- and grocery-store chains built stores in many cities. By 1930 US direct investment in Canada was over 5 times that of the UK.

The 1929 stock market crash and the GREAT DEPRESSION brought practically all forms of foreign investment to a standstill that lasted throughout WWII. In the early 1950s US investment resumed substantially. US industrial corporations undertook enormous mining projects, and following the discovery of the LEDUC oil pool (1947), US firms spent enormous sums in OIL and gas exploration, and on PIPELINES and refineries. The increasing population and its growing affluence made the Canadian market highly attractive to US firms. Manufacturers of consumer products set up branches, as did retail and financial firms and suppliers of equipment and services required by business firms.

Canada was a relatively secure and familiar market for US companies' first ventures into foreign investment. When they had acquired experience they often expanded farther, into Europe and other countries. Conceivably, goods and services produced in the branch plants of US firms could have been provided by Canadian-owned enterprises, but US firms had the enormous advantages of much greater capital and experience and strongly established, valuable connections. The markets of many US-owned plants in resource industries were safely established, as parent plants in the US bought all their products. Many US products were already well advertised in Canada. Branch plants tended to buy equipment and materials from the US firms that supplied their parent organizations. Few Canadians could set up enterprises able to compete effectively against American firms with these advantages.

Presumably the role of US-controlled firms in the economy would not have grown so rapidly if authorities had restricted it or had provided special assistance to Canadian-owned firms, but they were anxious to achieve as much economic development as possible and were unconcerned by the large increase in US participation in the economy. As a matter of principle they treated US-owned and Canadian-owned firms with absolute impartiality. In a relatively small number

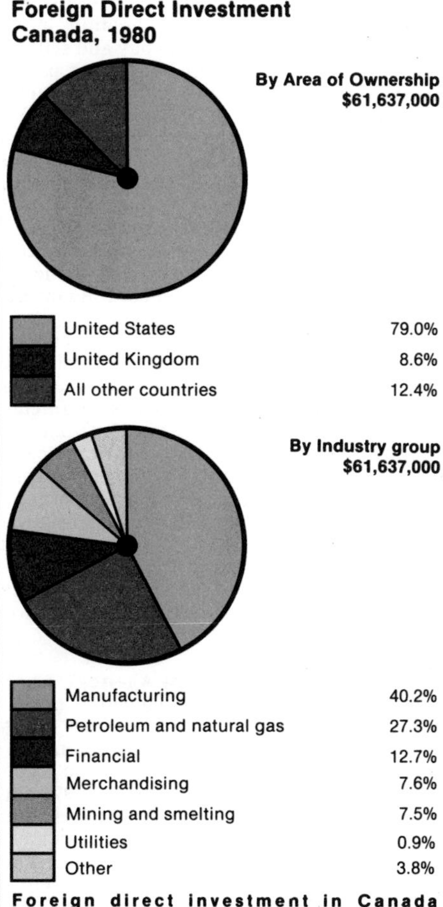

Foreign direct investment in Canada represents the book value, at a point in time, of long-term capital owned by foreign direct investors in incorporated or unincorporated entities in Canada, which are referred to as direct investment enterprises. The size and nature of the investment provide the foreign direct investor, on a lasting basis, the potential to influence or to have an effective voice in the management of the direct investment enterprise operating outside his own economy. This investment is normally identified by ownership of at least 10% of the equity of the concern in Canada. Direct investment covers the long-term capital provided by or accruing to foreign direct investors, comprising both long-term debt (bonds, debentures, loans, advances, etc.) and equity (common and preferred shares, and retained earnings).

Source: Statistics Canada Catalogue 67-202.

Distribution of Control of Capital in Nonfinancial Industries

	Total capital employed (Billions$)	*% controlled in Canada*	*% controlled in US*	*% controlled in other countries*
Manufacturing	44.8	45	42	13
Petroleum and natural gas	23.2	32	54	14
Mining and smelting	10.4	45	41	14
Railways	6.6	99	1	0
Other utilities	45.4	96	4	0

of instances, foreign firms licensed Canadian firms to use technology the former had developed so that goods and services using that technology were produced in Canadian-owned establishments. In addition to setting up branch plants in Canada, US firms bought established Canadian firms, incorporating them into their organizations. Many Canadian businesses sold to US corporations for considerably more than they would have received from Canadian buyers. In this way US direct investment, $3.4 billion in 1950, increased tenfold by 1977. Some of this increase was attributable to INFLATION, but a large portion of it reflected increased ownership of physical assets in Canada.

Although US-owned firms initiated the production here of many novel products and services and provided welcome job opportunities, there were problems. Huge and increasing amounts of money (nearly $2 billion by 1978) had to be remitted to US owners in the form of dividends on their investment. MULTINATIONAL CORPORATIONS carried on their Canadian operations to serve their own best interests, not those of Canada. Research and development, essential to industrial innovation and growth, was generally done not at subsidiary operations but in US facilities. When demand for the products of some international companies fell, they would reduce the scale of operation or close down the branch while maintaining operations in the parent plant. When an international firm uncovered a cheaper source of supplies or labour in another country, it might close down its Canadian operation. The presence of giant, foreign-owned companies made it difficult for the government to stabilize the economy. Possessing great financial power and having wide international interests, these firms could not be induced or pressured to alter the tempo of their Canadian operations to help keep the economy on an even keel. Subject to US legislation, which forbade US firms and their affiliates to trade with US enemies, plants here could not export their products to some countries that maintained normal trade relationships with Canada. Corporate strategy frequently had the same consequences; branch plants were generally designed to serve the domestic market and lacked the resources necessary to develop and sell products in export markets.

Aside from economic concerns, many Canadians (*see* COMMITTEE FOR AN INDEPENDENT CANADA) objected on nationalistic grounds to the scale of FOREIGN OWNERSHIP and control over the economy (*see* ECONOMIC NATIONALISM). The federal government responded in the 1960s with new legislation forbidding foreigners to own radio and television stations, and with restrictions on foreigners' rights to set up banks, insurance companies and other financial concerns, to enlarge established firms, to participate in the exploitation of oil, gas and mineral deposits or to acquire uranium mines. In 1974, the federal government established the FOREIGN INVESTMENT REVIEW AGENCY (FIRA) to control investments by nonresidents. FIRA approved about 90% of the proposals it reviewed and was not a significant barrier to the extension of foreign ownership. It was angrily criticized for its occasional rejec-

Direct Investment in Canada by Nonresidents							
	Total amount (Millions$)	*Owned in the US (Millions$)*	*% of total*	*Owned in the UK (Millions$)*	*% of total*	*Owned in all other countries (Millions$)*	*% of total*
1945	2 713	2 304	84.9	384	12.8	61	2.3
1950	3 975	3 426	86.2	468	11.8	81	2.0
1960	12 872	10 549	82.0	1 535	11.9	788	6.1
1970	26 423	21 403	81.0	2 503	9.5	2 517	9.5
1977	46 951	37 602	80.1	4 153	8.8	5 196	11.1
1978	48 228	38 348	79.5	4 476	9.3	5 404	11.2

Portfolio Investment in Canada by Nonresidents							
	Total amount (Millions$)	*Owned in the US (Millions$)*	*% of total*	*Owned in the UK (Millions$)*	*% of total*	*Owned in all other countries (Millions$)*	*% of total*
1946	4 073	2 590	63.6	1 260	30.9	222	5.4
1955	5 158	3 415	66.2	1 337	25.9	406	7.9
1964	9 456	7 349	77.7	1 324	14.0	783	8.3
1974	20 754	15 434	74.4	1 644	7.9	3 676	17.7
1978	57 746	31 813	66.4	2 385	5.0	13 548	28.6

tions and its slow response to proposals and was dismantled by the Conservative government in 1984. The federal government also created the CANADA DEVELOPMENT CORPORATION (1971) and PETRO-CANADA (1974), both of which have reduced foreign control by buying out a number of large foreign-owned concerns. The Saskatchewan government bought out large foreign-owned potash firms. These purchases by governments and a few takeovers by private groups slightly reduced the degree of foreign control over the economy by the end of the 1970s. In 1980 the Canadian government introduced its National Energy Program, under which it accorded special privileges and financial incentives to Canadian-owned and -controlled firms in the oil and gas industry.

These measures and actions to limit foreign ownership raised controversy. Businesses that profited from dealing with foreign-owned firms objected, and exponents of private enterprise decried the increasing role of the government in the economy. Provincial politicians, anxious for development that would broaden local economies and add to local employment, objected to federal restrictions that prevented such development. The US government protested the discrimination exercised against its nationals and threatened retaliatory action against Canadian firms operating in the US. In response to these pressures, the Liberal federal government began to loosen restrictions. The Conservative administration under Brian MULRONEY, elected Sept 1984, indicated that it planned to further reduce barriers to foreign investment in Canada.

In addition to direct investment, Americans invested comparable sums in portfolio investments. In 1978, when their direct investment totalled $38.3 billion, their portfolio investment — in bonds of government and private firms and shares in companies controlled by others — amounted to $31.5 billion, creating serious BALANCE OF PAYMENTS problems resulting from the very large amounts that had to be remitted each year to American bondholders and shareholders. These remittances — $2-3 billion in 1978 — actually exceeded those made because of US direct investment.

Americans are not the only investors in Canada. The investments, particularly portfolio, of countries such as West Germany, Japan and Belgium have been increasing recently at a faster rate than those of the US, although they are still only a fraction of US investment. British investment increased as well but by much less than that of other countries.

Foreign ownership of agricultural land and urban real estate is also important. British investors acquired large Canadian holdings in the 19th century and continued to buy and sell Canadian properties in the 20th. Europeans, particularly West Germans and Italians, acquired large amounts of agricultural land in the 1960s and 1970s, prompting provincial governments to pass legislation restricting the acquisition of land by nonresidents. Foreigners' investment in real estate, however, is very small compared with their investment in stocks and bonds. As of 1978, foreign long-term investment in the real-estate industry amounted to $1.3 billion; the aggregate of foreigners' direct and portfolio investments in that year was $95.7 billion.

The flow of investment funds has not been purely one-way. Canadians have been building mines and branch plants in foreign countries and buying the stocks and bonds of foreign firms. However, the aggregate of Canadian investment abroad has been insignificant compared with that of foreign investment in Canada. In 1978 the total direct and portfolio investment by Canadians in foreign countries was $22.6 billion, less than 24% of foreign direct and portfolio investment in Canada.

RUBEN C. BELLAN

Reading: K. Levitt, *Silent Surrender* (1970); Guy P.F. Steed, *Threshold Firms: Backing Canada's Winners* (1982).

Foreign Investment Review Agency (FIRA), federal agency formed by Parliament in 1973 as a result of concerns raised in the Gray report about foreign domination of the Canadian economy. The agency began screening foreign acquisitions of Canadian businesses in Apr 1974 and the establishment of new foreign businesses in Oct 1975. The agency advises the government (through the minister of industry, trade and commerce) on what action should be taken, if any. In making its recommendations, FIRA took the following factors into consideration: 1) the effect of the investment on employment and economic activity in Canada; 2) the effect on Canadian productivity, technological development and product variety; 3) the degree of Canadian participation in management; 4) the effect on competition; and 5) the compatability of the investment with national policies. From the point of view of ECONOMIC NATIONALISM, FIRA was criticised because it approved most of the applications it received. However, the agency was strongly opposed by many businessmen and in Dec 1984 Industrial Expansion minister Sinclair STEVENS revised its mandate to encourage rather than discourage FOREIGN INVESTMENT. Appropriately, the name of the agency was changed to Investment Canada.

Foreign Ownership and the Structure of Canadian Investment, Task Force on In 1967 the Liberal government under PM Lester Pearson was prodded by Walter GORDON into appointing a TASK FORCE on foreign ownership. There were 8 economists on the task force and the chairman was Mel Watkins. The Watkins Report (1968) documented the costs and benefits to Canadians of the high level of foreign ownership of the Canadian ECONOMY. Comprehensive recommendations included the setting up of a development corporation to facilitate Canadian ownership and an agency to co-ordinate policies with respect to multinational enterprise. The task force shifted the debate on foreign ownership toward more interventionist policy leading, in due course, to the creation of the Canada Development Corporation and the FOREIGN INVESTMENT REVIEW AGENCY (*see* FOREIGN INVESTMENT).

MEL WATKINS

Foreign Ownership, Task Force on, (the Gray Report) was established (1970) under the Hon Herb Gray to analyse the impact of the high degree of foreign control on Canadian development and its effect on the capacity of Canadians to control their national economic environment; and to examine policies that would enable Canadians to exercise greater control over their economy and to retain and increase Canadian ownership of business where feasible or desirable for economic, social, cultural or other reasons. In the 1960s, foreign control reached nearly 60% of total Canadian manufacturing, and 90% of industries such as rubber and petroleum.

The task force concluded (1972) that, in a highly qualified way, FOREIGN INVESTMENT had had a moderately favourable effect overall but that problems did exist, eg, "truncated firms" which performed only a narrow range of activities in Canada and were only dependent on foreign technology and management. It suggested that some problems could be handled through general economic policies, eg, tariffs, taxes and patents, but that others would be better solved through flexible administrative intervention on all new foreign investment, case by case. It rejected policies for a major push towards Canadian ownership.

C.E.S. FRANKS

Foreign Policy, White Paper on, a 6-volume review of foreign policy conducted 1968-70 by the Department of External Affairs with the involvement of many other departments and agencies, as well as invited academics, business people and others. The department had its initial overview rejected by Cabinet. A revised version, more in accord with the speeches and writings of PM Trudeau, was accepted. Besides a general paper there were sector papers on Europe, Latin America, the US, international development and the Pacific. The Paper recommended that foreign policy be related to 6 national interests: economic growth, social justice, quality of life, sovereignty and independence, peace and security, and harmonious natural environment — with emphasis on the first 3. Canada's role in PEACEKEEPING was to be downplayed, there was to be closer contact with Europe and the Third World, foreign aid was to be increased and the People's Republic of China was to be recognized diplomatically — all of which simply affirmed the redirection of foreign policy already initiated by the new Trudeau government. Canadian-American relations were not examined.

C.E.S. FRANKS

Foreign Relations, *see* EXTERNAL RELATIONS.

Forest, an ecosystem characterized by a more or less dense and extensive TREE cover. This definition views the forest as more than a simple collection of trees and takes into account shrubs, vines, herbs, mosses, microorganisms, insects and higher animals which interact among

Pacific rain forest *(photo by Tim Fitzharris).*

themselves and with their environment. This vastly complex pattern of life is a system in delicate balance. Natural or man-made alterations may trigger far-reaching and sometimes disastrous changes.

Worldwide there are 3 main forest types related directly to climatic zones: equatorial- and tropical-region forests, temperate-zone forests and forests associated with colder climates. Most of Canada's forest lies within the cold-climate boreal belt extending through Alaska, Siberia, Finland, Sweden and Norway. The boreal forest is composed predominantly of coniferous trees. Temperate-region forests extend into Canada only in milder areas along the Pacific coast and in SW Ontario. In BC the cool, temperate maritime climate supports a forest dominated by CONIFERS; in southern Ontario, under hot, humid summers, a deciduous forest has developed. Between this deciduous forest and the cold-climate boreal forest to the N exists a transitional mixed-wood forest, where coniferous and deciduous trees are about equally represented.

Canada's coniferous trees (31 species) include 9 species of PINE, 5 of SPRUCE, 3 of HEMLOCK, 3 of LARCH, 4 true FIRS, one DOUGLAS FIR, 2 of CEDAR, 2 of JUNIPER, one CYPRESS and one YEW. The conifers are variously known as softwoods, evergreens or needle-leaved trees. The mature conifer usually has a straight central trunk and short branches forming a distinctive, columnar crown. With the exception of larches, conifers retain their needlelike leaves for 2 or more years; the leaves are not shed all at once.

There are just over 100 species of deciduous trees in Canada, including 10 of MAPLE, 9 of OAK, 6 of BIRCH, 5 of POPLAR, 5 of hickory, 4 of ASH and 3 of ELM and members of 32 other genera. Deciduous trees, also known as hardwoods or broadleaf trees, vary considerably in form but often exhibit broad, rounded crowns with branches as long or longer than their short, tapered trunks. With the exception of arbutus, deciduous trees shed all their leaves annually.

The first appearance of trees occurred countless centuries before the advent of GRASSES and the age of DINOSAURS. According to paleobotanists, PLANT life originated in a marine environment more than 3 billion years ago; plants moved onto land only in the late Silurian and early Devonian periods (between 400 and 386 million years ago). These first land plants, less than one metre tall, were sporebearers tied to damp environments. In the relatively short Devonian period (395 and 345 million years ago) the first forests appeared. They were heavily stocked with treelike CLUB MOSSES having slender trunks and drooping branches. The earliest FOSSILS of gymnosperm seeds date to the late Devonian. Gymnosperms, of which modern coniferous trees are examples, produce seeds that are not enclosed by an ovary.

At the end of the Devonian, extensive, shallow ocean flooding occurred within the N American continent. Rivers poured sediments into this sea, producing great swamps from which eventually sprang the monumental forests of the Carboniferous period (between 345 and 280 million years ago). Here, tree-size ancestors of present-day, diminutive HORSETAILS flourished along with FERNS, seed ferns and dominant club mosses, some of which soared over 30 m. At the end of the Carboniferous, these junglelike forests succumbed to major climatic changes and were buried, compressed and ultimately converted into COAL, which has fueled a great part of modern industry. During the Carboniferous, gymnosperms predominated at higher elevations, and the passing of the period set the stage for a major proliferation of gymnosperms, prominent among which were primitive conifers and palmlike cycads. Fern and horsetail numbers decreased.

A still more dramatic advance occurred during the Mesozoic era (between 225 and 190 million years ago), when some plants developed the ability to produce flowers and to encase their seeds inside ovaries or fruits; these were the angiosperms (*see* SEED PLANTS). Many flowering trees (eg, WILLOW, POPLAR, MAPLE, magnolias) and flowering herbaceous plants appeared. By the end of the Cretaceous period (about 65 million years ago) angiosperms dominated the floral landscape. In parallel with their ascent, a rapidly expanding world of wildlife developed, with insects, birds and mammals drawing upon the forest and helping to sustain and expand it.

CLIMATE soon worked another change upon the N American forest. About 55 million years ago in the "modern" era of the Cenozoic, a long-term cooling trend began; as it intensified, forests that had thrived comfortably within the ARCTIC CIRCLE were pushed southwards. Then, just under 2 million years ago, all but a minute part of Canada was slowly covered by 4 successive, monstrous ice sheets, sometimes as much as 3 km thick. Great glacial tongues also penetrated deeply into the northeastern US (*see* GLACIATION). The advancing ice sheets scoured the forestland, but their slow movement enabled the forest to withdraw each time and find refuge in warmer southern environments. Following the retreat of the last ice sheets (7000-10 000 years ago), reestablishment of the forest began. In the vanguard of the northward march were the ALGAE and FUNGI, followed by higher plants, such as mosses, LICHENS and horsetails, capable of living on the cold, wet fringes of the land most recently vacated by ice. Next came the hardy gymnosperms: spruces, firs, pines and larches. Finally, the deciduous trees arrived: the oaks, ashes, maples and other species. These slow-moving belts of vegetation present the essential pattern of Canadian forests today. They may be growing in another interglacial period or may conceivably be in the early phase of a new tropical age. The passage of several centuries may begin to provide answers (*see* BIOGEOGRAPHY).

C.R. STANTON

Forest Economics, the application of economic principles to a wide range of subjects extending from the forest RESOURCE through the processing, marketing and consumption of forest products. Forest ECONOMICS has much in common with AGRICULTURAL ECONOMICS, but although the latter discipline has an established academic history in Canada, no departments of forest economics exist in this country. Forestry students may, however, emphasize economics subjects, supplementing a single forest-economics course with courses in rural sociology, agricultural economics, outdoor-recreation economics, general economics and forest policy. Forest economics courses *per se* concentrate on the evaluation of the forest resource, on business management principles as applied to the forest and forest-products industries, and on the relation of the forest resource and its exploitation to national economic and social policies. Thus the subject may be seen to address factors affecting the financial viability of a given operation and those affecting the objectives of society as a whole, as distinct from the interests of individuals or groups.

Fiscal factors that affect the success of a particular operation include the rulings and costs involved in licensing of public timberland; taxation (in 1983 the provincial and federal governments were expected to receive $3 billion in taxes, timber sale revenues and import duties from the forest industry and its employees); industrial legislation and regulation; costs of inputs and prices of commodities; geographic distribution of customers (as it affects transportation costs); marketing constraints; labour markets; and various federal and provincial policies. The forest economist must also be familiar with technical aspects of forest management and industrial production, and should have at least some knowledge of forest ecology, the processing of timber products, technological innovations and wildlife management.

Forestry resembles agriculture in that both deal with crops, but the differences between them point out some of the constraints that forest economists must consider. For example, agricultural land is usually cropped annually; forests must be managed over several years (the shortest crop cycle, that of hybrid poplar for pulpwood, is approximately 10 years) and failure to do so threatens the long-term viability of an operation, as well as having a negative effect on the ecosystem. This extended perspective also has advantages: it permits the industry to make management decisions, marketing arrangements and other plans for the longer term. Farmers own their land or rent it from private owners; most forestland is publicly owned (the provinces own 67%, the federal government 27%). Thus a real conflict may arise between the industry's desire to "mine" the resource for profit and society's desire to protect public land. This potential conflict is further complicated by the fact that the forest resource base provides several economic and social values that may in some locations conflict with timber harvesting, eg, grazing, HUNTING, recreation, watershed protection. The scale of operation is also a factor: while farms occupy a few square kilometres at most, forests cover almost half of Canada's land area and forest harvesting may affect very large areas.

Thus, while forest economists apply such general economic ideas as supply and demand and other market factors, financial rates of return, capital investment, development, conservation, etc, they must take great care when choosing the analytical framework within which they work. For example, the relative costs and benefits of forest management will differ depending on the length of time under consideration; on whether the calculation involves indirect as well as direct effects; on whether it is done from the perspective of an individual company, a provincial economy or a national economy, etc. An experienced forest economist can ensure the recognition of economic, social, environmental and political linkages.

Log booms in Howe Sound, north of Vancouver, BC. Forests cover almost half of Canada's land area and forest harvesting affects very large areas (*photo by J.A. Kraulis*).

One of the most important issues today is the apparent conflict among forestry investment criteria. The traditional approach in professional forestry was to emphasize biological growth. A forest was said to be mature and ready for harvesting when timber of sawlog size was available or when a timber stand ceased to add volume because annual growth was exceeded by disease, decay and mortality. In recent decades, support has grown for the concept of financial rotation, whereby the ideal harvest date is set by its calculated maximum value to the owner. A financial rotation age is based on economic efficiency as measured by market prices and costs. It assumes free competition and the absence of external costs to the ENVIRONMENT, wildlife, etc. This method tends to favour exploitation. As timber supply problems began to emerge worldwide in the past quarter century, the fairness of liquidating forest capital began to be questioned. This change in attitude has resulted in an increasing interest in CONSERVATION criteria that seek to keep the resource base essentially intact over time, a goal with particular appeal to managers of publicly owned land who do not operate by the profit motive and are not expected to apply corporate financial criteria. This approach does not mean a complete break from financial rates of return. Provincial land managers must still use financial methods to allocate funds budgeted for REFORESTATION, and they must choose among sites and silvicultural treatments to achieve the best growth and yield possible with limited funds. Economics aside, the only politically and socially acceptable policy, for public and private forest managers alike, is to replant promptly after harvest. But how much should be spent on more intensive silvicultural activities (eg, thinning and fertilizing)? For provincial foresters the answer is largely political, though it is based on expected long-term economic and social benefits. Private industry and small woodlot owners apply a variety of measures to determine the level of forest management, usually with a shorter time in mind than their public counterparts and with taxes playing a key role. The forest economist can determine the appropriate method of calculating the benefits of forest renewal and forest protection.

Forest economists also play a crucial role in formulating public policy. Such policy is firmly fixed on the goal of maintaining at least the present harvest in perpetuity. Unfortunately the record of forest-resource management in Canada is well below the level necessary to sustain existing harvest levels, let alone to provide for stable growth. Although Canada does have some of the best forestry performance in the world, it also has far too much that is below an acceptable level. As a result of decades of neglect, timber-supply deficits are emerging in many forest-based communities. In recognition of this threat the provinces and the federal government have begun to formulate new policies and programs that will double or triple spending on forest renewal. Federal government leadership is shown in the adoption of *A Forest Sector Strategy for Canada* in 1981 and 4 follow-up policies in 1982 and 1983. Priorities include increased funding for Canadian forestry faculties; increased research and development; joint programs with the provinces in such areas as replanting, timber-stand improvements, etc; and improved forest-fire suppression (eg, through establishment of a fire co-ordination centre in Winnipeg and a fleet of CANADAIR CL-215 water-bomber aircraft to be built in Montréal).

The case for forest renewal is based on the need to stabilize existing forest-industry employment as well as the estimated 2 indirect jobs associated with each person employed in the woods and mills. It is estimated that 25 000 new jobs could be created in forest renewal alone; an additional 75 000 could be generated through increased output and higher value added in processing. In addition there is the generation of billions of dollars in tax revenue, foreign-exchange earnings, watershed and wildlife protection and the support of a multi-billion recreation and tourism industry. The social costs of neglect are community dislocation, employee relocation and welfare. These costs are probably much higher than those of maintaining timber in scores of threatened forest-based towns.

Other issues for the forest economist are the social and economic impact of ACID RAIN on forests, the pricing of nontimber forest products, the trade-off between forestry and fishery values, the benefits flowing from forestry science and related new-product development, and national and international sector-development opportunities. F.L.C. REED

Reading: Jamie Swift, *Cut and Run: The Assault on Canada's Forests* (1983).

Emily Carr
Margaret Lauren
William Lyon Mackenzie King
Sir Alexander Mackenzie
Wayne Gretzky
OILERS
J.S. Woodsworth